# THE
# SOTHEBY'S
# WINE
# ENCYCLOPEDIA

## TOM STEVENSON

London, New York, Melbourne,
Munich, and Delhi

4TH EDITION, REVISED (2007)

## DORLING KINDERSLEY

MANAGING ART EDITOR Marianne Markham
MANAGING EDITOR Deirdre Headon
U.S. EDITOR Christine Heilman
INDEXER John Noble

Produced for Dorling Kindersley by

## COOLING BROWN LTD.

CREATIVE DIRECTOR Arthur Brown
DESIGN Peter Cooling, Elaine Hewson, Tish Jones, Elly King
SENIOR EDITOR Fiona Wild
COPY EDITOR Alyson Lacewing

This revised edition undertaken by

## SANDS PUBLISHING SOLUTIONS

PROJECT EDITOR David Tombesi-Walton

First American Edition, 2007

Published in the United States by
DK Publishing
375 Hudson Street
New York, New York 10014

10 11   10 9 8 7 6 5 4 3

SD351/Nov-07

DK books are available at special discounts when purchased in
bulk for sales promotions, premiums, fund-raising, or educational use.
For details, contact: DK Publishing Special Markets, 375 Hudson Street,
New York, New York 10014 or SpecialSales@dk.com.

Color reproduction by Colorscan, Singapore

Printed and bound by Toppan, China

Tom Stevenson can be found at www.wine-pages.com/guests/tom/intro.htm

Discover more at
**www.dk.com**

# CONTENTS

---

## FACTORS AFFECTING TASTE AND QUALITY

The Factors Affecting Taste and Quality boxes appear on the introductory pages of countries, regions, or districts. The taste guides (Appellations, Producers, and Wine Styles) follow these introductions.

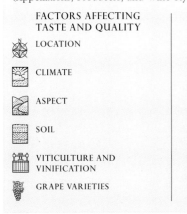

### FACTORS AFFECTING TASTE AND QUALITY

LOCATION

CLIMATE

ASPECT

SOIL

VITICULTURE AND VINIFICATION

GRAPE VARIETIES

### TASTE GUIDE SYMBOLS

When to drink for optimum enjoyment. This is usually given as a range (such as 3–7 years) from the date of the vintage. "Upon purchase" is for wines that should be both bought and drunk while young. "Upon opening" is for fortified wines that can keep for many years but, contrary to popular belief, do not keep well once opened.

Grape varieties used.

The 10 (or fewer) greatest wines for the type or style indicated.

Recommended producers, vineyards, and wines.

## STAR RATING SYSTEM

Stars are given for a producer's general quality and do not necessarily apply to each wine produced. When a producer has neither stars nor a cross, this indicates an acceptable but not outstanding standard.

Half-stars indicate intermediate ratings

★ Wines that excel within their class or style.

★★ Very exceptional wines. The local equivalent of a Bordeaux super-second. *See* Glossary, p638.

★★★ The best wines that money can buy, without any allowances made for limitations of local style and quality.

Ⓞ A producer of organic wines.

Ⓑ A producer of biodynamic wines.

Ⓥ Wines of exceptional value for money, whether they are inexpensive or not.

Ⓠ Wines that are inconsistent, or too rustic, or judgment has been reserved for a stated reason.

Ⓧ Underperformers for their category or style.

**Key to symbols**
How good a wine producer is and why a wine tastes the way it does are the twin pillars of this encyclopedia—thus, Factors Affecting Quality and Star Rating System are two of its two most regular features.

# FOREWORD

## by Serena Sutcliffe MW

THE WINE WORLD IS CONSTANTLY ON THE MOVE, and this is a reflection of market demand, climate change, and a vintage every year. The fundamentals hold good, grapes have taken root where they are best suited, more is known about ripeness and ecology, and faults are better understood, but still new producers emerge and areas refine traditions and adapt to changing circumstances.

The purpose of *The Sotheby's® Wine Encyclopedia* is to inform, stimulate, and, dare I say it, entertain, for wine should never be boring. You will find facts, preferences, and opinions, always based on experience and a considerable amount of tasting. If ever a book has been mulled over, this is it. Over the years, myriad questions have been asked of growers and winemakers, all adding to the mosaic of information, figures, and background knowledge. The aim of author Tom Stevenson has been to decant this material into a helpful form. We hope you will gain real pleasure from reading this revised edition, leading you to try new wines, to experiment, and to be adventurous, as well as to return to old favorites.

*The Sotheby's® Wine Encyclopedia* is, above all, accessible. It is designed both to be dipped into and, with a glass to hand, to provide longer reading when one wants to pursue a subject in depth. Whenever I use it, I go down alleyways and glean a mass of information for which I was not even looking—surely the purpose of an encyclopedia. No pebble, let alone any sand or clay, has been left unturned in the effort to put as much as possible on each page. Those who make the world's wines seem to be at your side as you leaf through the book, and I certainly feel the taste of hundreds of wines as I read their descriptions. The encyclopedia is, of course, a bedside book, but it is also a tabletop book and a companion in the car when touring wine regions. It obviously has its place in the cellar, too, and it would be fitting if it collected some wine stains over the years, as a true mark of its usefulness.

*Serena Sutcliffe*

# GOOD NEWS AND BAD NEWS

THE GOOD NEWS IS THE NUMBER OF TOP-PERFORMING wine producers throughout the world, which has swollen out of all proportion when compared with earlier editions of this encyclopedia. Despite deleting hundreds of previously recommended producers, there are now in excess of 6,000 wineries recommended over the following pages. I have never upgraded the star ratings of so many producers in any revision as I have for the California chapter in this edition. And, proportionately, the number of increased ratings for wineries in Australia and, my self-confessed favorite, New Zealand, was not far behind.

The bad news is the low number of top-performing organic wine producers. To be frank, I had no idea just how bad the situation was when I first decided to use ◉ and ❸ symbols to identify recommended organic and biodynamic wine producers, but the relative rarity of these symbols throughout the book rang alarm bells. It is one thing if someone gifted like Olivier Humbrecht of Domaine Zind-Humbrecht in Alsace or Lalou Bize-Leroy of Domaine Leroy in Burgundy goes organic or biodynamic. When great winemakers with exceptional *terroirs* "go green" they produce great organic or biodynamic wines. However, it is quite another matter when others less passionate about the quality of wine are organic. While they may well have a true passion for the environment, the majority of the world's organic producers clearly have no idea how to make a superior quality wine. And considering that many of them have been churning out their green gunge for years, they obviously could not care less. Just as worrying are the organizations that certify organic and biodynamic production, because it seems as if they could not care less either. It is not good enough to certify the method of production alone. They should acknowledge the importance of quality by introducing some sort of superior award on the label. Either that or the likes of Humbrecht and Bize-Leroy should set up international schools of organic and biodynamic excellence. Both ideas would be nice.

## Keeping it fresh

Researching the next major revision and expansion is an arduous but ultimately rewarding task, and it is one that necessarily takes a great deal of time. Everything from new appellations to additional varieties permitted in established appellations, or minute changes in the percentages of currently permitted varieties, must be noted. New appellations have to be mapped and alterations to existing ones taken in. New producers have to be evaluated and current recommendations reassessed. And much, much more. The problem is that by the time I finish a major revision, the information in the immediately previous edition of *Sotheby's Wine Encyclopedia* will be getting a bit tired. The only solution is what we have here: a minor revision that includes some references to new appellations, deleting some recommended producers and inserting a few new ones—but that is not its purpose because, frankly, I do not have the budget for a major revision and thus no additional pages into which to expand. The primary purpose of this minor revision is to update the vintage assessments and other time-sensitive information, to keep the book as fresh as possible while I work on the major revision.

September 2007

# WINE AUCTIONS AND COLLECTING WINE

### by Serena Sutcliffe MW

*There has never been a better time for a wine lover to be active in buying and selling wine. It is always, of course, the perfect time to be drinking wine, but an avid wine connoisseur needs to buy to keep up to date and may occasionally need to sell when short of space or money. The difference between a collector of wine and, say, a collector of furniture is that the wine lover will have new options every year, with the new vintage, at the same time as consuming some of the collection. A good cellar rotates, keeping pace with the wines' aging process. It should renew itself, like a planting program in a vineyard, so that everything does not reach maturity at the same time. And it should reflect the personal taste of the collector.*

SOTHEBY'S NEW YORK SALEROOM
*Jamie Ritchie, senior vice president, bringing down the gavel on a rare Nebuchadnezzar (equivalent to 20 standard bottles) of Château Mouton Rothschild 2000—one of only 69 produced. The bottle achieved a record price of $119,500 during the "Treasures from the Private Cellar of Baroness Philippine" sale of Château Mouton Rothschild held at Sotheby's New York Headquarters on Wednesday, February 28, 2007.*

## WINES FOR PLEASURE AND INVESTMENT

The first question to ask yourself when starting a collection is what it will be used for. Is it for early drinking, long-term keeping, or a mixture of the two, with wines of varying type and age, to ensure gradual consumption of bottles as they mature? With a clear idea of what is wanted, better advice can be gathered from experts in auction houses, reputable wine merchants, and stores.

My first advice would be not to buy modest, everyday wines to lay down. These can be bought hand to mouth and will be better and fresher as a result. Wines for storage, however short or long term, should be more interesting, better quality, and, of course, suitable for aging.

I also ask any prospective collector if the aim of acquiring a cellar is pleasure, investment, or a combination, which is both feasible and sensible. The more the collector favors the investment element, the more blue chip, and less adventurous, should be the wines bought. Most people who acquire modest wine collections do it purely for pleasure, their own and that of their friends, which is an added joy and very much part of wine culture: sharing bottles and opinions with like-minded wine lovers is convivial and life-enhancing. With a reasonable disposable income, an enthusiast can build up a collection that is large enough for investment wines to be sold from time to time in order to finance personal drinking—a solution that has a wisdom all of its own.

## PRACTICAL TIPS

Unless collecting for investment purposes only, everyone wishes to buy wines that they actually like. So, do taste as often as possible at restaurants, in-store tastings, presale tastings given by auction houses for catalog subscribers, with friends, or at wine courses. It is only by tasting that you discover your favorite wine-producing areas and grape varieties. Then, concentrate on collecting those types of wine. There are several practical aspects to consider before arriving at the store or saleroom. How much money is there to spend? How much storage space is available? And, if you are storing at home, is it suitably cold there?

The more information you can give an adviser on your vinous needs and tastes, the more pleasure you will derive from your collection. The most gifted of Masters of Wine cannot guide you to the wine of your dreams without being advised of your tastes: young or old, dry or sweet, gutsy and tannic, or light and floral. Of course, it is permitted to like them all. Read, discuss, and, above all, taste as much as possible as you build up your wine collection, and keep all your options open—new and exciting experiences lie around the corner.

## INVESTMENT WINES

A cellar that is laid down with the prime aim of providing an investment should be chosen with great care and with the advice of those who really know the fine-wine market. The field of wine investment is dominated by top clarets, the great red wines from Bordeaux's classed growths.

Those Médoc châteaux that were classified as First Growths in the 1855 classification are the blue chips of the wine-investment world, along with the First Growth from the Graves, Château Haut-Brion. Other châteaux that fall into this category are La Mission Haut-Brion, in Pessac-Léognan, and the most renowned of the Médoc Second Growths, such as Pichon Longueville Comtesse-de-Lalande, Cos d'Estournel, Ducru-Beaucaillou, Montrose, Léoville-Barton, and Léoville-Las-Cases. Then there are the châteaux from elsewhere in the *classement* that are also sure to increase in value: Palmer and Fifth Growths such as Grand-Puy-Lacoste and Lynch-Bages are classic examples.

However, precise advice is vital because the fortunes of châteaux can fluctuate—Pichon-Longueville Baron and Léoville Poyferré have advanced recently. There are also certain châteaux in Pomerol and St-Emilion that fall into the investment category, such as Pétrus, Cheval Blanc, Ausone, Latour à Pomerol, Lafleur, Angélus, and Le Pin.

Investment cellars might also include Sauternes, such as Château d'Yquem and Rieussec, and Vintage Port from houses such as Taylor, Fonseca, Graham, Warre, and Noval. The investment wines of Burgundy are fewer in number, because the estates are far smaller and the market fragmented and complex. This area is dominated by the seven wines of the Domaine de la Romanée-Conti, followed by estates such as Comtes de Vogüé, Armand Rousseau, Henri Jayer (for past vintages), and Leflaive and Coche-Dury for white wine. The Rhône investment wines would be headed by the Côte Rôties of Guigal, and Châteauneuf-du-Papes from Rayas and Beaucastel.

California's red wines may be part of an investment cellar, and the wines of Harlan, Colgin, Caymus, Ridge, Heitz Martha's Vineyard, Stag's Leap, and Opus One would be most likely to feature, especially their top reserve wines. The one Australian wine with international investment value is Grange, while Sassicaia, Ornellaia, and Masseto lead the field in Italy, and Pingus and L'Ermita in Spain.

## VINTAGES ARE VITAL
For investment purposes, stick to very good vintages, but keep an open mind and observe developments. For instance, 1998 started as a much-touted year for Right Bank wines (St-Emilion and Pomerol), but now the classics from the Left Bank—Médoc and Pessac-Léognan—are also in demand, confirming their majestic status.

## THE AUCTION SCENE
Starting in 2006, this market has "taken off," as has the art market. There is clearly a large amount of disposable income available worldwide, and new collectors are very active in East Asia, Eastern Europe, South America, and even India. However, Western Europeans and North Americans remain faithful clients, and there is no doubt that some of the greatest collections in the world are currently to be found in the United States. At the highest level, the market is polarized on a limited amount of châteaux and top estates, and it is to be hoped that, eventually, some of the newest buyers at auction will realize that there are splendid wines outside of this small selection.

## AUTHENTICITY
More than ever before, vigilance is necessary when buying precious wines. Keynote requirements are verifiable provenance, excellent condition, and genuine authenticity. Only buy wines from impeccable sources, where stock is actually checked by experts.

Thirty years ago, many "trophy" wines had almost disappeared. Gems, frequently in large formats, such as Mouton 1945, Cheval Blanc 1947, Lafleur 1947, Margaux 1900, Pétrus in a variety of vintages, and Latour 1961, as well as Yquem 1921 and 19th-century Lafite—that is, the usual litany (plus Romanée-Conti and La Tâche in various sizes and years, and more recent Henri Jayer Burgundies)—were very rarely found, and when they were, it was usually in old family cellars in the region of origin and in a few old country estates in Europe. Now, they are "made to order" and quite prevalent. A recorked trophy bottle can become 100: cloning at its most efficient. They are generally bought by less experienced collectors who rightly wish to "experience" these mythical wines. They mostly taste quite good and are pronounced "amazingly youthful" (very accurate). Some are bought to impress or as an "investment," and then they are sold on and scattered even more widely.

Genuine old wines are not powerful, lusty, robust, and consistent. They are often light-textured, ephemeral, very inconsistent, and aging every day. For example, the fabulous old Montroses I tasted recently, direct from the château, showed more age than they did 10 years ago. Real old wines are often lingering, lacy, ethereal, magic; they are also often volatile, acid, and mushroomy. The "surgically altered" monsters out on the block are great brutes that never age. They have trout lips and scars under the hairline. I do not like them; nor do I like those making fortunes trading in them.

## BORDEAUX REIGNS SUPREME IN LONDON
The results for highly prized Bordeaux speak for themselves: in some instances, prices doubled in 2006 compared to 2005, most notably for the fabled 2000 vintage. However, prices for the 1998 vintage also progressed significantly, riding the wave of demand for the more expensive vintages. An indication of the surge in prices for the 2000 vintage can be gauged by the First Growths: Château Mouton Rothschild (£2,760 in 2004; £4,255 in spring 2007), Château Lafite (£2,990 in 2004; £5,750 in spring 2007), Château Margaux (£2,875 in 2004; £5,980 in spring 2007), Château Latour (£5,060 in 2004; £6,900 in spring 2007) and Château Haut-Brion (£2,185 in 2004; £3,910 in spring 2007). The 1998s have risen from a more modest base: Château Mouton Rothschild at £943 in 2004 to £1,840 in spring 2007; Château Lafite, £1,150 in 2004 to £2,875 in spring 2007; Château Margaux, £897 in 2004 to £1,610 in spring 2007; Château Latour, £805 in 2004 to £1,208 in spring 2007; and Château Haut-Brion, £1,725 in 2004 to £2,530 in spring 2007.* The Left Bank 1999s remain good value for drinking, and at the moment, top Médoc 1996s are the best buys for investment purposes.

Top Right Bank wines tell a different story entirely, with Château Cheval Blanc 1998 doubling in price between 2005 and 2006, from £2,070 per case to £4,140 per case. Pétrus 2000 achieved new heights in 2006 at £29,900 per dozen. Château Pétrus is a special case based on its highly individual taste and the small amount made. Astronomic price increases have occurred over the past years, in particular for the 1982 and the twin 1989/1990 vintages. Pétrus 1982 clocked in at £14,950 in 2004 and £29,900 in spring 2007, while both Pétrus 1989 and 1990 rose from £10,120 in 2004 to £27,600 in spring 2007.*

## THE AMERICAN AUCTION SCENE
The North American market has mirrored the growth of interest in wine in the UK, with many newer and younger buyers coming into the market for the first time. This younger generation of buyers (and drinkers) has flourished and become the dominant force at the auctions, leaving those with already significant collections to sit on the sidelines and smile as the value of their collections has increased, sometimes doubling in just a two-year period. While there has been an enormous growth of interest from newly affluent North American buyers (mostly people from the financial world, such as those from hedge funds, private equity, investment banking, and private wealth management), there has also been increased interest worldwide, particularly from Asia. These new collectors seem to have a very healthy appetite for the top-flight wines and are building up very substantial collections. Their interest is mostly focused on the top Bordeaux châteaux, Burgundy domaines, and Rhône producers—and only the best vintages, which leaves some excellent buys for less affluent collectors, who buy slightly lesser-known properties and from more modest vintages. There is always value in the marketplace, and this is particularly relevant now, since the prices of the very top wines have reached such a high that the wines on tiers just below are good value in comparison. One interesting point to note is the appetite for buying wines, from excellent provenance, in quantity. Sotheby's sold its first, and the world's first, million-dollar lot when 50 cases of Château Mouton Rothschild 1982 sold for $1.05 million, and another 25 cases were subsequently sold by private sale (from one collector to another).

*prices quoted are highest aggregate price (including buyer's premium) per case of 12 bottles or equivalent*

# THE TASTE OF WINE

*The difference between tasting and drinking is similar to test-driving a car you may buy and the relish of driving it afterward. One is a matter of concentration, as you seek out merits and faults, while the other is a more relaxed and enjoyable experience. Almost anyone can learn to taste wine.*

WHEN TASTING A WINE it is important to eliminate all distractions, especially comments made by others; it is all too easy to be swayed. The wine should be tasted and an opinion registered before any ensuing discussions. Even at professionally led tastings, the expert's job is not to dictate but to educate, to "lead from behind," putting into perspective other people's natural responses to smells or tastes through clear and concise explanation. The three "basics" of wine-tasting are sight, smell, and taste, known as "eye," "nose," and "palate."

## THE SIGHT, OR "EYE," OF A WINE

The first step is to assess the wine's limpidity, which should be perfectly clear. Many wines throw a deposit, but this is harmless if it settles to yield a bright and clear wine. If it is cloudy or hazy, the wine should be discarded. Tiny bubbles that appear on the bowl or cling persistently to the edge of the glass are perfectly acceptable in a few wines, such as Muscadet *sur lie* and Vinho Verde, but probably indicate a flaw in most other still wines, particularly if red and from classic Old World regions.

The next step is to swirl the wine gently around the glass. So-called "legs" or "tears," thin sinewy threads of wine that run down the side of the glass, may appear. Contrary to popular belief, they are not indicative of high glycerol content, but are simply the effect of alcohol on wine's viscosity, or the way the wine flows. The greater the alcohol content, the less free-flowing, or more viscous, the wine actually becomes.

### The color of wine

Natural light is best for observing a wine's color, the first clue to its identity once its condition has been assessed. Look at the wine against a white background, holding the glass at the bottom of the stem and tilting it away from you slightly. Red wines vary in color from *clairet*, which is almost rosé, to tones so dark and opaque that they seem black. White wines range from a colorless water-white to deep gold, although the majority are a light straw-yellow color. For some reason, there are very few rosé wines that are truly pink in color, the tonal range extending from blue-pink, through purple-pink, to orange-pink. Disregard any impression about a wine's color under artificial lighting because it will never be true—fluorescent light, for example, makes a red wine appear brown.

### Factors affecting color

The color and tonal variation of any wine, whether red, white, or rosé, is determined by the grape variety. It is also influenced by the ripeness of the actual grapes, the area of production, the method of vinification, and the age of the wine. Dry, light-bodied wines from cooler climates are the lightest in color, while fuller-bodied or sweeter-styled wines from hotter regions are the deepest. Youthful red wines usually have a purple tone, whereas young white wines may hint of green, particularly if they are from a cooler climate. The aging process involves a slow oxidation that has a browning effect similar to the discoloration of a peeled apple that has been exposed to the air.

## THE SMELL, OR "NOSE," OF A WINE

Whenever an experienced taster claims to be able to recognize in excess of 1,000 different smells, many wine lovers give up all hope of acquiring even the most basic tasting skills. Yet they should not be discouraged. Almost everybody can detect and distinguish over 1,000 different smells, the majority of which are ordinary, everyday odors. Ask anyone to write down all the

VISUAL EXAMINATION
*Unless it has an extreme color or hue, the appearance of a wine is the least interesting aspect of a tasting note for most readers, which is why most authors use color descriptions sparingly. The eye is, however, one of the most important sensory organs for professional tasters, since even the most subtle shade or nuance can provide numerous clues to the wine's identity.*

NOSING A WINE
*As we smell most flavors, rather than taste them, a good sniff tells us a lot about a wine. But refrain from continuously sniffing, as this will dull your sense of smell. Take one good sniff, then pause for thought. Do not rush on to tasting the wine. Remember that no smells are specific to wine—they can all be compared to something familiar, but you need time to work out what they are.*

smells they can recognize and most will be able to list several hundred without really trying. Yet a far greater number of smells are locked away in our brains waiting to be triggered.

The wine-smelling procedure is quite simple. Give the glass a good swirl, put your nose into the glass, and take a deep sniff. While it is essential to take a substantial sniff, it is not practicable to sniff the same wine again for at least two minutes. This is because each wine activates a unique pattern of nerve ends in the olfactory bulb; these nerve ends are like small candles that are snuffed out when activated and take a little time to reactivate. As a result, subsequent sniffs of the same smell can reveal less and less, yet it is perfectly feasible to smell different smells, therefore different wines, one after the other.

## THE TASTE, OR "PALATE," OF A WINE

As soon as one sniffs a wine the natural reaction is to taste it, but do this only after all questions concerning the nose have been addressed. The procedure is simple, although it may look and sound rather strange to the uninitiated. Take a good mouthful and draw air into the mouth through the wine; this makes a gurgling sound, but it is essential to do it in order to magnify the wine's volatile characteristics in the back of the throat.

The tongue itself reveals very little; sweetness is detected on its tip, sourness or acidity on the sides, bitterness at the back and top, and saltiness on the front and sides. Apart from these four basic taste perceptions, we smell tastes rather than taste them. Any food or drink emits odorous vapors in the mouth that are automatically conveyed to the roof of the nasal passages. Here the olfactory bulb examines, discerns, and catalogs them—as they originate from the palate the natural inclination is to perceive them as tastes. For many of us it is difficult to believe that we taste with an organ located behind the eyes at the top of the nose, but when we eat ice cream too quickly, we painfully experience precisely where the olfactory bulb is, because the chilly aromas of the ice cream literally freeze this acutely delicate sensory organ. The texture of a wine also influences its taste; the prickly tactile sensation of carbon dioxide, for example, heightens our perception of acidity, while increased viscosity softens it.

MAGNIFYING THE TASTE OF A WINE
*The tongue discerns only sweetness, sourness, bitterness, and saltiness. Every other "taste" we smell. By drawing air through a mouthful of wine, the volatilized aromas are taken into the back of the throat, where they are picked up by the olfactory bulb, which automatically analyzes them and transmits the information to the brain as various so-called flavors. (See also "Umami," Glossary p.639)*

SPITTING OUT
*When tasting a large number of wines, each mouthful should be ejected after due assessment to prevent alcohol from affecting the ability to taste. Yet some wine will remain, even after spitting out, coating the inner surface of the mouth, where it is absorbed directly into the bloodstream. Contrary to popular belief, the more you taste the better you taste, but it is always a race between the wine sharpening the palate and the alcohol dulling the brain!*

## QUALITY AND TASTE: WHY OPINIONS DIFFER

Whether you are a novice or a Master of Wine, it is always personal preference that is the final arbiter when you are judging wine. The most experienced tasters can often argue endlessly over the relative merits and demerits of certain wines.

We all know that quality exists, and more often than not agree which wines have it, and yet we are not able to define it. Lacking a solid definition, most experienced tasters would happily accept that a fine wine must have natural balance and finesse and show a definite, distinctive, and individual character within its own type or style. If we occasionally differ on the question of the quality of wine, should we disagree on what it tastes like? We may love or hate a wine, but surely the taste we perceive is the same?

Conveying specific taste characteristics from the mind of one person to that of another is difficult enough, whether one is writing a book or simply discussing a wine at a tasting. Much of this difficulty lies in the words we choose, but the problem is not confined to semantics. In a world of perfect communication, conveying impressions of taste would still be an inexact art because of the different threshold levels at which we pick up elementary tastes and smells, and because of the various tolerance levels at which we enjoy them. If individuals require different quantities of acidity, tannin, alcohol, sugar, esters, and aldehydes in a wine before actually detecting them, then the same wine has, literally, a different taste for each of us. In the unlikely event of people having the same threshold for every constituent and combination of constituents, disagreement would probably ensue because we also have different tolerance levels; therefore, some of us would enjoy what others dislike because we actually like the tastes and smells they dislike. Thresholds and tolerance levels vary enormously; the threshold for detecting sweetness, for example, varies by a factor of five, which explains the "sweet tooth" phenomenon, and there are an infinite number of tolerance levels. Apply this to every basic aroma and flavor, and it is surprising that we agree on the description of any wine.

# HOW TO ASSESS A WINE

*It would be impossible to answer many of the following questions without a degree of experience. Likewise, it would be difficult to identify a particular wine, or type of wine, having never tasted it. But your knowledge will increase with every tasting.*

## SIGHT

Look at the color. Is it deep or pale? Is there a positive quality to it, a specific hue that reminds you of a particular grape variety, the growing climate, or the area of production? Is the color vivid and youthful, or is there browning that might suggest its age? What does the rim, or meniscus, indicate? Does it retain the intensity of colour to the rim of the glass, which suggests a high-quality product, or does it fade to an unimpressive, watery finish?

## SMELL

If the first impression is very heady, is the wine fortified? (Classic fortified wines, such as port, sherry, and Madeira, do have easily recognizable characteristics, but it can still be difficult to distinguish between a robust wine with a naturally high alcohol level produced in a hot country and a fortified wine.) Does the wine have any distinctive aromas, or are they obscure or bland,

## A SAMPLE TASTING

This chart provides a few examples from a whole range of the possible options that are open in the complex business of tasting. It also demonstrates that it is possible to approach the task systematically and rationally. When tasting it is important to keep your options open until you have assessed the sight, smell, and taste of the wine. At each stage you should be seeking to confirm at least one of the possibilities that has arisen during the previous stage. Be confident and do not be afraid to back your own judgement—it is the only way to learn.

**SIGHT**
The clear, well-defined garnet color of medium intensity suggests only moderately hot climatic origins. The tinge of purple on the meniscus could indicate youth.

**SMELL**
This is dominated by the distinctive pear-drop aroma of *macération carbonique*, hallmark of all but the best *cru* Beaujolais. Often mistaken for the varietal aroma of Gamay (from which Beaujolais is made), the aroma is characteristic of all wines fermented in this way. If this is a Beaujolais, the color suggests something more serious than a lighter basic Beaujolais or Nouveau.

**TASTE**
The balance between fruit, acidity, and alcohol confirms that this is Beaujolais. The good depth of spicy-grapey fruit beneath the pervasive pear-drop character indicates that it is better than average.

**CONCLUSION**
**Grape variety** Gamay
**Region** Beaujolais
**Age** 2 to 3 years old
**Comment** Beaujolais Villages

**SIGHT**
Water-white, this wine has obvious cool climatic origins, although the tiny bubbles collecting on the glass suggest it could be a Vinho Verde. But the palest usually have a tell-tale hint of straw color. Probably a modest *Qualitätswein* from the Mosel region of Germany.

**SMELL**
This is not Vinho Verde. Its crisp, youthful, sherbet aroma is typical Mosel Riesling. Considering its color, the nose would confirm that this is probably a *Qualitätswein*, or a *Kabinett* at most, of a modest vintage, but from a very good grower who is possibly as high up as the Saar tributary.

**TASTE**
Youthful, tangy fruit, the flower of the Riesling is still evident. More flavor than expected, and a nice dry, piquant finish with a hint of peach on the aftertaste.

**CONCLUSION**
**Grape variety** Riesling
**Region** Mosel
**Age** about 18 to 24 months
**Comment** *Kabinett*, top grower

**SIGHT**
Intense, almost black color that is virtually opaque. Obviously from a thick-skinned grape variety like the Syrah, which has ripened under a very hot sun. Australia's Swan Valley or France's Rhône Valley? California?

**SMELL**
As intense on the nose as on the eye. Definitely Syrah, and judging by its spicy aroma with hints of herbal scrub, almost certainly from the northern Rhône. Australia and California can now be ruled out. More massive than complex, it must be from an exceptional vintage.

**TASTE**
Powerful and tannic, the spicy-fruit flavor is rich with blackberries, blackcurrants, plums, and cinnamon. Beginning to develop, but has a long way to go. This is a high-quality Rhône Syrah, but without quite the class of Hermitage, or the finesse of Côte Rôtie.

**CONCLUSION**
**Grape variety** Syrah
**Region** Cornas, Rhône Valley
**Age** about 5 years old
**Comment** top grower, great year

**SIGHT**
The brick-red color and watery meniscus immediately suggest a young Bordeaux of *petit-château* quality. But first impressions can deceive—more evidence is needed.

**SMELL**
An attractive violet aroma with a restrained hint of soft, spicy fruit. Nothing contradicts my impressions, although the lack of blackcurrant suggests that the wine is a Bordeaux with a high proportion of Merlot rather than Cabernet Sauvignon.

**TASTE**
The palate perfectly reflects the nose. This is a medium-bodied, modest claret of no great age. However, the fruit is well rounded and the soft tannin structure indicates that in little more than another 2, possibly 3, years it will be at its peak.

**CONCLUSION**
**Grape variety** Merlot-dominated blend
**Region** Bordeaux
**Age** 2 years old
**Comment** *petit château* or good generic

or simply reticent? Does the wine smell as youthful or as mature as it appears to the eye? Is it smooth and harmonious, suggesting the wine is ready to drink? If so, should it be drunk? If it is not ready, can you estimate when it will be? Is there a recognizable grape variety aroma? Are there any creamy or vanilla hints to suggest that it has been fermented or aged in new oak? If so, which region ages such wine in oak? Is it a simple wine or is there a degree of complexity? Are there any hints as to the area of production? Is its quality obvious or do you need confirmation on the palate?

## TASTE

This should reflect the wine's smell and therefore confirm any judgements that you have already made. Should. But human organs are fallible, not least the brain, so keep an open mind. Be prepared to accept contradiction as well as confirmation. Ask yourself all the questions you asked on the nose, but before you do, ask what your palate tells you about the acidity, sweetness, and alcoholic strength.

If you are tasting a red wine, its tannin content can be revealing. Tannin is derived from the grape's skin, and the darker and thicker it is, and the longer the juice macerates with the skins, the more tannin there will be in the wine. A great red wine will contain so much tannin that it will literally pucker the mouth, while early-drinking wines will contain little.

If you are tasting a sparkling wine, on the other hand, its mousse, or effervescence, will give extra clues. The strength of the mousse will determine the style—whether it is fully sparkling, semi-sparkling, or merely *pétillant* – and the size of the bubbles will indicate the quality; the smaller they are, the better.

## CONCLUSION

Just try to name the grape variety and area of origin, and give some indication of the age and quality of the wine. Wise tasters will not risk their credibility by having a stab at anything more specific, such as the producer or vineyard, unless he or she is 100 percent sure. In the Master of Wine examination, marks are given for correct rationale, even if the conclusion that is drawn is wrong, while it has been known for a candidate to name the wine in precise detail but, because of defective reasoning, to receive no score at all. Wine tasting is not a matter of guessing. It is about deduction, and getting it wrong should be encouraged because that is the only way to learn.

**SIGHT**
This distinctive yellow-gold color retains its intensity to the rim. Various possibilities: a sweet wine, a full-bodied dry wine, a mature wine, or something obscure like Retsina. If none of these, it could be a Gewürztraminer.

**SMELL**
Gewürztraminer! Full, rich, and spicy, the aroma hits you between the eyes and the first instinct is to think of Alsace. Usually you will be right, but bear in mind the possibility of a top grower in the Rheinpfalz or Austria. If the aroma were muted, it might be Italian; if exotic, Californian or Australian. This, however, seems to be a classic example of a ripe Alsace vintage of perhaps 4 years of age.

**TASTE**
A rich-flavored wine; full, fat, and fruity with well-developed spice and a soft, succulent finish. Evidently made from very ripe grapes.

**CONCLUSION**
**Grape variety** Gewürztraminer
**Region** Alsace
**Age** about 4 to 5 years old
**Comment** very good quality

**SIGHT**
Stunning color, more distinctive even than the Gewürztraminer, the old gold immediately suggests a full, rich, and probably very sweet wine. Sauternes springs to mind, but Austria, or even an oddity from Australia are also possible.

**SMELL**
This has the amazingly full, rich, and opulent nose of a botrytized wine. Anyone who dislikes sweet wine should smell a wine like this before giving up on it altogether. A touch of creamy-spicy oak rules out Austria and its maturity, probably between 10 and 15 years, probably disposes of Australia.

**TASTE**
Everything is here from peaches, pineapple, and cream to the honeyed aromatics of a fairly mature wine. Only a classic Sauternes can have such intense flavors, yet possess such great finesse.

**CONCLUSION**
**Grape variety** mostly Sémillon
**Region** Sauternes
**Age** about 15 years old
**Comment** *Premier cru*, great vintage

**SIGHT**
The orange-pink of this wine almost certainly pins it to Provence or Tavel, although, if the orange hue is not indicative of the style and vinification of the wine, it could be almost any over-the-hill rosé.

**SMELL**
Put the dunce's hat on and stand in the corner! The high-toned Pinot Noir aroma dismisses the firm conviction of a Tavel or Provence rosé. But what is it? It is not oxidized, so it cannot be an otherwise obvious wine that has gone over. Is the orange hue a clue to its origin? More information is needed; must taste the wine.

**TASTE**
Definitely Burgundian, but with a very distinctive, piquant Pinot Noir taste. At its peak now, but certainly not on the way down. By eliminating what it cannot be, only Rosé de Marsannay fits the bill.

**CONCLUSION**
**Grape variety** Pinot Noir
**Region** Burgundy
**Age** 4 to 5 years old
**Comment** medium quality

**SIGHT**
This sparkling wine has an attractive, lively, lemon-yellow color. Not young, but not old, its mousse is evident, but its power and size of bubble cannot be assessed without tasting it. Its star-bright limpidity just makes it look like a fine wine.

**SMELL**
Its quality is immediately evident, with the autolytic characteristics of a wine with several years on its first cork (in contact with its lees prior to disgorgement), which eliminates every possibility other than a fine Champagne. It has the zippy tang of ripe Chardonnay grapes. This must be a Champagne *blanc de blancs* with a high proportion of wine from the Côte des Blancs.

**TASTE**
A gently persistent mousse of ultra-fine bubbles. The fresh, lively flavor has a long finish but needs five years more to reach perfection.

**CONCLUSION**
**Grape variety** Chardonnay
**Region** Champagne
**Age** about 5 years old
**Comment** top quality

# TERROIR

*The same grape grown in the same area can make two totally different wines, owing to seemingly inconsequential factors such as a different soil or aspect. And yet different grapes grown continents apart may produce two wines that are very similar.*

THERE ARE CERTAIN, CONSTANT FACTORS that affect the taste and quality of wine. These include location; climate, which determines the ability to grow grapes; vintage, the vagaries of which can make or break a harvest; aspect, responsible for enhancing or negating local conditions; and soil. All these factors are discussed in more detail below and can be classified as elements of *terroir*. Also important, of course, are viticulture, because the cultivation techniques used can stretch or concentrate varietal character (*see* pp.19–22); vinification, which, like cooking methods, can produce a range of options from the same basic ingredient (*see* pp.25–31); the winemaker, the idiosyncratic joker in the pack; and grape variety—always the most important factor (*see* pp.35–45).

## LOCATION
The location of a vineyard is fundamental in determining whether its climate is suitable for viticulture. Virtually all the world's wine-producing areas, in both hemispheres, are located in the temperate zones between 30° and 50° latitude, where the annual mean temperature is between 10°C (50°F) and 20°C (68°F). The most northerly vineyards of Germany are at the outermost limit of this range, between 50° and 51° latitude (almost 53° if we include the scattered vineyards of former East Germany), but they survive because of the continental climatic influence, which assures hotter summers. The shorter days also retard the cane growth in favor of fruit maturity, allowing the grapes to ripen before the harsh continental winter. Interestingly, most of the world's finest wines are produced in west-coast locations, which tend to be cooler and less humid than east-coast areas. Forests and mountain ranges protect the vines from wind and rain. A relatively close proximity to forests and large masses of water can influence the climate through transpiration and evaporation, providing welcome humidity in times of drought, although they can also encourage rot. Thus some factors can have both positive and negative effects.

APPLE TREE IN CALVADOS, NORMANDY
*Methods of vine-training are applicable to other cultivated fruits, as this spur-trained apple tree in Calvados illustrates.*

## CLIMATE
Climate and weather are the most important factors that influence the growth of grapes for high-quality wines. Climate is determined by geographical location, whereas weather is the result of how nature decides to affect that climate on a daily basis. In other words, climate is what it should be, weather is what it is. A grower must select a region with an amenable climate and hope that nature does not inflict too many anomalies.

Although some vines survive under extreme conditions, most—and all classic—winemaking vines are confined to two relatively narrow climatic bands between 30° and 50° latitude and require a combination of heat, sunshine, rain, and frost.

## HEAT
Vines will not provide grapes suitable for winemaking if the annual mean temperature is less than 50°F (10°C). The ideal

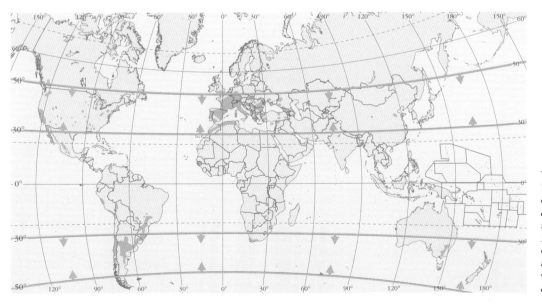

THE WORLD OF WINE
*The most important areas of cultivation in both the northern and southern hemispheres lie mainly between latitudes 30° and 50°. However, there are a number of smaller winemaking areas closer to the equator. Indeed, equatorial* vinifera *wines are produced in tiny quantities in Kenya and Peru.*

mean temperature is 57° to 59°F (14° to 15°C), with an average of no less than 66°F (19°C) in the summer and 30°F (-1°C) in the winter. In order for the vines to produce a good crop of ripe grapes, the minimum heat-summation, measured in "degree-days" with an average of above 50°F (10°C) over the growing season, is 1,800° (using °F to calculate) or 1,000° (using °C to calculate). Below are the degree-day totals over the growing season for a variety of vineyards from around the world.

| AREA/REGION | DEGREE-DAYS FAHRENHEIT (CELSIUS) |
|---|---|
| Trier, Mosel, Germany | 1,700 (945) |
| Bordeaux, France | 2,375 (1,320) |
| McLaren Vale, South Australia | 2,425 (1,350) |
| Russian River, California | 3,600 (2,000) |

## SUNSHINE
While light is required for photosynthesis, the most important biological process of green plants, there is sufficient light for this even in cloudy conditions. For vinegrowing, however, sunshine is needed more for its heat than its light. Approximately 1,300 hours is the minimum amount of sunshine required per growing season, but 1,500 hours is preferable.

## RAINFALL
A vine requires 27 inches (68 centimeters) of rain per year. Ideally, most of the rain should fall in the spring and the winter, but some is needed in the summer too. Vines can survive with less water if the temperature is higher, although rain in warm conditions is more harmful than rain in cool conditions. A little rain a few days before the harvest will wash the grapes of any sprays, and is therefore ideal if followed by sun and a gentle, drying breeze. Torrential rain, however, can split berries and cause fungus.

Below are annual rainfall figures for a variety of vineyards from around the world.

| AREA/REGION | RAINFALL |
|---|---|
| McLaren Vale, South Australia | 24 in (60 cm) |
| Trier, Mosel, Germany | 26 in (65 cm) |
| Bordeaux, France | 36 in (90 cm) |
| Russian River, California | 53 in (135 cm) |

PREPARING FOR RAIN
*In southern Spain, furrows are dug horizontally between rows of vines to provide channels for any rain.*

## FROST
Surprising as it may seem, some frost is desirable, providing it is in the winter, since it hardens the wood and kills spores and pests that the bark may be harboring. However, frost can literally kill a vine, particularly at bud-break and flowering (*see* p.23).

## VINTAGE
The anomalies of a vintage can bring disaster to reliable vineyards and produce miracles in unreliable ones. A vintage is made by weather, as opposed to climate. While the climate may be generally good, uncommon weather conditions can sometimes occur. In addition to this, the vintage's annual climatic adjustment can be very selective; on the edge of a summer hail storm, for example, some vineyards may be destroyed and produce no wine at all, while others are virtually unharmed and produce good wine. Vines situated between the two might be left with a partial crop of fruit that could result in wines of an exceptional quality if given a further two to three months of warm sunshine before the harvest, because reduced yields per vine produce grapes with a greater concentration of flavor.

## CLIMATIC CONDITIONS

### Favorable
• A fine, long summer with warm, rather than hot, sunshine ensures that the grapes ripen slowly. Such weather leads to a good acid–sugar balance.

• A dry, sunny fall is essential for ripening grapes and avoiding rot; but, again, it must not be too hot.

• The winter months from November to February (May to August in the southern hemisphere) are climatically flexible, with the vine able to withstand temperatures as low as -4°F (-20°C) and anything other than absolute flood or drought.

• Within the above parameters, the climate must suit the viticultural needs of specific grape varieties; for example a cooler climate for Riesling, hotter for Syrah, and so on.

### Unfavorable
• Major dangers are frost, hail, and strong winds, all of which can denude a vine and are particularly perilous when the vine is flowering or the grapes are ripening and at their most susceptible.

• Rain and/or cold temperatures during the flowering may cause imperfect fertilization, which results in a physiological disorder called *millerandage*. The affected grapes contain no seeds and will be small and only partially developed when the rest of the cluster is fully matured.

• Persistent rain at, or immediately before, the harvest can lead to rot or dilute the wine, both of which can cause vinification problems.

• Sun is not often thought of as a climatic danger, but, just as frost can be beneficial to the vine, so sun can be harmful. Too much sun encourages the sap to go straight past the embryo grape clusters to the leaves and shoots. This causes a physiological disorder called *coulure*, which is often confused with *millerandage*. It is totally different, although both disorders can appear together due to the vagaries of climate. Most seeds suffering from *coulure* drop to the ground, and those that remain do not develop.

• Excessive heat during the harvest rapidly decreases the acid level of grape juice and makes the grapes too hot, creating problems during fermentation. It is especially difficult to harvest grapes at an acceptable temperature in very hot areas, such as South Africa. As a result, some wine estates harvest the grapes at night when the grapes are at their coolest.

## ASPECT

The aspect of a vineyard refers to its general topography—which direction the vines face, the angle and height of any slope, and so on—and how this interrelates with the climate.

There are few places in the world where winemaking grapes—as opposed to table grapes—are successfully grown under the full effect of a prevailing climate. The basic climatic requirements of the vine are usually achieved by manipulating local conditions, keeping sunshine, sun strength, drainage, and temperature in mind.

### SUNSHINE

South-facing slopes (north-facing in the southern hemisphere) attract more hours of sunshine and are therefore cultivated in cooler areas. In hotter regions, the opposite facing slopes tend to be cultivated.

### SUN STRENGTH AND DRAINAGE

Because of the angle, vines on a slope absorb the greater strength of the sun's rays. In temperate regions the sun is not directly overhead, even at noon, and therefore its rays fall more or less perpendicular to a slope. Conversely, on flat ground the sun's rays are dissipated across a wider area, so their strength is diluted. (The plains are also susceptible to flooding and have soils that are usually too fertile, yielding larger crops of correspondingly inferior fruit). Lake- and river-valley slopes are particularly well suited for vines because they also receive rays reflected from the water.

A sloping vineyard also affords natural drainage. However, hilltop vines are too exposed to wind and rain and their presence, instead of a forest covering, deprives vines below of protection. Forested hilltops not only supply humidity in times of drought, but absorb the worst of any torrential rain that could wash away the topsoil below.

### TEMPERATURE

While slopes are very desirable sites, it must be remembered that every 330 feet (100 meters) above sea level, the temperature falls 1.8°F (1°C). This can result in an extra 10 to 15 days being needed for the grapes to ripen and, because of the extra time, the acidity will be relatively higher. Thus a vineyard's altitude can be a very effective way of manipulating the quality and character of its crop. Riverside and lakeside slopes also have the advantages of reflected sunlight and the water acting as a heat reservoir, releasing heat at night that has been stored during the day. This not only reduces sudden drops in temperature that can be harmful, but also the risk of frost. However, depressions in slopes and the very bottoms of valleys collect cold air, are frost-prone, and retard growth.

## SOIL

Topsoil is of primary importance to the vine because it supports most of its root system, including most of the feeding network. Subsoil always remains geologically true. Main roots penetrate several layers of subsoil, whose structure influences drainage, the root system's depth, and its ability to collect minerals.

The metabolism of the vine is well known, and the interaction between it and the soil is generally understood. The ideal medium in which to grow vines for wine production is one that has a relatively thin topsoil and an easily penetrable (and therefore well-drained) subsoil with good water-retaining characteristics. The vine does not like "wet feet," so drainage is vital, yet it needs access to moisture, so access to a soil with good water-retention is also important. The temperature potential of a soil, its heat-retaining capacity, and its heat-reflective characteristics affect the ripening period of grapes: warm soils (gravel, sand, loam) advance ripening, while cold soils (clay) retard it. Chalk falls between these two extremes, and dark, dry soils are obviously warmer than light, wet soils. High-pH (alkaline) soils, such as chalk, encourage the vine's metabolism to produce sap and grape juice with a relatively high acid content. The continual use of fertilizers has lowered the pH level of some viticultural areas in France, and these are now producing wines of higher pH (less acidity).

### THE MINERAL REQUIREMENTS OF THE VINE

Just as various garden flowers, shrubs, and vegetables perform better in one soil type as opposed to another, so too do different grape varieties. Certain minerals essential to plant growth are found in various soils. Apart from hydrogen and oxygen (which are supplied as water) the most important soil nutrients are nitrogen, which is used in the production of a plant's green matter; phosphate, which directly encourages root development and indirectly promotes an earlier ripening of the grapes (an excess inhibits the uptake of magnesium); potassium, which improves the vine's metabolism, enriches the sap, and is essential for the development of the following year's crop; iron, which is indispensable for photosynthesis (a lack of iron will cause chlorosis); magnesium, which is the only mineral constituent of the chlorophyll molecule (lack of magnesium also causes chlorosis); and calcium, which feeds the root system, neutralizes acidity, and helps create a friable soil structure (although an excess of calcium restricts the vine's ability to extract iron from the soil and therefore causes chlorosis). For information on specific soil types, *see* pp.17–18.

TERRACED VINEYARDS OVERLOOKING THE RHINE
*Vines beside bodies of water benefit from the sun's rays reflecting off the water, an advantage in areas where the climate is cooler.*

HILLS NEAR SANCERRE
*In the spring, vineyards give the rolling countryside in France's Loire Valley a speckled appearance. Most soils in the area are dominated by clay or limestone.*

# GUIDE TO VINEYARD SOILS

*To the wine amateur, the details of geology are not always important; what matters is how soil affects the growth of vines. If one clay soil is heavier or more silty, sandy, or calcareous, that is relevant. But there is enough jargon used when discussing wine to think of mixing it with rock-speak.*

**Aeolian soil** Sediments deposited by wind (e.g. loess).

**Albariza** White-surfaced soil formed by diatomaceous deposits, found in southern Spain.

**Alluvial deposits** (noun—alluvium) Material that has been transported by river and deposited. Most alluvial soils contain silt, sand, and gravel, and are highly fertile.

**Aqueous rocks** One of the three basic rock forms (*see* **Rock**). Also called sedimentary or stratified.

**Arenaceous rocks** Formed by the deposits of coarse-grained particles, usually siliceous and often decomposed from older rocks (e.g. sandstone).

**Argillaceous soils** This term covers a group of sedimentary soils, commonly clays, shales, mudstones, siltstones, and marls.

**Basalt material** accounts for as much as 90 percent of all lava-based volcanic rocks. It contains various minerals, is rich in lime and soda, but not quartz, the most abundant of all minerals, and it is poor in potash.

**Bastard soil** A *bordelais* name for medium-heavy, sandy-clay soil of variable fertility.

**Boulbènes** A *bordelais* name for a very fine siliceous soil that is easily compressed and hard to work. This "beaten" earth covers part of the Entre-Deux-Mers plateau.

**Boulder** *See* **Particle size**

**Calcareous clay** Argillaceous soil with carbonate of lime content that neutralizes the clay's intrinsic acidity. Its low temperature also delays ripening, so wines produced on this type of soil tend to be more acidic.

**Calcareous soil** Any soil, or mixture of soils, with an accumulation of calcium and magnesium carbonates. Essentially alkaline, it promotes the production of acidity in grapes, although the pH of each soil will vary according to its level of "active" lime. Calcareous soils are cool, with good water retention. With the exception of calcareous clays (*see* above), they allow the vine's root system to penetrate deeply and provide excellent drainage.

**Carbonaceous soil** Soil that is derived from rotting vegetation under anaerobic conditions. The most common carbonaceous soils are peat, lignite, coal, and anthracite.

**Chalk** A type of limestone, chalk is a soft, cool, porous, brilliant-white, sedimentary, alkaline rock that encourages grapes with a relatively high acidity level. It also allows the vine's roots to penetrate and provides excellent drainage, while at the same time retaining sufficient moisture for nourishment. One of the few finer geological points that should be adhered to is that which distinguishes chalk from the numerous hard limestone rocks that do not possess the same physical properties.

**Clay** A fine-grained argillaceous compound with malleable, plastic characteristics and excellent water-retention properties. It is, however, cold, acid, offers poor drainage, and, because of its cohesive quality, hard to work. An excess of clay can stifle the vine's root system, but a proportion of small clay particles mixed with other soils can be advantageous.

**Clayey-loam** A very fertile version of loam, but heavy to work under wet conditions with a tendency to become waterlogged.

**Cobble** *See* **Particle size**

**Colluvial deposits** (noun—colluvium) Weathered material transported by gravity or hill-wash.

**Crasse de fer** Iron-rich hardpan found in the Libournais area of France. Also called *machefer*.

**Crystalline** May either be igneous (e.g. granite) or metamorphic.

**Dolomite** A calcium-magnesium carbonate rock. Many limestones contain dolomite.

**Feldspar** or **Felspar** One of the most common minerals, feldspar is a white- or rose-colored silicate of either potassium-aluminum or sodium-calcium-aluminum and is present in a number of rocks, including granite and basalt.

**Ferruginous clay** Iron-rich clay.

**Flint** A siliceous stone that stores and reflects heat, and is often associated with a certain "gun-flint" smell that sometimes occurs in wines, although this is not actually proven and may simply be the taster's auto-suggestion.

**Galestro** Rocky, schistous soil commonly found in most of Tuscany's best vineyards.

**Glacial moraine** A gritty scree that has been deposited by glacial action.

**Gneiss** A coarse-grained form of granite.

**Granite** A hard, mineral-rich rock that warms quickly and retains its heat. Granite contains 40 to 60 percent quartz and 30 to 40 percent potassium feldspar, plus mica or hornblende, and various other minerals. It has a high pH, which reduces wine acidity. Thus, in Beaujolais, it is the best soil for the acidic Gamay grape. It is important to note that a soil formed from granite is a mixture of sand (partly derived from a disintegration of quartz and partly from the decomposition of feldspar with either mica or hornblende), clay, and various carbonates or silicates derived from the weathering of feldspar, mica, or hornblende.

**Gravel** A wide-ranging term that covers siliceous pebble of various sizes that are loose, granular, airy, and afford excellent drainage. Infertile, it encourages the vine to send its roots down deep in search of nutrients. Gravel beds above limestone subsoils produce wines with markedly more acidity than those above clay.

GRAVEL
*Château de France, Leognan, Gironde.*

**Greywacke** Argillaceous rocks that could have been formed as recently as a few thousand years ago by rivers depositing mudstone, quartz, and feldspar. Commonly found in Germany, South Africa, and New Zealand.

**Gypsum** Highly absorbent, hydrated calcium-sulfate that was formed during the evaporation of seawater.

**Gypsiferous marl** A marly soil permeated with Keuper or Muschelkalk gypsum fragments, which improve the soil's heat-retention and water-circulation properties.

**Hardpan** A dense layer of clay that forms if the subsoil is more clayey than the topsoil at certain depths. Because hardpans are impermeable to both water and roots, they are not desirable too close to the surface, but may provide an easily reachable watertable if located deep down. A sandy, iron-rich hardpan known as ironpan is commonly found in parts of Bordeaux.

**Hornblende** A silicate of iron, aluminum, calcium, and magnesium, it constitutes the main mineral found in basalt, and is a major component of granite and gneiss.

**Humus** Organic material that contains bacteria and other microorganisms capable of converting complex chemicals into simple plant foods. Humus makes soil fertile. Without it, soil is nothing more than finely ground rock.

**Igneous rock** One of the three basic rock forms (*see* **Rock**), igneous rocks are formed from molten or partially molten material. Most igneous rocks are crystalline.

**Ironpan** A sandy, iron-rich hardpan.

**Keuper** Often used when discussing wines in Alsace, Keuper is a stratigraphic name for the Upper Triassic period, and can mean marl (varicolored, saliferous gray or gypsiferous gray) or limestone (ammonoid).

**Kimmeridgian soil** A grayish-colored limestone originally identified in, and so named after, the village of Kimmeridge in Dorset, England. A sticky, calcareous clay containing this limestone is often called Kimmeridgian clay.

**Lignite** The "brown coal" of Germany and the "black gold" of Champagne, this is a brown

CHALK
*Pristine white chalk on the Côtes des Blancs.*

carbonaceous material intermediate between coal and peat. Warm and very fertile, it is mined and used as a natural fertilizer in Champagne.

**Limestone** Any sedimentary rock consisting essentially of carbonates. With the exception of chalk, few limestones are white, with gray- and buff-colored probably the most commonly found limestone in wine areas. The hardness and water retention of this rock varies, but being alkaline it generally encourages the production of grapes with a relatively high acidity level.

**Loam** A warm, soft, crumbly soil with roughly equal proportions of clay, sand, and silt. It is perfect for large-cropping wines of mediocre quality, but too fertile for fine wines.

**Loess** An accumulation of wind-borne, mainly silty material, sometimes calcareous, but usually weathered and decalcified. It warms up relatively quickly and also has good water-retention properties.

**Machefer** *See* **Crasse de fer**

**Marl** A cold, calcareous clay that delays ripening and adds acidity to wine.

**Marlstone** Clayey limestone that has a similar effect to marl.

**Metamorphic rocks** One of the three basic categories of rock (*see* **Rock**), it is caused by great heat or pressure, often both.

**Mica** A generic name encompassing various silicate minerals, usually in a fine, decomposed-rock format.

**Millstone** Siliceous, iron-rich, sedimentary rock.

**Moraine** *See* **Glacial moraine**

**Mudstone** A sedimentary soil similar to clay but without its plastic characteristics.

**Muschelkalk** Often used when discussing wines in Alsace, Muschelkalk is a stratigraphic name for the Middle Triassic period, and can mean anything from sandstone (shelly, dolomitic, calcareous, clayey, pink, yellow, or millstone) to marl (varicolored or fissile), dolomite, limestone (crinoidal or gray), and shingle.

**Oolite** A type of limestone.

**Oolith** A term used for small, round, calcareous pebbles that have grown through fusion of very tiny particles.

**Palus** A *bordelais* name for a very fertile soil of modern alluvial origin that produces medium-quality, well-colored, robust wines.

**Particle size** The size of a rock determines its descriptive name. No handful of soil will contain particles of a uniform size, unless it has been commercially graded, of course, so all such descriptions can only be guessed at, but it is worth noting what they should be, otherwise you will have nothing to base your guesses on. According to the Wentworth-Udden

scale, they are: boulder (greater than 256mm), cobble (64mm–256mm), pebble (4mm–64mm), gravel (2mm–4mm), sand (1/16mm–2mm), silt (1/256mm–1/16mm) and clay (smaller than 1/256mm). Notice that even by this precise scale, Wentworth and Udden have allowed overlaps, thus a 1/16mm particle might either be sand or silt and, of course, sub-divisions are possible within each group, as there is such a thing as fine, medium, or coarse sand and even gritty silt.

**Pebble** *See* **Particle size**

**Perlite** A fine, powdery, light, and lustrous substance of volcanic origin with similar properties to diatomaceous earth.

**Porphyry** A colored igneous rock with high pH.

**Precipitated salts** A sedimentary deposit. Water charged with acid or alkaline material, under pressure of great depth, dissolves various mineral substances from rocks on the seabed, which are then held in solution. When the water flows to a place of no great depth or is drained away or evaporates, the pressure is reduced, the minerals are no longer held in solution, and precipitate in deposits that may be just a few inches or several thousand yards deep. There are five groups: oxides, carbonates, sulfates, phosphates, and chlorides.

**Pudding stones** A term used for a large, heat-retaining conglomerate of pebbles.

**Quartz** The most common and abundant mineral found in various sizes and in almost all soils, although sand and coarse silt contain the largest amount. Quartz has a high pH, which reduces wine acidity, but quartz that is pebble-sized or larger, stores and reflects heat, which increases alcohol potential.

**Red earth** *See* **Terra rossa**

**Rock** A rock may be loosely described as a mass of mineral matter. There are three basic types of rock: igneous, metamorphic, and sedimentary (or aqueous or stratified).

**Sand** Tiny particles of weathered rocks and minerals that retain little water, but constitute a warm, airy soil that drains well and is supposedly phylloxera-free.

**Sandstone** Sedimentary rock composed of sand-sized particles that have either been formed by pressure or bound by various iron minerals.

**Sandy-loam** Warm, well-drained, sand-dominated loam that is easy to work and suitable for early-cropping grape varieties.

**Schist** Heat-retaining, coarse-grain, laminated, crystalline rock rich in potassium and magnesium, but poor in nitrogen and organic substances.

**Scree** Synonymous with colluvium deposits.

**Sedimentary rock** One of the three basic rock forms (*see* **Rock**), it includes arenaceous (e.g. sandstone), argillaceous (e.g. clay), calcareous (e.g. limestone), carbonaceous (e.g. peat, lignite, or coal), siliceous (e.g. quartz), and the five groups of precipitated salts, (oxides, carbonates, sulfates, phosphates, and chlorides). Sedimentary rocks are also called aqueous or stratified.

**Shale** Heat-retaining, fine-grain, laminated, moderately fertile sedimentary rock. Shale can turn into slate under pressure.

**Shingle** Pebble- or gravel-sized particle rounded by water-action.

**Siliceous soil** A generic term for acid rock of a crystalline nature. It may be organic (flint and kieselguhr) or inorganic (quartz) and have good heat retention, but no water retention unless found in a finely ground form in silt, clay, and

SLATE
*Slate soil of the Mosel valley.*

other sedimentary soils. Half of the Bordeaux region is covered with siliceous soils.

**Silt** A very fine deposit, with good water retention. Silt is more fertile than sand, but is cold and offers poor drainage.

**Slate** Hard, dark gray, fine-grain, platelike rock formed under pressure from clay, siltstone, shale, and other sediments. It warms up quickly, retains its heat well, and is responsible for many fine wines, most notably from the Mosel.

**Steige** A type of schist found on the north side of Andlau in Alsace, it has metamorphosed with the Andlau granite and is particularly hard and slaty. It has mixed with the granitic sand from the top of the Grand Cru Kastelberg and makes a dark, stony soil.

**Stone** This word should be used with rock types, such as limestone and sandstone, but is often used synonymously with pebble.

**Stratified rock** One of the three basic rock forms (*see* **Rock**), also called sedimentary or aqueous.

**Terra rossa** A red, claylike, sometimes flinty sedimentary soil deposited after carbonate has been leached out of limestone. It is often known as "Red earth."

**Tufa** Various vent-based volcanic rocks, the chalktufa of the Loire being the most important viticulturally speaking.

**Volcanic soils** Derived from two sources, volcanic soils are lava-based (the products of volcanic flow) and vent-based (material blown into the atmosphere). Some 90 percent of lava-based rocks and soils are comprised of basalt, while others include andesite, pitchstone, rhyolite, and trachyte. Vent-based matter has either been ejected as molten globules, cooled in the air, and dropped to Earth as solid particles (pumice), or as solid material and fractured through the explosive force with which it was flung (tufa).

PUDDING STONE
*Large stones (galettes), Château de Beaucastel, in Châteauneuf-du-Pape.*

TERRA ROSSA
*The red soil of Wynns, Coonawarra, South Australia.*

# VITICULTURE

*While it is the variety of grape that determines the basic flavor of a wine, it is the way in which the variety is grown that has the most profound effect on the quality of the wine.*

IN VINE TRAINING, it is absolutely crucial to ensure that no cane ever touches the ground. Should a cane find its way to the ground, its natural inclination is to send out suckers that will put down roots. Within two or three years the majority of the grafted vine's (*see* Phylloxera, p.35) above-ground network would be dependent not on grafted roots, but on the regenerated root system of the producing vine. Not only would this have the effect of putting the vine at the mercy of phylloxera, but, ironically, that part of the vine still receiving its principal nourishment from the grafted hybrid rootstock would send out its own shoots and, unchecked by any sort of pruning, these would produce hybrid fruit. Therefore, the fundamental reason for training and pruning a vine is to avoid phylloxera and to ensure that the purity of the fruiting stock is maintained.

The manner in which a vine is trained will guide the size, shape, and height of the plant toward reaping maximum benefits from the local conditions of aspect and climate. Vines can be trained high to avoid ground frost, or low to hug any heat that may be reflected by stony soils at night. There may be a generous amount of space between rows to attract the sun and avoid humidity. On the other hand, vines may be intensively cultivated to form a canopy of foliage to avoid too much sun.

## STYLES OF VINE TRAINING

Within the two basic systems of cane training and spur training, hundreds of different styles are employed, each developed for a reason, and all having their own advantages and disadvantages. In order to discern the style used in a particular vineyard, it is always best to look at the vines between late fall and early spring when the branches are not camouflaged with leaves. In the illustrations below, which are not drawn to scale, vines are shown as they appear during their winter dormancy, with the following season's fruiting canes shown in green. For cane-trained systems, a green-brown tint has been used to pick out the one-year-old wood used as next season's main branch.

### Bush vine—*Spur-training system*

An unsupported version of the Gobelet system (*see* below left), the term "bush vine" originated in Australia, where a few old vineyards—usually planted with Grenache—are still trained in this fashion. Bush vines are traditional in Beaujolais (where both supported and unsupported methods are referred to as Gobelet) and they are commonly found throughout the most arid areas of the Mediterranean. Being unsupported, the canes often flop downward when laden with fruit, giving the vine a sprawling, straggly look. In the Beaujolais *crus*, the total number of canes on a vine is restricted to between three and five, but in other, less controlled, wine areas a bush vine may have as many as 10 canes. This method is only suitable for training low-vigor vines.

### Chablis—*Spur-training system*

As the name implies, this style of vine training was originally developed in the Chablis district, although the method employed there now is, in fact, the Guyot Double. Champagne is the most important winemaking region to employ the Chablis system for training vines; there, it is used for more than 90 percent of all the Chardonnay grown. Either three, four, or five permanent branches may be cultivated, each one being grown at yearly intervals. This results in a three-year-old vine (the minimum age for AOC Champagne) having three branches, a four-year-old having four branches, and so forth. The distance between each

---

## BASIC SYSTEMS OF VINE TRAINING

There are two basic systems of vine training, cane training and spur training, of which there are many local variations. Cane-trained vines have no permanent branch because all but one of the strongest canes (which will be kept for next season's main branch) are pruned back each year to provide a vine consisting of almost entirely new growth. Apart from the trunk, the oldest wood on a cane-trained vine is the main branch and that is only ever one year old. This system gives a good spread of fruit over a large area, and allows easier regulation of annual production, because the number of fruiting buds can be increased or decreased. With spur training there is no annual replacement of the main branch, thus a solid framework is formed. It is easy, therefore, to know which basic training system has been applied to a vine simply by looking at the main branch. Even if you cannot recognize the specific style of training, if the main branch is thin and smooth, you will know that it has been cane trained, whereas if it is thick, dark, and gnarled, it has been spur trained.

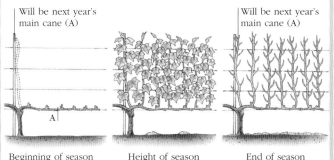

| Will be next year's main cane (A) | | Will be next year's main cane (A) |
|---|---|---|
| A | | |
| Beginning of season | Height of season | End of season |

GUYOT—AN EXAMPLE OF CANE-TRAINING
*In the winter, the main horizontal cane is cut off and the spare cane (A) is bent horizontally to be tied to the bottom wire, where it will become next season's main cane. Another shoot close to the trunk will be allowed to grow as next season's spare cane.*

| Beginning of season | Height of season | End of season |
|---|---|---|

GOBELET—AN EXAMPLE OF SPUR-TRAINING
*The main canes on a spur-trained vine are all permanent, and will only be replaced if they are damaged. Only the year-old shoots are pruned back.*

vine in the same row determines the eventual life of the oldest branch because, when it encroaches on the next vine, it is removed and a new one cultivated from a bud on the main trunk.

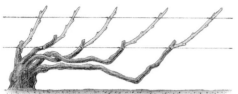

The Chablis spur-training system is, in effect, little more than a slanting bush vine unsupported by a central post.

### Cordon de Royat—*Spur-training system*
This is to Champagne's Pinot Noir what the Chablis system is to its Chardonnay and is nothing more complicated than a spur-trained version of Guyot Simple (*see below*). There is even a double variant, although this is rarely cultivated purely for its own ends, its primary reason for existence being to replace a missing vine on its blind side. When, after their winter pruning, they are silhouetted against the sky, Cordon de Royat vines look very much like columns of gnarled old men in perfect formation; they all face forward, bent almost double, as if with one arm dug into the pit of the back and the other seeking the support of a stick.

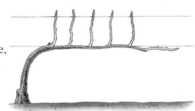

### Geneva Double Curtain—*Spur-training system*
This downward-growing, split-canopy system was developed by Professor Nelson Shaulis of the Geneva Experimental Station in New York State in the early 1960s to increase the volume and ripening of locally-grown Concord grapes. Since then, GDC, as it is often referred to, has been adopted all over the world (particularly in Italy). However, unlike Concord varieties, classic *vinifera* vines have an upward-growing tendency, which makes the system more difficult to apply. Successful results are obtained by shoot positioning, which can either be accomplished via a moveable wire (as in Scott Henry, *see opposite*), by hand, or even by machine. Yields from GDC are 50 percent higher than those from the standard VSP trellis (*see opposite*), and the system offers increased protection from frosts (due to height above ground). It is ideal for full mechanization of medium- to high-vigor vineyards on deep fertile soils (low-vigor vines do not benefit).

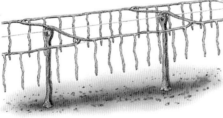

### Guyot—*Cane-training system*
Developed by Jules Guyot in 1860, both the double and simple forms shown here represent the most conservative style of cane training possible. It is the least complicated concept for growers to learn and, providing the number of fruiting canes and the number of buds on them are restricted, Guyot is the easiest means of restraining yields. Even when growers abuse the system, it is still the most difficult vine-training method with which to pump up production. This

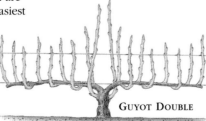

GUYOT DOUBLE

system is commonly used in Bordeaux, where the number of canes and buds are restricted by AOC rules (although, like most French bureaucratic systems, much depends on self-regulation. I have never seen an INAO inspector in the middle of a vineyard checking the variety of vines or counting them, let alone counting the number of canes or buds on canes!). Guyot is also used for some of the finest wines throughout the winemaking world, both Old and New.

GUYOT SIMPLE

### Lyre—*Spur-training system*
Also known as the "U" system, the canopy is divided, so as to allow a better penetration of light (thereby improving ripeness levels) and air (thereby reducing the incidence of cryptogamic disorders). Although it was developed in Bordeaux, the Lyre system is more common in the New World where vine vigor is a problem, although not a major one. As with all split-canopy systems, the Lyre method is of no use whatsoever for low-vigor vineyards. Some growers have successfully adapted Lyre to cane training.

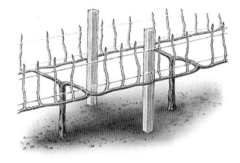

### Minimal Pruning—*Spur-training system*
A wild, unruly mass that contains a central thicket of unpruned dead wood, by definition it has no disciplined form and is therefore impossible to illustrate. Some of the central thicket may be mechanically removed in the winter, but will still be a tangled mass. Initially, several canes are wrapped loosely around a wire, either side of the trunk, about 5 to 6 feet (1.5 to 2 meters) off the ground. The vine is then left to its own devices, although if necessary some of the summer shoots will be trimmed to keep the fruit off the ground. Some growers give up very quickly because yields can initially be alarmingly high and as the volume increases, so the quality noticeably deteriorates. However, if they are patient, the vine eventually achieves a natural balance, reducing the length of its shoots and, consequently, the number of fruiting nodes on them. Although mature minimally pruned vines continue to give fairly high yields, the quality begins to improve after two or three years. By the sixth or seventh year the quality is usually significantly superior to the quality achieved before minimal pruning was introduced—and the quantity is substantially greater. The ripening time needed by the grapes also increases, which can be an advantage in a hot climate, but disastrous in a cool one, particularly if it is also wet. Furthermore, after a number of years, the mass of old wood in the central thicket and the split-ends of machine-pruned cane ends surrounding it can make the vine vulnerable to various pests and diseases, especially rot and mildew, which is why minimally pruned vines in wet areas like New Zealand are more heavily pruned than they are in the hotter areas of Australia—such as Coonawarra and Padthaway—where minimal pruning first emerged and is still used to great effect.

### Pendelbogen—*Cane-training system*
Also known as the "European Loop," or "Arc-Cane Training," this vine-training system, which is a variant of the Guyot Double (*see left*), is most popular in Switzerland and the flatter Rhine Valley areas of Germany and Alsace, although it can also be found in

Mâcon, British Columbia, and Oregon. By bending the canes in an arch, Pendelbogen has more fruit-bearing shoots than the Guyot Double system, thereby providing higher yields. The arching does promote better sap distribution, which helps the production of more fruit, but it can also reduce ripeness levels, making the prime motive for adopting Pendelbogen one of economy, not of quality.

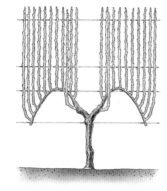

### Scott Henry—*Cane-training system*
Developed by Scott Henry at the Scott Henry Vineyard in Oregon, this system effectively doubles the fruiting area provided by Guyot Double. It also offers a 60 percent increase in fruiting area over the standard VSP Trellis system (*see right*). Scott Henry not only provides larger crops, but riper, better fruit. And because the canopy is split and, therefore, less dense, the wines are less herbaceous, with smoother tannins. Increased yields and increased quality may seem unlikely, but Kim Goldwater of Waiheke Island has records to prove it; and as Goldwater Estate is consistently one of New Zealand's best red wines, that is good enough for me. When I have asked growers who have tried the Scott Henry method why they have given it up, they invariably reply "Have you ever tried to grow vine shoots downward? It doesn't work!" However, the downward-growing shoots actually grow upward for most of the season. They are separated from the other upward-growing shoots by a moveable wire that levers half the canopy into a downward position. The secret of this system's success is to move the wire no earlier than two or three weeks before the harvest, which gives the canes no time to revert and, with the increasing weight of the fruit, no inclination. In areas where grazing animals coexist with vines (as sheep do in New Zealand, for instance), the fact that both halves of the canopy are about 3 feet (1 meter) above the ground most of the time allows under-vine weeds and water-shoots to be controlled without herbicides or manual labor, without fear of the crop being eaten in the process. Scott Henry is found mainly in the New World and is becoming increasingly popular.

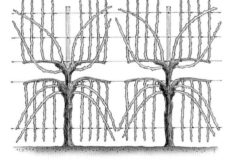

### Scott Henry—*Spur-training system*
When the Scott Henry cane-training system is adapted to spur training, each vine has two permanent spurs instead of four annual canes and produces either top canopies or bottom

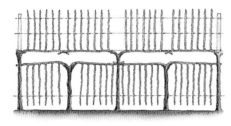

canopies, but not both. The vines are pruned at alternating heights to replicate the effect of cane training, and all canopies grow upward until those on the lower vines are eventually levered downward to the position shown here. The detailed structure of the Scott Henry system is almost impossible to identify when the vines are shrouded in foliage.

### Sylvos—*Spur-training system*
This is like Guyot Double, only the trunk is much longer—just over 6 feet (2 meters)—the main branches are permanent, and the fruiting canes are tied downward, not upward. Sylvos requires minimal pruning and is simple to maintain, lending itself to mechanization, but yields are low, unless pruned very lightly. *Vinifera* varieties do not like being forced downward, but shoot positioning has been introduced by growers in Australia (where it is called "Hanging Cane") and New Zealand. The system was originally conceived by Carlo Sylvos in Italy, where it is still very popular and is sometimes operated without a bottom wire, the canes falling downward under their own weight. The main disadvantage is the dense canopy, which makes the vines prone to bunch-rot.

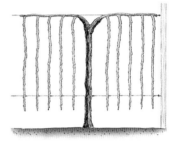

### Sylvos (Hawke's Bay variant)—*Spur-training system*
This version of the Sylvos system was developed by Gary Wood of Montana Wines in the early 1980s on a Hawke's Bay vineyard belonging to Mark Read. The difference between this and the similar Scott Henry system is that it has two main spurs instead of four. With alternate fruiting canes on the same spur trained upward then downward, the canopy is more open, and grape clusters are farther apart. This reduces bunch-rot significantly and facilitates better spray penetration. Yields are increased by as much as 100 percent. The only disadvantage is the longer ripening time needed, which is a risk in areas where late harvests have their dangers.

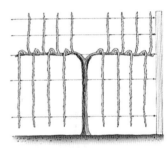

### VSP Trellis—*Cane-training system*
The VSP or Vertical Shoot Positioned trellis is widely used, particularly in New Zealand, where it is commonly referred to as the "standard" trellising system. With the fruiting area contained within one compact zone on wires of a narrow span, it is ideally suited to mechanized forms of pruning, leaf removal, harvesting, and spraying, but it is prone to high vigor and shading. This is a very economic method and, when properly maintained, it is capable of producing wines of good, but not top, quality. VSP is only suitable for low-vigor vines. A spur-trained version with just two main spurs is commonly encountered in France and Germany.

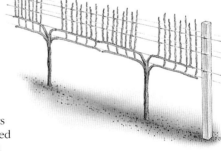

## VITICULTURAL SPRAYS
The use of sprays was once confined to protecting the vine against pests and diseases and for controlling weeds, but they now have additional uses. Foliar feeds supply nutrients direct to the vine, while other sprays halt the growth of foliage, rendering summer pruning unnecessary. Some sprays deliberately induce two disorders called *millerandage* and *coulure* to reduce the yield and, hopefully, increase the quality.

## PRUNING

Important for controlling quantity, pruning is equally important for producing a good quality of fruit. As with any crop, be it grapes or prize roses, if the quantity is reduced, the quality is increased. Reducing the number of fruiting buds lowers the quantity of fruit.

## FLOWERING

The most critical period of a vine's life is when it flowers—at this stage frost, hail, rain, wind, and excessively high or low temperatures could wipe out a crop before the growing season begins in earnest. Even quality-conscious growers usually leave a couple of extra buds on each vine in case of poor weather during flowering. It follows that if the weather permits a perfect flowering, even the best growers' vines end up with too many grape bunches.

## MAN: THE JOKER IN THE PACK

The winemaker, and that includes the winegrower, can maximize or minimize the fruits of nature by his or her skill. Time and again I have seen that neighboring winemakers can make totally different quality wine using virtually the same raw product and the same technology. Chemical analyzes of the wines in question may be virtually indistinguishable, yet one wine will have all the definition, vitality, and expression of character that the other lacks. Why does this occur? No doubt there are valid reasons that science may one day establish, but in our current state of ignorance I can only say that it is always the winemakers with passion who are able to produce the finer, more characterful wines. Of course, many inferior wines are made by the misuse of up-to-date technology, but I have seen dedicated winemakers produce absolutely spellbinding wines using what I would consider to be totally inadequate or inferior equipment. Some winemakers have even been known to sleep by their vats during a particularly difficult fermentation, so that they are on hand to make any adjustments immediately if anything goes wrong. From the grower who never hesitates to prune the vine for low yields, yet always agonizes over the optimum time to harvest, to the winemaker who literally nurses the wines through each and every stage of fermentation and maturation and bottles at precisely the right time and at exactly the correct temperature, the human element is most seriously the joker in the pack when it comes to factors affecting the taste and quality of the wines produced.

INSPECTING MATURING WINE
*Auguste Clape, one of the finest winemakers in France's Northern Rhône area, checks the progress of his oak-matured wine.*

The weather is not often so kind in classic areas, but when it is, the perfect solution is to remove some of the embryo bunches. Most growers wait until the beginning of *véraison* (the ripening period), when the grapes start to take on color and begin to ripen, before cutting off unwanted bunches. By now the vine has already wasted much of its energy on developing the clusters about to be discarded, but their removal will help the remaining bunches of grapes to ripen.

## THE TIMING OF THE GRAPE HARVEST

When to pick is one of the most crucial decisions a grower has to make each year. As grapes ripen, there is a reduction in their acidity (which is also converted from mostly malic acid to primarily tartaric acid) and an increase in sugar, color, various minerals, and essential aromatic compounds. The decision when to pick will vary according to the grape variety, the location of the vineyard, and the style of wine that is to be made. White wine generally benefits from the extra acidity of early-harvested grapes, but they also need the varietal aroma and richness that can only be found in ripe grapes. It is essential to get the balance right. Red wine requires relatively low acidity and profits from the increased color, sugar, and tannin content of grapes harvested later. The grower must also take the vagaries of the weather into account. Those who have the nerve to wait for perfectly ripe grapes every year can produce exceptional wines in even the poorest vintages, but run the risk of frost, rot, or hail damage. This can totally destroy not only an entire crop, but also an entire year's income. Those who never take a chance may always harvest healthy grapes, but in poor years the disadvantage of this approach is that the crop will be unripe and the wine mediocre.

## MECHANICAL HARVESTING

Mechanical harvesting is a contentious subject. The advantages of mechanization are dramatically reduced labor costs and a quick harvest of the entire crop at optimum ripeness, but the vineyard has to be adapted to the machine chosen and the reception and fermentation facilities must be enlarged to cope with the greater amounts and quicker throughput, which is costly. Disadvantages relate to the efficiency of the machinery and the quality of the wine.

As the machines beat the vine trunks with rubber sticks, the grapes drop onto a conveyor along with leaves and other matter, most of which is ejected as the fruit is sorted on its way to the hold. Apart from the rubbish that inevitably remains with the harvested grapes—which is becoming less as machines become more sophisticated—the main disadvantage of mechanical harvesting is the inability of a machine to distinguish between the ripe and the unripe, and the healthy and the diseased or plain rotten (the first thing to drop from any plant when shaken).

Despite these inadequacies, many excellent red wines have been made from mechanically harvested grapes. From a practical point of view it would seem that this method of harvesting is better for red wine than it is for white, particularly sparkling, wine because it splits the grapes. This encourages oxidation and a loss of aromatics and, when harvesting black grapes for white sparkling wine, results in an undesirable coloration of the juice.

## TRANSPORTING THE GRAPES

In the race against time to get the grapes from the vineyard to the winery, everything possible should be done to cosset the fruit. Ideally, the winery and the vineyards should be as close as possible and the grapes transported in plastic crates small enough to prevent damage from their own weight. The crates should be designed so that stacking one on top of the other does not crush the fruit. The fact that some of the best-value wines of Eastern Europe are dumped into huge skips and take hours to reach their destination is fine for red wine, but currently less useful for white. It splits the grapes, thereby encouraging oxidation and a loss of aromatics.

# ANNUAL LIFE CYCLE OF THE VINE

*The calendar of events by which any well-established vine seeks to reproduce, through the production of grapes, is outlined below, with a commentary on how the vine is cultivated to encourage the best grapes for winemaking. The vine's year starts and finishes with the end and approach of winter.*

### FEBRUARY Northern hemisphere
### AUGUST Southern hemisphere

#### 1. Weeping

Weeping is the first sign of the vine awakening after a winter of relative dormancy. When the soil at a depth of 10 inches (25 centimeters) reaches 50°F (10.2°C), the roots start collecting water and the sap in the vine rises, oozing out of the cane ends which were pruned in winter, in a manifestation called "weeping." This occurs suddenly, rapidly increases in intensity, and then decreases gradually. Each vine loses between half a quart and 11 pints (half and five-and-a-half liters) of sap. Weeping is the signal to prune for the spring growth. However, this poses a problem for the

*As the soil warms up the vine awakes, pushing sap out of its cane ends.*

grower because the vine, once pruned, is at its most vulnerable to frost. But waiting for the danger of frost to pass wastes the vine's preciously finite energy and retards its growth, delaying the ripening of the fruit by as much as 10 days, and thus risking exposure of the fruit to fall frosts later on.

### MARCH to APRIL Northern hemisphere
### SEPTEMBER to OCTOBER Southern hemisphere

#### 2. Bud-break

In the spring, some 20 to 30 days after the vine starts to weep, the buds open. Different varieties bud-break at different times; there are early bud-breakers and the same variety can bud-break at different times in different years due to climatic changes. The type of soil can also affect the timing. Clay, which is cold, will retard the process, while sand, which is warm, will promote it. Early bud-break varieties are susceptible to frost in northerly vineyards (southerly in the southern hemisphere), just as late-ripeners are vulnerable

*Buds begin to open at a time determined by variety and climate.*

to fall frosts. In the vineyard, pruning continues into March (September in the southern hemisphere). The vines are secured to their training frames, and the earth that was plowed over the grafting wound to protect it in the winter is plowed back, aerating the soil and leveling off the ground between the rows.

### APRIL to MAY Northern hemisphere
### OCTOBER to NOVEMBER Southern hemisphere

#### 3. Emergence of shoots, foliage, and embryo bunches

*Embryo bunches, the vine's flowers, form.*

Following bud-break, foliage develops and shoots are sent out. In mid-April (mid-October in the southern hemisphere), after the fourth or fifth leaf has emerged, tiny green clusters form. These are the flowers which, when they bloom, will develop into grapes. Commonly called embryo bunches, they are the first indication of the potential size of a crop. In the vineyard, spraying to ward off various vine pests, or cure diseases and other disorders, starts in May (November), and continues until the harvest. Many of these sprays are combined with systemic fertilizers to feed the vine directly through its foliage. These spraying operations are normally done by hand or tractor, but may sometimes be carried out by helicopter if the slopes are very steep or the vineyards too muddy to enter. At this time of year the vine can be affected by *coulure* or *millerandage (see p.15).*

### MAY to JUNE Northern hemisphere
### NOVEMBER to DECEMBER Southern hemisphere

#### 4. Flowering of the vine

The embryo bunches break into flower after the 15th or 16th leaf has emerged on the vine. This is normally about eight weeks after the bud-break and involves pollination and fertilization, and lasts for about 10 days. The weather must be dry and frost-free, but temperature is the most critical requirement. A daily average of at least 59°F (15°C) is needed to enable a vine to flower and between 68° and 77°F (20° and 25°C) is considered ideal. Heat summation, however, is more important than temperature levels, so the length of day has

*The 10 days in which the vine flowers is a vulnerable period.*

a great influence on the number of days the flowering will last. Soil temperature is more significant than air temperature, so the soil's heat-retaining capacity is a contributory factor. Frost is the greatest hazard, and many vineyards are protected by stoves or sprinkling systems.

**JUNE to JULY** Northern hemisphere
**DECEMBER to JANUARY** Southern hemisphere

### 5. Fruit set

After the flowering, the embryo bunches rapidly evolve into true clusters. Each fertilized berry expands into a grape, the first visible sign of the actual fruit that will produce the wine. This is called fruit set. The number of grapes per embryo bunch varies from variety to variety, as does the percentage that actually set into grapes. The panel below illustrates this. In the vineyard, spraying continues and summer pruning (cutting away some bunches) will concentrate the vine's energy on making fruit. In

*Clearly recognizable grapes begin to form.*

some vineyards this is the time for weeding, but in others the weeds are allowed to grow as high as 20 inches (50 centimeters) before they are mown and plowed into the soil to break up the soil and provide the vines with excellent green manure.

| VARIETY | BERRIES PER EMBRYO BUNCH | GRAPES IN A RIPE CLUSTER | PERCENTAGE OF FRUIT SET |
|---|---|---|---|
| Chasselas | 164 | 48 | 29% |
| Gewürztraminer | 100 | 40 | 40% |
| Pinot Gris | 149 | 41 | 28% |
| Riesling | 189 | 61 | 32% |
| Sylvaner | 95 | 50 | 53% |

**AUGUST** Northern hemisphere
**JANUARY** Southern hemisphere

### 6. Ripening of the grapes

As the grape develops its fleshy fruit, very little chemical change takes place inside the berry until its skin begins to turn a different color—the process known as *véraison*. Throughout the grape's green stage, the sugar and acid content remains the same, but during August (January in the southern hemisphere), the ripening process begins in earnest. The skin changes color, the sugar content dramatically increases, and the hard malic acid diminishes as the riper tartaric acid builds up. Although the tartaric acid content begins to

*The grapes begin to change color, the sign of true ripening.*

decline after about two weeks, it always remains the primary acid. It is at this stage that the grape's tannins are gradually hydrolyzed. This is a crucial moment because only hydrolyzed tannins are capable of softening as a wine matures. In the vineyard, spraying and weeding continue, and the vine's foliage is thinned to facilitate the circulation of air and thus reduce the risk of rot. Be careful not to remove too much foliage, since it is the effect of sunlight on the leaves, not the grapes, that causes the grapes to ripen.

**AUGUST to OCTOBER** Northern hemisphere
**FEBRUARY to MARCH** Southern hemisphere

### 7. Grape harvest

*Grapes are picked at a time determined by the winemaker.*

The harvest usually begins mid- to late September (mid- to late February in the southern hemisphere) and may last for a month or more, but, as is the case with all vineyard operations, the timing is earlier nearer to the equator and is dependent on the weather. Picking may, therefore, start as early as August (February) and finish as late as November (April). White grapes ripen before black grapes and must, in any case, be harvested that little bit earlier to achieve a higher acidity balance.

**NOVEMBER to DECEMBER** Northern hemisphere
**APRIL to MAY** Southern hemisphere

### 8. Grapes affected by Botrytis cinerea

*Rotting grapes, soon to be harvested for sweet botrytized wine.*

In November the sap retreats to the protection of the vine's root system. As a result, the year-old canes begin to harden and any remaining grapes, cut off from the vine's metabolic system, start to dehydrate. The concentrated pulp that they become is subject to severe cold. This induces complex chemical changes in a process known as *passerillage*. In specialist sweet-wine areas the grapes are deliberately left on the vine to undergo this quality-enhancing experience and, in certain vineyards with suitable climatic conditions, growers pray for the appearance of *Botrytis cinerea,* or "noble rot."

**DECEMBER to JANUARY** Northern hemisphere
**MAY to JUNE** Southern hemisphere

### 9. Eiswein

*Grapes still on the vine may yet become wine.*

In Germany and Canada you can see grapes on the vine in December and even January. In Germany this is often because the grower has hoped for *Botrytis cinerea,* or *Edelfäule* as it is called there, but it has failed to occur on some grapes. Should frost or snow freeze the grapes, they can be harvested to produced Eiswein, or Icewine, which is made in Canada. It is one of the world's most spectacular wines. Once the grapes are pressed the frozen water is skimmed off, leaving a super-concentrated unfrozen pulp to make Eiswein.

# VINIFICATION

*Although the internationalization of winemaking techniques is a topic that is always much discussed. Methods of production can still vary greatly not just from country to country, but from region to region, and quite commonly even from grower to grower within the same village.*

IN WINEMAKING, much depends on whether traditional values are upheld or innovations are sought and, for the latter, whether the technology is available. Whatever the winemaker decides, certain principles will, essentially, remain the same. These are described below, followed by sections on styles of wine and the processes common or unique to each one.

## THE DIMINISHING QUALITY FACTOR
The quality of the grapes when they are harvested represents the maximum potential of any wine that can be made from them. However, a winemaker will never be able to transfer 100 percent of this inherent quality to the wine, because deterioration sets in from the moment a grape is disconnected from the vine's metabolism. Furthermore, the very process of turning grapes into wine is necessarily a destructive one, so every action that the winemaker takes, however quality-conscious, will inevitably erode some of the wine's potential. Winemakers, therefore, can only attempt to minimize the loss of potential quality.

It is relatively easy to retain approximately 80 percent of the potential quality of a wine, but very difficult to claw back every percentile point after that. It is also relatively easy to double or even treble the basic grape quality by better selection of vineyard sites, improved training methods, the use of superior clones, correct rootstock, and a reduction in yields. As a result, research has now swung from the winery back to the vineyard.

That said, enological practices are still important and how they are employed will have a profound effect not only on quality, but also on the style of the wine produced.

## PRINCIPLES OF VINIFICATION
With modern technology, good everyday-drinking wines can be made anywhere that grapes are grown. When such wines are not made, the reason is invariably a lack of equipment and expertise. Wines of a finer quality require vineyards that have a certain potential and winemakers with a particular talent. When not even good everyday-drinking wines are made from fine-wine vineyards, it is usually due to a combination of excessive yields and poor winemaking, and there is no excuse for either.

## FERMENTATION
The biochemical process that transforms fresh grape juice into wine is called fermentation. Yeast cells excrete enzymes that convert natural fruit sugars into almost equal quantities of alcohol and carbonic gas. This process ceases when the supply of sugar is exhausted or when the alcoholic level reaches a point that is toxic for the yeast enzymes (usually 15 to 16 percent, although certain strains can survive at 20 to 22 percent). Traditionally, winemakers racked their wine from cask to cask (*see* p.26) until they were sure that fermentation had stopped, but there are now many other methods that halt fermentation artificially. These can involve the use of heat, sulfur dioxide, centrifugal filtration, alcohol, pressure, or carbonic gas.
- **Heat** There are various forms of pasteurization (for table wines), flash-pasteurization (for finer wines), and chilling operations that

are used to stabilize wine. These operate on the basis that yeast cells are incapacitated at temperatures above 97°F (36°C), or below 26°F (-3°C), and that yeast enzymes are destroyed above 149°F (65°C). Flash-pasteurization subjects wines to a temperature of about 176°F (80°C) for between 30 seconds and one minute, whereas fully fledged pasteurization involves lower temperatures of 122 to 140°F (50 to 60°C) for a longer period.
- **Addition of sulfur dioxide or sorbic acid** Dosing with one or more aseptic substances will kill off the yeasts.
- **Centrifugal filtration or filtration** Modern equipment is now capable of physically removing all the yeasts from a wine, either by filtration (simply pouring the wine through a medium that prevents certain substances from passing through) or by centrifugal filtration (a process that separates unwanted matter from wine—or grape juice, if used at an earlier stage—by so-called "centrifugal force").
- **Addition of alcohol** Fortification raises the alcohol content to a level toxic to yeast.
- **Pressure** Yeast cells are destroyed by pressure in excess of eight atmospheres (the pressure inside a Champagne bottle is around six atmospheres).
- **Addition of carbonic gas ($CO_2$)** Yeast cells are killed in the presence of .5 oz per quart (15 g per l) or more of carbonic gas.

## THE USE OF SULFUR
Sulfur is used in winemaking from the time the grapes arrive at the winery until just before the wine is bottled. It has several qualities, including antioxidant and aseptic qualities, that make it essential for commercial winemaking. To some extent, all wines are oxidized from the moment the grapes are pressed and the juice is exposed to the air, but the rate of oxidation must be controlled. This is where sulfur is useful, because it has a chemical attraction for the tiny amounts of oxygen that are present in wine. One molecule of sulfur will combine with two molecules of oxygen to form sulfur dioxide ($SO_2$), or fixed sulfur. Once it is combined with the sulfur, the oxygen is neutralized and can no longer oxidize the wine. More oxygen will be absorbed by wine during the vinification process, of course, and there will also be a small head of air between the wine and the cork after bottling. It is for this reason that wines are bottled with a set amount of free sulfur (the amount of the total sulfur content that is not fixed). On occasion a winemaker claims that sulfur is completely superfluous to the winemaking process, but whereas low-sulfur regimes are

---

### YEAST THE FERMENTER

The yeasts used for fermentation may be divided into two categories: cultured yeasts and natural yeasts.

**Cultured yeasts** are nothing more than thoroughbred strains of natural wine yeasts that have been raised in a laboratory. They may be used because the juice has been cleansed of all organisms, including its yeasts, prior to fermentation; or because the winemaker prefers their reliability, or for a specific purpose, such as withstanding higher alcohol levels or the increased osmotic pressure that affects bottle-fermented sparkling wines.

**Natural yeasts** are to be found adhering to the *pruina*, a waxy substance that covers the skin of ripe grapes and other fruits. By the time a grape has fully ripened, the coating of yeasts and other micro-organisms, commonly referred to as the "bloom," contains an average of 10 million yeast cells, although only one percent—or just 100,000 cells—are so-called "wine-yeasts." A yeast cell is only microscopic, yet under favorable conditions it has the ability to split 10,000 sugar molecules every second during fermentation.

actually to be encouraged, wines produced without it are usually dire or have a very short shelf-life.

One famous wine that claimed not to use any sulfur was so long-lived that I had a bottle independently analyzed, only to find that it did contain sulfur. The quantity was small, but far too significant to have been created during fermentation (which is possible in tiny amounts). It was, therefore, an example of how effective a low-sulfur regime can be. Methods of reducing the level of $SO_2$ are well known, the most important being a very judicious initial dosage because a resistance to sulfur gradually builds up and, as a result, later doses always have to be increased.

Some wines can be over-sulfured and, although they are less common than they used to be, they are by no means rare. Over-sulfured wines are easily recognizable by their smell, which ranges from the slight whiff of a recently ignited match (which is the clean smell of free sulfur) to the stench of rotten eggs (which is $H_2S$, where the sulfur has combined with hydrogen—literally the stuff of stinkbombs). When $H_2S$ reacts with ethyl alcohol or one of the higher alcohols, foul-smelling compounds called mercaptans are formed. They can smell of garlic, onion, burning rubber, or stale cabbage, depending on the exact nature of the compound. Mercaptans are extremely difficult for the winemaker to remove and can ruin a wine, which illustrates just how important it is to maintain a low-sulfur regime.

## MALOLACTIC FERMENTATION

Malolactic fermentation is sometimes known as the secondary fermentation, but this is an inappropriate description. The malolactic, or "malo" (as it is sometimes called), is a biochemical process that converts the "hard" malic acid of unripe grapes into two parts "soft" lactic, or "milk," acid (so-called because it is the acid that makes milk sour) and one part carbonic gas. Malic acid is a very strong-tasting acid, which reduces during the fruit's ripening process. However, a significant quantity persists in ripe grapes, and, although reduced by fermentation, also in wine.

The quantity of malic acid present in a wine may be considered too much and the smoothing effect of replacing it with just two-thirds the quantity of the much weaker lactic acid is often desirable. This smoothing effect is considered vital for red wine, beneficial for fuller, fatter, more complex whites, and optional for lighter, crisper whites and certain styles of sparkling wine.

To ensure that the malo can take place, it is essential that specific bacteria are present. These are found naturally on grape skins among the yeasts and other microorganisms, but commercially prepared bacteria may also be used. To undertake their task, they require a certain warmth, a low level of sulfur, a pH of between 3 and 4, and a supply of various nutrients found naturally in grapes.

## STAINLESS STEEL OR OAK?

The use of stainless steel and oak containers for fermentation and maturation is not simply dependent on the cost (see right). The two materials produce opposing effects on wine, so the choice is heavily dependent on whether the winemaker wants to add character to a wine or to keep its purity.

A stainless-steel vat is a long-lasting, easy-to-clean vessel made from an impervious and inert material that is ideally suited to all forms of temperature control. It has the capacity to produce the freshest wines with the purest varietal character. An oak cask has a comparatively limited life, is not easy to clean (it can never be sterilized), makes temperature control very difficult, and is neither impervious nor inert. It allows access to the air, which encourages a faster rate of oxidation, but also causes evaporation, which concentrates the flavour. Vanillin, the essential aromatic constituent of vanilla pods, is extracted from the oak by oxidation and, with various wood lactones and unfermentable sugars, imparts a distinctive, sweet and creamy vanilla nuance to wine. This oaky character takes on a smoky complexity if the wine is allowed to

STAINLESS-STEEL VATS
*Stainless steel is the cornerstone of modern winemaking technology. The bands around each tank contain a coolant to regulate fermentation temperatures.*

go through its malolactic fermentation in contact with the wood, and becomes even more complex, and certainly better integrated, if the wine has undergone all or most of its alcoholic fermentation in cask. Oak also imparts wood tannins to low tannin wine, absorbs tannins from tannic wine, and can exchange tannins with some wines. Oak tannins also act as catalysts, provoking desirable changes in grape tannins through a complex interplay of oxidations.

## POST-FERMENTATION PROCEDURES

Numerous procedures can take place in the winery after fermentation and, where applicable, malolactic fermentation, have ceased. However, the five most basic procedures are racking, fining, cold stabilization, filtration, and bottling.

### Racking

Draining the clear wine off its lees, or sediment, into another vat or cask is known as "racking" because of the different levels, or racks, on which the wine is run from one container into another. In modern vinification, this operation is usually conducted several times during vat or cask maturation. The wine gradually throws off less and less of a deposit. Some wines, such as Muscadet sur lie, are never racked.

### Fining

After fermentation, wine may look hazy to the eye. Even if it does not, it may still contain suspended matter that threatens cloudiness in the bottle. Fining usually assists the clarification of wine at this stage. In addition, special fining agents may be employed to remove unwanted characteristics. When a fining agent is added to wine, it adheres to cloudy matter by physical or electrolytic attraction,

---

### THE COST OF NEW OAK

Two hundred 59-gallon (225-liter) oak casks with a total capacity of 11,900 gallons (450 hectoliters) cost between four and 10 times the cost of a single 11,900-gallon (450-hectoliter) stainless-steel vat. After two years of much higher labor costs to operate and maintain the large number of small units, the volume of wine produced in the oak casks is 10 percent less because of evaporation, and the winemaker faces the prospect of purchasing another 200 casks.

creating tiny clusters (known as colloidal groups), which drop to the bottom of the vat as sediment. The most commonly encountered fining agents are egg white, tannin, gelatin, bentonite, isinglass, and casein. Winemakers have their preferences and individual fining agents also have their specific uses. Oositively charged egg white fines out negatively charged matter, such as unwanted tannins or anthocyanins, while negatively charged bentonite fines out positively charged matter, such as protein haze and other organic matter.

## Cold stabilization

When wines are subjected to low temperatures, a crystalline deposit of tartrates can form a deposit in the bottle. Should the wine be dropped to a very low temperature for a few days before bottling, this process can be precipitated, rendering the wine safe from the threat of a tartrate deposit in the bottle. For the past 20 years, cold stabilization has been almost obligatory for cheap commercial wines, and it is now increasingly used for those of better quality as well. This recent trend is a pity because the crystals are, in fact, entirely harmless and their presence is a completely welcome indication of a considerably more natural, rather than heavily processed, wine.

## Filtration

Various methods of filtration exist, and they all entail running wine through a medium that prevents particles of a certain size from passing through. Filtration has become a controversial subject in recent times, with some critics claiming that anything that removes something from wine must be bad. Depending on who you listen to, this "something" is responsible for a wine's complexity, body, or flavor. However, although it is undeniable that filtration strips something from a wine, if it is unfiltered, it will throw a much heavier deposit and do so relatively quickly. The mysterious "something" is, therefore, purged from all wines at some time or other, whether they are filtered or not, and whether the critics like it or not. Filtration, like so many things, is perfectly acceptable if it is applied in moderation. The fact that many of the world's greatest wines are filtered is a testament to this.

I prefer less or no filtration, as do most quality-conscious winemakers. This is not because of any romantic, unquantifiable ideal, it is simply because I prefer wine to be as unprocessed and as natural as possible. This is a state that can only be achieved through as much of a hands-off approach as the wine will allow. Generally the finer the wine, the less filtration required, as consumers of

## FROM GRAPE TO GLASS

Virtually every ingredient of a fresh grape can be found in the wine it makes, although additional compounds are produced when wine is made and any sedimented matter is disposed of before it is bottled. The most significant difference in the two lists below is the disappearance of fermentable sugar and the appearance of alcohol, although the constituents will vary according to the variety and ripeness of the grape and the style of wine produced.

### THE "INGREDIENTS" OF FRESH GRAPE JUICE
Percentage by volume

| | | |
|---|---|---|
| 73.5 | Water | |
| 25 | Carbohydrates, of which: | |
| | 20% | Sugar (plus pentoses, pectin, inositol) |
| | 5% | Cellulose |
| 0.8 | Organic acids, of which: | |
| | 0.54% | Tartaric acid |
| | 0.25% | Malic acid |
| | 0.01% | Citric acid (plus possible traces of succinic acid and lactic acid) |
| 0.5 | Minerals, of which: | |
| | 0.25% | Potassium |
| | 0.05% | Phosphate |
| | 0.035% | Sulfate |
| | 0.025% | Calcium |
| | 0.025% | Magnesium |
| | 0.01% | Chloride |
| | 0.005% | Silicic acid |
| | 0.1% | Others (aluminum, boron, copper, iron, molybdenum, rubidium, sodium, zinc) |
| 0.13 | Tannin and color pigments | |
| 0.07 | Nitrogenous matter, of which: | |
| | 0.05% | Amino acids (arginine, glutamic acid, proline, serine, threonine, and others) |
| | 0.005% | Protein |
| | 0.015% | Other nitrogenous matter (humin, amide, ammonia, and others) |
| Traces | Mainly vitamins (thiamine, riboflavin, pyridoxine, pantothenic acid, nicotinic acid, and ascorbic acid) | |

WATER INTO WINE
*The individual flavoring elements in any wine represent barely two percent of its content. Although we can determine with great accuracy the amount and identity of 99 percent of these constituents, the mystery is that if we assembled them and added the requisite volume of water and alcohol, the result would taste nothing like wine, let alone like the specific wine we would be trying to imitate.*

### THE "CONTENTS" OF WINE
Percentage by volume

| | | |
|---|---|---|
| 86 | Water | |
| 12 | Alcohol (ethyl alcohol) | |
| 1 | Glycerol | |
| 0.4 | Organic acids, of which: | |
| | 0.20% | Tartaric acid |
| | 0.15% | Lactic acid |
| | 0.05% | Succinic acid (plus traces of malic acid citric acid) |
| 0.2 | Carbohydrates (unfermentable sugar) | |
| 0.2 | Minerals, of which: | |
| | 0.075% | Potassium |
| | 0.05% | Phosphate |
| | 0.02% | Calcium |
| | 0.02% | Magnesium |
| | 0.02% | Sulfate |
| | 0.01% | Chloride |
| | 0.005% | Silicic acid |
| | Traces | Aluminum, boron, copper, iron, molybdenum, rubidium, sodium, zinc |
| 0.1 | Tannin and color pigments | |
| 0.045 | Volatile acids (mostly acetic acid) | |
| 0.025 | Nitrogenous matter, of which: | |
| | 0.01% | Amino acids (arginine, glutamic acid, proline, serine, threonine, and others) |
| | 0.015% | Protein and other nitrogenous matter (humin, amide, ammonia, and others) |
| 0.025 | Esters (mostly ethyl acetate, but traces of numerous others) | |
| 0.004 | Aldehydes (mostly acetaldehyde, some vanillin, and traces of others) | |
| 0.001 | Higher alcohols (minute quantities of amyl plus traces of isoamyl, butyl, isobutyl, hexyl, propyl, and methyl may be present) | |
| Traces | Vitamins (thiamine, riboflavin, pyridoxine, pantothenic acid, nicotinic acid, and ascorbic acid) | |

expensive wines expect sedimentation and are prepared to decant. Delicate reds, such as Pinot Noir, should be the least filtered of all, as I swear they lose fruit just by looking at them, and they certainly lose color—that, at least, is quantifiable. No wine with extended barrel-aging should ever require filtration—just a light, natural fining.

Each filtration is expensive and time-consuming, thus even producers of the most commercial, everyday wines (which even filtration critics accept must be filtered) should keep these operations to a minimum. The principle means of achieving this is by ensuring the best possible clarification by settling and racking. Fining (*see* p.26) should always take precedence, because it is both kinder on the wine and much cheaper than filtering. There are four basic types of filtration: Earth, Pad, Membrane, and Crossflow.

• **Earth Filtration** This system is primarily used after racking for filtering the wine-rich lees that collect at the bottom of the fermentation tank. A medium, usually kieselguhr (a form of diatomaceous earth), is continuously fed into the wine and used with either a Plate and Frame Filter or a Rotary Drum Vacuum Filter. Both types of filter are precoated with the medium, but in a Plate and Frame Filter, the wine and medium mix is forced, under pressure, through plates, or screens, of the medium, in a manner similar to that of any other filter. For the Rotary Drum Vacuum Filter, however, the precoat adheres to the outside of a large perforated drum by virtue of the vacuum that is maintained inside. The drum revolves through a shallow bath into which the wine is pumped and literally sucks the wine through the precoat into the center, where it is piped away. The advantage of this system is that on one side of the shallow bath there is a scraper that constantly shaves the coating on the drum to the desired thickness. The medium thus falls into the wine, with which it mixes, and is then sucked back onto, and through, the drum. It is a continuous process and a very economical one, since the amount of medium used is limited. In a Plate and Frame Filter, the medium is enclosed and eventually clogs up, requiring the operation to be stopped, and the equipment to be dismantled and cleaned before the process can resume.

• **Pad Filtration** Also called Sheet Filtration, this involves the use of a Plate and Frame Filter with a variable number of frames into which filter pads or sheets can slide. Before it was outlawed in the 1970s, these used to be made of asbestos. They now contain numerous filtration mediums, ranging from diatomaceous earth to regular cellulose pads, the latter of which are the most commonly used medium. Special filter formats include active carbon (to remove unwanted color, which is frowned upon for all but the most commercial, high-volume wines) and electrostatically charged pads. These are designed to attract any matter that is suspended in the wine, most of which will possess a negative or positive charge. It is claimed that these electrostatically charged pads are more effective in filtering out matter than the same pads without a charge.

• **Membrane Filtration** This is also called Millipore because the membranes contain microscopic holes capable of removing yeasts and other microorganisms. These holes account for 80 percent of the sheet's surface, so the throughput of wine can be extremely fast provided it has undergone a light prefiltration. Both filtration and prefiltration can now, however, be done at the same time with new Millipore cartridge filters. These contain two or more membranes of varying porosity, thus the coarser ones act as a screen for those with the most minuscule holes.

• **Crossflow Filtration** Originally designed to purify water, a crossflow filter varies from the others (with the exception of the Rotary Drum Vacuum Filter) because it is self-cleaning and never clogs up. The wine flows across the membrane, not into it, so only some of it penetrates. Most of it returns to the chamber from which it came and, because it flows very fast, takes with it any matter filtered out by the membrane.

## BOTTLING

When visiting larger producers, automated bottling lines are the wine journalist's *bête noire*. They get faster and more complex each year and, having invested vast sums in the very latest bottling line, it is understandable that proprietors are keen to show off their new high-tech toy. However, as John Arlott once told me, as he resolutely refused to set foot in the bottling hall of Piper-Heidsieck, "I have not written a single word about bottling lines in my life and I'm not going to start now." They make a very dull experience and inevitably break down just as one's host boasts that it is the fastest bottling line in the world, but their smooth

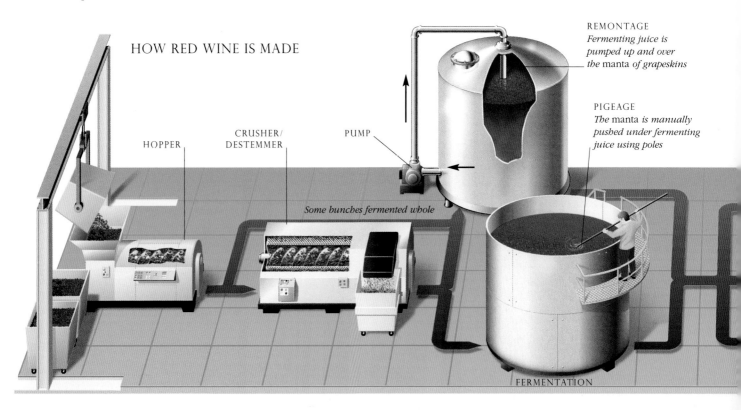

HOW RED WINE IS MADE

HOPPER

CRUSHER/
DESTEMMER

PUMP

*Some bunches fermented whole*

REMONTAGE
*Fermenting juice is pumped up and over the* manta *of grapeskins*

PIGEAGE
*The* manta *is manually pushed under fermenting juice using poles*

FERMENTATION

operation most days of the week is essential if the wine is to remain as fresh as possible in the bottle. All that readers need to know is that the bottles should be sterile; that fully-automated lines cork, capsule, label, and box the wines; and that there is a device to detect any impurities before the bottles are boxed. All European systems print a lot number identifying the date each batch was bottled either on the label or directly onto the bottle using a laser. Therefore, in an emergency, a specific batch can be recalled, rather than the entire production having to be cleared from every wholesaler and retailer stocking a particular line.

## RED WINES

On arrival at the winery the grapes are usually crushed and destemmed, although it was once accepted practice to leave the stems for a more tannic wine. However, stem tannins are too harsh and fail to soften as the wine matures. The modern winemaker can include a small quantity of stems if the grape variety requires extra structure or if the vintage needs firming up.

## FERMENTATION

After the grapes are destemmed and lightly crushed, they are pumped into a vat where fermentation may begin as early as 12 hours or as late as several days later. Even wines that will be cask-fermented must start off in vats, whether they are old-fashioned oak *foudres* or modern stainless-steel tanks. This is because they must be fermented along with a *manta*, or cap, of grapeskins. To encourage fermentation, the juice may be heated and selected yeast cultures or partially fermented wine from another vat added. During fermentation, the juice is often pumped from the bottom of the vat to the top and sprayed over the *manta* to keep the juice in contact with the grapeskins. This ensures that the maximum color is extracted. Other methods involve the *manta* being pushed under the fermenting juice with poles. Some vats are equipped with crude but effective grids that prevent the *manta* from rising, others rely on the carbonic gas given off during fermentation to build up pressure, releasing periodically and pushing the *manta* under the surface; another system keeps the *manta* submerged in a "vinimatic," a sealed, rotating stainless-steel tank, based on the cement-mixer principle.

The higher the temperature during fermentation, the more color and tannin will be extracted; the lower the temperature, the better the bouquet, freshness, and fruit will be. The optimum temperature for the fermentation of red wine is 85°F (29.4°C). If it is too hot, the yeasts produce certain substances (decanoic acid, octanoic acids, and corresponding esters) that inhibit their own ability to feed on nutrients and cause the yeasts to die. It is, however, far better to ferment hot fresh juice than to wait two weeks (which is normal in many cases) to ferment cooler but stale juice. The fuller, darker, more tannic and potentially longer-lived wines remain in contact with the skins for anything between 10 and 30 days. Lighter wines, on the other hand, are separated from the skins after only a few days.

## VIN DE GOUTTE AND VIN DE PRESSE

The moment the skins are separated from the juice, every wine is divided into two—free-run wine, or *vin de goutte*, and press wine, or *vin de presse*. The free-run juice runs out of the vat when the tap is opened. The remains—the *manta* of grapeskins, pips, and other solids—are put into a press to extract the very dark, extremely tannic "press wine." The free-run wine and the press wine are then pumped into separate vats or casks depending on the style of the wine being made. These wines then undergo their malolactic conversion separately and are racked several times, fined, racked again, blended, then fined and racked once more before bottling.

## MACÉRATION CARBONIQUE

There are several variations of *macération carbonique*, a technique used almost exclusively for making red wine, involving an initial fermentation under pressure of carbonic gas. The traditional method, dating back at least 200 years, was to put the uncrushed grapes in a closed container, where after a while, a natural fermentation would take place inside the grapes. When the grapes eventually exploded, filling the container with carbonic gas, a normal fermentation continued and the grapes macerated in their own skins. Today the grapes are often placed in vats filled with carbonic gas from a bottle. *Macération carbonique* produces light wines with good color, soft fruit, and a "pear-drop" aroma.

## WHITE WINES

Until fairly recently it could be said that two initial operations distinguished the white-winemaking process from the red one: first, an immediate pressing to extract the juice and separate the skins, and, second, the purging, or cleansing, of this juice. But for white wines of expressive varietal character the grapes are now often crushed and then macerated in a vinimatic for 12 to 48

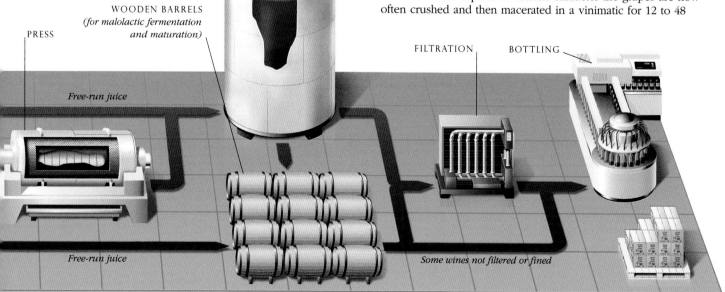

PRESS

WOODEN BARRELS
*(for malolactic fermentation
and maturation)*

STAINLESS-
STEEL TANK
*(for maturation)*

FILTRATION

BOTTLING

*Free-run juice*

*Free-run juice*

*Some wines not filtered or fined*

hours to extract the aromatics that are stored in the skins. The juice that is run out of the vinimatic, and the juice that is pressed out of the macerated pulp left inside it, then undergoes cleansing and fermentation like any other white wine.

With the exception of wines macerated in a vinimatic, the grapes are either pressed immediately on arrival at the winery or lightly crushed and then pressed. The juice from the last pressing is murky, bitter, and low in acidity and sugar, so only the first pressing, which is roughly equivalent to the free-run juice in red wine, together with the richest elements of the second pressing, should be used for white-wine production. Once pressed, the juice is pumped into a vat where it is purged, or cleansed, which in its simplest form means simply leaving the juice to settle so that particles of grapeskin and any other impurities fall to the bottom. This purging may be helped by chilling, adding sulfur dioxide and, possibly, a fining agent. Light filtration and centrifugation may also be applied during this process.

After cleansing, the juice is pumped into the fermenting vat or directly into barrels if the wine is to be cask-fermented. The addition of selected yeast cultures occurs more often in the production of white wine because of the wine's limited contact with the yeast-bearing skins and the additional cleansing that reduces the potential amount of wine yeasts available.

The optimum temperature for fermenting white wine is 64°F (18°C), although many winemakers opt for between 50°F and 63°F (10°C and 17°C), and it is actually possible to ferment wine at temperatures as low as 39°F (4°C). At the lower temperatures, more esters and other aromatics are created, less volatile acidity is produced, and a lower dose of sulfur dioxide is required; on the other hand, the resulting wines are lighter in body and contain less glycerol.

With acidity an essential factor in the balance of fruit and, where appropriate, sweetness in white wines, many products are not permitted to undergo malolactic conversion and are not bottled until some 12 months after the harvest. Oak-matured wines which, incidentally, always undergo malolactic conversion, may be bottled between 9 and 18 months, but wines that are made especially for early drinking are nearly always racked, fined, filtered, and bottled as quickly as the process will allow in order to retain as much freshness and fruitiness as possible.

## ROSÉ WINES

With the exception of pink Champagne, most of which is made by blending white wine with red, all good-quality rosés are produced either by bleeding, pressing, or limited maceration. A true-bled rosé is made from the juice that issues from black grapes pressed under their own weight. This is a sort of *tête de cuvée*, which, after fermentation, is a very pale *vin gris* color, but has a rich, fruity, and exquisitely fresh flavor. Pressed rosé is made by pressing black grapes until the juice takes on enough color. It, too, has a pale *vin gris* color, but lacks the true richness of a *tête de cuvée* rosé. Limited maceration is the most common method used in the production of rosé. During this process, rosé is made in exactly the same way as red wine, except that skin-contact is limited to what is sufficient to give the desired pink tint. (All shades of rosé exist, ranging from a barely perceptible hint of color to *clairet*, or almost red.) Some superior rosé wines that have been made using this last method are virtually by-products of red-wine production. In certain areas that lack the appropriate climate for deep red wines, some free-run juice might be run off in order to produce rosé, thus leaving a greater ratio of coloring pigment in the juice that remains.

## SPARKLING WINES

When grape juice is fermented, sugar is converted into alcohol and carbonic gas. For still wines the gas is allowed to escape, but if it is prevented from doing so—by putting a lid on a vat or a cork in a bottle—it will remain dissolved in the wine until the lid or cork is removed. When the gas is released it rushes out of the wine in the form of bubbles. The production of all natural sparkling wines is based on this essential principle, using one of four different methods: *méthode champenoise*, bottle-fermented, *méthode rurale*, and *cuve close*. They can also be made by injecting the bubbles.

### MÉTHODE CHAMPENOISE

Also referred to as *méthode traditionnelle* or *méthode classique* (France), *metodo classico* (Italy), and *Cap Classique* (South Africa), this term indicates a sparkling wine that has undergone a second fermentation in the bottle in which it is sold. A label may refer to a wine being "Individually fermented in this bottle," which is the beautifully simple American equivalent of *méthode champenoise*.

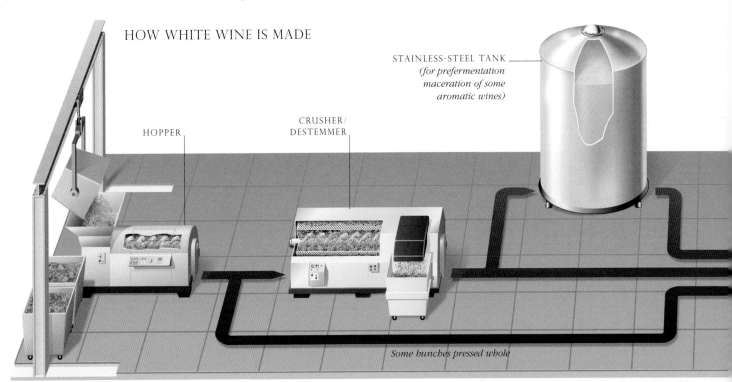

HOW WHITE WINE IS MADE

HOPPER

CRUSHER/
DESTEMMER

STAINLESS-STEEL TANK
*(for prefermentation
maceration of some
aromatic wines)*

*Some bunches pressed whole*

# BOTTLE-FERMENTED

This refers to a wine produced through a second fermentation in a bottle, but (and this is the catch) not necessarily in the bottle in which it is sold. It may have been fermented in one bottle, transferred to a vat and, under pressure at 26°F (-3°C), filtered into another bottle. This is also known as the "transfer method."

# MÉTHODE RURALE

This refers to the precursor of *méthode champenoise*, which is still used today, albeit only for a few obscure wines. It involves no second fermentation, the wine being bottled before the first alcoholic fermentation is finished.

# CUVE CLOSE, CHARMAT, OR TANK METHOD

This is used for the bulk production of inexpensive sparkling wines that have undergone a second fermentation in large tanks before being filtered and bottled under pressure at 26°F (-3°C). Contrary to popular belief, there is no evidence to suggest that this is an intrinsically inferior method of making sparkling wine. It is only because it is a bulk production method that it tends to attract mediocre base wines and encourage a quick throughput. I genuinely suspect that a *cuve close* produced from the finest base wines of Champagne and given the autolytic benefit of at least three years on its lees before bottling might well be indistinguishable from the "real thing."

# CARBONATION

This is the cheapest method of putting bubbles into wine and simply involves injecting it with carbon dioxide. Because this is the method used to make lemonade, it is incorrectly assumed that the bubbles achieved through carbonation are large and short-lived. They can be, and fully sparkling wines made by this method will indeed be cheapskates, but modern carbonation plants have the ability to induce the tiniest of bubbles, even to the point of imitating the "prickle" of wine bottled *sur lie*.

# FORTIFIED WINES

Any wine, dry or sweet, red or white, to which alcohol has been added is classified as a fortified wine, whatever the inherent differences of vinification may be. Still wines usually have a strength of 8.5 to 15 percent alcohol; fortified wines a strength of 17 to 24 percent. The spirit added is usually, but not always, brandy made from local wines. It is totally neutral, with no hint of a brandy flavor. The amount of alcohol added, and exactly when and how it is added, is as critical to the particular character of a fortified wine as is its grape variety or area of production. *Mutage*, early fortification, and late fortification are all methods that may be used to fortify wines.

# MUTAGE

This is the addition of alcohol to fresh grape juice. This prevents fermentation and produces fortified wines, known as *vins de liqueurs* in France, such as Pineau des Charentes in the Cognac region, Floc de Gascogne in Armagnac, and Ratafia in Champagne.

# EARLY FORTIFICATION

This is the addition of alcohol after fermentation has begun. This is often done in several small, carefully measured, timed doses spread over several hours or even days. The style of fortified wine being made will dictate exactly when the alcohol is added, and the style itself will be affected by the variable strength of the grapes from year to year. On average, however, alcohol is added to port after the alcohol level has reached 6 to 8 percent, and added to the *vins doux naturels* of France, such as Muscat de Beaumes de Venise, at any stage between 5 and 10 percent.

# LATE FORTIFICATION

This is the addition of alcohol after fermentation has ceased. The classic drink produced by this method is sherry, which is always vinified dry, with any sweetness added afterward.

# AROMATIZED WINES

With the exception of Retsina, the resinated Greek wine, aromatized wines are all fortified. They also all have aromatic ingredients added to them. The most important aromatized wine is vermouth, which is made from neutral white wines of 2 to 3 years of age, blended with an extract of wormwood (vermouth is a corruption of the German *wermut* meaning "wormwood"), vanilla, and various other herbs and spices. Italian vermouths are produced in Apulia and Sicily, and French vermouths in Languedoc and Roussillon. Chambéry is a delicate generic vermouth from the Savoie and Chambéryzette is a red-pink version flavored with alpine strawberries, but such precise geographical aromatized wines are rare. Most, in fact, are made and sold under internationally recognized brands such as Cinzano and Martini. Other well-known aromatized wines include Amer Picon, Byrrh, Dubonnet (both red and white), Punt e Mes, St.-Raphael, and Suze.

STAINLESS-STEEL
FERMENTATION TANK

PRESS     WOODEN BARRELS

FILTRATION     BOTTLING

FERMENTATION

*Some wines not filtered or fined*

# THE CHOICE OF OAK

*I have seen the question only once in print, yet it is the most fundamental question that could possibly be asked: why oak? Why out of all the woods around the world is oak, and to any significant degree, only oak, used for barrel-making?*

THE ANSWER IS THAT OTHER WOODS are either too porous or contain overpowering aromatic substances that unpleasantly taint the wine. It is not entirely true to say that only oak is used in winemaking. Chestnut, for example, is occasionally found in the Rhône and elsewhere, but it is so porous and so tannic that it is usually lined with a neutral substance, rendering the wood no different from any other lined construction material (such as concrete). A beech variety called *rauli* used to be popular in Chile until its winemakers, suddenly exposed to international markets, soon discovered they had become so used to the wood that they had not realized that it gave their wines a musty joss-stick character. Large, redwood tanks are still used in California and Oregon, but they are not greatly appreciated and, as the wood cannot be bent very easily, it is not practical for small barrels. Pine has a strong resinous character that the Greeks seem to enjoy, although they have had 3,000 years to acquire the taste. Most tourists try Retsina, but very few continue to drink it by choice when they return home. Moreover, it is made by adding resin, with no direct contact with the wood and, apart from an oddity called "Tea Wine," produced on La Palma in the Canary Islands, no wine to my knowledge is produced in barrels made of pine. Eucalyptus also has a resinous affect, acacia turns wine yellow, and hardwoods are impossible to bend and contain aromatic oils that are undesirable.

White oak, on the other hand, is easily bent, has a low porosity, acceptable tannin content, and mild, creamy aromatic substances that either have an intrinsic harmony with wine or, like the Greeks, we have grown accustomed to the effect.

## LARGE OR SMALL?
The size of the cask is critical to its influence. The smaller it is, the larger the oak-to-wine ratio, and the greater an oaky flavor it imparts. A 53-gallon (200-liter) *barrique* has 1.5 times the internal surface area of oak for every quart of wine as a 132-gallon (500-liter) cask. Traditional sizes for *barriques* range from 54 gallons (205 liters) in Champagne, to 59 gallons (225 liters) in Bordeaux and Spain, 60 gallons (228 liters) in Burgundy, and 79 to 83 gallons (300 to 315 liters) in Australia and New Zealand.

## AN OAK BARREL
The staves of a barrel are held together by metal hoops, which are sometimes positioned at slightly different distances, depending on the traditions of the cooper, or *tonnelier*, in question. There may be a red color between the two innermost hoops, but this is merely where some winemakers wish to conceal their own dribble marks

around the bung by dyeing the entire middle area with wine, which can look very impressive. When fermenting white wines, the bung is always uppermost and, even with a good ullage, or space, the hole may be left open during the most tumultuous period. It will be sealed with an air-lock valve when the fermentation process settles down to remain closed during the malolactic fermentation. After racking, when all wines mature for several months, the barrels are filled to the very top, and positioned so that the bung is to one side, visually reminding cellar-workers that the casks are full.

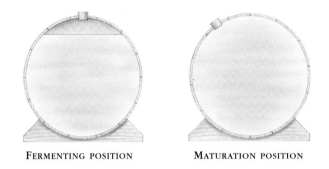

**FERMENTING POSITION**          **MATURATION POSITION**

Square barrels were even developed to increase the ratio of oak-to-wine. Although treated as a novelty, they were actually more practical and economical than normal casks. More practical because they made more efficient use of storage space and more economical because their straight sides could be reversed to create a new oak barrel from an old one. An Australian firm even built a square stainless-steel tank with two oak panels made from oak staves that could be replaced, reversed, and adjusted in size to give different oak-to-wine ratios. However, all such barrels became superfluous, with the advent and widespread use of oak chips.

## CHIPS OFF THE OLD BLOCK
Using old oak barrels for the finest *barrique*-fermented or *barrique*-matured wines is a question of style rather than a consideration of cost. But for less expensive wines, it is almost entirely a question of economics, because barrels can double, for example, the cost of a *vin de pays*.

The use of new oak *barriques* for just a small percentage of a wine blend can add a certain subliminal complexity to it, although not the overt oakiness that so many people find attractive, yet so few are willing to pay very much for. Oak chips or shavings are the answer. Although generally believed to be a recent phenomenon, the use of oak chips was sufficiently widespread by 1961 to warrant statutory controls in the United States. In fact, as a by-product of barrel-making, today's ubiquitous chip probably has an equally long, if somewhat more covert, history. Oak chips have been one of the most potent weapons in the New World's armory, producing relatively inexpensive, but distinctly premium-quality, wines to conquer international markets. This has been particularly evident in Australia, where flying winemakers have not only perfected oak

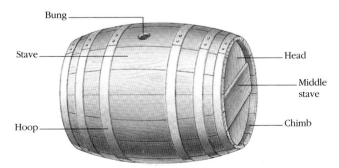

Bung

Stave

Head

Middle
stave

Hoop

Chimb

**AMERICAN OAK DUST**     **FRENCH OAK CHIPS**     **AMERICAN OAK CHIPS**
Light-toast                Medium-toast             High-toast

## FRENCH OAK "APPELLATIONS"

Some winemakers swear by a particular variety of French oak, but most are suspicious of barrels that claim to be from one specific forest. Tronçais, for example, is one of the most famous oak forests, but the Tronçais forest supplies just 2 percent of all French oak and, if every barrel claiming to be from there actually did so, the forest would have disappeared long ago.

Perhaps the Bordelais, who are the most experienced in buying new French oak, realized this centuries ago, as they have traditionally purchased barrels made from "mixed staves" (i.e. various forests).

Most winemakers buy from a particular cooper because they like their barrels. This usually has less to do with their construction, than with the seasoning of the wood and the toasting of the barrels. Most barrels are not only made on a mix-and-match basis, but the mix of staves is likely to vary from year to year. This is because oak is sold by auction and coopers buy on quality, not name. It is more important who owns the forest than where it is located, because known sources, such as the *Office National des Forêts*, which is the only purveyor of *Haute Futaie* oak and who only sells *Haute Futaie* oak, can guarantee a consistency that a private proprietor, even with good wood, cannot. Therefore, some companies, such as Seguin Moreau, follow a policy of buying only *Haute Futaie* oak.

---

chip wines, but by the early 1990s had exported the techniques to virtually every winemaking country in the world. Some experiments have demonstrated that wine matured with oak chips used in old barrels is "virtually indistinguishable" from the same wine stored in new oak. The range of oak chip products is now very comprehensive, covering the entire range of oak varieties and different toast levels. Some are even impregnated with malolactic bacteria. If a wine label mentions oak, but not *barriques*, barrels, or casks, it is probably a clue that oak chips have been employed in the winemaking and, if the wine is cheap, you can bet on it.

### ANYONE FOR TOAST?
Toasting is one operation in the barrel-making process that has a very direct effect on the taste of the wine. In order to bend the staves, heat is applied in three stages: warming-up (*pre-chauffrage*), shaping (*cintrage*), and toasting (*bousinage*), each of which browns, or chars, the internal surface of the barrel. However, it is only the last stage—*bousinage*—that determines the degree of toasting. During toasting, furanic aldehydes (responsible for "roasted" aromas) reach their maximum concentration, the vanilla aroma of vanillin is heightened, and various phenols, such as eugenol (the chief aromatic constituent of oil of cloves), add a smoky, spicy touch to the complexity of oak aromas in wine.

BOUSINAGE
*The final barrel-firing operation puts a light, medium, or heavy toast on the inner surface.*

There are three degrees of toasting: light, medium, and heavy. A light toasting is used by winemakers who seek the most natural oak character (although it is not as neutral as using staves that have been bent with steam); medium varies between a true medium, which suits most red wine demands, and the so-called medium-plus, which is the favorite for fermenting white wines; the third, a heavy toast, dramatically reduces the coconutty-lactones and leaves a distinctly charred-smoke character that can be overpowering unless used only as a small component in a blend. Furthermore, with time, the high carbon content of heavily toasted barrels can leach the color out of some wines, so they tend to be used for white wines (often big, brash Chardonnays), although heavy toast is best suited to maturing Bourbon whiskey.

### THE DIFFERENT OAKS
Both American and European oaks are used for winemaking. The aromatics of fast-growing, wide-grained American white oak, *Quercus alba*, are more pungent, while there are more tannins, finer in texture, in slow-growing, tight-grained European brown oaks, *Quercus robur* (*syn* pedunculate oak), and *Quercus sessilis* (*syn Quercus petraea* and *Quercus rouvre*). Much of the appealing, if obvious, coconut character in American oak is also due to the very different barrel-making techniques used in the U.S.

Unlike European oak, American is sawn, not split. This ruptures the wood cells, releasing aromatic substances, especially vanillin and up to seven different lactones, which together explain the coconut aroma. American oak is also kiln-dried, which concentrates the lactones, while European oak is seasoned outside for several years, a process that leaches out some of the most aromatic substances, and reduces the more aggressive tannins. The whole process tends to accentuate the character of American oak, while subduing that of European oak.

Many French winemakers consider American oak vulgar. Even so, a little-known fact is that in ultraconservative Bordeaux, at least 60 châteaux are experimenting with it. Coconut-flavored claret is by no means a foregone conclusion, but oak is expensive, a little sawn *Quercus alba* goes a long way, and a small percentage of American oak, either as barrels or mixed staves, could, in fact, significantly reduce the percentage of new oak needed each year.

**LIGHT TOAST**          **MEDIUM TOAST**          **HEAVY TOAST**

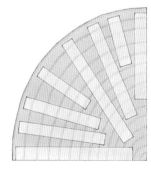
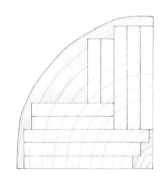

EUROPEAN SPLIT VERSUS AMERICAN SAWN
*After the bark has been stripped from a log destined for barrel-making, it will be split (in Europe) or sawn (in the United States) into quarters. The examples above clearly show that it is more economical to saw staves from a quarter, as opposed to splitting them. This is the major reason why American oak barrels cost half the price of European ones.*

# REGIONAL OAK VARIETIES

For winemaking, the tighter the size of the oak grain, the better. The slower the tree grows, the tighter the grain—thus, cooler-climate European oak is older and tighter-grained than warmer-climate American oak. Of the European oaks, forest oak (*Quercus sessilis*) is preferred to solitary oak trees (*Quercus robur*) because its branches start higher and the trunk is longer and straighter. Solitary oaks grow faster and have a larger grain because they tend to grow in fertile soil where there is more water. *Quercus sessilis* is also preferred to *Quercus robur* because it is four times richer in aromatic components.

## AMERICAN *Quercus alba*

This oak covers most of the eastern U.S. Some winemakers think that Minnesota and Wisconsin are the best, while others find them too tannic and consider Appalachian oak, particularly from Pennsylvania, to be superior. Other popular oaks are Ohio, Kentucky, Mississippi, and Missouri. All are white oaks, fast-growing, wide-grained, with lower tannin (except for Oregon) than any European brown oaks, but with higher, sweeter, more coconutty aromatics. *Quercus alba* is favored for traditional Rioja, Australian Shiraz, and California Zinfandel.

## OREGON *Quercus gariana*

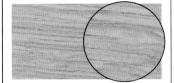

Although a white oak, *Quercus gariana* has a significantly tighter grain than *Quercus alba*. Relatively few barrels have been made from Oregon oak, and it has always been sawn, making it hard to evaluate the claim that it is similar to European oak. In 1996, however, barrels were made from split, open-air seasoned Oregon oak, so watch this space.

## ALLIER *Quercus sessilis*

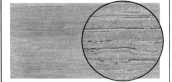

Tight-grained with well-balanced, medium tannin and aromatics, Allier is highly regarded.

## ARGONNE *Quercus sessilis*

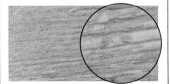

Tight-grained with low aromatics and tannin, this oak was used for Champagne before the advent of stainless-steel. Now seldom used.

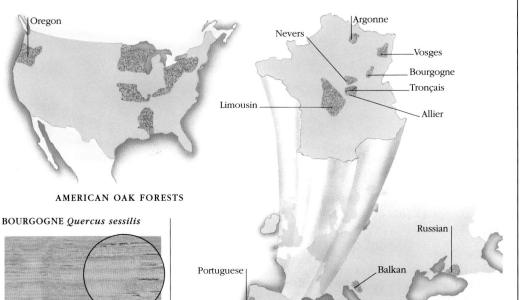

**AMERICAN OAK FORESTS**

**EUROPEAN OAK FORESTS**

## BOURGOGNE *Quercus sessilis*

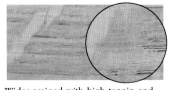

Tight-grained with high tannin and low aromatics, most of this oak goes to Burgundian cellars.

## LIMOUSIN *Quercus robur*

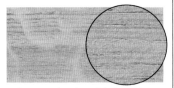

Wider-grained with high tannin and low aromatics, this oak used to be favored for Chardonnay, but is most widely used for brandy.

## NEVERS *Quercus sessilis*

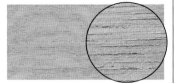

Tight-grained with well-balanced, medium tannin and aromatics, Nevers is highly regarded.

## TRONÇAIS *Quercus sessilis*

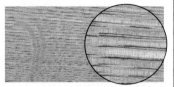

The tightest-grained and, with Vosges, the highest tannin content, Tronçais grows in the Allier forest. It is highly suitable for long-term maturation, owing to its understated aromatics, and has been long sought after.

## VOSGES *Quercus sessilis*

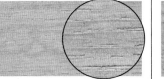

The tight grain, very high tannin content, and understated but slightly spicy aromatics make Vosges an especially well-balanced oak for winemaking. It is underrated, particularly in its home region of Alsace, where even though few winemakers use *barriques*, those who do ironically seem to experiment with virtually every French forest except the one that is actually on their own doorstep. Vosges is especially popular in California and New Zealand, where some winemakers think it is similar to Allier and Nevers. Vosges deserves to receive greater recognition.

## BALKAN *Quercus robur*

Often called Slavonian or Yugoslav oak, the grain is tight, with medium tannin and low aromatics. Balkan oak is popular for large oval casks, particularly in Italy. Use is diminishing because of recent troubles.

## PORTUGUESE *Quercus gariana*

Cooperage oak (*Quercus gariana*) is far less of a commercial concern in Portugal than stunted cork-industry oak (*Quercus suber*), but the former's medium-grain wood has good aromatic properties, making it preferable in Portugal itself, where it is much cheaper than French oak.

## RUSSIAN *Quercus sessilis*

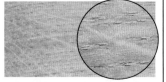

Tight-grained with low aromatics and easy to confuse with French oak under blind conditions, this was the major oak in Bordeaux during the 19th century and up until the 1930s. Thus all the great old vintages owe something to it. Thanks to investment from Seguin Moreau, which set up a cooperage in the Adygey region near the Black Sea, French producers have begun to use Russian oak again, although it is mysteriously just 10 percent cheaper than French.

# GRAPE VARIETIES

*The grape variety used for a wine is the most influential factor in determining its taste. The factors that determine the inherent flavor of any grape variety are the same as those that determine the varietal taste of any fruit. How they affect the taste of wine is outlined below.*

## SIZE

The smaller the fruit, the more concentrated the flavor will be. Thus most classic grape varieties, such as Cabernet Sauvignon and Riesling, have small berries, although some varieties that rely more on elegance than power of concentration, such as the Pinot Noir, may yield large berries. Many varieties are known as *petit-* or *gros-* something, and it is usually the *petit* that is the better variety—Petit Vidure is Cabernet Sauvignon; Gros Vidure, Cabernet Franc.

## SKIN STRUCTURE

The skin contains most of the aromatic characteristics with which we associate the varietal identity of any fruit. Its construction and thickness is, therefore, of paramount importance. For example, the thick-skinned Sauvignon Blanc produces an aromatic wine that, when ripe, varies in pungency from "peach" in a warm climate to "gooseberry" in a cool climate, and when underripe varies in herbaceousness, ranging from "grassy" to "elderflower" and even "cat's pee." Meanwhile the thin-skinned Sémillon produces a rather neutral wine, although its thin skin makes it susceptible to noble rot and is thus capable of producing one of the world's greatest botrytized sweet wines, with mind-blowing aromatics.

## SKIN COLOR AND THICKNESS

A dark-colored, thick-skinned grape, such as Cabernet Sauvignon, produces very deep-colored wines, while the lighter-colored, thin-skinned grapes, such as Merlot, produce a less intense color.

## ACID–SUGAR RATIO AND PRESENCE OF OTHER CONSTITUENTS

The grape's sugar content dictates the wine's alcohol level and the possibility of any natural sweetness; together with the acidity level, this determines the balance. The proportions of a grape's other constituents, or their products after fermentation, form the subtle nuances that differentiate the varietal characters. Although soil, rootstock, and climate have an effect on the ultimate flavor of the grape, the genetics of the vine dictate the end result.

## THE VITIS FAMILY

The vine family is a large and diverse family of plants ranging from the tiny pot-plant Kangaroo Vine to Virginia Creeper. The Wine Vine Tree, (*see below*), shows how the *Vitis vinifera*, the classic winemaking species, relates to the rest of the vine family. The *Vitis vinifera* is one of many belonging to the subgenus *Euvites*. Other species in this subgenus are used for rootstock.

## PHYLLOXERA VASTATRIX—PEST OR BLESSING?

The vine louse—*Phylloxera vastatrix*—that devastated the vineyards of Europe in the late 19th century still infests the soils of nearly all the world's winegrowing regions. At the time, it was considered the greatest disaster in the history of wine, but with hindsight, it was a blessing in disguise.

Before phylloxera arrived, many of Europe's greatest wine regions had gradually been devalued because of increased demand for their wines. This led to bulk-producing, inferior varieties being planted, and vineyards being extended into unsuitable lands. As phylloxera spread, it became apparent that every vine had to be grafted onto phylloxera-resistant American rootstock. This forced a much-needed rationalization, in which only the best sites in the classic regions were replanted and only noble vines were cultivated, a costly operation that vineyard owners in lesser areas could not afford. The grafting took France 50 years, and enabled the *Appellation d'Origine Contrôlée* system to be set up. It is hard to imagine what regional or varietal identities might now exist if phylloxera had not occurred.

## ROOTSTOCK

Hundreds of rootstock varieties have been developed from various vine species, usually *Vitis berlandieri*, *V. riparia*, or *V. rupestris*, because they are the most phylloxera-resistant. The precise choice of rootstock is dependent on its suitability to the vinestock on which it is to be grafted as well as on its adaptability to the geographical location and soil type. The choice can increase or decrease a vine's productivity, and thus has a strong effect on the quality of the wine produced from the grapes. Generally, the lower the quantity, the higher the quality.

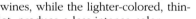

**VITIS VINIFERA** *Several thousand varieties*

Aligoté · Cabernet Franc · Cabernet Sauvignon · Chardonnay · Chenin Blanc · Gamay · Gewürztraminer · Grenache · Merlot · Muscat Blanc · Nebbiolo · Pinot Gris · Pinot Meunier · Pinot Noir · Riesling · Sangiovese · Sauvignon Blanc · Sémillon · Sylvaner · Syrah · Touriga Nacional · Viognier · Zinfandel · Others

*Vitis rotundifolia · Vitis munsoniana · Vitis popenoei · Vitis vinifera · Vitis riparia · Vitis labrusca · Vitis berlandieri · Vitis amurensis · Vitis rupestris · Vitis cariboea · Vitis argentifolia · Others*

**SUBGENUS MUSCADINIAE**

**SUBGENUS EUVITES** *60 species, but only* Vitis vinifera *is important for winemaking*

**GENUS VITIS** *Of the 10 genera belonging to the Vitaceae family, only the genus* Vitis *is important for winemaking*

**BOTANICAL FAMILY** *Vitaceae (also called Ampelidaceae)*

## THE WINE VINE TREE

*The green line running from the ground traces the parentage of* Vitis vinifera, *the species from which all classic winemaking grapes come. Although* Vitis vinifera *is the most important species of the subgenus* Euvites, *wine is made from grape varieties from other species, notably* Vitis labrusca, *native to North America.*

# GLOSSARY OF GRAPE VARIETIES

*There are thousands of winemaking grape varieties grown throughout the world. The varieties that are the most significant, to one degree or another, in the areas where they are cultivated are profiled over the following pages.*

## CROSSES AND HYBRIDS
A cross between grape varieties within one species is called a cross, whereas a cross between varieties from different species is called a hybrid. Cross the same grape varieties more than once and the odds are that the new strains produced will not be the same. Thus *Sylvaner x Riesling* is not only the parentage of the Rieslaner, but also the Scheurebe, two totally different grapes. It is also possible to cross a variety with itself and produce a different grape. In this glossary, the parentage of crosses and hybrids is always in italic.

## CLONES AND CLONING
Within varietal limitations, intensive selection can produce a vine to suit specific conditions, such as to increase yield, resist certain diseases, or to thrive in a particular climate. Identical clones of this vine can then be replicated an infinite number of times by microbiogenetic techniques. Clones are named by number and initial. For instance, "Riesling clone 88Gm" is the 88th clone of the Riesling variety produced at Geisenheim (Gm), the German viticultural research station. A "localized" clone is a vine that has evolved naturally under specific conditions within a particular environment. These may be named first by grape variety and then by locality and referred to as subvarieties. However, the name of the original variety is often entirely forgotten with the passing of time, so that the variety acquires a new name altogether.

## GRAPE COLOR
Most white wines are made from "white" grapes, which actually range from green to amber-yellow. On the other hand, most red or rosé wines are made from "black" grapes, which vary from red to blue-black. White wine can also be made from most black grapes because, with only a few exceptions (categorized as *teinturier*, literally "dyer," grapes) only the skin is colored, not the juice. But red wine can be made only from black grapes, because it is pigments in the skin, called anthocyanins, that give the wine its color. The acidity in the skin's sap also affects the color of its wine: high acid levels gives a ruddy color, while the lower the acidity the more purple, and eventually violet, the wine becomes.

# WHITE GRAPE VARIETIES

**Note** Some pink-colored varieties, such as Gewürztraminer and Pinot Gris, are included in this section because the wine they make is essentially white.

### ALBALONGA
A *Rieslaner x Sylvaner* cross developed and grown in Germany for its naturally high sugar level and early-ripening qualities.

### ALIGOTÉ
*See box, below.*

### ALTESSE
The finest of Savoie's traditional varieties, this grape makes delightfully rich and fragrant wines.

### ALVARINHO
The classic Vinho Verde grape, although it might not rank as a classic grape variety *per se.*

### ARINTO
The Arinto is one of Portugal's potentially excellent white grapes. Its use in the small district of Bucelas is to make a crisp, lemony wine that ages well.

### ARNEIS
Literally meaning "little rascal," this Piedmontese grape was so named because of its erratic ripening. Once threatened by commercial extinction, this delicately aromatic variety is now extremely fashionable.

### ASSYRTIKO
One of the better-quality indigenous varieties of Greece.

### AUXERROIS
At home in Alsace, Luxembourg, and England, Auxerrois makes a fatter wine than Pinot Blanc, so suits cooler situations. Its musky richness has immediate appeal, but it is inclined to low acidity and blowsiness in hotter climates.

### BACCHUS
A (*Riesling x Sylvaner*) x *Müller-Thurgau* cross that is one of Germany's more superior crosses.

### BORRADO DES MOSCAS
A Dão grape, literally called "fly droppings," Borrado des Moscas retains high natural acidity at high alcohol levels, making it well suited to white winemaking in hot areas.

### BOUVIER
A modest-quality variety in Austria and one which, as Ranina, produces the "Tiger's Milk" wine of Slovenia.

### BUAL
The richest and fattest of Madeira's four classic grape varieties.

### CHARDONEL
Known as "Chard in Hell" to many a wine judge forced to taste its wines, Chardonel is a *Seyval x Chardonnay* cross made by Cornell University in 1953, but not released until 1990. So far the wines produced have been more bland than even the most anonymous Chardonnay.

### CHARDONNAY
*See box, opposite.*

### CHASSELAS
Responsible for the best-forgotten Pouilly-sur-Loire wines (not to be confused with Pouilly-Blanc Fumé), this variety is at its modest best in Switzerland's Valais (where it is known as the Fendant) and Alsace. Primarily a good grape for eating.

### CHENIN BLANC
*See box, opposite.*

### CLAIRETTE
A sugar-rich, intrinsically flabby grape best known for its many wines of southern France. It is the Muscat though, not the Clairette, which is chiefly responsible for the "Clairette de Die" in the Rhône.

### COLOMBARD
This produces thin, acidic wine ideal for the distillation of Armagnac and Cognac. It has also adapted well to the hotter winelands of California and South Africa, where its high acidity is a positive attribute.

### CRUCHEN BLANC
Widely cultivated, this variety usually, but incorrectly, has the tag of Riesling attached to it, such as Cape Riesling and Clare Riesling.

### DELAWARE
This American hybrid of uncertain parentage was developed in Frenchtown, New Jersey, and propagated in Delaware, Ohio, in the mid-19th century. Although grown in New York State and Brazil, it is far more popular in Japan.

### ALIGOTÉ
*This is a thin-skinned grape of unexceptional quality grown in Burgundy and Bulgaria. It makes tart wines of moderate alcoholic content, but in exceptionally hot years they can have good weight and richness. The variety's best wines come from certain Burgundian villages, especially Bouzeron, where the quality may be improved by the addition of a little Chardonnay.*

## CHARDONNAY

*This is the greatest nonaromatic dry white wine grape in the world, despite the proliferation of cheap, identikit Chardonnay wines that are churned out around the world. This classic variety is responsible for producing the greatest white Burgundies and is one of the three major grape types used in the production of Champagne.*

## CHENIN BLANC

*A variety that acquired its name from Mont-Chenin in the Touraine district in about the 15th century, it can be traced back to Anjou, around A.D. 845. The grape has a good acidity level, thin skin, and a high natural sugar content, making it very suitable for either sparkling or sweet wines, although some dry wines, notably Savennières, are made from it.*

## EHRENFELSER
A *Riesling* x *Sylvaner* cross, the Ehrenfelser has turned out to be a *cul-de-sac* in British Columbia, Canada, where it remains the preserve of a few die-hards.

## ELBLING
This variety was once held in high esteem in Germany and France. The major Mosel grape in the 19th century, it is now mostly confined to the Ober-Mosel where its very acid, neutral flavor makes it useful for German *Sekt*. In Alsace it was *Knipperlé* and its former position was such that one of the *grand cru* Guebwiller slopes was named after it.

## EMERALD RIESLING
A *Muscadelle* x *Riesling* cross, this grape was developed for cultivation in California by a Professor Olmo of UC-Davis fame as the sister to his Ruby Cabernet cross.

## FABER
A *Weissburgunder* x *Müller-Thurgau* cross grown in Germany, where it produces a fruity wine with a distinctive light Muscat aroma.

## FOLLE BLANCHE
Traditionally used for the distillation of Armagnac and Cognac, the Folle Blanche grape also produces the Gros Plant wine of the Loire Valley.

## FORTA
A little of this *Madeleine Angevine* x *Sylvaner* cross is grown in Germany, where it produces good-quality grapes that are rich in sugar.

## FREISAMER
A *Sylvaner* x *Pinot Gris* cross that is grown in Germany and produces a full, neutral, Sylvaner-like wine.

## FURMINT
This strong, distinctively flavored grape is the most important variety used to make Tokaji in Hungary.

## GARGANEGA BIANCO
The principal grape used in the production of Soave.

## GEWÜRZTRAMINER
*See box, below.*

## GLORIA
A *Sylvaner* x *Müller-Thurgau* cross grown in Germany, where it yields grapes that are rich in sugar, but make rather neutral wines.

## GRENACHE BLANC
This is the white Grenache variant that is widely planted in France and

## GEWÜRZTRAMINER

*At its most clear-cut and varietally distinctive in Alsace (where it is never spelled with an umlaut), this variety produces very aromatic wines that are naturally low in acidity. The Gewürztraminer's famous spiciness is derived from terpenes, which are found in the grape's skins. The grapes have to be ripe, otherwise the wine will just have a soft rose-petal character, and the wine must not be acid-adjusted or the spice will lack breadth and potential complexity.*

Spain. It is an ancient Spanish variety with the potential to produce a good-quality, full-bodied wine.

## GRÜNER VELTLINER
This is the most important wine grape in Austria, where it produces fresh, well-balanced wines, with a light, fruity, sometimes slightly spicy, flavor. Top-quality Grüner Veltliner from the Wachau can have a penetrating pepperiness.

## GUTENBORNER
This *Müller-Thurgau* x *Chasselas* cross is grown in Germany and England. It produces grapes with intrinsically high sugar levels, but makes rather neutral wines.

## HARSLEVELŰ
A Hungarian grape that is the second most important Tokaji variety. It produces a full, rich, and powerfully perfumed wine.

## HUXELREBE
A *Chasselas* x *Muscat Courtillier* cross that is grown in Germany and England, and is capable of producing good-quality wine.

## JACQUÈRE
The workhorse grape of the Savoie, the Jacquère is subject to rot, has a neutral flavor and high acidity.

## JOHANNISBERG RIESLING
This is a synonym often used to distinguish a wine that is made from the true Riesling grape. Many people believe that the Riesling is at its classic best when grown in the Rheingau vineyards of Johannisberg, thus the synonym most probably evolved as a way of indicating that a wine contained Riesling grapes "as grown in Johannisberg."

## KANZLER
A *Müller-Thurgau* x *Sylvaner* cross that produces a good Sylvaner substitute in the Rheinhessen.

## KERNER
A *Trollinger* x *Riesling* cross that produces wines with a high natural sugar content and good acidity, but a very light aroma.

## LEN DE L'EL
Flavorsome, naturally sugar-rich grape that is used in Gaillac.

## MACABÉO
This is a Spanish variety used to "lift" a sparkling Cava blend and give it freshness. Bearing the name of Viura, it is also responsible for the "new wave" of fresh, unoaked white Rioja.

## MADELEINE ANGEVINE
This is a *Précoce de Malingre* x *Madeleine Royale* cross that is grown quite successfully in England, where it produces a characteristically light-bodied, aromatic wine.

## MANSENG
The Gros Manseng and Petit Manseng are grown in southwestern France, and are well known mainly for producing the legendary Jurançon Moelleux.

## MARIENSTEINER
A *Sylvaner* x *Rieslaner* cross that is grown in Germany and is generally considered superior to the Sylvaner.

## MARSANNE
This grape makes fat, rich, full wines and is one of the two major varieties used to produce the rare white wines of Hermitage and Châteauneuf-du-Pape.

## MAUZAC
A late-ripening grape with good acidity, grown in southwestern France, Mauzac is flexible in the wines it produces, but is particularly suitable for sparkling wine.

## MELON DE BOURGOGNE
This variety was transplanted from Burgundy to Nantais where it replaced less hardy vines after the terrible winter of 1709. Most famous for its production of Muscadet. When fully ripe, it makes very flabby wines, lacking in acidity, although curiously it can be successful in California's warmer climes.

## MORIO-MUSKAT
This *Sylvaner* x *Pinot Blanc* cross is widely grown in the Rheinpfalz and Rheinhessen of Germany. It has always been intriguing how such neutral parents could produce such

a powerfully aromatic offspring, but now we know that the Traminer is one of Sylvaner's parents, the answer is obviously in the genes.

### MÜLLER-THURGAU
This variety was bred at Geisenheim in 1882 by Professor Hermann Müller, who hailed from the canton of Thurgau in Switzerland, and was named after him by August Dern in 1891. It was originally believed to be a *Riesling* x *Sylvaner* cross, but not one single plant has ever reverted to Sylvaner, and the closest resemblance to it is the Rabaner, a *Riesling (clone 88Gm)* x *Riesling (clone 64Gm)*. This seems to confirm the theory that the Müller-Thurgau is, in fact, a self-pollinated Riesling seed. It is more prolific than the Riesling, has a typically flowery bouquet and good fruit, but lacks the Riesling's characteristic sharpness of definition. Although this variety has a justifiably important position in the production of cheap German *Tafelwein*, its cultivation in the classic Riesling vineyards of the Mosel does tend to devalue that

great wine region. It is widely planted in English and New Zealand vineyards, although in both cases the acreage devoted to it has shrunk markedly since the 1990s.

### MULTANER
A *Riesling* x *Sylvaner* cross, a small amount of this variety is grown in Germany. However, the area planted is declining because the grapes need to be very ripe.

### MUSCADELLE
A singular variety that has nothing to do with the Muscat family, although it does have a musky aroma and there is, confusingly, a South African synonym for the Muscat—the Muskadel. In Bordeaux, small quantities of this grape add a certain lingering "after-smell" to some of the sweet wines, but the Muscadelle is at its sublime best in Australia, where it is called the Tokay and produces a rich and sweet "liqueur wine."

### MUSCAT
A family name for numerous related varieties, subvarieties, and localized

clones of the same variety, all of which have a distinctive musky aroma and a pronounced grapey flavor. The wines that are produced range from dry to sweet, still to sparkling, and fortified.

### MUSCAT À PETITS GRAINS
*See box, left.*

### MUSCAT D'ALEXANDRIE
An extremely important grape in South Africa, where it makes mostly sweet, but some dry, wines. In France, it is responsible for the fortified wine Muscat de Rivesaltes (a very tiny production of unfortified dry Muscat is also made in Rivesaltes), and the grape is also used for both wine and raisin production in California.

### MUSCAT OTTONEL
An East European variety which, because of its relative hardiness, is now in the process of replacing the Muscat à Petits Grains in Alsace.

### NOBLESSA
This is a low-yielding *Madeleine Angevine* x *Sylvaner* cross grown in Germany, which produces grapes with a high sugar level.

### NOBLING
A *Sylvaner* x *Chasselas* cross grown in Baden, Germany, its grapes have high sugar and acidity levels.

### ONDENC
A grape once widely planted in southwestern France and popular in Bergerac, it is now grown more in Australia than in France. Its acidity makes it useful for sparkling wines.

### OPTIMA
Developed in 1970, this (*Riesling* x *Sylvaner*) x *Müller-Thurgau* cross is already widely grown in Germany because it ripens even earlier than the early-ripening Müller-Thurgau.

### ORTEGA
A *Müller-Thurgau* x *Siegerrebe* cross that is grown in both Germany and

England, its aromatic grapes have naturally high sugar and make a pleasantly fragrant and spicy wine.

### PALOMINO
The classic sherry grape variety.

### PARELLADA
The major white grape variety of Catalonia, used for still wines and sparkling Cava, in which it imparts a distinctive aroma and is used to soften the firm Xarel-lo grape.

### PERLE
A *Gewürztraminer* x *Müller-Thurgau* cross, this grape can survive winter temperatures as low as -22°F (-30°C), and produces a light, fragrant, and fruity wine, but in low yields.

### PINOT BLANC
A variety that is perhaps at its best in Alsace, where it is most successful, producing fruity, well-balanced wines with good grip and alcohol content. Plantings of the true Pinot Blanc are gradually diminishing worldwide.

### PINOT GRIS
*See box, below left.*

### POULSARD
The Jura's famous grape with pink skin and pink juice can produce a fine and aromatic *vin gris*.

### PROSECCO
This grape is responsible for producing a great deal of very ordinary Italian sparkling wine.

### RABANER
This *Riesling (clone 88Gm)* x *Riesling (clone 64Gm)* cross has the dubious honor of being the variety that most resembles the Müller-Thurgau.

### RABIGATO
This is the main white port grape variety. It is also known as Rabo da Ovelha, or "ewe's tail."

## REGNER

The parents of this *Luglienca Bianca* x *Gamay* cross are a curious combination. Why anyone would consider crossing a table grape with the red wine grape of Beaujolais to create a German white wine variety is a mystery. Predictably it produces sugar-rich grapes and mild, Müller-Thurgau-like wines.

## REICHENSTEINER

This *Müller-Thurgau* x *Madeleine Angevine* x *Calabreser-Fröhlich* cross is grown in Germany and England. Its sugar-rich grapes produce a mild, delicate, somewhat neutral, Sylvaner-like wine.

## RHODITIS

This grape is used as a supporting variety in the making of Retsina, a use only eclipsed by its suitability for the distilling pot!

## RIESLANER

A *Riesling* x *Sylvaner* cross mainly grown in Franken, Germany, where it produces sugar-rich grapes and full-bodied, rather neutral wines.

## RIESLING

*See box, opposite.*

## RKATSITELI

A grape variety that is grown extensively in Russia, on a scale that would cover the vineyards of Champagne at least 10 times over. The Soviets consider it to be a high-quality wine grape; it is also grown in Bulgaria, China, California, and New York State.

## ROBOLA

Confined to the island of Cephalonia, this is a good-quality Greek grape.

## ROMORANTIN

An obscure variety that is confined to the Loire Valley, Romorantin can produce a delicate, attractive, and flowery wine if it is not overcropped.

## ROUSSANNE

One of two major varieties used to produce the rare white wines of Hermitage and Châteauneuf-du-Pape in France's Rhône Valley, this grape makes the finer, more delicate wines, while those made from the Marsanne tend to be fatter and richer.

## SACY

A minor grape variety that produces bland "stretching" wine and is grown in small quantities in the Chablis district. Its high acidity could make it very useful in the production of sparkling wines.

## SAINT-ÉMILION

This is a synonym for the Ugni Blanc in France and for the Sémillon in Romania.

## SAUVIGNON BLANC

*See box, below.*

## SAUVIGNONASSE

This literally means "Sauvignon-like" and is, in fact, the Sauvignon Vert, which confusingly is no relation to the Sauvignon Blanc. According to Pierre Galet, this is the Tocai Friulano, although some find this hard to accept. The high-yielding Sauvignonasse is grown in Chile, where it used to masquerade as Sauvignon Blanc until the mid-1990s.

## SAVAGNIN

This grape is a nonaromatic Traminer, and it is responsible for the sherry-like *vin jaune* of the Jura, of which the best known is Château Chalon. The Savagnin Rosé is the nonaromatic Traminer Rosé (from which the highly aromatic Gewürztraminer evolved) and this grape grows in the village of Heiligenstein, Alsace, where it is known as the Klevener de Heiligenstein.

## SAVATIANO

This grape variety was used by the Greeks to make Retsina. A pure, unresinated Savatiano called Kanza is made in Attica, the heartland of Retsina.

### SÉMILLON

*In Sauternes and Barsac, this is the grape susceptible to "noble rot." Some say its aroma is reminiscent of lanolin, but as pure lanolin is virtually odorless, the comparison hardly conveys the Sémillon's distinctive bouquet. For dry wine, this grape is at its best in Australia, particularly the Hunter Valley, where its lime fruit takes to oak like a duck to water, whereas bottle-aged Sémillon can be sublime after several decades.*

## SCHEUREBE

A *Riesling* x *Sylvaner* cross, this is one of the best of Germany's new varieties. When ripe, it makes very good aromatic wines, but, if it is harvested too early, very herbaceous cat's-pee.

## SCHÖNBURGER

A *Spätburgunder* x (*Chasselas Rosé* x *Muscat Hamburg*) cross, this grape is grown in Germany and England. It produces sugar-rich grapes that make wine with good aromatic qualities but low acidity.

## SÉMILLON

*See box, above.*

## SEPTIMER

A *Gewürztraminer* x *Müller-Thurgau* cross grown in Germany, where it is early-ripening and produces sugar-rich grapes that are made into aromatic wines.

## SERCIAL

This classic grape of Madeira is reputed to be a distant relative of the Riesling. However, judging by its totally different leaf shape, this seems rather unlikely.

## SEYVAL BLANC

This *Seibel 5656* x *Seibel 4986* hybrid is the most successful of the many Seyve-Villard crosses. It is grown primarily in New York State and England, where it produces attractive wines.

## SIEGERREBE

This is a *Madeleine Angevine* x *Gewürztraminer* cross, a grape that is widely grown in Germany.

## SYLVANER

*See box, next page.*

## SYMPHONY

Plantations of this *Muscat d'Alexandrie* x *Grenache Gris* cross rapidly increased in California in the mid-1990s, althouth it was developed by Professor Olmo as long ago as 1940. The wine it makes is usually off-dry with a distinctly flowery-grapey Muscat aroma.

## TORRONTÉS

Various different clones of this lightly aromatic grape are found throughout South America, but particularly in Argentina. No relation to the Spanish Torrontés (which is a local synonym for the Monastrell Blanco) or Torrontés Riojano (which is a local synonym for the Malvoisie).

## TRAMINETTE

A *JS 23–416* x *Gewürztraminer* hybrid that was developed by Cornell University and released in 1996, since when it has become planted here and there throughout the Atlantic Northeast. Some American winemakers consider it superior to Gewürztraminer because of its significantly higher acidity, but this interferes with aromatics, which are more "spiky" than the Gewürztraminer's classic broad-spice bouquet. Notwithstanding this, there have been successes, even if they are few and far between. Generally perceived as a cool-climate grape, the Traminette's high acidity does however raise the question of whether it might not fare much better in the warmer climes of California.

## TROUSSEAU GRIS

This grape is now more widely grown in California and New Zealand than in its traditional home of the northern Jura, France. It is yet another grape that has been erroneously tagged with the Riesling name in the New World but does not resemble that grape in the slightest.

## UGNI BLANC

A variety that usually makes light, even thin, wines that have to be distilled, the Ugni Blanc is ideal for making Armagnac and Cognac. There are a few exceptions, but most wines are light, fresh, and quaffing at their very best.

### SAUVIGNON BLANC

*Sauvignon Blanc is at its best defined in New Zealand, particularly Marlborough, and is still a long way off achieving a similar level of quality and consistency in its home location of the Loire Valley. It is improving in Bordeaux, where it is also used in Sauternes and Barsac blends. Some exciting wines have begun to emerge from the Cape winelands, South Africa (ignoring those that are artificially flavored), but California remains hugely disappointing, even though its vines are the same Sauvignon Blanc clone as New Zealand.*

## SYLVANER

*Originally from Austria, this variety is widely planted throughout Central Europe. It is prolific, early maturing, and yields the dry wines of Franken and Alsace. It is also widely believed to be the Zierfandler of Austria. Sylvaner has a tart, earthy, yet neutral flavor, which takes on a tomato-like richness in the bottle. This grape is now known to be the offspring of the Österreichisch Weiss and Traminer.*

## VIOGNIER

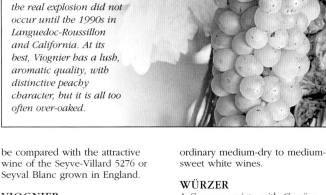

*This individual, shy-bearing variety was until relatively recently confined to a tiny part of the Rhône Valley, where it produced the famous wines of Condrieu and Château Grillet. Although this variety crept out to Australia in the 1970s, the real explosion did not occur until the 1990s in Languedoc-Roussillon and California. At its best, Viognier has a lush, aromatic quality, with distinctive peachy character, but it is all too often over-oaked.*

## VERDELHO

A successful grape variety for making white wines in Australia, the Verdelho is possibly connected to the Verdello of Italy. Verdelho is best known, however, as a classic grape variety that is grown on Madeira for the production of the island's fortified wine (a Verdelho *tinto* also exists on the island).

## VERDICCHIO

As well as being used to make Verdicchio wine, this grape is also employed for blending.

## VILLARD BLANC

This *Seibel 6468* x *Seibel 6905* hybrid is the widest cultivated of the Seyve-Villard crosses in France. Its slightly bitter, iron-rich wine cannot be compared with the attractive wine of the Seyve-Villard 5276 or Seyval Blanc grown in England.

## VIOGNIER

*See box, above.*

## WELSCHRIESLING

No relation whatsoever to the true Riesling, this variety is grown throughout Europe, producing ordinary medium-dry to medium-sweet white wines.

## WÜRZER

A German variety with *Gewürz-traminer* x *Müller-Thurgau* origins.

## XAREL-LO

A Spanish grape variety vital to the sparkling Cava industry, Xarel-lo makes firm, alcoholic wines.

# BLACK GRAPE VARIETIES

## AGIORGITIKO

An excellent indigenous Greek grape variety that is responsible for the rich and often oak-aged wines of Nemea.

## ALICANTE BOUSCHET

A *Petit Bouschet* x *Grenache* cross, this is a *teinturier* grape, with vivid, red juice. It was a favorite during Prohibition, when the rich color of its juice enabled bootleggers to stretch wines with water and sugar. Although the cultivation of this grape has increased by 42 percent since 1995, Alicante Bouschet is used primarily for port-style wines today, and is seldom seen as a varietal table wine. The secret of a good Alicante Bouschet table wine is in achieving the tannins, structure, and mouthfeel that are compatible with its naturally inky-purple color. Many moons ago, Angelo Papagni's death-defying Alicante Bouschet was not to be missed, and Coturri and Jim Clendenen (with Il Podere dell'Olivos) have at times dabbled very successfully with this variety. Rainbow Ridge ("the first gay-owned winery in the country") has yet to demonstrate that its 2001 is more than a flash in the pan. Which leaves the organically minded Topolos as the only consistently high-quality producer of Alicante Bouschet nowadays.

## BARBERA

A prolific Italian variety grown in Piedmont, the Barbera makes light, fresh, fruity wines that are sometimes very good.

## BASTARDO

This is the classic port grape and is identified as the Trousseau, an ancient variety once widely cultivated in the Jura, France.

## BLACK SPANISH

This grape is making something of a minor revival in Texas, where it was widely grown in the 1830s to make a portlike wine. This is, in fact, Lenoir or Jacquez, and contrary to those who believe it to be a natural *aestivalis-cinerea-vinifera* hybrid, 100 percent *vinifera*.

## CABERNET FRANC

*See box, right.*

## CABERNET PFEFFER

A grape of disputed origins. The French call this Pfeffer Cabernet (also called Fer Servadou), whereas the Americans have transposed the French name into Cabernet Pfeffer, which for Anglo-Saxons slips off the tongue easily and is more rational. There are various opinions as to its origins in the U.S., the most plausible being a 19th-century cross (but no one knows what with or who made the cross, and cannot be more precise than a 100-year-old span). Only two U.S. sources of this variety exist today: the 100-year-old Wirz Family vineyard in Monterey's Cienega Valley, California, and one of Casa Nuestra's vineyards in Oakville, where the vines were planted in the 1940s.

## CABERNET SAUVIGNON

*See box, opposite.*

## CARIGNAN

A Spanish grape grown extensively in southern France and California. One of its synonyms—Mataro—is a common name for the Mourvèdre, which also provides a well-colored wine, but one that is not quite as harsh. A Carignan Blanc and Gris also exist.

## CARMENÈRE

An old *bordelais* variety that was almost extinct, until it was discovered in Chile posing as Merlot, and then in Franciacorta, where it was pretending to be

## CABERNET FRANC

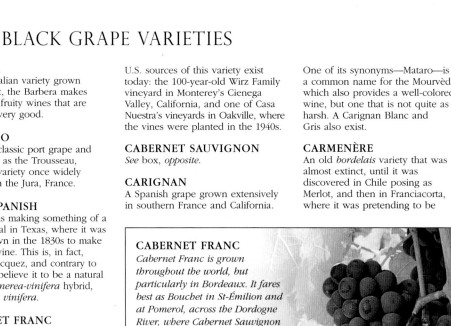

*Cabernet Franc is grown throughout the world, but particularly in Bordeaux. It fares best as Bouchet in St-Émilion and at Pomerol, across the Dordogne River, where Cabernet Sauvignon is less well represented. Grown under neutral conditions, it might not be easy to distinguish any significant varietal differences between the two Cabernets, but, suited as they are to different situations, the Cabernet Franc tends to produce a slightly earthy style of wine that is very aromatic, but has less fine characteristics on the palate when compared to the Cabernet Sauvignon.*

## CABERNET SAUVIGNON

*The noblest variety of Bordeaux, the Cabernet Sauvignon, rich in color, aroma, and depth, is vitally important to the classic Médoc wines. Many of its classical traits have been transplanted as far afield as California, Chile, and Australia. The complexities that this grape can achieve transcend simplistic comparisons to cedar, blackcurrants, or violets. The Cabernet Sauvignon's parents are now known to be Cabernet Franc and Sauvignon Blanc.*

## GAMAY

*The mass-produced wine of this famous grape from Beaujolais has a tell-tale "pear-drop" aroma, indicative of its macération carbonique style of vinification. These wines should be drunk very young and fresh, although traditionally vinified wines from Beaujolais' 10 classic crus can be aged like other red wines and, after 10 or 15 years, develop Pinot Noir traits. This may be because the grape is an ancient, natural clone of Pinot Noir. In France, Gamay Beaujolais is the synonym for true Gamay.*

Cabernet Franc (interestingly, one of Carmenère's synonyms is Grand Vidure, while one of Cabernet Franc's names is Gros Vidure). So far, the Carmenère produced in Franciacorta has more finesse than those in Chile, but overall there is a tendency to produce wines with a marked blackcurrant character that seldom develops complexity.

### CÉSAR

A minor grape variety of moderate quality that is still used in some areas of Burgundy, most notably for Bourgogne Irancy.

### CINSAULT

A prolific grape found mainly in southern Rhône and Languedoc-Roussillon vineyards, where it makes robust, well-colored wines. It is best blended, as happens at Châteauneuf-du-Pape, for example.

### CONCORD

The widest-cultivated variety in North America outside of California, this variety has an extremely pronounced "foxy" flavor.

### DOLCETTO

Underrated variety found in northwestern Italy, where it is often overcropped, but can be delightful when yields are restricted.

### GAMAY

*See box, above.*

### GRACIANO

An important variety used in the production of Rioja, where a small amount lends richness and fruit to a blend, Graciano could be the next pure varietal to grab the headlines.

### GRENACHE

*See box, right.*

### GROLLEAU

A prolific grape with a high natural sugar content, it is important for the bulk production of Anjou rosé, but rarely interesting in terms of quality.

### KADARKA

Hungary's most widely cultivated grape variety is grown throughout the Balkans. It was once thought to be the same as the Zinfandel, but this theory no longer persists. It makes pleasant, light, and fruity wine.

### LAMBRUSCO

An Italian variety, this is famous for its production of the medium-sweet, red, frothy wine of the same name in the Emilia-Romagna area.

### LIMBERGER

An Austrian variety (also called Blaufränkisch) that makes a relatively simple, light red wine. This grape is also grown in the Atlantic Northeast, where it is more commonly referred to as Lemberger (a name that is also used elsewhere, erroneously, as a synonym for the Gamay).

### MALBEC

This grape is traditionally used in Bordeaux blends in order to provide color and tannin. It is also grown in the Loire, Cahors, and Mediterranean regions, among many others, and was the grape responsible for the "black wine of Cahors"—a legendary name, if not wine, in the 19th century. However, Cahors is now made from a blend of grapes and is an infinitely superior wine to its predecessor.

### MAZUELO

A variety grown in Rioja, it is believed to be the Carignan, although it bears little resemblance to it, and produces wines of light, yet rich, fruit and low alcohol.

### MERLOT

*See box, next page.*

### MONTEPULCIANO

A late-ripening variety that performs best in the Abruzzi region of Italy, where its wines are very deep in color, and can either be full of soft, fat, luscious fruit, or made in a much firmer, more tannic, style.

### MONASTRELL

An underrated Spanish variety that is usually hidden in blends. However, it does have a full and distinctive flavor and could make individual wines of some appeal.

### MONDEUSE

This variety may have originally hailed from Friuli in northeastern Italy, where it is known as the Refosco. It is now planted as far afield as the Savoie in France, parts of the U.S., including California, and in Switzerland, Italy, the Argentine, and Australia, where it is often an important constituent of the fortified port-type wines.

### MOURVÈDRE

This excellent-quality grape has been used more than other lesser varieties in Châteauneuf-du-Pape blends in recent years. It is grown extensively throughout southern France, and, under the name of the Mataro, also in Spain. This is one of Australia's widest-cultivated black grapes, but a declining force in southern California.

### NEBBIOLO

*See box, next page.*

### NORTON

Also known as Cynthiana, although at one time Norton and Cynthiana were thought to be different varieties. Described accurately by some of its proponents as "The Real American Grape" because, unlike Zinfandel, Norton (or Cynthiana) is native to the U.S. It is pure *Vitis aestivalis*, not *vinifera*, but does not have any "foxy" character. Norton yields very small grapes with high pip ratio, necessitating *déstelage* to avoid excessively harsh tannins in the wine. Acidity is high, with an unusually high proportion of malic acidity, and the wine has the unnerving ability seemingly to "stain" glass! That said, it is the only wild grape capable of producing fine wine.

### PAMID

This is the most widely cultivated of Bulgaria's indigenous black grape varieties. It makes light and fruity quaffing wine.

## GRENACHE

*The Grenache is grown in southern France, where it is partly responsible for the wines of Châteauneuf-du-Pape, Tavel, and many others. It is the mainstay of Rioja, makes port-style and light rosé wines in California, and is also grown in South Africa. Its wines are rich, warm, and alcoholic, sometimes too much so, and require blending with other varieties. The true Grenache has nothing to do with the Grenache de Logroño of Spain, which is, in fact, the Tempranillo or Tinto de Rioja. Some sources say the Alicante (a synonym of the Grenache) is the Alicante Bouschet (or plain Bouschet in California), but this too is misleading.*

## MERLOT

*Merlot produces nicely colored wines, soft in fruit but capable of great richness. It is invaluable in Bordeaux, bringing fruity lusciousness and a velvet quality to wines that might otherwise be rather hard and austere. It is the chief grape in Château Pétrus, which is the top name in Pomerol.*

## PINOT MEUNIER

*An important variety in Champagne, where vinified white gives more upfront appeal of fruit than the Pinot Noir when young, and is therefore essential for early-drinking Champagnes. Its characteristics are more immediate, but less fine and somewhat earthier than those of the Pinot Noir. The Pinot Meunier is extensively cultivated in the Marne Valley area of Champagne, where its resistance to frost makes it the most suitable vine. Now cropping up all over the place, and can make a red wine very similar to Pinot Noir.*

### PETIT VERDOT
A grape that has been used to good effect in Bordeaux because it is a late ripener, bringing acidity to the overall balance of a wine. Certain modern techniques of viticulture and vinification have rendered it less valuable, which might prove to be a pity, because it also produces a characterful, long-lived, and tannic wine when it is sufficiently ripe.

### PETITE SIRAH
An ancient cross between Syrah and Peloursin, the Petite Sirah seems more at home in California than its native France.

### PINEAU D'AUNIS
This grape is best known for its supporting role in the production of Rosé d'Anjou.

### PINOTAGE
A *Pinot Noir* x *Cinsault* cross developed in 1925, it occupies an important position in South African viticulture, where its rustic and high-toned wine is greatly appreciated.

### PINOT MEUNIER
*See box, above.*

### PINOT NOIR
*See box, below.*

### PORTUGIESER
The most widely planted black grape variety in Germany, it originates in the Danube district of Austria, not in Portugal as its name suggests. It makes very ordinary and extremely light red wine, so it is often used in bad years to blend with the too acidic white wine.

### RONDINELLA
An Italian variety, secondary to the Corvina grape in terms of area planted, it is used in the production of Bardolino and Valpolicella.

### ROTBERGER
A *Trollinger* x *Riesling* cross, the parents seem an odd couple, but the offspring is surprisingly successful, producing some excellent rosé wines.

### RUBY CABERNET
An American *Carignan* x *Cabernet*

*Sauvignon* cross that originated in 1936, first fruited in 1940, and made its first wine in 1946.

### SANGIOVESE
This is the principal variety used in Chianti. In a pure varietal form it can lack fruit and have a metallic finish.

### SYRAH
*See box, opposite.*

### TANNAT
This grape originated from the Basque region, and has the potential to produce deeply colored, tannic wines of great longevity (although there are certain modern methods of vinification that often change the traditional character of Tannat wines). The variety's best-known wines are the attractive red Madiran and Irouléguy. A little Tannat wine is used for blending purposes in and around the town of Cahors.

### TEMPRANILLO
This is the most important variety in Rioja, where it is traditional to blend the grapes, although many pure

Tempranillo wines of excellent quality are made. It is capable of producing long-lived wines of some finesse and complexity. It is also an important variety in Argentina.

### TOURIGA FRANCESA
This classic port grape is no relation of the Touriga Nacional. Its wine is less concentrated, but of fine quality.

### TOURIGA NACIONAL
The finest port grape in the entire Douro, it produces fantastically rich and tannic wine, with masses of fruit, and is capable of great longevity and complexity.

### VERDELHO TINTO
A classic Madeira grape.

### XYNOMAVRO
Xyno means "acid" and "mavro" black, an indication of how dark and long-lived the wines of this excellent Greek variety can be.

### ZINFANDEL
*See box, opposite.*

## NEBBIOLO

*Famous for its production of Barolo, this grape is also responsible, totally or in part, for the other splendid wines of Piedmont in Italy, such as Gattinara, Barbaresco, Carema, and Donnaz. It often needs to be softened by the addition of Bonarda grapes, which have the same role as Merlot grapes in Bordeaux. In fact, Merlot is used in Lombardy to soften Nebbiolo for the production of Valtellina and Valtellina Superiore wines, of which Sassella can be the most velvety of all.*

## PINOT NOIR

*This is one of the classic varieties of Champagne, but its greatest fame lies in Burgundy. In the right place, and under ideal climatic conditions, the Pinot Noir can produce the richest, most velvet-smooth wines in the world. Depending on both climate and ripeness, its varietal flavor can range from cherries to strawberries. Great Pinot Noir is also made in California (notably Russian River and Santa Barbara), Oregon and Central Otago, New Zealand.*

## SYRAH

*Because the name of this grape derived from Shiraz (which Australia has adopted), the capital of Fars, the idea has sprung up that this variety must have originated in Persia. We now know that it is pure French in its breeding, being the progeny of two minor varieties, the Mondeuse Blanche and Dureza. The Syrah makes fashionably dark-colored red wines in many countries.*

## ZINFANDEL

*Once thought to be the only indigenous American Vitis vinifera grape, Zinfandel has now been positively identified by Isozyme "finger printing" as the Primitivo grape of southern Italy. However, the origins of this grape are Croatian, where it is known as the Crljenak Kastelanski. Depending on the vinification method used, Zinfandel can produce many different styles of wine, from rich and dark to light and fruity or nouveau style. They can be dry or sweet; white, rosé or red; dessert or sparkling.*

# GRAPE VARIETY SYNONYMS

*Many varieties of grape are known by several different synonyms. The Malbec grape, for example, has at least 34 different names, including Pressac, Auxerrois, Balouzet, Cot, Estrangey, and Grifforin. This would not be too confusing if the synonyms applied, uniquely, to the same grape variety, but unfortunately this is not the case. The Malbec is a good example. A black grape, it is known as the Auxerrois in Cahors, but in Alsace and Chablis, the Auxerrois is a white grape, while in other parts of France, the Malbec is known as the Cahors!*

SYNONYMS RELATING TO LOCALIZED clones or subvarieties are often regarded as singularly separate varieties in their own right. The Italian Trebbiano, itself a synonym for the French Ugni Blanc, has many subvarieties recognized by the Italian vine regulations. Also, many synonyms revolve around the name of another grape variety, although they are not necessarily related. Ampelographers distinguish between "erroneous" and "misleading" synonyms. The former refers to varieties that have mistakenly been given the name of another, totally different variety, whereas the latter refers to varieties whose names suggest, incorrectly, that they are related to another variety. For example, the Pinot Chardonnay, which is Chardonnay, is not remotely related to any Pinot variety whatsoever.

Albariño—Alvarinho
Alben—Elbling
Albig—Elbling
Alcaing—Macabéo
Alcabéo—Macabéo
Alicante—Grenache
Alicante Grenache—Grenache
Alva (in Portugal)—Elbling
Alzeýer Perle—Perle
Angélicant—Muscadelle
Angélico—Muscadelle
Aragad—Grenache
Aragonez—Tempranillo
Arnaison—Chardonnay
Aubaine—Chardonnay
Auvernat—Pinot Noir
Auvernat Blanc—Muscadelle
Auvernat Gris—Pinot Gris
Auvernat Gris—Pinot Meunier
Auxerrois—Malbec
Auxerrois Gris—Pinot Gris
Auxois—Pinot Gris

Baiyu—Rkatsitel
Balkan Kadarka—Kadarka
Balouzet—Malbec
Balzac—Mourvèdre
Banatski Rizling—Welschriesling
Beaunois—Chardonnay
Beaunois—Pinot Blanc
Beli Muscat—Muscat Blanc à Petits Grains
Beni Carlo—Mourvèdre
Béquin (in Bordeaux)—Ondenc
Bergeron—Roussanne
Bical Tinto—Touriga Nacional
Bidure—Cabernet Franc
Bidure—Cabernet Sauvignon
Biela Sladka Grasica—Welschriesling
Bigney—Merlot
Black Hamburg—Trollinger
Black Malvoisie—Cinsault
Blanc d'Anjou—Chenin Blanc
Blanc de Troyes—Aligoté
Blanc Doux—Sémillon

Blanc Fumé—Sauvignon Blanc
Blanc Select—Ondenc
Blanc Vert—Sacy
Blanche Feuille—Pinot Meunier
Blanc-lafitte—Mauzac
Blanquette—Clairette
Blanquette—Colombard
Blanquette—Ondenc
Blauburgunder—Pinot Noir
Blauer Limberger—Blaufränkisch
Blauer Malvasier—Trollinger
Blauer Spätburgunder—Pinot Noir
Blauer Trollinger—Trollinger
Blauer Zweigelt—Zweigelt
Blaufränkisch—Gamay
Bobal—Monastrell
Bois Dur—Carignan
Bordeleza Belcha—Tannat
Borgogna Crna—Gamay
Bötzinger—Sylvaner
Bouchet—Cabernet Franc
Bouchet—Cabernet Sauvignon
Bourdalès—Cinsault
Bourguignon Noir—Gamay
Bouschet Sauvignon—Cabernet Franc
Bouschet Sauvignon—Cabernet Sauvignon
Bouviertraube—Bouvier
Bovale—Monastrell
Breton—Cabernet Franc
Briesgaver—Elbling
Briesgaver Riesling—Elbling
Brown Muscat—Muscat Blanc à Petits Grains
Brunello (in Montalcino)—Sangiovese
Buisserate—Jacquère
Burger Elbling—Elbling
Burgundi Gamet—Gamay
Burgundi Kék—Gamay

Burgundi Lagrein—Lagrein
Burgundi Mic—Pinot Noir
Burgundi Nagyszemu—Gamay
Burgundske Sede—Pinot Gris
Burgundské Modré—Pinot Gris
Cabarnelle—Carmenère
Cabernet—Cabernet Franc
Cabernet Gris—Cabernet Franc
Cahors—Malbec
Calabrese—Sangiovese
Camobraque—Folle Blanche
Cape Riesling (in South Africa)—Cruchen Blanc
Carignan Noir—Carignan
Carignane—Carignan
Cariñena—Carignan
Carmelin—Petit Verdot
Carmenelle—Carmenère
Carmenet—Cabernet Franc
Catalan—Carignan
Catalan—Mourvèdre
Catape—Muscadelle
Cavalier—Len de l'El
Cencibel—Tempranillo
Chalosse—Folle Blanche
Chardonnay—Chasselas
Chardonnay—Pinot Blanc
Chasselas—Chardonnay
Chasselas Blanc—Chasselas
Chasselas Doré—Chasselas
Chaudenet Gras—Aligoté
Chenin Noir—Pineau d'Aunis
Chevier—Sémillon
Chevrier—Sémillon
Chiavennasca—Nebbiolo
Chira—Syrah
Christkindltraube—Gewürztraminer
Cinq-saou—Cinsault
Cinsaut—Cinsault
Clairette à Grains Ronds—Ugni Blanc

Clairette Blanc—Clairette
Clairette Blanche—Clairette
Clairette de Vence—Ugni Blanc
Clairette Ronde—Ugni Blanc
Clare Riesling (in Australia)—
   Cruchen Blanc
Clevner—Gewürztraminer
Clevner—Pinot Blanc
Codarka—Kadarka
Collemusquette—Muscadelle
Colombar—Colombard
Colombier—Colombard
Colombier—Sémillon
Cortaillod—Pinot Noir
Corvina Veronese—Corvina
Cot—Malbec
Cot à Queue Rouge—Pineau d'Aunis
Crabutet Noir—Merlot
Crna Moravka—Blaufränkisch
Crucillant—Sémillon
Cruina—Corvina
Crujillon—Carignan
Cugnette—Jacquère
Cuviller—Cinsault
Dannery—Romorantin
Dorin—Chasselas
Douce Noir—Dolcetto
Douzanelle—Muscadelle
Dreimanner—Gewürztraminer
Drumin—Gewürztraminer
Dusty Miller—Pinot Meunier
Edeltraube—Gewürztraminer
Elben—Elbling
Enragé—Folle Blanche
Enrageade—Folle Blanche
Entournerien—Syrah
Epinette Blanche—Chardonnay
Ermitage Blanc—Marsanne
Espagna—Cinsault
Espar—Mourvèdre
Esparte—Mourvèdre
Estrangey—Malbec
Estreito—Rabigato
Etaulier—Malbec
Etranger—Malbec
Farine—Sacy
Fauvet—Pinot Gris
Fehérburgundi—Pinot Blanc
Feiner Weisser Burgunder—
   Chardonnay
Fendant—Chasselas
Fendant Blanc—Chasselas
Fermin Rouge—Gewürztraminer
Fié dans le Neuvillois—
   Sauvignon Blanc
Flaischweiner—Gewürztraminer
Folle Enrageat—Folle Blanche
Formentin (in Hungary)—Savagnin
Franken—Sylvaner
Franken Riesling—Sylvaner
Frankenriesling—Sylvaner
Frankenthaler—Trollinger
Frankinja Crna—Gamay
Frankinja Modra—Gamay
Frankisch—Gewürztraminer
Frankovka—Limberger
Frankovka Modrá—Limberger
Frauentraube—Chasselas
Fréaux Hatif—a Gamay *teinturier*
French Colombard—Colombard
Frenscher—Gewürztraminer
Fromenté—Savagnin
Fromenteau Gris—Pinot Gris
Fromenteau Rouge—Gewürztraminer
Fromentot—Pinot Gris
Frontignac—Muscat Blanc à Petits Grains
Fumé Blanc—Sauvignon Blanc
Fuszeres—Gewürztraminer
Gaamez—Gamay
Gamai—Gamay
Gamay Beaujolais—Gamay
Gamay Blanc—Melon de Bourgogne
Gamay Blanc à Feuille Rond—
   Melon de Bourgogne
Gamay Castille—a Gamay *teinturier*

Gamay de Bouze—a Gamay *teinturier*
Gamay de Chaudenay—a Gamay
   *teinturier*
Gamay Fréaux—a Gamay *teinturier*
Gamay Noir—Gamay
Gamay Noir à Just Blanc—Gamay
Gamay Rond—Gamay
Gamay Teinturier Mouro—a Gamay
   *teinturier*
Gamé—Gamay
Gamza—Kadarka
Garnacha—Grenache
Garnacha Blanca—Grenache Blanc
Garnache—Grenache
Garnacho—Grenache
Garnacho Blanco—Grenache Blanc
Garnaxta—Grenache Blanc
Gelber Muscatel—Muscat Blanc
   à Petits Grains
Gelber Muscateller—Muscat Blanc
   à Petits Grains
Gelber Muskatel—Muscat Blanc à Petits
   Grains
Gelber Muskateller—Muscat Blanc
   à Petits Grains
Gelder Ortlieber—Elbling
Gentilduret Rouge—Gewürztraminer
Gentin à Romorantin—Sauvignon Blanc
Giboudot—Aligoté
Glera—Prosecco
Golden Chasselas—Chasselas
Gordo Blanco—Muscat d'Alexandrie
Goujan—Pinot Meunier
Gourdoux—Malbec
Graisse—Ugni Blanc
Graisse Blanc—Ugni Blanc
Granaccia—Grenache
Grand Picot—Mondeuse
Grande Vidure—Carmenère
Grasica—Welschriesling
Grassevina—Welschriesling
Grau Clevner—Pinot Blanc
Grauer Mönch—Pinot Gris
Grauerburgunder—Pinot Gris
Grauklevner—Pinot Gris
Gray Riesling—Trousseau Gris
Greffou—Roussanne
Grenache de Logroño—Tempranillo
Grenache Nera—Grenache
Grey Friar—Pinot Gris
Grey Pinot—Pinot Gris
Grey Riesling—Trousseau Gris
Grifforin—Malbec
Gris Cordelier—Pinot Gris
Gris Meunier—Pinot Meunier
Gris Rouge—Gewürztraminer
Gros Auxerrois—Melon de Bourgogne
Gros Blanc—Sacy
Gros Bouchet—Cabernet Franc
Gros Bouschet—Cabernet Franc
Gros Cabernet—Cabernet Franc
Gros Lot—Grolleau
Gros Monsieur—César
Gros Noir—César
Gros Noir Guillan Rouge—Malbec
Gros Plant—Folle Blanche
Gros Plant du Nantais—Folle Blanche
Gros Rhin—Sylvaner
Gros Rouge du Pays—Mondeuse
Gros Vidure—Cabernet Franc
Groslot—Grolleau
Grosse Roussette—Marsanne
Grosse Syrah—Mondeuse
Grossriesling—Elbling
Grossvernatsch—Trollinger
Grünedel—Sylvaner
Grüner—Grüner Veltliner
Grüner Silvaner—Sylvaner
Grünfrankisch—Sylvaner
Grünling—Sylvaner
Grünmuskateller—Grüner Veltliner
Guenille—Colombard
Guépie—Muscadelle
Guépie-catape—Muscadelle
Guillan—Muscadelle

Guillan-musqué—Muscadelle
Gutedel—Chasselas
Haiden—Gewürztraminer
Hanepoot—Muscat d'Alexandrie
Harriague—Tannat
Heida—Gewürztraminer
Hermitage—Cinsault
Hermitage Blanc—Marsanne
Hignin—Syrah
Hignin Noir—Syrah
Hocheimer—Riesling
Hunter Riesling (in Australia)—Sémillon
Hunter River Riesling (in Australia)—
   Sémillon
Ilegó—Macabéo
Iskendiriye Misketi—Muscat
   d'Alexandrie
Island Belle—Campbell's Early
Italianski Rizling—Welschriesling
Italiansky Rizling—Welschriesling
Jacobain—Malbec
Johannisberg Riesling—Riesling
Johannisberger—Riesling
Kadarska—Kadarka
Kékfrankos—Blaufränkisch
Kékfrankos—Gamay
Klavner—Gewürztraminer
Klein Reuschling—Elbling
Kleinberger—Elbling
Kleiner Räuschling—Elbling
Kleingelber—Elbling
Kleinweiner—Gewürztraminer
Klevener de Heiligenstein—
   Savagnin Rosé
Klevner—Pinot Blanc
Klevner—Pinot Noir
Knipperlé—Elbling
Kurztingel (in Austria)—Elbling
Lardot—Macabéo
Laski Rizling—Welschriesling
Laskiriesling—Welschriesling
Lemberger—Blaufränkisch
Lemberger—Gamay
Lemberger—Limberger
Len de lElh—Len de l'El
Lexia—Muscat d'Alexandrie
Limberger—Blaufränkisch
Limberger—Gamay
Limberger (in U.S.)—Lemberger
Liwora—Gewürztraminer
Luckens—Malbec
Lyonnaise Blanche—
   Melon de Bourgogne
Maccabeu—Macabéo
Mâconnais—Altesse
Madiran—Tannat
Magret—Malbec
Mala Dinka—Gewürztraminer
Malaga Morterille Noire—Cinsaut
Malbeck—Malbec
Malmsey—Pinot Gris
Malvagia—Pinot Gris
Malvasia—Pinot Gris
Malvasia Rey—Tinta Amarela
Malvoisie—Pinot Gris
Manseng Blanc—Manseng
Marchigiano—Verdicchio
Mataro—Carignan
Mataro—Mourvèdre
Mausat—Malbec
Maussac—Mauzac
Mauzac—Malbec
Mauzac Blanc—Mauzac
Mavrud—Mavroud
Mazuelo—Carignan
Médoc Noir—Merlot
Melon—Melon de Bourgogne
Melon Blanc—Chardonnay
Melon d'Arbois—Chardonnay
Menu Pineau—Arbois
Meunier—Pinot Meunier
Modrý Portugal—Portugieser
Moisac—Mauzac
Molette Noir—Mondeuse
Monemrasia—Pinot Gris

Monterey Riesling (in California)—
   Sylvaner
Montonec—Parellada
Montonech—Parellada
Moravka Silvanske (in Czech Republic) –
   Sylvaner
Morellino—Sangiovese
Morillon—Pinot Noir
Morillon Taconé—Pinot Meunier
Morrastel—Graciano
Moscata—Muscat Blanc à Petits Grains
Moscata Bianca—Muscat Blanc à Petits
   Grains
Moscatel—Muscat Blanc à Petits Grains
Moscatel—Muscat d'Alexandrie
Moscatel Bravo—Rabigato
Moscatel de Alejandria—Muscat
   d'Alexandrie
Moscatel de Grano Menudo—Muscat
   Blanc à Petits Grains
Moscatel de Málaga—Muscat d'Alexandrie
Moscatel de Setúbal—Muscat
   d'Alexandrie
Moscatel Dorado—Muscat Blanc à Petits
   Grains
Moscatel Gordo—Muscat d'Alexandrie
Moscatel Gordo Blanco—Muscat
   d'Alexandrie
Moscatel Menudo Bianco—Muscat Blanc
   à Petits Grains
Moscatel Romano—Muscat d'Alexandrie
Moscatel Rosé—Muscat Rosé à Petits
   Grains
Moscatel Samsó—Muscat d'Alexandrie
Moscatello—Muscat Blanc à Petits
   Grains
Moscatello Bianco—Muscat Blanc
   à Petits Grains
Moscato—Muscat Blanc à Petits Grains
Moscato d'Asti—Muscat Blanc à Petits
   Grains
Moscato di Canelli—Muscat Blanc
   à Petits Grains
Mosel Riesling—Riesling
Moselriesling—Riesling
Mosttraube—Chasselas
Mourane—Malbec
Moustère—Malbec
Moustrou—Tannat
Moustroun—Tannat
Mueller-Thurgau—Müller-Thurgau
Müller Rebe—Pinot Meunier
Müller Schwarzriesling—Pinot Meunier
Müllerrebe—Pinot Meunier
Muscade—Muscadelle
Muscadel Ottonel—Muscat Ottonel
Muscadet—Chardonnay
Muscadet—Melon de Bourgogne
Muscadet—Muscadelle
Muscadet Doux—Muscadelle
Muscat—Muscat Blanc à Petits Grains
Muscat Aigre—Ugni Blanc
Muscat Canelli—Muscat Blanc à Petits
   Grains
Muscat Cknelli—Muscat Blanc
   à Petits Grains
Muscat d'Alsace—Muscat Blanc
   à Petits Grains
Muscat d'Alsace—Muscat Rosé
   à Petits Grains
Muscat de Frontignan—Muscat Blanc
   à Petits Grains
Muscat Doré—Muscat Blanc
   à Petits Grains
Muscat Doré de Frontignan—
   Muscat Blanc à Petits Grains
Muscat Fou—Muscadelle
Muscat Gordo Blanco—Muscat
   d'Alexandrie
Muscat Rosé à Petits Grains d'Alsace—
   Muscat Rosé à Petits Grains
Muscat Roumain—Muscat d'Alexandrie
Muscatel—Muscat Blanc à Petits Grains
Muscatel Branco—Muscat Blanc
   à Petits Grains

Muscateller—Muscat Blanc à Petits Grains
Muskadel—Muscadelle
Muskat—Muscat Blanc à Petits Grains
Muskateller—Muscat Blanc à Petits Grains
Muskat-Silvaner—Sauvignon Blanc
Muskotaly—Muscat Blanc à Petits Grains
Muskotály—Muscat Ottonel
Muskuti—Muscat Blanc à Petits Grains
Musquette—Muscadelle
Nagi-Burgundi—Pinot Noir
Nagyburgundi—Pinot Noir
Napa Gamay—Gamay
Naturé—Savagnin
Nebbiolo Lampia—Nebbiolo
Nebbiolo Michet—Nebbiolo
Nebbiolo Rosé—Nebbiolo
Nebbiolo Spanna—Nebbiolo
Negri—Malbec
Negron—Mourvèdre
Nerino—Sangiovese
Neuburské—Neuburger
Noir de Pressac—Malbec
Noir Doux—Malbec
Noiren—Pinot Noir
Oesterreicher—Sylvaner
Ojo de Liebre—Tempranillo
Olasz Rizling—Welschriesling
Olaszriesling—Welschriesling
Olaszrizling—Welschriesling
Oporto—Portugieser
Ormeasco—Dolcetto
Ortlieber—Elbling
Paarl Riesling (in South Africa)—
  Cruchen Blanc
Pansa Blanca—Xarel-lo
Panse Musquée—Muscat d'Alexandrie
Parde—Malbec
Perpignanou—Graciano
Petit Bouschet—Cabernet Sauvignon
Petit Cabernet—Cabernet Sauvignon
Petit Dannezy—Romorantin
Petit Gamai—Gamay
Petit Mansenc—Manseng
Petit Merle—Merlot
Petit Pineau—Arbois
Petit Rhin—Riesling
Petit Riesling—Riesling
Petit Verdau—Petit Verdot
Petite Sainte-Marie—Chardonnay
Petite Syrah—Petite Sirah
Petite-Vidure—Cabernet Sauvignon
Petit-Fer—Cabernet Franc
Picardin Noir—Cinsault
Picotin Blanc—Roussanne
Picoutener—Nebbiolo
Picpoul—Folle Blanche
Picpoule—Folle Blanche
Picutener—Nebbiolo
Pied de Perdrix—Malbec
Pied Noir—Malbec
Pied Rouge—Malbec
Pied-Tendre—Colombard
Pinat Cervena—Gewürztraminer
Pineau—Pinot Noir
Pineau Blanche de Loire—Chenin
  Blanc
Pineau de la Loire—Chenin Blanc
Pineau de Saumur—Grolleau
Pineau Rouge—Pineau d'Aunis
Pinot Beurot—Pinot Gris
Pinot Blanc—Chardonnay
Pinot Blanc (in California)—
  Melon de Bourgogne
Pinot Blanc Chardonnay—Chardonnay
Pinot Blanc Vrai Auxerrois—Pinot Blanc
Pinot Chardonnay—Chardonnay
Pinot de la Loire—Chenin Blanc
Pinot Grigio—Pinot Gris
Pinot Vérot—Pinot Noir
Piperdy—Malbec
Pisse Vin—Aramon
Plant Boisnard—Grolleau
Plant d'Arles—Cinsault
Plant d'Aunis—Pineau d'Aunis

Plant de Brie—Pinot Meunier
Plant Dore—Pinot Noir
Ploussard—Poulsard
Portugais Bleu—Portugieser
Portugalka—Portugieser
Prèchat—Malbec
Pressac—Malbec
Preto Martinho—Negra Mole
Primativo—Primitivo
Primitivo—Crljenak Kastelanski
Prolongeau—Malbec
Prugnolo (in Montepulciano)—
  Sangiovese
Ptinc Crveny—Gewürztraminer
Pugnet—Nebbiolo
Puiechou—Sauvignon Blanc
Punechon—Sauvignon Blanc
PX—Pedro Ximénez
Quercy—Malbec
Queue-Tendre—Colombard
Queue-Verte—Colombard
Rabo da Ovelha—Rabigato
Rabo da Ovelha Tinto—Tinta Amarela
Raisinotte—Muscadelle
Rajinski Rizling—Riesling
Rajnai Rizling—Riesling
Ranfoliza—Gewürztraminer
Ranina—Bouvier
Räuschling—Elbling
Rcatzitelli—Rkatsiteli
Rdeci Traminac—Gewürztraminer
Red Trollinger—Trollinger
Refosco—Mondeuse
Reno—Riesling
Resinotte—Muscadelle
Rezlink—Riesling
Rezlink Rynsky—Riesling
Rhein Riesling—Riesling
Rheingau Riesling—Riesling
Rheingauer—Riesling
Rheinriesling—Riesling
Rhine Riesling—Riesling
Riesler—Riesling
Riesling (in Australia)—Sémillon
Riesling du Rhin—Riesling
Riesling Italianski—Welschriesling
Riesling Italico—Welschriesling
Riesling Italien—Welschriesling
Riesling Renano—Riesling
Rieslinger—Riesling
Riesling-Sylvaner—Müller-Thurgau
Rislig Rejnski—Riesling
Rismi—Welschriesling
Rivaner—Müller-Thurgau
Rizling Rajinski Bijeli—Riesling
Rizling Vlašsky—Welschriesling
Romain—César
Ronçain—César
Roriz—Tempranillo
Rössling—Riesling
Rossola—Ugni Blanc
Rotclevner—Gewürztraminer
Rotclevner—Pinot Noir
Rotedel—Gewürztraminer
Roter Nurnberger—Gewürztraminer
Roter Traminer—Gewürztraminer
Rotfranke—Gewürztraminer
Rotter Muscateller—Muscat Rosé
  à Petits Grains
Rotter Muskateller—Muscat Rosé
  à Petits Grains
Roussan—Ugni Blanc
Roussanne—Ugni Blanc
Rousselet—Gewürztraminer
Roussette—Altesse
Roussillon Tinto—Grenache
Roussillonen—Carignan
Royal Muscadine—Chasselas
Rulandské—Pinot Gris
Rulandské Bielé—Pinot Blanc
Rulandské Bílé—Pinot Blanc
Rulandské Modrý—Pinot Noir
Ruländer—Pinot Gris
Rulonski Szürkebarát—Pinot Gris
Rusa—Gewürztraminer

Rynski Rizling—Riesling
Ryzling Rynsky—Riesling
Ryzling Vlašsky—Welschriesling
Ryzlink Rýnsky—Riesling
Ryzlink Vlašsky—Welschriesling
Saint-Emilion (in Romania)—Sémillon
Saint-Emilion—Ugni Blanc
Salvagnin—Savagnin
Sangiovese di Lamole—Sangiovese
Sangiovese Dolce—Sangiovese
Sangiovese Gentile—Sangiovese
Sangiovese Toscano—Sangiovese
Sanvicetro—Sangiovese
Sargamuskotaly—Muscat Blanc à Petits
  Grains
Sauvagnin—Savagnin
Sauvignon Jaune—Sauvignon Blanc
Sauvignon Vert (in California)—
  Muscadelle
Sauvignon Vert—Sauvignonasse
Savagnin Blanc—Savagnin
Savagnin Musqué—Sauvignon Blanc
Savagnin Noir—Pinot Noir
Savagnin Rosé—Gewürztraminer
Savignan Rosé—Traminer Rosé
Savignin—Pinot Noir
Savoyanche—Mondeuse
Scharvaner—Sylvaner
Schiava—Trollinger
Schiavagrossa—Trollinger
Schiras—Syrah
Schwartz Klevner—Pinot Noir
Schwarze Frankishe—Blaufränkisch
Schwarze Melonetraube—Gamay
Schwarzriesling—Pinot Meunier
Séme—Malbec
Semijon—Sémillon
Sémillon Muscat—Sémillon
Sémillon Roux—Sémillon
Sercial (in Australia)—Ondenc
Serenne—Syrah
Seretonina (in Yugoslavia)—Elbling
Serine—Syrah
Serprina—Prosecco
Seyve-Villard—Seyval Blanc
Seyve-Villard 5276—Seyval Blanc
Shiraz—Syrah
Shyraz—Syrah
Silvain Vert—Sylvaner
Silván (in Czech Republic)—
  Sylvaner
Silvaner—Sylvaner
Silvaner Bianco—Sylvaner
Silvánske Zelené—Sylvaner
Sipon—Furmint
Sirac—Syrah
Sirah—Syrah
Sirrah—Syrah
Sirras—Syrah
Sonoma Riesling (in California)—Sylvaner
Soubirat-Parent—Malvasia
Spanna—Nebbiolo
Spätburgunder—Pinot Noir
Steen—Chenin Blanc
Surin—Sauvignon Blanc
Süssling—Chasselas
Svatovavrinéké—St. Laurent
Svätovavrinecké—St. Laurent
Syra—Syrah
Syrac—Syrah
Syras—Syrah
Szilváni (in Hungary)—Sylvaner
Szürkebarát—Pinot Gris
Talia—Ugni Blanc
Talijanski Rizling—Welschriesling
Tamyanka—Muscat Blanc
  à Petits Grains
Tanat—Tannat
Teinturier—Malbec
Tempranilla—Tempranillo
Tempranillo de la Rioja—Tempranillo
Termeno Aromatico—Gewürztraminer
Terranis—Malbec
Terrano—Mondeuse
Tinta Aragonez—Tempranillo

Tinta Bairrada—Baga
Tinta Fina—Baga
Tinta Miuda—Graciano
Tinta Roriz—Tempranillo
Tinto—Mourvèdre
Tinto Aragonés—Grenache
Tinto de la Rioja—Tempranillo
Tinto de Toro—Tempranillo
Tinto Fino—Tempranillo
Tinto Madrid—Tempranillo
Tinto Mazuela—Carignan
Tokaier—Pinot Gris
Tokay (in Australia)—Muscadelle
Tokay—Pinot Gris
Tokay d'Alsace—Pinot Gris
Tokayer—Pinot Gris
Tokay-Pinot Gris—Pinot Gris
Touriga—Touriga Nacional
Tramin—Savagnin
Traminac—Gewürztraminer
Traminac Creveni—Gewürztraminer
Traminer—Gewürztraminer
Traminer Aromatico—Gewürztraminer
Traminer Aromatique—Gewürztraminer
Traminer Musqué—Gewürztraminer
Traminer Parfumé—Gewürztraminer
Traminer Rosé—Gewürztraminer
Traminer Rosso—Gewürztraminer
Traminer Roz—Gewürztraminer
Traminer Rozovy—Gewürztraminer
Tramini—Gewürztraminer
Tramini Piros—Gewürztraminer
Trebbiano (often with local place name
  appendaged)—Ugni Blanc
Tresallier—Sacy
Trincadeira—Tinta Amarela
Ugni Noir—Aramon
Ull de Llebre—Tempranillo
Uva di Spagno—Grenache
Uva Marana—Verdicchio
Veltliner—Grüner Veltliner
Veltlini (in Hungary)—Grüner Veltliner
Veltlínské Cervene—Roter Veltliner
Veltlinske Zelene—Grüner Veltliner
Verdet—Arbois
Verdone—Verdicchio
Verdot—Petit Verdot
Verdot Rouge—Petit Verdot
Vernatsch—Trollinger
Verneuil—Romorantin
Véron—Cabernet Franc
Vert Doré—Pinot Noir
Vidure—Cabernet Sauvignon
Vionnier—Viognier
Vitraille—Merlot
Viura—Macabéo
Wälschriesling—Welschriesling
Weiss Clevner—Pinot Blanc
Weiss Musketraube—Muscat Blanc
  à Petits Grains
Weissburgunder—Pinot Blanc
Weisse Muskateller—Muscat Blanc
  à Petits Grains
Weissemuskateller—Muscat Blanc
  à Petits Grains
Weisser Clevner—Chardonnay
Weisser Elbling—Elbling
Weisser Riesling—Riesling
Weisserburgunder (in Germany)—Melon
  de Bourgogne
Weissgipfler—Grüner Veltliner
White Frontignan—Muscat Blanc
  à Petits Grains
White Hermitage—Ugni Blanc
White Pinot—Chenin Blanc
White Riesling—Riesling
Wrotham Pinot—Pinot Meunier
Xarel-lo—Xarello
Zibibbo—Muscat d'Alexandrie
Zinfandel—Crljenak Kastelanski
Zinfandel—Primitivo
Zingarello—Primitivo
Zingarello—Zinfandel
Zuti Muscat—Muscat Blanc
  à Petits Grains

# STORING WINE

*Do you have to worry about how and where to store wine? Not really. More than 95 percent of wine is ready to drink straight from the shelf and most is actually consumed within 24 hours of purchase. If you do not have a cellar—and most people do not—then there really is no need to store wine. However, if you want to keep a few bottles for convenience, common sense will tell you to place it somewhere relatively cool and dark. On the other hand, if you are determined to built up a cellar of wine (and for the enthusiast, there is nothing more enjoyable), then there are some very important factors to consider, principally temperature and light.*

## TEMPERATURE

While 52°F (11°C) is supposed to be the perfect storage temperature for wine, anything between 40°F and 65°F (5°C and 18°C) will in fact suffice for most styles of wines, providing there is no great temperature variation over a relatively short period of time. Higher temperatures increase the rate of oxidation in a wine, therefore a bottle of wine stored at 65°F (18°C) will gradually get "older" than the same wine stored at 52°F (11°C). However, a constant 59°F (15°C) is far kinder to a wine than erratic temperatures that often hit 52°F (11°C), but fluctuate between 40°F and 65°F (5°C and 18°C) from one day to the next. Such rapid changes in temperature cause the cork to shrink and expand, which can loosen the closure's grip on the inner surface of the bottle's neck, rendering the wine liable to oxidation through exposure to the air.

## LIGHT

All wines are affected negatively by the ultraviolet end of the light spectrum, but some of the harmful photo-chemical effects this causes can be reversed by cellaring a light-affected wine in darkness for a few months. Brown or dead-leaf colored wine bottles offer more natural protection from ultraviolet light than those that are made of traditional green glass. But dark green is better than light green, whereas blue and clear are the most vulnerable (which is why Roederer Cristal is wrapped in protective yellow cellophane).

While it is perfectly okay to buy a wine for everyday drinking (or even for keeping a few months) off a well-lit supermarket shelf, if you want to keep a wine much longer, you should avoid any bottles displayed in sunlight or under artificial lighting. Ask instead for bottles of the same wine that are still in their cartons in the storeroom.

## OTHER FACTORS

A certain humidity (between 60 and 70 percent) is essential to keep the cork moist and flexible, thereby avoiding oxidation. This is one reason why long-term storage in a

THE THURN AND TAXIS CELLAR
*The contents of this wine cellar in Regensburg, Germany, were sold by Sotheby's in October 1993, when the 75,000 bottles on offer constituted the world's largest wine auction.*

domestic refrigerator should be avoided—the refrigeration process dehumidifies. Several days in a refrigerator is okay, but much longer than this, and the cork will start to dry out. Wines should also be stored under vibration-free conditions, but this only becomes a significant factor over a long period for sparkling wines and mature wines with sediment.

The position in which a wine bottle is stored is also extremely important. Most wines should be stacked on their sides to keep their corks moist, and therefore fully swollen and airtight. Exceptions to this rule are sparkling wines and any wine that has been sealed with a screwtop lid. Champagne and any other sparkling wine may be safely stored in an upright position because the carbonic gas ($CO_2$) trapped in the space between the top of the wine and the base of the cork provides more-than-sufficient humidity to keep a sparkling-wine cork moist and swollen. Screwtop lids require no moistening, of course.

SYDMONTON COURT
*The wine cellar in Sydmonton Court in Hampshire, England, is owned by Sir Andrew Lloyd Webber. He sold most of its contents in 1997 when he realized that he had far more wine than he could possibly drink in his lifetime.*

# SERVING WINE

*Traditionally, white wines have been served chilled and red wines at room temperature, or* chambré. *At higher temperatures, the odorous compounds found in all wines are more volatile, so the practice of serving full-bodied red wines* chambré *has the effect of releasing more aromatics into the bouquet.*

ONE MAJOR EFFECT OF CHILLING WINE is that more carbonic gas is retained at lower temperatures. This enhances the crispness and freshness and tends to liven the impression of fruit on the palate. It is thus vital to serve a sparkling wine sufficiently chilled, since this keeps it bubbling longer. However, the widespread use of refrigerators and central heating means that white wines are all too frequently served too cold, and red wines too warm.

Controversy surrounds the subject of the temperature at which wines are served. Over-chilling wine kills its flavor and aroma as well as making the cork difficult to remove because the wax on a cork adheres to the bottle. Over-warm wine, on the other hand, is bland to taste. The rough guide below is more than you need to know. I prefer not to complicate life with specific temperatures and simply think in terms of "putting a chill on" white or rosé wines and "taking the chill off" red wines.

| WINE TYPE | SERVING TEMPERATURE |
| --- | --- |
| Sparkling (red, white, and rosé) | 40–45°F (4.5–7°C) |
| White | 45–50°F (7–10°C) |
| Rosé and light-bodied red | 50–55°F (10–12.5°C) |
| Medium-bodied red | 55–60°F (12.5–15.5°C) |
| Full-bodied red | 60–65°F (15.5–18°C) |

## RAPID CHILLING AND INSTANT CHAMBRÉ
It is fine to chill wine in a refrigerator for a couple of hours, but not for much longer because the cork may stick. Unlike the cumulative effect of wide temperature variations, 10 or 15 minutes in the deep-freeze has never done a wine any harm. The belief that this practice "burns" a wine is unfounded; the cold creeps evenly into the bottle. The rapid-chill sheaths that can be kept in the freezer and slid over a bottle when needed are a great innovation.

Unlike cooling, warming a wine by direct heat is not an even process; whether standing a bottle by an open fire or putting it under a hot faucet, some of the wine gets too hot, leaving the rest too cold. The best way of "taking the chill off" is 60 to 90 seconds in a microwave on medium power.

## DECANTING
With increasing age, many wines—especially red wines—throw a natural deposit of tannins and coloring pigments that collect in the base of the bottle. Both red and white wines, particularly white, can also shed a crystalline deposit due to a precipitation of tartrates. Although all these deposits are harmless, their appearance is distracting and decanting will be necessary to remove them.

### Preparing the bottle and pouring the wine
Several hours prior to decanting, move the bottle into an upright position. So doing allows the sediment lying along the side of the bottle to fall to the bottom. Cut away the top quarter-inch so of the foil capsule. This could well reveal a penicillin growth or, if the wine is an old vintage, a fine black deposit, neither of which will have had contact with the wine, but to avoid any unintentional contamination when removing the cork it is wise to wipe the lip of

the bottle neck and the top of the cork with a clean, damp cloth. Insert a corkscrew and gently withdraw the cork. Place a clean finger inside the top of the bottle and carefully remove any pieces of cork or any tartrate crystals adhering to the inside of the neck, then wipe the lip of the bottle neck with a clean, dry cloth.

Lift the bottle slowly in one hand and the decanter in the other and bring them together over a light source, such as a candle or torch, which will reveal any sediment as the wine is poured. Aim to pour the wine in a slow, steady flow so that the bottle does not jerk and wine does not "gulp for air." Such mishaps will disturb the sediment, spreading it through a greater volume of liquid.

### Filtering dregs
Personally, I flout tradition by pouring cloudy dregs through a fine-grade coffee filter paper. I always attempt to decant the maximum volume, thereby filtering the minimum, and I have never been able to tell the difference between pure-decanted wine and that augmented by a small volume of filtered wine. In fact, none of my friends and colleagues who have doubted my assertion have been able to score higher than 50 percent in blind tastings.

## ALLOWING WINE TO BREATHE
As soon as you open a bottle of wine, it will be "breathing" (exposed to the air). Wine "feeds" on the small amount of air trapped inside the bottle between the wine and the cork, and on the oxygen naturally absorbed by the wine itself. It is during this slow oxidation that various elements and compounds are formed or changed in a complex chemical process known as maturation. Allowing a wine to breathe is, in effect, creating a rapid, but less sophisticated, maturation. This artificial aging may be beneficial to certain still wines for several reasons, only some of which are known. The only generalization that tends to hold true is that breathing is likely to improve young, full-bodied, tannic red wines.

### OPENING A BOTTLE OF CHAMPAGNE

• Remove the foil from the bulbous top end of the neck. Quite often there is a little foil tail sticking out, which you merely pull. Failing this, you may have to look for the circular imprint of the end of the wire cage, which will have been twisted, folded upward, and pressed into the neck. When you find this, simply pull it outwards—this will rip the foil, enabling you to remove a section from just below the level of the wire cage.

• Holding the bottle upright at an angle, keep one hand firmly on the cork to make sure it will not surprise you by shooting out, untwist the wire with the other hand, and loosen the bottom of the wire cage so that there is a good space all round. A good tip is not to remove the wire cage, not only because that is when most bottles fire their corks unexpectedly, but also because it acts as a good grip, which you need when a Champagne cork is stuck tight.

• Transfer your grip on the cork to the other hand, which should completely enclose the cork and cage, and, holding the base of the bottle with your other hand, twist both ends in opposite directions. As soon as you feel pressure forcing the cork out try to hold it in, but continue the twisting operation until, almost reluctantly, you release the cork from the bottle. The mark of a professional is that the cork comes out with a sigh, not a bang.

Keep a firm grip on the cork and cage while twisting

Twist the bottle and cork in opposite directions, backward and forward

# The WINES of
# THE WORLD

FROM A GLOBAL PERSPECTIVE, wine consumers are
gradually moving upscale in quality. They are
also moving from white wine to red, and from
Old World to New. These shifts appear to be
long term. Old World wine consumers drink
considerably less than they did 15 years ago,
whereas New World wine consumers drink
significantly more. Ironically, the greatest decline
in wine consumption is in the world's three
largest wine-producing countries, France, Italy,
and Spain, where younger generations are
drinking more beer. However, wine consumption
continues to increase in the U.K., Belgium, and
the Scandinavian countries, which fit more into
New World drinking patterns than Old. Wine
consumption in Mediterranean countries fell by
40 per cent in the last two decades of the 20th
century, while wine production decreased by just
20 percent. The excess in Europe was not
mopped up by growing exports, highlighting the
most pressing problem at the beginning of the
21st century: surplus production. This excess
production has supposedly been targeted by
European Union policies, but not very
successfully so far.

RIPENING CABERNET FRANC GRAPES
*This traditional Bordeaux grape can now be found
in sites all over the winemaking world.*

# A WORLD OF WINE

*At just over 6.6 billion gallons (250 million hectoliters), world wine production has fluctuated very little over the past 10 years. It peaked at almost 8 billion gallons (300 million hl) in 2000, only slightly higher than it was a decade ago.*

GOOD WINE WILL ALWAYS SELL, but almost every country produces more wine than it can consume or export. These surpluses are inevitably at the very lowest end of the quality spectrum. The situation is at its worst in, but not confined to, the European Union (EU), where the Common Agricultural Policy (CAP) has encouraged a dismal tradition of deliberate overproduction over the second half of the 20th century. Even though the wine regime under CAP was altered in 1999 to combat this practice, it has had little impact on growers, who find it much easier and more profitable to grow grapes that are not meant to be turned into wine. Intervention still exists; EU authorities continue to buy the surplus grapes and wines that achieve the intervention price or less. These grapes are turned into rectified sugar for chaptalizing wines, while the undrinkable wines are carted off for distillation (called "crisis distillation" under the new regulations). On average, global wine production exceeds demand every year, peaking at 1.4 billion gallons (53 million hl) of surplus wine in 1999 and 2000, with France and Italy claiming the dubious joint honor of providing some 80 percent of it.

For France, the main problem is straightforward overproduction in historically identifiable areas, which cynics might label as a legalized scam. Italy, on the other hand, has a serious problem of too much cheap wine competing for the same, declining market, which can be illustrated by the fact that the average price per quart of the entire Italian wine production is only 46 percent of the average price of French wine. In both countries and, indeed, throughout the entire EU, there is supposed to be a move toward drinking less in volume, more in quality, but a Bordeaux campaign to "drink less, drink better" was banned in 2004, after the National Association for the Prevention of Alcoholism took the Conseil Interprofessionnel des Vins de Bordeaux to court, and it was judged to be illegal because it "incited people to purchase wine."

## BEWARE OF ALL-CONSUMING FACTS
Statistics for *per capita* wine consumption are notoriously unreliable. Even supposedly the same statistic (i.e., *per capita* consumption for the same country in the same year) can vary in different documents and tables from the same organization. There are many anomalies at work. The Luxembourgois, to quote one major reference, "leave everyone else standing" when it comes to wine consumption, but the Belgians and Germans use their country as a giant supermarket, buying wine, cigarettes, and gasoline in bulk because of the significantly lower taxes. The trade is so vast and Luxembourg's population so small that this cross-border trading distorts the imbibing prowess of the Luxembourgois, so precisely where they fit in the *per capita* scheme of things is debatable. In contrast, the population of France is so large that the trade makes no difference and would, in any case, be offset by cross-Channel transactions. Vacation islands with small populations, such as Cyprus, are prone to similar distortions, with much of the wine enjoyed by tourists rather than inhabitants. Small discrepancies may be due to the use of different 12-month periods, with some organizations using pure annual figures, while others use midyear to midyear and differing statistical adjustments. Such tables therefore generally provide a good overview, rather than a detailed picture.

## INTERNATIONALIZATION?
Some critics are obsessed by what they see as a growing internationalization of wine. This is often ascribed to the spread of such ubiquitous grapes as Chardonnay and Cabernet Sauvignon, especially into new and emerging regions, and often at the expense of indigenous varieties. It is also attributed to a perceived homogenization in style due to technology, flying winemakers, and schools of enology, where winemakers are all taught to sing from the same sheet. Anyone who has to taste thousands of wines for a living gets "Chardonnayed out" far too frequently these days, but I believe there are good reasons not to be so pessimistic.

### Those ubiquitous grapes
They were a necessary evil. It was not that long ago when it was a relief to taste a fresh young Chardonnay in parts of Languedoc-Roussillon, let alone Spain, southern Italy, Sardinia, Greece, and much more obscure wine-producing regions of the world. As recently as the early 1980s, it was almost impossible to discern whether many such areas had any potential whatsoever. Was the dire quality in these places caused by what were (then) unknown grape varieties, by the way that the vines were grown and harvested, a lack of experience of making wines of good quality, or the crude conditions under which the wines were produced? For anyone setting out to improve quality in these viticultural backwaters, the obvious place to start was in the vineyard and, equally obviously, Chardonnay was the best choice.

While Chardonnay might get a hard press these days, this was not always the case. If readers consult books and articles written a quarter of a century ago, they will discover Chardonnay to be universally revered as one of the greatest white wine grapes in the world. Furthermore, its ability to transplant varietal characteristics to myriad soils and climates throughout the world was considered uncanny and, if anything, served to confirm its nobility. Jancis Robinson waxed lyrical about Chardonnay in her seminal work *Vines, Grapes, and Wines* (1986), and even today only the most prejudiced wine drinker would deny that the best white Burgundies rank among the very greatest of dry white wines. If a winemaker in a lowly area of southern France, an Aegean island, or parts of China could not produce a half-decent wine out of the world's greatest, best-traveled grape variety, the vineyards in question would have been written off long ago.

### Decline of indigenous varieties
Far from being under the threat of decline, these varieties owe their survival to the likes of Chardonnay and Cabernet Sauvignon muscling in on their areas of production. Had the so-called "international varieties" not achieved a certain success, these areas would have been grubbed up long ago. Between 1980 and 1994, the area under vine worldwide plummeted from over 25 million acres to less than 19 million (10 million to 8 million hectares), this loss almost entirely stemming from the Old World. Having demonstrated a suitability for viticulture via yardsticks like Chardonnay, local winemakers started to apply the standards learned to the indigenous varieties. In the New World, of course, there are virtually no indigenous grapes suited to winemaking, but again the experience with benchmark international varieties has encouraged growers in emerging wine areas to experiment with other European varieties. In both Old and New Worlds, there is too much ordinary Chardonnay being made, but it is only too much for critics and wine enthusiasts—if it were too much for most consumers, the wines would not exist. If they develop a deeper interest, the market will adapt—so perhaps wine critics should spend more time communicating.

## Homogenization of style

Technology is what you make of it. It can enable vast volumes of technically correct wines to be produced with more fruit and fresher flavors, thus enticing greater numbers of consumers to explore finer wines, and that's not a bad thing. When the best technology is combined with the best traditions, it can also improve the quality and expressiveness of highly individual wines, and that's not bad either.

What about so-called flying winemakers? Are they responsible for homogenization in style? I cannot imagine how they can be, as they make less than one percent of one percent of the world's wine. What flying winemakers have done is to leave a certain level of cleanliness and competence in their wake, and to show winemakers in underperforming wineries what can be achieved. They have also created a reverse flow in terms of where winemakers go to seek practical experience. Over the past quarter century, New World winemakers had gone to Europe to pick up tips on fruit handling and winemaking techniques; now the most inquisitive Europeans go to Australia, New Zealand, or California to learn.

As for schools of enology, it used to be *de rigeur* to have the likes of Bordeaux, Dijon, or Montpellier on a winemaker's resumé, but now the university faculties at Roseworthy (Australia) and Davis are the fashion, as much in Europe as the New World itself. There might be a danger that these schools are producing technically correct enologists trained not to take risks, rather than winemakers whose passion is intimately entwined with the sort of risk-taking that can result in something truly special. However, ultimately, it is better for a winemaker to understand what he or she is doing, though even that statement has its exceptions, with many a self-taught winemaker who has never opened a book on enology producing some of the world's most stunning wines.

## MULTINATIONALS

With all the talk of an international style dominating the range of wines we can buy, should we be worried by multinationals and other large companies increasing this homogenization by controlling production and sales? Again, the figures do not support commonly held beliefs. Indeed, because of the fragmented nature of the wine industry, the world's top 10 wine marketers combined account for less than 14 percent of global wine volume, in direct contrast to the world's top 10 brewers and the world's top 10 spirits companies, which account for 54 percent of their respective markets. The top 10 wine companies in 2003 were:

1. Constellation
2. E & J Gallo
3. Pernod-Ricard
4. LVMH
5. Southcorp
6. Beringer Blass
7. Diageo
8. Castel Frères
9. Henkell & Co
10. Freixenet

## WORLD WINE PRODUCTION (THOUSAND HECTOLITERS)

| COUNTRY (POSITION 10 YEARS AGO) | 2005 | 2004 | 2003 | 2002 | 2001 | 2000 | 1999 | 1998 | 1997 | 1996 |
|---|---|---|---|---|---|---|---|---|---|---|
| 1. Italy (1) | 50556 | 53000 | 44090 | 44600 | 52290 | 54070 | 58070 | 54190 | 50890 | 587700 |
| 2. France (2) | 50500 | 57386 | 47350 | 52000 | 55770 | 59740 | 60240 | 52670 | 53560 | 570500 |
| 3. Spain (3) | 35300 | 43162 | 36000 | 34440 | 30940 | 41790 | 32680 | 31180 | 33220 | 310000 |
| 4. United States (4) | 23500 | 20109 | 23500 | 25400 | 23000 | 25000 | 20690 | 20500 | 22000 | 188800 |
| 5. Argentina (5) | 15222 | 15465 | 11200 | 12150 | 15840 | 12540 | 15890 | 12670 | 13500 | 126800 |
| 6. China (10) | 11050 | 12467 | 10860 | 10800 | 10800 | 10500 | 10260 | 10640 | 9000 | 75000 |
| 7. Australia (11) | 14001 | 13811 | 11800 | 12200 | 10770 | 8590 | 8510 | 7420 | 6170 | 67300 |
| 8. Germany (8) | 9100 | 10047 | 8290 | 10180 | 9080 | 10080 | 12290 | 10830 | 8500 | 86400 |
| 9. South Africa (7) | 8310 | 9279 | 7610 | 7610 | 7610 | 6950 | 7970 | 7700 | 8120 | 87400 |
| 10. Chile (14) | 7886 | 6301 | 5750 | 5750 | 5650 | 6670 | 4810 | 5480 | 4550 | 38200 |
| 11. Portugal (6) | 6645 | 7475 | 6800 | 6270 | 7430 | 6690 | 7810 | 3750 | 6120 | 97100 |
| 12. Russia (19) | 4200 | 4000 | 4100 | 3430 | 3430 | 3230 | 2903 | 2180 | 2230 | 2550 |
| 13. Greece (13) | 4093 | 4295 | 4950 | 5000 | 4280 | 4600 | 3680 | 3830 | 3990 | 41100 |
| 14. Romania (9) | 3800 | 6166 | 5460 | 5000 | 5500 | 5460 | 6500 | 5000 | 6690 | 76600 |
| 15. Hungary (12) | 3100 | 4340 | 4200 | 3800 | 5410 | 4300 | 3340 | 4330 | 4470 | 41900 |
| 16. Brazil (15) | 2850 | 3925 | 4000 | 3200 | 3200 | 3000 | 3190 | 2780 | 2740 | 31300 |
| 17. Croatia (17) | 2600 | 2600 | 2600 | 2200 | 2040 | 1890 | 2090 | 2280 | 2260 | 19600 |
| 18. Moldova (18) | 2400 | 2620 | 2400 | 2100 | 1400 | 2020 | 1332 | 1700 | 3123 | 3598 |
| 19. Austria (16) | 2259 | 2735 | 3250 | 2600 | 2530 | 2340 | 2800 | 2700 | 1800 | 21100 |
| Other | 21278 | 20200 | 18370 | 19130 | 20210 | 24040 | 24260 | 24790 | 28030 | 271000 |
| World | 278650 | 299383 | 262580 | 267870 | 277160 | 293500 | 280010 | 255660 | 259810 | 269290 |

**Source:** COPS & CIES—Global Wine Markets, 1961–2003
**Note:** Columns may not total due to rounding

## PER CAPITA CONSUMPTION—HIGHEST-CONSUMING COUNTRIES (LITERS PER PERSON PER YEAR)

| COUNTRY | 2003 | 2002 | 2001 | 2000 | 1999 | 1998 | 1997 | 1996 | 1995 | 1994 |
|---|---|---|---|---|---|---|---|---|---|---|
| 1. Luxembourg (4)* | 55.8 | 60.9 | 59.4 | 65.1 | 62.8 | 62.1 | 61.5 | 60.5 | 55.2 | 51.0 |
| 2. France (1) | 55.4 | 56.0 | 56.9 | 55.9 | 57.2 | 58.1 | 60.0 | 60.0 | 63.0 | 62.5 |
| 3. Portugal (2) | 52.6 | 43.0 | 47.0 | 46.0 | 48.0 | 51.0 | 54.5 | 56.6 | 58.1 | 58.9 |
| 4. Italy (3) | 51.1 | 51.0 | 50.0 | 51.0 | 51.5 | 52.0 | 53.5 | 54.2 | 55.7 | 57.8 |
| 5. Slovenia (5) | 44.4 | 31.2 | 31.1 | 35.4 | 28.3 | 41.5 | 51.9 | 56.2 | 47.6 | 47.7 |
| 6. Switzerland (7) | 41.4 | 41.8 | 43.1 | 43.5 | 43.5 | 43.1 | 43.5 | 43.3 | 43.6 | 44.3 |
| 7. Croatia (5) | 39.5 | 42.1 | 43.2 | 42.0 | 47.0 | 50.8 | 45.1 | 35.8 | 48.2 | 48.1 |
| 8. Spain (12) | 33.6 | 29.6 | 30.0 | 32.0 | 34.0 | 35.6 | 35.1 | 30.3 | 30.6 | 32.2 |
| 9. Argentina (8) | 32.1 | 36.1 | 36.3 | 37.8 | 38.7 | 38.8 | 40.3 | 41.1 | 41.1 | 43.2 |
| 10. Denmark (16) | 31.8 | 32.0 | 31.2 | 30.9 | 29.8 | 29.1 | 29.3 | 28.3 | 27.6 | 26.2 |
| 11. Hungary (14) | 31.6 | 36.0 | 35.1 | 34.0 | 32.0 | 31.0 | 29.0 | 30.3 | 26.6 | 29.2 |
| 12. Austria (11) | 29.4 | 29.8 | 28.5 | 30.5 | 30.6 | 30.9 | 30.0 | 31.5 | 32.0 | 32.8 |
| 13. Belgium (24) | 25.3 | 24.3 | 24.2 | 23.4 | 23.0 | 22.9 | 23.9 | 19.4 | 17.8 | 17.7 |
| 14. Germany (18) | 24.4 | 24.2 | 24.0 | 23.1 | 23.0 | 22.8 | 23.0 | 23.1 | 22.2 | 22.6 |
| 15. Romania (17) | 22.6 | 25.3 | 25.5 | 23.2 | 22.7 | 30.0 | 32.2 | 26.0 | 25.3 | 23.2 |
| 16. Greece (10) | 22.3 | 33.9 | 34.0 | 34.0 | 35.2 | 32.0 | 34.9 | 34.0 | 34.5 | 33.8 |
| 17=. Uruguay (13) | 22.1 | 32.8 | 31.9 | 32.0 | 32.0 | 30.5 | 30.7 | 30.1 | 29.8 | 31.1 |
| 17=. Netherlands (26) | 22.1 | 22.5 | 21.0 | 19.5 | 15.9 | 13.8 | 15.1 | 19.1 | 18.1 | 16.1 |
| 19. Australia (22) | 21.3 | 21.2 | 20.5 | 20.5 | 20.4 | 19.5 | 19.0 | 19.0 | 18.3 | 18.4 |
| 20. Cyprus (29) | 20.6 | 16.0 | 15.2 | 14.6 | 11.1 | 11.5 | 11.2 | 11.0 | 11.8 | 11.9 |
| 21. United Kingdom (27) | 17.9 | 17.6 | 17.0 | 15.3 | 17.2 | 16.9 | 15.8 | 14.9 | 14.3 | 14.5 |
| 22. Bulgaria (19) | 17.7 | 21.3 | 21.4 | 21.4 | 21.4 | 22.1 | 21.6 | 21.7 | 21.8 | 22.0 |
| 23. New Zealand (25) | 17.0 | 17.1 | 16.7 | 17.0 | 16.3 | 16.1 | 17.0 | 16.2 | 16.6 | 16.3 |
| 24. Sweden (28) | 16.9 | 16.0 | 15.9 | 13.5 | 13.6 | 12.4 | 11.8 | 12.9 | 13.0 | 13.9 |
| 25. Chile (20) | 16.1 | 15.9 | 16.0 | 18.8 | 18.6 | 17.7 | 12.5 | 15.8 | 21.7 | 21.4 |
| 26. Ireland (36) | 14.7 | 13.0 | 12.8 | 11.6 | 9.8 | 8.6 | 7.5 | 6.7 | 6.0 | 5.5 |
| 27. Norway (32) | 12.4 | 11.3 | 10.9 | 10.3 | 9.9 | 9.6 | 9.3 | 9.0 | 8.7 | 8.4 |
| 28. Czech Republic (N/A) | 11.5 | 10.6 | 8.7 | 6.6 | 6.3 | 6.4 | 6.4 | 6.2 | N/A | N/A |
| 29. Slovakia (33) | 11.0 | 11.9 | 11.8 | 11.7 | 8.2 | 6.7 | 7.8 | 6.8 | 8.1 | 8.0 |
| 30. Canada (35) | 10.9 | 9.1 | 9.0 | 8.8 | 8.6 | 7.5 | 6.7 | 6.9 | 7.0 | 6.2 |
| 31. Macedonia (15) | 10.8 | 23.7 | 23.8 | 23.8 | 23.8 | 23.8 | 28.4 | 18.7 | 27.2 | 27.1 |
| 32. Malta (N/A) | 10.2 | 8.9 | 7.7 | 6.4 | 9.5 | 5.7 | 8.5 | 8.4 | N/A | N/A |
| 33. Iceland (N/A) | 9.7 | 8.7 | 8.4 | 8.2 | 8.1 | 7.2 | 6.3 | 5.9 | N/A | N/A |
| 34. Finland (31) | 8.7 | 23.5 | 21.9 | 20.6 | 19.5 | 17.5 | 15.6 | 13.1 | 11.5 | 8.8 |
| 35. Yugoslavia (21) | 8.6 | 13.0 | 13.1 | 14.2 | 14.1 | 19.9 | 27.7 | 23.1 | 19.1 | 19.3 |
| 36. United States (34) | 8.1 | 9.7 | 9.3 | 8.3 | 8.3 | 7.8 | 6.9 | 6.7 | 6.9 | 7.0 |

**Sources:** Australian Wine Bureau; Wine Institute (US); Richard Cartier's *Wine Market Report*; CIES; OIV; IVV; Statec. * *See* Beware of all-consuming facts, p50

# The WINES of
# FRANCE

FRENCH WINES ARE REGARDED AS THE BEST in the world, and a thread of this belief is even shared by France's fiercest New World competitors. Although the winemakers of Australia and California, for instance, no longer try to copy famous French wine styles, they still consider them benchmarks. The great French wine regions are a fortunate accident of geography, climate, and *terroir*. No other winemaking country in the world has such a wide range of cool climates; this factor has enabled France to produce the entire spectrum of classic wine styles—from the crisp sparkling wines of Champagne through the smooth reds of Burgundy to the rich sweet wines of Sauternes. Over many centuries of trial and error, the French have discovered that specific grapes are suited to certain soils and, through this, distinctive regional wine styles have evolved, so that every wine drinker knows what to expect from a bottle of Bordeaux, Burgundy, Champagne, or Rhône. This has been the key to success for French wines.

THE MOON RISING OVER CHÂTEAU LATOUR
*The magnificent tower of Château Latour is bathed in moonlight, evoking the majesty of one of the world's greatest wines.*

# FRANCE

*The success of French wine has been built on deservedly famous regions that have been enshrined by* Appellation d'Origine Contrôlée (AOC) *laws, but the unwillingness to police this system in any meaningful sense has gradually debased historic reputations at the precise point in history when New World producers have been eager to establish their own wines.*

FRANCE HAS A TOTAL OF 2,153,800 acres (872,000 hectares) under vine, including 172,900 acres (70,000 hectares) for Cognac and 14,820 acres (6,000 hectares) for Armagnac, and produces an average of almost 630 million cases (57 million hectoliters) of wine every year. Since the mid-1980s, French wine production has dropped by 27 percent in response to a move away from the lower-quality end of the spectrum, as consumers have begun to drink less wine, but of better quality. How that quality is classified is the most contentious issue facing the French wine industry.

## HOW FRENCH WINE IS CLASSIFIED
In 1935, when the Institut National des Appellations d'Origine (INAO) was established, France became the first nation to set up a countrywide system for controlling the origin and quality of its wines, although individual wine areas outside France had put in place quality controls much earlier (Chianti in 1716 and Rioja in 1560). INAO's task was to devise the geographical limits of appellations and to enforce the regulations governing them.

### Appellation d'Origine Contrôlée (AOC)
There are now more than 470 separate AOCs, covering almost 1,210,300 acres (490,000 hectares), and producing just over 322 million cases (29 million hectoliters) of wine. The AOC laws regulate the grape varieties used, viticultural methods, harvest and yield restrictions, minimum alcohol content, and winemaking techniques for each area. Although the laws are supposed to control the quality of each wine by having it pass an official

CHÂTEAU GRUAUD-LAROSE
*One of the largest and most consistent of Bordeaux's second growths, this estate was established by the Gruaud family in 1757; the chateau was built in 1875.*

analysis and tasting, the latter of these has become something of a farce, since panels of tasting judges are composed of the very people who actually make the wine. Furthermore, the wines are not tasted and passed on a tank by tank basis, the absence of which is probably responsible for most of the very worst AOC wines on the shelf. Virtually all the producers I know admit that only those wines with faults—and obvious ones at that—are likely to be rejected, with no account taken of either quality or whether a wine reflects the character of the grapes used or expresses any particular regional style. Some were honest enough to explain that most people are too afraid to start the ball rolling on the issue of quality or style for fear that someone whose wine has already been rejected might seek revenge by rejecting other wines indiscriminately. It is little surprise, therefore, that only around 2 or 3 percent of wines fail to pass such sham tastings.

The tasting system is obviously deficient, as evidenced by the glut of very poor-quality AOCs that are put on the shelf every year. The best AOC wines are still superb, but without some sort of overhaul of the system (*see* Challenging Tradition, p58), the onus remains very much on the knowledge of consumers to discern the reputation of individual producers.

On a more positive note, INAO has instituted tougher controls in the vineyards that could result in distillation of the entire crop of any grower who exceeds the *Plafond Limité de Classement* (PLC). The PLC is the absolute maximum yield for any AOC. This is usually set at 20 percent above the base yield, which may itself be adjusted upward on an annual basis by, normally, some 10–15 percent. INAO has formed local "work committees" to visit vineyards, to detect any aberrations. Essentially, but not exclusively, they will be looking for signs of overproduction, and if found, they will tell the grower (depending on the time of year) to prune, green-harvest, or thin the bunches. Later in the year, the grower could have his entire crop declassified if he has not done as requested. In future years, such an offender might not be given the opportunity to rectify any overcropping and could have his entire crop carted

## FRENCH WINE AT A GLANCE

### BY CLASSIFICATION

**Appellation d'Origine Contrôlée (AOC or AC)**
Exactly 58% of total French wine production—25% exported, 75% consumed within France

**Vin Délimité de Qualité Supérieure (VDQS)**
Less than 1% of total French wine production—17% exported, 83% consumed within France

**Vin de Pays**
Almost 31% of total French wine production—10% exported, 90% consumed within France

**Vin de Table**
Just over 10% of total French wine production—16% exported, 84% consumed within France

### BY TYPE

**Red wine**
Just over 65% of total French wine production—30% exported, 70% consumed within France

**White wine**
21.5% of total French wine production—55% exported, 45% consumed within France

**Rosé wine**
6.5% of total French wine production—30% exported, 70% consumed within France

**Sparkling wine**
Just under 6% of total French wine production – 42% exported, 58% consumed within France

**Fortified wine**
Just under 1% of total French wine production—20% exported, 80% consumed within France

# FRANCE

*The colored areas on this map identify the 10 main wine-producing regions of France, where the areas of Appellation d'Origine Contrôlée, which cover 1.2 million acres (490,000 hectares), are concentrated. However, the country has almost 400,000 acres of vineyards in total, and many good, everyday-drinking wines are made in other parts of the country. See also Vin de Pays maps pp.248, 249.*

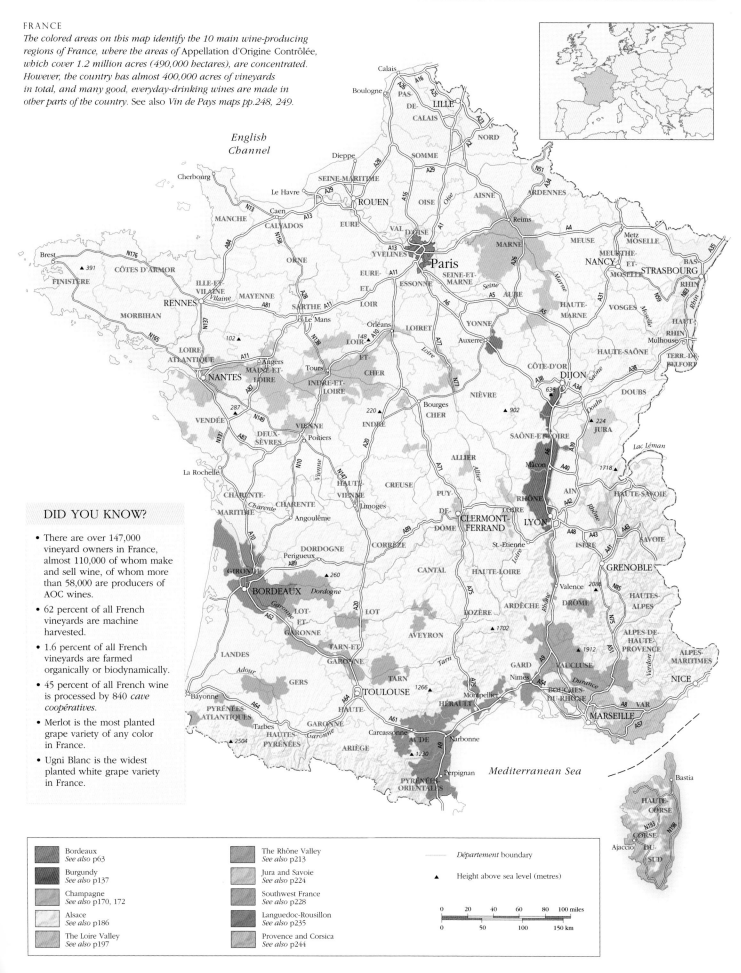

## DID YOU KNOW?

- There are over 147,000 vineyard owners in France, almost 110,000 of whom make and sell wine, of whom more than 58,000 are producers of AOC wines.

- 62 percent of all French vineyards are machine harvested.

- 1.6 percent of all French vineyards are farmed organically or biodynamically.

- 45 percent of all French wine is processed by 840 *cave coopératives*.

- Merlot is the most planted grape variety of any color in France.

- Ugni Blanc is the widest planted white grape variety in France.

| | | |
|---|---|---|
| Bordeaux *See also p63* | The Rhône Valley *See also p213* | *Département* boundary |
| Burgundy *See also p137* | Jura and Savoie *See also p224* | ▲ Height above sea level (metres) |
| Champagne *See also p170, 172* | Southwest France *See also p228* | |
| Alsace *See also p186* | Languedoc-Rousillon *See also p235* | |
| The Loire Valley *See also p197* | Provence and Corsica *See also p244* | |

0   20   40   60   80   100 miles

0        50        100        150 km

off for distillation for inadequate pruning. Of course, the efficacy of this initiative will be dependent upon how tough the "work committees" actually are, and, like AOC tasting panels, these will be composed of fellow winegrowers, so....

### Vin Délimité de Qualité Supérieure (VDQS)

There are just over 33 VDQS wines, covering almost 17,000 acres (approximately 6,800 hectares), and producing an annual average of just over 4.8 million cases (438,000 hectoliters) under similar controls to those applied to AOC wines, but with yields that may be higher and alcoholic strengths that are often lower. The overall quality standard is not as high, although it may be argued in certain cases that the quality is easily comparable.

Since the emergence of the *vins de pays* category in the 1970s, there have been persistent rumors of the imminent demise of VDQS, but the INAO, which is the regulatory body for both AOC and VDQS wines, has found this category to be such a convenient staging post for potential AOCs that its removal is unlikely. VDQS wines promoted to AOC status include Coteaux du Tricastin (promoted in 1973), St.-Chinian (1982), Coteaux du Lyonnais (1984), Costières de Nîmes (1986), Côtes du Marmandais (1990), Marcillac (1990), Cheverny and Cour-Cheverny (1993), Coteaux Varois (1993), Côtes Roannaises (1994), Coteaux de Pierrevert (1998), Coteaux du Giennois (1998), Côtes de Toul (1998), Côtes du Forez (2000), and Sauvignon de St.-Bris (2003).

It would be a mistake, however, to think of all VDQS wines as purely transitory. It is not a guaranteed halfway house to full AOC status, as can be demonstrated by those wines that still retain VDQS classification 40 years after this category came into fruition, and the fact that the majority of surviving VDQS wines actually date from the 1960s and 1970s. It is not beyond imagination that the French might elevate these crusty old VDQS wines at some date in the future, but most potential new AOC wines will be selected from those VDQS wines that have come up through the nicely matured *vin de pays* ranks.

### Vin de pays

There are 153 *vin de pays*, or "country wine," appellations, covering 494,200 acres (200,000 hectares), and producing an annual average of almost 166 million cases (15 million hectoliters). Officially established in 1968, the *vins de pays* did not become a marketable reality until 1973, when the rules for production were fixed. They were created, quite simply, by authorizing some *vins de table* to indicate their specific geographic origin and, if desired, the grape varieties used, but the effect was more profound than that. For a long while, it was even obligatory for these wines to carry the term "Vin de Table" in addition to their *vin de pays* appellation, but this regulation was discontinued in 1989. Allowing producers of potentially superior table wine areas to declare, for the first time, the origin and content of their wines gave back a long-lost pride to the best growers, who started to care more about how they tended their vines and made their wines, and began to uproot low-quality varieties, replant with better ones, and restrict yields.

There are four categories of *vin de pays*, each with its own controls, but all regulated by the Office National Interprofessionnel des Vins (ONIVINS). Although every *vin de pays* must have a specified origin on the label, a wide range of grape varieties can be used and high yields are allowed. A certain flexibility on choice of grape varieties allows innovation, a character-building trait that has been denied winemakers under the AOC regime, but the high yields permitted have also caused many an unprincipled producer to jump on the relatively lucrative *vin de pays* bandwagon, thus the quality can vary greatly. This is, nevertheless, a most interesting category of wines, often infiltrated by foreign winemakers—usually Australian—producing some of the most exciting, inexpensive, and upfront-fruity wines.

Many *vins de pays* are, of course, bland and will never improve, but some will make it up the hierarchical ladder to VDQS and, possibly, then full AOC status. Certain individual producers, such as the Guiberts of Mas de Daumas Gassac and the Dürrbachs of Domaine de Trévallon, could not care less about AOC status, as they happen to be making wines under the less draconian *vin de pays* system. They already have reputations as good as those of the finest French appellations and demand even higher prices than some expensive AOC wines. For a description of the various *vin de pays* categories, a map showing the areas producing *vins de pays*, and profiles of every *vin de pays* along with their finest producers, *see* pp.248–259.

### Vin de table

There are over 430,000 acres (175,000 hectares) of unclassified vineyards in France, producing an annual average of more than 75 million cases (nearly 5 million hectoliters) of *vins de table,*

---

## VINS DE PRIMEUR

We tend to think of Beaujolais Nouveau as the only *vin de primeur*, or "new wine," but there are no fewer than 55 different wines that are allowed by AOC regulations to be sold in the year they are harvested, and 25 of these must be labeled *primeur* or *nouveau*. They are made in a style that is at its peak in the first year of its life. So, for those who like drinking wine when it has only just stopped fermenting, why not look out for the following?

1. Anjou Gamay
2. Beaujolais (red or rosé)
3. Beaujolais Supérieur (red or rosé)
4. Beaujolais-Villages (red or rosé)
5. Beaujolais with village name but not *cru* (red or rosé)
6. Bourgogne (white only)
7. Bourgogne Aligoté (white only)
8. Bourgogne Grand Ordinaire (white only)
9. Cabernet d'Anjou (rosé)
10. Cabernet de Saumur (rosé)
11. Coteaux du Languedoc (red or rosé)
12. Coteaux du Lyonnais (red, white, or rosé)
13. Coteaux du Tricastin (red, white, or rosé)
14. Côtes-du-Rhône (red sold only as a *vin de café* or rosé)
15. Côtes du Roussillon (red, white, or rosé)
16. Côtes du Ventoux (red, white, or rosé)
17. Gaillac (red Gamay or white)
18. Mâcon (white or rosé)
19. Mâcon Supérieur (white only)
20. Macon-Villages (white only)
21. Macon with village name (white only)
22. Muscadet
23. Muscadet de Sèvre et Maine
24. Muscadet des Coteaux de la Loire
25. Muscadet Côtes de Grand-Lieu
26. Rosé d'Anjou
27. Tavel (rosé only)
28. Touraine Gamay (red only)
29. Touraine (rosé only)

The following wines may be sold from December 1 after the harvest without any mention of *primeur* or *nouveau*:

1. Anjou (white only)
2. Bergerac (white or rosé, but not red)
3. Blayais (white only)
4. Bordeaux (*sec, rosé,* or *clairet*)
5. Buzet (white or rosé)
6. Cabernet d'Anjou (rosé)
7. Cabernet de Saumur (rosé)
8. Corbières (white or rosé)
9. Costières de Nîmes (white or rosé)
10. Coteaux d'Aix-en-Provence (white or rosé)
11. Coteaux du Languedoc (white or rosé)
12. Coteaux Varois (white or rosé)
13. Côtes de Bourg (white only)
14. Côtes de Duras (white or rosé)
15. Côtes du Marmandais (white or rosé)
16. Côtes de Provence (white or rosé)
17. Côtes-du-Rhône (white or rosé)
18. Côtes du Ventoux (white or rosé)
19. Entre-Deux-Mers (white only)
20. Faugères (rosé only)
21. Graves (white only)
22. Graves de Vayres (white only)
23. Jurançon Sec
24. Minervois (white or rosé)
25. Montravel (white or rosé)
26. Muscadet
27. Muscadet de Sèvre et Maine
28. Muscadet des Coteaux de la Loire
29. Muscadet Côtes de Grand-Lieu
30. Premières Côtes de Blaye (white only)
31. Rosé d'Anjou
32. Rosé de Loire
33. St.-Chinian (rosé only)
34. Ste.-Foy-Bordeaux (white only)
35. Saumur (white only)
36. Touraine (white only)

## BREAKDOWN OF FRENCH WINE PRODUCTION MEASURED IN HECTOLITRES

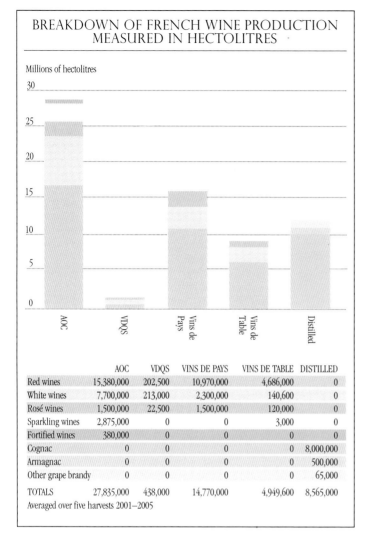

Millions of hectolitres

|  | AOC | VDQS | VINS DE PAYS | VINS DE TABLE | DISTILLED |
|---|---|---|---|---|---|
| Red wines | 15,380,000 | 202,500 | 10,970,000 | 4,686,000 | 0 |
| White wines | 7,700,000 | 213,000 | 2,300,000 | 140,600 | 0 |
| Rosé wines | 1,500,000 | 22,500 | 1,500,000 | 120,000 | 0 |
| Sparkling wines | 2,875,000 | 0 | 0 | 3,000 | 0 |
| Fortified wines | 380,000 | 0 | 0 | 0 | 0 |
| Cognac | 0 | 0 | 0 | 0 | 8,000,000 |
| Armagnac | 0 | 0 | 0 | 0 | 500,000 |
| Other grape brandy | 0 | 0 | 0 | 0 | 65,000 |
| TOTALS | 27,835,000 | 438,000 | 14,770,000 | 4,949,600 | 8,565,000 |

Averaged over five harvests 2001–2005

## FRENCH WINE PRODUCTION BY TYPE

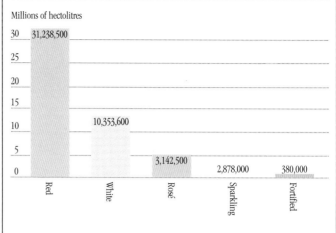

Millions of hectolitres

Red 31,238,500 · White 10,353,600 · Rosé 3,142,500 · Sparkling 2,878,000 · Fortified 380,000

### Zind

Produced by Domaine Zind-Humbrecht after the authorities finally made up their minds that Chardonnay should not be allowed in any AOC Alsace blend other than a Crémant d'Alsace. Not wishing to make a sparkling wine, Olivier Humbrecht MW was forced to sell the wine as a *vin de table*, which he has named simply Zind. He cannot put the year on this wine, so he numbers each *cuvée* starting with Z001. However, I can reveal that this is in fact the 2001 vintage, so Z002 is 2002, and so on. Humbrecht also cannot put the varietal content and origin on the label, but Zind is primarily Auxerrois (usually 50 percent of the blend, invariably from Clos Windsbuhl, Herrenweg, and Rotenberg), plus Pinot Blanc (15 percent, Herrenweg) and, of course, Chardonnay (35 percent, Clos Windsbuhl). The curious thing is that the maximum permitted yield for *vin de table* is 400 cases per acre (90 hectoliters per hectare), as opposed to 440 cases per acre (100 hectoliters per hectare) for the supposedly superior Alsace appellation. In addition, no *vin de table* is allowed to be chaptalized, whereas AOC Alsace is. Thus, in these two respects, *vin de table* is stricter than AOC Alsace!

### Libre Expression

Produced by Domaine Cazes, this rich, smooth white wine, which contains 16 percent alcohol, is effectively a late-harvest, nonfortified version of Rivesaltes, but one that finishes dry. It is vintaged, which is technically illegal, but by calling the wine "Libre Expression," the Cazes brothers are definitely making a statement.

(although this also includes a variable volume of grape juice, grape concentrate, and wine vinegar). This compares with a production of 510 million cases (34 million hectoliters) 10 years ago, and is evidence of the trend away from the lower end of the market.

The official use of *vin de table* (also designated as *vin de consommation courante*, or wine for immediate consumption) is contrary to the common usage, particularly in New World countries, of table wine to refer to those that are neither fortified nor sparkling. In the latter sense, table wines are, or can be, quality wines, but in official French terms, *vins de table* are *vins ordinaires*, and are cheap in every sense of the word. They are not intended for keeping, and some might argue that they are not fit for drinking either, since much of this wine is traditionally diluted with water before even the French can bring themselves to consume it.

*Vins de table* also come under the auspices of ONIVINS, but there are no controls apart from negative ones, such as not being allowed to mention any grape names or indicate an origin more specific than France. The address of the producer seldom has any bearing on the origin of the wine, although some producers do try to fabricate a style in accordance with their local image. Thus a *négociant* based in Nuits-St.-Georges might attempt to make a *vin de table* with some sort of Burgundian character, but the consumer cannot be sure that any of the wines used will be from Burgundy, and the likelihood is that they will not. Some wine merchants pride themselves on the quality of their basic *vin de table* brand, but this is a dead-end category as far as being able to discover useful information, let alone rely on it, is concerned. However, there are always exceptions. These currently include:

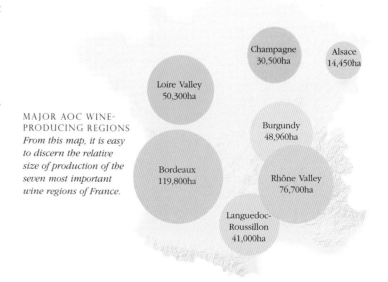

MAJOR AOC WINE-PRODUCING REGIONS
*From this map, it is easy to discern the relative size of production of the seven most important wine regions of France.*

Champagne 30,500ha
Alsace 14,450ha
Loire Valley 50,300ha
Burgundy 48,960ha
Bordeaux 119,800ha
Rhône Valley 76,700ha
Languedoc-Roussillon 41,000ha

**Muscat de Petit Grains Passerillé Vendange d'Octobre Elevée en Fûts de Chêne**
Produced by Mas de Bellevue from old vines, on which the grapes have been left to shrivel. In the 2000 vintage (again illegally indicated), the only year I have tasted, at least half the grapes had been botrytized prior to *passerillage*.

## CHALLENGING TRADITION

The French establishment has been slow to wake up to the fact that the AOC classification was not AOK, but they have started to think the unthinkable: change. When the late René Renou, director of INAO (the man in charge of running the entire French appellation system), proposed a super-appellation that would be bestowed on wines of "demonstrably superior quality," he shook the very foundations of French culture—tradition. This country produces both the best and the worst wines in the world because of its fixation with tradition, but whereas the French are always willing to preserve the best traditions, they are loath to banish the worst. Even when the need to do so is staring them in the face.

In 1995 Michel Bettane, one of France's top wine writers, was quoted as saying: "Today, *appellation contrôlée* guarantees neither quality nor authenticity." At the time, Alain Berger was the director of INAO, and when pressured he caused uproar by confessing that: "One can find on the market scandalously poor products with the *appellation contrôlée* halo." But was anything done? Of course not. For Renou to confirm the situation, and propose a solution, was a unique event. However, a fundamental shake-up to the system that gave birth to wine regimes throughout Europe threatened the moral authority of French wine, thus Renou's proposals have been met with hostility in some quarters, while in others they are viewed as absolutely necessary.

Those who support Renou are, essentially, a quality-conscious minority, while those who oppose include the worst of the worst, although the vast majority simply feel so safe with their traditions that they do not wish to rock the boat.

Initially, there was good news and bad news: the good news being that the Burgundians were for it, the bad being that the *bordelais* were not. However, the good news turned out to be bad, as evidenced by the supposedly pro-Renou Jean-François Delorme, who as president of the Bureau Interprofessionnel des Vins de Bourgogne (BIVB), commented: "Of course, all of Burgundy's AOCs would be super-AOCs." If all Burgundy were of the quality of Romanée Conti, Leroy, or Leflaive, no one would argue, but much too much is no better than *vin ordinaire*, while—as with every wine region—some wines can be almost undrinkable. So no, a pan-Burgundian application for super-AOCs would not be very super at all.

Being no fool, Renou allowed his historic proposal to "slip out" in London, where he could count on its radical goals receiving widespread objective approval, before presenting the plan in detail to the INAO's 80-member National Committee. He later provided more details about his superappellation, which he now called *Appellation d'Origine Contrôlée d'Excellence* (AOCE), and threw another monkey wrench in the traditionalist works by introducing the novel concept in the form of his proposed new *Site et Terroir d'Excellence* (STE) appellation.

On past experience, the odds always were that a compromise would be sought. That the goals would become so fudged, and the regulations so watered-down, that they will not simply be ineffective, but will probably be detrimental to the future of French wine. And that is precisely what has happened, but these new appellations and the reasons why they were rejected need exploring in more detail so that French wine lovers can at least know what Renou's good intentions were. Readers will then be able to appreciate how the French catastrophically missed this opportunity, and why the growers and government minister involved deserve to reap whatever ill fortune they have sown.

The BIVB was the first to support Renou's initiative, but Delorme's unrealistic position was disowned by its members, who turned out to be so hostile to the idea of AOCEs that

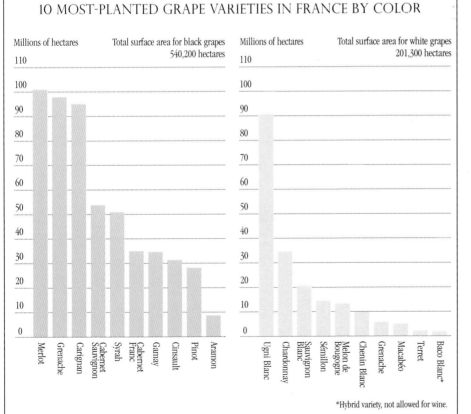

## 10 MOST-PLANTED GRAPE VARIETIES IN FRANCE BY COLOR

Millions of hectares — Total surface area for black grapes 540,200 hectares

Black grapes (left to right): Merlot, Grenache, Carignan, Cabernet Sauvignon, Syrah, Cabernet Franc, Gamay, Cinsault, Pinot, Aramon

Millions of hectares — Total surface area for white grapes 201,300 hectares

White grapes (left to right): Ugni Blanc, Chardonnay, Sauvignon Blanc, Sémillon, Melon de Bourgogne, Chenin Blanc, Grenache, Macabéo, Terret, Baco Blanc*

*Hybrid variety, not allowed for wine.

PINOT NOIR GRAPES
*The Holy Grail of red winemakers, the Pinot Noir is the most finicky of all black grapes to work with, but when successful, it can produce velvety red wines of stunning purity, finesse, and length.*

Burgundy was given until "early 2005 at the latest" to present the INAO's president with modifications and solid proposals for putting such plans in place. They would not get the chance. The chop would come much earlier than that.

But what exactly did the Burgundians, and, in fact, growers from almost every wine region, object to? The AOCE designation would be granted only to areas that committed to a series of strict regulations in virtually every facet of vineyard management and winemaking, including lower yields, higher planting density, harvesting (manual or machines), aging (oak barrels or chips), grape varieties, wines judged by tasting panels, and so on. To become eligible for an AOCE, a minimum of 75 percent of the producers in an appellation would have to approve the tighter regulations, at which point any unwilling grower would be coerced to follow the majority and abide by the new regulations. INAO would review each appellation's status as an AOCE every five years.

There were two obvious flaws. First, if it is up to the wine producers of an appellation to decide by voting whether it is to be an AOC or AOCE, it cannot work. A truly famous wine that is offered the opportunity of claiming superappellation status is one thing, but an ordinary wine that assumes superappellation status simply because the majority of its growers vote for it would be pointless. Equally, if the growers of a truly famous wine did not grab such a chance with both hands, they would deserve to suffer the decline that would inevitably ensue, although there were many objectors who did not think that far ahead. In Chablis, for example, which is a truly famous wine region, one person with a short-term view is Jean Durup. He sits on the INAO National Committee, and was reported as saying that he didn't think the AOC would want to change its standards and adopt stricter rules because "we are the world's most famous white wine, and there is no crisis in Chablis." What would the next generation of Chablis growers think in 20 years' time, once the AOCE status of other white Burgundies had become well established? It would surely not be unreasonable for consumers at that juncture to assume that plain old Chablis AOC was simply not in the same class as Burgundy's AOCEs. The second potential flaw in the system was the panel tastings, because if they were to be conducted by the producers themselves, the results would be as worthless as those for AOC wines (*see* p54).

## SITE ET TERROIR D'EXCELLENCE

As for the brand new STE classification, this was a truly inspired concept and, as such, its demise has been an even greater tragedy. STE was designed to recognize the exceptional effort put in by serious, quality-conscious producers in relatively modest or otherwise generally unambitious appellations. Individual wineries could receive the STE label if their wines are much better wines than those of most other producers in the appellation. Renou had intimated that INAO was likely to approve hundreds of STE wineries. What an opportunity the French have lost to fight back on the superpremium stage.

Jean-Michel Aubinel, who represents growers in Mâcon, clearly did not think so. He was reported as saying the scheme would entrench rivalry between neighboring properties, if applied to one and not the other. Well, that's the whole idea Monsieur: it is called competition. How else does anyone in any sphere strive to improve? But then, perhaps the AOC is meant only to guarantee mediocrity. Denis Dubourdieu of Château Reynon in Premières Côtes de Bordeaux was far more upbeat, pointing out that: "The STE concept appears to be the truly original point of the proposal. You can spend 20 years claiming you do better than most in one of Bordeaux's lesser-known satellite appellations, but the STE will give you status, and it will stimulate producers to make excellent wines." Well, Denis, my readers know about your top-performing wines, but it looks as though you'll have to spend another 20 years telling the rest of the world.

---

### FRANCE "SHOT IN FOOT"

A Bordeaux campaign to "drink less, drink better" was banned in 2004, after the National Association for the Prevention of Alcoholism (NAPA) took the Conseil Interprofessionnel des Vins de Bordeaux (CIVB) to court. Any rational person would have to question the motives of an organization that is so opposed to people drinking less, but better wine that it would drag them into a court of law. If NAPA seeks prohibition, it should do so openly. Furthermore any rational person would also have to question the motives behind a law under which a court is obliged to declare that "drink less, drink better" is illegal because it "incites people to purchase wine." Why should inciting people to purchase less, better-quality wine be against the law? One of the Bordeaux posters was also declared illegal because it depicted someone drinking wine. According to this warped law, it is legal to display an alcoholic product on a poster, but not legal to display that product being consumed. What are people supposed to think they should do with such a product after purchasing it?

The law in question is the Loi Evin, enacted in January 1991, and named after Claude Evin, a minister in the Rocard government. And so, finally, we must question this man's motives. Why, when Evin presented his proposal to the French parliament, did he do so under the banner of "In the case of alcohol, only abuse is dangerous"? Certainly not to mislead parliament. The National Assembly was informed precisely how far beyond the curbing of abuse this law extended, and was thus as guilty as the infamous Evin. So, if the minister was not hiding the draconian powers of his legislation behind such a misleading slogan from parliament, who was he hiding them from? The French people?

Other French governments have inherited the Loi Evin, but had done nothing to curb its excesses until July 2004, when to get around its advertising restrictions, Hervé Gaymard, the French agricultural minister, announced plans to reclassify wine as a "food." This was quickly followed by a report requested by Prime Minister Raffarin on how to boost the "struggling wine industry" through advertising "without undermining the principles of consumer protection" in the Loi Evin.

In fact, the Loi Evin has no principles of consumer protection—it has no principles, period. It is not of the making of any current French government, so they should stop trying to fudge a questionable compromise, and simply revoke the Loi Evin on the grounds of its being against the national interest.

---

In conclusion, AOCEs and STEs would have reinvented and reinvigorated the French appellation system. Renou's proposals represented one of just four options. The second was to fudge them, the third was to do nothing at all, and the fourth was to scrap the "control-freak" element of French appellations altogether, bringing them more in line with New World thinking. There are good reasons why the fourth option should have been considered, such as: Why shouldn't people grow what they like, where they like? What does it matter what system of vine training a grower employs? Why try to control yields when the consumer will be the final arbiter of whether a producer will survive? Surely all that is necessary is the New World concept of truth in labeling: if a wine claims to be made from a particular variety, grown in a specific place, in a certain year, then that is what the wine should be. All good reasons—but there is a little Francophile part of me that wants to see the AOC concept survive, and to do that it needs reinventing from time to time. So what did they choose? The fudge, of course. The French cannot resist fudge, particularly when it comes sugar-wrapped.

At a three-hour crisis meeting between the French minister of agriculture, Hervé Gaymard, and representatives of the French wine industry on July 21, 2004, Renou's proposals were discarded because they made French wine more complicated at a time when it needs to become more accessible (granted, sorting the chaff from the wheat does tend to make the chaff less accessible! —T. S.). Gaymard stressed that there would be "tighter" controls for the production of AOC wines, to ensure that they were genuine *vins de terroir*, which represented "the top of the range," and were product-driven rather than consumer-driven (a flaw-free implementation of AOCE and STE would have achieved these very goals—T. S.). Gaymard's proposals were presented to each regional interprofessional bodies with a view to becoming effective with the 2006 harvest, along with a 50 percent increase in government aid for wine promotion overseas (the sugar coating—T. S.).

# FRENCH LABEL LANGUAGE

*FRONT AND BACK LABEL DEFINITIONS*

**Année** Literally year, this will refer to the vintage.

**Appellation d'Origine Contrôlée** Top official classification, commonly referred to as AOC, immediately above *Vin Délimité de Qualité Supérieure* (*see* p.54).

**Barriques** Small oak barrels of approximately 225 liters (59 gallons) capacity.

**Blanc** White.

**Blanc de Blancs** Literally "white of whites," a white wine made from white grapes, a term that is often, but not exclusively, used for sparkling wines.

**Blanc de Noirs** Literally "white of blacks," a white wine made from black grapes, a term that is often, but not exclusively, used for sparkling wines. In the New World, the wines usually have a tinge of pink, often no different from a fully-fledged rosé, but a classic *blanc de noirs* should be as white as possible without artificial means.

**Brut** Normally reserved for sparkling wines, *brut* literally means raw or bone dry, but in practice there is always some sweetness and so can at the most only be termed dry.

**Cave coopérative** Cooperative cellars where members take their grapes at harvest time, and the wines produced are marketed under one label. Basic products will often be blended, but top-of-the-range wines can be from very specific locations. A lot of cooperative wines can be ordinary, but the best cooperatives usually offer exceptional value.

**Cépage** This means grape variety, and is sometimes used on the label immediately prior to the variety, thus "Cépage Mauzac" means that the wine is made from the Mauzac grape variety.

**Châtaignier** Chestnut (occasionally used to make barrels).

**Château** Literally "castle" or "mansion," but whereas many wines do actually come from magnificent edifices that could truly be described as châteaux, many that claim this description are merely modest one-story villas, some are no more than custom-built *cuveries*, while a few are actually tin sheds! The legal connotation of a château-bottled wine is the same as for any domaine-bottled wine.

**Chêne** Oak (commonly used to make barrels).

**Clairet** A wine that falls somewhere between a dark rosé and a light red wine.

**Climat** A single plot of land with its own name, located within a specific vineyard.

**Clos** Synonymous with *climat*, except this plot of land is either enclosed by walls, or was once.

**Côte, côtes** Literally slope(s) or hillside(s) of one contiguous slope or hill, but in practical terms often no different from Coteau, Coteaux.

**Coteau, Coteaux** Literally slope(s) or hillside(s) in a hilly area that is not contiguous, but in practical terms often no different from Côte, Côtes.

**Crémant** Although traditionally ascribed to a Champagne with a low-pressure and a soft, creamy mousse, the term has now been phased out in Champagne as part of the bargain struck with other French sparkling wines that have agreed to drop the term *méthode champenoise*. In return they have been exclusively permitted to use this old Champagne term to create their own appellations, such as Crémant de Bourgogne, Crémant d'Alsace, etc.

**Cru** or **Crû** Literally means a growth or plot of land, this term usually implies that it has been officially designated in some way, such as a *cru bourgeois*, *cru classé*, *premier cru*, or *grand cru*.

**Cru Bourgeois** An officially designated growth below *cru classé* in the Médoc.

**Cru Classé** An officially classified vineyard in the Médoc and Provence.

**Cuve** A vat, *cuve* should not be confused with *cuvée*.

**Cuve Close** A sparkling wine that has undergone second fermentation in a vat, *cuve close* is synonymous with Charmat or Tank Method.

**Cuvée** Originally the wine of one *cuve* or vat, but now refers to a specific blend or product which, in current commercial terms, will be from several vats, this term is used most commonly, but not exclusively, in Champagne.

**Dégorgé** or **dégorgement** Found on some sparkling wines, this term will be followed by the date when the wine was disgorged of the yeast sediment that has built up during its second fermentation in bottle.

**Demi-muid** A large oval barrel, usually made of oak, with a capacity of 300 liters (79 gallons)—600 liters (158 gallons) in Champagne.

**Demi-sec** Literally semi-dry, but actually tastes quite sweet.

**Domaine** Closer to estate than vineyard, as a domaine can consist of vineyards scattered over several appellations in one region. The wine in the bottle must come from the domaine indicated on the label. Some former "châteaux" have changed to "domaine" in recent years.

**Doux** A sweet wine.

**Encépagement** The proportion of grape varieties in a blend or *cuvée*.

**Elevage par X** or **Eleveur X** Refers to the traditional function of a *négociant* (X), who has not made the wine initially, but purchased it, after which the *négociant* will age, possibly blend, bottle, and sell the wine.

**Elevée en ...** Aged in ....

**Elevée et mise en bouteille par X** The wine was aged and bottled by X, but none or only part of the wine was produced by X.

**Foudre** A large wooden cask or vat.

**Fûts** Barrels, but not necessarily small ones.

**Grand cru** Literally "great growth," this term indicates the wine has come from a truly great vineyard (which, to put it in context, a lousy producer can make a hash of) in regions such as Burgundy and Alsace, where its use is strictly controlled. In Champagne, *grand cru* is much less meaningful, since it applies to entire villages, which might contain most of the best vineyards in the region, but where lesser vineyards also exist.

**Grand vin** This term has no legal connotation whatsoever, but when used properly in Bordeaux, *grand vin* applies to the main wine sold under the château's famous name, and will have been produced from only the finest barrels. Wines excluded during this process go into second, third, and sometimes fourth wines that are sold under different labels.

**Lie** French for lees: *sur lie* refers to a wine kept in contact with its lees.

**Lieu-dit** A named site, this term is commonly used for a wine from a specific, named site.

**Médaille** Medal: *médaille d'or* is gold medal, *médaille d'argent* is silver, and *médaille de bronze* is bronze.

**Méthode Ancestrale** A sweet sparkling wine from Limoux that is produced by a variant of *méthode rurale*, a process that involves no secondary fermentation, the wine being bottled before the first alcoholic fermentation has finished.

**Méthode Classique** One of the legal terms for a sparkling wine made by the *méthode champenoise*.

**Méthode Champenoise** Contrary to popular belief, this term is not banned in the EU. It is expressly reserved for Champagne, the producers of which seldom bother to use it. (I cannot say never because I saw it once!) *Méthode champenoise* is the process whereby an effervescence is produced through a secondary fermentation in the same bottle it is sold in.

**Méthode Deuxième Fermentation, Traditionnelle, Méthode Traditionnelle Classique** Legal terms for a sparkling wine made by the *méthode champenoise* (*méthode deuxième fermentation* is used only in Gaillac).

**Millésime, millésimé** Refers to the vintage year.

**Mis en bouteille au domaine** or **à la propriété** or **le château** Bottled at the domaine/property/

AOC

VDQS

## VIN DE PAYS

## CHAMPAGNE

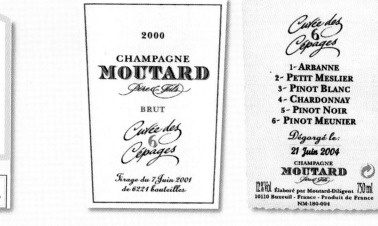

château indicated on the label (the wine must have been made exclusively from grapes grown there).

**Mis en bouteille par ...** Bottled by ... (not necessarily made by).

**Mistelle** Fresh grape juice that has been muted with alcohol before any fermentation can take place.

**Moelleux** Literally "soft" or "smooth," this term usually implies a rich, medium-sweet style in most French areas, except the Loire, where it is used to indicate a truly rich, sweet botrytis wine, thereby distinguishing it from *demi-sec*. This term was due to be obligatory in Alsace for wines that have a minimum residual sugar of 12g/l (9g/l for Riesling), but it was dropped after being vetoed by growers.

**Monopole** With one exception, this means that the wine comes from a single vineyard (usually a *grand cru*) that is under the sole ownership of the wine producer in question. The exception is Champagne Heidsieck & Co. Monopole, which is just a trading name.

**Mousse** The effervescence of a sparkling wine.

**Mousseux** Sparkling, found only on cheap fizz.

**Négociant** Literally a trader or merchant, this name is used by wine producers whose business depends on buying in raw materials. The name is derived from the traditional practice of negotiating with growers to buy grapes and/or wine, and with wholesalers and retailers to sell wine.

**Négociant-éleveur** Wine firm that buys in ready-made wines for *élevage*.

**Négociant-Propriétaire** A *négociant* who owns vineyards and probably offers a range of its own produced wines.

**Non filtré** The wine has not been filtered, thus liable to drop a sediment much earlier than most other wines, and should always be decanted.

**Oeil-de-perdrix** Literally "partridge eye" and refers to a rosé-colored wine.

**Perlant** Very slightly sparkling—less so than *pétillant*.

**Pétillance, pétillant** A wine with enough carbonic gas to create a light sparkle.

**Premier cru** Literally a "first growth," the status of a *premier cru* is beneath that of *grand cru* but only of relevance in areas where the term is controlled, such as Burgundy and Alsace. In Champagne, *premier cru* is much less meaningful, because it applies to entire villages, of which there are far too many, and in which much lesser vineyards also exist.

**Produit** Product, as in Product of ...

**Propriétaire-Récoltant** A grower-producer whose wine will be made exclusively from his own property.

**Récolte** Refers to the vintage year.

**Réserve** Ubiquitous and meaningless.

**Rosé** Pink.

**Rouge** Red.

**Rubis** Sometimes seen on rosé wines, particularly, but not exclusively, on darker styles.

**Saignée** A rosé wine produced by "bleeding" off surplus liquid from either the press or the fermenting vat.

**Sec** Dry, but in a sparkling wine this will have more sweetness than a *brut*.

**Sélection de Grains Nobles** A rare, intensely sweet, wine in Alsace made from selected botrytized grapes.

**Sélection par X** Selected, but not produced or bottled by X.

**Supérieur** As part of an appellation (e.g., Mâcon Supérieur as opposed to Mâcon plain and simple), this refers not so much to a superior quality than—possibly—a superior alcoholic strength (the minimum criteria being 0.5 percent ABV higher than the minimum for the same appellation without the Supérieur appendage).

**Sur lie** Refers to wines, usually Muscadets, that have been kept on their lees and have not been racked or filtered prior to bottling. This enhances the fruit of the normally bland Melon de Bourgogne grape used in Muscadet, often imparting a certain liveliness.

**Tête de cuvée** No legal obligation, but this term strongly suggests that a wine has been produced exclusively from the first flow of juice during the pressing, which is the highest in quality with the most acids, sugars, and minerals.

**Tonneau** A large barrel, traditionally four times the size of a *barrique*.

**Trie** Usually used to describe the harvesting of selected overripe or botrytized grapes by numerous sweeps (or *tries*) through the vineyard.

**Union Coopérative** A regional collective of local cooperatives.

**Vendange tardive** Late harvest; the term implies a sweet wine.

**Vieilles Vignes** Supposedly from old vines, implying lower yields and higher concentration, but no legal parameters apply, although most reputable producers would not dream of using the term unless the vines are at least 35 to 50 years old.

**Vieillissement** Aging.

**Vigneron** Literally a vineyard worker, but often used to denote the owner-winemaker.

**Vigne** Vine.

**Vignoble** Vineyard.

**Vin d'une nuit** A rosé or very pale red wine that is allowed contact with its grapeskins for one night only.

**Vin de glace** The French equivalent of *Eiswein* or Ice Wine.

**Vin** Wine.

**Vin de l'Année** Synonymous with *vin primeur*.

**Vin de liqueur** A fortified wine that is muted with alcohol before fermentation can begin.

**Vin de paille** Literally "straw wine," this is a complex sweet wine produced by leaving late-picked grapes to dry and shrivel while hanging from rafters over straw mats.

**Vin de Pays** Official classification, usually precedes the actual *vin de pays* name such as *Vin de Pays des Collines de la Moure*, *Vin de pays* is below VDQS and above *vin de table* (see p.56).

**Vin de Table** Lowest official classification, immediately below *vin de table* (see p.56).

**Vin Délimité de Qualité Supérieure** Official classification, commonly referred to as VDQS, below AOC and above *vin de pays* (see p.56).

**Vin Doux Naturel**. A fortified wine, such as Muscat de Beaumes de Venise, that has been muted during fermentation, after it has achieved between 5 and 8 percent alcohol.

**Vin gris** A delicate, pale version of rosé.

**Vin jaune** The famous "yellow wine" of the Jura derives its name from the honey-gold color that results from its deliberate oxidation beneath a sherry-like flor. The resulting *vin jaune* is similar to an aged fino sherry, although *vin jaune* is not fortified.

**Vin Mousseux** Literally means sparkling wine without any connotation of quality one way or the other, but because all fine sparkling wines in France utilize other terms, it should be taken to mean a cheap, low-quality fizz.

**Vin Nouveau** Synonymous with *vin primeur*.

**Vin primeur** A young wine that is sold within weeks of the harvest, and meant to be drunk within the year. Beaujolais Primeur is the most commonly known example of this type of wine, but numerous other AOCs are allowed to be sold in this fashion (see box, p.56), as are all *vins de pays*.

# BORDEAUX

*Bordeaux is an area in an almost-perfect viticultural situation on the west coast of France and benefits from the ultimate marketing tool—a château-based classification system that was established 150 years ago.*

THE NEW MILLENNIUM appears to be just as taxing for Bordeaux's reputation as the last decade of the 20th century turned out to be. Rain-drenched harvests toward the end of the 1990s challenged Bordeaux's claim to be the ultimate viticultural paradise, while the depressingly poor quality of its generic wines attracted almost as much bad publicity as the grossly inflated prices of modest vintages from the top châteaux. The weather might have improved in the first few years of the 21st century, but the quality of generic Bordeaux has remained abysmal, prices continue to rise almost in direct relation to the drop in sales—and then the unimaginable happened: the renowned US wine critic Robert Parker failed to appear for the *primeur* tastings in March 2003.

But all is not lost—Christian Delpeuch, the new head of the Conseil Interprofessionel des Vins de Bordeaux (CIVB), has mooted the possibility of declassifying some of the weaker Bordeaux wines into a wider *vin de pays*, which could then be bolstered by stronger wines from outside the region, but traditional to the southwest, such as the deep, dark Tannat. Delpeuch is the managing director of Ginestet, the region's biggest trader, and seems to have a good understanding of the more commercial end of Bordeaux's business. He has suggested the creation of a Vins des Cépages d'Aquitaine category for the Bordeaux region, under which varietal wines could be marketed. Far from detracting from the classic wines of Bordeaux, this would in fact improve their quality through stricter selection. As for the very top end of the market, the *bordelais* can once again sleep easy in their beds, as Robert Parker returned for the *primeur* tastings in 2004.

## OVERVIEW
The Bordeaux appellation and the Gironde *département* are geographically one and the same. Moreover, the Gironde is the largest *département* in France, and Bordeaux is the largest source of quality wines in the world. There are more than 22,000 vineyard proprietors working in excess of 280,000 acres (120,000 hectares), producing over 71 million cases (6.4 million hectoliters) of Bordeaux wine (85 percent red, 3 percent rosé, and 12 percent white) under 57 different appellations every year. Of these 22,000 properties, no fewer than 10,000 are châteaux and domaines producing wine. Of these 10,000 wine-producing properties, some 6,000 make and market wine under their own name (75 percent of total production), while the remaining 4,000 wine-producing properties are members of 53 cooperative wineries in Bordeaux (representing 25 percent of production, a little of which is sold under the producing property name).

## THE CHÂTEAU SYSTEM AND MERCHANT POWER
Prior to the concept of château wine estates, the land was worked on a crop-sharing basis. This feudal system slowly changed from the late 17th century onward. As the *Bordelais* brokers developed the habit of recording and classifying wines according to their *cru*, or growth (that is to say their geographical origin), and the prices they fetched, the reputations of individual properties became established.

The 19th century saw the rise of the *négociant*, or merchant, in Bordeaux. Many *négociants* were of English origin, and some

firms were established by Scottish, Irish, Dutch, or German businessmen. The best château wines were not consumed by the French themselves; they were the preserve of other northern European countries. Thus foreign merchants had an obvious advantage over their French counterparts. Yearly, in spring, these *négociants* took delivery of young wines in cask from the various châteaux and matured them in their cellars prior to shipping. They were, therefore, responsible for their *élevage*, or upbringing, and came to be known as *négociants-éleveurs*, eventually becoming the middlemen found in every aspect of wine trading. Many foreign buyers found it more convenient to deal through a *négociant* than directly with the wine producer, and often they had no alternative, since a number of châteaux were owned by, or were exclusive to, certain *négociants*.

CHÂTEAU PALMER
*This majestic turreted château is one of the finest in the Médoc.*

## THE MODERN BORDEAUX WINE TRADE
It was perhaps inevitable that the historically powerful and family-owned *négociant-éleveur* firms would eventually become a spent force. They lacked the resources required to finance adequately the huge increase in demand for Bordeaux in the 1960s, and those that did not founder during the oil crisis of the early to mid-1970s fell prey to the economic depressions of the following two decades.

As proud old firms were either taken over or went bankrupt, so the power shifted from the *négociants* to the châteaux, and in order to cope with a boom in world markets, many Bordeaux properties expanded their vineyards or added large, shiny new fermentation facilities. Many of these projects were financed with bank loans when interest rates were low. When sales slumped

## VOLUME VS. REPUTATION

Very few Bordeaux wines are produced from great vineyards. As the table below illustrates, the famous appellations represent a relatively small amount of the bordelais vignoble, and the classified growths a minuscule proportion of that. Yet it could be argued that the reputation of Bordeaux has been built upon a fraction of its *cru classé* or *grand cru classé*—the best performers. Bordeaux is a great wine region, but not all bordeaux is great wine.

| DISTRICTS | SURFACE AREA<br>Expressed as a percentage of<br>Bordeaux vineyards |
|---|---|
| Bordeaux (red) | 36.8 |
| Bordeaux Supérieur (red) | 10.0 |
| Médoc (red, non *cru classé*) | 11.0 |
| Médoc (red, *cru classé*) | 2.4 |
| Graves (red) | 3.1 |
| Saint-Émilion (red) | 4.2 |
| Saint-Émilion (red, *grand cru classé*) | 0.8 |
| Saint-Émilion satellites (red) | 2.7 |
| Pomerol (red) | 0.7 |
| Lalande de Pomerol (red) | 1.0 |
| Fronsac (red) | 1.1 |
| Various *côtes* (red) | 14.4 |
| Dry white | 8.3 |
| Sweet white | 3.4 |

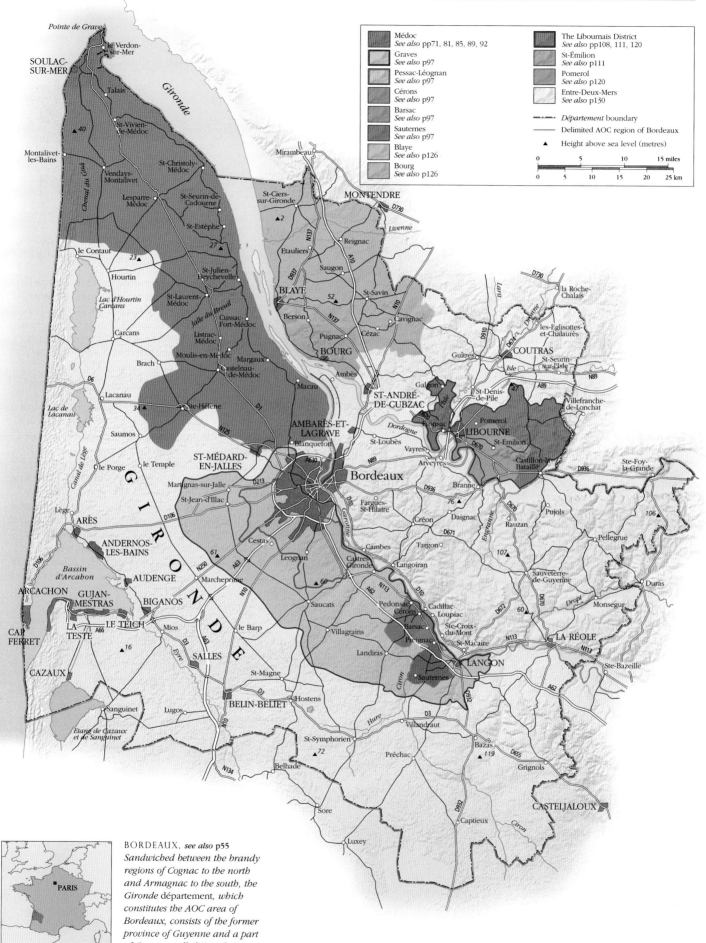

**Médoc**
See also pp71, 81, 85, 89, 92

**Graves**
See also p97

**Pessac-Léognan**
See also p97

**Cérons**
See also p97

**Barsac**
See also p97

**Sauternes**
See also p97

**Blaye**
See also p126

**Bourg**
See also p126

**The Libournais District**
See also pp108, 111, 120

**St-Émilion**
See also p111

**Pomerol**
See also p120

**Entre-Deux-Mers**
See also p130

– · – · –  *Département* boundary

————  Delimited AOC region of Bordeaux

▲  Height above sea level (metres)

0   5   10   15 miles

0  5  10  15  20  25 km

**BORDEAUX,** *see also p55*
*Sandwiched between the brandy regions of Cognac to the north and Armagnac to the south, the Gironde département, which constitutes the AOC area of Bordeaux, consists of the former province of Guyenne and a part of Gascony called Bazedais.*

PARIS

and interest rates shot up, the repayments became unbearable. Consequently, aside from a few entrepreneurial owners, power then shifted from châteaux to investors—not only banks but insurance groups, pension funds, and the like.

In today's market, therefore, the *négoce* has much less influence than before, with its *élevage* role primarily restricted to branded wines. The *élevage* of fine *cru classé* wine is either handled by the individual château itself or dispensed with by selling wines ridiculously young through French supermarkets or through the worldwide *en primeur* trade (*see* p66). Additionally, a number of château owners have carved out little empires, collecting estates or developing their own *négociant* businesses.

## THE CLASSIFICATION OF BORDEAUX WINES

Of all the Bordeaux classifications that exist, it is the 1855 Classification that is meant whenever anyone refers to "The Classification." It was commissioned by the Bordeaux Chamber of Commerce, which was required by the government of the Second Empire to present a selection of its wines at the 1855 Exposition Universelle in Paris. For their own ends, the brokers of the Bordeaux Stock Exchange traditionally categorized the most famous Bordeaux properties on the basis of the prices they fetched, so they were charged by the Chamber of Commerce to submit a "complete list of classified red Bordeaux wines, as well as our great white wines." The classifications listed above and to the right give the 19th-century names in the original form as listed by the brokers on April 18, 1855. The frequent absence of the word château has been followed, as has the circumflex in *crû*, and the use of *second crû* for red wines and *deuxième crû* for whites.

## THE CLASSIC GRAPE VARIETIES OF BORDEAUX

Contrary to what one might expect, it is Merlot, not Cabernet Sauvignon, that is the most important grape variety in Bordeaux. Cabernet Sauvignon represents only 27 percent of black grapes cultivated in Bordeaux, whereas Merlot accounts for more than 58 percent. It is nearer the truth, therefore, to say that Cabernet Sauvignon gives backbone to Merlot, rather than to suggest that Merlot softens Cabernet Sauvignon (which is the old adage). Although Château Mouton-Rothschild contains no less than 90 percent Cabernet Sauvignon, it is an exception, as even on the Médoc's hallowed ground, where it is blasphemy to mention the name of Merlot, 40 percent of the vines grown are of that variety. Château Pétrus (*see* p123), one of the most expensive wines in

THE MERLOT GRAPE VARIETY
*Almost twice as much Merlot as Cabernet Sauvignon grows in Bordeaux.*

### THE 1855 CLASSIFICATION OF THE WHITE WINES OF THE GIRONDE

**PREMIER CRU SUPÉRIEUR**
*(Superior First Growth)*
**Yquem**, Sauternes

**PREMIER CRUS**
*(First Growths)*
**Latour Blanche**, Bommes (now *Château La Tour Blanche*)
**Peyraguey**, Bommes (now two properties: *Château Lafaurie-Peyraguey* and *Château Clos Haut-Peyraguey*)
**Vigneau**, Bommes (now *Château Rayne-Vigneau*)
**Suduiraut**, Preignac
**Coutet**, Barsac
**Climens**, Barsac
**Bayle**, Sauternes (now *Château Guiraud*)
**Rieusec**, Sauternes (now *Château Rieussec*, Fargues)
**Rabaud**, Bomme (now two properties: *Château Rabaud-Promis* and *Château Sigalas-Rabaud*)

**DEUXIÈME CRUS**
*(Second Growths)*
**Mirat**, Barsac (now *Château Myrat*)
**Doisy**, Barsac (now three properties: *Château Doisy-Daëne, Château Doisy-Dubroca,* and *Château Doisy-Védrines*)
**Pexoto**, Bommes (now part of *Château Rabaud-Promis*)
**D'arche**, Sauternes (now *Château d'Arche*)
**Filhot**, Sauternes
**Broustet Nérac**, Barsac (now two properties: *Château Broustet* and *Château Nairac*)
**Caillou**, Barsac
**Suau**, Barsac
**Malle**, Preignac (now *Château de Malle*)
**Romer**, Preignac (now two properties: *Château Romer* and *Château Romer-du-Hayot*, Fargues)
**Lamothe**, Sauternes (now two properties: *Château Lamothe* and *Château Lamothe-Guignard*)

the world, contains 95 percent Merlot, without any Cabernet Sauvignon at all. Cabernet Sauvignon is a classic grape, quite possibly the greatest red-wine grape in the world, but its importance for Bordeaux is often overstated.

Sémillon is the most important white grape variety grown in Bordeaux. It is significant both in terms of its extent of cultivation and quality. This grape variety is susceptible to botrytis, the "noble rot" that results in classic Sauternes and Barsac. It is therefore considered to be the world's greatest sweet-wine grape. Sémillon also accounts for most of the fine dry white wines of Bordeaux, but these are relatively few and lack prestige. Sauvignon Blanc plays the supporting role in the production of sweet wines, and is used to a greater or lesser degree for dry wines. Many of the less expensive dry white wines are pure Sauvignon Blanc varietals.

## VARIETAL CONTRIBUTIONS TO A CUVÉE

The Cabernet Sauvignon is the most complex and distinctive of all black Bordeaux grapes. It has a firm tannic structure, yet with time reveals a powerful, rich, and long-lasting flavor. Wines from this grape can have great finesse; their bouquets often possess a "blackcurrant" or "violets" character. Cabernet Franc has similar characteristics to Cabernet Sauvignon, but may also have a leafy, sappy, or earthy taste, depending on where it is cultivated. It does, however, shine through as the superior variety when grown in St.-Émilion and Pomerol, and can compete on even terms with its more famous cousin in parts of Graves. Merlot is soft, silky, and sometimes opulent. It is a grape that charms and can make wines with lots of juicy-rich and spicy fruit. Petit Verdot is a late-ripener with a naturally high acidity, while Malbec has a thick skin that is rich in color pigments. Small amounts of Petit Verdot and Malbec were traditionally used to correct the color and acidity of a blended wine. The cultivation and use of these two varieties for this purpose has been on the decline for the last 20 years owing to the various modern techniques of viticulture and vinification.

The white Sémillon grape provides a wine naturally rich in flavor and high in alcohol. It makes succulent, sweet white wines that are capable of great longevity. Its intrinsically low acidity

## THE 1855 CLASSIFICATION OF THE RED WINES OF THE GIRONDE

**PREMIERS CRUS**
*(First Growths)*
Château Lafite, Pauillac
(now *Château Lafite-Rothschild*)
Château Margaux, Margaux
Château Latour, Pauillac
Haut-Brion, Pessac (Graves)

**SECONDS CRUS**
*(Second Growths)*
Mouton, Pauillac (now *Château Mouton-Rothschild* and a First Growth since 1973)
Rauzan-Ségla, Margaux
Rauzan-Gassies, Margaux
Léoville, St.-Julien (now three properties: *Châteaux Léoville-Las-Cases, Léoville-Poyferré,* and *Léoville-Barton*)
Vivens Durfort, Margaux
(now *Château Durfort-Vivens*)
Gruau-Laroze, St.-Julien
(now *Château Gruaud-Larose*)
Lascombe, Margaux
(now *Château Lascombes*)
Brane, Cantenac (now *Château Brane-Cantenac*)
Pichon Longueville, Pauillac
(now two properties: *Château Pichon-Longueville-Baron* and *Château Pichon-Longueville-Comtesse-de-Lalande*)
Ducru Beau Caillou, St.-Julien
(now *Château Ducru-Beaucaillou*)
Cos Destournel, St.-Estèphe
(now *Château Cos d'Estournel*)
Montrose, St.-Estèphe

**TROISIÈMES CRUS**
*(Third Growths)*
Kirwan, Cantenac
Château d'Issan, Cantenac
Lagrange, St.-Julien
Langoa, St.-Julien (now *Château Langoa-Barton*)
Giscours, Labarde
St.-Exupéry, Margaux (now *Château Malescot-St.-Exupéry*)
Boyd, Cantenac (now two properties: *Châteaux Boyd-Cantenac* and *Château Cantenac Brown*)
Palmer, Cantenac
Lalagune, Ludon (now *Château La Lagune*)
Desmirail, Margaux
Dubignon, Margaux (no longer in existence, but some of these original vineyards now belong to *Châteaux Malescot-St.-Exupéry, Château Palmer,* and *Château Margaux*)
Calon, St.-Estèphe (now *Château

Calon-Ségur*)
Ferrière, Margaux
Becker, Margaux (now *Château Marquis d'Alesme-Becker*)

**QUATRIÈMES CRUS**
*(Fourth Growths)*
St.-Pierre, St.-Julien (now *Château St.-Pierre-Sevaistre*)
Talbot, St.-Julien
Du-Luc, St.-Julien (now *Château Branaire-Ducru*)
Duhart, Pauillac (at one time *Château Duhart-Milon Rothschild,* but now *Château Duhart-Milon,* although still Rothschild-owned)
Pouget-Lassale, Cantenac
(now *Château Pouget*)
Pouget, Cantenac (now *Château Pouget*)
Carnet, St.-Laurent (now *Château La Tour-Carnet*)
Rochet, St.-Estèphe (now *Château Lafon-Rochet*)
Château de Beychevele, St.-Julien
(now *Château Beychevelle*)
Le Prieuré, Cantenac
(now *Château Prieuré-Lichine*)
Marquis de Thermes, Margaux
(now *Château Marquis-de-Terme*)

**CINQUIÈMES CRUS**
*(Fifth Growths)*
Canet, Pauillac (now *Château Pontet-Conet*)
Batailley, Pauillac (now two properties: *Château Batailley* and *Château Haut-Batailley*)
Grand Puy, Pauillac (now *Château Grand-Puy-Lacoste*)
Artigues Arnaud, Pauillac
(now *Château Grand-Puy-Ducasse*)
Lynch, Pauillac (now *Château Lynch-Bages*)
Lynch Moussas, Pauillac
Dauzac, Labarde
Darmailhac, Pauillac (now *Château d'Armailhac*)
Le Tertre, Arsac (now *Château du Tertre*)
Haut Bages, Pauillac (now *Château Haut-Bages-Libéral*)
Pédesclaux, Pauillac (now *Château Pédesclaux*)
Coutenceau, St.-Laurent
(now *Château Belgrave*)
Camensac, St.-Laurent
Cos Labory, St.-Estèphe
Clerc Milon, Pauillac
Croizet-Bages, Pauillac
Cantemerle, Macau

---

few years ago. Early harvesting, prefermentation maceration on the grape skins to draw out the aromatics, and longer, cooler fermentation in stainless steel, have all combined to produce a far more interesting, medium-quality, dry white wine.

## FERMENTATION AND MATURATION

Although some properties producing *crus classés* retain their wooden vats for the fermentation process (more because they lack the funds to reequip than for any idealistic reasons), hardly any of them actually invest in new oak vats, preferring those made of stainless steel. The one startling exception is Château Margaux. This great property has spent more money, following the advice of the legendary oenologist Professor Peynaud, than any other château in Bordeaux. This is puzzling because it was principally at his recommendation that virtually everyone else in Bordeaux invested in stainless steel.

## ADDING VIN DE PRESSE

One technique that is more characteristic of red winemaking in Bordeaux than in any other region is the addition of a certain amount of *vin de presse*. This is produced after the wine has completed its alcoholic fermentation and has undergone malolactic conversion. The wine is drawn off its lees into casks and the residue of skin and pips at the bottom of the vat is pressed. Normally this requires two pressings: the first *vin de presse* is the best and represents about 10 percent of the total wine produced, the second provides a further 5 percent. *Vin de presse* is relatively low in alcohol, very dark, and extremely tannic. In a wine made for early drinking, *vin de presse* would be harsh and unpleasant, but with the structure of a classic oak-matured Bordeaux, it gives extra body and increases longevity.

THE VINIFICATION PROCESS
*The proportion of grape varieties grown and the intrinsic potential of a château's terroir determine the basic quality and character of Bordeaux's finest wines. Manipulating the vinification process has, however, always been the method of honing the style of this region's best châteaux. Processes include adding up to 15 percent* vin de presse; *grape-skin contact (which can be for up to a month); maturation, which used to take 3 to 5 years, but now takes 15 to 18 months; and a percentage of new oak, always the hallmark of Bordeaux's premiers crus.*

---

makes it less suitable for producing dry wines, but in exceptional circumstances the highest quality Sémillon does make a fine dry white wine—if matured in new oak. This enhances the aromatic character of the wine and gives it a firm structure without which it would be too "fat" and "flabby."

The Sauvignon Blanc in Bordeaux is soft, delicate, and easy to drink. It does not have the same bite as it does in the Loire vineyards of Sancerre or Pouilly-Fumé, but the varietal character is more pronounced today, with a crisper, fresher style, than it was a

## BUYING EN PRIMEUR

### WHAT IS BUYING EN PRIMEUR?
This is a method of investing in Bordeaux wines by buying the wine before it is bottled. It is no longer something I subscribe to. Every château in Bordeaux attempts to presell a certain amount of its wine production in the first year of the wine's life, although it will not be bottled and shipped until it is three or, perhaps, four years old.

### APPROXIMATED BLENDS
The wines tasted by the trade and upon which *en primeur* offers are based will be approximated blends, which is to say that they will consist of several different casks in roughly the proportion of grape variety that will make up the final *grand vin*. Yet no matter how honest and accurate the winemaker tries to be, this can never be a true representation of the final wine. Winemakers do not know what the final proportions of grape varieties will be. Much depends on whether every

barrel matures as expected, and how strict the selection is when it comes to rejecting wines not fit for making *grand vin*.

### WINE SALES BY MAIL ORDER
The first sales usually go on sale in the spring after the vintage, shortly after merchants from all over the world have spent a hectic week tasting hundreds of wines barely six months old. Cask samples (wine bottled from the cask) of the best wines are taken back to their home markets for tasting by the trade and key private buyers. This can be as early as March, although June is the most popular month and it is at around then that mail-order offers go out with vivid descriptions of the wines and how they are likely to mature.

### WHY BUY EN PRIMEUR?
It is only worth buying a wine that you cannot touch for three or four years (and probably

should not drink for at least another three or four years after that), if you know it will be unavailable by any other means or, when it does become available, that it is likely to cost significantly more at that time.

### WHICH WINES SHOULD YOU BUY?
Wine lovers are better advised to take up offers to buy *en primeur* wines such as Cornas from the Rhône, which never seem to be available when it is ready to drink. As far as investments are concerned, there is only one piece of advice I can give, and that is to stick to "blue-chip" wines in top vintages. It does not matter whether cask samples of Latour, Mouton, Pétrus, Yquem, and so on bear any resemblance to the final bottled product, they will always be a good investment, and from a wine drinker's point of view, there is no point in gambling on any other Bordeaux *en primeur*.

## OAK CASK MATURATION
After fermentation and prior to bottling, all the best red Bordeaux are matured in 59-gallon (225-liter) Bordeaux oak casks called *barriques*. The duration of this operation and the percentage of new oak casks used should depend entirely on the quality and structure of the wine, and this will vary according to the vintage. The bigger the wine, the more new oak it can take and the longer maturation it will need. The greatest wines—all the *premiers crus*—require at least 18 to 24 months in 100 percent new oak to reach maturity. Other fine-quality Bordeaux wines do not need so much time, perhaps only 12 to 18 months, and do not benefit from 100 percent new oak; between 30 and 50 percent may be enough. If you get the chance, put your nose into a new oak cask before it has been used. The wonderful creamy-smoky, vanilla-and-charcoal aroma is the very essence of what should come through when a fine wine has been properly matured in oak.

## PAST, PRESENT, AND FUTURE
During the early 1980s, the idea of "second wines"—always a factor in the production of the finest Bordeaux growths—began to catch on among the properties producing *crus bourgeois*, enabling

**BARRELS IN A BORDEAUX CHAI**
*These new oak barriques at Château Langoa-Barton contain the wines of Château Léoville-Barton (Léoville-Barton has no chai of its own). Both properties belong to the Barton family (who are of British descent).*

modest properties to make much better wines through stricter selection of their *grands vins*. Toward the end of the 1980s, "green harvesting," or crop-thinning, became *de rigueur* for all quality-conscious châteaux (even though the Romans considered such practices essential 2,000 years ago!).

However, the most significant advance in Bordeaux over the last 20 years came in 1994, when a decision was made to harvest grapes according to tannin ripeness, rather than sugar-acidity ripeness. Unripe tannins are not hydrolyzed; they are hard and will never soften, whereas ripe tannins are hydrolyzed, have a certain suppleness from day one, and will always soften. This phenomenon has long been known, but precisely when it occurs can vary from region to region, and year to year. In Bordeaux tannin ripeness has been under study since 1986 by Vincent Dupuch, who discovered that grapes deemed physiologically ripe in Bordeaux by their sugar-acidity ratio actually possessed a high proportion of unripe tannins.

In 1994, many *bordelais* harvested according to Dupuch's tannin ripeness parameters and were surprised to discover the optimum moment to pick was in fact much later than they had previously thought. This means not only that many Bordeaux wines will be riper, but also that by determining ripeness in this way, the winemaker is aware of the precise phenolic content, and this allows the fine-tuning of maceration and fermentation for each batch of grapes.

The 21st century will see a continuation in the rise of super-premium boutique wines, particularly from St.-Émilion. However, the increase in the density of vines to raise general standards in several Bordeaux appellations has been delayed. According to decrees issued in 1994, these new standards were to be fast-tracked, but this was fudged by new decrees in 1998, which let some areas off the hook, making higher-density planting not legally enforceable until 2025.

Meanwhile, the volume of dry white Bordeaux has dropped, leaving fewer producers making superior wines. Once the poorest cousin in Bordeaux, dry whites are better today than they have ever been. This applies across the board, from the lowliest Entre-Deux-Mers to the finest classified growth, even to the point where the 1993 Château Couhins-Lurton became the first Bordeaux *cru classé* to be sealed with a screwcap.

In a move to inform the public, and increase the region's profile among consumers of wines that do not include the Bordeaux name in the appellation (from Bourg to Blaye, and Fronsac to Pauillac, *et. al.*), all wines must include "Vin de Bordeaux" or "Grand Vin de Bordeaux" on the label.

## RECENT BORDEAUX VINTAGES

**2006** A bizarre year in which July was too hot, August too cool, September much too wet, and the generally high humidity a pain for all, including the *sauternais* at times. With rot, unripe grapes, and raisined berries in abundance, strict selection during the harvest was essential. The best wines will be extremely elegant, but few and far between, with relatively modest natural alcohol levels. This year favored Merlot over Cabernet Sauvignon, thus Right Bank over Left, although those who restricted yields in the Médoc produced some excellent wines. Some good dry whites were also produced.

**2005** A great vintage, with drought and a touch of *coulure* and *millerandage* acting in unison to restrict, rather than reduce in any drastic way, the size of the harvest, which was only 10 percent below average, although well down on the bumper 2004 crop. The drought conditions were not due to excessive heat, as in 2003, but simply to the absence of any major rainfall between May and October, when the vineyards were bathed in beautiful sunshine. All areas prospered, but the oldest vines in Margaux and Pomerol fared best of all. On par, no doubt, with 2000, while the *coulure* and *millerandage* is a sufficiently intriguing echo of 1961 for some châteaux to set their sights even higher! A brilliant year for Sauternes and Barsac, both of which are marked by botrytis of great finesse.

**2004** This huge harvest was twice the size of the 2003 crop, achieved only by a massive green-pruning exercise across the entire region. Despite the size, the quality of the wine is truly excellent. Reds are excellent to great on both left and right banks, Sauternes and Barsac are almost as good, and the size of the crop even allowed some brilliant early-picked dry white wines. When you taste the wines and look at the figures, it's no wonder that the *bordelais* think they can get away with overcropping!

**2003** Unlike the rest of France, this was not a drought year. In fact, precipitation levels were slightly above average. However, as in other French wine regions, 2003 was a very hot and sunny vintage, with exceptional ripeness. Exceptionally, acidification was permitted, but although initial concerns about low acid musts were widespread, relatively few producers bothered to add acid. This is a great Bordeaux vintage, with good to superb wines produced throughout the region, but favoring the Right Bank and improving the farther north the vineyards are in the classic communal appellations of the Médoc. The most concentrated wines will be quite exotic and flamboyant. Great Sauternes were also made.

**2002** Hyped up immediately after the vintage, when the wines were tasted the following spring, this vintage turned out to be far more variable than anyone had imagined. Essentially, it is a Cabernet year, not Merlot, thus some very high-quality Médocs were produced, particularly in, but not restricted to, Pauillac. The farther up the *cru classé* scale you go, the better the wines are, with Lafite a match for the greatest wines of any Bordeaux vintage. Brilliant for Sauternes too.

## BORDEAUX'S BEST GENERIC BRANDS

Bordeaux has the greatest reputation for red wine in the world, but as in all regions, ordinary wines do exist. In fact, the majority of wines produced in any region is very ordinary, and Bordeaux is no exception. Remember that more than money separates Mouton Cadet from Château Mouton-Rothschild. While the former might be the most famous of all generic Bordeaux brands, it is merely the blended product of relatively inferior wines grown anywhere within the vast *départemental* appellation of Bordeaux, while the latter is a selection of one of the finest wines grown on a single estate—a *premier cru classé* in the small, communal AOC of Pauillac.

As a branded generic Bordeaux wine can be a disappointing introduction to the world's greatest wine region, the following brands are suggested as reliable choices:

**CHAMARRÉ TRADITION**
Ironically for the first French brand created to exploit the advantages of cross-regional blending, Chamarré's best wine by far is its AOC Bordeaux. This modern claret boasts well-rounded, juicy Merlot fruit that builds in the glass, and is marked by a satisfying, ripe-fruit sweetness on the finish.

**CORDIER**
What they used to call "good luncheon claret" in the old days.

**DOURTHE NUMÉRO 1**
Probably the best, largest-selling branded Bordeaux available.

**KRESSMAN MONOPOLE BLANC**
One of the few big white Bordeaux blends to show any distinctive character.

**LA COUR PAVILLON**
One of the most reliable and underrated generic Bordeaux wines on the market at the moment. Made at Château Loudenne, this wine always displays good fruit, but possesses enough structure to keep for a while.

**MAÎTRE D'ESTOURNEL**
This has the same connection to Château Cos d'Estournel as "Mouton Cadet" has to Château Mouton-Rothschild, which is absolutely nonexistent as far as the wine is concerned, but both brands hope to sell on the back of their respective château name. There is, however, a fundamental difference between the two, of course: "Maître d'Estournel" happens to be an expressive, early-drinking wine that can also take a few years in bottle, whereas "Mouton Cadet" is mutton dressed up as lamb.

**MICHEL LYNCH**
Produced by Michel Cazes of Château Lynch-Bages in an unashamedly up-front, fruity style. Red, white, and rosé are all thoroughly recommended.

**PREMIUS EXIGENCE**
Produced by Yvon Mau, the step up between the premium Premius and Premius Exigence is about as big as it can get for two wines sharing the same brand. The stricter selection of grapes and no-expense-spared handling shows through in the richer, oak-layered fruit.

**SICHEL SIRIUS**
This is as serious as it sounds. An excellent oak-aged generic Bordeaux, it will improve for a further year or two in bottle.

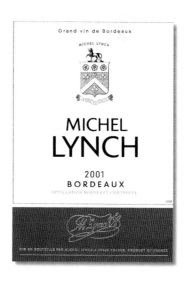

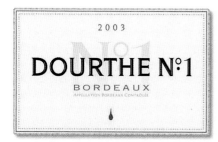

## THE APPELLATIONS OF GENERIC
# BORDEAUX

There are more than 50 appellations in Bordeaux and every one has its generic wines, produced by a *négociant* or local *coopérative*.

## BORDEAUX AOC

As with any large, and thus variable, appellation, the generic Bordeaux AOC is responsible for the good, bad, and ugly wines of the region. Overall, quality is of a decent standard, although the best wines are unlikely to fit the classic descriptions that have made the region famous. Wines carrying the generic appellation may come from any AOC vineyard in the entire Gironde. Some of the most interesting wines are from classic areas where the more specific appellation is confined to a precise style: such as a red Bordeaux produced by a château in Sauternes. If the wine is a brand, it should be ready to drink. If it is a château wine, the address should reveal its origin, and the price will be an indication of its quality and a guide to when it should be drunk.

**RED** Most are simply dry, luncheon claret styles, made for early drinking and usually softened by a high Merlot content.

🍇 Cabernet Sauvignon, Cabernet Franc, Carmenère, Merlot, Malbec, Petit Verdot

🍷 1–5 years

**WHITE** All medium-dry, basic white bordeaux contain at least 4 grams of residual sugar per liter, and have a certain sweetness. It is by far the most variable appellation category, with many dull wines. If the wine contains less than 4 grams of residual sugar per liter, the Bordeaux appellation must be qualified by "Sec." These dry whites are also variable, but most of the best wines of the appellation are found among them. They may be sold from December 1 without any mention of *primeur* or *nouveau*.

🍇 Sémillon, Sauvignon, Muscadelle plus up to 30% in total of Merlot Blanc, Colombard, Mauzac, Ondenc, Ugni Blanc

🍷 1–2 years

**ROSÉ** When made by individual properties, this medium-dry, medium-bodied wine can be attractive. These wines may be sold from December 1 following the harvest without any mention of *primeur* or *nouveau*.

🍇 Cabernet Sauvignon, Cabernet Franc, Carmenère, Merlot, Malbec, Petit Verdot

🍷 Immediately

## BORDEAUX CLAIRET AOC

"Clairet" is a term that refers to a red wine that is light in body and color. It derives from *vin claret* in Old French, a term of respect; this suggests that Bordeaux achieved a reputation for limpidity before other wines.

**ROSÉ** Rich, dark rosé or failed, feeble red? The best examples of this medium-dry, medium-bodied wine come from the village of Quinsac in the Premières Côtes de Bordeaux.

🍇 Cabernet Sauvignon, Cabernet Franc, Carmenère, Merlot, Malbec, Petit Verdot

🍷 1–2 years

## BORDEAUX ROSÉ AOC

The theory is that this appellation is reserved for wine deliberately produced as rosé, while "Bordeaux Clairet" is for a light-colored red wine. Both may simply be labeled "Bordeaux AOC." For technical details *see* Bordeaux AOC.

## BORDEAUX SEC AOC

White bordeaux with less than 4 grams of residual sugar per liter (*see* Bordeaux AOC).

## BORDEAUX SUPÉRIEUR AOC

Technically superior to Bordeaux AOC by only half a degree of alcohol, yet most of these wines do seem to have a greater consistency of quality, and, therefore, value. All generics are variable, but this one is less so than most.

**RED** These dry, light-bodied or medium- to full-bodied wines vary a lot but are generally fuller and richer than most red wines using the basic Bordeaux appellation.

🍇 Cabernet Sauvignon, Cabernet Franc, Carmenère, Merlot, Malbec, Petit Verdot

🍷 2–6 years

**WHITE** Dry or sometimes sweet, light- to medium-bodied white wines that are little seen.

🍇 Sémillon, Sauvignon, Muscadelle plus up to 30% in total Merlot Blanc, Colombard, Mauzac, Ondenc, Ugni Blanc; the proportion of Merlot Blanc must not exceed 15%

🍷 1–2 years

## BORDEAUX SUPÉRIEUR CLAIRET AOC

This is a little-seen appellation: the wines are sold either as "Bordeaux Supérieur" or "Bordeaux Clairet."

**ROSÉ** Medium-dry and medium-bodied as Bordeaux Clairet, but with an extra half degree of alcohol.

🍇 Cabernet Sauvignon, Cabernet Franc, Carmenère, Merlot, Malbec, Petit Verdot

🍷 1–2 years

## BORDEAUX SUPÉRIEUR ROSÉ AOC

This appellation has a small cast—and Château Lascombe's Rosé de Lascombes still tops the bill.

**ROSÉ** As few examples of these medium-dry, medium-bodied wines exist, it is possible to generalize and describe them as fuller, richer, and having more class than any Bordeaux Rosé AOC wines.

🍇 Cabernet Sauvignon, Cabernet Franc, Carmenère, Merlot, Malbec, Petit Verdot

🍷 1–2 years

## CRÉMANT DE BORDEAUX AOC

This was introduced in 1990 to replace the old Bordeaux Mousseux AOC (which was phased out on December 31, 1995). Although preferable to a lot of poorly produced Loire sparkling wines, there is nothing special about Bordeaux bubbly. Changing the appellation has done nothing to change the product because, like its predecessor, Crémant de Bordeaux is merely a modest and inoffensive fizz. It lacks the spirit and expressiveness to stand out from the sea of far cheaper, but equally boring, sparkling wines that exist almost everywhere. I have tasted much better from areas far less suited to sparkling wine than Bordeaux.

**SPARKLING WHITE** Varies from dry to sweet and light- to medium-bodied, but is almost always bland.

🍇 Sémillon, Sauvignon, Muscadelle, Ugni Blanc, Colombard, Cabernet Sauvignon, Cabernet Franc, Carmenère, Merlot, Malbec, Petit Verdot

🍷 1–2 years

**SPARKLING ROSÉ** The authorities should have taken advantage of the introduction of a new appellation to allow the inclusion of white grapes for this style, as this would potentially have improved the quality.

🍇 Cabernet Sauvignon, Cabernet Franc, Carmenère, Merlot, Malbec, Petit Verdot

🍷 2–3 years

---

## THE WINE PRODUCERS OF
# BORDEAUX AND BORDEAUX SUPÉRIEUR

Although many of the following properties are located within more specific appellations, at least a certain portion of their wine production is sold as either Bordeaux or Bordeaux Supérieur, and it is those particular wines that have been recommended by the author in this section.

## BORDEAUX

### CHÂTEAU BEAULIEU
**Le Gay**
★

Brilliant value until 2005, then a step up in quality. This is one to watch—definitely a future star. But make sure you get in before the price shoots up!

### CHÂTEAU BERTINERIE
**Cavignac**

A serious rosé, pleasantly romantic, with delicately rich, floral fruit on the palate and a smooth finish.

### CHÂTEAU BONHOSTE
**St.-Jean-de-Blaignac**
★ ⓥ

Classic white bordeaux at its best.

### DOMAINE DU BRU
**St.-Avit-St.-Nazaire**

Refreshing clairet: light in color and body and easy to drink.

### CHÂTEAU CARSIN
**Rions**

Popular in the UK, New World influenced.

## CHÂTEAU COURTEY
### St.-Macaire
**★ⓥ**

These are intensely flavored old-style wines, possessing quite a remarkable bouquet.

## CHÂTEAU FAUGAS
### Cadillac

Well-balanced reds with attractive berry-fruit flavors.

## CHÂTEAU DU GRAND MOUEYS
### Capian

Consistently elegant red wines.

## CHÂTEAU GRAND VILLAGE
### Mouillac

Rich and easy Merlot-dominated, oak-aged red, and a good second wine under the "Beau Village" label.

## CHÂTEAU DE HAUX
### Haux

Gorgeously ripe and dry white wine, with very fresh and elegant fruit.

## CHÂTEAU LAGROSSE
### Tabanac
**★ⓥ**

Elegant, ripe, and long, with lemony-rich, oaky fruit.

## CHÂTEAU LAPÉYÈRE
### Cadillac

Well-structured red, dominated by Cabernet Sauvignon.

## CHÂTEAU DE LUGUGNAC
### Pellegrue

Romantic 15th-century château making attractive, firm, and fleshy red that can show some finesse.

## CHÂTEAU MARJOSSE
### Branne
**★ⓥ**

This is Pierre Lurton's home, where he makes lush and up-front reds with creamy-silky fruit and a beautiful dry white.

## CHÂTEAU MORILLON
### Monségur
**★ⓥ**

Rich, fat, and juicy wines.

## CLOS DE PELIGON
### St-Loubès

Fine, full-bodied red with a hint of oak.

## CHÂTEAU PLAISANCE
### Capian

This château makes excellent, lightly rich Bordeaux Blanc Sec, made from 50-year-old vines and fermented in oak.

## CHÂTEAU DE PLASSAN
### Tabanac
**★ⓥ**

The basic Bordeaux Blanc Sec has fresh, sweeping Sauvignon fruit, while the more expensive Bordeaux Blanc Sec, which is fermented and aged in oak, has lovely creamy fruit and a fine, lemony-vanilla finish.

## CHÂTEAU POUCHAUD-LARQUEY
### La Réole

Full and rich red with lots of fruit.

## CAVE DE QUINSAC
### La Tresne

Delicately colored, light-bodied, rosé-style wines sold as clairet.

## CHÂTEAU RENON
### Langoiran
**★ⓥ**

This is a pleasantly fresh and floral Sauvignon-style wine.

## CHÂTEAU REYNON
### Cadillac
**★ⓥ**

This is a star-performing château that produces *cru classé* dry white wine under the auspices of Denis Dubourdieu. The elite Vieilles Vignes *cuvée* is quite extraordinary, but everything produced here can be relied upon, right down to the aptly named "Le Second de Reynon." Also very good red.

## CHÂTEAU ROC-DE-CAYLA
### Targon

Easy-drinking, well-balanced reds with good fruit and some finesse.

## LE ROSÉ DE CLARKE
### Castelnau-de-Médoc

From Château Clarke, this has all the fragrance expected from a classic dry rosé.

## CHÂTEAU THIEULEY
### Créon

These are medium-bodied, elegant reds that possess more than just a hint of cask-aging. Also fine, fresh, floral, and fruity white wines.

## CHÂTEAU TIMBERLAY
### St-André-de-Cubzac
**★ⓥ**

Deep-colored, full of flavor, but not without a certain elegance.

# BORDEAUX SUPÉRIEUR

## CHÂTEAU DES ARRAS
### St-André-de-Cubzac
**★ⓥ**

Deep-colored wines with good structure and lots of chunky fruit.

## CHÂTEAU LA COMBE-CADIOT
### Blanquefort
**★ⓥ**

Well-colored wines with a big bouquet; oaky with delicious fruit.

## CHÂTEAU FONCHEREAU
### St-Loubès
**★ⓥ**

Well-structured, finely balanced *vins de garde* of extremely good quality.

## CHÂTEAU FOUCHÉ
### Bourg-sur-Gironde

This wine is firm yet has fat, juicy fruit and a smooth finish.

## CHÂTEAU LA GRANGE-LES-TOURS
### St-André-de-Cubzac

Well-made, full, flavorsome wines.

## CHÂTEAU GREE LAROQUE
### St-Ciers-d'Abzac
**★**

Elegantly rich wines, with succulent, beautifully focused fruit supported by fine-grained tannins.

## CHÂTEAU GROSSOMBRE
### Branne
**★ⓥ**

Nicely concentrated, very good red wine that will improve for 12 to 18 months, and represents exceptional value.

## CHÂTEAU JEAN FAUX
### Ste-Radegonde
**★**

An ancient wine property that once belonged to the Knights Templars, Château Jean Faux has been brought back to life by wine-loving *tonnelier* Pascal Collotte, with the advice of top consultant Stéphane Derenoncourt.

## CHÂTEAU LATOUR
### Sauveterre-de-Guyenne

These medium-bodied wines have consistently good fruit, smooth flavor, and make a cheap punt to get the "latour" name on the table!

## CHÂTEAU LAVILLE
### St-Loubès

Rich, tannic, and powerfully structured wines with spicy fruit.

## MARQUIS DE BOIRAC
### Castillon-la-Batille
**★ⓥ**

Super value *coopérative* wine with a big, oaky aroma and fruit to match.

## CHÂTEAU MÉAUME
### Coutras

Alan Johnson-Hill used to be a UK wine merchant before settling north of Pomerol. Since then, he has gained a reputation for cleverly tailoring this red Bordeaux to young British palates.

## CHÂTEAU LA MICHELERIE
### St-André-de-Cubzac

Another property producing a big, tannic style of wine.

## CHÂTEAU LES MOINES-MARTIN
### Galgon

Well-made wine for reasonably early drinking, with an attractive bouquet, round fruit, and fine balance.

## CHÂTEAU DE PIERREDON
### Sauveterre-de-Guyenne
**★ⓥ**

Cabernet Sauvignon-dominated Bordeaux from the Haut-Benauge.

## CHÂTEAU LE PIN BEAUSOLEIL
### St-Ciers-d'Abzac
**★**

Originally named Le Pin, this ancient property was purchased in 1997 by Arnaud Pauchet, who renovated and renamed it. He soon started making a name for his wine, with the help of consultant Stéphane Derenoncourt. He sold it in 2002 to Dr. Michael Hallek, who retained Derenoncourt.

## CHÂTEAU PUYFROMAGE
### Lussac

Attractive, well-balanced, medium-bodied, and easy to drink.

## ROSÉ DE LASCOMBES
### Margaux

Refreshing, fruity rosé of excellent character, quality, and finesse.

## CHÂTEAU SARRAIL-LA-GUILLAMERIE
### St-Loubès

Rich and fleshy wine that softens nicely with age.

## CHÂTEAU DE SEGUIN
### La Tresne

Look out for the Cuvée Prestige, which is rich and smoother than the basic Château de Seguin.

## CHÂTEAU TOUR-DE-L'ESPÉRANCE
### Galgon
**★ⓥ**

This is soft and smooth wine, full of fat, ripe, and juicy fruit, yet not without finesse.

## CHÂTEAU TOUR PETIT PUCH
### St-Germain-du-Puch
**★ⓥ**

Attractively colored, well-made wines, with a touch of spice.

## CHÂTEAU DE LA VIEILLE TOUR
### St-Michel-Lapujade
**★ⓥ**

Consistently rich and smooth, even in notoriously harsh vintages.

## CHÂTEAU VIEUX MOULIN
### Villegouge

Well-rounded, long, supple wines, of consistently fine quality.

# THE MÉDOC

*The style of wine alters more radically over short distances in the Médoc than in any other French red wine district. The wines are mild and unexceptional immediately to the northwest of Bordeaux, but from Ludon onward, they become progressively more characterful, acquire finesse, and—after Margaux—gain considerable body. Beyond St.-Estèphe, the firmness of body of the wines eventually turns to coarseness, and their finesse fades.*

THE MÉDOC TAKES its name from the Latin phrase *medio aquae*—"between the waters"—referring to the Gironde estuary and the Atlantic Ocean. It is a long, thin strip of prized vines, extending northwest from the city limits of Bordeaux to the Pointe de Grave. At its center is the classic area of Bordeaux, where the vast majority of the most famous châteaux are located, and yet this was the last major district of Bordeaux to be cultivated. While winemaking in the Libournais district of St.-Émilion began as early as the Roman occupation, it was another thousand years before scattered plots of vines spread along the Médoc. Across the large, brown expanse of water called the Gironde, the Romans viewed Bourg and considered its hilly area far more suitable for growing vines. At that time the marshland of the Médoc was difficult to cross and impossible to cultivate. Today, the Médoc is the envy of winemakers the world over and Bourg is merely a source of inexpensive, if good-value, basic Bordeaux.

## THE MÉDOC STYLE: VARIATIONS ON A THEME

The four famous communes of Margaux, St.-Julien, Pauillac, and St.-Estèphe, plus the two lesser-known but developing communes of Listrac and Moulis, are to be found in a region within the Médoc known as the Haut-Médoc, where the wines are fine, firm, and fleshy. The Haut-Médoc begins at the southern outskirts of the city of Blanquefort, along the northern reaches of the Graves district, where the wines are fairly neutral. The greatest wines of the Haut-Médoc are found in the area beginning at Ludon with Château la Lagune—the first *cru classé* encountered moving north from Blanquefort. Fine *crus bourgeois* are to be found in this area as well.

The wines at Margaux are soft and velvety and full of charm, although they are very much *vins de garde* and will improve well with age. The wines of St.-Julien are elegant with a very pure flavor. They have the delicate touch of Margaux, yet lean closer to Pauillac in body. The wines of Pauillac are powerful, often having a rich blackcurrant flavor with hints of cedar and tobacco. These

## FACTORS AFFECTING TASTE AND QUALITY

**LOCATION**
The Médoc lies on the left bank of the Gironde estuary, stretching northwest from Bordeaux in the south to Soulac in the north.

**CLIMATE**
Two large masses of water on each side of the Médoc—the Atlantic and the Gironde—act as a heat-regulator and help provide a microclimate ideal for viticulture. The Gulf Stream generally gives the Médoc mild winters, warm summers, and long, sunny falls. The district is protected from westerly and northwesterly winds by the continuous coastal strip of pine forest that runs roughly parallel to the Médoc.

**ASPECT**
Undulating hillsides with knolls and gentle slopes are characteristic of the Médoc. The best vineyards can "see the river" and virtually all areas of the Haut-Médoc gradually slope from the watershed to the Gironde. Marshy areas, where vines cannot be grown, punctuate most communes.

**SOIL**
Similar topsoils lie over different subsoils in the Médoc. Its topsoils are typically outcrops of gravel, consisting of sand mixed with siliceous gravel of varying particle size. Subsoils may contain gravel and reach a depth of many feet, or may consist of sand, often rich in humus, and some limestone and clay.

**VITICULTURE AND VINIFICATION**
Only red wines can use the Médoc appellation. Mechanical harvesting is commonplace and all grapes are destalked prior to fermentation in tanks, or in vats increasingly made of stainless steel. Skin contact lasts for one to two weeks, although some châteaux have reverted to the once standard four weeks.

**GRAPE VARIETIES**
**Primary varieties**: Cabernet Sauvignon, Cabernet Franc, Merlot
**Secondary varieties**: Carmenère, Petit Verdot, Malbec

BARREL-MAKING AT
LAFITE ROTHSCHILD
*Wines are aged in new oak at Château Lafite-Rothschild, although for a shorter length of time than in the past. The barrels are made with great care in a time-honored, traditional manner.*

## DISTRIBUTION OF MÉDOC CRUS CLASSÉS THROUGHOUT THE APPELLATIONS

| APPELLATION | GROWTHS | | | | | |
|---|---|---|---|---|---|---|
| | 1ST | 2ND | 3RD | 4TH | 5TH | TOTAL |
| Haut-Médoc | 0 | 0 | 1 | 1 | 3 | 5 |
| St.-Estèphe | 0 | 2 | 1 | 1 | 1 | 5 |
| Pauillac | 3 | 2 | 0 | 1 | 12 | 18 |
| St.-Julien | 0 | 5 | 2 | 4 | 0 | 11 |
| Margaux | 1 | 5 | 10 | 3 | 2 | 21 |
| **TOTAL** | 4 | 14 | 14 | 10 | 18 | 60 |

are wines of great finesse, and Pauillac can be considered the greatest appellation of the Médoc. St.-Estèphe includes many minor growths of rustic charm and a few classic wines, and technology is changing the robustness of its spicy wines to richness.

Beyond St.-Estèphe lies the commune of St.-Seurin-de-Cadourne, whose wines are entitled to use the Haut-Médoc appellation, after which the appellation becomes simply AOC Médoc. This area, formerly known as the Bas-Médoc, has a lesser reputation than the Haut-Médoc. However, many exceptional wines are made here: the triangle formed by St.-Yzans, Lesparre, and Valeyrac contains such outstanding minor growths as Loudenne, Potensac, la Cardonne, Blaignan, les Ormes-Sorbet, la Tour-St-Bonnet, la Tour-de-By, and Patache d'Aux. In general the style is more simplistic than in the Haut-Médoc.

## PROPORTION OF AOC AREA UNDER VINE REPRESENTED BY CRUS CLASSÉS

| APPELLATION | TOTAL ACRES | TOTAL (HA) | TOTAL IN HA | (ACRES) | CRUS CLASSÉS REPRESENTS |
|---|---|---|---|---|---|
| Médoc | 3,240 | (5,358) | | | No crus classés |
| Haut-Médoc | 11,342 | (4,590) | 630 | (255) | 6% of AOC, 9% of crus classés |
| Listrac | 1,641 | (664) | – | | No crus classés |
| Moulis | 1,500 | (607) | – | | No crus classés |
| St.-Estèphe | 3,099 | (1,254) | 558 | (226) | 18% of AOC, 8% of crus classés |
| Pauillac | 2,988 | (1,209) | 2,081 | (842) | 70% of AOC, 30% of crus classés |
| St.-Julien | 2,246 | (909) | 1,552 | (628) | 68% of AOC, 22% of crus classés |
| Margaux | 3,464 | (1,402) | 2,110 | (854) | 61% of AOC, 31% of crus classés |
| TOTAL | 39,520 | (15,993) | 6,931 | (2,805) | 8% of Médoc AOCs, 100% of crus classés |

## THE FIGHT FOR GRAVEL

The best soils for vine-growing also happen to be the most suitable for gravel quarrying. After WWII, in the absence of any legislation, gravel quarrying started in abandoned vineyards. Once the gravel was gone, the opportunity to reclaim the area as a vineyard was lost. There is plenty of gravel in the Gironde estuary itself, but it is more profitable to take it from an open pit. Quarrying companies will continue to plunder the Médoc's finite resources until the government agrees to protect them, but past administrations have shown little interest.

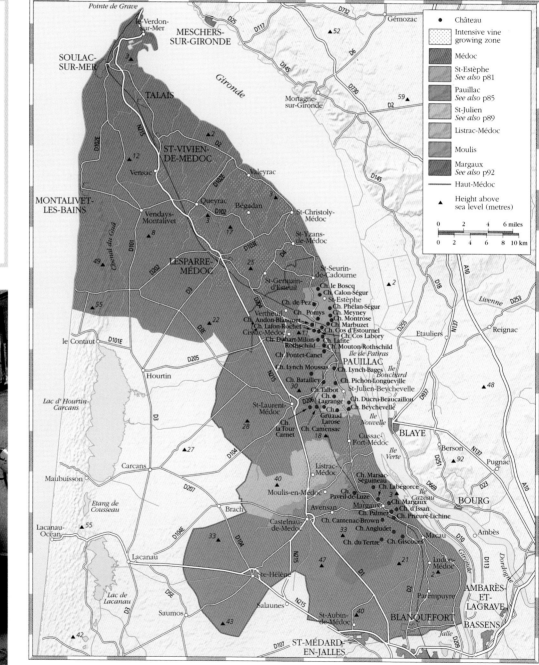

THE MÉDOC, *see also p63*
*The Médoc, a narrow strip of land between the Gironde estuary and the Atlantic Ocean, stretches northwards from the city of Bordeaux to the Pointe de Grave. The climate is Bordeaux's mildest, moderated by both the estuary and the ocean.*

# CLASS STRUGGLE

According to the new bourgeois growths law of November 2000, the classification of wines of the Médoc is to be reassessed every 12 years. The first reassessment under this legislation took place in June 2003, and of the 490 châteaux that applied for consideration, only 245 were successful in gaining *cru bourgeois* status. The high failure rate reflects a seriousness often lacking in recent French classifications, and I believe that in most cases the judging panel got it right. However, some château owners objected to the outcome, none more so that Jean-François Mau, who was "outraged" by the exclusion of his Château Preuillac. Mau had purchased this property as recently as 1998, but the panel tasted wines only from the vintages of 1994 to 1999, which is why he was so critical of the process, stating "It is a huge injustice to be judged on the past and not present performance." My initial reaction was that Mau was wrong, that for a classification to be taken seriously, the successful châteaux must display a firm track record, and that he was impatient, as he will surely do much better in the next reclassification. But on reflection, I think the wines tasted could have had a more recent emphasis. Part of the criteria established by the November 2000 law take into account the reputation of any proposed bourgeois growth, and that has to be established over a period of time that—objectively—precludes the classification of Château Preuillac. But rather than tasting six vintages, the youngest of which is almost four years old, every single vintage since the last vintage tasted at the previous reclassification should be sampled. Nothing less will do, if this law is to stand the test of time. And, whereas it might not be right to classify according to the latest vintages only, the system could be made sufficiently flexible to award some form of commended classification for those châteaux that have made a profound and demonstrable effort to improve quality in recent years. This would not only be fair to new owners, and established ones who have renewed their efforts, but it would also perform a service for consumers, pointing them in the direction of Médoc wines that are improving with each vintage. This presumes, of course, that the Syndicat des Crus Bourgeois du Médoc is organized for the benefit of consumers, and not just its own glorification. The current 2003 classification consists of 9 *Crus Bourgeois Exceptionnels*, 87 *Crus Bourgeois Supérieurs*, and 151 *Crus Bourgeois* as follows:

### CRUS BOURGEOIS EXCEPTIONNELS

Château Chasse-Spleen (Moulis-en-Médoc, Moulis-en-Médoc)

Château Haut-Marbuzet (Saint-Estèphe, Saint-Estèphe)

Château Labegorce Zédé (Soussans, Margaux)

Château Ormes-de-Pez (Saint-Estèphe, Saint-Estèphe)

Château de Pez (Saint-Estèphe, Saint-Estèphe)

Château Phélan Ségur (Saint-Estèphe, Saint-Estèphe)

Château Potensac (Ordonnac, Médoc)

Château Poujeaux (Moulis-en-Médoc, Moulis-en-Médoc)

Château Siran (Labarde, Margaux)

### CRUS BOURGEOIS SUPÉRIEURS

Château d'Agassac (Ludon-Médoc, Haut-Médoc)

Château d'Angludet (Cantenac, Margaux)

Château Anthonic (Moulis-en-Médoc, Moulis-en-Médoc)

Château d'Arche (Ludon-Médoc, Haut-Médoc)

Château Arnauld (Arcins, Haut-Médoc)

Château d'Arsac (Arsac, Margaux)

Château Beaumont (Cussac-Fort-Médoc, Haut-Médoc)

Château Beau-Site (Saint-Estèphe, Saint-Estèphe)

Château Biston-Brillette (Moulis-en-Médoc, Moulis-en-Médoc)

Château Le Boscq (Saint-Estèphe, Saint-Estèphe)

Château Bournac (Civrac, Médoc)

Château Brillette (Moulis-en-Médoc, Moulis-en-Médoc)

Château Cambon La Pelouse (Macau, Haut-Médoc)

Château Cap-Léon-Veyrin (Listrac-Médoc, Listrac-Médoc)

Château La Cardonne (Blaignan, Médoc)

Château Caronne Sainte-Gemme (Saint-Laurent-Médoc, Haut-Médoc)

Château Castera (Saint-Germain-d'Esteuil, Médoc)

Château Chambert-Marbuzet (Saint-Estèphe, Saint-Estèphe)

Château Charmail (Saint-Seurin-de-Cadourne, Haut-Médoc)

Château Cissac (Cissac-Médoc, Haut-Médoc)

Château Citran (Avensan, Haut-Médoc)

Château Clarke (Listrac-Médoc, Listrac-Médoc)

Château Clauzet (Saint-Estèphe, Saint-Estèphe)

Château Clément Pichon (Parempuyre, Haut-Médoc)

Château Colombier-Monpelou (Pauillac, Pauillac)

Château Coufran (Saint-Seurin-de-Cadourne, Haut-Médoc)

Château Le Crock (Saint-Estèphe, Saint-Estèphe)

Château Dutruch Grand Poujeaux (Moulis-en-Médoc, Moulis-en-Médoc)

Château d'Escurac (Civrac, Médoc)

Château Fonbadet (Pauillac, Pauillac)

Château Fonréaud (Listrac-Médoc, Listrac-Médoc)

Château Fourcas Dupré (Listrac-Médoc, Listrac-Médoc)

Château Fourcas Hosten (Listrac-Médoc, Listrac-Médoc)

Château Furcas Loubaney (Listrac-Médoc, Listrac-Médoc)

Château du Glana (Saint-Julien-Beychevelle, Saint-Julien)

Château Les Grands Chênes (Saint-Christoly-de-Médoc, Médoc)

Château Gressier Grand Poujeaux (Moulis-en-Médoc, Moulis-en-Médoc)

Château Greysac (Bégadan, Médoc)

Château La Gurgue (Margaux)

Château Hanteillan (Cissac-Médoc, Haut-Médoc)

Château Haut-Bages Monpelou (Pauillac, Pauillac)

Château La Haye (Saint-Estèphe, Saint-Estèphe)

Château Labegorce (Margaux, Margaux)

Château Lachesnaye (Cussac-Fort-Médoc, Haut-Médoc)

Château de Lamarque (Lamarque, Haut-Médoc)

Château Lamothe Bergeron (Cussac-Fort-Médoc, Haut-Médoc)

Château Lanessan (Cussac-Fort-Médoc, Haut-Médoc)

Château Larose Trintaudon (Saint-Laurent-Médoc, Haut-Médoc)

Château Lestage (Listrac-Médoc, Listrac-Médoc)

Château Lestage Simon (Saint-Seurin-de-Cadourne, Haut-Médoc)

Château Lilian Ladouys (Saint-Estèphe, Saint-Estèphe)

Château Liversan (Saint-Sauveur, Haut-Médoc)

Château Loudenne (Saint-Yzans-de-Médoc, Médoc)

Château Malescasse (Lamarque, Haut-Médoc)

Château de Malleret (Le Pian-Médoc, Haut-Médoc)

Château Maucaillou (Moulis-en-Médoc, Moulis-en-Médoc)

Château Maucamps (Macau, Haut-Médoc)

Château Mayne Lalande (Listrac-Médoc, Listrac-Médoc)

Château Meyney (Saint-Estèphe, Saint-Estèphe)

Château Monbrison (Arsac, Margaux)

Château Moulin à Vent (Moulis-en-Médoc, Moulis-en-Médoc)

Château Moulin de La Rose (Saint-Julien-de-Beychevelle, Saint-Julien)

Château Les Ormes Sorbet (Couquèques, Médoc)

Château Paloumey (Ludon-Médoc, Haut-Médoc)

Château Patache d'Aux (Bégadan, Médoc)

Château Paveil de Luze (Soussans, Margaux)

Château Petit Bocq (Saint-Estèphe, Saint-Estèphe)

Château Pibran (Pauillac, Pauillac)

Château Ramage La Batisse (Saint-Sauveur, Haut-Médoc)

Château Reysson (Vertheuil, Haut-Médoc)

Château Rollan de By (Bégadan, Médoc)

Château Saransot-Dupré (Listrac-Médoc, Listrac-Médoc)

Château Ségur (Parempuyre, Haut-Médoc)

Château Sénéjac (Le Pian-Médoc, Haut-Médoc)

Château Soudars (Saint-Seurin-de-Cadourne, Haut-Médoc)

Château du Taillan (Le Taillan-Médoc, Haut-Médoc)

Château Terrey Gros Cailloux (Saint-Julien-Beychevelle, Saint-Julien)

Château La Tour de By (Bégadan, Médoc)

Château La Tour de Mons (Soussans, Margaux)

Château Tour de Marbuzet (Saint-Estèphe, Saint-Estèphe)

Château Tour de Pez (Saint-Estèphe, Saint-Estèphe)

Château Tour du Haut Moulin (Cussac-Fort-Médoc, Haut-Médoc)

Château Tour Haut Caussan (Blaignan, Médoc)

Château Tronquoy-Lalande (Saint-Estèphe, Saint-Estèphe)

Château Verdignan (Saint-Seurin-de-Cadourne, Haut-Médoc)

Château Vieux Robin (Bégadan, Médoc)

Château Villegorge (Avensan, Haut-Médoc)

## CRUS BOURGEOIS

Château Andron Blanquet (Saint-Estèphe, Saint-Estèphe)

Château Aney (Cussac-Fort-Médoc, Haut-Médoc)

Château d'Arcins (Arcins, Haut-Médoc)

Château L'Argenteyre (Bégadan, Médoc)

Château d'Aurilhac (Saint-Seurin-de-Cadourne, Haut-Médoc)

Château Balac (Saint-Laurent-Médoc, Haut-Médoc)

Château Barateau (Saint-Laurent-Médoc, Haut-Médoc)

Château Bardis (Saint-Seurin-de-Cadourne, Haut-Médoc)

Château Barreyres (Arcins, Haut-Médoc)

Château Baudan (Listrac-Médoc, Listrac-Médoc)

Château Beau-Site Haut-Vignoble (Saint-Estèphe, Saint-Estèphe)

Château Bégadanet (Bégadan, Médoc)

Château Bel Air (Saint-Estèphe, Saint-Estèphe)

Château Bel Air (Cussac-Fort-Médoc, Haut-Médoc)

Château Bel Orme Tronquoy-de-Lalande (Saint-Seurin-de-Cadourne, Haut-Médoc)

Château Bel-Air Lagrave (Moulis-en-Médoc, Moulis-en-Médoc)

Château des Belles Graves (Ordonnac, Médoc)

Château Bessan Ségur (Civrac, Médoc)

Château Bibian (Listrac-Médoc, Listrac-Médoc)

Château Blaignan (Blaignan, Médoc)

Château Le Boscq (Bégadan, Médoc)

Château Le Bourdieu (Valeyrac, Médoc)

Château Le Bourdieu (Vertheuil, Haut-Médoc)

Château de Braude (Macau, Haut-Médoc)

Château du Breuil (Cissac-Médoc, Haut-Médoc)

Château La Bridane (Saint-Julien-Beychevelle, Saint-Julien)

Château des Brousteras (Saint-Yzans-de-Médoc, Médoc)

Château des Cabans (Bégadan, Médoc)

Château Cap de Haut (Lamarque, Haut-Médoc)

Château Capbern Gasqueton (Saint-Estèphe, Saint-Estèphe)

Château Chantelys (Prignac-en-Médoc, Médoc)

Château La Clare (Bégadan, Médoc)

Château La Commanderie (Saint-Estèphe, Saint-Estèphe)

Château Le Coteau (Arsac, Margaux)

Château Coutelin Merville (Saint-Estèphe, Saint-Estèphe)

Château de La Croix (Ordonnac, Médoc)

Château Dasvin-Bel-Air (Macau, Haut-Médoc)

Château David (Vensac, Médoc)

Château Devise d'Ardilley (Saint-Laurent-Médoc, Haut-Médoc)

Château Deyrem Valentin (Soussans, Margaux)

Château Dillon (Blanquefort, Haut-Médoc)

Château Domeyne (Saint-Estèphe, Saint-Estèphe)

Château Donissan (Listrac-Médoc, Listrac-Médoc)

Château Ducluzeau (Listrac-Médoc, Listrac-Médoc)

Château Duplessis (Moulis-en-Médoc, Moulis-en-Médoc)

Château Duplessis Fabre (Moulis-en-Médoc, Moulis-en-Médoc)

Château Duthil (Le Pian-Médoc, Haut-Médoc)

Château L'Ermitage (Listrac-Médoc, Listrac-Médoc)

Château d'Escot (Lesparre-Médoc, Médoc)

Château La Fleur Milon (Pauillac, Pauillac)

Château La Fleur Peyrabon (Saint-Sauveur, Pauillac)

Château La Fon du Berger (Saint-Sauveur, Haut-Médoc)

Château Fontesteau (Saint-Sauveur, Haut-Médoc)

Château Fontis (ʃʃOrdonnac, Médoc)

Château La Galiane (Soussans, Margaux)

Château de Gironville (Macau, Haut-Médoc)

Château La Gorce (Blaignan, Médoc)

Château La Gorre (Bégadan, Médoc)

Château Grand Clapeau Olivier (Blanquefort, Haut-Médoc)

Château Grandis (Saint-Seurin-de-Cadourne, Haut-Médoc)

Château Granins Grand Poujeaux (Moulis-en-Médoc, Moulis-en-Médoc)

Château Grivière (Blaignan, Médoc)

Château Haut-Beauséjour (Saint-Estèphe, Saint-Estèphe)

Château Haut-Bellevue (Lamarque, Haut-Médoc)

Château Haut Breton Larigaudière (Soussans, Margaux)

Château Haut-Canteloup (Saint-Christoly-de-Médoc, Médoc)

Château Haut-Madrac (Saint-Sauveur, Haut-Médoc)

Château Haut-Maurac (Saint-Yzans-de-Médoc, Médoc)

Château Houissant (Saint-Estèphe, Saint-Estèphe)

Château Hourbanon (Prignac-en-Médoc, Médoc)

Château Hourtin-Ducasse (Saint-Sauveur, Haut-Médoc)

Château Labadie (Bégadan, Médoc)

Château Ladouys (Saint-Estèphe, Saint-Estèphe)

Château Laffitte Carcasset (Saint-Estèphe, Saint-Estèphe)

Château Laffitte Laujac (Bégadan, Médoc)

Château Lafon (Prignac-en-Médoc, Médoc)

Château Lalande (Listrac-Médoc, Listrac-Médoc)

Château Lalande (Saint-Julien-Beychevelle, Saint-Julien)

Château Lamothe-Cissac (Cissac-Médoc, Haut-Médoc)

Château Larose Perganson (Saint-Laurent-Médoc, Haut-Médoc)

Château Larrivaux (Cissac-Médoc, Haut-Médoc)

Château Larruau (Margaux, Margaux)

Château Laujac (Bégadan, Médoc)

Château La Lauzette-Declercq (Listrac-Médoc, Listrac-Médoc)

Château Leyssac (Saint-Estèphe, Saint-Estèphe)

Château Lieujean (Saint-Sauveur, Haut-Médoc)

Château Liouner (Listrac-Médoc, Listrac-Médoc)

Château Lousteauneuf (Valeyrac, Médoc)

Château Magnol (Blanquefort, Haut-Médoc)

Château de Marbuzet (Saint-Estèphe, Saint-Estèphe)

Château Marsac Séguineau (Soussans, Margaux)

Château Martinens (Cantenac, Margaux)

Château Maurac (Saint-Seurin-de-Cadourne, Haut-Médoc)

Château Mazails (Saint-Yzans-de-Médoc, Médoc)

Château Le Meynieu (Vertheuil, Haut-Médoc)

Château Meyre (Avensan, Haut-Médoc)

Château Les Moines (Couquèques, Médoc)

Château Mongravey (Arsac, Margaux)

Château Le Monteil d'Arsac (Arsac, Haut-Médoc)

Château Morin (Saint-Estèphe, Saint-Estèphe)

Château de Moulin Rouge (Cussac-Fort-Médoc, Haut-Médoc)

Château La Mouline (Moulis-en-Médoc, Moulis-en-Médoc)

Château Muret (Saint-Seurin-de-Cadourne, Haut-Médoc)

Château Noaillac (Jau-Dignac-Loirac, Médoc)

Château du Perier (Saint-Christoly-de-Médoc, Médoc)

Château Le Pey (Bégadan, Médoc)

Château Peyrabon (Saint-Sauveur, Haut-Médoc)

Château Peyredon Lagravette (Listrac-Médoc, Listrac-Médoc)

Château Peyre-Lebade (Listrac-Médoc, Haut-Médoc)

Château Picard (Saint-Estèphe, Saint-Estèphe)

Château Plantey (Pauillac, Pauillac)

Château Poitevin (Jau-Dignac-Loirac, Médoc)

Château Pomys (Saint-Estèphe, Saint-Estèphe)

Château Pontac Lynch (Cantenac, Margaux)

Château Pontey (Blaignan, Médoc)

Château Pontoise Cabarrus (Saint-Seurin-de-Cadourne, Haut-Médoc)

Château Puy Castéra (Cissac-Médoc, Haut-Médoc)

Château Ramafort (Blaignan, Médoc)

Château du Raux (Cussac-Fort-Médoc, Haut-Médoc)

Château La Raze Beauvallet (Civrac, Médoc)

Château du Retout (Cussac-Fort-Médoc, Haut-Médoc)

Château Reverdi (Listrac-Médoc, Listrac-Médoc)

Château Roquegrave (Valeyrac, Médoc)

Château Saint-Ahon (Blanquefort, Haut-Médoc)

Château Saint-Aubin (Saint-Sauveur, Médoc)

Château Saint-Christophe (Saint-Christoly-de-Médoc, Médoc)

Château Saint-Estèphe (Saint-Estèphe, Saint-Estèphe)

Château Saint-Hilaire (Queyrac, Médoc)

Château Saint-Paul (Saint-Seurin-de-Cadourne, Haut-Médoc)

Château Segue Longue (Jau-Dignac-Loirac, Médoc)

Château Ségur de Cabanac (Saint-Estèphe, Saint-Estèphe)

Château Semeillan Mazeau (Listrac-Médoc, Listrac-Médoc)

Château Senilhac (Saint-Seurin-de-Cadourne, Haut-Médoc)

Château Sipian (Valeyrac, Médoc)

Château Tayac (Soussans, Margaux)

Château Le Temple (Valeyrac, Médoc)

Château Teynac (Saint-Julien-Beychevelle, Saint-Julien)

Château La Tonnelle (Cissac-Médoc, Haut-Médoc)

Château Tour Blanche (Saint-Christoly-de-Médoc, Médoc)

Château La Tour de Bessan (Cantenac, Margaux)

Château Tour des Termes (Saint-Estèphe, Saint-Estèphe)

Château Tour-du-Roc (Arcins, Haut-Médoc)

Château Tour Prignac (Prignac-en-Médoc, Médoc)

Château Tour Saint-Bonnet (Saint-Christoly-de-Médoc, Médoc)

Château Tour Saint-Fort (Saint-Estèphe, Saint-Estèphe)

Château Tour Saint-Joseph (Cissac-Médoc, Haut-Médoc)

Château Trois Moulins (Macau, Haut-Médoc)

Château Les Tuileries (Saint-Yzans-de-Médoc, Médoc)

Château Vernous (Lesparre, Médoc)

Château Vieux Château Landon (Bégadan, Médoc)

Château de Villambis (Cissac-Médoc, Haut-Médoc)

# THE APPELLATIONS OF
# THE MÉDOC

## HAUT-MÉDOC AOC

This AOC encompasses the Médoc's four finest communes—Margaux, St.-Julien, Pauillac, and St.-Estèphe—as well as the less well-known Listrac and Moulis communes. Wines produced outside these six appellations but within the Haut-Médoc are not generally as thrilling, although infinitely superior to those of Médoc. Among these very reliable wines are a few great-value *crus classés* and many high-quality *crus bourgeois*, but although Haut-Médoc is a name to look out for on the label of château-bottled wines, it counts for little on a generic.

**RED** These dry wines have a generosity of fruit tempered by a firm structure, and are medium- to full-bodied.

🍇 Cabernet Sauvignon, Cabernet Franc, Merlot, Malbec, Petit Verdot, Carmenère

🍷 6–15 years (*crus classés*);
5–8 years (others)

## LISTRAC-MÉDOC AOC

Significant funds have been invested in a number of high-performance châteaux in this commune, although its heavy clay soil does not have anything like as much potential as the gravel ridges found in the most famous Médoc appellations.

**RED** These dry, medium- to full-bodied wines have the fruit and finesse of St.-Julien combined with the firmness of St.-Estèphe. The most successful wines tend to have a large proportion of Merlot, which enjoys the Haut-Médoc's clay soil.

🍇 Cabernet Sauvignon, Cabernet Franc, Carmenère, Merlot, Malbec, Petit Verdot

🍷 5–10 years

## MARGAUX AOC

The best Margaux are potentially the greatest wines in the whole of Bordeaux, but this is an appellation that covers five communes encompassing a great diversity of soil and some of its wines not unnaturally have a tendency to disappoint. Margaux benefits enormously from having a namesake château, which is unique in Bordeaux, and the fact that this property sets the most extraordinarily high standards has done no harm to the reputation and price of these wines generally. The phenomenal success of Château Margaux has, however, unfairly raised expectations of many lesser-quality châteaux in the area, but those critics who widely accuse proprietors of sacrificing quality for quantity could not be further from the truth. There are individual châteaux that overproduce and therefore fail to achieve their full potential, but excessive volume is not typically the problem with this appellation, since it has the

lowest yield per acre of the four famous Médoc AOCs.

**RED** Exquisite, dry, medium-bodied, and sometimes full-bodied, wines that can be deep-colored and fabulously rich, yet they have great finesse and a silky finish.

🍇 Cabernet Sauvignon, Cabernet Franc, Carmenère, Merlot, Malbec, Petit Verdot

🍷 5–20 years (*crus classés*);
5–10 years (others)

## MÉDOC AOC

Technically, this appellation covers the entire Médoc, but most wines actually come from north of the Haut-Médoc in the area that was formerly called the Bas-Médoc. Its vineyards have undergone a rapid and extensive expansion since the mid-1970s.

**RED** The best of these dry, medium-bodied wines are similar in style to good Haut-Médocs, although the style is less sophisticated.

🍇 Cabernet Sauvignon, Cabernet Franc, Carmenère, Merlot, Malbec, Petit Verdot

🍷 4–8 years

## MOULIS AOC OR
## MOULIS-EN-MÉDOC AOC

One of the two communal appellations located on the Atlantic side of the Médoc, Moulis-en-Médoc is smaller and potentially more interesting than its neighbor Listrac. Like Listrac, it has no *cru classé* châteaux, despite adjoining Margaux, the appellation that has the highest number of such properties in the Médoc.

**RED** These dry, medium-bodied, sometimes full-bodied, wines have more power than those of Margaux, but far less finesse.

🍇 Cabernet Sauvignon, Cabernet Franc, Carmenère, Merlot, Malbec, Petit Verdot

🍷 5–12 years

## PAUILLAC AOC

This commune vies with Margaux as the most famous appellation, but is without doubt the most rock solid and consistent of Bordeaux AOCs, while its *premiers crus* of Latour, Lafite, and Mouton make it the most important.

**RED** Dark and virtually opaque, great Pauillac is a dry, powerfully constructed wine, typically redolent of blackcurrants and new oak. It might be unapproachable when young, but is always rich with fruit when mature. Although it does not have the grace of great Margaux, Pauillac

brings power and style together to produce wines of incomparable finesse for their size.

🍇 Cabernet Sauvignon, Cabernet Franc, Carmenère, Merlot, Malbec, Petit Verdot

🍷 9–25 years (*crus classés*);
5–12 years (others)

## ST-ESTÈPHE AOC

The potential of St-Estèphe is exemplified by Cos d'Estournel, which is one of the best *deuxièmes crus* in the Médoc, but the strength of this appellation lies in its range of *crus bourgeois*. The area under vine is slightly less than that of Margaux, which has the largest area, but St.-Estèphe has far more unclassified châteaux, and even the best wines are wonderfully cheap.

**RED** If Pauillac is the stallion of the four famous appellations, St.-Estèphe must be the dray horse. These dry, full-bodied wines are big and strong, yet not without dignity. St-Estèphe demands affection and, with the rich fruit of a sunny year, deserves it. These most enjoyable, sweet-spice and cedary wines can have lots of honest, chunky fruit. Cos d'Estournel is the thoroughbred of the commune.

🍇 Cabernet Sauvignon, Cabernet Franc, Carmenère, Merlot, Malbec, Petit Verdot

🍷 8–25 years (*crus classés*);
5–12 years (others)

## ST-JULIEN AOC

St-Julien is the smallest of the four famous appellations and the most intensively cultivated, with almost 50 percent of the commune under vine. There are no first growths, but there are as many as five seconds, and the standard and consistency of style is very high. This AOC overlaps part of the commune of Pauillac, and, historically, châteaux Latour and Pichon-Longueville-Comtesse-de-Lalande could easily have become St-Julien AOC as Pauillac AOC.

**RED** These are dry, medium-bodied, sometimes full-bodied, wines that have purity of style, varietal flavor, and can be long-lived. Well balanced and elegant, these wines fall somewhere between the lushness that is typical of Margaux and the firmer structure of Pauillac.

🍇 Cabernet Sauvignon, Cabernet Franc, Carmenère, Merlot, Malbec, Petit Verdot

🍷 6–20 years (*crus classés*);
5–12 years (others)

THE WINE PRODUCERS OF

# THE MÉDOC

## CHÂTEAU D'AGASSAC
AOC Haut-Médoc
Cru Bourgeois Supérieur
★☆ⓥ

This is one of the best unclassified wines in the Haut-Médoc. The wine is matured in wood for 15 months, with one-third new oak.

**RED** Dark-colored, plummy wine, with a lot of soft, ripe fruit.

🍇 Cabernet Sauvignon 47%, Merlot 50%, Petit Verdot 3%

🍷 4–10 years

**Second wine:** *Château Pomiès-Agassac*

## CHÂTEAU D'AURILHAC
AOC Haut-Médoc Cru Bourgeois
★

A relative newcomer that has quickly developed a cult following. The grapes are machine harvested, and the wine is matured in wood for 12 months, with 35 percent new oak.

**RED** A flashy, huge, dark, and dense wine with masses of fruit to balance the ripe tannins and extrovert oak.

🍇 Cabernet Sauvignon 56%, Merlot 38%, Cabernet Franc 3%, Petit Verdot 3%

🍷 5–15 years

**Second wine:** *Château La Fagotte*

## CHÂTEAU BEAUMONT
AOC Haut-Médoc
Cru Bourgeois Supérieur
☆ⓥ

A large property that consistently produces wines of good quality. This wine is matured in wood for 12 months, with 30 percent new oak.

**RED** These are aromatically attractive wines with elegant fruit and supple tannin.

🍇 Cabernet Sauvignon 60%, Merlot 35%, Cabernet Franc 2%, Petit Verdot 3%

🍷 4–8 years

**Second wine:** *Château d'Arvigny*
**Other wine:** *Tours de Beaumont*

## CHÂTEAU BEL-AIR LAGRAVE
AOC Moulis, Cru Bourgeois
☆ⓥ

This growth was classified *cru bourgeois* in 1932, but not included in the Syndicat's 1978 list. The wine is matured in wood for 18 to 20 months, with 70 percent new oak.

**RED** These vividly colored wines have a fine bouquet and firm tannic structure.

🍇 Cabernet Sauvignon 60%, Merlot 35%, Petit Verdot 5%

🍷 8–20 years

**Second wine:** *Château Peyvigneau*

## CHÂTEAU BELGRAVE
AOC Haut-Médoc 5ème Cru Classé
★☆ⓥ

Situated on a good gravel bank behind Château Lagrange, the wine, which is matured in wood for 24 months with up to 50 percent new oak, has improved consistently throughout the 1990s.

**RED** A good balance of blackcurrant fruit and ripe acidity, with much more supple tannin structure than used to be the case, and vanilla overtones of new oak.

🍇 Cabernet Sauvignon 55%, Merlot 32%, Cabernet Franc 12%, Petit Verdot 1%

🍷 8–16 years

**Second wine:** *Diane de Belgrave*

## CHÂTEAU BEL-ORME-TRONQUOY-DE-LALANDE
AOC Haut-Médoc Cru Bourgeois
★

This property has a confusingly similar name to Château Tronquoy-Lalande, St.-Estèphe. Steady improvement since the mid-1990s has turned the once four-square character of these wines into a more classically structured style. This wine is matured in wood for 12 to 14 months, with 10 percent new oak.

**RED** These are firm, fruity, classically structured wines.

🍇 Cabernet Sauvignon 35%, Merlot 55%, Cabernet Franc 10%

🍷 7–15 years

## CHÂTEAU BERNADOTTE
AOC Haut-Médoc
★☆ⓥ

Consistently performing above its class, this château is situated on fine, gravelly ground that once had the right to the Pauillac appellation and formed part of a *cru classé*. The quality has improved since the property was purchased in 1996 by the redoubtable Madame Lencquesaing, who also owns Pichon-Longueville-Comtesse-de-Lalande. This wine is now matured in

wood for 12 months, with 30 percent new oak.

**RED** These wines are very stylish, with lush Cabernet fruit backed up by the creamy richness of new oak.

🍇 Cabernet Sauvignon 62%, Merlot 36%, Cabernet Franc and Petit Verdot 2%

🍷 6–12 years

**Second wine:** *Château Le Fournas Bernadotte*

## CHÂTEAU BISTON-BRILLETTE
AOC Moulis
Cru Bourgeois Supérieur
★☆ⓥ

This top-quality Moulis property ages its wines in wood for 12 to 15 months, with up to 35 percent new oak.

**RED** Wines that are very rich in color and fruit with a full, spicy-cassis character and a supple tannin structure.

🍇 Cabernet Sauvignon 55%, Merlot 40%, Malbec 2%, Petit Verdot 3%

🍷 5–15 years

**Second wine:** *Château Biston*
**Other wine:** *Château Graveyron*

## CHÂTEAU BOUQUEYRAN
AOC Moulis
☆ⓥ

A big improvement in quality and value since this 32-acre (13-hectare) property was leased by Philippe Porcheron of nearby Château Rose Saint-Croix. Wines are matured in wood for 18 months with up to 50 percent new oak. La Fleur de Bouqueyran is a superior *cuvée*.

**RED** Lovely deep-colored, deep-flavored wines of not inconsiderable style and finesse.

🍇 Cabernet Sauvignon 41%, Merlot 57%, Petit Verdot 2%

🍷 5–10 years

**Second wine:** *Les Tourelles de Bouqueyran*

## CHÂTEAU LE BOURDIEU VERTHEUIL
AOC Haut-Médoc Cru Bourgeois

Situated between Vertheuil and St.-Estèphe, this château was classified *cru bourgeois* in 1932, but not included in the Syndicat's 1978 list. This wine is matured in wood for 12 months, with 30 per cent new oak.

**RED** Well-colored, full-bodied wines of robust character that are not lacking in charm.

🍇 Cabernet Sauvignon 60%, Merlot 25%, Cabernet Franc 10%, Petit Verdot 5%

🍷 7–15 years

**Second wine:** *Château Haut-Brignays*
**Other wines:** *Château La Croix des Sablons, Château Victoria-Picourneau*

## CHÂTEAU BRANAS GRANDPOUJEAUX
AOC Moulis
★☆ⓥ

These excellent and rapidly improving wines are aged in wood for 18 months, with 100 percent new oak.

**RED** Thanks to an increase in Merlot, this wine has plenty of accessible fruit, charming aromatic properties, and increasing finesse.

🍇 Cabernet Sauvignon 50%, Merlot 45%, Petit Verdot 5%

🍷 5–12 years

**Second wine:** *Clos des Demoiselles*

## CHÂTEAU BRILLETTE
AOC Moulis
Cru Bourgeois Supérieur
★☆ⓥ

This château's name reputedly derives from its glinting, pebbly soil. The wine is matured in wood for 12 months, with 40 percent new oak.

**RED** These are attractively colored wines of full but supple body, with delightful summer-fruit and vanilla aromas. Easily equivalent to *cru classé* quality.

🍇 Cabernet Sauvignon 40%, Merlot 48%, Cabernet Sauvignon 9%, Petit Verdot 3%

🍷 5–12 years

## CHÂTEAU CAMBON-LA-PELOUSE
AOC Haut-Médoc
Cru Bourgeois Supérieur
☆

Under the same ownership as Château Grand Barrail-Lamarzelle-

Figeac, this estate was classified *cru bourgeois* in 1932, but not included in the Syndicat's 1978 list. This wine is matured in wood for 12 months, with 45 percent new oak.

**RED** Soft, medium- to full-bodied wines with fresh and juicy flavors.

Cabernet Sauvignon 30%, Merlot 50%, Cabernet Franc 20%

⌛ 3–8 years

**Other wine:** *Château Trois Moulins*

## CHÂTEAU CAMENSAC
### AOC Haut-Médoc 5ème Cru Classé
★ⓥ

Situated behind Château Belgrave, this property was renovated in the mid-1960s by the new owners, the Forner brothers, who are of Spanish origin, and later established Marquès de Cáceres in Rioja. Camensac began making wine equivalent to its classification in the late 1970s, and since 1995 has been performing beyond its class. It is matured in wood for 17 to 20 months, with 35–70 percent new oak.

**RED** Well-structured wine, with a medium weight of fruit and a certain amount of finesse.

Cabernet Sauvignon 60%, Merlot 40%

⌛ 8–20 years

**Second wine:** *La Closerie de Camensac*

**Other wine:** *Le Bailly de Camensac*

## CHÂTEAU CANTEMERLE
### AOC Haut-Médoc 5ème Cru Classé
★✦ⓥ

In 1980, new stainless-steel fermentation vats replaced the old wooden ones that had been responsible for some stingy vintages. Also discarded were all the old casks, so the 1980 vintage was uniquely matured in 100 percent new oak. The wine is normally matured in wood for 18 to 20 months, with one-third new oak. It is currently performing above its classification.

**RED** Deliciously rich wines of fine color, creamy-oaky fruit, beautiful balance, and increasing finesse.

Cabernet Sauvignon 50%, Merlot 40%, Cabernet Franc 5%, Petit Verdot 5%

⌛ 8–20 years

**Second wine:** *Villeneuve de Cantemerle*

## CHÂTEAU CAP-LÉON-VEYRIN
### AOC Listrac
### Cru Bourgeois Supérieur
★

Simply called Château Cap-Léon originally, the vines of this property are planted in two plots of clay-gravel soil over marl.

**RED** Deep-colored, full-bodied, richly flavored wines with high extract levels and a good balance of tannin.

Cabernet Sauvignon 35%, Merlot 60%, Petit Verdot 5%

⌛ 5–12 years

## CHÂTEAU LA CARDONNE
### AOC Médoc
### Cru Bourgeois Supérieur
★ⓥ

This property was purchased by the Rothschilds of Lafite in 1973 and has since been expanded and renovated. This wine is matured in wood for 12 months, with 50 percent new oak.

**RED** These are attractive, medium-bodied wines with a good, grapey perfume and a silky texture, made in an elegant style.

Cabernet Sauvignon 45%, Merlot 50%, Cabernet Franc 5%

⌛ 6–10 years

## CHÂTEAU CARONNE-STE.-GEMME
### AOC Haut-Médoc
### Cru Bourgeois Supérieur
★✦ⓥ

This property is situated south of Château Lagrange—a superb island of vines on a gravel plateau. Matured in wood for 12 months, with 25 percent new oak.

**RED** Full-bodied wines rich in flavor with undertones of creamy oak, and a supple, tannin structure.

Cabernet Sauvignon 65%, Merlot 33%, Petit Verdot 2%

⌛ 8–20 years

**Second wine:** *Château Labat*

## CHÂTEAU CASTÉRA
### AOC Médoc
### Cru Bourgeois Supérieur
★ⓥ

The original château was reduced to ruins by the Black Prince in the 14th century. This wine is matured in wood for 12 months, with one-third new oak.

**RED** Soft-textured, medium-bodied wines best drunk relatively young.

Cabernet Sauvignon 45%, Merlot 45%, Cabernet Franc 7%, Petit Verdot 3%

⌛ 4–8 years

**Second wine:** *Château Bourbon La Chapelle*

**Other wines:** *Château Moulin de Buscateau, La Chapelle du Castera*

## CHÂTEAU CHANTELYS
### AOC Médoc Cru Bourgeois
★ⓥ

Owner Christine Courrian Braquissac brings a gentle touch to the naturally firm wines of this district.

**RED** Well-colored, medium-bodied, gently rich-flavored wines of some elegance.

Cabernet Sauvignon 55%, Merlot 40%, Petit Verdot 5%

⌛ 3–8 years

**Second wine:** *Château Gauthier*

## CHÂTEAU CHARMAIL
### AOC Haut-Médoc
### Cru Bourgeois Supérieur
★✦ⓥ

The wines from this château have improved dramatically since its excellent 1996 vintage, and continue to perform well in recent blind tastings. This wine is matured in wood for 12 months, with 30 percent new oak.

**RED** Rich, spicy, and long, with well-rounded, ripe tannins.

Cabernet Sauvignon 30%, Cabernet Franc 20%, Merlot 48%, Petit Verdot 2%

⌛ 3–7 years

**Second wine:** *Château Tours de Charmail*

## CHÂTEAU CHASSE-SPLEEN
### AOC Moulis
### Cru Bourgeois Exceptionnel
★★ⓥ

The proprietor of this quality-conscious property also owns the *cru classé* Château Haut-Bages-Libéral and the excellent unclassified growth of Château la Gurgue in Margaux. The wine is matured in wood for 18 months with 40 percent new oak, and is usually of *cru classé* quality. Certainly, it well deserves being recently classified as one of only nine *crus bourgeois exceptionnels*.

**RED** Full-bodied wines of great finesse, vivid color, with a luxuriant, creamy-rich flavor of cassis and chocolate with warm, spicy-vanilla undertones. Easily equivalent to *cru classé* quality.

Cabernet Sauvignon 70%, Merlot 25%, Petit Verdot 5%

⌛ 8–20 years

**Second wines:** *L'Oratoire de Chasse-Spleen, L'Ermitage de Chasse-Spleen, L'Orangeraie de Chasse-Spleen*

## CHÂTEAU CISSAC
### AOC Haut-Médoc
### Cru Bourgeois Supérieur
★ⓥ

Château Cissac is always good value, especially in hot years. It is fermented in wood and matured in cask with no *vin de presse*. This wine is matured in wood for 18 months, with up to 50 percent new oak.

**RED** These are deep-colored, well-

flavored, full-bodied wines made in a *vin de garde* style.

Cabernet Sauvignon 75%, Merlot 20%, Petit Verdot 5%

⌛ 8–20 years

**Second wine:** *Château Les Reflets du Cissac*

**Other wine:** *Château Abiet*

## CHÂTEAU CITRAN
### AOC Haut-Médoc
### Cru Bourgeois Supérieur

This substantial-sized property was once run by Château Coufran, then passed into Japanese ownership, under the Fujimoto company, which invested in improvements in the vineyard and winery. In 1997, it was taken back into French ownership, under the auspices of Groupe Taillan, and is run primarily by Céline Villars. This wine is matured in wood for 12 to 14 months, with 40 percent new oak.

**RED** A once solid, if plodding, Médoc of robust character, the style has become more accessible since the mid-1990s, and since the new millennium has shown a true plumpness of fruit, with not inconsiderable finesse.

Cabernet Sauvignon 58%, Merlot 42%

⌛ 5–15 years

**Second wine:** *Moulins de Citran*

## CHÂTEAU LA CLARE
### AOC Médoc Cru Bourgeois
★ⓥ

A well-established property that is receiving renewed attention of late. Approximately 30 percent of the wine is matured in wood for 23 months, with 5–10 percent new oak.

**RED** A rich, nicely colored, medium-bodied wine with some spicy finesse.

Cabernet Sauvignon 57%, Merlot 36%, Cabernet Franc 7%

⌛ 4-8 years

**Second wines:** *Laveline, Gentilhomme*

## CHÂTEAU CLARKE
### AOC Listrac
### Cru Bourgeois Supérieur
★ⓥ

This estate's vines were dug up and its château pulled down in 1950. All was abandoned until 1973, when it was purchased by Baron Edmund de Rothschild. He completely restored the vineyard and installed an ultramodern winery. Since the 1981 vintage, it has become one of the Médoc's fastest-rising stars. The wine is fermented in stainless steel and matured in wood for 12 to 18 months, with up to 80 percent new oak.

**RED** Well-colored wines have a good measure of creamy-smoky oak, soft fruit, and increasing finesse.

🍇 Cabernet Sauvignon 40%, Merlot 60%

🍷 7–25 years

**Second wine:** *Château Granges des Domaines Edmond de Rothschild*

## CHÂTEAU COUFRAN
### AOC Haut-Médoc
### Cru Bourgeois Supérieur
### ★🅥

These wines are matured in wood for 13 to 18 months, with 25 percent new oak.

**RED** Frank and fruity, this medium- to full-bodied wine has a chunky, chocolaty flavor, which is dominated by Merlot.

🍇 Cabernet Sauvignon 15%, Merlot 85%, Petit Verdot 5%

🍷 4–12 years

**Second wine:** *Domaine de la Rose-Maréchale*

## CHÂTEAU DUTRUCH GRAND POUJEAUX
### AOC Moulis
### Cru Bourgeois Supérieur
### ★🅥

Dutruch is one of the best Grand Poujeaux satellite properties. It also makes two other wines from the specific-named plots "La Bernède" and "La Gravière." Matured in wood for 12 months, with 25 percent new oak.

**RED** These are fine, full-bodied wines of excellent color, fruit, and finesse.

🍇 Cabernet Sauvignon 45%, Merlot 50%, Petit Verdot 5%

🍷 7–15 years

**Other wines:** *La Bernède-Grand-Poujeaux, La Gravière-Grand-Poujeaux*

## CHÂTEAU FONRÉAUD
### AOC Listrac
### Cru Bourgeois Supérieur

This splendid château has south-facing vineyards situated on and around a knoll, Puy-de-Menjon. This wine is matured in wood for 12 to 18 months, with one-third new oak.

**RED** Attractive medium- to full-bodied wines of good fruit and some style.

🍇 Cabernet Sauvignon 55%, Merlot 42%, Petit Verdot 3%

🍷 6–12 years

**Second wine:** *La Tourelle de Château Fonréaud*

## CHÂTEAU FOURCAS DUPRÉ
### AOC Listrac
### Cru Bourgeois Supérieur
### ★🅥

A charming house, with vineyards situated on gravel over iron-pan

soil, which can excel in hot years. This wine is matured in wood for 12 months, with one-third oak.

**RED** The good color, bouquet, and tannic structure of these wines is rewarded with rich fruit in good years.

🍇 Cabernet Sauvignon 44%, Merlot 44%, Cabernet Franc 10%, Petit Verdot 2%

🍷 6–12 years

## CHÂTEAU FOURCAS HOSTEN
### AOC Listrac
### Cru Bourgeois Supérieur
### ★🅥

Under multinational ownership (French, Danish, and American) since 1972, the winemaking facilities here have been renovated. The wines are matured in wood for 12 months, with one-third new oak.

**RED** Deeply colored and full-bodied wines, rich in fruit and supported by a firm tannic structure, although the style is becoming more supple, and can even be quite fat in ripe years like 1982.

🍇 Cabernet Sauvignon 45%, Merlot 45%, Cabernet Franc 10%

🍷 8–20 years

**Second wine:** *Les Cèdres d'Hosten*

## CHÂTEAU LES GRANDS CHÊNES
### AOC Médoc
### Cru Bourgeois Supérieur
### ★🅥

The quality here has been excellent since the mid-1990s, but has taken another step up since 1999, when the château was purchased by Bernard Magrez, one of the joint owners of Château Pape Clément. Magrez runs this property personally. The wine is matured in wood for 12 to 15 months, with one-third new oak (except for its 100 percent new oak "Prestige Cuvée").

**RED** Lush and charming, with opulent fruit and fine acidity balance.

🍇 Cabernet Sauvignon 65%, Merlot 30%, Cabernet Franc 5%

🍷 6–15 years

**Other wine:** 🗸 *Château Les Grands Chênes Prestige Cuvée*

## CHÂTEAU GRESSIER GRAND POUJEAUX
### AOC Moulis
### Cru Bourgeois Supérieur
### ★🅥

This château was classified *cru bourgeois* in 1932, but not in 1978. It has in recent years produced successful wines that compare well with good *crus classés*. This wine is matured in wood for 24 months, with one-third new oak.

**RED** Full-bodied wines with plenty of fruit and flavor. Well worth laying down.

🍇 Cabernet Sauvignon 50%,

Merlot 30%, Cabernet Franc 10%, Petit Verdot 10%

🍷 6–12 years

## CHÂTEAU GREYSAC
### AOC Médoc Cru Bourgeois Supérieur
### ★🅥

Since it was purchased by the late Baron de Gunzbourg in 1973, the facilities of this château have undergone extensive modernization. The quality of the wine is excellent and its future promising. This wine is matured in wood for 12 months, with 25 percent new oak.

**RED** Stylish, medium-bodied wines with silky-textured, ripe-fruit flavors.

🍇 Cabernet Sauvignon 45%, Merlot 45%, Cabernet Franc 5%, Petit Verdot 5%

🍷 6–10 years

## CHÂTEAU HANTEILLAN
### AOC Haut-Médoc
### Cru Bourgeois Supérieur
### ★🅥

Under the enthusiastic direction of Catherine Blasco, this large property produces a consistently fine wine, and her achievements have been consolidated by the new winemaking facilities. This wine is matured in wood for 12 months, with 30 percent new oak.

**RED** The wine has a fine color, spicy bouquet with underlying vanilla-oak tones, ripe fruit, and supple tannins.

🍇 Cabernet Sauvignon 50%, Merlot 41%, Cabernet Franc 5%, Petit Verdot 4%

🍷 6–12 years

**Second wine:** *Château Larrivaux Hanteillan*

## CHÂTEAU LACOMBE-NOILLAC
### AOC Haut-Médoc
### ★🅥

Jean-Michel Lapalu's property boasts some of the most northerly vines in the Médoc. The wine is matured in wood for 6 months, with 15 percent new oak.

**RED** Elegant, medium-bodied wines of surprising style and finesse for the location.

🍇 Cabernet Sauvignon 58%, Cabernet Franc 6%, Merlot 32%, Petit Verdot 4%

🍷 4–10 years

**Second wine:** *Château Les Traverses*

**Other wine:** *Château Les Traverses La Franque*

## CHÂTEAU LA LAGUNE
### AOC Haut-Médoc 3ème Cru Classé
### ★★🅥

Owned by the Ducellier family of Champagne Ayala, the immaculate vineyard of this fine château is the first *cru classé* encountered after leaving Bordeaux, and is situated on sand and gravel soil. The château itself was completely renovated in

2003. This wine is matured in wood for 16 to 18 months, with 100 percent new oak.

**RED** These wines are deep-colored with complex cassis and stone-fruit flavors intermingled with rich, creamy-vanilla oak nuances. They are full-bodied but supple.

🍇 Cabernet Sauvignon 60%, Merlot 20%, Cabernet Franc 10%, Petit Verdot 10%

🍷 5–30 years

**Second wine:** *Moulin de Lagune*

## CHÂTEAU DE LAMARQUE
### AOC Haut-Médoc
### Cru Bourgeois Supérieur
### ★🅥

This large and constantly improving property is owned and run by Pierre-Gilles and Marie-Hélène Gromand-Brunet d'Évry. The vineyard was systematically replanted in the 1960s and is currently at its optimum age for both quality and volume. While it will gradually decline in yield, the quality should continue to improve. The wine is matured in wood for 12 to 15 months, with one-third new oak.

**RED** This wine has the supple style of a modern Médoc, with plenty of real fruit flavor, and an enticingly perfumed bouquet.

🍇 Cabernet Sauvignon 46%, Merlot 25%, Cabernet Franc 24%, Petit Verdot 5%

🍷 5–12 years

**Second wine:** *D de Lamarque*

**Other wines:** *Réserve du Marquis d'Évry, Noblesse Oblige (saigné rosé)*

## CHÂTEAU LAMOTHE-CISSAC
### AOC Haut-Médoc
### Cru Bourgeois
### ★🅥

An up-and-coming wine from one of Bordeaux's oldest properties, Lamothe-Cissac is matured in wood for 12 to 14 months, with 20 percent new oak. It has recently started to outperform Cissac.

**RED** Classically proportioned, Cabernet-dominated wines of excellent potential longevity.

🍇 Cabernet Sauvignon 70%, Merlot 26%, Petit Verdot 4%

🍷 4–16 years

## CHÂTEAU LANESSAN
### AOC Haut-Médoc Cru Bourgeois Supérieur
### ★★🅥

Supposedly missed out from the 1855 classification because the owner forgot to submit samples, or could not be bothered, this château was later classified *cru bourgeois* in 1932, but not included in the Syndicat's 1978 list. The grapes are machine harvested, and the wines are matured in wood for 15 months, with no claim of any new oak.

**RED** Big, intensely flavored wines of deep, often opaque, color and a quality that closely approaches that of a *cru classé*, requiring a similar minimum aging before its fruit shows through.

🍇 Cabernet Sauvignon 75%, Merlot 20%, Cabernet Franc 1%, Petit Verdot 4%

🍷 7–20 years

**Second wine:** *Domaine de Ste-Gemme*

### CHÂTEAU LAROSE-TRINTAUDON
AOC Haut-Médoc Cru Bourgeois Supérieur
★☆Ⓥ

This is the largest estate in the Médoc and was under the same ownership as Château Camensac until 1986, during which time vast sums were spent on renovation. The standard of these wines, which are matured in wood for 12 months with 25 percent new oak, is as high as it has ever been.

**RED** Medium-bodied, and sometimes full-bodied, wines with an elegantly rich flavor of juicy summer fruits, vanilla, and truffles, backed up by supple tannins. Larose-Perganson is more of a *tête de cuvée* than a second wine. Representing just 15 percent of the total production, this wine is exclusively from the oldest vines and the grapes are all handpicked, in contrast to Larose-Trintaudon, which is machine-picked.

🍇 Cabernet Sauvignon 65%, Merlot 30%, Cabernet Franc 5%

🍷 6–15 years

**Second wine:** *Larose Saint-Laurent*
**Other wines:** ✓ *Château Larose-Perganson, Les Hauts de Trintaudon*

### CHÂTEAU LESTAGE-DARQUIER
AOC Moulis
★Ⓥ

This is the least encountered of the many Poujeaux châteaux (formerly sold as Château Lestage-Darquier-Grand-Poujeaux), but well worth digging out. This wine is matured in wood for 9 to 12 months, with 100 percent year-old oak.

**RED** Densely colored wines, rich in bouquet and fruit, with a powerful structure.

🍇 Cabernet Sauvignon 50%, Merlot 45%, Cabernet Franc 2%, Petit Verdot 2%

🍷 8–20 years

### CHÂTEAU LIVERSAN
AOC Haut-Médoc Cru Bourgeois Supérieur
★Ⓥ

The estate of Château Liversan was purchased in 1984 by Prince Guy de Polignac, when it was inexorably linked with Champagne Pommery, but was first leased and then sold to the owners of Patache d'Aux. The vineyard is on fine, sandy gravel over a limestone subsoil, just under 2 miles (3 kilometers) from Lafite

and Mouton-Rothschild. The wine is fermented in stainless steel and matured in wood for 12 months, with 25 percent new oak.

**RED** Rich and flavorful wines, of full body and some style. They are gaining in class with each vintage.

🍇 Cabernet Sauvignon 49%, Merlot 38%, Cabernet Franc 10%, Petit Verdot 3%

🍷 7–20 years

**Second wine:** *Les Charmes des Liversan*

### CHÂTEAU LOUDENNE
AOC Médoc Cru Bourgeois Supérieur
★Ⓥ

This pink-washed, Chartreuse-style château, with its lawns running down to the Gironde, once belonged to W. and A. Gilbey, who ran it in a style that harkened back to the last days of the British Empire. It was sold to Jean-Paul Lafgragette in 1999. The wine is matured in wood for 15 to 18 months, with 25 percent new oak. Loudenne also produces a dry white wine that is attractive when drunk one to two years after the harvest.

**RED** Full-bodied wines with a spicy-blackcurrant bouquet, sometimes silky and hinting of violets, with underlying vanilla oak, a big mouthful of rich and ripe fruit, excellent extract, and great length.

🍇 Cabernet Sauvignon 45%, Merlot 45%, Cabernet Franc 7%, Malbec 2%, Petit Verdot 1%

🍷 5–15 years

**Second wines:** *Château Lestagne, Pavillon de Loudenne*

### CHÂTEAU MALESCASSE
AOC Haut-Médoc Cru Bourgeois Supérieur
★Ⓥ

Entirely replanted between 1970 and 1992, Château Malescasse was purchased midway through this process by the owner of Pontet-Canet and Lafon-Rochet, only to be sold to Alcatel Alsthon once completed. The wine is matured in wood for 16 months, with 30 percent new oak.

**RED** Firm, dependable, good-value

claret, getting better with each vintage.

🍇 Cabernet Sauvignon 55%, Merlot 35%, Cabernet Franc 10%

🍷 4–8 years

**Second wine:** *Le Closerie de Malescasse*

### CHÂTEAU DE MALLERET
AOC Haut-Médoc Cru Bourgeois Supérieur

Château de Malleret is a vast estate, which incorporates a stud farm with two training racetracks and stables for both hunting and racing. The vineyard boasts 148 acres (60 hectares). This wine is matured in wood for 12 to 16 months, with up to 50 percent new oak.

**RED** Delightful wines of good bouquet, medium body, and juicy-rich fruit. Improving.

🍇 Cabernet Sauvignon 65%, Merlot 30%, Cabernet Franc 3%, Petit Verdot 2%

🍷 5–12 years

### CHÂTEAU MAUCAILLOU
AOC Moulis Cru Bourgeois Supérieur
★☆Ⓥ

Château Maucaillou is consistently one of the best-value wines produced in Bordeaux. This wine is matured in wood for 18 months, with up to 80 percent new oak.

**RED** Deep-colored, full-bodied wine with masses of velvety-textured fruit, beautiful cassis and vanilla flavors, and supple tannins.

🍇 Cabernet Sauvignon 55%, Merlot 36%, Cabernet Franc 2%, Petit Verdot 7%

🍷 6–15 years

**Second wine:** *Château Cap de Haut-Maucaillou*
**Other wine:** *Château Duplessis-Fabre*

### CHÂTEAU MAUCAMPS
AOC Haut-Médoc Cru Bourgeois Supérieur
★Ⓥ

Situated between Macau itself and the *cru classé* Cantemerle to the south, this château makes superb use of its 37 acres (15 hectares) of fine, gravelly vineyards. This wine is matured in wood for 16 months, with up to 40 percent new oak.

**RED** Always a deep-colored, full-bodied wine with plenty of fruit flavor supported by supple tannins.

🍇 Cabernet Sauvignon 50%, Merlot 40%, Petit Verdot 10%

🍷 5–12 years

**Second wine:** *Clos de May*

### CHÂTEAU LE MEYNIEU AOC
Haut-Médoc Cru Bourgeois
★Ⓥ

This property is under the same ownership as Château Lavillotte, which is situated in St.-Estèphe. The

deep-colored wine is not filtered before it is bottled.

**RED** This is a deep, dark, brooding wine of dense bouquet and solid fruit which promises much for the future.

🍇 Cabernet Sauvignon 62%, Merlot 30%, Cabernet Franc 8%

🍷 7–15 years

### CHÂTEAU MOULIN-À-VENT
AOC Moulis Cru Bourgeois Supérieur

One-third of the property of Château Moulin-à-Vent overlaps the commune of Listrac, but its appellation is still Moulis. This wine is matured in wood for 20 months, with 25 percent new oak.

**RED** Medium-bodied wines with an elegant bouquet and a full flavor.

🍇 Cabernet Sauvignon 60%, Merlot 35%, Petit Verdot 5%

🍷 7–15 years

**Second wine:** *Moulin-de-St.-Vincent*

### CHÂTEAU NOAILLAC
AOC Médoc Cru Bourgeois
★Ⓥ

Under the same ownership as Château La Tour de By. The wine is matured in wood for up to 12 months, with 15 percent new oak.

**RED** Deliciously fruity style, underpinned by a discreet use of oak.

🍇 Cabernet Sauvignon 55%, Merlot 40%, Petit Verdot 5%

🍷 3-8 years

**Second wines:** *Moulin de Noaillac, La Rose Noaillac, Les Palombes de Noaillac*

### CHÂTEAU LES ORMES-SORBET
AOC Médoc Cru Bourgeois Supérieur
★Ⓥ

Owned by the Boivert family since 1764. The wine today is matured in wood for 18 to 20 months, with one-third new oak.

**RED** Once reputed for its characterful wines of substantial body, dense fruit, and positive flavor, this château has made an increasingly opulent style, with fine aromatics, since the early 1990s, fully justifying its 2003 *cru bourgeois supérieur* classification.

🍇 Cabernet Sauvignon 65%, Merlot 30%, Petit Verdot 2%, Carmenère 1%

🍷 4–15 years

**Second wine:** *Château de Conques*

### CHÂTEAU PALOUMEY
AOC Haut-Médoc Cru Bourgeois Supérieur
★Ⓥ

An old property that enjoyed fame in the 19th century, but was left rundown and forgotten until the current owner, Martine Cazeneuve, replanted it in 1990. The wine is matured in wood for 12 to 15 months, with one-third new oak.

**RED** Deliciously rich and ripe, fruit-driven style that is underpinned by a nicely restrained use of oak, with exceptional finesse for such young vines. Can only get better!

Cabernet Sauvignon 55%, Merlot 40%, Cabernet Franc 5%

4–8 years

**Second wines:** *Les Ailes de Paloumey, Château Haut-Carmaillet*

### CHÂTEAU PATACHE-D'AUX
#### AOC Médoc
#### Cru Bourgeois Supérieur
★ ✪

This old property once belonged to the Aux family, descendants of the counts of Armagnac, but was purchased by a syndicate headed by Claude Lapalu in 1964. Although Patache-d'Aux is always reliable, it has performed particularly well since its stunning 1990 vintage. The wine is matured in wood for 12 months, with 25 percent new oak.

**RED** Stylish, highly perfumed, medium-bodied wine with very accessible fruit.

Cabernet Sauvignon 70%, Merlot 20%, Cabernet Franc 7%, Petit Verdot 3%

4–8 years

**Second wine:** *Le Relais de Patache-d'Aux*

**Other wines:** *Les Chevaux de Patache-d'Aux*

### CHÂTEAU PEYRABON
#### AOC Haut-Médoc Cru Bourgeois
★ ✪

Virtually unknown until 1998, when it was purchased by Millesima (formerly Les Vins des Grands Vignobles), Château Peyrabon is matured in wood for 18 months, with one-third new oak.

**RED** Sturdy style, but not lacking in fruit, and usually very good value.

Cabernet Sauvignon 57%, Merlot 37%, Cabernet Franc 5%, Petit Verdot 1%

5–10 years

**Second wines:** *Lapiey, Château Le Fleur Peyrabon*

**Other wines:** *Château Pierbone, Domaine du Roman*

### CHÂTEAU PLAGNAC
#### AOC Médoc

Owned by Domaines Cordier since 1972, this property has produced consistently good-value red Bordeaux since the end of that decade. The wine is matured in wood for 12 months.

**RED** Full-bodied and full-flavored, with some breed; lots of up-front Merlot fruit, and a smooth finish.

Cabernet Sauvignon 65%, Merlot 35%,

4–10 years

**Second wine:** *Château Haut de Plagnac*

### CHÂTEAU PONTEY
#### AOC Médoc Cru Bourgeois
★ ✬ ✪

Owned by the Bordeaux *négociant* Quancard family, this château occupies an excellent location on a gravel plateau. The wines are matured in wood for 12 months, with one-third new oak.

**RED** These wines have always been cleverly constructed and brimming with lush, oaky fruit, but they are even more lush than before.

Cabernet Sauvignon 45%, Merlot 55%

3–12 years

**Second wine:** *Château Vieux Prezat*

**Other wine:** *Château Pontey Caussan*

### CHÂTEAU POTENSAC
#### AOC Médoc
#### Cru Bourgeois Exceptionnel
★ ✬ ✪

This property is under the same ownership as Château Léoville-Las-Cases in St.-Julien, and its wines often aspire to *cru classé* quality, fully justifying the *cru bourgeois exceptionnel* classification in 2003. The wine is fermented in stainless steel, then matured in wood for 18 months, with 20 percent new oak.

**RED** Classy, full-bodied wines of a lovely, brick-red color, with lots of fruit and underlying chocolate and spice flavors.

Cabernet Sauvignon 60%, Merlot 25%, Cabernet Franc 15%

6–15 years

**Second wine:** *Château Lassalle*

**Other wines:** *Château Gallais-Bellevue, Goudy la Cardonne*

### CHÂTEAUX POUJEAUX
#### AOC Moulis
#### Cru Bourgeois Exceptionnel
★★ ✪

After Chasse-Spleen, this château produces the best wine in Moulis and is easily the equivalent of a good *cru classé*. Hence, it was no surprise that it was classified as one of only nine *crus bourgeois exceptionnels* in 2003.

**RED** Full-bodied and deep-colored wine with a very expansive bouquet and creamy-rich, spicy fruit.

Cabernet Sauvignon 50%, Merlot 40%, Cabernet Franc 5%, Petit Verdot 2%

10–25 years

**Second wine:** Château La Salle-de-Poujeaux

### CHÂTEAU PREUILLAC
#### AOC Médoc
★ ✪

Purchased in 1998 by Yvon Mau, who has sold his eponymously named *négociant* business to Freixenet in a bid to build up a portfolio of estate properties. Mau devoted a lot of money and attention to renovating this

property, reducing yields, and updating the vinification facilities, which is why he was so upset not to have been included in the 2003 *cru bourgeois* classification (see p72), although there is no doubt that it will succeed at the next reclassification in 2015. Certainly, if the current rate of improvement can be maintained, this château will do very well. The grapes are all handpicked, then sorted on tables, while the wines are fermented in stainless steel (2001 being the first such vintage), then matured in wood for 18 months, with 20 percent new oak.

**RED** The creamy cassis and chocolaty fruit in these wines is a testament to Mau's efforts. Preuillac used to be rather rustic, but now shows more finesse with each and every vintage, particularly from 2003.

Cabernet Sauvignon 54%, Merlot 44%, Cabernet Franc 2%

4–12 years

### CHÂTEAU RAMAGE-LA-BATISSE
#### AOC Haut-Médoc
#### Cru Bourgeois Supérieur
★ ✪

This property has excelled itself since the late 1980s, making wines of remarkable quality–price ratio which are matured in wood for 14 months, with 50 percent new oak.

**RED** Rich, well-flavored, oaky wines that are immediately attractive in light years and ridiculously inexpensive *vins de garde* in the best vintages. Not unlike a poor man's Lynch-Bages (which, in turn, I have called a poor man's Latour!).

Cabernet Sauvignon 70%, Merlot 23%, Cabernet Franc 5%, Petit Verdot 2%

7–15 years

**Second wine:** *Le Terrey*

**Other wine:** *Château Dutellier*

### CHÂTEAU ROLLAN DE BY
#### AOC Médoc
#### Cru Bourgeois Supérieur
★★

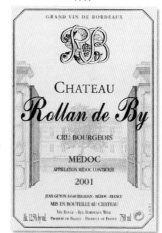

A new cult wine on the Bordeaux scene, it is matured in wood for 18 months, with 60 percent new oak. The wine has a string of blind

tasting victories. The Château Haut-Condessas is a super-selection, with 100 percent new oak.

**RED** Lots of up-front fruit, but long and classy, with plenty of finesse. Not big and, surprisingly, not overoaked.

Cabernet Sauvignon 20%, Merlot 70%, Petit Verdot 10%

4–12 years

**Other wine:** *Château Fleur de By*

### CHÂTEAU ST-BONNET
#### AOC Médoc
★

Some 130 of this important estate's 210 acres are planted with vines (53 of 85 hectares). The wine is matured in wood for 18 months, with 25 percent new oak.

**RED** Full-flavored wines of promising quality and immediate aromatic appeal.

Merlot 50%, Cabernet Sauvignon 28%, Cabernet Franc 22%

5–10 years

### CHÂTEAU ST-PAUL
#### AOC Haut-Médoc
#### Cru Bourgeois
★ ✪

Up-and-coming vineyard pieced together from parcels previously owned by two St.-Estèphe châteaus. This wine is matured in wood for 18 months, with 25 percent new oak.

**RED** Plump, fruit-driven reds of good class and finesse, with a long finish.

Cabernet Sauvignon 60%, Merlot 35%, Cabernet Franc 5%

4–12 years

### CHÂTEAU SÉNÉJAC
#### AOC Médoc
#### Cru Bourgeois Supérieur
★ ✪

This property changed hands in 1999. The wine is matured in wood for 18 months, with 25 percent new oak (up to 100 percent for its prestige *cuvée* Karolus).

**RED** A firm, full-flavored wine of excellent longevity, Sénéjac is not, however, for the faint-hearted, especially in its rather stern youthful years. The Karolus is bigger, richer, and more concentrated.

Cabernet Sauvignon 60%, Merlot 25%, Cabernet Franc 14%, Petit Verdot 1%

5–15 years

**Second wine:** *Artique de Sénac*

**Other wine:** ✔ *Karolus*

### CHÂTEAU SIGOGNAC
#### AOC Médoc
✪

Owned by Colette Bonny, this wine is matured in wood for 12 months, with 20 percent new oak.

**RED** Consistently good-value, lunchtime claret of some elegance.

🍇 Merlot 50%, Cabernet Sauvignon 28%, Cabernet Franc 22%

🍷 3–8 years

**Second wine:** *Château La Croix du Chevalier*

## CHÂTEAU SOCIANDO-MALLET
### AOC Haut-Médoc
### ★★ⓥ

This property has been making a name for itself since 1970, when Jean Gautreau raised standards to near *cru classé* quality. The quality of Sociando-Mallet has continued to increase throughout the 1990s, when between 80 and 100 percent new oak became the norm. Its owners did not bother to submit wines for the 2003 reclassification, since it already achieves a higher price than a number of *cru classé* wines, but it is undoubtedly at least *cru bourgeois exceptionnel* in quality, if not in name.

**RED** These are powerfully built wines that are rich in color and extract. Often totally dominated by vanilla oak in their youth, they are backed up with plenty of concentrated cassis fruit.

🍇 Cabernet Sauvignon 55%, Merlot 42%, Cabernet Franc 2%, Petit Verdot 1%

🍷 10–25 years

**Second wine:** *La Demoiselle de Sociando-Mallet*

## CHÂTEAU SOUDARS
### AOC Médoc
### Cru Bourgeois Supérieur
### ★ⓥ

Soudars was formed by the combination of several parcels of rock-strewn land that had become overgrown with brambles until Eric Miailhe took over the property in 1973 and spent several years clearing it. The wine is fermented in stainless steel, and matured in wood for 12 to 14 months, with up to 40 percent new oak.

**RED** Excellent, well-colored wines of good structure and accessible fruit.

🍇 Cabernet Sauvignon 49%, Merlot 50%, Cabernet Franc 1%

🍷 5–10 years

**Second wine:** *Château Marquis de Cadourne*

## CHÂTEAU LE TEMPLE
### AOC Médoc Cru Bourgeois
### ★★ⓥ

Starting to live up to its reputation in the early 1900s, when it was known as "Lafite of the Bas-Médoc," this wine is matured in wood for 12 months, with 22 percent new oak.

**RED** Increasingly lush and fruit-dominant, without losing its classic, tannin structure.

🍇 Cabernet Sauvignon 60%, Merlot 35%, Petit Verdot 5%

🍷 7–15 years

**Second wine:** *Château Bairac*
**Other wine:** *Château La Croix des Sablons*

## CHÂTEAU LA TOUR DE BY
### AOC Médoc Cru Bourgeois Supérieur
### ★ⓥ

The tower of Tour de By was once a lighthouse. The wine is of very good quality; it is matured in wood for 16 months, with up to 30 percent new oak.

**RED** These deeply colored, full-bodied, richly flavored wines have good spicy fruit, backed up by a firm tannic structure.

🍇 Cabernet Sauvignon 60%, Merlot 36%, Cabernet Franc 4%

🍷 6–12 years

**Second wine:** *Château La Roque-de-By*
**Other wines:** *Château Moulin de Roque, Château Moulin de la Roque*

## CHÂTEAU LA TOUR-CARNET
### AOC Haut-Médoc
### 4ème Cru Classé
### ★

This charming, 13th-century miniature moated castle has a well-kept vineyard. Its wines used to be lackluster, but have been transformed by the new owner, Bernard Magez of Pape-Clément, who purchased the property in 1999. The wine is now matured in wood for 12 to 18 months, with 60 percent new oak.

**RED** Much riper, more opulent fruit, with some lush new oak in a supporting role, this wine has the richness of flavor it used to lack, with improvements noticeable from one year to the next.

🍇 Cabernet Sauvignon 53%, Merlot 33%, Cabernet Franc 10%, Petit Verdot 4%

🍷 5–15 years

**Second wine:** *Douves de Carnet*

## CHÂTEAU TOUR HAUT-CAUSSAN
### AOC Médoc
### Cru Bourgeois Supérieur
### ★★

An up-and-coming property owned by Philippe Courrian, who also makes wine in Corbières. The grapes are all hand-harvested, and the wine is matured in wood for 12 months, with one-third new oak.

**RED** Rich, well-colored wines with a great concentration of fruit and nicely integrated, creamy oak.

🍇 Cabernet Sauvignon 50%, Merlot 50%

🍷 4–10 years

**Second wine:** *Château Landotte*

## CHÂTEAU TOUR SAINT-BONNET
### AOC Médoc
### ★ⓥ

Situated on fine, gravely ridges, this property was known as Château la Tour Saint-Bonnet-Cazenave in the 19th century. This wine is matured in wood for 18 months, with 50 percent new oak.

**RED** Firm, full-flavored, well-colored wines of consistent quality.

🍇 Cabernet Sauvignon 45%, Merlot 45%, Malbec 5%, Petit Verdot 5%

🍷 7–15 years

**Second wine:** *Château La Fuie-Saint-Bonnet*

## CHÂTEAU VERDIGNAN
### AOC Haut-Médoc
### Cru Bourgeois Supérieur
### ★ⓥ

Since 1972, the property of the Miailhe family, who continue to improve the quality. The wine is fermented in stainless steel and matured in wood for 12 to 14 months, with 30 percent new oak.

**RED** Medium-bodied, fruity wines, made in a soft and silky style.

🍇 Cabernet Sauvignon 50%, Merlot 45%, Cabernet Franc 5%

🍷 5–10 years

**Second wine:** *Château Plantey-de-la-Croix*

## CHÂTEAU VILLEGORGE
### AOC Haut-Médoc
### Cru Bourgeois Supérieur
### ★ⓥ

This château was classified *cru bourgeois* in 1932. It was purchased by Lucien Lurton in 1973, but he then resigned from the Syndicat and, therefore, the château was not included in its 1978 list, although it is superior to a few that were. He was succeeded by his daughter, Marie-Louise, the present incumbent, who has continued improving the quality, achieving *supérieur* status in the 2003 reclassification. The wine is matured in wood for 10 to 24 months, with up to 30 percent new oak.

**RED** Full-bodied wines, with a lovely color, increasingly lush and opulent fruit, understated, creamy oak, and an increasing spicy finesse.

🍇 Cabernet Sauvignon 40%, Merlot 60%

🍷 6–12 years

**Second wine:** *Reflet de Villegeorge*

**VINEYARDS THRIVING IN THE MEDOC**
*In Ancient Roman times this area was considered too marshy for cultivation, yet today it is one of the most prized areas under vine in the world, envied by winemakers worldwide.*

# SAINT-ESTÈPHE

*Although St.-Estèphe can be considered the least sexy of the Médoc's famous four appellations, it has an abundance of high-quality bourgeois growths, which make it indubitably the "bargain basement" of Bordeaux wines.*

WITH ONLY FIVE *CRUS CLASSÉS* covering a mere 6 percent of the commune, St.-Estèphe is a rich source of undervalued clarets, where the prices paid by wine drinkers are unlikely to be outbid by wine investors. Enthusiasts rather than speculators will benefit from the fact that no fewer than 4 of the Médoc's 9 *crus bourgeois exceptionnels* are to be found in this commune.

## CHÂTEAU COS D'ESTOURNEL

St.-Estèphe might lack *crus classés*, but it is not lacking in class. If it had only one *cru classé*—the stunning, stylish Château Cos d'Estournel—St.-Estèphe would still be famous. The reputation of this château soared after Bruno Prats took over control in 1971. Essentially, this success can be put down to his maximizing the true potential of Cos d'Estournel's exceptional *terroir*, a superb, south-facing ridge of gravel with perfect

HARVEST, CHÂTEAU
COS D'ESTOURNEL
*The bizarre eastern façade of this specially built winery overlooks the vineyards. The château was owned by perfectionist Bruno Prats before it was sold to the Bernard Taillan group in October 1998.*

## FACTORS AFFECTING TASTE AND QUALITY

### LOCATION
St.-Estèphe is the most northerly of the four classic communes of the Médoc. It is situated 11 miles (18 kilometers) south of Lesparre, bordering the Gironde.

### CLIMATE
As for the Médoc (*see* p.00).

### ASPECT
St.-Estèphe has well-drained, well-sited, softly sloping vineyards. The southeast-facing crest of gravel overlooks Château Lafite-Rothschild in Pauillac and is relatively steep for the Médoc.

### SOIL
The topsoil is gravelly and more fertile than in communes farther south, with clay subsoil exposed in parts, consisting of clay beds, stony-clay, and limestone over iron-pan.

### VITICULTURE AND VINIFICATION
Only the red wines have the right to the appellation in this commune. With increasing emphasis placed on the Merlot grape, which can now account for up to 50 percent of the vines cultivated in some châteaux, reduced use of *vin de presse*, and improved vinification techniques, these wines are becoming far more accessible in less sunny years. During the vinification, all grapes must be destalked, and duration of skin contact averages three weeks. Maturation in cask currently varies between 15 and 24 months.

### GRAPE VARIETIES
**Primary varieties:** Cabernet Sauvignon, Cabernet Franc, Merlot
**Secondary varieties:** Carmenère, Malbec, Petit Verdot

drainage. Those vineyards on heavier soil with less gravel and more clay tend to produce more rustic wines.

## MODERN ST.-ESTÈPHE

Most wines from St.-Estèphe have always been well structured, with natural longevity, but they now have more lushness of fruit, which allows the wines to be accessible when relatively young. It was once essential to buy only the greatest vintages and wait 20 years or more before drinking them. The increasing use of the Merlot grape as well as Cabernet Sauvignon and Cabernet Franc, and a tendency to favor vinification techniques that extract color and fruit in preference to the harsher tannins, provide richer, fruitier, and eminently drinkable wines in most vintages.

ST.-ESTÈPHE, *see also* p63
*Of the Haut-Médoc's four best-known communes, St.-Estèphe is the most northerly, although the actual AOC area covers only part of the commune.*

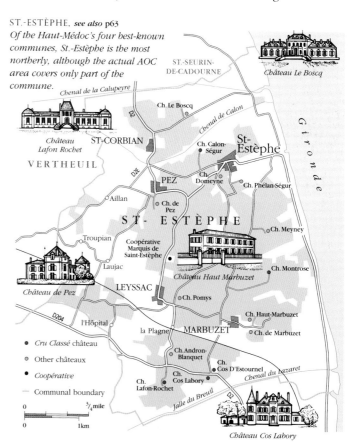

*Château Cos Labory*

## ST.-ESTÈPHE PROFILE

**Appellation area**
Covers parts of the commune of St.-Estèphe only

**Size of commune**
9,284 acres (3,757 ha)

**AOC area under vine**
3,099 acres (1,254 ha), 33% of commune

**Surface area of *crus classés***
558 acres (226 ha ), 6% of commune, 16% of AOC

**Special comments**
Approximately 12.5 acres (5 ha) of vineyards within St.-Estèphe are classified as AOC Pauillac

## ST.-ESTÈPHE CRU CLASSÉ STATISTICS

***Crus classés* in AOC St.-Estèphe**
5 châteaux (by number: 8% of *crus classés* in the Médoc) with 558 acres (226 ha) of vineyards (by area: 8% of *crus classés* in the Médoc and 18% of this AOC)

**1er *crus classés***
None

**2ème *crus classés***
2 châteaux (by number: 14% of 2ème *crus classés* in the Médoc) with 299 acres (121 ha) of vineyards (by area: 15% of 2ème *crus classés* in the Médoc)

**3ème *crus classés***
1 château (by number: 7% of 3ème

*crus classés* in the Médoc) with 119 acres (48 ha) of vineyards (by area: 11% of 3ème *crus classés* in the Médoc)

**4ème *crus classés***
1 château (by number: 10% of 4ème *crus classés* in the Médoc) with 111 acres (45 ha) of vineyards (by area: 10% of 4ème *crus classés* in the Médoc)

**5ème *crus classés***
1 château (by number: 6% of 5ème *crus classés* in the Médoc) with 30 acres (12 ha) of vineyards (by area: 2% of 5ème *crus classés* in the Médoc)

# THE WINE PRODUCERS OF
# SAINT-ESTÈPHE

### CHÂTEAU ANDRON-BLANQUET
**Cru Bourgeois**
★✩Ⓥ

Under the same ownership as Château Cos Labory, the vineyards of this property are situated above the gravel crest of *cru classé* châteaux that overlook Château Lafite-Rothschild in Pauillac. This wine is matured in wood for 12 months, with 25 percent new oak.

**RED** An exceptionally well-made wine that consistently rises above its *petit château* status. Fermented and matured in cask, it has good fruit and a distinctive style.

🍇 Cabernet Sauvignon 40%, Merlot 35%, Cabernet Franc 25%

🍷 4–10 years

**Second wine:** *Château St.-Roch*
**Other wine:** *Château Blanquet*

### CHÂTEAU BEAU-SITE
**Cru Bourgeois Supérieur**
★✩Ⓥ

This property should not be confused with Château Beau-Site Haut-Vignoble, a lesser St.-Estèphe. This wine is matured in wood for 16 to 18 months, with 50 percent new oak.

**RED** A stylish, medium-bodied, sometimes full-bodied, wine that often has an elegant finish reminiscent of violets.

🍇 Cabernet Sauvignon 70%, Merlot 30%

🍷 3–10 years

### CHÂTEAU LE BOSCQ
**Cru Bourgeois Supérieur**
★✩Ⓥ

This property has always produced good wine, but quality increased dramatically in the 1980s. It was taken over by Dourthe-Kressman in 1995.

**RED** Superbly aromatic, almost exotic, full-bodied wine that is elegant and rich with the flavor of summer fruits, and is nicely backed up with new oak.

🍇 Cabernet Sauvignon 42%, Merlot 51%, Petit Verdot 7%

🍷 5–12 years

**Second wine:** *Héritage de Le Boscq*

### CHÂTEAU CALON-SÉGUR
**3ème Cru Classé**
★✩Ⓥ

From the Gallo-Roman origins of this château grew the community of St.-Estèphe. The first wine estate in the commune, it used to boast "*Premier Cru de St.-Estèphe*" on its label until other producers objected. This wine is matured in wood for 18 months, with 50 percent new oak.

**RED** Full, fruity, well-structured wine that has a creamy, rich flavor. It is of consistently good quality and improves well in bottle.

🍇 Cabernet Sauvignon 50%, Merlot 35%, Cabernet Franc 10%, Petit Verdot 5%

🍷 3–20 years

**Second wine:** *Marquis de Ségur*

### CHÂTEAU CAPBERN GASQUETON
**Cru Bourgeois**
★✩Ⓥ

This property is under the same ownership as Château Calon-Ségur. The vineyards are found north and south of the village of St.-Estèphe. This wine is matured in wood for 18 months, with 30 percent new oak.

**RED** Medium-weight, ripe, and fruity wine of consistent quality; it is mellowed by 24 months in wood.

🍇 Cabernet Sauvignon 50%, Merlot 35%, Cabernet Franc 15%

🍷 4–12 years

### CHÂTEAU CHAMBERT-MARBUZET
**Cru Bourgeois Supérieur**
★✩Ⓥ

Technically faultless, hand-harvested wine produced in limited quantities from the sister château of Haut-Marbuzet. Many would rate it easily equivalent to a *cru classé*. This wine is matured in wood for 18 months, with 50 per cent new oak.

**RED** Aromatically attractive, medium-bodied, sometimes full-bodied, wine. It is rich, ripe, and fruity, with plenty of caramel-oak and sufficient tannin to age well.

🍇 Cabernet Sauvignon 70%, Merlot 30%

🍷 3–10 years

**Second wine:** *Château Grand-Village Capbern*

### CHÂTEAU COS D'ESTOURNEL
**2ème Cru Classé**
★★★Ⓥ

This was one of the very first super-seconds to emerge and this was the achievement of one man, Bruno Prats, although he would claim it to be teamwork. In 1998 Prats was forced by French tax laws to sell out to Groupe Taillan, who in 2001 sold it on to Michel Reybier, a Geneva-based food manufacturer. Cos d'Estournel has no château as such, merely a bizarre façade to the winery with huge, elaborately carved oak doors that once adorned the palace of the Sultan of Zanzibar. Bruno Prats' son Jean-Guillaume manages the property for Reybier, and the wine is made in the same careful way that his father introduced. This involves some of the wine being fermented in stainless steel, but all of it is matured in cask for 18 to 24 months, with 100 percent new oak for big years, and up to 70 percent for lighter vintages.

**RED** A rich, flavorsome, and attractive wine of full body, great class, and distinction; without doubt the finest wine in St.-Estèphe. It is uniquely generous for the appellation and capable of amazing longevity, even in the poorest years. This is a complex wine with silky fruit and great finesse.

🍇 Cabernet Sauvignon 60%, Merlot 40%

🍷 8–20 years

**Second wine:** *Les Pagodes de Cos*

### CHÂTEAU COS LABORY
**5ème Cru Classé**
★

Until the late 19th century, this property formed part of Château Cos d'Estournel. During the 1920s, it was purchased by distant cousins of Madame Audoy, the current owner. The wine is matured in wood for 15 to 18 months, with one-third new oak.

**RED** These wines used to be merely light and elegant with a certain degree of finesse, even when at their best. However, recent vintages have displayed a very welcome change to a distinctly fuller, fruitier, and fatter style.

🍇 Cabernet Sauvignon 55%, Merlot 35%, Cabernet Franc 5%, Petit Verdot 5%

🍷 5–15 years

**Second wine:** *Château Charme Labory*

### CHÂTEAU LE CROCK
**Cru Bourgeois Supérieur**
★✩Ⓥ

This property is under the same ownership as Château Léoville-Poyferré of St-Julien, and was promoted to *supérieur* status in the 2003 reclassification. This hand-harvested wine is matured in wood for 18 months, with 20 percent new oak.

**RED** These dark-colored, substantial wines have surged in quality since 1995 under the personal guidance of Michel Rolland.

🍇 Cabernet Sauvignon 58%, Merlot 24%, Cabernet Franc 12%, Petit Verdot 6%

🍷 6–15 years

**Second wine:** *Château Croix Saint-Estèphe*
**Other wine:** *Château Fatin*

### CHÂTEAU DOMEYNE
**Cru Bourgeois**
★Ⓥ

This property was not classified *cru bourgeois* in 1932, nor was it listed by the Syndicat in 1978, but it certainly should have been. This wine is matured in wood for 18 months, with 40 percent new oak.

**RED** These are typically deep-colored, rich-flavored wines that have an excellent marriage of fruit and oak. They are smooth and well-rounded wines that can be drunk while fairly young.

🍇 Cabernet Sauvignon 60%, Merlot 35%, Cabernet Franc 5%

🍷 3–8 years

### CHÂTEAU FAGET
★✩Ⓥ

Château Faget was classified *cru bourgeois* in 1932, but was not included in the Syndicat's 1978 list. However, this *coopérative*-produced wine is now superior to some that were included. This hand-harvested wine is matured in wood for 12 months, with one-third new oak.

**RED** This is a well-made wine that gives a solid mouthful of flavor, and ages well.

🍇 Cabernet Sauvignon 60%, Merlot 30%, Cabernet Franc 10%

🍷 6–10 years

### CHÂTEAU HAUT-MARBUZET
**Cru Bourgeois Exceptionnel**
★★✩Ⓥ

This is one of several properties belonging to Henri Duboscq. These wines receive 18 months in 100 percent new oak, which is extremely rare even for *cru classé* châteaux.

**RED** These full-bodied, deep-colored wines are packed with juicy fruit, backed up by supple tannin. They are marked by a generous buttered-toast and creamy-vanilla character.

🍇 Merlot 50%, Cabernet Sauvignon 40%, Cabernet Franc 10%

🍷 4–12 years

**Second wine:** *Tour de Marbuzet*

### CHÂTEAU LA HAYE
**Cru Bourgeois Supérieur**
★Ⓥ

New equipment, 25 percent new oak casks every year, and a fair proportion of old vines combine to produce some exciting vintages at this property.

**RED** Always limpid, this medium-bodied, sometimes full-bodied, wine is rich in color and flavour, well balanced, and lengthy, with vanilla-oak evident on the finish.

Cabernet Sauvignon 50%, Merlot 42%, Petit Verdot 8%

5–8 years

**Second wine:** *Fief de la Haye*

## CHÂTEAU LAFON-ROCHET
### 4ème Cru Classé
★ ✔

When Guy Tesseron purchased this vineyard, which is situated on the borders of Pauillac, in 1959, he embarked on a project to increase the proportion of Cabernet Sauvignon grapes used in the wine. However, this proved to be a mistake for Lafon-Rochet's *terroir* and has been rectified in recent years. The wine produced here is matured in wood for 18 months, with up to 50 percent new oak.

**RED** More fruit and finesse from the mid-1990s onward.

Cabernet Sauvignon 55%, Merlot 40%, Cabernet Franc 5%

5–12 years

**Second wine:** ✔ *Numero 2*

## CHÂTEAU LAVILLOTTE
★ ★ ✔

This star-performing *petit château* gives good value. This wine is matured in wood for 16 months, with up to 40 percent new oak.

**RED** These are dark-colored wines with a deep and distinctive bouquet. Smoky, full-bodied, intense, and complex.

Cabernet Sauvignon 72%, Merlot 25%, Petit Verdot 3%

5–12 years

**Second wine:** *Château Aillan*

## CHÂTEAU DE MARBUZET
### Cru Bourgeois
★

Under the same ownership as Cos d'Estournel, Marbuzet used to include the wines rejected from the *grand vin* of that "super-second." However, all the wine from this château has been produced exclusively from its own 42-acre (17-hectare) vineyard since 1994. The wine is matured in wood for 12 to 14 months in used barrels.

**RED** These elegant, medium-bodied, and sometimes full-bodied, wines are well balanced and have good fruit and a supple finish.

Cabernet Sauvignon 40%, Merlot 60%

4–10 years

**Second wine:** *Château Charme Labory*

## LE MARQUIS DE SAINT-ESTÈPHE
★ ✔

This wine is produced by the conscientious Cave Coopérative Marquis de Saint-Estèphe, who mature it in wood for 12 months, with a whopping 70 percent new oak.

**RED** A consistently well-made,

good-value, usually medium-bodied (although sometimes full-bodied) wine, with increasingly more noticeable oak.

Cabernet Sauvignon 65%, Merlot 25%, Cabernet Franc 3%, Malbec 3%, Petit Verdot 4%

3–6 years

## CHÂTEAU MEYNEY
### Cru Bourgeois Supérieur
★ ✔

This château is consistent in managing to produce fine wines in virtually every vintage.

**RED** These wines used to be big, beefy, chunky, and chewy, and required at least 10 years in bottle. They have changed, and for the better, acquiring a silky-textured finesse and aging gracefully without so many years in bottle.

Cabernet Sauvignon 67%, Merlot 25%, Cabernet Franc 5%, Petit Verdot 3%

5–25 years

**Second wine:** *Prieuré de Meyney*

## CHÂTEAU MONTROSE
### 2ème Cru Classé
★ ★ ✔

This "youngest" of the *cru classé* vineyards, this property grew out of an inconsequential plot of vines retained by a Mr. Dumoulin, the former owner of Calon-Ségur, when he sold that château in 1824. These vines were on a 12–15 acre (5–6 hectare) plot of land called Escargeon, which for some reason he changed to Montrose the very next year. There are rumors about the origin of this new name, but no one really knows the true story. What we do know, however, is that by 1855, Montrose had grown to 237 acres (96 hectares), as Dumoulin bought and exchanged parcels of land from and with his neighbors. Despite the newfound importance of Montrose, Calon-Ségur was still considered by locals to be its superior, thus there was much surprise when Montrose was classified as a *deuxième cru classé*, above *troisième cru* Calon-Ségur. The wines are matured in wood for 19 months, with 50 percent new oak.

**RED** The inhibiting factor at Montrose had always been its "stemmy" tannins. A vintage of exceptional richness and fatness was required to overcome the aggressive character produced by these tannins. The excellent 1994 gave me hope that this château has started to harvest the grapes when they are tannin-ripe (*see* p66) and was applying more specific maceration techniques. Happily, my hopes were not dashed, and Montrose's performance since the mid-1990s has clearly demonstrated that this wine is a true *deuxième cru classé*.

Cabernet Sauvignon 65%, Merlot 25%,

Cabernet Franc 10%

8–25 years

**Second wine:** ✔ *La Dame de Montrose*

## CHÂTEAU LES ORMES DE PEZ
### Cru Bourgeois Exceptionnel
★ ★ ✔

Owner Jean-Michel Cazes of Château Lynch-Bages in Pauillac installed new stainless-steel vats in 1981 and has raised the quality of these wines from good to sensational. Matured in wood for at least 12 to 15 months, with 50 percent new oak, this relatively cheap wine is easily equivalent to a good *cru classé*.

**RED** Dark and fruity, yet capable of aging with a herbal complexity.

Cabernet Sauvignon 65%, Merlot 25%, Cabernet Franc 10%

3–15 years

## CHÂTEAU DE PEZ
### Cru Bourgeois Exceptionnel
★ ★ ✔

This property was purchased by Louis Roederer of Champagne in 1995. The wines are fermented in wooden vats, then matured in small casks for 18 months, with 40 percent new oak. These wines are easily the equivalent of *cru classé* quality.

**RED** Consistently one of the best *bourgeois* growths in the entire Médoc. A medium-bodied wine, it has a rich fruit flavor and good tannic structure, and can mature into a sublime, cedary wine.

Cabernet Sauvignon 45%, Merlot 44%, Cabernet Franc 8%, Petit Verdot 3%

6–20 years

## CHÂTEAU PHÉLAN-SÉGUR
### Cru Bourgeois Exceptionnel
★ ★ ✔

This château was purchased in 1984 by its present owners, the Gardinier family, one year after selling Champagnes Pommery and Lanson. In retrospect, it is quite clear to see that there have been two steps up in quality; the first in 1988 and the second in 1999, with obvious consolidation achieved during the

intervening decade, with serious investment going into the infrastructure of vineyard and winery. Now one of the best-value wines in the Médoc, this wine is matured in wood for 16 months, with 50 percent new oak.

**RED** Increasingly stylish wines of good color and a certain plumpness of fruit, without loss of true St.-Estèphe structure. Unlike most other success stories in the commune, this has not been achieved by increasing Merlot; the reverse, in fact.

Cabernet Sauvignon 60%, Merlot 35%, Cabernet Franc 5%

5–10 years

**Second wine:** *Franck Phélan*

**Other wine:** *Croix Bonis*

## CHÂTEAU POMYS
### Cru Bourgeois
★ ✔

This property was classified *cru bourgeois* in 1932, but was not included in the 1978 list, although it is superior to a few that were. This hand-harvested wine is matured in wood for 15 months, with 30 percent new oak.

**RED** Substantial wines with good fruit and tannin balance.

Cabernet Sauvignon 50%, Merlot 35%, Cabernet Franc 15%

3–10 years

**Other wine:** *Château Saint-Louis*

## CHÂTEAU TOUR DE PEZ
### Cru Bourgeois Supérieur
★ ★ ✔

The huge investments made since this château changed hands in 1989 paid off in 2003 when it was promoted to *crus bourgeois supérieur*. This wine is matured in wood for 16 to 18 months, with 50 percent new oak.

**RED** Consistently elegant, medium-bodied wine with good, plump, fleshy fruit.

Cabernet Sauvignon 45%, Cabernet Franc 10%, Merlot 40%, Petit Verdot 5%

3–7 years

**Second wine:** *T de Tour de Pez*

**Other wines:** *Château les Hauts de Pez, Château L'Hereteyre Château Haut-Coutelin*

## CHÂTEAU TRONQUOY-LALANDE
### Cru Bourgeois Supérieur
★ ✔

Owned by Arlette Castéja-Texier with active input from the Dourthe-Kressman winemaking team.

**RED** This wine can be dark and tannic, but as from the 1996 vintage it has displayed more fruit and finesse.

Cabernet Sauvignon 45%, Merlot 45%, Petit Verdot 10%

3–7 years

# PAUILLAC

*If any Bordeaux appellation can be described as "big, black, and beautiful," it is Pauillac—the commune most famous for the three* premiers crus *crus of Latour, Lafite, and Mouton. If the wine is allowed to evolve slowly, it achieves an astonishing degree of finesse for its weight.*

PAUILLAC IS, HOWEVER, an appellation of quite surprising contrasts. Although it boasts three-quarters of the Médoc's *premiers crus*, it also contains two-thirds of the region's *cinquièmes crus*. Very little lies between these two extremes, and *crus bourgeois* are, therefore, the exception rather than the rule. Cabernet Sauvignon is at its most majestic in Pauillac, and while the much-vaunted blackcurrant character of this grape may be elusive in many clarets, it is certainly very much in evidence in Pauillac. In this wine, the cassis character is always beautifully balanced by a tannic structure.

## PAUILLAC CRU CLASSÉ STATISTICS

*Crus classés* **in AOC Pauillac**
18 châteaux (by number: 30% of *crus classés* in the Médoc) with 2,080 acres (842 ha) of vineyards (by area: 30% of *crus classés* in the Médoc and 70% of this AOC)

*1er crus classés*
3 châteaux (by number: 75% of *1er crus classés* in the Médoc) with 568 acres (230 ha ) of vineyards (by area: 75% of *1er crus classés* in the Médoc)

*2ème crus classés*
2 châteaux (by number: 14% of *2ème crus classés* in the Médoc) with 222 acres (90 ha) of vineyards (by area: 11% of *2ème crus classés* in the Médoc)

*3ème crus classés*
None

*4ème crus classés*
1 château (by number: 10% of *4ème crus classés* in the Médoc) with 111 acres (45 ha) of vineyards (by area: 10% of *4ème crus classés* in the Médoc)

*5ème crus classés*
12 châteaux (by number: 67% of *5ème crus classés* in the Médoc) with 1,179 acres (477 ha) of vineyards (by area: 63% of *5ème crus classés* in the Médoc)

**Note:** Only Margaux has more *cru classé* châteaux than Pauillac, and no communal AOC has a greater concentration of *cru classé* vines.

CHÂTEAU LATOUR
*Due to radical changes in vinification techniques introduced in the 1960s, Château Latour became the most consistent of Bordeaux's great* premiers crus classés. *It produces the archetypal Pauillac wine, which is full of finesse.*

# FACTORS AFFECTING TASTE AND QUALITY

## LOCATION
Pauillac is sandwiched between St.-Estèphe to the north and St.-Julien to the south.

## CLIMATE
As for the Médoc (*see* p.00

## ASPECT
Pauillac consists of two large, low-lying plateaux, one to the northwest of the town of Pauillac, the other to the southwest. Exposure is excellent, and both drain down gentle slopes, eastward to the Gironde, westward to the forest, or north and south to canals and streams.

## SOIL
Pauillac's two plateaux are massive gravel beds, reaching a greater depth than any found elsewhere in the Médoc. The water drains away before the iron-pan subsoil is reached. St.-Sauveur consists of shallow sand over a stony subsoil to the west, and gravel over iron-pan (or more gravel) in the center and south.

## VITICULTURE AND VINIFICATION
Only red wines have the right to the Pauillac appellation. Some *vin de presse* is traditionally used by most châteaux. Skin contact duration averages between 3 and 4 weeks, and maturation in cask currently varies between 18 and 24 months.

## GRAPE VARIETIES
**Primary varieties**: Cabernet Sauvignon, Cabernet Franc, Merlot
**Secondary varieties**: Carmenère, Petit Verdot, Malbec

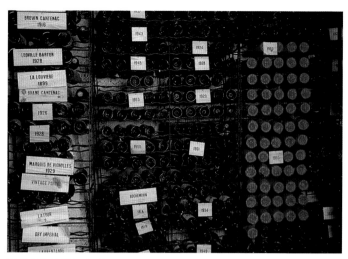

CAVEAU PRIVÉ, CHÂTEAU PICHON-LONGUEVILLE-COMTESSE-DE-LALANDE
*One wall of the château's private cellars encapsulates a winemaking history, particularly of Bordeaux, stretching back nearly 200 years.*

# PAUILLAC PROFILE

### Appellation area
Covers parts of the commune of Pauillac, plus 84 acres (34 ha) in St.-Sauveur, 40 acres (16 ha) in St.-Julien, 12.4 acres (5 ha) in St.-Estèphe, a nd 2.5 acres (1 ha) in Cissac

### Size of commune
6,274 acres (2,539 ha)

### AOC area under vine
2,988 acres (1,209 ha), 48% of commune

### Surface area of *crus classés*
2,080 acres (842 ha), 3% of commune, 70% of AOC

PAUILLAC
*The town of Pauillac, the largest of the Médoc, sits on the west bank of the Gironde. Despite its size and position, it retains a quiet, rural character.*

PAUILLAC, *see also* p63
*Blessed with three premiers crus, Lafite-Rothschild and Mouton-Rothschild in the north, and Latour to the south, Pauillac is sandwiched between St.-Estèphe and St.-Julien.*

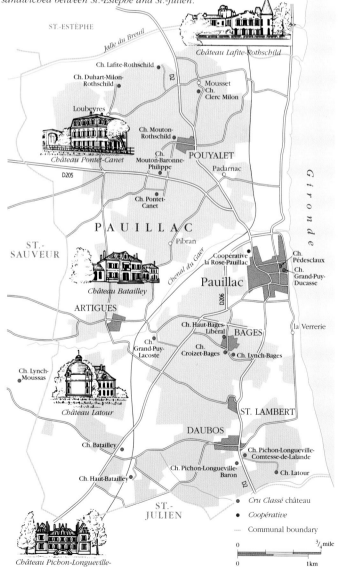

Château Pichon-Longueville-Comtesse-de-Lalande

THE WINE PRODUCERS OF
# PAUILLAC

## CHÂTEAU D'ARMAILHAC
### 5ème Cru Classé
★★☆

Baron Philippe de Rothschild purchased Château Mouton d'Armailhac in 1933. In 1956 he renamed it Château Mouton Baron-Philippe. In 1975 it was changed to Mouton-Baronne-Philippe in honor of the baron's late wife. In 1991 it reverted to d'Armailhac, but without the Mouton tag because the baron believed the wine to be in danger of assuming second wine status due to the overwhelming prestige of Mouton-Rothschild. This property borders that of Mouton, and one of Baron Philippe's reasons for acquiring it was to provide an easier, more impressive access to the famous *premier cru*. The wines, which are matured in wood for 16 months, with 25 percent new oak, are produced with the same care and consideration. Despite this attention, I have criticized the "austere, light, and attenuated style" of Château d'Armailhac in the past, which "proves that even money cannot buy *terroir*," but within limits improvements can always be made, and by tweaking harvesting and vinification techniques, owners Baron Philippe de Rothschild S.A. produced the greatest wine this property has ever known in 2000. That was an extraordinary vintage, but the style shift and giant stride in quality continued in 2001, 2002, and 2003.

**RED** Since 2000, much riper tannins, and a more supple structure has given this wine more velvety fruit than previous vintages had established. The start of a new era.

🍇 Cabernet Sauvignon 52%, Merlot 26%, Cabernet Franc 20%, Petit Verdot 2%

🍷 6–15 years

## CHÂTEAU BATAILLEY
### 5ème Cru Classé
★★☆ ⓥ

This is a château that responds well to sunny years and produces underrated and undervalued wine.

The 1985 was possibly the best bargain in Bordeaux, and the 1986 is probably even better. This wine is matured in wood for 18 months, with 60 percent new oak.

**RED** This wine has sometimes been rustic and too assertive in the past, but now shows its class with fine, succulent fruit supported by a ripe tannic structure and a complex creamy-oak aftertaste.

🍇 Cabernet Sauvignon 70%, Merlot 25%, Cabernet Franc 3%, Petit Verdot 2%

🍷 10–25 years

**Second wine:** *Château Haut-Bages Monpelou*

## CHÂTEAU CLERC MILON
### 5ème Cru Classé
★

This property was purchased by Baron Philippe de Rothschild in 1970. After more than a decade of investment and quite a few disappointing vintages along the way, it came good in 1981, achieved sensational quality in 1982, and now consistently performs well above its classification. This wine, which is matured in wood for 18 months with one-third new oak, is one worth watching.

**RED** A deep-colored, medium-bodied, sometimes full-bodied, wine with cassis-cum-spicy-oak aromas and rich berry flavors well balanced by ripe acidity.

🍇 Cabernet Sauvignon 70%, Merlot 20%, Cabernet Franc 10%

🍷 10–20 years

## CHÂTEAU COLOMBIER-MONPELOU
### Cru Bourgeois Supérieur
★★ ⓥ

In the third edition of *Bordeaux and its Wines*, published in 1874, this property was described as a *quatrième cru*. Of course, it was never classified as such, but its recent *cru bourgeois supérieur* achievement is about right. This wine is matured in wood for 16 months, with 40 percent new oak.

**RED** Rich, spicy, fruit with fine Cabernet characteristics, backed up by good, ripe tannic structure and vanilla-oaky undertones.

🍇 Cabernet Sauvignon 55%, Merlot 35%, Cabernet Franc 5%, Petit Verdot 5%

🍷 5–12 years

**Other wines:** *Château Grand Canyon, Château Pey la Rose, Château Coubersant, Château de Puy la Rose*

## CHÂTEAU CORDEILLAN-BAGES
★

Jean-Michel Cazes of Château Lynch-Bages was the driving force behind the group of growers from the Médoc who renovated Château de Cordeillan, turning it into an extensive complex comprising a hotel, restaurant, and wine school. With only a very small production from just five acres of vineyard this hand-harvested wine that is produced by the Lynch-Bages winemaking team, is matured in wood for up to 15 months, with a massive 100 percent new oak.

**RED** As dark and as dense as might be expected from a wine produced with the Lynch-Bages influence, with smoky oak, tobacco plant, and violet aromas weaving their way through the chocolaty Cabernet fruit.

🍇 Cabernet Sauvignon 70%, Merlot 20%, Cabernet Franc 10%

🍷 3–8 years

## CHÂTEAU CROIZET-BAGES
### 5ème Cru Classé
★ ⓥ

Under the same ownership as Château Rauzan-Gassies of Margaux, and situated on the Bages plateau, Croizet-Bages is a classic example of a "château with no château." Its wine is matured in wood for 18 months and although not unattractive, it lacks class and rarely excites. Improvements started slowly in the mid-1990s, then stepped up a gear at the turn of the millennium.

**RED** Not one of the most deeply colored Pauillacs, this medium-bodied wine has always been easy-drinking, but has been more stylish since 1999, gaining both in gravitas and finesse.

🍇 Cabernet Sauvignon 37%, Cabernet Franc 30%, Merlot 30%, Malbec and Petit Verdot 3%

🍷 6–12 years

**Second wine:** *Enclos de Moncabon*

## CHÂTEAU DUHART-MILON-ROTHSCHILD
### 4ème Cru Classé
★★☆

Another "château with no château," Duhart-Milon was purchased by the Lafite branch of the Rothschild family in 1962. Its wines prior to this date were almost entirely Petit Verdot, and so only in abnormally hot years did it excel with this late-ripening grape, which is traditionally cultivated for its acidity. Interestingly, in the near-tropical heat of 1947, Duhart-Milon managed to produce a wine that many considered to be the best of the vintage. The Rothschilds expanded these vineyards bordering Lafite and replanted them with the correct combination of varieties to suit *terroir*. In 1994 Charles Chevalier arrived, and since 1996 he has moved these wines up a gear. The wine is matured for at least 18 months in wood, with 50 percent new oak.

**RED** These wines are elegantly perfumed, deliciously rich in creamy-oaky fruit, and have exceptional balance and finesse.

🍇 Cabernet Sauvignon 80%, Merlot 20%

🍷 8–16 years

**Second wine:** *Moulin de Duhart*

## CHÂTEAU LA FLEUR-MILON
### Cru Bourgeois

A "château with no château," La Fleur-Milon produces a wine accumulated from various parcels of vines bordering such prestigious properties as Lafite, Mouton, and Duhart-Milon. This wine is matured in wood for 18 months, with one-third new oak.

**RED** A consistently firm, solid, and decent kind of wine, which somehow fails to live up to the favored origins of its vines.

🍇 Cabernet Sauvignon 45%, Cabernet Franc 20%, Merlot 35%

🍷 4–10 years

**Other wines:** *Château Chanteclerc-Milon, Château Buisson-Milon*

## CHÂTEAU FONBADET
### Cru Bourgeois Supérieur
### ★ⓥ

This growth was classified *cru bourgeois* in 1932, but was not included in the Syndicat's 1978 list, although it is superior to a few that were, and achieved due recognition in the 2003 reclassification. Many of the vines are in excess of 80 years old, with an average age of 50 years for the entire 50-acre (20-hectare) vineyard. This hand-harvested wine is matured in wood for 18 months, with 30 percent new oak. Great-value Pauillac.

**RED** This typical Pauillac has a deep, almost opaque color, an intense cassis, cigar-box, and cedarwood bouquet, a concentrated spicy, fruit flavor with creamy-oak undertones, and a long finish.

🍇 Cabernet Sauvignon 60%, Merlot 20%, Cabernet Franc 15%, Malbec and Petit Verdot 5%

🍷 6–15 years

**Other wines:** *Château Haut-Pauillac, Château Padarnac, Château Montgrand-Milon, Château Tour du Roc-Milon, Pauillac*

## CHÂTEAU GRAND-PUY-DUCASSE
### 5ème Cru Classé
### ★✲ⓥ

Under the same owners as Château Rayne-Vigneau in Sauternes, this property produces an undervalued wine that comes from various plots scattered across half the commune. One of the best value, improving *cru classé* wines available, this wine is matured in wood for 18 to 24 months, with up to 40 percent

new oak.

**RED** Well-balanced, relatively early-drinking, medium-bodied, sometimes full-bodied, wine of classic Pauillac cassis character and more suppleness than is usual for this commune.

🍇 Cabernet Sauvignon 61%, Merlot 39%

🍷 5–10 years

**Second wine:** *Prélude à Grand-Puy Ducasse*

**Other wine:** *Château Artigues-Arnaud*

## CHÂTEAU GRAND-PUY-LACOSTE
### 5ème Cru Classé
### ★★ⓥ

Under the same ownership as Château Ducru-Beaucaillou, Grand-Puy-Lacoste is going from strength to strength under the skillful guidance of François-Xavier Borie. The wine is matured in wood for 18 months, with 50 percent new oak.

**RED** Deep-colored with complex cassis, cigar-box spice, and vanilla bouquet, with lots of fruit, length, and finesse.

🍇 Cabernet Sauvignon 75%, Merlot 25%

🍷 10–20 years

**Second wine:** *Lacoste-Borie*

## CHÂTEAU HAUT-BAGES-LIBÉRAL
### 5ème Cru Classé
### ★

Under the same ownership as the bourgeois growth of Château Chasse-Spleen in Moulis and the excellent unclassified Château la Gurgue in Margaux, this dynamic property is currently producing sensational wines. They are matured for 16 months in wood, with up to 40 percent new oak.

**RED** Dark, full-bodied wines with masses of concentrated spicy-cassis fruit, great tannic structure, and ripe, vanilla oak. In a word—complete.

🍇 Cabernet Sauvignon 80%, Merlot 17%, Petit Verdot 3%

🍷 8–20 years

**Second wine:** *Chapelle de Bages*

## CHÂTEAU HAUT-BATAILLEY
### 5ème Cru Classé
### ★ⓥ

This property is under the same ownership as châteaux Grand-Puy-Lacoste and, in St.-Julien, Ducru-Beaucaillou. When the Borie family purchased Château Batailley in 1942, this part of the vineyard was given to one son, while the bulk of the property, including the château itself, was given to the other. The wine is matured in wood for 20 months, with one-third new oak.

**RED** Haut-Batailley is well-colored and medium-bodied and shows more elegance and finesse than Batailley, although it can lack the latter's fullness of fruit.

🍇 Cabernet Sauvignon 65%, Merlot 25%, Cabernet Franc 10%

🍷 7–15 years

**Second wine:** *Château La Tour l'Aspic*

**Other wine:** *Château La Couronne*

## CHÂTEAU LAFITE-ROTHSCHILD
### 1er Cru Classé
### ★★★

Since 1994 this famous château, the vineyard of which includes a small plot in St.-Estèphe, has been run along traditional lines and with fastidious care by Charles Chevalier for Baron Eric of the French branch of the Rothschilds. The St.-Estèphe portion of the Lafite vineyard is allowed to bear the Pauillac appellation, having been part of the Lafite-Rothschild estate for several hundred years. A change of style occurred in the mid-1970s, when the decision was made to give the wines less time in cask, but under Chevalier they have gone into hyperdrive and are often the very best of the *premiers crus*. Well into

the first decade of the new millennium, Lafite is arguably the best performing of all *premiers crus*. This hand-harvested wine is matured in wood for 20 months, with 100 percent new oak.

**RED** Not the biggest of the *premiers crus*, but Lafite is nevertheless textbook stuff: a rich delicacy of spicy fruit flavors, continuously unfolding, supported by an array of creamy-oak and ripe tannins; a wine with incomparable finesse.

🍇 Cabernet Sauvignon 70%, Merlot 25%, Cabernet Franc 3%, Petit Verdot 2%

🍷 25–50 years

**Second wine:** ☑ *Carruades de Lafite*

**Other wine:** *Moulin des Carruades*

## CHÂTEAU LATOUR
### 1er Cru Classé
### ★★★

The Pearson Group (which now owns the publisher of this book) was accused by the French of turning a Bordeaux *premier cru* into a dairy when temperature-controlled, stainless-steel vats were installed in 1964. These French critics conveniently ignored the fact that Château Haut-Brion had done the same three years earlier. Pearson actually owned just over half of Latour at the time and Harveys of Bristol owned a quarter. Together they paid less than three million dollars for almost 80 percent of this *premier cru*. It was a bargain, for although they invested heavily in renovating the vineyards and winery, Allied-Lyons (owners of Harvey's) paid almost $110 million in 1989 for Pearson's share, valuing the entire property at $180 million. Allied-Lyons lost out, however, when in 1993 they needed to liquidate various shareholdings to finance takeovers and sold Latour to François Pinault, the French industrialist, for $130 million. Pinault appointed Frédéric Engerer, a graduate of one of France's top business schools, as the new young president of Latour. He has revolutionized working practices in both the vineyard and winery and with Frédéric Ardouin, his new, even younger winemaker at his side, the change in gear at Latour promised to be as dramatic as it was at Margaux. This hand-harvested wine is matured in wood for 18 months, with 100 percent new oak.

**RED** Despite its close proximity to the neighboring commune of St.-Julien, Latour is the archetypal Pauillac. Its ink-black color accurately reflects the immense structure and hugely concentrated flavor of this wine. If Lafite is the ultimate example of finesse, then Latour is the ideal illustration of how massive a wine can be while still retaining great finesse.

🍇 Cabernet Sauvignon 75%, Merlot 20%, Cabernet Franc and Petit Verdot 5%

🍷 15–60 years
**Second wine:** ✓ *Les Forts de Latour*
**Other wine:** *Pauillac de Latour*

## CHÂTEAU LYNCH-BAGES
### 5ème Cru Classé
### ★★✪

This château is sited on the edge of the Bages plateau, a little way out of Pauillac. It is on the southern fringe of the small town of Bages. Jean-Michel Cazes produces wines that some people describe as "poor man's Latour (or Mouton)." Well, that cannot be such a bad thing, but if I were rich, I would drink as many *cinquièmes crus* from this château as *premiers crus* from elsewhere. No expense was spared in building the new vinification and storage facilities at this château, and since 1980 the successes in off-vintages have been extraordinary, making it more consistent than some *deuxièmes crus*. This hand-harvested wine is matured in wood for 12 to 15 months, with 50 percent new oak.

**RED** An intensely deep purple-colored wine of seductive character that is packed with fruit and has obvious class. It has a degree of complexity on the nose, a rich, plummy flavor, supple tannin structure, and a spicy, blackcurrant and vanilla aftertaste.

🍇 Cabernet Sauvignon 75%, Merlot 15%, Cabernet Franc 10%

🍷 8–30 years
**Second wine:** ✓ *Château Haut-Bages-Avérous*
**Other wine:** *Blanc de Lynch-Bages (rare "Médoc" white wine)*

## CHÂTEAU LYNCH-MOUSSAS
### 5ème Cru Classé
### ★

Owned by Emile Castéja of Borie-Manoux, this property has been renovated and the wines could well improve. The wine is matured in wood for 18 months, with 60 percent new oak.

**RED** After a false start in the mid-1980s, when an exceptionally stylish 1985 turned out to be exactly that (an exception), this château continued to produce light, rather insubstantial wines of no specific character or quality, but with better selection, riper fruit, less time in cask, and more than twice the

amount of new oak Lynch-Moussas used to receive, it has made significantly better wines since the mid-1990s.

🍇 Cabernet Sauvignon 75%, Merlot 25%

🍷 4–8 years
**Second wine:** *Château Haut-Madrac*

## CHÂTEAU MOUTON-ROTHSCHILD
### 1er Cru Classé
### ★★★

The famous case of the only wine ever to be officially reclassified since 1855, Baron Philippe de Rothschild's plight ended with Mouton's status being justly raised to *premier cru* in 1973. Through promotion of Mouton's unique character, he was probably responsible for elevating the Cabernet Sauvignon grape to its present high profile. Part of his campaign to keep this château in the headlines was the introduction of a specially commissioned painting for the label of each new vintage. The hand-harvested wine is matured in wood for up to 22 months, with 100 percent new oak.

**RED** It is difficult to describe this wine without using the same descriptive terms as those used for Latour, but perhaps the color of Mouton reminds one more of damsons and the underlying character is more herbal, sometimes even minty. And although it ages just as well as Latour, it becomes accessible slightly earlier.

🍇 Cabernet Sauvignon 77%, Merlot 11%, Cabernet Franc 10%, Petit Verdot 2%

🍷 12–60 years
**Second wine:** *Le Petit Mouton de Mouton-Rothschild*
**Other wines:** *Aile d'Argent* (another rare "Médoc" white)

## CHÂTEAU PEDESCLAUX
### 5ème Cru Classé

Little-seen *cru classé* produced from two very well-situated plots of vines, one bordering Lynch-Bages, the other between Mouton-

Rothschild and Pontet-Canet. Most of its exported production goes to Belgium. It is matured in wood for 18 months, with 50 percent new oak. Wine rejected for the *grand vin* is blended into the wine of Château Belle Rose, a *cru bourgeois* under the same ownership.

**RED** Full, firm, traditional style of Pauillac that is slow-maturing and long-lasting.

🍇 Cabernet Sauvignon 65%, Merlot 25%, Cabernet Franc 5%, Petit Verdot 5%

🍷 15–40 years
**Second wine:** *Château Haut-Pardanac*

## CHÂTEAU PICHON-LONGUEVILLE BARON PICHON-LONGUEVILLE
### 2ème Cru Classé
### ★★☆

The smaller of the two Pichon vineyards and until very recently the less inspiring, although many experts reckoned the *terroir* of Pichon-Baron to be intrinsically superior to that of its neighbor, the star-performing Pichon-Comtesse. Indeed, 10 years ago, I even suggested that Madame de Lencquesaing should buy this château and cast her seemingly irresistible spell on what would inevitably be the still greater *terroir* of the two properties combined. Whether she had such an ambition, or even the cash to consider it, AXA-Millesimes got there first, and has been remarkably successful at conjuring the most incredible quality from Pichon-Baron. Essentially by reducing Cabernet Sauvignon in favor of Merlot and almost tripling the amount of new oak used, AXA has ensured that Pichon-Baron now lives up to its potential. The wine is matured in wood for 15 to 18 months, with 80 percent new oak.

**RED** Intensely colored, full-bodied wine with concentrated spicy-cassis fruit backed up by supple tannins, which are rich and heady with smoky-creamy oak and complexity. True super-second quality.

🍇 Cabernet Sauvignon 60%, Merlot 35%, Cabernet Franc 4%, Petit Verdot 1%

🍷 8–25 years
**Second wine:** ✓ *Les Tourelles de Longueville*

## CHÂTEAU PICHON LONGUEVILLE COMTESSE-DE-LALANDE
### 2ème Cru Classé
### ★★☆

There is a limit to the quality of any wine and this is determined by the potential quality of its grapes. But at Pichon-Comtesse (as it is known), the formidable Madame de Lencquesaing demands the maximum from her *terroir*—and consistently gets it. The wine is matured in wood for 20 months, with 50 percent new oak.

**RED** This temptress is the Château Margaux of Pauillac. It is silky-textured, beautifully balanced, and seductive. A wine of great finesse, even in humble vintages.

🍇 Cabernet Sauvignon 45%, Merlot 35%, Cabernet Franc 12%, Petit Verdot 8%

🍷 10–30 years
**Second wine:** ✓ *Réserve de la Comtesse*
**Other wines:** *Les Gartieux*

## CHÂTEAU PONTET-CANET
### 5ème Cru Classé
### ★★☆

The reputation of this château has suffered in recent decades, but many thought the situation would be reversed when Guy Tesseron purchased the property in 1975. The 1985 vintage gave a glimmer of hope, but it was not until 1995 that the breakthrough occurred, and the 1998 vintage is nothing less than outstanding. Definitely one to watch, this hand-harvested wine is matured in wood for 15 to 20 months, with 60 percent new oak.

**RED** Since the mid-1990s, these wines have been fruity and graceful with a rich, smooth, oaky touch.

🍇 Cabernet Sauvignon 68%, Merlot 20%, Cabernet Franc 10%, Malbec 2%

🍷 6–12 years
**Other wine:** *Les Hauts de Pontet*

## CHÂTEAU LA TOUR-PIBRAN
### ★✪

This growth was classified *cru bourgeois* in 1932, but was not in the Syndicat's 1978 list, although it is superior to a few that were.

**RED** This wine has bags of blackcurranty fruit, yet retains the characteristic Pauillac structure and firm finish. The superb 1985 is not unlike a "mini-Mouton."

🍇 Cabernet Sauvignon 75%, Merlot 15%, Cabernet Franc 10%

🍷 6–16 years

# SAINT-JULIEN

*The commune's fame is disproportionate to its size, since it is smaller than any of the other three classic Médoc appellations—St.-Estèphe, Pauillac, or Margaux.*

ST-JULIEN HAS NO *PREMIERS CRUS*, although some châteaux sometimes produce wines that are undeniably of *premier cru* quality, and no *cinquièmes crus*. The concentration of its 11 *crus classés* in the middle of the classification is St.-Julien's real strength, enabling this commune justly to claim that it is the most consistent of the Médoc appellations; these quintessential clarets have a vivid color, elegant fruit, superb balance, and great finesse.

It is perhaps surprising that wines from 40 acres (16 hectares) inside St.-Julien's borders may be classified as AOC Pauillac, particularly in view of the perceived difference in style between these appellations. This illustrates the "gray area" that exists when communal boundaries overlap the historical borders of great wine estates, and highlights the existence and importance of blending, even in a region reputed for its single-vineyard wines. We should not be too pedantic about communal differences of style: if these borders of the Médoc followed local history, Château Latour, the most famous château of Pauillac, would today be in St.-Julien—and that makes me wonder how the wines of this commune might be described under such circumstances?

## ST.-JULIEN PROFILE

**Appellation area**
Covers part of the commune of St.-Julien only

**Size of commune**
3,840 acres (1,554 ha)

**AOC area under vine**
2,246 acres (909 ha), 59% of commune

**Surface area of *crus classés***
1,552 acres (628 ha), 40% of commune, 68 of AOC

**Special comments**
Some 40 acres (16 ha) of St.-Julien are classified as AOC Pauillac

## FACTORS AFFECTING TASTE AND QUALITY

**LOCATION**
St.-Julien lies in the center of the Haut-Médoc, 2.5 miles (4 kilometers) south of Pauillac.

**CLIMATE**
As for the Médoc (*see* p70).

**ASPECT**
The gravel crest of St.-Julien slopes almost imperceptibly eastward toward the village and drains into the Gironde.

**SOIL**
Fine, gravel topsoil of good-sized pebbles in vineyards within sight of the Gironde. Farther inland, the particle size decreases and the soil begins to mix with sandy loess.

The subsoil consists of iron-pan, marl, and gravel.

**VITICULTURE & VINIFICATION**
Only red wines have the right to the appellation. All grapes must be destalked. Some *vin de presse* may be used according to the needs of the vintage. Skin contact duration averages 2 to 3 weeks and most châteaux allow 18 to 22 months' maturation in cask.

**GRAPE VARIETIES**
**Primary varieties:** Cabernet Sauvignon, Cabernet Franc, Merlot **Secondary varieties:** Carmenère, Malbec, Petit Verdot

## ST.-JULIEN CRU CLASSÉ STATISTICS

**Crus classés** in AOC St.-Julien
11 châteaux (by number: 18% of *crus classés* in the Médoc) with 1,552 acres (628 ha) of vineyards (by area: 22% of *crus classés* in the Médoc and 68% of this AOC)

**1er crus classés**
None

**2ème crus classés**
5 châteaux (by number: 36% of *2ème crus classés* in the Médoc) with 786 acres (318 ha) of vineyards (by area: 40% of *2ème crus classés* in the Médoc)

**3ème crus classés**
2 châteaux (by number: 14% of *3ème crus classés* in the Médoc) with 170 acres (69 ha) of vineyards (by area: 16% of *3ème crus classés* in the Médoc)

**4ème crus classés**
4 châteaux (by number: 40% of *4ème crus classés* in the Médoc) with 596 acres (241 ha) of vineyards (by area: 51% of *4ème crus classés* in the Médoc)

**5ème crus classés**
None

ST.-JULIEN-BEYCHEVELLE
*The Médoc's most consistent appellation has two small villages as its major centers, St.-Julien-Beychevelle itself and, to the south, Beychevelle.*

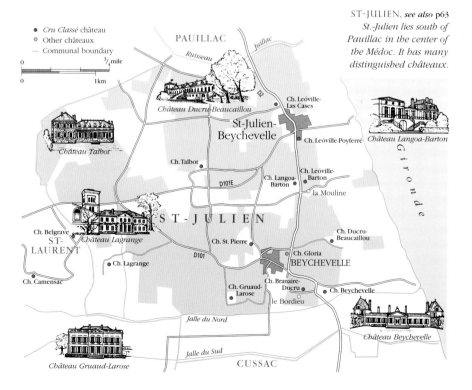

ST-JULIEN, *see also* p63
*St.-Julien lies south of Pauillac in the center of the Médoc. It has many distinguished châteaux.*

- ● Cru Classé château
- ◎ Other châteaux
- — Communal boundary

# THE WINE PRODUCERS OF
# SAINT-JULIEN

### CHÂTEAU BEYCHEVELLE
#### 4ème Cru Classé
#### ★★

The immaculate and colorful gardens of this château never fail to catch the breath of passers-by. Beychevelle also boasts one of the most famous legends of Bordeaux: its name is said to be a corruption of *"basse-voile,"* the command to "lower sail." This arose because the Duc d'Épernon, a former owner who was also an admiral of France, apparently required the ships that passed through the Gironde to lower their sails in respect. His wife would then wave her kerchief in reply. This story, however, is not true. Épernon actually held the title of Baron de Beychevelle prior to being made the Amiral de Valette, and did not actually live at Beychevelle. I prefer the story of the sailors who lowered their pants and revealed their sterns, which shocked the duchess but made her children laugh. The wines are matured in wood for 20 months with 40 percent new oak.

**RED** Medium- to full-bodied wines of good color, ripe fruit, and an elegant oak and tannin structure. They can be quite fat in big years.

🍇 Cabernet Sauvignon 59%, Merlot 30%, Cabernet Franc 8%, Petit Verdot 3%

🍷 12–20 years

**Second wine:** ✓ *Réserve de l'Amiral*

**Other wine:** *Les Brulières de Beychevelle*

### CHÂTEAU
### BRANAIRE-DUCRU
#### 4ème Cru Classé
#### ★ ❤

The vineyards of this château are situated farther inland than those of Beychevelle and Ducru-Beaucaillou and its soil contains more clay and iron-pan than theirs, so the wine here is fuller and can be assertive, although never austere. It is matured in wood for 18 months, with up to 50 percent new oak, and is remarkably consistent.

**RED** This is a quite full-bodied wine, which is richly flavored and can show a certain chocolate character in big years. It has a distinctive bouquet that sets it apart from other St.-Juliens.

🍇 Cabernet Sauvignon 75%, Merlot 20%, Cabernet Franc 5%

🍷 12–25 years

**Second wine:** *Duluc*

### CHÂTEAU LA BRIDANE
#### Cru Bourgeois

The owners of this property have maintained a vineyard here since the 14th century.

**RED** Attractive, fruity, medium-bodied wine that is easy to drink.

🍇 Cabernet Sauvignon 55%, Merlot 45%

🍷 3–6 years

### CHÂTEAU DUCRU-
### BEAUCAILLOU
#### 2ème Cru Classé
#### ★★★¼

One of the super-seconds, the quality of this classic St.-Julien château, the flagship property of the Borie empire, is both legendary and inimitable. In both good years and bad it remains remarkably consistent and, although relatively expensive, the price fetched falls short of those demanded by *premiers crus*, making it a relative bargain. The wine is matured in wood for 20 months, with 50 percent new oak.

**RED** This wine has a fine, deep color that can belie its deft elegance of style. There is richness of fruit, complex spiciness of oak, great finesse, and exquisite balance.

🍇 Cabernet Sauvignon 65%, Merlot 25%, Cabernet Franc 10%

🍷 15–30 years

**Second wine:** *La Croix*

### CHÂTEAU DU GLANA
#### Cru Bourgeois Supérieur
#### ★★ ❤

This property is under the same ownership as Château Plantey in Pauillac and Château la Commanderie in St.-Estèphe.

**RED** Du Glana is normally an unpretentious and medium-weight wine, but it excels in really hot years, when it can be deliciously ripe and juicy.

🍇 Cabernet Sauvignon 68%, Merlot 25%, Petit Verdot 5%, Cabernet Franc 2%

🍷 3–6 years

### CHÂTEAU GLORIA
#### ★

Gloria excites opposite passions in wine drinkers: some consider it the equal of several *cru classé* wines— even superior in some cases—while others believe it earns an exaggerated price based on the reputation of merely a handful of vintages. Certainly the owners saw nothing to be gained by entering this wine for consideration in the 2003 reclassification, although it should have easily made *cru bourgeois supérieur* status had they done so. The wine is matured in wood for 12 months, with 40 percent new oak.

**RED** A deep plum-colored, full-bodied wine with masses of fruit and a rich, exuberant character.

🍇 Cabernet Sauvignon 65%, Merlot 25%, Cabernet Franc 5%, Petit Verdot 5%

🍷 12–30 years

**Second wine:** *Peymartin*
**Other wine:** *Haut-Beychevelle-Gloria*

### CHÂTEAU
### GRUAUD-LAROSE
#### 2ème Cru Classé
#### ★★ ❤

This large property produces consistently great wines of a far more solid structure than most other St.-Julien wines. Anyone who has tasted the supposedly mediocre 1980 Sarget de Gruaud-Larose (made from the wines rejected from the *grand vin*) will realize the true potential of Château Gruaud-Larose in any year. If anything, the quality of Gruaud-Larose is still improving.

**RED** Full-bodied, rich, and plummy wine with masses of fruit. Its spicy blackcurrant flavor is supported by a structure of ripe tannins.

🍇 Cabernet Sauvignon 57%, Merlot 30%, Cabernet Franc 7%, Petit Verdot 4%, Malbec 2%

🍷 10–40 years

**Second wine:** ✓ *Sarget de Gruaud-Larose*
**Other wines:** *La Roseraie de Gruaud-Larose, Chevalier de Gruaud-Larose*

### CHÂTEAU HORTEVIE
#### ★★¼ ❤

There is no château as such on this property. This tiny vineyard's wine is made at Château Terrey-Gros-Caillou by Henri Pradère, the owner of both properties.

**RED** This is a silky-soft, rich, and succulent wine of excellent quality. This great-value wine is easily equivalent to *cru classé* quality.

🍇 Cabernet Franc and Cabernet Sauvignon 70%, Merlot 25%, Petit Verdot 5%

🍷 7–15 years

### CHÂTEAU DE
### LACOUFOURQUE

This tiny 3-acre (1.25-hectare) vineyard is mentioned not because of its past performance but because it is unique in Bordeaux in being a 100 percent Cabernet Franc varietal, and it should be preserved.

**RED** This wine is sold in bulk as generic St.-Julien, which makes it impossible to make generalizations about its character.

🍇 Cabernet Franc 100%

### CHÂTEAU LAGRANGE
#### 3ème Cru Classé
#### ★★★¼ ❤

When the *Ban de Vendanges* was held at this Japanese-owned château in 1986, everyone realized that the Japanese were not simply content to apply state-of-the-art technology; they seriously intended to make Lagrange the best-quality wine in St.-Julien. They could very well succeed in this ambition. The formidable Bordeaux oenologist Professor Peynaud has dubbed Lagrange a "dream estate," and describes its vinification center as "unlike any other in the whole of Bordeaux." Each vat is, according to Peynaud, a "winemaking laboratory." The wine spends 18 months in wood, with up to 60 percent new oak.

**RED** A deeply colored wine with intense spicy-fruit aromas. It is full-bodied, silky-textured, and rich, with an exquisite balance and finish.

🍇 Cabernet Sauvignon 65%, Merlot 28%, Cabernet Franc and Petit Verdot 7%

🍷 8–25 years

**Second wine:** ✓ *Les Fiefs de Lagrange*

### CHÂTEAU LALANDE-BORIE
#### ★ ❤

Under the same ownership as the illustrious Château Ducru-Beaucaillou, Lalande-Borie is an inexpensive introduction to the wines of St.-Julien.

**RED** These are well-colored wines, dominated by rich, blackcurranty Cabernet Sauvignon flavors. Some vintages are fat and juicy, while others are more ethereal and tannic.

🍇 Cabernet Sauvignon 65%, Merlot 25%, Cabernet Franc 10%

⌛ 5–10 years

## CHÂTEAU LANGOA-BARTON

### 3ème Cru Classé
★ V

This beautiful château was known as Pontet-Langlois until 1821, when it was purchased by Hugh Barton, grandson of "French Tom" Barton, the founder of Bordeaux *négociant* Barton & Guestier, and is now run by Anthony Barton. Both Langoa-Barton and Léoville-Barton are made here using very traditional techniques. The wine is matured in wood for 24 months, with a minimum of one-third new oak.

**RED** Attractive, easy-drinking wine with good fruit and acidity. It is lighter than the Léoville and can sometimes taste a little rustic in comparison, but has gained a degree of extra elegance and finesse in recent years.

🍇 Cabernet Sauvignon 70%, Merlot 20%, Cabernet Franc 8%, Petit Verdot 2%

⌛ 10–25 years

**Second wine:** ✓ *Lady Langoa* (a blend of Langoa-Barton and Léoville-Barton formerly sold simply as "St.-Julien")

## CHÂTEAU LÉOVILLE-BARTON

### 2ème Cru Classé
★★★ V

A quarter of the original Léoville estate was sold to Hugh Barton in 1826, but the château remained in the hands of the Léoville estate and is now called Château Léoville-Las Cases (*see below*). This wine is made by Anthony Barton at Langoa-Barton (*see above*). It is matured in wood for 24 months, with a minimum of one-third new oak. Although it is the better of the two Barton estates, it has been considered significantly beneath the standard set by Léoville-Las Cases—since the late 1980s, however, it has performed equally well. A great château in ascendancy.

**RED** Excellent wines of great finesse and breeding; they are darker, deeper, and richer than the Langoa-Barton, which is itself of very good quality. With maturity, a certain cedarwood complexity develops in this wine and gradually overwhelms its youthful cassis and vanilla character.

🍇 Cabernet Sauvignon 70%, Merlot 20%, Cabernet Franc 8%, Petit Verdot 2%

⌛ 15–30 years

**Second wine:** ✓ *Lady Langoa* (a blend of Langoa-Barton and Léoville-Barton formerly sold simply as "St.-Julien")

## CHÂTEAU LÉOVILLE-LAS CASES

### 2ème Cru Classé
★★★⯨

The label reads "*Grand Vin* de Léoville du Marquis de Las Cases," although this wine is commonly referred to as "Château Léoville-Las Cases." This estate represents the largest portion of the original Léoville estate. This is a great wine, and it certainly qualifies as one of the super-seconds, while "Clos du Marquis" is one of the finest second wines available and probably the best value St.-Julien. The *grand vin* spends 18 months in wood, with 50 percent new oak.

**RED** This dark, damson-colored, full-bodied, and intensely flavored wine is complex, classy, and aromatically stunning. A skillful amalgam of power and finesse.

🍇 Cabernet Sauvignon 65%, Merlot 19%, Cabernet Franc 13%, Petit Verdot 3%

⌛ 15–35 years

**Second wine:** ✓ *Clos du Marquis*
**Other wines:** *Domaine de Bigarnon*

## CHÂTEAU LÉOVILLE POYFERRÉ

### 2ème Cru Classé
★★⯨

This property once formed a quarter of the original Léoville estate, and probably suffers from being compared to the other two châteaux, whose properties were also part of Léoville—Léoville-Barton and Léoville-Las Cases. Yet in the context of St.-Julien as a whole, it fares very well, and since

1982 it has had some extraordinary successes. Since the involvement of Michel Rolland from the mid-1990s, quality has gone up another notch. Wine is matured in wood for 18 months, with one-third new oak.

**RED** This wine has always been tannic, but is now much fuller in fruit, richer in flavor, and darker in color, with oaky nuances.

🍇 Cabernet Sauvignon 65%, Merlot 30%, Cabernet Franc 5%

⌛ 12–25 years
**Second wine:** *Moulin-Riche*

## CHÂTEAU MOULIN-DE-LA-ROSE

### Cru Bourgeois Supérieur
★ V

This vineyard is well situated, being surrounded by *crus classés* on virtually all sides. Its wine is fermented in stainless steel and aged in cask for 18 months, with 25 percent new oak.

**RED** This attractively aromatic wine is unusually concentrated and firm for a minor St.-Julien, but rounds out well after a few years in bottle.

🍇 Cabernet Sauvignon 65%, Merlot 25%, Petit Verdot 8%, Cabernet Franc 2%

⌛ 6–12 years

## CHÂTEAU ST.-PIERRE

### 4ème Cru Classé
★⯨ V

This property was bought in 1982 by Henri Martin, who owns the *bourgeois* growth Château Gloria. The wine is matured in wood for between 18 and 20 months, with 50 percent new oak.

**RED** Once an astringent, coarse wine; now ripe, fat, and full of cedarwood, spice, and fruit.

🍇 Cabernet Sauvignon 70%, Merlot 20%, Cabernet Franc 10%

⌛ 8–25 years

**Second wine:** *Saint-Louis-le-Bosq*
**Other wine:** *Clos d'Uza*

## CHÂTEAU TALBOT

### 4ème Cru Classé
★⯨ V

Named after the English Commander who fell at the Battle of Castillon in 1453, this property remains under Cordier family ownership, while its sister château Gruaud-Larose now belongs to Groupe Taillan. To contrast the style

of these two St.-Juliens is justifiable, but to compare their quality is not: Château Talbot is a great wine and closer to the style of a classic St.-Julien, but intrinsically it does not have the quality nor the consistency of Château Gruaud-Larose. Talbot is matured in wood for between 15 and 18 months, with one-third new oak.

**RED** A graceful wine, medium-bodied, with elegant fruit, gently structured by ripe oak tannins and capable of considerable finesse.

🍇 Cabernet Sauvignon 66%, Merlot 24%, Cabernet Franc 3%, Petit Verdot 5%, Malbec 2%

⌛ 8–30 years

**Second wine:** ✓ *Connétable Talbot*

**Other wine:** *Caillou Blanc*

## CHÂTEAU TERREY-GROS-CAILLOU

### Cru Bourgeois Supérieur
★★ V

This establishment is under the same ownership as Château Hortevie (whose wine it also makes), and is itself a top-performing property.

**RED** This beautifully colored, medium- to full-bodied wine always has rich fruit and is often equivalent to a good *cru classé*.

🍇 Cabernet Sauvignon 65%, Merlot 30%, Petit Verdot 5%

⌛ 5–12 years

## CHÂTEAU TEYNAC

### Cru Bourgeois
★ V

This fine gravel vineyard once formed part of *cru classé* Château Saint-Pierre.

**RED** Well-balanced, medium- to full-bodied wine with good spice and a firm tannin structure.

🍇 Cabernet Sauvignon 65%, Merlot 35%

⌛ 6–10 years

# MARGAUX

*Situated in the south of the Médoc district, Margaux is the most famous of all Bordeaux appellations. While it bathes in the reflected glory of its name-sake* premier cru, *it is also the largest and least consistent of the four classic Médoc appellations.*

WHILE THE OTHER THREE great Médoc AOCs—St.-Estèphe, Pauillac, and St.-Julien—are connected in one unbroken chain of vineyards, Margaux stands alone to the south, with its vines spread across five communes—Labarde, Arsac, and Cantenac to the south, Margaux in the center, and Soussans to the north. Margaux and Cantenac are the most important communes and, of course, Margaux contains the *premier cru* of Château Margaux itself. Cantenac has a slightly larger area under vine and no fewer than eight classified growths, including the star-performing Château Palmer, which was partly owned by the late Peter Sichel.

Margaux and Pauillac are the only appellations in the Médoc with *premier cru* vineyards, but only Margaux can boast vineyards in all five categories of the classification. It also has more *cru classé* châteaux than any other Médoc appellation, including an impressive total of 10 *troisièmes crus*.

## FACTORS AFFECTING TASTE AND QUALITY

### ⊞ LOCATION
In the center of the Haut-Médoc, some 17 miles (28 kilometers) northwest of Bordeaux, encompassing the communes of Cantenac, Soussans, Arsac, and Labarde, in addition to Margaux itself.

### ▨ CLIMATE
As for the Médoc (*see* p70).

### ▧ ASPECT
One large, low-lying plateau centering on Margaux, plus several modest outcrops that slope west toward the forest.

### ▦ SOIL
Shallow, pebbly, siliceous gravel over a gravel subsoil interbedded with limestone.

### ⊞ VITICULTURE AND VINIFICATION
Only red wines have the right to the appellation. All grapes must be destalked. On average, between 5 and 10 percent *vin de presse* may be used in the wine, according to the needs of the vintage. Skin contact duration averages 15 to 25 days, with the period of maturation in cask currently varying between 18 and 24 months.

### ⊕ GRAPE VARIETIES
**Primary varieties:** Cabernet Sauvignon, Cabernet Franc, Merlot
**Secondary varieties:** Carmenère, Malbec, Petit Verdot

## MARGAUX CRU CLASSÉ STATISTICS

**Crus classés in AOC Margaux**
21 châteaux (by number: 35% of *crus classés* in the Médoc) with 2,110 acres (854 ha) of vineyards (by area: 35% of *crus classés* in the Médoc and 61% of this AOC)

**1er crus classés**
1 château (by number: 25% of *1er crus classés* in the Médoc) with 185 acres (75 ha) of vineyards (by area: 25% of *1er crus classés* in the Médoc)

**2ème crus classés**
5 châteaux (by number: 36% of *2ème crus classés* in the Médoc) with 670 acres (271 ha) of vineyards (by area: 34% of *2ème crus classés* in the Médoc)

**3ème crus classés**
10 châteaux (by number: 72% of *3ème crus classés* in the Médoc) with 754 acres (305 ha) of vineyards (by area: 72% of *3ème crus classés* in the Médoc)

**4ème crus classés**
3 châteaux (by number: 30% of *4ème crus classés* in the Médoc) with 259 acres (105 ha) of vineyards (by area: 22% of *4ème crus classés* in the Médoc)

**5ème crus classés**
2 châteaux (by number: 11% of *5ème crus classés* in the Médoc) with 242 acres (98 ha) of vineyards (by area: 13% of *5ème crus classés* in the Médoc)

*Château Durfort-Vivens*

● Cru Classé château
○ Other châteaux
— Communal boundary

*Château Palmer*

*Château Prieuré-Lichine*

*Château D'Issan*

*Château Cantenac-Brown*

*Château Siran*

CHÂTEAU MARGAUX
*Margaux's celebrated* premier cru *vineyards are matched by the grandeur of the building itself. Both the building and the wine are justifiably famous.*

MARGAUX, *see also* p63

*Of the classic Médoc appellations, Margaux—the most famous—stands alone to the south, and can boast more* cru classé *châteaux than any of the others.*

## MARGAUX PROFILE

Appellation covers: parts of the communes of Arsac, Cantenac, Labarde, Margaux, and Soussans as follows.

| REGION | SIZE OF COMMUNE | AOC AREA UNDER VINE | VINE AREA AS PROPORTION OF COMMUNE | VINE AREA AS PROPORTION OF APPELLATION |
|---|---|---|---|---|
| Arsac | 7,954 acres (3,219 ha) | 524 acres (212 ha) | 7% | 15% |
| Cantenac | 3,502 acres (1,417 ha) | 963 acres (387 ha) | 27% | 28% |
| Labarde | 1,174 acres (475 ha) | 279 acres (113 ha) | 24% | 8% |
| Margaux | 2,083 acres (843 ha) | 1,006 acres (407 ha) | 48% | 29% |
| Soussans | 3,850 acres (1,558 ha) | 699 acres (283 ha) | 18% | 20% |
| TOTAL | 18,562 acres (7,512 ha) | 3,464 acres (1,402 ha) | 19% | 100% |

Total size of all five communes: 18,562 acres (7,512 ha)
Total AOC area under vine: 3,311 acres (1,402 ha) (19% of communes)
Surface area of crus classés: 2,110 acres (854 ha) (11% of communes, 64% of AOC)

## AN OUTSTANDING WINE

If the massive Pauillac wines of Château Latour and Château Mouton are an object lesson in how it is possible to bombard the senses with power and flavor, and yet retain quite remarkable finesse, then the exquisite wines of Margaux at their very best are perfect proof that complexity does not necessarily issue from an intense concentration of flavor.

However, this is not to suggest that Margaux wines do not actually possess some concentration; indeed, Château Margaux has a particularly remarkable concentration of flavor, and it remains the quintessential wine of this appellation.

NEW CELLAR AT CHÂTEAU MARGAUX
*Evidence of the investment made in Château Margaux since the late 1970s is the refurbished wine store and its full complement of new oak barrels.*

SOUTIRAGE CHÂTEAU MARGAUX
*As the wine matures in the barrel its clarity is checked regularly. It spends between 18 and 24 months in new oak.*

CHÂTEAU CANTENAC BROWN
*This third growth was originally part of Château Boyd, but after the Boyds and Browns—who were joined by marriage in the late 18th century—had a family crisis, the property was divided into Château Boyd-Cantenac and Château Cantenac Brown.*

CHÂTEAU D'ANGLUDET
*Angludet, home of the Sichel family, dates back to Bertrand d'Angludet, who in 1313 swore allegiance to Edward II of England. Owned by Sichel from 1960 till 1999, this property exudes its English heritage, with swans gliding on the brook at the bottom of the property.*

# THE WINE PRODUCERS OF
# MARGAUX

### CHÂTEAU D'ANGLUDET
**Cru Bourgeois Supérieur**
★☆

This château is owned by the Sichel family, who are also part-owners of the star-performing Château Palmer. Since the late 1980s this château has established itself as *cru classé* quality. It will be interesting to see what the next decade brings. The wine is matured in wood for 12 months, with up to one-third new oak.

**RED** Vividly colored, medium- to full-bodied wines with excellent fruit, finesse, and finish—classic Margaux.

🍇 Cabernet Sauvignon 55%, Merlot 35%, Petit Verdot 10%

🍷 10–20 years

**Second wine:** *La Ferme d'Angludet*
**Other wine:** *Clairet d'Angludet*

### CHÂTEAU D'ARSAC
**Cru Bourgeois Supérieur**

Until recently this was the only property in Arsac not to benefit from the Margaux appellation. Since a change in ownership this estate has expanded its vineyards from just over 27 acres (11 hectares) to 252 acres (102 hectares), of which 100 (40 hectares) are now classified as Margaux. The wines are matured in wood for 12 to 18 months, with 20 percent new oak.

**RED** These are deep-colored, full-bodied wines.

🍇 Cabernet Sauvignon 80%, Merlot 15%, Cabernet Franc 5%

🍷 7–15 years

**Second wine:** *Château Ségur-d'Arsac*
**Other wine:** *Château Le Monteil-d'Arsac*

### CHÂTEAU BEL-AIR MARQUIS D'ALIGRE
ⓥ

Château Bel-Air Marquis d'Aligre was classified *cru bourgeois* in 1932, but was not included in the Syndicat's 1978 list, although it is superior to a few that were. The vineyard has limestone subsoil and only organic fertilizers are used.

**RED** Well-made wines of fine color, elegant fruit, with a distinctive style are produced by Château Bel-Air Marquis d'Aligre.

🍇 Merlot 35%, Cabernet Sauvignon 30%, Cabernet Franc 20%, Petit Verdot 15%

🍷 6–12 years

**Second wine:** *Château Bel-Air-Marquis-de-Pomereu*

### CHÂTEAU BOYD-CANTENAC
**3ème Cru Classé**

Château Boyd-Cantenac is a property producing traditional-style wines from old vines. The wine is made at owner Mr. Guillemet's other property, Château Pouget, under the supervision of Professor Peynaud. It is matured in wood for 24 months, with 30 percent new oak and, in my opinion, would benefit from more Merlot and no Petit Verdot.

**RED** Full-bodied, firm wine of good color that needs a long time in bottle to soften. The mediocre 1980 was particularly successful.

🍇 Cabernet Sauvignon 70%, Merlot 20%, Cabernet Franc 5%, Petit Verdot 5%

🍷 12–20 years

### CHÂTEAU BRANE-CANTENAC
**2ème Cru Classé**
★☆ⓥ

This property is a superb plateau of immaculately kept vines situated on gravel over limestone and is owned and run by Henri Lurton. The wine is matured in wood for 18 months, with 25 to 30 percent new oak.

**RED** These stylish wines have a smoky-cream and new-oak bouquet, deliciously rich fruit, and finesse on the palate. They are top-quality wines, velvety and beautifully balanced.

🍇 Cabernet Sauvignon 70%, Cabernet Franc 15%, Merlot 13%, Petit Verdot 2%

🍷 8–25 years

**Second wine:** *Le Baron de Brane*
**Other wines:** *Domaine de Fontarney, Château Notton*

### CHÂTEAU CANTENAC BROWN
**3ème Cru Classé**

Ever since I drank a 50-year-old half-bottle of 1926 Cantenac Brown in splendid condition, I have had a soft spot for this château, which has, frankly, been disproportionate to the quality of its wines. Despite heavy investment after being purchased by AXA in 1989, these wines have not noticeably improved. However, that did not stop Syrian-born, British-based property billionaire Simon Halabi from snapping up this château for a rumored £50 million ($90 million) in 2006. At the time, he insisted that the aim was to invest further in Cantenac Brown, to make it one of the best wines in Margaux.

**RED** Similar in weight to Brane-Cantenac, but with a less velvety and generally more rustic style.

🍇 Cabernet Sauvignon 65%, Merlot 25%, Cabernet Franc 10%

🍷 10–25 years

**Second wine:** *Canuet*
**Other wine:** *Lamartine*

### CHÂTEAU CHARMANT

This property was not classified as a *cru bourgeois* in 1932, nor listed by the Syndicat in 1978, but it certainly deserves recognition today.

**RED** An elegant wine with plenty of fruit and a soft finish, it makes delightful drinking when young.

🍇 Cabernet Sauvignon 60%, Merlot 35%, Cabernet Franc 5%

🍷 3–8 years

### CHÂTEAU DAUZAC
**5ème Cru Classé**
★

Now owned by MAIF and managed by Vignobles André Lurton, the quality of the wines from this château has steadily increased since the mid-1990s. The wine, which is matured in wood for 16 to 18 months with one-third new oak, is steadily improving.

**RED** Ruby-colored, medium-bodied, round, and attractively fruity wines that are easy to drink.

🍇 Cabernet Sauvignon 65%, Merlot 25%, Cabernet Franc 5%, Petit Verdot 5%

🍷 6–12 years

**Second wine:** *Labarde*
**Other wine:** *La Bastide*

### CHÂTEAU DESMIRAIL
**3ème Cru Classé**
☆

A "château with no château" (because the building that was its château was purchased by Château Marquis d'Alesme-Becker), Desmirail has been on the ascent since its purchase by the Lurton family, but it still has some way to go before it becomes a true *troisième cru*. It is owned and run by Denis Lurton, while oenologist Professor Peynaud advises. The wine is matured in wood for 20 months, with 25 to 50 percent new oak.

**RED** A medium-bodied wine that is nicely balanced, with gentle fruit flavors and supple tannins. It is well-made and gradually gaining in finesse.

🍇 Cabernet Sauvignon 80%, Merlot 10%, Cabernet Franc 9%, Petit Verdot 1%

🍷 7–15 years

**Second wine:** *Château Baudry*
**Other wine:** *Domaine de Fontarney*

### CHÂTEAU DEYREM-VALENTIN
**Cru Bourgeois**

This château was classified *cru bourgeois* in 1932, but was not included in the Syndicat's 1978 list, although it is superior to a few that were. Its vineyards adjoin those of Château Lascombes.

**RED** Honest, medium-bodied, fruity wine of some elegance.

🍇 Cabernet Sauvignon 45%, Merlot 45%, Cabernet Franc 5%, Petit Verdot 5%

🍷 4–10 years

### CHÂTEAU DURFORT-VIVENS
**2ème Cru Classé**
★ⓥ

Owned by Gonzague Lurton, who is married to Claire Villars, the administrator of châteaux Chasse-Spleen and Haut-Bages-Libéral. Dufort-Vivens has become one of the best-value *cru classé* wines of Margaux since the mid-1990s. This property matures its wine in wood for 18 to 20 months, with up to one-third new oak.

**RED** Higher tannic structure than Brane-Cantenac, but without the luxurious new-oak character, and with less fruit and charm. The 1985 was particularly rich and impressive.

🍇 Cabernet Sauvignon 82%, Cabernet Franc 10%, Merlot 8%

🍷 10–25 years

**Second wine:** *Second de Durfort*
**Other wine:** *Domaine de Curé-Bourse*

### CHÂTEAU FERRIÈRE
**3ème Cru Classé**
★ⓥ

When managed by Château Lascombes this was little more than second-label status, but it has gained in both exposure and quality since this property was purchased by the Villars family.

**RED** Quick-maturing wine of medium weight and accessible fruit.

🍇 Cabernet Sauvignon 75%, Merlot 20%, Petit Verdot 5%

🍷 4–8 years

**Second wine:** *Les Remparts de Ferrière*

## CHÂTEAU GISCOURS
### 3ème Cru Classé
★★⯪

This property is situated in the commune of Labarde. It was purchased in 1952 by the Tari family, who have restored the château, the vineyard, and the quality of its wine to their former glory. In 1995 the château was sold to Eric Albada Jelgersma, a Dutch businessman who has at least maintained the quality and, arguably, improved it. The wine is matured in wood for 20 to 34 months, with 50 percent new oak.

**RED** Vividly colored wine, rich in fruit and finesse. Its vibrant style keeps it remarkably fresh for years.

Cabernet Sauvignon 75%, Merlot 22%, Cabernet Franc 2%, Petit Verdot 1%

8–30 years

**Second wine:** *La Sirène de Giscours*
**Other wine:** *Cantelaude*

## CHÂTEAU LA GURGUE
### Cru Bourgeois Supérieur

This property was classified *cru bourgeois* in 1932, but not included in the 1978 list, although it is superior to a few that were. Its proprietor also owns *cru classé* Haut-Bages-Libéral and *cru bourgeois exceptionnel* Chasse-Spleen.

**RED** Soft, elegant, medium-bodied wine of attractive flavor and some finesse, improving since 2000.

Cabernet Sauvignon 70%, Merlot 25%, Petit Verdot 5%

4–12 years

## CHÂTEAU D'ISSAN
### 3ème Cru Classé
★★

This beautiful 17th-century château is frequently cited as the most impressive in the entire Médoc, and its remarkable wines, matured in wood for 18 months, with up to one-third new oak, are consistently just as spectacular.

**RED** This wine really is glorious! Its luxuriant bouquet is immediately seductive, its fruit is unbelievably rich and sumptuous. A great wine of great finesse.

Cabernet Sauvignon 85%, Merlot 15%

10–40 years

**Second wine:** *Blason d'Issan*
**Other wine:** *De Candel*

## CHÂTEAU KIRWAN
### 3ème Cru Classé
★★⯪ⓥ

Château Kirwan is a well-run and improving property owned by the Bordeaux négociant Schröder & Schÿler with Michel Rolland consulting. The wine is matured in wood for 18 to 24 months, with up to 50 percent new oak.

**RED** Deep-colored, full-bodied, rich and concentrated wines that are well-made and gaining in generosity, riper tannins, and new oak influence with each passing vintage.

Cabernet Sauvignon 40%, Merlot 30%, Cabernet Franc 20%, Petit Verdot 10%

10–35 years

**Second wine:** *Les Charmes de Kirwan*

## CHÂTEAU LABÉGORCE
### Cru Bourgeois Supérieur
★ⓥ

This château was classified *cru bourgeois* in 1932, but not included in the 1978 list. Since Hubert Perrodo, a wine-loving oil tycoon, purchased Labégorce in 1989, the quality and price of its wines have increased steadily. Matured in wood for 18 months, with up to one-third new oak.

**RED** Well-colored wine with good balance of concentration and finesse.

Cabernet Sauvignon 55%, Merlot 40%, Cabernet Franc 5%

5–15 years

## CHÂTEAU LABÉGORCE-ZÉDÉ
### Cru Bourgeois Exceptionnel
★★⯪ⓥ

Classified *cru bourgeois* in 1932, but not included in the 1978 list, although it is one of the best non-*cru classé* wines of the commune.

**RED** Fine flavor and great length, combined with a certain complexity, give the wines of this château an edge over those of Labégorce.

Cabernet Sauvignon 50%, Merlot 35%, Cabernet Franc 10%, Petit Verdot 5%

5–15 years

**Second wine:** *Château de l'Amiral*

## CHÂTEAU LASCOMBES
### 2ème Cru Classé
★★

Owned by Bass Group, the wines of this large property have always been good, yet they have improved dramatically under René Vanatelle. It was Vanatelle who recognized that only 125 of Lascombes' 208 acres (50 of 83 hectares) were of authentic *deuxième cru* potential. He therefore segregated the vineyard and sold the lesser wines as Château Segonnes. This accounted for the noticeable step up in quality in the 1980s. Then in 1997, the year before he retired,

Vanatelle introduced a true second wine, Chevalier des Lascombes, which has pushed standards up yet another notch, before handing over to Bruno Lemoine, formerly of Montrose. The wine is matured in wood for 14 to 20 months, with one-third new oak.

**RED** Full-bodied, rich, and concentrated wine with ripe fruit, a lovely cedarwood complexity, and supple tannin.

Cabernet Sauvignon 55%, Merlot 40%, Petit Verdot 5%

8–30 years

**Second wine:** *Chevalier Lascombes*
**Other wines:** *Château Segonnes, Gombaud, Rosé de Lascombes, Vin Sec Chevalier Lascombes*

## CHÂTEAU MALESCOT ST-EXUPÉRY
### 3ème Cru Classé
★

English-owned until 1955, when it was purchased by Roger Zuger, whose brother owns Château Marquis-d'Alesme-Becker. The wine is matured in wood for 18 months, with 20 percent new oak.

**RED** Richer, more complex wines have been produced since 1996.

Cabernet Sauvignon 50%, Merlot 35%, Cabernet Franc 10%, Petit Verdot 5%

8–25 years

**Second wines:** *Château De Loyac, La Dame de Malescot*
**Other wine:** *Balardin*

## CHÂTEAU MARGAUX
### 1er Cru Classé
★★★ⓥ

This is the most famous wine in the world and, since its glorious rebirth in 1978, the greatest. Its quality may occasionally be matched, but it is never surpassed. Purchased in 1977 for 72 million francs ($14.5 million) by the late André Mentzelopoulos, who spent an equal sum renovating it, this fabulous jewel in the crown of the Médoc is now run by his daughter, Corinne Mentzelopoulos. Both Château Margaux and its second wine, "Pavillon Rouge," are vinified in oak vats and matured for 18 to 24 months in 100 percent new oak.

**RED** If finesse can be picked up on the nose, then the stunning, complex bouquet of Château Margaux is the yardstick. The softness, finesse, and velvety texture of this wine belie its depth. Amazingly rich and concentrated, with an elegant, long, and complex finish supported by ripe tannins and wonderful smoky-

creamy oak aromas. This is as near perfection as we will ever get.

Cabernet Sauvignon 75%, Merlot 20%, Cabernet Franc and Petit Verdot 5%

15–50 years

**Second wine:** *Pavillon Rouge du Château Margaux*
**Other wine:** *Pavillon Blanc du Château Margaux*

## CHÂTEAU MARQUIS D'ALESME-BECKER
### 3ème Cru Classé

Like Château Malescot St.-Exupéry, this was English-owned until purchased by Jean-Claude Zuger, who also purchased the maison of neighboring Desmirail to act as its château. The wine is matured in wood for 12 months, with one-sixth new oak.

**RED** Austere and charmless wines from my point of view, although they have their admirers. They are well-made, but lack sufficient selection, although the terroir has potential.

Cabernet Sauvignon 40%, Merlot 30%, Cabernet Franc 20%, Petit Verdot 10%

8–20 years

**Second wine:** *Marquise d'Alesme*

## CHÂTEAU MARQUIS-DE-TERME
### 4ème Cru Classé

Situated next to Château Margaux, this once majestic estate developed the reputation for producing tight, tannic, one-dimensional wines, but its quality has picked up since the late 1970s and has been performing extremely well since 1983. The wine is matured in wood for 24 months, with one-third new oak.

**RED** Appears to be developing a style that is ripe and rich, with definite and delightful signs of new oak. The 1984 was quite a revelation.

Cabernet Sauvignon 60%, Merlot 30%, Petit Verdot 7%, Cabernet Franc 3%

10–25 years

**Second wine:** *Terme des Goudat*

## CHÂTEAU MARSAC-SÉGUINEAU
### Cru Bourgeois

This property was classified *cru bourgeois* in 1932, but not included in the Syndicat's 1978 list, although it is superior to a few that were. The vineyards of this château include some plots that originally belonged to a *cru classé*.

**RED** Medium- to full-bodied wines of good bouquet and a soft style.

Cabernet Sauvignon 65%, Merlot 35%

5–12 years

**Second wine:** *Château Gravières-de-Marsac*

## CHÂTEAU MONBRISON
### Cru Bourgeois Supérieur
★ ✿

These vineyards used to be part of *cru classé* Château Desmirail; the wines were excellent 10 years ago, and now vie with those of true *cru classé* standard.

**RED** This château's second label offers a brilliant selection of beautifully deep-colored wines with spicy-oak, superrich juicy fruit, and a fine structure of supple tannin.

🍇 Merlot 35%, Cabernet Franc 30%, Cabernet Sauvignon 30%, Petit Verdot 5%

🍷 8–15 years

**Second wine:** *Château Cordat*

## CHÂTEAU MONTBRUN

Château Montbrun was classified *cru bourgeois* in 1932, but not included in the Syndicat's 1978 list, although it is superior to a few that were. This used to be part of *cru classé* Château Palmer.

**RED** Beautifully made, ripe, and juicy, medium- to full-bodied, Merlot-dominated wines.

🍇 Merlot 75%, Cabernet Franc and Cabernet Sauvignon 25%

🍷 5–12 years

## CHÂTEAU PALMER
### 3ème Cru Classé
★★☆

Only Château Margaux outshines this property, jointly owned by Belgian, French, and British (the Sichel family) interests. Château Palmer 1961 and 1966 regularly fetch prices at auction that equal those fetched by the *premiers crus*. Judged at the very highest level, it could be more consistent. It is usually excellent, but not always astonishing—although when it is, it can stand shoulder to shoulder with *premiers crus* in a blind tasting. A true supersecond that promises to achieve even greater heights since the introduction of Alto Ego, a sort of superpremium of second wines, in 1998. The wine is matured in wood for 18 to 24 months, with one-third new oak.

**RED** Almost opaque-colored, with masses of cassis fruit and an exceedingly rich, intense, and complex construction of creamy, spicy, cedarwood, and vanilla flavors.

🍇 Cabernet Sauvignon 50%, Merlot 40%, Cabernet Franc 7%, Petit Verdot 3%

🍷 12–35 years

**Second wines:** *Alto Ego, Réserve du Général*

## CHÂTEAU PONTAC-LYNCH
### Cru Bourgeois
★ ✿

This property was classified *cru bourgeois* in 1932, but not included in the Syndicat's 1978 list, although it is superior to a few that were. The vineyards are well-situated, and surrounded by *crus classés*.

**RED** Richly perfumed, deeply colored, full-bodied wines of good structure.

🍇 Cabernet Sauvignon and Merlot 47%, Cabernet Franc 45%, Petit Verdot 8%

🍷 6–15 years

**Second wine:** *Pontac-Phénix*

## CHÂTEAU POUGET
### 4ème Cru Classé
❓

Under the same ownership as Boyd-Cantenac, this property houses the winemaking and storage facilities for both châteaux. The wine is matured in wood for 22 to 24 months, with 30 percent new oak.

**RED** Well-colored, full-bodied wine with good depth of flavor. Good, but not great, and could be more consistent.

🍇 Cabernet Sauvignon 70%, Merlot 17%, Cabernet Franc 8%, Petit Verdot 5%

🍷 10–25 years

## CHÂTEAU PRIEURÉ-LICHINE
### 4ème Cru Classé
★

The late Alexis Lichine purchased Château Prieuré in 1951 and added his name to it. To develop the small rundown vineyard, he bought various prized plots of vines from Palmer, Kirwan, Giscours, Boyd-Cantenac, Brane-Cantenac, and Durfort-Vivens—some 148 acres (60 hectares). The composite classification must be higher than its official status—the wines certainly are. Lichine's son Sacha ran the property until 1999, when he sold it. The current owners, the Ballande family, have steadily improved the quality under top consultant Stéphane Derenoncourt. The wines are matured in wood for 19 months, with one-third new oak.

**RED** Well-colored, full-bodied wines, plummy and rich, with good blackcurrant fruit supported by supple tannins and a touch of vanilla-oak.

🍇 Cabernet Sauvignon 54%, Merlot 39%, Cabernet Franc 2%, Petit Verdot 5%

🍷 7–20 years

**Second wine:** *Château De Clairefont*

## CHÂTEAU RAUZAN-GASSIES
### 2ème Cru Classé
★☆

Until the French Revolution of 1789, this property and Château Rauzan-Ségla were one large estate. The globe-trotting Professor Peynaud was brought in to steer this wine back on course in the early 1980s, but he failed miserably. Jean-Louis Camp, formerly of Loudenne, seems to be having more success. The wine is matured in wood for 17 to 20 months, with 20 percent new oak, although there is little evidence of it on the palate.

**RED** The 1996 and 1998 suggested an upturn in quality, and this has been partly realized in vintages like 2000 and 2002, but the quality is still frustratingly patchy.

🍇 Cabernet Sauvignon 40%, Merlot 39%, Cabernet Franc 20%, Petit Verdot 1%

🍷 7–15 years

**Second wine:** *Enclos de Moncabon*

## CHÂTEAU RAUZAN-SÉGLA
### 2ème Cru Classé

★★☆

The quality of this once-disappointing château began to lift in the 1980s due to significant investment in the property from its owner, the Bordeaux négociant house of Eschenauer, which also instigated a far stricter selection of the *grand vin*. In 1994 Rauzan-Ségla was sold to Chanel, the underbidder for Latour (sold by Allied-Lyons to the French industrialist François Pinault). Since then key personnel from the *premier cru* have been brought in to keep the improvements in full swing. The wine is matured in wood for 20 months, with 50 percent new oak, and is currently one of Bordeaux's top-performing *deuxièmes crus*.

**RED** In classic years, this wine is deep and dark, with a powerful tannic construction, and more than enough intensely flavored fruit to match. Lesser vintages are dark for the year, but much more lush, with softer tannins.

🍇 Cabernet Sauvignon 65%, Merlot 30%, Cabernet Franc 5%

🍷 15–30 years

**Second wine:** *Ségla*
**Other wines:** *Lamouroux*

## CHÂTEAU SIRAN
### Cru Bourgeois Exceptionnel
★★☆ ✿

The vineyard is well situated, with immaculately manicured vines that border those of châteaux Giscours and Dauzac. The wine is matured in wood for 24 months, with one-third new oak, in air-conditioned cellars. Owned by the Miailhe de Burgh family, who are direct descendants of Sir Patrick Sarsfield, the daring Irish Jacobite who gave William of Orange such a bloody nose.

**RED** Stylish, aromatic wines of good body, creamy-spicy fruit,

length, and obvious class. Easily equivalent to *cru classé* quality.

🍇 Cabernet Sauvignon 40%, Merlot 35%, Petit Verdot 20%, Cabernet Franc 5%

🍷 8–20 years

**Second wine:** *Château Bellegarde*
**Other wines:** *Château St-Jacques*

## CHÂTEAU TAYAC
### Cru Bourgeois

As Bernard Ginestet, whose family owned Château Margaux for 40 years, once wrote, "this is one of the largest of the smaller properties, and one of the smallest of the larger."

**RED** Firm, medium- to full-bodied wines of good character, although somewhat rustic; they tend to be coarse in lesser years.

🍇 Cabernet Sauvignon 65%, Merlot 25%, Cabernet Franc 5%, Petit Verdot 5%

🍷 6–12 years

## CHÂTEAU DU TERTRE
### 5ème Cru Classé
★★☆

An underrated *cru classé*, this château has well-situated vineyards. It is under the same ownership as Giscours since 1998. The wine is matured in wood for 24 months, with 25 percent new oak.

**RED** Although the scent of violets is supposed to be common to Margaux wines, this is one of the few in which I pick it up. The wine is medium- to full-bodied, rich in fragrant fruit, and has excellent balance, with obvious class.

🍇 Cabernet Sauvignon 85%, Cabernet Franc 5%, Merlot 10%

🍷 8–25 years

## CHÂTEAU LA TOUR DE MONS
### Cru Bourgeois Supérieur

These wines are aged in wood for 22 months, with 20 percent new oak and have improved enormously since the late 1980s. Easily equivalent to *cru classé* quality.

**RED** As richly flavored as ever, but without the tannins or acidity that used to be this wine's pitfall.

🍇 Cabernet Sauvignon 45%, Merlot 40%, Cabernet Franc 10%, Petit Verdot 5%

🍷 10–30 years

**Second wine:** *Château Rucheterre*

## CHÂTEAU DES TROIS-CHARDONS
★☆ ✿

A tiny production of very high-quality wine from a château named after the current owner, a Monsieur Chardon, and his two sons.

**RED** Ultraclean, soft, fruity but serious wines of some finesse and well-defined Margaux character.

🍇 Cabernet Sauvignon 50%, Merlot 40%, Cabernet Franc 10%

🍷 6–15 years

# GRAVES, CÉRONS, SAUTERNES, AND BARSAC

*The finest red Graves wines are produced in Pessac-Léognan, good red and improving dry white wines in the center of Graves, and the great sweet wines of Sauternes and Barsac in the south. The emphasis in production is on classic red wines.*

THE SILKY-SMOOTH red wines of the Graves district have been famous since the Middle Ages, when they were protected by local laws that punished those who dared to blend them with other Bordeaux wines. Château Haut-Brion was the only red wine outside the Médoc to be classified in 1855, and such was its reputation that it was placed alongside the *premiers crus* of Latour, Lafite, and Margaux. Beneath Haut-Brion, there are a few great wines equivalent in quality to *deuxième* or *troisième cru*, but only a few.

The relative lack of superstars in Graves is offset by a higher base quality of wine and greater consistency of performance in the red wines at least. There are 43 communes in this appellation. Much the best are Léognan, Talence, and Pessac, after which Martillac and Portets are the most outstanding, followed by Illats and Podensac. All the greatest wines are therefore in the north of the Graves district, amid the urban sprawl of Bordeaux, and this presents something of a problem. The once-peaceful left bank of the Garonne is slowly and inexorably disappearing. As the city bursts outward, more rural vineyards are encircled by the concrete jungle, and many quite simply vanish. How many Bordeaux

aficionados who fly directly to the airport in Mérignac stop to consider the cost of such progress? In 1908 there were 30 winemaking properties in the commune of Mérignac; today there is just one—Château Picque-Caillou. The conurbated communes of Cadaujac, Gradignan, Léognan, Martillac, Mérignac, Pessac, Talence, and Villenave d'Ornon have lost 214 wine châteaux over the same period.

## THE PROBLEM OF WHITE GRAVES SOLVED

Well almost! While the quality and reputation of the red wines have always been well established, white Graves had a serious identity problem that came to a crisis point in the mid-1980s. Although fine white Graves were being produced, most of it was in the northern communes, but they were tarred with the same brush as the worst white wines from farther south. It was not simply a north–south divide; there was also an identity problem— should they be making rich, oak-aged blends or light and fluffy Sauvignon Blanc? Paradoxically, the worst wines came from some of the best properties in the north, produced by winemakers who either did not know how to, or did not care to, clean up their act, as they continued to sell tired, oversulfured, oxidized, and flabby wines on the backs of their decaying reputations.

An official north-south divide, however, proved to be the solution for, since 1987, when the Pessac-Léognan AOC was introduced, things have never looked better for Graves. The Pessac-Léognan appellation is a single appellation for both red and white wines from the communes Cadaujac, Canéjan, Gradignan, Léognan, Martillac, Mérignac, Pessac, St.-Médard-d'Eyrans, Talence, and Villenave d'Ornon. This has had the effect of giving the northern châteaux the official quality recognition

GRAVES, CÉRONS, SAUTERNES, AND BARSAC, *see also p63*
*The winemaking area that includes Graves, Cérons, Sauternes, and Barsac forms a swathe that sweeps down from Bordeaux, parallel with the Garonne.*

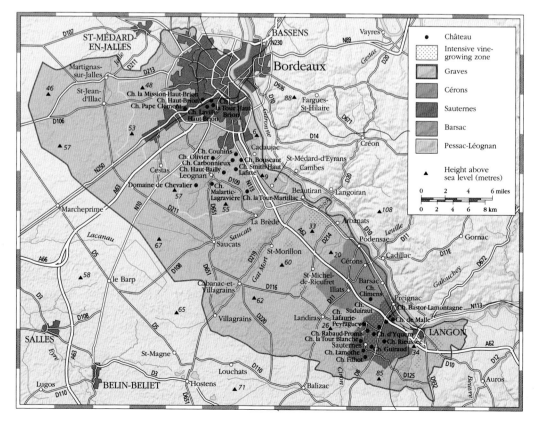

VINES AT HAUT-BRION
*Rose bushes at the end of each row act as a pest early-warning system.*

## THE CLASSIFICATION OF GRAVES

The only Graves property to be classified in 1855 was Château Haut-Brion. The Syndicat, for the defense of the Graves appellation, wanted to create its own classification, but was prevented from doing so until the 1921 law was changed in 1949. The first classification was not made until 1953, and this itself was later modified in 1959.

Distinction is made between red wines and white wines, but no attempt at ranking between the various growths is made—they all have the right to use the term *cru classé*. It can be seen from the 1,320 acres (535 hectares) of classified properties listed below that this represents not much more than 13 percent of the total 1,745 acres (4,350 hectares) of delimited vineyards planted in the Graves and Pessac-Léognan appellation.

| RED WINES | COMMUNE | AREA CURRENTLY UNDER VINE | AREA CURRENTLY UNDER VINE |
|---|---|---|---|
| Château Bouscaut | Cadaujac | 96 acres | (39 ha) |
| Château Carbonnieux | Léognan | 124 acres | (50 ha) |
| Domaine de Chevalier | Léognan | 82 acres | (33 ha) |
| Château de Fieuzal | Léognan | 96 acres | (39 ha) |
| Château Haut-Bailly | Léognan | 69 acres | (28 ha) |
| Château Haut-Brion | Pessac | 106 acres | (43 ha) |
| Château La Mission -Haut-Brion | Pessac | 52 acres | (21 ha) |
| Château Latour-Haut- Brion | Talence | 12 acres | (5 ha) |
| Château La Tour- Martillac | Martillac | 69 acres | (28 ha) |
| Château Malartic- Lagravière | Léognan | 91 acres | (37 ha) |
| Château Olivier | Léognan | 94 acres | (38 ha) |
| Château Pape-Clément | Pessac | 74 acres | (30 ha) |
| Château Smith-Haut- Lafite | Martillac | 109 acres | (44 ha) |
| TOTAL AREA UNDER VINE | | 1,075*ACRES | (435 HA) |

| WHITE WINES | COMMUNE | AREA CURRENTLY UNDER VINE | AREA CURRENTLY UNDER VINE |
|---|---|---|---|
| Château Bouscaut | Cadaujac | 20 acres | (8 ha) |
| Château Carbonnieux | Léognan | 104 acres | (42 ha) |
| Domaine de Chevalier | Léognan | 12 acres | (5 ha) |
| Château de Fieuzal | Léognan | 20 acres | (8 ha) |
| Château Couhins- Lurton | Villenave | 13 ha | (32 acres) |
| Château Haut-Brion | Pessac | 10 acres | (3 ha) |
| Château La Tour- Martillac | Martillac | 25 acres | (10 ha) |
| Château Laville- Haut-Brion | Talence | 10 acres | (4 ha) |
| Château Malartic- Lagravière | Léognan | 17 acres | (7 ha) |
| TOTAL AREA UNDER VINE | | 250*ACRES | (100 HA) |

*Note—These figures are not precise conversions of the hectare totals, but are column totals and differ because of rounding up.

VINEYARDS AT CHÂTEAU D'YQUEM
*Here, the winter vineyard shows the characteristic sandy-pebbly clay topsoil and the system of wires and stakes that supports the vines. Yquem's clay subsoil contains 62 miles (100 kilometers) of terra-cotta pipes, which were laid down at the end of the 19th century to provide perfect drainage.*

THE GLOWING TINTS OF CHÂTEAU D'YQUEM
*Château d'Yquem vintages, stretching back from a bottle of the 1980. The younger wines are a rich gold with a greenish tinge, deepening to old gold and amber with the older vintages.*

CHÂTEAU D'YQUEM: THE INNER COURTYARD
*A huge stone well dominates the square central courtyard of this beautiful château, which comprises disparate elements dating from the 15th, 16th, and 17th centuries.*

they both wanted and deserved. It was a bit slow to start off—after all, Pessac-Léognan hardly trips off the tongue and there were worries about its marketability. There is still a tendency to put Graves on labels, and use Pessac-Léognan to qualify the wine as if it were a higher classification of Graves, which for all practical purposes it is.

Once the châteaux realized that foreign markets were picking up on the superior connotation of Pessac-Léognan, use of the appellation soon became widespread. Whether by their own volition or due to peer pressure, many of the underperformers have become the most quality-conscious châteaux in the appellation, and it has spurred producers in the south to improve their wines. They do not like being considered inferior, and as they intend to prove they are not, the consumer can only gain.

## CÉRONS

This is an area situated within the boundaries of Graves. It is the stepping stone between dry white Graves, and sweet white Sauternes and Barsac. The châteaux of Cérons have been given the official right to make both red and white Graves, Graves Supérieur (which may be dry but is usually sweet) and, of course, the sweet wine of Cérons—a wine that has enjoyed a modest reputation for nearly 200 years. In fact, only 20 percent of the production in this area is sold as Cérons since the appellation covers three communes, those of Illats, Podensac, and Cérons itself. Many of the vineyards comprise scattered plots, some of which are partially planted with acacias.

## SAUTERNES AND BARSAC

The gap between ordinary sweet white wines and the great wines of Sauternes and Barsac is as wide as that between sweet and dry wines. What creates this gap is something called "complexity"—to

TRADITIONAL HORSE-DRAWN PLOW
*At Château d'Yquem workhorses are used to help plow the topsoil between the rows, both after the harvest and again in March.*

find out what that is, sample the aroma of a glass of mature Sauternes. The wines produced in Sauternes are not only the world's most luscious, but also the most complex wines. I have seen hardened men who resolutely refuse to drink anything sweeter than lemon juice go weak at the knees after one sniff of Château Suduiraut, and I defy the most stubborn and bigoted anti-sweet wine drinker not to drool over a glass of Château d'Yquem 1967. Astonishingly, there are dissenters, but for me Yquem is by far the best wine of these two appellations, Sauternes and Barsac. The battle for second place is always between the soft, luscious style of Suduiraut, and the rich, powerful character of Rieussec, with Climens, Nairac, and the nonclassified growths of Gilette and de Fargues in close pursuit. Guiraud has the potential to go right to the top, and with so many châteaux seriously improving, they could all end up chasing each other for the number two spot.

### The "noble rot"

Yquem might be the ultimate sweet white wine, but many other great wines are made in these two small areas tucked away in the Bordeaux backwaters. What gives all these wines their hallmark of complexity is, literally, a lot of rot—namely "noble rot," or the fungal growth *Botrytis cinerea*. The low-lying hills of Sauternes and, to a lesser extent, of Barsac, together with a naturally warm but humid climate, provide a natural breeding ground for botrytis, the spores of which are indigenous to the area. They remain dormant in the vineyard soil and on vine bark until they are activated by suitable conditions—alternate moisture and heat (the early-morning mist being followed by hot, mid-morning sunshine). The spores latch on to the skin of each grape, replacing its structure with a fungal growth and feeding on moisture from within the grape. They also devour five-sixths of the grape's acidity and one-third of its sugar, but as the amount of water consumed is between one-half and two-thirds, the effect is to concentrate the juice into a sticky, sugar-rich pulp. A healthy, ripe grape with a potential of 13 percent alcohol is thus converted into a mangy-looking mess with a potential of between 17.5

percent and 26 percent. The spread of botrytis through a vineyard is neither orderly nor regular, and the harvest may take as long as 10 weeks to complete, with the pickers making various sorties, or *tries*, through the vineyard. On each *trie*, only the affected grapes should be picked, but care must be taken to leave some rot on each bunch to facilitate its spread. The longer the growers await the miraculous "noble rot," the more the vines are prone to the ravages of frost, snow, hail, and rain, any of which could destroy an entire crop

The viticulture of Sauternes and Barsac is the most labor-intensive of any region. The yield is very low, officially a maximum of 112 cases per acre (25 hectoliters per hectare), about half that in the Médoc, and the levels achieved in the best châteaux are much lower, around 67 to 90 cases per acre (15 to 20 hectoliters per hectare). At Yquem it is even less, the equivalent of one glass per vine. On top of all this, the vinification is, at the very least, difficult to handle, and maturation of a fine sweet wine demands a good proportion of very expensive new oak.

### Variations in character

Not all the sugar is used up during fermentation, even when a wine of perhaps 14 to 15 percent alcohol is made. The remaining unfermented sugar, often between 50 and 120 grams per liter, gives the wine its natural sweetness. However, unlike Sauternes' German counterparts, its alcohol level is crucial to its character. Its strength, in harmony with the wine's sweetness, acidity, and fruit give it a lusciousness of concentration that simply cannot be matched. Its complexity is not, however, the effect of concentration, although an increased mineral level is no doubt an influence. Complexity is created by certain new elements that are introduced into the grape's juice during the metabolic activities of its botrytis—glycerol, gluconic acid, saccharic acid, dextrin, various oxidizing enzymes, and an elusive antibiotic substance called "botrycine."

It is easy to explain how these components of a botrytized wine that form its inimitably complex character can vary. When tasting wine from different *tries* at the same château, the intensity of botrytized character varies according to the "age" of the fungus when the grapes are harvested. Wines made from the same percentage of botrytized grapes collected at the beginning and end of the harvest are noticeably mute compared to those in the middle when the rot is at its most rampant. If it is not surprising that youthful *Botrytis cinerea* has an undeveloped character, the same cannot be said of late-harvested. Many people believe that the longer botrytis establishes itself, the more potent its effect, but this is not true.

CHÂTEAU DE FARGUES
*The original family home of the Lur-Saluces family is now a ghostly ruin. The family moved to Yquem in 1785 upon its union with the De Sauvage family.*

**THE "POURRITURE NOBLE," OR NOBLE ROT**
*A bunch of Sémillon grapes ready for the first* trie. *Some of the grapes are still unaffected by the fungus, some are affected and discolored but not shriveled, others are dried, withered, and covered with the fungus bloom.*

## FACTORS AFFECTING TASTE AND QUALITY

### LOCATION
The left bank of the Garonne river, stretching southeast from just north of Bordeaux to 6 miles (10 kilometers) east of Langon. Cérons, Sauternes, and Barsac are tucked into the southern section of the Graves district.

### CLIMATE
Very similar to the Médoc, but fractionally hotter and with slightly more rainfall. In Sauternes and Barsac it is mild and humid, with an all-important fall alternation of misty mornings and later sunshine, the ideal conditions for "noble rot."

### ASPECT
The suburbs of Bordeaux sprawl across the northern section of this district, becoming more rural beyond Cadaujac. Graves has a much hillier terrain than the Médoc, with little valleys cut out by myriad streams that drain into the Garonne. Some of the vineyards here are very steep. The communes of Sauternes, Bommes, and Fargues are hilly, but Preignac and Barsac, on either side of the Ciron—a small tributary of the Garonne—have gentler slopes.

### SOIL
Traveling south through the district, the gravelly topsoil of Graves gradually becomes mixed with sand, then with weathered limestone and eventually with clay. The subsoil also varies, but basically it is iron-pan, limestone, and clay, either pure or mixed. Cérons has a stony soil, mostly flint and gravel, over marl; there is reddish clay-gravel over clay, or gravelly iron-pan in Sauternes, and clay-limestone over clay-gravel in Fargues. The gravel slopes of Bommes are sometimes mixed with heavy clay soils, while the plain is sandy clay with a reddish clay or limestone subsoil. Preignac is sand, gravel, and clay over clay-gravel in the south, becoming more alluvial over sand, clay, and limestone closer to Barsac. Where the classified growths of Barsac are situated, the soil is clay-limestone over limestone, elsewhere the topsoil mingles with sandy gravel.

### VITICULTURE AND VINIFICATION
Some châteaux add a certain amount of *vin de presse* to the red wine. The *cuvaison* varies between eight and 15 days, although some Graves châteaux permit 15–25 days. Maturation in cask is generally between 15 and 18 months. The sweet white wines of Sauternes and Barsac are made from several *tries* of late-harvested, overripe grapes which, ideally, have "noble rot." Destalking is usually unnecessary. The fermentation of grape juice so high in sugar content is difficult to start and awkward to control, but it is usually over within two to eight weeks. The exact period of fermentation depends upon the style desired. Many of the best wines are matured in cask for one and a half to three and a half years.

### GRAPE VARIETIES
**Primary varieties:** Cabernet Sauvignon, Cabernet Franc, Merlot, Sémillon, Sauvignon Blanc.
**Secondary varieties:** Malbec, Petit Verdot, Muscadelle.

### The rewards, the reality, and the future
A good Sauternes is the most arduous, expensive, and frustrating wine in the world to produce—and what is the winemaker's reward? Very little, I'm afraid. Aside from Château d'Yquem— not only the greatest Sauternes but some would argue the greatest wine *per se*—the wines of this region fail to realize their true worth. This is predictable in a world where the trend is toward lighter and drier styles of wine, and may have a positive short-term effect for Sauternes *aficionados*, for it means a cheaper supply of their favorite wine. In the long term, however, this is not a positive way to operate, and some proprietors simply cannot afford to go on. The Comte de Pontac uprooted all the vines at his *deuxième cru* Château de Myrat in Barsac, and even the ever-optimistic Tom Heeter, former owner of Château Nairac, once said, "You have to be at least half-crazy to make a living out of these wines." We certainly do not deserve the luscious wines of Sauternes and Barsac if we continue to ignore them, but if the authorities had more sense, and the owners more business acumen, these wines could literally become "liquid gold."

### The only way ahead
The vineyards of Sauternes and Barsac should also be allowed to sell red and dry white wines under the Graves appellation. If this is a right accorded to modest Cérons, why not to its illustrious neighbors? Many châteaux already make red and dry white wines, but they are sold under the cheaper "Bordeaux" appellation. Tom Heeter was right, the proprietors must be half-crazy, because their motivation for producing these alternative products is to subsidize the cost of making their botrytized wine, when they should be trying to supplement their incomes. Given the incentive of a superior appellation, the châteaux should concentrate on making the finest red and dry white wines every year. Only when conditions appear favorable should some of the white grape crop be left on the vine, with fingers crossed for an abundance of *Botrytis cinerea*. Instead of these châteaux investing in new oak for modest vintages, they should utilize the casks for the red and the dry white. The result would be a tiny amount of the world's most luscious wine, maybe three or four years in 10. It would no longer be necessary to attempt the impossible task of selling an old-fashioned image to young wine drinkers; the limited supply would outstrip the current demand. After 30 years of watching this area's vain attempts to win over popular support for its wines, I have come to accept the view of Comte Alexandre de Lur-Saluces, proprietor of Château d'Yquem. When asked to justify the price of Yquem, he simply said his wines are not made for everyone; they are made for those who can afford them.

THE APPELLATIONS OF
# GRAVES, CÉRONS, SAUTERNES, AND BARSAC

## BARSAC AOC

The commune of Barsac is one of five that have the right to the Sauternes appellation. (The others are Preignac, Fargues, Bommes, and Sauternes itself.) Some generic wines sold in bulk may take advantage of this, but all individual properties are sold as Barsac. The wine must include overripe botrytized grapes harvested in *tries*.

**WHITE** Luscious, intensely sweet wines similar in style to Sauternes, but perhaps lighter in weight, slightly drier, and less rich. As in Sauternes, 1983 is one of the best vintages of the 20th century.

🍇 Sémillon, Sauvignon Blanc, Muscadelle

🍷 6–25 years for most wines; between 15–60 years for the greatest

## CÉRONS AOC

These inexpensive wines from an area adjacent to Barsac are the best value-for-money sweet wines in Bordeaux. They must include overripe botrytized grapes harvested in *tries*.

**WHITE** Lighter than Barsac, but often just as luscious, the best of these wines can show true botrytis complexity.

🍇 Sémillon, Sauvignon Blanc, Muscadelle

🍷 6–15 years for most wines

## GRAVES AOC

This appellation begins at the Jalle de Blanquefort, where the Médoc finishes and runs for 37 miles (60 kilometers) along the left bank of the Garonne. Almost two-thirds of the wine is red, and is consistently high in quality and value.

**RED** I was brought up on the notion that with full maturity a Graves reveals itself through a certain earthiness of character. Experience has taught me the opposite. The biggest Graves from hot years can have a denseness that may combine with the smoky character of new oak to give the wine a roasted or tobaccolike

complexity, but Graves is intrinsically clean. Its hallmark is its vivid fruit, clarity of style, silky texture, and hints of violets.

🍇 Cabernet Sauvignon, Cabernet Franc, Merlot Secondary grape varieties: Malbec, Petit Verdot

🍷 6–15 years

**WHITE** This is the disappointing half of the appellation: light- to full-bodied, from pure Sauvignon to pure Sémillon (with all proportions of blends in between, flabby to zingy, and unoaked to heavily oaked). Pay strict attention to the château profiles on the following pages. These wines may be sold from December 1 following the harvest without any mention of *primeur* or *nouveau*.

🍇 Sémillon, Sauvignon Blanc, Muscadelle

🍷 1–2 years for modest wines; 8–20 years for the best

## GRAVES SUPÉRIEUR AOC

Some surprisingly good would-be Barsacs lurk beneath this appellation that is rarely seen, yet accounts for more than one-fifth of all white Graves produced.

**WHITE** This wine can be dry, but most is a sweet style, similar to Barsac.

🍇 Sémillon, Sauvignon Blanc, Muscadelle

🍷 6–15 years

## PESSAC-LÉOGNAN AOC

Introduced in September 1987, this appellation covers the 10 best communes that have the right to the Graves AOC, and it is not by chance that it also encompasses 55 of the best estates, including all the *crus classés*. The technical requirements are similar to Graves except that the Carmenère may be used for red wines; white wines must contain at least 25 percent Sauvignon Blanc and a slightly stricter yield. If you are not sure which château to buy in the Graves, it is worth remembering this appellation

and paying a premium for it.

**RED** Soft, silky reds of great violety elegance, and not lacking either concentration or length. Most have been aged in a percentage of new oak, which adds a smoky or tobaccolike complexity.

🍇 Cabernet Sauvignon, Cabernet Franc, Merlot, Malbec, Petit Verdot, Carmenère

🍷 6–20 years

**WHITE** The serious styles are invariably oaked these days, with oodles of flavor, often tropical and fruity, with a firm acid structure. These wines may be sold from December 1 following the harvest without any mention of *primeur* or *nouveau*.

🍇 A minimum of 25% Sauvignon Blanc, plus Sémillon, Muscadelle

🍷 Usually 3–8 years, but up to 20 years for the best

## SAUTERNES AOC

The much hillier communes of Bommes, Fargues, and Sauternes produce the richest of all Bordeaux's dessert wines, while the châteaux in the lower-lying, flatter Preignac make wines very close in style to Barsac. The wine must include overripe botrytized grapes harvested in tries.

**WHITE** Golden, intense, powerful, and complex wines that defy the senses and boggle the mind. They are rich in texture, with masses of rich, ripe, and fat fruit. Pineapple, peach, apricot, and strawberry are some of the lush flavors that can be found, and the creamy-vanilla character of fruit and new oak matures into a splendid honeyed sumptuousness that is spicy and complex. Above all, these wines are marked by the distinctive botrytis character.

🍇 Sémillon, Sauvignon Blanc, Muscadelle

🍷 10–30 years for most wines; between 20 and 70 years for the greatest

---

THE GENERIC APPELLATIONS OF
# GRAVES AND CÉRONS

### CHÂTEAU D'ARCHAMBEAU
**Illats**
★ ☆ ♥

Sited in Podensac, one of the communes of Cérons, this fine property is owned by Dr. Jean Dubourdieu, nephew of Pierre Dubourdieu of Doisy-Daëne, a *deuxième cru* in Barsac. He produces a fine-quality, fragrant, and attractively aromatic red wine, which has the typical silky Graves texture. The deliciously fresh, crisp, and fruity dry white Graves is better than some efforts by certain *cru classé* châteaux. His soft, fruity Cérons is *moelleux* with the emphasis more on perfume than richness.

**Second wines:** *Château Mourlet, Château La Citadelle*

### CHÂTEAU LA BLANCHERIE
**La Brède**
◎ ★ ♥

This fresh and lively dry white Graves is cool fermented, and has plenty of juicy fruit flavor balanced with ripe acidity.

### CHÂTEAU LA BLANCHERIE-PEYRAT
**La Brède**
◎ ★ ♥

The red wine of La Blancherie is sold under this label. It is a medium- to full-bodied wine that is matured in casks and has an engaging, spicy bouquet and a rich, fruity flavor.

### CHÂTEAU BOUSCAUT
**Cadaujac**
**Cru Classé (red and white)**
★ ★ ☆

Belongs to Sophie and Louis Lurton. The red wine is matured in wood for 18 months, with 25 percent new oak. The white wine is fermented and matured for up to six months in 100 percent new oak.

**RED** Until the 1980s this wine was big, tough, and tannic with little charm. Recent vintages have shown increasing suppleness, but the wine still struggles to find form. The second wine, Château Valoux, is a really excellent wine for its class.

🍇 Merlot 55%, Cabernet Sauvignon 35%, Cabernet Franc 5%, Malbec 5%

🍷 8–20 years

**Second wine:** *Château Valoux*

**WHITE** This dry, medium-bodied white wine has exotic fruit flavors supported by gentle oak.

🍇 Sémillon 70%, Sauvignon 30%

🍷 5–10 years

### CHÂTEAU CARBONNIEUX
**Léognan**
**Cru Classé (red and white)**
★ ☆ ♥

This is the largest wine estate in Graves. The white wine, the better known of the two styles, is cool-fermented in stainless steel and matured in 100 percent new oak for three months.

**RED** I frankly did not care for this wine until the splendid 1985

vintage, which seduced me with its creamy-oak nose, silky-textured fruit, and supple tannin, but similar joys have been few and far between.

Cabernet Sauvignon 55%, Merlot 30%, Cabernet Franc 10%, Malbec, and Petit Verdot 5%

6–18 years

**WHITE** Once solid and uninspiring, this wine has really come into its own since the early 1990s. From this time Château Carbonnieux has been lush and creamy with well-integrated new oak and not a little finesse.

Sauvignon 60%, Sémillon 40%

2–5 years

**Second wine:** *Château La Tour Léognan*

## CHÂTEAU DE CARDAILLAN
### Toulenne
### ★☆❤

Under the same ownership as Château de Malle, this is a *deuxième cru* Sauternes in the commune of Preignac. This excellent property produces a technically brilliant red Graves with a voluptuous blackcurrant flavor, which develops quickly, yet ages well.

Cabernet Sauvignon 80%, Merlot 20%

## CHÂTEAU LES CARMES-HAUT-BRION
### Pessac
### ★

From 1584 until the French Revolution in 1789, this property belonged to the white friars Carmes, hence the name. This soft, Merlot-dominated wine has always been in the shadow of its more famous neighbor, Haut-Brion, and always will, but there has been a noticeable shift upward in quality.

## CHÂTEAU DE CÉRONS
### Cérons

This 17th-century château, which makes an attractively light, sweet white Cérons, is owned by Jean Perromat, owner of Mayne-Binet, de Bessanes, Ferbos, Ferbos-Lalanette in Cérons, and Prost in Barsac.

## CHÂTEAU DE CHANTEGRIVE
### Podensac
### ★☆❤

This château produces a substantial quantity of an excellent, soft, and fruity red Graves (Cabernet Sauvignon 50 percent, Merlot 40 percent, Cabernet Franc 10 percent) that is matured in wooden vats for six months and then transferred to casks for a further 12 months with 20 percent new oak. It also produces an elegant, aromatic, cool-fermented dry white Graves that is produced entirely from the first pressing (Sémillon 60 percent, Sauvignon 30 percent,

Muscadelle 10 percent). The proprietor also owns Château d'Anice.

**Second wine:** *Château Mayne-Lévêque*

**Other wine:** *Château Bon-Dieu-des-Vignes*

## DOMAINE DE CHEVALIER
### Léognan
### Cru Classé (red and white)
### ★★★❤

One of the top three Graves after Haut-Brion, this extraordinary property gives me more pleasure than any other in this AOC. It utilizes the most traditional methods to produce outstanding red and dry white wine. Fermenting red wine at a temperature as high as 89°F (32°C) might encourage some problems elsewhere, but under the meticulous care of those at the Domaine de Chevalier, this practice, designed to extract the maximum tannins and coloring material, is a positive advantage. The red wine is matured in wood for up to 24 months, with 50 percent new oak. The white wine is fermented and matured in wood for 18 months, with up to 25 percent new oak. Stéphane Derenoncourt has been consulting (red wine) since 2003.

**RED** Deep-colored, medium-to-full or full-bodied wines, stunningly rich in fruit and oak, with intense cedarwood and tobacco overtones, yet subtle, seductive, and full of finesse. These are wines of great quality, longevity, and complexity.

Cabernet Sauvignon 65%, Merlot 30%, Cabernet Franc 5%

15–40 years

**WHITE** Even better than the red, but produced in frustratingly small quantities, this star-bright, intensely flavored dry wine is almost fat with exotic fruit and epitomizes finesse.

Sauvignon 70%, Sémillon 30%

8–20 years

## CHÂTEAU CHICANE
### Toulenne

This châteaux is typical of the large number of properties in the area that consistently make an excellent basic Graves. Here is an elegant, medium-bodied red wine, with a bouquet of violets, and heaps of clean, silky-smooth fruit.

## CLOS FLORIDÈNE
### Pujols-sur-Ciron
### ★★❤

Owned by Bordeaux's white wine revolutionary, Denis Dubourdieu, who is producing a sensational dry white Graves (Sémillon 70 percent, Sauvignon 30 percent) from this small estate. The red Clos Floridène (Cabernet Sauvignon 80%, Merlot 20%) possesses an extraordinary combination of rich fruit and elegant new oak, and is the equivalent of a top *cru classé*.

**Second wine:** *Second de Floridène*

## CLOS SAINT-GEORGES
### Illats
### ★❤

This property produces a small amount of red Graves, but is most famous for its scintillating sweet Graves Supérieur. A stunningly rich and flavorsome wine, full of botrytis complexity.

## CHÂTEAU COUHINS
### Villenave-d'Ornon
### Cru Classé (white only)

The Institut National de La Réchèrche Agronomique (INRA) and Lucien Lurton share this estate. INRA produces a separate wine, which is cool fermented with no maturation in wood.

**WHITE** Clean, crisp, and fruity dry white wines that are well made.

Sauvignon 50%, Sémillon 50%

2–4 years

**Note** Château also produces a red Graves, but it is not a *cru classé*.

## CHÂTEAU COUHINS-LURTON
### Villenave-d'Ornon
### Cru Classé (white only)
### ★☆❤

The highest-performing half of the Couhins estate owned by André Lurton. The wine is fermented and matured in 100 percent new oak.

**WHITE** Delicious dry wines that have all the advantages of freshness and fruitiness, plus the complexity of oak. Surprisingly fat for pure Sauvignon.

Sauvignon 100%

3–8 years

**Second wine:** *Château Cantebau*

## CHÂTEAU DE CRUZEAU
### St.-Médard-d'Eyrans
### ★❤

Situated on a high, south-facing crest of deep, gravel soil, this property belongs to André Lurton, owner of Château Couhins-Lurton, the high-performance white Graves *cru classé*. De Cruzeau makes 18,000 cases of full-bodied red Graves (Cabernet Sauvignon 60 percent, Merlot 40 percent) that is ripe and velvety with a spicy-cedarwood complexity.

This château also produces around 5,000 cases of a fine-quality white Graves (Sauvignon 90 percent, Sémillon 10 percent) that after some five years of maturation develops an intense citrous bouquet and flavor.

## CHÂTEAU FERRANDE
### Castres

A large property that, like so many in Graves, makes better red wine than white. The red wine (Cabernet Sauvignon 35 percent, Merlot 35 percent, Cabernet Franc 30 percent) is a consistently good-quality, chocolaty Graves that is matured in

wood for 15 to 18 months, with 10 to 15 percent new oak. The dry white Graves (Sémillon 60 percent, Sauvignon 35 percent, Muscadelle 5 percent) is somewhat less inspiring.

## CHÂTEAU DE FIEUZAL
### Léognan
### Cru Classé (red only)
### ★★

This property occupies the highest and best exposed gravel crest in the commune. The vineyard and the château are immaculate, which is reflected in the style of its wines.

**RED** A deeply colored, full-bodied, rich, stylish wine with typical Graves silky texture and ample finesse.

Cabernet Sauvignon 60%, Merlot 30%, Malbec 5%, Petit Verdot 5%

12–30 years

**Second wine:** *L'Abeille de Fieuzal*

**Note** De Fieuzal also produces a rich, exotic, and dry white wine that is not *cru classé*, yet is one of the finest white Graves produced.

## GRAND ENCLOS DU CHÂTEAU DE CÉRONS
### Cérons
### ★☆❤

This property, entirely enclosed by a wall, once formed the largest part of the estate of Château de Cérons. The wines produced here—far superior to those of Château de Cérons, and possibly the best of the appellation—are fat and rich, with good aging potential and some complexity. The proprietor also makes dry white wines at nearby Château Lamouroux.

## DOMAINE DE LA GRAVE
### Portets
### ★❤

Formerly owned by maestro Peter Vinding-Diers, the Danish-born, Australian-trained winemaker who isolated the famous "RZ" yeast strain. Vinding-Diers sold this property along with Landiras to Van Quikelberg in 1998. The wines are for medium-term consumption, with a very soft, vibrantly fruity, easy-to-drink red and a lovely oak-aged white.

## CHÂTEAU HAURA
### Illats

Château Haura produces wines under the Cérons appellation. Although not as consistent as it should be, it can sometimes produce a fine, honey-sweet wine with some distinction and concentration. The residence on this property is known as Château Hillot and red and dry white Graves are sold under this name that come from vines contiguous with those of Haura. The proprietor also owns Château Tucau in Barsac.

## CHÂTEAU HAUT-BAILLY
Léognan
Cru Classé (red only)
★★☆ⓥ

This château's well-kept vineyard is located on an excellent gravel crest bordering the eastern suburbs of Léognan. This red Graves is matured in wood for up to 20 months, with 50 percent new oak.

**RED** The class of fruit and quality of new oak is immediately noticeable on the creamy-ripe nose of this medium-bodied wine. Never block-busting stuff, but always elegant and stylish.

🍇 Cabernet Sauvignon 60%, Merlot 30%, Cabernet Franc 10%

🍷— 12–25 years

**Second wine:** *Le Pardre de Haut-Bailly*

## CHÂTEAU HAUT-BRION
Pessac
Cru Classé (red and white)
★★★

In 1663 this famous château was mentioned in Pepys's Diary as "Ho Bryan." It has been under American ownership since 1935, when it was purchased by Clarence Dillon, the banker. The parent company is called Domaine Clarence Dillon, and Dillon's granddaughter, the Duchesse de Mouchy, is the president. Jean Delmas is the technical director. The red wine is fermented in stainless steel and matured in wood for 24 to 27 months, with 100 percent new oak. The white wine is fermented and matured in 100 percent new oak.

**RED** This supple, stylish, medium- to full-bodied wine has a surprisingly dense flavor for the weight, and a chocolaty-violet character. The ideal commercial product, it develops quickly and ages gracefully.

🍇 Cabernet Sauvignon 55%, Merlot 25%, Cabernet Franc 20%

🍷— 10–40 years

**Second wine:** ⓥ *Bahans-Haut-Brion*

**WHITE** This is not one of the biggest white Graves, but it is built to last. It is sumptuous, oaky, and teeming with citrous and more exotic fruit flavors.

🍇 Sauvignon 50%, Sémillon 50%

🍷— 5–20 years

## CHÂTEAU LANDIRAS
Landiras

Mr. and Mrs. van Quikelberg purchased this property in 1998. Production is four-fifths white and potentially of *cru classé* quality.

## CHÂTEAU LARRIVET-HAUT-BRION
Léognan
★★

Originally called Château Canolle, the name was at one point changed to Château Haut-Brion-Larrivet. Larrivet is a small stream that flows through the property, and Haut-Brion means "high gravel," referring to the gravel plateau west of Léognan on which the vineyard is situated.

Château Haut-Brion took legal action over the renaming, and since 1941 the property and its wines have been known as Château Larrivet-Haut-Brion. The red wine (Cabernet Sauvignon 55 percent, Merlot 45 percent), which is matured in wood for 18 months with 25 percent new oak, is certainly *cru classé* standard, being a well-colored and full-bodied Graves with good flavor, spicy-cedarwood undertones, and a firm tannic structure. The white wine (Sauvignon Blanc 85 percent, Sémillon 15 percent) has leapt in quality since 1996.

## CHÂTEAU LAVILLE-HAUT-BRION
Talence
Cru Classé (white only)
★★

Since 1983, this small vineyard has been owned by Clarence Dillon, American proprietor of Château Haut-Brion. This "château with no château" is thought of as the white wine of La Mission. The wine is fermented and matured in cask.

**WHITE** Until 1982, the style was full, rich, oaky, and exuberant, tending to be more honeyed and spicy with a floral finesse since 1983. Both styles are stunning and complex.

🍇 Sauvignon 60%, Sémillon 40%

🍷— 6–20 years

## CHÂTEAU LA LOUVIÈRE
Léognan
★★ⓥ

Part of André Lurton's Graves empire, this château has made a clear about-face since 1985 as far as the quality of its red wine goes. A string of dull, lifeless vintages has come to an end with the beautiful, deep, and vividly colored wines of the years 1985 and 1986. There was another step up in quality in the mid-1990s, since when this has been a truly splendid, full-bodied red Graves that is rich in spicy-blackcurrany fruit and new oak (Cabernet Sauvignon 70 percent, Merlot 20 percent, Cabernet Franc 10 percent). The white wines of Château La Louvière have always

been excellent, but even here there has been a gigantic leap in quality. These are exciting and complex wines that deserve to be among the very best *crus classés*.

**Second wine:** *Château Coucheroy*

**Other wines:** *"L" de Louvière* (dry white), *Château Les Agunelles, Château Cantebau, Château Clos-du-Roy, Château Le Vieux-Moulin*

## CHÂTEAU MAGENCE
St.-Pierre-de-Mons
★☆ⓥ

A good property making 5,000 cases of a supple, well-perfumed, red wine (Cabernet Sauvignon 40 percent, Cabernet Franc 30 percent, Merlot 30 percent) and 10,000 cases of attractive, aromatic, cool-fermented dry white Graves (Sauvignon 64 percent, Sémillon 36 percent).

## CHÂTEAU MALARTIC-LAGRAVIÈRE
Léognan
Cru Classé (red and white)
★★

This 50-acre (20-hectare) vineyard forms a single block around the château. An underrated property, which has consistently produced much higher quality wines since the 1980s. The red wine is fermented in stainless steel at a low temperature (61°F/16°C), and matured in wood for 20 to 22 months, with one-third new oak. The white wine is now matured in 100 percent new oak for seven to eight months.

**RED** Rich, garnet-colored with an opulent sweet-oak nose, penetrating flavor, and supple tannin structure.

🍇 Cabernet Sauvignon 50%, Cabernet Franc 25%, Merlot 25%

🍷— 7–25 years

**WHITE** Recent vintages of this once lackluster white Graves prove the worth of new oak. It is not difficult to mistake this honey-rich, ripe, and succulent wine for pure Sémillon.

🍇 Sauvignon 100%

🍷— 5–12 years

## CHÂTEAU MAYNE-BINET
Cérons

Proprietor Jean Perromat also owns several other châteaux, namely De Cérons, De Bessanes, Ferbos, and Ferbos-Lalanette in Cérons and Château Prost in Barsac. At Mayne-Binet he produces a fine sweet white Cérons.

## CHÂTEAU MILLET
Portets
★ⓥ(red only)

The red is a deep, dark-colored wine made in a traditional style with a dense flavor of concentrated spicy fruit. Although it has a firm tannin structure, this quickly rounds out with a few years in bottle. There is a dry white Graves, but it lacks the boldness and character of the red.

**Other wine:** *Château Du Clos Renon*

## CHÂTEAU LA MISSION-HAUT-BRION
Pessac
*Cru Classé* (red only)
★★★

Under the ownership of Henri Woltner, this was the pretender to the throne of Graves. Little wonder, then, that Clarence Dillon of Haut-Brion snapped it up when the opportunity arose in 1983. The red wine is matured in wood for 24 months, with 50 percent new oak.

**RED** Despite different winemaking techniques, Dillon's La Mission is no less stunning than Woltner's. Both styles are deeper, darker, and denser than any other wine Graves can manage. They are essentially powerful wines that require great bottle-age, but they do lack finesse.

🍇 Cabernet Sauvignon 60%, Merlot 30%, Cabernet Franc 10%

🍷— 15–45 years

**Second wine:** *La Chapelle de la Mission-Haut-Brion*

## CHÂTEAU OLIVIER
Léognan
Cru Classé (red and white)
★☆

There has never been any doubt about this château's *terroir*, which has as much potential as any Graves *cru classé*, but it was one of the appellation's most disappointing producers until 1990. Since then progress has been agonizingly slow and patchy, but recent vintages have revived hopes that this remains a château to watch. The red wine is matured in wood for 18 months; the white wine up to three months, with 100 percent new oak.

**RED** The fruit is now easier-drinking and the oak, which used to be aggressive, more supple and creamy.

🍇 Cabernet Sauvignon 70%, Merlot 30%

**WHITE** This wine actually began to sparkle as early as 1985, with some quite outstanding vintages in the 1990s, since when has been an added freshness, real fruit flavor, and some positive character developing.

🍇 Sémillon 65%, Sauvignon 30%, Muscadelle 5%

🍷— 3–7 years

## CHÂTEAU PAPE-CLÉMENT
Pessac
Cru Classé (red only)
★★

After a disastrous period in the 1970s and early 1980s, Pape-Clément began to improve in 1985 and 1986, due to stricter selection of the *grand vin* and the introduction of a Second Wine. Some critics rate these two vintages highly, and they were very good wines, but when examined in the context of the enormous potential of this vineyard, my brain tells me they were not at all special, even if my heart wants them to be.

The trio of 1988, 1989, and 1990 wines turned out to be the best this château has produced since 1953, although they are nowhere near as great and still not special at the very highest level of Graves wine. However, even in the string of lesser vintages Bordeaux experienced in the early 1990s, Pape-Clément managed to produce good wines, and with 1995, 1996, 1998, and 1999, it has truly regained the reputation of its former glory years. The red wine from this château is matured in wood for 24 months, with a minimum of 50 percent new oak.

**RED** Medium-bodied wines of excellent deep color, a distinctive style, and capable of much finesse.

🍇 Cabernet Sauvignon 67%, Merlot 33%

**Second Wine:** Le Clémentin

Note This château also produces a little non-*cru classé* white Graves, made from equal proportions of Sémillon, Sauvignon, and Muscadelle.

### CHÂTEAU RAHOUL
**Portets**

The wine produced by Château Rahoul is not quite as exciting as it was in the 1980s, when the property was home to—although never owned by—the maestro, Peter Vinding-Diers (see Domaine de la Graves and Château Landiras). However, both red and white wines are still reliable sources of very good value oak-aged Graves.

**Second wine:** *Château Constantin*
**Other wine:** *Petit Rahoul*

### CHÂTEAU RESPIDE-MÉDEVILLE
**Toulenne**
★🇻

Christian Médeville, the man responsible for Château Gilette, the rising star of Sauternes, produces excellent wines here using a totally different wine philosophy. Both the red and the white are fine examples of the best of modern vinification combined with new oak. The red is

a well-colored wine with rich, ripe fruit, some spice, and a creamy, new-oak aftertaste, good for early drinking. The white is a rich, creamy-vanilla concoction with soft, succulent fruit and a fat finish.

### CHÂTEAU DU ROCHEMORIN
**Martillac**
★🇻

Originally called "La Roche Morine," (the Moorish rock) this estate has a history that extends at least as far back as the eighth century, when Bordeaux was defended by the Moors from attacking Saracens. Another château belonging to André Lurton, Rochemorin produces a fine, elegant, fruity red Graves that is well0balanced and has a good spicy finish (Cabernet Sauvignon 60 percent, Merlot 40 percent). Rochemorin also produces a very clean and correct dry white Graves.

### CHÂTEAU DE ROQUETAILLADE LA GRANGE
**Mazères**
★☆🇻

This is a very old property, that produces some 12,000 cases of an attractive, well-colored red Graves that has an aromatic bouquet and a delicious spicy-cassis flavor. This wine is made from Merlot 40 percent, Cabernet Sauvignon 25 percent, Cabernet Franc 25 percent, Malbec 5 percent, and Petit Verdot 5 percent. Its firm, tannic structure means it matures gracefully over 15 or more years. The white wine, which is made from Sémillon 80 percent, Sauvignon 20 percent, is less successful.

**Second wine:** *Château de Carolle*
**Other wines:** *Château de Roquetaillade-le-Bernet*

### CHÂTEAU DU SEUIL
**Cérons**

Up-and-coming Graves property producing fine, elegant reds and fruity, oak-aged whites, both proving to be of increasingly excellent value.

### CHÂTEAU SMITH-HAUT-LAFITTE
**Martillac**
**Cru Classé (red only)**
★★☆🇻

The reputation of these wines began to soar under consultant Michel Rolland, but the quality has stepped up another gear since 2001, when Stéphane Derenoncourt took over. The red wine matures in wood for 18 months, with 50 percent new oak.

**RED** These wines are now in a richer style with creamy-oak undertones and up-front fruit,.

🍇 Cabernet Sauvignon 69%, Merlot 20% Cabernet Franc 11%

🍷— 8–20 years

**Second wine:** *Les Hauts-de-Smith-Haut-Lafitte*

Note A white Graves is also made. It is not a *cru classé*, yet ironically now considered one of the finest white wines in Pessac-Léognan.

### CHÂTEAU LA TOUR-HAUT-BRION
**Talence Cru Classé (red only)**
★★

This château is situated close to Château La Mission-Haut-Brion. By 1980 wine sold under the label of this château was merely regarded as the Second Wine of Château La Mission-Haut-Brion. All the grapes from both vineyards were vinified together, and the two wines made

by selection. However, after acquisition by Domaine Clarence Dillon in 1983, some 11 acres (4.5 hectares) of vines were delimited as Château La Tour-Haut-Brion, and from 1984 all its wines can be said to be from one specific site. The wine is matured in wood for 24 months, with 50 percent new oak.

**RED** This very dark, tannic, full-bodied wine is full of chocolaty, tannic fruit above an earthy-smoky bitterness of undeveloped extract. Despite its awesome attack of flavor it shows great finesse.

🍇 Cabernet Sauvignon 60%, Merlot 30%, Cabernet Franc 10%

🍷— 20–40 years

### CHÂTEAU LA TOUR-MARTILLAC
**Martillac**
**Cru Classé (red and white)**
◎ ★☆

This property has its own herd of cattle to supply manure for the château's strictly "organic" wine. Its red wine is not as consistent as the very best Graves and tends to lack charm in cask. These factors make it an underrated wine. It is matured in wood for 18 to 22 months with one-third new oak. The white is fermented in stainless steel and matured in 100 percent new oak.

**RED** Not big or bold wines with immediate appeal; the reds are elegant with some finesse. The fruit in recent vintages has tended to be a bit plumper, but it is in bottle that these wines take on richness, developing creamy-oak flavor.

🍇 Cabernet Sauvignon 60%, Merlot 25%, Cabernet Franc 6%, Malbec 5%, Petit Verdot 4%

🍷— 8–20 years

**Second wine:** *Château La Grave-Martillac*

**WHITE** The stunning 1986 vintage heralded a new era of exciting dry whites. This is very fresh, elegant wine, the fruit gently balanced by complex nuances of oak.

🍇 Sémillon 55%, Sauvignon 35%, Muscadelle 3%, old diverse

🍷— 4–8 years

---

THE WINE PRODUCERS OF
# SAUTERNES AND BARSAC

### CHÂTEAU D'ARCHE
**Sauternes**
**2ème Cru Classé**
★🇻

This property dates from 1530. It was known as Cru de Bran-Eyre until it was bought by the Comte d'Arche in the 18th century. It has been inconsistent. The wine sees up to 50 percent new oak.

**WHITE** The successful Château d'Arche is an elegantly balanced wine that is more in the style of

Barsac than Sauternes. It is sweet, rich, and has complex botrytis flavors, which often puts it on par with a *premier cru*, although it is less plump than most Sauternes. Easily equivalent to a classed growth in quality and the Crème de Tête is even better.

🍇 Sémillon 80%, Sauvignon 15%, Muscadelle 5%

🍷— 8–25 years

**Second wine:** *Cru de Braneyre*
**Other wine:** *d'Arche-Lafaurie*

### CHÂTEAU BASTOR-LAMONTAGNE
**Preignac**
★🇻

A large property that deserves *deuxième cru* status. The wine is matured in wood for up to 36 months, with 10 to 15 percent new oak. Lighter years such as 1980, 1982, and 1985 lack botrytis but are successful in an attractive mellow, citrus style. Big years such as 1983 lack nothing: the wines are full,

rich, and stylish with concentrated botrytis flavor and ample class. 1989, 1990, 1996, 1997, 1998, and 1999 all very successful.

**Second wine:** *Les Remparts du Bastor*

### CHÂTEAU BOUYOT
**Barsac**
★☆🇻

Jammy Fonbeney, the winemaker at this little-known property, is producing some stunning wines that deserve recognition. They have classic Barsac elegance, light in body, but not in flavor, with rich pineapple and creamy botrytis fruit, some spice, and fine length.

### CHÂTEAU BROUSTET
**Barsac 2ème Cru Classé**
★ ♥

The wine produced at Château Broustet is matured in wood for 20 months with what was until recently just 10 percent new oak, but this increased to 40 percent after the 1986 vintage.

**WHITE** Chateau Broustet can be a delightful wine, with a fruit-salad-and-cream taste, a very elegant balance, and some spicy-botrytis complexity.

🍇 Sémillon 63%, Sauvignon 25%, Muscadelle 12%

🍷 8–25 years

**Second wine:** *Château de Ségur*

### CHÂTEAU CAILLOU
**Barsac**
**2ème Cru Classé**
★ ✭ ♥

This château gets its name from the *cailloux*, the stones that are brought to the surface during plowing. These have been used to enclose the entire 37-acre (15-hectare) vineyard and to provide hardcore for the tennis courts. Mr. Bravo, the owner, has run out of uses but he is still churning them up. This is not one of the better-known *deuxièmes crus*, but it consistently produces wines of a very high standard, and so deserves to be.

**WHITE** A rich, ripe, and spicy-sweet Barsac with concentrated botrytis flavors underscored by refined oak. Not the fattest of Barsacs, but made in the richer rather than lighter style.

🍇 Sémillon 90%, Sauvignon 10%

🍷 8–30 years

**Second wine:** *Petit-Mayne*

**Other wines:** *Cru du Clocher (red), Château Caillou Sec (dry white), Rosé St.-Vincent (dry rosé)*

### CHÂTEAU DE LA CHARTREUSE
**Preignac**
★ ♥

This is the same stunning wine as Château Saint-Amande, but under a different exclusive label. *See also* Château Saint-Amande.

### CHÂTEAU CLIMENS
**Barsac**
**1er Cru Classé**
★★★ ✭

Under the ownership of Bérénice Lurton, this property has long been considered one of the top wines of both appellations. The wine is matured in wood for 24 months with up to one-third new oak.

**WHITE** The fattest of Barsacs, yet its superb acidity and characteristic citrous style give it an amazingly fresh and zippy balance. This wine has masses of creamy-ripe botrytis fruit supported by good cinnamon and vanilla-oak flavors.

🍇 Sémillon 98%, Sauvignon 2%

🍷 10–40 years

**Second wine:** *Les Cyprès de Climens*

### CHÂTEAU CLOS HAUT-PEYRAGUEY
**Bommes**
**1er Cru Classé**
★★

Originally part of Château Lafaurie-Peyraguey, this property has been owned by the Pauly family since 1934. A good dose of sulfur dioxide used to be the method of stopping fermentation at Clos Haut-Peyragey and the bouquet was often marred by an excess of sulfur. Thankfully, this has not been evident since the 1985 vintage, when coincidentally, the wines began to benefit from some new oak. The wine is now matured in wood for 18 months, with up to 25 percent new oak.

**WHITE** This wine now flaunts a positively eloquent bouquet, and has a rich flavor with complex botrytis creamy-oak nuances—very stylish.

🍇 Sémillon 83%, Sauvignon 15%, Muscadelle 2%

🍷 8–25 years

**Second wine:** *Château Haut-Bommes*

### CHÂTEAU COUTET
**Barsac**
**1er Cru Classé**
★★

This château is usually rated a close second to Climens, but in fact it is capable of matching it in some vintages and its occasional production of tiny quantities of *tête de cuvée* called "Cuvée Madame" often surpasses it. It is fermented and matured for 24 months in cask with 30 to 50 percent new oak. The dry white "Vin Sec" is an AOC Graves and very disappointing.

**WHITE** This wine has a creamy vanilla-and-spice bouquet, an

initially delicate richness that builds on the palate, good botrytis character, and oaky fruit.

🍇 Sémillon 75%, Sauvignon 23%, Muscadelle 2%

🍷 8–25 years (15–40 years for *Cuvée Madame*)

**Other wines:** *Cuvée Madame, Vin Sec du Château Coutet*

### CHÂTEAU DOISY-DAËNE
**Barsac**
**2ème Cru Classé**
★★ ♥

Owner Pierre Dubourdieu cool ferments this wine in stainless steel until the desired balance of alcohol and sweetness is achieved, and then matures it in 100 percent new oak for a short while. The wine also undergoes various low-sulfur techniques. The result is a wine equal to a Barsac *premier cru*.

**WHITE** This is a wine of great floral freshness and elegance, with a delightful honeyed fragrance of deliciously sweet fruit, delicate botrytis character, hints of creamy oak, and perfect balance.

🍇 Sémillon 100%

🍷 8–20 years

**Second wine:** *Château Cantegril*
**Other wine:** *Vin Sec de Doisy-Daëne*

### CHÂTEAU DOISY-DUBROCA
**Barsac**
**2ème Cru Classé**

This property is run in conjunction with Climens, and is the smallest part of the original Doisy estate. But the wine, although consistent, is not in the same class as Doisy-Daëne, let alone Climens. It is matured in cask for 24 to 30 months with 25 percent new oak.

🍇 Sémillon 90%, Sauvignon 10%

🍷 6–15 years

**Second wine:** *La Demoiselle de Doisy*

### CHÂTEAU DOISY-VÉDRINES
**Barsac**
**2ème Cru Classé**
★ ✭ ♥

This is the original and largest of the three Doisy châteaux. It is owned by Olivier Castéja, the head of Bordeaux *négociant* Roger Joanne. The wine is matured in wood for 18 months with one-third new oak.

**WHITE** This wine was somewhat lackluster until 1983, since when it has exploded with character. Rich, ripe, and oaky, with a concentrated botrytis complexity.

🍇 Sémillon 80%, Sauvignon 20%

🍷 8–25 years

**Other wine:** *Château La Tour-Védrines*

### CHÂTEAU DE FARGUES
**Fargues**
★★

The eerie ruin of Château de Fargues is the ancestral home of the Lur-Saluces family. The small production of ultrahigh-quality wine is made by essentially the same fastidious methods as Yquem, including fermentation and maturation in 100 percent new oak. It is powerful and viscous, very rich, succulent, and complex, with a fat, toasty character (Sémillon 80 percent, Sauvignon 20 percent). Easily equivalent to a classed growth.

### CHÂTEAU FILHOT
**Sauternes**
**2ème Cru Classé**
★

The beautiful Château Filhot was built between 1780 and 1850. This splendid château has a potentially great vineyard that consistently produces boring wine. Investment is required on a large scale in nearly every department: the proportion of Sémillon should be increased, the number of *tries* should be increased, the wine should contain more botrytized grapes and should be matured in cask, with some new oak.

**WHITE** At best these are well-made, simply fruity, and sweet.

🍇 Sémillon 60%, Sauvignon 37%, Muscadelle 3%

### CHÂTEAU GILETTE
**Preignac**
★

Christian Médeville rejects modern marketing methods, preferring instead to keep his precious nectar (made from Sémillon 94 percent, Sauvignon 4 percent, Muscadelle 2 percent) in vats under anaerobic conditions for an amazing 20 years before bottling and selling it. The Crème de Tête is *premier cru* quality with a powerful bouquet and intense flavor of liquorice and peaches and cream, followed by a long barley-sugar aftertaste. The Crème de Tête deserves ★★, but I am less impressed with Château Gilette's regular bottlings (if, indeed, any bottling at this property can be so described!).

### CHÂTEAU GUIRAUD
**Sauternes**
**1er Cru Classé**
★★

This property has been on the up since 1981, when the Narby family of Canada purchased it. The château and vineyards were in a very rundown state. Narby dug up much of the Sauvignon and planted Sémillon, then totally reequipped the winery and renovated the château. Only Yquem is on as high ground as Guiraud and since drainage is a key factor affecting the quality of the greatest Sauternes, where heavy clay soils dominate, the potential for this wine is very exciting and one that has been skillfully exploited with the help of Xavier Plantey, ex-manager of Château la Gaffelière. The wine is matured in wood for 30 months with at least 50 percent new oak. The first vintages of the dry white Vin Blanc Sec "G" were dull, but subsequent efforts have improved.

**WHITE** After two dismal decades, great Sauternes arrived at this château with the classic 1983 vintage, the first true botrytis wine under Narby's ownership. Guiraud is now plump with Sémillon fruit and fat with botrytis character. A deliciously sweet wine with luxuriant new oak, complexity, and considerable finesse.

🍇 Sémillon 70%, Sauvignon 30%

🍷 12–35 years

**Second wine:** *Le Dauphin*
**Other wine:** *Vin Blanc Sec "G"* (dry white)

## CHATEAU HAUT-BOMMES
### Bommes

The owner, Jacques Pauly, prefers to live here rather than at his *premier cru* Château Clos Haut-Peyraguey. Occasionally the wine used to excel for an unclassified growth; the recent improvements at Château Clos Haut-Peyraguey augur well for the future.

## CHÂTEAU LES JUSTICES
### Preignac
### ★ V

Under the same ownership as the star-performing Château Gilette, but here Christian Médeville gives his wines only four years of aging in vats. Les Justices is a consistent wine of excellent quality that is riper and fruitier than Gilette and the equivalent of a *deuxième cru*.

## CHATEAU LAFAURIE-PEYRAGUEY
### Bommes
### 1er Cru Classé
### ★★★ V

As with Cordier properties, this wine shows remarkable consistency. It is matured in wood for between 18 and 20 months with up to 50 percent new oak.

**WHITE** The combination of botrytis and oak is like pineapples and peaches and cream in this elegant wine that keeps fresh and retains an incredibly light color in old age.

🍇 Sémillon 98%, Sauvignon 2%

🍷 8–30 years

## CHÂTEAU LAMOTHE-DESPUJOLS
### Sauternes
### 2ème Cru Classé

In 1961 the Lamothe vineyard was split in two. The section belonging to Jean Despujols has been the most disappointing half up until the 1985 vintage, but it has really come into its own since 1990.

**WHITE** Fuller, richer, and sweeter than previously expected, and in an oily, fuller-bodied style, with overtly attractive tropical fruit character.

🍇 Sémillon 70%, Sauvignon 20%, Muscadelle 10%

## CHÂTEAU LAMOTHE-GUIGNARD
### Sauternes
### 2ème Cru Classé
### ★ V

The Guignards are really trying to achieve something with their section of the Lamothe vineyard. It was called Lamothe-Bergey until the name was changed in 1981. The wine is matured in wood for 24 months with 20 percent new oak.

**WHITE** Rich, spicy, and concentrated wines of full body and good botrytis character.

🍇 Sémillon 85%, Muscadelle 10%, Sauvignon 5%

🍷 7–20 years

## CHÂTEAU LIOT
### Barsac
### ★ V

This wine is elegant, with light but fine botrytis character and creamy vanilla of new oak—probably the equivalent of a *deuxième cru* in quality and is excellent value. Owner Jean-Nicol David also produces Château Saint-Jean, a dry white Graves, and Château Pinsas, a fruity red Graves.

## CHÂTEAU DE MALLE
### Preignac
### 2ème Cru Classé

Dry white wine is produced under the "Chevalier de Malle" label, and red Graves from contiguous vineyards under the Château du Cardaillan label. While this vineyard does not shine every year (1989 and 1990 are its best-ever vintages), when it does, it can be superb value.

**WHITE** These are firm, well-concentrated wines often influenced more by *passerillage* than botrytis. Delicious, rich, and luscious.

🍇 Sémillon 75%, Sauvignon 22%, Muscadelle 3%

🍷 7–20 years

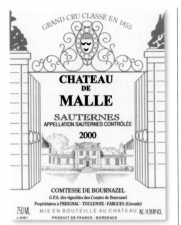

GRAND CRU CLASSÉ EN 1855

CHATEAU DE MALLE

SAUTERNES
APPELLATION SAUTERNES CONTRÔLÉE

2000

COMTESSE DE BOURNAZEL
G.F.A. des vignobles des Comtes de Bournazel
Propriétaires à PREIGNAC - TOULENNE - FARGUES (Gironde)
750 ML    MIS EN BOUTEILLE AU CHATEAU  ALC 14,5% BY VOL
L-M-001          PRODUIT DE FRANCE - BORDEAUX

**Second wine:** *Château St.-Hélène*
**Other wine:** *Chevalier de Malle*

## CHÂTEAU DU MAYNE
### Barsac
### V

There is a good proportion of old vines at this property which adds concentration and weight to these wines, which are fatter than the norm for Barsac. Owned by the Sanders family of the splendid Château Haut-Bailly of Graves.

## CHÂTEAU MÉNOTA
### Barsac
### V

This quaint old property—with its historic towers and ramparts—has exported its wines to England since the 16th century. Château Ménota produces very good Barsac, despite the unusually high proportion of Sauvignon Blanc (60 percent).

## CHÂTEAU NAIRAC
### Barsac
### 2ème Cru Classé
### ★★

Tom Heeter established the practice of fermenting and maturing his wine in up to 100 percent new oak—Nevers for vanilla and Limousin for backbone—and his perfectionist ex-wife, Nicole Tari, has continued this format with great success.

**WHITE** These are rich and oaky wines that require ample aging to show true finesse. With enough bottle maturity the tannin and vanilla harmonize with the fruit, and the rich botrytis complexity emerges.

🍇 Sémillon 90%, Sauvignon 6%, Muscadelle 4%

🍷 8–25 years

## CHÂTEAU PERNAUD
### Barsac
### ★ V

This property was once part of the Sauvage d'Yquem estate. It was then owned by the Lur-Saluces family, but was abandoned after the oidium fungus devastated Bordeaux in the late 18th century. It has been completely replanted and renovated, and is now building up something of a reputation. This slightly richer style of Barsac (Sémillon 70 percent,

Sauvignon 25 percent, Muscadelle 5 percent) has a typically elegant balance and is certainly a wine to watch.

## CHÂTEAU RABAUD-PROMIS
### Bommes
### 1er Cru Classé
### ★★

The wines of this once-grand property used to be awful. It was sad to see the vineyard, château, and wine so neglected. What a joy to witness such a dramatic change. It began with the 1983; and the vintages are now something special.

**WHITE** A lovely gold-colored wine with full, fat, and ripe botrytis character on the bouquet and palate.

🍇 Sémillon 80%, Sauvignon 18%, Muscadelle 2%

🍷 8–25 years

## CHÂTEAU RAYMOND-LAFON
### Sauternes

As I wrote in the last edition, it is easy to understand how people can get carried away by the idea of a vineyard so close to Yquem as Raymond-Lafon, especially when its owner, Pierre Meslier, was régisseur at Yquem. This was, however, an overrated and overpriced wine in the mid-1980s, and although things have improved since the 1989 and 1990 vintages, it is performing at only *deuxième cru* level and is consequently overrated and overpriced. Now that the style has been cleaned up and plumped out, Raymond-Lafon (Sémillon 80 percent, Sauvignon 20 percent) is a nice Sauternes, but not worth three times the price of Rieussec or two-and-a-half times as much as Climens.

## CHÂTEAU RAYNE-VIGNEAU
### Bommes
### 1er Cru Classé
### ★

The quality of Rayne-Vigneau had plummeted to dismal depths until as recently as 1985. The wine is now matured in wood for 24 months with 50 percent new oak. It has a higher Sémillon content than the statistics would suggest, due to the 5,000 cases of dry Sauvignon Blanc that are sold as "Rayne Sec."

**WHITE** Château Rayne-Vigneau is now a very high-quality wine that has an elegant peachy ripeness to its botrytis character.

🍇 Sémillon 65%, Sauvignon 35%

🍷 8–25 years

**Second wine:** *Clos l'Abeilley*
**Other wines:** *Rayne Sec*

## CHÂTEAU RIEUSSSEC
### Fargues
### 1er Cru Classé
### ★★★

This fine property promises to make even better wine since its acquisition by Domaines Rothschild in 1984. None of the Sauvignon

produced here is used for Château Rieussec (it goes in the "R"), effectively making the wine 96 percent Sémillon. It is barrel-fermented and cask matured for 18 to 30 months with 50 percent new oak.

**WHITE** This wine is one of the richest and most opulent of Sauternes, with intense pineapple fruit and a heavily botrytized character.

🍇 Sémillon 75%, Sauvignon 22%, Muscadelle 3%

🍷 12–35 years

**Second wines:** *Clos Labère, Mayne des Carmes*

**Other wine:** *"R" de Château Rieussec* (dry white)

### CHÂTEAU DE ROLLAND
Barsac
★☆

Buy at leisure at Château de Rolland, where you can stop over at the B&B in the vineyard and relax in the swimming pool.

**WHITE** Fresh and elegant, with a particular emphasis on fruit. An improving Barsac, produced by the Guignard family, which also owns the excellent Château de Roquetaillade-La-Grange at Mazères in Graves.

🍇 Sémillon 80%, Sauvignon 15%, Muscadelle 5%

🍷 5–8 years

### CHÂTEAU ROMER
Fargues
2ème Cru Classé
❓

The original Romer estate was divided in 1881, and at just 13 acres (five hectares) this is the smallest part. I have never come across the wine.

🍇 Sémillon 50%, Sauvignon 40%, Muscadelle 10%

### CHÂTEAU ROMER-DU-HAYOT
Fargues
2ème Cru Classé
☑

Monsieur André du Hayot owns these 25 acres (10 hectares) of vines on a fine clayey-gravel crest that was once part of the original Romer estate. The wines are little seen, but represent very good value.

**WHITE** Fresh, not oversweet, fruit-salad and cream style, with light botrytis character and an elegant balance.

🍇 Sémillon 70%, Sauvignon 25%, Muscadelle 5%

🍷 5–12 years

### CHÂTEAU ROUMIEU
Barsac
★☑

This property, which borders the classified growths of Climens and Doisy-Védrines, has produced luscious sweet wines of a richer than normal style in some vintages (Sémillon 90 percent, Sauvignon 10 percent).

### CHÂTEAU ROUMIEU-LACOSTE
Barsac
★☑

A Dubourdieu property producing consistently fine Barsac (Sémillon 80 percent, Sauvignon 20 percent) with good botrytis concentration.

### CHÂTEAU SAINT-AMANDE
Preignac
★☑

An elegant and stylish wine (Sémillon 67 percent, Sauvignon 33 percent) that is very attractive when young, yet some vintages have potentially excellent longevity and are often equivalent to a classed growth in quality. Part of the production of this property is sold under the Château de la Chartreuse label.

**Second wine:** *Château de la Chartreuse*

### CHÂTEAU SIGALAS-RABAUD
Bommes
1er Cru Classé
★★

This is the largest part of the original Rabaud estate. The proprietor contracted Cordier to manage this property as from 1995 and the wines have already shown a marked improvement.

**WHITE** A stylish early-drinking wine with an elegant botrytis bouquet and deliciously fresh fruit on the palate.

🍇 Sémillon 85%, Sauvignon 15%

🍷 6–15 years

### CHÂTEAU SIMON
Barsac
2ème Cru Classé

A combination of modern and traditional methods produces a mildly sweet wine from Sémillon 70 percent, Sauvignon 30 percent. Most Sauternes and Barsacs are aged in Nevers or Limousin oak. Sometimes Allier is used, but at Simon they mature the wine in Merrain oak for two years.

### CHÂTEAU SUAU
Barsac
2ème Cru Classé

The vineyard belongs to Roger Biarnès, who makes the wine at his Château Navarro in Cérons because the original château is under different ownership. Furthermore, this is not the same property as Château Suau at Capian, on the opposite bank of the Garonne,

almost directly north.

**WHITE** This attractive, fresh, and fragrantly fruity wine has a gentle citrus-and-spice botrytis complexity. Improvement noted in the 2005 vintage.

🍇 Sémillon 80%, Sauvignon 10%, Muscadelle 10%

🍷 6–12 years

### CHÂTEAU SUDUIRAUT
Preignac
1er Cru Classé
★★★☆

This splendid 17th-century château, with its picturesque parkland, effectively evokes the graceful beauty found in its luscious wines. Suduiraut's superb 245-acre (100-hectare) vineyard enjoys a good susceptibility to "noble rot," and adjoins that of Yquem. The wines went through an inconsistent patch in the 1980s, but have improved dramatically under the watchful eye of Jean-Michel Cazes's AXA insurance group. The wines are fermented and matured in cask for 24 months, with at least one-third new oak.

**WHITE** Soft, succulent, and sublime, this is an intensely sweet wine of classic stature. It is rich, ripe, and viscous, with great botrytis complexity that benefits from good bottle-age.

🍇 Sémillon 80%, Sauvignon 20%

🍷 8–35 years

**Second wine:** *Castelnau de Suduiraut*

### CHÂTEAU LA TOUR BLANCHE
Sauternes
1er Cru Classé
★★☆

This property was placed at the head of the *premiers crus* in 1855, when only Yquem was deemed to be superior, but until relatively recently it failed to live up to this reputation. Even at its lowest ebb, few critics would have denied that these vineyards possessed truly great potential, but the wines were ordinary. This was made all the more embarrassing by the fact that the state-owned La Tour Blanche was a school of agriculture and oenology that was supposed to teach others how to make Sauternes. This depressing situation began to change, however, in the mid-1980s when Château la Tour Blanche started increasing the proportion of Sémillon, picking much riper grapes, and implementing stricter selection in both vineyard and chais. Fermentation is in wood (with up to 90 percent new oak but averaging 25 percent in most years), and the results have been exciting with excellent wines produced in 1988, 1989, 1990, (its greatest ever) 1994, 1995, 1996, 1997, and 1998.

**WHITE** These are now so rich they are almost fat and bursting with

plump, ripe, juicy fruit and oodles of complex botrytis character.

🍇 Sémillon 78%, Sauvignon 19%, Muscadelle 3%

🍷 8–20 years

**Second wine:** *Mademoiselle de Saint-Marc*

### CHÂTEAU D'YQUEM
Sauternes
1er Cru Supérieur
★★★

This most famous of all châteaux belonged to the English crown from 1152 to 1453. It then passed into the hands of Charles VII, King of France. In 1593 Jacques de Sauvage acquired tenant's rights to the royal property and in 1711 his descendants purchased the fiefdom of Yquem. In 1785 it passed into the hands of the Lur-Saluces family. The *tries* tradition was kept alive at Yquem when it was long forgotten by other noble châteaux. Like Pétrus, one of Yquem's "secrets" is its pickers. They are all skilled; they know what to pick and, just as important, what to leave. The gap between *tries* can vary from three days to several weeks. Housing and feeding 120 pickers for several weeks of inactivity is not cheap.

The property has been run with passionate care by succeeding generations, although LVMH (which owns Moët & Chandon in Champagne) purchased a majority shareholding in 1999 (after three years of acrimony between members of the Lur-Saluces family). Alexandre Lur-Saluces lost his independence, but won a handsome contract to remain in his former home. He is still very much in charge

In 1972 the harvest consisted of 11 *tries* spread over 71 days. In that year no wine was sold as Château d'Yquem. This is not to say that Yquem's fastidious attention to selection and quality does not pay off in some poor vintages. But in good years, because of the strict selection in the vineyard, the amount of wine that is finally used is as high as 80 to 90 percent. The wines are matured for up to 42 months with 100 percent new oak. Other *terroirs* in Sauternes and Barsac are potentially comparable, but, no matter how conscientious their owners, none makes the same sacrifices as Yquem.

**WHITE** This wine represents the ultimate in richness, complexity, and class. No other botrytis wine of equal body and concentration has a comparable finesse, breeding, and balance. Some of the characteristic aromas and flavors include peach, pineapple, coconut, nutmeg, and cinnamon, with toasty-creamy vanilla and caramel flavors of new oak.

🍇 Sémillon 80%, Sauvignon 20%

🍷 20–60 years

**Other wines:** *"Y" de Château d'Yquem* (dry white)

# THE LIBOURNAIS AND FRONSADAIS

*The right bank of the Dordogne River, known as the Libournais district, is red-wine country. Dominated by the Merlot grape, the vineyards here produce deep-colored, silky- or velvety-rich wines of classic quality in the St.-Émilion and Pomerol regions, in addition to wines of modest quality, but excellent value and character, in the "satellite" appellations that surround them.*

IN THE MID-1950S, many Libournais wines were harsh, and even the best AOCs did not enjoy the reputation they do today. Most growers believed that they were cultivating too much Cabernet Sauvignon and Malbec for their particular *terroir* and decided that they should plant more vines of Cabernet Franc. A few growers argued for the introduction of Merlot, which was allowed by the regulations, because it would give their wines the suppleness they desired. Even if they could have agreed on united action, changing the *encépagement* of an entire district would have been very a very long-term project, as well as being extremely expensive. However, in 1956, frost devastated the vineyards, forcing the Libournais growers into action. With poor, short crops inevitable for some years to come, prices soared, enabling them to carry out the massive replanting which, ironically, they could not have afforded prior to the crisis. This devastation led to the wholesale cultivation of Merlot and Cabernet Franc, which established a completely different style of wines, providing the catalyst for the spectacular postwar success of St.-Émilion and Pomerol.

## THE GARAGISTE EFFECT

In 1979, Jacques Thienpont, owner of Pomerol's classy Vieux Château Certan, unintentionally created what would become the *"vin de garagiste"* craze, when he purchased a neighboring plot of land and created a new wine called Le Pin. With a very low yield, 100 percent Merlot, and 100 percent new oak, the decadently rich Le Pin directly challenged Pétrus, less than a mile away. It was widely known that Thienpont considered Vieux Château Certan to be at least the equal of Pétrus, and he could certainly claim it to be historically more famous, but Pétrus regularly got much the higher price, which dented his pride. So Le Pin was born, and although he did not offer his fledgling wine at the same price as Pétrus, it soon trounced it on the auction market. In 1999, a case of 1982 Le Pin was trading at a massive $19,000, while a case of 1982 Château Pétrus could be snapped up for a "mere" $13,000. By 2003, the Pétrus had traded up to a mind-boggling $26,000 and yet Le Pin sold for $44,000. Unfortunately, Jacques Thienpont died in 1985, long before his little experiment yielded such crazy prices. By the late 1980s, however, Le Pin's extraordinary financial success had became so obvious to a number of *vignerons* in neighboring St.-Emilion that they attempted to replicate it with small plots of land in their own appellation: Jean-Luc Thunevin with Château de Valandraud (first vintage 1991), Gérard and Dominique Bécot with Château La Gomerie (first vintage 1995), Von Neippberg with Château La Mondotte (first vintage 1996), Francis Gaboriaud with Château L'Hermitage (first vintage 1997), Alain and Françoise Raynaud with Château Quinault l'Enclos (first vintage 1997), and Château

THE LIBOURNAIS DISTRICT *See also p63*
*This great red-wine area includes St.-Émilion, Pomerol, and their satellites. In the Libournais district, the Merlot grape reigns supreme, its succulent fruit essential to the local style.*

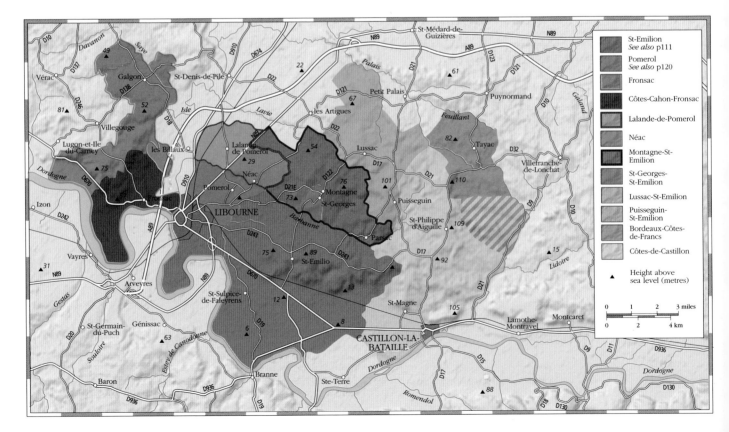

Legend:
- St-Emilion *See also p111*
- Pomerol *See also p120*
- Fronsac
- Côtes-Cahon-Fronsac
- Lalande-de-Pomerol
- Néac
- Montagne-St-Emilion
- St-Georges-St-Emilion
- Lussac-St-Emilion
- Puisseguin-St-Emilion
- Bordeaux-Côtes-de-Francs
- Côtes-de-Castillon
- ▲ Height above sea level (metres)

0   1   2   3 miles
0       2       4 km

Teyssier with Le Dôme (first vintage 1998). But it was Le Pin's cellar, which is truly a garage under a battered farmhouse, that inspired French wine writer Michel Bettane to coin the phrase "*vins de garage*." It is interesting how this new breed of wines has polarized critics into opposite camps, as if there is something intrinsically right or wrong with producing wine on a small scale. Because that is all it is, and the *garagistes* are popping up in the Graves, the Médoc, and well beyond the borders of Bordeaux. While some consumers (all wealthy) are happy to pay any price demanded for these wines, others seem to take offense at the very mention of the word *garagiste*. Both positions are bizarre. Besides, where do you draw the line between a *vin de garage* and an honest *lieu-dit* wine? Oh dear Jacques and Michel: what have you started?

## THE SATELLITE APPELLATIONS OF ST.-ÉMILION AND POMEROL
The wines of Lussac, Montagne, Parsac, Puisseguin, Sables, and St.-Georges were once sold as St.-Émilion, but in 1936 these outer areas were given their own AOCs. This was done to protect the

image of the greatest St.-Émilion châteaux, but through the historical use of this famous name these areas won the right to attach the name of St.-Émilion to theirs. The tiny Sables area was later reclaimed by the St.-Émilion AOC, and in 1972 a new appellation, Montagne-St.-Émilion, was created. This appellation, which covered a large region, could be adopted by growers who had previously used either Parsac-St.-Émilion AOC or St.-Georges-St.-Émilion AOC, but the executive order that created Montagne-St.-Émilion AOC in 1972 did not disband either of these smaller appellations.

So, a situation arose in which growers could choose between two very similar AOCs. In 1993, however, Parsac-St.-Émilion was finally disbanded, since it was noticed that virtually all the producers of Parsac-St.-Émilion were not using the original AOC but opting for Montagne-St.-Émilion AOC. Many growers in St.-Georges-St.-Émilion, however, were still using the original appellation, and so disbanding this would not have been so simple. All five combined St.-Émilion AOCs would in fact benefit from merging, since they all produce wines of essentially similar nature, under identical regulations.

---

THE GENERIC APPELLATIONS OF
# THE LIBOURNAIS AND FRONSADAIS

## BORDEAUX SUPÉRIEUR CÔTES-DE-FRANCS AOC
*See* **Bordeaux-Côtes-de-Francs AOC**

## BORDEAUX-CÔTES-DE-FRANCS AOC
This forgotten area's vineyards are contiguous with those of Puisseguin-St.-Émilion and Lussac-St.-Émilion, and have a very similar clay-limestone over limestone and iron-pan soil. The Bordeaux Supérieur version of these wines differs only in its higher alcohol level.

**RED** These are essentially robust, rustic, full-bodied wines that are softened by their high Merlot content.

🍇 Cabernet Franc, Cabernet Sauvignon, Malbec, Merlot

🍷 5–10 years

**WHITE** Little-seen dry, semisweet, and sweet wines of clean, fruity character.

🍇 Sauvignon Blanc, Sémillon, Muscadelle

🍷 5–10 years

## BORDEAUX-CÔTES-DE-FRANCS LIQUOREUX AOC
This style of Bordeaux-Côtes-de-Francs wine must by law be naturally sweet and made from overripe grapes that possess at least 223 grams of sugar per liter. The wines must have a minimum level of 11.5 percent alcohol and 27 grams of residual sugar per liter.

**WHITE** Rich, genuinely *liquoreux* wines; only tiny amounts are made.

🍇 Sauvignon Blanc, Sémillon, Muscadelle

🍷 5–15 years

## CANON-FRONSAC AOC
*See* **Côtes-Canon-Fronsac AOC**

## CÔTES-CANON-FRONSAC AOC
Fronsac AOC and Côtes-Canon-Fronsac AOC will no doubt be the next wines to be "discovered" by budget-minded Bordeaux drinkers. The best of these wines are Côtes-Canon-Fronsac AOC, sometimes called Canon-Fronsac AOC. With lower yields and stricter selection, these wines could equal all but the best of St.-Émilion and Pomerol.

**RED** Full-bodied, deep-colored, rich, and vigorous wines with dense fruit, fine spicy character, plenty of finesse, and good length.

🍇 Cabernet Franc, Cabernet Sauvignon, Malbec, Merlot

🍷 7–20 years

## CÔTES-DE-CASTILLON AOC
This is an attractive hilly area squeezed between St.-Émilion, the Dordogne River, and the Dordogne *département*. Its wine has long been appreciated for quality, consistency, and value. These wines used to be sold as Bordeaux and Bordeaux Supérieur wine until the 1989 vintage, when Côtes-de-Castillon received its own AOC status.

**RED** Firm, full-bodied, fine-colored wines with dense fruit and finesse.

🍇 Cabernet Franc, Cabernet Sauvignon, Carmenère, Malbec, Merlot, Petit Verdot

🍷 5–15 years

## FRONSAC AOC
This generic appellation covers the communes of La Rivière, St.-Germain-la-Rivière, St.-Aignan, Saillans, St.-Michel-de-Fronsac, Galgon, and Fronsac.

**RED** These full-bodied, well-colored wines have good chunky fruit and a fulsome, chocolaty character. Not quite the spice or finesse of Côtes-Canon-Fronsac, but splendid value.

GRAND VIN DE BORDEAUX

*Château Dalem*

FRONSAC

**2002**

APPELLATION FRONSAC CONTRÔLÉE

S.C.E.A. DU CHÂTEAU DALEM, PROPRIÉTAIRE À SAILLANS · GIRONDE · FRANCE

13,5% vol. MIS EN BOUTEILLE AU CHATEAU 75cl

🍇 Cabernet Franc, Cabernet Sauvignon, Malbec, Merlot

🍷 6–15 years

## LALANDE-DE-POMEROL AOC
This good-value appellation covers the communes of Lalande-de-Pomerol and Néac. No matter how good they are, even the best are but pale reflections of classic Pomerol.

**RED** Firm, meaty Merlots with lots of character but without Pomerol's texture and richness.

🍇 Cabernet Franc, Cabernet Sauvignon, Malbec, Merlot

🍷 7–20 years

## LUSSAC-ST.-ÉMILION AOC
A single-commune appellation 5.5 miles (9 kilometers) northeast of St.-Émilion.

**RED** The wines produced on the small gravelly plateau to the west of this commune are the lightest, but have the most finesse. Those produced on the cold, clayey lands to the north are robust and earthy, while those from the

clay-limestone in the southeast have the best balance of color, richness, and finesse.

🍇 Cabernet Franc, Cabernet Sauvignon, Carmenère, Malbec, Merlot

🍷 5–12 years

## MONTAGNE-ST.-ÉMILION AOC

This appellation includes St.-Georges-St-Émilion, a former commune that is today part of Montagne-St.-Émilion. St.-Georges-St.-Émilion AOC and Montagne-St.-Émilion AOC are the best of all the appellations that append "St.-Émilion" to their names.

**RED** Full, rich, and intensely flavored wines that mature well.

🍇 Cabernet Franc, Cabernet Sauvignon, Malbec, Merlot

🍷 5–15 years

## NÉAC AOC

This appellation has not been employed since the proprietors have been allowed to use the Lalande-de-Pomerol appellation. *See* Lalande-de-Pomerol AOC.

## POMEROL AOC

The basic wines of Pomerol fetch higher prices than those of any other Bordeaux appellation. The average Merlot content of a typical Pomerol is around 80 percent.

**RED** It is often said that these are the most velvety-rich of the world's classic wines, but they also have the firm tannin structure that is necessary for successful long-term maturation and development. The finest also have surprisingly deep color, masses of spicy-oak complexity, and great finesse.

🍇 Cabernet Franc, Cabernet Sauvignon, Malbec, Merlot

🍷 5–10 years (modest growths);
    10–30 years (great growths)

## PUISSEGUIN-ST.-ÉMILION AOC

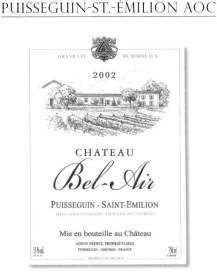

This commune has a clay-limestone topsoil over a stony subsoil and the wines it produces tend to be more rustic than those of the Montagne-St.-Émilion AOC.

**RED** These are rich and robust wines with a deep flavor and lots of fruit and color, but they are usually lacking in finesse.

🍇 Cabernet Franc, Cabernet Sauvignon, Carmenère, Malbec, Merlot

🍷 5–10 years

## ST.-ÉMILION AOC

These wines must have a minimum of 10.5 percent alcohol, but in years when chaptalization (the addition of sugar to grape juice to increase alcohol content) is allowed, there is also a maximum level of 13 percent.

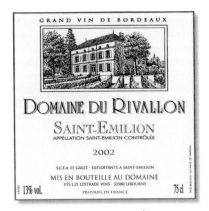

**RED** Even in the most basic St.-Émilions the ripe, spicy-juiciness of the Merlot grape should be supported by the firmness and finesse of the Cabernet Franc. The great châteaux achieve this superbly: they are full, rich, and concentrated, chocolaty and fruitcakey.

🍇 Cabernet Franc, Cabernet Sauvignon, Carmenère, Malbec, Merlot

🍷 6–12 years (modest growths);
    12–35 years (great growths)

## ST.-GEORGES-ST.-ÉMILION AOC

Along with the Montagne region of Montagne-St-Émilion, this is the best parish of the outer areas.

**RED** These are deep-colored, plummy wines with juicy, spicy fruit, and good supporting tannic structure.

🍇 Cabernet Franc, Cabernet Sauvignon, Malbec, Merlot

🍷 5–15 years

SATELLITE APPELLATIONS IN THE ST.-EMILION AREA
*It would make sound commercial sense if all the St.-Émilion satellites (Lussac-St.-Émilion, Puisseguin-St.-Émilion, and St.0-Georges-St. Émilion) were combined under the Montagne St.-Émilion appellation.*

# SAINT-ÉMILION

*The Romans were the first to cultivate the vine in St.-Émilion, a small area that has exported its wines to various parts of the world for over eight hundred years. In the first half of the twentieth century it lapsed into obscurity, but in the last fifty years it has risen like a phoenix.*

ST.-ÉMILION AS WE KNOW IT is a phenomenon of the postwar era, but there are many reminders of this wine's ancient past—from the famous Château Ausone, named after the Roman poet Ausonius, to the walled hilltop village of St.-Émilion itself, which has survived almost unchanged since the Middle Ages. In contrast, the Union des Producteurs, the largest single-appellation *coopérative* in France, is a graphic illustration of the best in modern, technologically sophisticated wine production. Today, there are over a thousand *crus* within 6 miles (10 kilometers) of the village of St.-Émilion that may use this appellation.

## THE APPEAL OF ST.-ÉMILION WINES

For those who find red wines too harsh or too bitter, St.-Émilion, with its elegance and finesse, is one of the easiest with which to make the transition from white to red. The difference between the wines of St.-Émilion and those of its satellites is comparable to the difference between silk and satin, whereas the difference between St.-Émilion and Pomerol is like the difference between silk and

velvet: the quality is similar, but the texture is not—although, of course, we must be humble about categorizing such complex entities as wine areas. It could justifiably be argued that the *graves* (gravelly terrain) that produces two of the very best St.-Émilions—Châteaux Cheval-Blanc and Figeac—has more in common with Pomerol than with the rest of the appellation.

**CHÂTEAU FIGEAC**
*Without doubt in a class of its own within Class B of premiers grands crus classés, Château Figeac has long fought to be classified with Ausone and Cheval Blanc.*

## A LARGE PRODUCTION

If you look at the map of the entire Bordeaux region (*see* p63) you will be amazed by how small this appellation of a thousand châteaux really is. It is a surprising but regular occurrence that an appellation as small as St.-Émilion produces more wine than all the famous appellations of the Médoc combined—St.-Estèphe, Pauillac, St.-Julien, and Margaux.

**CHÂTEAU AUSONE**
*From its hilltop perch, this ancient château commands a spectacular view of the sweeping vineyards below.*

# THE CLASSIFICATION OF ST.-ÉMILION

St-Émilion wines were first classified in 1958, with the intention that the classification be revised every 10 years according to the performance of properties during the previous decade. Three basic categories were established: *premier grand cru classé*, *grand cru classé*, and *grand cru*. Of the 12 châteaux that were originally classified *premiers grands crus classés*, Ausone and Cheval-Blanc were placed in a superior subsection. The rest were listed alphabetically, not qualitatively, as were the 64 *grands crus classés*. The classification was revised in 1969, 1985 (some six years late), and again in 1996 and 2006—which brought the reclassification period back to that anticipated. Beware the distinction between *grand cru* (unclassified growths) and *grand cru classé* (classified growths) because the difference is considerable. In St-Émilion, *grand cru* merely indicates a minimum alcoholic strength 0.5% higher than that required by the basic St-Émilion appellation, and a slightly lower yield. Any producer may apply for a *grand cru*, and hundreds do so. It is not a classification, but merely an adjunct to the appellation, and would be more accurately conveyed as a new appellation called St-Émilion Supérieur, since the difference between St-Émilion and *grand cru* is akin to that between basic Bordeaux and Bordeaux Supérieur.

## ST-ÉMILION CLASSIFICATIONS OF 1958, 1969, 1985, 1996, AND 2006
### Incorporating vineyard soil classification

### PREMIER GRAND CRU CLASSÉ CLASS A
1 Château Ausone
   Soil: *Côte and St-Émilion plateau*
22 Château Cheval Blanc
   Soil: *Graves and ancient sand*

### PREMIER GRAND CRU CLASSÉ CLASS B
3 Château l'Angélus [7]
   Soil: *Pied de côte and ancient sand*
4 Château Beau-Séjour Bécot [1, 7]
   Soil: *St-Émilion plateau and côte*
5 Château Beauséjour (Duffau Lagarosse)
   Soil: *Côte*
6 Château Belair Soil: *St-Émilion plateau and côte*
7 Château Canon
   Soil: *St-Émilion plateau and côte*
8 Château-Figeac
   Soil: *Graves and ancient sand*
9 Clos Fourtet
   Soil: *St-Émilion plateau and ancient sand*
10 Château la Gaffelière
   Soil: *Côte, pied de côte*
11 Château Magdelaine
   Soil: *St-Émilion plateau, côte, and pied de côte*
12 Château Pavie
   Soil: *Côte and St-Émilion plateau*
64 Château Pavie Macquin [10]
   Soil: *St-Émilion plateau, côte, and sandy gravel*
79 Château Troplong Mondot [10]
   Soil: *St-Émilion plateau*
13 Château Trottevieille
   Soil: *St-Émilion plateau*

### GRAND CRU CLASSÉ
14 Château l'Arrosée
   Soil: *Côte*
15 Château Baleau (now Château Côte de Baleau) [1, 3]
   Soil: *Côte and ancient sand*
16 Château Balestard la Tonnelle
   Soil: *St-Émilion plateau*
- Château Bellefont-Belcier
   Soil: *St-Émilion plateau*
17 Château Bellevue [11]
   Soil: *Côte and St-Émilion plateau*
18 Château Bergat
   Soil: *Côte and St-Émilion plateau*
19 Château Berliquet [2]
   Soil: *Côte and pied de côte*
20 Château Cadet-Bon [1, 8, 11]
   Soil: *St-Émilion plateau and côte*
21 Château Cadet-Piola
   Soil: *St-Émilion plateau and côte*
22 Château Canon-la-Gaffelière
   Soil: *Pied de côte and sandy-gravel*

23 Château Cap de Mourlin
   Soil: *Côte and ancient sand*
- Château la Carte [4]
   Soil: *St-Émilion plateau and ancient sand*
- Château Chapelle-Madeleine [5]
   Soil: *Côte and St-Émilion plateau*
24 Château le Châtelet [9]
   Soil: *Côte and ancient sand*
25 Château Chauvin
   Soil: *Ancient sand*
26 Château Clos des Jacobins
   Soil: *Côte and ancient sand*
27 Château la Clotte
   Soil: *Côte*
28 Château la Clusière
   Soil: *Côte*
29 Château Corbin
   Soil: *Ancient sand*
30 Château Corbin Michotte
   Soil: *Ancient sand*
31 Château la Couspaude [1, 8]
   Soil: *St-Émilion plateau*
32 Château Coutet [1]
   Soil: *Côte*
- Château le Couvent [6]
   Soil: *St-Émilion plateau*
33 Couvent des Jacobins [3]
   Soil: *Ancient sand and pied de côte*
34 Château Croque Michotte [9]
   Soil: *Ancient sand and graves*
35 Château Curé Bon la Madeleine
   Soil: *St-Émilion plateau and côte*
36 Château Dassault [3]
   Soil: *Ancient sand*
- Château Destieux
   Soil: *Côte*
37 Château la Dominique
   Soil: *Ancient sand and graves*
38 Château Faurie de Souchard [11]
   Soil: *Pied de côte*
- Château Fleur Cardinale
   Soil: *St-Émilion plateau*
39 Château Fonplégade
   Soil: *Côte*
40 Château Fonroque
   Soil: *Côte and ancient sand*
41 Château Franc-Mayne
   Soil: *Côte*
42 Château Grand Barrail Lamarzelle Figeac [9]
   Soil: *Ancient sand*
43 Château Grand Corbin [9]
   Soil: *Ancient sand*
44 Château Grand-Corbin-Despagne [9]
   Soil: *Ancient sand*
45 Château Grand Mayne
   Soil: *Côte and ancient sand*
46 Château Grandes Murailles [1, 8]
   Soil: *Côte and ancient sand*
47 Château Grand-Pontet
   Soil: *Côte and ancient sand*

48 Château Guadet St-Julien
   Soil: *St-Émilion plateau*
49 Château Haut-Corbin
   Soil: *Ancient sand*
50 Château Haut-Sarpe [3]
   Soil: *St-Émilion and St-Christophe plateaux and côtes*
51 Château Jean Faure [1]
   Soil: *Ancient sand*
52 Château Laniote [3]
   Soil: *Ancient sand and pied de côte*
53 Château Larcis Ducasse
   Soil: *Côte and pied de côte*
54 Château Larmande Soil: *Ancient sand*
55 Château Laroque [8]
   Soil: *St-Émilion plateau and côte*
56 Château Laroze
   Soil: *Ancient sand*
57 Clos la Madeleine [9]
   Soil: *St-Émilion plateau and côte*
58 Château la Marzelle [11] (now Château Lamarzelle)
   Soil: *Ancient sand and graves*
59 Château Matras [3]
   Soil: *Pied de côte*
60 Château Mauvezin
   Soil: *St-Émilion plateau and côte*
- Château Monbousquet
   Soil: *Côte*
61 Château Moulin du Cadet
   Soil: *Côte and ancient sand*
62 Clos de l'Oratoire [3]
   Soil: *Pied de côte*
63 Château Pavie Décesse
   Soil: *St-Émilion plateau and côte*
65 Château Pavillon-Cadet [9]
   Soil: *Côte and ancient sand*
66 Château Petit-Faurie-de-Soutard [11]
   Soil: *Ancient sand and côte*
67 Château le Prieuré
   Soil: *St-Émilion plateau and côte*
68 Château Ripeau
   Soil: *Ancient sand*
69 Château St-Georges (Côte Pavie)
   Soil: *Côte and pied de côte*
70 Clos St-Martin
   Soil: *Côte and ancient sand*
71 Château Sansonnet [9]
   Soil: *St-Émilion plateau*
72 Château la Serre
   Soil: *St-Émilion plateau*
73 Château Soutard
   Soil: *St-Émilion plateau and côte*
74 Château Tertre Daugay [3, 11]
   Soil: *St-Émilion plateau and côte*
75 Château la Tour Figeac
   Soil: *Ancient sand and graves*
76 Château la Tour du Pin Figeac [11] (Owner: Giraud-Belivier)
   Soil: *Ancient sand and graves*
77 Château la Tour du Pin Figeac [11] (Owner: Moueix)
   Soil: *Ancient sand and graves*

78 Château Trimoulet
   Soil: *Ancient sand and graves*
- Château Trois-Moulins [4]
   Soil: *St-Émilion plateau and côte*
80 Château Villemaurine [11]
   Soil: *St-Émilion plateau*
81 Château Yon-Figeac [11]
   Soil: *Ancient sand*

*See opposite* for an explanation of soil types.

### NOTES
[1] One *premier grand cru classé* and six *grands crus classés* demoted in the 1985 revision.
[2] This property was not in the original 1958 classification, nor was it included in the 1969 revision, but was awarded *grand cru classé* status in 1985.
[3] These properties were not in the original 1958 classification, but were awarded *grand cru classé* status in the 1969 revision.
[4] These two properties were merged with *premier grand cru classé* Château Beau-Séjour-Bécot in 1979. Wines bearing both labels can be found up to the 1978 vintage, and it is possible that they might reappear sometime in the future, particularly as the expansion of Château Beau-Séjour-Bécot vineyard was primarily responsible for its demotion in the 1985 classification.
[5] This property was merged with *premier grand cru classé* Château Ausone in 1970. Wines with this label can be found up to the 1969 vintage.
[6] This property changed hands prior to the 1985 revision and did not apply to be considered; it was not demoted, but simply ignored.
[7] Properties promoted to *premier grand cru classé* (B) in 1996.
[8] Properties promoted to *grand cru classé* in 1996.
[9] Properties demoted in 1996.
[10] Properties promoted to *premier grand cru classé* (B) in 2006.
[11] Properties demoted in 2006.

## FACTORS AFFECTING TASTE AND QUALITY

### LOCATION
St.-Émilion is on the right bank of the Dordogne, 80 miles (50 kilometers) east of Bordeaux.

### CLIMATE
The climate is less maritime and more continental than that of the Médoc, with a greater variation in daily temperatures—there is also slightly more rain during spring, and substantially less during summer and winter.

### ASPECT
The village of St.-Émilion sits on a plateau where vines grow at an altitude of 80–330 ft (25–100 m). These vineyards are quite steep, particularly south of the village where two slopes face each other. The plateau continues eastward in the form of hilly knolls. North and west of the village, the vineyards are on flatter ground.

### SOIL
St.-Émilion's soil is extremely complex (see "The question of quality," right) and is part of the area known as "Pomerol-Figeac graves" that encompasses the châteaux Cheval Blanc and Figeac.

### VITICULTURE AND VINIFICATION
Some of the vin de presse, usually the first pressing only, is considered necessary by many châteaux. Skin-contact usually lasts for 15–21 days, but may last up to four weeks. Some wines spend as little as 12 months in cask, but the average is nearer to 15–22 months.

### GRAPE VARIETIES
**Primary varieties:** Cabernet Franc, Cabernet Sauvignon, Merlot
**Secondary varieties:** Malbec, Carmenère

## THE QUESTION OF QUALITY

The diverse nature of St.-Émilion's soil has led to many generalizations that attempt to relate the quantity and character of the wines produced to the soils from which they come. Initially the wines were lumped into two crude categories, côtes (literally "hillside" or "slope") and graves (literally "gravelly terrain"). The term côtes was supposed to describe fairly full-bodied wines that develop quickly; the term graves, fuller, firmer, and richer wines that take longer to mature.

The simplicity was appealing, but it ignored the many wines produced on the stretch of deep sand between St.-Émilion and Pomerol, and those of the plateau, which has a heavier topsoil than the côtes. It also failed to distinguish between the eroded côtes and the deep-soiled bottom slopes. But most importantly, it ignored the fact that many châteaux are spread across more than one soil type (see the list of classified growths opposite) and that they have various other factors of terroir, such as aspect and drainage, which affect the character and quality of a wine (see Soil Survey of St.-Émilion, below).

The map below shows the positions of the 81 classified châteaux of St.-Émilion, listed with their soil types (see opposite). Châteaux la Carte, Chapelle-Madeleine, le Couvent, and Trois-Moulins are listed but do not appear on the map (see notes opposite).

## SOIL SURVEY OF ST-ÉMILION

The map below shows the area covered by premier grand cru classé and grand cru classé châteaux. Each soil type is described (right) and color keyed on the map. The numbers of the châteaux are listed opposite.

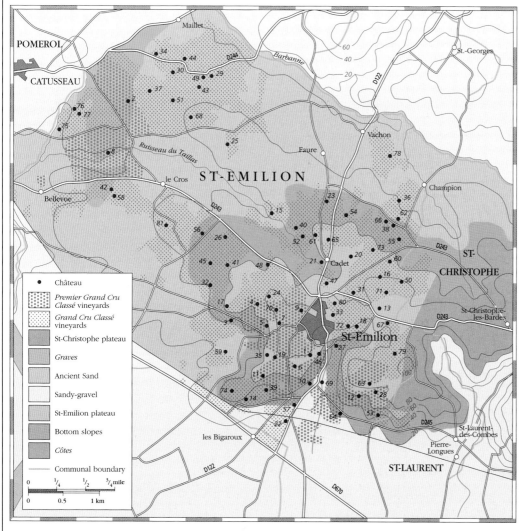

**Château**
- Premier Grand Cru Classé vineyards
- Grand Cru Classé vineyards
- St-Christophe plateau
- Graves
- Ancient Sand
- Sandy-gravel
- St-Emilion plateau
- Bottom slopes
- Côtes
- Communal boundary

**ST.-CHRISTOPHE PLATEAU**
Clay-limestone and clay-sand topsoil over limestone and terra rossa subsoil (a red, claylike, limestone soil).

**GRAVES**
Deep gravel topsoil with a subsoil of large-grain sand over a very deep, hard, and impermeable sedimentary rock called molasse. The gravel is similar to that found in the Médoc.

**ANCIENT SAND**
Thick blanket of large-grain sand over a subsoil of molasse. The bulk of this sand extends northeast from the village of St.-Émilion toward Pomerol. Although this area seems to have a gentle slope all around it, and the sand is very permeable, the molasse below is flat and impermeable. The water collects, saturating root systems and increasing soil acidity. Some châteaux benefit greatly from underground drainage pipes.

**SANDY-GRAVEL**
Sandy and sandy-gravel topsoil over sandy-gravel, ferruginous gravel, and iron-pan.

**ST.-ÉMILION PLATEAU**
Shallow clay-limestone and clay sand, shell debris, and silt topsoil over eroded limestone subsoil.

**BOTTOM SLOPES**
The gentler bottom slopes of the côtes have a deep, reddish-brown, sandy-loam topsoil over yellow sand subsoil.

**CÔTES**
The lower-middle to upper slopes of the côtes have a shallow, calcareous, clay-silty-loam topsoil with a high active lime content. Quite sandy on the middle slopes, the topsoil thins out higher up. The subsoil is mostly molasse, not the impermeable type found under the ancient sand and graves, but a weathered, absorbent molasse of limestone or sandstone.

# THE WINE PRODUCERS OF
# SAINT-ÉMILION

## CHÂTEAU ANGÉLUS
### Premier Grand Cru Classé (B)
### ★★

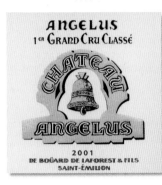

ANGELUS
1ᴱᴿ GRAND CRU CLASSÉ
CHÂTEAU
ANGELUS
2001
DE BOÜARD DE LAFOREST & FILS
SAINT-ÉMILION

This is a large property with a single plot of vines on the south-facing *côtes*. At one time the château produced wines in the old "farmyard" style, but that ended with the 1980 vintage. Two-thirds of the wine is matured for 14 to 16 months in wood with 100 per cent new oak. This château is a rising star, and was promoted to *premier grand cru classé* (B) in 1996.

**RED** This is a soft, silky, and seductive wine. The luxury of new oak is having a positive effect on the quality, character, and aging potential of this wine.

Cabernet Franc 50%, Merlot 45%, Cabernet Sauvignon 5%

7–20 years

**Second wine:** *Carillon de l'Angélus*

## CHÂTEAU L'ARROSÉE
### Grand Cru Classé
### ★☆❻

This property sits on the *côtes* above the local *coopérative*. Through excellent selection of only its finest grapes, it has consistently produced wines that are a class above those of many of its peers. Under new ownership (Roger Caille) since 2003.

**RED** A voluptuous bouquet, and soft, creamy-rich fruit backed up by supple oak tannin.

Merlot 50%, Cabernet Sauvignon 35%, Cabernet Franc 15%

5–15 years

**Second wine:** *Les Coteaux du Château l'Arrosée*

## CHÂTEAU AUSONE
### Premier Grand Cru Classé (A)
### ★★★

After gifted winemaker Pascal Delbeck took control of Château Ausone in 1975, this prestigious property produced wines of stunning quality, and it now deserves its superstar status. In 1997, after a power struggle between the two owners, Alain Vauthier took control

and fired Delbeck and hired Michel Rolland as consultant. The vineyard of Château Ausone has a privileged southeast exposure and its vines are fairly established at between 40 and 45 years of age. They are capable of yielding very concentrated wines, which are then matured in wood for between 16 and 22 months, with 100 percent new oak.

**RED** These rich, well-colored wines have opulent aromas and scintillating flavors. They are full in body, compact in structure, and refined in character, with masses of spicy-cassis fruit and creamy-oak undertones. These wines are the quintessence of class, complexity, and finesse.

Cabernet Franc 50%, Merlot 50%

15–45 years

## CHÂTEAU BALESTARD LA TONNELLE
### Grand Cru Classé
### ★

The label of this wine bears a 15th-century poem by François Villon that cites the name of the château. One-third of the wine is matured in 100 percent new oak for up to 24 months, one-third is aged in two-year-old barrels, and the remainder rests in stainless-steel vats until bottling, when it is all blended together.

**RED** The gentle, ripe aromas of this wine belie its staunchly traditional style. It is a full-bodied wine of great extract, tannin, and acidity that requires time to soften, but it has masses of fruit, and so matures gracefully.

Merlot 65%, Cabernet Franc 20%, Cabernet Sauvignon 10%, Malbec 5%

10–30 years

**Second wine:** *Les Tourelles de Balestard*

## CHÂTEAU BEAUSÉJOUR
### (Owner: Duffau-Lagarosse)
### Premier Grand Cru Classé (B)
### ★★

These little-seen wines consistently underwhelmed critics until the 1980s, since when Château Beauséjour began to produce darker, fuller wines with more class, but I was not that impressed until the stellar class 2000 vintage.

**RED** Lovely rich wine, with concentrated fruit, and great potential longevity from 2000 onward.

Merlot 50%, Cabernet Franc 25%, Cabernet Sauvignon 25%

7–15 years

**Second wine:** *La Croix de Mazerat*

## CHÂTEAU BEAU-SÉJOUR BÉCOT
### Premier Grand Cru Classé (B)
### ★★

Since 1979, this property has almost doubled in size by merging with two *grands crus classés*, Château la Carte and Château Trois Moulins. In 1985, Beau-Séjour Bécot was the only *premier grand cru classé* to be demoted in the revision of the St-Émilion classification. The demotion was not due to its quality or performance, which were consistently excellent, but because of its expansion. In 1996 this château was promoted and is once again a *premier grand cru classé* (B). The wine is fermented in stainless steel and matured in wood for 18 months, with 90 percent new oak.

**RED** Once lightweight and high-tone, this wine is now full, rich, and truly characterful. The silky Merlot fruit develops quickly, but is backed up with creamy new oak.

Merlot 70%, Cabernet Franc 15%, Cabernet Sauvignon 15%

7–25 years

**Second wine:** *La Tournelle des Moines*

## CHÂTEAU BELAIR
### Premier Grand Cru Classé (B)
### ★★

Pascal Delbeck, the winemaker formerly of Château Ausone, lives here and makes the wine with the same care and attention that he used to apply at Ausone. The wine is matured in wood for 16 to 20 months. Up to half is aged in new oak. This is one of the very best *premiers grands crus*.

**RED** This is a deep-colored, full-bodied wine with a rich flavor of plums, chocolate, black cherries, and cassis. It has great finesse.

Merlot 60%, Cabernet Franc 40%

10–35 years

**Second wine:** *Roc Blanquet*

## CHÂTEAU BELLEVUE
### ★★☆

This small property was originally called Fief-de-Bellevue and belonged to the Lacaze family from 1642 to 1938. Up to and through the 1990s, Bellevue was an underperformer at best, but since 2000 the wines have shown their true class under manager Nicolas Thienpont and ace consultant Stéphane Derenoncourt. So to be demoted from Grand Cru Classé in 2006 was perverse.

**RED** Beautifully ripe fruit, sleek, with great finesse, and remarkably evocative of its *terroir*.

Merlot 67%, Cabernet Franc 16.5%, Cabernet Sauvignon 16.5%

5–10 years

## CHÂTEAU BERGAT
### Grand Cru Classé
### ❷

This small vineyard is jointly owned by Emile Castéja and the Preben Hansen family.

**RED** Medium-bodied, with ample fruit for easy drinking, and hints of oak on the finish.

Merlot 50%, Cabernet Franc 40%, Cabernet Sauvignon 10%

4–6 years

## CHÂTEAU BERLIQUET
### Grand Cru Classé
### ★★☆

The only property upgraded to *grand cru classé* in 1985. The wine is fermented in stainless steel vats and matured in wood for 18 months, with 30 percent new oak.

**RED** These are deep, dark, and dense wines with spicy-cassis fruit and good vanilla oak.

Merlot 70%, Cabernet Franc and Cabernet Sauvignon 30%

10–30 years

## CHÂTEAU CADET-BON
### ★

This property was demoted from *grand cru classé* in 1985, reinstated in 1996, then demoted again in 2006! The last demotion was not as bewildering as Bellevue, but it was surprising nonetheless. However, under the wine wizardry of Stéphane Derenoncourt these wines stepped up another gear from 2004, ensuring that Cadet-Bon will be promoted once again in 2016.

**RED** From the 1990s until 2003, this wine was not the richest on the block, but it had an ampleness that made for easy, early drinking. Since 2004 there has been increasing richness, with a very fine, elegant tannin structure.

Merlot 60%, Cabernet Franc 40%

7–20 years

## CHÂTEAU CADET-PIOLA
### Grand Cru Classé
### ★

This property usually shows great consistency and exquisite style. Up to 50 percent of the wine is matured in new oak.

**RED** These are full-bodied, intensely flavored wines with powerful, new-oak character and great tannic strength.

Merlot 51%, Cabernet Sauvignon 28%, Cabernet Franc 18%, Malbec 3%

12–25 years

**Second wine:** *Chevalier de Malte*

## CHÂTEAU CANON
### Premier Grand Cru Classé (B)
### ★★ⓥ

Many years ago this château used to produce a second wine called "St.-Martin-de-Mazerat," which was the old parish name before Château Canon was absorbed by St.-Émilion. Excellent wines were made under Eric Forner and although he sold out in 1996 the quality has been maintained. In summer 2000 the new owners, Chanel Inc., bought the nearby property Curé Bon la Madeleine with INAO agreement to incorporate it into Canon from the 2000 vintage. So goodbye Curé Bon! The *grand vin*, fermented in oak vats and matured in wood for 20 months with 50 percent new oak, is one of the best of St.-Émilion's *premiers grands crus classés*.

**RED** These wines have a deep purple color, an opulent cassis bouquet, and are very rich and voluptuous on the palate with masses of juicy Merlot fruit and spicy complexity.

🍇 Merlot 55%, Cabernet Franc 40%, Cabernet Sauvignon 4%

🍷 8–30 years

**Second wine:** *Clos J. Kanon*

## CHÂTEAU CANON-LA-GAFFELIÈRE
### Grand Cru Classé
### ★★☆

Owned since 1985 by Comte Von Neippberg, Château Canon-la Gaffeliére is one of the oldest properties in St.-Émilion. Its wine was fermented in stainless-steel vats until wooden vats were installed in 1997, and the quality soared the very next year. Malolactic fermentation is carried out in barrel and the wines matured for 18 months, with up to 50 percent new oak.

**RED** This wine has been on form since 1998. It has been really plump, displaying vivid, concentrated, spicy fruit, finishing with creamy oak.

🍇 Merlot 65%, Cabernet Franc 30%, Cabernet Sauvignon 5%

🍷 8–20 years

**Other wines:** *Côte Mignon-la-Gaffelière*

## CHÂTEAU CAP DE MOURLIN
### Grand Cru Classé
### ★

Until 1982 there were two versions of this wine, one bearing the name of Jacques Capdemourlin and one that of Jean Capdemourlin. This property is run by Jacques. The wine is matured in wood for up to 24 months, with one-third new oak.

**RED** An improving, attractive, well-made, medium-bodied wine, with exquisitely fresh fruit, and a smooth finish.

🍇 Merlot 60%, Cabernet Franc 25%, Cabernet Sauvignon 12%, Malbec 3%

🍷 6–15 years

**Second wine:** *Mayne d'Artagnon*

## CHÂTEAU LA CARTE
### Grand Cru Classé

Since 1980, the vineyards of this property have been merged with those of *premier grand cru classé* Château Beau-Séjour-Bécot.

## CHÂTEAU CHAPELLE-MADELEINE
### Grand Cru Classé until 1996

Since 1971, these vineyards have been merged with those of *premier grand cru classé* Château Ausone.

## CHÂTEAU CHAUVIN
### Grand Cru Classé
### ★

This property's wine is matured in wood for 18 months, with one-third new oak. It is difficult to find, but its quality makes it deserving of better distribution.

**RED** When on form, Château Chauvin can have excellent color, an aromatic bouquet, full body, and plummy fruit. More hits than misses these days, as the wines are made with an increasing degree of finesse.

🍇 Merlot 60%, Cabernet Franc 30%, Cabernet Sauvignon 10%

🍷 4–10 years

**Second wine:** *Chauvin Variation*

## CHÂTEAU CHEVAL BLANC
### Premier Grand Cru Classé (A)
### ★★★

The unusual aspect of this great wine is its high proportion of Cabernet Franc, which harks back to the pre-1956 era. Switching to a majority of Merlot vines was advantageous for most Libournais properties but keeping a proportion of 60 percent Cabernet Franc was even better for Château Cheval Blanc. In 1998 this château was bought by two businessmen, Albert Frère from Belgium and Bernard Arnault, the head of LVMH. The wine is matured in wood for 20 months, with 100 percent new oak.

**RED** These wines have all the sweet, spicy richness one expects from a classic St.-Émilion property situated on *graves*.

🍇 Cabernet Franc 60%, Merlot 37%, Malbec 2%, Cabernet Sauvignon 1%

🍷 12–40 years

**Second wine:** *Le Petit Cheval*

## CLOS FOURTET
### Premier Grand Cru Classé (B)
### ★☆ⓥ

This property had an inconsistent record, but has steadily improved throughout the 1990s. The wines are matured in wood for 12 to 18 months, using 70 percent new oak.

**RED** Opulent and medium-bodied with silky Merlot fruit, gaining in complexity and finesse.

🍇 Merlot 60%, Cabernet Franc 20%, Cabernet Sauvignon 20%

🍷 6–12 years

**Second wine:** *Domaine de Martialis*

## CHÂTEAU CLOS DES JACOBINS
### Grand Cru Classé
### ★

Clos des Jacobins, which is kept in the impeccable style to which all the Cordier properties are accustomed, is impressive even during "off vintages."

**RED** These are rich, fat wines, bursting with chocolate and black-cherry flavors.

🍇 Merlot 85%, Cabernet Franc 10%, Cabernet Sauvignon 5%

🍷 8–25 years

## CLOS DE L'ORATOIRE
### Grand Cru Classé
### ★★

This property belongs to Stephan von Neipperg, who has developed a cult following for this wine. The wine is matured in wood for 18 months, with one-third new oak.

**RED** These fine, full-flavored wines tend to have great concentration and style.

🍇 Merlot 75%, Cabernet Franc 25%

🍷 7–15 years

## CLOS ST.-MARTIN
### Grand Cru Classé
### ★

These wines are made at Château Côte Baleau alongside those of that property and those of Château Grandes Murailles. Of these three wines, only Clos St.-Martin retained *grand cru classé* status after the reclassification of 1985. It is aged in wood with 25 percent new barrels every four years.

**RED** Vivid color with ripe Merlot fruit, silky texture, and elegant style.

🍇 Merlot 75%, Cabernet Franc 25%

🍷 6–15 years

## CHÂTEAU LA CLOTTE
### Grand Cru Classé
### ❓

This property is under the same ownership as the Logis de la Cadène restaurant in St.-Émilion, where much of its wine is sold. The Libournais *négociant* Jean-Pierre Moueix takes three-quarters of the crop.

**RED** Although not as consistent as some *grands crus classés*, when successful this estate can make attractive and elegant wines with lots of soft, silky fruit that are a match for its peers.

🍇 Merlot 70%, Cabernet Franc 30%

🍷 5–12 years

## CHÂTEAU LA CLUSIÈRE
### Grand Cru Classé
### ❓

This is a small enclave within the property of Château Pavie and is under the same ownership as Pavie and Château Pavie Décesse. This wine is fermented in stainless-steel vats and matured in wood (two-year-old barrels from Château Pavie) for up to 24 months.

**RED** This wine has a certain elegance, but lacks finesse and has a high-tone style that does not appeal to me. To be fair, I must point out that those who appreciate this style often find la Clusière solid and characterful.

🍇 Merlot 70%, Cabernet Franc 20%, Cabernet Sauvignon 10%

🍷 5–10 years

## CHÂTEAU CORBIN
### Grand Cru Classé
### ★☆

This property has the same owners as Château Grand Corbin—the Corbin estate, which is now divided into five separate properties bordering the Pomerol district. The wine is fermented in stainless steel and one-third of the production is matured in 100 percent new oak.

**RED** Deep-colored, full-bodied, and deliciously rich, but rather rustic for a classified growth.

🍇 Merlot 67%, Cabernet Franc and Cabernet Sauvignon 33%

🍷 6–12 years

**Other wines:** *Latour Corbin, Château Corbin-Vieille-Tour*

## CHÂTEAU CORBIN MICHOTTE
### Grand Cru Classé
### ★

This is one of five Corbin and two Michotte estates! This wine is fermented in stainless steel and some is matured in wood, with one-third new oak.

**RED** A dark, deeply flavored, full-bodied wine that has rich, juicy Merlot fruit and some finesse.

🍇 Merlot 65%, Cabernet Franc 30%, Cabernet Sauvignon 5%

🍷 6–15 years

**Second wine:** *Les Abeilles*

## CHÂTEAU CÔTE DE BALEAU
### Grand Cru Classé until 1985
★

This property was unjustly demoted from its *grand cru classé* status in the 1985 revision. Côte de Baleau deserves its former classification and is under the same ownership as Château Grandes Murailles and Clos St.-Martin, the former of which was also unfairly demoted. This wine is aged in wood and 25 percent of the barrels are renewed every four years.

**RED** Full, rich, and well-balanced wines that have good fruit, some fat, and an attractive underlying vanilla character.

🍇 Merlot 70%, Cabernet Sauvignon 20%, Cabernet Franc 10%

🍷 4–12 years

**Second wine:** *Des Roches Blanches*

## CHÂTEAU LA COUSPAUDE
### Grand Cru Classé
★

This property was demoted from its *grand cru classé* status in 1985 but, following a string of good vintages, was promoted back to its original classification in 1996, since when the quality has continued to improve. The wine is matured in wood, with up to 80 percent new oak.

**RED** This wine now has lots of upfront, juicy-Merlot fruit with an increasing amount of finesse.

🍇 Merlot 60%, Cabernet Franc and Cabernet Sauvignon 40%

🍷 3–7 years

**Second wine:** *Hubert*

## CHÂTEAU COUTET
### Grand Cru Classé until 1985
❓

This property was demoted from its *grand cru classé* status in 1985. It has a record of producing finer wines than la Couspaude (see previous entry), but, unfortunately, has the same lack of consistency.

**RED** Most vintages have a light but elegant style, with a firm tannin structure.

🍇 Cabernet Franc 45%, Merlot 45%, Cabernet Sauvignon 5%, Malbec 5%

🍷 4–8 years

## COUVENT DES JACOBINS
### Grand Cru Classé
★

The wine from the young vines of this property is not included in its *grand vin*, but is used to make a second wine called "Château Beau Mayne." One-third of the production is matured in wood, with 100 percent new oak.

**RED** The delicious, silky-seductive fruit in this consistently well-made wine is very stylish and harmonious.

## CHÂTEAU CROQUE MICHOTTE
### Grand Cru Classé until 1996
◉★

This property certainly deserves its former *grand cru classé* status. The wine is fermented in stainless steel and matured in wood for between 18 and 24 months, with up to one-third new oak.

**RED** A delightful and elegant style of wine, brimming with juicy, soft, and silky Merlot fruit.

🍇 Merlot 80%, Cabernet Franc and Cabernet Sauvignon 20%

🍷 5–12 years

## CHÂTEAU CURÉ BON LA MADELEINE
### Grand Cru Classé

Surrounded by *premiers grus classés* such as Ausone, Belair, and Canon, this property has had an excellent record, but was absorbed by Château Canon in the summer of 2000.

## CHÂTEAU DASSAULT
### Grand Cru Classé
★⯪

This property was promoted to *grand cru classé* in the 1969 revision of the 1954 St.-Émilion classification. It has an excellent record and more than deserves its classification. The wine is fermented in stainless steel and matured in wood for 12 months, with one-third of the casks being new oak, and undergoes as many as six rackings. With its beautifully understated Lafite-like label, Dassault's presentation is perfect.

**RED** Supremely elegant wines that always display a delicate marriage of fruit and oak in perfect balance, with fine acidity and supple tannin.

🍇 Merlot 65%, Cabernet Franc 20%, Cabernet Sauvignon 15%

🍷 8–25 years

**Second wine:** *Merissac*

## CHÂTEAU LA DOMINIQUE
### Grand Cru Classé
★★

This property, one of the best of the *grands crus classés*, is situated close to Château Cheval Blanc on the *graves* in the extreme west of St.-Émilion. The wine is fermented in stainless-steel vats that are equipped with grilles to keep the *marc* (residue of pips, stalks, and skin) submerged during the *cuvaison* (skin-contact fermentation). It is matured in wood for 24 months, with 50 percent new oak.

**RED** Very open and expressive wines that are plump and attractive, full of ripe, creamy fruit with elegant underlying oak.

🍇 Merlot 60%, Cabernet Franc 15%, Cabernet Sauvignon 15%, Malbec 10%

🍷 8–25 years

**Second wine:** *St.-Paul de la Dominique*

## CHÂTEAU FAURIE DE SOUCHARD

This lackluster underperformer was demoted from *grand cru classé* in 2006.

**RED** Recent vintages have increased in concentration and color, but the wines are not special.

🍇 Merlot 65%, Cabernet Franc 26%, Cabernet Sauvignon 9%

🍷 4–7 years

**Other wines:** *Cadet-Peychez*

## CHÂTEAU-FIGEAC
### Premier Grand Cru Classé (B)
★★★

Some critics suggest that the unusually high proportion of Cabernet Sauvignon in the *encépagement* (varietal blend) of this great château is wrong, but owner Thierry de Manoncourt refutes this. He has bottles of pure varietal wines produced at Figeac going back 30 years. As far as I am concerned, his blended *grand vin* says it all every year. This château belongs with the elite of Ausone and its *graves* neighbor, Cheval Blanc. The wine is matured in wood for 18 to 20 months, with 100 percent new oak.

**RED** Impressively ripe, rich, and concentrated wines with fine color, a beautiful bouquet, stunning creamy-ripe fruit, great finesse, and a wonderful spicy complexity.

🍇 Merlot 30%, Cabernet Franc 35%, Cabernet Sauvignon 35%

🍷 12–30 years

**Second wine:** *La Grange Neuve*

## CHÂTEAU FONPLÉGADE
### Grand Cru Classé

Under the same ownership as Château la Tour du Pin Figeac, this property belongs to Armand Moueix, cousin of Jean-Pierre Moueix of Château Pétrus *et al.* The wine is matured in wood for 12 to 15 months, using one-third new oak.

**RED** I used to find this wine astringent and vegetal, earthy even, but then it appeared to pick up, only to lapse. There have been so many false starts in its perceived improvement that I no longer expect any consistency. Even though the best vintages (1982, 1990, 2000, and 2001) have been delightfully clean and attractive, literally bursting with the soft, ripe, juicy flavors of raspberries and strawberries, mostly this is an

austere, tannic wine with attenuated fruit, and lacking style.

🍇 Merlot 60%, Cabernet Franc 35%, Cabernet Sauvignon 5%

🍷 5–12 years

**Second wine:** *Clos Goudichaud*

## CHÂTEAU FONROQUE
### Grand Cru Classé
★

Located just northwest of St.-Émilion itself, this secluded property has belonged to the négociant J.-P. Moueix since 1931. The wine is matured in wood for 24 months.

**RED** This is a deep-colored, well-made wine with a fine plummy character that shows better on the bouquet and the initial and middle palate than on the finish.

🍇 Merlot 70%, Cabernet Franc 30%

🍷 6–15 years

## CHÂTEAU LA GAFFELIÈRE
### Premier Grand Cru Classé (B)
★★⯪

This property belongs to Comte Léo de Malet-Roquefort, who also owns the very old estate of Château Tertre Daugay, a *grand cru classé*. After a string of aggressive, ungenerous vintages, Gaffelière has produced increasingly excellent wines since the mid-1980s. The wine is matured in wood for 18 months, with 100 percent new oak.

**RED** These wines are concentrated and tannic, but they now have much more finesse, fat, and mouth-tingling richness than previously.

🍇 Merlot 65%, Cabernet Franc 20%, Cabernet Sauvignon 15%

🍷 12–35 years

**Second wine:** *Clos la Gaffelière*
**Other wines:** *Roquefort*

## CHÂTEAU LA GOMERIE
### Grand Cru
★★

Owned by Gérard and Dominique Bécot of Beau-Séjour-Bécot fame, I rather get the impression that the tiny production of this 100 percent Merlot vinified in 100 percent new oak is the vinous equivalent of giving the finger to the authorities. The unfair demotion of Beau-Séjour-Bécot in 1985 (rectified in 1996) was a cruel and unjustified blow to the Bécots, who had improved the quality of their wine. By producing an unclassified superpremium St.-Émilion that demands and receives a higher price than its own *premier grand cru classé*, the Bécots have demonstrated that the classification is meaningless.

**RED** Masses of rich, ripe Merlot fruit dominate this wine, despite its 100 percent new oak. A stunning wine that deserves its cult following.

🍇 Merlot 100%

🍷 4–18 years

## CHÂTEAU GRAND-CORBIN-DESPAGNE
**Grand Cru Classé**
★ ✪

This part of the Corbin estate was bought by the Despagne family—hence the name. It was demoted in the 1996 St-Émilion Classification but reinstated in 2006. The wine is fermented in stainless steel and matured in wood for up to 18 months, with some new oak.

**RED** A well-colored wine of full and rich body with plenty of creamy fruit and oak, supported by supple tannin.

🍇 Merlot 90%, Cabernet Franc 10%

🍷 7–25 years

**Second wine:** *Reine-Blanche*

## CHÂTEAU GRANDES MURAILLES
**Grand Cru Classé**
★

This property was demoted from its *grand cru classé* status in 1985, unjustly I think. The wines produced here are better and more consistent than those of many châteaux that were not demoted at that time. Château Grandes Murailles was, however, promoted back to its previous status in the 1996 St.-Émilion Classification. It is under the same ownership as Château Côte de Baleau and Clos St.-Martin, the former of which was also unfairly demoted. The wine is fermented in stainless-steel vats and matured in wood for 20 months, using up to 25 percent new oak.

**RED** These elegant, harmonious wines have good extract and a supple tannin structure that quickly softens. They are a delight to drink when relatively young, although they also age gracefully.

🍇 Merlot 60%, Cabernet Franc 20%, Cabernet Sauvignon 20%

🍷 5–20 years

## CHÂTEAU GRAND MAYNE
**Grand Cru Classé**
★ ✫ ✪

This château ferments its wine in stainless-steel vats and ages it in wood with 80 percent new oak.

**RED** This is a firm, fresh, and fruity style of wine that had a rather inconsistent reputation until the 1990s, when the wines have had much more richness than in previous years.

🍇 Merlot 50%, Cabernet Franc 40%, Cabernet Sauvignon 10%

🍷 4–10 years

**Second wine:** *Les Plantes du Mayne*
**Other wines:** *Cassevert, Château Beau Mazerat*

## CHÂTEAU GRAND-PONTET
**Grand Cru Classé**
★ ✫ ✪

Since 1980 this property has been under the same ownership as

Château Beau-Séjour Bécot. The wine is matured in wood for 12–18 months with 50 percent new oak.

**RED** After a string of very dull vintages, this property is now producing full-bodied wines of fine quality and character. They are fat and ripe, rich in fruit and tannin, with delightful underlying creamy-oak flavors.

🍇 Merlot 60%, Cabernet Franc and Cabernet Sauvignon 40%

🍷 6–15 years

## CHÂTEAU GUADET ST.-JULIEN
**Grand Cru Classé**
✫

This property deserves its status. The wines are matured in wood for 18 to 20 months, using up to one-third new oak.

**RED** These are wines that show the silky charms of Merlot very early, and then tighten up for a few years before blossoming into finer and fuller wines.

🍇 Merlot 75%, Cabernet Franc and Cabernet Sauvignon 25%

🍷 7–20 years

## CHÂTEAU HAUT-CORBIN
**Grand Cru Classé**
★

This wine is matured in wood for 24 months, with up to 20 percent new oak. Same ownership as Canteneste, with a string of good vintages since the 1990s.

🍇 Merlot 70%, Cabernet Franc and Cabernet Sauvignon 30%

**Second wine:** *Vin d'Edouard*

## CHÂTEAU HAUT-SARPE
**Grand Cru Classé**
★

Although not one of the top performers, this château certainly deserves its status. The wine is matured in wood for 20 to 22 months, using 25 percent new oak.

**RED** Elegant, silky, and stylish medium-bodied wines that are best appreciated when young.

🍇 Merlot 70%, Cabernet Franc 30%

🍷 4–8 years

## CHÂTEAU JEAN FAURE
**Grand Cru Classé until 1985**

This property was demoted from its *grand cru classé* status in 1985. I have not tasted vintages beyond 1983. The wine is matured in wood for 24 months, with 25 percent new oak.

**RED** These wines have good color and easy, attractive, supple fruit.

🍇 Cabernet Franc 60%, Merlot 30%, Malbec 10%

🍷 3–8 years

## CHÂTEAU L'HERMITAGE
★

Owned by Véronique Gaboriaud, a friend of *garagiste* Jean-Luc

Thunevin, this well-sited property produces just 750 cases annually, with wines matured in 100 percent new oak.

**RED** So succulent and luscious is the fruit, and so supple the tannins, that this wine is accessible from a remarkably youthful age, yet will still improve.

🍇 Merlot 60%, Cabernet Sauvignon 40%

🍷 5–15 years

## CHÂTEAU LAMARZELLE
✫

Under the same ownership as Grand Barrail Lamarzelle Figeac, this property preserved its classification in 1996, while the other château was demoted—only to follow suit in 2006.

**RED** Forward, fruity wines that have improved throughout the 1990s.

🍇 Cabernet Franc 80%, Merlot 20%

🍷 3–7 years

## CHÂTEAU LANIOTE
**Grand Cru Classé**
✫

An old property that incorporates the "Holy Grotto" where St.-Émilion lived in the 8th century. The wine is fermented and matured in wood with 25 percent new oak.

**RED** Stylish medium-bodied wines, with plenty of fresh, elegant fruit.

🍇 Merlot 70%, Cabernet Franc 20%, Cabernet Sauvignon 10%

🍷 6–12 years

## CHÂTEAU LARCIS DUCASSE
**Grand Cru Classé**
★ ✫

This property, whose vineyard is situated on the Côte de Pavie, matures its wine in vat and wood for 24 months.

**RED** Fuller, richer wines in the 1990s, particularly in the best years.

🍇 Merlot 65%, Cabernet Franc and Cabernet Sauvignon 35%

🍷 4–8 years

## CHÂTEAU LARMANDE
**Grand Cru Classé**
★ ✫

Consistently one of the best *grands crus classés* in St.-Émilion, fermented in stainless-steel vats and matured in wood for 12 to 18 months, with 35 to 50 percent new oak.

**RED** These superb wines are typified by their great concentration of color and fruit. They are rich and ripe with an abundance of creamy cassis and vanilla flavors that develop into a cedarwood complexity.

🍇 Merlot 65%, Cabernet Franc 30%, Cabernet Sauvignon 5%

🍷 8–25 years

**Second wine:** *Le Cadet de Larmande*
**Other wines:** *Des Templiers*

## CHÂTEAU LAROQUE
**Grand Cru Classé**
★

Made a *grand cru classé* in 1996, this is one of three *grands crus classés* châteaux that are not situated in the commune of St.-Émilion itself.

**RED** As smooth and fruity as might be expected, with good tannic edge and increasing oak influence.

🍇 Merlot 80%, Cabernet Franc 15%, Cabernet Sauvignon 5%

🍷 4–16 years

**Second wine:** *Les Tours de Laroque*

## CHÂTEAU LAROZE
**Grand Cru Classé**
★ ✪

This 19th-century château was named Laroze after a "characteristic scent of roses" was found in its wines. The wine is matured in wood for one to three years.

**RED** The wine does have a soft and seductive bouquet, although I have yet to find "roses" in it. It is an immediately appealing wine of some finesse that is always a delight to drink early.

🍇 Merlot 50%, Cabernet Franc 45%, Cabernet Sauvignon 5%

🍷 4–10 years

## CHÂTEAU MAGDELAINE
**Premier Grand Cru Classé (B)**
★★ ✪

This could be considered the Pétrus of St.-Émilion. It is the grandest St.-Émilion estate in the Jean-Pierre Moueix Libournais empire, but as fine as the *terroir* is, and as much as Moueix does to extract maximum quality, the wine falls short of Pétrus. The wine matures in wood for 18 months, with a third new oak.

**RED** These well-colored wines have excellent concentration, yet great finesse and a certain delicacy. The flavor is multilayered with a long, elegant, and complex finish.

🍇 Merlot 80%, Cabernet Franc 20%

🍷 10–35 years

## CHÂTEAU MATRAS
**Grand Cru Classé**
✫

This wine is matured in tank for 12 months, followed by 12 months in one-third new oak.

**RED** Fine, floral, and firm.

🍇 Cabernet Franc 60%, Merlot 40%

🍷 6–15 years

## CHÂTEAU MAUVEZIN
### Grand Cru Classé
### ☆

This property deserves its *grand cru classé* status. The wine is fermented and matured in new oak.

**RED** Some stunningly supple vintages since 2001, showing great oak-laden, aromatic finesse.

🍇 Cabernet Franc 50%, Merlot 40%, Cabernet Sauvignon 10%

🍷 7–15 years

## CHÂTEAU MONBOUSQUET
### Grand Cru
### ★☆

This was hypermarket owner Gérard Perse's first venture into wine and he openly admits that he bought the property because of its beauty, rather than out of any detailed analysis of its viticultural potential. That said, he has, with the help of consultant Michel Rolland, taken this château to unbelievable heights and, having done so, set about analyzing what could and should be purchased in St.-Émilion from a purely viticultural perspective. He set his sights on Pavie and Pavie Décesse, which he purchased in 1998 and 1997. Monbousquet remains his home.

**RED** Voluptuous, velvety, and hedonistic, these wines lack neither complexity nor finesse, but they are so delicious to drink that their more profound qualities easily slip by. Or should that be slip down?

🍇 Cabernet Sauvignon 10%, Cabernet Franc 40%, Merlot 50%

🍷 4–15 years

## CHÂTEAU MONDOTTE
### Grand Cru
### ★★

Since the 1996 vintage, Stephan Von Neipperg's unclassified *vin de garage* has surpassed the quality and price of his excellent *grand cru classé* Château Canon-la-Gaffelière. Low yield, 100 percent oak, and ludicrous prices.

**RED** Extraordinary color, density, and complexity for a wine that is not in the slightest bit heavy and makes such charming and easy drinking.

🍇 Cabernet Franc 10%, Merlot 90%

🍷 5–20 years

## CHÂTEAU MOULIN DU CADET
### Grand Cru Classé
### ⓞ★Ⓥ

This château, which is farmed by the Libournais *négociant* J.-P. Moueix, is consistently one of the best *grands crus classés*. The wine is matured in wood for 18 months, with a small proportion of new oak.

**RED** These wines have good color, a fine bouquet, delightfully perfumed Merlot fruit, excellent finesse, and some complexity. They are not full or powerful, but what they lack in size, they more than make up for in style.

🍇 Merlot 85%, Cabernet Franc 15%

🍷 6–15 years

## CHÂTEAU PAVIE
### Premier Grand Cru Classé (B)
### ★★Ⓥ

This top-performing château was purchased in 1998 along with Pavie Décesse and La Clusière by Gérard Perse. Perse used to own a group of hypermarkets, but his love of fine wine began to take over his working life in 1993, when he purchased Monbousquet. The link between Pavie under its previous owners, the Valette family, and now is Michel Rolland, who has been retained as consultant. Although Pavie has produced some of the greatest wines of St.-Émilion in recent decades, the obvious advantage for Rolland is that Perse has poured a small fortune into new installations. The wine is matured in wood for 18 to 24 months, with 100 percent new oak.

**RED** Great, stylish wines packed with creamy fruit and lifted by exquisite new oak. Fabulous concentration since 1998, without losing any finesse, although I will keep an open mind about the 2003 for a decade or so!

🍇 Merlot 60%, Cabernet Franc 30%, Cabernet Sauvignon 10%

🍷 8–30 years

## CHÂTEAU PAVIE DÉCESSE
### Grand Cru Classé
### ★☆

This property was under the same ownership as Château Pavie when the Valette family were the owners, and still is under Perse. Although it is not one of the top *grands crus classés*, it is consistent and certainly worthy of its status.

**RED** Huge seachange in color, quality, and concentration in the 1998 and 1999 vintage.

🍇 Merlot 60%, Cabernet Franc 25%, Cabernet Sauvignon 15%

🍷 6–12 years

## CHÂTEAU PAVIE MACQUIN
### Premier Grand Cru Classé (B)
### ★☆

This property was named after Albert Macquin, a local grower who pioneered work to graft European vines on to American rootstock.

These wines have noticeably improved throughout the 1990s, when Nicolas Thienpont of Vieux Château Certan has overseen the production.

**RED** Much richer, with more fruit and new oak in recent years.

🍇 Merlot 75%, Cabernet Franc and Cabernet Sauvignon 25%

🍷 4–8 years

## CHÂTEAU PETIT-FAURIE-DE-SOUTARD
### ★☆

Some poor wines produced in the mid-1990s and at the turn of the millennium resulted in demotion from *grand cru classé* in 2006, but great improvements from 2003 to 2005 should mean reinstatement in 2016. Half of its production is matured in wood for up to a year.

**RED** This wine has soft, creamy aromas on the bouquet, some concentration of smooth Merlot fruit on the palate, a silky texture, and a dry, tannic finish. It is absolutely delicious when young but gains a lot from a little bottle-age.

🍇 Merlot 60%, Cabernet Franc 30%, Cabernet Sauvignon 10%

🍷 3–8 years

## CHÂTEAU PIPEAU
### Grand Cru
### ★Ⓥ

Up and coming château Pipeau is matured in wood for 18 months, with 50 percent new oak.

**RED** Rich, stylish, and quite striking wines that are full of fruit, underpinned by creamy-smoky oak, and easier to drink younger than most St.-Émilions.

🍇 Merlot 80%, Cabernet Franc 10%, Cabernet Sauvignon 10%

🍷 4–10 years

## CHÂTEAU LE PRIEURÉ
### Grand Cru Classé
### ☆

This property is under the same ownership as Château Vray Croix de Gay in Pomerol and Château Siaurac in Lalande-de-Pomerol. The wine produced here is matured in wood for 18 to 24 months, with 25 percent new oak.

**RED** Light but lengthy wines of some elegance that are best enjoyed when young and fresh.

🍇 Merlot 60%, Cabernet Franc 30%, Cabernet Sauvignon 10%

🍷 4–8 years

**Second wine:** *L'Olivier*

## QUINAULT L'ENCLOS
### Grand Cru
### ★Ⓥ

Increasingly impressive since being purchased by Dr. Alain Raynaud in 1997, this wine is matured in wood for 18 months, with 100 percent new oak.

**RED** Exceptionally concentrated and complex.

🍇 Merlot 80%, Cabernet Franc 10%, Cabernet Sauvignon 5%, Malbec 5%

🍷 6–20 years

## CHÂTEAU ST.-GEORGES (CÔTE PAVIE)
### Grand Cru Classé
### ★

Owned by Jacques Masson, this small property's vineyard is well situated, lying close to those of châteaux Pavie and la Gaffelière. The wine is fermented in stainless steel and matured in wooden casks for 24 months.

**RED** This is a delicious, medium-bodied wine with plump, spicy-juicy Merlot fruit, made in an attractive early-drinking style that does not lack finesse.

🍇 Merlot 50%, Cabernet Franc 25%, Cabernet Sauvignon 25%

🍷 4–8 years

## CHÂTEAU SANSONNET
### Grand Cru Classé until 1996
### ❓

Supposedly purchased in 1999 by François d'Aulan, the former owner of Piper-Heidsieck and the master puppeteer behind numerous wine-related deals ever since. One of my spies reports that the previous owner is still there. If d'Aulan is serious about taking this château on, then we can expect some investment and improvement. However, if it's just part of one of his deals, don't hold your breath.

**RED** This wine is inconsistent and many vintages lack concentration, but the 1982, even though it was very light for the year, remains supple and attractive.

🍇 Merlot 60%, Cabernet Franc 20%, Cabernet Sauvignon 20%

🍷 3–7 years

## CHÂTEAU LA SERRE
### Grand Cru Classé
### ★Ⓥ

This is another property that is improving tremendously in quality. It occupies two terraces on St.-Émilion's limestone plateau, one in front of the château and one behind. The wine is fermented in lined concrete tanks and matured in wood for 16 months with a small proportion of new oak.

**RED** This wine initially charms, then goes through a tight and sullen period, making it reminiscent of Château Guadet St.-Julien. Their styles, however, are very different. When young, this is quite a ripe and plump wine, totally dominated by new oak. In time, the fruit emerges to form a luscious, stylish wine of some finesse and complexity.

🍇 Merlot 80%, Cabernet Franc 20%

🍷 8–25 years

**Second wine:** *Menuts de la Serre*

## CHÂTEAU SOUTARD
### Grand Cru Classé
### ★✦♥

The large and very fine château on this estate was built in 1740 for the use of the Soutard family in the summer. Vines have grown here since Roman times. The wine of Soutard is matured in wood for 18 months, with up to one-third new oak casks.

**RED** This dark, muscular, and full-bodied wine is made in true *vin de garde* style, which means it improves greatly while aging. It has great concentrations of color, fruit, tannin, and extract. With time it can also achieve great finesse and complexity.

🍇 Merlot 65%, Cabernet Franc 30%, Cabernet Sauvignon 5%

🍷 12–35 years

**Second wine:** *Clos de la Tonnelle*

## CHÂTEAU TERTRE DAUGAY
### Grand Cru Classé
### ★✦

This property was purchased in 1978 by Comte Léo de Malet-Roquefort, the owner of *premier grand cru classé* Château la Gaffelière. The wine of Château Tertre Daugay, which is matured in wood with one-third new oak, is excellent and is getting better by the vintage.

**RED** These wines are rich, plump, and fruity with a fine bouquet, ripe underlying oak, great finesse, and surprising longevity.

🍇 Merlot 60%, Cabernet Franc 30%, Cabernet Sauvignon 10%

🍷 7–20 years

**Second wine:** *De Roquefort*
**Other wines:** *Moulin du Biguey*

## CHÂTEAU TERTRE-RÔTEBOEUF
### ★★

François Mitjavile's cult wine is yet more proof that the only important classification is made by the consumer. This was considered to be outrageously expensive before Mondotte. The price has not gone down, but in France you can get four or five bottles of Tertre-Rôteboeuf for the cost of one bottle of Mondotte.

**RED** Huge, oaky, complex, and cultish: the Leonetti of St.-Émilion!

🍇 Cabernet Franc 20%, Merlot 80%

🍷 5–20 years

## CHÂTEAU LA TOUR FIGEAC
### Grand Cru Classé
### ★✦

This property was attached to Château Figeac in 1879 and today it is one of the best of the *grands crus classés*. The wine is matured in wood for 18 months, with one-third new oak.

**RED** These are fat and supple wines with a very alluring bouquet and masses of rich, ripe cassis fruit gently supported by smoky-creamy oak.

🍇 Merlot 60%, Cabernet Franc 40%

🍷 4–8 years

## CHÂTEAU LA TOUR DU PIN FIGEAC
### (Giraud-Bélivier)
### ❷

This property is run by André Giraud, who also owns Château le Caillou in Pomerol. Unfortunately, these wines have never impressed me and so I am unable to recommend them.

🍇 Merlot 75%, Cabernet Franc 25%

## CHÂTEAU LA TOUR DU PIN FIGEAC
### (Moueix)
### ★✦

This property is one of the best of the *grands crus classés*. It is now part of the Armand Moueix stable of châteaux. The wine is matured in wood for 12 to 15 months, with one-third new oak.

**RED** These consistently well-made wines always show a beautiful balance of spicy-juicy Merlot fruit, creamy oak, and supple tannin.

🍇 Merlot 60%, Cabernet Franc 30%, Cabernet Sauvignon and Malbec 10%

🍷 6–15 years

## CHÂTEAU TRIMOULET
### Grand Cru Classé
### ★

This is an old property overlooking St.-Georges–St.-Émilion. The wine is matured in wood for 12 months, with 100 percent new oak.

**RED** This well-colored wine has an overtly ripe and fruity aroma, lots of creamy-oaky character, a fruit flavor, and supple tannin.

🍇 Merlot 60%, Cabernet Franc 20%, Cabernet Sauvignon 20%

🍷 7–20 years

## CHÂTEAU TROIS-MOULINS
### Grand Cru Classé

These vineyards have been incorporated with those of Château Beau-Séjour Bécot since 1979.

## CHÂTEAU TROPLONG MONDOT
### Premier Grand Cru Classé (B)
### ★★

This property is owned by Claude Valette and is run by his daughter Christine. Half the production is matured in wood for 18 months with 80 percent new oak.

**RED** Since the introduction of temperature-controlled fermentation and a second wine in 1985, some critics have believed the quality of this wine to be on a par with that of a *premier grand cru classé*, but for me, Troplong Mondot came on board with the sensational 1988, 1989, 1990, 1992, and 1996 (those in between being merely excellent!).

🍇 Merlot 65%, Cabernet Franc and Malbec 20%, Cabernet Sauvignon 15%

🍷 4–8 years

**Second wine:** *Mondot*

## CHÂTEAU TROTTEVIEILLE
### Premier Grand Cru Classé (B)
### ★✦

This property has the reputation of producing a star wine every five years or so, interspersed by very mediocre wines indeed, but has been made very consistent since 1985, and now makes true *premier grand cru classé* quality wine every year. The wine is matured in wood for 18 months, with up to 100 percent new oak.

**RED** The quality has dramatically improved since the mid-1980s. It has fabulous Merlot-fruit richness with new oak and the power of a true *premier grand cru classé*.

🍇 Merlot 50%, Cabernet Franc 40%, Cabernet Sauvignon 10%

🍷 8–25 years (successful years only)

## CHÂTEAU VALANDRAUD
### Grand Cru
### ★★

Owned by Jean-Luc Thunevin, Château Valandraud is one of St.-Émilion's best-known *vins de garage*, although it has grown from its original small plot of 1½ acres to 11 acres (0.6 hectares to 4.5 hectares), making it more of a *parc de stationnement*.

**RED** Wines that even Gary Figgins of Leonetti in Washington state might complain were too oaky!

🍇 Merlot 70%, Cabernet Franc 30%

🍷 6–25 years

## CHÂTEAU VILLEMAURINE

Château Villemaurine belongs to Robert Giraud, which is a *négociant* concern owning not only this property, but also some 20 other *petits châteaux* in various Bordeaux districts. The wine is matured in wood for 18 to 24 months, with 50 percent new oak. Demoted from *grand cru classé* in 2006.

**RED** These are full-bodied wines of excellent, spicy Merlot fruit, good underlying oak, and firm structure.

🍇 Merlot 70%, Cabernet Sauvignon 30%

🍷 8–25 years

**Other wines:** *Maurinus, Beausoleil*

## CHÂTEAU YON-FIGEAC
### ★

This important property situated near Pomerol was demoted, surprisingly, in 2006. The wine is matured for 18 months with 100 percent new oak.

**RED** This wine was merely attractive and easy-to-drink until 1997, since when it has shown admirable concentration of rich, spicy fruit of increasing complexity and finesse.

🍇 Merlot 80%, Cabernet Franc 20%

🍷 6–20 years

# THE BEST OF THE REST

With more than a thousand châteaux in this one district, it not practical to feature every recommendable wine, thus I list here the best of the rest: châteaux that consistently make wine that stands out for either for quality or value, sometimes both. Those marked with a star sometimes produce wines that are better than many *grands crus classés*.

*Château Bellefont-Belcier†
*Château Belregard-Figeac
*Château La Bienfaisance
*Château Cantenac (since 2002)
*Château Carteau Côtes Daugay
*Château Le Castelot
*Château Le Châtelet
Château Cheval Noir
*Château la Commanderie
*Château Destieux†
*Château Faugères
*Château Ferrand-Lartique (since 2003)

*Château la Fleur
*Château Fleur Cardinale†
*Château Fleur-Cravignac
Château la Fleur Pourret
*Château Fombrauge
*Château Fourtet (since 2001)
Château Franc Bigoroux
Château Grand Barrail Lamarzelle-Figeac
Château Grand Champs
*Château la Grave Figeac
*Château Haut Brisson
*Château Haut Plantey
*Château Haut-Pontet
*Haut-Quercus

Clos Labarde
Château Lapelletrie
*Château Laroque
*Lucia
*Château Magnan la Gaffelière
*Château Monbousquet
*Château Moulin-St-Georges
Château Patris
*Château Pavillon Figeac
*Château Petit-Figeac
Château Petit-Gravet
*Château Petit Val
Château Peyreau
*Château Pindefleurs

*Château Plaisance
Château de Pressac
Château Puy Razac
Château Roc Blanquant
*Château Rol Valentin (since 1999)
*Château Rolland
*Château Rolland-Maillet
Château Sansonnet
*Château Teyssier
Château Tour St-Christophe

† Promoted to *grand cru classé* in 2006.

# POMEROL

*The most velvety and sensuous clarets are produced in Pomerol, yet the traveler passing through this small and rural area, with its dilapidated farmhouses at every turn, few true châteaux and no really splendid ones, must wonder how this uninspiring area can produce such magnificently expensive wines.*

THE PROSPERITY OF RECENT YEARS has enabled Pomerol's properties to indulge in more than just an extra lick of paint, but renovation can only restore, not create, and Pomerol essentially remains an area with an air of obscurity. Even Château Pétrus, which is the greatest growth of Pomerol and produces what for the last 20 years has been consistently the world's most expensive wine, is nothing more than a simple farmhouse.

There has been no attempt to publish an official classification of Pomerol wines, but Vieux Château Certan was considered to be its best wine in the 19th century. Today, however, Pétrus is universally accepted as the leading growth. It commands prices that dwarf those of wines such as Mouton and Margaux, so could not be denied a status equivalent to that of a *premier cru*. Indeed, Le Pin has become considerably more expensive than Pétrus itself. If, like the 1885 classification, we classify Pomerol according to price, next would come Lafleur, followed by a group including L'Evangile, La Fleur Pétrus, La Conseillante, Trotanoy, and a few others, all of which can cost as much as a Médoc First Growth. It is difficult to imagine, but Pomerol was ranked as an inferior sub-appellation of St.-Émilion until it obtained its independent status in 1900. Even then it was a long hard struggle, since even Pétrus did not become sought after until the mid-1960s.

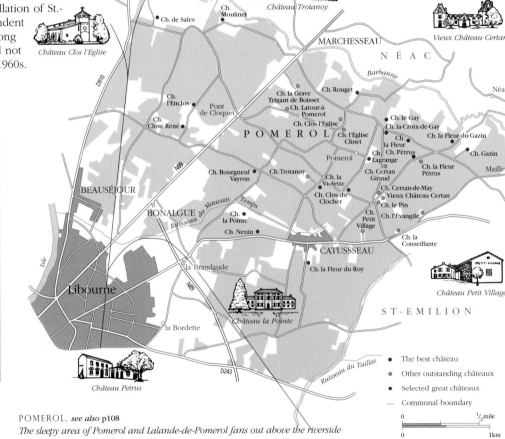

THE VINEYARDS OF VIEUX CHÂTEAU CERTAN
*After Château Pétrus, this is one of the best wine-producing properties in Pomerol. A quaint signpost marks the boundary of the vineyard.*

POMEROL, *see also* p108
*The sleepy area of Pomerol and Lalande-de-Pomerol fans out above the riverside town of Libourne. None of the so-called "châteaux" is particularly imposing: among the most attractive are Château Nénin and Vieux Château Certan.*

THE WINE PRODUCERS OF
# POMEROL

## CHÂTEAU BEAUREGARD
★★☆

An American architect who visited Pomerol after World War I built a replica of Beauregard called "Mille Fleurs" on Long Island, New York. Quality changed dramatically at Beauregard in 1985, two years before the arrival of Michel Rolland, who followed 1985's superb wine with others and was generally responsible for turning this château around. The wine is matured in wood for 24 months with 60 percent new oak.

**RED** Firm, elegant, and lightly rich wine with floral-cedarwood fruit.

Merlot 48%, Cabernet Franc 44%, Cabernet Sauvignon 6%, Malbec 2%

5–10 years

**Second wine:** *Le Benjamin de Beauregard*

## CHÂTEAU BONALGUE

This small property lies on gravel and sand northwest of Libourne. The wine is matured in wood.

**RED** This medium- to full-bodied wine has always been of respectable quality with a frank attack of refreshing fruit flavors, a supple tannin structure, and a crisp finish.

Merlot 65%, Cabernet Franc and Cabernet Sauvignon 30%, Malbec 5%

5–10 years

**Second wine:** *Burgrave*

## CHÂTEAU LE BON PASTEUR
★

This good and steadily improving wine is matured in wood for 24 months, with 35 percent new oak.

**RED** These intensely colored, full-bodied, complex wines are packed with cassis, plum, and black-cherry flavors.

Merlot 75%, Cabernet Franc 25%

8–25 years

## CHÂTEAU BOURGNEUF-VAYRON
★❤

This property is situated close to Château Trotanoy. It has an honorable, if not exciting, record and a 25-acre (10-hectare) vineyard.

**RED** Made in a quick-maturing style with soft fruit and a light herbal finish.

Merlot 85%, Cabernet Franc 15%

4–8 years

## CHÂTEAU LA CABANNE
★

This is a fine estate producing increasingly better wine. The wine is matured in wood for 18 months, with one-third new oak.

**RED** These medium-bodied, sometimes full-bodied, wines have fine, rich, chocolaty fruit.

Merlot 60%, Cabernet Franc 30%, Malbec 10%

7–20 years

**Second wine:** *Domaine de Compostelle*

## CHÂTEAU CERTAN DE MAY DE CERTAN
★★

This can be a confusing wine to identify because the "De May de Certan" part of its name is in very small type on the label and it is usually referred to as "Château Certan de May." It is matured in wood for 24 months, with 50 percent new oak.

**RED** This is a firm and tannic wine that has a powerful bouquet bursting with fruit, spice, and vanilla.

Merlot 65%, Cabernet Franc 25%, Cabernet Sauvignon and Malbec 10%

15–35 years

## CHÂTEAU CLINET
★☆

This wine, which is matured in wood with one-third new oak, has undergone a revolution in recent years. It used to disappoint those looking for the typically fat, gushy-juicy style of Pomerol, and critics often blamed this on the wine's high proportion of Cabernet Sauvignon. The 1985 vintage was more promising (a touch plumper than previous vintages, with more juicy character), so Clinet's previous lack of typical Pomerol character was evidently not entirely due to the blend of grape varieties, although the vineyard has since undergone a radical change in varietal proportions. There was talk of a turnaround in quality beginning with the 1986 vintage, but it was not until the stunning 1989 and 1990 vintages that we really saw this wine take off. There has, however, been inconsistency, going through phases of better, and not so good, quality, although currently on the up.

**RED** Château Clinet is now producing exceedingly fine, rich, ripe wine with ample, yet supple tannin structure mixed with oaky tannins to produce a creamy-herbal-menthol complexity.

Merlot 75%, Cabernet Sauvignon 15%, Cabernet Franc 10%

7–20 years

## CLOS DU CLOCHER
★★❤

This belongs to the Libournais négociant Audy. The wine is rotated in thirds between new oak, one-year-old casks, and vat, and is one of the most undervalued Pomerols.

**RED** These are deliciously deep-colored, attractive, medium-bodied, sometimes full-bodied, wines that have plenty of plump, ripe fruit, a supple structure, intriguing vanilla undertones, and plenty of finesse.

Merlot 80%, Cabernet 20%

8–20 years

**Second wine:** *Esprit de Clocher*
**Other wine:** *Château Monregard-Lacroix*

## CLOS L'ÉGLISE
★★☆

There are several "Église" properties in Pomerol. The wine from this one is matured in wood for 24 months, with some new oak.

**RED** A consistently attractive wine with elegant, spicy Merlot fruit and firm structure; it is eventually dominated by violet Cabernet perfumes.

Merlot 55%, Cabernet Sauvignon 25%, Cabernet Franc 20%

6–15 years

**Second wine:** *La Petite Église*

## CLOS RENÉ
★❤

This property is situated just south of l'Enclos on the western side of the N89. The wine is matured in wood for 24 months with up to 15 percent new oak. An underrated wine, it represents good value.

**RED** These wines have a splendid spicy-blackcurrant bouquet, plenty of fine plummy fruit on the palate, and a great deal of finesse. They are sometimes complex in structure, and are always of excellent quality.

Merlot 60%, Cabernet Franc 30%, Malbec 10%

6–12 years

**Other wine:** *Moulinet-Lasserre*

## CHÂTEAU LA CONSEILLANTE
★★★

If Pétrus is rated a "megastar," this property must be rated at least a "superstar" in the interests of fairness. The wine is matured in wood for 20 to 24 months, with 50 percent new oak.

**RED** This wine has all the power and concentration of the greatest wines of Pomerol, but its priorities are its mindblowing finesse and complexity.

Cabernet Franc 45%, Merlot 45%, Malbec 10%

10–30 years

## CHÂTEAU LA CROIX
★

This property's wine is matured in wood for 20 to 24 months.

**RED** These attractive wines are quite full-bodied, yet elegant and quick-maturing, with fine, spicy Merlot fruit.

Merlot 60%, Cabernet Sauvignon 20%, Cabernet Franc 20%

5–10 years

**Second wine:** *Le Gabachot*

## CHÂTEAU LA CROIX DE GAY
★

This property is situated in the north of Pomerol on sandy-gravel soil, and the wine is matured in wood for 18 months, with up to 100 percent new oak.

**RED** Used to be somewhat lightweight, but attractive, with easy-drinking qualities, the fruit in Croix de Gay has plumped-up in recent vintages.

Merlot 80%, Cabernet Sauvignon 10%, Cabernet Franc 10%

4–8 years

**Other wines:** *Château le Commandeur, Vieux-Château-Groupey*

## CHÂTEAU LA CROIX-ST-GEORGES
★

Under the same ownership as Château La Croix-de-Gay, this wine is matured in wood for 18 months, with 100 percent new oak.

**RED** Rich, soft and seductive.

Merlot 95%, Cabernet Franc 5%

4–10 years

**Other wines:** *Château le Commandeur, Vieux-Château-Groupey*

## CHÂTEAU DU DOMAINE DE L'ÉGLISE

This is the oldest estate in Pomerol. The wine is matured in wood for 18 to 24 months, with one-third new oak.

**RED** This is another attractive, essentially elegant wine that is light in weight and fruit.

🍇 Merlot 90%, Cabernet Franc 10%

🍷 4–8 years

## CHÂTEAU L'ÉGLISE-CLINET
★★

The wine produced by Château L'Église-Clinet, which is matured in wood for up to 24 months with as much as 50 percent new oak, is fast becoming one of the most exciting Pomerols. Quality in overdrive since the 1990s.

**RED** These are deeply colored wines with a rich, seductive bouquet and a big, fat flavr bursting with spicy blackcurrant fruit and filled with creamy-vanilla oak complexity.

🍇 Merlot 80%, Cabernet Franc 20%

🍷 8–30 years

**Second Wine:** *La Petite l'Église*

## CHÂTEAU L'ENCLOS
★ⓥ

The vineyard is situated on an extension of the sandy-gravel soil from the better side of the N89. The wine is matured in wood for 20 months, with a little new oak.

**RED** These are deliciously soft, rich, and voluptuous wines, full of plump, juicy Merlot fruit and spice.

🍇 Merlot 80%, Cabernet Franc 19%, Malbec 1%

🍷 7–15 years

## CHÂTEAU L'ÉVANGILE
★★★

Situated close to two superstars of Pomerol, Vieux Château Certan and Château la Conseillante, this château produces stunning wines that are matured in wood for 15 months with 40 percent new oak.

**RED** Dark but not brooding, these fruity wines are rich and packed with summer fruits and cedarwood. More Merlot and new oak since 1998 has given the wine more generosity.

🍇 Merlot 78%, Cabernet Franc 22%

🍷 8–20 years

## CHÂTEAU FEYTIT-CLINET
★

J.-P. Moueix, who is not this château's owner, does produce the wine and sells it on an exclusivity basis. Some vines are over 70 years old. The wine is matured in wood for 18 to 22 months.

**RED** Consistently well-colored and stylish wines that are full of juicy plum and black-cherry flavors.

🍇 Merlot 80%, Cabernet Franc 20%

🍷 7–15 years

## CHÂTEAU LA FLEUR-DE-GAY
★★

Owned by the Raynaud family, with the ubiquitous Michel Rolland consulting, this wine is matured in wood for 18 months, with 100 percent new oak.

**RED** Big, concentrated fuit underpinned by firm tannic structure.

🍇 Merlot 100%

🍷 8–20 years

## CHÂTEAU LA FLEUR-PÉTRUS
★★

Château La Fleur-Pétrus, producer of one of the best Pomerols, is situated close to Château Pétrus, but on soil that is more gravelly. Ten acres (four hectares) of Château le Gay were purchased in 1994 and incorporated in this property, fattening out the style. The wine is matured in wood for 18 to 22 months.

**RED** Although recent vintages are relatively big and fat, these essentially elegant wines rely more on exquisiteness than richness. They are silky, soft, and supple.

🍇 Merlot 80%, Cabernet Franc 20%

🍷 6–20 years

## CHÂTEAU LE GAY
★ⓥ

This is another château exclusive to the Libournais négociant J.-P. Moueix. The wine is matured in wood for 18 to 22 months.

**RED** Firm and ripe, this big wine is packed with dense fruit and coffee-toffee oak.

🍇 Merlot 70%, Cabernet Franc 30%

🍷 10–25 years

## CHÂTEAU GAZIN
★★ⓥ

This château's record was disappointing until the stunning 1985 vintage, and it has been on a roll ever since, having abandoned harvesting by machine, introduced new, thermostatically controlled vats, and employed various quality-enhancing practices, not the least being a second wine, which enables stricter selection of grapes. The wine is matured in wood for 18 months

with up to one-third new oak.

**RED** Marvelously ripe and rich wine with plump fruit. It should have a great future.

🍇 Merlot 80%, Cabernet Franc 15%, Cabernet Sauvignon 5%

🍷 8–20 years

**Second Wine:** *Hospitalet de Gazin*

## CHÂTEAU LA GRAVE
★

The gravelly vineyard of this property has an excellent location. The Trignant de Boisset element of this château's name has been dropped. It is owned by Christian Moueix and farmed by J.-P. Moueix. The wine is matured in wood with 25 percent new oak.

**RED** Supple, rich and fruity, medium-bodied wines of increasing finesse.

🍇 Merlot 85%, Cabernet Franc 15%

🍷 7–15 years

## CHÂTEAU HOSANNA
★★⭒ⓥ

This property was called Château Certan-Marzelle until 1956 and was purchased in 1999 by Jean-Paul Moueix, with Christian Moueix in control. Almost immediately 10 acres (four hectares) of less well-positioned vineyards were sold to Nénin and strict selection imposed on the 1999 vintage. Watch this space! The wine is matured in wood for 24 months, with 15 percent new oak.

**RED** These ripe, voluptuous wines become darker and denser since 1999.

🍇 Merlot 67%, Cabernet Franc and Cabernet Sauvignon 33%

🍷 8–20 years

**Second Wine:** *Clos du Roy*

**Other wines:** *Château Certan-Marzelle*

## CHÂTEAU LAFLEUR
★★⭒

This property has a potential for quality second only to Château Pétrus itself, but it has a very inconsistent record. The quality and concentration of the wines have soared since 1985.

**RED** This is a well-colored wine with a rich, plummy-porty bouquet, cassis fruit, a toasty-coffee oak complexity and great finesse.

🍇 Cabernet Franc 50%, Merlot 50%

🍷 10–25 years

**Second Wine:** 🗸 *Les Pensées de Lafleur*

## CHÂTEAU LAFLEUR-GAZIN
★

This property has been run by the J.-P. Moueix team on behalf of its owners since 1976. It produces a wine that is matured in wood for 18 to 22 months.

**RED** Well-made wines of good color and bouquet, supple structure, and some richness and concentration.

🍇 Merlot 70%, Cabernet Franc 30%

🍷 6–15 years

## CHÂTEAU LAGRANGE
★ⓥ

Not to be confused with its namesake in St.-Julien, this property belongs to the firm J.-P. Moueix. The wine is aged in wood for 18 to 22 months, with some new oak.

**RED** The recent vintages of this full-bodied wine have been very impressive, with an attractive and accessible style.

🍇 Merlot 90%, Cabernet Franc 10%

🍷 8–20 years

## CHÂTEAU LATOUR À POMEROL
★★ⓥ

Château Latour à Pomerol now belongs to the last surviving sister of Madame Loubat, Madame Lily Lacoste (owner of one-third of Château Pétrus). The wine is matured in wood with 25 percent new oak.

**RED** These deep, dark wines are luscious, voluptuous, and velvety. They have a great concentration of fruit and a sensational complexity of flavors.

🍇 Merlot 90%, Cabernet Franc 10%

🍷 12–35 years

## CHÂTEAU MAZEYRES
★

Two-thirds of this wine is matured in wood with 40 percent new oak, and one-third is aged in vat.

**RED** These elegant wines are rich, ripe, and juicy, and have silky Merlot fruit and some oaky finesse.

🍇 Merlot 70%, Cabernet Franc 30%

🍷 5–12 year

## CHÂTEAU MOULINET
★ⓥ

This large estate belongs to Armand Moueix. The wine is matured for 18 months, with one-third new oak.

**RED** These red wines are attractively supple with a light, creamy-ripe fruit and oak flavor.

🍇 Merlot 60%, Cabernet Sauvignon 30%, Cabernet Franc 10%

🍷 5–10 years

## CHÂTEAU NÉNIN
★

A large and well-known property between Catussau and the outskirts of Libourne. The wine has had a disappointing record, but there has been a noticeable improvement since this property was purchased by Jean-Hubert Delon in 1997, who added 10 acres (four hectares) from Certan-Giraud.

**RED** No similarity to Nenin of the past, vintages from 1998 onward have been increasingly full, deep, and concentrated, with a lush, opulent fruit, and a silky finish.

🍇 Merlot 75%, Cabernet Franc 25%

🍷 5–18 years

**Second Wine:** ✓ *Fugue de Nenin*

## CHÂTEAU PETIT-VILLAGE
★★

This property borders Vieux Château Certan and Château La Conseillante, and it therefore has the advantage of a superb terroir and a meticulous owner. The result is a wine of superstar quality, even in poor years. Petit-Village is matured in wood for 18 months with at least 50 percent of the casks made from new oak.

**RED** These wines seem to have everything. Full and rich with lots of color and unctuous fruit, they have a firm structure of ripe and supple tannins and a luscious, velvety texture. Classic, complex, and complete.

🍇 Merlot 80%, Cabernet Franc 10%, Cabernet Sauvignon 10%

🍷 8–30 years

## CHÂTEAU PÉTRUS
★★★

The Libournais *négociant* Jean-Pierre Moueix was in technical control of this estate from 1947 until his death at the age of 90 in March 2003. Before the previous owner, Madame Loubat, died in 1961, she gave one-third of Pétrus to Monsieur Moueix. She had no children, just two sisters who were not on the best of terms, so Madame Loubat wisely gave Moueix the means of ensuring that family disagreements would not be able to harm the day-to-day running of Château Pétrus. In 1964 Moueix purchased one of the other two shares and his family has controlled the destiny of this world-famous château ever since.

**RED** The low acidity of Château Pétrus makes it an intrinsically soft wine which, when combined with the inherent lusciousness of the Merlot grape, enables Pétrus to

produce intensely colored, superconcentrated wines that would otherwise be too harsh to drink.

🍇 Merlot 95%, Cabernet Franc 5%

🍷 20–50 years

## CHÂTEAU LE PIN
★★

This tiny property was purchased in 1979 by the late Jacques Thienpont. The yield is very low, the wine is fermented in stainless steel and matured in wood for 18 months with 100 percent new oak.

**RED** These oaky wines are very full-bodied, and powerfully aromatic with a sensational spicy-cassis flavor dominated by decadently rich, creamy-toffee, toasty-coffee oak. Those who are not convinced by Le Pin keep asking whether there is enough concentration in these wines to match the oak; my guess is that there is, and that their wonderfully voluptuous style belies their true size and structure, but it will be a long time before we really know the answer.

🍇 Merlot 100%

🍷 10–40 years

## CHÂTEAU PLINCE
★⊙

This property is owned by the Moreau family, but its wines are sold by the Libournais négociant J.-P. Moueix. It is matured in vats for six months and in wood for 18 months, with 15 percent new oak.

**RED** These wines are fat, ripe, and simply ooze with juicy Merlot flavor. Although they could not be described as aristocratic, they are simply delicious.

🍇 Merlot 75%, Cabernet Franc 20%, Cabernet Sauvignon 5%

🍷 4–8 years

## CHÂTEAU LA POINTE
⊙

After hoping that the mid-1980s would prove to be a turning point in the reputation of this important château, it now seems that this did not happen until 1998, although there is still a lot of room for improvement before La Pointe can be described as a truly lush Pomerol.

**RED** Lightweight, lackluster wines until 1998, when they have shown more fruit, with plummy-chocolaty overtones. Getting there.

🍇 Merlot 80%, Cabernet Franc 15%, Malbec 5%

🍷 5–12 years

**Second wine:** *La Pointe Riffat*

## CHÂTEAU ROUGET
★⊙

One of the oldest properties in Pomerol. The proprietor also owns the neighboring estate of Vieux Château des Templiers. The wine is matured in wood for 24 months.

**RED** Château Rouget produces excellent red wines with a fine

bouquet and elegant flavor. Fat and rich, with good structure and lots of ripe fruit, they are at their most impressive when mature.

🍇 Merlot 90%, Cabernet Franc 10%

🍷 10–25 years

## CHÂTEAU DE SALES
★⊙

At 119 acres (48 hectares), this is easily the largest property in the Pomerol appellation. It is situated in the very northwest of the district. Despite an uneven record, it has demonstrated its potential and inherent qualities on many occasions and the wine, which is matured in wood for 18 months with 35 percent new oak, is one to watch for the future.

**RED** When successful, these wines have a penetrating bouquet and a palate jam-packed with deliciously juicy flavors of succulent stone fruits such as plums, black cherries, and apricots.

🍇 Merlot 70%, Cabernet Franc 15%, Cabernet Sauvignon 15%

🍷 7–20 years

**Second wine:** *Château Chantalouette*

**Other wine:** *Château de Délias*

## CHÂTEAU DU TAILHAS

The wines of this château are matured in wood for 18 months with 50 percent new oak.

**RED** Consistently attractive, with silky Merlot fruit and creamy oak.

🍇 Merlot 80%, Cabernet Franc 10%, Cabernet Sauvignon 10%

🍷 5–12 years

## CHÂTEAU TAILLEFER

This potentially excellent property belongs to Bernard Moueix. The wines are matured in wood for between 18 and 22 months, with the addition of some new oak.

**RED** At best these wines are attractively light and fruity, revealing their potential, but more often than not they are simply light and dilute. The 2000 was the best vintage this château has produced, but it was very difficult not to make fine wine that year.

🍇 Merlot 55%, Cabernet Franc 30%, Cabernet Sauvignon 15%

🍷 4–8 years

**Second wine:** *Clos Toulifaut*

## CHÂTEAU TROTANOY
★★★

Some consider this to be second only to Château Pétrus, although in terms of price L'Évangile and Lafleur have overtaken it. The wine is matured in wood for up to 24 months, with 50 percent new oak.

**RED** This inky-black, brooding wine has a powerful bouquet and a rich flavor, which is supported by a firm tannin structure and a complex, creamy-toffee, spicy-coffee oak character.

🍇 Merlot 90%, Cabernet Franc 10%

🍷 15–35 years

## VIEUX CHÂTEAU CERTAN
★★★

This was once regarded as the finest-quality growth in Pomerol. It has not so much dropped its standards as witnessed the rapid rise of a new star—Pétrus—and all its pretenders. Vieux Château Certan remains one of Bordeaux's great wines. This wine is matured in wood for 18 to 24 months with up to 60 percent new oak.

**RED** This is an attractive, garnet-colored, full-bodied wine that has a smouldering, smooth, and mellow flavor. It displays great finesse and complexity of structure.

🍇 Merlot 50%, Cabernet Franc 25%, Cabernet Sauvignon 20%, Malbec 5%

🍷 12–35 years

**Second wine:** *La Gravette de Certan*

## CHÂTEAU LA VIOLETTE
★

In the same way as Château Laroze in St.-Émilion is said to be named after its aroma of roses, so this château is named after its aroma of violets—or so the story goes. It is located in Catussau and its vineyards are scattered around the commune. The wine, matured in wood for up to 24 months, can be inconsistent, but I think it has great potential.

**RED** I have not tasted this wine as frequently as I would like, but I can enthusiastically recommend the best vintages, when they have a rich and jubilant flavor of Merlot fruit, which is ripe and fat.

🍇 Merlot 95%, Cabernet Franc 5%

🍷 5–15 years

## CHÂTEAU VRAY CROIX DE GAY

A small property on good gravelly soil next to Château le Gay and under the same ownership as Château le Prieuré. The wine is matured in wood in 18 months.

**RED** The wine can be full, rich, chocolate- and black-cherry-flavored, with the best vintages showing more fat and oak.

🍇 Merlot 80%, Cabernet Franc 15%, Cabernet Sauvignon 5%

🍷 5–10 years

## THE WINE PRODUCERS OF THE FRONSADAIS AND THE
# SAINT-ÉMILION AND POMEROL SATELLITES

### DOMAINE DE L'A
AOC Bordeaux-Côtes-de-Castillon
★☆B

The home of ace consultant Stéphane Derenoncourt, and unlike plumbers and decorators, he does not neglect his own property. Sleek and rich, early drinking, yet benefits from several years' additional aging, and it's biodynamic. A future star!

### CHÂTEAU D'AIGUILHE
AOC Bordeaux-Côtes-de-Castillon
★☆V

Purchased in 1998 by Stephan von Neipperg, who has restored the property. Super since 1999.
**Second wine:** *Seigneurs d'Aiguihle*

### CHÂTEAU DES ANNEREAUX
AOC Lalande-de-Pomerol

Attractive, fruity, medium-bodied wines of some elegance.

### CHÂTEAU BARRABAQUE
AOC Côtes Canon-Fronsac
★☆V

Situated on the mid-*côte*, this 80 percent Merlot has really shone since the late 1990s. Excellent Cuvée Prestige is the *crème de la crème* here.

### CHÂTEAU BEL-AIR
AOC Puisseguin-St-Émilion

This property makes generous, fruity, early-drinking wines.

### CHÂTEAU DE BEL-AIR
AOC Lalande-de-Pomerol
★V

One of the best of the appellation, this property has fine, sandy gravel.

### CHÂTEAU BELAIR-MONTAIGUILLON
AOC St-Georges-St-Émilion
★V

Consistently rich, deliciously fruity. The best wine selected from old vines and matured in cask, including some new oak, is sold as Château Belair-St-Georges.

### CHÂTEAU DE BELCIER
AOC Bordeaux-Côtes-de-Francs and Bordeaux Supérieur Côtes-de-Francs

This property produces fruity wines that can claim the Côtes de Castillon or Côtes de Francs appellations.

### CHÂTEAU CALON
AOC Montagne-St-Émilion and AOC St-George-St-Émilion
★

This château is under the same ownership as the *grand cru classé* Château Corbin-Michotte. The wine is good-quality, with a juicy style, and very Merlot in character. Part of this vineyard falls within the St-George-St-Émilion area and this produces the best wine.

### CHÂTEAU CANON
AOC Côtes Canon-Fronsac
★☆V

This is one of several Fronsadais properties formerly owned, and still managed, by J-P Moueix. It was sold to Jean Galland in September 2000. It produces one of the best wines in this appellation from 100 percent Merlot (40 years old).

### CHÂTEAU CANON DE BREM
AOC Côtes Canon-Fronsac

No longer owned by J-P Moueix, Château Canon de Brem was sold to Jean Halley, the CEO of, and major shareholder in, Carrefour, in September 2000. It produces fine, firm, and flavorsome *vins de garde* that are deep colored and powerful, yet complex and spicy.

### CHÂTEAU CAP DE MERLE
AOC Lussac-St-Émilion
★V

Château Cap de Merle is wine guru Robert Parker's best Lussac performer for the 1981, 1982, and 1983 vintages. These wines today remain consistently good value.

### CHÂTEAU CARLES
AOC Fronsac
★V

This producer's primary wine is attractive and juicy, but it is the 1.5 blockbusting 95 percent Merlot selection, sold as Château Haut Carles, that really stands out here.
**Other wine:** *Château Haut Carles*

### CHÂTEAU CASSAGNE-HAUT-CANON
AOC Côtes Canon-Fronsac
★V

Château Cassagne-Haut-Canon produces a selection of rich, full, fat, fruitcake-flavored wines that are especially attractive when they are still young.

### CHÂTEAU LES CHARMES-GODARD
AOC Bordeaux-Côtes-de-Castillon
★V

Brilliant, soft, silky wines of elegance and richness since 1999.

### CHÂTEAU DE CLOTTE
AOC Bordeaux-Côtes-de-Castillon and AOC Bordeaux Supérieur Côtes-de-Castillon
★V

This property has the right to both the Côtes-de-Castillon and Côtes-de-Francs appellations, but uses only the former.

### CHÂTEAU LA CROIX CANON
AOC Côtes Canon-Fronsac
☆V

Another former Moueix property that was sold to Jean Halley, the CEO of, and major shareholder in, Carrefour, yet it is managed by the established team. Attractive, Merlot-dominated wines are full of juicy fruit.

### CHÂTEAU DU COURLAT
AOC Lussac-St-Émilion

These are spicy-tannic wines with good fruit flavors.

### CHÂTEAU COUSTOLLE VINCENT
AOC Côtes Canon-Fronsac

Château Coustolle Vincent's wines are well-flavored, and matured in up to 20 percent new oak.

### CHÂTEAU DALEM
AOC Fronsac
★☆V

These soft and velvety wines develop quickly but have finesse and are among the very best of their appellation.

### CHÂTEAU DE LA DAUPHINE
AOC Fronsac
☆

This property has been sold to Jean Halley, the CEO of, and major shareholder in, Carrefour, but is still run by the Moueix team, which produces fresh and fruity wines that mature in oak, 20 percent of which is new.

### CHÂTEAU DURAND LAPLAIGNE
AOC Puisseguin-St-Émilion
★V

The excellent-quality wine produced by Château Durand Laplaigne is grown using clay-and-limestone soil, with a strict selection of grapes, and modern vinification techniques.

### CHÂTEAU LA FLEUR DE BOÜARD
AOC Lalande-de-Pomerol
★V

Very good wines, getting much better since this property was purchased by the owner of Angelus in 1998.
**Second wine:** *Château La Fleur St-Georges*

### CHÂTEAU FONTENIL
AOC Fronsac
★☆V

This rich, velvety 90 percent Merlot high-flyer has lots of new oak and is from Michel Rolland's own property.

### CHÂTEAU GRAND ORMEAU
AOC Lalande-de-Pomerol
★V

A rich and lusciously fruity wine that is matured in 50 percent new oak, Grand Ormeau is very classy for its appellation.
**Second wine:** *Château d'Haurange*

### CHÂTEAU GRAND-BARIL
AOC Montagne-St-Émilion

Attractive, fruity wine made by the agricultural school in Libourne.

### CHÂTEAU GUIBEAU-LA FOURVIEILLE
AOC Puisseguin-St-Emilion
★☆V

Much investment has gone into this property, the wines of which are now considered to be the best in Puisseguin.
**Second wines:** *Le Vieux Château Guibeau, Château La Fourvieille*

### CHÂTEAU HAUT-CHAIGNEAU
AOC Lalande-de-Pomerol
★V

Look out for Château Le Sergue 1.5, which is selected from this property's best wines and matured in 80 percent new oak. A poor man's Mondotte?
**Other wines:** *Château Le Sergue*

### CHÂTEAU HAUT-CHATAIN
AOC Lalande-de-Pomerol
★☆V

Fat, rich, and juicy wines with definite hints of new-oak vanilla are made by Château Haut-Chatain.

### CHÂTEAU LES HAUTS-CONSEILLANTS
AOC Lalande-de-Pomerol

Château les Hauts-Conseillants is another fine Néac property.
**Other wines:** *Château les Hauts-Tuileries* (export label)

## CHÂTEAU HAUT-TUQUET
AOC Bordeaux-Côtes-de-Castillon and AOC Bordeaux Supérieur Côtes-de-Castillon

This wine is consistently good.

## CHÂTEAU JEANDEMAN
AOC Fronsac

This château produces fresh, fruity wine with good aroma.

## CHÂTEAU JUNAYME
AOC Côtes Canon-Fronsac
★ⓥ

Well-known wines of finesse.

## CHÂTEAU DES LAURETS
AOC Puisseguin-St-Émilion

The appellation's largest property.
**Other wines:** *Château la Rochette, Château Maison Rose*

## CHÂTEAU DE LUSSAC
AOC Lussac-St-Émilion

Château de Lussac produces well-balanced, early-drinking wine.

## CHÂTEAU DU LYONNAT
AOC Lussac-St-Émilion

The appellation's largest property.
**Other wines:** *La Rose Peruchon*

## CHÂTEAU MAISON BLANCHE
AOC Montagne-St-Émilion

Château Maison Blanche produces attractive wine that is easy to drink.

## CHÂTEAU MAQUIN-ST-GEORGES
AOC St-Georges-St-Émilion

This wine is 70 percent Merlot.
**Other wines:** *Château Bellonne-St-Georges*

## CHÂTEAU MAUSSE
AOC Côtes Canon-Fronsac

Wines with good aroma and flavor.

## CHÂTEAU MAYNE-VIEIL
AOC Fronsac

Easy-drinking wines with good Merlot spice and fruit.

## CHÂTEAU MAZERIS
AOC Côtes Canon-Fronsac

There is an unusually high proportion of Cabernet Sauvignon in these wines.

## CHÂTEAU MILON
AOC Lussac-St-Émilion
★ⓥ

A château that produces a fine-quality, full, yet fragrant, wine.

## CHÂTEAU MONCETS
AOC Lalande-de-Pomerol
★ⓥ

This Néac property makes a fine, rich, and elegant Pomerol lookalike.

## CHÂTEAU MOULIN HAUT-LAROQUE
AOC Fronsac

Well-perfumed, quite fat wines with lots of fruit and good tannin.

## CHÂTEAU MOULIN NEUF
AOC Bordeaux-Côtes-de-Castillon and AOC Bordeaux Supérieur Côtes-de-Castillon
★ⓥ

These wines regularly win medals.

## CHÂTEAU LA PAPETERIE
AOC Montagne-St-Émilion

Wines with a rich nose and a big fruit-filled palate.

## CHÂTEAU DU PONT DE GUESTRES
AOC Lalande-de-Pomerol
★ⓥ

This château produces full, ripe, fat wines of good quality.

## CHÂTEAU LA PRADE
AOC Bordeaux-Côtes-de-Francs
★

Increasing quality since 2000.

## CHÂTEAU DU PUY
AOC Bordeaux-Côtes-de-Francs and AOC Bordeaux Supérieur Côtes-de-Francs
★ⓥ

Red wines from this property are rustic and overtly fruity.

## CLOS PUY ARNAUD
AOC Bordeaux-Côtes-de-Castillon
★

Owner-winemaker Thierry Valette produces increasingly concentrated, yet extremely approachable wines since 2000.

## CHÂTEAU PUYCARPIN
AOC Bordeaux-Côtes-de-Castillon and AOC Bordeaux Supérieur Côtes-de-Castillon

This property produces a well-made red, and a little dry white.

## CHÂTEAU PUYGUERAUD
AOC Bordeaux-Côtes-de-Francs and AOC Bordeaux Supérieur Côtes-de-Francs
★

Aromatically attractive wines with good color and supple fruit.

## CHÂTEAU RICHELIEU
AOC Fronsac
★Ⓑ

Excellent since 2003. The 2005 is stunning, especially the wonderfully lush and satisfying prestige cuvée "La Favorite de Richelieu".
**Second wine:** *Trois Musketeers*

## CHÂTEAU DE LA RIVIÈRE
AOC Fronsac
★

Magnificent wines that are built to last: they are rich, tannic, and fruity, and matured in up to 40 percent new oak.

## CHÂTEAU ROBIN
AOC Bordeaux-Côtes-de-Castillon and AOC Bordeaux Supérieur Côtes-de-Castillon
★ⓥ

Château Robin produces award-winning red wines.

## CHÂTEAU LA ROCHE-GABY
AOC Côtes Canon-Fronsac
★

Château La Roche-Gaby produces intensely flavored, attractive, and well-structured wines, which are designed to have a long life.

## CHÂTEAU ROCHER-BELLEVUE
AOC Bordeaux-Côtes-de-Castillon and AOC Bordeaux Supérieur Côtes-de-Castillon

A good St-Émilion lookalike that regularly wins medals.
**Other wines:** *La Palène, Coutet-St-Magne*

## CHÂTEAU ROUDIER
AOC Montagne-St-Émilion
★★

Quality wines that are well-colored, richly flavored, finely balanced, and long and supple.

## CHÂTEAU LA ROUSSELLE
AOC Fronsac
ⓥ

Lovely rich, ripe, elegant wines since 2003.

## CHÂTEAU SIAURAC
AOC Lalande-de-Pomerol

Fine, firm, and fruity wines.

## CHÂTEAU ST.-GEORGES
AOC St-Georges-St-Émilion
★★ⓥ

Super quality wine of great finesse.

## CHÂTEAU STE-COLOMBE
AOC Bordeaux-Côtes-de-Castillon
★ⓥ

This château was purchased in 1999 by Gérard Perse of Pavie *et al* and Alain Reynaud of La Croix-de-Gay. These wines look very promising indeed.

## CHÂTEAU TARREYO
AOC Bordeaux-Côtes-de-Castillon and AOC Bordeaux Supérieur Côtes-de-Castillon

Château Tarreyo (Gascon for "knoll of stones") is sited on a limestone mound, as its name suggests.

## CHÂTEAU THIBAUD-BELLEVUE
AOC Bordeaux-Côtes-de-Castillon and AOC Bordeaux Supérieur Côtes-de-Castillon

Medium-bodied, fruity red wine.

## CHÂTEAU TOUMALIN
AOC Côtes Canon-Fronsac

Fresh, fruity wine from a property under the same ownership as Château La Pointe in Pomerol.

## CHÂTEAU TOUR-DU-PAS-ST-GEORGES
AOC St-Georges-St-Émilion
★ⓥ

An excellent and inexpensive *entrée* into the world of *premier cru* claret.

## CHÂTEAU DES TOURELLES
AOC Lalande-de-Pomerol
★ⓥ

Fine wines with vanilla undertones.

## CHÂTEAU TOURNEFEUILLE
AOC Lalande-de-Pomerol
★★★ⓥ

This rich, long-lived wine is the best of the appellation.

## CHÂTEAU DES TOURS
AOC Montagne-St-Émilion
★ⓥ

The largest property in the appellation. The wine is big, full, and fleshy, yet soft and easy to drink.

## CHÂTEAU LA VALADE
AOC Fronsac
★ⓥ

Elegant, aromatic, and silky-textured wines, which are made exclusively from Merlot grapes.

## CHÂTEAU LA VIEILLE CURE
AOC Fronsac
★★

Very fresh and velvety with delightful floral, summer fruit aromas, these wines are at the very top of their appellation. The 1998 is stunning.

## VIEUX-CHÂTEAU-ST-ANDRÉ
AOC Montagne-St-Émilion
★★★

A soft, exciting wine, full of cherry, vanilla, and spice flavors.

## CHÂTEAU LA VILLARS
AOC Fronsac
★ⓥ

Soft, fat, and juicy wines of excellent quality, one-third of which are matured in new oak.

## CHÂTEAU VRAY-CANON-BOYER
AOC Côtes Canon-Fronsac

This château produces a fruity, medium-bodied wine that is attractive for early drinking from 90 percent Merlot grapes.

# BOURG AND BLAYE

*Ninety-five percent of the wine produced in Bourg and Blaye is good-value red. Tiny Bourg makes more wine than its five-times-larger neighbor, Blaye, and most of the vines grown in Blaye come from a cluster of châteaux close to the borders of Bourg.*

AS ONE WOULD EXPECT of an area that has supported a settlement for 400,000 years, Bourg has a close-knit community. Comparatively recently, the Romans used neighboring Blaye as a *castrum*, a fortified area in the defense system that shielded Bordeaux. According to some sources, the vine was cultivated in Bourg and Blaye as soon as the Romans arrived. Vineyards were certainly flourishing here long before those of the Médoc, just on the other side of the Gironde.

Bourg is a compact, heavily cultivated area with pretty hillside vineyards at every turn. The vine is less important in Blaye, which has other interests, including a caviare industry based at its ancient fishing port where sturgeon is still a major catch. The south-facing vineyards of Blaye are mostly clustered in the countryside immediately bordering Bourg and, despite the similarity of the countryside, traditionally produce slightly inferior

## FACTORS AFFECTING TASTE AND QUALITY

### LOCATION
The vineyards fan out behind the town of Bourg, which is situated on the right bank of the confluence of the Dordogne and the Garonne, some 12.5 miles (20 kilometers) north of Bordeaux. Blaye is a larger district that unfolds beyond Bourg.

### CLIMATE
These two areas are less protected than the Médoc from westerly and northwesterly winds, and have a higher rainfall.

### ASPECT
Bourg is very hilly with vines cultivated on steep limestone hills and knolls up to a height of 260 ft (80 m). In the southern section of Blaye the country is rich and hilly, with steep slopes overlooking the Gironde that are really just a continuation of those in Bourg. The northern areas are gentle and the hills lower, with marshes bordering the viticultural areas.

### SOIL
In Bourg the topsoil is clay-limestone or clay-gravel over a hard limestone subsoil, although in the east the subsoil sometimes gives way to gravel and clay. The soil in Blaye is clay or clay-limestone over hard limestone on the hills overlooking the Gironde, getting progressively sandier going east.

### VITICULTURE AND VINIFICATION
There are many grape varieties here, some of which are far too inferior or unreliable to contribute to the quality of these wines, particularly the whites. Bourg produces the best reds, Blaye the best whites, but there is relatively little white wine made in both appellations—even Blaye is 90 percent red and Bourg is in excess of 99 percent red. Very few *petits châteaux* in both areas can afford the use of casks, let alone new ones, and much of the wine in Bourg is made by one of its five *coopératives*.

### GRAPE VARIETIES
**Primary varieties:** Cabernet Franc, Cabernet Sauvignon, Merlot, Sauvignon Blanc, Sémillon
**Secondary varieties:** Malbec, Prolongeau, Cahors, Béguignol (Fer), Petit Verdot, Merlot Blanc, Folle Blanche, Colombard, Chenin blanc, Muscadelle, Ugni Blanc

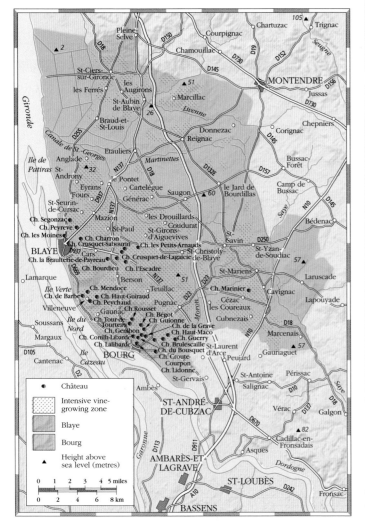

| Legend | |
|---|---|
| ● | Château |
| ▦ | Intensive vine-growing zone |
| ▩ | Blaye |
| ▨ | Bourg |
| ▲ | Height above sea level (metres) |

0   1   2   3   4   5 miles
0   2   4   6   8 km

THE TOWN OF BLAYE
*The attractive fishing port of Blaye with, in the foreground, the ruins of its ancient citadel guarding against the approach of marauders from the sea.*

BOURG AND BLAYE, *see also* p63
*Most of the best growths of Bourg and Blaye are clustered behind the respective ports that give this wine-producing area its name. Bourg, the smaller area, has a higher concentration of vineyards and generally produces the better wines.*

wines to those of Bourg. The D18 highway appears to be a barrier beyond which the less intensely cultivated hinterland takes on a totally different topography, where the more expansive scenery is dotted with isolated forests.

## THE POTENTIAL OF BOURG AND BLAYE

To the Romans, these south-facing vineyards overlooking the Gironde seemed the ideal place to plant vines. Indeed, the quality achieved today in these vineyards would have surpassed the most optimistic hopes of those past masters of the vine. However, by today's expectations, Bourg and Blaye have been relegated to a viticultural backwater. This is a pity, since there are some exciting quality wines being made here. Perhaps when the world has woken up to the gems in Canon-Fronsac, more curious consumers might turn their attention to the better producers in this district. As soon as wine lovers are prepared to pay higher prices for these wines, so its proprietors will be able to restrict yields, improve vinification techniques, and indulge in a percentage of new oak.

### CHENIN BLANC IN BORDEAUX

The Chenin Blanc of Loire fame (or infamy, as the case may be) is allowed in the white wines of Bourg, albeit restricted to a maximum of 10 percent. However, in the AOCs of Blayais and Côtes de Blaye (but not Premières Côtes de Blaye), this interloper from the north has a free run, or could have, if a producer wanted to market a pure Chenin Blanc varietal wine. I have never been a fan of Chenin Blanc in the Loire, except in those idyllic vintages when the sublime *moelleux* style can be produced in quantity, and it is very hard not to produce liquid magic. The problem with Chenin in the Loire is that it grows like a weed, but rarely has the degree of sunshine this grape likes to luxuriate in. Combine that with the inclination of far too many growers to overyield and season it with those who have less than clinically clean vinification habits, and it is clear why Loire Chenin, particularly dry Loire Chenin, has such a poor reputation. On the other hand, even cheap, mass-produced Chenin Blanc wines in the New World have lovely ripe, tropical fruit flavors. Not all of them, of course, the New World has its good, bad, and ugly too, but I believe that the longer hours of warmer sunshine in Bordeaux could produce some excellent dry Chenin wines. A pure Chenin Blanc Bordeaux would indeed be a novelty.

VINEYARDS ALONG THE DORDOGNE AT BOURG
*The Romans planted these south-facing vineyards, believing this to be a far more ideal place to grow vines than on the other side of the confluence of the Dordogne and Garonne estuaries where, understandably, they failed to realize the possibilities of the Médoc concealed beyond its virtually impenetrable marshes.*

CHÂTEAU SEGONZAC, ST.-GENÈS-DE-BLAYE
*A short distance from the fortress of Blaye, these sweeping vineyards belong to Château Segonzac, a wine estate created in 1887 by Jean Dupuy, the owner of the* Petit Parisiane, *the largest-circulation newspaper in the world at the time.*

# THE APPELLATIONS OF
# BOURG AND BLAYE

The number of appellations in this area, and their various differences, are very confusing for the consumer. The system should be neatened up and there is no reason why just two AOCs—Côtes de Blaye and Côtes de Bourg—could not be used for all the wines produced here.

## BLAYAIS AOC
### *See* Blaye AOC

## BLAYE AOC

Blaye or Blayais is a large and diverse appellation of variable quality.

**RED** Few properties cultivate obscure varieties such as Prolongeau and Béguignol, thus many utilize the prestigious sounding Premières Côtes de Blaye AOC; hence, hardly anyone bothers to sell the wine under this plain appellation.

%% Cabernet Sauvignon, Cabernet Franc, Merlot, Malbec, Prolongeau, Béguignol, Petit Verdot

⌇⤳ 3–7 years

**WHITE** Since 1997 Ugni Blanc has dominated, with Merlot Blanc and Folle Blanche banned. The ripeness level has been lowered from 170 to 153 grams of sugar, with no more than four grams residual allowed in the finished wine, and a maximum of 12.5 percent alcohol imposed, thus ensuring fresher, crisper wines. These wines may be sold from December 1 following the harvest without any mention of *primeur* or *nouveau*.

%% Ugni Blanc plus up to 10% in total of Folle Blanche, Colombard, Chenin Blanc, Sémillon, Sauvignon Blanc, Muscadelle

⌇⤳ 1–2 years

## BOURG AOC

Also called Bourgeais, this appellation, which covers both red and white wines, has fallen into disuse because the growers prefer to use the Côtes de Bourg AOC, which is easier to market but conforms to the same regulations. *See also* Côtes de Bourg AOC.

## BOURGEAIS AOC
### *See* Bourg AOC

## CÔTES DE BLAYE AOC

Unlike the Bourg and Côtes de Bourg appellations, which cover red and white wines, Côtes de Blaye is white only. Blaye, however, may be red or white.

**WHITE** As much white Côtes de Blaye is produced as basic Blaye. The wines are similar in style and quality.

%% Merlot Blanc, Folle Blanche, Colombard, Chenin Blanc, Sémillon, Sauvignon Blanc, Muscadelle

⌇⤳ 1–2 years

## CÔTES DE BOURG AOC

Bourg is one-fifth the size of Blaye, yet it traditionally produces a greater quantity and, more importantly, a much finer quality of wine than that produced at Blaye.

**RED** Excellent value wines of good color, which are full of solid, fruity flavor. Many are very stylish indeed.

%% Cabernet Sauvignon, Cabernet Franc, Merlot, Malbec

⌇⤳ 3–10 years

**WHITE** A very small quantity of this light, dry wine is produced and sold each year. It may be sold from December 1 following the harvest without any mention of *primeur* or *nouveau*.

%% Sémillon, Sauvignon Blanc, Muscadelle, Merlot Blanc, Colombard, plus a maximum of 10% Chenin Blanc

⌇⤳ 1–2 years

## PREMIÈRES CÔTES DE BLAYE AOC

This covers the same area as Blaye and Côtes de Blaye, but only classic grapes are used and the minimum alcoholic strength is higher. The area has very good potential for producing quality wines.

**RED** There are one or two excellent properties that use a little new oak.

%% Cabernet Sauvignon, Cabernet Franc, Merlot, Malbec

⌇⤳ 4–10 years

**WHITE** Dry, light-bodied wines that may have a fresh, lively, grapey flavor.

%% Sémillon, Sauvignon Blanc, Muscadelle

⌇⤳ 1–2 years

---

# THE WINE PRODUCERS OF
# BOURG

### CHÂTEAU DE BARBE
**Villeneuve**

Château de Barbe is a property that makes substantial quantities of light-styled, Merlot-dominated, gently fruity red wines that are easy to drink.

### CHÂTEAU BÉGOT
**Lansac**

This property produces some 5,000 cases of agreeably fruity red wine, which is best drunk young.

### CHÂTEAU DU BOUSQUET
**Bourg-sur-Gironde**
★ ⓥ

This large, well-known château produces some 40,000 cases of red wine of excellent value for money. The wine is fermented in stainless steel and aged in oak, has a big bouquet, and a smooth feel.

### CHÂTEAU BRULESCAILLE
**Tauriac**

Château Brulescaille's vineyards are very well-sited and produce agreeable wines for early drinking.

### CHÂTEAU CONILH-LIBARDE
**Bourg-sur-Gironde**

Soft, fruity red wines are made at this small vineyard overlooking Bourg-sur-Gironde and the river.

### CHÂTEAU CROUTE-COURPON
**Bourg-sur-Gironde**

A small but recently enlarged estate, it produces honest, fruity red wines.

### CHÂTEAU EYQUEM
**Bayon-sur-Gironde**

Owned by the serious winemaking Bayle-Carreau family, which also owns several other properties, this wine is not normally, however, purchased for its quality. It is enjoyable as a light luncheon claret, but the real joy is in the spoof of serving a red "Yquem."

### CHÂTEAU FALFAS
**Bourg-sur-Gironde**
Ⓑ ★ ⓥ

Owned by John and Vonique Cochran, whose biodynamic wines are consistently rich, midterm drinkers of no little finesse.

### CHÂTEAU GÉNIBON
**Bourg-sur-Gironde**

This small vineyard produces attractive wines that have all the enjoyment upfront and are easy to drink.

### CHÂTEAU GRAND-LAUNAY
**Teuillac**
★ ⓥ

This property has been developed from the vineyards of three estates: Domaine Haut-Launay, Château Launay, and Domaine les Hermats. Mainly red wine is produced, although a very tiny amount of white is also made. The star-performing wine at this château is a superb, special reserve *cuvée* of red that is sold under the Château Lion Noir label.

### CHÂTEAU DE LA GRAVE
**Bourg-sur-Gironde**
★ ⓥ

An important property situated on one of the highest points of Bourg-sur-Gironde, it produces a large quantity of light, fruity Malbec-influenced red wine and a very tiny amount of white.

### CHÂTEAU GUERRY
**Tauriac**
★ ⓥ

Some 10,000 cases of really fine wood-aged red wines are produced at this château. The wines have good structure, bags of fruit, and a smooth, elegant flavor.

### CHÂTEAU GUIONNE
**Lansac**

These are easy-drinking wines, full of attractive Merlot fruit, good juicy flavor, and some finesse. A little white wine of some interest and depth is also made.

### CHÂTEAU HAUT-MACÔ
**Tauriac**

This rustic red wine is full of rich, fruity flavors, and good acidity. The proprietors also own a property called Domaine de Lilotte in Bourg-sur-Gironde producing attractive, early-drinking red wines under the

Bordeaux Supérieur appellation.
**Other wine:** Les Bascauds

### CHÂTEAU HAUT-ROUSSET
**Bourg-sur-Gironde**

Some 12,000 cases of decent, everyday-drinking red wine and 1,000 cases of white are produced at this fairly large property. The red wines from a small vineyard close by are sold under the Château la Renardière label.

### CHÂTEAU DE LIDONNE
**Bourg-sur-Gironde**
★

This very old property produces an excellent-quality red wine, powerfully aromatic and full of Cabernet character. Its name comes from the 15th-century monks who looked after the estate and offered lodgings to passing pilgrims: "Lit-Donne" or "Give Bed."

### CHÂTEAU PEYCHAUD
**Teuillac**
★ Ⓥ

These fruity red wines are easy to drink when young. A little white is also made. It is under the same ownership as Château Peyredoulle and Château le Peuy-Saincrit.

### CHÂTEAU ROC DE CAMBES
**Bourg-sur-Gironde**
★★

You can expect to pay five times the price of any other Côtes de Bourg for this blockbuster, which is made by François Mitjavile, the owner of Tertre-Rôteboeuf. However, some vintages are worth it.

### CHÂTEAU ROUSSET
**Samonac**
★ Ⓥ

A fine estate of gravel vineyards producing lightly rich, juicy, Merlot-dominated wines of some finesse; they are perfect to drink when two or three years old.

### CHÂTEAU SAUMAN
**Villeneuve**

These immaculate vineyards produce a good-quality red wine for medium-term maturity. The proprietor also owns the red-wine producing Domaine du Moulin de Mendoce in the same commune.

### CHÂTEAU TOUR-DE-TOURTEAU
**Samonac**
★ Ⓥ

This property was once part of Château Rousset. However, the wines are definitely bigger and richer than those of Rousset.

## THE WINE PRODUCERS OF
# BLAYE

### CHÂTEAU BARBÉ
**Cars**
★ Ⓥ

This château produces well-made and overtly fruity red and white wines. Château Barbé is one of several properties owned by the Bayle-Carreau family (*see also* La Carelle).

### CHÂTEAU BOURDIEU
**Berson**

This old and well-known property produces Cabernet-dominated red wines of a very firm structure that receive time in oak. Seven hundred years ago this estate was accorded the privilege of selling "clairet," a tradition it maintains today by aging the blended production of various vineyards in oak. The white wines are of improving quality.

### CHÂTEAU LA CARELLE
**St-Paul**

More than 11,000 cases of agreeable red wines and just 1,500 cases of white are made at this property. The owner also runs Châteaux Barbé.

### CHÂTEAU CHARRON
**St-Martin-Lacaussade**
★ Ⓥ

These very attractive, well-made, juicy-rich, Merlot-dominated red wines are matured in oak, some of which is new. A small amount of white wine is also made.

### CHÂTEAU CRUSQUET-DE-LAGARCIE
**Cars**
★★ Ⓥ

A tremendously exciting, richly styled red wine, which is deep-colored, bright, big, full of fruit, vanilla, and spice. A small amount of dry white wine is sold under the name "Clos-des-Rudel" and an even smaller quantity of sweet white wine as "Clos-Blanc de Lagarcie." The châteaux Les-Princesses-de-Lagarcie and Touzignan, also in Cars, are under the same ownership.

### CHÂTEAU L'ESCADRE
**Cars**
★ Ⓥ

These elegant red wines are well-colored, full, and fruity. They can be enjoyed young, but also improve with age. A small amount of fruity white wine is produced.
**Second wine:** *Château la Croix*

### CHÂTEAU GIGAULT CUVÉE VIVA
**Mazion**
★★ Ⓥ

Amazing richness and opulence of fruit for the price.

### DOMAINE DU GRAND BARRAIL
**Plassac**
★ Ⓥ

This château makes a fine-quality red wine that attracts by its purity of fruit. A little white wine is produced. The proprietor also owns Château Gardut-Haut-Cluzeau and Domaine du Cavalier in Cars.

### CHÂTEAU DU GRAND PIERRE
**Berson**
★ Ⓥ

This property can produce tremendous-value medium- to full-bodied red wine with sweet, ripe fruit. Fresh, zesty, dry white wine of agreeable quality is also made.

### CHÂTEAU LES GRANDS MARÉCHAUX
**St-Girons d'Aiguevives**
★ Ⓥ

Bags of black fruit for your bucks.

### CHÂTEAU HAUT BERTINERIE
**Cubnezais**
★★ Ⓥ

The consistent class of this wine, with its silky fruit and beautifully integrated oak, makes it stand out above the rest as the best-value dry white currently made in Bordeaux.

### CHÂTEAU DE HAUT SOCIONDO
**Cars**

Agreeably light and fruity red and white wines are made here.

### CHÂTEAU LES JONQUEYRES
**St-Paul-de-Blaye**
★★ Ⓥ

This château produces lush Merlot-dominated reds with lots of well-integrated creamy oak. The wines are impeccably produced.

### CHÂTEAU LACAUSSADE SAINT MARTIN "TROIS MOULINS"
**St-Martin Lacaussade**
★ Ⓥ

Owned by Jacques Chardat, but managed and marketed by Vignobles Germain, both the sumptuous red and classy dry white benefit from 100 percent new oak.

### CHÂTEAU LAMANCEAU
**St-Androny**

Production at this property is entirely red and of an excellent standard: richly colored wine full of the juicy spice of Merlot.

### CHÂTEAU LES MOINES
**Blaye**

A red-only château, producing a light- to medium-bodied, fresh and fruity wine for easy drinking

### CHÂTEAU MARINIER
**Cézac**
★ Ⓥ

Twice as much red wine as white is produced. The red is agreeably fruity, but the white is much the better wine: smooth, well balanced, lightly rich, and elegant. Red and rosé wines are also produced under the Bordeaux appellation.

### CHÂTEAU MAINE-GAZIN "LEVENNE" VIEILLES VIGNES
**Plassac**
★ Ⓥ

With one-third new oak, this 90 percent Merlot wine is rich, sumptuous, and above its class.

### CHÂTEAU MENAUDAT
**St-Androny**
★ Ⓥ

These are extremely attractive, full, and fruity red wines.

### CHÂTEAU LES PETITS ARNAUDS
**Cars**
★ Ⓥ

Attractively aromatic red wines, pleasingly round and fruity. Dry white Blaye and a *moelleux* white.

### CHÂTEAU PEYREDOULLE
**Berson**
★ Ⓥ

This 15th-century property produces mainly good-quality red wine, although some white is made. The proprietors also own Château Peychaud in the Bourgeais commune of Teuillac and the Bordeaux AOC of Château le Peuy-Saincrit.

### CHÂTEAU PEYREYRE
**St-Martin-Lacaussade**
★ Ⓥ

This château produces rich-flavored reds of some finesse. Bordeaux Rosé is also made.

### CHÂTEAU SEGONZAC
**St-Genès-de-Blaye**
★ Ⓥ

Château Segonzac's easy-drinking red wines are light, well made, fresh, firm, and agreeably fruity.

# ENTRE-DEUX-MERS

*Entre-Deux-Mers, which literally means "between two seas" is situated between the Dordogne and Garonne rivers. It is Bordeaux's largest district, and produces inexpensive dry white wines and an increasing volume of excellent value-for-money red wines that are entitled to the Bordeaux, Bordeaux Supérieur, and Premières-Côtes-de-Bordeaux appellations.*

TECHNOLOGICAL PROGRESS in winemaking occurred earlier and more quickly in Entre-Deux-Mers than in any other district of Bordeaux. As early as the 1950s and 1960s, there was a grassroots viticultural movement to drop the traditional low vine-training systems and adopt the revolutionary "high-culture" system contrasted with the low vine-training methods common throughout Bordeaux. These new vineyard techniques were followed in the 1970s by a widespread adoption of cool-fermentation techniques. With fresh, light, and attractively dry white wines being made at many châteaux, the major export markets suddenly realized it would be easier to sell the name Entre-Deux-Mers rather than continue to sell what had become boring Bordeaux Blanc. This was even better if the wine could boast some sort of individual *petit château* personality.

## THE "HIGH-CULTURE" SYSTEM OF VINE TRAINING

Entre-Deux-Mers in the late 1940s and early 1950s was a sorry place. The wines were sold in bulk, ending up as anonymous Bordeaux Blanc, and much of the decline in the Bordeaux region was centered on this district. But the new postwar generation of

CHÂTEAU BONNET
*In 1898 this vineyard was acquired by Léonce Recapet, one of the first to carry out replanting after the devastation of the Gironde vineyard by phylloxera at the turn of the century. His son-in-law, François Lurton, succeeded him, and in 1956 his grandson, André Lurton, became the owner.*

winegrowers were not content with this state of affairs. Although times were difficult and the economy was deteriorating, the young, technically minded *vignerons* realized that the district's compressed *boulbènes* soil, which was choking the vines, could not be worked by their ancestors' outdated methods, and they therefore took a considerable financial risk to rectify the situation. They grubbed up every other row of vines, thus increasing the spacing between the rows, and trained the plants on a "high-culture" system similar to that practiced farther south in Madiran and Jurançon (also in Austria where it was originally conceived

LOUPIAC CHURCH
*The local church neighbors the vineyards of Château Loupiac, which are situated on the right bank of the Garonne.*

ENTRE-DEUX-MERS
*See also p55*
*The varied countryside of this district spreads out between the rivers Dordogne and Garonne as their paths diverge. The Premières Côtes form a narrow strip along the south side.*

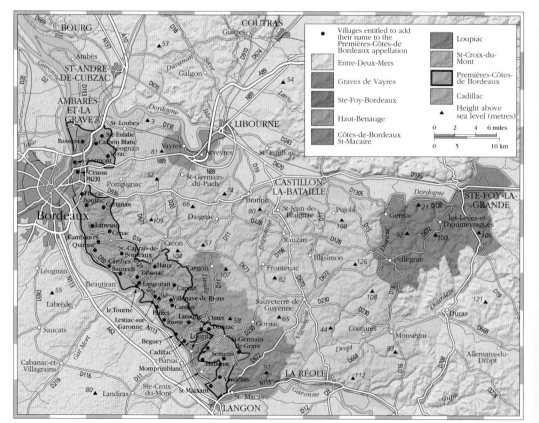

## FACTORS AFFECTING TASTE AND QUALITY

**LOCATION**
A large area east of Bordeaux between the Garonne and Dordogne rivers.

**CLIMATE**
More windy and wetter than the Médoc; areas near the rivers are liable to flood.

**ASPECT**
Quiet and very attractive countryside of vine-covered hillsides, orchards, and meadows.

**SOIL**
Very varied topsoils, ranging from alluvium by the river to gravel on some hillsides and crests, and clay-gravel or clay-limestone on various plateaus. At the western end of the district a soil called *boulbènes* dominates. This is extremely fine and sandy and has a tendency to compress into an impermeable barrier. Vines must be grafted on to special rootstock in order to be productive in such soil. Much of the subsoil is limestone or limestone-based, but sandy-clay, clay-and-limestone rubble, a quarry stone called *aslar*, and *ribot*—a sandstone containing gravel and iron deposits—are also found.

**VITICULTURE AND VINIFICATION**
This area is famed for its "high and wide" method of vine training, which was developed in the early 1950s and is similar to the Lenz Moser system used in Austria. Greater emphasis is now placed on the Sauvignon grape and cool fermentation in stainless-steel vats.

**GRAPE VARIETIES**
**Primary varieties:** Sémillon, Sauvignon Blanc, Muscadelle
**Secondary varieties:** Merlot Blanc, Colombard, Mauzac, Ugni Blanc

and was called the Lenz Moser system). This system allowed machinery to work the land and break up the soil. It also increased the canopy of foliage, which intensified chlorophyll assimilation and improved ripening.

## COOL FERMENTATION

In the 1970s, university-trained personnel at the well-funded Entre-Deux-Mers *coopératives* invested in temperature-controlled stainless-steel vats and led the way in cool-fermentation techniques. Prior to this, fermentation temperatures were often in excess of 83°F (28°C), but it was soon discovered that the lower the temperature, the more aromatic the compounds released. They discovered that fermentation could take place at temperatures as low as 39°F (4°C), although the risk of stuck-fermentation (when the fermentation process stops) was greater at such low temperatures. It soon became clear that the ideal fermentation temperature was somewhere between 50°F (10°C) and 64°F (18°C). This increased the yield of alcohol and important aromatic and flavor compounds. It also reduced both the loss of carbonic gas and the presence of volatile acidity and required less sulfur dioxide. In the mid-1980s it was confirmed that 64°F (18°C) is the optimum temperature for fermentation. Lower temperatures also produce amylic aromas, which in small quantities are fine, but the lower the temperature, the more the wine is dominated by these nail-polish aromas.

---

THE APPELLATIONS OF

# ENTRE-DEUX-MERS

## BORDEAUX HAUT-BENAUGE AOC

Situated above the Premières Côtes, opposite Cérons, this area corresponds to the ancient and tiny county of Benauge. To claim this appellation, as opposed to Entre-Deux-Mers-Haut-Benauge, the grapes are restricted to the three classic varieties and must be riper, with a minimum sugar level of 195 grams per liter instead of 170 grams per liter. The yield is 10 percent lower and the minimum alcoholic level 1.5 percent higher.

**WHITE** Dry, medium-sweet, and sweet versions of this light-bodied, fruity wine may be made.

Sémillon, Sauvignon Blanc, Muscadelle

1–3 years for dry and medium-sweet wines; 3–6 years for sweet wines

## CADILLAC AOC

Of the trio of sweet-wine areas on the right bank of the Garonne, Cadillac is the least known. It encompasses 21 communes, 16 of which form the canton of Cadillac, yet very little wine is produced under this appellation—ust one-fifth of that made in Loupiac, or one-tenth of that made in Ste.-Croix-du-Mont. The regulations state that the wines must be made from botrytized grapes harvested in successive *tries*, but there is little evidence of this in the wines, which at best have the character of *passerillage*. The *terroir* could produce wines of a much superior quality, but it would be costly to do so, and sadly, this appellation does not fetch a high enough price to justify the substantial investment needed.

**WHITE** Attractive honey-gold wines with fresh, floral aromas and a semisweet, or sweet, fruity flavor.

Sémillon, Sauvignon Blanc, Muscadelle

3–8 years

## CÔTES-DE-BORDEAUX-ST.-MACAIRE AOC

These little-seen wines come from an area at the eastern extremity of the Premières-Côtes-de-Bordeaux. Of the 6,000 acres (2,300 hectares) of vineyards that may use this appellation, barely 75 acres (30 hectares) bother to do so.

**WHITE** Medium-bodied, medium-sweet, or sweet wines that are attractive in a fruity way, but unpretentious.

Sémillon, Sauvignon Blanc, Muscadelle

1–3 years

## ENTRE-DEUX-MERS AOC

This is the largest district in the region, and after the generic Bordeaux Blanc, it is its greatest-volume white-wine appellation. Entre-Deux-Mers has a growing reputation for exceptional-value wines of a high technical standard.

**WHITE** Crisp, dry, light-bodied wines that are fragrant, aromatic, and usually predominantly Sauvignon Blanc. These are clean, cool-fermented wines. They may be sold from December 1 following the harvest without any mention of *primeur* or *nouveau*.

At least 70 percent Sémillon, Sauvignon Blanc, and Muscadelle, plus a maximum of 30 percent Merlot Blanc and up to 10 percent in total of Colombard, Mauzac, and Ugni Blanc

1–2 years

## ENTRE-DEUX-MERS-HAUT-BENAUGE AOC

These wines are drier than those of the Bordeaux-Haut-Benauge appellation, and their blends may include a greater number of grape varieties, although the same nine communes comprise both appellations. The wines comply with the less rigorous regulations of Entre-Deux-Mers and, consequently, this AOC produces four times the volume of wine than does Bordeaux-Haut-Benauge. Entre-Deux-Mers-Haut-Benauge has so far produced only dry wines, with the exception of 1983, when a luscious vintage arrived that was easy to make into sweet wines.

**WHITE** These dry wines are very similar to those of Entre-Deux-Mers.

At least 70 percent Sémillon, Sauvignon Blanc, and Muscadelle, plus a maximum of 30 percent Merlot Blanc and up to 10 percent in total of Colombard, Mauzac, and Ugni Blanc

1–3 years

## GRAVES DE VAYRES AOC

An enclave of gravelly soil on the left bank of the Dordogne, this appellation produces a substantial quantity of excellent-value red and white wines.

**RED** These are well-colored, aromatic, medium-bodied wines with fragrant, juicy-spicy, predominantly Merlot fruit. They are richer than those found elsewhere in Entre-Deux-Mers.

Cabernet Sauvignon, Cabernet Franc, Carmenère, Merlot, Malbec, Petit Verdot

4–10 years

**WHITE** Mostly dry and off-dry styles of fresh, fragrant, and fruity wines made for early drinking. Occasionally, sweeter styles are made. These wines may be sold from December 1 following the harvest without any mention of *primeur* or *nouveau*.

Sémillon, Sauvignon Blanc, and Muscadelle plus a maximum of 30 percent Merlot Blanc

1–3 years

## LOUPIAC AOC

This appellation is located on the right bank of the Garonne, opposite Barsac. It is by far the best sweet-wine appellation in Entre-Deux-Mers and its wines are always excellent value. According to the regulations, Loupiac must be made with the "assistance" of overripe botrytized grapes and, unlike Cadillac, these wines often have the honeyed complexity of "noble rot." The best Loupiac wines come from vineyards with clay-and-limestone soil.

**WHITE** Luscious medium- to full-bodied wines that are sweet or intensely sweet, honey-rich, and full of flavor. They can be quite complex, and in suitable years have evident botrytis character.

🍇 Sémillon, Sauvignon Blanc, Muscadelle

🍷 5–15 years (25 in exceptional cases)

## PREMIÈRES-CÔTES-DE-BORDEAUX AOC

A 37-mile (60-kilometer) strip of southwest-facing slopes covering 420 acres (170 hectares) of vines scattered through 37 communes, each of which has the right to add its name to this appellation. They are: Bassens, Baurech, Béguey, Bouliac, Cadillac, Cambes, Camblanes, Capian, Carbon Blanc, Cardan, Carignan, Cenac, Cenon, Donzac, Floirac, Gabarnac, Haux, Langoiran, Laroque, Lestiac, Lormont, Monprimblanc, Omet, Paillet, Quinsac, Rions, Sémens, St.-Caprais-de-Bordeaux, St.-Germain-de-Graves, St.-Maixant, Ste.-Eulalie, Tabanac, Le Tourne, La Tresne, Verdelais, Ville-nave de Rions, and Yvrac.

**RED** The best red wines come from the northern communes. These well-colored, soft, and fruity wines are a cut above basic Bordeaux AOC.

🍇 Cabernet Sauvignon, Cabernet Franc, Carmenère, Merlot, Malbec, Petit Verdot

🍷 4–8 years

**WHITE** Since the 1981 harvest, no dry wines have been allowed under this generally unexciting appellation. They must have at least some sweetness, and most are in fact semisweet. Simple, fruity wines, well-made for the most part, but lacking character.

🍇 Sémillon, Sauvignon Blanc, Muscadelle

🍷 3–7 years

## STE.-CROIX-DU-MONT AOC

This is the second-best sweet-white appellation on the right bank of the Garonne, and it regularly produces more wine than Barsac. Like Loupiac wines, these wines must be made with the "assistance" of overripe botrytized grapes. They have less honeyed complexity of "noble rot" than Loupiac wines, but often have more finesse.

**WHITE** Fine, viscous, honey-sweet wines that are lighter in body and color than Loupiac wines. Excellent value when they have rich botrytis character.

🍇 Sémillon, Sauvignon Blanc, Muscadelle

🍷 5–15 years (25 in exceptional cases)

## STE.-FOY-BORDEAUX AOC

Until relatively recently, Ste.-Foy-Bordeaux was known primarily for its white wines, but it now produces as much red as white. There is a high proportion of "organic" winemakers in this area.

**RED** Ruby-colored, medium-bodied wines made in a soft, easy-drinking style.

🍇 Cabernet Sauvignon, Cabernet Franc, Merlot, Malbec, Petit Verdot

🍷 3–7 years

**WHITE** Mellow, semisweet wines of uninspiring quality, and fresh, crisp dry white wines that have good aroma and make attractive early drinking. These wines may be sold from December 1 following the harvest without any mention of *primeur* or *nouveau*.

🍇 Sémillon, Sauvignon Blanc, and Muscadelle, and up 10 percent in total of Merlot Blanc, Colombard, Mauzac, and Ugni Blanc

🍷 1–3 years

---

THE WINE PRODUCERS OF

# ENTRE-DEUX-MERS

### CHÂTEAU ARNAUD-JOUAN
**Cadillac**
AOC Premières-Côtes-de-Bordeaux and AOC Cadillac
☆Ⓥ

This large, well-situated vineyard makes interesting, attractive wines.

### DOMAINE DU BARRAIL
**Monprimblanc**
AOC Premières-Côtes-de-Bordeaux and AOC Cadillac
☆Ⓥ

Both the red Premières Côtes and sweet white Cadillac produced at this property are worth watching.

### CHÂTEAU DE BEAUREGARD
AOC Entre-Deux-Mers and AOC Bordeaux-Haut-Benauge

The red and white wines are well-made. The red has good structure, but is softened by the spice of the Merlot.

### CHÂTEAU BEL-AIR
**Vayres**
AOC Graves de Vayres

Most of the wines made here are red and well-colored. They are aromatic wines of a Cabernet character.

### CHÂTEAU BIROT
**Béguey**
AOC Premières-Côtes-de-Bordeaux and AOC Cadillac
★Ⓥ

Popular for its easy-drinking whites, this property also produces well-balanced red wines of some finesse.

### CHÂTEAU LA BLANQUERIE
**Mérignas**
AOC Entre-Deux-Mers

Dry white wine with a Sauvignon character and a fine finish.

### CHÂTEAU BONNET
**Grézillac**
AOC Entre-Deux-Mers
★★☆

This top-performing Entre-Deux-Mers château is owned by André Lurton. It produces crisp, fresh, and characterful white wines, and soft, fruity, extremely successful

(Bordeaux Supérieur) red.
**Second wine:** *Le Colombey*
**Other wines:** *Tour-de-Bonnet, Château Gourmin, Château Peyraud*

### CHÂTEAU BRÉTHOUS
**Camblanes-et-Meynac**
AOC Premières-Côtes-de-Bordeaux and AOC Cadillac
★Ⓥ

The red wines are forward and attractive, yet well-structured, while the whites are succulent and sweet.

### CHÂTEAU CANET
**Guillac**
AOC Entre-Deux-Mers
★Ⓥ

These excellent white wines are clean and crisp, with good fruit and an elegant balance.

### CHÂTEAU CAYLA
**Rions**
AOC Premières-Côtes-de-Bordeaux
★Ⓥ

The reds are elegant and accessible with just a touch of new oak.

### CHÂTEAU DE CÉRONS
**Cérons**
AOC Cérons

Jean Perromat also owns Château d'Arche, and consistently produces superb, white botrytized wines.
**Other wine:** *De Calvimont* (dry white)

### DOMAINE DE CHASTELET
**Quinsac**
AOC Premières-Côtes-de-Bordeaux and AOC Cadillac

Domaine de Chastelet produces red wine that is delicious, yet firm and complex, with very well-balanced blackcurrant fruit flavors and a hint of vanilla oak.

### CLOS BOURGELAT
**Cérons**
AOC Cérons
★☆Ⓥ

These botrytized wines have great aroma, finesse, and complexity.

## CLOS JEAN
### Loupiac
### AOC Loupiac

The wines produced by Clos Jean are similar quality to those of Château du Cros, but more refined and ethereal in character.

## CHÂTEAU LA CLYDE
### Tabanac
### AOC Premières-Côtes-de-Bordeaux and AOC Cadillac
### ★ ⓥ

These aromatic, deep-colored, ruby-red wines show good spice and fruit. The white has finesse and balance.

## CHÂTEAU DU CROS
### Loupiac
### AOC Loupiac
### ★ ⓥ

The fine, fat, succulent sweet wines of this château are among the best of the appellation.

## CHÂTEAU DINTRANS
### Ste.-Eulalie
### AOC Premières-Côtes-de-Bordeaux and AOC Cadillac

This château produces attractive, nicely colored, fruity red wines.

## CHÂTEAU DE L'ESPLANADE
### Capian
### AOC Premières-Côtes-de-Bordeaux

Produced by Patrick and Sabine Bayle of Château Plaisance, these primarily Merlot wines are cheaper and simpler than those of Château Plaisance, but are easy-drinking nevertheless. They are also sold under the Château Florestan label.

## CHÂTEAU FAYAU
### Cadillac
### AOC Premières-Côtes-de-Bordeaux and AOC Cadilla

This château produces succulent sweet wines in addition to red, clairet, and dry white wines.

**Other wine:** *Clos des Capucins*

## CHÂTEAU FLORESTAN
### *See* Château de l'Esplanade

## CHÂTEAU FONGRAVE
### Gornac
### AOC Entre-Deux-Mers

These dry white wines have a fresh and tangy taste.

**Second wine:** *Château de la Sablière Fongrave* (red wines)

## CHÂTEAU DE GORCE
### Haux
### AOC Premières-Côtes-de-Bordeaux and AOC Cadillac

This château produces fruity reds and fresh, floral whites.

## CHÂTEAU GOUDICHAUD
### Vayres
### AOC Graves de Vayres

This property also extends into St-Germain-du-Puch in Entre-Deux-Mers, where it produces some very respectable wines.

## CHÂTEAU GOUMIN
### Dardenac
### AOC Entre-Deux-Mers

Goumin is another successful André Lurton château. It produces up to 10,000 cases of pleasant, soft, fruity red wine and 5,000 cases of white wine that is slightly fuller than other similar Lurton products.

## GRAND ENCLOS DU CHÂTEAU DE CÉRONS
### Cérons
### AOC Cérons
### ☆

Although historically part of Château de Cérons, this is not under the same ownership. The original estate belonged to the Marquis de Calvimont, but was split in two by the route from Bordeaux to Spain, which was constructed in 1875. The marquis then sold the property in three separate lots, one of which was called Grand Enclos and was purchased by the Lataste family, who are still the owners today. The white wines of Grand Enclos are equally as rich and potentially complex as those of Château de Cérons itself (which is so called because it retains the marquis' château).

## CHÂTEAU GRAND MONEIL
### Salleboeuf
### AOC Entre-Deux-Mers
### ★ ⓥ

Barely more than a thousand cases of white, but 35,000 cases of excellent-quality, soft, quaffing red.

## CHÂTEAU DU GRAND-MOÜEYS
### Capian
### AOC Premières-Côtes-de-Bordeaux
### ★ ⓥ

Excellent-value reds for medium-term aging are currently made at this château.

## CHÂTEAU GRAVELINES
### Sémens
### AOC Premières-Côtes-de-Bordeaux and AOC Cadillac
### ★ ⓥ

This large property produces equal quantities of excellent red and white wines.

## CHÂTEAU GROSSOMBRE
### Branne
### AOC Entre-Deux-Mers
### ★ ⓥ

The daughter of André Lurton runs this property, which produces lush yet elegant white wines and a beautifully concentrated red, the latter of which is sold under the Bordeaux Supérieur AOC and must be one of Bordeaux's greatest bargains.

## CHÂTEAU DU GUA
### Ambarès-et-Lagrave
### AOC Premières-Côtes-de-Bordeaux and AOC Cadillac
### ☆

An attractive, well-structured red wine is produced from this 20-acre (8-hectare) vineyard of fine gravel.

## CHÂTEAU HAUT-BRIGNON
### Cénac
### AOC Premières-Côtes-de-Bordeaux and AOC Cadillac
### ☆

This property has been steadily improving since the late 1980s, producing a soft, velvety red and crisp, dry white, plus one of Cadillac's better wines.

## CHÂTEAU DE HAUX
### Haux
### AOC Premières-Côtes-de-Bordeaux
### ★☆ ⓥ

These red and white wines are gorgeously ripe and ready to drink, absolutely fresh, and very elegant, and, under the Château Frère label, a fabulous oak-fermented white is also produced. Probably the top-performing château in the Premières Côtes for both red and white.

## CHÂTEAU HOSTENS PICANT
### Grangeneuve Nord
### ★ ⓥ

Since the current owners Nadine and Yves Picant purchased this property in 1986, broke off relations with the local cooperative, and built their own winery, this château has not looked back. The top wine, LVCVLLVS Cuvée d'Exception, is ★☆ quality, but the "basic" *grand vin* is excellent, and the refreshing dry white and rosé (sold as the seldom-seen AOC Bordeaux Clairet) offer deliciously good value.

## CHÂTEAU DU JUGE
### Haux
### AOC Premières-Côtes-de-Bordeaux and AOC Cadillac

These promising red wines are easy drinking, and full of juicy fruit flavors. Decent, if unexciting whites are also made.

## CHÂTEAU DU JUGE
### Cadillac
### AOC Premières-Côtes-de-Bordeaux and AOC Cadillac

Respectable red and dry white wines are produced at Château du Juge, and in some years, a little sweet white wine of high quality is also made. Both red and white wines are extraordinarily good value.

## CHÂTEAU LABATUT
### St-Maixant
### AOC Premières-Côtes-de-Bordeaux and AOC Cadillac
### ☆

The red wines are aromatic and full of flavor, while the sweet white wines are exceptional quality. Decent dry white is also produced.

## CHÂTEAU LAFITTE
### Camblanes-et-Meynac
### AOC Premières-Côtes-de-Bordeaux and AOC Cadillac

Nothing like the real thing (the famous *premier cru*), of course, but the wine is decent, well structured, and capable of improving with age— a cheap way to get a Château Lafitte on the table, even if it is not *the* Château Lafite.

## CHÂTEAU LAFUE
### Cadillac
### AOC Ste-Croix-du-Mont
### ☆

Attractive, sweet white wines with more of a fruity than a botrytis character. Nearly a quarter of the production is red wine.

## CHÂTEAU LAMOTHE
### Haux
### AOC Premières-Côtes-de-Bordeaux and AOC Cadillac

Some exceptionally good wines have been produced in recent years at this château, which derives its name from "La Motte," a rocky spur that protects the vineyard.

## CHÂTEAU LAROCHE BEL AIR
### Baurech
### AOC Premières-Côtes-de-Bordeaux

Absolutely delicious-drinking reds under the basic Château Laroche label, and an even better selection of oak-aged reds under Laroche Bel Air.

## CHÂTEAU LATOUR
### St.-Martin-du-Puy
### AOC Entre-Deux-Mers

From this ancient château, parts of which date back to the 14th century, 10,000 cases of attractive, well-balanced, smooth red Bordeaux Supérieur are produced every year. This château's technically sound wines often win prizes and enable its devotees to claim that they can afford to drink Château Latour every day, at minimum expense.

## CHÂTEAU LATOUR
### Camblanes-et-Meynac
### AOC Premières-Côtes-de-Bordeaux and AOC Cadillac

This is another everyday-drinking claret with this prestigious name.

## CHÂTEAU LAUNAY
### Soussac
### AOC Entre-Deux-Mers

This large property produces 40,000 cases of a fresh dry white wine and 15,000 cases of a red wine sold under the "Haut-Castanet" label.

**Other wines:** *Bradoire, Château Dubory, Château Haut-Courgeaux, Château La Vaillante*

## CHÂTEAU LAURETTE
### Cadillac
### AOC Ste.-Croix-du-Mont
### ☆

This property is under the same ownership as Château Lafue and runs along similar lines.

## CHÂTEAU LOUBENS
### Cadillac
### AOC Ste.-Croix-du-Mont
### ★

This château produces rich, liquorous, superbly balanced sweet white wines. Dry white wines are sold as "Fleur Blanc," and a little red wine is also made.

**Other wine:** *Fleur Blanc de Château Loubens*

## CHÂTEAU LOUPIAC-GAUDIET
### Loupiac
### AOC Loupiac

Fine, honey-rich sweet wines hinting of crystallized fruit are produced here.

## CHÂTEAU LOUSTEAU-VIEIL
### Cadillac
### AOC Ste.-Croix-du-Mont
### ★

This property produces richly flavoured, high-quality sweet wines.

## CHÂTEAU MACHORRE
### St.-Martin-de-Sescas
### AOC Côtes-de-Bordeaux-St.-Macaire
### ☆

The sweet white wine of this château has an attractive, fresh, fruit-salad flavor and is one of the best examples of the appellation. Very respectable red and dry Sauvignon wines are also produced, which are sold under the Bordeaux appellations.

## CHÂTEAU DES MAILLES
### Cadillac
### AOC Ste.-Croix-du-Mont

Some outstanding sweet wines are produced at Château des Mailles, but the wines can occasionally be disappointing.

## CHÂTEAU LA MAUBASTIT
### AOC Ste.-Foy-de-Bordeaux

Some 5,000 cases of white and 2,000 of red, both "organic" wines, are sold under the Bordeaux appellation.

## CHÂTEAU MORLAN-TUILIÈRE
### St.-Pierre-de-Bat
### AOC Entre-Deux-Mers-Haut-Benauge and Bordeaux Haut-Benauge

One of the best properties of the area, producing a vibrant, crystal-clear Entre-Deux-Mers-Haut-Benauge, a Bordeaux Supérieur in the *moelleux* style, and a fairly full-bodied red AOC Bordeaux.

## CHÂTEAU MOULIN DE LAUNAY
### Soussac
### AOC Entre-Deux-Mers

Despite the vast quantity produced, the dry white wine is crisp and fruity, and of a very fine standard. A little red is also produced.

**Other wines:** *Plessis, Château Tertre-de-Launay, Château de Tuilerie, Château la Vigerie*

## CHÂTEAU MOULIN DE ROMAGE
### AOC Ste.-Foy-de-Bordeaux

This château produces equal quantities of "organic" red and white.

## DOMAINE DU NOBLE
### Loupiac
### AOC Loupiac

This property consistently produces fine botrytized wines that combine sweetness and strength with elegance and a fresh, long finish.

## CHÂTEAU PETIT-PEY
### St.-André-du-Bois
### AOC Côtes-de-Bordeaux-St.-Macaire

Good, sweet white St.-Macaire and agreeably soft red AOC Bordeaux are made at this property.

## CHÂTEAU PEYREBON
### Grézillac
### AOC Entre-Deux-Mers

Produces red and white wine in almost equal quantities. The dry white is fine and flavorsome.

## CHÂTEAU PEYRINES
### Mourens
### AOC Entre-Deux-Mers-Haut-Benauge and Bordeaux Haut-Benauge
### ★★☆

The vineyard of this château has an excellent southern exposure and produces fruity red and white wines.

## CHÂTEAU DE PIC
### Le Tourne
### AOC Premières-Côtes-de-Bordeaux

The basic red is a lovely, creamy-sweet, easy-drinking, fruity wine. A superb oak-aged red under the *Cuvée* Tradition label is also made.

## CHÂTEAU PICHON-BELLEVUE
### Vayres
### AOC Graves de Vayres

The red wines are variable, but the dry whites are delicate and refined.

## CHÂTEAU PLAISANCE
### Capian
### AOC Premières-Côtes-de-Bordeaux

The *Cuvée* Tradition, in which the wine is aged in oak and is unfiltered, gives rich, ripe fruit with supple tannin structure and smoky oak.

**Other wines:** *De l'Esplanade, Château Florestin*

## CHÂTEAU DE PLASSAN
### Tabanac
### AOC Premières-Côtes-de-Bordeaux

The basic red has a lot of character, with cherry-minty undertones in riper years. However, the fuller, more complex *cuvée spéciale* is worth paying for, particularly if you want a wine to accompany food.

## CHÂTEAU PONTETTE-BELLEGRAVE
### Vayres
### AOC Graves de Vayres

This property has a reputation for subtly flavored, dry white wines.

## CHÂTEAU PUY BARDENS
### Cambes
### AOC Premières-Côtes-de-Bordeaux

This top-performing château produces reds with sweet, ripe, fat fruit and a soft, velvety finish.

## CHÂTEAU LA RAME
### Cadillac
### AOC Ste.-Croix-du-Mont

One of the top wines of the appellation, La Rame can have fruit, with cream and honey flavors.

## CHÂTEAU REYNON-PEYRAT
### Béguey
### AOC Premières-Côtes-de-Bordeaux

This property produces a superb, oak-aged Premières Côtes red wine, and two dry white wines under the Château Reynon label.

## CHÂTEAU RICAUD
### Loupiac
### AOC Loupiac

The wines of Château Ricaud are once again the best in the Loupiac appellation. They suffered a significant decline under the previous proprietor, but have at last recovered, and now display great class under new ownership.

## CHÂTEAU DE LA SABLIÈRE-FONGRAVE
### Gornac
### AOC Entre-Deux-Mers-Haut-Benauge and Bordeaux Haut-Benauge

Sold as a Bordeaux Supérieur, the red wine of Château de la Sablière-Fongrave is fairly robust and requires time in bottle to soften. A much better quality dry white is produced and sold under the Entre-Deux-Mers appellation.

## CHÂTEAU TANESSE
### Langoiran
### AOC Premières-Côtes-de-Bordeaux and AOC Cadillac

A Cordier property, Château Tanesse produces a decent Cabernet-dominated red, and fine-quality, Sauvignon-style dry white.

## CHÂTEAU DES TASTES
### Cadillac
### AOC Ste.-Croix-du-Mont
### ★ Ⓥ

The sweet white wine is truly exciting; luxurious in texture, with creamy-rich flavors showing the classic complex character of botrytis.

## CHÂTEAU TERFORT
### Cadillac
### AOC Ste.-Croix-du-Mont
### ☆

A small amount of excellent sweet white wine is produced by Château Terfort.

## CHÂTEAU THIEULEY
### La Sauve
### AOC Entre-Deux-Mers
### ☆

Château Thieuley is owned by Professor Courselle, a former Médoc professor of viticulture and oenology. His dry white combines good fruit flavor with a fine Sauvignon style, while the red is good and silky.

## CHÂTEAU DE TOUTIGEAC
### Targon
### AOC Entre-Deux-Mers-Haut-Benauge and Bordeaux Haut-Benauge
### ☆ Ⓥ

Château de Toutigeac is a well-known property that produces full, rich red wine. It is made for early drinking, and is the best the château produces.

# BURGUNDY

*Villages with double-barreled names are the key to Burgundy's greatest wines. This is because these villages hijacked the names of their most famous vineyards, so that humble village wines could sell on the backs of the finest grands crus. The village of Gevrey was the first to do this when in 1848 it took the name of its Chambertin vineyard to become Gevrey-Chambertin. You cannot become a Burgundy expert overnight, but if you remember the second part of every double-barreled Burgundian village is one of its best vineyards, you will instantly know some of Burgundy's greatest wines.*

SAY "BURGUNDY" AND most people think of the famous wines of the Côtes de Nuits and Côtes de Beaune, but Burgundy in fact stretches from Chablis in the north, which is close to the Aube vineyards of Champagne, down to Beaujolais in the south, in the Rhône *département*. In fact, the Côtes de Nuits and Côtes de Beaune account for less than 10 percent of Burgundy, while Beaujolais represents almost half of the region's entire production.

Burgundy still produces the world's greatest Chardonnay and Pinot Noir wines, and the only Gamay wines ever to achieve classic status, but it is increasingly debased by a growing number of lackluster, sometimes quite disgusting, supermarket wines that rely solely upon the reputation of the famous Burgundian names, which their producers abuse to sell low-quality wines at high prices.

Burgundy, or *Bourgogne* as it is known in French, is an area rich in history, gastronomy, and wine, but unlike the great estates of Bordeaux, the finest Burgundian vineyards are owned by a proliferation of smallholders. Prior to 1789, the church owned most of the vineyards in Burgundy, but these were seized and broken up as a direct result of the Revolution, which was as much antichurch as antiaristocracy. While in Bordeaux, although some of the large wine estates were owned by the aristocracy, many were owned by the *bourgeoisie*, who, because of their long association with the English, were antipapist, and so escaped the

**VIRÉ, MÂCONNAIS**
*Viré is the most ubiquitous of Mâcon's village appellations, but makes consistently fine wines. There are moves to upgrade this village and Clessé to superior appellations.*

full wrath of the Revolution. In Burgundy the great vineyards were further fragmented by inheritance laws, which divided the plots into smaller and smaller parcels. Consequently, many *crus*, or growths, are now owned by as many as 85 individual growers. The initial effect of this proprietorial carve-up was to encourage the supremacy of le négoce. Few commercial houses had been established prior to the mid-18th century because of the difficulty of exporting from a land-locked area, but with better transportation and no opposition from land-owning aristocracy, merchant power grew rapidly. A network of brokers evolved in which dealers became experts on very small, localized areas.

As ownership diversified even further, it became a very specialized, and therefore rewarding, job to keep an up-to-date and comprehensive knowledge of a complex situation. The brokers were vital to the success of a *négociant*, and the *négoce* himself was essential to the success of international trade and therefore responsible for establishing the reputation of Burgundy.

## RECENT BURGUNDY VINTAGES

**2006** Some great wines have been produced in Chablis, the most successful Burgundian district in 2006. Generally it's a white-wine vintage all around, with whites outperforming reds in the Côte de Beaune, Côte de Nuits, Côtes Chalonnaise, and, as to be expected, the Mâconnais. Best reds are in the early-drinking style with only a modest capacity to age, and most are to be found in the Côtes Chalonnaise. Beaujolais did well, too.

**2005** A medium-sized harvest of ripe, intensely flavored fruit resulted in one of the most consistently fine Burgundy vintages in recent years—equally successful in Chablis, the Côte Chalonnaise, the Mâconnais, and Beaujolais as it was in the Côte d'Or. The very best wines are the reds that were produced in the Côte

de Nuits. The white wines are generally on the fat side, which is more of a stylistic call than a qualitative comment.

**2004** An above-average to good-quality vintage that is highlighted by a streak of malic acidity. Although 2004 was better for whites than reds, the latter are plumping out in bottle, which could benefit the most aromatically fragrant examples. Some excellent Chablis, good to very good in the Côte Chalonnaise, and above average in the Mâconnais and Beaujolais.

**2003** The year of the never-ending heatwave took its toll on Burgundy, where hopes and hype were high, but the results are of variable quality at best, with red wine generally

showing huge, exaggerated flavors, high alcohol levels, and low acidity in the Côte d'Or. This is not a year for true connoisseurs of Pinot Noir, who adore the elegance and finesse of that great grape. However, this is one of those vintages where variability is the savior, and some delightful exceptions are to be found in the Côte de Nuits. Most white wines are heavy, alcoholic, and lacking in both freshness and acidity (some of Michel Laroche's Chablis *grands crus* being among the exceptions).

**2002** A very good vintage where a lovely ripeness of fruit has given the reds a slight edge over the excellent whites. One of the most interesting aspects of this vintage is how well the relatively modest village wines have excelled, especially in the hands of top growers.

## THE ROLE OF THE NÉGOCIANT

Until as recently as the early 1980s, virtually all Burgundy would be sold through *négociants* and, although many of them had their own vineyards, these wines were seldom domaine-bottled. Faced with the rise of domaine-bottled Burgundies from small growers, most of the old-fashioned merchants were devoured by Boisset (*see* Did You Know? box), which has become the largest merchant of its kind. Boisset might survive by marketing a mass of different labels, particularly in the supermarket sector or at the bottom end of the restaurant market, but the recent hiring of Pascal Marchand indicates that it has changed its strategy. Marchand is the French-Canadian whose wine-wizardry enabled the quality at Domaine Comte Armand to soar in the second half of the 1990s. By enticing him away to set up and run Domaine de la Vougeraie, Boisset has shown a determination to join the ranks of the few traditional *négociants* who can be said to be top-performing. These currently include Bouchard Père, Drouhin, Louis Jadot, and Leroy, who have not only enlarged their own domaines but have also taken an increasingly proactive role in the vineyards of their suppliers, tending now to buy in grapes or must rather than wines. Until this new strategy evolved, the purchase of wine rather than grapes was the major difference between the old-style *négociant* and the new-wave growers-cum-merchants. The best of the latter include the likes of Jean-Marc Boillot, Michel Colin, Bernard Morey, and Sauzet, who tend to buy grapes to expand their range of single-vineyard wines, in contrast to the old-style merchant, who still churns out examples from nearly every village under the Burgundian sun.

The decline of the old-style merchant is clearly highlighted by domaine-bottling statistics. Today, as much as 90 percent of all *grand cru* wines (and 50 percent of all *premiers crus*) are domaine bottled, although—tellingly—only 24 percent of the entire production of Burgundy is domaine bottled.

## BURGUNDY'S RICH DIVERSITY

Chablis in the north of Burgundy produces the crispest white Chardonnay wines in the world and is geographically closer to Champagne, of which it was once a part, than to the rest of Burgundy. After traveling more than 60 miles (100 kilometers)

GRAND CRU VALMUR, CHABLIS
*At the very heart of Chablis' grands crus lies Valmur. Bordered by Grenouilles and Vaudésir on one side and Les Clos on the other, this vineyard is renowned for the fine bouquet and rich flavor of its wines.*

CORTON, CÔTE DE BEAUNE
*Capped by the Bois de Corton, this magnificent slope produces the Côte de Beaune's most famous red wines and minuscule amounts of Corton Charlemagne, possibly the greatest of all white Burgundies.*

southwest from Champagne, we reach the great Burgundy districts of the Côte d'Or: the Côte de Nuits is encountered first and followed by the Côte de Beaune. If you associate Nuits with "night" or "darkness" and Beaune with "bone-white," then you will easily remember which area is most famous for which wine: for although both *côtes* make excellent red and white wines, most of the greatest red burgundies come from the Côte de Nuits, whereas most of the greatest white burgundies come from the Côte de Beaune.

The Côte Chalonnaise, or Mercurey, region—probably the least-known, but certainly the best-value, wine district of Burgundy—produces similar, if somewhat less classic, styles of red and white wines to those in the Côte de Beaune. Softer still are the primarily white wines of Mâcon, where Pouilly Fuissé AOC rules supreme. (Note that this wine should never be confused with Pouilly Fumé AOC in the Loire.)

Still in Burgundy, but farther south, is the Beaujolais region, which is in the Rhône *département*, although its soft, light, fluffy, fruity red wines are far removed from the archetypal full-bodied red wines that we immediately think of as coming from the Rhône Valley.

Beaujolais can be delicious, but most of it is not. Whereas Beaujolais Nouveau was never meant to be considered as a serious wine, it is now a joke, and far too many of even the best Beaujolais *cru* wines are simply overpriced, but that is all part of Burgundy's rich tapestry.

## GREAT PINOT AND CHARDONNAY

I was pleased to read in the second edition of Anthony Hanson's book *Burgundy* that he had revised his opinion that "Great burgundy smells of shit." Although semisubliminal faults can add to the complexity, interest, and enjoyment of a wine, they should never dominate, particularly in a Pinot Noir wine, in which purity of fruit and varietal character play such an important role. Just as the once-celebrated "sweaty saddle" smell of Australia's Hunter

PARIS

BURGUNDY, *see also* p55
*The route between Dijon and Lyon is studded with the illustrious names of the great growths of Burgundy. Above this north-south band are the Yonne appellations that include Chablis.*

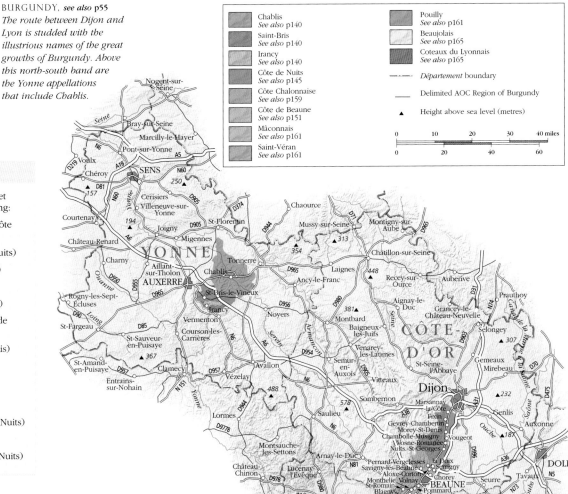

Chablis
*See also* p140

Saint-Bris
*See also* p140

Irancy
*See also* p140

Côte de Nuits
*See also* p145

Côte Chalonnaise
*See also* p159

Côte de Beaune
*See also* p151

Mâconnais
*See also* p161

Saint-Véran
*See also* p161

Pouilly
*See also* p161

Beaujolais
*See also* p165

Coteaux du Lyonnais
*See also* p165

— · — · — · Département boundary

———— Delimited AOC Region of Burgundy

▲ Height above sea level (metres)

## DID YOU KNOW?

The super-*négociant* Boisset currently owns the following:

- Bouchard Aîné & Fils (Côte de Beaune)
- F. Chauvenet (Côte de Nuits)
- Jaffelin (Côte de Beaune)
- Mommessin (Beaujolais)
- J. Moreau & Fils (Chablis)
- Morin Père & Fils (Côte de Nuits)
- Joseph Pellerin (Beaujolais)
- Pierre Ponnelle (Côte de Beaune)
- Ropiteau Frères (Côte de Beaune)
- Thomas-Bassot (Côte de Nuits)
- Thorin (Beaujolais)
- Charles Vienot (Côte de Nuits)

## BURGUNDY AT A GLANCE

| % OF ALL BURGUNDY | DISTRICT | CASES (HECTOLITERS) | PRODUCTION RED/ROSÉ | WHITE | (GRANDS CRUS) |
|---|---|---|---|---|---|
| 16.7% | Generic AOCs | 5,122,000 (461,000) | 46% | 54% | – |
| 9.0% | Chablis | 2,778,000 (250,000) | – | 100% | i2% |
| 3% | Côte de Nuits | 922,000 (83,000) | 95% | 5% | 12% |
| 1% | Hautes-Côtes de Nuits | 333,000 (30,000) | 83% | 17% | – |
| 6.7% | Côte de Beaune | 2,022,000 (182,000) | 83% | 17% | 2% |
| 1.4% | Hautes-Côtes de Beaune | 444,000 (40,000) | 83% | 17% | – |
| 2.8% | Côte Chalonnaise | 856,000 (77,000) | 53% | 47% | – |
| 12.4% | Mâconnais | 3,800,000 (342,000) | 12% | 88% | – |
| 47% | Beaujolais | 14,444,000 (1,300,000) | 99% | 1% | – |
| 100% | TOTAL | 30,731,000[1] (2,765,000[1]) | 74%[2] | 26%[2] | 0.8%[2] |

[1]These totals might not tally with each other due to rounding of numbers above
[2]Average percentage for region

**VINEYARD AND CHÂTEAU OF RULLY**
*With the most northerly AOC vineyards of the Côte Chalonnaise, Rully produces excellent dry Chardonnay wines and some pleasant red wines as well.*

While the California wineries of Santa Barbara, Carneros, and Russian River lead the way in the search for the winemaker's Holy Grail—successful Pinot Noir—and individual wineries in other parts of California, and in Oregon and New Zealand, are not far behind, rarely can anyone outside Burgundy manage to produce a deep-colored, full-bodied example of Pinot Noir and still retain its varietal purity, finesse, and elegance. Even in Burgundy it does not come easy and cannot be attempted on grapes coming from anywhere but the best *cru* vineyards. Yet, despite the inherent difficulty, it remains a relatively common occurrence in Burgundy. Just as common as poor-quality Burgundian Pinot, in fact!

Valley Shiraz turned out to be a fault, so has "*ça sent la merde.*" Hanson now admits: "I certainly oversimplified the case when I wrote in 1982 that great Burgundy smells of shit... if I perceive decaying vegetable and animal smells, I now mostly find them unacceptable".

Chardonnay is so ubiquitous it is probably cultivated in every wine-producing country in the world. Australian versions of this varietal are consistent and quaffable, even at the lowest level, but more expensive Chardonnays exist in Australia, just as they do in New Zealand, South Africa, Chile, California, Oregon, and lots of other places. This is why it is easy to forget just how different great white Burgundy is. When it is right, good white Burgundy is in a class of its own, and the incomparable richness, complexity, and longevity of the very greatest *grands crus* must be experienced to be believed.

# THE GENERIC APPELLATIONS OF
# BURGUNDY

## BOURGOGNE AOC

Many writers consider Bourgogne AOC to be too basic and boring to warrant serious attention, but for me it is the most instructive of all Burgundy's appellations. If a producer cares about the quality of the *Bourgogne*, how much more effort does that producer put into making higher-quality wines? I delight in finding a delicious, easy-to-drink *Bourgogne*, and I often get more of a kick discovering one that will improve for several years than I do from a superior appellation that should age well, considering its famous name and high price. Light-red/dark-rosé wines may be sold as Bourgogne Clairet AOC, but the style is outmoded and the appellation rarely seen.

**RED** Despite the grape varieties that may be used to make this wine, the only *Bourgogne* worth seeking out is that with the flavor and aroma of pure Pinot Noir. Many producers indicate the grape variety on the label.

🍇 Pinot Noir, Pinot Gris, Pinot Liébault plus, in the Yonne district, César, Tressot, and Gamay (if from one of the original nine *crus Beaujolais*—but not Régnié)

🍷 *2–5 years*

**WHITE** There are a lot of boring white wines made under this appellation, and unless you

have access to something more interesting like the wine from J.-F. Coche-Dury or another top grower, it is probably safer to buy an inexpensive Mâcon AOC. The once overperforming Bourgogne Blanc Clos du Château du Meursault, which was often better than Château du Meursault itself (which is Meursault AOC), is now one of Burgundy's underperformers (along with Château de Meursault!). These wines may be sold as *primeur* or *nouveau* as from the third Thursday of November following the harvest.

🍇 Chardonnay, Pinot Blanc

🍷 *1–4 years*

**ROSÉ** The wines produced under this appellation are acceptable, but they are never special—it is the least exciting category of *Bourgogne*.

🍇 Pinot Noir, Pinot Gris, Pinot Liébault, plus, in the Yonne district, César and Tressot

🍷 1–4 years

✓ **Bourgogne Rouge** Robert Arnoux • Ghislaine Barthod • Bertagna • Jean-Marc Boillot • Pascal Bouley • Carré-Courbin • Sylvain Cathiard • Château de Chamilly • Philippe Charlopin • Christian Clerget • J.-F. Coche-Dury • de la Combe • Joseph Drouhin • Alex Gambal • Anne Gros • Henri Jayer • Michel Juillot • Pierre Labet • Labouré-Roi • Michel Lafarge • Marie-Hélène Laugrotte • Dominique

Laurent • Olivier Leflaive • Lucien Lemoine • Leroy ❽ Hubert Lignier • Catherine et Claude Maréchal (Cathérine, Gravel) • Jean-Philippe Marchand • Mauperthuis (Grande Réserve) • Denis Mortet • Lucien Mouzard • de Perdrix • des Pitoux • de la Pousse d'Or • Daniel Rion & Fils • Michel & Patrice Rion • Nicolas Rossignol • Emmanuel Rouget • Tollot-Beaut • Vallet Frères • A. & P. de Villaine ❾• de la Vougeraie ❽ (Terres de Familles)
**Bourgogne Blanc** Jean-Baptiste Béjot • Simon Bize & Fils • Jean-Marc Boillot • Jean-Marc Brocard (Cuvée Jurassique) • J.-F. Coche-Dury • Coste-Caumartin • Alex Gambal • Patrick Javillier • François Jobard • Labouré-Roi • Michel Lafarge • Hubert Lamy • Leflaive ❽ • Olivier Leflaive • Lucien Lemoine • Lorenzon • Catherine et Claude Maréchal • Bátrice & Gilles Mathias • Pierre Morey ❽ • Antonin Rodet • Georges Roumier • Michel Rouyer (Domaine du Petit-Béru) • Tollot-Beaut • Henry de Vézelay • A. & P. de Villaine ❾
**Bourgogne Rosé** Abbaye du Petit Quincy • Philippe Defrance • Elise Villiers

Note: For other local generic wines *see*:
**Chablis** Bourgogne Chitry AOC, Bourgogne Coulanges-la-Vineuse AOC, Bourgogne Côtes d'Auxerre AOC, Bourgogne Côte Saint-Jacques AOC, Bourgogne Épineuil AOC, Bourgogne Vézelay AOC (p143)

• **Côte de Nuits** and **Hautes-Côtes de Nuits** Bourgogne Hautes-Côtes de Nuits AOC, Bourgogne Le Chapitre AOC, Bourgogne Montrecul AOC (p.140)

• **Côte de Beaune** and **Hautes-Côtes de Beaune** Bourgogne La Chapelle Notre-Dame AOC, Bourgogne Hautes-Côtes de Beaune AOC (p.140)

• **Côte Chalonnaise** Bourgogne Côte Chalonnaise AOC, Bourgogne Côtes du Couchois AOC (p.153)

## BOURGOGNE ALIGOTÉ AOC

The finest Bourgogne-Aligoté wines come from the village of Bouzeron in the Mercurey region, which has its own appellation (*see also* Bouzeron

AOC, p.160). With the exception of the wines below, the remaining Aligoté can be improved by adding *crème de cassis*, a local blackcurrant liqueur, to create an aperitif known as a "Kir."

**WHITE** Dry wines that are usually thin, acid, and not very pleasant: bad examples are even worse and are becoming widespread. When good, however, Aligoté can make a refreshing change from Burgundy's ubiquitous Chardonnay wines. However, even among the top producers, this grape seems to inflict its own inconsistency. Any one of the following recommended producers could make the greatest Aligoté of the vintage one year, then turn out something very ordinary the next year. Bourgogne Aligoté may be sold as *primeur* or *nouveau* from the third Thursday of November following the harvest.

🍇 Aligoté and a maximum of 15% Chardonnay

🍷 1–4 years

✓ *d'Auvenay* ❸ • *Bersan* • *Marc Brocard* • *Arnaud Ente* • *Naudin-Ferrand* • *de la Folie* • *Alex Gambal* • *Ghislaine et Jean-Hugues Goisot* • *François Jobard* • *Daniel Largeot* • *Catherine et Claude Maréchal* • *Edmond Monot* • *Alice et Olivier Moor* • *Jacky Renard* • *Thévenot-le-Brun & Fils* • *A. & P. de Villaine* ⓞ

## BOURGOGNE GRAND-ORDINAIRE AOC

In English-speaking markets the "*Grand*" sounds very grand indeed, and the fact that it qualifies "*Ordinaire*," not "*Bourgogne*," seems to get lost in the translation. Light-red/dark-rosé wines may be sold as Bourgogne Clairet Grand-Ordinaire AOC, but the style is outmoded and the appellation is rarely encountered.

**RED** These are mostly inferior wines made from the Gamay grape, but there are some interesting Pinot Noir-dominated versions.

🍇 Pinot Noir, Gamay, plus, in the Yonne district, César and Tressot

🍷 2–6 years

**WHITE** These dry wines are even more dismal than standard-issue *Bourgogne blanc*. Buy Mâcon blanc instead! These wines may be sold as *primeur* or *nouveau* as from the third Thursday of November following the harvest.

🍇 Chardonnay, Pinot Blanc, Aligoté, Melon de Bourgogne, plus, in the Yonne district, Sacy

🍷 1–4 years

**ROSÉ** The Hautes-Côtes *coopérative* produces a dry, light but elegant wine under this appellation, Rosé d'Orches.

🍇 Pinot Noir, Gamay, plus, in the Yonne district, César and Tressot

🍷 1–3 years

✓ *Jean-Paul Brun* (Terres Dorées) • *Edmond Cornu & Fils* • *Michel Lafarge* • *Emmanuel Rouget*

## BOURGOGNE MOUSSEUX AOC

Since December 1985 this appellation has been limited to, and remains the only outlet for, sparkling red Burgundy.

**SPARKLING RED** A favorite fizzy tipple in the pubs of prewar Britain. This wine's sweet flavor is very much out of step with today's sophisticated consumers.

🍇 Pinot Noir, Gamay, plus, in the Yonne district, César and Tressot

🍷 Upon purchase

## BOURGOGNE ORDINAIRE AOC

*See* Bourgogne Grand-Ordinaire AOC

## BOURGOGNE PASSE-TOUT-GRAINS AOC

Made from a *mélange* of Pinot Noir and Gamay grapes, *passe-tout-grains* is the descendant of an authentic peasant wine. A grower would fill his vat with anything growing in his vineyard and ferment it all together. Thus *passe-tout-grains* once contained numerous grape varieties. The Pinot Noir and Gamay varieties were, however, the most widely planted, and the wine naturally evolved as a two-grape product. Up until 1943 a minimum of one-fifth Pinot Noir was enforced by law; now the minimum is one-third.

**RED** Many *passe-tout-grains* used to be drunk too early, as the better-quality examples require a few years of bottle-aging to show the aristocratic influence of their Pinot Noir content. With an increase in Pinot Noir production and

more modern vinification techniques, more producers have begun making softer, less rustic *passe-tout-grains*, which are easier to drink when young. They remain relatively modest wines.

🍇 Pinot Noir plus a maximum of one-third Gamay and a combined maximum of 15% Chardonnay, Pinot Blanc, and Pinot Gris

🍷 2–6 years

**ROSÉ** This dry, pink version is worth trying.

🍇 A maximum of one-third Gamay plus Pinot Noir and Pinot Liébault

🍷 1–3 years

✓ *Robert Chevillon* • *Edmond Cornu & Fils* • *Michel Lafarge* • *Laurent Ponsot* (former Volpato old vines) • *Lejeune* • *Daniel Rion & Fils*

## CRÉMANT DE BOURGOGNE AOC

This appellation was created in 1975 to supersede the Bourgogne Mousseux AOC, which failed to inspire a quality image because the term "*mousseux*" also applied to cheap sparkling wines. Bourgogne Mousseux is now for red wines only. The major production centers for Crémant de Bourgogne are the Yonne, Region de Mercurey, and the Mâconnais. There are already many exciting wines, and the quality is certain to improve as more producers specialize in cultivating grapes specifically for sparkling wines, rather than relying on excess or inferior grapes, as was traditional in Burgundy.

**SPARKLING WHITE** Dry but round, the styles range from fresh and light to rich and toasty.

🍇 Pinot Noir, Pinot Gris, Pinot Blanc, Chardonnay, Sacy, Aligoté, Melon de Bourgogne, and a maximum of 20% Gamay

🍷 3–7 years

**SPARKLING ROSÉ** Until now the best pink Crémant produced outside of Champagne has come from Alsace. Good examples are made in Burgundy, but have not realized their potential.

🍇 Pinot Noir, Pinot Gris, Pinot Blanc, Chardonnay, Sacy, Aligoté, Melon de Bourgogne, and a maximum of 20% Gamay

🍷 2–5 years

✓ *Caves de Bailly* • *André Bonhomme* • *Paul Chollet* • *André Delorme* • *Roux Père* • *Caves de Viré*

# THE CHABLIS DISTRICT

*Chablis is one of Burgundy's two classic white-wine areas, yet this island of vines is closer to Champagne than to the rest of Burgundy, and its Chardonnay grape is grown on soils and under climatic conditions that are more* champenois *than* bourguignon.

LIKE CHAMPAGNE, CHABLIS owes much of its success to a cool and uncertain northern climate that puts viticulture on a knife-edge. This is a source of constant worry and not a little diabolical wine, but when everything comes together just right, Chablis can produce the most electrifying Chardonnay in the world.

Known as the "Golden Gate," this area has the advantage of being the inevitable first stop for anyone visiting the Burgundy region by car, whether directly from Paris or via Champagne. Situated in the Yonne *département*, much of which once formed part of the ancient province of Champagne, Chablis gives the distinct impression of an area cut off not simply from the rest of Burgundy but from the rest of France. Indeed, the great *négociants* of the Côte d'Or rarely visit Chablis and have never made any significant penetration into what appears to be a closed-shop trade.

THE TOWN OF CHABLIS
*Above the town of Chablis, the vines face southeast and southwest, clinging to hills along the banks of the Serein, a small tributary of the Yonne. These are the* grand cru *vineyards that make this district's finest wines.*

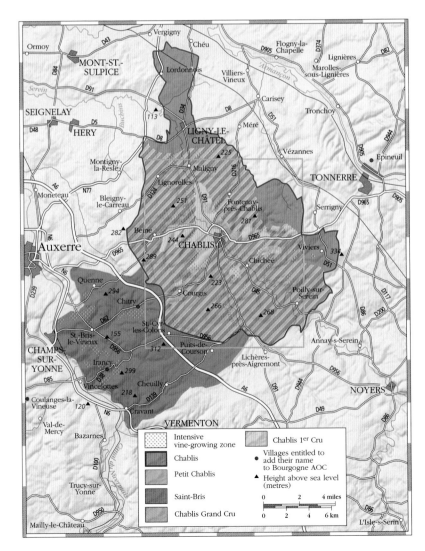

FOURCHAUME
*Just north of Chablis itself, Fourchaume is one of only two premier* cru *slopes that face southwest. The other is Montée de Tonnerre. It is probably no coincidence that, out of a total of 17 Chablis* premiers crus, *these vineyards are always among the top three.*

CHABLIS DISTRICT
*Overlooked by its grands crus and surrounded by* premiers crus, *Chablis (highlighted on the map) lies at the center of its eponymous wine-producing area, which is geographically and climatically closer to Champagne than to the rest of Burgundy.*

## FACTORS AFFECTING TASTE AND QUALITY

### ✦ LOCATION
Chablis is halfway between Beaune and Paris, 19 miles (30 kilometers) from the southernmost vineyards of Champagne, but 60 miles (100 kilometers) from the rest of Burgundy.

### ☁ CLIMATE
This area has a semicontinental climate with minimal Atlantic influence, which results in a long, cold winter, a humid spring, and a fairly hot, very sunny summer. Hail storms and spring frosts are the greatest hazards.

### ⬒ ASPECT
All the *grands crus* are located on one stretch of southwest-facing slopes just north of Chablis itself, where the vineyards are at a height of between 490 to 660 feet (150 and 200 meters). Apart from the southwest-facing slopes of Fourchaume and Montée de Tonnerre, the *premier cru* slopes face southeast.

### ▦ SOIL
This area is predominantly covered with calcareous clay, and the traditional view is that of the two major types, Kimmeridgian and Portlandian, only the former is suitable for classic Chablis; but this

is neither proven nor likely. Geologically they have the same Upper Jurassic origin. Any intrinsic geographical differences should be put down to aspect, microclimate, and the varied nature of the sedimentary beds that underlie and interbed with the Kimmeridgian and Portlandian soils.

### ⬚ VITICULTURE AND VINIFICATION
The vineyards in Chablis have undergone rapid expansion, most particularly in the generic appellation and the *premiers crus*, both of which have doubled in size since the early 1970s. Mechanical harvesting has now found its way to the *grands crus* slopes of Chablis, but smaller producers still pick by hand. Most Chablis is fermented in stainless steel, but oak barrels are making a comeback, although too much new oak fights against the lean, austere intensity of the Chardonnay grown in this district.

### 🍇 GRAPE VARIETIES
**Primary varieties:** Chardonnay
**Secondary varieties:** Pinot Noir, Pinot Blanc, Pinot Gris (*syn.* Pinot Beurot), Pinot Liébault, Sauvignon Blanc, Gamay, César, Tressot, Sacy, Aligoté, Melon de Bourgogne

## THE VARYING STYLES OF CHABLIS

The traditional description of Chablis is of a wine of clear, pale color with a green hue around the rim. It is very straight and positive, with an aggressive, steely character, very direct attack, and a high level of acidity that needs a few years to round out. This description, however, rarely applies, as much has changed in the way these wines are made at both ends of the quality spectrum.

Thirty years ago most Chablis did not undergo malolactic fermentation. The wines that resulted had a naturally high acidity, and were hard, green, and ungenerous in their youth, although they often matured into wines of incomparable finesse. Now, most Chablis wines undergo malolactic fermentation and cold stabilization, which is used to precipitate tartrates (although some wines fermented or matured in small oak casks do not), making the wine fuller, softer, and rounder.

At the top end of the market, there are two distinctly different schools. Some wines are fermented in stainless steel and bottled early to produce the most direct and attacking style, while others are fermented in wood and matured in casks with an increasing amount of new oak. Writers often describe the unoaked, stainless-steel-fermented Chablis as traditional, but these vats were introduced in the 1960s, so it cannot be a well-established tradition. The oak barrel is much older, of course, and thus far more traditional, but what the critics really mean is that new oak has never been a feature of Chablis winemaking, therefore the crisp, clean style of Chablis fermented in stainless steel is closer to the original style: traditional by default. Obviously, the most authentic style of Chablis is the wine that is made in old or, more accurately, well-used casks. The traditional Chablisienne cask, known as a *feuillette*, is only half the size of a normal Burgundian barrel, thus has twice the effect, but not being new oak, this would be an oxidative effect, not creamy-vanilla or other aromatics. However, the more rapid oxidative effect of the *feuillette* does explain why the wines were traditionally bottled

early, retaining the minerality of the fruit, and invariably imparting a slight spritz, further separating the style of these wines from Chardonnay produced in the Côte d'Or.

What makes the divide between oaked and unoaked Chablis even wider is the fact that the leaner, more mineral style of wine produced in this district can fight against the effects of new oak, whereas the fatter, softer, more seductive wines of the Côte d'Or embrace it with open arms. Recognizing that some people enjoy new oak characteristics, the recommendations in this book include producers of the best oaky Chablis. However, the trend for new oak peaked sometime in the late 1990s. Today, even producers known for the oakiest Chablis have been holding back, to promote the minerality meant to be expressive of the *terroir*.

There has always been a certain inconsistency about Chablis, which is only to be expected given its uncertain climate, and this has never deterred its devotees. However, things have gone from bad to worse over the past 15 years, and it is not the weather that has always been to blame—it is the increasing yields by greedy producers and sloppy winemaking. There are still great joys to be had with the best and most passionately produced of Chablis, from the lowliest appellation to the greatest *grands crus*, but wine buyers must be increasingly vigilant.

## OTHER WINES OF YONNE

Other than Chablis, the two best-known wines of the Yonne are the red wines of Bourgogne Irancy AOC and the white Saint-Bris AOC, made from the Sauvignon Blanc grape—a trespasser from the Loire. Other grapes peculiar to the Yonne are the César and Tressot, which are black, and the Sacy, which is white. None is permitted in any Burgundian appellation other than AOC Bourgogne from Yonne, and they are not even widely cultivated here. César is the most interesting of these varieties, albeit rather rustic. It is a low-yielding vine that produces a thick, dark, tannic

MACHINE-HARVESTING AT DOMAINE STE.-CLAIRE IN PRÉHY
*Machine-harvesting, which can lower the quality of white wines in particular, is widespread in Chablis, even on the* grands crus. *The technique is most appropriate at Préhy, where the vineyards are of lesser quality.*

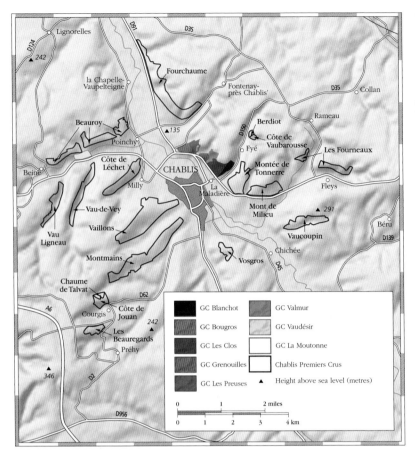

**THE GRANDS CRUS OF CHABLIS**
*The slopes of the district's greatest vineyards rise quietly and majestically on the other side of the Serein River beyond the northern outskirts of Chablis itself.*

**CHABLIS PREMIERS AND GRANDS CRUS**
*This map clearly illustrates that all seven grands crus are huddled together on one contiguous southwest-facing slope of exceptional situation and aspect, whereas the 17 premiers crus are scattered across the surrounding area on isolated slopes of excellent, but secondary, exposure.*

wine, although Simonnet-Febvre makes one of the better examples. César grows best at Irancy and can make a positive contribution when it is carefully blended with Pinot Noir. Just 5 or 10 percent of César is required, but a few growers use as much as 20 percent and this tends to knock all the elegance out of the light-bodied local Pinot Noir. The Tressot is thin, weak, and without any merit, but this blank canvas together with the advantage of its typically high yield made it the obvious partner to the César in bygone times. Occasionally encountered, it usually tastes like a thin, coarse Beaujolais. This district's other viticultural oddity is the steadily declining Sacy, a high-yielding white grape that produces acidic, neutrally flavored wines best used in Crémant de Bourgogne, although most of it has traditionally been sold to Germany for making *Sekt*.

## THE APPELLATIONS OF
# THE CHABLIS DISTRICT

### BOURGOGNE CHITRY AOC

A true single-village appellation, in that only vines in Chitry qualify. This village neighbors St.-Bris-le-Vineux to the northeast, and its vineyards are comprised of 67 acres (27 hectares) of black grapes, and 67 acres (27 hectares) of white grapes. Generally, the reds are least interesting, whereas the whites can be modestly successful, with their attractive, fresh-lemony fruit and an occasional aromatic hint on the nose and finish. Chalmeau and Thibaut are the best performers here.

🍇 Pinot Noir, Pinot Liébault, Pinot Gris, César, Tressot, Chardonnay, Pinot Blanc

🍶 Upon purchase

✓ *Patrick & Christine Chalmeau* (blanc only) • *Griffe* (blanc only) • *Jean-Baptiste Thibaut* (rouge only) • *Marcel Giraudon* (rouge only)

### BOURGOGNE CÔTE SAINT-JACQUES AOC

One of four Bourgogne *lieux-dits* created in the 1990s (*see also* Bourgogne La Chapelle Notre Dame, p.154, Bourgogne Le Chapitre, p.146, and Bourgogne Montrecul, p.146). Côte Saint-

Jacques overlooks Joigny, which has the most northerly vineyards in Burgundy. Vines were first permitted to grow here for basic Bourgogne AOC in 1975, but just a few hectares were planted. Currently the largest vineyard owner is Alain Vignot, whose father pioneered winemaking in the area, but the local *coopérative*, which also has vineyards here, is planting a large proportion of the 220 acres (90 hectares) that were officially classified as Côte Saint-Jacques. At the present time, the area barely manages to produce a light-bodied white wine, although Vignot makes a *vin gris* from Pinot Noir and Pinot Gris, which Joigny was famous for in pre-phylloxera times. What they need here is the true Auxerrois of Alsace (which has no connection with nearby Auxerre). The reasoning would be exactly the same as for Alsace, where more Auxerrois is used to make so-called Pinot Blanc wine the farther north the vineyards are situated. In the Côte de Nuits it would be too fat and spicy, but in Joigny it would simply bring some generosity to the wines.

**RED** Michel Lorain's Clos des Capucins outclasses the rest of this appellation with its good color and truly expressive fruit.

🍇 Pinot Noir, Pinot Liébault, Pinot Gris, César, Tressot

🍶 1–3 years

**WHITE** Not worth buying.

🍇 Chardonnay, Pinot Blanc

🍶 Upon purchase

**ROSÉ** There are a handful of pure Pinot Gris wines made elsewhere in Burgundy, but they are usually white wines, whereas the tradition here is to make a rosé or *vin gris* from this variety, either pure (Alain Vignot) or blended.

🍇 Pinot Noir, Pinot Liébault, Pinot Gris, César, Tressot

🍶 Upon purchase

✓ *Michel Lorain* (rouge only) • *Alain Vignot* (rouge and rosé only)

### BOURGOGNE CÔTES D'AUXERRE AOC

Overlapping the Saint-Bris appellation, Côte d'Auxerre covers various parcels of vines scattered throughout the hillsides overlooking Augy, Auxerre-Vaux, Quenne, St.-Bris-le-Vineux, and in part of Vincelottes that does not qualify for Irancy.

**RED** With the exception of Bersan or Ghislaine & Jean-Hugues Goisot in a good vintage, these wines are invariably disappointingly light and dilute.

🍇 Pinot Noir, Pinot Liébault, Pinot Gris, César, Tressot

🍷 Upon purchase

**WHITE** Ghislaine & Jean-Hugues Goisot make a range of different Côtes d'Auxerre, and their Corps de Garde and Gondonne *cuvées* usually outclass the rest of the competition, although Bailly-Lapierre gives Goisot a good run for its money in some years (such as 2002).

🍇 Chardonnay, Pinot Blanc

🍷 Upon purchase

**ROSÉ** Light, fresh, easy-drinking rosé that is better than a lot of supposedly finer AOCs.

🍇 Pinot Noir, Pinot Liébault, Pinot Gris, César, Tressot

🍷 Upon purchase

✓ *Bailly-Lapierre • Bersan • Patrice Fort • Ghislaine & Jean-Hugues Goisot • Tabit & Fils*

## BOURGOGNE COULANGES-LA-VINEUSE AOC

The far-flung borders of Coulanges-la-Vineuse encompass no fewer than six communes in addition to its own: Charentenay, Escolives-Sainte-Camille, Migé, Mouffy, Jussy, and Val-de-Mercy. Vines cover almost 148 acres (60 hectares), of which only 10 acres (4 hectares) are planted with white varieties.

**RED** Most of these wines are primarily Pinot Noir with a small dash of César. Most are simply frank and fruity, although the best can be quite rich, with truly expressive fruit.

🍇 Pinot Noir, Pinot Liébault, Pinot Gris, César, Tressot

🍷 1–3 years

**WHITE** Not worth buying.

🍇 Chardonnay, Pinot Blanc

🍷 Upon purchase

**ROSÉ** Not tasted.

🍇 Pinot Noir, Pinot Liébault, Pinot Gris, César, Tressot

🍷 Upon purchase

✓ *Le Clos du Roi (rouge only) • Jean-Luc Houblin (rouge only) • Jean-Pierre Maltoff (rouge only) • Alain Rigoutat (rouge only)*

## BOURGOGNE ÉPINEUIL AOC

A true single-village appellation, Épineuil consists of 210 acres (85 hectares) of hillside vineyards on the banks of the Amançon River, overlooking Tonnerre, northeast of Chablis. Planted mostly with Pinot Noir, there are just 15 acres (6 hectares) of white grapes, with La Chablisienne the most important producer.

**RED** Most are light and undistinguished, but the Domaine de l'Abbaye du Petit Quincy makes a much darker version, especially its Côte de Grisey and Côte de Grisey Cuvée Juliette, which many consider to be the finest wines of Épineuil. Neither light nor dark, the ruby-colored wine produced by the local *coopérative*, La Chablisienne, is probably the most consistent wine in the appellation.

🍇 Pinot Noir, Pinot Liébault, Pinot Gris, César, Tressot

🍷 1–5 years

**WHITE** Few wines deliver more than a straightforward fresh, crisp, dry white of fairly neutral character.

🍇 Chardonnay, Pinot Blanc

🍷 Upon purchase

**ROSÉ** At its best, this can be a deliciously fresh, easy-drinking rosé.

🍇 Pinot Noir, Pinot Liébault, Pinot Gris, César, Tressot

🍷 Upon purchase

✓ *Abbaye du Petit Quincy • La Chablisienne • Eric Dampt (white only) • Dominique Grubier • Alain Mathias*

## BOURGOGNE VÉZELAY AOC

This appellation southeast of the main Chablis district covers some 158 acres (64 hectares) of vines on the steep upper slopes (above the frost-line) overlooking the village of Vézelay itself.

**WHITE** At its most basic level, not worth buying, but top-performing white wines from these appellations are superior to the lower end of Chablis, which is relatively much more expensive. They are invariably pure Chardonnay, yet rarely taste like Chablis, being softer and smoother. Marc Meneau is the top producer here.

🍇 Chardonnay, Pinot Blanc

🍷 1–3 years

✓ *Marc Meneau • Elise Villiers*

## CHABLIS AOC

With careful selection, basic Chablis can be a source of tremendous-value, classic 100 percent Chardonnay wine, particularly in the best vintages. However, the appellation covers a relatively large area with many vineyards that do not perform well, and there are far too many mediocre winemakers. Basic Chablis needs to come from the most favorable locations, where the grower restricts the yield and the winemaker selects only the best wines; it is not an appellation in which short cuts can be taken. Cheap Chablis can be dire, even in superior appellations; better, therefore, to pay for a top *cuvée* of basic Chablis than to be seduced by a cut-price *premier cru*. However, La Chablisienne's Vieilles Vignes is not the consistent superstar it used to be. (*See also* Chablis *premier cru* AOC and Petit Chablis AOC.)

**WHITE** When successful, these wines have the quintessential character of true Chablis—dry, clean, green, and expressive, with just enough fruit to balance the "steel."

🍇 Chardonnay

🍷 2–6 years

✓ *Christian Adine • Baillard • Billaud-Simon • Jean-Marc Brocard • La Chablisienne*

• *de Chantemerle • Jean Collet • de la Concierge • Jean Defaix • René & Vincent Dauvissat • Jean-Paul Droin (especially Vieilles Vignes) • Gérard Duplessis • William Fèvre de la Maladière • des Malandes (especially Tour de Roi) • Jean-Pierre Grossot • Michel Laroche • Olivier Leflaive • Louis & Anne Moreau (especially Domaines de Biéville and Cèdre Doré) • Sylvain Mosnier (Vieilles Vignes) • Gilbert Picq (Vieilles Vignes) • François Raveneau*

## CHABLIS GRAND CRU AOC

The seven *grands crus* of Chablis are all located on one hill that overlooks the town of Chablis itself. They are Blanchot, Bougros, Les Clos, Grenouilles, Les Preuses, Valmur, and Vaudésir. One vineyard called La Moutonne is not classified in the appellation as a *grand cru*, but the authorities permit the use of the coveted status on the label because it is physically part of other *grands crus*. In the 18th century La Moutonne was in fact a 2½-acre (1-hectare) *climat* of Vaudésir, but under the ownership of Louis Long-Depaquit its wines were blended with those of three other *grands crus* (namely, Les Preuses, Les Clos, and Valmur). This practice came to a halt in 1950 when, in a bid to get La Moutonne classified as a separate *grand cru*, Long-Depaquit agreed to limit its production to its current location, which cuts across parts of Vaudésir and Les Preuses. Its classification never actually took place, but the two *grands crus* that it overlaps are probably the finest of all.

**WHITE** Always totally dry, the *grands crus* are the biggest, richest, most complex of all Chablis and should always boast great minerality. However, many are overwhelmed by new oak. Their individual styles depend very much on how the winemaker vinifies and matures the wine, but when well made they are essentially as follows: **Blanchot** has a floral aroma and is the most delicate of the *grands crus* (Michel Laroche's Réserve de l'Obédiance is the greatest Chablis *grand cru* I have tasted, taking richness to the very limit, while not losing sight of true Chablis structure, crispness, minerality, and finesse); **Bougros** has the least frills of all the *grands crus*, but is vibrant with a penetrating flavor; **Les Clos** is rich, luscious, and complex with great mineral finesse and beautiful balance; **Grenouilles** should be long and satisfying, yet elegant, racy, and aromatic; **Les Preuses** gets the most sun and is vivid, sometimes exotic, quite fat for Chablis, yet still expressive and definitely complex, with great finesse; **Valmur** has a fine bouquet, rich flavor, and smooth texture; **Vaudésir** has complex, intense flavors that display great finesse and spicy complexity; and **La Moutonne** is fine, long-flavored, and wonderfully expressive.

🍇 Chardonnay

8— 6–20 years

✓ **Blanchot** *Billaud-Simon* (Vieilles Vignes)
• *Michel Laroche* • *Raveneau* • *Domaine
Vocoret* **Bougros** *William Fèvre* • *Joseph
Drouhin* • *de la Maladière* • *Michel Laroche*
**Les Clos** *Billaud-Simon* • *La Chablisienne*
• *René & Vincent Dauvissat* • *Jean-Paul
Droin* • *Joseph Drouhin* • *Caves Duplessis* •
*William Fèvre* • *Michel Laroche* • *de la
Maladière* • *Domaines des Malandes* •
*Louis Michel* • *J. Moreau* (lieu-dit Clos des
Hospices) • *Pinson* • *Raveneau* • *Servin*
**Grenouilles** *La Chablisienne* (Château
Grenouilles) • *Louis Michel* **La Moutonne**
*Long-Depaquit* **Les Preuses** *Billaud-Simon*
• *Joseph Drouhin, René & Vincent Dauvissat*
• *William Fèvre* **Valmur** *Jean Collet* • *Jean-
Paul Droin* • *William Fèvre* • *Olivier
Leflaive* • *Raveneau* **Vaudésir** *Billaud-
Simon* • *La Chablisienne* • *Jean-Paul Droin*
• *Joseph Drouhin* • *William Fèvre* • *Michel
Laroche* • *des Malandes* • *Louis Michel*

## CHABLIS PREMIER CRU

*Premiers crus*: Les Beauregards, Beauroy,
Berdiot, Chaume de Talvat, Côte de Jouan,
Côte de Léchet, Côte de Vaubarousse,
Fourchaume, Les Fourneaux, Montée de
Tonnerre, Montmains, Mont de Milieu, Vaillons,
Vaucoupin, Vau-de-Vey (or Vaudevey), Vau
Ligneau, and Vosgros. Unlike the *grands crus*,
the 17 *premiers crus* of Chablis are scattered
among the vineyards of 15 surrounding
communes, and the quality and style is patchy.
Montée de Tonnerre is the best *premier cru*
throughout the different producers and across
the many vintages. One of its *lieux-dits*,
Chapelot, is considered by many to be the
equivalent of a *grand cru*. After Montée de
Tonnerre, Côte de Léchet, Les Forêts (which is
a *climat* within Montmains), Fourchaume, Mont
de Milieu, and Vaillons vie for second place.

**WHITE** Dry wines that can vary from light- to
fairly full-bodied, but should always be finer
and longer-lasting than wines of the basic Chablis
appellation, although without the concentration
of flavor expected from a *grand cru*.

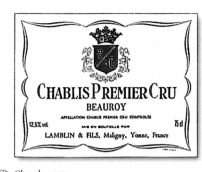

🍇 Chardonnay

8— 4–15 years

✓ **Les Beauregards** *Jean-Marc Brocard*
**Beauroy** *Sylvain Mosnier* **Berdiot** *None*
**Chaume de Talvat** *None* **Côte de Jouan**
*Michel Cobois* **Côte de Léchet** *Jean-Paul
Droin* • *Jean Defaix* • *Sylvain Mosnier* **Côte
de Vaubarousse** *None* **Fourchaume**
*Billaud-Simon* • *La Chablisienne* • *de
Chantemerle* • *Jean-Paul Droin* • *Gérard
Duplessis* • *Jean Durup* • *William Fèvre*
(Côte de Vaulorent) • *Lamblin & Fils*
• *Michel Laroche* (Vieilles Vignes) • *des
Malandes* • *Louis Michel* • *Francine &
Olivier Savary* • *Verget* **Les Fourneaux**
*Jean-Pierre Grossot* • *Louis & Anne Moreau*
**Montée de Tonnerre** *Billaud-Simon* •
*Jean-Paul Droin* (Vieilles Vignes) • *Caves
Duplessis, William Fèvre* • *Louis Michel* •
*Raveneau* (including Chapelot and Pied
d'Aloue *lieux-dits*) • *Guy Robin* **Montmains**
*La Chablisienne* • *René & Vincent Dauvissat*
(La Forest [sic] *lieu-dit*) • *Jean-Paul Droin,
Caves Duplessis* • *des Malandes* • *des
Marronniers* • *Louis Michel* • *Georges Pico,
Pinson* • *Raveneau* (Butteaux *lieu-dit*) •
*Guy Robin* (Butteaux *lieu-dit*) • *Robert
Vocoret* (La Fôret *lieu-dit*) **Mont de Milieu**
*Barat* • *Billaud-Simon* (especially Vieilles
Vignes) • *La Chablisienne* • *Jean Collet* •
*Jean-Pierre Grossot* • *de Meulière* • *Pinson*
**Vaillons** *Barat* • *Billaud-Simon* • *R & V
Dauvissat* (Séchet *lieu-dit*) • *Jean Defaix* •
*Jean-Paul Droin* • *Gérard Duplessis* •
*Michel Laroche* (Vieilles Vignes) • *François
Raveneau* • *Verget* **Vaucoupin** *Jean-Pierre
Grossot* **Vau-de-Vey** *Jean Durup* • *Michel
Laroche* **Vau Ligneau** *Thierry Hamelin* •
*Louis & Anne Moreau* **Vosgros** *Jean-Paul
Droin* • *Gilbert Picq*

## IRANCY AOC

Irancy was promoted from Bourgogne Irancy to
full village AOC status in its own right in 1999.
This red-wine-only appellation encompasses 395
acres (160 hectares) in Irancy and neighboring
villages of Cravant and Vincelottes.

**RED** Irancy is supposed to be the "famous" red
wine of Chablis, but it is not really that well
known and is not even the best local red wine.
Michel Lorain's Côte Saint-Jacques Clos des
Capucins, and Domaine de l'Abbaye du Petit
Quincy's Côte de Grisey Cuvée Juliette are both
consistently superior to the best Irancy, though
the latter do possess a certain richness of fruit
that most examples of this modest appellation
lack. Original Irancy was a pure César wine:
Anita and Jean-Pierre Colinot make the most
interesting example (Les Mazelots César).

🍇 Pinot Noir, Pinot Gris, César

8— 1–3 years

✓ *Léon Bienvenu* • *Benoît Cantin* (Cuvée
Emiline) • *Roger Delaloge* • *Anita & Jean-*

*Pierre Colinot* (Palotte, Les Mazelots, Les
Mazelots César, Les Bessys, Côte-de-Moutier)
• *Roger Delalogue* • *Christophe Ferrari*
(*rouge* only) • *Félix* • *Saint-Germain*
(La Bergère)

## PETIT CHABLIS AOC

A depreciatory appellation that covers inferior
soils and expositions within the same area as
generic Chablis, with the exception of Ligny-le-
Châtel, Viviers, and Collan. Although I have
found four more reliable producers than last
time, this appellation should be downgraded
to VDQS or uprooted. The rumor is that it
will be phased out, but do not misunderstand:
this does not mean that they will uproot the
vines, simply that this inferior land will instead
produce Chablis, albeit of a *petit vin* quality.

**WHITE** Aside from the occasional pleasant
surprise, most are mean and meager dry wines
of light to medium body. The producers below
provide most of the pleasant surprises.

🍇 Chardonnay

8— 2–3 years

✓ *Jean-Marc Brocard* • *Jean Durup* • *Vincent
Gallois* • *Thierry Hamelin* • *Francine &
Olivier Savary*

## SAINT-BRIS AOC

This wine is as good as most Sauvignon Blanc
AOCs, and considerably better than many other
white AOCs made from lesser grape varieties.
Twenty years ago I did not believe it possible
that Sauvignon de St.-Bris would ever overcome
Burgundy's Chardonnay-chauvinism to rise
to the ranks of Appellation Contrôlée, but
in 2003, Sauvignon de St-Bris VDQS was
promoted to Saint-Bris AOC (retrospectively
applied to the 2001 vintage).

**WHITE** Fine wet-grass or herbaceous aromas,
full smoky-Sauvignon flavors, and a correct,
crisp, dry finish. Made from the rare Sauvignon
Gris, Ghislaine & Jean-Hugues Goisot's Cuvée
du Corps de Garde Gourmand Fié Gris is the
best, most consistent, and most unusual wine
in this appellation, while the same producer's
"straight" Sauvignon is easily the top
thoroughbred Sauvignon Blanc.

🍇 Sauvignon Blanc, Sauvignon Gris

8— 2–5 years

✓ *Jean-Marc Brocard* • *Robert Defrance*
• *Félix* • *Ghislaine & Jean-Hugues Goisot*
• *Erick Lavallée* • *Jacky Renard*

# CÔTE DE NUITS AND HAUTES-CÔTES DE NUITS

*The Côte de Nuits is essentially a red-wine area (with one or two extraordinary whites), and with 22 of Burgundy's 23 red* grands crus, *it is the place par excellence for Pinot Noir.*

THE CÔTE D'OR, or "golden slope," is the departmental name for both the Côte de Nuits and the Côte de Beaune. Firmness and weight are the key words to describe the wines produced here, and these characteristics intensify as the vineyards progress north. A string of villages with some of the richest names in Burgundy— Gevrey-Chambertin, Chambolle-Musigny, Vosne-Romanée, and Nuits-St.-Georges—these slopes ring up dollar signs in the minds of merchants throughout the world. Ironically, the most famous appellations also produce some of Burgundy's worst wines.

CLOS ARLOT OF DOMAINE DE L'ARLOT
*Purchased in 1987 by the dynamic AXA group, Domaine de l'Arlot is one of the most consistent, high-quality producers in Nuits-St.-Georges, making textbook Pinot Noir and, from its monopole Clos Arlot, minuscule amounts of sublime white wine.*

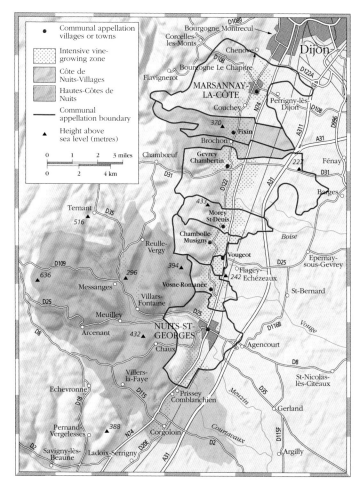

CÔTE DE NUITS AND HAUTES-CÔTES DE NUITS, *see also p137*
*The best vineyards of the Côte de Nuits form a tighter, more compact strip than those of the Côte de Beaune, (see also p151), and the wines produced are, coincidentally, tighter, with more compact fruit.*

## FACTORS AFFECTING TASTE AND QUALITY

### LOCATION
The Côte de Nuits is a narrow, continuous strip of vines stretching from Dijon to just north of Beaune, with the Hautes-Côtes de Nuits in the southwestern hinterland.

### CLIMATE
Semicontinental climate with minimal Atlantic influence, which results in a long, cold winter, a humid spring, and a fairly hot, very sunny summer. Hail is its greatest natural hazard and heavy rain is often responsible for diluting the wines and causing rampant rot.

### ASPECT
A series of east-facing slopes that curve in and out to give some vineyards northeastern, some southeastern aspects. The vines grow at an altitude of between 740 and 1,150 feet (225 to 350 meters) and, asode from Gevrey-Chambertin and Prémeaux-Prissey, those vineyards that have the right to the village and higher appellations rarely extend eastward beyond the RN 74 road.

### SOIL
A subsoil of sandy-limestone, which is exposed in places but usually covered by a chalky scree mixed with marl and clay particles on higher slopes and richer alluvial deposits on lower slopes. Higher slopes sometimes have red clay.

### VITICULTURE AND VINIFICATION
The vines are trained low to benefit from heat reflected from the soil at night. For red wines, the grapes are almost always destemmed and the juice is kept in contact with the skins for between eight and 10 days. Less than three percent of the wine produced is white, but this is mostly high quality and traditionally cask fermented. The best wines are matured in oak.

### GRAPE VARIETIES
**Primary varieties:** Pinot Noir, Chardonnay
**Secondary varieties:** Pinot Gris (known locally as Pinot Beurot), Pinot Liébault, Pinot Blanc, Aligoté, Melon de Bourgogne, Gamay

## CONFRÉRIE DES CHEVALIERS DU TASTEVIN

After the three terrible vintages of 1930, 1931, and 1932, and four years of world slump following the Wall Street Crash of 1929, Camille Rodier and Georges Faiveley formed the Confrérie des Chevaliers du Tastevin to revive Burgundy's fortunes. They named the brotherhood after the traditional Burgundian *tastevin*, a shallow, dimpled, silver tasting-cup with a fluted edge.

The first investitures took place on November 16, 1934, in a cellar in Nuits-St.-Georges; the Confrérie now boasts thousands of members in numerous foreign chapters and averages 20 banquets a year at Château du Clos de Vougeot. Until the late 1980s, wines bearing the distinctive Tastevinage label used to be a useful means of quickly identifying wines within basic appellations that have risen above their modest status, but the selection gradually became less rigorous, with some decidedly underperforming wines slipping through. In recent years, however, there appears to be more consistency, once again making the Tastevinage label worth watching out for.

On average only one-third of the wines submitted for the Tastevinage receive the coveted label. No charge is made for entering. The minimum quantity for commercial availability is just 900 bottles, and there is no maximum. The wines are tasted blind, and most importantly, the tasters include hoteliers, restaurateurs, sommeliers, wine merchants, and wine press, as well as producers. A wine can also be rejected on the basis of laboratory analysis alone (if, for example, it has elevated levels of volatile acidity). Another plus point is the random checks that are carried out at the point of sale on all markets.

# CÔTE DE NUITS AND HAUTES-CÔTES DE NUITS

**Note** Each *grand cru* of Côte de Nuits has its own appellation and is listed individually below. However, the *premiers crus* do not, and are therefore listed under the appellation of the village in which the vineyards are situated. *Premiers crus* that are virtually contiguous with *grand cru* vineyards are in *italics*; they are possibly superior to those that do not share a boundary with one or more *grand crus*, and generally superior to those that share boundaries with village AOC vineyards.

## BONNES MARES AOC
### Grand Cru

Bonnes Mares is the largest of the two *grands crus* of Chambolle-Musigny. It covers 34 acres (13.5 hectares) in the north of the village, on the opposite side to Musigny, the village's other *grand cru*, and extends a further 3.5 acres (1.5 hectares) into Morey-St.-Denis.

**RED** A fabulous femininity of style with sheer depth of flavor gives something rich and luscious, yet complex and complete.

🍇 Pinot Noir, Pinot Gris, Pinot Liébault

🍷— 12–25 years

✓ *d'Auvenay* ❷ • *Bouchard Père & Fils* • *Dujac* • *R Groffier* • *Dominique Laurent* • *J F Mugnier* • *Christophe Roumier* • *Georges Roumier* • *Nicolas Potel* • *Comte Georges de Vogüé*

## BOURGOGNE LA CHAPITRE AOC

One of the Côte de Nuits' two Bourgogne *lieux-dits* created in 1993, La Chapitre is located at Chenove, between Marsannay and Dijon. According to Anthony Hanson (in his book *Burgundy*), the wines of Chenove once fetched higher prices than those of Gevrey (Chenove's most famous vineyard is Clos du Roi, of which Labouré-Roi took management in 1994), but the only example I have tasted (Domaine Bouvier) was not special.

## BOURGOGNE HAUTES-CÔTES DE NUITS AOC

A source of good-value wines, these vineyards have expanded since the 1970s, and the quality is improving noticeably. Half-red/half-rosé wines may be sold as Bourgogne Clairet Hautes-Côtes de Nuits AOC, but the style is outmoded and the appellation rarely encountered.

**RED** Medium-bodied and medium- to full-bodied wines with good fruit and some true Côte de Nuits character. The wines from some growers have fine oak nuances.

🍇 Pinot Noir, Pinot Liébault, Pinot Gris

🍷— 4–10 years

**WHITE** Just 5 percent of the production is dry white. Most have a good weight of fruit, but little finesse.

🍇 Chardonnay, Pinot Blanc

🍷— 1–4 years

**ROSÉ** Little-seen, but those that have cropped up have been dry, fruity, and delicious wines of some richness.

🍇 Pinot Noir, Pinot Liébault, Pinot Gris

🍷— 1–3 years

✓ *Bertagna* • *J.-C. Boisset* • *Yves Chaley* • *Guy*

*Dufouleur* • *Michel Gros* • *Robert Jayer-Gilles* • *de Montmain* • *Naudin-Ferrand* • *Thévenot-le-Brun & Fils* • *Alain Verdet* ❷ • *Thierry Vigot-Battault*

## BOURGOGNE MONTRECUL OR MONTRE-CUL OR EN MONTRE-CUL AOC

The other Bourgogne *lieu-dit* in this district is actually located on the outskirts of Dijon. Some might think this is a wine to moon over, but the only wine I have tasted (again Domaine Bouvier) was again not special. If no one is going to produce something exciting under these Bourgogne *lieux-dits*, why bother with them in the first place?

## CHAMBERTIN AOC
### Grand Cru

This is one of the nine *grands crus* of Gevrey-Chambertin. All of them (quite legally) add the name Gevrey-Chambertin to their own and one, Clos de Bèze, actually has the right to sell its wines as Chambertin.

**RED** Always full in body and rich in extract, Chambertin is not, however, powerful like Corton, but graceful and feminine with a vivid color, stunning flavor, impeccable balance, and lush, velvety texture.

🍇 Pinot Noir, Pinot Gris, Pinot Liébault

🍷— 12–30 years

✓ *Bouchard Père & Fils* • *Vincent Girardin* • *Leroy* ❷ • *Denis Mortet* • *Henri Rebourseau* • *Armand Rousseau* • *Jean Trapet Père & Fils*

## CHAMBERTIN-CLOS DE BÈZE AOC
### Grand Cru

Another Gevrey-Chambertin *grand cru*. The wine may be sold simply as Chambertin, the name of a neighboring *grand cru*, but Chambertin may not call itself Clos de Bèze.

**RED** This wine is reputed to have a greater finesse than Chambertin but slightly less body. It is just as sublime.

🍇 Pinot Noir, Pinot Gris, Pinot Liébault

🍷— 12–30 years

✓ *Bouchard Père & Fils* • *Bruno Clair* • *Faiveley* • *R. Groffier* • *Louis Jadot* • *Dominique Laurent* • *Lucien Lemoine* • *Armand Rousseau*

## CHAMBOLLE-MUSIGNY AOC

This village is very favorably positioned, with a solid block of vines nestled in the shelter of a geological fold.

**RED** Many of these medium- to fairly full-bodied wines have surprising finesse and fragrance for mere village wines.

🍇 Pinot Noir, Pinot Gris, Pinot Liébault

🍷— 8–15 years

✓ *Ghislaine Barthod* • *Sylvain Cathiard* (Les Clos de L'Orme) • *Dujac Père* • *J. F. Mugnier* • *Géantet Pansiot* • *Perrot-Minot* • *Daniel Rion & Fils* • *Georges Roumier* • *Comte Georges de Vogüé*

## CHAMBOLLE-MUSIGNY PREMIER CRU AOC

*Premiers crus:* Les Amoureuses, Les Baudes, Aux Beaux Bruns, *Les Borniques*, Les Carrières, Les Chabiots, Les Charmes, *Les Châtelots*, *La Combe d'Orveau*, Aux Combottes, Les Combottes, Les Cras, Derrière la Grange, Aux Echanges, Les Feusselottes, *Les Fuées*, Les Grands Murs, Les Groseilles, Les Gruenchers, Les Hauts Doix, *Les Lavrottes*, Les Noirots, Les Plantes, Les Sentiers.

The outstanding *premier cru* is Les Amoureuses, with Les Charmes a very respectable second.

**RED** The best have a seductive bouquet and deliciously fragrant flavor.

🍇 Pinot Noir, Pinot Gris, Pinot Liébault

🍷— 10–20 years

✓ *Amiot-Servelle* (Amoureuses) • *Ghislaine Barthod* • *Jean-Claude Boisset* • *Confuron-Cotétidot* • *R Groffier* • *Moine Hudelot* • *Dominique Laurent* • *Lucien Lemoine* • *Leroy* ❷ • *Denis Mortet* • *Mugnier* • *Perrot-Minot* • *Laurent Ponsot* • *Michelle & Patrice Rion* • *Christophe Roumier* • *Georges Roumier* • *Comte Georges de Vogüé*

## CHAPELLE-CHAMBERTIN AOC
### Grand Cru

This is one of the nine *grands crus* of Gevrey-Chambertin, comprised of two *climats* called En la Chapelle and Les Gémeaux.

**RED** The lightest of all the *grands crus*, with a delightful bouquet and flavor.

🍇 Pinot Noir, Pinot Gris, Pinot Liébault

🍷— 8–20 years

✓ *Louis Jadot* • *Jean Trapet Père & Fils*

## CHARMES-CHAMBERTIN AOC
### Grand Cru

The largest Gevrey-Chambertin *grand cru*, part of the vineyard is known as Mazoyères, from which Mazoyères-Chambertin has evolved.

**RED** Soft, sumptuous wines with ripe-fruit flavors and pure Pinot character, although some slightly lack finesse.

🍇 Pinot Noir, Pinot Gris, Pinot Liébault

🍷 10–20 years

✓ *Denis Bachelet • Confuron-Cotétidot • Claude Dugat • Bernard Dugat-Py • Frederic Magnien • Géantet-Pansiot • Vincent Girardin • Perrot-Minot • Sérafin Père & Fils • Joseph Roty • Christophe Roumier • Armand Rousseau • Taupenot-Merme • de la Vougeraie* B

## CLOS DE BÈZE AOC

An alternative appellation for Chambertin-Clos de Bèze. *See* Chambertin-Clos de Bèze AOC.

## CLOS DES LAMBRAYS AOC
### Grand Cru

This vineyard was classified as one of the four *grands crus* of Morey-St.-Denis only as recently as 1981, although the previous owner used to put "*grand cru classé* " (illegally) on the label.

**RED** The vineyard was replanted under new ownership and now produces fine, elegant wines with silky fruit of a good, easily recommendable quality.

🍇 Pinot Noir, Pinot Gris, Pinot Liébault

🍷 10–20 years

✓ *des Lambrays*

## CLOS DE LA ROCHE AOC
### Grand Cru

Covering an area of almost 42 acres (17 hectares), Clos de La Roche is twice the size of the other *grands crus* of Morey-St.-Denis.

**RED** A deep-colored, rich, and powerfully flavored *vin de garde* with a silky texture. Many consider it the greatest *grand cru* of Morey-St.-Denis.

🍇 Pinot Noir, Pinot Gris, Pinot Liébault

🍷 10–20 years

✓ *Jean-Claude Boisset • Dujac • Leroy* B *• Lucien Lemoine • Hubert Lignier • Michel Magnien & Fils • Ponsot • Armand Rousseau*

## CLOS ST.-DENIS AOC
### Grand Cru

This is the *grand cru* that the village of Morey attached to its name when it was the best growth in the village, a position now contested by Clos de la Roche and Clos de Tart.

**RED** Strong, fine, and firm wines with rich liquorice and berry flavors that require time to come together.

🍇 Pinot Noir, Pinot Gris, Pinot Liébault

🍷 10–25 years

✓ *Bertagna • Philippe Charlopin-Parizot • Philippe Charlopin • Dujac • Louis Jadot • Lucien Lemoine • Michel Magnien & Fils • Ponsot • Nicolas Potel*

## CLOS DE TART AOC
### Grand Cru

This is one of the four *grands crus* of Morey-St.-Denis. It is entirely owned by the *négociant* Mommessin. In addition to Clos de Tart itself, a tiny part of the Bonnes Mares *grand cru* also has the right to this appellation.

**RED** This *monopole* yields wines with a penetrating Pinot flavor, to which Mommessin adds such a spicy-vanilla character from 100 percent new oak that great bottle maturity is required for a completely harmonious flavor.

🍇 Pinot Noir, Pinot Gris, Pinot Liébault

🍷 15–30 years

✓ *Mommessin*

## CLOS DE VOUGEOT AOC
### Grand Cru

The only *grand cru* of Vougeot, it is a massive 123-acre (50-hectare) block of vines with no fewer than 85 registered owners. It has been described as "an impressive sight, but a not very impressive site." This mass ownership situation has often been used to illustrate the classic difference between Burgundy and Bordeaux, where an entire vineyard belongs to one château and so the wine can be blended to a standard quality and style every year.

**RED** With individual plots ranging in quality from truly great to very ordinary, operated by growers of varying skills, it is virtually impossible to unravel the intrinsic characteristics of this *cru*. Its best wines, however, have lots of silky Pinot fruit, an elegant balance, and a tendency toward finesse rather than fullness.

🍇 Pinot Noir, Pinot Gris, Pinot Liébault

🍷 10–25 years

✓ *Robert Arnoux • Joseph Drouhin • René Engel • Faiveley • Jean Grivot • Anne Gros • Michel Gros • Alain Hudelot-Noëllat • Louis Jadot • Dominique Laurent • Leroy* B *• Méo-Camuzet • Mugneret-Gibourg • Nicolas Potel • Château la Tour • de la Vougeraie* B

## CLOS VOUGEOT AOC

*See* Clos de Vougeot AOC

## CÔTE DE NUITS-VILLAGES AOC

This appellation covers the wines produced in one or more of five communes: Fixin and Brochon situated in the north of the district and Comblanchien, Corgoloin, and Prissy in the south.

**RED** Firm, fruity, and distinctive wines made in true, well-structured Côte de Nuits style.

🍇 Pinot Noir, Pinot Gris, Pinot Liébault

🍷 6–10 years

**WHITE** Very little is made—just 44 cases (4 hectoliters) in 1985—and I have never encountered it.

🍇 Chardonnay, Pinot Blanc

✓ *de l'Arlot • Michel Esmonin • Gachot-Monot • Naudin-Ferrand • Daniel Rion & Fils* (Le Vaucrain)

## ECHÉZEAUX AOC
### Grand Cru

This 74-acre (30-hectare) vineyard is the larger of the two *grands crus* of Flagey-Echézeaux and is comprised of 11 *climats* owned by no fewer than 84 smallholders.

**RED** The best have a fine and fragrant flavor that relies more on delicacy than power, but too many deserve no more than a village appellation.

🍇 Pinot Noir, Pinot Gris, Pinot Liébault

🍷 10–20 years

✓ *Robert Arnoux • Albert Bichot* (Clos Frantin) *• Confuron-Cotétidot • Dujac • Engel • Faiveley • Forey Père & Fils • Vincent Girardin • Jean Grivot • A.-F. Gros • Louis Jadot • Robert Jayer-Gilles • Lucien Lemoine • Mongeard-Mugneret • Mugneret-Gibourg • de la Romanée-Conti • Emmanuel Rouget • Fabrice Vigot*

## FIXIN AOC

Fixin was at one time the summer residence of the dukes of Burgundy.

**RED** Well-colored wines that can be firm, tannic *vins de garde* of excellent quality and even better value.

🍇 Pinot Noir, Pinot Gris, Pinot Liébault

🍷 6–12 years

**WHITE** Rich, dry, and concentrated wines that are rare, but exciting and well worth seeking out. Bruno Clair shows what Pinot Blanc can produce when it is not overcropped.

🍇 Chardonnay, Pinot Blanc

🍷 3–8 years

✓ *Bart • Berthaut • Bruno Clair • Pierre Gelin • Philippe Joliet • Mongeard-Mugneret*

## FIXIN PREMIER CRU AOC

***Premiers crus:*** Les Arvelets, Clos du Chapitre, Aux Cheusots, Les Hervelets, Le Meix Bas, La Perrière, Queue de Hareng (located in neighboring Brochon), En Suchot, Le Village.

The best *premiers crus* are La Perrière and Clos du Chapitre. Clos de la Perrière is a monopoly owned by Philippe Joliet that encompasses En Souchot and Queue de Hareng as well as La Perrière itself.

**RED** Splendidly deep in color and full in body with masses of blackcurrant and redcurrant fruit, supported by a good tannic structure.

🍇 Pinot Noir, Pinot Gris, Pinot Liébault

🍷 10–20 years

**WHITE** I have not encountered any but it would not be unreasonable to assume that it might be at least as good as a basic Fixin *blanc*.

✓ *Berthaut • Pierre Gelin • Philippe Joliet • Mongeard-Mugneret*

## GEVREY-CHAMBERTIN AOC

Famous for its *grand cru* of Chambertin, the best growers also produce superb wines under this appellation. Some vineyards overlap the village of Brochon.

**RED** These well-colored wines are full, rich, and elegant, with a silky texture and a perfumed aftertaste reminiscent of the pure fruit of Pinot Noir.

🍇 Pinot Noir, Pinot Gris, Pinot Liébault

🍷 7–15 years

✓ *Denis Bachelet • Alain Burguet • Philippe Charlopin • Confuron-Cotétidot • Drouhin-Laroze • Bernard Dugat-Py • Dujac • Dujac Père • Labouré-Roi • Marc Roy (Vieilles Vignes, Clos Prieur) • Denis Mortet • Géantet Pansiot*

## GEVREY-CHAMBERTIN PREMIER CRU AOC

**Premiers crus:** *Bel Air*, La Bossière, Les

Cazetiers, Champeaux, *Champitennois*, Champonnet, Clos du Chapitre, *Cherbandes, Au Closeau*, Combe au Moine, *Aux Combottes, Les Corbeaux*, Craipillot, En Ergot, Etournelles (or Estournelles), Fonteny, Les Goulots, Lavaut (or Lavaut St.-Jacques), *La Perrière, Petite Chapelle*, Petits Cazetiers, *Plantigone* (or *Issarts*), Poissenot, *Clos Prieur-Haut* (or *Clos Prieure*), La Romanée, Le Clos St.-Jacques, Les Varoilles.

**RED** These wines generally have more color, concentration, and finesse than the village wines, but, with the possible exception of Clos St.-Jacques, do not quite match the *grands crus*.

🍇 Pinot Noir, Pinot Gris, Pinot Liébault

🍷 10–20 years

✓ *Alain Burguet • Bruno Clair • Drouhin-Laroze • Claude Dugat • Bernard Dugat-Py • Dujac • Frédéric Esmonin • Michel Esmonin • Faiveley • Jean-Claude Fourrier • Herezstyn • Louis Jadot • Lucien Lemoine • Denis Mortet • Philippe Nadeff • Géantet Pansiot • Michelle & Patrice Rion • Joseph Roty • Armand Rousseau • Sérafin • Jean Trapet Père & Fils*

## GRANDS ECHÉZEAUX AOC
### Grand Cru

The smaller and superior of the two *grands crus* of Flagey-Echézeaux, this area is separated from the upper slopes of the Clos de Vougeot by a village boundary.

**RED** Fine and complex wines that should have a silky bouquet, often reminiscent of violets. The flavor can be very round and rich, but is balanced by a certain delicacy of fruit.

🍇 Pinot Noir, Pinot Gris, Pinot Liébault

🍷 10–20 years

✓ *Engel • Gros Frère & Sœur • François Lamarche • Mongeard-Mugneret • de la Romanée-Conti*

## LA GRANDE RUE AOC
### Grand Cru

The newest *grand cru* of Vosne-Romanée, La Grande Rue was generally considered to have the best potential of all the *premiers crus* in this village. Officially upgraded in 1992, although the quality of wine produced by its sole owner, François Lamarche, was erratic to say the least. The *terroir* is, however, undeniably superior for

a *premier cru* and as Lamarche has been on form since its promotion, perhaps the cart should come before the horse sometimes.

**RED** When Lamarche gets this right, the wine is well colored with deep, spicy-floral, black cherry fruit.

🍇 Pinot Noir, Pinot Gris, Pinot Liébault

🍷 7–15 years

✓ *Lamarche*

## GRIOTTES-CHAMBERTIN AOC
### Grand Cru

The smallest of the nine *grands crus* of Gevrey-Chambertin.

**RED** The best growers produce deep-colored, delicious wines with masses of soft-fruit flavors and all the velvety texture that could be expected of Chambertin itself.

🍇 Pinot Noir, Pinot Gris, Pinot Liébault

🍷 10–20 years

✓ *Joseph Drouhin • Claude Dugat • Frédéric Esmonin • Jean-Claude Fourrier • Louis Jadot • Ponsot • Joseph Roty*

## LATRICIÈRES-CHAMBERTIN AOC
### Grand Cru

One of the nine *grands crus* of Gevrey-Chambertin, situated above the Mazoyères *climat* of Charmes-Chambertin. A tiny part of the adjoining *premier cru*, Aux Combottes, also has the right to use this AOC.

**RED** Solid structure and a certain austerity connect the two different styles of this wine (early-drinking and long-maturing). They sometimes lack fruit and generosity, but wines from the top growers recommended below are always the finest to be found.

🍇 Pinot Noir, Pinot Gris, Pinot Liébault

🍷 10–20 years

✓ *Drouhin-Laroze • Faiveley • Leroy* ⑬ *• Ponsot • Jean Trapet Père & Fils*

## MARSANNAY AOC

This village, situated in the very north of the Côte de Nuits, has long been famous for its rosé and has recently developed a reputation for its red wines. In May 1987 it was upgraded to full village AOC status from its previous appellation of Bourgogne Marsannay. There is talk of a classification of Marsannay that would result in a new Marsannay *premier cru* AOC. This would be at least as justifiable as Maranges *premier cru* in the Côte de Beaune, not so much in the sense that either village has vineyards of truly *premier cru* quality, but it is at least useful in highlighting the better vineyards.

**RED** Firm and fruity wines with juicy redcurrant flavors, hints of liquorice, cinnamon and, if new oak has been used, vanilla.

🍇 Pinot Noir, Pinot Gris, Pinot Liébault

🍷 4-8 years

**WHITE** Mostly light and tangy, early-drinking wines, although the top wines made in a suitable vintage, by the likes of Charles Audoin and Louis Jadot, are a lot richer, creamier and offer serious aging potential.

🍇 Chardonnay

🍷 2–5 years

**ROSÉ** These dry wines are rich, rather than light and fragrant. Packed with ripe fruit flavors that can include blackberry, blackcurrant, raspberry and cherry, they are best consumed young,

although people do enjoy them when the wine has an orange tinge and the fruit is overmature.

🍇 Pinot Noir, Pinot Gris, Pinot Liébault

🍷 1–3 years

✓ *Charles Audoin • René Bouvier • Bernard Coillot (Les Boivins) • Louis Jadot • Denis Mortet (Les Longeroies) • Géantet Pansiot (Champ Perdrix)*

## MAZIS-CHAMBERTIN AOC
### Grand Cru

Sometimes known as Mazy-Chambertin. One of the nine *grands crus* of Gevrey-Chambertin.

**RED** These complex wines have a stature second only to Chambertin and Clos de Bèze. They have a fine, bright color, supersilky finesse, and a delicate flavor that lasts.

🍇 Pinot Noir, Pinot Gris, Pinot Liébault

🍷 10–20 years

✓ *d'Auvenay* ⑬ *• Bernard Dugat-Py • Frédéric Esmonin • Faiveley • Jean-Michel Guillon • Lucien Lemoine • Leroy* ⑬ *• Bernard Maume • Philippe Nadeff • Joseph Roty • Armand Rousseau*

## MAZOYÈRES-CHAMBERTIN AOC

An alternative appellation for Charmes-Chambertin. *See* Charmes-Chambertin AOC.

## MOREY-ST.-DENIS AOC

This excellent little wine village tends to be overlooked. The fact that it is situated between two world-famous places, Gevrey-Chambertin and Chambolle-Musigny, coupled with the fact that Clos St.-Denis is no longer considered to be Gevrey-Chambertin's top *grand cru*, does little to promote the name of this village.

**RED** The best of these village wines have a vivid color, a very expressive bouquet, and a smooth flavor with lots of finesse. A Morey-St.-Denis from a domaine such as Dujac can have the quality of a top *premier cru*.

🍇 Pinot Noir, Pinot Gris, Pinot Liébault

🍷 8–15 years

**WHITE** Dujac produces an excellent Morey-St.-Denis *blanc*, but more interesting, although less consistent, is Ponsot's Monts Luisants *blanc*. Although Monts Luisants is a *premier cru*, the upper section from which this wine comes is part of the village appellation (the southeastern corner is classified *grand cru* and sold as Clos de la Roche!). When Ponsot gets the Monts Luisants *blanc* right, it can be a superbly fresh, dry, buttery-rich wine and some writers have compared it to a Meursault.

🍇 Chardonnay, Pinot Blanc

🍷 3–8 years

✓ *Pierre Amiot • Philippe Charlopin • Dujac • Dujac Père • Hubert Lignier • Michel Magnien • Perrot-Minot • Ponsot • Georges Roumier*

## MOREY-ST.-DENIS PREMIER CRU AOC

**Premiers crus:** Clos Baulet, Les Blanchards, La Bussière, *Les Chaffots, Aux Charmes, Les Charrières*, Les Chénevery, Aux Cheseaux, *Les Faconnières, Les Genevrières*, Les Gruenchers, *Les Millandes*, Monts Luisants, Clos des Ormes, Clos Sorbè, Les Sorbès, Côte Rôtie, La Riotte, *Les Ruchots*, Le Village.

**RED** These wines should have all the color, bouquet, flavor, and finesse of the excellent village wines plus an added expression of *terroir*. The best *premiers crus* are: Clos des Ormes, Clos Sorbè, and Les Sorbès.

🍇 Pinot Noir, Pinot Gris, Pinot Liébault

🍷 10–20 years

**WHITE** The only white Morey-St.-Denis I know is from the upper section of Monts Luisants belonging to Ponsot (*see* Morey-St.-Denis AOC above). To my knowledge, no other white Morey-St.-Denis *premier cru* is made.

🍇 Chardonnay

✓ *Pierre Amiot • Dujac • Herezstyn • Hubert Lignier • Frédic Magnien* (Les Ruchots) • *Perrot-Minot • Georges Roumier*

## MUSIGNY AOC
### Grand Cru

Musigny is the smaller of Chambolle-Musigny's two *grands crus*. It covers some 25 acres (10 hectares) on the opposite side of the village to Bonnes Mares.

**RED** These most stylish of wines have a fabulous color and a smooth, seductive, and spicy bouquet. The velvet-rich fruit flavor constantly unfolds to reveal a succession of taste experiences.

🍇 Pinot Noir, Pinot Gris, Pinot Liébault

🍷 10–30 years

**WHITE** Musigny *blanc* is a rare and expensive dry wine produced solely at Comte Georges de Vogüé. It combines the steel of a Chablis with the richness of a Montrachet, although it never quite achieves the quality of either.

🍇 Chardonnay

🍷 8–20 years

✓ *Joseph Drouhin • Louis Jadot • Leroy* **B** • *J.-F. Mugnier* (Château de Chambolle-Musigny) • *Christophe Roumier • Georges Roumier • Comte Georges de Vogüé*

## NUITS AOC
*See* Nuits-St.-Georges AOC

## NUITS PREMIER CRU AOC
*See* Nuits-St.-Georges Premier Cru AOC

## NUITS-ST.-GEORGES AOC

More than any other, the name of this town graphically projects the image of full flavor and sturdy structure for which the wines of the Côte de Nuits are justly famous.

**RED** These are deep-colored, full, and firm wines, but they can sometimes lack the style and character of wines from Gevrey, Chambolle, and Morey.

🍇 Pinot Noir, Pinot Gris, Pinot Liébault

🍷 7–15 years

**WHITE** I have not tasted this wine. (*See* white Nuits-St.-Georges *premier cru*).

✓ de l'Arlot • R. Chevillon • J. Chauvenet • J.-J. Confuron • Confuron-Cotétidot • Thibault Liger-Belair • Bertrand Marchard de Gramont • A. Michelot • des Perdrix • Daniel Rion & Fils

## NUITS-ST.-GEORGES PREMIER CRU AOC

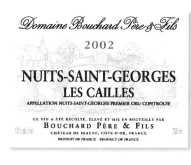

**Premiers crus:** Les Argillats, Les Argillières*, Clos Arlot*, Aux Boudots, Aux Bousselots, Les Cailles, Les Chaboeufs, Aux Chaignots, Chaine-Carteau (or Chaines-Carteaux), Aux Champs Perdrix, Clos des Corvées*, Clos des Corvées Pagets*, Aux Cras, Les Crots, Les Damodes, Les Didiers, Les Forêts* (or Clos des Forêts St.-Georges*), Les Grandes Vignes*, Château Gris, Les Hauts Pruliers, Clos de la Maréchale*, Aux Murgers, Aux Perdrix*, En la Perrière Noblet (or En la Perrière Noblot), Les Perrières, Les Porets, Les Poulettes, Les Procès, Les Pruliers, La Richemone, La Roncière, Rue de Chaux, Les St.-Georges, Clos St.-Marc (or Aux Corvées), Les Terres Blanches, Aux Thorey, Les Vallerots, Les Vaucrains, Aux Vignerondes.
*In the village of Prémeaux-Prissey.

**RED** These wines have a splendid color, a spicy-rich bouquet, and a vibrant fruit flavor which can be nicely underpinned with vanilla.

🍇 Pinot Noir, Pinot Gris, Pinot Liébault

🍷 10–20 years

**WHITE** Henri Gouges's La Perrière is dry, powerful, almost fat, with a spicy-rich aftertaste. The vines for this wine were propagated from a mutant Pinot Noir that produced bunches of both black and white grapes. Gouges cut a shoot from a white-grape-producing branch of the mutant vine in the mid-1930s, and there is now just over one acre (just under half a hectare) of the vines planted by Gouges, none of which have ever reverted to producing black grapes.

🍇 Chardonnay, Pinot Blanc

🍷 5–10 years

✓ *Bertrand Ambroise • de l'Arlot • Robert Arnoux • Bouchard Père & Fils • Jean Chauvenet* (Les Perrières) • *Robert Chevillon • J.-J. Confuron • Confuron-Cotétidot • Dubois & Fils • Faiveley • Forey Père & Fils • Henri Gouges • Jean Grivot • Alain Hudelot-Noëllat • Robert Jayer-Gilles • Dominique Laurent • Philippe & Vincent Léchenaut • Leroy* **B** • *Thibault Liger-Belair • Alain Michelot • Mugneret-Gibourg • Gérard Mugneret • Gilles Remoriquet • Daniel Rion & Fils • Michelle & Patrice Rion • Patrice Rion • Antonin Rodet • Jean Tardy • de la Vougeraie* **B**

## RICHEBOURG AOC
### Grand Cru

One of the six *grands crus* at the heart of Vosne-Romanée's vineyards.

**RED** This is a gloriously rich wine that has a heavenly bouquet and is full of velvety and voluptuous fruit flavors.

🍇 Pinot Noir, Pinot Gris, Pinot Liébault

🍷 12–30 years

✓ *Jean Grivot • Anne Gros • Alain Hudelot-Noëllat • Leroy* **B** • *Méo-Camuzet • de la Romanée-Conti*

## LA ROMANÉE AOC
### Grand Cru

This vineyard is owned by the Liger-Belair family, but the wine was matured, bottled, and sold by Bouchard Père & Fils until 2002, when Louis-Michel Liger-Belair took over. Less than 2½ acres (1 hectare), it is the smallest *grand cru* of Vosne-Romanée.

**RED** This is a full, fine, and complex wine that might not have the voluptuous appeal of a Richebourg, but that certainly has the class to age gracefully.

🍇 Pinot Noir, Pinot Gris, Pinot Liébault

🍷 12–30 years

✓ *Bouchard Père & Fils • Vicomte Liger-Belair*

## ROMANÉE-CONTI AOC
### Grand Cru

This Vosne-Romanée *grand cru* is under 5 acres (2 hectares) in size and belongs solely to the famous Domaine de la Romanée-Conti.

**RED** As the most expensive burgundy in the world, this wine must always be judged by higher standards than all the rest. Yet I must admit that I never fail to be amazed by the stunning array of flavors that continuously unfold in this fabulously concentrated and utterly complex wine.

🍇 Pinot Noir, Pinot Gris, Pinot Liébault

🍷 15–35 years

✓ *de la Romanée-Conti*

## ROMANÉE-ST.-VIVANT AOC
### Grand Cru

The largest of the six *grands crus* on the lowest slopes and closest to the village.

**RED** This is the lightest of the fabulous *grands crus* of Vosne-Romanée, but what it lacks in power and weight it makes up for in finesse.

🍇 Pinot Noir, Pinot Gris, Pinot Liébault

🍷 10–25 years

VINEYARDS OF CLOS DE VOUGEOT ON THE COTE DE NUITS
*The Château du Clos de Vougeot has played a big part in the region's wine industry for many years.
However, the 124 acres (50 hectares) of vineyards surrounding the château are split into more than 80 plots.*

☑ *Robert Arnoux • Sylvain Cathiard • J.-J. Confuron • Joseph Drouhin • Follin-Arbelet • Alain Hudelot-Noëllat • Lucien Lemoine • Leroy* ❸ *• de la Romanée-Conti*

## RUCHOTTES-CHAMBERTIN AOC
### Grand Cru

This is the second-smallest of the nine *grands crus* of Gevrey-Chambertin. It is situated above Mazis-Chambertin and is the last *grand cru* before the slope turns to face north.

**RED** Normally one of the lighter Chambertin look-alikes, but top growers like Roumier and Rousseau seem to achieve a bagful of added ingredients in their splendidly rich wines.

🍇 Pinot Noir, Pinot Gris, Pinot Liébault

🍷 8–20 years

☑ *Frédéric Esmonin • Mugneret-Gibourg • Christophe Roumier • Georges Roumier • Armand Rousseau*

## LA TÂCHE AOC
### Grand Cru

SOCIÉTÉ CIVILE DU DOMAINE DE LA ROMANÉE-CONTI
PROPRIÉTAIRE A VOSNE-ROMANÉE (COTE-D'OR) FRANCE

# LA TÂCHE
APPELLATION LA TÂCHE CONTROLÉE
1989 Bouteilles Récoltées
LES ASSOCIÉS-GÉRANTS
BOUTEILLE Nº 00000
ANNÉE 2001
Mise en bouteille au domaine

One of Vosne-Romanée's six *grands crus*, this fabulous vineyard belongs to the world-famous Domaine de la Romanée-Conti (DRC), which also owns the Romanée-Conti *grand cru.*

**RED** While this wine is indeed extremely rich and very complex, it does not in comparative terms quite have the richness of Richebourg, nor the complexity of Romanée-Conti. It does, however, have all the silky texture anyone could expect from the finest of burgundies, and no other wine surpasses La Tâche for finesse.

🍇 Pinot Noir, Pinot Gris, Pinot Liébault

🍷 12–30 years

☑ *de la Romanée-Conti*

## VOSNE-ROMANÉE AOC

This is the most southerly of the great villages of the Côte de Nuits. Some Vosne-Romanée vineyards are in neighboring Flagey-Echézeaux. This village includes the Romanée-Conti vineyard.

**RED** Sleek, stylish, medium-bodied wines of the purest Pinot Noir character and with the silky texture so typical of the wines of this village.

🍇 Pinot Noir, Pinot Gris, Pinot Liébault

🍷 10–15 years

☑ *Robert Arnoux • Sylvain Cathiard • Bruno Clavelier • Engel • Confuron-Contédidot • Bernard Dugat-Py* (Vieilles Vignes) *• Forey Père & Fils • Jean Grivot • Anne Gros • Michel Gros • Méo-Camuzet • Mugneret-Gibourg • Perrot-Minot • Emmanuel Rouget • Fabrice Vigot*

## VOSNE-ROMANÉE PREMIER CRU AOC

**Premiers crus:** *Les Beaux Monts*, Les Beaux Monts Bas\*, Les Beaux Monts Hauts\*, *Les Brûlées*, Les Chaumes, La Combe Brûlées, *La Croix Rameau*, *Cros-Parantoux*, *Les Gaudichots*, Les Hauts Beaux Monts, *Aux Malconsorts*, En Orveaux\*, *Les Petits Monts*, Clos des Réas, *Aux Reignots, Les Rouges du Dessus* \*, *Les Suchots*. \*These *premier cru* vineyards of Vosne-Romanée are actually in Flagey-Echézeaux.

**RED** These are well-colored wines with fine aromatic qualities that are often reminiscent of violets and blackberries. They have a silky texture and a stylish flavor that is pure Pinot Noir. The best *premiers crus* to look out for are: Les Brûlées, Cros-Parantoux, Les Petits-Monts, Les Suchots, and Les Beaumonts (an umbrella name for the various Beaux Monts, high and low).

🍇 Pinot Noir, Pinot Gris, Pinot Liébault

🍷 10–20 years

☑ *de l'Arlot • Robert Arnoux • Albert Bichot* (Clos Frantin) *• Sylvain Cathiard • Confuron-Cotétidot • Engel • Jean Grivot • Alain Hudelot-Noëllat • S. Javoubey • Henri Jayer • Lamarche • Lucien Lemoine • Leroy* ❸ *• Vicomte Liger-Belair • Méo-Camuzet • Gérard Mugneret • Perrot-Minot • Nicolas Potel • Daniel Rion & Fils • Michelle & Patrice Rion • Emmanuel Rouget*

## VOUGEOT AOC

The modest village wines of Vougeot are a relative rarity, this appellation covering less than 12 acres (5 hectares), which is less than one-tenth of the area encompassed by the Clos de Vougeot *grand cru* itself.

**RED** Little-seen, fine-flavored, well-balanced wines that are overpriced due to their scarcity. It is better to buy a *premier cru.*

🍇 Pinot Noir, Pinot Gris, Pinot Liébault

🍷 8–20 years

**WHITE** A rarity.

☑ *Bertagna • Mongeard-Mugneret*

## VOUGEOT PREMIER CRU AOC

**Premiers crus:** Les Crâs, Clos de la Perrière, Les Petits Vougeots, La Vigne Blanche.

The *premiers crus* are located between Clos de Vougeot and Musigny and, from a *terroir* point of view, should produce much better wines.

**RED** Can be nicely colored, medium bodied, and have an attractive flavoᵒr with a good balance and a certain finesse.

🍇 Pinot Noir, Pinot Gris, Pinot Liébault

🍷 10–20 years

**WHITE** A clean, rich, and crisp wine of variable quality, called Clos Blanc de Vougeot, is produced by L'Héritier Guyot from the *premier cru* of La Vigne Blanche.

🍇 Chardonnay, Pinot Blanc

🍷 4–10 years

☑ *Bertagna* (Clos de la Perrière *monopole*) *• Lamarche • de la Vougeraie* ❸ (Clos du Prieuré *monopole*)

# CÔTE DE BEAUNE AND HAUTES-CÔTES DE BEAUNE

*Pinot Noir in the Côte de Beaune is renowned for its softness and finesse, characteristics that become more evident as one progresses south through the region, but with seven of Burgundy's eight white* grands crus *this is really Chardonnay country, and the wines produced are the richest, longest-lived, most complex, and stylish white wines in the world.*

ENTERING THE CÔTE DE BEAUNE from the Nuits-St.-Georges end, the most immediately visible viticultural differences are its more expansive look and the much greater contrast between the deep, dark, and so obviously rich soil found on the inferior eastern side of the RN 74 road and the scanty patches of pebble-strewn thick drift that cover the classic slopes west of the road.

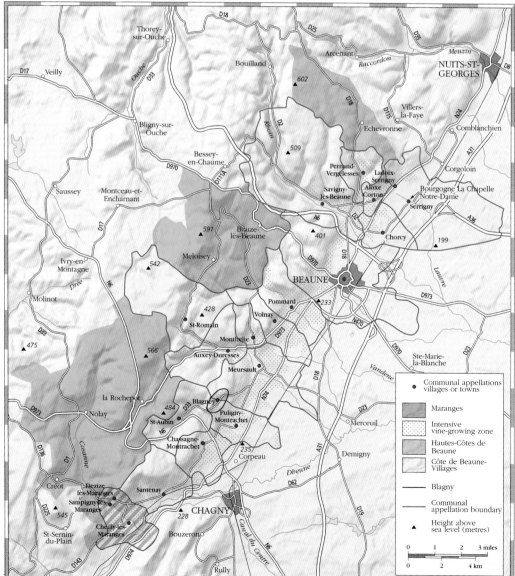

**CÔTE DE BEAUNE VINEYARDS**
*The slopes of the Côte de Beaune vineyards are generally a little gentler than those of the Côte de Nuits. In both areas, Pinot Noir and Chardonnay vines are planted, but it is here that Chardonnay is king.*

**LADOIX-SERRIGNY**
*Situated to the west of Aloxe-Corton, parts of Ladoix-Serrigny are encompassed by that village's appellations, including the* grands crus *of Corton and Corton-Charlemagne.*

**CÔTE DE BEAUNE AND HAUTES-CÔTES DE BEAUNE** *See also p137*
*The Côte d'Or is a hilly ridge that follows the trajectory of the Autoroute du Soleil. Most of the village and Hautes-Côtes appellations are clustered between Nuits-St.-Georges in the north and Chagny in the south.*

It is often said that the slopes of the Côte de Beaune are gentler than those of the Côte de Nuits, but there are many parts that are just as sheer, although the best vineyards of the Côte de Beaune are located on the middle slopes, which have a gentler incline. The steeper upper slopes produce good but generally lesser wines in all cases, except the vineyards of Aloxe-Corton—which are, anyway, more logically part of the Côte de Nuits than the Côte de Beaune.

## FACTORS AFFECTING TASTE AND QUALITY

### LOCATION
The Côte de Beaune abuts the Côte de Nuits on its southern tip and stretches almost 18 miles (30 kilometers) past the town of Beaune to Cheilly-lès-Maranges. Its vines are contiguous, although those of the Hautes-Côtes de Beaune in the western hinterland are divided into two by the Côte de Beaune vineyards of St.-Romain.

### CLIMATE
This area has a slightly wetter, more temperate, climate than the Côte de Nuits and the grapes tend to ripen a little earlier. Hail is still a potential hazard, but less so, with wet winds and heavy rain being a greater nuisance.

### ASPECT
Comprised of a series of east-facing slopes, just over 1 mile (2 kilometers) wide, which curve in and out to give some of the vineyards northeastern and others southeastern aspects. Here the vines grow at an altitude of between 740 to 1,250 feet (225 and 380 meters) on slightly less steep slopes than those of the Côte de Nuits. South of Beaune, no vines with the right to the village (and higher) appellations extend past the RN 74 road on to the flat and fertile ground beyond.

### SOIL
A limestone subsoil with sporadic beds of oolitic ironstones with flinty clay and calcareous topsoils. Light-colored marl topsoil is found in the vineyards of Chassagne and Puligny.

### VITICULTURE AND VINIFICATION
The vines are trained low to benefit from heat reflected from the soil at night. In the south of the district, the system employed is similar to that used in parts of Champagne and slightly different from elsewhere on the Côte de Beaune. For red wines, the grapes are almost always destemmed and the juice kept in contact with the skins for between eight and 10 days. Classic white wines are cask fermented and the best wines, both red and white, matured in oak. The flavor of the Pinot Noir grape can easily be overwhelmed by oak so it always receives less new-oak maturation than Chardonnay does.

### GRAPE VARIETIES
**Primary varieties:** Pinot Noir, Chardonnay
**Secondary varieties:** Pinot Gris (syn. Pinot Beurot), Pinot Liébault, Pinot Blanc, Aligoté, Melon de Bourgogne, Gamay

## THE HOSPICES DE BEAUNE LABEL

This distinctive label indicates that the wine comes from vineyards belonging to the Hospices de Beaune, a charitable institution that has cared for the sick and poor of Beaune since 1443. Half a millennium of gifts and legacies has seen the accumulation of vineyards that now total some 153 acres (62 hectares) of *premiers crus* and *grands crus*.

Since 1859 these wines have been sold by auction and, because of the publicity gained by this annual event, the prices fetched are now generally much higher than the going rate. We consumers must be prepared to pay a relatively higher price for these wines and help the cause.

After some criticism of the unreliability of certain wines, a new *cuverie* was built at the rear of the famous Hôtel-Dieu, known for its magnificent Flemish-crafted roof. All the wines are now matured in new oak casks. There remain, however, the variations that result from the different *élevages* of the various casks of the same *cuvée*. At the most innocent level, these may result from one *négociant* giving his wine more or less cask-maturation than another, and temperature and humidity levels can also radically change the wine's alcohol and extract content. The cellar management of less scrupulous firms may also be a consideration.

After the wines have been auctioned they become the full responsibility of the purchaser.

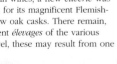

## THE HOSPICES DE BEAUNE CUVÉES

### RED WINES

**CUVÉE CLOS DES AVAUX**
AOC Beaune
*Unblended Les Avaux*

**CUVÉE BILLARDET**
AOC Pommard
*A blend of Petits Epenots, Les Noizons, Les Arvelets, Les Rugiens*

**CUVÉE BLONDEAU**
AOC Volnay
*A blend of Champans, Taille Pieds, Ronceret, En l'Ormeau*

**CUVÉE BOILLOT**
AOC Auxey-Duresses
*Unblended Les Duresses*

**CUVÉE BRUNET**
AOC Beaune
*A blend of Les Teurons, La Mignotte, Les Bressandes, Les Cents Vignes*

**CUVÉE SUZANNE CHAUDRON**
AOC Pommard
*Unblended Pommard*

**CUVÉE MADELEINE COLLIGNON**
AOC Mazis-Chambertin
*Unblended Mazis-Chambertin*

**CUVÉE RAYMOND CYROT**
AOC Pommard
*A blend of Pommard and Pommard premier cru*

**CUVÉE CYROT-CHAUDRON**
AOC Beaune
*Unblended Beaune Les Montrevenots*

**CUVÉE GEORGES KRITTER**
AOC Pommard
*Unblended Clos de la Roche*

**CUVÉE DAMES DE LA CHARITÉ**
AOC Pommard
*A blend of Les Epenots, Les Rugiens, Les Noizons, La Refène, Les Combes Dessus*

**CUVÉE DAMES HOSPITALIÈRES**
AOC Beaune
*A blend of Les Bressandes, La Mignotte, Les Teurons, Les Grèves*

**CUVÉE MAURICE DROUHIN**
AOC Beaune
*A blend of Les Avaux, Les Grèves, Les Boucherottes, Champs Pimont*

**CUVÉE CHARLOTTE DUMAY**
AOC Corton
*A blend of Renardes, Les Bressandes, Clos du Roi*

**CUVÉE FORNERET**
AOC Savigny-lès-Beaune
*A blend of Les Vergelesses, Aux Gravains*

**CUVÉE FOUQUERAND**
AOC Savigny-lès-Beaune
*A blend of Basses Vergelesses, Les Talmettes, Aux Gravains, Aux Serpentières*

**CUVÉE GAUVAIN**
AOC Volnay
*A blend of Les Santenots, Les Pitures*

**CUVÉE ARTHUR GIRARD**
AOC Savigny-lès-Beaune
*A blend of Les Peuillets, Les Marconnets*

**CUVÉE GUIGONE DE SALINS**
AOC Beaune
*A blend of Les Bressandes, En Sebrey, Champs Pimont*

**CUVÉE HUGUES ET LOUIS BÉTAULT**
AOC Beaune
*A blend of Les Grèves, La Mignotte, Les Aigrots, Les Sizies, Les Vignes Franches*

**CUVÉE LEBELIN**
AOC Monthélie
*Unblended Les Duresses*

**CUVÉE JEHAN DE MASSOL**
AOC Volnay-Santenots
*Unblended Les Santenots*

**CUVÉE GÉNÉRAL MUTEAU**
AOC Volnay
*A blend of Volnay-le-Village, Carelle sous la Chapelle, Cailleret Dessus, Les Frémiets, Taille Pieds*

**CUVÉE DOCTEUR PESTE**
AOC Corton
*A blend of Les Bressandes, Les Chaumes et la Voierosse, Clos du Roi, Les Fiètres, Les Grèves*

**CUVÉE RAMEAU-LAMAROSSE**
AOC Pernand-Vergelesses
*Unblended Les Basses Vergelesses*

**CUVÉE NICOLAS ROLIN**
AOC Beaune
*A blend of Les Cents Vignes, Les Grèves, En Genêt*

**CUVÉE ROUSSEAU-DESLANDES**
AOC Beaune
*A blend of Les Cent Vignes, Les Montrevenots, La Mignotte, Les Avaux*

### WHITE WINES

**CUVÉE DE BAHÈZRE DE LANLAY**
AOC Meursault-Charmes
*A blend of Les Charmes Dessus, Les Charmes Dessous*

**CUVÉE BAUDOT**
AOC Meursault-Genevrières
*A blend of Genevrières Dessus, Les Genevrières Dessous*

**CUVÉE PHILIPPE LE BON**
AOC Meursault-Genevrières
*A blend of Genevrières Dessus Les Genevrières Dessous*

**CUVÉE PAUL CHANSON**
AOC Corton-Vergennes
*Unblended Corton-Vergennes*

**CUVÉE DAMES DE FLANDRES**
AOC Bâtard-Montrachet
*Unblended Bâtard-Montrachet*

**CUVÉE GOUREAU**
AOC Meursault
*A blend of Le Poruzot, Les Pitures, Les Cras*

**CUVÉE ALBERT GRIVAULT**
AOC Meursault-Charmes
Unblended Les Charmes Dessus

**CUVÉE JEHAN HUMBLOT**
AOC Meursault
*A blend of Le Poruzot, Grands Charrons*

**CUVÉE LOPPIN**
AOC Meursault
*Unblended Les Criots*

**CUVÉE FRANÇOISE POISARD**
AOC Pouilly-Fuissé
*Unblended Pouilly-Fuissé*

**CUVÉE FRANÇOISE-DE-SALINS**
AOC Corton-Charlemagne
*Unblended Corton-Charlemagne*

THE APPELLATIONS OF

# THE CÔTE DE BEAUNE AND HAUTES-CÔTES DE BEAUNE

**Notes: 1.** All the *grands crus* of Côte de Beaune have their own separate appellations and are therefore listed individually below. However, the *premiers crus* do not, and are therefore listed under the appellation of the village in which the vineyards are situated. *Premiers crus* that are virtually contiguous with *grand cru* vineyards are italicized; they are possibly superior to those that do not share a boundary with one or more *grands crus*, and generally superior to those that share boundaries with village AOC vineyards.
**2.** Leflaive plain and simple refers to Domaine Leflaive, while Olivier Leflaive is the *négociant*.

## ALOXE-CORTON AOC

This village is more Côte de Nuits than Côte de Beaune, as its 99 percent red-wine production suggests.

**RED** These deeply colored, firm-structured wines with compact fruit are reminiscent of reds from northern Côte de Nuits. They are excellent value for money.

🍇 Pinot Noir, Pinot Gris, Pinot Liébault

🍷 10–20 years

**WHITE** Very little Aloxe-Corton *blanc* is made, but Daniel Senard makes a lovely buttery-rich, concentrated pure Pinot Gris wine (which, although it is definitely a white wine, makes it red according to the regulations!).

🍇 Chardonnay

🍷 4–8 years

✓ *Edmond Cornu & Fils* • *P. Dubreuil-Fontaine* • *Follin-Arbelet* • *Maurice Martray* • *Daniel Senard* • *Tollot-Beaut*

## ALOXE-CORTON PREMIER CRU AOC

**Premiers crus:** *Les Chaillots, La Coutière\**, Les Fournières, Les Guérets, *La Maréchaude\**, *Clos des Maréchaudes, Les Maréchaudes*, Les Meix (or Clos du Chapitre), *Les Moutottes\**, *Les Paulands, Les Petites Lolières\**, *La Toppe au Vert\**, *Les Valozières*, Les Vercots.

*\*Premier cru* vineyards of Aloxe-Corton in Ladoix-Serrigny.

**RED** These wines can have an intense bouquet and a firm, spicy fruit flavor. The best *premiers crus* are Les Fournières, Les Valozières, Les Paulands, and Les Maréchaudes.

🍇 Pinot Noir, Pinot Gris, Pinot Liébault

🍷 10–20 years

**WHITE** I have never encountered any.

✓ *Cachat-Ocquidant & Fils* (Les Machaudes) • *Capitain-Gagnerot* • *Antonin Guyon* • *André Masson* • *Prince Florent de Mérode*

## AUXEY-DURESSES AOC

A beautiful village, set in an idyllic valley behind Monthélie and Meursault.

**RED** Attractive wines not very deep in color, but with a softness of fruit and a little finesse.

🍇 Pinot Noir, Pinot Gris, Pinot Liébault

🍷 6–12 years

**WHITE** Medium-bodied wines with a full, spicy-nutty flavor, like that of a modest Meursault.

🍇 Chardonnay, Pinot Blanc

🍷 3–7 years

✓ *Robert Ampeau* • *d'Auvenay* **B** • *Jean-Pierre Diconne* • *Alain Gras* • *Louis Jadot* • *Henri Latour* • *Olivier Leflaive* • *Leroy* **B** • *Prunier* (all and sundry) • *Dominique & Vincent Roy* • *Jean-Marc Vincent* (Les Hautes)

## AUXEY-DURESSES PREMIER CRU AOC

**Premiers crus:** Bas des Duresses, Les Bretterins, La Chapelle, Climat du Val, Les Duresses, Les Écusseaux, Les Grands-Champs, Reugne.

**RED** The *premiers crus* provide nicely colored soft wines with good finesse. The best have fine redcurrant Pinot character with the creamy-oak of cask maturity.

🍇 Pinot Noir, Pinot Gris, Pinot Liébault

🍷 7–15 years

**WHITE** Excellent value, smooth, and stylish wines in the Meursault mould.

🍇 Chardonnay, Pinot Blanc

🍷 4–10 years

✓ *Armand* • *Jean-Pierre Diconne* • *Michel Prunier* • *Vincent Prunier*

## AUXEY-DURESSES-CÔTES DE BEAUNE AOC

Alternative appellation for red wines only. *See* Auxey-Duresses AOC.

## BÂTARD-MONTRACHET AOC
### Grand Cru

This *grand cru* is situated on the slope beneath Le Montrachet and overlaps both Chassagne-Montrachet and Puligny-Montrachet.

**WHITE** Full-bodied, intensely rich wine with masses of nutty, honey-and-toast flavors. It is one of the best dry white wines in the world.

🍇 Pinot chardonnay (*sic*)

🍷 8–20 years

✓ *Jean-Marc Boillot* • *Bouchard Père & Fils* • *Jean-Noël Gagnard* • *Vincent Girardin* • *Louis Latour* • *Leflaive* **B** • *Marc Morey* • *Pierre Morey* **B** • *Michel Niellon* • *Paul Pernot* • *Ramonet* • *Antonin Rodet* • *Étienne Sauzet*

## BEAUNE AOC

Beaune gives its name to village wines and *premiers crus*, but not to any *grands crus*.

**RED** These soft-scented, gently fruity wines are consistent and good value.

🍇 Pinot Noir, Pinot Gris, Pinot Liébault

🍷 6–14 years

**WHITE** An uncomplicated dry Chardonnay wine with a characteristic soft finish.

🍇 Chardonnay, Pinot Blanc

🍷 3–7 years

✓ *Bouchard Père & Fils* • *Bertrand Darviot* • *Dominique Laurent* (Vieilles Vignes) • *Machard de Gramont* • *Tollot-Beaut* • *de la Vougeraie* **B**

## BEAUNE PREMIER CRU AOC

**Premiers crus:** Les Aigrots, Aux Coucherias (or Clos de la Féguine), Aux Cras, Clos des Avaux, Les Avaux, Le Bas des Teurons, Les Beaux Fougets, Belissand, Les Blanches Fleurs, Les Boucherottes, Les Bressandes, Les Cents Vignes, Champs Pimont, Les Chouacheux, l'Écu (or Clos de l'Écu), Les Epenottes (or Les Epenotes), Les Fèves, En Genêt, Les Grèves, Clos Landry (Clos Ste.-Landry),Les Longes, Le Clos des Mouches, Le Clos de la Mousse, Les Marconnets, La Mignotte, Montée Rouge, Les Montrevenots, En l'Orme, Les Perrières, Pertuisots, Les Reversées, Clos du Roi, Les Seurey, Les Sizies, Clos Ste.-Anne (or Sur les Grèves), Les Teurons, Les Toussaints, Les Tuvilains, La Vigne de l'Enfant Jésus, Les Vignes Franches (or Clos des Ursules).

**RED** The best *crus* are medium-bodied with a delightfully soft rendition of Pinot fruit and lots of finesse. Look out for Faiveley's Clos de L'Écu, a *monopole* purchased at the time of writing. I expect Faiveley will want to make some sort of quality statement here.

🍇 Pinot Noir, Pinot Gris, Pinot Liébault

🍷 10–20 years

**WHITE** These wines have lovely finesse and can display a toasty flavor more common to richer growths. Domaine Jacques Prieur's Champs Pimont has stood out lately.

🍇 Chardonnay, Pinot Blanc

🍷 5–12 years

✓ *Arnoux Père & Fils* • *Bouchard Père & Fils* • *Chanson Père & Fils* (Clos de Fèves, Clos des Mouches) • *Joseph Drouhin* • *Camille Giroud* • *Louis Jadot* • *Jaffelin* • *Michel Lafarge* • *Louis Latour* • *René Monnier* • *Bernard Morey* • *Albert Morot* • *Michel Picard* • *Jacques Prieur* • *Tollot-Beaut*

## BIENVENUES-BÂTARD-MONTRACHET AOC
### Grand Cru

This is one of Puligny-Montrachet's four *grands crus*.

**WHITE** Not the fattest dry wines from this village, but they have great finesse, immaculate balance, and some of the nuttiness and honey-and-toast flavors expected in all Montrachets.

🍇 Chardonnay

🍷 8–20 years

✓ *Louis Carillon & Fils* • *Chartron et Trebuchet* • *Vincent Girardin* • *Louis Latour* • *Leflaive* **B** • *Paul Pernot* • *Ramonet* • *Étienne Sauzet*

## BLAGNY AOC

A red-only appellation from Blagny, a tiny hamlet shared by the communes of Meursault and Puligny-Montrachet.

**RED** These rich, full-flavored, Meursault-like red wines are underrated.

🍇 Pinot Noir, Pinot Gris, Pinot Liébault

🍷 8–15 years

✓ *Robert Ampeau* • *Matrot*

## BLAGNY PREMIER CRU AOC

**Premiers crus:** La Garenne (or Sur la Garenne), Hameau de Blagny (in Puligny-Montrachet), La Jeunelotte, La Pièce sous le Bois, Sous Blagny (in Meursault), Sous le Dos d'Ane, Sous le Puits.

**RED** These rich wines have even more grip and attack than basic Blagny.

🍇 Pinot Noir, Pinot Gris, Pinot Liébault

🍷 10–20 years

✓ *Robert Ampeau* • *François Jobard* • *Larue* (Sous le Puits) • *Leflaive* ❸ • *Matrot*

## BLAGNY-CÔTE DE BEAUNE AOC

Alternative appellation for Blagny. *See* Blagny AOC.

## BOURGOGNE LA CHAPELLE NOTRE-DAME AOC

One of three Bourgogne *lieux-dits* created in 1993. La Chapelle Notre Dame is located in Serrigny, which is just east of Ladoix. Red, white, and rosé may be produced according to the same grapes and rules as for Bourgogne AOC (*see* p.133). P. Dubreuil-Fontaine has produced a wine from this *lieu-dit* for many years. It has always been decent, not special, but capable of improving in bottle. André and Jean-René Nudant also makes a light, fresh red from this appellation.

## BOURGOGNE HAUTES-CÔTES DE BEAUNE AOC

This appellation is larger and more varied than Hautes-Côtes de Nuits. Half-red/half-rosé wines may be sold as Bourgogne Clairet Hautes-Côtes de Beaune AOC, but the style is outmoded and the appellation rarely encountered.

**RED** Ruby-colored, medium-bodied wines with a Pinot perfume and a creamy-fruit finish.

🍇 Pinot Noir, Pinot Gris, Pinot Liébault

🍷 4–10 years

**WHITE** Not very frequently encountered, but Guillemard-Dupont's pure Pinot Beurot (Pinot Gris) is rich, dry, and expressive. Its grape variety makes it a very pale white, red, or rosé according to the regulations!

🍇 Chardonnay, Pinot Blanc

🍷 1–4 years

**ROSÉ** Pleasantly dry and fruity wines with some richness and a soft finish.

🍇 Pinot Noir, Pinot Gris, Pinot Liébault

🍷 1–3 years

✓ *Contat-Grange* • *Jean Joliot & Fils* • *Didier Montchovet* • *Claude Nouveau* • *Naudin-Ferrand*

## CHARLEMAGNE AOC
### Grand Cru

This white-only *grand cru* of Aloxe-Corton overlaps Pernand-Vergelesses and is almost, but not quite, identical to the *grand cru* of Corton-Charlemagne.

## CHASSAGNE-MONTRACHET AOC

These village wines have a lesser reputation than those of Puligny-Montrachet.

**RED** Firm, dry wines with more color and less softness than most Côte de Beaune reds.

🍇 Pinot Noir, Pinot Gris, Pinot Liébault

🍷 10–20 years

**WHITE** An affordable introduction to the great wines of Montrachet.

🍇 Chardonnay, Pinot Blanc

🍷 5–10 years

✓ *Bernard Colin & Fils* • *Fontaine-Gagnard* • *Jean-Noël Gagnard* • *Marquis de Laguiche* • *Château de la Maltroye* • *Bernard Morey* • *Jean-Marc Morey*

## CHASSAGNE-MONTRACHET PREMIER CRU AOC

**Premiers crus:** Abbaye de Morgeot, Les Baudines, *Blanchot Dessus*, Les Boirettes, Bois de Chassagne, Les Bondues, La Boudriotte, Les Brussonnes, En Cailleret, La Cardeuse, Champ Jendreau, Les Champs Gain, La Chapelle, Clos Chareau, Les Chaumées, Les Chaumes, Les Chenevottes, Les Combards, Les Commes, Ez Crets, Ez Crottes, *Dent de Chien*, Les Embrazées, Les Fairendes, Francemont, La Grande Borne, La Grande Montagne, Les Grandes Ruchottes, Les Grands Clos, Guerchère, Les Macherelles, *La Maltroie*, Les Morgeots, Les Murées, Les Pasquelles, Petingeret, Les Petites Fairendes, Les Petits Clos, Clos Pitois, Les Places, Les Rebichets, En Remilly, La Romanée, La Roquemaure, Clos St.-Jean, Tête du Clos, Tonton Marcel, Les Vergers, *Vide Bourse*, Vigne Blanche, Vigne Derrière, En Virondot.

**RED** The wines of Chassagne-Montrachet have the weight of a Côte de Nuits and the softness of a Côte de Beaune.

🍇 Pinot Noir, Pinot Gris, Pinot Liébault

🍷 10–25 years

**WHITE** Flavorsome dry wines, but lacking the finesse of those in the neighboring appellation of Puligny.

🍇 Chardonnay, Pinot Blanc

🍷 6–15 years

✓ *Guy Amiot & Fils* • *Roger Belland* (Morgeot Clos Pitois *monopole*) • *Blain-Gagnard* • *Bernard Colin & Fils* • *Marc Colin* • *Vincent Dancer* • *Michel Colin-Deléger* (due to a split in this domaine, look for Bruno Colin and Philippe Coil) • *Fontaine-Gagnard* • *Jean-Noël Gagnard* • *Gagnard-Delagrange* • *Vincent Girardin* • *Gabriel et Paul Jouard* • *Vincent et François Jouard* • *Louis Latour* • *Olivier Leflaive* • *Lucien Lemoine* • *Château de la Maltroye* • *Bernard Moreau & Fils* • *Marc Morey* • *Michel Niellon* • *Roux* • *Verget*

## CHASSAGNE-MONTRACHET-CÔTE DE BEAUNE AOC

Alternative appellation for red wines only. *See* Chassagne Montrachet AOC.

## CHEVALIER-MONTRACHET AOC
### Grand Cru

This is one of Puligny-Montrachet's four *grands crus.*

**WHITE** Fatter and richer than Bienvenues-Bâtard-Montrachet, this wine has more explosive flavor than Bâtard-Montrachet.

🍇 Chardonnay

🍷 10–20 years

✓ *d'Auvenay* ❸ • *Bouchard Père & Fils* • *Vincent Dancer* • *Georges Déléger* • *Vincent Girardin* • *Louis Jadot* • *Leflaive* ❸ • *Marc Morey* • *Michel Niellon*

## CHOREY-LÈS-BEAUNE AOC

This satellite appellation of Beaune produces exciting, underrated wines.

**RED** Although next to Aloxe-Corton, Chorey has all the soft and sensuous charms that are quintessentially Beaune.

🍇 Pinot Noir, Pinot Gris, Pinot Liébault

🍷 7–15 years

**WHITE** Less than one percent of the wines produced in this village are white.

✓ *Arnoux Père & Fils* • *Maillard Père & Fils* • *Maurice Martray* • *Tollot-Beaut*

## CHOREY-LÈS-BEAUNE CÔTE DE BEAUNE AOC

Alternative appellation for red wines only. *See* Chorey-lès-Beaune AOC.

## CORTON AOC
### Grand Cru

This is one of the *grands crus* of Aloxe-Corton (it extends into Ladoix-Serrigny and Pernand-Vergelesses). Corton is the only *grand cru* in the Côte de Beaune that includes red and white wines and thus parallels the Côte de Nuits *grand cru* of Musigny. The following 20 *climats* may hyphenate their names (with or without the prefix) to the Corton appellation: Les Bressandes, Le Charlemagne, Les Chaumes, Les Chaumes et la Voierosse, Les Combes, Le Corton, Les Fiètres, Les Grèves, Les Languettes, Les Maréchaudes, Les Miex, Les Meix Lallemand, Les Paulands, Les Perrières, Les Pougets, Les Renardes, Le Rognet-Corton, Le Clos de Roi, Les Vergennes, La Vigne au Saint. So it is possible to get a red Corton-Charlemagne. Beware: Corton is one of the least dependable *grands crus* for quality. When it is great, it is wicked, but production is vast (38,850 to 42,180 cases/3,500 to 3,800 hectoliters per year)—more than twice the volume of the huge, overproducing Clos de Vougeot, and over one-quarter of all the red *grand cru* wine produced in both the Côte de Nuits and Côte de Beaune.

**RED** These wines may sometimes appear intense and broody in their youth, but, when fully mature, a great Corton has such finesse and complexity that it can stun the senses.

🍇 Pinot Noir, Pinot Gris, Pinot Liébault

🍷 12–30 years

**WHITE** A medium- to full-bodied wine with a fine, rich flavor.

🍇 Chardonnay

🍷 10–25 years

✓ *Arnoux Père & Fils* • *Bouchard Père & Fils* • *Chevalier Père & Fils* (Rognet) • *Vincent Girardin* • *Antonin Guyon* • *Louis Jadot* • *Leroy* ❸ • *Bonneau du Martray* • *Faiveley* • *Michel Juillot* • *Prince Florent de Mérode* • *Jacques Prieur* • *Rapet Père & Fils* • *Comte Daniel Senard* • *Tollot-Beaut*

## CORTON-CHARLEMAGNE AOC
### Grand Cru

This famous *grand cru* of Aloxe-Corton extends into Ladoix-Serrigny and Pernand-Vergelesses. Although the best Corton-Charlmagne is incomparable, there is so much produced that consumers can pay a lot of money for relatively disappointing wine. At an average of 25,300 cases (2,280 hectoliters), the production of Corton-Charlemagne represent more than two out of every three bottles of all the *grand cru* white wines produced in both the Côte de Nuits and Côte de Beaune.

**WHITE** At its natural best, this is the most sumptuous of all white Burgundies. It has a fabulous concentration of rich, buttery fruit flavors, a dazzling balance of acidity, and delicious overtones of vanilla, honey, and cinnamon.

🍇 Chardonnay

🍷 5–25 years

✓ *Bertrand Ambroise • Bonneau du Martray • Bouchard Père & Fils • J.-F. Coche-Dury • Joseph Drouhin • Genot-Boulanger • Vincent Girardin • Antonin Guyon • Louis Jadot • Patrick Javillier • Michel Juillot • Louis Latour • Olivier Leflaive • Lucien Lemoine • Jacques Prieur • Rapet Père & Fils • Remoissenet Père & Fils • Christophe Roumier*

## CÔTE DE BEAUNE AOC

Wines that are entitled to the actual Côte de Beaune appellation are restricted to a few plots on the Montagne de Beaune above Beaune itself.

**RED** These are fine, stylish wines that reveal the purest of Pinot Noir fruit. They are produced in the soft Beaune style.

🍇 Pinot Noir, Pinot Gris, Pinot Liébault

🍷 10–20 years

**WHITE** Little-seen, dry basic Beaune.

🍇 Chardonnay, Pinot Blanc

🍷 3–8 years

✓ *Lycée Agricole & Viticole de Beaune*

## CÔTE DE BEAUNE-VILLAGES AOC

While AOC Côte de Nuits-Villages covers red and white wines in a predominantly red-wine district, AOC Côte de Beaune-Villages applies only to red wines in a district that produces the greatest white Burgundies!

**RED** Excellent-value fruity wines, made in true soft Beaune style.

🍇 Pinot Noir, Pinot Gris, Pinot Liébault

🍷 7–15 years

✓ *Bernard Bachelet & Fils • Coron Père & Fils • Lequin Roussot*

## CRIOTS-BÂTARD-MONTRACHET AOC
### Grand Cru

The smallest of Chassagne-Montrachet's three *grands crus*.

**WHITE** This wine has some of the weight of its great neighbors and a lovely hint of honey-and-toast richness, but it is essentially the palest and most fragrant of all the Montrachets.

🍇 Pinot chardonnay (*sic*)

🍷 8–20 years

✓ *d'Auvenay* 🅑 *• Joseph Belland • Blain-Gagnard • Vincent Girardin • Olivier Lam*

## LADOIX AOC

Parts of Ladoix-Serrigny have the right to use the Aloxe-Corton Premier Cru appellation or the *grands crus* of Corton and Corton-Charlemagne. Ladoix AOC covers the rest of the wine produced in the area.

**RED** Many wines are rustic versions of Aloxe-Corton, but there are some fine grower wines that combine the compact fruit and structure of a Nuits with the softness of a Beaune.

🍇 Pinot Noir, Pinot Gris, Pinot Liébault

🍷 7–20 years

**WHITE** Just 5 percent of the production is white and it is not very well distributed.

🍇 Chardonnay, Pinot Blanc

🍷 4–8 years

✓ *Capitain-Gagnerot • Edmond Cornu & Fils • François Gay & Fils • Maurice Martray • Prince Florent de Mérode*

## LADOIX PREMIER CRU AOC

**Premiers crus:** Basses Mourottes, Bois Roussot, Les Buis, Le Clou d'Orge, La Corvée, Les Gréchons, *Hautes Mourottes*, Les Joyeuses, La Micaude, En Naget, *Rognet et Corton*.

These *premiers cru* vineyards were expanded from 35 to 59 acres (14 to 24 hectares) in 2000.

**RED** These wines are decidedly finer in quality and deeper in color than those with the basic village appellation.

🍇 Pinot Noir, Pinot Gris, Pinot Liébault

🍷 7–20 years

**WHITE** Prince Florent de Mérode of de Serrigny makes the only white Ladoix Premier Cru I know: Ladoix Hautes Mourottes blanc.

✓ *Bertrand Ambroise • Capitain-Gagnerot • Edmond Cornu & Fils • Prince Florent de Mérode • Naudin-Ferrand • André Nudant & Fils • G & P Ravaut*

## LADOIX-CÔTE DE BEAUNE AOC
### See Ladoix AOC

Alternative appellation for red wines only.

## MARANGES AOC

In 1989 Maranges AOC replaced three separate appellations: Cheilly-lès-Maranges AOC, Dézize-lès-Maranges AOC, and Sampigny-lès-Maranges AOC, a trio of villages sharing the once moderately famous *cru* of Marange, which is on a well-exposed hillside immediately southwest of Santenay. The red wines may also be sold as Côte de Beaune AOC or Côte de Beaune-Villages AOC. Production used to be erratic, with most of the wine (including much of that qualifying for *premier cru*) sold to *négociants* for blending into Côte de Beaune-Villages, but two or three dedicated growers are beginning to get the name around.

**RED** Wines with a very pure Pinot perfume, which are developing good color and body.

🍇 Pinot Noir, Pinot Gris, Pinot Liébault

🍷 2–7 years

**WHITE** Rarely produced in any of the three villages and never in Dézize-lès-Maranges, as far as I am aware, although it is allowed.

✓ *Fernand Chevrot • Contat-Grange • Jaffelin • René Martin • Edward Monnot • Claude Nouveau*

## MARANGES CÔTE DE BEAUNE AOC

Alternative appellation for red wines only. *See* Maranges AOC.

## MARANGES PREMIER CRU AOC

**Premiers crus:** Clos de la Boutière, La Croix aux Moines, La Fussière, Le Clos des Loyères, Le Clos des Rois, Les Clos Roussots.

Some of these *climats* officially designated as *premiers crus* are a bit of a puzzle. Clos de la Boutière, for example, was originally just plain old La Boutière, and Les Clos Roussots once adjoined a *premier cru* called Les Plantes de Marange, but was never classified as one itself. According to maps prior to the merging of the three appellations, Les Plantes de Marange, Maranges, and En Maranges were the authentic names of the most important vineyards in the area classified as *premier cru*, but they have since adopted less repetitive *lieux-dits*, and such revisionism is probably justified from a marketing aspect.

**RED** The best examples are well colored, with a good balance of fruit, often red fruits, and a richer, longer finish than those wines bearing the basic Maranges appellation.

🍇 Pinot Noir, Pinot Gris, Pinot Liébault

**WHITE** Rarely encountered.

🍇 Chardonnay, Pinot Blanc

✓ *Bernard Bachelet & Fils • Fernand Chevrot • Contat-Grangé • Edward Monnot • Claude Nouveau*

## MEURSAULT AOC

While the greatest white Côte de Beaune is either Montrachet or Corton-Charlemagne, Meursault is probably better known and is certainly more popular.

**RED** This is often treated as a novelty, but it is a fine wine in its own right, with a firm edge.

🍇 Pinot Noir, Pinot Gris, Pinot Liébault

🍷 8–20 years

**WHITE** Even the most basic Meursault should be deliciously dry with a nutty-buttery-spice quality added to its typically rich flavor.

🍇 Chardonnay, Pinot Blanc

🍷 5–12 years

✓ *Robert Ampeau • d'Auvenay* 🅑 *• Pierre Boisson • Bouchard Père & Fils • Boyer-Martenot • Alain Coche-Bizouard • J-F Coche-Dury • Vincent Dancer • Jean-Philippe Fichet • Henri Germain* (Limozin) *• Albert Grivault • Patrick Javillier • François Jobard • Rémy Jobard • Comte Lafon* 🅑 *• Michelot* (any Michelot, hyphenated or otherwise, with a Meursault address) *• François Mikulski • Pierre Morey* 🅑 *• Guy Roulot*

## MEURSAULT PREMIER CRU AOC

*Domaine Bouchard Père & Fils*
2002
**MEURSAULT PERRIÈRES**
APPELLATION MEURSAULT PREMIER CRU CONTRÔLÉE

CE VIN A ÉTÉ RÉCOLTÉ, ÉLEVÉ ET MIS EN BOUTEILLE PAR
**BOUCHARD PÈRE & FILS**
CHÂTEAU DE BEAUNE, CÔTE D'OR, FRANCE
PRODUIT DE FRANCE • PRODUCT OF FRANCE

**Premiers crus:** Aux Perrières, Les Bouchères, Les Caillerets, Les Charmes-Dessous (or Les Charmes-Dessus), Les Chaumes de Narvaux, Les Chaumes des Perrières, Les Cras, Les Genevrières-Dessous (or Les Genevrières-Dessus), Les Gouttes d'Or, La Jeunelotte, Clos des Perrières, Les Perrières-Dessous (or Les Perrières-Dessus), La Pièce sous le Bois, Les Plures, Le Porusot, Les Porusot-Dessous (or Le Porusot-Dessus), Clos des Richemont (or Cras), Les Santenots Blancs, Les Santenots du Milieu, Sous Blagny, Sous le Dos d'Âne.

**RED** Finer and firmer than the basic village wines, these reds need plenty of time to soften.

🍇 Pinot Noir, Pinot Gris, Pinot Liébault

🍷 10–20 years

**WHITE** Great Meursault should always be rich. Their various permutations of nutty, buttery, and spicy Chardonnay flavours may often be submerged by the honey, cinnamon, and vanilla of new oak until considerably mature.

🍇 Chardonnay, Pinot Blanc

🍷 6–15 years

✓ d'Auvenay **B** • Bouchard Père & Fils • Michel Bouzereau & Fils • J.-F. Coche-Dury • Vincent Dancer • Henri Germain • Vincent Girardin • Albert Grivault (Clos des Perrières) • Patrick Javillier • François Jobard • Comte Lafon **B** • Leroy **B** • Martelet de Cherisey (Meursault-Blagny) • Matrot • Mazilly Père & Fils (Les Meurgers) • Michelot (any Michelot, hyphenated or otherwise, with a Meursault address) • Pierre Morey **B** • Alain Patriarche (Les Grands Charrons) • Jacques Prieur • Hubert de Montille (Château de Puligny-Montrachet, Les Pruzots) • Remoissenet Père & Fils • Guy Roulot

## MEURSAULT-BLAGNY PREMIER CRU AOC

**Premiers crus:** La Jeunelotte, La Pièce sous le Bois, Sous Blagny, Sous le Dos d'Âne.

An alternative appellation for Meursault wines from vineyards in the neighboring village of Blagny. The wines must be white, otherwise they claim the Blagny Premier Cru appellation. See Meursault Premier Cru AOC.

## MEURSAULT-CÔTE DE BEAUNE AOC

Alternative red-wine-only appellation for Meursault. See Meursault AOC.

## MEURSAULT-SANTENOTS AOC

This is an alternative appellation for Meursault Premier Cru that comes from a part of the Volnay-Santenots appellation. See Volnay-Santenots AOC.

## MONTHÉLIE AOC

Monthélie's wines, especially the premiers crus, are probably the most underrated in Burgundy. A few years ago there was a silly fuss over whether there should be an accent on the first "e" in Monthélie, and sure enough, a number of very authoritive references differ. The definitive answer—in black and white from the mayor of the village, and the president of the local syndicat for Monthélie—is yes, there should be.

**RED** These excellent wines have a vivid color, expressive fruit, a firm structure, and a lingering, silky finish.

🍇 Pinot Noir, Pinot Gris, Pinot Liébault

🍷 7–15 years

**WHITE** Relatively little white wine is produced.

🍇 Chardonnay, Pinot Blanc

🍷 3–7 years

✓ Eric Boigelot • Denis Boussey • Eric Boussey • J.-F. Coche-Dury • Paul Garaudet • Comte Lafon **B** • Monthélie-Douhairet • Annick Parent

## MONTHÉLIE PREMIER CRU AOC

**Premiers crus:** Le Cas Rougeot, Les Champs Fulliot, Les Duresses, La Château Gaillard, Le Clos Gauthey, Le Meix Bataille, Les Riottes, Sur la Velle, La Taupine, Les Vignes Rondes, Le Village de Monthélie.

**RED** Monthélie's premiers crus are hard to find, but worth the effort.

🍇 Pinot Noir, Pinot Gris, Pinot Liébault

🍷 8–20 years

**WHITE** Paul Garaudet's delicately perfumed Champs-Fulliot blanc is the only white premier cru I have come across.

✓ Eric Boigelot • Denis Boussey (Les Champs Fulliots) • Jehan Changarnier • Gérard Doreau • Paul Garaudet • Château de Monthélie **B** • Annick Parent

## MONTHELIE-CÔTE DE BEAUNE AOC

Alternative appellation for red wines only. See Monthélie AOC.

## LE MONTRACHET AOC

*See* Montrachet AOC

## MONTRACHET AOC

### Grand Cru

Many consider Montrachet to be the greatest dry white wine in the world. On the other hand, I do remember reading somewhere that its flavors can be so intense that it is difficult to know whether it is a joy to drink or whether you are giving your palate an end-of-year exam. It definitely is a joy to drink, but I know what the writer means.

**WHITE** When it is fully mature, Montrachet has the most glorious and expressive character of all dry white wines. Its honeyed, toasty, floral, nutty, creamy, and spicy aromas are simply stunning.

🍇 Pinot Chardonnay (sic)

🍷 10–30 years

✓ Guy Amiot & Fils • Amiot-Bonfils • Bouchard Père & Fils • Chartron et Trebuchet • Marc Colin • Louis Jadot • Comte Lafon **B** • Leflaive **B** • Marquis de Laguiche (made and sold by Joseph Drouhin) • Pierre Morey **B** • Jacques Prieur • de la Romanée-Conti

## PERNAND-VERGELESSES AOC

This village, near Aloxe-Corton, is the most northerly appellation of the Côte de Beaune.

**RED** With the exception of the silky wines recommended below, too many of these are rustic and overrated and would be better off in a négociant Côte de Beaune-Villages blend.

🍇 Pinot Noir, Pinot Gris, Pinot Liébault

🍷 7–15 years

**WHITE** Although this village is famous for its Aligoté, growers such as Jacques Germain

produce smooth, deliciously balanced wines that deserve more recognition.

🍇 Chardonnay, Pinot Blanc

🍷 4–8 years

✓ Denis Père & Fils • P. Dubreuil-Fontaine • Jacques Germain • Olivier Leflaive

## PERNAND-VERGELESSES-CÔTE DE BEAUNE AOC

Alternative appellation for red wines only. See Pernand-Vergelesses AOC.

## PERNAND-VERGELESSES PREMIER CRU AOC

**Premiers crus:** En Caradeux, Creux de la Net, Les Fichots, Île des Hautes Vergelesses, Les Basses Vergelesses.

**RED** These wines repay keeping until the fruit develops a silkiness that hangs gracefully on the wine's structure and gives Pernand's premiers crus the class its village wines lack.

🍇 Pinot Noir, Pinot Gris, Pinot Liébault

🍷 10–20 years

**WHITE** The Beaune firm of Chanson Père & Fils produces a consistent wine of medium body, which is dry but mellow. However, Pavelot is the best white premier cru from this village I have tasted.

🍇 Chardonnay, Pinot Blanc

🍷 4–8 years

✓ Delarche • P Dubreuil-Fontaine • Roger Jaffelin & Fils (Creux de la Net) • Pavelot • Rapet Père & Fils • Rollin Père & Fils

## POMMARD AOC

A very famous village with a "reborn" image built up by a group of dedicated and skillful winemakers.

**RED** The "famous" dark, alcoholic, and soupy wines of Pommard are now mostly a thing of the past, having been replaced by exciting fine wines.

🍇 Pinot Noir, Pinot Gris, Pinot Liébault

🍷 8–16 years

✓ Robert Ampeau • Comte Armand • Billard-Gonnet • Jean-Marc Boillot • Bernard & Louis Glantenay • Leroy **B** • Aleth Leroyer-Girardin • Hubert de Montille • F Parent • Château de Pommard • Vaudoisey-Creusefond (Croix Blanche)

## POMMARD PREMIER CRU AOC

**Premiers crus:** Les Arvelets, Les Bertins, Clos Blanc, Les Boucherottes, La Chanière, Les Chanlins-Bas, Les Chaponnières, Les Charmots, Les Combes-Dessus, Clos de la Commaraine, Les Croix Noires, Derrière St.-Jean, Clos des Epeneaux, Les Fremiers, Les Grands Epenots, Les Jarolières, En Largillière (or Les Argillières), Clos Micot, Les Petits Epenots, Les Pézerolles, La Platière, Les Poutures, La Refène, Les Rugiens-Bas, Les Rugiens-Hauts, Les Saussilles,

Clos de Verger, Village.

**RED** The best *crus* are the various *climats* of Les Rugiens (deep and voluptuous) and Les Epenots (soft, fragrant, and rich).

🌱 Pinot Noir, Pinot Gris, Pinot Liébault

🍷 10–20 years

✓ *Comte Armand (Les Petits Epenots* 🅱*) • Denis Carré • Billard-Gonnet • Jean-Marc Boillot • de Courcel (Les Vaumuriens) • Vincent Dancer • Lejeune • Leroy* 🅱 *• Olivier Leflaive • Catherine et Claude Maréchal • Moissenet-Bonnard (Les Epenots) • Hubert de Montille • Pierre Morey* 🅱 *• Parent • Nicolas Potel • Pothier-Rieusset • de la Pousse d'Or • de la Vougeraie* 🅱

# PULIGNY-MONTRACHET AOC

One of two Montrachet villages producing some of the greatest dry whites in the world.

**RED** Although some fine wines are made, Puligny-Montrachet *rouge* demands a premium for its scarcity.

🌱 Pinot Noir, Pinot Gris, Pinot Liébault

🍷 10–20 years

**WHITE** Basic Puligny-Montrachet from a top grower is a very high-quality wine: full bodied, fine, and steely, requiring a few years to develop a nutty honey-and-toast flavor.

🌱 Chardonnay, Pinot Blanc

🍷 5–12 years

✓ *Robert Ampeau • Jean-Marc Boillot • Louis Carillon & Fils • des Lambrays (Clos du Cailleret) • Leflaive* 🅱 *• Olivier Leflaive • Étienne Sauzet*

## PULIGNY-MONTRACHET PREMIER CRU AOC

***Premiers crus:*** Le Cailleret (or *Demoiselles*), Les Chalumeaux, Champ Canet, Champ Gain, Au Chaniot, Clavaillon, Les Combettes, Ez Folatières, Les Folatières, La Garenne (or Sur la Garenne), Clos de la Garenne, Hameau de Blagny, La Jaquelotte, Clos des Meix, Clos de la Mouchère (or Les Perrières), Peux Bois, *Les Pucelles,* Les Referts, En la Richarde, Sous le Courthil, Sous le Puits, La Truffière.

**RED** I have never encountered any.

🌱 Pinot Noir, Pinot Gris, Pinot Liébault

**WHITE** A *premier cru* Puligny by a top grower such as Étienne Sauzet is one of the most flavor-packed taste experiences imaginable.

🌱 Chardonnay, Pinot Blanc

🍷 7–15 years

✓ *Guy Amiot & Fils • Robert Ampeau • d'Auvenay* 🅱 *• Jean-Marc Boillot • Jean-Claude Boisset • Michel Bouzereau & Fils (Les Champs Gains) • Louis Carillon & Fils • Joseph Drouhin • Louis Jadot (La Garenne) • Leflaive* 🅱 *• Lucien Lemoine • Martelet de Cherisey • Hubert de Montille • Marc Morey • Jacques Prieur • Étienne Sauzet*

# PULIGNY-MONTRACHET-CÔTE DE BEAUNE AOC

Alternative appellation for red wines only. *See* Puligny-Montrachet AOC.

# ST.-AUBIN AOC

This underrated village has many talented winemakers and is an excellent source for good-value wines.

**RED** Delicious, ripe but light, fragrant, and fruity red wines that quickly develop a taste of wild strawberries.

🌱 Pinot Noir, Pinot Gris, Pinot Liébault

🍷 4–8 years

**WHITE** Supervalue white wines—a sort of "Hautes-Côtes Montrachet"!

🌱 Chardonnay, Pinot Blanc

🍷 3–8 years

✓ *Jean-Claude Bachelet • Françoise & Denis Clair • Clerget • Marc Colin • Hubert Lamy & Fils*

## ST.-AUBIN PREMIER CRU AOC

***Premiers crus:*** Le Bas de Gamay à l'Est, Bas de Vermarain à l'Est, Les Castets, Les Champlots, Es Champs, Le Charmois, La Chatenière, Les Combes au Sud, Les Cortons, En Créot, Derrière chez Edouard, Derrière la Tour, Echaille, Les Frionnes, Sur Gamay, Marinot, En Montceau, Les Murgers des Dents de Chien, Les Perrières, Pitangeret, Le Puits, En la Ranché, En Remilly, Sous Roche Dumay, Sur le Sentier du Clou, Les Travers de Marinot, Vignes Moingeon, Le Village, En Vollon à l'Est.

The best of these *premiers crus* are Les Frionnes and Les Murgers des Dents de Chien, followed by La Chatenière, Les Castets, En Remilly, and Le Charmois.

**RED** Very appealing strawberry and oaky-vanilla wines that are delicious young, yet improve further with age.

🌱 Pinot Noir, Pinot Gris, Pinot Liébault

🍷 5–15 years

**WHITE** These dry wines are often superior to the village wines of Puligny-Montrachet and always much cheaper.

🌱 Chardonnay, Pinot Blanc

🍷 4–10 years

✓ *Guy Amiot & Fils • Jean-Claude Bachelet • Clerget • Marc Colin • Vincent Girardin • Hubert Lamy • Olivier Lamy • Patrick Miolane • Bernard Morey • Marc Morey • Henri Prudhon & Fils • Gérard Thomas*

## ST.-AUBIN-CÔTE DE BEAUNE AOC

Alternative appellation for red wines only. *See* St.-Aubin AOC.

# ST.-ROMAIN AOC

A little village amid picturesque surroundings in the hills above Auxey-Duresses.

**RED** Good-value, medium-bodied, rustic reds that have a good, characterful flavor.

🌱 Pinot Noir, Pinot Gris, Pinot Liébault

🍷 4–8 years

**WHITE** Fresh and lively, light- to medium-bodied dry white wines of an honest Chardonnay style.

🌱 Chardonnay, Pinot Blanc

🍷 3–7 years

✓ *Ambroise Bertrand • de Chassorney • Joseph Drouhin • Alain Gras • Thévenin-Monthélie*

## ST.-ROMAIN-CÔTE DE BEAUNE AOC

Alternative appellation for red wines only. *See* St.-Romain AOC.

# SANTENAY AOC

This most southerly village appellation of the Côte d'Or (but not of the Côte de Beaune) is a source of good-value burgundy.

**RED** These wines are fresh and frank, with a clean rendition of Pinot Noir fruit supported by a firm structure.

🌱 Pinot Noir, Pinot Gris, Pinot Liébault

🍷 7–15 years

**WHITE** Only 2 percent of Santenay is white, but some good buys can be found among the top growers.

🌱 Chardonnay, Pinot Blanc

🍷 4–8 years

✓ *Bernard Bachelet & Fils • Roger Belland • Françoise & Denis Clair • Vincent Girardin • Alain Gras • Prieur-Brunet*

## SANTENAY PREMIER CRU AOC

***Premiers crus:*** Beauregard, Le Chainey, La Comme, La Comme Dessus, Clos Faubard, Les Fourneaux, Grand Clos Rousseau, Les Gravières, La Maladière, Clos des Mouches, Passetemps, Petit Clos Rousseau, Clos de Tavannes.

The best are Clos de Tavannes, Les Gravières, La Maladière, and La Comme Dessus.

**RED** In the pure and frank mold of Pinot Noir wines, but with an added expression of *terroir*.

🌱 Pinot Noir, Pinot Gris, Pinot Liébault

🍷 6–15 years

**WHITE** Rarely encountered.

🌱 Chardonnay, Pinot Blanc

🍷 5–10 years

✓ *Roger Belland • Françoise & Denis Clair • Vincent Girardin • Alain Gras (also sold as René Gras-Boisson) • Lecquin-Colin (Vieilles Vignes) • Bernard Morey • Lucien Muzard & Fils • de la Pousse d'Or • Jean-Marc Vincent (Beaurepaire, Passetemps)*

## SANTENAY-CÔTE DE BEAUNE AOC

Alternative appellation for red wines only. *See* Santenay AOC.

## SAVIGNY AOC

*See* Savigny-lès- Beaune AOC

## SAVIGNY PREMIER CRU AOC

*See* Savigny-lès-Beaune Premier Cru AOC

## SAVIGNY-CÔTE DE BEAUNE AOC

Alternative appellation for red wine only. *See* Savigny-lès-Beaune AOC.

## SAVIGNY-LÈS-BEAUNE AOC

This village has gifted winemakers producing very underrated and undervalued wines.

**RED** Delicious, easy-to-drink, medium-bodied wines that are very soft and Beaune-like in style.

🍇 Pinot Noir, Pinot Gris, Pinot Liébault

🍷 7–15 years

**WHITE** Some excellent dry wines with good concentration of flavor, a smooth texture and some finesse, but they are difficult to find.

🍇 Chardonnay, Pinot Blanc

🍷 4–10 years

✓ *Robert Ampeau • Simon Bize & Fils • Bouchard Père & Fils • Camus-Brochon • Philippe Delagrange* (white) *• Maurice Giboulot • Girard-Vollot • Pierre Guillemot • Lucien Jacob • Maréchal-Caillot • Parent • Jean-Marc Pavelot • du Prieuré • Rollin Père & Fils • Tollot-Beaut*

## SAVIGNY-LÈS-BEAUNE PREMIER CRU AOC

**Premiers crus:** Aux Clous, Aux Fournaux, Aux Gravains, Aux Guettes, Aux Serpentières, Bas Marconnets, Basses Vergelesses, Clos la Bataillères (*or* Aux *or* Les Vergelesses), Champ Chevrey (*or* Aux Fournaux), Les Charnières, Hauts Jarrons, Les Hauts Marconnets, Les Jarrons (*or* La Dominode), Les Lavières, Les Narbantons, Petits Godeaux, Les Peuillets, Redrescut, Les Rouvrettes, Les Talmettes

**RED** These wines have a very elegant, soft, and stylish Pinot flavor that hints of strawberries, cherries, and violets. The best are: Les Lavières, La Dominode, Aux Vergelesses, Les Marconnets, and Aux Guettes.

🍇 Pinot Noir, Pinot Gris, Pinot Liébault

🍷 7–20 years

**WHITE** Domaine des Terregelesses produces a splendidly rich, dry Les Vergelesses.

🍇 Chardonnay, Pinot Blanc

🍷 5–15 years

✓ *Simon Bize & Fils • Bouchard Père & Fils • Camus-Brochon • Chandon de Briailles •*

*Chanson Père & Fils • Bruno Clair • Maurice Ecard • François Gay & Fils • Machard de Gramont • A.-F. Gros* (Clos des Guettes) *• Louis Jadot • Leroy* 🅑 *• Albert Morot* (La Bataillère aux Vergelesses) *• Olivier Père & Fils* (Les Peuillets) *• Pavelot • des Terregelesses* (Les Vergelesses) *• Tollot-Beaut*

## SAVIGNY-LÈS-BEAUNE-CÔTE DE BEAUNE AOC

Alternative appellation for red wines only. *See* Savigny-lès-Beaune AOC.

## VOLNAY AOC

Volnay ranks in performance with such great *crus* as Gevrey-Chambertin and Chambolle-Musigny. It is the most southerly red-wine-only appellation in the Côte d'Or, and the only great wine village located above its vineyards.

**RED** These wines are not cheap, but they are firm and well colored with more silky finesse than should be expected from a village appellation.

🍇 Pinot Noir, Pinot Gris, Pinot Liébault

🍷 6–15 years

✓ *Marquis d'Angerville • Michel Lafarge • Régis Rossignol*

## VOLNAY PREMIER CRU AOC

**Premiers crus:** Les Angles, Les Aussy, La Barre, Bousse d'Or (or Clos de la Bousse d'Or), Les Brouillards, En Cailleret, Les Caillerets, Cailleret Dessus (part of which may be called Clos des 60 Ouvrées), Carelles Dessous, Carelle sous la Chapelle, Clos de la Caves de Ducs, En Champans, Chanlin, En Chevret, Clos de la Chapelle, Clos des Chênes (or Clos des Chânes), Clos de Ducs, Clos du Château des Ducs, Frémiets (or Clos de la Rougeotte), La Gigotte, Les Grands Champs, Lassolle, Les Lurets, Les Mitans, En l'Ormeau, Pitures Dessus, Pointes d'Angles, Robardelle, Le Ronceret, Taille Pieds, En Verseuil (or Clos du Verseuil), Le Village.

**RED** No *grands crus*, but its silky-smooth and fragrant *premiers crus* are great wines, showing

tremendous finesse. The best are: Clos des Chêne, Taille Pieds, Bousse d'Or, Clos de Ducs, the various *climats* of Cailleret, Clos des 60 Ouvrées, and En Champans.

🍇 Pinot Noir, Pinot Gris, Pinot Liébault

🍷 8–20 years

✓ *Marquis d'Angerville • Jean-Marc Boillot • Jean-Marc Bouley* (Les Carelles) *• Antonin Guyon • Louis Jadot • Michel Lafarge • Comte Lafon* 🅑 *• Olivier Leflaive • Leroy* 🅑 *• Hubert de Montille • Nicolas Potel • de la Pousse d'Or • Régis Rossignol*

## VOLNAY-SANTENOTS PREMIER CRU AOC

This confusing appellation is in Meursault, not Volnay, although it does run up to the boundary of that village. It dates back to the 19th century, when the Meursault *lieu-dit* of Les Santenots du Milieu became famous for its red wines. White wines cannot be called Volnay-Santenots and must be sold as Meursault or, if produced from the two-thirds of this vineyard farthest from the Volnay border, they may be sold as Meursault Premier Cru AOC or Meursault-Santenots. The right to the Volnay-Santenots appellation was accorded by Tribunal at Beaune in 1924.

**RED** These wines, which are not often found, are similar to Volnay with good color and weight, but can lack its silky elegance.

🍇 Pinot Noir, Pinot Gris, Pinot Liébault

🍷 8–20 years

✓ *Robert Ampeau • Comte Lafon* 🅑 *• Leroy* 🅑 *• Matrot • François Mikulski • Jacques Prieur • Prieur-Brunet*

GRAND CRU VINEYARD CORTON CLOS DES VERGENNES
*The tiny vineyard of Corton Clos des Vergennes is under single ownership and the wines are distributed by Moillard-Grivot.*

# THE CÔTE CHALONNAISE

*This is a simple district in wine terms, with just five appellations, two exclusively white and three red or white. Despite the fact that many of the wines are little known, their quality in all appellations is very good, and the value for money is even better.*

THE CÔTE CHALONNAISE, or Région de Mercurey, as it is sometimes called, was once the forgotten area of Burgundy, perceived as too serious for its own good. Because its flavorsome reds and buttery whites have more in common with the wines of the Côte de Beaune than elsewhere, merchants categorized them as inferior or pretentious. Perhaps the Côte Chalonnaise need not have been forgotten had merchants thought of it more as a superior Mâconnais than as an inferior Côte de Beaune. However, over the last 10 years, as merchants across the world have become more willing to seek out lesser-known wines, the area has built up a reputation as one of Burgundy's best sources of quality wines.

## EXCELLENT NÉGOCIANTS
The Burgundy drinker is blessed with a fine choice of *négociants* in the Côte Chalonnaise, including Chandesais, Delorme, and Faiveley. There is a good *coopérative* at Buxy, and an increasing number of talented growers. This area produces fine Crémant de Bourgogne and, in Bouzeron, has the only single-village appellation of Aligoté wine.

## FACTORS AFFECTING TASTE AND QUALITY

**LOCATION**
These three islands of vines are situated to the west of Châlon-sur-Saône, 217 miles (350 kilometers) southeast of Paris, between the Côte de Beaune in the north and the Mâconnais in the south.

**CLIMATE**
Slightly drier than that of the Côte d'Or, with many of the best slopes protected from the worst ravages of frost and hail.

**ASPECT**
This is a disjointed district in which the great plateau of the Côte d'Or peters out into a complex chain of small hills with vines clinging to the most favorable slopes, at an altitude of between 750 and 1,050 feet (230 to 320 meters), in a far more sporadic fashion than those in the Côte d'Or.

**SOIL**
Limestone subsoil with clay-sand topsoils that are sometimes enriched with iron deposits. At Mercurey there are limestone ooliths mixed with iron-enriched marl.

**VITICULTURE AND VINIFICATION**
The wines are produced in an identical way to those of the Côte de Beaune, with no exceptional viticultural or vinification techniques involved, *see p152*.

**GRAPE VARIETIES**
**Primary varieties:** Pinot Noir, Chardonnay
**Secondary varieties:** Pinot Gris (syn. Pinot Beurot), Pinot Liébault, Pinot Blanc, Aligoté, Melon de Bourgogne, Gamay

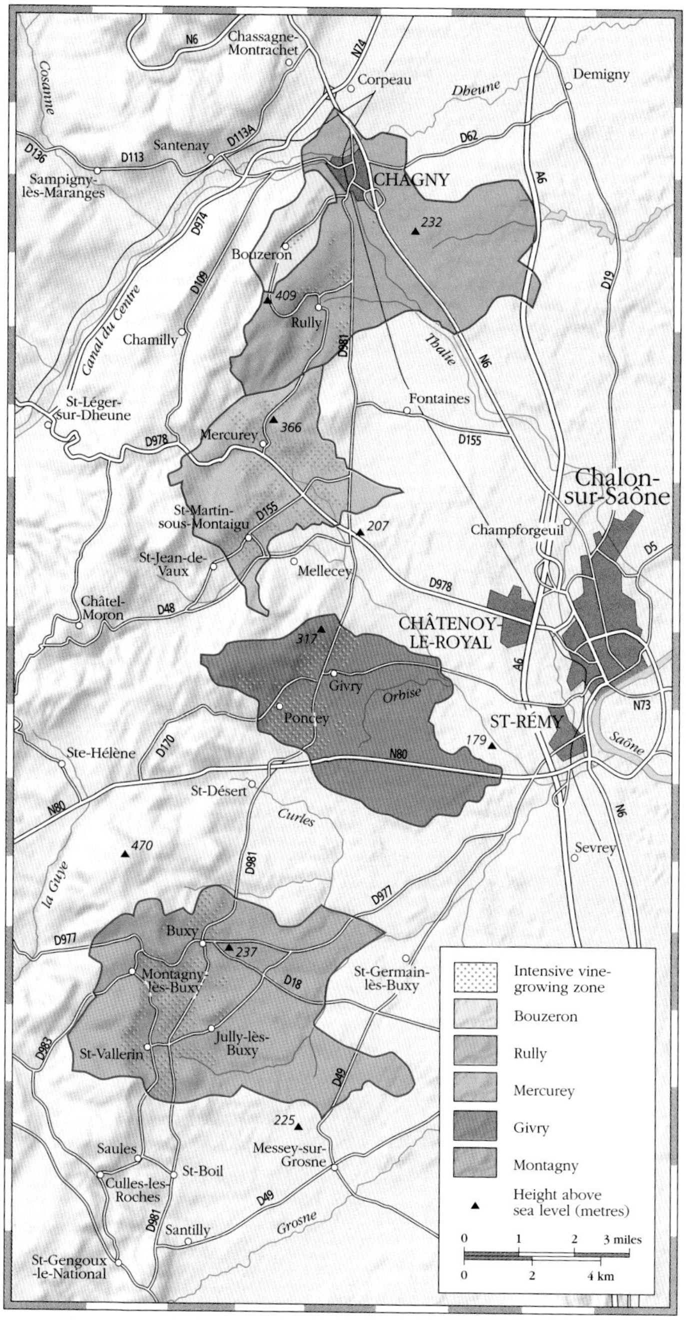

THE CÔTE CHALONNAISE, *see also* p137
*The vine-growing zones form three separate "islands" west of Chalon, between the Côte de Beaune to the north and the Mâconnais to the south.*

Map legend:
- Intensive vine-growing zone
- Bouzeron
- Rully
- Mercurey
- Givry
- Montagny
- ▲ Height above sea level (metres)

## THE APPELLATIONS OF
# THE CÔTE CHALONNAISE

## BOURGOGNE CÔTE CHALONNAISE AOC
As from the 1990 vintage, basic Bourgogne made exclusively from grapes harvested in the region may bear this specific appellation.

**RED** A. & P. de Villaine's Digoine has outstanding fruit and finesse for such a modest appellation.

Only Michel Goubard's Mont-Avril comes close in richness, and can be truly excellent, but is not in the same class. Both are terrific value.
🍇 Pinot Noir, Pinot Liébault, Pinot Gris
⏳ 1–3 years

**WHITE** Normally softer and fuller than a Mâcon, but not particularly rich in fruit, except for A. &

P. de Villaine's Clous, which is the best white wine in the appellation, and Venot's La Corvée, the number two.
🍇 Chardonnay, Pinot Blanc
⏳ Upon purchase

**ROSÉ** Seldom encountered and not special; no reason though why it should not be successful.

🍇 Pinot Noir, Pinot Liébault, Pinot Gris

🍷 Upon purchase

✓ *René Bourgeon • Caves de Buxy • André Delorme • Michel Derain • Michel Goubard (Mont Avril) • Guy Narjoux • Venot (La Corvée) • A. & P. de Villaine* ◉

## BOURGOGNE CÔTES DU COUCHOIS AOC

Although the Côtes du Couchois extends across five communes (Dracy-Lès-Couches, Saint-Jean-de-Trézy, Saint-Maurice-Lès-Couches, Saint-Pierre-de-Varennes, and Saint-Cernin-du-Plain) in addition to Couches itself, at just 50 acres (20 hectares) this appellation is nowhere near as large as the Côte Chalonnaise, which comprises 1,643 acres (665 hectares) of vines. The wines I have tasted (Domaine des Trois Monts, Bichot's Château de Dracy, and Serge Prost), although restricted in number and style (red only, although white and rosé are also permitted), have not been special.

## BOUZERON AOC

In 1979 Bouzeron became the only *cru* to have its own appellation specifically for the Aligoté grape, as Bourgogne Aligoté Bouzeron AOC, and in 1998 achieved full village status.

**WHITE** This excellent and interesting dry wine is much the fullest version of Aligoté available. In weight, fruit, and spice its style is nearer to Pinot Gris than to Chardonnay. The Bouzeron produced by A. & P. de Villaine is a class apart.

🍇 Aligoté

🍷 1–5 years

✓ *Bougeot • Ancien Carnot (sold by Bouchard Père & Fils) • Chanzy Frères • André Delorme • A & P de Villaine* ◉

## GIVRY AOC

Underrated wines from just south of Mercurey.

**RED** Light- to medium-bodied, soft, and fruity wine with delightful nuances of cherry and redcurrant.

🍇 Pinot Noir, Pinot Gris, Pinot Liébault

🍷 5–12 years

**WHITE** Just 10 percent of Givry is white—a deliciously clean, dry Chardonnay that can have an attractive spicy-buttery hint on the aftertaste.

🍇 Chardonnay, Pinot Blanc

🍷 3–8 years

✓ *René Bourgeon • Chofflet-Vaudenaire • Michel Derain • Didier Erker (En Chenèvre) • Mme du Jardin • Joblot • Louis Latour • François Lumpp • Parize Père & Fils (Champ Nalot) • Jean-Paul Ragot • R. Remoissenet & Fils • Baron Thénard*

## GIVRY PREMIER CRU AOC

**Premiers crus:** Clos de la Barraude, Les Berges, Bois Chevaux, Bois Gauthier, Clos de Cellier aux Moines, Clos Charlé, Clos du Cras Long, Les Grandes Vignes, Grand Prétants, Clos Jus, Clos Marceaux, Marole, Petit Marole, Petit Prétants, Clos St.-Paul, Clos St.-Pierre, Clos Salomon, Clos de la Servoisine, Vaux, Clos du Vernoy, En Vignes Rouge, Le Vigron.

**RED** Best examples are medium bodied, soft, rich, and fruity with delightful nuances of cherry and redcurrant.

🍇 Pinot Noir, Pinot Gris, Pinot Liébault

🍷 5–12 years

**WHITE** Similar in character to Givry AOC, the

deliciously clean, dry Chardonnay can have an attractive spicy-buttery hint on the aftertaste.

🍇 Chardonnay, Pinot Blanc

🍷 3–8 years

✓ *René Bourgeon • Chofflet-Vaudenaire • Michel Derain • Mme du Jardin • Joblot • Louis Latour • François Lumpp • Parize & Fils • Jean-Paul Ragot • R. Remoissenet & Fils • Baron Thénard*

## MERCUREY AOC

The wines of Mercurey, including the *premiers crus*, account for two-thirds of the production of the entire Côte Chalonnaise.

**RED** Medium-bodied wines with excellent color and fine varietal character that have an exceptional quality-for-price ratio.

🍇 Pinot Noir, Pinot Gris, Pinot Liébault

🍷 5–12 years

**WHITE** Dry wines that combine the lightness and freshness of the Mâconnais with some of the fatness and butteriness of the Côte de Beaune.

🍇 Pinot Chardonnay (*sic*)

🍷 3–8 years

✓ *Brintet (white Vieilles Vignes) • Château de Chamilly • Louis Desfontaine • Lorenzon • Antonin Rodet*

## MERCUREY PREMIER CRU AOC

**Premiers crus:** La Bondue, Les Byots, La Cailloute, Champs Martins, La Chassière, Le Clos, Clos des Barraults, Clos Château de Montaigu, Clos l'Evêque, Clos des Myglands, Clos du Roi, Clos Tonnerre, Clos Voyens (or Les Voyens), Les Combins, Les Crêts, Les Croichots, Les Fourneaux (or Clos des Fourneaux), Grand Clos Fortoul, Les Grands Voyens, Griffères, Le Levrière, Le Marcilly (or Clos Marcilly), La Mission, Les Montaigus (or Clos des Montaigus), Les Naugues, Les Petits Voyens, Les Ruelles, Sazenay, Les Vasées, Les Velley.

**RED** These *premiers crus* have increased in number from 5 to 27 and in area from 37 to over 250 acres (15 to 100 hectares).

🍇 Pinot Noir, Pinot Gris, Pinot Liébault

🍷 5–15 years

**WHITE** I have encountered white Mercurey only at the basic village level.

✓ *Brintet • Faiveley • Jeannin-Nastet • Émile Juillot • Michel Juillot • Lorenzon • Guy Narjoux • François Raquillet • Antonin Rodet (Château de Chamirey)*

## MONTAGNY AOC

As all the vineyards in this AOC are *premiers crus*, the only wines that appear under the basic village appellation are those that fail to meet the technical requirement of 11.5 percent alcohol before chaptalization.

**WHITE** These dry white wines are good-value, fuller versions of the white Mâcon type.

🍇 Chardonnay

🍷 3–10 years

✓ *Maurice Bertrand & François Juillot • Caves de Buxy • Faiveley • Louis Latour • Antonin Rodet*

## MONTAGNY PREMIER CRU AOC

**Premiers crus:** Les Bassets, Les Beaux Champs, Les Bonnevaux, Les Bordes, Les Bouchots, Le Breuil, Les Burnins, Les Carlins,

Les Champs-Toiseau, Les Charmelottes, Les Chandits, Les Chazelles, Clos Chaudron, Le Choux, Les Clouzeaux, Les Coères, Les Combes, La Condemine, Cornevent, La Corvée, Les Coudrettes, Les Craboulettes, Les Crets, Creux des Beaux Champs, L'Epaule, Les Garchères, Les Gouresses, La Grand Pièce, Les Jardins, Les Las, Les Males, Les Marais, Les Marocs, Les Monts Cuchots, Le Mont Laurent, La Mouillère, Moulin l'Echenaud, Les Pandars, Les Pasquiers, Les Pidans, Les Platières, Les Resses, Les St.-Mortille, Les St-Ytages, Sous les Roches, Les Thilles, La Tillonne, Les Treufferes, Les Varignys, Le Vieux Château, Vignes Blanches, Vignes sur le Clou, Les Vignes Couland, Les Vignes Derrière, Les Vignes Dessous, La Vigne Devant, Vignes Longues, Vignes du Puits, Les Vignes St.-Pierre, Les Vignes du Soleil.

With every one of its 60 vineyards classified as *premier cru*, Montagny is unique among the villages of Burgundy.

**WHITE** These delicious dry wines have a Chardonnay flavor that is more akin to that of the Côte de Beaune than it is to Mâconnais.

🍇 Chardonnay

🍷 4–12 years

✓ *Stéphane Aladame • Arnoux Père & Fils • Caves de Buxy • Château de Davenay (white) • Maurice Bertrand & François Juillot • Château de la Saule • Jean Vachet*

## RULLY AOC

The Côte Chalonnaise's northernmost appellation produces wines that are closest in character to those from the southern Côte de Beaune.

**RED** Delightfully fresh and fruity wines of light to medium body and some finesse which are uncomplicated when young but develop well.

🍇 Pinot Noir, Pinot Gris, Pinot Liébault

🍷 5–12 years

**WHITE** Serious dry wines that tend to have a crisper balance than wines made farther south in Montagny, although a few can be quite fat.

🍇 Chardonnay

🍷 3–8 years

✓ *Chanzy Frères • André Delorme • Joseph Drouhin • Raymond Dureuil-Janthial • de Folie • des Fromanges • H et P Jacqueson • de la Renard • Antonin Rodet (Château de Rully)*

## RULLY PREMIER CRU AOC

**Premiers crus:** Agneux, Bas de Vauvry, La Bressaude, Champ-Clou, Chapitre, Clos du Chaigne, Clos St.-Jacques, Les Cloux (or Cloux), Ecloseaux, La Fosse, Grésigny, Margotey (or Margoté), Marissou, Meix-Caillet, Mont-Palais, Moulesne (or Molesme), Phillot, Les Pieres, Pillot, Préau, La Pucelle, Raboursay (or Rabourcé), Raclot, La Renarde, Vauvry.

**RED** Fine-quality, medium-bodied wines with a silky texture added to the summer-fruit flavor.

🍇 Pinot Noir, Pinot Gris, Pinot Liébault

🍷 5–15 years

**WHITE** Generally finer, fuller, and richer dry wines, many with excellent finesse.

🍇 Chardonnay

🍷 4–12 years

✓ *Belleville • Jean-Claude Brelière • Michel Briday • André Delorme • de Folie • Vincent Girardin • H et P Jacqueson • Laborde-Juillot • Albert Sounit*

# THE MÂCONNAIS

*The Mâconnais produces three times more white wine than the rest of Burgundy put together and, although it never quite matches the high quality achieved in the Côte d'Or, its best producers make the world's greatest-value pure Chardonnay wines.*

THE MÂCONNAIS IS AN ANCIENT viticultural area that was renowned as long as 1,600 years ago when Ausonius, the Roman poet of St.-Émilion, mentioned its wines. Today, it makes sense to couple it with the Beaujolais because, while Chardonnay is the dominant white grape in both districts (as it is in the rest of Burgundy), the Gamay is the dominant black grape, which it is not elsewhere; this forms a link between the two. The Mâconnais can be seen as essentially a white-wine producing area, while the Beaujolais is almost entirely red.

## MÂCON ROUGE—A RELIC OF THE PAST?

Although the Mâconnais is a white-wine district in essence, some 25 percent of the vines planted here are in fact Gamay; and a further 7.5 percent are Pinot Noir. The Gamay does not, however, perform very well on the limestone soils of the Mâconnais, and

## FACTORS AFFECTING TASTE AND QUALITY

Situated halfway between Lyon and Beaune, the vineyards of the Mâconnais adjoin those of the Côte Chalonnaise to the north and overlap with those of Beaujolais to the south.

### CLIMATE
The climate is similar to that of the Côte Chalonnaise, but with a Mediterranean influence gradually creeping in toward the south, so occasional storms are more likely.

### ASPECT
The soft, rolling hills in the north of the Mâconnais, which are a continuation of those in the Côte Chalonnaise, give way to a more closely knit topography with steeper slopes and sharper contours becoming increasingly prominent as one travels farther south into the area that overlaps the Beaujolais.

### SOIL
The topsoil consists of scree and alluvium, or clay and clay-sand, and covers a limestone subsoil.

### VITICULTURE AND VINIFICATION
Some exceptional wines (such as the "Vieilles Vignes" Château de Fuissé made in Pouilly Fuissé) can stand a very heavy oak influence, but most of the white wines are fermented in stainless steel and bottled very early to retain as much freshness as possible. The red wines are vinified by *macération carbonique*, either fully or in part.

### GRAPE VARIETIES
**Primary varieties:** Chardonnay, Gamay
**Secondary varieties:** Pinot Noir, Pinot Gris (*syn.* Pinot Beurot), Pinot Liébault, Pinot Blanc, Aligoté, Melon de Bourgogne

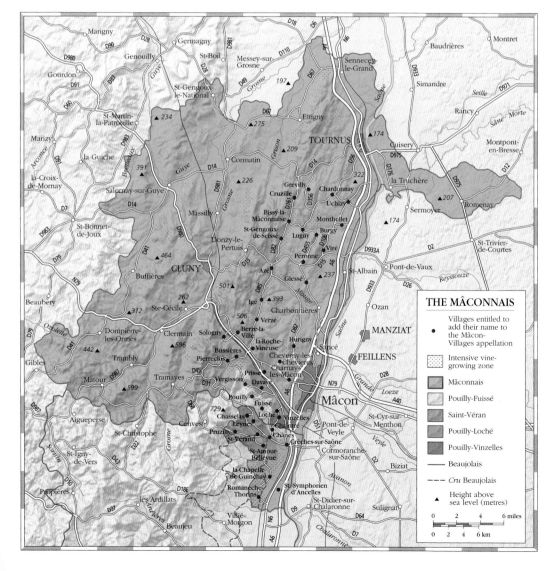

THE ROCK OF SOLUTRÉ
*The dramatic shape of the Rock of Solutré towers over the village's vineyard. Solutré is one of the 42 villages of the Mâcon-Villages appellation, and a commune of Pouilly-Fuissé.*

THE MÂCONNAIS
*See also p137*
*Concentrated to the west of the river Saône, the famous appellations of the Mâconnais interlace with those of Beaujolais to the south and spread out over the area northwest of itself.*

THE MÂCONNAIS

- Villages entitled to add their name to the Mâcon-Villages appellation
- Intensive vine-growing zone
- Mâconnais
- Pouilly-Fuissé
- Saint-Véran
- Pouilly-Loché
- Pouilly-Vinzelles
- Beaujolais
- Cru Beaujolais
- ▲ Height above sea level (metres)

0    2    4    6 miles
0  2  4  6 km

despite the smoothing effect of modern vinification techniques, these wines will always be of rustic quality with a characteristic hard edge. I well remember a blind tasting I once organized as editor of *The Sunday Telegraph Good Wine Guide*. All that the tasters knew was that the wines were produced from the Gamay grape and were thus most probably Beaujolais. British Master of Wine Christopher Tatham simply wrote "Limestone's the trouble!" about one wine. It turned out to be the only non-Beaujolais wine; it was Mâcon Rouge, which meant that limestone was indeed the problem. Such an accurate observation under blind conditions highlights how inappropriate the Gamay is in the Mâconnais.

It is possible to make a pure Pinot Noir Mâcon *rouge*, but because the market assumes that this appellation is pure Gamay, there is little incentive for producers to plant the more noble grape. It is, however, far more suitable and capable of producing wines of some finesse in the limestone vineyards of the Mâconnais. Perhaps it is time to introduce a Mâcon Rouge Pinot Noir appellation, or maybe producers should print the grape variety boldly on the label of the existing appellation?

BERZÉ-LE-CHÂTEL, SAÔNE-ET-LOIRE, MÂCONNAIS
*The massive fortifications of Berzé-le-Châtel, the seat of the first feudal barony of Mâcon, boast 13 medieval towers.*

# THE APPELLATIONS OF
# THE MÂCONNAIS

## MÂCON AOC

Most wines from this district-wide appellation are produced in the area north of the Mâcon-Villages area.

**RED** Better vinification techniques have improved these essentially Gamay wines, but Gamay is still a grape that does not like limestone.

🍇 Gamay, Pinot Noir, Pinot Gris

🍷— 2–6 years

**WHITE** These are basic-quality Chardonnay wines that are also fresh, frank, tasty, and dry; easy to drink and superb value. They may be sold as *primeur* or *nouveau* from the third Thursday of November following the harvest.

🍇 Chardonnay, Pinot Blanc

🍷— 1–4 years

**ROSÉ** These lightweight wines have an attractive, pale raspberry color and light fruit flavor, and are more successful than their counterparts. They may be sold as *primeur* or *nouveau* from the third Thursday of November after the harvest.

🍇 Gamay, Pinot Noir, Pinot Gris

🍷— 1–3 years

🍷 *Bénas Frères* • *E. Brocard* (red) • *Desvignes* • *des Deux Roches* (Pierreclos red & Chavigne red) • *Maurice Gonon* (red) • *Guffens-Heynen* • *Jean Thévenet* • *Henri Lafarge* (Braye red) • *Saumaize-Michelin* (Les Bruyères red) • *Valette*

## MÂCON SUPÉRIEUR AOC

All of France's so-called "*Supérieur*" appellations merely demand extra alcohol (usually one degree more than the basic appellation), which does not necessarily make a superior wine.

**RED** Aside from those listed, these well-colored, medium-bodied wines are nothing special.

🍇 Gamay, Pinot Noir, Pinot Gris

🍷— 3–8 years

**WHITE** It is curious that almost a quarter of Mâcon Supérieur is white. The wines could just

as easily sell as Mâcon AOC plain and simple. These wines may be sold as *primeur* or *nouveau* from the third Thursday of November following the harvest.

🍇 Chardonnay, Pinot Blanc

🍷— 1–4 years

**ROSÉ** These are attractively colored wines with a fresh and tasty fruit flavor.

🍇 Gamay, Pinot Noir, Pinot Gris

🍷— 1–2 years

🍷 *Paul Beaudet* (Terres Rouges) • *Père Tienne* (Elevé en Fût)

## MÂCON-SUPÉRIEUR (VILLAGE NAME) AOC
### *See* Mâcon (village name) AOC

## MÂCON-VILLAGES AOC

This white-only appellation covers 41 villages, 8 of which also fall within the Beaujolais-Villages appellation (*see* p.167); four of these have the additional right to the Saint-Véran AOC (*see* p.164). If the wine comes from a single village, it may replace the "Villages" part of this appellation with the name of that specific village (*see* the list below for details of all 41 villages).

**WHITE** These are some of the world's most delicious, thirst-quenching, easy-drinking, dry Chardonnay wines. They also represent tremendous value. These wines may be sold as *primeur* or *nouveau* commencing from the third Thursday of November following the harvest.

🍇 Chardonnay, Pinot Blanc

🍷— 1–4 years

🍷 **Mâcon-Villages** (*without a named village*) Gonon • *René Michel* (Vieilles Vignes)

## THE 41 VILLAGES OF MÂCON-VILLAGES

The single-village version of Mâcon-Villages AOC covers the white wines from 41 villages (originally 43 villages, but Mâcon-Clessé and Mâcon-Viré were replaced by Viré-Clessé in 1999, *see* Viré-Clessé AOC):

## MÂCON-AZÉ AOC

This village has a good *coopérative*, and its wines a reputation for fatness and consistency.

🍷 *Cave d'Azé* (Cuvée Jules Ricard) • *Georges Blanc* (d'Azenay) • *des Grand Bruyères* • *Duvergey-Taboureau* (de la Garonne)

## MÂCON-BERZÉ-LE-CHÂTEL AOC

The only wine I have tasted here has been Paul Beaudet's Château de Berzé.

## MÂCON-BERZÉ-LE-VILLE AOC

I have not encountered these wines.

## MÂCON-BISSY-LA-MÂCONNAISE AOC

Rijckaert's delicious wine is the only Mâcon-Bissy-La-Mâconnaise I have encountered.

🍷 *Jean Rijckeart*

## MÂCON-BURGY AOC

I have very rarely encountered these wines, but elegant examples from de Chervin demonstrate its potential.

🍷 *de Chervin* • *Verget*

## MÂCON-BUSIÈRES AOC

Rarely encountered.

🍷 *du Terroir de Jocelyn*

## MÂCON-CHAINTRE AOC

Chaintre is home to Georges Duboeuf's older brother, Roger. Since this village is one of five that form the appellation of Pouilly-Fuissé, its wines are entitled to two appellations.

🍷 *Cave Coopérative de Chaintre* • *Roger Duboeuf* • *des Granges* • *Valette*

## MÂCON-CHÂNES AOC

This village is also part of the Beaujolais-Villages and Saint-Véran areas, so its wines have a choice of three appellations.

🍷 *de Lalande* (Les Serraudières)

## MÂCON-LA CHAPELLE-DE-GUINCHAY AOC

This village is also part of the Beaujolais-Villages area and its wines therefore have the right to both appellations.

## MÂCON-CHARDONNAY AOC

These wines have a certain following due in part, no doubt, to the novelty of their name. The *coopérative*, however, produces fine wines.

✓ *Cave de Lugny* (L'Originel)

## MÂCON-CHARNAY-LÈS-MÂCON AOC

Excellent wines produced east of Pouilly-Fuissé.

✓ *E. Chevalier & Fils • Jean Manciat • Manciat-Poncet • Didier Tripoz* (Clos des Tournons)

## MÂCON-CHASSELAS AOC

Unfortunately, Chasselas is also the name of a table grape known for producing inferior wines, thus growers here usually sell their wines as basic Mâcon or as Saint-Véran. The only Mâcon-Chasselas I have come across was a decent, but not special red wine from Château de Chasselas.

## MÂCON-CHEVAGNY-LÈS-CHEVRIÈRES AOC

Reasonable wines, but not easy to find.

✓ *Groupement de Producteurs de Prissé*

## MÂCON-CLESSÉ AOC

This appellation lapsed as of 2002. *See* Viré-Clessé AOC.

## MÂCON-CRÈCHES-SUR-SAÔNE AOC

I have not encountered these wines.

## MÂCON-CRUZILLE AOC

These are rare wines from a tiny hamlet in the extreme north of the *villages* appellation area.

✓ *Demessy* (Château de Messy) • *Guillot-Broux* **B**

## MÂCON-DAVAYÉ AOC

Some excellent wines are made here, although they are usually sold as Saint-Véran AOC.

✓ *des Deux Roches • Lycée Viticole de Davayé*

## MÂCON-FUISSÉ AOC

This village is one of five communes that form Pouilly-Fuissé AOC.

✓ *Cordier • de Fussiacus • Yves Giroux • Le Moulin du Pont • La Soufrandise • Jean-Paul Thibert*

## MÂCON-GRÉVILLY AOC

A village with a good reputation, Mâcon-Grévilly is located in the extreme north of the

*villages* appellation area.

✓ *Guillot-Broux* **B**

## MÂCON-HURIGNY AOC

I have not encountered these wines.

## MÂCON-IGÉ AOC

The wines from this village are not very often seen, but have a good reputation.

✓ *Les Vignerons d'Igé*

## MÂCON-LEYNES AOC

This village is also part of the Beaujolais-Villages and Saint-Véran AOCs and its wines therefore have a choice of all three appellations.

✓ *André Depardon*

## MÂCON-LOCHÉ AOC

This village also has the right to the Pouilly-Loché and Pouilly-Vinzelles AOCs, and its wines therefore have a choice of all three appellations.

✓ *Caves des Grands Crus Blancs • Château de Loché*

## MÂCON-LUGNY AOC

Louis Latour has done much to promote the wines of this village.

✓ *Louis Latour • Cave de Lugny • du Prieuré*

## MÂCON-MILLY-LAMARTINE AOC

Dominique Lafon makes a delicious Milly-Lamartine, particularly from the Clos du Four.

✓ *Comte Lafon* **B**

## MÂCON-MONTBELLET AOC

Rarely encountered wines that develop well after a couple of years in bottle.

✓ *Henri Goyard* (de Roally) • *Jean Rijckaert* (En Pottes Vieilles Vignes)

## MÂCON-PÉRONNE AOC

These wines seem to be fuller on the nose and stronger on the palate than those of most villages, but with less charm, although their producers say this is because they take longer than most Mâcon to "come around."

✓ *Maurice Josserand • de Lanques* (Les Berthelots) • *des Légères • Cave de Lugny • du Mortier • Daniel Rousset*

## MÂCON-PIERRECLOS AOC

Guffens-Heynen is by far the best producer here.

✓ *Guffens-Heynen • Henri de Villamont*

## MÂCON-PRISSÉ AOC

This village is also part of the Saint-Véran area and its wines therefore have a choice of two appellations.

✓ *Groupement de Producteurs de Prissé • de Thibert Père & Fils*

## MÂCON-PRUZILLY AOC

This village is situated in the Beaujolais-Villages area and its wines therefore have a choice of two appellations.

## MÂCON-LA ROCHE VINEUSE AOC

These underrated wines of Mâcon-La Roche Vineuse are produced on west- and south-facing slopes north of Pouilly-Fuissé, the potential of which is pushed to the very limits by Olivier

Merlin, one of Mâcon's greatest winemakers.

✓ *Olivier Merlin • Groupement de Producteurs de Prissé • Verget*

## MÂCON-ROMANÈCHE-THORINS AOC

The village of Mâcon-Romanèche-Thorins is also part of the Beaujolais-Villages area, so its wines have a choice of two appellations. Most of its production is red.

## MÂCON-SOLOGNY AOC

The village of Mâcon-Sologny lies just north of Pouilly-Fuissé AOC and produces a fresh, crisp, herbaceous wine.

✓ *Ets Bertrand • Cave de Sologny*

## MÂCON-SOLUTRÉ AOC

This village is one of the five communes of Pouilly-Fuissé and also forms part of the Saint-Véran area. Its wines therefore have a choice of three appellations.

✓ *André Depardon • Jean-Michel & Béatrice Drouhin • Chantal & Dominique Vaupré*

## MÂCON-ST.-AMOUR-BELLEVUE AOC

Mâcon-St.-Amour Bellevue is a village famous for its *cru* Beaujolais St.-Amour and also forms part of the Beaujolais-Villages and Saint-Véran areas. Some of its vineyards therefore have a choice of four appellations and this one is the least appealing.

## MÂCON-ST.-GENGOUX-DE-SCISSÉ AOC

I have not encountered these wines.

## MÂCON-ST.-SYMPHORIEN-D'ANCELLES AOC

As Mâcon-St.-Symphorien-d'Ancelles is also part of the Beaujolais-Villages area, its wines therefore have the advantage of a choice between two appellations.

## MÂCON-ST.-VÉRAND AOC

This village is in an area that is also part of the Beaujolais-Villages and the similarly spelled Saint-Véran areas and its wines therefore have a choice of all three appellations.

## MÂCON-UCHIZY AOC

More commonly seen than a few years ago, the wines from this village, which is adjacent to Chardonnay, are usually of a good, thirst-quenching quality.

✓ *Raphaël et Gard Sallet* (Clos des Ravières) • *Paul & Philebert Talmard*

## MÂCON-VERGISSON AOC

This village of Mâcon-Vergisson is one of five communes that form the Pouilly-Fuissé AOC. Its wines are richer than most, and can be aged a few years in bottle.

✓ *Daniel Barraut • Michel Forest • Verget*

## MÂCON-VERZÉ AOC

Rarely encountered.

✓ *du Clos Gandin*

## MÂCON-VINZELLES AOC

This village also has the right to Pouilly-Vinzelles AOC and its wines therefore have a choice of two appellations.

✓ *Caves des Crus Blancs*

## MÂCON-VIRÉ AOC

This appellation is due to lapse as of 2002. *See* Viré-Clessé AOC.

## MÂCON (VILLAGE NAME) AOC

This appellation differs from the Mâcon-Villages AOC above (which may attach a village name and has to be white) in that it covers a slightly larger range of villages, the names of which must (rather than may) be indicated on the label, and it applies only to red and rosé wines. In addition to 41 villages listed under the white-only Mâcon-Villages appellation, the full list for this sister AOC also includes Boyer, Bray, Bresse sur Grosne, Champagny-sous-Uxelles, Champlieu, Etrigny, Jugy, Laives, Mancey, Montceaux-Ragny, Nanton, Quintaine, Sennecey-le-Grand, Serrières, and Vers.

**RED** There is some indication that a few growers with isolated plots of vines growing in favorable soils within a few villages can make better-balanced wines than the Gamay has hitherto been expected to produce in Mâcon.

🍇 Gamay, Pinot Noir, Pinot Gris

**ROSÉ** I have not encountered these wines.

🍇 Gamay, Pinot Noir, Pinot Gris

✓ *Jean-Michel Combier* (Serrières) • *Michel Guillemot* (Quintaine) • *Henri Lafarge* (Bray) • *Thierry Morot* (Pierreclos Vieilles Vignes) • *Jean-Claude Thevenet* (Quintaine)

## PINOT CHARDONNAY-MÂCON AOC

This is an alternative appellation for white Mâcon. *See* Mâcon AOC.

## POUILLY-FUISSÉ AOC

This pure Chardonnay wine should not be confused with Pouilly-Fumé, the Sauvignon Blanc wine from the Loire. This appellation covers a wide area of prime vineyards, but there is considerable variation.

**WHITE** These dry wines range from typical Mâcon *blanc* style, through slightly firmer versions, to the power-packed, rich oaky flavors of Michel Forest and Vincent's Château Fuissé Vieilles Vignes. Although these last two are widely regarded as the finest in Pouilly-Fuissé, they are by no means typical of Mâcon, leaning more toward the Côte Chalonnaise, sometimes even the Côte de Beaune, and ardent admirers of the more traditional, light, and fluffy Mâcon will not even touch them. On the other hand, wines from producers such as Guffens-Heynen can be just as rich and intense as either Forest or Château Fuissé, but without any oak whatsoever.

🍇 Chardonnay

🍷 3–8 years

✓ *Daniel et Martine Barraud* • *Cordier* •

VILLAGE OF FUISSÉ SURROUNDED BY ITS VINEYARDS
*Fuissé, which dates back to Neanderthal settlements, sits at the center of an amphitheater of vineyards.*

*Nadine Ferrand* (Prestige) • *Des Gerbeaux* (Cuvée Jacques Charvet) • *Guffens-Heynen* • *Jeandeau* (Terre Jeanduc) • *Roger Lassarat* • *Pascal Rollet* (Clos de la Chapelle) • *Jean Rijckaert* • *Thibert Père & Fils* (Vignes de la Cote) • *Pierre Vessigaud* (Vieilles Vignes) • *Valette* • *Verget* • *Vincent & Fils* (Château de Fuissé Vieilles Vignes)

## POUILLY-LOCHÉ AOC

One of Pouilly-Fuissé's two satellite appellations.

**WHITE** This village may produce Mâcon-Loché AOC, Pouilly-Loché AOC, or Pouilly-Vinzelles AOC. The dry wines of this village are more of the Mâcon style, whatever the AOC.

🍇 Chardonnay

🍷 1–4 years

✓ *Louis Jadot* (Château de Loché) • *Cordier*

## POUILLY-VINZELLES AOC

One of Pouilly-Fuissé's two satellite appellations.

**WHITE** More the Mâcon-type of Pouilly-Fuissé, for similar reasons to those of Pouilly-Loché.

🍇 Chardonnay

🍷 1–4 years

✓ *La Soufrandière* (X Taste) • *Thibert Père & Fils* (aka Thibert-Parisse) • *Valette* • *Verget*

## SAINT-VÉRAN AOC

This appellation overlaps the Mâconnais and Beaujolais districts, and is itself bisected by the Pouilly-Fuissé AOC, with two villages to the north (Davayé and Prissé) and five to the south (Chânes, Chasselas, Leynes, Saint-Amour, and Saint-Vérand). Saint-Véran was named after Saint-Vérand, but the "d" was dropped in deference to the growers in certain other villages, who it was feared would not support the new appellation if they felt their wines were

being sold under the name of another village. This appellation was introduced in 1971 to provide a more suitable outlet for white wines produced in Beaujolais than the Beaujolais Blanc appellation.

**WHITE** Excellent value, fresh, dry, and fruity Chardonnay wines that are very much in the Mâcon-Villages style. Vincent, the proprietor of Château Fuissé, produces an amazingly rich wine that is far closer to Pouilly-Fuissé than to Macon-Villages, with hints of oak and honey.

🍇 Chardonnay

🍷 1–4 years

✓ *Daniel et Martine Barraud* • *Cordier* • *Pierre Janny* • *Roger Lassarat* • *Michel Paquet* (Cuvée Hors Class) • *Jean Rijckaert* • *Verget*

## VIRÉ-CLESSÉ AOC

This appellation was created in February 1999, by combining the Mâcon-Viré and Mâcon-Clessé subappellations, and recognizing the wines from Viré-Clessé in their own right, above and beyond those of Mâcon-Villages. The appellation was retrospectively applied to the 1998 vintage, but producers could continue using either of the original two AOCs up to and including the 2002 vintage. Viré was always the most ubiquitous of the Mâcon-Villages wines, but it was also the most consistent and one of the best, while Clessé showed the most finesse. The regulations are slightly stricter in terms of syield, with an increased minimum natural sugar content for wines bearing a *lieu-dit* name.

🍇 Chardonnay

🍷 1–4 years

✓ All those recommended under Mâcon-Viré and Mâcon-Clessé are potential recommendations here, but those that have actually excelled are:
*André Bonhomme* • *Jean Rijckaert* (L'Epinet) • *La Soufrandière* (Les Plantes) • *Jean Thévenet* • *Verget* (Vieilles Vignes) • *Cave de Viré* (Cuvée Spéciale)

# THE BEAUJOLAIS

*This huge district is famous for producing the only Gamay wine to gain classic status—a purple-colored, fresh, light, and quaffing wine that accounts for almost half of all the Burgundy produced each year.*

THE BEST PRODUCERS in the 10 *crus* Beaujolais make a Gamay wine that truly deserves its classic status. Basic Beaujolais, however, should be simply fresh, purple-colored, juicy-fruit wine. The problem is that most Beaujolais falls short of even these basic standards: the majority of it, including bad *cru* Beaujolais, smells of bubble gum or bananas and tastes of pear drops. The trade calls it "lollipop" wine and it is ideal for anyone who does not actually enjoy the characteristics of real wine.

The factors that make most Beaujolais the lollipop wine it is are the method of vinification and the sheer volume of production—the grape variety has nothing to do with it. A massive amount of Beaujolais is produced each year: two-and-a-

HARVESTING IN FLEURIE
*To encourage semicarbonic maceration, the Gamay grapes must arrive at the cuverie in whole bunches, on their stalks, and as uncrushed as possible.*

half times the entire red- and white-wine production of the rest of Burgundy put together! More than half is sold only a few weeks after the harvest as Beaujolais Nouveau or Primeur and all of this, plus a great chunk of Beaujolais, Beaujolais Supérieur, and Beaujolais-Villages, not to mention rip-off *cru* Beaujolais, is made by semicarbonic maceration (a variant of *macération carbonique*, see p.00), which creates a preponderance of the same chemical compounds (amyl acetate and ethyl acetate) that give bubble gum, bananas, and pear drops their trademark aroma. This process also creates the pungent aroma of nail polish, of which some of the worst Beaujolais Nouveau can smell, although I

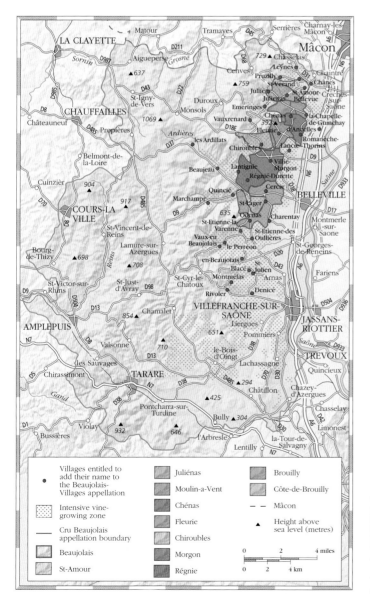

Villages entitled to add their name to the Beaujolais-Villages appellation

Intensive vine-growing zone

Cru Beaujolais appellation boundary

Beaujolais

St-Amour

Juliénas

Moulin-a-Vent

Chénas

Fleurie

Chiroubles

Morgon

Régnié

Brouilly

Côte-de-Brouilly

— — Mâcon

▲ Height above sea level (metres)

0    2    4 miles
0    2    4 km

THE BEAUJOLAIS, *see also* p137
*Forming the southernmost part of the Burgundy region, the Beaujolais area is planted almost entirely with Gamay vines, the best vineyards being on granite soil.*

## FACTORS AFFECTING TASTE AND QUALITY

**LOCATION**
Beaujolais, the most southerly of Burgundy's districts, is located in the Rhône *département*, 250 miles (400 kilometers) southeast of Paris.

**CLIMATE**
Beaujolais has an essentially sunny climate tempered by the Atlantic and Mediterranean, as well as by continental influences. Although the annual rainfall and temperature averages are ideal for winegrowing, they are subject to sudden stormy changes due to the influence of the Mediterranean.

**ASPECT**
A hilly district where vines grow at between 500 and 2,000 feet (150 to 550 meters) on slopes facing all points of the compass.

**SOIL**
The northern Beaujolais, which encompasses the famous *crus* and those communes entitled to the Beaujolais-Villages AOC, is an area renowned for its granite-based soil, the only type on which the Gamay has so far excelled. The topsoils are often schistous or comprised of decomposed granite mixed with

sand and clay. The southern section is essentially limestone-based and this is a problem for the Gamay grape, which accordingly produces much lighter wines, which lack the class of those in the north.

**VITICULTURE AND VINIFICATION**
The vines are trained and pruned to the Gobelet system (*see* p.00), which gives them a totally different appearance from those in the rest of Burgundy. Grapes are hand-harvested and undergo whole-bunch fermentation by semicarbonic maceration, which encourages the accumulation of carbon dioxide in the top half of the vat, although *cru* Beaujolais are more traditionally produced, have greater skin contact (around seven days as opposed to just two days for Beaujolais Nouveau), and may be matured with some new oak.

**GRAPE VARIETIES**
**Primary varieties**: Gamay
**Secondary varieties**: Chardonnay, Pinot Noir, Pinot Gris (*syn.* Pinot Beurot), Pinot Liébault, Pinot Blanc, Aligoté, Melon de Bourgogne

## THE LEGEND OF "PISSE VIEILLE"

The vineyard of Pisse Vieille in Brouilly amuses English-speaking consumers, who are dismayed by those writers who dare only to print the vineyard's story in French. It goes like this:

One day, an old woman called Mariette went to confession. The priest was new to the village and unaware of its dialect. He also did not know that Mariette was hard of hearing. When he heard her confession, he merely said "Allez! Et ne péchez plus!" ("Go! And do not sin again!"). Mariette misheard this as "Allez! Et ne piché plus!"—which in the dialect meant "Go! And do not piss again!" (*piché* being the local form of *pisser*). Being a devout Catholic, Mariette did exactly as she was told. When her husband asked what terrible sin she had committed she refused to tell and, after several days, he went to ask the new priest. When he found out the truth he hurried home, and as soon as he was within shouting distance, began yelling "Pisse, vieille!" ("Piss, old woman!").

## VIN DE MERDE OR "THE SHIT WINE CASE"

After 1,100,000 cases (100,000 hectoliters) of Beaujolais had to be distilled in 2001, a French wine critic by the name of François Mauss claimed in *Lyon Mag*, a small French magazine, that poor-quality Beaujolais of this ilk was "not proper wine, but rather a sort of lightly fermented and alcoholic fruit juice." No wonder they could not sell it. Mauss blamed the need for distillation on the craze for Beaujolais Nouveau, which is rushed to market barely two months after the harvest. Beaujolais producers, he claimed, had ignored all warning signs that consumers were no longer willing to buy such wine, which he branded as *vin de merde* or "shit wine," and the proverbial hit the fan.

Even though this description was not the assessment of *Lyon Mag per se*, but a quote from someone being interviewed, and despite the fact that the publication balanced these comments with those of a Beaujolais representative defending the wine, an association of 56 Beaujolais cooperative producers decided to sue the magazine, not for libel, but under a rarely used French law that protects products from being denigrated. A cynic might ask why these producers did not feel able to sue for libel, but even more disturbing is the fact that a modern-day court in a supposedly civilized society could actually find what this magazine published to be illegal in any way. But it did, and more disturbingly, the court (in Villefranche-sur-Saône, the heart of Beaujolais country) considered this quote to be so serious a wrongdoing that it ordered *Lyon Mag* to pay $350,000, which for such a small, employee-owned publication would have put it out of business. On appeal, this was reduced to $113,000 and, after a backlash of bad publicity around the world, the Beaujolais cooperatives decided not to pursue any damages, just their costs, which amounted to $2,800.

At the time of writing, *Lyon Mag* was planning to appeal on a point of principle, and was intent on taking it all the way to the European Court of Human Rights if necessary. If the association of 56 cooperative producers started this case to protect the reputation of Beaujolais Nouveau, it clearly achieved the opposite result, since its reputation has been dealt a more severe blow by the worldwide coverage of "The Shit Wine Case." If the cooperatives don't like wine critics describing Beaujolais Nouveau as crap, they should make it delicious and fruity to drink. Is that too much to ask?

hasten to add that it is not harmful. The amount of antipathy, even in Burgundy, to this style of Gamay is revealed by Anthony Hanson, who, in his book *Burgundy*, quotes Jean-Marie Guffens as describing the fermentation method used in much Beaujolais as "carbonic masturbation."

The profit generated by Beaujolais Nouveau is considerable, but the wine itself should not be taken too seriously by anyone. No producer of Beaujolais Nouveau claims it is a fine wine. Such a claim would destroy the carefully marketed image of a young, unpretentious wine intended to be consumed in copious quantities. Beaujolais Nouveau should be fun and used to promote a greater awareness of wine *per se*, just as Liebfraumilch can attract new wine drinkers, although readers should be aware that these "lollipop" wines are not good-quality Gamay, whereas the best *crus* of Beaujolais are the world's greatest Gamay wines.

## THE APPELLATIONS OF
# THE BEAUJOLAIS

## BEAUJOLAIS AOC

This generic Beaujolais appellation accounts for half the wine produced in the district and more than half of this is sold as Beaujolais "Primeur." The basic quality of these wines means that they cannot be bought from the great *négociants* of the Côte d'Or, although *cru* Beaujolais can be.

**RED** Due to their method of vinification, most of these wines have a "pear-drop" character to their fruitiness. The best also have a delightful freshness and frankness that beg for the wine to be consumed in large quantities.

🍇 Gamay, Pinot Noir, Pinot Gris

🍷 1–3 years

**WHITE** Less than half of one percent of the production of this basic appellation consists of dry white wine, and the specialized producers of this usually make very fine wines. Pierre Charmet's Beaujolais *blanc* is aromatic and peachy.

🍇 Chardonnay, Aligoté

🍷 1–3 years

**ROSÉ** Fresh, "pretty," and fruity.

🍇 Gamay, Pinot Noir, Pinot Gris

🍷 1–3 years

✓ *Jean-Paul Brun* (Terres Dorées) • *Jean-Jacques Martin* (white) • *Cave Sain-Bel* (Les Bruyères) • *Cave Saint-Vérand* (Vieilles Vignes) • *Terres Morel* • *Vissoux* (Traditionnelle)

## BEAUJOLAIS NOUVEAU AOC
*See* Beaujolais Primeur AOC

## BEAUJOLAIS PRIMEUR AOC

More than half of all the Beaujolais produced is sold as *vin de primeur*, a wine made by intensive semicarbonic maceration methods that enable it to be consumed in export markets from the third Thursday of each November. "Beaujolais Nouveau" is synonymous with "Beaujolais Primeur" and the former is the name more often seen on export market labels, while the latter is more popular on the French market itself. Beaujolais Nouveau is supposed to be a fun wine, but the merrymaking wears a bit thin when it smells like nail polish and tastes of bubble gum. What else can you expect from something that was swinging from the vine just a few weeks before? "Lollipop" wine is how it is known in the trade. There is no such thing as good-quality Beaujolais Nouveau, and that is "official." While organizing tastings for the preparation of the 2005 revised edition of this book, the Union Interprofessionnelle des Vins du Beaujolais (UIVB) conveyed to me that it was eager to assist. One of the challenges I gave the UIVB was to show me, if such wines existed, a serious-quality Beaujolais Nouveau from a producer with a successful track record with this style, rather than the exception. Of all the wines the UIVB submitted for my consideration, there was not one Beaujolais Nouveau or Primeur. It was not as if it were bad timing, as the UIVB had the 2003 vintage to choose from, and that was supposed one of the best vintages ever for *nouveau*. The only conclusion I can draw is that even the local authorities think there is no such thing as good-quality Beaujolais Nouveau. The regulation for this AOC should be totally overhauled, or the wine should be banned altogether. If the regulations are overhauled, then the one thing that must be tackled above everything else is the method of production. With today's technology, there are numerous ways to make a serious-quality red wine drinkable within weeks without inducing the pear-drop aroma of full-scale carbonic maceration. As one of several tools, carbonic maceration can have a positive effect, but its use has to be restricted to no more than 10 to 20 percent of the wine, so that the grape is allowed to express itself (many consumers unwittingly believe that pear drops are the varietal aroma of Gamay!). If the authorities and, ultimately, producers are not willing to take this on, then Beaujolais Nouveau will continue being a joke, and not a very funny one at that. For real Beaujolais and great Gamay, then readers must be prepared to pay for the wines recommended under any of the other appellations.

## BEAUJOLAIS SUPÉRIEUR AOC

Only 1 percent of all Beaujolais wines carry this appellation. It is very rare to find a

Beaujolais Supérieur that is superior in anything other than strength to basic Beaujolais AOC, since this appellation merely indicates that the wines contain an extra 1 percent alcohol. Red and rosé Beaujolais Supérieur may be sold as *primeur* or *nouveau* from the third Thursday of November following the harvest.

**RED** By no means superior to Beaujolais AOC—buy basic Beaujolais for fun or *cru* Beaujolais for more serious drinking.

🍇 Gamay, Pinot Noir, Pinot Gris

🍷 3–8 years

**WHITE** Barely 5 percent of this tiny appellation produces white wine. Fine as it may be, it has no intrinsic superiority over the quaffing quality of basic Beaujolais *blanc*.

🍇 Chardonnay, Aligoté

🍷 1–3 years

**ROSÉ** I have not encountered any pink versions of this appellation.

✓ *Cave Beaujolais du Bois-d'Oingt* • *Cave Saint-Vérand*

## BEAUJOLAIS-VILLAGES AOC

The 38 villages that may add their names to the Beaujolais AOC (*see* Beaujolais [village name] AOC) also have the right to this appellation and must use it if the wine is a blend of wines from two or more villages.

**RED** If you find a good example, these wines are well coloured with a rich Gamay flavor and should have all the superiority that Beaujolais Supérieur wines mysteriously lack.

🍇 Gamay, Pinot Noir, Pinot Gris

🍷 3–8 years

**WHITE** Very little encountered, but more Villages *blanc* is produced than Beaujolais *blanc*. These wines may be sold as *primeur* or *nouveau* from the third Thursday of November following the harvest.

🍇 Chardonnay, Aligoté

🍷 1–3 years

**ROSÉ** Seldom encountered, but the Cave Beaujolais du Bois-d'Oingt makes an attractive wine. These wines may be sold as *primeur* or *nouveau* from the third Thursday of November following the harvest.

🍇 Gamay, Pinot Noir, Pinot Gris

🍷 1–3 years

✓ *Accoeur* • *Philippe Deschamps* • *des Duc* • *Stephane Gardette* • *Jean-Claude Lapalu* (Vieilles Vignes) • *Manoir du Pavé* • *Sermezy* • *Michel Tête* (Clos du Fief)

## BEAUJOLAIS (VILLAGE NAME) AOC

Of the 38 villages that may add their names to this appellation, very few do. One reason is that all or part of 15 of these villages (asterisked below) qualify for one of the superior *cru* Beaujolais appellations and it makes no sense to use a less famous name to market the wines. Another is that eight of the villages are entitled to the Mâcon-Villages AOC (marked "M") and four of these are also within the St.-Véran AOC (*see also* p.164), marked "S.-V.," which overlaps with Mâconnais and Beaujolais; some of these villages, of course, produce more white wine than red. These village names are also underexploited because,

apart from a few that are famous (the best wines of which will claim *cru* Beaujolais status), the rest are either unknown or more suggestive of Mâcon than Beaujolais, thus it is easier to sell them as nothing more specific than Beaujolais-Villages. The wines may be sold as *primeur* or *nouveau* from the third Thursday of November following the harvest.

The following is a complete list of villages that may use the appellation: Arbuisonnas; Les Ardillats; Beaujeu; Blacé; Cercié*; Chânes (M., S.-V.); La Chapelle-de-Guinchay* (M.); Charentay; Chénas; Chiroubles*; Denicé; Durette; Emeringes*; Fleurie*; Jullié*; Juliénas*; Lancié; Lantignié; Leynes (M., S.-V.); Marchampt; Montmelas; Odenas; Le Perréon; Pruzilly* (M.); Quincié*; Régnié*; Rivolet; Romanèche-Thorins* (M); St-Amour-Bellevue* (M., S.-V.); St.-Étienne-des-Ouillères; St.-Étienne-la Varenne*; St.-Julien; St.-Lager; St.-Symphorien-d'Ancelles (M.); St.-Vérand (M., S.-V.); Salles; Vaux; Vauxrenard; Villié-Morgon*

**RED** When you find good examples, they should be richly flavored Gamay wines that are similar in quality to nonspecific Beaujolais-Villages, but with more personality.

🍇 Gamay, Pinot Noir, Pinot Gris

🍷 3–8 years

**WHITE** I have rarely encountered these wines.

🍇 Chardonnay, Aligoté

🍷 1–3 years

**ROSÉ** Rarely encountered, and uninspiring when they are.

🍇 Gamay, Pinot Noir, Pinot Gris

🍷 1–3 years

## BROUILLY AOC
### Cru Beaujolais

The largest and most southerly of the 10 *cru* villages, this is the only one, with Côte de Brouilly, to permit grapes other than Gamay.

**RED** Most Brouilly are serious wines, even if they do not rank among the best *cru* Beaujolais. They are not quite as intense as Côte de Brouilly wines, but they are full, fruity, and supple, if a little earthy. They should be rich and can be quite tannic.

🍇 Gamay, Chardonnay, Aligoté, Melon de Bourgogne

🍷 2–7 years (4–12 years for *vin de garde* styles produced in the very best vintages)

✓ *de la Chanaise* (Château du Prieuré) • *Daniel Guillet* • *Jean-Claude Lapalu* (Vieilles Vignes) • *Joseph Pellerin* • *Château Thivin*

## CHÉNAS AOC
### Cru Beaujolais

The smallest of the *cru* Beaujolais, situated on the slopes above Moulin-à-Vent. These slopes used to be occupied by oak trees, and so its

name derives from *chêne*, the French for oak.

**RED** Although most Chénas cannot match the power of the wines from neighbouring Moulin-à-Vent, they are nevertheless in the full and generous mold, and wines made by gifted growers such as Jean Benon and Champagnon are seductively rich and powerful, the former oaked, the latter not.

🍇 Gamay

🍷 3–8 years (5–15 years for *vin de garde* styles produced in the very best vintages)

✓ *Jean Benon* (especially Vieillis en Fût de Chêne) • *Champagnon* • *des Duc* (Chante Grilles) • *Hubert Lapierre* (Vieilles Vignes)

## CHIROUBLES AOC
### Cru Beaujolais

Situated high in the hills above the Beaujolais plain, the terrace of Chiroubles produces the most fragrant of all the *cru* Beaujolais.

**RED** These light-bodied wines have a perfumed bouquet and a deliciously delicate, crushed-grape flavor. They are charming to drink when young, but exceptional examples can improve with age.

🍇 Gamay

🍷 1–8 years (5–15 years for *vin de garde* styles produced in the very best vintages)

✓ *Alain Passot* • *Bernard Métrat* • *Céline & Gilles Méziat* (Petit Puits) • *Maison des Vignerons de Chiroubles* (Cuvée Vidame de Rocsain) • *Château de Raousset*

## CÔTE DE BROUILLY AOC
### Cru Beaujolais

If there were such things as *grands crus* in Beaujolais, Côte de Brouilly would undoubtedly be classified as the *grand cru* of Brouilly (the vineyards of which practically surround those of this appellation).

**RED** A fine Côte de Brouilly is full, rich, and flavorsome. Its fruit should be vivid and intense, with none of the earthiness that may be found in a Brouilly.

🍇 Gamay, Pinot Noir, Pinot Gris

🍷 3–8 years (5–15 years for *vin de garde* styles produced in the very best vintages)

✓ *Jean-Paul Brun* (Terres Dorées) • *Georges Duboeuf* • *Franchet* • *Griffon* • *Château Thivin* (especially Cuvée Zacharie) • *Bernadette et Gilles Vincent*

## COTEAUX DU LYONNAIS AOC

This is not part of the true Beaujolais district, but it falls within its sphere of influence and certainly utilizes classic Beaujolais grapes. In May 1984, this wine was upgraded from VDQS to full AOC status.

**RED** Light-bodied wines with fresh Gamay fruit and a soft balance. These wines may be sold as *primeur* or *nouveau* from the third Thursday of November following the harvest.

🍇 Gamay

⌛ 2–5 years

**WHITE** Fresh and dry Chardonnay wine that is softer than a Mâcon and lacks the definition of a Beaujolais *blanc*. These wines may be sold as *primeur* or *nouveau* from the third Thursday of November following the harvest.

🍇 Chardonnay, Aligoté

⌛ 1–3 years

**ROSÉ** I have not encountered these wines.

✓ *Ris Descotes* (blanc) • *de Prapin* (blanc) • *Clos du Saint-Marc*

## FLEURIE AOC
### Cru Beaujolais

The evocatively named Fleurie is the most expensive of the *crus* and its finest wines are the quintessence of classic Beaujolais.

**RED** The wines of Fleurie quickly develop a fresh, floral, and fragrant style. Not as light and delicate as some writers suggest, their initial charm belies a positive structure and a depth of fruit that can sustain the wines for many years.

🍇 Gamay

⌛ 2–8 years (4–16 years for *vin de garde* styles produced in the very best vintages)

✓ *Christian Bernard* • *Michel Chignard* • *Jean-Marc Despres* (Cuvée Spéciale Vieilles Vignes) • *Georges Duboeuf* (Château des Bachelards, Prestige) • *de la Madone* • *Bernard Métrat* • *Alain Passot* • *Vissoux* (Garants)

## JULIÉNAS AOC
### Cru Beaujolais

Situated in the hills above St.-Amour, Juliénas is named after Julius Caesar and, according to local legend, was the first Beaujolais village to be planted. It is probably the most underrated of the 10 Beaujolais *crus*.

**RED** The spicy-rich, chunky-textured fruit of a youthful Juliénas will develop a classy, satin-smooth appeal if given time to develop in bottle.

🍇 Gamay

⌛ 3–8 years (5–15 years for *vin de garde* styles produced in the very best vintages)

✓ *Mme Ernest Aujas* • *Jean Benon* • *François Condemine* • *J. M. Coquenlorge* • *Georges Duboeuf* (La Trinquée) • *Château de Juliénas* • *Henri Lespinasse* • *Cellier de la Vieille Église* (Cuvée fût de chêne)

## MORGON AOC
### Cru Beaujolais

Just as the Côte de Brouilly is a finer and more concentrated form of Brouilly, so the wines of Mont du Py in the center of Morgon are far more powerful than those of the surrounding vineyards in this commune.

**RED** Although these wines are variable in character and quality, the best of them rank with those of Moulin-à-Vent as the most sturdy of all Beaujolais. They have a singularly

penetrating bouquet and very compact fruit.

🍇 Gamay

⌛ 4–9 years (6–20 years for *vin de garde* styles produced in the very best vintages)

✓ *Aucoeur* • *Daniel Bouland* • *Jean-Marc Burgaud* • *de la Chanaise* • *de la Chaponne* • *François Condemine* • *Louis-Claude Desvignes* • *Donzel* (Cuvée Prestige) • *Foillard* • *J Gonard & Fils* • *Marcel Lapierre* • *Jacques Lespinasse* (Maupas) • *Michel Tête* (Clos du Fief)

## MOULIN-À-VENT AOC
### Cru Beaujolais

Because of its sheer size, power, and reputation for longevity, Moulin-à-Vent is known as the "King of Beaujolais." The exceptionally powerful character of Moulin-à-Vent has been attributed to the high manganese content of its soil. The availability of manganese to the vine's metabolic system depends on the pH of the soil, and in the acid, granite soil of Beaujolais, manganese is all too readily available. For a healthy metabolism, however, the vine requires only the tiniest trace of manganese, so its abundance at Moulin-à-Vent could be toxic (to the vine, that is, not the consumer!), may well cause chlorosis, and would certainly affect the vine's metabolism. This naturally restricts yields and could alter the composition of the grapes produced.

**RED** These well-colored wines have intense fruit, excellent tannic structure, and, in many cases, a spicy-rich oak flavor.

🍇 Gamay

⌛ 4–9 years (6–20 years for *vin de garde* styles produced in the very best vintages)

✓ *Christian Bernard* • *de la Chanaise* • *Château de Chénas* • *Desperrier Père & Fils*

(Clos de la Pierre) • *Georges Duboeuf* (Carquelin, Prestige, Rosiers) • *Gay-Coperet* • *Château des Jacques* (lieu-dit cuvées only) • *Paul Janin* (Clos du Tremblay) • *Château du Moulin-à-Vent* (Cuvée Exceptionnelle) • *du Visoux* (Rochegès, Rochelles)

## RÉGNIÉ AOC
### Cru Beaujolais

The growers claim this village was the first to be planted with vines in Beaujolais, but so do the growers of Juliénas. Régnié was upgraded to full *cru* Beaujolais status in December 1988. Too many half-hearted efforts nearly sank the ship while it was being launched, but the best growers are gradually carving a reputation for this fledgling *cru*.

**RED** There are two distinct styles of red wine here: one is light and fragrant, the other much fuller and more meaty, but all the best examples are fruity and supple, showing a fresh, invigorating aroma.

🍇 Gamay

⌛ 2–7 years (4–12 years for *vin de garde* styles produced in the very best vintages)

✓ *Lydie et Lucien Grandjean* • *Jacky Gauthier* • *Les Petit Pierres* • *Michel Rampon & Fils*

## ST.-AMOUR AOC
### Cru Beaujolais

This is the most northerly of the 10 *crus*, and is more famous for its Mâcon wines than for its *cru* Beaujolais. Despite its modern-day connotations, St.-Amour has nothing to do with love, but derives from St.-Amateur, a Roman soldier who was converted to Christianity and founded a monastery in the locality.

**RED** Charming wines of fine color, seductive bouquet, and soft, fragrant, fruity flavor. They will also repay a little aging.

🍇 Gamay

⌛ 2–8 years (4–12 years for *vin de garde* styles produced in the very best vintages)

✓ *des Duc* (especially Cuvée Saint Valentin) • *Jean-Marc Monnet* (Chataignier Durand) • *André Poitevin* • *Michel Tête* • *Georges Trichard*

BARRELS AND FLOWERS AT ST.-AMOUR, BEAUJOLAIS
*Just five* cru *Beaujolais were originally classified in 1936 (Chénas, Chiroubles, Fleurie, Morgon, and Moulin-à-Vent), a further three (Brouilly, Côte de Brouilly, and Juliénas) in 1938, while St.-Amour became the ninth* cru *in 1946 and Régnié the tenth in 1988.*

# CHAMPAGNE

*If you have become accustomed to the quality and character of good Champagne, there really are few other sparkling wines that will satisfy you—and when you do find one to rival Champagne, it will be just as expensive as the real thing.*

NO OTHER VINE-GROWING region can challenge Champagne's claim to produce the world's greatest sparkling wine because no other area resembles this viticultural twilight zone where the vine struggles to ripen grapes each year. In order to produce a truly great sparkling wine in the classic *brut* sense, the grapes must be harvested with a certain balance of richness, extract, and acidity, which can be achieved only through the long-drawn-out ripening process that occurs when the vine is grown on a knife-edge between success and failure. The Champagne *terroir*, which includes a cold, sometimes mean, northern climate and lime-rich chalk soil, is the key to the wine's intrinsic superiority, yet if such an area were to be discovered today, modern wine experts would quickly dismiss it as unsuitable for viticulture, thus economically unsound for winemaking.

## A SPECIFIC WINE, NOT A STYLE

Champagne is not a generic term for any sparkling wine but the protected name of a sparkling wine produced from grapes grown within a specific, legally defined area of northern France.

In Europe and various countries throughout the world, strict laws ensure that only true Champagne may be sold under the name "Champagne," but this principle is not respected in a number of places. The most blatant misuse in the developed world is in the US, although the Americans are not entirely to blame, since the *Champenois* have stubbornly refused even to consider a compromise, such as "Champagne-style." Considering this intransigence and the fact that for many years some of the most powerful Champagne houses have sold the sparkling wines they produce in South America under the name "Champaña," which is Spanish for Champagne, the *Champenois* deserve the treatment they get in the US. In 1985, the term *méthode champenoise* was

AUTUMNAL VIEW OF VILLEDOMMANGE
*The premier cru vineyards of Villedommange completely surround the village, which is located in the Petite Montagne, a few miles southwest of Reims. Pinot Meunier reigns supreme, although the Pinot Noir, shown above, accounts for 30 percent of the vines grown.*

banned for all wines produced or sold in the European Economic Community (now the European Union). The term, while not a guarantee, had proved useful for separating the wheat from the chaff, since the quality of the product must warrant the cost of fermenting in bottle. Now consumers have to look for linguistic variations along the *méthode traditionnelle* or *classique* theme. In addition, there are Crémant AOCs in France, Cava DO in Spain, as well as new terms (for example Talento in Italy), which crop up all the time.

## THE FIVE MAJOR DISTRICTS

There are five major districts in Champagne, and each produces numerous base wines that differ distinctly within a region as well as between regions. When these wines are blended in various proportions, many contrasting styles are produced. The best way to appreciate regional influences is to seek out grower-producer Champagnes.

### MONTAGNE DE REIMS
The vineyards of the northern *montagne* face north and would not ripen grapes but for the fact that the *montagne* itself is a free-standing formation, which allows the chilled night air to slip down the slopes on to the plain, to be replaced by warmer air from a thermal zone that builds up above the *montagne* during the day.

The vines here generally produce darker-colored, bigger-bodied wines than those from the southern *montagne*, which often have a deeper flavor, a more aromatic character, and greater finesse.
**Primary grape variety** Pinot Noir
**Best villages** Ambonnay, Aÿ-Champagne, Bouzy, Verzenay, Verzy

### CÔTE DES BLANCS
The name of this area is derived from its almost exclusive cultivation of white Chardonnay grapes. The wines produced from these grapes have become the most sought-after wines in the whole of Champagne. They contribute finesse and delicacy yet they mature to an unequaled intensity of flavor.
**Primary grape variety** Chardonnay
**Best villages** Cramant, Avize, le Mesnil-sur-Oger

### VALLÉE DE LA MARNE
Essentially easy-drinking, fruity, and forward wines produced from an extremely high proportion of Pinot Meunier, which is cultivated in the frost-prone valley vineyards due to its late bud-break and early ripening.
**Primary grape variety** Pinot Meunier
**Best villages** Mareuil-sur-Aÿ (for Pinot Noir), Dizy and Hautvillers (for both Pinot Noir and Pinot Meunier), Cumières, Leuvrigny, and Ste-Gemme (for Pinot Meunier)

### THE AUBE
Ripe, fruity wines are produced in this southern part of Champagne, which is closer to Chablis than to the classic vineyards of the Marne. The wines are better in quality than those of the outer areas of the Vallée de la Marne around Château-Thierry.

**Primary grape variety** Pinot Noir
**Best village** les Riceys Arrivey-Lingey

### CÔTE DE SÉZANNE
The Sézannais is a rapidly developing area 10 miles (16 kilometers) southwest of the Côte des Blancs. Like its neighbor, the Sézannais favors Chardonnay, but its wines are fruitier, with less finesse, than those of the Côte des Blancs, and can be quite exotic and musky. These wines are ideal for people who enjoy New World sparkling wines but may have difficulty coming to terms with the more classic style of Champagne.
**Primary grape variety** Chardonnay
**Best villages** Bethon, Villenauxe-la-Grande

**CHAMPAGNE,** *see also* p.55
*In the European Union, only
those wines produced within
the delimited Champagne
AOC region may be called
Champagne. It is the most
northerly wine-producing
region of France.*

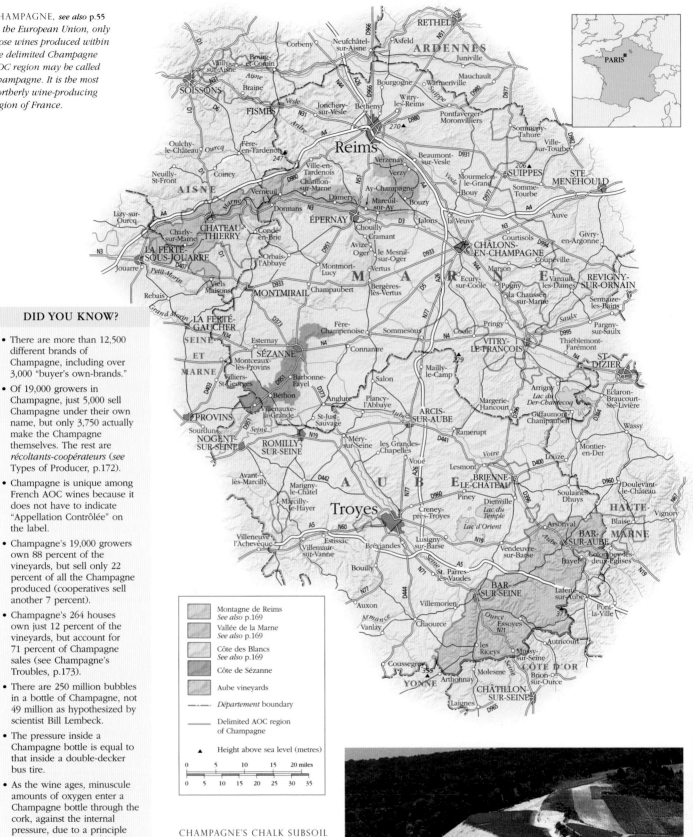

## DID YOU KNOW?

- There are more than 12,500 different brands of Champagne, including over 3,000 "buyer's own-brands."

- Of 19,000 growers in Champagne, just 5,000 sell Champagne under their own name, but only 3,750 actually make the Champagne themselves. The rest are *récoltants-coopérateurs* (*see* Types of Producer, p.172).

- Champagne is unique among French AOC wines because it does not have to indicate "Appellation Contrôlée" on the label.

- Champagne's 19,000 growers own 88 percent of the vineyards, but sell only 22 percent of all the Champagne produced (cooperatives sell another 7 percent).

- Champagne's 264 houses own just 12 percent of the vineyards, but account for 71 percent of Champagne sales (see Champagne's Troubles, p.173).

- There are 250 million bubbles in a bottle of Champagne, not 49 million as hypothesized by scientist Bill Lembeck.

- The pressure inside a Champagne bottle is equal to that inside a double-decker bus tire.

- As the wine ages, minuscule amounts of oxygen enter a Champagne bottle through the cork, against the internal pressure, due to a principle known as exchange of gases.

- The chalk bed that surfaces in Champagne's Côte des Blancs is contiguous with the seam of chalk that extends westward, beneath Paris, to emerge as the White Cliffs of Dover in the UK.

|  | Montagne de Reims *See also* p.169 |
| --- | --- |
|  | Vallée de la Marne *See also* p.169 |
|  | Côte des Blancs *See also* p.169 |
|  | Côte de Sézanne |
|  | Aube vineyards |

·—·—· *Département* boundary

———— Delimited AOC region of Champagne

▲ Height above sea level (metres)

```
0    5    10    15    20 miles
0   5  10  15  20  25  30  35
```

CHAMPAGNE'S CHALK SUBSOIL
*This subsoil is part of a seabed that
dried up 65 million years ago and is
part of the same bed of chalk as the
White Cliffs of Dover. It was formed
by the slow accumulation of coccoliths,
a calcareous matter secreted by sea
organisms. It took 1,000 billion
coccoliths to produce each cubic inch
of this pure-white chalk.*

# FACTORS AFFECTING TASTE AND QUALITY

### ⬡ LOCATION
This most northerly of the AOC wine regions of France lies some 90 miles (145 kilometers) northeast of Paris, and is separated from Belgium by the forested hills of the Ardennes. Four-fifths of the region is in the Marne, and the balance is spread over the Aube, Aisne, Seine-et-Marne, and the Haute-Marne.

### ▨ CLIMATE
This cold and wet northern climate is greatly influenced by the Atlantic, which has a cooling effect on its summer and makes the seasons generally more variable. Its position at the northern edge of the winemaking belt stretches the duration of the vine's growth cycle to the limit, making frost a major problem during spring and fall.

### ◿ ASPECT
Vineyards are planted on the gently rolling east- and southeast-facing slopes of the Côte des Blancs at altitudes of 380 to 640 feet (120 to 200 meters). On the slopes of the Montagne de Reims (a plateau) the vines grow at altitudes similar to those on the Côte. The best valley vineyards lie in sheltered situations on the right bank of the Marne.

### ▦ SOIL
The vineyards of the Côte des Blancs, Montagne de Reims, Marne Valley, and Côte de Sézanne are all situated on a porous chalk subsoil up to 960 feet (300 meters) thick, which is covered by a thin layer of drift derived in various proportions from sand, lignite, marl, loam, clay, and chalk rubble. The pure-white chalk in Champagne's soil drains well, yet retains enough water for the vines to survive a drought. The chalk's high active lime content encourages the vines to produce grapes that have relatively high acid when they become ripe.

### ▥ VITICULTURE AND VINIFICATION
Jacquesson is leading the way to improve quality from the ground up, operating a very expensive form of viticulture, from cover-cropping to plowing, leaving off herbicides, short pruning, double-debudding, and so on. This house is the first Champagne grower to train Pinot Noir and Meunier on a permanent cordon, as opposed to employing a replacement branch, and growing the vines much closer together to restrict the branch length. This means fewer fruiting canes, but entails a lot more work to improve exposure and ventilation. The resultant grapes actually looked like grapes even in the obscenely huge, largely rotten, and underripe 2001

vintage, something that not many others managed to achieve. No mechanical harvesting is allowed, hence the entire Champagne crop is gathered by hand. Picking usually starts around mid-October. Contrary to popular belief, the grapes are not early-picked, but are on average picked two weeks later than Bordeaux. In exceptional years the harvest has commenced as early as August and as late as November. Rain invariably interrupts the flowering, resulting in at least two crops, although the second, known in *champenois* as the *bouvreux*, rarely ripens and is traditionally left for the birds. The once-traditional sorting into shallow trays called *osiers* is rarely carried out today. Roederer and Bollinger both sort their grapes on occasions, but not so thoroughly as in the past, and most houses do not use any form of selection, although some small growers have started. With rot being a regular problem, intensive sorting should be a legal requirement. If a minimum percentage of grapes must be discarded for Châteauneuf-du-Pape in the sunny south of France, logic dictates that a similar law would be even more beneficial in rainy Reims. Most grapes are still pressed using the traditional, vertical Champagne press or *pressoir coquard*, although pneumatic presses are fairly common. Increasing use is being made of stainless-steel vats with temperature-controlled conditions for the first fermentation, but a few houses and many growers still ferment part or all of their wines in cask, with the younger generation employing a percentage of new oak. The second fermentation gives the wine its sparkle, and this always takes place in the bottle in which it is sold. A nonvintage Champagne must not be sold until at least 15 months after January 1 following the harvest (of the youngest wines in the blend), although most nonvintage Champagnes spend 18 to 24 months of yeast. A vintaged Champagne must not be sold for at least 36 months but most are aged for much longer. Aging improves Champagne because the sediment contains dead yeast cells that break down through autolysis, which contributes to the wine's inimitable "champagny" character.

### 🍇 GRAPE VARIETIES
**Primary varieties:** Chardonnay, Pinot Noir, Pinot Meunier
**Secondary varieties:** Arbanne, Petit Meslier, Pinot Blanc Vrai

CHAMPAGNE PRESS
*The design of the pressoir coquard is basically the same as it was in the 17th century, when Dom Pérignon devised several winemaking methods still practiced in Champagne today.*

## THE MÉTHODE CHAMPENOISE
The techniques used to create Champagne—essentially the second fermentation inside the bottle in which the wine is subsequently sold—have defined the production method for the best sparkling wines worldwide (*see* Making sparkling wine, pp.30–31). There is nothing mysterious about the initial fermentation, which results in a dry, still wine, very acid to taste and seemingly quite unremarkable in character. It must be neutral in character for the subtle influence of the second fermentation (and the process of autolysis that follows it) to work their effect on the flavor.

## ASSEMBLAGE—THE BLENDER'S ART
In other wine regions blending is frowned upon, and the best wines made on one estate come from a single vintage. The traditional view in Champagne could not be a greater contrast, since a nonvintage blend of different grapes, from many different areas and several harvests, is the most classic of Champagnes. The critical operation of *assemblage*, or blending, is highly skilled and painstaking. To blend from as many as 70 different base wines—each of which changes in character from year to year—a consistent nonvintage *cuvée* of a specific house style is a remarkable feat and one that is more successful in some years than in others. The *assemblage* takes place in the first few months of the year following the harvest. At its most basic, and without taking into consideration any particular house style, it is a matter of balancing the characteristics of two or more of the three available grape varieties. The Chardonnay is often steely in its youth, but has the greatest finesse and potential longevity. Pinot Noir provides much of the backbone and body of a Champagne, and real depth and richness of fruit. The Pinot Meunier is a grape of immediate fruity-flowery appeal and in a

BLENDING
*The highly skillful art of blending a fine Champagne can be compared to the game of chess: the winemaker, like the chess player, must think several moves ahead—this is necessary in order to predict how the wine will react to each addition to the blend.*

blend of all three varieties in equal parts it is the first to dominate the wine, particularly on the nose.

The blender can also draw on stocks of reserve wines (quite literally wines kept in reserve from previous years). These are essential for, indeed restricted to, the production of nonvintage Champagne. The job of reserves is, like that of the *dosage*, to make Champagne easier to drink at a younger age. Reserve wines also provide a certain richness, fullness, and mellowed complexity.

## THE SECOND FERMENTATION AND REMUAGE

The second fermentation is the essence of the *méthode champenoise*, and is the only way to produce a fully sparkling wine. After the blended wine has undergone its final racking, the *liqueur de tirage*, or bottling liquor, is added. This is a mixture of still Champagne, sugar, selected yeasts, yeast nutrients, and a clarifying agent. The amount of sugar added depends on the degree of effervescence required and the amount of natural sugar in the wine. The wines are bottled (usually in May or thereabouts) and capped with a temporary closure. The second fermentation can take between 10 days and three months, after which the bottles can be transferred to *pupitres* to undergo *remuage*. A *pupitre* consists of a pair of heavy, hinged, rectangular boards, each containing 60 holes, which have been cut at an angle to enable the bottle to be held by the neck in any position between horizontal and vertical (neck pointing downward).

*Remuage* is a method of riddling the bottles to loosen sediment, encouraging it to move to the neck of the bottle, where it collects. By hand this takes about eight weeks, although many companies now have computerized 504-bottle pallets that perform the task in just eight days. A technique involving the use of porous yeast

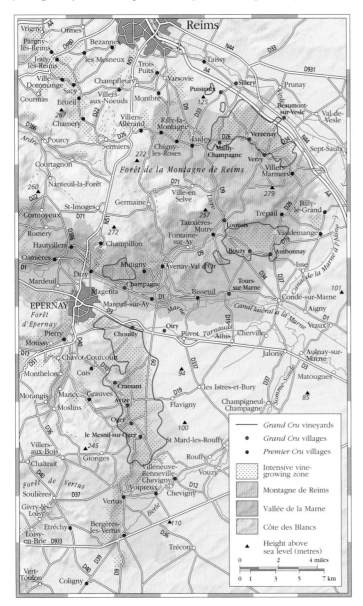

**THE GRAND CRU AND PREMIER CRU VILLAGES**
*Within the three important districts surrounding Épernay, 17 villages have grand cru status and 40 the status of premier cru.*

---

## TYPES OF PRODUCER

The label on a bottle of Champagne will include some initials, usually found at the bottom and preceding a small code or number. These initials are the key to the type of producer who has made the Champagne.

**NM = Négociant-Manipulant**
Traditionally referred to as a "house," a *négociant-manipulant* is a producer that is allowed to purchase grapes and *vins clairs* in large volumes from growers, cooperatives, and other houses. A few houses, such as Bollinger and Louis Roederer, own sufficient vineyards to supply as much as two-thirds of their own needs, whereas some own none or hardly any at all (Alfred Gratien).

**RM = Récoltant-Manipulant**
Otherwise known as a grower-producer, or grower for short. In principle, a grower is not allowed to buy grapes or *vins clairs*, as the Champagne sold under their label is supposed to be 100 percent from their own vineyards. However, growers are legally permitted to purchase grapes or wines from each other, up to a maximum of 5 percent of their total production. The reasoning behind this is to enable those with exclusively

Chardonnay vines to buy Pinot Noir for the production of rosé.

**CM = Coopérative-Manipulant**
A cooperative of growers that makes and sells Champagne under one or more brands that it owns.

**RC = Récoltant-Coopérateur**
A grower who delivers grapes to a cooperative and, in part or full payment, receives back ready-made Champagne, which they sell under their own name. Although more than 4,000 RC brands are registered, they are seldom encountered even in France, and many of these cooperative clones are still sold with RM numbers. Moves to rectify this are ongoing.

**SR = Société de Récoltants**
A publicly registered firm set up by two or more growers—often related—who share premises to make and market their Champagne under more than one brand.

**ND = Négociant-Distributeur**
A company that sells Champagne it did not make to others, who then retail it.

**MA = Marque d'Acheteur**
A brand name owned by the purchaser, such as a restaurant, supermarket, or wine merchant.

---

## WHO OWNS THE BRANDS?

| GROUP | TOTAL PRODUCTION | BRANDS |
|---|---|---|
| LVMH | 60 million bottles | Moët & Chandon, Mercier, Ruinart, Veuve Clicquot, Krug |
| BCC | 25 million bottles | Chanoine, Boizel (including Camuset, Kremer, Montoy, Veuve Borodin, Veuve Delaroy), Philipponnat (including Abel-Lepitre), De Venoge, Alexandre Bonnet, F Bonnet Père et Fils, Brossault, Lanson (including Massé), Besserat de Bellefon [plus 200 low-profile brands] |
| Vranken Monopole | 15 million bottles | Vranken, Pommery, Charles Lafitte Demoiselle, Heidsieck & Co Monopole Barancourt, Collin, Charbaut, Germain |
| Laurent-Perrier | 14 million bottles | Laurent-Perrier (including Lemoine), De Castellane (including Chaurey, Freminet, Ettore Bugatti, Jacques Cattier, A Mérand), Salon, Delamotte, Beaumet, Jeanmaire, Oudinot |
| Pernod-Ricard | 10 million bottles | Mumm, Perrier-Jouët |
| Rapeneau | 10 million bottles | GH Martel (including De Noiron, Rapeneau, Charles du Roy, Charles Oban, P L Martin, Balahu, Mortas, Comte de Lamotte, Marcel Pierre), De Cazenove (including Baudry, J Lanvin, Magenta, Marguerite Christel), Mansard-Baillet, Château de Bligny |
| Rémy-Cointreau | 8 million bottles | Piper-Heidsieck, Charles Heidsieck, Heidsieck |
| Duval-Leroy | 7 million bottles | Duval-Leroy (including Baron de Beaupré, E Michel, Henri de Varlane, Paul Vertay) |
| Taittinger | 5 million bottles | Taittinger (including Irroy, Saint-Eyremond) |
| Thienot | 6 million bottles | Alain Thienot (including Billiard, Castille, Petitjean), Marie Stuart, Joseph-Perrier, Canard-Duchêne, Malard (including Georges Goulet, Gobillard) |
| Roederer | 4 million bottles | Louis Roederer, Théophile Roederer, Deutz |

**SEDIMENT**
*The Champagne's second fermentation creates a sediment that falls in separate sticky layers; it must be worked down the bottle by an operation called* remuage.

capsules, which trap the sediment inside them, reduces *remuage* to a mere eight seconds. After *remuage*, the wine undergoes a period of aging *sur point* (in a fully inverted position) before the sediment is removed.

## DISGORGEMENT AND DOSAGE

Disgorgement is the removal of the sediment from the wine, which is usually collected in a plastic pot. The method usually used today is known as *dégorgement à la glace*, which involves the immersion of the bottle neck in a shallow bath of freezing brine. This causes the sediment to adhere to the base of the plastic pot, enabling the bottle to be turned upright without disturbing the sediment. When the crown-cap is removed, the semifrozen sediment is ejected by the internal pressure of the bottle. Only a little wine is lost, as the wine's pressure is reduced by its lowered temperature.

Before corking, bottles are topped off to their previous level and *liqueur d'expédition* is added. In all cases except for *Extra Brut*, this *liqueur* includes a small amount of sugar: the younger the wine, the greater the *dosage* of sugar required to balance its youthful acidity. High acidity is crucial to a fine Champagne, since it keeps the wine fresh during its lengthy bottle-aging method of production and also during any additional cellaring by the consumer. High acidity is also necessary to carry the flavor to the palate through the tactile effect caused by thousands of minuscule bursting bubbles. This acidity rounds out with age, thus the older the Champagne, the smaller the *dosage* required.

## CHAMPAGNE'S TROUBLES

Champagne sales are notoriously cyclical, going from boom to bust and back to boom again. This is due partly to achieving worldwide fame at a time when the Industrial Revolution created new money, and partly because of the intrinsic imbalance of vineyard ownership. For centuries the fashionability of Champagne had vied with that of Burgundy, so it was only by chance that Champagne happened to be in vogue in the 1870s, when the *nouveau riche* were on the rise. The pop of the cork and liveliness of the bubbles captured the imagination and suited the celebratory lives of the *nouveau riche*, who quickly made Champagne the most chic drink in London, Paris, and New York, doubling its sales in the process. That is why Champagne is inextricably linked to celebration and happiness. Champagne sales are thus extremely sensitive to the mood of consumers, making fluctuations unavoidable. Any well-organized industry should be able to cope with such fluctuations, but the disparity in vineyard ownership creates tensions in supply and demand that convert what would otherwise be relatively harmless fluctuations into damaging booms and busts. Just 12 percent of the vineyards are owned by the houses, which are responsible for over 70 percent of Champagne sales. When Champagne sales boom, the houses are desperate for grapes, which the growers withhold, selling only a fraction of what they normally would, demanding as much as they can in the process. The pressure created by disproportionate vineyard ownership causes an artificially high demand, which is inevitably followed by a crash. When the bubble bursts, the houses do not want to buy grapes, and will ignore all but those growers with whom they have long-term relationships, especially those who have speculated at their expense.

This boom-bust recipe for commercial disaster could be consigned to history, but the system is rigged to keep vineyards under the ownership of small growers. It would be an equal travesty if growers were forced to sell any vineyards to the *négoce*, but it should at least be possible for houses to buy or rent vineyards. In theory they can, but only in theory. Ostensibly, there is nothing stopping anyone from buying any land in France, but in practice, Champagne's strict adherence to certain controls ensures that the growers maintain ownership of the vineyards. The only realistic

## RECENT CHAMPAGNE VINTAGES

**2006** Definitely a "Chardonnay vintage," with some excellent base wines produced on the Côte des Blancs, but the Pinot Noir suffered rather more rot in 2006 than most producers were inclined to admit, and the Meunier was even worse. With nearly 16 percent affected, the normally hardy Meunier was exceptionally rot-prone for the second year running.

**2005** Not the universally fine vintage it was elsewhere, 2005 saw significant rot (14 percent) among the black varieties, particularly the Meunier, although some very good Pinot Noir was produced in Verzy and Verzenay. Chardonnay excelled on the Côte des Blancs, especially in Le Mesnil-sur-Oger. Some surprisingly good 2005s have been made.

**2004** Elsewhere in the country—and, indeed, the rest of Europe—2005 was a great vintage, while 2004 was surprisingly good at best, yet in Champagne it was the reverse. The 2004

*vins clairs* were classic, with the best acids I have tasted in years. At the end of a cold and wet August, the *champenois* returned from their annual vacation to find their vineyards creaking at the seams with a massive crop of unripe grapes. They were staring disaster in the face when the region was miraculously blessed with beautiful sunny days and clear, cool nights. One *chef de caves* emailed me to say, "Another 10 days of this, and we'll have a great vintage," to which I replied: "Another 10 days of rain, and you'll have another 2001." They got their sunshine, and due to abnormally high reserves of plant sugars residing in the roots of the vine (unused thanks to frost decimating the crop in 2003), the grapes ripened at twice the rate, delivering a superior vintage for truly exceptional reasons, and despite an average yield of 23,000 kg per hectare (equivalent to 146.5 hl/ha)!

**2003** Thanks to the pan-European heatwave, this was the earliest Champagne harvest since at least 1822 and, with 50 percent of the potential crop destroyed by spring frosts, it was also the smallest harvest since 1981. There were concerns over the worst acidity and highest pH readings on record. There will be some truly special Champagnes (Bollinger, Moët, Roederer, and Jacquesson stand out), but they will be mixed in with a motley crew of the weird and ugly.

**2002** This is without doubt a vintage year and a very special one too, marked by a *passerillage* that reduced the crop in some vineyards by up to 40 percent, and endowed the wines with the highest natural alcohol level since 1990 (which itself was the highest since 1959). It is definitely a Pinot Noir year, with Aÿ-Champagne the most successful village.

**COMBATTING FROST**
*Vines are protected from frost, the most harmful of Champagne's natural hazards, by aspersion. Aspersion (water-sprinkling) is performed by a system that operates automatically whenever the vineyard temperature drops below freezing. The frost expends its energy in freezing the water, leaving the delicate shoots and buds safely cocooned in ice.*

way for a house to acquire more vineyards is to take over ailing companies that owned land prior to the Contrôlée des Structures, a law that forbids any firm from farming more than 37 acres (15 hectares), whether owned or rented. This law applies throughout France, but Champagne is very stringent in its application, which has not only maintained an artificial imbalance in vineyard ownership, but has encouraged the industry's polarization.

## CLASSIFICATION OF CHAMPAGNE VINEYARDS

Champagne's vineyards are quality-rated on a village-by-village basis using a percentile system known as the *Échelle des Crus*, which constitutes a pro-rata basis for grape prices. Villages with the maximum *échelle* of 100 percent are *grands crus*, while those rated between 90 and 99 percent are *premiers crus* and receive a correspondingly lower price for their grapes. The lowest-rated villages are currently classified at 80 percent, but the *Échelle des Crus* was originally a true percentile system, starting at just 22.5 percent. It would be unrealistic for any such system to commence at 1 percent, since no village with merely one-hundredth the potential of a *grand cru* should even be part of the Champagne appellation, but when first conceived, the *Échelle des Crus* had a comprehensive structure of *crus* covering the middle ground, which is something that it lacks today. Due to various *ad hoc* reclassifications and political posturing, the minimum *échelle* has gradually increased from 22.5 per cent to 80 percent, and in truth the present system is nothing more than a 20-point scale.

### CHAMPAGNE CORKS

1. A crown-cap to seal the wine during second fermentation.
2. The plastic pot in which the deposit is collected after a successful *remuage*.
3. A cork before insertion, which is cylindrical.
4. A cork from a youthful Champagne, which shows the mushroom head achieved when ramming it into the bottle.
5. The cork of a more mature Champagne, which has shrunk and straightened through age.

There are 17 villages possessing official *grand cru* status. Until 1985 there were only 12. The five villages elevated to *grand cru* in 1985 were Chouilly, le Mesnil-sur-Oger, Oger, Oiry, and Verzy.

## HOMEGROWN

Is it better for a Champagne producer to grow its own grapes? Does this guarantee a better quality and greater consistency of style? As the table below demonstrates, the answer is "maybe" to the first question and "no" to the second. Own grapes do not guarantee a better quality or a greater consistency of style. They make it easier to achieve these ends, but there are more than enough cooperatives and growers making poor Champagne exclusively from their own vineyards to realize that own grapes do not guarantee quality, whereas the likes of Alfred Gratien and Gosset, neither of whom own a single vine, demonstrate that the highest levels of quality and consistency can be achieved exclusively from purchased grapes. Economically, it is cheaper to grow grapes than to buy them, unless yields are deliberately reduced, and other quality-enhancing viticultural techniques are practiced.

### VINEYARDS BELONGING TO THE HOUSES

| PRODUCER | VINEYARDS OWNED | PROPORTION OF PRODUCTION[1] | CHAMPAGNES MADE FROM OWN GRAPES[2] |
|---|---|---|---|
| Billecart-Salmon[3] | 240 acres | ?% | Entire range (?%) |
| Bollinger | 395 acres | 67% | Vieilles Vignes Françaises (100%) Grande Année (80–90%) Grande Année Rosé (80–90%) |
| Deutz | 104 acres | 30% | Entire range (30%) |
| Gosset | None | Zero | None |
| Alfred Gratien | None | Zero | None |
| Henriot | 67 acres | 20% | Entire range (20%) |
| Jacquesson | 64 acres | 60% | Avize Grand Cru (100%) Grand Vin Signature (67%) NV cuvées (40–60%) In the pipeline: Aÿ Grand Cru (100%) Dizy Premier Cru (100%) Forthcoming Grand Vin Signature (75%) |
| Krug | 50 acres | 40% | Clos du Mesnil (100%) Rest of range (40%) |
| Lanson | 2.5 acres | 0.08% | Entire range (0.08%) |
| Moët & Chandon | 1,850 acres | up to 25% | Dom Pérignon (100%) Trilogie des Grands Crus (100%) Vintage cuvées (50–75%) |
| Mumm | 544 acres | 25% | Entire range (25%) |
| Perrier-Jouët | 160 acres | 25% | Entire range (25%) |
| Bruno Paillard | 59 acres | 14% | Most used in Brut Première Cuvée, but sometimes part in Chardonnay Réserve Privée or Vintage or NPU. |
| Philipponnat | 42 acres | 33% | Clos des Goisses (100%) Réserve Millésimée (75%) Cuvée 1522 (65%) |
| Pol Roger | 210 acres | over 50% | Chardonnay ("largely") Rest of the range (over 50%) |
| Pommery | 133 acres | 10% | N/A (current cuvées and those due to be sold for several years to come were made when Pommery owned 307 hectares, supplying 40% of needs) |
| Roederer | 504 acres | 67% | Vintage cuvées (100%) NV cuvées (50%) |
| Taittinger | 667 acres | 50% | Entire range (50%) |
| Veuve Clicquot | 944 acres | up to 30% | Grande Dame (up to 100%) Grande Dame Rosé (up to 100%) vintage cuvées (predominantly) |

**Notes**

[1] Represented by own grapes. An average figure that very much depends on the harvest.

[2] An average figure that very much depends on the harvest (especially when no vintage wines are produced) and, of course, the ultimate freedom to construct each cuvée according to the judgment of the house rather than to any set formula that dictates a certain percentage.

[3] Includes 222 acres (90 hectares) belonging to Frey, a major shareholder in Billecart-Salmon, which has first refusal on all grapes grown as of October 2004.

# WHO INVENTED CHAMPAGNE?

Originally Champagne was a still wine (a "faintly reddish" *vin gris*); any incidental fizziness would have been considered a fault back then, as it would be in, say, a *cru classé* claret today. To find the first sparkling wine, we must ignore accidents and faults, and look for the earliest deliberate rendering of a wine in the sparkling format: the precursor to the evolutionary process we know as the *méthode champenoise*.

## PÉRIGNON THE PRETENDER

The French would have us believe that Dom Pérignon invented Champagne in the late 1690s, but there is no evidence that he made a single bottle of sparkling wine, and every suggestion that he regarded fizziness as a fault. If anything, the legendary Benedictine monk spent his life trying to rid Champagne of bubbles. So what do the French traditionalists base their belief on? They rely on a French document, *Mémoire sur le Manière de cultiver la Vigne et de faire le Vin de en Champagne*, written in 1718 by an anonymous author (believed to be Jean Godinot), which contains the first use of the term "vin mousseux" and refers to its popularity having been established "more than 20 years earlier." This is not proof, of course, but if we accept it as an accurate account, sparkling wines became mainstream in France circa 1697.

## LACK OF TECHNOLOGY

It could not possibly have been much earlier than this because the French did not have the technology. They did not have a strong enough glass bottle to withstand the internal pressure of a sparkling wine, or an effective seal to maintain it. French glass was wood-fired, and thus too weak, while cork-stoppers had been "lost" during the decline of the Roman Empire and replaced by wooden bungs wrapped in hemp, which would hardly keep the draft out, let alone the fizz in.

## INVENTION OF INVENTOR

There is no mention in Godinot's *mémoire* of Dom Pérignon. Incredible though it may seem, the first documented claim that Dom Pérignon made sparkling Champagne was made in 1821, more than a century after his death, by Dom Grossard, who wrote "As you know, it was the celebrated Dom Pérignon who found the secret of making white sparkling wine." But there was no secret process. The manifestation of effervescence in wine was a capricious and ephemeral effect that Godinot attributed to the phases of the moon! However, despite his claim of sparkling Champagne's popularity in France from the late 1690s, the 1721 edition of *Dictionnaire Universel* did not refer to any wine as "mousseux," an adjective that would not appear in this context until the 1724 edition.

## ENGLISH CHAMPAGNE

Yet sparkling Champagne was not only available in England much earlier than this, but it had also become so popular that dramatists were mentioning it by 1676,

DOM PÉRIGNON
*How could Dom Pérignon have invented Champagne when "sparkling Champaign" was mentioned in English literature six years before the famous monk arrived in the region?*

when Sir George Etherege wrote in The Man of Mode:
*To the Mall and the Park*
*Where we love till 'tis dark,*
*Then sparkling Champaign*
*Puts an end to their reign;*
*It quickly recovers*
*Poor languishing lovers,*
*Makes us frolic and gay,*
*And drowns all sorrow;*
*But, Alas,*
*We relapse again on the morrow.*

## ENGLISH PARADOX

How could sparkling Champagne be recorded in English literature two decades before even the French admit the first sparkling Champagne was made? Because, whereas the French did not have the technology, the English did, and, being inveterate meddlers, they used it to make still French wines fizzy. Although the French did not rediscover cork until 1685 at the earliest (almost a decade after Etherege's "sparkling Champaign"), the English, who also lost the cork after the Romans left, came across it more than 130 years before the French. All wines in Shakespeare's time were shipped to England in casks, but the English habitually bottled their wines, sealing them with corks, from the late 16th century onward. And whereas French glass was wood-fired and intrinsically weak, English glass was coal-fired at a much higher temperature, making it a vastly stronger product.

It is clear that the English had the means to preserve the effervescence of a sparkling Champagne long before its first recorded mention by Sir George Etherege, but how and why did still wine from Champagne end up sparkling?

## IRRELEVANCE OF NATURAL FIZZ

Obviously there were many occurrences of accidental refermentation causing a wine to become fizzy. The most common cause for such faulty wines was the cold northerly situation of Champagne, where we can be sure that fermentation would have prematurely stopped at the first snap of winter, only for it to recommence once bottled and stored in the

warmth of an English tavern. However, accidentally sparkling wines have been a fact of life since Biblical times, and such incidents are an irrelevance to historians searching for the first intentionally sparkling wine.

## MÉTHODE MERRET

Conclusive proof can only be demonstrated by documentary evidence describing the most rudimentary element of the *méthode champenoise*: the addition of sugar to a finished wine to induce a second fermentation with the specific intention of making it not just "gay," "brisk," or "lively" (words often thought to imply effervescence), but unequivocally sparkling. Such a document exists, not in Reims or Épernay, but in London, where an eight-page paper entitled "Some observations concerning the ordering of wines" was presented on December 17, 1662, to the newly formed Royal Society by Christopher Merret, who stated "our wine-coopers of recent times use vast quantities of sugar and molasses to all sorts of wines to make them drink brisk and sparkling."

## PROOF POSITIVE

Merret goes on to state that this process was also "… to give them spirit as also to mend their bad tastes, all which raisins and cure and stum perform." His use of "spirit" denotes increased alcohol content, while his "stum perform" describes precisely in 17th-century English a new fermentation. Although Merret does not mention Champagne specifically, he does state "all wines" and this would surely have included Champagne. Furthermore, we can deduce that of "all wines" it was Champagne that suited the process better than any other because, within a very short while, all efforts were concentrated on that wine. If not, then "sparkling Champaign" could not have achieved the level of fame required for Etherege to wax lyrical about it just 14 years later.

Thus the English invented the Champagne process, and did so six years before Dom Pérignon set foot in Champagne, more than 30 years before the French made their first sparkling Champagne, over 60 years before *mousseux* was first mentioned in a French dictionary, and almost 80 years before the first Champagne house was established.

# THE WINE STYLES OF
# CHAMPAGNE

## NONVINTAGE BRUT

No wine depends upon the winemaker's blending skills more than nonvintage Champagne, which accounts for more than 75 percent of all Champagne sold. Although nonvintage Champagnes are not usually the finest Champagnes, they are capable of being so. Their base wine, to which reserve wines may be added, will always be from the last harvest. Most producers make up between 10 and 15 percent of their blends from reserves from the previous two or three years, but some utilize as much as 40 percent, while a few will add much less reserve wine in volume, but from a greater number of much older vintages. Many growers have no reserve wines, thus their nonvintage will in fact be from one year, but of a lesser quality than the *cuvée* selected for their vintage Champagne. All but the most dynamic coopératives typically make up just 5 percent of their blends from reserves from the year immediately preceding that of the base wine—and they seldom excel.

🏆 *Billecart-Salmon • Deutz* (Classic) • *Gosset* (Grande Réserve) • *Charles Heidsieck* (Mis en Cave) • *Jacquesson* (Cuvée No XXX) • *Henri Mandois •* • *Serge Mathieu* (Tête de Cuvée Select) *Bruno Paillard • Louis Roederer • Vilmart & Cie* (Grand Cellier d'Or)

## VINTAGE BRUT

Not more than 80 percent of any year's harvest may be sold as vintage Champagne, so at least 20 percent of the best years' harvests are conserved for the future blending of nonvintage wines. Some houses stick rigidly to declaring a vintage in only the greatest years, but many, sadly, do not, which is why we have seen vintage Champagnes from less than ideal years such as 1980, 1987, and even 1984. Most *coopératives* and a large number of grower-producers produce a vintage virtually every year, which is possible, of course, but rather defeats the object and debases the value of the product. However, even in great years, a vintage Champagne is more the result of tightly controlled selection of base wines than a reflection of the year in question, and this makes these wines exceptionally good value. The character of a vintage Champagne is more autolytic, giving it an acacialike floweriness, than that of a nonvintage of the same age because it has no reserve-wine mellowness. If you like those biscuity or toasty bottle-aromas, you should keep vintage for a few years. For those who have read about me trumpeting Henri Giraud's 1993 Fût de Chêne, despite its ludicrous price (five euros ($6.50) more than Cristal, at the time of writing), I have not tasted another vintage from this producer that comes remotely close to the special quality of his 1993.

🏆 *Billecart-Salmon* (Cuvée Nicolas-François Billecart) • *Bollinger* (Grande Année) • *Deutz • Alfred Gratien • Krug • Lanson • Pol Roger • Louis Roederer • Veuve Clicquot • Vilmart & Cie* (Grand Cellier d'Or)

## BLANC DE BLANCS
### Non-vintage, vintage, and prestige

Literally meaning "white of whites," this wine is produced entirely from white Chardonnay grapes and possesses the greatest aging potential of all Champagnes. *Blanc de blancs* may be made in any district of Champagne, but the best examples come from a small part of the Côte des Blancs between Cramant and Le Mesnil-sur-Oger. If consumed too early, a classic *blanc de blancs* can be austere and seem to lack fruit and generosity, yet with proper maturity this style of Champagne can be very succulent. Given a few years' bottle aging after purchase, most *blanc de blancs* develop a toasty-lemony bouquet together with intense, beautifully focused fruit. If the first blend of Lenoble's nonvintage Cuvée Les Aventures (1990/5/6) is anything to go by, it will be fighting for a place in the top 10 nonvintage *blanc de blancs*.

🏆 **Nonvintage** *Billecart-Salmon • Boizel • Bonnaire • Gaston Chicquet • Delamotte • Pierre Gimonnet • Moncuit • Joseph Perrier • Jacques Sélosse* (Tradition) • *Vilmart & Cie • Vintage Billecart-Salmon • Bonnaire • Deutz • Duval-Leroy • Pierre Gimonnet* (Collection *en magnum*) • *Jacquesson* (Avize) • *Henri Mandois* (Chardonnay Brut) • *Le Mesnil* (Vigne Sélectionnée) • *Pol Roger • Louis Roederer* • **Prestige *cuvée*** *Boizel* (Joyeau) • *Deutz* (Amour de Deutz) • *Charles Heidsieck* (Cuvée de Millénaires) • *Krug* (Clos du Mesnil) • *Ruinart* (Dom Ruinart) • *Salon* ("S") • *Taittinger* (Comtes de Champagne)

## BLANC DE NOIRS
### Nonvintage, vintage, and prestige

Literally translated as "white of blacks," these Champagnes are made entirely from black grapes, either Pinot Noir or Pinot Meunier, or a blend of the two. The most famous and most expensive is Bollinger's Vieilles Vignes Françaises, which is a unique example of pure Pinot Noir Champagne made from two tiny plots of ungrafted vines, which between them cannot produce more than 3,000 bottles, hence the hefty price tag. Aside from Bollinger, few producers have traditionally used the term *blanc de noirs*, but the Vieilles Vignes Françaises has given it a certain cachet and a few commercially minded houses have begun to cash in on the term (Beaumet, Jeanmaire, Mailly Grand Cru, Oudinot, and De Venoge, for example). Many supermarkets now sell their own-label brand of *blanc de noirs*. Bollinger inadvertently created the myth that a *blanc de noirs* is intrinsically a big, full, and muscular Champagne, but it is generally little different in style from the other *cuvées* a house may produce. If you try Serge Mathieu's Champagne,

you will discover a wine so elegant that you would never guess it is made only from Pinot Noir, let alone that it is grown in the Aube. Pommery's Wintertime and the Mailly cooperative's basic nonvintage Blanc de Noirs Grand Cru just miss the cut, but deserve an honorary mention. Another cooperative, Veuve A. Devaux, has just come back on track with its nonvintage Blanc de Noirs, which should make the list next time around if standards are maintained.

🏆 *Bollinger* (Vieilles Vignes Françaises) • *Canard-Duchêne* (Charles VII) • *Serge Mathieu* (Cuvée Tradition) • *Moët & Chandon* (Les Sarments d'Aÿ)

## EXTRA SEC, SEC, AND DEMI-SEC (RICH)
### Nonvintage and vintage

In theory, *doux* is the sweetest Champagne style available, with a residual sugar level in excess of 50 grams per liter. However, this style is no longer used. The last *doux* sold was a 1983-based Louis Roederer Carte Blanche. That cuvée is now a *demi-sec*, although 100 years ago it contained a fabulous 180 grams per liter of sugar.

The extinction of *doux* has meant that *demi-sec* has, for all practical purposes, become the sweetest of the Champagne categories. A *demi-*

---

### SWEETNESS CHART

The sweetness of a Champagne can be accurately indicated by its residual sugar level, which is measured in grams per liter. The percentage *dosage* applied, which some books refer to, is not an accurate indicator because the *liqueur* added in the *dosage* itself varies in sweetness. The legal levels are as follows:

**BRUT NATURE 0–3 GRAMS PER LITER** Absolutely bone dry!

**EXTRA BRUT 0–6 GRAMS PER LITER** Bone dry

**BRUT 0–15 GRAMS PER LITRE** Dry to very dry, but should never be austere

**EXTRA SEC OR EXTRA DRY 12–20 GRAMS PER LITER** A misnomer—dry to medium-dry

**SEC OR DRY 17–35 GRAMS PER LITER** A bigger misnomer—medium to medium-sweet

**DEMI-SEC 33–50 GRAMS PER LITER** Definitely sweet, but not true dessert sweetness

**DOUX 50+ GRAMS PER LITER** Very sweet; this style was favored by the czars, but is no longer commercially produced

**Note** Under the old Champagne laws, *rich* or *riche* was strictly used as an official alternative designation for *demi-sec*, but is currently used for anything between *sec* and *demi-sec*.

*sec* may contain between 33 and 50 grams per liter of residual sugar, although most of them contain 35 grams, and only a few contain as much as 45 grams.

While these wines are not dry, they certainly are not sweet and are nothing like a top Sauternes, which in great years will average between 90 and 108 grams per liter. A *demi-sec* thus falls between two stools and, because it is primarily sold to an unsophisticated market, the *champenois* have been able to get away with using wines of decreasing quality. There are exceptions, of course, but Champagne *demi-sec* is now so adulterated that few *champenois* take the style seriously.

The exceptions that do exist are not sweet enough to accompany desserts and are best served with the main course, or even with starters, with fruit elements in the sauce or garnish that present a little natural sweetness, requiring a balancing sweetness in the wine.

🏆 **Nonvintage** *Billecart-Salmon* (Demi-Sec Réserve) • *Gatinois* (Demi-Sec) • *Lanson* (Ivory Label) • *Moët & Chandon* (Nectar) • *Philipponnat* (Sublime) • *Piper-Heidsieck* (Sublime) • *Pol Roger* (Demi-Sec) • *Louis Roederer* (Rich Sec) • *Jacques Sélosse* (Cuvée Exquise Sec) • *Veuve Clicquot* (Demi-Sec) • **Vintage** *Veuve Clicquot* (Rich)

## ROSÉ
### Nonvintage, vintage, and prestige

The first record of a commercially produced rosé Champagne is by Clicquot in 1777 and this style has enjoyed ephemeral bursts of popularity ever since. It is the only European rosé that may be made by blending white wine with a little red; all other rosé, whether still or sparkling, must be produced by macerating the skins and juice to extract pigments. More pink Champagne is produced by blending than through skin contact, and in blind tasting it has been impossible to tell the difference. Both methods produce good and bad wine that can be light or dark in color and rich or delicate in flavor. A good pink Champagne will have an attractive color, perfect limpidity, and a snow-white mousse. Why no Krug Rosé? Intrinsically it would come very close to the top of my list of "multivintage" rosés, but Krug either makes too much or it does not sell quickly enough—or they don't make it often enough. It is the only wine in the Krug range that does not merit keeping, and there have been too many occasions when a tired Krug Rosé was the only Krug Rosé available. Laurent-Perrier's Cuvée Grand Siècle Alexandra, the first couple of vintages of which were to die for, is edged out of the top 10 prestige *cuvée* rosés for having no track record between the 1990 and 1997 vintages. On the other hand, Chanoine's 1999 Tsarine Rosé was not only a beautifully elegant start for this new vintaged wine, but it was also exceptionally fine for a 1999; but will Chanoine maintain this standard?

🏆 **Nonvintage** *Billecart-Salmon* • *Château de Boursault* • *Egly-Ouriet* • *Gosset* (Grand Rosé) • *Jacquesson* (Perfection) • *Henri Mandois* • *Serge Mathieu* • *Piper-Heidsieck* (Rosé Sauvage) • *François Secondé* • **Vintage** *Bollinger* • *Jacquesson* (Signature) • *Pol Roger* • *Louis Roederer* • *Veuve Clicquot* • **Prestige cuvée** *Billecart-Salmon* (Cuvée Elisabeth) • *Deutz* (Cuvée William Deutz) • *Gosset* (Celebris) • *Moët & Chandon* (Dom Pérignon) • *Perrier-Jouët* (Belle Epoque) • *Pommery* (Cuvée Louise Pommery) • *Louis Roederer* (Cristal) • *Ruinart* (Dom Ruinart) • *Taittinger* (Comtes de Champagne) • *Veuve Clicquot* (Grande Dame)

## NON-DOSAGE
### Nonvintage and vintage

The first non-*dosage* Champagne to be sold was Laurent-Perrier's Grand Vin Sans Sucre in 1889. Officially Brut Extra, but commercially labeled variously as Brut Zéro, Brut Sauvage, Ultra Brut, or Sans Sucre, these wines became fashionable in the early 1980s, when consumers began seeking lighter, drier wines. This trend was driven by critics who had been privileged to taste wonderful old vintages straight off their lees, which led them to believe that a Champagne without any *dosage* was somehow intrinsically superior to a Champagne with a *dosage*. It is, of course, if it is of superior quality and at least 10 years old before disgorgement. It is not superior, however, when the Champagne is of normal commercial age, when it can only be austere, tart, and unpleasant to drink, which is why the fashion was so short-lived. Sometimes, even I think that I have discovered a great non-*dosage* Champagne, only to discover most of the follow-up releases disappointing. These include De Bruyne, Mailly (Cassiopee), and Philipponnat (Cuvée 1522 Extra Brut). I enjoyed Delouvin Nowack 1996 Brut Extra Selection, but nothing before or since. I could have died for the first release of André et Michel Drappier NV Pinot Noir Zero Dosage, but later shipments fell a long way short. Even Billecart-Salmon reduced a great Champagne to merely a good to very good one when launching its single-vineyard Les Clos St.-Hilaire with no *dosage* in the inaugural 1995 vintage. I could say the same about Jacquesson Corne Beautray.

🏆 **Vintage** *Bollinger* (R. D. Extra Brut) • *Duval-Leroy* (Fleur de Champagne Extra Brut) • *Pierre Gimonnet* (Cuvée Oenophile Extra-Brut) • *Pommery* (Flacon d'Excellence Nature *en magnum*)

## CUVÉE DE PRESTIGE
### Brut style—Nonvintage and vintage

Also known as special or deluxe *cuvées*, Cuvées de Prestige should be the best that Champagne has to offer, regardless of the price. Dom Pérignon was the first commercial example of these Champagnes, launched in 1936, although Louis Roederer's Cristal has a far longer history, having first been produced in 1876, but that was made exclusively for Czar Alexander II. The first commercially available Cristal *cuvée* was not produced until 1945.

A typical prestige *cuvée* may be made entirely of wines from a firm's own vineyards, and the blend is often restricted to grapes from *grand cru* villages. Most of these are vintage Champagnes, and many are produced by the most traditional methods (fermented in wood,

sealed with a cork and *agrafe*, rather than a crown-cap, then hand-disgorged), aged for longer than normal, and sold in special bottles at very high prices. Some are clearly overpriced, others are overrefined, having so much mellowness that all the excitement has been squeezed out of them, but a good number are truly exceptional Champagnes and worth every penny.

In addition to true deluxe *cuvées*, there are many more premium *cuvées* that are probably far better value, but are not included below. These are the special selections of vintage and nonvintage *brut* that for a relatively modest increase, as opposed to a doubling or tripling in price, offer a distinctive step up in quality.

🏆 **Nonvintage** *Krug* (Grande Cuvée) • *Laurent-Perrier* (Grand Siècle La Cuvée) • *Piper-Heidsieck* (Cuvée Rare) • **Vintage** *Billecart-Salmon* (Grande Cuvée) • *Deutz* (Cuvée William Deutz—since 1995) • *Jacquesson* (Grand Signature) • *Moët & Chandon* (Dom Pérignon) • *Perrier-Jouët* (Belle Epoque) • *Pol Roger* (Cuvée Sir Winston Churchill) • *Pommery* (Cuvée Louise Pommery) • *Louis Roederer* (Cristal) • *Veuve Clicquot* (Grande Dame) • *Vilmart* (Coeur de Cuvée)

**Note** Top-performing prestige *cuvées* that are *blanc de blancs*, *blanc de noirs*, *rosé*, or single-vineyard Champagnes are not recommended above, but under their respective headings. For those who might wonder about the absence of Krug Vintage, it was a matter of juggling the top 10 selections, so I have included that under Vintage Brut.

## SINGLE VINEYARD
### Nonvintage and vintage

Although the winemakers of Champagne are gradually becoming aware of the concept of single-vineyard sparkling wines, it is only a handful of houses that are doing this and not the growers, who are those best equipped to take advantage of and promote the concept of wines that are expressive of *terroir*. The trio of nonvintage single-vineyard Champagnes sold under Leclerc-Briant's Les Authentiques label have not lived up to their initial promise, and only one of Moët's three single-vineyard *grand cru* Champagnes stands out, but keep your eye out for Lenoble's nonvintage Cuvée Les Aventures, which might, if the initial 1990/5/6 blend is anything to go by. Billecart-Salmon's Les Clos St.-Hilaire is very good, but needs a *dosage* to achieve a listing below. Also watch out for a whole raft of single-vineyard Champagnes from top-performing Jacquesson.

🏆 **Nonvintage** *Cattier* (Clos du Moulin) • *Moët & Chandon* (Sarments d'Aÿ) • **Vintage** *Drappier* (Grande Sendrée Brut and Rosé) • *Krug* (Clos du Mesnil) • *Philipponnat* (Clos des Goisses)

## COTEAUX CHAMPENOIS AOC
### Nonvintage and vintage

The still wines (red, white, and rosé) that are produced in Champagne are low in quality and high in price. The white and rosé are the least interesting, although with modern technology they should be more successful in a fresh, easy-to-drink style. Château Saran from Moët & Chandon is a Coteaux Champenois *blanc* that has to achieve a certain minimum standard, since it comes from some of the vines reserved for Dom Pérignon, which is a 50/50 blend, thus for every bottle of Château Saran produced, two bottles of Dom Pérignon must be sacrificed! Regrettably, the minimum standard is not that special, and, although it is a nice enough, smooth, dry white wine when released, it does not improve after a year in bottle.

Although Champagne's notorious climate is very punishing on those who try to make a red wine every year, it is the Coteaux Champenois *rouge* that can be the most fascinating of all. Black grapes rarely ripen sufficiently to obtain a good color without overextraction, which merely brings out the harsh, unripe tannins. Most reds are, therefore, light- to medium-bodied wines that barely hint at the flush of fruit found in a good Burgundy at the most basic level.

However, the all-too-rare exceptions can be singly impressive in their deep color and rich fruit. Such wines often have a slightly smoky style distinctly reminiscent of Pinot Noir. Bouzy is the most famous of these wines, but a good vintage rarely occurs in the same village more than once in 10 years and various other growths can be just as good. The best reds from a successful vintage in Ambonnay, Aÿ, or any other winegrowing village in Champagne can certainly be compared to Bouzy.

Because of this intrinsic unreliability, it is impossible to recommend any Coteaux Champenois on a regular basis. However, virtually all the famous houses have a bottle or two of an amazing rouge—usually Bouzy from venerable vintages such as 1929, 1947, or 1959—but their current commercial bottlings are usually pretty mediocre. Bollinger is the exception, with a *barrique*-matured Aÿ rouge from the *lieu-dit* La Côte aux Enfants, which consistently tries hard, even if it is more successful in some years than others. Joseph Perrier's Cumières Rouge is also worth keeping an eye on. I cannot in all honesty list a top 10 of such a variable product, but to give readers a starting point, in addition to La Côte aux Enfants listed below and Joseph Perrier's Cumières Rouge already mentioned, the Coteaux Champenois I have had most joy from over the years include Paul Bara (Bouzy), Edmond Barnault (Bouzy), André Clouet (Bouzy), Denois (Cumières), Paul Déthune (Ambonnay), Egly-Ouriet (Bouzy), Fresnet-baudot (Sillery), Gatinois (Aÿ), René Geoffroy (Cumières), Gosset-Brabant (Aÿ), Patrick Soutiran (Ambonnay), and Emmanuel Tassin (Celles-sur-Ource). The largest producer of Coteaux Champenois in all three denominations is Laurent Perrier, but the quality is seldom more exciting than acceptable.

*Bollinger* (La Côte aux Enfants)

## ROSÉ DES RICEYS AOC

This is not part of the Coteaux Champenois AOC, but is a totally separate appellation. This pure Pinot Noir, still, pink wine is made in the commune of Les Riceys in the Aube *département* and is something of a legend locally, its fame dating back to the 17th century and Louis XIV, who is said to have served it as often as he could. It should be dark pink, medium bodied, and aromatic. The best are often reminiscent of chocolate, herbs, and even mint, and can possess a penetrating, fruity flavor with a long, smooth finish. Production has greatly increased in recent years, with even Vranken, the most commercial of commercial houses, producing one, but quality is erratic, and I have never tasted an example anywhere near Horiot's 1971. Try Veuve A. Devaux, Gallimard, and Morel—but be prepared for more disappointments than successes.

# THE WINE PRODUCERS OF
# CHAMPAGNE

**Notes**

**GM** Former *grande marque*

**NV** Nonvintage

**V** Vintage

**PC** Prestige *cuvée* (see p177)

**SV** Single vineyard

Where "entire range" is recommended, this applies to Champagne only, not to Coteaux Champenois.

## MICHEL ARNOULD
### 28 rue de Mailly
### 51360 Verzenay
### ★★✓**V**

Arnould is a traditional grower specializing in pure Verzenay Champagne, including a very rich but exquisitely balanced *blanc de noirs* Grand Cru Brut Réserve.

✓ *Grand Cru Brut* (**NV**) • *Grand Cru Brut Rosé* (**NV**) • *Grand Cru Brut Réserve* (**NV**)

## AYALA & CO (GM)
### Château d'Aÿ
### 51160 Aÿ-Champagne
### ★✓**V**

Now owned by Bollinger, Ayala is under the direct control of Hervé Augustin, former head of De Castellane. Initial signs are that he will be allowed the same freedom to compete at the highest level as Roederer's Rouzaud family has allowed Fabrice Rosset at Deutz.

✓ *Brut* (**NV**) • *Brut* (**V**) • *Grande Cuvée* (**V**) • *Perle d'Ayala*

## BEAUMONT DES CRAYÈRES
### 64 rue de la Liberté
### 51318 Mardeuil
### ★✓**V**

This cooperative's 210 members own just 200 acres (80 hectares) of vineyards and they are mostly of modest origin, but they are tended like gardens, without resort to machines or chemical treatments. Winemaker Jean-Paul Bertus regularly produces richly flavored Champagne with a light *dosage*.

✓ *Fleur de Rosé* (**V**) • *Fleur de Prestige* (**V**)

## BILLECART-SALMON (GM)
### 40 rue Carnot
### 51160 Mareuil-sur-Aÿ
### ★★★✓

Billecart-Salmon is a small, family-owned (55 percent), *grande marque* of exceptionally high quality. This house has an excellent reputation for the delicate, silky style of its rosé Champagnes, which it has been producing since 1830, and its top-of-the-line Cuvée Elisabeth Salmon Rosé really is exquisite. All the Champagnes here have a delicious richness of fruit, with an accent on elegance and finesse. The single-vineyard Clos St-Hilaire is very good, but has the potential to be much greater with a true *dosage*.

✓ *Entire range*

## BOIZEL
### 14 rue de Bernon
### 51200 Epernay
### ★★✓**V**

Boizel is now part of BCC (Boizel-Chanoine Champagne), one of the industry's youngest and most dynamic companies (of which Bruno Paillard is the chairman and the largest shareholder, although the Roques-Boizel family and Philippe Baijot of Chanoine are almost equal partners). Although the nonvintage Boizel has occasionally been prone to the ubiquitous pear-drop style, quality has been more consistent since 1995 and the *blanc de blancs*, rosé, and prestige *cuvée* have always stood out.

✓ *Brut* (**NV**) • *Blanc de Blancs* (**NV**) • *Rosé* (**V**) • *Joyau de France* (**PC**) • *Joyau de Chardonnay* (**V**)

## BOLLINGER (GM)
### Rue Jules Lobet
### 51160 Aÿ-Champagne
### ★★★✓

If you find the nonvintage Special Cuvée too austere, try it in magnums, which are always fruitier. Bollinger is, however, a house *par excellence* for vintage Champagne and, although famous for its R. D. (exactly the same Champagne as the Grande Année, but with longer yeast contact), I prefer buying the Grande Année when released, and aging after disgorgement.

✓ *Entire range*

## BONNAIRE
### 120 rue d'Epernay
### 51530 Cramant
### ★★✓**V**

Although occasionally spoiled by dominant malolactic or the whisper of lifted fruit, most wines are a pure joy, with beautifully focused fruit, and a luxuriantly creamy finish. When on form, these are stunningly rich, crisp, and vivacious wines, with intense, zippy-zingy fruit supported by great acidity, offering great potential longevity.

✓ *Brut Blanc de Blancs* (**NV**) • *Cuvée Prestige* (**V**) • *Cramant Grand Cru* (**V**)

## RAYMOND BOULARD
### Route Nationale 44
### 51220 Cauroy-les-Hermonville
### ★★✓**V**

Run by Francis Boulard, whose style tends to be lifted fruit with oxidative complexity and, like most export-conscious growers these days, he is dabbling with new oak.

✓ *Cuvée Rosé Brut* (**NV**) • *Brut Tradition* (**NV**)

## CHÂTEAU DE BOURSAULT

**Boursault**

**51480 prés Epernay**

★✰ⓥ

Château de Boursault NV has started to develop a real finesse since 1995, and the rosé has always been a joy. Made by owner Harald Fringhian, these Champagnes are now outperforming the château's modest 84 percent *échelle*, which is probably helped by the fact that the vineyards are a genuine *clos* (an enclosed plot of land).

✓ *Rosé* (**NV**)

## CANARD DUCHÊNE (GM)

**1 rue Edmond Canard**

**51500 Ludes**

★✰ⓥ

Owned by Veuve Clicquot from 1978 until 2003, when it was sold to the Alain Thienot group, these value-for-money, easy-drinking Champagnes have improved significantly since the mid-1990s. The Blanc de Noirs version of Charles VII prestige *cuvée* is serious quality.

✓ *Brut* (**NV**) • *Rosé* (**NV**) • *Charles VII Blanc de Noirs* (**NV**)

## DE CASTELLANE

**57 rue Verdun**

**51200 Epernay**

★ⓥ

Part of the Laurent-Perrier group, this is an excellent source of undervalued, ripe, exotic *blanc de blancs*, as are the more expensive Cuvée Commodore and Cuvée Florens de Castellane, despite their presentation—the former looks like its from the 1950s, while the latter is decidedly kitsch.

✓ *Chardonnay* (**NV**) • *Cuvée Royale Chardonnay* (**V**) • *Cuvée Commodore* (**PC**) • *Cuvée Florens de Castellane* (**PC**)

## CATTIER

**6 et 11 rue Dom Pérignon**

**51500 Chigny-les-Roses**

★ⓥ

I have always respected Clos du Moulin, Cattier's great single-vineyard Champagne, but have not been impressed—or depressed for that matter—by any of the other *cuvées*, until I first tasted its trio of particularly stunning vintages: 1988, 1989, and 1990.

✓ *Brut* (**V**) • *Clos du Moulin* (**SV**)

## CHANOINE

**avenue de Champagne**

**51100 Reims**

★ⓥ

This marque was established in 1730 (just one year after Ruinart, the oldest house in Champagne) but was relaunched by Philippe Baijot in 1991. I was greatly impressed with the first *cuvées* following the relaunch, but their brilliant quality has never been recaptured. Well, not in the basic vintage and nonvintage, but the more recent

Tsarine *cuvées* promise to grab attention (and I don't only mean because of the convoluted bottle shape, which comes out of the same mold as a certain brand of Asti!). The first vintage (1999) of Tsarine Rosé is of exceptional quality and elegance.

✓ *Tsarine* (**NV**) • *Tsarine* (**V**)

## CHAUVET

**41 avenue de Champagne**

**51150 Tours-sur-Marne**

★ⓥ

A small, quality-conscious house situated opposite Laurent Perrier, Champagne Chauvet is owned by the Paillard-Chauvet family, who are wonderfully eccentric. They are related to Pierre Paillard in Bouzy, Bruno Paillard in Reims, and the Gossets of Aÿ. I have always enjoyed Chauvet's Carte Vert *blanc de blancs*, which is an excellent nonvintage blend of exclusively *grand cru* wines, and I have also greatly admired the consistency and quality of their entire range since the early 1990s.

✓ *Entire range*

## GASTON CHIQUET

**890-912 avenue du Général-Leclerc**

**51310 Dizy**

★✰ⓥ

Antoine and Nicolas Chiquet are grower cousins of *négociants* Jean-Hervé and Laurent Chiquet of Jacquesson, which is also in Dizy. The style here is succulent and creamy, with moreish juicy fruit. Only a tendency to use volatile acidity to lift the fruit holds this producer back from a two-star rating.

✓ *Entire range*

## ANDRÉ CLOUET

**8 rue Gambetta**

**51150 Bouzy**

★

André Clouet, a small, quality-conscious grower, produces a very large range of attractive, rich, and beautifully made Champagnes.

✓ *Brut Grande Réserve* (**NV**) • *Brut Millésime* (**V**)

## COMTE AUDOIN DE DAMPIERRE

**5 Grande Rue**

**51140 Chenay**

★ⓥ

This Anglophile, lovingly eccentric, classic car fanatic of an aristocrat is one of those larger than life characters who are simply too charming and polite to ignore.

Elegant and fruity, most *cuvées* are nicely made for current drinking. The cork on Dampierre's late disgorged *grand cru blanc de blancs* is tied down in the old style with hemp, and even comes with a pair of scissors in the box!

✓ *Entire range*

## DELAMOTTE PÈRE & FILS

**5 rue de la Brèche**

**51190 Le Mesnil-sur-Oger**

★ⓥ

Part of the Laurent-Perrier group and situated next door to Champagne Salon, which also belongs to Laurent-Perrier, Delamotte is a small, underrated, high-quality, good-value house that has been privately owned by the Nonancourt family (the owners of Laurent-Perrier) since the end of World War I, when it was purchased by Marie Louise de Nonancourt, the sister of Victor and Henri Lanson.

✓ *Brut* (**NV**) • *Blanc de Blancs* (**NV**) • *Blanc de Blancs* (**V**) • *Nicolas Louis Delamotte* (**PC**)

## PAUL DÉTHUNE

**2 rue du Moulin**

**51150 Ambonnay**

★✰ⓥ

As one of the more consistent growers, Paul Déthune always makes good vintage and rosé, but is best known for his prestige *cuvée*, the luxuriously rich, big, deliciously creamy Princesse des Thunes, which is made from an assemblage of mature vintages. Try his fascinating, educational, and quality-driven Trilogy Ambonnay Grand Cru: three bottles labeled Cuvée 1, 2, and 3—each one being made from the same Pinot Noir and Chardonnay wines, but in different proportions. Decide which one you prefer (they are all excellent), then discover why. Also, from 2005, look out for Cuvée à l'Ancienne.

✓ *Grand Cru Rosé* (**NV**) • *Millésimé* (**V**) • *Trilogy* (**V**) • *Princesse des Thunes* (**PC**)

## DEUTZ (GM)

**16 rue Jeanson**

**51160 Aÿ-Champagne**

★★★✰ⓥ

The profitability and quality of Deutz suffered from underfunding until Roederer acquired it in 1983. Its resurgence began a little shakily with the 1985 vintage but was firmly established by 1988, when it returned to making very stylish Champagnes. Now on stunning form. Deutz also owns Delas Frères in the Rhône and Château Vernous in the Médoc, and has a partnership

Montana to produce Deutz Marlborough in New Zealand (owned by Pernod-Ricard, which owns Mumm and Perrier-Jouët).

✓ *Entire range*

## DRAPPIER

**Grande rue**

**10200 Urville**

★★✰ⓥ

Drappier's Champagnes are brilliantly consistent, ultrafruity, and rapidly acquire mellow biscuity complexity.

✓ *Entire range*

## J. DUMANGIN

**3 rue de Rilly**

**51500 Chigny-les-Roses**

★ⓥ

Run by Gilles Dumangin, who makes soft, fruit-driven Champagnes that tend to go biscuity rather than, or as well as, toasty.

✓ *Brut Grande Réserve* (**NV**)

## DUVAL-LEROY

**65 avenue de Bammental**

**51130 Vertus**

★★✰ⓥ

Duval-Leroy has achieved a great consistency of quality for its fresh, light, and elegant house style, thanks to Hervé Jestin, Duval-Leroy's former winemaker. Couple this with Carol Duval's focus on the primary brand—to the detriment, thankfully, of the firm's BOB business (once its staple)—and it is easy to appreciate just how close Duval-Leroy was to rubbing shoulders with the elite group of famous names at the turn of the millennium. The quietly spoken Jestin, however, kept his blending recipes a secret, which unfortunately led to his departure in December 2005. He is succeeded by Sandrine Logette, an oenologist who has worked for Duval-Leroy since 1991. She has a hard act to follow.

✓ *Entire range*

## NICOLAS FEUILLATTE

**CV de Chouilly**

**51206 Chouilly**

★ⓥ

Some of this giant cooperative's customers seem to be under the impression that Nicolas Feuillatte is a small, lone grower. The guy exists, but he just represents this super-cooperative brand. Aside from a couple of special wines (the 1985 Palmes d'Or Brut, and the 1992 Palmes d'Or Brut in magnums), I was never enamoured of the quality here until the splendid 1995s and 1996s. The trio of 1995 single-village grand cru Champagnes was as inspired and as innovative as any cooperative has achieved, including the very best (Devaux, Palmer, and Jacquart), and I was delighted to hear that the range had been extended to six for the 1996 vintage. But despite the greatness of that year, and Feuillatte's success with other 1996s, the quality was not as exciting. Perhaps they just need more time on yeast? They are worth keeping an eye on, even if I cannot give them *carte blanche* approval below. And Feuillatte's newfound quality has continued into the 1997 vintage, so it is good to know that the surge in quality is not a flash in the pan due more to vintage than intrinsic improvements.

☑ *Cuvée Speciale* (**V**) • *Palmes d'Or* (**V**) • *Palmes d'Or Rosé* (**V**)

## FLEURY
### 43 Grande rue
### 10250 Courteron
### Ⓑ★Ⓥ

One of the more readily available biodynamic Champagnes on export markets, Fleury was nothing more than acceptable until the 1996 vintage, when this grower produced a classic *barrique*-fermented Champagne with a mind-blowing barrage of aromas and flavors.

☑ *Fleur de l'Europe Brut* (**NV**) • *Brut* (**V**)

## FLUTEAU
### 5 rue de la Nation
### 10250 Gyé-sur-Seine
### ★Ⓥ

Thierry Fluteau and his American wife Jennifer tend to release their Champagnes one year ahead of most others, when they are very fruity and easy to drink. Vintaged *cuvées* are worth keeping and should be purchased in magnums, which are at their beautiful best in their seventh or eighth year.

☑ *Entire range*

## GARDET & CIE
### 13 rue Georges Legros
### 51500 Chigny-les-Roses
### ★Ⓥ

This Champagne used to be sold as Georges Gardet in the UK and Charles Gardet in France, but the emphasis is now on Gardet plain and simple. Gardet has always prided itself on the longevity of its wines, but I prefer the vintage almost before it is even released, although the greatest Gardet I have ever tasted was the 1964 in 1995. A very welcome addition to the range is the succulent new *blanc de blancs*, the first vintage of which was 1990.

☑ *Brut Spécial* (**NV**) • *Brut* (**V**) • *Blanc de Blancs* (**V**)

## RENÉ GEOFFROY
### 150 rue du Bois-des-Jots
### 51480 Cumières
### ★Ⓥ

The Geoffroy family have been growers in Cumières since 1600 and they conscientiously harvest grapes in *tries*. The Champagne, which does not go through malolactic fermentation and may be matured in oak *foudres*, is classic in style, long-lived, and capable of great complexity.

☑ *Cuvée Prestige* (**NV**) • *Cuvée de Réserve Brut* (**NV**) • *Cuvée*

*Sélectionnée Brut* (**V**) • *Brut Rosé* (**NV**)

## PIERRE GIMONNET
### 1 rue de la République
### 51530 Cuis
### ★☆Ⓥ

This excellent grower's vineyards are all planted with Chardonnay, hence every wine is a *blanc de blancs*, which is a very rare phenomenon, even among growers on the Côte des Blancs. Quality is exceptionally high and prices very reasonable.

☑ *Entire range*

## PAUL GOERG
### 4 Place du Mont Chenil
### 51130 Vertus
### ★Ⓥ

This small but superior *coopérative* produces very fine and elegant yet rich, concentrated Champagnes.

☑ *Blanc de Blancs* (**NV**) • *Brut* (**V**) • *Cuvée Lady C* (**V**)

## GOSSET (**GM**)
### 69 rue Jules Blondeau
### 51160 Aÿ-Champagne

Established in 1584, Gosset is the oldest house in the region, but for still wines, not sparkling. In 1992, Gosset became the first new *grande marque* for more than 30 years; then, in 1994, after 400 years of family ownership, the house was sold to the Cointreau family, and is now under the direct control of Jean-Pierre Cointreau. The *chef de caves* and oenologist remain the same, as do the winemaking techniques. I have always rated the Grande Réserve, the Grand Millésimé, and the Grand Millésimé Rosé as three of the consistently greatest Champagnes available, and they have since been accompanied by the prestige vintage *brut* and rosé under the Celebris label.

☑ *Entire range* (except Brut Excellence)

## HENRI GOUTORBE
### 11 rue Jeanson
### 51160 Aÿ-Champagne
### ★☆Ⓥ

With 37 acres (15 hectares) of vineyards and half a million bottles in stock, this is one of the larger wine growers. Henri Goutorbe produces some rich, classic, and well-structured Champagnes that become very satisfying with age.

☑ *Entire range*

## ALFRED GRATIEN
### 30 rue Maurice-Cerveaux
### 51201 Epernay
### ★☆Ⓥ

This house is part of Gratien, Meyer, Seydoux & Cie, who also sell a range of Loire traditional method wines under the Gratien & Meyer brand. Alfred Gratien is one of the most traditionally produced Champagnes available. The old

vintages never fail to amaze, as they are brilliant in quality and retain a remarkable freshness for decades. The nonvintage wine is beautifully fresh with mature reserves coming through on the palate, making it a wine to drink now, yet one that will improve with age.

☑ *Vintage Brut*

## CHARLES HEIDSIECK (**GM**)
### 12 allée du Vignoble
### 51061 Reims
### ★★Ⓥ

Charles Heidsieck is part of Rémy-Cointreau's Champagne group, which also includes Piper-Heidsieck. The superb quality of the house of Charles Heidsieck was guided by the masterly hand of Daniel Thibault until his untimely demise in 2002. As his creation of Mis en Cave demonstrated, Thibault was one of Champagne's greatest winemakers. Mis en Cave is still the best-value, most consistent Champagne in the richly flavored style, regularly achieving a standard few vintage Champagnes can match. Thibault will be a hard act to follow, but for a few years he had been grooming Régis Camus, the former *chef de caves* at Jacquart, to do just that. Due to the long lead time required before a Champagne reaches the shelf, it will not be until the year following publication of this edition of the encyclopedia that we will begin to know whether he is succeeding. This Champagne is rated on the hope that he is.

☑ *Entire range*

## HENRIOT
### 3 place des Droits-de-l'Homme
### 51100 Reims
### ★

Under family ownership since 1994, when Joseph Henriot left Clicquot, the house he had famously performed a reverse-takeover on prior to the formation of LVMH. Henriot's son, Stanislaus, is now in day-to-day control, while Odilon de Varenne has moved from Deutz to take over as *chef de caves*. Aside from the fact that the Enchanteleurs is more often than not released far too late, there is not much to criticize here.

☑ *Cuvée des Enchanteleurs* (**V**) • *Brut Millésime* (**V**) • *Blanc de Blancs Brut* (**NV**)

## JACQUART
### 5 rue Gosset
### 51066 Reims
### ★☆Ⓥ

This CRVC (Coopérative Régionale des Vins de Champagne) *coopérative* cleverly converted its primary brand into a *négociant-manipulant* Champagne by making its members shareholders. The quality of Jacquart is always acceptable at the very least, and some vintages, such as the 1985, can be outstanding, while the 1987 turned out to be one of the four best wines of that year.

☑ *Cuvée Mosaïque Brut* (**V**) • *Cuvée Mosaïque Blanc de Blancs* (**V**) • *Cuvée Mosaïque Rosé* (**V**) • *Brut de Nominée* (**NV**) • *Cuvée Onctueuse Rosé* (**NV**)

## JACQUESSON & FILS
### 68 rue du Colonel Fabien
### 51310 Dizy
### ★★★☆

This small, family-owned house is run by the Chiquet brothers, two of the most charming people you are likely to meet. Michael McKenzie of Mayfair Cellars is a shareholder. Jacquesson makes utterly sublime Champagnes, on the same quality level as Billecart-Salmon, but in a bigger, fuller style. Both houses make Champagnes of complexity and finesse, but Jacquesson has more complexity, while Billecart-Salmon has more finesse. Jacquesson has pioneered various quality-enhancing practices in the vineyards, while in the winery it has turned Champagne's traditional nonvintage concept on its head by not attempting any consistency in style. Rather than smooth out the differences presented by each harvest, the new concept is to produce the best possible nonvintage Champagne each year. It is something that no large *grande marque* would dare contemplate, but it is a very clever move for a small house, as it effectively creates a second vintage wine and one that is easier to make, given the flexibility of blending in wine from other years. The first new nonvintage was named Cuvée No. 728 and was 2000-based, Cuvée No. 729 is 2001-based, and so on. Another innovation is a whole raft of single-vineyard Champagnes, the best of which will take several vintages to discern, although the 1998 Le Clos de Jacquesson, a pure Pinot Meunier Champagne, has been the most exciting so far. And the 2003 Oiry Champ Braux *vin clair* was so delicious that I ordered a case bottled as a still wine!

☑ *Entire range*

## ANDRÉ JARRY
### Rue Principale
### 51260 Bethon
### ★Ⓥ

Excellent Champagne in a style that is midway between the classic character of Champagnes from the Marne *département* and the exotic character of Sézannais Champagnes, full of biscuity richness yet with an aftertaste of vanilla and peaches.

☑ *Cuvée Special* (**NV**)

## KRUG & CO. (**GM**)
### 5 rue Coquebert
### 51051 Reims
### ★★★

Krug puts quality first and makes Champagne in its own individual style, regardless of popular taste or production costs. With the possible exception of Salon, this sort of quality is not equaled by any other

Champagne house, although it could be if they were willing to sell tiny quantities at very high prices. If everyone did this, it would be a disaster—Champagne has to be affordable—but that at least one house does is not just laudable, it is very important for Champagne.

✓ *Entire range*

## LANSON INTERNATIONAL
### 22 rue Maurice-Cerveaux
### 51205 Epernay
### ★ ⓥ

Formerly known as Marne et Champagne, Lanson International was acquired by BCC in 2006. It is likely that the new owners will cull some of the more obscure brands among the company's portfolio of 200 labels. Like Lanson, all these Champagnes are produced without malolactic fermentation, and the quality, even under the most obscure label or BOBs, can be very good, particularly if cellared for an additional 12 months. The best Champagnes are to be found under the Besserat de Bellefon, Alfred Rothschild (restricted to the French market), Pol Gessner, Eugène Cliquot, Geismann & Co, and Gauthier labels. Other top-selling brands include Pol Albert, Bourgeois, Baron de Brou, De Bracieux, Colligny Père & Fils, Delacoste & Fils, Laurence Duvivier, Leprince-Royer, Georges Martel, Mary Martin, Veuve Pasquier & Fils, Roger Perreau, Roger Perroy, Marquis de Prevel, and Veuve Guérin.

## LANSON PÈRE & FILS (GM)
### 12 boulevard Lundy
### 51056 Reims
### ★ ★ ⓥ

This house was purchased in 1991 by Marne et Champagne (now Lanson International) and is now owned by BCC (Boizel Chanoine Champagne). Lanson famously eschewed malolactic, excelling at classic, slow-maturing, biscuity vintage Champagnes, but the deal did not include the vineyards that this *grande marque* had relied upon, so the jury was out for a while. Even when Lanson had vineyards, the vintages were sometimes ordinary at best when released, but devotees got to know a good vintage when they saw one (some stunning old vintages *en magnum* are still commercially available: 1989, 1988, 1981, 1979, 1976). When the 1993 was first released, it was a creditable wine, but not special, and this was put down to the good, but not exceptional, year. However, it attained much more gravitas with an additional 12 months on yeast, and today the magnums with 4 years postdisgorgement aging are unbelievably classic in quality. The 1995 was obviously excellent from the start, but the 1996 is singularly special—the greatest value, classic quality Champagne of that very particular year. Lanson is back!

✓ *Entire range*

## GUY LARMANDIER
### 30 rue du Général Koenig
### 51130 Vertus
### ★

Guy and François Larmandier have a well-earned reputation for finely balanced wines of surprising depth and obvious finesse.

✓ *Blanc de Blancs Cramant* (**NV**)

## LARMANDIER-BERNIER
### 43 rue du 28 août
### 51130 Vertus
### Ⓑ ★

These high-quality *blanc de blancs* Champagnes are made by Pierre Larmandier, the president of the Young Winegrowers of Champagne.

✓ *Entire range*

## LAURENT-PERRIER (GM)
### Avenue de Champagne
### 51150 Tours-sur-Marne
### ★ ★ ⓥ

This house used to head a sprawling vinous empire until its outposts in Burgundy and Bordeaux were sold off to concentrate Laurent-Perrier's efforts and finances on its Champagne holdings, including De Castellane, Delamotte, Lemoine, and Salon, and in 2003 it took over Château Malakoff (Champagnes Beaumet, Jeanmaire, and Oudinot, plus the Michelin-starred La Briqueterie in Vinay). Michel Fauconnet took over as *chef de caves* in early 2004.

✓ *Entire range* (except Ultra Brut)

## LECLERC BRIANT
### 67 rue de la Chaude-Ruelle
### 51204 Epernay
### Ⓑ ⓥ

Pascal Leclerc can come up with the odd Champagne to dumbfound people, such as his blood-red Rubis Rosé des Noirs, which excels in some vintages. When he does, they represent excellent value for money, but there could be more consistency here. His Les Authentiques range of single-vineyard Champagnes was a brilliant marketing concept, but the wines, while enjoyable enough when launched, have failed to display any consistent and distinctive *terroir* character. A *cuvée* called Divine is the best of the range, despite its gaudy label.

✓ *Divine* (**PC**)

## LILBERT FILS
### 223 rue du Moutier
### 51200 Cramant
### ★

This house is a consistent producer of firm *blancs de blancs* that show finesse and age gracefully.

✓ *Entire range*

## MAILLY GRAND CRU
### 28 rue de la Liberation
### 51500 Mailly-Champagne
### ★ ½ ⓥ

I have never been so impressed by this mono-*cru* cooperative than I am now. The quality and innovation has been on a roll for a few years.

✓ *Cassiopée* (**NV**) • *Brut Millésime* (**V**) • *Cuvée des Echansons* (**V**) • *Cuvée l'Intemporelle* (**V**) • *Cuvée du 60e Anniversaire* (**V**)

## HENRI MANDOIS
### 66 rue du Gal-de-Gaulle
### 51200 Pierry
### ★ ½ ⓥ

The house style of Henri Mandois is for elegant Champagnes that have a very satisfying length of attractive, creamy fruit, and a fine balance. Most *cuvées* peak at between five and six years of age and do not attain great complexity. However, they do represent great value and give much satisfaction. Jimmy Boyle's favorite Champagne!

✓ *Entire range*

## SERGE MATHIEU
### Les Riceys
### 10340 Avirey-Lingey
### ★ ★ ⓥ

Mathieu, a small grower in the Aube, consistently produces excellent Champagnes that are beautifully focused, have much finesse, and a real richness of fruit for such light and elegantly balanced wines.

✓ *Entire range*

## MERCIER (GM)
### 75 avenue de Champagne
### 51200 Epernay
### ⓥ

Mercier, established by Eugène Mercier in 1858, was the original owner of the Dom Pérignon brand, although it never utilized it and, in a strange twist of fate, sold it to Moët & Chandon in 1930. Moët liked the product so much that it bought Mercier, albeit some 40 years later. Mercier is still the best-selling brand in France, no matter how hard the parent company tries to make Moët number one, although Moët is way ahead in global sales. There are rumors that LVMH wants shot of Mercier like it did Canard-Duchêne (the reasoning being that it would increase the vineyards-to-sales ratio, the average price of LVMH brands, and gross profit percentage), and it would not surprise me if this house were to be snapped up by Lanson International.

✓ *Brut* (**V**)

## DE MERIC
### 17 rue Gambetta
### 51160 Aÿ-Champagne
### ★ ⓥ

De Meric, whose wines are made by Christian Besserat, ranges from the simple but elegant and fruity nonvintage Brut to the sublime and very special Cuvée Cathérine de Medicis, with various fine and fragrant *cuvées* in between.

✓ *Blanc de Blancs* (**NV**) • *Rosé* (**NV**) • *Cuvée Cathérine de Medicis* (**PC**)

## LE MESNIL
### Union des Propriétaires Récoltants
### 51390 Le Mesnil-sur-Oger
### ★ ⓥ

If only this cooperative's basic Champagnes were as stunning as those recommended below.

✓ *Vigne Sélectionnée Blanc de Blancs* (**V**) • *Réserve Sélection, Blanc de Blancs* (**V**) • *Sublime* (**V**)

## MOËT & CHANDON (GM)
### 20 avenue de Champagne
### 54120 Epernay
### ★ ½

The largest Champagne house by a mile, Moët is also the leading company in the LVMH group, which also includes Mercier, Krug, Ruinart, Pommery, and Veuve Clicquot. When first released, the soft style of Brut Impérial makes it amenable to everyone and offensive to no one, but after a further 12 months bottle-age, it mellows into a much fuller, toasty-rich Champagne that has won many a competitive tasting. Between the unfairly criticized nonvintage and the universally praised Dom Pérignon, the vintage Brut Impérial and Brut Impérial Rosé have both been ignored and underrated. With sales of Dom Pérignon approaching two million bottles, and a group ethos that is pushing the premium *cuvée* envelope (by cutting out lower-priced brands, increasing the vineyard-to-sales ratio, and introducing innovative, premium-priced *cuvées*), the obvious move would be to add another 247 acres (100 hectares) to the 494 (200 hectares) currently reserved for this most famous of Champagnes, invest in a showcase winery exclusively devoted to Dom Pérignon, and develop a range of wines under this label, which is already perceived as a brand in its own right.

✓ *Brut Impérial* (**V**) • *Dom Pérignon* (**PC**) • *Dom Pérignon Rosé* (**PC**)

## MONCUIT
### 11 rue Persault-Maheu
### 51190 Le Mesnil-sur-Oger
### ★ ⓥ

Some years (or disgorgements of apparently the same wine) can have overly dominant buttery-malo aromas, while others are fresh and crisp, with lively rich fruit that is tasty and satisfying. Usually matures into a creamy-biscuity style.

✓ *Cuvée Nicole Moncuit Vieille Vigne* (**V**)

## G. H. MUMM & CO. (GM)
### 29 & 34 rue du Champ-de-Mars
### 51053 Reims
### ★

Now owned by Pernod-Ricard, Mumm has successfully pulled its act together, thanks to a young winemaker by the name of Dominique Demarville, who was put in charge of winemaking at this large *grande marque* house back in 1998. He was so successful, so quickly and so efficiently, that he was promoted to wines and vines director for both Mumm and Perrier-Jouët, yet such is his modesty that he accepted a lower position—assistant *chef de caves* at Veuve Clicquot—just to learn from his winemaking idol Jacques Peters. Hopefully Demarville's replacement, Didier Mariotti, will continue to improve the quality at Mumm, returning to its authentic house style of freshness, light balance, fragrance, and elegance.

✓ *Brut Rosé* (**NV**) • *Demi-Sec* (**NV**) • *Mumm de Cramant* (**NV**) • *Cordon Rouge* (**V**)

## BRUNO PAILLARD
### avenue du Champagne
### 51100 Reims
### ★✰❤

Bruno Paillard is Champagne's fastest-rising star. He opts for elegance rather than body or character, and his Première Cuvée is not just elegant, but one of the most consistent nonvintage Champagnes on the market. This house belongs personally to Bruno Paillard and is not part of the BCC group, which he also heads.

✓ *Entire range*

## PALMER & CO.
### 67 rue Jacquart
### 51100 Reims
### ★❤

Palmer is generally acknowledged to be one of the highest-quality and most reliable *coopératives* in Champagne, on top of which it has a growing reputation for the excellent Champagnes sold under its own label and is particularly well known for its mature vintages.

✓ *Entire range*

## PANNIER
### 23 rue Roger Catillon
### 02400 Château-Thierry
### ★❤

For some time now this coopérative has been able to produce some very good vintage Champagne, especially its prestige *cuvée* Egérie de Pannier, but the basic Brut Tradition was always forthright. This changed with the 1990-based Brut Tradition. Although this was and still is Pannier's best *cuvée*, due no doubt to the year in question, it also marked a general increase in finesse and this promises better quality ahead.

✓ *Brut Tradition* (**NV**) • *Brut Vintage* (**V**) • *Egérie de Pannier* (**V**)

## JOSEPH PERRIER (GM)
### 69 avenue de Paris
### 51005 Châlons-sur-Marne
### ★❤

This house is still run by Jean-Claude Fourmon, even though he has sold a 51 percent share in the business to his cousin Alain Thienot via an ephemeral interest by Laurent-Perrier. The style of these Champagnes is rich and mellow, although the difference when switching from one *cuvée* or vintage to the next can be quite severe, and the wines need to be laid down for 12 months or so.

✓ *Cuvée Royale* (**NV**) • *Cuvée Royale Rosé* (**NV**) • *Cuvée Royale Blanc de Blancs* (**NV**) • *Cuvée Royale* (**V**) • *Cuvée Joséphine* (**PC**)

## PERRIER-JOUËT (GM)
### 26/28 avenue de Champagne
### 51200 Epernay
### ★✰

Now owned by Pernod-Ricard, along with its sister house Mumm. The straight vintage here has always been one of Champagne's longest-lived, and this standard has been maintained by the current *chef de caves*, Hervé Deschamps.

✓ *Grand Brut* (**V**) • *Belle Époque Brut* (**PC**) • *Belle Époque Rosé* (**PC**) • *Belle Époque Blanc de Blancs* (**PC**)

## PHILIPPONNAT
### 13 rue du Pont
### 51160 Mareuil-sur-Aÿ
### ★✰

Part of the BCC group, under the day-to-day control of Charles Philipponnat, a direct descendant and a sharp player in the grape-buying business. Philipponnat has built new facilities, with space for up to 500 barrels. Clos des Goisses is already 35 to 45 percent wood and will stay that way; vintages are 15 to 20 percent wood and will increase to about 30 to 35 percent; nonvintage is 5 to 10 percent and will increase to 20 to 25 percent. Clos des Goisses remains Philipponnat's jewel in the crown—one of the greatest Champagnes available, Clos des Goisses is a fully south-facing vineyard on a very steep incline overlooking the Marne canal.

✓ *Grand Blanc* (**V**) • *Clos des Goisses* (**PC**) • *Abel Lepitre* (Cuvée No. 134, Brut Millésime)

## PIPER-HEIDSIECK (GM)
### 51 boulevard Henri Vasnier
### 51100 Reims
### ★✰❤

After working his miracles on Charles Heidsieck, the late Daniel Thibault upgraded the quality of Piper-Heidsieck without upsetting the supremacy of its sister brand. He achieved this by pouring more fruit into the blend and sourcing much of it from the warm Aube vineyards, giving the wine a soft but simple, fruity aroma, and very tempting fruit on the palate. New *chef de caves* Régis Camus launched a quartet of delicious new *cuvées* in 2004, the same year that the 1996 vintage (made by Thibault) scooped the Champagne Trophy at the first Decanter World Wine Awards.

✓ *Rosé Sauvage* (**NV**) • *Divin Blanc de Blancs* (**NV**) • *Brut Millésimé* (**V**) • *Cuvée Rare* (**PC**) • *Sublime* (**NV**)

## PLOYEZ-JACQUEMART
### 51500 Ludes
### ★❤

Although the prestige *cuvée* L. d'Harbonville has always been excellent, it has jumped up a class since the 1989 vintage, when it was first fermented in small oak barrels and not put through its malolactic fermentation. This made it even more succulent and mouthwatering than usual, with ample *dosage* to balance its electrifying acidity.

✓ *Entire range*

## POL ROGER & CO. (GM)
### 1 rue Henri Lelarge
### 51206 Epernay
### ★★★✰❤

If I were to choose just one house from which to source a vintage Champagne to lay down, there is no question that I would choose Pol Roger. There are always exceptions, of course, but, generally speaking, these Champagnes last longer and remain fresher than those of any other house, however justified their great reputations may be, and I base this opinion on tasting a good number of vintages spanning back a century or more at many houses.

✓ *Entire range*

## POMMERY (GM)
### 5 place Général-Gouraud
### 51053 Reims
### ★★

Owned by Vranken, Pommery has been on a roll since 1995, which is no mean feat for such a light and elegant Champagne with a production of almost seven million bottles, because the lighter the wine's style, the more difficult it is to maintain the quality as production increases.

✓ *Entire range*

## LOUIS ROEDERER (GM)
### 21 boulevard Lundy
### 51100 Reims
### ★★★✰❤

Louis Roederer is the most profitable house in Champagne, and should be an object lesson for those houses that count success in terms of the number of bottles they sell. The keys to real success in Champagne are an impeccable reputation, which guarantees a premium price; sufficient vineyards to guarantee consistent quality for a production large enough to rake in the money; and the self-discipline required not to go beyond that level. Jean-Claude Rouzaud knows that if he goes too far beyond Roederer's current production of 2.5 million bottles, he will be unable to guarantee the quality he demands and his brand would soon lose the cachet of relative exclusiveness. He does not, however, like to see his capital lie idle, which is why he would rather take over Deutz than increase his own production. Jean-Baptiste Lecaillon has slipped seamlessly into the position of *chef de cave* previously occupied by the talented Michel Pansu.

✓ *Entire range*

## RUINART (GM)
### 4 rue de Crayères
### 51053 Reims
### ★★

Established in 1729 by Nicolas Ruinart, this is the oldest commercial producer of sparkling Champagne. This house was taken over in 1963 by Moët & Chandon, but has managed to maintain the image of an independent, premium-quality Champagne in spite of it being part of LVMH, the largest Champagne group, and tripling its production in the meantime. The house style tends to develop very toasty aromas.

✓ *Entire range*

## SALON (GM)
### 5 rue de la Brèche
### 51190 Le Mesnil-sur-Oger
### ★★★

Owned by Laurent-Perrier, located next door to Delamotte (also owned by Laurent-Perrier), Salon is one of the greatest Champagnes available, and possibly the rarest, since only one *cuvée* is produced and it is exclusively vintage, thus it is not produced every year. The wine does not usually undergo malolactic fermentation, is often kept on its sediment for 10 years or more, and continues to benefit from at least an equal amount of aging after disgorgement.

✓ *"S"* (**V**)

## JACQUES SÉLOSSE
### 22 rue Ernest Vallée
### 51190 Avize
### ★★

Anselme Sélosse has found a niche in the market for *barrique*-fermented, nonmalolactic wines that receive minimal *dosage* and usually require several years extra postdisgorgement cellarage to show their full potential, by which time they have lost much of the finesse that would have been present with a normal *dosage*. Generally far too much raw oak for my liking, but there is no denying the quality of the wine underneath, and rated for those who like the style.

✓ *Entire range* (but with care)

## TAITTINGER (GM)
9 place Saint-Niçaise
51061 Reims
★★

This house uses a high proportion of Chardonnay in its nonvintage Brut Réserve, making it one of the most elegant and delicate of *grande marque* Champagnes. Comtes de Champagne *blanc de blancs* is one of the greatest Champagnes produced.
✓ *Entire range*

## ALAIN THIENOT
14 rue des Moissons
51100 Reims
★☉

A very savvy financier who has quietly built up a significant group (including Joseph Perrier, Canard-Duchêne, George Goulet, and Marie Stuart), Alain Thienot also produces good-value, fruit-driven Champagnes under his own label, ranging from a successful pouring-quality nonvintage, through good-quality vintage *brut* and rosé, to an excellent Cuvée Stanislas.
✓ *Brut Rosé* (**V**) • *Grand Cuvée Brut* (**V**) • *Cuvée Stanislas* (**V**)

## UNION CHAMPAGNE
7 rue Pasteur
51190 Avize
☉

Champagne de St.-Gall is this cooperative's primary brand, with Cuvée Orpale its prestige *cuvée*. There are two ranges, Grands Crus and Premiers Crus, and wines in the former range are not always superior. The quality of Champagnes released by this cooperative has improved considerably over the last five years or so.
✓ *Grands Crus Millésime* (**N**) • *Cuvée Orpale* (**PC**)

## DE VENOGE
30 avenue de Champagne
51200 Epernay
★☉

Part of BCC (Boizel-Chanoine Champagne) group, this remains a good-value, well-made brand, but its one top-quality Champagne, the

often truly excellent Cuvée des Princes, looks ridiculous in its novelty, tear-shaped bottle.
✓ *Blanc de Noirs* (**V**) • *Brut* (**V**) • *Cuvée des Princes* (**PC**)

## VEUVE CLICQUOT-PONSARDIN (GM)
12 rue du Temple
51054 Reims
★★★☆

The quality and image of this producer is surprisingly high and upmarket for such a large house. The Clicquot style is not just big, but beautiful. This is achieved by the excellence of its Pinot Noir vineyards on the Montagne de Reims, with Bouzy often dominating the selection of grapes from these vineyards, and the relatively hands-off approach to winemaking. The fermentation temperature is not excessively low at Veuve Clicquot-Ponsardin, there is no filtering before blending, and only a light filtration prior to bottling, with reserves stored on their lees.
✓ *Entire range*

## VEUVE A. DEVAUX
Domaine de Villeneuve
10110 Bar-sur-Seine
★☉

This was the most dynamic cooperative in Champagne from the late 1980s and throughout the 1990s, producing richer, crisper, fruitier Champagnes than some Marne-based cooperatives with a large percentage of *grand cru* vineyards. The quality took a dip at the turn of the millennium, but is now back on track.
✓ *Grande Réserve Brut* (**NV**) • *Cuvée D Brut* (**NV**) • *Blanc de Noirs* (**NV**) • *Cuvée Distinction Rosé* (**V**) • *D. de Devaux* (**V**)

## VILMART
4 rue de la République
51500 Rilly-la-Montagne
◉★★☆

The top *cuvées* became too oaky, but Vilmart has now gone through this heavy-handed phase, and emerged all the better for it as from the 1996 vintage.
✓ *Entire range*

## VRANKEN
42 avenue de Champagne
51200 Epernay
☉

The house of Vranken is owned by Belgian Paul Vranken, whose ideas on quality I do not share but who undoubtedly has one of the most clever commercial brains in the region. His brands include Charles Lafitte, René Lallement, Demoiselle, Vranken, Barancourt, and Heidsieck & Co. Monopole, but his masterstroke was the purchase of Pommery in 2002. Marne et Champagne bought Lanson at the top of the market, and watched its assets dwindle, whereas Vranken bought Pommery at the bottom of the market, and watched his assets grow. He paid 150–180 million ($180–215 million), which was some 50 million ($60 million) less than LVMH were asking at one time. Although sales inevitably sank after the millennium blip, Vranken knew they were about to rise, and very quickly saw the value of Pommery jump 50 million ($60 million). In addition, Pommery sells at a premium compared to other Vranken brands, thus his group's profit margin increased overnight. Some critics believed the Belgian business maestro would have to sell more bottles of Pommery to meet his bank repayments, and the only way he could do that would be by cutting prices, but he has in fact increased both sales and price! Vranken also owns subsidiaries in Portugal (Port: Quinta do Convento, Quinta do Paco, and São Pedro) and Spain (Cava: Senora and Vranken).

## BEST OF THE REST

The following producers have produced at least some wines of excellence since the early 2000s.

Ch de l'Auche (CM, Janvry)
Barnaut (RC, Bouzy)
Baron Albert (NM, Charly-sur-Marne)
Besserat de Bellefon (NM, Epernay)
Henri Billiot (RM, Ambonnay)
H. Blin (RC, Vincelles)
Brice (NM, Aÿ-Champagne)
Louise Brison (RC, Noé-les-Mallets)
P. Brugnon (RM, Rilly-la-Montagne)
Roger Brun (RC, Aÿ-Champagne)
Le Brun de Neuville (CM, Bethon)
Christian Bourmault (RM, Avize)
Guy Cadel (RM, Mardeuil)
Pierre Callot (RM, Avize)
Guy Charbaut (RM, Mareuil-sur-Aÿ)
Guy Charlemagne (RM, Le Mesnil-sur-Oger)
J. Charpentier (RM, Villers-sous-Châtillon)
Collard-Chardelle (RM, Viller-sous-Châtillon)
Chartogne-Taillet (RC, Merfy)
Raoul Collet (CM, Aÿ-Champagne)
Delouvin Nowack (RM, Vandières)
Doquet-Jeanmaire (RM, Vertus)
Didier Doué (RM, Montguex)
Charles Ellner (NM, Epernay)
Gatinois (RM, Aÿ-Champagne)
Henri Giraud (NM, Aÿ-Champagne)
Michel Gonet (RM, Avize)
Gosset Brabant (RM, Aÿ-Champagne)
George Goulet (NM, Epernay)
Goussard & Dauphin (RM, Avirey-Lingey)
Jacquinot (NM, Epernay)
Pierre Jamain (RM, La Celle-sous-Chantemerle)
R. C. Lemaire (RM, Villers-sous-Châtillon)
Lancelot-Pienne (RM, Cramant)
Lenoble (NM, Damery)
Michel Loriot (RM, Festigny)
A. Margaine (RM, Villers-Marmery)
Rémy Massin (RM, Villé-sur-Arce)
Milan (RM, Oger)
Jean Moutardier (RM, Le Breuil)
Pierre Paillard (RM, Bouzy)
Fabrice Payelle (RM, Ambonnay)
Pehu-Simonet (RM, Verzenay)
Petit-Camusat (RM, Noé-les-Mallets)
Alain Robert (RM, Le Mesnil-sur-Oger)
Tarlant (RM, Oeuilly)
De Telmont (NM, Epernay)
Tribaut (RM, Hautvillers)
J. L. Vergnon (RM, Le Mesnil-sur-Oger)
Jean Vesselle (RM, Bouzy)
Maurice Vesselle (RM, Bouzy)

## MORE GREEN CHAMPAGNES

In addition to the few Champagnes listed in this directory that are biodynamic or organic, there are also the following. No negative inference of quality should be taken from the fact that they are not featured among the recommended Champagne producers. The truth is that there are over 12,500 brands, and I have no experience of the Champagnes produced by many of the following.

**Biodynamic**
Champagne Françoise Bedel (Crouttes-sur-Marne)
Champagne Benoît Lahaye (Bouzy)
Champagne Thierry Demarne (Villé-sur-Arce)
Champagne David Léclapart (Trépail)
Champagne Réaut-Noirot (Courteron)
Champagne Ruffin (Avenay)
Champagne Schreiber (Courteron)
Champagne Vouette & Sorbée (Buxieres-sur-Arce)

**Organic**
Champagne Jacques Beaufort (Ambonnay)
Champagne Bénard-Pitois (Mareuil-sur-Aÿ)
Champagne Jean Bliard (Hautvillers)
Champagne Vincent Bliard (Hautvillers)
Champagne Serge Faust (Vandières)
Champagne José Ardinat (Vandières)
Champagne Roger Fransoret (Mancy)
Champagne Vincent Laval (Cumières)
Champagne Lefèvre (Bonneil)
Champagne Régis Poirrier (Venteuil)

# ALSACE

*Contrary to the New World's belief that they invented the concept, Alsace has built its reputation on varietal wines. This is a region that traditionally produces rich, dry white wines, but they have in recent years become increasingly sweet.*

A FASCINATING MIXTURE of French and German characteristics pervades this northeastern fragment of France, cut off from the rest of the country by the barrier of the Vosges mountains, and separated from neighboring Germany by the mighty Rhine. The colorful combination of cultures is the result of wars and border squabbles that have plagued the ancient province since the Treaty of Westphalia put an end to the Thirty Years' War in 1648. This gave the French sovereignty over Alsace, and royal edicts issued in 1662, 1682, and 1687 proffered free land to anyone willing to restore it to full productivity. As a result of this, Swiss, Germans, Tyroleans, and Lorrainers poured into the region. In 1871, at the end of the Franco-Prussian War, the region once again came under German control, and remained so until the end of World War I, when it once again became French. At this juncture, Alsace began to reorganize the administration of its vineyards in line with the new French AOC system, but in 1940 Germany reclaimed the province from France before this process was complete. Only after World War II, when Alsace reverted to France, was the quest for AOC status resumed, finally being realized in 1962.

The vineyards of Alsace are dotted with medieval towns of cobbled streets and timbered buildings, reflecting—as do the wines—the region's myriad Gallic and Prussian influences. The grapes are a mixture of German, French, and the exotic, with the German Riesling and Gewurztraminer (written without an umlaut in Alsace), the French Pinot Gris, and the decidedly exotic Muscat comprising the four principal varieties. Sylvaner, another German grape, also features to some extent, while other French varieties include Pinot Noir, Pinot Blanc, Auxerrois, and Chasselas. While Gewurztraminer is definitely German (and fine examples are still to be found in the Pfalz, its area of origin), only in Alsace is it quite so spicy. And only in Alsace do you find spicy Pinot Gris, a grape that is neutral elsewhere. Even the Pinot Blanc may produce spicy wines in Alsace, although this is normally due to the inclusion of the fat-spicy Auxerrois grape.

Very little red wine is made in Alsace. What is produced is intended principally for local restaurants and *Weinstuben*. Ninety percent of the wine in Alsace is white. Traditionally, the style of these very fruity wines is dry, although some varieties, such as the Gewurztraminer, have always been made less dry than others. With the introduction of Vendange Tardive and Sélection de Grains Nobles wines, growers have deliberately reduced yields to chase high sugar levels. This practice has resulted in even the most basic *cuvées* being too rich for a truly dry style, so the tendency to produce less dry wine has now spread to other grape varieties.

## VENDANGE TARDIVE AND SELECTION DE GRAINS NOBLES

"Vendange Tardive," or late-harvested wines, have occasionally been made by a handful of quality-conscious producers throughout the history of Alsace, among them Hugel & Fils, who had long sold such wines under the German descriptions:

---

### RECENT ALSACE VINTAGES

**2006** As with most of France, this was a very strange year, with a baking hot, very sunny July (the hottest on record for Alsace), which pushed the vine's growth cycle way ahead of the norm, only for the *véraison* to be stopped dead its tracks by a cool August. Then there was rain in September that not even the Vosges could stop, and rot set in. But it was the downpour on October 3–4 that caused the biggest problems. The crop ripened, however, thanks to a beautiful Indian summer soon thereafter. Strict selection in the vineyard was vital, but some excellent wines have been made, including VT and SGN.

**2005** Overall, 2005 is better than 2004, with brighter fruit flavors, possibly vying with 2001 and 2002—but the wines need time to confirm their precise qualities. Gewurztraminer was the best all-around performer, while Riesling was the most variable (though some Rieslings were as good as the best Gewurztraminers) and the Pinot Gris was excellent. All other varieties, good to very good. Ideal conditions for botrytis suggests excellent botrytized (as opposed to *passerillé*) VT and SGN.

**2004** An almighty relief after the exhausting task of tasting the mostly acid-deficient (some poorly acidified) 2003s. This is definitely a more classic vintage, with good fruit and excellent acidity levels. Not in the same class as 2002 or 2001, but it has a distinct edge over 2000 and is certainly fresher, fruitier, and more classic than 2003.

**2003** The hottest summer since 1540 (and they really do have records going back that far). Rainfall was virtually nonexistent (4½ inches between May and September) and temperatures were relentlessly hot, at one point exceeding 104°F (40°C) for almost two weeks continuously. Heat and drought stress caused many vines to shut down their metabolic system during the *véraison*, especially the Riesling, which does not like hot weather. Remarkable as it might seem for such a hot year, some Riesling failed to ripen beyond 8 percent ABV. Indeed, most growers had picked the greater part of their crop by mid-September, whereas the grapes were not physiologically ripe until mid-October. There is no doubt that 2003 was an exceptional and extraordinary vintage, but apart from Pinot Noir (for which this is a benchmark year), and a handful of anomalies, the quality will be neither exceptional nor extraordinary.

**2002** The best 2002s have the weight of the 2000s, but with higher alcohol levels and, more importantly, even higher acidity, thus have far more focus and finesse. Riesling definitely fared best, and will benefit from several years' bottle age, but Gewurztraminer and Muscat also performed well. The Gewurztraminers are very aromatic, with broad spice notes, whereas the Muscats are exceptionally fresh and floral. Pinot Gris was less successful. Some extraordinary Sélections de Grains Nobles (*see opposite*) have been produced.

---

HEADQUARTERS OF HUGEL & FILS
*The small wine shop, cellars, and offices of the merchants Hugel & Fils in Riquewihr are marked by a typically Alsatian sign.*

LA PETITE VENISE, COLMAR
*This charming town, closely associated with the wine trade, boasts
many architectural delights as well as a picturesque canal district.*

"Auslese" and "Beerenauslese." Wanting to introduce Francophile
terms, the firm pioneered the decree authorizing and controlling
the commercial designations of Vendange Tardive (VT) and
Sélection de Grains Nobles (SGN). The decree was passed in
March 1984, and these styles have been universally produced
since the botrytis-rich vintage of 1989.

## DISAPPEARING DRY WINES

Although there has been an explosion in the numbers of
producers making and selling VT and SGN wines—from just two
or three prior to the decree to literally hundreds—the production
of these late-harvest wines remains minute, at just 2 percent of
Alsace wines as a whole. The vast bulk of Alsace wines have
traditionally been dry, but these so-called dry wines have become
increasingly sweet over the last 10 years or so, and some are very
sweet indeed. So much so that it has become almost impossible
for the wine-drinking public to tell whether the wine they are
buying is dry or sweet. This is not because Alsace producers
deliberately chose to create sweeter wines; it is merely the
regrettable by-product of good intentions and worshipping the
false concept of "physiological ripeness."

All the best producers, including many of the names most
commonly encountered on export shelves, have dramatically
cut their yields, particularly in the *grand cru* vineyards. Reduced
yields produce higher must weights, and in sun-blessed Alsace
this soon leads to a choice between over-alcoholic wines or
significant amounts of residual sugar. However, the *grands crus*
and other prized sites are not so much sun-blessed as sun-traps.

Grammatically, "physiological ripeness" is a nonsense because
the ripening process is, in any case, intrinsically a physiological one,
but a lot of winemakers have been brainwashed into believing that
"physiological ripeness" involves a certain skin color, stem maturity,
tannin ripeness, aroma development, berry shrivel, pulp texture, and
seed ripeness. The truth is that these factors, with the conventional
parameters of sugar, acidity, and pH, are all indicators of the
progress of grape ripeness, not of grape ripeness *per se*. The only
ripeness that matters is flavor ripeness, and that usually begins
when tartaric acid starts to dominate. The decision when to pick
after this point is a quality judgment that, subject to weather
considerations, is based purely on the style of wine to be produced.
If winemakers want to delay harvesting, that is their prerogative, but
they cannot claim that earlier-picked grapes are not ripe. There are
some very famous winemakers in Alsace who maintain that Riesling
grapes grown on limestone or calcareous clay are far too sugar-rich
to make a dry wine by the time they are "physiologically ripe." Well,
Trimbach's Clos Ste-Hune and Cuvée Frédéric-Émile are both grown

## FACTORS AFFECTING TASTE AND QUALITY

### LOCATION
The northeast corner of France,
flanked by the Vosges mountains
and bordered by the Rhine and
Germany's Black Forest. Six rivers
rise in the fir-capped Vosges,
flowing through the 60-mile (97-
kilometer) strip of vineyards to feed
the River Ill.

### CLIMATE
Protected from the full effect of
Atlantic influences by the Vosges
mountains, these vineyards are
endowed with an exceptional
amount of warm sunshine and a
very low rainfall. The rain clouds
tend to shed their load on the
western side of the Vosges as they
climb over the mountain range.

### ASPECT
The vineyards nestle on the
lower east-facing slopes of the
Vosges at a relatively high altitude
of about 600–1,200 feet (180–360
meters), and at an angle ranging
between 25° on the lower slopes
and 65° on the higher ones. The
best vineyards have a south or
southeast aspect, but many good
growths are also found on north-
and northeast-facing slopes. In
many cases the vines are cultivated
on the top as well as the sides of a
spur, but the best sites are always
protected by forested tops. Too
much cultivation of the fertile plains
in the 1970s has led to recent
overproduction problems. However,
some vineyards on the plains do
yield very good-quality wines due
to favorable soil types.

### SOIL
Alsace has the most complex
geological and solumological
situation of all the great wine areas
of France. The three basic

morphological and structural areas
are: the siliceous edge of the
Vosges; limestone hills; and the
hydrous alluvial plain. The soils of
the first include: colluvium and
fertile sand over granite, stony-clay
soil over schist, various fertile soils
over volcanic sedimentary rock,
and poor, light, sandy soil over
sandstone; of the second, dry,
stony, and brown alkaline soil over
limestone, brown sandy calcareous
soils over sandstone and limestone,
heavy fertile soils over clay-and-
limestone, and brown alkaline soil
over chalky marl; and of the
third, sandy-clay and gravel over
alluvium, brown decalcified
loess, and dark calcareous soils
over loess.

### VITICULTURE AND VINIFICATION
The vines are trained high on wires
to avoid spring ground frost. There
are a high number of organic and
biodynamic producers. Traditionally,
the wines are fermented as dry as
possible (*see below*). Although very
few have a strict no-malolactic
policy (Trimbach being one of the
exceptions), the general trend is to
avoid it if possible. In years like
2001, however, it happens
spontaneously during the
fermentation process and is
widespread, although the results
are more creamy-tactile than
buttery aromas.

### GRAPE VARIETIES
**Primary varieties:**
Gewurztraminer, Muscat
(Blanc/Rosé à Petits Grains, and
Ottonel), Pinot Gris, Riesling
**Secondary varieties:** Auxerrois,
Chardonnay, Chasselas, Pinot Blanc,
Pinot Noir, Savagnin Rosé, Sylvaner

PINOT GRIS, ROTENBERG
*A view of Turckheim from the steep slopes of Rotenberg vineyard in
Wintzenheim, where Domaine Zind Humbrecht produces fabulously
fat Pinot Gris wines with powerful aromatic qualities.*

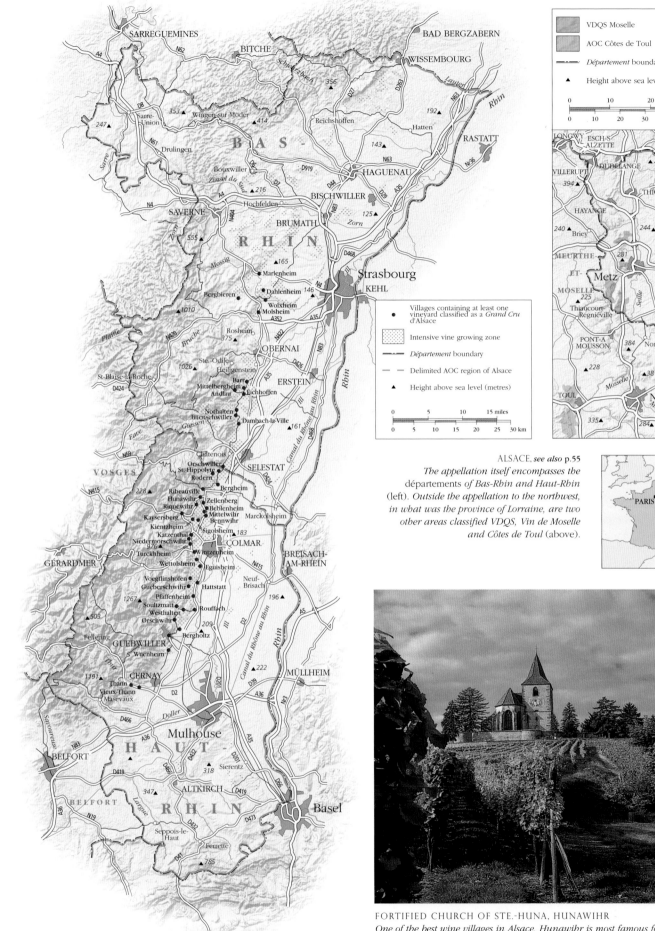

SARREGUEMINES
BITCHE
BAD BERGZABERN
WISSEMBOURG

356
353
Wingen-sur-Moder
414
Reichshoffen
192
Hatten
RASTATT
247
Sarre-
Union
Drulingen
143

BAS-

Bouxwiller
216
Hochfelden
HAGUENAU
BISCHWILLER
125
SAVERNE
BRUMATH
Zorn

RHIN

165
Marlenheim
Dahlenheim
146
Strasbourg
Bergbieren
Wolxheim
KEHL
Molsheim
1010

Rosheim
375
OBERNAI
ERSTEIN
Ste.-Odile
Heiligenstein
1026
Barr
St.-Blaise-la-Roche
Mittelbergheim
Andlau
Eichhoffen
Nothalten
Blienschwiller
Dambach-la-Ville
161

Châtenois
Orschwiller
St.-Hippolyte
SELESTAT
Rodern
Bergheim
VOSGES
Ribeauvillé
228
Hunawihr
Zellenberg
Riquewihr
Beblenheim
Kaysersberg
Mittelwihr
Bennwihr
Marckolsheim
Kientzheim
Sigolsheim
183
Katzenthal
Niedermorschwihr
COLMAR
976
Turckheim
Winzenheim
BREISACH-
GÉRARDMER
Wettolsheim
Eguisheim
AM-RHEIN
Voegtlinshofen
Hattstatt
Neuf-
Gueberschwihr
Brisach
1267
Pfaffenheim
196
Soultzmatt
Rouffach
Westhalten
Orschwihr
209
503
Bergholtz
Felleringen
GUEBWILLER
Wuenheim
222
MÜLLHEIM
1191
CERNAY
Thann
Vieux-Thann
Masevaux

Mulhouse

HAUT-

BELFORT
318
Sierentz
BELFORT
347
ALTKIRCH
RHIN
Basel
Seppois-le-
Haut
Ferrette
785

● Villages containing at least one
   vineyard classified as a *Grand Cru*
   d'Alsace
▨ Intensive vine growing zone
— *Département* boundary
-- Delimited AOC region of Alsace
▲ Height above sea level (metres)

0    5    10    15 miles
0  5  10  15  20  25  30 km

0   10   20   30 miles
0  10  20  30  40  50 km

LONGWY
ESCH-S-
ALZETTE
240
VILLERUPT
DUDELANGE
394
THIONVILLE
290
HAYANGE
Bouzonville
240
Briey
244
271
MEURTHE-
MOSELLE
281
ET-
Metz
MOSELLE
225
Courcelles-
Chaussy
Thiaucourt-
Regniéville
308
PONT-A-
Delme
MOUSSON
384
Nomeny
228
Château-
Salins
381
TOUL
335
Nancy
284
LUNÉVILLE

ALSACE, *see also* p.55
*The appellation itself encompasses the*
départements *of Bas-Rhin and Haut-Rhin*
(left). *Outside the appellation to the northwest,*
*in what was the province of Lorraine, are two*
*other areas classified VDQS, Vin de Moselle*
*and Côtes de Toul* (above).

PARIS

FORTIFIED CHURCH OF STE.-HUNA, HUNAWIHR
*One of the best wine villages in Alsace, Hunawihr is most famous for its Clos*
*Ste.-Hune vineyard, from which Trimbach consistently produces great Riesling.*

on calcareous clay, and both are beautifully dry. If they are made from unripe grapes, then I'll eat my hat.

Lowering yields and adherence to "physiological ripeness" have increased must weights to the point where, even at 15 percent alcohol, the wines have so much residual sugar that they are really quite sweet. Throughout Alsace, Gewurztraminer and Tokay-Pinot Gris frequently contain residual sugar of 30 to 40 grams per liter, with 50 grams per liter or more not unusual. To give a few specific examples, Zind Humbrecht's Gewurztraminer 2001 Clos Windsbuhl weighed in at 35 grams per liter, while its Pinot Gris 2001 Heimbourg had 50 grams per liter, and the Pinot Gris 2001 Clos Windsbuhl no less than 70 grams per liter, yet none of these wines is classified as a Vendange Tardive. As I wrote in *The Wines of Alsace* (1993), "Few people command the respect that Léonard Humbrecht does. There is not one *négociant* too large or lofty to acknowledge his tireless enthusiasm and almost evangelical crusade for lower yields." Zind Humbrecht pioneered low yields, then other growers saw the extraordinary plaudits and prices the wines attracted and followed suit. The result is a market full of sweet Alsace wine today. Or so it seems. The situation is not quite as bad as it appears in restaurants and on the best export markets. This is because the phenomenon applies primarily to the best producers and vineyards, particularly *grands crus*. These are the wines that make the headlines, are reviewed and entered into competitions. However, putting the problem into perspective does not help those who buy the best Alsace wines, or order a Riesling in a restaurant to go with fish only to find it is as sweet as Sauternes.

The simple solution would have been to introduce an obligatory dry-wine designation, but in 2004 the opposite was attempted, with the proposed introduction of a *moelleux* style. However, the trouble with defining minimum residual-sugar content for any sweet designation is that it does not necessarily follow that all wines failing to qualify will in fact be dry. Alsace consumers still await an obligatory dry-wine designation. It's not much to ask, is it?

THE GRANDS CRUS OF

# ALSACE

In the 2001 revised edition of this encyclopedia, I wrote: "The original *grand cru* legislation was introduced in 1975, but it was not until 1983 that the first list of 25 *grand cru* sites appeared. Three years later a further 23 were added, and there are now 50, although this number is the subject of much controversy, not least because it excludes what is acknowledged as one of the most famous, truly great *crus* of Alsace—Kaefferkopf in Ammerschwihr. While the *grands crus* will be of long-term benefit to both Alsace and the consumer, the limitation of *grand cru* to pure varietal wines of just four grapes—Muscat, Riesling, Pinot Gris, and Gewurztraminer—robs us of the chance to drink the finest quality Pinot Noir, Pinot Blanc, Sylvaner, and Chasselas.

"Even if these wines might not be in the same league as the big four, it seems wholly unreasonable to prevent their cultivation for AOC Alsace Grand Cru when market forces dictate that most growers will, in any case, plant the four classic varieties in their most prized *grand cru* sites because they fetch the highest prices. If, however, a grower on a *grand cru* is determined to make the best possible wine from any of the less lucrative varieties or, indeed, to produce a classic blend, why should we, the buyers, be prevented from knowing where the grapes came from because the law prevents the grower from mentioning *grand cru* on the label of such wines?"

I have been aware of these shortcomings since the publication of *The Wines of Alsace* (1993), so it was particularly heartening when in 2000 various impeccable sources informed me that the *grand cru* appellation would shortly be opened up to include varieties other than the so-called noble grapes. In 2004 Zotzenberg became the first (for Sylvaner), followed by Altenberg de Bergheim (for a blend of grapes), and, having cleared that hurdle, the INAO was forced to give the go-ahead for *grand cru* application.

It will not stop there. There is talk of allowing Pinot Noir for Steinklotz, and if Steinklotz is classified for Pinot Noir, then Vorbourg cannot be far behind. The ball will just keep rolling because if Sylvaner from Zotzenberg, why not Chasselas from Hengst? There will be fears that these wines will dilute the status of *grand cru*, and that may indeed happen, but it does not matter. In the long term, it is the market that dictates status, not a decree. Reputations have to be earned, not bestowed. That is why the cheapest wine from Zind Humbrecht is more expensive than some producers' *grands crus*. The classification Alsace Grand Cru was late in coming, but happened in a rush, leapfrogging any thought of an intermediate *premier cru* appellation, and the delimitation of many sites was a joke. However, the market is already starting to seaparate the chaff from the wheat and the same will happen to classified wines made from less classic varieties and grape blends.

Under the same law that permits local *syndicats* of growers to press for different wine styles under their own particular *grand cru*, they are also permitted to impose more stringent quality criteria on a growth-by-growth basis. Where the *syndicats* have actually done this, you will find the new specifications listed below. Where there are no new specifications, the criteria laid down in the *grand cru* decree applies, and that is as follows. Riesling and Muscat: maximum yield of 66hl/ha (basic limit of 55hl/ha plus 11hl/ha PLC); minimum ripeness equivalent to 11% at time of harvest, and chaptalization up to 1.5% allowed. Pinot Gris and Gewurztraminer: maximum yield of 66hl/ha (basic limit of 55hl/ha plus 11hl/ha PLC); minimum ripeness equivalent to 12.5% at time of harvest, and chaptalization up to 1.5% allowed. Note that all ripeness levels are expressed as percent ABV.

## ALTENBERG DE BERGBIETEN
### Bergbieten

An exceptional growth, but not a truly great one. Its gypsum-permeated, clayey-marl soil is best for Gewurztraminer, which has a very floral character with immediate appeal, yet can improve for several years in bottle. The wines are now allowed to be blended from different varieties. The local *syndicat* has renounced the PLC, limiting the yield to an absolute maximum of 55hl/ha. It has also outlawed all chaptalization, and has increased the minimum ripeness of Riesling and Muscat from 11% to 12%, and that of Pinot Gris and Gewurztraminer from 12.5% to 14%.

⚜ *Etienne Loew • Frédéric Mochel*

## ALTENBERG DE BERGHEIM
### Bergheim

This Altenberg has been a true *grand cru* since the 12th century. Its calcareous clay soil is best suited to Gewurztraminer, which is tight and austere in youth, but gains in depth and bouquet with aging. This *cru* now permits wines made from a blend of grapes.

⚜ *Marcel Deiss* ❸ *• Georges et Claude Freyburger • Louis Freyburger* ❸ *• Charles Koehly*

## ALTENBERG DE WOLXHEIM
### Wolxheim

Although appreciated by Napoleon, this calcareous clay *cru* cannot honestly be described as one of the greatest growths of Alsace, but it does have a certain reputation for its Riesling.

⚜ *Zoeller*

## BRAND
### Turckheim

This *cru* might legitimately be called Brand New, the original Brand being a tiny *cru* of little more than 7½ acres (3 hectares). In 1924 it was expanded to include surrounding sites: Steinglitz, Kirchthal, Schneckenberg, Weingarten, and Jebsal, each with its own fine reputation. By 1980 it had grown to 74 acres (30 hectares) and it is now almost double that. This confederation of *lieux-dits* is one of the most magnificent sites in the entire region, and the quality of the wines consistently excites me—great Riesling, Pinot Gris, and Gewurztraminer. The local *syndicat* has reduced chaptalization of Riesling and Muscat from the allowable 1.5% to 1%, and that of Pinot Gris and Gewurztraminer from 1.5% to 0.5%. It has also increased the minimum ripeness of Riesling and Muscat from 11% to 11.5%, and that of Pinot Gris and Gewurztraminer from 12.5% to 13.5%.

♈ *Albert Boxler* **B** • *Dopff Au Moulin* • *JosMeyer* **B** • *Preiss-Zimmer* • *Zind Humbrecht* **B**

## BRUDERTHAL
### Molsheim

Riesling and Gewurztraminer—reputedly the best varieties—occupy most of this calcareous clay *cru*. I have tasted good, fruity Riesling from Bernard Weber, which was elegant, but not really top stuff. Gérard Neumeyer used not to impress me at all, but his genuinely dry 2001 Pinot Gris was one of the best Bruderthal I have tasted. The local *syndicat* has renounced all chaptalization. It has also increased the minimum ripeness of Riesling and Muscat from 11% to 12%, and that of Pinot Gris and Gewurztraminer from 12.5% to 13%.

♈ *Alain Klingenfus* • *Gérard Neumeyer*

## EICHBERG
### Eguisheim

This calcareous clay *cru* has the lowest rainfall in Colmar and produces very aromatic wines of exceptional delicacy, yet great longevity. Famous for Gewurztraminer, which is potentially the finest in Alsace, Eichberg is also capable of making superb long-lasting Riesling and Pinot Gris. The local *syndicat* has reduced chaptalization of Riesling from 1.5% to 1%, and outlawed it completely for Pinot Gris and Gewurztraminer. It has also increased the minimum ripeness of Riesling from 11% to 11.5%, and Pinot Gris and Gewurztraminer from 12.5% to 13%. The chaptalization and minimum ripeness of Muscat remain the same.

♈ *Charles Baur* **B** • *Emile Beyer* • *Léon Beyer* (not sold as such, Beyer's Cuvée des Comtes d'Eguisheim is 100% pure Eichberg) • *Paul Ginglinger* • *Albert Hertz*

## ENGELBERG
### Dahlenheim and Scharrachbergheim

One of the least-encountered *grands crus*, this vineyard gets long hours of sunshine and is supposed to favor Gewurztraminer and Riesling; but few of the wines I have tasted suggest anything special.

♈ *Jean-Pierre Bechtold*

## FLORIMONT
### Ingersheim and Katzenthal

Mediterranean flora abounds on the sun-blessed, calcareous clay slopes of this *cru*—hence its name, meaning "hill of flowers"—the excellent microclimate producing some stunning Riesling and Gewurztraminer.

♈ *François Bohn* • *René Meyer* • *Bruno Sorg*

## FRANKSTEIN
### Dambach-la-Ville

Not so much one vineyard as four separate spurs, the warm, well-drained, granite soil of this *cru* is best suited to the production of delicate, racy Riesling, and elegant Gewurztraminer. J. Hauller used to be by far and away the best producer of Frankstein, for both the Riesling and Gewurztraminer.

♈ *Charles & Dominique Frey* **B** • *Ruhlman* • *Schaeffer-Woerly*

## FROEHN
### Zellenberg

This *cru* sweeps up and around the southern half of the hill upon which Zellenberg is situated. The marly-clay soil suits Muscat, Gewurztraminer, and Pinot Gris, in that order, and the wines are typically rich and long-lived. The local *syndicat* has outlawed all chaptalization, and increased the minimum ripeness of Riesling and Muscat from 11% to 12%, and that of Pinot Gris and Gewurztraminer from 12.5% to 13.5%.

♈ *J. .P & J. F. Becker* **B**

## FURSTENTUM
### Kientzheim and Sigolsheim

This estate is best for Riesling, although the vines have to be well established to take full advantage of the calcareous soil. Gewurztraminer can also be fabulous—in an elegant, more floral, less spicy style—and Pinot Gris excels even when the vines are very young. The local *syndicat* has reduced all chaptalization from the allowable 1.5% to 0.5%. It has also increased the minimum ripeness of Riesling and Muscat from 11% to 11.5%, and Pinot Gris and Gewurztraminer from 12.5% to 13%.

♈ *Paul Blanck* **O** • *Bott-Geyl* • *Albert Mann* • *Weinbach/Faller*

## GEISBERG
### Ribeauvillé

Geisberg has been well documented since as long ago as 1308 as Riesling country par excellence. The calcareous, stony-and-clayey sandstone soil produces fragrant, powerful, and long-lived wines of great finesse. Trimbach owns vines here, and in a contiguous plot with vines in Osterberg, the whole of which produces the superb Riesling Cuvée Frédéric Émile. The local *syndicat* has reduced the chaptalization of Riesling, Pinot Gris, and Gewurztraminer from 1.5% to 0.5%. It has also increased the minimum ripeness of Riesling from 11% to 11.5%, and that of Pinot Gris and Gewurztraminer from 12.5% to 13%. The chaptalization and minimum ripeness of Muscat remain the same.

♈ *Robert Faller* • *André Kientzler*

## GLOECKELBERG
### Rodern and St-Hippolyte

This clay-granite *cru* is known for its light, elegant, and yet persistent style of wine, with Gewurztraminer and Pinot Gris the most successful varieties. The local *syndicat* has halved the PLC, thereby reducing the absolute maximum yield allowed to 60.5hl/ha.

♈ *Koberlé-Kreyer*

## GOLDERT
### Gueberschwihr

Dating back to the year 750, and recognized on export markets as long ago as 1728, Goldert derives its name from the color of its wines, the most famous of which is the golden Gewurztraminer. The Muscat grape variety also excels on the calcareous clay soil, and whatever the varietal style of wine is rich and spicy with a luscious creaminess.

♈ *Ernest Burn* (Clos St-Imer) • *Zind Humbrecht* **B**

## HATSCHBOURG
### Hattstatt and Voegtlinshoffen

Gewurztraminer from this south-facing, calcareous marl soil slope excels, but Pinot Gris and Riesling are also excellent.

♈ *Buecher-Fix* • *André Hartmann* • *Lucien Meyer*

## HENGST
### Wintzenheim

Hengst Gewurztraminer is a very special, complex wine, seeming to combine the classic qualities of this variety with the orange zest and rose-petal aromas more characteristic of the Muscat grape variety. But Hengst is a very flexible *cru*. Besides Gewurztraminer, its calcareous marl soil also produces top-quality Muscat, Riesling, and Pinot Gris. The local *syndicat* has renounced all chaptalization. It has also increased the minimum ripeness of Riesling and Muscat from 11% to 12%, and that of Pinot Gris and Gewurztraminer from 12.5% to 13%.

♈ *JosMeyer* **B** • *Albert Mann* • *Zind Humbrecht* **B**

## KAEFFERKOPF
### Ammerschwihr

The saga of Kaefferkopf's classification finally ended in 2006, when it became the 51st *grand cru*. The first list of potential *grands crus* was published in 1975, and although Kaefferkopf had been the very first named site in Alsace to have its boundaries delimited (in 1932, by a Colmar tribunal) and was also the only named site to be recognized in the original AOC Alsace of 1962, it was not included in the 50 *grands crus* delimited between 1983 and 1992. Kaefferkopf's traditional practice of blending two or more grape varieties was in direct conflict with the pure varietal connotation of AOC Alsace Grand Cru. Furthermore, it was claimed that the original 1932 delimitation covered an area of geologically diverse soils. However, the concept of *grand cru* wine consisting of more than one variety was accepted in principle by 2005, following the changes to Altenberg de Bergheim, and the question of geological uniformity, so often spouted by pedants of the *grand cru* system, can only be true to the subsoil, not the topsoil, and the subsoil across the entire area originally classifed by the tribunal is pure granite. All in all, some 70 ha have been delimited, compared to the 67.81 ha delimited in 1932. This not only includes vineyards that were not previously classified as Kaefferkopf; it also excludes some vineyards that were (however, their owners have the right to use the Kaefferkopf name for the next 25 years!). Authorized grape varieties are Gewurztraminer, Riesling, and Pinot Gris (each of which may be either a single variety or part of a blend) plus Muscat (only as part of a blend).

🏆 *J B Adam* (Jean-Baptiste) • *Marcel Freyburger* Ⓑ • *Meyer-Fonné* (Nicolas) • *Martin Schaetzel* Ⓑ • *Maurice Schoech*

## KANZLERBERG
### Bergheim

Although this tiny *cru* adjoins the western edge of Altenberg de Bergheim, the wines of its gypsum-permeated, clayey-marl *terroir* are so different from those of the Altenberg growth that the vinification of the two sites has always been kept separate. The wines have the same potential longevity, but the Kanzlerbergs are fuller and fatter. Kanzlerberg has a reputation for both Riesling and Gewurztraminer, but their ample weight can be at odds with their varietal aromas when young, and both wines require plenty of bottle age to achieve their true finesse. The local *syndicat* has renounced the PLC, limiting the yield to an absolute maximum of 55hl/ha. It has also outlawed all chaptalization, and increased the minimum ripeness of Riesling and Muscat from 11% to 12%, and that of Pinot Gris and Gewurztraminer from 12.5% to 14%.

🏆 *Louis Freyburger* Ⓑ • *Sylvie Spielmann* Ⓑ

## KASTELBERG
### Andlau

One of the oldest vineyards in Alsace, Kastelberg has been planted with vines since the Roman occupation. Situated on a small hill next to Wiebelsberg, Andlau's other *grand cru*, the very steep, schistous *terroir* has long proved to be an excellent site for racy and delicate Riesling, although the wines can be very closed when young and require a few years to develop their lovely bottle aromas. Kastelberg wines remain youthful for 20 years or more, and even show true *grand cru* quality in so-called "off" years.

🏆 *Guy Wach*

## KESSLER
### Guebwiller

Though a *cru* more premier than grand (the truly famous sites of Guebwiller being Kitterlé and Wanne, the latter not classified), the central part of Kessler is certainly deserving of *grand cru* status. Here, the vines grow in a well-protected, valleylike depression, one side of which has a very steep, south-southeast facing slope. Kessler is renowned for its full, spicy, and mellow Gewurztraminer, but Riesling can be much the greater wine. The local *syndicat* has renounced the PLC, limiting the yield to an absolute maximum of 55hl/ha. It has also outlawed all chaptalization, and increased the minimum ripeness of Riesling and Muscat from 11% to 11.5%, and that of Pinot Gris and Gewurztraminer from 12.5% to 13.5%.

🏆 *Dirler-Cadé* Ⓑ • *Schlumberger*

## KIRCHBERG DE BARR
### Barr

The true *grands crus* of Barr are Gaensbroennel and Zisser, but these have been incorporated into the calcareous marl *terroir* of Kirchberg, which is known for its full-bodied yet delicate wines that exhibit exotic spicy fruit, a characteristic that applies not only to Pinot Gris and Gewurztraminer but also to Riesling.

🏆 *Stoeffler* Ⓞ

## KIRCHBERG DE RIBEAUVILLÉ
### Ribeauvillé

One of the few *lieux-dits* that has regularly been used to market Alsace wine over the centuries. It is famous for Riesling, which typically is firm, totally dry, and long-lived, developing intense gasoline characteristics with age. Kirchberg de Ribeauvillé also produces great Muscat with a discreet, yet very specific, orange-and-musk aroma, excellent acidity, and lots of finesse. The local *syndicat* has reduced the chaptalization of Riesling, Pinot Gris and Gewurztraminer from 1.5% to 0.5%. It has also increased the minimum ripeness of Riesling from 11% to 11.5%, and that of Pinot Gris and Gewurztraminer from 12.5% to 13%. The chaptalization and minimum ripeness of Muscat remain the same.

🏆 *André Kientzler* • *Jean Sipp* • *Louis Sipp*

## KITTERLÉ
### Guebwiller

Of all the grape varieties that are grown on this volcanic sandstone *terroir*, it is the crisp, gasolinelike Riesling that shows greatest finesse. Gewurztraminer and Pinot Gris are also very good in a gently rich, supple, and smoky-mellow style. The local *syndicat* has renounced

the PLC, limiting the yield to an absolute maximum of 55hl/ha. It has also outlawed all chaptalization, and has increased the minimum ripeness of Riesling and Muscat from 11% to 11.5%, and that of Pinot Gris and Gewurztraminer from 12.5% to 13.5%.

🏆 *Schlumberger*

## MAMBOURG
### Sigolsheim

The reputation of this *cru* has been documented since 783, when it was known as the "Sigolttesberg." A limestone *coteau*, with calcareous clay topsoil, Mambourg stretches for three-quarters of a mile (over a kilometer), penetrating farther into the plain than any other spur of the Vosges foothills. Its vineyards, supposedly the warmest in Alsace, produce wines that tend to be rich and warm, mellow and liquorous. Both the Gewurztraminer and the Pinot Gris have plenty of smoky-rich spice in them.The local *syndicat* has reduced chaptalization of Riesling, Pinot Gris and Gewurztraminer from 1.5% to 0.5% and increased the minimum ripeness of Riesling from 11% to 12%, and that of Pinot Gris and Gewurztraminer from 12.5% to 13%.

🏆 *Jean-Marc Bernhard* • *Marcel Deiss* Ⓑ • *Daniel Fritz* • *Pierre Sparr* • *Marc Tempé* Ⓑ

## MANDELBERG
### Mittelwihr and Beblenheim

Mandelberg—"almond tree hill"—has been planted with vines since Gallo-Roman times, and used as an appellation since 1925. Its reputation has been built on Riesling, although today more Gewurztraminer is planted; high-quality Pinot Gris and Muscat is also produced. The local *syndicat* has renounced the PLC, limiting the yield to an absolute maximum of 55hl/ha. It has also outlawed chaptalization for Pinot Gris and Gewurztraminer, increasing the minimum ripeness for these two grapes from 12.5% to 13%. The minimum ripeness for Riesling and Muscat remains at 11%, and the possibility of chaptalization is retained exclusively for these two varieties.

🏆 *Hartweg* • *Frédéric Mallo* • *André Stentz* Ⓞ

## MARCKRAIN
### Bennwihr and Sigolsheim

Markrain is the east-facing slope of the Mambourg, which overlooks Sigolsheim. The soil is a limestone-marl with oolite pebbles interlaying the marl beds. It is mostly planted with Gewurztraminer, with some Pinot Gris and a few Muscat vines. The Bennewihr *coopérative* usually makes a decent Pinot Gris under the Bestheim label. The local *syndicat* has reduced the chaptalization of Pinot Gris and Gewurztraminer from an allowable 1.5% to 1%, and increased the minimum ripeness of these grapes from 12.5% to 13%. The chaptalization and minimum ripeness of Riesling and Muscat remain the same.

🏆 *Bestheim* • *Stirn*

## MOENCHBERG
### Andlau and Eichhoffen

Moenchberg—"monk's hill"—was owned by a Benedictine order until 1097, when it was taken over by the inhabitants of Eichhoffen. With its clayey-marl soil, excellent exposure to the sun, and very hot, dry microclimate, this *cru* has built up a reputation for firm, intensely fruity, and very racy Riesling. Excellent though it is, however, the finest Moenchberg wines I have tasted have been Pinot Gris. Not to be confused with the equally excellent *grand cru* Muenchberg of Nothalten.

☙ *André & Rémy Gresser*

## MUENCHBERG
### Nothalten

This sunny vineyard belonging to the abbey of Baumgarten, whose monks tended vines in the 12th century, nestles under the protection of the Undersberg, a 2,950-feet (900-meter) peak in the Vosges mountains. The striking style of Muenchberg's wines is due in part to the special microclimate it enjoys, and also to the ancient, unique, and pebbly volcanic sandstone soil. The wines are now allowed to be blended from different varieties. The local *syndicat* has renounced the PLC, limiting the yield to an absolute maximum of 55hl/ha. It has also outlawed all chaptalization and has increased the minimum ripeness of Riesling and Muscat from 11% to 12%, and that of Pinot Gris and Gewurztraminer from 12.5% to 14%.

☙ *André Ostertag* ⓑ • *Jean-Luc Schwartz*

## OLLWILLER
### Wuenheim

Ollwiller's annual rainfall is one of the lowest in France, with Riesling and Gewurztraminer faring best on its clayey-sand soil—although it is not one of the greatest *grands crus*, and the recommended wines are rated in that context.

☙ *Château Ollwiller* • *CV Vieil Armand*

## OSTERBERG
### Ribeauvillé

This stony-clay growth abuts Geisberg, another Ribeauvillé *grand cru*, and makes equally superb Riesling country. The wines age very well, developing the gasoline nose of a fine Riesling. Trimbach owns vines here, and in a contiguous plot with vines in Geisberg, the whole of which produces the superb Riesling Cuvée Frédéric Émile. Gewurztraminer and Pinot Gris also fare well.

☙ *André Kientzler* • *Louis Sipp*

## PFERSIGBERG *also spelled* PFERSICHBERG & PFIRSIGBERG
### Eguisheim and Wettolsheim

A calcareous sandstone soil well-known for its full, aromatic, and long-lived Gewurztraminer—although Pinot Gris, Riesling, and Muscat also fare well here. The wines all share a common succulence of fruit acidity, and possess exceptional aromas. The local *syndicat* has reduced chaptalization of Riesling from 1.5% to 1% and outlawed it completely for Pinot Gris and Gewurztraminer. It has also increased the minimum ripeness of Riesling from 11% to 11.5%, and that of Pinot Gris and Gewurztraminer from 12.5% to 13%. The chaptalization and minimum ripeness of Muscat remain the same.

☙ *Charles Baur* ⓑ • *Emile Beyer* • *Léon Beyer* (not sold as such, but Beyer's Cuvée Particulière is 100% pure Pfersigberg) • *Pierre Freudenreich* • *Bruno Sorg*

## PFINGSTBERG
### Orschwihr

All four *grand cru* varieties grow well on the calcareous-marl and clayey-sandstone of this *cru*, producing wines of typically floral aroma, combined with rich, honeyed fruit. The local *syndicat* has renounced all chaptalization. It has also increased the minimum ripeness of Riesling and Muscat from 11% to 12%, and that of Pinot Gris and Gewurztraminer from 12.5% to 13.5%.

☙ *Lucien Albrecht* • *François Braun* • *François Schmitt* • *Albert Ziegler*

## PRAELATENBERG
### Kintzheim and Orschwiller

Although Praelatenberg dominates the north side of the village of Orschwiller, virtually all the *cru* actually falls within the boundary of Kintzheim, 1 mile (1.5 kilometers) away. The locals say that all four varieties grow to perfection here, but Pinot Gris has been best in my experience, followed by Riesling, and then Gewurztraminer. The local *syndicat* has reduced all chaptalization from an allowable 1.5% to 1%. It has also increased the minimum ripeness of Riesling and Muscat from 11% to 11.5%, and that of Pinot Gris and Gewurztraminer from 12.5% to 13%.

☙ *Allimant-Laugner* • *Jean Becker* • *Engel Frères* • *Siffert*

## RANGEN
### Thann and Vieux-Thann

The 15th-century satirist Sebastian Brant, writing about the little-known travels of Hercules through Alsace, reveals that the mythical strongman once drank so much Rangen that he fell asleep. So ashamed was he on waking that he ran away, leaving behind his bludgeon—the club which today appears on Colmar's coat of arms.

So steep that it can be cultivated only when terraced, Rangen's volcanic soil is very poor organically, but extremely fertile minerally. It also drains very quickly, and its dark color makes it almost too efficient in retaining the immense

heat that pours into this sweltering sun-trap. However, this fierce heat and rapid drainage are essentially responsible for the regular stressing of the vine, which is what gives the wines their famed power and pungency. Rangen produces great wines even in the poorest years, making it a true *grand cru* in every sense.

☙ *Schoffit* • *Wolfberger* • *Zind Humbrecht* ⓑ

## ROSACKER
### Hunawihr

First mentioned in the 15th century, this *cru* has built up a fine reputation for Riesling, but one wine—Trimbach's Clos Ste.-Hune—is almost every year far and away the finest Riesling in Alsace. Occasionally other producers make an exceptional vintage that may challenge it, but none has consistently matched Clos Ste.-Hune's excellence. Trimbach makes no mention of Rosacker on its label because the family believes, as do a small number of internationally known producers, who avoid using the term, that much of Rosacker should not be classified as *grand cru* (although Trimbach used to sell Clos Ste.-Hune *grand cru* in the 1940s). Rosacker's calcareous and marly-clay soil is rich in magnesium and makes fine Gewurztraminer as well as top Riesling. The local *syndicat* has reduced chaptalization of Riesling, Pinot Gris, and Gewurztraminer from 1.5% to 1%. It has also increased the minimum ripeness of Riesling from 11% to 11.5%, and that of Pinot Gris and Gewurztraminer from 12.5% to 13%. The chaptalization and minimum ripeness of Muscat remain the same.

❖*C. V. de Hunawihr* • *Roger Jung* • *F. E. Trimbach* (Clos Ste.-Hune)

## SAERING
### Guebwiller

This vineyard, first documented in 1250 and marketed since 1830, is situated below Kessler and Kitterlé, Guebwiller's other two *grands crus*. Like Kessler, this *cru* is more *premier* than *grand* (yet still better than many of the *grands crus*). The floral, fruity, and elegant Riesling is best, especially in hot years, when it becomes exotically peachy, but Muscat and Gewurztraminer can also be fine.

☙ *Dirler-Cadé* ⓑ • *Loberger* • *Schlumberger*

THE VILLAGE OF RIQUEWIHR
*Alsace is full of beautiful villages, but Riquewihr is one of the most delightful, having avoided much of the commercial exploitation that has made nearby Ribeauvillé a more thriving yet less intimate place.*

## SCHLOSSBERG
### Kientzheim and Kaysersberg

The production of Schlossberg was controlled by charter in 1928, and in 1975 it became the first Alsace *grand cru*. Although its granite *terroir* looks equally shared by the two sites, 1¼ acres (less than half a hectare) belongs to Kaysersberg. Schlossberg is best for Riesling, but Gewurztraminer can be successful in so-called "off" vintages. The wine is full of elegance and finesse, whether produced in a classic, restrained style, as Blanck often is, or with the more exuberant fruit that typifies Weinbach/Faller. The local *syndicat* has reduced the chaptalization of Pinot Gris and Gewurztraminer from an allowable 1.5% to 0.5%, and increased the minimum ripeness of these grapes from 12.5% to 13%. The chaptalization and minimum ripeness of Riesling and Muscat remain the same.

ℒ *Paul Blanck* ⓞ • *Joseph Fritsch* • *Albert Mann* • *Weinbach/Faller* • *Ziegler-Mauler*

## SCHOENENBOURG
### Riquewihr

This vineyard has always had a reputation for producing great Riesling and Muscat, although modern wines show Riesling to be supreme, with Pinot Gris vying with Muscat for the number two spot. Schoenenbourg's gypsum-permeated, marly-and-sandy soil produces very rich, aromatic wines in a *terroir* that has potential for VT and SGN.

ℒ *J. P. & J. F. Becker* ⓑ • *Marcel Deiss* ⓑ • *Roger Jung*

## SOMMERBERG
### Niedermorschwihr and Katzenthal

Known since 1214, the fame of this *cru* was such that a strict delimitation was in force by the 17th century. Situated in the foothills leading up to Trois-Épis, its granite soil is supposed to be equally excellent for all four classic varieties, although Riesling stands out in my experience. Sommerberg wines are typically aromatic, with an elegant succulence of fruit.

ℒ *Albert Boxler*

## SONNENGLANZ
### Beblenheim

In 1935, two years after Kaefferkopf was defined by tribunal at Colmar, Sonnenglanz received a similar certification. Unlike at Kaefferkopf, however, its producers failed to exploit the appellation until 1952, when the local cooperative was formed. But Sonnenglanz is a *grand cru* and Kaefferkopf technically is not. Once renowned for its Sylvaner, the calcareous clay soil of Sonnenglanz is best suited to Gewurztraminer and Pinot Gris, which can be very ripe and golden in color.

ℒ *J. P. & J. F. Becker* ⓑ • *Bott-Geyl* • *Hartweg*

## SPIEGEL
### Bergholtz and Guebwiller

Known for only 50 years or so, this is not one of the great *grands crus* of Alsace. However, its sandstone and marl *terroir* can produce fine, racy Riesling with a delicate bouquet and good, though not great, Gewurztraminer and Muscat. The local *syndicat* has renounced all chaptalization of Pinot Gris and Gewurztraminer, but permissible chaptalization of Riesling and Muscat remains at 1.5%. It has also increased the minimum ripeness of Pinot Gris and Gewurztraminer from 12.5% to 13.5%, but that of Riesling and Muscat remains 11%.

ℒ *Dirler-Cadé* • *Loberger* • *Eugène Meyer* ⓑ • *Wolfberger*

## SPOREN
### Riquewihr

Sporen is one of the truly great *grands crus*, its stony, clayey-marl soil producing wines of remarkable finesse. Historically, this *terroir* is famous for Gewurztraminer and Pinot Gris, which occupy virtually all of its vineyard today, but it was also traditional to grow a mix of varieties and vinify them together to produce a classic nonvarietal wine, such as Hugel's Sporen Gentil, which was capable of aging 30 years or more (and in a totally different class from that firm's own Gentil, which does not come from Sporen and is a blend of separately vinified wines).

ℒ *Dopff Au Moulin* • *Roger Jung* • *Mittnacht-Klack*

## STEINERT
### Pfaffenheim and Westhalten

Pinot Gris is the king of this stony, calcareous *cru*, although historically Schneckenberg (now part of Steinert) was always renowned for producing a Pinot Blanc that tasted more like Pinot Gris. The Pfaffenheim cooperative still produces a Pinot Blanc Schneckenberg (although not a *grand cru*, of course), and its stunning Pinot Gris steals the show. Steinert's Pinot Blanc-cum-Gris reputation illustrates the exceptional concentration of these wines. Gewurztraminer fares best on the lower slopes, Riesling on the higher, more sandy slopes. The local *syndicat* has reduced chaptalization of Riesling and Muscat from the allowable 1.5% to 1%, and that of Pinot Gris and Gewurztraminer

from 1.5% to 0.5%. It has also increased the minimum ripeness of Riesling and Muscat from 11% to 12%, and that of Pinot Gris and Gewurztraminer from 12.5% to 13.5%.

ℒ *C. V. Pfaffenheim* • *Rieflé* • *François Runner* • *Pierre Paul Zink*

## STEINGRUBLER
### Wettolsheim

Although this calcareous-marl and sandstone *cru* is not one of the great names of Alsace, I have enjoyed some excellent Steingrubler wines, particularly Pinot Gris. This can be very rich, yet show great finesse. Certainly Steingrubler is one of the better lesser-known *grands crus*, and it could well be a great growth of the future. The local *syndicat* has reduced all chaptalization from an allowable 1.5% to 1%. It has also increased the minimum ripeness of Riesling and Muscat from 11% to 11.5%, and that of Pinot Gris and Gewurztraminer from 12.5% to 13%.

ℒ *Barmès-Buecher* ⓑ • *Robert Dietrich* • *Albert Mann* • *Wolfberger* • *Wunsch & Mann* (Collection Joseph Mann)

## STEINKLOTZ
### Marlenheim

Steinklotz ("block of stone") was part of the estate of the Merovingian king Childebert II, from which Marlenheim derives its reputation for Pinot Noir, but since it has flown the *grand cru* flag, Steinklotz is supposed to be good for Pinot Gris, Riesling, and Gewurztraminer. However, local growers are determined to have their Pinot Noir recognized and will be applying for *grand cru* status for these wines.

ℒ *Romain Fritsch*

## VORBOURG
### Rouffach and Westhalten

All four varieties excel in this calcareous sandstone *terroir*, whose wines are said to develop a bouquet of peaches, apricots, mint, and hazelnut—but Riesling and Pinot Gris fare best. Muscat favors warmer vintages, when its wines positively explode with flavor, and Gewurztraminer excels in some years but not in others. Vorbourg catches the full glare of the sun from dawn to dusk and so is also well suited to Pinot Noir, which is consequently heavy with pigment. The local *syndicat* has renounced all chaptalization. It has also increased the minimum ripeness of Riesling and Muscat from 11% to 12%, and that of Pinot Gris and Gewurztraminer from 12.5% to 13.5%.

ℒ *de l'École* (Fleuron de Vorbourg) • *Muré* ⓞ (Clos St.-Landelin)

## WIEBELSBERG
### Andlau

This vineyard has very good sun exposure, and its siliceous soil retains heat and drains well. Riesling does well, producing wines that can be very fine and floral, slowly developing a delicate, ripe-peachy fruit on the palate.

🏆 *André & Rémy Gresser* • *André Rieffel*

## WINECK-SCHLOSSBERG
### Katzenthal and Ammerschwihr

Wineck-Schlossberg's granite vineyards enjoy a sheltered microclimate that primarily favors Riesling, followed by Gewurztraminer. The wines are light and delicate, with a fragrant aroma.

🏆 *J B Adam* (Jean-Baptiste) • *Clément-Klur* • *Meyer-Fonné*

## WINZENBERG
### Blienschwiller

Locals claim that this *cru* is cited in "old documents" and that Riesling and Gewurz-traminer fare best in its granite vineyards. The Riesling I have encountered has been light and

charming, but not special. Gewurztraminer has definitely been much the superior wine, showing fine, fresh aromas with a refined spiciness of some complexity.

🏆 *Auther*

## ZINNKOEPFLÉ
### Soultzmatt and Westhalten

Zinnkoepflé's hot, dry microclimate gives rise to a rare concentration of Mediterranean and Caspian fauna and flora near its exposed summit. The heat and the arid, calcareous sandstone soil are what gives it its reputation for strong, spicy, and fiery styles of Pinot Gris and Gewurztraminer. The Riesling is a delicate and most discreet wine, but this is deceptive and it can, given decent bottle-age, be just as powerful. Mention should be made of Seppi Landmann, who has produced some

stunning Zinnkoepflé, but also far too many ordinary wines, and a few absolute bummers, thus does not get a wholehearted recommendation below.

🏆 *Léon Boesch* ⊙ • *Agathe Bursin* • *Jean-Marie Haag* • *Schlegel-Boeglin*

## ZOTZENBERG
### Mittelbergheim

First mentioned in 1364, when it was known as Zoczenberg, the wines of this calcareous clay *terroir* have been sold under its own *lieu-dit* since the beginning of the 20th century. It is historically the finest site in Alsace for Sylvaner, and in 2004 became the first *grand cru* to be officially recognized for this supposedly lowly grape variety. Gewurztraminer and Riesling show a creamy richness of fruit.

🏆 *Agathe Bursin* • *André Rieffel*

---

# THE APPELLATIONS OF
# ALSACE AND LORRAINE

## ALSACE AOC

This appellation covers all the wines of Alsace (with the exception of Alsace Grand Cru and Crémant d'Alsace), but 95 percent of the wines are often sold according to grape variety. These are: Pinot (which may also be labeled Pinot Blanc, Clevner, or Klevner), Pinot Gris, Pinot Noir, Riesling, Gewurztraminer, Muscat, Sylvaner, Chasselas (which may also be labeled Gutedel), and Auxerrois. This practice effectively creates nine "varietal" AOCs under the one umbrella appellation, and these are listed separately.

## ALSACE GRAND CRU AOC

The current production of *grand cru* wine is approximately 4 percent of the total volume of AOC Alsace. Because every *cru*, or growth, makes a wine of a specific character, it is impossible to give a generalized description.

**WHITE** *See* The Grands Crus of Alsace, *p.187*

🍇 Muscat, Riesling, Gewurztraminer, Pinot Gris, Sylvaner (Zotzenberg only)

## ALSACE SÉLECTION DE GRAINS NOBLES AOC

This is not an AOC in itself, but a subordinate designation that may be appended either to the basic appellation or to Alsace Grand Cru AOC. Its production is strictly controlled, and the regulations are far tougher than for any AOC elsewhere. In theory, these wines are harvested after VT, but in practice they are picked in several tries prior to the best VT, which will be produced from what remains on the vine after a further period of ripening.

This is not an AOC in itself, but a subordinate designation that may be appended either to the basic appellation or to Alsace Grand Cru AOC. Its production is strictly controlled, and the regulations are far tougher than for any AOC elsewhere. In theory, these wines are harvested after VT, but in practice they are picked in several tries prior to the best VT, which will be produced from what remains on the vine after a further period of ripening.

These rare and sought-after wines are made from botrytis-affected grapes; unlike Sauternes, however, Alsace is no haven for "noble rot," which occurs haphazardly and in much reduced concentrations. The wines are, therefore, produced in tiny quantities and sold at very high prices. The *sauternais* are often amazed not only by the high sugar levels (while chaptalization is not permitted in Alsace, it has become almost mandatory in Sauternes), but also by how little sulfur is used, highlighting why SGN has become one of the world's greatest dessert wines.

**WHITE** Now made with less alcohol and higher sugar than when first introduced, these wines possess even more finesse than before. While Gewurztraminer is almost too easy to make, Pinot Gris offers the ideal balance between quality and price; just a couple of Muscat have been produced, and Riesling SGN is in a class of its own. Check the appropriate varietal entry for the best producers.

🍇 Gewurztraminer, Pinot Gris, Riesling, Muscat

⏳ 5–30 years

## ALSACE VENDANGE TARDIVE AOC

This is not an AOC in itself, but a subordinate designation that may be appended either to the basic appellation or to Alsace Grand Cru AOC. Its production is controlled, and the regulations are far stricter than for any AOC elsewhere in France. VT is far less consistent in quality and character than SGN. This is because some producers make these wines from grapes that have the correct minimum sugar content, but that were picked with the rest of the crop, not late-harvested. Such VT lacks the true character of a late-harvested wine, which is only brought

temperatures (the norm) and those that have enjoyed a late Indian summer (not uncommon) will produce entirely different wines. Until the regulations are changed to ensure that VT is always harvested after a certain specified date, choose recommended wines and look for a date of harvest on the back label.

Another aspect that requires regulating is the relative sweetness of the wine, as VT can be anything from almost dry to sweeter than some SGN. Refer to the appropriate varietal entry for the best producers.

**WHITE** Whether dry, medium-sweet, or sweet, this relatively full-bodied wine should always have the true character of *passerillage*—although sometimes this will be overwhelmed by botrytis. Gewurztraminer is the most commonly encountered variety, but only the best have the right balance; Pinot Gris and Riesling both offer an ideal balance between quality, availability, and price. Muscat is almost as rare for VT as it is for SGN, as it tends to go very flabby when overripe.

🍇 Gewurztraminer, Pinot Gris, Riesling, Muscat

⏳ 5–20 years

## AUXERROIS AOC

**JOSMEYER**
VIN D'ALSACE
APPELLATION ALSACE CONTRÔLÉE

2002
PINOT AUXERROIS
"H"® Vieilles Vignes

mis en bouteille par JOSMEYER à F 68920 WINTZENHEIM
ALC.13% BY VOL. PRODUCT OF FRANCE 750 ml

Theoretically this designation does not exist, but Auxerrois is one of the varieties permitted for the production of Pinot wine and makes such a distinctly different product that it has often been labeled separately. This practice, currently on the increase, is "officially tolerated."

**WHITE** Fatter than Pinot Blanc, with a more buttery, honeyed, and spicy character to the fruit, the greatest asset of Auxerrois is its natural richness and immediate appeal. Inclined to low acidity, it can easily become flabby and so musky it tastes almost foxy, but the best Auxerrois can give Pinot Gris a run for its money.

🍇 Auxerrois

🍷 Up to 5 years

✓ *Emile Beyer* • *Rolly Gassmann* • *JosMeyer* **B** • *André Kientzler* • *Julien Rieffel* (the Klevner Vieilles Vignes is pure Auxerrois despite the Pinot Blanc synonym) • *Bruno Sorg* • *Marc Tempé* **B** (Vieilles Vignes)

## CHASSELAS AOC

Rarely seen, but enjoying something of a revival among a few specialized growers.

**WHITE** The best Chasselas wines are not actually bottled, but sit in vats waiting to be blended into anonymous *cuvées* of Edelzwicker. They are neither profound nor complex, but teem with fresh, fragrant fruit and are an absolute joy to drink; they taste better, however, before they are bottled than after. The fruit is so delicate that it needs a lift to survive the shock of being bottled, and the wine would probably benefit from being left on lees and bottled very cold to retain a bit of tongue-tingling carbonic gas.

🍇 Chasselas

🍷 Upon purchase

✓ *JosMeyer* **B** • *André Kientzler* • *Schoffit*

## CLASSIC ALSACE BLENDS

Despite the varietal wine hype, Alsace is more than capable of producing the finest-quality classic blends, but their number is small and dwindles every year because so few consumers realize their true quality. It is difficult for producers to make potential customers appreciate why their blends are more expensive than ordinary Edelzwicker, but classic Alsace blends should no more be categorized with Edelzwicker than *crus classés* compared with generic Bordeaux. This category focuses attention on the region's top-performing blends which, whether or not they fetch them, deserve *grand cru* prices. Unlike the blending of Edelzwicker, for which various wines are mixed together—and where there is always the temptation to get rid of unwanted wines—the different varieties in most classic Alsace blends always come from the same vineyard and are traditionally harvested and vinified together. *See also* Kaefferkopf, p.189

**WHITE** Most of these wines improve with age, but go through phases when one or other grape variety dominates, which is interesting to observe and should help you to understand why you prefer to drink a particular blend. Depending on the amounts involved, Gewurztraminer typically dominates in the young wine, followed by Pinot Gris then, many years later, Riesling, but other varieties may also be involved when overripe.

🍇 Chasselas, Sylvaner, Pinot Blanc, Pinot Gris, Pinot Noir, Auxerrois, Gewurztraminer, Muscat Blanc à Petits Grains, Muscat Rosé à Petits Grains, Muscat Ottonel, Riesling

✓ *Marcel Deiss* **B** (Grand Vin de Schoenbourg, Altenberg de Bergheim Assemblage, Burg, Engelgarten) • *Marcel Freyburger* **B** (Kaefferkopf) • *C. V. Ribeauvillé* (Clos du Zahnacker equal parts Gewurztraminer, Pinot Gris, and Riesling) • *Jean Sipp* (Clos du Schlossberg 50% Riesling, 20% Gewurztraminer, 20% Tokay-Pinot Gris, 10% Muscat) • *Louis Sipp* (Côtes de Ribeauvillé 40% Pinot Blanc plus 60% Sylvaner, Riesling, and Gewurztraminer)

## CLEVNER AOC

Commonly used synonym under which Pinot is marketed, sometimes spelled Klevner, but not to be confused with Klevener. *See* Pinot AOC

## CÔTES DE TOUL AOC

Part of the once-flourishing vineyards of Lorraine, these *côtes* are located in eight communes west of Toul, in the *département* of Meurthe-et-Moselle, and were elevated to AOC status in 2003. Although the best are merely ready-drinking country wines, Laroppe easily outclasses the competition.

**RED** The Pinot Noir is the most successful, and the wine is usually sold as a pure varietal. It can have surprisingly good color for wine from such a northerly region, and good cherry-Pinot character.

🍇 Pinot Meunier, Pinot Noir

🍷 1–4 years

**WHITE** These wines represent less than two percent of the VDQS, just 844 cases (76 hectoliters). Nevertheless, the Auxerrois is the best grape, its fatness making it ideal for such a northerly area with a calcareous soil.

🍇 Aligoté, Aubin, Auxerrois

🍷 1–3 years

**ROSÉ** Most Côtes de Toul is made and sold as *vin gris*. This pale rosé is delicious when it is still youthful.

🍇 Gamay, Pinot Meunier, Pinot Noir, plus a maximum of 15% Aligoté, Aubin, and Auxerrois

🍷 Upon purchase

✓ *Vincent Gorny* • *Michel & Marcel Laroppe* • *de la Linotte* • *Isabelle et Jean-Michel Mangeot* • *CV du Toulouis*

## CRÉMANT D'ALSACE AOC

Although small growers like Dirler had made Vin Mousseux d'Alsace as early as 1880, it was not until 1900 that Dopff Au Moulin created a sparkling wine industry on a commercial scale, and 1976 before an AOC was established. The quality is good, and is improving. Good to see the Hartenberg Pinot Gris back on track.

**SPARKLING WHITE** Although the Pinot Blanc has perfect acidity for this sort of wine, it can

lack sufficient richness, and after intensive tastings I have come to the conclusion that the Pinot Gris has the right acidity and richness.

🍇 Pinot Blanc, Pinot Gris, Pinot Noir, Auxerrois, Chardonnay, Riesling

🍷 5–8 years

**SPARKING ROSÉ** These delightful wines can have a finer purity of perfume and flavor than many pink Champagnes.

🍇 Pinot Noir

🍷 3–5 years

✓ *René Barth* • *Bernard Becht* • *Joseph Gruss* • *Klein-Brand* • *C. V. Pfaffenheim* (Hartenberg Pinot Gris) • *Rieflé* • *Wolfberger*

## EDELZWICKER AOC

This appellation—its name means "noble blend"—is reserved for wines blended from two or more of the authorized grape varieties, and it was indeed once noble. However, since the banning of AOC Zwicker, which was never meant to be noble, and due to the fact that there has never been a legal definition of which varieties are noble, producers simply renamed their Zwicker blends Edelzwicker. Consequently, this appellation has become so tarnished that many producers prefer to sell their cheaper AOC Alsace wines under brand names or simply AOC Alsace, rather than put the debased Edelzwicker name on the label. *See also* Classic Alsace Blends

**WHITE** Essentially dry, light-bodied wines that have a clean flavor and are best drunk young. Most Edelzwickers are either Sylvaner or Pinot Blanc-based. Better or slightly more expensive products have a generous touch of Gewurztraminer to fatten up the blend, but most of these have forsaken the Edelzwicker designation, and there are now no examples that can be recommended with confidence.

🍇 Chasselas, Sylvaner, Pinot Blanc, Pinot Gris, Pinot Noir, Auxerrois, Gewurztraminer, Muscat Blanc à Petits Grains, Muscat Rosé à Petits Grains, Muscat Ottonel, Riesling

🍷 Upon purchase

## GEWURZTRAMINER AOC

No other wine region in the world has managed to produce Gewurztraminer with any real spice, which is probably why this is usually the first Alsace wine people taste. Its voluptuous, up-front style is always immediately appealing.

**WHITE** The fattest and most full-bodied of Alsace wines. Classic renditions of this grape typically have the aroma of banana when young and take 3 to 4 years in bottle to build up a pungent spiciness of terpene-laden aromas, often achieving a rich gingerbread character when mature.

🍇 Gewurztraminer

🍷 3–10 years (20–30 years for great examples)

✓ *Barmès-Buecher* **B** • *Charles Baur* **B** • *Léon Beyer* • *Paul Blanck* **O** • *Bott-Geyl* • *Albert Boxler* • *Camille Braun* (Cuvée Annabelle) • *Brobecker* (Cuvée Spéciale) • *Hugel & Fils* (Jubilée) • *André Kientzler* • *Meyer-Fonné* (Réserve Particulière) • *Muré* **O** (Clos St-Landelin) • *Rolly Gassmann* • *Georges et Claude Humbrecht* (Vieilles Vignes) • *Martin Schaetzel* **B** • *A Scherer* • *François Schmitt* (Pfingstberg) • *Jean Sipp* • *Bruno Sorg* (Pfersigberg) • *Sylvie Spielmann* **B** • *Antoine Stoffel* • *F E Trimbach* • *Weinbach/Faller* • *Zind Humbrecht* **B**

**VT** *J B Adam* • *Léon Beyer* • *Léon Boesch* **O** • *René Fleith-Eschard* • *Louis Freyburger* **B** (Kanzlerberg) • *Geschikt* • *Hugel & Fils* • *Jean Huttard* (Burgreben) • *Roger Jung* • *André Kientzler* • *Ostertag* **B** • *Pierre Meyer* • *Maurice Schoech* • *André Thomas* **B** • *Weinbach/Faller* • *Zind Humbrecht* **B**

**SGN** *Léon Beyer* (especially Quintessence) • *Paul Blanck* **O** • *Léon Boesch* **O** • *Albert Boxler* • *Dirler-Cadé* **B** • *Hugel & Fils* • *André Kleinknecht* **B** • *Albert Mann* • *Muré* **O** (Clos St-Landelin) • *Rolly Gassmann* • *Seppi Landmann* • *Damien Schlegel* • *Schlumberger* (Cuvée Anne) • *Sick-Dreyer* • *F E Trimbach* • *Weinbach/Faller* • *Zind Humbrecht* **B**

## GUTEDEL AOC

Synonym under which Chasselas may be marketed. *See* Chasselas AOC

## KLEVENER DE HEILIGENSTEIN AOC

An oddity in Alsace for three reasons: first, the wine is made from a grape variety that is native to the Jura farther south and not found anywhere else in Alsace; second, of all the famous village appellations (Rouge d'Ottrott, Rouge de Rodern, etc.), it is the only one specifically defined in the regulations; third, it is the only grape confined by law to a fixed area within Alsace (the village of Heiligenstein). It is not to be confused with Klevner, a common synonym for the Pinot Blanc.

**WHITE** Dry, light-bodied wines of a subdued, spicy aroma, and delicate, fruity flavor. Sadly, no wines worth recommending.

🍇 Savagnin Rosé

🍷 2–4 years

## KLEVNER AOC

*See* Pinot Blanc AOC

## MOSELLE VDQS

This VDQS was called Vins de Moselle until 1995, when it became simply Moselle. Although many restaurants list German Mosel as "Moselle," the river and the wine it produces are called Mosel in Germany, only becoming Moselle when crossing the border into France (and Luxembourg). Gamay is limited by law to a maximum of 30 percent of the surface area of this appellation. A maximum of 12.5 percent alcohol is applied to prevent producers from overchaptalizing.

**RED** Château de Vaux produces a surprisingly good Pinot Noir.

🍇 Gamay, Pinot Meunier, Pinot Noir

🍷 Upon purchase

**WHITE** There has been an improvement in these wines, particularly the Pinot Gris.

🍇 Auxerrois, Müller-Thurgau, Pinot Blanc, Pinot Gris, Riesling, Gewurztraminer

🍷 Upon purchase

✓ *Michel Maurice* (Pinot Gris) • *Oury-Schreiber* • *Château de Vaux* (Pinot Noir Les Hautes Bassières)

## MUSCAT AOC

The best Muscat wine, some growers believe, is made from the Muscat d'Alsace, a synonym for both the white and pink strains of the rich, full Muscat à Petits Grains. Others are convinced that the lighter, more floral Muscat Ottonel is best. A blend of the two is probably preferable. These wines are better in average years, or at least in fine years that have good acidity, rather than in truly great vintages.

**WHITE** Dry, aromatic wines with fine floral characteristics that often smell of orange-flower water and taste of peaches. A top-quality Muscat that is expressive of its *terroir* is a great wine.

🍇 Muscat Blanc à Petits Grains, Muscat Rosé à Petits Grains, Muscat Ottonel

🍷 Upon purchase

✓ *Jean Becker* • *Emile Beyer* • *Ernest Burn* (Clos St-Imer) • *Pierre Henri Ginglinger* **B** • *Roger Jung* • *André Kientzler* • *Frédéric Mochel* • *Muré* **O** (Clos St-Landelin) • *Rolly Gassmann* • *Sylvain Hertzog* • *Bruno Sorg* • *Sylvie Spielmann* **B** • *Weinbach/Faller* • *Zind Humbrecht* **B** (Goldert)

**VT** *Jean-Marc et Frédéric Bernhard* • *Barmès-Buecher* **B**

**SGN** *Claude Bleger* • *Fernand Engel* **O** • *Romain Fritsch* • *Albert Mann* (Le Tri)

## PINOT AOC

Not necessarily pure Pinot Blanc, this white wine may be made from any of the Pinot grape varieties, including Auxerrois (often confused with Pinot Blanc but in fact a totally separate variety). Most Pinot wines are a blend of Pinot Blanc and Auxerrois; the farther north the vines are cultivated, the more Auxerrois is used to plump out the Pinot Blanc. Zind is included under Zind Humbrecht below because this luscious, effectively dry blend of 50 percent Auxerrois, 35 percent Chardonnay, and 15 percent Pinot Blanc used to be sold under the Pinot designation. When the authorities enforced the regulations that state Chardonnay may only be used in Crémant d'Alsace, not a still wine under the AOC, Zind Humbrecht was forced to sell

the wine as *vin de table*. Since it is not allowed to indicate a vintage on a *vin de table* (the European Union wine regime obviously does not believe in greater transparency), Olivier Humbrecht used a code, and it does not take a genius to figure out Z001 stands for 2001, or that the next NV will be numbered Z002, and so on. The funny thing is that the maximum permitted yield for *vin de table* is 90 hectoliters per hectare as opposed to 100 hectoliters per hectare for the Alsace appellation, and chaptalization is banned. Silly us for thinking that an AOC is supposed to be superior to a *vin de table*!

**WHITE** Some Pinot wines are occasionally spineless, but lackluster examples are not as common as they used to be, as it is the plump and juicy *cuvées* that have made this the fastest-growing category of Alsace wine.

🍇 Pinot Blanc, Auxerrois, Pinot Noir (vinified white), Pinot Gris

🍷 2–4 years

✓ *J B Adam* • *Camille Braun* • *CV Cléebourg* • *Pierre Frick* **O** (Précieuse) • *JosMeyer* **B** • *Koeberlé-Kreyer* • *Albert Mann* • *CV Pfaffenheim* • *Rolly Gassmann* • *Sylvie Spielmann* **B** • *Zind Humbrecht* **B** (including Zin *vin de table*)

## PINOT BLANC AOC

This designation should only be used if the wine is made from 100 percent Pinot Blanc. *See also* Pinot AOC

## PINOT GRIS AOC

This designation is now the most common way of marketing wine from the rich Pinot Gris grape. For hundreds of years, it has been known locally as Tokay d'Alsace. Legend had it that the Pinot Gris was brought back to Alsace from Hungary by Baron Lazare de Schwendi in the 1560s, and as Tokay or Tokaji was the only famous Hungarian wine, it was assumed that this was the grape Tokay was made from, and the name stuck. But they got it all wrong: this grape came to Alsace from Burgundy, Schwendi had nothing to do with it, and Pinot Gris has nothing to do with Tokay/Tokaji. In the 1980s, the Hungarians wanted their name back, and initially the French agreed, but after counterarguments from Alsace producers, alleging over 400 years' use of the name, the French reneged, and agreed instead to change the name from Tokay d'Alsace to Tokay-Pinot Gris, with vague promises that they might drop the Tokay at some time in the future. That did not happen, but the fall of communism did, and with Hungary's entry to the European Union, the French were forced to honor their partner's historic appellation, so all bottles will have to be labeled Pinot Gris, with no reference to Tokay, no later than the end of 2006.

**WHITE** This full-bodied, off-dry wine is decadently rich, but has excellent acidity, and its fullness of flavor never tires the palate.

A young Pinot Gris can taste or smell of banana, and sometimes be smoky, with little or no spice, but as it matures it increasingly develops a smoky-spice, toasty-creamy richness, finally achieving a big, honeyed walnut-brazil complexity with good bottle age. Top Alsace Riesling can be much finer, but the variety is so sensitive to soil conditions and handling that the quality is nowhere near as consistent as Pinot Gris across the board.

🍇 Pinot Gris

⌇— 5–10 years

✓ *Lucien Albrecht • Barmès-Buecher* 🅱 *• J P & J F Becker* 🅱 *(Froehn) • Albert Boxler • CV Cléebourg • Robert Faller* (Bénédicte) *• CV de Hunawihr (Rosacker) • André Kientzler • Henri Klée • Albert Mann • Mittnacht-Klack • Muller-Koeberle • Ostertag* 🅱 *• Antoine Stoffel • Bernard Weber* (Finkenberg) *• Weinbach/Faller • Zind Humbrecht* 🅱

**VT** *Lucien Albrecht • Joseph Cattin • Jean-Marie Koehly • Marc Kreydenweiss • Hugel & Fils • Vignobles Reinhart • Zind Humbrecht* 🅱

**SGN** *J B Adam • Léon Beyer* (Quintessence) *• Albert Boxler • Marcel Deiss* 🅱 *• Louis Freyburger* 🅱 (Altenberg de Bergheim) *• Hugel & Fils • Marc Kreydenweiss • Koberlé-Kreyer • Kuentz-Bas • Albert Mann* (Altenbourg Le Tri) *• F E Trimbach • Weinbach/Faller • Zind Humbrecht* 🅱 *• Pierre Paul Zink* (Barrique)

## PINOT NOIR AOC

Not so long ago, Pinot Noir d'Alsace was synonymous in style with rosé, but the trend has swung hard over toward a true red wine. After a steep learning curve, during which many wines were overextracted, lacked elegance, were prone to rapid oxidation, and bore the most ungainly caramelized characteristics, Alsace winemakers have now managed to master the handling of oak and red-wine techniques. Alsace producers are now allowed to use a fatter bottle of almost Burgundian proportions for Pinot Noir instead of the Flûte d'Alsace, the use of which has been enshrined in law since 1959. This is a positive move, and although strictly confined to Pinot Noir, I hear rumors that it will be used for other Pinot varieties, which would also be good.

**RED** Most are unsatisfactory (overextracted, too tannic, or too oaky—sometimes all three), but Marcel Deiss's Burlenberg is in a different class and is comparable to a good Burgundy. A step down, but still good, is Domaine Weinbach Réserve in a good year, and the most commercial of all, Hugel Jubilée Pinot Noir, with its special selection Le Neveaux, is a serious contender for Deiss's crown. And that is about it. You can find perhaps another four or five wines each year that are delightful on the nose, but do not live up to the promise on the palate. Why is it that although both Alsace and Germany started at the same time (mid-1980s) to develop Pinot Noir as a serious red wine style (as opposed to rosé), only Germany has succeeded? The cadre of top-performing German Pinot Noir producers includes the likes of Deutzerhof, Kreuzberg, Huber, Johner, Knipser, Philipp Kuhn, Bernhart, Fürst, August Kesseler, and Aldinger, yet the only Alsace producer who would not be shown up in such company is Deiss, and the very best of Hugel's wines.

🍇 Pinot Noir

## MORE GREEN ALSACE

In addition to the Alsace producers recommended above, and which are either biodynamic or organic, there are also the following. No negative inference of quality should be taken from the fact that they are not featured among my recommended Alsace producers. There are a number that have been recommended in other editions, and still make some fine wines, but have been culled out to make room for others.

**Biodynamic**
Geschickt (Ammerschwihr)
Jean Ginglinger (Pfaffenheim)
Pierre-Paul Humbrecht (Pfaffenheim)
Marc Kreydenweiss (Andlau)
Jean Schaetzel (Ammerschwihr)
Trapet Alsace (Beblenheim)
Valentin Zusslin Fils (Orschwihr)
**Organic**
Yves Amberg (Epfig)
Yannick et Jean Baltenweck (Ribeauvillé)
Maurice Barthelme (Wettolsheim)
Rémy Biwand (Mackenheim)
Lucien et Théo Dietrich (Sigolsheim)
Yves Dietrich (Sigolsheim)
André Durrmann (Andlau)
Eblin-Fuchs (Zellenberg)

Gilg (Wettolsheim)
Philippe & Fernand Heitz (Molsheim)
Annick Hummel (St-Léonard Boersch)
Bernard Hummel (St-Léonard Boersch)
Martin Jund (Colmar)
Clément Klur (Katzenthal)
Mathieu Knecht (Dambach la Ville)
Pierre Martin (Scherwiller)
Mischler (Bennwihr)
Mittnacht Frères (Hunawihr)
Charles Muller & Fils (Traenheim)
François-Joseph Munsch (Jungholtz)
André Rohrer (Mittelbergheim)
Albert Staehle (Wintzenheim)
Philippe Vorburger (Voegtlinshoffen)
Odile & Danielle Weber (Eguisheim)

⌇— 2–6 years (12 years for exceptional *cuvées*)

**ROSÉ** At its best, this dry, light-bodied wine has a deliciously fragrant aroma and flavor, which is reminiscent of strawberries, raspberries, or cherries. Seldom seen on export markets, but still commonly encountered by the *pichet* in local *winstubs*.

🍇 Pinot Noir

⌇— 1–2 years

✓ *Marcel Deiss* 🅱 (Burlenberg) *• Hugel & Fils* (Jubilée Le Neveux) *• Weinbach/Faller* (Réserve)

## RIESLING AOC

Of all Alsace grape varieties, Riesling is the most susceptible to differences in soil: clay soils give fatness and richness; granite Riesling is also rich, but with more finesse; limestone adds obvious finesse but less richness; and volcanic soil gives a well-flavored, spicy style.

**WHITE** In youth, fine Rieslings can show hints of apple, fennel, citrus, and peach, but can be so firm and austere that they give no hint of the beautiful wines into which they can evolve.

🍇 Riesling

⌇— 4–20 years

✓ *J B Adam • Lucien Albrecht* (Clos Schild) *• Barmès-Buecher* 🅱 *• Léon Baur* 🅱 *• Léon Beyer • Paul Blanck* 🅾 (Furstentum, Schlossberg) *• Albert Boxler* (Sommerberg Vieilles Vignes) *• Albert Hertz • JosMeyer* 🅱 (Hengst) *• Mader • Albert Mann* (Schlossberg) *• Frédéric Mochel • Muré* 🅾 (Clos St-Landelin) *• Rolly Gassmann • Martin Schaetzel • Roland Schmitt • Schoffit • Jean Sipp • Louis Sipp • Sipp-Mack • Bruno Sorg • Sylvie Spielmann* 🅱 *•*

*Bernard Schwach • F E Trimbach* (Cuvée Frédéric Emile, Clos Ste-Hune, Réserve) *• Weinbach/Faller • Wunsch & Mann • Zind Humbrecht* 🅱

**VT** *Jean Becker • Hugel & Fils • JosMeyer* 🅱 *• André Kientzler • Weinbach/Faller • Zind Humbrecht* 🅱

**SGN** *Hugel & Fils • Fernand Engel* 🅾 *• André Kientzler • F E Trimbach • Weinbach/Faller • Zind Humbrecht* 🅱

## SYLVANER AOC

Hugh Johnson once described the Sylvaner as "local tap-wine," and this is how it should be served—direct from the stainless-steel vat, with all the zip and zing of natural carbonic gas (normally filtered out during the bottling process). Like the Muscat, it does not take heat, and is a wine to buy in cooler years. Most attempts at late-harvest or botrytized styles (which cannot legally be sold as either VT or SGN) are diabolical. This does not mean that people should give up, just that they should not try to palm off these failures on the public. Better to add their tiny quantity to a much larger volume of an Edelzwicker—or whatever they like to call it—and sell more bottles of a turbocharged basic appellation at a much smaller premium, as this might result in better reviews and a better profit. Alsace producers should take a lesson from Angelo Publisi of Ballandean winery (*see* p596), who replicates the VT style by cutting the fruit-bearing canes just after *véraison*. This cuts the grape off from the vine's metabolism and the effect is much the same as when the leaves drop and sap returns to the roots after the first snap of winter. The resulting wine is consistently fabulous.

**WHITE** Sylvaner is an unpretentious, dry, light-to medium-bodied wine, with fragrance rather than fruitiness. It is generally best drunk young, but, like the Muscat, exceptionally long-living examples can always be found.

🍇 Sylvaner

⌇— Upon purchase

✓ *Agathe Bursin • JosMeyer* 🅱 (Rouge – sic) *• Rolly Gassmann • Weinbach/Faller • Zind Humbrecht* 🅱

## VIN D'ALSACE AOC

Alternative designation for Alsace AOC.

# THE LOIRE VALLEY

*In winemaking terms, the Loire Valley is best imagined as a long ribbon with crisp white wines at either end and fuller wines of all types in the middle. It is the home of Sauvignon Blanc, the only wine area in the world that specializes in Cabernet Franc and, in truly great vintages, makes some of the most sublime and sumptuous botrytized Chenin Blanc wines.*

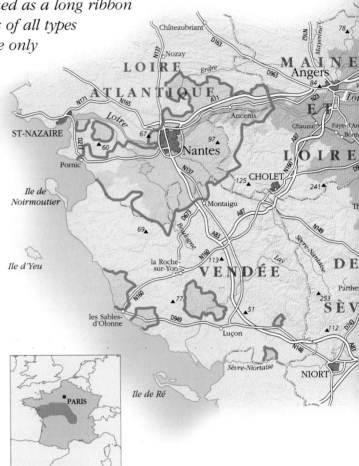

THE LOIRE IS THE LONGEST RIVER in France. From its source in the Cévennes Mountains, it flows 620 miles (1,000 kilometers) through 12 *départements*. The variations in soil, climate, and grape varieties found along its banks and those of its tributaries are reflected in the wide range of wines grown in the four major wine-producing districts. Red, white, and rosé; still, *pétillant*, and fully sparkling wines are produced in 87 different appellations ranging in style from bone dry to intensely sweet.

## THE LOIRE'S MOST IMPORTANT GRAPE

The Chenin Blanc grape produces four distinctly different styles of wine: dry, semisweet, sweet, and sparkling. This is due to traditional practices that have been forced on growers by the vagaries of climate. This grape has abundant natural acidity and, if it receives enough sun, a high sugar content. But the Loire is considered a northern area in viticultural terms, and growers must contend with late frosts, cold winds, and variable summers. Given a sunny year, the grower's natural inclination is to make the richest wine possible with this sweet and tangy grape; but in many vintages, only a medium or a dry style can be achieved. This variation in style is the root of the Loire's problems because it is difficult to build a reputation on uncertainty. If you take into account overproduction, the all too often debilitating effect of

VINEYARDS AT VOUVRAY
*In sunny years the area just to the east of Tours produces sweet, slow-maturing wines, valued for their longevity.*

## RECENT LOIRE VINTAGES

**2006** As with the rest of France, the July heatwave pushed vine growth on at a tremendous rate, but unlike most other regions, the August cold spell had minimal effect. The harvest in September was good, although the tail end of tropical storms dumped a lot of water, particularly on Muscadet. The result was an unbelievably good to excellent year for every wine style, particularly for those who decrease yields from the outset by rubbing off buds, and those who grass between the vines. Crispness, freshness, and good fruit will be the hallmark of most 2006s.

**2005** A beautiful year, from the fruity Muscadets, to crisp, concentrated Sauvignon Blancs from Sancerre, Pouilly Fumé, *et al.*, and the emergence of serious-quality dry Chenin Blanc in Anjou. The sweeter whites were mostly *demi-sec* level, although several really elegant *moelleux* were also produced. Some soft, deeply colored reds can also be found.

**2004** A great Muscadet vintage, but only the best producers who reduce their yields made something special in all other styles.

**2003** The vintage par excellence for Cabernet Franc and other Loire reds, which have an intensity of color and flavor seldom seen in the Loire, with a plumpness of fruit and, thanks to low acid levels, a seductively soft finish. Some very rich, incredibly sweet wines have been made, but through *passerillage*, not botrytis. Be very wary of all dry whites, with the possible exception of Muscadet, which might not be Muscadet as we know it, but has made some tremendous wines for those who like to see a more Burgundian style.

**2002** Top-class vintage for all styles in all districts, the wines have great ripeness levels, but pack more acidity than the 2003s.

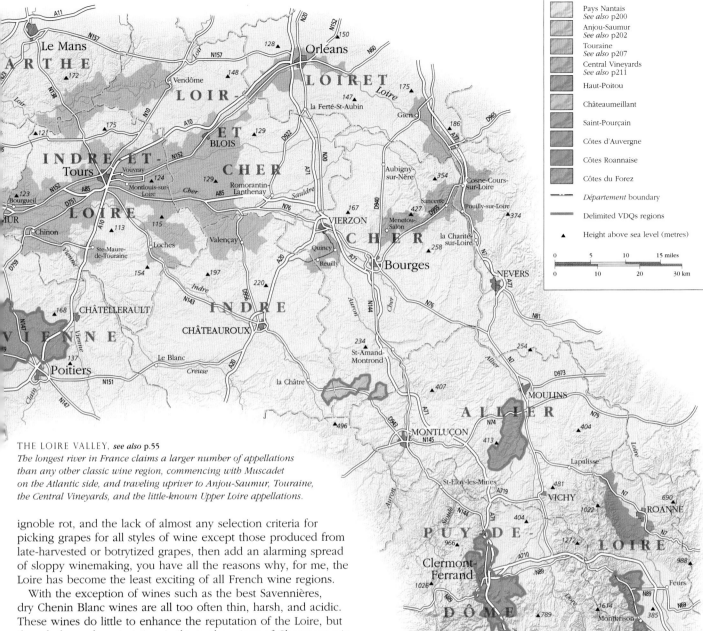

THE LOIRE VALLEY, *see also* p.55
*The longest river in France claims a larger number of appellations
than any other classic wine region, commencing with Muscadet
on the Atlantic side, and traveling upriver to Anjou-Saumur, Touraine,
the Central Vineyards, and the little-known Upper Loire appellations.*

ignoble rot, and the lack of almost any selection criteria for
picking grapes for all styles of wine except those produced from
late-harvested or botrytized grapes, then add an alarming spread
of sloppy winemaking, you have all the reasons why, for me, the
Loire has become the least exciting of all French wine regions.

With the exception of wines such as the best Savennières,
dry Chenin Blanc wines are all too often thin, harsh, and acidic.
These wines do little to enhance the reputation of the Loire, but
they do have characteristics similar to the wines of Champagne in
that they are disappointing when still, yet appear glamorous when
sparkling. It is little wonder, then, that as the Champagne trade
rapidly evolved in the 19th century, so the seeds of a sparkling-
wine industry were sown in Saumur.

THE LOIRE NEAR
SANCERRE
*In this area the ground
rises well above the river
and the neighboring
vineyards.*

## DID YOU KNOW?

- The Loire is the last wild river in Europe
  and designated a World Heritage Site by the
  United Nations Educational, Scientific, and
  Cultural Organization (UNESCO).

- As a wild river, the water level can vary by
  several yards within a few days, and its
  islands slowly move from year to year.

- The Loire Valley is known as the "Garden
  of France."

- The Loire Valley is the second-largest
  sparkling wine region in France (although
  Crémant d'Alsace is the second-largest
  individual appellation).

To suggest that the Chenin Blanc is fit only for fizzing up is to do the grape a great injustice. First, it is not in fact suited to the classic *brut* style of sparkling wine, as its aromatic qualities tend to fight rather than absorb the subtle effects of second fermentation. Second, it is this very character that makes Chenin Blanc one of the world's great wine grapes when botrytized. However, it is not the grape that is intrinsically disappointing when vinified as a still wine, but merely the methods employed by the grower and winemaker.

Chenin Blanc has been given pride of place in the Anjou-Saumur district, but unfortunately its cultivation has spread to unsuitable areas over the past 25 years. Producers more interested in making money than building a fine reputation have taken advantage of the Chenin Blanc's natural inclination to overcrop. It is a grape that should be harshly pruned, but most growers lack the courage to do this, and when the weather is unsettled it is these same growers who are the first to harvest. The heavier the crop, the less ripe the grapes, and the less ripe the grapes, the more washed out the flavors.

However, there are quality-conscious growers in the Loire, who restrict their yield and allow the grapes to ripen, yet still agonize over whether to risk the weather for one more day's maturity. It is from such top-performing growers as Domaine Baumard in the Coteaux du Layon, Clos Naudin and Huet in Vouvray, and Dominique Moyer in Montlouis that we get Chenin Blanc wines that dazzle our palates.

## FROM SOURCE TO SEA

For some inexplicable reason, most references restrict the Loire to its four major districts of Pays Nantais, Anjou-Saumur, Touraine, and Central Vineyards. Although some books incorporate the outlying areas of Fiefs Vendéens and Haut-Poitou, few mention the appellations of the Upper Loire, yet the wines of Côtes du Forez, Côte Roannaise, Côtes d'Auvergne, St.-Pourçain, and Châteaumeillant are equally legitimate members of the Loire's family of wines. And whereas the most famous appellations could and should rank among the most exciting wines of the world, there are so many underachievers that the major districts have become a minefield for wine lovers, while growers in the lesser-known areas of the Upper Loire have everything to prove.

THE GENERIC AND OUTLYING APPELLATIONS OF
# THE LOIRE VALLEY

## CHÂTEAUMEILLANT VDQS

Borders the Cher and Indre, around Bourges. Although only red-wine grapes are grown, white wine of some standing used to be made here, and its production is still permitted.

**RED** The Gamay grape usually dominates the red wines, which should be drunk as young as possible.

🍇 Gamay, Pinot Gris, Pinot Noir

🍷 6–12 months

**ROSÉ** The best Châteaumeillant wines. They are fresh, grapey, and delicately balanced.

🍇 Gamay, Pinot Gris, Pinot Noir

🍷 6–12 months

✓ *Du Chaillot • CV Châteaumeillant • Valérie et Frédéric Dallot • De Pavillon*

## CÔTES D'AUVERGNE VDQS

Côtes d'Auvergne is located south of Saint-Pourçain and west of Côtes du Forez on the edge of the Massif Central. This is the most remotely situated of all the outer areas that fall officially within the Loire region. The wines from certain villages are superior and have therefore been given the right to use the following communal appellations: Côtes d'Auvergne-Boudes (villages of Boudes, Chalus, and St.-Hérant); Côtes d'Auvergne-Chanturgues (villages of Clermont-Ferrand and Cézabat [part]); Côtes d'Auvergne-Châteaugay (villages of Châteaugay and Cézabat [part]); Côtes d'Auvergne-Corent (villages of Corent, Les Martres-de-Veyre, La Sauvetat, and Veyre-Monton); and Côtes d'Auvergne-Madargues (village of Riom).

**RED** The best of these dry, light-bodied, and fruity wines carry the Chanturgues appellation. Most are made from Gamay, a grape that has traditionally been grown in the area, and are very much in the style of Beaujolais.

🍇 Gamay, Pinot Noir

🍷 1–2 years

**WHITE** These dry, light-bodied wines made from Chardonnay have been overlooked but can be more accessible than the same variety grown in more classic areas of the Loire, thus they are surely a marketable commodity in view of Chardonnay's upmarket status.

🍇 Chardonnay

🍷 1–2 years

**ROSÉ** These are dry, light-bodied wines with an attractive cherry flavor. They are made in the village of Clermont-Ferrand, and carry the Chanturgues appellation.

🍇 Gamay, Pinot Noir

🍷 Within 1 year

✓ *Vignoble de l'Arbe Blanc • Pradier • Gilles Persilier*

## CÔTES DU FOREZ AOC

Similar to Beaujolais, this wine is produced in the Loire *département* adjacent to Lyon, and was upgraded from VDQS to AOC in 2000. The wines are improving through the efforts of the *coopérative* and a few quality-conscious growers, but they could be better.

**RED** These are dry, light-bodied wines with some fruit. They are best drunk young and at a cool temperature.

🍇 Gamay

🍷 Upon purchase

**ROSÉ** Simple, light-bodied, dry rosés that make attractive, unpretentious picnic wines.

🍇 Gamay

🍷 Upon purchase

✓ *Gilles Bonnefoy (La Madone) • Les Vignerons Foreziens • Odile Verdier et Jacky Logel*

## CÔTE ROANNAISE AOC

Red and rosé wines made from a localized Gamay clone called Gamay Saint-Romain. Grown on south- and southwest-facing slopes of volcanic soil on the left bank of the Loire some 25 miles (40 kilometers) west of the Mâconnais district of Burgundy. This appellation was promoted from VDQS to full AOC status in 1994.

**RED** Some of these dry, medium- to full-bodied wines are produced using a form of *macération carbonique*, and a few are given a little maturation in cask. The result can vary between well-colored wines that are firm and distinctive, and oaky and fruity Beaujolais-type versions for quaffing when young.

🍇 Gamay

🍷 1–5 years

**ROSÉ** Dry, medium-bodied, well-made wines that are crisp and fruity.

🍇 Gamay

🍷 2–3 years

✓ *Alain Baillon (Cuvée Monplaisir) • Paul et Jean-Pierre Benetère (Vieilles Vignes) • Des Pothiers • De la Rochette (Vieilles Vignes) • Robert Serol (Cuvée Troisgros)*

## CRÉMANT DE LOIRE AOC

Of all the Loire's sparkling wines, this is probably the most underrated, yet it has the greatest potential because it can be blended from the wines of Anjou-Saumur and Touraine and from the widest range of grape varieties.

**SPARKLING WHITE** The better-balanced *cuvées* of these dry to semisweet, light- to medium-bodied wines are normally a blend of Chenin Blanc in the main, with a good dash of Cabernet Franc and Chardonnay. The best Chardonnay clones are yet to be established in the Loire, but at least Chardonnay is widely utilized for sparkling wines, whereas Pinot Noir is not—this is a mystery, as it is a proven variety in the region.

🍇 Chenin Blanc, Cabernet Franc, Cabernet Sauvignon, Pineau d'Aunis, Pinot Noir, Chardonnay, Arbois, Grolleau Noir, and Grolleau Gris

🍷 1–3 years

**SPARKLING ROSÉ** The best of these light- to medium-bodied wines are *brut*, and usually contain a high proportion of Cabernet Franc and Grolleau Noir grapes. Cabernet Franc makes the most distinctive wine. A pure Pinot Noir *crémant* rosé would be interesting to taste.

🍇 Chenin Blanc, Cabernet Franc, Cabernet Sauvignon, Pineau d'Aunis, Pinot Noir, Chardonnay, Arbois, Grolleau Noir and Gris

🍷 Most are best consumed upon purchase, although some benefit if kept 1–2 years.

✓ *Baumard • Yves Lambert • Château de Montgueret • De Nerleux • Château de Putille • C. V. de Saumur*

## HAUT-POITOU VDQS

Situated 50 miles (80 kilometers) southwest of Tours, the Poitiers district produces wines that have achieved a remarkable reputation despite its hot, dry climate, and flat land that is more suited to arable farming than to viticulture. The local *cave coopérative* was responsible for this achievement, partly because of its high-tech establishment, which turned out clean wines during the late 1980s, when the rest of the Loire was going through its worst dirty wine period, and partly due to clever marketing. However, things went wrong on the financial side, Georges Duboeuf bought 40 percent of the cooperative, and it now operates as a *négociant*.

**RED** This is a wine to watch: although the really successful reds have until now been in short supply and confined mainly to Cabernet, there is a feeling that a general breakthrough is imminent. The quality of the entire appellation is likely to rise significantly, and there is promise of some exciting, pure varietal reds.

🍇 Pinot Noir, Gamay, Merlot, Malbec, Cabernet Franc, Cabernet Sauvignon, and a maximum of 20% each of Gamay de Chaudenay and Grolleau

🍷 Within 3 years

**WHITE** Dry, light- to medium-bodied, varietal wines. Those made from pure Sauvignon are softer and more floral than most of their northern counterparts, yet retain the freshness and vitality that is so important to this grape variety.

🍇 Sauvignon Blanc, Chardonnay, Pinot Blanc, and up to a maximum of 20% Chenin Blanc

🍷 Within 1 year

**ROSÉ** These dry, light- to medium-bodied wines are fresh and fruity.

🍇 Pinot Noir, Gamay, Merlot, Malbec, Cabernet Franc, Cabernet Sauvignon, and a maximum of 20% each of Gamay de Chaudenay and Grolleau

🍷 Within 3 years

✓ *Ampelidæ • Du Centaure • C. V. Haut-Poitou*

## ORLÉANS VDQS

Although made an appellation as recently as 2000, vines have been growing in this area since the 10th century. Legend has it that vines were originally brought from the Auvergne, hence the local synonyms of Auvernat Rouge for Pinot Noir and Auvernat Blanc for Chardonnay. The delimited area consists of 494 acres (200 hectares) in scattered parcels, of which 395 acres (160 hectares) are currently planted, encompassing the outskirts of Orléans, where the soil is silty, and 11 neighboring villages, stretching from the chalky soils of Saint Hilaire, and red, sandy-stony soils of Sologne, near Mézières, to clayey soils elsewhere.

**RED** Successful wines have good color and just about enough fruit to balance the tannins, affording a more supple finish. Montigny-Piel's Clos Saint-Fiacre stands out as the best wine of this appellation in all its color formats.

🍇 Minimum of 60% Pinot Meunier, plus Pinot Noir and Pinot Gris

🍷 Within 3 years

**WHITE** The least exciting wines so far, although it is very early days for these dry white wines, which must possess no more than 4 grams per liter of residual sugar.

🍇 Minimum of 60% Chardonnay, plus Pinot Gris

🍷 Within 1 year

**ROSÉ** The few encountered have been fresh, easy drinking with Meunier-cum-Pinot character, expressed more as red summer fruits than as cherries.

🍇 Minimum of 60% Pinot Meunier, plus Pinot Noir and Pinot Gris

🍷 Within 3 years

✓ *Montigny-Piel* (Clos Saint-Fiacre)

## ORLÉANS-CLÉRY VDQS

This subappellation was granted in 2002, and is restricted to red wines produced in Cléry-Saint-André and four neighboring villages southwest of Orléans, but confusingly from entirely different grapes from the main appellation.

**RED** The local *coopérative* (Grand Maison) makes a good wine from 25-year-old vines, which is old for this rediscovered part of the Loire, but most Cabernet-based wines from this area suffer too much from a herbaceous character.

🍇 Minimum of 75% Cabernet Franc, plus Cabernet Sauvignon planted before October 2002

🍷 Within 3 years

✓ *Jacky Legroux • C. V. de la Grand Maison*

## PINEAU DES CHARENTES AOC

A *vin de liqueur* produced in the Cognac region, which is between the Loire and Bordeaux (thus not really the Loire Valley, but it has to go somewhere!).

**WHITE** Few manage to rise above the typically dull, oxidative *vin de liqueur* style that goes *rancio* with age.

🍇 Cabernet Franc, Cabernet Sauvignon, Colombard, Folle Blanche, Jurançon Blanc, Meslier Saint-François, Merlot, Merlot Blanc, Montils, Sauvignon Blanc, Sémillon, Ugni Blanc

🍷 Upon opening

**ROSÉ** Few manage to rise above the typically dull, oxidative *vin de liqueur* style that goes *rancio* with age.

🍇 Cabernet Franc, Cabernet Sauvignon, Malbec, Merlot

🍷 Upon opening

✓ *Barbeau & Fils* (Tres Vieux Rosé Grand Réserve) • *Chais du Rouissoir* (Rosé) • *Vinet* (Félix-Marie de la Villière Blanc)

## ROSÉ DE LOIRE AOC

A dry rosé wine introduced in 1974 to exploit the international marketing success of Rosé d'Anjou and to take advantage of the trend for drier styles. The result has been very disappointing on the whole, although the few producers (recommended below) who have really tried demonstrate that very good-quality dry rosé can be made throughout the Loire.

**ROSÉ** Dry, light- to medium-bodied rosé from the Loire that could (and should) be the most attractive wine of its type—a few growers try, but most do not. These wines may be sold from December 1 following the harvest without any mention of *primeur* or *nouveau*.

🍇 Pineau d'Aunis, Pinot Noir, Gamay, Grolleau, and at least 30% Cabernet Franc and Cabernet Sauvignon

🍷 Upon purchase

✓ *De Chanteloup • Lecheteau • De Montgilet • Château de Passavant*

## ST.-POURÇAIN VDQS

The wines of Saint-Pourçain have a long and impressive history for what is, after all, an obscure VDQS, with vineyards first planted not by the Romans, as elsewhere in the Loire Valley, but by the Phoenicians. The Saint-Pourçain area covers 19 communes southeast of the Bourges appellations of the Central Vineyards in the Allier *département*. The growers are quite ambitious, and many people think that these wines have a particularly promising future. There are 1,235 acres (500 hectares) of vineyards.

**RED** Dry, light- to medium-bodied wines, but they can vary from very light Beaujolais look-alikes to imitations of Bourgogne Passetoutgrains, depending on the grape varieties in the blend.

🍇 Gamay, Pinot Noir, and up to a maximum of 10% Gamay Teinturier

🍷 1–2 years

**WHITE** Dry, light- to medium-bodied wines. The Tresallier grape (which is known as the Sacy in Chablis), when blended with Chardonnay and Sauvignon, produces a crisp, toasty, full-flavored wine that does have some merit. Very little is known about the Saint-Pierre-Doré, except that locals say it makes a "filthy wine," according to Master of Wine Rosemary George in *French Country Wines*.

🍇 A maximum of 50% Tresallier and 10% Saint-Pierre-Doré, plus Aligoté, Chardonnay, and Sauvignon Blanc

🍷 1–2 years

**ROSÉ** Crisp, dry, light- to medium-bodied wines that have a fragrance that is reminiscent of soft summer fruits. The rosés are generally more successful than the red wines of the area, but both styles are particularly refreshing and thirst-quenching.

🍇 Gamay, Pinot Noir, and up to a maximum of 10% Gamay Teinturier

🍷 1–2 years

✓ *De Bellevue • Jallet* (Les Ceps Centenaires) • *C. V. de Saint-Pourçain* (Cuvée Réserve) • *Cave Touzain*

# PAYS NANTAIS

*Nantais is Muscadet country. The Sèvre-et-Maine district produces the richest Muscadet, while Côtes de Grandlieu, granted its own appellation in 1994, and the Coteaux de la Loire to the north produce wines with extra acidity.*

SOUTHEAST OF NANTES are the vineyards of Muscadet. The best are those of the Sèvre-et-Maine district, named after two rivers, which is much hillier than the surrounding countryside and protected from northwesterly winds by Nantes itself. Sèvre-et-Maine accounts for one-quarter of the general appellation area, yet 85 percent of all Muscadet produced. Only in unusually hot or dry years, when they contain extra natural acidity, can Muscadet grapes grown farther north in the Coteaux de la Loire sometimes surpass those of Sèvre-et-Maine.

## THE MUSCADET GRAPE AND ITS WINES
It is uncertain when the Muscadet grape, also known as the Melon de Bourgogne and the Gamay Blanc, was first planted in the area. There is a plaque at Château de la Cassemichère that claims that the first Muscadet vine was transplanted there from Burgundy in 1740. But Pierre Galet, the famous ampelographer (vine botanist), tells us that "following the terrible winter of 1709, Louis XIV ordered that the replanting of the frozen vineyards of Loire-Atlantique be with Muscadet blanc."

The wine produced from the Muscadet grape is neutral in flavor and bears no hint of the muskiness that some believe its name implies. Traditionally, it is harvested early to preserve acidity, and yet, in doing so, the grower risks making a wine that lacks fruit. But if the wine is left in contact with its sediment and bottled *sur lie*, this enhances the fruit, adds a yeasty roundness, and, by retaining more of the carbonic gas created during fermentation, imparts a certain liveliness and freshness.

There have always been rare examples of exceptionally ripe Muscadet, which tend to age like a modest Burgundy after a few years in bottle. More recently, however, there has been a trend among quality-conscious growers to pick riper grapes (which is a significant risk, given the weather), in order to produce fuller, richer wines. This practice has come under attack from more conservative growers, who believe that there should not only be a maximum alcoholic strength for the finished wine (currently 12 percent after any chaptalization), but also a high minimum total acidity.

I have some sympathy with these traditionalists, since the Melon de Bourgogne grape is intrinsically incapable of competing with Chardonnay at even modest levels, thus most of the wines produced in this manner, while being extraordinary for Muscadet, make disappointing "Burgundy." Furthermore, I like the way that a correctly lean structure and naturally high acidity yield a certain nervosity of fruit in good Muscadet. However, good Muscadet represents perhaps one out of every 10 bottles, and it is a lack—sometimes a total absence—of fruit that is the pitfall of the rest. The *sur lie* process cannot conjure fruit out of thin air. But, despite their initial concentration on richness rather than fruit, the new winemakers should be encouraged, as they need to experiment in every direction if they are to find a reliable way to impart a feather-light fruit and freshness to these wines. There is no need for traditionalists to worry about the classic Muscadet style being perverted by a few; they have already done much worse by allowing the majority to all but destroy its classic quality. They should give the rebels the chance to do better; they will not want a reputation for poor man's Burgundy, but rather for rich man's Muscadet.

## FACTORS AFFECTING TASTE AND QUALITY

### LOCATION
The Pays Nantais lies in the coastal area and the westernmost district of the Loire Valley, with vineyards occupying parts of the Loire-Atlantique and the Maine-et-Loire *départements*.

### CLIMATE
Mild and damp, but winters can be harsh and spring frosts troublesome. Summers are generally warm and sunny, although they are also rainy.

### ASPECT
Some of the vineyards are found on the flat land around the mouth of the Loire southwest of Nantes. There are rolling hills in the Sèvre-et-Maine and Coteaux de la Loire, with the best vineyards on gentle riverside slopes. Some of the smaller valleys are actually too steep for viticulture, and the vines in these areas occupy the hilltops.

### SOIL
The best vineyards of the Sèvre-et-Maine are light and stony, with varying proportions of sand, clay, and gravel above a granitic, schistous, and volcanic subsoil that is rich in potassium and magnesium. The Coteaux de la Loire is more schistous, while the Côtes de Grandlieu is schistous and granitic, and vineyards in the generic Muscadet appellation have sand with silt. These soils provide good drainage, essential here.

### VITICULTURE AND VINIFICATION
The Muscadet is a frost-resistant, early-ripening grape that adapts well to the damp conditions of the Pays Nantais. It is harvested early (mid- to late September) to preserve its acidity, although a number of growers have started to reduce yields and pick riper. The best Muscadet is left in vat or barrel on its sediment—*sur lie*—until it is bottled. This imparts a greater depth and fruitiness, and a faint prickle of natural carbonic gas.

### GRAPE VARIETIES
**Primary varieties:** Muscadet, Folle Blanche
**Secondary varieties:** Cabernet Franc, Cabernet Sauvignon, Gamay, Gamay de Chaudenay, Gamay de Bouze, Négrette, Pinot Noir, Groslot Gris, Chardonnay, Chenin Blanc

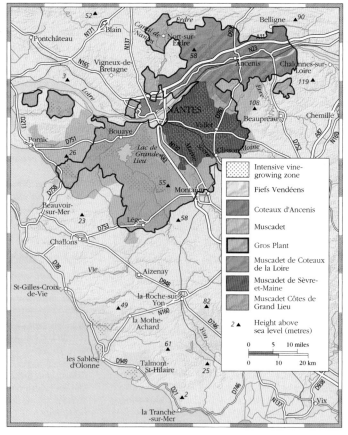

PAYS NANTAIS, *see also* p.196
*The finest wines in the Pays Nantais are produced to the east of Nantes in Sèvre-et-Maine and Coteaux de la Loire.*

Intensive vine-growing zone
Fiefs Vendéens
Coteaux d'Ancenis
Muscadet
Gros Plant
Muscadet de Coteaux de la Loire
Muscadet de Sèvre-et-Maine
Muscadet Côtes de Grand Lieu
Height above sea level (metres)

# THE APPELLATIONS OF
# PAYS NANTAIS

## COTEAUX D'ANCENIS VDQS

These varietal VDQS wines, which come from the same area as Muscadet Coteaux de la Loire, should be promoted to full AOC status.

**RED** Bone-dry to dry, and light- to medium-bodied wines that include Cabernets, made from both Cabernet Franc and Cabernet Sauvignon grapes. Surprisingly, they are not as successful as the juicy Gamay wines that represent no less than 80 percent of the total production of this appellation.

🌿 Cabernet Sauvignon, Cabernet Franc, Gamay, and up to a combined total of 5% Gamay de Chaudenay and Gamay de Bouze

🍷 2 years

**WHITE** Dry to medium-dry, light-bodied wines. The Pinot Gris, also sold as "Malvoisie," is not as alcoholic as its Alsatian cousin, yet can possess a light richness that will linger in the mouth. The Chenin Blanc, known locally as "Pineau de la Loire," is rarely very special.

🌿 Chenin Blanc, Pinot Gris

🍷 12–18 months

**ROSÉ** Bone-dry to dry, light- to medium-bodied wines, some of which are fresh, firm, and lively. Gamay is the most popular grape variety.

🌿 Cabernet Sauvignon, Cabernet Franc, Gamay, and up to a combined total of 5% Gamay de Chaudenay and Gamay de Bouze

🍷 2 years

✓ *CV des Terroirs de la Noëlle* • *Guindon* • *Du Haut Fresne*

## FIEFS VENDÉENS VDQS

A *vin de pays* until 1984, this appellation has been steadily improving and deserves its VDQS status. The regulations controlling the grape varieties permitted for this appellation are unique. They determine the proportion of each variety that must be cultivated in the vineyard, yet they do not limit the percentages of grapes contained in the final blend; thus blends and pure varietals are allowed.

**RED** The communes of Vix and Mareuil-sur-Lay-Disais produce the best wines. They are dry, medium-bodied, and firm, but not long-lived. They can have a grassy character, derived from the Cabernet Franc, which is the predominant grape grown in both these villages.

🌿 A minimum of 50% Gamay and Pinot Noir plus Cabernet Franc, Cabernet Sauvignon, Négrette, and up to a maximum of 15% Gamay de Chaudenay

🍷 Within 18 months

**WHITE** Bone-dry to dry, light-bodied wines which, apart from those of Vix and Pissotte, are of limited quality. This could be because the Chenin Blanc rarely ripens properly in a northerly coastal area. If some of the other permitted grape varieties were grown over a much wider area, quality might improve.

🌿 A minimum of 50% Chenin Blanc, plus Sauvignon Blanc and Chardonnay. A maximum of 20% Melon de Bourgogne in the communes of Vix and Pissotte and a maximum of 30% Groslot Gris in the coastal vineyards around Les Sables d'Olonne.

🍷 Upon purchase

**ROSÉ** Dry, light- to medium-bodied wines. The best wines of Vix and Mareuil-sur-Lay-Disais are soft, delicate, and underrated.

🌿 A minimum of 50% Gamay and Pinot Noir plus Cabernet Franc, Cabernet Sauvignon, Négrette, and a maximum of 15% Gamay de Chaudenay. A maximum of 30% (was as high as 30% until 1994) Groslot Gris in the coastal vineyards around Les Sables d'Olonne.

🍷 Within 18 months

✓ *Coirer* (Pissotte Sélection) • *Des Dames* (Les Aigues Marines) • *Saint Nicolas* (Brem Reflets)

## GROS PLANT VDQS OR GROS PLANT NANTAIS VDQS

Gros Plant is the local synonym for the Folle Blanche—one of the grapes used to make Cognac.

**WHITE** Gros Plant is normally so dry, tart, and devoid of fruit and body that it seems tough and sinewy to taste. I would rather drink lemon juice than 99 percent of the Gros Plant that I have had, but if yields are limited and the wine bottled *sur lie*, it can have sufficient depth to match its inherent bite.

🌿 Gros Plant

🍷 Usually upon purchase

✓ *De la Boitaudière* (Sur Lie) • *Guy Bossard* 🅱 (De l'Ecu) • *La Haut-Vrignais* (Sur Lie)

## MUSCADET AOC

This basic appellation covers the whole Muscadet area, yet the wines produced under it account for only 10 percent of the total production.

**WHITE** Bone-dry, light-bodied wines that, with very few exceptions, are ordinary at best, and often lack balance. Not one basic Muscadet has impressed me in recent years. These wines may be sold as *primeur* or *nouveau* as from the third Thursday of November following the harvest.

🌿 Muscadet

🍷 Upon purchase

## MUSCADET DES COTEAUX DE LA LOIRE AOC

The Coteaux de la Loire is the most northerly wine area on the French coast, above which it is almost impossible to grow grapes of sufficient ripeness for winemaking.

**WHITE** Bone-dry, light-bodied wines of variable quality, usually lacking in fruit, but can be the best balanced of all Muscadets in very hot years.

🌿 Muscadet

🍷 Upon purchase

✓ *Guindon* • *Du Moulin Giron* • *De la Varenne*

## MUSCADET CÔTES DE GRANDLIEU AOC

Delimited as recently as 1994, this area west of Sèvre-et-Maine once represented 73 percent of the basic Muscadet appellation. The wines now fetch a nice premium above that received when they were merely perceived as generic Muscadets and, while some deserve elevated price and status, many plainly do not.

**WHITE** Bone-dry, light-bodied wines that initially displayed considerable variation in quality, but the best are now showing a fine, floral-minerality of fruit.

🌿 Muscadet

🍷 Upon purchase

✓ *Du Fief Guerin* • *Gandais Père & Fils* • *Les Hautes Noëlles*

## MUSCADET DE SÈVRE-ET-MAINE AOC

Classic Muscadet from a small area containing most of the best wines. Some 45 percent of this appellation is bottled and sold as *sur lie*, having remained in contact with its sediment for at least one winter before bottling. There are so many groupings of Muscadet estates that I have decided to list them separately where I can.

**WHITE** Bone-dry to dry, light-bodied wines. The best should have fruit, acidity, and elegance, but although they can be reminiscent of a modest white Burgundy and exceptional wines can survive considerable aging, they seldom improve and always trade off finesse for depth.

🌿 Muscadet

🍷 2 years, although some may last 3–4 years

✓ *Guy Bossard* 🅱 (De l'Ecu) • *De la Braudière* • *Michel Bregeon* • *De la Chauvinière* • *Chasseloir* • *Coing de Saint-Fiacre* • *Comte Leloup de Chasseloir* • *Jean Douillard* • *Gandais Père & Fils* • *Grand Fief de la Cormeraie* • *La Haute Févrie* • *De la Louvetrie* • *Des Petites Cossardières* • *De la Quilla* • *Château des Roi* • *Abbaye de Ste Radegonde* • *Sauvion* 🅾

## MUSCADET SUR LIE AOC

Until recently there were no controls and unscrupulous producers would simply describe an ordinary filtered wine as *sur lie* and thereby demand a higher price. Since 1994, however, this term may be applied to only one of the three subappellations (Coteaux du Loire, Côtes de Grandlieu, and Sèvre-et-Maine) and may not be used on any wines bearing the generic Muscadet AOC. Quite what the logic is to this is uncertain, since Gros Plant VDQS is permitted to use *sur lie* and it is even more inferior than the generic Muscadet appellation. The lesser the wine, the more need for a *sur lie* boost, thus rather than limiting its use, more emphasis should be placed on stricter controls.

At the moment Muscadet *sur lie* must remain in contact with its sediment for one winter, and may not be bottled before the third week of March following the harvest, with a second bottling period of mid-October to mid-November for fuller styles. The wine must also be bottled directly off its lees, and must not be racked or filtered, but there is still no regulation on the size and type of vessel in which the wine should be kept *sur lie*. Some growers would like the term applied only to wines kept in wooden barrels, arguing that the effect of keeping a wine in contact with its lees in huge vats is negligible, but at the very least vats over a certain size should be equipped with paddles to circulate the lees.

# ANJOU-SAUMUR

*Anjou-Saumur is a microcosm of the entire Loire
Valley, with almost every grape available in the
Loire producing virtually every style of wine
imaginable—from dry to sweet, red through rosé
to white, and still wines to sparkling.*

**VINEYARDS, COTEAUX DU LAYON**
*In favorable sites, the vines are sometimes attacked by "noble rot."
The area is famous for its sweet white wines.*

SAUMUR IS THE LOIRE'S SPARKLING-WINE CENTER, where
tourists flock in the summer, visiting the numerous cellars hewn
out of the solid tufa subsoil. The magnificent white tufa-stone castle
that overlooks the town was built in the 14th century. It is regarded
as one of the finest of the Loire châteaux, and is used by the
Confrérie des Chevaliers du Sacavins (one of Anjou's several wine
fraternities) for various inaugural ceremonies and celebrations.

## THE WINES OF ANJOU

Rosé still represents as much as 45 percent of Anjou's total wine
output, even though it is on the decline. The figure was 55 percent
in the late 1980s. However, although rosé remains this district's
most popular wine, it has a down-market image and is essentially
a blend of minor grapes; thus its commercial success has not
propelled a specific variety to fame. Anjou's most celebrated
grape is the Chenin Blanc used to make white wines. This vine
has been cultivated in the area for well over a thousand years. It
has many synonyms, from "Pineau de la Loire" to "Franc-blanc,"
but its principal name, Chenin Blanc, stems from Mont-Chenin in
15th-century Touraine. Under other names it can be traced as far

back as the year 845, to the abbey of Glanfeuil (south of the river
in the Anjou district). The distinctive tang of the Chenin Blanc grape
comes from its inherently high tartaric acid content and this,
combined with a naturally high extract, makes for unacceptably
tart and often bitter styles of dry and medium-dry white. Exceptions
to this rule are few and mostly confined to the four sun-blessed,
southeast-facing slopes of Savennières. Anjou growers go by the
rule rather than the exception, and the common practice has
always been to leave the harvest of this variety until as late as

**ANJOU-SAUMUR,**
*see also* p.196-7
*Boasting sparkling wine, and
more, from Saumur, and a range
of wines from Angers's environs,
Anjou-Saumur produces most types
of wine found in the Loire as a whole.*

**BOTTLING AT
SAUMUR-CHAMPIGNY**
*The appellation produces some of
the Loire Valley's finest red wines
from Cabernet Franc.*

**Map legend:**

- Villages entitled to add their name to the Coteaux du Layon appellation
- Intensive vine-growing zone
- Anjou
- Anjou Coteaux de la Loire
- Savennières
- Coteaux de L'Aubance
- Coteaux de Saumur
- Saumur-Champigny
- Saumur
- Vins du Thouarsais
- Coteaux du Layon
- Anjou-Villages
- ▲ Height above sea level (metres)

0       5       10 miles
0          10          20 km

possible. This invites the risk of rain, but by going over the vines several times in the time-honored tradition of *tries*, picking only the ripest and healthiest grapes on each and every sweep of the vineyard, a miraculous wine may be made. Although this is a time-consuming, labor-intensive operation, the unique quality of overripe grapes produced can result in the most succulent and immaculately balanced of sweet wines. Unlike poor and boring dry Chenin Blanc wines that only deteriorate with age, these treasures are vinous investments that are capable of great maturity and can achieve wonderfully complex honeyed characteristics.

## THE SPARKLING SAUMUR INDUSTRY
With the rapid growth of the Champagne market in the 19th century, producers in the Loire began to copy effervescent winemaking practices, believing that here, at last, was a potential outlet for the surplus of thin, tart Chenin Blanc wines with which even the most quality-conscious growers were often lumbered. Saumur eventually turned into the largest French sparkling-wine industry outside Champagne. In many parts of the Loire the Chenin Blanc grape has the perfect acidity for a quality sparkling wine, although devotees of the true yeasty character of Champagne can find its bouquet sweet and aromatic, maintaining that its flavor is too assertive to be properly transmuted by the traditional method. However, the wines are hugely popular, and the mixture of Chardonnay and other neutral varieties can greatly improve the overall blend. The most ardent admirer of Champagne has been known to fall prey to the charms of a superior pure Chenin Blanc bubbly from this region, and even

**TUFA SUBSOIL CELLARS**
*The tufa-stone not only dominates the architecture; the subsoil is ideal for the sparkling-wine cellars.*

**THE TOWN OF SAUMUR**
*The 14th-century castle, one of the finest in the Loire, towers above the bustling town of Saumur, the buildings distinguished by the brilliant white tufa-stone typical of the area.*

I have been known to be besotted by Bouvet-Ladubay's luxuriously ripe, oak-fermented Trésor.

## THE REGION'S RED WINES
It is in Anjou, especially south of Saumur, that the Cabernet Franc emerges as the Loire's best red-wine grape. However, beyond neighboring Touraine, its cultivation rapidly diminishes. The Loire is the largest wine region in France, yet surprisingly it boasts just three classic red wines—Saumur-Champigny, Bourgueil, and Chinon—to which we might now add Anjou-Villages. It is no coincidence that most of the vineyards producing these wines are clustered together in a compact area around the confluence of the Vienne and the Loire—two rivers that long ago established the gravel terraces so prized for growing Cabernet Franc today.

## FACTORS AFFECTING TASTE AND QUALITY

### LOCATION
West-central district with mostly left-bank vineyards situated between Angers and Saumur.

### CLIMATE
A gentle Atlantic-influenced climate with light rainfall, warm summers, and mild falls, but frost is a problem in Savennières.

### ASPECT
Soft, rolling hills which hold back the westerly winds. The best sites are the south-facing rocky hillsides of Savennières and the steep-sided valley of the Layon River.

### SOIL
In the west and around Layon, the soil is schist with a dark, shallow topsoil that stores heat well and helps ripen the grapes, but some colder clay-soil areas produce heavier wines. The chalk-tufa soil in the east of the district around Saumur produces lighter wines, while the shale and gravel in Saumur-Champigny favors Cabernet Franc.

### VITICULTURE AND VINIFICATION
The Chenin Blanc is a particularly slow-ripening grape that is often left on the vine until November, especially in the Coteaux du Layon. The effect of the fall sun on the dew-drenched, overripe grapes can encourage "noble rot," particularly in Bonnezeaux and Quarts-de-Chaume. In good years, pickers go through the vineyards several times, selecting only the ripest or most rotten grapes—a tradition known as *tries*. Most wines are bottled in the spring following the vintage, but wines produced from such richly sweet grapes take at least three months to ferment and, for this reason, might not be bottled until the following fall.

### GRAPE VARIETIES
**Primary varieties:** Chenin Blanc, Cabernet Franc, Gamay, Grolleau
**Secondary varieties:** Chardonnay, Sauvignon Blanc, Cabernet Sauvignon, Malbec, Pineau d'Aunis

# THE APPELLATIONS OF
# ANJOU-SAUMUR

## ANJOU AOC

The Anjou district encompasses the vineyards of Saumur; thus Saumur may be sold as Anjou, but not vice versa. The red wines are by far the best, the whites the worst, and the rosé wines, although waning in popularity, remain the most famous. Because "mousseux" has "cheap bubbly" connotations, the wines officially designated as Anjou Mousseux appellation are often marketed simply as "Anjou."

**RED** Dry, medium- to full-bodied wines, made mostly from pure Cabernet Franc or with a touch of Cabernet Sauvignon. These delightful wines are best drunk young, although the odd oak-aged wine of surprising complexity can be found.

🍇 Cabernet Franc, Cabernet Sauvignon, Pineau d'Aunis

🍷 1–3 years

✓ *Des Baumard • Bouvet-Ladubay* (Non Pareils) *• Château de Fesles • Richard Leroy • Le Logis du Prieuré • D'Orgigné • Des Sablonnettes* (Genêts) *• Saint Arnoul • De la Sansonnière • Château Soucherie* (Champ aux Loups) *• De Terrebrune*

**WHITE** Although these wines vary from dry to sweet and from light- to full-bodied types, there are too many aggressively acid-dry or simply mediocre medium-sweet Chenin Blanc wines in the appellation. Some improvement has been made by growers maximizing the 20 percent Chardonnay and Sauvignon allowance, while Jacques Beaujeu and a few others use oak to smooth out Chenin's jagged edges, and Ogereau even ferments *en barrique*. These wines may be sold from December 1 following the harvest without any mention of *primeur* or *nouveau*.

🍇 A minimum of 80% Chenin Blanc and a maximum of 20% Chardonnay and Sauvignon Blanc

🍷 Upon purchase

✓ *Philippe Delesvaux • Les Grandes Vignes* (Varenne de Combre) *• Ogereau • Château de Passavant* ◉ *• Jo Pithon • Du Regain • Du Roy René* (Les Pierres) *• Richou • Château La Varière*

**ROSÉ** Once a marketing miracle, Anjou Rosé or Rosé d'Anjou sells less well in today's increasingly sophisticated markets. There is nothing intrinsically wrong with a wine that happens to be pink with some sweetness, although you would be forgiven for thinking this is exactly why some critics turn up their

noses at these wines. I prefer dry rosés, but I enjoy medium-sweet rosés when they are very fresh and fruity. The trouble with so many of these medium-sweet, light- to medium-bodied, coral-pink wines is that, while they can be delicious in the early spring following the vintage, an alarming number quickly tire in the bottle. The moral is, therefore, that even when you have found an Anjou rosé you like, never buy it by the case. These wines may be sold as *primeur* or *nouveau* from the third Thursday of November following the harvest or from December 1 without any mention of *primeur* or *nouveau*.

🍇 Predominantly Grolleau, with varying proportions of Cabernet Franc, Cabernet Sauvignon, Pineau d'Aunis, Gamay, Malbec

🍷 Upon purchase

✓ *C. V. de la Loire* (Elysis) *• Château La Varière*

## ANJOU COTEAUX DE LA LOIRE AOC

This rare, white-only appellation is situated southwest of Angers. Production is small and will dwindle even further as vineyards are replanted with Cabernet for the increasingly popular Anjou Rouge appellation. The minimum natural richness of the grapes at harvest is 221 grams per liter (the same as Sauternes), with a minimum residual sugar in the finished wine of 17 grams per liter.

**WHITE** Although currently produced in dry through to medium styles, this was originally legally defined in 1946 as a traditionally sweet wine. Today, producers following the trend for drier styles are hampered by out-of-date regulations that set the alcoholic strength too high and the yield too low.

🍇 Chenin Blanc

🍷 Within 1 year

✓ *Musset Roullier*

## ANJOU GAMAY AOC

Gamay is only allowed in Anjou AOC wines if the name of the grape is added to the appellation on the label.

**RED** Dry to medium-dry, light-bodied wines that are rarely of great interest. These wines may be sold as *primeur* or *nouveau* as from the third Thursday of November following the harvest.

🍇 Gamay

🍷 Upon purchase

✓ *De la Charmoise • Roy René* (La Creusette)

## ANJOU MOUSSEUX AOC

This traditional method wine is softer, but less popular than its Saumur equivalent, although it may come from the communes within Saumur itself.

**SPARKLING WHITE** These dry to sweet, light- to medium-bodied wines desperately need a change of regulation to allow a little Chardonnay in the blend. The Chardonnay's fatter, more neutral character would enable producers to make a more classic, less frivolous style of sparkling wine.

🍇 A minimum of 60% Chenin Blanc plus Cabernet Sauvignon, Cabernet Franc, Malbec, Gamay, Grolleau, Pineau d'Aunis

🍷 1–2 years

**SPARKLING ROSÉ** If you want to know what Anjou Rosé tastes like with bubbles, try this light- to medium-bodied wine, which is mostly sold as *demi-sec*.

🍇 Cabernet Sauvignon, Cabernet Franc, Malbec, Gamay, Grolleau, Pineau d'Aunis

🍷 Upon purchase

## ANJOU PÉTILLANT AOC

A little-used appellation for gently sparkling traditional method wines with a minimum of nine months' bottle age, which must be sold in ordinary still-wine bottles with regular corks.

**SEMI-SPARKLING WHITE** These are dry to *demi-sec*, light-bodied sparkling wines. Considering the variable quality of Anjou Blanc, many producers might be better advised to fizz it up and sell it under this appellation.

🍇 A minimum of 80% Chenin Blanc and a maximum of 20% Chardonnay and Sauvignon Blanc

🍷 Upon purchase

**SEMI-SPARKLING ROSÉ** Dry to medium, light-bodied wines which are rarely encountered outside the area and may be labeled "Anjou Pétillant," "Anjou Rosé Pétillant," or "Rosé d'Anjou Pétillant."

🍇 Grolleau, Cabernet Franc, Cabernet Sauvignon, Pineau d'Aunis, Gamay, Malbec

🍷 Upon purchase

## ANJOU ROSÉ AOC
### See Anjou AOC

## ANJOU-VILLAGES AOC

This superior, red-wine-only appellation was first delimited in 1986, but it did not come into effect until 1991. If you buy from the best growers, you will get some of the finest red wines that the Loire has to offer.

**RED** The very best wines can be deeply colored with a creamy-raspberry aroma and flavor.

🍇 Cabernet Franc, Cabernet Sauvignon

🍷 2–6 years

✓ *Patrick Baudoin • De la Bergerie • Château Pierre Bise • Des Griottes • L. & F. Martin • De la Motte • Ogereau • De la Poterie • De Putille • Des Quatre Quarres • Michel Robineau • Des Saulaies • Château La Varière*

## ANJOU–VILLAGES BRISSAC AOC

This village was singled out under the Anjou-Villages appellation in 1998 and backdated for wines from 1996 onward. It covers the area of Brissac-Quincé and nine surrounding communes.

✓ *Davieu* (Château de Brissac) *• De Haute-Perche • Du Prieuré • Richou • Des Rochelles* (La Croix de Mission) *• Château La Varière*

## BONNEZEAUX AOC

Grown on three south-facing river slopes of the commune of Thouarcé in the Coteaux du Layon, this is one of the undisputed great sweet wines of France. The grapes must be harvested in *tries* with the pickers collecting only the ripest, often botrytis-affected fruit, which can take up to two weeks. In 2003 the minimum natural richness of the grapes at harvest was increased from 204 to 238 grams per liter (compared to 221 grams per liter for Sauternes), and the minimum residual sugar increased from 17 to 34 grams per liter.

**WHITE** Intensely sweet, richer, and more full-bodied than Quarts-de-Chaume, the other great growth of the Layon Valley, this wine can have pineapple and liquorice fruit when young, often achieving a beautiful honeyed-vanilla complexity with age.

🌱 Chenin Blanc

🍷 Up to 20 years or more

☑️ *Philippe Delesvaux • Château de Fesles • Godineau/Des Petit Quarts • Claude Robin (Floriane) • De la Sansonnière • De Terrebrune • Château La Varière*

## CABERNET D'ANJOU AOC

This appellation includes Saumur, and it was a *saumurois* named Taveau who, in 1905, was the first person to make an Anjou Rosé from Cabernet grapes. Despite its classic Cabernet content and an extra degree of natural alcohol, this is not as superior to Anjou Rosé as it should be because bulk sales at cheap prices have devalued its reputation.

**ROSÉ** Good examples of these medium to medium-sweet, medium-bodied wines produced by the best domaines have a clean and fruity character with aromas of raspberries. These wines may be sold as *primeur* or *nouveau* from the third Thursday of November following the harvest or from December 1 without any mention of *primeur* or *nouveau*.

🌱 Cabernet Franc, Cabernet Sauvignon

🍷 Upon purchase

☑️ *La Croix des Loges • C. V. de la Loire (Elysis) • Des Petite Grouas • De Preville*

## CABERNET DE SAUMUR AOC

All Cabernet de Saumur wines have the right to claim the appellation Cabernet d'Anjou, but those sold as Saumur are usually finer in quality.

**ROSÉ** A delicate, medium-sweet, light- to medium-bodied wine with a hint of straw to its pink color and a distinctive raspberry aroma. These wines may be sold as *primeur* or *nouveau* from the third Thursday of November following the harvest or from December 1 without any mention of *primeur* or *nouveau*.

🌱 Cabernet Franc, Cabernet Sauvignon

🍷 Upon purchase

☑️ *Du Val Brun*

## CHAUME IER CRU DES COTEAUX DU LAYON AOC

This new appellation covers the south-facing vineyards on the *butte* de Chaume, and has been a long time in receiving recognition, as the original application dates back almost 50 years. The grapes must have a minimum natural sugar of 238 grams per liter (compared to 221 grams per liter for Sauternes) and are harvested by successive *tries*, with a maximum yield of 110 cases per acre (25 hectoliters per hectare) and a minimum residual sugar in the finished wine of 34 grams per liter. Because of the natural air-drainage on these slopes, *passerillage* is more widespread than *Botrytis cinerea*.

**WHITE** Big, rich, lusciously sweet wines that will make their mark in years to come.

🌱 Chenin Blanc

🍷 5–15 years

☑️ *Château Pierre Bise • Michel Blouin • Cady • Du Petit Metris • Du Rocher • De la Soucherie*

## COTEAUX DE L'AUBANCE AOC

These wines are made from old vines grown on the schistous banks of the Aubance River. To be entitled to this appellation growers must use grapes that are well ripened and harvested by *tries*, a labor-intensive system that is not cost-effective, thus until recently most growers produced Cabernet d'Anjou. A new generation of growers has transformed this appellation such that in 2003 the minimum natural sugar of the grapes at harvest was increased from 204 to 230 grams per liter (compared with 221 grams per liter for Sauternes) or 294 grams per liter for Coteaux l'Aubance "Sélection de Grains Nobles," as indicated on the label. The minimum residual sugar was increased from 17 to 34 grams per liter.

**WHITE** A few growers still make this rich and semisweet, medium- to full-bodied wine of excellent longevity and exceptional quality.

🌱 Chenin Blanc

🍷 5–10 years

☑️ *De Bablut ◉ • Davieu • De Montgilet (Clos Prieur) • Richou*

## COTEAUX DU LAYON AOC

This appellation, which overlaps Anjou Coteaux de la Loire in the northwest and Saumur in the southeast, has been famous for its sweet white wines since the fourth century. In favorable sites the vines are sometimes attacked by "noble rot," but in all cases the grapes must be extremely ripe and harvested by *tries* to a minimum of 12 percent alcohol from a maximum 132 cases per acre (30 hectoliters per hectare). Due to the relatively low price this appellation commands, harvesting by *tries* is viable only for the top domaines. In 2003 the minimum natural richness of the grapes at harvest was increased from 204 to 221 grams per liter (the same as Sauternes) or 294 grams per liter for Coteaux du Layon "Sélection de Grains Nobles." The minimum residual sugar was also increased from 17 to 34 grams per liter.

**WHITE** Green-gold- to yellow-gold-colored, soft-textured, sweet, medium- to full-bodied wines, rich in fruit, and potentially long lived.

🌱 Chenin Blanc

🍷 5–15 years

☑️ *Patrick Baudoin • Baumard (le Paon) • Château Pierre Bise • Philippe Delesvaux • Dhomme • Château de Fesles (Château de la Roulerie) • De la Gerfauderie (Les Hauts de la Gerfauderie) • Ogereau (Prestige) • Du Petit Val (Simon) • Du Portaille (Planche Mallet) • Du Regain (Le Paradis) • Des Sablonnettes (La Bohème)*

## COTEAUX DU LAYON VILLAGES AOC

Historically, these six villages have consistently produced the cream of all the wines in the Coteaux du Layon, and thus have the right to add their names to the basic appellation. In 2003 the minimum natural sugar of the grapes at harvest was increased from 204 to 238 grams per liter (compared to 221 grams per liter for Sauternes) or 294 grams per liter for Coteaux du

Layon Villages "Sélection de Grains Nobles." The minimum residual sugar was also increased from 17 to 34 grams per liter.

**WHITE** Sweet wines that are medium- to full-bodied. According to the "Club des Layon Villages," Beaulieu has a soft, light aroma; Faye has a scent reminiscent of brushwood; Rablay is big, bold, and round; Rochefort is full-bodied, tannic, and matures well; St.-Aubin has a delicate aroma that develops; and St.-Lambert is robust yet round.

🌱 Chenin Blanc

🍷 5–15 years

☑️ **Beaulieu** *Château de Breuil • Château Pierre Bise* • **Faye** *Château de Fresne (Clos de Cocus), Richard Leroy* • **Rablay** *Des Sablonettes ◉* • **Rochefort** *De la Motte* • **St.-Aubin** *Des Barres, Philippe Delesvaux, Jo Pithon, De la Roche Moreau* • **St.-Lambert** *Ogereau, Jo Pithon, Du Roy René (Les Cartelles), Michel Robineau*

## COTEAUX DU LAYON-CHAUME AOC

In many ways, there is very little that separates this single-village appellation from Coteaux du Layon, although it does have a lower maximum yield of 110 cases per acre (25 hectoliters per hectare) instead of 132 cases per acre (30 hectoliters per hectare), which itself is very low.

**WHITE** Sweet, medium- to full-bodied, fine, viscous wines that usually rank above most basic Coteaux du Layon.

🌱 Chenin Blanc

🍷 5–15 years

☑️ *Château de Fesles (Château de la Roulerie Aunis) • Des Forges (Les Onnis) • Château de la Guimonière • L. & F. Martin • Du Petit Metris*

## COTEAUX DE SAUMUR AOC

After the ban in 1985 on the use of the term *méthode champenoise* for wines produced or sold in the European Union (*see* p.169), there were moves to develop this little-used appellation as the principal still wine of the Saumur district in order to promote Saumur AOC as an exclusively sparkling wine. That idea has, it seems, ground to a halt.

**WHITE** Relatively rare, semisweet, medium- to full-bodied wines that are richly flavored and worth seeking out.

🌱 Chenin Blanc

🍷 5–10 years

☑️ *Champs Fleuris (Sarah) • De Nerleux • De Saint Just (La Valboisière)*

## QUARTS-DE-CHAUME AOC

These wines are grown on the plateau behind the village of Chaume in the Coteaux-du-Layon commune of Rochefort-sur-Loire. The vineyards of Quarts-de-Chaume used to be run by the abbey of Ronceray, whose landlord drew a quarter of the vintage as rent. In 2003 the minimum natural sugar of the grapes at harvest was increased from 204 to 238 grams per liter (compared to 221 grams per liter for Sauternes), and the minimum residual sugar increased from 17 to 34 grams per liter.

**WHITE** These are semisweet to sweet, medium- to full-bodied wines. Although harvested by *tries* and produced in the same manner as Bonnezeaux, Quarts-de-Chaume comes from a more northerly area and as a result is slightly lighter in body. It also tends to have a touch less sweetness.

🍇 Chenin Blanc

🍷 Up to 15 years or more

✓ *Des Baumard* • *Château de Bellerive* • *De Laffourcade* • *Château de la Roche Moreau* • *Château Pierre Bise* • *Château La Varière*

## ROSÉ D'ANJOU AOC
*See* Anjou AOC

## ROSÉ D'ANJOU PÉTILLANT AOC
*See* Anjou Pétillant AOC

## SAUMUR AOC

Saumur, situated within the borders of the Anjou appellation, is regarded as the pearl of Anjou. Its wine may be sold as Anjou, but Anjou does not automatically qualify as Saumur. Unless made from Cabernet grapes, all rosé wines must adopt the Anjou Rosé appellation. Like Anjou, its white wines are variable, yet its red wines are excellent.

**RED** These fine, bone-dry to dry, medium- to full-bodied wines are often similar to the red wines of Anjou, although they can vary from light and fruity to deep-colored and tannic.

🍇 Cabernet Franc, Cabernet Sauvignon, Pineau d'Aunis

🍷 1–10 years according to style

✓ *Du Bois Mignon* (La Belle Cave) • *Du Collier* • *De Fiervaux* • *De Château-Gaillard* ❸ • *Filliatreau* • *Guiberteau* • *Des Hautes Vignes* • *Langlois-Château* (Vieilles Vignes) • *Des Nerleux* • *Château de Passavant* • *Des Raynières* • *C. V. de Saumur* (Reserve) • *Château Yvonne*

**WHITE** Varying from bone-dry to sweet and from light- to full-bodied, these wines have a style more akin to Vouvray than Anjou, due to the limestone and the tufa soil. In poor-to-average years, however, a Saumur is easily distinguished by its lighter body, leaner fruit, and a tartness of flavor that can sometimes have a metallic edge on the aftertaste. These wines may be sold as from December 1 following the harvest without any mention of *primeur* or *nouveau*.

🍇 A minimum of 80% Chenin Blanc and a maximum of 20% Chardonnay and Sauvignon Blanc

🍷 Upon purchase

✓ *Du Collier* • *Guiberteau* (Le Clos) • *Château de Hureau* • *Langlois-Château* (Vieilles Vignes) • *Des Roches Neuves* • *Clos Rougeard* • *C. V. de Saumur* • *Château de Villeneuve*

**SPARKLING WHITE** Although the production per acre of this wine is one-third more than for its Anjou equivalent, Saumur is—or at least should be—better in quality and style due to its Chardonnay content and the tufa-limestone soil. Most wines are made in a true, bone-dry, *brut* style, although the full gamut is allowed and wines up to *demi-sec* sweetness are relatively common. The vast majority of these wines have a tart greengage character, lack finesse, and do not pick up bottle aromas. The wines indicated below have an elegance sadly lacking in most Saumur, and possess gentler, more neutral fruit, which will benefit from a little extra time in bottle, although after a while all these wines tend to age rather than mature gracefully. The creamy-rich *barrique*-fermented Bouvet Trésor

is the one significant exception as not only is it just the best sparkling wine in the Loire, it can be compared to very good-quality Champagne, although it is in a very different style.

🍇 Chenin Blanc plus a maximum of 20% Chardonnay and Sauvignon Blanc, and up to 60% Cabernet Sauvignon, Cabernet Franc, Malbec, Gamay, Grolleau, Pineau d'Aunis, and Pinot Noir

🍷 3–5 years

✓ *De Beauregard* • *De la Bessière* • *Bouvet-Ladubay* (Mlle Ladubay, Trésor) • *De Brizé* • *Gratien & Meyer* (Flamme) • *C. V. de Saumur* (Spéciale)

**SPARKLING ROSÉ** An increasing number of pink Saumurs are pure Cabernet Franc and an increasing number are showing very well. However, the aggressive potential of this grape can quickly turn a thrilling raspberry-flavored fizz into something hideous. Pure Cabernet Sauvignon rosés can be much smoother, less overt, and not as intrinsically Saumur as a Cabernet Franc *cuvée*.

🍇 Cabernet Sauvignon, Cabernet Franc, Malbec, Gamay, Grolleau, Pineau d'Aunis, Pinot Noir

🍷 Upon purchase

✓ *Bouvet-Ladubay* (Trésor) • *Gratien & Meyer* (Flamme)

## SAUMUR-CHAMPIGNY AOC

Many people believe that the vineyards southeast of Saumur entitled to add the village name of Champigny to their appellation produce the best red wines in the Loire.

**RED** Bone-dry to dry, full-bodied wines with a distinctive deep color and full and fragrant raspberry aromas, often tannic and long-lived.

🍇 Cabernet Franc, Cabernet Sauvignon, Pineau d'Aunis

🍷 5–10 years

✓ *Du Bois Moze Pasquier* • *La Bonnelière* • *Des Champs Fleuris* • *Filliatreau* • *Château du Hureau* (Lisagathe) • *René-Noël Legrand* • *Petit Saint Vincent* • *De Rocfontaine* (Vieilles Vignes) • *Des Roches Neuves* • *Clos Rougeard* • *De Saint Just* • *Château de Villeneuve* • *Château Yvonne*

## SAUMUR MOUSSEUX AOC

This is the technically correct appellation for all fully sparkling white and rosé Saumur wines made by the traditional method, but producers have shied away from the down-market term *mousseux*, selling the wines simply as Appellation Saumur Contrôlée. There is no allowance for this in the regulations, but it is a widespread practice. A significant amount of red traditional method wine is also produced, but this cannot claim AOC status. *See also* Saumur AOC

## SAUMUR D'ORIGINE AOC

When the European Union banned the term *méthode champenoise*, this marketing term was developed by the producers of sparkling Saumur to promote and advertise their wines. *See also* Saumur AOC

## SAUMURZ PÉTILLANT AOC

Little-used appellation for gently sparkling, traditional method wines with a minimum of nine months' bottle age, which must be sold in ordinary still-wine bottles with regular corks.

**SEMI-SPARKLING WHITE** These dry to *demi-sec*, light-bodied, and fruity wines are not

dissimilar to the fine wines of the Montlouis Pétillant appellation and should be revived.

🍇 A minimum of 80% Chenin Blanc and a maximum of 20% Chardonnay and Sauvignon Blanc

🍷 Upon purchase

## SAVENNIÈRES AOC

When this small portion of Anjou Coteaux de la Loire produced only sweet wines, the AOC regulations set a correspondingly low maximum yield. This concentrates the wines on four southeast-facing slopes of volcanic debris that produce the world's greatest dry Chenin Blanc.

**WHITE** Bone-dry to dry wines of great mineral intensity, Savennières can be some of the longest-lived dry white wines in the world. Most critics believe that the single greatest Savennières is Nicolas Joly's Clos de la Coulée de Serrant and, while I agree that it is one of the greatest wines of the Loire, I think that Baumard's Clos du Papillon (not to be confused with Clos du Papillon from other growers) consistently displays greater elegance and finesse. Over the past 15 years or so, a few producers have resurrected the semisweet style that used to be more popular in Savennières in the first half of the 20th century.

🍇 Chenin Blanc

🍷 5–8 years (10–15 years for Clos de la Coulée de Serrant)

✓ *Des Baumard* • *Du Closel* (Clos du Papillon) • *Château de Fesles* (Château de Varennes) • *Nicolas Joly* (Clos de la Coulée de Serrant) • *De la Monnaie* • *Château Pierre Bise* • *Pierre Soulez*

## SAVENNIÈRES COULÉE-DE-SERRANT AOC

One of just two single-vineyard designations authorized for Savennières, Coulée-de-Serrant is 17 acres (7 hectares) and a mono-*cru*, solely owned by Nicolas Joly of Château de la Roche-aux-Moines. Many consider this to be the single-greatest Loire dry white wine. *See also* Savennières AOC

## SAVENNIÈRES ROCHE-AUX-MOINES AOC

The second and largest of the two single-vineyard designations authorized for Savennières, Roche-aux-Moines is 42 acres (17 hectares) and owned by three producers: Nicolas Joly of Château de la Roche-aux-Moines, Pierre and Yves Soulez of Château de Chamboureau, and Madame Laroche of au Moines. *See also* Savennières AOC

## VINS DU THOUARSAIS VDQS

Michel Gigon is the sole producer of Vins du Thouarsais, a wine that could once boast over a hundred growers.

**RED** Dry, light- to medium-bodied, fruity reds, sometimes reminiscent of cherries and other stone fruit.

🍇 Cabernet Franc, Cabernet Sauvignon, Gamay

🍷 1–2 years

**WHITE** A lighter-bodied but far more fragrant version of dry and semisweet Anjou Blanc.

🍇 Chenin Blanc plus up to 20% Chardonnay

🍷 Upon purchase

**ROSÉ** This is a splendid dry, light-bodied or light- to medium-bodied picnic wine.

🍷 Upon purchase

✓ *Michel Gigon*

# TOURAINE

*Wines bearing Touraine appellations are prolific and capable of giving good value, but for the most part they are not great. However, there are notable exceptions, such as the wines from Vouvray and the less well-known but equally elite wines of Montlouis, Bourgueil, and Chinon.*

THE WINEGROWING DISTRICT around Tours dates back to Roman times, as does the town itself. The Cabernet Franc, known locally as Breton, was flourishing in the vineyards of the abbey of Bourgueil 1,000 years ago and, as recently as 500 years ago, the Chenin Blanc—today's predominant Touraine grape—acquired its name from Mont Chenin in the south of the district.

## TOURAINE'S WINE REGIONS

With the possible exception of Saumur-Champigny, the best red wines in the Loire come from the appellations of Chinon and Bourgueil, which face each other across the Loire River, just west of Tours. Made predominantly from Cabernet Franc, good vintages aged in oak may be complex and comparable to claret, while the more everyday wines have the aromas of fresh-picked raspberries and can be drunk young and cool. To the east, Vouvray and Montlouis produce rich, sweet, long-lived *moelleux* wines from overripe Chenin Blanc grapes in sunny years. North of Tours, the wines produced in Jasnières are from the same grape, but the dry style is distinctly different. Jasnières is a singular white subappellation within a wider red, white, and rosé AOC called the Coteaux du Loir. The "Loir" is not a typographical error for "Loire," but a tributary of the great river. Also grown on the banks of the Loir, Coteaux du Vendômois produces the full spectrum of still-wine styles, as does Cheverny to the east, including a distinctive dry white wine from the obscure Romorantin grape. Touraine Sauvignon Blanc makes an attractively priced, unassuming alternative to Sancerre, while the fruity Gamay makes easy-drinking reds and rosés. Chenin Blanc is still the dominant

variety here and, as in Anjou-Saumur, the tradition has been to produce naturally sweet wines in great years when these grapes are full of sugar, but lighter, not completely dry styles are more usual. The surplus of less-than-overripe grapes, like that in Anjou-Saumur, is traditionally utilized for sparkling wines.

TOURAINE, *see also* p.197
*Surrounded by different appellations, the ancient city of Tours is the focal point of an area rich in the variety of its wines.*

## FACTORS AFFECTING TASTE AND QUALITY

### LOCATION
East-central district with most of its vineyards in the *département* of Indre-et-Loire, but they extend into Loir-et-Cher, Indre, and Sarthe.

### CLIMATE
Touraine falls under some Atlantic influence, but the climate is less maritime than in the Nantes district and Anjou-Saumur. Protected from northerly winds by the Coteaux du Loir. Warm summer, low October rainfall.

### ASPECT
Attractively rolling land, flatter around Tours itself, hillier in the hinterland. Vines are planted on gently undulating slopes, which are often south-facing, at between 130 to 330 feet (40 and 100 meters) above sea level.

### SOIL
Clay and limestone over tufa subsoil east of Tours around Vouvray and Montlouis. Tufa is chalk boiled by volcanic action. It is full of minerals, retains water, and can be tunneled out to make large, cool cellars for storing wine. Sandy-gravel soils in low-lying Bourgueil and Chinon vineyards produce fruity, supple wines; the slopes or *coteaux* of sandy-clay produce firmer wines.

### VITICULTURE AND VINIFICATION
White-wine fermentation takes place at low temperatures and lasts for several weeks for dry wines, several months for sweet wines. The reds undergo malolactic fermentation. Some Bourgueil and Chinon is aged for up to 18 months in oak casks before bottling.

### GRAPE VARIETIES
**Primary varieties:** Chenin Blanc, Cabernet Franc, Sauvignon Blanc, Grolleau
**Secondary varieties:** Cabernet Sauvignon, Pinot Noir, Meslier, Gamay, Gamay Teinturier, Pineau d'Aunis, Romorantin, Arbois, Chardonnay, Malbec

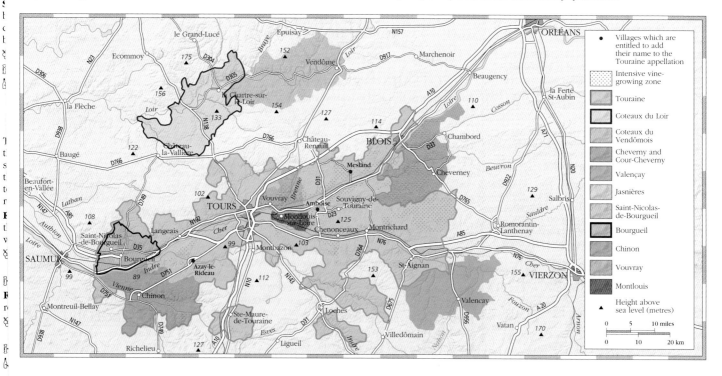

Map legend:
- Villages which are entitled to add their name to the Touraine appellation
- Intensive vine-growing zone
- Touraine
- Coteaux du Loir
- Coteaux du Vendômois
- Cheverny and Cour-Cheverny
- Valençay
- Jasnières
- Saint-Nicolas-de-Bourgueil
- Bourgueil
- Chinon
- Vouvray
- Montlouis
- Height above sea level (metres)

0 5 10 miles
0 10 20 km

**SPARKLING RED** Dry, light- to medium-bodied wines that are fruity and refreshing.

🍇 Cabernet Franc

🍷 Upon purchase

**SPARKLING WHITE** These light- to medium-bodied wines are made in dry and sweet styles, and the quality is consistent due to the large production area, which allows for complex blending.

🍇 Primarily Chenin Blanc but may also include Arbois and up to 20% Chardonnay and a combined maximum of 30% Cabernet, Pinot Noir, Pinot Gris, Pinot Meunier, Pineau d'Aunis, Malbec, and Grolleau

🍷 Upon purchase

**SPARKLING ROSÉ** Light- to medium-bodied wines that are attractive when *brut*, though a bit cloying if sweeter.

🍇 Cabernet Franc, Malbec, Noble, Gamay, and Grolleau

🍷 1–2 years

✔ *Blanc Foussy* (Robert de Schlumberger, Veuve Oudinot) • *Jean-Pierre Laissement* (Rosé) • *Monmousseau* (JM)

## TOURAINE NOBLE-JOUÉ AOC

A rosé-only appellation, this AOC was created in 2001 in recognition of the *vin gris* produced that was modestly famous in the 19th century, but its vineyards were gradually swallowed by the creeping urbanization southwest of Tours.

**ROSÉ** Yet to reestablish a reputation, the best of these wines so far have been fresh, light-bodied, elegantly fruity wines with smoky-floral minerality.

🍇 A minimum of 40% Pinot Gris, plus at least 20% Pinot Gris and a minimum of 10% Pinot Noir

🍷 Upon purchase

✔ *Bernard Blondeau*

## TOURAINE PÉTILLANT AOC

Refreshing, slightly effervescent white and rosé wines made from the same grape varieties as Touraine Mousseux. None are exported.

**SEMI-SPARKLING RED** Medium-dry, light-bodied wines that are not very popular.

🍇 Cabernet Franc

🍷 Upon purchase

**SEMI-SPARKLING WHITE** Well-made, refreshing, light-bodied wines, in dry and sweet styles.

🍇 Chenin Blanc, Arbois, Sauvignon Blanc, and up to 20% Chardonnay

🍷 Upon purchase

**SEMI-SPARKLING ROSÉ** Attractive, light, quaffing wines that are made in dry and sweet styles.

🍇 Cabernet Franc, Malbec, Noble, Gamay, and Grolleau

🍷 Upon purchase

## VALENÇAY AOC

Situated in the southeast of Touraine around the Cher River, these vineyards produce well-made, attractive wines. Promoted from VDQS to AOC in 2003, when the *encépagement* changed. Rarely seen outside France.

**RED** Dry, light-bodied, fragrant wines that can be very smooth and full of character. The Malbec, known locally as Cot, is particularly successful.

🍇 30–60% Gamay, with at least 30% in total of Pinot Noir and Malbec, plus optional

Cabernet Franc and Cabernet Sauvignon, which together must not exceed 10% of the entire blend (20% up to the 2003 vintage)

🍷 1–2 years

**WHITE** Simple, dry, light-bodied wines that are improved by the addition of Chardonnay.

🍇 A minimum of 70% Sauvignon Blanc, plus Arbois and Chardonnay

🍷 1–2 years

**ROSÉ** Dry to medium-dry, light-bodied wines that can be full of ripe soft-fruit flavors.

🍇 30–60% Gamay, with at least 30% in total of Pinot Noir and Malbec, plus an optional maximum of 30% Pinot d'Aunis, with or without Cabernet Franc and Cabernet Sauvignon, which together must not exceed 20% of the entire blend

🍷 Upon purchase

✔ *Chantal et Patrick Gibault* • *Jean-François Roy*

## VOUVRAY AOC

These white wines may be dry, medium-dry, or sweet depending on the vintage. In sunny years, the classic Vouvray that is made from overripe grapes affected by the "noble rot" is still produced by some growers. In cooler years, the wines are correspondingly drier and more acidic, and greater quantities of sparkling wine are produced.

**WHITE** At its best, sweet Vouvray can be the richest of all the Loire sweet wines. In good years, the wines are very full bodied, rich in texture, and have the honeyed taste of ripe Chenin Blanc grapes.

🍇 Chenin Blanc but may also contain Arbois

🍷 Usually 2–3 years; the sweeter wines can last up to 50 years

✔ *Des Aubuisières* (Giraudières) • *Champalou* (Le Clos du Portail Sec) • *Philippe Foreau* (Clos Naudin) • *De la Haute Borne* (Tendre) • *Huet* • *Clos de Nouys* • *Pichot* • *De la Taille au Loups* • *Vigneau Chevreau* ◉ • *Alain Robert* (La Sablonnière)

## VOUVRAY MOUSSEUX AOC

These sparkling wines are made from overripe grapes. In years when the grapes do not ripen properly they are converted into sparkling wines using the traditional method and blended with reserve wines from better years.

**SPARKLING WHITE** Medium- to full-bodied wines made in both dry and sweet styles. They are richer and softer than sparkling Saumur but have more edge than sparkling Montlouis.

🍇 Chenin Blanc and Arbois

🍷 Non-vintage 2–3 years, vintage *brut* and *sec* 3–5 years, vintage *demi-sec* 5–7 years

✔ *Marc Brédif* • *Champalou* • *Champion* • *Clos de l'Epinay* (Tête de Cuvée) • *Philippe Foreau* • *Domaine de la Galinière* (Cuvée Clément) • *Sylvain Gaudron* • *Huet* • *Laurent et Fabrice Maillet* • *Château de Moncontour* (Cuvée Prédilection)

## VOUVRAY PÉTILLANT AOC

These are stylish and consistent semi-sparkling versions of Vouvray, but very little is produced.

**SEMI-SPARKLING WHITE** Medium- to full-bodied wines made in dry and sweet styles. They should be drunk young.

🍇 Chenin Blanc and Arbois

🍷 Upon purchase

✔ *Gilles Champion* • *Jean-Charles Cathelineau* • *Huet*

## MORE GREEN WINES

In addition to the Loire producers recommended in this book that are either biodynamic or organic, there are also the following. They include a number that have been recommended in other editions, and still make some fine wines, but have been culled out to make room for others.

**PAYS NANTAIS**

**Biodynamic**

*St. Nicolas* (Brem sur Mer)

**Organic**

*Chevolleau-Goulpeau* (Aubigny), *De La Louvetrie* (La Haye-Fouassière), *De la Parentière* (Vallet), *Bruno Dejardin* (Rosnay)

**ANJOU-SAUMUR**

**Biodynamic**

*De la Charmeres se* (Faye d'Anjou), *De la Sansonnière* (Thouarcé), *Château La Tour Grise* (Le Pûy Notre Dame)

**Organic**

*Laurent Charrier* (Doué la Fontaine), *Collegiale des de Loire* (Le Puy Notre Dame), *Cousin Leduc* (Martigne Briand), *De Dreuillé* (Champ-sur-Layon), *De l'Echalier* (Rablay-sur-Layon), *Elliau* (Vaudelany), *Foucault* (Chacé), *Château Fouquet* (Dampierre-sur-Loire), *Des Frogères* (Chacé), *I. & J. Godineau Pithon* (St-Lambert du Lattay), *Anne Hacquet* (Beaulieu-sur-Layon), *Hauret* (Martigné Briand), *Henquinet-Pilhon* (Champ-sur-Layon), *Michel Joseph* (Chacé), *Du Layon* (St.-Georges du Layon), *Gérard Leroux* (Les Verchers-sur-Layon), *Manoir de la Tête Rouge* (Le Puy Notre Dame), *De Mosse* (St.-Lambert du Lattay), *Nouteau-Cerisier Père & Fils* (Faye d'Anjou), *Du Pas St. Martin* (Doué la Fontaine), *Régnier-David* (Meigné), *Rochais* (Rochefort-sur-Loire), *De Rochambeau* (Soulaines-sur-Aubance), *Rochard* (Chanzeaux), *Ste.-Barbe* (Saumur), *Patric Thomas* (St.-Georges-sur-Layon), *Val Brun* (Parnay), *Du Vieux Tuffeau* (Le Puy Notre Dame), *Vintrou* (St. Jean des Mauvrets)

**TOURAINE**

**Biodynamic**

*De Pontcher* (Thesée)

**Organic**

*Clos Roches Blanches* (Mareuil-sur-Cher), *Philippe Tessier* (Cheverny), *Michelle Thibault* (Bourgueil), *Du Clos Tue Boeuf* (Les Montils), *Breton* (Restigné), *Yves Lecocq* (Bourgueil), *Loquineau* (Cheverny), *De la Mabillière* (Vernou-sur-Brenne), *Joseph Moreau* (Vallères), *Du Mortier* (St. Nicolas de Bourgueil), *Château de la Roche* (Cheillé), *Les Cailloux du Paradis* (Soings en Sologne), *Alain Courtault* (Thésée), *Joël Courtault* (Thésée—in conversion to biodynamic), *Denis Père et Fils* (Civray de Touraine), *Des Deux Saintes* (St. Aubin le Dépeint), *Georget* (La Brosse-Touvois), *Guion* (Le Pontarin)

**CENTRAL VINEYARDS**

**Organic**

*Claude Prugnard* (Orcet), *Clos St. Jean*, *Clos de la Chapelle* (St. Jean St. Maurice), *Carroget Gautier* (Anetz), *Christian Chaput* (Prompsat), *Joël Lapalue* (St. Jean St. Maurice)

# CENTRAL VINEYARDS

*In this district of scattered vineyards, all the classic wines are dry variations of the Sauvignon Blanc, but there are some discernible differences between the best of them—the concentration of Sancerre, the elegance of Pouilly Fumé, the fresh-floral character of Menetou-Salon, the lightness of Reuilly, and the purity of Quincy.*

THE CENTRAL VINEYARDS are so called because they are in the center of France, not the center of the Loire Valley. This is a graphic indication of how far the Loire Valley extends and, while it might not be a surprise to discover the vineyards of Sancerre are quite close to Chablis, it does take a leap of the imagination to accept that they are nearer to the Champagne region than to Tours. And who could discern by taste alone that Sancerre is equidistant between the production areas of such diverse wines as Hermitage and Muscadet?

Best known of all the towns in this district is Orléans, famous for its liberation by Joan of Arc from the English in 1429. The other important town is Bourges, which is situated in the south between the wine villages of Reuilly, Quincy, and Menetou-Salon, and was once the capital of the Duchy of Berry.

## THE REGION'S SAUVIGNON BLANC WINES

The Sauvignon Blanc is to the Central Vineyards what Muscadet is to the Pays Nantais. It produces the classic wine of the district, which, like Muscadet, also happens to be both white and dry. But two dry white wines could not be more different in style and taste. In the best Muscadet *sur lie* there should be a yeasty fullness, which can sometimes be misread as the Chardonnay character of a modest Mâcon. In Central Vineyard Sauvignons, however, whether they come from Sancerre or Pouilly—or even from one of the lesser-known, but certainly not lesser-quality, villages around Bourges—the aroma is so striking it sometimes startles. The rasping dryness of the wine's flavor catches the breath and can come from only one grape variety.

CHÂTEAU DU NOZET, POUILLY-SUR-LOIRE
*This 19th-century château at Pouilly-sur-Loire is the home of Patrick de Ladoucette, the baron of Pouilly.*

## A BURGUNDIAN INFLUENCE

Historically, this district was part of the Duchy of Burgundy, which explains the presence of Pinot Noir vines. After the scourge of *phylloxera*, the area under vine shrank. That brought back into production was mostly replanted with Sauvignon Blanc, which began to dominate the vineyards, although isolated spots of Pinot Noir were maintained. Some of the wines these produce today can be good, although they are extremely delicate in style; and however fine the quality, they are but a shadow of great Burgundian Pinot.

## FACTORS AFFECTING TASTE AND QUALITY

**LOCATION**
The most easterly vineyards of the Loire are situated in the center of France, chiefly in the *départements* of Cher, Nièvre, and Indre.

**CLIMATE**
More continental than areas closer to the sea; the summers are shorter and hotter and the winters longer and colder. Spring frosts and hail are particular hazards in Pouilly. Harvests are irregular.

**ASPECT**
Chalk hills in a quiet, green landscape. Vines occupy the best sites on hills and plateaus. At Sancerre they are planted on steep, sunny, sheltered slopes at an altitude of 660 feet (200 meters).

**SOIL**
The soils are dominated by clay or limestone, topped with gravel and flinty pebbles. When mixed with chalk-tufa, gravelly soils produce lighter, finer styles of Sauvignon wines; when combined with Kimmeridgian clay, the result is firmer and more strongly flavored.

**VITICULTURE AND VINIFICATION**
Some of the vineyard slopes in Sancerre are very steep, so cultivation and picking are done by hand. Most properties are small and use the traditional wooden vats for fermentation, but some growers have stainless-steel tanks.

**GRAPE VARIETIES**
**Primary varieties:** Sauvignon Blanc, Pinot Noir
**Secondary varieties:** Chasselas, Pinot Blanc, Pinot Gris, Cabernet Franc, Chenin Blanc, Gamay

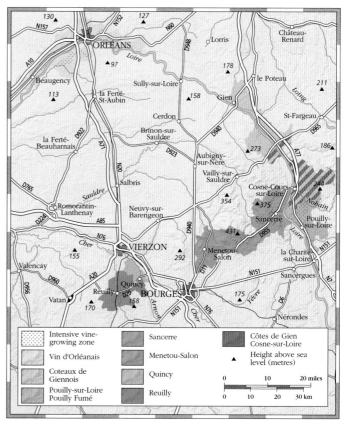

CENTRAL VINEYARDS, *see also p.197*
*The most easterly of the Loire's vineyards, and the most central of France, the Central Vineyards are famous for wines made from the Sauvignon Blanc grape.*

# THE APPELLATIONS OF
# CENTRAL VINEYARDS

## CÔTES DU GIEN COSNE-SUR-LOIRE AOC

Of the 16 communes that produce Coteaux du Giennois, only eight are entitled to add Cosne-sur-Loire to the appellation. It was promoted from VDQS to AOC in 1998.

**RED** Dry, bright ruby-colored wines. Often full-tasting, but rarely with the body to match and sometimes quite tannic.

🐝 Gamay, Pinot Noir—since 1992, neither variety may exceed 80% of the total blend

🍷 1–2 years

**WHITE** These are dry, medium-bodied, curiously aromatic white wines that develop a full, toasty flavor with a little bottle age.

🐝 Sauvignon Blanc

🍷 1–2 years

**ROSÉ** Light-salmon-colored wines, slightly fuller bodied than the Coteaux du Giennois made a little further to the north, but equally capable of the same citrous fragrance.

🐝 Gamay, Pinot Noir—since 1992, neither variety may exceed 80% of the total blend

🍷 1–4 years

✓ Alain Paulat ◉

## COTEAUX DU GIENNOIS AOC

This appellation could boast nearly a thousand growers at the turn of the 20th century when it was 40 times its current size. Promoted from VDQS to AOC in 1998.

**RED** Dry, light-bodied red wines that often have less color than many rosés.

🐝 Gamay, Pinot Noir—since 1992, neither variety may exceed 80% of the total blend

🍷 1–2 years

**WHITE** These very basic, dry, light-bodied wines lack interest. Chenin Blanc can no longer be used to make this wine.

🐝 Sauvignon Blanc

🍷 1–2 years

**ROSÉ** Light-salmon-colored, light-bodied wines that can have a fragrant citrous character.

🐝 Gamay, Pinot Noir—since 1992, neither variety may exceed 80% of the total blend

🍷 1 year

✓ Emile Balland • De Beaurois • De Villegeai

## MENETOU-SALON AOC

This underrated appellation covers Menetou-Salon and the nine surrounding villages.

**RED** These are dry, light-bodied, crisp, and fruity wines with fine varietal aroma. They are best drunk young, although some oak-matured examples can age well.

🐝 Pinot Noir

🍷 2–5 years

**WHITE** Bone-dry to dry wines. They are definitely Sauvignon in character, but the flavor can have an unexpected fragrance.

🐝 Sauvignon Blanc

🍷 1–2 years

**ROSÉ** Extremely good-quality, dry, light-bodied aromatic wines, full of straightforward fruit.

🐝 Pinot Noir

🍷 Within 1 year

✓ Georges Chavet & Fils • De Loye • Henry Pellé

## POUILLY BLANC FUMÉ AOC
### See Pouilly Fumé AOC

## POUILLY FUMÉ AOC

This used to be the world's most elegant Sauvignon Blanc wine, but too many wines of ordinary and often quite dire quality have debased this once-great appellation. In Pouilly-sur-Loire and its six surrounding communes, only pure Sauvignon wines have the right to use "Fumé" in the appellation name, a term that evokes the grape's gunsmoke character.

**WHITE** Great Pouilly Fumé is rare but when found, its crisp, gooseberry flavor will retain its finesse and delicacy in even the hottest years.

🐝 Sauvignon Blanc

🍷 2–5 years

✓ Bouchié-Chatellier • Jean-Claude Châtelain • Didier Dagueneau • Château Tracy

## POUILLY-SUR-LOIRE AOC

This wine comes from the same area as Pouilly Fumé, but it is made from the Chasselas grape, although Sauvignon Blanc is allowed for blending. Chasselas is a good dessert grape but makes very ordinary wine.

**WHITE** Dry, light-bodied wines. Most are neutral, tired, or downright poor.

🐝 Chasselas, Sauvignon Blanc

🍷 Upon purchase

✓ Guy Saget

## QUINCY AOC

These vineyards, on the left bank of the Cher, are situated on a gravelly plateau. Although located between two areas producing red, white, and rosé wines, Quincy produces only white wine, from Sauvignon Blanc.

**WHITE** Bone-dry to dry, quite full-bodied wines in which the varietal character of the Sauvignon Blanc is evident. There is a purity that rounds out the flavor and seems to remove the rasping finish usually expected in this type of wine.

🐝 Sauvignon Blanc

🍷 1–2 years

✓ Bailly • De Ballandors • Mardon • De Puy-Ferrand • Philippe Portier • Silice de Quincy

## REUILLY AOC

Due to the high lime content in the soil, Reuilly produces wines of higher acidity than those of neighboring Quincy.

**RED** These are dry, medium-bodied wines. Some are surprisingly good, although often tasting more of strawberries or raspberries than the more characteristic redcurrant flavor associated with Pinot Noir.

🐝 Pinot Noir, Pinot Gris

🍷 2–5 years

**WHITE** These are bone-dry to dry, medium-bodied wines of good quality with more of a grassy than a gooseberry flavor, yet possessing a typically austere dry finish.

🐝 Sauvignon Blanc

🍷 1–2 years

**ROSÉ** This bone-dry to dry, light-bodied wine is a pure Pinot Gris wine, although it is simply labeled Pinot.

🐝 Pinot Gris

🍷 2–5 years

✓ Aujard[1] • Claude Lafond • De Seresnes[1] • Jean-Michel Sorbe[1] • Pascal Desroches (Clos des Varennes)

[1]Also particularly recommended for red or rosé

## SANCERRE AOC

This appellation is famous for its white wines, although originally its reds were better known. Recently the reds and rosés have developed greater style.

**RED** These wines have been more variable in quality than the whites, but the consistency is improving rapidly. They are dry, light- to medium-bodied wines, with a pretty floral aroma and a delicate flavor.

🐝 Pinot Noir

🍷 2–3 years

**WHITE** Classic Sancerre should be bone dry, highly aromatic, and have an intense flavor, sometimes tasting of gooseberries or even peaches in a great year. However, too many growers overproduce, never get the correct ripeness, and make the most miserable wines.

🐝 Sauvignon Blanc

🍷 1–3 years

**ROSÉ** Attractive, dry, light-bodied rosés with strawberry and raspberry flavors.

🐝 Pinot Noir

🍷 Within 18 months

✓ Henri Bourgeois • Pascal Cotat • Lucien Crochet[1] • Vignoble Dauny ◉ • André Dezat[1] • Fouassier (Clos Paradis, Les Grands Groux) • Gitton • Alphonse Mellot • Henry Natter • Vincent Pinard • Christian Thirot (Des Vieux Pruniers)

[1]Also particularly recommended for red or rosé

## VINS DE L'ORLÉANAIS VDQS

These wines have been made for centuries, but only one-third of the appellation is worked now.

**RED** Dry, medium-bodied, fresh, and fruity wines that are given a short maceration, producing a surprisingly soft texture. They are usually sold as pure varietal wines: the Pinot can be delicate, the Cabernet Franc is fuller.

🐝 Pinot Noir, Pinot Meunier, Cabernet Franc

🍷 1–2 years

**WHITE** Very small quantities of interesting wines are made from Chardonnay, known locally as Auvernat Blanc. Dry, medium-bodied, and surprisingly smooth and fruity.

🐝 Chardonnay (syn. Auvernat Blanc), Pinot Gris (syn. Auvernat Gris)

🍷 1–2 years

**ROSÉ** The local speciality is a dry, light- to medium-bodied rosé known as Meunier Gris—an aromatic vin gris with a crisp, dry finish.

🐝 Pinot Noir, Pinot Meunier, Cabernet Franc

🍷 Within 1 year

✓ Clos St.-Fiacre • Vignerons de la Grand'Maison

# THE RHÔNE VALLEY

*Famous for its full, fiery, and spicy-rich red wines, the Rhône Valley also produces small quantities of rosé and white, and even some sparkling and fortified wines. Although essentially red-wine country, and great red-wine country at that, the Rhône has experienced a kind of revolution in white-wine production. There has been a growing number of exotic, world-class white wines in various appellations since the late 1980s, when just a few began to emerge in Châteauneuf-du-Pape.*

STRETCHING FROM VIENNE TO AVIGNON, the Côtes-du-Rhône appellation occupies a 125-mile (200-kilometer) length of the Rhône River. Beyond this great region other Rhône wines exist, and some are not even French. The banks of this mighty European river are clad with vines all the way from the Valais vineyards of Visp in Switzerland, just 30 miles (50 kilometers) from the Rhône's glacial origins in the Alps, to the *vin de pays* vineyards of the Bouches-du-Rhône, set amid the Rhône delta just west of Marseilles, where the river finally and sluggishly runs into the Mediterranean.

Only a tiny patch of vineyards in the very north of this region is in fact located within the Rhône *département* (which is a geographic misnomer as it actually accounts for 70 percent of Burgundy's output). Comparing the contrasting characters of Rhône

LA LANDONNE VINEYARD, CÔTE RÔTIE
*Syrah grapes are harvested on the steep slopes of Guigal's top-performing La Landonne vineyard in the Côte Brune area of Côte Rôtie, above Ampuis.*

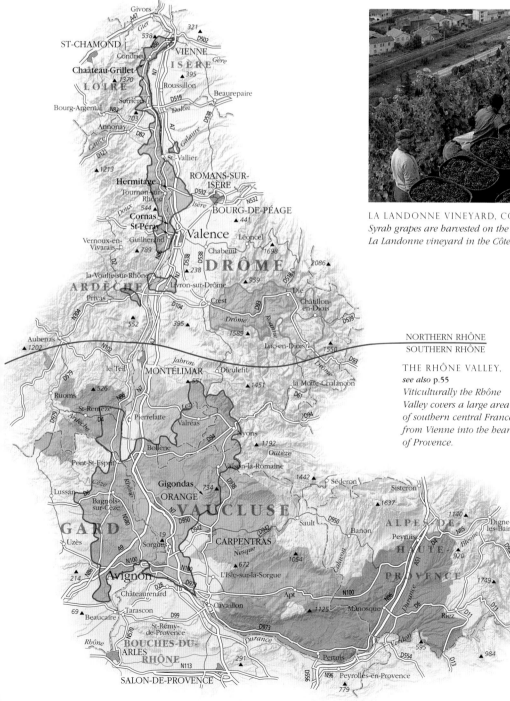

NORTHERN RHÔNE
SOUTHERN RHÔNE

THE RHÔNE VALLEY,
**see also** p.55
*Viticulturally the Rhône Valley covers a large area of southern central France, from Vienne into the heart of Provence.*

| | |
|---|---|
| | Côtes-du-Rhône *See also* pp215, 218 |
| | Côtes-du-Rhône-Villages *See also* p218 |
| | Clairette de Die *See also* p214 |
| | Châtillon-en-Diois *See also* p214 |
| | Coteaux du Tricastin *See also* p218 |
| | Coteaux de Pierrevert *See also* p218 |
| | Côtes du Lubéron *See also* p218 |
| | Côtes du Ventoux *See also* p218 |
| | Côtes du Vivarais *See also* p218 |
| ——— | Département boundary |
| ▲ | Height above sea level (metres) |

| 0 | 10 | 20 miles |
|---|---|---|
| 0 | 10 20 30 | 40 km |

CÔTE BRUNE ON THE CÔTE RÔTIE, NORTHERN RHÔNE
*The Côte Brune is an area of the Côte Rôtie where the rust color of the soil
is visible evidence of iron-rich elements in its granitic sandy soil.*

and Burgundy wines produced within the one *département* can
have a humbling effect on all those who glibly talk about regional
styles. For example, what could be further apart than a rich,
classic Condrieu and a fresh, light Mâcon, or an intense, ink-black
Côte Rôtie and a quaffing, cherry-colored Beaujolais? Yet all of
these wines are produced in the same *département* and could
thus be described as coming from the same region.

BEAUMES-DE-VENISE, SOUTHERN RHÔNE
*Home to one of the most elegant and consistent fortified Muscat wines in the
world, Beaumes-de-Venise also produces a soft, peppery red wine under the
Côtes-du-Rhône-Villages appellation.*

## RECENT RHÔNE VINTAGES

**2006** A cool August revived the vines after a scorching-hot July, and
the grapes were picked under sunny skies that provided far more
ideal conditions than in most other French regions. Hermitage and
Côte Rôtie are the standouts, but this year is an excellent vintage for
all styles in both northern and southern Rhône.

**2005** A great year, particularly for reds, and especially in the
northern Rhône, but the southern Rhône is almost as exceptional,
with Châteauneuf-du-Papes rivaling the best the north could provide.
Beautifully balanced wines that make for delicious early drinking
but will improve for many years in the bottle.

**2004** Another excellent year. Although concentrated with high alcohol
levels, the 2004s are much more classic than the 2003s, and lean
much more toward the 2005s, both stylistically and geographically,
with their clean lines and finer balance, resulting in standout wines
for Hermitage, Côte Rotie, and Châteauneuf-du-Papes.

**2003** Another classic region turned upside-down by the dramatic heat
wave, with unprecedented high sugar and low acidity levels that
provided the potential for great red wines only from those skilled
enough to cope with the challenge. There will be many flashes of
brilliance that will have the critics raving, only to find the wines will
shed their fruit relatively quickly to end up with the alcohol showing
through. The northern Rhône probably has the edge over the south, but
where the wines are properly balanced, the greatest reds across the
region will probably be a match for the best Rhônes from any vintage
in living memory. Generally you can forget the whites and rosés.

## A REGION DIVIDED

In terms of grape varieties, the Rhône divides neatly into two—
the Syrah-dominated north and the Grenache-influenced south—
although there are those who confuse the issue by separating the
southernmost section of the northern district and calling it the
Middle Rhône. The north and south differ not only in terrain and
climate, but also contrast socially, culturally, and gastronomically.

# THE NORTHERN RHÔNE

*The Northern Rhône is dominated by the ink-black wines of Syrah, the Rhône's only truly classic black grape. A small amount of white wine is also produced and, in the south of the district, at St.-Péray and Die, sparkling wines are made.*

THE NORTHERN RHÔNE might be the gateway to the south, but it has more in common with its northern neighbor, Burgundy, than it does with the rest of the Rhône, even though its wines cannot be compared with those from any other area. Indeed, it would be perfectly valid to isolate the north as a totally separate region called the Rhône, which would, therefore, allow the Southern Rhône to be more accurately defined as a high-quality extension of the Midi.

## THE QUALITY OF THE NORTHERN RHÔNE

The ink-black classic wines of Hermitage and Côte Rôtie stand shoulder to shoulder with the *crus classés* of Bordeaux in terms of pure quality, and the greatest Hermitage and Côte Rôtie deserve the respect given to *premiers crus* such as Latour, Mouton, or Lafite. Cornas can be even bigger and blacker than Hermitage or Côte Rôtie, and the top growers can rival the best of wines from its better-known neighbors. While the fine, dry white wines of Condrieu and (potentially) Château Grillet are unique in character, the presence of such a style in this part of France is not as surprising as that of the sparkling white wines of St.-Péray and Die, particularly the latter, which Francophiles would describe as a superior sort of Asti!

## FACTORS AFFECTING TASTE AND QUALITY

### LOCATION
The narrow strip of vineyards that belong to the Northern Rhône commences at Vienne, just south of Lyon, and extends southward to Valence.

### CLIMATE
The general effect of the Mediterranean is certainly felt in the Northern Rhône, but its climate has a distinctly continental influence. This results in the pattern of warmer summers and colder winters, which is closer to the climate of southern Burgundy, to the north, than to that of the Southern Rhône. The climatic factor that the area does have in common with the southern half of the Rhône is the Mistral, a bitterly cold wind that can reach up to 90 miles (145 kilometers) per hour and is capable of denuding a vine of its leaves, shoots, and fruit. As a result, many Mistral-prone vineyards are protected by poplar and cypress trees. The wind can, however, have a welcome drying effect in humid harvest conditions. The average summertime temperature is just two degrees Fahrenheit lower than in the south.

### ASPECT
The countryside is generally less harsh than that of the southern Rhône, with cherry, peach, chestnut, and other deciduous trees in evidence. The valley vineyards are cut far more steeply into the hillsides than they are in areas farther south.

### SOIL
The Northern Rhône's soil is generally light and dry, granitic and schistous. More specifically, it is made up of: granitic-sandy soil on the Côte-Rôtie (calcareous-sandy on the Côte Blonde and ruddy, iron-rich sand on the Côte Brune); granitic-sandy soil at Hermitage and Condrieu with a fine overlay of decomposed flint, chalk, and mica, known locally as *arzelle*; heavier soil in Crozes-Hermitage with patches of clay; granitic sand with some clay between St.-Joseph and St.-Péray, getting stonier toward the southern end of the region, with occasional outcrops of limestone; and limestone and clay over a solid rock base in the area that surrounds Die.

### VITICULTURE AND VINIFICATION
Unlike the Southern Rhône, most Northern Rhône wines are produced entirely or predominantly from a single grape variety, the Syrah, despite the long list of grapes that are occasionally used (*see* Secondary varieties, *below*). Viticultural operations are labor-intensive in the northern stretch of the district and, due to the cost, the vineyards were once under the threat of total abandonment. Since that threat we pay much more for Côte Rôtie, but at least it has remained available. Vinification techniques are very traditional and, when wines are aged in wood, there is less emphasis on new oak than is given in Bordeaux or Burgundy, although chestnut casks are sometimes used.

### GRAPE VARIETIES
**Primary varieties:** Syrah, Viognier
**Secondary varieties:** Aligoté, Bourboulenc, Calitor, Camarèse, Carignan, Chardonnay, Cinsault, Clairette, Counoise, Gamay, Grenache, Marsanne, Mauzac, Mourvèdre, Muscardin, Muscat Blanc à Petits Grains, Pascal Blanc, Picardan, Picpoul, Pinot Blanc, Pinot Noir, Roussanne, Terret Noir, Ugni Blanc, Vaccarèse

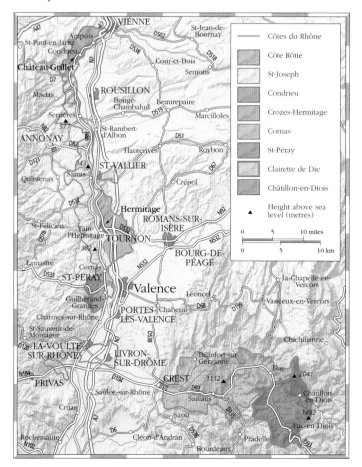

Côtes du Rhône
Côte Rôtie
St-Joseph
Condrieu
Crozes-Hermitage
Cornas
St-Péray
Clairette de Die
Châtillon-en-Diois
▲ Height above sea level (metres)

0   5   10 miles
0   5   10 km

THE NORTHERN RHÔNE,
*see also p.213*
*At the heart of this region the towns of Tain and Tournon face each other across the river.*

AMPUIS UNDER SNOW
*These southeast-facing vineyards of Côte Rôtie form a dramatic stretch of scenery on the west bank of the Rhône, 5 miles (9 kilometers) south of Vienne.*

# THE NORTHERN RHÔNE

## CHÂTEAU GRILLET AOC

Château Grillet has remained under the same family ownership (Neyret-Gachet) since 1830, and is one of only two single-estate appellations in France, the other being Romanée-Conti. Although it is often described as one of the world's great white wines, this is a legacy from more than a century ago. Château Grillet has not achieved anything like its full potential for at least the last few decades. There is no doubt that its sun-blessed terraces could produce Viognier of a singularly outstanding quality, but there is no inkling the proprietors can be bothered to pursue such a course. Who could blame them when Château Grillet could charge two or three times the price of Condrieu? But the price of some of the best Condrieu are now snapping at its heels, and unless there is a dramatic increase in quality, Château Grillet will drop in price. In today's more transparent market, fine wine consumers are no longer willing to drink labels.

**WHITE** This is, potentially, a wine of great finesse and complex character, but not one to keep in bottle as long as some would have you believe.

🍇 Viognier

🍷 3–7 years

## CHÂTILLON-EN-DIOIS AOC

This wine was raised to full AOC status in 1974, although it is hard to comprehend what merited such an elevation then or now.

**RED** Light in color and body, thin in fruit, with little discernible character.

🍇 Gamay, plus up to 25% Syrah and Pinot Noir

**WHITE** Sold as pure varietal wines, the light and fresh, gently aromatic Aligoté is as good as the richer, fuller, and rather angular Chardonnay.

🍇 Aligoté, Chardonnay

**ROSÉ** I have not encountered any.

🍇 Gamay, plus up to 25% Syrah and Pinot Noir

✓ *Didier Cornillon* (Clos de Beylière)

## CLAIRETTE DE DIE AOC

This dry sparkling wine is being phased out in favor of Crémant de Die from 1999 in what must be a classic example of Gallic logic—removing the name Clairette from an appellation of a wine that must be made from 100 percent Clairette grapes, yet retaining it for one (*see below*) that does not have to contain any!
*See also* Crémant de Die AOC

## CLAIRETTE DE DIE MÉTHODE DIOISE ANCESTRALE AOC

Formerly sold as Clairette de Die Tradition, this wine may contain Clairette, but it is not the primary grape. What makes it so different, however, is that it is produced from one fermentation only, as opposed to the two required by Crémant de Die, the old Clairette de Die Mousseux, and most other sparkling wines.

In the *Méthode Dioise Ancestrale*, the wine first undergoes a long, cold part-fermentation in bulk and when bottled must contain a minimum of 55 grams of residual sugar per liter and no *liqueur de tirage*. Fermentation continues inside the bottle, but when disgorged the wine must still retain at least 35 grams of residual sugar per liter. The wine undergoes *transvasage* (meaning it is filtered into a fresh bottle) and is corked without any addition of a *liqueur d'expédition*.

**SPARKLING WHITE** A very fresh, deliciously fruity, gently sparkling wine of at least *demi-sec* sweetness, with a ripe, peachy flavor.

🍇 At least 75% Muscat à Petits Grains (this went up in 1993 from a minimum of 50%), plus Clairette

🍷 Upon purchase

✓ *Buffardel Frères* • *C. V. du Diois* (Clairdie, Clairdissime)

## CONDRIEU AOC

This is the greatest white-wine appellation in the entire Rhône Valley, with more up-and-coming young talent among its producers than anywhere else in the world. Initially the trend was to produce sweet and medium-sweet wines, but Condrieu has tended to be a distinctly dry wine for a couple of decades now. When the vintage permits, late-harvested sweeter wines are produced, and these styles are very much part of Condrieu's recent revival as one of the undisputed great white wines of the world.

**WHITE** These pale-gold-colored wines are essentially dry, but can have such an exotic perfume that you might easily think they are sweet when you first breathe in their heavenly aroma. The bouquet is fine, floral, and fruity, with heady, opulent aromas that can include may-blossom, honeysuckle, violets, roses, peaches, lime, and apricot, and in especially rich vintages there can also be some youthful honey wafting through. The fruit on the palate is always very perfumed and can give the impression of sweetness, even when completely dry. A great Condrieu has a beguiling balance of fatness, freshness, and finesse that produces an elegant, peachy-apricoty coolness of fruit on the finish. Do not be fooled into cellaring these wines—the dry ones in any case—as their greatest asset is the freshness and purity of fruit, which can only be lost over the years.

🍇 Viognier

🍷 4–8 years

✓ *Yves Cuilleron* (Les Ayguets) • *Delas* (Clos Boucher) • *E. Guigal* (La Doriane) • *Vignobles du Monteillet* (Les Grandes Chaillées) • *Alain Paret* (Lys de Volan) •

*André Perret* (Clos Chanson) • *Georges Vernay* • *François Villard* (Le Grand Vallon)

## CORNAS AOC

The sun-trap vineyards of Cornas produce the best value of all the Rhône's quality red wines, but you have to buy it as soon as it is released as it is always sold far too young, so there is none left when it starts to show its true potential.

**RED** Ink-black, full-bodied, strong-flavored, pure Syrah wines with lots of blackcurrant and blackberry fruit, lacking only a little finesse if compared to a great Hermitage or Côte Rôtie.

🍇 Syrah

🍷 7–20 years

✓ *Thierry Allemand* • *Auguste Clape* • *Jean-Luc Colombo* • *Courbis* (Les Eygats) • *Eric & Joël Durand* • *Patrick Lesec* • *Paul Jaboulet Aîné* • *Tardieu-Laurent* (Vieilles Vignes)

## CÔTE RÔTIE AOC

The terraces and low walls of the "burnt" or "roasted" slopes of Côte Rôtie must be tended by hand, but the reward is a wine of great class that vies with Hermitage as the world's finest example of Syrah.

**RED** A garnet-colored wine of full body, fire, and power, made fragrant by the addition of Viognier grapes. The result is a long-living and complex wine with nuances of violets and spices, and great finesse.

🍇 Syrah, plus up to 20% Viognier

🍷 10–25 years

◉✓ *Patrick & Christophe Bonnefond* • *Clusel-Roch* ◉ • *Cuilleron-Gaillard-Villard* (Les Essartailles) • *Delas* (Seigneur de Maugiron) • *Jean-Michel Gerin* (Champin le Seigneur) • *E. Guigal* • *Paul Jaboulet Aîné* • *Joseph Jamet* • *Patrick Jasmin* • *Michel Ogier* • *René Rostaing* • *Vidal-Fleury* (La Chatilonne) • *François Villard* (La Brocarde)

## COTEAUX DE DIE AOC

This new appellation was created in 1993 to soak up wines from excess Clairette grape production that were formerly sold under previous sparkling-wine appellations.

**WHITE** Perhaps it is unfair to prejudge a wine that has had so little time to establish itself, but it is hard to imagine a quality wine made from this grape. In effect, Coteaux de Die is the still-wine version of Crémant de Die. It is easy to see why such a bland dry wine needs bubbles to lift it, yet so few make the transition successfully.

🍇 Clairette

🍷 Upon purchase

✓ *Jean-Claude Raspail*

## CÔTES DU RHÔNE AOC

Although generic to the entire region, relatively little Côtes du Rhône (CDR) is made in this district, where the only difference in technical criteria is that Syrah may replace Grenache as the principal red wine variety.

## CRÉMANT DE DIE AOC

This dry sparkling wine was introduced in 1993 to replace Clairette de Die Mousseux, which was phased out by January 1999. Like the old Clairette de Die Mousseux appellation, Crémant de Die must be made by the traditional method, but whereas the former could include up to 25 percent Muscat à Petit Grains, the latter must be made entirely from Clairette.

**SPARKLING WHITE** It is too early to make a definitive pronouncement, but it looks as if Crémant de Die will be every bit as neutral and lackluster as Clairette de Die.

🍇 Clairette

🍷 1–3 years

✓ Carod

## CROZES-ERMITAGE AOC
### *See* Crozes-Hermitage AOC

## CROZES-HERMITAGE AOC
Crozes-Hermitage is produced from a relatively large area surrounding Tain, hence the quality is very variable, but a good Crozes-Hermitage will always be a great bargain.

**RED** These well-colored, full-bodied wines are similar to Hermitage, but they are generally less intense and have a certain smoky-rustic-raspberry flavor that only deepens into blackcurrant in the hottest years. The finest wines do, however, have surprising finesse, and make fabulous bargains.

🍇 Syrah, plus up to 15% Roussanne and Marsanne

🍷 6–12 years
    8–20 years for top wines and great years

**WHITE** These dry white wines are improving and gradually acquiring more freshness, fruit, and acidity.

🍇 Roussanne, Marsanne

🍷 1–3 years

✓ *Chapoutier* ❸ (Les Varonnières) • *Yann Chave* (Tête de Cuvée) • *Les Chenets* • *C. V. des Clairmonts* (Pionniers) • *du Colombier* (Gaby) • *Combier* ❸ (Clos des Grives) • *Alain Graillot* • *Paul Jaboulet Aîné* (Thalabert) • *des Remizières*[1] (Emilie)

## ERMITAGE AOC
### *See* Hermitage AOC

## HERMITAGE AOC
One of the great classic French red wines, produced entirely from Syrah grapes in virtually all cases, although a small amount of Marsanne and Roussanne may be added. The vines are grown on a magnificent south-facing slope overlooking Tain.

**RED** These wines have a deep and sustained color, a very full body, and lovely, plummy, lip-smacking, spicy, silky, violety, blackcurrant fruit. A truly great Hermitage has boundless finesse, despite the weighty flavor.

🍇 Syrah, plus up to 15% Roussanne and Marsanne

🍷 12–30 years

**WHITE** These big, rich, dry white wines have a full, round, hazelnut and dried-apricot flavor. The wines have improved recently but are generally no more than curiosities.

🍇 Roussanne, Marsanne

🍷 6–12 years

✓ *M Chapoutier*[1] ❸ (Ermite, Méal, L'Orée, Pavillon) • *Jean-Louis Chave*[1] • *Emmanuel Darnaud* • *Delas* (Les Bassards) • *Alain Graillot* • *E. Guigal* (Ex Voto) • *Paul Jaboulet Aîné* (La Chapelle) • *des*

*Remizières*[1] (Emilie) • *Marc Sorrel* (Gréal) • *Tardieu-Laurent* (Vieilles Vignes)

[1]Particularly recommended for white as well as red.

## HERMITAGE
## VIN DE PAILLE AOC
In the first edition of this book (1988), I wrote "In 1974 Gérard Chave made the last *vin de paille* of Hermitage, a wine that is now confined to the Jura vineyards of eastern France. Monsieur Chave declares he made the wine for 'amusement.' Considering its success, it is extraordinary that some enterprising grower has not taken advantage of this appellation."

Chapoutier has since made several vintages of Hermitage *vin de paille* on a commercial basis—or as near commercial as you can get with this style of wine—and other producers include Michel Ferraton, Jean-Louis Grippat, and Guigal. Even the local *coopérative* has churned some out. At one time all Hermitage *blanc* was, in effect, *vin de paille*, a style that dates back in this locality to at least 1760. Marc Chapoutier apparently drank the last wine of that vintage in 1964 when it was 204 years old. The traditional *vin de paille* method in Hermitage is not as intensive as the one revived relatively recently in Alsace, in which the grapes are dried out over straw beds until more than 90 percent of the original juice has evaporated before they are pressed, as even Chave's legendary 1974 was made from grapes bearing as much as a third of their original juice, but some of the results have been equally stunning. Despite decades between production, this wine still has its own AOC.

**WHITE** Some *vins de paille* are rich and raisiny whereas others—the best—have a crisp, vivid freshness about them, with intense floral-citrous aromas and a huge, long, honeyed aftertaste. After his famed 1974 vintage, Chave made a 1986 and at least a couple more vintages since. His *vin de paille* is reputed to be the greatest, but is practically unobtainable and certainly not available on the open market. This wine is made in the most commercial quantity, yet this still amounts to hardly anything, since the wine is hard to find and very expensive. Jean-Louis Grippat made a *vin de paille* in 1985 and 1986, neither of which I have had the privilege to taste, but John Livingstone-Learmonth describes them as "not quite like late-harvest Gewurztraminer" in his seminal work *The Wines of the Rhône*.

🍇 Roussanne, Marsanne

🍷 Up to 30 years

✓ *Chapoutier* ❸

## L'ERMITAGE AOC
### *See* Hermitage AOC

## L'HERMITAGE AOC
### *See* Hermitage AOC

## ST.-JOSEPH AOC

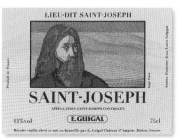

At last, some truly exciting wines are being produced under this appellation. St.-Joseph has now replaced Cornas as the bargain-seeker's treasure trove.

**RED** The best wines are dark, medium- to full-bodied, with intense blackberry and blackcurrant fruit aromas and plenty of soft fruit, whereas mediocre St.-Joseph remains much lighter-bodied with a pepperiness more reminiscent of the Southern Rhône.

🍇 Syrah, plus up to 10% Marsanne and Roussanne

🍷 3–8 years

**WHITE** At their best, clean, rich, and citrous-resinous dry wines.

🍇 Marsanne, Roussanne

🍷 1–3 years

✓ *Chapoutier* ❸ (Les Granits) • *Chave* • *Courbis*[1] (Les Roys) • *Pierre Coursodon* (Le Paradis Saint-Pierre) • *Yves Cuilleron* • *Pierre Gaillard* • *Gonan*[1] (Les Oliviers) • *E. Guigal* (Vignes de la Hospices) • *Vignobles du Monteilet* (Fortior) • *Tardieu-Laurent* (Vieilles Vignes) • *François Villard* (Reflet)

[1]Particularly recommended for white as well as red

## ST.-PÉRAY AOC
This white-wine-only village appellation is curiously out of step with the rest of the area.

**WHITE** Firm and fruity, with good acidity for a wine from the south of the region, but unfortunately it usually lacks charm. Even the best growers within this region, recommended below, struggle to produce anything of interest.

🍇 Marsanne, Roussanne

🍷 1–3 years

✓ *J.-F. Chaboud* • *Bernard Gripa* • *Jean Lionnet* • *Alain Voge*

## ST.-PÉRAY MOUSSEUX AOC
This is a traditional method sparkling wine made from the wrong grapes grown on the wrong soil. The growers would be advised to rip the whole lot up and replant with black grapes for a red Côtes du Rhône.

**SPARKLING WHITE** An overrated, dry sparkling wine with a coarse *mousse*.

🍇 Marsanne, Roussanne

# THE SOUTHERN RHÔNE

*While the mellow warmth of the Grenache is found in most Southern Rhône wines, this region is in fact a blender's paradise, with a choice of up to 23 different grape varieties.*

THE SOUTHERN RHÔNE is a district dominated by herbal scrubland, across which blows a sweet, spice-laden breeze. This is a far larger district than the slender northern *côtes*, and its production is, not unnaturally, much higher. Allowing the north a generous 10 percent of the generic Côtes du Rhône appellation, the southern Rhône still accounts for a staggering 95 percent of all the wines produced in the region.

## WINES OF THE MIDI OR PROVENCE?

At least half of the Southern Rhône is in what was once called the Midi, an area generally conceded to cover the *départements* of the Aude, Hérault, and Gard. This is never mentioned by those intent on marketing the Rhône's image of quality, because the Midi was infamous for its huge production of *vin ordinaire*. The Rhône River marks the eastern border of the Midi and its most famous appellations are geographically part of Provence. But, viticulturally, these areas do not possess the quasi-Italian varieties that dominate the vineyards of Provence and may, therefore, be more rationally defined as a high-quality extension of the Midi.

THE SOUTHERN RHÔNE, *see also* p.213
*The wider southern part of the Rhône Valley area stretches its fingers down toward Provence and eastwards to the Alps.*

## FACTORS AFFECTING TASTE AND QUALITY

### LOCATION
The Southern Rhône starts at Viviers, south of Valence, and runs south to Avignon.

### CLIMATE
The Southern Rhône's climate is unmistakably Mediterranean and its vineyards are far more susceptible to sudden change and abrupt, violent storms than are those of the Northern Rhône.

### ASPECT
The terrain in the south is noticeably Mediterranean, with olive groves, lavender fields, and herbal scrub amid rocky outcrops.

### SOIL
The limestone outcrops that begin to appear in the south of the Northern Rhône become more prolific and are often peppered with clay deposits, while the topsoil is noticeably stonier. Châteauneuf-du-Pape is famous for its creamy-colored drift boulders, which vary according to location. Stone-marl soils persist at Gigondas and weathered-gray sand in Lirac, Tavel, and Chusclan. The soils also incorporate limestone rubble, clay-sand, stone-clay, calcareous clay, and pebbles.

### VITICULTURE AND VINIFICATION
The vines are traditionally planted at an angle leaning into the wind so that the Mistral may blow them upright when they mature. The south is a district where blends reign supreme. However, pure varietal wines are gaining ground. Traditional methods of vinification are used on some estates, but modern techniques are common.

### GRAPE VARIETIES
**Primary varieties**: Carignan, Cinsault, Grenache, Mourvèdre, Muscat Blanc à Petits Grains, Muscat Rosé à Petits Grains
**Secondary varieties**: Aubun, Bourboulenc, Calitor, Camarèse, Clairette, Clairette Rosé, Counoise, Gamay, Grenache Blanc, Grenache Gris, Macabéo, Marsanne, Mauzac, Muscardin, Oeillade, Pascal Blanc, Picardan, Picpoul Blanc, Picpoul Noir, Pinot Blanc, Pinot Noir, Roussanne, Syrah, Terret Noir, Ugni Blanc, Vaccarèse, Vermentino (known locally as Rolle), Viognier

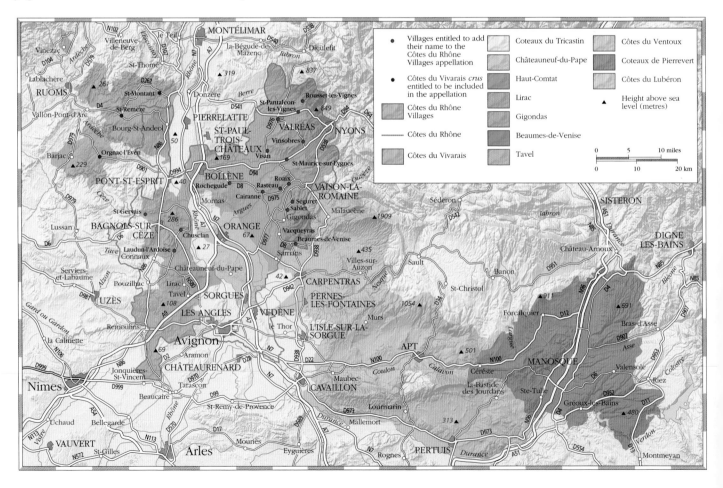

| | |
|---|---|
| ● | Villages entitled to add their name to the Côtes du Rhône Villages appellation |
| ● | Côtes du Vivarais *crus* entitled to be included in the appellation |
| | Côtes du Rhône Villages |
| | Côtes du Rhône |
| | Côtes du Vivarais |
| | Coteaux du Tricastin |
| | Châteauneuf-du-Pape |
| | Haut-Comtat |
| | Lirac |
| | Gigondas |
| | Beaumes-de-Venise |
| | Tavel |
| | Côtes du Ventoux |
| | Coteaux de Pierrevert |
| | Côtes du Lubéron |
| ▲ | Height above sea level (metres) |

THE APPELLATIONS OF
# THE SOUTHERN RHÔNE

## BRÉZÈME CÔTES DU RHÔNE AOC

A regulatory curiosity, Brézème is not one of the 16 Côtes du Rhône Villages, which may attach their name only to the end of that appellation, but an anomalous village that through a peculiarity in the AOC laws is allowed to put its name before the basic Côtes du Rhône appellation (although some prefer to place it after, in much larger letters). The story dates back to the mid-1800s, when the wines from Brézème almost rivaled those of Hermitage, and sold for nearly as much. In 1943, when Brézème was first allowed to add its own name to the Côtes du Rhône AOC, the vineyards amounted to a mere 25 acres (10 hectares). Shortly afterward, most of the vineyards were abandoned and the village was all but forgotten. By 1961 there were barely 2½ acres under cultivation, yet remarkably a few producers continued to make Brézème. According to Eric Texier, one of the most respected growers was a Monsieur Pouchoulin, who was known as the "Grandfather of Brézème." Texier, a former nuclear engineer, took over Pouchoulin's vines, which are all Syrah and range from 60 to 100 years old. Thanks to Pouchoulin and others like him, the Brézème AOC was extended to include 208 acres (84 hectares) and, with renewed interest in the wine, plantings have increased by a further 55 acres (22 hectares), with more vines going in each year.

**RED** This pure Syrah wine has been likened to a Crozes-Hermitage, but some *cuvées* (Lombard's Grand Chêne and Eugène, for example) are aged in a percentage of new oak and are not at all like a Northern Rhône wine.

🍇 The full spectrum of Côtes du Rhône grapes is allowed, but Syrah is the only red wine grape grown

🍷 3–10 years

**WHITE** Texier produces a pure Viognier and a pure Roussanne.

🍇 The full spectrum of Côtes du Rhône grapes is allowed, but only Marsanne, Roussanne, and Viognier are grown

🍷 3–10 years

✓ *Jean-Marie Lombard* • *Eric Texier* (Syrah, Viognier)

## CHÂTEAUNEUF-DU-PAPE AOC

The name Châteauneuf-du-Pape dates from the time of the dual papacy in the 14th century. The appellation is well known for its amazingly stony soil, which at night reflects the heat stored during the day, but the size, type, depth,

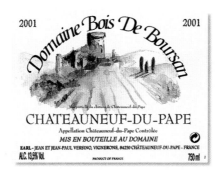

and distribution of the stones varies enormously, as does the aspect of the vineyards. These variations, plus the innumerable permutations of the 13 grape varieties that may be used, account for the diversity of its styles. In the early 1980s, some growers began to question the hitherto accepted concepts of *encépagement* and vinification; winemaking in Châteauneuf-du-Pape is still in an evolutionary state. The steady decline of the traditionally dominant Grenache has speeded up as more growers are convinced of the worth of the Syrah and Mourvèdre. The Cinsault and Terret Noir are still well appreciated, and the Counoise is beginning to be appreciated for its useful combination of fruit and firmness. The use of new oak is under experimentation and it already seems clear that it is better suited to white wine than red.

The regulations for this appellation have a unique safeguard designed to ensure that only fully ripe grapes in the healthiest condition are utilized: between 5 and 20 percent of the grapes harvested within the maximum yield for this AOC are rejected and may be used to make only *vin de table*. This process of exclusion is known as *le rapé*.

**RED** Due to the variations of *terroir* and almost limitless permutations of *encépagement*, it is impossible to describe a typical Châteauneuf-du-Pape, but there are two categories—the traditional, full, dark, spicy, long-lived style and the modern, easy-drinking Châteauneuf-du-Pape, the best of which are unashamedly upfront and brimming with lip-smacking, juicy-jammy fruit. Both are warmer and spicier than the greatest wines of Hermitage and Côte Rôtie.

🍇 Grenache, Syrah, Mourvèdre, Picpoul, Terret Noir, Counoise, Muscardin, Vaccarèse, Picardan, Cinsault, Clairette, Roussanne, Bourboulenc

🍷 6–25 years

**WHITE** Early harvesting has reduced sugar levels and increased acidity, while modern vinification techniques have encouraged a drop in fermentation temperatures, so these wines are not as full as those produced previously. They can still be very rich, albeit in a more opulent, exotic fruit style, with a much fresher, crisper finish. The very best white Châteauneuf-du-Pape is generally agreed to be Château de Beaucastel Vieilles Vignes.

🍇 Grenache, Syrah, Mourvèdre, Picpoul, Terret Noir, Counoise, Muscardin, Vaccarèse, Picardan, Cinsault, Clairette, Roussanne, Bourboulenc

🍷 1–3 years (4–6 years in exceptional cases)

✓ *Paul Autard* (Côte Ronde) • *Barville* • *Château de Beaucastel*[1] ⓞ • *de Beaurenard* (Boisrenard) • *Benedetti*[1] • *Bois de Boursan* (Felix) • *Bousquet des Papes* • *La Boutinière* • *Clos du Caillou* • *Les Cailloux* (Centenaire) • *Réserve des Célestins* • *Chapoutier* ⓑ (Barbe Rac, Croix de Bois) • *de la Charbonnière* • *Gérard Charvin* • *de Cistia* • *Font de Michelle* • *Château de la Gardine* • *Grand Veneur* • *de la Janasse* • *Lafond Roc-Epine* • *Patrick Lesec* • *de Marcoux* ⓑ • *Font de Michelle* (Etienne Gonet) • *Monpertuis* • *Château Mont-Redon* • *de la Mordorée* (Reine des Bois) • *de Nalys* • *Château la Nerthe*[1] • *de Panisse* • *Clos des Papes* • *du Pegaü* • *Château Rayas*[1] • *Roger Sabon* • *Clos St. Michel* (Grand Clos) • *de la Solitude* • *Tardieu-Laurent* (Vieilles Vignes) • *Pierre Usseglio* • *de la Vieille Julienne* • *du Vieux Télégraphe* • *de Villeneuve*

[1]Particularly recommended for white as well as red

## COTEAUX DE PIERREVERT AOC

This appellation consists of some 990 acres (400 hectares) and was upgraded from VDQS to full AOC status in 1998.

**RED** Dull, uninspiring wines with little original character to commend them.

🍇 Carignan, Cinsault, Grenache, Mourvèdre, Oeillade, Syrah, Terret Noir

🍷 2–5 years

**WHITE** Unspectacular, light, dry white wines with more body than fruit.

🍇 Clairette, Marsanne, Picpoul, Roussanne, Ugni Blanc

🍷 1–3 years

**ROSÉ** Well-made wines with a blue-pink color and a crisp, light, fine flavor.

🍇 Carignan, Cinsault, Grenache, Mourvèdre, Oeillade, Syrah, Terret Noir

🍷 1–3 years

✓ *La Blaque* (Réserve) • *Vignobles de Régusse* (Bastide des Oliviers)

## COTEAUX DU TRICASTIN AOC

Established as a VDQS in 1964, Tricastin was upgraded to full AOC status in 1973.

**RED** Very good wines, especially the deeply colored, peppery Syrah wines that are a delight after a few years in bottle. These wines may be sold as *primeur* or *nouveau* from the third Thursday of November following the harvest.

🍇 Grenache, Cinsault, Mourvèdre, Syrah, Picpoul Noir, and a maximum of 20% Carignan; and 20% (in total) of Grenache Blanc, Clairette, Bourboulenc, and Ugni Blanc

🍷 2–7 years

**WHITE** Although I was unable to recommend Tricastin *blanc* in the first edition of this book (1988), the variety of grapes permitted has since been expanded to include Roussanne, Marsanne, and Viognier, which has enabled some producers to make richer, crisper, more interesting wines.

Grenache Blanc, Clairette, Picpoul, Bourboulenc, and a maximum of 30% (in total) of Ugni Blanc, Roussanne, Marsanne, and Viognier

**ROSÉ** A small production of fresh and fruity dry rosé that occasionally yields an outstandingly good wine. These wines may be sold as *primeur* or *nouveau* as from the third Thursday of November following the harvest.

Grenache, Cinsault, Mourvèdre, Syrah, Picpoul Noir, and a maximum of 20% Carignan; and 20% (in total) of Grenache Blanc, Clairette, Bourboulenc, and Ugni Blanc

Upon purchase

✓ *Bour • des Estubiers • de Grangeneuve • de Montine • Saint-Luc*

## CÔTES DU LUBÉRON AOC

The wine of Côtes du Lubéron was promoted to full AOC status in February 1988. Much of the credit must go to Jean-Louis Chancel: his vineyards at Château Val-Joanis are still young, but the promise is such that this property has been described as the jewel in Lubéron's crown.

**RED** These are bright, well-colored wines with plenty of fruit and character, improving with every vintage.

A blend of two or more varieties to include a minimum of 60% Grenache and Syrah (in total)—of which Syrah must represent at least 10%; a maximum of 40% Mourvèdre; 20% (each) of Cinsault and Carignan; and 10% (either singly or in total) of Counoise, Pinot Noir, Gamay, and Picpoul

3–7 years

**WHITE** As white Lubéron has no established style or reputation, it seems bureaucratic nonsense to be so precise about the percentage of each grape variety that may or may not be included in its production. There was a feeling that some sort of quality and style was about to emerge in these wines in the late 1980s when Lubéron was merely a VDQS. Even then the regulation concerning grape varieties was unnecessarily complicated. Since its upgrade to full AOC status, the regulations have become even more confusing, and I doubt if it is a coincidence that Lubéron *blanc* has completely lost its way over the same period.

A blend of two or more varieties, which can include Grenache Blanc, Clairette, Bourboulenc, Vermentino, a maximum of 50% Ugni Blanc, and up to 20% (of the blend) of Roussanne and/or Marsanne

1–3 years

**ROSÉ** These attractively colored, fresh, fruity wines are much better quality than most Provence rosé.

A blend of two or more varieties to include

a minimum of 60% Grenache and Syrah (in total)—of which Syrah must represent at least 10%; a maximum of 40% Mourvèdre; 20% (each) of Cinsault and Carignan; 20% (in total) of Grenache Blanc, Clairette, Bourboulenc, Vermentino, Ugni Blanc, Roussanne, and Marsanne; plus 10% (either singly or in total) of Counoise, Pinot Noir, Gamay, and Picpoul

Upon purchase

✓ *de la Bastide de Rhodarès • Château la Canorgue • de la Citadelle • Château Constantin-Chevalier* (Fondateurs) • *de Fontenille* (Prestige) • *Cellier de Marrenon* (Grand Lubéron) • *de Mayol • de la Royere • Château Thouramme* ⊙ • *Château Val Joanis*

## CÔTES DU RHÔNE AOC

A generic appellation that covers the entire Rhône region, although the vast majority of wines are actually produced in the Southern Rhône. There are some superb Côtes du Rhônes, but there are also some disgusting wines. The quality and character varies to such an extent that it would be unrealistic to attempt any generalized description. The red and rosé may be sold as *primeur* or *nouveau* from the third Thursday of November following the harvest, although the reds can be sold only unbottled as *vin de café*. Red, white, and rosé wines can go on sale from December 1 without mention of *primeur* or *nouveau*.

**RED** The red wines are the most successful of this basic appellation, and often represent the best choice when dining in a modest French restaurant with a restricted wine list. Top *négociants* like Guigal consistently produce great-value Côtes du Rhône, but those below are all capable of very special quality.

A minimum of 40% Grenache (except in the Northern Rhône, where Syrah may be considered the principal variety), plus Syrah and/or Mourvèdre, with up to 30% in total of any of the following: Camarèse, Carignan, Cinsault, Clairette Rosé, Counoise, Grenache Gris, Muscardin, Vaccarèse, Picpoul Noir, Terret Noir, and no more than 5% in total of any of the following white varieties: Clairette, Grenache Blanc, Marsanne, Picpoul, Roussanne, Bourboulenc, Ugni Blanc, Viognier

3–10 years

**WHITE** These wines have improved tremendously in the past 5–10 years and continue to do so in encouraging fashion.

Bourboulenc, Clairette, Grenache Blanc, Marsanne, Roussanne, Viognier, and up to 20% Ugni Blanc and/or Picpoul

1–3 years

**ROSÉ** Many of the best rosés are superior in quality to those from more expensive Rhône appellations.

A minimum of 40% Grenache (except in the Northern Rhône, where Syrah may be considered the principal variety), plus Syrah and/or Mourvèdre, with up to 30% in total of any of the following: Camarèse, Carignan, Cinsault, Clairette Rosé, Counoise, Grenache Gris, Muscardin, Vaccarèse, Picpoul Noir, Terret Noir, and no more than 5% in total of any of the following white varieties: Clairette, Grenache Blanc, Marsanne, Picpoul, Roussanne, Bourboulenc, Ugni Blanc, Viognier

1–3 years

✓ *Max Aubert* (de la Présidente) • *Castan • Coudoulet de Beaucastel • Cuilleron-Gaillard-Villard • Fond Croze • Château de Fontsegune • Grand Veneur • Clos de l'Hermitage • Paul Jaboulet Aîné • Clos des Magnaneraie • Clos Martin • Château de Montfaucon • Château Mont-Redon • Rigot • des Roches Fortes* (Prestige) • *Xavier Vignon*

## CÔTES DU RHÔNE VILLAGES AOC

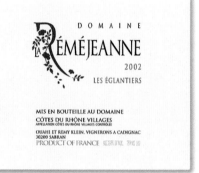

Compared with the generic Côtes du Rhône, these wines generally have greater depth, character, and quality. The area covered by the appellation is entirely within the Southern Rhône. If the wine comes from one commune only, then it has the right to append that name to the appellation.

Gigondas, Cairanne, Chusclan, and Laudun were the original Côtes du Rhône Villages (CDRV), an appellation that has waxed and waned over the years as some villages attained their own AOCs (Gigondas in 1971, Vacqueras in 1990, and Beaumes-de-Venise and Vinsobres in 2005) and others were added (the latest being Massif d'Uchaux, Plan de Dieu, Puymeras, and Sinargues in 2005).

The wines recommended below are for the Côtes du Rhône Villages appellation without any specified village, followed by separate entries for each of the 18 villages that are currently allowed to add their name to this AOC.

**RED** These wines are mostly excellent.

A minimum of 50% Grenache, plus a minimum of 20% Syrah and/or Mourvèdre, with up to 20% in total of Camarèse, Carignan, Cinsault, Clairette Rosé, Counoise, Grenache Gris, Muscardin, Vaccarèse, Picpoul Noir, Terret Noir

3–10 years

**WHITE** These wines are improving—Vieux Manoir du Frigoulas is the best.

🍇 Bourboulenc, Clairette, Grenache Blanc, Marsanne, Picpoul, Roussanne, Viognier

🍷 1–3 years

**ROSÉ** These wines can be very good.

🍇 A minimum of 50% Grenache, plus a minimum of 20% Syrah and/or Mourvèdre; up to 20% in total of Camarèse, Carignan, Cinsault, Clairette Rosé, Counoise, Grenache Gris, Muscardin, Vaccarèse, Picpoul Noir, Terret Noir; no more than 20% in total of any of the following white varieties: Bourboulenc, Clairette, Grenache Blanc, Marsanne, Picpoul, Roussanne, Viognier; and a maximum of 20% Ugni Blanc and/or Picpoul

🍷 1–3 years

✓ *Les Aphillanthes • Bouche • Le Clos du Caillou • Château la Gardine • Château d'Hugues* (L'Orée des Collines) • *de la Janasse* (Terre Argile) • *Mas de Libian • du Petit-Barbras* (Le Chemin de Barbras Sélection) • *La Réméjeanne* (Eglantiers) • *Dominique Rocher* (Monsieur Paul) • *St-Anne • Saint Estève d'Uchaux* (Vieilles Vignes) • *CV de St-Hilaire d'Ozilhan* (Saveur du Temps) • *Viret* (Emergence)

## THE 18 VILLAGES OF THE CÔTES DU RHÔNE VILLAGES

These single-villages versions of the above appellation wines can add their village name to the AOC Côtes du Rhône Villages.

### BEAUMES-DE-VENISE AOC

An appellation in its own right since 2005, AOC Beaumes-de-Venise must now be red only (except for the separate AOC Muscat de Beaumes-de-Venise, of course) and consist of at least 50% Grenache and 25% Syrah, plus other permitted CDR grape varieties (including a maximum of 5% white CDR grape varieties).

✓ *La Chapelle Notre Dame d'Aubune • Durban*

### CAIRANNE CÔTES DU RHÔNE VILLAGES AOC

Since Vacqueyras was promoted to its own AOC, Cairanne is now the top village in the appellation. It is an excellent source of rich, warm, and spicy red wines that age very well.

✓ *d'Aeria • Daniel et Denis Alary • Les Grand Bois* (Mireille) • *Les Hautes Cances • de l'Oratoire St-Martin • Marcel Richaud* (L'Ebrescade)

### CHUSCLAN CÔTES DU RHÔNE VILLAGES AOC

Chusclan may also be made from vines growing in Bagnols-sur-Cèze, Cadolet, Orsan, and St-Etienne-des-Sorts. These villages are situated just north of Lirac and Tavel, two

famous rosé appellations, and make an excellent rosé. However, most of the wines are red, and produced in a good, quaffing style. The white is fresh, lively, and reliable.

✓ *CV de Chusclan* (Esprit de Terroir) • *Château Signac*

### LAUDUN CÔTES DU RHÔNE VILLAGES AOC

Laudun can be made from vines grown outside the village in St-Victor-Lacoste and Tresques. Excelling in fine, fresh, and spicy red wines, Laudun also makes the best white wines in the CDRV appellation, and a small amount of quite delightful rosé wines.

✓ *Château St-Maurice*

### MASSIF D'UCHAUX CÔTES DU RHÔNE VILLAGES AOC

New CDRV-named village since 2005, for vines growing on sandstone hillsides at 330–920 ft (100–280 m) at Massif d'Uchaux and five surrounding communes, including Mondragon, the first wines of which were recorded in 1290.

✓ *Château du Grand Moulas*

### PLAN DE DIEU CÔTES DU RHÔNE VILLAGES AOC

New CDRV-named village since 2005, Plan de Dieu extends over four communes, where grapes grow on gravelly terraces under the shadow of Mont Ventoux, an area that was originally planted with vines by the Knights Templar.

✓ *Bernard Latour*

### PUYMERAS CÔTES DU RHÔNE VILLAGES AOC

New CDRV-named village since 2005. The wines are made from grapes grown in Puymeras and four surrounding communes, including two in the neighboring *département* of Drôme.

### RASTEAU CÔTES DU RHÔNE VILLAGES AOC

This village is best known for its sweet Rasteau "Rancio" (*see below*), yet it produces nearly four times as much dry red, white, and rosé as it does Rasteau. Deep-colored, full, and rich, with a spicy warmth, Rasteau *rouge* is a wine that can improve for up to 10 years.

✓ *de Beaurenard* (Argiles Bleus) • *Bressy-Masson • La Courançonne* (Magnificat) • *des Escaravailles* (La Ponce) • *La Soumade* (Confiance) • *Tardieu-Laurent*

### ROAIX CÔTES DU RHÔNE VILLAGES AOC

Adjoining the vineyards of Séguret, Roaix produces a similar dark-colored red wine that requires two or three years in bottle to mellow. A little rosé is also produced.

✓ *CV de Roaix-Séguret*

### ROCHEGUDE CÔTES DU RHÔNE VILLAGES AOC

Only the red wine of Rochegude may claim the CDRV appellation. The local *coopérative* wine is good quality, well colored, soft, and plummy. The white and rosé are sold as generic Côtes du Rhône.

✓ *CV de Rochegude*

### ROUSSET-LES-VIGNES CÔTES DU RHÔNE VILLAGES AOC

The neighboring villages of Rousset-les-Vignes

and St-Pantaléon-les-Vignes possess the most northerly vineyards of this appellation, close to the verdant Alpine foothills. With the coolest climate of all the Côtes du Rhône villages, the wines are light, but soft and quaffable.

✓ *La Bouvade*

### SABLET CÔTES DU RHÔNE VILLAGES AOC

This village's soft, fruity, and quick-maturing red and rosé wines are consistent in quality, and are always good value.

✓ *de Piaugier* (Montmartel)

### ST-GERVAIS CÔTES DU RHÔNE VILLAGES AOC

The valley vineyards of St-Gervais are not those of the great river itself, but belong to the Céze, one of its many tributaries. The red wines are deliciously deep and fruity, and the whites are fresh and aromatic with an excellent, crisp balance for wines from such a southerly location.

✓ *Clavel* (L'Étoile du Berger) • *CV de St-Gervais* (Prestige) • *Sainte-Anne*

### ST-MAURICE CÔTES DU RHÔNE VILLAGES AOC OR ST-MAURICE-SUR-EYGUES CÔTES DU RHÔNE VILLAGES AOC

Light, easy-drinking red and rosé wines. Production is dominated by the local *coopérative*.

✓ *CV des Coteaux St-Maurice*

### ST-PANTALÉON-LES-VIGNES CÔTES DU RHÔNE VILLAGES AOC

The neighboring villages of St-Pantaléon-les-Vignes and Rousset-les-Vignes possess the most northerly vineyards of this appellation. With the coolest climate of all the CDRV, the wines are light, but soft and quaffable. Production is monopolized by the local *coopérative*, which has yet to make anything special.

### SÉGURET CÔTES DU RHÔNE VILLAGES AOC

Séguret produces red wine that is firm and fruity with a good, bright, deep color. A little quantity of white and rosé is also made, but they seldom excel.

✓ *de Mourchon* (Grande Réserve) • *Eric Texier*

### SINARGUES CÔTES DU RHÔNE VILLAGES AOC

New CDRV-named village since 2005, for the most southerly named village in this appellation, encompassing vines grown in Domazan, Estézargues, Rochefort du Gard, and Saze to the east of Avignon.

### VALREAS CÔTES DU RHÔNE VILLAGES AOC

These are fine red wines with plenty of fruit flavor. A little rosé is also made.

✓ *Clos Petite Bellane • Comte Louis de Clermont-Tonnerre • des Grands Devers • Le Val des Rois*

### VINSOBRES AOC

Now an appellation in its own right since 2005, AOC Vinsobres must consist of at least 50% Grenache and 25% Syrah and/or Mourvedre, plus other permitted CDR grape varieties.

✓ *des Ausellons* • *du Coriançon* • *du Moulin* (Charles Joseph) • *Perrin*

## VISAN CÔTES DU RHÔNE VILLAGES AOC

These red wines have good color and true *vin de garde* character. Fresh, quaffing white wines are also made.

✓ *de la Coste Chaude* • *Olivier Cuilleras*

## CÔTES DU VENTOUX AOC

The limestone subsoil of this AOC produces a relatively lighter wine.

**RED** These fresh and fruity, easy-to-drink reds are the best wines in this AOC. The wines may be sold as *primeur* or *nouveau* from the third Thursday of November following the harvest.

🍇 Grenache, Syrah, Cinsault, and Mourvèdre, plus up to 30% Carignan, and a maximum of 20% (in total) of Picpoul Noir, Counoise, Clairette, Bourboulenc, Grenache Blanc, Roussanne, and—until the 2014 vintage— Ugni Blanc, Picpoul Blanc, and Pascal Blanc

🍾 2–5 years

**WHITE** A little white wine is produced, but it is seldom anything of interest. These wines may be sold as *primeur* or *nouveau* from the third Thursday of November following the harvest.

🍇 Clairette, Bourboulenc, plus up to 30% (in total) of Grenache Blanc, Roussanne, and— until the 2014 vintage—Ugni Blanc, Picpoul Blanc, and Pascal Blanc

**ROSÉ** Fresh character and deliciously delicate fruit. They may be sold as *primeur* or *nouveau* from the third Thursday of November following the harvest.

🍇 Same as red-wine grape varieties

🍾 Upon purchase

✓ *La Ferme Saint Pierre* (Roi Fainéant) • *Le Murmurium* • *Château Talaud* • *Les Terrasses d'Eole* (Lou Mistrau) • *Château Valcombe* • *de la Verrière* • *Xavier Vignon* (Xavier)

## CÔTES DU VIVARAIS AOC

The *côtes* of Vivarais look across the Rhône River to the *coteaux* of Tricastin. Its best *cru* villages (Orgnac, St-Montant, and St-Remèze) may add their names to the Côtes du Vivarais. Promoted from VDQS to AOC in 1999.

**RED** These light, quaffing reds are by far the best wines in the district.

🍇 A minimum of 90% in total of Syrah (minimum 40%) and Grenache (minimum 30%), with Cinsault and Carignan optional

🍾 1–3 years

**WHITE** These wines were always rather dull and disappointing but have improved in recent years.

🍇 At least two varieties from Clairette, Grenache Blanc, and Marsanne, with no variety accounting for more than 75%

🍾 1–3 years

**ROSÉ** Pretty pink, dry wines that can have a ripe, fruity flavor.

🍇 At least two varieties from Syrah, Grenache, and Cinsault, with no variety accounting for more than 80%

🍾 1–3 years

✓ *Les Chais du Vivarais*

## GIGONDAS AOC

Gigondas produces some of the most underrated red wines in the Rhône Valley.

**RED** The best have an intense black-red color with a full, plummy flavor.

🍇 A maximum of 80% Grenache, plus at least 15% Syrah and Mourvèdre, and a maximum of 10% (in total) of Clairette, Picpoul, Terret Noir, Picardan, Cinsault, Roussanne, Marsanne, Bourboulenc, Viognier, Counoise, Muscardin, Vaccarèse, Pinot Blanc, Mauzac, Pascal Blanc, Ugni Blanc, Calitor, Gamay, and Camarèse

🍾 7–20 years

**ROSÉ** Good-quality, dry rosé wines.

🍇 A maximum of 80% Grenache and a maximum of 25% (in total) of Clairette, Picpoul, Terret Noir, Picardan, Cinsault, Roussanne, Marsanne, Bourboulenc, Viognier, Counoise, Muscardin, Vaccarèse, Pinot Blanc, Mauzac, Pascal Blanc, Ugni Blanc, Calitor, Gamay, and Camarèse

🍾 2–5 years

✓ *La Bouissière* • *Brusset* (Le Grand Montmirail, Les Hauts des Montmirail) • *du Cayron* • *de la Gardette* • *Les Goubert* (Florence) • *Grapillon d'Or* (Elevé en Vieux Foudres) • *de Longue-Toque* • *Gabriel Meffre* (Château Raspail) • *L'Oustau Fauquet* (Secret de la Barrique) • *Saint Cosme* • *Saint-Damien* (Les Souteyrades) • *de St.-Gayan* (Fontmaria) • *Sainte Anne* • *Santa Duc* • *La Tourade*

## LIRAC AOC

This appellation was once the preserve of rosé, but the production of red is now on the increase.

**RED** In really great years, the Syrah and Mourvèdre can dominate despite the quite small quantities used, which produces a more plummy wine with silky-spicy finesse.

🍇 A minimum of 40% Grenache and 25% (in total) of Syrah and Mourvèdre, plus up to 10% Carignan and no limit on the amount of Cinsault (although this used to be restricted to 20%, and I suspect this

relaxation is due to clerical error when the regulations were rewritten in 1992)

🍾 4–10 years

**WHITE** A fragrant, dry white wine, the best of which has improved since 1992, when Marsanne, Roussanne, and Viognier were permitted for use in this appellation. The cheapest wines have declined in quality because the amount of Clairette allowed has been doubled. Macabéo and Calitor are no longer permitted.

🍇 Up to 60% (each) of Bourboulenc, Clairette, and Grenache Blanc; plus up to 25% (each) of Ugni Blanc, Picpoul, Marsanne, Roussanne, and Viognier (but these secondary varieties must not represent more than 30% of the blend in total)

🍾 1–3 years

**ROSÉ** Production is declining in favor of red wine, but these dry rosés can have a delightful summer-fruit flavor that is fresher than either Tavel or Provence.

🍇 A minimum of 40% Grenache and 25% (in total) of Syrah and Mourvèdre, plus up to 10% Carignan, no limit on the amount of Cinsault (but *see* red wine grapes above), and up to 20% (in total) of Bourboulenc, Clairette, Grenache Blanc, Ugni Blanc, Picpoul, Marsanne, Roussanne, and Viognier

🍾 1–3 years

✓ *Château d'Aquéria* • *Lafond Roc-Epine* • *Maby* (La Fermade) • *de la Mordorée*

## MUSCAT DE BEAUMES-DE-VENISE AOC

These wines from Muscat de Beaumes-de-Venise are the most elegant of the world's sweet fortified Muscat wines. Very little sweet Muscat was made before World War II. When the AOC was granted in 1945, the wine was classified as a *vin doux naturel*. The process by which this is made entails the addition of pure grape spirit, in an operation called *mutage*, after the must has achieved 5 percent alcohol by natural fermentation. The final wine must contain at least 15 percent alcohol, plus a minimum of 110 grams per liter of residual sugar. The Coopérative des Vins & Muscats, which was established in 1956, accounts for a formidable 90 percent of the wine produced. It is often said that this wine is always nonvintage, but in fact 10 percent is sold with a vintage on the label.

**WHITE/ROSÉ** The color varies between the rare pale gold and the common light apricot-gold, with an aromatic bouquet more akin to the perfume of dried flowers than fruit. You should expect Muscat de Beaumes-de-Venise to have hardly any acidity, which surprisingly does not make it cloying, despite its intense sweetness, but does enable it to be one of the very few wines to partner ice cream successfully.

🐝 Muscat Blanc à Petits Grains, Muscat Rosé à Petits Grains

🍷 1–2 years

☑ *de Coyeux* • *de Durban* • *Paul Jaboulet Aîné* • *Gabriel Meffre* (Laurus) • *Pigeade* • *de St.-Saveur* • *Vidal-Fleury*

## RASTEAU AOC

This appellation was first created in the early 1930s, and was promoted to full AOC status on January 1, 1944. Rasteau was the first of the Rhône's two *vin doux naturel* appellations. In popularity and quality it is, however, second to Muscat de Beaumes-de-Venise.

**RED** A rich, sweet, coarse, grapey-flavored concoction with plenty of grip, a rather awkward spirity aroma, and a pithy, apricot-skin aftertaste.

🐝 A minimum of 90% Grenache (Gris or Blanc), plus up to 10% (in total) of Clairette, Syrah, Mourvèdre, Picpoul, Terret Noir, Picardan, Cinsault, Roussanne, Marsanne, Bourboulenc, Viognier, Carignan, Counoise, Muscardin, Vaccarèse, Pinot Blanc, Mauzac, Pascal Blanc, Ugni Blanc, Calitor, Gamay, and Camarèse

🍷 1–5 years

**WHITE/TAWNY/ROSÉ** This wine can be white, tawny, or rosé depending on the technique used and on the degree of aging. It does not have the grip of the red, but has a mellower sweetness.

🐝 A minimum of 90% Grenache (Gris or Blanc), plus up to 10% (in total) of Clairette, Syrah, Mourvèdre, Picpoul, Terret Noir, Picardan, Cinsault, Clairette, Roussanne, Bourboulenc, Viognier, Carignan, Counoise, Muscardin, Vaccarèse, Pinot Blanc, Mauzac, Pascal Blanc, Ugni Blanc, Calitor, Gamay, and Camarèse

🍷 1–5 years

☑ *des Escaravailles*

## RASTEAU "RANCIO" AOC

These wines are similar to those of the Rasteau AOC (*see above*), except they must be stored in oak casks "according to local custom," which often means exposing the barrels to sunlight for a minimum of two years, which allows the wines to develop the "rancio" character.

## TAVEL AOC

Tavel is the most famous French dry rosé, but only the very best domaines live up to its reputation. In order to retain freshness, Tavel's alcoholic level is restricted to a maximum of 13 percent.

---

## MORE GREEN SOUTHERN RHÔNE

In addition to the producers recommended in this directory that are either biodynamic or organic, there are also the following. No negative inference of quality should be taken from the fact that they are not featured among my recommended producers. There are a number that have been recommended in other editions, and still make some fine wines, but have been cut out to make room for others.

### Biodynamic

*Pierre André* (Courthézon), *Château de Bastet* (Sabran), *des Estubiers* (Les Granges Gontardes), *Grande Bellane* (Domaine de la Grande Bellane), *Gaïa* (Saint-Marcellin), *Patrick Pélisson* (Goult), *Eric Saurel* (Sarrians), *St. Apollinaire* (Vaison-La-Romaine)

### Organic

*des Adrès* (Villedieu), *Arbre aux Soleils* (Faucon), *des Auzières* (Roaix), *de Balazut* (St. Paulet de Caisson), *des Carabiniers* (Roquemaure), *Catherine Le Goeuil* (Cairanne), *des Cèdres* (St. Nazaire), *Le Clos de Caveau* (Vacqueyras), *Clos du Joncuas* (Gigondas), *des Coccinelles* (Domazan), *Château de la Croix des Pins* (Mazan), *Jean David* (Séguret), *Michel Delacroix* (Theziers), *Duseigneur* (St. Laurent des Arbres), *de la Gautière* (La Penne-sur-Ouvèze), *Goisbault* (Saze), *Grange de Louiset* (Flassans), *Herbouze* (St. Alexandre), *de la Jasse* (Violès), *de Lumian* (Valreas), *Monastère de Solan* (La Bastide d'Engras), *C. V. du Nyonsais* (Nyons), *de la Roche Buissière* (Faucon St. Honorat (Domazan), *St. Pons* (Villars), *Terres de Solence* (Mazan), *C. V. des Vignerons de Vacqueyras* (Vacqueyras), *Val de Morcasse* (Montfrin), *Le Van* (Bedoin), *du Vieux Chêne* (Camaret-sur-Aigues), *La Vigneronne* (Vaison la Romaine)

---

**ROSÉ** Some properties still cling to the old-style vinification methods and, frankly, this means the wines are too old before they are sold. The top domaines in the appellation make clean-cut wines with freshly scented aromas and fine fruit flavors, which are invariably good food wines.

🐝 Grenache, Cinsault, Clairette, Clairette Rosé, Picpoul, Calitor, Bourboulenc, Mourvèdre, and Syrah (none of which may account for more than 60% of the blend), plus a maximum of 10% Carignan

🍷 1–3 years

☑ *Château d'Aquéria* • *Mireille Petit Roudil* • *de la Mordorée* (La Dame Rousse)

## VACQUEYRAS AOC

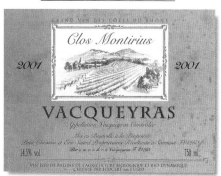

Formerly one of the single-village wines under the AOC Côtes du Rhône-Villages, Vacqueyras was elevated to full AOC status in 1990, without any mention of Côtes du Rhône or Côtes du Rhône-Villages, and is now theoretically on a par with Gigondas. The vines are spread over two communes, Vacqueyras and Sarrians, growing in the foothills of the Dentelles de Montmirail.

**RED** The best are dark, rich, and robust, with a warm, black-pepper spiciness.

🐝 At least 50% Grenache, plus up to 20% in total of Syrah and/or Mourvèdre, plus no more than 10% in total of any of the following: Camarèse, Carignan, Cinsault, Clairette Rosé, Counoise, Grenache Gris, Muscardin, Vaccarèse, Picpoul Noir, Terret Noir

🍷 4–12 years

**WHITE** This is the least successful style of the appellation; most tend to be either flabby or so dominated by modern, cool vinification methods that they are simply fresh and could come from anywhere.

🐝 Grenache Blanc, Clairette, and Bourboulenc, plus up to 50% in total of Marsanne, Roussanne, and Viognier

🍷 2–3 years

**ROSÉ** Can be lovely, fresh, and fruity.

🐝 At least 60% of Grenache, plus a minimum of Mourvèdre and/or Cinsault, with an optional maximum 10% of any of the following: Camarèse, Carignan, Cinsault, Clairette Rosé, Counoise, Grenache Gris, Muscardin, Vaccarèse, Picpoul Noir, Terret Noir

🍷 2–3 years

☑ *des Amouriers* • *de la Brunely* (Elevé en Fût de Chêne) • *de la Charbonnière* • *La Fourmone* • *Les Grands Cypres* • *de la Monardière* (Vieilles Vignes) • *Le Sang des Cailloux* (Lopy) • *Tardieu-Laurent* (Vieilles Vignes) • *Xavier Vignon* (Povidis)

# THE JURA AND SAVOIE

*White wines dominate the production from these picturesque vineyards set amid the ski slopes of the French Alps. Sparkling wines are the specialty of Savoie, while Jura can boast the rare, sweet vins de paille and the amazingly long-lived vins jaunes.*

THE JURA IS DOMINATED by the town of Arbois, a little alpine community reigned over by the winemaker Henri Maire. His infamous sparkling "Vin Fou," or "Mad Wine," has no appellation and comes in various different *cuvées*, of which some are better than others, but many taste the same. Despite the light-hearted approach to its consumption, "Vin Fou" has performed one admirable function: it has introduced wine drinkers to the district of Jura and Savoie and its many better wines. This could not have been achieved by the *vins de paille* and *vins jaunes*, due to their scarcity and high price. The very sweet *vin de paille*, or "straw wine," is so called because the grapes were traditionally dried on straw mats to concentrate the juice into a syrup. The *vin jaune*, or

"yellow wine," derives its name from the color that results from its deliberate oxidation under a yeast *flor* when matured in casks that are not topped up for six years. This region also produces a number of more ordinary wines, often pure varietals, that are seldom exciting. The Jura's other claim to fame is, of course, as the birthplace of Louis Pasteur (1822–1895), who for all intents and purposes invented oenology, having been requested by Napoléon III to investigate the changes already observed during the maturation of wine. Born in the Arbois, where a small museum dedicated to him exists today, Pasteur's discoveries included the vital role of yeast during fermentation—totally unsuspected in his day, but without the knowledge of which the branch of chemistry called oenology would not exist. His vineyard, just outside Arbois, is now owned by the firm of Henri Maire.

The vineyards in the area between Lake Geneva and Grenoble, known as the Savoie, should be far more of a success than they are. I cannot imagine a better way to promote these wines than through the Savoie's winter-sports business. The only obstacle to their greater success is the failure of foreign wine merchants to import the wines in sufficient quantities.

## THE SAVAGNIN CONSPIRACY

The Savagnin grape is none other than the Traminer or, to be more precise, the nonspicy Traminer as found in Tramin, Italy, and Heiligenstein in Alsace, where it is sold as Klevener de Heiligenstein. At best it has very delicate aromatics, but more often than not it is quite bland. In the Jura, however, it has

**CHÂTEAU-CHALON VINEYARDS**
*This commune produces the most famous of all the* vins jaunes *from 100 percent Savagnin. Best drunk very old, the wine takes its name from its deep honey-gold color.*

THE JURA AND SAVOIE,
*see also p.55*
*This region lies parallel to Burgundy, between Beaune and the southern limits of the Beaujolais. There are two mountain ranges.*

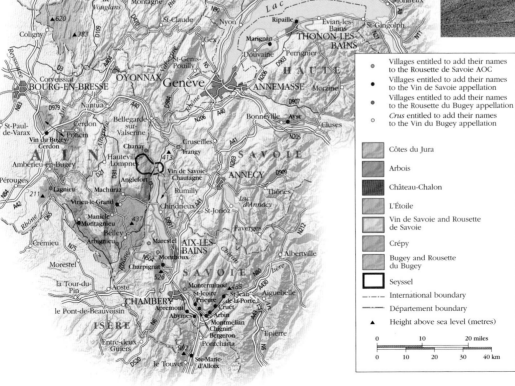

| | Villages entitled to add their names to the Rousette de Savoie AOC |
| --- | --- |
| | Villages entitled to add their names to the Vin de Savoie appellation |
| | Villages entitled to add their names to the Rousette du Bugey appellation |
| | *Crus* entitled to add their names to the Vin du Bugey appellation |

| | |
| --- | --- |
| | Côtes du Jura |
| | Arbois |
| | Château-Chalon |
| | L'Étoile |
| | Vin de Savoie and Rousette de Savoie |
| | Crépy |
| | Bugey and Rousette du Bugey |
| | Seyssel |
| --- | International boundary |
| --- | Département boundary |
| ▲ | Height above sea level (metres) |

0    10    20 miles
0  10  20  30  40 km

PARIS

## RECENT JURA AND SAVOIE VINTAGES

**2006** July's heatwave shut down the vines' metabolism, and a cold August did little to help, but a sunny September successfully completed the *véraison*, only to be ruined by rain in October. With only those growers who, alerted by advance weather reports, harvested early and produced reasonably good wines, consumers will have to be very selective in this generally poor and extremely mixed vintage.

**2005** Great quality for all styles in both the Jura and Savoie.

**2004** Large volume of mostly average quality.

**2003** A benchmark year for red wines in both regions, and for *vins de paille* in the Jura, but dry whites were problematic. There is a question mark over the *vins jaunes*, although the Jura has never experienced such Jerez-like heat, thus the quality could surprise everyone.

**2002** Much better in the Jura than in the Savoie. Although the harvest in Savoie was saved by good weather in the last few weeks, the best wines were early drinking, and would have been at their best as après ski before this edition was due to be published. All styles were good in the Jura.

## FACTORS AFFECTING TASTE AND QUALITY

**LOCATION**
Running down the mountainous eastern border of France, the Jura and Savoie are parallel to the Burgundy region.

**CLIMATE**
The climate is continental, with hot summers and cold winters. The close proximity of the Jura and the Savoie mountain ranges can provoke sudden changes, although these may sometimes be mitigated by the calming effect of lakes Geneva and Bourget.

**ASPECT**
The vineyards of the Jura are situated on the lower slopes of the Jura mountains. The vines grow at an altitude of 820–1,640 feet (250–500 meters). The Savoie vineyards lie lower than those of the Jura.

**SOIL**
The limestone of the Jura is generally mixed with clay over a subsoil of compacted marl. There are limestone and marl topsoils over a base of sandy and gravelly marls at Arbois and Château-Chalon and a limestone scree, calcareous sand, and claylike sand with alluvial deposits at Bugey and Seyssel.

**VITICULTURE AND VINIFICATION**
The Jura is famous for two special techniques: the viticultural practice responsible for *vin de paille* and the vinification procedure required to make *vin jaune*. For *vin de paille*, wicker trays or wire mesh may be used, but in most cases bunches of grapes are hung from the rafters of heated huts, after which the shriveled-up, highly concentrated, raisinlike grapes produce an amber-colored sweet wine of great potential longevity. *Vin jaune* is produced entirely from the Savagnin grape, which, after a normal fermentation, is left to age in wooden barrels for six years with no topping off. A yeast *flor* develops similar to that generated during the production of *fino* sherry and the results are not dissimilar. Light dry Jura white wines made from the traditional Savagnin grape used to be distinctly oxidized due to the common practice of blending in any *vin jaune* that failed to make the grade, but some producers have begun to make at least a few of these wines without any declassified *vin jaune*, thus in a totally fresh, nonoxidative style.

**GRAPE VARIETIES**
Aligoté, Cabernet Franc, Cabernet Sauvignon, Chardonnay (*syn.* Melon d'Arbois or Gamay Blanc), Chasselas, Chasselas Roux, Chasselas Vert, Etraire de la Dui, Frühroter Veltliner (*syn.* Malvoisie Rosé or Veltliner Rosé), Gamay, Gringet (close relation to Savagnin), Jacquère, Joubertin, Marsanne, Molette, Mondeuse, Mondeuse Blanche, Persan, Pinot Blanc, Pinot Noir (*syn.* Gros Noiren), Poulsard (*syn.* Ploussard), Roussette, Roussette d'Ayze, Savagnin (*syn.* Naturé), Serène, Trousseau, Verdesse

always had a tendency to oxidize. Or so we were told. Every time I tasted a pure Savagnin produced in a light table wine style, it always had at least a niggling oxidative hint. And every time I asked the producer, whether in the Jura or at tastings in London, why this should be so in a grape variety that is not oxidative elsewhere, I was always told "*C'est le Savagnin, il est un vin typé.*" And now I know that each time, every producer I spoke to lied. It is not the Savagnin. It is the *vin jaune* that fails to receive certification, or has been weeded out somewhere along its six-year route to certification, and that they have disposed of by blending it into their dry white table wines.

While I fully support a certification process that prevents inferior wines from bearing the *vin jaune* designation, and I understand the dilemma of producers faced with stocks of yellow, oxidized wine they are unable to sell as *vin jaune*, the answer is not to spoil fresh, light table wines. The only rational solution is to create a *vin de pays* for the *vin jaune* style. Consumers will understand that the *vin de pays* version is not supposed to be of the same standard and, indeed, this would be reflected in the price. However, although cheaper than *vin jaune* proper, a *vin de pays "vin jaune"* would probably attract a premium over the price of the Jura's light table wines, and without the rejected *vin jaune*, the light table wines would be fresher, crisper, cleaner, and fruitier, the sales and price of which could only increase. Better profits for producers, and better wines for consumers. A result all round, I would have thought. And no need to tell lies.

THE APPELLATIONS OF

# THE JURA AND SAVOIE

## ARBOIS AOC

This is the best-known appellation of the Jura, from in and around the town of Arbois.

**RED** Trousseau wines are rich, and sometimes coarse, and Pinot wines are light and rustic.

Trousseau, Poulsard, Pinot Noir

2–8 years

**WHITE** Light, fresh Chardonnays are best; pure Savagnin can be delicately aromatic when not blended with declassified *vin jaune*, good examples of which are world renowned.

Savagnin, Chardonnay, Pinot Blanc

1–3 years

**ROSÉ** Famous for its firm and distinctive dry rosé wines made in the pale *vin gris* style.

Poulsard, Trousseau, Pinot Noir

AQUARELLE

ARBOIS
Appellation Arbois Contrôlée
2003

DOMAINE
ROLET
PÈRE ET FILS
VIGNERONS
ARBOIS JURA FRANCE

1–3 years

Daniel Dugois • Raphaël Fumey & Adeline Chatelain • Michel Gahir (Trousseau Grands Vergers) • Labet Père & Fils • Henri Maire (Montbief Chardonnay) • De la Pinte ◉ (Terre Rouge) • Jacques Puffeney • Cave de la Reine Jeanne • Jean Rijckaert • André & Mireille Tissot ◉ • Jacques Tissot • De la Tournelle

## ARBOIS MOUSSEUX AOC

This is a traditional method sparkling wine seldom seen outside Arbois.

**SPARKLING WHITE** These fresh, dry sparkling wines show more potential than quality.

Savagnin, Chardonnay, Pinot Blanc

1–3 years

Foret • Fruitière Vinicole d'Arbois

## ARBOIS PUPILLIN AOC

This is a single-commune appellation for red, white, rosé, *vin jaune*, and *vin de paille* made to the same specification as Arbois AOC. *See* Arbois AOC, Arbois Vin de Paille AOC, and Arbois Vin Jaune AOC.

✓ *Désiré Petit & Fils* (Vin de Paille) • *De la Renardière*

## ARBOIS VIN JAUNE AOC

For details of production and style, *see* Château-Chalon AOC.

✓ *De la Pinte* ◉ • *Jacques Puffeney* • *Rolet* • *André & Mireille Tissot* ◉ • *Jacques Tissot*

## ARBOIS VIN DE PAILLE AOC

This wine is made from grapes that are dried to concentrate the juice, followed by a long fermentation and up to four years in wood.

**WHITE** These are very sweet wines with an old-gold color, complex bouquet, and a rich, nutty flavor.

🍇 Poulsard, Trousseau, Savagnin, Chardonnay

🍷 10–50 (or more) years

✓ *Rolet* • *André & Mireille Tissot* ◉

## BUGEY VDQS

Formerly called Vin de Bugey, the criteria for these wines has changed substantially since the decree of January 2004, particularly the *encépagement*. The village of Machuraz no longer has the right to add its name to this appellation. However, the following villages may still add their name: Manicle (for Chardonnay or Pinot Noir), Montagnieu (Mondeuse), Virieu-le-Grand (white only).

**RED** Fresh wines that range from the fruity Pinot to the rich Mondeuse.

🍇 Gamay, Mondeuse, Pinot Noir

🍷 2–8 years

**WHITE** Off-dry, fresh, light, and gently fruity.

🍇 A minimum of 50% Chardonnay, plus optional Aligoté, Altesse, Jacquère, Mondeuse Blanche, and Pinot Gris

🍷 1–3 years

**ROSÉ** Light and refreshing dry wines.

🍇 Gamay, Mondeuse, Pinot Noir

🍷 1–3 years

✓ *Monin* (Mondeuse: Les Griots, Les Perrailles)

## BUGEY CERDON VDQS

This appellation was a confusing mess until January 2004. Prior to this date, the wines could be still or sparkling, dry or sweet, and white or red. If sparkling they had to be white, but could be described as *mousseux* or *pétillant*, and had to be made by the traditional method. Now they must be rosé only, and made by *méthode ancestrale*, with a minimum

of 40 grams per liter of residual sugar, which puts it at the top side of *demi-sec*, thus could easily become *doux*. The appellation is restricted to Cerdon and seven surrounding villages.

**SPARKLING ROSÉ** Should be fresh and luscious, but true Cerdon Rosé Méthode Ancestrale has yet to establish a track record.

🍇 Gamay, Poulsard

🍷 Within 1 year

✓ *Daniel Boccard* • *Christian Bolliet*

## CHÂTEAU-CHALON AOC

The Jura's *vins jaunes* possess a unique style and Château-Chalon (which is the name of a commune) is its most legendary exponent. It is normally fermented, then left to age in sealed wooden barrels for six years with no topping up. During this time, a *flor* develops— a skin of yeast that floats on top of the wine. The changes induced by the *flor* give the acetaldehyde-dominated *vin jaune* a resemblance to a *fino* sherry, but the fact that it is not fortified (whereas sherry is) and is made from a different grape produces its unique character.

**WHITE** *Vin jaune* is something of an acquired taste and should be drunk when very old. The vast array of complex nuances of bouquet eventually subdue and transmute the sherrylike smell of acetaldehyde. It has a dry flavor.

🍇 Savagnin

🍷 10–100 years

✓ *Baud Père & Fils* • *Berthet-Bondet* • *Philippe Butin* • *Durand-Perron* • *Jean Macle*

## CÔTES DU JURA AOC

This generic appellation contains some of the most widely encountered Jura wines. Its larger area of production gives it an edge over Arbois, the better-known AOC within its boundaries.

**RED** Usually light in color and body, with elegant fruit and a little finesse.

🍇 Poulsard, Trousseau, Pinot Noir

🍷 2–8 years

**WHITE** Simple dry whites that make an ideal accompaniment to the local *raclette* cheese dish.

🍇 Savagnin, Chardonnay

🍷 1–3 years

**ROSÉ** These dry rosés have a fine and fragrant *vin gris* style, with solid fruit.

🍇 Poulsard, Trousseau, Pinot Noir, Pinot Gris, Savagnin, Chardonnay

🍷 1–3 years

✓ *Château d'Arlay* • *Daniel & Pascal Chalandard* (Cuvée Siloé) • *Charbonnier* • *Ganevat* (Florine Ganevat Chardonnay, Julien Ganevat Pinot Noir) • *Grand Frères* (Tradition) • *Labet* • *Jean Macle* • *Pignier* ⓑ (Trousseau) • *Jean Rijckaert* • *Rolet* (Chardonnay) • *André & Mireille Tissot* ◉

## CÔTES DU JURA MOUSSEUX AOC

Probably Jura's best sparkling-wine appellation.

**SPARKLING WHITE** These wines have a persistent *mousse* of tiny bubbles, excellent balance, surprising finesse, and great potential.

🍇 Savagnin, Chardonnay, Pinot Blanc

🍷 1–3 years

✓ *Château Gréa*

## CÔTES DU JURA VIN JAUNE AOC

For details of production and style, *see* Château-Chalon AOC.

✓ *Château d'Arlay* • *Philippe Butin*

## CÔTES DU JURA VIN DE PAILLE AOC

These wines are made from grapes that are dried to concentrate the juice, after which fermentation is long and the wine is given up to four years in wood.

**WHITE** These very sweet wines have old-gold, honey-gold, and amber-gold colors; a full, distinctive, and complex bouquet; a powerfully rich and nutty flavor; and a surprisingly crisp finish, with a raisiny, apricot-skin aftertaste.

🍇 Poulsard, Trousseau, Savagnin, Chardonnay

🍷 10–50 (or more) years

✓ *Berthet-Bondet* • *Denis & Marie Chevassu* • *Richard Delay* • *Château Gréa* • *Labet* • *Morel-Thibaut* • *Désiré Petit & Fils* • *Pignier* ⓑ *Père & Fils* • *Philippe Vandelle*

## CRÉMANT DU JURA AOC

This appellation was introduced in 1995. It can be used for any wine conforming to *vin mousseux* AOCs of the Côtes du Jura, Arbois, and L'Étoile, and may be applied retrospectively to any of these wines from 1991 onward. Part of the "*crémantization*" of French traditional method appellations, once most sparkling wines in the region are marketed as Crémant du Jura, the unwieldy bunch of *mousseux* appellations (*see below*) will be quietly dropped.

✓ *Richard Delay* • *Grand Frères* (Prestige) • *De Montebourgeau* • *Désiré Petit & Fils* (Cuvée Désiré) • *Rolet Père & Fils* (Coeur de Chardonnay) • *Jacques Tissot*

## CRÉPY AOC

These wines are well known to the skiing set, who enjoy them after a day on the *piste*.

**WHITE** Light, dry, and fruity wines, with a floral aroma and a slight spritz.

🍇 Chasselas Roux, Chasselas Vert

🍷 1–3 years

✓ *Goutte d'Or* (Tête de Cuvée)

## L'ÉTOILE AOC

These wines are named after the star-shaped fossils found in the local limestone.

**WHITE** Light, dry white wines whose aromas reveal the scents of alpine herbs and bracken.

🍇 Chardonnay, Poulsard, Savagnin

🍷 1–3 years

✓ *Baud Père & Fils*

## L'ÉTOILE MOUSSEUX AOC

Not quite up to the standard of Côtes du Jura Mousseux, but this traditional method wine has more potential than Arbois Mousseux.

**SPARKLING WHITE** De Montbourgeau makes a fine-quality, dry, sparkling wine.

🍇 Chardonnay, Poulsard, Savagnin

🍷 1–3 years

✓ *Château de l'Étoile*

## L'ÉTOILE VIN JAUNE AOC
*See Château-Chalon AOC*

🍇 Savagnin

🍷 10–100 years

☑️ *Château de l'Étoile • Claude & Cédric Joly*

## MACVIN AOC OR MACVIN DU JURA AOC

Macvin, a *vin de liqueur*, is made by adding *marc* (local brandy distilled from the residue of skins) to grape juice, preventing fermentation.

**RED** Typical dull *vin de liqueur* aroma, sweet and grapey.

🍇 Poulsard, Trousseau, Pinot Noir

🍷 Upon purchase or never

**WHITE** This has a typical dull *vin de liqueur* aroma, and is sweet and grapey. This is the most oxidative Macvin style.

🍇 Chardonnay, Poulsard, Savagnin

🍷 Never!

**ROSÉ** Typical dull *vin de liqueur* aroma, sweet and grapey.

🍇 Poulsard, Trousseau, Pinot Noir

🍷 Upon purchase or never

☑️ *Labet*

## ROUSSETTE DU BUGEY VDQS

The following villages may add their name to this appellation, if harvested within an extremely low yield: Anglefort, Arbignieu, Chanay, Lagnieu, Montagnieu, and Virieu-le-Grand.

**WHITE** Light, fresh, and agreeable off-dry wines with few pretensions.

🍇 A minimum of 50% Roussette, plus (until 2008) Chardonnay

🍷 1–3 years

☑️ *Jean Peillot*

## ROUSSETTE DE SAVOIE AOC

The following villages have the right to add their name to this appellation, if the wine is 100 percent Roussette: Frangy, Marestel (or Marestel-Altesse), Monterminod, and Monthoux.

**WHITE** Drier than Roussette de Bugey, these wines have fine, tangy fruit.

🍇 Roussette, Mondeuse Blanche, plus up to 50% Chardonnay

🍷 1–3 years

☑️ *Dupasquier • Château de Monterminod • André & Michel Quenard • De Saint-Germain*

## SEYSSEL AOC

This is a favorite après-ski wine.

**WHITE** These are fragrant, dry, refreshing wines.

🍇 Roussette

🍷 1–3 years

☑️ *Maison Mollex*

## SEYSSEL MOUSSEUX AOC

It was Varichon & Clerc that first carved a niche for Seyssel Mousseux in the export market.

**SPARKLING WHITE** With a full, yeasty nose, fine *mousse*, and elegant flavor, the Royal Seyssel Private Cuvée is a yardstick for other producers.

🍇 Molette, Chasselas, plus a minimum of 10% Roussette

🍷 1–3 years

☑️ *Maison Mollex • Royal Seyssel*

## VIN DE SAVOIE AOC

The wines in this generic appellation are produced to a high standard. The following villages have the right to add their name to the appellation: Abymes, Apremont, Arbin, Ayze, Chautagne, Chignin, Chignin-Bergeron (white Roussanne only), Cruet, Jongieux, Marignan (Chasselas white only), Marin, Montmélian, Ripaille (Chasselas white), St.-Jean de la Porte, St.-Jeoire Prieuré, and Sainte-Marie d'Alloix.

**RED** Blends and single-variety wines; the blended wines are usually better.

🍇 Gamay, Mondeuse, Pinot Noir, plus a maximum of 10% (in the Savoie *département*) of Cabernet Franc, and Cabernet Sauvignon, Persan, and (in the Isère *département*) Etraire de la Dui, Joubertin, Persan, and Serène

🍷 2–8 years

**WHITE** These dry wines are the best of the AOC, with Abymes, Apremont, and Chignin the best villages. All are fine, rich, and complex.

🍇 Aligoté, Altesse, Jacquère, Mondeuse Blanche, Roussette, Veltliner Précoce, plus a maximum of 10% (in the Ain and Haute-Savoie *départements*) of Chasselas, Gringet, Roussette d'Ayze, and (in the Isère *département*) Marsanne and Verdesse

🍷 1–3 years

**ROSÉ** Attractive, light, and fruity, dry to off-dry rosés made for early drinking.

🍇 Gamay, Mondeuse, Pinot Noir, plus a maximum of 10% (in the Savoie *département*) of Cabernet Franc, and Cabernet Sauvignon, Persan, and (in the Isère *département*) Etraire de la Dui, Joubertin, Persan, and Serène

🍷 1–3 years

☑️ *Pierre Boniface, Dupasquier, De L'Idylle (Mondeuse), Louis Magnin (Jacquère, Roussette), Jean Perrier & Fils (Mondeuse Vieilles Vignes), De Rouzan (Gamay), De Saint-Germain (Chardonnay)* • **Best single-*cru* wines: Abymes** *Frédéric Giachino;* **Apremont** *Philippe Betemps;* **Arbin** *Genoux, Louis Magnin, Charles Trosset (Mondeuse);* **Chignin** *André & Michel Quénard, Raymond Quénard (Mondeuse);* **Chignin-Bergeron** *Gilles Berlioz 🔴, Louis Magnin, André & Michel Quénard, Philippe Ravier, Jean Vullien;* **Jongieux** *Edmond Jacquin & Fils;* **Montmélian** *Louis Magnin*

## VIN DE SAVOIE AYZE PÉTILLANT OR MOUSSEUX AOC

These are very promising, single-commune, traditional method wines, but unfortunately are seldom encountered.

**SEMI-SPARKLING WHITE** Wispy-light wines with an Alpine-fresh, clean taste.

🍇 Gringet, Roussette, plus up to 30% Roussette d'Ayze

🍷 1–3 years

## VIN DE SAVOIE MOUSSEUX AOC

These are very consistent and undervalued generic traditional-method wines. The Savoie does not have a large-scale sparkling-wine industry as such, although it most certainly has the potential to build one. The tradition of making the effervescent wines in this part of eastern France dates back to 1910, when two growers, Messieurs Varichon and Clerc, joined together to make sparkling wine in Seyssel from the Roussette grape, the wines of which were naturally *pétillant*, just as the Swiss wines made from the Chasselas, just across Lake Geneva, were, and still are, today.

**SPARKLING WHITE** These dry and delicately fruity wines have a fragrant aroma, fine acidity, and a good balance.

🍇 Aligoté, Roussette, Jacquère, Chardonnay, Pinot Gris, Mondeuse Blanche, plus (in the Ain and Haute-Savoie *départements*) Chasselas, (in the Haute-Savoie and Isère *départements*) Molette, (in the Haute-Savoie *département*) Gringet and Roussette d'Ayze, (in the Isère) Marsanne and Verdesse

🍷 1–2 years

☑️ *Maison Mollex • Des Rocailles*

## VIN DE SAVOIE PÉTILLANT AOC

A very consistent and undervalued generic traditional method wine.

**SEMI-SPARKLING WHITE** Attractive, early-drinking dry wines with a gentle, light *mousse* and a fragrant flavor.

🍇 Aligoté, Roussette, Jacquère, Chardonnay, Pinot Gris, Mondeuse Blanche, plus Chasselas (in the Ain and Haute-Savoie *départements*), Gringet, Rousset d'Ayze (in the Haute-Savoie *département*), Marsanne, and (in the Isère *département*) Verdesse

🍷 Within 1 year

☑️ *Perrier & Fils • Varichon & Clerc*

# SOUTHWEST FRANCE

*This region encompasses numerous small, scattered areas that combine to produce an impressively wide range of excellent-value wines with diverse, but quite discernible, stylistic influences from Bordeaux, Spain, Languedoc-Roussillon, and the Rhône.*

AT THE HEART OF THE REGION lies Gascony, the great brandy district of Armagnac. It was from here that d'Artagnan set out in around 1630 to seek fame and fortune in the King's Musketeers. The narrow tracks upon which his eventful journey began still wind their lonely way around wooded hills and across bubbling brooks. Aside from brightly colored fields of cultivated sunflowers, surprisingly little has changed since Alexandre Dumas painted such a vivid and colorful picture of these parts, for they remain sparsely populated to this day. Time passes slowly even in the towns, where the main square is usually completely deserted all day long, except during the five o'clock rush hour, which can last for all of 10 minutes.

## THE DIVERSITY OF THE APPELLATIONS

The Southwest does not have a single wine of truly classic status, yet it probably offers more value for money and is a greater source of hidden bargains than any other French region. From the succulent, sweet Jurançon *moelleux* and Monbazillac to the fine wines of Bergerac, Buzet, and Marmandais, the revitalized "black wines" of Cahors, the up-and-coming Frontonnais, the tannic Madiran, and the highly individual Irouléguy of the Basque country, this part of France represents tremendous potential for knowing wine drinkers.

Perhaps because it is a collection of diverse areas, rather than one natural region, the appellations of the Southwest seem at first numerous and confusing—even within one area there appear to be needless duplications. In Bergerac, for example, the dry white wines and red wines are reasonably easy to understand, since there are three dry appellations (Bergerac, Bergerac sec, and

SOUTHWEST FRANCE, *see also* p.55
*This diverse region bridges the southwest corner of France. While it is mostly subject to the climatic influence of the Atlantic, areas such as Gaillac are also affected by the Mediterranean.*

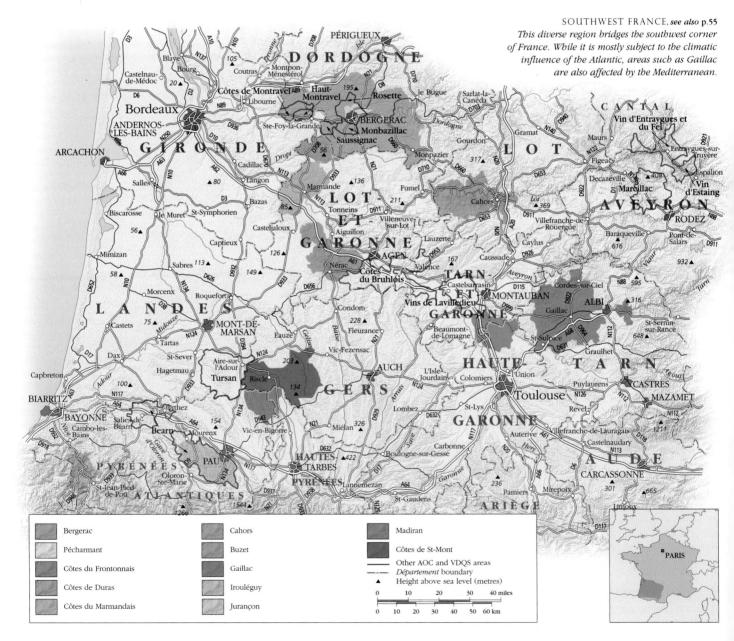

| | Bergerac | | Cahors | | Madiran |
|---|---|---|---|---|---|
| | Pécharmant | | Buzet | | Côtes de St-Mont |
| | Côtes du Frontonnais | | Gaillac | | Other AOC and VDQS areas |
| | Côtes de Duras | | Irouléguy | | *Département* boundary |
| | Côtes du Marmandais | | Jurançon | ▲ | Height above sea level (metres) |

**CÔTES DE BUZET VINEYARDS**
*This good-value Bordeaux satellite is barely 9 miles
(15 kilometers) from the Gironde département.*

Montravel) and three red-wine appellations (Bergerac, Côtes
de Bergerac, and Pécharmant), but there is a veritable galaxy of
sweet and semi-sweet appellations (Bergerac, Bergerac Moelleux,
Montbazillac, Côtes de Montravel, Haut-Montravel, Rosette, and
Saussignac). When such a small and relatively minor area as
Bergerac can develop so many different appellations, it is little
wonder that a large and famous region such as Bordeaux has
evolved into 50-odd appellations. It would surely be simpler to
have a single Bergerac appellation to which certain villages might
be allowed to add a communal name; if the same logic were
applied throughout this region, more of its wines could achieve
marketing success, rather than attracting only occasional attention
as hidden bargains. With a more cohesive image and some
enterprising wineries straddling the many different appellations,
Southwest France should be at least as exciting as Languedoc-
Roussillon has recently become. Flying winemakers have
occasionally come to roost here in the past few years, but it will
take a permanent New World winery for the exciting potential
of Southwest France to be fully recognized.

## RECENT SOUTHWEST FRANCE VINTAGES

**2006** Extremely variable, from poor to excellent, according to the
weather and when growers decided to harvest.

**2005** Despite widespread flooding in September from the tail end
of tropical storms coming in from the Atlantic, this is an excellent
vintage in all areas for all styles.

**2004** A very good vintage, particularly for reds and late-harvest whites.

**2003** As elsewhere in France, a vintage that was too hot and too early,
with some reds and late-picked sweet whites the only likely standouts.

**2002** Good to exceptional quality in Cahors particularly, but also
Bergerac and Buzet. Variable elsewhere.

## FACTORS AFFECTING TASTE AND QUALITY

### LOCATION
The southwest corner of France,
bordered by Bordeaux, the Atlantic,
the Pyrenees, and the Mediterranean
vineyards of Languedoc-Roussillon.

### CLIMATE
The climate of southwestern
France is Atlantic-influenced, with
wet winters and springs, warm
summers, and long, sunny falls. The
vineyards of Cahors, Fronton, and
Gaillac are subject to the greater
heat but more changeable
characteristics of the Mediterranean.

### ASPECT
Mostly east- and east-through-
to-south-facing slopes, affording
protection from the Atlantic, in a
varied countryside that can range
from rolling and gently undulating
to steep and heavily terraced.

### SOIL
This collection of diverse areas
has, not unexpectedly, a number of
different soils: sandy-and-calcareous
clay over gravel in the best vineyards
of Bergerac; sandy soils on the Côte
de Duras; calcareous and alluvial
soils in the *côtes* of Buzet and
Marmandais; gravel-clay and gravel
crests over marly bedrock in the
hilly hinterland of Cahors, and
alluvial soils peppered with pebbly
quartz, limestone, and gravel over a
calcareous bedrock in the Lot Valley;
limestone, clay-and-limestone, and
gravel at Gaillac; sandy soils in
Madiran, Tursan, and Irouléguy; and
stony and sandy soils in Jurançon.

### VITICULTURE AND VINIFICATION
The viticultural traditions and
vinification techniques of Bergerac,
Buzet, Marmandais, and, to some
extent, Cahors, are similar to those
of Bordeaux. Other districts of this
composite region have very much
their own distinctive, individual
practices: Béarn, Gaillac, and
Jurançon produce almost every
style of wine imaginable by many
vinification techniques, among them
the *méthode rurale* (known locally
as the *méthode gaillaçoise*).
Although the winemaking
technique in these areas is
generally very modern, the Basque
district of Irouléguy remains stoutly
traditional, allowing only the
introduction of Cabernet Sauvignon
and Cabernet Franc to intrude upon
its set ways.

### GRAPE VARIETIES
Abouriou, Arrufiac, Baroque,
Cabernet Franc, Cabernet
Sauvignon, Camaralet, Castet,
Chardonnay, Chenin Blanc,
Cinsault, Clairette, Claret de Gers,
Claverie, Colombard, Courbu Blanc,
Courbu Noir, Cruchinet, Duras, Fer,
Folle Blanche, Fuella, Gamay, Gros
Manseng, Jurançon Noir, Lauzet,
Len de l'El, Malbec (*syn.* Cot),
Manseng Noir, Mauzac, Mauzac
Rosé, Mérille, Merlot, Milgranet,
Mouyssaguès, Muscadelle, Négrette,
Ondenc, Petit Manseng, Picpoul,
Pinot Noir, Raffiat, Roussellou,
Sauvignon Blanc, Sémillon, Syrah,
Tannat, Ugni Blanc, Valdiguié

# THE APPELLATIONS OF
# SOUTHWEST FRANCE

## BÉARN AOC

This modest AOC shines in the local Basque area. Wines made in Bellocq, Lahontan, Orthez, and Saliès are allowed to add the communal designation Bellocq to the appellation.

**RED** Fresh, light, and fruity wines with a good balance, but lacking depth.

🅖 A maximum of 60% Tannat, plus Cabernet Franc, Cabernet Sauvignon, Fer, Manseng Noir, Courbu Noir

🍷 1–4 years

**WHITE** Light, dry, and aromatic wines.

🅖 Petit Manseng, Gros Manseng, Courbu Blanc, Lauzet, Camaralet, Raffiat, Sauvignon Blanc

🍷 1–2 years

**ROSÉ** Simple, fruity, dry rosés with a fresh floral aroma.

🅖 Tannat, Cabernet Franc, Cabernet Sauvignon, Fer, Manseng Noir, Courbu Noir

🍷 1–2 years

✓ *Bouscassé* (Rosé) • *C. V. de Jurançon* (Larribère)

## BÉARN-BELLOCQ AOC
### *See* Béarn AOC

## BERGERAC AOC

Adjoining Bordeaux, Bergerac produces wines that are sometimes mistaken for the modest appellations of its more famous neighbor. Its wines were shipped to London as early as 1250. Supplies dried up after the Hundred Years' War, which ended with the Battle of Castillon, and Castillon-la-Bataille marks the ancient English-French boundary between Bergerac and Bordeaux.

**RED** The best reds have a good garnet or ruby color, fine fruit, and an elegant balance.

🅖 Cabernet Sauvignon, Cabernet Franc, Merlot, Malbec, Fer, Mérille

🍷 2–8 years

**WHITE** Mostly dry Bordeaux-style wines, but semisweet wines with up to 54 grams per liter of residual sugar are permitted. Until 1993, such wines had to be described as *moelleux*; however, as this is no longer compulsory, we will not know whether some of these wines are *moelleux* or not. Bergerac Blanc may be sold from December 1 following the harvest without any mention of *primeur* or *nouveau*.

🅖 Sémillon, Sauvignon Blanc, Muscadelle, Ondenc, Chenin Blanc, and up to 25% Ugni Blanc (on the proviso that the quantity of Sauvignon Blanc used is at least equal)

🍷 1–3 years

**ROSÉ** These are light, easy, and attractive dry wines. They may be sold from December 1 following the harvest without mention of *primeur* or *nouveau*.

🅖 Cabernet Sauvignon, Cabernet Franc, Merlot, Malbec, Fer, Mérille

🍷 1–3 years

✓ *de l'Ancienne Cure* • *Julienne* (Casnova des Conti) • *Château Les Justices* • *Château Laulerie* • *Château Miaudoux* (Inspiration) • *Château Le Payral* (Héritage) • *Château Pion* • *Julien de Savignac* (Rosé) • *Château Tour des Gendres* • *Les Verdots* (Les Verdots selon David Fourtout)

## BERGERAC SEC AOC

These white wines are distinguished from Bergerac Blanc by having to be dry, with no more than 4 grams per liter of residual sugar.

**WHITE** Dry Bordeaux-style wines. They may be sold from December 1 following the harvest without any mention of *primeur* or *nouveau*.

🅖 Sémillon, Sauvignon Blanc, Muscadelle, Ondenc, Chenin Blanc, and up to 25% Ugni Blanc (on the proviso that the quantity of Sauvignon Blanc used is at least equal)

🍷 1–3 years

✓ *de l'Ancienne Cure* • *Château Cailevet* (Accent) • *Château Miaudoux* • *Château de Panisseau* (Divin) • *Michel Roche* (Le Top de Mazière) • *Julien de Savignac* (Les Jardins de Cyrano) • *Château Tour des Gendres* • *Château Tourmentine* (Barrique) • *Les Verdots* (Les Verdots selon David Fourtout)

## BUZET AOC

Formerly known as Côtes de Buzet, this supervalue Bordeaux satellite is located on the northern edge of the Armagnac region.

**RED** The best are always very good, with considerable finesse and charm.

🅖 Merlot, Cabernet Sauvignon, Cabernet Franc, Malbec

🍷 3–10 years (15 in exceptional cases)

**WHITE** These dry whites are the least interesting wines in this appellation. They may be sold from December 1 following the harvest without any mention of *primeur* or *nouveau*.

🅖 Sémillon, Sauvignon Blanc, Muscadelle

🍷 1–3 years

**ROSÉ** Ripe, fruity, dry rosés. They may be sold from December 1 following the harvest without any mention of *primeur* or *nouveau*.

🅖 Merlot, Cabernet Sauvignon, Cabernet Franc, Malbec

🍷 1–4 years

✓ *Baron d'Albret* • *C. V. de Buzet* • *Château Sauvagnères*

## CAHORS AOC

The once-famous "black wine" of Cahors got its name from the Malbec grape, which, prior to phylloxera, produced dark, inky-colored wines. But the vines did not graft well to the earliest American rootstocks and Cahors fell into decline. Compatible rootstocks were developed, and with the introduction of the Merlot and Tannat, Cahors has started to claw back its reputation. The sheer number of good producers now makes Cahors one of the most reliable red-wine appellations in France. Vieux Cahors must be aged in oak for at least three years.

**RED** Most Cahors wines have a deep color with a blackcurrant tinge. They are full of fruit and have a good, plummy, Bordeaux-like taste, with a silky texture and a distinctive violet-perfumed aftertaste.

🅖 A minimum of 70% Malbec, plus up to 30% (in total) of Merlot and Tannat—Jurançon Noir has not been permitted since 1996

🍷 3–12 years (20 in exceptional cases)

✓ *Château de Clasou* • *Château la Caminade* (Commandery, Esprit) • *Château de Cèdre* • *de la Coustarelle* • *Croix du Mayne* (Elevé en Fûts de Chêne) • *C. V. Côtes d'Olt* • *Château Gautoul* • *des Grauzils* • *Château Haut Monplaisir* (Pur Plaisir) • *Clos d'Un Jour* • *Château Lacapell Cabanac* (Prestige Elevé en Fûts de Chêne) • *Château Lagrezette* • *Château Lamartine* (Expression, Particulière) • *Primo Palatum du Prince* • *Château La Reyne* (Vente d'Ange) • *Clos Triguedina*

## COTEAUX DU QUERCY VDQS

Located just south of the Cahors area, and a *vin de pays* since 1976, Coteaux du Quercy was promoted to VDQS in 1999, when its *encépagement* changed (formerly Gamay- and Merlot-dominated wines).

**RED** Richly colored, full-bodied wines, the best of which have plenty of morello cherry and blackberry fruit.

🅖 Cabernet Sauvignon, Cabernet Franc, Merlot, Malbec, Fer, Mérille

🍷 1–4 years

**ROSÉ** Soft, easy-drinking, fresh, and fruity rosé, with a maximum of 3 grams per liter residual sugar, thus truly dry.

🅖 Cabernet Sauvignon, Cabernet Franc, Merlot, Malbec

🍷 Upon purchase

✓ *de Merchien*

## CÔTES DE BERGERAC AOC

Geographically, there are no *côtes*; the only difference between this appellation and Bergerac is an extra degree of alcohol. The appellation Côtes de Bergerac Moelleux was withdrawn in 1993 (wines from this appellation must now be sold as Bergerac or Bergerac Moelleux), thus any wine bearing Côtes de Bergerac must now be red.

**RED** Should be richer than Bergerac AOC.

🅖 Cabernet Sauvignon, Cabernet Franc, Merlot, Malbec, Fer, Mérille

🍷 3–10 years

✓ *Château La Bard Les Tendoux* (Elevé en Fûts de Chêne) • *Château Les Mailleries*

(Dany Moelleux) • *Château Masburel* • *Marlene & Alain Mayet* (Révelation du Bois de Pourquie) • *Château Tour des Verdots*

## CÔTES DU BRULHOIS VDQS

Elevated from *vin de pays* in November 1984, this appellation encompasses vineyards along the Garonne immediately west of Buzet.

**RED** Decent, if unexciting, Bordeaux-like wine, though more rustic in style.

🍇 Cabernet Franc, Cabernet Sauvignon, Fer, Merlot, Malbec, Tannat

🍷 2–4 years

**ROSÉ** Fresh, easy-to-drink dry wine.

🍇 Cabernet Franc, Cabernet Sauvignon, Fer, Merlot, Malbec, Tannat

🍷 1–3 years

✓ *Château Grand Chêne* (Elevé en Fûts de Chêne)

## CÔTES DE DURAS AOC

An appellation of increasing interest.

**RED** Light Bordeaux-style wines.

🍇 Cabernet Sauvignon and Franc, Merlot, Malbec

🍷 2–3 years

**WHITE** Clean, crisp, and dry wines, except for those designated *moelleux*, which must have a minimum of 4 grams per liter of residual sugar, although most good *moelleux*, such as Château Lafon, contain much more than this and are definitely sweet. With the exception of *moelleux*, these wines may be sold from December 1 following the harvest without any mention of *primeur* or *nouveau*.

🍇 Sauvignon Blanc, Sémillon, Muscadelle, Mauzac, Chenin Blanc, Ondenc, and up to 25% Ugni Blanc (provided that the quantity of Sauvignon Blanc used is at least equal)

🍷 1–3 years

**ROSÉ** These attractively colored, dry, crisp, fruity rosés are firm and fresh. They may be sold from December 1 following the harvest without any mention of *primeur* or *nouveau*.

🍇 Cabernet Sauvignon, Cabernet Franc, Merlot, Malbec

🍷 1–3 years

✓ *des Allergrets* (Elevé en Fûts de Chêne) • *Duc de Berticot* (Elevé en Fûts de Chêne) • *Château la Grave Bechade* (Alexandre Elevé en Fûts de Chêne) • *Château Laplace* • *Château Moulière* • *Château La Petite Bertrande* (Elevé en Fûts de Chêne) • *Château La Petit Malrome* (Sarah Elevé en Fûts de Chêne)

## CÔTES DU FRONTONNAIS AOC

Situated just west of Gaillac. The wines of two villages, Fronton and Villaudric, are allowed to add their own names to the appellation.

**RED** These medium- to full-bodied wines have excellent color and violet-perfumed fruit.

🍇 50–70% Négrette, up to 25% (in total) of Malbec, Mérille, Fer, Syrah, Cabernet Franc, and Cabernet Sauvignon, plus a maximum of 15% Gamay, Cinsault, and Mauzac

🍷 2–8 years

**ROSÉ** Overtly fruity wines.

🍇 50–70% Négrette, up to 25% (in total) of Malbec, Mérille, Fer, Syrah, Cabernet Franc, and Cabernet Sauvignon, plus a maximum of 15% Gamay, Cinsault, and Mauzac

🍷 1–3 years

✓ *Château Baudare* • *Château Bellevue la Forêt* • *Château Bouissel* • *Château Devès* (Allegro) • *Château Laurou* (Elevé en Fûts de Chêne) • *Château Plaisance* • *Château le Roc*

## CÔTES DU FRONTONNAIS FRONTON AOC
### See **Côtes du Frontonnais AOC**

## CÔTES DU FRONTONNAIS VILLAUDRIC AOC
### See **Côtes du Frontonnais AOC**

## CÔTES DU MARMANDAIS AOC

This successful Bordeaux imitation, upgraded from VDQS to AOC in 1990, is situated on the border of Bordeaux itself; its vines grow on both sides of the Garonne, on the left-bank Côtes de Cocumont and the right-bank Côtes de Beaupuy. Few French people outside the region know anything about these wines, but the English have shipped them since the 14th century.

**RED** Fresh, clean, and impeccably made wines.

🍇 A maximum of 75% (in total) of Cabernet Franc, Cabernet Sauvignon, and Merlot, plus up to 50% (in total) of Abouriou, Malbec, Fer, Gamay, and Syrah

🍷 2–5 years

**WHITE** These dry white wines are soft and delicious. They may be sold from December 1 following the harvest without any mention of *primeur* or *nouveau*.

🍇 At least 70% Sauvignon Blanc, plus Ugni Blanc and Sémillon

🍷 1–2 years

**ROSÉ** Ripe and dry wines. They may be sold from December 1 following the harvest without any mention of *primeur* or *nouveau*.

🍇 A maximum of 75% (in total) of Cabernet Franc, Cabernet Sauvignon, and Merlot, plus up to 50% (in total) of Abouriou, Malbec, Fer, Gamay, and Syrah

🍷 1–2 years

✓ *CV de Cocumont* (Beroy) • *Château La Gravette* (Elevé en Fûts de Chêne) • *Elian da Ros*

## CÔTES DE MILLAU VDQS

Upgraded to VDQS in 1994 from *vin de pays* status (Gorges et Côtes de Millau), this appellation has yet to establish any characteristic style or reputation. There is no intrinsic reason why it should not, but with just 124 acres (50 hectares) under vine and one dominant *coopérative* (Aguessac), it will not be easy.

**RED** *Vin primeur* is a specialty.

🍇 A blend of at least two varieties, including a minimum of 30% Gamay and Syrah, plus Fer, Duras, and up to 20% Cabernet Sauvignon

**WHITE** Very little is made and I have not encountered any.

🍇 Chenin Blanc, Mauzac

**ROSÉ** Very little is made and I have not encountered any.

🍇 A blend of at least two varieties, including a minimum of 50% Gamay, plus Syrah, Cabernet Sauvignon, Fer, and Duras

✓ *C. V. des Gorges du Tarn* (Maitre des Sampettes) • *du Vieux Noyer*

## CÔTES DE MONTRAVEL AOC

This wine must have a minimum residual sugar of 8 grams per litre and a maximum of 54 grams per liter in order to meet the requirements of the appellation. Any red wines produced here are sold as Bergerac AOC.

**WHITE** These fat, fruity wines are usually produced in a *moelleux* style.

🍇 Sémillon, Sauvignon Blanc, Muscadelle

🍷 3–8 years

✓ *Château du Bloy* • *Château Lespinassat* (Vieilles Vignes) • *Château Masburel*

## CÔTES DE SAINT-MONT VDQS

Situated within the Armagnac region, the vineyards of this appellation extend northward from Madiran. Wine production is dominated by the local *coopérative*.

THE DORDOGNE RIVER, SEEN FROM THE TOWN OF DOMME
*Southwest France includes appellations lying just east of Bordeaux, such as Côtes de Duras and Bergerac on the Dordogne, as well as areas of vineyard close to the Spanish border.*

**RED** Well-colored wines of good flavor and medium body. They are not dissimilar to a lightweight Madiran, although they could become deeper, darker, and more expressive if the *coopérative* were prepared to reduce yields and produce better-quality wine.

🍇 At least 70% Tannat, plus Cabernet Sauvignon, Cabernet Franc, Merlot, and Fer (which must constitute one-third of all the grapes other than the Tannat)

⌛ 2–5 years

**WHITE** Fruity, dry wines with a tangy finish.

🍇 At least 50% Arrufiac, Clairette, and Courbu, plus Gros Manseng and Petit Manseng

⌛ 1–2 years

**ROSÉ** Dry wines with a clean, fruity flavor.

🍇 At least 70% Tannat, plus Cabernet Sauvignon, Cabernet Franc, Merlot, and Fer (which must constitute one-third of all grapes other than the Tannat)

⌛ 1–3 years

✓ *Producteurs Plaimont* • *Château Saint-Go* (Elevé en Fûts de Chêne)

## FLOC DE GASCOGNE AOC

This *vin de liqueur* is produced in the Armagnac region.

**WHITE** Few manage to rise above the typically dull, oxidative *vin de liqueur* style that goes *rancio* with age.

🍇 A minimum of 70% Colombard, Gros Manseng, and Ugni Blanc, plus Baroque, Folle Blanche, Petit Manseng, Mauzac, Sauvignon Blanc, and Sémillon

⌛ Upon opening

**ROSÉ** Few manage to rise above the typically dull, oxidative *vin de liqueur* style that goes *rancio* with age.

🍇 A minimum of 50% Tannat, plus Cabernet Franc, Cabernet Sauvignon, Fer Servadou, Malbec, and Merlot

⌛ Upon opening

✓ *C. V. du Muscat de Lunel* (Prestige) • *Saint Pierre de Paradis* (Vendange d'Automne)

## GAILLAC AOC

These vineyards, among the oldest in France, have only recently begun to make their mark. In order to emphasize local styles, there has been a concerted move away from classic grapes toward different native varieties. Gaillac Liquoreux and Gaillac Moelleux are no longer permitted appellations, but such wines are still available under the Gaillac Doux appellation. The Gaillac Sec Perlé denomination for slightly *pétillant* dry white wines has been dropped (although Gaillac Perlé still seems to flourish), and the sparkling wines of Gaillac are now segregated by their method of production (*see* Gaillac Mousseux AOC and Gaillac Mousseux Méthode Gaillaçoise AOC). The required *encépagement* has always been confusingly complex, but became even more so with the new regulations introduced in 2001.

**RED** Wines made mostly in the fresh, soft but light *macération carbonique* style. They may be sold as *primeur* or *nouveau* from the third Thursday of November following the harvest.

🍇 At least 60% Duras, Fer, Gamay, and Syrah, of which Duras, Fer, and Syrah (or any two of these) must represent at least 30% of the entire blend; furthermore, there must be at least 10% each of Duras and Fer, plus optional Cabernet Franc, Cabernet Sauvignon, and Merlot

⌛ 1–3 years

**WHITE** Dry and fresh, these wines may be sold as *primeur* or *nouveau* as from the third Thursday of November following the harvest.

🍇 At least 15% of Len de l'El or Sauvignon Blanc (or a blend of the two), plus Mauzac, Mauzac Rosé, Muscadelle, Ondenc, and Sémillon

⌛ Upon purchase

**ROSÉ** Easy to drink, light, fresh, and dry rosés.

🍇 At least 60% Duras, Fer, Gamay, and Syrah, of which Duras, Fer, and Syrah (or any two of these) must represent at least 30% of the entire blend; furthermore. there must be at least 10% each of Duras and Fer, plus optional Cabernet Franc, Cabernet Sauvignon, and Merlot

⌛ 1–2 years

✓ *Causse Marines* (Délires d'Automne) • *Manoir de l'Émeille* (Tradition) • *d'Escausses* (La Vigne l'Oubli) • *de Gineste* (Aurore, Grand Cuvée) • *de Larroque* (Privilège d'Autan) • *Château de Lastours* • *Château Lecusse* (Spéciale) • *Château Montels* • *Paysels* (Tradition) • *Robert Plageoles* • *René Rieux* (Concerto) • *des Terrisses* (Saint-Laurent) • *Château La Tour Plantade*

## GAILLAC DOUX AOC

These are naturally sweet wines that must contain a minimum of 70 grams per liter of residual sugar.

**WHITE** Sweet to very sweet wines of ripe-peach, or richer, character.

🍇 At least 15% (each or in total) of Len de l'El and Sauvignon Blanc, plus Mauzac, Mauzac Rosé, Muscadelle, Ondenc, and Sémillon

⌛ 5–15 years

✓ *Barreau* (Caprice d'Automne) • *Château Palvie* (Les Secrets) • *Peyres-Combe* (Flaveurs d'Automne) • *Robert Plageoles* • *Rotier* (Renaissance) • *Sanbatan* (Muscadelle) • *de Vayssette* (Maxime) • *Les Vergnades*

## GAILLAC MOUSSEUX AOC

This is a sparkling wine made by the traditional method. Expect to see a phasing out of the term *mousseux* on these and other Gaillac sparkling-wine appellations.

**SPARKLING WHITE** These wines are fresh and fragrant with a fine sparkle.

🍇 At least 15% (each or in total) of Len de l'El and Sauvignon Blanc, plus Mauzac, Mauzac Rosé, Muscadelle, Ondenc, and Sémillon

⌛ 1–3 years

**SPARKLING ROSÉ** Attractive, fresh, fruity wines.

🍇 At least 60% Duras, Fer, Gamay, and Syrah, of which Duras, Fer, and Syrah (or any two of these) must represent at least 30% of the entire blend; furthermore, there must be at least 10% each of Duras and Fer, plus optional Cabernet Franc, Cabernet Sauvignon, and Merlot

⌛ 1–2 years

✓ *Manoir de l'Emeille* • *René Rieux*

## GAILLAC MOUSSEUX MÉTHODE GAILLAÇOISE AOC

Sparkling wines made by the *méthode rurale*, involving just one fermentation, with no addition of a *liqueur de tirage*. The wine is bottled before the fermentation stops and no *liqueur d'expédition* is added prior to distribution, thus any residual sweetness is entirely from the original grape sugars. Styles include *brut* and *demi-sec*. A *doux* is also available, but is governed by stricter rules and is given its own appellation (*see below*).

**SPARKLING WHITE** These very fresh, fragrant, and grapey wines have a fine natural sparkle.

🍇 At least 15% (each or in total) of Len de l'El and Sauvignon Blanc, plus Mauzac, Mauzac Rosé, Muscadelle, Ondenc, and Sémillon

⌛ 1–3 years

**SPARKLING ROSÉ** These wines are attractive, fresh, and deliciously fruity.

🍇 At least 60% Duras, plus Fer, Gamay, Syrah, Cabernet Sauvignon, Cabernet Franc, Merlot

⌛ 1–2 years

## GAILLAC MOUSSEUX MÉTHODE GAILLAÇOISE DOUX AOC

This is a sparkling wine made by the *méthode rurale* (*see above*) from riper grapes (minimum of 11 percent) than those of any other Gaillac sparkling-wine appellation, and with at least 45 grams per liter of residual natural sugar.

**SPARKLING WHITE** Not as exotic as, say, Clairette de Die Méthode Dioise Ancestrale, but delicious, grapey, and fragrant all the same.

🍇 At least 15% (each or in total) of Len de l'El and Sauvignon Blanc, plus Mauzac, Mauzac Rosé, Muscadelle, Ondenc, and Sémillon

⌛ 1–3 years

**SPARKLING ROSÉ** I have never come across a Gaillac Doux rosé, but if the white is anything to go by, it would be an interesting wine.

🍇 At least 60% Duras, Fer, Gamay, and Syrah, of which Duras, Fer, and Syrah (or any two of these) must represent at least 30% of the entire blend; furthermore, there must be at least 10% Cabernet Franc, Cabernet Sauvignon, and Merlot

⌛ 1–2 years

## GAILLAC PREMIÈRES CÔTES AOC

These are dry white wines that come from 11 communes. The grapes must be riper than for ordinary Gaillac AOC and the wine must conform to the technical requirements of Gaillac Doux in all but sweetness.

✓ *Robert Plageoles* • *Château de Salettes*

## HAUT-MONTRAVEL AOC

This wine must have a minimum residual sugar of 8 grams and a maximum of 54 grams per liter to meet the requirements of the appellation. Any red wines produced here are sold as Bergerac AOC.

**WHITE** Fat, fruity, and *moelleux* wines.

🍇 Sémillon, Sauvignon Blanc, Muscadelle

⌛ 3–8 years

✓ *Château Puy-Servain*

## IROULÉGUY AOC

The local *coopérative* dominates this Basque appellation, which makes some of the most distinctive red wines in Southwest France. Surprisingly, however, the production of rosé outweighs that of red.

**RED** These deep, dark, tannic wines have a rich and mellow flavor, with a distinctive earthy-and-spicy aftertaste.

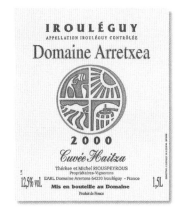

Tannat, plus at least 50% (in total) of Cabernet Sauvignon and Cabernet Franc

4–10 years

**WHITE** These modest dry whites are the least interesting of this appellation.

Courbu, Manseng

**ROSÉ** This salmon-colored, very fruity dry rosé is best drunk very young and fresh.

Tannat plus at least 50% (in total) of Cabernet Sauvignon and Cabernet Franc

Upon purchase

✓ *Arretxa* ◉ • *Etxegaraya*

## JURANÇON AOC

The sweet version of this wine from the Pyrénées-Atlantiques was used at Henri de Navarre's christening in 1553 and is often sold today as *vendanges tardives* or *moelleux*. Most production is, however, tart, dry, and nervy, and sold as Jurançon Sec (*see below*).

**WHITE** The best wines have a fine, spicy, and tangy bouquet and flavor, and can hint of pineapples and peaches, candied peel, and cinnamon.

Petit Manseng, Gros Manseng, Courbu, plus up to 15% (in total) of Camaralet and Lauzet

5–20 years

✓ *Bru-Baché* • *Cauhapé* • *Clos Lapeyre* • *Primo Palatum* • *Clos Thou* • *Clos Uroulat*

## JURANÇON SEC AOC

This wine has to meet the same requirements as Jurançon AOC, but less residual sugar is allowed, and the grapes may be less ripe. It is best drunk young. These wines may be sold from December 1 following the harvest without any mention of *primeur* or *nouveau*.

**WHITE** If any wine in the world habitually has a certain nervousness, it has to be Jurançon Sec.

Most lack any individual character that would make them stand out from other dry whites, and none has the complexity and richness of Jurançon's late-harvest wines, but the best can have an intensity that hints of grapefruit.

Petit Manseng, Gros Manseng, Courbu, plus up to 15% (in total) of Camaralet and Lauzet

2–5 years

✓ *Capdevieille* (Brise Océane) • *Cauhape* (Sève d'Automne) • *du Cinquau* • *C. V. de Jurançon* (Grain Sauvage) • *Lapeyre* • *Larredya* • *Nigri* • *Primo Palatum*

## MADIRAN AOC

One of the most individually expressive appellations in Southwest France, but there are as many disappointments as successes. Many domaines are trying new oak, and there is a trend toward more Cabernet Franc.

**RED** You literally have to chew your way through the tannin in these dark, rich, and meaty wines when young.

40–60% Tannat, plus Cabernet Franc, Cabernet Sauvignon, and Fer

5–15 years

✓ *Berthoumieu* • *Château Bouscassé* • *Château Labranche-Laffont* • *Château Laffitte-Teston* • *Laffont* • *Château Montus* • *Plaimont* (Arte Benedicte) • *Primo Palatum* • *Château de Viela*

## MARCILLAC AOC

This rarely encountered wine from the northeastern borderlands was upgraded from Vin de Marcillac VDQS to Marcillac AOC in 1990, when greater focus was placed on the local Fer and Gamay, while Jurançon Noir, Mouyssagués, and Valdiguié were disallowed.

**RED** Rough and rustic when young, these wines soften with age.

At least 90% Fer, plus Cabernet Franc, Cabernet Sauvignon, and Merlot

3–6 years

**ROSÉ** Full, ripe, and attractive dry rosés that have expressed more individual style since the minimum Fer content has tripled.

At least 90% Fer, plus Cabernet Franc, Cabernet Sauvignon, and Merlot

1–3 years

✓ *C. V. de Ladrecht*

## MONBAZILLAC AOC

An excellent value Sauternes-style appellation at the heart of Bergerac, these wines date back to 1080, when vines were planted by the abbey of St.-Martin on a hill called Mont Bazailhac.

**WHITE** These intensely sweet, rich wines are of a very high quality.

Sémillon, Sauvignon Blanc, Muscadelle

7–20 years

✓ *de l'Ancienne Cure* (Abbaye, L'Extase) • *Château Caillavel* • *Château Fonmorgues* • *Grande Maison* ◉ (Cuvée du Château) • *Château Tirecul La Gravière*

## MONTRAVEL AOC

The largest of the three Montravel appellations and the only one where the white wine can (and must) be dry.

**RED** Elegant, ruby-colored reds that are very much in the Bergerac style. These wines may be sold from December 1 following the harvest without any mention of *primeur* or *nouveau*.

A minimum of 50% Merlot, plus Cabernet Franc, Cabernet Sauvignon, and Malbec

2–8 years

**WHITE** Dry, crisp, and aromatic Sauvignon-dominated wines. These wines may be sold from December 1 following the harvest without any mention of *primeur* or *nouveau*.

A minimum 25% each of Sémillon and Sauvignon Blanc, plus optional Muscadelle (Chenin Blanc, Ondenc, and Ugni Blanc are no longer allowed)

1–2 years

✓ *Château du Bloy* (Le Bloy) • *Château Laulerie* • *Moulin Caresse* (Cent pour 100) • *Château Pagnon* • *Château Pique-Sègue* • *Portes du Bondieu* • *Château Puy-Servain* (Marjolaine)

## PACHERENC DU VIC-BILH AOC

New oak is being increasingly used in this white-only appellation, which covers the same area as Madiran.

**WHITE** Exotic floral aromas, a fruit salad of flavors, Pacherenc du Vic-Bilh is made in off-dry (sold as *sec*), medium-sweet (*moelleux*), and sweet (*doux*) styles.

A minimum of 30% Arrufiac, which with Courbu and Petit Manseng must represent at least 60% of the entire blend, plus Gros

Manseng and a maximum of 10% in total of Sauvignon Blanc and Sémillon

🍷— 3–7 years

✓ *Château Bouscassé • Berthoumieu • Château Labranche-Laffont • Château de Viela*

## PÉCHARMANT AOC

These are the finest red wines of Bergerac; all but one (Saint-Saveur) of the communes in this appellation are also within the Rosette AOC.

**RED** All the characteristics of Bergerac, but with a greater concentration of color, flavor, and tannin.

🍇 Cabernet Franc, Cabernet Sauvignon, Merlot, Malbec

🍷— 4–12 years

✓ *Château Beauportail • Château de Biran (Prestige de Bacchus) • Château Champarel • Château Hugon (Elevé en Fûts de Chêne)*

## ROSETTE AOC

A white-wine-only appellation. The wines must contain 8 to 54 grams per liter of residual sugar. Any red wines are sold as Bergerac AOC.

**WHITE** Soft and delicately fruity with a sweet, waxy flavor.

🍇 Sémillon, Sauvignon Blanc, Muscadelle

🍷— 4–8 years

✓ *Château de Contancie*

## SAUSSIGNAC AOC

A sweet-wine appellation; it must have a minimum of 18 grams per liter of residual sugar. Any red wines are sold as Bergerac AOC.

**WHITE** The best can be very rich, fat, and full.

🍇 Sémillon, Sauvignon Blanc, Muscadelle, Chenin Blanc

🍷— 5–15 years

✓ *Château Le Chabrier • Château Eyssards (Flavie) • Château Grinou (Elevé en Fûts de Chêne) • Château La Maurigne (La Maurigne) • Château Miaudoux*

## TURSAN VDQS

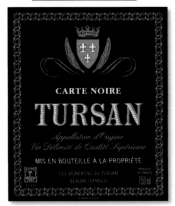

The reds rely on the Tannat, the same primary grape used in Madiran; the whites are essentially Baroque, a variety more at home in Tursan. There was a change of *encépagement* as from 2003.

**RED** Rich and chewy, or finer-flavored and aromatic, depending on the dominant grape.

🍇 A minimum of 30% Tannat and 30% Cabernet Franc, plus (until 2010) a maximum of 10% Cabernet Sauvignon and Fer

**WHITE** The *coopérative* traditionally makes a full-bodied white with a solid, somewhat rustic, rich flavor, but it is gradually being influenced by the growing reputation of the wine made under the relatively new Château de Bachen label, Baron de Bachen, which is far more aromatic and elegant.

🍇 A minimum of 30% Baroque, plus a maximum of 50% (in total) of Gros Manseng and Petit Manseng, of which Petit Manseng must not represent more than 20% of the entire blend; no more than 30% Sauvignon Blanc and 20% Chenin Blanc (Claverie, Raffiat, Claret du Gers, and Clairette no longer allowed)

🍷— 2–5 years

**ROSÉ** An unpretentious dry wine with good, juicy, fruit flavor.

🍇 A minimum of 50% Cabernet Franc and 10–30% Tannat, plus a maximum of 40% Cabernet Sauvignon and Fer

🍷— 1–3 years

✓ *Michel Guérard (Baron de Bachen) • C. V. de Landais (Haute Carte)*

## VINS D'ENTRAYGUES AND DU FEL VDQS

This area overlaps the Aveyron and Cantal *départements* in the northeast of the region, but only a tiny amount is made. The wines are rarely encountered and never exported.

**RED** Light, rustic wines that are best consumed locally because they need all the local ambience they can get.

🍇 Cabernet Franc, Cabernet Sauvignon, Fer, Gamay, Jurançon Noir, Merlot, Mouyssaguès, Négrette, Pinot Noir

🍷— 1–2 years

**WHITE** Light, dry, and crisp wines for unpretentious quaffing.

🍇 Chenin Blanc, Mauzac

🍷— Upon purchase

**ROSÉ** Light, fresh, and dry rosés.

🍇 Cabernet Franc, Cabernet Sauvignon, Fer, Gamay, Jurançon Noir, Merlot, Mouyssaguès, Négrette, Pinot Noir

🍷— 1–2 years

✓ *Jean-Marc Viguer*

## VINS D'ESTAING VDQS

This area is contiguous with the southern tip of the above VDQS and production is even more minuscule.

**RED** These wines are light bodied, attractive, and fruity.

🍇 Fer, Gamay, Abouriou, Jurançon Noir, Merlot, Cabernet Franc, Cabernet Sauvignon, Mouyssaguès, Négrette, Pinot Noir, Duras, Castet

🍷— 1–3 years

**WHITE** These are unpretentious, dry white wines with a crisp flavor and a rustic, tangy style.

🍇 Chenin Blanc, Roussellou, Mauzac

🍷— 1–2 years

**ROSÉ** These pleasant dry wines are probably the most interesting in the appellation.

🍇 Fer, Gamay, Abouriou, Jurançon Noir, Merlot, Cabernet Franc, Cabernet Sauvignon, Mouyssaguès, Négrette, Pinot Noir, Duras, Castet

🍷— Upon purchase

✓ *C. V. d'Olt (Prestige)*

## VINS DE LAVILLEDIEU VDQS

Situated south of Cahors, this VDQS is a northern extension of the Frontonnais, with vines growing on a *boulbènes* soil that is similar to that of Bordeaux's Entre-Deux-Mers district. Production is dominated by the local *coopérative*, and the wines are seldom seen outside the locality.

**RED** Nicely colored, medium-bodied wines with a fresh, fruity flavor.

🍇 A minimum of 80% (in total) of Mauzac, Mérille, Cinsault, Fuella, and Négrette (which must account for at least 35%), plus up to 20% (in total) of Syrah, Gamay, Jurançon Noir, Picpoul, Milgranet, and Fer

🍷— 3–6 years

**WHITE** Dry, crisp, aromatic wines.

🍇 Mauzac, Sauvignon Blanc, Sémillon, Muscadelle, Colombard, Ondenc, Folle Blanche

🍷— 1–3 years

✓ *C. V. de Lavilledieu du Temple*

# LANGUEDOC-ROUSSILLON

*The 1990s saw an influx of Australian winemakers, who have since played a not insignificant role in the raising of standards; but the sale in 2003 of the Australian-owned Domaine de la Baume could signal a swing back to a more homegrown stimulus. Domaine de la Baume is not significant in terms of the total production of this region, but there is no denying that its purchase by BRL Hardy in 1990, at the beginning of Australia's inexorable success on export markets, gave local wine producers a psychological boost.*

VINEYARDS AT BAGES
*The Mediterranean coastal vineyards of the Côtes du Roussillon, around Perpignan, are reputed to be some of the hottest in France.*

IN A STRANGE WAY, the presence of a top Australian group was viewed as a seal of approval for local winemakers, just as the presence of Moët & Chandon in Australia had been seen by that country's sparkling winemakers. It was all a matter of timing: Australian wines were surging, French wines were slowing down, and the south was all potential, with very few wineries taking advantage of it. And *vins de pays* were not, as yet, a force to be reckoned with. BRL Hardy, or Hardy's as it was known then, was leading the Australian charge on global exports, and yet it saw sufficient promise in a small domaine in an

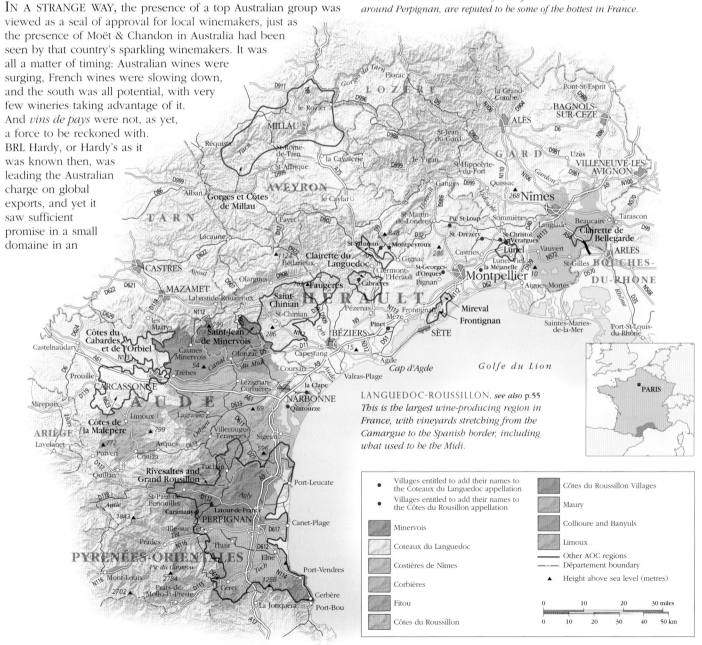

LANGUEDOC-ROUSSILLON, *see also p.55*
*This is the largest wine-producing region in France, with vineyards stretching from the Camargue to the Spanish border, including what used to be the Midi.*

| | |
|---|---|
| • Villages entitled to add their names to the Coteaux du Languedoc appellation | Côtes du Roussillon Villages |
| • Villages entitled to add their names to the Côtes du Rousillon appellation | Maury |
| Minervois | Collioure and Banyuls |
| Coteaux du Languedoc | Limoux |
| Costières de Nîmes | Other AOC regions |
| Corbières | Département boundary |
| Fitou | ▲ Height above sea level (metres) |
| Côtes du Roussillon | |

unknown part of France to be sidetracked into purchasing it outright. The next few years saw the rise of *vins de pays*, particularly Vin de Pays d'Oc, including those of Domaine de la Baume, which became a commercial success on the UK market, against the tide for most other inexpensive French wines. During this time, there was an internationalization of grape varieties and wine styles in the south of France, and, barring some unfortunate experiments in the late 1970s and the 1980s, this development was far from regrettable.

Some French producers had started putting their own houses in order long before the BRL Hardy purchased Domaine de la Baume. Indeed, a number of domaines began bottling their own wines in the late 1970s, when the government's *vins de pays* program was encouraging quality-conscious growers to reduce yields. The problem was that there were never enough "quality-conscious" growers. But those who were formed a new generation of elite winemakers. They combined modern technology with the best traditional practices, including the use of some aging with new oak, to create exciting new wines in the early 1980s. As other growers observed the vastly increased prices that their pioneering neighbors were attracting, more of them switched from selling in bulk to domaine-bottling, and it was this potential that attracted the Australians.

It was thus the French who created the newfound pride in this region, but it was the Australians who grabbed the limelight, focusing international attention on the fabulous potential. It is almost possible to give consumers an iron-clad guarantee that if they buy ultrapremium *cuvées* from Languedoc-Roussillon they will not only be delighted with the wines, but they will also be cheaper than and far superior to medium-priced wines bearing the most famous French appellations.

When BRL Hardy sold Domaine de la Baume to Les Grands Chais in 2003, the Australians left this wine region in a far better commercial position than they found it 13 years earlier; so the French in general, and Les Grands Chais in particular, have no excuse if they fail to take Languedoc-Roussillon to the next level of success. That will require a twin philosophy that does not restrict the planting of classic grapes and yet encourages a resurgence of the most interesting local varieties.

---

## RECENT LANGUEDOC-ROUSSILLON VINTAGES

**2006** Ripe but soft, making for easy drinking. Moderately good quality.

**2005** A sunny summer without the excessive heat experienced elsewhere gave rise to hopes of a great vintage, only to be dashed for early-ripening varieties when severe storms hit the region immediately prior to picking. The harvest itself was conducted in near-perfect conditions, auguring well for later-ripening varieties, particularly reds.

**2004** An excellent vintage for reds and whites. Grenache stood out.

**2003** Higher-altitude appellations, such as Pic-St-Loup, have fared best, but it will be a mishmash of good, bad, and ugly elsewhere, with a very small scattering of stunning reds.

**2002** The year of the floods, with only those areas that escaped (essentially western and southern extremities, and higher-altitude vineyards) managing to produce a decent quality.

---

## FACTORS AFFECTING TASTE AND QUALITY

**LOCATION**
A crescent of vineyards situated in southern France between the Rhône to the east and the Pyrenees to the southwest.

**CLIMATE**
The Mediterranean-influenced climate is generally well suited to the cultivation of the vine, although it is subject to occasional stormy weather. Two winds dominate: the cold and parching Mistral, which blows down from the heights of the Alpine glaciers, and the wet and warm Marin, which comes in from the sea and can cause rot at harvest time. There are many microclimates in this collection of isolated vine-growing areas.

**ASPECT**
Famous for its unending tracts of flat, *vin ordinaire* vineyards that stretch across the vast plains; the best sites of Languedoc-Roussillon, however, mostly occupy south-, southeast-, and east-facing *garrigues* and hillsides, or nestle beneath protective overhanging cliffs.

**SOIL**
In general terms, the plains and valleys have rich alluvial soils, while the hillsides are schist or limestone and the *garrigues*, or former moorlands, are comprised of stony, carbonaceous soils over fissured limestone. However, specific situations vary enormously.

**VITICULTURE AND VINIFICATION**
This remains the great *vin ordinaire* region of France, where everything is mechanized and the vines of the plain are farmed like wheat or corn. There is a trend toward developing single-domaine vineyards that have potentially expressive *terroirs*, growing classic varieties and combining various traditional methods with modern techniques. Limoux still practices the ancient *méthode rurale*—in Blanquette Méthode Ancestrale AOC (*see below*)—although the majority of the wines are pure traditional method and sold under the new *crémant* appellation.

**GRAPE VARIETIES**
Aspiran Noir, Aspiran Gris, Aubun (*syn.* Counoise), Bourboulenc (known in some areas as Malvoisie or Tourbat), Cabernet Franc, Cabernet Sauvignon, Carignan, Carignan Blanc, Cinsault, Clairette, Duras, Fer, Grenache, Grenache Blanc, Grenache Gris, Lladoner Pelut, Listan Negra (the black version of Spain's Palomino), Malbec, Macabéo, Marsanne, Merlot, Mourvèdre, Muscat d'Alexandrie, Muscat Blanc à Petits Grains, Muscat Doré de Frontignan, Muscat Rosé à Petits Grains, Négrette, Oeillade, Picpoul, Picpoul Noir, Roussanne, Syrah, Terret, Terret Noir, Ugni Blanc, Vermentino (*syn.* Rolle).

---

THE APPELLATIONS OF
# LANGUEDOC-ROUSSILLON

**Note** In the following entries, a wine described as a *vin doux naturel* (or VDN) is made from very ripe grapes and fortified with pure grape spirit after its fermentation has reached 5 or 6 percent. It has the natural sweetness of the grape. To be labeled "Rancio" a VDN must be stored in oak casks "according to local custom," which often means exposing the barrels to direct sunlight for a minimum of two years. This imparts the distinctive *rancio* flavor that is so prized in Roussillon. Depending on the color of the original wine, the wine technique used, and how long it has been aged, the style of the wine produced varies; it can be red, white, rosé, or tawny.

## BANYULS AOC

The most southerly appellation in France, the vineyards of this *vin doux naturel* are literally a stone's throw from those of Spain. The vines are grown on precipitous slopes of schist where man and mule have great difficulty in maintaining a foothold, mechanization is out of the question, yields are extremely low, and ripeness very high. You will often see "rimage" on labels; this word is derived from the Catalan *rime*, or "grape," and refers to the vintage.

**RED** This is the deepest and darkest of all VDNs. A rich, sweet, red Banyuls (without too much barrel-age) has a chocolaty, bottled-fruitiness, which is the nearest France gets to the great wines of Portugal's Douro region. It lacks the fire of a great port, but has its own immense charm. After 15 to 20 years in bottle a great Banyuls develops a curious but wonderful complexity that falls somewhere between the porty-plummy, dried-fruit spice of a mature vintage port and the coffee-caramel, nutty-raisiny smoothness of a fine old tawny.

 10–40 years

**WHITE/ROSÉ/TAWNY** Like all VDNs that may be made in red, white, and rosé style, they can all turn tawny with time, particularly "rancio" wines.

All wines: a minimum of 50% Grenache,

plus Grenache Gris, Grenache Blanc, Macabéo, Tourbat, Muscat Blanc à Petits Grains, Muscat d'Alexandrie, and a maximum 10% (in total) of Carignan, Cinsault, and Syrah

🍇— 10–20 years

✓ *Le Dominican* (Hanicotte) • *CV l'Étoile* (Extra Vieux) • *Du Mas Blanc* • *De la Tour Vieille* • *Du Traginer* ◉ (Rimage Mis Tardive)

## BANYULS GRAND CRU AOC

The requirements are the same as for Banyuls AOC, but a minimum of 75 percent Grenache is required. The grapes must be destemmed and macerated for a minimum of five days and the wine matured in oak for at least 30 months. The wines are similar in character to those of the basic, although not at all ordinary, Banyuls appellation, but in terms of classic port styles, they veer more toward the tawny than vintage.

✓ *L'Abbé Rous* (Christian Reynal) • *L'Étoile* (Réserve) • *Cellier des Templiers*

## BANYULS GRAND CRU "RANCIO" AOC

**See Banyuls Grand Cru AOC**

## BANYULS "RANCIO" AOC

**See Banyuls AOC**

## BERLOU ST-CHINIAN AOC

One of two multicommunal *terroirs* within the St-Chinian appellation, Berlou AOC was established in 2005, with the first wines (from 2004) not available until 2006. Most production monopolized by the Cave de Berlou cooperative. Schistous hillsides; compulsory hand-harvesting.

**RED** No experience, as yet, but there are some interesting old Carignan vines in the area.

🍇 A minimum of 30% Carignan, plus at least 60% in total of Grenache, Syrah, and Mourvèdre, of which both Grenache and Syrah must each represent a minimum of 20%. Impressively, all vines must be at least 10 years old

🍇— Estimated 2–6 years

## BLANQUETTE DE LIMOUX AOC

The best Blanquette de Limoux have improved but many are still somewhat rustic and must adopt a more refined style if they are to compete internationally.

**SPARKLING WHITE** These wines used to have the distinctive aroma of fresh-cut grass, but they are slowly developing finer aromas.

🍇 Mauzac, Chardonnay, Chenin Blanc

🍇— 1–3 years (up to 12 for vintages)

✓ *Antech* (Flascon des Maïstre) • *Robert* (Dame Robert, Maistre Blanquetiers) • *Sieur d'Arques* (Aimery Princesse)

## BLANQUETTE MÉTHODE ANCESTRALE AOC

Formerly called Vin de Blanquette, but still produced by the ancient *méthode rurale*.

**SPARKLING WHITE** These succulently sweet sparkling wines are a hedonist's dream and should be far more commercially available. The ancient *méthode rurale* should be perfected so that prestige *cuvées* can be sold at a premium, allowing Limoux to capitalize on its historical value and individual wines' reputation.

🍇 Mauzac

✓ *Sieur d'Arques* (Dame d'Arques)

## CABARDÈS AOC

An obscure appellation north of Carcassonne, these wines were once sold as Côtes du Cabardès et de l'Orbiel VDQS, but this hardly tripped off the tongue, thus the shortened form was in common usage long before the appellation was promoted to full AOC status in 1999, when the *encépagement* changed.

**RED** The best wines have elegant fruit and a leaner, more Bordeaux-like balance than most of the warmer, spicy-ripe southern French reds.

🍇 At least 40% Grenache and Syrah, plus a minimum of 40% Cabernet Franc, Cabernet Sauvignon, and Merlot (Aubun and Carignan are no longer allowed)

🍇— 3–8 years

**ROSÉ** A rich, fruity, well-colored rosé.

🍇 At least 40% Grenache and Syrah, plus a minimum of 40% Cabernet Franc, Cabernet Sauvignon, and Merlot (Aubun and Carignan are no longer allowed)

🍇— Between 2–3 years

✓ *Château de La Bastide* (L'Esprit) • *Claude et Michelle Carayol* (Cabrol Vent d'Est) • *Château de Pennautier* (L'Esprit) • *Château Ventenac* (Le Carla)

## CLAIRETTE DE BELLEGARDE AOC

When compared with all the best *vins de pays*, this appellation, which is dedicated to the lowly, intrinsically flabby Clairette grape, does not deserve to be a VDQS, let alone an AOC.

**WHITE** Unimpressive dry white wines.

🍇 Clairette

🍇— Before Christmas of the year of production

## CLAIRETTE DU LANGUEDOC AOC

The appellation of Clairette du Languedoc covers three basic wine types. These are natural, fortified, and *rancio*. The *rancio* must be aged in sealed casks for at least three years, and can be produced in both natural and fortified styles.

**WHITE** The natural wine is fuller and richer than Bellegarde, but has more alcohol and less sweetness in its *rancio* form. The fortified version is off-dry to medium-sweet, with a resinous flavor that is stronger in *rancio* character than the natural white.

🍇 Clairette

🍇— 1–3 years for naturally fermented wines, 8–20 years for fortified wines and *rancio* wines

✓ *Saint Rome* (Moelleux)

## CLAIRETTE DU LANGUEDOC "RANCIO" AOC

**See Clairette du Languedoc AOC**

## COLLIOURE AOC

An obscure but exciting appellation for unfortified wines from normally harvested grapes grown in Banyuls.

**RED** These deep, dark, and powerful wines have a full and concentrated fruit flavor, with a soft, spicy aftertaste.

🍇 At least 60% (in total) of Grenache,

Mourvèdre, and Syrah (no variety may exceed 90%), plus Cinsault and no more than 30% Carignan (Grenache Gris is no longer allowed)

🍇— 2–10 years

**WHITE** These wines had to be sold as Vin de Pays de la Côte Vermeille until 2002, when white Collioure was first allowed.

🍇 Minimum of 70% in total of Grenache Blanc and/or Grenache Gris, plus a maximum of 30% in total (and individually a maximum of 15%) of Malvoisie, Macabéo, Marsanne, Rousanne, and Velmentino

🍇— 1–3 years

**ROSÉ** I have not encountered these wines.

🍇 Same as for red

🍇— Upon purchase

✓ *Château des Abelles* • *Du Mas Blanc* (Les Junquets) • *Mas Cornet* • *Celliers des Templiers* (Abbaye de Valbonne) • *De la Tour Vieille* (Puig Oriol) • *Du Traginer* (Octobre)

## CORBIÈRES AOC

When this appellation was elevated to full AOC status in December 1985, its area of production was practically halved to its current realm of 57,000 acres (23,000 hectares). The top estates often use *macération carbonique*, followed by 12 months or so in new oak, and the results can be stunning. There is such a great diversity of *terroirs* in the appellation. This has led to the unofficial formation of 11 internal zones: Boutenac (central-north of Corbières, the first zone to achieve its own AOC status, Corbières-Boutenac is for red wines only, the grapes for which must be manually harvested and comprise at least two varieties, 30–50% of which must be Carignan; others are Grenache, Mourvèdre, and a maximum of 30% Syrah); Durban (wedged between the two hilly halves of Fitou, this zone is cut off from any Mediterranean influence); Fontfroide (extending from the northern tip of Durban to the western outskirts of Narbonne, this zone has a very low rainfall and is well suited to Mourvèdre); Lagrasse (protected limestone valley vineyards immediately west of Boutenac); Lézignan (a low plateau of gravelly vineyards in the most northerly zone of Corbières); Montagne d'Alaric (northerly zone just west of Lézignan, with vines growing on well-drained slopes of gravel over limestone); Quéribus (most southerly zone, with vineyards on high, stony slopes); St-Victor (the very heart of Corbières); Serviès (the northwestern perimeter, the wettest zone, with calcareous-clay soils particularly well suited to Syrah); Sigean (the coastal strip of Corbières, where Syrah performs best); Termenès (the western perimeter, between Serviès and Quéribus, with the highest vineyards in the appellation).

**RED** These wines have an excellent color, a

full, spicy-fruity nose, and a creamy-clean, soft palate that often hints of cherries, raspberries, and vanilla.

🍇 A minimum of 50% of Grenache, Lladoner Pelut, Mourvèdre, and Syrah, plus Carignan, Picpoul Noir, Terret, and a maximum of 20% Cinsault (Macabéo and Bourboulenc are no longer allowed)

🍷 2–5 years (3–8 years in exceptional cases)

**WHITE** Soft, almost clinically clean, dry wines that have acquired a more aromatic character in recent vintages—Château Meunier St.-Louis is probably the best example—but many of the wines should be more expressive. There have been some successful experiments with oak fermentation. These wines may be sold from December 1 following the harvest without any mention of *primeur* or *nouveau*.

🍇 Bourboulenc, Grenache Blanc, Macabéo, Marsanne, Roussanne, and Vermentino, plus a maximum of 10% Clairette, Muscat Blanc à Petit Grains, Picpoul, and Terret

🍷 1–3 years

**ROSÉ** The best of these dry wines have an attractive color and a pleasant, floral aroma, but are nothing special.

🍇 A minimum of 50% of Grenache, Lladoner Pelut, Mourvèdre, and Syrah, plus Carignan, Picpoul Noir, Terret Noir, a maximum of 20% Cinsault, and no more than 10% Bourboulenc, Grenache Blanc, Macabéo, Marsanne, Roussanne, and Vermentino, plus a maximum of 10% Clairette, Muscat Blanc à Petit Grains, Picpoul, and Terret

🍷 1–3 years

✓ *Clos de L'Anhel* • *Des Chandelles* • *Clos Canos* (Les Cocobirous) • *Desmoiselles* (Blanc de Blancs) • *Château des Erles* (La Recaoufa) • *CV de Gruissan* (Elevé en Fûts de Chêne) • *Château de Mansenoble* (Marie-Annick, Réserve) • *CV du Mont Ténarel d'Octaviana* (Sextant) • *Château de Romilhac* (Privilège) • *Rouire-Ségur* (Vieilles Vignes) • *Château la Voulte-Gasparets* (Romain Pauc)

## COSTIÈRES DE NÎMES AOC

Upgraded from a VDQS called Costières du Gard in 1986.

**RED** Simple, light, fruity wines are the norm, yet the best are round, aromatic, and spicy.

🍇 A maximum of 40% (each) Carignan and

Cinsault, a minimum of 25% Grenache, and at least 20% (in total or each) of Mourvèdre and Syrah

🍷 2–3 years (average wines), 3–8 years (better *cuvées*)

**WHITE** Fresh, soft, but uninspiring. These wines may be sold from December 1 following the harvest without any mention of *primeur* or *nouveau*.

🍇 A blend of at least two varieties, including Bourboulenc, Clairette, Grenache, Macabéo, Marsanne, Roussanne, a maximum of 30%

Ugni Blanc (not be permitted as of 2010), Vermentino, and a maximum of 10% Viognier

🍷 1–2 years

**ROSÉ** Good-value dry wine with a delightful color and ripe fruit. These wines may be sold from December 1 following the harvest without any mention of *primeur* or *nouveau*.

🍇 A maximum of 40% (each) of Carignan and Cinsault, a minimum of 25% Grenache, at least 20% (in total or each) of Mourvèdre and Syrah, plus up to 10% (in total) of Clairette, Grenache Blanc, Bourboulenc, Ugni Blanc, Marsanne, Roussanne, Macabéo, Vermentino, and Viognier

🍷 Within 1–2 years

✓ *Château Amphoux* (Les Galion des Crêtes Elevé en Fûts de Chêne) • *Barbe-Caillette* (Haut Jovis) • *Château Grande Cassagne* • *Château Lamargue* (Aegidiane) • *Château La Tour de Beraud* • *Château Tuilerie* (Carte Blanche) • *Château de Valcombe* (Garence)

## COTEAUX DU LANGUEDOC AOC

This appellation consists of a collection of areas strung out across three *départements*, which gives rise to a variation in style, but the quality is remarkably consistent.

**RED** Full and honest red wines that make excellent everyday drinking. These wines may be sold as *primeur* or *nouveau* from the third Thursday of November following the harvest.

🍇 A minimum of 50% Grenache (itself limited to maximum of 40%), Lladoner Pelut, Mourvèdre, and Syrah (these last two must represent at least 10% of the entire blend), no more than 40% of either Carignan or Cinsault, plus a maximum of 10% (in total) Counoise, Grenache Gris, Terret, and Picpoul Noir

🍷 1–4 years

**WHITE** Getting better by the day, some wonderfully fresh, aromatic, dry white wines are being made by the appellation's younger *vignerons*, often with a little new oak and not infrequently from very old vines. These wines may be sold from December 1 of the vintage indicated without any mention of *primeur* or *nouveau*.

🍇 Bourboulenc, Clairette, Grenache Blanc, Picpoul, Marsanne, Roussanne, Vermentino, plus a maximum of 30% Macabéo, Terret Blanc, Carignan Blanc, and Ugni Blanc (growers may no longer plant Carignan Blanc, Macabéo, or Ugni Blanc)

**ROSÉ** These dry wines have good fruit and are far more enjoyable than many a pricey Provence rosé. These wines may be sold as *primeur* or *nouveau* from the third Thursday of November following the harvest.

🍇 As for red, plus the following may be included with the optional maximum 10%: Bourboulenc, Carignan Blanc, Clairette, Grenache, Macabéo, Marsanne, Roussanne, Ugni Blanc, and Vermentino

🍷 1–2 years

✓ *De l'Aiguelière* • *Mas de Bayle* (Grande Cuvée) • *Château Chenaie* (Le Douves Blanches) • *Château La Clotte-Fontaine* (Mouton) • *Château des Crès Ricards* (Les Hauts de Milési) • *Dupéré-Barrera* (Chien de Prairie) • *Château Daurion* (Prestige Elevé en Fûts de Chêne) • *CV La Fontesole* (Prieuré Saint-Hippolyte) • *De Ganoupiac* (Les Cresses) • *Château Grès Saint Paul* (Antonin) • *Mas*

*Haut-Buis* (Costa Caoude) • *Virgile Joly* (Virgile) • *Château de Lascaux* (Les Secrets) • *Mas Lumen* (La Sylve) • *Paul Mas* • *Château de Montpezat* (La Pharaonne) • *Château de la Négly* (L'Ancely) • *Peyre Rose* ◉ • *Prieuré St-Jean de Bébian* • *De Roquemale* • *CV de Saint-Saturnin* • *Mas de la Seranne* (Les Griottiers) • *Le Clos du Serres* (Le Florilège) • *De Serres Cabanis* (Bos de Canna) • *Les Souls* • *Château Le Thou* (Georges et Clem)

## COTEAUX DU LANGUEDOC (VILLAGE NAME) AOC

Except where stated, the wines bearing the names of the following villages conform to the requirements of Coteaux du Languedoc AOC.

### CABRIÈRES AOC

This is a single commune of steep schistous slopes in the center of the Clairette du Languedoc subappellation. Cabrières's production is dominated by the local *coopérative*. This village produces mostly rosé: a fine, firm, and racy wine that contains more Cinsault than other Languedoc rosés. A little red is also produced, and its *vin vermeil*, so called because of its vivid vermilion color, is best known.

✓ *Du Temple* (Jacques de Molay)

### LA CLAPE AOC

These red, white, and rosé wines come from vineyards on a limestone outcrop extending across five communes of the Aude *département* where the appellations of Coteaux du Languedoc and Corbières overlap. One of only two whites allowed under the Coteaux du Languedoc Villages appellation, it must be made from at least 60 percent Bourboulenc and Grenache Blanc. White La Clape can be full, fine, and golden or firm, with an attractive Mediterranean spice, and is generally more expensive than the red. But the latter is easily best, with its full, rich flavor and *vin de garde* style. The rosé is refreshing, light, and well worth seeking out.

✓ *Ferri Arnaud* (Romain Elevé en Fûts de Chêne) • *Château de la Négly* (La Falaise) • *Château Pech Redon* • *Château Rouquette-sur-Mer* (Henry Lapierre)

### COTEAUX DE LA MÉJANELLE AOC
#### *See* La Méjanelle AOC

### COTEAUX DE ST-CHRISTOL AOC
#### *See* St-Christol AOC

### COTEAUX DE VÉRARGUES AOC
#### *See* Vérargues AOC

### GRÈS DE MONTPELLIER AOC

New red-wine-only appellation as of the 2002 vintage, Grès de Montpellier effectively encompasses the Coteaux du Languedoc Villages designations of St-Christol, St-Drézéry, St-Georges-d'Orques, and Vérargues. It must be produced from at least 70 percent in total of Grenache (itself a minimum of 20 percent), Mourvèdre, Syrah, and up to 30 percent Carignan. Too early to provide a critique.

### LA MÉJANELLE AOC

This appellation, which may also be sold as Coteaux de la Méjanelle, covers four communes in an area once part of the Rhône delta—

river-smoothed boulders litter the vineyards. Rosé is permitted, but La Méjanelle produces mostly red wines of a dark, rich, and well-structured *vin de garde* style. Château de Flaugergues consistently ranks as the best.

✓ *Château de Flaugergues (Sommelière)*

## MONTPEYROUX AOC

This village is located on schistous hills next to St-Saturnin, just north of the Clairette du Languedoc subappellation. The style of all but the best of these red and rosé wines is firm and somewhat rustic, but they are honest and pleasing, and those recommended below rank among the finest in Languedoc.

✓ *D'Aupilhac • Des Grecaux (Hêméra) • Château de Lancyre (Vieilles Vignes)*

## PÉZENAS AOC

Prieuré de Saint-Jean-de-Bébian, owned by Chantal Lecouty and Jean-Claude Le Brun, former editors of the *Revue du Vin*, demonstrate the potential here (although still sold as a straight Coteaux du Languedoc AOC).

✓ *Prieuré de Saint-Jean-de-Bébian*

## PICPOUL-DE-PINET AOC

Covering six communes, this white-wine-only appellation must be made, as the name suggests, from 100 percent Picpoul, which in Pinet produces a lively young white that quickly tires, and thus must be drunk as young as possible. Gaujal is undoubtedly the best.

✓ *Château Font-Mars • CV de Florensac (Ressac Prestige) • Des Lauriers*

## PIC-ST-LOUP AOC

Red and rosé wines from 12 communes in Hérault and one in Gard, all in the vicinity of the *pic*, or peak, of Pic St-Loup, including some high-altitude locations that must rank among the coolest vineyards in southern France. Permitted grape varieties for Pic-St-Loup break from the norm—red wines must be made from a blend of at least two of the following: Grenache, Mourvèdre, and Syrah (no minimum or maximum restrictions), plus up to 10 percent Carignan and Cinsault (Counoise, Grenache Gris, Terret Noir, Picpoul Noir, and Lladoner Pelut are not allowed). The grapes for rosé are the same, except that Carignan is excluded and as much as 30 percent Cinsault may be used.

✓ *Devois du Claus (Elevé en Fûts de Chêne) • Foulaquier (Les Chalades) • Mas Gourdou (Les Roches Blanches) • De l'Hortus • Clos Marie • Morties (Que Sera Sera) • Château Taurus-Montel (Prestige Elevé en Fûts de Chêne)*

## QUATOURZE AOC

These sandy-soil vineyards just south of Narbonne overlap the Corbières appellation, but the wines, mostly red with some rosé, are rather stern and four-square, although the best can fill out and soften up with a few years in bottle. I have tasted nothing recommendable from this village since the last edition.

## ST-CHRISTOL AOC

Just north of Lunel, the calcareous-clay soil of St-Christol produces ripe, spicy, well-balanced red and rosé wines that may also be sold as Coteaux de St-Christol AOC. The local *coopérative* dominates production.

✓ *De la Coste* (Sélectionné) • *Guinand* (Elevé en Fûts de Chêne) • *Gabriel Martin • CV de St-Christol*

## ST-DRÉZÉRY AOC

Both red and rosé wines are allowed under this village appellation north of Montpellier, but I have encountered only reds, and those have been of a very modest quality.

## ST-GEORGES-D'ORQUES AOC

Just west of Montpellier, the St-Georges-d'Orques appellation extends over five communes and produces mostly red wines of very good color, plenty of fruit, and no little finesse for this unpretentious Languedoc appellation. A small quantity of rosé is also made, the best having a bouquet of dried flowers and some summer fruits on the palate.

✓ *Château de l'Engarran* (Quetton Saint-Georges) • *Château Icard* (Elevé en Fûts de Chêne) • *Les Quatre Pilas*

## ST-SATURNIN AOC

Named after the first bishop of Toulouse, these red and rosé wines come from three communes in the foothills of the Cévennes Mountains, just west of Montpeyroux, where deep-colored, fine, and full-flavored red wines are possible, if not always evident. Production is dominated by the *coopératives* of St-Félix-de-Lodez and St-Saturnin, the former specializing in a pleasant, slightly *pétillant* rosé, while the latter makes a *vin d'une nuit*, a light-bodied red that has been macerated for only one night.

✓ *Lucian • Virgile Joly*

## TERRASSES DE BÉZIERS AOC

Although the *syndicat* representing this appellation has existed since 1990, the wines are still a case of work in progress!

## TERRASSES DU LARZAC AOC

Terrasses du Larzac is another *coteaux* appellation that still has to put wines on the shelf bearing its own individual name. However, Le Mas de l'Ecriture already produces some of the most exciting wines in the south of France from these vineyards, albeit under the straight Coteaux du Languedoc AOC.

✓ *Mas Cal Demoura • Le Mas de l'Ecriture • Mas Jullien*

## TERRES DE SOMMIÈRES AOC

Yet another work in progress!

## VÉRARGUES AOC

Vérargues produces large quantities of quaffing, but otherwise unexceptional red and rosé wines from nine communes, four of which also constitute the Muscat de Lunel appellation. They are also sold as Coteaux de Vérargues AOC.

✓ *Château du Grès-St-Paul*

## CÔTES DE LA MALEPÈRE VDQS

Between the Razès *coopérative* and Domaines Virginie (Des Bruyère), this is becoming one of the fastest-rising, value-for-money, superb-quality appellations in Languedoc-Roussillon. Should be made an AOC.

**RED** Well-colored wines of medium to full body, with elegant, deliciously spicy fruit.

🍇 A minimum of 50% Merlot, at least 20% Cabernet Franc and Malbec, plus optional Cabernet Sauvignon, Cinsault, Grenache,

and Lladoner Pelut (Syrah is no longer allowed)

🍷 3–7 years

**ROSÉ** These attractive dry wines are totally different from the reds, due to the greater use and mellow effect of Grenache.

🍇 A minimum of 70% Cabernet Franc, Cinsault, and Grenache, plus optional Cabernet Sauvignon, Malbec, Merlot, and Syrah (Lladoner Pelut is no longer allowed, and growers must not plant any more Syrah)

🍷 1–3 years

✓ *Château de Barthe • Girard* (Neri) • *Château Guilhem* (Prestige) • *Château Guiraud*

## CÔTES DU CABARDÈS ET DE L'ORBIEL VDQS
### See Cabardès AOC

## CÔTES DU ROUSSILLON AOC

Situated south of Corbières, this appellation began to shrug off the reputation that typified the wines of the Midi long before Languedoc.

**RED** The best of these wines have a good color and a generosity of southern fruit, with the tiniest hint of vanilla and spice. They may be sold as *primeur* or *nouveau* from the third Thursday of November following the harvest.

🍇 A blend of at least three of the following varieties, no two of which may exceed 90% of the total: Carignan (60% maximum), Cinsault, Grenache, Lladoner Pelut, Macabéo (10% maximum), Mourvèdre, and Syrah (there must be at least 20% of Syrah and/or Mourvèdre)

🍷 3–8 years

**WHITE** The best of these floral wines were fat, and all too often lacked acidity, prior to the change of *encépagement* in 2002. (So was 2003, but that was the vintage, rather than the varietal mix.) They may be sold as *primeur* or *nouveau* from the third Thursday of November following the harvest.

🍇 At least 50% of Grenache, Macabéo, and Tourbat, plus a minimum of 20% Marsanne, Roussanne, and Vermentino (all varieties obligatory)

🍷 1–2 years

**ROSÉ** Fresh and attractive dry wines, these rosés may be sold as *primeur* or *nouveau* from the third Thursday of November following the harvest.

🍇 As for red

🍷 1–2 years

✓ *Alquier* (Des Filles) • *Mas Amiel • Mas des Baux* (Soleil) • *De Casenove • CV Catalans* (Dédicace, La Llose) • *Cazes Frères • Jaubert-Noury* (Château Planères) • *Joliette* (André Mercier) • *Lafage* (Le Vignon) • *Du Mas Rous* (Elevé en Fûts de Chêne) • *Mosse* (Tradition) • *CV de Passa* (Mas d'en Badie) • *Piquemal • Primo Palatum • Pujols* (La Montadella) • *Château de Rey* (Les Galets Roulés) • *Sarda-Malet • Sol-Payre* (Scelerata Ame Noire)

## CÔTES DU ROUSSILLON LES ASPRES AOC

New red-wine-only designation for Côtes du Roussillon (not Villages), Les Aspres must be produced from at least three varieties, with a minimum of 50 percent Grenache, Mourvèdre, and Syrah (the latter two representing at least 20 percent of the entire blend), plus a maximum of 20 percent Carignan. Too early to critique.

## CÔTES DU ROUSSILLON VILLAGES AOC

This appellation encompasses exclusively red wines from 25 villages along the Agly River and its hinterland, in the best area of the Côtes du Roussillon. The *encépagement* changed in 2003.

**RED** Just as good value as basic Côtes du Roussillon, the best can have even more character and finesse.

🍇 A blend of at least three of the following varieties, no two of which may exceed 90% of the total: Carignan (60% maximum), Cinsault, Grenache, Lladoner Pelut, Macabéo (10% maximum), Mourvèdre, and Syrah (furthermore, there must be at least 30% of Syrah and/or Mourvèdre)

⌛ 3–10 years

✓ *Château Aymerich* (Général Joseph Aymerich) • *Château de Caladroy* (La Juliane) • *Clot de L'Oum* (Saint Bart Vieilles Vignes) • *Clos des Fées* • *Força Real* (Hauts de Força) • *Gardiés* • *Haute Coutume* (Schistes de Trémoine) • *Mas de Lavail* (Tradition) • *Château Planezes* (Elevé en Fûts de Chêne) • *Des Schistes* (Tradition)

## CÔTES DU ROUSSILLON VILLAGES CARAMANY AOC

This super-value red wine conforms to the requirements of Côtes du Roussillon Villages, except for a minimum Syrah content and the stipulation that the Carignan must be vinified by *macération carbonique*. (This seemingly strange criterion stems from the fact that, in 1964, the local *coopérative* claimed to be the first in France to use this technique.)

**RED** Simply the fullest, richest, and longest-living wines of Roussillon, despite the *macération carbonique*, which just goes to prove how useful that process can be when used to lift the natural fruit of a wine instead of dominating it with pear-drop aromas.

🍇 As for Côtes du Roussillon Villages except that there must be at least 25% Syrah

⌛ 3–15 years

✓ *CV Catalans*

## CÔTES DU ROUSSILLON VILLAGES LESQUERDE AOC

Restricted to vines growing in the villages of Lansac, Lesquerde, and Rasiguères. It conforms to the requirements of Côtes du Roussillon Villages, except for some of the *encépagement* and the stipulation that the Carignan must be vinified by *macération carbonique* (*see* Côtes du Roussillon Caramany for explanation).

**RED** Rich, well-colored wines that deserve their own village designation.

🍇 As for Côtes du Roussillon Villages except that Macabéo is not allowed, and there must be at least 30% Syrah and Mourvèdre

⌛ 3–15 years

✓ *Semper* (Voluptas) • *CV de Tautavel* (Tradition)

## CÔTES DU ROUSSILLON VILLAGES TAUTAVEL AOC

Restricted to vines growing in the villages of Tautavel and Vingrau. It conforms to the requirements of Côtes du Roussillon Villages, except for some of the *encépagement*, the stipulation that at least 50 percent of the Carignan content must be vinified by *macération carbonique* (*see* Côtes du Roussillon Caramany for explanation), and the fact that the wines may not be released for sale prior to October 1 following the year of harvest.

**RED** Rich, well-colored wines that deserve their own village designation.

🍇 As for Côtes du Roussillon Villages except that Macabéo is not allowed, and there must be at least 20% Grenache and Lladoner Pelut, and no more than 50% Carignan

⌛ 3–15 years

✓ *Des Chênes* (La Carissa) • *Fontanel* (Prieuré Elevé en Fûts de Chêne)

## CÔTES DU ROUSSILLON VILLAGES LATOUR-DE-FRANCE AOC

This is a fine-value red wine that conforms to the requirements of Côtes du Roussillon Villages. Virtually the entire production of Latour-de-France used to be sold to, and through, the national French wine-shop group Nicolas, which was a great advantage when this village obtained its own appellation, as its seemingly cheeky name was already known the length and breadth of the country.

**RED** Full in color and body, these fine-value wines have a fruity flavor.

⌛ 3–15 years

✓ *De L'Ausseil* (La Capitelle)

## CRÉMANT DE LIMOUX AOC

This sparkling wine was introduced in 1989 to allow producers to decide the future name of their appellation: Blanquette de Limoux or Crémant de Limoux. The former relied primarily on the Mauzac grape and Crémant de Limoux on Chardonnay and Chenin Blanc. The choice was not merely about a name, but what direction and style the wine should follow. It was thought that Mauzac-based Blanquette de Limoux would take the slow lane while Chardonnay-influenced Crémant would be in the fast lane. By law, they should have made this decision by the end of 1994, but Crémant de Limoux did not take off as anticipated. Both styles deserve to exist.

**SPARKLING WHITE** Chardonnay tends to be the main base, with just enough Mauzac retained to assure a certain style, and Chenin Blanc is used as a natural form of acid adjustment. The wines are generally more refined than Blanquette de Limoux, and the best have a finesse that the more traditional products cannot match.

🍇 A maximum of 90% in total of Chardonnay and Chenin Blanc, including at least 20% of the latter, plus a maximum of 20% in total of Mauzac and Pinot Noir, with the latter restricted to no more than 10%

✓ *De l'Aigle* • *Sieur d'Arques* • *Veuve Tailhan*

## FAUGÈRES AOC

Although fair-sized, Faugères is an obscure and overlooked appellation, probably due to the fact that it was formerly known for *eau-de-vie* and fortified Muscat, with red wine a postwar development. Despite the similarity between the schistous, hillside vineyards and grape varieties here and in neighboring St-Chinian, the two appellations make distinctly different wines.

**RED** These rustic wines have a deep color and are heavy with the spicy, warm flavors of Cinsault and Carignan.

⌛ 3–10 years

**WHITE** Fresh, exotic fruits with a touch of zest.

🍇 A minimum of two grape varieties, including at least 30% Roussanne, plus Grenache Blanc, Marsanne, and Vermentino. Also permitted up to a maximum of 10% each are Clairette and (if planted before 2005) Bourboulenc, and (if planted before 1998) Carignan or Macabéo

⌛ 1–3 years

**ROSÉ** Small production of attractively colored, ripe, and fruity dry rosés. These wines may be sold from December 1 following the harvest without any mention of *primeur* or *nouveau*.

🍇 A maximum of 40% Carignan, and no more than 20% Cinsault, plus at least 20% Grenache and/or Lladoner Pelut, a minimum of 15% Syrah, and at least 5% Mourvèdre (furthermore Grenache, Lladoner Pelut, Mourvèdre, and Syrah represent at least 50% of the entire blend)

⌛ 3–10 years

✓ *Alquier* • *Château des Estanilles* • *Abbaye de Sylva Plana*

## FITOU AOC

When it was made an AOC in 1948, Fitou was fast asleep. But wine buyers beat a path to its desolate door in the early 1980s, making it the fastest-rising star in the Mediterranean firmament. It seems to have returned to its dozing state. The *encépagement* changed in 2001.

**RED** Even at the lowest level, these wines have a fine color and a spicy warmth of Grenache that curbs and softens the concentrated fruit and tannin of low-yielding Carignan.

🍇 A minimum of 30% Carignan, plus Mourvèdre, Syrah, and at least 30% Grenache and Lladoner Pelut; within this Carignan, Grenache, and Lladoner Pelut must account for at least 70% of the entire blend; and until 2007 there must be at least 10% Cinsault, while as of 2008 there must be at least 10% Mourvèdre (Macabéo and Terret Noir are no longer allowed)

⌛ 3–6 years (4–10 years in exceptional cases)

✓ *Bertrand Bergé* • *Château des Erles* • *CV de Mont Tauch* (Seigneur de Don Neuve) • *Château de Nouvelles* • *De la Rochelière* (Noblesse du Temps) • *De Roland*

## FRONTIGNAN AOC
### *See* Muscat de Frontignan AOC

## GRAND ROUSSILLON AOC

The largest appellation producing the least amount of wine, Grand Roussillon is a VDN that encompasses 100 communes, yet produces as little as 330 cases (30 hectoliters) of wine per year. This has nothing to do with low yields or a strict selection process—the appellation is apparently used as a sort of *sous marque* or dumping ground for the inferior wines produced by the better VDNs within its boundaries.

🍇 Muscat d'Alexandrie, Muscat Petits Grains, Grenache (Gris, Blanc, and Noir), Macabéo, Tourbat, plus up to 10% (in total) of Carignan, Cinsault, Syrah, and Listan

## GRAND ROUSSILLON "RANCIO" AOC
### See Grand Roussillon AOC

## LIMOUX AOC
In 1993, Limoux became the first French AOC to insist on barrel fermentation, and some fabulous successes quickly established an enviable reputation for the Chardonnay-dominated wines of this appellation. The only question now is, will Limoux have equal success with Chenin Blanc? A new red Limoux was introduced in 2004.

**RED** Too early to tell. We need to see more wines made by different producers, since the cooperative Cave Anne de Joyeuse currently churns out some 70% of the total production.

🍇 Minimum of 50% Merlot, plus Cabernet Franc, Cabernet Sauvignon, Carignan, Grenache, Malbec and Syrah. Carignan must not exceed 10% and is due to be phased out by 2010. There must be at least three varieties, no two of which may exceed 90% of the blend.

🍷 3–6 years

**WHITE** Although every wine must contain at least 15 percent Mauzac, you will encounter supposedly pure Chardonnay and Chenin Blanc varietal wines (and Mauzac, of course). This is explained by the European Union law that requires that a pure varietal wine must contain at least 85 percent of the grape named. Chardonnay varietals are sherbetty-fresh with a zesty style at minimum; the best are beautifully rich, with succulent, lemony-oaky fruit and mouth-watering acidity. The pure Mauzac from Rives-Blanques makes me wonder whether it would not be better for producers to focus on this, their local grape, rather than resign themselves to making yet another Chardonnay in a world awash with that variety. This was not initially my view. Tasted when first released, the Chardonnay clearly outshines the Mauzac, thus it is little wonder that the Cuvée Occitania vacuums up so many medals for Rives-Blanques. However, follow them in bottle for just 12 months, and the Mauzac evolves into the more expressive wine.

🍇 A minimum of 15% Mauzac, plus Chardonnay and Chenin Blanc

🍷 1–2 years

✓ *D'Antugnac* (Gravas) • *Rives-Blanques* (Dédicace) • *Sieur d'Arques* (Toques et Clochers)

## MAURY AOC
Despite the long list of possibilities, these fortified wines are mostly pure Grenache, a fact that is recognized by the gradual increase in the compulsory percentage of this grape—the minimum was just 50 percent 10 years ago.

**RED/WHITE/ROSÉ/TAWNY** Pale and intricate wines, they have a combination of tangy, toasty, berry flavors and nutty-raisiny richness.

🍇 At least 75% Grenache (a minimum of 70% for pre-2000 vintages), a maximum of 10% Macabéo (15% for pre-2000 vintages), plus Grenache Gris, Grenache Blanc, Muscat à Petits Grains, Muscat d'Alexandrie, Tourbat, and a combined maximum of 10% of Carignan, Cinsault, Syrah, and Listan Negra

🍷 10–30 years

✓ *Mas Amiel* • *Jean-Louis Lafage* (Prestige Vieilli en Fûts de Chêne) • *Pouderoux*

## MAURY "RANCIO" AOC
### See Maury AOC

## MINERVOIS AOC
North of Corbières and adjoining the western extremity of the Coteaux du Languedoc, the rocky Minervois area has the typically hot and arid air of southern France. Elevated to full AOC status in February 1985, its vineyards are divided into zones. As in Corbières, these are not official, but one day they may in part or as a whole join La Livinière, which was recognized as a *cru* in its own right in 1999. The zones are: L'Argent Double (rough, rugged vineyards amid rocky outcrops in the arid heart of Minervois); La Clamoux (a cooler western area with a touch more rainfall than most Minervois zones, with Grenache and Syrah doing well, particularly on the higher-altitude vineyards); La Clause (rugged, mountain climate and stony, *terra rosa* soil combine to produce rather rustic *vins de garde* in the north of Minervois); Les Côtes Noires (under a harsh mountain climate, these high-altitude vineyards situated in the northwestern corner of Minervois are better suited to the production of white wine than of red); Le Petit Causse (when it can get enough moisture, Mourvèdre does well on these baking-hot, sheltered, limestone slopes in the arid heart of Minervois—La Livinière is located at the heart of Le Petit Causse); Les Serres (very dry, stony vineyards over limestone subsoil, mostly planted with Carignan). The *encépagement* for red and rosé changed in 2003.

**RED** At worst, these wines are rough and ready for an AOC, but some of the best domaines also produce *vins de pays* that are better than the Minervois of other properties, thus their Minervois can be very good indeed.

🍇 A minimum of 40% Grenache, Lladoner Pelut, Mourvèdre, and Syrah (these last two must represent at least 10% of the entire blend, and at least 20% as from 2006), plus optional Aspiran Noir, Carignan, Cinsault, Picpoul Noir, and Terret Noir

🍷 1–5 years

**WHITE** Less than one percent of Minervois is white. A simple, dry, and fruity wine fermented at cooler temperatures than was once standard, it is now fresher and more aromatic.

🍇 Bourboulenc, Grenache Blanc, Macabéo, Marsanne, Roussanne, Vermentino, plus not more than 20% Clairette, Muscat à Petits Grains (itself limited to a maximum of 10%), Picpoul, and Terret Blanc

🍷 Within 1 year

**ROSÉ** Most of these are good-value wines with a pretty pink color and a dry, fruity flavor.

🍇 A minimum of 40% Grenache, Lladoner Pelut, Mourvèdre, and Syrah (these last two must represent at least 10% of the entire blend, and at least 20% as from 2006), plus optional Aspiran Noir, Carignan, Cinsault, Picpoul Noir, and Terret Noir, with no more than 10% Bourboulenc, Clairette, Grenache Blanc, Macabéo, Marsanne, Roussanne, Muscat à Petits Grains, Picpoul, Terret Blanc, and Vermentino

🍷 Within 1 year

✓ *Des Aires Hautes* • *Borie de Maurel* (Sylla) • *Le Cazal* (Le Paps de Zarat) • *Château d'Oupia* (Oppius) • *Primo Palatum* • *Du Roc* (Passion) • *La Tour Buisse*

## MINERVOIS LA LIVINIÈRE AOC
Located in Le Petit Causse, the central-northern zone of Minervois, La Livinière was in 1999 the first *cru* in this appellation to be recognized in its own right. The vines grow on the best areas of the Petit Causse, the sheltered, limestone cliffs that skirt the foot of the Montagne Noir at a height of 460 feet (140 meters).

**RED** Where there is sufficient finesse to match the structure of these wines, they represent some of Minervois's best *vins de garde*.

🍇 A minimum of 40% Grenache, Lladoner Pelut, Mourvèdre, and Syrah (these last two must represent at least 10% of the entire blend, and at least 20% as from 2006), plus optional Aspiran Noir, Carignan, Cinsault, Picpoul Noir, and Terret Noir

🍷 2–10 years

✓ *Clos de L'Escandil* • *C. V. des Crus de Haut-Minervois* (Gaïa) • *Château Faiteau*

## MUSCAT DE FRONTIGNAN AOC
It is claimed that the Marquis de Lur-Saluces visited Frontignan in 1700 and it inspired him to make sweet wines at Château d'Yquem in Sauternes, but Muscat de Frontignan is no longer botrytized—it is a fortified wine. Muscat de Frontignan may either be a *vin doux naturel* (VDN) or a *vin de liqueur* (VDL). In the latter, the spirit is added to the grape juice before any fermentation whatsoever can take place. If the label does not differentiate between the two, the small green tax mark on the cap should bear the letters VDN or VDL.

**WHITE** The VDNs are delightful, golden-colored, raisiny-rich, sweet, and delicious wines that have a succulent, honeyed aftertaste with a somewhat fatter style than those of Beaumes, although many lack its finesse. The VDLs are much sweeter.

🍇 Muscat Doré de Frontignan

🍷 1–3 years

✓ *Château des Aresquiers* • *Château de la Peyrade*

## MUSCAT DE LUNEL AOC
Situated on limestone terraces northeast of Montpellier, this undervalued VDN approaches Frontignan in terms of pure quality.

**WHITE/ROSÉ** Lighter than Frontignan, these wines nevertheless have fine, fragrant Muscat aromas of great delicacy and length.

🐝 Muscat Blanc & Rosé à Petits Grains

🍷 1–3 years

✓ *Lacoste* (Clos Bellevue, Passerillé) • *CV du Muscat de Lunel* (Prestige)

## MUSCAT DE MIREVAL AOC

This is a little-seen VDN appellation.

**WHITE** Light and sweet wines that can have a better balance and (relatively) more acidity than those from neighboring Frontignan.

🐝 Muscat Blanc à Petits Grains

🍷 1–3 years

✓ *Château d'Exindre* (Vent d'Anges) • *Du Mas Neuf*

## MUSCAT DE RIVESALTES AOC

This appellation should not be confused with the blended Rivesaltes VDNs that bear no mention of the Muscat grape.

**WHITE/ROSÉ** Rich, ripe, grapey-raisiny wines that are very consistent in quality.

🐝 Muscat Blanc à Petits Grains, Muscat d'Alexandrie

🍷 1–3 years

🅱✓ *Cazes Frères* 🅑 • *Des Chênes* • *Cornelianum* • *Jean Estavel* (Prestige) • *Lafage* • *Laporte* • *Château de Nouvelles* • *Sarda-Malet* • *Des Schistes* • *Arnaud de Villeneuve*

## MUSCAT DE ST-JEAN-DE-MINERVOIS AOC

This tiny subappellation of Minervois produces a little *vin doux naturel* that used to be grossly underrated but can be excellent.

**WHITE/ROSÉ** These golden wines have a balanced sweetness and an apricot flavor.

🐝 Muscat Blanc & Rosé à Petits Grains

🍷 1–3 years

✓ *De Barroubio* • *La Muscat* (Petit Grain)

## RIVESALTES AOC

This appellation represents half of the *vin doux naturel* produced in France. Optional legally defined terms include *ambré* for an oxidative style of tawny-colored Rivesaltes; *tuilé* for an oxidative red; and *grenat* for a reductive-style red that must not be bottled any later than March 1 of the second year. *Hors d'age* requires a minimum of five years' aging.

**RED/ROSÉ** The warm, brick-red glow of these wines belies their astringent-sweet, chocolate, and cherry-liqueur flavor and drying, tannic finish.

🐝 A minimum of 50% (for oxidative style) or 75% (for reductive style) Grenache, plus Grenache Blanc, Grenache Gris, Tourbat, with a maximum of 10% Carignan, Cinsault, Palomino, and Syrah

🍷 10–40 years

**WHITE/TAWNY** Because much of the red version can be lightened after lengthy maturation in wood, all Rivesaltes eventually merge into one tawny style with time. The whites do not, of course, have any tannic astringency and are more oxidative and raisiny, with a resinous, candied-peel character.

🐝 Grenache Blanc, Grenache Gris, Macabéo, Muscat Blanc à Petits Grains, Muscat d'Alexandrie, Muscat Romain, Tourbat (the Muscat varieties must not exceed 20% of the entire blend in total or separately)

🍷 10–20 years

✓ *Du Mas Alart* (Ambré Hors d'Age) • *Des Chênes* • *Cazes Frères* 🅑 • *Gardies* •

*Château de Nouvelles* (Tuilé) • *Sarda-Malet* (La Carbasse) • *Château de Sau* (Ambré Hors d'Age) • *Terrassous* (Ambré Vinifié en Fûts de Chêne) • *Arnaud de Villeneuve* (Ambré Hors d'Age)

## RIVESALTES "RANCIO" AOC

*See* Rivesaltes AOC

## ROQUEBRUN ST-CHINIAN AOC

One of two multicommunal *terroirs* within the St-Chinian appellation, established in 2005. The first wines (from 2004) were not available until 2006. Most production monopolized by the Cave de Roquebrun cooperative. Schistous hillsides; compulsory hand-harvesting.

**RED** No experience, as yet, but will be more Syrah-influenced than the Berlou AOC.

🐝 A minimum of 70% Syrah, Grenache, and Mourvèdre, of which Syrah must be at least 25%, Grenache at least 20%, and Mourvèdre no more than 30%

🍷 2–7 years

## ST-CHINIAN AOC

This excellent-value appellation is the nearest that native southern French grapes come to Bordeaux. Similar varieties from comparable schistous hillsides in neighboring Faugères make an entirely different, far more rustic wine.

**RED** Relatively light in color and weight, these wines have an elegance that belies their Mediterranean origin.

🐝 At least 50% in total of Grenache, Lladoner Pelut, Mourvèdre, and Syrah, plus a maximum of 40% Carignan and no more than 30% Cinsault

🍷 2–6 years

**WHITE** Crisp, grassy fruits with more minerality than most whites made in Languedoc-Roussillon.

🐝 A minimum of two grape varieties, including at least 30% Grenache Blanc, plus Marsanne, Roussanne, and Vermentino. Bourboulenc, Carignan, Clairette, and Macabéo are allowed, but new plantations are not authorized.

🍷 1–2 years

**ROSÉ** Dry and delicately fruity rosés with an attractive, fragrant bouquet and flavor. May be sold from December 1 following the harvest without any mention of *primeur* or *nouveau*.

🐝 Same as red

🍷 1–3 years

✓ *Clos Bagatelle* • *Berloup* (Vignes Royales) • *Mas Canet Valette* • *De Canimals Le Haut* • *Mas Champart* • *Château La Dournie* • *Fontaine Marcousse* • *Des Jougla* (Vieihs Arrasics) • *Navare* (Olivier)

## VIN DE FRONTIGNAN AOC

*See* Muscat de Frontignan AOC

---

## MORE GREEN WINES

In addition to the producers recommended in this directory that are either biodynamic or organic, there are also the following. No negative inference of quality should be taken from the fact that they are not featured among my recommended producers. There are a number that have been recommended in other editions, and still make some fine wines, but have been culled out to make room for others.

**Biodynamic**

*Beau-Thorey* (Corconne), *De Bila-Haut* (Latour de France), *De Combebelle* (Villespassans), *Jean-Claude Daumond* (Vendargues), *De Fontedicto* (Caux), *De Malaïgue* (Uzés), *Des Perrières* (Manduel), *Le Petit Domaine de Gimios* (St Jean de Minervois), *St Julien* (Azille), *Sylvain Saux* (Lauraguel)

**Organic**

*Cabanis* (Beauvoisin), *De Caillan* (Bessan), *De Camplazens* (Combaillaux), *Château de Caraguilhes* (St Laurent de la Cabrerisse), *De Clairac* (Cazouls lès Béziers), *Combes-Giraud* (Valros), *Costeplane* (Cannes et Clairan), *CV les Côteaux de Creissan* (Creissan), *Jean Bigou* (Rouvenac), *Blanquette Beirieu* (Roquetaillade), *Bourguet* (Béziers), *Alain Bousquet* (St Etienne de Gourgas), *Couderc* (Neffies), *Mas Coutelou* (Puimisson), *Du Farlet* (Meze), *La Fon de Lacan* (St Pargoire), *Jacques Frélin Vignobles* (Villeneuve lès Béziers), *Grand Bourry* (Le Cailar), *La Grangette* (Castelnau de Guers), *De Gressac* (Verfeuil), *Mas de Janiny* (St Bauzille de la Sylve), *Mas Jullien* (Jonquières), *CV La Clairette* (Bellegarde), *La Tour* (Beaucaire), *Du Lac* (Montescot), *CV Languedoc Roussillon* (Montpellier), *Bernard Legoy* (Condat-en-Combrailles), *CV Les Gres* (Vendargues), *De Litenis* (St Jean de Fos), *Lou Pas d'Estrech* (St Christol de Rodières), *Loupia* (Pennautier), *Louvet/Cellier du Languedoc Vins Distribution* (Narbonne), *Château Maris* (La Livinière), *Maurel Vedeau* (Servian), *Antoine Maurel* (Conques-sur-Orbiel), *De Mayrac* (Couiza), *De Montahuc*

(St Jean de Minervois), *Croix de Bel-Air* (Marseillan), *De Montjouy* (Florensac), *CV de Montpeyroux* (Montpeyroux), *Ochre Rouge* (Dions), *Château du Parc* (Pezenas), *Pastouret* (Bellegarde), *Château Pech-Latt* (Lagrasse), *De Petit Roubié* (Pinet), *Château des Auzines* (Auzines), *Bannières* (Castries), *Du Mas Barjac* (Monteils), *Bassac* (Puissalicon), *De Malavieille* (Merifons), *Peyre-Rose* (St Pargoire), *De Picheral* (Mus), *Château Roubia* (Roubia), *La Solana* (Festes), *Des Soulié* (Assignan), *St Alban* (Neffies), *Château St Auriol* (Lézignan-Corbières), *De St Blaise* (Cessenon), *Ste Marie des Pins* (Verzeille), *Des Syles* (Béziers) *La Triballe* (Guzargues), *De Valescure* (Aimargues), *Abbaye de Valmagne* (Villeveyrac), *Château Ventaiolle* (Ventenac-Cabardes), *Château Veredus* (Cruscades), *Zumbaum-Tomasi* (Claret), *De l'Ametlier* (Pézenas), *Anthéa* (Sallès d'Aude), *La Batteuse* (Antugnac), *Château Bel Air La Côte* (Beauvoisin), *Château Belaussel* (Lagrasse), *Belles Croix Robin* (Guzargues), *Château Bousquette* (Cessenon-sur-Orb), *De Brau* (Villemoustaussou), *De Buzarens* (Assas), *Arnaudiés* (Ceret), *Batlle-Jacquet* (Fourques), *Carle-Courty* (Millas), *Henri-Albert Foxonet* (Toulouges), *Joliette* (Espira de l'Agly), *Franck Jorel* (St Paul de Fenouillet), *Château de L'Ou* (Montescot), *Laguerre* (St Martin de Fenouillet), *Le Casot de Mailloles* (Banyuls-sur-Mer), *Lenan* (Trouillas), *Nivet-Galinier* (Toulouges), *Jean-Michel Paraire* (Fourques), *Olivier Pithon* (Calce), *De la Rourède* (Fourques), *Du Soula* (St Martin de Fenouillet), *Clos St Martin* (Bompas)

# PROVENCE AND CORSICA

*If any wine does not travel, it has to be Provence rosé. But this probably has more to do with the romance surrounding the wine than with the wine itself. The best Provençal wines are red, and they can be truly splendid.*

YOU CAN FORGET MOST PROVENCE ROSÉ. It may come in an exotically shaped bottle, but exotic is the last word that could be used to describe its dull, flabby contents. They have been making wine here for more than 2,600 years, and by the time the Romans arrived, in 125BC, it was already so good that they immediately exported it back to Rome. But ask yourself this question: do you think that wine was a rosé? Of course not; Provence rosé is a relatively recent phenomenon and, some would cynically say, one that was deliberately designed to swindle the gold-draped *nouveau riche* who flock here.

Rosé still represents more than half of all Provençal production, although sales have declined in recent years, as the once-

CORSICAN VINEYARDS
*These vineyards of Domaine de Valrose at Borgo, near the east coast, are typical of the Corsican landscape. The east-coast plains are backed by dramatic mountains, and palm trees proliferate.*

exclusive resorts become more accessible to the sophisticated middle classes, who recognize how dull these wines are. Quality improved in the 1980s, but has reached a plateau and, without resorting to actually acidifying the wines, modern vinification techniques will never be able to rid them of the dusty flabbiness that is their sunny southern heritage.

## THE TRUE CLASSIC WINES OF PROVENCE

For most people, Provence evokes the beaches of St.-Tropez or the rich, *bouillabaisse*-laden aromas of backstreet Marseille, but there are other experiences to be had in this sun-blessed corner of southern France. For while the wines of Provence may not have the classic status of Burgundy or Bordeaux, the reds, such as the magnificent Bandol, the darkly promising Bellet, and the aptly named Cassis, have an abundance of spice-charged flavors that show more than a touch of class. Silly-shaped bottles are being discarded by the more serious winemakers who find the classic,

## FACTORS AFFECTING TASTE AND QUALITY

### LOCATION
Provence is situated in the southeast of France, between the Rhône delta and the Italian border. A farther 68 miles (110 kilometers) southeast lies Corsica.

### CLIMATE
Winters are mild, as are springs, which can also be humid. Summers are hot and stretch into long, sunny falls. A vine requires 1,300 hours of sunshine in one growing season—1,500 hours is preferable, but in Provence, it luxuriates in an average of 3,000 hours. The close proximity of the Mediterranean, however, is also capable of inducing sharp fluctuations in the weather. Rain is spread over a limited number of days in fall and winter.

### ASPECT
The vineyards run down hillsides and on to the plains.

### SOIL
The geology of Provence is complex. Many ancient soils have undergone chemical changes and numerous new soils have been created. Sand, red sandstone, and granite are, however, the most regular common denominators, with limestone outcrops that often determine the extent of superior *terroirs*: the Var *département* has mica-schist, chalky scree, and chalky tufa as well as granite hillsides; there are excellent flinty-limestone soils at Bandol; and pudding stones (conglomerate pebbles) that are rich in flint at Bellet. The south of Corsica is mostly granite, while the north is schistous, with a few limestone outcrops and deposits of sandy and alluvial soils in between.

### VITICULTURE AND VINIFICATION
All the vines used to be planted in *gobelet* fashion, but most are now trained on wires. The recent trend toward Cabernet Sauvignon has stopped, although many excellent wines are still made from this grape. The current vogue is to reestablish a true Provençal identity by relying exclusively (where possible) on local varieties, and the laws have been changed to encourage this particular evolution. Much of the rosé has been improved by modern cool-vinification techniques, although most remains tired and flabby.

### GRAPE VARIETIES
Aragnan, Aramon, Aramongris, Barbarossa, Barbaroux, Barbaroux Rosé, Bourboulenc, Braquet, Brun-Fourcat, Cabernet Sauvignon, Calitor (*syn.* Pecoui-touar), Carignan, Castets, Chardonnay, Cinsault (*syn.* Plant d'Arles), Clairette, Clairette à Gros Grains, Clairette à Petits Grains, Clairette de Trans, Colombard, Counoise, Doucillon, Durif, Fuella, Grenache, Grenache Blanc, Marsanne, Mayorquin, Mourvèdre, Muscat d'Aubagne, Muscat Blanc à Petits Grains, Muscat de Die, Muscat de Frontignan, Muscat de Hambourg, Muscat de Marseille, Muscat Noir de Provence, Muscat Rosé à Petits Grains, Nielluccio, Panse Muscade, Pascal Blanc, Petit-Brun, Picardan, Picpoul, Pignerol, Sauvignon Blanc, Sémillon, Sciacarello, Syrah, Téoulier (*syn.* Manosquin), Terret Blanc, Terret Gris (*syn.* Terret-Bourret), Terret Noir, Terret Ramenée, Tibouren (*syn.* Tibourenc), Ugni Blanc, Ugni Rosé, Vermentino (*syn.* Rolle)

## RECENT PROVENÇAL AND CORSICAN VINTAGES

**2006** No excessive heat, and no drought, resulted in an excellent vintage that is at least the equal of 2005, particularly for reds and rosés.

**2005** Whites and rosés are deeper-colored than usual, but very pure and fresh. Reds are also well colored, with plenty of fruit and finesse.

**2004** Soft, low-acid rosés, but much better, fuller reds.

**2003** The year of the heatwave meant extremely variable results in Provence, where even the best reds are all too often overalcoholic and lacking in elegance.

**2002** Wet at best, floods at worst, with few exceptional wines in Provence (a good rosé year!), but good in Corsica for Vin de Corse (particularly, though not exclusively, for whites), Patrimonio, and Muscat du Cap Corse.

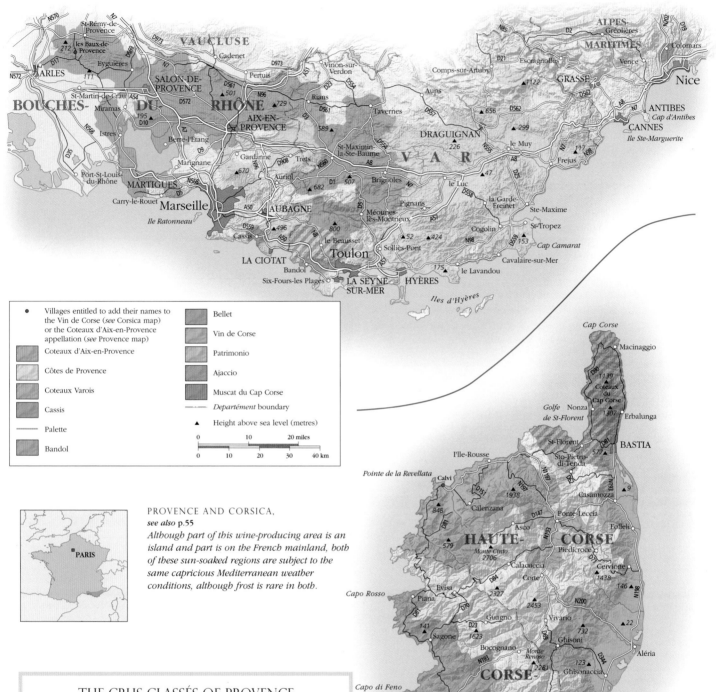

PROVENCE AND CORSICA,
see also p.55

*Although part of this wine-producing area is an island and part is on the French mainland, both of these sun-soaked regions are subject to the same capricious Mediterranean weather conditions, although frost is rare in both.*

## THE CRUS CLASSÉS OF PROVENCE

*Provence is the only region outside Bordeaux to boast a cru classé system. The cru classé concept was conceived by Napoléon III, hence the 1855 classification. One hundred years later, 14 domaines in the Côtes de Provence somehow managed to arrange their own classification, endorsed by ministerial decree on July 20, 1955. These domaines were selected on the basis of the following criteria: ancestral inheritance; family ownership; historic buildings and reputation; the soil, vineyard, winery, and cellar; the wine produced; and the quality sought for more than one century. The crus classés of Côtes de Provence are:*

• Château de Brégançon (Bormes les Mimosas): 124 acres/50ha • Clos Cibonne (Le Pradet): 34½ acres/14ha • Château du Galoupet (La Londe): 163 acres/66ha • Domaine du Jas d'Esclans (La Motte): 156 acres/63ha • Château de Mauvanne (Hyères): 124 acres/50ha • Château Minuty (Gassin): 161 acres/65ha • Clos Mireille (La Londe): 131 acres/53ha • Domaine de Rimauresq (Pignans): 91 acres/37ha • Château de Roubine (Lorgues): 173 acres/70ha • Château Ste. Marguerite (La Londe): 62 acres/25ha • Château de St. Martin (Taradeau): 94 acres/38ha • Château St. Maur (Cogolin): 119 acres/48ha • Château Ste. Roseline (Les Arcs-sur-Argens): 222 acres/90ha • Château de Selle (Taradeau): 151 acres/61ha

### Legend

• Villages entitled to add their names to the Vin de Corse (*see* Corsica map) or the Coteaux d'Aix-en-Provence appellation (*see* Provence map)

Coteaux d'Aix-en-Provence

Côtes de Provence

Coteaux Varois

Cassis

Palette

Bandol

Bellet

Vin de Corse

Patrimonio

Ajaccio

Muscat du Cap Corse

*Département* boundary

▲ Height above sea level (metres)

understated lines of Bordeaux- and Burgundy-style bottles better reflect the quality of their wines.

The top estates of the Riviera produce red wines of a far more serious caliber than might be expected from an area better known for its play than its work. Maximum yields are low, however, and the potential for quality can be high. The smaller AOCs of Bandol, Bellet, and Palette are restricted to a maximum of 180 cases per acre (40 hectoliters per hectare), which is very modest for a region that could easily average more than double this amount. Even the all-embracing AOCs of Côtes de Provence and Coteaux d'Aix-en-Provence are absolutely full of fine vineyards capable of producing the exciting red wine that must surely be Provence's future.

## CORSICA—"THE ISLE OF BEAUTY"
In Corsica, the advent of France's *vin de pays* system meant that around one-third of the island's vineyards were uprooted and put

to better use. If the *vin de pays* system was intended to encourage the production of superior-quality wines from the bottom of the market upward, then here at least it has been successful, for this island is no longer the generous contributor to Europe's "wine-lake" it used to be.

The days when Corsica's wines were fit only for turning into industrial spirit are long gone, but nor is this a potentially fine wine region. Just 15 percent of its vineyards are AOC, and these yield barely more than 5 percent of Corsica's total wine production. Although this is a fair and accurate reflection of its true potential, most critics agree that even within the modest limits of *vin de pays* production there should be many more individually expressive domaines. What has restricted their numbers is, however, something few are willing to talk about—intimidation and extortion by the local Mafia, which has caused more than one brave new Corsican venture to founder.

---

## THE APPELLATIONS OF
# PROVENCE AND CORSICA

**Note** * denotes producers who are particularly recommended for rosé.

## AJACCIO AOC
This is a predominantly red-wine appellation on the west coast of Corsica.

**RED** When successful, this will inevitably be a medium-bodied Sciacarello wine with a good bouquet.

🍇 At least 60% (in total) of Barbarossa, Nielluccio, Vermentino, and Sciacarello (the last of which must account for at least 40%), plus a maximum of 40% (in total) of Grenache, Cinsault, and Carignan (the last of which must not exceed 15%)

**WHITE** Decently dry and fruity, the best have a good edge of Ugni Blanc acidity.

**ROSÉ** Average to good-quality dry rosé with a typical southern roundness.

🍇 As for the red

🍷 All wines: 1–3 years

☑️ *Comte Abbatucci* (Faustine Abbatucci) • *Comte Peraldi*

## BANDOL AOC

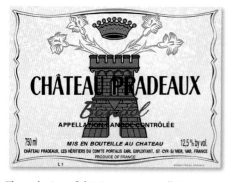

The red wine of this Provence appellation is a true *vin de garde* and deserves recognition. The white wine *encépagement* changed in 2003.

**RED** The best of these wines have a dark purple-black color, a deep and dense bouquet, masses of spicy-plummy Mourvèdre fruit, and complex after-aromas that include vanilla, cassis,

cinnamon, violets, and sweet herbs.

🍇 A blend of at least two of the following: Mourvèdre, Grenache, and Cinsault, of which a minimum of 50% Mourvèdre is obligatory, plus no more than 15% in total or 10% individually of Syrah and Carignan

🍷 3–12 years

**WHITE** These dry wines are now fresher and more fragrant than they were, but they are nothing special compared with the reds.

🍇 A minimum of 20% (50% as from 2011) Clairette, plus 40% (60% as from 2011) of Bourboulenc and/or Ugni Blanc (Sauvignon Blanc is no longer allowed)

🍷 Within 1 year

**ROSÉ** Well-made, attractive dry rosés, with body, structure, and a fine individual character.

🍇 As for red but no minimum Mourvèdre content

🍷 1–2 years

☑️ *Château des Baumelles* • *Bunan* (Moulin des Costes Charriage, Château la Rouvière, Mas de la Rouvière) • *Dupéré-Barrera* (India) • *du Gros'Noré* • *de l'Hermitage* • *de la Laidière* • *Lafran-Veyrolles* • *Château de Pibarnon* • *Château Pradeaux* • *Château Ste.-Anne* ◉ • *des Salettes* • *La Suffrene* (Les Lauves) • *Tempier* • *Terrebrune* • *Vannières*

## LES BAUX DE PROVENCE AOC
Excellent red and rosé wines, sold under the subappellation of Coteaux d'Aix-en-Provence Les Baux until 1995, when they were given their own AOC and the requirements changed.

**RED** Deep, dark, and rich, with creamy-spicy cherry and plum flavors.

🍇 A minimum of 60% Grenache, Mourvèdre and Syrah, no two varieties of which must account for more than 90% of the entire blend, plus a maximum 30% in total of one or more of the following: Carignan, Cinsault and Counoise, with a maximum of 20% Cabernet Sauvignon

🍷 4–10 years

**ROSÉ** De la Vallongue is rich and ripe.

🍇 A minimum of 60% Cinsault, Grenache, and Syrah, no two varieties of which must account for more than 90% of the entire blend, plus a maximum of 30% in total of one or more of the following: Carignan, Counoise, and Mourvèdre, with a maximum of 10% Cabernet Sauvignon

🍷 1–2 years

☑️ *Hauvette* ◉ • *Mas Sainte-Berthe* (Louis David) • *de la Vallongue** ◉

## BELLET AOC

This tiny Provence appellation is cooled by Alpine winds and produces exceptionally fragrant wines for such a southerly location.

**ROSÉ** Fine, floral, dry rosés that are exceptionally fresh and easy to drink.

🍇 Braquet, Fuella, Cinsault, plus up to 40% (in total) of Grenache, Rolle, Ugni Blanc, Mayorquin, Clairette, Bourboulenc, Chardonnay, Pignerol, and Muscat à Petits Grains

🍷 1–2 years

**RED** These wines have a good color and structure, with a well-perfumed bouquet.

🍇 Braquet, Fuella, Cinsault, plus up to 40% (in total) of Grenache, Rolle, Ugni Blanc, Mayorquin, Clairette, Bourboulenc, Chardonnay, Pignerol, and Muscat à Petits Grains

🍷 4–10 years

**WHITE** Fine, firm yet fragrant, and highly aromatic, dry white wines of unbelievable class and finesse.

Rolle, Ugni Blanc, Mayorquin, plus up to 40% Clairette, Bourboulenc, Chardonnay, Pignerol, and Muscat à Petits Grains

🍇 3–7 years

✓ *Château de Bellet* • *Clos Saint-Vincent* (Clos)

## CASSIS AOC

This is a decent but overpriced Provence appellation located around a beautiful rocky bay, a few miles east of Marseille. In all but a few enterprising estates, these vineyards are on the decline.

**RED** These solid, well-colored red wines can age, but most do not improve.

🍇 Grenache, Carignan, Mourvèdre, Cinsault, Barbaroux, plus up to 10% (in total) of Terret Noir, Terret Gris, Terret Blanc, Terret Ramenée, Aramon, and Aramon Gris

**WHITE** These dry white wines have an interesting bouquet of herby aromas of gorse and bracken, but are usually flabby and unbalanced on the palate. However, Bagnol and St.-Magdeleine produce excellent, racy whites for such southerly vineyards, and Ferme Blanche can be almost as good.

🍇 Ugni Blanc, Sauvignon Blanc, Doucillon, Clairette, Marsanne, Pascal Blanc

**ROSÉ** Pleasantly fresh, dry rosés of moderately interesting quality.

🍇 Grenache, Carignan, Mourvèdre, Cinsault, Barbaroux, plus up to 10% (in total) of Terret Noir, Terret Gris, Terret Blanc, Terret Ramenée, Aramon, and Aramon Gris

🍇 All wines: 1–3 years

✓ *du Bagnol* • *Clos Val Bruyère*

## CORSE AOC

Alternative appellation, *see* Vin de Corse AOC

## COTEAUX D'AIX-EN-PROVENCE AOC

This large appellation has many fine estates, several of which have been replanted and reequipped.

**RED** The best are deeply colored *vins de garde* with lots of creamy-cassis, spicy-vanilla, and cherry flavors of some complexity.

🍇 Grenache, plus a maximum of 40% of Cinsault, Counoise, Mourvèdre, Syrah, Cabernet

Sauvignon, and Carignan (the last two of which must not exceed 30%)

🍇 3–12 years

**WHITE** Dry and fruity white wines that are of moderate quality, and are certainly improving. These wines may be sold from December 1 following the harvest without any mention of *primeur* or *nouveau*.

🍇 A maximum of 70% (each) of Bourboulenc, Clairette, Grenache Blanc, Vermentino, up to 40% Ugni Blanc and no more than 30% (each) of Sauvignon Blanc and Sémillon

🍇 Upon purchase

**ROSÉ** Fine-quality dry rosés that are light in body, but bursting with deliciously fresh and ripe fruit. These wines may be sold from December 1 following the harvest without any mention of *primeur* or *nouveau*.

🍇 As for red, plus up to 10% (in total) of Bourboulenc, Clairette, Grenache Blanc, Vermentino, Ugni Blanc, Sauvignon Blanc, and Sémillon

🍇 1–2 years

✓ *des Béates* ❽ (Terra d'Or) • *Château de Beaupré* • *Château de Calissanne* • *de Camaissette* (Amadeus) • *Jean-Luc Colombo* (Pin Couchés) • *Château la Coste\** • *Hauvette* ❾ • *Château Pigoudet* (La Chapelle) • *Château St-Jean\**

## COTEAUX VAROIS AOC

Upgraded from *vin de pays* to VDQS in 1985 and to AOC in 1993, this appellation covers an area of pleasant country wines in the center of Provence. The *encépagement* changed in 2001.

**RED** The best have good color, a deep fruity flavor, and some finesse.

🍇 At least two of the following must represent 80 to 90% of the entire blend: Cinsault, Grenache, Mourvèdre, and Syrah, plus optional Cabernet Sauvignon, Carignan, and Tibouren (permitted since 2001)

**WHITE** Soft and fresh at best.

🍇 A minimum of 30% Vermentino, plus Clairette, Grenache Blanc, a maximum of 30% Sémillon, and no more than 25% Ugni Blanc

**ROSÉ** These attractive, easy-to-drink, dry rosés offer better value than some of the more famous, pretentious wines of Provence.

🍇 At least two of the following must represent 80 to 90% of the entire blend: Cinsault, Grenache, Mourvèdre, and Syrah, plus optional Cabernet Sauvignon, Carignan, and Tibouren (permitted since 2001), and no more than 10% Clairette, Grenache Blanc, Sémillon, Ugni Blanc, and Vermentino

🍇 All wines: 1–3 years

✓ *des Chaberts* (Prestige) • *de Garbelle* (Les Barriques de Barbelle) • *Château Lafoux* • *de Ramatuelle* • *Château Thuerry* (Les Abeillons) • *Château Trians*

## CÔTES DE PROVENCE AOC

While this AOC is famous for its rosés, it is the red wines of Côtes de Provence that have real potential, and they seem blessed with good vintages, fine estates, and talented winemakers. Inferior wines are made, but drink the best and you will rarely be disappointed. The major drawback of this all-embracing appellation is its very size. There are, however, several areas with peculiarities of soil and specific microclimates that would make a Côtes

de Provence Villages AOC a logical evolution and give the most expressive growers something to aim for.

**RED** There are too many exciting styles to generalize, but the best have a deep color and many show an exuberance of silky Syrah fruit and plummy Mourvèdre. Some have great finesse, others are more tannic and chewy. The southern spicy-cassis of Cabernet Sauvignon is often present and the Cinsault, Grenache, and Tibouren grapes also play important roles.

🍇 The following must represent at least 70% (80% as from 2015) of the entire blend: Cinsault, Grenache, Mourvèdre, Syrah, and Tibouren, but no two varieties may account for more than 90%; plus optional Barbaroux Rosé, Cabernet Sauvignon, Calitor, and Carignan, with no more than 10% of Clairette, Sémillon, Ugni Blanc, and Vermentino

🍇 3–10 years

**WHITE** Moderate but improving soft, dry, fragrant, and aromatic wines. These wines may be sold from December 1 following the harvest without any mention of *primeur* or *nouveau*.

🍇 Clairette, Sémillon, Ugni Blanc, and Vermentino

🍇 1–2 years

**ROSÉ** Mediterranean sun is integral to the enjoyment of these wines, which are without doubt made to accompany food, but even the best fail to perform against other rosés under blind conditions; their low acidity makes them seem flat and dull. These wines may be sold from December 1 following the harvest without any mention of *primeur* or *nouveau*.

🍇 The following must represent at least 70% (80% as from 2015) of the entire blend: Cinsault, Grenache, Mourvèdre, Syrah, and Tibouren, but no two varieties may account for more than 90%; plus optional Barbaroux Rosé, Cabernet Sauvignon, Calitor, and Carignan, with no more than 10% of Clairette, Sémillon, Ugni Blanc, and Vermentino

🍇 1–2 years

✓ *Clos d'Alari* (Manon) • *Château des Anglades* (Collection Privée) • *Château de l'Aumerade* (Louis Fabre) • *Château Barbeyrolles* • *de la Bastide Neuve* (d'Antan) • *Ludovic de Beauséjour* (Bacarras) • *de la Courtade* • *Château Coussin Sainte-Victoire* (César) • *Dupéré-Barrera* (En Caractère) • *Domaines Gavoty* • *du Grand Cros* (Nectar) • *de Jalle* (La Bouïsse) • *de La Lauzade* • *de la Malherbe\** • *Château Maravenne* • *Château Minuty* (Prestige) • *Commanderie de Peyrassol\** • *Château Requier\** (Tête de Cuvée) • *de Rimauresq* • *La Rouvade* (Prestige) • *Saint-André de Figuière* • *de St.-Baillon* • *Château Sainte-Roseline* • *Château Sarrins\** • *Château de Selles\** (also Clos Mireille) • *Château de la Tour l'Evêque* • *Vignerons Presqu'île St.-Tropez* (Château de Pampelonne, Carte Noire) • *Vannières* • *Vitis Alba* (Elevé en Fûts de Chêne)

## MUSCAT DU CAP CORSE AOC

When I first wrote this book in 1988, Corsica's only truly classic wine, the succulent sweet Muscat of Cap Corse, was not even recognized, let alone awarded the AOC status it deserved, and it took five more years to get it on the statute books. The Muscat du Cap Corse appellation overlaps Vin de Corse Coteaux du Cap Corse and five of the seven communes that

## MORE GREEN WINES

*In addition to the producers recommended in this directory that are either biodynamic or organic, there are also the following. No negative inference of quality should be taken from the fact that they are not featured among my recommended producers. There are a number that have been recommended in other editions, and still make some fine wines, but have been removed to make room for others.*

**Biodynamic**
*Château la Canorgue* (Bonnieux),
*Les Fouques* (Hyères),
*Château Romanin* (St Rémy de Provence),
*St Estève* (Lambesc)

**Organic**
*des Terres Blanches* (St Rémy-de-Provence),
*du Thouar* (Le Muy), *de l'Adret des Salettes*
(Lorgues), *des Alysses* (Pontevès),
*des Annibals* (Brignoles), *L'Attilon* (Mas Thibert),
*Les Bastides* (Le Puy Ste Réparade),
*de Beaujeu* (Arles), *Château de Beaulieu*
(Rognes), *Château La Calisse* (Pontevès),
*CV des Vignerons de Correns et du Val* (Correns),
*de Costebonne* (Eygalières),
*Mas de la Dame* (Les Baux de Provence),

*Chateau du Duvivier* (Pontevès),
*Château d'Esclans* (La Motte), *Château Les
Eydins* (Bonnieux), *Mas de Gourgonnier*
(Mouriès), *Hauvette* (St Rémy de Provence),
*de l'Isle des Sables* (Fourques), *du Jas d'Esclans*
(La Motte), *La Bastide du Puy*
(St Saturnin Lès Apt), *de Landue* (Solliés-Pont),
*Mas de Longchamp* (St Rémy de Provence),
*Château Miraval* (Correns), *de Pierrascas*
(La Garde), *de Pinchinat* (Pourrières),
*Rabiega* (Draguignan), *de Révaou*
(La Londes les Maures), *Richeaume*
(Puyloubier), *Robert* (Rognes), *de la Sanglière*
(Bormes Les Mimosas), *SCIEV* (Molleges),
*de Séoule* (St Saturnin Lès Apt),
*St André de Figuière* (La Londe des Maures),
*de St-Jean-de-Villecroze* (Villecroze)

comprise the Patrimonio AOC.

**WHITE** The wines of Clos Nicrosi (in particular) demonstrate that Corsica has the ability to produce one of the most fabulous Muscats in the world. These wines are so pure and succulent, with wonderful fresh aromas, that they have very little to gain through age.

🍇 Muscat Blanc à Petits Grains

🕯 Upon purchase

✓ *Clos Nicrosi • Leccia • Orenga de Gaffory*

## PALETTE AOC

The ridiculously long list of permissible grapes here illustrates one of the worst excesses of the AOC system. What is the point of such a large number of diverse grape varieties? Ignoring the fact that it includes some low-quality ones that should, if anything, be banned, it is obvious that no specific style could possibly result from the infinite permutation of varieties and percentages this AOC permits. Why not simply have an appellation that guarantees that Palette is from Palette? Despite this farce, Palette is one of the best in Provence. It can be considered the equivalent of a *grand cru* of Coteaux d'Aix-en-Provence, standing out from surrounding vineyards by virtue of its calcareous soil. Three-quarters of this appellation is occupied by just one property—Château Simone.

**RED** Though not in the blockbusting style, this is a high-quality wine with good color and firm structure, and can achieve finesse.

🍇 At least 50% (in total) of Mourvèdre, Grenache, and Cinsault, plus Téoulier, Durif, and Muscat (any variety planted), Carignan, Syrah, Castets, Brun-Fourcat, Terret Gris, Petit-Brun, Tibouren, Cabernet Sauvignon, and up to 15% (in total) of Clairette (any variety planted), Picardan, Ugni Blanc, Ugni Rosé, Grenache Blanc, Muscat (any variety planted), Picpoul, Pascal, Aragnan, Colombard, and Terret-Bourret

🕯 7–20 years

**WHITE** Firm but nervy dry wine with a pleasantly curious aromatic character.

🍇 At least 55% (in total) of Clairette (any

variety planted), plus Picardan, Ugni Blanc, Ugni Rosé, Grenache Blanc, Muscat (any variety planted), Picpoul, Pascal, Aragnan, Colombard, and a maximum of 20% Terret-Bourret

🕯 Upon purchase

**ROSÉ** A well-made but not exceptional wine, which is perhaps made too seriously for its level of quality.

🍇 At least 50% (in total) of Mourvèdre, Grenache, and Cinsault, plus Téoulier, Durif, and Muscat (any variety planted), Carignan, Syrah, Castets, Brun-Fourcat, Terret Gris, Petit-Brun, Tibouren, Cabernet Sauvignon, and up to 15% (in total) of Clairette (any variety planted), Picardan, Ugni Blanc, Ugni Rosé, Grenache Blanc, Muscat (any variety planted), Picpoul, Pascal, Aragnan, Colombard, and Terret-Bourret

🕯 1–3 years

✓ *Château Crémade • Château Simone*

## PATRIMONIO AOC

This is a small appellation situated west of Bastia in the north of Corsica. The *encépagement* changed in 2002.

**RED** Some fine-quality red wines of good color, body, and fruit are made.

🍇 At least 90% Nielluccio, plus Grenache, Sciacarello, and Vermentino

**WHITE** Light and dry wines of a remarkably fragrant and floral character for Corsica.

🍇 Vermentino

**ROSÉ** Good-value dry rosés that have a coral-pink color and an elegant flavor.

🍇 At least 75% Nielluccio, plus Grenache, Sciacarello, and Vermentino

🕯 All wines: 1–3 years

✓ *Aliso-Rossi • de Catarelli • Gentile* (Sélection Noble) *• Giacometti* (Cru des Agrigates) *• Leccia • Orenga de Gaffory • Pastricciola • Clos Teddi*

## VIN DE BANDOL AOC
### See **Bandol AOC**

## VIN DE BELLET AOC
### See **Bellet AOC**

## VIN DE CORSE AOC

Vin de Corse is a generic appellation covering the entire island. The *encépagement* changed in 2003.

**RED** These honest wines are full of fruit, round, and clean, with rustic charm.

🍇 At least 50% Grenache, Nielluccio, Sciacarello, and Grenache Noir, plus a maximum of 50% Barbarossa, Carignan, Cinsault, Mourvèdre, Syrah, and Vermentino (Carignan and/or Vermentino must not exceed 20% of the entire blend)

**WHITE** The best are well-made, clean, and fresh, but not of true AOC quality.

🍇 At least 75% Vermentino, plus optional Ugni Blanc

**ROSÉ** Attractive, dry, fruity, easy-to-drink wines.

🍇 At least 50% Grenache, Nielluccio, Sciacarello, and Grenache Noir, plus a maximum of 50% Barbarossa, Carignan, Cinsault, Mourvèdre, Syrah, and Vermentino (Carignan and/or Vermentino must not exceed 20% of the entire blend)

🕯 All wines: 1–3 years

✓ *Andriella • Casabianca • Clos Colombu • CV de L'Ile de Beauté* (Réserve du Président) *• Maestracci • Musoleu* (Monte Cristo) *• Clos de L'Orlea • Clos Poggiale*

## VIN DE CORSE CALVI AOC

Lying north of Ajaccio, this subappellation of Vin de Corse AOC requires the same grape varieties and meets the same technical level.

✓ *Colombu • Maestracci • Renucci*

## VIN DE CORSE COTEAUX DU CAP CORSE AOC

A subappellation of Vin de Corse, this requires the same varieties, except that Codivarta may be used with Ugni Blanc in support of Vermentino.

## VIN DE CORSE FIGARI AOC

Situated between Sartène and Porto Vecchio, Vin de Corse Figari is a subappellation of Vin de Corse AOC and requires the same grape varieties and technical level.

✓ *de Petra Bianca* (Vinti Legna)

## VIN DE CORSE PORTO VECCHIO AOC

The southeastern edge of Corsica, around Porto Vecchio, is a subappellation of Vin de Corse AOC and requires the same grape varieties and technical level.

## VIN DE CORSE SARTENE AOC

South of Ajaccio, this subappellation of Vin de Corse AOC requires the same grape varieties and conforms to the same technical level.

✓ *Clos d'Alzeto • Saparale*

# VINS DE PAYS

*This category of wine includes some of the most innovative and exciting wines being produced in the world today, yet most of the 153* vin de pays *denominations are superfluous and confusing. The success of the* vin de pays *system lies not in creating more appellations, but in freeing producers from them, which allows the most talented individuals to carve out their own reputations.*

VINS DE PAYS, OR "COUNTRY WINES," are supposed to be unpretentious, but many are better than average-quality AOC wines and the best rank as some of the finest wines that France can produce. This was never the intention; a *vin de pays* was merely meant to be a quaffing wine that should display, in a very rudimentary sense, the broadest characteristics of its region's greatest wines. However, because of this modest aim, *vin de pays* had fewer restrictions than higher appellations. This encouraged the more creative winemakers to produce wines that best expressed their *terroir* without being hampered by an overregulated AOC system and, in so doing, they managed to equal and occasionally surpass the quality of the more famous local appellations. As news of these exciting *vins de pays* hit the headlines of the international wine press, so the thought of shedding the shackles of AOC restrictions attracted a new generation of winemakers, including a number of Australians. The combination of French and foreign winemakers opened up the *vin de pays* system, turning it into something its creators had never imagined.

## COUNTRY ORIGINS
The expression "Vin de Pays" first appeared in the statute books in a decree dated February 8, 1930. The law in question merely allowed wines to refer to their canton of origin provided they attained a certain alcoholic degree; for example "Vin de Pays de Canton X." These cantons were not controlled appellations as such: there was no way of enforcing a minimum standard of quality, and the relatively small amounts of these so-called *vins de pays* were often the product of inferior hybrid grapes. It was not until 1973 that the concept was officially born of *vins de pays* that were a superior breed of *vins de table*, originating from a defined area and subject to strict controls. By 1976, a total of 75 *vins de pays* had been established, but all the formalities were not worked out until 1979, and between 1981 and 1982 every single existing *vin de pays* was redefined and another 20 created. Currently there are 153, although the number fluctuates as *vins de pays* are upgraded to VDQS, when new *vins de pays* are created, or, as has happened recently, when some *départements* are denied the right to produce a *vin de pays* (*see* Vins de Pays at a Glance, p.250).

Officially, a *vin de pays* is a *vin de table* from a specified area that conforms to quality-control laws that are very similar to those regulating AOC and VDQS wines, although obviously not quite as strict. *Vin de pays* came of age in 1989, prior to which all such wines had to carry the additional descriptor *Vin de Table Français* or *Vin de Table de France*. From time to time, *vins de pays* are upgraded to VDQS, which itself has become a staging post for AOC status. The last *vin de pays* to be promoted was Coteaux du Quercy, in 1999, which is now a VDQS, and others are expected to follow.

## VARIETY IS THE SPICE OF LIFE FOR VIN DE PAYS
While the universally recognized great wines produced in the most famous regions of France remain, very much, in a cozy market of their own, their volume in global terms is minute, and

**DOMAINE DE LA BAUME**
*This property was made famous by BRL Hardy, one of Australia's largest wine companies. Believing the French had not exploited varietal wines and seeing an opening in the market for Australian-made French wines, Hardy puchased Domaine de la Baume on the outskirts of Béziers just in time for the 1990 harvest.*

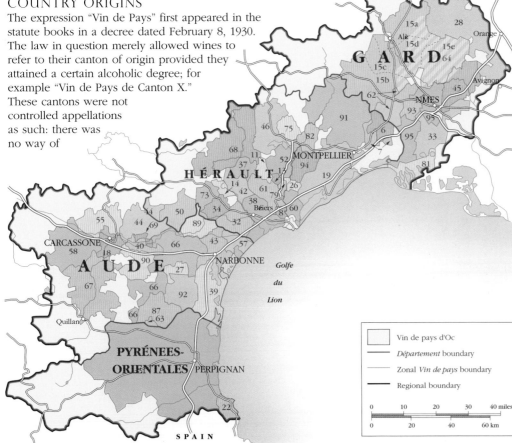

| | |
|---|---|
| ▨ | Vin de pays d'Oc |
| — | *Département* boundary |
| — | Zonal *Vin de pays* boundary |
| ▬ | Regional boundary |

0    10    20    30    40 miles
0      20      40      60 km

**VIN DE PAYS, MAP A,**
*see also* p.249 (opposite)
*Languedoc-Roussillon encompasses the greatest concentration of zonal* vins de pays *and is dominated by the regional* Vin de Pays d'Oc, *by far the most successful* vin de pays.

the average-quality AOC wines have been losing the export battle against the New World, particularly "Brand Australia." It was left to the up-and-coming *vins de pays* to fight a rear-guard action, while the AOC regions sort out their problems of perennial mediocrity (if indeed they can). However, even with fewer restrictions than AOCs, *vins de pays* have had to fight with one hand behind their back. The first and most important disadvantage was that *vins de pays* were marketing wines under names such as Coteaux du Littoral Audois or Comté Tolosan, while the opposition was simply selling Chardonnay or Cabernet Sauvignon. While

the varietal concept might cause a "sense of place" crisis for the New World's finer wines, when they try to ride the export surf into Europe, it matters not one bit in the US, and the *vins de pays* are not up against such wines. At the price point of most *vins de pays* and their New World opponents, the appellation *per se* is irrelevant. All readers of this encyclopedia will drink such wines, and delight in searching out those that are the best and most interesting, but the vast majority of consumers do not know or even care about appellations. They see

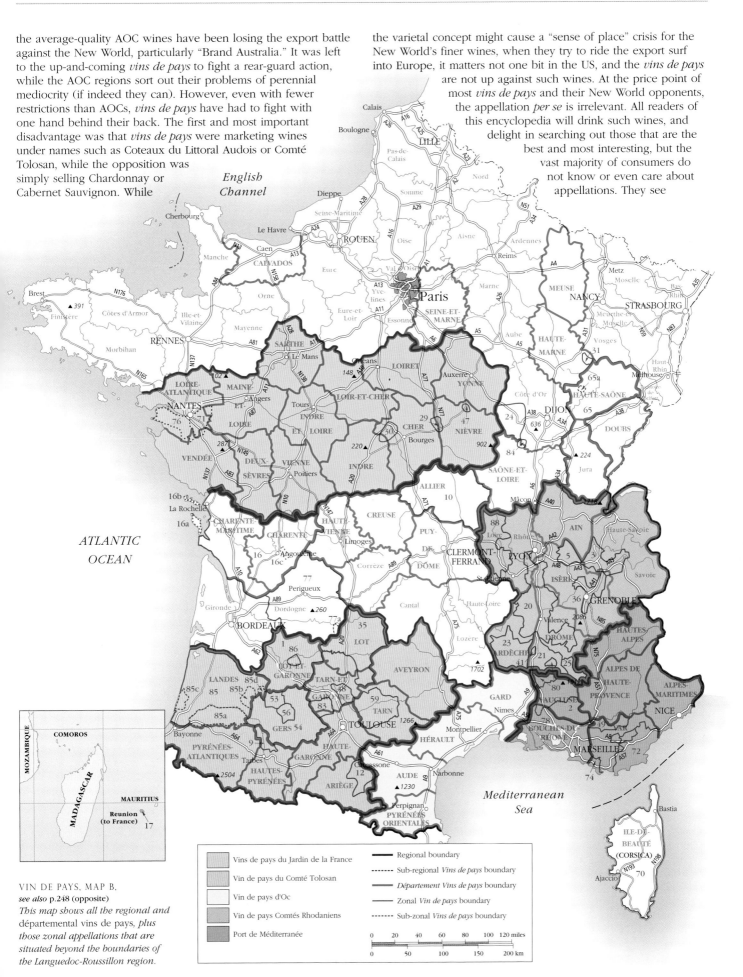

VIN DE PAYS, MAP B,
see also p.248 (opposite)
*This map shows all the regional and départemental vins de pays, plus those zonal appellations that are situated beyond the boundaries of the Languedoc-Roussillon region.*

Vins de pays du Jardin de la France

Vin de pays du Comté Tolosan

Vin de pays d'Oc

Vin de pays Comtés Rhodaniens

Port de Méditerranée

——— Regional boundary

- - - - Sub-regional *Vins de pays* boundary

——— *Département Vins de pays* boundary

——— Zonal *Vin de pays* boundary

- - - - Sub-zonal *Vins de pays* boundary

## VINS DE PAYS AT A GLANCE

### 153 VIN DE PAYS DENOMINATIONS IN TOTAL

Or 167 if the subregional and subzonal *vins de pays* are included. From virtually zero production in 1973 to an annual average of almost 166 million cases (15 million hectoliters), *vins de pays* now represent over 30 percent of the total French wine production, and this expansion is continuing.

### TYPES OF VINS DE PAYS

There are three basic categories of *vins de pays*: regional, *départementale*, and zonal. Although no official quality differences exist between these, it is not an unreasonable assumption that the zonal *vins de pays* may sometimes show more individual character than the much larger *vins de pays départementaux* or all-encompassing regional *vins de pays*, but this is not always so.

A grower within a specific zone may find it easier to sell wine under a more generic *vin de pays*, which explains why so many individual wines are to be found under the vast Vin de Pays d'Oc denomination. Also, the geographical size of a *vin de pays* can be deceptive, with many *départements* producing relatively little wine compared with some more prolific, relatively minute, zonal *vins de pays*. In the Loire few producers bother with the *départementale* denominations.

### REGIONAL VINS DE PAYS (45 percent of total *vin de pays* output)

There are five of these wide-ranging appellations: Comté Tolosan; Comtés Rhodaniens; Jardin de la France (which includes a further two subregional denominations); Oc; and Portes de Méditerranée. Each encompasses two or more *départements*. They represented only 12 percent of *vin de pays* production in 1990, yet Vin de Pays d'Oc alone accounts for 26 percent today.

### DÉPARTEMENTALE VINS DE PAYS (28 percent of total *vin de pays* output)

These cover entire *départements*, and although 52 are officially in use, some are effectively redundant as producers have opted for one of the more widely supported regional appellations, which are often easier to promote. In theory every *département* in France can claim a

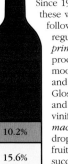

10.2%

15.6%

*vin de pays* under its own *départementale* denomination, but to avoid confusion with AOC wines the following were in 1995 expressly forbidden from exercising this right: the Marne and Aube (in Champagne), the Bas-Rhin and Haut-Rhin (in Alsace), the Côte-d'Or (in Burgundy), and the Rhône (which encompasses Beaujolais but is likely to cause confusion with the Côtes du Rhône AOC). Jura, Savoie, and Haut-Savoie have also been disenfranchised.

### ZONAL VINS DE PAYS (27 percent of total *vin de pays* production)

There are now 96 zonal *vins de pays*, plus 12 subzonal denominations, although many of the former and some of the latter are seldom encountered.

### VINS DE CÉPAGE

After a widespread authorization of pure varietal *vins de pays* in 2000, regulations for which lagged well behind the actual production, this category has taken off to such an extent that it now accounts for half of all the *vins de pays* produced each year, with 80 percent sold under one of five regional *vins de pays*, of which 70 percent is Vin de Pays d'Oc.

### VINS DE PAYS PRIMEUR

Since 1990, all *vin de pays* denominations have been permitted to produce these wines, which may be marketed from the third Thursday of October following the harvest (much earlier than Beaujolais Nouveau). The regulations allow for red and white wines to be made as *vins primeurs*, but strangely not rosé, although by the very nature of their production many reds are lighter than some rosés, so it is a somewhat moot point. White wines are vinified by cool-fermentation techniques and red wines by one of three methods: *macération carbonique* (see Glossary), part-*macération carbonique* (some of the grapes are crushed and mixed with the whole bunches), and "short-classic" (traditional vinification with minimum skin contact). Cool-fermented whites and *macération carbonique* reds are dominated by amylic aromas (pear drops, banana, nail polish). "Short-classic" rarely provides enough fruit, depth, or color, whereas part-*macération carbonique* can be very successful in enhancing the fruitiness of a wine without drowning it in amylic aromas, but it has to be expertly applied.

---

Chardonnay on two or three bottles, and grab one. Why? Probably because they have had it before, and it was okay, or for no other reason than the label looks nicer than the others—but the reason is immaterial. What is important is that in making their choice, they—that is, the vast majority—have gone straight past the Coteaux du Littoral Audois *et al.*

This is the old story of customers proclaiming, "I don't want Chablis, I want Chardonnay," and the French authorities have agonized about how to get around the problem. The French being French could not bring themselves to allow *vins de pays* to be sold as pure varietal wines. Instead, in 1996, they tried to divert consumer attention from single-varietal names with the twin-varietal concept, enabling producers to market wines as Cabernet-Merlot, Chardonnay-Sémillon, and so on. Although some very good wines were produced, the idea never really took off. It is fine in a New World country, where the varietal wine concept is all, and a twin-varietal is simply seen as a logical move, but for the *vins de pays* it was like learning to run before they could walk.

The French realized this, and in 2000 issued wide-sweeping decrees authorizing varietal wines for almost all *vins de pays*. It was still an unfair fight because the regulations insisted that such wines be made from 100 percent of the variety indicated, whereas New World imports merely had to comply with the European Union minimum of 85 percent. At the price point of most *vins de pays* and New World varietals, the flexibility to strengthen or soften a variety to one degree or another in a given year is a major advantage. Another advantage the opposition had was to use oak chips. It is one thing to expect a *cru classé* château to use casks rather than chips (although I cannot see why it actually has to be illegal), but it is impossible for *vins de pays* to compete at the same price as the New World wines if the French have to use oak casks or nothing. With casks, they cannot even get the wine on

the shelf at the same time, let alone the same price. Fortunately, Hervé Gaymard, the French Minister of Agriculture, finally agreed that it was unfair, and in July 2004 authorized producers to use oak chips and to blend up to 15 percent of another variety and vintage into a single-varietal *vin de pays*.

## VIN DE PAYS DES CÉPAGES DE FRANCE

At the same meeting, one thing that Gaymard refused to authorize was the proposed Vin de Pays des Cépages de France. The faction proposing this have only themselves to blame. Cross-regional blending is a good idea; the error was simply in the naming of the *vin de pays*, which doomed it to failure from the start. Those who objected in principle to cross-regional blending, including a number of UK shippers, claimed that it would "almost certainly become a dumping ground, especially in the current climate of oversupply." That was part of the attraction, from my viewpoint. How else do the classic AOC regions raise the quality of their most basic wines without some form of selection, i.e. dumping, of lesser quality wines? Furthermore, wines might be "dumped" by Bordeaux for different, sometimes opposite, reasons from the Rhône or Roussillon, and blending the two, together with wines from nonclassic areas, could produce something superior to its individual parts. And even when it does not, the shippers have nothing to fear because no one is making them buy the wines.

Where the cross-regional *vin de pays* went wrong was in naming it Vin de Pays des Cépages de France, sourcing the wine from anywhere in France, and expecting European Union legislation to be modified to allow this through. All they had to do was to draw a line from Vannes on the west coast to Roubaix on the Belgian border, name the wine Vin de Pays des Cépages de Sud-Est France (deliberate shades of southeastern Australia), and it would have been passed without anyone blinking an eye.

THE VINS DE PAYS OF
# FRANCE

## AGENAIS

**Zonal** *vin de pays* Map B, No.1

These red, white, and rosé wines are produced from a combination of classic *bordelais* grapes and some rustic regional varieties, including the Tannat and Fer. Although more than three-quarters of the output is red, it is the rosé made primarily from Abouriou that is best known.

✓ *de Cazeaux* (Tradition)

## AIGUES

**Zonal** *vin de pays* Map A, No.2

Created as recently as 1993, this *vin de pays* roughly corresponds to the Coteaux du Lubéron, and has a similar range of grape varieties.

## AIN

**Départementale** *vin de pays* Map B

This *départementale vin de pays* encompasses unclassified vineyards in southern Burgundy, and has relatively recently come into usage, but the level of production remains insignificant. Pure varietal wines have been allowed since 2000.

✓ *Jean-Christophe Pellerin* (Chardonnay Cép d'Argent)

## ALLIER

**Départementale** *vin de pays* Map B

Relatively recent *départementale vin de pays* for red and rosé wines, primarily from Cabernet Franc, Cabernet Sauvignon, Gamay, and Grolleau, but also Abouriou, Pinot d'Aunis, and Pinot Noir. Whites primarily from Chardonnay, Chenin Blanc, and Sauvignon Blanc, but also Arbois, Folle Blanche, Grolleau Gris, Melon de Bourgogne, and Pinot Blanc. Pure varietal wines have been allowed since 2000.

## ALLOBROGIE

**Zonal** *vin de pays* Map B, No.3

This is the *vin de pays* equivalent of the Vin de Savoie, although it extends beyond the borders of that AOC into cattle country, where the existence of vines is very sporadic. The wines are similar to Vin de Savoie, if somewhat lighter and more rustic in style. Almost 90 percent of production is white, made primarily from Jacquère, Chardonnay, and Chasselas, although Altesse, Mondeuse Blanche, Roussanne, and Molette can also be used. The balance of the production is essentially red and may be made from Gamay, Mondeuse, and Pinot Noir, with rosé accounting for less than 1 percent. Pure varietal wines have been allowed since 2000.

✓ *Demeure-Penet* (Jacquère)

## ALPES DE HAUTE-PROVENCE

**Départementale** *vin de pays* Map B

Most of these wines come from the Durance Valley in the east of the *département*. Production is mostly red, made from Carignan, Grenache, Cinsault, Cabernet Sauvignon, Merlot, and Syrah. Rosé accounts for 15 percent and white made from Ugni Blanc, Clairette, Chardonnay, and Muscat for just 7 percent. Pure varietal wines have been allowed since 2000.

✓ *La Madeleine* (Cabernet Sauvignon)
• *de Régusse* (Muscat Moelleux, Pinot Noir, Merlot)

## ALPES-MARITIMES

**Départementale** *vin de pays* Map B

Some 70 percent of production is red and 30 percent rosé, made from Carignan, Cinsault, Grenache, Ugni Blanc, and Vermentino grapes, mostly from the communes of Carros, Mandelieu, and Mougins. White wines may also be produced. Pure varietal wines have been allowed since 2000.

✓ *de Toasc* (Lou Vin d'Aqui)

## ARDÈCHE

**Départementale** *vin de pays* Map B

Red and white wines, from a range of Rhône and *bordelais* grapes. Pure varietal wines allowed.

✓ *de Champal* (Viognier Arzelle)

## ARGENS

**Zonal** *vin de pays* Map A, No.4

Almost 50/50 rosé and red are made from Carignan, Cinsault, Syrah, Roussanne du Var, Mourvèdre, and Cabernet Sauvignon. A little white is also produced.

## ARIÈGE

**Départementale** *vin de pays* Map B

A small production of red, white, and rosé, Ariège is from the foot of the Pyrenees, overlapping the notional borders of Southwest France and Languedoc-Roussillon. Pure varietals allowed.

## ATLANTIQUE

**New regional** *vin de pays*

Encompassing the *départements* of Charente, Charente-Maritime, Dordogne, Gironde, and the northwestern corner of Lot-et-Garonne. Red, white, and rosé wines made from varieties permitted for each respective *département*.

## AUDE

**Départementale** *vin de pays* Map B

Although still the second or third largest *vin de pays*, this used to boast almost exactly the same output as Vin de Pays d'Oc in 1993, but while the production of the latter appellation has more than tripled, Vin de Pays de L'Aude has virtually stood still. Nevertheless, a lot of fresh and fruity wine is made here, most of which is red, with just 5 percent each of rosé and white. Mediterranean grape varieties dominate. Pure varietal wines have been allowed since 2000.

✓ *de La Bouysse* ❽ (Merlot) • *de Fontannelles* (Poête Renaissance)

## AVEYRON

**Départementale** *vin de pays* Map B

Since most of the wines produced in this *département*, which is situated between Cahors and Hérault, used to claim the Vin de Pays des Gorges et Côtes de Millau (now Côtes de Millau VDQS) appellation, it will be interesting to see how many *vin de pays* producers utilize this denomination or prefer to use the wider Comté Tolosan appellation. Pure varietal wines have been allowed since 2000.

## BALMES DAUPHINOISES

**Zonal** *vin de pays* Map B, No.5

In the denomination of Balmes Dauphinoises, dry white, made from Jacquère and Chardonnay, accounts for 60 percent of production, and red, made from Gamay and Pinot Noir, accounts for 40 percent. Rosé may also be produced.

## BÉNOVIE

**Zonal** *vin de pays* Map A, No.6

This denomination is located at the eastern extremity of the Coteaux du Languedoc and overlaps part of the Muscat-de-Lunel area. Almost 80 percent of the production is a light, fruity red, made predominantly from Carignan, Grenache, Cinsault, and Syrah, although Merlot and Cabernet Sauvignon may also be used. A fair amount of attractive rosé is made, mostly by the *saignée* method, plus a small quantity of Ugni Blanc-based dry white. Pure varietal wines have been allowed since 2000.

✓ *des Hospitaliers* (Merlot)

## BÉRANGE

**Zonal** *vin de pays* Map A, No.7

Production in Bérange is 75 percent red, 20 percent rosé, and 5 percent white, made from a range of grape varieties very similar to those used in the Coteaux du Languedoc and neighboring Bénvoie.

## BESSAN

**Zonal** *vin de pays* Map A, No.8

This tiny, single-village denomination just east of Béziers is best known for its dry, aromatic rosé, which now accounts for 65 percent of production. Just 10 percent red is made, with simple Ugni Blanc-based white accounting for the balance.

## BIGORRE

**Zonal** *vin de pays* Map B, No.9

Mostly full, rich, Madiran-type red wine is made here, plus a little good crisp, dry white. Rosé may also be produced.

## BOUCHES-DU-RHÔNE
### *Départementale vin de pays* Map B

This denomination has one of the largest *vin de pays* productions in the country, some 80 percent of which is red and most of that comes from the Coteaux d'Aix-en-Provence area. These wines are warm, spicy, and often quite powerfully structured from Carignan, Grenache, Cinsaut, Cabernet Sauvignon, Merlot, and Syrah. The production of rosé is just 12 percent, which is a reasonable proportion for the style, and also in view of the absence of the mystique of a name (it cannot have Provence on the label). The quality is invariably much better than most of the AOC rosé from this area. A little white is also made from Ugni Blanc, Clairette, Bourboulenc, Vermentino, Chardonnay, and Chasan (a slightly aromatic Listan and Chardonnay cross). Domaine de Trévallon is not only the finest wine of the appellation, but one of the greatest *vins de pays*, producing a quality easily equal to some of best *crus classés* of Bordeaux. Pure varietal wines have been allowed since 2000.

✓ *Hauvette* ◉ • *de l'Île St.-Pierre* (Chardonnay) • *La Michelle* (Rouge) • *Jean-Paul Luc* (Minna Vineyard Rouge) • *de Trévallon*

## BOURBONNAIS
### *Zonal vin de pays* Map B, No.10

This is a rarely seen *vin de pays* from a white-only area of unclassified vines in the Loire Valley.

## CALVADOS
### *Départementale vin de pays* Map B

Growers are legally entitled to produce a *vin de pays* named after the *département* in which the vines are located, but after all the fuss about *départementale* names that could be construed to come from a classic wine region, it is surprising to see Calvados approved. Although a *départementale vin de pays*, the area of vines is very small, located at Grisy, west of St. Pierre-sur-Dives. The wines are varietal (Auxerrois, Pinot Gris, Melon, and Müller-Thurgau) made by Gérard Samson under the Arpents du Soleil label. Pure varietal wines have been allowed since 2000.

## CASSAN
### *Zonal vin de pays* Map A, No.11

This area is in the Coteaux du Languedoc north of Béziers and overlaps part of Faugères. Almost three-quarters of the wine is red and full bodied, from Carignan, Cinsaut, Grenache, Cabernet Sauvignon, Merlot, and Syrah. The balance is split between a well-flavored rosé and a crisp, dry white made primarily from Ugni Blanc, although Clairette and Terret may also be used. Since 2000, however, it has been permissible to market wines as pure varietals, without any specification in the new regulation as to what those varieties may be, hence the Tempranillo below.

✓ *de La Tour Penedesses* (Tempranillo Mas de Couy Elevé en Fûts de Chêne)

## CATHARE
### *Zonal vin de pays* Map A, No.12

This area overlapping the Aude and Ariège *départements* was made a *vin de pays* in 2001. Red wines are made from the following: Merlot, Cabernet Franc, Cabernet Sauvignon, and Merlot, one or more of which must represent 50 to 70 percent of the entire blend, plus at least two of the following must account for 30

to 50 percent: Arinarnoa, Caladoc, Carignan, Cinsaut, Chenanson, Eiodola, Grenache, Malbec, Marselan, Pinot Noir, Pinot Gris, Pinot Blanc, Portan, and Syrah. For white wine, there should be 60 to 80 percent of Chardonnay and/or Sauvignon Blanc, plus 20 to 40 percent Bourboulenc, Chasan, Chenin Blanc, Grenache, Grenache Blanc, Macabéo, Marsanne, Mauzac, Roussanne, Sémillon, Ugni Blanc, Vermentino, and Viognier. Rosé is made from Merlot, Cabernet Franc, Cabernet Sauvignon, and Syrah, one or more of which must represent 50 to 70 percent of the entire blend, plus one or more of the following, which must account for 30 to 50 percent: Caladoc, Cinsaut, Chanson, Grenache, and Portan.

✓ *de Sautes* (Signature Cathare)

## CAUX
### *Zonal vin de pays* Map A, No.13

This *vin de pays* produces a good, typical dry and fruity rosé in a Languedoc style from vines growing north of Béziers. Some 40 percent of the output is red, and a little white and rosé are also made. Pure varietal wines have been allowed since 2000.

✓ *Causses de Nizzas* (Carignan Vieilles Vignes)

## CESSENON
### *Zonal vin de pays* Map A, No.14

This appellation produces red wines of a rustic St.-Chinian style, plus a little rosé.

## CÉVENNES
### *Zonal vin de pays* Map A, No.15

This new appellation is an amalgamation of four former *vins de pays*, now subzones: Coteaux Cévenols (15a), Coteaux du Salavès (15b), Côtes du Libac (15c—originally Serre du Coiran), Mont Bouquet (15d), and Uzège (15e), each of which may add its subzonal name to the Vin de Pays des Cévennes. Most of the wines are red; 15 percent is rosé, with *saignée* rosé a specialty. Pure varietal wines have been allowed since 2000. Very small quantities of white *vin primeur* are also produced. Production is mostly of an honest, fruity Languedoc style. Pure varietal wines have been allowed since 2000.

✓ *Clos de La Roque* (Pinot Noir)

## CHARENTAIS
### *Zonal vin de pays* Map B, No.16

The dry white wines are really good, even though 50 percent of the grapes used are Ugni Blanc. It seems that this lowly variety and, indeed, the Colombard make light but very fresh, crisp, and tangy wine in the Charente, which is not only well suited to distilling Cognac, but makes a cheap, cheerful, quaffable wine. Some red and rosé wines from Gamay and *bordelais* grapes are also made. The following subzonal areas are allowed to add their names to Vin de Pays Charentais: Île d'Oléron (16a), Île de Ré (16b), and Saint Sornin (16c). Pure varietal wines have been allowed since 2000.

✓ *de La Chauvillière* (Chardonnay) • *Gardrat* (Colombard) • *Chai du Roussoir* (Cabernet Terroir de Fossiles) • *Terra Sana*

## CHARENTE
### *Départementale vin de pays* Map B

Hardly used *départementale vin de pays*, most producers preferring the wider-known Vin de

Pays Charentais. Pure varietal wines have been allowed since 2000.

## CHARENTE-MARITIMES
### *Départementale vin de pays* Map B

Hardly used *départementale vin de pays*, most producers preferring the wider-known Vin de Pays Charentais. Pure varietal wines have been allowed since 2000.

## CHER
### *Départementale vin de pays* Map B

Mostly Touraine-like, Gamay-based red wine, plus a small amount of dry rosé in a light *vin gris* style. Since 1997, an increasing amount of dry white Sauvignon Blanc has been made by the cooperative at Venesmes, which makes a wine comparable to a rustic Sancerre or Menetou-Salon. Pure varietal wines have been allowed since 2000.

## CILAOS
### *Zonal vin de pays* Map B, No.17

The most remote of all French wines, the Vin de Pays de Cilaos was created in January 2004 for vines growing on the island of Réunion, a French protectorate in the Indian Ocean, 420 miles (680 kilometers) east of Madagascar. Grape varieties already grown include Chenin Blanc, Pinot Noir, and Malbec, with plans to plant Gros Manseng, Pinotage, Syrah, and Verdelho. The styles produced are red, white, rosé, and, because the tendency is for grapes to overripen rather too easily, *moelleux*. The only wine producer currently is the local cooperative, which in January 2004 harvested 28 tons of grapes. "Cilaos" means "the place you never leave."

## CITÉ DE CARCASSONNE
### *Zonal vin de pays* Map A, No.18

Red wines account for over 90 percent of production, rosé 5 percent, and white wine barely 1 percent. The wines come from 11 communes around Carcassonne. Pure varietal wines have been allowed since 2000. If blended, red and rosé wines must include at least 20 percent of one or more of the following: Cabernet Franc, Cabernet Sauvignon, Malbec, Merlot, Pinot Noir, and Syrah, plus a maximum of 40 percent Alicante Bouschet, Arinarnoa, Caladoc, Carignan, Chenanson, Cinsault, Egiodola, Grenache, Marselan, and Portan. Red *vin de primeur* is restricted to Chenanson, Cinsaut, Merlot, Portan, and Syrah. White wine blends may be made from any of the following: Bourboulenc, Carignan Blanc, Chardonnay, Chasan, Chenin Blanc, Clairette, Colombard, Grenache Blanc, Macabéo, Marsanne, Mauzac, Muscat d'Alexandrie, Muscat à Petits Grains Blanc, Picpoul, Roussanne, Sauvignon Blanc, Sémillon, Terret, Turbat, Ugni Blanc, and Viognier.

✓ *Auzias* • *Sarrail* (Pech l'Estagnère)

## COLLINES DE LA MOURE
### *Zonal vin de pays* Map A, No.19

More than 80 percent of production is basic red, made from a choice of Carignan, Cinsault, Grenache, Syrah, Cabernet Sauvignon, and Merlot, the last two of which are often vinified separately. A light, dry rosé accounts for about 15 percent of production, but very little white is made and it is mostly from Ugni Blanc. Although late-harvest rather than a *vin doux naturel*, it should come as no surprise that this *vin de pays* denomination roughly corresponds to the AOCs Muscat de Mireval and Muscat de Frontignan.

✓ *Montlobre* (La Chapelle) • *de Mujolan* (Mas de Mante Vertige)

## COLLINES RHODANIENNES
### Zonal *vin de pays* Map B, No.20

A large denomination at the center of Comtés Rhodaniens, this *vin de pays* straddles five *départements* (Rhône, Isère, Drôme, Ardèche, and Loire) and produces primarily red wines from Gamay, Syrah, Merlot, and Pinot Noir. Some extremely small quantities are made of rosé and white, the latter coming from an interesting choice of Chardonnay, Marsanne, Roussanne, Viognier, Jacquère, Aligoté, and Clairette. With the range of body, fatness, aromatic complexity, and acidity that a successful blend of these varieties could bring, there is ample scope for Collines Rhodaniennes to develop a first-rate reputation for white wines. Pure varietal wines have been allowed since 2000.

✓ *Cuilleron-Gaillard-Villard* (Sotanum) • *François Villard* (Syrah)

## COMTÉ DE GRIGNAN
### Zonal *vin de pays* Map B, No.21

Virtually all the production of Comté de Grignan is red and most of that Grenache-dominated, although Syrah, Cinsault, Gamay, Carignan, Merlot, and Cabernet Sauvignon are also allowed. Rosé accounts for just 1 percent, and white is virtually nonexistent.

## COMTÉ TOLOSAN
### Regional *vin de pays* Map B

Modest quantities of mostly red wines are produced, with some rosé and a tiny amount of white (of which Daubert and Ribonnet stand out). The white wines should be made from the same grape varieties permitted for Armagnac (Blanc Dame, Colombard, Folle Blanche, Graisse, Jurançon Blanc, Mauzac, Mauzac Rosé, Meslier St.-François, Ugni Blanc, and until 2010 Baco Blanc). Red wine grapes are not specified beyond "what is growing"! Certainly the white wines are the most successful. Domaine de Ribonnet makes a very good stab at the Australian Chardonnay-Sauvignon Blanc style. Pure varietal wines have been allowed since 2004.

✓ *Baudave* (Rouge) • *François Daubert* (Madrigal sur le Mauzac) • *Plaimont* (Rive Haute Sauvignon Blanc) • *de Ribonnet*

## COMTÉS RHODANIENS
### Regional *vin de pays* Map B

Created in 1989, Comtés Rhodaniens encompasses eight *départements* and its name

can be given only to wines that have already qualified as a zonal *vin de pays*. It is the smallest of the five regional *vins de pays*, with just one-tenth of the production of the second-smallest regional *vin de pays* (Comté Tolosan), and a mere one-thousandth of the largest (Oc).

✓ *C. V. Ardechois*

## CORRÈZE
### Départementale *vin de pays* Map B

Mostly reds from Cabernet Franc, Merlot, and Gamay, grown on the stony, limestone *coteaux* of Branceilles, the vineyards of which flourished in the 19th century, but were restored as recently as the 1990s. Pure varietal wines have been allowed since 2000.

✓ *Mille et Une Pierre* (Elevé en Fûts de Chêne)

## CÔTE VERMEILLE
### Zonal *vin de pays* Map A, No.22

Mostly red and rosé, these wines are the *vin de pays* equivalent of Collioure, which in turn is the table-wine equivalent of Banyuls.

✓ *Vial Magnères*

## COTEAUX DE L'ARDÈCHE
### Zonal *vin de pays* Map B, No.23

This large denomination has a very significant output and is particularly well known for its dark, spicy red wine, which accounts for 80 percent of the total production. Often Syrah-dominated, this wine may also include Cabernet Sauvignon, Carignan, Cinsault, Grenache, Gamay, and Merlot. Louis Latour's Chardonnay put this *vin de pays* on the map during the 1990s, and the same firm's stunning Pinot Noir is proving to be an even greater success. Just over 10 percent of this denomination's total output is rosé, and just under 10 percent is white, the latter made from Bourboulenc, Marsanne, Viognier, Roussanne, Marsanne, Sauvignon Blanc, and Ugni Blanc. About 30 percent of all wines produced are sold as pure varietal.

✓ *C. V. Ardèchois* • *de Bournet* (Chris) • *Mas d'Intras* • *Louis Latour* • *des Louanes* (L'Encre de Sy)

## COTEAUX AUXOIS
### Zonal *vin de pays* Map B, No.24

This zonal *vin de pays* has replaced the *départementale* denomination Côte d'Or (which some growers want to utilize for a new AOC), and may produce red and rosé wines from one or more of Gamay, Pinot Gris, and Pinot Noir; while white wines are made from one or more of Aligoté, Auxerrois, Chardonnay, Pinot Gris, Melon de Bourgogne, Sauvignon Blanc, and Sauvignon Gris.

✓ *C. V. de Flavigny* (Chardonnay Fûts de Chêne)

## COTEAUX DES BARONNIES
### Zonal *vin de pays* Map B, No.25

Almost 90 percent of Coteaux des Baronnies wines are red and almost 10 percent rosé, made from Cabernet Sauvignon, Cinsault, Syrah, Grenache, Pinot Noir, Gamay, and Merlot. Less than 2 percent is white, with varietal wines generally increasing. Pure varietal wines have been allowed since 2000.

✓ *du Rieu Frais* (Cabernet Sauvignon) • *La Rosière* (Merlot)

## COTEAUX DE BESSILLES
### Zonal *vin de pays* Map A, No.26

Fresh, light, rustic-style wines from the Coteaux du Languedoc immediately north of Pinet. Production is two-thirds red, one-quarter rosé, and the balance white. Pure varietal wines have been allowed since 2000.

✓ *St.-Hilaire* (Vermentino)

## COTEAUX DE LA CABRERISSE
### Zonal *vin de pays* Map A, No.27

Mostly red wine, as might be expected from what is after all the heart of Corbières, with 10 percent rosé and just 3 percent white, including some *vins primeurs*. There is a wide range of grape varieties permitted, particularly for the red, which may be made from Carignan, Grenache, Cinsault, Syrah, Mourvèdre, Terret Noir, Cabernet Sauvignon, Cabernet Franc, Merlot, and the Teinturier grape Alicante Bouschet. White grapes include Terret, Grenache Blanc, Clairette, Ugni Blanc, and Macabéo.

## COTEAUX DE CEZE
### Zonal *vin de pays* Map A, No.28

This is a large denomination with a modest output of roughly 80 percent red and 20 percent rosé, with a minuscule amount of white.

✓ *Armand et Roger Maby*

## COTEAUX CHARITOIS
### Zonal *vin de pays* Map B, No.29

Basic white wines and light reds (Pinot Noir) from the Loire Valley.

✓ *de la Vernière* (Pinot Noir)

## COTEAUX DU CHER ET DE L'ARNON
### Zonal *vin de pays* Map B, No.29

The reds and *vin gris* are made from Gamay, and dry white from Sauvignon Blanc.

## COTEAUX DE COIFFY
### Zonal *vin de pays* Map A, No.31

A relatively new and as yet untested *vin de pays* from way up north, between Champagne and Alsace, in the southeastern corner of the Haute-Marne *département*. Red and rosé from Gamay and Pinot Noir; whites from Aligoté, Arbane, Auxerrois, Chardonnay, Pinot Blanc, Pinot Gris, and Petit Meslier. Pure varietal wines have been allowed since 2001.

✓ *C. V. les Coteaux de Coiffy* (Auxerrois)

## COTEAUX D'ENSÉRUNE
### Zonal *vin de pays* Map A, No.31

This *vin de pays* west of Béziers used to produce two-thirds red and one-third rosé, but red wines now account for almost 90 percent of the output, made from a typical range of Languedoc grapes. Just 10 percent rosé is produced, but hardly any white. However, Jeanjean makes a nice, soft, fruity dry white from Ugni Blanc, Marsanne, and Chardonnay.

✓ *Jeanjean*

## COTEAUX FLAVIENS
### Zonal *vin de pays* Map A, No.33

From hills named after the Roman Emperor Flavius, this *vin de pays* just south of Nîmes in the Costières de Nîmes produces a full, warm-hearted red which accounts for 85 percent of the output. Most of the rest is rosé, and just a small amount of white is made. Carignan, Grenache, Cinsault, Cabernet Sauvignon, Merlot, and Syrah are the main grape varieties used.

## COTEAUX DE FONTCAUDE
### Zonal *vin de pays* Map A, No.34

This area overlaps much of Saint-Chinian in the eastern section of the Coteaux du Languedoc. Almost 80 percent of the wines are red, and these are made in a light, fresh but interesting style from Carignan, Cinsault, Grenache, Cabernet Sauvignon, and Syrah. Rosé and a little white are also to be found.

## COTEAUX DE GLANES
### Zonal *vin de pays* Map B, No.35

This appellation produces mainly red wines, which are Gamay or Merlot dominated, plus a little rosé.

## COTEAUX DU GRÉSIVAUDAN
### Zonal *vin de pays* Map B, No.36

Red and rosé Savoie-style wines made from Gamay, Pinot, and Etraire de la Dui (a local grape variety), and Jacquère-based dry whites.

## COTEAUX DE LAURENS
### Zonal *vin de pays* Map A, No.37

Some 85 percent of these wines are a red *vin de pays* equivalent of Faugères, made mostly from Carignan, Cinsault, Syrah, and Grenache, but some of the better wines also include Cabernet Sauvignon and Merlot. A small amount of rosé and even less white is made.

✓ *de La Commanderie de St.-Jean*

## COTEAUX DU LIBRON
### Zonal *vin de pays* Map A, No.38

Situated around Béziers itself, this *vin de pays* produces mainly red wines, made from Carignan, Grenache, Cinsault, Cabernet Sauvignon, Merlot, and Syrah. Some 12 percent of the output is rosé, and less than 7 percent white, the latter being made mainly from Ugni Blanc, with a touch of Terret and Clairette. Pure varietal wines have been allowed since 2000.

✓ *de la Colombette* • *de Pierre-Belle* (Réserve)

## COTEAUX DU LITTORAL AUDOIS
### Zonal *vin de pays* Map A, No.39

This area corresponds geographically to the unofficial Sigean zone of Corbières, where Syrah performs best and is used, not surprisingly, in many of these *vins de pays*, of which red wine accounts for no less than 98 percent of the total output. Other black grape varieties permitted include Carignan, Grenache, Cinsault, Merlot, and Cabernet Sauvignon. Minuscule amounts of rosé and white are produced; the latter is made mainly from Grenache Blanc and Macabéo, but can also include Ugni Blanc, Terret, and Clairette.

## COTEAUX DE MIRAMONT
### Zonal *vin de pays* Map A, No.40

Red wines from a typically Mediterranean range of *bordelais* and southern-Rhône grapes dominate this denomination, which bridges the Côtes de La Malepère and Corbières. Rosé and white together account for less than 5 percent of output, including some *vins primeurs*.

✓ *Foncalieu*

## COTEAUX DE MONTÉLIMAR
### New zonal *vin de pays* Map B, No.41

This *vin de pays* was established in September 2004, and encompasses vineyards between Montélimar and Dieulefit in the Drôme *département*, just north of the Coteaux de Tricastin AOC. Pure varietal wines are allowed. Red and rosé must be made from one or more of the following: Cabernet Sauvignon, Carignan, Cinsault, Gamay, Grenache, Marselan, Merlot, Pinot Noir, and Syrah. White wines from one or more of Chardonnay, Clairette, Grenache Blanc, Marsanne, Muscat à Petits Grains, Roussanne, Sauvignon Blanc, and Viognier.

## COTEAUX DE MURVIEL
### Zonal *vin de pays* Map A, No.42

Just next to the Saint-Chinian area, this *vin de pays* produces some very good reds, which account for 85 percent of the output, made from Carignan, Cinsault, Grenache, Cabernet Sauvignon, Merlot, and Syrah. There are a number of rosés, but very few whites.

✓ *de Ciffre* (Val Taurou) • *de Ravanès* (Les Gravières du Taurou Grande Réserve)

## COTEAUX DE NARBONNE
### Zonal *vin de pays* Map A, No.43

Mostly soft red wines, and just 4 percent in total of white and rosé, come from this coastal edge of Corbières where the vines overlap with those of Coteaux du Languedoc.

✓ *Hospitalet*

## COTEAUX DE PEYRIAC
### Zonal *vin de pays* Map A, No.44

Full and rustic red wines, made from local grape varieties augmented by the Syrah, Cabernet, and Merlot, account for more than 80 percent of the production of this *vin de pays* in the heart of Minervois. The remainder is mostly rosé, with less than 1 percent white.

## COTEAUX DU PONT DU GARD
### Zonal *vin de pays* Map A, No.45

The Pont du Gard is a stunningly beautiful, three-tier Roman aqueduct from the 1st century BCE. Its bottom tier is still strong enough to support modern traffic 2,000 years later, but the wines of Coteaux du Pont du Gard, though mostly rich and powerful reds, are built for a considerably shorter life span. A small amount of white and rosé is also produced, with *vins primeurs* a local specialty.

✓ *Mas de Forton* • *Leyris Mazière*

## COTEAUX DU SALAGOU
### Zonal *vin de pays* Map A, No.46

Production is 80 percent red and 20 percent rosé, from a range of typical Languedoc grapes.

✓ *Mas d'Agalis*

## COTEAUX DE TANNAY
### Zonal *vin de pays* Map B, No.47

This relatively new *vin de pays* area east of Sancerre was created in 2001. White wines are made from Chardonnay or Melon de Bourgogne. Red and rosé come from Gamay and Pinot Noir, plus up to 20 percent of Gamay Teinturier de Bouze and Gamay de Chaudenay. Pure varietal wines are allowed.

✓ *Cyrille Raty* (Chardonnay)

## COTEAUX ET TERRASSES DE MONTAUBAN
### Zonal *vin de pays* Map B, No.48

Red and rosé wines from the Pays de La Garonne.

✓ *de Montels* (Louise)

## COTEAUX DU VERDON
### Zonal *vin de pays* Map B, No.49

This *vin de pays* in the northern hinterland of Côtes de Provence and Coteaux Varois was created as recently as 1992 and has no restriction on the grape varieties that may be used.

✓ *La Colline de Vignoble* (Merlot-Cabernet Sauvignon)

## CÔTES DU BRIAN
### Zonal *vin de pays* Map A, No.50

An area in Minervois, Côtes du Brian produces 90 percent red, from Carignan for the most part, although Grenache, Cinsault, Cabernet Sauvignon, Merlot, and Syrah may also be used. The balance of the production is principally rosé, with very few white wines. Pure varietal wines have been allowed since 2000.

✓ *la Combe Blanche* (Le Dessous de l'Enfer)

## CÔTES CATALANES
### Zonal *vin de pays* Map A, No.51

Much enlarged following the absorption of and merger with the former *vins de pays* of Catalan, Coteaux de Fenouillèdes, and Vals d'Agly. This nonsensical exercise of bureaucratic expediency has angered many, not least those in the Coteaux de Fenouillèdes, who were just beginning to make a name for themselves when their *vin de pays* was suppressed in September 2003. Furthermore, the inhabitants of the Fenouillèdes are not Catalan, nor do they speak Catalan. Pure varietal wines have been allowed since 2000.

✓ *Boudau* (Le Petit ClosRosé, Muscat Sec) • *Caves de Baixas* (Rozy) • *Cazes Frères* ❸ • *La Différence* (Carignan, Grenache Noir, Viognier Muscat) • *Galhaud* (Oenoalliance) • *Gauby* ❸ (La Soula) • *Mas Baux* (Velours Rouge) • *Mas Karolina* (Blanc Sec) • *de Pézilla* • *Salvat* (Fenouil Rouge) • *Arnaud de Villeneuve* (Muscat Moelleux)

## CÔTES DU CÉRESSOU
### Zonal *vin de pays* Map A, No.52

Typically light and fruity Languedoc wines are produced in fairly large amounts; 60 percent is red, 15 percent white, and 25 percent rosé.

## CÔTES DU CONDOMOIS
### Zonal *vin de pays* Map B, No.53

Production includes 60 percent red, dominated by the Tannat grape, and 40 percent white, from the Colombard or Ugni Blanc. A little rosé is also produced.

✓ *Plaimont* (Prestige du Condomois)

## CÔTES DE GASCOGNE
### Zonal *vin de pays* Map B, No.54

These deliciously tangy, dry white wines are the undistilled produce of Armagnac. Those made from the Colombard grape are the lightest, while those from the Ugni Blanc are fatter and more interesting. Manseng and Sauvignon Blanc are also used to good

aromatic effect in some blends. Less than 20 percent of production is red and barely 1 percent rosé. Pure varietal wines have been allowed since 2000.

✓ *Alain Brumont* (Les Menhirs) • *des Cassagnoles* (Gros Manseng Sélection) • *de Joy* (Sauvignon Gros Manseng) • *de Lartigue* • *Plaimont* • *du Tariquet* (Les Premières Gries, Les 4 Cépages)

## CÔTES DE LASTOURS
Zonal *vin de pays* Map A, No.55

This area roughly corresponds to the Cabardès VDQS and produces mostly red wines from a similar range of grapes. Just 4 percent rosé and 3 percent white (Mauzac, Chenin, Chardonnay, and Ugni Blanc) is made, with *vins primeurs* a local specialty.

✓ *Baron d'Ambres*

## CÔTES DE MONTESTRUC
Zonal *vin de pays* Map B, No.56

Production includes reds, made from Alicante Bouschet, Cabernets, Malbec, Merlot, and Jurançon Noir, and white wines, made from the Colombard, Mauzac, and Ugni Blanc.

## CÔTES DE PÉRIGNAN
Zonal *vin de pays* Map A, No.57

This area is within the southern extremity of the Coteaux du Languedoc, just north of La Clape AOC and incorporating some of La Clape's northern slopes. Almost 90 percent is red wine that is similar, if more rustic, in style to the wines of La Clape and made from a similar range of grape varieties, but with Grenache, Syrah, and Cinsault dominating. The fresh, dry rosé can be good quality and flavorsome too. Just 1 percent of white wine is made, mainly from Clairette and Ugni Blanc, but Terret and Macabéo are also permitted. *Vin primeur* is also made.

✓ *de La Negly* (Palazy Rosé)

## CÔTES DE PROUILLE
Zonal *vin de pays* Map A, No.58

These red, white, and rosé wines produced by the Côtes de Prouille appellation come from the Aude *département*.

## CÔTES DU TARN
Zonal *vin de pays* Map B, No.59

Côtes du Tarn is the *vin de pays* equivalent of Gaillac: some 60 percent is red, 30 percent white, and the rest rosé. These wines are made from *bordelais* and southwestern grape varieties, plus, uniquely for France, the Portugais Bleu. Gamay is often used for Côtes du Tarn Primeur, while together with Syrah it makes an appealing, delicate *saignée* rosé. Pure varietal wines have been allowed since 2000.

✓ *Chaumet Lagrange* (Braucol) • *Guy Fontaine* (Les Vignes des Garbasses Syrah) • *Sabrelle* (Chardonnay)

## CÔTES DE THAU
Zonal *vin de pays* Map A, No.60

A small denomination west of Béziers, producing almost equal quantities of red, white, and rosé from all the usual Languedoc varieties. These wines used to be used for vermouth until the upswing in *vin de pays*.

✓ *de Marie-Anais* (Syrano) • *Hugues de Beauvignac* (Syrah)

## CÔTES DE THONGUE
Zonal *vin de pays* Map A, No.61

Mostly red wine, from grapes including Grenache, Cinsault, Cabernet Sauvignon, Merlot, Syrah, and Carignan, with *vins primeurs* of the last three varieties a specialty. Emphasis is placed on pure varietal wines of all styles. Some 15 percent rosé and 10 percent white.

✓ *CV d'Alignan du Vent* (Icare, Montarels) • *Clos de l'Arjolle* • *de la Croix Belle* (Cascaïllou, No.7 Rouge) • *Deshenrys* (Lissac) • *Mont d'Hortes* (Sauvignon) • *Montplézy* (Félicité) • *Saint Rose* (Low Yield Roussanne)

## CÔTES DU VIDOURLE
Zonal *vin de pays* Map A, No.62

Wedged between the Coteaux du Languedoc and Costières de Nîmes, more than 80 percent of the wines produced are red, from Carignan, Grenache, Cinsault, Cabernet Sauvignon, Merlot, Cabernet Franc, and Syrah. About 15 percent rosé is made, but white is seldom seen.

## CREUSE
*Départementale vin de pays* Map B

Little-used *départementale vin de pays* right in the center of France. Red and rosé wines are made primarily from Cabernet Sauvignon, Cabernet Franc, Merlot and Tannat. White wines are primarily from Chenin Blanc, Sauvignon Blanc, and Sémillon. Pure varietal wines are allowed.

## CUCUGNAN
Zonal *vin de pays* Map A, No.63

A tiny denomination of essentially red wines in the midst of the Côtes du Roussillon Villages district, produced from Rhône varieties boosted by Cabernet Sauvignon and Merlot. Rosé may be made, but it seldom is, although there is an average of 1 percent dry white from Mauzac, Chenin Blanc, Chardonnay, and Ugni Blanc.

## DEUX-SÈVRES
*Départementale vin de pays* Map B

Simple wines of a frank nature, from the vineyards with the richest soil (and thus the poorest for wine production) in the Nantais. Pure varietal wines have been allowed since 2000.

✓ *Bouvet-Ladubay* (Non Pareils)

## DOUBS
*Départementale vin de pays* Map B

Recent *départementale vin de pays* with minute production, Doubs is in the very east of France, between the Jura and Alsace. Pure varietal wines have been allowed since 2000.

## DRÔME
*Départementale vin de pays* Map B

Red, white, and rosé wines are produced from typical Rhône varieties augmented by Gamay, Cabernet Sauvignon, and Merlot. More than 90 percent of the output is red and similar in style to Coteaux du Tricastin AOC. A small amount of decent rosé is made. Pure varietal wines have been allowed since 2000.

✓ *Le Plan* (Rouge) • *Sud-Est Appellations* (Syrah)

## DUCHÉ D'UZÈS
Zonal *vin de pays* Map A, No.64

This area overlaps all but 10 of the 131 villages in Vin de Pays des Cévennes.

✓ *les Collines du Bourdic* (La Rabassières)

## FRANCHE COMTÉ
Zonal *vin de pays* Map B, No.65

A vast area overlapping the Jura and Savoie, Franche Comté produces fresh, clean, crisp, but otherwise unremarkable red and rosé wines. Only the white, made from Chardonnay, Pinot Gris, and Pinot Blanc, is of any note. Wines produced in the village of Champlitte have the right to add the subzonal name Coteaux de Champlitte (65a) to the Franche Comté *vin de pays*.

✓ *Vignoble Guillaume* (Pinot Noir Collection Réservée)

## GARD
*Départementale vin de pays* Map B

A large production of mostly red wines made from Carignan, Grenache, Cinsault, Cabernet Sauvignon, Merlot, and Syrah. Some clean, fruity rosé and mainly Ugni Blanc-based white wines (with Viognier a growing niche within this small percentage). Pure varietal wines have been allowed since 2000.

✓ *Mas de Aveylands* • *Mas de Bressades* • *de Campuget* (Viognier Prestige) • *des Cantarelles* • *de Guiot* • *Saint-Antoine*

## GAULES
New zonal *vin de pays*

This covers "just" 95 villages in the Beaujolais district Revillages, and not the larger area that was originally envisaged. Red, white, and rosé wines made from Aligoté, Chardonnay, Gamay, Pinot Noir, Syrah, and Viognier. A minimum cellarage of three months prevents any *vin de primeur*, thereby protecting Beaujolais Nouveau.

## GERS

*Départementale vin de pays* Map B

Mostly white wines, similar in style to Côtes de Gascogne. Pure varietal wines have been allowed since 2000.

√ *Patrick Azcué* • *Château Bouscassé* • *Plaimont* (Rive Haute)

## GIRONDE

*Départementale vin de pays* Map B

Red and white wines made in isolated areas not classified for the production of Bordeaux. Pure varietal wines have been allowed since 2000.

## HAUTE GARONNE

*Départementale vin de pays* Map B

Robust red and rosé wines made from Jurançon Noir, Négrette, and Tannat grapes grown in old vineyards south of Toulouse, with a little Merlot, Cabernet, and Syrah. A minuscule amount of dry white is made, and total production of all styles is very small, but De Ribonnet has put this denomination on the viticultural map and is in a class apart from all the other producers. Pure varietal wines have been allowed since 2000.

√ *de Ribonnet*

## HAUTE MARNE

*Départementale vin de pays*

Located adjacent to Champagne's Aube and Burgundy's Côte d'Or, it is not surprising that Le Muid Montsaugeonnais has made some pretty good Pinot Noir. Pure varietal wines have been allowed since 2000.

√ *Le Muid Montsaugeonnais* (Pinot Noir Elevé en Fûts de Chêne)

## HAUTERIVE

Zonal *vin de pays* Map A, No.66

Formerly called Vin de Pays d'Hauterive en Pays d'Aude, this appellation was renamed in 2004, when it was merged with the former *vins de pays* of Coteaux de Termenès, Côtes de Lézignan, and Val d'Orbieu. Production is primarily red, made from a range of typical Languedoc and southwestern grapes in the Corbières. A little *vin primeur* is made, as well as small amounts of white and rosé.

## HAUTES-ALPES

*Départementale vin de pays* Map B

Very little wine is produced under this denomination, which is the *département* just south of the Savoie. Pure varietal wines have been allowed since 2000.

√ *de Trésbaudon* (Rouge)

## HAUTE-SAÔNE

*Départementale vin de pays* Map B

Rarely used, this is a minor *départementale vin de pays* for red, white, and rosé wines from unclassified vineyards in the south of Burgundy. Pure varietal wines have been allowed since 2000.

## HAUTE-VALLÉE DE L'AUDE

Zonal *vin de pays* Map A, No.67

Mostly dry whites, from Chardonnay, Chenin, Mauzac, and Terret grapes grown in the Limoux district. A quarter of the output is red, from *bordelais* grapes, with just 3 percent rosé. Pure varietal wines have been allowed since 2000.

DOMAINE
D'ANTUGNAC
· 2001 ·
*Chardonnay*
Mis en bouteille par · Christian COLLOVRAT · Jean-Luc TERRIER · à leur Domaine
VIN DE PAYS DE LA HAUTE-VALLÉE DE L'AUDE · PRODUCT OF FRANCE · WHITE WINE

√ *de l'Aigle* (Chardonnay Les Aigles, Pinot Noir Terres Rouges) • *Marc Ramires* (Prieuré d'Antugnac)

## HAUTE-VALLÉE DE L'ORB

Zonal *vin de pays* Map A, No.68

A limited amount of red, white, and rosé, primarily from Pinot Noir, Chardonnay, and Viognier. Pure varietal wines have been allowed since 2000.

√ *Marc Ramires* (Prieuré d'Antugnac) • *de Roquebrun* (Terres d'Orb)

## HAUTE-VIENNE

*Départementale vin de pays* Map B

Rarely used, minor *départementale vin de pays* for red, white, and rosé wines east of the Cognac region. Pure varietal wines have been allowed since 2000.

## HAUTS DE BADENS

Zonal *vin de pays* Map A, No.69

These red and rosé wines are produced in a rustic Minervois style.

## HÉRAULT

*Départementale vin de pays* Map B

Red wine accounts for 85 percent of production and is increasing. The choice of grapes is quite wide, but most blends are based on Carignan, Cinsault, Grenache, and Syrah, boosted by a small proportion of *bordelais* varieties. About 10 percent rosé and 5 percent white wine is produced, the latter made from Clairette, Macabéo, Grenache Blanc, and Ugni Blanc. Production is vast, over 11 million cases (one million hectoliters), making it the second or third largest *vin de pays*, together with Vin de Pays de l'Aude. Improved viticultural techniques have transformed what was once the heart of Midi mediocrity into delicious, brilliant-value wine in some cases. Pure varietal wines are allowed.

The most famous wine bearing this modest *vin de pays* denomination is, of course, Mas de Daumas Gassac. Situated northwest of Montpellier at Aniane, this property has been dubbed "the Lafite of the Languedoc," but when Aimé and Véronique Guibert purchased it, wine was the last thing on their minds. That was, however, before the visit of Professor Enjalbert, the Bordeaux geologist and author, who discovered Daumas Gassac had a rare, fine,

powdery volcanic soil that is an incredible 65 feet (20 meters) deep. Enjalbert predicted that it would yield a world-class wine if cultivated as a *grand cru*, and that is exactly what Aimé Guibert set out to do. I am not convinced about the rosé, and the white has been far too flabby in recent vintages, but the red is the equivalent of a Bordeaux *cru classé*. Even in lighter vintages, when Guibert gets slated by the critics, I think his red has a rare elegance that is missed just because it is not as big as people expect.

√ *Mas de Daumas Gassac* (Rouge) • *de la Fadèze* • *C. V. Frontignan* (Abeillon) • *La Grange des Pères* • *Mas de Janiny* (Cabernet Sauvignon) • *Les Quatre Pilas* (Mouchère)

## ÎLE DE BEAUTÉ

Zonal *vin de pays* Map B, No.70

With AOC wines accounting for just 15 percent of Corsica's wine output, its one all-encompassing (though technically not *départementale*) *vin de pays* has a huge impact on the perceived quality of this island's wine. Almost 60 percent of this *vin de pays* is red and 25 percent rosé, both made from a wide range of grapes, including many indigenous Corsican varieties, some of which may be related to certain Italian grapes. Grape varieties used include: Aleatico (red Muscat-like variety), Cabernet Sauvignon, Carignan, Cinsault, Grenache, Merlot, Syrah, Barbarossa, Nielluccio (the widest-planted on the island and said to be related to Sangiovese), Sciacarello (echoes of Provence's Tibouren), and Pinot Noir. A lot of effort is made to promote Corsican Pinot Noir, but at the time of writing this seems to be totally misguided. The best show decent varietal aroma, but lack an elegance of fruit and do not possess the essence of Pinot on the palate. Maybe someone will make good Corsican Pinot Noir, but it is a variety that requires a lot more care and attention in the vineyard and winery than is evident in any example I have tasted so far. Nielluccio has a reputation for good rosé, but as Orenga de Gaffory of Patrimonio in Corsica has shown, it also has the ability to produce a very fine red wine.

White wines from Chardonnay, Ugni Blanc, Muscat, and Vermentino are usually more demonstrative of clean, anaerobic handling and very cool fermentation than they are of any expression of *terroir*. Pure varietal wines have been allowed since 2000.

√ *Casabianca* (Nectar d'Automne) • *du Mont Saint-Jean* (Aleatico, Pinot Noir) • *de Patrapiana* (Nielluciu) • *de Saline* • *Terra Viecchia* (Rouge) • *Union des Vignerons* (Marestagno, Réserve du Président Muscat)

## INDRE

*Départementale vin de pays* Map B

Red, white, and rosé wines, including a pale *vin gris* style, from traditional Loire grape varieties are produced under this appellation. Pure varietal wines have been allowed since 2000.

## INDRE-ET-LOIRE

*Départementale vin de pays* Map B

From vineyards east of Tours, this *vin de pays* is 80 percent red, made primarily from Gamay, although Cabernet Franc and Grolleau are also used. A little white, but even less rosé, is made. Pure varietal wines are allowed.

## ISÈRE
### Départementale vin de pays Map B

Hardly used *départementale vin de pays*, most producers preferring one of a number of zonal appellations for the unclassified vineyards in this part of the northern Rhône Valley. Mostly red wine, a smattering of white, but no rosé. Pure varietal wines have been allowed since 2000.

## JARDIN DE LA FRANCE
### Regional *vin de pays* Map B

This *vin de pays* produces red, white, and rosé wines from 14 *départements* covering most of the Loire Valley. It would seem, from the wines most commonly encountered, that the majority of this vast output must be dry white, dominated by either Chenin Blanc or Sauvignon Blanc, but, according to the statistics, 60 percent is red. Generally a disappointing appellation, with the thin, acid Chardonnays being the most depressing, but the Cabernet Sauvignon from Pierre & Paul Freuchet is surprisingly soft and perfumed for this northerly denomination. Pure varietal wines have been allowed since 2000.

✓ *Paul Boutinot* (Signature Chardonnay) • *Adéa Consules* (Ligeria) • *Bruno Cormerais* (Elevé en Fûts de Chêne) • *de la Couperie* (Clyan Elevé en Fûts de Chêne) • *Levin* (Sauvignon Blanc) • *Manoir La Perrière* (Chardonnay) • *Henry Marionnet* (Provinage) • *du Petit Château* (Chardonnay) • *Château de La Ragotière* • *de la Saulze* (Gamay Rosé)

## LANDES
### Départementale *vin de pays* Map B

Red, white, and rosé wines are produced under this appellation. Approximately 80 percent is red, and the grapes used are traditional southwestern varieties. Pure varietal wines have been allowed since 2000.

✓ *Duprat Frères* (Cabernet-Tannat)

## LOIRE-ATLANTIQUE
### Départementale *vin de pays* Map B

Red and rosé wines, including a pale *vin gris*, are made from Gamay and Grolleau, while Folle Blanche and Melon are used for white, with some interesting developments using Chardonnay. Pure varietal wines are allowed.

✓ *Jean Douillard* (Melon)

## LOIRET
### Départementale *vin de pays* Map B

A small amount of red and rosé, including a pale *vin gris* style, made from Gamay. A Sauvignon Blanc white is also made. Pure varietal wines have been allowed since 2000.

## LOIR-ET-CHER
### Départementale *vin de pays* Map B

Red, white, and rosé wines, including a pale *vin gris*, are made from traditional Loire grape varieties, mostly from around Blois in the Cheverny area. Almost half the production is red and the rest white, but a touch more of the former is made, with very little rosé. Pure varietal wines have been allowed since 2000.

## LOT
### Départementale *vin de pays* Map B

Most wines are red, and claim either the regional Comté Tolosan denomination or Vin de Pays des Coteaux de Glanes. Pure varietal wines have been allowed since 2000.

✓ *des Ardailloux* (Chardonnay Tradition) • *Côtes d'Olt* (Terreo Malbec Réserve)

## LOT-ET-GARONNE
### Départementale *vin de pays* Map B

This denomination is seldom seen, as the wines in this *département* are mostly red and sold as Vin de Pays du Comté Tolosan, but a tiny amount of white wine is produced under the Vin de Pays du Lot-et-Garonne label. Pure varietal wines have been allowed since 2000.

✓ *C. V. des Coteaux du Mézinais* (Gros Manseng Moelleux)

## MAINE-ET-LOIRE
### Départementale *vin de pays* Map B

Production is 85 percent red, and white and rosé account for the rest, made from traditional Loire grape varieties in the Anjou-Saumur district. Substantial quantities are produced, but most are sold from the back door. Pure varietal wines have been allowed since 2000.

✓ *Gaillard* ❽

## MARCHES DE BRETAGNE
### Subregional *vin de pays* Map B, No.71

Wines from the Marches de Bretagne subregion have the right to add this name to the Vin de Pays du Jardin de la France. Production includes red and rosé wines, made predominantly from Abouriou, Gamay, and Cabernet Franc, plus a little white from Muscadet and Gros Plant.

## MAURES
### Zonal *vin de pays* Map B, No.72

This denomination has a very large production and covers most of the southern part of the Côtes de Provence. Almost half the wines are rosé of a similar style and quality to those of the *Vin de Pays du Var*. The rest is red, which is rich, warm, and spicy, while white wine accounts for just 5 percent of total output. Pure varietal wines have been allowed since 2000.

✓ *Borrely-Martin* (Le Carre de Laure) • *Dupéré-Barrera* (Nowat Syrah) • *Marouine* (Carignan Vieilles Vignes)

## MEUSE
### Départementale *vin de pays* Map B

This *vin de pays* produces red and rosé wines, including a pale *vin gris*, from Pinot Noir and Gamay. Some white wine from Chardonnay, Aligoté, and Auxerrois is also made. Pure varietal wines have been allowed since 2000.

✓ *de Coustille* (Pinot Gris) • *Laurent Degenève* (Auxerrois)

## MONT BAUDILE
### Zonal *vin de pays* Map A, No.73

Production is mostly red wine, from a typical Languedoc range of grapes grown in the foothills of the Causses de Larzac. Rosé and white account for less than 15 percent of the total output, although crisp, dry whites are on the increase.

✓ *d'Aupilhac* • *Cave de Mont Peyroux* (Ethnik)

## MONT-CAUME
### Zonal *vin de pays* Map B, No.74

Effectively the *vin de pays* of Bandol—it is indeed the red wines that are the best here, including some truly outstanding wines, such as Bunan's classic Cabernet Sauvignon. However, the main varieties for most red and rosé wines (which account for 45 percent of the total production) are Carignan, Grenache, Cinsault, Syrah, and Mourvèdre. A little white is produced, but it is of little interest. Pure varietal wines have been allowed since 2000.

✓ *Bunan* (Cabernet Sauvignon, Mourvèdre) • *Gauby* (Ginestre)

## MONTS DE LA GRAGE
### Zonal *vin de pays* Map A, No.75

These red and rosé wines are produced in a basic Languedoc style, often beefed up with Syrah grapes. White wines must be truly dry (less than 2.5 grams per liter residual sugar). Pure varietal wines have been allowed since 2000.

✓ *de la Bergerie d'Amilhac* (Syrah) • *Le Bosc* (Syrah) • *Condamine Bertrand* (Petit Verdot Gourmandise) • *de la Fadèze* (Merlot Elevé en Fûts de Chêne) • *Grange des Rouquette* (Agrippa) • *de Malleport* (Alexandre) • *Mas Montelle* (Jéricho) • *de Montlobre* (Tête de Cuvée) • *de Saint-Louis* • *du Soleil* (Solstice Merlot Réserve Barrique) • *des Soulie* (Merlot) • *de Terre Mégère* (Cabernet Sauvignon) • *Vigne Blanche* (Cabernet Sauvignon)

## NIÈVRE
### Départementale *vin de pays* Map B

Red, white, and rosé wines, production of which is mostly confined to the areas of Charité-sur-Loire, La Celle-sur-Nièvre, and Tannay. Pure varietal wines have been allowed since 2000.

## OC
### Regional *vin de pays* Map B

This vast appellation is the most successful of all *vins de pays*, commercially and qualitatively. It sells well because of the simplicity of its name, which even English speakers have no difficulty pronouncing, and it encompasses most of the best *vins de pays* produced in France. The "Oc" of this regional *vin de pays* is southern dialect for "yes," it being "oui" elsewhere in France; thus, Languedoc, the "tongue of Oc." Some 70 percent of production is red, with the balance split equally between

white and rosé. Even though most of the finest *vins de pays* are produced here, the volume of output is so vast that the quality will inevitably be variable. What has enabled so many truly fine wines to emerge in this denomination is the role of the so-called *cépages améliorateurs*. These grapes, such as Cabernet Sauvignon, Merlot, Syrah, Chardonnay, and Sauvignon Blanc, are not traditional in the region, but add greatly to the quality and finesse of more rustic local varieties. They also make excellent varietal wines. Viognier is on the increase as a varietal wine and makes a good-value, juicy-fruity, more exotic alternative to Chardonnay.

The quest for Pinot Noir du Vin de Pays d'Oc has been less satisfactory. They might succeed, but most efforts have been totally alien to any knowledgeable drinker's concept of this grape. Marselan (Cabernet Sauvignon x Grenache) has been authorized since December 2005.

✓ *de l'Aigle* (Chardonnay Les Aigles) • *des Aires Hautes* • *Astruc* (Chardonnay Réserve) • *de la Baume* • *Condamine Bertrand* (Cigalus, Elixir Rouge) • *Jean-Marc Boillot* (de la Truffière) • *des Bons Auspices* (Emparitz Cabernet Sauvignon) • *Chantovent* (Chardonnay Dolmen des Fées) • *Jean-Louis Denois* • *La Différence* • *Le Fort* (Blanche Chardonnay) • *Foncalieu* (Bouquet d'Oriane, Enseduna Réserve Syrah) • *de Gourgazaud* • *La Grange des Quatre Sous* • *de Granoupiac* (Merlot) • *James Herrick* • *Lalande* (Pinot Noir) • *Michel Laroche* (La Croix Chevalière) • *Paul Mas* (La Forge Merlot) • *Mas Carlot* (Syrah-Grenache) • *Mas Neuf* • *Gabriel Meffre* (Galet Vineyards) • *Montlobre* (Tête de Cuvée Rouge) • *de l'Orviel* (Chardonnay) • *Primo Palatum* (Chardonnay) • *Pavillon Blanc* (Les Collines du Bourdic) • *Peirière* (Elevé en Fûts de Chêne: Cabernet Sauvignon, Merlot, Syrah) • *Michel Picard* (Chardonnay) • *Preignes le Vieux* (Petit Verdot) • *Antonin Rodet* (Syrah) • *St-Hilaire* • *de Sérame* (Muscat Réserve) • *Skalli* (Réserve F: Cabernet Sauvignon or Merlot) • *du Soleil* (La Chasse du Pape: Chardonnay, Viognier, or Syrah) • *de Terre Mégère* • *CV des Trois Terroirs* (L'Esprit du Midi Viognier, XL Les Grès) • *Vedeau* (Chardonnay Terre d'Amandiers) • *Arnaud de Villeneuve* (Grenache, Syrah) • *Virginie* (Castel Chardonnay Réservée, Gold Label Cabernet Merlot Réserve) • *Les Yeuses* (Cuvée La Soure, Les Épices Syrah)

## PAYS DE RETZ
**Subregional *vin de pays* Map B, No.76**

This denomination may be added to the Vin de Pays du Jardin de la France. Best known for its rosé made from the Grolleau Gris (typified by Domaine du Parc), although red wines are also made from Grolleau, Gamay, and Cabernet Franc and account for as much as 70 percent of production. A tiny amount of white from Grolleau Gris can be found. Pure varietal wines have been allowed since 2000.

✓ *du Parc* (Grolleau)

## PÉRIGORD
**Zonal *vin de pays* Map B, No.77**

This name replaced the *départementale* Vin de Pays of Dordogne for vines growing on the *causse* or limestone region of Périgord, where vineyards flourished in the 19th century. Now there are just 45 acres (18 hectares), producing 35% rosé, 10% Perigord Noir, and 50% Tradition (an oak-matured red wine). The balance is sold as *vin primeur*. The subzonal Vin de Domme (77a) is allowed to add its name to this *vin de pays*.

✓ *CV des Coteaux du Céou* (Vin de Domme Tradition) • *Grand Gaillard* (Sauvignon Blanc)

## PETITE CRAU
**Zonal *vin de pays* Map B, No.78**

A small *vin de pays* south of Avignon, production is almost 80 percent red and 20 percent rosé from mostly Carignan, Grenache, Cinsault, and Syrah. Most rosé wines are made from, or dominated by, the Cinsault using the *saignée* method. Insignificant amounts of white from Ugni Blanc and Clairette are also produced. Pure varietal wines are allowed.

✓ *CV de Laure* (Cabernet Pétrarque et Laure)

## PORTES DE MÉDITERRANÉE
**Regional *vin de pays* Map B**

A vast regional *vin de pays*, but merely a modest production.

✓ *La Blaque* (Pinot Noir) • *de Régusse* (Muscat Moelleux)

## PÉZENAS
**Zonal *vin de pays* Map A, No.79**

Just south of Cabrières AOC, this single-village denomination produces mostly red wines. The grapes permitted are typical for Languedoc, with pure varietal wines on the increase, particularly Merlot, Cabernet Sauvignon, and Syrah. Rosé and white account for about 10 percent each, with crisp, dry whites on the increase, including a tiny amount sold as *vins primeurs*.

## PRINCIPAUTÉ D'ORANGE
**Zonal *vin de pays* Map B, No.80**

This is a full red wine, made predominantly from Rhône grape varieties grown around Orange, north of Avignon, in an area that bridges Châteauneuf-du-Pape and Côtes-du-Rhône Villages. Just 4 percent rosé and barely 1 percent white is made.

✓ • *de l'Ameillaud* • *Font Simian*

## PUY-DE-DÔME
**Départementale *vin de pays* Map B**

Red, white, and rosé wines of simple, rustic quality are made under this appellation. A *puy* is a volcano stack, a number of which are found in the Puy-de-Dôme *département*. Pure varietal wines have been allowed since 2000.

## PYRÉNÉES-ATLANTIQUES
**Départementale *vin de pays* Map B**

Two-thirds red and one-third white wine from traditional southwestern grape varieties is produced under this appellation. Pure varietal wines have been allowed since 2000.

## PYRÉNÉES-ORIENTALES
**Départementale *vin de pays* Map B**

From the most southerly French *département*, bordering Spain's Andorra region, much of the *vin de pays* in the Pyrénées-Orientales comes from the same area as the AOC Côtes-du-Roussillon and Vin de Pays Catalan. Most of the production consists of full, fruity reds, with just 10 percent rosé and 5 percent white. Pure varietal wines have been allowed since 2000.

✓ *The Fifteen* (Grenache)

## SABLES DU GOLFE DU LION
**Zonal *vin de pays* Map A, No.81**

A very go-ahead *vin de pays* situated along the Mediterranean coast of Gard, Hérault, and Bouches-du-Rhône, where the vines are mostly ungrafted and grown on an amazing sandbar with seawater on both sides. Production is, unusually, two-thirds rosé, including a large proportion in pale *vin gris* style, plus 30 percent red and a small amount of white wine. Pure varietal wines have been allowed since 2000.

✓ *Bosquet-Canet* (Cabernet Sauvignon) • *du Petit Chaumont* (Chardonnay) • *Listel* (Jarras Gris de Gris)

## SAINT BAUME
**New zonal *vin de pays***

Too recent to map, this *vin de pays* was established in September 2004 and encompasses vineyards in the villages of Bras, Brignoles, La Celle, Mazaugues, Méounes-lès-Montrieux, Nans-les-Pins, Néoules, Ollières, Plan-d'Aups, Riboux, La Roquebrussanne, Rougiers, Saint-Maximin, Saint-Zacharie, Signes, and Tourves in the Var *département*. No grape varieties are specified, but pure varietal wines are allowed.

## SAINT-GUILHEM-LE-DÉSERT
**Zonal *vin de pays* Map A, No.82**

Formerly called Vin de Pays des Gorges de L'Hérault, this denomination is in Coteaux du Languedoc and overlaps most of the Clairette du Languedoc appellation, yet less than 10 percent of its wines are white, with Ugni Blanc and Terret supporting Clairette. They are, however, better known than the reds, which account for over 80 percent of output. Some rosés are also made.

✓ *d'Aupilhac* (Plos des Baumes)

## SAINT-SARDOS
**Zonal *vin de pays* Map B, No.83**

This *vin de pays* produces wines from a typical hodgepodge of grape varieties, with reds and rosés from Cabernet Franc, Cabernet Sauvignon, Gamay, Syrah, and Tannat, plus a maximum of 30 percent in total of Gamay Teinturier de Bouze and Teinturier de Chaudenay, both of which have colored juice; while whites are made from Chardonnay, Mauzac, Muscadelle, Sauvignon Blanc, and Sémillon.

✓ *C. V. de Saint-Sardos* (Gilles de Morban Rouge)

## SAINTE-MARIE-LE-BLANCHE
**Zonal *vin de pays* Map A, No.84**

This *vin de pays* area straddles the border between Côte d'Or and Saône-et-Loire. Those in the Côte d'Or are just a few miles east of Beaune, and used to have the right to the Vin de Pays de la Côte d'Or until it was suppressed in 1998. Pure varietal wines are allowed. Red wines are made from one or more of Gamay, Pinot Gris, and Pinot Noir, while white wines are made from one of the following: Aligoté, Auxerrois, Chardonnay, Melon de Bourgogne, Pinot Blanc, and Pinot Gris.

☑ *Vincent Sauvestre* (Chardonnay)

## SAÔNE-ET-LOIRE
*Départementale vin de pays* Map B

Rarely exported *départementale vin de pays* for mostly red and white wines from unclassified vineyards in the Burgundy region. Pure varietal wines have been allowed since 2000.

## SARTHE
*Départementale vin de pays* Map B

Red, white, and rosé wines may be made, although production of this *vin de pays départementale* is minuscule and, as far as I am aware, limited to just one grower in Marçon. Pure varietal wines have been allowed since 2000.

## SEINE-ET-MARNE
*Départementale vin de pays* Map B

Recently created, rarely used, minor *départementale vin de pays* for red, white, and rosé wines from unclassified vineyards in between Champagne and Paris. Red and rosé wines from Gamay and Pinot Noir, white wines from Aligoté, Auxerrois, Chardonnay, and Sauvignon Blanc. Pure varietal wines have been allowed since 2000.

## TARN
*Départementale vin de pays* Map B

Relatively minor *départementale vin de pays* for red, white, and rosé wines produced outside the well-known Côtes du Tarn *vin de pays*. Pure varietal wines have been allowed since 2000.

☑ *C. V. de Labastide de Lévis* (Les Trois Bastides)

## TARN-ET-GARONNE
*Départementale vin de pays* Map B

Red wine accounts for 90 percent of the tiny production of this appellation, although some rosé and a minuscule amount of white is also made. Most of these vines are west of Montauban, in an area that can also claim the Vin de Pays Saint-Sardos, which overlaps part of a southwest VDQS called Vins de Lavilledieu. The grape varieties are similar to those for Lavilledieu, except for the fact that they can also include Merlot, Cabernet, and Tannat. Pure varietal wines have been allowed since 2000.

## TERROIRS LANDAIS
*Zonal vin de pays* Map B, No.85

These are red, white, and rosé wines from four separate subzonal areas in Aquitaine, each of which may be appended to this *vin de pays* denomination: Les Coteaux de Chalosse (85a—the largest area in the south of the Landes *département*, where vines grow in and around Dax and Murgon); Les Côtes de l'Adour (85b—from vines around Aire-sur-Adour and Geaune); Les Sables de l'Océan (85c—the romantic-sounding "Sands of the Ocean" refers to vines growing in the sand dunes around Messanges); and Les Sables Fauves (85d—the "Wild Sands" is a tiny enclave of vines west of Eauze). Reds and rosés are made from Tannat supported by *bordelais* varieties, while whites are primarily Ugni Blanc plus Colombard, Gros Manseng, and Baroque.

☑ *Michel Guérard* (Rouge de Bachen)

## THÉZAC-PERRICARD
*Zonal vin de pays* Map A, No.86

This is a small *vin de pays* adjoining the western extremity of Coteaux du Quercy, producing Cahors-like reds from Cabernet Franc, Cabernet Sauvignon, Gamay, Malbec, Merlot, and Tannat.

☑ *C. V. de Thézac-Perricard* (Vin du Tsar Le Bouquet)

## TORGAN
*Zonal vin de pays* Map A, No.87

As this is geographically the *vin de pays* equivalent of Fitou AOC, it is no surprise to discover that 98 percent of its wines are red. They are, in fact, made from a very similar range of grapes as that used to make Fitou, but certain other grapes are also permitted, including *bordelais* varieties and the Teinturier Alicante Bouschet. Rosé may be made, but seldom is, and the minuscule amount of aromatic dry white may be made from Clairette, Macabéo, and Marsanne. This *vin de pays* used to be known as Coteaux Cathares.

☑ *C. V. du Mont Tauch* (de Gardie)

## URFÉ
*Zonal vin de pays* Map B, No.88

Red wine is made in modest quantities. White and rosé may also be produced.

## VAL-DE-CESSE
*Zonal vin de pays* Map A, No.89

These are mostly red wines, plus 10 percent rosé, and 5 percent white from local grape varieties in the Minervois area.

## VAL-DE-DAGNE
*Zonal vin de pays* Map A, No.90

This area overlaps part of the Côtes de Malepère and produces almost entirely red wines from a choice of Carignan, Grenache, Terret Noir, Merlot, Cabernet Sauvignon, Cabernet Franc, and the Teinturier Alicante Bouschet. Very little rosé and white is made.

## VAL DE MONTFERRAND
*Zonal vin de pays* Map A, No.91

Mostly red wines, but rosé accounts for 25 percent of production, and white for 15 percent in this denomination, which encompasses the *garrigues* below the Cévennes. The usual Languedoc grapes are used. *Vin primeur* and *vin d'une nuit* are local specialities produced in relatively large quantities.

☑ *Mas de Martin* (Roi Patriote)

## VALLÉE DU PARADIS
*Zonal vin de pays* Map A, No.92

Mostly red wines from an area that overlaps Corbières and Fitou, made from Carignan, Syrah, Grenache, Cinsault, Cabernet Sauvignon, and Merlot. Very little white wine is made (usually as *vin primeur*) and even less rosé. A heavenly name, even to English-speakers' ears, which no doubt helps it on export markets, which account for almost half its sales.

☑ *Jeanjean*

## VAR
*Départementale vin de pays* Map B

This denomination is one of the largest producers of *vins de pays*. Covering the vast majority of the Côtes de Provence AOC, it not surprisingly produces a large quantity of rosé:

no less than 45 percent, in fact. The wines are usually made by the *saignée* method and range from a very pale *vin gris* style, through orange to almost cherry red. The quality is equally as variable. The big, rich, spicy reds are much better and of a more consistent quality, often using Syrah, Mourvèdre, and Cabernet Sauvignon to boost the Grenache, Cinsault, Carignan, and Roussane du Var, on which the rosés mainly rely. Some white wines are also made, but represent just 5 percent of production. They are not usually very exciting, and are mostly made from Ugni Blanc, Clairette, Bourboulenc, and Vermentino. The white from Rabiega is one of the exceptions, relying on Chardonnay for body and Viognier and Sauvignon Blanc to lift the Ugni Blanc base. Pure varietal wines have been allowed since 2000.

☑ *les Caves du Commandeur* (Syrah) • *de Garbelle* (Vermentino) • *le Saint André* • *Château Sarrins* • *Château Thuerry* (L'Exception)

## VAUCLUSE
*Départementale vin de pays* Map B

Three-quarters of output of this *vin de pays* is red, similar to basic Côtes-du-Rhone. Rosé can be fresh, and accounts for just 10 percent of output; white is generally the least interesting. Pure varietal wines are allowed.

☑ *de la Citadelle* (Cabernet Sauvignon) • *Fondacci* (Chasan) • *Fontaine du Clos* (Chardonnay) • *de Marotte*

## VAUNAGE
*Zonal vin de pays* Map A, No.93

Light red wines made in typical Languedoc style.

## VENDÉE
*Départementale vin de pays* Map B

Red, white, and rosé wines are produced in small quantities, in a style similar to Fiefs Vendéens (which was a *vin de pays* until it was promoted to VDQS status in December 1984). Pure varietal wines are allowed.

## VICOMTÉ D'AUMELAS
*Zonal vin de pays* Map A, No.94

Overlapping part of Cabrières, this *vin de pays* produces mostly red wines of a simple, fresh, fruity style, from traditional southwestern grape varieties, such as the typical Languedoc grape. Just over 10 percent of wines are rosé, and a tiny amount of crisp, dry white is produced.

## VIENNE
*Départementale vin de pays* Map B

This appellation produces red, white, and rosé wines, most of which are grown in and around the Haut-Poitou district. Pure varietal wines have been allowed since 2000.

☑ *Ampelidae*

## VISTRENQUE
*Zonal vin de pays* Map A, No.95

This appellation produces red and rosé wines, which are made in very small quantities. White wine may also be produced.

## YONNE
*Départementale vin de pays* Map B

The Yonne is a white-only appellation, and its production of wines is quite small. Pure varietal wines have been allowed since 2000.

# The WINES of
# ITALY

THE WINES OF ITALY ARE RICH IN POTENTIAL
but lack focus; consequently, the country's
image is muddled, when it should really be
diverse. In Italy, vines are so easy to grow
that one even expects them to shoot up from
cracks in the sidewalk after a Mediterranean
squall. Furthermore, the number of interesting
indigenous grape varieties is greater than can
be found in any other major winemaking country
of the world, including France. However, there
are no wine regions, great or otherwise, in
Italy—just provinces that abut each other.
Consumers cannot visualize Italian wines in the
maps of their minds as they can French wines.
Vine varieties and the types of wine they make
not only merge within provinces, but also
overlap their boundaries, blurring the already
confused picture. Despite this, Italy, like France,
makes a quarter of the world's wines, and Italian
exports are healthy. If and when Italy manages
to project a coherent image of distinct regional
styles, France will have a rival to worry about.

HILLSIDE VINES ABOVE FUMANE, VENETO
*The town of Fumane is situated in one of five valleys
that comprise the historic Valpolicella Classico area.*

# ITALY

*This country churns out new appellations as if there is no tomorrow, with far too many that are much too obscure. The trend also continues to promote ordinary DOCs to even-less-than-ordinary DOCGs. Italy has an extraordinary and exceptional potential to make some of the greatest wines in the world, yet seems even more inept than France at running its wine industry.*

IT IS STAGGERING TO THINK that a quarter of the world's wine is Italian yet, despite 4,000 years of Italian winemaking history, the Italian wine industry remains in a state of flux. Italy's enormous wine production has given many discerning wine drinkers a misleading impression of the country's true quality

### MONTALCINO
*With its famous Brunello vines in the foreground, Montalcino basks in Tuscan sunshine. Viticulturally, the surrounding area is highly prestigious; its tannic red wines generally need at least 10 years' maturation.*

potential. Italy can, and does, make many fine wines, but they have always been surrounded by so much *vin ordinaire* that finding them is a hit-and-miss affair. Like Italy, France churns out a huge volume of wine and its production can include a fair amount of plonk, but the names of great French wines roll off the tongue of even the uninitiated, and, rightly or wrongly, France has managed to get away with it, whereas Italy never has. Yet Italy has at least as much potential in terms of the diversity of its *terroir* and a plethora of native grape varieties. The key problem is identity: in Italy vines grow in every corner, whereas in France they are mostly confined to half a dozen major regions and each of these has its own recognizable style and reputation.

## ITALY'S LAW OF MEDIOCRITY
Italy's DOC legislation was introduced in 1963, but this law was fundamentally flawed because it failed to establish a small number of easily identifiable regions, each bearing an umbrella name and style. It also actively encouraged increased volume by officially recognizing the most productive grape varieties and classifying the highest-yielding areas on the edges of famous appellations. The late 1950s and early 1960s were crucial in the development of the modern wine industry in Europe, and Italy's DOC system

encouraged its largest bottlers to move out of the low-yielding, hilly, *classico* areas, which make better wines than the higher-yielding plains but are the more difficult and expensive to maintain. From this point, the Italian wine industry became increasingly dominated by mass production; most wineries became passionless factories and the quality of Italy's most famous wines sank as fast as the volume of production increased.

At first, out of respect for Senator Paolo Desana, who fathered the DOC concept, Italy ignored foreign criticism of its new wine regime. But by the early 1980s, its greatest wine names were so devalued that many of its best wines were being sold as *vini da tavola*, which made a mockery of the DOC system. In the end, even the most conservative Italians had to admit something must be done. Over the next 10 years, successive agricultural ministers tried to overhaul Italy's wine laws, but failed because of the political clout of the industrial bottlers, who had a lot to gain by flooding the market with cheap wines. When agricultural minister Giovanni Goria declared his intention to press for even more radical changes than any of his predecessors had, few took him seriously. No one would have bet a single lira on Goria's success, yet within 10 weeks of his appointment, a "New Disciplinary Code for Denomination of Wines of Origin" had been ratified by the Senate.

## GORIA'S LAW
In February 1992 Law 164, now known simply as Goria's Law or the Goria Law, replaced Desana's wine regime. When the law first

### ITALY
*As might be expected of a nation so geographically and culturally diverse, Italy produces a vast array of different types of wine. Away from the mainland, the islands of Sicily and Sardinia both have thriving wine industries.*

| | |
|---|---|
| | Northwest Italy *see also pp266,267* |
| | Northeast Italy *see also p275* |
| | West-Central Italy *see also pp282,283* |
| | East-Central Italy *see also p289* |
| | Southern Italy and the Islands *see also pp292, 293* |
| —— | *Provincia* boundary |
| ▲ | Height above sea level (meters) |

came into force, much attention was focused on the introduction of a brand new category called IGT (*Indicazioni Geografiche Tipiche*). The equivalent of French *vins de pays*, IGTs were supposed to form a buffer between the DOCs and *vini da tavola*, Goria having denied the latter the right to bear any geographical provenance other than Italy itself. Each IGT would come from an officially recognized zone of production, but could not claim to be anything more specific, such as the product of a village, microzone, estate, or single vineyard. Under Law 164 all such specific origins were restricted to DOC or DOCG wines.

In the euphoric first few months of this new law, it was predicted that there would be 150 to 200 IGTs, accounting for some 130 million cases (12 million hectoliters) of wine, which should—according to Goria's own plans—rise to 40 percent of the total Italian wine output, representing 10 percent of world production. For almost five years, no applications were received for IGT status. Without the right to mention the specific origins of these wines, yet being obliged to meet similar criteria to a DOC, why would producers bother, when they might as well opt for DOC or simply make *vino da tavola*? This is why the major thrust of Goria's groundbreaking law was considered, even in Italy, to have been stillborn. Then, with the 1996 harvest, the applications poured in, and there are now no fewer than 118 classified IGTs, in addition to the 309 DOCs and 30 DOCGs.

### NEW RESPECT FOR THE DOCS?

Did the Goria Law successfully reconfigure the fundamentally flawed DOCs and DOCGs? The answer is yes and no. "No" because Italy's wines will never achieve their true potential until, like those of France, they can be encapsulated within half a dozen major regions of recognizable style (*see* DOC's Lack of Specificity below) and reputation. Goria did not even attempt to tackle this problem. Furthermore, Italy's greatest wines will never receive the international acclaim they deserve until their delimited areas are reduced to the original hilly *classico* districts, about which Goria also did nothing.

Until Goria's Law, many wines were denied the *vini da tavola* status because Italy's appellation system defined the characteristics of each DOC, and in so doing did not take into account the foreign grapes and nontraditional vinification methods that most premium *vini da tavola* came to employ. Giovanni Goria had the sense to realize that any system that did not recognize some of the country's finest wines is a discredited system. He thus made it easier for such wines to be accepted within established DOCs.

To qualify for DOC status, the wine or wines must have a history of at least five years' production. Any DOC with a further

five years of recorded production can apply for a DOCG, providing it has acquired a "reputation and commercial impact both at home and at an international level."

### DOC'S LACK OF SPECIFICITY

Part of the problem of Italian wines being unable to project a readily discernible image is the number of ways in which a single DOC wine may be interpreted. An appellation system should project and protect a recognizable style (and, one hopes, quality) through detailed regulations, or it should simply make sure the provenance of a wine is as stated—guaranteeing where it comes from, even if it is a blend of different areas. The very last thing that any wine regime should do is insist on an intricate recipe of grape-variety percentages and precise geographical limitation, then say it can be dry, off-dry, medium sweet, sweet, still, *passito*, *frizzantino* (slightly sparkling), *frizzante* (semi-sparkling), or *spumante* (fully sparkling). All this does is foster the uncertain image with which Italian wines have long been lumbered.

### ALL THAT SPARKLES

No country has as many sparkling wine appellations as Italy, with its optional "may be *spumante*" clauses littering over 100 of its DOCs, including some of its truly greatest red wines. However, despite so many possibilities, Italy had no specific appellation for dry sparkling wine until 1995 when Franciacorta, the first and still the only appellation to insist on the traditional method, was given DOCG status. The rest of Italy's little-known, half-forgotten sparkling wine appellations are all *cuve close*. Bottle-fermentation does not guarantee quality, but it does encourage producers in the right direction, which is why it is a mistake for any dry sparkling DOC wine to be produced by any other process. Until all DOC *cuve close* is outlawed, no Italian dry sparkling wine will be taken seriously and Franciacorta's efforts to establish the country's first classic *brut* appellation will be frustrated.

### FUTURE SIMPLICITY

The solution to Italy's wine worries is very simple. Map out no more than half-a-dozen truly classic Italian wine regions, reduce the number of DOCs within these regions to a maximum of 100, all limited to historically authentic areas, and the most famous styles (no more multiple choice appellations!), with tough regulations and qualifying tastings performed by an independent

RIONERO, BASILICATA
*A 17th-century farm building on the Conca d'Oro estate in Vulture, where Fratelli d'Angelo produces a great red wine called Aglianico del Vulture.*

# ITALIAN LABEL LANGUAGE

**ABBOCCATO** Slightly sweet

**AMABILE** Sweeter than *abboccato*

**AMARO** Bitter or very dry

**ANNATA** This means "year" and often precedes or follows the vintage date. At least 85 percent of the wine must be from the vintage indicated. *See also Vendemmia*

**ASCIUTTO** Bone dry

**AUSLESE** German term used in the Alto Adige for wines from selected grapes

**AZIENDA, AZIENDA AGRICOLA, AZIENDA AGRARIA, OR AZIENDA VITIVINICOLA** Estate winery

**BIANCO** White

**CANTINA SOCIALE OR COOPERATIVA A** cooperative winery

**CASCINA** North Italian term for a farm or estate

**CASA VINICOLA** A commercial winery

**CERASUOLO** Cherry red, used for vividly colored rosés

**CHIARETTO** Wines falling between very light red and genuine rosé

**CLASSICO** The best, oldest, or most famous part of a DOC zone

**CONSORZIO** A group of producers who control and promote wine, usually insisting on higher standards than DOC regulations enforce

**DENOMINAZIONE DI ORIGINE CONTROLLATA, OR DOC** There are more than 250 DOCs, but some are multiple-varietal appellations covering as many as 12 different wines, resulting in more than

600 DOC names. This is similar, and just as worthless as, the French AOC system, as both merely guarantee mediocrity. The producer's name is still the best assurance of quality.

**DENOMINAZIONE DI ORIGINE CONTROLLATA E GARANTITA, OR DOCG** Theoretically the highest-quality official denomination, but encompasses a lot of very ordinary wine, as well as isolated pockets of truly fine wine. Again, the producer's name is the best assurance of quality.

**DOLCE** Very sweet

**FATTORIA** Farm

**FERMENTAZIONE NATURALE** Method of producing sparkling wine by natural refermentation in a tank or bottle

**FIORE** Term meaning "flower." Often part of a name, it indicates quality, as it implies that the first grape pressing has been used.

**FRIZZANTE** Semi-sparkling, the equivalent of *pétillant*

**FRIZZANTINO** Very lightly sparkling

**IMBOTTIGLIATO ALL'ORIGINE** Estate-bottled

**INDICAZIONE GEOGRAFICA TIPICA, OR IGT** The Italian equivalent of a French *vin de pays*

**LIQUOROSO** Usually fortified and sweet, but may also be dry wine that is simply high in alcohol

**LOCALITÀ, RONCO, OR VIGNETO** Indicates a single-vineyard wine

**MESSO IN BOTTIGLIA NELL'ORIGINE** Estate-bottled

**METODO CLASSICO OR METODO TRADIZIONALE** The Italian for traditional method

**PASSITO** Strong, often sweet wine made from semidried grapes

**PASTOSO** Medium-sweet

**PRODUTTORE ALL'ORIGINE** Estate-bottled

**RAMATO** Copper-colored wine made from Pinot Grigio grapes that are briefly macerated on their skins.

**RECIOTO** Strong, sweet wine made from semidried grapes

**RIPASSO** Wine refermented on the lees of a *recioto* wine

**RISERVA OR RISERVA SPECIALE** DOC or DOCG wines that have been matured for a statutory number of years (the *speciale* is older)

**ROSATO** Rosé

**ROSSO** Red

**SECCO** Dry

**SEMI-SECCO** Medium-sweet

**SPUMANTE** Fully sparkling

**STRAVECCHIO** Very old wines aged according to DOC or DOCG rules

**SUPERIORE** When part of the appellation, this usually refers to a longer minimum aging period before the wine can be sold

**TALENTO** A registered trademark signifying a sparkling wine made by the traditional method

**TENUTA** Estate

**UVAGGIO** Wine blended from various grape varieties

**VECCHIO** Old

**VENDEMMIA** This means "harvest" and often precedes or follows the vintage date. At least 85 percent of the wine must be from the vintage indicated. *See also Annata*

**VIGNA OR VIGNETO** Vineyard

**VIN SANTO OR VINO SANTO** Traditionally sweet, occasionally dry, white wine made from *passito* grapes stored in sealed casks, and not topped up for several years

**VINO** Wine

**VINO NOVELLO** Italian equivalent of Vin Primeur or Vin Nouveau

**VINO DA PASTO** Ordinary wine

**VINO DA TAVOLA** Literally "table wine," this is Italy's most basic category, but as well as including most of the country's plonk, it also includes some of its greatest wines, although many of the latter are gradually developing their own appellations

---

body with no vested interests. Set up a panel of experts to determine the 12 truly greatest wines to receive DOCG status, and set that in stone, so that no expansion can ever dilute the DOCG reputation. Within each DOCG, an Italian equivalent of *grand cru* and *premier cru* classification should be made. Then dispose of all the 118 IGTs except for the 12 regional IGTs (Basilicata, Toscana, Sicilia, etc.), and increase their number to 20, which would cover the entire country. There should be no other type of IGT. To balance this restriction, I would encourage the greatest flexibility in IGT regulations, including the use of single-village, single-estate, and individual site names. I would even allow the use of obsolete DOCs and IGTs (providing they are not classified as such, and their names are printed at no more than one-third the size of the regional IGT), so that no producer could claim that he had been prevented from selling his wine under the appellation for which it had become known, however obscure or meaningless that might have been to the outside world. The bureaucrats might squeal at the thought of such a thing, but it really does not matter. What matters is that these IGTs would have a recognizable name and therefore offer some sense of place

for drinkers in other countries. Just as important, a flexible IGT could be used both to preserve traditional values and promote innovation. And, finally, the clever part: the Italians should steal René Renou's concept of *Site et Terroir d'Excellence* (STE—*see* p.58). If the French authorities are too stupid to adopt such an ingenious idea, then the Italians should demonstrate what an opportunity they have missed. With the number of regional IGTs and DOCGs fixed, there must be another means of rewarding true standout quality, if any new system is to avoid the current wine regime's guarantee of mediocrity, and a nice big STE stamp on the label of an IGT or DOC wine would provide that. Imagine the difference it would make. A cluster of STE-awarded IGT wineries might one day elect to form a new DOC, but the flexibility of IGT and premium attracted by STE status should be sufficient to keep most wineries in the IGT system, thereby reducing any threat of a major expansion of the number of DOCs. And while the highest-flying STE-awarded DOCs should never be allowed to join the ranks of the DOCGs (all the best systems have something intrinsically unfair, yet inherently stable, built into them), they might well fetch the price of a top DOCG.

# NORTHWEST ITALY

*This area includes the great wine region of Piedmont as well as the regions of Liguria, Lombardy, and Valle d'Aosta. Generally, the wines are fuller and richer than those of northeastern Italy, which is a more mountainous area.*

FEW AREAS ENCOMPASS such contrasting topographies as northwest Italy, from the alpine *pistes* of the Valle d'Aosta and the Apennines of Liguria to the alluvial plains of the Po River. Contrast is also evident in the character of its two most famous wines—the big, black, and tannic Barolo DOCG and the light, water-white, effervescent, and grapey-sweet Asti DOCG.

## PIEDMONT (PIEMONTE)

Piedmont is dominated by two black grapes (Nebbiolo and Barbera) and one white (Moscato). Nebbiolo makes the magnificently rich and smoky Barolo and the elegant, more feminine, yet sometimes just as powerful, Barbaresco. The Barbera has a much greater yield than Nebbiolo but is potentially almost as fine. It is softer in tannin, at least as high in acidity, and

**NORTHWEST ITALY,** *see also p.263*
*The presence of the Alps gives this largely hilly region a hot growing season and a long fall. The finest wines come from the foothills of Piedmont, which provide ideal growing conditions for the late-ripening Nebbiolo grape.*

### AVERAGE ANNUAL PRODUCTION

| REGION | DOC PRODUCTION | TOTAL PRODUCTION |
|---|---|---|
| Piedmont | 11 million cases (1 million hl) | 44 million cases (4 million hl) |
| Lombardy | 4 million cases (400,000 hl) | 22 million cases (2 million hl) |
| Liguria | 78,000 cases (7,000 hl) | 4 million cases (400,000 hl) |
| Valle d'Aosta | 5,550 cases (500 hl) | 350,000 cases (30,000 hl) |

*Percentage of total Italian production: Piedmont, 5.2%; Lombardy, 2.6%; Liguria, 0.52%; Valle d'Aosta, 0.04%.*

excels around Alba and, to a slightly lesser extent, around Asti. White Asti, made from Moscato, is Italy's most popular fine wine. Whether still, *frizzantino*, or *spumante*, Asti is light and succulently sweet, with a mesmerizing grapey character. Fully sparkling Asti is no longer called Asti Spumante because the term, like *mousseux*, has a cheap, low-quality connotation and Asti is undeniably the world's greatest dessert-style sparkling wine.

## LOMBARDY (LOMBARDIA)

Northeast of Piedmont, Lombardy stretches from the flat plains of the Po Valley to snow-clad Alpine peaks. The region's finest wines

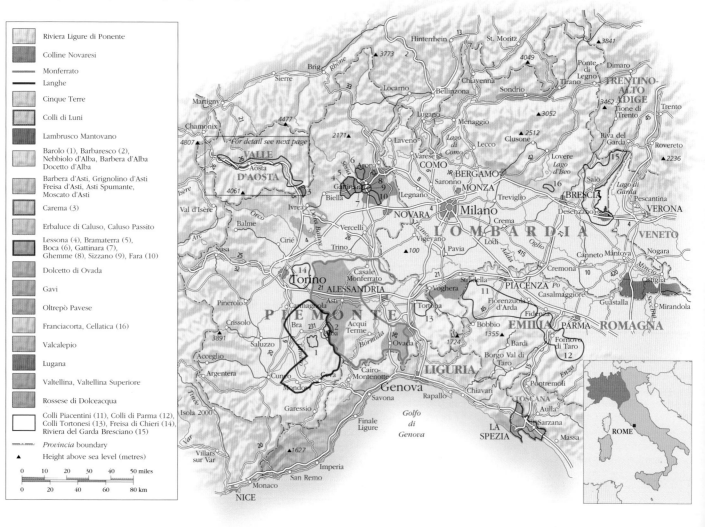

**Legend:**
- Riviera Ligure di Ponente
- Colline Novaresi
- Monferrato
- Langhe
- Cinque Terre
- Colli di Luni
- Lambrusco Mantovano
- Barolo (1), Barbaresco (2), Nebbiolo d'Alba, Barbera d'Alba Docetto d'Alba
- Barbera d'Asti, Grignolino d'Asti Freisa d'Asti, Asti Spumante, Moscato d'Asti
- Carema (3)
- Erbaluce di Caluso, Caluso Passito
- Lessona (4), Bramaterra (5), Boca (6), Gattinara (7), Ghemme (8), Sizzano (9), Fara (10)
- Dolcetto di Ovada
- Gavi
- Oltrepò Pavese
- Franciacorta, Cellatica (16)
- Valcalepio
- Lugana
- Valtellina, Valtellina Superiore
- Rossese di Dolceacqua
- Colli Piacentini (11), Colli di Parma (12), Colli Tortonesi (13), Freisa di Chieri (14), Riviera del Garda Bresciano (15)
- *Provincia* boundary
- ▲ Height above sea level (metres)

# FACTORS AFFECTING TASTE AND QUALITY

### ✦ LOCATION
Flanked to the north and west by the Alps and by the Ligurian Sea to the south, northwest Italy contains the provinces of Piedmont, Lombardy, Liguria, and Valle d'Aosta.

### CLIMATE
The winters are severe with frequent inversion fogs rising out of the valleys. Summers are hot, though not excessively so, but hail can damage the grapes at this time of year. Long falls enable the late-ripening Nebbiolo grape to be grown very successfully.

### ASPECT
This area covers mountains, foothills (*piedmont* means "foothill"), and the valley of Italy's longest river, the Po. Grapes are grown on hillsides that provide good drainage and exposure to the sun. In classic areas such as Barolo, every south-facing hillside is covered with vines, while in Lombardy many vineyards extend down to the rich, alluvial plains of the Po Valley.

### SOIL
A wide range of soils with many local variations, the predominant type is calcareous marl (*see* p.18), which may be interlayered or intermingled with sand and clay.

### VITICULTURE AND VINIFICATION
The great red wines of the region have suffered in the past from long aging in large wooden vats, as many growers bottled their wine only when they sold it. This practice dried up the fruit and oxidized the wine. However, many wines are bottled at the optimum time although there is still no consensus about the best aging vessels. The use of *cuve close* for sweet, grapey styles of wine from Asti has been very successful and these wines sell well internationally. Some of the same *spumante* houses have developed dry *spumante* from Pinot and Chardonnay grapes, using the traditional method, to produce fine-quality sparkling wines.

### 🍇 GRAPE VARIETIES
**Primary varieties**: Barbera, Muscat (*syn.* Moscato), Nebbiolo (*syn.* Chiavennasca)
**Secondary varieties**: Arneis, Blanc de Morgex, Bonarda, Brachetto, Brugnola, Cabernet Franc, Cabernet Sauvignon, Casalese, Chardonnay, Cortese, Croatina (*syn.* Bonarda in Lombardy, but not the true Bonarda of Piedmont), Dolcetto (*syn.* Ormeasco in Liguria), Erbaluce, Favorita, Freisa, Fumin, Gamay, Grenache, Grignolino, Gropello, Incrocio Terzi (Barbera **x** Cabernet Franc), Lambrusco, Malvasia, Marzemino, Mayolet, Merlot, Neyret, Petit Rouge (*syn.* Oriou), Petite Arvine, Pigato, Pignola Valtellina, Pinot Blanc (*syn.* Pinot Bianco), Pinot Gris (*syn.* Pinot Grigio, Malvoisie, not Malvasia), Pinot Noir (*syn.* Pinot Nero), Premetta, Riesling (*syn.* Riesling Renano), Rossese, Rossola, Ruché, Schiava Gentile, Syrah, Timorasso, Tocai Friulano (separate variety— neither Pinot Grigio nor Malvasia), Trebbiano (*syn.* Buzzetto), Ughetta, Uva Rara, Vermentino, Vespolina, Vien de Nus, Welschriesling (*syn.* Riesling Italico)

**PERGOLA-TRAINED VINES**
*These Nebbiolo vines, grown near Carema in Piedmont, are trained on a Pergola Piemontese. They are made into a fragrant, medium-bodied wine.*

include Franciacorta's full reds and its new DOCG for classic *brut* sparkling wines, plus the best of Valtellina's red Sassella. These wines are still relatively unknown compared with Piedmont's Barolo and Barbaresco and are good value.

## LIGURIA
One of Italy's smallest regions, Liguria is more famous for its Riviera, which is set against the dramatic and beautiful backdrop of the Maritime Alps, than it is for its wines. Cinque Terre, which is the best-known Ligurian wine, is named after the *Cinque Terre*, or five villages, which are perched along the Ligurian coast, above which the steep, intricately terraced vineyards tower like some great Aztec pyramid. Other than the Cinque Terre, interesting wines include the soft, spicy Rossese di Dolceacqua and the vividly colored Albenga rosé of the Riviera Ligure di Ponente DOC. The Colli di Luni is almost Tuscan, and part of this DOC even overlaps that region, so it is not surprising that it is capable of producing a decent Sangiovese. However, most Ligurian wines belong to the category of pleasant vacation drinking, and some of the best potential vineyards have been grubbed up to accommodate the tourists who drink them.

## VALLE D'AOSTA
If Liguria is a marginal wine region, then Valle d'Aosta is almost subliminal. High in the Alps, overlooked by Mont Blanc and the Matterhorn, the Valle d'Aosta looks at first as if it could as easily be a part of France or Switzerland as of Italy, but the only easy, natural access is from Piedmont along the Dora Baltea River. Italy's smallest and most mountainous wine region, the Valle d'Aosta has picturesque, high-altitude vineyards that produce some enjoyable wines, particularly Chambave, Nus, and Torrette, just three of the 20 wines within the Valle d'Aosta DOC. However, most are tourist wines; the best are easy-drinking and unpretentious.

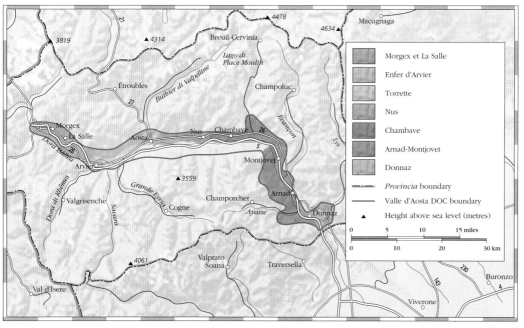

**VALLE D'AOSTA,** *see also opposite*
*The winters here are cold and snowy, but summers in the valley can be very hot with contrastingly cold nights, which should make for some exciting wines.*

Morgex et La Salle
Enfer d'Arvier
Torrette
Nus
Chambave
Arnad-Montjovet
Donnaz

- - - *Provincia* boundary
—— Valle d'Aosta DOC boundary
▲ Height above sea level (metres)

THE APPELLATIONS OF
# NORTHWEST ITALY

## CLASSIC BRUT SPARKLING WINES

All these wines are made by the traditional method.

🍷— Upon purchase—for all regions

✓ **Lombardy** *Bellavista Cuvée Brut*
  • *Bellavista Gran Cuvée pas Operé*
  • *Berlucchi Brut Cuvée Impériale*
  • *Berlucchi Brut Cuvée Impériale Millesimato* • *Berlucchi Brut Cuvée Impériale Max Rosé* • *Ca'del Bosco Franciacorta Pinot Brut* • *Ca'del Bosco Franciacorta pas Dose* • *Ca'del Bosco Franciacorta Crémant Brut* • *Doria Pinot Brut, Mirabella Franciacorta Brut* • *Villa Mazzucchelli Brut* • *Villa Mazzucchelli pas Dose*

  **Piedmont** *Stefano Barbero, Luigi Bosca Brut Nature, Contratto Brut*

## ALBENGA DOC
### Liguria

Vividly colored, dry, and characterful, Liguria's best-known rosés are now classified as part of the Riviera Ligure di Ponente DOC. *See* Riviera Ligure di Ponente DOC.

## ARENGO
### Piedmont

A soft, light-bodied, fruity non-DOC Barbera red made by several Asti producers.

## ARNAD-MONTJOVAT DOC
### Valle d'Aosta

A red-only subappellation of the regional Valle d'Aosta DOC producing Nebbiolo-based red wines, with up to 30 percent Dolcetto, Freisa, Neyret, Pinot Noir, and Vien de Nus. *See* Valle d'Aosta DOC.

## ARNEIS DI ROERO DOC
### Piedmont

These wines are produced from the ancient Arneis grape grown in the hills north of Alba. Formerly a *vino da tavola*, the high price and reputation of these wines ensured they would eventually become part of the Roero DOC. The best are amazingly rich and full-flavored white wines, yet soft and deftly balanced with a fine *frizzantino*. Essentially dry wines, some renditions are, however, less dry than others and Deltetto's Bric Tupin has started a trend for a lusciously sweet style. *See* Roero DOC.

🍷— 3–5 years

✓ *Ceretto* (Blangé) • *Carlo Deltetto* • *Bruno Giacosa* • *Castello di Neive* • *Vietti*

## ASTI DOCG
### Piedmont

Formerly sold as Asti Spumante, the *spumante* (which means "sparkling") has been removed because it has become tarnished by cheap products that also use the term. It is now known simply as Asti and has been promoted to full DOCG status, which the best wines deserve, but an increasing number of underperformers do not. Italy's finest sparkling wine, and one of the most famous wines in the world, Asti is made by *cuve close*, which is far superior to the traditional method when producing an aromatic, sweet sparkling wine. The grapes used are grown in 52 communes throughout the provinces of Asti, Cuneo, and Alessandria.

The best Asti has a fine *mousse* of tiny bubbles, a fresh and grapey aroma, a luscious sweetness, and a light, delicately rich flowery-fruitiness that hints at peaches. Asti should be consumed as young as possible primarily because one of the most important compounds contributing to the Moscato aroma is geraniol, which is wonderful when fresh, but with bottle-age assumes a pungent geranium odor. Gancia's special selection *cuvée* called Camilo Gancia (no longer produced) was the best Asti I ever tasted. *See also* Moscato d'Asti DOCG.

🍷— Upon purchase

✓ *Barbero* (Conte di Cavour) • *Walter Barbero* (Acini Dolce) • *Batasiolo* • *Bersano* • *Capetta* • *Villa Carlotta* • *Cerutti* (Cesare) • *Conte di Cavour* • *Giuseppe Contratto* • *Romano Dogliotti* (La Selvatica) • *Fontanafredda* (Millesimato) • *Marenco* ◉ • *De Miranda* • *Mondoro* • *Perlino* • *Sperone* • *Tosti* • *Cantina Sociale Vallebelbo*

## BARBACARLO
### Lombardy

Dry, *frizzante*, red *vin de garde* that was originally classified as part of the Oltrepò Pavese DOC. However, Lino Maga has been legally recognized as its exclusive producer and it has returned to being a *vino da tavola*.

## BARBARESCO DOCG
### Piedmont

Generally more feminine and elegant than Barolo, Barbaresco has a greater suppleness, softer fruit, and a more obvious charm, although some producers overlap the weightier Barolo style. Produced from Italy's greatest indigenous grape variety, Nebbiolo, these wines must be aged for a minimum of two years, one of which must be in oak or chestnut casks.

🍷— 5–20 years

✓ *Produttori di Barbaresco* • *Ceretto* • *Pio Cesare* • *Fratelli Cigliuti* • *Giuseppe Cortese* • *Angelo Gaja* • *Bruno Giacosa* • *Piero Busso* • *Cantina del Glicine* • *Marchesi di Gresy* • *Moccagatta* • *Castello di Neive* • *Alfredo Prunotto* • *Bruno Rocca* • *Scarpa*

## BARBERA
### Piedmont

Although this grape can be a bit rustic, overly acidic, and may lack elegance if not grown in a suitable *terroir*, stunning *vini da tavola*, often aged in a *barrique*, are made in classic areas by producers who do not want to be restricted by the DOC and thus do not claim it.

✓ *Braida* (Bricco dell'Uccellone) • *Castello di Neive* (Rocca del Mattarello)

## BARBERA D'ALBA DOC
### Piedmont

Barbera is the most prolific Piedmont vine and, as such, has suffered unfairly from a somewhat lowly image. But in fact, it is one of Italy's great grapes and the best Barbera from Alba are magnificently rich and full of flavor, and quite

capable of challenging Barolo and Barbaresco very closely in terms of intrinsic quality. The production of Barbera d'Alba is very small, in fact often minute, in comparison with that of Barbera d'Asti.

🍷— 5–12 years

✓ *Marziano Abbona* • *Pio Cesare* • *Fratelli Cigliuti* • *Clerico* • *Aldo Conterno* • *Giacomo Conterno* • *Conterno Fantino* • *Damonte* • *Franco Fiorina* • *Angelo Gaja* • *Gepin* • *Elio Grasso* • *Manzone* • *Giuseppe Mascarello* • *Prunotto* • *Renato Ratti* • *Bruno Rocca* • *Vajra* • *Vietti* • *Roberto Voerzio*

## BARBERA D'ALBA COLLINE NICESI DOC
### Piedmont

The lower yield of this proposed subzone of Barbara d'Alba is intended to lead the way to full DOCG status for part or all of the current Barbera d'Alba DOC classified wines.

## BARBERA D'ASTI DOC
### Piedmont

Similar in character to Barbera d'Alba, but softer and more supple, with simpler generic wines, but equally profound single-vineyard wines.

🍷— 3–8 years

✓ *Marchesi Alfieri* • *Cascina la Barbatella* • *Bava* (Stradivario) • *Alfiero Boffa* • *Braida* (Bricco della Figotta) • *Cascina Castelet* (Passum) • *Chiarlo* (Valle del Sole) • *Coppo* • *Cossetti* (Cascina Salomone) • *Neirano* (Le Croci) • *Antica Casa Vinicola Scarpa* • *Zonin* (Castello del Poggio)

## BARBERA DEL MONFERRATO DOC
### Piedmont

Most of the wines produced by Barbera Del Monferrato are lesser versions of Barbera d'Asti. Semisweet or *frizzante* styles may also be made.

✓ *C. S. di Castagnole Monferrato* (Barbera Vivace)

## BAROLO DOCG
### Piedmont

Barolo is unquestionably Italy's greatest wine appellation and its finest wines are the ultimate expression of the Nebbiolo grape. All the best vineyards of Barolo are located on a small, raised area of mostly gentle, but occasionally steep, slopes surrounded by the hills of the Langhe. The soil is essentially calcareous marl (*see* p.18), the northwestern half high in magnesium and manganese, the southeastern half more iron-rich. This small difference is deemed to be the reason why Barolo wines from the northwest have more elegance, while those from the southeast are fuller in body.

The biggest factor in the quality of Barolo has, however, been due more to man than to soil, especially with the trend over the past 10 years to isolate the very best Barolo and market them under single-vineyard names. A vineyard name will not necessarily guarantee excellence, but hardly any of the very top Barolo are blended these days, and quality should continue to rise under the Goria Law (*see* p.263), which requires significantly lower yields from any wine claiming single-vineyard status.

Great Barolo is incomparable, but there are still poor Barolo wines, although not as many as in the late 1980s. But even then the emergence of a new wave of fruit-driven Barolo was fairly evident. Initially, this split Barolo; the modern-style wines had more fruit, riper and more supple tannins, and were aged in small *barriques* of new oak, while the worst of the so-called traditionalists continued to produce thick, tannic, dried-out wines.

The popular belief that so many traditional Barolo are dried out because they are bottled late is only half right. The truth is that they are—or were—bottled to order. This meant that some of the shipments of the same vintage would be more dried-out than others. There is still a large number of producers who perceive themselves to be traditional, but this simply means that they eschew *barriques* and new oak. Most traditionalists now bottle their Barolo when the wines—not the orders—require it, which, in effect, is earlier than before. They also tend to pick later and began to drop their yields even before the Goria Law of 1992. Today, both the modern and traditional schools of producers make stunning Barolo.

Modern styles are riper and more creamy than traditional ones, supported by the vanilla of new oak, whereas the traditional styles are arguably more complex, with tobacco, tar, and smoky aromas replacing the clean-cut vanilla. The best of both, however, are deep, sometimes inky-deep, in color and share lashings of fruit. All Barolo should be powerfully built, even the more elegant, earlier-drinking styles, and the best have surprising finesse for such weighty wines.

⌇— 8–25 years

✓ *Marziano Abbona • Accomasso • Elio Altare • Abbazia dell'Annunziata • Azelia • Fratelli Barale • Giacomo Borgogno • Bricco Roche • Fratelli Brovia • Giuseppe Cappellano • Cavalotto • Ceretto • Clerico • Aldo Conterno • Giacomo Conterno*

• *Conterno-Fantino • Corino • Franco-Fiorina • Fratelli Oddero • Angelo Gaja • Bruno Giacosa • Manzone • Marcarini • Bartolo Mascarello • Giuseppe Mascarello • Alfredo Prunotto • Renato Ratti • Giuseppe Rinaldi • Luciano Sandrone • Antica Casa Vinicola Scarpa • Vietti • Roberto Voerzio*

## BAROLO CHINATO DOCG
### Piedmont

This Barolo, aromatized with quinine, is a DOCG, which is a bit like classifying Bordeaux's aperitif "Lillet" as a *cru classé*.

## BLANC DE COSSAN
### Valle d'Aosta

These are fresh, tart *blancs de noir* made by the Institut Agricole Régional from Grenache grapes grown at Cossan, just outside Aosta.

## BOCA DOC
### Piedmont

These are medium- to full-bodied, spicy red Nebbiolo wines. They are hard to find, but wines have been made here since Roman times and when found can be good value.

⌇— 3–6 years

✓ *Antonio Vallana • Podere ai Valloni*

## BOTTICINO DOC
### Lombardy

Full-bodied, Barbera-based red wines with a good level of alcohol and a light tannic structure.

⌇— 3–5 years

✓ *Miro Bonetti • Benedetto Tognazzi*

## BRACHETTO
### Piedmont

Sweet, red, non-DOC Brachetto is often made by Asti producers.

✓ *Batasiolo*

## BRACHETTO D'ACQUI DOCG
### Piedmont

Sweet, *frizzante* (semi-sparkling), and sparkling red wines that are grapey and Muscat-like.

## BRAMATERRA DOC
### Piedmont

Good value, full-bodied red wines produced primarily from Nebbiolo, but which may include Bonarda, Croatina, and Vespolina grapes.

⌇— 3–6 years

✓ *Luigi Perazzi • Fabrizio Sella*

## BUTTAFUOCO DOC
### Lombardy

*See* Oltrepò Pavese DOC.

## CABERNET FRANC
### Lombardy

This grape is far more traditional in Lombardy than Cabernet Sauvignon is, although the latter steals the limelight today. Mostly used in blends.

## CABERNET SAUVIGNON
### Piedmont

Thrives in Piedmont where *vini da tavola* can be excellent in quality as well as in value.

✓ *Angelo Gaja* (Darmagi)

## CABERNET-MERLOT
### Lombardy

A relative newcomer to Lombardy, this classic Bordeaux mix has shown outstanding potential.

✓ *Bellavista* (Solesine) • *Ca'del Bosco* (Maurizio Zanella)

## CALUSO PASSITO DOC
### Piedmont

Fragrant yet full-bodied, sweet white wines made from *passito* Erbaluce grapes.

⌇— 3–5 years

✓ *Vittorio Boratto*

## CAPRIANO DEL COLLE DOC
### Lombardy

Rarely encountered red wines made from the Sangiovese, which are blended with Marzemino, Barbera, and Merlot, and tart white wines made from the Trebbiano.

## CAREMA DOC
### Piedmont

Soft, medium-bodied Nebbiolo wines that are grown on the mountainous slopes close to the border with the Valle d'Aosta. They are good and reliable but rarely exciting.

⌇— 2–5 years

✓ *Luigi Ferrando*

## CASALESE
### Piedmont

A local grape capable of light, delicately dry white wine with a characteristic bitter finish, both as DOC and *vino da tavola*.

## CELLATICA DOC
### Lombardy

This aromatic and flavorsome red wine has been made in the hills overlooking Brescia for 400 years. Permitted grapes are Barbera, Marzemino, Schiava Gentile, and Incrocio Terzi.

⌇— 2–6 years

✓ *Barbi*

## CHAMBAVE DOC
### Valle d'Aosta

A subappellation of the regional Valle d'Aosta DOC, Chambave produces attractively scented, crisp red wines primarily from Petit Rouge grapes, plus up to 40 percent Dolcetto, Gamay, and Pinot Noir. Two white wines are also permitted; one sweet, long-lived, and *passito* in style, the other a highly perfumed, early-drinking, dry- to off-dry white—both from the Moscato grape. *See* Valle d'Aosta DOC.

⌇— 2–3 years (red and *passito*) • upon purchase (white)

✓ *La Crotta di Vegneron • Ezio Voyat*

## CHARDONNAY
### Lombardy, Piedmont, and the Valle d'Aosta

Most of the Chardonnay grown in Lombardy ends up in traditional method wines, many of no specific origin, or in the Franciacorta and Oltrepò Pavese DOCs. However, there are a growing number of excellent, pure varietal *barrique*-aged *vini da tavola*, many of which are surprisingly full and lusty in style.

In contrast to Valle d'Aosta below, pure Chardonnay *vini da tavola* are quite common in Piedmont. Although the quality is variable, when Piedmont Chardonnay is good, it is rich and lush, yet classically structured and of a quality that few other Italian wine regions can touch. Many will no doubt receive official DOC status in years to come.

A few *barrique*-aged examples have proved the worth of this grape in Valle d'Aosta, but it is not a frequently encountered varietal, even though it is recognized in the regional DOC.

✓ **Lombardy** *Bellavista • Ca'del Bosco • Cascina La Pertica • Tenuta Castello • Tronconero*

**Piedmont** *Angelo Gaja • Pio Cesare*

## CINQUE TERRE *or* CINQUETERRE DOC
### Liguria

These spectacular coastal vineyards produce good, though not exactly spectacular, delicately fruity dry white wines, and the somewhat more exciting Cinque Terre Sciacchetrà, which is a medium-sweet *passito* wine.

🕰 1–3 years

✓ *Forlini Cappellini*

## COLLI DI LUNI DOC
### Liguria

Sangiovese-based reds and Vermentino whites from the eastern extremity of Liguria, bordering and even overlapping part of Tuscany.

🕰 2–5 years (red) and 1–2 years (white)

✓ *La Colombiera*

## COLLI MORENICI MANTOVANI DEL GARDA DOC
### Lombardy

Although vines have been cultivated since ancient times in Lake Garda, today viticulture is one of the least important crops. The wines are dry, light-bodied, red, white, and rosé, produced from a mixture of grape varieties.

## COLLI TORTONESI DOC
### Piedmont

Robust and rather rustic, full-bodied Barbera reds, and crisp, dry, rather lightweight, and sometimes *frizzante* Cortese whites.

## COLLINE NOVARESI DOC
### Piedmont

A new DOC for red and white wines from the Novarese province northwest of Milan; the white is dry and made exclusively from the Erbaluce grape, whereas the red is a blend of at least 40 percent Uva Rara and 30 percent Nebbiolo, plus up to 30 percent Vespolina and Croatina.

## CORTESE DELL'ALTO MONFERRATO DOC
### Piedmont

Dry, crisp, still, *frizzante*, and fully sparkling white wines that often incline to a coarser style than expected for the Cortese grape.

## CORTESE DI GAVI DOCG

*See* Gavi DOCG.

## DIANO D'ALBA DOC

*See* Dolcetto di Diano d'Alba DOC.

## DOLCETTO
### Piedmont

Non-DOC Dolcetto can be excellent-value reds, gushing with soft, easy-drinking fruit.

✓ *Clerico • Corino • Marchesi di Gresy • Marcarini • Luciano Sandrone*

## DOLCETTO D'ACQUI DOC
### Piedmont

Dolcetto is a plump grape with a low acid content that is traditionally used to make cheerful, Beaujolais-type wines that are deep purple in color and best enjoyed young.

🕰 1–3 years

✓ *Viticoltori dell'Acquese • Villa Banficut*

## DOLCETTO D'ALBA DOC
### Piedmont

Dolcetto d'Alba DOC produces some soft, smooth, juicy wines that should be drunk while they are young, fresh, and fruity.

🕰 1–3 years

✓ *Elio Altare • Azelia • Batasiolo • Fratelli Brovia • Ceretto • Pio Cesare • Fratelli Cigliuti • Aldo Conterno • Cascina Drago • Franco Fiorina • Elio Grasso • Bartolo Mascarello • Pira • Roberto Voerzio*

## DOLCETTO D'ASTI DOC
### Piedmont

These wines are lighter than Dolcetto d'Alba.

## DOLCETTO DELLE LANGHE MONREGALESI DOC
### Piedmont

Rare wines produced in tiny quantities, reputed to have an exceptionally fine aroma.

## DOLCETTO DI DIANO D'ALBA *or* DIANO D'ALBA DOC
### Piedmont

Diano is a hilltop village just south of Alba, which produces wines that are slightly fuller and more grapey than most other Dolcetto wines.

🕰 3–5 years

✓ *Alario • Casavecchia • Colué • Fontanafredda • Giuseppe Mascarello • Cantina della Porta Rossa • Mario Savigliano • Veglio & Figlio*

## DOLCETTO DI DOGLIANI DOC
### Piedmont

Most Dolcetto from Dogliani used to be made to drink young and fruity, but more is now being made in a *vin de garde* style. The best attain a lovely perfumed finesse with a few years in bottle.

✓ *Chionetti • Luigi Einaudi • Angelo Gaja • Pira • Roberto Voerzio*

## DOLCETTO DI OVADA DOC
### Piedmont

These are the fullest and firmest of Dolcettos.

🕰 3–6 years (up to 10 for the very best)

✓ *Cascina Scarsi Olivi*

## DOLCETTO-NEBBIOLO
### Piedmont

When backed up by full, firm Nebbiolo, the soft, lush fruit of Dolcetto remains remarkably fresh for a considerable time in bottle.

✓ *Cascina Drago* (Bricco del Drago, especially Vigna le Mace)

## DONNAZ *or* DONNAS
### Valle d'Aosta

Formerly its own DOC, but now a subappellation of the regional Valle d'Aosta DOC, Donnaz produces soft, well-balanced, Nebbiolo-based red wines that have a pleasant, yet slightly bitter aftertaste. *See also* Valle d'Aosta DOC, p274.

## ENFER D'ARVIER
### Valle d'Aosta

Formerly its own DOC, but now a subappellation of the regional Valle d'Aosta DOC, Enfer d'Arvier is a low-key, medium-bodied red wine made primarily from the Petit Rouge grape, although Dolcetto, Gamay, Neyret, Pinot Noir, and Vien de Nus may also be used. *See also* Valle d'Aosta DOC, p274.

## ERBALUCE DI CALUSO *or* CALUSO DOC
### Piedmont

These are fresh, dry, light-bodied white wines made from the Erbaluce, which is a rather undistinguished grape. A far more interesting *passito* version exists and it is probably this that gave Erbaluce its overrated, albeit localized, reputation. *See also* Caluso Passito DOC.

🕰 1–3 years

✓ *Luigi Ferrando*

## FARA DOC
### Piedmont

In the hands of someone like Dessilani, Fara DOC proves to be an underrated, enjoyable, Nebbiolo-based wine with lots of fruit combined with a spicy-scented character.

✓ *Luigi Dessilani* (Caramino)

## FAVORITA
### Piedmont

Descended from the Vermentino, this was once a popular table grape, but now makes dry, crisp white *vini da tavola* and, since 1995, DOC Langhe Favorita. The best varietal wines have a delicate floral aroma and refreshing acidity.

## FLÉTRI
### Valle d'Aosta

In this bilingual region, the French *flétri*, which means "shriveled," may be used in preference to the Italian *passito*.

## FRANCIACORTA DOCG
### Lombardy

The sparkling white and rosé wines made by Franciacorta were promoted to DOCG status in September 1995. Produced by the traditional method with 25 months' aging on the lees (or 37 if *riserva*), Franciacorta had already shown its potential for producing fine, biscuity, *brut*, and lightly rich rosé sparkling wines when this book was first published. It not only deserves its prestigious classification, it is an object lesson for the rest of the Italian wine industry for two reasons. First, the still wines have retained their former DOC status (*see* Terre di Franciacorta DOC), making it one of Italy's more prestigious appellations. Meanwhile, the selection of only sparkling wines for DOCG enhances this new classification, whereas promoting an entire DOC devalues it. Not every region has a supercategory to promote as Franciacorta has, but others could, for example, restrict production to the original *classico* area and a reduced yield. This would result in both a DOC and DOCG for the same region and, in the mind of the consumer, it would ensure that the "G" did guarantee an elevated quality equivalent to *grand cru*, for example. The second lesson is that as the first Italian wine to insist on bottle-fermentation, Franciacorta is currently the only Italian dry sparkling-wine appellation that can demand respect from the rest of the world. *See* Terre di Franciacorta DOC for still wines.

⌐⊷ 2–5 years

☑ *Banfi • Bellavista • Fratelli Berlucchi • Bersi Serlini • Ca'del Bosco • Bredasole • Castelfaglia • Tenuta Castellino • Casteveder • Cavalleri • Cola • Ricci Curbastro • Faccoli • Lantieri de Paratico • Majolini • La Montina • Barone Pizzini • Lo Sparviere • Villa*

## FREISA
### Piedmont

The Freisa is a black grape of refreshing acidity, which makes ruby-red wines with characteristic raspberry and rose-petal aromas for early drinking. Non-DOC wines abound, particularly around Alba, where this variety excels in quality, despite the lack of official recognition.

⌐⊷ 3–6 years (up to 10 for the very best)

☑ *Clerico • Aldo Conterno • Coppo*

## FREISA D'ASTI DOC
### Piedmont

Known for centuries, and a favorite of King Victor Emmanuel, this is the original and most famous Freisa. These fruity red wines may be made fully sparkling, *frizzante*, or still, and in both dry and sweet styles.

⌐⊷ 3–6 years (up to 10 for the very best)

☑ *Gilli*

## FREISA DI CHIERI DOC
### Piedmont

Freisa di Chieri produces the same styles of wine as Freisa d'Asti from just outside Turin.

## FUMIN
### Valle d'Aosta

Very little is known about this grape, which is usually blended with others but occasionally makes a robust red on its own under the Valle d'Aosta DOC or as a *vino da tavola*.

## GABIANO DOC
### Piedmont

The full-bodied, red Barbera wines of Castello di Gabiano seemed to make this a promising DOC, but the appellation has not taken off and these wines are seldom encountered.

## GAMAY
### Valle d'Aosta

The non-DOC wines of Gamay are light-bodied with an attenuated earthy fruitiness.

## GAMAY-PINOT NERO
### Valle d'Aosta

A light and fruity *passetoutgrains* style.

## GATTINARA DOCG
### Piedmont

From Nebbiolo and up to 10 percent Bonarda grown on the right bank of the Sesia River in northern Piedmont, Gattinara can be a fine, though not a great, wine, especially now that overcropping problems have been reduced since Gattinara attained DOCG status. When young, the fruit can be chunky and rustic when compared with Barbaresco or Barolo, but the best Gattinara wines develop a fine, silky-textured flavor and a graceful, violet-perfumed finesse when mature. Gattinara earned its DOC and then full DOCG status through the almost single-handed efforts of Mario Antoniolo, whose wines have always been among the greatest produced in the area. Others have followed his example, but have been too few and too slow to give Gattinara the sort of reputation that a world-class wine appellation ought to have.

⌐⊷ 6–15 years

☑ *Mario Antoniolo • Le Colline • Travaglini*

## GAVI *or* CORTESE DI GAVI DOCG
### Piedmont

The quality and character of these highly fashionable wines is very uneven, although prices are uniformly high. At best, they are soft-textured, dry white wines with a slight *frizzantino* when young, and can develop a honey-rich flavor after a couple of years in bottle. Too many examples have all their character fermented out at low temperatures, which gives them an amylic peardrop aroma, and some are definitely *frizzante*.

⌐⊷ 2–3 years

☑ *Nicola Bergaglio • Chiarlo* (Fior di Rovere) *• Carlo Deltetto • La Scolca*

## GHEMME DOCG
### Piedmont

A Nebbiolo-based wine produced on the bank opposite Gattinara, Ghemme is usually seen as the inferior of the two appellations, but it has never been as persistently overcropped and is generally more consistent. Although not capable of reaching the heights of Antoniolo's Gattinara, for example, most Ghemme has just as much color, body, and flavor as Gattinara in general, and starts off with a much finer bouquet and more elegant fruit. In addition to Nebbiolo, Vespolina and Bonarda may be used.

⌐⊷ 4–15 years

☑ *Antichi Vigneti di Cantelupo • Le Colline • Luigi Dessilani*

## GRIGNOLINO D'ASTI DOC
### Piedmont

Grignolino d'Asti DOC produces lightly tannic red wines with a slightly bitter aftertaste.

## GRIGNOLINO DEL MONFERRATO CASALESE DOC
### Piedmont

These are light, crisp, fresh red wines made from Grignolino around the Casalese Monferrato.

## GRUMELLO DOC
### Lombardy

*See* Valtellina Superiore DOC.

## INFERNO DOC
### Lombardy

*See* Valtellina Superiore DOC.

## LAMBRUSCO MANTOVANO DOC
### Lombardy

Not all Lambrusco comes from Emilia-Romagna. This one is produced just across the border on the plains of Mantua (Mantova). Formerly a *vino da tavola*, Mantovano is red and *frizzante* with a pink foam and may be dry or sweet.

⌐⊷ Upon purchase

☑ *C. S. di Quistello*

## LANGHE DOC
### Piedmont

This area overlaps the DOCs Barbaresco, Barolo, Nebbiolo d'Alba, Dolcetto d'Alba, and Barbera d'Alba and, if used sensibly, through selection, could ensure the highest quality in those wines. White, red, and six varietal wines are permitted: Dolcetto, Freisa, and Nebbiolo for red; and Arneis, Favorita, and Chardonnay for white.

☑ *Chionetti • Aldo Conterno • Angelo Gaja • Giuseppe Mascarello*

## LESSONA DOC
### Piedmont

These are red wines that can be delightfully scented, with rich fruit and some finesse.

## LOAZZOLO DOC
### Piedmont

From the village of Loazzolo, south of Canelli, this Moscato *passito* is aged for two years, including six months in *barriques*, to produce a golden-hued, richly flavored, lusciously textured, exotically sweet wine. A wine that can age, but which is best drunk young.

⌐⊷ 2–4 years

✓ *Borgo Maragliano* • *Borgo Sambui*
• *Bricchi Mej* • *Giancarlo Scaglione*

## LUGANA DOC
### Lombardy

These are soft, smooth, dry white wines made from Trebbiano grown on the shores of Lake Garda, slightly overlapping Veneto in northeast Italy. There are many dullards, but the very best Lugana manage to transcend the lackluster level normally expected from this grape variety.

🍷 1–2 years

✓ *Cà dei Frati* • *Visconti*

## MALVASIA
### Lombardy

In many instances Malvasia, Malvoisie, and Pinot Gris are the same variety of grape, but the Malvasia of Lombardy is the true Malvasia and a very different grape from the Malvoisie of Valle d'Aosta. A dark-skinned grape, Malvasia makes both red and white wines, still and sparkling, dry and sweet, and, most puzzling of all, full- and light-bodied, and neutral and aromatic.

✓ *La Muiraghina*

## MALVASIA DI CASORZO D'ASTI DOC
### Piedmont

These are lightly aromatic, sweet, red, and rosé wines that may also be sparkling.

🍷 1–2 years

✓ *Bricco Mondalino*

## MALVASIA DI CASTELNUOVO DON BOSCO DOC
### Piedmont

The DOC of Malvasia di Castelnuovo Don Bosco produces attractive, lightly aromatic, sweet, red, still, and sparkling wines.

🍷 1–2 years

✓ *Bava*

## MALVOISIE
### Valle d'Aosta

The Malvoisie of Valle d'Aosta is in fact Pinot Gris, not Malvasia, and its dry, semisweet, and *passito* wines are, though not at all spicy, smooth and usually slightly bitter in both DOC and *vino da tavola* versions.

## MONFERRATO DOC
### Piedmont

This is a relatively new DOC, which was introduced in 1995 for red, white, and *ciaret* or *chiaretto* (rosé) Dolcetto, Casalese, and Freisa from a wide area overlapping the Asti region.

✓ *La Barbatella* • *Martinetti* • *Villa Sparina*

## MORGEX ET LA SALLE DOC
### Valle d'Aosta

A subappellation of the regional Valle d'Aosta DOC, the vineyards of these two communes reach as high as 4,265 feet (1,300 meters), which makes it one of the highest wine-growing areas in Europe. However, most vines in these two villages are grown between 2,952 and 3,280 feet (900 and 1,000 meters), although even this is remarkable as, in theory, grapes do not ripen above 2,625 feet (800 meters) in the Valle d'Aosta. However, in practice they ripen, and produce a fine, dry, *frizzantino* white. Brut, Extra Brut, and Demi Sec *spumante* versions are also made. *See also* Valle d'Aosta DOC.

🍷 1–3 years

✓ *Alberto Vevey*

## MOSCATO
### Lombardy and Piedmont

Good non-DOC is made in Lombardy and the Moscato di Scanzo is undoubtedly the best. In the Piedmont, non-DOC Moscato is prolific in many styles and formats, and even a crisp, dry version to challenge Alsace is available from Alasia (an alliance between the flying winemaker Martin Shaw and the Araldica consortium of cooperatives).

✓ **Lombardy** *Celinate Ronchello* • *Il Cipresso* • *La Cornasella*

**Piedmont** *Alasia* (especially Muscaté Sec)

## MOSCATO D'ASTI DOCG
### Piedmont

Wines similar in flavor to Asti, but with a minimum pressure of three atmospheres, as opposed to five. Still, slightly *frizzantino*, and positively *frizzante* examples of Moscato d'Asti exist. Those with some degree of effervescence are bottled without any *dosage*, while the first fermentation is still underway, as opposed to Asti plain and simple, which is made by the *cuve close* method. Compared with Asti, Moscato d'Asti is generally, though not necessarily, less alcoholic (5.5 to 8 percent instead of 7.5 to 9 percent) and almost always much sweeter. If there is any criticism of this luscious, heavenly nectar, it is the unfortunate trend to make these wines fizzier, as there is often little difference between modern Moscato d'Asti and Asti itself. Rarely does one find a still Moscato d'Asti with the barest prickle, as in the past. That said, this is the Asti DOC to pick. As there are fewer than 3 million bottles, as opposed to 85 million Asti, it is more expensive, and the best, such as Borgo Maragliano's La Caliera, which is in a completely different class from the rest, are definitely fine.

🍷 Upon purchase

✓ *Araldica* • *Castello Banfi* • *Alfiero Boffa* • *Borgo Maragliano* • *Redento Dogliotti* • *Gatti* • *Marchesi di Gresy* • *Villa Lanata* • *Luciana Rivella* • *La Spinetta-Rivetti*

## NEBBIOLO
### Piedmont

Most *vini da tavola* from this grape are relatively simple red wines, as the best areas for Nebbiolo have long been known and have become famous DOCGs. Exceptionally fine examples have, however, been made in great years by the best Barolo and Barbaresco producers. It remains to be seen whether or not they will continue to do so now that they also have the choice of Nebbiolo d'Alba and Langhe

Nebbiolo DOCs through which to sell such wines.

✓ *Elio Altare* • *Clerico* (Arté) • *Corino* • *Cascina Drago* • *I Paglieri* (Opera Prima)

## NEBBIOLO D'ALBA DOC
### Piedmont

Pure Nebbiolo wines come from between Barolo and Barbaresco. Most are fine, full, rich, and fruity. Sweet and sparkling versions are allowed.

🍷 4–10 years

✓ *Ascheri* • *Tenuta Carretta* • *Ceretto* • *Pio Cesare* • *Aldo Conterno* • *Giacomo Conterno* • *Franco Fiorina* • *Angelo Gaja* • *Bruno Giacosa* • *Hilberg-Pasquero* • *Giuseppe Mascarello* • *Val de Prete* • *Vietti*

## NEBBIOLO-BARBERA
### Piedmont

A strikingly successful *vino da tavola* blend that takes to *barrique*-aging like a duck to water, producing delicious yet classy red wines with plump, juicy fruit, held together by supple tannins and a touch of smoky-oak. Some wines, such as Conterno Fantino's Monprà, contain more Barbera than Nebbiolo. *See also* Petit Rouge.

✓ *Giacomo* (Bric Milieu) • *Chiarlo* (Barilot) • *Valentino Migliorini* (Bricco Manzoni) • *Conterno Fantino* (Monprà) • *Vietti* (Fioretto) • *Roberto Voerzio* (Vignaserra) • *Oriou* (Valle d'Aosta)

## NUS DOC
### Valle d'Aosta

A subappellation of the Valle d'Aosta DOC, Nus makes an interesting red from Vien de Nus, Petit Rouge, and Pinot Noir grapes. Dry and *passito* styles of white wine are made from Pinot Gris or Malvoisie de Nus. *See also* Valle d'Aosta DOC.

🍷 2–4 years

✓ *La Crotta di Vegneron*

## OLTREPÒ PAVESE DOC
### Lombardy

The Oltrepò Pavese covers 42 communes south of the Po River, although much of the production is not marketed under this DOC, but sold to specialized wineries in Piedmont. These wineries turn it into non-DOC *spumante* by the *cuve close* process or the traditional method. There used to be three geographical subappellations, but Barbacarlo has since been recognized as the exclusive product of Lino Maga, reverting to *vino da tavola* status. The two remaining subappellations are **Oltrepò Pavese Buttafuoco** ("sparks of fire"), a deep-colored, fruity, dry or semisweet *frizzante* red; and **Oltrepò Pavese Sangue di Giuda** (charmingly named "blood of Judas"), a soft, sweet, red *spumante*. Both wines are restricted to vineyards around the villages of Broni, Canetto Pavese, Castana, Cigognola, Montescano, Pietra de Giorgi, and Stradella. Aside from blended red, white, and rosé wines, Oltrepò Pavese permits 11 varietal wines: Barbera, Bonarda (made from Croatina), Cabernet Sauvignon, and Pinot Noir (still and *spumante*) for red; and Chardonnay, Cortese, Malvasia, Moscato (still, *spumante*, and *liquoroso*), Pinot Grigio, Riesling Italico, and Riesling Renano for white.

🍷 1–3 years (white, rosé, and sparkling)
  2–5 years (red)

✓ *Giacomo Agnes • Angelo Ballabio • Bianchina Alberici • Doria (Pinot Nero) • Lino Maga (see also Barbacarlo) • Monsupello • Piccolo Bacco dei Quaroni • Tronconero (Bonarda) • Zonin (Moscato spumante)*

## ORMEASCO
### Liguria

Ormeasco is the local Ligurian variant of Dolcetto, which can produce some deliciously easy-to-drink, soft, fruity red wines.

## PETIT ROUGE
### Valle d'Aosta

Deep, dark, and highly perfumed red wines from this low-yielding, local grape that can be met within both DOC and *vino da tavola* versions. There are many variants in the family of Petit Rouge, but they can all be traced back to the Oriou, which may in future be used for its varietal wines. Moves have been underway since the early 1990s to change the name of the Petit Rouge grape to Oriou owing to the supposedly belittling effect of *petit* in its name, even though this refers to the size of berry, not the quality of wine (most classic varieties have smaller, rather than larger, grapes and this should thus be seen as a positive attribute).

## PIEMONTE DOC
### Piedmont

Introduced in 1995, this DOC embraces all the other DOC areas in the Piedmont and, with the exception of Piemonte Moscato and Piemonte Moscato Passito, which must be made from 100 percent Moscato grapes, all wines claiming this appellation are required to contain at least 85 percent of the variety indicated. Permitted red wine varietals are Barbera, Bonarda, Brachetto, Dolcetto, and Pinot Noir, while in addition to the Moscato wines already mentioned above, white varietals include Cortese, Pinot Blanc, and Pinot Gris. The creation of this regional DOC probably explains why no IGT wines have been declared in Piedmont, and it is doubtful whether any IGT will be in the future.

## PINOT NERO
### Lombardy

Most Pinot Noir grown in northwest Italy goes into classic *brut spumante* wines. Still wines are made under the Oltrepò Pavese denomination (Doria being outstanding) and a small number of non-DOC examples are to be found. The two wines listed below are *barrique*-aged, and are exceptionally fine in quality.

✓ *Ca'del Bosco • Tenuta Mazzolino*

## PREMETTA
### Valle d'Aosta

Lightly tannic, bright cherry-red wines from this local grape, Premetta, can be encountered in both DOC and *vino da tavola* versions.

## RIVIERA DEL GARDA BRESCIANO *or* GARDA BRESCIANO DOC
### Lombardy

This area makes light, fruity, slightly bitter red wines that are no more interesting than the bulk of Valpolicella, produced on the opposite bank of Lake Garda. Most are blended from Gropello, Sangiovese, Marzemino, and Barbera, but some are pure varietal wines from the Gropello grape and these tend to be superior. Although the whites may be pure Riesling, this is taken to mean either Riesling Renano, which is true Riesling, or Riesling Italico, which is not. Furthermore, as up to 20 percent of other local grape varieties may be used, Garda Bresciano *bianco* has not been of much interest so far. The most successful wine here has been the rosé, or *chiaretto*, which, although it is made from exactly the same varieties as the *rosso*, can be much softer and easier to drink.

🍷 Upon purchase

✓ *Costaripa*

## RIVIERA LIGURE DI PONENTE DOC
### Liguria

Four former *vini da tavola* are grouped together under this appellation, which covers the western Riviera of Liguria. These are: *Ormeasco*, bright, cherry-red wines with juicy, raspberry, Dolcetto fruit; *Pigato*, full-flavored yet somewhat precocious red wines; *Rossese*, well-scented, characterful reds; and *Vermentino*, rich, full, and characterful dry white wines.

## ROERO DOCG
### Piedmont

This DOC covers light-bodied, easy-drinking, inexpensive Nebbiolo reds and the highly regarded, highly priced Arneis whites from the Roeri hills north of Alba. *See Arneis di Roero.*

🍷 1–2 years

✓ *Carlo Deltetto • Giovanni Almondo • Matteo Correggia • Monchero Carboni • Malvirà*

## ROSSESE DI DOLCEACQUA *or* DOLCEACQUA DOC
### Liguria

This DOC produces light, easy-drinking red wines that are capable of rich, lush fruit, a soft texture, and spicy-aromatic aftertaste.

🍷 1–4 years

✓ *Giobatta Cane • Lupi • Antonio Perrino*

## RUBINO DI CANTAVENNA DOC
### Piedmont

A full-bodied red wine blend of mostly Barbera, Grignolino, and sometimes Freisa. It is made by a *cooperativa* called Rubino, which was solely responsible for creating this appellation, but failed to interest other producers. As a result, the DOC has not taken off.

## RUCHÉ
### Piedmont

The Ruché is a rather mysterious grape of unknown origin that generally makes a light ruby-colored wine with an aromatic twist, although, through reduced yields, much darker, weightier, richer wines can be achieved.

✓ *Scarpa*

## RUCHÉ DI CASTAGNOLE MONFERRATO DOC
### Piedmont

When grown on the vineyards overlooking Castagnole Monferrato, the Ruché grape is supposed to produce an aromatic red wine that ages like Nebbiolo. Up to 10 percent Barbera and Brachetto may be used in production.

🍷 3–5 years

✓ *Piero Bruno • Ruché del Parrocco*

## SAN COLOMBANO AL LAMBRO *or* SAN COLOMBANO DOC
### Lombardy

Rich, robust, if somewhat rustic red wines made from Croatina, Barbera, and Uva Rara are produced by this DOC. San Colombano is the only DOC in the Milan province.

🍷 2–5 years

✓ *Carlo Pietrasanta*

## SAN MARTINO DELLA BATTAGLIA DOC
### Lombardy

Dry, full-flavored white wine with a flowery aroma and slightly bitter aftertaste, and a sweet, *liquoroso* wine, made from the Tocai Friulano.

## SANGUE DI GIUDA DOC

See Oltrepò Pavese DOC.

## SASSELLA DOC
### Lombardy

See Valtellina Superiore DOC.

## SAUVIGNON BLANC
### Piedmont

These wines are virtually unknown in the region, although the soil and climate seem favorable. Angelo Gaja's *barrique*-aged pure Sauvignon Alteni di Brassica shows potential.

✓ *Angelo Gaja* (Alteni di Brassica)

## SIZZANO DOC
### Piedmont

These are good, full-bodied red wines that are produced from a Gattinara-like blend on a bank of the Sesia River, just south of Ghemme.

## SPANNA
### Piedmont

The local name for the Nebbiolo, Spanna merely represents the most basic wines from this grape variety, although in the hands of some specialists it can surpass many generic Barolo and Barbaresco.

✓ *Luciano Brigatti • Villa Era*

## SYRAH
### Valle d'Aosta

The Institut Agricole Régional has produced very interesting *barrique* wine from this grape, the Syrah, since the late 1980s.

## TERRE DI FRANCIACORTA DOC
### Lombardy

Part of the original Franciacorta appellation since 1967, the still wines were renamed Terre di Franciacorta in 1995 when the name in its singular form, Terra di Franciacorta, was reserved for the new DOCG. Produced northeast of Milan, on hilly slopes near Lake Iseo, the red wines are typically well colored, medium- to full-bodied, made from Cabernet Franc and Cabernet Sauvignon, with the possible addition of Barbera, Nebbiolo, and

Merlot. Many are richly flavored and show some finesse. The dry white wines, primarily from Chardonnay with a little Pinot Blanc permissible, have improved tremendously.

⌑⏦ 3–8 years (red), 1–3 years (white)

☑ *Ca'del Bosco • Enrico Gatti • Ragnoli*

## TIMORASSO
### Piedmont

Tipped by some to be the next trendy white grape variety, Timorasso has until now been confined to *vini da tavola* and *grappa*, with more emphasis on the latter. Walter Massa in the upper Val Curone was the first to produce a varietal wine from Timorasso, almost by accident, when a *grappa* producer by the name of Antonella Bocchino became curious about this grape. She had seen it mentioned in 19th-century documents, but it was thought to be extinct until she tracked down a plot on Massa's estate. Since Bocchino was interested in making only *grappa* with the pressings, Massa was left with the wine on his hands and it turned out to be more than just a curiosity. Massa has supplied other estates with cuttings and several producers now make Timorasso, a varietal that could follow on the success of Gavi and Arneis.

## TORRETTE DOC
### Valle d'Aosta

A red-only subappellation of the regional Valle d'Aosta DOC, Torrette produces deep-colored wines of good bouquet and body from the Petit Rouge, plus up to 30 percent Dolcetto, Fumin, Gamay, Mayolet, Pinot Noir, Premetta, and Vien de Nus. *See also* Valle d'Aosta DOC.

☑ *Elio Cassol • Grosjean*

## VALCALEPIO DOC
### Lombardy

An up-and-coming appellation for well-colored, deeply flavored red wines made from a blend of Merlot and Cabernet Sauvignon, and for light, delicately dry white wines made from Pinot Blanc and Pinot Gris.

⌑⏦ 1–3 years (white), 3–7 years (red)

☑ *Tenuta Castello*

## VALGELLA DOC
### Lombardy

*See* Valtellina Superiore DOC.

## VALLE D'AOSTA *or* VALLÉE D'AOSTE DOC
### Valle d'Aosta

A regional DOC encompassing 20 different styles of wine, Valle d'Aosta took under its wings the only two DOCs formerly recognized in the region: Donnaz and Enfer d'Arvier. These are now two of the seven subappellations within this DOC, the other five being Arnad-Montjovat, Chambave, Morgex et La Salle, Nus, and Torrette (*see* individual entries). The Valle d'Aosta DOC has revitalized this region's tiny production of somewhat low-key wines.
Aside from blended red, white, and rosé, the following varietal wines are permitted: Fumin, Gamay, Nebbiolo, Petit Rouge, Pinot Noir, and Premetta for reds; and Chardonnay, Müller-Thurgau, Petit Arvine, and Pinot Gris for whites. There is also a Bianco di Pinot Nero, which you might see labeled as a Blanc de Noir de Pinot Noir, as all Valle d'Aosta wines have official alternative French designations.

**SPRINGTIME AT MORGEX, VALLE D'AOSTA**
*Grown at more than 3,000 feet (900 meters), these vines annually disprove the theory that grapes should not ripen above 2,600 feet (800 meters) in the Valle d'Aosta.*

⌑⏦ 1–3 years

☑ *Grosjean • La Crotta di Vegneron • Les Crêtes*

## VALTELLINA DOC
### Lombardy

Encompasses 19 communes of the province of Sondrio. Most are light-scented, medium-bodied red wines of simple, but pleasing, character. Many critics believe Valtellina to be very overrated, and the basic *appellation* certainly is, but the fine wines are virtually all classed as Valtellina Superiore. *See also* Valtellina Superiore DOC.

## VALTELLINA SUPERIORE DOCG
### Lombardy

The best wines of Valtellina are produced from a narrow strip of vineyards on the north bank of the Adda River near the Swiss border, and must contain a minimum of 12 percent alcohol, as opposed to the 11 percent required for Valtellina. Most of the wines come from four subdistricts: **Grumello** (the lightest), **Inferno** (supposedly the hottest, rockiest part of the valley), **Sassella** (the best), and **Valgella** (the most productive but least interesting). Essentially a Nebbiolo, but up to 10 percent Pinot Noir, Merlot, Rossola, Brugnola, and Pignola Valtellina may also be used. The richness of the best of these wines is belied by their elegance. They have good color and are capable of developing exquisite finesse after several years in bottle. *Sfursat* or *Sforzato*, which literally means "strained" and is made from shriveled grapes, is a dry, concentrated red wine that has a minimum of 14.5 percent alcohol (try Nino Negri's), which makes it the equivalent of *amarone*.

⌑⏦ 5–15 years

☑ *Enologica Valtellinese • Sandro Fay • Fondazione Fojanini • Nino Negri • Conti Sertoli-Salis • Fratelli Triacca • Mamete Prevostini*

## VIEN DE NUS
### Valle d'Aosta

A very similar grape to the Petit Rouge, but whereas the Petit Rouge is widely planted throughout the Valle d'Aosta, cultivation of the Vien de Nus is restricted to the vineyards around Nus itself.

## VIN DE CONSEIL
### Valle d'Aosta

Perfumed dry white made by the Institut Agricole Régional from Petite Arvine.

### NEW IGT WINES

The following Indicazioni Geografiche Tipiche wines were agreed to at the end of 1996, yet most have still to register with consumers, or establish any consistency of style or quality:

☑ **Liguria** *Colli Savonesi • Golfo del Tigullio • Val Polcevera*

**Lombardy** *Alto Mincio • Benaco Bresciano • Bergamasca • Collina del Milanese • Quistello • Ronchi di Brescia, Sabbioneta • Sebino • Terrazze Retiche di Sondrio*

**Piedmont** *none*

**Valle d'Aosta** *none*

# NORTHEAST ITALY

*Freshness, crisp acidity, and purity of varietal character personify the wines of the northeastern regions of Trentino-Alto Adige, Friuli-Venezia Giulia, and the Veneto; but beware the mass-produced wines, which are so clean and pure that they lack any fruit.*

THIS IS A MORE MOUNTAINOUS area than the northwest (with the exception of that region's Valle d'Aosta), as just over half the land is occupied by the Dolomites and their precipitous foothills. Some of the finest wines are grown in the lush, verdant vineyards of the South Tyrol (Alto Adige), just over the border from Austria. A great deal of wine is exported; the bulk of it is unexciting Soave and Valpolicella. Locally there is much greater variety and value to be had—a number of French and German grapes are grown in addition to fascinating local varieties, and dedicated

NORTHEAST ITALY, *see also p.263*
*The variety of sites offered by the mountains and the hills of this area enables many grape varieties to be grown in addition to local ones. The most exciting wines come from the high vineyards of the South Tyrol, the hills of Friuli, and around Vicenza in the Veneto.*

TERMENO VINEYARDS, ALTO ADIGE
*The town of Termeno, or Tramin, as it is also called, is situated between Bolzano and Trento, in the Alto Adige region. This is where the Traminer Aromatico, or Gewürztraminer, is supposed to have originated, but the local clone is far more restrained than the classic Alsace version, with hardly any spice to its character.*

| | |
|---|---|
| | Valdadige |
| | Casteller |
| | Teroldego Rotaliano |
| | Alto Adige encompassing Terlano, Santa Maddalena, Colli di Bolzano Lago di Caldaro, Valle Isarco (6) |
| | Trentino, Casteller, Sorni |
| | Bardolino, Bianco di Custoza, Bardolino Classico (7) |
| | Valpolicella, Valpolicella Classico (8) |
| | Soave |
| | Lessini Durello |
| | Gambellara |
| | Colli Berici |
| | Colli Euganei |
| | Montello e Colli Asolani |
| | Prosecco di Conegliano-Valdobbiadene |
| | Lison-Pramaggiore |
| | Friuli-Grave |
| | Collio |
| | Colli Orientali del Friuli |
| | Carso |
| 1 | Breganze |
| 2 | Piave |
| 3 | Friuli-Latisana |
| 4 | Friuli-Aquileia |
| 5 | Isonzo |
| | *Provincia* boundary |
| ▲ | Height above sea level (metres) |

## AVERAGE ANNUAL PRODUCTION

| REGION | DOC PRODUCTION | TOTAL PRODUCTION |
|---|---|---|
| Veneto | 17 million cases (1.5 million hl) | 110 million cases (10 million hl) |
| Trentino-Alto Adige | 8 million cases (700,000 hl) | 17 million cases (1.5 million hl) |
| Friuli-Venezia Giulia | 5 million cases (5 million cases) | 18 million cases (1.6 million hl) |

Percentage of total Italian production: Veneto, 13%; Trentino-Alto Adige, 2%; Friuli-Venezia Giulia, 1.5%.

producers continue to experiment. Austria to the north and Slovenia to the east have influenced the styles produced.

## TRENTINO-ALTO ADIGE
This is the most westerly and spectacular of the northeast's three regions, and more than 90 percent of its area is covered by mountainous countryside. It is made up of two autonomous provinces, the Italian-speaking Trento in the south and the German-speaking Bolzano, or South Tyrol, in the north. In Bolzano the wines may possess alternative German names and can carry a QbA (*Qualitätswein bestimmter Anbaugebiete*) designation. The generic Alto Adige DOC (*Südtiroler QbA*) is remarkably good and accounts for one-third of the region's total DOC output. There are also numerous fine wines produced in these cool, high vineyards.

## THE VENETO
The Veneto stretches from the Po River to the Austrian border, between Trentino-Alto Adige to the west and Friuli-Venezia Giulia to the east, and most of the wines are grown on alluvial plains in the south. Once famous, but more recently infamous, for its Valpolicella and Soave, the Veneto is also one of the most exciting hunting grounds for some of Italy's best Bordeaux-type blends, and there are signs that even the aforementioned abused wine names are beginning to regain a little of their former respectability.

## FRIULI-VENEZIA GIULIA
Situated in the northeastern corner of Italy, this predominantly mountainous region has grown many non-Italian varieties since phylloxera wiped out its vineyards in the late 19th century. The naturally innovative Friulians (and South Tyroleans) used the

BARDOLINO VINEYARDS
*Ripening grapes adorn rows of vines in the Veneto's Bardolino area, which has a good reputation for light, dry red, and rosé wines.*

opportunity to replant their vineyards with several better-quality foreign grape varieties, starting with the Merlot, which was brought to this region by Senator Pecile and Count Savorgnan in 1880. Over the past 100 years, the northeast has consistently demonstrated that the use of superior grape varieties and relatively lower yields can produce wines of dramatically improved quality. Friuli is the home of some of the country's finest wines, including many of its most complex Cabernet blends. Girolamo Dorigo's Montsclapade, which is the best of an exceptionally fine group of wines, is a typically Friulian blend of both Cabernets, Merlot, and Malbec. It is rare to find the Malbec variety on this side of the Alps, but it fares well in Friuli and might well be the key to the complexity of these wines. A few rather unconventional blends are found, the most unusual being Abbazia di Rosazzo's multinational Ronco dei Roseti, which mixes the four Bordeaux varieties with the German Limberger, the Italian Refosco, and the obscure Tazzelenghe. Another Abbazia di Rosazzo wine, Ronco delle Acacie, is a rare masterpiece in the new Italian school of "superdeluxe" *vini da tavola* white wines—a category of dry white Italian wine that is expensive but mostly disappointing.

The largest volume of fine wines produced in the northeast comes from Colli Orientali del Friuli, one of Friuli's two *colli*, or "hilly," areas. This one is situated close to the former Yugoslav border and encompasses many varietal wines. These wines are well worth looking out for—with the exception of the Picolit, which is a grossly overrated and horrendously overpriced sweet wine wherever it comes from. The Picolit produced in Colli Orientali del Friuli is the only one in Italy to have DOC status, but, in fact, the wine is no better than other examples to be found throughout the country.

## FACTORS AFFECTING TASTE AND QUALITY

**LOCATION**
The northeast is bounded by the Dolomites to the north and the Adriatic Sea to the south.

**CLIMATE**
Similar to the northwest in that summers are hot and winters cold and harsh, but fog is less of a problem and hail more frequent. There are unpredictable variations in the weather from year to year so vintages are important, particularly for red wines.

**ASPECT**
Vineyards are found on a variety of sites ranging from the steep, mountainous slopes of Trentino-Alto Adige to the flat, alluvial plains of the Veneto and Friuli-Venezia Giulia. The best vineyards are always sited in hilly countryside.

**SOIL**
Most vineyards are on glacial moraine—a gritty mixture of sand, gravel, and sediment deposited during the Ice Age. Most are clayey or sandy clay and the best sites are often marly and rich in calcium. The light, stony soil in the South Tyrol is rapidly leached by weathering and fertilizers have to be added annually.

**VITICULTURE AND VINIFICATION**
The northeast has led Italy's move toward more modern vinification

techniques and experimentation with foreign grape varieties. It was the first area to use cold fermentation and, initially, the wines produced were so clean that they lacked natural character. There is now much experimentation into how to increase intensity of flavor through the use of new oak.

**GRAPE VARIETIES**
Blauer Portugieser (*syn. Portoghese*), Cabernet Franc, Cabernet Sauvignon, Chardonnay, Cortese (*syn. Bianca Fernanda*), Corvina (*syn. Corvinone or Cruina*), Durello, Franconia (*syn. Limberger*), Garganega, Gewürztraminer, Incrocio Manzoni 215 (*Prosecco x Cabernet Sauvignon*), Incrocio Manzoni 6013 (*Riesling x Pinot Blanc*), Kerner, Lagrein, Lambrusco a Foglia Frastagliata, Malbec, Malvasia, Marzemino, Merlot, Molinara (*syn. Rossara or Rossanella*), Mondeuse (*syn. Refosco or Terrano*), Muscat (*syn. Moscato*), Nosiola, Petit Verdot, Picolit, Pinella (*Pinello*), Pinot Blanc (*syn. Pinot Bianco*), Pinot Gris (*syn. Pinot Grigio*), Pinot Noir (*syn. Pinot Nero*), Prosecco (*syn. Serprina or Serprino*), Raboso (*syn. Friularo*), Ribolla, Riesling, Rossola (*syn. Veltliner*), Sauvignonasse (*syn. Tocai Friulano*), Sauvignon Blanc, Schiava (*syn. Vernatsch*), Schioppettino, Tazzelenghe, Teroldego, Tocai, Ugni Blanc (*syn. Trebbiano*), Verduzzo, Vespaiolo,

# NORTHEAST ITALY

## THE BEST CLASSIC BRUT SPARKLING WINES

These wines all come from Trentino-Alto Adige and are made by the traditional method.

✓ *Equipe 5 Brut Riserva • Equipe 5 Brut Rosé • Ferrari Brut • Ferrari Brut de Brut • Ferrari Brut Rosé • Ferrari Nature • Ferrari Riserva Giulio Ferrari • Methius Brut • Methius Riserva • Spagnolli Brut • Vivaldi Brut • Vivaldi Extra Brut*

## ALTO ADIGE *or* SÜDTIROLER DOC

### Trentino-Alto Adige

This generic appellation covers the entire Alto Adige, or South Tyrol, which is the northern half of the Valdadige DOC.

There are seven red-wine varietals: Cabernet covers either Cabernet Sauvignon or Cabernet Franc, or both, and ranges from simple, but delightful, everyday wines to deeper-colored, fuller-bodied, richer wines that become warm, mellow, and spicy after five to 10 years; Lagrein Scuro, or *Lagrein Dunkel*, is made from an underrated, indigenous grape and can have a fine, distinctive character and good color; Malvasia, or *Malvasier*, is produced here as a red wine, although it would be better made into white or rosé; Merlot can be simply light and fruity or can attain greater heights, with a good spicy, sweet-pepper aroma and a fine, silky texture; Pinot Noir, or *Blauburgunder*, is a difficult varietal to perfect, but those from Mazzon are good and a specialty of this region (they will have Mazzoner on the label); Schiava, or *Vernatsch*, accounts for one in five bottles produced under this appellation and is the most popular tavern wine; Schiava Grigia, or *Grauervernatsch*, has recently been added to the list, as have two red-wine blends of Cabernet-Lagrein and Cabernet-Merlot.

There are no fewer than 10 different white-wine varietals: Chardonnay can range from light and neutral to delicately fruity, and even *frizzantino* or verging upon *spumante*—the fuller versions can have recognizable varietal characteristics, but still lack the weight and intensity of flavor of even basic Burgundy; Moscato Giallo, or *Goldenmuskateller*, is made into delicious dessert wines; Pinot Bianco, or *Weissburgunder*, is the most widely planted of all the white grape varieties and produces most of Alto Adige's finest white wines; Pinot Grigio, or *Ruländer*, is potentially as successful as Pinot Blanc, but does not always occupy the best sites; Riesling Italico, or *Welschriesling*, is insignificant in both quantity and quality; Riesling Renano, or Rheinriesling, is fine, delicate, and attractive at the lowest level, but can be extraordinarily good in exceptional vintages; Riesling x Silvaner, or *Müller-Thurgau*, is relatively rare, which is a pity because it achieves a lively spiciness in this region; Sauvignon was very scarce in the early 1980s, but as the vogue for this grape spread so its cultivation increased and the crisp, dry, varietally pure Sauvignon is now one of the most successful wines of the Alto Adige; Silvaner is made mostly to be drunk young and fresh; Traminer Aromatico, or *Gewürztraminer*, is far more restrained than the classic Alsace version, even if, as some claim, the variety

originated in the village of Tramin or Termeno, between Bolzano and Trento. If you can forget the full-blown spicy wine of Alsace, the delicate aroma and understated flavor of this wine can have a certain charm of its own.

Only three dry varietal *rosato*, or *Kretzer*, wines are allowed: Lagrein Rosato, or *Lagrein Kretzer*, is overtly fruity in a very round and smooth style; Merlot Rosato, or Merlot Kretzer, is a relatively recent addition and makes a curiously grassy or bell-pepper rosé; Pinot Nero Rosato, or *Blauburgunder Kretzer*, is more successful as a rosé than as a red.

Moscato Rosa, or *Rosenmuskateller*, are very flamboyant, deep-pink to scarlet-red, semisweet to sweet wines with an unusually high natural acidity, intense floral perfume, and an exaggerated Muscat flavor.

There is one sparkling-wine denomination for pure or blended Pinot Blanc and/or Chardonnay with up to 30 percent Pinot Gris and Pinot Noir, with both *cuve close* and the traditional method permissible.

In 1994 five former DOCs were incorporated into the Alto Adige, or Südtiroler, DOC as geographical subappellations. **Colli di Bolzano DOC**, or *Bozner Leiten*, for soft, fruity, early-drinking, Schiava-based red wines from the left bank of the Adige River, and both banks of the Isarco near Bolzano; **Meranese**, or **Meranese di Collina DOC**, or *Meraner Hügel*, from the hills around Merano, north of Bolzano, where the Schiava grape produces a light, delicately scented red wine, which may be labeled as Burgravio, or *Burggräfler*, if it comes from the part of the Meranese that was formerly part of the Contea di Tirol; **Santa Maddalena DOC**, or *Sankt Magdalener*, in the heart of the Colli di Bolzano (*see above*), where the Schiava-based red wines are just as soft and fruity, but fuller in body and smoother in texture—few Italian references today boast that Santa Maddalena was ranked by Mussolini (overoptimistically) as one of Italy's greatest wines; **Terlano DOC**, or *Terlaner*, which overlaps most of Caldaro DOC on the right bank of the Adige, running some 10 miles (16 kilometers) northwest of Bolzano to 15 miles (24 kilometers) south, and covers one blended, one *spumante*, and the following eight varietal white wines: Pinot Bianco (*Weissburgunder*), Chardonnay, Riesling Italico (*Welschriesling*), Riesling Renano (*Rheinriesling*), Silvaner, Müller-Thurgau, and Sauvignon; and, finally, **Valle Isarco DOC**, or *Eisacktaler*, which takes in both banks of the Isarco River from a few miles north of Bolzano to just north of Bressanone, where the vineyards are high in altitude and the vines trained low to absorb ground heat. Six white-wine varietals are produced: Kerner, Müller-Thurgau, Pinot Grigio, or *Ruländer*, Sylvaner, Traminer Aromatico, or *Gewürztraminer*, and Veltliner. Valle Isarco also includes a geographical blend called *Klausner Leitacher* for red wines from the villages of Chiusa (also known as *Klausen*), Barbiano, Velturno, and Villandro, which must be made from at least 60 percent Schiava plus up to 40 percent Portoghese and Lagrein. Furthermore, any Valle Isarco wine produced in Bressanone or Varna can be labeled "di Bressanone" or "*Brixner*."

🍷 2–10 years (red and rosé), 2–5 years (white), 1–3 years (sparkling)

✓ *Abbazia di Novacella • Cantina Gries-Bolzano • Cantina Terlano • Colterenzio • Cortaccia • Anton Gojer • Giorgio Grai • Franz Haas • Hofstätter • Kettmeir • Klosterkellerei Eisacktaler • Klosterkellerei Schreckbichl • Alois Lageder • Mazo Foradori • Muri-Gries • Nalles Niclara Magre • Stiftskellerei Neustift • Niedermayr • Peter Pliger • Plattner-Waldgries • Prima & Nuova • Heinrich Rottensteiner • San Michele* (Sanct Valentin) *• Santa Margherita • Schloss Rametz • Schloss Sallegg • Schloss Schwanburg • Termeno • Tiefenbrunner • Elena Walch • Baron Georg von Widmann*

## AMARONE DELLA VALPOLICELLA *or* RECIOTO DELLA VALPOLICELLA AMARONE DOC

### Veneto

*See* Valpolicella DOC.

## AQUILEA DOC

### Friuli-Venezia Giulia

*See* Friuli-Aquilea DOC.

## BARDOLINO SUPERIORE DOCG

### Veneto

Bardolino DOC produces dry, sometimes *frizzante*, red and rosé (*chiaretto*) wines from the southeastern shores of Lake Garda. The reds, made from Corvina, Molinara, and Negrara, could be very interesting, but unfortunately most producers tend to make rather bland, lightweight wines.

🍷 1–3 years

✓ *Guerrieri-Rizzardi*

## BIANCO DI CUSTOZA DOC

### Veneto

Effectively the white wines of Bardolino, they can be scented with a smooth aftertaste and may sometimes be sparkling. Some critics compare Bianco di Custoza to Soave, which neatly sums up the quality. The grapes are Trebbiano, Garganega, Tocai Friulano, Cortese, and Malvasia.

## BOZNER LEITEN *or* COLLI DI BOLZANO DOC

### Trentino-Alto Adige

*See* Alto Adige DOC.

## BREGANZE DOC
### Veneto

This is one of Italy's unsung DOC heroes, largely due to the excellence of Maculan. As a generic red, Breganze is an excellent Merlot-based wine with the possible addition of Pinot Noir, Freisa, Marzemino, Gropello Gentile, Cabernet Franc, and Cabernet Sauvignon. As a white, it is fresh, zesty, and dry and made from Tocai Friulano, with the possible addition of Pinot Blanc, Pinot Gris, Welschriesling, and Vespaiolo. But it is mostly sold as a varietal, of which there are two red (Cabernet and Pinot Nero) and three white (Pinot Bianco, Pinot Grigio, and Vespaiolo).

🍷— 2–5 years (red), 1–2 years (white)

✓ *Bartolomeo da Breganze* • *Maculan*

## CABERNET FRANC
### Veneto

Most Cabernet wines are DOC, but a few non-DOC exist and are invariably well worth seeking out as they tend to be *barrique*-aged selections of ripe, not too grassy fruit.

✓ *Quintarelli* (Alerzo)

## CABERNET SAUVIGNON
### Veneto

Less traditional in Veneto than Cabernet Franc, pure varietal wines of any real quality or concentration are rarely encountered, but Cabernet Sauvignon from Anselmi and Le Vigne di San Pietro can be superb.

🍷— 3–6 years

✓ *Anselmi* (Realda) • *Le Vigne di San Pietro* (Refolà)

## CABERNET-MERLOT
### Trentino-Alto Adige and Veneto

There are so many Cabernet DOCs available in this region that few bother to produce a *vino da tavola*, but of those that do, the hellishly expensive San Leonardo is the very best. In the Veneto, with one notable exception, Cabernet-based blends are not as common as one imagines they might be.

✓ **Trentino-Alto Adige** *Tenuta San Leonardo* (Vallagrina)

**Veneto** *Conte Loredan-Gasparini* (Venegazzù della Casa, Venegazzù Capo di Stato)

## CALDARO *or* LAGO DI CALDARO KALTERER KALTERERSEE DOC
### Trentino-Alto Adige

As this overlaps the heart of the Terlano area, Caldaro might as well be yet another subappellation of the Alto Adige DOC, along with Terlano and the other former DOCs that have now been absorbed. Schiava-based red wines with the possible addition of Lagrein and Pinot Noir, they are usually soft and fruity, with a hint of almond, and easy to drink.

## CARSO DOC
### Friuli-Venezia Giulia

Carso Terrano must consist of at least 85 percent Terrano (also known as Mondeuse or Refosco), which also makes a deep, dark, and full red wine that can be fat and juicy. Carso Malvasia is a rich and gently spicy, dry white wine.

🍷— 1–3 years

✓ *Edi Kante*

## CASTELLER DOC
### Trentino-Alto Adige

The thin strip of hilly vineyards that produces these wines is virtually identical to the Trentino DOC. Dry or semisweet, red and rosé wines for everyday drinking from Schiava, Merlot, and Lambrusco a Foglia Frastagliata grapes.

## CHARDONNAY
### Northeast Italy

A decade ago, only two pure Chardonnay DOCs existed in northeast Italy: Alto Adige and Grave del Friuli. Now it is one of the most ubiquitous varietals, but premium-priced non-DOC wines from this grape variety are still excellent quality.

✓ *Azienda Agricola Inama* (Campo dei Tovi) • *Jermann* (Where The Dreams Have No End)

## COLLI BERICI DOC
### Veneto

In addition to a sparkling Garganega-based white wine, this DOC includes three red varietals (Merlot, Tocai Rosso, and Cabernet) and five white (Garganega, Tocai Bianco, Pinot Bianco, Sauvignon, and Chardonnay). The Cabernet can be rich and grassy with chocolaty fruit, and the Merlot, in the right hands, is plump and juicy; the red Tocai is unusual and interesting, and the Chardonnay suffices as usual. However, the other wines from this area immediately south of Vicenza are less exciting.

🍷— 2–5 years (red), 1–2 years (white)

✓ *Castello di Belvedere* • *Villa dal Ferro*

## COLLI DI BOLZANO *or* BOZNER LEITEN DOC
### Trentino-Alto Adige

*See* Alto Adige DOC.

## COLLI EUGANEI DOC
### Veneto

Bordering Colli Berici to the southeast, this area produces soft, full-bodied, dry or semisweet red-wine blends (from Merlot plus Cabernet Franc, Cabernet Sauvignon, Barbera, and Raboso) and four red varietals: Cabernet, Cabernet Franc, Cabernet Sauvignon, and Merlot. There are dry or semisweet white-wine blends (from Prosecco, Garganega, and Tocai Friulano with the possible addition of Chardonnay, Pinot Blanc, Pinella, and Welschriesling) and seven white varietals: Chardonnay, Fior d'Arancio (from the Moscato Giallo grape in sweet *frizzantino*, *spumante*, and *liquoroso* styles), Moscato (sweet *frizzantino* and *spumante* styles), Pinella or Pinello, Pinot Bianco, Serprina or Serprino (dry

or sweet in still, *frizzantino*, *frizzante*, or *spumante* styles), and Tocai Italico.

🍷— 2–5 years (red), 1–2 years (white)

✓ *Villa Sceriman* ⊙ • *Vignalta*

## COLLI ORIENTALI DEL FRIULI DOC
### Friuli-Venezia Giulia

Larger than neighboring Collio and initially more prestigious, both DOCs have now shown their excellent potential. In addition to a generic *rosato* blend, there are seven red varietals (Cabernet, Cabernet Franc, Cabernet Sauvignon, Merlot, Pinot Noir, Refosco, and Schioppettino); and 12 white (Chardonnay, Malvasia, Picolit, Pinot Bianco, Pinot Grigio, Ramandolo (dessert-style Verduzzo), Ribolla, Riesling Renano, Sauvignon Blanc, Tocai Friulano, Traminer Aromatico, and Verduzzo Friulano). The whites are especially outstanding, but the most famous, Picolit, is overrated and overpriced, even though this used to be the only Picolit in Italy to have its own DOC and should, therefore, have a reputation to maintain.

🍷— 3–8 years (red), 1–3 years (white)

✓ *Borgo del Tiglio* • *Girolamo Dorigo* • *Le Due Terre* • *Livio Felluga* • *Dorino Livon* • *Miani* • *Scubla* • *Le Vigne di Zamó* • *Volpe Pasini*

## COLLIO *or* COLLIO GORIZIANO DOC
### Friuli-Venezia Giulia

A large range of mostly white wines from a hilly area close to the Slovenian border, Collio now encompasses 19 different wines. With some top producers making very high-quality wines, this appellation is clearly in line for full DOCG status in the near future. As well as a blended dry white (primarily from Ribolla, Malvasia, and Tocai Friulano), which can be slightly *frizzantino*, and blended red (Merlot, Cabernet Sauvignon, and Cabernet Franc, plus Pinot Noir and possibly one or two others), there are five red varietals (Cabernet, Cabernet Franc,

Cabernet Sauvignon, Merlot, and Pinot Nero); and 12 white (Chardonnay, Malvasia, Müller-Thurgau, Picolit, Pinot Bianco, Pinot Grigio, Riesling Italico, Riesling Renano, Tocai Friulano, Ribolla, Sauvignon, and Traminer Aromatico). Jerman makes some of the very greatest wines, but now markets his wines under the IGT Delle Venezie. They are included below for completeness.

🍷— 1–4 years (red), 1–3 years (white)

✓ • *Borgo del Tiglio* • *Castello di Spessa* • *Josko Gravner* • *Jermann* • *Edi Keber* • *Dorino Livon* • *Dario Roccaro* • *Russiz Superiore* • *Schiopetto* • *Franco Toros* • *Venicia & Venicia* • *Villa Russiz*

## CORVINA
### Veneto

Arguably the greatest grape in Veneto, Corvina is the key player in Bardolino and Valpolicella, particularly the *recioto* and *amarone* styles of the latter, but can also be found in a few premium *vini da tavola*.

✓ *Allegrini* (Pelara, La Poja)

## EISACKTALER *or* VALLE ISARCO DOC
### Trentino-Alto Adige

See Alto Adige DOC.

## ETSCHTALER DOC
### Trentino-Alto Adige

See Valdadige DOC.

## FRANCONIA *or* BLAUFRANKISCH
### Friuli-Venezia Giulia

Franconia is the synonym for the Limberger grape of Germany. The wine is made in a fuller, darker style than is possible in its homeland, yet it still possesses the same light, fruity flavor.

## FRIULI-AQUILEA DOC
### Friuli-Venezia Giulia

Formerly know simply as Aquilea, this is a wide-ranging appellation that covers five varietal red wines (Merlot, Cabernet, Cabernet Franc, Cabernet Sauvignon, and Refosco); eight white varietals (Chardonnay, Tocai Friulano, Pinot Bianco, Pinot Grigio, Riesling Renano, Sauvignon, Traminer, and Verduzzo Friulano); and a generic rosé of at least 70 percent Merlot plus Cabernet Franc, Cabernet Sauvignon, and Refosco. There is also a Chardonnay *spumante*. All are generally light, crisply balanced wines, although some producers excel in better years.

🍷— 1–4 years (red), 1–3 years (white, rosé, and sparkling)

✓ *Zonin* (Tenuta Cà Bolani)

## FRIULI-GRAVE DOC
### Friuli-Venezia Giulia

Formerly called Grave del Friuli, this massive appellation spreads out on both sides of the Tagliamento River between Sacile in the west and Cividale di Friuli in the east, and accounts for over half of the region's total production. It is a huge and complicated, but rapidly improving, multivarietal DOC in which several winemakers regularly produce fine wines. In addition to generic red and white blends, there are six red varietals (Cabernet, Cabernet Franc, Cabernet Sauvignon, Merlot, Refosco, and Pinot Noir); and eight white varietals (Chardonnay,

Pinot Bianco, Pinot Gris, Riesling Renano, Sauvignon, Tocai Friulano, Traminer Aromatico, and Verduzzo Friulano). There is a Chardonnay *frizzante*, Verduzzo *frizzante*, Chardonnay *spumante*, and a blended generic *spumante*.

🍷— 1–4 years (red), 1–3 years (white, rosé, and sparkling)

✓ *Borgo Magredo* • *Pighin* • *Vigneti le Monde* • *Vigneti Pittaro*

## FRIULI-LATISANA *or* LATISANA DOC
### Friuli-Venezia Giulia

An area that stretches from the central section of the Friuli-Grave to the Adriatic coast at Lignano Sabbiadoro. In addition to a generic, blended rosé (Bordeaux varieties) and *spumante* (Chardonnay and Pinot varieties) there are five red varietal wines (Merlot, Cabernet Sauvignon, Franconia (Limberger), Pinot Nero, and Refosco); and nine white varietals (Chardonnay, Malvasia, Pinot Bianco, Pinot Grigio, Riesling Renano, Sauvignon, Tocai Friulano, Traminer Aromatico, and Verduzzo Friulano). Chardonnay, Malvasia, and Pinot Nero may also be produced in a *frizzante* style.

## GAMBELLARA DOC
### Veneto

Produces scented, dry, or sometimes semisweet white wines and fruity, semisweet, still, *frizzante* or fully sparkling white *recioto*. A smooth, sweet *vin santo* is also produced here.

🍷— 2–5 years

✓ *La Biancara*

## GARGANEGA
### Veneto

The primary grape used for Soave—in skilled hands Garganega can produce a fabulously rich yet delicately balanced dry white, but it has a tendency to overcrop, and most Garganega wines turn out bland.

## GRAVE DEL FRIULI DOC
### Friuli-Venezia Giulia

See Friuli-Grave DOC.

## ISONZO *or* ISONZO DEL FRIULI DOC
### Friuli-Venezia Giulia

A small area south of Collio, producing a very good yet still improving quality wine. There are generic red- and white-wine blends, plus four red varietals (Cabernet, Merlot, Franconia (Limberger), and Refosco); and 10 white varietals (Chardonnay, Malvasia, Pinot Bianco, Pinot Grigio, Riesling Italico, Riesling Renano, Sauvignon, Tocai Friulano, Traminer Aromatico, and Verduzzo Friulano); and a Pinot *spumante*.

🍷— 1–4 years (red), 1–3 years (white)

✓ *Borgo Conventi* • *Lis Neris-Pecorari* • *Ronco del Gelso* • *Vie di Romans*

## KALTERER *or* KALTERERSEE DOC
### Trentino-Alto Adige

See Caldaro DOC.

## LAGREIN
### Trentino-Alto Adige

An ancient Alto Adige variety, it was well known to Pliny, who called it Lageos. Although

it is by no means the greatest grape grown in the region, Lagrein does, however, produce one of Alto Adige's most original and expressive wines, with rich, chunky, youthful fruit of relatively high acidity, but capable of developing a silky, violety finesse after a few years in bottle.

## LATISANA DOC
### Friuli-Venezia Giulia

See Friuli-Latisana DOC.

## LESSINI DURELLO DOC
### Veneto

Dry white wine from just northeast of Soave, in still, *frizzantino*, and fully sparkling styles, from the Durello grape with the possible addition of Garganega, Trebbiano, Pinot Blanc, Pinot Noir, and Chardonnay.

✓ *Marcato*

## LISON-PRAMAGGIORE DOC
### Veneto and Friuli-Venezia Giulia

This DOC, which is in the very east of the Veneto, and overlaps a small part of Friuli, originally combined three former DOCs (Cabernet di Pramaggiore, Merlot di Pramaggiore, and Tocai di Lison) into one. However, it has since been expanded to encompass a total of seven white varietal wines (Chardonnay, Pinot Bianco, Pinot Grigio, Riesling Italico, Sauvignon, Tocai Italico, and Verduzzo); and four reds (Cabernet, Cabernet Franc, Cabernet Sauvignon, and Refosco dal Peduncolo Rosso). Cabernet and Merlot are still the best in a rich, delicious, chocolaty style.

🍷— 3–8 years (red), 1–3 years (white)

✓ *Santa Margherita* • *Russola* • *Tenuta Sant'Anna* • *Villa Castalda* (Cabernet Franc)

## LUGANA DOC
### Veneto

See Lugana DOC (Lombardy) under Northwest Italy.

## MARZEMINO
### Trentino-Alto Adige

This grape variety was probably brought to Italy from Slovenia by the Romans. By the 18th century, it had achieved sufficient fame for Mozart to use it in his opera *Don Giovanni* as a preliminary to the seduction of Zerlina. A Marzemino cluster typically provides large, loosely bunched grapes, which make an aromatic, early-drinking red wine, either as DOC (Trentino) or *vino da tavola*.

## MERANESE *or* MERANESE DI COLLINA MERANER HÜGEL DOC
### Trentino-Alto Adige

See Alto Adige DOC.

## MERLOT
### Friuli-Venezia Giulia

A prolific grape in northeastern Italy, where it has been grown for almost 200 years. Far too many wishy-washy examples abound, but top producers achieve concentration and quality through low yields and strict selection. Although Merlot is a varietal wine in virtually all the DOCs of Friuli-Venezia Giulia, the only ones with any special reputation for it are Colli

Orientali, where the richest varietals are made, and Collio, which is less consistent, but the best are plump and juicy.

✓ *Borgo del Tiglio (Rosso della Centa)*

## MONTELLO E COLLI ASOLANI DOC
### Veneto

From vineyards at the foot of the aptly named Mount Grappa, most of wines are varietals, comprising two reds (Merlot and Cabernet); four whites (Prosecco, Chardonnay, Pinot Bianco, and Pinot Grigio); and three *spumante* (Chardonnay, Pinot Bianco, and Prosecco). Any red wines that do not carry a varietal name will be primarily Cabernet-Merlot blends.

⌐— 1–3 years

✓ *Fernando Berta* • *Abbazia di Nervesa*

## NOSIOLA
### Trentino-Alto Adige

Probably the least known of the Trentino's traditional grapes because it is mostly used for *vin santo*. However, dry white varietal wines are also made from this variety and, although it is best when blended with more aromatic varieties, as in Sorni DOC, it is even making a reputation as a premium *vino da tavola*.

✓ *Pravis (Le Frate)*

## PIAVE *or* VINI DEL PIAVE DOC
### Veneto

A large area to the west of Lison-Pramaggiore producing five red varietals (Merlot, Cabernet, Cabernet Sauvignon, Pinot Nero, and Raboso); and five whites (Chardonnay, Tocai Italico, Pinot Bianco, Pinot Grigio, and Verduzzo). The Cabernet and Raboso can be particularly good.

⌐— 1–3 years

✓ *Reichsteiner*

## PICOLIT DOC
### Friuli-Venezia Giulia

*See* Colli Orientali del Friuli DOC.

## PROSECCO
### Veneto

Although it is one of the most traditional of Veneto grape varieties, Prosecco originated in the village of that name in Friuli's Carso district. Latin-lovers adore the soft bubbly produced by this grape, but most of it is boring, and it will take a revolution in quality to convince me that this grape is suitable for dry sparkling wines.

## PROSECCO DI CONEGLIANO-VALDOBBIADENE DOC
### Veneto

Dry and semisweet fizzy white wines of passable quality, although most of them have large bubbles and a coarse, dull flavor. A still version is also produced.

⌐— Upon purchase

✓ *Adami Adriano* (Vigneto Giardino) • *Fratelli Bartolin Spumante* • *Bisol* • *Carpenè Malvolti*

## RABOSO
### Veneto

The indigenous Raboso grape has long made excellent-value red wines that are full of sunny fruit and capable of improving after two to

three years in bottle. There are two distinct, localized clones—Raboso del Piave, most often used as a pure varietal, and the more productive Raboso Veronese, which does not have the richness or such a positive character, and is merely a blending component. Most of the wines produced are *vini da tavola* but DOC wines are available under the Piave appellation.

## RAMANDOLO DOCG
### Friuli-Venezia Giulia

Sweet Verduzzo dessert wine.

## RECIOTO BIANCO DI CAMPOCIESA
### Veneto

Soft, sweet, well-scented, golden-colored, non-DOC white wines made from *passito* grapes.

## RECIOTO DELLA VALPOLICELLA *or* RECIOTO DELLA VALPOLICELLA AMARONE DOC
### Veneto

*See* Valpolicella DOC.

## RECIOTO DI SOAVE DOCG
### Veneto

Naturally sweet Soave made from *passito* grapes, to produce wines that are either *liquoroso* or *spumante*. Most are too oxidative, but Pieropan is excellent and Anselmi is outstanding—both as pure as driven snow.

✓ *Anselmi* (I Capitelli) • *Pieropan* (Le Colombare Vendemmia Tardiva)

## REFOSCO
### Friuli-Venezia Giulia

Known as Terrano in the Carso district, the Refosco is none other than the Mondeuse of France. It typically produces a deep-colored red wine with soft, juicy, low-acid fruit, which can be somewhat one-dimensional, but is at its best in the Colli Orientali and Friuli-Grave.

## SANTA MADDALENA *or* SANKT MAGDALENER DOC
### Trentino-Alto Adige

*See* Alto Adige DOC.

## SCHIAVA
### Trentino-Alto Adige

This is the most widely cultivated variety in the Alto Adige, where it accounts for 60 percent of the vines grown. In the Tyrol, where this grape is believed to have originated, it is known as Vernatsch, but most ampelographers refer to it as Schiava. There are four subvarieties: Schiava Grossa, Schiava Gentile, Schiava Grigia, and Schiava Meranese. Schiava wines are usually medium-bodied with an almond character to the fruit and a light bitterness on the finish.

## SCHIOPPETTINO
### Friuli-Venezia Giulia

An ancient Friulian variety, Schioppettino was nearly extinct until these wines suddenly became fashionable in the 1980s. It produces very ripe and round wines with a fine, spicy-scented bouquet and rich fruit flavor that attains great finesse only with maturity.

✓ *Ronchi di Cialla* • *Ronco del Gnemiz* • *Giuseppe Toti*

## SOAVE DOC
### Veneto

Most Soave is still overcropped, thin, and acidic, and in 2000, Roberto Anselmi took his greatly admired wines out of the Soave appellation in protest. Top producers continue to make immensely enjoyable wines from Garganega and Trebbiano, when they are grown to restricted yields in the central, hilly, *classico* area. Anselmi's wines are included below for completeness. *See also* Recioto di Soave DOC.

⌐— 1–4 years

✓ *Anselmi* (Capitel Foscarino, Capitel Croce) • *Bolla* (Castellaro, Vigneti di Froscà) • *Ca' Rugate* (Monte Alto) • *Cantina del Castello* (Monte Pressoni) • *Inama* (Vigneto du Lot) • *Pieropan* (Vigneto Calvarino, Vigneto la Rocca) • *Suavia* (Le Rive) • *Fratelli Tedeschi* (Monte Tenda)

## SORNI DOC
### Trentino-Alto Adige

This tiny DOC is situated just south of Mezzo-lombardo at the confluence of the Avisio and Adige rivers. Soft Schiava-based reds are often improved by the addition of Teroldego and Lagrein. Light, fresh, delicate Nosiola-based white wines are usually charged with a dollop of Müller-Thurgau, Silvaner, and Pinot Blanc.

⌐— 2–3 years (red), up to 18 months (white)

✓ *Maso Poli*

## SÜDTIROLER DOC
### Trentino-Alto Adige

*See* Alto Adige DOC.

## TACELENGHE *or* TAZZELENGHE
### Friuli-Venezia Giulia

This grape variety takes its name from the local dialect for *tazzalingua* which means "a sharpness in the tongue," and is indicative of the wine's tannic nature. However, it does soften after five or six years in bottle.

## TERLANO *or* TERLANER DOC
### Trentino-Alto Adige

*See* Alto Adige DOC.

## TEROLDEGO
### Trentino-Alto Adige

An indigenous black grape with a thick bluish skin, Teroldego is productive and makes a dark-colored red wine with a distinctive aroma and a chewy, tannic raspberry richness that softens with age, attaining a silky-violety finesse. This has made it a very useful blending component in the past. However, more varietal wines are gradually being made and it has even started to be marketed as a premium *vino da tavola*.

✓ *Foradori* (Granato)

## TEROLDEGO ROTALIANO DOC
### Trentino-Alto Adige

Full-bodied red wines made from the Teroldego in the Rotaliano area, where the grape is said to have originated. There is also a fuller *Superiore* version and an attractive rosé.

⟊— 1–4 years

✓ *Foradori* (Vigneto Morei) • *Conti Martini*

## TERRANO
### Friuli-Venezia Giulia

*See* Refosco.

## TREBBIANO
### Veneto

The Trebbiano of Soave and Lugana are supposedly superior to the Trebbiano of Tuscany, but there is much dross produced in both DOCs, and it is the producer who makes the real difference.

## TRENTINO DOC
### Trentino-Alto Adige

This appellation represents the southern half of the Valdadige DOC and its wines are generally softer and less racy than those from Alto Adige to the north, although there is an equally bewildering number of varietal wines. If no variety is shown, white wines will be Chardonnay-Pinot Blanc blends and reds Cabernet-Merlot. There are seven red-wine varietals (Cabernet, Cabernet Franc, Cabernet Sauvignon, Lagrein, Marzemino, Merlot, and Pinot Nero), and nine white (Chardonnay, Moscato Giallo, Müller-Thurgau, Nosiola, Pinot Bianco, Pinot Grigio, Riesling Italico, Riesling Renano, and Traminer Aromatico). Furthermore, the Nosiola can be made in *vin santo* style, while all Pinot (Blanc, Gris, and Noir) may be fully sparkling. There is also a bright scarlet, lusciously sweet Moscato Rosa, and both Moscato Rosa and Moscato Giallo may be made in *liquoroso* style.

✓ *Barone de Cles* • *Càvit* • *Cesconi* • *LaVis* • *Longariva* • *Madonna del Vittoria* • *Conti Martini* • *Pojer & Sandri* • *Giovanni Poli* • *Tenuta San Leonardo* • *Armando Simoncelli* • *de Tarczal* • *Vallarom* • *Roberto Zeni*

## VALDADIGE *or* ETSCHTALER DOC
### Trentino-Alto Adige and Veneto

This huge generic denomination encompasses both the Alto Adige and Trentino DOCs, a myriad of subappellations, and extends well into the Veneto. Few producers bother to use what is generally considered to be Trentino-Alto Adige's lowest quality DOC. If the IGTs proposed by the Goria Law actually existed and worked, the size and location of Valdadige would make it an ideal candidate, as producers could select their best wines to go out under Alto Adige, Trentino, or another label, selling off the balance as an unpretentious Valdadige country wine. As it is already a DOC, nobody would dare suggest downgrading it to IGT, so the result is that hardly anyone uses it anyway. And, of the few who do, the dry and

semisweet white and red wines that they sell inevitably attract a poor reputation as DOCs, whereas underselling the same products as IGTs would make them honest, good-value introductions to the finer wines of Trentino-Alto Adige.

## VALLE ISARCO *or* EISACKTALER DOC
### Trentino-Alto Adige

*See* Alto Adige DOC.

## VALPANTENA DOC
### Veneto

*See* Valpolicella DOC.

Subappellation for Valpolicella, in *recioto*, *amarone*, *spumante*, and regular *rosso* styles.

## VALPOLICELLA DOC
### Veneto

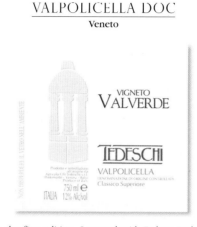

In the first edition, I agreed with Robert Parker, the American wine writer, when he described most Valpolicella as "insipid industrial garbage," but technology has changed things over the past 25 years. While most are still insipid and industrial, relatively few are as bad as garbage. Made from at least 80 percent Corvina with the possible addition of Rossignola, Negrara, Trentina, Barbera, and Sangiovese, most Valpolicella are simply light-red and light-bodied, with lackluster, attenuated fruit hinting of cherries, and a dry, slightly bitter finish. There are an increasing number of wines that are full of juicy cherry-fruit flavors, but they are still in a minority and for truly fine wines bearing the Valpolicella DOC you have to seek out exceptional wines from the tiny number of producers recommended below.

Valpolicella *recioto* is a bittersweet, yet very smooth, deep-colored, portlike wine made from *passito* grapes, although it may also be produced in a *spumante* style. *Amarone* is a derivative of *recioto*, with a similar deep color, but in a dry or off-dry style, which seems to make the flavors more powerful and chocolaty-spicy with a distinctly bitter finish. There is also something very specific that marks the fruit in *amarone* wines, which wine writer Oz Clarke once described—perfectly to my mind—as a "bruised sourness." This is an oxidative character that will not appeal to lovers of clean, precise, well-focused flavors, but its complexity is undeniable and such wines age wonderfully. Quintarelli is the most outstanding producer, with Allegrini hard on his heels.

⟊— Upon purchase for most, 2–5 years for recommendations

✓ **Valpolicella** *Allegrini* (La Grola) • *Bolla* (Vigneti di Jago) • *Guerrieri-Rizzardi* (Villa Rizzardi Poiega) • *Quintarelli* • *Le Ragose* •

*Serègo Alighieri* • *Fratelli Tedeschi* (Capitel delle Lucchine, Capitel dei Nicalò) • *Tommasi* (Vigneto del Campo Rafael) **Recioto della Valpolicella** *Stefano Accordini* (Acinatico) • *Allegrini* (Gardane) • *Lorenzo Begali* • *Tommaso Bussola* (TB) • *Masi* (Mazzanella) • *Quintarelli* • *Serègo Alighieri* (Casel dei Ronchi) • *Fratelli Tedeschi* (Capitel Monte Fontana) **Recioto della Valpolicella Amarone** *Allegrini* (Fieramonte) • *Bertani* • *Brigaldara* • *Tommaso Bussola* • *Masi* (Mazzone) • *Fratelli Pasqua* (Vigneti Casterna) • *Quintarelli* • *Romano Dal Forno* (Vigneto di Monte Lodoletta) • *Sant'Antonio* (Campo de Gigli) • *Serègo Alighieri* (Vaio Armoron) • *Speri* (Vigneto Monte Sant'Urbano) • *Fratelli Tedeschi* (Capitel Monte Olmi) • *Tommasi* • *Trabucchi* (Marchetto) • *Viviani* (Casa de Bepi)

## VALPOLICELLA "RIPASSO"
### Veneto

*Ripasso* ("re-passed") wine has long been traditional in the Veneto. The best young Valpolicella is put into tanks or barrels that still contain the lees of the *recioto* for which they were previously used. When mixed with the young wine, active yeast cells in this sediment precipitate a second fermentation. This increases the alcohol content and gives it some *recioto* character. After having undergone this process, the wines usually cannot carry the Valpolicella appellation and are therefore sold as *vino da tavola* under various brand names, although some Valpolicella wines are turbocharged by *ripasso* without any mention of it on the label.

⟊— 6–15 years

✓ *Allegrini* (Palazzo alla Torre) • *Boscaini* (Le Cane) • *Fratelli Tedeschi* (Capitel San Rocco) • *Masi* (Campo Fiorin)

## VINI DEL PIAVE DOC
### Veneto

*See* Piave DOC.

## WILDBACHER
### Veneto

This black grape seems to be restricted to the Veneto area and to Western Styria in Austria, where it is known as Blauer Wildbacher. Mostly used as a blending component, its distinctive, aromatic quality and high acidity are sometimes found in varietal form in non-DOC wines.

✓ *Le Case Bianche*

## NEW IGT WINES

The following Indicazioni Geografiche Tipiche wines were agreed at the end of 1996, yet most have still to register with consumers, or establish any consistency of style or quality:

✓ **Friuli-Venezia Giulia** *Alto Livenza* • *Delle Venezie* • *Venezia Giulia*

**Trentino-Alto Adige** *Atesino* • *Delle Venezie* • *Vallagarina*

**Veneto** *Alto Livenza* • *Colli Trevigiani* • *Conselvano* • *Delle Venezie* • *Marca Trevigiani* • *Provincia di Verona or Veronese* • *Vallagarina* • *Veneto* • *Veneto Orientale*

# WEST-CENTRAL ITALY

*The heart of Italy is also the center of the country's
most important quality-wine exports, which are
dominated by famous red Sangiovese wines from
the tiny Tuscan hills and valleys between Florence
and the Umbria-Latium border.*

## TUSCANY (TOSCANA)

The home of traditional winemaking, Tuscany has also been the
main focus of experimentation. Its powerful red Vino Nobile di
Montepulciano was Italy's first DOCG, and has been followed by
Brunello di Montalcino, Chianti, Carmignano, and Vernaccia di
San Gimignano. But not all of its finest wines bear these famous
appellations, a fact recognized by the Tuscan producers
themselves, who, on the one hand, sought the ideal DOCG
solution for Chianti, while on the other began to invest in
premium wines that were not restricted by the DOC. It was
the uncompromising quality of their Super-Tuscan wines that
encouraged premium *vini da tavola* throughout the rest of Italy.
Unfortunately, they were less successful
with the DOCG of Chianti. The
Tuscans had two sensible,

forward-thinking approaches: one was to apply DOCG to the
Chianti Classico area and other isolated areas, such as parts of
Rufina and the Colli Fiorentini, where most of the finest wines
have traditionally been made, and to leave the rest as DOC
Chianti; the other was to grant DOCG status to the best 10
percent, regardless of origin. Either would have made Chianti a
success. But the biggest Chianti producers had more political clout
than the best producers, and the new regulations gave DOCG
status to the whole area and all Chianti wines, regardless of their
origin or quality.

It is true that the Trebbiano Toscano, a localized clone, is an
intrinsically high-class Trebbiano and, indeed, it can make some
charming wines, but it is not a fine-wine grape. Currently,
Tuscany has no white-wine sister for its red Sangiovese grape.
Unfortunately, its best dry
white-wine grape so far has
been Chardonnay, a variety
that excels in almost every
half-decent wine area.
Vermentino might be Tuscany's
white-wine grape of the future,
although it is really a Sardinian
grape and currently mostly

Chianti including Carmignano (1),
Rufina (2), Colli Fiorentini (3),
Montespertoli (4), Colline Pisani (5),
Vernaccia di San Gimignano (6)
Vino Nobile di Montepulciano (7)

Chianti Classico

Bianco di Pitigliano

Montefalco

Orvieto

Est! Est!! Est!!! di Montefiascone

Colline Lucchesi

Montecarlo Bianco

Val di Cornia

Val d'Arbia

Bianco Vergine della Valdichiana

Colli Perugini

Colli Amerini

Colli Martani

Montalbano
Pomino
Aretini
Colli Senesi
Brunello di Montalcino
Candia dei Colli Apuani
Bianco della Val di Nievole
Bianco Pisano di San Torpe
Aleatico di Gradoli
Morellino di Scansano

| 8 | Montescudaio |
| 9 | Bolgheri |
| 10 | Monteri di Massa Marittima |
| 11 | Moscadello di Montalcino |
| 12 | Elba |
| 13 | Maremma Toscana |
| 14 | Slovana |
| 15 | Parrina |
| 16 | Colli del Trasimeno |
| 17 | Colli Altotiberini |
| 18 | Torgiano |

*See page opposite*

*Provincia* boundary

▲ Height above sea level (metres)

0   10   20   30   40   50 miles

0        20        40        60        80 km

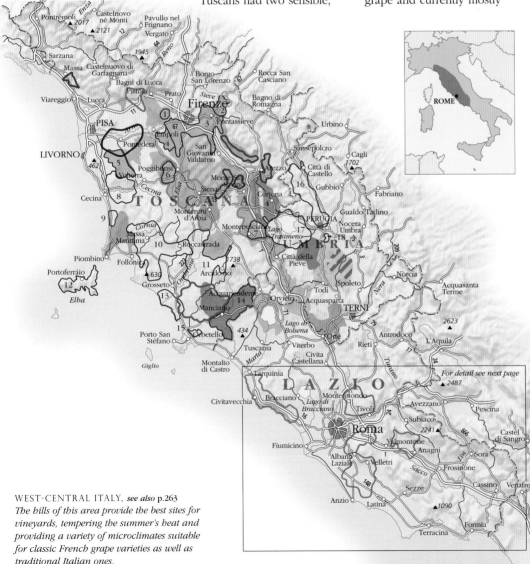

WEST-CENTRAL ITALY, *see also p.263*
*The hills of this area provide the best sites for
vineyards, tempering the summer's heat and
providing a variety of microclimates suitable
for classic French grape varieties as well as
traditional Italian ones.*

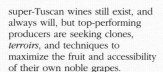

# FACTORS AFFECTING TASTE AND QUALITY

**LOCATION**
Located between the Apennines to the north and east and the Tyrrhenian Sea to the west.

**CLIMATE**
Summers are long and fairly dry and winters are less severe than in northern Italy. Heat and lack of rain can be a problem throughout the area during the growing season.

**ASPECT**
Vineyards are usually sited on hillsides for good drainage and exposure to the sun. Deliberate use is made of altitude to offset the heat, and black grapes grow at up to 1,800 feet (550 meters) and white grapes at up to 2,275 feet (700 meters). The higher the vines, the longer the ripening season and the greater the acidity of the grapes.

**SOIL**
These are very complex soils with gravel, limestone, and clay outcrops predominating. In Tuscany a rocky, schistose soil, known in some localities as *galestro*, covers most of the best vineyards.

**VITICULTURE AND VINIFICATION**
After much experimentation, particularly in Tuscany, with classic French grapes, the trend recently has been to develop the full potential of native varieties. Many stunning Cabernet-influenced,

super-Tuscan wines still exist, and always will, but top-performing producers are seeking clones, *terroirs*, and techniques to maximize the fruit and accessibility of their own noble grapes.

A traditional speciality is the sweet, white *vin santo*, which is made from *passito* grapes dried on straw mats in attics. It is aged for up to six years, often in a type of *solera* system.

**GRAPE VARIETIES**
**Primary varieties:** Sangiovese (*syn.* Brunello, Morellino, Prugnolo, Sangioveto, Tignolo, Uva Canina), Malvasia, Trebbiano (*syn.* Procanico)
**Secondary varieties:** Abbuoto, Aglianico, Albana (*syn.* Greco, but not Grechetto), Albarola, Aleatico, Barbera, Bellone, Bombino, Cabernet Franc, Cabernet Sauvignon, Canaiolo (*syn.* Drupeggio in Umbria), Carignan (*syn.* Uva di Spagna), Cesanese, Chardonnay, Ciliegiolo, Colorino, Gamay, Grechetto (*syn.* Greco, Pulciano), Inzolia (*syn.* Ansonica), Mammolo, Merlot, Montepulciano, Moscadelletto, Muscat (*syn.* Moscadello, Moscato), Nero Buono di Cori, Pinot Blanc (*syn.* Pinot Bianco), Pinot Gris (*syn.* Pinot Grigio), Roussanne, Sagrantino, Sauvignon Blanc, Sémillon, Syrah, Verdello, Vermentino, Vernaccia, Welschriesling

TRADITION AND INNOVATION
*This tranquil landscape appears to have remained unchanged for many centuries, but, while Tuscan winemaking is steeped in tradition, the area is now also experimenting with different grape varieties and* barrique *aging.*

restricted to Tuscany's coastal areas. It is time someone managed to rekindle an ancient, all-but-extinct Tuscan white grape and rescue it with commercial success, much as the *piemontesi* did with Arneis and, as I suspect, they will next try with Timorasso.

## BIRTH OF THE SUPER-TUSCANS
Ten years ago the largest number of exceptional Tuscan wines were the then relatively new *barrique*-aged Super-Tuscans. Their story began in 1948 when the now famous Sassicaia wine was produced for the first time by Incisa della Rochetta using Cabernet Sauvignon vines reputedly from Château Lafite-Rothschild. This was an unashamed attempt to produce a top-quality Italian wine from Bordeaux's greatest grape variety, decades before the idea became old hat in the wine world. It became so successful that in the wake of the 1971 vintage, a new red called Tignanello was

ROME AND ITS ENVIRONS, *see also* **opposite**
*The recent proliferation of appellations in the hills surrounding Italy's capital are evidence of a wine regime gone mad— this country's wines need cohesion, not further diversity.*

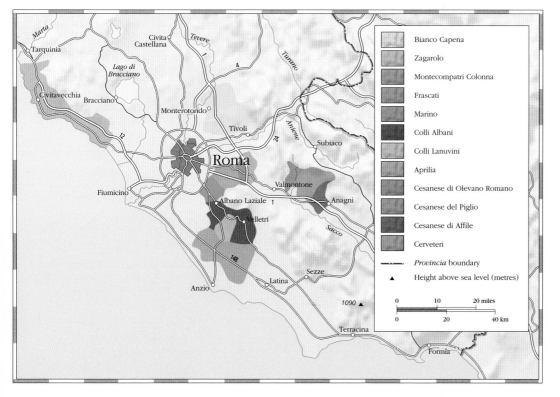

| | |
|---|---|
| | Bianco Capena |
| | Zagarolo |
| | Montecompatri Colonna |
| | Frascati |
| | Marino |
| | Colli Albani |
| | Colli Lanuvini |
| | Aprilia |
| | Cesanese di Olevano Romano |
| | Cesanese del Piglio |
| | Cesanese di Affile |
| | Cerveteri |

- - - *Provincia* boundary
▲ Height above sea level (metres)

VERNACCIA VINES IN FALL
*These vines grow exclusively around the medieval Tuscan town of San Gimignano, whose impressive towers can be seen here in the distance. When it comes from good producers, the white Vernaccia can be a deliciously crisp, fruity dry wine.*

introduced by Piero Antinori with a Sangiovese base and 20 percent Cabernet Sauvignon, as a compromise between Tuscany and Bordeaux. Although Frescobaldi had used Cabernet Sauvignon in its Nipozzano Chianti for over a century and it grew in the Carmignano area in the 18th century, nobody had truly appreciated the harmony that could be achieved between the two grapes until Tignanello appeared. The blend was akin to the natural balance of Cabernet and Merlot, only the Cabernet added weight to the Sangiovese and provided balance through a more satisfying flavor. Tignanello thus sparked off a new wave of Super-Tuscan *vini da tavola*. However, as the numbers grew, so they became an embarrassment, as observers realized that very few of the region's greatest wines actually qualified for DOC. But at the same time, many of the winemakers responsible for these French-influenced Super-Tuscans were also working hard to make the Sangiovese stand alone. After extensive clonal and site selection, reduced yields, improved viticultural practices and vinification techniques, a new

breed of Super-Tuscan emerged; first as Sangiovese-dominated blends, such as Tignanello, then as pure Sangiovese wines. Now that the Goria Law has opened the door for Italy's greatest *vini da tavola*, many who had resorted to making wines outside the DOC system are using their experience in remolding the Sangiovese to reestablish the great old names of the past (Chianti, Brunello di Montalcino, Vino Nobile di Montepulciano) by making wines that are complete without the help of foreign varieties.

## UMBRIA

Orvieto is Umbria's best-known and best-forgotten wine. Next to Frascati and Soave, it is the most used and abused name in the world's Italian restaurants. While there are a few good Orvieto wines, and tiny amounts of truly exciting *muffato* (a lusciously sweet botrytized version), they are in a lamentable minority. One of Umbria's few deservedly famous names is Lungarotti Rubesco Torgiano, whose reputation led to the Torgiano DOC and, more recently, to DOCG status for Torgiano Riserva. Lungarotti also leads in the production of Umbria's excellent new-wave wines. These use various grapes, both native and French, and are made in various styles, although nearly always aged in new-oak *barriques*.

## LATIUM (LAZIO)

One of Italy's largest regions, Latium appropriately boasts one of its largest-selling wines, Frascati, the Latin Liebfraumilch, and Est! Est!! Est!!!, probably the blandest tourist wine in existence. For a region responsible for Falernum, a classic wine of antiquity, it can now boast only two truly fine wines, Boncompagni Ludovisi's Fiorano Rosso and Cantina Colacicchi's Torre Ercolana, both innovative Cabernet-Merlot blends, which are very good.

THE APPELLATIONS OF

# WEST-CENTRAL ITALY

## CLASSIC BRUT SPARKLING WINES

The best sparkling *brut* wines are made in Tuscany by the traditional method.

✓ *Brut di Capezzana* • *Falchini Brut* • *Villa Banfi Brut*

## ALEATICO

### Tuscany

These are rare, rich, sweet red wines.

## ALEATICO DI GRADOLI DOC

### Latium

Sweet, sometimes fortified, red wines, without the reputation of the Aleatico di Puglia DOC.

## APRILIA DOC

### Latium

This DOC has two red varietals, Merlot and Sangiovese, and one white, Trebbiano, which is uninspiring. The washed-out flavors indicate that official yields are far too high.

## ASSISI

### Umbria

Assisi produces some soft, satisfying red, and fresh, easy-drinking white wines.

✓ *Sasso Rosso* • *Fratelli* • *Sportoletti* • *Tili*

## BARCO REALE DI CARMIGNANO DOC

### Tuscany

After Carmignano became a DOCG, this appellation was adopted for easy-drinking, Sangiovese-dominated (with a touch of Cabernet) red wines in order to retain simple DOC status. This acted as a selection instrument to increase and maintain quality for the superior denomination. *See also* Carmignano DOC and Carmignano DOCG.

## BIANCO CAPENA DOC

### Latium

Bianco Capena is a large DOC northeast of Rome producing dry and semisweet Trebbiano-based white wines of modest quality.

## BIANCO DELL'EMPOLESE DOC

### Tuscany

This is an overrated, overpriced, and uninspiring dry white Trebbiano from the Empoli hills, west of Florence. A *passito* may be sold as *vin santo* under the same denomination.

## BIANCO DELLA VAL DI NIEVOLE *or* BIANCO DELLA VALDINIEVOLE DOC

### Tuscany

Dry, slightly *frizzante* white wines and soft, white *vin santo*, made primarily from Trebbiano grapes.

## BIANCO DI PITIGLIANO DOC

### Tuscany

This DOC produces delicate, refreshing, dry, and easy-drinking Trebbiano-based white wines, which are improved by the possible inclusion of Malvasia, Grechetto, Verdello, Chardonnay, Sauvignon, Pinot Blanc, and Welschriesling. A *spumante* version is also allowed.

⌛ 1–2 years

✓ *La Stellata*

## BIANCO PISANO DI SAN TORPÉ DOC

### Tuscany

These dry white wines and dry or semisweet *vin santo* are made from Trebbiano grown in a large area southeast of Pisa.

## BIANCO VERGINE DELLA VALDICHIANA DOC

### Tuscany

This DOC produces off-dry, Trebbiano-based white wines with a bitter aftertaste. The best have a more delicate, floral fragrance.

⌛ 1–2 years

✓ *Poliziano*

## BOLGHERI DOC

### Tuscany

Until recently this was a relatively anonymous, pleasant, but hardly exciting DOC, producing delicate, dry whites and dry, slightly scented, Sangiovese *rosato*. Reds were ignored, even though it was home to Sassicaia, one of Italy's greatest wines. Now that reds are allowed, Sassicaia has its own subappellation, and two varietal whites (Sauvignon and Vermentino) and a pink *vin santo*, Occhio di Pernice, have been added. Sassicaia will surely be upgraded to full DOCG status shortly, and will probably leave behind a much healthier, better-known Bolgheri DOC with, hopefully, a number of aspiring new wines aiming to replicate its success. Look out for Piero Antinori's new Vermentino, which promises to be Tuscany's first great white wine from a native variety, and for established wines, such as Lodovico Antinori's Ornellaia.

🍷— 1–3 years (white), 3–7 years (most reds), 8–25 years (Sassicaia and *vin santo*)

✓ *Antinori* (Guado al Tasso) • *Angelo Gaja* (Ca' Marcanda Camarcanda) • *Le Macchiola* (Paleo) • *Colle Massari* (Grattamacco) • *Enrico Santini* • *Michele Satta* • *Tenuta dell'Ornellaia* • *Tenuta San Guido* (especially Sassicaia)

## BRUNELLO DI MONTALCINO DOCG
### Tuscany

One of Italy's most prestigious wines, made from Brunello, a localized clone of Sangiovese. Many relatively unknown producers offer classic wines. The idea is that the wines should be so thick with harsh tannins that they must be left for at least 20 years. If they are ripe skin tannins and there is enough fruit, this can be a formula for a wine of classic stature. But too many are macerated for too long and are not destemmed, leaving the tannins in even the most expensive wines incapable of softening. The producers below make wines requiring at least 10 years' maturation, but packed with fruit that develops into layers of complex, smoky-spicy, plummy-fruit flavors. Look out for new Frescobaldi-Mondavi wines from the Solaria estate.

🍷— 10–25 years

✓ *Altesino, Tenuta di Argiano* • *Villa Banfi* (especially Poggio all'Oro) • *Fattoria dei Barbi* (Vigna del Fiore) • *Campogiovanni* • *Tenuta Caparzo* • *Tenuta Carlina* (La Torgata) • *Casanova di Neri* • *Case Basse* • *Castelgiocondo* • *Castello Romitorio* • *Cerbaiona* • *Col d'Orcia* • *Conti Costanti* • *Frescobaldi* • *Eredi Fuligni* • *Fanti-La Palazzetta Fanti-San Filippo* • *Lisini* • *Mastrojanni* • *Pertimali* • *Podere Salicutti* • *La Poderina* (Poggio Banale) • *Poggio Antico Tenuta Il Poggione* • *Salvioni-La Cerbaiola* • *Tenuta Silvio Nardi* (Manachiara) • *Siro Pacenti* • *Solaria-Cencioni* • *Talenti* • *Uccelliera* • *Val di Suga*

## CABERNET SAUVIGNON
### Tuscany

Ideally suited to the Tuscan soil and climate.

✓ *Villa Banfi* (Tavernelle) • *Villa Cafaggio* (Cortaccio) • *Frescobaldi* (Mormoreto) • *Isole e Olena* • *Monsanto* (Nemo) • *Fattoria di Nozzole* (Il Pareto) • *Poliziano* (Le Stanze) • *Castello di Querceto* (Cignale)

## CABERNET-MERLOT
### West-central Italy

Cabernet-Merlot is a classic *bordelais* blend that is best suited to Tuscany.

✓ **Tuscany** *Il Paradis* (Saxa Calida) • *Villa di Capezzana* (Ghiaic della Furba) • *Podere Il*

*Carnasciale* • *Tenuta dell'Ornellaia* (Ornellaia)

**Latium** *Cantina Colacicchi* (Torre Ercolana), *Fiorano Rosso*, *Colle Picchioni* (Vigna del Vassello)

## CABERNET-SANGIOVESE BLENDS
### Tuscany

Most contain at least 80 percent Cabernet Sauvignon, 20 percent Sangiovese, and are the antithesis of the rising tide of Sangiovese blends.

✓ *Antinori* (Solaia) • *Tenuta di Bossi* (Mazzaferrata) • *Castellare di Castellina* (Coniale di Castellare) • *Castello di Gabbiano* (R e R) • *Lungarotti* (San Giorgio) • *Sette Ponti* (Oreno) • *Tenuta dell'Ornellaia* (Le Volte) • *Castello di Querceto* (Il Querciolaia) • *Poliziano* (Le Stanze) • *Castello dei Rampolla* (Sammarco, D'Alceo) • *Rocca delle Macie* (Roccato)

## CANAIOLO
### Tuscany

This is a native Tuscan grape, which is capable of soft, seductively fruity red wines.

## CANDIA DEI COLLI APUANI DOC
### Tuscany

Delicate, slightly aromatic, dry or semisweet whites from Vermentino and Albarola grapes.

## CARMIGNANO DOC
### Tuscany

Since Carmignano achieved DOCG status, the DOC has been used for *rosato*, *vin santo*, and *rosé vin santo*, called Occhio di Pernice (even though these styles were not allowed before the upgrading). The declassified Carmignano reds can now be sold as Barco Reale di Carmignano.

## CARMIGNANO DOCG
### Tuscany

Only traditional red Carmignano from this tiny appellation west of Florence may claim DOCG status. Other wines are classified as either Carmignano DOC or Barco Reale di Carmignano DOC. This DOCG is made from 45 to 65 percent Sangiovese, 10 to 20 percent Canaiolo Nero, 6 to 10 percent Cabernet Sauvignon, 10 to 20 percent Trebbiano, Canaiolo Bianco or Malvasia, and up to 5 percent Mammolo or Colorino. The result is similar to medium-bodied Chianti, but with less acidity, which, with its Cabernet content, gives a chocolaty-finesse to the fruit. *See also* Carmignano DOC and Barco Reale di Carmignano DOC.

🍷— 4–10 years

✓ *Fattoria di Ambra* • *di Artimino* • *Fattoria di Bacchereto* • *Contini Bonacossi* (Villa di Capezzana, Villa di Trefiano) • *Fattoria Il Poggiolo* • *Piaggia*

## CASTELLI ROMANI
### Latium

Castelli Romani are rarely exciting, dry and semisweet white, red, and rosé wines.

## CERVETERI DOC
### Latium

Rustic Sangiovese-based reds, dry and semisweet Trebbiano-Malvasia white wines of decent, everyday quality.

## CESANESE
### Latium

This local black grape variety makes medium-bodied red wines of no special quality in all styles from dry to sweet, and still to sparkling.

## CESANESE DEL PIGLIO *or* PIGLIO DOC
### Latium

This DOC covers a complicated range of basically simple red wines, from Cesanese grapes grown in a hilly area southeast of Rome. The styles include bone-dry, off-dry, medium-dry, semisweet, and sweet, and may be still, *frizzantino*, *frizzante*, or *spumante*.

## CESANESE DI AFFILE *or* AFFILE DOC
### Latium

This DOC produces the same styles as Cesanese del Piglio from a neighboring area.

## CESANESE DI OLEVANO ROMANO *or* OLEVANO ROMANO DOC
### Latium

Much smaller than the previous two nearby Cesanese DOCs, but covering the same styles.

## CHARDONNAY
### Tuscany and Umbria

The great, if ubiquitous, Chardonnay first squeezed into the official wines of Tuscany when it was adopted by the Pomino DOC, but the best renditions are still *vini da tavola*. In Umbria, although there are only a few great Chardonnay wines, it has great potential in the region, whether in the pure form, as made by Lungarotti, or blended with a little Grechetto, as in the case of Antinori's Cervaro della Sala.

✓ **Tuscany** *Castello di Ama* (Colline di Ama) • *Caparzo* (Le Grance) • *Villa Banfi* (Fontanelle) • *Felsina Berardenga* (I Sistri) • *Isole e Olena* • *Ruffino* (Cabreo Vigneto la Pietra)

**Umbria** *Antinori Castello della Sala* (Cervaro della Sala) • *Lungarotti* (Vigna I Palazzi)

## CHIANTI & CHIANTI CLASSICO DOCG
### Tuscany

When Chianti was granted DOCG status, its yields were reduced, the amount of white grapes allowed in Chianti Classico was cut, and up to 10 percent Cabernet Sauvignon was permitted in the blend. However, the DOCG was applied to the entire Chianti production area and thus has failed to be a guarantee of quality. Most Chianti is still garbage, albeit in a cleaner, more sanitized form than it used to be. The best basic Chianti, however, is full of juicy cherry, raspberry, and plummy fruit flavors, which makes an enjoyable quaffer, although it is not what DOCG should be about. Only the finest wines of Chianti deserve DOCG status and they are usually sold as *classico* (the original, hilly Chianti area), although Rufina (from a small area northeast of Florence, which should not be confused with Ruffino, the brand name) and Colli Fiorentini (which bridges the Classico and Rufina areas), which are both outside the *classico* district, also produce *classico*-like quality. Both also have lower yields than the rest of Chianti, with the exception of Classico, which demands the lowest yield of all.

Whatever the industrial bottlers do to continue debasing Chianti's reputation, readers must not forget that the best wines from these three areas rank among the greatest in the world. Rufina and Colli Fiorentini are, however, just two of six subappellations collectively known as the Chianti Putto, which covers the peripheral areas surrounding Chianti Classico itself. The other four are Colli Senesi (the largest and most varied, and so inconsistent that few wines claim this provenance, two portions of which are better known for Brunello di Montalcino and Vino Nobile di Montepulciano); Colli Pisani (lightest of all Chianti); Colli Aretini (young, lively Chianti); and Montalbano (in effect the second wine of Carmignano, although there are two of those, so maybe it is the third wine?).

All Chianti other than *classico* must contain between 75 and 90 percent Sangiovese plus the possibility of 5 to 10 percent Canaiolo Nero, 5 to 10 percent Trebbiano or Malvasia, and up to a maximum of 10 percent Cabernet or any other specified black grape varieties. This recipe applied to Chianti Classico until 1995, when it was changed to allow up to 100 percent Sangiovese, which should be a good move for those dedicated growers who are striving to get this difficult variety right. With the amount of Cabernet and other black grapes increased to 15 percent, this DOC is wide open to many of the so-called Super-Tuscans to be classified as Chianti Classico and thereby greatly enhance the reputation of this once great appellation.

🍷— 3–5 years (inexpensive, everyday drinking), 4–8 years (more serious Chianti), 6–20 years (finest *classico*)

✓ *Antinori* (Peppoli) • *Badia a Coltibuono* • *Barone Ricasoli* (Castello di Brolio) • *Carobbio* (Riserva) • *Caparsa* (Doccio a Matteo Riserva) • *Castellare di Castellina* (Vigna Il Poggiale) • *Castellini Villa* • *Castello di Ama* • *Castello di Cacchiano* • *Castello di Fonterutoli* • *Castello Querceto* • *Castello di Rampolla* • *Castello di San Polo in Rosso* • *Castello di Volpaia* • *Felsina* (Rancia) • *Fontodi* • *Isole e Olena* • *La Massa* (Giorgio Primo) • *Monsanto* (Il Poggio) • *Podere Il Palazzino* (Grosso Sanese) • *Poggerino* • *Poggio al Sole* (Casasilia) • *Riecine* (Riserva) • *Rocca della Macìe* (Roccato) • *San Fabiano Calcinaia* (Cellole Riserva) • *San Felice* (Poggio Rosso Riserva) • *San Giusto* (Gaio) • *San Vicente* (Riserva) • *Terrabianca* • *Uggiano* • *Vecchie Terre di Montefili* • *Villa Vignamaggio* (Mona Lisa Riserva)

## COLLI ALBANI DOC
### Latium

Soft and fruity, dry and semisweet white wines that can be *spumante*.

## COLLI ALTOTIBERINI DOC
### Umbria

An interesting DOC in the hilly upper Tiber Valley area, which produces dry white wines from Trebbiano and Malvasia, and firm, fruity reds from Sangiovese and Merlot. However, it is the crisp, fragrant rosés from the same red grape varieties that most people prefer.

## COLLI AMERINI DOC
### Umbria

Dry whites from Trebbiano with the possible addition of Grechetto, Verdello, Garganega, and Malvasia, with red and rosé from Sangiovese plus the possibility of Montepulciano, Ciliegiolo, Canaiolo, Merlot, and Barbera. A dry white pure Malvasia varietal may also be produced.

## COLLI DEL TRASIMENO DOC
### Umbria

A very large DOC area on the Tuscan border. The dry and off-dry whites are ordinary, but the reds, in which the bitter edge of Sangiovese is softened with Gamay, Ciliegiolo, Malvasia, and Trebbiano are more interesting.

🍷— 2–5 years

✓ *La Fiorita*

## COLLI DELL'ETRURIA CENTRALE DOC
### Tuscany

The idea was fine, to provide an alternative appellation for lesser red, white, and rosé wines produced in the Chianti area and thus improve the DOCG through selection. But the name hardly trips off the tongue and one might be forgiven for thinking it was agreed to by producers who wanted any excuse not to use it and so keep churning out as much Chianti as possible. Red wines may be referred to as *vermiglio*, which has historical connotations with Chianti, and *vin santo* may also be made.

## COLLI DI LUNI DOC
### Tuscany

*See* Colli di Luni DOC (Liguria, Northwest Italy).

## COLLI LANUVINI DOC
### Latium

Smooth, white wines, either dry or semisweet.

## COLLI MARTANI DOC
### Umbria

This covers four varietal wines from a large but promising area encompassing the Montefalco DOC: Sangiovese, Trebbiano, Grechetto, and the single-commune Grechetto di Todi.

## COLLI PERUGINI DOC
### Umbria

Dry, slightly fruity, Trebbiano-based white wines, full-bodied red wines, and dry, fresh rosé wines, primarily from Sangiovese grapes. Produced in a large area between Colli del Trasimeno and the Tiber, covering six communes in the province of Perugia and one in the province of Terni.

## COLLINE LUCCHESI DOC
### Tuscany

This DOC produces light, soft, Chianti-like reds and bland, dry, Trebbiano-based whites.

## CORI DOC
### Latium

Little-seen and rarely exciting, dry, semisweet, or sweet white wines and smooth, vinous reds.

## ELBA DOC
### Tuscany

The range of wines from the vacation isle of Elba have been expanded to include 10 types: Trebbiano-based dry white; Sangiovese-based red, and *riserva* red; *rosato*; Ansonica dell'Elba (dry white from the Ansonica, better known as the Inzolia grape of Sicily); Ansonica Passito dell'Elba; Aleatico dell'Elba; Vin Santo dell'Elba, Vin Santo dell'Elba Occhio di Pernice; and a white *spumante*. However, these wines are mostly made for tourists.

🍷— *In situ* only

✓ *Acquabona*

## EST! EST!! EST!!! DI MONTEFIASCONE DOC
### Latium

The name is the most memorable thing about these dry or semisweet white wines made from Trebbiano and Malvasia grapes grown around Lake Bolsena, adjacent to the Orvieto district. Traditionally, the name dates to the 12th century, when a fat German bishop called Johann Fugger had to go to Rome for the coronation of Henry V. In order to drink well on his journey, he sent his *majordomo* ahead to visit the inns along the route and mark those with the best wine with the word "Est," short for "*Vinum est bonum*." When he arrived at Montefiascone, the *majordomo* so liked the local wine that he chalked "Est! Est!! Est!!!." Fugger must have agreed with him, because once he had tasted the wine he canceled his trip and stayed in Montefiascone until his death. The truth of the story is uncertain, for, although a tomb in the village church bears Fugger's name, whether it contains his 800-year-old body or not is unknown. As for the wine, Hugh Johnson has accurately described it as an unextraordinary white wine that trades on its oddball name.

## FALERNO *or* FALERNUM
### Latium

Falernum was the famous wine of Ancient Rome. Its modern equivalent is a typically dark and rustically rich Aglianico wine, the best of which is the Villa Matilde *riserva*, which has a full aroma and a better balance than most. A dry white wine is also produced.

## FRASCATI DOC
### Latium

Most Frascati used to be flabby or oxidized, but with recent improvements in vinification techniques they are now invariably fresh and clean, although many still have a bland, peardrop aroma and taste. The few exceptions come from virtually the same group of top-performing producers as they did a decade ago and these wines stand out for their noticeably full flavor, albeit in a fresh, zippy-zingy style. Frascati is made from Trebbiano and Malvasia grapes, primarily dry, but semisweet, sweet, and *spumante* styles are also made.

🍷— 1–2 years

✓ *Colli di Catone* (especially Colle Gaio—other labels include Villa Catone and Villa Porziana) • *Fontana Candida* (Vigneti Santa Teresa) • *Villa Simone*

## GALESTRO
### Tuscany

This ultraclean, light, fresh, and delicately fruity, dry white wine is made by a *consorzio* of Chianti producers to agreed standards. It is shortly due to receive DOC recognition.

## GRECHETTO *or* GRECO
### Umbria and Tuscany

Clean, fresh, dry and sweet white wines with a pleasant floral aroma that can make interesting drinking, but seldom excel, with the exception of Bigi's Marrano, which is aged in oak.

⌛ 1–2 years

✓ *Bigi* (Marrano)

## MARINO DOC
### Latium

A typically light and unexciting Trebbiano and Malvasia blend that may be dry, semisweet, or *spumante*. Paola di Mauro's deliciously rich and caramelized Colle Picchioni Oro stands out due to its relatively high proportion of Malvasia grapes, and the fact that it receives a prefermentation maceration on its skins and is matured in *barriques*.

⌛ 1–4 years

✓ *Colle Picchioni* (Oro)

## MERLOT
### Tuscany

There is only one classic Merlot produced in Tuscany, Masseto, and although it is one of the most expensive red wines in Italy, some vintages can stand shoulder to shoulder with Pétrus, which might make it look like a bargain, depending on your perspective.

⌛ 3–8 years

✓ *Villa Banfi* (Mandrielle) • *Tenuta dell'Ornellaia* (Masseto) • *Petrolo* (Galatrona)

## MONTECARLO DOC
### Tuscany

Some interesting dry white wines are starting to appear in this area situated between Carmignano and the coast. Although based on the bland Trebbiano, supplementary varieties (Roussanne, Sémillon, Pinot Grigio, Pinot Bianco, Sauvignon Blanc, and Vermentino) may account for 30 to 40 percent of the blend, thus allowing growers to express individual styles, from light and delicate to full and rich, either with or without *barrique*-aging. Red wines may be made from Sangiovese, Canaiolo, Ciliegiolo, Colorino, Syrah, Malvasia, Cabernet Franc, Cabernet Sauvignon, and Merlot. A white *vin santo* and a pink Occhio di Pernice *vin santo* are also allowed.

⌛ 4–10 years

✓ *Fattoria dell Buonamico* • *Carmignani* • *Fattoria Michi* • *Vigna del Greppo*

## MONTECOMPATRI COLONNA *or* MONTECOMPATRI COLONNA DOC
### Latium

These dry or semisweet, Malvasia-based white wines may bear the name of one or both of the above towns on the label.

## MONTEFALCO DOCG
### Umbria

There is a significant difference in quality between these basic red and white wines and the more interesting, characterful DOCG Sagrantino of Montefalco.

## MONTEFALCO SAGRANTINO DOCG
### Umbria

Upgraded to DOCG in 1992 and detached from the basic Montefalco denomination, these distinctive red wines in dry and sweet *passito* styles are made exclusively from the Sagrantino grape, which has the advantage of being grown on the best-exposed hillside vineyards southwest of Perugia. The *passito* wines are the most authentic in style, dating back to the 15th century, but the dry table-wine style, which hints at ripe, fresh-picked blackberries, is the best and most consistent.

⌛ 3–12 years

✓ *Fratelli Adanti* • *Antonelli* • *Villa Antico* • *Arnaldo Caprai* • *Colpetrone*

## MONTEREGIO DI MASSA MARITTIMA DOC
### Tuscany

These are red, white, rosé, *novello*, and *vin santo* from the northern part of the province of Grosseto. A dry white Vermentino varietal wine and a pink *passito* called Occhio di Pernice are also included within Monteregio di Massa Marittima DOC.

## MONTESCUDAIO DOC
### Tuscany

A Trebbiano-based dry white wine, a soft, slightly fruity, Sangiovese-based red, and a *vin santo* from the Cecina Valley.

⌛ 1–3 years

✓ *Poggio Gagliardo* • *Sorbaiano*

## MORELLINO DI SCANSANO DOC
### Tuscany

This DOC produces some good Brunello-like wines from 100 percent Sangiovese, which are thick with tasty, ripe fruit and can age well.

⌛ 4–8 years

✓ *Erik Banti* • *Poggio Argentiera* (Capa Tosta) • *Motta* • *Fattoria Le Pupille*

## MOSCADELLO DI MONTALCINO DOC
### Tuscany

An ancient style of aromatic, sweet Muscat that was famous long before Brunello. Fortified versions and sweet *frizzante* are also possible.

⌛ Upon purchase

✓ *Villa Banfi* (Vendemmia Tardiva) • *Col d'Orcia* • *Tenuta Il Poggione*

## MOSCATO
### Tuscany

There is just one Tuscan Moscato DOC, Moscadello di Montalcino, but a few delicately sweet rosé *vini da tavola* are made from the Moscato Rosa grape. It is an exquisite wine well worth searching out.

⌛ Upon purchase

✓ *Castello di Farnatella* (Rosa Rosae)

## ORVIETO DOC
### Umbria and Latium

The vineyards for this popular, widely exported, dry or semisweet, Trebbiano-based white wine are primarily located in Umbria. In general, Orvieto is still disappointing, although Bigi's Vigneto Torricella remains outstanding and the number of wines aspiring to a similar quality is growing. The best semisweet, or *abboccato*, style will include a small proportion of botrytized grapes. Fully botrytized, or *muffato*, Orvieto are extremely rare, but well worth tracking down as they offer a fabulous combination of elegance, concentration, and youthful succulence.

⌛ Upon purchase

✓ *Antinori* (Campogrande) • *Barberani* (Castagnolo) • *Bigi* (Torricella) • *Decugnano dei Barbi* • *Palazzone* (Terre Vineate)

## PARRINA DOC
### Tuscany

The dry whites of Parrina, the most southerly of Tuscany's DOCs, are the least interesting. The Sangiovese-based reds used to be merely soft, light, and attractive, but of late have become much darker, fuller, and richer, like an oaky Chianti, with just a touch of vanillin sweetness on the finish, and even an occasional wisp of mint on the aftertaste.

⌛ 3–7 years

✓ *Franca Spinola*

## POMINO DOC
### Tuscany

This wine dates back to 1716, and a Pomino was marketed as a single-vineyard Chianti by Marchesi de' Frescobaldi long before it was resurrected as its own DOC in 1983. The white is a blend of Pinot Blanc, Chardonnay, and Trebbiano, although Frescobaldi's Il Benefizio is pure Chardonnay. The red is a blend of Sangiovese, Canaiolo, Merlot, Cabernet Franc, and Cabernet Sauvignon. A semisweet *vin santo* is also made in both red and white styles.

⌛ 1–3 years (blended white) 3–7 years (red and Il Benefizio)

✓ *Frescobaldi* • *Fattoria Petrognano*

## ROSATO DELLA LEGA
### Tuscany

Rosato della Lega are dry, Tuscan rosé wines, which are produced by members of the Chianti Classico *consorzio*.

## ROSSO DELLA LEGA
### Tuscany

These are reasonable, everyday red wines, which are produced by members of the Chianti Classico *consorzio*.

## ROSSO DI MONTALCINO DOC
### Tuscany

This appellation is for lesser or declassified wines of Brunello di Montalcino or for wines made from young vines. Although there has been a tendency in recent years to produce deeper, darker, more concentrated wines, as a rule the biggest Rosso di Montalcino wines are much more accessible in their youth than Brunello, which some readers may prefer.

🍷— 5–15 years

✓ *Altesino • Castelgiocondo • Conti Costanti • Lisini • Tenuta Il Poggione • Val di Suga*

## ROSSO DI MONTEPULCIANO DOC
### Tuscany

This DOC is for the so-called lesser wines of Vino Nobile di Montepulciano and, like Rosso di Montalcino DOC, its wines are softer and more approachable when young.

🍷— 5–15 years

✓ *Avignonesi • Bindella • Podere Boscarelli • Le Casalte • Contucci • Fattoria del Cerro • Poliziano • Tenuta Trerose*

## SAGRANTINO
### Umbria

Another local variety that almost died out but has seen a revival, Sagrantino traditionally makes both dry and sweet, *passito* reds. Some people believe its name is derived from *sagra*, ("festival") and suggest that the wines it yields were originally reserved for feast days.

## SANGIOVESE *or* SANGIOVESE-DOMINATED
### Tuscany and Umbria

Although just 10 years ago no one believed that Sangiovese could stand alone, its success was merely a matter of reduced yields and a suitable *terroir*. With good, but not overstated, *barrique*-aging, and bottling at the optimum moment for fruit retention, Sangiovese can be rich, lush, and satisfyingly complete, with a succulent, spicy-cedary oak complexity. It is commonly found in Umbria, but exceptional Sangiovese-based wines are relatively rare.

✓ **Tuscany** *Altesino* (Palazzo Altesi) • *Avignonesi* (I Grifi) • *Badia a Coltibuono* (Sangioveto) • *Calcinaia* (Cerviolo Rosso) • *Castello di Cacchiano* (RF, Rocca di Montegrossi) • *Villa Cafaggio* (San Martino) • *Podere Capaccia* (Querciagrande) • *Castiglione* (Giramonte) • *Felsina* (Fontalloro) • *Fontodi* (Flaccianello della Pieve) • *Isole e Olena* (Cepparello) • *Monsanto* (Bianchi Vigneti di Scanni) • *Montepeloso* (Nardo) • *Podere Il Palazzino* (Grosso Senese) • *Poliziano* (Elegia) • *Castello di Querceto* (La Corte) • *Ruffino* (Cabreo Il Borgo) • *Guicciardini Strozzi* (Sodole) • *Terrabianca* (Campaccio, Piano del Cipresso) • *Monte Vertine* (Le Pergole Torte) • *Viticcio* (Prunaio)

**Umbria** *Lungarotti*

## SANGIOVESE WITH OTHER ITALIAN GRAPES
### Tuscany

✓ *Castellare di Castellina* (I Sodi di San Niccolò) • *Ricasoli-Firidolfi* (Geremia) • *Monte Vertine* (Il Sodaccio)

## SANGIOVESE-CABERNET/MERLOT BLENDS
### Tuscany

Cabernet Sauvignon was originally blended with Sangiovese to supply fruit and accessibility within a classic fine-wine structure.

✓ *Altesino* (Alte d'Altesi) • *Antinori* (Tignanello) • *Caparzo* (Cà del Pazzo) • *Castello di Bossi* (Corbaia) • *Colombaio* (Il Futuro) • *Fonterutoli* (Siepi) • *Monsanto* (Tinscvil) • *Querciabella* (Camartina) • *Castello di Volpaia* (Balifico)

## SAUVIGNON
### Tuscany

The Sauvignon does not really seem at home in Tuscany, although judging by the remarkable success of Ornellaia's Poggio alle Gazze, you wouldn't think this was the case.

✓ *Tenuta dell'Ornellaia* (Poggio alle Gazze)

## SYRAH
### Tuscany

This classic Rhône grape shows tremendous potential, but at equally tremendous prices.

✓ *Fontodi* (Case Vie) • *Isole e Olena* (L'Eremo) • *Varramista*

## TORGIANO DOC
### Umbria

This DOC was built on the back of the reputation of one producer, Lungarotti (*see also* Torgiano Riserva DOCG). As before, Torgiano DOC covers generic blends for red and rosé (Sangiovese, Canaiolo, Trebbiano, Ciliegiolo, and Montepulciano) and white (Trebbiano, Grechetto, Malvasia, and Verdello), but also sparkling (Pinot Noir and Chardonnay) and five varietals: Chardonnay, Pinot Grigio, Riesling Italico, Cabernet Sauvignon, and Pinot Noir.

🍷— 3–8 years (red), 1–5 years (white and rosé)

✓ *Lungarotti*

## TORGIANO RISERVA DOCG
### Umbria

Lungarotti's best *rosso*, the *riserva* is a model of how all DOCG denominations should work, and has deservedly been upgraded from DOC.

🍷— 4–20 years

✓ *Lungarotti*

## VAL D'ARBIA DOC
### Tuscany

A large area south of the Chianti Classico district, producing a dry, fruity, Trebbiano-based white wine boosted by Malvasia and Chardonnay, which may be dried prior to fermentation for dry, semisweet, or sweet *vin santo*.

## VAL DI CORNIA DOC
### Tuscany

A large area of scattered vineyards in hills east of Piombino and south of Bolgheri. Rarely seen Trebbiano dry whites and Sangiovese reds and rosés, with the subappellations of Campiglia Marittima, Piombino, San Vincenzo, and Surveto.

✓ *Russo* (Barbicone)

## VELLETRI DOC
### Latium

Rather uninspiring, dry or semisweet white wines and reds from the Castelli Romani area.

## VERNACCIA DI SAN GIMIGNANO DOCG
### Tuscany

This dry white wine was Italy's first-ever DOC, so DOCG status was inevitable, even if most are bland. The best have always been deliciously crisp and full of vibrant fruit, which makes them well worth seeking out, but not seriously worthy of DOCG status if this is supposed to signify one of the world's finest wines.

🍷— 1–3 years

✓ *Falchini • Panizzi • Teruzzi & Puthod*

## VIGNANELLO DOC
### Latium

This is a new and untested DOC for red, white, and rosé blends, plus pure Grechetto dry white wine in still and fully sparkling formats.

## VIN SANTO
### Tuscany and Umbria

A red or white *passito* wine that may be sweet, semisweet, or dry.

✓ *Avignonesi* (Occhio di Pernice)

## VINO NOBILE DI MONTEPULCIANO DOCG
### Tuscany

Made largely from Prugnolo Gentile, a clone of Sangiovese, plus Canaiolo and other local grapes, including white varieties, these wines come from Montepulciano. Most wines used to be overrated and overpriced, and a number still are, but a growing number of producers make wines that deserve DOCG status. The best resemble a fine *riserva* Chianti Classico, but have a more exuberant character, with generous ripe-fruit flavors hinting of cherry and plum.

🍷— 6–25 years

✓ *Avignonesi • Bindella • Podere Boscarelli • Le Casalte • Contucci • Fattoria de Cerro • Poliziano • Tenuta Trerose*

## ZAGAROLO DOC
### Latium

This DOC has a tiny production of dry or semisweet white from Malvasia and Trebbiano grapes, which are grown east of Frascati in an area more famed for its wines half a millennium ago than it is now.

### NEW IGT WINES

The following Indicazioni Geografiche Tipiche wines were agreed to at the end of 1996, yet most have still to register with consumers, or establish any consistency of style or quality:

✓ **Latium** *Castelli Romani • Circeo • Civitella d'Agliano • Colli Cimini • Colli delle Sabina • Colli Etruschi Viterbesi • Frusinate or del Frusinate • Lazio • Nettuno*

**Tuscany** *Alta Valle Della Greve • Colli della Toscana Centrale • Maremma Toscana • Orcia • Toscana or Toscano • Val di Magra*

**Umbria** *Allerona • Assisi • Bettona • Cannara • Lago di Corbara • Narni • Spello • Umbria*

# EAST-CENTRAL ITALY

*This area comprises the regions of Emilia-Romagna, the Marches, the Abruzzi, and Molise. The best-quality wines come from the Marches and the Abruzzi, but the best-known is Emilia-Romagna's lollipop wine, Lambrusco, which is exported in vast quantities.*

IF THIS REGION, which extends across almost the entire width of northern Italy into Piedmont, appears geographically to wander off its central-east designation, it certainly does not do so topographically, for every acre lies east of the Apennines on initially hilly ground that flattens out into alluvial plains stretching toward the Adriatic.

## EMILIA-ROMAGNA

Emilia-Romagna is protected on its western flank by the Apennines, the source of seven major, and many minor, rivers.

## FACTORS AFFECTING TASTE AND QUALITY

**LOCATION**
This area stretches along the Adriatic coast, from Molise in the south right up to Emilia-Romagna.

**CLIMATE**
The influence of the Mediterranean provides generally hot and dry summers, which become progressively hotter as one travels south, and cool winters. In hilly regions microclimates are created by the effects of altitude and aspect.

**ASPECT**
The best vineyards are invariably to be found on well-drained, foothill sites, but viticulture is spread across every imaginable type of terrain, with a heavy concentration on flat plains, particularly along the Po Valley in Emilia-Romagna, where grapes are produced in abundance.

**SOIL**
The soil is mostly alluvial, with some outcrops of granite and limestone.

**VITICULTURE AND VINIFICATION**
A wide variety of viticultural practices and vinification techniques are used here. Much bulk-blended

wine originates here, but some producers retain the most worthwhile traditions and augment them with modern methods.

**GRAPE VARIETIES**
Aglianico, Albana (*syn.* Biancame, Bianchello, Greco di Ancona, or Passerina), Ancellotta, Barbarossa, Barbera, Beverdino, Bombino Bianco (*syn.* Pagadebit or Pagadebito), Cabernet Franc, Cabernet Sauvignon, Chardonnay, Ciliegiolo, Croatina (*syn.* Bonarda), Fortana (*syn.* Fruttana or Uva d'Oro), Incrocio Bruni 54 (Verdicchio x Sauvignon), Lacrima (*syn.* Gallioppa or Galloppo), Lambrusco, Maceratino, Malvasia, Merlot, Mondeuse (*syn.* Cagnina, Refosco or Terrano), Montepulciano, Montuni (*syn.* Montù or Bianchino), Moscato (*syn.* Muscat), Ortrugo (*syn.* Altra Uva), Pecorino, Perricone (*syn.* Pignoletto), Pinot Bianco (*syn.* Pinot Blanc), Pinot Grigio (*syn.* Pinot Gris), Pinot Nero (*syn.* Pinot Noir), Sangiovese, Sauvignon (*syn.* Spergola), Toscano, Trebbiano (*syn.* Campolese, Ugni Blanc or Albanella), Verdea, Verdicchio, Vernaccia Nera, Riesling Italico (*syn.* Welschriesling)

The rich soil results in abundant grape production, the most prolific varieties being Lambrusco, Trebbiano, and Albana, which produce rustic white wines that, unaccountably, have been given Italy's first DOCG for a white wine. Emilia-Romagna does, however, have some genuinely outstanding *vini da tavola*, such as Fattoria Paradiso's Vigna del Dosso, a red from the Barbarossa, and, especially, a classy Sangiovese-Cabernet blend from Fattoria Zerbina, called Marzeno di Marzeno.

## THE ABRUZZI (ABRUZZO)

Although its hills have a variety of soils and microclimates, and should be capable of producing many fine wines, the Abruzzi offers only one—Montepulciano d'Abruzzo. But winemakers are conservative here and only one producer, Santoro Corella, is experimenting with different grape varieties.

EAST-CENTRAL ITALY, *see also p.263 With the Apennines forming the region's western border, the eastern part of central Italy is dominated by their foothills and the plains.*

### Map legend

- Colli Piacentini
- Colli di Parma
- Bosco Eliceo
- Cagnina di Romagna, Pagadebit di Romagna
- Montuni del Reno
- Bianchello del Metauro, Falerio dei Colli Ascolani
- Lacrima di Morro d'Alba
- Colli Maceratesi
- Albana di Romagna
- Sangiovese di Romagna
- Lambrusco
- Trebbiano di Romagna
- Verdicchio dei Castelli di Jesi
- Rosso Piceno
- Verdicchio di Matelica
- Montepulciano d'Abruzzo, Trebbiano d'Abruzzo
- Biferno
- 1 Bianco di Scandiano
- 2 Colli Bolognesi
- 3 Colli Pesaresi
- 4 Pentro
- 5 Vernaccia di Serrapetrona
- 6 Rosso Conero
- 7 Falerio dei Colli Ascolani
- 8 Rosso Piceno Superiore
- *Provincia* boundary
- ▲ Height above sea level (metres)

0   10   20   30   40   50   60 miles
0      20      40      60      80      100 km

# SOUTHERN ITALY AND THE ISLANDS

*Hot and largely hilly, with volcanic soils, southern Italy is an ancient and prolific wine-growing area. Overproduction continues to be a problem, but well-made wines were starting to clean up Italy's southern-plonk image over a decade ago, since when a host of flying winemakers have made some remarkably expressive wines utilizing local varieties.*

JUTTING OUT INTO THE BLUE WATERS of the Mediterranean, the vineyards of southern Italy receive very little natural moisture and bake rather than bask in unrelenting sunshine. This explains the deep-colored wines with strong flavors and high alcoholic levels. Although these heavy wines do not suit modern tastes and southern Italy continues to produce a glut of these almost unsellable wines, the region is subtly changing course. Its

small but growing volume of cleaner, finer, more expressive wines may enable it to establish an identity capable of thriving in ever more sophisticated world-wine markets. In this respect it is being helped by foreign investment and flying winemakers, but the biggest obstacle to consolidating these isolated successes is the poverty that has for so long blighted southern Italy.

## APULIA (PUGLIA)

Apulia's exceptionally fertile plains make it one of Italy's largest wine-producing regions, but until the 1970s most of its wines were seen as fit only for blending or for making Vermouth. Because of this, most Apulian producers chose to try to rid themselves of this lowly reputation, bringing about a radical transformation of their industry. A great number of very ordinary wines are still produced, but various changes have greatly improved the situation. Irrigation programs, the introduction of lower-yielding, higher-quality grape varieties (including many classic French ones), and a move away from the single-bush cultivation, known as *alberello*, to modern wire-trained systems, have led to both new wines gaining favor and some traditional ones showing renewed promise. The two most important grape varieties are now the Primitivo, which has been identified as the Zinfandel of California and is the earliest-ripening grape grown in Italy, and the Uva di Troia, which

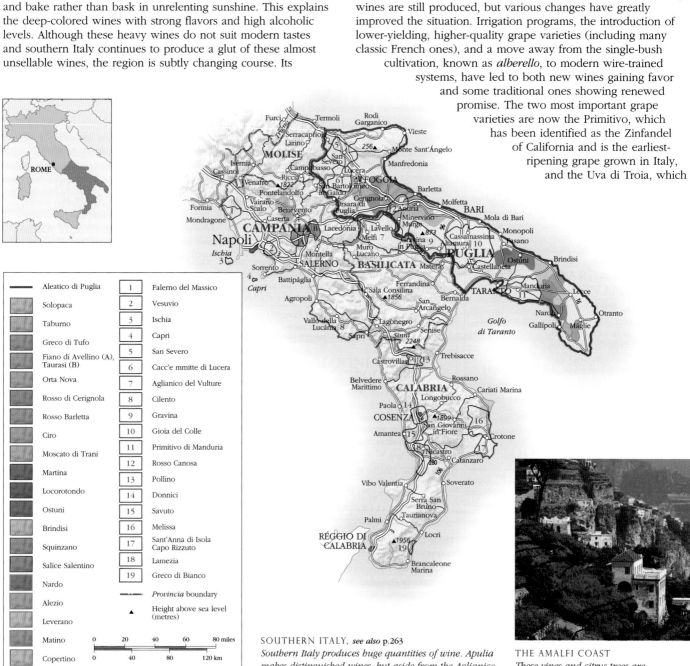

| | | |
|---|---|---|
| — Aleatico di Puglia | 1 | Falerno del Massico |
| Solopaca | 2 | Vesuvio |
| Taburno | 3 | Ischia |
| Greco di Tufo | 4 | Capri |
| Fiano di Avellino (A), Taurasi (B) | 5 | San Severo |
| Orta Nova | 6 | Cacc'e mmitte di Lucera |
| Rosso di Cerignola | 7 | Aglianico del Vulture |
| Rosso Barletta | 8 | Cilento |
| Ciro | 9 | Gravina |
| Moscato di Trani | 10 | Gioia del Colle |
| Martina | 11 | Primitivo di Manduria |
| Locorotondo | 12 | Rosso Canosa |
| Ostuni | 13 | Pollino |
| Brindisi | 14 | Donnici |
| Squinzano | 15 | Savuto |
| Salice Salentino | 16 | Melissa |
| Nardo | 17 | Sant'Anna di Isola Capo Rizzuto |
| Alezio | 18 | Lamezia |
| Leverano | 19 | Greco di Bianco |
| Matino | | *Provincia* boundary |
| Copertino | ▲ | Height above sea level (metres) |

0    20    40    60    80 miles
0    40    80    120 km

SOUTHERN ITALY, *see also p.263*
*Southern Italy produces huge quantities of wine. Apulia makes distinguished wines, but aside from the Aglianico wines of Basilicata and Campania, the quality is patchy.*

THE AMALFI COAST
*These vines and citrus trees are terraced on cliffs typical to this area.*

has no connection with the town of Troia in Apulia's northern province of Foggia, but refers to ancient Troy, whence the grape originates. It was brought to the region by the first Greeks to settle in the Taranto area.

## CAMPANIA

The best-known wine of Campania Felix, as the Romans called this area, is Lacryma Christi (Tears of Christ), but the best quality is the lesser-known Taurasi DOCG made from the underrated Aglianico grape. Falerno del Massico is an up-and-coming Aglianico-based DOC, but aside from wines made by individual producers such as Mastroberardino and Antica Masseria Venditti, there is little else of interest produced here.

## BASILICATA

Basilicata is a dramatic and wild region dominated by the extinct volcano Mount Vulture. Manufacturing industry is scarce here, accounting for less than one percent of the region's output, and the mountainous terrain makes mechanized agriculture extremely difficult. Lacking investment finance and with two in every three

### AVERAGE ANNUAL PRODUCTION

| REGION | DOC PRODUCTION | TOTAL PRODUCTION |
|---|---|---|
| Sicily | 3 million cases (270,000 hl) | 110 million cases (10 million hl) |
| Sardinia | 2.8 million cases (260,000 hl) | 28 million cases (2.5 million hl) |
| Apulia | 2.2 million cases (198,000 hl) | 2.5 million hl (11 million hl) |
| Calabria | 367,000 cases (33,000 hl) | 13 million cases (1.2 million hl) |
| Campania | 139,000 cases (12,500 hl) | 28 million cases (2.5 million hl) |
| Basilicata | 70,000 casesx (70,000 cases) | 4.7 million cases (0.42 million hl) |

*Percentage of total Italian production: Apulia, 14%; Sicily, 13%; Campania, 3.3%; Sardinia, 3.3%; Calabria, 1.6%; Basilicata, 0.6%.*

inhabitants unemployed, Basilicata has not had the means nor the incentive to modernize its wine industry. Consequently, with the exception of the first-class, if idiosyncratic, Aglianico del Vulture, (Basilicata's solitary DOC), a wonderful non-DOC Aglianico called Canneto from Fratelli d'Angelo, and delicious Moscato and Malvasia from Fratelli d'Angelo and Paternosta, the fine-wine scene in Basilicata is as barren as the landscape, although it should make fertile pastures for flying winemakers.

## CALABRIA

The decline in Calabria's viticultural output since the 1960s has been for the better in terms of quality. Since then, the most unsuitable land has been abandoned, and the 10 current DOCs, located in hilly and mountainous terrain, may eventually prove to be a source of quality wine. At the moment, however, improvement in wine technology is slow and, with the exception of Umberto Ceratti's succulent Greco di Bianco, a world-class dessert wine that is a relic of the past, and Odoardi's Vigna Vecchia, a fruity red from the obscure Gaglioppo variety, and a luscious Moscato *vino da tavola* from Guido Lojelo, this region also has little in the way of interesting wine.

## SICILY (SICILIA)

Sicily is the largest island in the Mediterranean and, in terms of quantity, is one of Italy's most important wine regions, annually producing a quantity roughly equal to the Veneto or Emilia-Romagna. Much of this is produced at high yields deliberately to take advantage of the EU's intervention program, which takes the wine off the market and distills it. The ancient port of Marsah-el-Allah, built under Arab rule, gives its name to Sicily's once popular classic wine, Marsala. By the mid-19th century, Marsala had evolved into a style between that of Madeira and sherry, but now finds itself as popular as bread and dripping, and just as likely to come back into fashion. Indeed, until recently, Sicilian wines were generally unfashionable. Then in 1995, the Planeta family established its winery, the wines started to attract attention and growing respect in the early 2000s, and Planeta is now not only the island's top producer, but also one of Italy's greatest. The stunning quality of these

THE ISLANDS, *see also p.263*
*Sicily and Sardinia are usually included with southern Italy because they are on the same latitude, but they had to be separated for mapping purposes in this edition because of the proliferation of new appellations, including the contentious DOCG status of Vermentino di Gallura in Sardinia.*

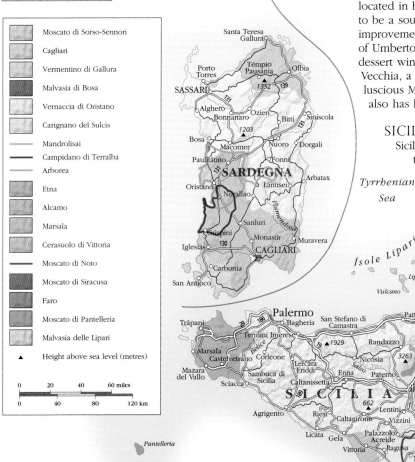

Moscato di Sorso-Sennori
Cagliari
Vermentino di Gallura
Malvasia di Bosa
Vernaccia di Oristano
Carignano del Sulcis
Mandrolisai
Campidano di Terralba
Arborea
Etna
Alcamo
Marsala
Cerasuolo di Vittoria
Moscato di Noto
Moscato di Siracusa
Faro
Moscato di Pantelleria
Malvasia delle Lipari
▲ Height above sea level (metres)

0    20    40    60 miles
0    40    80    120 km

THE POLLINO MOUNTAINS, CALABRIA
*Spring flowers carpet the slopes above Frascineto, in the foothills of the Pollino Mountains. This small mountain range gives its name to the fruity chiaretto-style wine made from Gaglioppo, Greco Nero, Malvasia, and Guarnaccia.*

wines encouraged some long-established wineries (such as Tasca d'Almerita and, when it was bought by Illva Saronno, Corvo) to raise standards, as well as investment from big mainland producers, such as Zonin, which established Feuda Principi di Butera.

## SARDINIA (SARDEGNA)

Sardinia is the second-largest island in the Mediterranean and, while it produces virtually all styles of wine, the modernization its wine industry has undergone since the late 1970s has had a more radical effect on its white wines than on any other style. Although Sardinia produces no "fine" wines in the classic sense, the wines are generally well made and easy to enjoy, and a small number of top-performing wineries make interesting wines under the Carignano del Sulcis

and Cagliari DOCs, while exceptional Malvasia *vini da tavola* are made by Gian Vittorio Naitana. Vermentino di Gallura was another enjoyable DOC, but its controversial promotion was the most ludicrous abuse of DOCG status since Albana di Romagna. Gallura does offer potential for fine wines, but more for reds, than whites. Indeed, much of the hilly terrain on this island is naturally suited to lower-yielding, black grape varieties, which if harvested fully ripe could produce intensely flavored, age-worthy reds, such as Turriga from Antonio Argiolas, an excellent Cannonau-based blend.

## FACTORS AFFECTING TASTE AND QUALITY

### LOCATION
This area includes the southern mainland regions of Apulia, Campania, Basilicata, Calabria, the islands of Sicily farther south, and Sardinia, across the Tyrrhenian Sea to the west.

### CLIMATE
The south is by far the hottest and driest region of Italy, although the coastal areas and islands are tempered by maritime winds.

### ASPECT
Most of the region is either mountainous or hilly, although vineyards are to be found on the flat land and gentle slopes of Apulia. The best sites are always found on the north-facing, higher slopes of hillsides where the vines receive less sun and benefit from the tempering effect of altitude, thus ensuring a longer growing season.

### SOIL
Soil is predominantly volcanic and granitic, but there are some isolated outcrops of clay and chalk.

### VITICULTURE AND VINIFICATION
This area, together with the Midi in France, is the principal source of Europe's infamous "wine lake." Nevertheless, producers using better-quality grape varieties grown on higher sites are making wines of a standard and style that deserve wider recognition. Flying winemakers have helped enormously by showing what can be done.

### GRAPE VARIETIES
Aglianico, Albana (*syn.* Greco, but this Greco is not Grechetto), Aleatico, Alicante Bouschet, Asprinio (*syn.* Asprino, Olivese, Ragusano, or Uva Asprina), Barbera, Bianco d'Alessano, Biancolella (*syn.* Biancolelle, Ianculillo, Ianculella,

Petit Blanche, or Teneddu), Bombino, Bombino Nero, Cabernet Franc, Calabrese (*syn.* Nero d'Avola or Niura d'Avola), Carignan (*syn.* Carignano or Uva di Spagna), Carricante, Catarratti (*syn.* Cataratto), Chardonnay, Cinsault (*syn.* Ottavianello), Coda del Volpe (Caprettone, Coda di Pecora, or Pallagrello Bianco), Damaschino, Falanghina, Fiano, Forastera, Francavidda (*syn.* Francavilla), Gaglioppo (*syn.* Arvino, Gaioppo, Lacrima Nera, Magliocco, Mantonico Nero, or Montonico Nero), Garganega (*syn.* Grecanico), Girò, Grechetto, Greco Nero, Grenache (*syn.* Cannonadu, Cannonatu, Cannonao, Cannonau, or Canonau), Grillo, Guarnaccia (*syn.* Cannamelu or Uarnaccia), Impigno, Incrocio Manzoni 6013 (Riesling x Pinot Blanc), Inzolia (*syn.* Ansolia, Ansonica or Nzolia), Malbec, Malvasia, Malvasia Nera,

Mantonico, Marsigliana, Monastrell (*syn.* Bovale or Muristrellu), Monica (*syn.* Monaca, Munica, Niedda, Pacali, Passale, or Tintilla), Montepulciano, Muscat (*syn.* Moscato), Nasco (*syn.* Nascu or Nusco), Negroamaro, Nerello (*syn.* Frappato), Nocera, Notar Domenico, Nuragus (*syn.* Abbondosa, Axina de Margiai, Axina de Poporus, Meragus, or Nuragus Trebbiana), Pampanuto (*syn.* Pampanino), Perricone (*syn.* Pignatello), Piedirosso (*syn.* Palombina Nera, Pedepalumbo, Per'e Palumme, Per'e Palummo, or Pied di Colombo), Pinot Blanc (*syn.* Pinot Bianco), Pinot Gris (Pinot Grigio), Pinot Noir (*syn.* Pinot Nero), Sangiovese, Sauvignon, Sciascinoso (*syn.* Olivella), Susumaniello, Torbato, Ugni Blanc (*syn.* Trebbiano), Uva di Troia, Verdeca, Vermentino, Vernaccia, Zibibbo (Moscato variant), Zinfandel (*syn.* Primitivo or Zagarese)

THE APPELLATIONS OF
# SOUTHERN ITALY AND THE ISLANDS

## AGLIANICO
### Basilicata

Many people think that this black grape is not dissimilar to the Barbera, and it has been respected since Ancient Roman times, when it produced the famed wine of Falernum. One of Italy's two greatest Aglianico wines today is Basilicata's Aglianico del Vulture (the other is Campania's Taurasi). Its best producer, Fratelli d'Angelo, is also the greatest producer of a non-DOC Aglianico.

⌽⤙ 6–20 years

⩗ *Fratelli d'Angelo* (Canneto)

## AGLIANICO DEL TABURNO DOC
### Campania

*See* Taburno DOC.

## AGLIANICO DEL VULTURE DOC
### Basilicata

This is the only DOC in Basilicata to encompass the volcanic slopes of Mount Vulture and its surrounding hills, which make the best growing areas for the Aglianico grape. A big but balanced red wine of warm color, rich, chocolate-cherry fruit, and firm tannin structure, Aglianico del Vulture can be slightly rustic in youth, yet develops a true silky finesse with age.

Some would argue that it is the greatest Aglianico and will doubtless achieve DOCG status. If described as *vecchio* (old), Aglianico del Vulture will have been aged for a minimum of three years, while *riserva* will have had five; both will have been aged for two years in wood. Aglianico del Vulture may also be sold as semisweet and *spumante*.

⌽⤙ 6–20 years

⩗ *Fratelli d'Angelo* • *Paternosta*

## ALCAMO *or* BIANCO ALCAMO DOC
### Sicily

Dry, slightly fruity white wines from the Catarratto grape with the possible addition of Damaschino, Garganega, and Trebbiano. The soil is too fertile and yields far too high to produce wines of any real quality or character.

## ALEATICO DI PUGLIA DOC
### Apulia

Produced in tiny quantities throughout the region, this wine is rarely exported. Opulent and aromatic wines with a full, warming, smooth, and exotic flavour, ranging from very sweet and fortified (*liquoroso* or *liquoroso dolce naturel*) to medium-sweet and unfortified (*dolce naturel*). A *riserva* must be aged for at least three years from the date of harvest or, in the case of *liquoroso*, the date of fortification.

⌽⤙ Upon purchase

⩗ *Francesco Candido*

## ALEZIO DOC
### Apulia

A DOC since 1983 for red and *rosato* wines made from Negroamaro, with the possible addition of Sangiovese, Montepulciano, and Malvasia Nera. The red is alcoholic, slightly tannic, and not very interesting, but the dry rosé can be soft and flavorful with delicate fruit.

⌽⤙ Upon purchase (rosé)

⩗ *Michele Calò* (Mjère)

## ARBOREA DOC
### Sardinia

Three varietal wines: Sangiovese red, Sangiovese *rosato*, and a dry or semisweet Trebbiano white.

## ASPRINIO
### Basilicata

This grape is always grown on its own rootstock and produces a green, often mean, dry white that is often *frizzante*.

## ASPRINIO DI AVERSA DOC
### Campania

Fresh, crisp, Vinho Verde-look-alike dry white wine from Asprinio grapes grown on vines trained to trees. Usually still, *frizzantino*, or *frizzante*, but sometimes fully sparkling.

## BIANCOLELLA
### Campania

Almost exclusively grown on the island of Ischia where D'Ambra does a pure varietal bottling.

## BRINDISI DOC
### Apulia

VIGNA FLAMINIO
Brindisi
Denominazione di Origine Controllata

Rosso 2000

AGRICOLE VALLONE

75 cl ℮          13% vol

Estate Bottled

Smooth, vinous red wines and dry, light, fruity rosés, both primarily from Negroamaro grapes, although Montepulciano, Malvasia Nera, Sangiovese, and Susumaniello may also be used.

⌽⤙ 3–6 years (red)

⩗ *Cosimo Taurino* (Patriglione)

## CABERNET BLENDS
### Calabria & Campania

Relatively few Cabernet-dominated wines stand out, but Gravello and Montevetrano are exceptionally fine.

⩗ *Silvio Imparato* (Montevetrano) • *Librandi* (Gravello)

## CACC'E MMITTE DI LUCERA DOC
### Apulia

The name of this full-bodied red *uvaggio*, which is made from seven grape varieties, loosely means "knock it back" (*cacc'e* means "drink" and *mmitte* means "pour"), which aptly applies to this simple, easy-drinking red wine.

## CAGLIARI DOC
### Sardinia

Four varietals: Malvasia (a smooth, delicately scented red wine in dry, sweet, and *liquoroso* styles); Moscato (rich, succulently sweet white wines that may be fortified); Nasco (finely scented, delicate, dry and sweet white wines that can also be *liquoroso*); and Nuragus (a large production of dry, semisweet, and *frizzante* white wines from the Nuragus grape).

⌽⤙ 1–2 years

⩗ *Meloni* ◉

## CAMPI FLEGREI DOC
### Campania

Two generic blends: red (Piedirosso, Aglianico, and Sciascinoso) and white (Falanghina, Biancolella, and Coda del Volpe); plus one red-wine varietal: Piedirosso (dry or *passito* dry-to-sweet); and one dry white varietal Falanghina (still or *spumante*).

## CAMPIDANO DI TERRALBA *or* TERRALBA DOC
### Sardinia

Soft yet full-bodied reds from the Monastrell, known locally as Bovale.

## CANNONAU DI SARDEGNA DOC
### Sardinia

A DOC of variable quality that throws up the occasional gem, Cannonau, better known as the Grenache, encompasses dry, semisweet, or sweet red, rosé, and *liquoroso* styles.

## CAPRI DOC
### Campania

Easy-to-drink, dry white wines seldom seen beyond the Isle of Capri. The island's soil and climate suggests that these wines should be much finer, but the land for vines is scarce and expensive, encouraging growers to extract far too much from those vineyards that do exist.

## CARIGNANO DEL SULCIS DOC
### Sardinia

Promising red and rosé wines from the Carignan grape, to which may be added a little Monica, Pascale, and Alicante Bouschet.

⌽⤙ 1–4 years

⩗ *CS di Santadi* (Riserva Rocca Rubia, Terre Brune)

## CASTEL DEL MONTE DOC
### Apulia

The region's best-known wine is named after the 13th-century castle built by Emperor Frederick von Hohenstaufen. With the exception of a red *riserva* made by Rivera and called Il Falcone (The Falcon), the wines are less lofty than the name of this DOC suggests. In addition to the generic red and rosé, which are made from Uva di Troia and Aglianico grapes, and the basic dry white from Pampanuto and Chardonnay, there are two red varietals, Pinot Nero and Aglianico; four white varietals, Chardonnay, Pinot Bianco, Pinot Bianco da Pinot Nero, and Sauvignon; plus a rose, Aglianico.

🍷 2–6 years (red, but 8–20 years for Il Falcone)

☑ *Rivera* (especially II Falcone and Terre al Monte)

## CASTEL SAN LORENZO DOC
### Campania

A relatively new DOC covering several communes in the province of Salerno, Castel San Lorenzo encompasses generic red and rosé (Barbera and Sangiovese), white (Trebbiano and Malvasia), one red wine varietal (Barbera) and one sweet white varietal (Moscato, still or *spumante*).

## CERASUOLO DI VITTORIA DOC
### Sicily

Cherry-colored Nerello-Calabrese wines from the southeastern corner of Sicily.

☑ *Planeta*

## CERDÈSER
### Sicily

Red, white, and rosé wines produced in and around Cerda, close to Palermo.

## CILENTO DOC
### Campania

Vines struggle in the rocky vineyards of Cilento, where generic red and rosé are made from Aglianico, Piedirosso, and Barbera, and generic white from Fiano, Trebbiano, Greco, and Malvasia. An Aglianico varietal also exists, but has yet to prove itself.

## CIRÒ DOC
### Calabria

Strong, alcoholic Gaglioppo-based red and rosé, and Greco-based dry white wines that rely too heavily on the Cirò name, which was famous in ancient times.

## CONTESSA ENTELLINA DOC
### Sicily

This new DOC encompasses vineyards in the commune of Contessa Entellina in the province of Palermo for a delicate dry white blend of Inzolia, Catarratto, Garganega, Chardonnay, Sauvignon, and Müller-Thurgau; and three dry white-wine varietals, Chardonnay, Grecanico (Garganega), and Sauvignon.

## COPERTINO DOC
### Apulia

This appellation is named after the town of Copertino, although the wines that qualify for this DOC can also come from five other villages. These smooth, rich red wines and dry, finely scented rosés are made primarily from the Negroamaro grape with the possible addition of Malvasia Nera, Montepulciano, and Sangiovese.

🍷 2–5 years

☑ *C. S. di Copertino* (riserva)

## CORVO
### Sicily

The brand name for red, white, *spumante*, and fortified "Stravecchio di Sicilia" wines of Duca di Salaparuta, Corvo has no DOC but is probably the most famous wine in Sicily. The full, smooth, fruity red is by far the most successful and consistent of the range.

## CREMOVO ZABAIONE VINO *or* CREMOVO ZABAIONE VINO AROMATIZZATO DOC
### Sicily

*See* Marsala DOC.

## DONNICI DOC
### Calabria

Fruity, cherry-colored red and rosé wines (traditionally *chiaretto*) from Gaglioppo and Greco Nero grapes grown in the province of Cosenza. They are best drunk young.

## ELORO DOC
### Sicily

This appellation straddles the provinces of Ragusa and Siracusa, where a generic red and rosé (Calabrese, Frappato, and Pignatello) are produced and, if the blend contains at least 80 percent Calabrese, it may be called Pachino. These grapes are also vinified separately to produce three varietal wines, the Calabrese being sold under its local synonym Nero d'Avola.

## ETNA DOC
### Sicily

According to Homer, this is the wine that Ulysses used to intoxicate the Cyclops. There are three basic styles: a full red and fruity rosé from the Nerello grape, and a soft but bland dry white from Carricante and Catarratto with the possible addition of Trebbiano.

☑ *Benanti* (Pietramarina)

## FALERNO DEL MASSICO DOC
### Campania

This appellation celebrates Falernum, the wine so enjoyed in Ancient Rome, which was made in the northwest of Campania and Latium. The deep-colored, full-bodied, and rustically robust red generic is a blend of Aglianico and Piedirosso with the possible addition of Primitivo and Barbera. The round, fruity dry white generic is, in fact, pure Falanghina. A red varietal Primitivo is also produced.

🍷 3–7 years (red) Upon purchase (white and rosé)

☑ *Villa Matilde* • *Michele Moio* (Primitivo)

## FARO DOC
### Sicily

Ruby-colored, medium-bodied but firmly flavored red wines from Nerello and Nocera grapes grown around Messina. Calabrese, Gaglioppo, and Sangiovese may also be used.

🍷 2–5 years

☑ *Bagni* • *Palari*

## FIANO DI AVELLINO DOCG
### Campania

Mastroberardino's Vignadora is the best wine in this unusual, but well above average, dry white wine DOCG, made from Fiano grapes grown in the hilly hinterland of Avellino.

🍷 1–3 years

☑ *Mastroberardino*

## GIOIA DEL COLLE DOC
### Apulia

For this large DOC in the province of Bari there are generic red and rosé blends (Primitivo, Montepulciano, Sangiovese, Negroamaro, and Malvasia Nera); a dry white (Trebbiano and anything else that moves); and two varietals, a sweetish Primitivo and an intensely sweet Aleatico (which can be fortified).

## GIRO DI CAGLIARI DOC
### Sardinia

Smooth, alcoholic, dry and sweet red wines and dry and sweet fortified wines.

## GRAGNANO DOC
### Campania

*See* Penisola Sorrentina DOC.

## GRAVINA DOC
### Apulia

Dry or semisweet, blended white wines that may be still or *spumante*, made from Malvasia, Greco, and Bianco d'Alessano, with the possible addition of Bombino, Trebbiano, and Verdeca.

## GRECO DI BIANCO DOC
### Calabria

Made on the very tip of Calabria, around Bianco, from the Grechetto grape, known locally as Greco Bianco. With the exception of Umberto Ceratti's exceptional rendition, Greco di Bianco is a simple *passito* wine. Ceratti harvests tiny, already shriveled grapes and, apparently, plunges them into boiling water immediately after picking (to flash pasteurize the wine, which removes or reduces the need to use sulfur). His Greco di Bianco is deceptively strong, succulently sweet and smooth, with a vivacious bouquet, exuberant fruit, and a luscious silk finish.

🍷 3–5 years

☑ *Umberto Ceratti*

## GRECO DI TUFO DOCG
### Campania

Delicate, dry, and soft white wines that may sometimes be *spumante*, from the true Greco grown north of Avellino.

🍷 Upon purchase

☑ *Mastroberardino* (Vignadangelo)

## GUARDIA SANFRAMONDI *or* GUARDIOLO DOC
### Campania

Located in the hilly terrain of the Benvento, this DOC consists of a generic dry white (Malvasia and Falanghina plus up to 30 percent pick-and-mix), generic Sangiovese-based red and rosé, one dry white varietal (Falanghina), which may be *spumante*, and one red varietal (Aglianico).

## ISCHIA DOC
### Campania

Vinous, medium-bodied generic red (Guarnaccia and Piedirosso, plus 20 percent pick-and-mix); a lightly aromatic, generic dry white (Forastera and Biancolella), which may be *spumante*; two dry white varietal wines (Biancolella and Forastera); and one red varietal (Piedirosso), which can be either dry or *passito*.

🍷 2–4 years (red), upon purchase (white and rosé)

✓ *D'Ambra*

## LAMEZIA DOC
### Calabria

Originally a one-wine DOC for a light, delicately fruity, but otherwise unexceptional blended red wine (Nerello, Gaglioppo, Greco Nero, and Marsigliana), Lamezia has now been expanded to include a generic, full dry white (Grechetto, Trebbiano, and Malvasia) and a white varietal called Greco, the local name for Grechetto. The light red has been split into red and rosé.

## LETTERE DOC
### Campania

*See* Penisola Sorrentina DOC.

## LEVERANO DOC
### Apulia

Alcoholic red wines and fresh, fruity rosés (Negroamaro with the possible addition of Sangiovese, Montepulciano, and Malvasia Nera), and soft, dry white wines (Malvasia plus Bombino and Trebbiano). Conti Zecca's elegant red Vigna del Sareceno stands out.

🍷 3–7 years (red)

✓ *Conti Zecca* (Vigna del Saraceno)

## LIZZANO DOC
### Apulia

Negroamaro-based red and rosé, still or *frizzante* generic wines, which may be boosted by the addition of Montepulciano, Sangiovese, Bombino Nero, Pinot Noir, and Malvasia Nera. The rosé can also be fully *spumante*, as can the generic white blend of Trebbiano and Chardonnay (with the possible addition of Malvasia, Sauvignon, and Bianco d'Alessano), which also comes in still or *frizzante* styles. There are two red varietal wines, Negroamaro and Malvasia Nera; and one rosé varietal, Negroamaro—all three in straightforward, dry still-wine styles.

## LOCOROTONDO DOC
### Apulia

Fresh, lightly fruity, dry white wines of improving quality from Verdeca and Bianco d'Alessano, with the possible addition of Fiano, Malvasia, and Bombino, made in still and *spumante* styles.

🍷 Upon purchase

✓ *C. S. di Locorotondo*

## MALVASIA
### Basilicata and Sardinia

This grape plays a respectable second fiddle to Moscato in the *vini da tavola* stakes. Usually sweet, sometimes fizzy. In Sardinia, the wines are mostly fortified and DOC, but Malvasia della Planargia is still *vino da tavola*, although many rank it as the finest in Sardinia.

✓ **Basilicata** *Fratelli d'Angelo* • *Paternosta*
**Sardinia** *Gian Vittorio Naitana* (Vigna Giagonìa, Vigna Murapiscados)

## MALVASIA DELLE LIPARI DOC
### Sicily

Sweet, aromatic, *passito* white wines.

🍷 2–5 years

✓ *Carlo Hauner*

## MALVASIA DI BOSA DOC
### Sardinia

Rich, sweet and dry white wines, and sweet and dry *liquoroso* wines. Generally fuller-bodied than Malvasia di Cagliari.

## MALVASIA DI CAGLIARI DOC
### Sardinia

Rich, sweet or dry, white wines, and dry or sweet, *liquoroso* wines. They are lighter but finer and more elegant wines than Malvasia di Bosa and traditionally are drier.

## MALVASIA NERA
### Apulia

Dark-skinned Malvasia is commonly found in the Salento district, and traditionally complements the local Negroamaro grape, although it is sometimes made into a pure varietal wine, both as DOC and *vini da tavola*. Alone, this grape produces a vivid red wine with slightly aromatic fruit and a dry but velvety-smooth finish.

## MANDROLISAI DOC
### Sardinia

Red and rosé wines with a bitter aftertaste blended from Bovale (Monastrell), Cannonau (Grenache), and Monica.

## MARSALA DOC
### Sicily

This wine was conceived by John Woodhouse, who began shipping it in 1773. Its name is Arabic, deriving from *Marsah-el-Allah*, the old name of the port of Marsala. The grapes used include Grillo (the original Marsala variety and still considered the best), Catarratto, Pignatello, Garganega, Calabrese, Damaschino, Nerello, and Inzolia. The wine is fortified by the adding of neutral spirit and, where appropriate, sweetened with grape concentrate made locally. Marsala can be dry (*secco*), semisweet (*semisecco*), or sweet (*dolce*); is further defined by color, gold (*oro*), amber (*ambra*), and red (*rubino*); and is made in four basic styles, *Fine*, *Superiore*, *Vergine*, and *Solera*.

Marsala Fine, the lowest category, is aged for just a year (not necessarily in wood) with at least 17 percent ABV. As Italian-wine expert David Gleave MW has put it, Marsala Fine is "usually anything but fine, being a cheap and rather nasty travesty of the name." Marsala Superiore is aged for at least two years in wood (four years if *riserva*), with a minimum 18 percent ABV. Marsala Vergine is aged for at least five years in wood, or 10 if *stravecchio* or *riserva*, is only *secco* (thus no grape concentrate allowed), and must have a minimum 18 percent ABV. Marsala Solera is also aged for at least five years in wood, or 10 years if *stravecchio* or *riserva*, is only *secco* (thus no grape concentrate allowed), and must have a minimum of 18 percent ABV. Some historical abbreviations are still found on labels: IP (stands for Italy

Particular—Marsala Fine), LP (London Particular—Marsala Superiore), SOM (Superior Old Marsala—Marsala Superiore), GD (Garibaldi Dolce—Marsala Superiore). Flavored Marsala may be sold as Cremovo Zabaione Vino or Cremovo Zabaione Vino Aromatizzato (sickly sweet eggnog containing at least 80 percent Marsala wine, eggs, and a minimum of 200 grams of residual sugar per liter), Preparato con l'impiego di Vino Marsala (for other Marsala-based products containing not less than 60 percent Marsala wine), and you will find non-DOC Marsala-based concoctions with all sorts of flavorings (banana, chocolate, orange, etc.). I must confess that, except for rare old bottlings of Vergine or Solera, most Marsala leaves me cold and the flavored versions horrify me, but the best producers are well known.

🍷 Upon purchase

✓ *Cantina de Bartoli* • *Florio* • *Carlo Pellegrino*

## MARTINA *or* MARTINA FRANCA DOC
### Apulia

These dry white wines in still or *spumante* styles are very similar to those of Locorotondo.

## MATINO DOC
### Apulia

Dry, robust red and slightly vinous rosé wines made from Negroamaro with the possible addition of Malvasia Nera.

## MELISSA DOC
### Calabria

An appellation of full-bodied reds (Gaglioppo, Greco Nero, Grechetto, Trebbiano, and Malvasia) and crisp, dry whites (Grechetto, Trebbiano, and Malvasia).

## MENFI
### Sicily

Decent red and white *vini da tavola* are made in and around Menfi at the western end of the south coast of the island.

## METAPONTUM
### Basilicata

Basic red and white *vini da tavola* are produced from the Ionian coastal plain either side of the Basento River around Metaponto in the eastern corner of Basilicata.

## MOSCATO
### Basilicata and Calabria

In Basilicata, the two best wine producers of these *vini da tavola* believe in the potential of Moscato, always sweet and usually fully *spumante*, from the Mount Vulture area. It is also grown all over Calabria, but is more often made into a *passito* wine than a *spumante* one.

✓ **Basilicata** *Fratelli d'Angelo* • *Paternosta*
**Calabria** *Guido Lojelo*

## MOSCATO DI CAGLIARI DOC
### Sardinia

*See* Cagliari DOC.

## MOSCATO DI NOTO DOC
### Sicily

Still, *spumante*, or fortified semisweet and sweet Moscato wines.

## MOSCATO DI PANTELLERIA DOC
### Sicily

Sicily's best still, *spumante*, and fortified semi-sweet and sweet Moscato are made on the island of Pantelleria, closer to Tunisia than to Sicily.

✓ *De Bartoli* (Passito Bukkuram) • *Cantine Florio* (Morsi di Luce) • *Salvatore Murana*

## MOSCATO DI SIRACUSA DOC
### Sicily

These sweet, smooth white wines are made from semi-*passito* grapes.

## MOSCATO DI SORSO-SENNORI DOC
### Sardinia

Sweet, rich, white Moscato and sweet, aromatic *liquoroso*. The wines are fuller than either Moscato di Cagliari or Moscato di Sardegna.

## MOSCATO DI TRANI DOC
### Apulia

Tiny production of luscious, ultrasmooth, sweet white Moscato wines, which may be fortified. These wines are high quality and distinctive.

⌛ Upon purchase
✓ *Fratelli Nugnes*

## NARDO DOC
### Apulia

Cherry-red rosés from Negroamaro, with Malvasia Nera and Montepulciano permitted.

## NASCO DI CAGLIARI DOC
### Sardinia

*See* Cagliari DOC.

## NEGROAMARO
### Apulia

A productive grape, the Negroamaro makes dark, potentially bitter red wines that used to be sold in bulk for blending, but used to acquire their own reputation. It makes a good rosé under the Alezio DOC, but unless vinified with care, the red wine it produces tends to be too alcoholic, coarse, and bitter, although Calò's *barrique*-aged Vigna Spano and Vallone's *passito* Graticcia are *vino da tavola* exceptions.

✓ *Michele Calò* (Vigna Spano) • *Vallone* (Graticcia)

## NEGROAMARO-MALVASIA NERO
### Apulia

The traditional red-wine blend of Salento.

✓ *Cosimo Taurino* (Notarpanaro)

## NURAGUS DI CAGLIARI DOC
### Sardinia

*See* Cagliari DOC.

## ORTA NOVA DOC
### Apulia

These are full-bodied red and dry rosé Sangiovese-based wines from the villages of Orta Nova and Ordona in the province of Foggia.

## OSTUNI DOC
### Apulia

A delicate, dry white made from Impigno and Francavidda and a light-bodied red from the

THE MARSALA PLAINS, SICILY
*Vines on the hot, arid plains of western Sicily grow on a low-yielding soil called sciari, producing the finest Marsala, while farther east, but still within the DOC, the soil is more fertile and the wines are of lower quality.*

Cinsault grape, known locally as Ottavianello, with the possible addition of Negroamaro, Notar Domenico, Malvasia Nera, and Susumaniello.

## OTTAVIANELLO DOC
### Apulia

*See* Ostuni DOC.

## PELLARO
### Campania

Ottavianello DOC produces powerful Alicante-based *chiaretto* wines from just south of Reggio di Calabria on the very toe of Italy.

## PENISOLA SORRENTINA DOC
### Campania

This is a relatively new DOC for former *vini da tavola* from the Sorrento peninsula, including a generic red (Piedirosso with the possible addition of Sciascinoso, Aglianico, and other unspecified nonaromatic varieties), which can also be made in a purple-colored *frizzante* style, and a dry white generic (Falanghina with the possible addition of Biancolella, Greco, and other nonaromatic varieties). If the subzones Sorrento (for white and still red), Gragnano, or Lettere (red *frizzante*) appear on the label, the wines must conform to higher standards, including extraripe grapes.

## PIEDIROSSO
### Campania

An ancient variety identified by Pliny, Piedirosso is usually blended with more noble varieties, but has been produced as a varietal wine by D'Ambra on the island of Ischia, where the grape is commonly known as Per'e Palummo.

## POLLINO DOC
### Calabria

Full, fruity, *chiaretto* wines from Gaglioppo, Greco Nero, Malvasia, and Guarnaccia.

## PRIMITIVO
### Apulia

Now proven to be the Zinfandel, although it generally makes a wine that has nowhere near Zinfandel's character, let alone its quality.

## PRIMITIVO DI MANDURIA DOC
### Apulia

Dry to semisweet, full-bodied red wines which may also be fortified and naturally sweet, and fortified and dry. Until I tasted Giordano's 1993 vintage in 1996, no Primitivo had shown any class.

⌛ 3–10 years (Giordano as from 1993)
✓ *Giordano* • *Vinicola Savese*

## ROSSO BARLETTA DOC
### Apulia

Medium-bodied, ruby-colored, everyday-quality red wines made from Uva di Troia with the possible addition of Montepulciano, Sangiovese, and a small amount of Malbec. Most Rosso Barletta is consumed locally when very young.

## ROSSO CANOSA DOC
### Apulia

Vinous, slightly tannic red wines made from Uva di Troia with the possible addition of Montepulciano and Sangiovese.

## ROSSO DI CERIGNOLA DOC
### Apulia

Rare, rustic reds from Negroamaro and Uva di Troia with the possible addition of Sangiovese, Barbera, Montepulciano, Malbec, and Trebbiano.

## SALICE SALENTINO DOC
### Apulia

Full-bodied reds and smooth, alcoholic rosés from Negroamaro with the possible addition of Malvasia Nera, and, more recently, two dry white wines: a Chardonnay, which may be *frizzante*, and a Pinot Bianco, which may be *spumante*; plus a sweet red Aleatico, which can be fortified. The Negroamaro-based red wines are still, however, the best wines in this DOC.

⌛ 3–7 years
✓ *Francesco Candido* • *Leone de Castris* • *Cosimo Taurino* • *Vallone*

## SAN SEVERO DOC
### Apulia

Dry, vinous red and rosé wines made from Montepulciano and Sangiovese, and dry, fresh whites from Bombino and Trebbiano, with the possible addition of Malvasia and Verdeca.

## SAN VITO DI LUZZI DOC
### Calabria

A new DOC covering generic red, rosé (Gaglioppo and Malvasia with the possible addition of Greco Nero and Sangiovese), and dry white (Malvasia, Grechetto, and Trebbiano) wines produced in and near the village of Luzzi in the province of Conseza.

## SANT'AGATA DEI GOTI DOC
### Campania

Relatively new DOC for generic red, dry white, and rosé from Aglianico and Piedirosso (thus the white is a *blanc de noirs*); two red wine varietals, Aglianico and Piedirosso; and two white varietals, Greco and Falanghina.

## SANT'ANNA DI ISOLA CAPO RIZZUTO DOC
### Calabria

Vinous red and rosé wines from Gaglioppo, Greco Nero, and Guarnaccia grapes grown in the Ionian hills.

## SARDEGNA DOC
### Sardinia

This DOC is for wines made from grapes grown throughout the island, although in practice they are generally restricted to traditional areas. For Moscato, vines must not be grown above 1,476 feet (450 meters). Moscato di Sardegna is sweet and surprisingly delicate, usually in a natural still-wine style, although *spumante* is produced and the subappellations Tempio Pausania, Tempio, and Gallura are reserved for sparkling wines in the Gallura area. Monica di Sardegna is a fragrant red wine that may be dry or sweet, still or *frizzante*, but unlike Monica di Cagliari, is never fortified. Vermentino di Sardegna is a light-bodied, soft, clean, unexciting dry white wine that all too often has its flavors washed out by cool fermentation techniques.

## SAVUTO DOC
### Calabria

Fresh, fruity red or rosé wines from Gaglioppo, Greco Nero, Nerello, Sangiovese, Malvasia, and Pecorino grapes grown in Catanzaro province.

⌛ 1–3 years

✓ *Odoardi* (Vigna Vecchia)

## SCAVIGNA DOC
### Calabria

Generic red, rosé (Gaglioppo, Nerello, and Aglianico) and a fruity dry white (Trebbiano, Chardonnay, Grechetto, and Malvasia) from the communes of Nocera Terinese and Falerna.

⌛ 1–3 years

✓ *Abbazia Sant'Anastasia* (Passomaggio)

## SICILIA IGT
### Sicily

All—not just most—of the very best wines produced on this island are sold under this IGT, and considering Sicily's reputation up to now, the prices that some of these wines achieve should be an object lesson to all the odd, obscure IGTs on the mainland.

✓ *Cottanera* (Sole di Sesta) • *Corvo* (Duca Enrico) • *Cusumano* (Noà, Sagana) • *Fatascià* (Almanera) • *Feuda Principi di Butera* (Deliella) • *Firriato* (Camalot, Harmonium) • *Morgante* (Don Antonio), *Planeta* (Burdese, Cometa, Merlot, Syrah), *Santa Anastasia* (Litra) • *Tasca d'Almerita* (Contea di Sciafani, Cabernet Sauvignon), *Tenute Rapitala* (Hugonis, Solinero) • *Trapani* (Forti Terre Cabernet Sauvignon)

## SOLOPACA DOC
### Campania

Smooth generic red and rosé (Sangiovese and Aglianico with the possible addition of Piedirosso, Sciascinoso, and up to 30 percent pick-and-mix), generic dry white (Trebbiano, Falanghina, Malvasia, and Coda di Volpe), one red wine varietal (Aglianico) and one white varietal (Falanghina—still or *spumante*). Solopaca comes from the Calore Valley.

⌛ 1–4 years

✓ *Antica Masseria Venditti*

## SORRENTO DOC
### Campania

*See* Penisola Sorrentina DOC.

## SQUINZANO DOC
### Apulia

Full-bodied red wines and lightly scented rosé wines from Negroamaro with the possible addition of Sangiovese and Malvasia Nera, grown in Squinzano and the surrounding communes.

⌛ 2–4 years (red), upon purchase (rosé)

✓ *Villa Valletta*

## TABURNO DOCG
### Campania

This DOC started out life as Aglianico del Taburno in red and rosé, but it is one of those DOCs that just grows. It now includes a generic red (Sangiovese and Aglianico); white (Trebbiano and Falanghina, plus 30 percent pick-and-mix); a *spumante* (Coda di Volpe and Falanghina, plus 40 percent pick-and-mix); three white wine varietals (Falanghina, Greco, and Coda di Volpe); and one red (Piedirosso).

## TAURASI DOCG
### Campania

Red wines made primarily from Aglianico grapes (up to 15 percent in total of Barbera, Piedirosso, and Sangiovese may be added) that are grown in Taurasi and 16 nearby villages. It was elevated to DOCG status in 1993. Along with Basilicata's thicker tasting Aglianico del Vulture, it is one of the country's greatest wines from this underrated grape variety, in an equally age-worthy style. Mastroberardino's *riserva* excels.

⌛ 5–10 years (some may last for as long as 20)

✓ *Mastroberardino* • *Giovanni Struzziero* • *Antonio Caggiano*

## TERRALBA DOC
### Sardinia

*See* Campidano di Terralba DOC.

## VERMENTINO DI GALLURA DOCG
### Sardinia

Despite cool fermentation, this is the best Vermentino Sardinia offers, the hilly *terroir* of Gallura producing intense flavors. Although this wine was elevated to DOCG status in 1997, it could be much better quality and cheaper to make if fermented at slightly higher temperatures.

⌛ 1–2 years

✓ *Tenuta di Capichera* • *C. S. di Gallura* • *C. S. del Vermentino*

## VERNACCIA DI ORISTANO DOC
### Sardinia

ANTICOGREGORI
VERNACCIA DI ORISTANO
V.Q.P.R.D.
CONTINI

The DOC of Vernaccia di Oristano makes dry and lightly bitter white wines, which are sherry-like in style. Also produced are *liquoroso* sweet and dry wines.

⌛ Upon purchase

✓ *Contini*

## VESUVIO DOC
### Campania

Restricted to vines on the volcanic slopes of Mount Vesuvius, a generic dry white (Coda di Volpe and Verdeca grapes, with the possible addition of Falanghina and Greco), and a generic rosé (Piedirosso and Sciascinoso with the possible addition of Aglianico) are produced by Vesuvio DOC. Those that are labeled Lacryma (or Lacrima) Christi del Vesuvio are usually dry white wines, but less commonly they may also be *spumante* or sweet and fortified.

## NEW IGT WINES

The following IGT wines were agreed at the end of 1996, but we have yet to see what style, quality, or consistency each one will establish:

✓ **Apulia** *Daunia • Murgia • Puglia • Salento • Tarantino • Valle d'Itria*

**Basilicata and Calabria** *Arghilli • Bivongi • Calabria • Condoleo • Costa Viola • Esaro • Lipuda • Locride • Palizzi • Scilla • Val di Neto • Valdamato • Valle del Crati*

**Campania** *Colli di Limvara • Isola dei Nuraghi • Marmilla • Nurra • Ogliastro • Parteolla • Planargia • Provincia di Nuoro • Romangia • Sibiola • Tharros • Trexenta • Valle del Tirso*

**Sicily** *Camarro • Colli Ericini • Della Nivolelli • Fontanarossa di Cerda • Salemi • Salina • Sciacca • Valle Belice*

# The WINES of
# SPAIN

SPAIN CONTINUES TO OVERPERFORM,
providing more wines of real interest and quality
than the most optimistic critic could reasonably
hope for. Why do I say that? For a start, as
indigenous grape varieties go, Tempranillo is
Spain's only class act. Furthermore, although
most Spanish vineyards are not totally lacking
in potential (otherwise we would not have
witnessed the revolution in Spanish wines that
we have), there are no really world-class *terroirs*
to be found beyond parts of Rioja, Penedés, and
the Ribera del Duero. Yet the number of truly
fine Spanish wines continues to increase, with
at least as much excitement at the lower end of
the quality scale as at the higher end. As recently
as the 1980s, with the general exception of
Rioja, most Spanish wines were either oxidized
or over-sulfured. Never has an established,
traditional winemaking nation gotten its act
together as quickly or as thoroughly as Spain.

FALL VINES AT LAROCO, VALDEORRAS
*Until Rías Baixas came on the scene, Laroco was
Galicia's up-and-coming white-wine district.*

# SPAIN

*In the early 1970s, Spanish wines had such a bad reputation that, by comparison, Italian wines seemed preferable. By the late 1980s, however, the wines of Spain were being taken seriously, whereas those of Italy generally were not.*

THAT SPAIN COULD ACHIEVE such a swift turnaround in the quality of its wines can be put down to its efforts to get out of the bulk wine market. The Spanish did not stop selling bulk wine altogether, but prevented this low-quality product from dominating exports. By its very volume, bulk wine dilutes and downgrades a country's winemaking reputation, and in the 1970s Spanish bulk wine was so bad that the country's worsening image threatened to undermine its share of global markets just as the culture of wine drinking was developing in the US, the UK, and other potentially lucrative markets. It was not as if there was a

## CONSEJO REGULADOR STAMPS

Every current DO and DOCa possesses its own stamp, which usually appears somewhere on the label, offering a guarantee of authenticity.

## SPANISH LABEL LANGUAGE

**AÑEJO** Aged for 12 months in cask or bottle

**BLANCO** White

**BODEGA** Literally a "wine cellar," commonly used as part of the name of a wine firm

**CAVA** A sparkling DO wine produced using the traditional method

**CLARETE** Midway between light red and dark rosado, synonymous with *tintillo*

**COSECHA** Means vintage, and indicates that a minimum of 85 percent of a wine thus labeled is produced in the year marked

**COSECHERO** A fresh, fruity, "new" or nouveau style wine, synonymous with *nuevo* and *vino joven*, and usually a *vino de mesa*

**CRIADO Y EMBOTELLADO POR** Blended and bottled by

**CRIANZA** A red *crianza* must be aged for a minimum of 2 years (of which at least 6 months must be in oak); a white or rosado *crianza* requires 1 year of aging (with at least 6 months in oak)

**CRIANZA CORTA** Wines that have less than the legal minimum cask-age for any cask-age designation. Synonymous with *sin crianza*

**DENOMINACIÓN DE ORIGEN (DO)** Wine that originates from a controlled-quality wine region

**DENOMINACIÓN DE ORIGEN CALIFICADA (DOCA)** The highest official classification, above *Denominación de Origen*

**DOBLE PASTA** This term refers to red wines that have been macerated with double the normal proportion of grape skins to juice during fermentation. Such wines are opaque, with an intense color, and may be sold in the bottle or for blending

**DULCE** Sweet

**EMBOTELLADO POR** Bottled by

**ESPUMOSO** A sparkling wine made by any method

**GENEROSO** A fortified or dessert wine

**GRAN RESERVA** Red wines must be at least 5 years old, with a minimum of 18 months in oak. White and rosado *gran reservas* must be at least 4 years old, with a minimum of 6 months in oak

**NOBLE** Aged for 2 years in cask or bottle

**NUEVO** A fresh, fruity, "new" or nouveau style

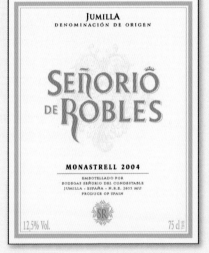

wine, synonymous with *cosechero* and *vino joven*, and usually a *vino de mesa*

**RESERVA** Red wines must be at least 3 years old, with a minimum of 12 months in oak. White and rosado *reservas* must be at least 2 years old, with a minimum of 6 months in oak

**ROSADO** Rosé

**SECO** Dry

**SEMIDULCE** Medium-sweet

**SIN CRIANZA** A wine without wood-aging, including all cool-fermented, early-bottled white and most rosado wines. The term *sin crianza* is falling out of use, in favor of *vino joven*

**TINTILLO** Midway between light red and dark rosado, synonymous with *clarete*

**TINTO** Red

**VIEJO** A term that literally means "old." Use of this term was not controlled by law until 2005, since which date such a wine must be aged for at least 3 years

**VIÑA OR VIÑEDO** Literally "vineyard," but often merely part of a brand name, and nothing to do with a specific vineyard

**VINO COMARCAL** A regional wine, above *Vino de mesa* and below *Vino de la tierra*

**VINO DE AGUJA** A semisparkling, or *pétillant*, wine

**VINO DE CALIDAD CON INDICACIÓN GEOGRÁFICA** A stepping stone between *Vino de la tierra* and *Denominación de Origen*

**VINO DE LA TIERRA** Literally "country wine"

**VINO DE MESA** Literally "table wine"; likely to be seen on the labels of very ordinary, inexpensive wines

**VINO DE PASTO** An ordinary, inexpensive, and often light style of wine

**VINO JOVEN** Wine made to be drunk within the year. There are moves to replace the term *sin crianza* with *vino joven*, but while wines in both categories must be without any wood-aging, some *sin crianza* wines are made to age well in bottle, unlike *vino joven*

**VINUM OPTIMUM RARE SIGNATUM, OR VERY OLD RARE SHERRY (VORS)** Minimum age of 30 years

**VINUM OPTIMUM SIGNATUM, OR VERY OLD SHERRY (VORS)** Minimum age of 20 years

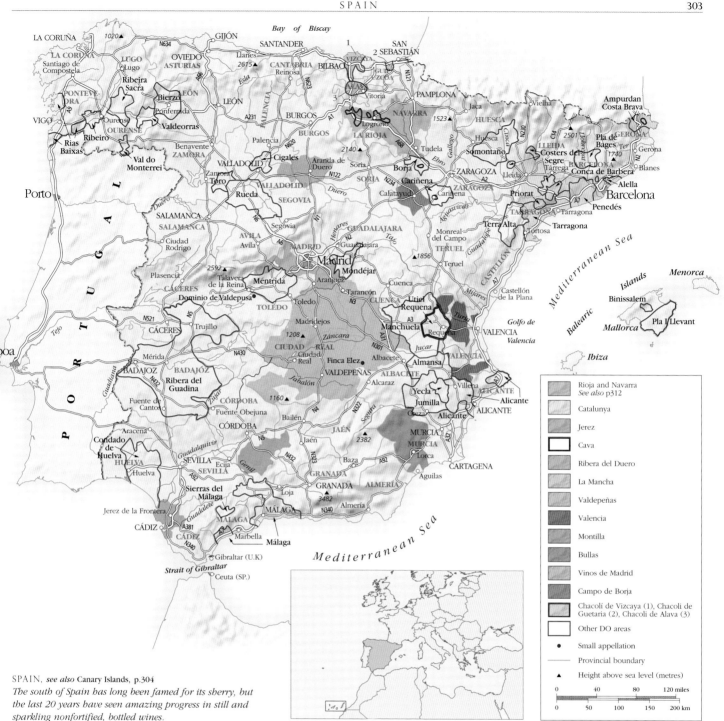

SPAIN, *see also* Canary Islands, p.304
*The south of Spain has long been famed for its sherry, but the last 20 years have seen amazing progress in still and sparkling nonfortified, bottled wines.*

meeting at which the entire Spanish wine industry took a vote to change things, but there must have been some sort of industry-wide determination to improve quality because the situation was reversed so quickly. Spain's reputation leapfrogged Italy's, despite having much less going for it in terms of native grape varieties and *terroirs*, establishing the country as one of the best-value sources in Europe.

## ANCIENT ORIGINS

Vines were first planted in Spain *c*.1100 BC around Cádiz by, it is believed, the Phoenicians. The earliest wines were by all accounts rich, sweet, and heavy, the precursors of modern-day sherry. However, from the start of the 8th century until the end of the 15th, southern Spain was under the rule of the Moors, and being Mohammedans, wine production was not a priority. This is not to say that the Moors never drank wine; indeed, Al-Motamid, the last Moorish king of Seville, enjoyed wine so much that he publicly

mocked anyone who drank water. The Moors also enjoyed the grape as a fruit and for its fresh, unfermented juice, but under a theoretically abstemious rule, winemaking stagnated. So, while Spain can claim a 3,000-year history of wine, the diversity of its wine areas and styles did not commence until the 1490s, just 30 years before the Spanish planted the first vines in the Americas. Some parts of the Old and New Worlds are much closer in age, in terms of winemaking, than these terms imply.

## SPAIN'S BEST WINES AND ITS APPELLATION SYSTEM

Vega Sicilia in the Ribera del Duero was once definitively Spain's most expensive wine, leading many to believe that it must be Spain's greatest. Others can now lay equal claim to be the most expensive and greatest of Spanish wines (Clos l'Ermita, Dominio de Pingus, and Cirsión are likely candidates), and many more are equal in quality if not quite as ridiculously priced, including

Pesquera, Rioja (Contino, Barón de Ley, Muga Prado Enea, Murrieta Castillo Ygay Gran Reserva), Penedès (Torres and Jean Léon), and even some nonappellation wines such as Marqués de Griñón.

The *Denominación de Origen* (DO) system is Spain's equivalent of the French *Appellation d'Origine Contrôlée* (AOC) or Italian *Denominazione di Origine Controllata* (DOC) systems. The only higher Spanish classification is *Denominación de Origen Calificada* (DOCa), and Rioja remains the only recipient of this superior status since its inception in 1981, although other high-quality wines may be promoted to DOCa in the future. Ribera del Duero, Navarra, Penedès, and Cava all spring to mind as candidates for such promotion. If there is a lesson the Spanish could learn from Italy, it is not to overlook outstanding nonappellation wines such as Marqués de Griñón's Cabernet Sauvignon and Syrah from south of Madrid. Indisputably two of Spain's great wines, they should jump from DO straight to DOCa status, if Spain's regime is to avoid the same fate as Italy's, whose best *vini da tavola* were forced to build up reputations at the expense of the official system.

## RECENT SPANISH VINTAGES

**2006** Some great wines, but generally good to very good, despite the hype in Rioja. Whites less successful.

**2005** An excellent vintage for both reds and whites. Well balanced.

**2004** A very good to excellent year for whites, but reds less great, with the exception of Rioja, where the quality is outstanding.

**2003** It might seem odd that Spain's baking-hot south fared better than the north of the country in this sweltering drought year, but as others have pointed out, the vineyards down there are prepared for the heat.

**2002** Variable quality, mostly average to poor, with somewhat better quality in the south.

## TRADITIONAL VERSUS MODERN STYLES

It used to be possible to speak of new-wave Spanish wines, as the tradition had been to leave wines in oak for longer than most modern winemakers consider wise and a younger generation of winemakers reacted by producing wines that were as fresh, clean, and unoaked as possible. However, although the old style for reds was dried-out and that for whites oxidized, the new style was so clean, it was clinical, and was no great improvement as such. The tendency now is to talk of modern style rather than new-wave, as the wines are much fruitier and the use of oak is not so much avoided, as restrained, with French casks more likely than American, and fermented rather than aged.

THE HILLTOP TOWN OF LAGUARDIA
*Set against the majestic backdrop of the Sierra de Cantabria is the hilltop town of Laguardia, which boasts some of the finest vineyards of the Rioja Alava.*

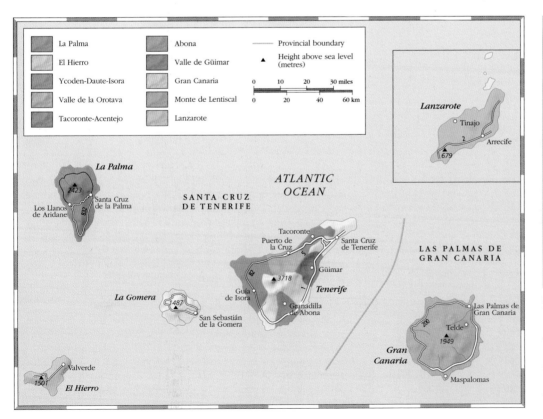

SAMPLING SHERRIES
USING A VENENCIA
*The development of a cask of sherry is of crucial importance in determining its eventual style.*

CANARY ISLANDS
*The first of these appellations was established in 1992, but "Canary Sack" was famous in Shakespeare's time.*

# APPELLATIONS BELOW DENOMINACIÓN DE ORIGEN

A baffling oddity in Spain's wine regime is the hierarchy of country-wine classifications, all of which are similar to the French *vin de pays* appellation. *Vino de la tierra* (VdT) literally means "country wine," while *vino comarcal* (VC) means "local wine" and comes from a larger area, effectively adding regional status to a *vino de mesa*. A new appellation called *Vino de Calidad con Indicación Geográfica* (VCIG) has been introduced for wines that aspire to *Denominación de Origen* (DO) and is thus seen as a stepping stone to it, making VCIG similar to the French *Vin Délimité de Qualité Supérieure*.

### ABANILLA VDLT
**Murcia** This flat, dry area has a scattering of vineyards whose wines have traditionally been blended with others in the Murcia region.

### ALJARAFE VC
**Andalucía** These fortified wines are effectively an extension of the Condado de Huelva appellation.

### ALTO JILOCA VC
**Aragón** Made mainly from Garnacha and Macabéo grapes, these wines were formerly sold with those of Daroca under the Alto Jiloca-Daroca appellation.

### ANOIA VC
**Catalonia** Mostly soft, bland rosado wines from the Sumoll grape, as the whites are usually sold in bulk to Cava producers in Penedès.

### BAGES VDLT
**Catalonia** Formerly the *vino comarcal* Artés, this area of Barcelona changed its appellation to Bages when it was upgraded to Catalonia's only *vino de la tierra*. Bages VdlT is now the DO Pla de Bages, although vintages of both are still available.

### BAJO ARAGON VDLT
**Aragón** These wines are mostly *tinto* or *blanco* from red and white Garnacha grapes, although a fair amount of Macabéo, Mazuelo, and even Cabernet Sauvignon grow in this very large area.

### BAJO-EBROE-MONTSIA VC
**Catalonia** Meseguera, known locally as Exquitxagos, is the widest-planted grape variety in this area.

### BENAVENTE VC
**Castilla-León** This region was once quite famous for its *pétillant* rosado, but has yet to reestablish its historical reputation.

### BENIARRÉS VC
**Valencia** This area produces robust, alcoholic reds and sweet Moscatel from Alicante.

### BETANZOS VC
**Galicia** A small amount of crisp, light-bodied, "Vinho Verde"-style wines are produced here.

### CADIZ VDLT
**Andalucía** These are light, white table wines of Jerez, pioneered and promoted by Barbadillo—they are fresh, but not special.

### CAMPO DE CARTAGENA VDLT
**Murcia** Mostly oxidized whites, plus some rustic reds, although quality is apparently improving.

### CAÑAMERO VDLT
**Extremadura** These rustic whites are produced in the foothills of the Sierra de Guadalupe. Now one of the six subregions of the DO Ribera del Guadiana, although some producers refused to join the DO and are still labeling their wines as Cañamero VdlT.

### CASTILLA VDLT
**Castilla-La Mancha** This VdlT was inaugurated in 1999 after lobbying by "maverick" winemakers in Castilla-La Mancha, headed by Carlos Falcó. It is a "Vin de Pays d'Oc"-type classification allowing people to make the wines they want with minimal regulation throughout a vast region.

### CEBREROS VDLT
**Castilla-León** A good source of cheap, fruity wines made from the Garnacha grape. Destined to achieve DO status.

### CONCA DE TREMP VC
**Catalonia** A once-famous wine area at the foot of the Pyrenees, Conca de Tremp has a warmer microclimate than surrounding areas and could produce some interesting wines.

### CONTRAVIESA-ALPUJARRA VDLT
**Andalucía** These rustic, fortified wines are from Granada and used to be called Costa-Albondón.

### DAROCA VC
**Aragón** Made mainly from Garnacha and Macabéo grapes, these wines were formerly sold with those of Alto Jiloca.

### FERMOSELLE-ARRIBES DEL DUERO VDLT
**Castilla-León** This is a large but shrinking viticultural area in which one of its secondary grape varieties, Juan García, could prove to be the most interesting. Destined to become the Arribes del Duero DO.

### GALVEZ VDLT
**Castilla-La Mancha** Grape varieties in this large area southwest of Toledo are Tempranillo and Garnacha.

### GRAN CANARIA-EL MONTE VDLT
**Canary Islands** These wines are made from the Negra Común grape grown on Gran Canaria. Recently promoted to DO status under the appellation of Monte Lentiscal, but vintages of both are still available.

### GRANDES PAGOS DE CASTILLA
**Castilla-La Mancha & Castilla-León** Literally meaning "Great Domains of Castile," this is a private designation utilized by an important group of producers throughout both parts of Castile. The wines they will make under this banner could be DO, VdlT, or without regulations, but the corporate designation will take pride of place. The founding members include Mariano García, formerly of Vega Sicilia, plus various local government dignitaries, and the wine writer Víctor de la Serna. The president is Carlos Falcó. One to watch.

### LA GOMERA VDLT
**Canary Islands** Wines made from Forastera and Palomino grapes grown on the steep hillsides of La Gomera.

### LA RIBERA DEL ARLANZA VC
**Castilla-León** This is a declining viticultural area, but high-altitude vineyards growing Tempranillo vines show potential.

### LA SIERRA DE SALAMANCA VC
**Castilla-León** This area has potential, but some 70 percent of its shallow granitic terraces overlooking the Alagón River are planted with Rufete, a high-yielding, low-quality Portuguese grape.

### LAUJAR VC
**Andalucía** These are mostly rosado wines from an area better suited to the production of table grapes.

### LOPERA VC
**Andalucía** These are unfortified Pedro Ximénez wines, sold in bulk.

### LOS PALACIOS VC
**Andalucía** These wines are mostly *mistela* (a combination of unfermented grape juice and alcohol) made from the Mollar grape, or light, attenuated, white wines from Airén grapes.

### MANCHUELA VDLT
**Castilla-La Mancha** These are effectively the lesser wines produced in the DO areas of Jumilla, La Mancha, and Utiel-Requena. This is now a DO, but vintages of both are still available.

### MATANEGRA VDLT
**Extremadura** A very large area, Matanegra produces rather lackluster whites, but interesting Tempranillo-based reds.

### MONTANCHEZ VDLT
**Extremadura** This is a sizeable area in the province of Cáceres, producing rustic reds and whites from a mixture of varieties.

### MUNIESA VC
**Aragón** This area is planted mostly with Garnacha, and the wines tend to be dark and tough.

### PLA I LLEVANT DE MALLORCA VDLT
**Balearic Islands** Mallorca is seeking to replicate the fame of Majorca's Binissalem, which itself is but local. This is now a DO, although vintages of both are still available.

### POZOHONDO VDLT
**Castilla-La Mancha** The reds are made from Monastrell grapes, the whites from Airén. They have yet to achieve any reputation.

### RIBEIRA DO ULLA VC
**Galicia** Albarella (*syn*. Albarello) is supposedly the best varietal to look for here.

### RIBERA ALTA DEL GUADIANA VDLT
**Extremadura** There is promising potential here from both indigenous and foreign grape varieties.

### SACEDÓN-MONDÉJAR VDLT
**Castilla-La Mancha** An area southwest of Madrid producing mostly young, Tempranillo-based reds that are deep in color and often sold in bulk. The area is also called Mondéjar-Sacedón. This is now the DO Mondéjar, although vintages of both are still available.

### SAN MATEO VC
**Valencia** No reputation, not encountered, and no connection with the San Mateo festival in Rioja.

### SIERRA DE ALCARAZ VDLT
**Castilla-La Mancha** No reputation, not encountered, but I hear that this area is starting to show some serious promise, mainly through Manuel Manzaneque, and could be a candidate for DO.

### TIERRA BAJA DE ARAGON VDLT
**Aragón** These rough and ready Garnacha-dominated reds could well be improved over the next few years through increased cultivation of Tempranillo and Cabernet Sauvignon.

### TIERRA DE BARROS VDLT
**Extremadura** Bodegas Inviosa is demonstrating this area's potential for inexpensive fruity reds.

### TIERRA DEL VINO DE ZAMORA VDLT
**Castilla-León** This traditional winegrowing area between Toro and Zamora is best known for its Tempranillo-based reds.

### VALDEJALÓN VDLT
**Aragón** This has a similar history to that of Calatayud, but lags behind and has not quite the same potential. This VdlT is about to become a DO.

### VALDEVIMBRE-LOS OTEROS VDLT
**Castilla-León** Of all the VdlTs in Castilla-León, this area holds the most promise. Rocky-clay terraces either side of the Elsa River are planted with the Prieto Picudo grape, which produces wines that are similar to Tempranillo, but without the color. They are traditionally blended to good effect with Garnacha and the underrated Mencía grape.

### VALLE DEL CINCA
**Aragón** Exciting new area being developed by Codorníu's high-tech Naviana winery and estate.

### VALLE DEL MIÑO VDLT
**Galicia** These wines used to be sold as Ribeira del Sil prior to the best vineyards receiving DO status, while the remaining areas were relegated to this *vino de la tierra*.

# THE APPELLATIONS OF
# SPAIN

**Note** Regions or provinces in which appellations are located are given in bold beneath each heading. "DO" is short for *Denominación de Origen*. A synonym for a particular grape variety is indicated by "*syn.*"

## ABONA DO
### Canary Islands

This new appellation was established in 1996 for white wines made in the south of Tenerife, where the vines are grown on terraces that are also planted with potatoes. Before they gained DO status, these wines were sold under the names of Granadilla, San Miguel, and Vilaflor.

🍇 Listán, Malvasia

✔ *Viña Peraza*

## ALELLA DO
### Catalonia

This is a tiny, predominantly white appellation just north of Barcelona, where grapes are traditionally grown on windy granite hills, but due to urban development the DO was extended in 1989 into the colder, limestone vallès of the Cordillera Catalana. The red wines of Alella have good color, medium body, and a soft, fruity flavor. White and *rosado* are pale-colored, fresh, and delicate, with good acidity when made with grapes from the best north-facing slopes.

🍇 Chardonnay, Chenin Blanc, Garnacha, Garnacha Blanca, Garnacha Peluda, Pansá Rosada, Tempranillo, Xarel-lo

🍷 1–5 years (red), 1–2 years (white and *rosado*), 1–4 years (sweet)

✔ *Alta Alella Chardonnay* • *Alellasol* • *Marfil* • *Marqués de Alella*

## ALICANTE DO
### Valencia

These mild-climate red, white, and *rosado* wines are grown on dark, limey soil in the hills behind Alicante. The red wines are naturally deep in color and, when made in a *doble pasta* style, they can be ink-black and astringent, but younger, fruitier styles are emerging, as indeed they are among *rosados* and whites. Fortified Moscatels from this region are light and refreshing. A fortified wine of local repute called Fondillón is made from Monastrell grapes in a tawny port style.

🍇 Airén, Bobal, Garnacha, Garnacha Tinta, Meseguera, Moscatel Romano, Monastrell, Planta Fina, Tempranillo, Viura

🍷 6–12 years (reds)

✔ *Enrique Mendoza* • *Hijo de Luís García Poveda* (Costa Blanca)

## ALMANSA DO
### Castilla-La Mancha

This red and *rosado* appellation, which lies north of Jumilla and Yecla, bridges the heights of the central plains of La Mancha and the lowlands of Valencia. The red wines produced here are full-bodied and richly colored, with the best examples being quite smooth and fruity. Good examples of *rosado* can be fruity and clean.

🍇 Airén, Garnacha, Meseguera, Monastrell, Tempranillo

🍷 3–10 years (red), 1–3 years (*rosado*)

✔ *Alfonso Abellan* • *Carrion* • *Piqueras*

## AMPURDAN-COSTA BRAVA DO
### Catalonia

Lying at the foot of the narrowest section of the Pyrenees, this is the closest Spanish wine appellation to France. Most of the production is *rosado* and aimed at tourists, but the reds are much better, having a fairly deep, cherry-red color, medium to full body, and a crisp, plummy flavor. Whites are fruity and may be off-dry or slightly sweet, with a pale, often greenish-tinged color, and are sometimes *pétillant* (lightly sparkling).

🍇 Cariñena, Garnacha, Garnacha Blanca, Viura

🍷 2–5 years (red), 9–18 months (white and *rosado*)

✔ *Cavas de Ampurdán* • *Convinosa* • *Oliveda*

## BIERZO DO
### Castilla-León

One of the more exciting of Spain's less traditional DOs, Bierzo includes red, white, and *rosado* wines. Young reds stand out, being made from a minimum of 70 percent Mencía, an underrated variety capable of attractively aromatic wines.

🍇 Doña Blanca, Garnacha, Godello, Malvasía, Mencía, Palomino

🍷 1–4 years (red), 9–18 months (white and *rosado*)

✔ *Bodegas C. A. del Bierzo* • *Bodegas Palacio de Arganza* (non-DO wines) • *Pérez Caramés* • *Casa Valdaiga*

## BINISSALEM DO
### Balearic Islands

This appellation owes its existence primarily to just one man, José Ferrer, but there are at least two other producers of Majorca's best-known wine who are worth searching out. The white and *rosado* are simple, but the reds are slightly more serious and show some potential.

🍇 A minimum of 50% Manto Negro (for reds) or 70% Moll for whites, plus Callet, Monastrell, Parellada, Tempranillo, and Viura

🍷 Upon purchase

✔ *José L Ferrer* • *Jaume Mesquida* • *Miguel Oliver*

## BULLAS DO
### Murcia

This is a large region just south of Jumilla where the soil is so poor that, aside from vines, only olives and almonds can survive. The young red wines here are made primarily from Monastrell grapes and seem to have the best potential, but white and *rosado* wines are also allowed. Bullas is, however, a new appellation that has yet to prove its quality.

🍇 Airén, Garnacha, Monastrell, Tempranillo

## CALATAYUD DO
### Aragón

A patchwork of vineyards, mostly planted with Garnacha vines, tussle with fruit trees for meager sustenance from the poor, buff-colored rocky soil. Increasing the amount of Tempranillo vines and temperature-controlled stainless-steel vats will eventually improve the potential here, but the best wines are still simple, fresh, fruity *rosados*.

🍇 Garnacha, Garnacha Blanca, Juan Ibáñez, Malvasía, Mazuelo, Miguel de Arco, Moscatel Romano, Monastrell, Tempranillo, Viura

🍷 Upon purchase

✔ *Jalón* • *Langa*

## CAMPO DE BORJA DO
### Aragón

This name derives from the notorious Borgia family, who used to run things here at the height of their power in the late 15th century. The whites are fresh, but somewhat neutral. The reds and *rosados* are full, robust, and can be alcoholic, but are they are improving. Their character is sometimes compared with that Navarra once had, and Campo de Borja is now experimenting with Cabernet Sauvignon in the same way as Navarra once did. This is a wine area to watch.

🍇 Garnacha, Garnacha Blanca, Viura

🍷 3–8 years (red), 9–15 months (white and *rosado*)

✔ *Bordeje* • *Agrícola de Borja* (Borsao) • *C. A. del Campo Union* • *Agraria del Santo Cristo* • *C. A. del Campo San Juan Bautista*

## CARIÑENA DO
### Aragón

Cariñena's low rainfall accounted for the traditionally high alcohol content of these wines, but modern vinification now makes a fresher, lighter, fruitier, more aromatic style. Reds are the best of this appellation, especially from parcels of old Garnacha. Some deliberately maderized *rancio* wines are still produced.

🍇 Cabernet Sauvignon, Cariñena, Garnacha, Garnacha Blanca, Juan Ibáñez, Moscatel Romano, Monastrell, Parellada, Tempranillo, Viura

🍷 11–5 years (red), 9–18 months (white and *rosado*)

✔ *Añadas* • *Covinca* • *Gran Ducay*

## CATALUNYA DO
### Catalonia

With all styles of red, white, *rosado*, and fortified wine allowed, this basic, regional appellation offers innovative winemakers more flexibility than the supposedly superior, smaller, more specific DOs.

🍇 Bobal, Cabernet Franc, Cabernet Sauvignon, Cariñena, Chardonnay, Chenin Blanc, Garnatxa Blanca, Garnatxa Negra, Garnatxa Tintorera, Gewürztraminer, Macabeu, Malvasia, Malvasia de Sitges, Mazuela, Merlot, Monastrell, Muscat d'Alexandrie,

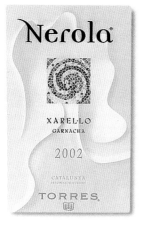

Parellada, Pedro Ximénez, Peluda, Picapoll, Pinot Blanc, Pinot Noir, Riesling, Sauvignon Blanc, Syrah, Tempranillo, Ull de Llebre, Xarel-lo

✓ *Mas Gil* (Clos d'Agon)

## CAVA DO
*See* Penedés: Cava Country p.318

## CHACOLÍ *or* TXAKOLINA DO
### Cantabria

This appellation is split into three areas: Chacolí de Alava (or Getariako Alava), Chacolí de Guetaria (or Getariako Txakolina), and Chacolí de Vizcaya (or Bizkaiko Txakolina). The alternative names are Basque and, as this is Basque country, these spellings will probably take precedence. The wines are mostly white, dry, and slightly *pétillant*, although a little red is also produced. As is typical of wines in the northeastern corner of the Iberian peninsula, they are high in acidity and low in alcohol.

Hondarribi Beltza, Hondarribi Zuri

✓ *Aretxondo* • *Txomin Etxaniz*

## CIGALES DO
### Castilla-Léon

This appellation is best known for fresh, fruity, light reds and *rosados*.

Albillo, Garnacha, Palomino, Tempranillo, Verdejo, Viura

✓ *C. A. de Cigales* (Escogido del Año, Viña Torondos) • *Emeterio Fernández* (La Legua Capricho) • *Frutos Villa* (Conde Ansurez, Viña Calderona) • *González Lara* (Fuente del Conde Rosado)

## CONCA DE BARBERA DO
### Catalonia

This once little-known appellation for red, white, and *rosado* wines from the hilly hinterland of Penedés promises to be one of Spain's most exciting areas. Chardonnay is outstanding here, as the rich, potentially complex Torres Milmanda demonstrates. Merlot is the most up-and-coming variety in the red department, but Trepat could mount a few surprises for fresh, easy-drinking styles of both red and *rosado*.

Cabernet Sauvignon, Garnacha, Merlot, Parellada, Tempranillo, Trepat, Viura

1–5 years

✓ *Torres* (Milmanda Chardonnay)

## CONDADO DE HUELVA DO
### Andalucía

The sweet dessert wines of this area, which is sandwiched between the sherry district of southwest Spain and the Algarve of Portugal, were mentioned by Chaucer in *The Canterbury Tales*. They ended up, however, as blending fodder for sherry. There are two basic types of fortified wine here: *pálido* (young, pale-straw color, dry, austere wines, of 14–17 percent alcohol) and *viejo* (solera-matured, mahogany-hued, in both dry and sweet styles that are deliberately oxidized, of 15–23 percent alcohol).

Garrido Fino, Palomino, Zalema

Upon purchase

## COSTERS DEL SEGRE DO
### Catalonia

This is a top-performing appellation taking in four areas of different viticultural character in the province of Lérida: Les Garrigues and Valls de Riu Corb (primarily white-grape districts); Artesa (planted almost entirely with black grapes); and Raimat (dominated by foreign grape varieties and has quickly assumed classic status through Codorníu's innovative Raimat Estate).

Cabernet Sauvignon, Cariñena, Chardonnay, Garnacha, Garnacha Blanca, Merlot, Monastrell, Parellada, Trepat, Ull de Llebre, Viura, Xarel-lo

2–6 years (red), 1–4 years (white)

✓ *Raïmat* • *Castell del Remei*

## DEHESA DEL CARRIZAL DO
### Castilla-La Mancha

In 2006 this became Spain's third *Pago*, or single-estate, appellation. Legend has it that Marcial Gómez Sequeira planted this semidesert area with Cabernet Sauvignon some 20 years ago on a bet, but it was so successful that he enlarged the vineyard to 54 acres (22 ha) with Chardonnay, Merlot, Syrah, and Tempranillo.

## DOMINIO DE VALDEPUSA DO
### Castilla-La Mancha

Owned by Carlos Falcó of Marqués de Griñón fame, Dominio de Valdepusa became Spain's first *Pago* appellation in 2001. It was Spain's first vineyard to use a new trellis system and drip-irrigation, both in 1973. More recently, Dominio de Valdepusa became the first vineyard in Europe to adopt the Australian PRD technique, and one of the first in the world to deploy dendrometers (*see* Glossary). Over the years, Falcó has employed a veritable gaggle of gurus (Lichine, Peynaud), with Rolland and Smart his current advisors. According to Smart, the red clay over limestone at Dominio de Valdepusa is identical to the famous *terra rossa* soil of Coonawarra.

Cabernet Sauvignon, Petit Verdot, Syrah

✓ *Marqués de Griñón* (Dominio de Valdepusa)

## EL HIERRO DO
### Canary Islands

El Hierro is the smallest and most westerly island in the archipelago, yet the local cooperative is one of the most advanced in the Canary Islands. Before gaining DO status, these wines were sold under the local names of Frontera and Valverde.

The Negramoll grape is best for reds and *rosados*, while the Verijadiego is best for whites.

Listán, Malvasía, Moscatel, Negramoll, Pedro Ximénez, Verdello, Verijadiego

✓ *Fontera*

## FINCA ELEZ DO
### Castilla-La Mancha

Located near the village of El Bonillo, in the heart of the Sierra de Alcaraz, this single-estate appellation was established in 2002 and is owned by Manuel Manzaneque, a theater director and producer.

Cabernet Sauvignon, Chardonnay, Merlot, Syrah, Tempranillo

✓ *Finca Elez*

## JEREZ *or* JEREZ-XÉRÈS-SHERRY DO
### *See* Sherry Country p.321

## JUMILLA DO
### Murcia

The high, hilly vineyards of Jumilla have never been affected by phylloxera, and most of the vines are still ungrafted. Almost all the wines produced here are red, and until recently were lackluster, unless made in a *doble pasta* style, which produces wines so thick and intense that they are in great demand for blending purposes throughout Spain and also abroad. The best reds carry the Jumilla Monastrell varietal appellation and can be very smooth, fruity, and aromatic, tending to improve with age. With earlier picking and temperature-controlled fermentation, lighter, more accessible wines are now being made that are best drunk when young and juicy, including some soft, fruity whites as well as some *rosados*.

Airén, Garnacha, Meseguera, Monastrell, Pedro Ximénez, Tempranillo

1–3 years (red, but up to 6 years for wines made in *doble pasta* style), 9–15 months (white and *rosado*)

✓ *Bleda* (Castillo Jumilla) • *Julia Roch e Hijos* • *Jumilla Union Vitivinícola* (Cerrillares, Incunable) • *Señorío del Condestable*

## LA MANCHA DO
### Castilla-La Mancha

Although its output remains enormous, accounting for some 40 percent of all Spanish wines produced, the wine land of Don Quixote has improved tremendously since the 1980s. Many producers now harvest much earlier than previously and ferment at cooler temperatures (sometimes too cool), achieving fresher, lighter, more aromatic wines. The best wines of La Mancha used to be made in Valdepeñas DO, and that appellation still boasts most of the best, but the arrival of Alejandro Fernández (El Vinculo) in 1999 has raised the stakes. Who would have thought that any wine bearing "La Mancha" could be considered up-and-coming?

🍇 Airén, Cabernet Sauvignon, Garnacha, Merlot, Moravia, Pardina, Tempranillo, Viura

🍷 1–4 years (red), 9–15 months (white and *rosado*)

✓ *Ayuso* (Estola Gran Reserva) • *Vinícola de Castilla* (Castillo de Alhambra, Señorío de Guadianeja) • *Jesús Diaz e Hijos* • *El Vinculo* • *C. Españolas* (Fuente del Ritmo) • *Hermanos Morales* (Gran Créacion) • *C. A. del Campo Nuestra Señora de Manjavacas* (Zagarrón) • *C. A. del Campo Nuestra Padre Jesús de Perdon* (Casa la Teja, Lazarillo, Yuntero) • *Rama Corta* • *Rodriguez y Berger* (Viña Santa Elena) • *Julián Santos* • *Torres Filoso* (Arboles de Castollejo)

## LA PALMA DO
### Canary Islands

This new appellation was established in 1995 for the island of La Palma. It was in Fuencaliente, in the south of the island, that the famed "Canary Sack" of Shakespeare's time was produced, and the grape responsible, Malvasia, still grows here, amid four smoking volcanoes, in the same sort of craterlike depressions that abound on Lanzarote. An oddity aged in pine casks and curiously called Vino del Tea ("Tea" being the local name for a particular species of pine) is available in the north of the island, but only the most ardent admirers of Retsina should search it out.

🍇 Bujariego, Gual, Listán, Malvasia, Negramoll

✓ *Hoyo de Mazo*

## LANZAROTE DO
### Canary Islands

This new appellation was established in 1995 for the island of Lanzarote, where the lunar landscape is dotted with vines in craterlike depressions, protected by low stone walls. The most spectacular example of this weirdly beautiful form of viticulture can be viewed at La Geria, an area west of Arrecife where no fewer than 5,000 acres (2,000 hectares) of such vineyards are to be found.

🍇 include: Caleta, Diego, Listán, Malvasia

## MÁLAGA DO
### Andalucía

Just northeast of Jerez in southern Spain, the coastal vineyards of Málaga produce one of the most underrated classic dessert wines in the world. Most of this is matured by the *solera* system, involving some six scales (*see* Sherry Country, p321) and may be blended in a sherrylike manner using various grape-based coloring and sweetening agents, such as *arrope*, *vino de color, vino tierno,* and *vino maestro.* The color of these fortified wines can range from gold through tawny to brown and red, depending on the style of Málaga, its age, and method of maturation, its degree of sweetness, and the grape variety used.

Málaga may be any one of the following. Dulce Color is a dark, medium-bodied Málaga that has been sweetened with *arrope.* Lágrima is made from free-run juice only, and is the most luscious of all Málaga styles. Moscatel is a sweet, rich, raisiny, medium- to full-bodied wine that is similar to the Jerez version, only more luscious. Old Solera has the most finesse, depth, and length of all Málagas and is capable of complexity rather than lusciousness. It is medium- to full-bodied, still sweet yet with a dry finish. Oscuro is a dark, sweet Málaga that has been sweetened with *arrope* and colored by *vino de color.* Pajarette or Paxarete is darkish in color, and less sweet, but more alcoholic, than other Málagas. Pedro Ximénez is a smooth, sweet, deliciously rich varietal wine with an intense flavor that is similar in character to the Jerez version. Seco is a pale, dry, tangy wine with a distinctive creamy hazelnut character.

🍇 Moscatel, Pedro Ximénez

🍷 Upon purchase (although it can last, but not improve, for several years)

✓ *Scholtz Hermanos* • *Pérez Texeira* • *Larios*

## MANCHUELA DO
### Castilla-La Mancha

This is a very large region, encompassing La Mancha, Ribera del Júcar, Utiel-Requena, and Almansa, with cooperatives accounting for two-thirds of the *bodegas,* and a quality that is seldom better than an acceptable quaff. Much is a lot worse. The delicious red wines of Finca Sandova are, however, a class apart, and the improving Gualberto may one day reach a similar level.

🍇 Albillo, Bobal, Cabernet Sauvignon, Cencibel, Chardonnay, Garnacha, Macabéo, Merlot, Monastrell, Moravia Dulce, Sauvignon Blanc, Syrah, Verdejo

✓ *Finca Sandoval* • *Gualberto*

## MANZANILLA DO
### See Sherry Country p.321

## MÉNTRIDA DO
### Castilla-La Mancha

Cheap wine, still mostly consumed locally, but yields have dropped, and a number of *bodegas* have improved their facilities, although it is too early to confirm a similar improvement in quality, as there are still too many deep-colored, coarse reds and alcoholic *rosados.*

🍇 Garnacha, Tempranillo

## MONDÉJAR DO
### Castilla-La Mancha

Although fewer bulk wines are being produced here since Mondéjar achieved DO status, the wines are still mostly uninspiring, with Mariscal the solitary producer that seems interested in improving quality.

🍇 Airen, Cabernet Sauvignon, Garnacha, Jaén, Macabéo, Malvar, Tempranillo, Torrontés

✓ *Mariscal*

## MONSTANT DO
### Catalonia

A new and potentially exciting appellation clasping the eastern, western, and southern edges of Priorat.

🍇 Cabernet Sauvignon, Cariñena, Garnacha, Merlot, Monastrell, Syrah, Tempranillo

✓ *Celler de Capéanes* (Mas Picosa) • *Fra Guerau* • *Laurona*

## MONTERREI DO
### Galicia

This area was first awarded a provisional DO in the early 1980s, but this was revoked when too few of its growers showed any interest in modernizing their estates. However, some progress was made in the late 1980s, and this appellation has now been granted full DO status.

🍇 Alicante, Doña Blanca, Godello, Gran Negro, Mencía, Mouratón, Palomino

✓ *Pazo Pondal* (Lenda Pondal)

## MONTILLA-MORILES DO
### Andalucía

The sherrylike wines of Montilla fall into three categories: *generosos* (fortified *finos, amontillados, olorosos,* and magnificent PX); unfortified traditional wines (cream, medium, and dry at 14.5 percent alcohol); and *jóvenes afrutados* (ghastly).

🍇 Airén, Baladí, Moscatel, Pedro Ximénez, Torrontés

🍷 Can be kept, but consume upon opening

✓ *Marqués de la Sierra* • *Alvear* • *Mora Chacon* • *Gracia Hermanos* • *Perez Barquero* • *Rodriguez Chiachio*

## NAVARRA DO
### See Rioja and Navarra p.312

## PENEDÈS DO
*See* Penedès: Cava Country p.318

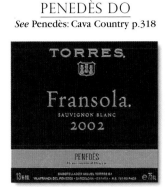

## PLA DE BAGES DO
### Catalonia

Winemaking is an old tradition in Bages, and yet this is an up-and-coming DO, with many newly planted vineyards and a small but growing band of modern *bodegas*, of which Massies d'Avinyó clearly leads the way. "Bages" is a derivative of Bacchus, the name of the Roman god of wine.

🍇 Chardonnay, Garnatxa, Macabéo, Malbec, Merlot, Picapoll, Pinot Noir, Sauvignon Blanc, Sumoll, Tempranillo

✓ *Massies d'Avinyó*

## PLA I LEVANT DO
### Mallorca

The island's newest appellation produces some of its best wines.

🍇 Cabernet Sauvignon, Callet, Chardonnay, Frogoneu, Manto Negro, Macabéo, Merlot, Moscatel, Parellada, Pinot Noir, Prensal Blanc, Syrah, Tempranillo

✓ *Miquel Geabert • Miquel Oliver*

## PRIORAT DOCA
### Catalonia

This area has a dry climate and poor soil, in which the vines' roots spread everywhere in search of moisture, the local saying being that Priorat vines can suck water out of stone. The best wines are currently being made around the hilltop town of Gratallops, by a group of young winemakers led by Bordeaux-trained Riojan oenologist Alvaro Palacios, who brought with him a wealth of experience from Château Pétrus to the Napa Valley. New-style reds are huge, serious, and stunningly rich, but those of the old style tend to be heavy, overalcoholic, and oxidized, although the best traditional wines fall somewhere in between. One of the country's oldest appellations, Priorat is one of the Spanish wine industry's superstars. The use of the spelling "Priorato" has been dropped on bottles in favor of the Catalan version "Priorat," and DOQ, the Catalan equivalent of DOCa, is now prevalent.

🍇 Cabernet Sauvignon, Cariñena, Garnacha, Garnacha Blanca, Merlot, Monastrell, Pedro Ximénez, Syrah, Viura

🍷 5–15 years (red)

✓ *Alvaro Palacios* ⓑ (Finca Dofí, Clos l'Ermita, Las Terrasses) • *René Barbier* (Clos Mogador) • *Clos Erasmus* • *Costers del Siurana* (Clos de l'Obac, Miserere) • *Masia Barril* • *De Muller* • *Scala Dei* (Cartoixa, El Cipres, Novell) • *Vinicola del Priorato* (Mas d'Alba, Onix)

## RÍAS BAIXAS DO
### Galicia

Spain's fastest-rising star in the DO firmament, the Rías Baixas appellation covers various red, white, and *rosado* wines, but the best-known and most enjoyable wines are the softly perfumed, zippy whites made from low-yielding Albariño grapes, which can have real depth and fruit, and a fresh, lively acidity. Although I have always admired the best of these wines, I did wonder whether they are worth what appeared to be an increasingly high price. At the table, however, they accompany fine food beautifully, which in my book makes even the most expensive Rías Baixas well worth the price demanded for it.

🍇 Albariño, Brancellao, Caíño Blanco, Caíño Tinto, Espadeiro, Loureira Blanca, Loureira Tinta, Mencía, Sousón, Torrontés, Treixadura

🍷 1–3 years

✓ *Albariño do Salnes • Pazo de Barrantes • Cardallal • Lagar de Cevera • del Palacio de Fefiñanes • Granxa Fillaboa • Morgadio-Agromiño • Pazo Pondal • de Vilariño Cambados* (Martín Códax, Organistrum) • *Santiago Ruíz*

## RIBEIRA SACRA DO
### Galicia

The most widely planted grape variety here is Palomino, but on the steep, terraced vineyards of Ribeira Sacra, Albariño is far more exciting, and the Mencía variety also shows promise for red wines.

🍇 Albariño, Brancellao, Caíño, Doña Blanca, Espadeiro, Ferrón, Godello, Garnacha, Loureira, Loureira Tinta, Mencía, Merenzao, Negrada, Palomino, Sousón, Torrontés

🍷 1–3 years

✓ *Adegas Moure* (Albariño Abadia da Cova)

## RIBEIRO DO
### Galicia

Due to the Atlantic-influenced climate of northwest Spain, the styles of Ribeiro's red and white wines reflect that of Portugal's Vinhos Verdes, except that they are somewhat more fruity and aromatic. The very best examples possess a wonderfully fresh, pure, vibrancy of fruit.

🍇 Albariño, Albillo, Brancellao, Caíño, Ferrón, Garnacha, Godello, Jerez, Loureira, Mencía, Sousón, Tempranillo, Torrontés, Treixadura, Viura

🍷 9–18 months

✓ *Alanis • Arsenio Paz • Rivera • C. A. del Ribeiro*

## RIBERA DEL DUERO DO
### Castilla-León

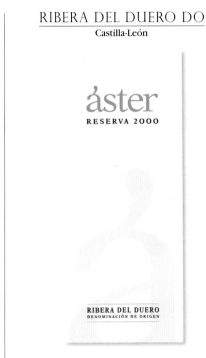

From the upper reaches of the Duero River (which becomes the Douro, once it crosses the Portuguese border), the *rosados* are fresh, dry, fruity wines of a *clarete* or *claro* style, but are nowhere near the class of the best reds, which have a truly dense, black color and are packed solid with rich, oaky-sweet, plummy-blackcurranty fruit flavors.

Ribera del Duero DO built its reputation on "Vega Sicilia," formerly Spain's most expensive wine. In the first edition of this book, I categorically stated that contrary to the informed opinion of many other wine critics, this was not Spain's greatest red wine, although it was potentially the best. The problem was that 10 or more years in wood took its toll on the fruit in a way that would destroy many of the greatest wines of Bordeaux.

There was also no logic to the duration and mode of aging at Vega Sicilia, which occurred in different sizes and ages of wooden casks, the various vintages being transferred from one vessel to another simply to fulfill the logistical necessity of moving the wines around in order to accommodate the incoming harvest. Since the first edition, however, Vega Sicilia has given its wines no more than six years in wood and now has a more disciplined approach to how long wines spend in various types and ages of casks, including new oak *barriques*. It is once again one of Spain's greatest wines, but not necessarily the greatest Ribera del Duero, with a handful of *bodegas* capable of matching, sometimes surpassing, the quality of Vega Sicilia. These include Aalto, Vega Sicilia's own Alion, Alejándro Fernández's Pesquera, Condado de Haza (also owned by Fernández), Domino de Pingus, and Pago de los Capellanes, with a few others waiting in the wings.

🍇 Cabernet Sauvignon, Garnacha, Malbec, Merlot, Pardina, Tinto del País

🍷 3–8 years (modern red), 5–25 years (traditional red), 1–2 years (*rosado*)

✓ *Aalto • Abadía Retuerta • Alión • Arzuaga Condado de Haza • Dominio de Pingus* ⓑ *• Emelio Moro • Ismael Arroyo • Julio Cesar Conde Delgado y Otros* (Neo) *• O Fournier* (Alfa Spiga) *• Legaris • Mauro • Pago de Carraovejas • Pago de los Capellanes •*

Pagos del Rey • Pérez Pascuas (Viña Pedrosa) • Pesquera • Pomar Vinédos • Real Sitio de Ventosilla (Prado Rey) • Reyes • Sastre • Uvaguilera Aguilera • Vega Sicilia (including Valbuena)

## RIBERA DEL GUADIANA DO
### Extramadura

A group of six *vinos de la tierra* (Cañamero, Matanegra, Montanchez, Ribera Alta, Ribera Baja, and Tierra de Barros), which retain this classification, but also form subzones of the Ribera del Guadiana DO, entitling them to make wines under two different origins of quality.

✓ *La de Barros* • *Santa Mariña*

## RIBERA DEL JÚCAR DO
### Castilla-La Mancha

This new red-wine DO since the 2003 vintage encompasses some of La Mancha's best vineyards. Although the grapes authorized include Cabernet Sauvignon, Merlot, Pinot Noir, and Syrah, most wines released so far are cheap Tempranillo or Tempranillo-based blends.

## RIOJA DOCA
### See Rioja and Navarra p.312

## RUEDA DO
### Castilla-León

This small district downriver from Ribeiro del Duero is known for fresh, crisp, dry white wines made almost entirely from Verdejo, but traditionally the wines were fortified *in fino* (Palido Rueda) and *rancio* (Dorado Rueda) styles, and these can still be found. A traditional method Rueda Espumoso is also allowed.

🍇 Palomino, Sauvignon Blanc, Verdejo, Viura
🍷 1–2 years

---

✓ *Agricola Castellana* • *Frutos Villa* (Viña Morejona) • *Marqués de Griñón* • *Marqués de Riscal*

## SHERRY *or* JEREZ-XÉRÈS-SHERRY DO
### See Sherry Country p.321

## SIERRAS DE MÁLAGA DO
### Andalucía

Although Málaga is one of Spain's oldest DOs, this appellation was granted in 2001, for an area that is higher in altitude than Málaga, and for red and white wines that cannot be fortified.

🍇 Airén, Cabernet Franc, Cabernet Sauvignon, Chardonnay, Colombard, Doradilla, Garnacha, Macabeo, Merlot, Moscatel d'Alejandrie, Moscatel Morisco, Pedro Ximénez, Petit Verdot, Pinot Noir, Romé, Sauvignon Blanc, Syrah, Tempranillo

✓ *F. Schatz* ◉

## SITGES
### Catalonia

This is a famous, but rare, non-DO fortified Malvasia and Moscatel wine that is made just south of the outskirts of Barcelona, from grapes that are allowed to shrivel on the vine.

✓ *Cellers Robert*

## SOMONTANO DO
### Aragón

Set at the foot of the Pyrenees mountains, between the regions of Penedés and Navarra, Somontano is destined to become one of Spain's greatest wine regions. Chardonnay is by far the best grape grown here for serious, barrel-fermented white wines, but both Tempranillo and Cabernet Sauvignon show superb potential for making fragrant reds with a lively richness of fruit.

🍇 Alcañón, Cabernet Sauvignon, Chardonnay, Garnacha, Garnacha Blanca, Moristel, Parreleta, Tempranillo, Viura
🍷 2–5 years (red), 1–3 years (white)

✓ *Aragonesa* • *Otto Bestué* • *Viñas del Vero* • *Enate* • *Lalanne* • *Pirineos*

---

## TACORONTE-ACENTEJO DO
### Canary Islands

Established in 1992, this is the oldest Canary Island appellation and, so far, it has proved to be the best, although it is too early to tell how the others will fare.

🍇 Castellano, Gual, Listán, Listán Negro, Malvasía, Marmajuelo, Moscatel, Negra Común, Negramoll, Pedro Ximénez, Tintillo, Torrontés, Verdello

✓ *El Lomo* • *Monje* • *Viña Norte*

## TARRAGONA DO
### Catalonia

This is the largest appellation in Catalonia, but its potential quality is modest compared with that of neighboring Penedés. Having said that, Australian winemakers Nick Butler and Mark Nairn have been quietly raising standards at Pedro Rovira, using hands-off methods to retain as much natural character in the wine as possible. The best red, white, and *rosado* from this region can all be fresh, fruity, and rewarding. Even the local fortified wine, which is sold as Tarragona Classico, can be worth looking out for.

🍇 Cariñena, Garnacha, Garnacha Blanca, Parellada, Tempranillo, Viura, Xarel-lo
🍷 1–5 years (red), 1–2 years (white and rosado)

✓ *C. A. de Valls* • *José Lopez Beltrán* (Don Beltrán) • *Pedro Masana* (non-DO wines) • *De Müller* (Moscatel Seco, Parxete) • *Pedro Rovira*

## TERRA ALTA DO
### Catalonia

This slowly improving appellation lies in the highlands well away from the coast. It produces some good, everyday-drinking red and white wines, but the best sites are not always planted with the most suitable varieties and have to compete with Cava growers. It is advisable to avoid the local sweet, fortified *mistela*.

🍇 Cabernet Sauvignon, Cariñena, Garnacha, Garnacha Blanca, Merlot, Moscatel, Parellada, Tempranillo, Viura
🍷 1–2 years

✓ *C. A. Gandesa* • *C. A. la Hermandad* • *Pedro Rovira* (Alta Mar, Viña d'Irto) • *Vinalba dels Arcs* (Vall de Berrús)

## TORO DO
### Castilla-León

The exciting quality of Toro wines today is a very recent phenomenon, built on a sudden influx of high-profile names, which has tripled the number of *bodegas* since 2000. When this DO was established in 1987, there were just four *bodegas*, the decrepit local cooperative dominated production, and the quality was really quite dire. By 2000, the number of *bodegas* had increased to 18, but, more importantly, the Álvarez family of Vega Sicilia fame had been purchasing land under an assumed name since 1997, and after this was announced in 2002, the floodgates opened, so that at the last count there were 40 *bodegas*. Consequently, land prices have soared, and the battle for Toro's true quality has only just begun. Vega Sicilia's rival, Alejándro Fernández of Pesquera, followed suit in 1998, but his great wine Dehesa La Granja is made from vines growing just outside this DO, near Zamora. I suspect this may be a single-estate DO in waiting.

🌿 Garnacha, Malvasía, Tinta de Toro, Verdejo Blanco

🍷 2–8 years (red), 1–3 years (white)

✓ *Alquiriz • Bajoz • Jacques & François Lurton (El Albar Excelencia, Campo Eliseo) • Numanthia • Fariña (Gran Colegiata, Gran Colegiata Campus) • Maurodós*

## TXAKOLINA DO
### *See* Chacolí DO

## UCLÉS DO
### Castilla-La Mancha

The first vintage allowed for this new red-wine DO was 2005. This DO encompasses some of La Mancha's best high-altitude vineyards, located on either side of the Altomira mountains. Authorized grapes include Cabernet Sauvignon, Garnacha, Merlot, Syrah, and Tempranillo, with a sliding scale of maximum yield ranging from 8,000 kg/ha for 6-year-old vines, down to 5,000 kg/ha for vines that are 40 years or older.

## UTIEL-REQUENA DO
### Valencia

This large and important, essentially red-wine district is situated in the extreme west of the province of Valencia. Although distilling wine and the *doble pasta* process were once the area's forte, softer, more palatable reds are now being made, and the best dry *rosados* are fresh and delicate for such sunny climes.

🌿 Bobal, Garnacha, Meseguera, Tardana, Tempranillo, Viura

🍷 2–5 years (red), 9–18 months (*rosados*)

✓ *Augusto Egli (Casa Lo Alto)*

## VALDEORRAS DO
### Galicia

Until Rías Baixas came on the scene, this was Galicia's most promising district. With vines planted on terraced, slaty hillsides flanking the Sil River and Valdeorras's northern, wet, Atlantic-influenced climate, these wines have never been overburdened with alcohol, as so much Spanish wine was once upon a time, and refreshing acidity is part of their charm. The best wineries have now been modernized and are even better than they used to be, particularly for white wines made from the Godello grape.

🌿 Doña Blanca, Garnacha, Godello, Gran Negro, Lado, María Ardoña, Mencía,

Merenzao, Palomino

🍷 1–4 years (red), 1 year (white and *rosado*)

✓ *Godeval • Guitián • Jesus Nazareno • Joaquín Rebolledo*

## VALDEPEÑAS DO
### Castilla-La Mancha

This was once Castilla-La Mancha's solitary fine-wine area. Despite the torrid heat (the climate has been described as nine months of winter, three months of hell) and an apathetic attitude held by far too many producers, some terrific wines are being made here by a minority of wineries, and they represent very good value. The rich, red, stony soil hides a water-retentive limestone base that helps offset the lack of rainfall. The best reds are medium- to full-bodied, pure Tempranillo, with a wonderfully rich yet well-balanced flavor, and more and more new-oak influence. The *rosados* can be smooth and fruity, but it would take a complete overhaul of the vineyards, replanting them with something decent, to make the white wines appealing, although there is really no excuse for their not being fresh.

🌿 Airén, Tempranillo

🍷 2–6 years (red), 9–18 months (*rosado*)

✓ *Miguel Calatayud • J A Megía • Los Llanos • Luis Megía (Marqués de Gastañaga) • Felix Solis (Viña Albali Reserva) • Casa de la Viña (Vega de Moriz)*

## VALENCIA DO
### Valencia

This area was once renowned for its heavy, alcoholic, and low-quality *vino de mesa*. However, most modern wineries produce much lighter wines than before, and they are at least fresh and drinkable. There are some good reds from the Monastrell grape, which are smooth and medium-bodied, and these wines may sometimes be aged in oak. The deliciously sweet and raisiny Moscatel is consistently excellent value, often performing well under blind conditions against French Muscat de Beaumes de Venise that sells for twice the price.

🌿 Forcayat, Garnacha, Malvasía, Meseguera, Monastrell, Moscatel, Pedro Ximénez, Planta Fina, Tempranillo, Tortosí, Viura

🍷 1–4 years (red), 9–18 months (white and *rosado*), upon opening (Moscatel)

✓ *C. A. de Villar • Vícente Gandía • Augusto Egli (particularly good-value Moscatel) • Schenk (Cavas Murviedro) • Tierra Hernández*

## VALLE DE GÜÍMAR DO
### Canary Islands

This appellation was established in 1996 for wines from the eastern side of Tenerife, just south of downtown Santa Cruz. The vineyards here abut cultivated fields, which are irrigated and thus indirectly feed these vines. Before gaining DO status, these wines were not even sold locally, but consumed by the people who produced them.

🌿 Listán, Listán Negro, Negramoll

## VALLE DE LA OROTAVA DO
### Canary Islands

Established in 1996, this appellation covers wines produced on the lush, northern side of Tenerife, between the appellations of Tacoronte-Acentejo and Ycoden-Daute-Isora. Before they were granted DO status, these wines were sold

under the *vino de la tierra* (literally "country wine") of La Orotava-Los Realos.

🌿 Listán, Listán Negro

## VINOS DE MADRID DO
### Madrid

Much admired by Casanova, who sought refuge in Madrid at a time when the capital was rapidly expanding at the expense of its vineyards, these wines probably assumed a rarity value that outshone their intrinsic quality. By extending the appellation well beyond its fast-disappearing 18th-century boundaries, Vinos de Madrid was resurrected in 1990, although you would have to be a greater lover of these wines than Casanova to declare your open admiration for them. There are, however, a couple of exceptions to the rule, and one of these, Jesús Díaz e Hijos, is exceptional by any standards.

🌿 Airén, Albillo, Garnacha, Malvar, Tinto Fino

🍷 Upon purchase (2–3 years for recommended wines)

✓ *Francisco Figuero • Jesús Díaz e Hijos*

## XÉRÈS *or* JEREZ-XÉRÈS-SHERRY DO
### *See* Sherry Country p.321

## YCODEN-DAUTE-ISORA DO
### Canary Islands

This DO was established in 1995 for the wines that are produced on the northwestern corner of the island of Tenerife. In this area, the grapes are usually grown on terraces, which are often irrigated. Before they gained DO status, these wines were sold under the *vino de la tierra* of Icod de Los Vinos, a name that recalls their long-lost fame. After the Battle of Trafalgar, the Canaries were a favorite watering hole with the British Royal Navy, and the orange-tinged white wines of this area were apparently enjoyed by all ranks.

🌿 Listán, Listán Negro

## YECLA CAMPO ARRIBA DO
### *See* Yecla DO

## YECLA DO
### Murcia

You might think that these stony-limestone vineyards between Alicante and Jumilla should do rather well in terms of quality, but although some decent wines can be found, nothing special stands out.

The reds produced here are either ink-black, *doble pasta*-style wines, or are cherry-colored, generally with good body and fruit. Wines from the Campo Arriba zone in the north of this appellation are permitted to add this name to the Yecla DO if they are either red or *rosado*, and are made from 100 percent Monastrell grapes harvested at almost half the yield required elsewhere in Yecla. The white wines produced in Yecla are at their best fresh, clean, and pleasantly fruity, but, again, tend not to be remarkable.

🌿 Garnacha, Meseguera, Monastrell, Verdil

🍷 2–5 years (red, but 3–6 years for Yecla Campo Arriba), 1–2 years (white and *rosado*)

✓ *Castaño (Pozuelo, Las Gruesas) • Ochoa Palao (Cuvée Prestige)*

# RIOJA AND NAVARRA

*The first wine to receive DOCa status, Spain's highest classification, Rioja is without doubt the country's greatest fine-wine region. Neighboring Navarra, which was once regarded as the country's best source of rosado but little else, is slowly developing a reputation for other styles, having upgraded its vineyards and wineries.*

ONLY A SHORT DRIVE from the shabby suburbs of the commercial city of Bilbao, and the dramatic beauty of an upland valley becomes apparent, rich with architectural treasures of the 12th century, isolated hilltop *pueblos*, a philanthropic people, a generous tradition, and a hearty cuisine.

## RIOJA

Rioja is oaky, and all attempts to rid the wine of oak are doomed to failure. Oak is the basis of its fame and the reason it became Spain's first and greatest red-wine success, and while critics who suggest that these wines are too oaky for today's more

sophisticated consumers may have a point, there is precious little left in most Rioja once you take away the oak.

It was the French who originally blessed the wines of this region with their unmistakable sweet-vanilla oak identity. As early as the 18th century, a few enlightened *Riojanos* had looked to France, Bordeaux particularly, to improve their winemaking skills. The transformation that resulted was subtle compared to the radical changes that occurred in Rioja in the 1840s and 1860s, after phylloxera, a louse that attacks vine roots, had wreaked havoc on French vineyards. A number of *vignerons*, mostly *Bordelais* but some Burgundian too, gave up hope of reviving their own vineyards and descended upon Rioja to set up new wineries. Their methods dramatically improved the quality and style of Rioja, while other Frenchmen, mostly merchants from Bordeaux, opened up an instantly lucrative trade for the wine, as they desperately sought to boost the dwindling produce of their own devastated vineyards.

## *Origins*

Wine has been made in Rioja since at least the 2nd century BC, when the Romans conquered the area. Rioja was sufficiently well respected by 1560 that its producers forbade the use of grapes from outside the region, guaranteeing the authenticity of their

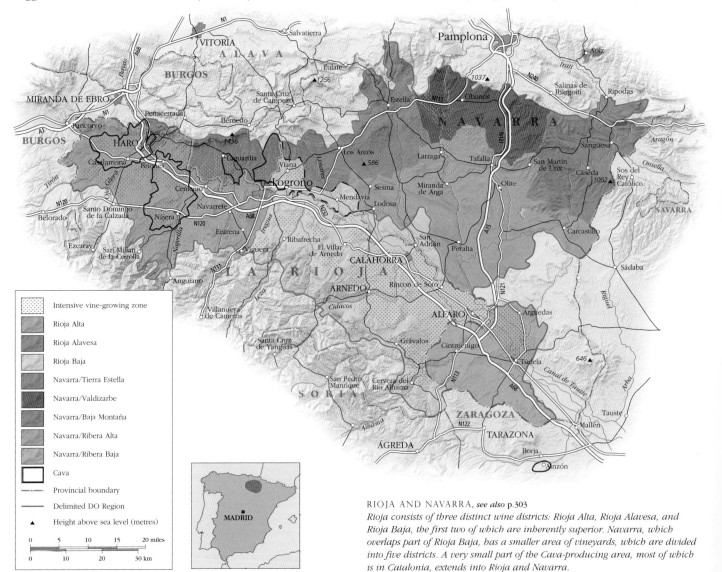

Intensive vine-growing zone

Rioja Alta

Rioja Alavesa

Rioja Baja

Navarra/Tierra Estella

Navarra/Valdizarbe

Navarra/Baja Montaña

Navarra/Ribera Alta

Navarra/Ribera Baja

Cava

— — — Provincial boundary

———— Delimited DO Region

▲ Height above sea level (metres)

0   5   10   15   20 miles
0   10   20   30 km

RIOJA AND NAVARRA, *see also p.303*
*Rioja consists of three distinct wine districts: Rioja Alta, Rioja Alavesa, and Rioja Baja, the first two of which are inherently superior. Navarra, which overlaps part of Rioja Baja, has a smaller area of vineyards, which are divided into five districts. A very small part of the Cava-producing area, most of which is in Catalonia, extends into Rioja and Navarra.*

wines with a brand on the *pellejos* (goat skins) in which they were transported. Wooden barrels came into use in the 18th century, but were five times the size of casks today and it was not until 1860 at Marqués de Riscal that the first Bordeaux *barriques* were used (although there seems to be evidence that Manuel Quintano was the first, *c.*1800). One particularly influential Frenchman, Jean Pineau, was employed to teach French methods to local growers. In 1868, upon completion of his contract, Pineau was employed by Don Camilo Hurtado de Amezaga, the Marqués de Riscal, who was an admirer of Médoc wines and had lived in Bordeaux for 15 years. He had planted Cabernet Sauvignon on his estate in 1863 and wanted Pineau to develop his new *bodega* in the manner of the most advanced wine châteaux in the Médoc.

## RIOJA'S CLASSIC WINE DISTRICTS

Rioja's vineyards are located along the Ebro Valley, between Haro and Alfaro, and throughout its hinterland, with vines clustered around many of the Ebro's tributaries, one of which, the Oja River, has given its name to the region. Most Rioja is red and blended from wines or grapes (primarily Tempranillo and Garnacha) originating from the region's three districts (Rioja Alta, Rioja Alavesa, and Rioja Baja), although many of the best-quality are single-district wines and a handful of single-estate Rioja have also emerged in recent years.

### Rioja Alta

Logroño and Haro, the principal towns of Rioja, are both in the Rioja Alta. Logroño is a very big town by Spanish standards, but Haro, at the western edge of the region, is an enclosed hilltop community and a much smaller, far more charming, older, and traditional place. The area's wine is Rioja's fullest in terms of fruit and concentration, and can be velvety smooth. Bodegas Muga makes fine examples of pure Rioja Alta, as do CVNE (Compañía Vinícola del Norte de España)—in the form of their Imperial line—in nine years out of every ten.

### Rioja Alavesa

There are no large towns in the Alavesa, a district that is similar in climate to the Alta. Wines produced here are Rioja's fullest in body and reveal a much firmer character than those of the Alta and the Baja, with greater acidity. It was to the Alavesa that Pedro Domecq came, after years of intensive research, to plant a vast estate of 985 acres (400 hectares), cultivating his vines on wires as opposed to

using the bush method traditional to the region. Aside from Bodegas Domecq, which produces mainly pure Alavesa wines, Remelluri and Contino, two single-estate Alavesas, are both typical of the district.

### Rioja Baja

Baja is a semiarid area influenced by the Mediterranean, and is hotter, sunnier, and drier than the Alta and the Alavesa, with rainfall averaging between 15 and 17 inches (38 and 43 centimeters) per year, but falling as low as 10 inches (25 centimeters) at Alfaro in the south. Some 20 percent of the vines growing here come within, and can claim, the Navarra appellation. The wines are deep-colored and very alcoholic, some as strong as 18 percent, but lack acidity, aroma, and finesse, and are best used for blending.

## NAVARRA

The wine-growing region of Navarra overlaps part of the Rioja Baja, but although not quite in the same league as Rioja in general, it is capable of producing some fine wines of exceptional value.

Recent marketing successes have halted the decline in Navarra's vineyards and encouraged various ambitious trials with foreign grapes such as Merlot, while previous experimental varieties such as Cabernet Sauvignon are now fully recommended. According to the Estación de Viticultura y Enología de Navarra (EVENA), Spain's most advanced viticultural and oenological research station, these Bordeaux varieties are ideally suited to Navarra's soil and climate.

### A rosy past

Navarra was once virtually synonymous with *rosado* and this style still accounts for almost half of total production, but what has really held back the reputation of this area has been the Garnacha (*syn.* Grenache) grape. This modest-quality grape variety can make good *rosado*, but except as part of a blend, rarely excels in red wines. Garnacha makes up more than 65 percent of Navarra's vines, so the region is ill equipped to develop beyond its *rosado* horizon. Furthermore, Tempranillo, the grape upon which Rioja's success has been built and indubitably Spain's finest red-wine variety, represents just 15 percent of Navarra's vines. This proportion has, however, doubled since 1990 and with Tempranillo and Cabernet Sauvignon making up 60 percent and 20 percent respectively of all new vines currently being planted, Navarra is set to achieve a tremendous boost in quality.

According to Javier Ochoa, former chief oenologist at EVENA, the perfect Navarra blend should be something in the order of

## GRAPE VARIETIES IN RIOJA

Although there has been a recent trend toward pure varietal wines (particularly Tempranillo for *tinto* and Viura for *blanco*), most Rioja is blended, thus its character and quality depend to a large extent upon the producer's own house style. In addition to blending the strengths and weaknesses of different *terroirs*, there is usually an attempt to balance the various varietal characteristics of one or more of the seven grapes that are permitted in Rioja. These grape varieties are: Tempranillo, Garnacha, Graciano, Mazuelo, Viura, Malvasia, and the little-utilized Garnacha Blanca.

### A TYPICAL RED RIOJA BLEND

**Tempranillo** 70 percent for its bouquet, acidity, and aging qualities. It ripens some two weeks before the Garnacha (*temprano* means "early") and is also known in Spain as the Cencibel, Tinto Fino, or Ull de Llebre. Tempranillo has a naturally low oxidizing enzyme content, giving its wines exceptional longevity.

**Garnacha** 15 percent for body and alcohol—too much can make the wine coarse. This is the Grenache of the Rhône, also known as the Lladoner and Aragonés. It is the major variety of the Rioja Baja, where it can produce wines of 16 percent alcohol.

**Graciano** 7.5 percent for freshness, flavor, and aroma. A singular variety with the unusual property of thin, yet tough, black skin.

**Mazuelo** 7.5 percent for color, tannin, and good aging characteristics. This is the Carignan of southern France and is also known in Spain as the Cariñena.

To the above a small proportion of white grapes, perhaps 5–10 percent of Viura, may sometimes be added, but this tradition is fading. Cabernet Sauvignon is not an authorized variety in Rioja, but is permitted by special dispensation for *bodegas* that have historically used the variety (such as Marqués de Riscal, which uses 15 to 60 percent) and those that are growing it on a trial basis. Although a number of *bodegas* have experimental plantations, Cabernet Sauvignon is not of any great significance for the vast majority of Rioja wines.

### A TYPICAL WHITE RIOJA BLEND

**Viura** 95 percent for freshness and fragrance. This grape has reasonable acidity and a good resistance to oxidation. It is also known as the Macabéo and Alcañón in other parts of Spain, and is one of three major Cava varieties.

**Malvasía** 5 percent for richness, fragrance, acidity, and complexity. Also known as the Rojal Blanco and Subirat, this grape has a tendency to color a patchy red when ripe, so pressing must be quick to avoid tainting the juice.

Most white wines are pure Viura, although some contain up to 50 percent Malvasía. Some *bodegas* use a tiny amount of Garnacha Blanca, particularly in lesser years, to increase alcohol levels, but they do so at the expense of a certain amount of freshness and aroma.

50 percent Tempranillo, 30 percent Garnacha, and 20 percent Cabernet Sauvignon, but I wonder if even this is tempered by the large amount of Garnacha that will still exist when the replanting program has concluded.

## NAVARRA'S DISTRICTS
The region is divided into five districts:

### *Baja Montaña*
Situated in the Montaña foothills, Baja Montaña is the highest and wettest area of Navarra and the vintage is considerably later here than in the south of the region, hence the greater importance placed on early-ripening Tempranillo. Extra rain causes the grape yield to be between 50 and 100 percent higher than that of any of the other four areas. The district produces some of Navarra's best *rosados*, fresh and fruity in aroma and flavor.

### *Ribera Alta*
With twice the number of vineyards as Baja Montaña and Tierra Estella, this is one of the two most important of Navarra's districts. Ribera Alta borders the Rioja Alta and produces some of the region's finest wines. The *rosados* are smooth and aromatic, and the reds soft and fruity, but with as much as 40 percent Viura planted, this is a major white-wine player and the style is soft, dry, and fresh.

TIERRA ESTELLA, NAVARRA
*The picturesque village of Maneru is situated near Estella, southwest of Pamplona. Tempranillo is the main variety grown in the area's vineyards.*

### *Ribera Baja*
One of the two most important wine districts of Navarra, Ribera Baja is very hot and dry and includes approximately 20 percent of what is effectively the Rioja Baja district. The wines produced are mostly red, made principally from the Garnacha (Grenache) grape, and typically deep-colored, full, and robust. Muscat à Petits Grains accounts for 10 percent of the vines planted and produces a sweet Moscatel-style wine.

### *Tierra Estella*
Viticulturally as important as Baja Montaña and climatically similar to Valdizarbe in the north, though gradually getting drier farther south, the Tierra Estella makes pleasant, fruity reds and *rosados* from the Tempranillo, which is heavily planted here. The Garnacha variety is less important since its wines tend to oxidize. Some crisp white wines from the Viura grape are also produced.

### *Valdizarbe*
The smallest of Navarra's five districts, Valdizarbe has a slightly drier climate than the Baja Montaña and is an excellent source of good-value red and *rosado* wines, although some of these have an unfortunate tendency to oxidize.

## FACTORS AFFECTING TASTE AND QUALITY

### LOCATION
Situated in northern Spain in the upper valley of the Ebro River, Rioja and Navarra are bounded to the northeast by the Pyrenees and to the southwest by the Sierra de la Demanda. Navarra has the second-most northerly vineyards in Spain.

### CLIMATE
The Cantabrian Mountains, a range that is modest in elevation yet impressive in structure, provide a major key to the quality of Rioja, protecting the region from the devastating winds whipped up over the Bay of Biscay and holding in precarious check the influence of the Atlantic and Mediterranean. That of the former is at its strongest in Navarra, and of the latter in the Rioja Baja. Temperature rises and rainfall decreases as one moves eastward to the Mediterranean. The Pyrenees also provide shelter from the north, but winters can be cold and foggy, particularly in Navarra. Rioja can suffer from hailstorms and the hot, dry *solano* wind.

### ASPECT
Vineyards are variously located, from the highest in the foothills of the Pyrenees in Navarra to those on the flatter lands of the Rioja Baja in the southeast. Generally, the best vineyards are in the central hill country of the Rioja Alta and the Alavesa.

### SOIL
Although soils do vary, the common denominator is limestone. In Navarra, limestone contains between 25 and 45 percent "active" lime, and is coated by a layer of silty-alluvium near the Ebro or by weathered limestone and sandstone topsoil in drier areas. Limestone with either sandstone or calcareous clay and slaty deposits dominate the Rioja Alavesa and Alta, while a ferruginous-clay and a silty-loam of alluvial origin cover a limestone base in the Rioja Baja.

### VITICULTURE AND VINIFICATION
Most wines are a blend of at least three grapes from different areas within a single appellation; very few are 100 percent pure varietal or single-estate wines. The traditional vinification process, which is still used to produce the local *vino nuevo*, is a crude form of *macération carbonique* carried out in open vats; the grapes are trodden after the first few days of intercellular fermentation. This is much as Beaujolais wines used to be made, but the result here is much coarser, with a dark-damson color and lots of youthful tannin. Most wines are, however, vinified in the normal manner, but aged longer than other commercial wines. Although recent trends favor shorter oak-aging and longer bottle-maturation, the character of Rioja still relies heavily on oak, and it is essential for its future that it should remain so.

### GRAPE VARIETIES
**Primary varieties:** Tempranillo, Viura (*syn.* Macabéo)
**Secondary varieties:** Cabernet Sauvignon, Carignan (*syn.* Mazuelo), Chardonnay, Cinsault, Garnacha (*syn.* Grenache), Garnacha Blanca (*syn.* Grenache Blanc), Graciano, Malvasia, Mourvèdre (*syn.* Monastrell), Muscat (*syn.* Moscatel)

## RIOJA'S DISTRICTS AT A GLANCE

### GRAPE VARIETIES GROWN (IN HECTARES)

| BLACK VARIETIES | RIOJA ALTA | RIOJA ALAVESA | RIOJA BAJA | REGIONAL TOTAL |
|---|---|---|---|---|
| Tempranillo | 19,768 | 11,607 | 16,896 | 48,270 |
| Garnacha | 3,894 | 160 | 3,328 | 7,381 |
| Mazuelo | 954 | 105 | 816 | 1,875 |
| Graciano | 313 | 137 | 268 | 718 |
| Others | 47 | 0 | 40 | 88 |
| Experimental | 65 | 47 | 55 | 166 |
| TOTAL | 25,041 | 12,055 | 21,402 | 58,498 |

| WHITE VARIETIES | RIOJA ALTA | RIOJA ALAVESA | RIOJA BAJA | REGIONAL TOTAL |
|---|---|---|---|---|
| Viura | 2,005 | 1,078 | 1,714 | 4,796 |
| Malvasia | 23 | 20 | 20 | 62 |
| Garnacho blanco | 9 | 0 | 8 | 17 |
| Others | 42 | 7 | 36 | 85 |
| Experimental | 7 | 1 | 6 | 15 |
| TOTAL | 2,087 | 1,106 | 1,783 | 4,976 |
| TOTAL (ALL VINES) | 27,128 | 13,161 | 23,186 | 63,475 |

### WINE PRODUCED (IN HECTOLITERS) AND BY ROUNDED PERCENTAGE

| | RIOJA ALTA | | RIOJA ALAVESA | | RIOJA BAJA | | TOTAL | |
|---|---|---|---|---|---|---|---|---|
| Red | 1,014,310 | 88% | 515,573 | 92% | 847,216 | 86% | 2,363,132 | 88% |
| White | 81,861 | 7% | 30,551 | 5% | 49,406 | 5% | 161,818 | 6% |
| Rosé | 56,454 | 5% | 13,066 | 3% | 88,513 | 9% | 158,033 | 6% |
| TOTAL | 1,152,625 | 100% | 559,190 | 100% | 985,135 | 100% | 2,696,950 | 100% |

# THE WINE PRODUCERS OF
# RIOJA AND NAVARRA

**Note** Unless specifically stated otherwise, all recommendations (including "Entire range") are for red wine only. Reds from both regions are generally drinking well in their third year, but top *cuvées* often improve for up to 10 years, and exceptional ones can age gracefully for decades, while most white and *rosado* wines are best fresh and should thus be consumed when purchased. *See* p.304 for details of the wine styles mentioned.

## BODEGAS AGE
### Rioja

*See also* Campo Viejo and Marques del Puerto

Part of Bebidas (formerly Savin), this *bodega* is now better known as Bodegas & Bebidas or ByB, and is under the same ownership as Campo Viejo and Marques del Puerto. The basic quality is rather uninspiring, but top of the line wines are usually very good value indeed. Labels include Agessimo, Azpilicueta Martínez, Credencial, Don Ernesto, Marqués del Romeral (traditional style and the best), and Siglo (modern style).

✓ *Reserva* • *Gran Reserva*

## BODEGAS ALAVESAS
### Rioja

This makes some long-lived *reserva* and *gran reserva* of surprising quality and elegance. Labels include Solar de Samaniego (primary) and Castillo de Bodala (secondary).

✓ *Reserva* • *Gran Reserva*

## FINCA ALLENDE
### Rioja
### ★★

One of the fastest-rising stars on the Riojan firmament.

✓ *Entire range*

## AMÉZOLA DE LA MORA
### Rioja
### ★

I have encountered a couple of interesting wines from this Rioja Alta estate. One to watch.

✓ *Viña Amézola* • *Señorío de Amézola*

## ARAEX
### Rioja

Formed in 1993, ARAEX is a group of nine *bodegas* selling Rioja under the following labels: Bodegas Don Balbino, Bodegas Luís Cañas (some excellent *reservas* that benefit from aging 10 years or more in bottle), Viña Diezmo, Bodegas Larchago (voluptuous fruit), Viña Lur, Bodegas Heredad de Baroja (heaps of fruit, firm tannin structure), Bodegas Muriel, Solagüen, and Valserano.

## BARÓN DE LEY
### Rioja
### ★★✫ⓥ

*See also* El Coto

An exciting single-estate Rioja, produced by Barón de Ley using exclusively French, rather than American, oak. It is currently one of the two greatest Riojas in production (the other being Contino).

✓ *Entire range*

## BARÓN DE OÑA
### Rioja
### ★★✫

*See also* La Rioja Alta

This small *bodega* at Paganos was established in the late 1980s but sold to La Rioja Alta in 1995, long before its wines had any chance of distribution in Spain, let alone abroad. With a high-tech, stainless-steel winery and use of 100 percent new French oak, Barón de Oña is a name to watch out for.

✓ *Entire range*

## BODEGAS BERBERANA
### Rioja
### ★✫ⓥ

This producer can be disappointing at the lower end, but makes good to very good *reserva* and *gran reserva* wines that are full, fat, and sometimes even blowsy, with soft, oaky fruit. Berberana is also good value for older vintages. Labels include Preferido (*joven* style), Carta de Plata (younger style), Carta de Oro (bigger, richer), and Berberana *reserva* and *gran reserva* (best).

✓ *Reserva* • *Gran Reserva* • *Tempranillo* • *Dragon Tempranillo*

## BODEGAS BERCEO
### Rioja

Berceo has few vineyards and makes ordinary basic wines, but good *reservas* and *gran reservas*. Bodegas Berceo, located at Haro in Rioja Alta, has the same owners as Bodegas Luís Gurpegui Muga at San Adrián, where Rioja Baja overlaps Navarra.

✓ *Gonzalo de Berceo Gran Reserva*

## BODEGAS BERONIA
### Rioja

These are firm, oaky reds and fresh whites from Gonzalez Byass.

✓ *Reserva* • *Gran Reserva*

## BODEGAS BILBAÍNAS
### Rioja
### ★

Major vineyard owners, Bilbaínas are producers of traditionally styled Rioja. Labels include Viña Pomal (deep, dark, and well-oaked with plummy fruit), Viña Zaco (oakier), Vendimia Especial (excellent older

vintages) and Royal Carlton (one of Rioja's Cava brands).

✓ *Reserva* • *Gran Reserva*

## BODEGAS CAMPILLO
### Rioja
### ★ⓥ

*See also* Faustino Martínez

Touted by many as a new Rioja, Campillo has been around for some years, initially as a second label of Faustino Martínez. Even at the time of the first edition of this encyclopedia in 1988, Campillo was "often better than the principal label." This was because these wines were used to break in Faustino's new barrels, a strategy that caused Campillo to outshine Faustino's flagship wines.

✓ *Entire range*

## BODEGAS CAMPO VIEJO
### Rioja
### ★★ⓥ

*See also* Bodegas AGE and Marqués del Puerto

A large producer with major vineyard holdings under the same ownership as Bodegas AGE and Marqués del Puerto, Campo Viejo has a well-earned reputation for good-quality wines of exceptional value. Its *tinto* wines are typically full-bodied and marked by a fatness of ripe fruit and rich vanilla-oak. Labels include Albor (*joven* style), Viña Alcorta (wood-aged pure varietals), San Asensio (exuberantly fruity) and Marqués de Villamagna (created for bottle-aging, classic and fine rather than fat).

✓ *Reserva* • *Gran Reserva* • *Marqués de Villamagna Gran Reserva*

## LUIS CAÑAS
### Rioja
### ★★★

Wine growers for more than two centuries and winemakers since 1928—but winemakers of great class since the late 1990s, when the effect of their new winery (1994) began to kick in. A tendency for high alcohol levels, especially in the horrendously expensive flagship wine Hiru 3 Racimos, but the fruit is so pure and the tannins so soft, ripe, and elegantly

structured that they are not big.

✓ *Hiru 3 Racimos*

## BODEGAS CARLOS SERRES
### Rioja

Carlos Serres was founded by Charles (later known as Carlos) Serres in 1869, one year after his fellow Frenchman Jean Pineau went to Marqués de Riscal. The house style tends to be on the light side, but the *reserva* and *gran reserva* wines often have an elegant richness.

✓ *Carlomagno* (Reserva) • *Carlos Serres* (Gran Reserva)

## BODEGAS CASTILLO DE MONJARDÍN
### Navarra
### ★

An up-and-coming new *bodega* growing a high proportion of Tempranillo and French varieties. Fresh, creamy-rich red and white wines, both with and without oak. Exciting potential.

✓ *Chardonnay* • *Tinto Crianza*

## CONTINO
### Rioja
### ★★★

Owned by CVNE and a group of growers (whose combined holdings comprise the vineyards of this single-estate Rioja), Contino was not the first single-vineyard Rioja, but its great success encouraged other boutique wineries to follow. It also stimulated interest in French oak as opposed to American.

✓ *Contino Rioja Reserva*

## BODEGAS CORRÁL
### Rioja

This improving *bodega* has relatively few vineyards and is best-known for its Don Jácobo range, although the underrated Corral Gran Reserva is by far its best wine.

✓ *Corral Gran Reserva*

## COSECHEROS ALAVESES
### Rioja
### ★✫ⓥ

Perhaps one reason why this is one of Rioja's better cooperatives is that it is so small that it is hardly a cooperative in the commonly accepted definition of the term. The other reason is the excellent location of their vines around Laguardia in Rioja Alavesa. The style is always bright and fruity.

✓ *Artadi* (including blanco) • *Orobio* • *Valdepomares*

## BODEGAS EL COTO
### Rioja
### ★★✫

*See also* Barón de Ley

These are wines of immaculate style, grace, and finesse, particularly the Coto de Imaz and, more recently, the single-vineyard Barón de Ley.

✓ *El Coto* • *Coto de Imaz Reserva*

## CVNE
### Compañía Vinícola del Norte de España Rioja
★
#### See also Contino

Also known as Cune (pronounced "coonay"), Compañía Vinícola del Norte de España Rioja was once the most old-fashioned and traditional of Rioja producers and its vintages were legendary, easily lasting 30 years or more. Ironically, these wines went through a dicey patch following the installation of a $23 million state-of-the-art winery, but CVNE seems to be coming to terms with this new technology. Recent vintages appear to be picking up, hence its half-star rating, and, hopefully, this *bodega* will return to its previous long-established quality, which should earn it two stars. Labels include Imperial (for finesse) and Viña Real (a plummier, fatter style) and Monopole (the best of the freshest, creamiest, oakiest style of *blanco*).

✓ *Gran Reserva* • *Monopole*

## BODEGAS DOMECQ
### Rioja
★ Ⓥ

Part of Pernod Ricard since 2005, this is just one of 11 Domecq wineries scattered over nine Spanish appellations. José Ignacio Domecq's original concept to create the largest contiguous vineyard in Rioja was daring, but one-time second brand Marqués de Arienzo has come out on top. It was impossible to establish Domecq Domaine (sold as Privilegio Rey Sancho on the Spanish market itself) as a super-sized, single-vineyard Rioja. Marqués de Arienzo is effectively the wine that Domecq Domaine once was, with Viña Eguia taking over as the cheaper brand.

✓ *Gran Reserva* • *Reserva*

## DOMINIO DE MONTALVO
### Rioja
★

This is an innovative barrel-fermented, pure Viura *blanco*.

✓ *Dominio de Montalvo Viura*

## BODEGAS FAUSTINO MARTÍNEZ
### Rioja
★

If given sufficient bottle-age (keeping five years will do no harm) Faustino *reserva* and *gran reserva* can attain exceptional finesse, but are often outshone by Campillo, which started out as a second brand tasked with soaking up the unwanted oakiness from the *bodega*'s new barrels.

✓ *Faustino V* (Reserva) • *Faustino I* (Gran Reserva)

## FEDERICO PATERNINA
### Rioja

These wines are generally light and lacking, especially Banda Azul, its best-known label. You must go up to *reserva* level to find real richness, although the *gran reserva* (Conde de Los Andes) is unpredictable, ranging from pure brilliance to absolute volatility.

✓ *Viña Vial* (Reserva)

## BODEGAS GUELBENZU
### Non-DO Navarra
★★★

Taken out of the DO in order to increase quality and consistency through less restrictive regulations, the basic, ridiculously cheap, Guelbenzu Jardín is a wonderfully delicious, easy-drinking wine made from 30–40 year-old Garnacha vines that is superior to 90 percent of "authentic" DO Navarra. Guelbenzu Azul (primarily Tempranillo-Cabernet Sauvignon with 10–20% Merlot) is where the class starts, Evo (Cabernet Sauvignon-Tempranillo reverses the emphasis, plus 10–20% Merlot) was once the top-of-the-line, but Guelbenzu has topped this with the truly magnificent Lautus (50% Tempranillo, 30% Merlot, 10% Cabernet Sauvignon, 10% Garnacha).

✓ *Entire range*

## BODEGAS GURPEGUI
### Rioja

Located at San Adrián in Rioja Baja, where it produces the Viñadrián and Dominio de la Plana ranges, Bodegas Gurpegui also owns Bodegas Berceo in Rioja Alta.

## BODEGAS IRACHE
### Navarra

This is a modern winery producing unpretentious, fruity wines.

✓ *Viña Irache* • *Gran Irache*

## BODEGAS JULIÁN CHIVITE
### Navarra

Bodegas Julián Chivite typically produces soft, mellow, smooth, oaky wines with plenty of creamy-coconutty fruit flavor.

✓ *Chivite Reserva* • *Gran Feudo* • *Viña Marcos*

## BODEGAS LAGUNILLA
### Rioja

Lagunilla is decent and dependable, but rarely exciting, even though the wines are usually pure Tempranillo and one of its labels, Viña Herminia, enjoys a good reputation in Spain itself. It is best to stick to older vintages and *gran reservas*.

## LEALTANZA
### Rioja
★★

High-tech winery blending the best of tradition to produce top-class, exclusively Tempranillo wines.

✓ *Entire range*

## BODEGAS MAGAÑA
### Navarra

Juan Magaña is best-known for varietal wines, particularly the excellent Merlot, but his Merlot-Tempranillo blend called Eventum has more finesse.

✓ *Eventum* • *Merlot*

## MANZANOS
### Rioja
★★

High-tech winery blending the best of tradition to produce a line of top-class, exclusively Tempranillo wines.

✓ *Entire range*

## MARQUÉS DE ARIENZO
#### See Bodegas Domecq

## MARQUÉS DE CÁCERES
### Rioja
★

Marqués de Cáceres is often quoted as part of the modern school of Rioja winemaking, but is more accurately described as a traditional Bordeaux style, and its wines benefit from bottle-aging. Antea is an excellent barrel-fermented white.

✓ *Antea* • *Reserva* • *Gran Reserva*

## MARQUÉS DE GRIÑÓN
### Rioja
★★ Ⓥ

Marqués de Griñón is perhaps better known for its outstanding Domino de Valdepusa, Spain's first *Pago* DO, from south of Madrid, but it also produces excellent modern-style Rioja, including some wines that incorporate "experimental" Syrah, Merlot, and Cabernet Sauvignon. Wines also sold under the Marqués de Concordia label.

✓ *Entire range*

## MARQUÉS DE MURRIETA
### Rioja
★★★

Owned by Dominos de Creixell, along with Pazo de Barrantes (see Rías Baixas DO under "The Appellations of Spain," p.309), Marqués de Murrieta is known for its pungently oxidative *blanco reserva*, which is impossible to criticize, even if some vintages taste like a cup of lemon-tea brewed in new oak, as it is considered to be the epitome of its style. Marqués de Murrieta whites contain more freshness and fruit than they used to, but it is the remarkable range of old red vintages that excel here, especially the venerable Castillo Ygay.

✓ *Ygay Etiqueta Blanca* • *Ygay Reserva* • *Castillo Ygay*

## MARQUÉS DE RISCAL
### Rioja
★★★

When the first edition of this book came out, Riscal's Swiss importer faxed Francisco Hurtado de Amexaga a copy of this page claiming "the red wines from Rioja's most famous *bodega* have an unpleasant musty-mushroom character," upon receipt of which Hurtado de Amexaga recalled his top winemaker from Riscal's Rueda outpost to investigate. These wines had gradually acquired a musty character since the 1960s, prior to which they were always among the top three Riojas produced, but since they had the oldest and greatest reputation in Rioja, no one had dared mention this until this book was published in 1988. Every one of Riscal's 20,000 barrels was tasted and 2,000 were immediately destroyed, with the equivalent of 600,000 bottles of wine poured away. Another 2,000 borderline barrels were earmarked for replacement the next year and a program instigated to renew all 20,000 over 10 years. In turning around the situation so quickly and with no expense spared, Hurtado de Amexaga ensured that Riscal would regain its position among the world's finest wines.

✓ *Reserva* • *Gran Reserva* • *Barón de Chirel*

## MARQUÉS DEL PUERTO
### Rioja
#### See also Bodegas AGE and Campo Viejo

Formerly known as Bodegas Lopez Agos, Marqués del Puerto is part of Bebidas (formerly Savin), along with Bodegas AGE and Campo Vieja, and produces an elegant style of Rioja, with ripe fruit and good acidity.

✓ *Reserva*

## BODEGAS MARTÍNEZ BUJANDA
### Rioja
★

This high-tech winery consistently produces pure, fresh *blanco* and fine, firm, fruit-driven *tinto*.

✓ *Conde de Valdemar*

## BODEGAS MONTECILLO
### Rioja
★

Owned by Osborne of Jerez, Montecillo covers the spread of styles, from fruity *crianza* reds, through zippy *blanco*, to great *gran reserva* reds.

✓ *Viña Cumbrero* (blanco) • *Reserva* • *Gran Reserva*

## BODEGAS MUERZA
### Rioja
❓

The cheapest reds made here are light, peppery wines that spoil the reputation of this *bodega*, which also produces relatively inexpensive *reservas* and *gran reservas* that are firm and oaky with good, old-fashioned, life-preserving acidity.

✓ *Rioja Vega* (Reserva, Gran Reserva)

## BODEGAS MUGA
### Rioja
★★★

Lovely *rosado* here, but the reds are really top-class, especially Prado Enea. The basic Muga crianza is much younger and fresher, but can be bottle-aged to obtain a similar elegance and seductive, silky finish to those found in the Prado Enea.

◊✓ *Entire range*

## BODEGAS MURUA
### Rioja
### ★

This is a small winery dedicated to producing pure Rioja Alta Tempranillo of some finesse.

◊✓ *Reserva* • *Gran Reserva*

## BODEGAS NEKEAS
### Navarra
### ★★

The amazing discovery of the 1996 International Wine Challenge, Nekeas defeated some of the greatest Chardonnays from Burgundy and the New World to win the coveted Chardonnay Trophy. Made by Spain's former agricultural minister, Francisco San Martin, who certainly knows his vines, and probably his onions, too.

◊✓ *Entire range*

## BODEGAS OCHOA
### Navarra
### ❷

The well-known Bodega Ochoa has been disappointing of late, but EVENA's (*see p.313*) former head oenologist certainly has the knowledge, equipment, and expertise to produce top-flight Navarra wines once again, so I will reserve my judgment.

## BODEGAS OLARRA
### Rioja
### ★

This ultramodern, high-tech winery always used to produce a good Rioja across the range, but vintages became erratic in the mid-1980s, then decidedly poor, but improvements were first noticed with the 1990 vintage in the mid-1990s, since when the quality has been consistent. Labels include La Catedral.

◊✓ *Añares and Cerro Añón ranges*

## BODEGAS PALACIO
### Rioja
### ★✫

An old *bodega* that has truly excelled since the early 1990s, Palacio uses both French and American oak, with wines ranging from the pure Tempranillo Cosme Palacio y Hermanos, a very traditional Rioja that is consistently Palacio's best wine, and Milflores, which gushes with delicious, juicy fruit, making it one of the better *joven* wines produced.

◊✓ *Cosme Palacio y Hermanos* • *Glorioso* • *Milflores*

## BODEGAS PALACIO REMONDO
### Rioja
### ★★

Class Rioja from the gifted hands of Alvaro Palacio.

◊✓ *Entire range*

## PALACIO DE LA VEGA
### Navarra
### ★✫

José María Nieves produces beautifully packaged, stylish wines that are brimming with fruit and finesse. He makes them exclusively from vines grown on this excellent estate.

◊✓ *Cabernet Sauvignon* (Reserva)

## BODEGAS PIEDEMONTE
### Navarra
### ★

This is an up-and-coming *bodega*, which produces excellent Cabernet Sauvignon with a silky texture and a spicy finesse.

◊✓ *Oligitum Cabernet Sauvignon*

## BODEGAS PRÍNCIPE DE VIANA
### Navarra
### ★❶

Formerly known as Agronavarra Cenal and having devoured and dispensed with Bodegas Canalsa, Príncipe de Viana, the firm's premium product, has been adopted as the name of the high-tech *bodega*. Bodegas Príncipe de Viana wines have become something of a bargain compared to those of other top Navarra *bodegas*, which have gained in price as they have achieved greater quality. Príncipe de Viana does not have the finesse of the best Navarra wines, but they are much cheaper and have oodles of rich, coconutty fruit, which I associate with American oak, although some of the wines claim to use French barrels. Labels include Agramont and Campo Nuevo.

◊✓ *Cabernet Sauvignon* • *Chardonnay*

## BODEGAS RAMÓN BILBAO
### Rioja
### ✫

With few of its own vineyards and a small production from mostly bought-in grapes, Ramón Bilbao's best wine is Viña Turzaballa. Its blend contains 90 percent Tempranillo, and the wine is given plenty of time in oak. Viña Turzaballa and also benefits from up to six years further aging in bottle.

◊✓ *Viña Turzaballa Gran Reserva*

## REMELLURI
### La Granja Nuestra Señora de Remelluri
### Rioja
### ★★

These single-vineyard Riojas of consistently high quality from Labastida de Alava possess exquisite balance, elegance, and finesse, great richness of ripe fruit, and a long creamy-vanilla oak finish.

◊✓ *Labastida de Alava*

## LA RIOJA ALTA
### Rioja
### ★★

The Viña Alberdi *crianza* is an excellent introduction to these wines, but the serious business begins with the elegant Viña Arana and Viña Ardanza *reservas*, which are remarkably complex wines considering that they account for more than half of the firm's production. The Gran Reserva 904 is an exceptionally concentrated and classy wine, while the Gran Reserva 890 is a rare product indeed.

◊✓ *Barón de Oña* • *Viña Alberdi* • *Viña Ardanza* (Reserva) • *Gran Reserva 904* • *Gran Reserva 890* • *Marqués de Horo*

## BODEGAS RIOJA SANTIAGO
### Rioja

Memories of excellent 1950s vintages from Rioja Santiago tasted in the 1970s are fading fast by today's acceptable, but hardly special, standards. Other labels these days include Vizconde de Ayala.

◊✓ *Gran Condal* (Reserva, Gran Reserva)

## BODEGAS RIOJANAS
### Rioja
### ★✫

This *bodega* has built its reputation on red wines, particularly the *reserva* and *gran reserva* versions of its rich-oaky Viña Albina and the dark, plummy Monte Real with its vanilla-spice aftertaste.

◊✓ *Canchales* (Vino Nuevo) • *Viña Albina* (Reserva) • *Monte Real* (Reserva)

## SAN VICENTE
### Rioja
### ★★

Top quality Rioja from the makers of Numanthia in Toro.

◊✓ *Entire range*

## BODEGA DE SARRÍA
### Navarra
### ★

A large, well-established estate with a modern winery, producing clean, fruity wines that are constantly improving despite the death of Francisco Morriones, the oenologist

responsible for establishing this *bodega*'s current reputation. Labels include Viña del Portillo, Viña Ecoyen, and Viña del Perdón.

◊✓ *Gran Vino del Señorió de Sarría* • *Viña del Perdon* • *Viña Ecoyen* • *Blanco seco* • *Rosado*

## BODEGAS SIERRA CANTABRIA
### Rioja
### ★

These are large vineyard owners producing an easy-drinking Rioja, with lush fruit, its fatness often lifted by an intense cherry tang. Other labels include Bodegas Eguran.

◊✓ *Codice* • *Reserva*

## VIÑA IJALBA
### Rioja
### ★

One of the smallest and potentially most exciting of Rioja *bodegas*, making startling wines in weird bottles, including a rare, pure Graciano. Warranting two stars by the next edition?

◊✓ *Ijalba* (Graciano) • *Solferino* (Tempranillo)

## VIÑA SALCEDA
### Rioja
### ★

Fresh, gluggy *crianza* reds, huge, rich, and serious *gran reservas*.

◊✓ *Gran Reserva*

## VIÑA TONDONIA
### López de Heredia Viña Tondonia
### Rioja
### ★★

Just up the hill from the very traditional Bodegas Muga is Tondonia, a firm that makes Muga look high-tech. It is impossible to find a more old-fashioned *bodega*, from the huge cobwebs in the tasting room to the religious dipping into wax of all bottle ends as if they contained port. The wines are rich and oaky, and capable of great age. Tondonia is the finest, Bosconia the fattest, and Cubillo the youngest.

◊✓ *Viña Bosconia* • *Viña Cubillo* • *Viña Tondonia* (including *blanco*)

## VINÍCOLA DE LABASTIDA
### Rioja
### ✫

This is probably the best cooperative in Rioja.

◊✓ *Gastrijo* (Reserva) • *Castillo Labastida* (Gran Reserva)

## VINÍCOLA NAVARRA
### Navarra
### ❶

Richly colored and flavored wines, sometimes a touch porty, but always cheap and good value, Vinicola Navarra is part of the sprawling ByB empire.

◊✓ *Las Campanas* • *Castillo de Tiebas* (Reserva)

# PENEDÈS: CAVA COUNTRY

*The worldwide popularity of Cava—Spain's only traditional method sparkling DO wine—together with the success of winemaking genius Miguel Torres, have made Penedès the most famous district in Catalonia, opening up the entire region's wine to export markets.*

PRIOR TO PHYLLOXERA, which struck Penedès in 1876, more than 80 percent of the vineyards here were planted with black grapes. When the vines were grafted on to American rootstock, white varieties were given priority due to the growing popularity of sparkling white wines. It is easy to recognize the classic imported varieties in the vineyards because they are trained along wires, whereas traditional Spanish vines grow in little bushes.

## THE DISTRICTS OF PENEDÈS

Penedès can be divided into three wine districts: Bajo Penedès, Medio Penedès, and Alta Penedès (also called Penedès Superior).

### Bajo (or Baix) Penedès

The following grape varieties are grown in the Bajo Penedès: Monastrell, Malvasía, Grenache (*syn.* Garnacha), Cariñena, and various other, mostly black, grape varieties.

This area occupies the coastal strip and is the warmest of all three areas. The land of the Bajo Penedès is low and flat, with vines growing on limestone, clay, and sandy soil. This area produces more and more full-bodied red wines such as Torres's Sangredetoro.

### Medio (or Mitja) Penedès

The grapes grown are mostly Xarello and Macabéo, but this is also the best area for Tempranillo, Cabernet Sauvignon, Merlot, and Monastrell.

The middle section of the Penedès is slightly hilly, occasionally flat land at an altitude of some 660 feet (200 meters) in the foothills west of Barcelona, on a soil of mostly limestone and clay. It has a cooler climate than the Bajo, with most areas equivalent to Regions II and III of the California Heat Summation System (*see* p.470). This is essentially Cava country, but it also produces the best of the new-style reds, including Torres's various Coronas wines.

### Alta (or Alt) Penedès

Grape varieties grown in this district are almost exclusively white, being mostly Parellada, plus Riesling, Gewürztraminer, and Muscat. A little Pinot Noir is also grown.

This area is the farthest inland, and the grapes are grown on chalky foothills at an altitude of between 1,640 and 2,620 feet (500 and 800 meters). Climatic conditions are the coolest in Penedès, equivalent to Regions I and II. It is so cool that Cabernet Sauvignon will not ripen here and almost all wines produced are white, although Pinot Noir for Torres's Mas Borras is grown at San Marti. Most pure Alta Penedès wines are fresh, of the cool-fermented type, and can show remarkably fine aroma and acidity.

## CAVA: SPAIN'S SPARKLING WINE

The first Spanish sparkling wine was made by Antoni Gali Comas some time prior to 1851, when he entered it in a competition in Madrid. He did not persevere, and the next milestone was with

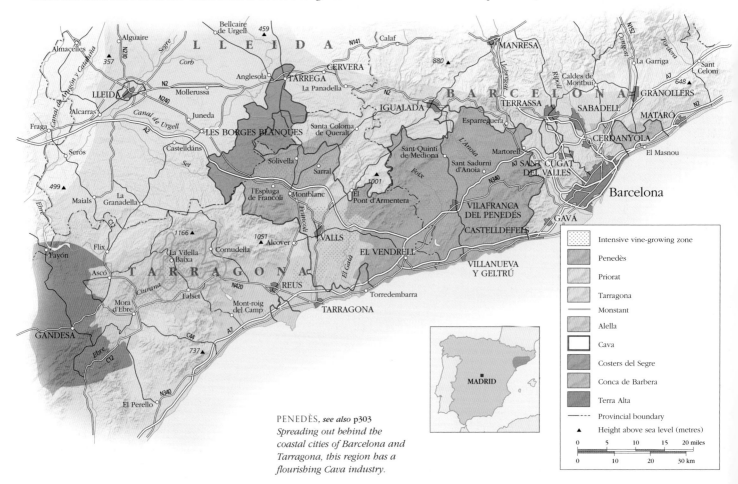

PENEDÈS, *see also* p303
*Spreading out behind the coastal cities of Barcelona and Tarragona, this region has a flourishing Cava industry.*

| | Intensive vine-growing zone |
| --- | --- |
| | Penedès |
| | Priorat |
| | Tarragona |
| | Monstant |
| | Alella |
| | Cava |
| | Costers del Segre |
| | Conca de Barbera |
| | Terra Alta |
| | Provincial boundary |
| ▲ | Height above sea level (metres) |

## FACTORS AFFECTING TASTE AND QUALITY

### LOCATION
Lying in the northeast corner of Spain, where Rioja's Ebro River enters the Mediterranean, Penedès is part of Catalonia, which also includes Alella, Tarragona, Priorat, and Terra Alta.

### CLIMATE
A mild Mediterranean climate prevails in Penedès, becoming more continental (hotter summers and colder winters) moving westward and inland toward Terra Alta. In the same way, problems with fog in the northeast are gradually replaced by the hazard of frost toward the southwestern inland areas. In the high vineyards of Alta Penedès, white and aromatic grape varieties are cultivated at greater altitudes than traditional ones; since they benefit from cooler temperatures.

### ASPECT
Vines are grown on all types of land, ranging from the flat plains of the Campo de Tarragona, through the 1,300-foot- (400-meter-) high plateaux of Terra Alta, to the highest vineyards in the Alta Penedès, which reach an altitude of 2,620 feet (800 meters). For every 330-foot (100-meter) rise in altitude, the temperature drops 0.56°F (1°C).

### SOIL
There is a wide variety of soils, ranging from granite in Alella, through limestone-dominated clay, chalk, and sand in Penedès, to a mixture of mainly limestone and chalk with granite and alluvial deposits in Tarragona. The soil in Priorat is an unusual reddish slate with particles of reflective mica in the north, and schistose rock in the south.

### VITICULTURE AND VINIFICATION
Catalonia is a hotbed of experimentation. Ultramodern winemaking techniques have been pioneered by Cava companies such as Codorníu and fine-wine specialists like Torres. Viticultural and vinification practices are generally quite modern throughout Catalonia. This is especially so at the Raimat Estate in Lérida, where the technology ranges from the latest and most efficient "Sernagiotto" continuous press for bulk production to the "Potter gravity crusher." Described as the simplest press ever designed, this extracts no more than 50–60 percent of the grape's potential juice.

### GRAPE VARIETIES
**Primary varieties:** Cabernet Sauvignon, Carignan (*syn.* Cariñena, Mazuelo), Garnacha (*syn.* Lladoner, Aragonés), Mourvèdre (*syn.* Alcayata, Monastrell), Samsó, Tempranillo (*syn.* Ull de Llebre), Viura (*syn.* Macabéo); Xarel-lo (*syn.* Pansá Blanca)
**Secondary varieties:** Cabernet Franc, Chardonnay, Chenin Blanc, Gewürztraminer, Merlot, Muscat d'Alsace, Parellada, Pinot Noir, Riesling, Sauvignon, Subirat-Parent (*syn.* Malvasía Riojana)

internationally renowned grapes like Chardonnay can only dilute the wine's identity. However, as Codorníu has shown, blending with Chardonnay can fill out a Cava in a way that the traditional varieties (Macabéo, Parellada, and Xarel-lo) cannot.

At a Cava shippers' dinner in 1991, when Manuel Duran, the chairman of Freixenet, admitted that they were still undecided as to whether Cava's varieties were ideally suited to sparkling wine, he was challenged not simply to find an indigenous substitute for Chardonnay, but also to try to experiment with black Spanish varieties. Cava's traditionalists have, for some bizarre reason, always considered black grapes in a white Cava to be sacrilegious, yet Duran picked up the gauntlet, producing a Monastrell-Xarel-lo *cuvée* (the first release was too flabby, but the second release in 1997 was much better—the Catalonians are not used to handling black grapes for white wines, and I expect this Cava to continue improving). Prior to Freixenet's project, Codorníu was the only house to try black grapes in white Cava and succeeded in producing one of the most sumptuous Spanish sparkling wines ever using Pinot Noir.

Whether it is Monastrell, Grenache (*syn.* Garnacha), Trepat, Tempranillo, or some other Spanish grape, I believe that Cava will one day benefit from the use of indigenous black varieties and when that happens, Codorníu will, I am sure, use them, just as they will use any Spanish white variety that is discovered to be as useful in plumping up a *cuvée* as Chardonnay.

CAVA AND PENEDÈS
*Although many Cava producers are either manual or computer-controlled* girasols, *which enable* remuage *to be performed by the pallet-load, some of the more traditional houses, such as the family-owned firm of Juvé y Camps, still use* pupitres.

Luis Justo i Villanueva, the Laboratory Director at the Agricultural Institute of Sant Isidre in Catalonia. It was under Villanueva that all the earliest commercial producers of Spanish sparkling wine learned the Champagne process. In 1872, three of his former students, Domenec Soberano, Francesc Gil, and Augusti Vilaret, entered their sparkling wines in a Barcelona competition. All used classic Champagne grapes grown in Catalonia. Soberano and Gil were awarded gold medals, while Vilaret, who used raspberry liqueur in the dosage, received a bronze. Vilaret's firm, Caves Mont-Ferrant, is the only one of these enterprises to have survived.

The above facts are fully documented and thus contradict Codorníu's claim that it was first to produce Spanish sparkling wine in 1872. Codorníu did not, in fact, sell its first sparkling wines until 1879, and it would not be until 1893 that its production hit 10,000 bottles, a level that the three original firms achieved in the 1870s. What everyone seems agreed on, however, is that José Raventós i Fatjó of Codorníu was the first to make bottle-fermented sparkling wine out of Parellada, Macabéo, and Xarel-lo and that these grapes came to form the basis of the entire Cava industry.

## CAVA'S SPANISH CHARACTER
The production of Cava is dominated by two firms: Codorníu and Freixenet. The latter has always been violently opposed to the invasion of Cava vineyards by foreign grape varieties. Freixenet's argument is certainly valid—that the introduction of foreign varieties could erode Cava's Spanish character. Cava is, after all, the only dry sparkling-wine appellation of any repute outside France and, of course, Spain has its own indigenous varieties, thus

# THE WINE PRODUCERS OF
# CAVA AND PENEDÈS

**Note** For recommended wines of all other Catalonian appellations, see the relevant DO under "The Appellations of Spain" on p.306. Included below are only those wines that come under Cava DO and Penedès DO. Reds from Penedès generally drink well in their third year, but top *cuvées* often improve for up to 10 years, and exceptional ones can age gracefully for decades. Penedès white and *rosado* wines and sparkling Cava are best fresh and should thus be consumed when purchased.

## ALBET I NOYA
★

Established as recently as 1981, Josep Albet i Noya soon became a respected producer of fresh, lively Cava and well-made white Penedès, but is now turning out some spectacular reds.

✓ *Cava* (Vintage) • *Blanc Novell* • *Cabernet Sauvignon* • *Tempranillo*

## CAN RAFOLS DELS CAUS
★

This is an up-and-coming small estate producing excellent Cabernet (Franc and Sauvignon), and a Merlot blend called Gran Caus. Other labels include Petit Caus.

✓ *Gran Caus*

## CASTELL DE VILARNAU
★

This producer is not as consistent as it should be, but has always been capable of richer, more complex Cava, even before the general improvement that lifted the industry in the mid-1990s.

✓ *Cava* (Vintage)

## CASTELLBLANCH
★ⓥ

Castellblanch is a firm owned by Freixenet, and it produces a remarkably consistent Cava wine.

✓ *Cava* (Brut Zero)

## CODORNÍU
★

The largest and most innovative Cava firm, its production dwarfs even that of Moët & Chandon in Champagne. Codorníu started the foreign grape controversy by introducing Chardonnay, first through Raimat Cava in Conca de Barberà, then in its own range. When grown in the right area, Chardonnay does plump up the quality, depth, and finesse of Cava, but there is opposition to nontraditional Spanish grape varieties from those who fear they will erode the intrinsically Spanish character of the wine.

✓ *Cava* (Anna de Codorníu Chardonnay, Jaume de Codorníu, Brut Rose)

## CONDE DE CARALT
★

This is a reliable Cava from part of the Freixenet group.

✓ *Cava* (Brut)

## COVIDES
★

This cooperative produces a surprisingly rich style of Cava.

✓ *Cava* (Duc de Foix Brut, Duc de Foix Vintage, Xenius)

## FREIXENET
★

Freixenet is the second-largest Cava firm, and produces probably the best known of all Cavas. Other labels include Castellblanch, Conde de Caralt, Paul Cheneau, and Segura Viudas.

✓ *Cava* (Brut Nature, Carta Nevada)

## GRAMONA
★

Of its tangy Cavas, Celler Battle shows rare vanilla-finesse on finish.

✓ *Celler Battle* • *Imperial III Lustros*

## CAVAS HILL
★

This old-established, family-owned estate produces elegant Cavas and some very good still wines.

✓ *Cava* (Reserva Oro Brut) • *Blanc Cru* • *Gran Civet* • *Gran Toc*

## JAUME SERRA
★

Jaume Serra produces good Cava, but even better Penedès still wines, made in modern, fruit-driven style in collaboration with Chilean winemaker Ignacio Recabarren.

✓ *Cava* (Cristalino) • *Viña de Mar*

## JEAN LÉON
★★

Following the death of Jean Léon, these wines are now made and marketed by Torres. These big, rich, oaky wines are stunning, but some vintages can disappoint. By no means infallible.

✓ *Cabernet Sauvignon* • *Chardonnay*

## JUVÉ Y CAMPS

I have failed to discern any of the intrinsically superior qualities in these wines that some Cava-infatuated critics have found. However, I do hasten to add that there is nothing wrong with the wines of this respected, traditional, family firm. They are just not special.

## MARQUÉS DE MONISTROL
★

This competent Cava firm, owned by Martini & Rossi, also makes a fine Reserva red Penedès wine and a fresh, youthful Merlot.

✓ *Cava* • *Penedès Reserva* • *Merlot*

## MAS RABASSA
★

Mas Rabassa makes fresh and quite delicious, new-style wines.

✓ *Xarello* • *Macabéo*

## CAVAS MASCARÓ
★

A small, family-owned producer founded in the immediate postwar era, Mascaró is best known for its Don Narciso brandy, but also makes an underrated line of wines.

✓ *Cava* (Brut) • *Anima Cabernet Sauvignon*

## MASÍA BACH
★

Renowned more for its sweet, oak-aged white Extrísimo Bach, than for its reds, which have always been merely soft and acceptable, this Codorníu-owned firm began to take its red winemaking seriously when it released a stunning 1985, simply labeled Masía Bach.

✓ *Masía Bach* (Reserva) • *Viña Extrísima* (Reserva)

## MESTRES
★

Mestres is a small, traditional, family-owned Cava business that produces numerous wines of fine autolytic character.

✓ *Cava* • *Clos Nostre Senyor* • *Mas-Via*

## MONT MARÇAL
★

This is a well-made Cava produced by a private family firm.

✓ *Cava* (Nature, Chardonnay)

## PARXET
★

Under the same ownership as Marqués de Alella, Parxet is capable of producing refined sparkling wines. Its pink-hued "Cuvée Dessert" is sweeter than a *demi-sec* and needs to be cellared for a couple of years. This firm is not afraid to go out on a limb.

✓ *Cava* (Brut Nature, Brut Reserva)

## CELLARS PUIG I ROCA
★★

Cellars Puig and Roca are exciting, estate-bottled wines from ex-Torres troubleshooter Josep Puig. The entrepreneurial Puig even produces a varietal vinegar from Cabernet Sauvignon, which is aged in chestnut casks for flavor.

✓ *Augustus* (Cabernet Sauvignon, Cabernet Sauvignon Rosado, Chardonnay, Merlot)

## RAÏMAT
★★ⓥ

In the Conca de Barberà, the Raïmat estate is owned by Codorníu and utilizes innovative equipment to make an excellent range of fine wines (Abadia, Tempranillo, Cabernet Sauvignon, and Merlot), using classic grape varieties, in addition to its Cava, which was Spain's first pure Chardonnay sparkling wine.

✓ *Abadia Reserva Cabernet Sauvignon* (Mas Castell) • *Chardonnay* (Seleccion Especial) • *Sparkling wine* (Chardonnay)

## RAVENTÓS I BLANC

Josep Maria, black sheep of the Raventós family, left Codorníu to set up his own Cava house, producing fresh, lively *cuvées*, sometimes of excellent quality.

✓ *Cava* (Brut)

## RENÉ BARBIER FILL
★★

Not the old-established firm of René Barbier, which belongs to Freixenet, but René Barbier fill (Catalan for "son"), which is the relatively new company that has been founded in Gratallops in Priorat.

✓ *Priorat* (Clos Mogador)

## SEGURA VIUDAS
★ⓥ

The best Cava house in the huge Freixenet group, the wines produced by Segura Viudas seem to have extra richness and relatively greater aging potential.

✓ *Cava* (Aria, Heredad, Vintage Brut)

## TORRES
★★

The Torres name conjures up French grape varieties and limited editions of world-class wines, but it is actually one of the largest family-owned wine producers in Spain, with 2,000 acres (800 hectares) of vineyard and annual sales of 1.4 million cases of wine. Considering that Sangre de Toro accounts for some 300,000 cases, which is almost a quarter of Torres' total production, this modest, hearty red wine is of a remarkable quality.

✓ *Entire range* (but especially Atrium Fransola, Viña Esmeralda, Mas la Plana Cabernet Sauvignon)

# SHERRY COUNTRY

*On January 1, 1996, sherry regained exclusive use in Europe of its own name, which had suffered decades of abuse by producers of so-called "sherry" in other countries, especially Great Britain and Ireland. The governments of these countries had shamelessly vetoed the protection of sherry's name when Spain joined the Common Market in 1986.*

SUCH ARE THE BLOCKS and checks of the European Union (EU) that it took 10 years for this legislation allowing the abuse of sherry's name to be reversed, ensuring that the name sherry (also known as Jerez or Xérès) may now be used only for the famous fortified wines made around Cádiz and Jerez de la Frontera in the south of Spain. Due to the sherry industry's own folly in trying to compete with these cheaper, fortified ripoffs, the vineyards of Jerez got into massive overproduction problems, but this was recognized in the early 1990s, when lesser-quality vineyards were uprooted, reducing the viticultural area from 43,000 acres (17,500 hectares) to the current 26,000 acres (10,600 hectares).

## SHERRY'S ANCIENT ORIGINS

The vinous roots of sherry penetrate three millennia of history, back to the Phoenicians who founded Gadir (today called Cádiz), in 1100 BC. They quickly deserted Gadir because of the hot, howling *levante* wind that is said to drive people mad, and they established a town farther inland called Xera, which some historians believe may be the Xérès or Jerez of today. It was probably the Phoenicians who introduced viticulture to the region. If they did not, then the Greeks certainly did, and it was the

JEREZ DE LA FRONTERA
*Palomino vines amid the brilliant white* albariza *soil of Montigillilo, Emilio Lustau's superb 300-acre (120-hectare) vineyard, just north of Jerez.*

Greeks who brought with them their *hepsema*, the precursor of the *arropes* and *vinos de color* that add sweetness, substance, and color to modern-day sweet or cream sherries. In the Middle Ages, the Moors introduced to Spain the *alembic*, a simple pot-still with which the people of Jerez were able to turn their excess wine production into grape spirit, which they added, along with *arrope* and *vino de color*, to their new wines each year to produce the first crude but true sherry. The repute of these wines gradually spread throughout the Western world, helped by the English merchants who had established wine-shipping businesses in Andalucía at the end of the 13th century. After Henry VIII broke with Rome, Englishmen in Spain were under constant threat from the Inquisition. The English merchants were rugged individualists and they survived, as they also did, remarkably, when Francis Drake set fire to the Spanish fleet in the Bay of Cádiz in 1587. Described as the day he singed the King of Spain's beard, it was the most outrageous of all Drake's raids, and when he returned home, he took with him a booty of 2,900 casks of sherry. The exact size of these casks is not known, but the total volume is estimated to be in excess of 150,000 cases, which makes it a vast shipment of one wine for that period in history. It was, however, eagerly consumed by a relatively small population that had been denied its normal quota of Spanish wines during the war. England has been by far the largest market for sherry ever since.

## THE UNIQUENESS OF JEREZ SHERRY

It is the combination of Jerez de la Frontera's soil and climate that makes this region uniquely equipped to produce sherry, a style of wine attempted in many countries around the world but never truly accomplished outside Spain. Sherry has much in common with champagne, as both regions are inherently superior to all others in their potential to produce a specific style of wine. The parallel can be taken further: both sherry and champagne are made from neutral, unbalanced base wines that are uninspiring to drink before they undergo the elaborate process that turns them into high-quality, perfectly balanced, finished products.

### The famous albariza soil
Jerez's *albariza* soil, which derives its name from its brilliant white surface, is not chalk but a soft marl of organic origin formed by the sedimentation of diatom algae during the Triassic period. The *albariza* begins to turn yellow at a depth of about

## FACTORS AFFECTING TASTE AND QUALITY

**LOCATION**
This winemaking region is situated in the province of Cádiz, around Jerez de la Frontera in the southwest of Spain.

**CLIMATE**
This is the hottest wine region in Spain. Generally, the climate is Mediterranean, but toward the Portuguese border, the Atlantic influence comes into play and, farther inland, around Montilla-Moriles, it becomes more continental. It is the Atlantic-driven *poniente* wind that produces the *flor* yeast of *fino* sherry.

**ASPECT**
Vines are grown on all types of land, from the virtually flat coastal plains producing *manzanilla*, through the slightly hillier sherry vineyards rising to 330 feet (100 meters), to the higher gentle inland slopes of Montilla-Moriles and the undulating Antequera plateau of Málaga at some 1,640 feet (500 meters).

**SOIL**
The predominant soil in Jerez is a deep lime-rich variety known as *albariza*, which soaks up and retains moisture. Its brilliant white color also reflects sun on to the lower parts of the vines. Sand and clay soils also occur but, although suitable for vine-growing, they produce second-rate Sherries. The equally bright soil to the east of Jerez is not *albariza*, but a schisto-calcareous clay.

**VITICULTURE AND VINIFICATION**
Vinification is the key to the production of the great fortified wines for which this area is justly famous. Development of a *flor* yeast and oxidation by deliberately underfilling casks are vital components of the vinification, as, of course, is the *solera* system that ensures a consistent product over the years. The larger the *solera* the more efficient it is, because there are more butts. Montilla is vinified using the same methods as for sherry, but is naturally strong in alcohol, and so less often fortified.

**GRAPE VARIETIES**
Palomino, Pedro Ximénez, Moscatel

3 feet (1 meter) and turns bluish after 16 feet (5 meters). It crumbles and is super-absorbent when wet, but extremely hard when dry. This is the key to the exceptional success of *albariza* as a vine-growing soil. Jerez is a region of baking heat and drought; there are about 70 days of rain each year, with a total precipitation of some 20 inches (50 centimeters). The *albariza* soaks up the rain like a sponge and, with the return of the drought, the soil surface is smoothed and hardened into a shell that is impermeable to evaporation. The winter and spring rains are imprisoned under this protective cap, and remain at the disposal of the vines, the roots of which penetrate some 13 feet (4 meters) beneath the surface. The *albariza* supplies just enough moisture to the vines, without making them too lazy or over-productive. Its high active-lime content encourages the ripening of grapes with a higher acidity level than would otherwise be the norm for such a hot climate. This acidity safeguards against unwanted oxidation prior to fortification.

three varieties are authorized: Palomino, Pedro Ximénez, and Moscatel Fino. The Palomino is considered the classic sherry grape and most sherries are, in fact, 100 percent Palomino, though they may be sweetened with Pedro Ximénez for export markets.

## HOW GREAT SHERRY IS MADE
### The harvest
Twenty or more years ago, it was traditional to begin the grape harvest in the first week of September. After picking, Palomino grapes were left in the sun for 12–24 hours, Pedro Ximénez and Moscatel for 10–21 days. Older vines were picked before younger ones, and Pedro Ximénez and Moscatel were picked first of all because they required longer sunning than Palomino. At night, the grapes were covered with *esparto* grass mats as a protection against dew. This sunning is called the *soleo*, and its primary purpose is to increase sugar content, while reducing the malic acid and tannin content. Although some producers still

OSBORNE,
PUERTO DE SANTA MARÍA
*The Bajamar solera of Osborne was established in 1772.*

### The levante *and* poniente *winds*
The hot, dry *levante* is one of Jerez de la Frontera's two alternating prevailing winds. This easterly wind blow-dries and vacuum-cooks the grapes on their stalks during the critical ripening stage. This results in a dramatically different metabolization of fruit sugars, acids, and aldehydes, which produces a wine with an unusual balance peculiar to Jerez. Alternating with the *levante* is the wet Atlantic *poniente* wind. This is of fundamental importance, as it allows the growth of several *Saccharomyces* strains in the microflora of the Palomino grape. This is the poetically named sherry *flor* (*see opposite*), without which there would be no *fino* in Jerez.

## SHERRY'S CLASSIC GRAPE VARIETIES
British sherry expert Julian Jeffs believes that as many as 100 different grape varieties were once traditionally used to make sherry and, in 1868, Diego Parada y Barreto listed 42 then in use. Today only

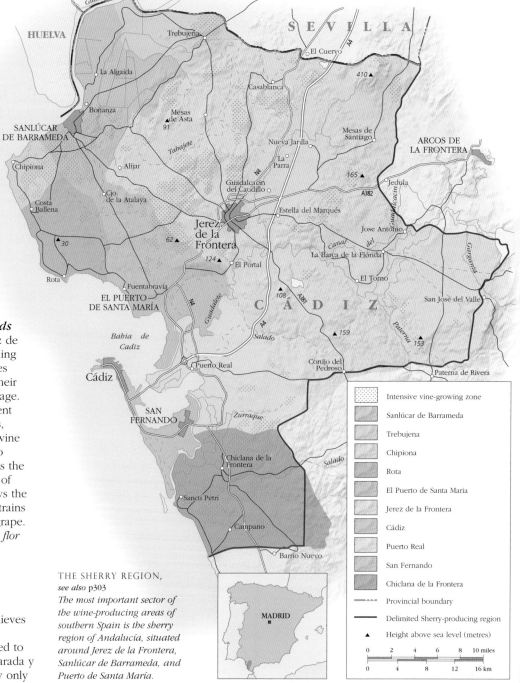

THE SHERRY REGION,
*see also p303*
*The most important sector of the wine-producing areas of southern Spain is the sherry region of Andalucía, situated around Jerez de la Frontera, Sanlúcar de Barrameda, and Puerto de Santa María.*

Legend:
- Intensive vine-growing zone
- Sanlúcar de Barrameda
- Trebujena
- Chipiona
- Rota
- El Puerto de Santa Maria
- Jerez de la Frontera
- Cádiz
- Puerto Real
- San Fernando
- Chiclana de la Frontera
- Provincial boundary
- Delimited Sherry-producing region
- ▲ Height above sea level (metres)

0  2  4  6  8  10 miles
0  4  8  12  16 km

carry out the *soleo*, most harvest in the second week of September and forgo the *soleo* for all grapes but Pedro Ximénez and Moscatel, used in the sweetest sherry. The grapes are now left in the sun for far fewer than the traditional 10–21 days.

### The yeso

Traditionally, prior to pressing the grapes, the stalks are removed and a small proportion of *yeso* (gypsum) is added to precipitate tartrate crystals. This practice, which is dying out, may have evolved when growers noticed that grapes covered by *albariza* dust produced better wine than clean ones. *Albariza* has a high calcium carbonate content that would crudely accomplish the task.

### The pressing

Traditionally, four laborers called *pisadores* were placed in each *lagar* (open receptacle) to tread the grapes, not barefoot but wearing *zapatos de pisar*, heavily nailed cowhide boots to trap the seeds and stalks undamaged between the nails. Each man tramped 36 miles (58 kilometres) in place during a typical session lasting from midnight to noon. Automatic horizontal, usually pneumatic, presses are now in common use.

### Fermentation

Some sherry houses still ferment their wine in small oak casks purposely filled to only 90 percent capacity. After 12 hours, the fermentation starts and continues for between 36 and 50 hours at 77–86°F (25–30°C), by which time as much as 99 percent of available sugar is converted to alcohol; after a further 40 or 50 days, the process is complete. Current methods often use stainless-steel fermentation vats, and yield wines that are approximately 1 percent higher in alcohol than those fermented in casks due to an absence of absorption and evaporation.

## THE MAGICAL FLOR

For the majority of sherry drinkers, *fino* is the quintessential sherry style. It is a natural phenomenon called *flor* that determines whether or not a sherry will become a *fino*. *Flor* is a strain of *Saccharomyces* yeast that appears as a gray-white film floating on a wine's surface, and it occurs naturally in the microflora of the Palomino grape grown in the Jerez district. It is found to one degree or another in every butt or vat of sherry and *manzanilla*, but whether or not it can dominate the wine and develop as a *flor* depends upon the strength of the *Saccharomyces* and the biochemical conditions. The effect of *flor* on sherry is to absorb remaining traces of sugar, diminish glycerine and volatile acids, and greatly increase esters and aldehydes. To flourish, *flor* requires:

- An alcoholic strength of between 13.5 and 17.5 percent. The optimum is 15.3 percent, the level at which vinegar-producing acetobacter is killed.
- A temperature of between 59 and 86°F (15 and 30°C).
- A sulfur dioxide content of less than 0.018 percent.
- A tannin content of less than 0.01 percent.
- A virtual absence of fermentable sugars.

## CASK CLASSIFICATION AND FORTIFICATION

The cellarmaster's job is to sniff all the casks of sherry and mark on each one in chalk how he believes it is developing, according to a recognized cask-classification system. At this stage, lower-grade wines (those with little or no *flor*) are fortified to 18 percent to kill any *flor*, thus determining their character once and for all and thereafter protecting the wine from the dangers of acetification. The *flor* itself is a protection against the acetobacter that threaten to turn the wine into vinegar, but it is by no means invincible and will be at great risk until it is fortified to 15.3 percent, or above, the norm for *fino*, and is not truly safe until it is bottled. A fifty-fifty mixture known as *mitad y mitad*, *miteado*, or *combinado* (half

## GRAPE-BASED SWEETENING AND COLORING AGENTS

The most traditional and most important sweetening agent in the production of sherry, although gradually giving way to other less expensive ones, is that made from pure, overripe, sun-dried Pedro Ximénez grapes, also known as PX. After the *soleo*, or sunning, of the grapes (*see* p322), the sugar content of the PX increases from around 23 percent to between 43 and 54 percent. The PX is pressed and run into casks containing pure grape spirit. This process, known as muting, produces a mixture with an alcohol level of about 9 percent and some 430 grams of sugar per liter. This mixture is tightly bunged and left for four months, during which time it undergoes a slight fermentation, increasing the alcohol by about one degree and reducing the sugar by some 18 grams per liter. Finally, the wine undergoes a second muting, raising the alcoholic strength to a final 13 percent but reducing the sugar content to about 380 grams per liter. Other sweetening agents are:

**MOSCATEL**
This is prepared in exactly the same way as PX, but the result is not as rich and its use, which has always been less widespread than PX, is technically not permitted under DO regulations.

**DULCE PASA**
Preparation is as for PX and Moscatel, but using Palomino, which achieves up to a 50 percent sugar concentration prior to muting. Its use is on the increase. This must not be confused with *dulce racimo* or *dulce apagado*, sweetening agents that were once brought in from outside the region and are now illegal.

**DULCE DE ALMIBAR *OR* DULCE BLANCO**
A combination of glucose and levulose blended with fino and matured, this agent is used to sweeten pale-colored sherries.

**SANCOCHO**
A dark-colored, sweet, and sticky nonalcoholic syrup that is made by reducing unfermented local

grape juice to one-fifth of its original volume by simmering over a low heat. It is used in the production of *vino de color*—a "coloring wine."

**ARROPE**
This dark-colored, sweet, and sticky nonalcoholic syrup, made by reducing unfermented local grape juice to one-fifth of its original volume, is also used in the production of *vino de color*.

**COLOR DE MACETILLA**
This is the finest *vino de color* and is produced by blending two parts *arrope* or *sancocho* with one part unfermented local grape juice. This results in a violent fermentation and, when the wine falls bright, it has an alcoholic strength of 9 percent and a sugar content of 235 grams per liter. Prized stocks are often matured by *solera*.

**COLOR REMENDADO**
This is a cheap, commonly used *vino de color*, which is made by blending *arrope* or *sancocho* with local wine.

## HOW THE FERMENTED SHERRY DEVELOPS

The larger *bodegas* like to make something of a mystery of the *flor*, declaring that they have no idea whether or not it will develop in a specific cask. There is some justification for this—one cask may have a fabulous froth of *flor* (looking like dirty soap suds), while the cask next to it may have none. Any cask with good signs of dominant *flor* will invariably end up as *fino*, but others with either no *flor* or ranging degrees of it may develop into one of many different styles. There is no way of guaranteeing the evolution of the wines, but it is well known that certain zones can generally be relied on to produce particular styles.

| ZONE | STYLE | ZONE | STYLE |
|---|---|---|---|
| Añina | *fino* | Madroñales | *Moscatel/sweet* |
| Balbaina | *fino* | Miraflores | *fino/manzanilla* |
| Carrascal | *oloroso* | Rota | *Moscatel/sweet* |
| Chipiona | *Moscatel/sweet* | Sanlúcar | *fino/manzanilla* |
| Los Tercios | *fino* | Tehigo | *colouring wines* |
| Macharnudo | *amontillado* | Torrebreba | *manzanilla* |

pure alcohol, half grape juice) is usually used for fortification. However, some producers prefer to use mature sherry for fortification instead of grape juice.

### Further cask-classification

The wines are often racked prior to fortification, and always after. Two weeks later, they undergo a second, more precise classification, but no further fortification, or other action, will take place until nine months have elapsed, after which they will be classified regularly over a period of two years to determine their final style.

## CASK CLASSIFICATION IN THE CELLAR

### FIRST CASK CLASSIFICATION

| CHALK MARK | CHARACTER OF WINE | PROBABLE STYLE OF SHERRY | ACTION TO TAKE |
|---|---|---|---|
| / *una raya* | light and good | *fino/amontillado* | fortify up to 15.5% |
| /' *raya y punto* | slightly less promising | undecided | fortify up to 15.5% |
| // *dos rayas* | less promising | *oloroso* | fortify up to 18% |
| /// *tres rayas* | coarse or acid | – | usually distill |
| Ⓥ *vinegar* | – | – | immediately remove to avoid infection |

### SECOND CASK CLASSIFICATION

| CHALK MARK | CHARACTER OF WINE | PROBABLE STYLE OF SHERRY | ACTION TO TAKE |
|---|---|---|---|
| Ⴟ *palma* | a wine with breeding | has *flor* | – |
| / *raya* | fuller | no *flor* | – |
| // *dos rayas* | tending to be coarse | no *flor* | – |
| # *gridiron* | no good at all | no *flor* | – |

### FURTHER CASK CLASSIFICATION

| CHALK MARK | CHARACTER OF WINE | PROBABLE STYLE OF SHERRY | ACTION TO TAKE |
|---|---|---|---|
| Ⴟ *palma* | Light and delicate | a *fino* sherry | – |
| Ⴟ̶ *palma cortada* | Fuller than a *fino* | *Fino-amontillado* or *amontillado* | – |
| + *palo cortado* | No *flor*, but exceptional, full-bodied, and delicate | *Palo cortado* | – |
| / *raya* | Darker, fuller, not breeding *flor* | Medium-quality *oloroso* | – |
| // *dos rayas* | Darker and fuller but coarser | Low-quality *oloroso*, for blending cheap sherries that are usually sweetened | – |
| ✓ *pata de gallina* | a *raya* that has developed the true fragrance of a fine *oloroso* | Top-quality *oloroso*, to be aged and kept dry | – |

### The solera blending system

Once the style of the sherry has been established, the wines are fed into fractional-blending systems called *soleras*. A *solera* consists of a stock of wine in cask, split into units of equal volume but different maturation. The oldest stage is called the *solera*; each of the younger stages that feed it is a *criadera*, or nursery. There are up to seven *criaderas* in a sherry *solera*, and up to 14 in a *manzanilla solera*. Up to one-third (the legal maximum) of the *solera* may be drawn off for blending and bottling, although some *bodegas* may restrict their very high-quality, old *soleras* to one-fifth. The amount drawn off from the mature *solera* is replaced by an equal volume from the first *criadera*, which is topped off by the second *criadera*, and so on. When the last *criadera* is emptied of its one-third, it is refreshed by an identical quantity of *añada*, or new wine. This comprises like-classified sherries from the current year's production, aged up to 36 months, depending on the style and exactly when they are finally classified.

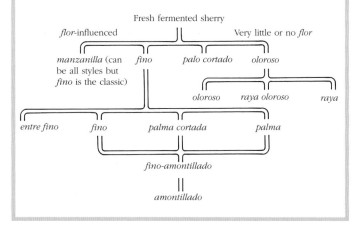

## THE EVOLUTION OF SHERRY STYLES

The tree shows the course taken by each sherry to become one of the well-known styles by which it is sold.

---

## THE STYLES OF

# SHERRY

The development of a sherry can be natural, so that a *fino* can, without the help of increased fortification, turn into an *oloroso* (thus a natural *oloroso* may have developed with the aid of *flor*, whereas the increased fortification usually used to turn a *fino* into an *oloroso* would prevent the development of *flor*). A *palo cortado* can develop from either an *amontillado* or an *oloroso*. A genuine old *fino* sherry can surprise everyone and turn into an *oloroso*.

## ALMACENISTA *or* BODEGAS DE ALMACENADO

This is not a style, but a category of increasing interest among sherry enthusiasts. An *almacenista* is a private stockholder whose pure, unblended sherries are held as an investment for 30 years or more, after which they are in great demand by large *bodegas*, who use them to improve their commercial blends. Lustau, itself an *almacenista* until the 1950s (and now part of the Caballero group), was the first firm to market the concept, making these purest of sherries available to consumers (and

they registered "Almacenista" as a trademark in the process). All styles of sherry and *manzanilla* exist in *almacenista* form and are, almost by definition, guaranteed to be of extraordinary quality. Fractions on the label such as ⅛, ½, or 1/40 indicate the number of barrels in the *solera* from which it was drawn, therefore the lower the denominator (the number below the line), the greater the rarity of the wine and consequently the more expensive it will be.

✓ *Lustau*

## AMONTILLADO

With age, a *fino* develops an amber color in cask and becomes a *fino-amontillado*, then, after at least eight years, a full *amontillado*, when it takes on a nutty character and acquires more body. A true *amontillado* is completely dry, with between 16 and 18 percent alcohol, but will often be sweetened to a medium style for export markets.

The term *amontillado* means "Montilla style"; it was originally used to distinguish a sherry with characteristics similar to those of Montilla

(then part of the Jerez region—*see* p321). Ironically, it was illegal for producers of Montilla to use the term *amontillado* under the Spanish republic, thus sherry could be made in a Montilla style, but not Montilla! Under the EU, however, the law has changed and once again Montilla houses are shipping Montilla *amontillado*.

✓ *Domecq* (Botaina) • *Gonzalez Byass* (Duque) • *Sandeman* (Bone Dry Old Amontillado) • *Valdespino* (Coliseo, Don Tomás) • *Wisdom & Warter* (Very Rare Solera Muy Viejo)

## BROWN

This sweetened *oloroso* is usually, but not always, of lesser quality than *oloroso*. High-quality Brown Sherries used to be very popular in Scotland.

✓ *Williams & Humbert* (Walnut Brown)

## CREAM *or* DARK CREAM

An *oloroso* style that is usually sweetened with Pedro Ximénez, the quality of which can range from the commercial to extremely good.

☑ *Diego Romero* (Jerezana) • *Lustau* (Premium Solera, Vendimia)

## EAST INDIA

Some sources believe that this rich, sweet, Madeira-like style of sherry dates back to as early as 1617, but the practice of shipping sherry to East Asia and back gradually disappeared during the 19th century with the advent of steam-driven ships. It was revived in 1958 by the owners of the Ben Line and Alastair Campbell, an Edinburgh wine merchant, when they sent a hogshead of Valdespino Oloroso on a 20,000-mile (32,000-kilometer) round trip to East Asia, but although the style survives, the effects of the sea voyage, as with Madeira, are now replicated in the cellar.

☑ *Lustau* (Old East India) • *Osborne* (India Rare Solera Oloroso)

## FINO

A *palma* is the highest quality of *fino* sherry and may be graded in a rising scale of quality: *dos palmas, tres palmas, cuatro palmas*. A *palma cortada* is a *fino* that has developed more body, has a very dry, but smooth, almondy flavor, and is veering toward *amontillado*. An *entre fino* has little merit. Few *finos* remain *fino* with age in cask, which is why genuine Old Fino Sherry is rare. A *fino* is light, dry, and delicate; its *flor* nose should overpower any acetaldehyde.

This style is best appreciated straight from the cask, when it is crisp and vital, as it quickly tires once bottled and further declines rapidly as soon as it is opened. Until producers are required to declare the bottling date on the label (fat chance), the only sensible advice is not to buy *fino* until the day you want to drink it and, once opened, consume the entire contents: don't keep it. The wines are invariably 100 percent Palomino with an alcoholic strength of between 15.5 and 17 percent.

☑ *Tomás Abad* • *Domecq* (La Ina) • *Gonzalez Byass* (Tio Pepe) • *La Riva* (Tres Palmas) • *Williams & Humbert* (Pando)

## MANZANILLA

Sea winds in the Sanlúcar de Barrameda area create a more even temperature and higher humidity than those found in Jerez itself, which, with the tradition of allowing more ullage (empty volume) in *manzanilla* casks, encourages the thickest, whitest, and most vigorous growth of *flor* in the region. Fino is therefore the most classic style, but *manzanilla*, too, has its *fino-amontillado* (called *pasada*)

and *amontillado*. *Oloroso* and various intermediary styles are also produced, but these are invariably sold as sherry, rather than *manzanilla*, even when they are exclusively composed of the latter.

## MANZANILLA AMONTILLADA

Fuller than a *pasada*, but lighter and more fragrant than Jerez *amontillado*, this is less common than the previous two, but can be excellent.

☑ *Barbadillo* (Principe) • *Lustau* (Manuel Cuevas Jurado)

## MANZANILLA FINA

Manzanilla (sherry made in Sanlúcar de Barrameda) is a relatively modern, early-picked, *fino*. Its production differs from that of a traditional *fino* in that its fortification is lower and the *solera* system more complex. A true *manzanilla fina* is pale, light-bodied, dry, and delicate with a definite *flor* nose, a touch of bitterness on the palate, and sometimes even a slightly saline tang. *See* general *fino* style below about freshness and when to consume. These wines are usually 100 percent Palomino with an alcoholic strength of 15.5–17 percent.

☑ *Barbadillo* (Eva) • *Diez-Mérito* (Don Zoilo) • *Duff Gordon* (Cabrera)

## MANZANILLA PASADA

When a *manzanilla* begins to age, it loses its *flor*, gains alcoholic strength, and becomes the equivalent of a *fino-amontillado*, known in Sanlúcar de Barrameda as a *pasada*. These wines are invariably 100 percent Palomino with an alcoholic strength of up to 20.5 percent.

☑ *Barbadillo* (Solear) • *Delgado Zuleta* (Amontillado Fino, La Goya) • *Hidalgo* (Pasada)

## MILK

Sweetened *amontillado*, usually of lesser quality.

## MOSCATEL

Occasionally, releases of this wine can be rich, raisiny delights.

☑ *Lustau* (Las Cruzes, Solera Reserva Emelin)

## OLOROSO

*Oloroso* means fragrant and, when genuinely dry, rich, and complex from age, I find it certainly has the greatest finesse, and is the most rewarding wine in Jerez. Much of its character is due to the relatively high fortification it receives and the generous glycerine content that develops without the aid of *flor*. The alcoholic strength of these

wines usually ranges between 18 and 20 percent. Some high-quality, sweeter, dessert-style *oloroso* wines are also produced.

☑ **Dry** *Barbadillo* (Oloroso Seco) • *Diez-Mérito* (Victoria Regina) • *Domecq* (Río Viejo) • *Gonzalez Byass* (Alfonso, Apostles) • *Hidalgo* (Oloroso Seco) • *Lustau* (Don Nuno, Emperatríz Eugenia, Principe Rio, Tonel) • *Osborne* (Bailén, Alonso el Sabio) • *Diego Romero* (Jerezana) • *Sandeman* (Dry Old Oloroso) • *Valdespino* (Don Gonzalo)
**Dessert style** *Gonzalez Byass* (Matúsalem) • *Sandeman* (Royal Corregedor) • *Valdespino* (Solera 1842)

## PALE CREAM

Pale cream is sweetened, usually lesser-quality, *fino* sherry.

## PALE DRY

This style is synonymous with *fino*.

## PALO CORTADO

This wine cannot be deliberately made, nor even encouraged (a *palo cortado solera* is very difficult to operate); only one butt in a thousand turns into a true *palo cortado*. A law unto itself, it is a naturally dry wine with a style somewhere between *amontillado* (on the nose) and *oloroso* (on the palate), but this description does not by any means convey the stunning richness, nutty complexity, and fabulous finesse, which really must be experienced to be believed.

It should be totally dry, but some sweeter dessert-style *palo cortado* wines are produced and can be wonderful. Like *palma*, *palo cortado* may be graded: *dos cortados, tres cortados, cuatro cortados*.

☑ *Domecq* (Sibarita) • *Hidalgo* (Jerez) • *Lustau* (Peninsula) • *Rosario Fantante* (Dos Cortados) • *Sandeman* (Dry Old) • *Valdespino* (Cardenal) • *Williams & Humbert* (Dos Cortados)
**Dessert style** *Osborne* (Abocado Solera) • *Sandeman* (Royal Ambrosante) • *Wisdom & Warter* (Tizón)

## PEDRO XIMÉNEZ

Although it is primarily produced as a sweetening agent, Pedro Ximénez is occasionally released in limited bottlings that are invariably very old and utterly stunning. These are huge, dark, deep, powerfully rich wines piled high with complex yet succulent, raisiny, Muscovado flavors. These bottlings of Pedro Ximénez can be compared in quality, weight, and intensity—though not in character—with only some of the oldest and rarest Australian liqueur Muscats.

☑ *Gonzalez Byass* (Noe) • *Lustau* (Murillo, San Emilio) • *Sanchez Romate* (Superior) • *Valdespino* (Solera Superior) • *Wisdom & Warter* (Viale Viejisimo)

## PUERTO FINO

This is a *manzanilla*-type sherry that is produced in El Puerto de Santa Maria, where the winds are almost as legendary as those of Sanlúcar de Barrameda.

☑ *Burdon* (Puerto Fino Superior Dry) • *Osborne* (Coquinera Amontillado)

# The WINES of
# PORTUGAL

THIS COUNTRY IS SLOWLY BUT SURELY
shaking off its image of tired white wines and
dusty-dry reds. Thanks to a bonanza of grants
during Portugal's honeymoon period of
European Union membership, its wine industry
underwent a massive technological upgrade in
the 1990s, and we are only just beginning to
reap the rewards. First came fresh, fruity,
inexpensive red wines, then a whole raft of
classy, upmarket reds hit the shelves. Over
the next few years, we will see similar
improvements in Portugal's white wines.
International varieties still have a role to play,
but it will be this country's indigenous grapes
that will establish its reputation in the third
millennium. And while Madeira suffers the
same woes as most other fortified wines, Port
remains by-and-large resistant to the modern
trend of ignoring this style of wine.

VINEYARDS IN THE DOURO VALLEY
*Vines grow on terraces overlooking the Douro River
near Pinhão, a town in the port region.*

# PORTUGAL

*Once devoid of anything interesting beyond its two classic fortified wines, port and Madeira, Portuguese winemakers have now woken up to the tremendous potential of the* terroirs *and native grape varieties that their country offers, making it a hotbed of innovation.*

THE JOINT VENTURE BETWEEN Bruno Prats, the former owner and winemaker of Château Cos d'Estournel, and the Symington family of port fame to produce premium red wine in the Douro will put the icing on the cake for Portugal's fine wine reputation. This testament to the top-end potential of Portugal's wine industry follows close on the heels of the red wine revolution that started to materialize in its more inexpensive reds in the mid-1990s.

In the past, Dão had always typified the sort of wines we had come to expect from Portugal, with its dried-out, fruitless reds and dull, heavy, oxidized whites. But in 1995 deliciously fruity, easily accessible reds and fresh, crisp whites came on stream and, like a true revolution, the change started at the lowest levels, with wines such as Alta Mesa and Ramada from Estremadura. At the time these were, and still are, some of the cheapest wines in the world. They had already turned heads by being clean, easy-drinking wines from what was formerly considered a lackluster wine country but, with the vintages of 1994 and 1995, they suddenly had twice the fruit, which gave them instant gulpability and gained them international recognition.

VINEYARDS, SETÚBAL
*The area's Moscatel vines (Muscat d'Alexandrie) produce a celebrated fortified wine that has its own* Denominação de Origem Controlada.

PORTUGAL
*It is in the north of the country that the most famous wines—port and* vinho verde—*are produced, along with the most upwardly mobile, those from Bairrada and Dão.*

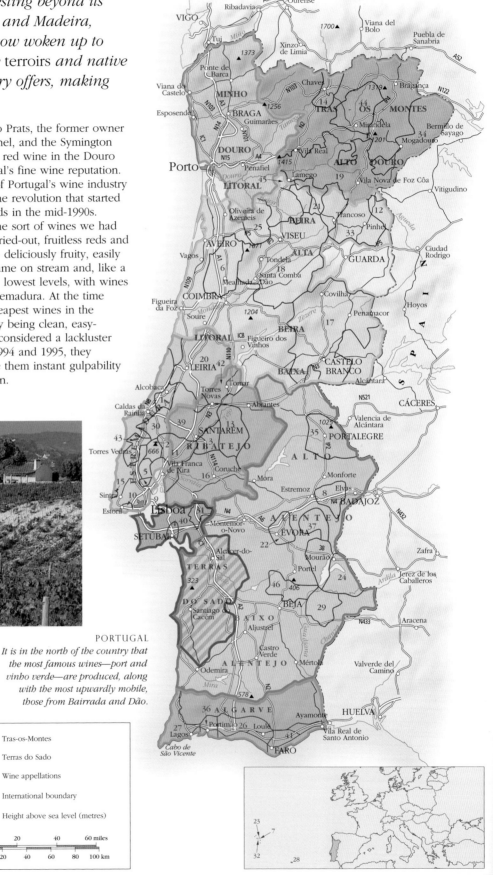

**Major Wine Regions**

- Alentejo
- Algarve
- Beiras
- Estremadura
- Ribatejo
- Rios do Minho
- Tras-os-Montes
- Terras do Sado
- 1　Wine appellations
- - - - International boundary
- ▲　Height above sea level (metres)

0　　20　　40　　60 miles
0　20　40　60　80　100 km

## CURRENT TRENDS

The rush of fruit has only just begun to filter its way upward through the quality scale. This was in part due to the fact that more serious wines took longer to reach the market, thus while we were gulping 1994s and 1995s from Estremadura and other lesser-known Vinhos Regionals, such as Alentejo and Terras do Sado, the 1991s and 1992s from Dão and Bairrada were only just reaching the shelves. A few producers, such as Duque de Viseu in Dão, had got their act together by the early 1990s, but most had not and we still had to get through the dismal 1993 vintage before these more famous regions could show us what they were doing while the likes of Alta Mesa and Ramada were being knocked out.

Another reason for the delayed action in Portugal's fine-wine regions is that producers had until relatively recently been forced to buy wines. Quite extraordinarily, it was illegal for them to buy grapes. Most growers involved in the bulk market barely have a grasp of how to cultivate vines, let alone ferment wines, so being able to buy grapes has enabled firms like Sogrape (which makes Duque de Viseu) to have much greater control over the quality of the final product. When and if the same growers ever learn to grow grapes properly, the recent surge in quality will seem nothing and Portugal's finest wine areas should be catapulted to superstardom.

### RECENT PORTUGUESE VINTAGES

**2006** Some excellent white wines, with Setúbal Moscatels standing out, but patchy for red wines due to ripening problems.

**2005** A smal crop of variable quality, except in Bairrada, Dão, and the Douro, where the best wines are excellent.

**2004** An excellent to great year for both reds and whites.

**2003** Some excellent reds, and should be a very good vintage port year.

**2002** A potentially outstanding red-wine vintage destroyed by pre-harvest rain almost everywhere, the exception being in the Douro, both for still reds, and for single-*quinta* port.

---

## PORTUGUESE LABEL LANGUAGE

**ADAMADO** Sweet

**ADEGA** Literally "cellar," and commonly used as part of the name of a company or cooperative, similar to the Spanish term *bodega*.

**APERITIVO** Apéritif

**BRANCO** White

**BRUTO** Portuguese adaptation of the French *brut*, used to describe a dry sparkling wine.

**CARVALHO** Oak

**CASA** Refers to the property or estate and may also indicate a single-vineyard wine.

**CASTA** Grape variety

**CASTA PREDOMINANTE** Refers to the major grape variety used in a wine.

**COLHEITA** This means vintage and is followed by the year of harvest.

**CLARETE** Bordeaux-style or deep rosé

**CLARO** New, or "nouveau," wine

**DOCE** Sweet

**DENOMINACÃO DE ORIGEM CÓNTROLADA (DOC)** Roughly equivalent to a French AOC.

**ENGARRAFADO POR** Bottled by

**ENGARRAFADO NA ORIGEM** Estate-bottled

**ESCOLHA** Choice or selection

**ESPUMANTE** A sparkling wine that may be made by any method unless qualified by another term.

**GARRAFA** Bottle

**GARRAFEIRA** This term may be used only for a vintage-dated wine that possesses an extra 0.5 percent of alcohol above the minimum requirement. Red wines must have a minimum of three years' maturation, including one year in bottle; white wines must have one year, with six months in bottle. The wine may come from a demarcated region, or be blended from various areas.

**GENEROSO** An apéritif or dessert wine rich in alcohol and usually sweet.

**INDICAÇÃO DE PROVENIÊNCIA REGULAMENTADA (IPR)** Roughly equivalent to a French VDQS

**LICOROSO** A fortified wine

**MADURO** Literally "matured"—it often refers to a wine that has been aged in a vat.

**PALÁCIO** Refers to the property or estate and may also indicate a single-vineyard wine.

**PRODUZIDO E ENGARRAFADO POR** Produced and bottled at or by

**QUINADO** Tonic wine

**QUINTA** Farm or estate

**ROSADO** Rosé

**RESERVA** A term that can be used only to qualify a vintage year of "outstanding quality," where the wine has an alcoholic strength of at least 0.5 percent above the minimum requirement. Wine may come from a demarcated region, but does not have to; it could be blended from different areas.

**SECO** Dry

**SOLAR** Refers to the property or estate and may also indicate a single-vineyard wine.

**TINTO** Red

**VELHO** Literally means "old" and, in the past, this term used not to have any legal definition. Now it can only be applied to wines with a strict minimum age: three years for red wines and two years for whites.

**VINHA** Vineyard

**VINHO REGIONAL (VR)** Similar to a large-sized *vin de pays*.

**VINHO DE MESA** The table wine equivalent to French *vin de table*. If the label does not state a specific DOC or Garrafeira, the wine will be a cheap blend.

---

## THE APPELLATIONS OF
# PORTUGAL

**Note DOC** stands for *Denominação de Origem Controlada*, Portugal's equivalent of France's AOC, Spain's DO, etc.

**IPR** stands for *Indicação de Proveniência Regulamentada*, roughly equivalent to VDQS or a "DOC in waiting", a number having been promoted to DOC status in recent years.

**VR** stands for *Vinho Regional*, a sort of large-sized *vin de pays*.

### ALCOBAÇA IPR
**Map (No. 1)**

These wines from the hills surrounding the old monastic town of Alcobaça are predominantly white. Yields are unfavorably high, producing thin reds and light whites significantly lower in alcohol than wines from surrounding areas.

🍇 For all wines: Arinto, Baga, Fernão Pires, Malvasia, Periquita, Tamarêz, Trincadeira, Vital

### ALENQUER IPR
**Map (No. 2)**

The valley-side vineyards of Alenquer are well-suited to viticulture, ripening grapes easily and producing full, ripe-flavored reds, with peppery-spicy aromas and soft, easy-going, creamy-dry whites.

🍇 Arinto, Camarate (possibly the same as Castelão Nacional), Fernão Pires, Graciano (*syn.* Tinta Miuda), Jampal, Mortágua, Periquita, Preto Martinho, Vital

🍷 1–3 years (new-wave, fruity style) 2–5 years (others)

✔ *Quinta de Abrigada • Quinta de Plantos • Quinta do Carneiro*

### ALENTEJO VR

Stretching up from the Algarve, the plains of Alto and Baixo Alentejo cover about one-third of Portugal. A sparsely populated area with large estates and a scattering of vines, Alentejo is better known for cork than vineyards, even though it has produced some of the country's most outstanding one-off wines and has achieved this with both indigenous and imported grape varieties.

🍇 Abundante, Alfrocheiro Preto, Alicante Bouschet, Antão Vaz, Arinto, Cabernet Sauvignon, Carignan, Chardonnay, Diagalves, Fernão Pires, Grand Noir, Manteudo, Moreto, Palomino (*syn.* Perrum), Periquita, Rabo de Ovelha, Tempranillo (*syn.* Aragonez), Trincadeira

🍶 1–3 years (new-wave, fruity style), 2–5 years (others)

✓ *Apostolo • Cortes de Cima • Esporão* (other brands include Monte Velha) • *J. P. Vinhos* (Quinta da Anfora) • *Herdade de Mouchão • José de Sousa • Pêra Manca • A. C. de Reguengos • Quinta do Carmo • Sogrape* (Vinha do Monte) • *Tapada do Chaves*

## ALGARVE VR

The downgrading of Algarve to Vinho Regional was just a smoke-screen to gain acceptance for its four new internal DOCs: Lagos, Portimão, Lagoa, and Tavira. Lagoa used to have a reputation for fortified whites, which is not surprising considering its proximity to Jerez, but although wine is still produced, none of any interest, fortified or not, is made in the Algarve these days. It is wise to remember that the tourist economy, not quality, regulates wine appellations in the Algarve.

🍇 Arinto, Bastardo, Diagalves, Moreto, Negra Mole, Periquita, Perrum, Rabo de Ovelha, Tamarêz d'Algarve (possibly the same as Roupeiro)

✓ *Adega do Cantor*

## ALMEIRIM IPR
### Map (No. 3)

An up-and-coming area in the Ribatejo region, rapidly becoming known as a source for cheap, fruity red and white wines, often from the plains, known locally as *lezíria* and simply sold as *vinho de mesa*. Terraced vines on the left bank of the Tagus apparently have more potential.

🍇 Arinto, Baga (*syn.* Poeirinha), Castelão Nacional, Fernão Pires, Periquita, Rabo de Ovelha, Tinta Amarela (*syn.* Trincadeira Preta), Trincadeira das Pratas (*syn.* Tamarêz d'Azeitão), Ugni Blanc (*syn.* Tália), Vital

🍶 6–18 months

✓ *A. C. de Almeirim* (including wines under Falcoaria and Quinta das Verandas labels)

## ARRABIDA IPR
### Map (No. 4)

This area on the Setúbal peninsula has well-drained limestone soil and great quality potential, particularly for reds, but whether it takes off as an appellation, when the much wider, more flexible

Terras do Sado VR is doing so well, remains to be seen.

🍇 Alfrocheiro, Arinto, Cabernet Sauvignon, Periquita (Castelão Francês), Fernão Pires, Muscat d'Alexandrie (*syn.* Moscatel de Setúbal), Rabo de Ovelha, Roupeiro

## ARRUDA IPR
### Map (No. 5)

From intensively cultivated hillsides surrounding the town of Arruda in the Estremadura region, come some of Portugal's cheapest, yet reliable, fruity reds.

🍇 Camarate (possibly the same as Castelão Nacional), Fernão Pires, Graciano (*syn.* Tinta Miuda), Jampal, Trincadeira, Vital

🍶 1–3 years (new-wave, fruity style), 2–5 years (others)

✓ *A. C. de Arruda*

## BAIRRADA DOC
### Map (No. 6)

This area produces one of Portugal's two most important red wines and the best have a deep color with good tannin and fine, bell pepper-blackcurranty fruit. However, it is only just beginning to demonstrate its potential for white wines. Sogrape's Nobilis exemplifies Bairrada's fast-emerging rosé style, which really hits the spot with its freshness and depth of fruit.

🍇 Baga, Borrado das Moscas (*syn.* Bical), Castelão Francês, Fernão Pires (*syn.* Maria Gomes), Rabo de Ovelha, Tinta Pinheira

🍶 3–12 years (reds) 1–3 years (rosés and whites)

✓ *José Maria da Fonseca • Gonçalves Faria* (Reserva) • *Luis Pato* (especially Quinta do Ribeirinho Vinhos Velhos) • *Quinta de Pedralvites • Casa de Saima • Caves São João • Sogrape* (Reserva, Nobilis Rosé) • *Terra Franca* (tinto)

## BEIRAS VR

Located in the north of Portugal, encompassing the three Beira provinces of Alta, Baixa, and Litoral, containing the DOCs of Dão and Bairrada, plus the IPRs of Castelo Rodrigo, Cova de Beira, Lafões, Lamego, Pinhel, Varosa, Encostas da Nave, and most of Encostas d'Aire, Beiras produces virtually every imaginable style of wine made, but standards vary enormously.

🍇 Arinto, Baga, Bastardo, Borrado das Moscas (*syn.* Bical), Camarate (possibly the same as Castelão Nacional), Cerceal, Esgana Cão, Fernão Pires, Jaen, Malvasia, Marufo, Monvedro, Periquita, Rabo de Ovelha, Rufete, Tinta Amarela (Trincadeira Preta), Touriga Nacional, Verdelho, Vital

🍶 1–3 years (new-wave, fruity style) 2–5 years (others)

✓ *Bright Brothers* (Baga) • *Buçaco • Conde de Santar* (Reserva) • *Entre Serras • João Pato • Quinta de Foz de Arouce*

## BISCOITOS IPR
### Map (No. 7)

Rarely encountered fortified wines produced on the island of Terceira in the Azores.

🍇 Arinto, Terrantez, Verdelho

## BORBA DOC
### Map (No. 8)

The first subappellation of the Alentejo region to gain recognition outside of Portugal itself,

especially for its inexpensive, juicy red wines.

🍇 Aragonez, Periquita, Perrum, Rabo de Ovelha, Roupeiro, Tamarêz, Trincadeira

🍶 1–3 years

✓ *A. C. de Borba* (Reserva)

## BUCELAS DOC
### Map (No. 9)

The Arinto grape grows particularly well on the loam soil of this small district, but the antiquated winemaking methods are still holding back what is obviously a potentially fine white-wine appellation. Cool fermentation, early bottling, and a delicate touch of new oak would make this wine an international superstar, but so many wines are dried-out and overacidic. Quinta da Romeira is the most consistent Bucelas, and is recommended in this context, but has failed to live up to its promise.

🍇 Arinto, Esgana Cão

🍶 Upon purchase

✓ *Quinta da Romeira* (Prova Régia)

## CARCAVELOS DOC
### Map (No. 10)

Famous in Portugal itself since the late 18th century when the Marquis of Pombal owned a large vineyard and winery here. This area's oldest surviving vineyard, Quinta do Barão, stopped production in 1991, but a relatively new one, Quinta dos Pesos, is trying desperately to rekindle interest in Carcavelos. Rarely seen on export markets, it is a topaz-colored, off-dry fortified wine with a nutty aroma, delicate almondy flavor, and a velvety texture.

🍇 Arinto, Boal, Galego Dourado, Negra Mole, Trincadeira, Torneiro

🍶 5–20 years

✓ *Quinta dos Pesos*

## CARTAXO IPR
### Map (No. 11)

This flat, fertile area overlaps the Estremadura and Ribatejo regions, producing good, fruity, value-for-money reds and whites.

🍇 Arinto, Castelão Nacional, Fernão Pires, Periquita, Preto Martinho, Tinta Amarela (Trincadeira Preta), Trincadeira das Pratas (*syn.* Tamarêz d'Azeitão), Ugni Blanc (*syn.* Tália), Vital

🍶 1–3 years

✓ *Almeida*

## CASTELO RODRIGO IPR
### Map (No. 12)

These full, spicy reds on the border with Spain, south of the Douro, in the Beiras region, show excellent potential, but have yet to establish an international reputation.

🍇 Arinto, Assario Branco (*syn.* Arinto do Dão), Bastardo, Codo, Fonte Cal, Marufo, Rufete, Touriga Nacional

🍶 1–3 years (new-wave, fruity style) 2–5 years (others)

✓ *Quinta do Cardo*

## CHAMUSCA IPR
### Map (No. 13)

This subappellation of the Ribatejo region is adjacent to Almeirim and produces similar wines, but not quite of the same potential.

🍇 Arinto, Castelão Nacional, Fernão Pires,

Periquita, Tinta Amarela (Trincadeira Preta), Trincadeira das Pratas (*syn.* Tamarêz d'Azeitão), Ugni Blanc (*syn.* Tália), Vital

## CHAVES IPR
### Map (No. 14)

From the upper reaches of the Tâmega River in the Trás-os-Montes VR, this appellation tends to produce a similar but lighter style to that of the Douro DOC.

🍇 Bastardo, Boal, Codega (possibly the same as Roupeiro), Gouveio, Malvasia Fina, Tinta Carvalha, Tinta Amarela

## COLARES DOC
### Map (No. 15)

This small wine area is famous for its ungrafted Ramisco vines planted in trenches dug out of the sandy dunes of Sintra, which not only protects them from salt-blighting Atlantic winds, but also from the dreaded phylloxera louse. This is a historic wine, but should not be vinified in such an antiquated fashion if it is going to appeal to modern consumers. If the greatest Bordeaux châteaux have moved with the times, why not Colares? The reds are well-colored and full-bodied, but have so much tannin that they are mouth-puckeringly astringent, smoothing out to a silky finish only with great age, when there is no fruit left. If the grapes could be picked according to tannin-ripeness, rather than fruit-ripeness, and more careful fermentation techniques employed, Colares could be world class. The dry whites are traditional *maduro*-style and not recommended.

🍇 Arinto, Jampal, Galego Dourado, Malvasia, Ramisco

🍷 15–30 years (red)

✓ *Antonio Bernardino Paulo da Silva* (Chitas)

## CORUCHE IPR
### Map (No. 16)

This appellation covers wines made from sandy, well-irrigated plains covering the southern half of the Ribatejo region, but Coruche is seldom encountered and has yet to make its mark.

🍇 Fernão Pires, Periquita, Preto Martinho, Tinta Amarela (Trincadeira Preta), Trincadeira das Pratas (*syn.* Tamarêz d'Azeitão), Ugni Blanc (*syn.* Tália), Vital

## COVA DE BEIRA IPR
### Map (No. 17)

Located in the Beira Alta, between the Vinho Verde and Dão districts, Cova de Beira is the largest of Portugal's IPRs. As with the Beiras VR, every style of wine is produced in varying quality, but the area is best-known for its lightweight reds.

🍇 Arinto, Assario Branco (*syn.* Arinto do Dão), Jaen, Marufo, Periquita, Pérola, Rabo de Ovelha, Rufete, Tinta Amarela

## DÃO DOC
### Map (No. 18)

For 20 years there have been rumors that Dão wines have more fruit and less tannin, but only over the past five have we seen this promise fulfilled in the glass, as fruit-filled Dão have begun to emerge.

They have sufficient fruit to drink much earlier than the old-style Dão wines, but have a certain structure and dry, spicy-finesse that expresses their Portuguese origins. The best whites can be clean and fresh, but not yet truly special, although the Quinta de Saes branco is surprisingly good, especially when consumed with food.

🍇 Alfrocheiro Preto, Assario Branco (*syn.* Arinto do Dão), Barcelo, Bastardo, Borrado das Moscas, Cercial, Encruzado, Jaen, Tempranillo (*syn.* Tinta Roriz), Tinta Pinheira, Touriga Nacional, Verdelho

🍷 3–8 years (reds), 1–3 years (whites)

✓ *José Maria da Fonseca* (Garrafeira P) • *Campos da Silva Olivera* • *Casa da Insua* • *Duque de Viseu*

## DOURO DOC
### Map (No. 19)

Known principally for its port, the Douro Valley in fact makes as much table wine as fortified wine. Because the finest Port is produced on schist soils, most table wines are relegated to areas of the region's other dominant soil, granite. I remain surprised that the Syrah, which thrives in the Northern Rhône's hot, granite soil, has not been tried here, even though it has been experimented with in the Alentejo, where there is much less potential for this variety. The Douro's table wine quality potential is highlighted by Barca Velha, Portugal's most expensive table wine, made by Ferreira at Quinta do Vale de Meão, although its second wine, Reserva Especial, is often just as good, if not better. Is it a coincidence that across the Spanish frontier, where the Douro becomes the Duero, Vega Sicilia, Spain's most expensive wine, grows on its banks? There is nothing porty about these table wines, which range from the lighter, claret types to the fuller, richer Burgundian style. New oak is almost *de rigueur* for premium quality wines.

🍇 Bastardo, Donzelinho Branco, Gouveio, Malvasia Fina, Rabigato (probably not the same as Rabigato *syn.* Rabo de Ovelha), Mourisco Tinto, Tempranillo (*syn.* Tinta Roriz), Tinta Amarela, Tinta Barroca, Tinta Cão, Touriga Nacional, Touriga Francesa, Viosinho

🍷 2–10 years (red, but up to 25 for Barca Velha), 1–4 years (white)

✓ *Bright Brothers* • *Ferreirinha* (Barca Velha, Reserva Especial) • *Niepoort* (Redoma and especially Charme Douro) • *Quinta do Côtto* (Grande Escolha) • *Quinta do Crasto* • *Quinta de Passadouro* • *Quinta de la Rosa* • *Quinta do Vale da Raposa* • *Ramos-Pinto* (Duas Quintas) • *Sogrape* (Reserva) • *Vale do Bomfim* (Reserva)

## ENCOSTAS DA AIRE IPR
### Map (No. 20)

Overlapping the Beiras and Estremadura region, the limestone hills of this appellation should produce some excellent wines, but most have so far been light and rather dried-out.

🍇 Arinto, Baga, Fernão Pires, Periquita, Tamarêz, Tinta Amarela (Trincadeira Preta), Vital

## ENCOSTAS DA NAVE IPR
### Map (No. 21)

Not to be confused with Encostas da Aire, this is a much smaller appellation, located entirely within the Beiras region, adjacent to Varosa, and its wines are much fuller, resembling those of the Douro immediately north, but have yet to establish themselves.

🍇 Folgosão, Gouveio, Malvasia Fina, Mourisco Tinto, Tinta Barroca, Touriga Francesa, Touriga Nacional

## ESTREMADURA VR

From Lisbon, Estremadura stretches north to the Bairrada region and encompasses the DOCs of Bucelas, Carcavelos, and Colares, plus the IPRs of Alenquer, Arruda, Obidos, Torres Vedras, and, in part, Encostas d'Aire (which overlaps Beiras) and Cartaxo (which overlaps Ribatejo). This is Portugal's largest wine-producing region in terms of volume (although Beiras and Alentejo are much larger geographically) and, as such, Estremadura is often perceived as a source of cheap, uninteresting wine. While there are indeed cheap wines made here, they are good guzzlers and far from uninteresting, with a few *quintas* making much finer, more serious wines that are not remotely expensive.

🍇 Alfrocheiro Preto, Antão Vaz, Arinto, Baga, Bastardo, Borrado das Moscas (*syn.* Bical), Cabernet Sauvignon, Camarate (possibly the same as Castelão Nacional), Chardonnay, Esgana Cão, Fernão Pires, Graciano (*syn.* Tinta Miuda), Jampal, Malvasia, Moreto, Periquita, Rabo de Ovelha, Ramisco, Tamarêz, Tinta Amarela (Trincadeira Preta), Trincadeira das Pratas (*syn.* Tamarêz d'Azeitão), Ugni Blanc (*syn.* Tália), Vital

🍷 2–4 years (reds, 4–8 years for better wines), 1–3 years (whites)

✓ *A. C. do Arruda* (selected cuvées) • *A. C. de São Mamede da Ventosa* • *A. C. do Torres Vedras* (selected cuvées) • *Espiga* • *Quinta da Folgorosa* • *Quinta de Pancas* • *Palha Canas*

## EVORA IPR
### Map (No. 22)

This area of the Alentejo region is destined to be one of Portugal's most exciting appellations, especially for full-bodied, creamy-rich red.

🍇 Aragonez, Arinto, Periquita, Rabo de Ovelha, Roupeiro, Tamarêz, Tinta Caida, Trincadeira

🍷 2–5 years

✓ *Heredad de Cartuxa* • *Pêra Manca* (branco)

## GRACIOSA IPR
### Map (No. 23)

Rarely encountered light table wines produced on the island of Graciosa in the Azores.

🍇 Arinto, Fernão Pires, Terrantez, Verdelho

## GRANJA AMARELEJA IPR
### Map (No. 24)

The harsh climate and schistous soils of this subappellation of the Alentejo region can produce powerful, spicy reds, but it has yet to establish itself on export markets.

🍇 Manteudo, Moreto, Periquita, Rabo de Ovelha, Roupeiro, Trincadeira

## LAFÕES IPR
### Map (No. 25)

Light, acidic, red and white wines produced in a small area straddling the Vinho Verde and Dão regions.

🍇 Amaral, Arinto, Cerceal, Jaen

## LAGOA DOC
### Map (No. 26)

Formerly known for fortified white wines, which are still made, but are not of interest, this subappellation of the Algarve does not deserve its DOC classification.

🍇 Crato Branco, Negra Mole, Periquita

## LAGOS DOC
### Map (No. 27)

These Algarve wines do not deserve their DOC classification.

🍇 Boal Branco, Negra Mole, Periquita

## MADEIRA DOC
### Map (No. 28)

*See* The styles of Madeira, p.341

## MOURA IPR
### Map (No. 29)

Cool, red clay soil stretches out the grape's ripening period in this hot patch of the Alentejo, adding a certain finesse to the lush, plump fruit in these wines, which promise great things, but the appellation has not yet established itself.

🍇 Alfrocheiro, Antão Vaz, Fernão Pires, Moreto, Periquita, Rabo de Ovelha, Roupeiro, Trincadeira

## OBIDOS IPR
### Map (No. 30)

The white wines from this area have traditionally been distilled, but the firm, cedary-oaky reds might have potential.

🍇 Arinto, Bastardo, Camarate (possibly the same as Castelão Nacional), Fernão Pires, Periquita, Rabo de Ovelha, Tinta Miuda, Vital

## PALMELA IPR
### Map (No. 31)

The Palmela area was first made famous by the João Pires off-dry white made from early-picked Muscat grapes, but it is equally good for full-bodied reds and the inspired, high-volume João Pires now claims the much larger Terras do Sado appellation, as have others, hence there are no

recommendations, despite the excellent wines made here.

🍇 Alfrocheiro, Arinto, Fernão Pires, Muscat d'Alexandrie (*syn*. Moscatel de Setúbal), Periquita, Rabo de Ovelha, Tamarêz, Tinta Amarela (*syn*. Espadeiro, but no connection with the Espadeiro of Vinho Verde)

## PICO IPR
### Map (No. 32)

Rarely encountered fortified wines produced on the island of Pico in the Azores.

🍇 Arinto, Terrantez, Verdelho

## PINHEL IPR
### Map (No. 33)

In the Beiras region, just south of the Douro, Pinhel makes dry, full, and earthy-tasting white wines, mostly sold to sparkling-wine producers.

🍇 Arinto, Assario Branco (*syn*. Arinto do Dão), Bastardo, Codo, Fonte Cal, Marufo, Rufete, Touriga Nacional

## PLANALTO MIRANDÊS IPR
### Map (No. 34)

In the Trás-os-Montes region, in the very northeastern corner of Portugal, Planalto Mirandês borders Spain, producing full-bodied reds and heavy whites.

🍇 Bastardo, Gouveio, Malvasia Fina, Mourisco Tinto, Rabo de Ovelha (*syn*. Rabigato), Tinta Amarela, Touriga Francesa, Touriga Nacional, Viosinho

## PORT DOC

*See* The styles of Port, p.337

## PORTALEGRE DOC
### Map (No. 35)

Powerful, yet elegant, spicy reds, and rather heavy, alcoholic whites produced in the Alentejo region, adjacent to the Spanish frontier.

🍇 Aragonez, Arinto, Assário, Fernão Pires, Galego, Grand Noir, Manteudo, Periquita, Roupeiro, Trincadeira

## PORTIMÃO DOC
### Map (No. 36)

These Algarve wines do not deserve their DOC classification.

🍇 Crato Branco, Negra Mole, Periquita

## REDONDO DOC
### Map (No. 37)

A subappellation within the progressive Alentejo region, Redondo shows promise for the sort of gushy, upfront, fruity reds that are popping up all over Portugal at grassroots level.

🍇 Aragonez, Fernão Pires, Manteudo, Moreto, Periquita, Rabo de Ovelha, Roupeiro, Tamarez, Trincadeira

🍷 1–3 years

✓ *A. C. de Redondo*

## REGUENGOS DOC
### Map (No. 38)

An up-and-coming DOC in the Alentejo, Reguengos is already producing both gluggy and much finer reds, plus increasingly good whites, making it an appellation to watch.

🍇 Aragonez, Manteudo, Moreto, Periquita, Perrum, Rabo de Ovelha, Roupeiro, Trincadeira

🍷 1–3 years (new-wave, fruity style), 2–5 years (others)

✓ *A. C. de Reguengos* (tinto) • *J. P. Vinhos* (Quinta da Anfora)

## RIBATEJO VR

This large province is sandwiched between Estremadura and Alentejo, and includes the following IPRs: Almeirim, Cartaxo (in part), Chamusca, Coruche, Santarém, Tomar, and Valada do Ribatejo. The temperate climate and rich alluvial plains of the Tagus River encourage high yields, making this the second most important wine region in Portugal. Some very good wines are made by those who restrict yields, particularly by Peter Bright in collaboration with the Fuiza family's vineyards.

🍇 Arinto, Cabernet Sauvignon, Camarate (possibly the same as Castelão Nacional), Carignan, Chardonnay, Esgana Cão, Fernão Pires, Jampal, Malvasia Fina, Malvasia Rei (possibly the same as Palomino), Merlot, Periquita, Pinot Noir, Rabo de Ovelha, Sauvignon, Syrah, Tamarêz, Tinta Amarela (Trincadeira Preta), Tinta Miuda, Touriga Nacional, Trincadeira das Pratas (*syn* Tamarêz d'Azeitão), Ugni Blanc (*syn*. Tália), Vital

🍷 1–5 years (reds), 1–3 years (whites)

✓ *Bright Brothers* • *Falua* • *Fuiza* • *Quinta da Lagoalva* • *Terra de Lobos*

## RIOS DO MINHO VR

A sort of *vin de pays* Vinhos Verdes, except that this appellation also allows for still table wines from foreign varieties. Predictably lightweight.

🍇 Alvarinho, Arinto (*syn*. Paderna), Avesso, Azal Branco, Azal Tinto, Batoca, Borracal, Brancelho (*syn*. Alvarelho), Cabernet Sauvignon, Chardonnay, Espadeiro, Loureiro, Merlot, Padreiro de Basto, Pedral, Rabo de Ovelha, Riesling, Trajadura, Vinhão (possibly the same as Sousão)

## SANTARÉM IPR
### Map (No. 39)

A new appellation for the area around the capital of the Ribatejo region, Santarém should begin to establish itself over the next few years.

🍇 Arinto, Castelão Nacional, Fernão Pires, Periquita, Preto Martinho, Rabo de Ovelha, Tinta Amarela (Trincadeira Preta), Trincadeira das Pratas (*syn*. Tamarêz d'Azeitão), Ugni Blanc (*syn*. Tália), Vital

## SETÚBAL DOC
### Moscatel de Setúbal
### Map (No. 40)

This style of fortified Muscat wine is believed to have been created by José-Maria da Fonseca, the old-established company that still has a quasi-monopoly over its production today. There are various wood-aged styles (5- or 6-Year-Old is best for freshness and the grapey-apricoty varietal character, while 20- or 25-Year-Old is darker and far more complex with a raisiny-nutty-caramel-apricoty intensity), but single-vintage Setúbal is top of the range.

🍇 Muscat d'Alexandrie (*syn.* Moscatel de Setúbal), Moscatel do Douro, Moscatel Roxo plus up to 30 percent Arinto, Boais, Diagalves, Fernão Pires, Malvasia, Olho de Lebre, Rabo de Ovelha, Roupeiro, Tália, Tamarêz, Vital

🍂 Upon purchase (but will last many years)

⚗✓ *J. M. Fonseca*

## TAVIRA DOC
### Map (No. 41)

These Algarve wines do not deserve their DOC classification.

🍇 Crato Branco, Negra Mole, Periquita

## TERRAS DO SADO VR

Probably the most clever appellation the Portuguese could conjure up, Terras do Sado covers a fairly large area fanning out from the Sado estuary far beyond the Setúbal peninsula, where a good many innovative wines originated, but their development had been threatened by the urban sprawl south of Lisbon. If such wines take up the Terras do Sado appellation, they can be sourced from a much wider area. João Pires, Periquita, Quinta de Camarate, and Quinta da Bacalhôa have all claimed this humble VR status without it affecting the prices they command, which has made Terras do Sado an attractive appellation for future new wines.

🍇 **RED** At least 50 percent Aragonez, Cabernet Sauvignon, Merlot, Moscatel Roxo, Periquita (Castelão Francês), Tinta Amarela (Trincadeira Preta) and Touriga Nacional, plus up to 50 percent Alfrocheiro Preto, Alicante Bouschet, Bastardo, Carignan, Grand Noir, Monvedro, Moreto, Tinto Miuda

🍇 **WHITE** At least 50 percent Arinto, Chardonnay, Fernão Pires, Malvasia Fina, Muscat d'Alexandrie (*syn.* Moscatel de Setúbal) and Roupeiro, plus up to 50 percent Antão Vaz, Esgana Cão, Sauvignon, Rabo de Ovelha, Trincadeira das Pratas (*syn.* Tamarêz d'Azeitão), Ugni Blanc (*syn.* Tália)

🍂 1–3 years (new-wave style), 2–5 years (others)

⚗✓ *J. M. Fonseca* (João Pires, Periquita, Quinta de Camarate Tinto) • *J. P. Vinhos* (Quinta da Bacalhôa, Cova da Ursa)

## TOMAR IPR
### Map (No. 42)

Red and white wines grown on limestone slopes of the right bank of the Tagus River in the Ribatejo region.

🍇 Arinto, Baga, Castelão Nacional, Fernão Pires, Malvasia, Periquita, Rabo de Ovelha, Ugni Blanc (*syn.* Tália)

## TORRES VEDRAS IPR
### Map (No. 43)

Originally called simply "Torres" until Miguel Torres objected, these high-yielding vineyards in the Estremadura region of Portugal have traditionally supplied the largest producers with bulk wines for their high-volume branded *vinho de mesa*.

🍇 Arinto, Camarate (possibly the same as Castelão Nacional), Fernão Pires, Graciano (*syn.* Tinta Miuda), Jampal, Mortágua, Periquita, Rabo de Ovelha, Seara Nova, Vital

## TRÁS-OS-MONTES VR

The province of Trás-os-Montes is situated in northeastern Portugal, and encompasses the IPRs of Chaves, Valpaços, and Planalto-Mirandês. The style of wine ranges from light-bodied in the higher altitude vineyards to full-bodied and alcoholic in the south. But the most important wine made in terms of volume is semisweet, semi-sparkling *rosado*.

🍇 Bastardo, Cabernet Franc, Cabernet Sauvignon, Chardonnay, Donzelinho, Gewürztraminer, Gouveio, Malvasia Fina, Merlot, Mourisco Tinto, Pinot Noir, Rabo de Ovelha (*syn.* Rabigato), Sauvignon Blanc, Sémillon, Tempranillo (*syn.* Tinta Roriz), Tinta Amarela, Tinta Barroca, Tinta Cão, Touriga Francesa, Touriga Nacional, Viosinho

🍂 1–3 years (new-wave style), 2–5 years (others)

⚗✓ *Casal de Valle Pradinhos* • *Quintas dos Bons Ares*

## VALPAÇOS IPR
### Map (No. 44)

Firm reds and slightly *pétillant* rosés from the upper reaches of the Tua, a tributary of the Douro, in the Trás-os-Montes region.

🍇 Bastardo, Boal, Codega (possibly the same as Roupeiro), Cornifesto, Fernão Pires, Gouveio, Malvasia Fina, Mourisco Tinto, Rabo de Ovelha (*syn.* Rabigato), Tempranillo (*syn.* Tinta Roriz), Tinta Amarela, Tinta Carvalha, Touriga Francesa, Touriga Nacional

## VAROSA IPR
### Map (No. 45)

Like Pinhel, this Beiras subappellation has yet to establish a reputation above that of being a traditional source of base wines for the sparkling-wine industry.

🍇 Alvarelhão, Arinto, Borrado das Moscas, Cercial, Chardonnay, Fernão Pires, Folgosão, Gouveio, Malvasia Fina, Pinot Blanc, Pinot Noir, Tempranillo (*syn.* Tinta Roriz), Tinta Barroca, Touriga Francesa, Touriga Nacional

## VIDIGUEIRA DOC
### Map (No. 46)

This appellation takes its name from one of three towns around which vineyards flourish on volcanic soils, while the name of the town itself is derived from the word *videira*, meaning "wine," illustrating how long vines have been growing in this part of the Alentejo.

🍇 Alfrocheiro, Antão Vaz, Manteudo, Moreto, Periquita, Perrum, Rabo de Ovelha, Roupeiro, Trincadeira

## VINHO VERDE DOC

The vines literally grow on trees, up telephone poles, and along fences—on anything that takes them above the ground. Training the vine in such a way enables the smallholders—and there are more than 60,000 of them in the Minho—to grow the cabbages, corn, and beans that the families survive on, and to produce grapes, which are either sold to large wineries or made into wine locally and sold to tourists. Genuine Vinho Verde is sharp, may be slightly fizzy, but should always be totally dry, either delicately or raspingly dry, depending primarily on the grape varieties used. The best two grape varieties are Alvarinho and Loureiro. The Alvarinho is a low-cropping variety that is more at home in the northern part of the Minho, between the Lima Valley and the Spanish border. It produces the most substantial Vinhos Verdes, with alcohol levels of 12.5 percent ABV, compared to the norm of 9.5–10 percent. Palácio da Brejoeira is the yardstick for this grape, and widely considered to be a class apart from any other Vinho Verde. The Loureiro is a heavier-cropping variety, producing aromatic wines. Vinhão is the most successful grape for red Vinho Verde, followed by Azal Tinto and Espadeiro, and the best examples of these deep-purple wines have a peppery smack to them, even if it is quickly washed down the throat in a fizzy rush.

🍇 Alvarinho, Arinto (*syn.* Paderna), Avesso, Azal, Azal Tinto, Brancelho (*syn.* Alvarelho), Borracal, Espadeiro, Loureiro, Perdal, Trajadura, Vinhão (possibly the same as Sousão)

🍂 Upon purchase (9–18 months maximum)

⚗✓ **Red single-quintas** *Casa do Valle* • *Ponte de Lima*

**White single-quintas** *Casa de Sezim* • *Morgadio de Torre* • *Palácio da Brejoeira* • *Ponte de Lima* • *Quinta de Azevedo* • *Quinta de Franqueira* • *Quinta da Tamariz* • *Solar de Bouças*

**White commercial blends** *Cepa Velha* (Alvarinho) • *Chello* • *Gazela* • *Grinalda*

# PORT: THE DOURO VALLEY

*No two neighboring districts could produce wines of more contrasting styles than the deep-colored, rich, sweet, warm, and spicy fortified port of Portugal's Douro Valley, and the light, water-white, sharply dry, semi-sparkling Vinho Verde of the Minho region.*

"IT SHOULD FEEL LIKE liquid fire in the stomach... it should burn like inflamed gunpowder... should have the tint of ink... it should be like the sugar of Brazil in sweetness and the spices of India in aromatic flavor." Written in 1754 by the agents for the Association of Port Wine Shippers, such vivid accounts of port remain a fair description of the great after-dinner wine we know today.

## THE ORIGIN OF PORT

It is hard to imagine how such a wonderful winter-warming drink as port could ever have been conceived in such a hot and sunny country as Portugal. Popular belief has it that that it was not the Portuguese but the British who were responsible for port; however, this is not entirely accurate. We can thank the Portuguese for dreaming up this most classic of fortified wines; the British merely capitalized on their original idea.

In 1678, two Englishmen were sent by a Liverpool wine merchant to Viana do Castello, north of Oporto, to learn the wine business. Vacationing up the Douro River, they were regally entertained by the Abbot of Lamego. Finding his wine "very agreeable, sweetish, and extremely smooth," they asked what made it exceptional among all others tasted on their journey. The Abbot

confessed to doctoring the wine with brandy, but the Englishmen were so pleased with the result this had that they purchased the entire stock and shipped it home.

## THE ORIGIN OF THE PORT TRADE

The ancient house of C. N. Kopke & Co. had been trading in Douro wines for nearly 40 years by the time the above encounter took place. Eight years before they stumbled upon the Abbot of Lamego, another Englishman named John Clark was busy building up a business that would become Warre & Co. In 1678, the same year as the encounter, Croft & Co. was established, and this was followed by Quarles Harris in 1680 and Taylor's in 1692. By the time the Methuen Treaty of 1703 gave Portuguese wines preferential rates of duty in Britain, many British firms had set up business in Oporto. Firms of other nationalities—Dutch, German, and French—followed, but it was the British shippers who virtually monopolized the trade, frequently abusing their power. In 1755, the Marquis of Pombal, who had assumed almost dictatorial powers over Portugal some five years before, put a curb on their activities through the Board of Trade. The privileges enjoyed by British merchants under two 100-year-old treaties were restricted. He also established the Oporto Wine Company, endowing it with the sort of powers to which the British had been accustomed.

This infuriated the British, but their protests were to no avail and Pombal went on to instigate many worthy, if unpopular, reforms, including limiting the Douro's production area to the finest vineyards, the banning of elderberries for coloring the wine, and the outlawing of manure, which reduced yields but greatly improved quality.

THE DOURO AND THE MINHO, *see also* p.328
*These two northern areas produce the celebrated port and vinho verde. The Douro River has long been crucial to the port trade.*

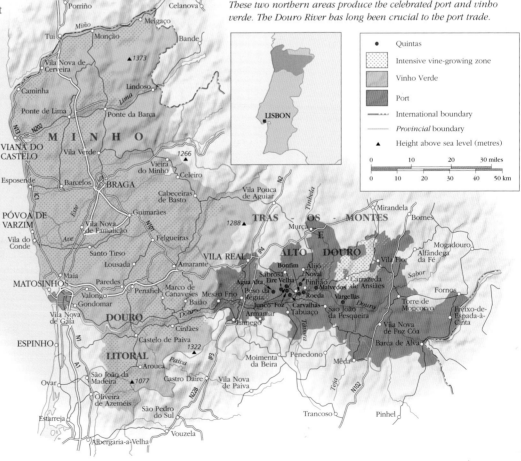

Quintas

Intensive vine-growing zone

Vinho Verde

Port

International boundary

*Provincial* boundary

▲ Height above sea level (metres)

0    10    20    30 miles

0    10    20    30    40    50 km

GRAPE PICKERS NEAR AMARANTE, SOUTHERN MINHO
*Grape pickers use ladders with buckets attached to them to harvest the overhead bunches.*

## PORT GRAPE VARIETIES

There are 48 grape varieties permitted in the production of port. This simple fact goes a long way toward explaining the great variation in quality and character of ports within the same basic style. The official classification of the grapes is as follows:

### VERY GOOD BLACK GRAPES
Bastardo, Donzelinho Tinto, Mourisco, Tinta Cão, Tinta Francisca, Tinta Roriz, Touriga Francesa, Touriga Nacional

### GOOD BLACK GRAPES
Cornifesto, Malvasia Preta, Mourisco de Semente, Periquita, Rufete, Samarrinho, Sousão, Tinta Amarela, Tinta da Barca, Tinta Barroca, Tinta Carvalha, Touriga Brasileira

### AVERAGE BLACK GRAPES
Alvarelhão, Avesso, Casculho, Castela, Coucieira, Moreto, Tinta Bairrada, Tinto Martins

### VERY GOOD WHITE GRAPES
Donzelinho, Esgana Cão, Folgosão, Gouveio (or Verdelho), Malvasia Fina, Malvasia Rei, Rabigato, Viosinho

### GOOD WHITE GRAPES
Arinto, Boal, Cercial, Côdega, Malvasia Corada, Moscatel Galego

### AVERAGE WHITE GRAPES
Branco sem Nome, Fernão Pires, Malvasia Parda, Pedernã, Praça, Touriga Branca

### THE SIX BEST PORT GRAPE VARIETIES
The six port grape varieties currently considered by growers and winemakers to be the best are:

#### Touriga Nacional
Almost universally agreed to be the very best of all port grapes, this has tiny berries and produces pitch-black wine with intense aromatic properties, great extract, and high tannin content. It prefers hotter situations, but is a poor pollinator and does not yield a large crop. Cloning is underway to increase production by 15 percent and sugar content by 10 percent, the most successful clone so far being R110.

#### Tinta Cão
This variety can add finesse and complexity to a blend, but it enjoys a cooler environment and requires training on wires to produce a decent crop. Since traditional cultivation methods make it a poor producer, growers are not overly eager to cultivate it; the grape's survival will depend upon the willingness of port shippers to maintain the variety on their large, managed estates.

#### Tinta Roriz
Not really a member of the Tinta family, this grape is sometimes simply called the Roriz. It is, in fact, the well-known Spanish variety, Tempranillo, the mainstay of Rioja. In the Douro it likes heat and fares best on the sunniest front rows of terraces cut into south- or west-facing slopes. Its dark grapes have thick skins, high sugar content, and low acidity, providing great color, tannin, and succulence in a blend. Some believe this to be better than the Touriga Nacional.

#### Tinta Barroca
The wine produced by this grape variety is quite precocious and is therefore useful in younger-drinking ports, or to dilute wines that are too tannic and distinctive. Like Tinta Cão, this grape variety prefers cooler situations and particularly enjoys north-facing slopes.

#### Touriga Francesa
A member of the Touriga family, this grape has no connection with the similarly named Tinta Francisca, a member of the Tinta family. According to Bruce Guimaraens of Fonseca and Taylor's, this high-quality variety is useful for "filling in the gaps" in vineyards between those areas occupied by vines that like either hot or cool situations. It gives fruit and aroma to a blend.

#### Tinta Amarela
This grape variety is dark-colored and very productive. Its importance has been on the increase in recent years. As this high-quality vine is susceptible to rot, it performs best in the hottest, driest areas.

## FACTORS AFFECTING TASTE AND QUALITY

### LOCATION
Port is made in the Cima Corgo, Baixo Corgo, and Douro Superior districts of the Douro Valley in the north of Portugal.

### CLIMATE
The summers are dry and hot, the winters mild and wet, becoming more continental in the upper Douro Valley, where the summers are extremely hot, rainfall is high—20½ inches(52 centimeters)—and winters can be very cold.

### ASPECT
Vines are planted on generally hilly land that becomes very steep in some parts.

### SOIL
The Douro is a patchwork of hard, sun-baked, granite, and schist soils, with the finest ports originating from the schist vineyards that dominate upriver. Because of the importance of schist to port production, Douro table wines are relegated to granite soils.

### VITICULTURE AND VINIFICATION
Terracing in the Douro is widespread to maximize the use of the land, although the current trend is to make wider terraces, thus enabling mechanization. Some of the less precipitous slopes are now cultivated in vertical rows. Steep terraces mean labor-intensive viticulture, and the hard Douro soil often requires blasting to enable planting. Port wines are made and fortified in the Douro, but most are blended and bottled at lodges in Vila Nova de Gaia.

### GRAPE VARIETIES
*See* Port Grape Varieties, left

by the British. It is even possible to generalize about the stylistic difference between the wines of British- and Portuguese-owned port houses. The British tend to go for bigger, darker, sweeter, fruit-driven wines and have made vintage port their particular niche, while the Portuguese opt for lighter, elegant, more mellow styles, the best of which are exquisitely aged tawnies. At one time, some Portuguese houses rarely even declared a vintage, since they focused on tawny. When they did, the wines were so much lighter in style that export countries often dismissed them as inferior. Although a few were indeed inferior, many were just different. Now, of course, world markets demand that if they are to survive, the Portuguese houses must declare vintages as often as British-owned houses.

When considering stylistic differences between vintage port and the lighter, tawny styles, it is probably more accurate to categorize the fuller, fatter vintage port as North European, not simply British, because this style is also preferred by Dutch, German, and French port houses.

## HOW PORT IS MADE
If any wine is perceived as having been "trodden," then it is port. This is perhaps because the pressing and winemaking traditionally takes place in the vineyards where, until relatively recently, affairs

The production of port had not been perfected at this time. Fifty years after the encounter with the Abbot of Lamego, the industry had widely accepted the practice of brandying, but the importance of when, and in what quantity, to administer the brandy had not been recognized. Ironically, the Abbot's wine was superior because he had added the brandy during, and not after, the fermentation, thus interrupting, or "muting," the process with the natural sweetness that had so attracted the two Englishmen. Even after several centuries, the port trade is still dominated

THE HISTORIC BARCO RABELO
*Based on the Viking warship, these flat-bottomed boats, loaded with pipes of port, would sail for Oporto on the hazardous journey from the upper Douro.*

were conducted on farms in a rather rustic style. Today, few ports are trodden, although several houses have showpiece *lagars*—troughs used for crushing grapes—for tourists. Many houses have "autovinificators"—rather antiquated devices that rely on the build-up of carbonic gas pressure given off during fermentation to force the juice up and over the *manta* (cap) of grape skins. The object is to extract the maximum amount of coloring matter from the skins, because so much is lost by fortification. It is possible also to achieve this using special vats and several have been installed throughout the port industry.

## FERMENTATION AND FORTIFICATION

The initial fermentation phase of port differs little from that in the rest of the world, except that vinification temperatures are often as high as 90°F (32°C). This has no detrimental effect on port, and in fact probably accounts for its chocolaty, high-pH complexity. When a level of about 6 to 8 percent alcohol has been achieved, the wine is fortified, unlike sherry, for which the fermentation process is allowed to complete its natural course. Port derives its sweetness from unfermented sugars, whereas sweet sherries are totally dry wines to which a syrupy concentrate is added. The timing of the addition of brandy is dependent upon the sugar reading, not the alcohol level. When the sweetness of the fermenting juice has dropped to approximately 90 grams per liter of sugar , the alcoholic strength will normally be between 6 and 8 percent, but this varies according to the richness of the juice, which in turn is dependent upon the grape variety, where it is grown, and the year.

The use of the word "brandy" is somewhat misleading. It is not, in fact, brandy, but a clear, flavorless, grape-distilled spirit of 77 percent alcohol, known in Portugal as *aguardente*. It adds alcoholic strength to a port, but not aroma or flavor. *Aguardente* is produced either from wines made in southern Portugal or from excess production in the Douro itself. Its price and distribution to each shipper are strictly rationed. On average 29 gallons (110 liters) is added for every 116 gallons (440 liters) of wine, making a total of 145 gallons (550 liters)—the capacity of a Douro pipe, a specific size of cask used for shipping wine from the valley to the lodges at Vila Nova de Gaia. A drier port has a slightly longer fermentation and requires less than 26 gallons (100 liters) of *aguardente*, while a particularly sweet (or *geropiga*) port is muted with as much as 36 gallons (135 liters). If gauged correctly, the brandy which has been added to arrest the fermentation will eventually harmonize with the fruit and the natural sweetness of the wine. Our conception of balance between fruit, alcohol, and sweetness is, of course, greatly affected by what we are used to drinking. In deepest Douro a local farmer is likely to use a far higher proportion of alcohol for port he intends to drink himself than for the port he makes for export. Generally, British shippers prefer more fruit and less brandy, but all commercial shippers, British or Portuguese, would consider the domestic port of a Douro farmer to lack sufficient body to match the brandy.

## MATURATION AND BLENDING

Until 1986, all port had by law to be matured and bottled at Vila Nova de Gaia on the left bank of the Douro estuary opposite Oporto. At some 47 miles (75 kilometers) from the region of production, this was like insisting that all Champagne be blended, bottled, and disgorged at Le Havre. The law bestowing Vila Nova de Gaia was made in 1756 and it was ostensibly created by and for the big shippers, as it effectively prevented small growers from exporting their wine, since they could not possibly afford the expense of a lodge at Vila Nova de Gaia. By the late 18th century, most of the famous port names were already established, and this restrictive law enabled them to maintain the status quo, especially on the lucrative international markets. All this has changed, and though most ports still come from the big shippers' lodges, many new ports now find their way on to the market direct from privately owned Douro *quintas*.

## THE QUINTA CLASSIFICATION

A *quinta* is a wine-producing estate or vineyard. The Douro Valley covers 600,000 acres (243,000 hectares), of which 82,000 acres (33,000 hectares) are cultivated. Within this area, there are approximately 80,000 individual vineyards or *quintas* owned by 29,620 growers. Each vineyard is classified according to a points system allocated for the categories listed below. The better the classification, the higher official price a vineyard receives for its grapes and the greater its permitted production.

| CATEGORY | MINIMUM | MAXIMUM |
|---|---|---|
| Location | -50 | +600 |
| Aspect | 1,000 | +250 |
| Altitude; lowest is best | (-900) | (+150) |
| Gradient; steepest is best | (-100) | (+100) |
| Soil | (-350) | (+100) |
| Schist | (N/A) | (+100) |
| Granite | (-350) | (N/A) |
| Mixture | (-150) | (N/A) |
| Microclimate; sheltered is best | 0+ | 60 |
| Vine varieties; official classification | -300 | +150 |
| Age of vines; oldest is best | 0 | +60 |
| Vine density; lowest is best | -50 | +50 |
| Productivity; lowest is best | -900 | +120 |
| Vineyard maintenance | -500 | +100 |
| Total | -3,150 | +1,490 |

Vineyards are classified from **A**, for best, to **F**, for worst, as follows: • **Class A** (1,200 points or more); **Class B** (1,001–1,199 points); **Class C** (801–1,000 points); **Class D** (601–800 points); **Class E** (400–600 points); **Class F** (400 points or below).

### CLASS A
*Aciprestes* (Royal Oporto), *Atayde* (Cockburn), *Bomfin* (Dow), *Bom-Retiro* (Ramos-Pinto), *Carvalhas* (Royal Oporto), *Carvalheira* (Calem & Filho), *Boa vista* (Offley Forrester), *Corte* (privately owned, managed by Delaforce), *Corval* (Royal Oporto), *Cruzeiro St. Antonio* (Guimaraens), *Cavadinha* (Warre), *Eira Velha* (privately owned, managed by Cockburn), *Ervamoira* (Ramos-Pinto), *Fontela* (Cockburn), *Fonte Santa* (Kopke), *Foz* (Calem & Filho), *La Rosa* (privately owned), *Lobata* (Barros, Almeida), *Madalena* (Warre), *Malvedos* (Graham), *Mesquita* (Barroa, Almeida), *Monte Bravo* (privately owned, managed by Dow), *Nova* (privately owned, managed by Warre), *Panascal* (Guimaraens), *Passa Douro* (Sandeman), *Sagrado* (Càlem & Filho), *Santo Antonio* (Càlem & Filho), *Sibio* (Royal Oporto), *St Luiz* (Kopke), *Terra Feita* (Taylor's), *Tua* (Cockburn), *Vale de Mendiz* (Sandeman), *Vale Dona Maria* (Smith Woodhouse), *Vargellas* (Taylor's), *Vedial* (Càlem & Filho), *Zimbro* (privately owned, managed by Dow)

### CLASS A-B
*Aradas* (Noval), *Avidagos* (Da Silva), *Casa Nova* (Borges & Irmao), *Ferra dosa* (Borges & Irmao), *Hortos* (Borges & Irmao), *Junco* (Borges & Irmao), *Leda* (Ferreira), *Marco* (Noval), *Meao* (Ferreira family), *Noval* (Noval), *Porto* (Ferreira), *Roeda* (Croft), *Seixo* (Ferreira), *Silho* (Borges & Irmao), *Silval* (Noval), *Soalheira* (Borges & Irmao), *Urqueiras* (Noval), *Velho Roncao* (Pocas), *Vezuvio* (Symington family)

### CLASS B
*Carvoeira* (Barros, Almeida), *Dona Matilde* (Barros, Almeida), *Laranjeira* (Sandeman), *San Domingos* (Ramos-Pinto), *Urtiga* (Ramos-Pinto)

### CLASS B-C
*Sta Barbara* (Pocas)

### CLASS C
*Porrais* (Ferreira family), *Quartas* (Pocas), *Valado* (Ferreira family)

### CLASS C AND D
*Sidro* (Royal Oporto)

### CLASS C, D AND E
*Granja* (Royal Oporto)

### CLASS D
*Casal* (Sandeman), *Confradeiro* (Sandeman)

### CLASS NOT DISCLOSED
*Agua Alta* (Churchill), *Alegria* (Santos), *Cachão* (Messias), *Côtto* (Champalimaud), *Crasto* (privately owned), *Fojo* (privately owned), *Forte* (Delaforce), *Infantado* (privately owned), *Rosa* (privately owned), *Val de Figueria* (Càlem & Filho), *Vau* (Sandeman)

THE STYLES OF
# PORT

**Note** With the exception of white port, there are just two basic styles from which all variants stem: ruby and tawny. What distinguishes these two styles is bottle-aging for rubies and cask-aging for tawnies.

## WHITE PORT

Most dry white ports taste like flabby sherry, but there are some interesting sweet ones, such as Ferreira's Superior White, which is creamy-soft and delicious. Truly sweet white port is often labeled Lagrima. Niepoort pure Moscatel can make an nice alternative to Moscatel de Setúbal.

🍷 Upon purchase

✓ *Ferreira's Superior White*

## BASIC RUBY PORT

The cheapest red ports are rubies with less than a year in cask and often no time at all. Sold soon after bottling, they do not improve if kept. Inexpensive rubies have a basic, pepper-grapey flavor that can be quite fiery. Superior-quality wines are blended from various vintages with up to four years in cask, giving a more homogenous taste, though they should still have the fruity spice and warmth of a young ruby.

🍷 Upon purchase

✓ *Cockburn's* (Special Reserve) • *Fonseca* (Bin 27) • *Graham's* (Six Grapes) • *Quinta de la Rosa* (Finest Reserve) • *Warre's* (Warrior)

## CRUSTED PORT *or* CRUSTING PORT

The greatest nonvintage ruby port, this is a blend of very high-quality wines from two or more years, given up to four years in cask and, ideally, at least three years in bottle. Like vintage, it throws a deposit in bottle, hence the name. Ready to drink when purchased, providing it is carefully decanted, crusting port benefits from acclimatizing to new storage conditions, when it will shed further sedimentation before resuming the much slower process of maturation.

🍷 1–10 years

✓ *Churchill's* • *Martinez* • *Smith Woodhouse*

## LATE-BOTTLED VINTAGE PORT (LBV)

A late-bottled vintage is a pure vintage port from a good, but not necessarily great year. LBVs are usually made in lighter, generally undeclared years. Lighter, more precocious vintages are usually chosen for this less expensive category, and the wines are given between four and six years in cask to bring them on even more quickly. LBVs are thus ready for drinking when sold, but continue to improve in bottle for another five or six years.

🍷 5–10 years

✓ *Burmester* • *Churchill's* • *Graham's* • *Quinta de la Rosa* • *Ramos-Pinto* • *Smith Woodhouse* • *Warre's*

## SINGLE-QUINTA PORT

A wine from a single vineyard, this may be a classic vintage port from an established house or a special release from an undeclared vintage.

Most single-*quinta* ports are as accessible as LBV because, after bottling, the wines are stored until more or less ready to drink. Many single-*quinta* and LBV ports are the same age, although the former is aged longer *after* bottling, while the latter is aged longer *before*. With interest in these ports increasing, the change in the law allowing port to be matured at the *quintas*, and the fact that individual domaine wines are seen as more prestigious, this category could one day become more esteemed than vintage port itself.

🍷 8–25 years

✓ *Cálem* (Quinta de Foz) • *Champalimaud* (Quinta do Cotto) • *Churchill's* (Quinta de Agua Alta) • *Ferreira* (Quinta do Seixo) • *Fonseca* (Quinta do Panascal) • *Niepoort* (Quinta do Passadouro) • *Quinta de la Rosa* • *Quinta de Vesuvio* • *Quinta do Noval* • *Quinta do Sagrado* • *Ramos-Pinto* (Quinta da Urtiga) • *Taylor's* (Quinta de Vargellas) • *Warre's* (Quinta da Cavadinha)

## VINTAGE CHARACTER PORT

The suggestion that these wines, blended from various years and matured in cask for up to four years, have a "vintage" character is misleading. They may be fine ports, but the character is that of a genuine fine old ruby, not a vintage port.

🍷 Upon purchase

✓ *Cálem* • *Churchill's* • *Ferreira* • *Royal Oporto* (The Navigator's) • *Sandeman's* (Signature)

## VINTAGE PORT

By law, a vintage port must be bottled within two years. Maturation in bottle is more reductive than cask-aging and the wine that results has a certain fruitiness that will not be found in any fine old tawny. When mature, a fine vintage port is a unique taste experience with a heady bouquet and a sultry flavor. A warming feeling seems to follow the wine down the throat—more an "afterglow" than an aftertaste. The grape and spirit are totally integrated and the palate is nearly bursting with warm, spicy-fruit flavors.

🍷 12–30 years (but see individual producers)

✓ *Churchill's* • *Champalimaud* (Quinta do Cotto) • *Ferreira* • *Fonseca* • *Fonseca Guimaraens* • *Gould Campbell* • *Niepoort* • *Quinta do Noval* (especially Nacional) • *Taylor's*

## AGED TAWNY PORT

These 10-, 20-, 30-year-old and over-40-years-old ports are traditionally known as "fine old tawnies," but like fine old rubies, there are no legal requirements. By constant racking over a period of 10, 20, or more years, port fades to a tawny color, falls bright, and will throw no further deposit. It assumes a smooth, silky texture, a voluptuous, mellow, nutty flavor, and complex after-aromas that can include freshly ground coffee, caramel, chocolate, raisins, nutmeg, and cinnamon. The years are merely an indication of age; in theory, a 20-year-old tawny could be just a year old, if it could fool the Port Wine Institute. In practice, most blends probably have an age close to that indicated.

Most tawny port experts find 20-year-old the ideal tawny, but 30- and over-40-years-old tawnies are not necessarily past it. The only relatively negative aspect of a good 30- or over-40-years-old is that it will be more like a liqueur than a port.

🍷 Upon purchase

✓ **10-Year-Old** *Cálem* • *Churchill's* • *Cockburn's* • *Croft* • *Dow's* • *Ferreira* (Quinta do Porto) • *Fonseca* • *Graham's* • *Niepoort* • *Offley* (Baron Forrester) • *Ramos-Pinto* • *Robertson's* (Pyramid) • *Smith Woodhouse* • *Taylor's* • *Warre's* (Sir William)

**20-Year-Old** *Barros Almeida* • *Burmester* • *Cálem* • *Cockburn's* • *Croft* (Director's Reserve) • *Dow's* • *Ferreira* (Duque de Bragança) • *Fonseca* • *Graham's* • *Niepoort* • *Noval* • *Offley* (Baron Forrester) • *Robertson's* (Private Reserve) • *Sandeman* (Imperial) • *Taylor's*

**30-Year-Old** *Cálem* • *Croft* • *Dow's* • *Fonseca* • *Niepoort* • *Ramos-Pinto*

**Over 40 Years Old** *Cálem* • *Fonseca* • *Graham's* • *Noval* • *Taylor's*

## BASIC TAWNY PORT

These are often a blend of red and white ports. Some skillful blends can be very good and have even the most experienced port-tasters guessing whether they are tawny by definition or by blending. On the whole, it is wise to pay more to ensure that you buy an authentically aged product. The best tawnies are usually eight years old, although this is seldom indicated.

🍷 Upon purchase

✓ *Delaforce* (His Eminence's Choice) • *Dow's* (Boardroom) • *Warre's* (Nimrod)

## SINGLE-QUINTA TAWNY PORT

Although most single-vineyard ports are vintage and ruby in style, some are made as tawny, either with an indicated age or vintage-dated.

🍷 Upon purchase

✓ **10-Year-Old:** *Quinta do Sagrado* • *Ramos-Pinto* (Quinta da Ervamoira)

**20-Year-Old:** *Ramos-Pinto* (Quinta do Bom-Retiro)

**Vintage-Dated:** *Borges' Quinta do Junco*

## VINTAGE-DATED TAWNY *or* COLHEITA PORT

These excellent-value, often sublime, cask-aged wines are from a single vintage, and may have 20 or 50 years in cask. They must not be confused with the plumper, fruitier vintage ports. There should be an indication of when the wine was bottled or a term such as "Matured in Wood." Some vintage ports are simply labeled "vintage" and tawnies "Colheita." Other clues are "Reserve," "Reserva," or "Bottled in" dates.

🍷 Upon purchase

✓ *Barros Almeida* • *Burmester* • *Cálem* • *Offley* (Baron Forrester) • *Niepoort* • *Noval*

# THE WINE PRODUCERS OF
# THE DOURO VALLEY

**Note** The age range for "when to drink" refers to the optimal enjoyment of vintage ports and appears only when this style is recommended. When the entire range is recommended, this includes all wines with the exception of the most basic ruby and tawny or any white port, unless otherwise stated.

## BARROS
### Barros Almeida
★☆ ⓥ

Manuel de Barros started work as an office boy at Almeida & Co., ending up not only owning the company, but also building a port empire, as he and his descendants took over Douro Wine Shippers and Growers, Feist, Feuerheerd, Hutcheson, Kopke, Santos Junior, and Viera de Sousa. Only Kopke and Barros Almeida itself retain any form of independence. In 2006, Barros Almeida was taken over by Sogevinus, the drinks arm of the Spanish Caixanova bank and owners of port houses Burmester, Cálem, and Gilberts.

✓ *20-Year-Old Tawny • Vintage-Dated Tawny • Colheitas*

## BORGES & IRMÃO
❂

Established in 1884, the Portuguese-owned house of Borges & Irmão is best known for its Soalheira 10-Year-Old and Roncão 20-Year-Old Tawnies, but the quality of their port has suffered under a lack of direction from Portuguese government ownership.

## BURMESTER
★☆ ⓥ

Of Anglo-German origin, Burmester is an underrated house that is best for mature tawny styles, but also makes good vintage. *See* Cálem.

✓ *Late-Bottled • Vintage • 20-Year-Old Tawny • Colheitas • Vintage*

## CÁLEM
★

Cálem was established in 1859 and today is owned by Sogevinus. Consistently elegant tawny, single-*quinta*, and vintage port. Also owns Barros, Burmester, and Gilberts.

☷ 15–25 years

✓ *10-, 20-, 30-, and 40-Year-Old Tawny • Vintage Character • Quinta de Foz • Vintage*

## CHAMPALIMAUD
### Quinta do Cotto
★☆

Although Miguel Montez Champalimaud can trace his family's viticultural roots in the Douro Valley back to the 13th century, he did not produce his first port until 1982,

when it became the world's first estate-bottled single-*quinta* port, making him the fastest-rising star among the new wave of privately owned grower ports.

☷ 12–25 years

✓ *Quinta do Cotto*

## CHURCHILL'S
★★☆

Established in 1981 by Johnny Graham, a member of the Graham's port family who was married to Caroline (*née* Churchill), this was the first port shipper to be established in recent times, and it has quickly risen to the top.

☷ 12–25 years

✓ *Entire range*

## COCKBURN'S
★★

Founded in 1815 by Robert Cockburn, who married Mary Duff, a lady much admired by Lord Byron. The Cockburn's brand is owned by Jim Beam Global, but the port is produced the Symington Group. Cockburn's best-selling Special Reserve and Fine Old Ruby are surprisingly good despite being produced in vast quantities. The vintage ports are consistently excellent in quality.

☷ 15–30 years

✓ *Entire range*

## CROFT
★☆

To many people, Croft is best known for its Sherries, yet it is one of the oldest port houses, having started production in 1678. Croft's elegant style best suits fine old tawnies. In all but a few years, its vintage ports are among the lightest. Now part of Taylor's.

✓ *10-, 20-, and 30-Year-Old Tawny*

## CRUZ
❂

The lackluster quality of Cruz says a lot about the average Frenchman's appreciation of the world's greatest fortified wine. France takes nearly half of all the port currently exported and this is the best-selling brand. The French could be forgiven if they cooked with it, but they actually drink the stuff. Now under the same ownership as C. da Silva.

## DELAFORCE
★☆

The style of Delaforce is very much on the lighter-bodied side, which particularly suits His Eminence's Choice, an exquisite old tawny with a succulent balance as well as a lingering fragrance.

✓ *His Eminence's Choice Superb Old Tawny*

## DIEZ
### Diez Hermanos
❓

Interesting recent vintages make this low-key producer one to watch.

## DOURO WINE SHIPPERS AND GROWERS
*See* Barros

## DOW'S
### Silva & Cosens
★★

Although the brand is Dow's, this firm is actually called Silva & Cosens. It was established in 1862 and James Ramsay Dow was made a partner in 1877, when his firm, Dow & Co., which had been shipping port since 1798, was merged with Silva & Cosens. Dow's is now one of the many brands belonging to the Symington family, but consistently makes one of the very greatest vintage ports. *See also* Gould Campbell, Graham's, Quarles Harris, Smith Woodhouse, Warre's.

☷ 18–35 years

✓ *Entire range*

## FEIST
*See* Barros

## FERREIRA
★★

This house was established in 1761 and was family-owned until 1988, when it was taken over by Sogrape, the largest wine shipper in Portugal. The brand leader in Portugal itself, Ferreira did not establish its present reputation until the mid-19th century, when it was under the control of Dona Antonia Adelaide Ferreira, who was so successful that when she died she left an estate of $16 million, valued at 1896 rates. Ever mindful of its Portuguese roots, it is not surprising that elegantly rich tawny port is Ferreira's forte. Equally consistent is the style of its vintage port. While this wine is typically light, smooth, and mellow, it does age beautifully.

☷ 12–30 years

✓ *Entire range*

## FEUERHEERD
*See* Barros

## FONSECA
### Fonseca Guimaraens
★★★

This house was originally called Fonseca, Monteiro & Co., but changed its name when it was purchased by Manuel Pedro Guimaraens in 1822. Although it has been part of Taylor, Fladgate & Yeatman since 1948, it operates in a totally independent fashion, utilizing its own *quintas* and contracted suppliers. Fonseca has always been the top-quality brand, but even its second wine, Fonseca Guimaraens, puts many port houses to shame.

☷ 15–30 years

✓ *Entire range*

## GOULD CAMPBELL
★

Although at the cheaper end of the Symington group, Gould Campbell, which was established in about 1797, produces fine, sometimes stunningly fine, vintage ports. *See also* Dow's, Graham's, Smith Woodhouse, Quarles Harris, Warre's.

☷ 12–25 years

✓ *vintage*

## GRAHAM'S
### W. & J. Graham & Co.
★★★☆

Graham's was founded as a textile business and only entered the port trade when, in 1826, its Oporto office accepted wine in payment of a debt. Along the way, Graham's took over the firm of Smith Woodhouse and both of them became part of the Symington port empire in 1970. Although it is the vintage port that earned Graham's its reputation, the entire range is of an equally high quality, category for category. *See also* Dow's, Gould Campbell, Quarles Harris, Smith Woodhouse, Warre's.

☷ 18–40 years

✓ *Entire range, including basic Six Grapes Ruby*

## GUIMARAENS
*See* Fonseca

## HUTCHESON
*See* Barros

## KOPKE
*See* Barros

## MARTINEZ
### Martinez Gassiot
★★☆ ⓥ

Martinez was founded in 1797 by Sebastian González Martinez, a

Spaniard, but became affiliated with Cockburn in the early 1960s. Rather underrated, it produces small quantities of high-quality vintage and great-value crusted, and is also a source of extraordinarily good own-label port. *See also* Cockburn's.

🍷⎯ 12–20 years
✓ *Entire Range*

## MORGAN
### ★⍟

One of the oldest port houses, Morgan was acquired by Croft in 1952, but Croft itself was sold by Diageo to Taylor's in 2001. The Morgan brand was retained by Diageo (owners of Captain Morgan Rum), but its production has stopped and its future remains uncertain. A number of excellent own-label ports have filtered onto the market bearing the Morgan Brothers name in small type, and Taylor's sold off a large cache of excellent Morgan vintages at auction in 2007.

## NIEPOORT
### ★★

This small Dutch-owned firm is best known for its elegantly rich tawnies, especially the colheitas, but also makes fine, underrated vintage port.

🍷⎯ 12–25 years
✓ *Entire range*

## NOVAL
### Quinta do Noval
### ★★⍟
### *Nacional* ★★★

Originally a Portuguese house, having been founded in 1813 by Antonio José da Silva, Quinta do Noval was controlled by the Dutch van Zeller family for four generations until it was purchased by the French AXA group. Although officially known as Quinta do Noval, it carefully markets most products under the Noval brand, reserving the *quinta* name for those ports made exclusively from the property itself.

🍷⎯ 15–35 years (25–70 years for Nacional)
✓ *Vintage • Nacional • 20- and 40-Year-Old Tawny*

## OFFLEY
### Offley Forrester
### ★★⍟

Established in 1737, this firm once belonged to the famous Baron Forrester, but is now owned by Sogrape. Offley makes excellent-quality colheitas, elegant vintage ports, and a deeper-colored single-*quinta* Boa Vista.

🍷⎯ 12–25 years
✓ *Vintage • Boa Vista • Colheita • 10- and 20-Year-Old Tawny*

## POÇAS
### Poças Junior

Established in 1918, like many Portuguese-owned firms, Poças Junior started declaring vintage ports relatively recently (1960s) and is primarily known for its tawnies

and colheitas. Second labels include Lopes, Pousada, and Seguro.

## QUARLES HARRIS

Established in 1680 and the second-largest port house in the 18th century, when it was taken over by Warre's, Quarles Harris is now one of the smallest port brands under the control of the progressive Symington Group. *See also* Dow's, Gould Campbell, Graham's, Quarles Harris, Smith Woodhouse, Warre's.

## QUINTA DE LA ROSA
### ★

Promising new estate-bottled, single-*quinta* port. Look for the new 10-year-old tawny.

🍷⎯ 8–25 years
✓ *Finest Reserve • Late Bottled Vintage • Vintage*

## QUINTA DO COTTO
### *See* Champalimaud

## QUINTA DO INFANTADO
### ★⍟

The vintage port from this estate-bottled single-*quinta* have been rather lightweight, but the 1991 late-bottled vintage was a real gem, so it might be worth keeping an eye on future releases from this independent producer.

## QUINTA DO NOVAL
### *See* Noval

## QUINTA DO VESUVIO

This massive, 990-acre (400-hectare) former Ferreira property was considered to be the greatest *quinta* in the Douro when planted in the 19th century. Owned since 1989 by the Symington group, which has already established its vintage port as exceptional, but how exceptional remains to be seen.

🍷⎯ 12–30 years
✓ *Vintage*

## RAMOS-PINTO
### ★★⍟

Established in 1880 by Adriano Ramos-Pinto, when he was 20 years old, this firm remained in family ownership until 1990, when it was purchased by Champagne Louis Roederer. Ramos-Pinto always has produced excellent tawnies, particularly the single-*quintas* 10- and 20-year-old and its colheitas, but if the 1994 is anything to go by, vintage port could be its future *forte*.

🍷⎯ 12–25 years
✓ *Late-Bottled Vintage • Single-Quinta* (Quinta da Ervamoira 10-Year-Old, Quinta do Bom-Retiro 20-Year-Old) *• Colheitas • Vintage* (from 1994)

## REBELLO VALENTE
### *See* Robertson Brothers and Co

## ROBERTSON BROTHERS AND CO
### ⍟

Established in 1881, this small port house is now a subsidiary of

Sandeman and thus owned by Sogrape. Best known for its tawnies and, under the famous Rebello Valente label, very traditional vintage ports.

🍷⎯ 12–25 years
✓ *10- and 20-Year-Old Tawnies • Vintage*

## ROYAL OPORTO
### Real Companhia Velha
### ★⍟

Founded in 1756 by the Marquis de Pombal to regulate the port trade. Its reputation as a good source of inexpensive tawny and vintage character ports has ensured its survival, but it is focusing its greatest efforts on nonfortified Douro wines.

✓ *Vintage Character* (The Navigator's)

## ROZES
### ⍟

Part of the giant Moët-Hennessy group, Rozes has yet to establish a reputation beyond France.

## SANDEMAN
### ⍟

Also known for its sherry and Madeira, Sandeman was established in 1790 and took over Robertson's and Rebello Valente in 1881, after which it acquired Diez and Offley, and is itself owned by Sogrape. The quality of Sandeman's vintage port is variable and seldom blockbusting, but its tawnies are reliable, especially Imperial 20-Year-Old.

✓ *20-Year-Old Tawny* (Imperial) *• Vintage Character* (Signature)

## SANTOS JUNIOR
### *See* Barros

## SILVA & COSENS
### *See* Dow & Co

## SILVA, C. DA
Now under the same ownership as Cruz.

## SMITH WOODHOUSE
### ★⍟⍟
The products of this famous British port house are not as well known

in Portugal as they are on export markets, where they are much appreciated for tremendous value across the entire range, and also for some of the very greatest vintage ports ever made. *See also* Dow's, Gould Campbell, Graham's, Smith Woodhouse, Warre's.

🍷⎯ 12–25 years
✓ *Entire range*

## SYMINGTON GROUP

The Symingtons are one of the most well-known and successful of all port families, owning six brands, yet not one of these boasts the family name. *See also* Dow's, Gould Campbell, Graham's, Quarles Harris, Smith Woodhouse, Warre's.

## TAYLOR'S
### Taylor, Fladgate & Yeatman
### ★★★

Founded in 1692 by Job Bearsley, this house underwent no fewer than 21 changes of title before adopting its present one, which derives from the names of various partners: Joseph Taylor in 1816, John Fladgate in 1837, and Morgan Yeatman in 1844. At one time the firm was known as Webb, Campbell, Gray & Cano (Joseph Cano was, as it happens, the only American ever to be admitted into the partnership of a port house). In 1744, Taylor's became the first shipper to buy a property in the Douro, but its most famous acquisition was Quinta de Vargellas in 1890, a prestigious property that provides the heart and soul of every Taylor's vintage port.

🍷⎯ 20–40 years
✓ *Entire range*

## VIERA DE SOUSA
### *See* Barros

## WARRE'S
### ★★★⍟

Only the German-founded house of Kopke can claim to be older than Warre's, which was established in 1670, although it only assumed its present name in 1729 when William Warre entered the business. This house, which now belongs to the entrepreneurial Symington family, normally vies with Graham's, another Symington brand, as the darkest and most concentrated vintage port after that of Taylor's. *See also* Dow's, Gould Campbell, Graham's, Quarles Harris, Smith Woodhouse.

🍷⎯ 18–35 years
✓ *Entire range*

## WEISE & KROHN

Weise & Krohn port house was originally founded in 1865 by two Norwegians of German extraction, Theodore Weise and Dankert Krohn. It has been owned by the Portuguese Carneiro family since the 1930s. It makes rather insubstantial vintage port, and is best known for its tawnies.

✓ *Colheitas*

# MADEIRA

*The island of Madeira gives its name to the only wine in the world that must be baked in an oven! This fortified wine is deliberately heated to replicate the voyages of old during which the wine accidentally underwent maderization at equatorial temperatures.*

PRINCE HENRY THE NAVIGATOR sent Captain João Gonçalves in search of new lands in the 15th century. The Captain's nickname was Zarco, or "squinter," because he had been wounded in one eye while fighting the Moors. Although "squinter" seems an odd name for someone whose job it is to keep his eyes peeled for events on the horizon, particularly at that time, when every sailor was worried about falling off the edge of the world, this nickname is fact not fiction. Indeed, he was so proud of being called the "squinter" that he adopted it as a surname, becoming João Gonçalves Zarco. Despite this impediment to his sight, Zarco not only navigated his ship safely, but he actually managed to discover places. In 1418, for example, he found Madeira, although it must be admitted that he was searching for Guinea at the time. Zarco actually thought it was a cloud, but the more he squinted, the more suspicious he became: it was always in the same position.

One day he chased the cloud, sailed through it and bumped into an island. It was entirely covered in dense forest and the cloud was merely the mist of transpiration given off in the morning sun. The forest was impenetrable (Madeira means "island of woods"), so Zarco lit fires to denude areas of the island, sat back, and waited. By all accounts he had a long wait, as the fires raged for seven years and consumed every bit of vegetation, infusing the permeable volcanic soil with potash, which by chance rendered it particularly suitable for vine-growing.

## THE ORIGIN OF MADEIRA'S DISTINCTIVE WINE

As a source of fresh food and water, the island soon became a regular port of call for east-bound ships, which would often transport barrels of Madeira wine for sale in the Far East or Australia. As the ships journeyed through the tropics, the wine was heated to a maximum of 113°F (45°C) and cooled again during the six-month voyage, giving it a very distinctive character. The winemakers of Madeira were totally unaware of this until one unsold shipment returned to the island. Since then, special ovens, called *estufas*, have evolved in order that this heating and cooling can be replicated in the *estufagem* process (cheaper wines do this in large concrete vats, while the casks of better-quality wines experience a much longer, gentler process in warm rooms). All Madeiras undergo a normal fermentation prior to the *estufagem* process. Drier wines are fortified prior to *estufagem*, the sweeter styles afterward.

## THE FUTURE OF MADEIRA

Although sales of Madeira are growing, they are doing so from a relatively low base. Madeira has fallen a long way from its height of fame in the 19th century, when Russia was its greatest market and one Grand Duke alone purchased the equivalent of 76,000 cases a year. Far too much Madeira today is cheap, made from the lowly Tinta Negra Mole grape, and sold in bulk to France, Germany, and Belgium, where the natural impulse is to cook with it. If Madeira is to survive, it must concentrate on quality by replanting with classic varieties, encouraging a new wave of independent producers, banning bulk wines, and updating the concept of Vintage Madeira. Pushing Madeira upmarket is not merely required to reestablish its reputation, it is simple logic—viticulture on this precipitous island is so labor-intensive that cheap wine makes no economic sense.

COASTAL VIEW, MADEIRA
*Terraced vineyards cling to Madeira's rocky terrain, where irrigation is accomplished via a network of aqueducts.*

MADEIRA, *see also* p.328
*The island of Madeira, in the Atlantic Ocean west of Morocco, is famed for its fortified wine. Funchal is the capital of the island, where many wine lodges are found.*

LISBON

MADEIRA

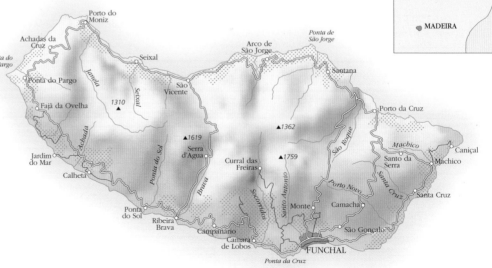

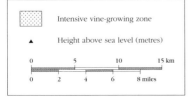

Intensive vine-growing zone

▲ Height above sea level (metres)

0   5   10   15 km

0   2   4   6   8 miles

# THE STYLES OF
# MADEIRA

There have traditionally been four basic styles of Madeira, named after the following grape varieties: Sercial, Verdelho, Bual, and Malmsey. During the 20th century, however, the majority of Madeira produced was blended with a high proportion of Tinta Negra Mole (or its variant Complexa) or of American hybrids. Since 1990, however, no hybrids have been allowed, and since 1993, those wines made from Tinta Negra Mole may use only generic terms of sweetness (and not the stylistic terms listed below), such as *seco* (dry), *meio seco* (medium dry), *meio doce* (medium sweet), and *doce* (sweet), accompanied by descriptors such as pale, dark, full, or rich, while at least 85 percent of a varietal wine must be made from the grape indicated.

**Note** Madeira should be ready to drink when sold and good Madeira will keep indefinitely, so no optimal drinking periods are given below.

## BASTARDO

Another rarity from Madeira's once glittering past, there is some question as to whether this black grape variety is related to the Douro variety of the same name, but there is no doubting its great potential quality, making it yet another golden oldie that is long overdue a revival.

## BUAL

Definitely sweeter and darker than the styles above, Bual can often be recognized under blind conditions by its khaki-colored meniscus. This style has soft, gentle fruit with noticeable fatness and ripeness, underscored by a baked, smoky complexity. The legal limit for residual sugar is 78–96 grams per liter.

✓ *See styles by age*

## EXTRA RESERVE *or* OVER-15-YEAR-OLD MADEIRA

This style is rarely encountered, but is always significantly richer and more complex than 10-Year-Old Madeira. The 15 years reference is excluded from some wines that are much older.

✓ *Barbeito* (25-Year-Old Bual) • *Cossart* (Malmsey 15-Year-Old Malmsey, Very Old Duo Centenary Celebration Bual, Very Old Duo Centenary Celebration Sercial)

## FINEST *or* 3-YEAR-OLD MADEIRA

This, the lowest level of Madeira, will be the style of any Madeira whose age is not given. It consists primarily of Tinta Negra Mole, and some Moscatel. Three years is too short a time for any decent wine to evolve into a true Madeira and much is sold in bulk for cooking, and cannot be recommended.

## MALMSEY

Made from both white and black varieties of Malvasia grown on the island's lowest and warmest regions, Malmsey is the ultimate Madeira and my own favorite. It is the most luscious, the sweetest, and most honeyed of all Madeira styles. Potentially the most complex and long-lived Madeira, Malmsey matures to an ultrasmooth, coffee-caramel succulence, which lasts forever in the mouth. The legal limit for residual sugar is 96–135 grams per liter.

✓ *See styles by age*

## MOSCATEL

Madeira has made some interesting Moscatel, but only a few remain available for tasting today. However, with so many fortified Muscats of superb quality made throughout the world, Madeira's Moscatel should perhaps be reserved for blending purposes only.

## RAINWATER

This is effectively a paler, softer version of a medium-dry Verdelho but, because varietal names are never used, making Rainwater with Verdelho would be a waste of this good-quality classic grape. Rainwater is more likely to be a paler, softer version of Tinta Negra Mole trying to emulate Verdelho. There are two theories about the origin of this curiously named Madeira style. One is that it came from the vines, which were grown on hillsides where it was impossible to irrigate, thus growers had to rely on rainwater. The other theory concerns a shipment that was bound for Boston in the US: even though the wine was accidentally diluted by rain en route, the Madeira house in question had hoped to get away with it, and were shocked when the Americans loved it so much they wanted more!

## RESERVE *or* 5-YEAR-OLD MADEIRA

This is the youngest age at which the noble varieties (Sercial, Verdelho, Bual, Malmsey, Bastardo, and Terrantez) may be used, so if no single variety is claimed, you can be sure that it is mostly, if not entirely, Tinta Negra Mole. Five years was once far too young for a classic Madeira from noble grapes, but they are much better than they used to be and some bargain five-year-old varietals can be found.

✓ *Barbeito* (Malmsey) • *Blandy's* (Sercial, Bual, Malmsey) • *Cossart* (Sercial)

## SERCIAL

This grape is known on the Portuguese mainland as Esgana Cão, or "dog strangler," and is grown in the island's coolest vineyards. Sercial is the palest, lightest, and driest Madeira, but matures to a rich, yet crisp, savory flavor with the sharp tang of acidic spices and citrus fruits. The legal limit for residual sugar is 18–65 grams per liter (the bottom end of this range tastes bone dry when balanced against an alcohol level of 17 percent in such an intensely flavored wine, and even 40 grams per liter can seem dry).

✓ *See styles by age*

## SOLERA MADEIRA

Although an old *solera* will contain barely a few molecules from the year on which it was based and which it boasts on the label, the best examples of authentic Madeira *soleras* (there have been several frauds) are soft, sensuous, and delicious.

✓ *Blandy's Solera 1863 Malmsey • Blandy's Solera 1880 Verdelho • Cossart Solera 1845 Bual*

## SPECIAL RESERVE *or* 10-YEAR-OLD MADEIRA

This is where serious Madeira begins, and even nonvarietals may be worthy of consideration because, although some wines in this style may be made with Tinta Negra Mole, producers will risk only superior wines from this grape for such extended aging.

✓ *Blandy's* (Sercial, Malmsey) • *Cossart* (Verdelho, Malmsey) • *Henriques & Henriques* (Sercial, Malmsey) • *Power Drury* (Malmsey) • *Rutherford & Miles* (Bual, Malmsey)

## TERRANTEZ

This white grape variety is virtually extinct on the island, but the highly perfumed, rich, powerfully flavored, and tangy-sweet Madeira wine it produced is so highly regarded that old vintages can still attract top prices at auction. If and when the Young Turks ever reach Madeira, this is one variety they will be replanting in earnest.

## VERDELHO

Some modern renditions of this style are almost as pale as Sercial, but Verdelho, both white and black varieties of which are grown on the island, traditionally produces a golden Madeira whose color deepens with age. It is, however, always made in a medium-dry to medium-sweet style, which gives it somewhat more body than Sercial, and this can make it seem softer and riper than it actually is, although its true astringency is revealed on the finish. The legal limit for residual sugar in these wines is 49–78 grams per liter.

✓ *See styles by age*

## VINTAGE MADEIRA

All Madeira wines at one time bore a vintage, but this practice is unusual today, since most are blends or products of *solera* systems. Current regulations stipulate that vintage Madeira must spend at least 20 years in cask, but if Madeira is to prosper, this outdated approach must be discarded and a system similar to that used for vintage port must be adopted. This is not to suggest that vintage Madeira should not spend 20 years in cask, just that this rather lengthy process ought not to be mandatory. Consumers worldwide perceive vintage wines to be superior to nonvintage ones, and it does not seem to matter that the opposite is sometimes true: if Madeira is to reclaim the world stage and capture international imaginations, producers simply must put the spotlight on vintage Madeira, and the world is unlikely to wait 20 years for this to happen. Madeira must therefore release some of its vintages when they are much younger and put the onus on consumers to age the wines themselves. This would have the added advantage of feeding the auction circuit with a new investment and, as the different vintages are successively tasted and retasted, reported and discussed by critics, this would raise consumer awareness of these wines, thus very usefully enhancing the reputation of Madeira in general.

# The WINES of
# GERMANY, AUSTRIA, AND SWITZERLAND

CLASSIC GERMAN RIESLING IS INCOMPARABLE. No other wine can offer in a single sip as much finesse, purity of fruit, intensity of flavor, and thrilling acidity as a fine Riesling, yet it remains underrated. German Pinot Noir (Spätburgunder) is even more underrated. Few people have even heard of it. Yet, almost one-third of Germany's vineyards are planted with black grapes and, of that, one-third is Pinot Noir. Top Spätburgunder from the Ahr, Baden, and the Pfalz can be compared in quality with some of the best *premiers crus* in Burgundy. The only question is whether such wines can be produced at prices that do not make good Burgundy seem cheap by comparison! Austria also makes beautiful, underappreciated Riesling and Pinot Noir, in addition to which, top quality examples of one of its indigenous varieties, the highly distinctive Grüner Veltliner, are at last being taken seriously. And if German red wine is a surprise, nearly half of all Swiss wine is red, with smooth Pinot Noir and dense-yet-velvety Merlot the up-and-coming stars. These three countries will offer consumers some of the most exciting and diverse wine experiences of the new millennium.

THE RHEINGAU DISTRICT
*A fall view of the quaint Hallgarten chapel, which lies between the Schönhell and Würzgarten vineyards.*

# GERMANY

*The best German wines (Riesling and Pinot Noir) are better than ever, but the worst have never been as bad, and the German wine law passed in 1994 to replace the flawed law of 1971 has unfortunately not improved matters. On top of this, we now have a befuddled Großes Gewächs classification muddying the water at the very top end of the market, and wine labels with Anglicized fantasy names at the bottom end of the market. The latter are supposed to simplify labeling, yet make the wines look as if they were made in Eastern Europe.*

EVERY GERMAN WINE is graded by the natural sugar content of its grapes; the more sugar, the higher the quality, therefore the greatest German wines are inevitably the sweetest. Although the philosophy that equates ripeness with greatness is misguided and has proved harmful to Germany's reputation, it is not an unreasonable one, for ripe grapes are required to make fine wine, and in Germany's northerly climate it is usually only the best sites that can fully ripen grapes. Nonetheless, taken to its ultimate conclusion, the German ideal implies, nonsensically, that a drier wine is inherently inferior to a sweeter wine. In the quest for sweetness and greater volume, the Riesling was gradually discarded in favor of German crosses such as Müller-Thurgau and Kerner, which easily ripened at much higher sugar levels and yielded far larger crops.

## A GERMAN ESTATE-WINE REVIVAL?

In the 18th and 19th centuries, German wines from the Rhine were as famous and as expensive as the wines of Bordeaux, and Germany's system of aristocratic wine estates was on a par with the great wine châteaux of France. Today, almost every wine critic agrees that Germany's best estates must reassert their position, if this country wants to regain its reputation for quality. But this is not currently possible because each estate makes far too many wines to project any sort of unified image, let alone reputation.

## QUALITY STRUCTURE OVERVIEW

This is a simplistic overview because each category varies according to the grape variety and its area of origin. More detailed analyses are given under each region (*see* Quality Requirements and Harvest Percentages box, p.346).

| QUALITY CATEGORY | MINIMUM OECHSLE | MINIMUM POTENTIAL ALCOHOL |
|---|---|---|
| Deutscher Tafelwein* | 44–50° | 5.0–5.9% |
| Landwein* | 47–55° | 5.6–6.7% |
| Qualitätswein bestimmter Anbaugebiete (QbA)* | 50–72° | 5.9–9.4% |
| **QUALITÄTSWEIN MIT PRÄDIKAT (QmP):** | | |
| Kabinett | 67–85° | 8.6–11.4% |
| Spätlese | 76–95° | 10.0–13.0% |
| Auslese | 83–105° | 11.1–14.5% |
| Beerenauslese | 110–128° | 15.3–18.1% |
| Eiswein | 110–128° | 15.3–18.1% |
| Trockenbeerenauslese (TBA) | 150–154° | 21.5–22.1% |

*Chaptalization is allowed, and will be necessary if the wine has a potential alcoholic strength of less than 8.5 percent.*

SCHLOSS JOHANNISBERG
*This historic, mansion-style* schloss, *which dominates the Rheingau slope between Winkel and Geisenheim, was built in 1563.*

In Bordeaux one can speak of the style and quality of, say, Château Margaux *vis-à-vis* Château Latour, but what can be said about any top German estate, when the wines range from QbA, through *Kabinett, Spätlese, Auslese, Beerenauslese,* and *Trockenbeerenauslese* to *Eiswein* for each grape variety grown? At one time Germany's top wine estates did not market a vast number of *Prädikat* wines. Instead, they built their reputations on a single, flagship *cuvée*, which was invariably pure Riesling and, no matter how many times the vineyards were combed for

## THE WINE REGIONS OF GERMANY

Viticulturally, Germany is made up of four large *Deutscher Tafelwein* regions encompassing eight *Tafelwein* subregions, within which there are separate infrastructures for 13 *Qualitätswein* and 20 *Landwein* regions. (The two *Qualitätswein* and two *Landwein* regions in former Eastern Germany fall outside the *Tafelwein* structure.) The *Qualitätswein* regions encompass 39 *Bereiche* (districts), containing 160 *Grosslagen* (collective sites), which in turn encapsulate 2,632 *Einzellagen* (single sites).

| DEUTSCHER TAFELWEIN REGIONS | DEUTSCHER TAFELWEIN SUB-REGIONS | LANDWEIN REGIONS | QUALITÄTSWEIN REGIONS |
|---|---|---|---|
| Rhein-Mosel | Rhein | Ahrtaler Landwein | Ahr |
| | | Starkenburger Landwein | Hessische Bergstrasse |
| | | Rheinburgen Landwein | Mittelrhein |
| | | Nahegauer Landwein | Nahe |
| | | Altrheingauer Landwein | Rheingau |
| | | Rheinischer Landwein | Rheinhessen |
| | | Pfälzer Landwein | Pfalz |
| | Mosel | Landwein der Mosel | |
| | Saar | Saarländischer Landwein | Mosel |
| | | Landwein der Ruwer | |
| Bayern | Main | Fränkischer Landwein | Franken |
| | Donau | Regensburger Landwein | |
| | Lindau | Bayerischer Bodensee Landwein | Württemberg |
| Neckar | - | Schwäbischer Landwein | |
| Oberrhein | Römertor | Südbadischer Landwein | Baden |
| | Burgengau | Unterbadischer Landwein | |
| | | Taubertäler Landwein | |
| | | Mitteldeutscher Landwein | Saale-Unstrut |
| | | Sächsischer Landwein | Sachsen |
| Stargarder Land | | Mecklenburger Landwein | |

grapes, just one wine was produced. It would be like combining all the different *Prädikat* wines into one superrich blend today. In the days of Germany's illustrious wine estates, the wines were fermented more fully, rather than being arrested at artificially low alcohol levels in order to retain sweetness. Thus, these flagship *cuvées* were not just richer than today's wines, but drier, fuller-bodied, and more alcoholic. It was this sort of wine that made Germany's finest wine estates famous throughout the world, and

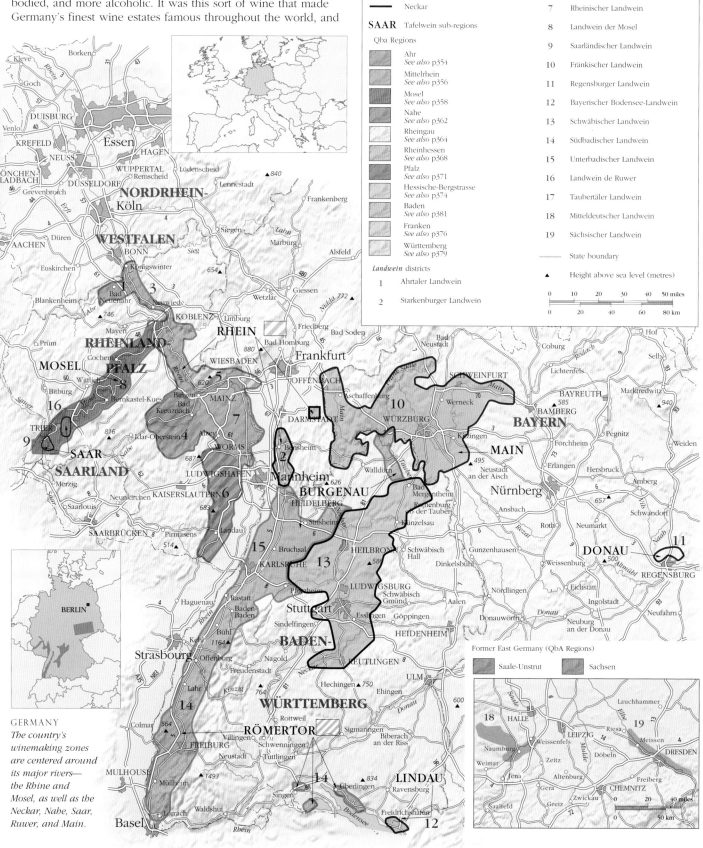

**GERMANY**

*The country's winemaking zones are centered around its major rivers—the Rhine and Mosel, as well as the Neckar, Nahe, Saar, Ruwer, and Main.*

**Tafelwein districts**

| | |
|---|---|
| —— | Rhein-Mosel |
| —— | Oberrhein |
| —— | Bayern |
| —— | Neckar |

**SAAR** Tafelwein sub-regions

**Qba Regions**

- Ahr *See also p354*
- Mittelrhein *See also p356*
- Mosel *See also p358*
- Nahe *See also p362*
- Rheingau *See also p364*
- Rheinhessen *See also p368*
- Pfalz *See also p371*
- Hessische-Bergstrasse *See also p374*
- Baden *See also p381*
- Franken *See also p376*
- Württemberg *See also p379*

**Landwein districts**

1 Ahrtaler Landwein
2 Starkenburger Landwein
3 Rheinburger Landwein
4 Nahegauer Landwein
5 Altrheingauer Landwein
6 Pfälzer Landwein
7 Rheinischer Landwein
8 Landwein der Mosel
9 Saarländischer Landwein
10 Fränkischer Landwein
11 Regensburger Landwein
12 Bayerischer Bodensee-Landwein
13 Schwäbischer Landwein
14 Südbadischer Landwein
15 Unterbadischer Landwein
16 Landwein de Ruwer
17 Taubertäler Landwein
18 Mitteldeutscher Landwein
19 Sächsischer Landwein

—— State boundary

▲ Height above sea level (metres)

**Former East Germany (QbA Regions)**

Saale-Unstrut    Sachsen

## QUALITY REQUIREMENTS AND HARVEST PERCENTAGES

Germany is notorious for the variation of its vintages. Therefore, as a form of insurance, , most of the crop is harvested early. This secures a minimum income from Deutscher Tafelwein and QbA wines, with those grapes that remain on the vine providing a possibility of higher-quality wines from late harvests. If, when, and how much these grapes ripen is the most basic indication of the nature of any vintage. The degree of ripeness attained is expressed in degrees *Oechsle* and the minimum level for each QmP can vary according to the region and grape variety in question. Each degree of *Oechsle* is the equivalent of 2–2.5 per liter grams of sugar. The exact amount of sugar varies according to the level of unfermentable extract also present. (For a survey of each region, see the individual charts in the regional sections.)

only when they return to the same basic philosophy will they be able to rebuild their reputations.

## THE 1971 GERMAN WINE LAW

In 1971 a wine law was established to take account of EEC legislation regulating wine production. The main aspect of the law was to reduce 30,000 *Einzellagen* (individually named vineyards) to 2,600. The law allowed the boundaries of each of the original *Einzellagen* to be extended in order to cover a minimum area of five hectares (12⅓ acres). The solution appeared efficient, but missed the point of why any plot of land evolves a name or reputation to distinguish it from neighboring vineyards: *terroir* (*see* pp.14–16). The enshrining of these amalgamated vineyards in law has duped the public into believing that highly priced wines come from specific, historical sites when in fact they may originate from the surrounding areas that, on average, are more than 10 times the size.

This was nothing less than legalized fraud, but the bureaucratic bungling did not end there. The lawmakers went on to create an entirely new geographical appellation called the *"Grosslage,"* which has turned out to be an even greater deception. In fact, once this law's capacity to deceive was fully understood, it became known on English-speaking markets as the "Gross lie." A *Grosslage,* or "collective site," is a very large area, not merely encompassing several *Einzellagen* (single sites as the term literally means) but many villages, each of which comprises a large number of *Einzellagen*. On average, each *Grosslage* consists of 17 post-1971 *Einzellagen* or 197 pre-1971 *Einzellagen*. Such wines are widely blended and of modest quality, but this in itself would not have been a problem had it been obligatory for the term *"Grosslage"* to appear on the label before the name of the

## COMPARISON OF GERMAN HARVESTS 2000–2003

Production varies enormously in Germany—from as much as 171 million cases (15.4 million hectoliters) in 1982 to as little as 58 million cases (5.2 million hectoliters) in 1985—as does the spread of wines across the range of quality categories, shown by the table below:

|  | 2000 | 2001 | 2002 | 2003 |
|---|---|---|---|---|
| **QUALITY CATEGORY** | | | | |
| Tafelwein to Landwein | 2% | 0.5% | 0.5% | 3% |
| QbA | 54% | 45.5% | 43.5% | 33% |
| QmP | 44% | 54% | 56% | 64% |
| **SIZE OF HARVEST** | | | | |
| Millions of hectolitres | 10.1 | 9.1 | 10.1 | 8.3 |
| (Millions of cases) | 112 | 101 | 112 | 92 |
| Hectares under vine | 101,546 | 99,714 | 98,772 | 98,270 |
| (Acres) | 250,926 | 246,399 | 244,071 | 242,830 |
| Hectolitres per hectare | 99.3 | 91.1 | 102.6 | 84.3 |

## DECODING THE AP NUMBER

All QbAs and QmPs, including *Deutscher Sekt*, must carry an AP number (*Amtliche Prüfnummer*). This proves that a wine has undergone and passed various tasting and analytical tests and its origin has been established to the board's satisfaction. Each time a producer applies for an AP number, specially sealed samples of the approved wine are kept by both the board and the producer. Should there be a fault or a fraud enquiry, these samples are analyzed and checked against a sample of the product on the market that has given rise to complaint or investigation. This sounds foolproof, and it is indeed more stringent than the EU's Lot Number, which has been in operation since 1989. But like all systems it can be abused, which in this case would simply mean printing fictitious AP numbers on the label, although if noticed the penalty for this would be imprisonment, plus a ban from operating for the company, and a large fine. Understanding the AP number can be very useful. If the wine is a nonvintage QbA, it can give you some idea of how long it has been in bottle.

**2002 "Weingut Müller-Catoir" Riesling Spätlese Qualitätswein mit Prädikat (QmP)**

**5** = Examination Board number

**174** = number of the commune where the wine was bottled

**079** = the bottler's registered number

**16** = the bottler's application number

**03** = the year in which the bottler made the application

AP Nr. 5 174 079 16 03

The communes' and bottlers' numbers run into thousands and are of the least significance to the consumer. It is the last two sets of numbers that provide the most useful information. In this instance, the 16 and 03 reveal that this is Weingut Müller-Catoir's 16th application made in 2003. The application numbers are sequential, but do not necessarily apply to the same wine, i.e., none of the 15 previous applications made by Weingut Müller-Catoir in 2003 need necessarily apply to its 2002 Riesling Spätlese QmP. You will find that some references state that the application number actually refers to a specific cask the wine came from (which in this case would be *fuder* 16), but although this is so in some cases (Fritz Haag, and Von Schubert's Maximin Grünhaus, for example), this is only because the producer in question will number his cask to coincide with the application number. What the last two sets of digits tell us is that if they are the same, then the wine is *exactly* the same. If you find two bottles of 2002 Weingut Müller-Catoir Riesling Spätlese QmP both bearing the AP number 5 174 079 16 03, then you know beyond any doubt that the contents of both bottles swam with each other before being bottled together. If you find two bottles of 2002 Weingut Müller-Catoir Riesling Spätlese QmP both bearing the AP number where either or both of the last two sets of digits are different, then you know that the contents are, at the very least, subtly different. They might simply be bottled on a different date, or from a different cask, but when the designation is as broad as Riesling Spätlese QmP, the grapes could have been grown miles apart, picked on different days, vinified in different tanks, with radically different sugar, alcohol, and acidity readings.

*Grosslage* itself, as *"Bereich"* (district) has to. Not only does the term *Grosslage* not have to appear anywhere on the label, but the name of the *Grosslage* appears after that of the village, in precisely the same way as the name of an *Einzellage* does, constantly leading consumers to believe that a *Grosslage* wine is from a single *Einzellage*. The criteria that originally established Germany as one of the great wine-producing countries of the world—the preeminence and defining quality of the Riesling grape, the famous villages or estates where it was grown, and the legendary quality of the individually named vineyards, or true *Einzellagen*—no longer applied after 1971.

## THE 1994 WINE LAW

In 1994, when Germany was required to bring its wine law into line with those of other EU member states, it had a chance to remedy the flaws in the 1971 wine law. Those who cared about

## GERMAN LABEL LANGUAGE

**ABFÜLLUNG** Bottling.

**AUSLESE** A category of German QmP wine that is very sweet, made from late-picked grapes, and which may also contain some botrytized grapes, *Auslese* is one step of sweetness above *Spätlese*, but one below *Beerenauslese*, and most of the best lean upward rather than downward.

**BADISCH ROTGOLD** A specialty rosé wine made from a blend of Ruländer and Spätburgunder, Badischer Rotgold must be of at least QbA level, and can be produced only in Baden.

**BARIQUEWEIN** Fermented or matured in new oak casks.

**BEERENAUSLESE** A category of German QmP wine that comes above *Auslese* in sweetness, but beneath *Trockenbeerenauslese* and is made from botrytized grapes. It has more finesse and elegance than any other intensely sweet wine, with the possible exception of *Eiswein*.

**BEREICH** If the wine carries the appellation of a *Bereich*, it will simply state this—"Bereich Burg Cochem," for example.

**DEUTSCHER** German.

**DEUTSCHER QUALITÄTS-SCHAUMWEIN OR DEUTSCHER SEKT BESTIMMTER ANBAUGEBIETE** A sparkling wine made by any method (but probably *cuve close*), from 100 percent German grapes grown in one specified region, although it may indicate an even smaller area of origin if at least 85 percent of the grapes come from that named area.

**DEUTSCHER SEKT OR DEUTSCHER QUALITÄTSSCHAUMWEIN** A sparkling wine made by any method (but probably *cuve close*), from 100 percent German grapes. It may indicate a maximum of two grape names and should be at least 10 months old when sold.

**DEUTSCHER WEINSIEGEL** An official seal of quality awarded to wines that receive a higher score than the minimum required for an AP number, Deutscher Weinsiegels use a color-coding system: *trocken* wines bear a bright yellow seal; *halbtrocken* a lime green seal, and sweeter wines a red seal.

**EDELFÄULE** The German term for noble rot.

**EINZELLAGE** A single-vineyard wine area; the smallest geographical unit allowed under German wine law.

**EISWEIN** A rare wine resulting from the tradition of leaving grapes on the vine in the hope of attracting *Botrytis cinerea*. The grapes are frozen by frost or snow, then harvested, and pressed while frozen. This is done because only the ice freezes and, as

this rises to the top of the vat, it can be scraped off to leave a concentrated juice that produces a wine with a unique balance of sweetness, acidity, and extract.

**ERSTES LAGE** *See* Grosses Gewächs

**ERSTES GEWÄCHS** *See* Grosses Gewächs

**ERZEUGERABFÜLLUNG** At one time this was considered to mean estate-bottled, but so many cooperatives use it (because, they claim, their members' estates are the cooperative's estates) that it now means no more producer-bottled, thus some estates now use *Gutsabfüllung*. See *Gutsabfüllung*

**FLASCHENGÄRUNG** A bottle-fermented *Sekt* that is not necessarily made by the traditional method.

**FLASCHENGÄRUNG NACH DEM TRADITIONELLEN VERFAHREN** A *Sekt* made by the traditional method, although it is not likely to show much autolytic character.

**FÜDER** A large oval cask that holds 1,000 liters (265 gallons); more prevalent in the Mosel than the Rhine.

**FÜR DIABETIKER GEEIGNET** Suitable for diabetics, the wines must be *trocken* (dry), contain less than 1.5 grams per liter of sulfur dioxide (as opposed to the legal maximum of 2.25 grams per liter), and no more than 12 percent alcohol.

**GROSSES GEWÄCHS** (Great Growth), **ERSTES GEWÄCHS** (First Growth—Rheingau only), and **ERSTE LAGE** (First Site—Mosel only) are reserved for wines from the most highly rated vineyards. Only *Auslese, Beerenauslese, Trockenbeerenauslese,* or *Eiswein prädikate* are allowed, except in Mosel, where *Kabinett* and *Spätlese prädikate* and various other designations may also be used. When not qualified by any *prädikat, Grosses Gewächs* must be a dry wine made from grapes with a minimum *Spätlese* must weight. In the Ahr, only dry Pinot Noir or Frühburgunder of a minimum *Auslese* must weight qualify for *Grosses Gewächs*. All *Grosses/Erstes Gewächs* and *Erste Lage* wines must be hand harvested to a maximum yield of 50hl/ha (220 cases/acre), subjected to a VDP taste test, and cannot be released until September of the year following that of the harvest (two years for red wines).

**GROSSLAGE** A *Grosslage*, or "collective site," is a large area under which name cheap, bulk-blended wines are sold.

**GUTSABFÜLLUNG** This term literally means "bottled on the property" and has been taken up by those who feel that *Erzeugerabfüllung* has been so debased by the the cooperatives that it no longer stands for a wine that is

truly estate-bottled. *Gutsabfüllung* can only be used by a winemaker who holds a diploma in oenology. This means any naturally gifted winemaker who has not sat the examination, but owns an estate and makes brilliant wines, has no legal way of indicating his or her wine is an authentic product that has been grown on, fermented at, and bottled on a individual wine estate.

**GUTSWEIN AND ORTSWEIN** (estate wine and commune wine) is applicable to wines observing the VDP's general standards, which include viticultural methods adhering to strict controls, regular inspection of vineyards, higher must weights than those prescribed by law, and a maximum yield of 75hl/ha (330 cases/acre).

**HALBTROCKEN** Literally "half-dry," although practically semisweet on most occasions, this wine does not contain more than 18 grams per liter of residual sugar and 10 grams per liter of acid .

**JAHRGANG** Vintage year.

**KLASSIFIZIERTER LAGENWEIN** (wine from a classified site) is restricted to wines from classified vineyards that impart site-specific traits, with a maximum yield of 65hl/ha (285 cases/acre).

**KABINETT** The predicate at the end of this wine's name (it can come either before or after the grape variety) reveals that it is the lightest and driest of the QmP wines.

**LANDWEIN** This Teutonic version of the French *vin de pays* is not only a failure in commercial terms (unlike its Gallic compatriot), but is also rather strange in that it may be produced in only *trocken* and *halbtrocken* styles.

**LIEBLICH** Technically medium-sweet, although nearer to the French *moelleux*, this wine may have up to 45 grams per liter of residual sugar.

**ORTSWEIN** *See* Gutswein

**QUALITÄTSWEIN MIT PRÄDIKAT** (QmP) The wine comes from the highest quality category of German wine and will carry one of the predicates that range from *Kabinett* up to *Trockenbeerenauslese*.

**PERLWEIN** Cheap, semi-sparkling wines made by carbonating a still wine. Mostly white, but may be red or rosé.

**QBA** *Qualitätswein bestimmter Anbaugebiete*, this is the theoretical equivalent of the French AOC.

**QMP** *Qualitätswein mit Prädikat*, this literally means a "quality wine with predication," and is a term used for any German wine above QbA, from *Kabinett* upward. The predication carried by a QmP wine depends upon the level of ripeness of the grapes used in the wine.

**QUALITÄTSSCHAUMWEIN** A "quality sparkling wine" can be produced by any member state of the EU, but the term should be qualified by the country of origin (of the wine). Only *Deutscher Qualitätsschaumwein* will necessarily be from Germany.

**REBE** Grape variety.

**RESTUSSE** Residual sugar.

**ROSEWEIN OR ROSEEWEIN** Rosé.

**ROTLING** A rosé wine that may be made from black grapes or a mixture of black and white. This designation must be indicated on the label of any category of *Tafelwein* up to and including *Landwein*, and must also be featured on the label of QbA wine, although it is optional for QmP.

**ROTWEIN** Red wine. This designation must be indicated on the label of any category of *Tafelwein* up to and including *Landwein*, and must also be featured on the label of QbA wine, although it is optional for QmP.

**SCHAUMWEIN** With no further qualification, such as *Qualitätsschaumwein*, this indicates the cheapest form of sparkling wine, probably a carbonated blend of wines from various EU countries.

**SCHILLERWEIN** A style of wine produced in Württemberg that is the same as a *Rotling*.

**SEKT** Sparkling wine.

**SPÄTLESE** A QmP wine that is one step of sweetness above *Kabinett*, but one below *Auslese*. It is fairly sweet and made from late-picked grapes.

**SÜSS** A sweet wine with in excess of 45 grams per liter of residual sugar.

**TAFELWEIN** A lowly table wine or *vin de table*.

**TROCKEN** Literally "dry," a *trocken* wine must not contain more than 4 grams per liter of residual sugar, although up to 9 grams per liter is permitted if the acidity is 2 grams per liter or more.

**TROCKENBEERENAUSLESE** A wine produced from individually picked, botrytized grapes that have been left on the vine to shrivel, it is typically golden-amber to amber in color, intensely sweet, viscous, very complex and as different from *Beerenauslese* as that wine is from *Kabinett*.

**VDP** Verband Deutscher Prädikats- und Qualitätsweingüter, an association of top wine estates.

**WEISSHERBST** A single-variety rosé produced from black grapes only, the variety of which must be indicated.

**WEISSWEIN** White wine. This designation must be indicated on the label of any category of *Tafelwein* up to and including *Landwein*. It may also be featured on the label of QbA and higher-quality wines, but this is not mandatory.

## SÜSSRESERVE

*Süssreserve* is sterilized grape juice that may have just one or two degrees of alcohol, but has none if processed before fermentation can commence. It not only contributes the grapey freshness and sweetness for which German wines are famous, but also provides the winemaker with a convenient last-minute ingredient with which he can correct the balance of a wine. The origin of *Süssreserve* must, in essence, be the same as the wine to which it is added. Its quality, or degree of ripeness, should by law be at least the equivalent of the wine itself. The quantity added is not in itself restricted, but is indirectly controlled by the overall ratio of sugar to alcohol.

| QUALITY | GRAMS OF ALCOHOL FOR EVERY GRAM OF RESIDUAL SUGAR PER LITRE | EXCEPTIONS |
|---|---|---|
| Tafelwein | 3g | Franconian red 5g |
| Qualitätswein | 3g | Franconian red 5g |
| | | Franconian white and rosé 3.5g |
| | | Württemberg red 4g |
| | | Rheingau white |
| Kabinett | no controls | Franconian red 5g |
| | | Franconian white 3g and rosé |

quality bravely attempted reforms, but the large private and cooperative bottlers of inferior wine were too powerful, thus the bad law of 1971 was replaced by the even worse law of 1994. *Grosslagen* and *Bereiche* could and should have been disposed of because they are unnecessary appellations that do not enhance the reputation of German wines. But if such a simple yet radical move was too difficult to accomplish, then a temporary and perfectly adequate means of stopping the rot would have been to focus on reforming the *Grosslagen*, which are a deception as well as a distraction. This would have been easy to achieve simply by making it mandatory to print the term *Grosslage* on the label, in the same way that *Bereich* must appear. Until there is a consensus on the reform or eradication of the *Grosslagen*, there is no hope of reinstating the authentic names and boundaries of the *Einzellagen*, yet this is the only hope Germany has of reclaiming equal fine-wine status with France. Only a hierarchical classification of Germany's greatest vineyards will put this country back among the elite winemaking nations of the world, but it would be pointless to build one on the current tissue of lies. The number of *Einzellagen* was reduced to 2,600 in 1971 because, it was claimed, 30,000 was too confusing to contemplate;

## RECENT GERMAN VINTAGES

**2006** Erratic weather kept growers on their toes, and an Indian summer led to excellent results for most quality-conscious producers.

**2005** The vintage of the century, some said. Well, perhaps of this century, but not the last 100 years. Mosel vineyards outperformed most Rhine regions, but the Nahe and Mittelrhein made equally great wines, as did Franken. With a few amazing exceptions, the new-wave dry whites failed to maximize the advantages of the vintage, essentially because most were not truly dry. Excellent reds.

**2004** Classic whites, particularly Riesling, but some reds lack plumpness of fruit.

**2003** Like 1976 all over again, but growers were permitted to irrigate the vines this time (water stress having turned that potentially great vintage into a hodgepodge of the good, the bad, and the ugly). Only no one was set up for irrigation, and bowsers were seen all over the vineyard, although what good they did is debatable. So 2003 is probably a slightly more successful version of 1976, and still they won't waste money on irrigation. The best Rieslings have turned out to be a good buy for those who adore bottle-developed terpenes dominating young, fruity wines. Some excellent reds, but a number lack fruit.

**2002** A great vintage, despite rain at the start of the harvest. Perfect for everything from reds and QbAs to the upper end of the QmP scale.

**WEINGUT MAX FERD RICHTER, MÜLHEIM**
*A producer of great Riesling, particularly from Juffer Sonnenuhr in Braunberg, Dr. Richter is justly famous for his superb* Eiswein.

but this claim was without justification. It does not matter whether there are 30,000 or 300,000—there are as many *Einzellagen* as there are; they all have the same right to exist, but only the outstanding ones will ever earn a reputation, so where is the potential for confusion? No one has suggested that all 30,000 should be classified. If the Germans ever conduct an official classification, and it is done properly, it would probably consist of no more than the best 250 *Einzellagen* and only the top 10 percent of these would need to create the sort of international reputation that Bordeaux's *premiers crus* have so effectively achieved.

## VDP CLASSIFICATION

Without the will or authority to impose a legally recognized nationwide classification, this task has been left to voluntary, quality-conscious organizations. The earliest response was in 1983 in the Rheingau, where the late George Breuer pushed through the now famous Charta (pronounced "karta"), whereby vineyards were classified as *Erstes Gewächs* (First Growths), a designation that could only be used for wines that are essentially dry in style and comply with strict quality criteria. The most important aspect of the Charta, however, was its reclassification of the *Einzellagen*. It demonstrated that some famous sites had been inflated by as much as 806 percent under the 1971 wine law. It was hoped this example would be copied on a panregional basis by the largest organization of wine estates, the *Verband Deutscher Prädikatsweingüter* (VDP). Unfortunately, the VDP did not pick up the gauntlet until June 2002, when it announced its *Grosses Gewächs* (Great Growths) classification for all regions, except the Ahr and Mosel (the Mosel joined the program in March 2003, and the Ahr in August 2003).

The delay was much less of a worry than what had prompted

## A LITTLE GERMAN

Those who don't speak German may find it helpful to know that the plural of German words ending in "e" is achieved by adding an "n," thus, one *Grosslage*, two or more *Grosslagen*. For the plural of words ending with a consonant, an "e" is added, thus, one *Bereich*, two or more *Bereiche*.

the VDP into action in the first place. It was not so much vineyard classification, as the new dry wine designations of Classic and Selection. The VDP agreed with most of the criteria for the top Selection designation, which is restricted to *Einzellage* wines, but objected to the lack of any vineyard classification, other than the mostly bloated and meaningless *Einzellage* created by the 1971 wine law. It therefore withdrew its support of Classic and Selection designations, and launched instead its *Grosses Gewächs* concept. Thus the whole *Grosses Gewächs* concept has become irrevocably and unnecessarily entangled in stylistic issues, instead of setting out with blinding simplicity the true boundaries of Germany's greatest vineyards.

By not concentrating on a sense of place, the VDP became engrossed in ridiculous arguments as to what wine styles should be permitted to use the *Grosses Gewächs* classification, with definitions differing from region to region, not to mention the designation itself, which now accommodates the already established *Erstes Gewächs* in the Rheingau and *Erstes Lage* (First Site) in the Mosel, plus, of course, *Grosses Gewächs*.

## CHANGING IDEAS ABOUT GERMAN WINES

The modern idea of which German wines to drink, and how and when to drink them, is based on a tradition that is over a hundred years old. Outside Germany itself, the predilection for Rhine and Mosel is essentially a British one. Historically, this has always been so. Even two world wars failed to diminish the British fondness for these wines, and despite a 25 percent drop in exports in the early 1990s, Britain remains Germany's biggest customer.

At one time, the British, whose tastes influenced the rest of the world, drank only Hock, a name that originally applied only to the wines of Hochheim in Rheingau, but soon became generic for all white Rhine wines. Unlike the light, grapey Rhine wines we know today, the passion in the 19th century was for mature, full-flavoured, amber-colored wines. In fact, Hock glasses traditionally have brown stems because they were deliberately made to reflect the desired amber hue of age into the wine. The Christie's auction of May 1777 listed "Excellent Genuine Old Hock" of the 1719 vintage, and another London sale offered "Hock Hocheim" 1726 in August of 1792. How a modern Hock might taste in 60 years or so is anyone's guess, but mine is that it would not be very pleasant by today's standards—unless it happened to be a *Trockenbeerenauslese*.

## FROM HOCK TO MOSEL

By the time Mosel wines became popular, the trend was for lighter, younger wines, hence traditional green-stemmed Mosel glasses were manufactured. The green stem reflected the verdancy of youth from the glass into the wine. (Incidentally, "Moselle" is the name of the river in France's most northerly wine area, producing VDQS Vins de Moselle, and as soon as the river crosses the border it becomes "Mosel." Surprisingly, too many English-labeled German wines mistakenly use the spelling "Moselle".) The brown- or amber-stemmed "Hock" glass was introduced in the 18th century, when it had become fashionable to drink Rhine of great maturity; the colored glass was intended to reflect the desired hues of honeyed-richness and maturity in the wine.

## LIEBFRAUMILCH—NOT A WINE THE GERMANS DRINK OR EVEN KNOW!

More than one-third of all German wine exports are sold as Liebfraumilch, an inexpensive, bulk-blended product that few Germans have even heard of, let alone tasted. Less than 0.01 percent of the 12 million cases (1.1 million hectoliters) produced each year is consumed in Germany itself, and most of that is sold to foreign tourists and servicemen. Virtually 100 percent of all Liebfraumilch is consumed by non-Germans and, although it is no

PICKING GRAPES IN THE MOSEL
*Harvesting the Riesling in this region's steep vineyards is labor-intensive, due to precipitous slopes and treacherous loose slate soil.*

longer fashionable among the new generation of drinkers in the UK, it nevertheless remains the number one best-selling wine in Britain's largest supermarket groups. While the two largest markets, the UK and US, continue to consume such vast quantities of Liebfraumilch, I am duty bound to tell the full story.

Myriad theories surround the origin of the name Liebfraumilch (or Liebfrauenmilch), but many agree that it means "milk of Our Lady" and refers to the wine produced from one small and fairly indifferent vineyard in the suburbs of Worms that was once called Liebfrauenkirche, or "Church of Our Lady." This is now part of Liebfrauenstift-Kirchenstück, which in turn is part of the 2,470-acre (1,000-hectare) *Grosslage* Liebfrauenmorgen. The single-vineyard wine that gave birth to the name of Liebfraumilch has no bearing whatsoever on the bulk-blended wine of today, nor, for that matter, any connection with the Liebfraumilch that was sold more than 100 years ago. What is interesting, however, is the nature of those early Liebfraumilch wines that gave the blended product of today its worldwide reputation and huge sales. The blurred and nonspecific character of this wine was officially classified by the Worms Chamber of Commerce in 1910, when it stated that Liebfraumilch was merely "a fancy name" that merchants "have made use of," applying it to "Rhine wines of good quality and character." The ill-defined use of this "fancy name" widened during the following 20 years. Even between 1945 and the advent of the new German wine laws in 1971, one-third of the wines blended into Liebfraumilch came from German regions other than the Rhine.

This should have ended when Liebfraumilch was granted *Qualitätswein* status under the 1971 German wine law because the law further stated that a *Qualitätswein* could come only from one specified region. However, the regulations also specified that Liebfraumilch could be made only from Rheinhessen, Pfalz,

## SEKT SWEETNESS CHART

| SWEETNESS RATING | RESIDUAL SUGAR (GRAMS PER LITRE) |
| --- | --- |
| Extra Herb or Extra Brut | 0–6 |
| Herb or Brut | 0–15 |
| Extra Trocken or Extra Dry | 12–20 |
| Trocken* or Dry | 17–35 |
| Halbtrocken* or Demi-Sec | 33–50 |
| Süss, Drux, Doux, or Sweet | 50+ |

*Not to be confused with still-wine limits, which are no more than 9 grams per liter for trocken and 18 grams per liter for halbtrocken.*

BERNKASTEL-KUES, MOSEL
*Looking across the Mosel to Bernkastel-Kues, above which is the famous
Doctor vineyard, from which some of Germany's greatest wines come.*

Rheingau, and Nahe grapes and, although few people doubted
the spirit of the law, many producers interpreted this quite
literally. They considered Liebfraumilch to be an umbrella
designation that entitled the wine to come from any one or more
of the four specified regions. Now, however, at least 85 percent
of every Liebfraumilch has to come from just one region, which
must be indicated on the label.

There have been many moves to reclassify Liebfraumilch as a
*Tafelwein*, which would permit it to be blended with grape
varieties from the much wider *Tafelwein* regions and this would
be more in keeping with its quality, which is not poor or bad *per
se*, simply unpretentious and of nonspecific character. However,
Liebfraumilch producers disliked the idea of the *Tafelwein*
classification—a misguided view in my opinion, not least because
Liebfraumilch sells on its brand name. Although not intrinsically
poor quality, far too many Liebfraumilch are bad wines, just as far
too many cheap German wines in general are. Taken at its best, a
decent Liebfraumilch should possess a fresh, flowery aroma and
sweet, grapey taste. It has proved to be a good stepping-stone, with
statistics showing that the vast majority of seasoned wine drinkers
originally "cut their teeth" on this accessible wine, but there will
always be some Liebfraumilch drinkers who never stray beyond it.
Those drinkers, if honest, dislike the taste of alcohol, but enjoy
the effect it has and most of them are not too fond of tannin,
acidity, and the assertively dry taste found in most "real" wines.
There is no reason why they should—it is all a matter of taste.

## WHAT IS LIEBFRAUMILCH?

Ironically, Germany's most criticized wine is the only one to be
defined by taste and sweetness in its wine laws. According to
the regulations, the minimum residual sugar allowed is 18 grams
per liter, equivalent to the maximum allowed for a *halbtrocken*,
although few are actually this low, and some are twice as high.
Producers have their own idea of what level of sweetness is right
for the market and make their wines accordingly. Many buyers
insist on a certain ratio of sugar to acidity; most brands contain
between 22–35 grams per liter of sugar, with 27–28 grams per liter
of sugar  as a good average. Liebfraumilch labels must now show
one of the four permitted regions; at least 85 percent of the wine
must come from the region stated. On average, the Rheinhessen
and the Pfalz produce more than nine out of every 10 bottles of
Liebfraumilch, while the Nahe makes very little and the Rheingau
virtually none. Any grape permitted for German QbA wine may
be used for the production of Liebfraumilch, the only control
being that at least 51 percent of the blend must be composed of
one or more of the following varieties: Riesling, Silvaner, Müller-
Thurgau, and Kerner. According to the present regulations, the
wine should taste of these grapes, although I have so far met
no expert who can either describe or detect a definitive blend of
four such different varieties in the wine. What I have discovered,
however, is that some of the best blends have actually been
denied their AP numbers because they have received a beneficial
*Süssreserve* of aromatic Morio-Muskat. The Liebfraumilch
examining board apparently believes these eminently more
attractive wines to be atypical of the appellation.

## SEKT—GERMANY'S SPARKLING WINE

Germany's *Sekt* or sparkling wine industry is very important,
producing almost half a billion bottles a year, more than twice that
of Champagne. This is almost entirely made by *cuve close* and over
85 percent is not *Deutscher Sekt* at all, but *Sekt* plain and simple,
made from imported wines. Despite a fourfold increase in exports
over the past 15 years, foreign markets still represent barely 8
percent of sales. In general, Germans make *Sekt* for themselves
and its bland, off-dry style with a very young tartness to it has a
peculiarly domestic appeal that sparkling wine drinkers in most
international markets cannot comprehend, whether they are used
to Champagne or New World bubbly. *Deutscher Sekt* is little better,
and the best *Deutscher Sekt* is seldom encountered. On those rare
occasions when bottle-fermented wines are produced, *Sekt* will not
appeal to most sparkling wine drinkers outside Germany itself
because the grapes are too aromatic for the expected mellow biscuity
character to develop. However, there are Pinot Noir-based *Sekt*
rosés that cross the barrier, and the best mature Riesling *Sekt* can
appeal to a niche market, just as Australia's sparkling Shiraz does.

## HOW TO USE THE "APPELLATIONS OF..." SECTIONS

The entries that follow for each of Germany's wine regions are set out in a
logical order. In each of these regions, or *Anbaugebiete*, every *Bereich* is
listed and the wine styles are described; this is followed by the *Grosslagen*
within that particular *Bereich*. Under each *Grosslage*, the best villages are
listed where applicable and, within each of these, the finest *Einzellagen*, or
vineyards, are named.

In Germany, vineyards are rarely owned only by one estate, as they are in
Bordeaux, for example. It is therefore important to be aware of not only
which are the top vineyards, but also who makes the best wines there,
which is why I recommend growers and estates within each of the finest
vineyards. The term "village" covers both *Gemeinden*—communes, which
may be anything from a tiny village to a large, bustling town—and *Ortsteile*,
which are villages absorbed within the suburbs of a larger *Gemeinde*. The
term *"Grosslagenfrei"* refers to villages and *Einzellagen* within one *Bereich*
that are not part of any of its *Grosslagen*.

Where it is stated that there are no outstanding villages, estates, growers,
or growers in a particular *Grosslage*, excellent estates and growers might well

own vineyards there, but the wine produced in these vineyards may not
actually be of the highest standard.

All styles and descriptions of wines refer to Riesling, unless otherwise
stated. The following sample entry is given from the Franken region.

| | |
|---|---|
| **BEREICH** ............................................... | # BEREICH STEIGERWALD |
| **GROSSLAGE** ......................... | GROSSLAGE SCHLOSSBERG |
| **BEST VILLAGE** ............................ | **RÖDELSEE** |
| **BEST VINEYARD AND/OR** ... **BEST GROWERS** | ☑ **Vineyard** *Küchenmeister* **Grower** *Juliusspital Würzburg* • **Vineyard** *Schwanleite* **Grower** *Johann Ruck* |

THE WINE STYLES OF

# GERMANY

**Note** From *Wein* to *Trockenbeerenauslese*, the categories below are in ascending order of quality, and not in alphabetical order, after which different styles are listed. Only the broadest character can be given for each category, since so much depends upon the grape variety. The grape variety can even determine the color of a wine, although some 90 percent of the production is white. Most grape varieties likely to be encountered, including all the most important crosses, are included in the Glossary of Major Grape Varieties (see pp.36–45).

The area of origin also has a strong influence on the type of wine a particular grape variety will produce. A winemaker can either make the most of what nature brings, or fail. For full details on these two aspects, see the regional chapters in which styles are described and growers recommended.

## WEIN

The existence of this term without the qualification "Tafel-," indicates a cheap, blended wine made from grapes grown outside the EU.

## TAFELWEIN

Table wine may be a blend from different EU countries or wine made in one member country from grapes harvested in another. Known as "Euroblends," these products are sometimes dressed up to look like German wines, but the wine beneath the Gothic writing and German language usually turns out to be an Italian or multistate blend. This practice, once prolific, now less so, is tantamount to deception and contrary to EU regulations. To be sure of drinking a genuine German product, check that "Tafelwein" is qualified by the all-important "Deutscher." The more successful of these wines are made in years when Germany is overburdened by such a huge yield of basic-quality wines that the wineries turn back the convoy of tankers from Italy and dump the excess production in their bulk-selling Euroblends. The best have a good dose of fresh and flowery Morio-Muskat *Süssreserve*.

🍷 Upon purchase

## DEUTSCHER TAFELWEIN

This is the lowest grade of pure German wine, which about 10 years ago represented between 3 and 5 percent of the country's total production, but now, when added to *Landwein*, it accounts for between 1 and 2 percent. The quality of production has not dramatically improved at the bottom end of the German wine market and the cheapest QbAs have actually deteriorated in quality—now you know why.

This wine must be 100 percent German and, if at least 75 percent comes from any one of the *Tafelwein* regions or subregions indicated earlier in the table, the label is allowed to show that name. These regional names are the most specific geographic location permitted, although, prior to the introduction of *Landwein* legislation, it was permissible sometimes to include the name of a *Bereich*.

A *Deutscher Tafelwein* should convey the basic characteristics of the region from which it comes, so a Rhein, for example, might be expected to have a more flowery aroma, but less acidity than a Mosel. In practice, however, the wines are blended from such a hodgepodge of grape varieties, mostly crosses, that all one can hope for is something fresh and fruity in a medium-dry "Germanic" style!

🍷 Upon purchase

## LANDWEIN

*Landwein* is a *Deutscher Tafelwein* from a specific region and the label must contain both terms. The major difference is that the former must be made either as *trocken*, with up to 9 grams per liter residual sugar, or as *halbtrocken*, with a maximum of 18 grams per liter.

*Landwein* was introduced in 1982 to parallel the French *vin de pays* system, although there are significant differences. The 153 or so *vins de pays* represent a group of wines that aspire to VDQS and, theoretically, AOC status, and it has become one of the most exciting categories of wine in the world (see p.248). The German category is not a transitional one, it consists of 20 fixed areas that have no hope of achieving anything more illustrious than a "dressed-up" *Tafelwein* status.

Although *Landwein* can never be the same as a *vin de pays*, it could and should serve a very useful, one might even say essential, purpose: to improve the quality of German wines in the QbA (primarily) and QmP categories through selection. By siphoning off the lesser elements of these wines of superior status, it could have improved not only their quality, but the quality of *Landwein* itself. It would be great to think that the biggest producers had taken this category to heart and, through a genuine desire to raise standards all round, reduced yields and used *Landwein* to mop-up 15 or 20 percent of total German production. However, the authorities have instead opted to use this category to increase yields, which is why the country's best winemakers have not been attracted to the notion of *Landwein* as a legitimate means to increase the quality of their other wines, thus there have been no special *Landweins* to attract critics and consumers. The wines have not taken off and, together with *Deutscher Tafelwein*, account for less than 2 percent of Germany's total production, which has not helped this country's wine reputation one iota.

🍷 Upon purchase

## QUALITÄTSWEIN BESTIMMTER ANBAUGEBIETE OR QBA

A QbA is literally a quality wine from one of the 13 specified regions. These wines may be (and invariably are) chaptalized to increase the alcohol content, and sweetened with *Süssreserve*. The legal minimum potential alcoholic strength of a QbA is merely 5.9 percent, so it can be understood why the alcohol level is not increased for its own sake, but to give the wine a reasonable shelf life. The category includes Liebfraumilch and the vast majority of Niersteiner Gutes Domtal, Piesporter Michelsberg, and other generic wines. Most *Grosslage* and *Bereich* wines are sold as QbAs. There is no technical or legal reason why this is so, but it makes marketing sense if more specific wines, such as *Einzellagen* or estate-bottled wines, are sold as prestigious QmPs, as they can demand higher prices. Although a QbA has a lower *Oechsle* than a *Kabinett*, it is a more commercial product and therefore often distinctly sweeter.

🍷 1–3 years (up to 10 years for exceptional wines)

## QUALITÄTSWEIN GARANTIERTEN URSPRUNGS OR QGU

*Qualitätswein garantierten Ursprungs* is a QbA from a specific district, vineyard or village that has a consistent taste profile associated with its appellation of origin. Such wines are subject to more stringent sensory and analytical requirements than QbAs generally. Some Mosel vintners near the Luxembourg border were the first to make use of QgU status with an Obermosel Elbling Trocken.

🍷 1–3 years

## QUALITÄTSWEIN MIT PRÄDIKAT OR QMP

This means "a quality wine affirmed (predicated) by ripeness" and covers the categories *Kabinett*, *Spätlese*, *Auslese*, *Beerenauslese*, *Eiswein*, and *Trockenbeerenauslese*. The grower must give the authorities prior notice of his intention to harvest for any QmP wine and, whereas a QbA can be blended from grapes gathered from all four corners of an *Anbaugebiet*, providing it carries only the name of that region, the origin of a QmP must be a geographical unit of no greater size than a *Bereich*. A QbA can be chaptalized, but a QmP can not. A certain very highly respected estate owner who believes he could make much better QmP wines if he were allowed to chaptalize them, once made the interesting observation that the French chaptalize their best wines, while Germans chaptalize only their poorest! It is, however, permissible to add *Süssreserve*, although many growers maintain that it is not the traditional method and claim that sweetness is best achieved by stopping the fermentation before all the natural grape sugars have been converted to alcohol. (*See* the various QmP entries.)

## KABINETT QMP

The term *Kabinett* once referred to wines that were stored for their rare and exceptional qualities, much as "Reserve" is commonly used today. In this context, it originated at Kloster Eberbach in the Rheingau in the early 18th century. The first documented existence of this word appeared as "Cabernedt" on an invoice from the Elville master cooper, Ferdinand Ritter, to the Abbot of Eberbach in 1730. Just six years later, another bill in Ritter's hand refers to the "Cabinet-Keller." (The meaning of "Cabinet" as a treasured store found its way into the French language as early as 1547, and is found in German literature in 1677.) *Kabinett* is the first of the predicates in the *Oechsle* scale. Its grapes must reach an *Oechsle* level of 67–85°, the exact minimum varying according to the grape variety concerned and its geographical origin. With no chaptalization, this means that the wine has a minimum potential alcoholic strength of between 8.6 and 11.4 percent by volume.

Although made from riper (thus sweeter) grapes than a QbA, a *Kabinett* is usually, though not necessarily, made in a slightly drier style. Some producers resolutely refuse to bolster the wine with *Süssreserve*. This makes *Kabinett* the lightest and, for some, the purest of German wine styles.

🍷— 2–5 years (up to 10 years in exceptional cases)

🏆 **Riesling** Mittelrhein: *Didinger* • **Rheingau:** *Leitz, Künstler* • **Mosel:** *Dr Loosen, Vollenweider* • **Nahe:** *Göttelmann, Kruger-Rumpf* • **Pfalz:** *Koehler-Ruprecht, Mosbacher* • **Rheinhessen:** *Kühling-Gillot, Manz* • **Baden:** *Bercher*

## SPÄTLESE QMP

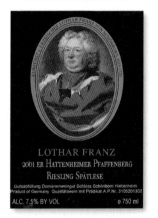

Technically, "*Spätlese*" implies that a wine is made from late-harvested grapes, but it is important to remember that "late" is relative to the normal (early) occurrence of a harvest in Germany. As both QbA and *Kabinett* are produced from grapes that have not fully ripened, *Spätlese* can more accurately be seen as the first level of German wine to be produced from ripe grapes. The minimum *Oechsle* level of 76–95°, which would give a minimum potential strength of between 10 and 13 percent by volume, is hardly an indication of overripe grapes. Although a *Spätlese* is made from grapes that merely have a modest degree of ripeness, the style of wine produced is traditionally sweet, with excellent balancing acidity.

🍷— 3–8 years (up to 15 in exceptional cases)

🏆 **Mittelrhein:** *Didinger, Weingart* • **Mosel:** *J J Prüm, Fritz Haag, Grans-Fassian, Molitor* • **Nahe:** *Dr Crusius, Dönnhoff, Emrich-Schönleber* • **Rheingau:** *Künstler, Leitz* • **Rheinhessen:** *Gunderloch, Keller, Wittmann* • **Pfalz:** *A Christmann, Müller-Catoir* • **Baden:** *Andreas Laible* • **Württemberg:** *Graf Adelmann, Karl Haidle*

## AUSLESE QMP

This predicated wine is made from bunches left on the vines after the *Spätlese* harvest and as such is truly late-harvested. The regulations state that bunches of fully ripe to very ripe grapes free from disease or damage must be selected for this wine—how this can be achieved by machine-harvesting, which has been permitted for *Auslese* since the new German wine laws of 1994, is beyond the imagination of every quality-conscious German winemaker I have spoken to.

*Auslese* must also possess an *Oechsle* reading of 83–105°, the exact minimum varying according to the grape variety concerned and its geographical origin. With no chaptalization, this means that the wine has a minimum potential strength of between 11.1 and 14.5 percent by volume.

Traditionally, this rich and sweet wine is made in exceptional vintages only. There may be some hint of *Edelfäule* (botrytis), especially if the wine comes from a top estate that has a policy of underdeclaring its wines, and thus an *Auslese* might be borderline *Beerenauslese*, but even without *Edelfäule*, an *Auslese* is capable of considerable complexity. It is possible to find totally dry *Auslese* wine and this may or may not be labelled *Auslese trocken*, depending on the whim of the winemaker. *Auslese* is the perfect ripeness level for *trocken* wines, but ideally a different designation should be found for these wines to distinguish them from their sweet counterparts.

🍷— 5–20 years

🏆 **Sweet style** Franken: *Horst Sauer* • **Rheingau:** *Leitz, Dr Weil* • **Mittelrhein:** *Weingart* • **Mosel:** *Dr Loosen, Fritz Haag, J J Prüm, Egon Müller, Molitor, Grans Fassian, Knebel* • **Nahe:** *Dönnhoff, Emrich-Schönleber* • **Pfalz:** *Bassermann-Jordan, Bürklin-Wolf, A Christmann, Müller-Catoir* • **Rheinhessen:** *Gunderloch, Keller, Wittmann*

## BEERENAUSLESE QMP

A very rare wine made only in truly exceptional circumstances from overripe grapes that have been affected by *Edelfäule*. According to the regulations, each berry should be shriveled, and be individually selected on a grape-by-grape basis. They must achieve an *Oechsle* level of 110–128°, the exact minimum varying according to the grape variety concerned and its geographical origin. With no chaptalization, this means that the wine has a minimum potential strength of between 15.3 and 18.1 percent by volume, but only 5.5 percent need actually be alcohol, with residual sugar accounting for the rest.

These intensely sweet, full-bodied wines are remarkably complex and elegant. I actually prefer *Beerenauslese* to the technically superior *Trockenbeerenauslese*—it is easier to drink and be delighted by the former, whereas the latter requires concentration and appraisal.

🍷— 10–35 years (up to 50 years in exceptional cases)

🏆 **Baden:** *Andreas Laible* • **Mosel:** *Molitor, Fritz Haag, J J Prüm, Dr Loosen* • **Nahe:** *Dönnhoff, Emrich-Schönleber* • **Rheingau:** *Fritz Allendorf, August Kesseler, Dr Weil* • **Rheinhessen:** *Keller* • **Pfalz:** *Müller-Catoir*

## EISWEIN QMP

Until 1982 this was a qualification used in conjunction with one of the other predicates. It was previously possible to obtain *Spätlese Eiswein, Auslese Eiswein* and so on; but *Eiswein* is now a predicate in its own right, with a minimum *Oechsle* level for its grapes equivalent to *Beerenauslese*. An *Eiswein* occurs through extremely unusual circumstances whereby grapes left on the vine to be affected by *Edelfäule* are frozen by frost or snow. They are harvested, rushed to the winery, and pressed in their frozen state. Only the water inside the grape actually freezes; this either remains caked inside the press or rises to the top of the vat in the form of ice, which is then skimmed off. What remains available for fermentation is a freeze-condensed juice that is rich, concentrated, and capable of producing wines that are the equivalent of, but totally different from, *Beerenauslese* or *Trockenbeerenauslese*.

This icy harvest can be very late. It seldom occurs before December and often takes place in January of the following year (although it must carry the previous year's vintage). The *Oechsle* level of an *Eiswein*, which must be at least the equivalent of a *Beerenauslese*, can be every bit as high as a *Trockenbeerenauslese*. Its quality is also comparable, although of an entirely different character, due essentially to its far higher acidity balance. For me, it is the zippy, racy, tangy vitality of this acidity that makes it superior. The finest *Eiswein* has a finesse unequaled by other botrytis wine. The quality-minded wanted the new law to demand hand-picking for *Eiswein*, which would bring it in line with *Auslese, Beerenauslese*, and *Trockenbeerenauslese*, but the industrial bottlers fended this off, making it legal for it to be machine-harvested, although it is impossible to collect authentic *Eiswein* grapes this way.

🍷— 0–50 years

🏆 **Ahr:** *Deutzerhof* • **Mittelrhein:** *Didinger* • **Mosel:** *Molitor, Max Ferd Richter, Karthäuserhof (Ruwer), Egon Müller (Saar)* • **Nahe:** *Schlossgut Diel, Dönnhoff, Emrich-Schönleber, Schäfer-Fröhlich* • **Rheingau:** *Weil* • **Rheinhessen:** *Keller, Manz* • **Franken:** *Fürstlich Castellsches Domäneamt, Horst Sauer* • **Württemberg:** *Aldinger*

## TROCKENBEERENAUSLESE QMP OR TBA

Germany's legendary TBA is produced from heavily botrytized grapes, left on the vine to shrivel into raisinlike berries that must be individually picked. These grapes must reach an *Oechsle* level of 150–154°. With no chaptalization, the wine will have a minimum potential strength of between 21.5 and 22.1 percent by volume, although only 5.5 percent need be alcohol, the rest being residual sugar.

Consulting charts, however, does little to highlight the difference in style that exists between a *Beerenauslese* and a TBA, which is every bit as great as that between a *Kabinett* and a *Beerenauslese*. The first noticeable difference is often the color. Going from *Auslese* to *Beerenauslese* is merely to progress from a light to a rich gold or buttercup yellow. The TBA color range extends from a raisin khaki through various shades of brown, to dark iodine, with some distinctly odd orange-tawny hues in between. The texture is very viscous and its liqueurlike consistency is just one of many reasons why it is impossible to drink TBA. Taking a good mouthful of TBA is about as easy as swigging cough syrup—one can merely sip it. Its intensity and complexity, and the profundity of its aromas and flavors really must be experienced. It demands attention and provokes discussion, but is not really a wine to enjoy, and is difficult to relax with.

🍷— 12–50 years

🏆 Mittelrhein: *Weingart* • Mosel: *Fritz Haag, Egon Müller (Saar), Heymann-Löwenstein, Molitor* • Nahe: *Dönnhoff, Emrich-Schönleber* • Rheingau: *Weil* • Franken: *Horst Sauer, Staatlicher Hofkeller Würzburg* • Rheinhessen: *Gunderloch, Keller* • Pfalz: *A Christmann, Ökonomierat Rebholz, Müller-Catoir*

## RED WINE

Even members of the wine trade find it surprising that almost 37 percent of German vineyards are planted with black grape varieties. The most commonly encountered German red wines are Dornfelder, Regent, and Spätburgunder (Pinot Noir), and many of the best are sold simply as Qualitätswein or even Tafelwein, to allow producers a greater freedom of expression. Dornfelder is grown mostly in the Pfalz, Rheinhessen, and Württemberg, and producers have developed three basic styles: *barrique*-aged for serious drinking; early-drinking Beaujolais-style; and an off-dry grapey style. Regent is a relatively new hybrid ([Silvaner x Müller-Thurgau] x Chambourcin), grown for its resistance to rot and mildew, and though mainly produced in a quaffing style, it can also yield wines with serious quality aspirations. Spätburgunder (Pinot Noir) is the most-planted black grape variety in the country, and over the past 15–20 years some talented winemakers have produced truly beautiful, silky-smooth, well-colored red wines from it. A few growers have been almost as successful with with Frühburgunder, a lighter mutation of Pinot Noir that has evolved in and around the village of Bürgstadt in the Franken, where it has been grown for at least 150 years. The Frühburgunder nearly became extinct in the 1970s because it was considered uneconomical due to its low and variable yields, but dedicated growers such as Rudolf Fürst have coaxed exquisitely elegant wines from it by lowering yields. Contrary to some international misconceptions, Germany has clearly demonstrated that it is a world-class producer of quality Pinot Noir. The only question that remains is whether German producers can put them on the shelf at generally affordable prices.

🍷— 2–8 years

🏆 **Spätburgunder** Ahr: *Meyer-Näkel, Deutzerhof, Stodden* • Pfalz: *Friedrich Becker, Bernhart, A Christmann* • Baden: *Huber, Duijn, Johner* • Rheingau: *August Kesseler*

**Frühburgunder** Franken: *Fürst*

**Dornfelder** Pfalz: *Knipser*

## SPARKLING WINE

The common method of production for this anonymous sparkling wine is *cuve close*, although when the industry was born in the 1820s, all *Sekt* was bottle-fermented. Today, not only is it an industrialized product, but most is made from grapes grown outside Germany, usually from Italy or the Loire Valley in France. Furthermore, until 1986, this Euro-fizz could be called *Deutscher Sekt*. This was because *Sekt* was considered to be a method of production and, so it was argued, if production took place in Germany, it must logically be German or *Deutscher Sekt*. As the vast majority of Germany's huge *Sekt* industry used imported grapes, juice, or wine (and still does), this was more a matter of lobbying by those with vested interests, than of logic. However, much of the effort to dispose of this false logic came from honorable sectors within the German wine industry itself. Common sense finally won out on September 1, 1986, when an EU directive brought this appellation into line with the general philosophy of the EU's wine regime. There has been a noticeable upsurge in the numbers of what are now genuine German *Deutscher Sekt*, although *Sekt* plain and simple still dominates the market.

### DEUTSCHER SEKT

*Deutscher Sekt* must be made from 100 percent German grapes. The best are usually Riesling-based and do not allow autolysis (the enzymatic

breakdown of yeast) to interfere with the pure varietal aroma and flavor of the wine, characteristics that are held in the greatest esteem by its producers and the vast majority of its German consumers. Try Max Ferdinand. The best *Sekt* I have ever tasted was Wegeler-Deinhard Bernkasteler Doctor, but it is rarely produced and very expensive. See also Deutscher Qualitätsschaumwein bestimmter Anbaugebiete.

🍷— 3–8 years

### DEUTSCHER SEKT BESTIMMTER ANBAUGEBIETE OR DEUTSCHER SEKT BA

*See* Deutscher Qualitätsschaumwein bestimmter Anbaugebiete

### DEUTSCHER QUALITÄTSSCHAUMWEIN BESTIMMTER ANBAUGEBIETE OR DEUTSCHER QUALITÄTSSCHAUMWEIN BA

This *Deutscher Sekt* must be made entirely from grapes grown within one specified wine region and may come from a smaller geographical unit, such as a *Bereich, Grosslage*, or *Einzellage*, providing that at least 85 percent of the grapes used come from the area indicated. An alternative appellation is Deutscher Sekt bestimmter Anbaugebiete.

🍷— 3–8 years

### TROCKEN/ HALBTROCKEN WINES

Wines of the *trocken* category must not contain more than 9 grams per liter of residual sugar, or 18 grams for the off-dry *halbtrocken* category. National demand for drier style wines really started to take off in the early 1990s and now accounts for more than 50 percent of all German wines produced, but some of these can be thin, weak, and disappointing. There are some terrific *trocken* wines, but to be any good, *trocken* really has to be made from grapes of Auslese ripeness. Only then does it have the body, structure, and weight that most dry wine drinkers are used to. The VDP's *Grosses Gewächs* classification considers *Spätlese trocken* ripe enough, but some of the wines released under this banner do not really meet the standard expected from a *grand cru* designation. The former practice of quality-conscious growers to make and sell *trocken* offerings as Deutscher Tafelwein has more or less ceased except for one or two producers of red wines.

🍷— 2–6 years

🏆 **Riesling Trocken** Baden: *Dr Heger, Bercher* • Nahe: *Emrich-Schönleber, Schlossgut Diel* • Pfalz: *Bürklin-Wolf, A Christmann* • Rheingau: *August Eser, Breuer* • Rheinhessen: *Keller, Wittmann*

**Riesling Halbtrocken** Mittelrhein: *Matthias Müller, Weingart* • Mosel: *Knebel, Molitor* • Nahe: *Emrich-Schönleber, Kruger-Rumpf* • Rheingau: *Leitz, Künstler*

**Grau- and Weissburgunder Trocken** Baden: *Bercher, Huber, Johner, R u C Schneider* • Franken: *Fürst* • Pfalz: *Münzberg, Dr Wehrheim, Ökonomierat Rebholz*

**Gewürztraminer Trocken** Pfalz: *Bernhart*

**Silvaner Trocken** Franken: *Horst Sauer*

IMMACULATE VINEYARDS, BADEN
*Baden's greatest wines are produced around the extinct volcano of Kaiserstuhl, in neat vineyards that are perfect examples of* Flurbereinigung.

# THE AHR

*It may seem surprising that black grapes can be cultivated here at all, considering the Ahr is one of Europe's most northerly wine regions, yet varieties such as Spätburgunder and Portugieser account for three-quarters of the Ahr's vines.*

SPÄTBURGUNDER AND PORTUGIESER can grow here because the Ahr is a deep valley—protected by the Hohe Eifel hills—this captures sunlight in its rocky, slaty soil. The cumulative effect of the heat allows black grapes to ripen, but until recently few growers took advantage of these favorable conditions. Consequently the Ahr became known for mild, dilute red wines, popular with social clubs on weekend outings.

A change in winemaking philosophy, however, has propelled a good number of the region's Spätburgunders into contention for Germany's red wine crown. Unfortunately, quantities will always be too small to quench the international wine community's thirst, thus readers are unlikely to find the Ahr's best reds in their local wine store. These remain the preserve of knowledgeable consumers willing to put on walking boots and take a trip to the Ahr to buy them direct. Not that the wines are cheap. The likes of Meyer-Näkel, Deutzerhof, and Kreuzberg produce some of Germany's greatest Pinot Noirs, and the wines are priced accordingly. The region takes the name of the river that flows parallel to, and north of, the lower Mosel and joins the Rhine just south of Bonn. It is one of the world's most beautiful and serene viticultural landscapes, as anyone who has ever traveled along the *Rotweinwanderweg*, the Ahr's red-wine route, will verify.

## FACTORS AFFECTING TASTE AND QUALITY

### LOCATION
The Ahr is one of Germany's northernmost wine regions, with vineyards extending only 15 miles (24 km) along the lower reaches of the Ahr River, 6 miles (10 kilometers) south of Bonn.

### CLIMATE
Despite its northerly position, the deep Ahr valley is sheltered by the surrounding Hohe Eifel hills and maintains temperatures that are favorable for viticulture, with a greenhouselike climate on some of the steeper sites.

### ASPECT
The best vineyards of the Ahr are sited on steeply terraced rocky valley sides, with higher yielding vineyards on gentler slopes in the broader, eastern end of the valley.

### SOIL
Deep, rich, loess soils in the lower Ahr valley (eastern) and basalt and slaty stone soils with some tufa in the upper Ahr valley (western).

### VITICULTURE AND VINIFICATION
Three-quarters of vineyards are worked by part-time farmers, whose wines are sold by cooperatives. Most vines are cultivated under labour-intensive conditions, hence the wines are expensive to produce. Nearly all of the region's wine is consumed locally or sold to tourists. Pure varietal Weissherbst, usually Spätburgunder, is a speciality, but in terms of pure quality, this easy-drinking rosé has given way to fully red styles. As Riesling vines diminish, so the Spätburgunder is taking over as the classic Ahr variety.

### GRAPE VARIETIES
**Primary varieties:** Portugieser, Riesling, Spätburgunder
**Secondary varieties:** Domina, Dornfelder, Frühburgunder, Kerner, Müller-Thurgau

## RIESLING

Riesling grapes can produce fresh, racy, aromatic wines here, but over the years have given way to black grapes and now comprise just 8 percent of the region's vines. Given the healthy prices that Ahr reds command, Riesling is unlikely to regain its share.

HARVESTING IN THE AHR
*These steeply sloping vineyards at Marienthal are planted with the black grape varieties Spätburgunder and a little Portugieser, and 80 percent of the region's wines are, in fact, red.*

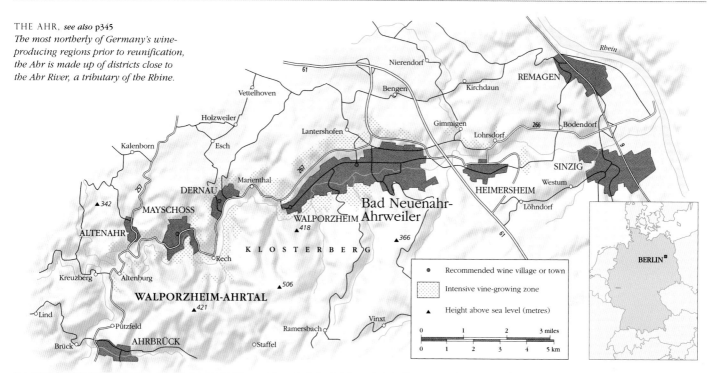

THE AHR, *see also p345*
*The most northerly of Germany's wine-producing regions prior to reunification, the Ahr is made up of districts close to the Ahr River, a tributary of the Rhine.*

- ● Recommended wine village or town
- ▒ Intensive vine-growing zone
- ▲ Height above sea level (metres)

BERLIN

## QUALITY REQUIREMENTS AND AVERAGE QMP PRODUCTION

| AHR'S MINIMUM OECHSLE | QUALITY CATEGORY | HARVEST BREAKDOWN |
|---|---|---|
| 44° | Deutscher Tafelwein | 0.5% |
| 47° | Landwein | 0.5% |
| 50–60° | * QbA | 80% |
| 67–73° | * Kabinett | 12.5% |
| 76–85° | * Spätlese | 6% |
| 83–88° | * Auslese | 0.5% |
| 110° | Beerenauslese | – |
| 110° | Eiswein | – |
| 150° | Trockenbeerenauslese | – |

*Minimum Oechsle levels vary according to grape variety; those that have a naturally lower sugar content may qualify at a correspondingly lower level.*

## THE REGION AT A GLANCE

**Area under vine**
1,245 acres or 504 ha (decreasing)

**Average yield**
350 cases/acre or 81 hl/ha (increasing)

**Red wine**
82% (increasing)

**White wine**
18% (decreasing)

**Dry & semidry wine**
41% Trocken, 31% Halbtrocken

**Most important grape varieties**
59% Spätburgunder, 13% Portugieser, 8% Riesling, 20% Others

**Infrastructure**
Bereich 1; Grosslage 1; Einzellagen 43

**Note:** The vineyards of the Ahr straddle 11 *Gemeinden* (communes), the names of which may appear on the label.

---

## THE APPELLATIONS OF
# THE AHR

### BEREICH WALPORZHEIM-AHRTAL

This is the only *Bereich* in the Ahr region. Walporzheim-Ahrtal produces many kinds of wines, from light, ruby-colored Portugiesers to Dornfelders with great intensity, but the real class is provided by some of Germany's finest Spätburgunders. Those areas in the *Bereich* with slaty soil give a vigorous wine, while those situated on rich loess soil produce a softer style. At one time, the wines used to be fairly sweet, but the trend today is for drier wines. The Weissherbst is a soft and fruity wine, and the Riesling fresh and racy. Try the Rotwein with *Rauchfleisch* (smoked meats), the Weissherbst with *Schinken* (ham), and the Riesling with trout or with the salmon that have recently been reintroduced into the river.

### GROSSLAGE KLOSTERBERG

The only *Grosslage* in the *Bereich*, Klosterberg is thus identical to that of Walporzheim-Ahrtal.

#### AHRWEILER
☼✓ **Vineyard** *Silberberg* **Growers** *Kreuzberg* (red)

#### ALTENAHR
☼✓ **Vineyard** *Eck* **Growers** *Deutzerhof* (red and white), *Winzergenossenschaft Mayschoss-Altenahr*

#### DERNAU
☼✓ **Vineyard** *Pfarrwingert* **Growers** *Kreuzberg* (red), *Meyer-Näkel* (red)

#### MAYSCHOSS
☼✓ **Vineyard** *Moenchberg* **Grower** *Deutzerhof* (red)

#### NEUENAHR
☼✓ **Vineyard** *Schieferlay* **Grower** *Kreuzberg* (red) • **Vineyard** *Sonnenberg* **Growers** *Kreuzberg* (red), W. G. *Mayschoss-Altenahr* (red)

#### RECH
☼✓ **Vineyard** *Herrenberg* **Grower** *Jean Stodden* (red)

#### WALPORZHEIM
☼✓ **Vineyard** *Gärkammer* **Grower** *J. J. Adeneuer* (red) • **Vineyard** *Kräuterberg* **Grower** *Meyer-Näkel* (red) • **Premium Red Wine Blends: Growers** *Deutzerhof* (Melchior, Apollo, Grand Duc) • *Meyer-Näkel* (S, Goldkapsel) • *Nelles* (B48, B52, B59), *H. J. Kreuzberg* (Devonschiefer), *Winzergenossenschaft Mayschoss-Altenahr* (Ponsart, Selection XII), *J. J. Adeneuer* (No.1)

### CERTIFIED ORGANIC WINEMAKERS

Christoph Bäcker (Mayschoss)
Ursula & Christoph Richter (Ahrweiler)

# THE MITTELRHEIN

*Possessing precariously perched vineyards that have declined by almost 50 percent since 1965, the Mittelrhein is a region that is all too often overlooked by serious wine drinkers. Yet it offers some of Germany's finest and most underrated wines.*

IT WAS FROM THE MITTELRHEIN that the Celts spread out across Europe. With such ancient roots, it is not surprising that this region is so steeped in Germany's mythical history. It was at the Drachenfels in Königswinter, for instance, that Siegfried slew the dragon, and, in fact, the vineyards in this area produce a red Spätburgunder wine known as Drachenblut, or "Dragon's blood." The Rhine River, associated with many myths and fables, flows past numerous medieval castles and towers, and rushes through the Rhine Gorge, past the famous "Loreley" rock on to which the siren lured many ships to their final and fatal destination.

## SHRINKING VINEYARDS, GROWING TOURISM

The difficulty of working the steepest of the Mittelrhein's vineyard slopes has encouraged many of the workforce to forsake them and seek higher wages for easier work in Germany's industrial cities. This has led to a decline in the number of vineyards, although the Mittelrhein is by no means deserted, as its dramatic beauty makes it one of Germany's favorite tourist spots. In this region, where many tiny tributaries provide valley vineyards of a superior natural aspect for viticulture than most others on the Rhine, there is much potential for producing high-quality Riesling on its slaty soil. There

## QUALITY REQUIREMENTS AND AVERAGE QMP PRODUCTION

| MITTELRHEIN'S MINIMUM OECHSLE | QUALITY CATEGORY | HARVEST |
|---|---|---|
| 44° | Deutscher Tafelwein | 1% |
| 47° | Landwein | 1% |
| 50–60° | * QbA | 68% |
| 67–73° | * Kabinett | 18% |
| 76–85° | * Spätlese | 4% |
| 83–88° | * Auslese | 2% |
| 110° | Beerenauslese | 2% |
| 110° | Eiswein | 2% |
| 150° | Trockenbeerenauslese | 2% |

*Minimum Oechsle levels vary according to grape variety; those that have a naturally lower sugar content may quality at a correspondingly lower level.*

THE MITTELRHEIN, *see also p.345*
*North and south of Koblenz, the Mittelrhein's vineyards run up toward the steep, rocky escarpments that closely border this stretch of the Rhine.*

| | |
|---|---|
| ● | Recommended wine village or town |
| ▦ | Intensive vine-growing zone |
| — | *Bereich* boundary |
| — | *Grosslage* boundary |
| ▲ | Height above sea level (metres) |

0   2   4   6   8   10 miles
0   4   8   12   16 km

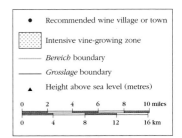

BERLIN

## FACTORS AFFECTING TASTE AND QUALITY

### LOCATION
A 100-mile (160-kilometer) stretch of the Rhine Valley between Bonn and Bingen.

### CLIMATE
The benefits of the sun are maximized by the steep valley sides that afford protection from cold winds. The river acts as a heat-reservoir, tempering the low night and winter temperatures.

### ASPECT
Vines on the steep valley sides benefit from any available sunshine. North of Koblenz the vineyards are on the east bank, while to the south most are on the west bank.

### SOIL
Primarily clayish slaty soil and graywacke. There are also small, scattered deposits of loess and,

toward the north, some vineyards are of volcanic origin.

### VITICULTURE AND VINIFICATION
Virtually all remaining vineyards have been *flurbereinigt* (modernized by abolishing terraces) and many slopes are a patchwork of steep vineyards. With a high proportion of Riesling giving an average yield that is very low by German standards, quality is generally high. About 80 percent of growers are part-time and a quarter of the harvest is processed by the coops using normal white-wine techniques.

### GRAPE VARIETIES
**Primary varieties:** Riesling
**Secondary varieties:** Bacchus, Kerner, Müller-Thurgau, Optima, Portugieser, Scheurebe, Silvaner, Spätburgunder

## THE REGION AT A GLANCE

**Area under vine**
1,260 acres or 510 ha (decreasing)

**Average yield**
290 cases/acre or 66 hl/ha (decreasing)

**Red wine**
7% (increasing)

**White wine**
93% (decreasing)

**Dry & semidry wine**
44% Trocken, 34% Halbtrocken

**Most important grape varieties**
71% Riesling (decreasing), 7%
Müller-Thurgau (decreasing), 7%
Kerner (increasing), 12% Others

**Infrastructure**
*Bereiche* 2; *Grosslagen* 11;
*Einzellagen* 111

**Note** The vineyards of the
Mittelrhein straddle 59 *Gemeinden*
(communes), the names of which
may appear on the label.

**MITTELRHEIN VINEYARDS**
*The region's weekend winegrowers have plenty to do to maintain these slopes, which include some of the steepest vineyards in Germany.*

are a few excellent estates making exciting wines that display a vigorous varietal character, intense flavor, and splendid acidity. The acidity, so prized that *Sekt* houses try to buy as much of the lesser quality and surplus wines as possible, makes the rare occurrence of *Auslese* and higher QmP wines something special.

THE APPELLATIONS OF

# THE MITTELRHEIN

## BEREICH LORELEY

This new *Bereich* is formed from the two former *Bereiche* of Bacharach (the very small but heavily cultivated southern end of the Mittelrhein, restricted to the west bank and named after the beautiful old market town of Bacharach) and Rheinburgengau (a very large, successful area bordering the Rheingau).

## GROSSLAGE BURG HAMMERSTEIN

Starting south of Königswinter and stretching along the right bank, almost as far as Koblenz, this long, scenic *Grosslage* comprises scattered vineyards, with the only unbroken stretch of fine Riesling vines at Hammerstein itself.

## GROSSLAGE BURG RHEINFELS

A village-sized *Grosslage* on the west bank, with its best vineyards situated on the southeast-facing banks of a small tributary at Werlau, an *Ortsteil* of Sankt Goar.

## GROSSLAGE GEDEONSECK

A top-performing *Grosslage* where a bend in the river allows for good east- and south-facing vineyards, the best of which are situated within an *Ortsteil* of Boppard.

### BOPPARD HAMM

☑ **Vineyard** *Feuerlay* **Growers** *Didinger* (Oberspay), *Matthias Müller, Weingart* (Spay) • **Vineyard** *Mandelstein* **Growers** *Matthias Müller, August Perll, Weingart* (Spay) • **Vineyard** *Ohlenberg* **Growers** *Weingart* (Spay), *Matthias Müller*

## GROSSLAGE HERRENBERG

The southeastern end of this *Grosslage* abuts the western edge of the Rheingau, but all of the *Einzellagen* are located in the north, between Dörscheid and Kaub, just downstream from Bacharach on the opposite bank.

## GROSSLAGE LAHNTAL

There are no outstanding villages, vineyards, estates, or growers in this *Grosslage*, which has been in a state of decline for years.

## GROSSLAGE LORELEYFELSEN

Some fine Riesling vineyards set amid dramatic scenery that includes the famous "Loreley" rock.

## GROSSLAGE MARKSBURG

The vineyards on the Mittelrhein side of Koblenz have mostly been overtaken by urban sprawl, but one of the best remains in the *Ortsteil* of Ehrenbreitstein. The others in this *Grosslage* are located to the north and south of the city. There is a natural similarity between these wines and those of the lower Mosel.

## GROSSLAGE PETERSBERG

The same area as *Bereich* Siebengebirge. There are no outstanding villages, vineyards, estates, or growers, although good wines are made in the Drachenfels vineyard of Königswinter.

## GROSSLAGE SCHLOSS REICHENSTEIN

There are no outstanding villages, vineyards, estates, or growers in this *Grosslage* that faces the Rheingau across the river and neighbors the Nahe to the south, but good wines are made in the village of Niederheimbach, especially the vineyard of Froher Weingarten.

## GROSSLAGE SCHLOSS SCHÖNBURG

The reputation of the fine Riesling vineyards in this *Grosslage* rests on two growers.

### ENGELHÖLL

☑ **Vineyard** *Bernstein* **Grower** *Lanius-Knab*

### OBERWESEL

☑ **Vineyard** *Römerkrug* **Growers** *Goswin Lambrich*

## GROSSLAGE SCHLOSS STAHLECK

There is perhaps more potential here, in the south-facing vineyards that belong to tributaries of the Rhine, than in the east-facing vineyards on the great river itself. Yet it is wines from Hahn and Posten at Bacharach, with both easterly and southerly aspects, that excel.

### BACHARACH

☑ **Vineyard** *Hahn* **Grower** *Toni Jost-Hahnenhof* • **Vineyard** *Kloster Fürstental* **Grower** *Ratzenberger* • **Vineyard** *Posten* **Grower** *Fritz Bastian* • **Vineyard** *Wolfshöhle* **Grower** *Ratzenberger*

## SIEBENGEBIRG

A single-*Grosslage Bereich* covering the vineyards of Königswinter Siebengebirge.

## CERTIFIED ORGANIC PRODUCERS

Dr. Randolph Kauer (Bacharach-Steeg)
Edelfaul (Manubach); Gerd Lang (Rodenbach)
Hof Wildeck (Urbar); Joachim Scherer (Manubach)

# MOSEL

*The greatest Rieslings grown along the Mosel River have an excruciating, but delightful, acidity that can only be relieved through a knife-edge balance of sweetness. Unlike in the warmer Rhine regions, the Riesling grape is at its best here in hot vintages.*

IF ANY GRAPE IS INTRINSICALLY RACY, it is the vigorous Riesling; and if any region can be singled out for emphasizing this raciness, it must be Mosel. Grown on the steepest, slaty slopes, Riesling combines a relatively high acidity with an irrefutable suggestion of lightness and elegance. But a fine Mosel is never thin, as these wines have surprisingly high extract levels that, together with the acidity, intensify the characteristics of flavor.

In even the hottest vintages, the best *Auslesen* and *Beerenauslesen* remain racy, while those from the other regions appear fat and overblown by contrast. Even the most modest wines retain a freshness and vitality in sunblessed years that will be lacking in those from the warmer regions.

## THE GOOD DOCTOR

There are many great vineyards in this region, but none so famous as the legendary Bernkasteler Doctor, which produces Germany's most expensive wine. The story is that Boemund II, Archbishop of Trier in the 14th century, was so ill that his doctors could do nothing for him. A winegrower from Bernkastel recommended the restorative powers of the wine from his vineyard. Boemund drank some, made a miraculous recovery, and declared "The best doctor grows in this vineyard in Bernkastel." More recently, the Doctor vineyard has been the subject of a lengthy court case. The original vineyard comprised 3⅓ acres (1.35 hectares), but in 1971 the new German wine law proscribed a ban on all vineyards of less than 12⅓ acres (5 hectares). The authorities planned to expand the Doctor almost equally to the

west (into the *Einzellage* Graben) and to the east (into an area classified merely as Grosslage Badstube). This enabled 13 different producers to make and sell Bernkasteler Doctor, whereas only three owners of the true Doctor vineyards had existed before. It is not surprising that the owners of the original Doctor vineyard felt strongly enough to take their objections to court. The case continued until finally, in 1984, after an exhaustive study had

---

## FACTORS AFFECTING TASTE AND QUALITY

### LOCATION
This region follows the Mosel River, as it meanders for 150 miles (250 km) from Koblenz south to the border with France. It includes the vineyards of two major tributaries, the Saar and the Ruwer, that flow into the Mosel from the south.

### CLIMATE
The moderate rainfall and rapid warming of the steep and protective valley sides provide ideal conditions for vines to flourish and produce grapes with high acidity, even when late harvested.

### ASPECT
The Mosel has more loops and bends than any other German river, and most of the vines grow at an altitude of between 330 and 1,150 feet (100 and 350 meters). This valley provides slopes of every aspect, with many that are spectacularly steep, boasting gradients as high as 70 degrees.

### SOIL
Soils in this region vary from sandstone, shell-limestone, and red marl in the upper Mosel, to Devon slate in the middle Mosel, Saar, and Ruwer, and clay slate and gray stony soil in the lower Mosel. Alluvial sand and gravel soils are also found in lower sites. Classic Riesling sites are slaty; the Elbling prefers limestone.

### VITICULTURE AND VINIFICATION
Many of the greatest German wines come from the highest and steepest

vineyards in this area, most of which are situated in the upper reaches of the valleys. In these notoriously difficult sites, each vine has to be tied to its own eight-foot wooden stake, and the slate soil that is washed down to the bottom of the slope by the winter rains has to be carried back up every year. Tending the vines is thus unavoidably labor-intensive and this, combined with a longer winter than experienced elsewhere in Germany, accounts for the higher prices asked for fine Mosel wines. The early onset of winter causes fermentation to take place at cool temperatures, and when the wines are bottled early they retain more carbonic gas, which emphasizes the crisp, steely character of the Riesling grape. There are about 13,750 growers owning very small plots of land. The regional cooperative in Bernkastel-Kues alone processes one-fifth of the entire crop, but much is sold on to the commercial wineries, which sell 60 percent of the total wine produced, whereas the cooperatives sell just 13 percent and this figure is declining. On the other hand, growers and estates account for 28 percent of sales, and are increasing their share.

### GRAPE VARIETIES
**Primary varieties:** Müller-Thurgau, Riesling
**Secondary varieties:** Auxerrois, Bacchus, Elbling, Kerner, Optima, Ortega, Spätburgunder

---

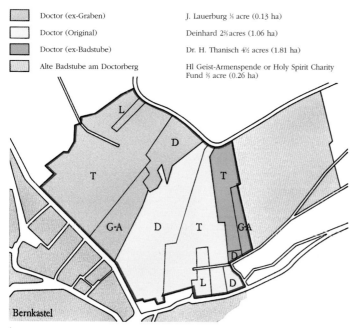

| | |
|---|---|
| Doctor (ex-Graben) | J. Lauerburg ⅓ acre (0.13 ha) |
| Doctor (Original) | Deinhard 2⅔ acres (1.06 ha) |
| Doctor (ex-Badstube) | Dr. H. Thanisch 4½ acres (1.81 ha) |
| Alte Badstube am Doctorberg | Hl Geist-Armenspende or Holy Spirit Charity Fund ⅔ acre (0.26 ha) |

Bernkastel

**THE BERNKASTELER DOCTOR VINEYARD TODAY**
*The red outline encloses the area of the original vineyard (yellow) and those areas finally adopted in 1984 (light and medium green). The area excluded in 1984 is pink.*

**BERNKASTEL FROM THE DOCTOR VINEYARD**
*Bernkasteler Doctor wines are some of Germany's most prestigious and expensive. Bernkastel lies in the Badstube Grosslage.*

# QUALITY REQUIREMENTS AND AVERAGE QMP PRODUCTION

| MOSEL'S MINIMUM OECHSLE | QUALITY CATEGORY | HARVEST BREAKDOWN |
|---|---|---|
| 44° | Deutscher Tafelwein | 1% |
| 47° | Landwein | 1% |
| 50–60° | * QbA | 72% |
| 67–73° | * Kabinett | 18% |
| 76–85° | * Spätlese | 4% |
| 83–88° | * Auslese | 1% |
| 110° | Beerenauslese | 1% |
| 110° | Eiswein | 1% |
| 150° | Trockenbeerenauslese | 1% |

*Minimum Oechsle levels vary according to grape variety; those that have a naturally lower sugar content may qualify at a correspondingly lower level.*

MOSEL, *see also* p345

*Formerly known as the Mosel-Saar-Ruwer, this region underwent a name change, being simplified to Mosel, as of the 2007 vintage according to the latest wine-legislation update.*

**Legend:**
- Recommended wine village or town
- Intensive vine-growing zone
- *Bereich* boundary
- *Grosslage* boundary
- ▲ Height above sea level (metres)

# THE REGION AT A GLANCE

**Area under vine**
25,079 acres or 10,149 ha
(decreasing)

**Average yield**
395 cases/acre or 90 hl/ha
(decreasing)

**Red wine**
2% (increasing)

**White wine**
98% (decreasing)

**Dry & semidry wine**
15% Trocken, 11% Halbtrocken

**Most important grape varieties**
55% Riesling (increasing), 18% Müller-Thurgau (decreasing), 8% Elbling (decreasing), 7% Kerner (decreasing), 12% Others

**Infrastructure**
*Bereiche* 6; *Grosslagen* 19; *Einzellagen* 523

**Note** *The vineyards of Mosel straddle 192 Gemeinden (communes), the names of which may appear on the label.*

been made of the vineyard's *terroir*, the court decided that the Doctor vineyard could legitimately be stretched to include all the Graben element and a small portion of the Badstube, making a total of 8 acres (3.26 hectares). The main reason why the Doctor vineyard was primarily expanded westward, rather than eastward, is that these westerly exposures benefit from longer hours of sunshine. However, the 10 owners of the Badstube section excluded from the Doctor vineyard found themselves in possession of vineyards that, having for 13 years been accorded the status of Germany's most prestigious wine, were now nameless. They proposed that they should be allowed to use the *Einzellage* name of Alte Badstube am Doctorberg (Old Badstube on the Doctor's Hill) and, despite protests from the original owners, this was accepted by officials.

Not only was the expansion of the *terroir* open to question in this case, but the general directive that a single vineyard should be of a stipulated minimum size was sheer folly and illustrative of one of the fundamental flaws in the 1971 German wine law (*see also* p.346). It would have been much more effective to have amended the law to allow any genuine vineyard name the right to appear in small print on a label, and to establish a register of perhaps 100 or more (but certainly not 2,600) truly great vineyards that would have the right to appear on the label in a dominant size of print with an appropriate designation of elevated status. If the greatest German wines could trade on a reputation similar to that of the finest wines of France, the Mosel would probably have more *"grands crus"* than any other region, although the Rheingau would give it a good fight.

# THE APPELLATIONS OF
# MOSEL

## BEREICH BERNKASTEL

This covers the entire Mittelmosel, encompassing all of the river's most famous villages and towns, and most of its best vineyards. Much wine is sold under this *Bereich* appellation, but unfortunately most of it is disappointing.

### GROSSLAGE BADSTUBE

Badstube must be the grandest *Grosslage* in Germany, encompassing as it does the most famous of all *Einzellagen*, the Doctor vineyard, as well as the almost equally well-known Lay, the superb Graben, and six other good sites. The quality of even the surplus wine from such great vineyards is so high that it is practically impossible to find poor Badstube, and the *Grosslage* wines are especially good in relatively poor years when grapes from the Doctor vineyard fail to achieve *Kabinett* level and are included in these blends.

#### GROSSLAGE BLEND

⚬✓ **Grower** *Selbach-Oster*

#### BERNKASTEL

⚬✓ **Vineyard** *Doctor* **Growers** *Wwe. Dr. H. Thanisch-Erben Thanisch, Wegeler-Gutshaus Bernkastel* • **Vineyard** *Alte Badstube am Doctorberg* **Grower** *Dr. Pauly-Bergweiler/Peter Nicolay* • **Vineyard** *Lay* **Growers** *Dr. Loosen*

## GROSSLAGE KURFÜRSTLAY

This includes the lesser wines of Bernkastel and the superior wines of Brauneberg, the best of which come from the fabulous vineyards on the south-southeast-facing Juffer hill that rises from the river opposite the village of Brauneberg. Its wines are remarkably racy considering their exceptional fullness of body and some prefer them to those of the Doctor, although I find it impossible to choose, and delight in their differences.

#### BRAUNEBERG

⚬✓ **Vineyard** *Juffer* **Growers** *Max Ferd Richter* • **Vineyard** *Juffer Sonnenuhr* **Growers** *Fritz Haag, Reichsgraf von Kesselstatt, Schloss Lieser, Max Ferd Richter, Paulinshof* • **Vineyard** *Mandelgraben* **Grower** *Markus Molitor*

#### LIESER

⚬✓ **Vineyard** *Niederberg Helden* **Grower** *Schloss Lieser*

#### MÜHLHEIM

⚬✓ **Vineyard** *Helenenkloster* **Grower** *Max Ferd Richter*

#### WINTRICH

⚬✓ **Vineyard** *Ohligsberg* **Grower** *Reinhold Haart*

## GROSSLAGE MICHELSBERG

There are some great wines made in the village of Piesport in the Michelsberg *Grosslage*, but the thin, characterless Piesporter Michelsberg is not one of them. It is a *Grosslage* wine that comes not from steep, slaty slopes such as Goldtröpfchen or Domherr, but from very high-yielding, flat, alluvial land. No great grower would contemplate cultivating such fertile soil, the low-quality wines of which have unfairly debased the Piesporter village name to such a degree that its wine in the industry has become known as Piss-pot. The great wines of Trittenheim have not had to suffer from such great indignities, and the village of Dhron especially should not be forgotten for its produce.

#### PIESPORT

⚬✓ **Vineyard** *Domherr* **Growers** *Kurt Hain, Reinhold Haart* • **Vineyard** *Goldtröpfchen* **Growers** *Reinhold Haart, Kurt Hain, Grans-Fassian, Weller-Lehnert, Sankt Urbans-Hof, Vereinigte Hospitien* • **Vineyard** *Treppchen* **Grower** *Weller-Lehnert*

#### TRITTENHEIM

⚬✓ **Vineyard** *Apotheke* **Growers** *Ernst Clüsserath, Ansgar Clüsserath, Clüsserath-Eifel, Clüsserath-Weiler, Grans-Fassian, Josef Rosch, Milz Laurentiushof* • **Vineyard** *Altärchen* **Grower** *Franz-Josef Eifel*

## GROSSLAGE MÜNZLAY

The three villages in this *Grosslage* may lack the fame of Bernkastel and the popularity of Piesport, but they possess truly superb Mosel vineyards and boast an incomparable number of great growers and estates.

#### GRAACH

⚬✓ **Vineyard** *Domprobst* **Growers** *Kees-Kieren, S. A. Prüm, Willi Schaefer, Philipps-Eckstein, Dr. Weins-Prüm* • **Vineyard** *Himmelreich* **Growers** *Kees-Kieren, Markus Molitor (red), J. J. Prüm, S. A. Prüm, Max Ferd Richter, Selbach-Oster, Weins-Prüm, Philipps-Eckstein* • **Vineyard** *Josephshof* **Grower** *Reichsgraf von Kesselstatt*

#### WEHLEN

⚬✓ **Vineyard** *Sonnenuhr* **Growers** *Dr. Loosen, J. J. Prüm, S. A. Prüm, Dr. Weins-Prüm, Wegeler-Gutshaus Bernkastel*

#### ZELTINGEN

⚬✓ **Vineyard** *Sonnenuhr* **Growers** *Markus Molitor, Selbach-Oster* • **Vineyard** *Himmelreich* **Grower** *Selbach-Oster*

## GROSSLAGE NACKTARSCH

The labels of this *Grosslage* are collectors' items because of the naked bottoms featured on many of them—reflecting not only the name but also the quality of most of the wine.

## GROSSLAGE PROBSTBERG

There are no outstanding villages or vineyards, except at Longuic and Sweich, that face each other at the confluence with the Ruwer at Eitelsbach.

## GROSSLAGE ST. MICHAEL

Popular but generally overrated wines come from Klüsserath these days, although the wonderful wines of Kirsten and Franz-Josef Regnery are bringing back the glory days. Detzem, Mehring, and Schleich all have good potential, but it is Leiwen that truly excels, especially in its steepest and sunniest vineyards of Laurentiuslay and Klostergarten, which stretch up above the village, exposing their superb southwesterly aspect.

#### KLÜSSERATH

⚬✓ **Vineyard** *Bruderschaft* **Growers** *Kirsten, Franz-Josef Regnery*

#### LEIWEN

⚬✓ **Vineyard** *Klostergarten* **Growers** *Heinz Schmitt, St. Urbanshof, Josef Rosch, Carl Loewen* • **Vineyard** *Laurentiuslay* **Growers** *Carl Loewen, Grans-Fassian, Josef Rosch*

#### MEHRING

⚬✓ **Vineyard** *Blattenberg* **Grower** *Heinz Schmitt*

## GROSSLAGE SCHWARZLAY

Erden and Ürzig are two of the Mittelmosel's most underrated villages. Their spectacular vineyards cling to clifflike slopes in defiance of gravity and are capable of producing rich, racy wines of rapierlike acidity, stunning intensity, and immaculate style.

#### BURG

⚬✓ **Vineyard** *Wendelstück* **Grower** *Paul Knod*

#### ENKIRCH

⚬✓ **Vineyard** *Batterieberg* **Grower** *Immich-Batterieberg* • **Vineyard** *Steffensberg* **Grower** *Immich-Batterieberg*

#### ERDEN

⚬✓ **Vineyard** *Treppchen* **Growers** *Jos Christoffel Jun, Joh Jos Christoffel Erben, Stephan Ehlen, Dr. Loosen, Mönchhof-Robert Eymael, Dr. Weins-Prüm, Kees-Kieren, Andreas Schmitges, Klaus Lotz* • **Vineyard** *Prälat* **Growers** *Dr. Loosen, Mönchhof-Robert Eymael, Dr. Pauly Bergweiler/Peter Nicolay, Andreas Schmitges*

#### TRARBACH

⚬✓ **Vineyard** *Schlossberg* (red) **Grower** *Markus Molitor*

#### ÜRZIG

⚬✓ **Vineyard** *Würzgarten* **Growers** *J. J. Christoffel Erben, Jos Christoffel Jun, Dr. Loosen, Merkelbach, Mönchhof-Robert Eymael*

**WOLF**

✓ **Vineyard** *Goldgrube* **Grower** *Vollenweider*

## GROSSLAGE VOM HEISSEN STEIN

There are two growers who excel in this otherwise modest *Grosslage*.

**PÜNDERICH**

✓ **Vineyard** *Marienburg* **Grower** *Clemens Busch* ◉

**REIL**

✓ **Vineyard** *Goldlay* **Grower** *Paul Knod*

# BEREICH BURG COCHEM

Formerly Bereich Zell, this covers the lower Mosel and is generally regarded as an area of unexciting wines, yet there are some good ones to be found.

## GROSSLAGE GOLDBÄUMCHEN

There are few outstanding villages, vineyards, or growers in this *Grosslage*, although good wines are made in the village of Eller at Pommern.

## GROSSLAGE GRAFSCHAFT

Good wines are made in the villages of Alf and Bullay, but the Riesling of Neef stands out from the rest.

## GROSSLAGE ROSENHANG

This is a promising *Grosslage*, which winds along the right bank of the Mosel downstream from *Grosslage* Schwarze Katz.

## GROSSLAGE SCHWARZE KATZ

The village of Zell has some good *Einzellagen*, with officially classified slopes that can make fine and aromatic Riesling, but it is best known for its *Grosslage* label that carries the famous Schwarze Katz "Black Cat" logo. In 1863, three merchants from Aachen were selecting wines in cellar in Zell, but could not decide which of three casks to buy. When the grower tried to take a second sample of one of the wines, his black cat leaped on to the barrel, arched its back, and hissed. The merchants thought that the cat was perhaps defending the best wine, thus purchased it, returning each year for what they dubbed the "Schwarze Katz" wine. As this story spread, it became customary for other producers in Zell to label their best wines with the insignia of the black cat, but since Merl and Kaimt have been merged with Zell, it has become merely a blended *Grosslage* wine.

## GROSSLAGE WEINHEX

This *Grosslage* extends over both banks of the Mosel and into the suburbs of Koblenz, encompassing some very steep slopes planted entirely with Riesling. Three growers coax some world-class Riesling from this tourist-unfashionable end of the river.

**WINNINGEN**

✓ **Vineyard** *Uhlen* **Growers** *Heymann-Löwenstein, Knebel, Freiherr von Heddersdorf* • **Vineyard** *Röttgen* **Growers** *Knebel, Freiherr von Heddersdorf, Heymann-Löwenstein*

**PREMIUM WHITES WITHOUT VINEYARD DESIGNATION**

✓ **Growers** *Heymann-Löwenstein* (Schieferterassen, von blauem Schiefer)

# BEREICH MOSELTOR

This is the most southerly *Bereich* on the Mosel. It encompasses the upper reaches of the river that flows from its source in the Vosges mountains of France through Luxembourg and into Germany, hence the name Moseltor or "Mosel gate." Its wines are very light and acidic, and of little significance except to the *Sekt* houses.

## GROSSLAGE SCHLOSS BÜBINGER

Haven of the less than heavenly Elbling. While colleagues across the river in Luxembourg earn a good living out of wine and tourism, the acidic Elbling wines of this *Grosslage* do not make it easy for its growers to survive.

# BEREICH OBERMOSEL

The Obermosel, or Upper Mosel, runs parallel to the Luxembourg border and is planted mostly with Elbling. The wines are thin, acidic, and mostly made into *Sekt*.

## GROSSLAGE GIPFEL

No outstanding villages, vineyards, or growers, although respectable wines are made in the village of Nittel.

## GROSSLAGE KÖNIGSBERG

No outstanding villages, vineyards, or growers.

# BEREICH RUWERTAL

The northern half of the former Bereich Saar-Ruwer.

## GROSSLAGE RÖMERLAY

This covers the vineyards of the Ruwer and incorporates the ancient Roman city of Trier, as well as a few scattered plots on the Mosel, including one on the left bank facing Trier. The Ruwer is much the smaller of the two tributaries, yet it has its share of exceptional vineyards owned by gifted growers who make very aromatic, vital wines that are as racy as any on the Mosel, but not quite as biting as those of the Saar. The quality is high and few wines are seen under the *Grosslage* appellation.

**EITELSBACH**

✓ **Vineyard** *Karthäuserhofberg* **Grower** *Karthäuserhof*

**KASEL**

✓ **Vineyard** *Kehrnagel* **Growers** *Karlsmühle* • **Vineyard** *Nieschen* **Growers** *Erben von Beulwitz, Reichsgraf von Kesselstatt,*

*Karlsmühle*

**LORENZHOF**

✓ **Non-Einzellage wines** • **Grower** *Karlsmühle*

**MERTESDORF**

✓ **Vineyard** *Maximin Grünhäuser Abtsberg* **Grower** *Gutsverwaltung von Schubert-Maximin Grünhaus*

# BEREICH SAAR

The southern half of the former Bereich Saar-Ruwer.

## GROSSLAGE SCHARZBERG

This covers the Saar and a small section of the Mosel between Konz and Trier to the north. These wines are so racy that they are positively biting and steely in their youth, but they age gracefully, harmonizing into exquisitely piquant flavors. Very modest Saar wines can be too thin and unripe to enjoy, but *Kabinett* and higher predicates from great growers are almost sure to please. Unlike the Ruwer's Römerlay, this *Grosslage* appellation is often used.

**KANZEM**

✓ **Vineyard** *Altenberg* **Grower** *Von Othegraven* • *Johann Peter Reinert*

**OBEREMMEL**

✓ **Vineyard** *Karlsberg* **Grower** *Reichsgraf von Kesselstatt* • **Vineyard** *Hütte* **Grower** *Von Hövel*

**OCKFEN**

✓ **Vineyard** *Bockstein* **Growers** *Weinhof Herrenberg* (Schoden) ◉, *St. Urbanshof* (Leiwen)

**SERRIG**

✓ **Vineyard** *Schloss Saarstein* **Grower** *Schloss Saarstein*

**SAARBURG**

✓ **Vineyard** *Rausch* **Grower** *Forstmeister Geltz Zilliken*

**SCHARZHOFBERG**

✓ **Vineyard** *Scharzhofberger* **Growers** *Reichsgraf von Kesselstatt, von Hövel, Vereinigte Hospitien, Egon Müller*

**SCHODEN**

✓ **Vineyard** *Herrenberg* **Grower** *Weinhof Herrenberg*

**WILTINGEN**

✓ **Vineyard** *Klosterberg* **Grower** *Johann Peter Reinert* • **Vineyard** *Schlangengraben* **Growers** *Weinhof Herrenberg, Johann Peter Reinert* • **Vineyard** *Braune Kupp* **Grower** *Egon Müller*

# THE NAHE

*In the Nahe region, a sunny microclimate and varied soils combine to produce wines that have the elegance of a Rheingau, the body of a light Rheinhessen, and the acidity of a Mosel. The perfumed aroma of a Nahe wine is unique, as are its extremely fragrant flavor and soft, smooth style.*

DESPITE AN ABUNDANCE of Roman roads and villas, viticulture came relatively late to the Nahe, in the eighth century. As in the rest of Germany, the vineyards underwent expansion in the 12th and 13th centuries, and by the 19th century the Nahe was universally considered to be on a par with the Rheingau. Strangely, by World War II it had become Germany's least-known region. This had nothing to do with a loss of either quantity or quality: excellent vineyards such as Kupfergrube at Schlossböckelheim, today widely acclaimed as the greatest of all Nahe vineyards, did not even exist before 1900. The decline was probably due instead to the fact that the region was a relatively small area of scattered vineyards, and as such it was difficult to compete with larger, more compact ones. When those larger competitors also became industrialized, they prospered and developed sophisticated transportation systems, edging the Nahe further into the cold. As a region with an essentially rural, nonindustrialized, mixed-agricultural economy,

it looked inward. Its own population could consume most of its production with little trouble, and so the Nahe's wines adopted a lower profile on national and international markets.

## SMALL COULD BE SO BEAUTIFUL
If the majority of the grape varieties cultivated in the Nahe were Riesling, the region would be able to capitalize on its limited size, and market the exclusive quality of its fine-wine production.

## THE REGION AT A GLANCE

**Area under vine**
10,433 acres or 4,222 ha (decreasing)

**Average yield**
325 cases/acre or 74 hl/ha (decreasing)

**Red wine**
10% (increasing)

**White wine**
90% (decreasing)

**Dry & semidry wine**
23% Trocken, 11% Halbtrocken

**Most important grape varieties**
26% Riesling (decreasing), 18% Müller-Thurgau (decreasing), 9% Silvaner (decreasing), 31% Others

**Infrastructure**
*Bereich* 1; *Grosslagen* 7; *Einzellagen* 328

**Note** The vineyards straddle 80 *Gemeinden* (communes), the names of which may appear on the label.

## QUALITY REQUIREMENTS AND AVERAGE QMP PRODUCTION

| NAHE'S MINIMUM OECHSLE | QUALITY CATEGORY | HARVEST BREAKDOWN |
|---|---|---|
| 44° | Deutscher Tafelwein | 1% |
| 47° | Landwein | 1% |
| 50–60° | * QbA | 76% |
| 67–73° | * Kabinett | 17% |
| 76–85° | * Spätlese | 1% |
| 83–88° | * Auslese | 1% |
| 110° | Beerenauslese | 1% |
| 110° | Eiswein | 1% |
| 150° | Trockenbeerenauslese | 1% |

*Minimum Oechsle levels vary according to grape variety; those that have a naturally lower sugar content may qualify at a correspondingly lower level.*

THE NAHE, *see also p.345*
*Between Rheinhessen and the Mittelrhein nestles the self-contained wine-producing region of the Nahe. Its namesake river has many tributaries running between spectacular overhanging cliffs.*

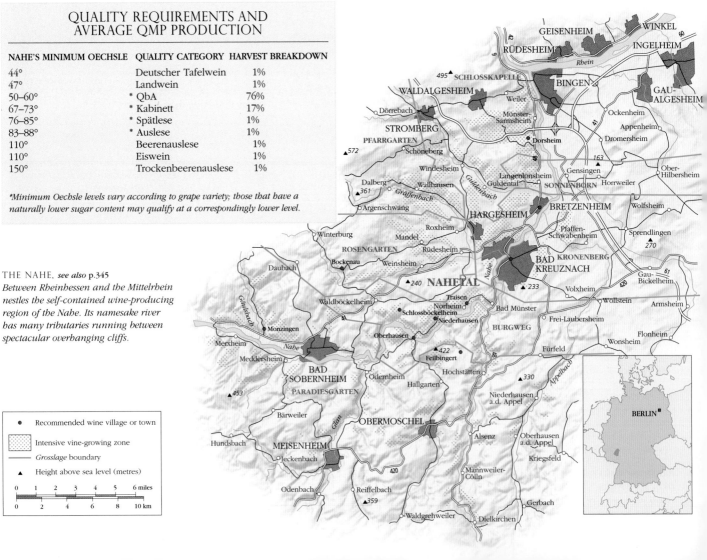

- ● Recommended wine village or town
- ▦ Intensive vine-growing zone
- — *Grosslage* boundary
- ▲ Height above sea level (metres)

0  1  2  3  4  5  6 miles
0  2  4  6  8  10 km

---

## FACTORS AFFECTING TASTE AND QUALITY

### LOCATION
The region balloons out from between Rheinhessen and Mittelrhein around the Nahe River, which runs parallel to, and 25 miles (40 kilometers) southeast of, the Mosel.

### CLIMATE
A temperate, sunny climate with adequate rainfall and no frosts. Local conditions are influenced by the Soonwald forest to the northeast and heat-retaining, rocky hills to the east. Protected south-facing vineyards enjoy microclimates that are almost Mediterranean.

### ASPECT
Vineyards are found on both the gentle and steep slopes of the Nahe and its hinterland of many small tributary river valleys. Vines grow at altitudes of between 330 and 985 feet (100 and 300 meters).

### SOIL
Diverse soils ranging from quartzite and slate along the lower reaches to porphyry (hard rock poor in lime), melaphyry (hard rock rich in lime), and colored sandstone in the middle and upper reaches. Near Bad Kreuznach, weathered clay, sandstone, limestone, loess, and loam soil may also be found. The greatest Riesling wines grow on sandstone.

### VITICULTURE AND VINIFICATION
Since the mid-1960s, cultivation of Riesling and Silvaner has declined by 20 and 15 percent respectively, yet Riesling is still the most widely planted variety, accounting for some 26 percent of the Nahe's vineyards. This is due to the increased cultivation of crosses such as Kerner, Scheurebe, and Bacchus. In the cellar, methods remain traditional but very efficient, with technically up-to-date cooperatives processing just 20 percent of the crop. As much as 40 percent of all Nahe wine is processed by small growers who sell directly to passing customers, with the remaining 40 percent belonging to the traditional industrial and export houses.

### GRAPE VARIETIES
**Primary varieties:** Müller-Thurgau, Riesling, Silvaner
**Secondary varieties:** Bacchus, Faberrebe, Kerner, Scheurebe, Ruländer, Weissburgunder

---

THE APPELLATIONS OF
# THE NAHE

## BEREICH NAHETAL

This region-wide *Bereich* replaces the former *Bereich* of Kreuznach, which covered the area once called Untere Nahe, or Lower Nahe, and Schlossböckelheim, which is the most famous.

### GROSSLAGE BURGWEG

Not to be confused with the *Grosslagen* of the same name in the Rheingau and Franken, this Burgweg produces the Nahe's greatest range of fine Riesling wines. For many years Schlossböckelheimer Kupfergrube was regarded as the best of all, but today the Oberhäuser Brücke gets most of the rave reviews.

#### NIEDERHAUSEN
✓ **Vineyard** *Hermannshöhle* **Grower** *Hermann Dönnhoff, Gutsverwaltung Niederhausen-Schlossböckelheim* • **Vineyard** *Hermannsberg* **Growers** *Gutsverwaltung Niederhausen-Schlossböckelheim*

#### NORHEIM
✓ **Vineyard** *Kirschheck* **Grower** *Dr. Crusius, Hermann Dönnhoff* • **Vineyard** *Kafels* **Grower** *Staatsweingut Bad Kreuznach*

#### OBERHAUSEN
✓ **Vineyard** *Brücke* **Grower** *Hermann Dönnhof*

#### SCHLOSSBÖCKELHEIM
✓ **Vineyard** *Kupfergrube* **Grower** *Gutsverwaltung Niederhausen-Schlossböckelheim, Hermann Dönnhoff* • **Vineyard** *Felsenberg* **Grower** *Dr. Crusius, Hermann Dönnhoff*

#### TRAISEN
✓ **Vineyard** *Bastei* **Grower** *Dr. Crusius* • **Vineyard** *Rotenfels* **Grower** *Dr. Crusius*

### GROSSLAGE KRONENBERG

This is not a branded beer, but one of the best *Grosslagen* in the Nahe, although all its finest wines, invariably Rieslings with a magical blend of perfumed fragrance and soft yet racy acidity, carry *Einzellage* names.

#### BAD KREUZNACH
✓ **Vineyard** *Paradies* **Grower** *Korrell-Johanneshof* • **Vineyard** *St. Martin* **Grower** *Korrell-Johanneshof*

## GROSSLAGE PARADIESGARTEN

This *Grosslage* consists of many scattered vineyards of very variable quality. Aside from Oberndorf, all its finest wines come from the very eastern edge of the Nahe. One grower, Emrich-Schönleber, has raised the Rieslings of Monzingen from relative obscurity to cult status.

#### MEDDERSHEIM
✓ **Vineyard** *Rheingrafenberg* **Grower** *Hexamer*

#### MONZINGEN
✓ **Vineyard** *Frühlingsplätzchen* **Grower** *Emrich-Schönleber* • **Vineyard** *Halenberg* **Grower** *Emrich-Schönleber, Schäfer-Fröhlich*

#### SOBERNHEIM
✓ **Vineyard** *Marbach* **Grower** *Hexamer*

### GROSSLAGE PFARRGARTEN

Although the *Grosslage* of Pfarrgarten is relatively small, it is intensively cultivated. Grosslage Pfarrgarten lies west and slightly north of Bad Kreuznach. Wallhausen wines are the best.

#### WALLHAUSEN
✓ **Vineyard** *Johannisberg* **Grower** *Prinz zu Salm* ◉ • **Vineyard** *Felseneck* **Grower** *Prinz zu Salm* ◉

### GROSSLAGE ROSENGARTEN

The true, original, and famous Rüdesheimer Rosengarten is a great Rheingau Riesling from an *Einzellage* called Rosengarten. The Nahe version may be honest enough, but it is not particularly special, being merely a modest *Grosslage* wine and, in all probability, a blend of Müller-Thurgau and Silvaner.

#### BOCKENAU
✓ **Vineyard** *Felseneck* **Grower** *Schäfer-Fröhlich*

#### ROXHEIM
✓ **Vineyard** *Berg* **Grower** *Prinz zu Salm*

### GROSSLAGE SCHLOSSKAPELLE

In this *Grosslage* there are a number of attractive, good-quality wines from Münster-Sarmsheim and Dorsheim that are excellent value. In addition to some full and rich Riesling, the Weisser and Grauer Burgunder are also making a name for themselves.

#### DORSHEIM
✓ **Vineyard** *Burgberg* **Grower** *Schlossgut Diel* • **Vineyard** *Goldloch* **Grower** *Schlossgut Diel, J. B. Schäfer* • **Vineyard** *Pittermännchen* **Grower** *J. B. Schäfer, Schlossgut Diel*

#### LAUBENHEIM
✓ **Vineyard** *Karthäuser* **Grower** *Tesch* • **Vineyard** *St. Remigiusberg* **Grower** *Tesch*

#### WINDESHEIM
✓ **Vineyard** *Rosenberg* **Grower** *Rudolf Sinß* (red) **Non-Einzellagewein Grower** *Lindenhof* (red)

#### MÜNSTER (-SARMSHEIM)
✓ **Vineyard** *Dautenpflänzer* **Growers** *Göttelmann* • *Kruger-Rumpf* • **Vineyard** *Rheinberg* **Grower** *Göttelmann* • **Vineyard** *Pittersberg* **Grower** *Kruger-Rumpf* • **Non-Einzellagen wine** *Kruger-Rumpf*

### GROSSLAGE SONNENBORN

Sonnenborn is a one-village *Grosslage* and at least one grower in Langenlonsheim produces some interesting and fulsome wines.

#### LANGENLONSHEIM
✓ **Vineyard** *Löhrer Berg* **Growers** *Tesch*

---

## OTHER CERTIFIED ORGANIC WINEMAKERS

**Biodynamic**
Fuchs Jacobus (Waldaubersheim)
Im Zwölberich (Langenlonsheim)
Klaus Krost (Waldlaubersheim)
Wolfgang Hermes/Hermeshof (Bretzenheim)

**Organic**
Aloys Müller (Pfaffen-Schwabenheim)
Anke Eckes (Windesheim)
Anni & Hermann Steitz (Dielkirchen)
Brühler Hof (Volxheim)
Georg Forster (Rümmelsheim)
Gutshöfe FVA Ernst Anhauser (Bad Kreuznach)
Hans-Gerhard Hamann (Guldental-Heddenheim)
Hanmühle (Mannweiler-Cölln)
Häussling (Laubenheim)
Konrad Knodel (Windesheim)
Rheinhold Grossmann (Windesheim)
Schillingshof (Waldlaubersheim)

# THE RHEINGAU

*There can be no doubt that Riesling, the king of Germany's grapes, is more at home in and around the village of Johannisberg in the Rheingau than anywhere else in the world. Nowhere else can it produce such lush, juicy-ripe wines with distinctive, silky-smooth peach fruit.*

MANY COUNTRIES OF THE WORLD use the synonym "Johannisberg Riesling" to distinguish the true Riesling grape variety from the many false and inferior Rieslings that claim the name. There can be no doubt that the Riesling grape luxuriates on this single sun-blessed slope of the Johannisberg vineyard in a most unique way.

Even at QbA level, the relaxed and confident style of a good Rheingau wine will leave a soft, satisfying, and elegant taste of peaches in the mouth. This gradually merges into a youthful, honeyed character that has nothing to do with *Edelfäule* (botrytis,

VITICULTURE IN THE RHEINGAU
*Just under 80 percent of the vines are Riesling, and it is here that Riesling has historically ripened to such perfection that the wines have a juicy peachiness.*

## THE REGION AT A GLANCE

**Area under vine**
8,125 acres or 3,129 ha (decreasing)

**Average yield**
295 cases/acre or 67 hl/ha (increasing)

**Red wine**
12% (increasing)

**White wine**
88% (decreasing)

**Dry & semidry wine**
66% Trocken, 22% Halbtrocken

**Most important grape varieties**
79% Riesling (decreasing), 12% Spätburgunder (increasing), 2% Müller-Thurgau (decreasing), 7% Others

**Infrastructure**
*Bereich* 1; *Grosslagen* 10; *Einzellagen* 118

**Note** The vineyards of Rheingau straddle 28 *Gemeinden* (communes), the names of which may appear on the label.

or noble rot), overripeness, or bottle-aging. One can prefer other stylistic renditions of the Riesling grape, but it is impossible to find finer, more graceful examples.

## THE RHEINGAU'S INITIAL CHARTA FOR QUALITY
In the midst of the excitement generated by Germany's new *trocken* wines, it became evident to various top Rheingau estates that most of the wines exported were bulk blended and of low commercial quality. Since these properties had traditionally produced naturally drier wines, they believed that a continuance

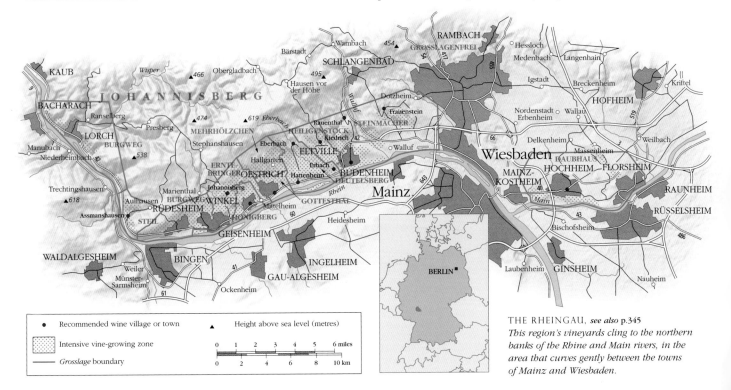

| • | Recommended wine village or town |
| | Intensive vine-growing zone |
| — | *Grosslage* boundary |

▲ Height above sea level (metres)

0 1 2 3 4 5 6 miles
0 2 4 6 8 10 km

THE RHEINGAU, *see also p.345*
*This region's vineyards cling to the northern banks of the Rhine and Main rivers, in the area that curves gently between the towns of Mainz and Wiesbaden.*

## QUALITY REQUIREMENTS AND AVERAGE QMP PRODUCTION

| RHEINGAU'S MINIMUM OECHSLE | QUALITY CATEGORY | HARVEST BREAKDOWN |
|---|---|---|
| 44° | Deutscher Tafelwein | 0.5% |
| 53° | Landwein | 0.5% |
| 57–60° | * QbA | 70% |
| 73–80° | * Kabinett | 20% |
| 85–95° | * Spätlese | 5% |
| 95–105° | * Auslese | 1% |
| 125° | Beerenauslese | 1% |
| 125° | Eiswein | 1% |
| 150° | Trockenbeerenauslese | 1% |

*Minimum Oechsle levels vary according to grape variety; those that have a naturally lower sugar content may qualify at a correspondingly lower level.*

of poor *trocken* wines could damage their own image, so they banded together to protect it. In 1983, the Association of Charta (pronounced "karta") Estates was launched to "further the classic Rheingau Riesling style, to upgrade the quality of Rheingau wines, and to make them unique among wines from other growing areas." Although this could not have succeeded without the active support of almost all the best Rheingau producers, the engine that relentlessly drove the Charta organization was, until his untimely death, Georg Breuer. Under his direction, Charta became the antithesis of any official quality-control system, as it aspired to the highest possible quality, rather than succumbing to the lowest common denominator. When first drawn up, the Charta's rules were uncommonly stiff; yet every few years, Breuer would tighten the ratchet a bit more by issuing even tougher rules.

### TROCKEN WINES

One in every five bottles of German wine is *trocken,* or dry, but many of these are thin and short. The intrinsically riper grapes grown by the Rheingau's Charta estates produce a fatter, fuller style of wine that adapts naturally to the *trocken* style, especially with food; but *trocken* wines produced in other regions have come on in leaps and bounds since the early 1990s. They are now well balanced, with an elegance that was missing from even the best of the best in the late 1980s. Due to the botrytis found in *Spätlese* and *Auslese* grapes used, they also possess a level of youthful complexity that is seldom encountered in other wines. They are very accessible when young, but rarely improve after their first flush of youth.

SCHLOSS VOLLRADS
*This famous wine schloss was built circa 1300 by the Knights of Greiffenclau.*

## THE CHARTA RULES

I have tasted many Charta wines and am convinced that they are indeed superior to other Rheingau wines. It must be emphasized, however, that it is only dry styles that are subject to the Charta organization's regulations—great QmP Rheingau wines of sweet styles from *Auslese* upward are not affected. A Charta wine may be recognized by the traditional tall, slim, brown bottle typical of the Rheingau region and by the distinctive "Charta capsule" consisting of a Romanesque double-arch on a white background. There is also a label on the back with the same insignia.

Charta wines are examined organoleptically (using only the senses of taste, smell, and sight) before and after bottling. There is a second examination to check the authenticity of the original sample. Wines destined to receive the Charta imprimatur must be accompanied by official analysis documents and must also satisfy certain criteria laid down by the Association of Charta Estates, as follows:

The wines that are submitted for examination must be made in a "dry" style and conform to the following:

- 100 percent own-estate production
- 100 percent Riesling grapes
- Grapes handpicked by *tries*
- Minimum of 12 percent potential alcohol
- Maximum production of 50 hl/ha (220 cases/acre)
- No *Prädikat* may be mentioned*

The wines must have the true characteristics of a Riesling, of the specific vintage, and of the vineyard where the grapes were grown.

Registration has to be made four weeks prior to the date of examination, indicating the vintage and category.

*Older vintages of Prädikat wines may be encountered. These will not have been produced according to the above rules if only for the simple reason that they have not been made in a dry style, but they will have undergone the same exhaustive tasting and, if selected, become "Charta Designated," rather than "Charta Approved."

As a control, normal wines of comparable location and category are tasted blind alongside wines submitted for examination. Charta wines have to surpass the quality of these standard wines in each of the required aspects. The wines provided for the second tasting, as well as being a control, have to be accompanied by the analysis of the AP number (*see* p.346). The results of these tests are lodged with the association and can be used in the eventuality of any subsequent claim that a member is passing off an inferior wine as a Charta wine.

Charta bottle

RHEINGAU RIESLING

CHARTA

Nur Rheingauer Rieslinge, die den strengen Anforderungen der Vereinigung der CHARTA-Weingüter entsprechen, tragen das Zeichen CHARTA® auf dem Etikett. Dieser klassisch herbe Riesling eignet sich besonders als Essenbegleiter.

Charta capsule                    Back label

#### CAPSULE AND BACK LABEL
*All wines that have passed the Charta examination are sealed with a capsule bearing the organization's logo consisting of a Romanesque double-arch that also appears on the back label.*

#### CHARTA BOTTLE
*Originally all bottles were embossed with the Charta logo similar to the example here. However, the cost of embossing proved prohibitive for some of the smaller producers, and it is now optional.*

**BERG SCHLOSSBERG VINEYARDS, RÜDESHEIM**
*These south-facing vineyards on the slopes of Berg Schlossberg
are blessed with perfect exposure to the sun's rays.*

## FACTORS AFFECTING TASTE AND QUALITY

### LOCATION
The Rheingau is a compact region only 22 miles (36 kilometers) long, situated on the northern banks of the Rhine and Main rivers between Bingen and Mainz.

### CLIMATE
Vines are protected from cold by the tempering effect of the rivers and the shelter provided by the Taunus Mountains. The region receives above-average hours of sunshine during the growth period of May to October.

### ASPECT
The vines grow at an altitude of 330 to 985 feet (100 to 300 meters) on a superb, fully south-facing slope.

### SOIL
Quartzite and weathered slate-stone in the higher situated sites produce the greatest Riesling, while loam, loess, various types of clay, and sandy gravel soils of the lower vineyards give a fuller, more robust style. The blue phyllite-slate around Assmannshausen is traditionally thought to favor the Spätburgunder.

### VITICULTURE AND VINIFICATION
In contrast to other German regions, the Rheingau consists of a large number of independent wine estates (500 odd) in a relatively compact area. There are approximately 2,600 private growers, many of whom make and market their own wines, while others supply the region's 10 cooperatives. The Riesling grape variety represents almost 80 percent of the vines cultivated and it is traditional in this region to vinify all but the sweetest wines in a drier style than would be used in other regions. Assmannshausen is famous for its red wine, one of Germany's best.

### GRAPE VARIETIES
**Primary varieties:** Riesling
**Secondary varieties:** Ehrenfelser, Kerner, Müller-Thurgau, Silvaner, Spätburgunder, Weissburgunder

## THE CHARTA'S NEW CLASSIFIED VINEYARD WINES

Look out for Charta *Einzellage* wines with a black bottom border bearing not one but three Romanesque double-arches on the front label. This is verification that the wine comes not from the grossly inflated official *Einzellagen*, but from the original, authentic site, which Charta has called *Erstes Gewächs* or First Growths. They must conform to the same rules (i.e., dry style with no mention of *Prädikat*), although new regulations to cover botrytis and even Spätburgunder *Erstes Gewächs* are under study. The difference between official and authentic *Einzellage* size can be, as you can see, quite enormous. In fact, the 1971 German wine law is nothing less than the promotion of legalized fraud on a massive and widespread scale.

| VILLAGE | EINZELLAGE | VINEYARD SIZE Official | Charta | 1971 EXPANSION |
|---------|------------|----------|--------|----------------|
| Lorch | Bodenthal-Steinberg | 28.1 | 12.3 | 128% |
| Lorch | Kapellenberg | 56.9 | 17.9 | 218% |
| Lorch | Krone | 14.5 | 7.5 | 93% |
| Assmannshausen | Höllenberg | 43.4 | 20 | 117% |
| Rüdesheim | Berg Schlossberg | 25.5 | 23.2 | 10% |
| Rüdesheim | Berg Roseneck | 26.7 | 16.2 | 65% |
| Rüdesheim | Berg Rottland | 36.2 | 32.3 | 12% |
| Geisenheim | Fuchsberg | 44.4 | 5.6 | 693% |
| Geisenheim | Rothenberg | 26.8 | 9 | 198% |
| Geisenheim | Kläuserweg | 57.6 | 14.3 | 303% |
| Geisenheim | Mäuerchen | 32.6 | 3.6 | 8.60% |
| Johannisberg | Schloss Johannisberg | 21.9 | 16.6 | 32% |
| Johannisberg | Klaus | 2 | 2 | 0% |
| Johannisberg | Hölle | 20.9 | 6.2 | 237% |
| Johannisberg | Mittelhölle | 6.5 | 6.5 | 0% |
| Winkel | Jesuitengarten | 31.2 | 26 | 20% |
| Winkel | Hasensprung | 103.8 | 19.9 | 421% |
| Winkel | Schloss Vollrads | 37.7 | 15 | 151% |
| Mittelheim | St Nikolaus | 44.8 | 6.7 | 569% |
| Oestrich | Lenchen | 130.6 | 35.8 | 265% |
| Oestrich | Doosberg | 137.9 | 38.4 | 259% |
| Hattenheim | Engelmannsberg | 14.1 | 10.5 | 34% |
| Hattenheim | Mannberg | 8.1 | 8.1 | 0% |
| Hattenheim | Pfaffenberg | 6.6 | 6.6 | 0% |
| Hattenheim | Nussbrunnen | 10.8 | 10.8 | 0% |
| Hattenheim | Wisselbrunnen | 16.9 | 9.7 | 74% |
| Hattenheim | Steinberg | 36.7 | 26.9 | 36% |
| Hallgarten | Schönhell | 52.1 | 18.9 | 176% |
| Erbach | Marcobrunn | 5.2 | 5.2 | 0% |
| Erbach | Steinmorgen | 28.2 | 8.6 | 228% |
| Erbach | Siegelsberg | 15.1 | 13.7 | 10% |
| Erbach | Hohenrain | 17.1 | 5.8 | 195% |

| VILLAGE | EINZELLAGE | VINEYARD SIZE Official | Charta | 1971 EXPANSION |
|---------|------------|----------|--------|----------------|
| Erbach | Schlossberg | 28.1 | 12.3 | 128% |
| Kiedrich | Gräfenberg | 56.9 | 17.9 | 218% |
| Kiedrich | Wasseros | 14.5 | 7.5 | 93% |
| Eltville | Sonnenberg | 43.4 | 20 | 117% |
| Rauenthal | Baiken | 25.5 | 23.2 | 10% |
| Rauenthal | Gehrn | 26.7 | 16.2 | 65% |
| Rauenthal | Rothenberg | 36.2 | 32.3 | 12% |
| Rauenthal | Nonnenberg | 44.4 | 5.6 | 693% |
| Rauenthal | Wülfen | 26.8 | 9 | 198% |
| Rauenthal | Wildsau | 57.6 | 14.3 | 303% |
| Martinsthal | Langenberg | 32.6 | 3.6 | 806% |
| Walluf | Walkenberg | 21.9 | 16.6 | 32% |
| Wiesbaden | Neroberg | 2 | 2 | 0% |
| Hochheim | Domdechaney | 20.9 | 6.2 | 237% |
| Hochheim | Kirchenstück | 6.5 | 6.5 | 0% |
| Hochheim | Hölle | 31.2 | 26 | 20% |
| Hochheim | Königin Victoria Ber | 103.8 | 19.9 | 421% |

GEORG BREUER
RÜDESHEIM
BERG SCHLOSSBERG
RHEINGAU

GEORG BREUER
RÜDESHEIM
BERG SCHLOSSBERG
RHEINGAU

THE APPELLATIONS OF
# THE RHEINGAU

## BEREICH JOHANNISBERG

This *Bereich* covers the entire Rheingau. Trading off the famous village of Johannisberg, situated behind Schloss Johannisberg, lesser wines sell well under it. However, some producers have started using *Grosslage* names on labels and because they do not use the word "*Grosslage*," this implies the wine might be from one specific site, and perhaps of better quality.

### GROSSLAGE BURGWEG

This is the westernmost *Grosslage*. If a wine bears its name on the label and clearly shows "Riesling," it may well be good, but it will not in any way compare with Burgweg's superb *Einzellage* wines that are produced by the great estates or small growers.

**GEISENHEIM**

✓ **Vineyard** *Rothenberg* **Grower** *Wegeler-Gutshaus Oestrich*

**RÜDESHEIM**

✓ **Vineyard** *Berg Roseneck* **Grower** *Josef Leitz, August Kesseler* • **Vineyard** *Berg Rottland* **Growers** *Georg Breuer, Johannishof, Josef Leitz, Wegeler-Gutshaus Oestrich* • **Vineyard** *Berg Schlossberg* **Growers** *Georg Breuer, August Kesseler* (red and white), *Josef Leitz* • **Vineyard** *Bischofsberg* **Growers** *Georg Breuer, August Kesseler* • **Premium Red Wine Blends Growers** *Breuer* (Spätburgunder "S")

### GROSSLAGE DAUBHAUS

The best vines of Daubhaus, which is the most easterly *Grosslage* in *Bereich* Johannisberg, grow in just one tiny, isolated, but excellent strip at Hochheim. The wines are firm and full, but do not quite match the elegance of the Rheingau's very best.

**HOCHHEIM**

✓ **Vineyard** *Domdechaney* **Grower** *Domdechant Werner'sches Weingut* • **Vineyard** *Kirchenstück* **Grower** *Domdechant Werner'sches Weingut, Franz Künstler* • **Vineyard** *Hölle* **Growers** *Franz Künstler* • **Vineyard** *Reichestal* **Grower** *Franz Künstler* (red)

**WICKER**

✓ **Vineyard** *Mönchsgewann* **Grower** *Joachim Flick*

### GROSSLAGE DEUTELSBERG

Grosslage Deutelsberg encompasses the great Erbach vineyards as well as the rather underrated wines of Hattenheim, which have great strength and longevity. It also includes the famous Kloster Eberbach and Mariannenau Island vineyard, where there is a little Chardonnay grown.

**HATTENHEIM**

✓ **Vineyard** *Pfaffenberg* **Grower** *Domäne Schloss Schönborn* • **Vineyard** *Wisselbrunnen* **Growers** *Josef Spreitzer, Hans Lang, Schloss Reinhartshausen*

## GROSSLAGE ERNTEBRINGER

The most often-seen of the Rheingau's *Grosslagen*, Erntebringer is also its best, although not comparable to the *Einzellagen*, particularly the legendary Schloss Johannisberg and the grossly underrated Klaus.

**GEISENHEIM**

✓ **Vineyard** *Klaus* **Grower** *Prinz von Hessen*

**JOHANNISBERG**

✓ **Vineyard** *Hölle* **Grower** *Johannishof* • **Vineyard** *Schloss Johannisberg* **Grower** *Schloss Johannisberg* • **Vineyard** *Klaus* **Growers** *Prinz von Hessen*

**WINKEL**

✓ **Vineyard** *Hasensprung* **Grower** *Prinz von Hessen* • **Vineyard** *Schloss Vollrads* **Grower** *Schloss Vollrads*

## GROSSLAGE GOTTESTHAL

It is strange that this *Grosslage*, sandwiched between the superb Deutelsberg and Honigberg, should be disappointing in the wines it produces. However, some excellent, long-lived Riesling can be found.

**OESTRICH**

✓ **Vineyard** *Lenchen* **Growers** *Wegeler-Gutshaus Oestrich, Peter Jakob Kühn, Josef Spreitzer*

## GROSSLAGE HEILIGENSTOCK

The best product of this small *Grosslage* is the fabulous, peach-and-honey Riesling of Kiedrich, often culminating in some of the world's most noble sweet wines. The *Grosslage* wine can also be good.

**KIEDRICH**

✓ **Vineyard** *Gräfenberg* **Grower** *Robert Weil*

## GROSSLAGE HONIGBERG

Wines of great vitality, finesse; all the elegant, mouthwatering, peachy fruit, and youthful honey you could expect from top Rheingau wines.

**ERBACH**

✓ **Vineyard** *Hohenrain* **Grower** *Jakob Jung* • **Vineyard** *Marcobrunn* **Growers** *Schloss Schönborn* • *Schloss Reinhartshausen* ⊙ • **Vineyard** *Michelmark* **Grower** *Jakob Jung* • **Vineyard** *Steinmorgen* **Grower** *Heinz Nikolai* • **Vineyard** *Schlossberg* **Grower** *Schloss Reinhartshausen*

**WINKEL**

✓ **Vineyard** *Hasensprung* **Growers** *Prinz von Hessen* • **Vineyard** *Jesuitengarten* **Growers** *Prinz von Hessen, J. Wegeler Erben*

## GROSSLAGE MEHRHÖLZCHEN

The *Grosslage* of Mehrhölzchen, on higher, steeper slopes than the rest of the Rheingau, is tucked up beneath the Taunus hills. The area is planted almost entirely with Riesling, and the wine is fat, almost heavy. It is sometimes full of fruit, displaying a unique spicy aroma.

**HALLGARTEN**

✓ **Vineyard** *Jungfer* **Grower** *Prinz*

## GROSSLAGE STEIL

The tiny *Grosslage* of Steil divides the *Grosslage* of Burgweg. Steil is famous for the red wines of Assmannshausen. These are soft and delicate, and have a pure varietal style, but possess neither the body nor the tannin one is accustomed to finding to some degree in any red wine, whatever its grape variety or provenance. The majority of the vineyards in Grosslage Steil are situated on steep, southwest-facing slopes, but those of Höllenberg, which notably produce the best wine, are situated on a tiny, south-facing tributary.

**ASSMANNSHAUSEN**

✓ **Vineyard** *Höllenberg* **Growers** *August Kesseler* (red), *Staatsweingüter Assmannshausen, Robert König* (red), *Weingut Krone* (red)

## GROSSLAGE STEINMÄCHER

The vineyards of Grosslage Steinmächer are less intensively cultivated than those situated in the main body of the Rheingau's vine-growing area, but this does not mean that the wines they produce are in any way less impressive.

**WALLUF**

✓ **Vineyard** *Walkenberg* **Grower** *J. B. Becker*

---

## OTHER CERTIFIED ORGANIC WINEMAKERS

**Organic**
Altenkirch & Schmidt (Lorch im Rheingau)
Asbach-Kretschmar (Rüdesheim)
Bernd J Richter (Hochheim)
Graf von Kanitz (Lorch im Rheingau)
Hans-Josef Engelmann (Kiedrich)
Hirt-Albrecht (Eltville)
Jakob Hamm (Oestrich-Winkel)
Rheinhard Glassner (Lorch im Rheingau)
Stefan Muskat (Geisenheim)
Troitzsch-Pusinelli (Lorch)

# RHEINHESSEN

*Rheinhessen is the most heavily cultivated of all Germany's* Qualitätswein *regions. The diversity of its soils and grape varieties makes it impossible to convey a uniform impression of its wines. Riesling is planted in just eight percent of its vineyards. Most vineyards produce cheap, unpretentious wines, ranging from mild Silvaner to aromatic Müller-Thurgau, but some truly fine wines are to be found.*

RHEINHESSEN IS INDISPUTABLY LINKED with the ubiquitous Liebfraumilch. This is partly because the area is responsible for producing one in every two bottles, partly because of the famous Liebfraumilch-Kirchenstück in Worms, where the Liebfraumilch story began; and partly because Sichel & Co. brews up perhaps the most famous Liebfraumilch ("Blue Nun") in sleepy Alzey. Nierstein carries a similar stigma to that of Liebfraumilch in the minds of many experienced drinkers,

## FACTORS AFFECTING TASTE AND QUALITY

### LOCATION
This region is situated between the towns of Bingen, Mainz, and Worms, immediately south of the Rheingau.

### CLIMATE
Rheinhessen enjoys a temperate climate and is protected from cold winds by the Taunus hills to the north and the Odenwald forest to the east. Vineyards that slope down to the river are protected by the Rhine terrace itself.

### ASPECT
On the river slopes of the Rhine Terrace vines grow on east- and southeast-facing slopes at an altitude of between 330 and 660 feet (100 and 200 meters), while those in Rheinhessen's hinterland are found at various heights and with every possible aspect.

### SOIL
Mainly loess deposited during interglacial sandstorms, but also limestone, sandy-marl, quartzite, porphyry-sand, and silty-clay. Riesling growers favor heavier marl soil, except near Bingen, where there is an outcropping of quartzite-slate. A red, slaty-sandy clay soil known as *rotliegendes* is found on the best, steep riverfront vineyards of Nackenheim and Nierstein.

### VITICULTURE AND VINIFICATION
Due to the large number of part-time growers, much of the wine is made from vast vineyard yields and bulk-blended into cheap generic wines such as Bereich Nierstein, and, of course, Liebfraumilch. At the other extreme, small quantities of some fine wines are produced on the best estates.

### GRAPE VARIETIES
**Primary varieties:** Müller-Thurgau, Silvaner, Riesling
**Secondary varieties:** Bacchus, Faberrebe, Huxelrebe, Kerner, Morio-Muskat, Portugieser, Scheurebe

due to the huge quantities of the cheap Bereich Nierstein and Niersteiner Gutes Domtal that flood the market and which downgrade the reputation of the high-quality Niersteiner *Einzellagen*.

## THE RHINE TERRACE
Despite the high volume of indifferent wines, there are many great growers and estates producing good wine in this region. If you are looking for an initial increase

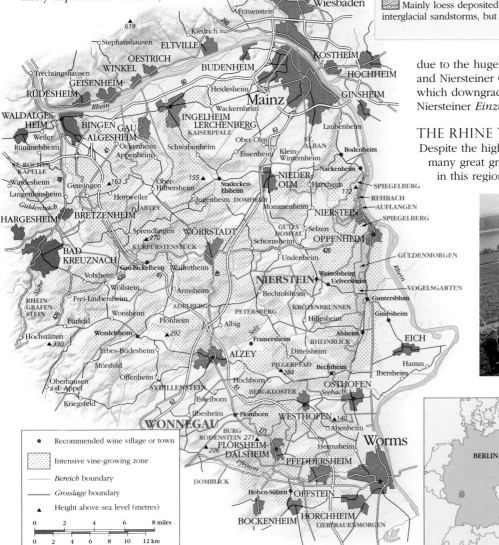

RHINE TERRACE
VINEYARDS AT NIERSTEIN
*Nierstein is one of the nine member villages of the "Rhein Terrasse" group, which offers good-value, quality wines. New grape crosses are a feature of this area.*

RHEINHESSEN, see also p.345
*One of Germany's largest regions in terms of acres under vine, this is an area of great variety where several different grapes are grown.*

in quality for a modest price, look out for the "Rhein Terrasse" sticker on bottles of Rheinhessen wine.

The Rhine Terrace comprises nine villages on the slopes that descend from Rheinhessen's plateau to the Rhine River. These villages and their *Grosslagen* are as follows: Bodenheim in the St. Alban *Grosslage*; Nackenheim in the Gutes Domtal *Grosslage*; Nierstein, which is shared by the *Grosslagen* of Gutes Domtal, Spiegelberg, Rehbach, and Auflangen; Oppenheim in the *Grosslagen* of Güldenmorgen and Krötenbrunnen; Dienheim, also in the Krötenbrunnen *Grosslage*; Guntersblum and Ludwigshöhe, both of which are in the Krötenbrunnen and Vogelsgarten *Grosslagen*; and Alsheim and Mattenheim, in the *Grosslage* of Rheinblick.

**LIEBFRAUMILCH COUNTRY IN THE SPRING**
*The village of Grau-Heppenheim, near Alzey, the home of Blue Nun, in the large Petersberg Grosslage.*

## QUALITY REQUIREMENTS AND AVERAGE QMP PRODUCTION

| RHEINHESSEN'S MINIMUM OECHSLE | QUALITY CATEGORY | HARVEST BREAKDOWN |
|---|---|---|
| 44° | Deutscher Tafelwein | 0.5% |
| 53° | Landwein | 0.5% |
| 60–62° | * QbA | 69% |
| 73–76° | * Kabinett | 17% |
| 85–90° | * Spätlese | 8% |
| 92–100° | * Auslese | 1% |
| 125° | Beerenauslese | 2% |
| 125° | Eiswein | 1% |
| 150° | Trockenbeerenauslese | 1% |

*Minimum Oechsle levels vary according to grape variety; those that have a naturally lower sugar content may qualify at a correspondingly lower level.*

## THE REGION AT A GLANCE

**Area under vine**
62,269 acres or 25,199 ha (decreasing)

**Average yield**
415 case/acre or 95 hl/ha (increasing)

**Red wine**
13% (increasing)

**White wine**
87% (decreasing)

**Dry & semidry wine**
22% Trocken, 8% Halbtrocken

**Most important grape varieties**
20% Müller-Thurgau (decreasing), 11% Silvaner (decreasing), 10% Riesling (increasing), 8% Dornfelder (increasing), 8% Kerner (decreasing), 7% Portugieser (increasing), 6% Scheurebe (decreasing), 6% Bacchus (decreasing), 24% Others

**Infrastructure**
*Bereiche* 3; *Grosslagen* 24; *Einzellagen* 434

**Note** The vineyards of Rheinhessen straddle 167 *Gemeinden* (communes), the names of which may appear on the label.

---

## THE APPELLATIONS OF
# RHEINHESSEN

## BEREICH BINGEN

Abutting the Nahe region to the west and separated by the Rhine from the Rheingau to the north, Bereich Bingen is the smallest of Rheinhessen's three *Bereiche* and the least important in terms of both the quantity and quality of the wine produced.

## GROSSLAGE ABTEY

The *Grosslage* of Abtey does not have any outstanding villages, vineyards, or growers, although good-quality wines are produced in the village of St. Johann.

## GROSSLAGE ADELBERG

Some good value wines can be found in the small town of Wörrstadt, but in terms of quality no vineyards or growers stand out.

## GROSSLAGE KAISERPFALZ

Kaiserpfalz is a *Grosslage* consisting mainly of Bingen and Mainz, with vineyards facing to both the east and west. This *Grosslage* produces some of the region's most promising red wines from the Portugieser and Spätburgunder grapes. The village of Ingelheim is one of the places that claim to be the birthplace of the emperor Charlemagne.

**INGELHEIM**
☑ **Vineyard** *Steinacker* **Grower** *Arndt F. Werner* ◉ (red and white)

## GROSSLAGE KURFÜRSTENSTÜCK

Gau-Bickelheim is the home of Rheinhessen's huge central cooperative, but it has been the good growers or excellent *Staatsdomäne* from the *Einzellage* of Kapelle that have produced superior wines in the past.

## GROSSLAGE RHEINGRAFENSTEIN

Some exciting efforts from a new shooting star demonstrate the potential of this *Grosslage*.

**SIEFERSHEIM**
☑ **Vineyard** *Heerkretz* **Grower** *Wagner-Stempel* • **Vineyard** *Höllberg* **Grower** *Wagner-Stempel* • **Premium Red Wine Blend Grower** *Wagner-Stempel* (Spaetburgunder "R")

## GROSSLAGE SANKT ROCHUSKAPELLE

Bingen is often thought to belong more to the Nahe region than to Rheinhessen, but 14 of its 18 *Einzellagen* belong to this Rheinhessen *Grosslage*, which is among the best in *Bereich* Bingen.

**HORRWEILER**
☑ **Vineyard** *Gewürzgärtchen* **Grower** *Huf-Doll*

## BEREICH NIERSTEIN

Although this is a famous *Bereich* with many superb sites and great growers, most wines sold under its label include some of the most dull, characterless, and lackluster in all of Germany. Wine enthusiasts will find it best to choose the great *Einzellagen* and leave these *Grosslage* products alone.

## GROSSLAGE AUFLANGEN

This is the best of the three *Grosslagen* that encompass some parts of Nierstein (the other two are Rehbach and Spiegelberg). Its vineyard area actually begins in the center of the town, then stretches west to include the south- and southeast-facing vineyards of the tiny tributary of the Rhine that flows through Schwabsburg, and then north to the Kranzberg, which overlooks the Rhine itself.

**NIERSTEIN**

✓ **Vineyard** *Oelberg* **Growers** *Heyl zu Herrnsheim* ⊙ • *St. Antony, Seebrich*

## GROSSLAGE DOMHERR

Once forming ecclesiastical vineyards (Domherr means "Canon of the Cathedral") this *Grosslage* has good vineyards on steep slopes, but there are few outstanding growers.

## GROSSLAGE GÜLDENMORGEN

Güldenmorgen was once a fine-quality *Einzellage* belonging to Oppenheim, but now encompasses three villages. The best wines come from the Sackträger site. Please note that although the village of Uelversheim is clearly situated in the *Grosslage* of Krotenbrunnen, the eastern tail end of its vineyards actually overlaps Güldenmorgen.

**OPPENHEIM**

✓ **Vineyard** *Sackträger* **Grower** *Manz* • *Kühling-Gillot*

## GROSSLAGE GUTES DOMTAL

This district covers a vast area of Rhine hinterland behind the better *Grosslagen* of Nierstein. Although it encompasses 15 villages, most is sold under the ubiquitous Niersteiner Gutes Domtal (sometimes Domthal) name. Much is decidedly inferior and cheapens the reputation of Nierstein's truly great wines. The most famous village is Dexheim, because of its so-called Doktor, named after the old spelling of the great Bernkasteler Doctor vineyard. But neither Dexheim generally, nor Dexheimer Doktor specifically, warrant the attention.

**WEINOLSHEIM**

✓ **Vineyard** *Kehr* **Grower** *Manz*

## GROSSLAGE KRÖTENBRUNNEN

This district encompasses those parts of Oppenheim's vineyards that are not included in the *Grosslage* Güldenmorgen, and the wide-ranging vineyards of Guntersblum.

## GROSSLAGE PETERSBERG

This *Grosslage* lies behind Gutes Domtal and is wedged between the *Bereiche* of Bingen and Wonnegau. Although large, this *Grosslage* has few, if any, exciting sites or growers.

## GROSSLAGE REHBACH

Rehbach is one of the greatest *Grosslagen* in Rheinhessen, consisting of a long, thin strip of very steep terraced slopes overlooking the Rhine, just north of Nierstein. Riesling wines produced by these vineyards are aromatic, intense, and delightfully mellow, yet have a definite raciness on the finish.

**NIERSTEIN**

✓ **Vineyard** *Hipping* **Growers** *Georg Albrecht Schneider, St. Antony* • **Vineyard** *Pettenthal* **Growers** *Heyl zu Herrnsheim* ⊙*, St. Antony, Gunderloch, Kühling-Gillot*

## GROSSLAGE RHEINBLICK

This district produces better-than-average Grosslage wines.

## GROSSLAGE ST. ALBAN

Named after the St. Alban monastery, which once owned most of the land in this underrated *Grosslage* situated between Mainz and Nierstein.

The *Einzellage* wines have fine, positive character and usually represent excellent value for money.

## GROSSLAGE SPIEGELBERG

The largest of Nierstein's riverside districts, its vineyards stretch to the north and south of both the famous town and the Grosslage Auflangen. Ignore the ubiquitous, mild, and neutral-flavored *Grosslagen* wines and choose the wines of the finer *Einzellagen* that are situated between Nierstein and Oppenheim.

**NACKENHEIM**

✓ **Vineyard** *Rothenberg* **Grower** *Gunderloch*

## GROSSLAGE VOGELSGARTEN

This is not, in fact, one of the best Rheinhessen districts, although Weingut Ohnacker makes fine, rich, sometimes powerful wines that are well worth seeking out.

# BEREICH WONNEGAU

The least-known of Rheinhessen's three *Bereiche*, Wonnegau contains the world-famous (although not world-class) Liebfrauenstift *Einzellage*, which had the rather dubious honor of giving birth to Liebfraumilch. Wonnegau means "province of great joy."

## GROSSLAGE BERGKLOSTER

Some of Germany's top dry Riesling comes from Westhofen.

**WESTHOFEN**

✓ **Vineyard** *Aulerde* **Grower** *Wittmann* ⊙ • **Vineyard** *Morstein* **Grower** *Wittmann, Gerhard Gutzler* (red), *Keller* • **Vineyard** *Kirchspiel* **Grower** *Wittmann K. F. Groebe* • **Premium red wine blends Growers** *Gerhard Gutzler* ("GS" barrique)

## GROSSLAGE BURG RODENSTEIN

A large proportion of the wines made in the Grosslage Burg Rodenstein district are sold under its *Grosslage* name. Most of it is well above average quality, although not in the same class as its best *Einzellage* wines. Since the mid-1990s Keller has been considered by many critics to be Germany's top wine estate.

**DAHLSHEIM (an *Ortsteil* of Flörsheim-Dahlsheim)**

✓ **Vineyard** *Hubacker* **Grower** *Keller*

**Vineyard** *Bürgel* (red) **Growers** *Keller* **Non-Einzellage Premium White Grower** *Keller* (G-Max, varietals)

**NIEDERFLÖRSHEIM (an *Ortsteil* of Flörsheim-Dahlsheim)**

✓ **Vineyard** *Frauenberg* **Growers** *Scherner-Kleinhanns*

## GROSSLAGE DOMBLICK

There are few outstanding growers here, although good wines are made in the village of Monsheim, and the *Grosslage* label usually offers sound value.

**MONSHEIM**

✓ **Vineyard** *Silberberg* **Grower** *Keller* (Flörsheim-Dahlsheim)

**OFFSTEIN**

✓ **Non-Einzellage Premium Red Grower** *Georg Jakob Keth*

## GROSSLAGE GOTTESHILFE

A tiny district encompassing the excellent wine village of Bechtheim. Very little wine is seen on export markets under the *Grosslage* label.

**BECHTHEIM**

✓ **Vineyard** *Geyersberg* **Grower** *Riedenbacher Hof-Spiess* (red)

## GROSSLAGE LIEBFRAUENMORGEN

This familiar sounding *Grosslage* includes the famous Liebfrauenstift-Kirchenstück vineyard in Worms, the birthplace of Liebfraumilch.

**WORMS**

✓ **Vineyard** *Liebfrauenstift-Kirchenstück* **Grower** *Gerhard Gutzler*

## GROSSLAGE PILGERPFAD

This *Grosslage* stretches from the lesser vineyards of Bechtheim to the large Petersberg district in Bereich Nierstein.

## GROSSLAGE SYBILLENSTEIN

There are no outstanding villages, vineyards, or growers in this *Grosslage*, although some valid efforts with Silvaner can be reported from the Kappellenberg vineyard. Alzey is the location of Sichel & Co., master blenders of "Blue Nun" Liebfraumilch.

**WEINHEIM**

✓ **Vineyard** *Kapellenberg* **Grower** *Meiser*

---

# OTHER CERTIFIED ORGANIC WINEMAKERS

**Biodynamic**
Armin Ackermann (Mettenheim)
Helmut and Walfried Sander (Gau-Odernheim)
Volker Feth (Flörsheim-Dahlsheim) (Ortsteil Dalsheim)

**Organic**
Adam Schmitt (Mommenheim)
Albrecht Schütte (Alsheim)
Axel (Ober-Hilbersheim)
Bardo Kneib (Zornheim)
Berthold Ferstl (Zwingenberg)
Birkenhof (Armsheim)
Brüder Dr. Becker (Ludwigshöhe)
Dieter Klein (Offstein)
Dr. Helmut Scholl (Bornheim)

Dr. Schnell (Guntersblum)
E. Weidenbach (Ingelheim)
Eckhard (Ingelheim)
Eckhard Weitzel (Ingelheim)
Eugen Schönhals (Bieblenheim)
Gerhard Huf (Ingelheim)
Gerhard Sander (Mettenheim)
Goldberg (Osthofen)
Hans L. Spanier (Hohen-Sülzen)
Harald Scholl (Gau-Heppenheim)
Haxthäuser Hof (Ingelheim (Wackernheim))
Heinz-Walter Metzler (Bermersheim)
Helmut Kloos (Worms-Horchheim)
Hirschof (Westhofen)
Hollerhof (Fürfeld)

Jakob Neumer (Uelversheim)
Jutta & Raimund Huster (Ingelheim-Grosswinternheim)
Klaus Knobloch (Ober-Flörsheim)
Lehnerhof (Mettenhein)
Lunkenheimer (Ingelheim-Groswinternheim)
Marienhof (Dienheim)
Reh Kendermann (Bingen am Rhein)
Rösch-Spies (Guntersblum)
Rothes (Aspisheim)
Schäfer (Armsheim)
Villa Sachsen (Bingen)
Villa Waldorf Schulz (Biebelsheim)
Wambolderhof (Stadecken-Elsheim)

# THE PFALZ

*Germany's rising star, the Pfalz, or Rheinpfalz, as it was called until recently, has always been capable of producing world-class wines, but it has only just started doing so on any widespread scale. The best winemakers of the Pfalz now tend to make rich, powerful, spicy wines that are more reminiscent of Alsace than those of Alsace's mirror image, Baden.*

RARE PHYSICAL EVIDENCE of ancient German wines exists in the Pfalz at the wine museum in Speyer. Here, a glass amphora contains genuine, golden 1,600-year-old wine, made by the Romans. By the 12th century, the Bishop of Speyer owned the best vineyards in the Pfalz and they remained the property of the Church until acquired by Napoleon.

After the great Corsican emperor somewhat reluctantly left the region, the socioeconomic composition of the Pfalz changed dramatically and irrevocably. With the restructuring came a considerably less monopolistic form of land ownership.

## THE PFALZ TODAY

Sometimes referred to as the Palatinate, the Pfalz covers 50 miles (80 kilometers) of the sun-blessed vineyards of the Haardt Mountains and the Pfalz forest. It has some 25,000 smallholders, each of whom works less than about two-and-a-half acres (one hectare) on average; most are part-time. Many sell their grapes to cooperatives, who process about 25 percent of the Pfalz's output. There is, however, still a minority of estates that have larger land-holdings. The vast

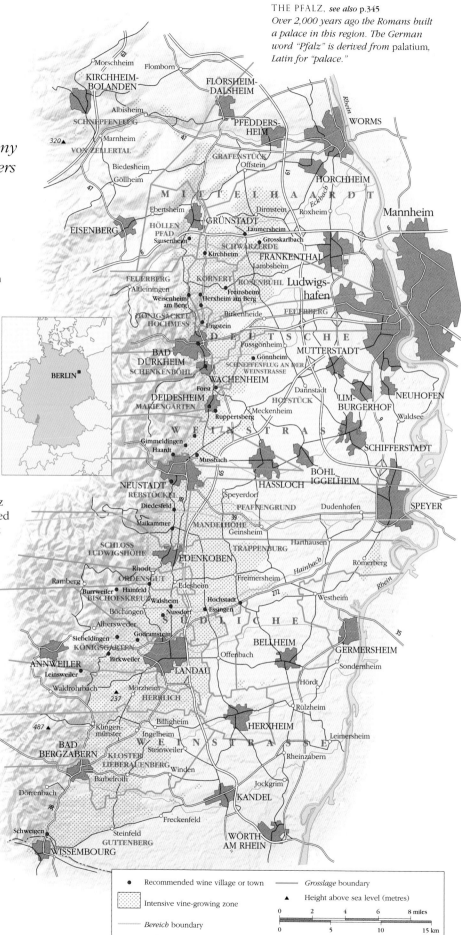

THE PFALZ, *see also p.345*
*Over 2,000 years ago the Romans built a palace in this region. The German word "Pfalz" is derived from palatium, Latin for "palace."*

## THE REGION AT A GLANCE

**Area under vine**
54,967 acres or 22,244 ha (decreasing)

**Average yield**
440 cases/acre or 102 hl/ha (increasing)

**Red wine**
21% (increasing)

**White wine**
79% (decreasing)

**Dry & semidry wine**
46% Trocken, 16% Halbtrocken

**Most important grape varieties**
21% Riesling (static), 15% Müller-Thurgau (decreasing), 11% Portugieser (increasing), 10% Dornfelder (increasing), 8% Kerner (decreasing), 5% Silvaner (decreasing), 5% Spätburgunder (increasing), 25% Others

**Infrastructure**
*Bereiche* 2; *Grosslagen* 25; *Einzellagen* 335

Note: The vineyards straddle 170 communities, the names of which may appear on the label.

**Legend:**
- Recommended wine village or town
- Intensive vine-growing zone
- Bereich boundary
- Grosslage boundary
- ▲ Height above sea level (metres)

0   2   4   6   8 miles
0   5   10   15 km

numbers of growers, grapes, soil types, and microclimates combine to create a diversity of wine styles, from close to half of all Liebfraumilch produced (Rheinhessen accounts for most of the other half) to a wealth of expressive pure varietals. This region yields more wine than any other in Germany, and it is the smallest growers who make it such a great one.

## QUALITY REQUIREMENTS AND AVERAGE QMP PRODUCTION

| PFALZ'S MINIMUM OECHSLE | QUALITY CATEGORY | HARVEST BREAKDOWN |
|---|---|---|
| 44° | Deutscher Tafelwein | 1% |
| 50–53° | Landwein | 0.5% |
| 60–62° | * QbA | 70% |
| 73–76° | * Kabinett | 19.5% |
| 85–90° | * Spätlese | 5% |
| 92–100° | * Auslese | 1% |
| 120° | Beerenauslese | 1% |
| 120° | Eiswein | 1% |
| 150° | Trockenbeerenauslese | 1% |

*Minimum Oechsle levels vary according to grape variety; those that have a naturally lower sugar content may qualify at a correspondingly lower level.

## FACTORS AFFECTING TASTE AND QUALITY

### LOCATION
The second-largest German wine region, stretching 50 miles (80 km) from Rheinhessen to Alsace, bounded by the Rhine on the east and Haardt Mountains on the west.

### CLIMATE
The Pfalz is the sunniest and driest wine-producing region in Germany, sheltered by the Haardt Mountains and Donnersberg hills.

### ASPECT
Vineyards are sited mainly on flat land or gentle slopes, at an altitude of between 330 and 820 feet (100 and 250 meters).

### SOIL
Although loam is prevalent, it is often interspersed with a wide range of other soils, from loess, sand, and weathered sandstone to widely dispersed "islands" of limestone, granite, porphyry, and clayish slate.

### VITICULTURE AND VINIFICATION
The Pfalz vies with Rheinhessen as the largest wine producer among Germany's wine regions. The leading estates have a relatively high proportion of Riesling in their vineyards and produce wines of the very highest quality, although specialty Gewürztraminers and Muskatellers can be extraordinarily good when vinified dry. One-third of Pfalz wine is sold directly to consumers, and half is marketed through large commercial wineries and two dozen or so cooperatives.

### GRAPE VARIETIES
**Primary varieties:** Müller-Thurgau, Riesling
**Secondary varieties:** Bacchus, Dornfelder, Gewürztraminer, Huxelrebe, Kerner, Morio-Muskat, Muskateller, Portugieser, Ruländer, Scheurebe, Silvaner, Spätburgunder

## THE APPELLATIONS OF
# THE PFALZ

**Note** In the Pfalz wine region, each *Grosslage* can be prefixed only by a specified village name. The village name has been listed here under the name of the *Grosslage*.

# BEREICH MITTELHAARDT-DEUTSCHE WEINSTRASSE

The quality of wines from this *Bereich* is so high, few are sold as anything less than *Einzellagen*.

## GROSSLAGE FEUERBERG
### Bad Dürkheim
A versatile *Grosslage*, producing a wide range of wines from full, spicy Gewürztraminers to soft, velvety Spätburgunders.

#### BAD DÜRKHEIM
✓ **Premium Red Wine Blends: Grower** *Egon Schmitt* (Taurus, Thur, Duca XI)

#### ELLERSTADT
✓ **Vineyard** *Kirchenstück* **Grower** *Klaus Schneider* (also red and white *cuvées*)

## GROSSLAGE GRAFENSTÜCK
Producer Ludi Neiss stands out with some excellent Spätburgunder and Frühburgunder.

#### KINDENHEIM
✓ **Non-Einzellagen red wines: Grower** *Ludi Neiss*

#### MÜHLHEIM
✓ **Vineyard** *Sonnenburg* **Grower** *Matthias Gaul*

## GROSSLAGE HOCHMESS
### Bad Dürkheim
This is a small, but high-performance *Grosslage*. It includes the best vineyards of Bad Dürkheim,

although some fine wines are also produced within the boundaries of the two neighboring *Grosslagen* of Feuerberg and Schenkenböhl. The attractive wines of Grosslage Hochmess display a perfect harmony of full flavor and flowery fragrance.

#### BAD DÜRKHEIM
✓ **Vineyard** *Michelsberg* **Growers** *Karl Schaefer* • **Vineyard** *Spielberg* **Growers** *Karl Schaefer*

## GROSSLAGE HOFSTÜCK
### Deidesheim
Grosslage Hofstück produces homogeneous, noble, and elegant wines. The outstanding quality of these wines owes a great deal to the vineyard's favorable soil conditions.

#### DEIDESHEIM
✓ **Vineyard** *Nonnenstück* **Growers** *Bürklin-Wolf, Reichsrat Von Buhl*

#### RUPPERTSBERG
✓ **Vineyard** *Gaisböhl* **Grower** *Bürklin-Wolf* • **Vineyard** *Reiterpfad* **Growers** *Bassermann-Jordan, Bergdolt, A. Christmann, Dr. Deinhard, Bürklin-Wolf*

## GROSSLAGE HÖLLENPFAD
### Grünstadt
Produces a range of wines that are full and substantial in body but lack finesse.

## GROSSLAGE HONIGSÄCKEL
### Ungstein
This is a small *Grosslage* composed of varied soil and making full-bodied wines of intense flavor, especially Scheurebe.

#### UNGSTEIN
✓ **Vineyard** *Herrenberg* **Grower** *Pfeffingen-Fuhrmann-Eymael* • **Vineyard** *Weilberg* **Grower** *Pfeffingen-Fuhrmann-Eymael*

## GROSSLAGE KOBNERT
### Kallstadt
A single vineyard prior to the 1971 wine law, this is now a *Grosslage*, but a very good one.

#### KALLSTADT
✓ **Vineyard** *Saumagen* **Growers** *Koehler-Ruprecht, Koehler-Ruprecht* (Philippi), *Landhaus Kronenberg-Familie Bender*

## GROSSLAGE MARIENGARTEN
### Forst an der Weinstrasse
Nowhere in the Pfalz can Riesling wines of such incomparable finesse and intensity be found.

#### DEIDESHEIM
✓ **Vineyard** *Kalkofen* **Growers** *Dr. Deinhard • Bassermann-Jordan, Bürklin-Wolf •* **Vineyard** *Kieselberg* **Growers** *Josef Biffar, Georg Mosbacher •* **Vineyard** *Herrgottsacker* **Grower** *Dr. Deinhard •* **Vineyard** *Leinhöhle* **Grower** *Bassermann-Jordan •* **Vineyard** *Hohenmorgen* **Growers** *Bassermann-Jordan, Bürklin-Wolf, A. Christmann •* **Vineyard** *Langenmorgen* **Grower** *Dr. Deinhard*

#### FORST
✓ **Vineyard** *Freundstück* **Grower** *Georg Mosbacher •* **Vineyard** *Ungeheuer* **Growers** *Bassermann-Jordan, J. L. Wolf, Lucashof, Georg Mosbacher, Eugen Müller, Dr. Deinhard •* **Vineyard** *Jesuitengarten* **Growers** *Bassermann-Jordan, von Buhl, Bürklin-Wolf, Dr. Deinhard •* **Vineyard** *Kirchenstück* **Grower** *Bassermann-Jordan, Bürklin-Wolf •* **Vineyard** *Pechstein* **Growers** *Bassermann-Jordan, von Buhl, Bürklin-Wolf, J. L. Wolf*

#### WACHENHEIM
✓ **Vineyard** *Gerümpel* **Growers** *Bürklin-Wolf, Karl Schaefer, Josef Biffar, J. L. Wolf •* **Vineyard** *Goldbächel* **Growers** *Josef Biffar, Bürklin-Wolf •* **Vineyard** *Rechbächel* **Grower** *Bürklin-Wolf*

## GROSSLAGE MEERSPINNE
### Neustadt-Gimmeldingen

These climatically pampered vineyards, on the sheltered slopes of the Haardt Mountains, produce some of the very finest Pfalz wines.

#### GIMMELDINGEN
☑ **Vineyard** *Mandelgarten* **Growers** *A. Christmann, Müller-Catoir* • **Vineyard** *Schlössel* **Growers** *Müller-Catoir*

#### HAARDT
☑ **Vineyard** *Bürgergarten* **Grower** *Müller-Catoir* • **Vineyard** *Herrenletten* **Growers** *Müller-Catoir* • **Vineyard** *Mandelring* **Growers** *Müller-Catoir*

#### KÖNIGSBACH
☑ **Vineyard** *Idig* **Growers** *A. Christmann* (red and white) • **Vineyard** *Ölberg* **Grower** *A. Christmann* (red)

#### MUSSBACH
☑ **Vineyard** *Eselshaut* **Grower** *Müller-Catoir* • *A. Christmann* (red)

#### NEUSTADT
☑ **Vineyard** *Mönchgarten* **Grower** *Müller-Catoir*

## GROSSLAGE PFAFFENGRUND
### Neustadt-Diedesfeld

This is not an exceptional *Grosslage*.

#### DUTTWEILER
☑ **Vineyard** *Kalkberg* **Grower** *Bergdolt* (red and white)

## GROSSLAGE REBSTÖCKEL
### Neustadt-Diedesfeld

No outstanding villages, vineyards, or growers.

## GROSSLAGE ROSENBÜHL
### Freinsheim

No outstanding villages, vineyards, or growers.

## GROSSLAGE SCHENKENBÖHL
### Wachenheim

The third *Grosslage* to share the vineyards of Bad Dürkheim.

#### WACHENHEIM
☑ **Vineyard** *Königswingert* **Grower** *Emil Zimmermann*

## GROSSLAGE SCHNEPFENFLUG AN DER WEINSTRASSE
### Forst an der Weinstrasse

Except for a small part of Forst's vineyards (the rest belong to Grosslage Mariengarten), few outstanding growers are to be found here.

#### FORST
☑ **Vineyard** *Stift* **Grower** *Georg Mosbacher*

## GROSSLAGE SCHNEPFENFLUG VOM ZELLERTAL
### Zell

No outstanding villages, vineyards, or growers.

## GROSSLAGE SCHWARZERDE
### Kirchheim

Mediocre Silvaner-based wines are standard here, but there are a couple of excellent growers in obscure villages that offer good value.

#### DIRMSTEIN
☑ **Vineyard** *Mandelpfad* **Grower** *Knipser*

#### GROSSKARLBACH
☑ **Vineyards** *Burgweg* (red and white)

**Grower** *Knipser*

#### LAUMERSHEIM
☑ **Vineyards** *Kirschgarten* (red) **Grower** *Knipser, Philipp Kuhn*

# BEREICH SÜDLICHE WEINSTRASSE

Dominated by rather dull and neutral Müller-Thurgau, but younger winemakers are beginning to excel.

## GROSSLAGE BISCHOFSKREUZ
### Walsheim

Improving quality.

#### BURRWEILER
☑ **Vineyard** *Schlossgarten* **Grower** *Herbert Messmer*

#### WALSHEIM
☑ **Vineyard** *Silberberg* **Grower** *Karl Pfaffmann*

## GROSSLAGE GUTTENBERG
### Schweigen

When is a German wine not German? When it's grown in France, of course, where 321 acres (130 ha) of Schweigen's "sovereign" vineyards are located. Every year the growers pick their grapes in France and trundle across the border to vinify them. Weird as it might sound, the grapes are German if pressed in Germany, but French if pressed in France! The *terroir* of this *Grosslage* is most suited to the Burgunder varietals and Gewürztraminer, reflecting the area's northern extension of the Alsace vineyards.

#### SCHWEIGEN
☑ **Vineyard** *Sonnenberg* **Growers** *Friedrich Becker* (red and white), *Bernhart* (red and white) • **Premium Red Wine Blend Grower** *Friedrich Becker* (Tafelwein Reserve)

## GROSSLAGE HERRLICH
### Eschbach

An area easily capable of producing good QmP wines. The *Auslese* can be astonishingly cheap.

#### LEINSWEILER
☑ **Vineyard** *Sonnenberg* **Grower** *Siegrist* • **Non-Einzellagen red and white wines Grower** *Siegrist*

## GROSSLAGE KLOSTER LIEBFRAUENBERG
### Bad Bergzabern

One grower is beginning to break the mold.

#### PLEISWEILER-OBERHOFEN

☑ **Premium red wine Grower** *Wilker* (Frühburgunder)

## GROSSLAGE KÖNIGSGARTEN
### Godramstein

This *Grosslage* consists of some excellent wine villages and several talented winemakers.

#### ALBERSWEILER
☑ **Vineyard** *Latt* **Grower** *Ökonomierat Rebholz*

#### BIRKWEILER
☑ **Vineyard** *Kastanienbusch* **Growers** *Ökonomierat Rebholz, Dr. Wehrheim* (red and white) • **Vineyard** *Mandelberg* **Growers** *Schneider, Albersweiler* (red), *Dr. Wehrheim*

#### GODRAMSTEIN
☑ **Vineyard** *Münzberg* **Growers** *Münzberg* **Vineyard** *Schlangenpfiff* **Grower** *Münzberg*

#### SIEBELDINGEN
☑ **Vineyard** *Im Sonnenschein* **Growers** *Ökonomierat Rebholz* (red and white), *Wilhelmshof* (red and white) • **Premium Red Wine Blend Grower** *Ökonomierat Rebholz* (Tradition)

## GROSSLAGE MANDELHÖHE
### Maikammer

Some pleasant, attractive Rieslings.

#### KIRRWEILER
☑ **Vineyard** *Mandelberg* **Grower** *Bergdolt*

#### MAIKAMMER
☑ **Vineyard** *Heiligenberg* **Grower** *Ullrichshof-Familie Faubel* • **Vineyard** *Kapellenberg* **Grower** *Ullrichshof-Familie Faubel*

## GROSSLAGE ORDENSGUT
### Edesheim

Rising red wine star!

#### HAINFELD
☑ **Vineyard** *Kapelle* **Grower** *Gerhard Klein* **Premium red wines Grower** *Gerhard Klein* ("B," "S," Theatrum Vinum "R")

## GROSSLAGE SCHLOSS LUDWIGSHÖHE
### Edenkoben

No outstanding villages, vineyards, or growers.

## GROSSLAGE TRAPPENBERG
### Hochstadt

Few outstanding vineyards in this *Grosslage*.

#### ESSINGEN
☑ **Non-Einzellagen wines: Grower** *Weingut Frey & Soehne*

---

## CERTIFIED ORGANIC PRODUCERS

Andreas Kopf (Landau)
Brigitte Hohl (Freinsheim)
Dr. Helmut Scholl (Bornheim)
Feitig-Richter (Siebeldingen)
Fippinger-Wick (Zell)
Franz Braun (Ranschbach)
Franz Krahl (Heinfeld)
Friedrich Graf (Edesheim)
G. Schwarztrauber (Mußbach)
Georg Siben Erben (Deidesheim)
Hans Clödy (Niederotterbach)
Hans Manck (Freinsheim)
Hans Pflüger (Bad Dürkheim)
Hartmut Risser (Kerzenheim)

Hartmut Stauch (Kallstadt)
Heiner Sauer (Böchingen)
Helmut Krauss (Zellertal/Zell)
Hoffmann (Göcklingen)
Isegrim-Hof, Klaus Wolf (Bad Dürkheim-Ungstein)
Janson Bernhard (Zellertal-Harxheim)
Karin Deutscher (Klein-Bockenheim)
Klaus Hohlreiter (Göcklingen)
Kurt Weber (Böchingen)
Lebenshilfe (Bad Dürkheim)
Ludwig Seiler (Weyher)

Martinshof (Böbingen)
Marzolph (Landau-Wollmesh)
Rudolf Eymann (Gönnheim)
Rummel (Landau-Nussdorf)
Schneider-Beiwinkel (Edenkoben)
Spinnrädel (Kaiserslautern)
Stefan Kuntz (Landau)
Stephanshof (St Martin)
Walhbacherhof (Contwig)
Walter Merk (Ellerstadt)
Winfried Seeber (St Martin)
Wöhrle (Bockenheim)

# THE HESSISCHE BERGSTRASSE

*Situated between the Rheinhessen and Franken, the northern tip of Baden's vineyards is the Hessische Bergstrasse. This is the smallest and least-known of Germany's Qualitätswein regions, and its fruity wines are marked by a pronounced earthy acidity, with almost 60 percent made in a dry style.*

THIS REGION CORRESPONDS to the northern section of the old Roman *strata montana*, or "mountain road," hence Bergstrasse. This ancient trade route ran from Darmstadt to Wiesloch, which is south of Heidelberg in what is now the Baden region. The Romans brought viticulture to this area, but without the monasteries, which developed, spread, and maintained the vineyards throughout the medieval period, the tradition of winemaking would have ceased long ago.

The vineyards of the Hessische Bergstrasse are dotted among orchards in a strip of foothills along the western edge of Odenwald. Protected by the Odenwald, the fragrance of fruit trees in full bloom hangs noticeably over these hills in springtime. Indeed, Odenwald's forested mountains offer such effective protection that the sun-trap vineyards of Bensheim boast the

UNTERHAMBACH
*A vineyard above Unterhambach, where small-scale winemaking is the norm. The cooperative in nearby Heppenheim receives 70 percent of the region's grapes.*

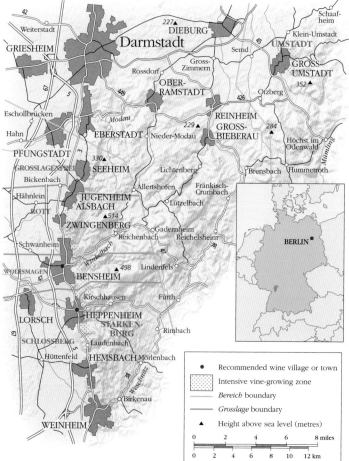

THE HESSISCHE BERGSTRASSE, *see also p.345*
*This area is called the " spring garden," because of the early flowering of its fruit and almond orchards, between which vineyards are planted.*

## THE REGION AT A GLANCE

**Area under vine**
1,087 acres or 440 ha (decreasing)

**Average yield**
315 cases/acre or 72 hl/ha (static)

**Red wine**
8% (increasing)

**White wine**
92% (decreasing)

**Dry & semidry wine**
58% Trocken, 29% Halbtrocken

**Most important grape varieties**
53% Riesling (decreasing), 10% Müller-Thurgau (decreasing), 8% Grauburgunder (increasing), 29% Others

**Infrastructure**
*Bereiche* 2
*Grosslagen* 3
*Einzellagen* 22

**Note** The vineyards of the Hessische Bergstrasse straddle 10 *Gemeinden* (communes), the names of which may appear on the label.

highest annual mean temperatures in Germany. This exceptional heat is, of course, relative to Germany's cool northern climate, and the wines produced here have an excellent level of acidity, but there is a definite peachiness to the finest Rieslings, which is an indication of their ripeness. The Hessische Bergstrasse is planted with a relatively high proportion of Riesling, particularly in the *Bereich* Starkenburg, where the best wines are grown.

The vines, which grow on relatively rich soils, produce very fruity wines that have a typical and easily recognized, earthy acidity, with a style that is richer than most Rheinhessen wines and more reminiscent of a somewhat rustic Rheingau. The Müller-Thurgau is not Germany's best, but it can be fragrant; the Silvaner lacks the assertive character found in Franken to the east; but the Gewürztraminer can have a fine, subdued style.

The vineyards are farmed by more than 1,000 individual growers with the average-sized plot being barely more than four-fifths of an acre (one-third of a hectare). Most of these growers are part-timers who tend their plots on the weekends. This helps to explain the anonymity of the area's wines, and this will remain until a number of large, quality-minded estates are established.

GRONAU HESSISCHE BERGSTRASSE
*Looking down the south-facing slopes of the Hemsburg vineyard toward Gronau, an Ortsteil of Bensheim.*

## FACTORS AFFECTING TASTE AND QUALITY

### ⊕ LOCATION
Between Darmstadt and Heppenheim, beside the Odenwald Mountains, with the Rhine to the west and the Main to the north.

### ❄ CLIMATE
The vineyards on the southern slopes of the valleys flanking the Bergstrasse benefit from an average temperature of over 48°F (9°C). Combined with an annual rainfall of 30 inches (75.5 centimeters), this produces ideal conditions. Bensheim is supposed to be the hottest place in Germany.

### ⊿ ASPECT
The best vineyards are generally on southwest-facing slopes in the *grosslagen* of Schlossberg and Wolfsmagen (particularly Kalkgasse in Bensheim and Centrericht in Heppenheim).The terrain is more one of hilly hinterland than steep valleys.

### ▦ SOIL
Most of the soil consists of varying amounts of light, finely structured loess and basalt.

### ▦ VITICULTURE AND VINIFICATION
The vineyards are not contiguous, but are planted rather haphazardly, sometimes on old-established terraces among orchards. Although a great many individuals grow grapes, more than half the crop is processed by the regional cooperative in Heppenheim. Müller-Thurgau is giving way to Grauburgunder, and almost 60 percent of the total wines produced in this region are technically dry (*trocken*). The State Wine Domain in Bensheim is the region's largest vineyard owner, but given the small size of this region, almost all of its wines are consumed locally.

### 🍇 GRAPE VARIETIES
**Primary varieties:** Müller-Thurgau, Riesling
**Secondary varieties:** Ehrenfelser, Gewürztraminer, Grauburgunder, Kerner, Ruländer, Scheurebe, Silvaner, Weissburgunder

## QUALITY REQUIREMENTS AND AVERAGE QMP PRODUCTION

| HESSISCHE BERGSTRASSE'S MINIMUM OECHSLE | QUALITY CATEGORY | HARVEST BREAKDOWN |
|---|---|---|
| 44° | Deutscher Tafelwein | 0.5% |
| 53° | Landwein | 0.5% |
| 57–66° | * QbA | 68% |
| 73–80° | * Kabinett | 23% |
| 85–95° | * Spätlese | 6% |
| 95–105° | * Auslese | 1% |
| 125° | Beerenauslese | 1% |
| 125° | Eiswein | – |
| 150° | Trockenbeerenauslese | – |

*Minimum Oechsle levels vary according to grape variety; those that have a naturally lower sugar content may qualify at a correspondingly lower level.*

## THE APPELLATIONS OF
# THE HESSISCHE BERGSTRASSE

## BEREICH STARKENBURG

This is the larger of this region's *Bereiche*, and the best in terms of quality. Riesling is planted in most of its vineyards.

### GROSSLAGE ROTT

The largest of Starkenburg's three *Grosslagen*, this includes the northern section of Bensheim, one of the region's two best communes. The finest wine comes from its south-facing Herrnwingert vineyard.

### GROSSLAGE SCHLOSSBERG

This *Grosslage* covers part of Bensheim and three villages to the south, with Heppenheim the most highly rated. A unique peachiness is associated with the sun-drenched Stemmler and Centgericht vineyards.

**HEPPENHEIM**
✓ **Vineyard** *Centgericht* **Grower** *Staatsweingut Bergstrasse*

### GROSSLAGE WOLFSMAGEN

This includes the southern section of Bensheim with the two *Ortsteile* of Zell and Gronau.

**BENSHEIM**
✓ **Vineyard** *Kalkgasse* **Grower** *Staatsweingut Bergstrasse, Weingut der Stadt Bensheim*

## BEREICH UMSTADT

There are no remarkable villages, vineyards, or *Grosslagen* in this *Bereich*.

ZELL VINEYARD
*Vineyard in the Streichling Einzellage at Zell, near Bensheim, Hessen.*

# FRANKEN

*Classic Franconian Silvaner wine is distinctly dry with an earthy or smoky aroma and is bottled in the traditional flask-shaped* Bocksbeutel. *In this region, the Silvaner grape variety has, to a certain extent, given way to Müller-Thurgau, among others, although this trend is now being reversed.*

THERE IS ALMOST twice as much land under vine in Franken as there is in the Rheingau, for instance, but the vineyards are scattered over a far greater area and they are interspersed with meadows and forests. Franken is also a beer-producing region, and many say that more pleasure can be had from a Stein of

INTERIOR OF THE RESIDENZ, WÜRZBURG
*The Residency in Würzburg, with its Baroque grand staircase, is now part of the Bavarian State Domain.*

## QUALITY REQUIREMENTS AND AVERAGE QMP PRODUCTION

| FRANKEN'S MINIMUM OECHSLE | QUALITY CATEGORY | HARVEST BREAKDOWN |
|---|---|---|
| 44° | Deutscher Tafelwein | 1% |
| 50° | Landwein | 1% |
| 60° | * QbA | 69% |
| 76–80° | * Kabinett | 21% |
| 85–90° | * Spätlese | 4% |
| 100° | * Auslese | 1% |
| 125° | Beerenauslese | 1% |
| 125° | Eiswein | 1% |
| 150° | Trockenbeerenauslese | 1% |

*Minimum Oechsle levels vary according to grape variety; those that have a naturally lower sugar content may qualify at a correspondingly lower level.*

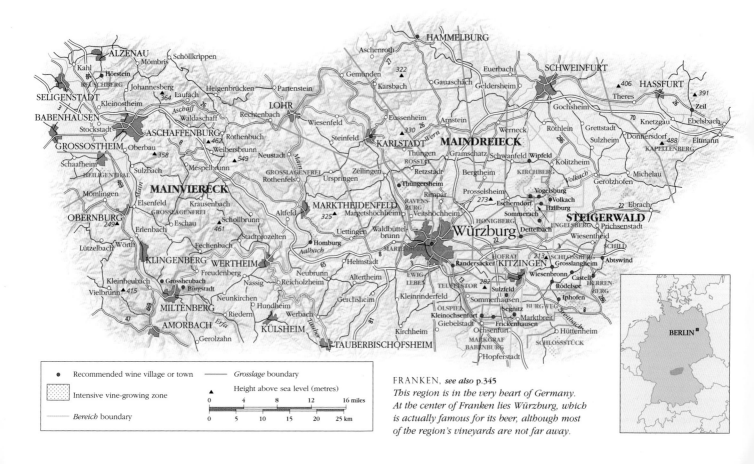

FRANKEN, *see also p.345*
*This region is in the very heart of Germany. At the center of Franken lies Würzburg, which is actually famous for its beer, although most of the region's vineyards are not far away.*

Recommended wine village or town
Intensive vine-growing zone
*Bereich* boundary
*Grosslage* boundary
Height above sea level (metres)
0   4   8   12   16 miles
0   5   10   15   20   25 km

## THE REGION AT A GLANCE

**Area under vine**
5,907 ha or 14,597 acres (decreasing)

**Average yield**
75 cases/acre or 85 hl/ha (static)

**Red wine**
8% (increasing)

**White wine**
92% (decreasing)

**Dry & semidry wine**
55% Trocken, 34% Halbtrocken

**Most important grape varieties**
39% Müller-Thurgau (decreasing), 21% Silvaner (increasing), 12% Bacchus (increasing), 28% Others

**Infrastructure**
*Bereiche* 3; *Grosslagen* 20; *Einzellagen* 171

**Note:** The vineyards of Franken straddle 125 *Gemeinden* (communes), the names of which may appear on labels.

THE CELLAR AT THE RESIDENZ, WÜRZBURG
*The magnificent cellar under the Baroque Residency at Würzburg has been state run since 1803.*

Würzburger beer than from a glass of Würzburger Stein, Franken's most famous wine. Exported wine invariably comes from the better estates and it is relatively expensive, particularly if bottled in the traditional *Bocksbeutel*.

Wines made from this region's Silvaner grape have a full taste and an earthy bite, sometimes attaining smoky complexity, making it far more interesting than most examples of this variety. However, my favorite Franconian wine is Riesling, because,

although it accounts for less than 3 percent of the vines grown and often fails to ripen here, it can be made into exceptional wines in sunny years. Rieslaner (Riesling x Silvaner cross), Bacchus, and Kerner are all successful, particularly as QmP, although it is rare to find a wine above *Auslese* level.

## FACTORS AFFECTING TASTE AND QUALITY

**LOCATION**
Situated in Bavaria, Franken is the most northeasterly of the wine regions of former West Germany.

**CLIMATE**
The most continental climate of Germany's wine regions, with dry warm summers and cold winters. Severe frosts affect yields.

**ASPECT**
Many vineyards face south and are located on the slopes of the valleys of the Main and its

tributaries, as well as on sheltered sites of the Steigerwald.

**SOIL**
Franken's three *Bereiche* have different soil structures: Mainviereck has predominantly weathered colored sandstone; Maindreieck limestone with clay and loess; and Steigerwald, weathered red marl.

**VITICULTURE AND VINIFICATION**
The classic Franconian vine, the Silvaner, has become less widely

planted than the Müller-Thurgau, although the pendulum has started to swing back the other way. Rieslaner is something of a local specialty. Franken wines generally are usually drier than most in Germany and accompany food well. There are 6,000 growers, allowing for a great range of styles, although 40 percent of the wines are processed by the regional cooperative in Kitzingen and smaller cooperatives. Exports are insignificant, with four out of

every five bottles of Franken wine consumed within a 150 mile radius of where they were produced.

**GRAPE VARIETIES**
**Primary varieties:** Müller-Thurgau, Silvaner
**Secondary varieties:** Bacchus, Kerner, Ortega, Perle, Rieslaner, Riesling, Scheurebe, Spätburgunder, Traminer

## THE APPELLATIONS OF
# FRANKEN

**Note** In Franken, certain *Grosslagen* can be prefixed only by a specified village name, which is listed immediately beneath the relevant *Grosslage* name.

## BEREICH MAINDREIECK

Most of the vineyards in this *Bereich* are in the vicinity of Würzburg. Grapes grown on the limestone soils can produce exceptional wines.

### GROSSLAGE BURG
#### Hammelburg

Robust, earthy Silvaners and the lighter, fragrant Müller-Thurgaus are the main attractions.

### GROSSLAGE ENGELSBERG

A new *Grosslage*, God forbid, encompassing part of two *Einzellagen* formerly in the

*Grosslage* Kirchberg, the Sommeracher vineyards of Katzenkopf and Rosenberg.

#### SOMMERACH
☑ **Vineyard** *Katzenkopf* **Grower** *Glaser-Himmelstoss*

### GROSSLAGE EWIG LEBEN

This *Grosslage* contains the greatest concentration of fine vineyards in Franken and some fine wines are available under its generic designation. Ewig Leben has the advantage of a particularly favorable microclimate, which helps create wines of a rare harmony. Rieslings from this area possess an original natural charm complemented by a bouquet often reminiscent of peaches.

#### RANDERSACKER
☑ **Vineyard** *Sonnenstuhl* **Growers** *Schmitt's Kinder, Schloss Sommerhausen* • **Vineyard** *Marsberg* **Growers** *Schmitt's Kinder*

### GROSSLAGE HOFRAT
#### Kintzingen

This is one of Franken's few relatively large *Grosslagen*, where the *Einzellagen* seldom excel, except for the vineyards on the lazy bend of the Main River north and south of Sulzfeld.

#### SULZFELD
☑ **Vineyard** *Cyriakusberg* **Grower** *Zehnthof Theo Luckert*

## FACTORS AFFECTING TASTE AND QUALITY

**LOCATION**
Württemberg is situated between Frankfurt to the north and Lake Constance to the south.

**CLIMATE**
Sheltered by the Black Forest to the west and the hilly Swabian Alb to the east, this area has an especially warm growing season.

**ASPECT**
Vineyards are widely scattered either side of the Neckar River.

**SOIL**
Soils vary, but red marl, clay, loess, keuper and loam dominate, with scatterings of shell-limestone in the Neckar Valley area. Topsoils are deep and well drained, producing full wines with a firm acidity.

**VITICULTURE AND VINIFICATION**
Most of Württemberg's 16,500 growers own tiny plots and tend them part-time, taking their grapes to the cooperatives for processing. Most of the production is consumed locally. Trollinger has overtaken Riesling as the leading grape, while Lemberger and Spätburgunder are the fastest expanding. Another major variety, Schwarzriesling, is the same as Pinot Meunier. Over half the wine is made in *halbtrocken* style.

**GRAPE VARIETIES**
**Primary varieties:** Lemberger, Riesling, Schwarzriesling, Trollinger
**Secondary varieties:** Kerner, Müller-Thurgau, Pinot Meunier, Portugieser, Ruländer, Silvaner, Spätburgunder

## THE APPELLATIONS OF
# WÜRTTEMBERG

### BEREICH BAYERISCHER BODENSEE
Climatic conditions are not suited to Riesling.

### GROSSLAGE LINDAUER SEEGARTEN
Politically part of Bavaria (QbA Franken), but classified by wine law as part of Württemberg.

### BEREICH KOCHER-JAGST-TAUBER
White wines that rarely excel.

### GROSSLAGE KOCHERBERG
Modest wines are made in Criesbach.

### GROSSLAGE TAUBERBERG
Some good Rieslings, Traminers, and Muscats.

### BEREICH OBERER NECKAR
A tiny *Bereich* with no outstanding vineyards.

### BEREICH REMSTAL-STUTTGART
The second-largest *Bereich*.

### GROSSLAGE HOHENNEUFFEN
Good wines are made in Metzingen.

### GROSSLAGE KOPF
Improvements in a once uninspiring *Grosslage*.

**WINTERBACH**
- **Vineyard** *Hungerberg* **Grower** *Ellwanger*
- **Non-Einzellagen premium blends: Growers** *Ellwanger* ("Hades," red and white), *Albrecht Schwegler* ("Saphir," "Granat," both red)

### GROSSLAGE SONNENBÜHL
No outstanding villages, vineyards, or growers.

### GROSSLAGE WARTBÜHL
Superior wines from between the unremarkable *Grosslagen* of Kopf and Sonnenbühl.

**STETTEN**
- **Vineyard** *Pulvermächer* **Growers** *Karl Haidle, Beurer* • **Premium red blends Grower** *Karl Haidle* ("Ypsilon," and *trocken barrique* wines)

### GROSSLAGE WEINSTEIGE
An up-and-coming *Grosslage*.

**UNTERTÜRKHEIM**
- **Vineyard** *Herzogenberg* (red and white) **Grower** *Wöhrwag* • **Non-Einzellagen premium red blends Grower** *Wöhrwag* (cuvées "X" and "Philipp"), *Weinmanufaktur Untertürkheim*

### BEREICH WÜRTTEMBERGISCH BODENSEE
A one-*Einzellage Bereich* on Lake Constance.

### BEREICH WÜRTTEMBERGISCH UNTERLAND
This *Bereich* encompasses more than 70 percent of Württemberg's vineyards.

### GROSSLAGE HEUCHELBERG
Some of Württemberg's finest wines.

**NEIPPERG**
- **Vineyard** *Schlossberg* **Grower** *Graf zu Neipperg* • **Premium red wine blend Grower** *Graf zu Neipperg* (Cuvee SE)

**PFAFFENHOFEN**
- **Vineyard** *Hohenberg* **Grower** *Wachtstetter* (also Cuvée Ernst Combe premium red and white wines)

**SCHWAIGERN**
- **Vineyard** *Ruthe* **Grower** *Graf zu Neipperg*

### GROSSLAGE KIRCHENWEINBERG
Pinot Meunier dominates in this area.

### GROSSLAGE LINDELBERG
A small, scattered area east of Heilbronn.

### GROSSLAGE SALZBERG
Sandwiched between Heilbronn and Lindelberg.

### GROSSLAGE SCHALKSTEIN
Käsberg vineyard is the finest in this *Grosslage*. It specializes in full, dark red wines.

### GROSSLAGE SCHOZACHTAL
Mostly white wines, including fine Riesling, but also some encouraging *barrique*-matured Lemberger and Spätburgunder.

### GROSSLAGE STAUFENBERG
This covers the town of Heilbronn, its *Ortsteile*, and several outlying villages.

**HEILBRONN**
- **Non-Einzellagen wines: Grower** *Drautz-Able* (red and white varietals)

**WEINSBERG**
- **Non-Einzellagen wines: Grower** *Staatsweingut Weinsberg* ◉ (red and white varietals and *cuvées*)

### GROSSLAGE STROMBERG
A predominantly black-grape area.

**BÖNNIGHEIM**
- **Vineyard** *Sonnenberg* **Grower** *Ernst Dautel* • **Premium red wine blend: Grower** *Ernst Dautel* (Kreation)

### GROSSLAGE WUNNENSTEIN
For many years now Graf Adelmann has carried the torch for an area that could otherwise be regarded as vinous hinterland.

**KLEINBOTTWAR**
- **Vineyard** *Süssmund* **Grower** *Graf Adelmann*

### OTHER CERTIFIED ORGANIC PRODUCERS

**Biodynamic**
*Ernst-Friedrich Haller (Remshalden-Rohrbronn)*
*Siegfried Setzer (Vaihingen)*
*Werner Gienger (Illingen)*
*Werner und Bernd Lieberherr (Kirchheim am Neckar)*

**Organic**
*Andreas Stutz (Heilbronn)*
*Gen Brackenheim (Brackenheim)*
*Häberlen (Weinsberg)*
*Häusser (Bönnigheim)*
*Hermann Schmalzried (Korb)*
*Jürgen Winkler (Brackenheim)*
*Klaus Halter (Neckarsulm)*

*Muck (Bietigheim)*
*Reiner Döbler (Brackenheim)*
*Schäfer-Heinrich (Heilbronn)*
*Schloßgut Hohenbeilsten/ Hartmann Dippon (Beilstein)*
*Siglinger (Weinstadt-Grossheppach)*
*St. Urban (Ilsfeld-Schozach)*
*Stromberg Kellerei (Bönnigheim)*

# BADEN

*Often described as Germany's southernmost wine-producing region, Baden is not so much one region as a hadgepodge of politically diverse districts that once produced wine in the now defunct Grand Duchy of Baden.*

THE MOST NORTHERLY SECTION OF BADEN is parallel with the Mosel, bridging Franconia and Württemberg, while south from Baden-Baden, the vineyards are the mirror-image of Alsace across the border, and three pockets of vines on the shores of Bodensee are almost the most southerly in Germany; that dubious honor goes to Württemberg's nearby *Grosslage* of Lindauer Seegarten.

This variation of geographical, geological, and climatic conditions produces a wide range of wines, from mild Silvaner, through light, spicy Gutedel, to the full-bodied Ruländer, the attractive pink-colored Weissherbst, a specialty of the region, and

## QUALITY REQUIREMENTS AND AVERAGE QMP PRODUCTION

| BADEN'S MINIMUM OECHSLE | QUALITY CATEGORY | HARVEST BREAKDOWN |
|---|---|---|
| 50–55° | Deutscher Tafelwein | 0.5% |
| 55° | Landwein | 0.5% |
| 60–72° | * QbA | 81% |
| 76–85° | * Kabinett | 10% |
| 86–92° | * Spätlese | 5% |
| 100–105° | * Auslese | 1% |
| 128° | Beerenauslese | 1% |
| 128° | Eiswein | – |
| 154° | Trockenbeerenauslese | 1% |

*Minimum Oechsle levels vary according to grape variety; those that have a naturally lower sugar content may qualify at a correspondingly lower level.*

## THE REGION AT A GLANCE

**Area under vine**
37,906 acres or 15,340 ha (decreasing)

**Average yield**
335 cases/acre or 76 hl/ha (increasing)

**Red wine**
32% (increasing)

**White wine**
68% (decreasing)

**Dry & semidry wine**
55% Trocken, 26% Halbtrocken

**Most important grape varieties**
33% Spätburgunder (increasing), 24% Müller-Thurgau (decreasing), 9% Grauerburgunder (static), 8% Riesling, 7% Gutedel (decreasing), 7% Weissburgunder, 12% Others

**Infrastructure**
*Bereiche* 8; *Grosslagen* 16; *Einzellagen* 306

**Note** The vineyards of Baden straddle 315 *Gemeinden* (communes). Their names may appear on the label.

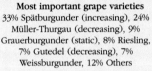

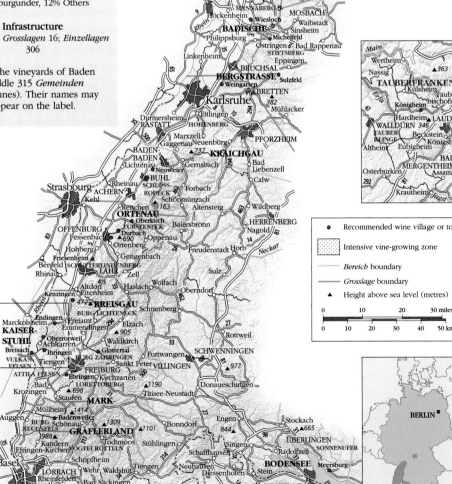

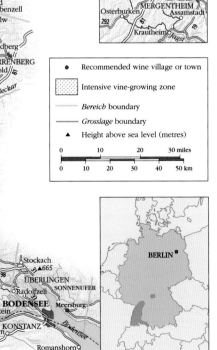

BADEN, *see also p.345*
*The vineyards of this huge wine-producing region are mostly spread along a strip extending beside the western boundary of the Black Forest, between it and the border with France. Inset (right) is the northerly area of the Bereich of Tauberfranken, while inset (above) is the Grosslage of Vulkanfelsen, which has been magnified to reveal all the recommended wine villages of this first-class wine district.*

RIESCHEN VINEYARD
*The old and new castles above the Rieschen vineyard,*
*on the north shore of the Bodensee at Meersburg.*

a good deal of Germany's best red wines. If, however, anything can be said to be the mark of a Baden wine it must be a certain warmth, roundness, and mellowness.

Baden is considered to be one of Germany's newest wine regions, yet by 1800 it had become its largest, possessing more than 66,700 acres (27,000 hectares) of vines, almost twice the amount grown today. Ironically, it was when Germany acquired a wealthy and viticulturally prolific Alsace in 1871, as one of the spoils of the Franco-Prussian War, that Baden's vineyards began to decline. The downward trend continued, despite the formation of the Baden Wine Growers' Association, founded by the priest and winemaker Heinrich Hansjakob in Hagnau in 1881. Even after the return of Alsace to French sovereignty in 1918, Baden's wine production continued to decline, primarily through lack of investment. In the 1920s wine production was adversely affected by inheritance laws that split Baden's vineyards into smaller and smaller units. By 1950, with barely 14,800 acres (6,000 hectares) of vines, Baden's wine industry was at its lowest ebb.

The eventual resurgence of Baden's wine industry began in 1952 with the formation of the Zentralkellerei Kaiserstuhler Winzergenossenschaften (Central Winery of Kaiserstuhl), which two years later expanded into the Zentralkellerei Badischer Winzergenossenschaften (Central Winery of Baden), or ZBW for short. ZBW built a $120 million vinification and storage plant at Breisach that helped to raise quality standards throughout the

region and adopted an aggressive marketing policy on the domestic scene. Baden established itself as Germany's third-largest wine producing region, yet its wines were virtually unknown outside the country until ZBW made a serious effort to export its products in the early 1980s. Sadly, Baden is now a victim of its own success, for ZBW, which accounts for some 90 percent of the region's output, has established such a clear-cut identity for its wines that Baden is generally perceived to produce one style of well-made, but rather basic, characterless wine. The truth is that while this one style represents the bulk of ZBW's, and thus Baden's, production, both ZBW and the region's independent producers have a wealth of other wines that are seldom seen or spoken about outside their locality. It is now time for ZBW to turn its marketing expertise to the relatively small number of very high-quality wines within its region, and promote them as independent wine estates for the benefit of all.

## FACTORS AFFECTING TASTE AND QUALITY

### LOCATION
The longest *Anbaugebiete*, Baden stretches for approximately 250 miles (400 km), from Franken in the north, past Württemberg and the Badische Bergstrasse to Bodensee, or Lake Constance, some of Germany's most southerly vineyards.

### CLIMATE
Compared with the rest of Germany, the bulk of Baden's vineyards have a sunny and warm climate, due in part to the shelter afforded by the Black Forest and the Odenwald Mountains.

### ASPECT
Most vineyards are on level or gently sloping ground. Some, however, are to be found higher up the hillsides, and these avoid the frosts of the valley floors.

### SOIL
Baden's soils are rich and fertile, varying from heat-retaining gravel near Lake Constance, through limestone, clay, marl, loam, granite, and loess deposits to limestone and keuper, a sandy-marl, in the Kraichgau and Taubergrund. Volcanic bedrock forms the main subsoil structure throughout most of the region.

### VITICULTURE AND VINIFICATION
The relatively flat and fertile vineyards of this region are easily mechanized. Although the geographical spread and variety of soils has led to a large number of different, traditional styles of wine, they are overshadowed by the mild and neutrally fruity, bulk-produced Baden QbA marketed by ZBW. More than 90 percent of the winemaking in Baden is conducted by its 54 cooperatives, but there are several independent and top-quality estates among the region's 26,000 growers. Spätburgunder has now officially taken over from Müller-Thurgau as Baden's most important grape, and more than half the wines produced from all varieties in this region are made in a dry or *trocken* style. A specialty that is unique to Baden is Badisch Rotgold, a soft, delicately-flavored rosé made from pressing Ruländer and Spätburgunder grapes together.

### GRAPE VARIETIES
**Primary varieties**: Müller-Thurgau, Ruländer, Spätburgunder
**Secondary varieties**: Gutedel, Kerner, Nobling, Riesling, Silvaner, Traminer, Weissburgunder

BODENSEE (LAKE CONSTANCE)
*These vines are in the south of Baden, at Meersburg, the best village of the*
*Sonnenufer Grosslage, with some of the most southerly vineyards in Germany.*

THE APPELLATIONS OF
# BADEN

## BEREICH BADISCHE BERGSTRASSE-KRAICHGAU

This *Bereich* has four *Grosslagen*, two in the Badische Bergstrasse, north and south of Heidelberg, and two in the Kraichgau, a larger but sparsely cultivated area farther south. Only one *Grosslage*, Stiftsberg, in the Kraichgau, has any reputation at all. Half the *Bereich* is planted with Müller-Thurgau grapes, but it makes mostly dull and lackluster wine. When successful, the best wines are Ruländer and Riesling.

### GROSSLAGE HOHENBERG

In this *Grosslage* there are no outstanding villages, vineyards, or growers, although good wines are made in the village of Weingarten.

### GROSSLAGE MANNABERG

This *Grosslage* is situated just southeast of Mannheim and it encompasses the historic university town of Heidelberg, which has some fine steep vineyard slopes overlooking the Neckar River.

**HEIDELBERG**

**Vineyard** *Herrenberg* (red and white) **Grower** *Seeger/Leimen* • **Premium red wine blends: Grower** *Seeger* (Leimen—"R," "S," "RR")

### GROSSLAGE RITTERSBERG

There are no outstanding villages, vineyards, or growers here, although good wines are made in the villages of Leutershausen, Lützelsachen, Schriesheim, and Weinheim.

### GROSSLAGE STIFTSBERG

Situated in the Kraichgau, this is the *Bereich's* most successful *Grosslage*. Nearly half of its vineyards are classified as "steep," which officially means sloping at more than 20 degrees, and this contributes to the extreme fruitiness of the Ruländer and the relatively racy character of the Riesling.

**SULZFELD**

**Non-Einzellagen premium red: Growers** *Burg Ravensburg*

## BEREICH BODENSEE

In the Hochrhein of Bodensee, or the Upper Rhine of Bodensee (known in English as Lake Constance), the wines are not great, but can be very acceptable. They range from the fruity and lively Müller-Thurgau to Rotwein and Weissherbst, both produced from Spätburgunder.

### GROSSLAGE SONNENUFER

The steep sides of Lake Constance around Meersburg are the most spectacular vineyards here. The brothers Aufricht have brought a new dimension to the wines of this district, taking over the lead from Winzerverein Meersburg, Germany's first state domain (since 1802).

**MEERSBURG**

**Vineyard** *Sängerhalde* **Grower** *Aufricht*

## BEREICH BREISGAU

Strangely, the old city of Breisach is not part of the *Bereich* that takes its name; it is, in fact, situated in the *Bereich* of Kaiserstuhl-Tuniberg to the south. The wines of *Bereich* Breisgau have narrowed the gap on the better-known Kaiserstuhl-Tuniberg, with fruity, off-dry Müller-Thurgau balanced by some excellent Weissburgunder, Grauburgunder, and Spätburgunder.

### GROSSLAGE BURG LICHTENECK

Besides those of the villages recommended below, good wines are also made in Altdorf.

**MALTERDINGEN**

**Vineyard** *Bienenberg* **Grower** *Bernhard Huber* ⊙ • **Premium red wine blends: Grower** *Bernhard Huber* (R, S, Alte Reben)

### GROSSLAGE BURG ZÄHRINGEN

There are no outstanding villages, vineyards, or growers in this *Grosslage*, although good wines are made in the village of Glottertal.

### GROSSLAGE SCHUTTER-LINDENBERG

There are no outstanding villages, vineyards, or growers in this *Grosslage*, although good wines are made in the village of Friesenheim.

## BEREICH KAISERSTUHL

Formerly part of Kaiserstuhl-Tuniberg, this *Bereich* is dominated by the extinct volcano of Kaiserstuhl, whose immaculate slopes are textbook examples of *Flurbereinigung* (growing vines in rows up and down slopes).

In this, Germany's warmest and driest *Bereich*, there are microclimates that favor certain sites protected by the volcano. Some of Baden's best wines come from these *Einzellagen*, although most of the wine is sold under the *Bereich* name, usually with the grape name attached; Bereich Kaiserstuhl Müller-Thurgau dominates. But it is the very full white Ruländer and the assertive Weissherbst Ruländer that made the reputation of the *Bereich*. Some fine, rich Spätburgunder wines enhance this reputation.

### GROSSLAGE VULKANFELSEN

Vulkanfelsen is the largest and most successful of the two *Grosslagen* that belonged to the now defunct Kaiserstuhl-Tuniberg. As its name implies (Vulkanfelsen means volcano rock), it covers the superior, high volcanic vineyards of the Kaiserstuhl mound itself. Above all else, it is the full, fiery intensity of Ruländer wines from the Kaiserstuhl that give this district its reputation.

**ACHKARREN**

**Vineyard** *Schlossberg* **Growers** *Dr. Heger* (red and white), *Michel* (red and white) • **Non-Einzellagen Premium red and white wines Grower** *Johner* (SJ)

**BURKHEIM**

**Vineyard** *Feuerberg* **Grower** *Bercher* (red and white), *Winzergenossenschaft Burkheim*

**ENDINGEN**

**Grower** *Reinhold und Cornelia Schneider*

**IHRINGEN**

**Vineyard** *Winklerberg* **Growers** *Dr. Heger* (red and white), *Stigler*

**JECHTINGEN**

**Vineyard** *Eichert* **Grower** *Bercher*

**KÖNIGSSCHAFFHAUSEN**

**Vineyard** *Steingrüble* **Grower** *Winzergenossenschaft Königschaffhausen* (red)

**NIMBURG-BOTTINGEN**

**Vineyard** *Steingrube* **Grower** *Fischer*

**OBERBERGEN**

**Vineyard** *Bassgeige* **Grower** *Winzergenossenschaft Oberbergen* • **Premium red and white blends Grower** *Franz Keller-Schwarzer Adler* (Selection A and S)

**OBERROTTWEIL**

**Vineyard** *Eichberg* **Growers** *Freiherr von Gleichenstein, Salwey* (red and white) • **Vineyard** *Kirchberg* **Grower** *Salwey* (red and white)

**SASBACH**

**Vineyard** *Limburg* **Grower** *Bercher* • **Vineyard** *Rote Halde* **Grower** *Winzergenossenschaft Sasbach*

**SCHELINGEN**

**Vineyard** *Kirchberg* **Grower** *Schätzle*

## BEREICH MARKGRÄFLERLAND

This is the second-most important *Bereich* in Baden. The principal grape variety is, unusually, Gutedel, which makes a light, dryish, and neutral wine that benefits from a slight spritz and can be most attractive when very youthful. Other prominent varieties include Nobling, an up-and-coming cross between Gutedel and Silvaner that makes a more characterful wine than the light Müller-Thurgau. The latter can be attractive nevertheless. Spätburgunder can be full and successful, and Gewürztraminer also fares well.

## GROSSLAGE ATTILAFELSEN

Not enough is made of the potential for good wines at this small volcanic outcrop of the Tuniberg.

## GROSSLAGE BURG NEUENFELS

The vast majority of vineyards in this *Grosslage* are on steep ground. These vineyards make some of Germany's most delicious Gutedel, although the greatest potential lies in the Burgunder varietals.

### BADENWEILER

✓ **Vineyard** *Römerberg* **Grower** *Winzergenossenschaft Britzingen*

### LAUFEN

✓ **Non-Einzellagen wines: Grower** *Schlumberger* (red and white)

### MAUCHEN

✓ **Vineyard** *Sonnenstück* **Grower** *Lämmlin-Schindler* ◉ • **Vineyard Frauenberg Grower** *Lämmlin-Schindler*

## GROSSLAGE LORETTOBERG

A cooperative, a part-time asparagus grower and a Chardonnay specialist have brought some credibility to a long-underestimated Grosslage.

### PFAFFENWEILER

✓ **Vineyard** *Oberdürrenberg* **Grower** *Winzergenossenschaft Pfaffenweiler*

### SCHERZINGEN

✓ **Vineyard** *Batzenberg* **Grower** *Heinemann*

### SCHLATT

✓ **Vineyard** *Maltesergarten* **Grower** *Martin Wassmer* (red and white)

## GROSSLAGE VOGTEI RÖTTELN

Although much wine is sold under this *Grosslage*, its exceptional vineyards are known for Gutedel and, to a lesser extent, Spätburgunder.

## BEREICH ORTENAU

Sheltered by the Black Forest, the two *Grosslagen* in this *Bereich* produce some of Baden's greatest wines. They are generally full, fruity, and often very spicy. The Riesling, known locally as Klingelberger, is extremely fine for such a powerful and spicy variation of this normally racy variety. Müller-Thurgau is particularly good and full, and a successful Ruländer-Spätburgunder blend called Badisch Rotgold is also produced. Confusingly, the Gewürztraminer is often called Clevner, which is usually a synonym for Pinot Blanc.

## GROSSLAGE FÜRSTENECK

This *Grosslage* sports some of Baden's finest estates. The range of grape varieties is greater here than anywhere else within Baden and the wines include Rieslings that range from firm and spicy to fine and delicate; powerful Gewürztraminer; some of Germany's best Müller-Thurgau; and some extraordinary Gutedel. Many of the wines are made in increasingly drier styles, although some estates are famous for their sweeter, late-harvested products.

### DURBACH

✓ **Vineyard** *Schloss Grohl* **Grower** *Gräflich Wolff Metternich'sches Weingut* • **Vineyard** *Schlossberg* **Growers** *Gräflich Wolff Metternich'sches Weingut* • **Vineyard** *Plauelrain* **Growers** *Andreas Laible, Durbacher Winzergenossenschaft*

### ORTENBERG

✓ **Non-Einzellagen wines: Grower** *Schloss Ortenberg*

## GROSSLAGE SCHLOSS RODECK

For many years Schloss Neuweier was the undisputed number one in this *Grosslage*, but a Dutch newcomer has propelled himself to the forefront of developments with Spätburgunder in *barriques*.

### BÜHL

✓ **Non-Einzellagen premium red wines Grower** *Duijn*

### NEUWEIER

✓ **Vineyard** *Mauerberg* **Grower** *Schloss Neuweier* • **Vineyard** *Schlossberg* **Grower** *Schloss Neuweier*

## BEREICH TAUBERFRANKEN

The most northerly of Baden's vineyards, Bereich Tauberfranken bridges Franken and Württemberg. The wines have a similar style to those produced in both regions. If anything, the crisp, dry, aromatic, and slightly earthy Müller-Thurgau and Silvaner wines bear more resemblance to Franken wines rather than to Württemberg wines. Only that part of the *Bereich* outside Franken itself is allowed to use Franken's famous *Bocksbeutel* bottle.

## GROSSLAGE TAUBERKLINGE

As well as at Reicholzheim, good wines are also made in the villages of Beckstein, Königshofen, and Tauberbischofsheim.

### REICHHOLZHEIM

✓ **Vineyard** *First* **Grower** *Konrad Schlör*

## BEREICH TUNIBERG

Formerly part of Kaiserstuhl-Tuniberg, this *Bereich* is to the south of the mighty Kaiserstuhl and it is the far less awesome sight of the Tuniberg, another volcanic outcrop, that provides the only other topographical and viticultural relief. The Tuniberg's steeper, west-facing slopes are cultivated, but neither its reputation nor its bulk can match those of Kaiserstuhl's fabulous recommendations above.

---

## OTHER CERTIFIED ORGANIC PRODUCERS

**Biodynamic**
Alfons Schüber (Sasbach-Jechtingen)
Breitehof Hubert Schies (Vogtsburg-Burkheim a Kaiserstuhl)
Christoph Brenneisen (Sulburg-Laufen)
Guido Friderich (Sasbach)
Josef u Klara Vögtle (Sasbach-Jechtingen a Kaiserstuhl)
Josef Wörner (Durbach)
Markus Bürgin (Fischingen)
Max und Alice Schneider (Sasbach)

**Organic**
Andrea und Heiner Renn (Hagnau)
Andreas Fritz (Bühlertal)
Bettina Beck (Bahlingen)
Daniel Feuerstein (Heitersheim)
Edmund Eisele/Schelb (Ehrenkirchen)
Eduard Mannsperger (Sinsheim-Dühren)
Erwin Mick (Nimburg)
Freiburg (Heiliggeist Freiburg im Breisgau)
Friedhelm Rinklin (Eichstetten)
Friedrich & Bärbel Ruesch (Buggingen)
Fritz Lampp (Heitersheim)
Gallushof/Hügle (Teningen-Heimbach)
Geier (Königheim)
Gerd Köpfer (Staufen-Grunern)

Gerhard Aenis (Binzen)
Gretzmeier (Merdingen)
Gudrun Lauerbach (Tauberbischofsheim-Impfingen)
Günther Kaufmann (Efringen-Kirchen)
H. & J. Sprich (Weil-Haltingen)
Hans Hardt (Herbolzheim)
Harald Süssle (Merdingen)
Harteneck (Schliengen)
Hermann Helde & Sohne (Jechtingen)
Hermann Neuner-Jehle (Immenstaad)
H. P. & Helmut Grether (Laufen-Sulzburg)
Hubert Lay (Ihringen)
Jette Krumm (Auggen)
Joachim Netzhammer (Klettgau-Erzingen)
Johannes Haug (Nonnenhorn)
Kirchberghof (Kenzingen-Bombach)
Klaus Benz (Ballrechten-Dottingen)
Klaus Bischoff (Kellern)
Klaus Vorgrimmler (Freiburg-Munzingen)
Koehly-Harteneck (Bad Bellingen)
Kuckuckshof (Karlsbad-Ittersbach)
Kurt Breisacher (Riegel)
Langwerth Öko-Wein (Esselbach)
Ludwig Missbach (Ebringen)
Manfred & Eva Maria Schmidt (Vogtsburg-Bischoffingen)
Manfred Dannmeyer (Bamlach)
Markgräfler Wyhus (Efringen-

Kirchen)
Martin Hämmerlin (Buggingen)
Martin Küchlin (Buggingen-Betberg)
Martina Heitzmann (Bahlingen)
Matthias Höfflin/Schambachhof (Bötzingen)
Matthias Seywald (Ballrechten-Dottingen)
Matthias Wolff (Riedlingen)
Peter Kaiser (Bahnbrücken)
Philip Isele (Achkarren)
Pix (Ihringen A. K.)
Rabenhof (Vogtsburg-Bischofingen)
Reblandhof (Sulzfeld)
Reinhard Burs (March)
Richard G Schmidt (Eichstetten)
Siegfried Frei (Wasenweiler)
Sonnenbrunnen (Freiburg-Opfingen)
Stadt Lahr (Lahr/Schwarzwald)
Stränglehof (Leiselheim)
Thomas Schaffner (Bötzingen am Kaiserstuhl)
Thomas Selinger (Merdingen)
Tobias Kehnel (Broggingen)
Trautwein (Bahlingen)
Ulrich Klumpp (Bruchsal)
Walter J Schür (Vogtsburg-Oberrotweil)
Wendelin Brugger (Laufen)
Wilhelm Zähringer (Heitersheim)
Willi Frey (Freiburg-Tiengen)
Winzerhof Leber (Vogtsburg-Schelingen)
Wolfgang Ibert (Wallburg)

# SAALE-UNSTRUT AND SACHSEN

*These two eastern outposts of viticulture are the most northerly in Germany. Even though their terraced vineyards are being renovated and replanted, and modern vinification facilities installed, their wines can never be more than a tourist curiosity.*

PARADOXICALLY THIS LIMITATION may be the saving grace for the wines of Saale-Unstrut and Sachsen because they are far too small and rustically structured to stand any chance of competing with the large volumes of cheap plonk churned out by cooperatives in Germany's more intensively cultivated wine regions. Furthermore, as Meissen and Dresden are lucrative tourist areas, the wines must adhere to a certain standard if they are to satisfy tourists with far more sophisticated palates than those who consumed them under former GDR mismanagement. Most of the vineyards are between Dresden and Diesbar-Seusslitz, with a few vineyards that have been restored on the southern outskirts of Dresden itself. The state-owned cellars in historic Schloss Wackerbarth in Radebeul and the region's oldest (and privately owned) estate at Schloss Proschwitz are Sachsen's largest estates. The largest estate in Saale-Unstrut is Kloster Pforta, which was named after the 12th-century monastery between Bad Kösen and Naumburg.

## THE FUTURE—VARIETAL EVOLUTION

When Germany was reunified in 1989, the most commonly cultivated grape variety in the former GDR's rundown vineyards was Müller-Thurgau, and although it remains an important grape, it is on the

decline, and its days must be numbered. Riesling has increased from five to seven percent of the vines grown, but it is Germany's greatest variety, thus more will be planted, if only for the sake of national pride. The area is, however, more suited to the full, rich, and distinctively earthy wine produced by Silvaner and, perhaps surprisingly for such a northerly, frost-prone region, also to red wine grape varieties. But of all the varieties to choose from, who would have predicted the rise of Weisserburgunder when the Berlin Wall came down? Very few, I think, but it is the best placed to succeed Müller-Thurgau as this region's more important variety, although it will take a few years yet.

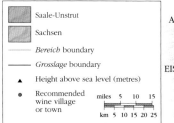

**SAALE-UNSTRUT AND SACHSEN,**
*see also p.345*
*More than 2,500 acres (1,000 hectares) of vines grow in these areas, formerly part of East Germany. Production is centered in Bad Kösen, Freyburg, and near the confluence of the Saale and Unstrut rivers at Naumberg.*

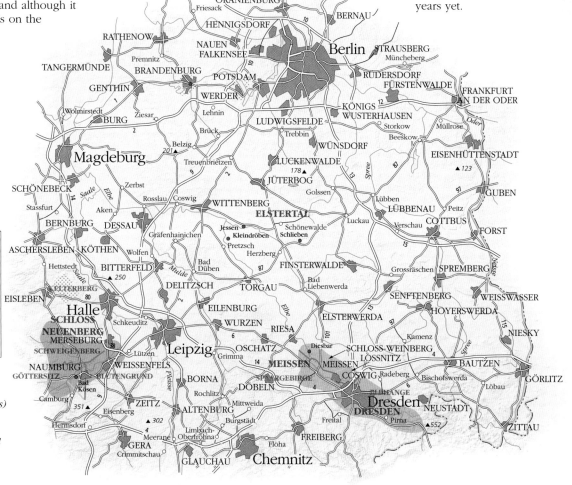

## FACTORS AFFECTING TASTE AND QUALITY

**LOCATION**
The most northerly wine regions in Germany, Saale-Unstrut is equidistant between Berlin and the Franken region, while Sachsen is about 80 miles (128 kilometers) east, around Dresden, close to the border with the Czech Republic.

**CLIMATE**
Despite their northerly position, the continental climate ensures high summer temperatures. However, winters are long and very cold, resulting in a short and dry growing season compared with other German regions. Spring and fall frosts are a particular danger, often cutting yields by 20–70 percent in Saale-Unstrut and as much as 90 percent in Sachsen.

**ASPECT**
Vineyards are on south and southeast facing valley slopes, but much of the terracing has deteriorated under Communist rule and the current reconstruction will take some time to complete.

**SOIL**
Limestone and a tiny amount of sandstone in Saale-Unstrut, with loam and loess over granite and volcanic subsoils in most of Sachsen, and weathered granite and gneiss on its steepest slopes.

**VITICULTURE AND VINIFICATION**
Many of the small parcels are planted on steep, labor-intensive stone terraces, most of which are cultivated by part-time growers who deliver their crop to Saale-Unstrut's regional cooperative in Freyburg or Sachsen's regional cooperative in Meissen. Yields were very low prior to reunification, but although production has since increased, yields remain very low due to the northerly situation. There are problems such as decimation of production by fierce attacks of frost, decaying terracing, dead vines, and rustic production methods, but it would be a pity if old vines were replaced and if the hardy but highest-yielding characterless crosses were introduced in place of classic varieties. Weissburgunder and Riesling are the fastest expanding grape varieties. Mostly dry wines are produced, with only four percent of the production sweeter than *Halbtrocken*, and as much as 86 percent sold as *Trocken*.

**GRAPE VARIETIES**
**Primary varieties:** Müller-Thurgau, Weissburgunder
**Secondary varieties:** Bacchus, Dornfelder, Elbling, Gewürztraminer, Grauburgunder, Gutedel, Kerner, Morio-Muscat, Portugieser

## THE APPELLATIONS OF
# SAALE-UNSTRUT AND SACHSEN

## ANBAUGEBIET SAALE-UNSTRUT

Wines have been produced in this area for nearly 1,000 years, but it took the GDR less than 50 years to erase these once-well-known names from the memory of wine drinkers. This region comprises two *Bereiche*, and Müller-Thurgau is the most important grape variety. It accounts for some 35 percent of the vines planted and black grapes account for some 10 percent.

## BEREICH SCHLOSSNEUENBURG

By far the largest of Saale-Unstrut's two *Bereiche*, Schloss Neuenburg encompasses all but a tiny section in the very south of the Saale-Unstrut region, plus the island of vines just west of Halle.

### GROSSLAGE BLÜTENGRUND

Some respectable wines have appeared on the market under the designation of this *Grosslage*.

### GROSSLAGE GÖTTERSITZ

Previous expectations in this Grosslage have not been quite fulfilled.

**NAUMBURG**
☑ **Vineyard** *Steinmeister* **Grower** *Gussek*

### GROSSLAGE KELTERBERG

No outstanding villages, vineyards, or growers.

### GROSSLAGE SCHWEIGENBERG

Two growers have made this the most respected *Grosslage* of the Saale-Unstrut region.

**FREYBURG**
☑ **Vineyard** *Edelacker* **Grower** *Pawis*
**KARSDORF**
☑ **Vineyard** *Hohe Gräte* **Grower** *Weingut Lützkendorf*

## BEREICH THÜRINGEN

The southern tip of the Saale-Unstrut region does not contain any *Grosslagen*, just two *Einzellagen*, one in Grossheringen, the other in Bad Sulza.

## BEREICHEFREI AND GROSSLAGENFREI MARK BRANDEBURG

Mark Brandenburg covers the vineyards around Werder, from which no outstanding wines have so far been made.

## ANBAUGEBIET SACHSEN

Incorporating Dresden and Meissen, this *Aubaugebiet* produces wines that are grown along the Elbe River (Sachsen was formerly known as Elbethal). The area is even more prone to frost damage than Saale-Unstrut, with Riesling relatively more important (13 percent as opposed to Saale-Unstrut's 5 percent). The quantity of black grapes is minuscule.

## BEREICH DRESDEN

This *Bereich* covers most of the southern half of Sachsen.

### GROSSLAGE ELBHÄNGE

Continuous efforts have finally paid off for one grower in this otherwise unremarkable *Grosslage*.

**PILLNITZ**
☑ **Vineyard** *Königlicher Weinberg* **Grower** *Klaus Zimmerling*

### GROSSLAGE LÖSSNITZ

There are no outstanding villages or vineyards, and no remarkable growers to be recommended in this *Grosslage*.

## BEREICH ELSTERTAL

This is a *Bereich* consisting of three villages at the southern end of Sachsen. There are relatively few vines and, so far, no village has produced any outstanding wines.

## BEREICH MEISSEN

The northern end of the Sachsen region, Meissen itself will always be more well known for the porcelain it once produced than its wine. This area, however, did have something of a name for producing fine wine at the beginning of the 19th century. Wine drinkers can only wait and see if there is sufficient potential for that reputation to be recaptured sometime in the future.

### GROSSLAGE SCHLOSS-WEINBERG

North of Meissen, some decent wines can come from a bend in the Elbe at Diesbar-Seusslitz where the vineyards face south.

**SEUSSLITZ**
☑ **Vineyard** *Heinrichsburg* **Grower** *Schloss Proschwitz*

### GROSSLAGE SPAARGEBIRGE

Substantial investments have helped to bring at least one estate's shine back to this *Grosslage*.

**PROSCHWITZ**
☑ **Vineyard** *Schloss Proschwitz* **Grower** *Schloss Proschwitz*

## CERTIFIED ORGANIC PRODUCERS

**Organic**
Hof Loessnitz (Dresden)

# AUSTRIA

*Austria used to be seen as a clone of Germany but has slowly yet surely established its own unique wine identity. It now produces some exceptionally fine red wines in addition to its classic Riesling and traditional Grüner Veltliner.*

IN THE LATE 1970S, Austrian wine production increased as domestic consumption declined, resulting in the largest wine lake outside the EC. Austria's wine industry was designed chiefly for exports to Germany, traditionally its only significant customer. After a succession of bumper harvests in both Germany and Austria, sales to Germany dried up, but overproduction in Austria continued. With hindsight, the so-called "antifreeze" scandal that took place in 1985 can be seen as a godsend for Austrian wine. Call it a scam or a scandal, but it was not the health

## RECENT AUSTRIAN VINTAGES

**2006** Variable quantity and quality, but some good to excellent reds (particularly Blaufränkisch, but also Cabernet Sauvignon and Pinot Noir), sweet and dry whites (Riesling and Grüner Veltliner). A very good year for Styrian Sauvignon Blanc.

**2005** Some top-quality red and sweet whites were made.

**2004** An extremely variable year, but quality-conscious producers have made some good reds and stunning dry white wines.

**2003** Best reds for a decade; brilliant dry whites; sweet wines lack finesse.

**2002** Fabulous white wines in the south, and great reds from all over. Good sweet wines, but not special.

**Weinbauregion Niederösterreich**

- Wachau
- Kremstal
- Kamtal
- Weinviertel
- Traisental
- Donauland
- Carnuntum
- Thermenregion

**Weinbauregion Wien**

- Wien

**Weinbauregion Burgenland**

- Neusiedler See
- Neusiedler See-Hügelland
- Mittelburgenland
- Südburgenland

**Weinbauregion Steierland**

- Weststeiermark
- Süd-Oststeiermark
- Südsteiermark
- Intensive vine-growing zone
- ● Best wine villages
- Provincial boundary
- International boundary
- ▲ Height above sea level (metres)

0 5 10 15 10 25 30 miles
0 10 20 30 40 50 km

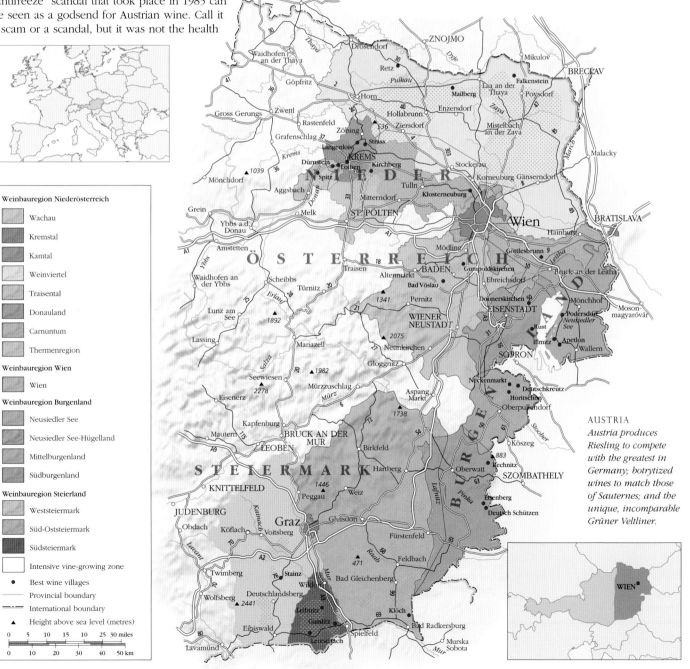

AUSTRIA
*Austria produces Riesling to compete with the greatest in Germany; botrytized wines to match those of Sauternes; and the unique, incomparable Grüner Veltliner.*

THE WACHAU
*Much of Austria is very picturesque, making it a popular vacation destination; here the lush vineyards complement this typical Lower Austrian landscape.*

## FACTORS AFFECTING TASTE AND QUALITY

**LOCATION**
The vineyards are in the east of the country, north and south of Vienna, bordering the Czech Republic, Hungary, and Yugoslavia.

**CLIMATE**
The climate is warm, dry, and continental, with annual rainfall between 23 to 31 inches (57 and 77 centimeters). The hottest and driest area is Burgenland, where in the warm falls, mists rising from the Neusiedlersee help promote *Botrytis cinerea* (the "noble rot" beloved by winegrowers).

**ASPECT**
Vines are grown on all types of land, from the plains of the Danube to its valley sides—which are often very steep and terraced—and from the hilly Burgenland to the slopes of mountainous Styria.

**SOIL**
Soils vary from generally stony schist, limestone, and gravel (though occasionally loamy) in the north, through predominantly sandy soils on the shores of the Neusiedlersee in Burgenland, to mainly clay with some volcanic soils in Styria.

**VITICULTURE AND VINIFICATION**
Not surprisingly, Austria's methods are similar to those of Germany, but, although modern techniques have been introduced here, far more Austrian wine is produced by traditional methods than is the case in Germany. More than 85 percent of the country's vines are cultivated by the Lenz Moser system. This is a method of training vines to twice their normal height, thereby achieving a comparatively higher ratio of quality to cost, by enabling the use of mechanized harvesting. This system brought fame to its Austrian inventor, Lenz Moser, and has been adopted by at least one grower in most winemaking countries. Harvesting is traditionally accomplished in *tries*, particularly on steeper slopes and for sweeter styles.

**GRAPE VARIETIES**
Blauberger, Blauer Portugieser, Blauer Wildbacher, Blaufränkisch, Bouviertraube, Cabernet Franc, Cabernet Sauvignon, Chardonnay, Frühroter Veltliner (*syn.* Malvasia), Furmint, Gewürztraminer, Goldburger, Grüner Veltliner, Pinot Blanc, Pinot Noir, Merlot, Müller-Thurgau, Muskateller, Muskatottonel, Neuburger, Pinot Gris, Roter Veltliner, Rotgipfler, Sauvignon Blanc, Scheurebe, St. Laurent, Silvaner, Trollinger, Riesling, Welschriesling, Zierfandler, Zweigelt.

scare it was made out to be. It did, however, have the effect of putting the Austrian government under enormous pressure to tighten up controls, with the result that Austria now has the most strictly controlled, safest wine industry in the world.

## WHAT WAS THE ANTI-FREEZE SCANDAL?

In 1985, a handful of Austria's 40,000 wine producers used diethylene glycol to sweeten their wines artificially. The media throughout the world claimed that Austrian wines had been poisoned with antifreeze, but it was not antifreeze, of course (ethylene glycol is). Diethylene glycol is, in fact, less toxic than alcohol, so adding it actually made the wines less poisonous.

## AUSTRIA VERSUS GERMANY

Both countries operate wine regimes that base levels of quality on degrees of ripeness by measuring the amount of sugar found in the grapes at the time of harvest. As in Germany, Austrian wines range from *Tafelwein*, through *Qualitätswein*, to *Trockenbeerenauslese*. The overview below shows that most Austrian wines conform to higher minimum standards than their German counterparts. More significant, however, is the fact that the minimum level for each category is rigid, so it has a distinctive style. This gives the consumer a clear idea of what to expect, whereas a German category varies according to the variety of grape and its area of origin. In Germany, only experience can reveal that a Mosel *Auslese*, for example, tastes no sweeter than a *Spätlese* from other regions. Also, *Süssreserve* is not allowed for any *Prädikat* wines, whereas in Germany this is permitted for *Kabinett*.

### MINIMUM OECHSLE LEVELS

| QUALITY CATEGORY | AUSTRIA | GERMANY |
|---|---|---|
| Tafelwein | 63° | 44–50° |
| Landwein | 63° | 47–55° |
| Qualitätswein | 73° | 50–72° |
| Kabinett | 83.5° | 67–85° |
| Spätlese | 94° | 76–95° |
| Auslese | 105° | 83–105° |
| Beerenauslese | 127° | 110–128° |
| Eiswein | 127° | 110–128° |
| Ausbruch | 138° | N/A |
| Trockenbeerenauslese | 156° | 150–154° |

## THE MODERN WINE TRADE

Enthusiasts have always known that Austria produces some of the greatest botrytized wines in the world, yet just how electrifying these wines can be became clear when Willy Opitz, one of the smallest, but truly greatest, dessert wine producers, took the trouble to tour world markets and speak to people about his products.

Over the past few years, Austria has produced Cabernet Sauvignon and Chardonnay to a very high standard, and even St. Laurent, an obscure local variety of grape, has proved to be quite stunning. What Austria must do now is to promote its greatest Riesling wines, which can compare with the best from Germany, and export its top Grüner Veltliner, and keep pushing these wines onto the international markets.

## AUSBRUCH—A RELIC OF THE AUSTRO-HUNGARIAN EMPIRE

*Ausbruch* is a still-popular style of wine that harks back to the days of the Austro-Hungarian Empire (and is also still produced in Hungary). At 138° *Oechsle* (*see left*), *Ausbruch* falls between the sweetness levels of *Beerenauslese* (127°) and *Trockenbeerenauslese* (156°). In terms of character, however, *Ausbruch* should be totally different from either a *Beerenauslese* or *Trockenbeerenauslese*. The name means "to break up"; the wine is made traditionally from the richest and sweetest botrytized grapes that are so shriveled and dried-out that to press them is virtually impossible without first moistening the mass (breaking it up) with a more liquescent juice (the regulation stipulates *Spätlese* quality). A true *Ausbruch* is overwhelmed by an intensely raisiny aroma and flavor that may be even more botrytized than a *Trockenbeerenauslese*, yet the wine itself need not necessarily be as rich.

THE WINE STYLES OF
# AUSTRIA

## BLAUBURGER

**RED** A Blauer Portugieser/Blaufränkisch cross that produces a well-colored wine of little distinction, but tends to improve in bottle.

↓— 1–3 years

♗ *Weingut Schützenhof Fam Faulhammer-Körper • Willi Opitz*

## BLAUER PORTUGIESER

**RED** This used to be Austria's most widely planted black grape variety and is still commonly found in Lower Austria, particularly Paulkautal, Retz, and the Thermen region, where it makes a light-bodied but well-colored red wine with a mild flavor, hinting of violets.

↓— 1–2 years

♗ *Johann Gipsberg • H. V. Reinisch*

## BLAUER WILDBACHER

**RED/ROSÉ** Otherwise known as Schilcher, this variety traditionally produces a light, dry, crisp, and fruity, pale rosé wine.

↓— 1–2 years

♗ *E. & M. Müller*

## BLAUFRÄNKISCH

**RED** Known as Lemberger in Germany and Kékfrankos in Hungary, this variety is popular in Neusiedlersee-Hügelland Burgenland, where it produces tart, fruity wine with good tannin and an underlying hint of cherries and spice. The best examples of Blaufränkisch are fat and sometimes given time in oak.

↓— 2–4 years

♗ *Weingut Gessellmann* (Creitzer) • *Feiler-Artinger • Weingut Fam Igler • Weingut H. und M. Krutzler*

## BOUVIER

**WHITE** An early-ripening table grape that has a low natural acidity and is often used for high-quality *Prädikatswein*.

↓— 1–3 year (*Qualitätswein*), 2–8 years (*Prädikatswein*)

♗ *Willi Opitz*

## CABERNET SAUVIGNON

**RED** Very little of this variety used to be grown in Austria. Until 1982 the only commercial cultivation was by Schlumberger at Bad Vöslau. Then Lenz Moser received special permission to cultivate 6 acres (2.5 hectares) at Mailberg, and the first Cabernet Sauvignon was grown in 1986 in Lower Austria. Today, everyone seems to be growing Cabernet Sauvignon.

↓— 5–6 years (*Qualitätswein*), 10–15 years (*Prädikatswein*)

♗ *Lenz Moser* (Siegendorf Prestige) • *Weingut Fam Igler • Weingut Gessellmann*

## CHARDONNAY

**WHITE** Also known in Austria as Feinburgunder, this grape variety has been grown for decades in Styria, where it is known as Morillon. Cultivation of this grape has risen rapidly since the early 1990s, producing some fat, rich wines.

↓— 2–5 years

♗ *Weingut Bründlmayer* (Kabinett) • *Juris-Stiegelmar* (Classic) • *H. V. Reinisch • Andreas Schafler • Weingut Gottfried Schellmann • Weingut Tement*

## FRÜHROTER VELTLINER

**WHITE** Sometimes labeled Malvasia, this dry Frühroter Veltliner has more alcohol and body than Austria's most widely grown white wine, Grüner Veltliner.

↓— 1–2 years

♗ *Weingut Leth*

## FURMINT

**WHITE** This is a rarely encountered Hungarian dry, medium- to full-bodied, rich, and fruity varietal that does well at Rust in Burgenland.

↓— 3–5 years

♗ *Weinbau Ladislaus und Robert Wenzel*

## GEWÜRZTRAMINER

**WHITE** Usually labeled Traminer or Roter Traminer, the wines from this variety range from light and floral to intensely aromatic. They may be dry or have one of various shades of sweetness. They are the fullest, richest, and most pungent of *Trockenbeerenauslesen*.

↓— 3–6 years

♗ *Weingut Rheinhold Polz • Andreas Schafler* (Traminer)

## GOLDBURGER

**WHITE** This is a Welschriesling/Orangetraube cross that produces white wines that are used for blending purposes.

↓— 1–3 years

## GRÜNER VELTLINER

**WHITE** Most Grüner Veltliners are bland or fat at best, but the finest examples now boast an astonishing minerality, and this is further enhanced by a racy acidity that was not associated with this grape before terroir-inspired growers began experimenting. When made by the best producers, this minerality can even be found in the sweetest Grüner Veltliner. The fiery, freshly ground pepper varietal character is now usually confined to the finish.

↓— 1–4 years (*Qualitätswein*), 3–10 years (*Prädikatswein*)

♗ *Weingut Bründlmayer* (Langenloiser Berg Vogelsang Kabinett, Ried Lamm, Spätlese

Trocken) • *Freie Weingärtner Wachau* (Weissenkirchner Achleiten "Smaragd") • *Graf Hardegg* (Dreikreuzen Kabinett, Maximilian Kabinett) • *Weingut Hirtzberger* (Rotes Tor "Smaragd," Spitzer Honifogl) • *Lenz Moser* (Knights of Malta) • *Loimer* (Kaferberg) • *Weingut Mantlerhhof* (older vintages) • *Metternich-Sandor* (Princess) • *Weingut Franz Prager • Weingut Wieninger* (Ried Herrenholz)

## JUBLINÄ UMSREBE

**WHITE** A Blauer Portugieser/Blaufränkisch cross, this is allowed for *Prädikatswein* only, as its mild character is transformed by botrytis.

↓— 3–7 years

## MERLOT

**RED** Small amounts are grown in Krems, Mailberg, and Furth in Lower Austria, plus in a few scattered plots in Burgenland. This variety has potential in Austria, as it can produce richly colored red wines with soft, spicy-juicy fruit, but has been underexploited until quite recently.

↓— 1–3 years (*Qualitätswein*), 3–5 years (*Prädikatswein*)

♗ *Hofkellerei des Fürsten von Liechtenstein* (Herrenbaumgärtner Spätlese)

## MÜLLER-THURGAU

**WHITE** Often labeled as Riesler x Silvaner, this is Austria's second most prolific grape variety. The best of Austria's pure varietal Müller-Thurgaus have a fine, spicy character that is superior to the average German version.

↓— 1–2 years

♗ *Weingut Hirtzberger • Weingut Schützenhof Fam Korper*

## MUSKATELLER

**WHITE** This is an underexploited variety that makes some of Burgenland's best *Prädikatswein* and excels in the sheltered sites of Styria.

↓— 1–3 years (*Qualitätswein*), 2–10 years (*Prädikatswein*)

♗ *Weingut Leth • Weinhof Platzer • Weinbau Ladislaus und Robert Wenzel*

## MUSKAT-OTTONEL

**WHITE** Less weighty than the Muskateller, the Muskat-Ottonel variety has more immediate aromatic appeal and is best drunk when young.

↓— 2–4 years

♗ *Willi Opitz*

## NEUBURGER

**WHITE** An Austrian variety that excels on chalky soil, making full-bodied wines with a typically nutty flavor in all categories of sweetness.

↓— 2–4 years (*Qualitätswein*), 3–8 years (*Prädikatswein*)

♗ *Dipl Ing Karl Alphart • H V Reinisch*

## PINOT BLANC

**WHITE** Often called Klevner or Weisser Burgunder, this produces a fresh, light-bodied, easy-to-drink wine at lower quality levels. In exceptional years, it can develop a fine spicy-richness in the upper *Prädikatswein* categories.

# SWITZERLAND

*At their best, Swiss wines are as fresh and clean as the Alpine air. Although many grape varieties are cultivated in Switzerland, the most famous grape grown here is the Chasselas. In France this variety is perceived as a table grape, yet the Swiss make it into a light, dry, spritzy, and delicately delicious wine that is the perfect partner to the Swiss cheese fondue.*

THE CHASSELAS CAN BE FOUND under the guise of the Dorin in the Vaud region, the Perlan in Geneva, and, most famous of all, the Fendant in the Valais. However, although this country's most popular grape variety represents 40 percent of the vines cultivated, nearly half of all Swiss wine produced is, rather surprisingly, red.

There is, in fact, as much as 27 percent Pinot Noir, 14 percent Gamay, and, nowhere near as important, but very much on the increase, Merlot, which currently accounts for 6 percent, leaving all the other varieties just 13 percent of the vineyards.

The quality of Swiss wines has certainly improved over the last decade, but yields have always been much too high in general (350 cases per acre/80 hectoliters per hectare on average, with some cantons producing as much as 530 cases per acre/120 hectoliters per hectare) for Switzerland to achieve a serious international reputation as a quality wine-producing country.

## RECENT SWISS VINTAGES

**2006** An excellent red-wine vintage, but not quite so good for the whites.

**2005** The best vintage of the new century, for all areas, varieties, and styles.

**2004** A great vintage for both red and white wines—more consistent than 2003, and superior to 2002, especially for whites.

**2003** A great year, particularly for red wines. The best wines overall since 2000, although the exceptionally hot weather did cause some problems for less experienced winemakers.

**2002** An excellent vintage that is probably more consistent across the regions, grape varieties, and wine styles than 2003, but without as many high spots.

Producers who keep their yields low make some splendid wines, but, unfortunately, they are at present too few to change the reputation of the country as a whole. The accepted wisdom on this issue is that the value of the Swiss franc and the high cost of living inevitably makes these wines expensive in international terms, especially the very best wines. Since the Swiss drink twice as much wine as they can produce and are conditioned to high prices, there is no need to export and little incentive, therefore, to develop better-value wines. Price aside, the finest Swiss whites can be delightful, and the best reds are getting deeper and more velvety by the vintage.

SWITZERLAND

*Switzerland is divided into three basic areas: French-speaking, German-speaking, and Italian-speaking. Some of the wine-producing cantons cross these "international" boundaries and possess alternative names, with most vineyards concentrated around the country's lakes and rivers.*

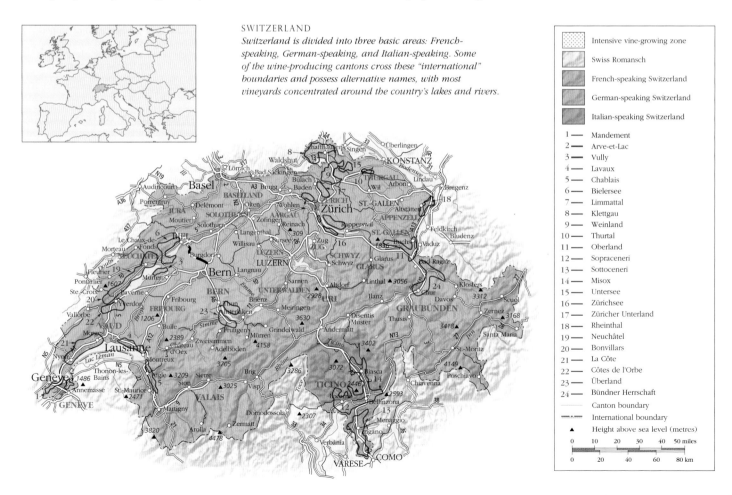

Intensive vine-growing zone

Swiss Romansch

French-speaking Switzerland

German-speaking Switzerland

Italian-speaking Switzerland

1 — Mandement
2 — Arve-et-Lac
3 — Vully
4 — Lavaux
5 — Chablais
6 — Bielersee
7 — Limmattal
8 — Klettgau
9 — Weinland
10 — Thurtal
11 — Oberland
12 — Sopraceneri
13 — Sottoceneri
14 — Misox
15 — Untersee
16 — Zürichsee
17 — Züricher Unterland
18 — Rheinthal
19 — Neuchâtel
20 — Bonvillars
21 — La Côte
22 — Côtes de l'Orbe
23 — Überland
24 — Bündner Herrschaft
        Canton boundary
        International boundary
▲       Height above sea level (metres)

0    10    20    30    40   50 miles
0    20    40    60    80 km

## FACTORS AFFECTING TASTE AND QUALITY

### ⊕ LOCATION
Situated between the south of Germany, north of Italy, and the central-east French border.

### CLIMATE
Continental Alpine conditions prevail, with local variations due to altitude, the tempering influence of lakes, and the sheltering effects of the various mountain ranges. An Alpine wind called the Foehn raises, rather than lowers, temperatures in some valleys. Rainfall is relatively low, and a number of areas, such as the Valais in the south, are very dry indeed. Spring frosts are a perennial threat in most areas.

### ASPECT
Vines are grown in areas ranging from valley floors and lake shores to the steep Alpine foothill sites, which have an average altitude of 2,460 feet (750 meters), although just south of Visp, they reach nearly 3,940 feet (1,200 meters) and are reputedly the highest vineyards in Europe. The best sites are found on south-facing slopes, which maximize exposure to sun, and where the incline is too steep to encourage high yields.

### SOIL
Mostly a glacial moraine (scree) of decomposed slate and schist, often with limestone over sedimented bedrock of limestone, clay, and sand. In the Vaud, Dézaley is famous for its "pudding stones," Chablais has limestone and marl, and Ollon and Bex both benefit from gypsum deposits.

### VITICULTURE AND VINIFICATION
Terracing is required on the steeper sites, and so too is irrigation (with mountain water) in dry areas such as the Valais. Most vineyard work is labor-intensive, except in a few more gently sloping vineyards such as those around Lake Geneva (Lac Léman), where mechanical harvesting is practical. Careful vinification produces remarkably high yields. The last three decades have seen a growth in the production of red wine in what is generally a white-wine-dominated region.

### GRAPE VARIETIES
Aligoté, Amigne, Ancellotta, Bacchus, Bonarda, Bondola, Cabernet Franc, Cabernet Sauvignon, Chardonnay, Charmont, Chasselas (*syn.* Dorin, Fendant, Gutedel, Perlan), Chenin Blanc, Completer, Cornalin (*syn.* Landroter), Diolinoir, Doral, Elbling (*syn.* Räuschling), Freisa, Freishamer (*syn.* Freiburger), Gamaret, Gamay, Gewürztraminer (*syn.* Païen), Gouais (*syn.* Gwäss), Himbertscha, Humagne Blanc, Humagne Rouge, Kerner, Lafnetscha (possibly the same variety as Completer), Malbec, Marsanne (*syn.* Ermitage), Merlot, Müller-Thurgau (*syn.* Riesling x Sylvaner), Muscat à Petits Grains, Petite Arvine, Pinot Blanc, Pinot Gris (*syn.* Malvoisie, Ruländer), Pinot Noir (*syn.* Blauburgunder, Clevner), Rèze, Riesling, Sauvignon Blanc, Seibel (*syn.* Plantet), Sémillon, Seyval Blanc, Sylvaner (*syn.* Silvaner), Syrah, Traminer (*syn.* Heida, Païn, Savagnin).

---

# THE APPELLATIONS OF
# SWITZERLAND

**Note** Under the federal appellation system, all cantons have the right to their own appellation and each winemaking village within each canton can register its own appellation. Geneva was the first canton to comply in 1988, followed by Valais in 1991, Neuchâtel in 1993, and Vaud in 1995. Along with these village appellations, each canton may also designate generic district and stylistic appellations, the number of which is increasing all the time.

## FRENCH-SPEAKING SWITZERLAND

**Cantons** *Fribourg, Gea, Jura, Neuchâtel, Valais, Vaud*

**District appellations** *Vully* (part in Fribourg, part in Neuchâtel); *Arve-et-Lac, Arve-et-Rhône, Mandement* (Geneva); *Bonvillars, Chablais, La Côte, Côtes de l'Orbe, Lavaux* (Vaud)

French-speaking Switzerland represents only 16 percent of the country by area, yet manages to boast more than 80 percent of its vineyards. Two-thirds of the wines are white, with Chasselas accounting for 90 percent, while the Pinot Noir and Gamay together represent 99 percent of the black grapes planted. Valais is the longest-established, most famous, and by far the most intensively cultivated of Switzerland's cantons, with vineyards stretching along 30 miles (50 kilometers) of the Rhône, from Lac Léman (Lake Geneva) to Brig (in the German-speaking sector). The Valais canton accounts for more than one-third of the country's wines, and even its lowliest wine villages are at least as good as the best villages of other Swiss cantons. The Vaud canton encompasses almost one-quarter of Switzerland's vineyards, which makes it the second most intensively cultivated canton in the country. The village of Salgesch is a fast-rising star for red wines—everything from elegant Pinot Noir to muscular Syrah.

☑ **Villages** *Auvernier, Cortaillod* (Neuchâtel)
• *Salgesch* • *St.-Léonard, Vétroz* (Valais)
• *Calamin* • *Dézaley* (Vaud)

**Growers** *Adrian Mathier • Alain Gerber, Albert Mathier & Söhne • Alphonse Orsat • André Ruedin • Antoine et Christophe Bétrisey • Cave de Champ de Clos • Cave de la Madelaine/André Fontannaz • Cave Emery • Cave Saint-Pierre • Caves Cidis • Caves de Riondaz • Caves du Château d'Auvernier • Caves Fernand Cina • Chanton • Charles Bonvin • Charles Favre • Château d'Allaman • Château de Vaumarcus • Château de Vinzel • Château Lichten • Château Maison Blanche • Christine & Stéphanie Delarze-Baud • Claudy Clavien • Clos de la George • C. V. Bonvillars • Denis Mercier • Didier Joris • Domaine de la Lance • Domaine E. de Montmollin Fils • Domaine de Riencourt • Domaine des Abeilles d'Or • Domaine des Graves • Domaine des Muses • Domaine du Martheray • Domaine du Mont d'Or • Domaine Saint-Raphaël • Dominique Passaquay • Dubuis et Rudaz • François et Dominique Giroud • Frédéric Dumoulin • Gérald Besse • Gérard Pinget • Germanier-Balavaud • Gilles & Joell Cina • Hammel • Henri Badoux • J. & P. Testuz • Jean-René Germaner • Jean-Michel Novelle • Jean-Pierre Walther • Jean-Yves Crettenand • Kuntzer & Fils • Louis Bovard • Louis Vuignier • Madeleine et Jean-Yves Mabillard-Fuchs • Marie-Thérèse Chappaz • Maurice Dupraz • Maurice Gay • Maurice Zufferey • Pierre-Alain Meylan • Philippe Rossier • Raphaël Vergère • René Favre • Robert Isoz • Roger Burgdorfer • Romain Papilloud • Rouvinez • Stéphane Clavien • Vincent Favre*

## GERMAN-SPEAKING SWITZERLAND

**Cantons** *Aargau, Basel, Bern, Graubünden* (part), *St.-Gallen, Schwyz, Schaffhausen, Thurgau*

**District appellations** *Bielersee, Uberland* (Bern); *Bündner Herrschaft* (Graubünden); *Oberland,* *Rheinthal* (St.-Gallen); *Klettgau* (Schaffhausen); *Thurtal, Untersee* (Thurgau); *Flaachtal, Limmattal, Rafzerfelder, Züricher Unterland, Weinland* (Zürich)

By far the largest of the three cultural divisions, German-speaking Switzerland (eastern Switzerland) covers almost two-thirds of the country, yet encompasses only one-sixth of its total viticultural area. Aargau is best known for its red wines, but also produces off-dry, light, fragrant white wines of low alcohol content. Basel is a producer of white wine only. Although some rather thin and mean red wines are produced in Bern, the majority of grapes grown are white and produce wines that are fragrant and lively, with refreshing acidity. In Graubünden vineyards on the upper reaches of the Rhine, the Pinot Noir ripens well and provides wines made from it with comparatively good color and body. Saint-Gallen also encompasses the upper reaches of the Rhine and produces mostly red wine. The southern fringes of Graubünden fall within the Italian-speaking sector of Switzerland, where the canton is referred to locally as Grigioni. The vines of Schaffhausen grow within sight of the famous falls of the Rhine. Thurgau is, of course, home of the famous Dr. Müller, who left his mark on world viticulture with his prolific Müller-Thurgau cross, and inevitably the grape grows there, although more than 50 percent of the vines are Pinot Noir and the fruity wine that grape produces is far superior. Zürich is the most important canton in German-speaking Switzerland, but it produces some of the most expensive, least impressive wines in the entire country, although Pinot Noir grown on sheltered slopes with a good exposure to the sun can produce attractive fruity wines.

☑ **Villages** *Brestenberger • Goldwand • Netteler* (Aargau) • *Schafis* (Bern) • *Fläsch, Jenins, Maenfeld • Malans* (Graubünden) • *Leutschen* (Schwyz)

• *Hallau* • *Schaffhausen* (Schaffhausen)
**Growers** *Adelheid von Randenburg* •
*Adolf Boner* • *Daniel & Martha Gantenbein*
• *Georg & Ruth Fromm* • *Christian*
*Hermann* • *Graaf von Spiegelberg* •
*Hans Schlatter* • *Schlossgut Bachtobel/*
*Hans Ulrich Kesselring* • *Peter & Rosi*
*Hermann* • *Peter Graf, Peter Wegelin* •
*Urs Pircher Stadtberg* • *Weingut am*
*Worrenberg* • *Weingut Picher*

## ITALIAN-SPEAKING SWITZERLAND

**Cantons** *Ticino, Grigioni* (part)
**District appellations** *Misox* (Grigioni);
*Sopraceneri, Sottoceneri* (Ticino)

Italian-speaking Switzerland consists of the cantons of Ticino (also known as Tessin) and the southern fringes of Graubünden (known in Italian as Grigioni) and more than 80 percent of the vineyards are planted with the Merlot grape variety. Merlot del Ticino is consistently one of the best wines produced in Switzerland. Labor costs are nowhere near as high as they are in the rest of the country, which also makes Merlot del Ticino the least expensive of Switzerland's finest wines.

✓ **Village** *Misox* (Grigioni)
**Growers** *Adriano Kaufmann,*
*Carlo Tamborini* • *Christian Zündel*
• *Huber Vini* • *Johanniterkeller* • *Luigi*
*Zanini* • *Tamborini* • *Werner Stucky*

# THE WINE STYLES OF
# SWITZERLAND

## AMIGNE

**WHITE** Old Valais variety mostly grown at Vétroz, the Amigne usually makes a full, rustic, smooth, dry white, although Germanier-Balavaud makes a sweet, luscious, late-harvest style.

🍂 1–2 years

🏆 *Cave de la Madelaine/André Fontannaz*
• *Germanier-Balavaud* (Mitis)

## ARVINE

**WHITE** Another old Valais variety that makes an even richer, dry white, with a distinctive grapefruit character and good acidity. The Petite Arvine (to distinguish it from the lesser-quality Grosse Arvine) adapts well to late-harvest styles and is highly regarded by Swiss wine lovers in both dry and sweet styles.

🍂 1–3 years

🏆 *François et Dominique Giroud* • *Jean-Yves Crettenand* • *René Favre*

## BONDOLA

**RED** An indigenous grape producing rustic reds on its own, Bondola is at its best in a wine called Nostrano, in which it is blended with Bonarda, Freisa, and other local varieties.

## BONVILLARS

**WHITE** Restricted to Chasselas grown around Lac de Neuchâtel in the villages of Côtes de l'Orbe and Vully, Bonvillars is lighter and more delicate and lively than Vaud wines of this variety grown farther south.

🏆 *C. V. Bonvillars* (Vin des Croisés)

## CABERNET SAUVIGNON

**RED** A relatively new variety that does well in the Chablais district and Ticino, both pure and blended.

🍂 2–6 years

🏆 *Christine & Stéphanie Delarze-Baud* •
*Pierre-Alain Meylan*

## CHARDONNAY

**WHITE** Just what the world needs, another Chardonnay, and at Swiss prices! However, the very best are worth a try.

🍂 1–4 years

🏆 *Caves Cidis* • *Gilles & Joell Cina* • *Johanniter-keller* • *Kuntzer & Fils* • *Peter Graf*

## CHASSELAS

**WHITE** Called Fendant in the Valais, Dorin in the Vaud, and Perlan in Geneva, this is the most important Swiss grape variety and can be nicely flavored, often having a charming *pétillance*. When grown on light, sandy soils it may have a lime-tree blossom aroma. The grape is sensitive to soil, with different characteristics depending on whether the soil is limestone, flint, gypsum, marl, schist, or whatever. Although it is possible to find relatively full, potentially long-lived wines from this variety, it is a wine best enjoyed young.

🍂 1–3 years

🏆 *Henri Badoux* (Cuvée Prestige) •
*Louis Bovard*

## CLASSIC RED BLEND

**RED** Although Ticino grows Switzerland's best Merlot and up-and-coming Cabernet Sauvignon, it also makes the best Bordeaux-style blends.

🍂 3–10 years

🏆 *Huber Vini* (Montagna Magica)

## COMPLETER

**WHITE** The Completer is rare grape variety of ancient origin that makes a fascinating, rich, *Auslese*-style of wine from scattered plots found in Graubünden.

🍂 3–7 years

🏆 *Adolf Boner* • *Peter & Rosi Hermann*

## CORNALIN

**RED** Most vines of this indigenous Swiss variety are very old, and restricted to the Valais, where they make dark, powerful red wines that are rich and concentrated, with a full, spicy complexity.

🍂 3–7 years

🏆 *Denis Mercier* • *Maurice Zufferey*

## DÔLE

**RED** A light red comprised of at least 50 percent Pinot Noir plus up to 50 percent Gamay, Dôle is the Swiss (Valais) equivalent of Burgundy's Passetoutgrains.

🍂 1–3 years

🏆 *Dubuis et Rudaz*

## DÔLE BLANCHE

**WHITE** The *blanc de noirs* version is popular, but does not carry its own appellation.

## ERMITAGE

**WHITE** A synonym for the Marsanne used in the Valais, where it makes a delicately rich, dry white wine that is often aged too long in bottle by its aficionados.

🍂 1–4 years

🏆 *Adrian Mathier* • *Marie-Thérèse Chappaz*

## FENDANT

**WHITE** This Chasselas synonym is used in the Valais, where it produces a fleshy-styled, dry white wine, the best of which can have a flinty, lime-tree-blossom aroma and a crisp, minerality of fruit. Ideal with cheese fondue.

🍂 1–3 years

🏆 *Adrian Mathier* • *Dubuis et Rudaz* • *Frédéric Dumoulin* (L'Orpailleur) • *Raphaël Vergère*

## GAMAY

**RED** Until recently, this Beaujolais grape rarely made red wines of distinction in its pure varietal form, and was much more successful when blended with Pinot Noir (*see* Dôle).

🍂 1–3 years

🏆 *Gérald Besse* • *Madeleine et Jean-Yves Mabillard-Fuchs*

## GEWÜRZTRAMINER

**WHITE** Rarely encountered.

🍂 1–5 years

🏆 *Dominique Passaquay* (Passerillé) •
*Maurice Dupraz*

## HEIDA

**WHITE** Fresh, lightly aromatic, dry and off-dry wine made from the Savagnin (Traminer) grape.

🍂 1–2 years

🏆 *Chanton*

## HUMAGNE BLANC

**WHITE** The Humagne Blanc is a wine with a relatively high iron content, which could be the reason it used to be given to babies, although it is probable that the dear little things cried when allowed to suck on Humagne Blanc. It has a green bean or capsicum aroma, hints of exotic fruit on the palate, and a touch of bitterness on the finish.

## HUMAGNE ROUGE

**RED** An old Valais variety, this dark-skinned grape hails from Italy's Valle d'Aosta and makes big, rich, rustic reds that traditionally go well with feathered game.

🍷— 1–4 years

🏆 *Jean-René Germaner*

## JOHANNISBERG

**WHITE** This is not the Johannisberg Riesling, but the official synonym for Sylvaner in the Valais, where it is supposedly musky, although they are usually sappy and savory with some sweetness.

🍷— Upon purchase

🏆 *Adrian Mathier • Albert Mathier & Söhne • Claudy Clavien • Domaine du Mont d'Or • François et Dominique Giroud*

## LA CÔTE

**RED & WHITE** Grown exclusively at La Côte (which encompasses the villages of Aubonne, Begnins, Bursinel, Coteau de Vincy, Féchy, Luins, Mont-sur-Rolle, Morges, Nyon, Perroy, and Vinze, as well as La Côte itself), where the Chasselas grape is at its most floral and aromatic, and fruity reds are often blended from two or more varieties, including Gamay, Gamaret, and Garanoir.

🍷— 1–2 years

🏆 *Caves Cidis (Gamaret/Garanoir/Gamay, Garanoir) • Philippe Rossier (Aubonne Merlot)*

## LAVAUX

**WHITE** Grown exclusively at Lavaux (which encompasses the villages of Calamin, Chardonne, Dézaley, Epesses, Lutry, Saint-Saphorin, Vevey-Montreux, and Villette, as well as Lavaux itself), the Chasselas is at its softest yet fullest.

🍷— 1–2 years

## MERLOT DEL TICINO

**RED** The Merlot grape accounts for more than 80 percent of the vines planted in Italian-speaking Switzerland, where it produces red wines that range from young and light-bodied to fuller, better-colored wines that have a nice varietal perfume and are often aged in *barriques*. The VITI classification on a bottle of Merlot del Ticino used to be seen as a guarantee of superior quality, but now merely indicates the wine has had one year's aging before being bottled.

🍷— 2–4 years (lighter styles), 3–10 years (*barrique* wines)

🏆 *Adriano Kaufmann • Carlo Tamborini • Christian Zündel • Huber Vini • Luigi Zanini • Werner Stucky*

## MÜLLER-THURGAU

**WHITE** This most prolific (supposedly) *Riesling\Sylvaner* cross was created in 1882 by Dr. Hermann Müller, who hailed from the canton of Thurgau, hence the name, which makes it rather ironic that the Swiss should call this grape *Riesling x Sylvaner* rather than by the name that honors its Swiss origins! However, the mild, grapey wine this variety produces even in its home canton is no more exciting than it is elsewhere, although relatively superior examples are produced in Aargau.

🍷— 1–2 years

🏆 *Schlossgut Bachtobel/Hans Ulrich Kesselring*

## MUSCAT

**WHITE** The Muscat à Petits Grains is traditionally grown in the Valais, in small quantities. It makes wines of very light body, with the grape's unmistakable varietal flowery aroma. Some interesting late-harvest styles are beginning to emerge.

🍷— 2–4 years

🏆 *Cave Emery (Grains Nobles de la Saint Nicolas—Séduction) • Domaine des Muses • Stéphane Clavien (Coteaux de Sierre)*

## NOSTRANO

**RED** This used to be an inexpensive blend of *vin ordinaire* quality, produced from grapes that failed to reach appellation standard, but now it has its own official classification and the quality has certainly improved. Nostrano means "our" and literally refers to the local varieties used, as opposed to American hybrids.

## OEIL DE PERDRIX

**ROSÉ** Oeil de Perdrix, which literally means "partridge eye," is a French term for pale, dry rosé wines made from free-run Pinot Noir.

🍷— Upon purchase

🏆 *Alain Gerber • Cave de Champ de Clos*

## PERLAN

**WHITE** In the canton of Geneva the Chasselas makes a slightly spritzy flowery wine that is sold as Perlan. Geneva must be mentioned on the label, or a village name: L'Allondon, Bardonnex, Dardagny, Jussy, Lully, Peissy, Russin, or Satigny.

## PINOT BLANC

**WHITE** Recently planted, fashionable variety, but few wines stand out.

🍷— 1–3 years

🏆 *Domaine des Abeilles d'Or • Domaine Saint-Raphaël*

## PINOT GRIS

**WHITE** This famous Alsace grape is becoming quite fashionable in Switzerland, where it makes more of a Pinot Grigio style, with some very successful *vendange tardive* emerging.

🍷— 1–3 years

🏆 *Cave Saint-Pierre • Caves du Château d'Auvernier (Vendange Tardive) • Domaine E. de Montmollin Fils (Vendange Tardive) • Schlossgut Bachtobel/Hans Ulrich Kesselring • Urs Pircher Stadtberg (Egfisauer Stadtberger)*

## PINOT NOIR

**RED** In a country like Switzerland, which adores Burgundy, it is not surprising that top producers make some of Switzerland's most serious wines with this grape variety—well colored, velvety, with soft, cherry fruit and a touch of oak. Although this wine is sold as Blauburgunder in German-speaking Switzerland, and Pinot Nero in Italian-speaking Switzerland, there are moves toward harmonizing under the internationally recognizable Pinot Noir name.

🍷— 3–6 years (up to 10 years in exceptional cases)

🏆 *Agriloro • Caves Fernand Cina • Christian Hermann • Daniel & Martha Gantenbein • Georg & Ruth Fromm • Peter Wegelin • Weingut am Worrenberg*

## RÄUSCHLING

**WHITE** This rarely seen variety is in decline and is now found only along the shore of Lake Zurich, where it is appreciated for its very fresh scents and fine acidity.

🍷— Upon purchase

🏆 *Weingut Picher*

## RIESLING

**WHITE** Aside from exceptional botrytized wines, Swiss Riesling does not have the quality or varietal intensity of Germany or Austria.

## SALVAGNIN

**WHITE** A light, supple red-wine blend of Pinot Noir and Gamay, this is the Vaud's equivalent of the more famous Dôle.

🍷— 1–3 years

🏆 *Jean-Pierre Walther*

## SÜSSDRUCK

**ROSÉ** A soft, fresh, dry rosé produced in eastern Switzerland from free-run Pinot Noir.

## SYRAH

**RED** This grape is at home in the heat and exposure of the northern Côtes du Rhône, and in Valais the Rhône River is as northerly as it gets. Peppery black fruits distinguish these fast-improving, increasingly fashionable wines.

🍷— 3–10 years

🏆 *Antoine et Christophe Bétrisey • Caves Fernand Cina • Domaine des Graves • Dubuis et Rudaz • François et Dominique Giroud • J. & P. Testuz (Les Oenocrates) • Jean-René Germaner • Roger Burgdorfer (Diable) • Romain Papilloud*

## VIN DE PAIN

**WHITE** A fresh, gently aromatic, dry white wine made from the Traminer in the Valais.

## VIN DU GLACIER

### Valais

Although Switzerland's equivalent of Germany's Eiswein tends to be oxidative, this rare product does have its enthusiastic followers.

## CERTIFIED ORGANIC PRODUCERS

**Biodynamic**
Ca di Ciser (Mergoscia)
Domaine de Beaudon (Fully)
Liesch-Hiestand (Malans)

# The WINES of
# NORTHWESTERN EUROPE

IF ENGLISH WINE COMES AS A SURPRISE TO SOME,
then the thought of commercial vineyards in
Belgium, the Netherlands, and even on a
Danish island north of Poland will beggar
belief—yet they exist. Their scope will
always be limited because of the combination
of northerly latitude and the uncertain climatic
effect of the northern Atlantic. However,
sparkling wines produced by Nyetimber and
Ridgeview demonstrate that world-class quality
can be achieved in England. The success
enjoyed by these producers has encouraged
the English wine industry to focus its efforts
on perfecting sparkling wines, and other
countries in northwestern Europe would be
well advised to follow this lead.

VINEYARDS IN THE WINTER, SURREY, BRITISH ISLES
*While winters can sometimes be cold, vineyards in
southeastern England generally enjoy a relatively mild climate
and soil types that range from clay to chalk.*

# THE BRITISH ISLES

*The future of English wine literally is sparkling. Forget the Müller-Thurgau, Seyval Blanc, and other odd-sounding French hybrids and German crosses that have provided local consumers with mostly forgettable wines. Nyetimber and Ridgeview are world-class sparkling wine producers, and as such represent a blueprint for all quality-conscious English and Welsh winemakers.*

AND NOW WE HAVE CHAMPAGNE PRODUCERS planting vineyards in this country (for English sparkling wine, of course, not Champagne!), and one of the world's two leading sparkling-wine consultants exclusively contracted to a former Formula 1 world-champion racecar driver, who is determined to produce the UK's first iconic sparkling wine. Any English or Welsh vineyard owners who do not have the courage to replace their hybrids and crosses with classic grape varieties and follow the fizz trailblazers will become marginalized. Although this country's winemaking efforts are destined to remain a cottage industry, this is not because England and Wales lack serious or successful producers; it is due to two simple facts: British vineyards are a very recent phenomenon, and Great Britain is a densely populated island. It will always be difficult to find suitable land for vineyards; therefore, the potential growth of English and Welsh wine* is severely limited. Furthermore, if any *grand cru* sites ever existed, they would be under concrete or asphalt today. It is a bit like starting up the French wine industry from scratch in a country that is half the size, twice as densely populated, and burdened with a severely unfavorable climate.

## ANCIENT BRITONS
Winemaking in Britain is not new, but dates back to AD 43, when every important villa had a garden of vines. It was not until 1995, however, when a 20-acre (8-hectare) Roman vineyard was excavated at Wollaston in Northamptonshire, that the true scale of this early viticulture was realized. The Domesday Book reveals the existence of some 40 vineyards of significance during the reign of William the

*\*British wine is neither British, nor wine made from fresh grapes, let alone fresh grapes grown in British vineyards: it is a legal misnomer for wines made from reconstituted grape concentrate sourced from anywhere in the world.*

THE DELL ON DENBIES, DORKING, SURREY
*Set amid Surrey countryside, Denbies Estate is the largest winery in Great Britain, surrounded by more than 107 hectares (265 acres) of vineyards.*

## FACTORS AFFECTING TASTE AND QUALITY

### LOCATION
Most of the vineyards are located in England and Wales, south of a line drawn through Birmingham and the Wash.

### CLIMATE
Great Britain is at the northerly extreme of climates suitable for the vine, but the warm Gulf Stream tempers the weather sufficiently to make viticulture possible. Rainfall is relatively high and conditions vary greatly from year to year, making harvests somewhat unreliable. High winds can be a problem, but winter frosts are less troublesome than in many wine regions.

### ASPECT
Vines are planted on all types of land, but the best sites are usually sheltered, south-facing slopes with the consequent microclimate advantages that can be crucial for wine production in this marginal viticultural region.

### SOIL
Vines are grown on a wide variety of different soils ranging from granite through limestone, chalk, and gravel to clay.

### VITICULTURE AND VINIFICATION
The commonly encountered high-trained vine systems indicate that many vineyards are poorly sited in frost-prone areas. Vigor is also a problem, as sap bypasses the fruit to produce an excessively luxuriant canopy of leaves, resulting in unnecessarily small grape clusters, delayed ripening, and overly herbaceous flavors. This problem is exacerbated by the use of rootstocks that actually promote vigor, but the New World influence that has already had its effect on English winemaking techniques will hopefully encourage the introduction of low-vigor rootstock. Although the British climate is least favorable for growing black grapes, an increasing amount of red and rosé has been produced since the early 1990s, but bottle-fermented sparkling wine is clearly the most up-and-coming of all the English wine styles.

### GRAPE VARIETIES
**Primary varieties:** Bacchus, Chardonnay, Dornfelder, Pinot Noir, Regent, Rondo, Seyval Blanc
**Secondary varieties:** Auxerrois, Blauberger, Blauer Portugieser, Cabernet Sauvignon, Cascade, Chasselas, Dunkelfelder, Ehrenfelser, Faberebe (*syn* Faber), Findling, Gagarin Blue, Gamay, Gewürztraminer, Gutenborner, Huxelrebe, Kanzler, Kerner, Kernling, Léon Millot, Madeleine Angevine, Müller-Thurgau, Optima, Ortega, Perle, Pinot Blanc, Pinot Gris, Pinot Meunier, Regner, Reichensteiner, Riesling, Sauvignon Blanc, Scheurebe, Schönburger, Seibel, Siegerrebe, Triomphe d'Alsace, Wrotham Pinot, Würzer, Zweigeltrebe

Conqueror; by medieval times the number had risen to 300, most of which were run by monks. The Black Death took its toll in the mid-14th century and, almost 200 years later, the dissolution of the monasteries virtually brought an end to English winemaking. Apart from a couple of vineyards in the mid-18th century and two more in the late 19th century, winemaking on a commercial scale was almost nonexistent until Hambledon was established in 1951. English vineyards began to boom in the late 1960s and peaked in the early 1970s. Since then almost 500 have been planted, although just over 300 survive today, and only 109 of these have their own winery.

Few vineyards in the UK can reasonably expect more than an average of 1,440 degree-days Fahrenheit (800 degree-days Celsius)—well below the accepted winemaking minimum of 1,800 degree-days Fahrenheit (1,000 degree-days Celsius), so even the best-situated vineyards risked failure when first established. Some vineyards were unsuccessful, but those in existence today have proved the theoretical conditions to be just that—theoretical.

## FUTURE TRENDS
Although English wine will remain forever a cottage industry, this does not mean it cannot earn a reputation for quality. High duty rates do mean, however, that it is difficult for the smallest vineyards, which have the highest overheads, to establish sales of a new product. Initially, this problem was overcome by contract winemaking, with virtually all the oldest and largest vineyards

providing a service. Since the early 1990s, however, cooperative groups have formed to produce large volumes of relatively inexpensive wines by blending wines from their members, all of whom also make and market their own single-vineyard products.

The next step in the development of English wine is to rid the country of most of its crosses and hybrids. The reason these funny grapes with funny names must go is because they have a negative impact on most serious wine consumers. Wine drinkers are attracted to classic varieties and even willing to dabble with more obscure *vinifera* grapes, particularly when indigenous to the wine-producing area of origin, but they either do not understand hybrids or find them a turnoff. As for German crosses, how can producers expect to establish an English or Welsh wine reputation with names like Reichensteiner or Siegerrebe?

## HERE COMES THE CAVALRY!

It took two Americans, Stuart and Sandy Moss, the original owners of Nyetimber, to shake the English out of their lethargy. The pioneering Mosses had a crazy ambition to make a top-quality English fizz from classic Champagne varieties, but when they sought so-called expert advice, they were told that Chardonnay would not ripen and Pinot Noir would just rot. Believing most English experts might be prejudiced by their training (most went to Guisenheim, where many of the crosses occupying most English vineyards originated), they did something nobody had bothered to do: they asked the *champenois* for help. They arrived, examined the soil, and advised what clones should be planted and how they should be trained. They even helped make the wine. Consequently, the Mosses created this country's first world-class wine, kick-started the English sparkling-wine industry, and, in the process, demonstrated that bottle-fermented sparkling wine is the only way forward for all English and Welsh vineyards with any ambition of a reputation. They have since retired, but Nyetimber continued to be the UK's flagship wine, first under songwriter Andy Hill and more recently Dutchman Eric Hereema. Mike Roberts at Ridgeview was the first to

snap at Nyetimber's heels with his aptly named Cuvée Merret (*see* p175). Bob Lindo's multi-award-winning Camel Valley is next in line, but Will Davenport's Limney Brut and Peter Hall's Breaky Bottom are also serious contenders. Didier Whitaker of Champagne Pierson Whitaker planted vines on the Hampshire Downs in 2005; and in 2006, wine writer Steven Spurrier announced that he was discussing a possible joint venture with Champagne Duval-Leroy to develop his wife's Bride Valley farm in Dorset for English sparkling-wine production. Meanwhile, Michel Salgue was signed up by Jody Scheckter, the former world-champion racing-car driver, to oversee the planting of an exclusively sparkling-wine vineyard and state-of-the-art winery at Scheckter's Laverstoke Park in Hampshire (billed as "The Largest Smallholding in the World"). Salgue established Roederer Estate in California's Anderson Valley and is widely recognized as having produced the first great sparkling wine outside of Champagne in 1987. His input in the UK is likely to be seminal.

---

THE WINE REGIONS OF
# THE BRITISH ISLES

Regional characteristics have not yet been established in the wine regions of the British Isles, and I am not sure that they ever will be, but it is very difficult to build up a proper spatial awareness of where English vineyards are located without first breaking them down into a small number of workable areas.

The following regions are all officially recognized by the United Kingdom Vineyard Association, or UKVA (which took over from the English Vineyard Association in 1996) and it would help if more vineyard owners were to utilize these regions on their labels in addition to a more specific location. Until they do, British consumers will be less informed about their own wines than they are about those of France or Australia.

### EAST ANGLIA

**Bedfordshire, Cambridgeshire, Essex, Hertfordshire, Norfolk, Suffolk**

The flattest and most exposed of all the regions, East Anglia is subject to bitterly cold easterly and northeasterly winds, but has fertile soils, which can encourage significantly higher yields than in some areas of England. Quite often this has the effect of trading off quality for an attempt to preserve consistency.

### MERCIA

**Cheshire, Derbyshire, Lancashire, Leicestershire, Lincolnshire, Northamptonshire, Nottinghamshire, Rutland, Shropshire, Staffordshire, Warwickshire, West Midlands, West Yorkshire**

This is a very large and naturally diverse region, with vineyards planted both on flat ground and slopes, with soils ranging from light sand to heavy clay. About the only common factor is Madeleine Angevine, which seems to be the most reliable variety. At the time of writing, another ten vineyards have been planted, but are not yet in production.

### SOUTHEAST

**East and West Sussex, Kent, Surrey**

This region covers the "Garden of England," which probably says it all. It is not as wet as the West Country, and milder than East Anglia, but not as warm as Thames and Chiltern. Soils range from clay to chalk. The latter forms the same basin that creates the chalk cliffs at Dover and goes under the Channel to rise in Champagne.

### SOUTHWEST

**Bristol, Cornwall, Devon, Gloucestershire, Herefordshire, Isles of Scilly, Republic of Ireland, Somerset, South Wales, Worcestershire**

Geographically the largest region, with vineyards as far apart as Cornwall, where the Gulf Stream has its greatest effect, but there is also a tendency to wet weather, and North Wales, which takes the brunt of weather systems from the Atlantic. Although prevailing westerly winds make conditions difficult in the west of Cornwall and Wales, the region is generally milder than the east coast. The topography of the region ranges from mountainous to flat, with some areas below sea level. Soils vary tremendously from limestone through shale, clay, and peat to granite.

### THAMES AND CHILTERN

**Berkshire, Buckinghamshire, Oxfordshire**

This large area is the warmest of all the regions, and most vineyards are located on slopes of moisture-retaining soils. There are also many aquifers in the area, which prevent stress during drought conditions.

### WESSEX

**Channel Islands, Dorset, Hampshire, Isle of Wight, Wiltshire**

The major factor linking these counties together is the interesting pattern of isotherms that form south of the Isle of Wight and provide a more temperate climate than the surrounding regions.

THE WINE PRODUCERS OF
# THE BRITISH ISLES

## 1 ADGESTONE
**Adgestone, Isle of Wight (Wessex)**

Estate-bottled wines from a south-facing chalk slope that was first planted in 1962.

## 2 ASTLEY
**Stourport on Severn, Worcestershire (Southwest)**
★ 🅥

An award-winning vineyard established in 1979 by Jonty Daniels and Janet Baldwin.

🖊 *Classic white blend* (Dry Reserve) • *Late Harvest*

## 3 BEARSTED
**Beardsted, Kent (Southeast)**

Small boutique winery with 4 acres planted in the late 1980s by former research chemist John Gibson.

🖊 *Sparkling* (Brut Vintage)

## 4 BEAULIEU
**Nr Brockenhurst, Hampshire (Wessex)**

This enthusiastic, aristocratic venture has been running since 1958.

## 5 BEECHES HILL
**Upton Bishop, Herefordshire (Southwest)**

Established in 1991, Beeches Hill grows Madeleine Angevine and Seyval Blanc grapes, but the wines are made by Three Choirs.

## 6 BIDDENDEN
**Biddenden, Kent (Southeast)**
★ 🅥

A former orchard on a gentle south-facing slope in a shallow, sheltered valley, Biddenden is principally known for its Ortega. Wines produced in part or whole from grapes grown elsewhere are sold under the Gribble Bridge label.

🖊 *Ortega* • *Rosé* (Gribble Bridge) • *Sparkling* (Gribble Bridge Vintage)

## 7 BINFIELD
**Wokingham, Berkshire (Thames and Chiltern)**

A dry white wine and a light red are produced here, but the emphasis is on a fizz under the Champion label, which is linked to the Bob Champion Cancer Fund, a charity that receives a percentage of the price of every bottle sold.

## 8 BOOKERS
**Bolney, Sussex (Southeast)**
★ 🅥

The first vines were planted in 1973, but initially the Pratt family sold their grapes, and only started making their own wine in 1983, with red wine unusually accounting for as much as half the output.

🖊 *Classic red blend* (Dark Harvest)

## 9 BOTHY
**Frilford Health, Oxfordshire (Thames and Chiltern)**
★ 🅥

The most successful wine produced by new owners Sian and Richard Liwicki is their Oxford Dry. Although from a typically English hodgepodge of grape varieties, it is a refreshing dry white that anyone partial to Sauvignon Blanc would enjoy.

🖊 *Oxford Dry*

## 10 BOZE DOWN
**Whitchurch-on-Thames, Oxfordshire (Thames and Chiltern)**

Established in 1985 by Dick and Sandra Conn, Boze Down Vineyard lies on the sheltered southern slopes of the Chiltern Hills overlooking the Thames River between Reading and Oxford.

🖊 *Classic white blend* (Skippetts)

## 11 BOW-IN-THE-CLOUD
**Malmesbury, Wiltshire (Wessex)**

Bow-in-the-Cloud vineyard was planted in 1992 and has been producing wine since 1995. Pure varietal wines are sold under the Arkadian label, while blends are sold under the Cloud Nine label.

## 12 BREAKY BOTTOM
**Northtease, Sussex (Southeast)**
★ 🅥

Peter Hall used to release his Seyval-based fizz far too young, but now he is running the risk of holding on to them for too long. The two *cuvées* below are best to buy and drink when Hall offers them at 5–6 years of age.

🖊 *Müller-Thurgau* • *Seyval Blanc* • *Sparkling* (Cuvée Maman Mercier, Cuvée Remy Alexandre)

## 13 CAMEL VALLEY
**Nanstallon, Cornwall (Southwest)**
★ 🅥

Former RAF pilot Bob Lindo gave up the high life for the more down-to-earth task of working the soil on the sunny slopes of the Camel River valley, midway between the Atlantic and Channel coasts. Local celebrity chef Rick Stein so enjoyed eating Lindo's Reichensteiner grapes off the vine that he renamed the variety "Ricksteiner" on his television program. Cornwall Brut is a rather too easy to drink sparkling wine with a potted history of Christopher Merret on the back label.

🖊 *Bacchus* • *Seyval Blanc* • *Pinot Noir* • *Sparkling* (Cornwall Brut)

## 14 CANTERBURY CHOICE
**Ash, Kent (Southeast)**
★ 🅥

The label under which the wines from Barnsole Vineyard are sold.

🖊 *Dry Reserve* • *Pilgrim's Harvest*

## 15 CARR TAYLOR
**Westfield, Sussex (Southeast)**

Established in 1971 by David and Linda Carr Taylor, with Alexander Carr Taylor the second-generation winemaker.

🖊 *Reichensteiner* (Alexis)

## 16 CHATEAU LE CATILLON
**Jersey, Channel Islands (Wessex)**

Chateau le Catillon has been bought by La Mare.

## 17 CHIDDINGSTONE
**Chiddingstone, Kent (Southeast)**

This vineyard was established by the late Dudley Quirk, whose two sons run Chiddingstone today.

## 18 CHILFORD HUNDRED
**Linton, Cambridgeshire (East Anglia)**
★ 🅥

This large vineyard was established in 1972, but it did not produce its first sparkling wine until 1994.

🖊 *Sparkling* (Aluric de Norsehide)

## 19 CHILTERN VALLEY
**Hambledon, Oxfordshire (Thames and Chiltern)**

Also known as Luxters, because owner David Ealand established his winery on the site of Old Luxters pig farm. Has produced some interesting wines in the past, although they have a lower profile these days.

## 20 COACH HOUSE
**Romsey, Hampshire (Wessex)**

This vineyard is owned by Roger Marchbank, who is better known as the chairman of UKVA, and cannot be accused of using his position to promote his wine, as I have never tasted Coach House wine, and seldom heard mention of it!

## 21 COURT LANE
**Alresford, Hampshire (Wessex)**

Stephen Flook must have broken a record when he took 12 years to plant just over one acre of vines.

## 22 DANEBURY
**Stockbridge, Hampshire (Wessex)**

Anne Bishop named her fizz Cossack after the controversial winner of the 1847 Derby.

## 23 DAVENPORT
**Rotherfield, East Sussex & Horsmonden, Kent (Southeast)**
◉ ★ 🅥

Will Davenport is a graduate of Roseworthy College in Australia, and has worked for wineries in Alsace, California, and South Australia before setting up in England in 1990. He has a still wine vineyard at Horsmonden in Kent, but his Rotherfield vineyard is primarily for sparkling wine. Planted in 1993 with Pinot Noir and Auxerrois, Davenport's Rotherfield vineyard came into production in 1997. His 1999 Limney Brut was brilliant, and the 2000 almost as good, suggesting that Davenport will soon be a third force to reckon with in the establishment of world-class English wine from a dedicated sparkling wine estate, following in the footsteps of Nyetimber and Ridgeview.

🖊 *Limney Brut* • *Limney Fumé* • *Red wine* (Pinot Noir)

## 24 DENBIES WINE ESTATE
**Dorking, Surrey (Southeast)**
★ 🅥

With 265 acres (106 hectares) of vines, Denbies Wine Estate is the largest English vineyard. Its Tesco-looking winery is also designed and equipped to receive tourists by the bus-load; consequently Denbies is also the most visited of English vineyards. Capable of producing award-winning wines, but not consistent throughout the range.

🖊 *Rosé* (Rose Hill)

## 25 EGLANTINE
**Costock, Nottinghamshire (Mercia)**

Readers might think that Tony Skuriat's vineyard is northerly enough, without deliberately freezing his grapes, but this is how he produces his award-winning wine North Star.

🖊 *Dessert wine* (North Star)

## 26 FAWLEY
**Henley-on-Thames, Oxfordshire (Thames and Chiltern)**

Nick and Wendy Sargent are just beginning to establish a reputation for Bacchus.

🖊 *Bacchus*

## 27 GIFFORD'S HALL
**Hartest, Suffolk (East Anglia)**

John and Jeanie Kemp claim to tread their grapes, and they also produce a variety of homemade liqueurs, but Gifford's Hall was up for sale in 2004.

## 28 GREAT STOCKS
**Stock, Essex (East Anglia)**

This vineyard was established between 1993 and 1999 by Brian and Gillian Barnard, who are hoping that Rondo will provide good red wine.

## 29 HALE VALLEY
**Boddington, Buckinghamshire (Thames and Chiltern)**

Sparkling wine has been Antony and Carol Chapman's most successful wine so far.

🖊 *Sparkling* (Brut Vintage)

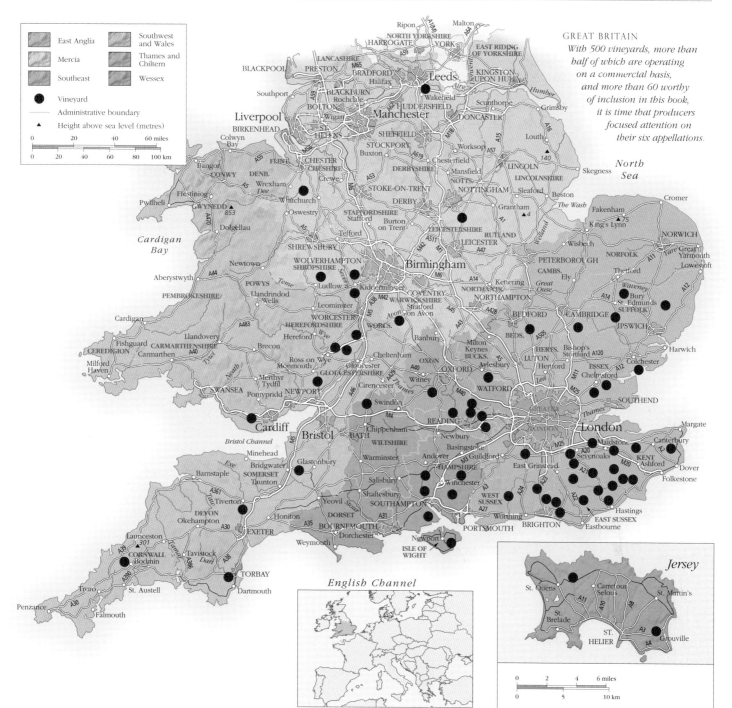

GREAT BRITAIN
*With 500 vineyards, more than
half of which are operating
on a commercial basis,
and more than 60 worthy
of inclusion in this book,
it is time that producers
focused attention on
their six appellations.*

**Legend:**
- East Anglia
- Mercia
- Southeast
- Southwest and Wales
- Thames and Chiltern
- Wessex
- ● Vineyard
- — Administrative boundary
- ▲ Height above sea level (metres)

*English Channel*

*Jersey*

## 30 HALFPENNY GREEN

**Halfpenny Green, Staffordshire (Mercia)**

★ **V**

Just over 22 acres (9 hectares) were planted between 1983 and 1991, then a winery was built in 1994. As with most northerly English vineyards, Madeleine Angevine has proved the most reliable variety.

✓ *Classic white blend* (Penny Black) • *Huxelrebe* • *Madeleine Angevine*

## 31 HEART OF ENGLAND

**Welford-on-Avon, Warwickshire (Mercia)**

★ **V**

David Stanley planted this vineyard in "Shakespeare Country" in 1995

but did not achieve his first commercial harvest until 2000.

✓ *Classic red blend* (Oberon)

## 32 HIDDEN SPRINGS

**Horsham, Sussex (Southeast)**

★ **V**

Although Martyn Doubleday and Chris Cammel make some trophy-winning wines, devotees would kill for Hidden Springs Art Deco labels, even if they put nothing inside the bottles!

✓ *Classic red blend* (Dark Fields) • *Classic white blend* (Decadence) • *Rosé* (Sussex Sunset) • *Sparkling wine* (Vintage Brut)

## 33 LA MARE

**Jersey, Channel Islands (Wessex)**

★ **V**

The Channel Islands' first vineyard and the only one open to visitors, La Mare now also owns Chateau le Catillon. Also produces a Norman-style cider and has installed a small Calvados pot still for apple brandy.

✓ *Classic white blend* (Domaine de La Mare) • *Sparkling wine* (Brut, Lily)

## 34 LAMBERHURST

**Lamberhurst, Kent (Southeast)**

★ **V**

Merged with Chapel Down in 2001 to form English Wines Plc.

✓ *Classic white blend* (Fumé)

## 35 LEVENTHORPE VINEYARD

**Woodlesford, West Yorkshire (Mercia)**

Established by chemist-turned-winemaker George Bowden in 1986, Leventhorpe vineyard is just a stone's throw away from the historic stately home of Temple Newsome. This is the country's most northerly vineyard and it is no mere curiosity, since it crops ripe grapes every year, and has its own winery.

## 36 LLANERCH VINEYARD

**Hensol, Vale of Glamorgan, Wales (Southwest)**

★ **V**

Wines are sold under the Cariad label. The fizz is improving.

✓ *Classic white blend* (Cariad Celtic Dry) • *Sparkling* (Cariad Blush)

### 37 LUDLOW VINEYARD
**Clee St. Margaret, Shropshire (Mercia)**
★ ✓

An up-and-coming, new vineyard, Ludlow might have struck it lucky with 2003 as its inaugural vintage, but it was an impressive start nonetheless. Clee Moonlight is a blend of Madeleine Angevine, Seyval, and Phoenix with a slight hint of oak. Only 200 bottles were made.

✓ *Clee Moonlight*

### 38 MEOPHAM
**Wrotham, Kent (Southeast)**

Part organic production, including an organic medium-sweet Pinot Noir.

### 39 MERSEA
**Mersea Island, Essex (East Anglia)**

On an island 9 miles (15 kilometers) south of Colchester, halfway between West Mersea and East Mersea, this vineyard and winery also boasts a microbrewery.

### 40 MOORLYNCH
**Bridgwater, Somerset (Southwest)**

This vineyard is located on a sunny south-facing hillside that has, surprisingly for England, a somewhat dry microclimate. Owner-winemaker Peter Farmer's most successful wine so far has been his 1996 Vintage Reserve Brut sparkling wine.

### 41 NEW HALL
**Purleigh, Essex (East Anglia)**

Established by the Greenwood family in 1969, this 91-acre (37-hectare) vineyard is one of the oldest and largest English wine producers, and the first to be planted in Essex.

### 42 NEW WAVE WINES
**Tenterden, Kent (Southeast)**
★ ✓

One of the country's four largest wine producers, this company was formed in early 2001, when Chapel Down Wines at Tenterden Vineyard merged with Lamberhurst Vineyard. Also referred to as English Wines Plc, the multi-award-winning New Wave Wines still has the feel of a large and expanding winery that is finding its way, which indeed it is, but the quality and consistency has greatly improved since the merger. Improvements continue under Owen Elias, who was named Winemaker of the Year in 2002 and 2003.

✓ *Curious Grape* (Bacchus, Ortega, Pinot Blanc, Pinot Noir, Schönburger)

### 43 NORTHBROOK SPRINGS
**Bishop Waltham, Hampshire (Wessex)**

Owner-winemaker Brian Cable Young has made some good-value fizz and noble rot dessert wines in the past.

### 44 NYETIMBER
**Pulborough, Sussex (Southeast)**
★ ★

Established in 1988 by American couple Stuart and Sandy Moss, who created the first world-class English sparkling wine before selling Nyetimber to English songwriter Andy Hill. He was as serious about maintaining the same very highest standards as the Mosses, but sold up following the breakdown of his marriage. After three changes of ownership and three changes of winemaker, the latest owner, Eric Heerema, moved swiftly to stabilize production by hiring Cherie Spriggs and Brad Greatrix, a Canadian-born married couple, as the new winemaking team for the UK's flagship sparkling wine. As Hereema's own website states, Nyetimber owes its reputation and awards to the high quality and distinctive fruit characters emanating from its ideal location and unique microclimate. So, whether his expansion of the vineyards from 35 to 360 acres (14 to 105 hectares) by planting outside the original estate is equally wise, only time and the wine in the bottle will tell.

✓ *Entire range*

### 45 PARVA FARM
**Tintern, Monmouthshire, Wales (Southwest)**
★ ✓

Emerging Pinot Noir potential from steep vineyards set within a working farm environment.

✓ *Pinot Noir*

### 46 PENSHURST
**Penshurst, Kent (Southeast)**

First planted in 1972 on a south-facing slope, the first crop was promising, and some excellent wines have been produced here. The picturesque label is charming and very English, except for the hidden kangaroo!

### 47 PLUMPTON COLLEGE
**Plumpton, East Sussex (Southeast)**

The only educational facility in the UK to provide courses in all aspects of wine, Plumpton College also possesses a well-equipped, commercial winery.

### 48 RIDGEVIEW ESTATE
**Ditchling, Sussex (Southeast)**
★ ★ ✓

Owned by Christine and Mike Roberts, this 16-acre (6-hectare) vineyard did not come into full production until 1997, yet quickly started snapping at the heels of Nyetimber for the English sparkling wine crown, and some *cuvées* are superior. In honor of Christopher Merret, the first person to document the process that eventually became known as the traditional method, all Ridgeview wines are marketed as "Cuvée Merret," a name the Roberts have registered. Furthermore, to maintain Merret's association with London, each style of "Cuvée Merret" is named after an area of London.

✓ *Entire range*

### 49 SANDHURST VINEYARDS
**Sandhurst, Kent (Southeast)**

A 25-acre (10-hectare) vineyard established in 1988 by the Nicholas family on Hoads Farm.

### 50 SEDLESCOMBE
**Robertsbridge, Sussex (Southeast)**
◎

In 1994 Sedlescombe became Britain's first organic vineyard, and in this rain-swept country, there have not been many brave enough to follow.

✓ *Classic white blend* (Dry White)

### 51 SHARPHAM
**Asprington, Devon (Southwest)**
★ ✓

Sharpham makes and markets wine from Beenleigh Manor Vineyard in Harbertonford, which was Britain's first "real" red wine in the 1980s. Since then, it has become a multi-award-winning wine.

✓ *Classic red blend* (Beenleigh) • *Classic white blend* (Dart Valley Reserve) • *Madeleine Angevine* (Barrel Fermented Dry) • *Pinot Noir*

### 52 SHAWSGATE
**Framlingham, Suffolk (East Anglia)**
★ ✓

One intriguing offer from this vineyard, which was established in 1973, is the chance to rent a row of vines, from which wine will be made for you—because they are "your" vines, the wine will be tax-free!

✓ *Rosé*

### 53 TENTERDEN
**Tenterden, Kent (Southeast)**
★ ✓

Originally planted and owned by Stephen Skelton, Tenterden is now the home of New Wave Wines, as well as one of its better labels.

✓ *Classic white blend* (Tenterden Estate)

### 54 THREE CHOIRS
**Newent, Gloucestershire (Southwest)**
★ ✓

One of the country's four largest wine producers, Three Choirs has always had potential, but was disappointing until the 2002/03 vintages.

✓ *Bacchus* (Estate Reserve) • *Desert* (Estate Reserve Noble Rot) • *Siegerrebe* (Estate Reserve)

### 55 THROWLEY
**Throwley, Kent (Southeast)**
★ ✓

A southwest-facing slope of the North Downs that is developing a reputation for Ortega.

✓ *Ortega* (Reserve)

### 56 TILTRIDGE
**Upton-on-Severn, Worcestershire (Southwest)**
★ ✓

Peter and Sandy Barker have not been very successful with their Elgar sparkling wine, the grapes for which obviously have more potential for still wines.

✓ *Schönburger* (Cello) • *Seyval* (Oaked)

### 57 STANLAKE PARK
**Stanlake Park, Berkshire (Thames and Chiltern)**
★ ✓

This vineyard was established by Jon Leighton in 1979. Originally called Thames Valley Vineyards, then simply Valley Vineyards, the name changed again when Leighton sold up and returned to the warmer climes of Australia. The new owners have retained winemaker Vince Gower.

✓ *Classic white blend* (Fumé) • *Rosé* (Pinot Blush) • *Schönburger* (Hinton Grove) • *Sparkling* (Ascot Brut, Heritage Rose)

### 58 WARDEN ABBEY
**Biggleswade, Bedfordshire (East Anglia)**

Established in 1986 by Jane Whitbread at the Abbey of Warden, founded by Cistercian monks in 1135 as the "daughter abbey" to Rievaulx Abbey in Yorkshire.

✓ *Bacchus*

### 59 WORTHENBURY
**Worthenbury, Wrexham, Wales (Southwest)**

The most northerly cultivation of Chardonnay, Pinot Noir, and Sauvignon Blanc, the grapes have to be trucked 170 to 260 miles (272 to 420 kilometers) (depending on the destination winery) to be vinified.

✓ *Classic white blend* (Chardonnay/Sauvignon)

### 60 WYKEN
**Stanton, Suffolk (East Anglia)**

Established in 1988 by Carla and Ken Carlisle, whose Bacchus has been winning awards since the inaugural 1991 vintage.

✓ *Bacchus*

### 61 YEARLSTONE
**Bickleigh, Devon (Southwest)**

Originally established by the late, lamented Gillian Pearkes, who planted her first vineyard in 1963 at the age of 18, and whose pioneering book *Growing Grapes in Britain* (1969) was used as a blueprint by many of today's vineyards. Yearlstone vineyard in the Exe Valley was taken over by Roger White, a BBC presenter, when Pearkes died in 1993.

✓ *Classic white blend* (Number 5)

---

## OTHER CERTIFIED ORGANIC PRODUCERS

Avalon (Pennard)
Carter's Vineyards (Colchester)

THE WINE STYLES OF
# THE BRITISH ISLES

## AUXERROIS

This grape variety is capable of producing fresh, creamy-rich wine that adapts well to oak and can also be a useful blending component for classic bottle-fermented sparkling wine.

## BACCHUS

Fat and grapey with rich, Muscatlike fruit when ripe, this grape provides high sugar levels even in cool climates, making it one of Great Britain's more successful German crosses. It does, however, develop an intensely herbaceous, elderflower style in cooler years and is downright catty when unripe.

♟ *Camel Valley* • *New Wave* (Curious Grape)

## CABERNET

Grown with Merlot in plastic tunnels at Beenleigh, this has promised deep, plummy fruit but has always been ruined during vinification.

## CHARDONNAY

Mostly planted for sparkling wine, but some still wine versions are beginning to emerge. Winemakers need to look to Champagne for the best clones (95, 96, 75, and 121) and to New Zealand for advice on how to handle this variety in a maritime-influenced growing environment.

♟ *Nyetimber* (Premier Cuvée)

## EHRENFELSER

Penshurst specializes in this grape, which is the darling of British Columbia in Canada, but to my mind it performs much better in Kent, where in warm years it is soft and ripe with a Riesling-like peach-stone intensity that develops well.

## GAMAY

The climate in Great Britain might not have the warmth to make good red wine from this grape, but if Thames Valley's effort iin 1992 (Clocktower Gamay) was not an anomaly, it could well be one of the most useful grapes for bottle-fermented sparkling wine.

## HUXELREBE

Easy-going fruit that sometimes has a herbaceous-grapefruit bite and can become elderflower-tasting or catty in poor years.

## KERNER

More aromatic in Great Britain than in Germany, where it was developed, Kerner is unsuitable for oak and is often grown for its late budding (thus frost avoidance) and high sugar level.

## MADELEINE ANGEVINE

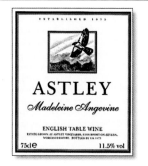

This grape has a light, floral aroma and after-perfume, and can have apricoty fruit, but often fights against an elderflower pungency.

♟ *Halfpenny Green* • *Sharpham* (Barrel Fermented Dry)

## MÜLLER-THURGAU

Müller-Thurgau is a typically German style that can become elderflower-tasting or catty, although wines of real flavor are possible.

♟ *Breaky Bottom*

## ORTEGA

Fat and jammy when ripe, becoming herbaceous in cooler years, with an elderflower, white currant character when unripe.

♟ *Biddenden* • *New Wave* (Curious Grape) • *Throwley*

## PINOT BLANC

Can be delicious, easy-drinking, and reminiscent of what Alsace does with this variety.

♟ *New Wave* (Curious Grape)

## PINOT GRIS

England's Pinot Gris is not the spiciest in the world, but it does offer richer fruit per ounce of acidity than either Pinot Blanc or Chardonnay. It can be successfully oaked, although the best-known example, Denbies 1995 Special Release, was over-oaked and would have been better if blended with another variety.

## PINOT NOIR

Some vineyard owners fear that English weather and this variety's susceptibility to rot will not mix, but those growers who have chosen the right clone (115, 114, 779, and 927) have been successful. In a good year, this grape is capable of making an elegant English red with a very attractive cherry and raspberry flavor. In less ripe years, color extraction can be a problem, and a school of thought reckons that such grapes should be used for sparkling wine, but Pinot Noir that cannot produce a light red will not make good fizz, and would be better used making off-dry, New World-style *blanc de noirs*.

♟ *Hidden Springs* (Dark Fields) • *New Wave* (Curious Grape) • *Parva Farm* (Rosé)

## REICHENSTEINER

Appreciated by growers for its resistance to rot and by winemakers for its high sugar levels, but its neutral character is seldom enjoyed by wine enthusiasts, although exceptions exist.

## SCHÖNBURGER

Soft and peachy when ripe, good examples should have at least a light spiciness. There is nothing worse than a dry Schönburger from a cool year, when it smells like a tomcat's spray.

♟ *New Wave* (Curious Grape) • *Valley Vineyards* (Hinton Grove)

## SEYVAL BLANC

Relatively neutral and capable of oak-aging, but classic English style is crisp and unoaked, with a grassy-elderflowery intensity that is very tangy and almost Sauvignonlike, although unlike

Sauvignon, good Seyval ages well in bottle. However, it can be catty with less ripeness.

♟ *Breaky Bottom* • *Camel Blanc*

## SIEGERREBE

A Madeleine Angevine/Gewürztraminer cross that can produce fat wines with tangy fruit.

♟ *Three Choirs* (Estate Reserve)

## TRIOMPHE

Triomphe is a red-wine hybrid with a hint of foxiness on the aftertaste, but this can be hidden in a clever blend.

# OTHER STYLES

### BOTRYTIS *or* LATE-HARVEST

There's no doubt that the UK can guarantee sufficiently damp mornings to encourage rot, but it requires a strong burn-off from mid-morning sun for two weeks to encourage noble rot, which is not that common. When it occurs, however, these wines can have a stunning piquance of mouthwatering fruit and acidity.

♟ *Three Choirs* (Estate Reserve Noble Rot)

### BOTTLE-FERMENTED SPARKLING WINE

The best wines use nonaromatic varieties, preferably classic Champagne grapes. Nyetimber has shown that these varieties can succeed.

♟ *Nyetimber* • *Ridgeview*

### CLASSIC RED BLENDS

Most English red wines are light and insubstantial, but New World influence has encouraged softer, more upfront, fruity styles.

♟ *Sharpham* (Beenleigh) • *Hidden Springs* (Dark Fields)

### CLASSIC WHITE BLENDS

One way to ignore the funny-sounding grape names of hybrids and crosses is to blend them into a wine sold under a proprietary label.

♟ *Hidden Springs* (Decadence) • *Sharpham* (Dart Valley Reserve) • *Valley Vineyards* (Fumé)

### OAKED WHITES

As in the US, some producers have adopted the term *fumé* to indicate oak-aging. Marginal climatic conditions produce wines of leaner structure than those of Europe or the New World, thus oak can easily overwhelm, and winemakers tend to restrain its use. Normally only nonaromatic varieties such as Seyval Blanc are oaked.

♟ *New Wave Wines* (Curious Grape Ortega) • *Sharpham* (Madeleine Angevine Barrel Fermented Dry) • *Valley Vineyards* (Fumé)

### ROSÉ

Although the British climate makes it difficult to produce a true red wine year in and year out, the viticultural fringe should be ideal for making crisp, ultrafresh, off-dry rosés and a few vineyards are beginning to realize the potential.

♟ *Denbies* (Rose Hill) • *Hidden Springs* (Sussex Sunset) • *Valley Vineyards* (Pinot Blush)

# LUXEMBOURG

*A small but varietally diverse wine-producing country on the northern cusp of commercially viable viticulture, Luxembourg's best vineyards consistently produce wonderfully fresh and pure dry white wines that are delicious to drink with food or without, and they fit conveniently into the niche vacated by so many Alsace producers as they make sweeter and sweeter wines.*

LUXEMBOURG DERIVES ITS NAME from Lucilinburhuc, or "Little Fortress," which is the Saxon name for a defensive position originally built by the Romans on a rocky promontory around which the city of Luxembourg was destined to grow. Under the Romans, this area held no geopolitical identity, but was part of the Trier region, where vines were grown 2,000 years ago. Today, the vineyards are scattered around and between 28 towns and villages, stretching from Wasserbillig in the north to Schengen in the south. This viticultural area is the mirror image across the Moselle River of the German *Bereiche* of Obermosel and Moseltor, which are located on the right bank, and generally produce less exciting wines than those from Luxembourg's vineyards opposite. It is from the German side of the river that the topography of Luxembourg's vineyards can best be observed, especially when the river bends north and south. This strip of the Moselle's left bank is officially designated *Appellation Moselle Luxembourgoise Contrôlée*, and vines are not allowed to be planted anywhere else in Luxembourg.

## TERROIR?

These vineyards are at their narrowest in the northern half of Luxembourg's Moselle valley, where the dolomite limestone subsoil has resisted erosion, leaving a narrower valley with steeper slopes. This pinkish-brown bedrock can be seen overhanging the old Caves St. Martin—now owned by the firm of Gales—which were carved out of the dolomite in 1919–21. Going south from Remich, much softer marly and clayey soils dominate; consequently, the area has been prone to erosion, which has widened the valley, leaving a softer landscape of gently rolling hills. It is said in Luxembourg itself that the wines in the south are soft, mellow, and best drunk young, whereas those in the north are crisper and finer, requiring

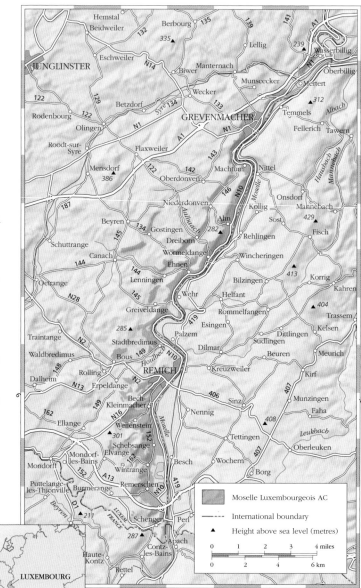

LUXEMBOURG
*A country united by other tongues: French is used by its government and courts, with most newspapers published in German, leaving the national dialect with no official role.*

## THE LIEUX-DITS—LUXEMBOURG'S BEST-KEPT SECRET

The *lieux-dits* represent Luxembourg's richest source of fine, expressive wines, and a joint project between the Institut Viti-Vinicole (IVV) and the German Weather Institute could be this country's key to international success. This project is identifying the best areas in each *lieu-dit* according to meteorological criteria (rain, sunshine, heat, etc.), which some believe could be the basis of a future *grand cru*-type classification. Weather is an infinitely better way of discerning which *parts* of a vineyard (rather than vineyards *per se*) should be classified than the French system. The French claim to isolate an individual *terroir* by its geological homogeneity compared with the surrounding area within a historically established

named site. As the relatively recent classification of Alsace's *grands crus* illustrates, not only does the geological homogeneity fly out of the window in the process, but so does the extent of the historically established named site. As growers on the periphery of a historically established named site realize the premium that can be demanded by a wine with *grand cru* on the label, they ask, "If his plot is going to be classified *grand cru*, why not mine?" And, of course, once they are allowed, their own neighbors—who were previously separated by unclassified land—want in. Thus it was that *grands crus* like Brand in Turckheim grew from less than 7 acres to almost 143! Such corrupt behavior would kill Luxembourg's

fledgling reputation. This is the one area where the IVV needs a firm hand. Its hardest task will be to establish in law the true historical boundary of every *lieu-dit*, after which the meteorological data cannot be argued with—growers cannot claim to have more or less rain, sunshine, or heat than the records show. So it should be possible, not merely to use this data to classify *grands crus*, but also to subdivide each *lieu-dit* so that, for example, parts of the *lieu-dit* of Greiveldange Fels are officially designated Greiveldange Fels *grand cru* and Greiveldange Fels *premier cru*, while the rest remains Greiveldange Fels *lieu-dit* plain and simple, albeit a single-vineyard wine in its own right.

## RECENT LUXEMBOURG VINTAGES

**2006** One of the earliest and shortest harvests on record, and one that was blighted by a lot of rot, this is a vintage in which the growers had to be very strict in selecting only the cleanest fruit. Consumers should also be very strict in what they select.

**2005** With low yields and perfect harvest conditions, this is probably Luxembourg's finest vintage ever across the board. Only an unseasonably wet July and a cool, cloudy August prevented this from being a perfect vintage, although the threat of unripened fruit was saved by the reduced demand of lower yields—something that all Luxembourg growers should ponder.

**2004** Extreme diurnal differences during the *véraison* extended the ripening period, with only those who risked delayed picking producing truly ripe fruit. On the face of it, not the best year for red wine, but there are always exceptions, and Cep d'Or's 2007 Pinot Noir Stadtbredimus Goldberg is the best that I've tasted from this country.

**2003** The hottest year on record meant very ripe grapes with very low acidity due to high yields. Probably not the best year for Luxembourg's typically refreshing styles of Pinot Blanc, Pinot Gris, and Auxerrois.

**2002** A very good vintage indeed for all styles and varieties other than Gewürztraminer and Pinot Noir.

## LUXEMBOURG'S GRAPE VARIETIES

*Based on 2002 statistics*

Growers not to exceed a maximum yield of 616 cases/acre for Elbling and Rivaner, 528 cases/acre for all the other varieties, but since average yields for four varieties exceed these parameters, the law is obviously being flouted on a wide scale.

| VARIETY | ACRES | % VINES | CASE/ACRE | CASES | % OF WINES |
|---|---|---|---|---|---|
| Rivaner | 1,016.70 | 31.4% | 621.30 | 631,676 | 37.32% |
| Auxerrois | 423.14 | 13.1% | 504.26 | 213,373 | 12.61% |
| Riesling | 417.63 | 12.9% | 431.32 | 180,132 | 10.64% |
| Pinot Gris | 411.70 | 12.7% | 419.11 | 172,548 | 10.19% |
| Elbling | 353.28 | 10.9% | 648.69 | 229,169 | 13.54% |
| Pinot Blanc | 338.29 | 10.5% | 511.92 | 173,177 | 10.23% |
| Pinot Noir | 201.72 | 6.2% | 356.19 | 71,851 | 4.25% |
| Gewürztraminer | 35.44 | 1.1% | 287.07 | 10,174 | 0.60% |
| Chardonnay | 29.07 | 0.9% | 348.84 | 10,141 | 0.60% |
| Others (Gamay, Muscat) | 6.47 | 0.2% | 54.38 | 352 | 0.02% |
| TOTAL | 3,233.44 | 100.0% | 523.47* | 1,692,593 | 100.00% |

\* Average yield

more time in bottle, but I have found little evidence of this in the wines. If yields averaged 176 cases per acre rather than the current greedy 528, provenance might become a factor in determining two contrasting styles of wine, but the differences that exist at the moment are more likely to be due to the stylistic preference of individual growers.

## LUXEMBOURG: THE NEW ALSACE?

Although this country has a tiny, emerging production of *vendange tardive*, *vin de glace*, and *vin de paille*, it will take a decade or more for any producer to establish a lasting reputation like that of Hugel's Riesling Vendange Tardive. Luxembourg certainly has nothing to compare with great dry wines like those of Trimbach's Clos Ste-Hûne, or any producers with reputations that come near those of Zind-Humbrecht, Weinbach, or Deiss. And there are wines such as Gewürztraminer and Pinot Noir at which Luxembourg will never be successful in anything other than heat-wave years like 2003. But what Luxembourg does have is what Alsace no longer offers, and that is a large range of uncomplicated, refreshing, easy-drinking, fine-quality varietal wines that consumers know to be dry without asking. This country's wines were boring in the 1980s, but underwent a quiet revolution in the 1990s, and have been attracting disenfranchised Alsace consumers since the turn of the century. The consistency in quality is already remarkable.

## FACTORS AFFECTING TASTE AND QUALITY

### LOCATION
A 26-mile (42-kilometer) strip of land along the country's southeastern flank, where 3,200 acres (1,300 hectares) of vines grow on the left bank of the Moselle River, overlooking the southernmost section of Germany's Mosel region.

### CLIMATE
A modified continental climate with mild winters and cool summers, the rainiest months coinciding with ripening and harvest. Frost can be dangerous, reducing yields by 80 percent on rare occasions, but rain and cold temperatures at flowering more commonly reduce yields.

### ASPECT
Going south from Remich, the valley widens, facilitating the growth of vines. Going north from Remich, it narrows and the slopes become steeper. More than 1,000 acres (400 hectares) of vines are grown on slopes of above 30 percent incline.

### SOIL
Marly and clayey in the south, with pinkish-brown dolomite limestone in the north.

### VITICULTURE AND VINIFICATION
Luxembourg's vineyards have undergone a restructuring, replacing traditional terracing with wider-spaced, vertically sloping rows. Called *remembrement*, this started in Wormeldange in 1970 and is nearly complete. Most vines are trained using a single Guyot system, though some are trained using the Trierer Rebenrad. Average yields are much too high (3,170 gallons/acre), but individual producers prune for smaller yields. There is a closed-shop system of 60 wine producers, including 6 commercial shippers and 6 cooperatives. Some *barriques* are used, and a number of traditional producers have large, old oak *fûdres,* but stainless-steel predominates, and the new *crémant* facility of Caves Gales at Ellange-Gare is state of the art.

### GRAPE VARIETIES
**Primary varieties:** Auxerrois, Elbling, Pinot Blanc, Pinot Gris, Riesling, Rivaner
**Secondary varieties:** Chardonnay, Gamay, Gewürztraminer, Muscat, Pinot Noir

## APPELLATION MOSELLE LUXEMBOURGOISE CONTRÔLÉE

There is just one appellation, and all *Appellation Contrôlée* wines must carry a state-controlled Marque Nationale mini-label. To get the Marque Nationale, wines are submitted to the Institut Viti-Vinicole (IVV) for chemical analysis and a blind-tasting test. The basic Marque Nationale is open to all varieties and styles, and is awarded to any wine scoring 12–13.9 points (out of 20) from the IVV tasting panel. For most grape varieties, a wine scoring 16–17.9 points is classified as a *premier cru,* while a wine scoring 18–20 points is deemed a *grand premier cru.* Any wine achieving fewer than 12 points is declassified into *vin de table.* This is a significant selection process, with as many as 32 percent of the wines submitted declassified.

Classifying a wine as a *cru* (growth) of any sort on the basis of tasting, regardless of whether the wine comes from a single site, is irrational

and contrary to the spirit of the European Union's wine regime. There are only two logical options: either all wines submitted must be the product of a *lieu-dit* (named site) or the designation should be altered to something like *premier vin* and *grand premier vin.* The latter would make it possible to reserve the terms *premier cru* and *grand cru* for any future classifications for the existing *lieux-dits* (see box).

If a Rivaner scores 14–15.9 points, it is designated as a *vin classé,* the highest classification any wine from this grape can achieve. The Elbling, Pinot Noir, and Crémant de Luxembourg may aspire to no more than the basic appellation. This is more nonsense, although it should be noted that, as with the *premier cru* and *grand premier cru* misnomers, these practices date from times when even French wine regions like Alsace were

blending *grands crus* and unfairly discriminating against wines because of the varietal content, rather than intrinsic quality. Things moved on in the world of wine, and the IVV's tasting panel needs to recalibrate its palate to modern standards. Many *premier cru* wines are no more than basic in quality, and even some of *grand premier cru* are little better. They might have stood out against other Luxembourg wines in the 1980s, but such standards do not apply today. I have tasted some groundbreaking wines that have failed to pass even the basic appellation, being rejected on stylistic grounds. The IVV is repeating the mistakes made by French and German official tasting panels, which denied the appellation to many of the most forward-thinking winemakers, resulting in an annihilation of their exports by New World rivals. Luxembourg cannot afford to follow suit.

THE WINE STYLES OF
# LUXEMBOURG

## ÄISWÄIN

*See* Vin de Glace

## AUXERROIS

**Minimum natural ripeness (2003):**
**63° Oechsle (8%ABV)**
**Maximum yield:528 cases/acre.**

One of Luxembourg's most successful grape varieties, which is amazing considering that its yield is second only to the rampant Rivaner. Yet Auxerrois ranks with the best you can find in the Haut-Rhin. Some producers leave a little residual sugar in these wines, but essentially they are light, dry, and delicious to drink.

↳ 1–2 years

🏆 *Aly Duhr* (Wormeldange Koeppchen) • *Max-Lahr et Fils* (Wormeldange Heiligenhäuschen) • *Pundel-Hoffeld* (Machtum Alwengert) • *R Kohll-Leuck* (Ehnen Ehnerberg) • *Vinsmoselle Caves de Stadtbredimus* (Stadtbredimus Primerberg)

## CHARDONNAY

**Minimum natural ripeness (2003):**
**63° Oechsle (8%ABV)**
**Maximum yield:528 cases/acre.**

The clones planted are 95 and 96, which are good for both still and sparkling wines, although 96 fares better at the latter, and this far north, growers should really be trying 75 and 121. Everyone who had this variety told me that their Chardonnay had been planted for sparkling wine, yet they all just happened to be making a still wine from it, none of which was any better than a Belgian Chardonnay (Clermont, Genoels-Elderen, and others). A certain warmth is required to make premium-quality Chardonnay, and Luxembourg just does not have this on any regular basis. If decent-quality, non-sparkling Chardonnay is extremely rare in Champagne, what chance does Luxembourg have?

↳ 1–2 years

🏆 *Gales* (Coteaux de Stadtbredimus)

## ELBLING

**Minimum natural ripeness (2003):**
**57° Oechsle (7%ABV)**
**Maximum yield:616 cases/acre.**

Traditionally grown as low-quality, low-tax fodder for Germany's *Sekt* industry, Elbling typically provides a neutral-flavored, high-acid wine. I once thought that it might be interesting to look out for the odd wine made from low-yield Elbling, but gave up when it became patently clear that no such thing exists.

## GEWÜRZTRAMINER

**Minimum natural ripeness (2003):**
**63° Oechsle (8%ABV)**
**Maximum yield:528 cases/acre.**

This grape is not as abundant as it is in Alsace, and it lacks the gravitas and broader notes found in the latter region's truly classic examples. The significantly lower level of ripeness reduces the availability of spice-laden terpenes, while its lower alcohol content (3 to 4 percent lower) gives an entirely different, much lighter, less viscous, mouthfeel. If anyone in Luxembourg is really serious about this grape, it must be grown on the very best, south-facing sites that have been traditionally reserved for Riesling, with yields halved, and harvested as late as possible.

↳ 1–2 years

🏆 *A Gloden* (Schengen Markusberg) • *Charles Decker* (Remerschen Kreitzberg) • *Domaine Mathis Bastian* ◉ (Domaine et Tradition) • *Schmit-Fohl* (Ahn Goellebour)

## PINOT BLANC

**Minimum natural ripeness (2003):**
**63° Oechsle (8%ABV)**
**Maximum yield:528 cases/acre.**

The crystal-clear, refreshing, light, dry and fruity, entry-level wine for any half-serious Luxembourg wine drinker. The sooner that plantings of Rivaner and Elbling are reduced to a statistical insignificance, the sooner that Auxerrois will be the entry-level wine for all consumers, with Pinot Blanc the flagship, and the better Luxembourg's wine reputation will be.

↳ 1–2 years

🏆 *Cep d'Or* (Stadtbredimus Goldberg) • *Domaine Gales* (Domaine et Tradition) • *Domaine Gales* (Bech-Macher Rëtschelt) • *Häremillen* (Wormeldange Weinbour) • *Mathes* (Wormeldange Mohrberg) • *Mathis Bastian* (Coteau de Remich) • *Pundel-Hoffeld* (Machtum Gëllebour) • *R Kohll-Leuck* (Ehnen Rousemen) • *Schram & Fils* (Bech-Kleinmacher Falkenberg) • *Schumacher-Lethal* (Wormeldange Heiligenhäuschen)

## PINOT GRIS

**Minimum natural ripeness (2003):**
**63° Oechsle (8%ABV)**
**Maximum yield:528 cases/acre.**

Luxembourg's Pinot Gris has none of the spice found in Alsace, and is simply a slightly richer, equally delicious version of Pinot Blanc—everything Italy's Pinot Grigio should be, yet seldom is. It is probably impossible for Pinot Gris to ripen sufficiently in Luxembourg's climate to create enough terpenes in the grape's skin for these to develop into spicy bottle-aromas.

↳ 1–4 years

🏆 *A Gloden & Fils* (Wellenstein Foulschette) • *Cep d'Or* (Stadtbredimus Primerberg Signature Terroir et Cépage) • *Häremillen* (Mertert Herrenberg) • *Jean Schlink-Hoffeld* (Machtum Ongkâf "Arômes et Couleurs") • *Krier Welbes* (Bech-Kleinmacher Naumberg) • *Pundel-Hoffeld* (Machtum Widdem) • *Mathes* (Wormeldange Woûsselt) • *R Kohll-Leuck* (Ehnen Kelterberg) • *Schmit-Fohl* (Ahn Goellebour)

## PINOT NOIR

**Minimum natural ripeness (2003):**
**63° Oechsle (8%ABV)**
**Maximum yield:528 cases/acre.**

The clones planted are 115 and 114, which are good, but also 375, which is not (overcropper, low quality, poor varietal character), and this far north, growers should be trying 779 and 927. I tasted nothing interesting from 2002, which was a riper than normal vintage. The wines have a certain sour-cherry varietal character, but lack fruit, structure, finesse, and complexity. If nothing special is produced from the 2003 vintage, then they should give up on Pinot Noir as a red varietal wine (although it would make a useful sparkling wine component).

🏆 *Cep d'Or* (Stadtbredimus Goldberg)

## RIESLING

**Minimum natural ripeness (2003):**
**63° Oechsle (8%ABV)**
**Maximum yield:120hl/ha.**

This is Luxembourg's finest potential wine, but most Riesling growers are not realizing this potential. In such a northern, Atlantic-influenced area, it is madness to average almost 100 hectoliters per hectare. It is widely understood that Riesling can be successfully cultivated only on fully south-facing sites in Luxembourg, yet the growers throw away the potential of the country's greatest sites by squeezing every last drop from the vines. They should be aiming for 12–13 percent alcohol without chaptalization, but they are averaging barely 9 percent. Luxembourg Riesling is dry, and if some are surprisingly good, it should not be taken as vindication of such ridiculously high yields. If all Riesling vines grown on the best slopes of Luxembourg's finest *lieux-dits* were cropped at a maximum of 35 hectoliters per hectare, this country's wines would have an international reputation. Riesling is tailor-made for Luxembourg: it adores cold October nights and is the only grape that can keep ripening at 54° F (12°C) (Pinot and Gewürztraminer stop at 65°F [18°C]). A few specialists produce excellent wines at reduced yields, but even they need to crop lower; unlike in Alsace, there is no danger inducing overripe grapes that the wines will become sweet.

↳ 1–8 years

🏆 *Aly Duhr* (Domaine et Tradition) • *Cep d'Or Riesling* (Stadtbredimus Fels "Signature Terroir et Cépage") • *Domaine Alice Hartmann* (Wormeldange Koeppchen and Les Terrasses de la Koeppchen la Chapelle) • *Domaine Gales* (Wellenstein Kurschells) • *Pundel-Hoffeld Riesling* (Wormeldange Elterberg "Cuvée Spéciale") • *Schumacher-Knepper* (Wintrage Felsberg) • *Steinmetz-Jungers* (Grevenmacher Fels) • *Vinsmoselle* (Coteaux de Schengen) • *Vinsmoselle Caves de Grevenmacher* (Mertert Herrenberg)

## RIVANER

**Minimum natural ripeness (2003):**
**57° Oechsle (7%ABV)**
**Maximum yield:616 cases/acre.**

Also known as Müller-Thurgau. Although this ubiquitous grape accounts for almost one-third of all the vines growing in Luxembourg today, it is definitely on the decline. Twenty years ago, every other bottle of wine produced in the Grand Duchy was made from Rivaner. This grape is grown at very high yields and turned into a sweetish, Liebfraumilch-type wine, making it Luxembourg's least interesting variety, but one that enjoys high-volume sales. Rivaner prices are low, and the popularity of this style of wine extends beyond the domestic market to Belgium, where it accounts for more than half of global exports of Vins Moselle Luxembourgoise. As long as the cultivated area of this variety continues to decline, there seems little point in getting high-minded about its yield. It will eventually bottom-out, and lowering yield will hardly produce a noticeably finer quality of wine.

✶⌐ Upon purchase

♈ *Aly Duhr* (Sélection Ahn Hohfels) • *Cep d'Or* (Stadtbredimus Goldberg) • *Domaine Viticole Kox* (Remich Primerberg) • *Krier-Welbes* (Bech-Kleinmacher Naumberg)

## OTHER GRAPE VARIETIES
**Minimum natural ripeness (2003): 63° Oechsle (8%ABV)**
**Maximum yield:528 cases/acre.**

Gamay did not impress me, although the three Muscats demonstrated that it might be worth persevering with this variety, especially Charles Decker's Muscat Ottonel (deliciously creamy 2001, and evocatively strawberry 1997).

✶⌐ 1–4 years

♈ *Charles Decker* (Muscat Ottonel, Remerschen Kreitzberg )

# OTHER STYLES
## CRÉMANT DE LUXEMBOURG
**Maximum yield:528 cases/acre.**

Champagne—real Champagne—was in fact produced in Luxembourg by Mercier from 1886 up to almost the beginning of World War II. During this time, Mercier was known as "Champagne Mercier, Epernay-Luxembourg," and both establishments were famous for being completely powered by 19th-century electricity. Today, of course, Champagne is a prohibited term, and the Crémant de Luxembourg appellation was created as part of the deal with Champagne not to use the term *méthode champenoise*. Curiously, it gets lumped in with French Crémant appellations (Alsace, Bordeaux, Bourgogne, Die, Jura, Limoux, Loire, and Luxembourg) at the annual Concours des Crémants. Most Crémant de Luxembourg encountered outside the country is boring, but the general standard is much higher, primarily because it is much fresher, and these sparkling wines are a delight to drink young. The style is fresh, soft, and elegant, with good acids providing a crisp, fruity finish. The only exception is Domaine Alice Hartmann Brut, which is chock-full of flavor and character, perhaps at the expense of finesse, and could be criticized for being too big and too oaky, but has to be admired, and is currently Luxembourg's greatest sparkling wine. However, it's a style that I would not like to see more than two or three other producers emulate, as Luxembourg is more naturally attuned to the Gales style of freshness and finesse. Whereas Crémant de Luxembourg must be made exclusively from grapes grown within the appellation Moselle Luxembourgoise, readers should be aware that any Luxembourg wines labelled Vin Mousseux, Vin Pétillant, Perlwein, or sold as "boissons effervescents à base de vin" may be blended from imported grapes, juice, or wine.

✶⌐ 1–2 years

♈ *Domaine Alice Hartmann* (Brut) • *Gales* (Heritage) • *Gales* (Jubilée) • *Gales* (Cuvée Premier Rosé) • *Vinsmoselle* (Poll-Fabaire Cuvée Art Collection)

## VENDANGE TARDIVE
Only Auxerrois, Pinot Blanc, Pinot Gris, Riesling, and Gewürztraminer are authorized. The minimum ripeness level of 243 grams per liter (220 for Riesling) of natural sugar content, is as tough as the *vendange tardive* law introduced in Alsace in 1984, and raising ripeness levels is more difficult in Luxembourg's colder, more northerly climate. Alsace raised the bar in 2001 (to 235–257 grams per liter), and Luxembourg should do likewise, confident in the knowledge that its vineyards are nothing like the suntraps in Alsace, thus the Grand Duchy will never be in danger of losing its primary crop of dry wine grapes. Vendange Tardive is a new, emerging category of wine, and too many of the wines are noticeably high VA, with a bitter finish. This will change, as producers get used to the style. Some, like Domaine Thill Frères, already are.

✶⌐ 1–8 years

♈ *Domaine Thill* (Château de Shengen Riesling)

## VIN DE GLACE OR ÄISWÄIN
Only Pinot Blanc, Pinot Gris, and Riesling are authorized. The minimum ripeness level is 292 grams per liter of natural sugar content. Luxembourg would seem to be more climatically adept at *vin de glace* than *vendange tardive*, but it is a style that generally attracts a high VA level and the Grand Duchy is no exception.

✶⌐ 1–8 years

♈ *Charles Decker* • *Domaine Gales*

## VIN DE PAILLE
Only Auxerrois, Pinot Blanc, Pinot Gris, and Gewürztraminer are authorized. The minimum ripeness level is 317 grams per liter of natural sugar. Only one outstanding example so far.

✶⌐ 1–8 years

♈ *Caves Sunnen-Hoffmann* ⓞ ⓑ (Auxerrois)

---

THE APPELLATIONS OF
# LUXEMBOURG

Due to the varying usage of all three languages (Luxembourgish, German, French, and sometimes Dutch/Low German), spellings of some villages and *lieux-dits* can vary. The most common variations are shown below. To list all the villages and all the *lieux-dits* in use today in all languages, not to mention the odd variant in each language, would confuse more than it would inform. It is obvious that Luxembourg must clean up its labelling act, obliging everyone to use the same nomenclature, and most observers would agree that Luxembourgish should be the dialect of choice.

## AHN
**Lieux-dits *Palmberg, Vogelsang, Elterberg, Hohfels/Houfels, Göllebour, Pietert, Nussbaum***

Warmer vineyards enable Gewürztraminer to succeed in exceptionally hot years. It is said that Luxembourg's first Traminer and Muscat vines were grown here at the beginning of the 20th century. Also good for Pinot Gris, Auxerrois, Riesling, and occasionally Crémant de Luxembourg. Domaine Viticole Mme Aly Duhr & Fils is the most famous producer here, but I have been at least as pleased by Schmit-Fohl,

followed by Steinmetz-Duhr. Other Ahn wines that have impressed me on occasions have been Clos du Rochers (Bernard-Massard) and Jean Ley-Schartz.

## BECH-KLEINMACHER
**Lieux-dits *Enschberg, Jongeberg, Falkenberg, Naumberg, Fuusslach, Gaalgeberg, Brauneberg, Gottesgôf, Kurschels, Rëtschelt***

Two villages, Bech and Macher, merged 100 years or so ago, when they built a communal church. Just two producers resident in the town (Krier-Bisenius and Schram et Fils), but growers sell most grapes to the cooperative at Wellenstein and Caves Gales for their sparkling wine (they also grow their own grapes here). Naumberg has been the most successful *lieu-dit* in my tasting, with fine Pinot Gris from Krier Welbes and the cooperative at Wellenstein. Schram makes a very good Pinot Blanc on both Falkenberg and Kurschells.

## BOUS
**Lieux-dits *Johannisberg, Fels***

Just one local producer (Caves Beissel) and nothing outstanding so far.

## EHNEN
**Lieux-dits *Kelterberg, Mesteschberg, Ebnerberg/Einerberg, Rousemen, Bromelt, Wousselt***

Ehnen is one of the prettiest villages on the Luxembourg wine route. I have enjoyed wines from Jean Linden-Heinisch and M Kohll-Reuland. Pinot Gris and Auxerrois fare well, with Mesteschberg and Kelterberg among the most successful *lieux-dits*.

## ELLINGEN/ELLANGE
**Lieux-dits *None***

Two very good producers are located here, Caves Gales and Krier Welbes, but no mono-*cru* wines produced. Growers either deliver their grapes to the cooperative or sell them to one of the six commercial wineries.

## ELVANGE/ELVINGEN
**Lieux-dits *None***

No producers are located here. Although there is one grower who owns three plots within this village that are delimited for the production of

Appellation Moselle Luxembourgoise Contrôlée, and have been exploited in the recent past, there are no vines growing here at the moment.

## ERPELDINGEN
**Lieux-dits** *None*

No producers are located here. Growers either deliver to the cooperative or sell to one of the six commercial wineries.

## GOSTINGEN
**Lieux-dits** *Bocksberg, Häreberg*

Just one local producer (Caves Fernand Rhein) and nothing outstanding so far.

## GREIVELDANGE/ GREIWELDIGEN
**Lieux-dits** *Hutte/Hëtt, Dieffert, Herrenberg/Häreberg, Hëttermillen*

The village is one mile from the Moselle, but the vineyards extend down to the river's banks. Of the two local producers, Beck-Franck and Stronck-Pinnel, the latter makes one of Greiveldange's best Rieslings from the Hëtt *lieu-dit*, while the former makes better wines from other villages. However, most of the growers belong to the village cooperative, and Vinsmoselle makes most of the best wines here, especially Dieffert Pinot Gris and Herrenberg Auxerrois.

## GREVENMACHER
**Lieux-dits** *Fels, Rosenberg/Rouseberg, Leitschberg/Leiteschberg, Pietert, Groaerd/Groärd*

The best-known producer here is Bernard Massard, one of Luxembourg's truly international exporters. The Fels *lieu-dit* is for Riesling, Leitschberg, and Pietert for Pinot Blanc. Steinmetz-Jungers, Vinsmoselle's Caves de Grevenmacher, and Fédération Viticole make the finest local wines.

## LENNINGEN
**Lieux-dits** *Häreberg*

Just one local producer (Caves Fernand Rhein) and nothing outstanding so far.

## MACHTUM
**Lieux-dits** *Alwengert, Hobenfels, Ongkâf, Goellebour/Göllebour, Widdem*

Matchum is supposedly known for its Ongkâf Riesling, but it produces better Pinot Gris, and to be truthful, Göllebour vies with Ongkâf as the top *lieu-dit* in the village. Matchum also makes good Pinot Blanc. The Riesling is good, but no better than Auxerrois and, in hotter years, Gewürztraminer. The two local producers, Jean Schlink-Hoffeld and Pundel-Hoffeld, are both very good, with Vinsmoselle and Cep d'Or the best producers from outside the village.

## MERTERT
**Lieux-dits** *Bocksberg, Herrenberg/Häreberg*

The best *lieu-dit* in this ugly, industrial port is Herrenberg, which thankfully is closer to Wasserbillig. Pinot Gris is Herrenberg's most successful variety, with Häremillen and the local Vinsmoselle Caves de Grevenmacher the top-performing producers.

## MONDORF
**Lieux-dits** *None*

No producers are located here. Growers either deliver to the cooperative or sell to one of the six commercial wineries.

## NIEDERDONVEN
**Lieux-dits** *Fels, Gölleberg, Diedenacker*

No producers are located here. Growers either deliver to the cooperative or sell to one of the six commercial wineries.

## OBER-WORMELDINGEN
**Lieux-dits** *None*

No producers are located here. Growers either deliver to the cooperative or sell to one of the six commercial wineries.

## OBERDONVEN
**Lieux-dits** *None*

No producers are located here. Growers either deliver to the cooperative or sell to one of the six commercial wineries.

## REMERSCHEN
**Lieux-dits** *Jongeberg, Kräitchen, Kreitzberg, Rodernberg/Roudeberg, Reidt*

Charles Decker is the award-winning producer here; many of his medals are for wines that were denied the most lowly appellation, having been rejected by the IVV. In the best years, Decker can produce good Muscat Ottonel and Gewürztraminer on the Kreitzberg *lieu-dit*, while Krier Frères has made good Riesling on Jongeberg.

## REMICH
**Lieux-dits** *Fels, Goldberg, Gaalgeberg, Hélwéngert, Hôpertsbour, Primerberg, Scheuerberg*

Primerberg is the most important *lieu-dit* here, and Riesling its best variety, with Krier Frères and Mathis Bastian the top producers, but this vineyard also makes fine Pinot Blanc and Auxerrois (St Remy Desom), and Pinot Gris (Gales). Overall Remich is most successful for Pinot Blanc, with Mathis Bastian (Coteau de Remich) and Krier Frères (Hôpertsbour) both vying with St. Remy Desom.

## ROLLING
**Lieux-dits** *None*

No producers are located here. Growers either deliver to the cooperative or sell to one of the six commercial wineries.

## ROSPORT
**Lieux-dits** *None*

Everyone in the Luxembourg wine trade will tell you that Wasserbillig is the very northern limit of *Appellation Moselle Luxembourgois Controlée*, yet I found these vines seven miles further north, and they are officially within the delimited region, even though they are not on the Moselle or even in its hinterland, but located on a tributary called the Sauer.

## SCHENGEN
**Lieux-dits** *Fels, Markusberg*

Although Fels Riesling is supposed to be best known, this most southerly of Luxembourg's wine villages is definitely Pinot country (Blanc and Gris), with Vinsmoselle dominating, though A Gloden & Fils also makes some fine wines.

## SCHWEBSINGEN/ SCHWEBSANGE
**Lieux-dits** *Letscheberg, Steilberg, Hehberg, Kolteschberg*

Supposedly good for Gewürztraminer, but I have yet to confirm that. The best *lieu-dit* is

Kolteschberg, where Vinsmoselle Caves de Wellenstein and Laurent & Benoît Kox produce some good Pinot Gris and Riesling.

## STADTBREDIMUS
**Lieux-dits** *Primerberg, Goldberg, Dieffert, Fels*

Only Wormeldingen produces more top-quality Luxembourg wines than Stadtbredimus. Most of the best come from Vinsmoselle Caves de Stadtbredimus and and Cep d'Or, but some also from Gales and Laurent & Benoît Kox. The largest *lieu-dit* is the Primerberg, but Dieffert and Fels are the best, producing some of the finest Rieslings in the country. Pinot Gris is the second best variety in Stadbredimus, and Primerberg, Goldberg, and Fels the most successful *lieu-dit* for this grape.

## WASSERBILLIG
**Lieux-dits** *Bocksberg, Häreberg*

Supposedly the most northerly of Luxembourg's main drag of vineyards, but not strictly so (*see* Rosport).

## WELLENSTEIN
**Lieux-dits:** *Foulschette, Kurschels, Veilchenberg, Roetchelt, Brauneberg, Knipp, St Annaberg*

Kurschels stands out as the best *lieu-dit*, and the best *lieu-dit* for Riesling. Foulschette is the second-best *lieu-dit*, and the best *lieu-dit* for Pinot Gris. Krier Welbes and Gales are the top producers in this region, followed closely by Mathis Bastian and Vinsmoselle (Série Limitée Art).

## WINTRANGE/WINTRINGEN
**Lieux-dits** *Hommelsberg, Felsberg*

Felsberg is the best-known *lieu-dit*, with its statue of St. Donatus crowning the hill, where Pinot Gris and Riesling are supposed to be among the best in Luxemboug, although I have tasted only one wine that matches up to that sort of reputation (and that is Vinsmoselle Caves de Remerschen Riesling Grand Premier Cru Wintrange Felsberg).

## WORMELDANGE/ WORMELDINGEN
**Lieux-dits** *Elterberg, Heiligenhäuschen, Koeppchen/Köppchen, Moorberg, Nidert, Nussbaum, Péiteschwengert, Pietert, Weinbour, Wousselt*

Wormeldingen is the superstar of Luxembourg's wine villages, Koeppchen its greatest *lieu-dit*, Domaine Alice Hartmann its best producer, and Riesling its king of grapes. Domaine Alice Hartmann is by no means the only top producer making wines from this village. I have also been impressed by Wormeldingen wines from Aly Duhr, Fédération Viticole, Häremillen, Jean Schlink-Hoffeld, Mathes, Pundel-Hoffeld, Schumacher-Lethal, St. Remy Desom, Steinmetz-Jungers, and Vinsmoselle Caves de Wormeldange. I have tasted some good Pinot Gris, Pinot Blanc, and Auxerrois from these producers, but with one exception (Aly Duhr), they have all been from other *lieux-dits*. If I have learned anything about the wines of Luxembourg, it is that the best parts of Koeppchen produce the country's finest Riesling, and it would be a great shame to plant this *terroir* with any other variety.

# OTHER WINEMAKING COUNTRIES OF NORTHWESTERN EUROPE

*In the northern hemisphere, the farther north a vine grows, the fewer hours of daylight it receives and the greater the angle at which the sunlight is spread out, thus the longer it takes to ripen grapes. Factor in the wet, windy, and uncertain climes of the Atlantic, and it may seem surprising that these countries do in fact manage to produce wine.*

THERE ARE ONLY TWO WAYS of looking at these frontier wine countries—outside looking in or inside looking out. Those with a purely quality-oriented perspective and a fascination for expressive wines would argue that growing conditions are less favorable in Belgium than in the Pas de Calais, and more tricky in Ireland than Finistère. They would point out that there are no vines growing in the Pas de Calais or in Finistère, and that the French would think anyone who suggested planting them there out of their mind.

But if you are on the inside looking out, you probably think, why not? Such is the attitude that makes this page possible. Irrational, unnecessary, and half-crazy, almost certainly—but still possible.

## BELGIUM

**Appellations:** *Côtes de Sambres et Meuse VQPRD, Hagelandse or Hageland VQPRD, Haspengouwse or Hespaye VQPRD, Vin de Pays des Flandres, Vin de Pays du Walloon*
In Belgium, winegrowing dates back to Roman times. Today, over 250 acres (100 hectares) of vineyards are cultivated by more than 100 growers. Most of these growers are part-time or hobbyists, although there are around 20 who could be described as commercial to one extent or another.
√ *Genoels-Elderen* (Chardonnay Goud Zwarte Parel), *Peter Colemont* (Chardonnay Clos d Opleeuw)

A VINEYARD IN LIECHTENSTEIN
*The Prince of Liechtenstein's vineyards in Vaduz, the capital of this tiny European principality.*

## DENMARK

There are 62 acres (25 hectares) of vines in this country. Even more amazingly, the EU has limited growth to no more than 245 acres (99 hectares). There are nine commercial producers, the oldest of which is Domain Aalsgaard, which was established in 1975. Chateau Lille Gadegard produced its first vintage in 2003 on Bornholm, a Danish island in Eastsee, to the north of Poland.

## IRELAND

Better suited to stout and whiskey, Ireland had absolutely no winemaking history when, in 1972, Michael O'Callaghan planted Müller-Thurgau vines at Mallow in County Cork. O'Callaghan has just over 2.5 acres (1 hectare) of exclusively Reichensteiner vines nowadays, and his wine is sold exclusively in the restaurant of his country house hotel, Longueville House. Just 3 miles (5 kilometers) away from Mallow is another Irish vineyard, called Blackwater Valley, where owner Dr. Christopher has 12 acres (5 hectares), growing Reichensteiner, Madeleine Angevine, and Seyval Blanc. Another venture, West Waterford Vineyards at Cappoquin, was not in production at the time of writing.

## LATVIA

Jukka Huttunen tends 160 wine-producing vines planted in 2001 on ground warmed by buried coolant pipes from Olkiluoto nuclear power station. At 61° 13' latitude, this is the most northerly vineyard in the world.

## LIECHTENSTEIN

Situated between Germany and Switzerland, Liechtenstein is a tiny principality of 62 square miles (160 square kilometers), with just 15 hectares (37 acres) of planted vines. They are primarily Pinot Noir and Chardonnay varieties, and are mostly owned by the Crown Prince through his private winery, the Hofkellerei Fürsten von Liechtenstein.

## NETHERLANDS

**Appellation:** *Nederlandse Landwijn (basic* vin de pays*)*
Although the Netherlands is north of Belgium, and therefore would seem an even more unlikely location for growing vines, almost all its vines grow east of Maastricht, so they are actually situated farther south than the vineyards in the Belgian part of Brabant. There are over 100 growers farming 124 acres (50 hectares) of vines, primarily consisting of Riesling, Müller-Thurgau, Auxerrois, and the inevitable German crosses.
√ *Apostelhoeve* (Auxerrois Riesling)

## NORWAY

The wine-producing Hallingstad vineyard was planted close to Harten (59° 24') in 1992 by Sveier Hansen, who exports to the United States.

## SWEDEN

Although Akessons has produced sparkling wine since 1985, the grapes were not grown in Sweden. The first three vineyards to be established in this country are Blaxta Vingård (planted in 2000, first wines in 2002) southwest of Stockholm near Flen (59° 03'), and two in the Skåne region farther south: Kullabygden Vingård (planted in 2000, first wines in 2002) near Helsingborg, and the Nangijala Vingård (planted in 2001, first wines in 2003) near Malmö.

# The WINES of
# SOUTHEASTERN EUROPE

ALMOST ALL THE COUNTRIES IN
Southeastern Europe have the capacity to
become major players in the global wine
market, but Hungary has the lead and, probably,
the most potential of all. It has the lead because
Tokaji is already regarded as one of the world's
greatest classic wines and because its government
had been dabbling in a mixed-market economy
long before the collapse of Communism, whereas
the other countries in the Eastern Bloc and former
USSR were—and still are—struggling. Tokaji gives
Hungary instant status in the wine world and this
attracts international investors, but the role of a
botrytized wine is very small in the scheme of
things. Red wine is Hungary's future, and it has
a long way to go in honing regional styles and
developing markets for this wine. Indeed, all the
countries in this region should be exploiting their
red wine potential, as their various *terroirs* are
better suited to it than to white wine, whatever
they happen to be making at the moment.

4,750-GALLON BARRELS IN SUHINDOL WINERY, BULGARIA
*The Suhindol Winery started the Bulgarian wine
bandwagon rolling in the mid-1970s with cheap
but reliable Cabernet Sauvignon.*

# BULGARIA

*Once the most dependable wine-producing state in Eastern Europe, Bulgaria was fashionable in the West for its cheap Cabernet Sauvignon as early as 1975, but by the mid-1990s, this country was no longer a consistent source of reliable quality. The privatization of the industry has not been as successful as hoped, partly due to an inefficiently large number of tiny plots that have been mismanaged, and partly because arguments over their ownership have dragged on while the vines have been left to wither. Some foreign investment has helped, but more is needed to buy up thousands of these ailing vineyards and consolidate them into a smaller number of larger, well-maintained estates. Unfortunately, much of the investment already at work has gone into faux New World brand names such as Blueridge and Stork Nest. Such Anglicized names undermine Bulgaria's identity and do nothing for its reputation, whatever the quality of the individual wines.*

## FACTORS AFFECTING TASTE AND QUALITY

**LOCATION**
Located in the center of the Balkan Peninsula, Bulgaria's eastern border is formed by the Black Sea, while its neighbors to the north, west, and south are respectively Romania, Serbia/Macedonia, and Greece/Turkey.

**CLIMATE**
The climate is warm continental, although it is cooler in the north and more temperate toward the east due to the influence of the Black Sea. Annual rainfall averages between 19 and 38 inches (47 and 95 centimeters).

**ASPECT**
Vines are grown largely on the flat valley floors and coastal plains.

**SOIL**
Predominantly fertile alluvium in the valleys, with dark-gray and brown forest soils in the northern region, and rich, black carbonate soils in the southern region, becoming sandy in the vineyards of the southeast coastal area.

**VITICULTURE AND VINIFICATION**
Most vineyards are concentrated in the valleys of the Danube and Maritsa Rivers. The disruption of privatization has not been a positive factor for Bulgaria, whose vineyards are highly fractured, with many that are poorly maintained. The wineries are comparatively well equipped, and vinification methods have been updated; there is a state-of-the-art facility at Sliven (Blueridge).

**GRAPE VARIETIES**
**Primary varieties:** Cabernet Sauvignon, Gamza, Mavrud, Merlot, Pamid, Rkatsiteli, Red Misket, Ugni Blanc, Welschriesling
**Secondary varieties:** Aligoté, Bolgar, Cabernet Franc, Chardonnay, Dimiat, Fetjaska, Gamay, Mavrud, Melnik (also called Shiroka Melnishka loza), Muskat Ottonel, Pinot Gris, Pinot Noir, Rubin (Nebbiolo x Syrah), Sylvaner, Syrah, Riesling, Sauvignon Blanc, Tamianka, Traminer

ALTHOUGH BULGARIANS HAVE been cultivating vines for more than 3,000 years, winemaking came to a halt when the Turks imposed Muslim rule between 1396 and 1878. It was not until 1918 that winemaking began again in earnest, and it was only in the 1970s that the Bulgarians made any real effort to export their wines. Bizarrely, it was PepsiCo who started this export drive. The company wanted to open up sales of its cola and, not interested in Bulgarian currency, needed something marketable in exchange. Wine seemed a good idea, so PepsiCo supplied the Sliven Winery with expertise from UC Davis to bring the domestic product up to modern standards. During the mid-1970s, the economic depression that was affecting most Western countries meant that consumers were on the look-out for cheaper alternatives to Bordeaux, and Bulgaria was suddenly in a position to oblige, thanks to PepsiCo.

## EXPORTING WINE
Cabernet Sauvignon from Bulgaria's Suhindol region was not simply cheap in the 1970s, it was extraordinarily well made, had a deep color, full body, soft fruit, rich blackcurrant varietal flavor, and just a hint of wood-aging on the finish.

Spurred on by the success of Cabernet Sauvignon, Bulgaria soon became the world's fourth-largest exporter of wine, and state subsidies ensured that prices remained attractive. For many years, Bulgarian wine was well known for its consistency and value for money, but Gorbachov's alcohol reforms in the mid-1980s resulted in the uprooting of many vineyards, which was the first factor to have a detrimental effect on quality. Ironically, the second factor was democracy, as this was the precursor to privatization, which denied many of the largest former state-owned wineries some of their best sources of grapes. The result has been a rather mixed bag, as some wineries have gone completely private, while most remain local cooperatives, and a large number of private growers have put their products (grapes now, but surely single-vineyard wines in the future) on the market for the very first time. In 1991, Domaine Boyar in Sofia became the first private wine company to be established in Bulgaria since 1947, and this has put it one step ahead of the rest in terms of sourcing by enabling it to forge links with ten of the best wineries in the country.

## BULGARIAN LABEL LANGUAGE

BJALO VINO White wine
BUTILIRAM To bottle
CHERVENO VINO Red wine
CONTROLIRAN These wines constitute just 2 percent of the total production of quality wines, and are made from grapes that originate from strictly defined and controlled microregional vineyards, with a limited maximum yield of grapes per acre and defined minimum sugar content.
COUNTRY WINE Inexpensive blended wine on a par with French *vins de pays*.
DESERTNO Dessert or sweet wine

ISKRIASHTO VINO Sparkling wine
KOLEKTZIONO Reserve
LOZIA Vineyard
LOZOVA PRACHKA Vine or vine variety
NATURALNO Natural
SLADKO VINO Sweet wine
RESERVE This term is restricted to DGO and Controliran wines, and indicates ageing in oak of at least three years for white and four for red, although after an intitial, indeterminate period the wines may be transferred from small *barriques* to large wooden vats.

SOSTATACHNA ZAKAR Semidry or medium wine
SUHO VINO Dry wine
TRADITZIONI REGIONALNI Vino Country Wine
VINO KONTROLIRANO NAIMENOVANIE ZA PROIZHOD Controliran wine (*see Controliran*)
VINO OT DEKLARIRAN GEOGRAFSKI OR DGO Wine of Declared Geographical Origin. This category constitutes 70 percent of all Bulgarian quality wines, those made from selected grapes originating from a particular geographical region.
VINOPROIZUODITEL Wine producer

## RECENT BULGARIAN VINTAGES

**2006** Possibly the best vintage of the 2000s.

**2005** Even less impressive than 2004, although the most successful wines are light and ready to drink.

**2004** Not the best of vintages, with particularly poor-quality, underripe reds. Some useful, early-drinking whites were made.

**2003** An excellent red and white wine vintage yielded very ripe grapes with relatively high acidity levels.

**2002** Poor-quality vintage for both red and white wines.

## NEW LAWS

On November 14, 2000, the Association of Producers and Merchants of Wines and Spirits of Bulgaria (APMWSB) was disbanded and, in line with the new Bulgarian Wine Law, its role was transferred to the newly established National Vineyard and Wine Chamber (NVWC), which is aligned with European Union structures, and is designed to facilitate European integration in 2007, if economic and other factors are met. The new Bulgarian Wine Law has been described by its opponents in Bulgaria as "French law" and, not unreasonably, they claim that a more flexible law would enable them to compete with New World rivals. By flexible, they do not mean anything underhand or corner-cutting, simply the sort of "truth in labelling" philosophy that their New World opponents tend to adopt. If a Bulgarian wine states that it is from a particular grape grown in a specific area, then that is what should be in the bottle. Eminently sensible, but if Bulgaria is to be a part of the European Union, then it must obey its wine regime, which is indeed very much based on French wine law at present. Once in the Union, Bulgarians can argue for fundamental changes to the pan-European wine regime until they are blue in the face. That will be their right. And they will discover that it is a very minor cog in a vast machine called the Common Agricultural Policy, which itself has such a history of corruption and kick-backs that there are far too many vested interests, both open and shadowy, to have a hope in hell of changing, as so many other, far more powerful, countries have found out.

There are other good producers in Bulgaria, of course, and, although many more dull wines exist than before, and handling of oak by some wineries has been very clumsy indeed, there has also been much progress. The introduction of young, unvatted Cabernet and Merlot at the behest of a certain British supermarket group has shown what these wines can be like if bottled before the first flush of wonderfully fresh fruit is lost in vat. For all those who still like a lot of oak, some of the top Reserve wines are very good indeed. And huge strides have been made in white winemaking, thanks to Australian flying winemakers.

This internationalization of Bulgarian wine was already well underway before Domaine Boyar launched its Blueridge export brand. Blueridge was designed to lull supermarket shoppers into a false sense of New World security; as they scanned the shelves, consumers would not realize that they had strayed out of familiar territory. The new Blueridge Winery in Sliven cost over 5 million euros in 1999, but it has contributed nothing to the world's awareness of Bulgarian wine. Its balance sheets might look fine now, but ultimately the value of its wines and the profitability of its operation will depend on the public's perception of its geographical origin. If its Anglicized abomination of a name is kept and customers continue to have their attention diverted from the wine's true origin, Blueridge might as well move to India, where costs are even cheaper, and make wines from imported grape concentrate. Domaine Boyar's Blueridge is not alone in its Westernization of Bulgarian wine. In 2003, a group of Australian investors purchased the Svichtov Winery and renamed it Stork Nest. The Australians are performing miracles in the vineyard, but doing nothing to promote Bulgarian wine *per se*.

It is about time that Bulgarians realize there is a difference between international input and internationalization. Thanks to international input, there is absolutely no doubt that Bulgaria can make world-class wines, but its winemakers must look to their roots. There is no reason to forsake international varieties such as Cabernet Sauvignon and Merlot, but they should also experiment intensively with indigenous varieties. The obvious strategy would

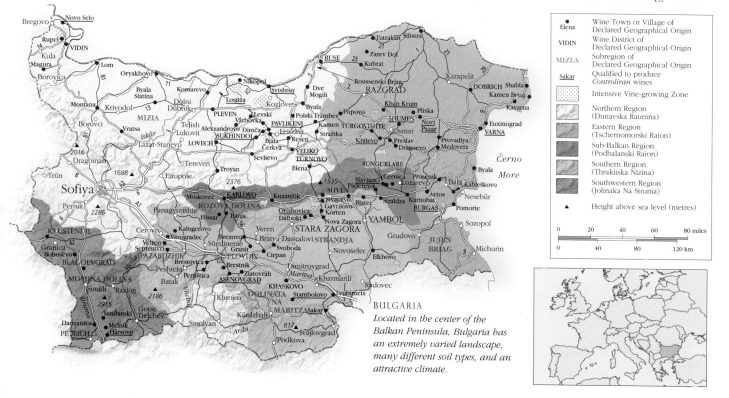

**BULGARIA**
*Located in the center of the Balkan Peninsula, Bulgaria has an extremely varied landscape, many different soil types, and an attractive climate.*

be to work with clones of Gamza, Mavrud, and Melnik, all easy enough to pronounce on export markets, planting them in the best *terroirs,* at high densities, pruning them to ultra-low yields to remove the leafy character, and building these grapes into Bulgaria's flagship wines. Utilizing the same practices, other intrinsically Bulgarian grapes could rise above their current reputation. For example, is Pamid the simple, light-bodied variety we imagine it to be, or is that merely the result of high-yield production? The new governing body, the National Vineyard and Wine Chamber, should use its honeymoon period to institute strong measures to combat the deterioration of Bulgaria's vineyards. A three-year ban, perhaps, on grapes from poorly maintained vineyards being allowed

in any wine other than an anonymous table wine. The threat of such a severe reduction in earnings would either force real changes in vineyard practices, or the sale of vineyards to more quality-conscious estates. Ironically, although too many vineyards are allowed to produce very high yields, poor standards of vineyard maintenance has reduced overall output, and some wineries are operating at less than half capacity. When vines are not looked after properly and allowed to bear a greater burden of fruit, they become vulnerable to climatic excesses and diseases throughout the growing season. However, above all, Bulgarians must take back their individuality, treating the use of New World technology as a means to carve out a unique Bulgarian identity.

## THE APPELLATIONS OF
# BULGARIA

**Note** Bulgaria's quality wines are divided into two categories: wines of Declared Geographical Origin, or DGOs, which carry subregional, district, town, or village appellations, and *Controliran* wines, the highest-quality category, which have to be made from specified grape varieties grown in certain DGOs.

## EASTERN REGION (TSCHERNOMORSKI RAION)

**DGO regions** *Burgas, Razgrad, Targovischte, Tolbuhin*

**DGO villages** *Ajtos, Bjala, Dragoevo, Euxinograd, Kabelskovo, Kavarna, Kamen Brjag, Kubrat, Medovetz, Pliska, Pomorie, Popovo, Preslav, Prosenik, Provadija, Sabla/Shabla, Shumen/Sumen, Silistra, Tutraken, Zarev Dol*

**Controliran wines** *Jujen Briag* (South Coast), *Khan Krum, Kralevo, Novi Pazar, Varna*

This region accounts for 30 percent of Bulgaria's vineyards and includes four regional DGOs. The Schumen district has long been noted for white wines, particularly those from Khan Krum, but it was only recently that they rose to international standards, thanks to Australian expertise. Other well-known Schumen Chardonnays come from Novi Pazar and Preslav. Preslav now makes good, gluggy Chardonnay-Sauvignon blends. Khan Krum is also known for its Riesling and Dimiat, which has become very fresh and tangy. South Coast Rosé is an off-dry Cabernet Sauvignon blush wine from Burgas, an underrated district that produces many inexpensive yet very drinkable Country Wines.

🍇 Aligoté, Bolgar, Cabernet Sauvignon, Chardonnay, Dimiat, Gewürztraminer (*syn* Traminer), Pamid, Rkatsiteli, Red Misket, Riesling (*syn* Rheinriesling), Sauvignon Blanc, Tamianka, Ugni Blanc, Varneski Misket, Welschriesling (*syn* Italian Riesling)

✓ *Domaine Boyar • Pomorie • Shumen • Targovischte*

## NORTHERN REGION (DUNAVSKA RAUNINA)

**DGO regions** *Pleven, Vidin*

**DGO districts** *Aleksandrovo, Bjala, Bjala Cerkva, Bjala Slatina, Dimca, Dve Mogili, Dolni Dâbnik, Elena, Kamen, Komarevo, Krivodol, Levski, Lom, Magura, Mihajlovgrad, Nikopol, Orahovo, Polski Trâmbes, Resen, Rupci, Sevlievo, Strakika, Trojan, Varbovka, Vraca*

**Controliran wines** *Lyaskovetz, Lositza, Novo Selo, Pavlikeni, Russe, Suhindol, Svichtov*

This region accounts for 35 percent of Bulgaria's vineyards, encompassing two subregional DGOs. Suhindol's reputation is based on Bulgaria's best-selling Cabernet Sauvignon, but two others from the district are worth trying: the grapey-oaky Gamza, which is a *Controliran* wine, and the interesting, soft-textured Merlot-Gamza blend, which is of equal quality but only a DGO. Russe has produced gorgeously fruity, so-called "unvatted" reds and, under the guidance of winemaker Kym Milne, Lyaskovetz is now making easy-drinking, inexpensive blended whites.

🍇 Cabernet Sauvignon, Chardonnay, Gamza, Gamay, Muskat Ottonel, Pinot Noir, Red Misket, Rkatsiteli, Sauvignon Blanc, Traminer, Vrachanski Misket

✓ *Stork Nest* (formerly Svichtov winery) *• Maxima • Tellish* (Merlot)

## SOUTHERN REGION (THRAKIISKA NIZINA)

**DGO regions** *Cirpan/Chirpan, Dolinata na Maritza, Haskovo, Iambol, Pazardzik, Plovdiv, Stara Zagora, Strandja*

**DGO villages** *Blatec, Brestovica, Brezovo, Dalboki, Elhovo, Gavrilovo, Granit, Kalugerovo, Korten, Liubimec, Nova Zagora, Perustica, Septemvri, Sivacevo, Svoboda, Vetren, Vinogradec, Zlatovrah*

**Controliran wines** *Assenovgrad, Brestnik, Oriachovitza, Sakar, Stambolovo*

This region accounts for 22 percent of Bulgaria's vineyards and encompasses eight regional DGOs. Assenovgrad is justly famous for its dark, dry, plummy-spicy Mavrud wine, which can age well for 10 or more years. Plovdiv makes fine, firm, blackcurranty Cabernet Sauvignon, as does Stara Zagora, a district that boasts a superb Cabernet Sauvignon-Merlot *Controliran* wine from Oriachovitza. Oriachovitza also makes a classy Cabernet Sauvignon Reserve. From the Strandja region comes Sakar Mountain Cabernet, one of the first wines to establish a reputation on export markets, although it is the Merlot from this area that has *Controliran* status. East of Stara Zagora is Iambol, which produces a very rich Cabernet Sauvignon Reserve in which the oak can take on a spicy-caramel complexity, while in the southeast, Elhovo churns out a much cheaper Cabernet with obvious coconutty aromas that should suit budget-conscious oak-lovers. Bessa Valley is an exciting joint venture between the Damianitza Winery, Count von Neipperg of Pomerol fame, French oenologist Mark Dworkin, and a couple of investors, who are building a Bordeaux-type

wine estate with over 250 acres (100 hectares) of grapes (Malbec, Merlot, Petit Verdot, and Syrah).

🍇 Aligoté, Cabernet Sauvignon, Dimiat, Gamay, Malbec, Mavrud, Merlot, Pamid, Petit Vardot, Pinot Noir, Red Misket, Sauvignon Blanc, Syrah

✓ *Assenovgrad • Bessa Valley • Domaine Saker • Ententa • Haskovo • Iambol • Korten • Oriachovitza • Todoroff* (Terres) *• Yamantievs* (King Leo, Parallel 41)

## SOUTHWESTERN REGION (JOLINAKA NA STRUMA)

**DGO regions** *Blagoevgrad, Kjustendil, Molina Dolina, Petric*

**DGO villages** *Bobosevo, Damjanica, Melnik, Sandanski*

**Controliran wines** *Harsovo*

This region accounts for 6 percent of Bulgaria's vineyards and includes four regional DGOs. The most famous wine is Melnik, which is generally well-colored, rich, and warm, and may be tannic or soft, depending on how it is made. Damianitza Melnik is very smooth and rich. No Mans Land is pure Cabernet Sauvignon. Re Dark is aptly named for a dense-colored, super-premium wine made from Merlot. Uniquato is made from a unique early-ripening clone of Melnik known locally as Shiroka Melnishka Loza.

🍇 Cabernet Sauvignon, Chardonnay, Melnik, Merlot, Shiroka Melnishka Loza, Tamianka

✓ *Damianitza* (No Man's Land, Re Dark, Uniquato) *• Santa Sarah Estate*

## SUB-BALKAN REGION (PODBALANSKI RAION)

**DGO regions** *Sliven*

**DGO villages** *Banja, Cernica, Hissar, Karnobat, Kasanlak, Pâderevo, Straldza* **Controliran wines** *Karlovo, Rozova Dolina* (Rose Valley)*, Slaviantzi, Sungurlare*

This region accounts for 7 percent of vineyards and encompasses one regional DGO. The Rozova Domina Misket is made in the Karlovo district, and Sungurlare Misket in Slaviantzi. Both are light-golden, floral-scented, musky wines. Sliven makes one of the world's cheapest Merlot blends, using Pinot Noir to add a touch of elegance to what is a very gluggy wine indeed.

🍇 Cabernet Sauvignon, Chardonnay, Merlot, Red Misket, Riesling, Ugni Blanc

✓ *Blueridge • Slaviantzi • VINI*

# HUNGARY

*Although potentially the most exciting winemaking country among the former Iron Curtain states, and despite there being a quality-focused movement afoot in some quarters, Hungary has a long way to go if it is to become a serious world player. Even in Tokaj, undisputedly one of the greatest botrytis regions in the world, improvements since the collapse of Communism have been sporadic, despite the example set by foreign investors, and local hero István Szepsy. If every wine producer in every region was as gifted and as committed as Szepsy, Hungary would be the greatest wine-producing country in the world. Perhaps the Hungarian government should give Szepsy prime sites in every single wine region in the country?*

WHEN DEMOCRACY ARRIVED in 1989, Hungary had a clear advantage over other former Eastern Bloc countries because even under Communist rule, it had long been dabbling with a mixed economy. Exploiting this to the full, the transition from a centrally planned economy to a market-driven one has been relatively smooth, with the private sector now accounting for more than 80 percent of Hungary's economic output, and foreign investment totaling in excess of $23 billion. This provides most Hungarian industries with the economic success and stability required to attract further investment to expand and improve, but although

## FACTORS AFFECTING TASTE AND QUALITY

**LOCATION**
Hungary is sandwiched between Austria and Romania, north of Yugoslavia, in the Carpathian basin south of Slovakia.

**CLIMATE**
Generally a continental climate, with some Mediterranean influence in the southern wine districts. The annual mean temperature is 51°F (10.5°C), with an average rainfall of 23 inches (60 centimeters). In the Carpathian foothills of Tokaj, in northeastern Hungary, long misty autumns encourage botrytis.

**ASPECT**
Almost half of the country's vines are grown on the Great Plain, where the land is flat or gently undulating river plains. The rest of the country is hilly.

**SOIL**
Slate, basalt, clay, and loess in the west, through the sandy soils of the Great Plain, to the clay, loess, and volcanic rock in the northeast, and volcanic, slate, and sandy soils in the south.

**VITICULTURE AND VINIFICATION**
Tokaji necessitates the harvesting and sorting of botrytized grapes. Otherwise, all Hungarian red and white wines are produced using standard vinification techniques, with no exceptional practices. However, a steady modernization of winemaking facilities has taken place since the 1990s.

**GRAPE VARIETIES**
Cabernet Franc, Cabernet Sauvignon, Chardonnay, Ezerjó, Furmint, Hárslevelű, Irsai Olivér, Kadarka, Kékfrankos (Limberger), Kékporto (Portugieser), Leányka, Olaszrizling (Welschriesling), Pinot Blanc, Pinot Gris, Sauvignon Blanc, Tramini (Traminer), Zweigelt

### DID YOU KNOW?

- Tokaj is the place, Tokaji is the wine, and Tokay is the old, Anglicized spelling, which is no longer used.
- *Szamorodni* is Polish, not Hungarian, for "the way it comes" and indicates a wine to which *aszú* (overripe grapes for sweetening) has not been added.

HUNGARY
*A country that has great potential for red wine, although this is overshadowed by the history and fame of Tokaji, one of the world's classic botrytized wines.*

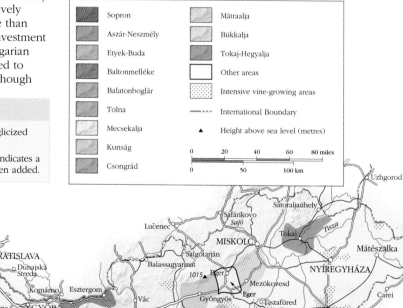

| | | |
|---|---|---|
| Sopron | | Mátraalja |
| Aszár-Neszmély | | Bükkalja |
| Etyek-Buda | | Tokaj-Hegyalja |
| Balatonmelléke | | Other areas |
| Balatonboglár | | Intensive vine-growing areas |
| Tolna | | International Boundary |
| Mecsekalja | | Height above sea level (metres) |
| Kunság | | |
| Csongrád | | |

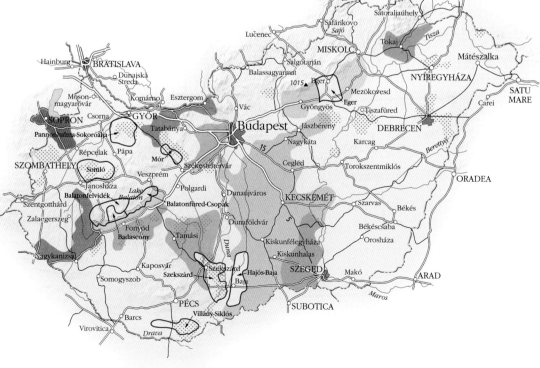

## THE DANGER OF INTERNATIONALIZED BRANDS

As with other former Eastern Bloc wine-producing countries, Hungary has more than its fair share of Anglicized brand names, each of which has been concocted to attract Western wine consumers who might not otherwise consider buying Hungarian wines, but should feel comfortable with the New World style of labelling. Whatever reputation the likes of Chapel Hill and Hilltop (including Riverview and Woodcutters White) earn, they do nothing to establish an identity for Hungarian wines, except perhaps the wrong one.

## TOKAJI TABLE

*Pre-1991 criteria are provided because many vintages from that era are still available on primary (retail) and secondary (auction) markets.*

| WINE STYLE | PRE-1991 WINE ACT | | POST-1991/7 WINE ACT | | |
| --- | --- | --- | --- | --- | --- |
| | RESIDUAL SUGAR | MINIMUM AGING IN WOOD | ALCOHOL | RESIDUAL SUGAR | MINIMUM AGING IN WOOD |
| Varietal wines (*Furmint, Hárslevelű Sárga Muskotály, Zéta*) | N/A | N/A | N/A | N/A | 1 |
| Máslás | N/A | N/A | 13% | N/A | 1 |
| Fordítás | N/A | N/A | 13% | N/A | 1 |
| Száraz Szamorodni | 0–4 g/l | 2 years | 13% | N/A | 1 |
| Edes Szamorodni | 20–50 g/l | 2 years | 13% | 30 g/l | 1 year |
| Aszú 2 puttonyos [2] | 50–60 g/l | 2 years | N/A | N/A | 2 years |
| Aszú 3 puttonyos | 60–90 g/l | 3 years | N/A | 60 g/l | 2 years |
| Aszú 4 puttonyos | 90–120 g/l | 4 years | N/A | 90 g/l | 2 years |
| Aszú 5 puttonyos | 120–150 g/l | 5 years | N/A | 120 g/l | 2 years |
| Aszú 6 puttonyos | 150–180 g/l | 6 years | N/A | 150 g/l | 2 years |
| Aszúesszencia (7–8 puttonyos) | 200–240 g/l | 7–8 years | N/A | 180 g/l | 2 years |
| Esszencia or Natúresszencia | N/A | N/A | N/A | 250 g/l | 2 years |

**Notes**

[1] Aging in wood allowed, and normal practice, but no prescribed minimum.

[2] Aszú 2 *puttonyos* is allowed, but for some reason has not been made since 1938.

the wine industry has enjoyed some foreign investment, it has not expanded and improved across the board. Why? Because finance alone cannot create a range of fine wines. It takes quality-conscious growers and inspirational winemakers, something that Hungary does not appear to have in any great number at the moment. It is probably a symptom of the country's past, and it might take a complete generation born in and bred under the ideals of a free, democratic state to nurture the sort of spirit needed to make something as decadent as fine wine. Certainly, there is no one who comes within a mile of István Szepsy's genius for winemaking. My suggestion, in the introduction, that the Hungarian government should give him prime sites in every single wine region in the country was only partly in jest. It would at least demonstrate the quality that is ultimately possible in each wine region, and that would attract foreign investors to those parts of the country.

## INVESTMENT IN TOKAJ

The first area that received investment was Tokaj. This is understandable, as Tokaji is the only classic wine of authentic historical reputation in all Eastern Europe. Hugh Johnson and the Australian-trained, Anglo-Danish maestro winemaker Peter Vinding-Diers (no longer involved) purchased the Royal Tokaji Wine Company in Mád and 156 acres (63 hectares) of vineyards. Interestingly, the Royal Tokaji vineyards have never been state-owned (all other investors have been forced to buy vineyards from Borkombinat, the State Wine Farm), and almost 60 percent are classified (dating back to 1700), including three first growths (Nyulaszo, Szt Tamas, and Betsek) and one second growth (Birsalmas). After this dynamic duo came a number of others:

• **Chateau Dereszla** Established in 1992 by CANA (France), but bought by the d'Aulan family (former owners of Champagne Piper-Heidsieck) in 1999, Chateau Dereszla has 37 acres (15 hectares) in Henye, and 49 acres (20 hectares) in Csirke, processing another 370 acres (150 hectares) of bought-in grapes.

• **Disznókõ** A new winery built by AXA, the most prominent French investor, led at the time by the redoubtable Jean-Michel Cazes, who purchased 320 acres (130 hectares) of vineyards.

• **Királyudvar** A joint venture funded by Philippine-born American businessman Anthony Hwang, with the winemaking talents of István Szepsy, who is also involved with Hwang in the purchase of Huet in the Loire. This renovated historic winery owns 222 acres (90 hectares) spread over 12 vineyards, mostly in Heyne, Lapis, and Danczka.

• **Chateau Megyer** Purchased in 2000 by Jean-Louis Laborde of Chateau Pajzos, Chateau Megyer comprises 193 acres (78 hectares) of vineyards.

• **Chateau Pajzos** Established in 1991 as a French-funded joint venture between Jean-Louis Laborde and the late Jean-Michel Arcaute, with Michel Rolland consulting. Chateau Pajzos owns 198 acres (80 hectares) of vineyards.

• **Tokaj Classic** A joint venture between Hungarian and German investors, Tokaj Classic was established in 1998, and consists of just over 17 acres (7 hectares) of vineyards, mostly in Betsek.

• **Tokaj Oremus** Spanish-owned by the famous Vega Sicilia, Tokaj Oremus own 272 acres (110 hectares) of vineyards, mostly in Mandúlas, Kútpatka, Budaház, Heyne, Máriássy, and Deák.

## HUNGARIAN LABEL LANGUAGE

**ASZTALI BOR** Table wine, the lowest quality of wine.

**ASZÚ** Overripe grapes for sweetening Tokaji, equivalent of German *Auslese*

**BOR** Wine

**BORKÜLÖNLEGESSÉGE SZÖLÖGAZDASÁGÁNAK** A speciality from the vineyards of the region named

**BORVIDÉK** Wine region

**DŰLÓ** Vineyard    check

**ÉDES** Sweet

**FEHÉR** White

**FORDÍTÁS** A sweet Tokaji produced from reused *aszúpaste*, drained from a *gönc* of *aszú* wine, rekneaded and macerated in fresh must. The result is comparable to a 4 or 5 *puttonyos* in

sweetness, but more tannic. They say that a Fordítás from a very good year is often better than an *aszú* from a poor vintage, but I have yet to see this difference demonstrated by the same Tokaji producer.

**HABZÓ** Sparkling

**HORDÓ** Cask or barrel

**JEGBOR** Ice wine, or Eiswein

**KÉSÖI SZÜRETELÉSŰ** Late harvest

**KÍMERT BOR** Ordinary wine

**KÖTNYÉKI BOR** Country wine

**KÜLÖNLEGES MINÓSÉGŰ** Official denomination denoting "special quality," placing it above Minösegi bor.

**MÁSLÁS** A dry version of Fordítás

(*see* Fordítás above), but fermented on the unpressed lees of an *aszú* wine, with much less lees to wine ratio. Máslás literally means "copy."

**MINÓSEGI BOR** Quality wine, equivalent to French AOC.

**ORSZÁGOS BORMINÓSÍTÓ BIZOTTSÁG** OR **OBB** National Wine Qualification Board

**ORSZÁGOS BORMINÓSÍTÓ INTÉZET** OR **OBI** State Wine Qualification Institute

**PALACK** Bottle

**PALACKZÁS** Bottling

**PALACKOZOTT** Bottled

**PEZSGO** Sparkling

**PINCE** Cellar

**SILLER** A dark rosé or light red

**SZAMORODNI** Literally "as it comes," the term often refers to Tokaji that has not been specially treated with *aszú* and is therefore usually dry, though it can be used for other wines.

**SZÁRAZ** Dry

**SZÓLÓ** Grapes

**SZÓLÓBIRTOK** Wine estate

**SZÓLÓSKERT** Vineyard

**TÁJBOR** Country wine, equivalent to a French *vin de pays*

**TERMELÓ** Production

**TÓKE** Vine

**TÖPPEDT SZÓLÓBÓL KÉSZÜLT** Botrytis selection

**VÖRÖS** Red

## RECENT HUNGARIAN VINTAGES

**2006** Excellent quality for red, white, and Tokaji styles. Extreme diurnal differences resulted in exceptionally good acids and aromatics.

**2005** Due to rain at the beginning of the harvest, late-picked wines fared best, making for very good Tokaji and reds from Villány, Szekszárd, and Sopron, but moderate elsewhere.

**2004** Good Tokaji and fruity whites.

**2003** An outstanding vintage for Tokaji and red wines. Hungary also produced its best-ever white wines, though mostly for ready drinking.

**2002** Good Tokaji, but best for dry whites.

The one thing these investors have in common is a change in the methods used to produce Tokaji. It was suggested that the French were intent on making Sauternes in Hungary, and this rankled local pride, with some critics wondering "whether Tokaji should not legitimately remain an oxidative wine." Old-style Tokaji was not, however, merely oxidative; it was deliberately oxidized. The only possible comparison is sherry and *vin jaune*, since they are the only wines that are deliberately left in part-filled barrels to oxidize, as Tokaji producers did in the Communist era. However, sherry and *vin jaune* casks are part-filled for a purpose: the ullage allows for the growth of *flor*, a froth of rare yeast that is responsible for the particular character and style of those wines. In the Tokaji process, there is no guarantee of *flor* and thus no justification for exposing the wine to the air—in which it merely oxidizes.

### Tokaji old and new
It would be wrong to divide old and new style between Hungarian and foreign producers. Firstly, old style is only as old as the Communist era. There is no evidence of half-filled casks in the 19th century; this practice is not mentioned in the meticulously detailed *Tokaj-Hegyaljai Album* (1867). Secondly, not all foreign-funded ventures are successful at the new style. Some have not gone the full distance—or they have old-style stocks they are gradually disposing of by fractional blending. Even those who went the full distance reined back on new style in the 1990s, when too many of their wines were refused the Tokaji appellation because of lack of typicity. And it is wrong to suggest that only foreign winemakers pioneered new-wave Tokaji. The first and the best by far was István Szepsy. No one has ever made Tokaji with the purity, precision, and finesse that Szepsy can manage.

So what is the difference between the so-called new and old styles? Most importantly, it is no longer a requirement to leave Tokaji Aszú in barrels for up to a decade with at least one-third air-space. This is still permitted for those who believe that oxidation is Tokaji's most essential character, but it is no longer obligatory. However, fortification was banned, even for those who persist with the old style. Fortification was common practice when Hungary was part of the Eastern Bloc (as was pasteurization), but the Communists cannot be blamed, as it was originally a late 19th-century "innovation," and officially recognized in law in 1936. Two years is the minimum aging period in wood under the new law, but although there is a lot of new or relatively new oak in use today, it has not so much been a conscious move as a necessity to replace ancient, leaking, and often diseased wood.

The other major change that has occurred since the decentralization of Tokaji cellars is the emergence of two fundamentally different, but mutually admirable, production philosophies—those who make wine based on a single estate (the Bordeaux concept), and those who make single-vineyard wines, which might or might not belong to the winery in question (the Burgundian route).

The official tasting committees should have changed their decision-making process after the 1991 Wine Act, or at least by the changes introduced in 1997, but they had difficulty shaking off the old ways. A number of new wineries were frustrated as their more pristine products were rejected throughout the 1990s for their lack of typicity (i.e., no "sherrylike" character). After a decade of stylistic debate, the authorities caught up with the times in 2000.

### How Tokaji is made today
As with all great sweet wines, Tokaji owes its quality and character to semidried, extremely rich grapes (Furmint and Hárslevelű) that have been affected by *Botrytis cinerea*, or "noble rot." These shriveled grapes, called *aszú* (pronounced "ossu") are put into a wooden hod called a *puttony* for six to eight days, and under their own weight a highly concentrated, thick, syrupy juice slowly drains out of holes at the bottom of the container into glass vessels called balloons. This is pure Esszencia, also called *nectar*. Each *puttony* holds 50 lb (25 kilograms) of *aszú* grapes but yields only a quarter of a pint (0.2 liters) of pure Esszencia. After the Esszencia has been removed, the *puttony* of *aszú* grapes is kneaded into a paste and added to a 36-gallon cask called a *gönc*, or a stainless-steel vat, of unfermented must or dry base wine. This is made from a blend of nonbotrytized Furmint and Hárslevelű grapes (though wines labelled Muskotály Aszú contain 100 percent Muskotály grapes). The sweetness of the wine depended upon how many *puttonyos* (plural of *puttony*) were added to the must or dry base wine, and wines are still marketed with *puttonyos* designations.

Tokaji Aszúesszencia is the equivalent of at least seven *puttonyos*, whereas Esszencia or Natúresszencia is pure Esszencia, and is the closest thing to the legendary drink of the tsars. It is so rich in sugar (up to 850 grams per liter) that it requires a special strain of yeast to ferment it, and even then it can take many decades to reach 5 or 6 percent of alcohol. Until privatization, it was made only for sweetening, and even now it is extremely rare and expensive (Oremus 1997 Esszencia was over $750 per bottle in 2005). I will never forget the first pure Esszencia, back in the days of Communist rule, at the state cellars at Tolcsva. It had been fermenting for 13 years, yet had achieved less than 2 percent of alcohol. With 640 grams of residual sugar per liter, it poured like oil, and had the most incredible bouquet, like the scent of a fresh rose in full morning bloom. It was intensely sweet and very grapey, but with a clean, almost crisp, finish thanks to an astonishing 38 grams per liter of acidity.

## BEYOND TOKAJI
Hungary is generally recognized as a potentially exciting red wine country, yet only 25 percent of its vineyards are planted with black grapes. One of Hungary's biggest problems is that its flagship wine, Tokaji, is an intensely sweet wine, and it is very difficult to promote any winemaking region on the back of a wine that is consumed very occasionally by a tiny minority of consumers. It will be essential, therefore, for the industry to concentrate its efforts on improving, experimenting with, and expanding the quality and styles of wines of Eger, Villány, Hajós-Baja, Szekszárd, and Sopron, the areas where the greatest red wine promise exists.

## IMPERIAL TOKAJI

The most famous wine is Imperial Tokaji, an elixir so prized by the tsars of Russia that they maintained a detachment of Cossacks solely for the purpose of escorting convoys of the precious liquid from Hungary to the royal cellars at St. Petersburg. Reputed to last at least three hundred years, it must surely have been considered an elixir of eternal youth. Until World War II, Fukier, the ancient wine merchants of Warsaw, had 328 bottles of Tokaji 1606 but, to my knowledge, none has emerged at auction since 1945. What is sold today as Tokaji Aszú and Tokaji Aszúesszencia does not have quite the same character, but can still be great wine.

# THE APPELLATIONS OF
# HUNGARY

## ASZÁR-NESZMÉLY

**Area under vine:** *3,460 acres*
**Subregions** *Aszár, Neszmély*

Winemaking traditions date back to the Middle Ages. Vineyards were cultivated along the lines of large estates as from the 18th century, with the famous Esterházi Csákvári estate considered to be a model vineyard and cellars in the 19th century. Most soils are loess-based. The climate is milder than the surrounding Great Plains area, with less risk of spring and fall frost. Mostly fresh, fragrant, lively white wines. The internationally known Hilltops winery produces over 50 different wines every year in Neszmély.

🍇 Chardonnay, Cserszegi Fûszeres, Királylányka, Irsai Olivér, Olaszrizling, Pinot Gris, Sauvignon Blanc, Szürkebarát

✓ *Hilltops* (Cserszegi Fûszeres, Riverview Cabernet Sauvignon, Virgin Vintage Chardonnay, Virgin Vintage Sauvignon Blanc)

## BADACSONY

**Area under vine:** *4,000 acres*

With its south-facing volcanic slopes on the northerly shores of Lake Balaton, Europe's largest lake, Badacsony is noted for its own indigenous grape called Kéknyelû. This increasingly rare white variety has excellent potential for full-bodied white wines, with a fiery palate, fine acids, and an intensive, aromatic bouquet, but often produces a disappointing quality.

🍇 Kékfrankos, Kéknyelu, Olaszrizling, Szürkebarát

✓ *Szent Orbán Pince* (Sz≥l≥sgyöröki Olaszrizling) • *Szeremley* (Kéknyelu, Szürkebarát, Tihanyi Kékfrankos)

## BALATONBOGLÁR

**Area under vine:** *6,400 acres*
**Subregions** *Csáfordi, Szentgyörgyvári, and Muravidéki*

The winemaking potential of Lake Balaton's south shore was seldom fulfilled until the early 1990s, when Australian flying winemaker Kym Milne started producing extremely rich, oak-aged Chardonnay at the Balatonboglár Winery under the Chapel Hill label. With Master of Wine Milne still in charge, ably assisted by Kiwi Clive Hartnell, and fellow Australian Richard Smart advising in the vineyard, the quality at Chapel Hill has strengthened in the 2000s. Other products from the Balatonboglár Winery are far less exciting, and some producers churn out a lot of very second-rate wines, particularly in the semisweet Olaszrizling category.

🍇 Chardonnay, Cserszegi Fûszeres, Kékfrankos, Királyleányka, Merlot, Olaszrizling, Rizlingszilváni, Szürkebarát, Sauvignon Blanc

✓ *Chapel Hill* (Chardonnay, Chardonnay-Pinot Noir Brut, Merlot, plus entire Winemaker's Selection and Single Vineyard Selection ranges) • *Ottó Légli* (Sz≥l≥skislaki Barrique Chardonnay)

## BALATONFELVIDÉK

**Area under vine:** *6,200 acres*
**Subregions** *Cserszeg, Kál, Balatonederics-Lesence*

With its hot, sunny, Mediterranean climate, and the extraordinary beauty of this area, it is no surprise that so many artists have set up home here. The best wines are full-bodied, with a fine fragrance and crisp acidity.

🍇 Chardonnay, Olaszrizling, Szürkebarát

## BALATONFÜRED-CSOPAK

**Area under vine:** *4,200 acres*
**Sub-regions** *Balatonfüred, Csopak, Zánka*

On the northern shore of Lake Balaton, viticulture and winemaking have prospered here since Roman times. The wines are full-bodied yet fragrant, with fine acidity.

🍇 Cabernet Sauvignon, Chardonnay, Merlot, Olaszrizling, Rizlingszilváni, Tramini

✓ *Isván Jásdi* (Csopaki Olaszrizling)

## BALATONMELLÉKE

**Area under vine:** *5,400 acres*
**Subregions** *Balatonmellék, Muravidéki*

On the eastern and northeastern flank of Lake Balaton. The Zalla hills are known for their so-called harrow-cellars, made in the 19th century from timbers and plastered inside and out with clay. The Balatonmelléke, with its brown forest soils and mild, wet climate, has been revived as a wine region as recently as 1998.

🍇 Chardonnay, Kékfrankos, Müller-Thurgau, Olaszrizling, Oportó, Rizlingszilváni, Tramini, Zöld Veltelini (Veltliner), Zweigelt

✓ *László Bussay* (Csörnyeföldi Szürkebarát)

## BÜKKALJA

**Area under vine:** *2,400 acres*

Grown on the southern and southwestern slopes of the Bükk Mountains, where Kékfrankos and Leányka are the major varieties, but produce wines that are lighter than those of neighboring Eger. As in Eger and Tokaj further east, cellars have long been hewn out of rhyolite-tuffa rock, with more than 1,000 such cellars carved out of the slopes of Avas.

🍇 Cserszegi Fûszeres, Kékfrankos, Olaszrizling, Leányka

## CSONGRÁD

**Area under vine:** *4,600 acres*
**Sub-regions** *Csongrád, Kistelek, Mórahalom, Pusztamérges*

This Great Plain wine region is the warmest and sunniest part of the country during the vegetation period of the vine. Principally, the red and rosé wines are renowned. The white wines of the region contain moderate acids and are rich in fragrance and aroma. The red wines are characterized by richness in coloring agents, pleasant acerbity, and excellent aroma.

🍇 Kadarka, Kékfrankos, Olaszrizling, Zweigelt

## EGER

**Area under vine:** *7,900 acres*
**Subregions** *Debr≥, Eger*

Located halfway between Budapest and Tokaj is Eger, a region famous for the legend of Egri Bikavér, or "Bull's Blood of Eger." The story dates from 1552, when the fortress of Eger, fiercely defended by István Dobó and his Magyars, was besieged by the numerically superior force of the Turkish army, led by Ali Pasha. It is said that, throughout the battle, the Magyars drank copious quantities of the local wine and that when the Turks saw the beards of their ferocious enemies stained red with wine, they ran in terror, thinking that all Magyars gained their strength by drinking the blood of bulls. Hence the name of this wine was born. Other regions produce Bikavér, but Egri Bikavér is the Bull's Blood that is most famously associated with the legend. It was never a pretentious wine, but it was traditionally a robust, Kadarka-based red of firm structure and fiery flavor. Since the early 1980s, however, Bull's Blood has been notoriously variable in both quality and character, as indeed has its varietal composition, with Kékfrankos now the most dominant grape, and others such as Cabernet Franc, Cabernet Sauvignon, Kékoportó, and Merlot playing minor roles. Hungary will never earn a reputation for the depth and breadth of its wines until the quality and consistency of its second most famous wine is something to write home about. Egri Bormives Céh, a group of quality-conscious Bikavér producers, are trying to raise standards, but they have had trouble with the largest producers of the most mediocre Egri Bikavér.

Leányka can make a decent gold-colored, medium-sweet white wine, but it is too soft and understated to grab the headlines, and Eger is really red wine country. The successes here with Merlot and Cabernet Sauvignon, even Pinot Noir, should encourage producers to explore their own red wine grapes. Before his untimely death in February 2005, Tibor Gál was the best local producer. He teamed up with Antinori to produce good-value, international-style wines under the GIA label, but his own wines—especially his single-vineyard Pinot Noirs and Bikavér Reserve—were superior.

🍇 Cabernet Franc, Cabernet Sauvignon, Kadarka, Kékfrankos, Kékoportó, Leányka, Merlot, Olaszrizling

✓ *GIA* (Bikavér, Cabernet Sauvignon, Chardonnay) • *István Balla* (Barrique Olaszrizling) • *József Hagymási* (Cabernet Sauvignon) • *Thummerer* (Bikavér, Kékfrankos, Vili Papa Cuvee) • *Tibor Gál* (Bikavér) • *Béla Vincze* (Cabernet Franc)

## ETYEK-BUDA

**Area under vine:** *4,400 acres*
**Subregions** *Etyek, Buda*

Etyek-Buda is supposedly Hungary's sparkling wine region, but the quality of its largest producer, Törley, leaves much to be desired, and more vineyards are moving over to still, dry white wines from individual estates, but since this region overlaps the prettier, hilly half of Budapest, it receives a lot of attention. The vines grow on a black loess soil over a limestone base, in a dry, sunny, but windy climate.

🍇 Chardonnay, Királyleányka, Olaszrizling, Pinot Blanc, Pinot Gris, Sauvignon Blanc

✓ *Nyakashegy* (Budai Chardonnay)

## HAJÓS-BOAJA

**Area under vine:** *3,500 acres*
**Subregions** *Hajós, Baja*

The white wines of this Great Plains region are rich in fragrance and aroma, while the reds rival the highly ranked wines produced in hilly regions.

🍇 Cabernet Franc, Cabernet Sauvignon, Kadarka, Kékfrankos, Merlot, Olaszrizling, Riesling

## KUNSÁG

**Area under vine:** *63,300 acres*

**Subregions** *Bácska, Cegléd, Dunamente, Izsák, Jászság, Kecskemét-Kiskunfélegyház, Kiskőrös, Kiskunhalas-Kiskunmajsa, Monor, Tiszamente*

This Great Plain wine region is the largest wine region in Hungary. The wines of this region can be rich in fragrance and flavors.

🍇 Ezerjó, Cserszegi Fûszeres, Kékfrankos, Olaszrizling

## MÁTRAALJA

**Area under vine:** *18,000 acres*

At Gyöngyös, the first truly excellent Hungarian dry white wine was produced in the early 1980s, and no prizes for guessing that it was made from Chardonnay. But it was essential to demonstrate what could be done with grapes of a certain quality and the right technology. That particular Chardonnay steadily improved until 1995, when it jumped up another notch in quality, and Sauvignon Blanc can be almost as successful, but nowadays, winemakers are looking at achieving at least the same general quality with local varieties, such as Chardonnay, Hárslevelű, and Muskotály.

🍇 Chardonnay, Hárslevelű, Kékfrankos, Müller-Thurgau, Muscat Ottonel, Muskotály, Olaszrizling, Tramini, Rizlingszilváni, Sauvignon Blanc, Zweigelt

## MECSEKALJA

**Area under vine:** *1,200 acres*
**Sub-regions** *Pécs, Szigetvár, Versend*

Vineyards here scattered over more than 50 miles (80 kilometers) of warm slopes around the historic city of Pécs, which has long been noted for Olaszrizling, although the traditional Furmint and Cirfandli vines are giving way to international varieties.

🍇 Cabernet Franc, Cabernet Sauvignon, Chardonnay, Cirfandli, Furmint, Merlot, Olaszrizling, Pinot Noir, Riesling, Rizlingszilváni, Sauvignon Blanc

✓ *Ebner Andreas* (Cosmo Cuvée)

## MÓR

**Area under vine:** *2,200 acres*

Ezerjó is the best grape variety suited to this region, where it makes one of Hungary's most distinctive dry white wines.

🍇 Ezerjó, Leanyka, Olaszrizling, Rizlingszilvani, Tramini

## PANNONHALMA-SOKORÓALJA

**Area under vine:** *1,600 acres*
**Subregions** *Pannonhalma, Sokoróalja*

Viticulture dates back to 996, when Benedictines settled on St. Martin Mountain, and established Hungary's first monastery at Pannonhalma. The first document mentioning vinegrowing is the deed of foundation of this monastery. The fresh, crisp, varietally pure Pannonhalmi Sauvignon Blanc from Szőllősi Mihály Pricészette winery is the best dry Hungarian white wine I have tasted.

🍇 Chardonnay, Cserszegi Fûszeres, Irsai Olivér, Királyleányka, Müller-Thurgau, Olaszrizling, Riesling, Tramini

✓ *Szőllősi Mihály Pricészette* (Sauvignon Blanc)

## SOMLÓ

**Area under vine:** *1,200 acres*
**Subregions** *Kissomlyó-Sághegy, Somló*

This is the smallest wine region of Hungary. Its wines are fiery, with a heavy, masculine character, and they have high acid and alcohol content. The long aging in wooden barrels produces a fine, elegant harmony of fragrance, taste, and aroma. According to popular memory, in the imperial court of Vienna, the newlyweds drank Somló wines on their wedding night to promote the birth of a male heir to the throne.

🍇 Chardonnay, Furmint, Hárslevelű, Juhfark, Olaszrizling, Tramini

✓ *Béla Fekete* (Chardonnay) • *József Laposa* (Bazalt Borhaz Olaszrizling)

## SOPRON

**Area under vine:** *3,400 acres*
**Subregions** *Kőszeg, Sopron*

One of the most ancient wine regions of Hungary, the Sopron lies on the foothills of the Alps in the northwestern corner of the country. For centuries, the city of Sopron itself enjoyed thriving trade and, surprisingly, until the 18th century Sopron was reputedly the largest wine-trading center in central Europe. Sopron is a potentially fine wine region, where the Kékfrankos grape is most famous, although the quality in the vineyard and the bottle could and should be significantly superior to the light, everyday-drinking wines that are commonplace in this region. Although essentially a red wine region, Sopron does also produce some interesting whites.

🍇 Cabernet Franc, Kékfrankos, Leányka, Sauvignon Blanc, Zöld Veltelini, Zweigelt

✓ *Franz Weninger* (Kékfrankos, Merlot, Rosé, Syrah) • *Hilltop* (Soproni Sauvignon Blanc)

## SZEKSZÁRD

**Area under vine:** *4,700 acres*

The Szekszárd vineyards have been noted for their wines since Roman times and for red wines since the 15th century. In this sunny wine region with its greater Mediterranean influence, excellent red wines can be produced, which are known for their velvety texture, and

often show more elegance than the red wines of Villány. The Szekszárdi Bikavér (Bull's Blood of Szekszárd) is ranked outstandingly high. The indigenous Kadarka variety gives excellent flavored, deep red wine, plus a local speciality, Nemes Kadar, made from botrytized grapes. Very good Kékfrankos, Cabernet Sauvignon, and some stunning Merlot are also produced.

🍇 Cabernet Sauvignon, Kadarka, Kékfrankos, Merlot, Olaszrizling, Rizlingszilváni

✓ *Dúzsi Tamás* (Kékfrankos Rozé) • *Péter Vida* (Cabernet Franc-Merlot) • *Szent Gaál Kastély* (Merlot) • *Takler Pince* (Cabernet Sauvignon Selection, Primarius Merlot, Regnum Monarchia Gold Selection) • *Vesztergombi* (Cabernet Sauvignon)

## TOKAJ-HEGYALJA

**Area under vine:** *13,000 acres*
**Subregions** *Tokaj, Hegyalja*

For full details about the classic sweet wines and other styles of wine produced in Tokaj, please see the main text on pp416–417.

🍇 Furmint, Hárslevelű, Sárga Muskotály, Zeta (formerly Oremus)

✓ *Arvay és Társa* • *Borok Úri* • *István Szepsy* • *Királyudvar* • *Oremus* • *Pajzos*

## TOLNA

**Area under vine:** *5,300 acres*
**Subregions** *Tamási, Tolna, Völgység*

Although Tolna became a wine region in its own right as recently as 1998, winemaking traditions go back centuries, and were strengthened in the 16th century, when the area was settled by Germans.

🍇 Chardonnay, Grüner Veltliner, Kadarka, Kékfrankos, Müller-Thurgau, Olaszrizling

## VILLÁNY-SIKLÓS

**Area under vine:** *4,000 acres*
**Subregions** *Villány, Siklós*

Vines have been growing here since this region was part of the Roman province of Pannonia. In Villány, the more Mediterranean climate produces some of Hungary's best red wines, including dark, spicy Kadarka and more velvety Bordeaux varietals. The red wine potential of Villány is probably the greatest of all of the 22 Hungarian wine regions. At the time of writing, a new two-tier appellation system called Hungaricus Districtus Controllatus (HDC for short), created for and by Villány, was due to be in place as from the 2005 vintage. HDC will have two superior quality levels, Classic and Premium, with stricter maximum yields and quality controls that will be monitored by a committee. Some growers in Villány still train their vines to a single pole, instead of along wires, which is four times as labor-intensive, and yields are reduced to as little as 413 or 550 cases per acre, rather than the normal 1,650. The wines of Siklós are white and fiery, including those that have been produced from late-harvested grapes, although they are more *passerillé* in style than botrytized.

🍇 Cabernet Sauvignon, Cabernet Franc, Hárslevelű, Kékporto, Olaszrizling, Pinot Noir, Zweigelt

✓ *Attila Gere* (Kopár Villanyi Cuvée, Merlot Solus) • *Gere Tamás Pincészet* (Gere Tamás Cuvée) • *Tiffán* (Villányi Cuvée) • *Vylyan Pincészet* (Kadarka, Merlot, Pinot Noir, Zweigelt)

# ROMANIA

*Romania has at least as much potential as any other Eastern European winemaking country. It has a growing reputation for Pinot Noir, particularly from the Dealul Mare region, but has received a fraction of the foreign investment that Hungary has enjoyed, and needs both financial and technical expertise to compete internationally.*

THE BIGGEST PROBLEM IN ROMANIA has been a lack of consistency. Since the early 1990s, we have seen flashes of promise—from exciting Gewürztraminer from Transilvania to deep, dark, brooding Cabernet Sauvignon from Dealul Mare, only to see some of these wines followed up by vintages of barely *vin de table* quality. Only a handful of wineries have received significant foreign investment and expertise, and it is no coincidence that they generally make the best wines in Romania today.

## MORE IMPORTANT THAN RUSSIA

Viticulture and winemaking is an old tradition in Romania, dating back 4,000 years. In Europe, only France, Italy, Spain, and Germany are bigger wine-producing countries. Romania is significantly more important than Hungary or Russia in winemaking terms. As in Bulgaria, there was a massive planting program in the 1960s, when the country was geared up to supply Comecon states with bulk-blending fodder, but most wine today is purchased and consumed on the home market. After the fall of Ceausescu in December 1989, the area under vine increased, going against the trend of other Eastern Bloc wine-producing countries. However, much of the replanting saw *vinifera* varieties being replaced with

LOW-TECH VINEYARDS
*Rickety pergolas providing support for vines and old thatched-roofed buildings reflect the conditions that most of Romania's agricultural industry has survived on since medieval times.*

hybrids, as the new private owners did not know how to look after their vineyards—or if they did, they could not care less—and hybrids are much hardier, yielding the highest volumes for the least effort. This expansion continued until 1995, when it started to decline. Both new planting and the replanting of old vineyards now represent less than two percent of the total area under vine, with a staggering amount of land planted with hybrids (estimates vary

## ROMANIA

*The main winemaking areas in Romania are scattered throughout the country: in the Carpathian foothills, on the plateau lands of Dobrudja, and on the plains.*

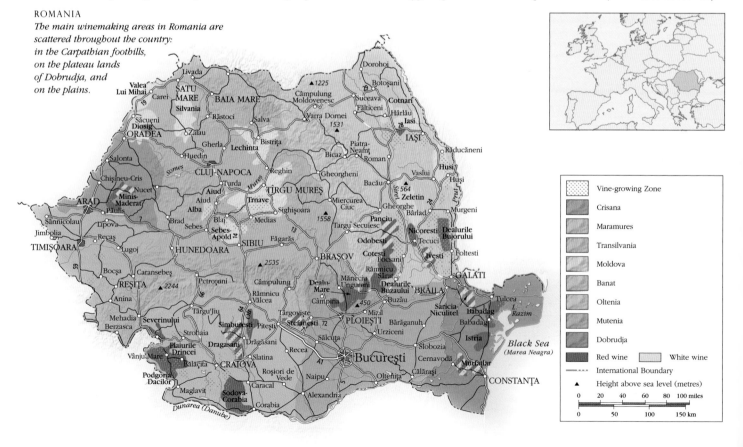

| | Vine-growing Zone |
| --- | --- |
| | Crisana |
| | Maramures |
| | Transilvania |
| | Moldova |
| | Banat |
| | Oltenia |
| | Mutenia |
| | Dobrudja |
| | Red wine / White wine |

--- International Boundary

▲ Height above sea level (metres)

0   20   40   60   80   100 miles
0        50        100       150 km

## RECENT ROMANIAN VINTAGES

**2006** A good, solid vintage.

**2005** Small harvest of dilute, unripe grapes, but some decent whites produced in Cotnari.

**2004** A lightweight but fresh, early-drinking vintage.

**2003** Severely reduced yields, due to spring frosts and summer droughts, but excellent quality, especially in reds.

**2002** Variable quality; mostly average to poor, with the excellent white wines of Transilvania the exception.

wildly between the official 75,000 acres and external observers' 297,500 acres). Furthermore, despite privatization, almost 23 percent of the vineyards still belong to the Romanian state. There are now eight wine regions encompassing 37 winegrowing districts, and vineyard registration is slowly coming into operation in preparation for Romania's EU membership in 2007–2010. The two largest wine-producing regions, Moldova and Mutenia, together account for more than 60 percent of all Romanian wines.

## THE FUTURE

Despite the difficulties of the past and accession to the EU, which will present the growers with as many problems as solutions, Romania has an excellent future—if it can be grasped. According to pre-membership agreements between Romania and the EU, all hybrids must be removed by 2014; although, on past experience, this will no doubt be extended. And extended. And extended. Far more important than replanting hybrid vines with *vinifera* is to ensure that only the best vineyards are replanted and that an emphasis is put on growing the best indigenous varieties, such as those of the Fetească family: Fetească Albă, Fetească Neagră, and Reglă. Other potentially interesting local varieties include Băbească, Busuioaca, Francusa, Galbenă, Grasă, and Tămaîoasă. Most wines currently produced from these grapes are a bit rustic, but they do show promise. Once the clones are sorted out; the vines are grown in the best-suited sites, at low yields; and skilful winemakers are employed to hone the style of the wines they produce, there will be no stopping Romania taking its rightful place in the world of wine.

NEW VINEYARDS IN DEALUL MARE
*A vineyard is staked out, waiting to support new vine growth in the Dealul Mare district of Mutenia.*

## FACTORS AFFECTING TASTE AND QUALITY

**LOCATION**
The main wine-producing areas in Romania spread from Iaşi in the northeast of the country down through the Carpathian foothills to the Danube river.

**CLIMATE**
A continental climate, with hot summers and cold winters, which are tempered only in the southeast by the Black Sea.

**ASPECT**
Vines are grown on all types of land—from the plains through the plateau land of Dobrudja to the slopes of the foothills of the Carpathian Mountains.

**SOIL**
A wide variety of soil types, including the generally sandy-alluvial plains and the stony, hillside soils of Banat; the limestone of Dobrudja; the oolitic limestone of Mutenia's Pietroasele vineyards; and the stony fringes of the Carpathian Mountains.

**VITICULTURE AND VINIFICATION**
Although some modernization of facilities has taken place since the 1990s, and a few new wineries have been established, at least half the wines are produced in antiquated conditions, and almost two-thirds must be made from hybrids, whatever the official statistics state.

**GRAPE VARIETIES**
Hybrids plus Băbească, Băbească Neagră, Cabernet Sauvignon, Fetească Albă, Fetească Neagră, Fetească Regălă, Galbenă, Grasă, Merlot, Pinot Gris, Pinot Noir, Riesling, Tămaîoasă, Welschriesling

## ROMANIAN LABEL LANGUAGE

**CULES LA INNOBILAREA BOABELOR (CIB)** Equivalent to *Beerenauslese* or above (a minimum of 112° *Oechsle*)
**CULES LA MATURIATE DEPLINA (CMD)** Similar to a high *Spätlese* (a minimum of 95° *Oechsle*)
**CULES LA MATURIATE INNOBILAREA (CMI)** Similar to a high Auslese (a minimum of 100° *Oechsle*)
**DULCE** Sweet
**EDELBEERENLESE** Equivalent to *Beerenauslese* or above (a minimum of 112° *Oechsle*)
**EDELREIFLESE** Equivalent to *Auslese* or above (a minimum of 100° *Oechsle*)
**IMBUTELIAT** Bottled
**IVV** This stands for cooperative and should be followed by its name or location.
**PIVNITĂ** Cellar
**RECOLTA** Vintage
**SEC** Dry
**SPUMOS** Sparkling
**STRUGURE** Grape
**VIE** Vine
**VIILE** Vineyard
**VIN ALB** White wine

**VIN DE MASĂ** Table wine
**VIN ROSE** Rosé wine
**VIN ROSU** Red wine
**VIN SUPERIOR** Superior wine
**VIN USOR** Light wine
**VOLLREIFLESE** Similar to a high *Spätlese* (a minimum of 95° *Oechsle*)
**VSO** Basic quality-wine designation
**VSOC** Categorized-quality wine designation similar to Germany's QmP and covering *Edelbeerenlese* (CIB), *Edelreiflese* (CMI) and *Vollreiflese* (CMD)

# THE APPELLATIONS OF
# ROMANIA

## BANAT

**Wine districts** *Buzias, Dealul Tirolului, Moldova Noua, Recaş, Teremia*

Although Banat is one of the better known wine regions in Romania—and has been since the 1980s—it is the smallest by a large margin, representing less than two percent of the country's vineyards. The sandy plain of the Teremia district is best known for its large production of eminently drinkable white wines, while the mountain slopes of Recaş-Tirol produce Valea Lunga, a pleasant, light-bodied red wine.

🍇 Cabernet Sauvignon, Cadarca, Fetească Regălă, Merlot, Mustoasă, Pinot Noir, Riesling

✓ *Recaş*

## CRIŞANA

**Wine districts** *Minis-Maderat*

Formerly part of the Banat region, the hilly Minis-Maderat area provides excellent, inexpensive reds from Cadarca, Pinot Noir, Cabernet Sauvignon, and Merlot grapes grown on stony terraces.

🍇 Cabernet Sauvignon, Cadarca, Fetească Regălă, Merlot, Mustoasă, Pinot Noir, Riesling

## DOBRUDJA

**Wine districts** *Babadag, Istria, Murfatlar, Saricia-Niculitel*

Murfatlar is the most important and oldest winemaking district in Dobrudja (or Dobrogea), with well-organized vineyards on hills close to the Black Sea and an experimental state research station that has introduced many classic western varieties. Once reliant on the region's prestigious past, the wines used to be too old, oxidized, and heavy, but they are beginning to receive the attention they deserve now that they are clean and well balanced; the lovely, late-picked, softly sweet, and stylish Gewürztraminer is a good example of this style.

🍇 Cabernet Sauvignon, Chardonnay, Gewürztraminer, Muscat Ottonel, Pinot Gris, Riesling

✓ *The Carpathian Winery* • *Murfatlar* (Ferma Noua, Trei Hectare)

## MARAMURES

**Wine districts** *Diosig, Silvania, Valea lui Mihai*

A breathtakingly wild and beautiful mountainous area full of rather strange but friendly people living a folksy, arts-and-crafts life in a place that time forgot. Maramures is a white-wine-only region. Diosig produces acidic wines that are ideal for brandy distillation.

🍇 Burgund Mare, Cabernet Sauvignon, Cadarca, Fetească Regălă, Mcrlot, Muscat Ottonel, Pinot Noir, Welschrieling

## MOLDOVA

**Wine districts** *Catchiest, Cotesti, Cotnari, Dealurile Bujorului, Dealurile Moldovei, Husi, Iaşi, Ivesti, Nicoresti, Odobesti, Panciu, Zeletin*

The vineyards of Odobesti surrounding the industrial town of Focsani produce quantities of rather ordinary red and white wine. There are, however, exceptions: Cotesti, for example, has a good reputation for Pinot Noir and Merlot, while Nicoresti is known for its full-colored,

spicy red wine produced from the Băbeaskă grape. The vineyards of Cotnari are the most famous in Romania; their reputation dates back to the 15th century. The wine is a rich dessert wine, not unlike Tokaji but not as complex. The Bucium hills of Visan and Doi Peri overlook the city of Iaşi and the cool conditions are reflected in Cabernet Sauvignon wines that have crisp, leafy characteristics.

🍇 Băbeaskă, Cabernet Sauvignon, Fetească Albă, Fetească Neagră, Grasă, Merlot, Pinot Noir, Welschriesling

## MUTENIA

**Wine districts** *Dealul Mare, Dealurile Suzaului, Pietroasele*

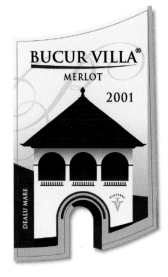

Dealul Mare is located to the north of Bucharest, stretching across the lower, southeast-facing slopes of the Carpathian Mountains. It is famous for Pinot Noir, Cabernet Sauvignon, and Merlot. There is a small area of chalky soil within this district that has a special microclimate best suited to the production of sweet white wines with fine, balancing acidity. It is here that the vineyards of Pietroasele are located. The area's Tămaîoasă or "Frankincense" grape is a Muscat-related variety that makes a lusciously sweet, gold-colored wine of very expressive quality. One of the most remarkable Romanian wines I have tasted was a beautiful, botrytized rosé

*Edelbeerenlese* version of the normally lackluster Fetească Neagră grape.

🍇 Băbeaskă Neagră, Cabernet Sauvignon, Fetească Neagră, Fetească Regălă, Galbenă, Merlot, Pinot Gris, Pinot Noir, Riesling, Tămaîoasă

✓ *Prahova Valley* (Cabernet Sauvignon, Merlot)
   • *S E R V E* (Cuvée Charlotte, Terra Romana)
   • *Vinarte* (Castel Bolovanu, Villa Zorilor)

## OLTENIA

**Wine districts** *Drăgasăni, Plaiurile Drincei, Podguria Dagilor, Sadova Corabia, Samburesti/ Simburesti, Severinului, Segarcea, Stefănesti, Vanju Mare*

Simburesti in the Drăgasăni district produces Oltenia's best reds. It is also known for a full, dry red wine from the Fetească Neagră grape, as well as for Cabernet Sauvignon. The Segarcea district also produces red wines. The Pinot Noir produced here is good, although it is not as well known as the Cabernet Sauvignon. Interesting sweet wines are found on the west side of the River Oltul.

🍇 Cabernet Sauvignon, Fetească Neagră, Fetească Regălă, Muscat Ottonel, Pinot Noir, Riesling, Sauvignon Blanc, Tămaîoasă

## TRANSILVANIA

**Wine districts** *Aiud, Albă, Iulia-Aiud, Bistrita, Lechinta, Sebes-Apold, Tarnave*

Of all the winegrowing regions of Romania, Transilvania is perhaps the most exciting. The crisp fruit and good acidity of its white wines lies somewhere between the styles of Alsace and South Tyrol. The steep Tirnave vineyards produce good-quality white wines with more than just a hint of Germanic style and delicacy. Not surprisingly, German settlers in Transilvania introduced many of their own grape varieties to the region. The native Fetească grape is also successful.

🍇 Fetească Albă, Fetească Regălă, Muscat Ottonel, Pinot Gris, Riesling, Sauvignon Blanc, Traminer, Welschriesling

✓ *Carl Reh* • *Vinarte* (Terasse Danubiane)

# SLOVAKIA AND THE CZECH REPUBLIC

*Slovakia has twice as much area under vine as the Czech Republic, even though it is much smaller. However, Slovakia's vineyards are in a state of decline, and the Czech Republic is rightly better known for its beer than its wine.*

ALTHOUGH THE FIRST VINES were planted in Moravia (now part of the Czech Republic) by the Romans as early as the third century CE, and winemaking in Slovakia is supposed to date back 3,000 years, none of the wines from anywhere encompassed by the borders of these countries today has ever gained sufficient repute to warrant significant exports, let alone worldwide fame. And, as with the rest of the former Eastern Bloc wine-producing countries, the period of centralized processing under Communist rule obscured whatever local reputations there were and cast a gray shadow over any individual efforts, as the vineyards were replanted high and wide for mass production.

## SLOVAKIA

Most Slovakian wine is classified as lowly table wine, which would be a good thing if this were the result of a quality-conscious culling of the total production to produce stunning quality top wines, but that is not the case—the wines are naturally of a dismal quality. Potentially the quality of Slovakian wine is greater than that of the Czech Republic, but the decline in the state of the Slovakian wine industry is greater, so it will be an even tougher job to turn around. More than 85 percent of Slovakian wine is white, with Müller-Thurgau, Ryzlink Vlašsky (Welschriesling), and Veltlinske Zelene (Grüner Veltliner) together accounting for over 60 percent of all the vines growing in this country. Sparkling wines have been made since 1825 at Sered and are still marketed under the "Hubert" brand, but quality is not high.

## CZECH AND SLOVAK LABEL LANGUAGE

**BIELE VÍNO** White wine
**ČERVENÉ VÍNO** Red wine
**DEZERTNÉ KORENENÉ VÍNO** Aromatized dessert wine
**DEZERTNÉ VÍNO** Dessert wine
**DIA** Suitable for diabetics (in other words, sugar-free)
**JAKOSTNÍ VÍNO** The equivalent of a *vin de pays*; must have a natural alcoholic potential of 8–11%
**KABINET** Equivalent to the German term Kabinett; must have a natural alcoholic potential of 11–12%
**LEDOVÉ VÍNO** The equivalent of Eiswein, which not only must have a natural alcoholic potential of at least 16%, but the grapes must be picked at below 21°F and must remain frozen throughout pressing
**ODRODOVÉ VÍNA** Grape variety
**OBSAH CUKRU** Sugar content
**POLOSLADKÉ** Semi-sweet
**POZDNÍ SBĚR** Literally "late harvest;" must have a natural alcoholic potential of 12–14%
**RUŽOVÉ VÍNO** Rosé wine
**SLADKÉ** Sweet

**SLÁMOVÉ VÍNO** Literally a "straw wine," which not only must have a natural alcoholic potential of at least 16%, but, for 3 months prior to being pressed, must also be stored on straw or reeds or hung in a well-aired place
**STOLNÍ VÍNO** Table wine, the lowest quality; must have a natural alcoholic potential of 5.5–8%
**SUCHÉ** Dry
**ŠUMIVÉ VÍNO** Sparkling wine
**VÍNA S PŘÍVLASTKEM** A wine of appellation, thus the equivalent of a French AOC
**VINÁRSKYCH ZÁVODOV** Wine producer
**VÍNO** Wine
**VÝBĚR** A wine predicated by selection; must have a natural alcoholic potential of at least 14%
**VÝBĚR Z HROZNŮ** A wine predicated by selection of individual grapes; must have a natural alcoholic potential of at least 16%
**ZVYŠKOVYM CUKROM** Residual sugar

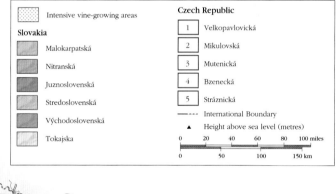

| | | |
|---|---|---|
| ⠿ Intensive vine-growing areas | | **Czech Republic** |
| **Slovakia** | | 1   Velkopavlovická |
|    Malokarpatská | | 2   Mikulovská |
|    Nitranská | | 3   Mutenická |
|    Juznoslovenská | | 4   Bzenecká |
|    Stredoslovenská | | 5   Stráznická |
|    Východoslovenská | | ---- International Boundary |
|    Tokajska | | ▲   Height above sea level (metres) |

0  20  40  60  80  100 miles
0  50  100  150 km

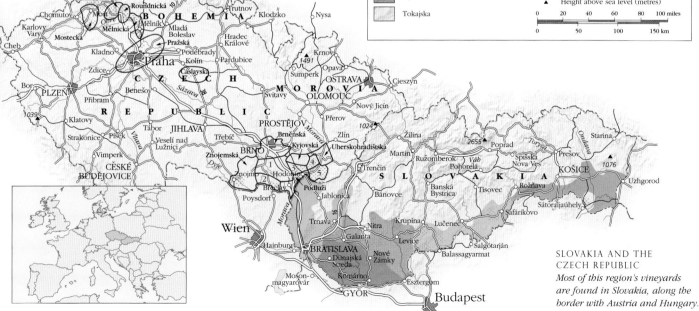

SLOVAKIA AND THE CZECH REPUBLIC
*Most of this region's vineyards are found in Slovakia, along the border with Austria and Hungary.*

CZECH VINES
*A vineyard at Ratíškovice, near Hodonin in the Czech Republic.*

## FACTORS AFFECTING TASTE AND QUALITY

**LOCATION**
The Czech Republic is an inland central European country north of Austria and its vines are mostly located in Moravia. There are also vineyards in Bohemia, mainly to the north and northeast of Prague. Slovakia is located south of Moravia.

**CLIMATE**
Generally a continental climate with occasional maritime influences from the Atlantic. In the Czech Republic, Moravia is significantly sunnier (1,760 hours) than Bohemia (1,450 hours), but Slovakia is even more favorable (2,000 hours), with less precipitation.

**ASPECT**
In the Czech Republic, vines are grown on rolling hills in Bohemia, and on mountain foothills in Moravia. Generally steeper and hillier in Slovakia.

**SOIL**
The primarily loess topsoils found in most Czech vineyards cover the acidic crystalline slate of the Bohemian Massive, the exception being in the Bohemian limestone basin around Prague. Sandy or rocky soils, with scattered alluvial deposits, dominate Slovakia.

**VITICULTURE AND VINIFICATION**
Although some modernization of facilities has taken place in the Czech Republic since the 1990s, and a few new wineries have been set up, at least half the production occurs under antiquated conditions, and far too much wine is made from hybrids for the country to be able to build a reputation. While the situation in Slovakia is worse, the potential quality is greater.

**GRAPE VARIETIES**
**Slovakian Primary Grape varieties:** Chardonnay, Devín, Frankovka Modrá (Limberger), Ryzlink Vlašsky (Welschriesling), Sauvignon Blanc, Svätovavrinecké (St-Laurent), Veltlinske Zelene (Grüner Veltliner)
**Slovakian Secondary Grape varieties:** Cabernet Sauvignon, Dievčie Hrozno, Furmint, Lipovina (Hárslevelű), Rulandské Bílé (Pinot Blanc), Ryzlink Rýnsky (Riesling), Silvánske Zelené (Sylvaner)
**Czech Primary Grape varieties:** Frankovka (Limberger), Müller-Thurgau, Rulandské Bílé (Pinot Blanc), Ryzlink Rýnsky (Riesling), Ryzlink Vlašsky (Welschriesling), Veltlínské Červene (Roter Veltliner), Svatovavřineké (St-Laurent)
**Czech Secondary Grape varieties:** André, Chardonnay, Modrý Portugal (Portugieser), Muskat Moravské, Neuburské (Neuburger), Rulandské Modrý (Pinot Noir), Rulandské Šedé (Pinot Gris), Sauvignon Blanc, Tramín (Savagnin), Zweigeltrebe

The most intriguing wine from this country is Slovakian Tokaji, produced in the small part of the world-famous district that falls within Slovak borders. The same grapes are grown as in the rest of the Tokaji-producing region (Furmint, Hárslevelű, and Muscat), and the wine is supposedly made in a very similar style to the great Hungarian version. In truth they do not compare, but there is no reason why, with properly maintained vineyards, adequately equipped producers of Slovakian Tokaji should not compete with their famous neighbors. With a little imagination, this wine has the potential to be so lucrative that it must surely be the door-opener for that much-needed foreign investment.

## THE CZECH REPUBLIC

Most Czech wines are produced in Moravia, where the majority of the vineyards are located. The two major areas of production are Hustopěce-Hodonin on the Morava River and Znojmo-Mikulov on the Dyje River. Around 80 percent of all the wine produced is white, with a good level of winemaking expertise for light, elegant, and aromatically fresh whites. Although the climate does not generally suit red-wine production, some interesting reds (such as the Cabernet Sauvignon from Pavlovice) are produced. Sparkling wines are made in the towns of Mikulov and Bzenec by *cuve close* and continuous methods. Since the 1995 Czech Wine Law was introduced, wines are categorized according to the grapes' sugar contents: effectively table wine, *vin de pays*, and AOC equivalents, followed by German-style predicated wines: Kabinet, Pozdní sběr, Výběr z hroznů, Výběr z bobulí, Ledová vína, and Slámová vína (*see* label language, p423).

(*see* label language, p423)

### RECENT CZECH VINTAGES

**2006** A great vintage all around, for both Slovakia and the Czech Republic.

**2005** A good, ripe vintage, with excellent acid levels.

**2004** Very good, particularly for botrytis wines.

**2003** The best Czech vintage in living memory. Also excellent in Slovakia, particularly for reds and late-harvest whites.

**2002** Variable quality, with some good white wines in the Czech Republic, but rain during the harvest affected some Slovak wines.

## THE APPELLATIONS OF
# SLOVAKIA AND THE CZECH REPUBLIC

### SLOVAKIA

#### JUŽNOSLOVENSKÁ
**Internal regions:** *Dunajskostredský, Galantský, Hurbanovský, Komárňanský, Palárikovský, Šamorinský, Strekovský, Stúrovský*

The Južnoslovenská or Southern Slovak region is warm and sunny; rich clay soils encourage late-harvest whites and well-colored reds.

🍇 Cabernet Franc, Cabernet Sauvignon, Frankovka Modrá, Muškat Moravsky, Ryzlink Rýnsky, Rulandské, Rulandské

Bílé, Rulandské Modré, Tramín Červný (Red Traminer)

✓ *Château Belá • Karpatská Perla • Vino-Masaryk*

#### MALOKARPATSKÁ
**Internal regions:** *Bratislavský, Dolanský, Hlovecký, Modranský, Orešanský, Pezinský, Senecký, Skalický, Stupavský, Trnavský, Vrbovský, Záborský*

The Malokarpatská or "Little Carpathian" region has a winemaking tradition of almost 3,000 years. Riesling from Limbach has the greatest reputation,

followed by Modrý Portugal (Blauer Portugieser) from Oresany.

🍇 Chardonnay, Modrý Portugal, Veltlinske Zelene, Ryzlink Rýnsky, Ryzlink Vlašsky

✓ *Karpatská Perla • Mrva & Stanko*

#### NITRANSKÁ
**Internal regions:** *Nitranský, Pukanský, Radošinský, Šintavský, Tekovský, Vrábel´ský, Želiezovský, Žitavský, Zlatomoravský*

This region produces a mixed bag of red and white, dry and sweet, still, and sparkling wines.

🐝 Cabernet Sauvignon, Frankovka Modrá, Müller-Thurgau, Pálava, Ryzlink Vlašsky, Rulandské Modré, Svätovavřinecké, Veltlinske Zelene

✓ *Mrva & Stanko • Vinanza*

## STREDOSLOVENSKÁ

**Internal regions:** *Fil´akovský, Gemerský, Hotiansky, Ipel´ský, Modrokamenský, Tornal´ský, Vinický*

In the Stredoslovenská, otherwise known simply as the Central Slovakian wine region, Tramín is considered to be the best variety.

🐝 Cabernet Sauvignon, Chardonnay, Ryzling Vlašsky, Svätovavřinecké, Tramín, Veltlinske Zelene

✓ *Mrva & Stanko*

## TOKAJSKÁ

This tiny region is surrounded on three sides by the Východoslovenská region, and on one by the Tokaj region in Hungary. Slovakian Tokajské is made from the same varieties as Hungarian Tokaji (Furmint, Lipovina, or Hárslevelů, and Muškát Žltý or Sárga Muskotály). Wines made from other varieties are not sold as Tokajské.

🐝 Devín, Furmint, Lipovina, Muškát Žltý, Rulandské Bílé, Tramín Červený (Red Traminer)

✓ *J. & J. Ostrožovič*

## VÝCHODOSLOVENSKÁ

**Internal regions:** *Král´ovskochlmecký, Michalovský, Moldavský, Sobranský*

The heavy clay soils of the Východoslovenská, or Eastern Slovakian, wine region are mostly thought to be suitable for white grapes, although red wines are made.

🐝 Frankovka Modrá, Müller-Thurgau, Ryzling Vlašsky, Svätovavřinecké, Tramín, Veltlinske Zelene

# THE CZECH REPUBLIC

## BRNĚNSKÁ

With two basic soil types, white grapes are mostly grown on lighter sandy soils, with black grapes grown on gravelly soils. Dolní Kounice is the most important wine town.

🐝 Frankovka, Modrý Portugal, Müller-Thurgau, Muskat Moravské, Palava, Svatovavřineké, Tramín, Veltlinske Zelene

## BZENECKÁ

Orechov, Bzenec, Polesovice, and Vracov are the most important wine villages in Bzenecká, the Czech Republic's smallest wine region. Clayey, sandy, and gravelly soils predominate. The local specialty is Bzenecká Lipká, made from Ryzlink Rýnsky. Olsava and Vitra are new varieties created by Cultivation Station at Polesovice.

🐝 Frankovka, Muskat Moravské, Olsava, Rulandské Bílé, Ryzlink Rýnsky, Svatovavřineké, Veltlinske Zelene, Vitra

## CÁSLAVSKÁ

A small enclave of vines growing at the foot of the Kutna Hora Mountain.

🐝 Modrý Portugal, Müller-Thurgau, Svatovavřineké, Sylvanske Zelene

## KYJOVSKÁ

The best wines are made from vines grown at Vresovice, on south-facing slopes, at 1,800 feet

in altitude; the grapes produced in this region have a pronounced acidity.

🐝 Müller-Thurgau, Svatovavřineké, Veltlinske Zelene

## MĚLNICKÁ

The largest wine region in Bohemia, Mělnická has a certain reputation for oak-aged reds, but produces better Chardonnay.

🐝 Chardonnay, Rulandské Bílé, Rulandské Modré, Rulandské Šedé, Ryzlink Rýnsky, Svatovavřineké, Zweigeltrebe

## MIKULOVSKÁ

With 6,180 acres (2,500 hectares) under vine, Mikulovská is the largest wine region in the country. Most wines produced are white, with the best coming from limestone soils, although sandy and marly soils are also quite common. The new Palava variety (Tramin x Müller-Thurgau) was developed here.

🐝 Chardonnay, Müller-Thurgau, Neuburské, Palava, Ryzlink Vlašsky, Silvánske Zelené, Tramin, Veltlinske Zelene

✓ *Sklepy • Tanzberg*

## MOSTECKÁ

This region has an extremely dry climate and volcanic (basalt) soils. A significant portion of the wine is traditionally produced under strictly Kosher conditions.

🐝 Müller-Thurgau, Ryzlink Rýnsky, Svatovavřineké, Zweigeltrebe

## MUTĚNICKÁ

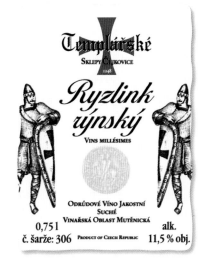

The vines grow on various clayey, sandy soils, with the best on calcareous clay. Although Mutěnická encompasses 14 communes, almost 90 percent of the vineyards are located in Cejkovice, where the wines have pronounced acidity. Most of the rest of the vines are located in Mutěnice, the location of Moravia's premier viticultural research station.

🐝 Frankovka, Müller-Thurgau, Ryzlink Vlašsky, Svatovavřineké, Veltlinske Zelene

## PODLUŽÍ

The vines grow in mineral-deficient clayey, sandy, and gravelly soils on frost-prone sites in this small region bordering Austria and Slovakia. The best wines are made from Veltlinske Zelene and originate in the clayey soils of Prušánsky.

🐝 Frankovka, Rulandské Bílé, Rulandské Šedé, Ryzlink Rýnsky, Ryzlink Vlašsky, Svatovavřineké, Veltlinske Zelene, Zweigeltrebe

## PRAŽSKÁ (PRAGUE)

Although this is the smallest region in the Czech Republic, Prague used to be the largest wine-producing town in Bohemia in centuries past. Modrý Portugal is the most widely planted variety, but the best wines are made from Riesling and Pinot Blanc, while colder, less-suitable sites are planted with Kerner and Müller-Thurgau.

🐝 Chardonnay, Modrý Portugal, Müller-Thurgau, Muskat Moravské, Rulandské Šedé, Ryzlink Rýnsky, Tramín, Svatovavřineké, Zweigeltrebe

## ROUDNICKÁ

Once famous for Sylvaner, Roudnická now grows a considerable amount of Müller-Thurgau, and has had some success with red wines produced on the valley slopes, with gold medal Rulandské Modré (Pinot Noir) giving short-lived hope in the mid-1990s. Most vines are grown on a marly limestone and chalk plateau, covered by loess and gravelly sand, near the Elbe river.

🐝 Modrý Portugal, Müller-Thurgau, Rulandské Modré, Svatovavřineké

## STRÁZNICKÁ

The vineyards in this region are located on the heavy clay slopes of the Bilé Karpaty, where red wines can be hard. Growers therefore mainly grow white-wine varieties.

🐝 Müller-Thurgau, Rulandské Šedé, Veltlinske Zelene

## USHERSKOHRADIŠTSKÁ

Vines grow on the banks of the Morava river and in its hinterland, on sandy and gravelly sand slopes of Chirby and Bilé Karpaty. Primarily white wines.

🐝 Müller-Thurgau, Rulandské Šedé

## VELKOPAVLOVICKÁ

The best wines are made from Neuburské and Veltlinske Zelene grown in the north of Velkopavlovická, the Czech Republic's second-largest wine region (5,810 acres/2,350 hectares).

🐝 Frankovka, Modrý Portugal, Müller-Thurgau, Neuburské, Ryzlink Vlašsky, Veltlinske Zelene

✓ *Vinum*

## ZERNOSECKÁ

Typical of Bohemia's sporadic viticultural character today, Zernosecká has just 16 wine producers (owning in total just 175 acres of vineyards spread over five wine villages), whereas the village of Litoměřice alone was once surrounded by more than 1,235 acres (500 hectares) of vines.

🐝 Müller-Thurgau, Rulandské Bílé, Rulandské Modré, Ryzlink Rýnsky, Svatovavřineké

## ZNOJEMSKÁ

This region's best wines come from Znojmo, which is not so much a city as two cities in one. Znojmo resides above its own underground city, comprising 19mi of interconnecting catacombs.

🐝 Müller-Thurgau, Ryzlink Rýnsky, Sauvignon Blanc, Veltlinske Zelene

✓ *Znovín*

# THE WESTERN BALKANS

*Few regions in the world have undergone so much political turmoil and human tragedy over such a relatively short period as the Western Balkans. Until the early 1990s, the entire region was supposedly just one country—Yugoslavia. However, Yugoslavia comprised at least seven one-time sovereign nations and was populated by five ethnic groups.*

FOLLOWING THE DEATH OF TITO, and the general collapse of Communism, it was inevitable that this artificial edifice would start to unravel, and the powder-keg of centuries of resentment would one day explode into bloody conflict. In these more peaceful times, newly independent countries at least have a chance to establish their own wine reputations. The fact that Slovenia, which for the most part avoided the skirmishes of war, is already competing on the world market with its wines should encourage other states that they could be equally successful once their wine industries return to their peacetime potential.

## ALBANIA
Winemaking in Albania dates back to pre-Roman times. However, since most Albanians are Muslim, wine production has not been of great importance in recent historical terms, and, under a xenophobic Communist government for 46 years, there were no exports. Thus the potential for this country's wine industry has been severely restricted. Since democracy was established between 1990 and 1992, successive governments have sought viticultural expert advice from the West, but the area under vine in Albania is now less than 14,800 acres (6,000 hectares), which is actually less than one-fifth of the area that was planted under Communist rule. Only a small fraction of vines are grown for wine, and they are located around the capital of Tirana, and in five surrounding disctricts: Durres, Berät, Korcë, Skoder, and Lushnje. Although well-known varieties such as Cabernet Franc, Mavrud, Merlot, and Welschriesling are to be found, indigenous varieties such as Shesh i Zi, Shesh i Barhe, and Kalmet (otherwise known as Kadarka) represent almost 60 percent of all Albanian vines, and three other local grapes (Vlosh, Serine, and Debine) account for most of the rest.

## BOSNIA-HERZEGOVINA
Vines are restricted to the south, in the Brotnjo hills around Mostar, where the climate and rocky soil favor two indigenous varieties, Zilavka for white wine and Blatina for red. There are currently 3,460 acres (1,400 hectares) planted. Other significant varieties grown are Bena, Dobrogostina, Krkoshia, Podbil, and Rkaciteli for white wines, and Alicante Bouschet, Cabernet Sauvignon, Gamay, Merlot, Plavka, Trnjak, and Vranac for reds.

## CROATIA
Prior to hostilities, Croatia was one of the two most prosperous states in Yugoslavia. Although it is today in a relatively stable

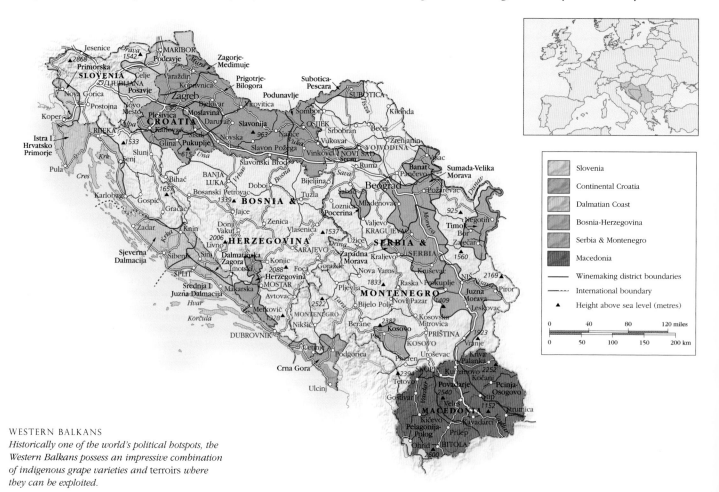

**WESTERN BALKANS**
*Historically one of the world's political hotspots, the Western Balkans possess an impressive combination of indigenous grape varieties and* terroirs *where they can be exploited.*

condition, many vineyards were destroyed during the worst upheavals of the Croatian war, when one million landmines were sown, and it will take until 2020 to clear them all. Massive replanting programs created new vineyards in the late 1990s. There are two main regions: Continental Croatia and the Dalmatian Coast. Watch out for the emergence of this wine country as it rides tail-winds of Dalmatia's newly found fame as home of the Zinfandel grape (which was originally known as Crljenak Kastelanski).

### Inland Croatia
More than 90 percent of the production is white wine, with over half of the vineyards planted with Graševina (Welschriesling). Of the few black grape varieties, Frankova (Lemberger) is probably the most important. Other grapes grown here include Chardonnay, Gewürztraminer, Muscat Ottonel, Riesling, Traminer, and Sauvignon Blanc.

### Coastal Croatia
White wine is also important here, accounting for no less than 70 percent of total production. The grape varieties grown are more diverse, with Malvasia the most widely planted, yet accounting for less than 10 percent of the vineyards. Other grape varieties include Debit-Grk (Ugni Blanc), Marastina, Plavać Mali, Pošip (Furmint), Vugava (Viognier), and Zlahtina (Chasselas). New plantations in this region include Cabernet Sauvignon and Merlot, and there have been serious attempts to revive Crljenak Kastelanski (Zinfandel).
✓ *Grgić Vina Winery*

## MACEDONIA
Following the secession of Slovenia and Croatia in 1991, Macedonia received full international recognition in 1993. The grape varieties grown in this country include Grenache, Kadarka, Kratošija, Plovdina, Prokupac, Temjanika, and Vranac. Phylloxera, which devastated European vineyards in the late 19th century, did not reach Macedonia until 1912.

The most popular Macedonian wine is Kratošija, which is a deep-colored red made from native Vranac and Kratošija varieties. It has a distinctive taste and aroma, full body, and a smooth flavor. It is bottled in its second year, when the bouquet is at its fullest, and is best drunk when very young. Prokupac and Kadarka make interesting reds, Belan produces a neutral white Grenache wine, and Temjanika an aromatic white.

## SERBIA AND MONTENEGRO
Although the Federal Army made abortive attempts to put down independence in Slovenia and Croatia, and supported the Bosnian Serbs, it did not fight any battles on its home ground until the Kosovo conflict. Most Serbian vineyards thus remain unaffected. There are four major viticultural regions: Kosovo, Vojvodina, Montenegro, and Serbia itself.

### Kosovo
Although part of Serbia, Kosovo is governed by the United Nations Interim Administration Mission, and this is set to continue until its future status has been confirmed by the international community. Until the conflict, the Rahovic winery had a lucrative contract to supply the German Racke group with over 5–7 million gallons of light red Kosovar wine, which was sold under the Amselfelder brand, but due to the uncertain political situation, production was transferred elsewhere. In these more peaceful times, Kosovo finds itself with a substantial wine industry, but no ready market.

### Montenegro
There are three winegrowing districts in Montenegro: Crnogorsko, Titogradski, and Primorje. The main grape varieties grown here

DALMATIAN VINES PROTECTED BY DRY-STONE WALLS, CROATIA
*Many vineyards built on the stony coastal hillsides of Croatia are protected by low dry-stone walls. These walls are painstakingly constructed by peasant farmers to protect low-growing vines from the cold north winds and to keep them cool in the heat of summer. Without such techniques, it would be impossible to cultivate this difficult ground.*

are Kratošija, Krstač, Merlot, and Vranac. The best-known vineyards of this region are those that are located on the terraced southern slopes of Lake Skadar. The Vranac and Merlot wines can be good, but Montenegro is better known for its grape brandy than for its wine.

### Serbia
I think that the best potential here is for Cabernet Sauvignon and Merlot when grown in Južna Morava and, possibly, Timok, but the best level of quality currently being achieved is by producers of the snappy, fresh Sauvignon Blanc from Kruševac in Zapadna Morava.
✓ *Rubin* (Sauvignon Blanc)

### Vojvodina (Voivodina)
North of Serbia, bordering Croatia, Hungary, and Romania, the vines grown include Ezerjó, Graševina (Welschriesling), Kadarka, Merlot, Riesling, Sauvignon Blanc, Sémillon, and Traminer. The Traminer is a more interesting alternative and the soft, fruity Merlot a good buy for red-wine drinkers.

## SLOVENIA
By far the wealthiest part of former Yugoslavia, with per capita income close to that of Austria, Slovenia is the rising star among the winemaking countries of the Western Balkans.

### Inland Slovenia (Kontinentalna Slovenija)
Squeezed between Austria, Hungary, and Croatia are two winegrowing districts, each comprising several smaller areas: Podravina (Bela Krajina, Haloze, Lutomer-Ororske, Maribor, Prekmurje, Radgona-Kapela, Slovenske) and Posavina (Belakrajina, Bizeljsko-Sremic, Dolenjska, Smarje-Virstajn).
✓ *Curin* (Sauvignon) • *Meranovo* (Sauvignon) • *Jožef Prus* (Ledeno Vino Renski Rizling)

### Coastal Slovenia (Primorska Slovenija)
This region is close to the Italian border and consists of four winegrowing districts: Brda, Karst, Koper, and Vipava. The climate of Coastal Slovenia is of a mild Mediterranean type, except in Vipara and Briški Okoliš, which come under the moderating influence of the Alps.
✓ *Movia* (Veliko Belo) • *Simčič* (Teodor Rdeče Reserve) • *Stojan Ščucrek* (Stara Brajda—white) • *Vipava* (Lathieri Sauvignon Zemono)

# THE BLACK AND CASPIAN SEAS

*Although Russia is the largest wine-producing country in this region, the wines of Moldova are better known internationally, while the legendary wines of Krym in the Ukraine boast the most illustrious history.*

GEORGIA AND ARMENIA have at least equivalent winemaking potential as these countries, but they are at the back of the line when it comes to heavy-duty international investment, and that is what it will take to upgrade the wine industries in this region. Without a radical overhaul of the technologies deployed in the vineyards and wineries, none of these countries will be able to produce wines of export quality.

## ARMENIA
At the height of the Soviet Union's hegemony, Armenia's vineyards covered 90,150 acres (36,500 hectares), but this declined following the collapse of Communism, and by 2003 amounted to just 29,650 acres (12,000 hectares). More than 200 grape varieties are grown here, many of them indigenous, but only 30 are wine grapes, and these include Adisi, Anait, Areni, Azateni, Dmak, Garan, Kahet, Karmrayut, Megrabuir, Mskhali, Muscat (various), Nerkeni, Rkatsiteli, Tokun, and Voskeat. The Ararat Valley is the most important winegrowing region, claiming up to 60 percent of the country's vineyards, but as with Armenian wine in general, most of the production is distilled. High-strength table wines and strong dessert wines are made, but grape brandy is this country's most important alcoholic product.

## AZERBAIJAN
Official statistics for the area under vine are notoriously inaccurate, having gone from 447,000 acres (181,000 hectares) in 1990 to less than 29,650 acres (12,000 hectares) in 2001. In 2004 the French Castel Group was hired to consult on expanding these vineyards, in the hope of exporting an improved quality of Azerbaijan wine to Russia. Azerbaijan has yet to resolve its conflict with Armenia over the largely Armenian-populated Azerbaijani Nagorno-Karabakh enclave, where vines are also planted.

## GEORGIA
Georgia has one of the oldest winemaking traditions in the world. There is evidence that the first vines could have spread from here or, at least, been preserved in this area during the last major ice age. Georgia has numerous valleys, each with its own favorable microclimate, and it is said that they contain 1,000 indigenous grape varieties. This should one day propel this country to the forefront of the East European wine scene, but isolated pockets of enthusiasm have yet to be translated into a solid range of quality wines on the shelf.

## KAZAKHSTAN
This is the country made famous by Borat, a character played by British comic genius Sacha Baron Cohen, who claims that in Kazakhstan, wine is made from horses' urine! The wine is not in fact that bad, but if any Kazakh entrepreneur decided to sell a wine labelled "Horses' Urine" (not too far away from the New Zealand "Cat's Pee"), they would probably double their country's exports overnight. The largest concentration of Kazakhstan's vineyards is in the extreme east, between Chimkent and Alma-Ata, in the foothills of the Tien Shan Mountains.

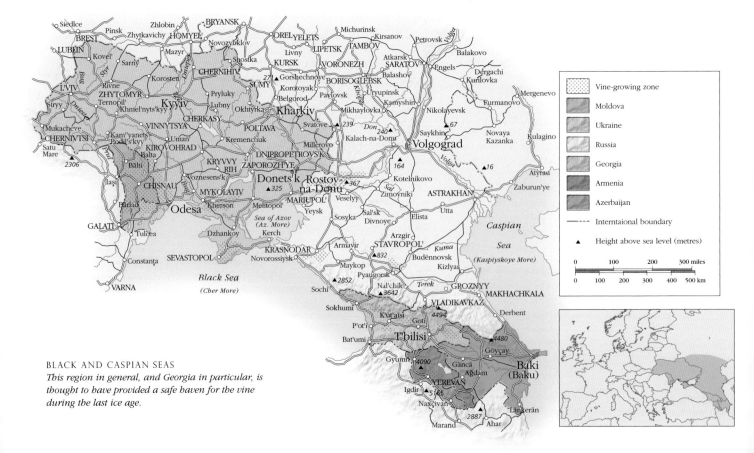

**BLACK AND CASPIAN SEAS**
*This region in general, and Georgia in particular, is thought to have provided a safe haven for the vine during the last ice age.*

## MOLDOVA

A small country the size of Belgium, Moldova is, in fact, an extension of Romania's Moldova and, historically, the two parts were one. There are six winemaking districts: Pucari, Balti, Ialoveni, Stauceni, Hincesti, Romanesti, and Cricova.

Pucari is 100 miles (160 kilometers) south of the capital in the heart of red wine country. Negru de Pucari is a deep-colored and firm-structured red wine blended from Cabernet Sauvignon and Saperavi; Purpuruiu de Pucari is a softer Pinot-Merlot blend; and Rosu de Pucari is a dark rosé made from Cabernet Sauvignon, Merlot, and Malbec. Romanesti's vineyards lie 30 miles (50 kilometers) farther north. Romanesti was named after the Romanov Tzar Alexander I, who restarted the Moldovan wine industry by establishing his own winery here. Vines include Aligoté, Cabernet Sauvignon, Malbec, Merlot, Pinot Noir, and Rkatsiteli, but it is the Bordeaux varieties that tend to fare best.

Halfway between Kishinev and Romanesti is Cricova, where unremarkable and often faulty sparkling wines are made in the most remarkable and elaborate underground city. Its entrance is a massive pair of steel doors in a rock face, through which the largest eighteen-wheelers can drive, winding their way 262 feet (80 meters) below the surface, where a city has been hewn out of solid rock. Its size corresponds to the area covered by 25 villages on the surface and it is serviced by 40 miles (65 kilometers) of underground roads, complete with stop lights and road signs. In addition to these roads, there are 75 miles (120 kilometers) of galleries, which almost equals the entire storage capacity of the Champagne region of France. Why, I asked myself, is this workplace equipped with opulent reception halls, a dining room the like of which I have not seen anywhere else during the Eastern Bloc era, and a cellar containing priceless old vintages of Mouton Rothschild, Latour, Romanée-Conti, and so on? I had absolutely no doubts that this was where the Politburo would head in a nuclear exchange.

✓ *AurVin* (Firebird) • *Cricova-Acorex* • *Dioysis Mereni*

## RUSSIA

Climate is something of an obstacle to vinegrowing in Russia, as winters are generally very cold indeed, often -22°F (-30°C), and the vines in many regions have to be buried in the earth to survive the bitterly cold months. Summers are very hot and dry and, but for the tempering effect of the Black and Caspian Seas, climatic conditions would probably be impossible for viticulture. There are five major winegrowing districts in Russia: Checheno-Ingush, Dagestan, Krasnodar, Rostov-na-Donu, and Stavropol, with grape varieties that include Aligoté, Cabernet, Muscatel, Pinot Gris, Pinot Noir, Plechistik, Pukhljakovsky, Rizling, Rkatsiteli, Sylvaner, and Tsimlyansky. In general, Russian producers concentrate on white and sparkling wines in the north and west, and red in the south and east.

In the mid-1950s, a system that has become known as the "Russian Continuous Flow Method" was developed for producing sparkling wine cheaply, easily, and quickly by a natural second fermentation. Krasnodar's most reputable vineyards are on southwest-facing coastal slopes overlooking the Black Sea. Abrau is known for its dry Rizling (Riesling), Cabernet, and Durso sparkling wine. Anapa, just along the coast to the north, also makes Rizling, while down the coast at Gelendzhik, Aligoté is the local specialty. To the east of Krasnodar and north of the Caucasus, Stavropol is known for its dry Rizling and Silvaner, as well as the Muscatel Praskoveiski dessert wines. Other dessert wines include the spicy Mountain Flower; and Rostov-na-Donu, located around the confluence of the rivers Don and Kan and the Taganrogskiy Zaliv estuary, is famous for its rich Ruby of the Don dessert wines. Plechistik is a grape variety that is used to lend backbone to Tsimlyansky and, throughout the state, it also makes decent, dry red wines.

On the east-facing slopes of the Caucasus Mountains, overlooking the Caspian Sea, are the vineyards of the Republic of Dagestan. This is a black grape area that is known for the full body and flavor of its dry red wines; the best come from Derbent in the south. Checheno-Ingush is another republic with vineyards on the Caucasus, but these are found inland, along its northern slopes, to the southeast of Stavropol. Most of the wines produced in this area are of the port type.

✓ *Château le Grand Vostock*

## UKRAINE

As viticulture represents one-fifth of this recently re-established nation's agricultural economy, it will be instrumental in building up overseas trade. This is necessary to replace Ukraine's trade with Russia, upon which it is still dependent. The state's wine industry is mainly concerned with producing still white wines, although red wines and white sparkling wines are also produced in the Crimea, and dessert wines are a local specialty. Crimea (Krym) is the peninsula that encloses the Sea of Azov. Sparkling "Krim" is a traditional method wine made in five styles, from Brut through to Sweet, and in a semi-sweet red version. The grapes used include Chardonnay, Pinot Noir, Rizling, Aligoté, and Cabernet. The wines are coarse, and the traditional addition of brandy does not help, but the Brut and Demi-Sec Red are widely available on export markets and sell on novelty value. The Ruby of Crimea, which is a blend of Saperavi, Matrassa, Aleatika, Cabernet, and Malbec, is a robust, rustic, full-bodied red that is quite commonly encountered in various countries.

Nikolayev-Kherson, just northeast of Crimea, and Odessa, near the Moldova state border, produce various white, sparkling, and dessert wines. The best known local wines are dry white wines such as Perlina Stepu, Tropjanda Zakarpatja, and Oksamit Ukrainy.

That this region is capable of not merely good but great wines of exceptional longevity is beyond doubt. In 1990, David Molyneux-Berry MW brought back some extraordinary wines for auction at Sotheby's in London. These came from the famous Massandra cellars, which were built on the outskirts of Yalta in the Crimea for the Russian imperial court at the end of the 19th century. This was not a winery, merely an aging facility acting as the central hub to a complex of 25 satellite wineries. The wineries were in the surrounding hills of Krymskiye Gory, where the vineyards were located, thus the grapes did not have to be transported, and almost every ounce of their potential quality was retained. This would be an ambitious project even by today's standards.

The wines Molyneux-Berry showed at a pre-auction tasting were nothing less than sensational. The Massandra Collection, as it has become known, consisted of fortified wines and I do not mean to be disparaging when I say that their maker deliberately mimicked classic styles such as Madeira, port, and so on. How could you put down a 1932 white-port-style wine that had more class, fragrance, and finesse at almost 60 years old than anything white and fortified that has ever been made in Oporto? The 1940 was let down by a spirity nose, but I would not keep a genuine white port five years, let alone 50, and it blew away the 1932 on the palate anyway. The 1929 Muscat had as much toffee, caramel, and exotic fruit as the best Australian Muscats, but a balance that undeniably placed it in the northern hemisphere. The best Massandra wines I tasted that day were both Madeiras, a 1937 and a 1922 (No.31), but although I would like to see such wines made again (fortified wines are still made, but not of comparable quality), I do not for one moment suggest that the entire Crimea should be turned over to the production of classic-quality fortified wines. What I do mean, however, is that great wines can be made in the Ukraine, in certain parts, given the right vines, yield, and proper winemaking expertise.

# The WINES of
# THE EASTERN
# MEDITERRANEAN

When this encyclopedia was first published in 1988, you could count the recommended wine producers in Greece on the fingers of one hand. There was general despair at how the first civilization to develop viticulture and winemaking could be reduced to such a pathetic state. Now it is one of Europe's most exciting wine-producing countries and, with thousands of unidentified ancient grape varieties preserved in its nurseries, it should be able to delight and surprise wine lovers for centuries to come. Turkey has the potential to rival Greece, but its political and religious constraints will not allow that to happen in our lifetime. The two most up-and-coming wine-producing countries are Lebanon and Israel; wines from here have flourished since the new millennium, as new boutique wineries have started to blossom—quite miraculously, all things considered. There is even improvement in the quality of Egyptian wine, not that it could have become much worse!

VINEYARDS ON THE ISLAND OF CEPHALONIA, GREECE
*The wines of origin produced in this appellation range from fresh and fruity dry whites to sweet red liqueur wines.*

Perhaps understandably, his first wine, Gentilini, started out so clean it was clinical, but it has moved on to become one of the country's finest, zippiest whites. Squeaky-cleanliness was a problem for Calligas, too, but its top white, Château Calligas, has been fatter since the early 1990s and this has been lifted by a nifty touch of residual gas. In recent years, numerous small wineries of exceptional talent have cropped up. Some have been around for a while, others are very new, but the best of these include names such as Aidarinis, Antonopoulou, Castanioti, Chrisohoou, Emery, Hatzimichali, Château Lazaridi, Mercouri, Oenoforos, Papaioannou, Château Pegasus, Semeli, Sigalas, and Skouras, with many others, no doubt, waiting in the wings.

## RETSINA—BOON OR BURDEN?

Retsina is wine (usually white) to which pine resin is added during fermentation. This practice dates back to antiquity, when wine was stored in jars and amphorae. As they were not airtight, the wines rapidly deteriorated. In the course of time, people learned to seal the jars with a mixture of plaster and resin and the wines lasted longer. This increased longevity was attributed to the antiseptic effect of resin, the aroma and flavor of which quickly tainted the stored wine. It was, of course, a false assumption, but in the absence of Pasteur's discoveries (then some twenty-five centuries in the future), it appeared to be supported by the fact that the more resinous the wine, the less it deteriorated. Within a short time, the resin was being added directly to the wine and the only difference between modern and ancient Retsina is that the resin is now added directly to the wine during fermentation, rather than after. The best Retsina is said to come from three areas, Attica, Evia, and Viota, and the best resin, which must be from the Alep or Aleppo pine, comes from Attica.

Strictly speaking, Retsina is not wine. It would be if its pine character were the result of maturation in pine casks, but having pine resin added makes it an aromatized wine, like vermouth. In the first edition, I joked about the possibility of a wine matured in pine casks, but I have since discovered on La Palma "Tea Wine," which is exactly that. Insignificant in volume—and oddity though it is—if it can be done in the Canary Islands, why not in Greece?

DOMAINE PORTO CARRAS
*Looking out across the blue waters of the Aegean to the fishing village of Maramas from the vineyards of Domaine Porto Carras, which also consists of a luxurious leisure and sports complex.*

## THE APPELLATIONS OF
# GREECE

**AO** = Appellation of Origin
**TA** = Traditional Appellation
**TI** = Topikos Inos (Regional Wine, similar to the French *vin de pays*)

### AMYNDEO AO *or* AMYNTAION AO
#### Macedonia

One of the most exciting, up-and-coming wine regions in Greece, Amyndeo is also the most northerly of this country's appellations, with vines growing at an altitude of 2,046 to 2,343 feet (620 to 710 meters). Until relatively recently, virtually all the output has been from the Amyntaion cooperative, and although the quality has been sporadic, the occasional gem has given hope of what might be. That hope has now been realized by the brilliant, *terroir*-driven Alpha Estate, which planted 11 international and indigenous grape varieties in the late 1990s, using the latest partial rootzone drying techniques and low yields to produce some beautifully structured wines. Most of these wines are not pure Xinomavro, thus cannot claim the Amyndeo appellation, but they are all outstanding. The non-appellation reds are particularly impressive, although I have a feeling that the wines released so far offer only an inkling of the quality that is to come. Yannis Boutaris is also trying hard at the Vegoritis winery, established in 1997.

🍇 Xinomavro

🍷 2–12 years (non-AO whites 1–3 years)

✓ *Alpha Estate* (Unfiltered Xinomavro)

### ANCHIALOS AO *or* ANHIALOS AO
#### Thessaly

This is a medium-bodied, dry white wine from the Nea Anchialos area on the Gulf of Pegassitikos near Volos. The local cooperative wine is clean, though unexciting. Babatzim wines are clean, acceptable, and improving.

🍇 Savatiano, Rhoditis, Sykiotis

🍷 1–2 years

### ARCHANES AO *or* ARHÁNES AO
#### Crete

The local cooperative makes the usual range of clean but unexceptional table wines, including a very ordinary red under the Archánes appellation. Vangelis Lidakis's non-appellation blend of Kotsifáli and Cabernet is the stand-out in this region.

🍇 Kotsifáli, Mandilariá

🍷 2–7 years

✓ *Boutari* (Domaine Fantaxometocho) • *Vangelis Lidakis*

### CÔTES DE MELITON AO *or* PLAYIES MELITONA AO
#### Macedonia

This appellation covers the red, white, and rosé wines of Sithonia, the middle of Halkidiki's three peninsulas, and was established by Domaine Porto Carras, the brainchild of the late

John Carras. Although secondary to the tourist resort of Porto Carras, the winery was profitable, whereas the tourist resort swallowed all the money, eventually bankrupting both ventures, which were sold to the Technical Olympic group in 2000. In the early 1980s, Domaine Porto Carras and, in particular, its flagship Château Porto Carras, became the first Greek wines of modern times to establish a truly international reputation. This was thanks to the aspirations of John Carras, which urged him to hire Bordeaux consultant Professor Peynaud, and Peynaud's choice of his ex-pupil Evangelos Gerovassiliou (see Epanomi TI, below) as winemaker. With the exception of the rich, classy Syrah, the Domaine wines are generally light, and are best enjoyed young, whereas the top-of-the-range Château Porto Carras has always been a rich-flavored, full-bodied, deep-colored red wine of true *vin-de-garde* quality.

🍇 Assyrtico, Athiri, Cabernet Franc, Cabernet Sauvignon, Cinsault, Grenache, Limnio, Petite Sirah, Rhoditis, Sauvignon Blanc, Savatiano, Ugni Blanc, Xinomavro

🍷 1–2 years (Château Porto Carras: 5–8 years for lighter vintages; 10–20 years for bigger)

✓ *Domaine Porto Carras*

## DAFNÉS AO
### Crete

Douloufakis is the best-known producer of these red wines, which may be dry or sweet.

🍇 *Liatiko*

## DRAMA TI
### Macedonia

Huddled between the Falakro, Menekio, and Peggio mountains, this regional appellation is grabbing attention primarily due to the huge investment in two of its wineries—Domaine Constantin Lazaridi (also known as Kosta or Kostas Lazaridis) at Adriani and Château Niko Lazaridi (also known as Nico or Nicos Lazaridis) at Agora—and the excellent, sometimes superb, wines that they have produced. But they are by no means the only excellent producers in this exciting new area.

🍇 Agiorgitiko, Assyrtico, Cabernet Sauvignon, Chardonnay, Limnio, Merlot, Rhoditis, Sauvignon Blanc, Sémillon, Ugni Blanc

🍷 2–7 years (red), 1–2 years (white)

✓ *Kostas Lazaridis* (Cava Amethystos) • *Château Nico Lazaridi* (Maghiko Vuono red & white) • *Pavlidis* (Assyrtiko) • *Wine Art Estate* (Idisma Drios Merlot, Techni Alipias Chardonnay and roze)

## EPANOMI TI
### Macedonia

This wine region has been put on the map single-handedly by Evangelos Gerovassiliou, the winemaker who made the first great Greek wine of modern times: Château Porto Carras. Gerovassiliou planted experimental vines on his family's property in 1981, while still working for Domaine Porto Carras, and has had no formal relationship with that winery since the Carras family relinquished ownership (see Côtes de Meliton) in 1999. The low, hilly land of Epanomi might not be the greatest place in Greece to grow wine grapes, but under Gerovassiliou, it definitely produces some of the country's greatest wines, both red and—particularly—white. The outstanding red is Syrah, while excellent whites include Fumé,

Malagousia, and Viognier, but all Domaine Gerovassiliou wines come highly recommended.

🍇 Negoska, Xinomavro

🍷 3–8 years

✓ *Gerovassiliou*

## GOUMENISSA AO
### Macedonia

A light-bodied red wine from the Goumenissa district, northeast of Naoussa. Usually a wine of good fruit and a certain elegance, the best undergo a light maturation in cask and can be relatively rich in flavor.

🍇 Negoska, Xinomavro

🍷 3–8 years

✓ *Aidarini* • *Boutari* (Filliria)

## KEFALONIA AO *or* CEPHALONIA AO
### Ionian Islands

There are three wines of origin in this appellation: Kefalonia or Robola of Kefalonia, Mavrodaphne of Kefalonia, and Muscat of Kefalonia. Kefalonia or Robola of Kefalonia is a dry white wine that can be fresh and floral, with an almost racy nose and a tangy, lightly rich, delicate-lemon fruity flavor. In the past, this wine has all too often been spoiled by sloppy winemaking, but most producers have cleaned up their act. The Mavrodaphne of Kefalonia is a sweet red liqueur wine similar in character to the Mavrodaphne of Patras (but not quite in the same class), while Muscat of Kefalonia is one of the lesser-known, sweet liqueur wines from the Muscat grape. Gentilini's non-appellation Syrah is probably the best single wine produced here.

🍇 Mavrodaphne, Muscat Blanc à Petits Grains, Robola

🍷 1–2 years (Robola), 1–10 years (Mavrodaphne), upon purchase (Muscat), 2–7 years (Syrah)

✓ *Gentilini* ◉

## KRANIA TI
### Thessaly

Dimitrios Katsaros produces a godlike Cabernet-Merlot blend and a very good, improving Chardonnay from vines growing on the slopes of Mount Olympus.

🍇 Cabernet Sauvignon, Chardonnay, Merlot

🍷 2–7 years (reds), 2–4 years (whites)

✓ *Katsaros*

## LIMNOS AO *or* LEMNOS AO
### The Aegean

There are two wines of origin produced in this appellation: Limnos and Muscat of Limnos. Limnos is an unfortified Muscat wine that may be made in dry, off-dry, and semi-sweet styles. It is usually soft and flowery, with an attractive Muscat aroma, followed by clean fruit. Muscat of Limnos is a superior liqueur Muscat wine that is richer and sweeter than Patras, though not in the class of Samos. So-called Muscat of Limnos Grand Cru is its sweetest style.

🍷 Upon purchase

✓ *Limnos Cooperative* • *Tsantali*

## MANTINÍA AO
### Peloponnese

This is a dry white wine from mountain vineyards in the center of the Peloponnese. The vines grow at an altitude of 2,130 feet (650

meters) and there are some very fresh, young wines with nice, lively fruit. Tselepos's non-appellation wines, such as Vareli, Cabernet-Merlot blend, and Merlot, are at least as good as its Mantinia.

🍇 Minimum of 85% Moschophilero, plus optional Asproúdes

🍷 Upon purchase

✓ *Antonopoulos* • *Cambas* • *Spyropoulos* • *Tselepos*

## MESSENIKOLA AO
### Peloponnese

This appellation was introduced in 1994, but has not exactly taken off. The primary variety, Mavro Messenikola, is grown at between 825 and 990 feet (250 and 300 meters).

🍇 70% Mavro Messenikola, 30% Carignane and Syrah

## NAOUSSA AO
### Macedonia

These generally reliable wines are grown west of Thessalonika, at a height of 1,150 feet (350 meters) on the southeastern slopes of Mount Velia. Although I give only rock-solid recommendations, I cautiously suggest that almost any Naoussa could be worth the gamble; the growers took a pride in their wine long before their peers did elsewhere. Good Naoussa is well-colored, rich, and aromatic, with heaps of spicy fruit and a long finish. Great Naoussa is world class. Yannis Boutaris's Kyr-Yanni is one of Naoussa's greatest, up-and-coming wineries, and his Yanakohori—a Xinomavro-Merlot blend—is at least as good as his excellent Xinomavro Ramnistas.

🍇 Xinomavro

🍷 4–15 years

✓ *Chrisohoou* • *Dalamaras* • *Karydas* • *Kyr-Yanni* (Xinomavro Ramnistas)

## NEMEA AO
### Peloponnese

This is a relatively reliable appellation and there is a local pride similar to that in Naoussa. Grown in the Corinth district at an altitude of between 820 and 2,620 feet (250 and 800 meters), the Agiorgitiko grape provides a deep-colored, full, and spicy red wine that can be spoiled by dried-out fruit, or by a lack of fruit. Known locally as the Blood of Hercules, because his blood was shed when he killed the Nemean lion, this wine has been produced for 2,500 years. Kokotos's *vins de pays* under his Château Semeli label are even better than his Semeli Nemea, and Skouras's Megas Oenos (see Other Wines, p436) is at least as classy as its Nemea.

🍇 Agiorgitiko

🍷 5–20 years

✓ *Gaia* (Estate) • *Kokotos* (Semeli) • *Kourtakis* (Kouros) • *Papaïoannou* (Palea Klimata) • *Parparoussis* (Epilegmenos) • *Skouras* (Aghiorghitiko, Grande Cuvée)

## PANGEON TI
### Macedonia

This regional wine area is south of Drama, in an ocean-influenced, mountainous microclimate, the elevation and weather of which result in a significantly longer growing season. Pangeon was effectively discovered and established by Vassilis Tsaktsarlis and Evangelos Gerovassiliou (see Côtes de Meliton AO and Epanomi TI), who started planting their vineyard at Kokkinohori as recently as 1999. Pangeon promises an even more exciting quality than Drama.

🍇 Agiorgitiko, Cabernet Sauvignon, Chardonnay, Merlot, Sémillon, Syrah

🍷 3–8 years

✓ *Biblia Chora*

## PAROS AO
### The Cyclades

This is a deep-colored, light-bodied red wine from the Mandilaria grape, which I have tasted only once. My notes record a very strange, but difficult to describe, taste. A rich, dry, white wine from the Monemvassia grape (which some believe to be the original Malvasia), is also produced, but I have not tasted it.

🍇 *Mandilaria, Monemvassia*

## PATRAS AO
### Peloponnese

There are four different wines of origin produced in this appellation in the hilly hinterland of Patras in the Peloponnese: Patras, Mavrodaphne of Patras, Muscat of Patras, and Muscat Rion of Patras. Patras plain and simple is a light, dry white wine made exclusively from the Rhoditis grape. These wines were once dull and flabby, but are now clean and crisp, although seldom excite, with Antonopoulos's Alepou about as good as it gets (and nowhere near the quality of its non-appellation Cabernet-Nea Dris; *see* Other Wines, below). Mavrodaphne of Patras is a rich, sweet, red liqueur wine with a velvety smooth, sweet-oak finish. Often compared to a Recioto della Valpolicella, a good Mavrodaphne is in my opinion far better, although it does have a similar raisiny-sherry oxidative aroma. One delightful aspect of this wine is that it can be drunk with equal pleasure when it is either young and fruity or smooth and mature. Muscat of Patras is a gold-colored, sweet, liqueur Muscat wine that can be delicious in its typically raisiny way, as can the Muscat Rion (or Rio) of Patras, which comes from Rion/Rio in Patras.

🍇 Mavrodaphne, Muscat Blanc à Petits Grains, Rhoditis

🍷 1–2 years (Patras), 1–20 years (Mavrodaphne), upon purchase (Muscat)

✓ **Patras** *Antonopoulos* (Adoli Ghis) • *Oenoforos* (Asprolithi) **Muscat of Patras** *Achaia Clauss* (Collector Series) **Muscat Rion (or Rio) of Patras** *Parparousis*

## PEZA AO
### Crete

The white wines are made from the Vilána grape and lack crispness, and the red wines, which are made from the Kotsifáli and Mandilaria grapes, are usually dried-out and could be fresher.

🍇 Kotsifáli, Mandilaria, Vilána

## RAPSANI AO
### Thessaly

Uninspiring dry red wines from flat, uninspiring land in the vicinity of Mount Olympus.

🍇 Krasáto, Stavrotó, Xinomavro

## RETSINA TA
### Central Greece

Although rosé is not unknown, Retsina is almost invariably white, with 85 percent of the blend

coming from the Savatiano grape. It may be blended from various areas or can have a specific, usually superior, origin, but in every case, Retsina carries the unique Traditional Appellation. This designation recognizes the ancient practice of resinating wine and the EU has confined its use to Greece.

There are degrees of resination, ranging from relatively light to heavy, and the quality of the pine resin itself can range from poor to fine; the better-quality pine resin makes better-quality Retsina. Despite its penetrating aroma and flavor, pine resin cannot hide a tired, flabby, oxidized, or simply bad wine. Personally, I do not like Retsina, but I have to admit that the aroma of fine pine resin is refreshing and I also agree that this aromatized wine has a useful cutting quality when drunk with oily Greek food.

🍇 Rhoditis, Savatiano

🍷 As young and as fresh as possible

✓ **Appellations** *Attica* • *Evia* • *Thebes* • *Viota* **Brands** *Gaia* (Ritinitis Nobilis)

## RODOS AO *or* RHODES AO
### The Dodecanese

Reds are 100 percent Mandilaria, whites are 100 percent Athiri; neither of which has so far amounted to much. The best wines are the sweet, golden, liqueur Muscat, the best of which are on a par with the Muscat of Patras. Other non-appellation wines produced on this island include the *méthode champenoise* wines of CAIR, the local cooperative, but they are rather coarse with an overly assertive mousse.

🍇 Amorgiano (aka Mandilaria), Athiri, Muscat Blanc à Petits Grains, Trani Muscat

🍷 Upon purchase

✓ *CAIR* (Muscat of Rhodes)

## SAMOS AO
### The Aegean

One of the great sweet wines of the world, the local cooperative's Samos, Samos Grand Cru, Samos Nectar, and Samos Anthemis, in order of increasing complexity and sweetness, are all superb, perfectly-balanced, rich, and mellifluous wines. The cooperative also produces a deliciously dry and fresh non-appellation version called Doryssa, and two that are off-dry: Samena and Samena Gold, which are both as clean as a whistle with a

delightful orange flower-water aroma and delicate fruit.

🍇 Muscat Blanc à Petits Grains

🍷 Upon purchase

✓ *Cambas* • *Samos cooperative*

## SANTORINI AO
### The Cyclades

This full-bodied, dry white wine can have an intruiging combination of high natural alcohol and a high acidity level. Sweet *vin de liqueur*, *vin doux naturel*, and *vin de paille* styles are also produced. Sigalas makes the best quality, most complete range within this appellation.

🍇 Aidani, Assyrtiko

🍷 2–5 years

✓ *Boutaris* (Nyhteri) • *Gaia* (Thalassitis) • *Kostas Antoniou* (Vareli, Vinsanto) • *Sigalas* (Bareli)

## SITIA AO
### Crete

The red wines in this appellation can be dry or sweet, fortified or not. White wines must be dry and cannot be fortified. They have traditionally been somewhat rustic in character, but the Sitia cooperative has improved out of all recognition, and Yannis Economou has been working hard since the mid-1990s to bring some elegance and finesse to his wines.

🍇 80% Liatiko plus 20% Mandilaria (reds), minimum 70% Vilána plus optional Thrapsathíri (whites)

✓ *Economou* • *Sitia cooperative*

## ZITSA AO
### Epirus

Dry and semi-sweet, slightly spritzy, clean, and fruity white wine from six villages around Zitsa, northwest of Ioánnina, where the vines grow at an altitude of 1,970 feet (600 meters). Most of this appellation's production is processed by the cooperative.

🍇 Debina

🍷 Upon purchase

✓ *Ioánninan cooperative* (Orion)

## OTHER WINES
Some of the country's best wines do not claim any of the above appellations.

**RED**

✓ *Alpha Estate* (Ktima Alpha) • *Antonopoulos* (Cabernet Nea-Dris) • *Boutaris* (Grande Reserve) • *Calligas* (Nostos) • *Evharis* (Estate Red, Merlot) • *Hatzimichali* (Cava) • *Mercouri* (Antaris, Cava) • *Parparoussis* (Oenofilos) • *Skouras* (Mega Oenos) • *Tsantalis* (Merlot) • *Tselepos* (Kokkinomylos Merlot) • *Voyatzis* (Erythros)

**WHITE**

✓ *Alpha Estate* (Ktima Alpha, Sauvignon Blanc) • *Antonopoulos* (Chardonnay) • *Chrisohoou* (Prekniáriko) • *Gentilini* (Fumé) • *Oenoforos* (Asprolithi, Lagorthi) • *Papaïoannou* (Chardonnay) • *Tsantali* (Ampelonas) • *Voyatzi* (Malvasia)

**DRY ROSÉ**

✓ *Emery* (Granrosé) • *Gentilini* (Rosé) • *Oenoforos* (Esperitis)

**SPARKLING WHITE**

✓ *Spiroloulos* (Oude Panos) • *Tselepos* (Villa Amalia)

# THE LEVANT

*In 1988, when this encyclopedia was first published, I wrote that aside from two wineries in Lebanon and one in Israel, "fine wine is nonexistent in the Levant." Who would have thought that after all the bloody troubles those two war-torn countries have been through since, we would find such growth, diversification, and exhilarating promise in the wines from Lebanon and Israel as we do today? But we do, and, essentially, this is down to the boom in boutique wineries in these two countries over the past decade.*

WINE WAS FIRST PRODUCED in Mesopotamia (an area roughly equivalent to modern-day Iraq) circa 4000 BCE. In recent times, most vineyards throughout this region have been used for the production of table grapes, raisins, and currants. The 1960s were a golden age for Lebanese wine and, indeed, Lebanon in general, but the outside world did not really know anything about wines from the Levant until the early 1980s. It was the success of Serge Hochar at Château Musar in Lebanon that drew our attention to the wine potential of this region. In the 1960s, Hochar's wines had been the favorite of certain French colonial officers, attracting them away from Château Ksara, their previous Lebanese favorite; but 1979 was the seminal year, as it was then that he showed his wines at the Bristol Wine Fair in England. In the late 1980s, Yarden put Israel on the wine map, but it was not until the early 2000s that more than a hundred boutique wineries gave these two pioneering Levant wine-producing countries real credibility.

## CYPRUS

**Wine districts:** *Marathassa Afames, Pitsilia, Maheras Mountains, Troödos Mountains, Mesaoria*
**Total area under vine:** *4,520 acres (18,300 hectares)*
Wines have been made on this beautiful island for at least 4,000

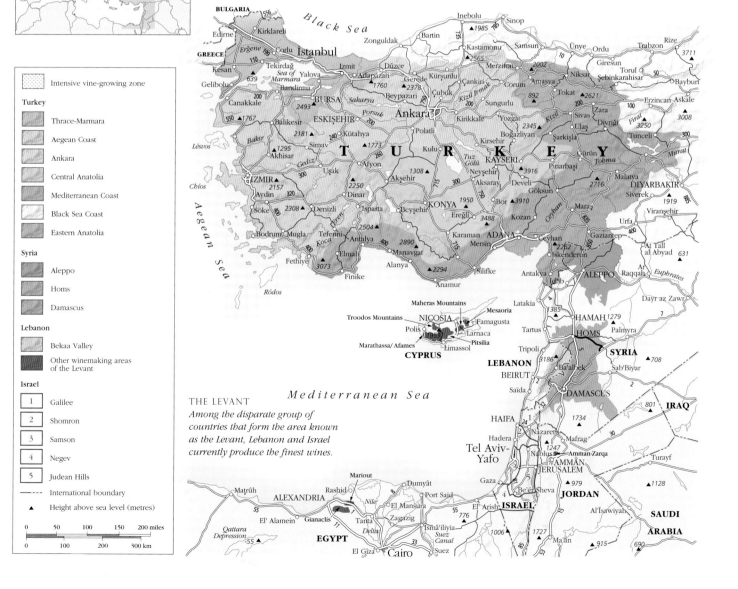

**Legend:**

Intensive vine-growing zone

**Turkey**
- Thrace-Marmara
- Aegean Coast
- Ankara
- Central Anatolia
- Mediterranean Coast
- Black Sea Coast
- Eastern Anatolia

**Syria**
- Aleppo
- Homs
- Damascus

**Lebanon**
- Bekaa Valley
- Other winemaking areas of the Levant

**Israel**
1. Galilee
2. Shomron
3. Samson
4. Negev
5. Judean Hills

--- International boundary
▲ Height above sea level (metres)

0  50  100  150  200 miles
0  100  200  300 km

THE LEVANT
*Among the disparate group of countries that form the area known as the Levant, Lebanon and Israel currently produce the finest wines.*

years and Cyprus's historically famous wine, Commanderie St John, is one of a handful that claim to be the world's oldest wine. It can be traced back to 1191, when Richard the Lionheart, King of England, acquired the island during the Crusades. He subsequently sold it to the Order of the Knights of the Temple, who established themselves as Commanderies and later became known as the Knights of the Order of St. John. Commanderie St John is a *solera*-matured, sweet dessert wine, which is made from a blend of black and white grapes that have been left in the sun for between 10 and 15 days after the harvest to shrivel and concentrate the grape sugars. It used to be rich and luscious with a fine, toasty fullness, but there is nothing special about the wine produced today. Those privileged enough to taste rarities dating back to the turn of the 20th century will recognize just how great these wines once were.

In recent years, early harvesting, temperature-controlled stainless-steel vats, and various modern vinification techniques have revolutionized Cypriot winemaking, producing much lighter, cleaner, and crisper wines. The large cooperative producers are cutting down the time taken to get the harvest to the winery, delays which were detrimental to the quality of their wines at one time. KEO, the island's largest and most advanced winery, is making the greatest strides toward improving quality, while the emergence of small, independent wineries since the early 1990s is only just beginning to offer consumers real choice.

*Fikardos* (Achillas, Chardonnay Xilogefiro) • *K & K Vasilikon* (Ayios Onoufrios, Xynisteri) • *KEO* (Domaine d'Ahera, Fino, Heritage, Othello, Rosella)

## EGYPT

**Wine district:** *Nile Delta*
**Total area under vine:** *165,490 acres (67,000 hectares)*
The world's earliest documented wine is from King Den's Horus vineyard, sometime between 3000 BC and 2890 BC, but winemaking in this country came to an abrupt end in AD 641, when it was conquered by Muslim Arabs. The first winery in more recent terms was established in 1882 by Nestor Gianaclis, a Greek-born Egyptian cigarette manufacturer. The Gianaclis (pronounced "jaana-cleesse") winery was nationalized in 1963 and privatized in 1999. During its nationalization, the wines became increasingly undrinkable, due to its ambient production and storage temperatures exceeding a mind-boggling 104°F (40°C). However, under private ownership of the Al-Ahram Beverages Company (ABC), air conditioning and temperature-controlled stainless-steel vats were installed. Gianaclis had a monopoly on wine production when privatized, but this was brushed aside by El Gouna Beverages Company, which undercut ABC's prices, marketing its Obelisk brand so aggressively that it quickly captured 40 percent of domestic wine sales. ABC could not compete, so it bought out El Gouna in 2001, following which ABC was itself taken over by Heineken in 2002. El Gouna's former managing director, André Hadji-Thomas, formed another company, the Egyptian International Beverage Company (EIBCO), which launched the Shahrazade and Jardin du Nil brands at the end of 2005. Rumors about Gianaclis buying in grapes from Lebanon and South Africa turned out to be true, although the provenance of those wines is clearly stated on the label. At the moment, white Egyptian wines are best, but for Gianaclis Pinot Blanc read Thompson Seedless, and for EIBCO's Chardonnay read Vermentino-Chardonnay. Steer clear of the Keg wines in "all-inclusive" resorts, particularly the red, which is made from reconstituted Spanish Bobal concentrate! Lots of classic varieties, black and white, at both ABC and EIBCO vineyards are due to come on stream as of 2008, so quality and range should improve.

## ISRAEL

**Wine districts:** *Galilee/Galil, Shomron/Samaria, Samson/Shimshon, Judean Hills, Negev*
**Total area under vine:** *14,820 acres (6,000 hectares)*
Over the last five years, we have seen a raft of small, independent wineries come on stream, forcing the biggest producers, notably Golan Heights (Yarden), Carmel (including the new Yatir winery), and Barkan, constantly to raise their game. This boutique boom started in the 1990s, and by the turn of the new millennium, there were 70 or so small new wineries on the scene, but by 2005 this had increased to no fewer than 140. Yet, paradoxically, while this is the most exciting time ever for the quality and diversity of Israeli wines, it is also financially the most precarious period in the wine industry's history, with huge losses incurred by a number of wineries, large and small. However, a series of sell-outs and mergers should see the Israeli wine industry settle down over the next five years.

*Castel* (Grand Vin) • *Chateau Golan* (Eliad, Merlot, Syrah) • *Flam* (Cabernet Sauvignon Reserve) • *Yarden* (Cabernet Sauvignon, Cabernet Sauvignon Elrom Vineyard, Katzrin Red, Merlot Ortel Vineyard) • *Yatir* (Forest)

## JORDAN

**Wine district:** *Amman-Zarqua*
**Total area under vine:** *9,880 acres (4,000 hectares)*
A country where the vine once flourished, Jordan's fast-diminishing vineyards now cover barely more than one-quarter of the area they did as recently as the late 1990s, and only a small percentage of these vines produce wine, averaging just 67,000 cases (6,000 hectoliters) a year. Jordanians are not wine drinkers, preferring Arrack, the aniseed-flavored spirit ubiquitous in the Levant.

## FACTORS AFFECTING TASTE AND QUALITY

**LOCATION**
Technically, the Levant comprises the countries along the eastern Mediterranean shores, which for practical reasons this encyclopedia has extended northwest to Turkey, southwest to Egypt, east to Jordan, and this necessitates that Cyprus is also included.

**CLIMATE**
Hot and dry for the most part, with a minority of cooler microclimates due to their proximity to the Mediterranean, or high altitude. Vines in Lebanon's Bekaa Valley receive an amazing 300 days of sunshine per year and no rain during the harvest.

**ASPECT**
Vines grow on all types of land from coastal plains to higher mountain slopes.

**SOIL**
Soils vary greatly from volcanic origin on Cyprus, through the alluvial river and sandy coastal plains to the Bekaa Valley's gravel over limestone.

**VITICULTURE AND VINIFICATION**
Better-quality vineyards are being planted on higher mountain slopes, grapes are being harvested at lower sugar levels, and the resulting wines are being fermented at cooler temperatures, with increasing use of new French oak for top-of-the-range wines.

**GRAPE VARIETIES**
**Cypriot Grape Varieties:**
Cabernet Sauvignon, Chardonnay, Grenache, Maratheftiko, Mavro, Opthalmo, Xineisteri
**Israeli Grape Varieties:**
Cabernet Franc, Cabernet Sauvignon, Carignan, Chardonnay, Colombard, Merlot, Riesling, Sauvignon Blanc
**Note** The Argaman, an Israeli *Souzão* x *Carignan* cross of disappointing quality, is being removed
**Lebanese Grape Varieties:**
Cabernet Sauvignon, Carignan, Chardonnay, Chasselas, Cinsault, Clairette, Gamay, Grenache, Muscat (various), Obaideh, Pinot Noir, Riesling, Sémillon, Syrah, Ugni Blanc
**Turkish Grape Varieties:**
Adakarasi, Ak Dimrit, Alicante Bouschet, Beylerce, Boğazkere, Burdur Dirmiti, Cabernet Sauvignon, Calkarasi, Carignan, Clairette, Dökülgen, Emir, Gamay, Kalecik Karasi, Misket, Narince, Oküzgözü, Semillon, Sultaniye

# LEBANON

**Wine district:** *Bekaa Valley*
**Total area under vine:** *37,000 acres (15,000 hectares)*

Although Lebanon's vineyards have shrunk from 66,690 acres (27,000 hectares) since the mid-1990s, the vines used for wine-making are actually on the increase. Only 10 percent of Lebanon's vineyards are used for wine, and they are mostly confined to the Bekaa Valley, where there is a tenfold potential for expansion. The Bekaa Valley was put on the wine map by Serge Hochar, owner of Château Musar, during the 15-year civil war, when he had to contend with Syrian tanks, Israeli jets, and all sorts of militia to get his grapes from the vineyards to his winery. At one time, Musar and Lebanese wine were synonymous, but its high volatile-acidity (VA) style makes Musar a yesterday wine. I have read that Hochar reduced VA levels in 1995, yet when tasting with him in 2001, he admitted that he has actually given instructions that the wines must have high minimum VA levels! It would be sad if Serge Hochar, who has been such a great ambassador for Lebanese wine, learns

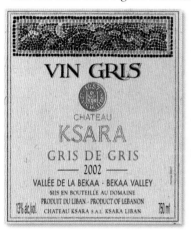

the hard way that reputations do not last indefinitely and are easier to lose than gain. No wineries or vineyards were damaged in 2006, which is no consolation to the dead and homeless left in the wake of Israel's targeting Hizbullah, which led to the destruction of Lebanon's infrastructure.

✓ *Chateau Belle-Vue* (La Renaissance) • *Chateau Kefraya* (Chateau Kefraya, Comte de M) • *Chateau Ksara* (Chardonnay, Cuvee de Printemps, Vin Gris) • *Clos St. Thomas* (Chateau St. Thomas) • *Massaya* (Selection) • *Wardy* (Private Selection)

# SYRIA

**Wine districts:** *Aleppo, Homs, Damascus*
**Total area under vine:** *185,250 acres (75,000 hectares)*

In ancient times, wine was second only to olives in terms of agricultural production in Syria. However, since Muslims now account for 90 percent of the country's population, the vines planted are mostly used for table grapes, raisins, and currants, with wine production rarely exceeding 90,000 cases (8,000 hectoliters) a year. The above-mentioned winegrowing districts are located on lower mountain slopes.

It was, apparently, French troops stationed in the country during World War II who were the catalyst for the wine industry that does exist today—because the French, being French, demanded wine. And if you want to taste Syrian wines, visit France, where an increasing number of Syrian-made "Lebanese" wines are finding their way onto Lebanese and North African restaurant wine lists!

# TURKEY

**Wine districts:** *Thrace-Marmara, Ankara, Mediterranean Coast, Black Sea Coast, Central Anatolia, Central-South Anatolia, East Anatolia*
**Total area under vine:** *1,383,200 acres (560,000 hectares)*

This country has the fourth-largest area under vine in the world (after Spain, Italy, and France), but because its population is predominantly Muslim, most vines produce table grapes, raisins, or currants. Just 2.5 percent of Turkish vineyards produce wine. Perhaps surprisingly, there are over 100 wineries in Turkey, but their wines are generally flabby, too alcoholic, heavy, over-sulfured, and all too often oxidized. The best known are Trakya (dry white Sémillon from Thrace), Trakya Kirmisi (a red blend of native grapes that also comes from Thrace), and the amusingly named Duo Hosbag (red Gamay, from Thrace) and Buzbag (red

wine made from native grapes grown in southeast Anatolia), but despite local fame, these wines should be avoided. The right varieties in well-selected sites could have a much greater potential in Turkey than the same grapes grown in either Lebanon or Israel, and with sufficient investment, technology, and passion, Turkey could even compete with Greece in terms of quality. There has been some investment since the second half of the 1990s, but media claims in early 2005 that Turkish wine production had enjoyed a "20 percent year-on-year growth" over the previous 10 years were a case of gross exaggeration. The latest reliable statistics available at the time of writing show a 27 percent decline between 1996 and 2001.

Political and religious considerations make significant foreign investment unlikely in the near future. However, it is worth noting that the best Turkish wine boasting any track record is Villa Doluca, and until the firm of Doluca was founded in 1926 by Nihat Kutman, the entire wine industry in this country was non-Muslim. Obviously, the religious dimension is not the brick wall that some might think. Kutman's son, Davis-trained Ahmet Kutman, teamed up with his old school buddy Güven Nil to establish Sarafin, a project involving the establishment of Sauvignon Blanc, Chardonnay, Cabernet Sauvignon, and Merlot vineyards at Saroz Bay on the Gallipoli Peninsula. That these wines have set new standards in Turkish winemaking is just a hint of what might lie in store.

✓ *Doluca* (Kav, Villa Doluca) • *Safarin* (Chardonnay, Merlot)

**CYPRIOT VINEYARDS**
*One of the island's thriving winemaking areas is located in the foothills of the Troödos Mountains.*

# The WINES of
# THE AFRICAS

THE OLD WORLD MEETS THE NEW WORLD
on the African continent, although they are
thousands of miles apart. There is no interest, let
alone excitement, in the former French colonies
of Algeria, Morocco, or Tunisia. The wine
industries in these increasingly fundamentalist
Islamic countries face difficult times, but if they
can survive, there is certainly potential and it is
only a matter of time before a flock of flying
winemakers arrives to exploit it. If and when this
happens, our perception of North African wine
could change profoundly. There are a number of
commercial wineries on Madagascar and a few
curiosities found in Ethiopia, Kenya, Namibia,
and Tanzania. The French even have a *vins de
pays* on the island of Réunion. But the class act
in Africa is, of course, South African wine. We
saw its exports soar in the Mandela years, but
that was merely filling the void created by its
isolation under apartheid. Sales of South African
wine in the second half of the 1990s were little
more than an international expression of
solidarity with the new Rainbow State. Since
2000, however, a technological revolution has
transformed the quality and diversity of Cape
wine, putting this country on a firm footing as
a New World player that is second to none.

FRANSCHOEK VALLEY IN THE PAARL REGION, SOUTH AFRICA
*An aerial view of vineyards that are higher and steeper than most
of the Paarl region, and well suited to red wines.*

# SOUTH AFRICA

*As export markets opened up in the mid-1990s, so the quality of South African wine started to blossom, but by the turn of the millennium it had gone into overdrive, as new vineyards got on board, and winemakers grasped every opportunity to hone their skills in the full glare of international attention. Some observers have called on South Africa to focus its attention on those varieties it grows best, but this country has only just come in from the cold, and the next couple of decades will see plenty of experimentation.*

AT FIRST, BETTER QUALITY simply meant stricter selection and, where appropriate, a massive investment in new oak, but an increasing amount of South Africa's growing export income has been plowed into the industry's Vine Improvement Programme (VIP). Phase one of VIP concentrates on clonal selection and rootstock improvement, while phase two analyzes the suitability to specific *terroirs* of various combinations of the clones and rootstocks the plan develops. It is so ambitious that the project will probably never end, but after such a lengthy period of international isolation it was essential to revitalize the country's vineyards. However, VIP has already manifested itself in wines of richer varietal character and greater complexity than ever before, and South Africa, which was once 10 years behind the rest of the world, is now at the forefront of viticultural research.

## IN THE BEGINNING

Virtually all South Africa's vineyards are found within 100 miles (160 kilometers) of Cape Town. The first vines were planted in 1655 and the wines were not, by all accounts, particularly successful. Simon van der Stel, who arrived in 1679, complained about the "revolting sourness" of the local wines. He proceeded to remedy the situation by founding Constantia, the most illustrious wine farm in the country's history (this has since split into three properties: Groot Constantia, Klein Constantia, and Buitenverwachting).

---

### RECENT SOUTH AFRICAN VINTAGES

**2007** The heatwave at the end of January was balanced by a cooler February, resulting in fresh, fruity whites and intense, well-structured reds.

**2006** A fabulous vintage for both white and red wines, the whites possessing outstanding crispness and exceptional aromatics, while the reds show an abundance of plump fleshy fruit.

**2005** Very variable, with most wines ranging from average to good quality.

**2004** An excellent vintage for both reds and whites, due to a long, drawn-out ripening period, providing ripe grapes with exceptional extract and acidity. However, the delayed maturity of early-ripening varieties meant that they were picked at the same time as some late-ripening varieties, which caused a congestion in many wineries.

**2003** Very good quality across the board, with some standout reds, but some late-ripening varieties proved difficult.

---

### Three centuries of winemaking

The arrival of French Huguenots, with their viticultural and winemaking expertise, greatly improved the quality of Cape wines, and by the early 1700s they were beginning to be held in high esteem. When French Revolutionary forces entered the Netherlands in 1806, the British occupied the Cape and, cut off from supplies of French wines, began exporting South African wines to the many corners of their empire, enhancing the wines' growing reputation there.

By 1859, the export of Cape wines to Britain alone had reached 1 million gallons (45,000 hectoliters) per year. However, in Britain, Richard Cobden (the "apostle of the free market") and William Gladstone secretly negotiated a commercial treaty with the French that had a devastating effect on this wine industry. In 1860, Cape wine exports fell to 22,000 hectoliters; the next year this dropped to 5,700 hectoliters; and by 1865 as little as 4,200 hectoliters were being exported.

---

### FACTORS AFFECTING TASTE AND QUALITY

**LOCATION**
South Africa is on the southernmost tip of the African continent.

**CLIMATE**
The climate is generally mild Mediterranean, but coastal areas have a much higher rainfall and are cooler than inland parts in spring and fall. All coastal areas are cooled by sea breezes chilled by the icy Benguela current from Antarctica. The coolest, Constantia, like Stellenbosch, rates as low Region III. Klein Karoo, Tulbagh, Olifants River, and parts of Paarl (Dal Josaphat) are the hottest, falling between high Region IV and low Region V (*see* p.470).

**ASPECT**
Most vines are cultivated flat on gently undulating valley floors. More recently, higher slopes have been increasingly cultivated and Klein Constantia, Thelema Mountain Vineyard, Bellingham, and Boschendal all have very steep vineyards.

**SOIL**
Soils range from gravel and heavy loams of sandstone, shale, and granitic origin on the coastal plain, to the deep alluvial, sandy, and lime-rich, red-shale soils of Klein Karoo and other river valleys.

**VITICULTURE AND VINIFICATION**
Contrary to popular belief, Cape vineyards sometimes fail even to ripen their grapes, although there are, of course, many hot areas where vines may suffer from heat-stress and grapes can quickly overripen. Irrigation is often necessary in Robertson, Worcester, and Vredendal, where successful cultivation depends on the availability of water. Where the heat factor is critical, some estates may conduct the harvest at night, under floodlight. South Africa has a history of overproduction, due to having too great an area under vine, too little emphasis on high-quality varieties, poor clones, and undesirably high yields, but is quickly upgrading its vineyards, and is now at the forefront of research on new clones and rootstock. Yields are also being lowered to appeal to export markets. Until the early 1990s, estates were slow to cultivate higher, cooler slopes, but this has changed, especially with emergence of a new breed of winery that buys in from single vineyards, often over a large area. There is a trend for each estate or winery to develop one "flagship" wine, usually a classic red blend.

**GRAPE VARIETIES**
**Primary varieties:** Cabernet Franc, Cabernet Sauvignon, Chardonnay, Chenin Blanc (*syn.* Steen), Cinsault, Colombard, Crouchen, Merlot, Muscat à Petit Grains (*syn.* White Muscadel), Muscat d'Alexandrie (*syn.* Hanepoot), Pinot Noir, Pinotage, Riesling (*syn.* Rhine Riesling, Weisser Riesling), Ruby Cabernet, Sauvignon Blanc, Sémillon, Syrah (*syn.* Shiraz)

**Secondary varieties:** Barbera, Bukettraube, Carignan, Chenel (*syn.* Chenin Blanc x Trebbiano), Emerald Riesling, Fernão Pires, Gamay, Gewürztraminer, Grenache (*syn.* Rooi Grenache), Hárslevelü, Malbec, Mourvèdre, Muscat Rosé à Petit Grains (*syn.* Red Muscadel), Nebbiolo, Petit Verdot, Pinot Gris, Sangiovese, Souzão, Tinta Barocca, Touriga Nacional, Ugni Blanc, Viognier, Zinfandel

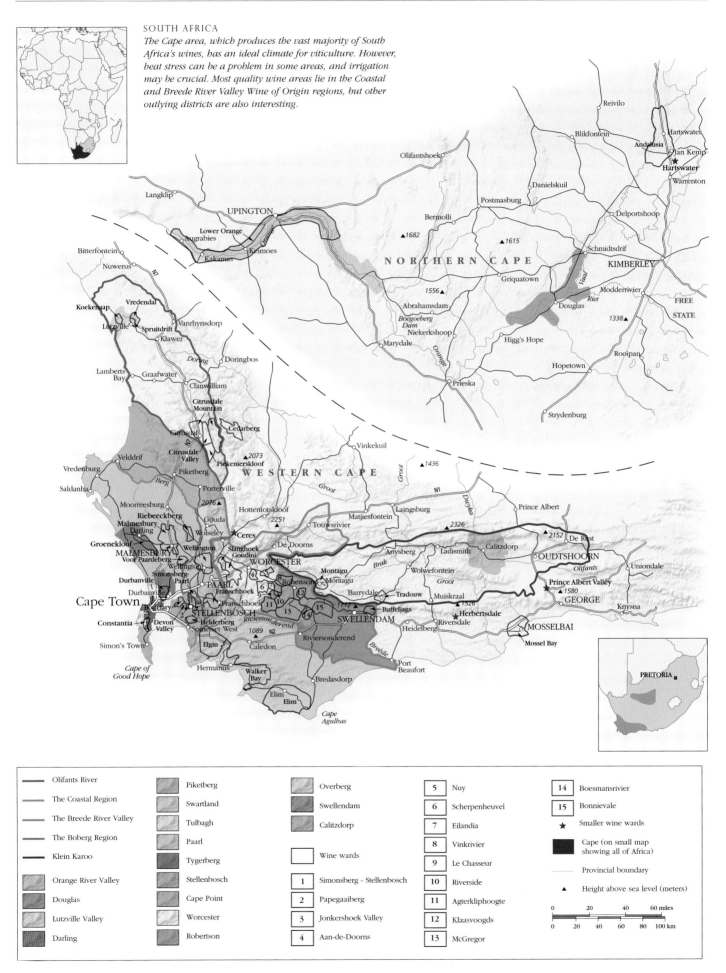

SOUTH AFRICA
*The Cape area, which produces the vast majority of South Africa's wines, has an ideal climate for viticulture. However, heat stress can be a problem in some areas, and irrigation may be crucial. Most quality wine areas lie in the Coastal and Breede River Valley Wine of Origin regions, but other outlying districts are also interesting.*

NORTHERN CAPE

WESTERN CAPE

FREE STATE

KIMBERLEY

UPINGTON

Cape Town

MALMESBURY

STELLENBOSCH

PAARL

WORCESTER

SWELLENDAM

OUDTSHOORN

MOSSELBAI

GEORGE

PRETORIA

Reivilo
Blikfontein
Hartswater
Andalusia
Jan Kemp
Hartswater
Warrenton
Olifantshoek
Postmasburg
Danielskuil
Delportshoop
Schmidtsdrif
Bermolli
▲1682
▲1615
Griquatown
Vaal
Modderrivier
1338▲
1556▲
Abrahamsdam
Riet
Douglas
Boegoeberg Dam
Niekerkshoop
Higg's Hope
Rooipan
Marydale
Hopetown
Orange
Prieska
Strydenburg

Langklip
Bitterfontein
Nuwerus
N7
Lower Orange
Augrabies
Keimoes
Kakamas
Orange
Koekenaap
Vredendal
Spruitdrift
Vanrhynsdorp
Lutzville
Klawer
Doring
Doringbos
Lamberts Bay
Graafwater
Clanwilliam
Citrusdale Mountain
Cedarberg
Vinkekuil
▲1436
Velddrif
Citrusdal
Citrusdale Valley
▲2073
Piekenierskloof
Vredenburg
Piketberg
Groot
Groot
Saldanha
Berg
Porterville
2076▲
Moorreesburg
Hottentotskloof
Laingsburg
Prince Albert
Riebeeckberg
Gouda
2251▲
Matjiesfontein
Duyka
▲2326
De Rust
Malmesbury
Darling
Wolseley
Touwsriver
Calitzdorp
▲2152
Groenekloof
Ceres
Slanghoek
Goudini
De Doorns
Anysberg
Ladismith
Olifants
Uniondale
Voor Paardeberg
Wellington
Brak
Wolwefontein
Prince Albert Valley
Wellington
Montagu
Groot
▲1580
Durbanville
Paarl
Robertson
Montagu
Muiskraal
Herbertsdale
GEORGE
Durbanville
Franschhoek
Barrydale
Tradouw
1526▲
Knysna
Bottelary
Franschhoek
Riviersonderend
1712▲
Buffeljags
Constantia
Devon Valley
Helderberg
Swellendam
Riversdale
Simonsberg
Somerset West
Riviersonderend
Heidelberg
Mossel Bay
Elgin
1089
Caledon
Breede
Hermanus
Riviersonderend
Port Beaufort
Walker Bay
Bredasdorp
Simon's Town
Cape of Good Hope
Elim
Elim
Cape Agulhas

**Legend:**

| | |
|---|---|
| ══ Olifants River | |
| ── The Coastal Region | |
| ── The Breede River Valley | |
| ── The Boberg Region | |
| ━━ Klein Karoo | |

Orange River Valley
Douglas
Lutzville Valley
Darling

Piketberg
Swartland
Tulbagh
Paarl
Tygerberg
Stellenbosch
Cape Point
Worcester
Robertson

Overberg
Swellendam
Calitzdorp

Wine wards

1 Simonsberg - Stellenbosch
2 Papegaaiberg
3 Jonkershoek Valley
4 Aan-de-Doorns

5 Nuy
6 Scherpenheuvel
7 Eilandia
8 Vinkrivier
9 Le Chasseur
10 Riverside
11 Agterkliphoogte
12 Klaasvoogds
13 McGregor

14 Boesmansrivier
15 Bonnievale
★ Smaller wine wards
■ Cape (on small map showing all of Africa)
── Provincial boundary
▲ Height above sea level (meters)

0   20   40   60 miles
0  20  40  60  80  100 km

## *A time of struggle for South African wine*

Despite this setback to the wine industry, production was not checked. In fact, the large influx of immigrants, attracted by the discovery of gold and diamonds in the late 19th century, prompted a rapid expansion of vineyards in anticipation of a vastly increased demand. This increase in demand was realized, but the sudden wealth of these immigrants sparked off the Boer War, and sales of wine decreased at home and abroad. Yet unsellable wine continued to be made.

In 1905, the Cape government encouraged the formation of cooperatives, but nothing constructive was done either to reduce production or stimulate demand. Thus, when the Koöperatiewe Wijnbouwers Vereniging, or KWV, as it is now known, was formed in 1918 with government-backed powers, its decision to distill half the country's annual wine production into brandy immediately and very effectively improved the quality of Cape wines. Its policy of blending the rest of the surplus into marketable export products did no less than save the South African wine industry.

## NEW AREAS AND BETTER WINES

Stellenbosch and Paarl are traditionally viewed as the country's two greatest wine districts, but since the establishment of Hamilton Russell's top-performing vineyard at Hermanus, many other areas are now considered to be potentially as fine for winemaking. Although there are just eight wine estates in Hermanus at the moment, Elgin has developed into another startlingly good wine area. Elgin is the Cape's apple-growing capital, and, as Washington State quickly learned, wherever apple growers choose to go, fine-quality wine grapes will follow. Even farther east, there is great hope for Plettenberg Bay, even though it was first planted as recently as 2000. This mountainous terrain some 12 miles (20 kilometers) east of Plettenberg Bay itself is thought to be a premium Sauvignon Blanc area. Other promising new areas include: Cape Agulhas (which encompasses Elgin, with Sauvignon Blanc, Sémillon, and Shiraz the most successful contenders); Philadelphia (a new ward north of Durbanville, where vines on hilly terrain up to 850 ft [260 m] in altitude benefit from cooling Atlantic influences and high diurnal differences, currently noted for Cabernet Sauvignon, Merlots, and red blends); Bamboes Bay (Olifants River area on the west coast, with exciting Sauvignon Blanc potential); Outeniqua (hopes for Pinot Noir in Little Karoo Region); and Langeberg-Garcia (the most recently demarcated ward). There is even a KwaZulu-Natal WO (planted in 2000, and demarcated in 2005, with the first certified WO wines released in 2006, this area in the province of KwaZulu-Natal north of Durban stretches from Greytown to Oribi Flats and the Midlands, where vines grow at altitudes of up to 4,920 ft [1,500 ml]).

In 1995, South African wine estates were allowed, for the first time, to buy grapes from outside their own domain to produce non-estate wines, and in 2005 to offer single-vineyard wines from other locations. This should lead to a certain polarizing of varieties in the areas where each performs best, which ties in with the second phase of the Vine Improvement Program, and the results can only be good for the future of South African wine.

# SOUTH AFRICAN LABEL LANGUAGE

*Although an increasing number of South African wine labels are in English or in English and Afrikaans, Afrikaans-only terms may be found on labels.*

**CAPE DATED TAWNY PORT** Wine of a single year that must have the character of a tawny port, and the label must include the year of vintage, the words "matured in wood" and the words "Tawny Port."

**CAPE LATE BOTTLED VINTAGE (LBV) PORT** Should be a port-style of a single year of quality, and be dark and full-bodied with signs of going tawny in color. The main label could indicate the year of bottling as well as the vintage, and the description "Late Bottled Vintage" or "LBV" must appear on the label. The port will be aged for three to six years, of which at least two years in oak, before bottling.

**CAPE RUBY PORT** A blend of young, full-bodied, round, and fruity port-style wine. Components could be aged in wood for up to three years, depending on the size of wood used, but no components should be aged for less than six months. The average age should not be less than one year.

**CAPE TAWNY PORT** A blend of wine that has been wood matured, this port-style wine must be amber/orange (tawny) in color and must have acquired a smooth, light, slightly nutty flavor. Blending of white and red port for tawny port is not allowed.

**CAPE VINTAGE PORT** A port-style wine from one harvest, dark and full-bodied, aged in wood of any size. The words "Vintage Port" and date of vintage may appear on the label.

**CAPE VINTAGE RESERVE PORT** A port-style wine from one harvest, produced in a year of recognized quality, with exceptional organoleptic characteristics, dark and full-bodied, with very fine aroma and palate. The producer can be assisted by a tasting panel set up by the Association. The wine should preferably be aged for an average of at least one year or more in wood of any size. The wine must be sold exclusively in glass. The words "Vintage Reserve Port" and date of vintage must appear on the label.

**CAPE WHITE PORT** Made from a non-Muscat white cultivar, aged in wood of any size for a minimum period of six months.

**CULTIVAR** Cultivar derives from a shortened form of "cultivated variety" and is the South African term for grape variety.

**EDEL LAAT-OES** Noble late harvest. Botrytized grapes must be used for this style, which must have a minimum of 50 grams of residual sugar per liter.

**EDELKEUR** This literally means "noble rot."

**FORTIFIED WINE, LIQUEUR WINE** This style of wine must have an alcoholic strength of no less than 16.5 percent by volume and no more than 22 percent. This category includes port and sherry, plus such uniquely South African wines as Jerepigo or Jerepiko.

**GEBOTTEL IN...** Bottled in...

**GEKWEEK EN GEMAAK OP...** Grown and made on... (i.e., but not bottled on).

**GEKWEEK, GEMAAK EN GEBOTTEL OP...** Grown, made, and bottled on... (i.e., estate-bottled).

**GEPRODUSER EN GEBOTTEL IN...** Produced and bottled in...

**GEPRODUSER EN GEBOTTEL IN DIE REPUBLIEK VAN SUD-AFRIKA** Produced and bottled in the Republic of South Africa.

**GRAPE VARIETY** Since 2005, wine must contain at least 85 percent of the grape variety or varieties indicated.

**JEREPIGO OR JEREPIKO** A very sweet liqueur wine with at least 220 grams per liter of residual sugar. All Muscadels are Jerepigos, but not all Jerepigos are Muscadels, since some are made from varieties other than Muscat de Frontignan.

**KOÖPERATIEWE, KÖPERATIEVE, KOÖPERASIE, KOÖPERATIEF** Cooperative.

**LAAT-OES** Late harvest, with natural alcoholic strength of at least 10 percent and 20 grams of residual sugar per liter.

**LANDGOEDWYN** Estate wine.

**MÉTHODE CAP CLASSIQUE** A general term that is used to describe a bottle-fermented sparkling wine.

**MOSKONFYT** Concentrated grape paste.

**OESJAAR** Vintage.

**ORIGIN OF THE WINE (WO)** The Wine of Origin (or *Wyn van Oorsprong*) is South Africa's equivalent of *Appellation d'Origine Contrôlée*. WO wines must be 100 percent from the appellation area indicated.

**SEMI-SOET** The Afrikaans term for "semisweet."

**SPESIALE LAAT-OES** Special late harvest. This usually, but not necessarily, implies that some botrytized grapes have been used; there is a minimum natural alcoholic strength of 11 percent by volume, and no restrictions on residual sugar.

**STEIN** A semisweet style of wine that is normally Chenin-based.

**VINTAGE** A vintage must contain at least 75 percent of the year indicated or 85 percent for exported wines (the balance must come from either the preceding or succeeding vintage).

**WYN VAN OORSPRONG (WO)** Dutch for Wine of Origin, South Africa's equivalent of *Appellation d'Origine Contrôlée*. WO wines must be 100 percent from the appellation area indicated.

THELEMA MOUNTAIN VINEYARDS
*These beautifully tended vineyards on the Simonsberg in Stellenbosch belong to Thelema Mountain, one of South Africa's youngest and most exciting wineries.*

## Pinotage and the "Cape Blend"

There are those who think that a "Cape Blend" with an obligatory Pinotage component should become the flagship of South Africa's export drive in the 21st century. And then there are those who are less than enamored of the Cape's own grape. It might be possible to play down this grape's typically high-toned, estery character and, in particular, iron out its high acetate (often incorrectly referred to as acetone) content with appropriate vinification techniques. And if it is cultivated on the Cape's higher slopes, it should be possible to utilize extended hang-time to harvest Pinotage on tannin ripeness without running the risk of producing wines that are big and cumbersome, with too much alcohol. In this way, Pinotage does not have to have its rough edges, green tannins, or the banana and nail-polish aroma of acetate-laden fruit. But, as its detractors inside South Africa point out, they will still be left with a rustic 1920s cross that has not attracted anyone to plant the variety widely anywhere else in the world—there are 232 acres (94 hectares) in New Zealand, but that is as good as it gets, because outside of that country it is found only in the US and Canada, where it is grown in such minuscule quantities that there are no official statistics.

Is Pinotage as bad as it is made out to be, and are they right not to want South Africa's reputation to depend on a blend that

must contain this grape? Yes and no. Of course, Pinotage has a poor track record, otherwise South Africa's Pinotage diehards would be right, and the rest of the world wrong, but blending it is a good idea. Pinotage is a good team player. With the right support, it is better at improving some blends than intrinsically finer grapes would be. We can see this in everything from sparkling wine *cuvées*, such as Villiera Tradition Brut, to some of South Africa's most stunning classic red blends, including Flagstone Dragon, Kaapzicht Steytler Vision, and Meinert Synchronicity. And who knows, perhaps they will make a prince out of this pauper's grape in the process. It is not as if there are absolutely no fine-quality pure Pinotage wines. Although I am a declared sceptic when it comes to this variety, you will find a number of excellent Pinotage wines listed on the following pages. And in my humble opinion, most Pinotage vineyards are on the wrong sites, so these successes must be encouraging. Diverting the bulk of this variety's production into blends while truly objective winemakers trial Pinotage on higher, cooler slopes for longer hang-times, to ripen its notoriously harsh tannins without increasing alcohol levels, can only be good for the long-term reputation of the Cape's own cultivar.

---

# THE APPELLATIONS OF
# SOUTH AFRICA

**Note** Although estates and single vineyards are the smallest demarcated WO (Wine of Origin), wine wards are the most specific type of WO appellation listed here. One or more WO wards may be contained in a larger WO district, and one or more WO districts may be contained in a WO region, but not all districts are necessarily attached to a larger region, and not all wards are attached to either a district or a region.

## BOBERG WO

**Wine districts** *Paarl WO, Tulbagh WO*

This regional WO is restricted to fortified wine from the Paarl and Tulbagh districts.

## BREEDE RIVER VALLEY WO

**Wine districts** *Robertson WO, Swellendam WO, Worcester WO*

**Wine wards** *Agterkliphoogte WO, Bonnievale WO, Boesmansrivier WO, Eilandia WO, Hoopsrivier WO, Klaasvoogds WO, Le Chasseur WO, McGregor WO, Vinkrivier WO, Aan-de-Doorns WO, Goudini WO, Nuy WO, Scherpenheuvel WO, Slangboek WO, Buffeljags WO, Stormsvlei WO*

Although Robertson is known as "the valley of vines and roses," its hot climate relegated this region to largely bulk-produced wine until the emergence of fine-wine hotspots on its lime-rich soils. It now has a number of top-performing estates with well-established reputations for white wines, particularly Chardonnay and sparkling wines, and an emerging one for reds, including several up-and-coming Syrahs. Swellendam is just east of Robertson, in an area where few wineries and vineyards exist, although it is suited to Muscadel and other

fortified wines, and plantations of Chenin Blanc can be found. Worcester is on the western edge of Little Karoo, adjoining the eastern border of Paarl, in the Breede River catchment area, which is intensively cultivated with vines. The hot climate is tempered in the west by high rainfall, while in the east rainfall is very low, with soils that are derived from Table Mountain sandstone and the fertile red shale of Little Karoo. Although there are some good wine estates in Worcester, including the excellent Bergsig, the real stars of this district are the high-performing cooperatives (Du Toitskloof, Goudini, and Nuy), which make exceptionally fine white and fortified wines.

## CEDERBERG WO

This up-and-coming ward comprises the Cederberg Wilderness Area, which lies within the Cape's famous "fynbos" region, one of the world's six floral kingdoms, an outlying area just east of the southern part of the Olifants River region. Cederberg Cellars is owned by the Nieuwoudt family and is one of the South African wine industry's fastest-rising superstars, with vineyards planted at an altitude of 3,280 feet (1,000 meters), the highest in the country, producing a raft of recently award-winning wines, including a coveted Veritas Double Gold.

## COASTAL REGION WO

**Wine districts** *Cape Point WO, Darling WO, Paarl WO, Stellenbosch WO, Swartland WO, Tulbagh WO, Tygerberg WO*

**Wine wards** *Bottelary WO, Constantia WO, Devon Valley WO, Durbanville WO, Franschhoek Valley WO, Groenekloof WO, Jonkershoek Valley WO, Malmesbury WO, Papegaaiberg WO, Philadelphia WO, Riebeekberg WO, Simonsberg-Paarl WO, Simonsberg-Stellenbosch WO, Voor Paardeberg WO, Wellington WO*

The most frequently encountered appellation, the Coastal Region comprises one external ward (Constantia WO) in addition to the above seven districts and their wards. Cape Point is a challenging new cool-climate district on the western and southern slopes of the Cape Peninsula that has demonstrated its potential for white wines, although the jury is still out for its red. Darling was part of Swartland, but its vineyards, particularly in the higher Groenekloof area, are too good not to have their own appellation. The Paarl district embraces the fertile Berg River valley and vineyards surrounding the towns of Franschhoek, Wellington, and Paarl itself. The vineyards are located on three main types of soil: granite in the Paarl district, Table Mountain sandstone along the Berg River, and Malmesbury slate to the north. The climate is Mediterranean, with wet winters and hot, dry summers. Average annual rainfall is about 26 inches (65 centimeters), but this declines toward the northwest of the district. Although this used to be a white wine area, it is now more of a red wine area, with high vineyards that are well suited to the production of fine-quality reds. The Stellenbosch district is located between False Bay to the south and Paarl to the north. This is where the greatest concentration of South Africa's finest wine estates have traditionally been situated. There are three types of soil: granite-based in the east (considered best for red wines), Table Mountain sandstone in the west (favored for white wines), and alluvial soils around the Eerste River. With warm, dry summers, cool, moist winters, and an average annual rainfall of 20 inches (50 centimeters), irrigation is usually unnecessary, except in some situations at the height of the summer season. Helderberg is the current hotspot. Of the vast area covered by Swartland, most is arable land, with viticulture confined to the southern

section around Darling, Malmesbury, and Riebeek. The soils are Table Mountain sandstone and Malmesbury slate, and rainfall is light, at around 9 inches (24 centimeters), which makes irrigation generally necessary, although some vineyards surprisingly manage without it. Within the Swartland district, Philadelphia is the latest, most exciting wine ward to emerge, with the reds from Havana Hills grabbing the headlines. Tulbagh is bordered to the south by the Riversonderend Mountains and to the north by Langeberg Range. Soil, climate, and topography are, for the most part, similar to those of the Karoo, although somewhat more temperate. Readers might not have heard of the Tygerberg district, but most will know Meerendal Estate, which sits on the southeastern slopes of the Tygerberg, where rich, red soils combine with moderated temperatures and airflow from the cool summer winds to provide the vines with an excellent growing environment. The vineyards of Constantia are situated on the eastern, red-granitic slopes of Constantia Mountain, south of Cape Town. Bordered by sea on two sides, the climate is very moderate, of Mediterranean character, but it is quite wet, with up to 47 inches (120 centimeters) of annual rainfall. Durbanville is located in the lowlands of the Tygerberg hills and, although the rainfall is less than half that of Constantia, the deep, well-weathered, red granite-based soils have a particularly good water retention, and the vines are cooled and dried by the sea breezes coming in from Table Bay.

## KLEIN KAROO WO

**Wine districts** *Calitzdorp WO*

**Wine wards** *Montagu WO, Outeniqua WO, Tradouw WO, Upper Langkloof WO*

This appellation is a long, narrow strip that stretches from Montagu in the west to De Rust in the east. The vineyards require irrigation to survive the hot and arid climate. The famous red shale-based Karoo soil and the deep alluvium closer to the various rivers are very fertile and are well suited to growing grapes to make the Jerepigo, Muscadel, and other dessert wines for which this area is well known. Calitzdorp is a semiarid desert region, with summer temperatures of up to 104°F (40°C). These temperatures are moderated by afternoon sea breezes and cool nights, providing a beneficial diurnal effect to ensure better acidity levels. Calitzdorp is, quite literally, the hottest place in South Africa for Port-style fortified wines, with Boplaas, De Krans, and Axe Hill all producing some of the country's finest Port-style wines.

## NORTHERN CAPE WO

**Wine districts** *Douglas WO*

**Wine wards** *Hartswater WO, Lower Orange WO, Rietrivier (Free State) WO*

This region encompasses Hartswater, South Africa's northernmost viticultural area, 50 miles (80 kilometers) north of Kimberley, encompassing the town of Jan Kempdorp, which was formerly known as Andalusia. Northern Cape is totally divorced from the rest of the country's vineyards. No fine wines as such are made in this region, but good fortified wines and an improving quality of good-value, fruity varietal wines are being made at Hartswater Wine Cellar, Landzicht, Oranjerivier Wine Cellars, and Douglas Winery.

## OLIFANTS RIVER

**Wine districts** *Citrusdal Mountain WO, Citrusdal Valley, Lutzville Valley WO*

**Wine wards** *Bamboes Bay, Koekenaap WO, Piekenierskloof WO, Spruitdrift WO, Vredendal WO*

The vines in this long, narrow district grow on sandstone or lime-rich alluvial soil. The climate is hot and dry, with rainfall averaging just 10 inches (26 centimeters) per year and decreasing closer to the coast. This is a large region where you will find few wineries, but two of those wineries are huge. Westcorp's Vredendal is South Africa's largest wine producer, and Lutzville, the country's second-largest winery, is now bigger than KWV, Fleur du Cap, and Nederburg, the former colossi of the Cape wine industry, put together.

## OVERBERG WO

**Wine districts** *Walker Bay WO*

**Wine wards** *Elgin WO, Elim WO, Kleinrivier WO*

Overberg WO consists of a huge, recently cultivated area southeast of Paarl and Stellenbosch. Fifteen years ago, there was only one estate here, Hamilton Russell Vineyards in Walker Bay, but this was obviously one of South Africa's most potentially exciting wine districts. Walker Bay is now one of the hottest spots on South Africa's wine map. Hottest meaning coolest, of course. This is considered the benchmark district for South Africa's Chardonnay and Pinot Noir, Hamilton Russell's success having attracted several highly reputed wineries to set up here, the highest flyers of which include Bartho Eksteen, Bouchard Finlayson, Newton Johnson, Sumaridge, and Whalehaven. Many more wineries are, at the time of writing, about to begin production in both areas.

## PICKETBERG

**Wine wards** *none*

This large district lies between Swartland and Tulbagh to the south and Olifants River district to the north. With very hot temperatures and annual rainfall as low as 7 inches (17.5 centimeters ) in places, it is really not suited to viticulture, yet is starting to produce some interesting fruit.

## WESTERN CAPE WO

A vast multiregional appellation covering all South African WO appellations except Northern Cape WO.

## OTHER ISOLATED WINE AREAS

**Wine wards** *Ceres WO, Herbertsdale WO, Prince Albert Valley WO, Ruiterbosch WO, Swartberg WO*

Ceres is located just east of the Tulbagh WO; Herbertsdale is 28 miles (45 kilometers) northwest of the potentially exciting Mossel Bay area, just south of the Klein Karoo, and it contains two wineries, Die Poort and Nietverloren; Prince Albert Valley is a 12-mile- (20-kilometer-) long valley at the foot of the Swartberg Mountain Nature Reserve, north of Klein Karoo, in an area previously better known for its olives than for its wine (although it has attracted considerable investments recently, including the Dutch-funded Bergwater Winery, which is irrigated by pure mountain water); and Swartberg is a promising wine ward that overlooks Prince Albert Valley.

THE WINE STYLES OF
# SOUTH AFRICA

## CABERNET SAUVIGNON

Traditional, firm, assertive styles are made here, but the trend is toward more up-front wines driven by ripe, juicy *cassis* fruit with cedary, spicy-vanilla oak complexity. New-wave wines are often enjoyable when young, but some also develop in bottle. Cabernet blends rank as one of South Africa's finest red wine styles. Other constituents are usually Cabernet Franc and Merlot, but may include Malbec, or, in the case of Boschendal Lanoy, even a dash of Shiraz (Shiraz-dominated blends are dealt with below).

🍷 3–7 years (modern style), 5–10 years (traditional style, exceptional modern style)

🏆 *Boekenhoutskloof* • *Cederberg* (V Generations) • *Kanonkop* • *Le Riche* (Reserve) • *Morgenhof* (Reserve) • *Neil Ellis* (Jonkershoek) • *Rustenberg* (Peter Barlow) • *Thelema* • *De Trafford* • *Vergelegen*

## CHARDONNAY

Although this is South Africa's most improved varietal, it was originally so bland that it could only get better. The trouble was that as soon as new oak became widely available for the first time, many winemakers went over the top, producing heavy, overwooded Chardonnays. These wines also suffered from poor raw material, but this situation improved with clonal selection and matching this variety to more suitable *terroirs*. The best oaked Chardonnays are often barrel-fermented, rather than just oak-aged, with just a kiss of creamy new oak, although some less refined, if just as lip-smacking, wines dominated by yummy, coconutty-oak are also to be found. The top unoaked Chardonnays are very pure and exquisitely balanced, and they often belie their hot-climate origins.

🍷 1–3 years (unoaked), 1–5 years (oaked)

🏆 *Bouchard Finlayson* (Kaaimansgat, Missionvale) • *Durbanville Hills* (Rhinofields) • *Eikendal Vineyards* • *Hamilton Russell* • *Jordan* • *Mulderbosch* (Barrel Fermented) • *Rustenberg* (Five Soldiers) • *Thelema* (Ed's Reserve) • *Vergelegen* (Reserve) • *De Wetshof* (Bateleur)

## CHENIN BLANC

Not so long ago this grape covered almost one-third of South Africa's vineyards. Yields were very high, producing wines that were generally off-dry to semisweet and considered cheap and cheerful for their day. Now it accounts for just over 17 percent, and most of the wines produced are still cheap, but although the

quality is generally the same, "cheerful" translates more as "dull, boring, and mediocre" by today's standards. In recent years, as this country's wines have come on by leaps and bounds, there has been much hype about the special quality of South African Chenin Blanc, and very little fulfillment in the bottle. It should be possible for the best sites of oldest vines to produce bone-dry wines of greater intensity than commonly found in the Loire, but truly special Chenin Blanc, such as Jean Daneel's Signature (I am thinking of the 2003 here), are few and far between.

🍷 Upon purchase

🏆 *Avontuur* (Barrel Select) • *Cederberg* (V Generations) • *Fort Simon Estate* (Barrel Fermented) • *Jean Daneel* (Signature) • *Kanu* (Wooded) • *Ken Forrester* • *Old Vines* • *Spice Route* • *Villiera*

## MERLOT
### Pure and blended

Cape winemakers are following in California's footsteps, having started with pure Cabernet Sauvignon, they then moved on to Cabernet blends and then pure Merlot wines. Cape Merlot is often spoiled by green tannins, but the best have a persistence of flavor that belies their softness. This softness can be anything from the simple, fruit-driven delight of, say, a Veenwouden Merlot to the very classy, silky smoothness of Du Plessis Havana Hills.

🍷 2–5 years

🏆 *Avondale* (Les Pleurs) • *Du Preez* (Reserve) • *Havana Hills* • *KWV* (Cathedral Cellar) • *Morgenhof* (Reserve) • *Overgaauw* • *Spice Route* (Flagship) • *Thelema* (Reserve) • *De Trafford* • *Vergelegen*

## PINOT NOIR

South Africa is not likely to challenge Burgundy or, for that matter, California, Oregon, or New Zealand when it comes to this fussy variety, but a few highly talented winemakers are crafting some elegant exceptions.

🍷 2–5 years

🏆 *Bouchard Finlayson* (Galpin Peak Tête de Cuvée) • *Cabrière* (Haut Cabrière) • *Flagstone* (The Poetry Collection) • *Glen Carlou* • *Hamilton Russell* • *Meerlust* • *Newton Johnson*

## PINOTAGE

This Cinsault x Pinot Noir cross is to South Africa what Zinfandel is to California and Shiraz to Australia. Or at least it should be. The problem is that it does not have half the potential of either of the other two grapes, but if anyone has the audacity to criticize this grape on its home turf, the South Africans become very touchy indeed. Yet, even after all these years, this country's winemakers still seem to be in a bit of a quandary about how it should be produced and that, if nothing else, puts Pinotage in the same league as Zinfandel because the Americans produce a hodgepodge of styles from that grape too. South African Pinotage can be found in all shades between the big, baked, earthy brews with volatile aromas, to the Beaujolais look-alikes with a touch of bubble-gummy oak. The trend for the best wines seems to be leaning toward the bigger styles, but too many are overly big or spoiled by green phenolics. Although the development of this cross was supposed to provide Burgundy-like elegance in the baking-hot vineyards of North Africa, the genes have transmitted more Cinsault than Pinot Noir. However, rather than baking-hot vineyards, I would like to see Pinotage grown in places like Cederberg, where the altitude can draw out the hang-time, resulting in full tannin ripeness without excessively high levels of sugar. Those who prefer length with delicacy and finesse to size and weight will find Hamilton Russell's Ashbourne a class apart. And it is no coincidence that this wine is grown under the truly cool-climate conditions of Walker Bay.

🍷 Upon purchase

🏆 *Ashbourne* • *Bellevue Estate* (PK Morkel) • *Clos Malverne* (Basket pressed) • *Diemersfontein* (Carpe Diem) • *Graham Beck* (The Old Road) • *Kaapzicht* (Steytler) • *KWV* (Cathedral Cellar) • *Morgenhof* • *Môreson* • *Thelema*

## RIESLING

Unless produced in a late-harvest or botrytized style, Riesling in South Africa just does not seem to have the fruit-acidity elegance I expect from this variety, but I find that I am similarly picky about Riesling throughout most of the New World. Others find far more satisfaction in these wines than I do, so perhaps I am being too harsh in my judgment, but where we do agree, I think, is on the exceptional style and quality of the wines below.

🏆 *De Wetshof* (Rhine Riesling) • *Klein Constantia* (Rhine Riesling) • *Thelema* (Rhine Riesling)

## SAUVIGNON BLANC

This is not this country's most successful varietal, despite the number of recommendations that are listed below. Their success is, however, disproportionate to the intrinsic quality that

Sauvignon has established in South Africa. The reason for this is that much of the industry seems to be committed to trying every which way in order to master this grape variety and, although the results show there are many overachievers out there, I had to drink my way through a sea of dross to find them. There are too many overherbaceous wines from those who are trying too hard with this varietal, and a great many dull wines from those who are jumping on the Sauvignon bandwagon.

With the exception of Flagstone, most of these producers have no hope of competing with the expressiveness of New Zealand Sauvignon Blanc, although if there is such a thing as South Africa's answer to Marlborough, it could be Elim (where Bruce Jack of Flagstone collaborates with wine grower Francis Pratt on the so-called Berrio Project) or Elgin. Note that "Fumé Blanc" or "Blanc Fumé" is used for barrel-fermented or oak-aged Sauvignon Blanc.

🍶 Upon purchase

🏆 *Bellevue* (Morkel) • *Cederberg* • *Flagstone* (Berrio) • *Mulderbosch* • *Neil Ellis* (Groenekloof) • *Nitida Cellars* (Club Select) • *Springfield* (Life from Stone) • *Steenberg* (Reserve) • *Vergelegen* (Schaapenburg Reserve) • *Villiera* (Traditional Bush Vine)

## SÉMILLON

Sémillon has great potential in South Africa, where it can produce rich yet refined wines on to which skilled winemakers can graft a lovely leesy complexity. However, the number of recommendations below is meager because few producers take the potential of this grape seriously. If the industry applied half the effort to this variety that they have to Sauvignon Blanc, Sémillon would quickly become one of South Africa's most fashionable wines.

🍶 18 months to 5 years

🏆 *Boekenhoutskloof* • *Boschendal* (Jean de Long) • *Constantia Uitsig* (Reserve) • *Fairview* (Oom Pagel) • *Rihk's* • *Nitida* • *Steenberg* • *Stellenzicht* (Reserve)

## SYRAH
### Pure and blended

Syrah is planted far less widely than in Australia, but it is South Africa's second-fastest-expanding red wine variety. It has come from virtually nothing in the 1990s to equal-sixth most widely planted black grape, placing it on a par with the Cape's beloved Pinotage, and not only do the best examples knock the socks off the best Pinotage, but they can give most Australian Shiraz a run for their money. This must now be regarded as South Africa's most exciting red wine variety.

🍶 2–8 years

🏆 *Avondale* (Les Pleurs) • *Boekenhoutskloof* • *Cederberg* (Shiraz) • *Fairview* (Solitude) • *Graham Beck* (The Ridge) • *Rust en Vrede* (Shiraz) • *Sentinel* • *Stellenbosch* (Genesis Shiraz) • *Stellenzicht* • *Vergelegen* (Shiraz)

## OTHER REDS

This section lists the best examples I have found of South Africa's less frequently encountered red varietals, some of which will no doubt become more widely established in this country one day.

🏆 **Barbera** *Altydgedacht*

**Cabernet Franc** *Bellingham* (Spitz)

• *Neethlingshof* (Lord Neethlingshof) • *Warwick Estate*

**Carignan** *Fairview* (Pegleg)

**Malbec** *Bellevue* (Limited Release)

**Nebbiolo** *Steenberg*

**Petit Verdot** *Du Preez* (Hendrik Lodewyk) • *Signal Hill* • *Simonsig* (Auction Reserve)

**Ruby Cabernet** *Flagstone* (Ruby in the Dust)

**Tinta Barocca** *Allesverloren*

**Zinfandel** *Blaauwklippen* (Vineyard Selection)

## OTHER WHITES

This section lists the best examples I have found of South Africa's less frequently encountered white wine varietals, some of which will no doubt become more widely established in this country one day.

🏆 **Grenache Blanc** *Signal Hill*

**Viognier** *Backsberg* (Babylons Toren) • *Bellingham* (Maverick) • *Fairview* • *Spier* (Private Collection)

# OTHER WINE STYLES
## CAP CLASSIQUE

This is South Africa's own term for "traditional method." Sparkling wine is generally less exciting here than in most other New World countries, which is probably due to the longer learning curve these wines demand. Most are merely in the fruity-fizz category, and only those recommended below show promise of anything more serious, but we could well see a revolution for sparkling wines as we have for Chardonnay. Two wines that should be represented below are Graham Beck's Synergy (a 70 percent Pinot Noir *cuvée* that I previewed in 2003, but have never seen on sale, although it is one of the two greatest sparkling wines produced in this country) and Graham Beck's Sparkling Pinotage (which was discontinued after the first release was not understood locally).

🍶 Upon purchase

🏆 *Graham Beck* (Blanc de Blancs) • *J. C. Le Roux* (Pinot Noir) • *Twee Jonge Gezellen* (Private Vintners Limited Release Pinot Noir) • *Villiera* (Brut Natural Chardonnay)

## CLASSIC RED BLENDS

These blends, particularly the Bordeaux-style red blends, are gradually establishing a solid superiority over their pure varietal counterparts in this country.

🍶 3–10 years

🏆 *De Toren* (Fusion V) • *Grangehurst* (Nikela) • *Havana Hills* (Du Plessis Reserve) • *Kanonkop* (Paul Sauer) • *Meerlust* (Rubicon) • *Morgenhof* (Première Sélection) • *Rust en Vrede* (Estate Wine) • *Rustenberg* (John X Merriman) • *Vergelegen* (Vergelegen V) • *Warwick* (Trilogy)

## CLASSIC WHITE BLENDS

This category encompasses white wine blends that are made from too many permutations of grapes to be able to record them all here. However, Sémillon, Chardonnay, Chenin Blanc, and Sauvignon Blanc are the most commonly featured grape varieties.

🍶 Mostly upon purchase (exceptional examples 2–3 years)

🏆 *Constantia Uitsig* (Sémillon-Sauvignon Blanc) • *Dornier* (Donatus White) • *The Company of Wine People* (VVS) • *Vergelegen* (Vergelegen White) • *Zevenwacht* (Tin Mine White)

## FORTIFIED WINES

Other high-performance fortified wine styles include red and white Muscadel, which is often called Hanepoot when made from Muscat d'Alexandrie (also in red and white styles). Jerepigo (or Jerepiko) is the South African equivalent of *vin de liqueur*, in which grape spirit is added to grape juice before fermentation can begin (as opposed to *vin doux naturel*, in which the grape spirit is added after fermentation has achieved an alcohol level of between 5 and 8 percent). Red styles range in color from cherry-bright to orange-gold and grow lighter with age, whereas white styles deepen with age (venerable vintages of both styles can become indistinguishable if they both assume an old-gold hue). Authentic Port is made only in the Douro Valley of northern Portugal, but Port-type fortified wines are made the world over, and South Africa has proved itself to be particularly adept at this style.

🏆 **Red** *Boplass* (Red Muscadel) • *Nuy* (Red Muscadel) • *Du Preez* (Hanepoot) • *Du Toitskloof* (Hanepoot Jerepigo) • *KWV* (White Muscadel) • *Rietvallei* (Muscadel 1908) • **White** *De Wetshof* (Muscadel) • *Jonkheer* (Muscatheer Family Reserve Muscat de Frontignan) • *KWV* (Red Muscadel) • *Monis* (Muscadel) • *Nuy* (White Muscadel) • **Port** *Allesverloren* • *Axe Hill* (Vintage) *Boplaas* (Vintage Reserve) • *KWV* (Tawny) • *Monis* (Very Old Tawny) • *Overgaauw* (Cape Vintage Reserve) • *Vergenoegd* (Old Cape Colony Vintage Port)

## LATE HARVEST

There are various categories of this style: Late Harvest must contain between 10 and 30 grams per liter of residual sugar; Special Late Harvest contains at least 20 grams and usually, but not necessarily, implies that some botrytized grapes have been used; for Noble Late Harvest there are no restrictions on residual sugar, but they are usually from botrytized grapes. Other naturally sweet, unfortified, non-botrytis dessert-style wines exist, including such marvelous oddities as Klein Constantia's Vin de Constance and Boschendal's Vin d'Or. All these styles will be seductive as soon as they are released, yet most will gain complexity over a great period of time.

🍶 Upon release and up to 20 years for Late Harvest; possibly 50 years or more for richer styles

🏆 *Boekenhoutskloof* (Noble Late Harvest Sémillon) • *Fleur du Cap* (Noble Late Harvest Riesling) • *Ken Forrester* (T Noble) • *Robertson Winery* (Wide River Reserve) • *Vergelegen* (Sémillon Noble Late Harvest) • *De Wetshof* (Edeloes) • **Other unfortified dessert wines** *Fairview* (La Beryl Blanc) • *Klein Constantia* (Vin de Constance) • *Signal Hill* (Mathilde Aszú 6 Puttonyos) • *Signal Hill* (Vin de Glacière) • *Signal Hill* (Vin de l'Empereur)

## SPARKLING WINES

🏆 *See Cap Classique.*

## THE WINE PRODUCERS OF
# SOUTH AFRICA

### ALLESVERLOREN
**Swartland**
★★☆

Traditionally one of the Cape's greatest port producers, the latest generation owner-winemaker Danie Malan has stepped up a gear over the last few years.

✓ *Cabernet Sauvignon • Fortified* (Port) • *Syrah* (Shiraz) • *Tinta Barocca*

### ALTO
**Stellenbosch**
★★☆

This estate has improved greatly in the 2000s, thanks to a new winemaker and new viticultural and winemaking consultants.

✓ *Cabernet Sauvignon • Classic red blend* (Alto Estate) • *Syrah* (Shiraz)

### ALTYDGEDACHT
**Durbanville**
★

Owned by the Parker family, who learned their winemaking skills in California and New Zealand.

✓ *Barbera • Pinotage • Syrah* (Shiraz)

### ASARA
**Stellenbosch**
★★☆

Formerly sold under the Verdun estate label, Asara has produced some of South Africa's most exciting wines under Markus Rahmann, who purchased this property in 2001.

✓ *Cabernet Sauvignon • Chardonnay • Classic red blend* (Bell Tower, Cape Blend, Carillon) • *Late Harvest* (Noble Late Harvest Chenin Blanc) • *Syrah* (Shiraz)

### ASHBOURNE
**Walker Bay**
★★★

By a long, stretched-out *véraison* under true, cool-climate conditions, Hamilton Russell demonstrates the delicacy, fragrance, and finesse that Pinotage can achieve. Restricted production, with no varietal name mentioned on the label.

✓ *Entire range*

### L'AVENIR
**Stellenbosch**
★★☆ Ⓥ

L'Avenir shot to fame when François Naudé became winemaker in 1992. In 2005 it was taken over by Michel Laroche (Chablis).

✓ *Cabernet Sauvignon • Chardonnay • Chenin Blanc • Classic red blend* (Black Label Reserve) • *Fortified* (Cape Port) • *Pinotage*

### AVONDALE
**Paarl**
Ⓞ★★

The as-yet-uncertified wines here have shown that organic wines from this country have double-gold potential. Soon to become one of South Africa's few organic producers.

✓ *Cabernet Sauvignon • Classic red blend* (Avondale) • *Merlot* (Les Pleurs) • *Sauvignon Blanc • Syrah* (Les Pleurs)

### AVONTUUR
**Stellenbosch**
★★☆ Ⓥ

This is the winery that gave the world pink Chardonnay.

✓ *Chardonnay* (Luna de Miel) • *Chenin Blanc* (Barrel Select) • *Classic red blend* (Baccarat)

### AXE HILL
**Calitzdorp**
★★☆

Bought in 1993 by the late and much-loved Tony Mossop, who quickly established Axe Hill as one of South Africa's iconic Port-style wines.

✓ *Entire range*

### BACKSBERG
**Paarl**
★★

This estate is owned by Michael Back and it produces some of South Africa's most consistent and classy wines, combining richness, finesse, and complexity with great success.

✓ *Chardonnay* (Babylons Toren) • *Classic red blend* (Babylons Toren Cabernet Sauvignon Merlot, Klein Babylons Toren) • *Viognier* (Babylons Toren)

### BARTHO EKSTEEN
**Walker Bay**
★★☆

One of the fast-rising stars of the up-and-coming Walker Bay district.

✓ *Sauvignon Blanc • Syrah* (Shiraz)

### GRAHAM BECK
**Robertson & Franschhoek**
★★★☆ Ⓥ

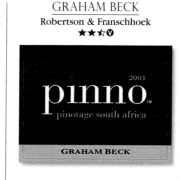

Graham Beck's senior winemaker is Pieter Ferreira, one of South Africa's top sparkling winemakers. This fact was confirmed at the Diners Club Winemaker Awards in 2004, its Cap Classique year, when Ferreira received the much coveted Winemaker Award. But he's a genius with other styles too.

✓ *Classic red blend* (The Joshua, The William) • *Pinotage* (The Old Road) • *Sparkling wine* (Blanc de Blancs, Brut Rosé) • *Syrah* (Shiraz, The Ridge Syrah)

### BELLEVUE ESTATE
**Stellenbosch**
★★☆

Long-time grape farmers, the Morkel family released the first wines under their own label with the 1999 vintage, to resounding success.

✓ *Classic red blend* (Tumara) • *Malbec* (Limited Release) • *Pinotage* (PK Morkel) • *Sauvignon Blanc* (Morkel) • *Syrah* (Shiraz)

### BELLINGHAM
**Franschhoek**
★★☆ Ⓥ

Owned by Douglas Green, Bellingham is a totally separate, standalone operation that makes some pretty remarkable wines.

✓ *Cabernet Franc* (Spitz) • *Cabernet Sauvignon* (Maverick) • *Chardonnay* (Spitz) • *Chenin Blanc* (Maverick) • *Merlot* (Spitz) • *Syrah* (Founder's Shiraz, Maverick Syrah) • *Viognier* (Maverick)

### BEYERSKLOOF
**Stellenbosch**
★★☆

Part-owned by Beyers Truter, who earned his reputation for Pinotage at Kanonkop.

✓ *Classic red blend* (Synergy) • *Pinotage*

### BILTON
**Stellenbosch**
★★☆

Another name to watch, Mark Bilton established this operation on the Helderberg with his first vintage in 1998.

✓ *Cabernet Sauvignon • Merlot • Syrah* (Shiraz)

### BLAAUWKLIPPEN
**Stellenbosch**
★

Nowadays Blaauwklippen seems a rather traditional winery, yet it was a pioneer of maturation in new oak, and one of the Cape's first great innovators. If you thought that Zinfandel was relatively new to South Africa, you should think again, as Blaauwklippen has been making it since the 1970s.

✓ *Cabernet Sauvignon* (Vineyard Selection) • *Zinfandel* (Vineyard Selection)

### BOEKENHOUTSKLOOF
**Franschhoek**
★★★☆

This rapidly rising star continues to make good. Entry-level wines are also sold under the Porcupine Ridge label, with the Syrah punching well above its weight.

✓ *Cabernet Sauvignon • Classic red blend* (The Chocolate Box) • *Late Harvest* (Noble Late Harvest Sémillon) • *Syrah • Sémillon*

### BOLAND WINE CELLAR
**Paarl**
★★☆ Ⓥ

This former cooperative has greatly improved since going private.

✓ *Cabernet Sauvignon* (No.1 Reserve) • *Chardonnay* (No.1 Reserve) • *Fortified* (Red Muscadel) • *Pinotage* (Winemaker's Selection) • *Syrah* (Shiraz No.1 Reserve)

### BOPLAAS
**Calitzdorp**
★★☆ Ⓥ

Lurking in a large range of commercially acceptable products are a number of extremely fine fortified wines, including one, the Vintage Reserve Port, one of South Africa's very greatest "ports."

✓ *Fortified* (Cape Tawny Port, Red Muscadel, Vintage Reserve Port)

### BOSCHENDAL
**Paarl**
★

Although this large producer is best known as the Cape's pioneering traditional method producer, Boschendal Estate also makes a large range of still wines, many of which, particularly the reds, are more exciting than the fizz.

✓ *Cabernet Sauvignon • Syrah*

## BOUCHARD-FINLAYSON
### Walker Bay
★★★

This small, deluxe enterprise was started by Hamilton Russell's winemaker Peter Finlayson, who was joined by Paul Bouchard from Burgundy. In 2001, however, controlling interest in the winery was taken over by Bea and Stanley Tollman. Bouchard remains a partner and Finlayson continues as winemaker. Finlayson is a bit of a gentle giant, and his wines reflect that, building quietly in the mouth to a remarkable elegance and depth of flavor. Galpin Peak Pinot Noir and Galpin Peak Tête de Cuvée Pinot Noir are the standouts here.

✓ *Chardonnay* (Kaaimansgat, Missionvale, Sans Barrique) • *Classic red blend* (Hannibal) • *Pinot Noir*

## J. P. BREDELL
### Stellenbosch
★★

This "port" specialist has always made varietal wines, but these have improved of late, particularly the Merlot.

✓ *Fortified* (Port: Late Bottled Vintage, Cape Vintage Reserve) • *Merlot*

## BUITENVERWACHTING
### Constantia
★★

Part of the historical Constantia estate, Buitenverwachting was renovated and replanted in the 1970s. It produced its first vintage in 1985, and was already showing promise by 1988. Throughout the 1990s it has been outstanding in virtually every style produced.

✓ *Cabernet Sauvignon* • *Chardonnay* • *Classic red blend* (Christine) • *Late Harvest* (Rhine Riesling Noble Late Harvest) • *Merlot* • *Sauvignon Blanc*

## CABRIÈRE
### Franschhoek
★★

This estate belongs to Achim von Arnim, formerly the winemaker at Boschendal, and, not surprisingly, he has carved out his initial reputation by specializing in Cap Classique, but also produces a very good Pinot Noir.

✓ *Sparkling wine* (Pierre Jourdan: Blanc de Blancs, Brut, Cuvée Belle Rose, Cuvée Reserve) • *Pinot Noir* (Haut Cabrière)

## CEDERBERG
### Cederberg
★★

South Africa's highest-altitude vineyards produce wines of great length and finesse, rather than heavy in weight and alcohol.

✓ *Cabernet Sauvignon* •

*Chenin Blanc* • *Classic red blend* (Cederberger) • *Sauvignon Blanc*

## CLOOF
### Darling
★★ Ⓥ

Too big for me, but these massively structured, high-alcohol wines are highly regarded award-winners within South Africa.

✓ *Pinotage* • *Syrah* (Crucible Shiraz)

## CLOS MALVERNE
### Stellenbosch
★★

Noted for its deep-colored, powerful, slow-developing wines.

✓ *Cabernet Sauvignon* • *Classic red blend* (Auret Cape Blend, Cabernet Sauvignon Pinotage Cape Blend, Cabernet Sauvignon Shiraz) • *Pinotage* (Reserve)

## PAUL CLUVER
### Elgin
★★

Pioneering Elgin wines from the first vintage in 1997.

✓ *Cabernet Sauvignon* • *Chardonnay* • *Late Harvest* (Weisser Riesling Noble Late Harvest) • *Pinot Noir* • *Riesling* (Weisser Riesling)

## CONSTANTIA UITSIG
### Constantia
★★

Owned by Dave and Marlene McCay, Constantia Uitsig makes one of South Africa's most lush red wines.

✓ *Chardonnay* (Reserve) • *Classic red blend* (Cabernet Sauvignon-Merlot) • *Classic white blend* (Sémillon-Sauvignon Blanc) • *Sémillon* (Reserve)

## CORDOBA
### Stellenbosch
★★

These high mountain vineyards produce some of South Africa's

finest reds, showing great length and finesse.

✓ *Classic red blend* (Crescendo) • *Merlot*

## JEAN DANEEL
### Napier
★★

A promising start for the former Morgenhof winemaker, who has just started releasing small volumes of exceptionally expressive wines from his own winery.

✓ *Chenin Blanc* (Signature) • *Classic red blend* (Cabernet Sauvignon-Merlot)

## DARLING CELLARS
### Darling
★★ Ⓥ

Abé Beukes produces increasingly fine wines at this former cooperative, although the alcohol levels can be alarmingly high.

✓ *Cabernet Sauvignon* (Onyx) • *Classic red blend* (Onyx Croon) • *Late Harvest* (Noble Late Harvest Chenin Blanc) • *Pinotage* (Onyx) • *Syrah* (DC Black Granite Shiraz)

## DELAIRE
### Stellenbosch
★★

Established by John Platter, South Africa's best-known wine writer; has since changed hands a couple of times. Delaire seems most consistent with Bordeaux-style blends and scintillating botrytized Riesling.

✓ *Chardonnay* • *Dessert* (Edeloes)

## DELHEIM
### Stellenbosch
★★ Ⓥ

Always a good buy, but until recently the quality is more good than great, and more consistent than outstanding. In recent years, however, Delheim has shown a dramatic improvement in quality.

✓ *Cabernet Sauvignon* (Grand Reserve) • *Merlot* • *Late Harvest* (Edelspatz) • *Syrah* (Vera Cruz Estate Shiraz)

## DEVON HILL
### Stellenbosch
★★

An up-and-coming winery, Devon Hill was established in 1997, with Erhard Roux taking over as winemaker in 2002.

✓ *Classic red blend* (Blue Bird) • *Syrah* (Shiraz)

## DIEMERSDAL
### Durbanville
★★ Ⓥ

Although the 14-percent-plus alcoholic strength of these wines is not unusual for a premium South African producer, the surprisingly elegant style is.

✓ *Cabernet Sauvignon* • *Chardonnay* • *Classic red blend* (Private Collection) • *Pinotage*

## DIEMERSFONTEIN
### Wellington
★★ Ⓥ

Full-throttle Pinotage in the style adored by South Africans.

✓ *Pinotage* (Carpe Diem)

## DISTELL
### Stellenbosch

Created in 2000 by the merger of Stellenbosch Farmers' Winery (SFW) and Distillers Corporation, bringing together Fleur du Cap and Nederburg (two competing, high-quality wine brands), making this South Africa's largest wine and liquor group. Another excellent-value brand owned by Distell is Zonnenbloem. It also owns the good-value Drosdy-Hof wines; the successful, fast-selling sparkling wines of J. C. Le Roux; and the award-winning fortified wines of Monis. Chateau Libertas is viewed as one of the Cape's largest-volume, "quality" red wines, and figures prominently in the turnover of this group. Distell has sole ownership of Plaisir de Merle, its flagship wine estate, and joint ownership of Durbanville Hills, Hill & Dale, and Tukulu (a black empowerment project). Five wine estates owned jointly with German industrialist Hans Schreiber—through Lusan Holdings—are Alto, Le Bonheur, Neethlingshof, Stellenzicht, and Uitkyk. Recently launched good-value brands, which are essentially export-oriented but also available on the home market, include African Skies, Obikwa, Oracle, Table Mountain, and Two Oceans. Other good-value Distell brands include Grünberger, Kupferberger Auslese, and Ship Sherry. And there are dozens of decent, if run-of-the-mill, commercial wine brands, such as Autumn Harvest, Capenheimer, Cellar Cask, Graça, Grand Mousseux, Kellerprinz, Oom Tas, Overmeer Cellars, Sedgewick's, Tassenberg, and Taverna. Jacobsdal and Theuniskraal are often associated with Distell, but are both privately owned estates, with Distell merely providing exclusive distribution.

## DORNIER
### Stellenbosch
★★

Dornier shows astonishing quality and consistency for a winery whose first vintage was 2002.

✓ *Classic red blend* (Donatus) • *Classic white blend* (Donatus White)

## DURBANVILLE HILLS
### Durbanville
★★

Apparently, it is so cold during the harvest that the Durbanville Hills pickers have to wear thick wool sweaters. No doubt this is the explanation for the excellent, bracing quality of the white wines at this up-and-coming joint venture between Distell and seven leading Durbanville growers.

✓ *Chardonnay* (Rhinofields)
• *Classic red blend* (Caapmans Cabernet Sauvignon-Merlot)
• *Sauvignon Blanc*

## EIKENDAL
### Stellenbosch
### ★★☆

This Swiss-owned producer is perhaps best known on export markets for its blockbuster Chardonnay, but it actually produces finer reds, and even manages to make a fine-quality Cinsault-dominated blend.

✓ *Cabernet Sauvignon* (Reserve)
• *Chardonnay* • *Classic red blend* (Classique, Rossini)
• *Sémillon*

## NEIL ELLIS
### Stellenbosch
### ★★

The Cape's first and foremost winemaker-négociant, Ellis's uncanny skill in sourcing grapes from cutting-edge viticultural areas, and equal expertise in crafting some of South Africa's classiest wines from them, has sparked off a whole raft of wineries that buy in from selected vineyards.

✓ *Cabernet Sauvignon* (Stellenbosch, Jonkershoek)
• *Classic red blend* (Cabernet Sauvignon-Merlot)
• *Chardonnay* (Aenigma, Elgin) • *Pinotage* (Stellenbosch) • *Sauvignon Blanc* (Groenekloof) • *Syrah* (Jonkershoek Shiraz)

## FAIRVIEW
### Paarl
### ★★★☆

This estate is run by Charles Back, one of the most innovative wine producers in South Africa, offering a large and constantly expanding range of wine styles. The poorest wines here are good, and the best are sensational.

✓ *Carignan* (Pegleg)
• *Chardonnay* (Akkerbos)
• *Classic red blend* (Caldera)
• *Dessert* (La Beryl Blanc)
• *Pinotage* (Primo)
• *Sauvignon Blanc* • *Sémillon* (Oom Pagel) • *Shiraz* (Cyril Back, Solitude) • *Viognier*

## FLAGSTONE
### Somerset West
### ★★

Owner-winemaker Bruce Jack was quick off the block with a stunning quality range of wines from his first vintage in 1999. A master at classic red blends, Jack has also produced South Africa's finest Sauvignon Blanc to date (Berrio).

✓ *Cabernet Sauvignon* (Berrio)

• *Classic red blend* (Bowwood, Dragon Tree, Foundation Longtitude, Mary Le Bon)
• *Pinot Noir* (The Poetry Collection) • *Ruby Cabernet* (Ruby in the Dust)
• *Sauvignon Blanc* (Berrio)

## FLEUR DU CAP
### Stellenbosch
### ★★★ Ⓥ

Made and marketed by the Bergkelder at Stellenbosch, Fleur du Cap has established a high standard of quality for its basic wines, but has reinvented itself with spectacular success with its "Unfiltered" range.

✓ *Cabernet Sauvignon* (Unfiltered) • *Chardonnay* (Unfiltered) • *Chenin Blanc*
• *Classic white blend* (Unfiltered Viognier-Chardonnay-Sauvignon Blanc-Sémillon)
• *Late Harvest* (Noble Riesling)
• *Merlot* (Unfiltered)
• *Sauvignon* (Unfiltered Limited Release) • *Sémillon* (Unfiltered)

## KEN FORRESTER
### Stellenbosch
### ★★☆

This property dates back to 1689, when the farm was called Zandberg, and by 1692 some 12,000 vines had been planted. But the first wine in modern times was produced in 1994, when owners Ken and Teresa Forrester pressed a small quantity of Sauvignon Blanc grapes to produce a Blanc Fumé. They also own the wonderful restaurant opposite the vineyard called 96 Winery Road.

✓ *Chenin Blanc* • *Classic red blend* (Gypsy) • *Late Harvest* (T Noble)

## FORT SIMON
### Stellenbosch
### ★★☆

Since its first vintage in 1998, Fort Simon Estate has impressed with the elegance of its wines.

✓ *Chardonnay* • *Chenin Blanc* (Barrel Fermented)

## THE FOUNDRY
### Stellenbosch
### ★★

Although made at Meerlust, this is the private label of Chris Williams and his business partner James Reid of Kumala fame. In 2004 Chris Williams took over from the legendary Giorgio Dalla Cia, as Meerlust's winemaker, and brought The Foundry label with him.

✓ *Syrah*

## GLEN CARLOU
### Paarl
### ★★

Donald Hess of The Hess Collection in Napa was the co-owner, until he bought out David Finlayson. Finlayson remains as winemaker, continuing to produce some of South Africa's finest Chardonnay.

✓ *Chardonnay* • *Classic red*

• *Pinot Noir* • *Syrah*

## GOEDE HOOP
### Stellenbosch
### ★ Ⓥ

Under owner Pieter Bestbier, this former Bergkelder estate offers an expanded range of wines of improving quality.

✓ *Cabernet Sauvignon* • *Classic red blend* (Merlot-Cabernet Sauvignon)

## GRANDE PROVENCE
### Franschhoek
### ★★☆

These wines were once marketed as Augusta, but they have since reverted to the original name of the restaurant that makes them. Top-class wines.

✓ *Cabernet Sauvignon* • *Chardonnay*

## GRANGEHURST
### Stellenbosch
### ★★

One of the new breed of winemakers who source grapes from various other growers, Grangehurst makes exciting, well-crafted, elegant yet substantive wines.

✓ *Cabernet Sauvignon* (Chairman's Reserve) • *Classic red blend* (Cabernet Sauvignon-Merlot, Nikela) • *Pinotage*

## GROOT CONSTANTIA
### Constantia
### ★★☆

This property is part of the original Constantia farm, the oldest and most famous of Cape estates, and is currently being run with passion and great skill.

✓ *Classic red blend* (Gouverneurs Reserve) • *Merlot* (Gouverneurs) • *Syrah* (Gouverneurs Shiraz)

## HAMILTON RUSSELL
### Walker Bay
### ★★★☆

Established by Tim Hamilton Russell, this was once Africa's most southerly vineyard. Now there are many this far south and some farther still. No expense was spared to ensure that this would become one of the finest wineries in the Cape, and winemaker

Peter Finlayson helped make that dream come true. Finlayson left to establish his own winery, Bouchard-Finlayson (which is just next door), but his replacement, Kevin Grant, continued to make some of the Cape's most spellbinding Burgundian varietals. Hannes Storm became the new winemaker at the Hamilton Russell vineyard in 2004.

✓ *Entire range*

## HARTENBERG
### Stellenbosch
### ★★

Some stunning wines, but what a pity they ripped out the Zinfandel!

✓ *Cabernet Sauvignon*
• *Chardonnay* • *Merlot*
• *Syrah* (Shiraz)

## HAVANA HILLS
### Philadelphia
### ★★☆

The winery that has single-handedly established the reputation of the new Philadelphia wine ward for top-performing red wines.

✓ *Cabernet Sauvignon* (Du Plessis Reserve) • *Classic red blend* (Du Plessis Reserve)
• *Merlot* (Du Plessis Reserve)
• *Shiraz* (Du Plessis Reserve)

## HILLCREST
### Durbanville
### ★★☆ Ⓥ

This estate's first vintage was as recent as 2002, yet the deftly sculptured wines scream out for attention.

✓ *Classic red blend* (Merlot-Cabernet Sauvignon)
• *Sauvignon Blanc*

## JONKHEER
### Robertson
### ★★☆ Ⓥ

The Madonna of the Cape wine industry, Jonkheer was established as long ago as 1912, and was known as Jonkheer Boere Wynmakery, when they were known for semisweet white wines called Edelweiss, but they have not only economized their trading name, but have also reinvented their wines, which are exemplary by any standards.

✓ *Chardonnay* (Dead Frogge, Family Reserve) • *Fortified* (Bakenskop White Muscadel, Muscatheer Family Reserve Muscat de Frontignan)

## JORDAN
### Stellenbosch
### ★★

This property is now a Cape front-ranker, especially for Cobblers Hill classic red wine blend (a three-barrel selection called Jordan Sophia is sold exclusively at the CWG Auction), but its primary reputation is for rich and vibrant white wines.

✓ *Chardonnay* (Nine Yards)

• *Classic red Blend* (Cobblers Hill) • *Sauvignon Blanc* • *Merlot*

## KAAPZICHT
### Stellenbosch
★★

Established in 1984, Kaapzicht Estate has only just awoken to provide a number of exciting wines in recent years. Although the Pinotage is usually a big wine, it is so well balanced that it belies its 15-point-something of alcohol.

✓ *Cabernet Sauvignon* • *Classic red blend* (Steytler Vision) • *Pinotage* (Steytler) • *Shiraz*

## KANONKOP
### Stellenbosch
★★

Winemaker Beyers Truter is generally considered to be one of the greatest Stellenbosch red wine exponents, and more specifically the king of Pinotage.

✓ *Cabernet Sauvignon* • *Classic red blend* (Paul Sauer) • *Pinotage*

## KANU
### Stellenbosch
★★✫ ✔

Delightful, easy-drinking, good-value standard range, and serious to stunning Limited Release wines from this winery that has captured much attention since it was established in 1998.

✓ *Cabernet Sauvignon* (Limited Release) • *Chardonnay* (Limited Release) • *Chenin Blanc* (Wooded) • *Classic red blend* (Keystone) • *Merlot* (Limited Release)

## KLEIN CONSTANTIA
### Constantia
★★✫

This property was part of Simon van der Stel's original Constantia Estate, but after centuries of neglect it was replanted as recently as 1982. Note that Vin de Constance is not a botrytis wine, nor is it fortified; it is supposedly a faithful replication of the famous Constantia of old.

✓ *Cabernet Sauvignon (Reserve)* • *Dessert* (Vin de Constance) • *Late Harvest* (Noble Late Harvest Sauvignon Blanc) • *Riesling* (Rhine Riesling) • *Sauvignon Blanc*

## KLEINE ZALZE
### Stellenbosch
★ ✔

This former Gilbeys property was purchased by Kobus Basson and Jan Malan in 1996, since when its wines have been put on the map and its reputation has been rising fast.

✓ *Cabernet Sauvignon* (Barrel Matured) • *Chardonnay* (Barrel Fermented) • *Merlot* (Barrel Matured, Cellar Selection)

## KWV
### Paarl
★★★ ✔

This was a super-sized cooperative that controlled the entire South African wine industry until 1995, when it was stripped of its legislative powers, and privatized. Extraordinary as it might seem to external observers, KWV wines were not allowed to be sold in South Africa itself. However, with legal and structural changes, this was due to change in 2001, although certain obstacles prevented these wines from reaching the shelf locally until 2004. As it turned out, 2004 was a year when the KWV hit the headlines for reasons its management would rather forget—it was discovered that two of its winemakers had added illegal (but harmless) flavorants to two Sauvignon Blanc wines (2004 Laborie and 2004 KWV Reserve). They were dismissed, and 60,000 liters of wine had to be destroyed. Looking on the bright side, the quality and value of KWV wines (especially in the Cathedral Cellar and Reserve ranges) have never been higher, and if such trickery were to occur anywhere else in South Africa, the one thing we can be sure about is that it will not be at KWV. There are just too many official eyes looking at everything they do.

✓ *Cabernet Sauvignon* (Cathedral Cellar, KWV Reserve, Laborie) • *Chardonnay* (Cathedral Cellar) • *Classic red blend* (Cathedral Cellar Triptych) • *Classic white blend* (Robert's Rock Chardonnay-Sémillon) • *Fortified* (Tawny Port, Vintage Port, Vintage Red Muscadel) • *Merlot* (Cathedral Cellar, KWV Reserve) • *Pinotage* (Cathedral Cellar) • *Sauvignon Blanc* (Laborie, KWV Reserve) • *Syrah* (Cathedral Cellar Shiraz, Laborie Cabernet Merlot Reserve, Laborie Jean Taillefert)

## LAIBACH
### Stellenbosch
★

This farm was called Good Success until it was purchased by Swiss-based German businessman Friedrich Laibach, who built a new cellar and bottled these wines for the first time in 1997. Almost 15 percent of the Laibach vineyard is farmed organically.

✓ *Classic red blend* (Friedrich Laibach, The Ladybird) ○ • *Pinotage*

## LANDSKROON
### Paarl
★★✫ ✔

This is a very large estate at 148 acres (600 hectares), of which 74 acres (300 hectares) are under vine.

✓ *Cabernet Sauvignon* • *Port* • *Shiraz* (Paul de Villiers)

## LOUISVALE
### Stellenbosch
★

Louisvale offers a solid range of well-made wines, but is best known for its big, leesy Chardonnay.

✓ *Chardonnay* • *Classic red bend* (Dominique)

## MEERLUST
### Stellenbosch
★★★✫

For more than 30 years this has been one of the Cape's most consistent wine estates. Meerlust is owned by the Myburgh family, who have been assisted from the very start by the visionary winemaker Giorgio Dalla Cia. Dalla Cia retired in 2004, handing over to Chris Williams, who worked with Michel Rolland, and was Dalla Cia's assistant winemaker between 1995 and 2000, when he set up The Foundry. All wines produced are among the very best in the country for their particular styles, but with eighth-generation Hannes Myburgh in overall charge, and such a talented, inquisitive new winemaker at the helm, Meerlust is set to go from high gear into overdrive.

✓ *Chardonnay* • *Classic red blend* (Rubicon) • *Merlot* • *Pinot Noir*

## MEINERT
### Stellenbosch
★★

Since 1997, Ken Forrester's winemaking partner Martin Meinert has made some splendid wines under his own label.

✓ *Classic red blend* (Devon Crest, Synchronicity) • *Merlot*

## MIDDELVLEI
### Stellenbosch
★

This estate made its reputation with Pinotage, but has recently been producing stunning Syrah.

✓ *Pinotage* • *Syrah* (Shiraz)

## MONIS
### Paarl
★★✫ ✔

This famous old Cape fortified brand belongs to Distell (*see* separate entry).

✓ *Fortified* (Cream Sherry, Muscadel, Very Old Tawny Port)

## MOOIPLAAS
### Stellenbosch
★★✫ ✔

After making and selling wine in bulk for 30 years, the owners started selling wines under their Mooiplaas label in 1995.

✓ *Cabernet Sauvignon* • *Pinotage* • *Syrah* (Shiraz)

## MÔRESON
### Franschhoek
★★✫

Acquired by Richard Friedmann in 1985, this estate initially developed

a reputation for its white wines, although it is its reds that have shone out in recent vintages.

✓ *Cabernet Sauvignon* • *Chardonnay* (Premium) • *Classic red blend* (Magia) • *Pinotage* • *Sauvignon Blanc*

## MORGENHOF
### Stellenbosch
★★★✫ ✔

This historic wine estate is owned by Anne Cointreau-Huchon, whose *cognaçais* family own Champagne Gosset. Morgenhof makes some truly stylish wines, with excellent-value entry-level wines sold under the Fantail label. I have not tasted New Cap Classique, but I would be surprised and disappointed if it is not one of the country's best.

✓ *Cabernet Sauvignon* (Reserve) • *Chardonnay* • *Classic red blend* (Première Sélection) • *Merlot* (Reserve) • *Pinotage* • *Sauvignon Blanc*

## MORGENSTER
### Stellenbosch
★★

Another new name to watch, Morgenster was established in 1993, but did not produce any wine under its own label until the 1998 vintage. Morgenster grows just four Bordeaux varieties (Merlot, Cabernet Sauvignon, Cabernet Franc, and Petit Verdot), and specializes in classic red blends. Pierre Lurton consults.

✓ *Classic red blend* (Lourens River Valley, Morgenster)

## LA MOTTE
### Franschhoek
★★

Owned by Hanneli Koegelenberg, the daughter of Anton Rupert, the second-richest man in South Africa, La Motte's wines have been made by Edmund Terblanche since 2001.

✓ *Classic red blend* (Shiraz-Viognier) • *Syrah* (Shiraz)

## MULDERBOSCH
### Stellenbosch
★★

These are top-flight wines from superbly sited mountain vineyards, with moves toward organic viticulture, and crafted by skillful winemaking.

✓ *Chardonnay* • *Chenin Blanc* (Steen-op-Hout) • *Classic red blend* (Beta Centauri, Faithful Hound) • *Sauvignon Blanc*

## MURATIE
### Stellenbosch
★★✫

Owned by the Melck family, who have made some brilliant wines since 2000. Guillaume Nell is the new winemaker since 2003.

✓ *Cabernet Sauvignon* • *Classic red blend* (Ansela) • *Fortified* (Cape Vintage) • *Syrah* (Shiraz)

## NEDERBURG
### Paarl
### ★☆🅥

Owned by Distell. As with Fleur du Cap, the consistency is remarkable for such a commercial range, on top of which the quality improves with each year. The entire 20-plus range of Private Bin wines sold exclusively at the annual Nederburg Auction is recommended, but they become available only should a retailer successfully bid for a lot, and later decide to market them.

✔ *Cabernet Sauvignon* (Private Bin) • *Classic red blend* (Edelrood) • *Classic red blend* (Prelude) • *Late Harvest* (Noble Late Harvest) • *Sauvignon Blanc* (Private Bin) • *Shiraz* (Private Bin)

## NEETHLINGSHOF
### Stellenbosch
### ★☆🅥

Owned by Lusan Holdings, this vineyard's wines have greatly improved in quality since the 1990s.

✔ *Cabernet Franc* (Lord Neethlingshof) • *Cabernet Sauvignon* (Lord Neethlingshof) • *Chardonnay* (Lord Neethlingshof) • *Classic red blend* (Cape Blend, Lord Neethlingshof Laurentius) • *Late Harvest* (Weisser Riesling Noble Late Harvest) • *Syrah* (Shiraz)

## NELSON
### Paarl
### ★☆

Established in 1993 by the Nelson family, this estate has moved up a gear since the new millennium.

✔ *Classic red blend* (Cabernet Sauvignon-Merlot) • *Chardonnay* • *Syrah* (Shiraz)

## NEWTON JOHNSON
### Walker Bay
### ★★🅥

One of the brightest new stars in the exciting Walker Bay wine scene.

✔ *Cabernet Sauvignon* • *Chardonnay* • *Classic red blend* (Shiraz-Mourvèdre) • *Pinot Noir* • *Sauvignon Blanc*

## NITIDA CELLARS
### Durbanville
### ★☆🅥

Small, up-and-coming boutique in the Durbanville Kloof, where there is a distinct intensity to the wines.

✔ *Cabernet Sauvignon* • *Sauvignon Blanc* • *Sémillon*

## NUY WINE CELLAR
### Worcester
### ★🅥

South Africa's best cooperative has a more private-sounding name these days, but the secret of its success is the same—it selects just 3 percent of the 10,000 tons processed every year to sell under its own label.

✔ *Colombard* (Dry) • *Fortified* (Red Muscadel, White Muscadel)

## THE OBSERVATORY
### Swartland
### ★★

The Lubbe family has made an indelible impact with minuscule releases from vines growing on the slopes of the Paardeberg.

✔ *Classic red blend* (Carignan-Syrah) • *Syrah*

## OLD VINES
### Rosebank
### ★☆🅥

South Africa's only women's empowerment winery, Old Vines was established in 1995 by mother and daughter Irina von Holdt and Françoise Botha, whose primary aim is to raise awareness of Chenin Blanc as the Cape's white-wine flagbearer.

✔ *Chenin Blanc*

## L'ORMARINS
### Franschhoek
### ★☆

Restored by the late Toni Rupert, son of Anton Rupert. With virtually unlimited finance at his disposal, Toni quickly established L'Ormarins at the very top of Cape winemaking. L'Ormarins is now owned by Toni's brother, Johann.

✔ *Cabernet Sauvignon* • *Classic red blend* (Optima) • *Merlot*

## OVERGAAUW
### Stellenbosch
### ★☆

This is a technically superior operation that produces exciting wines. With lots of class and very little sulfur dioxide, Overgaauw has been a pioneering wine estate for a quarter of a century.

✔ *Cabernet Sauvignon* • *Chardonnay* • *Classic red blend* (Shiraz-Cabernet Sauvignon, Tria Corda) • *Fortified* (Cape Vintage, Cape Vintage Reserve) • *Merlot*

## PLAISIR DE MERLE
### Simonsberg-Paarl
### ★★

Grapes from Plaisir de Merle formed the heart of many Nederburg wines until 1993, when, with the help of consultant Paul Pontallier of Château Margaux, owner-winemaker Niel Bester launched a range of estate-bottled wines that are worthy of Distell's flagship domaine.

✔ *Classic red blend* (Grand Plaisir) • *Merlot* • *Sauvignon Blanc*

## DU PREEZ
### Goudini
### ★☆🅥

An up-and-coming new star from an unlikely part of the Breede River Valley, with less expensive wines sold under Rockfields and Dry Creek labels.

---

✔ *Classic red blend* (Polla's Red) • *Fortified* (Hanepoot) • *Merlot* (Reserve) • *Petit Verdot* (Hendrik Lodewyk)

## REMHOOGTE
### Stellenbosch
### ★★☆

A rapidly improving winery whose inaugural vintage was 1995. Michel Rolland is a partner-consultant.

✔ *Classic red blend* (Bonne Nouvelle)

## RHEBOKSLOOF
### Paarl
### ★★☆

My, my, how the quality here has rocketed since the late 1990s.

✔ *Cabernet Sauvignon* • *Chardonnay* (Grand Reserve) • *Classic red blend* (Cabernet Sauvignon-Merlot)

## LE RICHE
### Stellenbosch
### ★★

The first vintage was 1997 for this small, up-and-coming winery that has focused on making a limited range of highly polished reds.

✔ *Cabernet Sauvignon* • *Cabernet Sauvignon-Merlot*

## RIETVALLEI
### Robertson
### ★

Classic Muscadel.

✔ *Chardonnay* • *Fortified* (Muscadel 1908, Red Muscadel) • *Syrah* (Shiraz)

## RIJK'S PRIVATE CELLAR
### Tulbagh
### ★☆

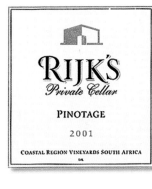

Fast-rising, potential star winery, Rijk's inaugural vintage was as recent as 2000.

✔ *Classic red blend* (Bravado) • *Sémillon*

## ROBERTSON WINERY
### Robertson
### ★☆🅥

For a cooperative that could be relied upon for little more than fortified wine, the Robertson Winery

---

has developed an exciting range of modern, finely honed table wines, and these have been on a roll since the early 2000s.

✔ *Chardonnay* (Kings River) • *Classic red blend* (No.1 Constitution Road) • *Late Harvest* (Wide River Reserve) • *Syrah* (Wolfkloof Shiraz)

## J. C. LE ROUX
### Stellenbosch
### ★

This Bergkelder label is used exclusively for sparkling wines.

✔ *Sparkling* (Pinot Noir)

## RUDERA
### Stellenbosch
### ★★

With his first vintage as recent as 2001, owner-winemaker Teddy Hall has rapidly established a broad and convincing reputation as one of the names to watch in the future of South African wine, particularly for Chenin Blanc.

✔ *Cabernet Sauvignon* • *Chenin Blanc* • *Late Harvest* (Noble Late Harvest Chenin Blanc) • *Syrah*

## RUST EN VREDE
### Stellenbosch
### ★

Owned by Jannie Engelbrecht, a former Springbok, who produces only wines he likes to drink—rich, red, dense, well balanced, and not sold until they are ready.

✔ *Cabernet Sauvignon* • *Classic red blend* (Estate Wine) • *Merlot* • *Syrah* (Shiraz)

## RUSTENBERG
### Stellenbosch
### ★★☆

Once heralded as the very best of South Africa's top growths, the quality at Rustenberg faltered in the early 1990s, only for it to be picked up as of the 1996 vintage, and pushed higher than it has ever been. Rustenberg Estate is now under the direct control of Simon Barlow, who installed a brand-new winery and has done everything necessary to ensure that Rustenberg's reputation remains impeccable. Wines sold under the entry-level Brampton label sometimes rival Rustenberg at its best.

✔ *Cabernet Sauvignon* (Peter Barlow) • *Chardonnay* (Five Soldiers, Stellenbosch) • *Classic red blend* (John X Merriman) • *Late Harvest* (QF)

## SAXENBURG
### Stellenbosch
### ★★

This Swiss-owned winery has been a rising star for wines of increasingly high quality and complexity since the late 1990s.

☑ *Cabernet Sauvignon* (Private Collection) • *Chardonnay* (Private Collection) • *Classic red blend* (Gwendolyn, Manuel) • *Merlot* (Private Collection) • *Pinotage* (Private Collection) • *Sauvignon Blanc* (Private Collection) • *Syrah* (Shiraz Select)

## SEIDELBERG
### Paarl
### ★★☆

Brilliant wines since the early 2000s.

☑ *Classic red blend* (Un Deux Trois) • *Fortified* (Red Muscadel) • *Merlot* (Roland's Reserve) • *Syrah* (Roland's Reserve)

## SENTINEL
### Stellenbosch
### ★★☆

Established by Rob Coppoolse, Walter Finlayson, and Viv Grater in 1995, the quality of these wines really began to take off with the 2002 vintage.

☑ *Merlot* • *Pinotage* • *Syrah* (Shiraz)

## SIGNAL HILL
### Cape Town
### ★★☆

Jean-Vincent Ridon is in the process of planting a vineyard on Signal Hill, next to Table Mountain, by renting every square inch he can find. Until these vines come on stream, he buys in grapes to produce a mostly splendid range of wines.

☑ *Chardonnay* (Corsaire) • *Classic red blend* (Frans Malan, Tiara) • *Dessert* (Mathilde Azú 6 Puttonyos, Vin de Glacière, Vin de l'Empereur) • *Grenache Blanc* • *Late Harvest* (Muscat d'Alexandrie Noble Late Harvest) • *Petit Verdot* • *Pinotage* (Malwenn) • *Sparkling* (Kaapse Vonkel) • *Syrah* (Merindol)

## SIMONSIG
### Stellenbosch
### ★★☆

This winery has a huge production, and its wines range from the

sensational down to pretty standard stuff, with an increasing proportion of the former.

☑ *Classic red blend* (Frans Malan, Tiara) • *Late Harvest* (Vin de Liza) • *Petit Verdot* (Auction Reserve) • *Sparkling* (Kaapse Vonkel) • *Syrah* (Merindol)

## SPICE ROUTE
### Swartland
### ★★

This estate was originally owned by a consortium of Charles Back, Jabulani Ntshangase, John Platter, and Gyles Webb, but it is now solely owned by Back. Spice Route excels at red wines, and its signature style is typically deep, dark, rich, and spicy, with masses of black fruit. Its Flagship Syrah is still one of the best I have tasted from South Africa.

☑ *Chenin Blanc* • *Classic red blend* (Malabar) • *Merlot* (Flagship) • *Syrah* (Flagship)

## SPIER
### Stellenbosch
### ★★

A winery has been added to this deluxe, classy hotel complex, which now belongs to Winecorp. The first vintage produced here was in 1996. The very best wines are sold under Spier's Private Collection label (which is a considerable step up in quality).

☑ *Cabernet Sauvignon* (Private Collection) • *Chenin Blanc* (Private Collection) • *Late Harvest* (Noble Late Harvest) • *Merlot* (Private Collection) • *Pinotage* • *Sauvignon Blanc* (Private Collection) • *Viognier* (Private Collection)

## SPRINGFIELD
### Robertson
### ◉★☆

Owner-winemaker Abrie Bruwer is considered a bit of an eccentric in his own country, but virtually all of his practices merely represent an organic approach.

☑ *Cabernet Sauvignon* (Méthode Ancienne, Whole Berry) • *Chardonnay* (Méthode Ancienne, Wild Yeast) • *Classic red blend* (The Work of Time) • *Sauvignon Blanc* (Life From Stone)

## STARK-CONDÉ
### Stellenbosch
### ★★

Condé wines are named after the winemaker José Conde, and are

single-vineyard wines made from Stark-Condé's best blocks. Stark wines are named after Franciska Stark, the late family matriarch, and are blended from more than one of Stark-Condé's vineyard blocks; given the same hand treatment as the Condé wines, they differ simply by being blends of multiple vineyard blocks.

☑ *Cabernet Sauvignon* (Condé, Stark) • *Shiraz* (Stark)

## STEENBERG
### Constantia
### ★★

From small quantities of gorgeously fresh Sauvignon Blanc to a fabulous range of stunning wines in a myriad of styles, including the country's best Sémillon.

☑ *Classic red blend* (Catharina) • *Nebbiolo* • *Sauvignon Blanc* • *Sémillon*

## STELLENZICHT
### Stellenbosch
### ★★☆

Under the same ownership as Neethlingshof, Stellenzicht's mountain vineyards produce some of the finest new arrivals on the South African fine-wine scene.

☑ *Classic red blend* (Stellenzicht) • *Sémillon* (Reserve) • *Syrah*

## THE COMPANY OF WINE PEOPLE
### Stellenbosch
### ★ⓥ

This is the latest reinvention of what was recently known as Omnia and, before that, Stellenbosch Vineyards. In 1996 the cooperatives of Helderberg, Welmoed, Bottelary, and Eersterivier amalgamated into a commercial entity called the Stellenbosch Exchange. The 150 growers who originally owned these three cooperatives converted their memberships into shareholdings and relaunched themselves in 1997 as Stellenbosch Vineyards. In October 2004, Stellenbosch Vineyards merged with Vinfruco, of which they already owned 34 percent. This new venture was called Omnia, and its purpose was to focus on brand marketing to those customers, mostly on export markets, that they had jointly been supplying. The most important of these brands was and still is Arniston Bay, followed by Thandi, Kumkani, Shamwari, Versus, Welmoed, and Inglewood (a joint venture with Neil Ellis). Omni changed to the quirky but rather splendid name of The Company of Wine People in 2006. Used to make some excellent-value reds under the old Genesis label, but now excels at white.

☑ *Classic white blend* (Arniston Bay Chenin-Chardonnay, Kumkani Chardonnay-Viognier, Kumkani VVS, Thandi Sauvignon-Sémillon) • *Pinotage* (Kumkani) • *Syrah* (Kumkani Shiraz) • *Sauvignon Blanc* (Kumkani, Kumkani Lanner Hill) • *Viognier* (Kumkani)

## THELEMA MOUNTAIN
### Stellenbosch
### ★★★☆

Under the steady hand of owner-winemaker Gyles Webb, Thelema Mountain has become one of the country's most exciting producers, producing stunningly rich, refined, and complex wines.

☑ *Cabernet Sauvignon* • *Cabernet Sauvignon-Merlot* • *Chardonnay* • *Merlot* • *Pinotage* • *Riesling* (Rhine Riesling) • *Sauvignon Blanc* • *Syrah* (Shiraz)

## DU TOITSKLOOF WINERY
### Worcester
### ★☆ⓥ

The Du Toitskloof Winery, a cooperative, has a long record of award-winning table wines and now produces top-flight dessert wines.

☑ *Fortified* (Hanepoot Jerepigo, Red Muscadel)

## DE TOREN
### Stellenbosch
### ★★

Although this winery's first vintage was as recent as 1999, it already has a cult following for its stunningly successful Fusion V, a classic blend of five varieties (Cabernet Sauvignon, Cabernet Franc, Merlot, Malbec, and Petit Verdot).

☑ *Classic red blend* (Diversity Beta, Fusion V)

## DE TRAFFORD
### Stellenbosch
### ★★

This ultra-small boutique winery has established a reputation for beautifully crafted Cabernet, with whispers in the wind of things to come, including serious, *barrique*-fermented Chenin Blanc.

☑ *Cabernet Sauvignon* • *Merlot*

## TUKULU
### Groenekloof
### ★☆ⓥ

This is a black empowerment joint venture with Distell, which will divest itself of its shareholding as the start-up capital is repaid through the sale of grapes in about 12 years' time (from 1998, its date of establishment).

☑ *Chenin Blanc* • *Pinotage*

## TWEE JONGEGEZELLEN
### Tulbagh
### ★ⓥ

Having endured horrendous bottle quality problems, Nicky Krone's

Krone Borealis is back on form, particularly because he is now giving it greater bottle-age. His greatest Cap Classique wine is, however, Private Vintners Limited Release 1995 Pinot Noir.

✓ *Sparkling wine* (Krone Borealis, Private Vintners Limited Release)

## VEENWOUDEN
### Paarl
### ★★✮Ⓥ

This boutique winery enjoyed its first vintage in 1993. Since then it has built up a compact range of increasingly fine quality.

✓ *Chardonnay* (Special Reserve) • *Classic red blend* (Classic, Vivat Bacchus) • *Merlot* • *Veenwouden* (Cabernet blend)

## VERGELEGEN
### Stellenbosch
### ★★★✮

This immaculately restored, historic wine estate must be everyone's choice as the leading South African wine producer, thanks to the meticulous efforts of its winemaker André van Rensburg.

✓ *Cabernet Sauvignon* • *Chardonnay* • *Classic red blend* (Vergelegen, Vergelegen V) • *Merlot* • *Sauvignon Blanc* • *Syrah* (Shiraz)

## VERGENOEGD
### Stellenbosch
### ★★✮Ⓥ

Owner-winemaker John Faure has gradually focused the quality of these wines since the 1990s.

✓ *Cabernet Sauvignon* • *Classic red blend* (Vergenoegd) • *Fortified* (Old Cape Colony Vintage Port) • *Merlot* • *Syrah* (Shiraz)

## VILAFONTÉ
### Paarl-Simonsberg
### ★★✮Ⓥ

This is a brand-new joint venture between winemaking guru Zelma Long, viticulturist Phillip Freese, Warwick Estate's Mike Ratcliffe, and Bartholomew Broadbent, the American wine merchant son of Michael Broadbent. Vilafonté is taken from the name *vilafontes*, the gray, sandy soil on the property, which its owners believe to have a significant impact on the flavor profile and development of their wines. The vineyards are in Paarl-Simonsberg district, on the northern side of the Simonsberg Mountains, and planted in high density with four Bordeaux varieties (Cabernet Franc, Cabernet Sauvignon, Malbec, and Merlot). All of the farming is carried out with four-wheel-drive ATVs to reduce soil compaction. Series C is Cabernet Sauvignon based, whereas Series M is Merlot-based.

✓ *Classic red blend* (Series C, Series M)

## VILLIERA
### Paarl
### ★★★Ⓥ

Villiera Estate was a rapidly rising star when the first edition of this encyclopedia was published 17 years ago, and it is now a well-established producer by current Cape wine standards.

✓ *Chenin Blanc* • *Classic red blend* (Monro) • *Classic white blend* (Down to Earth) • *Late Harvest* (Chenin Blanc Noble Late Harvest) • *Sparkling* (Brut Natural Chardonnay, Monro Brut, Tradition Brut, Tradition Rosé) • *Sauvignon Blanc* (Traditional Bush Vine)

## WARWICK
### Stellenbosch
### ★★

Michael Ratcliffe is doing a masterly job of filling his father's shoes, following Stan Ratcliffe's untimely death. Innovations include moving away from some varietals into the classic red "flagship" blend, and holding back five cases of every wine for re-release five years later. I can't help wondering why other wineries around the world do not hold back limited quantities like this, particularly for those wines in the range that tend to sell out well before their prime.

✓ *Cabernet Franc* • *Chardonnay* • *Classic red blend* (Three Cape Ladies, Trilogy)

## WATERFORD
### Stellenbosch
### ★★✮

The first Waterford vintage was in 1998, and already this winery promises to be one of South Africa's star wineries.

✓ *Cabernet Sauvignon* • *Chardonnay* • *Classic red blend* (Cape Winemaker's Guild Blend) • *Syrah* (Kevin Arnold Shiraz)

## WELGEMEEND
### Paarl
### ★★✮

A small, high-quality red wine specialist that was established in the 1970s, Welgemeend was one of the first boutique wineries in South Africa. The winemaker at Welgemeende is aiming more for finesse and length than they are for alcohol and weight.

✓ *Classic red blend* (Douelle, Estate Reserve, Pinotage Shiraz)

## WELTEVREDE
### Robertson
### ★★✮

Weltevrede means "well satisfied," which I am glad to say is still an apt description of anyone who has sampled the wines.

✓ *Chardonnay* (Poet's Prayer) • *Riesling* (Rhine Riesling) • *Sauvignon Blanc* (The Travelling Stone)

## DE WETSHOF
### Robertson
### ★★✮

Quite how Danie de Wet can make such exquisite Chardonnay wines when you can cook an egg on the rocks in his vineyard is a mystery; such mysteries are part of the eternal fascination that wine holds for enthusiasts.

✓ *Riesling* (Rhine Riesling) • *Chardonnay* • *Fortified* (Muscadel) • *Edeloes* (botrytis)

## THE WINERY
### Stellenbosch
### ★★

With partners from the Rhône, Barossa, and the Cape, The Winery has crafted some of South Africa's most stylish wines since its inception in 1998.

✓ *Cabernet Sauvignon* (Vinum) • *Chardonnay* (Radford Dale) • *Chenin Blanc* (Vinum) • *Classic red blend* (Radford Dale Gravity) • *Merlot* (Radford Dale) • *Syrah* (Radford Dale Shiraz)

## WOOLWORTHS
### No fixed region
### ★★

Readers should be aware that Woolworths in South Africa does not have any of the connotations of the Woolworths chain of stores in the UK. This winery produces wines that are stylish and generally good value. Much of the extraordinary in Woolworths' range can be attributed to Allan Mullins, who is one of this country's good guys, and possessor of a gifted palate. In addition to those wines recommended below, the Limited Release range can stand out, but the producer for each wine tends to change more often than those in other ranges. There is also a decent-quality organic range of wines here.

✓ *Cabernet Sauvignon* • *Chardonnay* (Limestone Hill, Reserve, Signature) • *Chenin Blanc* (Barrel) • *Classic red blend* (Cabernet Sauvignon Merlot Reserve, Signature Cabernet Sauvignon) • *Pinotage* (Reserve) • *Sauvignon Blanc* (Reserve) • *Sparkling wine* (Vintage Reserve Brut) • *Syrah* (Groenkloof Shiraz)

## YONDER HILL
### Stellenbosch
### ★

Yonder Hill produces a couple of beautifully crafted wines made from grapes grown in mountain vineyards on the Helderberg. The name of their classic red blend, iNanda, is Zulu for "beautiful place."

✓ *Classic red blend* (iNanda) • *Merlot*

## ZANDVLIET
### Robertson
### ★

Zandvliet is famous for its Syrah, and its new Hill of Eon wine is certainly the best yet. Astonvale is its second label.

✓ *Shiraz*

## ZEVENWACHT
### Stellenbosch
### ★Ⓥ

Zevenwacht grew rapidly in the 1980s, making wines that were fresh, frank, and aromatic, but perhaps not all that exciting. Recently, however, there have been considerable improvements in quality, and these wines can represent great value.

✓ *Classic white blend* (Tin Mine White) • *Merlot* • *Sauvignon Blanc* • *Syrah*

## ZONNEBLOEM
### No fixed region
### ★★✮Ⓥ

Although Zonnebloem, Distell's upmarket range, has always been strong on reds, they have noticeably more "oomph" in recent vintages, and even the Chardonnay has become quite exciting.

✓ *Cabernet Sauvignon* • *Chardonnay* • *Classic red blend* (Lauréat) • *Merlot* • *Pinotage* • *Syrah* (Shiraz) • *Rozendal* (Stellenbosch) • *Stellar Winery* (Olifants River)

## OTHER CERTIFIED ORGANIC WINE PRODUCERS

Rozendal (Stellenbosch)
Stellar Winery (Olifants River)

# NORTH AFRICA

*The wine industries of Algeria, Morocco, and Tunisia, and the appellation systems within which they work, are all based on the structure left behind by the colonial French. Although some good wines can be found, and a trickle of foreign investment exists, the development of wine industries in these countries has been held back by their governments, which do not promote alcohol in Islamic states. Furthermore, their laws do not allow direct sales by wineries to the public, making wine tourism impossible, cutting out an important source of revenue and feedback.*

CULTIVATION OF THE VINE flourished in Algeria, Morocco, and Tunisia as far back as 1000 BC, and winemaking was firmly established by at least the 6th century BC. Under French rule, North Africa was one of the most important winemaking regions

BERBER WOMEN WORKING IN A TUNISIAN VINEYARD
*The best and most reliable AOC wines in Tunisia are Muscats, although rosé enjoyed an ephemeral fashion just after World War II.*

## AVERAGE ANNUAL PRODUCTION

| COUNTRY | VINEYARDS TOTAL Acres | VINEYARDS WINE GRAPES Acres | WINE PRODUCTION Cases | Hectoliters | MAJOR GRAPE VARIETIES |
|---|---|---|---|---|---|
| Algeria | 40,000 | 10,000 | 5.0m | 450,000 | Alicante Bouschet, Carignan, Cinsault, Grenache, Muscat d'Alexandria |
| Morocco | 20,000 | 4,000 | 3.3m | 300,000 | Alicante Bouschet, Cabernet Sauvignon, Carignan, Cinsault, Grenache |
| Tunisia | 10,000 | 6,000 | 4.6m | 412,000 | Alicante Bouschet, Carignan, Cinsault, Grenache, Sangiovese |

NORTH AFRICA
*Morocco, Algeria, and Tunisia are all wine-producing countries. Most vineyards are concentrated along the coastal belts.*

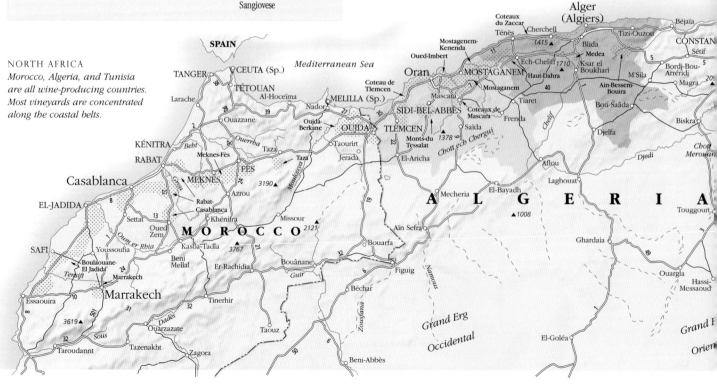

in the world. Yet today it is difficult to see how the quality of wine can progress in any of these countries, where wine production is at best tolerated, and even that level of forbearance is often undermined by government officials who would personally like to see a total ban.

## ALGERIA

**Wine districts of the *Département* of Oran** *Coteaux de Mascara, Coteaux de Tlemcen, Monts du Tessala, Mostaganem, Mostaganem-Kenenda, Oued-Imbert*

**Wine districts of the *Département* of Alger** *Aïn-Bessem-Bouïra, Coteaux du Zaccar, Coteau de Médéa, Dahra*

**Other wine areas of note**
*Alicante d'Oranie, Fontaine du Genie, Khayyam, Montagne des Lions, Nadim, Trappe*

In 1830, Algeria became the first North African country to be colonized by the French, which gave it a head start in viticulture over other North African countries. Algeria has always dominated North African viticulture in terms of quantity, if not quality. The demise of the country's wine industry after it gained independence in 1962 made it clear that cynical remarks about the use of its wine in bolstering Burgundies were true, but the ironic fact is that both the Algerian and the Burgundian wines benefited from being blended together. It was not the best Burgundies that were enhanced with dark Algerian red, but the poorest, thinnest, and least attractive wines. After the blending, they were not Burgundian in character, but were superior to the original Burgundy. By 1938 the Algerian wine

KHEMIS MILIANA, ALGERIA
*Gently undulating vineyards south of Cherchell in the Alger region, just west of Haut-Dahra district.*

industry had reached a peak of 988,000 acres (400,000 hectares) and 244 million cases (22 million hectoliters). Since independence, these vineyards have shrunk, and the number of wineries has plummeted from more than 3,000 to fewer than 50. Algeria has never known phylloxera, thus its varieties retain their own rootstock. Of the few reds that can honestly be recommended, the best are from Château Tellagh in Coteaux de Médéa and Cave de Bourkika in Coteaux de Mascara. Other wineries that produce reasonably good wine include: Coteaux de Mascara (Domaine El Bordj, Domaine Mamounia, Domaine Beni Chougrane); Coteaux de Tlemcen (Domaine de Sebra); Coteaux du Zaccar (Chateau Romain); and Dahra (Domaine de Khadra). Algeria has dropped further behind its wine-producing neighbors, but with the recent involvement of Jabulani Ntshangase, South Africa's only black winery owner (Thabani), and a real mover and shaker, it could be a sign that the future might be brighter than anticipated.

## MOROCCO

**Wine districts** *Berkane, Boufekrane, El Jadida, Les Coteaux de l'Atlas, Meknès-Fez, Mjat, Rabat-Casablanca, Marrakech, Sidi-Slimane, Skhirate*

Wines were made here during Roman times, but after more than 1,000 years of Muslim rule, viticulture died out. In 1912, however, most of Morocco came under either French or Spanish control (with an international zone encompassing Tangiers) and it once more became an active winemaking country. When Morocco gained independence in 1956, the new government introduced a quality-control regime similar to the French AOC (*Appellation d'Origine Contrôlée*) system and, in 1973, it nationalized the wine industry. However, few wines carry the official *Appellation d'Origine Garantie* designation. In 1998, the first *Appellation d'Origine Contrôlée* was created, Les Coteaux

de l'Atlas, encompassing the districts of Sidi-Slimane, Mjat, and Boufekrane, on the cool slopes of the Atlas Mountains, where

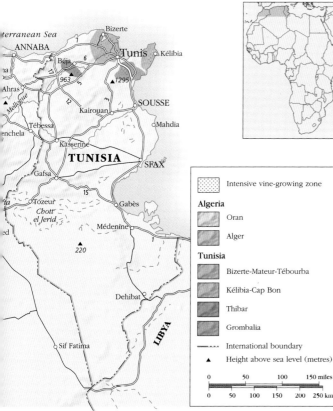

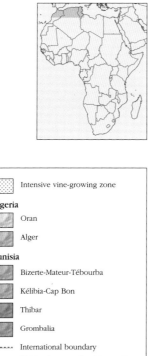

Intensive vine-growing zone

**Algeria**
Oran
Alger

**Tunisia**
Bizerte-Mateur-Tébourba
Kélibia-Cap Bon
Thibar
Grombalia

----- International boundary
▲ Height above sea level (metres)

0  50  100  150 miles
0  50  100  150  200  250 km

OLD MUSCAT VINES
*Vineyards at Bizerte in the Bizerte-Mateur-Tébourba region at the northern tip of Tunisia.*

the lime-rich clayey soils over dry, siliceous subsoil is particularly suitable for viticulture. Here we find Cabernet Sauvignon, Chardonnay, Merlot, and Syrah growing, and the wines produced by Les Celliers de Meknès, particularly the classic red blend, are the finest that Morocco currently has to offer. The country's more tradtional wines are made from Carignan, Cinsault, and Grenache, usually in a pale rosé style, and often sold as *vin gris*. These can be pleasant when served chilled, but the best of even the traditional wines are red, and the most successful of these are also produced by Les Celliers de Meknès, but sold under the Les Trois Domaines label. Owned by Reda Zniber, who is regarded as something of a "godfather" in Morocco, Les Celliers de Meknès produces 90 percent of the country's wine, and most of it is at least drinkable. Or it is when it leaves the cellars. Most is sold on the home market, and much of this is at undeservedly high prices, to tourists who are not willing to pay the even more exorbitant prices demanded for heavily taxed imported wines. Poor storage conditions inevitably spoil both Moroccan and imported wines. Moroccans themselves do drink wine, although there is a notable discrepancy between international per capita consumption figures (one quart) and Morocco's own religiously sensitive official estimation (zero!).

## TUNISIA
**Wine districts** *Grombalia, Bizerte-Mateur-Tébourba, Kélibia-Cap Bon, Thibar*
Wines were first made around the Carthage area in Punic times, but production was forbidden for 1,000 years under Muslim rule. After French colonization in 1881, viticulture resumed, and by Tunisian independence in 1955, the foundations of a thriving wine industry had been laid. At this time two basic appellations had been established—*Vin Supérieur de Tunisie*, for table wines, and *Appellation Contrôlée Vin Muscat de Tunisie*, for liqueur Muscat. These designations did not, however, incorporate any controls to safeguard origin, and in 1957 the government introduced a classification system that established four levels as follows: *Vins de Consommation Courante, Vins Supérieurs, Vins de Qualité Supérieure*, and *Appellation d'Origine Contrôlée*.

The best traditional Tunisian wines are those made from the Muscat grape, ranging from the lusciously sweet, rich, and viscous Vin de Muscat de Tunisie, to fresh, delicate, dry Muscats such as the Muscat de Kelibia. There are also a small number of good red wines, such as Château Feriani, Domaine Karim, and Royal Tardi, with Carignan and Cinsault the most important black grape varieties. The finest new-wave wines are made by the partly German-owned Domaine Magon, which is working proficiently with Cabernet Sauvignon, Merlot, Pinot Noir, and Syrah. There is also encouraging news of progress from research scientist Amor Jaziri, who produces organic wines under the Almory label, from his 35-acre (14-hectare) vineyard near Jedeida.

---

OTHER WINEMAKING COUNTRIES OF
# AFRICA

## ETHIOPIA
Grape-growing in Ethiopia? In fact, viticulture has existed here for many centuries. This country converted to Christianity in the 4th century, and locally grown Communion wine has been used by the Ethiopian Orthodox Church since at least the 12th century. So entrenched is grape-growing in Ethiopian history that it has entered the language as a specific term. Ethiopians distinguish three altitude-defined climatic zones: dega, wayna-dega, and kola. Dega means "cold" and indicates areas that are higher than 8,200 feet (2,500 meters) above sea level. Kola means "hot place," and applies to areas below 5,900 feet (1,800 meters). Wayna-dega literally means "grape elevation," or "place where you grow grapes," and refers to areas between 5,900 and 8,200 feet (1,800 and 2,500 meters) in height.

Ethiopia's largest vineyard is located at Awash, 100 miles (160 kilometers) east of Addis Ababa, in the Harar province, where some 74 acres (30 hectares) of Aleatico, Barbera, Chenin Blanc, Grenache, Petit Sirah, and Ugni Blanc are grown. There are also 185 acres (75 hectares) of so-called "local" varieties, including Debulbul Attere, Key Dubbi, Nech Debulbul, and Tiku Weyn. There are two harvests each year, and the grapes are trucked to the Awash Winery in the outskirts of Addis Ababa, where reasonable-quality red and white wines are produced. The most commonly encountered wines are Axumite (sweetish white), Crystals (dry white), Dukam (red), and Gouder (Ethiopia's best red, from the Gouder vineyard, 84 miles (135 kilometers) west of Addis Ababa). However, the Awash Winery is located next to the Awash River, which irrigates the Awash vineyards 100 miles (160 kilometers) downstream, and in 1998 researchers from the University of Turku found the Awash River to be polluted downstream from the winery's own effluent discharge, but not upstream. This situation will have to be rectified before any serious thoughts of export can be entertained, as will its practice of using rehydrated imported raisins in some of the wines. Currently, the most exported wine is made from honey, not grapes. Called Tej, it is made all over the country, and is much more famous than its grape-based counterparts. The Awash Winery exports Tej to Sweden and the US, but Ethiopia is not really wine country, whether from honey or grapes. It is coffee country, to the point of giving the world the name itself—the province of Kaffa was the etymological origin of the word "coffee."

## KENYA
Lake Naivasha Vineyards are located on volcanic soils beside Lake Naivasha, situated 6,200 feet (1,900 meters) above sea level in the Rift Valley. The Rift Valley is the Flower Garden of Africa, the blooms of which are flown to florists all over the world. In fact, you can grow absolutely anything here, and grow it twice a year too. You can certainly grow grapes, as John and Elli D'Olier did between 1982 and 1992, with cuttings they brought back from California. They ripped out most of the vines in 1992 when overnight hikes in local taxes made Kenyan wine economically unviable, making just the odd wine for home consumption, only

to replant in earnest in 2002. The economics are not much better now than they were in 1992, but the d'Oliers just cannot give up on the idea of Kenyan wine.

Richard Leakey is famous for finding a 2.5-million-year-old human skull in Kenya, but he is also one of this country's newest winemakers. He might have lost both legs below the knee in a plane crash, and have only one kidney (and that the gift of Philip Leakey, his younger brother and sometime political foe), but this anthropologist, paleontologist, bruised politician, great African patriot, and tireless warrior against the ivory trade is still game for a new challenge. Leakey is not the sort of person to settle for Kenyan Carignan or Cardinal, but who would have thought that he, or anyone else in this country, could set their sights on Pinot Noir, the Holy Grail of winemaking? Well Leakey has, and by 2001 he had succeeded in cropping Pinot Noir at his Ol Choro Onyore vineyard in Ngong, and putting it (and Sauvignon Blanc) in bottle.

## MADAGASCAR

Affectionately known as "Mad" to Anglo-Saxon inhabitants of the African continent, Madagascans have been growing grapes and making wine since the 19th century. Most of the vines growing on the island today are hybrids. With not a little tongue in cheek, John and Erica Platter write in *Africa Uncorked* (2002) that Stéphane Chan Foa Tong's sparkling Grand Cru d'Antsirabe is "Unquestionably the best sparkling wine in all Madagascar. Probably the finest Couderc Blanc *méthode champenoise* in the world!" and certainly it seems better than his still wines. The clean and decent, but hardly exciting, wines of Clos Malaza in the Ambatomena area are generally agreed by the locals to be the best that Madagascar currently produces, from 74 acres (30 hectares) of well-trained Chambourcin, Couderc Blanc, Petit Bouchet, Villardin, Varousset, and Villard Noir vines. From an outsider's point of view, the Chan brothers in Ambalavao produce more promising wine under the Côte de Fiana appellation (their best wine is sold as an exclusivity under the Tsara be label). Domaine Manomisoa is also known as Soavita Estate, and even more confusingly, its best wine is sold as Château Verger. Other wines are produced under the following labels: Clos de la Maromby (from the Masina Maria monastery, near Fiana) and Lazan'i Betsileo (a small cooperative in Fiana). Nothing really stands out among these wines, but with better grape varieties growing at altitude on the drier, eastern side of the island, and pruned to yield less than half the current average crop, Madagascar does have the potential to produce very much more interesting wines.

## MAURITIUS

Beware Mauritian-looking wine sold under the Oxenham label, which is made from imported grape concentrate. While there is nothing wrong with that, the fact should be made clear.

## NAMIBIA

Commercial Namibian wine is a very recent phenomenon, dating back to 1994, when Helmuth Kluge established Kristall Kellerei at Omaruru, on the periphery of the Namib desert. All wines are clean and well made, with fresh, zesty Colombard the best.

## RÉUNION

This African island is, believe it or not, the most far-flung of all French wines areas: Vin de Pays de Cilaos. Created as recently as 2004, the *vin de pays* regulations forced the removal of the hybrids that used to grow here. Hybrids are still the mainstay of viticulture on Madagascar, which arguably offers greater potential, but the performance of the classic *vinifera* varieties growing on Réunion (Chenin Blanc, Pinot Noir, and Malbec) could well change the mind of those "Mad" people. There are plans to plant Gros Manseng, Pinotage, Syrah, and Verdelho. The styles produced are red, white, rosé, and, because the tendency is for grapes to overripen rather too easily, Moelleux. The only wine producer currently is the local cooperative, Chais du Cilaos, which harvested just 28 tons of grapes in 2004. The vines grow at an altitude of 3,930 feet (1,200 meters) on volcanic soil, cropping in January. The wines are fresh, crisp, and well-made, fermented in new, temperature-controlled, stainless-steel vats.

## TANZANIA

There is only one winery, Tanganyika Vineyards, in Tanzania but two harvests a year, producing a decent, but not exciting, Chenin Blanc, and a Makutupora red and white.

## ZIMBABWE

Although the first production of wine began in the early 1950s under the labels of Worringham and Lorraine, these semisweet wines were made from table grapes. It was not until UDI that this most beautiful country in Africa gave birth to a

truly commercial wine industry. During the mid-1960s, when sanctions bit deep, and anything that could be produced locally was produced locally, Rhodesian farmers grew the grapes to make the wines they could no longer import. In the 1990s, many low-quality grape varieties were ripped up, and replaced by classic *vinifera*, with drip irrigation. The grape varieties grown in Zimbabwe today include Bukettraube, Cabernet Sauvignon, Cinsault, Clairette Blanche, Colombard, Chenin Blanc, Cruchen, Gewürztraminer, Merlot, Pinotage, Pinot Noir, Riesling, Ruby Cabernet, Sauvignon Blanc, and Seneca (*Lignan Blanc x Ontario* hybrid), but many wine farms have been occupied by "war vets." Worringham still exists, both as a wine farm (111 acres; 45 hectares) and as a brand, and is owned by African Distillers (also known as Stapleford Wines), but other familiar wine names from the early days, such as Philips and Monis, no longer exist, having been absorbed by the Mukuyu Winery. Export brands such as Flame Lily, which made an ephemeral appearance on the UK market, have also fallen by the wayside. Meadows Estate used to be a shining example of cutting-edge viticulture in the 1980s, growing Gewürztraminer, Riesling, Chardonnay, and Pinot Noir, but it is a rose farm now, although Mukuyu still sell wines under the Meadows Estate brand. The 1990s also witnessed the installation of cool-fermentation technology, and internationally trained winemakers deployed on flying visits, with New Zealander Clive Hartnell (of Hungary's Chapel Hill renown) currently winging his way around the wineries of African Distillers. The late Peter Raynor and his son Humpfrey established Zimbabwe's largest private vineyard near Wedza, but its once impeccably trained vines have been unattended since the Raynor family was evicted by Minister of Youth Brigadier Ambrose Mutinhiri in December 2004. The family had been forcibly removed in July of that year, only to be herded back three weeks later and told to produce a crop. They are trying to get back in, but sadly the current situation seems ominously more permanent. In addition to the human tragedy, this sadly marks the end of the brief promise shown by Zimbabwe's first and, now, only single-vineyard, pure varietal wines—Fighill 2002 Chardonnay and Fighill 2003 Shiraz, which the Raynors made from a superselected five percent of their own production. Most of their crop used to be split 50/50 between African Distillers (which bottled their domain wines) and Mukuyu (which is 65 percent government-owned, thus escaped its threatened compulsory acquisition in December 2001). Private farms have been so vulnerable to compulsory acquisition (i.e., occupation by "war vets") that African Distillers and Mukuyu are now the only producers here.

# The WINES of
# THE AMERICAS

ALL OF THE MOST FAMOUS WINE REGIONS—
California, Washington, Oregon, and Chile—are
found on or inland from the western coast. This is
because eastern seaboards are generally too humid
and prone to severely cold winters. Of the famous
regions in the Americas, California is, of course, the
most important. It is staggering to think that the 25
largest wineries in this state on their own produce
twice the output of Argentina (which itself is the
fifth-largest winemaking country in the world).
However, California is actually more about quality
than quantity. It produces some of the world's
greatest Cabernet Sauvignon, Merlot, Zinfandel,
Pinot Noir, and Chardonnay wines. Although
Washington has always been a considerably
larger wine-producing state than Oregon, from
an international perspective it used to live in the
shadow of the latter's excellent-but-overhyped
Pinot Noir. Well, no more. Washington is now justly
famous for powerful *bordelais* varietals, not to
mention its up-and-coming Syrah. British Columbia
has far more in common with Washington state
than it does with Ontario, and is creating at least
as much of a buzz in the wine world. Chile still
rules in South America, but a small number of
quality-conscious Argentinian producers are
giving their old rival a good run for its money.

MUSTARD FLOWERS IN CARNEROS, NAPA, CALIFORNIA
*Mustard planted near vines provides a habitat for predators of
vine pests and also prevents the evaporation of moisture.*

# NORTH AMERICA

*The US is the fourth-largest wine-producing country in the world, and the output of California alone is more than double that of the fifth-largest wine-producing country (Australia), yet almost every state in this vast country produces wine. And, of course, North America does not consist of just the US; it also encompasses the viticultural areas of Ontario and British Columbia in Canada (see also pp.532–7), and the Baja California and Sierra Madre in Mexico (see also pp.538–9).*

IN 1521, WITHIN ONE YEAR of invading Mexico, the Spanish planted vines and set about making the first North American wines. Fourteen years later, when French explorer Jacques Cartier sailed down the St. Lawrence to New France, he discovered a large island overrun by wild vines and decided to call it the Île de Bacchus. He had second thoughts, however, and later renamed it the Île d'Orléans, a calculated move in view of the fact that the then Duke of Orléans was the son of King Francis I of France. It is assumed that, circa 1564, the Jesuit settlers who followed in the wake of Cartier's explorations were the first winemakers in what was to become Canada. The earliest wines made in what is now the United States of America came from Florida. Between 1562 and 1564, French Huguenot settlers produced wines from native Scuppernong grapes on a site that would become Jacksonville.

JEKEL VINEYARDS, CALIFORNIA
*An irrigation pipe skirts rows of vines in one of the drier parts of Monterey County. Conditions are a far cry from those around the Finger Lakes, New York.*

## NATIVE NORTH AMERICAN GRAPE VARIETIES

All classic grape varieties belong to one species, *Vitis vinifera*, but North America's native varieties belong to several different species, not one of which happens to be *Vitis vinifera*. There were plenty of native vines growing wild wherever the early settlers traveled, and so they came to rely on them for their initial wine production. Settlers in Australia, on the other hand, were forced to wait for precious shipments of classic European vines before they could plant vineyards. Although various European varieties were taken across the Atlantic in the 19th century, nearly all North American wines, aside from California ones, remained products of native varieties until relatively recently.

The most common native North American species, *Vitis labrusca*, has such a distinctive aroma and flavor that it seems truly amazing that those pioneers who were also winemakers did not pester their home countries for supplies of more acceptable vines. The *labrusca* character, commonly referred to as "foxy," is so exotic, it cloys at the back of the throat, and is generally not appreciated by European and antipodean palates.

## PROHIBITION IN THE UNITED STATES

Although total Prohibition in the United States was confined to 1920–1933, the first "dry legislation" was passed as early as 1816, and the first state to go completely dry was Maine, in 1846. By the time the 18th Amendment to the Constitution was put into effect in 1920, forbidding "the manufacture, sale, or transport of intoxicating liquors," more than 30 states were already totally dry.

The result of Prohibition was chaos. It denied the government legitimate revenue and encouraged bootleggers to amass fortunes. The number of illicit stills multiplied quicker than the authorities could find and dismantle them, and the speakeasy became a way of life in the cities. Not only did the authorities often realize that it was much easier to turn a blind eye to what was going on, but the federal government actually found it useful to open its own speakeasy in New York! Many vineyards were uprooted, but those grapes that were produced were often concentrated, pressed, and sold as "grape bricks." These came complete with a yeast capsule and instructions to dissolve the brick in one gallon of water, but warned against adding the yeast because it would start a fermentation! This would turn the grape juice into wine "and that would be illegal," the warning pointed out.

### Prohibition and the wine industry

By the mid- to late 19th century, the California wine industry had such a reputation that great French wine areas, such as Champagne, began to form syndicats to protect themselves, in part, from the potential of California's marketing threat. However, the 13 years of Prohibition coincided with a vital point in the evolution of wine, and set the California wine industry back a hundred years, since other wine regions had just recovered from the effects of phylloxera (*see* p.471), and were busily reestablishing their reputations and carving out future markets. In Europe, World War I had robbed every industry of its young, up-and-coming generation, but the rich tradition of the wine industry enabled it to survive until the arrival of a new generation. The early 1900s were also the era of the foundation of the French *Appellation Contrôlée* laws, a quality-control system that many other serious winemaking countries would eventually copy.

The United States also lost much of one generation in World War I, but it had less of a winemaking tradition to fall back on and, by 1920, there was virtually no wine industry whatsoever to preserve. After Prohibition came one of the worst economic depressions in history, followed by World War II, which took yet

### Map Labels

**ALASKA**
▲1707 Fairbanks
ANCHORAGE
▲6193

**YUKON TERRITORY**
Inuvik
Dawson
Whitehorse
Skagway
▲472
2966

**NORTHWEST TERRITORIES**
Great Bear L.
Kugluktuk
Yellowknife
Great Slave L.
▲610

**Beaufort Sea**
Victoria Island
Victoria Island

**NUNAVUT**
▲240

**Hudson Bay**
Churchill

**Hudson Strait**

**Labrador Sea**

**NEWFOUNDLAND**
Kuujjuaq
Goose Bay
Schefferville
St John's

**BRITISH COLUMBIA**
Prince Rupert
Prince George
Fort Nelson
Fort McMurray
▲4042 Kamloops
VANCOUVER
Victoria
SEATTLE
Penticton

**ALBERTA**
EDMONTON
CALGARY
▲16
▲747

**SASKATCHEWAN**
Saskatoon
Regina
▲747

**MANITOBA**
Lake Winnipeg
WINNIPEG
▲305

**ONTARIO**
Fort George
Kapuskasing
Sudbury
Albany ▲259

**QUÉBEC**
Sept-Îles
QUÉBEC
Montréal
OTTAWA

**N.B.** **P.E.I.** **NOVA SCOTIA**
Halifax

PACIFIC OCEAN

**WASH.**
Spokane
PORTLAND
Eugene
▲4316
**OREGON**

Kamloops
Great Falls
**MONTANA**
Missouri

**IDAHO**
Boise ▲3857
Snake

**WYOMING**
Rapid City

**NORTH DAKOTA**
Grand Forks
▲693
**SOUTH DAKOTA**

**MINN.**
Duluth
MINNEAPOLIS
Lake Superior

**WISC.**
Lake Wisconsin
MILWAUKEE

**MICH.**
Lake Michigan
Lake Huron
Detroit
Toronto
Lake Ontario

SACRAMENTO
San Francisco
SAN JOSE
**CALIFORNIA**
Bakersfield
Los Angeles
SAN DIEGO
▲5

Reno
**NEVADA**
▲3982
Las Vegas
▲-86

SALT LAKE CITY ▲4114
**UTAH**

**COLORADO**
Grand Valley
DENVER
Colorado
Cheyenne
▲2008

**NEBRASKA**
OMAHA
Platte

**IOWA**
Des Moines

**ILL.**
Chicago
INDIANAPOLIS
**IND.**

Albany
**N.Y.**
New York
**PENN.**
▲777
**VT.** **N.H.**
Boston
**MASS.**
**R.I.** **CONN.**

**ATLANTIC OCEAN**

**KANSAS**
KANSAS CITY
Wichita
▲2008
Arkansas

**MISSOURI**
Hermann
ST. LOUIS
Augusta
Arkansas Mtn.

CLEVELAND
PITTSBURGH
**OHIO**
**W. VA.**
LOUISVILLE
**VIRGINIA**
Greensboro
**N.TH. CAROLINA**

Philadelphia
Washington D.C.
**MD.** **DEL.**

**KENTUCKY**
**TENN.**
MEMPHIS
**ARK.**
Little Rock
Tulsa
Altus
**OKLA.**
OKLAHOMA CITY
Red

**ARIZONA**
PHOENIX
Gila

**NEW MEXICO**
Middle Rio Grande
ALBUQUERQUE
Mimbres Valley
Mesilla Valley
El Paso
Pecos

**TEXAS**
Brazos
Escondido Valley
Bell Mtn.
▲2389 Fredericksburg
Austin
San Antonio
DALLAS
Houston

**LOUISIANA**
NEW ORLEANS

**MISS.** **ALABAMA**
Birmingham
Mississippi Delta
ATLANTA
**GEORGIA**
**STH CAROLINA**
Savannah
Jacksonville

**FLORIDA**
Tampa
St. Petersburg
MIAMI

Northern Baja California
▲3055
Sonoita
Caborca ▲3200
Nogales
Hermosillo

**CHIHUAHUA**
Delicias ▲2445
Laguna
Torreón
Parras
Saltillo
Culiacán
La Paz
Mazatlán

MONTERREY
**Gulf of Mexico**

Zacatecas
Aguascalientes
Tampico
GUADALAJARA
San Juan del Río
Mexico City
▲5452
Veracruz
Villahermosa
Mérida
Cancún
Oaxaca
ACAPULCO

PACIFIC OCEAN

### Hawaiian Islands Inset

**Hawaiian Islands**
Kauai
Lihue
Niihau
Oahu
Molokai
Lanai
Maui ▲3033
Hilo
Volcano Winery ▲4169
**Hawaii**
PACIFIC OCEAN

● State/Provincial boundary
▲ Height above sea level (metres)

| 0 | 100 | 200 | 300 miles |
| 0 | 100 | 200 | 300 | 400 | 500 km |

### Legend

| | |
|---|---|
| | California *See also* p469 |
| | Pacific Northwest *See also* p507 |
| | Atlantic Northeast *See also* p517 |
| | Canada *See also* pp532, 533 |
| | Ozark Mountain |
| | Ozark Highlands |
| | Texas High Plains |
| | Texas Hill Country |
| | Other winemaking areas |
| ● | Mexican winemaking areas |
| — | International boundary |
| — | State/Provincial boundary |
| ▲ | Height above sea level (metres) |

| 0 | 200 | 400 | 600 miles |
| 0 | 200 | 400 | 600 | 800 | 1000 km |

## NORTH AMERICA

*Wine is produced across the entire continent of North America, in Canada, the United States, and Mexico, whether from native grapes or vinifera varieties. Winemakers work in enormously varied conditions according to climate.*

MOUNT PLEASANT VINEYARDS
*These vineyards in Augusta, Missouri, were the first Approved Viticultural Area in the United States.*

another generation of bright young minds. It was, therefore, little wonder that by the late 1940s the wine industry of the United States was so out of date. It had lost touch with European progress and resorted to the production of awful *labrusca* wines that had been the wine drinker's staple diet in pre-Prohibition days. California produced relatively little *labrusca* compared to the eastern states, but its winemakers also resorted to old-fashioned styles, making heavy, sweet, fortified wines.

The fact that Californian wine today is a match for the best of its European counterparts and that its industry is healthy, growing fast, and looking to compete on foreign markets, clearly proves that in the United States opportunity is boundless.

## THE APPELLATION SYSTEM OF THE UNITED STATES

The older generation of appellations of the United States is based on political boundaries such as counties or states, and still exists. However, during the mid-1970s, the Department of Treasury's Bureau of Alcohol, Tobacco, and Firearms (BATF) considered the concept of specific controlled appellations based on geography and climate, and in September 1978 BATF published its first laws and regulations designed to introduce a system of Approved Viticultural Areas (AVAs), to supplement the old system, which is now run by the Alcohol and Tobacco Tax and Trade Bureau (TTB). Every state, from Hawaii to Alaska, and the counties they contain, are recognized in law as their own individual appellations of origin, but other generic appellations are also recognized:

**American or United States** This appellation classifies blended and varietal wines from anywhere in the US, including the District of Columbia and the Commonwealth of Puerto Rico. These wines, like *vins de tables* in France, are not allowed to carry a vintage, which is, in my opinion, irrational. It is the only appellation allowed for wines shipped in bulk to other countries.

**Multistate Appellation** This appellation is used to classify a wine from any two or three contiguous states. The percentage of wine from each state must be clearly indicated on the label.

**State Appellation** A wine from any state may use this appellation; at least 75 percent of grapes must come from grapes grown within the one state indicated (except for Texas, which is 85 percent, and California, which is 100 per cent). Thus, wine claiming the appellation of Oregon may contain up to 25 percent produce of other states. The grapes can be shipped to a neighboring state and

still be given the originating state name, but not to any state that does not share a border. Grapes can therefore be shipped from California to Oregon, where they are turned into wine, and may be called California wine (as long as the wine is at least 75 percent from those grapes), but the same grapes cannot be shipped to Washington State and be called California wine (although such a wine could be labeled California-Oregon-Washington, if it contained grapes from all three states, see Multistate Appellation). The same principles apply to County Appellations and Multicounty Appellations.

**Multicounty Appellation** This appellation classifies a wine from any two or three contiguous counties. The percentage of wine from each county must be clearly indicated on the label.

**County Appellation** A wine from any county within any state may use this appellation: at least 75 percent of the wine must come from grapes grown within the one county indicated.

### DID YOU KNOW?

- America's third president, Thomas Jefferson, was the country's greatest wine connoisseur, and even tried to grow vines at Monticello.

- There is a winery in every state of the US, even Alaska (though the grapes have to be trucked in, of course).

- Although almost every state in the US grows wine grapes, California accounts for more than 90 percent of the wines produced.

- It is legal to produce and sell American Champagne or Burgundy, but not American Bordeaux or Rhône.

- There are still "dry" counties in some US states.

- The oldest winery in the US is the Brotherhood Winery (1839) at Washingtonville in the foothills of the Catskills of New York State.

### THE SEMI-GENERIC SAGA

It is not only easy to understand how the misuse of famous European wine names started in the US, it is also perfectly understandable. As European immigrants poured into this land, some brought vines with them and when they made different styles of wine, it was inevitable that they would use the only wine names they knew to distinguish between them. Names like Burgundy, Chablis, Champagne, *et. al.* There is nothing to forgive. Until now, that is. Ever since the California wine industry became a significant exporter, opening the door for other wine-producing states, it was incumbent upon the US to respect all other legitimate geographical appellations, however well entrenched the usage might have become within the US itself. However, in 1978, well after California wines had stepped onto the international stage, the director of the Department of Treasury's Bureau of Alcohol, Tobacco, and Firearms (BATF) legally enshrined the concept of semi-generic wine names within Federal Regulations, citing, but not restricting itself to, 14 such examples: "Burgundy, Claret, Chablis, Champagne, Chianti, Madeira, Malaga, Marsala, Moselle, Port, Rhine Wine, Sauterne, Sherry, Tokay." The regulations state that these so-called semi-generic names must be qualified by their true place of origin: American Chablis, California Champagne, and so on. However, American regulations are not only unfair, they are decidedly quirky. While it is perfectly legal for US wineries to sell wines labeled as Champagne or Chablis, the name Liebfraumilch is protected by the full might of Federal Law. And whereas Burgundy is permitted, Bordeaux or Rhône are not. Where is the logic? As the most abused wine names were French, it was left initially to that country to redress the situation, but they got nowhere and, frankly, were not helped by their own antics in South America, where the *champenois* were abusing the Champagne appellation. The French were also chronically shortsighted when turning down an under-the-table deal that would have seen "Champagne" dropped in favor of "Champagne Style." Since then, the production of American wine sold under famous Italian appellations has become a substantial industry in itself, which with the use of other European wine names has seen the European Union take up the fight. Its negotiators have been hammering away at the US through the World Trade Organization, but they have not been any more successful than the French. What they have failed to understand is that they have nothing to bring to the negotiating table that the US is in the slightest bit bothered about, but when they recognize this, it should provide the European authorities with the obvious solution. If the French, Italians, Spanish, Portuguese, and Hungarians officially created a few new appellations, like Napa Valley, Sonoma County Green Valley, and, to catch the attention of the East Coast elite, North Fork of Long Island and Northern Neck George Washington Birthplace, the EU would soon find that it had something to bargain with, and the US might at least understand why Europeans are so protective of their appellations. The irony is that should such appellations be formally adopted and the wines put into distribution in their country of origin, they would be automatically eligible for sale in the US, where the law defines an acceptable foreign appellation on an imported wine to be "a delimited place or region the boundaries of which have been recognized and defined by the country of origin for use on labels of wine available for consumption within the country of origin." Perhaps the wine-producing countries who feel that they have been treated unfairly by the US will realize that sometimes it does take a wrong to right another wrong. Virtually all self-respecting, quality wine producers in the US will be on their side because they are proud of their own products, which do not need any famous European names as a crutch.

## AMERICAN WINE LABEL LANGUAGE

**ALCOHOL** It is obligatory to indicate the alcoholic strength of a US wine, and this is expressed as a percentage by volume.

**ANGELICA** An authentic American fortified wine style of 17–24 percent, traditionally made from Mission grapes, typically blended 50/50 wine and brandy, with the liquor added after fermentation has achieved just 5 percent alcohol, resulting in excess of 100g/l of residual sugar. If the strength is less than 18 percent, the wine must be labeled "Light Angelica." Other grapes that are sometimes used include Grenache, Muscat, and Palomino. The quality can be extremely high. Angelica was named after Los Angeles by Spanish Missionary winemakers in the 18th century, when the city was just a town and its name in full was El Pueblo de Nuestra Señora Reina de los Ángeles de la Porciuncula.

**BOTTLE FERMENTED** A sparkling wine derived through a second fermentation in "glass containers of not greater than one (US) gallon capacity." Usually refers to a wine that, after second fermentation, is decanted and filtered under pressure before rebottling.

**BURGUNDY** A semi-generic name allowed under US Federal Law for a red wine of legally undefined "Burgundy-style," such products today are inevitably of basic quality and made from almost anything, although high-yielding Carignane, Grenache, and Zinfandel are traditional. American Burgundy is typically dark in color, and full in body, but with some residual sweetness to give an impression of softness.

**CARBONATED WINE** Still wine made bubbly through the addition of carbon dioxide from a bottle of gas, the method used to produce carbonated drinks such as lemonade or cola.

**CHAMPAGNE** A semi-generic name allowed under US Federal Law for a wine rendered sparkling through a second fermentation in "glass containers of not greater than one (US) gallon capacity."

**CHIANTI** A semi-generic name allowed under US Federal Law for a red wine of legally undefined style, American Chianti is generally medium-bodied, falling somewhere between American claret and American Burgundy in color, character, and residual sweetness, with a more pronounced fruitiness, but is equally basic in quality.

**CLARET** A semi-generic name allowed under US Federal Law for a red wine of legally undefined style, American claret is a very basic wine that is generally drier than American Burgundy, as well as being somewhat lighter in color and in body.

**CRACKLING WINE** A sparkling wine derived through a second fermentation in "glass containers of not greater than one (US) gallon capacity," thus the same as for American "Champagne," although with less effervescence. This type of wine may also be called *pétillant*, *frizzante*, or *crémant*.

**CRACKLING WINE—BULK METHOD** I have not actually seen "Bulk Method" on a wine label, but it does exist, and it

means the same as for "Crackling Wine" but made by the *cuve close* method.

**DESSERT WINE** A wine, usually fortified, with an alcohol content of 14–24 percent. If less than 18 percent, the wine must be labeled "Light Dessert Wine."

**FERMENTED IN THE BOTTLE** A simple and smart way of describing a wine made by the *méthode champenoise*.

**FUMÉ BLANC** Widely used term for oak-aged Sauvignon Blanc.

**GRAPE VARIETY** If a single grape variety is mentioned on a label, the wine must contain at least 75 percent of the grape variety indicated (90 percent in Oregon). Although the potential of varietal labeling was recognized in Alsace in the 1920s, the international marketing phenomenon these wines represent today was brought about by the widespread application of the concept by California wineries.

**HAUTE SAUTERNE** (*sic*) Rarely encountered, highly questionable, semi-generic name allowed and misspelled under US Federal Law for medium-sweet and sweet variants of Sauterne (*sic*).

**HEALTH WARNING** Health warnings are required by federal law, yet none of the proven health advantages are permitted on the label (*see* p.634).

**HOCK** A semi-generic name allowed under US Federal Law for an undefined style of wine that, curiously, is light and dry, rather than vaguely approximating some sort of German Rhine wine. The grapes used are often the same as for American Chablis, but are blended to produce something lighter (which is correct) and drier (which is not).

**LIGHT WINE** A wine with an alcohol level not in excess of 14 percent (synonymous with Table Wine).

**MADEIRA** A semi-generic name allowed under US Federal Law for any fortified wine of 17–24 percent, made in a legally undefined "Madeira-style" that is usually sweet to some degree. If it contains less than 18 percent alcohol, the wine must be labeled "Light Madeira." This slowly diminishing style of wine is primarily Californian and is traditionally produced by blending American sherry with Angelica.

**MALAGA** A semi-generic name allowed under US Federal Law for any fortified wine of 17–24 percent, made in a legally undefined "Malaga-style" that is usually sweet to some degree. If it contains less than 18 percent alcohol, the wine must be labeled "Light Malaga." Made primarily from Concord grapes, American Malaga is often a kosher product and is used for sacramental rites.

**MARSALA** A semi-generic name allowed under US Federal Law for any fortified wine of 17–24 percent, made in a legally undefined "Marsala-style" that is amber or brown in color, usually sweet to some degree, and sometimes flavored with herbs. If it contains less than 18 percent alcohol, the wine must be labeled "Light Marsala."

**MOSELLE** A semi-generic name allowed under US Federal Law for an undefined style of wine that is traditionally made from Chenin Blanc and Riesling grapes.

American Moselle is light in body, pale in color, medium sweet to taste, and sometimes very lightly *pétillant*. It is softer and lighter than American hock.

**MUSCATEL** Generally a more basic quality version of sweet Muscat wine (which is usually sold varietally as Muscat Frontignan or Muscat Canelli), Muscatel is usually a blend of two or more of the following: Aleatico, Malvasia Bianca, and Muscat (Alexandria, Canelli, and Frontignan). Black Muscatel is a blend of Aleatico and Black Muscat (also known as Muscat Hamburg).

**NATURAL WINE** A wine may be called "natural" only if it has not been fortified with grape brandy or alcohol.

**PORT** A semi-generic name allowed under US Federal Law for any fortified wine of 17–24 percent that has been made in a legally undefined "port style." If it contains less than 18 percent alcohol, the wine must be labeled "Light Port." Zinfandel, Petite Sirah, and Cabernet Sauvignon are the most common grapes to be declared on a label, but others widely used include Alicante Bouschet, Carignane, Grenache, and Mission. Additionally, there is a small but growing category of quality ports, blended and varietal, that are made from various Portuguese varieties such as Tinta Madeira, Tinta Cão, Alvarelhão, Touriga, and Bastardo or Trousseau. When blended from different Portuguese varieties, the wine is often sold as a Tinta port. Whichever grapes are used, the wines are usually sweet to some degree, and often qualified by traditional port terminology such as Ruby, Tawny, and Vintage. Some examples can be very good indeed, particularly from specialists.

**RHINE WINE** Synonymous with American hock.

**SAUTERNE** (*sic*) A semi-generic name allowed and misspelled under US Federal Law for a wine that is usually of basic quality, less sweet than genuine Sauternes, and with no hint of botrytis. A few better-quality Sauterne wines are made, usually from Semillon and Sauvignon Blanc, but most Sauterne are nothing more than bland blends of Palomino, Sauvignon Vert, Thompson Seedless, and other even less respectable varieties. Amazingly for a semi-generic wine that should by definition be intensely sweet, Sauterne wines range from dry to very sweet, and are often qualified by "Dry" or "Sweet," with "Chateau" weirdly used for the sweetest styles. The cheapest dry Sauterne wines are not dissimilar to American Chablis. Some California producers spell Sauternes correctly, but it is difficult to work out which spelling constitutes the worst insult.

**SEMI-GENERIC** A semi-generic name is a geographical designation that has, in the opinion of the Director of the Department of Treasury's Alcohol and Tobacco Tax and Trade Bureau (TTB), become at least as well known for a specific style of wine, wherever it might happen to be produced, and is thus allowed under US Federal Law to be used by any wine producer in the US.

Thus, it is entirely legal within the borders of the US to abuse the appellations of Burgundy, Chablis, Champagne, Chianti, and many others.

**SHERRY** A semi-generic name allowed under US Federal Law for any fortified wine of 17–24 percent that has been made in a legally undefined "sherry style," usually sweet to some degree. If the alcohol content is less than 18 percent, the wine must be labeled "Light Sherry." Palomino is the favored variety for high-class sherries, and is also known in California as the Golden Chasselas or Napa Golden Chasselas. Palomino is the only varietally labeled sherry that is likely to be encountered, since the other grapes used (Mission, Thompson Seedless, and *labrusca*) are hardly worth shouting about. Although legally undefined by Federal Law, the best sherries will often involve the use of flor and will be blended under a solera system. However, the most common production method is to heat the wines for several months in order to replicate sherry's oxidative style, and some efforts are worse than others. Whatever method of production used, there are numerous substyles produced. Some sherries are actually labeled Dry, Medium, or Sweet, in addition to which there are Pale Dry (closer to fino) or Cocktail sherries, which are dry; Golden or Amber sherries, which are medium sweet; and Cream, which is sweet. The best American sherries can be very fine indeed.

**SPARKLING WINE** This term may be used to describe "carbonated," *cuve close*, "bottle-fermented," or *méthode champenoise* wine. If the label bears no other information, the consumer should fear the worst (carbonated or *cuve close*). However, the label may indicate any of the following terms: Champagne, Bottle Fermented, Fermented in this Bottle, Crackling Wine (including Crackling Wine—Bulk Method), and Carbonated Wine.

**SULFITES** It is obligatory for all American wines to state "Contains sulfites" or "Contains sulfiting agent/s" when sulfur dioxide or a sulfuring agent can be detected at a level of 10 or more parts per million.

**TABLE WINE** A wine with an alcohol level not in excess of 14 percent (synonymous with Light Wine).

**TOKAY** All-American blend of Angelica, Dry Sherry (to reduce the sweetness), and a dash of port to provide its characteristic tawny-pink color, Tokay is a medium-sweet dessert wine with a slightly nutty flavor, and 17–24 percent in strength. If less than 18 percent, the wine must be labeled "Light Tokay."

**VINTAGE** At least 95 percent of the wine must be from the vintage indicated. Until the early 1970s, federal regulations demanded that the figure was 100 percent, but winemakers, particularly those producing higher-quality wines aged in small oak barrels, petitioned for a limited margin to enable topping off, and this was granted.

**VOLUME** This must be stated somewhere on the bottle by law.

**Approved Viticultural Areas** There are no AVA rules governing the varieties grown, the methods of vine-training employed, the yields allowed, or the style of wines produced, and AVAs are all the better for it. Although some have evolved to a point where they can be said to favor certain grape varieties and produce identifiable styles, many have not and probably never will. America's AVAs are much maligned by various American critics, yet they are the healthy product of New World free enterprise. The *raison d'être* of the AVA system is truthful labeling: a wine comes from where it says it comes from (or, at least, a minimum of 85 percent must). The AVA process merely establishes the boundary of what must be demonstrated to be a fairly homogenous growing zone, whether small or large. Unfortunately, the law does not insist that the AVA name should be immediately followed by the term "Approved Viticultural Area." As a result, who is to know if a geographical area (or a seemingly geographical area) on a wine label has any official connotation whatsoever?

## HEALTH WARNINGS ON AMERICAN WINE LABELS

The following "Government Warning" must appear on every bottle of wine sold in the United States: 1. According to the Surgeon General, "women should not drink alcoholic beverages during pregnancy because of the risk of birth defects"; 2. "Consumption of alcoholic beverages impairs your ability to drive a car or operate machinery and may cause health problems." In my opinion, however, the warning is grossly misleading and contains half-truths and unsubstantiated claims, while proven health benefits are not included on the label.

As to the first part of the warning, women alcoholics can give birth to children deformed by "fetal alcohol syndrome," but a study of 2,000 Australian women concluded (in line with other reports) that "there is no significant relationship between light and moderate maternal alcohol intake and fetal growth effect." There can be no argument with the first part of the second warning because the "consumption of alcoholic beverages" does "impair" the ability to "drive a car or operate machinery," but, while the second part is true—that alcohol may cause health problems—it is grossly misleading because it does not put into context the word "may." The US government was forced to use this word because only excessive alcohol consumption is a potential health hazard, whereas tests and studies throughout the world, many of them carried out by America's most respected institutions, have shown various benefits to health of drinking alcohol in moderation (*see* Health Benefits of Wine, p.634).

## THE AVAS OF THE UNITED STATES

The very first AVA was, strangely enough, not Napa, but Augusta in Missouri, which was established in June 1980. There are now 188 AVAs and the number continues to rise. Although the establishment of any proposed AVA cannot be taken for granted, very few are likely to be rejected, if the growers making the proposals have done their homework. The boundary might be tweaked, and occasionally the proposed named has been altered, but the only denial in recent memory was for a proposed California Coast AVA, which was not only 650 miles (1,050 kilometers) long, but also penetrated inland, encompassing interior basins and valleys and 5,000-foot- (1,500-meter-) high mountain ranges, as well as shorelines and coastal plains, thus providing no homogeneity of climate. Most applications are, however, more sensibly prepared, and there will, no doubt, be many more AVA proposals to come. For an explanation of why this encyclopedia uses "Approved Viticultural Areas" rather than "American Viticultural Areas," see "AVA" in the Glossary.

**Alexander Valley** California
Est. November 23, 1984
**Alexandria Lakes** Minnesota
Est. August 1, 2005
**Alta Mesa** California
Est. August 16, 2006
**Altus** Arkansas  Est. June 29, 1984
**Anderson Valley** California
Est. September 19, 1983
**Applegate Valley** Oregon
Est. February 12, 2001
**Arkansas Mountain** Arkansas
Est. October 27, 1986
**Arroyo Grande Valley** California
Est. February 5, 1990
**Arroyo Seco** California
Est. May 16, 1983
**Atlas Peak** California
Est. January 23, 1992
**Augusta** Missouri  Est. June 20, 1980
**Bell Mountain** Texas
Est. November 10, 1986
**Ben Lomond Mountain** California
Est. January 8, 1988
**Benmore Valley** California
Est. October 18, 1991
**Bennett Valley** California
Est. December 29, 2003
**Borden Ranch** California
Est. August 16, 2006
**California Shenandoah Valley**
California  Est. January 27, 1983
**Capay Valley** California
Est. February 18, 2003
**Carmel Valley** California
Est. January 15, 1983
**Carneros** or **Los Carneros** California
Est. September 19, 1983
**Catoctin** Maryland
Est. November 14, 1983
**Cayuga Lake** New York
Est. March 25, 1988

**Central Coast** California
Est. November 25, 1985
**Central Delaware Valley**
Pennsylvania and New Jersey
Est. April 18, 1984
**Chalk Hill** California
Est. November 21, 1983
**Chalone** California  Est. July 14, 1982
**Chehalem Mountains** Oregon
Est. December 27, 2006
**Chiles Valley** Caliornia
Est. April 19, 1999
**Cienega Valley** California
Est. September 20, 1982
**Clarksburg** California
Est. February 22, 1984
**Clear Lake** California  Est. June 7, 1984
**Clements Hill** California
Est. August 16, 2006
**Cole Ranch** California
Est. March 16, 1983
**Columbia Gorge** Oregon and
Washington  Est. July 9, 2004
**Columbia Valley** Oregon and
Washington  Est. December 13, 1984
**Cosumnes River**  Est. August 16, 2006
**Covella** California  Est. March 20, 2006
**Cucamonga Valley** California
Est. March 31, 1995
**Cumberland Valley** Maryland and
Pennsylvania  Est. August 26, 1985
**Diablo Grande** California
Est. August 21, 1998
**Diamond Mountain District**
California  Est. July 31, 2001
**Dos Rios** California
Est. November 14, 2005
**Dry Creek Valley** California
Est. September 6, 1983
**Dundee Hills** Oregon
Est. January 31, 2005
**Dunnigan Hills** California

Est. May 13, 1993
**Edna Valley** California
Est. June 11, 1982
**El Dorado** California
Est. November 14, 1983
**Eola-Amity Hills**  Est. August 16, 2006
**Escondido Valley** Texas
Est. May 15, 1992
**Fair Play** California  Est. April 27, 2001
**Fennville** Michigan
Est. October 19, 1981
**Fiddletown** California
Est. November 3, 1983
**Finger Lakes** New York
Est. October 1, 1982
**Fredericksburg** Texas
Est. December 22, 1988
**Grand River Valley** Ohio
Est. November 21, 1983
**Grand Valley** Colorado
Est. November 25, 1991
**Green Valley of Russian River**
California  Est. April 23, 2007
**Guenoc Valley** California
Est. December 21, 1981
**Hames Valley** California
Est. March 27, 1994
**Hermann** Missouri
Est. September 10, 1983
**High Valley** California
Est. August 1, 2005
**Horse Heaven Hills** Washington
Est. August 1, 2005
**Howell Mountain** California
Est. January 30, 1984
**Hudson River Region** New York
Est. July 6, 1982
**Isle St. George** Ohio
Est. September 20, 1982
**Jahant** California
Est. August 16, 2006
**Kanawha River Valley** West Virginia

Est. May 8, 1986
**Knights Valley** California
Est. November 21, 1983
**Lake Erie** New York, Pennsylvania,
and Ohio  Est. November 21, 1983
**Lake Michigan Shore** Michigan
Est. November 14, 1983
**Lake Wisconsin** Wisconsin
Est. January 5, 1994
**Lancaster Valley** Pennsylvania
Est. June 11, 1982
**Leelanau Peninsula** Michigan
Est. April 29, 1982
**Lime Kiln Valley** California
Est. July 6, 1982
**Linganore** Maryland
Est. September 19, 1983
**Livermore Valley** California
Est. October 1, 1982
**Lodi** California  Est. March 7, 1986
**Long Island** New York
Est. July 16, 2001
**Loramie Creek** Ohio
Est. December 27, 1982
**Madera** California  Est. January 7, 1985
**Malibu-Newton Canyon** California
Est. June 13, 1996
**Martha's Vineyard** Massachusetts
Est. February 4, 1985
**McDowell Valley** California
Est. January 4, 1982
**McMinnville** Oregon
Est. March 21, 2005
**Mendocino** California
Est. July 16, 1984
**Mendocino Ridge** California
Est. December 26, 1997
**Merritt Island** California
Est. June 16, 1983
**Mesilla Valley**
New Mexico and Texas
Est. March 18, 1985

What truly amazes me is that a country regarded by the rest of the world as litigation-crazy has a wine industry that does not have the conviction to stand up for itself. I am informed that it would be impossible to prove the Surgeon General's unsubstantiated claim about birth defects in a court of law, so why not hire the largest firm of first-rate lawyers in the country and sue the Surgeon General for $50 billion in lost revenue? Instead, they welcomed with open arms the recently won (1999) right to put the following message on a bottle of wine: "The proud people who made this wine encourage you to consult your family doctor about the health effects of wine consumption." Such is the unempowered state of the US wine industry that some of its members have been absolutely euphoric about this statement, declaring it a small victory in the quest to redress the negative effect of the health warning, but what does it actually say? Wine is so good for you that you should consult your doctor? That sounds more like a warning than a benefit to me. No wonder the Surgeon General approved it.

VINEYARDS, UPSTATE NEW YORK
*Rows of vines combine to form an emerald-green patchwork on the gently sloping countryside near Hammondsport. In the distance is Keuka Lake, one of the finger-shaped lakes that have a moderating influence on the area's climate.*

**Middle Rio Grande Valley** New Mexico Est. February 2, 1988
**Mimbres Valley** New Mexico Est. December 23, 1985
**Mississippi Delta** Louisiana, Mississippi, and Tennessee Est. October 1, 1984
**Mockelumne River** California Est. August 16, 2006
**Monterey** California Est. July 16, 1984
**Monticello** Virginia Est. February 22, 1984
**Mt Harlan** California Est. November 29, 1990
**Mt Veeder** California Est. March 22, 1990
**Napa Valley** California Est. February 27, 1981
**Niagara Escarpment** New York Est. October 11, 2005
**North Coast** California Est. October 21, 1983
**North Fork of Long Island** New York Est. November 10, 1986
**North Fork of Roanoke** Virginia Est. May 16, 1983
**North Yuba** California Est. August 30, 1985
**Northern Neck—George Washington Birthplace** Virginia Est. May 21, 1987
**Northern Sonoma** California Est. June 17, 1985
**Oak Knoll District of Napa Valley** California Est. April 26, 2004
**Oakville** California Est. July 2, 1993
**Ohio River Valley** Indiana, Ohio, West Virginia, and Kentucky Est. October 7, 1983
**Old Mission Peninsula** Michigan Est. July 8, 1987
**Outer Coastal Plain** New Jersey Est. March 12, 2007
**Ozark Highlands** Missouri Est. September 30, 1987
**Ozark Mountain** Arkansas, Missouri, and Oklahoma Est. August 1, 1986
**Pacheco Pass** California Est. April 11, 1984
**Paicines** California Est. September 15, 1982

**Paso Robles** California Est. November 3, 1983
**Potter Valley** California Est. November 14, 1983
**Puget Sound** Washington Est. October 4, 1995
**Ramona Valley** California Est. January 6, 2006
**Rattlesnake Hills** Est. March 20, 2006
**Red Hill Douglas County** Oregon Est. November 14, 2005
**Red Hills Lake County** California Est. September 10, 2004
**Red Mountain** Washington Est. June 11, 2001
**Redwood Valley** California Est. December 23, 1996
**Ribbon Ridge** Oregon Est. July 1, 2005
**River Junction** California Est. July 9, 2001
**Rock Pile** California Est. April 29, 2002
**Rocky Knob** Virginia Est. February 11, 1983
**Rogue Valley** Oregon Est. February 22, 1992
**Russian River Valley** California Est. November 21, 1983
**Rutherford** California Est. July 2, 1993
**Saddle Rock–Malibu** California Est. August 16, 2006
**Salado Creek** California Est. August 30, 2004
**San Antonio Valley** California Est. July 14, 2006
**San Benito** California Est. November 4, 1983
**San Bernabe** California Est. August 30, 2004
**San Francisco Bay** California Est. March 22, 1999
**San Lucas** California Est. March 2, 1987
**San Pasqual Valley** California Est. September 16, 1981
**San Ysidro District** California Est. June 5, 1990
**Santa Clara Valley** California Est. March 28, 1989
**Santa Cruz Mountains** California Est. January 4, 1982

**Santa Lucia Highlands** California Est. June 15, 1992
**Santa Maria Valley** California Est. September 4, 1981
**Santa Rita Hills** California Est. July 30, 2001
**Santa Ynez Valley** California Est. May 16, 1983
**Seaid Valley** California Est. June 20, 1994
**Seneca Lake** New York Est. September 2, 2003
**Shawnee Hills** Illinois Est. December 27, 2006
**Shenandoah Valley** Virginia and West Virginia Est. January 27, 1983
**Sierra Foothills** California Est. December 18, 1987
**Slaughhouse** California Est. August 16, 2006
**Snake River Valley** Idaho & Oregon Est. April 9, 2007
**Solano Country Green Valley** California Est. January 28, 1983
**Sonoita** Arizona Est. November 26, 1984
**Sonoma Coast** California Est. July 13, 1987
**Sonoma Mountain** California Est. February 22, 1985
**Sonoma Valley** California Est. January 4, 1982
**South Coast** California Est. December 23, 1985
**Southeastern New England** Connecticut, Rhode Island, and Massachusetts Est. April 27, 1984
**Southern Oregon** Oregon Est. February 7, 2005
**Spring Mountain District** California Est. May 13, 1993
**St. Helena** California Est. September 11, 1995
**Stag's Leap District** California Est. January 27, 1989
**Suisun Valley** California Est. December 27, 1982
**Temecula Valley** California Est. November 23, 1984
**Texas Davis Mountain** Texas Est. May 11, 1998
**Texas High Plains** Texas Est. March 2, 1992

**Texas Hill Country** Texas Est. November 29, 1991
**Texoma** Texas Est. January 6, 2006
**The Hamptons Long Island,** New York Est. June 17, 1985
**Tracy Hills** California Est. December 8, 2006
**Trinity Lakes** California Est. April 29, 2005
**Umpqua Valley** Oregon Est. April 30, 1984
**Virginia's Eastern Shore** Virginia Est. January 2, 1991
**Wahluke Slope** Washington Est. January 6, 2006

**Walla Walla Valley** Washington and Oregon Est. March 7, 1984
**Warren Hills** New Jersey Est. August 8, 1988
**West Elks** Colorado Est. May 7, 2001
**Western Connecticut Highlands** Connecticut Est. February 9, 1988
**Wild Horse Valley** California Est. November 30, 1988
**Willamette Valley** Oregon Est. January 3, 1984
**Willow Creek** California Est. September 9, 1983
**Yadkin Valley** North Carolina Est. February 7, 2003
**Yakima Valley** Washington Est. May 4, 1983
**Yamhill-Carlton District** Oregon Est. February 7, 2005
**York Mountain** California Est. September 23, 1983
**Yorkville Highlands** California Est. June 8, 1998
**Yountville** California Est. May 18, 1998

# THE LARGEST US WINE GROUPS

*When the New York-based Canandaigua group merged with Australia's BRL Hardy to form Constellation Brands, it replaced E. & J. Gallo as the world's largest wine producer, but it is nowhere near the biggest producer of American wines.*

## 1. E. & J. GALLO

Accounting for more than one-quarter of all US wine sales, this company was founded by Ernest and Julio Gallo, who were driven by tragedy, division and a legendary zeal for hard work to create—in their own words—the "Campbell Soup Company of the wine industry." Elder brother Ernest became head of the family in 1933, after his father, a grape grower, inexplicably killed Ernest's mother and then shot himself. With the end of Prohibition, the brothers began winemaking, selling in bulk until 1940, when the first wines to carry the Gallo label appeared. The Gallo brothers had achieved their ambition by the 1960s, when theirs was easily the most popular wine brand in the US, but they wanted to conquer the world, and the only way to do that was with a profusion of inexpensive brands. By the 1980s, Gallo was the world's largest wine producer, churning out more wine than the annual output of countries like Australia. Ernest and Julio divided everything. Ernest ran the business and marketing, while Julio looked after the production.

Production is estimated at 75 million cases, mostly under penny-pinching labels such as Ernest & Julio Twin Valley Vineyards, Totts, Carlo Rossi, Ballatore, André, Gossamer Bay, Livingston Cellars, Peter Vella, and Wild Vines. Brands sold exclusively to hotels and restaurants (Burlwood, Copperridge, Liberty Creek, and William Wycliff) also represent a significant proportion, whereas mid-priced wines such as Indigo Hills, Turning Leaf, and Redwood Creek do not. The combined turnover of Gallo of Sonoma and the following other authentic wineries (as opposed to "homeless" brands) belonging to E. & J. Gallo is relatively tiny: Anapamu Cellars, Bridlewood, Frei Brothers, Louis Martini, MacMurray Ranch, Marcelina Vineyards, Mirassou Vineyards, and Rancho Zabacca.

## 2. CONSTELLATION BRANDS

Formed by the merger between Canandaigua Wine and BRL Hardy, Constellation Brands produces more than 90 million cases worldwide, some 58 million of which are made by American wineries. Almost 19 million are inexpensive wines from the Mission Bell Winery, 8 million from Vincor (the fifth-largest wine group in the US before it was taken over in 2006), 7 million from Canandaigua, 7 million under Turner Road Vintners, 2.5 million from Widmer Wine Cellars, and 1.8 million from Batavia Wine Cellars. The balance is Mondavi, taken over by Constellation in November 2004, and Columbia Winery, Covey Run, Dunnewood Vineyards, Franciscan Vineyards, Paul Thomas Winery, Simi Vineyards, Ste. Chapelle Winery, and Viña Santa Carolina (Chile).

## 3. THE WINE GROUP

The annual production of this San Francisco–based group is estimated to be over 25 million cases by the following wineries: Colony, Concannon, Corbett Canyon, Franzia, Glen Ellen, Golden State Vintners (Pacific Peak and numerous other brands), Lejon, M.G. Vallejo, Morgan David, Summit, and Alamonte (Argentina).

## 4. JFJ BRONCO

This is the company that gave the world "Two Buck Chuck" and it did so through one of its wineries, Charles Shaw, which accounts for about 5 million of Bronco's 9-million-case production. While other groups were uprooting vineyards, Charles Shaw was siphoning off the excess production from Bronco's other wineries (CC Vineyard, Coastal Ridge, Forest Glen, Hacienda, JFJ, and Napa Ridge), feeding it on to the market exclusively through Trader Joe's in a brilliant marketing coup. Bronco still has its assets in the ground, and instead of paying money out, they have raked it in. Other Bronco brands include: Albertoni Vineyards, Antares Cellar, Bear's Lair, Black Mountain, The California Winery, Cedar Brook, Domaine Napa, Douglas Hill, Estrella, Forestville, Fox Hollow, Gibson Winery, Grand Cru, JJJ, Laurier, J. W. Morris, Montpellier, Salmon Creek, and Silver Ridge.

## 5. DIAGEO

This UK-based group is the largest spirit company in the world. It has a 7-million-case wine portfolio, 90 percent of which is US-based, with wineries that include Beaulieu Vineyards, Blossom Hill, Painted Hills, Sterling Vineyards, and The Monterey Vineyard. In December 2004, Diageo acquired the Chalone Group, which, in addition to Chalone Vineyards itself, includes the California wineries of Acacia Vineyard, Provenance Vineyards, Hewitt Vineyard, Jade Mountain, Moon Mountain Vineyard, Dynamite Vineyards, Orogeny Vineyards, and Echelon Vineyards. Chalone is also joint owner of Edna Valley Vineyard and, in Washington, owns Sagelands Vineyard and Canoe Ridge Vineyard.

## 6. BROWN-FORMAN

Generally perceived to be a Kentucky-based wine and spirits company, Brown-Forman is in fact much more than that, manufacturing everything from china and crystal, through stainless steel and pewter products, to leather and luggage. Its American wine production totals some 6 million cases from the following wineries: Bel Arbor, Bonterra, Fetzer (including the Jekel brand), Korbel, Mariah, One.9, and Sonoma-Cutrer.

## 7. BERINGER BLASS

The wine division of Fosters, the Australian beer group, Beringer Blass's global wine production amounts to 17 million cases, although just 5.5 million are American. Wineries include Beringer Vineyards, Chateau St Jean, Chateau Souverain, Etude, Meridan Vineyards, Stag's Leap Winery, St. Clement, and Windsor.

## 8. JACKSON WINE ESTATES

With interests in Australia, Italy, and Chile as well as the US, annual sales are just over 4 million cases, and the vast majority are under Jess Jackson's core brand, Kendall-Jackson. Other American wineries in this group include Edmeades, La Crema, Stonestreet, Robert Pecota Winery, Murphy Goode, Arrowood Winery, Byron, and Freemark Abbey.

## 9. BEAM WINE ESTATES

Owned by the Australian fine-wine group Lion Nathan, Beam Wine Estates sells 4 million cases globally, thus fewer than that in the US but probably more than the 3 million that Allied-Domecq used to sell, since Beam already owned Geyser Peak, Jakes Fault, XYZin, Gary Farrell Vineyards & Winery, Wattle Creek, and Wild Horse Winery & Vineyards prior to acquiring Atlas Peak Vineyards, Buena Vista, Clos du Bois, J. Garcia, Haywood Estate, and William Hill Winery from Allied-Domecq following its takeover by Pernod-Ricard.

## 10. CORBETT CANYON

Most from this 3-million-case California brand are boxed wines.

# CALIFORNIA

*California's finest wines have become a victim of their own success. Ignoring the ridiculously priced iconic wines, the vast majority of California's greatest wines can stand shoulder-to-shoulder with equivalently priced wines from the classic regions of France, yet while the international market is willing to pay such prices for famous names from Bordeaux, Burgundy, and the Rhône, it is either unwilling or lacks the knowledge to pay the same price for the California wines. This has resulted in midpriced California wines filling the top end of the available line on even the most open-minded export markets. Thus, what is perceived to be the best that California has to offer is not really its best at all.*

CALIFORNIA WAS FIRST SETTLED by the Spanish in 1769 and formed part of Mexico until 1848, when it was ceded to the United States, becoming a state of the Union in 1850. The first California wine was made in 1782 at San Juan Capistrano, by Fathers Pablo de Mugártegui and Gregorio Amurrió. Mission grapes, from vines brought to California by Don José Camacho on the *San Antonio*, which docked at San Diego on May 16, 1778, were used to make the wine. However, it was not until 1833 that *Bordelais* Jean-Louis Vignes established California's first commercial winery. He was the first California winemaker to import European vines and, in 1840, he also became the first to export California wines.

## THE AMAZING HARASZTHY

Eight years before California passed from Mexican to American sovereignty, a certain Hungarian political exile called Agoston Haraszthy de Mokesa settled in Wisconsin. Haraszthy was a colorful, flamboyant entrepreneur in the mold of Barnum or Champagne Charlie. Among other things, he founded a town in Wisconsin and modestly called it Haraszthy (it was later renamed

NAPA VALLEY VINEYARDS
*Of all California's winemaking regions, the Napa Valley is perhaps the best known, and its wines are the most sought after. The first vines were planted here in 1838, and today the valley boasts a vast area under vine, with a bewildering array of grape varieties.*

Sauk City), ran a Mississippi steamboat, and cultivated the first vineyard in Wisconsin—all within two years of beginning a new life in a strange country.

In 1849, Haraszthy moved to San Diego, leaving his business interests in the hands of a partner, who promptly took advantage of a rumor that he had perished during his transcontinental trek, sold all the business and properties, and vanished with the money. Haraszthy was broke, yet within six months he was farming his own 160-acre (65-hectare) fruit and vegetable ranch. Such rapid success followed by disaster then an even greater triumph was to become Haraszthy's trademark. Within a few months of acquiring his ranch, he also became the owner of a butcher's shop and a livery stable in Middleton, a part of San Diego that still boasts a Haraszthy Street. In addition, he ran an omnibus company, started a construction business, was elected the first sheriff of San Diego, was made a judge, and became a lieutenant in the volunteer militia. He also began importing cuttings of numerous European vine varieties.

### The Buena Vista Winery

Having imported no fewer than 165 different vine varieties from Europe, in 1857 Haraszthy purchased 560 acres (230 hectares) of land near the town of Sonoma, in an area called the Valley of the Moon. Here, he built a winery, which he named Buena Vista, and dug six cellars out of the sandstone hill. With north California's

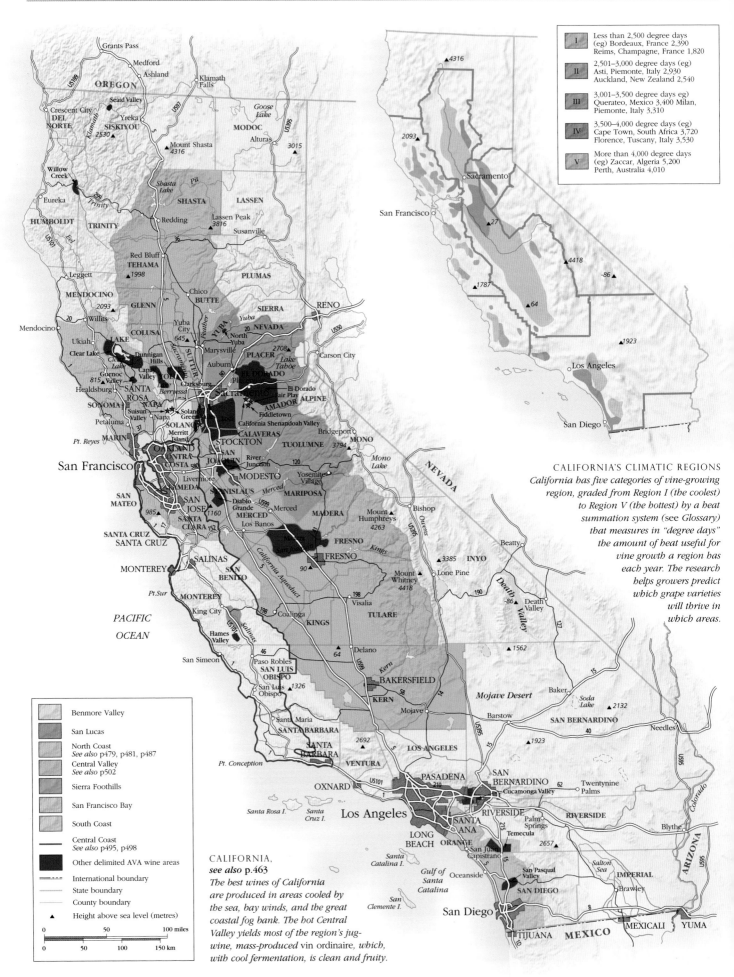

Less than 2,500 degree days
(eg) Bordeaux, France 2,390
Reims, Champagne, France 1,820

2,501–3,000 degree days (eg)
Asti, Piemonte, Italy 2,930
Auckland, New Zealand 2,540

3,001–3,500 degree days eg)
Querateo, Mexico 3,400 Milan,
Piemonte, Italy 3,310

3,500–4,000 degree days (eg)
Cape Town, South Africa 3,720
Florence, Tuscany, Italy 3,530

More than 4,000 degree days
(eg) Zaccar, Algeria 5,200
Perth, Australia 4,010

## CALIFORNIA'S CLIMATIC REGIONS

*California has five categories of vine-growing
region, graded from Region I (the coolest)
to Region V (the hottest) by a heat
summation system (see Glossary)
that measures in "degree days"
the amount of heat useful for
vine growth a region has
each year. The research
helps growers predict
which grape varieties
will thrive in
which areas.*

Benmore Valley

San Lucas

North Coast
*See also p479, p481, p487*

Central Valley
*See also p502*

Sierra Foothills

San Francisco Bay

South Coast

Central Coast
*See also p495, p498*

Other delimited AVA wine areas

International boundary

State boundary

County boundary

▲ Height above sea level (metres)

0        50        100 miles

0     50      100      150 km

## CALIFORNIA,
### see also p.463

*The best wines of California
are produced in areas cooled by
the sea, bay winds, and the great
coastal fog bank. The hot Central
Valley yields most of the region's jug-
wine, mass-produced vin ordinaire, which,
with cool fermentation, is clean and fruity.*

## THE SECOND COMING

Because phylloxera, a root-feeding insect, came from the US to destroy European vineyards, which were saved only when the vines were grafted on to phylloxera-resistant native American varieties, there is a widespread belief that California's vineyards have always been safe. Nothing could be further from the truth. Phylloxera's home was east of the Rockies, where over eons native vines, such as *Vitis berlandieri* and *V riparia*, developed a natural resistance to phylloxera. When European *vinifera* vines were introduced to California, phylloxera was bound to follow, via the wagon trains across the Rockies or on the vines themselves, and *vinifera* varieties proved to be as vulnerable in California as anywhere else.

### THE ANTI-BEAST

Phylloxera was first identified at Sonoma in 1873, coincidentally at the same time as another native American bug, *Tyroglyphus*, was deliberately being shipped to France. The idea of using *Tyroglyphus*, which was harmless to the vine but a deadly enemy of phylloxera, to infect phylloxera-infested vineyards was an imaginative one. Unfortunately, unlike phylloxera, *Tyroglyphus* did not care for the European climate and failed to settle.

In California, the effect of phylloxera was devastating. By 1891, Napa could boast 18,000 acres (7,200 hectares) of vines, but phylloxera multiplies at a terrifying rate (one female bug can be responsible for one billion offspring in twelve, 30-day generation cycles every year) that this had been reduced to a mere 3,000 acres (1,200 hectares). Under the auspices of Professor Hilgard, Head of Agriculture at the Department of Viticulture and Enology in the University of California at Berkeley (established in 1880, moved to Davis in 1906), California's growers eventually adopted the same method as the Europeans to control the pest, grafting *vinifera* vines on to phylloxera-resistant varieties. Ironically, it was some time before Californians realized these wonder vines originated from eastern American states and initially imported them from France! Only half the vineyards had been grafted when they were hit by another, even more lethal, plague—Prohibition. By the late 1940s, UC Davis had assembled one of the most formidable teams of viticultural and oenological experts in the world. Headed by such legendary figures as Amerine, Olmo, and Winkler, the university was primarily responsible for making California the wine force it is today. Along the way, however, they made some errors, such as placing too much emphasis on volume and technical correctness, but the biggest mistake of all was to recommend the widespread use of AxR#1 rootstock.

### ROOT CAUSE

Despite warnings from various European sources about its susceptibility to phylloxera (all acknowledged but brushed aside by numerous university textbooks), UC Davis recommended AxR's use on fertile valley floors, such as Napa, because of its ability to increase yields. As Winkler *et. al.* put it in *General Viticulture*: "This is a case where the choice of (root) stock cannot be based entirely on its resistance to phylloxera."

These words came back to haunt the faculty at Davis in the 1980s, when, slowly but inexorably, vineyards grafted on to AxR failed and the culprit, phylloxera, was identified. Three out of every four vines in California will have to be replaced, which will bring financial ruin to many, although for the California wine industry as a whole, it will ultimately be recognized as a blessing in disguise as undesirable grapes will not only be replaced by selected clones of better-quality varieties, but will also be grafted on to less productive rootstocks and planted at higher densities. The estimated cost of replanting the Napa and Sonoma districts alone is $1.2 billion. Napa was the worst hit, but has tackled the problem far more quickly and effectively than has Sonoma.

### SHARPSHOOTERS

Just as California's growers were counting the cost of dealing with phylloxera, so their vineyards were being invaded by another, possibly more dangerous, bug—*Homalodisca coagulata,* or the Glassy-Winged Sharpshooter. This leaf-hopper is not harmful in itself, but it carries the bacterium that infects vines with Pierce's disease. This disease is considerably faster-acting than phylloxera, killing vines in just one to five years, but what really frightens the industry is that there is no known cure. With no way to defeat Pierce's disease, most efforts have been focused on trying to control its vector, the Glassy-Winged Sharpshooter. In August 2000, David Morgan, a post-doctoral research scientist at the Riverside campus of the University of California, began a program to control the spread of Sharpshooters by releasing their natural enemy, *Gonatocerus triguttatus.* This tiny, stingless wasp had been effective in reducing populations in Texas and Mexico, but has yet to turn the tide in the Golden State, the southern and central counties of which are already infected. Despite Morgan's efforts, it is still predicted that the Glassy-Winged Sharpshooter will probably become a "permanent part of various habitats throughout northern California."

first significant wine estate, Haraszthy won several awards, and he attracted much publicity for both his vineyard and his wine. This venture drew so much attention that, in 1861, the governor of California commissioned Haraszthy to visit Europe and report on its winegrowing areas. Haraszthy's trip took him to every wine region in France, Germany, Italy, Spain, and Switzerland, where he interviewed thousands of winegrowers, took notes, consulted foreign literature, and so accumulated a library of reference material. He returned to the US with a staggering 100,000 cuttings of 300 different vine varieties, only to have the state Senate plead poverty when he presented them with a bill for $12,000 for his trip, although the cuttings alone were worth three times that amount. He was never reimbursed for his trouble and many of the cuttings, which he had expected to be distributed among the state's other winegrowers, simply rotted away.

## CALIFORNIA WINERIES

There are at least 1,367 wineries in California, over half of which sell fewer than 5,000 cases each, while the largest 25 account for 90 percent of all California wine sold on markets worldwide. According to the TTB, there were as many as 2,445 wineries in California in 2006, but there are various reasons why several "virtual" winery names might be located at the same physical address, whereas the Wine Institute's list below is a reliable source of bricks-and-mortar wineries on a county-by-county basis.

| COUNTY | 1990 | 2006 | DIFFERENCE |
|---|---|---|---|
| Alameda | 19 | 32 | 13 |
| Amador | 17 | 26 | 9 |
| Butte | 3 | 4 | 1 |
| Calaveras | 5 | 14 | 9 |
| Contra Costa | 6 | 2 | −4 |
| El Dorado | 11 | 38 | 27 |
| Fresno | 19 | 10 | −9 |
| Humboldt | 4 | 10 | 6 |
| Kern | 7 | 4 | −3 |
| Lake | 8 | 14 | 6 |
| Los Angeles | 16 | 11 | −5 |
| Madera | 5 | 9 | 4 |
| Marin | 8 | 13 | 5 |
| Mariposa | 0 | 3 | 3 |
| Mendocino | 41 | 56 | 15 |
| Merced | 1 | 1 | 0 |
| Modoc | 1 | 0 | −1 |
| Monterey | 20 | 75 | 55 |
| Napa | 211 | 391 | 180 |
| Nevada | 3 | 6 | 3 |
| Orange | 1 | 2 | 1 |
| Placer | 1 | 6 | 5 |
| Riverside | 16 | 24 | 8 |
| Sacramento | 5 | 4 | −1 |
| San Benito | 6 | 8 | 2 |
| San Bernardino | 5 | 3 | −2 |
| San Diego | 7 | 16 | 9 |
| San Francisco | 10 | 1 | −9 |
| San Joaquin | 22 | 37 | 15 |
| San Luis Obispo | 40 | 109 | 69 |
| San Mateo | 10 | 8 | −2 |
| Santa Barbara | 24 | 69 | 45 |
| Santa Clara | 35 | 36 | 1 |
| Santa Cruz | 23 | 25 | 2 |
| Shasta | 1 | 3 | 2 |
| Siskiyou | 0 | 1 | 1 |
| Solano | 9 | 3 | −6 |
| Sonoma | 160 | 260 | 100 |
| Stanislaus | 6 | 7 | 1 |
| Tehama | 0 | 1 | 1 |
| Trinity | 1 | 1 | 0 |
| Tulare | 4 | 3 | −1 |
| Tuolumne | 3 | 3 | 0 |
| Ventura | 5 | 8 | 3 |
| Yolo | 8 | 8 | 0 |
| Yuba | 1 | 2 | 1 |
| **Total** | **808** | **1,367** | **559** |

Haraszthy was not deterred: within seven years he managed to expand Buena Vista to 6,000 acres (2,430 hectares). In doing so, he totally changed the course of Californian viticulture, transferring the focus of attention from the south of the state to the north. At the height of its fame Buena Vista had offices in San Francisco, Philadelphia, Chicago, New York, and London. However, this success was purely superficial, for the vineyard was described in 1864 as "the largest wine-growing estate in the world and the most unprofitable." Haraszthy also suffered a number of losses on the stock exchange and was faced with a new tax on brandy, which resulted in further loss of income. A fire at the winery then destroyed much of his stock and the bank proceeded to cut off his credit.

Enough was enough, even for Agoston Haraszthy de Mokesa. He left California for Nicaragua, where he was successful in obtaining a government contract to distill rum from sugar. An enigmatic character to the end, Haraszthy disappeared altogether in 1869, presumed drowned while trying to cross an alligator-infested stream on his plantation.

## LEARNING CURVE

With California's natural abundance of sun and what to most Europeans seems like America's preoccupation with size, it was perhaps inevitable that the 1950s and early 1960s saw a series of massive, ink-black, tannic Cabernet Sauvignon blockbusters hitting the shelves. The late 1960s witnessed the introduction of high-tech wineries and the use of 100 percent new oak, and the precision of style and focus of fruit that resulted were welcomed at the time, as were the supple tannins that replaced harsh ones. The mid-1970s saw the irresistible rise of Chardonnay, but the wines were blatantly too rich and oaky. Sidetracked by the quest for finesse, the wines went too far in the wishy-washy vintages of 1982 and 1983, when overacidified, tart, and downright stingy wines were made. Some winemakers wanted to sacrifice the voluptuousness that is inherent in this sunny state in a fruitless bid to fabricate some sort of European-styled, slower-developing, longer-lived wine (a number still pursue this misguided idea), but the truly magnificent 1985 vintage, the best year since 1974, was a turning point for California's wine industry. Virtually everyone got it right. Since then, the wines of all those who sought elegance without stripping away their natural expression have deliciously demonstrated that the original quest for finesse was no folly.

This learning curve has established in California, as it has elsewhere, that the secret of fine wine is merely a matter of balance. The difficulty is in achieving it, for perfect balance is by definition a natural state that can be achieved only in the vineyard, not in the winery.

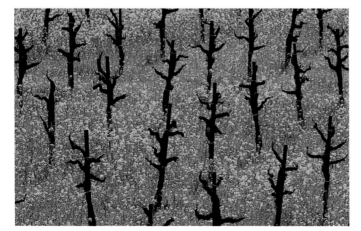

SPRING MUSTARD FLOWERS IN THE NAPA VALLEY
*This bright yellow carpet of mustard seed in full bloom will soon be plowed in as a "green manure" to feed the vines.*

## LONGEVITY

Now that most of California's makers of fine wines have found their direction, the only obstacle to prevent them from achieving their full potential (aside from the vagaries of vintage and occasional overzealousness), is the problem of cellarage temperature. Air conditioning is vital in California, but few people seem to realize that at 57°F (14°C), which seems to be the norm here, potentially fine white wines will fall over after two or three years and the longevity of even the best-quality red wines will be halved. The additional cost of maintaining a temperature just a few degrees lower can be considerable, but once the bottle maturation process has set in, it can only be speeded up, not slowed down, so it is a cost that cannot be cut. The *champenois* know this more than anyone else, since even their cheapest products must spend years in their cellars prior to distribution, which is why they are stored at between 50 and 52°F (10 and 11°C). Once most California cellars are kept at no more than 53.5°F (12°C), the notion that these wines rapidly mature will be shown to be a myth.

## TOO MUCH OF A GOOD THING?

Investors overestimated public demand for sparkling wines in the 1980s, when they copied Domaine Chandon in a number of new dedicated sparkling wine operations (Piper-Sonoma in 1980, Maison Deutz in 1981, Freixenet's Gloria Ferrar in 1982, Roederer Estate in 1982, Mumm Napa in 1985, Taittinger's Domaine Carneros in 1987, and Codorníu in 1991), only to release their products onto a market plateau, sparkling off a bubbly war, as they tried to grab a slice of the shrinking pie. The only real winner was Domaine Chandon, which had already recouped its capital outlay and was the only one that could afford to play the discount game and still make a profit. Also Roederer Estate, which refused to participate, and has subsequently built up a reputation as one of the greatest sparkling wine producers outside of Champagne itself. Domaine Carneros and Mumm Napa have both survived by discounting their entry-level wines, while creating awareness for some of their higher-quality *cuvées*, but Piper-Sonoma is just a label operating out of a small corner of what was once its own proud winery, but was purchased by Judy Jordan for the production of her premium-quality "J" sparkling wine. Maison Deutz has been defunct since 1997, and Codorníu was renamed Artesa and now specializes in upmarket still wines.

History repeated itself on a grander scale at the turn of the 21st century. In the mid-1990s, California was riding on the crest of the French Paradox wave, which started with the *60 Minutes* television program in 1991 and increased per capita wine consumption in the US by almost one third. In 1995, California experienced the largest growth in its wine sales for 20 years, when the industry was hit by a small crop. Sales continued to soar in 1996, and that year's crop was also down. Faced with the prospect of increasing sales and diminishing crops, growers commenced planting new vineyards at such a rate that by 2001 the acreage under vine had increased by more than 60 percent—then global economic decline was heightened by September 11. Wine drinking did not slow down, but consumers became more sensitive to price points. This resulted in $10 wines being discounted to $6, and cheaper wines being sold off anonymously. The ripple effect caused tens of thousands of acres to be grubbed up. This may not have been such a bad thing, since they were mostly fit for little more than blending, but it did seem a bit backward that while vines were being planted at the fastest rate ever in marginal areas like the Atlantic Northeast, vineyards were actually disappearing in sunny California. There was even talk that California's wine glut was affecting sales of its ultrapremium products, but although their prices have dropped, this was not the result of a general sensitivity to price points. The minuscule tip of the California wine market had become overcrowded with $100-plus wines, and their primary patrons, California's new money, eventually realized the value of scarcity.

# CALIFORNIA'S GRAPE VARIETIES

The area under vine in California has increased by almost 165,000 acres since 1995, but obscured by a modest increase in table grapes, and the fact that raisin varieties have actually decreased, this includes an even larger expansion of wine grapes (nearly 175,000 acres). The breakdown of vines in 2003 was as follows:

| VINE TYPE | 1995 ACRES | 2003 ACRES | INCREASED ACREAGE | PERCENTAGE GROWTH |
|---|---|---|---|---|
| Wine grape varieties | 354,417 | 529,000 | 174,583 | 49% |
| Raisin grape varieties | 277,190 | 260,000 | -17,190 | -6% |
| Table grape varieties | 85,539 | 93,000 | 7,461 | 9% |
| TOTAL | 717,146 | 882,000 | 164,854 | 23% |

From the breakdown below of wine grape varieties by color, the swing from red to white wine varieties continues to gather pace. In the 1980s, when the demand for Chardonnay was at its height and most people in the US believed that lighter meant healthier, white wine grapes accounted for as much as 57 percent, but the dominance of white wine sales in the US changed that fateful day in November 1991, when the so-called "French Paradox" (*see* Glossary) was much publicized on CBS television's *60 Minutes* program. It now appears clear that growers took advantage of the costly replanting of phylloxera-ravaged vineyards to swing the pendulum from white grape varieties to black.

| GRAPE COLOR | 1995 ACRES | % | 2003 ACRES | % | INCREASED ACREAGE | PERCENTAGE GROWTH |
|---|---|---|---|---|---|---|
| Black | 142,546 | 55% | 287,075 | 61% | 144,529 | 101% |
| White | 116,979 | 45% | 185,373 | 39% | 68,394 | 58% |
| TOTAL | 259,525 | 100% | 472,448 | 100% | 212,923 | 82% |

## CALIFORNIA'S WHITE GRAPE VARIETIES

In 2003 there were 185,373 acres of white grapes growing in California, with just 12 varieties accounting for almost 96 percent of this total. Again, no surprise which white grape is the fastest growing in the state, but it is strange to see the Burger (a.k.a. Monbadon) coming back into favor, having once been a very widely planted alternative to the Mission grape. It is good to see so much interest in Pinot Gris, even if the imported clones bear very little varietal relation to the spice-laden *sélection massal* from the best established vineyards in Alsace. Latin lovers should be interested to note an almost 7,000% increase (albeit from a minuscule base) in plantings of Catarratto, the prolific Sicilian grape.

| LE5 | FG5 | GRAPE VARIETY | 1995 ACREAGE | 2003 ACREAGE | INCREASED ACREAGE | PERCENTAGE GROWTH |
|---|---|---|---|---|---|---|
| 1. | | Chardonnay | 53,228 | 97,680 | 44,452 | 84% |
| | | French Colombard | 31,325 | 31,865 | 540 | 2% |
| 2. | | Sauvignon Blanc | 7,122 | 15,308 | 8,186 | 115% |
| | | Chenin Blanc | 12,658 | 13,416 | 758 | 6% |
| 3. | 2. | Pinot Gris | 590 | 5,908 | 5,318 | 901% |
| | | Muscat of Alexandria | 3,213 | 3,775 | 562 | 17% |
| 4. | | Viognier | 547 | 2,089 | 1,542 | 282% |
| | | Malvasia Bianca (Vermentino) | 1,616 | 1,857 | 241 | 15% |
| | | Riesling | 1,399 | 1,844 | 445 | 32% |
| 5. | | Burger | 716 | 1,500 | 784 | 109% |
| | | Gewürztraminer | 832 | 1,358 | 526 | 63% |
| | | Semillon 610 | 1,255 | 645 | 106% | |
| | | Muscat Canelli | 638 | 970 | 332 | 52% |
| | | Pinot Blanc | 461 | 627 | 166 | 36% |
| | | Palomino | 573 | 623 | 50 | 9% |
| | | Symphony | 372 | 612 | 240 | 65% |
| | | Ugni Blanc | 274 | 275 | 1 | 0% |
| | | Emerald Riesling | 267 | 267 | 0 | 0% |
| | 5. | Sauvignon Musque | 41 | 184 | 143 | 349% |
| | 3. | Roussanne | 18 | 176 | 158 | 878% |
| | | Muscat Orange | 83 | 163 | 80 | 96% |
| | | Tocai Friulano | 110 | 128 | 18 | 16% |
| | 1. | Catarratto | 1 | 70 | 69 | 6900% |
| | | Marsanne | 39 | 68 | 29 | 74% |
| | 4. | Grenache Blanc | 7 | 64 | 57 | 814% |
| | | Other | 239 | 3,291 | 3,052 | 1277% |
| | | **WHITE WINE TOTAL** | **116,979** | **185,373** | **68,394** | **58%** |

## CALIFORNIA'S BLACK GRAPE VARIETIES

In 2003 there were 287,075 acres of black grapes growing in California, with just 15 varieties accounting for more than 96 percent of this total. It is amazing to think that Zinfandel, which has been the most widely planted classic black variety for decades, could increase acreage by 36 percent, yet be nudged down to third place. Little surprise, however, to see that Cabernet Sauvignon is the fasting-growing black grape in the state, widening the gap between it and Merlot, despite the fashionability of softer-styled red wines from the latter variety. Interesting to note that Primitivo is listed separately from Zinfandel (*see* Zinfandel under The Wine Styles of California, p.478), although combining the two would not affect its positioning, despite the relatively small gap between second and third largest planted black varieties. However, Syrah looks as if it could be the dark horse, expanding from barely more than 2,000 acres to over 17,000 in just eight years.

| LE5 | FG5 | GRAPE VARIETY | 1995 ACREAGE | 2003 ACREAGE | INCREASED ACREAGE | PERCENTAGE GROWTH |
|---|---|---|---|---|---|---|
| 1. | | Cabernet Sauvignon | 27,385 | 75,154 | 47,769 | 174% |
| 2. | | Merlot | 26,605 | 51,973 | 25,368 | 95% |
| 5. | | Zinfandel | 37,032 | 50,199 | 13,167 | 36% |
| 3. | | Pinot Noir | 6,096 | 23,950 | 17,854 | 293% |
| 4. | 3. | Syrah | 2,206 | 17,140 | 14,934 | 677% |
| | | Rubired | 7,039 | 12,467 | 5,428 | 77% |
| | | Barbera | 8,164 | 8,851 | 687 | 8% |
| | | Grenache | 7,057 | 8,668 | 1,611 | 23% |
| | | Ruby Cabernet | 4,972 | 7,472 | 2,500 | 50% |
| | | Petite Sirah | 1,738 | 5,166 | 3,428 | 197% |
| | | Carignane | 5,033 | 5,132 | 99 | 2% |
| | | Cabernet Franc | 1,435 | 3,547 | 2,112 | 147% |
| | | Sangiovese | 881 | 2,603 | 1,722 | 195% |
| | | Carnelian | 882 | 1,637 | 755 | 86% |
| 4. | | Petit Verdot | 144 | 1,096 | 952 | 661% |
| | | Alicante Bouschet | 755 | 1,074 | 319 | 42% |
| 5. | | Malbec | 161 | 1,065 | 904 | 561% |
| | | Tempranillo | 380 | 767 | 387 | 102% |
| | | Mission | 447 | 656 | 209 | 47% |
| | | Mataro (Mourvèdre) | 288 | 644 | 356 | 124% |
| | | Salvador | 554 | 555 | 1 | 0% |
| | | Gamay | 474 | 539 | 65 | 14% |
| | | Royalty | 479 | 480 | 1 | 0% |
| | | Gamay Beaujolais | 362 | 403 | 41 | 11% |
| | | Centurion | 236 | 305 | 69 | 29% |
| | 1. | Primitivo | 18 | 240 | 222 | 1233% |
| | | Meunier | 163 | 207 | 44 | 27% |
| | | Nebbiolo | 113 | 177 | 64 | 57% |
| | | Cinsaut | 57 | 144 | 87 | 153% |
| | | Lambrusco | 103 | 103 | 0 | 0% |
| | | Dolcetto | 47 | 89 | 42 | 89% |
| | | Lagrein | 60 | 86 | 26 | 43% |
| | | Charbono | 40 | 81 | 41 | 103% |
| | | Touriga Naçional | 19 | 81 | 62 | 326 |
| | 2. | Counoise | 5 | 51 | 46 | 920% |
| | | Souzão | 16 | 51 | 35 | 219% |
| | | Other | 1,100 | 4,222 | 3,122 | 284% |
| | | **RED WINE TOTAL** | **142,546** | **287,075** | **144,529** | **101%** |

**Notes**

LE5 = Five largest-expanding varieties by increased acreage.

FG5 = Five fastest-growing varieties by percentage difference.

## THE WINE STYLES OF
# CALIFORNIA

### BARBERA

This Italian grape is mostly cultivated in the Central Valley, where its high natural acidity makes it useful for blending purposes. This said, it is cultivated on a much smaller scale in fine-wine areas, particularly Sonoma, Mendocino, and Sierra Foothills, where a number of wineries produce a pure varietal Barbera in one form or another. Although L'Uvaggio di Giacomo's best Barbera is La Pantera, its Il Gufo is extraordinarily good for a Central Valley wine.

🍷 *3–6 years* (up to 10 in exceptional cases)

🏆 *Eberle • Kunde Estate • L'Uvaggio di Giacomo* (La Pantera) • *Palmina • Preston • Renwood* (Sierra Series) • *Thornton* (Curran Ranch)

### BOTRYTIZED AND LATE HARVEST STYLES

Some of the world's most succulent botrytized and late-harvest wines are made in California. The "sunshine state" brings a wonderfully ripe peachiness to Riesling and mouthwatering tropical fruit freshness to Chenin and Muscat. Several excellent Icewines have been made, including one from Bonny Doon's irrepressible Randall Grahm, even though he openly admits to storing the grapes in his freezer before pressing them! I cannot write this section without mentioning the legendary wines of Sine Qua Non in the Edna Valley, which I have never visited because it is between Pinot Noir wineries, and I have always feared that a stop there could very well kill my dry wine palate for a couple of days. However, it would be unfair to suggest anything other than that its wines should be included on this page.

🍷 *Ready when released* (but last well in bottle)

🏆 *Arrowood* (Riesling Owl Hoot) • *Beringer* (Nightingale) • *Bonny Doon* (Muscat Vin de Glaciere) • *Dolce • Domaine de la Terre Rouge* (Muscat à Petits Grains) • *Château St. Jean* (Special Late Harvest Johannisberg Riesling) • *J. C. Cellars* (Ripken Late Harvest Viognier) • *Martinelli* (Jackass Hill) • *The Ojai Vineyard* (Late Harvest Viognier)

### BOTTLE-FERMENTED SPARKLING WINES

California used to be notorious for its cheap sparkling wine until Schramsberg and Domaine Chandon led the way in the early 1970s. Then in 1991, by dint of tasting back, it could be discerned that a number of houses had come of age with the wines that were made only four years earlier. Roederer Estate, in particular, was in a class of its own, and still is, but so many other producers dramatically improved the style and finesse of their wines that the quality of California sparkling wine in general had quadrupled by 1995.

🍷 *2–5 years* (up to 10 in very exceptional cases)

🏆 *Domaine Carneros* (Le Rêve) • *Gloria Ferrer* (Royal Cuvée) • *Handley* (Vintage Blanc de Blancs, Vintage Brut, Vintage Rosé) • *Robert Hunter* (Vintage Brut de Noirs) • *Iron Horse* (Classic Vintage Brut) • *J* (magnums) • *Mumm* (DVX) • *Roederer Estate*

### CABERNET FRANC

California's cultivation of this Bordeaux variety tripled between 1983 and 1988. At that time, it was primarily used for effecting better-balanced Cabernet Sauvignon blends, and the only pure varietal versions readers were likely to encounter were rosés from the North Coast area. Since then, the area occupied by Cabernet Franc vines has doubled and pure varietals will shortly become commonplace. Top California Cabernet Franc seems to have a fragrance and finesse not dissimilar to the way it performs in the best St.-Émilion vineyards.

🍷 *1–4 years*

🏆 *Detert Family Vineyards • Nevada City Winery • Peju • Pride • Rancho Sisquoc • Raymond Burr Vineyards • Reverie • Gainey Vineyard* (Limited Selection) • *Titus*

### CABERNET SAUVIGNON

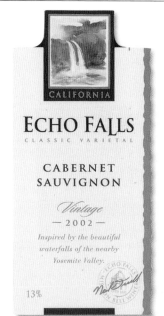

California's most widely planted, and probably potentially its finest, black grape variety. In areas that are too cool, Cabernet Sauvignon wines can have bell-pepper character, or even green bean, but in most other areas they tend to produce saturated, purple-hued wines with a smooth texture, deliciously ripe blackcurrant fruit, and oak-derived notes of vanilla, mocha, cedar, and spice. Oak is now used intelligently and some of the most exciting Cabernet wines are blended with Merlot, Cabernet Franc, and/or Petit Verdot, although not to the extent of a classic blend (*see* Classic Red Blends, and Meritage). At their best, these wines are a match for all but the very greatest vintages of Bordeaux *premiers crus*. Indeed, California is so blessed with Cabernet Sauvignon that it is impossible to come up with a definitive top 10, just 10 of the best, and in compiling the list below I have tried not to go overboard on too many fabulously expensive, virtually unobtainable iconic wines.

🍷 *3–5 years* (inexpensive), *5–12 years* (top wineries), *8–25 (or more) years* (exceptional wines)

🏆 *Abreu • Atalon • Behrens and Hitchcock • Caymus* (Special Selection) • *Colgin* (Tychson Hill) • *Duckhorn* (Estate Grown) • *Dunn • Lewelling Vineyards • Lokoya • Robert Mondavi* (Reserve)

### CARIGNANE

Surprisingly, this rarely sighted varietal is the 11th most widely grown black grape in California, well ahead of more prestigious varieties such as Cabernet Franc. Carignan, or Carignane as it is spelled in the US, provides a high yield of well-colored, strongly flavored wine that can be quite coarse and tannic. It is useful for blending both in California and in its native south of France, where it is one of the 13 grapes permitted in Châteauneuf-du-Pape. It has a less harsh character in California's coastal districts, where some wineries produce a pure varietal version, and very old vines can lose the coarse character, yielding wines of extraordinary depth and quality.

🍷 *3–6 years* (up to 10 years in exceptional cases)

🏆 *Cline* (Ancient Vines) • *Jessie's Grove* (Ancient Vine) • *Ravenswood • Ridge • Windsor* (Oat Valley Vineyards)

### CHARBONO

This variety is the Corbeau, an almost extinct French variety that is also known as the Charbonneau. It produces a wine with vibrant cherry fruit and tingling ripe acidity, in a not dissimilar style to Barbera. Indeed, Inglenook Vineyards, which was the first winery to make a pure varietal wine from this grape, labeled it Barbera until Dr. Winkler of the UC-Davis nursery identified it properly as Charbono.

🍷 *2–4 years*

🏆 *Duxoup • Robert Foley • Turley* (Tofanelli)

### CHARDONNAY

California might be awash with dreadful Chardonnay, but it also boasts more great-quality and/or great-value Chardonnay than ever. Although massive, blockbusting Chardonnays still abound, the best have improved and there have never been so many Chardonnay wines showing as much finesse as they do today. It is at the bottom end of the market where much of the dregs exists. Unlike the readers of this and other wine books, most consumers are no more interested in learning about wine than most drivers are in understanding cars. There is no reason why they should be, but this has resulted in most consumers budgeting for Chardonnay as they would canned goods, and within this price-banding they have come to think of Chardonnay as a brand with recognizable characteristics like butter and vanilla. They do not realize that butter is diacetyl produced by malolactic or that the vanilla is vanillin from oak. Because Chardonnay was the first, biggest, and, for a long time, practically the only wine that most American consumers drank, the signature notes of methods used at that time have become mistaken in consumer psyche as Chardonnay's varietal character. This misconception has prevented Chardonnay as a whole from progressing, particularly at the bottom end of the market. This phenomenon is not unique to the US, but it does seem to be stronger and longer lasting. If the country could only go through a trend for zippy, zingy, unoaked Chardonnay, then it would help raise standards from the basement upward, and this would percolate through to even the most expensive Chardonnay wines, in which it would then become commercially acceptable to allow more fruit to show through. It has to be said that far too many of the most widely acclaimed California Chardonnay wines betray their production techniques on the nose long before they express their fruit or origin. Beware, also, the residual sugar level in some of these wines. There could be dozens of top 10 best California Chardonnays, all of them arguably correct, thus when I have had to make a choice, I have opted for the wine with the most harmonious acidity balance, which provides the longest, most beautifully focused, and graceful finish.

🕐 *2–8 years* (15 or more years in very exceptional cases)

🏆 *Au Bon Climat* (Harmony Nuits-Blanches au Bouge) • *Beringer* (Sbragia) • *Blackjack Ranch* • *Brewer-Clifton* (Sweeney Canyon) • *Cuvaison* (Carneros Estate) • *Du Mol* (Chloe) • *Hartford Court* (Three Jacks) • *Kistler* (Vine Hill Road) • *Martinelli* (Three Sisters Vineyard) • *Walter Hansel* (Cahill Lane)

## CHENIN BLANC

This Loire Valley grape is famous for wines such as the sweet, honey-rich Vouvray and the very dry, searingly flavored Savennières. In California it is the fourth most widely planted white wine grape, yet it is seldom spoken of. Although the recent trend to improve the acidity balance has raised the standard of California Chenin Blanc, it fares less well in this state than it does in France. Since I am not a fan of any but the greatest Chenin Blancs, it is hard for me to work up much enthusiasm for the Chenin Blanc in California. I have long wondered about the veracity of all those books that carry the same spiel—that Clarksburg is the only area to produce a regionally identifiable Chenin Blanc, especially as finding wines with any Central Valley AVA is something of a quest. The now defunct R. & J. Cook winery used to be the most prolific producer of wines bearing the Clarksburg appellation, but produced better Petite Sirah than Chenin. Dry Creek Vineyard is considered by some to produce the best Chenin Blanc, but it used to blend Clarksburg with Sonoma fruit until relatively recently, thus it was never possible to assess Dry Creek Clarksburg Chenin Blanc in its own right. Now we can, of course, and the quality is at least as good as it ever was, so more than 20 years after the Clarksburg AVA was established, we are finally

seeing this appellation make a name for itself. However, although Dry Creek is one of California's best Chenin Blanc wines, collecting more awards for this variety than any other winery in the US, it is not always that special, and others can make much finer wines on occasions. Furthermore, because of the lack of consistency for this varietal and, indeed, the small number of producers, it is sometimes worth checking out the following: Callaway Coastal, Chapellet, Foxen Vineyard, Meador Estate, Sutter Home. All the best wines below are dry or off-dry. *See* Botrytized and Late-Harvest Wines for sweeter styles.

🕐 *1–4 years*

🏆 *Baron Herzog* (Clarksburg) • *Beringer* • *Casa Nuestra* • *Chalone* • *Dry Creek* (Clarksburg) • *Husch* (La Ribera) • *Windsor Vineyards*

## CINSAUT

Until the Rhône-style wine revolution in California, this variety was better known as the Black Malvoisie. There is precious little Cinsault or Cinsaut in the state, even though plantings have increased by more than 150 percent since 1995, and what does exist is mostly used in blends, although Frick continues to make a statement with 30-year-old Cinsaut vines in Sonoma's Dry Creek. There are very few pure Cinsaut wines produced in California; the only others I have come across are Castle (Sonoma), Domaine de la Terre Rouge, and Preston.

🕐 *2–5 years*

🏆 *Frick*

## CLASSIC RED BLEND

On balance I would say that Bordeaux-style blends are more successful in California than pure Cabernet Sauvignon varietals. However, it has proved very difficult to persuade California wine drinkers that they should pay the same price, let alone a premium, for such wines. For this reason the Meritage Association was formed (*see* Meritage), but not all wineries are members and some of the greatest Bordeaux-style blends do not actually use the *portmanteau*. Therefore, many of the best Bordeaux-style blends recommended here and under the producer profiles do not necessarily carry the Meritage designation. Furthermore, this encyclopedia's definition of a Classic Red Blend is not restricted to Bordeaux varieties, and California has experienced a substantial growth in Rhône-style blends since the mid-1990s. In American usage, this encyclopedia's Classic Red Blend can be taken as synonymous with a "Proprietary" red blend, but only from a certain classic quality and upward.

🕐 *3–5 years* (inexpensive), *5–12 years* (top wineries), *8–25* (or more) *years* (exceptional wines)

🏆 *Beringer* (Alluvium) • *Blackjack Ranch* (Harmonie) • *Colgin* (Cariad) • *Dalla Vale* (Maya) • *Harlan* • *L'Aventure* (Cuvée) • *Lewis* (Cuvée L) • *Peter Michael* (Les Pavots) • *Niebaum-Coppola* (Rubicon) • *Pride Mountain Vineyards* (Reserve Claret)

## CLASSIC WHITE BLEND

The combination of Sauvignon and Sémillon is a good one, the traditional view being that the Sauvignon provides the aromatics, freshness, acidity, and crispness, while the Sémillon adds the necessary fat, weight, depth, and

complexity. In some New World areas, however, including California, the Sauvignon is too soft and neutral for this philosophy to work successfully and is much better used to play the Sémillon's role, whereas a small quantity of that grape can, if harvested early enough, provide a grassy herbaceousness that is more like Sauvignon than Sauvignon. The effect is similar, but the reasoning somewhat back to front. This category includes all high-quality white wine blends, not just Bordeaux-style (*see* Meritage). Having found it difficult to whittle down the Classic Red Blends below 30-odd wines, all arguably top-10 material, it is clear that California is far better blessed for its red blends than its whites, as I have failed to find 10 worthy inclusions!

🕐 *2–4 years*

🏆 *Andrew Murray* (Enchanté) • *Beringer* (Alluvium) • *Luna Vineyards* (Bianco) • *Ojai* (Vin du Soleil) • *Signorello* (Seta) • *St Supéry* (Virtú)

## COLOMBARD

Amazingly, this is the second most widely planted white grape in California, and it is not even shrinking, having seen another 540 acres (200 hectares) planted since 1995. Colombard, also known as French Colombard, has always been more than adequate, but its true potential was realized only with the advent of cool fermentation techniques. A pure-varietal Colombard is not a fine-quality wine, but it can be superb value in a totally unpretentious and absolutely delicious way, if it is consumed young and fresh.

🕐 *Upon purchase*

🏆 *De Loach*

## FORTIFIED STYLES

A small number of California wineries are fast catching up with Australia in the fortified wine category. Port is the most successful style. Long before its demise, Inglenook used to be the yardstick for California Palomino Sherry.

🕐 *Ready when released* (but last well in bottle)

🏆 *Bellow Wine Company* (Touriga Nacional Vintage Reserve Port) • *Cedar Mountain* (Chardonnay del Sol) • *Ficklin* (Vintage Port) • *Geyser Peak Winery* (Henry's Reserve Shiraz Vintage Port) • *Guenoc* (Vintage Port) • *Joseph Filippi* (Angelica Elena) • *Joseph Filippi* (Oloroso Sherry Library Reserve) • *V. Sattui* (Madeira) • *Windsor* (Distinguished Cream Sherry)

## FUMÉ BLANC

This term was first coined by Mondavi in the 1970s, who stole and transposed two words from the French appellation Pouilly Blanc Fumé. It was very simple, yet very clever, and by fermenting the wines in oak *barriques*, he was able to sell what was then a very unfashionable grape variety under a new and catchy name. Fumé Blanc is now used as a generic name for a Sauvignon Blanc wine that has been fermented and/or aged in oak, with the results ranging from a subtle, *barrique*-fermented influence to a heavily oaked character. *See also* Sauvignon Blanc.

🕐 *1–3 years*

🏆 *Château St. Jean* (La Petite Étoile) • *De Loach* (Russian River Valley) • *Grgich Hills*

*Cellar* (Estate Grown) • *Robert Mondavi* (To Kalon I Block) • *Murphy-Goode* (Reserve)

## GEWÜRZTRAMINER

Although by no means one of California's commonly encountered varietal wines, Gewürztraminer must be one of its most overrated. The hype surrounding California's Gewürztraminers baffles me—most of them lack not only the varietal definition I expect of any classic grape, but their winemakers will insist on acidifying what is an intrinsically low-acid variety. The only way to extract the true pungency of spice that admirers of this varietal expect is through a prefermentation maceration. The spice will not be immediately apparent when bottled, but requires additional aging for the terpene-laden bottle-aromas to develop. The phenolics picked up from the skins during the prefermentation maceration are essential to the balance and length of such low-acid wines, providing a tactile impression that literally sears the spice on to the palate in its later life. It also gives such wines surprising longevity. The problem is that virtually every winemaker in California has been brainwashed into avoiding phenolics in white wine as if they were the plague. In case American readers should think I am taking an unreasonably European viewpoint, I quote Robert Parker: "Anyone who has tasted fine French Gewürztraminer must be appalled by what is sold under this name in California." About the only thing most California Gewürztraminer has in common with its French counterparts is that classic dry renditions are equally rare.

🍐 *1–3 years*

🍷 *Claiborne & Churchill* (Dry Alsatian Style) • *Fetzer* (Echo Ridge) • *Navarro* • *Windsor Vineyards*

## GRENACHE

Although cultivation of this variety has been in decline in recent years, it still accounts for some 10 percent of California's black grapes and, despite being traditionally associated in this state with medium-dry rosé and tawny-port-type dessert wines, some truly delicious, high-quality pure varietals have surfaced.

🍐 *1–3 years*

🍷 *Alban Vineyards* • *Bonny Doon* (Clos de Gilroy) • *Epiphany* (Revelation Rodney's Vineyard) • *Holly's Hill* (El Dorado) • *Wild Horse* (Equus James Berry Vineyard)

## MALBEC

Although a few wineries are now making good pure varietals from this grape, it has never really caught on in California, where, if it is not ignored entirely, Malbec is merely regarded as a blending component, much as it is in Bordeaux. Perhaps California's winemakers should look more to the 19th-century Black Wines of Cahors than to Bordeaux when considering this variety. When grown ungrafted or on low-yield rootstock, Malbec can produce excellent deep-colored red wines with soft, chewy fruit and has demonstrated the capability of developing much individuality and complexity in most warm climes, particularly when grown on gravelly-clay and marly-clay soils.

🍐 *2–5 years*

🍷 *Arrowood* • *Benzinger* • *Clos du Bois* (L'Étranger) • *Rancho Sisquoc* (Flood Family Vineyard) • *River Run* (Mannstand Vineyard)

## MERITAGE

Concocted from "merit" and "heritage," the term "Meritage" was devised as a designation for upmarket Bordeaux-style blends in 1988, and trademarked the following year. Meritage was first coined by Neil Edgar, who was one of 6,000 entrants in an international contest to come up with a name. There are no rules or regulations governing wines that use this trademark, other than that the wineries must be paid-up members of the Meritage Association, and the blends conform to very simple rules of varietal content. Such blends must consist of two or more of the following varieties: Cabernet Sauvignon, Merlot, Cabernet Franc, Petit Verdot, St. Macaire, Gros Verdot, Carmenère, and Malbec for reds; and Sauvignon Blanc, Sémillon, Muscadelle, Sauvignon Vert, and Sauvignon Musque for whites; with no single variety making up more than 90 percent of the blend. Certainly not the most inspired of American marketing terms, it has nevertheless been adopted by a wide range of wineries and restaurants, which often list these wines separately. The most outstanding, plus the many first-class blends that are not marketed as Meritage, are recommended under the Classic Red Blend and Classic White Blend categories.

## MERLOT

It has always been obvious that Merlot possessed everything required to make it one of California's most fashionable and sought-after

varietals, and that is exactly what it became in the early 1990s. Its lush fruit and velvety texture are tailormade for this sunshine state, although up to 25 percent Cabernet Sauvignon may be blended into supposedly pure varietals in order to give the wines added structure (25 percent if exported to EU countries).

🍐 *3–8 years*

🍷 *Beringer* (Founders' Estate) • *Blackjack Ranch* (Billy Goat Hill) • *Cosentino* (Reserve) • *Gainey Vineyards* (Limited Edition) • *Hartwell* • *Havens Wine Cellar* (Reserve) • *Napa Cellars* • *Newton* (Epic) • *Paloma* • *Pride* (Mountaintop Vineyard)

## MOURVÈDRE

Sometimes known as Mataro, this is one of the most underrated Rhône varieties, and can produce dark, silky-soft, smooth wines that compare to the Syrah, but are not as rich or dense. In California, Mourvèdre can easily acquire a raspberry-jam flavor, which is fine for inexpensive wines and even better as a blending component, although it is possible to find some exciting pure varietals.

🍐 *2–5 years*

🍷 *Bonny Doon* (Old Telegram) • *Cline Cellars* (Ancient Vines) • *Jade Mountain* (Evangelho Vineyard) • *Joseph Filippi* (Library Reserve) • *Ridge* (Mataro) • *Rosenblum Cellars* (Continente Vineyard) • *Sean Thackrey* (Taurus)

## MUSCAT BLANC

*See* Muscat Canelli.

## MUSCAT CANELLI

Also known as Muscat de Frontignan, Muscat Blanc, and Moscato Canelli, this grape is in fact the Muscat Blanc à Petits Grains, and it is surprisingly successful in California, producing some delightfully perfumed, flowery-flavored wines in off-dry through to very sweet and dessert styles. *See* Botrytized and Late-Harvest Wines for even sweeter styles.

🍐 *Upon purchase*

🍷 *Bonny Doon* (Vin de Glaciere) • *Eberle* • *Fresno State Winery* (John Diener Vineyard) • *Maurice Car'rie* • *Rosenblum* (Muscat de Glacier) • *Robert Pecota* (Muscato di Andrea) • *St. Supéry* (Moscato)

## OTHER VARIETALS

This section lists the best examples found of California's rarely encountered varietals, some of which will no doubt become more widely established one day.

🍷 **Albariño** *Havens* • *Verdad*
**Alicante Bouschet** *Topolos*
**Dolcetto** *Mosby*
**Grignolino** *Emilio Guglielmo* (Santa Clara Valley Reserve)*
**Nebbiolo** *Palmina* • *Santa Barbara Winery* (Stolpman Vineyard) • *Thornton* (Curran Ranch)
**Negrette** *De Rose* (Cienega Valley)*
**Orange Muscat** *Quady* (Electra) • *Renwood*
**Pinot Meunier** *Domaine Chandon*
**Sémillon** *St. Supéry* (Dollarhide Ranch)
**Sylvaner** *Rancho Sisquoc*
**Symphony** *Ironstone*
**Teroldego** *Mosby*
**Tempranillo** *Clos du Bois* (Alexander Valley Reserve) • *Gundlach-Bundschu* (Rhinefarm Vineyard) • *Verdad*

(Santa Ynez Valley)
**Trousseau** *Fanucchi Vineyards* (Wood Road Vineyard Gris)*

*Wineries not featured in the following pages.

## PETITE SIRAH

In the first edition I suggested that ignorance was perhaps bliss in the case of California's Petite Sirah. Although California growers had referred to this grape as Petite Sirah since the 19th century, it was unknown to consumers until the 1960s, when varietal wines began to take off. Petite Sirah quickly gained in popularity on the back of the Rhône's Syrah, only for prices to plummet ridiculously in the 1970s, when it was identified as the Durif, a lowly French variety. It was the same wine, but its humble origins obviously lacked cachet for budding new wine consumers of that era. In 1997, Dr. Carole Meredith used DNA "fingerprinting" to determine that only four of the seven Petite Sirahs in the UC Davis collection were in fact Durif, and that one was identified as true Syrah. As consumers began to wonder if their favorite Petite Sirah might not in fact be Syrah, the prestige and price of this varietal wine began to soar. But while 10 percent of Petite Sirah is indeed Syrah, the mix is found on a vine-by-vine basis. Rather than find one vineyard of Syrah for every nine vineyards of Durif, growers find they have 10 percent Syrah in their Petite Sirah vineyards. And not just Syrah. Petite Sirah vines are mostly found in old vineyards, planted with perhaps the odd Peloursin, Carignane, Grenache, Barbera, or Alicante Bouschet, in what is known as a "field blend." Despite increased prices, the purple-colored wine made by Petite Sirah, with its floral, blackfruit aromas, is not considered the equal of a true Syrah (although Switchback Ridge and Turley Cellars Petite Syrah—*sic*—definitely are), thus it remains one of California's most underrated varietals.

ⴑ⤳ *4–8 years*

🏆 *Biale* (Thomann Station) • *Delectus* • *Girard Winery* • *J. C. Cellars* (Frediani Vineyard) • *Jeff Runquist* ("R" Enver Salmon Vineyard) • *La Jota* • *Lava Cap* • *Rosenblum* (Rockpile) • *Switchback Ridge* • *Turley Cellars* (Petite Syrah)

## PINOT BLANC

When grown with care and barrel-fermented, it is virtually impossible to tell Pinot Blanc from a Chardonnay, particularly the examples from Napa, Monterey, and Sonoma. There are some excellent, very serious makers of pure varietal Pinot Blancs, but essentially this is one of California's most underexploited varieties.

ⴑ⤳ *1–3 years*

🏆 *Arrowood* (Saralee's Vineyard) • *Chalone* • *Etude* (Carneros) • *Michel-Schlumberger* (Dry Creek Valley) • *Navarro* • *Steele* (Santa Barbara)

## PINOT GRIS

Even at its best, California Pinot Gris is not at all the spicy heavyweight of Alsace fame, but more like a superior Pinot Grigio, with riper, purer fruit. Many of these wines are in fact sold as Pinot Grigio, which is preferable, as Pinot Gris implies a definite spicy element to the fruit and that is almost impossible to find outside of Alsace.

ⴑ⤳ *Upon purchase*

🏆 *Etude* (Carneros Pinot Gris) • *Gallo of*

*Sonoma* (Sonoma Coast Pinot Gris) • *Luna* (Pinot Grigio) • *Monteviña* (Pinot Grigio) • *Navarro* (Pinot Gris) • *Palmina* (Alisos Vineyard Pinot Grigio)

## PINOT NOIR

Beyond all expectations, this Burgundian grape has found a natural home in parts of California, most notably in Sonoma's Russian River Valley, the Carneros area straddling Sonoma and Napa, and the Santa Ynez Valley in Santa Barbara. Santa Barbara does, I think, have the greatest potential of all; equally fine Pinot Noir will be made elsewhere, but the largest number of Pinot Noir producers will eventually be seen to come from this southerly district. Other areas also show promise, particularly San Benito, Monterey, and the Arroyo Grande.

ⴑ⤳ *2–5 years*

🏆 *Au Bon Climat* (La Bauge Au-dessus) • *Brewer-Clifton* (Melville) • *Gary Farrell* (Rochioli-Allen Vineyards) • *Gainey Vineyards* (Limited Edition) • *Kistler* (Occidental Vineyard Cuvée Elizabeth) • *Martinelli* (Blue Slide Ridge) • *J. Rochioli* (West Block) • *Siduri* (Pisoni Vineyard) • *Talley Vineyards* (Rosemary's Vineyard) • *Williams Selyem* (Rochioli Riverblock Vineyard)

## RIESLING

Also known as Johannisberg Riesling and White Riesling, this grape covers more than 10 percent of California's white-grape vineyards. Aside from a small, but increasing number of sensational, tangy-dry exceptions, most wines are made in a slightly sweet, commercial style to placate consumer demand. I have tried, wherever possible, to shortlist only the drier styles below, as the sweeter ones are found elsewhere. *See* Botrytized and Late-Harvest Wines for sweeter styles.

ⴑ⤳ *1–3 years*

🏆 *Château Montelena* (Potter Valley) • *Claiborne & Churchill* (Dry Alsatian Style) • *Fetzer* (Echo Ridge) • *Kendall-Jackson* (Vintner's Reserve) • *Navarro* • *Rancho Sisquoc* (Flood Family Vineyard) • *Robert Mondavi* (Private Selection) • *Sanford Winery* (Vin Gris Santa Rita Hills) • *Windsor Vineyards* (California)

## ROSÉ OR BLANC DE NOIRS

One of the most overlooked wine styles in California, its well-made, unpretentious rosés can be delicious. All the wines recommended below are dry or off-dry.

ⴑ⤳ *Upon purchase*

🏆 *Bonny Doon* (Vin Gris de Cigare) • *Eberle* (Syrah Rosé) • *Heitz* (Grignolino Rosé) • *Thornton* (Grenache Rosé) • *V. Sattui* (Gamay Rouge—*sic*) • *Verdad*

## SANGIOVESE

Cultivation of this variety has increased over 20-fold since the late 1980s, and much of this is due to the number of winemakers and grape-growers who have Italian ancestry. Its success will depend on the choice of site, where the vine should struggle, so there is no need to employ labor-intensive methods to reduce yields through green pruning.

ⴑ⤳ *3–7 years* (15 years or more in exceptional cases)

🏆 *Atlas Peak* • *Beringer* (Knights Valley) •

*Coturri* (Jessandre Vineyard) • *Luna* (Riserva) • *Pride Mountain Vineyards* • *Saddleback* (Penny Lane Vineyard) • *Seghesio* • *Silverado Vineyards*

## SAUVIGNON BLANC

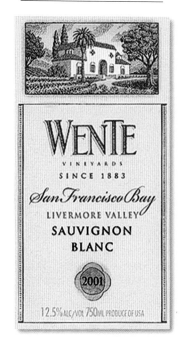

Also known as the Fumé Blanc, a synonym now adopted for an oaked style that is dealt with separately. Many wines labeled Sauvignon Blanc rather than Fumé Blanc are also oaked, but it would be too confusing to list them in this category, so all recommended wines are listed according to their labels, whether they adhere to that style or not. A straight California Sauvignon Blanc should have a crisp style, with the vibrancy of its varietal fruit picked up by, and highlighted with, abundant ripe acidity. California Sauvignon Blanc has, however, an identity problem, as most are soft and neutral, and some are downright wishy-washy. Although there has been a move toward better, more racy acidity by California's best winemakers, the greatest wines from this grape definitely lean more toward a Graves style than varietal purity. There is none of the turbocharged vibrancy of fruit found in New Zealand's Marlborough Sauvignon Blanc, let alone any gooseberry or passionfruit intensity, yet that country built its reputation on the UCD1 clone imported from the US, and until recently, UCD1 was the only clone available for planting in the US. It is about time that Davis reimported UCD1 back from New Zealand, performed comparative trials with the UCD1 motherstock, and made available the Kiwi-evolved UCD1 to growers in the US.

ⴑ⤳ *Upon purchase*

🏆 *Araujo Estate* (Eisele Vineyard) • *Artesa* (Napa Valley Reserve) • *Atalon* • *Gary Farrell* (Redwood Ranch) • *Geyser Peak Winery* (Block Collection) • *Lail* (Georgia) • *Peter Michael* (L'Après-Midi) • *Peju Province* • *J. Rochioli* • *Spottswoode*

## SYRAH

This classic Rhône grape illustrates how quickly things move in California. In the first edition I mentioned how surprised I was that the Syrah

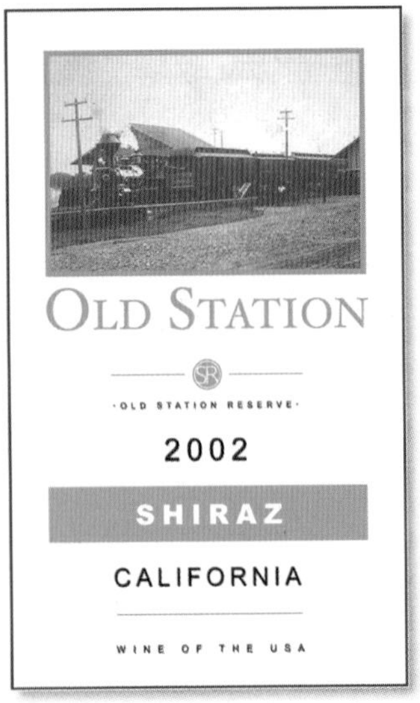


was not more widely planted. Since then it has increased from a modest 110 acres (45 hectares) to a massive 14,934 acres (6,403 hectares), making it the fourth most widely planted variety in California. There is a sumptuousness about California Syrah that makes it a totally different wine from either French Syrah or Australian Shiraz, although when full and ripe all three versions share the silky-*cassis* fruit and have the potential to develop a fine smoky-spicy complexity. From the top Syrahs listed below, it is obvious that this grape can be successfully grown in several areas of California.

*3–10 years*

*Alban* (Lorraine Vineyard) • *Araujo* (Eisel Vineyards) • *Arrowood* (Saralee's Vineyard) • *Blackjack* (Maximus) • *Du Mol* (Eddie's Patch) • *J. C. Cellars* • *Kongsgaard* (Hudson Vineyard) •*Martinelli* • *The Ojai Vineyard* (Thompson Vineyard) • *Pax* (Adler Springs The Terraces)

## VIOGNIER

This great Rhône white-wine grape was nonexistent in California until 1985, when the first vines were planted by Joseph Phelps, thus when the first edition of this book was published in 1988 they were not even bearing fruit. At that time, just 11 acres (4.5 hectares) of these vines existed. Now there are more than 2,000 acres (800 hectares), and it is the fourth largest-expanding white varietal in the state. While the vine seems to thrive in California, the wines seldom capture its elusive character. The same could be said about Château Grillet, of course, but if Condrieu has been able to overcome Viognier's inherent difficulties, there was no reason why more California winemakers could not follow suit. And in a way they have, as it is one of California's most successful white wines. What does bother me, however, is that the notoriously difficult Viognier should thrive so well in the golden state: not only is there no problem with flowered vines failing to fruit, but the yield is exceptionally high even by the greediest French grower's standard. This leads me to suspect the authenticity of the vines being sold as Viognier in California. Or, if indeed they are genuine, to wonder what else might have been eradicated during the eight years it took UC Davis to remove the virus from its Viognier bud stock before release. Perhaps the exquisiteness that makes the best Viognier wines great can be achieved only through debilitated vines? Because, although very successful, far too many are overtly floral, instead of being peachy-floral or, at least, fruity-floral, with too much residual sweetness (aside from those that are made in a Late-Harvest style, and should be sweet), and too little acidity, making them flabby. Authentic Viognier is not overblessed with acidity, but when it is grown at low yields, and harvested physiologically ripe, rather than sugar-ripe, there is a certain acid balance that, together with the proper fruit structure, will provide sufficient grip and length to avoid any connotation of flabbiness.

*Upon purchase*

*Alban* (Alban Estate Vineyard) • • *Alan Murray* (Calzada Vineyard) *Arrowood* (Saralee's Vineyard) • *Calera* • *Cold Heaven* • *Eberle* (Mill Road Vineyard) • *Failla* (Alban Vineyard) • *Foxen* (Rothberg Vineyard) • *J. C. Cellars* (Ripken Vineyard) • *Pride Mountain Vineyards*

## ZINFANDEL

This was once thought to be America's only indigenous *Vitis vinifera* grape, but was later positively identified by Dr. Carole Meredith as the Primitivo grape of southern Italy by Isozyme "fingerprinting," a method of recording the unique pattern created by the molecular structure of enzymes found within specific varieties. However, this led to a conundrum because the earliest records of Primitivo in Italy date from the late 19th century, whereas the Zinfandel name appears in the nursery catalog of William Prince of Long Island, dated 1830. One clue was that Italian growers often referred to their Primitivo as a foreign variety. This led Meredith farther afield and, with the help of Croatian researchers, she was able to announce in 2002 that the Zinfandel and Primitivo are in fact an obscure variety called Crljenak Kastelanski (pronounced Sirl-YEN-ak Kastel-ARN-ski). Referred to as Crljenak, for short, this grape was once widely planted throughout Dalmatia and on more than 1,000 islands, but has mostly been replaced by Croatia's best-known variety, Plavac Mali (the result of a cross-pollination of Crljenak and Dobricic). Nothing special has been produced so far by Crljenak in its homeland, but there will no doubt be efforts to see what can be achieved with it in the future. In the meantime, UC Davis has imported Crljenak and when it has gone through the regulated clean-up process (possibly by 2008), they intend growing it side by side with Primitivo and Zinfandel, to see which local characteristics these "localized clones" of the same variety might possess. Since the Crljenak gave way to Plavak Mali in Croatia because its tight grape clusters attracted rot, it would seem to be much closer to the tight-clustered Zinfandel than Primitivo, which has much looser fruit clusters. It is not unreasonable to surmise that the Primitivo clone probably adapted to the much hotter, drier local conditions in southern Italy by developing looser-hung berries.

Some growers have already started to vinify Primitivo separately from Zinfandel, and one day we shall probably see the emergence of California Crljenak. When this happens, it would make sense also to develop a blend of all three, and it strikes me that the new UC Davis classication for these grapes—ZPC—would be the ideal name for such *cuvées*. Depending on the way it is vinified, Zinfandel produces many different styles of wine, from rich and dark to light and fruity, or *nouveau* style, from dry to sweet, white to rosé, dessert wine or sparkling. The reason for such a variation in styles is that it is virtually impossible to harvest Zinfandel when all the grapes have an even ripeness. When most of the bunch achieves perfect ripeness, some grapes are green, but if the grower waits for these to ripen, the shoulder clusters quickly raisin. There are several ways to overcome this, but they are all labor-intensive, seemingly wasteful, and inevitably costly, which is why great Zinfandel is never cheap. Great Zinfandel is as rich and deep-colored as only California could produce, with ripe, peppery-spicy fruit, liquorice intensity, and a chocolate-herb complexity. When young, such wines are chewy and have classic berry-fruit flavors, which can swing toward black-cherry or simply have a gluggy-jamminess. It is the only varietal that positively demands the coconutty aromas of American oak, and it is often improved when blended with Petite Sirah for increased backbone. This is a wine that requires a certain amount of bottle-aging to bring out the dried-fruit spiciness.

Zinfandel is not one of California's longest-lived wines, but without sufficient time in bottle, the wine will merely have a richness of oak and berry fruits, and lack complexity. Massive, black, opaque Zinfandels with 16.5 percent plus of alcohol are on the increase, but they are grotesque abominations, and certainly do not stir my soul as they obviously do those of numerous American critics. I don't know what difference in style Crljenak might possess on California soil, but when Primitivo is vinified by the same winemaker, it is usually less alcoholic (just a 0.5 percent reduction), and a little softer, with less berry fruit and less "sweet and sour" flavor.

*2–5 years* (good but inexpensive wines), *5–15 years* (expensive, more serious styles)

*DeLoach* (OFS) • *Edmeades* (Zeni Vineyard) • *Gary Farrell* (Maple Vineyard) • *Hartford Court* (Hartford Vineyard) • *Martinelli* • *Nalle* (Reserve) • *Rosenblum* • *Storybook Mountain* (Estate Reserve) • *Turley Cellars* (Hayne Vineyard) • *Williams-Selyem* (Forchini Vineyard)

# MENDOCINO COUNTY

*The best vineyards here are located on the fork of the Navarro and Russian rivers in the south of Mendocino, a district that has become a byword for top-quality California sparkling wine since the emergence of Roederer Estate. Such is the climatic variation here that some excellent Zinfandel is made, and aromatic varieties may also do very well.*

IN THE EARLY 1980S, Champagne Louis Roederer sunk some $15 million into a 500-acre (200-hectare) vineyard and winery in the Anderson Valley, where the climate is considerably cooler than that of surrounding areas. A nonvintage wine in the *champenois* tradition, the first, 1986-based release was nothing special and has not improved over the years, yet the 1987-based release was the best sparkling wine produced anywhere in the world outside of Champagne itself, a quality that has been maintained ever since. The diversity of *terroir* within the sparkling-wine growing areas of Mendocino provides a fascinating contrast of styles, for Scharffenberger, just around the corner from Roederer, could hardly make a wine more different from Roederer. Whereas Roederer is rich, well-structured, and potentially complex in a style that leans decidedly toward Champagne, Scharffenberger is all lightness and elegance with a purity of fruit that gains in finesse every year. There are lots of reasons for this over and above that of *terroir*, including the good old joker in the pack—man—but it does suggest that we are witnessing the very earliest stages of development in California's sparkling-wine industry. In 20 years' time there is every chance that the state's best sparkling-wine areas will be known, planted, and exploited to the extent that each will have many producers making contrasting styles from neighboring vineyards.

## GROWTH OF MENDOCINO'S WINE INDUSTRY

Because parts of Mendocino are too hot for classic wine production, there has been a tendency in the past to plant highly productive vines for jug-wine blends. However, the county has a complex climate, and there are some areas where coastal influences dominate and cooler Region I and II climates (*see* p.470) prevail. This has been recognized by the substantial amount of premium-quality varietals that were planted in the late 1970s, and by the rise in the number of wineries in the area, from 16 in 1981 to 29 in 1985 and 41 in 1995.

## FACTORS AFFECTING TASTE AND QUALITY

### LOCATION
100 miles (160km) northwest of San Francisco, Mendocino is the most northerly of the major viticultural coastal counties.

### CLIMATE
The mountain ridges surrounding the Upper Russian and Navarro rivers climb as high as 3,500ft (1,070m) and form a natural boundary that creates the reputed transitional climate of Mendocino. This climate is unusual in that either coastal or inland influences can dominate for long or short periods, although it generally has relatively warm winters and cool summers. This provides for a growing season with many warm, dry days and cool nights. The Ukiah Valley has the shortest, warmest growing season north of San Francisco.

### ASPECT
Mainly flat ground on valley bottoms or gentle, lower slopes at a height of 250 to 1,460ft (76 to 445m), with some rising to 1,600ft (490m). The vines generally face east, though just south of Ukiah they face west.

### SOIL
Deep, diverse alluvial soils in the flat riverside vineyards, gravelly-loam in parts of the Russian River Valley, and a thin scree on the surrounding slopes.

### VITICULTURE AND VINIFICATION
The average growing season is 268 days, compared with 308 in Sonoma (bud-break is 10 days earlier here), and 223 days in Lake County.

### GRAPE VARIETIES
**Primary varieties**: Cabernet Sauvignon, Carignan, Chardonnay, Chenin Blanc, Colombard, Sauvignon Blanc, Zinfandel
**Secondary varieties**: Barbera, Burger, Cabernet Franc, Charbono, Early Burgundy, Flora, Folle Blanche, Gamay, Gamay Beaujolais, Gewürztraminer, Grenache, Gray Riesling, Green Hungarian, Malvasia Bianca, Merlot, Muscat Blanc, Palomino, Petite Sirah, Pinot Blanc, Pinot Noir, Ruby Cabernet, Sauvignon Vert, Sémillon, Sylvaner, Syrah, White Riesling

MENDOCINO, *see also* p.470
*This area's northerly location need not mean harsher microclimates. Inland regions are protected by the mountains, although the Anderson Valley is cooler.*

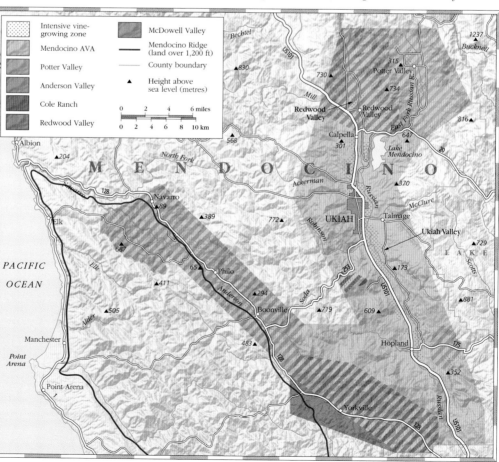

Intensive vine-growing zone
Mendocino AVA
Potter Valley
Anderson Valley
Cole Ranch
Redwood Valley
McDowell Valley
Mendocino Ridge (land over 1,200 ft)
County boundary
▲ Height above sea level (metres)

0 2 4 6 miles
0 2 4 6 8 10 km

## THE APPELLATIONS OF
# MENDOCINO COUNTY

### ANDERSON VALLEY AVA

Of some 57,600 acres (23,300 hectares) in this area, a mere 600 acres (240 hectares) have been planted with vines. Anderson Valley's coastal-influenced microclimate is cooler than in the rest of Mendocino. This is seen as one of California's coolest wine-growing areas, but temperatures do rise the frther southwest that vines are grown. The valley's soil consists of more than 20 alluvial soils, providing the diversity required for wineries such as Roederer Estate and Scharffenberger to produce a variety of base wines, the building blocks of any fine-quality sparkling wine. This area is also suitable for aromatic varieties such as Gewürztraminer and Pinot Gris, and farther inland Cabernet Sauvignon and Zinfandel are possible.

### COLE RANCH AVA

Situated in a small, narrow valley, this appellation consists of just 62 acres (25 hectares) of Cabernet Sauvignon, Chardonnay, and Johannisberg Riesling vineyards, all owned by the Cole family. Soils range from gravelly-clay loam to gravelly-silty clay.

### MCDOWELL VALLEY AVA

The McDowell Valley enjoys the protection of the mountains encircling it. Its vineyards are restricted to the gravelly-loam soils at around 1,000 feet (300 meters), other soils being unsuitable for vines. The microclimate here warms up when other areas are having spring frosts, although it is slightly cooler in the growing season.

### MENDOCINO AVA

This may only be used for wines produced from grapes that are grown in the southernmost third of the county. It encompasses four other smaller AVAs plus surrounding vineyards.

### MENDOCINO COUNTY AO

This appellation (not an AVA) covers the wines from anywhere within the county of Mendocino.

### POTTER VALLEY AVA

This appellation consists of 27,500 acres (11,130 hectares) situated northwest of Clear Lake, some 11,000 acres (4,450 hectares) of which are under vine. Vines grow on the valley floor and are protected by the surrounding hills.

### REDWOOD VALLEY AVA

This area is where the first Mendocino vines were planted. It has been known as Redwood Valley since it was settled in the mid-1850s and covers 35 square miles (90 square kilometers), with some 2,300 acres (930 hectares) of area under vine already in existence. The grapes ripen later than in the hotter and drier Ukiah area, providing higher acidity, color, and tannin.

### YORKVILLE HIGHLANDS AVA

Geographically, but not topographically, this appears to be an extension of the Anderson Valley AVA. Yorkville Highlands has a rocky soil with high gravel content, and a cool climate that is comparable to the middle of the Anderson Valley. Sauvignon Blanc does well here, and this AVA could also favor red Bordeaux varieties.

## THE WINE PRODUCERS OF
# MENDOCINO COUNTY

### ONTERRA
**Ukiah**
◉★✫Ⓥ

Part of the Brown-Forman group, but its organic philosophy proves that big business can be good guys too.

🗸 *Chardonnay • Merlot*

### EDMEADES VINEYARDS
**Philo**
★★✫

Part of the Kendall-Jackson group.

🗸 *Zinfandel*

### FETZER VINEYARDS
**Redwood Valley**
★Ⓥ

Owned by Brown-Forman, Fetzer produces good-value wines.

🗸 *Cabernet Sauvignon • Gewürztraminer • Merlot • Pinot Noir* (Ben Nacido Vineyard Reserve, Five Rivers Ranch) *• Syrah • Zinfandel*

### FREY
**Redwood Valley**
Ⓑ✫

The oldest and largest fully organic winery in the US, Frey was set up in 1980 and was the first US winery to produce biodynamic wines. Just over 10 percent of its wine is biodynamic.

🗸 *Petite Sirah* Ⓑ *• Sangiovese • Syrah*

### GREENWOOD RIDGE VINEYARDS
**Philo**
✫Ⓥ

An underrated winery best known for its Riesling, particularly its Late Harvest, although other varieties are well worth a look.

🗸 *Cabernet Sauvignon • Classic red blend* (Home Run Red) *• Pinot Noir • White Riesling* (Late Harvest)

### HANDLEY
**Philo**
★Ⓥ

An excellent, underrated *méthode champenoise* specialist. Handley's crisp Vintage Brut has creamy-vanilla richness, but he also makes flavorful Pinot Noir and Sauvignon Blanc of increasing elegance.

🗸 *Pinot Noir* (Estate Reserve) *• Sauvignon Blanc* (Handley Vineyard) *• Sparkling wine* (Vintage Brut) *• Syrah*

### HUSCH VINEYARDS
**Philo**
✫Ⓥ

Founded by Tony Husch, this winery was sold in 1979 to Hugo Oswald, the current owner and winemaker, who also has large vineyard holdings in the Anderson and Ukiah Valleys, from which his unpretentious white-wine varietals always stand out.

🗸 *Chardonnay • Chenin Blanc* (La Ribera) *• Muscat Canelli* (La Ribera) *• Sauvignon Blanc* (La Ribera)

### NAVARRO VINEYARDS
**Philo**
★Ⓥ

Some critics believe these vineyards produce some of California's best Gewürztraminer, although I think they have the potential to do much better. If I had to name the worst varietal for a sparkling wine, it would probably be Gewürztraminer, and I've only come across four producers stupid enough to try. Yet Navarro is the exception that proves the rule. It has nothing to do with classic sparkling wine as we generally perceive it, but there are far more spicy bottle-aromas in Navarro's fizzy Gewürztraminer than there are in its regular still wine. If you can appreciate the finest Riesling Sekt and sparkling Shiraz, then you really should try Navarro Sparkling Gewürztraminer. Otherwise, it's the purity of fruit found in the Pinot wines that most attracts me to this producer at the moment.

🗸 *Pinot Blanc • Pinot Gris • Pinot Noir • Riesling* (Riesling Cluster Select) *• Sparkling wine* (Gewürztraminer)

### PARDUCCI WINE CELLARS
**Ukiah**
✫Ⓥ

Parducci is a large winery, with over 351 acres (142 hectares), which was founded in Sonoma in 1918 and moved to Ukiah in 1931, where a new winery was built in preparation for the end of Prohibition. The wines are clean and fruity, and possess a good depth of flavor for their price.

🗸 *Petite Sirah • Zinfandel* (Zingaro)

### ROEDERER ESTATE
**Philo**
★★★✫Ⓥ

The first New World venture to achieve a quality of sparkling wine comparable not just to Champagne, but to very good Champagne, Roederer Estate (or Quartet as it is known on export markets) ages like no other California sparkling wine. L'Ermitage is the greatest wine here, but the standard nonvintage Brut can be almost as stunning. A bottle of the 1994-based nonvintage, which was disgorged in February 1997 and matured in my own cellar until 2002, still displayed beautifully pristine fruit of great finesse, when most California sparkling wines of a similar age would be as dead as a dodo.

🗸 *Entire range*

### SCHARFFENBERGER CELLARS
**Ukiah**
★✫Ⓥ

Founded by John Scharffenberger in 1981 and part-owned by Pommery until it was transferred to Veuve Clicquot. After it was decided to change the name to Pacific Echo, a soulless name with no sense of place, the writing was on the wall. Veuve Clicquot did nothing to encourage exports and even thwarted efforts to promote the brand abroad. It came as no surprise when Pacific Echo was purchased in July 2004 by the Roederer-owned Maisons Marques & Domaines USA, and announced that it would drop Pacific Echo in favor of a return to the original Scharffenberger name. The company has retained Tex Sawyer, who has been the winemaker from the start; he has slowly and consistently increased the elegance and finesse of these sparkling wines.

🗸 *Sparkling wine* (Blanc de Blancs, Rosé)

# SONOMA COUNTY

*Six fertile valleys combine to make Sonoma County California's most prolific wine-producing area, with an output comprising equal quantities of red and white wine, and a reputation for quality now fast approaching that of Napa County.*

BECAUSE OF THE VOLUME of its production, Sonoma County was classed as little more than a source of blending wine until the late 1960s. It produced better-quality blending wine than the Central Valley, admittedly, but that wine was still nothing more than pep-up fodder for the bulk-produced anonymous generics. Then, in 1969, Russell Green, a former oil mogul and owner of a fast-growing vineyard in the Alexander Valley, purchased Simi, a once-famous winery founded in 1876, but at the time in decline. Green had great plans for Simi, many of which he successfully carried out, but soaring costs forced him to sell up in 1973. During those four brief years, however, he managed to restore the pre-Prohibition reputation of the old winery by creating a new genre of high-quality varietal Sonoma wines. With this achievement, he made other winemakers in the district ambitious to improve the quality of their own wines.

Not only did this result in a very pleasing plethora of interesting vinous delights, but Green's activity also attracted new blood to the area. By 1985 there was a remarkable total of 93 wineries, and since then the number has increased to a staggering 210.

## FACTORS AFFECTING TASTE AND QUALITY

**LOCATION**
North of San Francisco, between Napa and the Pacific.

**CLIMATE**
Extremes of climate range from warm (Region III, *see* p.470) in the north of the county to cool (Region I, *see* p.000) in the south, mainly due to ocean breezes. Fog is prevalent around Petaluma.

**ASPECT**
Sonoma Valley creek drains into the San Francisco Bay, and the Russian River flows directly into the Pacific. The vines grow at an altitude of approximately 400 feet (120 meters) on flatland, or on the gentle lower slopes. Steeper slopes are being cultivated in the Sonoma Valley.

**SOIL**
The soil situation varies greatly, from low-fertile loams in the Sonoma Valley and Santa Rosa areas, to highly fertile alluvial soils in the Russian River Valley, with limestone at Cazadera, a gravelly soil in Dry Creek, and vent-based volcanic soils within the fallout vicinity of Mount St. Helena.

**VITICULTURE AND VINIFICATION**
Bulk winemaking is no longer important in the Russian River Valley; boutique wineries specializing in premium varietals have taken over.

**GRAPE VARIETIES**
**Primary varieties:** Cabernet Sauvignon, Chardonnay, Chenin Blanc, Colombard, Gewürztraminer, Merlot, Petite Sirah, Pinot Noir, Pinot Blanc, Sauvignon Blanc, White Riesling, Zinfandel
**Secondary varieties:** Aleatico, Alicante Bouschet, Barbera, Cabernet Franc, Carignan, Chasselas Doré, Folle Blanche, Gamay, Gamay Beaujolais, Grenache, Malbec, Malvasia, Muscat Blanc, Palomino, Pinot St. George, Ruby Cabernet, Sauvignon Vert, Sémillon, Sylvaner, Syrah

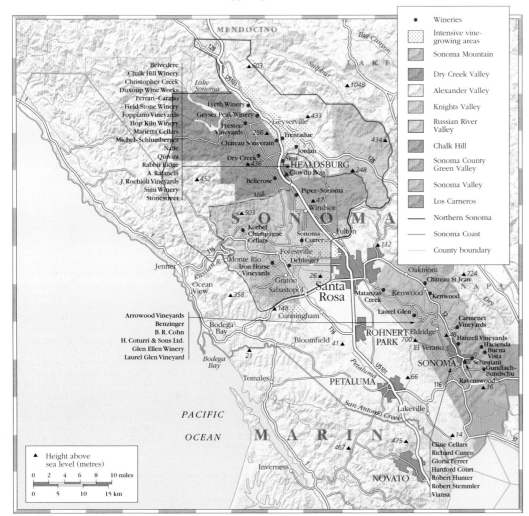

**DRY CREEK VALLEY**
*Sonoma's Dry Creek lies close to the Russian River, of which Dry Creek is a tributary. Moist and fertile, the valley has a gravelly soil unique to the area, enabling it to claim AVA status.*

**SONOMA COUNTY** *See also p.470*
*One of California's most important wine regions, Sonoma has a varied climate with different soils, which produce a broad spectrum of wines. It is perhaps aptly named, as Sonoma is derived from the local Wintun Native American word for "nose."*

# THE APPELLATIONS OF
# SONOMA COUNTY

## ALEXANDER VALLEY AVA

Located in the northeast of the county, this appellation extends from the banks of the Russian River into the foothills of the Mayacamas Mountains. In 1986 its boundaries were extended so that it overlapped the Russian River AVA, and were further extended in 1990 to incorporate Sir Peter Michael's Gauer Ranch and Ellis Alden's Chestnut Springs vineyards in the foothills east of Geyserville. Cabernet Sauvignon and Merlot are ideally suited to this area, where very fine Nebbiolo, Sangiovese, and Chardonnay can also be produced. Formerly part of Dry Creek AVA, the Gill Creek watershed area was reclassified as Alexander Valley AVA in 2001.

## CHALK HILL AVA

This appellation covers 33 square miles (85 square kilometers) and encompasses 1,600 acres (650 hectares) of vineyards rising in altitude from 200 to 1,300 feet (60 to 400 meters). There is no chalk here; the soil's whiteness is in fact derived from volcanic ash with a high quartzite content. Emitted by Mount St. Helena over many centuries, the ash has mixed with local sandy and silty loams to provide a deep soil that is not particularly fertile. This area is protected by a thermal belt that promotes a September harvest, compared with October in surrounding areas.

## DRY CREEK VALLEY AVA

This appellation faces that of the Alexander Valley across the Russian River. Its climate is generally wetter and warmer than surrounding areas, with a longer growing season than the Russian River appellation to the south, and varietal suitability is very flexible, stretching from Sauvignon Blanc to Zinfandel. The Gill Creek watershed area was declassified as Dry Creek in 2001, and reclassified under the Alexander Valley AVA.

## KNIGHTS VALLEY AVA

Knight's valley covers an area of approximately 55 square miles (140 square kilometers) containing 1,000 acres (400 hectares) of vineyards. The vines grow on rocky and gravelly soil of low fertility at altitudes that are generally higher than those in the adjacent AVAs, making it ideal Cabernet country.

## LOS CARNEROS AVA

The Los Carneros, or simply Carneros, appellation covers an area of low, rolling hills that straddle the counties of Sonoma and Napa. This was originally sheep country, but the cool sea breezes that come off San Pablo Bay to the south provide an excellent fine-wine growing climate, especially for Chardonnay, Pinot Noir, and sparkling-wine varieties.

## NORTHERN SONOMA AVA

The large appellation of Northern Sonoma completely encapsulates six other AVAs, those of Alexander Valley, Chalk Hill, Dry Creek Valley, Knights Valley, Russian River Valley, and Sonoma County Green Valley, and is separated from the Sonoma Valley appellation to the south by the city of Santa Rosa.

## RUSSIAN RIVER VALLEY AVA

The name Russian River began appearing on wine labels as recently as 1970, although vineyards in this region date from the 19th

century. The early-morning coastal fog provides a cooler growing season than that of neighboring areas, making the Russian River Valley very well suited to Pinot Noir—and indeed it produces some of California's finest Pinot Noir wines. In September 2003, this AVA was expanded to include 767 acres (307 hectares) south of Fulton.

## SONOMA COAST AVA

An appellation covering 750 square miles (1,940 square kilometers), Sonoma Coast AVA is made up of the area directly inland from the length of Sonoma's Pacific coastline—the AVA's western boundary. It is significantly cooler than other areas because of the persistent fog that envelops the Coast Ranges, the mountains that are within sight of the Pacific Ocean.

## SONOMA COUNTY GREEN VALLEY AVA

Originally it was proposed that this area within the Russian River Valley AVA be called, simply, Green Valley, but to avoid confusion with Solano County's Green Valley appellation, it was decided to add "Sonoma County." The climate here is one of the coolest in the Russian River Valley and the soil is mostly fine sandy loam, well suited to sparkling wine.

## SONOMA MOUNTAIN AVA

This tiny appellation is within the Sonoma Valley AVA. Sonoma Mountain AVA has a thermal belt phenomenon that drains cold air and fog from its steep terrain to the slopes below, creating a climate that is characterized by more moderate temperatures than the surrounding areas.

## SONOMA VALLEY AVA

The first vines were planted here in 1825 by the Mission San Francisco de Sonoma. Rainfall is lower than elsewhere in the county and fog rarely penetrates the Sonoma Mountains. It is red-wine country; particularly for Cabernet Sauvignon and Zinfandel.

# THE WINE PRODUCERS OF
# SONOMA COUNTY

### A. RAFANELLI
#### Healdsburg
★

It was always said that Americo Rafanelli, who died in 1987, made wine "as they used to in the olden days." Well, he would be proud of the blockbusters made by his son David from this small, unirrigated, hillside vineyard.

✓ *Zinfandel*

### ALEXANDER VALLEY VINEYARDS
#### Healdsburg
★ⓥ

An underrated winery built on the original homestead of Cyrus

Alexander, who gave his name to the Alexander Valley, now a famed AVA. Most products are well worth buying as value-for-money, everyday drinking wines, but some are much finer than that, despite their modest prices, and the Cyrus comes precariously close to making the top 10 classic red blends in California.

✓ *Cabernet Sauvignon • Chardonnay* (Wetzel Family Estate) • *Classic red blend* (Cyrus) • *Merlot • Pinot Noir*

### ARROWOOD VINEYARDS
#### Glen Ellen
★★ⓥ

Richard Arrowood makes very stylish wines and the quality gets

better each year, as he hones down his varietals. Excellent-value second label (Grand Archer). Now part of Jackson Family Wine Estates.

✓ *Cabernet Sauvignon* (Grand Archer, Réserve Spéciale) • *Chardonnay* (Cuvée Michel Berthod) • *Merlot* (Grand Archer, Réserve Spéciale) • *Pinot Blanc • Riesling* (Special Select Late Harvest Riesling Hoot Owl) • *Syrah • Viognier*

### B R COHN
#### Glen Ellen
⭐

Sometimes you have to spit the splinters out of these wines, but you

cannot deny the quality and have to admire the enthusiasm.

✓ *Cabernet Sauvignon* (Olive Hill) • *Merlot* (Sonoma Valley)

### BELVEDERE
#### Healdsburg
★ⓥ

Large vineyards enable owner Bill Hambrecht to make a wide range of wines. He used to excel at Chardonnay, but his best and most consistent wines are now Merlot and Zinfandel.

✓ *Merlot* (Healdsburg Ranches) • *Zinfandel* (Healdsburg Ranches)

## BENZIGER
### Glen Ellen
**B★★♥**

Since selling its Glen Ellen and M. G. Vallejo high-volume brands to Heublein, Mike Benziger now concentrates on producing more focused, quality wines under the family name. His highly successful Imagery series now has its own winery off Highway 12.

✓ *Cabernet Sauvignon* (Sonoma Coast) • *Chardonnay* (Carneros) • *Pinot Noir* (Sonoma Coast) • *Syrah* (California)

## BUENA VISTA WINERY
### Sonoma
**★♥**

Haraszthy's original winery (*see* p.469) is now owned by Allied-Domecq. Buena Vista's Carneros Estate wines are usually good value, particularly the Cabernet Sauvignon and Pinot Noir.

✓ *Cabernet Sauvignon* (Carneros Estate, Grand Reserve)

## CARMENET VINEYARD
### Sonoma
**★♥**

Owned by Chalone Vineyards of Monterey, Carmenet offers some excellent-value wines.

✓ *Cabernet Sauvignon* (North Coast Dynamite) • *Merlot* • *Sauvignon Blanc* (Reserve)

## CHALK HILL WINERY
### Healdsburg
**★**

This excellent operation was known as Donna Maria Vineyards when the owner only grew and sold grapes, but became Chalk Hill Winery when it first began to make and sell wines in 1981. Chardonnay has always been a major focus, and in the 2000 vintage Chalk Hill released a fascinating collection of six single-clone versions of this varietal.

✓ *Cabernet Sauvignon* (Estate Bottled) • *Chardonnay* (Estate Bottled)

## CHÂTEAU SOUVERAIN
### Geyserville
**★♥**

Good-value basic range, but the Winemaker's Reserve is seldom any better.

✓ *Merlot* (Alexander Valley) • *Sauvignon Blanc* (Alexander Valley) • *Zinfandel* (Dry Creek Valley)

## CHATEAU ST JEAN
### Kenwood
**★♥**

Prior to former Japanese owners (Suntory) selling this prestigious winery to Beringer, the style of some of these wines had already swung from overt richness to elegance. The quality remains, but some American critics are less appreciative of the change.

✓ *Cabernet Sauvignon* (Sonoma Coast, Sonoma Coast Reserve) • *Chardonnay* (Robert Young Vineyard Reserve) • *Classic red blend* (Cinq Cépages) • *Merlot* (Sonoma Coast) • *Riesling* (Special Late-Harvest) • *Sauvignon Blanc* (Fumé Blanc La Petite Étoile)

## CHRISTOPHER CREEK
### Healdsburg
**★★**

Formerly known as the Sotoyme Winery, Christopher Creek was snapped up by Englishman John Mitchell, who makes a wonderfully deep, rich, smoky Petite Sirah and, even better, a silky, stylish Syrah.

✓ *Petite Sirah* (Russian River Estate Bottled) • *Syrah* (Reserve, Russian River Estate Bottled) • *Zinfandel* (Dry Creek Valley)

## CLINE CELLARS
### Sonoma
**★★♥**

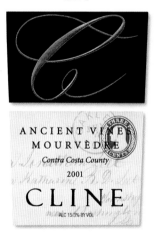

These excellent Rhône-style wines range from the jammy Côtes d'Oakly to the serious, oaky Mourvèdre, but it is the superb range of full-throttle, all-American Zinfandel wines that Cline is truly famous for.

✓ *Carignane* (Ancient Vines) • *Mourvèdre* (Ancient Vines, Late Harvest) • *Syrah* (Los Carneros) • *Zinfandel* (Ancient Vines)

## CLOS DU BOIS
### Healdsburg
**★★♥**

Owned by Allied-Domecq, Clos du Bois has made fleshy, well-textured, medal-winning wines from its

impressive 925 acres (370 hectares) of vineyards under a variety of highly talented winemakers.

✓ *Cabernet Sauvignon* (Alexander Valley Reserve, Winemaker's Reserve) • *Chardonnay* (Flintwood) • *Classic red blend* (Marlstone) • *Malbec* (Winemaker's Reserve) • *Merlot* (Winemaker's Reserve) • *Pinot Noir* (Sonoma Coast) • *Syrah* (Shiraz) • *Tempranillo* (Alexander Valley Reserve) • *Zinfandel* (Dry Creek Valley Reserve, Russian River)

## H. COTURRI & SONS LTD.
### Glen Ellen
**●★♥**

A wide range of sometimes excellent varietals, but as is often the case with organic winemaking, the quality ranges between rustic and brilliant. If they are drunk on release, the best examples of the following can be mind-blowing. The Albarello is essentially Zinfandel and Petite Sirah field-blend that includes a hodgepodge of other varieties.

✓ *Carignane* • *Charbono* • *Classic red blend* (Albarello) • *Sangiovese* • *Zinfandel* (Chauvet, Freiberg, Workingman's)

## DE LOACH VINEYARDS
### Santa Rosa
**★★♥**

This winery's signature wine used to be Chardonnay, but the reputation of De Loach is now firmly embedded in its exceptional range of Zinfandel wines. Anyone who does not like Zinfandel or is hard to please should really try De Loach, as these wines are the smoothest you are ever likely to encounter. Top of the range wines are sold as OFS (Our Finest Selection). De Loach was acquired by Burgundy's Jean-Claude Boisset in 2003.

✓ *French Colombard* • *Pinot Noir* (OFS) • *Sauvignon Blanc* (Russian River Valley Fumé Blanc) • *Zinfandel*

## DRY CREEK VINEYARD
### Healdsburg
**★★♥**

Not all of David Stare's elegant Dry Creek Vineyard wines actually come from the Dry Creek Valley AVA.

✓ *Cabernet Sauvignon* • *Chenin*

*Blanc* (Clarksburg) • *Fumé Blanc* • *Zinfandel* (Heritage, Old Vines)

## DU MOL
### Orinda
**★★**

Although based in Orinda, this small operation produces some of the classiest Chardonnay and Pinot Noir in the Russian River Valley, not to mention one of California's finest Syrahs.

✓ *Chardonnay* • *Pinot Noir* • *Syrah*

## DUXOUP
### Healdsburg
**★★**

The first time I visited Duxoup managed to get lost and asked to be excused for being over two hours late, but Andy Cutter waved away my apology with "Don't worry, when your colleagues Robert Joseph and Charles Metcalfe paid a visit, they were two days late," and I am very happy to say the wines are equally laid-back.

✓ *Charbono* • *Sangiovese* (Gennaio) • *Syrah*

## FERRARI-CARANO
### Healdsburg
**★★♥**

Don and Rhonda Carano sold up their Reno casino and hotel to buy 500 acres (200 hectares) of Sonoma vineyards in 1981, and their Italian-styled wines have always been a special feature.

✓ *Classic red blend* (Sienna, Tresor) • *Dessert style* (Eldorado Noir) • *Fumé Blanc*

## FISHER VINEYARDS
### Santa Rosa
**★★♥**

With two hillside vineyards situated in the Mayacamas Mountains and another one on the Napa Valley floor, Fred Fisher has always crafted some high-quality wines, but in particular from his Cabernet Sauvignon grapes.

✓ *Cabernet Sauvignon* (Lamb Vineyard, Wedding Vineyard) • *Chardonnay* (Unity, Whitney's Vineyard) • *Merlot* (RCF Vineyard)

## FRITZ CELLARS
### Cloverdale
**★♥**

This winery is best known for Chardonnay and Sauvignon, but it is the intense, extraordinarily long-lived Zinfandel that excites most. Particularly the Old Vine, made from a combination of 50-, 60-, and 80-year-old vines, and Rogers Reserve, from 100-year-old vines.

✓ *Cabernet Sauvignon* • *Zinfandel* (Old Vines)

## GARY FARRELL
### Healdsburg
★★

Gary Farrell makes truly special Russian River Pinot Noir, full of style, and rich in fruit, with amazing finesse and complexity.

✓ *Chardonnay* (Redwood Ranch) • *Classic red blend* (Encounter) • *Pinot Noir* • *Sauvignon Blanc* (Redwood Ranch) • *Zinfandel* (Maple Vineyard)

## GALLO OF SONOMA
### Healdsburg
❂★★Ⓥ

Gina and Matt Gallo literally moved hillsides to create this estate, but they have been unable to bulldoze away the prejudice that exists in some quarters against anything remotely connected with the Gallo empire, while true enthusiasts just let the wine do the talking.

✓ *Barbera* (Barrelli Creek) • *Cabernet Sauvignon* • *Chardonnay* • *Pinot Gris* (Sonoma Coast) • *Zinfandel* (Frei Ranch Vineyard)

## GEYSER PEAK WINERY
### Geyserville
★★★Ⓥ

Hugely underrated because of low price points, but the Block Collection range is a stunning success, and Australian winemaker Daryl Groom is a magician with even the least expensive, most modest of wines.

✓ *Cabernet Sauvignon* (Block Collection) • *Chardonnay* (Alexander Valley Reserve, Block Collection, Ricci Vineyard, Sonoma County) • *Classic red blend* (Reserve Alexandre Meritage) • *Fortified* (Henry's Reserve Shiraz Vintage Port, Tawny Port) • *Merlot* (Sonoma County) • *Riesling* (Late Harvest Reserve) • *Sauvignon Blanc* (Block Collection, California, Russian River Valley) • *Shiraz* (Sonoma County Reserve) • *Viognier* (Block Collection) • *Zinfandel* (Sonoma County)

## GLORIA FERRER
### Sonoma
★★Ⓥ

Established by Cava-giant Freixenet in 1982 and named after the wife of José Ferrer, the Spanish firm's president, Gloria Ferrer. Bob Iantosca, Gloria Ferrer's ponytailed winemaker might look as if he was left behind when the hippies trecked north to Oregon, but he is very much at home in the new millennium California, as his outstanding Royal Cuvée testifies. Royal Cuvée might not be the most expensive wine in the range, but it is certainly the best.

✓ *Sparkling wine* (Blanc de Noirs, Carneros Rosé, Royal Cuvée, Sonoma Brut)

## GUNDLACH-BUNDSCHU WINERY
### Sonoma
★

High-quality Cabernet and Zinfandel from the fifth generation of the family of the founder, Jacob Gundlach, this winery also shows promising signs for other varietals.

✓ *Cabernet Sauvignon* (Rhinefarm Vineyard) • *Tempranillo* (Rhinefarm Vineyard) • *Zinfandel* (Rhinefarm Vineyard)

## HACIENDA WINE CELLARS
### Sonoma
★Ⓥ

This operation used to encompass part of Haraszthy's original Buena Vista vineyard, but the brand was sold in 1993 to the Bronco Wine Company. Although little more than a label for pan-California wine blends, there are some amazing bargains.

✓ *Chardonnay* (Claire de Lune) • *Dry Chenin Blanc*

## HANZELL VINEYARDS
### Sonoma
★★

James Zellerbach, the founder of Hanzell Vineyards, revolutionized the California wine industry in 1957 by aging a Chardonnay wine in imported Burgundian *barriques*. The emphasis today of the 100 percent estate-bottled wines is *terroir*, rather than oak.

✓ *Chardonnay* • *Pinot Noir*

## HARTFORD COURT
### Sonoma
★★½

Owned by Don Hartford, who is married to the daughter of Jess Jackson of Kendall-Jackson fame, Hartford Court makes extremely classy Pinot Noir and Chardonnay, and a huge, oaky Zinfandel that is definitely out to grab attention.

✓ *Chardonnay* (Arrendell Vineyard) • *Pinot Noir* (Arrendell Vineyard) • *Zinfandel* (Hartford Vineyard)

## HOP KILN
### Healdsburg
★★Ⓥ

The hop-drying barn that houses Hop Kiln winery was built in 1905, and has been declared a national historic landmark. A Thousand Flowers is a very inexpensive, unpretentious, soft, flowery, off-dry blend of Riesling, Chardonnay and Gewürztraminer.

✓ *Classic white blend* (A Thousand Flowers) • *Zinfandel* (Old Windmill Vineyard, Primitivo Vineyard)

## IMAGERY ESTATE
### Glen Ellen
★★Ⓥ

Mike Benziger's Imagery series now has its own dedicated winery, and has branched out into single-vineyard varietals.

✓ *Cabernet Franc* (BlueRock Vineyard) • *Cabernet Sauvignon* (Ash Creek Vineyard) • *Merlot* (Sunny Slope Vineyard)

## IRON HORSE VINEYARDS
### Sebastopol
★★½

Once the only railroad stop in Sonoma Green Valley, hence the name (it also gave rise to its second label, Tin Pony), Iron Horse is famous for its textbook *méthode champenoise*, but also makes some elegant Pinot Noir wines that only reveal their hidden depth with food.

✓ *Pinot Noir* • *Sparkling wine* (Blanc de Blancs, Blanc de Blancs LD, Classic Vintage Brut, Rosé, Russian Cuvée)

## J. ROCHIOLI VINEYARDS
### Healdsburg
★★

The Rochioli family has been growing grapes at this long-established vineyard since the 1930s, but did not build a winery until 1984, making their first wine the following year. They now offer a large range of all too drinkable estate-bottled wines, including some of the most velvet-textured, varietally pure Pinot Noirs in all of California.

✓ *Pinot Noir* • *Sauvignon Blanc*

## J. WINE COMPANY
### Healdsburg
★★½

Established in 1986 by Judy Jordan, who rented space in her father's Jordan Winery until 1997, when she purchased Piper Sonoma's specialist sparkling wine facility, renaming it the J Wine Company. J sparkling wine was fundamentally perfected by the 1990/1991 vintage, and magnums have a particularly noticeable effect on these wines, thus well worth the investment. Like all sparkling wine ventures that diversify into still wines, the crossover was not entirely smooth, as such wineries are designed for something entirely different. However, following extensions to the winery, including new equipment and a barrel room, the still wines have become more polished in recent years.

✓ *Pinot Gris* (Russian River Valley) • *Pinot Noir* (Nicole's Vineyard, Russian River Valley) • *Sparkling wine* (Brut)

## JORDAN
### Healdsburg
★★½

This winery majors on rich, complex Cabernet Sauvignon, and is gradually honing its Chardonnay into a much finer wine than it used to be.

✓ *Cabernet Sauvignon* • *Chardonnay*

## JOSEPH SWAN VINEYARDS
### Forestville
★

For the son of teetotal parents, the late Joe Swan was an extraordinary winemaker in many senses, and his son-in-law, Rod Berglund, has continued his tradition of producing very small batches of high-quality wines, with Zinfandel his most consistent style.

✓ *Zinfandel*

## KENWOOD VINEYARDS
### Kenwood
★Ⓥ

Concentrated wines with good attack are consistently produced at these vineyards.

✓ *Cabernet Sauvignon* (Art Series, Jack London Vineyard) • *Chardonnay* (Russian River Reserve) • *Pinot Noir* (Olivet Reserve, Russian River Reserve) • *Sauvignon Blanc* (Sonoma County)

## KISTLER VINEYARDS
### Trenton
★★★½Ⓥ

Mark Bixler and Steve Kistler are outstanding single-vineyard Chardonnay specialists, who also turn out masterly Pinot Noir. No apologies for the value rating. Put these Sonoma Coast wines side by side with Burgundies of the same price, and Kistler wins more often than not.

✓ *Chardonnay* • *Pinot Noir*

## KORBEL CHAMPAGNE CELLARS
### Guerneville
❓

No wine encyclopedia would be complete without mention of California's leading sparkling-wine specialist in the popular sector, even though I have been able to recommend only one of its wines on a consistent basis. While the odd blend of this and that *cuvée* might rise above the norm, only Korbel Rouge is worthy of recommending year in, year out. The irony is, of course, that this medium-sweet red bubbly is usually the one that most critics turn their noses up at, yet its bold color and equally bold flavors, enhanced with some sweetness, would not fare too badly in a blind tasting of highly respected Australian sparkling reds. Owned by Brown-Forman.

✓ *Sparkling red* (Rouge)

## KUNDE ESTATE
### Kenwood
★★½

Kunde Estate winery was set up by a well-established group of Sonoma growers who started selling their own wines in 1990, and have rapidly made a huge impact with critics and consumers alike.

✓ *Cabernet Sauvignon* (Drummond) • *Chardonnay*

(Kinneybrook Wildwood) • *Sauvignon Blanc* (Magnolia Lane) • *Zinfandel* (Robusto)

## LA CREMA
### Geyserville
### ★☆♥

With a well-deserved reputation for reasonably priced, high-quality Chardonnay and Pinot Noir from the Russian River (9 Barrel being top of the range), La Crema also produces less expensive wines of reliable quality from the Sonoma Coast AVA.

✓ *Chardonnay* (9 Barrel, Russian River) • *Pinot Noir* (9 Barrel, Anderson Valley, Carneros, Russian River)

## LANDMARK VINEYARDS
### Windsor
### ★

These vineyards are best known for Chardonnay of a much fatter, richer, more complex style than they used to be, and are now developing a growing reputation for Pinot Noir.

✓ *Chardonnay* (Lorenzo) • *Pinot Noir* (Kastania Vineyard)

## LAUREL GLEN VINEYARD
### Glen Ellen
### ★☆

Laurel Glen offers a succulent Sonoma Mountain Cabernet Sauvignon, with Counterpoint as a half-price version. Reds is a seriously underrated classic red sold for under $10 a bottle. The 2002, for example, contained 60 percent Zinfandel from 80-year-old vines, 30 percent Carignane from 117-year-old vines, plus 10 percent Petite Sirah.

✓ *Cabernet Sauvignon* • *Classic red blend* (Reds)

## LAURIER
### Forestville
### ★♥

Formerly called Domaine Laurier, with production restricted to a 30-acre (12-hectare) vineyard, this is now a brand belonging to the Bronco Wine Company.

✓ *Cabernet Sauvignon* (Dry Creek Valley) • *Chardonnay* (Los Carneros) • *Merlot* (Dry Creek Valley)

## LYETH WINERY
### Geyserville
### ☆

Pronounced "Leeth," this was an exciting new winery in the 1980s, but when the founder died in a plane crash in 1988, it was sold off and is now owned by Burgundian *négociant* Boisset. The second label is Christophe.

✓ *Classic red blend* (Lyeth) • *Classic white blend* (Lyeth)

## MARIETTA CELLARS
### Healdsburg
### ★

Owner-winemaker Chris Bilbro started up this operation in 1980,

after selling off his share in the Bandeira Winery, which he had established while still working as an administrator for Sonoma State Hospital. He built his reputation on lush Merlot and great-value wines.

✓ *Classic red blend* (Old Vine Red) • *Petite Sirah* • *Zinfandel* (Cuvée Angeli)

## MARIMAR ESTATE
### Sebastopol
### ★☆

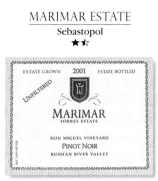

Miguel Torres planted his sister's vineyard with Chardonnay and Pinot Noir, at three to four times the normal density for California. These high-density vines work best for Pinot Noir, which has a combination of silky fruit, finesse, and age-worthiness that is uncommon in California.

✓ *Chardonnay* (Dobles Lias) • *Pinot Noir*

## MARTINELLI VINEYARDS
### Fulton
### ★★

Experienced grape growers, who turned winemakers in the early 1990s, the Martinelli family turns out limited quantities of lush, stylish wines under the guidance of Helen Turley. The range includes wonderfully classy Pinot Noir, stunning Syrah and Zinfandel, and sumptuous late-harvest Muscat Alexandria.

✓ *Entire range*

## MATANZAS CREEK WINERY
### Santa Rosa
### ★☆

This small, highly reputed winery has been owned by Jess Jackson and Barbara Banke of Kendall-Jackson since 2000, when the founding McIver family retired and sold up. The style is fine, rich, and elegant, with a signature of good fruit-acidity, probably better suited to European palates than American.

✓ *Cabernet Sauvignon* • *Chardonnay* • *Sauvignon Blanc*

## MICHEL-SCHLUMBERGER
### Healdsburg
### ☆

Formerly known as Domaine Michel Winery, under the ownership of Swiss-born Jean-Jacques Michel, but it is now in collaboration with Jacques Schlumberger, whose family comes from Alsace.

✓ *Cabernet Sauvignon* • *Chardonnay* (La Brume) •

*Merlot* (Dry Creek Valley) • *Pinot Blanc* (Dry Creek Valley)

## NALLE
### Healdsburg
### ★★

Doug Nalle was winemaker at Quivira, when he started making Zinfandel under his own label in 1984. His Zinfandel wines are usually augmented with 6–12 percent of Petite Sirah, Syrah, Carignane, Alicante Bouchet, and Gamay, and aged exclusively in French oak. They are not the massive monsters that win gold after gold or make national headlines, but the British appreciate them.

✓ *Zinfandel*

## PAX
### Santa Rosa
### ★★★☆

Former Dean and Deluca wine-buyer Pax Mahle established California's fastest-rising Syrah superstar as recently as 2000, and the mesmerizing quality of his low-yield, hands-off, single-vineyard wines has charmed the critics off their perch.

✓ *Entire range*

## PELLEGRINI FAMILY VINEYARDS
### South San Francisco
### ★♥

These vineyards produce delicious, vividly flavored red wines, with oodles of fresh fruit.

✓ *Cabernet Sauvignon* (Cloverdale Ranch) • *Merlot* (Cloverdale Ranch) • *Pinot Noir* (Olivet Lane Estate) • *Zinfandel* (Eight Cousins)

## PETER MICHAEL WINERY
### Calistoga
### ★★

With no expense spared, Englishman Sir Peter Michael has applied New World technology to the very best of traditional methods to produce some of the classiest wines in California. Air conditioning is vital in California, but this winery has computer-controlled steam jets to maintain sufficient humidity to reduce evaporation through the staves of new oak to virtually zero. The goal is for the wines not to overwhelm when served with food, but to build in finesse and complexity in the glass, and this is achieved most of the time. Some of the Chardonnays can be far too soft, flabby even, but when this varietal has a good acidity balance (such as the 2001 and 2002 Point Rouge, or the 2002 Cuvée Indigène), they are a match for the greatest Chardonnays from California and the Côte d'Or.

✓ *Chardonnay* (Cuvée Indigène, Pointe Rouge for power) • *Classic red blend* (Les Pavots) • *Sauvignon Blanc* (L'Après-Midi)

## PIPER SONOMA
### Windsor
### ★☆♥

When will someone give Raphael Brisbois the home he deserves? For years he has had to make do with a corner of the winery that was once Piper Sonoma's own facility. Since 1997, however, it has been the J Wine Company, owned by Judy Jordan. If I were Oded Shakked, J's winemaker, I would not want a lodger in my winery, and if I were Brisbois, I would be pretty miffed about being the master of my own premises. Not only does Brisbois not have a proper home for his wine, but he is subject to one of the most miserly budgets for grape supplies and time on yeast I have seen at any half-decent *méthode champenoise* producer, yet Piper Sonoma is better than many California sparkling wines that sell for two or three times the price. If Rémy-Cointreau (owners of Piper-Heidsieck, the Reims-based *grande marque* Champagne house) cannot afford or be bothered to do this operation justice, they should sell the brand to someone who can and will.

✓ *Sparkling wine* (Blanc de Noirs, Brut)

## PRESTON VINEYARDS
### Healdsburg
### ★☆♥

These Dry Creek vineyards are planted with an amazing and successful mix of varieties and are capable of making high-quality wines. Carignane, Cinsault, and Mourvèdre are worth keeping an eye on.

✓ *Barbera* • *Classic red blend* (L. Preston Red) • *Syrah* • *Viognier* • *Zinfandel*

## PRIDE MOUNTAIN VINEYARDS
### Santa Rosa
### ★★

Established in 1990 by the late Jim Pride, who transformed a rundown, underperforming vineyard into the current immaculate wine estate, which produces equally immaculate red wines and one of California's finest Viogniers under the skillful guidance of winemaker Bob Foley.

✓ *Cabernet Franc* • *Cabernet Sauvignon* • *Classic red blend* (Reserve Claret) • *Merlot* • *Sangiovese* • *Viognier*

## QUIVIRA
### Healdsburg
### ★☆♥

Quivira was named after a legendary American kingdom that Europeans spent 200 years searching for. Not able to locate Quivira, the earliest settlers apparently used the name for this part of northern California before it was called Sonoma.

✓ *Classic red blend* (Dry Creek Cuvée) • *Zinfandel*

### RAVENSWOOD
#### Sonoma
#### ★★

Joel Peterson is the master when it comes to monstrous Zinfandel. Some growers of tiny mountainside plots produce such low yields that their wines would be too intense to drink on their own, which is why even Ravenswood's Zinfandel blends can be quite sensational. Peterson's other first-class varietals should not be overlooked.

✓ *Cabernet Sauvignon* (Gregory) • *Carignane* • *Classic red blend* (Pickberry) • *Merlot* (Sangiacomo) • *Zinfandel* (Belloni, Cooke, Dickerson, Old Hill)

### RAYMOND BURR VINEYARDS
#### Geyserville
#### ✰Ⓥ

Named after the late actor, who was a partner, but he died three years before the first wines were released. Best known for Cabernet Sauvignon, yet makes one of California's best Cabernet Francs.

✓ *Cabernet Franc* • *Cabernet Sauvignon*

### ROBERT STEMMLER
#### Sonoma
#### ★

This winery formerly produced a full range of wines at Robert Stemmler's own winery in Healdsburg, when Pinot Noir was its biggest seller, and that variety is still its best wine, even though Robert Stemmler is now produced at and marketed by Buena Vista.

✓ *Chardonnay* (Three Clone) • *Pinot Noir*

### RODNEY STRONG VINEYARDS
#### Windsor
#### ★Ⓥ

Rodney Strong Vineyards produces rich Cabernet Sauvignon and soft-styled Chardonnay, but the fresh, easy-drinking Sauvignon is now emerging as his best wine. Constantly improving.

✓ *Cabernet Sauvignon* (Alden Vineyards) • *Chardonnay* (Chalk Hill) • *Sauvignon Blanc* (Charlotte's Home Vineyard) • *Zinfandel* (Knotty Vines Estate)

### SEBASTIANI
#### Sonoma
#### ✰Ⓥ

Even Sebastiani's top of the range wines are inexpensive, and although this winery has suffered from an inconsistent performance in the past, the quality is improving and leveling, with some real bargains to be found. Other labels include Pepperwood Grove, Talus, August Sebastiani, Vendange, and Richard Cuneo. *See also* Richard Cuneo.

✓ *Barbera* • *Cabernet Sauvignon* (Alexander Valley) • *Chardonnay* (Dutton Ranch) • *Classic red blend* (Cherryblock) • *Pinot Noir* (Russian River Valley) • *Zinfandel* (Domenici Vineyard, Sonoma County)

### SEGHESIO
#### Healdsburg
#### ★✰Ⓥ

This family-owned and -operated winery owns a considerable spread of well-established vineyards, the oldest of which date back to 1895, when Edoardo Seghesio planted his first vineyard in the Alexander Valley. Although he made and sold wine in bulk, it was not until 1983 that his grandchildren were persuaded by their own children to sell wines under the Seghesio label.

✓ *Sangiovese* • *Zinfandel*

### SIDURI
#### Santa Rosa
#### ★★

Named after the Babylonian goddess of wine by Adam and Diana Lee, a couple of Pinot Noir fanatics who source their wines from as far north as Oregon's Willamette Valley to as far south as Santa Barbara's Santa Rita Hills.

✓ *Pinot Noir*

### SIMI WINERY
#### Healdsburg
#### ✰

Simi's one-time dependability seems to have disappeared, with extreme variability playing havoc with what was once a power-packed line of ultra-California character. Some wines are still first class, such as the 1999 Alexander Valley Cabernet Sauvignon, but no one line has shown consistency of late. The only wine that stands out year after year is the Goldfields Vineyard Chardonnay.

✓ *Chardonnay* (Goldfields Vineyard Reserve)

### SONOMA-CUTRER VINEYARDS
#### Windsor
#### ★

Now owned by Brown-Forman, Sonoma-Cutrer continues to specialize in producing high-quality, single-vineyard Chardonnays.

✓ *Chardonnay* (Les Pierres, Founder's Reserve)

### SONOMA-LOEB
#### Geyserville
#### ✰

This producer is owned by John Loeb, a former American Ambassador to Denmark, who has grown grapes here since the early 1970s. However, he did not start making and selling wine under his own label until 1988.

✓ *Chardonnay* (Private Reserve)

### ST. FRANCIS VINEYARD
#### Kenwood
#### ★Ⓥ

Situated just across the road from Château St. Jean, this was an underrated winery, but is not producing as many cellar wines as it used to.

✓ *Cabernet Sauvignon* (Reserve Nuns Canyon) • *Chardonnay* (Reserve Behler) • *Zinfandel* (Reserve Pagani Vineyard)

### STARRY NIGHT WINERY
#### Novato
#### ★Ⓥ

This could be one to watch, having started as recently as 1999, yet achieving some very polished wines almost immediately. The bulk of the production is Zinfandel, and the Russian River Old Vine stands out, but my favorite wine of all is a Rhône-style blend of Carignane, Grenache, and Syrah called Adara.

✓ *Classic red wine blend* (Adara) • *Zinfandel* (Russian River Valley Old Vine)

### STONESTREET
#### Healdsburg
#### ★✰

One of the wineries in Kendal-Jackson's "Artisans & Estates" group, Stonestreet produces good Chardonnay, brilliant Sauvignon, and gorgeously sumptuous Cabernet and Merlot, but truly excels with its classy Legacy blend.

✓ *Cabernet Sauvignon* (Christopher's) • *Chardonnay* (Upper Barn Vineyard) • *Classic red blend* (Legacy) • *Merlot* (Sonoma County) • *Sauvignon Blanc* (Upper Barn Vineyard)

### TOPOLOS AT RUSSIAN RIVER VINEYARDS
#### North Forestville
#### Ⓥ✰❷

From good vineyards around the winery and on Sonoma Mountain, Topolos sometimes comes up with a gem in what can be an alarmingly wayward (hence rating) bunch of wines, including a bewildering array of Zinfandel.

✓ *Alicante Bouschet* • *Petite Sirah* • *Zinfandel*

### TRENTADUE WINERY
#### Geyserville
#### ★Ⓥ

The fast-improving Trentadue Winery produces a characterful

selection of good-value varietal wines that are rarely, if ever, filtered.

✓ *Classic red blend* (Old Patch) • *Petite Sirah* • *Zinfandel* (La Storia)

### WALTER HANSEL
#### Santa Rosa
#### ★★

A Burgundian specialist who uses wild yeast and does not fine or filter, resulting in some of California's finest Chardonnay and Pinot Noir wines.

✓ *Chardonnay* • *Pinot Noir*

### WILLIAMS SELYEM
#### Fulton
#### ★★✰

Established in 1981 by Burt Williams and Ed Selyem (since retired), William Selyem has carefully carved out a reputation for tiny quantities of some of the most sought-after Pinot Noir in California. The signature note of these wines is their beautiful balance and finesse.

✓ *Chardonnay* • *Pinot Noir* • *Zinfandel*

### WINDSOR VINEYARDS
#### Asti
#### ★✰Ⓥ

This producer is grossly underrated because it is corporate-owned and offers so many wines at such inexpensive prices that many think there cannot possibly be anything worth drinking. Yet on the competition circuit, Windsor Vineyards is very well known and highly respected, ranking as one of the three most award-winning wineries in the US every year for the last two decades. One reason to take a look at these wines is that Toni Stockhausen has been chief winemaker since 1999. Not only is she the daughter of Karl Stockhausen, who was quite probably Lindemans' (Australia) greatest-ever winemaker, but Toni started as an oenologist at Lindemans and went on to win awards at Australia's top wine shows before being sent to the US to head this operation. So, if you rate Australian wines, you should at least try some of these California wines made with an Aussie touch.

✓ *Cabernet Sauvignon* (Private Reserve, Signature Series, Simoneau Ranch) • *Carignane* • *Chenin Blanc* • *Classic red blend* (Signature Series Meritage) • *Gewürztraminer* • *Merlot* (Signature Series) • *Petite Sirah* (Mendocino County) • *Pinot Noir* (Private Reserve, Russian River Valley—Signature Series) • *Sauvignon Blanc* (Middle Ridge Vineyard) • *Syrah* • *Zinfandel* (North Coast, Signature Series)

# NAPA COUNTY

*Napa County is the heart and soul of the California wine industry. Its vineyards are the most concentrated in the state, it has more wineries than any other county, and they produce the greatest number and variety of fine wines in the entire North American continent.*

IT IS HARD TO BELIEVE that Napa was planted after Sonoma, but it was, and by some 13 years; in 1838 a trapper from North Carolina, George Yount, acquired a few Mission vines from General Mariano Vallejo's Sonoma vineyard and planted them outside his log cabin, 2 miles (3 kilometers) north of present-day Yountville. He merely wished to make a little wine for his own use. Little did he know that the entire Napa Valley would one day be carpeted with a lush green sea of vines. Within six years Yount himself was harvesting an annual average of 200 gallons (900 liters); by the turn of the decade other vineyards had sprung up and, in 1859, Samuel Brannan, an ex-Mormon millionaire, purchased 3 square miles

NAPA VINEYARDS
*In this, the most famous of all California wine regions, vines grow mostly on the fertile valley floors, although more and more vineyards are being established in the wooded foothills, where the earliest settlers first planted vines.*

(8 square kilometers) of valley land and planted cuttings of various European vine varieties he had collected on his travels. Within another 20 years there would be 18,000 acres (7,300 hectares) of vines in the county, more than half the amount currently cultivated and almost twice the area now covering Mendocino.

Today, the Napa Valley's vinous reputation is well established throughout the world. Napa wines, particularly Chardonnay and Cabernet Sauvignon, are the most sought-after and highly prized in the Americas, and will continue to be so for the foreseeable future.

NAPA COUNTY, *see also p.470*
*The intensive winegrowing areas of this illustrious California district occupy a long, narrow strip running roughly parallel to those of Sonoma County. Many famous names are crowded around Route 29.*

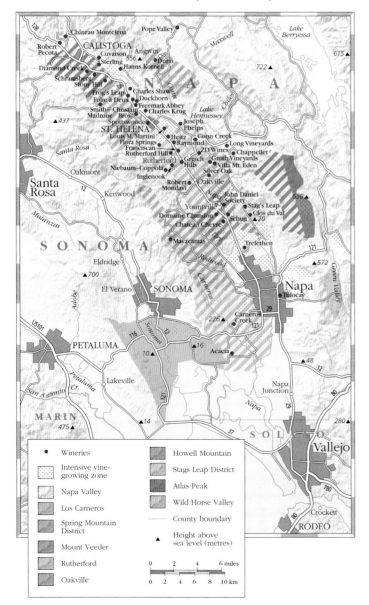

## FACTORS AFFECTING TASTE AND QUALITY

### LOCATION
Starting from San Francisco Bay, Napa runs 34 miles (54 kilometers) north and west to the foothills of Mount St. Helena. Flanking it are the Sonoma Valley to the west and Lake Berryessa to the east.

### CLIMATE
This ranges from cool (Region I, *see* p.470) near the Bay, in the often foggy Carneros District, to warm (Region III, *see* p.470) in the northern section of the Napa Valley and in Pope Valley.

### ASPECT
Vines are mostly planted on the valley floors but some are cultivated on slopes. The altitude of the valley floors ranges from barely 17 feet (5 meters) above sea level at Napa itself, to 230 feet (70 meters) at St. Helena, and 400 feet (122 meters) at Calistoga in the north. The wooded western slopes provide afternoon shade, which adds to the tempering effect of altitude and so favors white grapes, whereas the eastern slopes favor red varieties.

### SOIL
Fertile clay and silt loams in the south of the region, and gravel

loams of better drainage and lower fertility in the north.

### VITICULTURE AND VINIFICATION
There is a vast range of wineries here, from a small number of large firms employing the latest high-tech methods, to an increasing number of small boutique wineries. The latter have limited production, based on traditional methods, although often with judicious use of modern techniques.

### GRAPE VARIETIES
**Primary varieties:** Cabernet Sauvignon, Chardonnay, Chenin Blanc, Merlot, Pinot Noir, Sauvignon Blanc, White Riesling, Zinfandel
**Secondary varieties:** Aleatico, Alicante Bouschet, Barbera, Black Malvoisie, Burger, Cabernet Franc, Carignane, Early Burgundy, Colombard, Flora, Folle Blanche, Gamay, Gamay Beaujolais, Gewürztraminer, Gray Riesling, Green Hungarian, Grenache, Malbec, Malvasia Bianca, Mataro, Mission, Muscat Blanc, Palomino, Petite Sirah, Pinot Blanc, Pinot St. George, Ruby Cabernet, Sauvignon Vert, Sémillon, Sylvaner, Syrah

## THE APPELLATIONS OF
# NAPA COUNTY

### ATLAS PEAK AVA

The Atlas Peak appellation consists of 11,400 acres (4,600 hectares) on and around Atlas Peak mountain, where more than a quarter of California's Sangiovese vines are planted.

### CARNEROS AVA

Also known as Los Carneros, this AVA overlaps Napa and Sonoma counties. *See also* Los Carneros, Sonoma.

### CHILES VALLEY AVA

A narrow area of vines in the Vaca Mountains overlapping the northeast edge of the Napa Valley, the Chiles Valley was named after Joseph Ballinger Chiles, who was given a land grant for this area from the Mexican government in the middle of the 19th century. The cooling bay breezes that moderate the Napa Valley do not reach Chiles Valley, but its altitude of 800 to 1,000 feet (240 to 300 meters) and the prevailing northwesterly winds that funnel dry air through the valley, in combination with the airflow from the Vaca Mountains, tend to cool the grapes down more quickly than in the main areas of the Napa Valley itself. The vines growing here are primarily Zinfandel, Cabernet Sauvignon, Chardonnay, and Sauvignon Blanc.

### DIAMOND MOUNTAIN AVA

Just one-tenth of this appellation's 5,000 acres (2,000 hectares) are planted. Diamond Mountain AVA can be found in the Mayacamas Range on the northeastern corner of Napa Valley, where porous volcanic soils and extended exposure to the sun are the key to its legendary success for Cabernet Sauvignon. Other varieties, such as Cabernet Franc and Zinfandel, are almost as successful, and this is also the home of Schramsberg sparkling wine.

### HOWELL MOUNTAIN AVA

The relatively flat table-top of Howell Mountain is a sub-appellation of the Napa Valley, covering 22 square miles (57 square kilometers) and encompassing some 81 hectares (200 acres) of vineyards at an altitude of between 1,400 and 2,200 feet (420 and 890 meters). Vines were first planted here in 1880. It is best for Cabernet Sauvignon but also capable of top-flight Zinfandel and Chardonnay.

### MOUNT VEEDER AVA

Situated on the east-facing slopes of the Mayacamas Mountains and named after the volcanic peak that dominates this AVA, Mount Veeder is one of the hilly areas where winemakers went to escape the Napa Valley's fertile valley floor. Cool sea breezes from San Pablo Bay and occasional marine fogs temper the climate, while air-drainage prevents frost. Chardonnay and Cabernet Sauvignon are the two dominant varieties, the latter being quite exceptional in its varietal intensity and completely different in structure from the lush valley-floor Cabernets.

### NAPA COUNTY AO

This is an appellation that covers grapes grown anywhere in the entire county.

### NAPA VALLEY AVA

This AVA includes all of the county with the exception of the area around Putah Creek and Lake Berryessa. The Napa Valley appellation is 25 miles (40 kilometers) long and between 12 and 8 and 10 miles (16 kilometers) wide, and is sheltered by two parallel mountain ranges. The majority of vineyards occupy the flat valley floor in a continuous strip from Napa to Calistoga, although the slopes are also beginning to be cultivated.

### OAKVILLE AVA

If Rutherford has the greatest concentration of famous Cabernet Sauvignon vineyards, then neighboring Oakville, which is equally Napa's heartland, excels by its very diversity. Great Cabernet Sauvignon, Merlot, and Chardonnay are made here, and even the Sauvignon Blanc from these vineyards can be extraordinary.

### RUTHERFORD AVA

One of the most famous names in Napa, yet one of the last to gain AVA status because many growers feared that dividing the Napa Valley's heartland into smaller, possibly more prestigious subappellations would gradually have the effect of diluting the reputation of Napa itself. This AVA encompasses more than 30 wineries, including some of California's most famous, and contains many of Napa's greatest Cabernet Sauvignon vineyards.

### SPRING MOUNTAIN DISTRICT AVA

Originally proposed as Spring Mountain, but as this was already a brand name, the AVA was changed to Spring Mountain District to prevent confusion. This appellation is located within the Napa Valley AVA, just west of St. Helena, on the eastern flank of the Mayacamas Mountains, and comprises 8,600 acres (3,480 hectares), of which approximately 1,980 acres (800 hectares) are planted with vines.

### ST. HELENA AVA

The latest AVA to be established in a bid to carve up the Napa Valley into communal districts in a similar manner to the Médoc, St. Helena is immediately north of Rutherford.

### STAGS LEAP DISTRICT AVA

Confusingly, Stags Leap is spelled in three slightly different ways: with an apostrophe before the "s" in the famous Stag's Leap Wine Cellar; with an apostrophe after the "s" in the lesser-known Stags' Leap Winery; and without an apostrophe in the AVA name. Stag's Leap Wine Cellar shot to fame in 1976 when its Cabernet Sauvignon trumped top Bordeaux wines at a blind tasting in Paris. Stags Leap District vies with Rutherford as the crème of Napa Valley Cabernet Sauvignon, but also makes good Petite Sirah, excellent Merlot, and stunning red Bordeaux-style blends.

### WILD HORSE VALLEY AVA

Technically attached to Napa, Wild Horse Valley actually straddles the county line, occupying more of Solano than Napa.

### YOUNTVILLE AVA

Although less famous than Rutherford or Oakville, this AVA does have one of the Napa Valley's coolest vineyard exposures, which is why some people rate its Cabernet Sauvignon above those of its neighbors.

## THE WINE PRODUCERS OF
# NAPA COUNTY

### ABREU
**Napa**
★★☆

I often wondered what would happen when an immovable object (such as the density of the fruit used to make these wines) met an irresistible force like David Abreu's passion for great class and finesse, and here we have it in the form of Cabernet Sauvignon taken to another dimension (for where else could it go?). If you like massive, you must try Abreu.
 *Cabernet Sauvignon*

### ACACIA
WINERY
**Napa**
★★

Wines of increasing finesse, from a fine Chardonnay, which has a touch of spice, to a lovely Pinot Noir that is silky textured, and all cherries and vanilla.
✓ *Chardonnay* (Sangiacomo Vineyard) • *Pinot Noir* (Beckstoffer Vineyard, Carneros, Field Blend)

### ARAUJO
ESTATE
**Calistoga**
❽★★

Bart and Daphne Araujo now own the highly regarded Eisele vineyard, which is located north of Cuvaison, and makes Cabernet Sauvignon of outstanding quality.
 *Cabernet Sauvignon* (Eisele Vineyard) • *Sauvignon Blanc* (Eisele Vineyard) • *Syrah* (Eisele Vineyard)

### ARTESA
**Napa**
★☆

Formerly called Codorníu Napa, this is the California arm of the famous Catalan Cava producer, and originally opened in 1991. Although the quality increased as the years went by, Codorníu found it difficult to sell a sparkling wine at California prices, as consumers obviously wondered why they should pay twice the price for Codorníu with California on the label. It did not help that Codorníu was synonymous with Cava, one of the cheapest sparkling wines on the US market. The decision to pull the plug was taken in 1996, the winery was totally transformed into one suited for the production of classic varietal wines, and Artesa was born.

✓ *Cabernet Sauvignon • Sauvignon Blanc* (Napa Valley Reserve)

## ATALON
### Oakville
★★✪

Even the entry-level Cabernet Sauvignon is a stunning, classic structured wine of great class and supreme elegance. And relatively inexpensive for such quality—but for how long? Also fine Merlot.

✓ *Cabernet Sauvignon • Merlot*

## ATLAS PEAK
### Atlas Peak
★✫

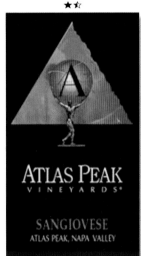

This exciting venture is backed with big bucks from Allied-Domecq (which also owns Clos du Bois and William Hill) with expertise provided by Champagne Bollinger and the famous Chianti house of Antinori. Sangiovese is the star here, and invariably the standard bottling that excels above that of the Sangiovese Reserve.

✓ *Cabernet Sauvignon* (Consenso) • *Sangiovese*

## BARNETT VINEYARDS
### St. Helena
★✫

These mountain vineyards make intense yet delicious, very elegant Cabernet Sauvignon, among other wines.

✓ *Cabernet Sauvignon* (Rattlesnake Hill)

## BEAULIEU VINEYARD
### Rutherford
★

This was the center of Californian innovation under the legendary winemaker André Tchelistcheff, but has long since passed into corporate hands, and is currently owned by

the UK-based Diageo group. Not the force it was, although on its own, the legendary Georges de Latour would easily rate as a two-star entry. Other wines have their day (such as the 2000 Pinot Noir Carneros Reserve), but lack consistency.

✓ *Cabernet Sauvignon* (Georges de Latour)

## BEHRENS AND HITCHCOCK
### Oakville
★★

Born in the middle of nowhere, viticulturally speaking, of Arcata, Humboldt County, not far from the Oregon border, where they made 175 cases a year from trucked-in grapes in 1991, Behrens and Hitchcock moved to a rented winery in Napa in 1997, before building their own winery in 1999. When I first nosed around Humboldt and Siskiou counties in 1994, this was just one of a handful of such producers, none of whom were taken very seriously, yet they now craft some of California's finest Cabernet Sauvignon.

✓ *Cabernet Sauvignon • Petite Sirah*

## BELO WINE COMPANY
### St. Helena
★✪

This fortified wine specialist grows traditional Portuguese grape varieties, and makes great vintage port, both blended and varietal.

✓ *Fortified* (Vintage Port)

## BERINGER VINEYARDS
### St. Helena
★★✪

Although all the products from Beringer Vineyards are among the finest in California, you do get proportionately more for your money if you pay extra for the better wines, with the singular exception of the Founders' Estate Merlot, which can offer extraordinary finesse for so few dollars. Indeed, if all vintages were as brilliant as the 2000, I would not hestitate to claim it to be one of California's 10 greatest Merlots. However, I must take issue with the name of this entry-level line. Beringer might be open about its diverse origins, hence the California AVA, but Founders' Estate does imply that the vineyards in question are part of a single estate of historic origins, and I'm not so sure that Jacob and Frederick Beringer owned vineyards stretching from Santa Barbara to Mendocino!

✓ *Botrytized* (Nightingale) • *Cabernet Sauvignon • Chardonnay* (Sbragia) • *Chenin Blanc • Classic red blend* (Alluvium) • *Classic white blend* (Alluvium) • *Merlot* (Bancroft Ranch, Founders' Reserve)

## BIALE VINEYARDS
### Napa
★★

Amazing, huge, rich, and gorgeously ripe, single-vineyard Zinfandel, and one of California's greatest Petite Sirah.

✓ *Zinfandel* (Aldo's Vineyard)

## BOUCHAINE VINEYARDS
### Napa
★

Noticeable by its absence from most American critics' thoughts, Bouchaine's Pinot Noir and Chardonnay are probably too light and elegant to stir up much opinion in the US, but have a purity and finesse much appreciated by European palates.

✓ *Pinot Noir*

## BRYANT FAMILY VINEYARD
### Calistoga
❷

This relatively new boutique winery is reputedly turning out masterly Cabernet Sauvignon.

## BUEHLER VINEYARDS
### St. Helena
★★

This estate is again producing Cabernet Sauvignon reminiscent of the size and quality that once made it legendary.

✓ *Cabernet Sauvignon*

## BURGESS CELLARS
### St. Helena
★★✪

Owner Tom Burgess and winemaker Bill Sorenson often produce well-weighted, oaky wines of fine quality.

✓ *Syrah • Zinfandel*

## CAIN CELLARS
### St. Helena
★✫

These are interesting, innovative, and well-made wines.

✓ *Classic red blend* (Cain Concept, Cain Five) • *Sauvignon Blanc* (Cain Musqué Ventana Vineyar)

## CAKEBREAD CELLARS
### Rutherford
★✫

Bruce Cakebread has a well-deserved reputation for producing one of the most delicious Sauvignon Blanc wines in California.

✓ *Cabernet Sauvignon* (Three Sisters, Vine Hill Ranch) • *Sauvignon Blanc • Syrah*

## CASA NUESTRA
### St. Helena
★✫✪

A tiny, high-quality winery that is up and coming, although it has been in existence since 1979. This makes its wines great value now,

but demand could change all that by a future edition, so best to taste them while you can still afford to. Casa Nuestra produces classic styles such as Merlot and Meritage, but some quirky ones too, such as one of California's finest Chenin Blanc and a classic red blend (Tinto) made from nine varieties, including Cabernet Pfeffer. Cabernet what? That's right: Cabernet Pfeffer (see Glossary of Grape Varieties).

✓ *Chenin Blanc • Classic red blend* (Tinto)

## CAYMUS VINEYARDS
### Rutherford
★★★✫

This extraordinary winery now focuses exclusively on deep, dark brooding Cabernet Sauvignon of superb quality. The classic white wine blend Conundrum is now sold under that name alone, and will shortly have its own dedicated winery in Monterey (see Conundrum).

✓ *Cabernet Sauvignon* (Napa Valley, Special Selection)

## CHAPPELLET VINEYARDS
### St. Helena
★★✫

Chappellet is an excellent winery with a range of skilfully produced wines that show great finesse.

✓ *Cabernet Sauvignon • Chardonnay • Chenin Blanc • Johannisberg Riesling • Merlot* (Napa Valley)

## CHARLES KRUG
### St. Helena
★✫✪

Purchased by the Mondavi family in 1943 and run by Bob Mondavi's less prominent brother Peter, this winery used to be known for its Cabernet Sauvignon, but Krug's reputation is diluted by its production of jug wine and generics sold under a second label—C. K. Mondavi.

✓ *Cabernet Sauvignon • Merlot* (Reserve)

## CHÂTEAU MONTELENA WINERY
### Calistoga
★★✫

The style of this small, prestigious winery has changed over the years, but the quality has always been high, especially for Cabernet Sauvignon, although the Chardonnay has been almost as good in recent years.

✓ *Cabernet Sauvignon • Chardonnay*

## CHÂTEAU POTELLE
### Mount Veeder
★

This winery was established in 1985 by a *bordelais* couple, who ironically were best known in their early days for their slow-evolving Chardonnay, but have since developed a reputation for other age-worthy varietals.

✓ *Cabernet Sauvignon* (VGS) •
*Chardonnay* (VGS) •
*Zinfandel* (VGS)

## CHIMNEY ROCK
### Napa
★

Part of the Terlato Wine Group
(which includes Sandford,
Rutherford Hill, and Alder Brook),
this was originally Chimney Rock
Golf Club, until its nine holes were
bulldozed and a vineyard planted.

✓ *Cabernet Sauvignon* • *Classic
red blend* (Elevage)

## CLIFF LEDE VINEYARD
### Napa
★

Cliff Lede took over S. Anderson in
2002, and uses that label exclusively
for the traditional method wines that
Carol Anderson had garnered such
a reputation for. The style is as
elegant as the labeling, with layers
of intense, finely poised fruit.

✓ *Cabernet Sauvignon* •
*Sauvignon Blanc* • *Sparkling
wine* (Blanc de Blancs, Brut,
Rosé)

## CLOS DU VAL
### Napa
★ Ⓥ

Bernard Portet still makes some
fine wines, but there is less of a
buzz about these wines.

✓ *Cabernet Sauvignon* (Stags
Leap District) • *Chardonnay*
(Carneros) • *Zinfandel* (Stags
Leap District Reserve)

## CLOS PEGASE
### Calistoga
★

A welcome, understated use of oak
coupled with lush fruit produces
wines of some elegance.

✓ *Cabernet Sauvignon* •
*Chardonnay* • *Classic red
blend* (Hommage) • *Merlot*

## COLGIN
### Napa
★★★☆

Tiny production of huge-priced,
high-class Cabernet Sauvignon,
with sufficient structure to support
the weight.

✓ *Cabernet Sauvignon* • *Classic
red blend* (Cariad)

## CONN CREEK WINERY
### St. Helena
☆

Owned by Stimson Lane (which
also owns Château Ste. Michelle,
Columbia Crest, and Villa Mount
Eden), Conn Creek is best known
for its supple, fruity Cabernet
Sauvignon, but does not have
the cachet it once had.

✓ *Cabernet Sauvignon* • *Classic
red blend* (Anthology) • *Merlot*

## CORISON
### St. Helena
★ ☆

After 10 years as Chappellet's
winemaker, Cathy Corison struck
out on her own, and has not looked
back since, purchasing small parcels
of the finest Napa Valley grapes to
produce lush, supple Cabernet
wines of surprising longevity.

✓ *Cabernet Sauvignon*

## CORNERSTONE CELLARS
### Oakville
★★Ⓥ

Owned by two Memphis doctors,
Michael Dragutsky and David Sloas.
In 1991, Sloas happened to be
tasting on Howell Mountain with
Randy Dunn, who mentioned that
he had received almost 5 tons of
grapes more than he needed from
one of his farmers. Sloas telephoned
his friend Dragutsky in Memphis,
they agreed they had both lost their
minds and purchased the grapes,
thus going from wine consumers to
wine producers in a few minutes.

✓ *Cabernet Sauvignon* • *Merlot*

## COSENTINO
### Yountville
★★☆

Mitch Cosentino has more wines on
his list than there are dishes on a
Chinese menu. The once hit-you-
between-the-eyes styles have been
toned down and, although the wines
are still exuberant in their fruit, they
now have much more finesse. Some
brilliant Merlot of late (2000 Reserve
is simply stunning). CE2V is an
ultrapremium brand, while Crystal
Valley is Cosentino's second label.

✓ *Classic red blend* (CE2V
Meritage, M. Coz, The Poet
Meritage) • *Dessert* (Viognier
Vin Doux Kay) • *Dolcetto*
(Celle Vineyard) • *Merlot*
(Reserve) • *Petite Sirah* (Knoll
Vineyard) • *Sangiovese* (CE2V
Napa Valley, Il Chiaretto) •
*Zinfandel* (Cigarzin, The Zin)

## CUVAISON
### Calistoga
Ⓥ

This Swiss-owned winery is making
better reds than whites.

✓ *Chardonnay* (Carneros Estate
Selection) • *Pinot Noir*
(Carneros Estate Selection) •
*Syrah* (Carneros)

## DALLA VALLE
### Oakville
★★☆

Dalla Valle produces great Cabernet
in addition to a truly heroic
Cabernet-based blend.

✓ *Cabernet Sauvignon* • *Classic
red blend* (Maya)

## DELECTUS
### Oakville
★★☆

Small, ultrahigh-quality operation
established in 1989 by Austrian-born

Gerhard Reisacher and his
wife Linda.

✓ *Classic red blend* (Cuvée Julia)
• *Petite Sirah*

## DETERT FAMILY VINEYARDS
### Oakville
★★Ⓥ

Former Opus One Cabernet Franc
vines produce this relatively new
winery's best and cheapest wine,
but don't let that put you off
Detert's beautifully focused
Cabernet Sauvignon.

✓ *Cabernet Franc* • *Cabernet
Sauvignon*

## DIAMOND CREEK VINEYARDS
### Calistoga
★☆

This small winery specializes in
awesomely long-lived, awesomely
priced Cabernet Sauvignon.

✓ *Cabernet Sauvignon* (Red Rock
Terrace, Gravelly Meadow,
Volcanic Hill)

## DOLCE
### Oakville
★★★☆

Established by Far Niente as
the only winery in the US solely
devoted to producing a single late-
harvest wine, Dolce is a lusciously
sweet, heavily botrytized, Sauternes-
styled dessert wine made from
approximately 90 percent Sémillon
and 10 percent Sauvignon Blanc.
The only pity is that they went
for such a kitsch, *nouveau riche*
presentation, instead of the
understated elegance that such
a classy, unique wine deserves.

✓ *Botrytized* (Dolce)

## DOMAINE CARNEROS
### Napa
★★

This winery has the pristine façade
of Taittinger's 17th-century Château
de la Marquetterie in Champagne,
and Le Rêve is one of the greatest
21st-century sparkling wines
produced outside Champagne.

✓ *Pinot Noir* (Avant-Garde) •
*Sparkling wine* (Brut, Brut
Rosé, Le Rêve)

## DOMAINE CHANDON
### Yountville
Ⓥ

Moët & Chandon's seal of approval
kickstarted California's sparkling
wine industry, which until then
had consisted of just one producer,
Schramsberg. Although the style of
its sparkling wine has lacked finesse
in the past, there has been a
noticeably lighter hand in recent
years. The same could be said for
its Pinot Noir, but that all changed
with the 2000 vintage, which is
impressive by any yardstick, while
the Pinot Meunier has always
been a delight.

✓ *Chardonnay* (Carneros) •

*Pinot Meunier* • *Pinot Noir*
(Carneros) • *Sparkling wine*
(Mt. Veeder, Riche, Vintage)

## DOMINUS
### Yountville
★★

Christian Moueix of Château Pétrus
joined forces with the daughters of
John Daniel to produce Dominus, a
massively structured Bordeaux-like
blend from the historic Napanook
vineyard. The best vintages are from
1990 onward, with the most recent
being the most impressive.

✓ *Classic red blend* (Dominus)

## DUCKHORN VINEYARDS
### St. Helena
★★☆

These superb, dark, rich, and tannic
wines have a cult following. Also
owns the Goldeneye winery in
Mendocino. Other labels include
Paraduxx (Zinfandel-Cabernet
Sauvignon blend), Decoy
(Bordeaux-style blend) and
Migration (Pinot Noir).

✓ *Cabernet Sauvignon* • *Merlot*
(Three Palms) • *Sauvignon
Blanc*

## DUNN VINEYARDS
### Angwin
★★

Randy Dunn makes a very small
quantity of majestic Cabernet
Sauvignon from his Howell
Mountain vineyard.

✓ *Cabernet Sauvignon*

## ELYSE
### Napa
★☆

These wines have always had
richness of fruit and expressive style,
but increasingly show greater finesse.

✓ *Cabernet Sauvignon* (Morisoli
Vineyard, Tietjen Vineyard) •
*Zinfandel* (Howell Mountain,
Morisoli Vineyard)

## ETUDE
### Oakville
★★

Tony Soter has eased back on his
consultancy work to spend more
time crafting some beautifully
proportioned, silky-smooth,

succulent, and stylish wines at the venture he established, and Beringer Blass now owns.

 *Cabernet Sauvignon* (Napa Valley) • *Merlot* (Napa Valley) • *Pinot Blanc* (Carneros ) • *Pinot Gris* (Carneros) • *Pinot Noir* (Heirloom)

## FAILLA
### Calistoga
### ★★

In the short history of this winery, which was established as recently as 1998, husband and wife team Ehren Jordan and Anne-Marie Failla have found themselves in hot water, as the original name for their winery—Failla Jordan—came under heavy legal barrage from the Jordan winery for infringement of its trademark. They had no option but to drop their own family name in favor of what is, I think, a much better, more elegant label.

✓ *Chardonnay* (Keefer Ranch) • *Pinot Noir* (Hirsch, Keefer Ranch) • *Syrah* • *Viognier* (Alban Vineyard)

## FAR NIENTE
### Oakville
### ★

A revitalized pre-Prohibition winery that made its mark with fine Chardonnay in the 1980s, but that wine can sometimes be overblown, and Cabernet Sauvignon is the more consistent and classier bet.

✓ *Cabernet Sauvignon* • *Chardonnay*

## FLORA SPRINGS
### St. Helena
### ★★🅥

This winery produces an exciting Trilogy, a blend of Merlot with two Cabernets, and a Soliloquy, a barrel-fermented Sauvignon Blanc bottled *sur lie*.

✓ *Cabernet Sauvignon* (Rutherford Hillside Reserve, Wild Boar Vineyard) • *Classic red blend* (Poggio del Papa, Trilogy) • *Merlot* (Napa Valley) • *Sauvignon Blanc* (Soliloquy)

## FORMAN VINEYARDS
### St. Helena
### ★

Rick Forman, formerly of Sterling Vineyard, set up this small winery in 1983. He has a following for classic yet opulent wines from his own vineyard, which sits on a gravel bed as deep as 56 feet (17 meters).

✓ *Cabernet Sauvignon* • *Chardonnay*

## FRANCISCAN VINEYARDS
### Rutherford
### ★★🅥

A consistent producer since the mid-1980s of smooth, stylish, premium-quality wines.

✓ *Chardonnay* (Cuvée Sauvage) • *Classic red blend* (Magnificat Meritage)

## FREEMARK ABBEY
### St. Helena
### ★★🅥

When it comes to its Cabernet Bosché and Chardonnay in general, Freemark Abbey consistently combines high quality and good value. Now part of Jackson Family Wine Estates.

✓ *Cabernet Sauvignon* (Bosché) • *Chardonnay*

## FROG'S LEAP WINERY
### St. Helena
### 🅞★

One of California's best-known organic producers, Frog's Leap was established in 1981 by John Williams, who had taken inspiration from his first Napa Valley winemaking post at Stag's Leap Cellars as the name for his new venture.

✓ *Chardonnay* • *Merlot* • *Sauvignon Blanc* • *Zinfandel*

## GIRARD WINERY
### Oakville
### ★★☆

Top-quality, smooth, and stylish Napa Valley Red boasts seamlessly integrated oak, and is the top wine here, although Girard's Petite Sirah is one of California's finest.

✓ *Chardonnay* (Russian River) • *Classic red blend* (Napa Valley Red) • *Petite Sirah*

## GRACE FAMILY VINEYARDS
### St. Helena
### ★★

Produces minuscule amounts of huge, dark, extremely expensive Cabernet Sauvignon wine, with wonderfully multilayered fruit, oak, and *terroir* flavors.

✓ *Cabernet Sauvignon*

## GRGICH HILLS CELLAR
### Rutherford
### ★☆🅥

Owned and run by Mike Grgich, once winemaker at Château Montelena, this winery produces intense, rich, and vibrant styles of high-quality wine.

✓ *Cabernet Sauvignon* (Napa Valley) • *Merlot* (Napa Valley) • *Sauvignon Blanc* (Estate Grown Fumé Blanc) • *Zinfandel* (Miljenko's Old Vine)

## GROTH VINEYARDS
### Oakville
### ★★

Although these wines are not as consistent as they used to be, Groth's Cabernet Sauvignon can still hack it with the finest in California.

✓ *Cabernet Sauvignon* (Oakville)

## HARLAN ESTATE
### Napa
### ★★★☆

Classic quality from the hills above Oakville, but you have to pay for it!

✓ *Bordeaux-style red* (Napa Valley)

## HARTWELL VINEYARDS
### Napa
### ★★

From a one-acre harvest in 1990, Bob and Blanca Hartwell's vineyard has become one of the fastest-rising stars in the Stags Leap District, and is now known for immaculate grapes and the deep, full, lush style of the wines produced.

✓ *Cabernet Sauvignon* • *Merlot*

## HAVENS
### Napa
### ★★🅥

For 20 years Mike Havens has attracted an enviable reputation for his supremely rich Merlot Reserve, which is certainly one of California's finest, but he also makes Syrah that is in a class of its own and a masterly Bordeaux-style red wine blend called Bourriquot. There is also an interesting, authentically dry Albariño.

✓ *Albariño* • *Classic red blend* (Bourriquot) • *Merlot* • *Syrah*

## HEITZ WINE CELLARS
### St. Helena
### ★★

The TCA of the 1990s (or bacterial infection as some have claimed) appears to have been overcome, although too few American critics dared tell the late king that he had no clothes on at the time. It will be a surprise to some, but Heitz is a master of Grignolino, making a delightful, quaffing red and a gorgeous rosé, not to mention a very appealing port-style fortified wine, which leans closer to the lighter, traditional Portuguese style than the Ink Grade Vineyard.

✓ *Cabernet Sauvignon* (Martha's Vineyard, Trailside Vineyard) • *Fortified* (Grignolino Port, Ink Grade Vineyard Port) • *Grignolino* (Rosé)

## JADE MOUNTAIN
### Angwin
### ★★☆

These high-quality Rhône-style wines are achieving increasingly well integrated oak of late. The Mourvèdre Ancient Vines from the Evangelho Vineyard were planted in 1890.

✓ *Classic red blend* (La Provençale) • *Mourvèdre* (Ancient Vines Evangelho Vineyard) • *Syrah* (Paras Vineyard, Paras Vineyard Block P-10)

## JOSEPH PHELPS VINEYARDS
### St. Helena
### ★★

This prestigious winery continues to make a large range of top-quality

wines, with an increasing emphasis on exciting Rhône-style wines, including the excellent Le Mistral blend, although Insignia remains its very greatest product.

✓ *Cabernet Sauvignon* (Backus) • *Chardonnay* (Ovation) • *Classic red blend* (Insignia, Le Mistral) • *Merlot* (Napa Valley) • *Syrah* (Napa Valley)

## KENT RASMUSSEN
### Napa
### ★★

As a librarian, Kent Rasmussen loved wine and yearned, so he took a B.Sc. in oenology at UC Davis in 1983, picked up some useful experience at Robert Mondavi Winery and Domaine Chandon, took a *stage* at Stellenbosch Farmers' Winery in South Africa, then at Saltram's Wine Estate in Australia, before setting up his own winery in 1986. Since then he has created a reputation for producing Carneros Pinot Noir at its most luscious.

✓ *Chardonnay* (Napa Valley) • *Pinot Noir* (Carneros)

## KONGSGAARD
### Oakville
### ★★☆

Many small wineries claim to make handcrafted wines, but John and Maggy Kongsgaard's is one of the few that actually does, as they limit their production—literally—to the wine they can make with their own hands. This and their nigh-fanatical minimalist approach yield wines of exceptional richness, balance, and finesse.

✓ *Entire range*

## LA JOTA
### Angwin
### ★★☆

La Jota is best known for lavishly flavored Cabernet Sauvignon, but produces a much smaller quantity of equally fine Petite Sirah.

✓ *Cabernet Sauvignon* • *Petite Sirah*

## ROBERT KEENAN WINERY
### St. Helena
### ★

This Spring Mountain hillside winery produces admirably restrained Cabernet Sauvignon and Merlot.

✓ *Cabernet Sauvignon* • *Merlot*

## LAIL
### Napa
### ★★

Established in 1995 by Robin Lail, the daughter of John Daniel, the great-nephew of the legendary Gustave Niebaum. Lail trained at Mondavi, and was the co-founder of Dominus and Merryvale, before selling her share in those businesses to set up on her own.

 *Classic red blend* (Blueprint, J. Daniel Cuvée) • *Sauvignon Blanc* (Georgia)

## LARKIN
### St. Helena
★★

After representing a number of small, high-quality wineries, Sean Larkin made his first wine in 1999 and achieved instant critical success from all the biggest names in the business.

✓ *Cabernet Franc*

## LEWELLING VINEYARDS
### St. Helena
★★ⓥ

The Lewelling family established these vineyards in 1864 and after the usual Prohibition hiatus, developed a reputation for supplying some of Napa's greatest wineries with grapes. These wines, however, date from just 1992, when the Wright family, descendants of the Lewellings, decided to produce wine under their own vineyard designation, and now produce some of California's greatest Cabernet Sauvignon.

✓ *Cabernet Sauvignon*

## LEWIS CELLARS
### Napa
★★

A small, hands-on winery run by ex-racing car driver Randy Lewis and his wife Debbie. The Merlot could be called a Californian version of top-class Pomerol.

✓ *Chardonnay • Classic red blend* (Alec's Blend, Cuvée L) *• Merlot • Syrah*

## LOKOYA
### Oakville
★★★

Named after a Native American tribe that lived on Mount Veeder, Lokoya is a Napa Cabernet Sauvignon specialist *par excellence*. All three styles are outstanding, from the Howell Mountain, which is the most lush, through the Mount Veeder, which packs the most complex fruit, to Diamond Mountain, which is probably the closest to Bordeaux in style.

✓ *Cabernet Sauvignon*

## LONG VINEYARDS
### St. Helena
★★

This operation was established in the 1970s by Robert and Zelma Long, who have since divorced, but are still joint owners. Amazingly, they not only continue to run this winery together, they do so with their respective new partners. The wines are equally smooth, stylish, and sophisticated.

✓ *Botrytis* (Johannisberg Riesling Estate Grown) *• Cabernet Sauvignon* (Estate Grown) *• Chardonnay* (Old Vines)

## LOUIS M MARTINI
### St. Helena
★ⓥ

The quality of this winery had been slowly turning around for the better

when it was purchased by E. & J. Gallo in 2002, although its reputation is still very patchy from vintage to vintage, even for its most successful wines.

✓ *Cabernet Sauvignon* (Monte Rosso) *• Chardonnay* (RVS) *• Fortified* (Cream Sherry, Dry Sherry) *• Sangiovese* (Dunnigan Hills) *• Zinfandel* (Monte Rosso)

## LUNA VINEYARDS
### Napa
★ⓥ

An artisanal winery with an Italian bent, located at the southern tip of the Silverado Trail.

✓ *Classic red blend* (Canto) *• Classic white blend* (Bianco) *• Pinot Grigio • Sangiovese* (Riserva)

## MARCASSIN
### Calistoga
★★

This small operation belongs to Helen Turley, who made her name at B. R Cohn and the Peter Michael Winery, and is one of California's most sought-after consultants. Marcassin produces highly desirable, nigh-unobtainable, extraordinarily lavish, yet extremely stylish wines.

✓ *Chardonnay • Pinot Noir*

## MARKHAM VINEYARDS
### St. Helena
★★ⓥ

This underrated Japanese-owned (Mercian Corporation) winery is best known for Merlot and Cabernet from its Napa Valley vineyards situated at Calistoga, Yountville, and Oakville, but other varietals are beginning to emerge. Good-value wines are also produced under Markham's second label, Glass Mountain.

✓ *Cabernet Sauvignon • Merlot • Petite Sirah • Zinfandel*

## MAYACAMAS VINEYARDS
### Napa

This prestigious small winery is renowned for its tannic, long-lived Cabernet, but actually produces much better, more user-friendly Chardonnay as well.

✓ *Chardonnay*

## MERRYVALE VINEYARDS
### St. Helena
★★

These are classy, stylish wines, particularly the Bordeaux-style blends.

✓ *Cabernet Sauvignon* (Beckstoffer Vineyard X) *• Chardonnay* (Silhouette) *• Classic red blend* (Profile)

## MONTICELLO CELLARS
### Napa
★

This producer used to be better for whites than reds, but although Monticello still receives many

plaudits for its Chardonnay, it is the red wines that are now established as its most exciting.

✓ *Cabernet Sauvignon* (Corley Reserve, Jefferson Cuvée) *• Classic red blend* (Corley Proprietary Red) *• Merlot* (Estate Grown)

## MUMM NAPA WINERY
### Rutherford
★★

This impeccably run sparkling-wine operation is under the helm of Greg Fowler, who was the winemaker at Schramsberg for seven years. Fowler really lets his winemaking skill fly with his Sparkling Pinot Noir, which has an outrageous deep cerise color, an aroma of strawberries, and intensely perfumed Pinot fruit.

✓ *Sparkling wine* (Blanc de Blancs, DVX, Sparkling Pinot Noir, Winery Lake)

## MURPHY-GOODE
### Geyserville
★ⓥ

The top wines are all rich, oaky blockbusters, but I get the most pleasure from Murphy-Goode's Fumé Blanc.

✓ *Fumé Blanc* (Alexander Valley Reserve)

## NAPA CELLARS
### Oakville
★★ⓥ

A brilliant source of great-value, great-quality wines that hit well above their weight, often outclassing famous brands at two or three times the price.

✓ *Cabernet Sauvignon • Chardonnay • Merlot*

## NEYERS
### Rutherford
★★ⓥ

Bruce and Barbara Neyers have been producing classy wines since 1992, but seem to have stepped up a gear since moving to their current renovated winery in 2000. Part of the production is from the Neyers' own 50-acre (20-hectare) Conn Ranch vineyard, but most is bought in from selected growers.

✓ *Chardonnay • Grenache • Merlot • Syrah*

## NEWTON VINEYARDS
### St. Helena
★★ⓥ

This top-notch estate has a track record for wines with impeccable oak integration, silky smooth fruit, and supple-tannin structure.

✓ *Cabernet Sauvignon • Chardonnay • Classic red blend* (Claret) *• Merlot*

## NIEBAUM-COPPOLA
### Rutherford
★★★

Hollywood movie director Francis Ford Coppola purchased the old

Gustave Niebaum homestead and half of the original Inglenook vineyards in 1975, producing his first wine, a classic red Bordeaux-style blend called Rubicon, in 1978. He bought almost all of the remaining Inglenook vineyards in 1995, plus the Inglenook winery, but not the brand (now the property of Mission Bell Winery, which belongs to Constellation Brands), and in 2002 Coppola paid out a record $31.5 million for the 60-acre (24-hectare) J. J. Cohn vineyard (no connection with B. R. Cohn in Sonoma, which adjoined the southern section of his own property). The Cabernet and Merlot grapes from this Rutherford vineyard should not only allow for increased production of Rubicon, but should also plug some holes that occasionally appeared in the quality of wines made in whole or part with bought-in fruit. Note that only pure estate wines are made exclusively from organically grown grapes.

✓ *Cabernet Sauvignon* (Cask Cabernet) *• Classic red blend* (Rubicon) *• Merlot* (Estate) *• Zinfandel* (Edizione Pennino)

## OPUS ONE
### Oakville
★★

The product of collaboration between Robert Mondavi and the late Baron Philippe de Rothschild, Opus One was the first Bordeaux–California joint venture and there is no denying the quality of this Cabernet-Merlot blend, just as there is no getting away from its outlandish price.

✓ *Opus One*

## PAHLMEYER
### Napa
★★

Typical of the boutique wineries established by America's affluent professional class, this operation was founded in 1985 by lawyer Jayson Pahlmeyer, who has hired various consultants, such as Randy Dunn, Helen Turley, and David Abreu, in his pursuit of varietal concentration allied to an expression of *terroir*. The Jayson is a blend of the wines that did not make the cut for Pahlmeyer's Proprietary Red.

✓ *Chardonnay • Classic red blend* (Jayson, Proprietary Red) *• Merlot*

## PALOMA
### Spring Mountain District
★★

This reclaimed 19th-century vineyard is located at an altitude of between 2,060 and 2,240 feet (618 and 672 meters) on Spring Mountain, and the difference between these wines and valley floor wines is that you get more complexity and length for the same weight of wine.

✓ *Cabernet Sauvignon • Merlot • Syrah*

## PATZ AND HALL
### Napa
### ★ ⊬

This winery specializes in rich, lush, single-vineyard Burgundian-style varietals.

✓ *Chardonnay* • *Pinot Noir* (Alder Springs, Pisioni Vineyard)

## PEJU PROVINCE
### Rutherford
### ★★

Established by Tony and Herta Peju as long ago as 1982, but with 90 percent of sales going through its tasting room, it has only been in the last five to eight years that Peju Province has really started to grab wider attention.

✓ *Cabernet Franc* • *Merlot* (Napa Valley Estate) • *Sauvignon Blanc*

## PHILIP TOGNI VINEYARD
### St. Helena
### ★★ ⊬

Philip Togni earned great respect at Chalone, Chappellet, Cuvaison, Mayacamus, and Chimney Rock, before establishing this vineyard.

✓ *Cabernet Sauvignon*

## PINE RIDGE WINERY
### Napa
### ★ ⊬ ❶

These are interesting wines of exciting quality that are in the midprice range.

✓ *Cabernet Sauvignon* (Stags Leap District) • *Classic red blend* (Andrus Reserve) • *Classic white blend* (Chenin-Viognier) • *Merlot* (Crimson Creek)

## PLUMPJACK
### Napa
### ★ ⊬

Owned by the Getty family and Gavin Newsom, Plumpjack is named after the roguish spirit of Shakespeare's Sir John Falstaff, dubbed "Plump Jack" by Queen Elizabeth. There's a whole Plumpjack empire out there, starting with shops and cafés before the Plumpjack winery was established in 1997. Plumpjack made headlines in 2000, when it sold its 1997 Reserve Cabernet Sauvignon under screwcap at $135 a bottle, while the regular cork-sealed version retailed for $125. Not only was Newsom making a statement, but he was also years ahead of his time in making it as far as red wines are concerned.

✓ *Cabernet Sauvignon*

## RAYMOND
### St. Helena
### ⊬ ❶

The Raymond family remain true to their reputation for vividly fruity Chardonnay and stylish Bordeaux-style reds. The cheaper Amberhill label is not to be overlooked.

✓ *Cabernet Sauvignon* (Amberhill, Napa Valley Reserve, Raymond Estates) • *Chardonnay* (Amberhill, Napa Valley Reserve) • *Merlot* (Amberhill, Raymond Estates)

## ROBERT CRAIG
### Mount Veeder
### ★★ ❶

Capable of classy, purple-hearted Cabernet Sauvignon.

✓ *Cabernet Sauvignon* • *Chardonnay*

## ROBERT FOLEY
### Angwin
### ★★ ❶

This red wine specialist makes just two wines, a classic blend (essentially Cabernet Sauvignon, plus a little Merlot and Petit Verdot) from his own vineyard on Candlestick Ridge, and Charbono grown by Gary Heitz.

✓ *Charbono* • *Red wine blend* (Claret)

## ROBERT MONDAVI
### Oakville
### ★ ⊬

ROBERT MONDAVI WINERY
NAPA VALLEY
FUMÉ BLANC

Established in 1966 by Bob Mondavi, who hoped to build a wine dynasty, and appeared to have succeeded beyond his wildest dreams by the 1980s. However, the Mondavi brand struggled to maintain its value in the new millennium, when profits plunged by 40 percent, and the company was sold to Constellation Brands in November 2004. The irony is that the top Robert Mondavi wines remain as great as they have ever been. Cabernet Sauvignon is Mondavi's greatest strength, even at the basic Napa Valley appellation, which can be very special in years such as 2000 and 2002. This winery has been rightly accused of turning out large volumes of very ordinary wine, yet it would be rated ★★⊬ if judged on Cabernet Sauvignon alone, as its Stags Leap District *cuvée*, and single-vineyard wines from To Kalon, Vine Hill, and Moffet are all on the same top quality level as the Reserve. The Io is not sold under the Mondavi name and its Santa Barbara mix (Syrah, Grenache, Mourvèdre) often contains more Syrah than some supposedly pure Syrah varietals.

✓ *Cabernet Sauvignon* • *Classic red blend* (Boomerang! Io) • *Riesling* (Private Selection) • *Sauvignon Blanc* (To Kalon I Block Fumé Blanc)

## ROBERT PECOTA WINERY
### Calistoga
### ★ ❶

This underrated winery always made ravishing white wines, and now has an excellent Cabernet.

✓ *Cabernet Sauvignon* (Kara's Vineyard) • *Muscat Canelli* (Moscato di Andrea)

## ROBERT PEPI WINERY
### Oakville
### ★ ⊬ ❶

This winery is still excellent value for Sauvignon Blanc, but is developing a reputation for interesting Italian-based blends.

✓ *Barbera* • *Classic red blend* (Colline di Sassi) • *Sangiovese* • *Sauvignon Blanc*

## ROBERT SINSKEY VINEYARDS
### Napa
### ❽ ★ ⊬

These vineyards produce vividly flavored Pinot, classy Vineyard Reserve, luscious Vin Gris, and crisp, age-worthy Chardonnay.

✓ *Chardonnay* • *Classic red blend* (Vineyard Reserve) • *Pinot Noir* • *Rosé* (Vin Gris of Pinot Noir)

## SADDLEBACK
### Oakville
### ★ ⊬

Nils Venge, formerly at Groth, is a master of the massive, old-fashioned, portlike style of Zinfandel.

✓ *Sangiovese* (Penny Lane Vineyard) • *Zinfandel*

## SAINTSBURY
### Napa
### ★ ⊬

David Graves and Dick Ward continue to make plump, juicy Pinot Noir at this increasingly impressive winery.

✓ *Chardonnay* • *Pinot Noir*

## SCHRAMSBERG VINEYARDS
### Calistoga
### ★

This prestigious winery started the modern Californian sparkling-wine industry rolling in 1965 and, until Domaine Chandon was set up some eight years later, was the only producer of serious-quality, bottle-fermented sparkling wine in the US. The head winemakers at Codorníu, Franciscan, Kristone, Mumm Napa Valley, and Piper-Sonoma all cut their teeth at Schramsberg.

✓ *Sparkling wine* (Blanc de Noirs, Crémant, J. Schram)

## SCREAMING EAGLE
### Oakville
### ★★ ⊬

Tiny quantities of cult Cabernet Sauvignon, always excruciatingly expensive, and mostly of exceptional quality, although I have found the odd underperformer at blind tastings.

✓ *Cabernet Sauvignon*

## SEAVEY
### St. Helena
### ★

Small quantities of beautifully crafted Cabernet Sauvignon wines are produced here. The Merlot is good, but less intense.

✓ *Cabernet Sauvignon* • *Merlot*

## SEQUOIA GROVE
### Napa

Jim and Steve Allen have been producing great Cabernet Sauvignon since 1978, and are now sourcing fine Chardonnay from Carneros.

✓ *Cabernet Sauvignon* • *Chardonnay*

## SHAFER VINEYARDS
### Napa
### ★ ⊬

Although the Cabernet Sauvignon Hillside Select is definitely the best wine, Shafer also makes very stylish Merlot and Chardonnay. The deliciously smooth Firebreak is a sort of Californian Super-Tuscan, while Relentless is a powerful blend of Syrah and Petite Sirah.

✓ *Cabernet Sauvignon* (Hillside Select) • *Chardonnay* • *Classic red blend* (Firebreak, Relentless) • *Merlot*

## SIGNORELLO VINEYARDS
### Napa
### ★ ⊬ ❶

The late Ray "Padrone" Signorello bought a vineyard on the Silverado Trail as long ago as 1970s, but only came to the fore with a bewildering display of fruity yet complex wines in the 1990s. If anything, the quality and consistency have stepped up a gear under Ray Signorello, Jr.

✓ *Cabernet Sauvignon* (Estate) • *Chardonnay* (Hope's Cuvée, Vieilles Vignes) • *Classic red blend* (Padrone) • *Classic white blend* (Seta) • *Zinfandel* (Luvisi Vineyard)

## SILVER OAK CELLARS
### Oakville
### ★

Concentrates solely on one variety, Cabernet Sauvignon, but there are three *cuvées*—Napa Valley, Bonny's Vineyard (also Napa Valley AVA), and Alexander Valley. I prefer the latter because it has the least oak and the most finesse.

✓ *Cabernet Sauvignon* (Alexander Valley)

## SILVERADO VINEYARDS
### Napa
### ★ ⊬

Silverado is owned by the widow of the late Walt Disney, but it has never produced a Mickey Mouse wine.

✓ *Cabernet Sauvignon* (Limited Reserve, Stags Leap Vineyard) • *Sangiovese* • *Sauvignon Blanc*

## SMITH-MADRONE
### St. Helena
### ★ ✩

This winery consists of some 40 acres (16 hectares) of high-altitude vines producing a small, high-quality range of wines.

✓ *Cabernet Sauvignon • Chardonnay • Riesling*

## SPOTTSWOODE
### St. Helena
### ◉ ★ ★

On benchland in the Mayacamas Mountains, the Novak family produce just two wines—tiny amounts of powerful but stylish Cabernet Sauvignon, and a deliciously fresh Sauvignon Blanc.

✓ *Cabernet Sauvignon • Sauvignon Blanc*

## SPRING MOUNTAIN VINEYARDS
### St. Helena
### ★ ✩

Known to millions as "Falcon Crest," this winery can produce wines that require aging and develop finesse.

✓ *Classic red blend (Elivette—formerly sold as Reserve) • Sauvignon Blanc • Syrah*

## ST. CLEMENT VINEYARDS
### St. Helena
### ★ ✩

One of the best-performing California wineries in the Beringer-Blass group.

✓ *Cabernet Sauvignon • Chardonnay • Classic red blend (Oroppas) • Merlot*

## ST. SUPÉRY
### Rutherford
### ★ ✩ Ⓥ

Capable of producing Cabernet of a rare level of finesse, and a deliciously tangy, yet inexpensive Sauvignon Blanc. Owned by Robert Skalli of South of France fame.

✓ *Cabernet Sauvignon (Dollarhide Ranch, Napa Valley) • Classic red blend (Elú Meritage, Rutherford Limited Edition) • Merlot • Muscat Canelli (Moscato) • Sauvignon Blanc • Sémillon (Dollarhide Ranch)*

## STAG'S LEAP WINE CELLARS
### Napa
### ★ ★

This is the famous Stag's Leap, with the apostrophe before the "s" and its legendary, ultraexpensive Cabernet Sauvignon Cask 23, although its Fay Vineyard and SLV can sometimes rival it in quality. Artemis is a lighter, easier-drinking, highly recommendable, less expensive blend of the Stag's Leap Arcadia vineyard with the leftovers from the selection of the three top Cabernet Sauvignons. Its second label is Hawk Crest.

✓ *Cabernet Sauvignon • Chardonnay (Arcadia)*

## STAGS' LEAP WINERY
### Napa
### ★

This is the other Stags' Leap winery, with the apostrophe after the "s" and less well known, although, ironically, the first to be established, as long ago as 1893. Stags' Leap Winery makes good Cabernet Sauvignon, particularly the Reserve, but it is not in the same class as the better-known Stag's Leap, whereas it does make one of California's finest Petite Sirah wines.

✓ *Cabernet Sauvignon • Petite Sirah (Petite Syrah)*

## STERLING VINEYARDS
### Calistoga
### ★

Astonishingly high quality in the mid-1970s, Sterling's standards dropped after Coca-Cola purchased it in 1978, but started a revival when Seagram took over in 1983 and has continued to improve.

✓ *Cabernet Sauvignon (Napa Valley Reserve) • Chardonnay (Napa Valley Reserve, Carneros Winery Lake) • Merlot (Three Palms, Napa Vy Reservealle)*

## STONY HILL VINEYARD
### St. Helena
### ★

The Chardonnays here are still world-class, but fatter than before.

✓ *Chardonnay*

## STORYBOOK MOUNTAIN VINEYARDS
### Calistoga
### ★ ★

Jerry Seps, a former college professor, has created a reputation for one of California's finest Zinfandels on this mountain vineyard, originally established by Adam and Jacob Grimm in 1880.

✓ *Zinfandel*

## SUTTER HOME WINERY
### St. Helena
### ✩ Ⓥ

Zinfandel of one style or another accounts for the majority of this winery's vast production under the state-wide California AVA. Some wines are brilliant one year (such as the 2002 Pinot Grigio), but nothing special the next, making recommendations difficult, but when the wines are good, the value is always great.

✓ *Chenin Blanc • Sauvignon Blanc*

## SWITCHBACK RIDGE
### Calistoga
### ★ ★

This converted orchard on the Peterson Ranch at the northern end of the Silverado Trail makes some of Napa's best and biggest reds.

✓ *Cabernet Sauvignon • Merlot • Petite Sirah*

## THE HESS COLLECTION
### Napa
### ★ ✩

Swiss-born art collector David Hess makes wines to be consumed not collected, although they do last well. Readers should note that Hess Select is a second label, not a premium *cuvée*.

✓ *Cabernet Sauvignon (Mount Veeder)*

## TITUS
### St. Helena
### ★ ★

Lee Titus brought his family from Minnesota to Napa, where he purchased this vineyard in separate lots in 1967. He replanted with classic varieties, and began to supply some of the top Napa Valley brands until the next generation decided to make and sell their own wine. With Phillip Titus as winemaker, and his brother Eric running both the business and the vineyard, Titus now threatens to become "the most fashionable new name in California winedom," according to Robert Parker.

✓ *Cabernet Franc*

## TREFETHEN VINEYARDS
### Napa
### ✩

This winery combines quality and consistency with good value.

✓ *Cabernet Sauvignon • Chardonnay (Library Selection) • Riesling*

## TRINCHERO WINERY
### Napa
### ★ Ⓥ

Although Sutter Home is the bigger brand and gets all the press, it has been owned by the Trinchero family since 1947, and they make sure that some pretty good wines go out under their own label.

✓ *Cabernet Sauvignon (Mario's Vineyard) • Classic red blend (Mario's Reserve Meritage) • Sauvignon Blanc (Family Reserve)*

## TURLEY
### Napa
### ★ ★ ✩

Talented brother and sister winemakers Larry and Helen Turley produce a raft of spectacular Zinfandel, with Petite Syrah (*sic*) and other interesting odds and ends.

✓ *Charbono (Tofanelli Vineyard) • Petite Syrah (sic) • Zinfandel*

## V. SATTUI
### St. Helena
### ★ ✩ Ⓥ

This underrated winery boasts a large range of relatively inexpensive, award-winning wines, but is let down by its rustic, 1950s labeling and presentation. Understated label would do wonders.

✓ *Cabernet Sauvignon (Morisoli Vineyard, Suzanne's Vineyard) • Chardonnay (Napa Valley) • Classic red blend (Family Red) • Fortified (Madeira) • Merlot (Napa Valley) • Riesling (Dry Johannisberg, Off-Dry Johannisberg) • Rosé (Gamay Rouge) • Zinfandel (Duarte Vineyard "Old Vine")*

## VIADER
### St. Helena
### ◉ ★ ✩

Tiny quantities of deeply colored, concentrated, red Bordeaux-style wine blended from vines grown on the slopes of Howell Mountain. Viader is a blend of 55–70 percent Cabernet Sauvignon with Cabernet Franc, while the firmer V is typically 58 percent Petit Verdot, 34 percent Cabernet Sauvignon, 8 percent Cabernet Franc.

✓ *Classic red blend (V, Viader)*

## VILLA MT EDEN WINERY
### Oakville
### ★ Ⓥ

Owned by Stimson Lane, Villa Mt. Eden established a high reputation in the 1980s, but has become less exciting since branching into a wider range of wines, although the wines that do excel are always great value.

✓ *Cabernet Sauvignon (Grand Reserve, Signature) • Chardonnay (Grand Reserve, Signature)*

## WHITEHALL LANE WINERY
### St. Helena
### ★ ✩

Despite various owners, Whitehall Lane consistently produces inspired wines, as endorsed by the Decanter World Wine Awards, when its 2001 Reserve Cabernet Sauvignon swept the boards to carry off the North American Bordeaux Varietal Trophy.

✓ *Cabernet Sauvignon • Merlot*

## WILLIAM HILL WINERY
### Napa
### ★ ✩

An improving winery in the Allied-Domecq stable.

✓ *Cabernet Sauvignon • Chardonnay • Merlot*

## ZD WINES
### Napa
### ★ ✩

Pronounced "Zee Dee", this winery used to make variable Cabernet Sauvignons, but is now very consistent; this wine now challenges Chardonnay's position as ZD's best varietal, and ZD sometimes comes out with a killer Pinot Noir (the 2000 Carneros Reserve).

✓ *Cabernet Sauvignon • Chardonnay • Pinot Noir (Carneros Reserve)*

# THE CENTRAL COAST (NORTH)

*Originally a district where a small number of big companies produced a vast quantity of inexpensive wines, the northern Central Coast can now boast a large number of top-quality, highly individual wineries.*

WINEMAKING IN THE northern Central Coast district dates from the 1830s, when virtually all the vineyards were located in and around Santa Clara County, and this remained the situation until the late 1950s and early 1960s, when the growing urban sprawl of San Jose forced the wine industry to search out new areas for vine-growing. Happily, this search coincided with the publication of a climatic report based on heat-summation (*see* p.470) by the University of California. This report pinpointed cooler areas farther south, particularly in Monterey, that should support fine-wine vineyards.

## THE MOVE TO MONTEREY

In 1957, two companies, Mirassou and Paul Masson, were the first to make the move, purchasing some 1,300 acres (530 hectares) in the Salinas Valley. In the ensuing rush to plant the land, some areas were used that were too cool or exposed to excessive coastal winds. These failures were not the fault of the heat-summation maps, but were due to producers who could not conceive that grapes would not ripen in California.

In October 1966, the two authors of the heat-summation study, Professors Winkler and Amerine, were honored at a special luncheon where a toast was made to "the world's first fine-wine district established as the direct result of scientific temperature research." Although this might have seemed premature, it has been substantiated by Monterey's viticultural growth. It was Bill Jekel who first brought the quality potential of this area to international fame, but this winery has been eclipsed by an eclectic bunch of wineries such as Bonny Doon, David Bruce, Calera, Chalone, Edmunds St. John, Frick, Morgan, Mount Eden, Ridge, Rosenblum, and Tamas.

JEKEL VINEYARDS
*Oak barrels wait to be filled at one of the Central Coast's pioneering wineries. Vineyards stretch out across the flat plain of Salinas Valley, where intensive irrigation systems have made this hot and dry area more synonymous with crisp salad vegetables than with wines, and the new pioneering wineries have moved up into the hills.*

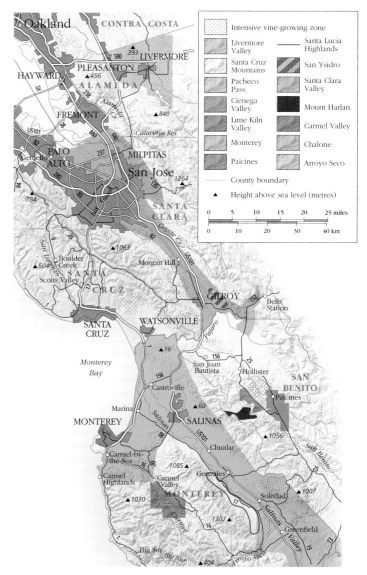

THE CENTRAL COAST (NORTH), *see also* p.470
*Until the late 1950s, most wineries were in Santa Clara County. Although this is still the Central Coast's northern heartland, it has long been in a slow decline, while Monterey and Santa Cruz are the area's fastest-growing counties.*

## FACTORS AFFECTING TASTE AND QUALITY

 **LOCATION**
The Central Coast's northern sector stretches from the San Francisco Bay area to Monterey.

**CLIMATE**
Generally warm (Region III, *see* p.470), but with variations such as the cooler (Region I, *see* p.470) areas of the Santa Cruz Mountains and the northern part of the Salinas Valley. Low rainfall in the south necessitates much irrigation, but there are microclimates with higher rainfall.

**ASPECT**
Vines are planted mainly on the flat and sloping lands of the various valleys. Variations are found: on the steep slopes of the Santa Cruz Mountains and the high benchland of the Pinnacles above Soledad, for example.

**SOIL**
A wide variety of gravel loams, often high in stone content and rich in limestone, in the Livermore Valley;

clay and gravel loams in Santa Clara; sandy and gravelly loams over granite or limestone in San Benito; and gravelly, well-drained, low-fertility soils in Monterey.

**VITICULTURE AND VINIFICATION**
A small number of big wine companies produce a vast quantity of inexpensive wines utilizing high-tech, production-line methods. The number of small wineries is growing. Many of these are quality-conscious and some are justifiably famous.

**GRAPE VARIETIES**
Barbera, Cabernet Sauvignon, Carignane, Chardonnay, Chenin Blanc, Colombard, Gamay, Gewürztraminer, Grenache, Gray Riesling, Mourvèdre, Muscat, Pinot Blanc, Pinot Gris (*syn.* Pinot Grigio), Pinot Noir, Petite Sirah, Riesling, Sauvignon Blanc, Sémillon, Syrah, Trebbiano, Viognier, Zinfandel

THE APPELLATIONS OF

# THE CENTRAL COAST (NORTH)

## ALAMEDA COUNTY AO

This appellation covers grapes grown anywhere within Alameda County.

## ARROYO SECO AVA

### Monterey County

Triangular-shaped, sloping benchland, with frost-free vineyards of coarse sandy loam.

## BEN LOMOND MOUNTAIN AVA

### Santa Cruz County

This AVA covers 60 square miles (155 square kilometers) on Ben Lomond Mountain, encompassing just 70 acres (28 hectares) of vines.

## CARMEL VALLEY AVA

### Monterey County

This appellation covers 30 square miles (78 square kilometers) around the Carmel River and Cachagua Creek. A distinctive microclimate is created by the valley's elevation and the northeastern Tularcitos Ridge, which curbs the marine fog and provides more sunny days.

## CHALONE AVA

### Monterey County

Benchland vineyards at 1,650 feet (500 meters) above sea level, with volcanic and granitic soils of high limestone content. The soil combines with an arid climate to stress the vines. Suited to Chardonnay, Pinot Noir, and Pinot Blanc.

## CIENEGA VALLEY AVA

### San Benito County

The Cienega valley is located at the base of the Gabilan (or Gavilan) Mountain Range where the Pescadero Creek is used artificially to augment the area's rainfall. The soil is loamy, well-drained, and often lies over weathered granite.

## CONTRA COSTA COUNTY AO

An appellation covering grape varieties grown anywhere within Contra Costa County.

## HAMES VALLEY AVA

### Monterey County

North of Lake Nacimiento, where more than 600 acres (250 hectares) of vineyards already exist.

## LIME KILN VALLEY AVA

### San Benito County

Annual rainfall ranges from 16 inches (41 centimeters) on the valley floor to 40 inches (102 centimeters) in the mountainous west. Soils are sandy and gravelly loams over limestone, with a high magnesium carbonate content.

## LIVERMORE VALLEY AVA

### Alameda County

One of the coastal intermountain valleys surrounding San Francisco, the Livermore Valley has a moderate climate, cooled by sea breezes and morning fog, with very little spring frost.

## MONTEREY AVA

### Monterey County

This AVA is distinguished by a very dry climate, although the watersheds of the Santa Lucia, Gabilan, and Diablo Mountain Ranges provide sufficient water, through the presence of underground aquifers, to irrigate the vineyards.

## MONTEREY COUNTY AO

An appellation covering grapes that are grown anywhere within Monterey County.

## MOUNT HARLAN AVA

### San Benito County

Like Chalone, Mount Harlan is, for all intents and purposes, a single-winery AVA (Calera in this instance), and is situated on rare limestone outcrops in the same range of hills (the San Benito Range), albeit at the other end and on the opposite-facing flank, and higher—2,200 feet (670 meters).

## PACHECO PASS AVA

### Santa Clara and San Benito Counties

The terrain sets this area apart from its neighbors. It is a small valley, with a flat or gently sloping topography that contrasts with the rugged hills of the Diablo Range to the east and west. The climate is moderate and wetter than that of the Hollister Basin to the south.

## PAICINES AVA

### San Benito County

Here the days are warm and the nights cool, and the annual rainfall ranges between 12 and 15 inches (30 and 38 centimeters). This AVA has fallen into disuse since Almadén, the winery that proposed it, moved to Santa Clara.

## SAN BENITO AVA

### San Benito County

Not to be confused with San Benito County, this AVA encapsulates the smaller AVAs of Paicines, Cienega Valley, and Lime Kiln Valley.

## SAN BENITO COUNTY AO

This is an appellation covering grapes grown anywhere within San Benito County.

## SAN FRANCISCO BAY AVA

This appellation encompasses more than 1.5 million acres that are, to some degree, affected by coastal fog and winds from San Francisco Bay. It also includes the city of San Francisco, apparently to justify the appellation name, but this could lead to the emergence of Moraga-like vineyards (see p.506).

## SAN LUCAS AVA

### Monterey County

This AVA consists of a 10-mile (16-kilometer) segment of the Salinas Valley between King City and San Ardo, in the southern section of Monterey County. The soils in this area are mostly alluvial loams.

## SAN MATEO COUNTY AO

This is an appellation covering grapes grown anywhere within San Mateo County.

## SAN YSIDRO AVA

### Santa Clara County

The appellation covers a small enclave of vineyards at the southeastern end of the Santa Clara AVA. San Ysidro sits between two hills that channel the sea breezes coming up the Pajaro River, and is particularly noted for Chardonnay.

## SANTA CLARA COUNTY AO

This is an appellation covering grapes grown anywhere within Santa Clara County.

## SANTA CLARA VALLEY AVA

### Santa Clara County

Encompassing the entire municipality of San Jose to the north and better known as Silicon Valley in the south, this AVA must qualify as the most built-up wine appellation in the world.

## SANTA CRUZ MOUNTAINS AVA

### Santa Clara County

The name "Santa Cruz Mountains" was first recorded in 1838. Its climate is influenced in the west by ocean breezes and maritime fog, while the east is moderated by San Francisco Bay. Cool air coming down from the mountains forces warmer air up, lengthening the growing season to a full 300 days. The soils are forms of shale that are peculiar to the area.

THE WINE PRODUCERS OF

# THE NORTH-CENTRAL COAST

## BONNY DOON VINEYARD

### Santa Cruz County

### ★★♥

This is one of California's brightest, most bizarre, and most innovative stars, with wines that are electrifying in their brilliance and style, often showing surprising finesse. I have gotten lost trying to find Bonny Doon on two occasions, but it was worth the effort just to meet the wacky winemaker, Randall Grahm. In 2001, Grahm officially declared himself "off his rocker" when he macerated three wines on ground-up rocks from three different parcels of his Cigare Volant red wine. If the experiment is deemed successful, it could lead to "The Rock Quartet." I'm still watching this space… In 2006, Grahm sold off his best-selling Cardinal Zin and Big House brands to The Wine Group—"Doonsizing," as he termed it, from 400,000 cases to just 40,000. He also announced plans to phase out Old Telegram (heaven forbid) and the hiving off of his Pacific Rim label, which will operate from a brand-new winery to be built in Washington State.

✓ Entire range

## BURNSTEIN-REMARK WINERY
### Monterey County
### ❷

Established as recently as 2003, and not tasted, thus not rated, but the first releases have stirred up such critical acclaim that readers should be made aware of their existence.

✓ *Grenache* (Marilyn Remark Wild Horse Vineyards) • *Marsanne* (Marilyn Remark Loma Pacific Vineyard)

## DAVID BRUCE
### Santa Cruz County
### ★ Ⓥ

Having gone through a learning curve, David Bruce now produces far more elegant wines than he used to. Pinot Noir has emerged as his consistently finest style.

✓ *Merlot* (Central Coast) • *Petite Syrah* (sic) (Central Coast, Shell Creek Vineyard) • *Pinot Noir* • *Zinfandel* (Paso Robles)

## CALERA WINE COMPANY
### San Benito County
### ★★

One of California's premier pioneers in the continuing quest for perfect Pinot Noir, Calera continues to produce some of the state's greatest examples of this wine, although the focus on varietal purity can sometimes result in overly pretty fruit.

✓ *Pinot Noir* • *Viognier*

## CEDAR MOUNTAIN
### Alameda County
### ★ Ⓥ

This boutique winery was established in 1990 and early vintages are promising, if a little too correct and in need of a personal signature.

✓ *Cabernet Sauvignon* • *Fortified* (Chardonnay del Sol) • *Zinfandel*

## CHALONE VINEYARD
### Monterey County
### ★★

This winery's 155-acre (63-hectare) vineyard has its own AVA. Chalone Vineyard is dedicated to, and astonishingly successful at, producing a range of fine, complex wines of the most exquisite style. The Chenin Blanc is from the Gavilan Mountain ridge, 1,800 feet (540 meters) above the Salinas Valley, where the vines were planted as long ago as 1919. These venerable vines have the capacity to make California's finest Chenin Blanc, and in some years they succeed in doing so, although there is variation in quality.

✓ *Chardonnay* • *Chenin Blanc* • *Pinot Blanc* • *Pinot Noir*

## CONCANNON VINEYARD
### Alameda County
### ★

This winery continues to make fine Petite Sirah wines, but is also getting a name for its Merlot.

✓ *Merlot* (Selected Vineyard) *Petite Sirah* (Heritage)

## CONUNDRUM
### Monterey County
### ★★

Under the same ownership as Caymus Vineyard, where Conundrum started out as a new addition to the range in 1989. Conundrum was created by Jon Bolta, who had assisted in the making of Caymus wines, and who has made every vintage to date. The idea behind Conundrum was to make a blended white wine to suit the new Pacific cuisine of coastal California. Jon originally experimented with 11 white grapes before deciding on the five that have been used ever since: Sauvignon Blanc, Chardonnay, Muscat Canelli, Sémillon, and Viognier.

✓ *Classic white blend* (Conundrum)

## EDMUNDS ST JOHN
### Alameda County
### ★★

Steven Edmunds and Cornelia St John established this exciting winery in 1985 in what used to be the East Bay Wine Works, where they have honed some of California's most beautifully balanced wines, with a particular penchant for classy Syrah.

✓ *Syrah* • *Viognier* (Rozet Vineyard)

## FRICK WINERY
### Santa Cruz County
### ★

This winery is an up-and-coming Rhône-style specialist with a hands-off approach to winemaking.

✓ *Cinsaut* • *Classic red blend* (C2) • *Syrah*

## HAHN ESTATES
### Monterey County
### ★★ Ⓥ

Nicky Hahn of Smith & Hook launched this label in 1991, and his flavour-packed, bargain wines now have their own dedicated winery.

✓ *Cabernet Franc* • *Classic red blend* (Meritage) • *Merlot* (Central Coast, Cycles Gladiator) • *Syrah*

## HELLER VINEYARDS
### Monterey County
### ❶★★

Although under new ownership since the death of Bill Durney, this winery continues to produce heroically dark, rich, densely flavoured Cabernet Sauvignon, and splendidly long-lived Chardonnay, with Celebration the standout wine.

✓ *Cabernet Sauvignon* • *Chardonnay* • *Classic red blend* (Celebration Meritage) • *Merlot*

## J C CELLARS
### Alameda County
### ★★

The personal label of Jeff "Rhône-in-his-Bones" Cohn specializes in single-vineyard, hillside-grown Syrah, Petite Syrah (one of California's best), Viognier, and Zinfandel.

✓ *Petite Sirah* • *Syrah* • *Viognier*

## JEKEL VINEYARD
### Monterey County
### ★ Ⓥ

Once known for its fascinating range of Riesling, owners Brown-Forman closed this winery in February 2004, but the vineyards have been retained and production of wines under this label continues. Even before the closure, this was no longer the force it used to be in Bill Jekel's heyday, although some wines still excite.

✓ *Classic red blend* (Sanctuary) • *Syrah* (Monterey County)

## J LOHR
### Santa Clara County
### ★ Ⓥ

The Valdigué used to be labelled Gamay until correctly identified by UC Davis. It is made in a fruity Gamay style that is not just a good quaffer, but really quite elegant and well perfumed with plenty of refreshing acidity.

✓ *Cabernet Sauvignon* (Crosspoint) • *Chardonnay* (Arroyo Vista Vineyard) • *Classic red blend* (Cuvée Pom Meritage) • *Valdigué* (Wildflower)

## MORGAN WINERY
### Monterey County
### ★★ Ⓥ

Possibly California's most underrated, age-worthy Pinot Noir and Chardonnay are produced here. Although plenty of Americans love good Burgundy, such consumers are by and large not avid fans of west-coast wines, and regular California wine drinkers are often put off by Morgan's Burgundian-like character. Those of you who fall between these stalls should give these wines a try. The fresh, zesty Sauvignon Blanc is consistently good, but the Rhône-style wines need some work.

✓ *Chardonnay* • *Pinot Noir* • *Sauvignon Blanc*

## MOUNT EDEN VINEYARDS
### Santa Clara County
### ★

This winery produces just three varietals. The range of Chardonnay excels, but the deep, dark, chocolaty Old Vines Cabernet comes a close second.

✓ *Cabernet Sauvignon* (Cuvée Saratoga, Old Vine Reserve) • *Chardonnay*

## MURRIETA'S WELL
### Alameda County

Run by Phil Wente, whose blends are significantly better than his pure varietal wines. His style is generally understated, but finer than that of his more prominent brother, Eric of Wente Bros. The red Vendimia is a classic Bordeaux-style blend, while Zarzuela is Tempranillo-based.

✓ *Classic red blend* (Vendimia, Zarzuela) • *Classic white blend* (Vendimia)

## RIDGE VINEYARDS
### Santa Clara County
### ★★

Those who wonder about the long-term maturation potential of California wines should taste these stunning ones, some of which need between 10 and 20 years in bottle before they are even approachable.

✓ *Cabernet Sauvignon* (Monte Bello) • *Chardonnay* (Howell Mountain, Santa Cruz Mountains) • *Classic red blend* (Geyserville) • *Mourvèdre* (Mataro) • *Petite Sirah* (York Creek) • *Zinfandel*

## ROSENBLUM CELLARS
### Alameda County
### ★★ Ⓥ

Established in 1978 by Kent Rosenblum, a Minnesotan who came to California to set up a veterinary practice, but got sidetracked by a sudden infatuation with the local wines. In its first year, Rosenblum made 400 cases of a Zinfandel that won a gold medal at the Orange County Fair. Now he produces over 100,000 cases of over 40 different wines from more than 75 vineyards throughout California, plus a few in Australia, and still finds time to run his veterinary practice. Excellent-value wines also sold under the Chateau La Paws label, particularly Mourvèdre, Syrah, Zinfandel (Amador), and Cote de Bone (Blanc and Roan).

✓ *Cabernet Sauvignon* • *Classic red blend* (Holbrook Mitchell Trio) • *Dessert style* (Rosie Rabbit Zinfandel) • *Marsanne* (Dry Creek) • *Merlot* (Mountain Selection) • *Mourvèdre* (Continente Vineyard) • *Muscat Canelli* (Muscat de Glacier) • *Petite Sirah* (Rockpile) • *Syrah* (England Shaw, Hillside Vineyards) • *Viognier* (Ripken Ranch Late Harvest) • *Zinfandel*

## ROBERT TALBOTT VINEYARDS
### Monterey County
### ★

Run by the son of the late founder, the Talbott family is best known for the internationally renowned Monterey-based Talbott Tie Company.

✓ *Chardonnay*

## WENTE BROS
### Alameda County
### ★ Ⓥ

Established for more than a century, Wente's wines used to range from overtly fruity to distinctly dull, but have improved in recent years.

✓ *Chardonnay* (Riva Ranch Reserve) • *Sauvignon Blanc* (Livermore Valley)

# THE CENTRAL COAST (SOUTH)

*An up-and-coming wine district in general, the southern Central Coast has very rapidly become one of the very best areas in the world, outside of Burgundy itself, for Pinot Noir. Chardonnay is equally exciting, and Italian varietals could well be the most prized wines of the new millennium.*

PASO ROBLES in San Luis Obispo county was originally planted with vines in the late 18th century; the Santa Ynez Valley, in Santa Barbara County, had a flourishing wine industry in pre-Prohibition times; Santa Barbara town itself was once dotted with vineyards. Yet both counties were virtually devoid of vines in the early 1960s; it was not until Estrella, in Paso Robles, and Firestone, in Santa Ynez Valley, established vineyards in 1972 that others followed.

Quite why Santa Barbara of all areas in the southern Central Coast has suddenly become the mecca for Pinot Noir specialists is difficult to unravel. In the late 1980s, California seemed the least likely place to be in a position to challenge Burgundy for the Holy Grail of winemaking. Oregon and New Zealand looked much more likely, but they have both since proved too small and prone to inconsistency. If it was going to be California, no one a decade ago would have put their money on Santa Barbara, way down south, just a stone's throw from Los Angeles; Carneros or Russian River seemed a more likely bet. The foundations for Santa Barbara's sudden surge of wonderful Pinot Noir wines were laid innocently in the 1970s, when the land was relatively cheap and planted with this variety in order to supply the sparkling-wine

industry in the north of the state. It is impossible to pinpoint exactly when local winemakers realized the potential of making their own still wine, but much of California's finest, purest, and most consistent Pinot Noir wines now come from this valley.

The Santa Ynez Valley makes the best Santa Barbara Pinot, yet the area where it excels is restricted: 9 miles (14 kilometers) from the ocean and the valley is too cool to ripen grapes; 16 miles (26 kilometers) and it is ideal for Pinot Noir; but for every 1 mile (1.5 kilometers) farther from the ocean the grapes gain an extra degree (ABV) of ripeness, and by 20 miles (32 kilometers) from the coast, this is Cabernet country. The best Pinot Noir vineyard in the Santa Ynez Valley is Sanford & Benedict. In the Santa Maria Valley, also well suited to Pinot Noir, the best vineyard is Bien Nacido.

## FACTORS AFFECTING TASTE AND QUALITY

### LOCATION
This stretches southward along the coast from Monterey, and includes the counties of San Luis Obispo and Santa Barbara.

### CLIMATE
Generally warm (Region III, *see* p.470), except for areas near the sea, particularly around Santa Maria in the middle of the region where Regions I and II (*see* p.470) prevail because of the regular incursion of the tail of the great coastal fog bank. Annual rainfall ranges from 10 inches (25 centimeters) to 45 inches (114 centimeters).

### ASPECT
Most vines grow on hillsides in San Luis Obispo and southern-facing benchland in Santa Barbara County, at altitudes from 120 to 600 feet (37 to 180 meters) in the Edna Valley, to 600 to 1,000 feet (180 to 305 meters) in Paso Robles, and 1,500 feet (460 meters) on York Mountain.

### SOIL
Mostly sandy, silty, or clay loams, but soil can be more alkaline, as in the gravelly lime soils on the Santa Lucia Mountains foothills.

### VITICULTURE AND VINIFICATION
By the mid-1980s, the cooler areas had invited experimentation with the Burgundian varieties planted in the early 1970s to supply sparkling-wine producers in the north of the state, and by the late 1980s a number of world-class Pinot Noirs had been produced. This variety is the region's main claim to fame, although viticultural methods are still developing, as indeed are vinification processes. Open-top fermenters are commonly used, the cap being punched down frequently. Some producers have incorporated 15–30 percent whole-cluster, but most have shied away from this. A cold maceration is followed by natural yeast fermentation, the temperatures of which run nice and high. After a gentle pressing, the wines are matured in *barriques* with 25–50 percent new oak. The oak is all French, and nearly everyone prefers tight-grain, with many going for a heavy toast.

### GRAPE VARIETIES
Barbera, Cabernet Franc, Cabernet Sauvignon, Chardonnay, Chenin Blanc, Gewürztraminer, Malvasia, Muscat, Pinot Blanc, Pinot Noir, Riesling, Sangiovese, Sauvignon Blanc, Sémillon, Sylvaner, Syrah, Tocai Friulano, Zinfandel

### Map Legend

- • Wineries
- ⬜ Intensive vine-growing zone
- York Mountain
- Paso Robles
- Edna Valley
- Santa Maria Valley
- Santa Ynez Valley
- Arroyo Grande
- County boundary
- ▲ Height above sea level (metres)

0   5   10   15   20   25   30 miles
0   10   20   30   40   50 km

THE CENTRAL COAST (SOUTH), *see also* p.470
*Based on San Luis Obispo and Santa Barbara counties, this area has a fine reputation for top-quality Pinot Noir.*

THE APPELLATIONS OF
# THE CENTRAL COAST (SOUTH)

## ARROYO GRANDE VALLEY AVA
### San Luis Obispo County

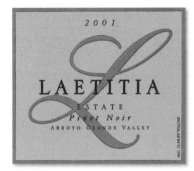

An area of 67 square miles (173 square kilometers) some 12 miles (19 kilometers) southeast of the town of San Luis Obispo, the Arroyo Grande Valley enjoys a Region I to II climate (see p.470), thanks primarily to its proximity to the ocean and the frequent fog produced by marine air in the mornings and evenings. Planted at an altitude of between 300 and 1,000 feet (90 and 300 meters), vines grow at much higher altitudes than those in the neighboring Edna Valley AVA, and also receive slightly more rain. The hillsides cultivated range from moderate to very steep slopes, with deep, well-drained, sandy-clay and silty-clay loam soils. With a 30°F (30°F) drop in nighttime temperatures, relatively high acidity levels are maintained throughout ripening. The potential for sparkling wine is considerable, so it is perhaps not surprising that Maison Deutz is the best-known winery here, with the largest vineyards in the appellation. Deutz has also produced some still Chardonnay and Pinot Noir,

and although rather strange, disjointed, and hardly indicative of any potential for such wines, Au Bon Climat has had stunning success with these varieties.

## EDNA VALLEY AVA
### San Luis Obispo County

This elongated valley is located just south of Paso Robles, and is well defined by the Santa Lucia Mountains to the northeast, the San Luis Range to the southwest, and a low hilly complex to the southeast. In the northwest, the Edna Valley merges with the Los Osos Valley, forming what is, in effect, a wide-mouthed funnel that sucks in ocean air from Morro Bay. This marine air flows unobstructed into the valley, where it is captured by the pocket of mountains and hills, providing a moderate summer climate that differentiates it from surrounding areas. The vines grow on the valley floor, rising to 600 feet (120 meters) in the Santa Lucia Mountains, on soils that are mostly sandy-clay loam, clay loam, and clay.

## PASO ROBLES AVA
### San Luis Obispo County

This area was given its name in the 18th century, when travelers passed through it on their way from the San Miguel to the San Luis Obispo missions. It is one of California's oldest winegrowing regions: grapes have been harvested in this area of rolling hills and valleys since c.1797. There is no penetration by coastal winds or marine fog and, consequently, there is the equivalent of an additional 500 to 1,000 degree-days here compared to viticultural areas to the west and east. This obviously has a considerable effect on grape-ripening patterns

making Paso Robles red-wine country, particularly for Zinfandel and Rhône varieties.

## SAN LUIS OBISPO AO
An appellation covering grapes grown anywhere within the entire county of San Luis Obispo.

## SANTA BARBARA AO
An appellation covering grapes grown anywhere within the entire county of Santa Barbara.

## SANTA MARIA VALLEY AVA
### Santa Barbara County

The Pacific winds blow along this funnel-shaped valley, causing cooler summers and winters and warmer falls than in the surrounding areas. The terrain climbs from 200 to 800 feet (60 to 240 meters), with most of the vineyards concentrated at 300 feet (90 meters). The soil is sandy and clay loam, and is free from the adverse effects of salts. This is top-quality Pinot Noir country and Bien Nacido (to which many winemakers have access) in the Tepesquet Bench area is far and away its best vineyard. Noises about Bien Nacido in the 1990s are reminiscent of the fuss made a decade earlier about the Sanford & Benedict vineyard in

RUGGED MOUNTAINS IN THE VAST LOS PADRES NATIONAL FOREST, CALIFORNIA
*California's best wines are produced in areas cooled by the sea, bay winds, and the great coastal fog bank. The Central Coast (South) has rapidly acquired a good reputation for its Pinot Noir.*

the Santa Ynez Valley. The Santa Maria Valley also grows top-quality Chardonnay and even one of California's best Syrahs.

## SANTA RITA HILLS AVA
### Santa Barbara County

This appellation is located almost entirely within the preexisting Santa Ynez Valley AVA and includes all the latter's coolest areas. The Santa Rita Hills is primarily planted with Chardonnay and Pinot Noir, although Syrah and Riesling are on the increase.

## SANTA YNEZ VALLEY AVA
### Santa Barbara County

The Santa Ynez Valley is bounded by mountains to the north and south, by Lake Cachuma to the east, and by a series of low hills to the west. The valley's close proximity to the ocean serves

to moderate the weather with maritime fog, and this tends to lower the temperatures. The Santa Rita Hills block penetration of the coldest of the sea winds, however, so the middle and eastern end of the valley do not have the coolest of coastal climates (2,680 degree-days), while Lompoc, which is just 2 miles (3 kilometers) outside the appellation's western boundary, has just 1,970 degree days. The vineyards are located at an altitude of between 200 and 400 feet (60 and 120 metres) in the foothills of the San Rafael Mountains, and the vines are grown on soils that are mostly well drained, sandy, silty, clay, and shale loam. Santa Barbara's finest Pinot Noir wines come from the Sanford & Benedict vineyard (to which a number of winemakers have access) in the west, yet just a few miles farther up the valley it is Cabernet and Zinfandel country. The Santa Ynez Valley also grows top-quality Chardonnay.

## TEMPLETON
### San Luis Obispo County

Templeton is situated within Paso Robles. It is not an AVA, but I have included it for the purposes of clarification, because various sources have stated that it is. Even official publications from California's Wine Institute have made the same error.

## YORK MOUNTAIN AVA
### San Luis Obispo County

This small appellation is just 7 miles (11 kilometers) from the sea, situated at an altitude of 1,500 feet (450 meters) in the Santa Lucia Mountains, close to the western border of Paso Robles. Its Region I (see p.470) climatic classification, and 45 inches (114 centimeters) of rain per year, set it apart from the warmer, and considerably drier, surrounding areas.

---

## THE WINE PRODUCERS OF
# THE CENTRAL COAST (SOUTH)

### ALBAN VINEYARDS
#### San Luis Obispo County
★★

John Alban claims that his family-owned vineyard, founded in 1989, was "the first American winery and vineyard established exclusively for Rhône varieties." He certainly produces some of the best California Rhône varietals.

✓ *Classic red blend* (Pandora) • *Grenache* • *Syrah* • *Viognier*

### ANDREW MURRAY
#### Santa Barbara County
★★

Up-and-coming, Rhône-style specialist, producing immaculately crafted wines from hillside vineyards.

✓ *Classic white blend* (Enchanté) • *Syrah* • *Viognier*

### AU BON CLIMAT
#### Santa Barbara County
★★

It was Jim Clendenen's wines of the 1980s that convinced me of Santa Barbara's suitability to Pinot Noir, since when, of course, this area has established a soaring reputation for Rhône varieties as well as Burgundian.

✓ *Chardonnay* (especially Sanford & Benedict) • *Pinot Noir*

### BABCOCK VINEYARDS
#### Santa Barbara County
★☆

Best for succulent Pinot Noir and, deep, dark, rewarding Syrah.

✓ *Chardonnay* (Grand Cuvee) • *Pinot Noir* • *Sauvignon Blanc* • *Syrah*

### BARON HERZOG
#### Santa Barbara County
★❤

A story of riches to rags and back to riches again. Eugene Herzog was born into an aristocratic family that was renowned as suppliers of wine since the days of the Austro-Hungarian Empire. Having survived the Nazis only to see his property confiscated by the Communists, he fled Czechoslovakia in 1948, taking his family to New York, where he came down to earth with a bump, working as a driver and salesman for the Royal Wine Company. The company was short of cash flow, and paid part of his salary in shares, but Herzog's selling acumen was such that he became the majority shareholder, purchasing the rest of the company within 10 years of setting foot in the US. The Baron Herzog winery was established in 1986, since when it has not been one of the flashy highfliers, but has steadily produced a number of modestly priced, award-winning wines.

✓ *Chenin Blanc* (Clarksburg) • *Sauvignon Blanc* (California) • *Zinfandel* (Lodi Old Vines)

### BLACKJACK RANCH
#### Santa Barbara County
★★☆

In 1989, Roger Wisted invented, patented, copyrighted, and trademarked "California Blackjack," the proceeds of which enabled him to indulge in his lifelong fantasy to plant his own vineyard. His first vintage was 1997, since when his wine have displayed a structure and acidity balance that sets them apart.

✓ *Chardonnay* • *Classic red blend* (Harmonie) • *Merlot* • *Syrah*

### BONACCORSI
#### Santa Barbara County
★★

Master Sommelier Michael Bonaccorsi, formerly of Spago Restaurant in Beverly Hills, which has won the *Wine Spectator's* Best of Award of Excellence each year since 1995. In 1999, Bonaccorsi set up his own winery, which has swiftly achieved an enviable reputation for the highly polished style of its wines.

✓ *Chardonnay* • *Pinot Noir* • *Syrah*

### BREWER-CLIFTON
#### Santa Barbara County
★★

Specialists in sourcing top-class Burgundian varietals from single-vineyards in the best areas of Santa Rita Hills AVA.

✓ *Chardonnay* • *Pinot Noir*

### BYRON
#### Santa Barbara County
★☆

Under Mondavi ownership since 1990, and now part of Jackson Family Wine Estates, these wines are still made by founder Byron Ken Brown, whose white wines are even better than his Pinot Noir.

✓ *Chardonnay* • *Pinot Blanc* • *Pinot Gris* • *Pinot Noir*

### CAMBRIA
#### Santa Barbara County
★☆

Personally owned by Jess Jackson's wife, Barbara Banke, rather than the Kendall-Jackson company, Cambria's strength is its extraordinary line of high-quality Chardonnay. Also produces interesting single-clone Pinot Noir wines from the same vineyard and vintage.

✓ *Chardonnay* • *Pinot Noir* (Rae's)

### CLAIBORNE & CHURCHILL
#### San Luis Obispo County
★☆❤

Alsatian specialists, with 20 years' experience, Claiborne Thompson and Fredericka Churchill are particularly enthusiastic about genuinely dry, classically structured Gewürztraminer. When I first heard of these wines I was sceptical, but as soon as I tasted them, I was convinced. Drink on purchase.

✓ *Gewürztraminer* (Dry Alsatian Style) • *Riesling* (Dry Alsatian Style)

### COLD HEAVEN
#### Santa Barbara County
★☆

Made by Jim Clendenen's wife, Morgan, whose main focus is on Viognier, but also produces an increasingly silky-stylish Pinot Noir.

✓ *Pinot Noir* (Le Bon Climat Vineyard) • *Viognier*

### EBERLE WINERY
#### San Luis Obispo County
★☆

Look no farther if you want massively built Zinfandel, but the Cabernet is the better-balanced, much classier wine, while the Steinbeck Syrah is the best of both worlds.

✓ *Barbera* • *Cabernet Sauvignon* • *Muscat Canelli* • *Sangiovese* (Fillipponi & Thompson Vineyard) • *Syrah* (Steinbeck) • *Viognier* (Glenrose Vineyard)

### EDNA VALLEY VINEYARD
#### San Luis Obispo County
★☆

A joint venture between Chalone and the Niven family, which owns the Paragon Vineyard, Edna Valley Vineyard still produces rich, toasty Chardonnay and very good Pinot Noir, but now also turns out a refreshing Pinot Gris that has a certain spicy potential if given a couple of years' aging. The Syrah has yet to find its feet, but other varieties are beginning to show promise.

✓ *Chardonnay* (Paragon Vineyard) • *Pinot Gris* (Paragon Vineyard) • *Pinot Noir* (Paragon Vineyard)

## EPIPHANY VINEYARDS
### Santa Barbara County
★ ✓

The personal winery of Eli Parker, son of Fess (*see* below).

✓ *Grenache* (Revelation Rodney's Vineyard) • *Pinot Gris*

## FESS PARKER WINERY
### Santa Barbara County
★ ✓ ✓

Unless you enjoyed a 1950s childhood, the name of actor Fess Parker is not likely to mean anything to you, but for me it will always be synonymous with his role as Davy Crockett, so it was quite amusing to see a fat American lady at least twice my age swoon in front of this still imposing figure. Unfortunately, she found all the wines too dry, even the excellent off-dry Riesling failed to please, but she did buy a poster of Mr. Crockett taking a bath wearing just his coonskin hat. These wines get better with each vintage.

✓ *Chardonnay* (Marcella's Vineyard) • *Pinot Noir* • *Syrah* • *Viognier*

## FIRESTONE VINEYARD
### Santa Barbara County
★ ✓

Although Firestone can occasionally lapse, the wines are usually rich and ripe, and are gradually assuming more finesse.

✓ *Johannisberg Riesling* • *Merlot* • *Sauvignon Blanc* • *Syrah*

## FOXEN VINEYARD
### Santa Barbara County
★ ✓ ✓

I am not as enamored as some by this winery's Pinot Noir, but have great respect for virtually everything else produced here.

✓ *Classic red blend* (Foothills Reserve) • *Pinot Noir* • *Syrah* • *Viognier*

## GAINEY VINEYARDS
### Santa Barbara County
★ ★ ✓

This winery still makes one of Santa Barbara's best Pinots, but is now best known for its Merlot, and turns out a number of amazing bargains.

✓ *Chardonnay* (Limited Selection) • *Merlot* (Limited Selection) • *Pinot Noir* (Limited Selection Santa Rita Hills) • *Riesling* (Santa Ynez Valley) • *Sauvignon Blanc* (Limited Selection) • *Syrah* (Limited Selection)

## THE HITCHING POST
### Santa Barbara County
★ ✓ ✓

Frank Ostini is the soft-spoken, friendly, fun-loving chef-owner of the Hitching Post restaurant in Santa Maria, which serves tasteful, unpretentious American barbecue food at its best. Frank also enjoys making wines with his fisherman friend, Gray Hartley. They started out in a corner of Jim Clendenen's Au Bon Climat winery, but in 2001 moved to Central Coast Wine Services in Santa Maria, and continue to make a number of excellent wines, particularly the polished Pinot Noirs.

✓ *Pinot Noir* • *Syrah* (Purisima Mountain)

## L'AVENTURE
### San Luis Obispo County
★ ★ ✓

Monstrous wines from *Bordelais* Stephan Asseo, whose vision of Bordeaux with Rhône in Pas Robles has attracted rave reviews. Second label: Stephan Ridge.

✓ *Classic red blend* (Côte-à-Côte, Cuvée) • *Syrah*

## LANE TANNER
### Santa Barbara County
★ ✓ ✓

The eponymous Lane Tanner established this small winery in 1989, since when she has honed a deliciously deep style of ripe, pure-flavored Pinot Noir.

✓ *Pinot Noir* • *Syrah*

## LONGORIA
### Santa Barbara County
★ ★

Rick Longoria started making tiny quantities under his own label while he was at Gainey Vineyard, which he put on the map as winemaker there for 12 years. Now he has his own winery, he still produces small batches of wine (ranging between 70 and 850 cases), but the quantities are massive by comparison with his early years. The quality is, however, even better—especially the Pinot Noir.

✓ *Chardonnay* • *Pinot Noir* • *Syrah* (Alisos Vineyard)

## MOSBY WINERY
### Santa Barbara County
★ ✓ ✓

Bill and Jeri Mosby run this interesting, sometimes provocative, Italian-style specialty operation.

✓ *Dolcetto* • *Pinot Grigio* • *Teroldego*

## PALMINA
### Santa Barbara County
★ ★ ✓

Some of California's greatest Italian style wines, especially the single-vineyard offerings, from the owners of Brewer-Clifton.

✓ *Barbera* • *Classic red blend* (Savoia) • *Nebbiolo* • *Pinot Grigio*

## QUPÉ
### Santa Barbara County
★ ✓ ✓

Owned by Bob Lindquist, who operates out of the Au Bon Climat winery. Great for Rhône-style reds, particularly the various single-vineyard Syrahs. Lindquist also owns Verdad with his wife, Louisa.

✓ *Classic red blend* (Los Olivos) • *Grenache* (Purisma Mountain Vineyard) • *Syrah*

## RANCHO SISQUOC
### Santa Barbara County
★ ★ ✓

These vividly fruity wines come from one of Santa Barbara's first vineyards. Rancho Sisquoc covers 200 acres (80 hectares) of the massive 36,000-acre (14,500-hectare) Flood Ranch.

✓ *Cabernet Franc* • *Classic red blend* (Sisquoc River Red Meritage) • *Chardonnay* (Flood Vineyard) *Malbec* (Flood Family Vineyard) • *Riesling* (Flood Family Vineyard) • *Sylvaner*

## RIVER RUN
### Santa Clara County
✓ ✓

After more than 25 years of continuous production, River Run has finally grabbed attention with an exciting quality, sharp-priced Malbec.

✓ *Malbec* (Mannstand Vineyard)

## SANFORD WINERY
### Santa Barbara County
✓ ★ ★ ✓

One of the twin founders of the eponymous Sanford & Benedict vineyard, and modern-day pioneer of Santa Barbara winemaking in general, Richard Sanford released his first wine in 1976, and it is now hard to imagine why that should be Riesling. However, he quickly gained a stellar reputation for Pinot Noir, attracting dozens of crusading wineries to open up around him.

✓ *Pinot Noir* (La Riconada, Sanford & Benedict, Vin Gris Santa Rita Hills) • *Sauvignon Blanc*

## SANTA BARBARA WINERY
### Santa Barbara County
★ ✓ ✓

Although this is the oldest Santa Barbara winery, dating back to the early 1960s, it did not get interested in premium-quality wines until a decade later, after the Sanford &

Benedict revolution. It soon began producing a number of great-value Burgundian varietals, and has since moved into Rhône-style wines, making some of the region's most impressive Syrah.

✓ *Chardonnay* (Lafond Vineyard, SRH) • *Nebbiolo* (Stolpman Vineyard) • *Pinot Noir* (Lafond Vineyard, SRH) • *Sauvignon Blanc* (Lafond Vineyard Late Harvest) • *Syrah* • *Zinfandel* (Beaujour, Essence)

## TALLEY VINEYARDS
### Santa Clara County
✓ ✓

Burgundian-style specialists with 100 percent estate-bottled production.

✓ *Chardonnay* • *Pinot Noir*

## VERDAD
### Santa Barbara County
★ ✓ ✓

Owned by Bob and Louisa Lindquist of Qupé, Verdad is, however, very much Louisa's baby, and she is starting to make waves with these Spanish-style wines.

✓ *Albariño* • *Rosé* • *Tempranillo* (Santa Ynez Valley)

## WILD HORSE
### San Luis Obispo County
✓ ✓

Established in 1982 by Ken Volk, Wild Horse was acquired in 2003 by Fortune Brands, the owners of Geyser Peak. Wild Horse crushes some 30-odd grape varieties and has something of a reputation for coming up with lesser-known varieties such as Arneis, Lagrein, Negrette, Tocai Friulano, Trousseau Gris, and Verdelho. There is a tendency to diversify into different brands, rather than create various ranges under the same label, Equus being the latest and most successful of such ventures.

✓ *Blaufrankisch* • *Grenache* (Equus James Berry Vineyard) • *Zinfandel*

## ZACA MESA WINERY
### Santa Barbara County
★ ✓

Best for inexpensive, refreshing Chardonnay, and exciting, low-yield Syrah.

✓ *Chardonnay* (Zaca Vineyard) • *Grenache* (Late Bottled) • *Roussanne* (Estate Bottled) • *Syrah* (Black Bear Block, Eight Barrel, The Mesa O & N)

# THE CENTRAL VALLEY

*While California's coastal areas are its most famous wine districts and those most capable of producing fine wines, they are not as significant in terms of quantity as the baking-hot, flat, and dry Central Valley, which accounts for three-quarters of all California wine; one company, Gallo, produces half of that.*

IF I HAD ANY PLANS at all for the California section of this new edition, it was to shine a light on the Central Valley, which has always been brushed to one side by authors because of its jug-wine reputation. Looking through the first edition of this book, I was nagged by the same question—"Surely the source of three out of every four bottles of California wine is worthy of some attention?" To find an answer, I made two visits specifically to look for the wines of the Central Valley. I wanted to establish whether any areas or wines truly stood out and the reasons why.

Why do AVAs such as Clarksburg, Merritt Island, and Lodi exist, if they do not mean something? Clarksburg is supposed to be good for Chenin Blanc, and Lodi has an even greater, older reputation for Zinfandel, but if this is true, why aren't the UK and other price-conscious, value-minded markets flooded with such wines? Perhaps in this valley of giant producers there are a number of small wineries making some stunning wines for the price, but lacking the money or marketing muscle to get them noticed?

To find some answers, I asked a local expert to set up a tasting of the best Central Valley AVA wines. I imagined there would be well over a hundred different wines, but he was able to assemble only 36, and a number of those were old vintages from wineries that no longer exist. After discounting those that were supposedly produced from pure or mostly Central Valley grapes but did not make any such claims on the bottle and were not very interesting in any case, there were just eight wines currently available that proudly proclaimed their origins. Maybe more will be available by the time this book is published, but it was evident that there were few individually expressive wines waiting to be discovered in the Central Valley. I tasted some passable Chenin from Clarksburg, but

FRANZIA WINERY IN RIPON, NEAR MODESTO
*Looking more like oil refineries than wineries, firms such as Franzia have perfected the art of industrialized winemaking.*

nothing special, and the best were only supposedly from Clarksburg, as they did not claim the AVA.

The wines from Bogle Vineyards on Merritt Island, at the heart of Clarksburg, were not particularly impressive at the tasting but, having had the opportunity to taste younger vintages at the winery itself, it was obviously one of the few independent Central Valley producers likely to succeed. I came away feeling that Bogle makes much better red than white wine, particularly Merlot, but it blends in up to 60 percent bought-in grapes, using the generic Californian appellation. As for the Lodi Zinfandel, the few examples claiming the AVA were big, old-fashioned, tasted maderized, and sometimes stank quite fouly.

Although I failed to find any outstanding wines, the experience taught me that the Central Valley AVAs are an irrelevance because the state's largest wineries (particularly Gallo, but also Mondavi in Woodbridge, in the heart of Lodi) have ignored them. When they select exceptional wines to bear and show off these AVAs, perhaps consumers will no longer be dismissive of the Central Valley?

HARVESTED CABERNET SAUVIGNON GRAPES
*Despite its huge output, premium-quality wines can be produced in Central Valley.*

## FACTORS AFFECTING TASTE AND QUALITY

### LOCATION
The viticultural area of this huge fertile valley stretches 400 miles (640 kilometers) from Redding in the north to Bakersfield in the south, running between the Coastal Ranges to the west and the Sierra Nevada to the east.

### CLIMATE
Generally homogenous from end to end, warming steadily from Region IV (*see* p.470) in the north to Region V (*see* p.470) in the south. The area around Lodi is the only exception, being cooled by sea air sweeping up the Sacramento River.

### ASPECT
The vines are grown on the vast flat area of the valley floors, intersected and irrigated by a network of levees.

### SOIL
Very fertile sandy loam dominates the length and breadth of the valley.

### VITICULTURE AND VINIFICATION
Production of vast quantities of reliable-quality jug wine, using the latest techniques of mechanization and irrigation, and a virtually continuous fermentation and bottling process. Somewhat higher-quality Zinfandel and sweet dessert wines are produced around Lodi.

### GRAPE VARIETIES
Barbera, Cabernet Sauvignon, Carnelian, Carignane, Chenin Blanc, Colombard, Grenache, Merlot, Mourvèdre, Muscat, Petite Sirah, Ruby Cabernet, Sauvignon Blanc, Sémillon, Zinfandel

THE APPELLATIONS OF
# THE CENTRAL VALLEY

## CAPAY VALLEY AVA
### Yolo County

Established as recently as 2003, this appellation is located 80 miles (130 kilometers) northeast of San Francisco, just east of Napa over the Blue Ridge Mountains, bordering Napa, Lake, and Colusa counties. Currently, the grapes grown are Tempranillo, Syrah, and Viognier.

## CLARKSBURG AVA
### Sacramento County

A large area south of Sacramento encompassing the AVA of Merritt Island, Clarksburg is cooled by the breezes that roll in off Suisun Bay. The average annual rainfall is 16 inches (41 centimeters), which is greater than the precipitation experienced in areas to the south and west, but less than that which occurs north and east. The area is crisscrossed by more than 1,000 miles (1,600 kilometers) of river and irrigation channels.

## DIABLO GRANDE AVA
### Sacramento County

This AVA, which is owned entirely by the Diablo Grande Resort Community, encompasses 30,000 acres (12,000 hectares), although only 36 (15 hectares) are planted with vines. The Diablo Grande AVA is named after Mount Diablo, the highest peak in the Pacific Coast Range; the

appellation is in its western foothills where, due to the elevation of 1,000 to 1,800 feet (300 to 540 meters), there is greater rainfall and lower average temperatures than in surrounding areas.

## DUNNIGAN HILLS AVA
### Yolo County

This is a new AVA located northwest of Sacramento in the rolling Dunnigan Hills. Much of the 1,100 acres (445 hectares) of vineyards cultivated in this area belongs to R. H. Phillips, a go-getting winery that has led the Dunnigan Hills reputation for easy-drinking varietals.

## LODI AVA
### Sacramento and San Joaquin Counties

An inland area that comprises alluvial fan, plains that are prone to flooding, and terrace lands both above and below the levees. This AVA expanded its southern and western boundaries in August 2002, increasing the viticultural area by 17 percent.

## MADERA AVA
### Madera and Fresno Counties

A viticultural area not to be confused with Madera County, Madera AVA is located in both Madera and Fresno counties and contains more than 36,000 acres (14,500 hectares) of wine grapes, plus substantial areas of raisin and table grapes.

## MERRITT ISLAND AVA
### San Joaquin County

An island bounded on the west and north by Elk Slough, by Sutter Slough on the south, and the Sacramento River on the east. Its climate is tempered by cooling southwesterly breezes from the Carquinez Straits, near San Francisco, which reduce the temperature substantially compared with that of the city of Sacramento, located just 14,500 hectares (10 kilometers) north. The soil is primarily sandy loam, while areas to the west have clay-type soil, and to the south, an organically structured, moderately fertile peat dirt.

## RIVER JUNCTION AVA
### San Joaquin County

As the name suggests, River Junction AVA is located at the confluence of two rivers: the San Joaquin and Stanislaus rivers. It is an area where cool maritime air collects, causing land surrounding the river junction to be significantly cooler than other Central Valley areas, and it is the only place in which a substantial amount of Grangeville fine sandy loam can be found. River Junction AVA is entirely owned by McManis Family Vineyards, which has already planted three-quarters of the appellation's 1,300 acres (520 hectares), with Chardonnay accounting for 90 percent of the planting.

THE WINE PRODUCERS OF
# THE CENTRAL VALLEY

## BOGLE VINEYARDS
### Sacramento County

Chris Smith, a former assistant winemaker at Kendall-Jackson in Lake County, is improving the quality at this winery, which has large vineyards on Merritt Island.

✓ *Merlot • Petite Sirah*

## DELICATO
### San Joaquin County
### ★ ✔

From penny-pinching jug wines to real quality bargains, with pure fruit and focus presented in smart blue livery. How this Central Valley winery has come up in the world!

✓ *Merlot • Syrah (Shiraz)*

## E. & J. GALLO WINERY
### Stanislaus County
### ❷

From the air, Gallo's Modesto premises might look like an oil refinery, but from the ground you see peacocks roaming freely over well-manicured lawns, and inside the building there is a marble-bedecked lobby, with waterfalls cascading into large pools surrounded by lush tropical vegetation, and containing carp the size of submarines. Gallo not only makes a lot of cheap plonk, it also produces inexpensive, yet

drinkable varietal wines. The plonk comes under a variety of labels (such as Totts, André, Bartles & James, Carlo Rossi), which encompass coolers, sweet wines from foxy-flavored native grapes such as Concord, and most of the generics (Burgundy, Chablis, Rhine), while the varietals bear the Gallo name itself (the nonvintage Cabernet Sauvignon is a real penny-saver). Some generics such as Hearty Burgundy and Chablis Blanc can cross the divide into the reasonably drinkable (sometimes amazingly drinkable) category, and the better generics also carry the Gallo name; there is a big difference between Gallo Hearty Burgundy or Chablis Blanc and Carlo Rossi Burgundy or Chablis. This is how the brothers Ernest and Julio Gallo, two struggling grape-growers who had to borrow money to buy a crusher when Prohibition ended, built up their business to become the most powerful wine producers in the world. This commercial success was not enough, however, as both brothers also wanted the critical acclaim of making some of California's finest wines, which is why they literally moved mountains to terraform their prized Sonoma estate. But if the Gallo family is

satisfied, it should not be. To create Gallo Sonoma with the money it threw at a single project was no challenge at all. If the Gallo family really does want respect and critical acclaim, then I repeat my challenge: give your winemakers at Modesto a free rein to do two things: bottle off small batches of anything exceptional, and allow them to develop pet projects.

I have never been one to condemn the huge wineries because of size. The bigger they are, the more likely it is that they will come across an outstanding batch of grapes or wine. The choice of losing these little gems in some mega-blend or of giving them due recognition is what separates the best large wineries from the worst. That Gallo has an army of highly qualified oenologists is beyond question, but it is obvious that those with any creativity will want to express that talent. If Gallo allowed its winemakers to propose and carry out their own projects (such as working with Lodi growers to make the best local Zinfandel possible), this would induce them to stay.

By following these two strategies, Gallo could very quickly attract rave reviews from the most hardened critics for limited bottlings of truly

exciting wines. It would reveal the best that can be expected from California's Central Valley vineyards, verify whether the AVAs that exist deserve to be recognized, and pin-point any other potential appellations that might exist. That would be a fitting achievement for a company that has benefited more than any other from the Central Valley, and an ideal legacy for which Gallo would always be remembered.

✓ *Cabernet Sauvignon* (Turning Leaf Coastal Reserve) • *Sauvignon Blanc* (Turning Leaf California)

## FICKLIN VINEYARDS
### Madera County
### ★ ✔

Ficklin is California's leading estate-bottled port-style specialist. The vineyards are planted with authentic Douro varieties such as Touriga Nacional and Tinta Cão, plus Sousão, which is used for Dão.

✓ *Fortified* (Old Vine Tinta Port, Touriga Nacional Vintage Reserve, Vintage Port)

## FRESNO STATE WINERY
### Fresno County
### ★ ✔

While Davis has the best-known university wine course in the US, Fresno is the only one with a commercial winery on its campus, and a very successful one it is too, having amassed a large number of medals since its inception in 1997. However, presentation is of fundamental importance to any wine venture its students might be running in the future, and the new Fresno Winery label launched in 2004 wins no medals!

✓ *Barbera* (California, Duarte Linden Hills Vineyard) • *Muscat Canelli* • *Syrah* • *Viognier* (John Berghold Vineyard)

### JEFF RUNQUIST
**Amador County**
★ ✮ ⓥ

Standout wines from a grossly underrated producer who majors on Zinfandel from the Shenandoah Valley, but also produces stunning Central Valley wines.

✓ *Barbera* ("R" Nostro Vino Vineyard) • *Cabernet Sauvignon* ("R" Colina Poca Vineyard) • *Petite Sirah* ("R" Enver Salmon Vineyard) • *Pinot Noir* ("R" Sisters Vineyard) • *Primitivo*

("R" Nostro Vino Vineyard) • *Sangiovese* • *Syrah* ("R" Paso Robles) • *Zinfandel* ("Z" Masoni Rach)

### JESSIE'S GROVE
**San Joaquin County**
★ ✮ ⓥ

Tiny production of high-quality Lodi varietals, with especially noteworthy Zinfandel and one of California's few tip-top Carignane wines, made from 115-year-old vines.

✓ *Carignane* (Ancient Vines) • *Zinfandel*

### KLINKER BRICK WINERY
**Lodi**
★ ⓥ

I came across Steve and Lori Felten's sleek, elegant, beautiful Zinfandel at the IEC wine competition in 2006. These fifth-generation growers and their 100-year-old Zinfandel vines should be treasured.

✓ *Zinfandel (Old Vines)* • *Syrah (Farah)*

### QUADY WINERY
**Madera County**
★

Quady is an eclectic fortified wine specialist *par excellence*, although I am not so fond of the Vya vermouth-style offerings. By contrast, Electra is a low-alcohol (4 percent) Moscato d'Asti-style light wine.

✓ *Fortified* (Muscat—Elysium, Essensia; Port—Starboard) • *Muscat* (Electra)

### R H PHILLIPS
**Sacramento County**
★ ✮ ⓥ

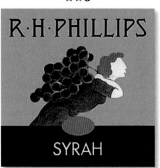

A spotless, hard-to-find winery on the Diamond G Ranch in the rolling Dunnigan Hills, R. H. Phillips is well worth searching out for supreme-value wines that are wickedly easy to drink.

✓ *Cabernet Sauvignon* (Dunnigan Hills) • *Alliance* (red Rhône style) • *Diamond G* (Sémillon-Sauvignon) • *Mourvèdre* (EXP) • *Night Harvest Cuvée Rouge*

---

## OTHER APPELLATIONS OF
# CALIFORNIA

**Note** This section contains a round-up of the various California wine areas that are not dealt with in the preceding pages. Each of the AVAs listed below can be found on the regional California map (*see* p.470).

### SIERRA FOOTHILLS AVA

In the 1850s, this land of majestic vistas was California's gold-rush country, but since the 1970s scores of new wineries have opened up, mostly of the one-man "boutique" ilk. The Sierra Foothills is a quality-wine area that is definitely not part of the Central Valley. It attracts rugged specialists who, not content with the safe option of farming fertile valley floors, want the challenge of making expressive wine in limited quantities in one of the few areas of California where, owing to the altitude, cultivating grapes is not always possible. In the 19th century, Zinfandel was the king of these mountain vineyards, and quickly reestablished itself as the big, blockbusting, spicy star of the 1980s. However, Sauvignon Blanc and Riesling were quick to take up the challenge, with Barbera and, predictably, Cabernet Sauvignon and Merlot not far behind.

### CALIFORNIA SHENANDOAH VALLEY AVA
**Amador County**

The famous Shenandoah Valley is, of course, in Virginia and, like this AVA, received its status in 1983. The California Shenandoah Valley AVA, which is set amid the Sierra Foothills, was named by Virginia settlers who migrated to California during the gold rush. Vines were first grown here in 1881 when the miners ran out of gold, and, as a result, turned to making wine instead. The soil is well drained, moderately

deep, and consists mostly of coarse sandy loams formed from weathered granitic rock over heavy, often clayey, loam.

### EL DORADO AVA
**El Dorado County**

The soil is mostly decomposed granite, except on Apple Hill, east of Placerville, where an old lava flow exists (*see* Lava Cap winery). Apple Hill is one of two main winegrowing areas and, as the name suggests, the area is covered with orchards. Orchards invariably predate vineyards in the US and vines always do extremely well wherever apples have grown best. The other main vineyard is located in the southeast of the AVA, between Quitingdale and Fairplay. Go any farther east and not only is it too cold for grapes, but grizzly bears become a real pest.

### FIDDLETOWN AVA
**Amador County**

The Fiddletown viticultural area is located in the eastern Sierra Foothills of Amador County. It differs from the neighboring Shenandoah Valley of California area because of its higher elevations, colder temperatures at night, and greater rainfall. Grapes are grown without any irrigation and the vineyards are located on deep, moderately well-drained, sandy loams.

## NORTHERN CALIFORNIA

### SEIAD VALLEY
**Siskiyou County**

Located just 15 miles (21 kilometers) south of the Oregon border, the Seiad Valley AVA is

comprised of 2,165 acres (877 hectares), of which just over 2½ (1 hectare) are planted with vines.

### WILLOW CREEK AVA
**Humboldt County**

This area is influenced primarily by two major climatic forces: the Pacific Ocean and the warmer climate of the Sacramento Valley, 100 miles (160 kilometers) to the east. These create easterly winds that give Willow Creek fairly cool temperatures in the summer and infrequent freezes in the winter. The area to the east of Willow Creek experiences colder temperatures in winter and hotter temperatures in summer.

## SOUTHERN CALIFORNIA
### CUCAMONGA VALLEY AVA
**Los Angeles and San Bernardino Counties**

An area of more than 100,000 acres (40,500 hectares), some 45 miles (72 kilometers) from Los Angeles, the Cucamonga Valley was first planted with Mission grapes in about 1840. Despite Prohibition, the vineyards reached their peak in the 1950s, when more than 35,000 acres (14,000 hectares) were under vine. As the viticultural emphasis in California moved northward, these vineyards declined, but there are still five operational wineries and some 2,000 acres (800 hectares) of vine.

### MALIBU-NEWTON CANYON AVA
**Los Angeles County**

A one-vineyard appellation on the south-facing slopes of the Santa Monica Mountains.

## SAN PASQUAL AVA
### San Diego County

A natural valley located in the Santa Ysabel watershed, the San Pasqual Valley is fed by natural streams that feed the San Diequito River, and is substantially affected by coastal influences. Temperatures are warm in the summer, but seldom very hot, and ocean breezes cool the area, especially during the nighttime. The surrounding areas have a variety of very different climates ranging from tropical, through desertlike, to mountainous.

## TEMECULA AVA
### Riverside County

Temecula is located in Riverside County, southern California, and includes Murrieta and Rancho California. Marine breezes entering the area through the Deluz and Rainbow Gaps cool the area to moderate temperatures. Sauvignon Blanc and Chardonnay are the most widely planted varieties, and Chenin Blanc and Cabernet Sauvignon the least successful.

# LAKE, MARIN, AND SOLANO COUNTIES

The only other counties of significance are Lake, Marin, and Solano, all of which are part of the North Coast AVA. Of these, Lake is the only area of real repute.

## BENMORE VALLEY AVA
### Lake County

Surrounded by the 2,900-foot (1,000-meter) peaks of the Mayacamas Mountains, this AVA encompasses 125 acres (50 hectares) of vines, but no wineries.

## CLEAR LAKE AVA
### Lake County

Located between the Mayacamas Mountains and the Mendocino National Forest, Clear Lake's large water mass moderates the AVA's climate. Although this area is best for Chardonnay and Sauvignon Blanc, well-textured Cabernet Sauvignon is also produced.

## FAIR PLAY AVA
### Amador County

Named after an old gold-mining camp, Fair Play is located in rolling hills at an altitude of 2,000 to 3,000 feet (600 to 900 meters), which, averaged, makes it the highest elevation of any California AVA. Low rainfall and loam soils favor Zinfandel, followed by Rhône and Italian varietals.

## GUENOC VALLEY AVA
### Lake County

This appellation lies south of McCreary Lake and east of Detert Reservoir. Situated within the North Coast AVA, the valley has a more extreme climate, lower rainfall, and less severe fog than the nearby Middletown area.

## NORTH YUBA AVA
### Yuba County

North Yuba is located in the middle and upper foothills of Yuba County, immediately west of the Sierra Nevada and north of the Yuba River. This area escapes both the early frosts and the snow of higher elevations in the Sierra Nevada and the heat, humidity, and fog common to the Sacramento Valley lowlands, and the climate is therefore relatively temperate compared with the rest of the AVA.

## SOLANO COUNTY GREEN VALLEY AVA
### Solano County

Green Valley is sandwiched between the Napa Valley to the west and the Suisun Valley to the east. The soil here is a clay loam and the climate is influenced by the cool, moist winds that blow inland from the Pacific and San Francisco Bay almost continuously from spring through to fall.

## SUISUN VALLEY AVA
### Solano County

Adjacent to Solano County Green Valley, and a stone's throw from the Central Valley, Suisun Valley AVA enjoys the same cool, moist winds that blow from spring until fall in both of these areas. The soils consist of various forms of clay, and silty and sandy loams.

---

OTHER WINE PRODUCERS OF

# CALIFORNIA

## SIERRA FOOTHILLS

### AMADOR FOOTHILL WINERY
#### Amador County

The wines from this winery, with its small Shenandoah Valley vineyards, are made by owner and ex-NASA chemist Ben Zeitman.

✓ *Zinfandel*

### BOEGER WINERY
#### El Dorado County
★

The first winery to reopen the pre-Prohibition Sierra Foothill vineyards, Boeger has established itself as a producer of understated fine wines that take time to flesh out in bottle, more appealing perhaps to European palates than to Californian ones.

✓ *Barbera* • *Classic red blend* (Mourvèdre/Syrah, Reserve El Dorado Meritage) • *Zinfandel*

### DOMAINE DE LA TERRE ROUGE
#### Amador County
★★

Billed as the winery where the Rhône Valley meets the Sierra Nevada, Domaine de la Terre Rouge produces elegant, stylish Syrah and an exotically sweet late-harvest Muscat à Petits Grains.

✓ *Muscat à Petits Grains* • *Syrah* (Ascent) • *Zinfandel*

### HOLLY'S HILL
#### El Dorado County
★ ♥

A boutique winery concentrating to a large degree on Rhône-style wines, Holly's Hill is planted with the latest French clones from Beaucastel and Rayas.

✓ *Grenache* (El Dorado) • *Syrah* (Wylie-Fenaughty) • *Zinfandel* (Sierra Foothills)

### IRONSTONE
#### Calaveras County
★ ♥

Opened in 1994, John Kautz's winery in gold-rush country has already shown a capability for smooth, lush Cabernet Franc and rich, oaky Syrah (labeled Shiraz, as in Australia).

✓ *Cabernet Franc* (Reserve) • *Cabernet Sauvignon* (Reserve) • *Syrah* (California Shiraz—sic) • *Zinfandel* (Reserve)

### LAVA CAP
#### Placerville
★★ ♥

This underrated producer just gets better and better. Excellent-value wines, including one of California's finest Petite Sirahs, grown on the volcanic soils, some 2,500 feet (760 meters) up Apple Hill in the El Dorado AVA.

✓ *Cabernet Franc* • *Mourvèdre* • *Petite Sirah* • *Syrah* (Reserve) • *Viognier* • *Zinfandel*

### MONTEVIÑA
#### Amador County
★ ♥

Part of Trinchero Family Estates, together with Sutter Home, Monteviña is best known for Zinfandel, but has also helped the Latino trend with its Italian varieties planted in the Shenandoah Valley.

✓ *Barbera* (Amador) • *Pinot Grigio* • *Sauvignon Blanc* (California) • *Zinfandel*

### NEVADA CITY WINERY
#### Nevada County

The ultimate garage winery, Nevada City Winery is located in the historic Miners Foundry Garage, on Spring Street in downtown Nevada City. It was founded in the early 1980s and has gone from strength to strength, winning several awards. red, white, rosé and dessert wines are produced.

✓ *Cabernet Franc* • *Zinfandel*

### RENAISSANCE
#### Yuba County
★

Founded by the Fellowship of Friends, Renaissance is a self-sufficient community of like-minded people dedicated to the fine arts, whose wines are made in a circular winery surrounded by an amphitheater of vines in one of the most idyllic spots on earth. Although the quality at Renaissance has always been patchy, due to its reliance on *terroir* and a relatively hands-off approach to winemaking, it has to be said that the high-quality peaks seem to be getting fewer and the best wines today fall a long way short of the world-class 1985 Riesling Special Select Late Harvest.

✓ *Late Harvest* (Riesling, Sauvignon Blanc Select, Sémillon) • *Pinot Noir* • *Riesling* • *Syrah*

### RENWOOD
#### Amador County
★ ♥

These well-made, good-value wines have just started to appear on my radar. The hillside location has produced some fine results.

✓ *Barbera* (Sierra Series) • *Viognier* (Sierra Series) • *Zinfandel* (Fiddleton, Jack Rabbit Flat)

# SOUTHERN CALIFORNIA

Southern California, site of the state's first vineyard, has even less land under vine than the Sierra Foothills. Since 1977 it has undergone a revival, particularly in Riverside and, to a lesser extent, San Diego counties.

## CALLAWAY
### Riverside County
### ✩✩ ⓥ

One of the first wineries to prove that parts of southern California have, in fact, excellent microclimates for producing fine-wine grapes.

✓ *Dolcetto* (Temecula Special Selection) • *Merlot* (Coastal)

## JOSEPH FILIPPI
### San Bernadino County
### ✩✩ ⓥ

This 30-year-old winery has recently moved from Fontana to Ranch Cucamonga, where it continues to produce a wide range of wines, including a number of very successful fortified styles.

✓ *Fortified* (Alicante Bouschet Port, Ciello Port Reserve, Oloroso Sherry Library Reserve) • *Mourvèdre* (Library Reserve) • *Muscat Canelli* (Library Reserve)

## MAURICE CAR'RIE WINERY
### Riverside County
### ✩✩ ⓥ

The Van Roekels came to Temecula to retire in 1984, but were sidetracked into just "one more venture" and haven't stopped since.

✓ *Muscat Canelli* • *Sauvignon Blanc*

## MORAGA
### Los Angeles County
### ✩✩

This winery is owned by Tom Jones. Not the singer, but the one who made his millions through Stealth technology. Six acres of Bel-Air real estate worth $3 million seems an odd place to grow vines when each bottle would have to retail at $50 for 22 years in order to gross—not cover—the original investment. Viticulturally, however, this tiny sandstone and limestone canyon is a good choice. It has a discernible microclimate with 24 inches (61 centimeters) of rain each year, compared with 15 inches (38 centimeters) on nearby properties, and the wines are also truly fine by any standards. Bel Air is a soft, deep-colored red, Bordeaux-style blend with seamless oak integration and beautifully layered fruit, the flavor building in the mouth. He also makes a tiny amount of fresh, soft, delicately rich Sauvignon Blanc.

✓ *Moraga* (Bel Air) • *Sauvignon Blanc*

## THE OJAI VINEYARD
### Ventura County
### ✩✩✩✫

Adam Tolmach, a former partner in Au Bon Climat, teamed up with Helen Hardenbergh to create this boutique winery. Stylish, smoky-blackcurrant Syrah stands out, but some great Pinot Noir too, all wines of all designations can be top-notch. The white Vin du Soleil is a nonmalolactic Roussanne-Viognier blend.

✓ *Chardonnay* • *Classic white blend* (Vin du Soleil) • *Pinot Noir* • *Sauvignon Blanc* • *Syrah* • *Viognier* (Late Harvest)

## THORNTON
### San Diego County
### ✩✩ ⓥ

Best known for its sparkling wine, particularly its Cuvée Rouge (although not my favorite), but these wines would be much better if sold younger and fresher. In recent years, however, the quality of Thornton's table wines has far exceeded that of its bubbly, and its Nebbiolo can rival the best that California has to offer.

✓ *Classic red blend* (Côte Red) • *Muscat Canelli* • *Nebbiolo* (Curran Ranch) • *Rosé* (Grenache) • *Sémillon* (Miramonte Vineyard) • *Sparkling wine* (Brut Rosé, Cuvée de Frontignan) • *Zinfandel* (Lopez Vineyard, Old Vine)

# LAKE, MARIN, AND SOLANO COUNTIES

## GUENOC WINERY
### Lake County
### ✩✩ ⓥ

This was once the property of Lillie Langtry (a mistress of Edward VII, when he was the Prince of Wales), and her picture is used to market one of these excellent-value wines.

✓ *Cabernet Sauvignon* • *Chardonnay* • *Classic red blend* (Langtry Meritage, Victorian Claret) • *Classic white blend* (Langtry Meritage) • *Petite Sirah* (North Coast, Serpentine Meadow) • *Zinfandel*

## KALIN CELLARS
### Marin County
### ❓

After waiting for four years before selling his 1990 Chardonnay, only to attract great acclaim, microbiologist Terry Leighton has stretched his late-release philosophy to bizarre lengths. In October 2004, for example, Leighton decided the time was right to release his 1996 Potter Valley Sauvignon Blanc! On average, he puts his whites on the market when they are six years old, and his reds when they are eight years old. This works better for some styles than others. While Leighton was initially to be applauded, it is always best to err on the side of youth, as the wine buying public can always cellar a wine, but cannot turn back the clock.

## KENDALL-JACKSON
### Lake County
### ✩✩ ⓥ

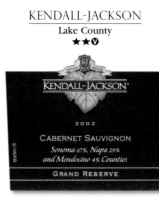

It's amazing to think that when I started researching the first edition of this encyclopedia, the Kendall-Jackson brand was barely 12 months old. Since then, K-J has become one of California's best-selling brands, although its impact on export markets has been minimal. In the US this company has become so successful that some critics now love to bash the brand they helped to create, when really it is only the obviousness of the entry-level Vintner's Reserve and cheaper subsidiary brands they object to. Yet it is the obviousness of these wines that make them so popular, and the people who buy Vintner's Reserve seldom read a wine critic's column, so what's the point of putting question marks in the minds of those who do? Better instead to point out the plus points, and K-J has plenty of those, not least in its higher level offerings, where the wines pack in one hell of a lot of quality at what are relatively inexpensive prices. K-J is a private company belonging to Jess Jackson, who also owns Cambria (which is run by his wife, Barbara Banke), La Crema, Edmeades, and Stonestreet. Other brands include Camelot, and Pepi.

✓ *Cabernet Sauvignon* (Great Estates, Hawkeye Mountain, Napa Mountain, Stature) • *Chardonnay* (Camelot, Clark, Durell, Stature, Grand Reserve) • *Classic red blend* (Stature Meritage) • *Muscat Canelli* (Vintner's Reserve) • *Pinot Noir* (Great Estates, Stature) • *Riesling* (Vintner's Reserve) • *Zinfandel* (Great Estates)

## ORFILA VINEYARDS & WINERY
### San Diego County
### ✩✩ ⓥ

Good value wines, including the odd gem that punches well above its weight, from the winery of Argentinian Alejandro Orfila, who was twice elected Secretary General of the Organization of American States.

✓ *Muscat Canelli* • *Sangiovese* (Collina Estate) • *Syrah* (San Pasqual Valley) • *Viognier* (Lotus)

## SEAN THACKREY AND COMPANY
### Marin County
### ✩✫

San Francisco art dealer Sean Thackrey loved Burgundy, which led him to establish this winery in 1980 and, naturally enough, try his hand at sculpting Pinot Noir. It was not until the late 1980s that his big, thick, richly flavored wines began to appear and quickly attracted attention. Since then Thackrey's obsession for fermenting under the stars, along with several other artisanal quirks of ancient winemaking, have intrigued critics and consumers alike.

✓ *Petite Sirah* (Sirius) • *Syrah* (Orion)

## STEELE
### Lake County
### ✩✩

This is the personal label of Jed Steele, who is a former Kendall-Jackson winemaker and a highly regarded wine consultant. His debut vintage was 1991, and his brightly flavored, brilliantly stylish wines made an instant impact. Excellent all around, but truly excels in his single-vineyard Pinot Noir range. The second label is Jed Steele's Shooting Star.

✓ *Chardonnay* • *Pinot Blanc* (Santa Barbara) • *Pinot Noir* • *Zinfandel* (Catfish Vineyard)

# THE PACIFIC NORTHWEST

*Oregon has a wet, maritime climate and has long been noted for its Pinot Noir, whereas Washington is a dry, semidesert wine area that has relatively recently become known for its muscular Bordeaux and Rhône varieties. After decades of needing to ride the Pacific Northwest denomination, both states are now emerging with their own clear identity.*

FOR MOST OF its winegrowing history, Washington has not had a reputation for any specific style, which is probably why its wines have taken so long to register with wine drinkers, even though it has always produced a vastly larger volumes of wine than Oregon. The contrary is true for Oregon, which has had a disproportionately high profile for such a small output of wine, due no doubt to its focus on one variety: Pinot Noir.

## WASHINGTON STATE

In 1775 the Spanish declared the land now known as Washington State to be theirs, but 17 years later, Robert Gray, captain of the first US ship to circumnavigate the globe, claimed it for the Americans. To further confuse the issue of sovereignty, George Vancouver had actually claimed it for the British a month before Gray had even reached the area. However, it remained Spanish until 1819, although it was effectively controlled by America through its domination of the fur trade, and American authority was irrevocably recognized in 1889, when Washington became the 42nd state.

### The early wine trade

The first planting of vines in Washington was in about 1825, at Fort Vancouver on the Columbia River, by traders working for the Hudson's Bay Company, though it is not known whether wine was actually produced. Washington's earliest winery was established at Walla Walla in the 1860s, and the first *vinifera* vines were planted at Yakima in 1871, although the production of wine

THE PACIFIC NORTHWEST,
*see also p.463*
*Encompassing thousands of square miles, the Pacific Northwest is a collection of well-dispersed winemaking areas. The ocean defines its western border from northern California in the south to the Canadian border in the north. The sea moderates the climate, although it has little effect on inland Idaho.*

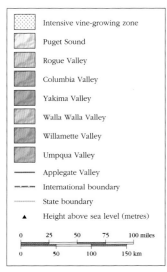

Intensive vine-growing zone

Puget Sound

Rogue Valley

Columbia Valley

Yakima Valley

Walla Walla Valley

Willamette Valley

Umpqua Valley

——— Applegate Valley

----- International boundary

——— State boundary

▲ Height above sea level (metres)

| 0 | 25 | 50 | 75 | 100 miles |
| 0 | 50 | 100 | | 150 km |

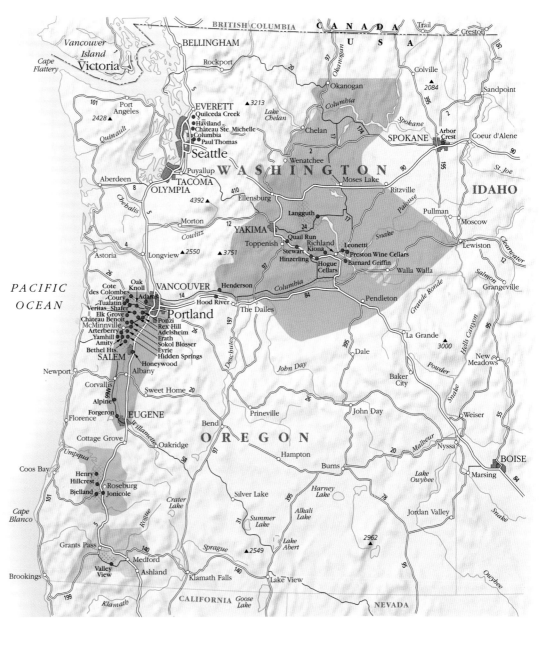

on a truly commercial scale was not effected until the post-Prohibition New Deal era allowed funding of the Columbia River irrigation project, which transformed an arid desert into an agricultural paradise.

Washington's wine industry grew rapidly, and 42 wineries were in operation by 1937, but the vineyards, like those in the rest of North America, were essentially *Vitis labrusca*-based. In addition to supplying California wineries with base wines for their abysmal "Cold Duck" blends (*see alos* Andrés Wines, p.535), the industry produced its own cheap, sweet, and often fortified wines from Concord, Island Belle, and other cloyingly foxy-tasting grapes.

## FACTORS AFFECTING TASTE AND QUALITY

### LOCATION
An arbitrary grouping of three northwestern states: Washington, Oregon, and Idaho. The Yakima Valley, running through Washington, is at roughly the same latitude as northern Bordeaux and southern Burgundy. Washington is more logically a southern extension of British Columbia's inland, desert-based vineyards than a northern extension of Oregon's coastal, rainswept hills.

### CLIMATE
The temperatures generated by continental air masses are moderated in Washington and Oregon by westerly winds from the Pacific Ocean. Oregon is the coolest state, and Washington the wettest but, with the exception of Puget Sound, all the viticultural areas of Washington are not only hotter, but much drier than those of Oregon, with plentiful sunshine (averaging over 17 hours per day in June) and crisp, cool nights during the critical ripening period. Climatic conditions are generally more continental toward Idaho.

### ASPECT
The vines are located in valleys, usually planted on low-lying slopes, but also on the valley floors and, in Oregon, in the hilly hinterland.

### SOIL
The soils are deep, fertile, light-textured, silty, sandy, or clay loams over volcanic bedrock, and sometimes more clayey in Oregon.

### VITICULTURE AND VINIFICATION
Washington vines are ungrafted, irrigation is widely practiced, with the oldest vines protected by cutting off the water supply prior to winter, thus allowing them to become dormant before the cold sets in. According to various surveys, Washington's viticultural areas are almost phylloxera-free, but some growers say it is rife in the state's Concord vines, which are resistant to the pest, yet for some mysterious reason it has not attacked *vinifera* vines growing on the same soil in adjacent vineyards. There is a general belief that Washington will have to graft over its vines, but it is difficult

from a survival point of view in areas where the winters are so cold.

Oregon is also looking at clonal and rootstock selection, but with much of Domaine Drouhin Oregon's success put down to the tight spacing of its vines, the big issue is whether to go for high-density vineyards. More than 50 percent of Oregon's Pinot Noir is planted at a density of less than 800 vines per acre (2,000 vines per hectare), and 30 percent are between 800 and 1,200 (2,000 and 3,000). A small number have tried increasing the density to between 1,200 and 1,800 per acre (3,000 and 4,500 vines per hectare), but claim there is no discernible advantage. However, the benefits do not kick in until vine density gets above 1,800 per acre (4,500 per hectare), and Drouhin's vines are planted at just under 3,000 per acre (7,450 per hectare). A good proportion of Oregon wine producers who are not certified organic manage both their vineyards and winery using sustainable and environmentally friendly practices.

### GRAPE VARIETIES
**Oregon**
**Primary varieties:** Pinot Noir, Pinot Gris, Chardonnay
**Secondary varieties:** Cabernet Franc, Cabernet Sauvignon, Gewürztraminer, Merlot, Müller-Thurgau, Pinot Blanc, Riesling, Sauvignon Blanc, Sémillon, Syrah, Zinfandel

**Washington**
**Primary varieties:** Cabernet Sauvignon, Chardonnay, Merlot, Riesling, Syrah
**Secondary varieties:** Cabernet Franc, Sangiovese, Sauvignon Blanc, Sémillon, Viognier

**Idaho**
**Primary varieties:** Cabernet Sauvignon, Chardonnay, Riesling
**Secondary varieties:** Cabernet Franc, Chenin Blanc, Fumé Blanc, Gewürztraminer, Lemberger, Merlot, Pinot Gris, Pinot Noir, Sauvignon Blanc, Sémillon, Syrah

Yakima was making Muscat, Riesling, and Sémillon wines as early as 1934. It was not until 1951 that the first commercial plantings of *vinifera* vines of the post-Prohibition period took place, but the example was not followed. Trial studies of *vinifera* varieties were conducted in the late 1950s at the Washington State University by Dr. Walter Clore. Clore's enthusiasm for these grapes earned him the nickname "Grandpa Grape" and encouraged the American Wine Growers (now called Château Ste. Michelle) to start the *vinifera* ball rolling with the first of several considerable plantings in the early 1960s. By 1978, 2,500 acres (1,000 hectares) of *vinifera* vines were being grown in Washington. Today, there are more than 30,000 acres (12,000 hectares), producing almost 7 million cases of wine, making Washington the second-largest producer of premium wines in the US.

### *More recent developments*
It is amazing to think that when I visited Washington State to research the first edition of this book, Alex Golitzen's Quilceda Creek was the only red wine of consistently great quality that I could find, and that was produced in minuscule amounts with ricketty equipment that he kept stashed away in the back of a

## RECENT PACIFIC NORTHWEST VINTAGES

**2006** Excellent to great for all varieties in both states.

**2005** Very good Pinot Noir in Oregon, but white wines were disappointing. Washington was disappointing, although some producers made standout reds in isolated cases.

**2004** Average quality in Oregon, but very good to excellent in Washington, especially for Merlot and Syrah.

**2003** Excellent Washington reds, but more for earlier drinking than keeping. Weather-induced mediocrity in Oregon.

**2002** Washington produced stunning reds, almost as special as the 1999s, while Oregon was extremely variable due to harvest rain, with only those winemakers who waited making riper, richer wines from longer-hung grapes.

IRRIGATION IN WASHINGTON
*Although some parts of the state have a notoriously wet climate, much of eastern Washington, where most of the vineyards are located, relies on irrigation.*

## WASHINGTON VERSUS OREGON

The contrast of natural factors affecting viticulture in these two contiguous coastal states offers a fascinating insight into why the wines they produce are so different:

| | WASHINGTON | OREGON |
|---|---|---|
| Vinifera vines | 30,000 acres/12,000 hectares | 13,500acres/5,420 hectares |
| Black varieties | 60% | 57% |
| White varieties | 40% | 43% |
| Major varieties | 24% Chardonnay | 53% Pinot Noir |
| | 22% Cabernet Sauvignon | 13% Pinot Gris |
| | 21% Merlot | 9% Chardonnay |
| | 23% Others | 25% Others |

• All but 1 percent of Washington vineyards are located on the hot, desert-dry, eastern side of the Cascades, whereas all of Oregon's vineyards are west of the Cascades where it is cooler, but where rain can be problematic.
• Washington irrigates, Oregon does not.
• Oregon's climate is marine-influenced, Washington's is more continental.
• Only the sturdiest varieties can withstand the cold of Washington's winter, which can kill grafted vines.
• It is Washington's extraordinary amount of sunshine (2,021 hours compared to Oregon's 1,660), rather than heat (1,240 degree days Celsius compared to Oregon's 1,179) that gives Washington State vines the photosynthetic capability of ripening Cabernet and other thick-skinned varieties that struggle in Oregon.
• Washington has no cryptogamic diseases, whereas bunch-rot is a major problem in Oregon.

garage. Now there are more than 320 wineries, with every one of them producing red wines.

As recently as 1996, almost 70 percent of all wine grapes grown in Washington were white varieties, yet by 2002 nearly 60 percent were black varieties. But it is not just the number that makes Washington a quintessentially red-wine region today. From a red-wine perspective, Washington stands shoulder to shoulder with California in terms of sheer quality.

## OREGON

The first *vinifera* vines were planted in Oregon's Rogue River Valley as early as 1854. These and other *vinifera* vineyards were still in existence at the time of Prohibition, but, as in Washington, the wine industry in Oregon relied almost entirely on *labrusca* grapes of the Concord variety until the 1970s. Change began in a small way in the 1960s and 1970s, when wineries were established by California dropouts such as Richard Sommer (Hill Crest, 1961), David Lett (The Eyrie Vineyards, 1965), and Bill Fuller (Tualatin, 1973).

Oregon's overnight fame came in 1979, when Lett entered his 1975 Pinot Noir in a blind wine-tasting competition organized by Robert Drouhin. Drouhin's Chambolle-Musigny 1959 had won, but Lett's The Eyrie Vineyards 1975 Pinot Noir came second, trouncing Drouhin's fabulous 1961 Clos-de-Bèze and many other prestigious Burgundies in the process. Since that eventful day, most critics have believed that it would only be a matter of time before the Pinot Noirs of Oregon would rival those of Burgundy.

By the mid-1980s, such success seemed imminent, and the Oregon wine industry, with more than one eye on hyping up the publicity, declared McMinnville host to an annual World Pinot Noir Conference, thereby endorsing the perception that Oregon is Pinot country. This state's vineyards have increased from a total of 5,950 acres (2,380 hectares) in 1992 to 13,400 acres (5,420 hectares) in 2004. Most of the expansion has been due to Pinot Noir, which had almost tripled over the same period, and by 2004 was in excess of 7,000 acres (2,800 hectares), and Pinot Gris, which has almost quadrupled, although from a much lower base, to 1,740 acres (696 hectares) by 2004. Apart from Merlot, most other varieties have virtually stood still. Riesling has actually decreased, as, surprisingly, has Chardonnay.

Oregon's reputation for patchy quality is being left behind as producers learn how to cope with the wet climate, and stop making wines for short-term success at competitions. At one time, almost all the production was consumed locally, but half of the wines are now being sold to other US states. There is room for improvement in exports, which are less than 4 percent, and should be at least half the total production if consumers around the world are to find these wines. Oregon Pinot Noir needs to be exported, not only to raise its international standing, but also because its producers need to spread their risk over as many markets as possible, enabling them to focus sales on the healthiest economies when others are in decline.

## IDAHO

At the Chicago World Fair in 1898, a prize was awarded to a wine produced by Robert Schleiser, from his vineyard near Lewiston in Idaho's Clearwater River Valley. In more modern times, grape-growing spread from Washington and Oregon to Idaho in 1969. This state's vineyards today are effectively an extension of Washington State's Snake River, and the altitude of these volcanic-soil vineyards—up to 3,500 feet (1,050 meters)—is the highest in the Pacific Northwest. Such extreme elevation ensures that the vines enjoy sunny days but extremely cold nights, and it is this extreme diurnal difference that produces wines with an unusually high acidity and alcohol balance.

---

### THE WINEMAKING STATES AND APPELLATIONS OF
# THE PACIFIC NORTHWEST

## IDAHO

There are a couple of wineries well north of the Snake River region, in Idaho's Panhandle area, around Coeur d'Alene, the state's largest, deepest, and, quite possibly, most beautiful lake, just a stone's throw from Spokane in Washington. There are now almost 20 wineries in Idaho, but its wine industry remains embryonic, and since Ste Chapelle is one of the largest wineries in the entire northwest, there is no real competition. However, there are many smaller, even more embryonic winemaking states in the US, so it is quite surprising that not one AVA has been proposed for Idaho, especially as there are locally defined areas, and the growing environment is such that the wines are renowned for their distinctive style of vivid fruit flavors heightened by intrinsically high acidity.

## OREGON

### APPLEGATE VALLEY AVA

Completely encased within the Rogue Valley AVA, this appellation has higher elevations than surrounding areas, and is largely protected from cooling coastal influences, resulting in a warmer, drier climate that encourages growers to cultivate Chardonnay, Syrah, and black Bordeaux varieties, in addition to Oregon's ubiquitous Pinot Noir.

### COLUMBIA VALLEY AVA
**Oregon and Washington**

*See* Washington.

### ROGUE VALLEY AVA

Within a short distance of California, this is the most southerly and warmest of Oregon's wine regions. With a mixture of elevations and exposures, and soil types ranging from loam to clay and some decomposed granite, it has been difficult for growers to decide what grape to focus on, hence the mishmash of varieties planted. Not surprisingly, Chardonnay is the most consistent, after which Cabernet Sauvignon and Pinot Noir are the most widely cultivated, which illustrates how undecided everyone is.

Even though the elevation of the Rogue Valley AVA is very high, it is the only area in Oregon where Bordeaux varieties ripen regularly.

## UMPQUA VALLEY AVA

A great variation in altitude, exposure, and other topographical factors has led to a much greater range of varieties than are grown elsewhere, with such diverse grapes as Riesling and Cabernet every bit as popular as both Pinot Noir and Chardonnay.

## WALLA WALLA VALLEY AVA
**Washington and Oregon**

*See* Washington.

## WILLAMETTE VALLEY AVA

The Willamette Valley is well known for Pinot Noir, although this reputation was founded as recently as 1970, when David Lett planted The Eyrie Vineyards in the Red Hills of Dundee. After Lett's 1975 Pinot Noir embarrassed Drouhin's 1961 Clos-de-Bèze, and Drouhin became serious about founding a winery in Oregon, it was no surprise that the Burgundian chose the Red Hills for the location. The Eola Hills, also in the Willamette Valley, which share the same volcanic soil as the hills of Dundee and straddle Yamhill and Polk counties, is an up-and-coming area within the Willamette Valley.

# WASHINGTON

## COLUMBIA VALLEY AVA
**Oregon and Washington**

Columbia Valley is Washington's largest appellation, encompassing two other AVAs, the Yakima Valley and Walla Walla Valley, and no fewer than 99 percent of the state's *vinifera* vines. At approximately 18,000 square miles (46,500 square kilometers), it is one-and-a-half times the size of Belgium, and consists of a large, treeless basin surrounding the Columbia, Yakima, and Snake rivers. There is a vast, undulating, semiarid plateau of between 1,000–2,000 feet (300 and 600 metres) in altitude, through which these three rivers cut many dramatic gorges, particularly just south of their confluence, where the Columbia makes a 180-degree turn to follow the Oregon border, creating some of America's most vivid, striking, and contrasting scenery.

The Columbia Valley encompasses numerous microclimates, but they mostly fall between 1,240 and 1,440 degree-days Celsius, which overlaps regions I and II on the California heat summation system (*see* p.470). Due to its northerly latitude and cloudless climate, the

Columbia Valley averages two hours' more sunlight during midsummer than the Napa Valley, a state and a half farther south. Astonishingly, there are more than 300 cloud-free days every year, and, although Washington as a whole is the wettest state in the nation, annual rainfall in the Columbia Valley is usually no more than 15 inches (38 centimeters).

Aside from the two subappellations of Yakima and Walla Walla, dealt with later, there are a number of other recognized areas within the Columbia Valley AVA. Without doubt, the most exciting of these is Canoe Ridge, which some people seem to think is in Walla Walla because that is where the Canoe Ridge winery is, but it is, in fact, 50 miles (80 kilometers) to the west, just beyond Paterson. The vines grow on the right bank of the Columbia, where there are great hopes for world-class Merlot, Cabernet, and Chardonnay, although some of its vineyards are prone to winds in excess of 25 miles per hour, the point at which viticulturists have recently discovered the vine temporarily shuts down its metabolism, hindering the ripening process. Other areas of note within the vast Columbia Valley AVA include Northern Columbia Valley (a convenient umbrella appellation for a collection of disparate wine regions, including Saddle Mountain, Wahluke Slope, Royal Slope, and Skookumchuck Creek, where the scenery is often breathtaking, but the wine seldom is) and Snake River (located between Red Mountain—*see* Yakima—and the Walla Walla, in the broad hills each side of the lower reaches of the Snake River, just a few miles east of Pasco, where it would seem that Cabernet and Merlot fare best).

## PUGET SOUND AVA

Seattle has a reputation as one of the world's wettest cities ("They don't tan in Seattle," Californians claim, "they rust!"), and rainfall initially put severe restrictions on what was grown. Bainbridge Island Winery boasts the nearest vines to downtown Seattle, with Müller-Thurgau and Siegerrebe growing just a couple of miles away by ferry, while farther south on the mainland, Johnson Creek Winery grows Müller-Thurgau. Bainbridge Island was the first vineyard in Puget Sound to grow Pinot Noir.

This AVA is a climatic contradiction, since it is significantly drier than Burgundy and sunnier than Bordeaux, yet as cool as the Loire. And, in a state of such homogenous soil, the basin drained by rivers and streams that flow into the Sound is marked by a glacial moraine not seen anywhere else in the Pacific Northwest. However, these statistics are a little like those used by Atlanta to secure the 100th Anniversary Olympics in 1996, as the annual rainfall within Puget Sound ranges between 17 and 45 inches (43 and 114 centimeters), so many areas are a lot wetter than Burgundy, even if the average is drier. Recognized areas within Puget Sound include Mount Baker and Lopez Island.

## RED MOUNTAIN AVA

Washington's smallest appellation, Red Mountain, overlaps Yakima AVA, encompassing 4,040 acres (1,616 hectares), of which more than 700 (280 hectares) are under vine. This AVA has a full southern exposure, with gentle slopes that are protected from frost by excellent air-drainage. The sandy loam soil has a high calcium content, which with the diurnal inflence of warm summer days and cool nights, encourages increased acidity levels in the grapes grown (Cabernet Franc, Cabernet Sauvignon, Sangiovese, and Syrah).

## WALLA WALLA VALLEY AVA

This area has been called the Walla Walla Valley since it was settled in the 1850s, before the creation of either Oregon or Washington. With less than half of one percent of the state's vineyards, Walla Walla would not perhaps seem to warrant its own AVA, but it can receive up to 20 inches (50 centimeters) of rain, which is more than twice as much as the rest of the Columbia Valley, and this makes Walla Walla a truly distinctive viticultural area with the potential to produce outstanding nonirrigated wine. For every mile you travel east from Walla Walla toward the Blue Mountains, you get another inch of rain.

Although viticulture is growing fast in Walla Walla, from just a dozen wineries cultivating 170 acres of vines in 1998, to more than 60 wineries growing over 1,500 acres in 2005, wine remains very much small beer compared to Walla Walla's wheat country, which still runs to almost a quarter of a million acres. But Walla Walla wine punches well above its weight when it comes to the excitement factor. At one time, Mountain Dome was one of the few outsiders to buy grapes from this AVA, traditionally sourcing a third of its Chardonnay and almost all of its Pinot noir from Whisky Creek vineyard. Nowadays Walla Walla is all the rage, with wineries from all over the state queueing up to get their hands on some of its production. A novel experience for local producers who until recently relied heavily on fruit purchased from outside the area. The Walla Walla AVA also encompasses a small chunk of Oregon.

## YAKIMA VALLEY AVA

One of the Columbia Valley's two subappellations, the Yakima Valley contains the greatest concentration of Washington's wineries and 40 percent of the state's vineyards. It is in every sense the home and historical center of the Washington wine industry. Most vineyards are on the southeast-facing slopes of the Rattlesnake Hills, especially in the mid-valley area from Sunnyside to Prosser, and intermingle with the apple, cherry, and peach orchards that are found between two irrigation canals, the Roza and the Sunnyside. The Roza is higher up the slopes and sometimes an odd plot of vines, a windbreak of trees, or an orchard can be seen above this canal, where the deep, lush green of irrigated vegetation stands out in contrast to the yellow-ocher starkness of semiarid desert. In this way, the Yakima is representative of the agricultural success brought to eastern Washington by irrigation projects dating back to the turn of the century, although real prosperity occurred under the great Columbia irrigation project funded by the New Deal. Everything grows here: apples, apricots, asparagus, cherries, hops, pears, lentils, mint, peas, plums, potatoes, and raspberries. The apple farmers arrived first and took all the best vineyard sites (apple trees and vines prefer a similar growing environment). In recent years, vineyards have slowly encroached on prime apple orchards. Old cherry orchards have also proved quite favorable for the vine, but former apple sites have proven superior and those chosen for Red Delicious the best of all (because this variety needs a warm site and is susceptible to frost). Other recognized areas that are located within the Yakima Valley AVA are Red Mountain, Red Willow, and Cold Creek. Red Mountain is just northeast of Benton City, where the wild west is at its wildest and reminiscent of the Australian outback. Despite this, Red Mountain Cabernet Sauvignon has been an ingredient in such award-winning wines as Quilceda Creek and Woodward Canyon and it is therefore an area for future viticultural development. Red Willow is located 24 kilometers (24 kilometers) southwest of Yakima itself, on Ahtanum Ridge, which is on the opposite side of the valley to the Roza and Sunnyside canals. It has a steep slope, particularly on the west side, where there is little topsoil, most of it having been dispersed by the winds that blow across the ridge. The west side produces small, thick-skinned berries,

whereas the east side, which has less of a slope and a deep topsoil, produces larger berries and softer, less tannic wines. Mike Sauer, who first planted Red Willow in 1973, claims that the complexity of the east-slope soils and the different air movements that occur over the various blocks of the vineyard create eight distinctly different microclimates. Red Willow is the source of Columbia Winery's best Cabernet Sauvignon, its top-class Syrah, and Milestone Merlot, and at least one winery is trying Nebbiolo there. Cold Creek is close to being the driest, warmest spot in the state and

one of the first vineyards to start harvest, yet when the vineyards around Prosser are covered in an autumnal carpet of leaves, just over the low Rattlesnake Hills, the vines of Cold Ridge are still verdant. This is because it has one of the longest growing seasons in Washington, so it is not only the first to start harvesting, but the last to finish, whereas the explanation for its name is that it is one of the most bitterly cold places in the state in winter. Originally noted for Chardonnay, Cold Creek Vineyard has matured into the consistent source for most of Château Ste. Michelle's premium varietal.

THE WINE PRODUCERS OF

# THE PACIFIC NORTHWEST

## IDAHO

### HELLS CANYON
#### Caldwell
#### ★ Ⓥ

One of the older boutique wineries, Hells Canyon Winery was founded in 1980 by Steve and Leslie Robertson, whose longer experience makes their wines stand out from most of the rest in this state.

✓ *Merlot* (Reserve) • *Syrah* (Deer Slayer, Falcons Fall Vineyard)

### INDIAN CREEK
#### Kuna
#### ★ Ⓥ

The owner of Indian Creek, Bill Stowe, is a Pinot Noir fanatic stuck in Riesling country!

✓ *Pinot Noir* • *White Riesling*

### KOENIG
#### Caldwell
#### ★ Ⓥ

Andy and Greg Koenig run an award-winning distillery and are beginning to get noticed for their wines.

✓ *Cabernet Sauvignon* (Bitner Vineyard) • *Riesling* (Ice Wine, Late Harvest) • *Syrah* (Three Vineyard Cuvée)

### PARMA RIDGE VINEYARDS
#### Parma
#### ★ Ⓥ

Dick and Shirley Dickstein grow Chardonnay, Gewürztraminer, Merlot, Syrah, Viognier, and even Zinfandel at an altitude of 2,400 feet (720 meters) on his 9½-acre (4-hectare) vineyard overlooking the Boise River.

✓ *Chardonnay* (Reserve)

### PEND D'OREILLE WINERY
#### Sandpoint
#### ★ Ⓥ

Julie and Stephen Meyer have a good reputation for their Vickers Vineyard Chardonnay and were judged "Idaho Winery of the Year" in 2003.

✓ *Chardonnay* (Vickers Vineyard)

### ROSE CREEK VINEYARDS
#### Hagerman
#### ★ Ⓥ

Former Ste. Chapelle employee Jamie Martin makes some very creditable wine at Rose Creek Vineyards, from both Idaho and Washington fruit, pure and mixed.

✓ *Chardonnay* • *Riesling*

### STE. CHAPELLE
#### Caldwell
#### ★ Ⓥ

Let's face it, these wines are not cheap. No, they're practically given away! Established in 1976 and named after the Gothic Ste. Chapelle in Paris, Idaho's largest and oldest winery has set a particularly fine standard for others to follow. Ste. Chapelle is, in fact, the fourth-largest winery in the Northwest, and part of Constellation Brands, the largest wine group in the world.

✓ *Cabernet Sauvignon* • *Riesling* (Ice Wine)

### SAWTOOTH WINERY
#### Nampa
#### ★ Ⓥ

Part of Corus Vineyards, Sawtooth draws on a south-facing vineyard on their large ranch just west of Boise.

✓ *Cabernet Sauvignon* • *Merlot* • *Roussanne* • *Syrah* • *Viognier*

### SNAKE RIVER WINERY
#### Parma
#### ★ Ⓥ

Improvised canopy management has yielded positive results since 1999.

✓ *Cabernet Sauvignon* (Arena Valley Vineyard) • *Merlot*

## OREGON

### A TO Z
#### Dundee
#### ★ Ⓥ

If A to Z has any address, it is a post office box in Dundee, but if you wanted to find its winemakers, Sam Tannahill (former Archery Summit winemaker) or his wife Cheryl Francis (former Chehalem

winemaker), you would have to search a number of wineries in Yamhill county. Together with their partners William Hatcher, who developed and managed Domaine Drouhin, and his wife Debra, these two families have established a *négociant*-style business to mop up any excess production from the wineries they work with. Although the individual wines purchased by A to Z are theoretically inferior or, at best, unwanted, Tannahill and Francis should be able to blend them into a harmonious product that is greater than the sum of its parts, if they are gifted at this particular oenological discipline. And it seems that they are. *Food & Wine* magazine named their 2001 Pinot Noir Willamette Valley "the best American Pinot Noir under $20," and since then A to Z has been set to become Oregon's fastest-growing brand.

✓ *Pinot Noir* (Willamette Valley)

### ABACELA VINEYARDS
#### Roseburg
#### ★★

A small, family-owned and -operated winery, with an interesting gaggle of grapes, including Tempranillo, Syrah, Merlot, Dolcetto, Malbec, Cabernet Franc, Grenache, Viognier, and Albariño, growing on sunny south-sloping rocky hillsides.

✓ *Albariño* • *Tempranillo* (South East Block Reserve) • *Syrah* • *Viognier*

### ADEA
#### Gaston
#### ★★

Known as Fisher Family Vineyards until this name was subject to a trademark conflict, when ADEA was adopted. It is always written in capital letters, since it was formed from the first letter of the first names of the Fisher family members, Ann, Dean, Erica, and Adam, who together produce delightful, velvety-textured Pinot Noir wines that are brimming with juicy fruit.

✓ *Pinot Noir*

### ADELSHEIM VINEYARD
#### Newberg
#### ★★

Fine wines across the range, and most successful for Pinot Noir, which are consistently among the best half-dozen in Oregon.

✓ *Chardonnay* • *Pinot Gris* • *Merlot* (Layne Vineyards Grant's Pass) • *Pinot Noir* • *Sauvignon Blanc*

### AMITY VINEYARDS
#### Amity
#### ★ Ⓥ

Most famous for Pinot Noir, yet this can be Myron Redford's least consistent varietal, as it is always well structured and can sometimes lack the fruit to support the tannin. However, when there is plenty of fruit, Amity makes one of the best-value Pinot Noirs in Oregon. Produces some sulfite-free wines.

✓ *Pinot Blanc* • *Pinot Noir* • *Riesling*

### ARCHERY SUMMIT
#### Dundee
#### ★★

Californian Gary Andrus put Archery Summit on the map with his gorgeously plump, infinitely classy Pinot Noir, but lost ownership of this winery following a very public divorce (*see also* Gypsy Dancer). Biodynamic experimentation under way.

✓ *Pinot Noir*

### ARGYLE WINERY
#### Dundee
#### ★★ Ⓥ

Part of the Australian Lion Nathan group, Argyle's exceptional sparkling wine performance is solely due to three people: Allen Holstein, who runs Domaine Drouhin's vineyards as well as Argyle's; Rollin Sole, who is this winery's gifted, laid-back winemaker; and Brian Croser, who was one of the original partners and whose intellectual curiosity into the hows and whys of everything that sparkles was the very catalyst of Argyle's success. Some excellent still wines are made, even though the Pinot Noir was once dire.

✓ *Chardonnay* (Nuthouse) • *Pinot Noir* • *Riesling* • *Sparkling wine* • *Syrah* (Nuthouse)

## BEAUX FRÈRES
### Dundee
### ★★☆

Wine critic Robert Parker owns a share of this vineyard and winery, which is run by his partner Mike Etzel. At approximately 2,400 vines per acre (6,000 per hectare), only Domaine Drouhin is planted at a higher density. These wines were very good when I wrote the previous revision of this book, but now they are sensational. Biodynamic experimentation under way.

✓ *Pinot Noir*

## BENTON-LANE
### Sunnymount Ranch
### ★☆

A joint venture between Stephen Girard of Girard Winery and Carl Doumani of Stag's Leap, whose vineyard has been certified for its sustainable viticulture by LIVE (Low Impact Viticulture and Enology).

✓ *Pinot Noir* (Reserve, Sunnymount Cuvee)

## BERGSTRÖM
### Dundee
### ★★☆

Established in 1997 by the Bergström family, who sent son Josh to France for a postgraduate course in Viticulture and Oenology at Beaune. The standard has been nothing less than exemplary since the first vintage in 1999. Their own winery was built in 2001.

✓ *Pinot Noir*

## BETHEL HEIGHTS VINEYARD
### Salem
### ★★Ⓥ

One of the best half-dozen wineries in the state, Bethel Heights' basic Pinot Noir (not the cheaper First Release) is often as good as the individual block bottlings and sometimes can even be better balanced, so it not only ranks as one of Oregon's best-quality Pinot Noirs, it also ranks as one of the best value.

✓ *Pinot Noir*

## BRICK HOUSE VINEYARD
### Newburg
### Ⓞ★★

These organic wines have shown a dramatic increase in elegance and finesse in recent years. Biodynamic experimentation underway.

✓ *Gamay* • *Pinot Noir*

## BRIDGEVIEW
### Cave Junction

Located in the Illinois Valley in the Cascades, where the Chardonnay

benefits from a fairly dense cultivation of just over 1,780 per acre (4,450 vines per hectare).

✓ *Chardonnay* • *Pinot Noir* (since 1994)

## CAMERON WINERY
### Dundee
### ★Ⓥ

An underrated winery with a good, easy-drinking, if sometimes bizarre, style.

✓ *Chardonnay* • *Pinot Blanc* • *Pinot Noir*

## CHÂTEAU LORANE
### Lorane
### ★Ⓥ

Linde and Sharon Kester produce a wide range of varietals that is eclectic, bordering on bizarre, with crosses and hybrids mingling with classic to obscure *vinifera*. The Marechal Foch is highly regarded by lovers of that hybrid. Some organic wines are made.

✓ *Chardonnay* • *Pinot Gris*

## CHEHALAM
### Newburg
### ★★

One of Oregon's most exciting, up-and-coming wineries, Chehalam draws its fruit from three vineyards, two of which belong to Harry Peterson-Nedry, the major shareholder, while his partners Bill and Cathy Stoller own the other one.

✓ *Chardonnay* (Ian's Reserve) • *Pinot Noir*

## COOPER MOUNTAIN
### Beaverton
### Ⓑ★

This winery produces fine-quality, barrel-fermented Chardonnay from an extinct volcano overlooking the Tualatin Valley. Cooper Mountain was certified organic in 1995, and biodynamic in 1999. Some wines are sulfite-free.

✓ *Chardonnay* • *Pinot Gris* • *Pinot Noir*

## CRISTOM
### Salem
### ★★

Native yeast fermentations produce some of Oregon's most gluggy Pinot Noirs.

✓ *Pinot Noir* • *Viognier*

## DOMAINE DROUHIN
### Dundee
### ★★☆

Joseph Drouhin has been intrigued by Oregon's potential since Oregon winemaker David Lett entered his 1975 Pinot Noir in a blind wine tasting Drouhin had organized. Although Drouhin's Chambolle-Musigny 1959 won, Lett's wine came second, trouncing Drouhin's Clos-de-Bèze 1961 and many other Burgundies. Ever since Domaine Drouhin's first vintage, 1988, was

released, locals and critics alike have marveled at how Drouhin's wine instantly possessed more color, depth, and complexity than any other Oregon Pinot Noir, yet still maintained the grape's varietal purity and finesse. It appeared that Drouhin had planted his vines three-and-a-half times closer than the average in Oregon. The notion that higher-density vines give better quality more quickly became established on the international grapevine as the reason for Drouhin's success. The locals knew, however, that the wine contained not a single grape from his own vineyard, which was too young. It was all down to the way that Drouhin had handled the grapes, which itself was ironic, because the only reason he started making wine in 1988 with bought grapes was because he wanted hands-on experience of Oregon fruit before committing himself with his own produce.

The 1989 vintage was a revelation and the 1990 was almost as good, but the stunning 1991 (the first made completely by Drouhin's daughter Véronique) was of such a significantly higher order that it led many to believe it was the first 100 percent estate wine, but just one-third of the grapes were from Drouhin's own vineyards. This is hotly disputed by some critics, so I will identify where the balance, in roughly equal parts, came from: Bethel Heights, Canary Hill, Durant, Knudsen, Hyland, and Seven Springs. The 1991 has such structure, weight, and color, yet nothing but the luscious fruit of pure Pinot Noir all the way to the bottom of the glass. I did not think that Oregon Pinot Noir could possibly get any better, until, that is, I tasted it against the 1992 and was dumbfounded.

✓ *Pinot Noir*

## DOMAINE SERENE
### Carlton
### ★★

This winery made an excellent debut with the 1992 vintage, but a shaky period followed. It is now finding its feet again.

✓ *Pinot Noir*

## ELK COVE VINEYARDS
### Gaston
### ★★

Joe and Pat Campbell can produce easy-going, varietally pure Pinot Noir, but the quality is still a little erratic.

✓ *Pinot Noir* • *Riesling* (Ultima)

## EOLA HILLS
### Rickreall
### ★★

Founded in 1986 by Tom Huggins, Eola Hills has made great improvements over the last 10 years, and is now at least as good for Chardonnay as for Pinot Noir.

✓ *Chardonnay* • *Pinot Noir* •

*Sauvignon Blanc* (Vin d'Or Late Harvest)

## ERATH WINERY
### Dundee
### ★★☆

Formerly Knudsen Erath, this is sometimes one of the best wineries in Oregon for Pinot Noir, but vintages can lurch between firm-tannic and soft, creamy, and voluptuous.

✓ *Chardonnay* • *Pinot Gris* • *Pinot Noir*

## EVESHAM WOOD
### Salem
### Ⓞ★☆

Evesham Wood is a small but expanding winery and is one of Oregon's rising stars.

✓ *Pinot Gris* • *Pinot Noir*

## FIRESTEED
### Rickreall
### ★Ⓥ

This soft, delicious, easy-drinking wine offers brilliant value and is sourced from Oregon vineyards by Washington-based *négociant* Howard Rossbach. Originally devised to satisfy the demands of his mother, Eleanor, whose drinking prowess once featured in *Vogue* magazine, Firesteed is now a brand in its own right

✓ *Pinot Noir*

## GYPSY DANCER
### Hillsboro
### ★★

Get in on the ground floor of these great Pinot Noir wines from Californian Gary Andrus, who made some stunning vintages at Archery Summit before losing the winery in a divorce settlement.

✓ *Pinot Noir*

## HENRY ESTATE
### Umpqua
### ★Ⓥ

The Henry Estate is not the most consistent of producers, but when on form can produce one of Oregon's best Pinot Noir wines.

✓ *Classic red blend* (Henry V) • *Riesling* (Select Clusters)

## KEN WRIGHT CELLARS
### McMinnville
### ★★★

High-performance winery founded by the former Panther Creek owner Ken Wright, who has established a reputation for sumptuous, stylish, expressive Pinot Noir sold under single-vineyard names.

✓ *Chardonnay* (Celio Vineyard) • *Pinot Noir*

## KING ESTATE
### Eugene
### Ⓞ★Ⓥ

This vast and still-expanding vineyard surrounds a high-tech, hilltop winery that promises to put

Oregon on the commercial map with a 200,000-case capacity.

 *Pinot Gris* (Vin Glacé) • *Pinot Noir*

## LA BÊTE
### McMinnville
### ★

Unfiltered wines made in an uncompromising style.

 *Aligoté* • *Pinot Noir*

## LEMELSON
### Carlton
### ◉★★

The Lemelson family is as organic-minded as certified organic producers, but does it out of respect for the land, rather than to parade an organically produced sticker on its bottles. The Lemelsons make vividly expressive Pinot Noir wines that brim with bright fruit flavor. Lemelson was certified organic just before the 2004 harvest.

 *Pinot Noir*

## MONTINORE VINEYARDS
### Forest Grove
### ★◕

A large project by Oregon standards, with all wines 100 percent estate grown, Montinore is at long last beginning to reflect its true potential.

 *Pinot Gris* (Entre Deux) • *Pinot Noir* (Parson's Ridge, Winemaker's Reserve)

## OAK KNOLL WINERY
### Hillsboro
### ★

This winery used to produce one of Oregon's finest Pinot Noirs, and has been trying very hard since the late 1990s to reclaim that reputation. And if you ever want a pure *labrusca* Oregon wine, this winery has not lost its reputation for that outdated varietal since the 1970s!

 *Pinot Noir*

## OWEN ROE
### Newberg
### ★★

This winery is the result of a collaboration between Jerry Owen, who looks after the vineyards, and David O'Reilly, who makes and sells these Oregon and Washington wines. The top-of-the-line wines are beautifully presented with photogravure labels bearing the inspired photography of fellow Irishman David Brunn. Entry-level wines are sold under the O'Reilly label. For other David O'Reilly wines, see Sineann.

 *Cabernet Sauvignon* (DuBrul Vineyard) • *Chardonnay* (Casa Blanca Vineyard) • *Merlot* (DuBrul Vineyard) • *Pinot Noir* • *Syrah* (DuBrul Vineyard)

## PANTHER CREEK
### McMinnville
### ★★

This tiny winery specializes in opulent Pinot Noir wines that rank

among the very finest in Oregon. It also makes a delicious white wine from the Muscadet grape, sold under its synonym of Melon.

 *Melon* • *Pinot Noir*

## PATRICIA GREEN
### Newberg
### ★★◐

Green is a long-time Oregon winemaker who launched her own operation in 2000, and makes remarkably consistent, delicious, elegant Pinot Noir.

 *Pinot Noir*

## PENNER-ASH
### Newberg
### ★★

Established by former CEO of Rex Hill winery, Lynn Penner-Ash, who has quickly established a reputation for stylish Pinot Noir.

 *Pinot Noir* • *Syrah*

## PONZI VINEYARDS
### Beaverton
### ★★

One of Oregon's top-performing Pinot Noirs for more than a decade.

 *Pinot Noir*

## RAPTOR RIDGE
### Cheshire
### ◐

"Raptor" is synonymous with bird of prey, and the name was chosen because of the large number of hawks, kestrels, and owls that hunt within the vicinity of this winery and vineyards. The bright, fruity wines produced here are also worth chasing down.

 *Pinot Noir*

## REDHAWK VINEYARD
### Salem
### ★◐

Proud winner of *Decanter* magazine's Worst Wine Label Awards, Redhawk has an uncanny knack with Bordeaux varieties, and is now moving into Italian and Rhône styles. The most expensive wines here cost less than the cheapest wines at some other wineries.

 *Cabernet Franc* • *Cabernet Sauvignon* (Safari Vineyard)

## REX HILL VINEYARDS
### Newberg
### ★★

Best known for its line of fine, stylish Pinot Noir wines, which consistently rank in the top half-dozen in Oregon.

 *Pinot Gris* • *Pinot Noir*

## SHEA WINE CELLARS
### Yamhill
### ★★★◐

You could not get two more diametrically opposed worlds than Wall Street and farming in Oregon, but Dick Shea made the transition with ease in 1996, and quickly achieved huge respect from local winemakers for his long, classy, complex Pinot Noir.

 *Cabernet Sauvignon* • *Merlot*

## SIDURI
### Santa Rosa
### ★★

Named after the Babylonian goddess of wine by Adam and Diana Lee, a couple of Pinot Noir fanatics who are based as far south as Santa Barbara's Santa Rita hills, but source their wines from as far north as Oregon's Willamette Valley. The Oregon Pinot Noir is grown at their Archery Summit vineyard, where they reduce yields, yet still end up rejecting up to 85 percent of the barrels made.

 *Pinot Noir*

## SINEANN
### Santa Rosa
### ★★

Winemaker Peter Rosback and his business partner David O'Reilly source wines for their own label from all over the northwest: Pinot Noir and Pinot Gris from the Willamette and the Hood River valleys; Cabernet Sauvignon, Merlot, and Zinfandel from the Columbia Valley; and Gewürztraminer from the Willamette Valley and the Columbia Gorge. For other David O'Reilly wines, see Owen Roe.

 *Cabernet Sauvignon* ("Block One" Champoux Vineyard, Baby Poux Vineyard) • *Fortified* (CJ Port) • *Merlot* (Columbia Valley) • *Pinot Noir* (all Oregon wines) • *Zinfandel* (Old Vine Columbia Valley)

## SILVAN RIDGE
### Eugene
### ★

Erratic Pinot Noir lurches between bizarre and brilliant, but surprisingly good Cabernet Sauvignon. Early Muscat Semi-Sparkling is always gorgeously peachy, and occasionally there are some extraordinary late-harvest styles.

 *Cabernet Sauvignon* • *Muscat* (Early Muscat Semi-Sparkling) • *Merlot*

## SOKOL BLOSSER WINERY
### Dundee
### ★★

This winery produces some lush, seductive, early-drinking Pinot Noirs that regularly rank among some of Oregon's finest. Biodynamic experimentation underway.

 *Chardonnay* • *Pinot Noir*

## SOTER
### Yamhill
### ★★

Tony Soter's Oregon venture was established in 1997, and abuts properties such as Beaux Frères and Brick House. In 2003, this vineyard was awarded a LIVE Farming Certificate, which is not organic as such, but recognizes the "sustainable farming practices" that have been employed since the Soter's purchase of the land.

 *Chardonnay* • *Pinot Noir*

## ST. INNOCENT
### Salem
### ★★

Vineyard-designated wines made from purchased grapes grown in the Eola Hills that rank as some of Oregon's greatest Pinot Noirs.

 *Chardonnay* • *Pinot Noir*

## THE EYRIE VINEYARDS
### McMinnville
### ★★◐

The man who started it all, David Lett, also makes Pinot Noir to age, Chardonnay for medium-term storage, and Pinot Gris that is best drunk young.

 *Chardonnay* • *Pinot Gris* • *Pinot Noir* (Reserve)

## TORI MOR
### Dundee
### ★★

An up-and-coming producer of nicely oaked, fat, juicy Pinot Noir.

 *Pinot Gris* • *Pinot Noir*

## TUALATIN VINEYARDS
### Forest Grove
### ★◐

Classically structured, yet elegant Pinot Noir.

 *Pinot Noir*

## VALLEY VIEW VINEYARD
### Jacksonville
### ★

This is one of the few consistent producers of Cabernet in Oregon. Jacksonville in the Rogue Valley is one of those idyllic towns everyone should visit. The Anna Maria *cuvée* is a reserve produced only in the best years, thus not available for all varietals in every year.

 *Chardonnay* (Anna Maria) • *Cabernet Sauvignon* (Anna Maria) • *Reserve* (Anna Maria) • *Sauvignon Blanc* (Anna Maria)

## VAN DUZER
### Dallas
### ★★◐

This vineyard is located in the foothills of the Van Duzer corridor, where the vines are affected by the cool Pacific air that flows inward to the Willamette Valley, and the ripening process benefits from the diurnal effect of warm days chased by cool nights. Van Duzer's sustainable farming practices have been endorsed by LIVE.

✓ *Pinot Noir*

## WILLAKENZIE ESTATE
### Turner
★★

Located on the rolling hillsides on the Chehalem Mountains, this winery was named after the Willakenzie soil, on which the vineyards are planted, and these vineyards are maintained today by sustainable viticulture.

✓ *Pinot Noir*

## WITNESS TREE
### Salem
★★☆

This vineyard takes its name from an ancient oak tree used as a surveyor's landmark as far back as 1854, during the Oregon Trail era. All wines produced are 100 percent estate grown.

✓ *Pinot Noir*

# WASHINGTON

## ANDREW WILL
### Vachon
★★★☆

Andrew Will as a person does not actually exist, as Chris and Annie Camarda, owners of this winery, named it after their nephew Andrew and son Will. These wines are superb, especially the line of beautifully crafted classic red blends.

✓ *Cabernet Franc* (Sheridan) • *Cabernet Sauvignon* (Klipsun) • *Classic red blend* (Champoux, Ciel du Cheval, Seven Hills, Sheridan, Sorella) • *Merlot* (Klipsun) • *Sangiovese* (Ciel du Cheval)

## APEX CELLARS
### Sunnyside
★★

Also known as Washington Hills, this venture was established in the 1980s by Harry Alhadeff, who owned a chain of wine shops and restaurants, and Brian Carter, whose winemaking skills brought the Paul Thomas winery to international attention when there were only 16 wineries in the entire state. Since 1990, Carter has produced a string of superb wines, particularly under the Apex label, which has put this winery among the very elite of Washington's producers.

✓ *Cabernet Franc* (Bridgman) • *Cabernet Sauvignon* (Apex) • *Chardonnay* (Apex) • *Gewurztraminer* (Apex Ice Wine) • *Merlot* (Apex) • *Riesling* (Apex Late Harvest) • *Syrah* (Apex)

## ARBOR CREST
### Spokane
★★Ⓥ

Formerly a cherry winery, Arbor Crest is owned by the Mielke family, with Kristina Mielke van Lvben Sels the winemaker since 1999. The vines growing around the Cliff House winery, with its spectacular view, are the only ones you are likely to see in or around Spokane, although there are a number of other wineries in the locality. Spokane is not the best place in the world to grow vines. All the best wines from Arbor Crest and its neighboring wineries are made from grapes sourced elsewhere.

✓ *Cabernet Sauvignon* (Columbia Valley) • *Chardonnay* (Conner Lee Vineyard) • *Classic red blend* (Dionysus)

## BADGER MOUNTAIN
### Kennewick
Ⓞ★Ⓥ

Established in 1983 by Greg and Bill Powers, Badger Mountain became Washington's first certified organic vineyard in 1990. One of the more consistent organic producers, especially in recent years, this winery uses its Powers label to produce wines from grapes that are not grown in its own 100 percent organic farmed vineyards. All Vintners Estate Series wines are organic, and heartily recommended, but those with "No Sulfites Added" are not as consistent.

✓ *Syrah* (Vintners Estate Series)

## BARNARD GRIFFIN
### Kennewick
★Ⓥ

Owners Deborah Barnard and Rob Griffin have a track record for Merlot, but have made some splendid Cabernets since the early 1990s and some stunning Syrahs since the late 1990s.

✓ *Merlot* (Red Mountain Ciel du Cheval) • *Sauvignon Blanc* (Fumé Blanc) • *Syrah* (Handcrafted Selection)

## BETZ FAMILY VINEYARDS
### Woodinville
★★

When I first met Bob Betz, he was a director at Château Ste. Michelle. I thought that here was someone who was good at connecting with visitors, but also a person who, I realized, would be happier with his hands in the soil, getting back to his winemaking roots. Over the years he has become the second only Master of Wine in the Pacific Northwest, and in 1997 he began releasing wine under his own label, while still at Château Ste. Michelle. At that first meeting, Betz was full of enthusiasm for Red Mountain, and that was long before any Washington wine drinkers had heard of it. He left Château Ste. Michelle in 2003, and it is no surprise to find that he now sources

many of his wines from Red Mountain. Production is tiny, just 200 cases or so of each wine.

✓ *Cabernet Sauvignon* (Père de Famille) • *Classic red blend* (Clos de Betz) • *Syrah* (La Côte Rousse, La Serenne)

## BOOKWALTER
### Pasco
★☆

Jerry Bookwalter graduated from UC Davis in 1962, but did not start up on his own until 1983, after 20 years' experience with Sagemoor Farms and various other vineyards in Washington and Oregon. this winery is now run by his son, John.

✓ *Cabernet Sauvignon* • *Merlot*

## BUTY
### Walla Walla
★☆

Up-and-coming, artisanal winery established as recently as 2000 by Nina Buty Foster and Caleb Foster, whose Chardonnay and Syrah reflect Calab's eight years at Woodward Canyon Winery, followed by overseas winemaking experience in New Zealand and South Africa. This should be one to keep an eye on.

✓ *Chardonnay* • *Syrah* (Rediviva of the Stones)

## CADENCE
### Seattle
★★

Gaye McNutt and Ben Smith produce small lots of classy red blends: Bel Canto (Merlot-based), Coda (Cabernet Franc-based), Ciel du Cheval (Cabernet Sauvignon-based), Klipsun (Merlot-based), and Tapteil (Cabernet Sauvignon-based). I like all five of these wines, but four are a class apart, and of those, Ciel du Cheval and Tapteil stand out.

✓ *Classic red blend* (Bel Canto, Ciel du Cheval, Klipsun, Tapteil)

## CANOE RIDGE
### Walla Walla
★☆

Owned by Chalone Vineyards of California, Canoe Ridge used Woodward Canyon and Hyatt Vineyards to make wines before setting up this winery to the east of its Canoe Ridge vineyards.

✓ *Merlot* (Reserve)

## CAYUSE
### Walla Walla
Ⓑ★★☆

This exciting boutique winery is owned by Christophe Baron of Champagne Baron Albert. Baron has always been a very enthusiastic Champagne producer, but due to the far too westerly location of his vineyards, he has not been the most consistent. Now he has gone as far west as he can without doubling back on himself, and his wines are extremely consistent. He has planted five vineyards totaling 41

acres (16 hectares), all on stony ground, which prompted Baron to name his venture after one of three local Native American tribes, as a play on the French word for stony "cailloux." Mostly planted with Syrah, plus a few other Rhône varieties. Look out for a future release of Tempranillo. Most of Baron 's wines have single-vineyard designations, while those that don't are usually of a humorous ilk; this is a Frenchman with a self-depricating sense of humor, as his top-performing "Bionic Frog" Syrah demonstrates.

✓ *Syrah*

## CHÂTEAU STE. MICHELLE
### Woodinville
★★Ⓥ

If rated on the top-of-the-line wines alone, Château Ste Michelle would deserve 2½ stars. However, to increase its overall rating to two full stars since 1997 indicates that this Stimson Lane-owned winery has made huge strides even at entry level. Col Solare is a Cabernet-Merlot blend with a dash of Syrah and Malbec, made in partnership with Piero Antinori. Eroica is the result of a collaboration with Ernest Loosen, and it has caused such a renaissance for this grape in Washington that growers are having to replant it as quickly as they can.

✓ *Cabernet Sauvignon* (Canoe Ridge Estate, Cold Creek) • *Chardonnay* (Canoe Ridge Estate, Indian Wells) • *Classic red blend* (Artist Series Meritage, Col Solare) • *Merlot* (Cold Creek) • *Riesling* (Eroica, Ice Wine, Single Berry Select) • *Syrah* (Reserve)

## COLUMBIA CREST
### Prosser
★★☆Ⓥ

Owned by Stimson Lane, this winery continues to impress, but is in the middle of nowhere, and will never realize its tourist potential. As tourism not only provides profit, but also increases the reputation of a wine area, it seems odd that Stimson Lane did not build its wine wonder-palace in the Yakima Valley, which has the greatest concentration of wineries and almost half the state's vineyards.

✓ *Cabernet Sauvignon* (Reserve) • *Classic red blend* (Walter Clore Reserve) • *Merlot* (Grand Estates, Reserve) • *Syrah* (Shiraz, Two Vines Shiraz)

## COLUMBIA WINERY
### Bellevue
### ★ ❂ ♥

Formerly Associated Vintners, these wines are made by Master of Wine David Lake, who makes some of Washington's best-value red wines.

✓ *Cabernet Sauvignon* (Red Willow Vineyard) • *Merlot* (Milestone) • *Syrah* (Red Willow Vineyard)

## COUGAR CREST
### Walla Walla
### ★ ✫ ♥

Deborah and David Hansen own 50 acres (20 hectares) of vineyards in the Walla Walla AVA, and had sold their grapes to other wineries for many years when, in 2001, they established this winery at Walla Walla airport. Very strong in red wine generally, with Cabernet Sauvignon the very best performer.

✓ *Cabernet Franc* • *Cabernet Sauvignon* • *Merlot* • *Syrah*

## COVEY RUN
### Zillah
### ✫

This winery started as a partnership between several Yakima farmers as an outlet for their grapes using the Quail Run label, but they soon fell foul of Quail Ridge in California, and changed the name to Covey Run. Capable of good value, rather than special quality.

✓ *Cabernet Sauvignon* • *Chardonnay* • *Classic red blend* (Cabernet-Merlot) • *Riesling* (Ice Wine) • *Syrah* (Barrel Select)

## DE LILLE CELLARS
### Woodinville
### ★★✫

If anything is proof of the strength of Washington's classic red wine blends, it is Chris Upchurch, a self-confessed inveterate blender, who has swiftly realized the potential of this state's vineyards with his line of top-performing blends. Even its second wine, D2, is so good that he had to name it twice (the D stands for Deuxième!), as if to emphasize its modest aspirations, yet it regularly knocks seven bells out of most other proprietary reds. All percentages vary from vintage to vintage, of course, but the D2 is usually around 50 percent Merlot, 35 percent Cabernet Sauvignon, 10 percent Cabernet Franc, and 5 percent Petit Verdot, while both Harrison Hill and Chaleur Estate are effectively 65 percent Cabernet Sauvignon, 25 percent Merlot, and 10 percent Cabernet Franc, the difference being that Harrison Hill is a single vineyard, whereas Chaleur Estate is an *assemblage* of half-a-dozen different vineyards.

✓ *Classic red blend* (D2, Harrison Hill, Chaleur Estate) • *Syrah* (Doyenne)

## DISTEFANO
### Woodinville
### ★★✫♥

Owner-winemaker Mark Newton was a mechanical and nuclear engineer, who first turned his hand to sparkling winemaking in the 1980s, under the Newton & Newton label, but has really begun to shine since 1990, when he started making still wines to honor a wedding vow to his bride, Donna DiStefano.

✓ *Cabernet Franc* (Sogno) • *Cabernet Sauvignon* • *Classic red blend* (Ottimo) • *Merlot*

## DUNHAM CELLARS
### Walla Walla
### ★★

Established in 1995 by Eric Dunham, who was born and brought up in Walla Walla, and served his winemaking apprenticeship under Marty Clubb at L'Ecole No. 41.

✓ *Cabernet Sauvignon* (Columbia Valley, Roman numeral series) • *Classic red blend* (Trutina) • *Syrah* (Columbia Valley, Lewis Vineyard)

## FIDELITAS
### Kennewick
### ★♥

When flight test engineer Charlie Hoppes gave up his job to set up this winery, his life really took off. Smart, minimalist presentation for far from minimalist wines.

✓ *Classic red blend* (Columbia Valley Meritage) • *Syrah* (Yakima Valley)

## FIELDING HILLS
### Wenatchee
### ★♥

Although this is only a small boutique winery and established as recently as 2000, co-owner/winemaker Mike Wade has quickly made a big splash with the serious quality of these wines, which are ready to drink as soon as released, yet can easily age a decade or so.

✓ *Classic red blend* (Riverben Red) • *Cabernet Sauvignon* (Columbia Valley)

## FIVE STARS CELLARS
### Walla Walla
### ★✫♥

Another up-and-coming Walla Walla boutique winery.

✓ *Cabernet Sauvignon* (Walla Walla Valley) • *Merlot* (Walla Walla Valley)

## GORDON BROTHERS
### Pasco
### ★✫♥

One of the more mature Washington wineries, with a large line of exclusively estate-produced wines. Bill Gordon retired in 1998, the same year that a new winery was built on the vineyard. In 2003, Jeff Gordon hired David Harvey as winemaker.

✓ *Chardonnay* • *Classic red blend* (Tradition) • *Syrah*

## HEDGES CELLARS
### Benton City
### ★★♥

I have never tasted a Hedges wine I would not want to drink. Tom Hedges has the amazing knack of being able to produce premium-quality Bordeaux-style reds that are lush, drinkable, and not lacking complexity and finesse within less than a year of the grapes being picked.

✓ *Classic red blend* (CMS, Red Mountain Reserve) • *Classic white blend* (Fumé Chardonnay)

## HOGUE CELLARS
### Prosser
### ★✫♥

Part of the Canadian-based Vincor group since 2001, Hogue Cellars has reinvented itself in recent years and the image today is one of a higher, more focused quality than before.

✓ *Cabernet Sauvignon* (Reserve) • *Chardonnay* (Reserve) • *Fumé Blanc* • *Merlot* (Reserve) • *Viognier* (Genesis)

## ISENHOWER CELLARS
### Walla Walla
### ★

Former pharmacists Brett and Denise Isenhower made their first wine in 2000, but began to build their reputation for great Syrah in 2001, and constructed their own winery in 2002.

✓ *Cabernet Sauvignon* (Batchelor's Button) • *Syrah* (River Beauty, Wild Alfalfa)

## JANUIK
### Woodinville
### ★★

Owned and run by Mike Januik, former Head Winemaker at Château Ste. Michelle. Both "basic" and single-vineyard wines of each varietal are of equally fabulous quality.

✓ *Cabernet Sauvignon* • *Merlot*

## K VINTNERS
### Walla Walla
### ★★

A raunchy line of silky, sensuous, saturated Syrah at prices that must surely double, so buy while you can. Some wonderfully eclectic classic red blends emerging too. Second wines sold under The Magnificent Wine Co. label.

✓ *Syrah*

## KESTREL
### Prosser
### ★♥

Established in 1999, Kestrel has rapidly created a reputation for good-value, flavorful wines that are ripe and easy to drink.

✓ *Chardonnay* • *Syrah*

## KIONA VINEYARDS
### Benton City
### ★

The arid backdrop to this lush vineyard illustrates how irrigation can transform a desert. Kiona is the most important vineyard on Red Mountain and, although it might not always hit the bull's eye in the Kiona wines themselves, the same fruit has consistently shown its potential in the wines of Woodward Canyon and has been one of three main ingredients of Quilceda Creek.

✓ *Cabernet Sauvignon* (Red Mountain) • *Chenin Blanc* • *Gewürztraminer* (Late Harvest) • *Merlot* (Red Mountain Reserve) • *Riesling* • *Sangiovese*

## L'ECOLE NO. 41
### Lowden
### ★★♥

Marty Clubb has carved out quite a reputation from the wines made at this old schoolhouse. L'Ecole No. 41 is primarily known for its Sémillon, but, although this is very good (particularly the Fries Vineyard), Marty's red wines are a class apart.

✓ *Cabernet Sauvignon* (Walla Walla Valley) • *Classic red blend* (Pepperbridge Vineyard Apogee) • *Merlot* (Columbia Valley, Walla Walla Valley) • *Sémillon* • *Syrah* (Seven Hills Vineyard)

## LEONETTI CELLAR
### Walla Walla
### ★★★✫

Owner-winemaker Gary Figgins has a cult following that is matched only by Quilceda Creek, and asking devotees of either wine which is best is a bit like asking a young kid in the 1960s to choose between the Beatles and the Rolling Stones. Figgins has never swayed from his convictions, but it is clear to see that over time he has perfected his handling of oak to match the distinctive style of his wines. While some of the earlier vintages could be criticized for showing too much oak, any objective observer must acknowledge that for some time now they have been beautifully balanced, highly polished, finely focused wines of great complexity, finesse, and longevity.

✓ *Entire range*

## LONG SHADOW VINTNERS
### Walla Walla
### ❓

The rating is undecided because this is such a new venture that only one wine from the inaugural 2003 vintage had been released at the time of writing, but if this ambitious project is only half successful, it should produce truly exciting results. Long Shadow is the culmination of all the dreams and fantasies Allen Shoup had during the 20 years he ran Stimson Lane (Château Ste. Michelle, Columbia Crest, *et. al.*). It was his collaboration with Piero Antinori and, particularly, Ernst Loosen (which led to Eroica), that convinced Shoup his idea could work. After retiring from Stimson Lane in 2000, he invited several of the world's most iconic winemakers to the sunny slopes where the Snake River and the Yakima River flow into the mighty Columbia, and explained his vision. He wanted them to tour the region, run the soil through their fingers, survey the leafy trellises that spill down the hillsides of the Columbia Valley appellation, and decide where ideally they would grow those varieties they had had a lifetime's experience with. The objective is to create seven or eight stand-alone, ultrapremium wineries, producing no more than 5,000 cases or so, with a focus on a single varietal or blend, made under the supervision of world-famous winemakers, comparable in stature to those they crafted in their native wine regions. Long Shadow Vintners is so named in tribute to the reputation of Shoup's select group of winemakers. So far, only Armin Diel's Poet's Leap Riesling has been released. Watch out for forthcoming wines: Randy Dunn's Feather Cabernet, John Duval's Sequel Syrah, Augustin Huneeus and Philippe Melka's Pirouette (Cabernet-Merlot blend), Allen Shoup and Gilles Nicault's Chester-Kidder (Merlot-Cabernet blend with a classic Washington twist of Syrah), and Michel Rolland's Pedestal (Merlot-Cabernet blend).

✓ *Riesling* (Poet's Leap)

## MATTHEWS
**Woodinville**
★✫🅥

Very young, exclusively Yakima Valley operation, Matthews demonstrates an innate sense of class in the quality of wine produced and its presentation in bottle.

✓ *Cabernet Sauvignon* (Elerding Vineyard) • *Syrah* (Hedges Estate)

## MCCREA
**Rainier**
★🅥

Promoted as "Washington State's first winery dedicated to Rhône varietals," McCrea's efforts were rather patchy initially, as he tried to understand a number of varieties, some of which might never have the potential in this state, but he was one of the first to perfect Syrah.

✓ *Classic red blend* (Sirocco) • *Syrah*

## MOUNTAIN DOME
**Spokane**
★🅥

Dr. Michael Manz and his family live in a dome that is cut into the side of a mountain. He is one of half a dozen people dotted around the world who have the potential to make truly exceptional sparkling wine.

✓ *Entire range*

## NORTHSTAR
**Walla Walla**
★★🅥

Consistently one of the finest Merlots in the Pacific Northwest.

✓ *Classic red blend* (Stella Maris) • *Merlot*

## OWEN SULLIVAN
**Tukwilla**
★★🅥

From a first vintage of a paltry 80 cases in 1997, Bill Owen and Rob Sullivan have quickly built up their sales on a reputation for Bordeaux-style reds full of sultry fruit and a long, lingering finish.

✓ *Cabernet Franc* (Champoux Vineyard) • *Classic red blend* (R3, Ulysses)

## PAUL THOMAS
**Bellevue**
★✫🅥

Underrated because it began with fruit wines, Paul Thomas now makes brilliant-value, vividly fruity wines.

✓ *Classic red blend* (Cabernet-Merlot) • *Chardonnay*

## PEPPER BRIDGE
**Walla Walla**
★★🅥

Having supplied grapes for some of Washington's greatest wines from its Pepper Bridge and Seven Hills vineyards, Norm McKibben built a classic gravity-fed winery on his property just in time for the 2000 harvest.

✓ *Cabernet Sauvignon* • *Merlot*

## PRECEPT BRANDS
**Seattle**
★✫🅥

Established as recently as 2003, Precept Brands is headed by Andrew Browne, who was the CEO of Corus until it was sold for $52 million to Canandaigua in 2001. Browne is attempting to repeat the success of Corus, but without the overheads and on an even larger scale. Whereas Corus owned wineries such as Covey Run, Columbia Winery, and Paul Thomas, Precept Brands has no winery as such. Browne is taking advantage of excess production, producing *négociant*-style wines under seven Washington labels (Avery Lane, Barrelstone, Painted Stone, Pavin & Riley, Pine & Post, Sockeye, and Washington Hills) in the wineries where he buys the wine. At the same time, Precept Brands launched four Australian labels (Outback Chase, Red Knot, Shingleback, and The Gate) and one Spanish brand (El Paseo).

✓ *Cabernet Sauvignon* (Sockeye) • *Merlot* (Avery Lane, Pavin & Riley) • *Riesling* (Avery Lane, Washington Hills) • *Sauvignon Blanc* (Avery Lane) • *Syrah* (Barrelstone, Washington Hills)

## PRESTON WINE CELLARS
**Pasco**
★🅥

Bill Preston turned his retirement home into what was, in the 1970s, the largest privately owned winery in the Pacific Northwest.

✓ *Cabernet Sauvignon* (Reserve) • *Syrah* (Preston Vineyards)

## QUILCEDA CREEK
**Seattle**
★★★

Washington's first truly great red wine, Quilceda Creek is still produced in tiny quantities and remains one of this state's very elite. After 25 years of authentic garage winemaking, Alex Golitzen and his son Paul built a state-of-the-art winery in time for the 2004 vintage.

✓ *Entire range*

## REININGER
**Walla Walla**
★★✫

Since Chuck Reininger established this up-and-coming Walla Walla boutique winery in 1997, he has hardly put a foot wrong.

✓ *Cabernet Sauvignon* • *Merlot* • *Syrah*

## RUSSELL CREEK
**Walla Walla**
★★🅥

Larry Krivoshein made smooth progress from five-gallon jars of homemade wine in 1988 to fine and sophisticated red wines from a fully bonded winery in 1998.

✓ *Cabernet Sauvignon* (Winemaker's Select) • *Classic red blend* (Tributary) • *Syrah* (Walla Walla)

## SAGELANDS VINEYARDS
**Wapato**
★✫🅥

Formerly known as Staton Hills, this winery and its vineyards were taken over by the Chalone Group in 1999 and relaunched as Sagelands in 2000.

✓ *Cabernet Sauvignon* (Four Corners) • *Merlot* (Four Corners)

## SEVEN HILLS WINERY
**Walla Walla**
★★🅥

Grapegrowers since 1980, Casey McClellan has some of Washington's best vineyards at his fingertips, and it shows in the wonderfully expressive wines he produces.

✓ *Cabernet Sauvignon* (Klipsun, Seven Hills, Walla Walla Reserve) • *Merlot* (Seven Hills)

## SPRING VALLEY
**Walla Walla**
★★🅥

These wines are made exclusively from Spring's own 40 acres (16 hectares) of vineyards, situated in the midst of over 600 acres (240 hectares) of wheat land that the Derby family has been farming for over a century.

✓ *Cabernet Sauvignon* (Derby) • *Classic red blend* (Frederick, Uriah) • *Merlot* (Muleskinner) • *Syrah* (Nina Lee)

## TAMARACK CELLARS
**Walla Walla**
★★🅥

Another up-and-coming Walla Walla boutique winery, Tamarack Cellars was established in 1998 by Ron and Jamie Coleman, whose rich, ripe, opulent Cabernet Sauvignon has quickly earned them a reputation.

✓ *Cabernet Sauvignon* (Columbia Valley) • *Classic red blend* (Firehouse Red)

## THREE RIVERS
**Walla Walla**
★

Established in 1999 by Steve Ahler, Bud Stocking, and Duane Wollmuth, Three Rivers has produced a raft of brilliant, award-winning wines in a very short time.

✓ *Cabernet Sauvignon* (Champoux Vineyard) • *Classic red blend* (Meritage) • *Classic white blend* (Meritage) • *Merlot* • *Sangiovese* (Pepper Bridge) • *Syrah* (Boushey Vineyard)

## WALLA WALLA VINTNERS
**Walla Walla**
★★

Owner-winemakers Myles Anderson and Gordon Venneri have established a thriving business, yet still hang on to their day jobs, as an insurance agent and a psychology teacher.

✓ *Cabernet Sauvignon* (Columbia Valley, Walla Walla Valley) • *Merlot* (Columbia Valley, Walla Walla Valley)

## WATERBROOK
**Walla Walla**
★✫🅥

Founded in 1984 by Eric and Janet Rindal, who named this winery to reflect that of Walla Walla itself, which means "running water."

✓ *Cabernet Sauvignon* (Columbia Valley) • *Classic red blend* (Mélange, Red Mountain Meritage) • *Merlot* (Columbia Valley) • *Viognier* (Columbia Valley)

## WOODWARD CANYON WINERY
**Lowden**
★★

This Walla Walla winery has hardly put a foot wrong since it was set up in 1981, making some of the state's most consistent and most elegant, award-winning red wines, showing great finesse and focus.

✓ *Cabernet Sauvignon* • *Classic red blend* (Charbonneau) • *Classic white blend* (Charbonneau) • *Chardonnay* (Celilo Vineyard, Conner Lee Vineyard) • *Merlot* (Columbia Valley)

# THE ATLANTIC NORTHEAST

*Michigan is currently outclassing New York, despite having only 90 wineries compared with the latter's 203, and nothing like its financial resources. The general consensus is that New York has the greatest potential of all northeastern states, but only a handful of its wineries are working hard to achieve that potential. Virginia promises to be the east coast's Washington State, while Pennsylvania and Ohio are the dark horses.*

ALL THAT HOLDS the Atlantic Northeast back is its harsh winters. Although this does not prevent the cultivation of classic grape varieties, it does make grafting wounds highly vulnerable, and this dictates where such grafted vines are planted. If vineyards could be chosen for their ripening potential, rather than for winter survival, the eastern seaboard could rival California, as it has a much greater variation of soils and microclimates. Since the first transgenic vines were produced, only the identity of two genes has stood in the way of the Atlantic Northeast achieving its full potential—the gene that makes *Vitis amurensis* immune to Siberian winters, together with the one that enables native American vines to resist phylloxera.

## AMERICA'S OLDEST WINE INDUSTRY

Wines have been made in America's Northeast since the middle of the 17th century, when vineyards were first established on Manhattan and Long Island. The emphasis, however, has always

LONG ISLAND, NEW YORK
*These rows of vines are widely spaced to accommodate vineyard machinery, and are a far cry from the mid-17th century, when Long Island was one of the first places in the Atlantic Northeast to be planted.*

THE ATLANTIC NORTHEAST, *see also* p.463
*The most prominent state in the Atlantic Northeast, New York has established this area's reputation for* vinifera *wines, but Virginia and Michigan are now rivaling this supremacy. The wine industries of many of the other states are dominated almost entirely by native* labrusca.

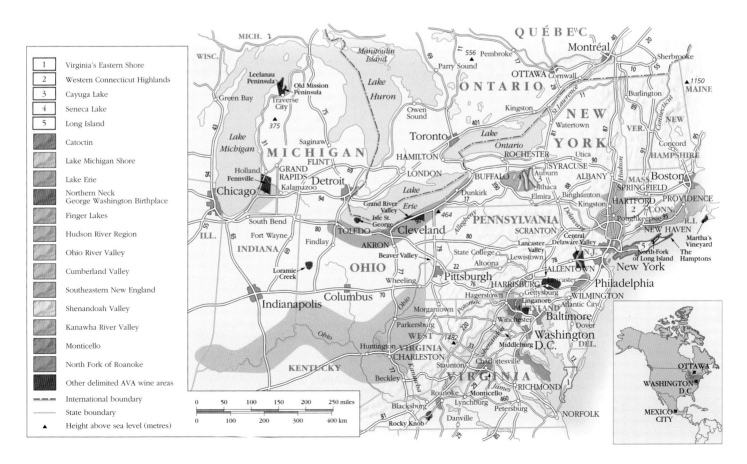

| | |
|---|---|
| 1 | Virginia's Eastern Shore |
| 2 | Western Connecticut Highlands |
| 3 | Cayuga Lake |
| 4 | Seneca Lake |
| 5 | Long Island |

- Catoctin
- Lake Michigan Shore
- Lake Erie
- Northern Neck George Washington Birthplace
- Finger Lakes
- Hudson River Region
- Ohio River Valley
- Cumberland Valley
- Southeastern New England
- Shenandoah Valley
- Kanawha River Valley
- Monticello
- North Fork of Roanoke
- Other delimited AVA wine areas
- --- International boundary
- State boundary
- ▲ Height above sea level (metres)

0   50   100   150   200   250 miles
0   100   200   300   400 km

MECHANICAL HARVESTING
*Grapes are picked by machine at vineyards belonging to the Taylor Wine Company.*
*Based at Hammondsport, the winery is one of New York State's most successful.*

## FACTORS AFFECTING TASTE AND QUALITY

### LOCATION
An arbitrary grouping of states situated between the Great Lakes and the Atlantic Ocean.

### CLIMATE
Despite severe winters, the moderating effect of large masses of inland water, such as the Great Lakes or the Finger Lakes, creates microclimates that make cultivation of *vinifera* vines possible. Harsh winter temperatures represent the most prevalent factor holding back the wine industry in the Atlantic Northeast. There are other more localized drawbacks, such as Virginia's heat and humidity at harvest time, which can cause rapid acidity drop and encourage cryptogamic diseases, but these problems can and will be overcome by viticultural practices.

### ASPECT
Many of the vineyards are planted on flat ground around the various lake shores, and on the nearby lower slopes of the various mountain ranges.

### SOIL
**New York:** shale, slate, schist, and limestone in the Hudson River Region. **Virginia:** silty loam and gravel at Rocky Knob, limestone and sandstone at North Fork of Roanoke. **Michigan:** glacial scree in

Fennville. **Ohio:** shallow drift soil over fissured limestone bedrock on Isle St. George. **Pennsylvania:** deep limestone-derived soils in the Lancaster Valley.

### VITICULTURE AND VINIFICATION
In many areas, despite some advantageous microclimates, *vinifera* vines can survive the harsh winters only by being buried under several feet of earth before the winter arrives. Sparkling wines are a specialty of New York State and of the Finger Lakes area in particular. Through very careful vineyard practices, the use of the latest sprays, and the aid of new technology in vinification, the number of *vinifera* varietals produced is increasing and their reputation growing.

### GRAPE VARIETIES
Native grapes such as Concord, Catawba, Delaware, Muscadine, and Norton predominate; French-American hybrids such as Vidal Blanc, Seyval Blanc, Chelois, Baco Noir, Maréchal Foch, and Aurore are important; and the quantity of *vinifera* varieties, such as Cabernet Franc, Cabernet Sauvignon, Chardonnay, Gewürztraminer, Pinot Blanc, Pinot Gris, Pinot Noir, Riesling, Sauvignon Blanc, Syrah, and Viognier is increasing.

been on the notoriously "foxy" *labrusca* varieties. *Vinifera* vines were not cultivated until as recently as 1957, although the series of events that culminated in this most important development in the Atlantic Northeast's quest for quality wines began in 1934.

Immediately after Prohibition, Edwin Underhill, the president of Gold Seal Vineyards, went to Champagne and persuaded Charles Fournier, the *chef de cave* at Veuve Clicquot, to return with him to the United States. But Fournier found the *labrusca* grape varieties planted in New York State's Finger Lake vineyards far too aromatic. Persuaded by local wine growers that *vinifera* vines could not survive the harsh winters, he began planting hybrid vines (crosses between French and native American varieties). These were initially shipped from France, and then acquired from a winemaker by the name of Philip Wagner, who had already established a considerable collection of hybrids at his Boordy Vineyard in Maryland.

In 1953 Fournier heard that one Konstantin Frank, a Ukrainian viticulturist who had arrived in the US in 1951, had been criticizing the industry for not planting European *vinifera* vines. On his arrival in the US, Frank, who spoke no English and had no money, had washed dishes to support his wife and three children. However, as soon as he had learned enough English to get by, he applied for a job at the New York State viticultural research station in Geneva, informing his prospective employers of his studies in viticulture in Odessa, and his experience in organizing collective farms in the Ukraine, teaching viticulture and oenology at an agricultural institute, and managing farms in Austria and Bavaria. When told that the winters were too harsh for European vines, he dismissed the idea as absurd. Two years later, when Fournier heard Frank's claims, he employed him, taking the chance that his theory would prove correct. Frank's claims were justified, particularly after the great freeze of February 1957. Later that year, some of the hardiest *labrusca* vines failed to bear a single grape, yet fewer than 10 percent of the buds on Frank's Riesling and Chardonnay vines were damaged and they produced a bumper crop of fully ripe grapes.

In the 1980s Frank was still battling with the Geneva viticultural station. *Vinifera* had not taken off in New York State, despite Frank's success. He blamed this on the "Genevians," who maintained that *vinifera* was too risky to be cultivated by anyone other than an expert. Frank had, however, become articulate in his new language: "The poor Italian and Russian peasants with their shovels can do it, but the American farmer with his push-button tools cannot."

## RECENT ATLANTIC NORTHEAST VINTAGES

**2003** A very difficult year at best, with Michigan suffering the worst, as spring frosts devastated vineyards, reducing yields by 50 to 100 percent, causing some wineries to truck in grapes from the west coast. The quality of Northeast-grown wines was extremely variable, with far more lows than highs.

**2002** Great red wines produced everywhere except Virginia, but this vintage was even better for white wines, especially Riesling (although not in New York's Finger Lakes).

**2001** One of the best ever all-around vintages for the region, with good acidity as well as ripeness. The only exceptions were New Jersey, which endured heavy rains during the harvest, and Ohio, where many vineyards were infested by ladybugs, which tainted some of the wines.

**2000** Generally a poor vintage that is best forgotten, although there are always exceptions, and in 2000 these were mostly Michigan wines, such as Ciccone Vineyards Pinot Noir, Black Star Farm's Leorie Vineyard Merlot-Cabernet Franc, Chateau de Leelanau Adante Sparkling Riesling, and Tabor Hill Riesling.

**1999** An early flowering and a long, hot growing season produced great Northeast red wines for the second year running, but the whites lacked acidity.

THE WINEMAKING STATES AND APPELLATIONS OF
# THE ATLANTIC NORTHEAST

## CONNECTICUT

No documented evidence exists of the first vineyard in this state, but from the great seal of Connecticut it seems certain that its earliest settlers at least attempted to plant vines. The great seal today depicts three grapevines bearing fruit, but the original seal, carried over from England in 1639, had 15 grapevines and the motto *Sustinet Qui Transtulit* ("who transplants sustains"). It soon became clear, however, that tobacco was the farm crop of choice. The first Connecticut wines of modern times were made by Ciro Buonocore, who planted various French hybrid varieties at North Haven.

### SOUTHEASTERN NEW ENGLAND AVA
**Connecticut, Rhode Island, and Massachusetts**
An area distinguished in New England by the moderate climate, caused by its proximity to various coastal bodies of water.

### WESTERN CONNECTICUT HIGHLANDS AVA
A vast 1,500-square-mile (3,900-square-kilometer) area of rolling hills that rise to 500 feet (150 meters) above sea level, and the Western Connecticut Highlands, small mountains that reach to 1,500 feet (460 meters).

## DELAWARE

The Swedes encouraged their settlers to plant vines and make wine in 1638, as did the Dutch, after they conquered the Swedes in 1655, but they found it easier to grow apples. Nassau Valley Vineyards was the first winery in this state, but it has not shown any distinction so far.

## DISTRICT OF COLUMBIA

John Adlum, the author of America's first book on winemaking, tried unsuccessfully to persuade the federal government in the 1820s to support a national experimental vineyard with every variety of native vine in existence "to ascertain their growth, soil, and produce."

## INDIANA

The first vines were planted by Jean-Jacques Dufour in 1804, at what would be Vevay in Switzerland county, 12 years before Indiana became a state. Dufour was a Swiss immigrant who had been sent by his family from war-torn Europe to search the newly opened lands of America for a location where they could establish a Swiss colony dedicated to winemaking. He landed in 1796, and by 1799 had already planted a vineyard at Big Bend, near Lexington, in Kentucky, but it was not a success, so he purchased land north of the Ohio River, in the newly surveyed Indiana Territory. The wines made by this Swiss colony achieved two firsts: they were made from the first American hybrid (commonly known as Alexander or Cape), and they were the very first American-grown wines sold to the public. However, this state was also the first to introduce a Prohibition law, which went on the books in Indiana in 1816, forbidding the sale of any alcohol on Sunday (still enforced to this day). By the 1840s numerous towns and whole counties throughout Indiana had gone totally "dry," as indeed they had in Georgia, Iowa, Michigan, New Hampshire, New York, and Ohio. Currently contemplating introducing IQ (Indiana Quality alliance) to elevate the quality and reputation of these wines.

### OHIO RIVER VALLEY AVA
**Indiana, Ohio, West Virginia, and Kentucky**
This is a vast AVA. Until 1859, Ohio was the leading wine-producing state. However, during the Civil War, black rot and powdery mildew took hold and destroyed nearly all its vineyards.

## MAINE

With vintners relying on *vinifera* grapes shipped in from as far afield as Washington, and only just steeling themselves to make the transition from fruit wines to own-grown French hybrids, there is hardly even an embryonic wine industry in this most northerly of America's eastern seaboard states. Maine's most important date in wine history was 1851, when it enacted the first state-wide law prohibiting the manufacture and sale of liquor. Within four years 13 of the then 31 states of the US had followed suit. In 2004 there were 10 wineries, but although native and hybrid vines are grown, most of the production is fruit wine, and Bartlett Estate Winemaker's Reserve Blueberry is deservedly better known than any grape-based wines.

## MARYLAND

In 1662, Lord Baltimore owned Maryland, and he instructed his son, Charles Calvert, the governor, to plant a vineyard and make wine. He planted 240 acres (96 hectares), and another 100 acres (40 hectares) three years later. The vines were native, not European, but the wine was reportedly "as good as the best Burgundy." Taking heart from this success, Lord Baltimore sent his son European vines in 1672, but they all failed to survive their first year. This state now grows no fewer than 140 different grape varieties, although many are French hybrids.

### CATOCTIN AVA
Situated west of the town of Frederick, this area's specific *terroir* was well known before the AVA was established, due to the fact that it roughly coincides with the Maryland Land Resource Area. This was determined by the US Soil Conservation Service on the basis of identifiable patterns of soil, climate, water availability, land use, and topography.

### CUMBERLAND VALLEY AVA
**Maryland and Pennsylvania**
The Cumberland Valley is situated between the South Mountains and the Allegheny Mountains and is 80 miles (120 kilometers) long, bending in a northeasterly direction. Although this AVA covers approximately 1,200 square miles (3,100 square kilometers), its vines are confined to small areas where the soil, drainage, rainfall, and protection from lethal winter temperatures permit viticulture. Vineyards are found on high terraces along the north bank of the Potomac River, on the hills and ridges in the basin of the valley, and in the upland areas of the South Mountains.

### LINGANORE AVA
Linganore, Maryland's first viticultural area, lies east of Frederick. It is generally warmer and wetter than the areas to the east, and slightly cooler and drier than those to the west.

## MASSACHUSETTS

Wines were made from native grapes in the very first summer of the Massachusetts Bay Colony in 1630, but its dubious quality was probably the reason why the settlers immediately petitioned the Massachusetts Bay Company for Frenchmen experienced in planting vines. Two years later, as part of an agreement with the Colonial Legislature, Governor John Winthrop planted a vineyard on Governor's Island, from which he was supposed to supply as annual rent "a hogshead of the best wine." However, there is no evidence that he succeeded and, as his rent was changed to "two bushels of apples" within just a few years, there is every reason to suspect that he had failed. In modern times, the first *vinifera* vines were planted in 1971 by the Mathieson family on, appropriately, Martha's Vineyard.

### MARTHA'S VINEYARD AVA
This AVA is an island of Massachusetts, and is surrounded to the north by Vineyard Sound, to the east by Nantucket Sound, and to the south and west by the Atlantic Ocean. The boundaries of the viticultural area include an area known as Chappaquiddick, which is connected to Martha's Vineyard by a sand bar. Ocean winds delay the coming of spring and make for a cooler fall, extending the growing season to an average of 210 days, compared with 180 days on the mainland.

### SOUTHEASTERN NEW ENGLAND AVA
**Connecticut, Rhode Island, and Massachusetts**
An area distinguished in New England by the moderate climate, caused by its proximity to various coastal bodies of water.

## MICHIGAN

Michigan was already a mature winemaking region by 1880, when the first national winegrowing census was taken, but the grapes used were native varieties, and they were grown in the southeast of the state, on the shore of Lake Erie, where virtually no vines exist today. Michigan made the transition to French hybrids in the 1950s and 1960s, although it was not in full swing until the mid-1970s. Meanwhile, the first European varieties were planted at Tabor Hill Vineyard by Len Olsen and Carl Banholzer in 1970, although 20 years later 85–90 percent of Tabor Hill wines were still being made from hybrids. However, that was in the southwest, in what is now Lake Michigan Shore AVA, and the future as far as quality and diversity of *vinifera* wines was concerned, and a whole raft of new boutique wineries that were about to emerge, lay in the Old Mission Peninsula and Leelanau Peninsula in the northwest of the state. Only one man was crazy enough to plant *vinifera* 140 miles (225 kilometers) north of Canada's Niagara District in 1974, and that was Ed O'Keefe of Château Grand Traverse, where not one single hybrid has ever been planted. O'Keefe is the only person in the entire Michigan wine industry who has been 100 percent committed to *vinifera* from the very start. His constant arguing of his case did not made him many friends among his fellow winegrowers, particularly those of the old school, who were clinging on to their hybrids, but he was right, and in the end he did everyone in the Michigan wine industry a big favor. Today, Michigan has 13,500 acres (5,400 hectares) of vineyards, making it the fourth-largest grape-growing state, but most of this area is still devoted to juice grapes such as Concord and Niagara. Only 1,500 acres (600 hectares) are devoted to wine grapes, making Michigan the eighth largest state for wine grape production.

## FENNVILLE AVA

Lake Michigan moderates this area's climate, providing slightly warmer winters and cooler summers than other areas within a 30-mile (48-kilometer) radius. Fennville covers 120 square miles (310 square kilometres) and has been cultivating various fruits for well over a century, including grapes for wine production. The soil is mostly scree of glacial origin.

## LAKE MICHIGAN SHORE AVA

Located in the southwest corner of Michigan, this AVA is a geographically and climatically uniform region, although it does encapsulate smaller, very specific *terroirs* such as Fennville, which has its own AVA.

## LEELANAU PENINSULA AVA

This AVA is on the western shore of Lake Michigan, northwest of Traverse City. The lake delays fruit development beyond the most serious frost period in the spring, and prevents sudden temperature drops in the fall. Most of Michigan's boutique wineries are located here.

## OLD MISSION PENINSULA AVA

This AVA is surrounded on three sides by Grand Traverse Bay, and connected to the mainland at Traverse City. The waters, coupled with warm southwesterly winds, provide a unique climate that makes cultivation of *vinifera* vines possible. The longer established of the two peninsulas, Old Mission houses the smallest number of wineries, but there is renewed interest in the area since Black Star Farms has sourced so many award-winning red wines from here, particularly the Leori Vineyard, and the success of white wines from Peninsula Cellars.

# NEW HAMPSHIRE

The first European vines were planted at the mouth of the Piscataqua River by Ambrose Gibbons in 1623, although from his diary we know he suspected that, unlike the native vines that prospered in the wild, they would not survive: "The vines that were planted will come to nothing. They prosper not in the ground where they were set, but them that grow naturally are very good of divers sorts." It would be almost another 250 years before

anyone managed to grow wine grapes in this state. In 1965, John J. Canepa planted 800 Maréchal Foch vines and, although some died in the severe winter of 1965/66, they yielded a thousand pounds of grapes in 1967, whereupon a photograph of the Canepa vineyard appeared in the *Boston Sunday Globe* with the caption "Soon, Yankee Wine"; the impossibility of this feat drew visitors from far and wide, including baffled university professors. In 1968, Canepa yielded three tons of Maréchal Foch grapes with a potential alcoholic strength of between 18 and 20 percent. He gave up the day job and built a commercial winery, which was bonded in 1969, but there are still no more than a handful of wine producers in New Hampshire.

# NEW JERSEY

Although far more famous for cider than wine, New Jersey does in fact boast the first American-grown wine to win an international award. It was as early as 1767 that London's Royal Society of the Arts recognized two New Jersey vintners for producing the first quality wine derived from colonial agriculture, although they were from wild vines, not *vinifera*. This state also gave birth to Dr. Thomas Bramwell Welch, the wine-hating dentist who curiously read Pasteur's studies of fermentation, which he turned on their head to sterilize grape juice. It was "Dr. Welch's Grape Juice" that established the grape-juice industry, though it was first sold as "Dr. Welch's Unfermented Wine." By 2004 there were eight wineries in this state, where native and hybrid vines are beginning to make inroads, although fruit wines dominate. The most successful New Hampshire winery for hybrids is the Jewell Town Vineyard at South Hampton.

## CENTRAL DELAWARE VALLEY AVA
### Pennsylvania and New Jersey

This appellation covers 150 square miles (388 square kilometers), although very little of it is actually planted with vines. The Delaware River modifies the climate.

## WARREN HILLS AVA

Wines made in the eastern half of the Central Delaware Valley AVA, which consists of five narrow valleys rather than one broad one, may use this subappellation. The narrow valleys provide hillsides that are exposed and funnel the winds, reducing the risk of frost and rot.

# NEW YORK

The first vineyard in what is now New York State was cultivated by the Dutch, when it was still New Amsterdam, in 1642. Very little is known about it other than that it failed to survive the winter, so it was probably *vinifera*. Long Island was an important nursery for imported vines in the late 18th and early 19th centuries. At one time, New York was second only to California in terms of area of vines, but this peaked in 1975 and had dropped to 31,000 acres (12,400 hectares) by 2003, while the area in trailing states has increased significantly since the late 1990s. Furthermore, of New York's 31,000 acres, more than 80 percent is comprised of nine native varieties (one-third being Concord), with only 3,000 acres (1,200 hectares) of *vinifera* and 1,700 acres (680 hectares) of hybrids. Its total, therefore, of (1,880 hectares)

4,700 acres places New York in fourth place after California (529,000 acres; 211,600 hectares), Washington (30,000 acres; 12,000 hectares), and Oregon (13,400 acres; 5,360 hectares). New York is still the number two in terms of wine production, churning out 12.7 million cases compared to Washington's 7.4 million. As New York has just one-tenth of Washington's *vinifera* area, yet makes almost twice as much wine, the bulk of New York's production can only be from native grapes. Only a bigot believes it impossible for native grapes ever to make a fine wine, but they are few and far between—certainly not even half of one per cent; it is the 99.5 per cent of New York's native grape wines that are ruining the efforts of this state's best *vinifera* wineries to create an international reputation for New York wine.

## CAYUGA LAKE AVA

This area encompasses vines along the shores of Lake Cayuga, making it part of the Finger Lakes AVA. The soil is predominantly shale and the growing season approximately one month longer than that of most of the Finger Lakes area.

## FINGER LAKES AVA

This name is derived from the 11 finger-shaped lakes in west-central New York State. These inland water masses temper the climate, and the topography of the surrounding land creates "air drainage," which moderates extremes of temperature in winter and summer.

## HUDSON RIVER REGION AVA

This AVA encompasses all of Columbia, Dutchess, and Putnam Counties, the eastern parts of Ulster and Sullivan Counties, almost all of Orange County, and the northern parts of Rockland and Westchester Counties. This is the Taconic Province, one of the most complex geological divisions where the soil is made up of glacial deposits of shale, slate, schist, and limestone.

## LAKE ERIE AVA
### New York, Pennsylvania, and Ohio

Overlapping three states, and encompassing the AVAs of Isle St. George and Grand River Valley, Lake Erie moderates the climate and is the fundamental factor that permits viticulture.

## LONG ISLAND AVA

The Long Island AVA covers the entire island, encompassing the two preexisting AVAs of North Fork of Long Island and The Hamptons, Long Island.

## NORTH FORK OF LONG ISLAND AVA

Although the climate of this AVA is classified as "humid continental," the sea that surrounds it makes it more temperate than many other places of the same latitude in the interior of the US. The growing season is about one to three weeks longer than in the South Fork of the Island and, in general, the sandy soils contain less silt and loam, but are slightly higher in natural fertility.

## SENECA LAKE AVA

Because Seneca Lake is the deepest of New York's 11 finger lakes, it is in permanent use by the US Navy's sonar testing platform. With a maximum depth of 678 feet (203 meters), this 35-mile- (56-kilometer-) long body of water in the heart of New York wine country does not freeze, its stored heat warms the surrounding area, and this effect is largely responsible for its success as a wine-growing region. Although best known for Riesling—the steep, slate slopes are ideal for this variety—it is often planted on silty, sandy, or loamy soils, while other varieties such as Pinot Noir are wasted on slate-rich soils, when they would do much better elsewhere.

## THE HAMPTONS, LONG ISLAND AVA

The Hamptons has been a productive agricultural area for 300 years. It lies within Suffolk County, next to North Fork of Long Island, with the Peconic River and Peconic Bay its northern boundary. This AVA includes Gardiners Island.

# OHIO

When Nicholas Longworth arrived in Cincinnati in the early 1820s, he studied law for a mere six months before setting up in a practice that made him a millionaire. As a hobby, he planted a vineyard in a part of Cincinnati known as Tusculum, but many of the vines he imported from Europe died. Longworth thus turned to native American varieties and quickly discovered Catawba, the so-called "wonder grape," which he planted in 1825. Three years later he made his first Catawba wine and was so impressed that he retired from law to devote his energy to viticulture and winemaking, planting hundreds of acres. At first he produced still wine, but as soon as he made sparkling Catawba, it took off. In 1854, Henry Longfellow even wrote an Ode to Catawba Wine in which he compared it with two of the most famous growths of Champagne, and by 1858 the fame of Catawba had spread as far as Europe, where the *Illustrated London News* reported that "Sparkling Catawba, of the pure, unadulterated juice of the Catawba grape, transcends the Champagne of France." By 1860, one-third of all the vines in America were planted along the banks of the Ohio, which boasted twice the acreage of California's vineyards, making Ohio the wine center of the New World prior to the Civil War. Between 1980 and 2000, the number of wineries in this state hardly wavered, moving from 44 to an equally sedate 47, but it has more than doubled since, reaching 100 by 2004, and indicating that some people now think that Ohio could regain its past glories.

## GRAND RIVER VALLEY AVA

Located within the Lake Erie AVA, the lake protects these vines from frost damage and forces a longer growing season than vineyards situated in inland areas. The river valley

increases "air drainage," giving this AVA a sufficiently different microclimate to warrant its distinction from the Lake Erie AVA.

## ISLE ST. GEORGE AVA

The northernmost of the Bass Islands, vines have been grown here since 1853. Today they cover over half the island. Although tempered by Lake Erie, the climate is cooler in the spring and summer, and warmer in the winter, than mainland Ohio. The region is frost-free for 206 days a year, which is longer than for any other area in Ohio. The shallow drift soil over fissured limestone bedrock is well suited to viticulture.

## LORAMIE CREEK AVA

This small AVA covers only 3,600 acres (1,460 hectares ) in Shelby County, west-central Ohio. Moderate-to-poor drainage means vines must be grown on slopes and ridges to prevent "wet feet."

## LAKE ERIE AVA
### New York, Pennsylvania, and Ohio

Overlapping three states, and encompassing the AVAs of Isle St. George and Grand River Valley, Lake Erie moderates the climate and is the fundamental factor that permits viticulture.

## OHIO RIVER VALLEY AVA
### Indiana, Ohio, West Virginia, and Kentucky

This is a vast AVA. Until 1859, Ohio was the leading wine-producing state. However, during the Civil War, black rot and powdery mildew took hold and destroyed nearly all its vineyards.

# PENNSYLVANIA

In 1683 William Penn established a vineyard with French and Spanish varieties he had brought with him, but they failed. However, Conrad Weiser, who arrived at the Penn colony in 1729, and became the greatest Indian interpreter of his time, was spectacularly successful with his vineyard, planted near Womelsdorf in the Tulpehocken Valley. Chambourcin is widely regarded as the most successful variety in this state today, although some good *vinifera* wines are also produced. In 2003, 14 Pennsylvania Limited Wineries established the Pennsylvania's Premium Wine Group, which introduced its PQA (Pennsylvania Quality Assurance) certification system. In order to be awarded a PQA seal, a wine has to be "made to prescribed quality standards as well as be approved by a professional tasting panel." Its success will depend on how stiff the selection process is, and that will take time for critics to assess, but in 2003 a total of 44 wines from member wineries were awarded the PQA seal.

## CENTRAL DELAWARE VALLEY AVA
### Pennsylvania and New Jersey

This appellation covers 150 square miles (388 square kilometers), although very little of it is actually planted with vines. The Delaware River modifies the climate.

## CUMBERLAND VALLEY AVA
### Maryland and Pennsylvania

The Cumberland Valley is situated between the South Mountains and the Allegheny Mountains and is 80 miles (120 kilometers) long, bending

in a northeasterly direction. Although this AVA covers approximately 1,200 square miles (3,100 square kilometers), its vineyards are confined to the relatively small areas where the soil, drainage, rainfall, and protection from the lethal winter temperatures permit viticulture. Vineyards are found on high terraces along the north bank of the Potomac River, on the hills and ridges in the basin of the valley, and in the upland areas of the South Mountains.

## LAKE ERIE AVA
### New York, Pennsylvania, and Ohio

Lake Erie AVA overlaps three US states and encompasses the AVAs of Isle St. George and Grand River Valley. Lake Erie itself moderates the climate and is the fundamental factor that permits viticulture.

## LANCASTER VALLEY AVA

Grapes have been grown in Lancaster County since the early 19th century but have only recently provoked outside interest. The vines are grown on a virtually level valley floor, at an average altitude of 400 feet (120 meters), where the deep, limestone-derived soils are well drained. Even so, they have good moisture retention, are highly productive, and differ sharply from those in the surrounding hills and uplands.

# RHODE ISLAND

The smallest and most densely populated US state, Rhode Island is not, of course, an island, but is surrounded on three sides by two other states, Connecticut and Massachusetts. The first vines were planted in Rhode Island in the 1820s by Huguenot settlers who successfully made wine, but these settlers were driven out by legal difficulties, after which viticulture did not continue in the state.

## SOUTHEASTERN NEW ENGLAND AVA
### Connecticut, Rhode Island, and Massachusetts

An area distinguished in New England by the moderate climate, caused by its proximity to various coastal bodies of water.

# VERMONT

Although the home of two native grape varieties, Vergennes and Green Mountain, which were commercially significant in the 19th century, Vermont is now more cider country than wine country, which explains why there were no more than two wineries until 1990, and only nine by 2004. Most of these wineries make fruit wines, although a few of them produce wine from own-grown native or hybrid grapes.

# VIRGINIA

This was not the first state to make wine. Strangely enough, that honor goes to Florida, where wine was made from wild grapes *circa* 1563; the first settlers in Virginia made wine from "hedge grapes" in 1609. However, Virginia was the first state to attempt the cultivation of *vinifera* grapes for wine, although not by its first governor, Lord De La Warre (which later became corrupted to Delaware), as many sources claim. The first documented attempt to transplant European vines to eastern America was recorded by S. M. Kingbury of the Virginia Company of London, who reported that French vines and eight French vignerons from Languedoc had been sent out to Virginia in 1619, one year after De La Warre had died at sea. The Virginia Company caused a law to be enacted requiring every householder to plant 10 vines a year "until they have attained the art and experience of dressing a vineyard," but all efforts to cultivate vineyards failed, even though native grapes were rampant in the wild. So desperate was Virginia to succeed that an Act of Assembly was passed in 1658 offering 10,000 pounds of tobacco to the first person to make "two tunne of wine raised out of a vineyard made in this colony." No one ever claimed the prize and, almost 30 years later, the offer was quietly dropped. Today, Virginia has the ability to be the Washington State of America's Northeast, but the negative influence of its hot and humid weather during the growing season, particularly toward the end of *véraison* and at harvest time, must first be overcome. There are two main difficulties. First, the sugar-ripeness of the grapes tends to soar away from the rate at which physiological ripeness progresses, resulting in the production of wines bearing green tannins and depleted acidity. Second, the humidity encourages cryptogamic diseases. Various oenological practices are employed to combat the harsh tannins, but the goal must ultimately be to produce grapes with ripe tannins and a good sugar-acidity balance, rather than to sift out unripe pips (*délistage*). The only way to achieve this is by improving canopy management.

## MONTICELLO AVA

Monticello is well known as the home of Thomas Jefferson, who is recorded as having planted wine grapes here. Most of Virginia's best wineries are found in this AVA.

## NORTH FORK OF ROANOKE AVA

A valley protected from excessive rainfall in the growing season by mountains to the west and east. The vines are on the limestone southeast-facing slopes and limestone-with-sandstone north-facing slopes. These soils are very different from those in the surrounding hills and ridges.

## NORTHERN NECK GEORGE WASHINGTON BIRTHPLACE AVA

This AVA lies on a peninsula 100 miles (160 kilometers) long, between the Potomac and Rappahannock rivers in the tidewater district of Virginia, which runs from Chesapeake Bay in the east to a few miles from the town of Fredericksburg to the west. The vines grow in sandy clay soils on the slopes and hills, and in alluvial soils on the river flats. The favorable climate, with excellent air-drainage, is moderated by the surrounding water.

## ROCKY KNOB AVA

This AVA is in the Blue Ridge Mountains, and in spring is colder than nearby areas. This means the vines flower later, enabling them to survive the erratic, very cold early spring temperatures. It also causes a late fruit-set, extending the growing season by about a week. The silty-loam and gravel soil provides good drainage.

## SHENANDOAH VALLEY AVA
### Virginia and West Virginia

The Shenandoah Valley lies between the Blue Ridge Mountains, and the Allegheny Mountains. This AVA extends south beyond the Shenandoah Valley almost as far as Roanoke.

## VIRGINIA'S EASTERN SHORE AVA

This is located in Accomack and Northampton counties along the 75-mile (120-kilometer) narrow tip of the Delmarva Peninsula, with the Atlantic to the east and Chesapeake Bay to the west. The climatic influence of these two large bodies of water helps to alleviate the most severe winter temperatures, but retards the ripening process and can be problematic at harvesttime.

# WEST VIRGINIA

Grape-growing began here, along the Ohio River, in the 1830s, when this state was still part of Virginia, and continued after West Virginia had been created during the Civil War. In 2004 there were 17 wineries, mostly producing native, hybrid, and fruit wines, with none standing out as yet.

## KANAWHA RIVER VALLEY AVA

This approved viticultural area covers 1,000 square miles (2,600 square kilometers), yet contains just 2½ acres of vines and one bonded winery.

## OHIO RIVER VALLEY AVA
### Indiana, Ohio, West Virginia, and Kentucky

This is a vast AVA. Until 1859, Ohio was the leading wine-producing state. However, during the Civil War, black rot and powdery mildew took hold and destroyed nearly all its vineyards.

## SHENANDOAH VALLEY AVA
### Virginia and West Virginia

The Shenandoah Valley lies between the Blue Ridge Mountains, and the Allegheny Mountains. This AVA extends south beyond the Shenandoah Valley almost as far as Roanoke.

---

THE WINE PRODUCERS OF
# THE ATLANTIC NORTHEAST

# CONNECTICUT
### 21 wineries in 2004

### CHAMARD
**Clinton**
★ⓥ

This is a modern winery just 3 kilometres from Long Island Sound.

✓ *Chardonnay* (Estate Reserve)

### STONINGTON VINEYARDS
**Stonington**
★ⓥ

This small vineyard and winery was set up in 1986, and produces wines from both hybrid and *vinifera* grapes.

✓ *Chardonnay* (Estate)

# INDIANA
### 35 wineries in 2004

### CHÂTEAU THOMAS WINERY
**Indianapolis**
★ⓥ

Dr Charles Thomas is so passionate about the wine he drinks, and the

cellar of fine European wines that he has built up, that he refuses to grow or buy grapes locally. If these wines seem special, it is because he buys grapes from only the best areas of the Napa Valley.

✓ *Chardonnay* • *Cabernet Sauvignon* • *Merlot*

### HUBER
**Indianapolis**
★ⓥ

One of Indiana's fastest-rising, award-winning wineries.

✓ *Classic red blend* (Heritage) • *Classic white blend* (Lakeside White) • *Vignoles*

# MARYLAND
### 19 wineries in 2004

### BASIGNANI
**Sparks**
★ⓥ

This small winery makes excellent Cabernet Sauvignon and its Merlot is good enough to attract attention.

✓ *Cabernet Sauvignon* •

*Lorenzino* (red Bordeaux style) • *Merlot*

### CATOCTIN VINEYARDS
**Brookeville**
★ⓥ

These vineyards are owned by a partnership that includes Bob Lyon.

✓ *Cabernet Sauvignon* (Reserve) • *Chardonnay* (Oak Fermented) • *Johannisberg Riesling*

### ELK RUN VINEYARD
**Mount Airy**
★ⓥ

The owner-winemaker, Fred Wilson, trained with the legendary Dr Konstantin Frank (see p518).

✓ *Cabernet Sauvignon* • *Chardonnay*

# MASSACHUSETTS
### 29 wineries in 2004

### WESTPORT RIVERS
**Westport**
★ⓥ

Bob and Carol Russell converted a

17th-century turnip farm into the largest vineyard in New England in 1986, establishing the Westport Rivers winery in 1989.

✓ *Chardonnay*

# MICHIGAN
### 90 wineries in 2004

### BEL LAGO
**Cedar**
★ⓥ

Charlie Edson has no fewer than 30 different clones of Pinot Noir growing in his vineyard, but it is the Cabernet Franc-Merlot-based Tempesta that is his best wine. Under clinical tasting conditions, the American oak is too dominant, but at Hattie's in Suttons Bay (the best restaurant in the region), I was having dinner with several producers, and numerous bottles were being passed around, yet I consumed an undue amount of Tempesta. In fact, I was accused of hogging the bottle! The 2002 Gewürztraminer was the first to show any real promise.

✓ *Auxerrois* • *Chardonnay* (Leelanau Peninsula) • *Classic red blend* (Tempesta) • *Classic white blend* (Crystal) • *Dessert* (Pinot Grigio Ice Wine) • *Pinot Gris* • *Riesling* • *Sparkling* (Brut)

## BLACK STAR FARMS
### Lake Leelanau
### ★★ Ⓥ

Michigan's superstar boutique winery (artisanal creamery and luxury B&B inn) has risen to the top under the skillful guidance of Lee Lutes, this state's most gifted red-winemaker. Lutes even manages to bring a touch of class to hybrids, making a yummy Red House Red from a blend of Maréchal Foch, Dornfelder, Regent, and Cabernet Franc.

✓ *Classic red blend* (Leorie Vineyard Merlot-Cabernet Franc, Red House Red) • *Pinot Gris* (Arcturos) • *Pinot Noir* (Arcturos) • *Riesling* (Arcturos Late Harvest)

## BOWYER'S HARBOUR
### Traverse City
### ❓

One of those wineries where the dog is the most famous member of the staff, Bowyer's Harbour is potentially a class act, but has had an unfortunate experience with TCA-tainted corks. The level of taint was mostly low, and would not be noticeable to many customers, but it would be unfair to rate Bowyer's Harbour at this juncture. I can imagine this to be an exciting venture in the near future, so do not be put off.

## CHÂTEAU CHANTAL
### Traverse City
### ★ Ⓥ

Owned by a priest who fell in love with a nun and got married. Robert and Nadine Begin gave up their church, but not their beliefs, to live out the ultimate love story. In 1983, they established Château Chantal, with spectacular views of both east and west Grand Traverse Bays, and a guest house so that visitors may enjoy the sun rising and setting over the water.

✓ *Riesling* (Late Harvest)

## CHÂTEAU DE LEELANAU
### Sutton's Bay
### ★ Ⓥ

The only Michigan winery to be owned by women (Roberta Kurtz and Joanne Smart), Château de Leelanau's 2000 Adante was everything German Riesling Sekt should be, but rarely is.

✓ *Sparkling* (Adante Sparkling Riesling) • *Rosé* (Rosé de Cabernet Franc)

## CHÂTEAU FONTAINE
### Lake Leelanau
### ★ Ⓥ

Dan Matthies came across a potato farm in the 1970s, and saw it as a vineyard in his mind's eye. After selling grapes to Good Harbour for 10 years, he used his wife's middle name (Fontaine) as his own label, which was launched in 2000, with 1998 as the inaugural vintage. Initially, Château Fontaine wines were made at Good Harbour, but the Matthies family now has its own winery.

✓ *Pinot Gris*

## CHÂTEAU GRAND TRAVERSE
### Traverse City
### ★ Ⓥ

Château Grand Traverse was established in 1974 by Ed O'Keefe, the first person in Michigan exclusively to plant *vinifera* vines, ruffling many feathers among the locals in the process. And a good thing it was too, for Michigan wine would not be where it is if he had not been as forceful as he was. The first time I had a couple of pints of Guinness with Ed at his local bar, his life story grew wilder the more we drank. I thought it was just blarney, but back at Château Grand Traverse I did indeed find a scrapbook with old brown cuttings of Ed the Olympic gymnast and Ed the Green Beret colonel being decorated. There was nothing about some of his other stories, but it was more than enough to understand that such a man has no need to fabricate anything.

✓ *Classic white blend* (Ship of Fools) • *Riesling* (Botrytized Select Harvest, Dry Icewine, Late Harvest)

## CICCONE VINEYARD
### Suttons Bay
### ★ Ⓥ

Tony Ciccone may be the father of rockstar Madonna, but he has eight children, and they are all equal in his eyes. Only one of them, however, is following in their father's viticultural footsteps, and that is Paula, who has studied oenology at Michigan State University. The best-known wine from the Ciccone Vineyard is Gewürztraminer, but the acid is too high, and it has yet to please me, although it will certainly be interesting to see how this variety develops following Paula's *stage* with Maison Trimbach in Alsace in 2004. The finest wine produced here so far has been Pinot Noir, which is light-bodied, but in vintages like 2000 can be extremely elegant, with a lovely length of beautifully pure varietal fruit. I also enjoy Ciccone's Pinot Gris, even though I like to give the man a hard time by asking for a glass of his "orange" wine. In some vintages (notably 2002), he lets this wine pick up a bit of color from the skins. It is more of a peach color than orange in truth, and should really be labeled Blanc de Noirs de Pinot Gris.

✓ *Chardonnay* • *Dolcetto* • *Pinot Gris* • *Pinot Noir*

## DOMAINE BERRIEN
### Berrien Creek
### ★ Ⓥ

It is worth a visit to this southwestern winery in the Lake Michigan Shore AVA, just to run a hand over the glossy wooden counter.

✓ *Viognier*

## FENN VALLEY VINEYARDS
### Fennville
### ★ Ⓥ

Established in 1973, this was the first winery to produce wines under the Fennville AVA. The 2002 Late Harvest Vignoles, with its high-voltage acidity, is the best example of that grape I have tasted from any producer anywhere.

✓ *Vignoles* (Late Harvest)

## GOOD HARBOUR
### Lake Leelanau

Owner-winemaker Bruce Simpson is one of Michigan's most prolific medal winners.

✓ *Chardonnay* • *Riesling* • *Sparkling* (Moonstruck)

## L. MAWBY
### Suttons Bay
### ★ Ⓥ

I have been following Larry Mawby since the mid-1990s, in which time he has gone from erratic (making one decent bubbly for every four failures) to remarkably consistent in a surprisingly elegant house style. Not at any time, however, has he had difficulty selling his products. Others saw this and brought out their own bubblies, but in most cases the wines did not sell, so they asked Larry whether he would take the stock off their hands. In the meantime, he had half-jokingly applied for permission to sell a wine called "Sex," and when this was approved, he said yes to his colleagues, took back the fizz they couldn't sell, added a little red wine to make it pink, relabeled it as Sex, and it flew off the shelves quicker than he could stack it. Sex is now made by *cuve close*, thus it comes under his second M. Lawrence label. It is not a great-quality bubbly, but it is clean, eminently drinkable and the ultimate novelty wine.

✓ *Sparkling* (L. Mawby: Blanc de Blancs, Mille, Redd; M. Lawrence: Sex)

## LEELANAU CELLARS
### Omena
### ★ Ⓥ

Established in 1974 by father and son Michael and Bob Jacobson, this winery had a brisk business in hybrid wines, and its *vinifera* wines have improved year after year since the late 1990s.

✓ *Chardonnay* (Tall Ship) • *Classic red wine* (Meritage) • *Pinot Gris* (Pinot Grigio) • *Riesling* (Late Harvest)

## PENINSULA CELLARS
### Traverse City
### ★★ Ⓥ

Owned by cherry farmers David and Joan Kroupa, who saw a chance to expand the diversity of their 250-acre (100-hectare) farm on Old Mission Peninsula and planted their first vineyard in 1991. This winery was initially known for its Cabernet-Merlot blend, the first hint that red wines were viable in northern Michigan, and the winemaker, Lee Lutes, was lured away by the new Black Star Farms winery. His assistant, Bryan Ulbrich, took over and produced the first world-class Gewürztraminer outside of Alsace in 2002. Ulbrich is a very talented white-wine maker. His Pinot Blanc is also uncannily Alsace-like. Ulbrich left Peninsula Cellars in 2007 to devote his full attention to his own Left Foot Charley winery in Traverse City.

✓ *Gewürztraminer* (Manigold Vineyard) • *Pinot Blanc*

## SHADY LANE
### Suttons Bay
### ★ Ⓥ

Bill Stouten and Joe O'Donnell planted this vineyard in 1989. Initially, Larry Mawby made the wine, but since 2000 the winemaker has been Adam Satchwell, who studied winemaking under his famous uncle, Jed Steele, at Edmeades.

✓ *Chardonnay* • *Pinot Noir*

## ST. JULIAN WINE COMPANY
### Paw Paw
### ★ Ⓥ

Founded in 1921 by Mariano Meconi, this winery was established in Canada, where it was called Border City Wine Cellars for a short while, before being renamed Meconi Wine Cellars. It did not become American until 1934, when Meconi moved his business to Detroit. In 1936 he moved the business to its current location, changing its name once again, to the Italian Wine Company. When the US entered World War II, Meconi sought to avoid antifascist sentiment by changing his company's name for the third and final time. The St. Julian Wine Company is thus the oldest continuously operating winery in Michigan. It is also by far the largest, producing almost as much as all the state's other wineries put together. Although the St. Julian Wine Company is rated ★, one of its products would rate ★★ on its own. The perpetually award-winning Solera Cream Sherry is world-class, which would be achievement enough for any winery outside of Jerez, but the fact that it is made exclusively from the Niagara grape makes it all the more miraculous. What lets St. Julian down is the winery itself, which should be condemned, yet the company actually shows it off to tourists! It's about time that owner David Braganini built an entirely new, state-of-the-art facility.

✓ *Fortified* (Solera Cream Sherry) • *Riesling*

## TABOR HILL
### Buchanam
★♥

Owned by David Upton, son of the founder of Whirlpool (washing machines), this is one of a small handful of wineries in the Fennville AVA of southwestern Michigan. Tabor Hill also boasts an excellent restaurant.

✓ *Cabernet Franc • Riesling*

## TABOR HILL BRONTE WINES
### Hartford

This winery was originally founded in Detroit as the Bronte Winery, which became the first firm to market the infamous sparkling wine called "Cold Duck," a carbonated-Concord concoction that enjoyed an extraordinary vogue in the 1960s. With such an ignominious history, it is little wonder that the firm moved to a different neighborhood and assumed another identity!

## THE ROUND BARN WINERY
### Baroda
★♥

Established in 1992 by the Moersch family, who were the first to make wines under the Fennville AVA, this winery was known as the Heart of the Vineyard until 2004, when the name was changed to The Round Barn Winery. This was in deference to the historic round barn that was transported 90 miles (145 kilometers) from Rochester, Indiana, by Amish carpenters. They dismantled the barn into a total of just six beams and then reassembled it, without nails, exactly as it had been originally built. These old barns were round so that the devil could not hide in a corner.

✓ *Muscat* (Muscat Ottonel) • *Pinot Meunier*

## WILLOW VINEYARDS
### Suttons Bay
★♥

Just down the road from Ciccone Vineyards, this boutique vineyard and winery was built from scratch (including their home), on a shoestring, by John and Jo Crampton. John worked as a carpenter, while establishing Willow Vineyards, and Jo waitressed at night to make ends meet. A lovelier couple it would be hard to find, and this comes through in the friendliness of their fruit-filled wines.

✓ *Chardonnay • Pinot Gris • Pinot Noir*

## WYNCROFT
### Buchanan
★♥

The most southerly of Michigan's wineries, and one of the smallest, Wyncroft is little heard of, even in state. The style is noticeably fatter than most other Michigan wines.

✓ *Chardonnay • Pinot Noir*

# NEW JERSEY
### 33 wineries in 2004

## ALBA VINEYARD
### Milford
★♥

This vineyard has occasionally made good Cabernet, but is best for rich, sweet, plummy port-style wines.

✓ *Vintage Port*

## TOMASELLO
### Hammonton
★♥

This winery, which opened up immediately after Prohibition was repealed, has had 50 years' decent sparkling-wine experience.

✓ *Cabernet Sauvignon* (Atlantic County) • *Chambourcin* (Atlantic County)

## UNIONVILLE VINEYARDS
### Ringoes
★♥

This is one of New Jersey's newest and fastest-rising wineries.

✓ *Classic red blend* (Nielson Proprietary Reserve) • *Riesling*

# NEW YORK
### 203 wineries in 2004

## ANTHONY ROAD
### Penn Yan
★♥

After 15 years of selling their grapes to other wineries, Ann and John Martini established Anthony Road in 1990 with wines made from the 1989 harvest.

✓ *Cabernet Franc • Chardonnay • Riesling*

## BEDELL
### Cutchogue
★♥

The first harvest of this Long Island winery coincided with Hurricane Gloria in 1985. However, subsequent Bedell vintages have stood the test of time.

✓ *Chardonnay* (Reserve) • *Classic red blend* (Cupola) • *Merlot* (Reserve)

## BENMARL WINE COMPANY
### Marlboro
★♥

One of the state's most successful wineries. "Benmarl" is Gaelic for the vineyard's slate-marl soil, and although hybrids are much less trouble, *vinifera* is grown, including award-winning Zinfandel.

✓ *Baco Noir • Zinfandel*

## BRIDGEHAMPTON
### Bridgehampton
★★♥

Long Island's fastest-rising star, Bridgehampton's wines have an intensity of fruit and a fine structure.

✓ *Chardonnay • Meritage* (red Bordeaux style) • *Merlot • Riesling • Sauvignon Blanc*

## BROTHERHOOD WINERY
### Washingtonville

The oldest winery in continuous operation in the US, Brotherhood Winery was established by a shoemaker called Jean Jacques, who initially sold wine to the First Presbyterian Church. The wines used to be very much of the old school, but are now fresher and crisper in character.

## CANANDAIGUA WINE COMPANY
### Canandaigua

The Seneca Native American word "canandaigua" means "chosen place." Even in the late 1980s, this firm had a huge production, but it is now second only in size to Gallo in terms of American production, and its merger with Australia's BRL Hardy to form Constellation Brands makes it the largest wine producer in the world. Various Atlantic Northeast labels include Richards, J. Roget, and Virginia Dare.

## CHANNING DAUGHTER
### Bridgehampton
★♥

This winery has been on the fast track since Walter and Molly Channing, and partner Larry Perrine, launched their first wines with the 1997 vintage.

✓ *Classic white blend* (Silvanus) • *Merlot* (The Sculptor) • *Tocai Friulano*

## FOX RUN
### Hamport
★♥

Owner Scott Osborn is one of the movers and shakers in the Finger Lakes wine industry.

✓ *Lemburger • Pinot Noir* (Reserve) • *Riesling* (Dry)

## DR. FRANK'S VINIFERA WINE CELLARS
### Hammondsport

Run today by Willy Frank, the son of the legendary Konstantin Frank.

✓ *Riesling* (Dry) • *Sparkling* (Blanc de Blancs)

## GALLUCCIO FAMILY WINERIES
### Cutchogue
★♥

Vince Galluccio took over Gristina Vineyards in August 2000, since when both brands have been made here.

✓ *Chardonnay* (Galluccio Cru George Allaire) • *Classic red blend* (Galluccio Cru George Allaire) • *Merlot* (Gristina)

## GLENORA WINE CELLARS
### Dundee
★♥

Named after the nearby Glenora waterfall, this winery consistently produces crisp and stylish wines.

✓ *Riesling • Seyval Blanc • Sparkling Wine* (Vintage Blanc de Blancs)

## GOLD SEAL
### Hammondsport

Originally called the Imperial Winery, this historic firm built its reputation on "New York Champagne." The quality of this sparkling wine was based on 100 years of Champagne expertise, in the form of Charles le Breton of Louis Roederer, Jules Crance of Moët & Chandon, Charles Fournier of Veuve Clicquot, and Guy Davaux of Marne & Champagne, who all worked at Gold Seal. Of these, it was Fournier who stood out, and his name lives on as the brand of this firm's quaffing bubbly.

## GOOSE WATCH WINERY
### Romulus
★♥

Under the same ownership as Swedish Hill winery, Goose Watch is an up-and-coming departure from the typical Finger Lakes mold, featuring grapes such as Diamond (*labrusca*), Lemberger, Melody, Merlot, Pinot Gris, and Viognier.

✓ *Lemberger • Viognier*

## GREAT WESTERN WINERY
### Hammondsport

Another historic winery, Great Western is now a subsidiary of The Taylor Wine Company. Its wines are less innovative, despite the occasional good *vinifera*.

## HARGRAVE VINEYARD
### Cutchogue
★♥

After looking at wine areas nationwide, Alex and Louisa Hargrave established Long Island's first vineyard in 1973, on what used to be a potato farm.

✓ *Cabernet Franc* (Reserve)

## HAZLITT'S 1852 VINEYARDS
### Hector

The late Jerry Hazlitt replanted the old family vineyards in 1984.

✓ *Riesling*

## HERMANN J WEIMER VINEYARD
### Dundee
### ☆ⓥ

While working for a certain hybrid aficionado, Weimer produced some outstanding *vinifera* wines from his own vineyard. They received rave reviews, and he has not looked back.

ᗷ✓ *Gewürztraminer* (Dry) • *Riesling* (Dry) • *Sparkling* (Cuvée Brut)

## HERON HILL VINEYARDS
### Hammondsport
### ☆ⓥ

The name "Heron Hill" is a flight of fancy on the part of advertising copywriter Peter Johnstone, who so liked Finger Lake on a visit in 1968 that he stayed, set up in business with major shareholder John Ingle, and turned winemaker in 1977.

ᗷ✓ *Classic red blend* (Eclipse, Game Bird Red) • *Riesling*

## HUNT COUNTRY
### Branchport
### ☆ⓥ

Owned and operated by Art and Joyce Hunt, the sixth generation to farm this land, but the first to make wine under their own name.

ᗷ✓ *Vignoles* (Late Harvest)

## KEUKA SPRING WINERY
### Penn Yan
### ☆ⓥ

After more than 20 years in the business, Len and Judy Wiltberger are beginning to produce wines that are getting noticed outside the Finger Lakes district. In 1999, they even won the Governor's Cup for their 1998 Cabernet Franc, which is remarkable for this part of the wine world.

ᗷ✓ *Cayuga* • *Vignoles* • *Riesling*

## KNAPP VINEYARD
### Romulus
### ☆ⓥ

This producer has always made wines from *vinifera* as well as hybrid varieties, including one of the state's best Seyval Blancs.

ᗷ✓ *Cabernet Franc* • *Chardonnay* (Barrel Reserve) • *Merlot*

## LAKEWOOD VINEYARDS
### Watkins Glen
### ★ⓥ

Owned and run by the Stamp family, which has farmed this land for four generations.

ᗷ✓ *Cabernet Franc* • *Dessert* (Glaciavinum) • *Fortified* (Port) • *Pinot Noir* • *Riesling* • *Sparkling* (Brut) • *Vignoles*

## LAMOREAUX LANDING
### Lodi
### ★☆ⓥ

There has always been something about this Finger Lakes winery, its design, and the people who run it that makes it a class act.

ᗷ✓ *Cabernet Franc* • *Chardonnay* (Reserve) • *Merlot* • *Riesling* • *Sparkling wine* (Blanc de Blanc—sic, Brut)

## LENZ
### Peconic
### ★ⓥ

While running a restaurant, Patricia and Peter Lenz developed a passion for wine, which led them to establish this winery on a potato farm.

ᗷ✓ *Cabernet Sauvignon* • *Chardonnay* • *Merlot*

## MARTHA CLARA
### Riverhead
### ☆ⓥ

Interesting wines from this recent start-up, whose first vintage was 1998.

ᗷ✓ *Dessert* (Ciel) • *Sémillon*

## MCGREGOR VINEYARD WINERY
### Dundee
### ☆ⓥ

Established by the McGregor family in 1980, this vineyard began making Chardonnay, Riesling, Gewürztraminer, and Pinot Noir that year, but their heart is obviously in sparkling wine.

ᗷ✓ *Sparkling* (Blanc de Noirs, Riesling)

## PALMER
### Aquebogue
### ☆ⓥ

The vineyard was converted from a potato and pumpkin farm in 1983, and the winery, built three years later, quickly started producing attention-grabbing wines. The reds, in particular, simply have more richness than other New York wineries can manage.

ᗷ✓ *Cabernet Franc* • *Chardonnay* • *Merlot*

## PAUMANOK VINEYARDS
### Aquebogue
### ★☆ⓥ

Another of Long Island's up-and-coming stars.

ᗷ✓ *Cabernet Sauvignon* • *Classic red blend* (Assemblage) • *Merlot*

## PECONIC BAY WINERY
### Cutchogue
### ☆ⓥ

Established in 1979, Peconic Bay was one of the first vineyards on the North Fork, producing its first commercial crop in 1984. The Merlot is particularly outstanding.

ᗷ✓ *Chardonnay* (La Barrique) • *Merlot*

## PELLEGRINI VINEYARDS
### Cutchogue
### ★☆ⓥ

A recently established Long Island winery, Pellegrini is one of the most promising North Fork producers.

ᗷ✓ *Cabernet Sauvignon* • *Chardonnay* • *Merlot*

## PINDAR VINEYARDS
### Peconic
### ★ⓥ

With the intention of growing grapes, Dr. Herodotus Damianos converted a potato farm on Long Island into a vineyard. In 1982 he built a winery, named it after the Greek lyric poet, and it is now Long Island's largest producer, and also one of the best.

ᗷ✓ *Chardonnay* • *Classic red blend* (Mythology) • *Merlot*

## RAPHAEL
### Peconic
### ★☆

Established in 1996, Raphael obviously has the money to make it one of the top two or three East Coast wineries. With Paul Pontallier of Château Margaux consulting, there is no reason why this potential should not be realized.

ᗷ✓ *Classic red blend* (La Fontana) • *Merlot*

## SHELDRAKE POINT VINEYARDS
### Ovid
### ☆ⓥ

Some 40 acres (16 hectares) of *vinifera* vines on the shores of Lake Cayuga.

ᗷ✓ *Riesling* (Ice Wine) • *Cabernet Franc*

## SILVER THREAD VINEYARDS
### Lodi
### ☉☆ⓥ

One of the first organic producers in the Atlantic Northeast, owner-winemaker Richard Figiel makes one of the Finger Lakes' better Pinot Noirs.

ᗷ✓ *Pinot Noir*

## SWEDISH HILL WINERY
### Romulus
### ☆ⓥ

Founded in 1986 by Dick and Cindy Peterson, Swedish Hill has become one of the largest wineries in the region, producing nearly 40,000 cases of wine a year. *See also* Goose Watch.

ᗷ✓ *Riesling* • *Sparkling Wine* (R Cuvée, Spumante Blush, Vintage Brut) • *Vidal Blanc*

## TRELEAVEN WINES
### King Ferry
### ☆ⓥ

Technically the King Ferry Winery, but owners Peter and Tracie Saltonstall sell their wines under the Treleaven label.

ᗷ✓ *Riesling* (Semi Dry)

## WAGNER VINEYARDS
### Lodi
### ☆

Consistently high-quality wines for a quarter of a century.

ᗷ✓ *Chardonnay* (Barrel Fermented) • *Riesling* (Dry, Icewine) • *Sparkling* (Riesling Champagne)

## WARM LAKE ESTATE
### Cambria
### ☆ⓥ

With the largest plantation of Dijon Clone Pinot Noir in New York, Michael Von Heckler produces one of this state's better Pinot Noir wines.

ᗷ✓ *Pinot Noir*

## WÖLFFER ESTATE
### Cambria
### ★ⓥ

Wölffer Estate made history with its 2000 Premier Cru Merlot when it was released as Long Island's first $100 wine.

ᗷ✓ *Merlot* • *Cabernet Franc*

# OHIO
### 100 wineries in 2004

## BUSCH-HARRIS
### Mount Victory
### ★ⓥ

Exciting new winery making waves with classy, award-winning Cabernet Sauvignon.

ᗷ✓ *Cabernet Sauvignon*

## FIRELANDS WINERY
### Sandusky
### ☆ⓥ

This winery occupies the original Mantey Vineyard site, which was planted in 1880, and manages to attract 40,000 visitors a year.

ᗷ✓ *Chardonnay* (Barrel Select) • *Riesling*

## MARKKO VINEYARD
### Ridge Road, Conneaut
### ★ⓥ

This vineyard is owned by Arnulf Esterer, the first of Konstantin Frank's followers to plant *vinifera* grapes in Ohio.

ᗷ✓ *Cabernet Sauvignon* • *Chardonnay* • *Riesling*

## TROUTMAN
### Wooster
### ☆ⓥ

Established as recently as 2001, Troutman produces a clutch of guzzlers that should attract wider attention.

ᗷ✓ *Cabernet Franc* • *Syval Blanc* (White Menagerie) • *Vidal* (Farmer's White)

# PENNSYLVANIA
### 99 wineries in 2004

## ALLEGRO VINEYARDS
### Brogue
### ☆ⓥ

John Crouch is a well-established producer of Cabernet, and is currently on form with Cadenza.

ᗷ✓ *Cabernet Sauvignon* • *Cadenza* (red Bordeaux-style)

## CHADDSFORD WINERY
### Chaddsford
★ Ⓥ

Eric and Lee Miller have established Chaddsford as one of the Atlantic Northeast's most successful wineries.

✓ *Chardonnay* (Barrel Select) • *Merlot*

## CLOVER HILL VINEYARDS
### Breinigsville
★ ☆ Ⓥ

Owner-winemaker John Scrips III is starting to pick up gold medals at his substantial 20,000-case winery.

✓ *Pinot Gris* (Pinot Grigio) • *Vignoles*

# RHODE ISLAND
### 7 wineries in 2004

## SAKONNET VINEYARDS
### Little Compton
★ ☆ Ⓥ

The first winery to open on Rhode Island after Prohibition. New wine called Rhode Island Red not tasted.

✓ *Gewürztraminer* • *Vidal Blanc*

# VIRGINIA
### 97 wineries in 2004

## BARBOURSVILLE VINEYARDS
### Barboursville
★ ★☆ Ⓥ

Once the property of James Barbour, a former governor of Virginia, this estate is now owned by Zonin of Piedmont in Italy. The wines possess a remarkable elegance, balance, and finesse and this is increasing as Luca Paschina comes to terms with the growing environment. Many seem to think that Virginia's best grape is Cabernet Franc, but Barboursville's Cabernet Sauvignon outperforms its Cabernet Franc most years. The Octagon requires aging after release.

✓ *Barbera* (Reserve) • *Cabernet Franc* (Reserve) • *Cabernet Sauvignon* (Reserve) • *Classic red blend* (Octagon) • *Nebbiolo* (Reserve) • *Viognier*

## BREAUX VINEYARDS
### Hillsboro
★ ☆ Ⓥ

Established in 1994 by Paul and Alexis Breaux, who bought a 3-acre vineyard planted in 1985, so these are mature vines by Virginia standards. The Late Harvest Alexis is a blend of Sauvignon Blanc, Sémillon, and Vidal Blanc.

✓ *Late Harvest* (Alexis) • *Sauvignon Blanc* • *Seyval Blanc* • *Viognier*

## CHÂTEAU MORISETTE
### Rocky Mount
★ ☆ Ⓥ

A relatively well established (1982), but recently up-and-coming winery.

✓ *Cabernet Sauvignon* • *Merlot* (Reserve)

## CHRYSALIS VINEYARDS
### Middleburg
★ ☆ Ⓥ

Chrysalis produces the most consistent quality Norton I have come across, but don't ask owner Jennifer McCloud about this All-American grape. Not unless you really want to know, because she's probably the world's foremost expert on the subject! The Rubiana is a blend of Tempranillo, Graciano, Fer Servadou, and Norton.

✓ *Classic red blend* (Rubiana) • *Norton* • *Petit Verdot* (Hollin Reserve) • *Viognier*

## HORTON
### Charlottesville
★ ☆ Ⓥ

At one time Dennis Horton was known as Virginia's lone Rhone Ranger, but he is currently performing best with grapes that are more at home in the southwest of France. Even though there is an inconsistency in Horton's Norton, I have to recommend it because the highlights are minor classics, and everyone just loves the alliteration.

✓ *Cabernet Franc* • *Norton* • *Petit Manseng* • *Tannat*

## JEFFERSON VINEYARDS
### Charlottesville
★ ☆ Ⓥ

Located just outside Charlottesville, a mile from Monticello, on vineyard sites chosen and planted by Thomas Jefferson in 1774, but obviously more successful, as these bear fruit!

✓ *Merlot* (Reserve)

## KESWICK VINEYARDS
### Keswick
★ ☆ Ⓥ

Located at the historic Edgewood Estate, part of the original 1727 Nicholas Meriwether Crown Grant. Al and Cindy Schornberg planted a vineyard here and produced their first wines in 2002, winning "Best White Wine in the US" at the Atlanta International Wine Summit with their Reserve Viognier.

✓ *Classic red blend* (Trevillian) • *Viognier* (Reserve)

## KING FAMILY VINEYARDS
### Crozet
★ ☆ Ⓥ

Michael Shaps is considered to be one of Virginia's most talented winemakers, and King Vineyards is one of the most beautiful locations in the scenic state of Virginia. One barrel of 2002 Merlot was by leaps and bounds the greatest red wine component I have ever tasted from any Virginia winery. Pity it was not bottled in its pure format, as it would have acted as a goal for all other wineries. Wines are sold under both King Family Vineyards and Michael Shaps labels.

## KLUGE ESTATE
### Charlottesville
★ ☆ Ⓥ

If any winery is destined to become Virginia's first ★★ winery, it's Kluge. Owned by Patricia Kluge (pronounced Klugee) and her husband Bill Moses, they have spared no expense from grape to glass, including the acquisition of such top international consultants as Michel Rolland (Bordeaux) and Claude Thibaut (sparkling). The Cru is a beautifully focused, Vin Doux Naturel style of sweet wine that knocks the socks off most Muscat de Beaumes de Venise. Second wines are sold under the Albemarle label.

✓ *Chardonnay* (Cru) • *Classic red blend* (New World Red) • *Sparkling Wine*

## OAKENCROFT
### Charlottesville
★ ☆ Ⓥ

Felicia Warburg Rogan started this venture in 1983, and is treated with love and respect as something of a *grande dame* by her younger neighbors.

✓ *Petit Verdot*

## OASIS VINEYARD
### Hume
★ ☆ Ⓥ

When Dirgham Salahi planted this vineyard in 1975, he was warned, like everyone else, against *vinifera* varieties, and the locals thought he was crazy when he not only ignored this advice, but also decided to gamble exclusively on premium varieties. He was proved right and has since become one of the state's more consistent producers.

✓ *Chardonnay* (Barrel Select)

## PIEDMONT VINEYARDS AND WINERY INC.
### Middleburg
★ ★

When Elizabeth Furness planted *vinifera* grapes in 1973, no one advised her otherwise, presumably because anyone who is crazy enough to start a new career at the age of 75 wouldn't listen anyway. Mrs. Furness proved to be one of Virginia's best winemakers and reveled in her new job until her death in 1986. Since then her daughter, Elizabeth Worrell, has carried on admirably.

✓ *Cabernet Sauvignon* • *Chardonnay* (Native Yeast) • *Merlot*

## PRINCE MICHAEL
### Culpeper
★ ☆ Ⓥ

Owned by French industrialist Jean Leducq, Prince Michael is the largest vineyard in Virginia, and its production is supplemented with grapes from the company's own vineyards in Napa. Wines are also sold under the Madison and Rapidan River labels.

✓ *Chardonnay* • *Classic red blend* (Symbius) • *Classic white blend* (Rapidan River Harmony) • *Shiraz* (Madison)

## RAPPAHANNOCK CELLARS
### Huntly
★ ☆ Ⓥ

John Delmare moved from California and built this winery in 2000.

✓ *Cabernet Sauvignon* • *Classic red blend* (Meritage)

## ROCKBRIDGE
### Raphine
★ ☆ Ⓥ

Owner-winemaker Shepherd Rouse earned a Masters degree in oenology at UC Davis while working at Schramsberg, Chateau St. Jean, and Carneros Creek. Returning to his native Virginia in 1986, he was the winemaker at Montdomaine Cellars when its 1990 Cabernet Sauvignon won the 1993 Virginia Governor's Cup. Rouse established Rockbridge Vineyard in 1988, since when he has won the Governor's Cup twice (1995 and 2001).

✓ *Chardonnay* (DeChiel Vineyard)

## TARARA
### Leesburg
★ ☆ Ⓥ

Established in 1989, this 40-acre (16-hectare) vineyard and winery started to shine almost immediately.

✓ *Chambourcin* • *Chardonnay* (Reserve) • *Classic red blend* (Meritage) • *Vidal Blanc*

## VALHALLA VINEYARDS
### Roanoke
★ ☆ Ⓥ

Since the Vascick family established Valhalla Vineyards in 1999, the wines have won over 125 medals in national and international competitions.

✓ *Classic red blend* (Valkyrie)

## VERITAS
### Afton
★ ☆ Ⓥ

British-born neurologist Andrew Hodson is in the process of establishing something special at this ambitious, but stylish and well-considered, family-run winery.

✓ *Merlot* • *Petit Verdot*

## WHITE HALL
### White Hall
★ ☆ Ⓥ

In 1991, Tony Champ planted 6 acres (2.5 hectares) with Chardonnay, Cabernet Sauvignon, Cabernet Franc, and Merlot near the Blue Ridge Mountains. He later added other varieties, and now has 25 acres 10 hectares) of vines and a state-of-the-art winery.

✓ *Classic red blend* (Cuvée des Champs) • *Petit Verdot* • *Viognier*

OTHER WINEMAKING AREAS OF
# THE UNITED STATES

## ALABAMA

The first commercially cultivated vines were planted here in the 1830s, and the state had a flourishing wine industry prior to Prohibition. However, as many as half its counties remained "dry" until as recently as 1975, and legislation licensing farm wineries was not passed until 1978. There are just five Alabama wineries, and the wines are made from Muscadine. Other varieties are trucked in from out of state.

## ALASKA

How do they do it? Well, not with Alaskan-grown grapes, that's for certain. There are six wineries, mostly making wines from locally grown soft fruits, although the Denali Winery produces a range of *vinifera* wines (Cabernet Sauvignon, Chardonnay, Merlot, Riesling, and the inevitable Alaska Icewine), albeit from trucked-in juice diluted with "crystal clear mountain water."

## ARIZONA

Surprisingly, table grapes have long thrived in the irrigated Arizona deserts, but recently classic wine-grape varieties have been cultivated in this state's solitary AVA of Sonoita, which is made possible only through its altitude of between 4,000 and 5,000 feet (1,200 and 1,500 meters).

### SONOITA AVA

The Santa Rita, Huachuca, and Whetstone mountain ranges isolate this AVA. Geologically, this appellation is an upland basin rather than a valley, because it comprises the headwaters for three distinct drainages: Sonoita Creek to the south, Cienega Creek to the north, and the Babocamari River to the east. Local growers believe their *terra rosa* soil will determine the potential of this area.

## ARKANSAS

More than 100 wineries sprang up in Arkansas after Prohibition, but lack of winemaking skills meant that barely half a dozen survived (seven in 2004). A fortified wine made by Cowie Wine Cellars and called Robert's Port is well respected, as is this winery's Cynthiana.

### ALTUS AVA

This plateau lies between the Arkansas River bottomlands and the climatically protective high peaks of the Boston Mountains.

### ARKANSAS MOUNTAIN AVA

This covers a huge area in the mountainous region of Arkansas. The Arkansas mountains moderate winter temperatures and provide shelter from violent northerly winds and sudden changes in temperature. Classic European grape varieties are grown here, but cannot survive in the area immediately south because of Pierce's disease, a vine-destroying condition associated with warm climates that attacks *Vitis vinifera*.

### OZARK MOUNTAIN AVA

Five major rivers make up this AVA's boundaries: the Mississippi, the Missouri, the Osage, the Neosho, and the Arkansas, and the area includes Mt. Magazine, the highest mountain in Arkansas. The Ozark Mountain appellation straddles parts of Missouri and Oklahoma, and is hilly-to-mountainous. The soils are stony, well drained, and contain clay from deeply weathered, well-consolidated sedimentary volcanic rocks.

## COLORADO

The growing season in most of Colorado is too short to permit grape-growing, but the number of wineries has grown from just 5 in 1995 to 54 by 2004, and there are more in the pipeline. Chardonnay and Merlot are the most popular *vinifera* varieties.

### GRAND VALLEY AVA

Grand Valley is located just west of Grand Junction, and incorporates three localities known as Orchard Mesa, Redlands, and Vinelands.

## FLORIDA

The very first wine made in what is now the US was made by French Huguenots at Fort Caroline in 1564, but the only viticulture of any significance occurred after the Civil War, when Florida was settled by dispossessed northerners and southerners alike. The northerners planted their beloved *labrusca* vines, while the southerners competed with their even more bizarre Muscadine. Some 500 acres (200 hectares) were cultivated toward the end of the 19th century, and it was the southerners who won this battle of the grapes, as *labrusca* succumbed to Florida's extreme heat and humidity. Amid this north–south viticultural divide, a Frenchman by the name of Emile Dubois produced Norton and Cynthiana (then believed to be two different varieties) of sufficient quality to win a medal at the Paris Exposition of 1900, but virtually all of Florida's vineyards disappeared shortly thereafter, as it was widely acknowledged that this semitropical state was better suited to citrus groves. Not surprisingly, a lot of "orange wine" is made today, not to mention the wines made from Key Lime, Mango, and Passion Fruit. However odd though these concoctions might be, they are superior to the wine made from the local Muscadine grapes. Florida's growers have tried to grow *vinifera* again and again throughout the 20th century, only to discover that they were being killed by Pierce's disease (PD), for which there is no cure, although Muscadine varieties are unaffected. Since the 1950s, the University of Florida has released a number of complex PD-resistant hybrids created by crossing French hybrids with American ones, with Lake Emerald (developed in 1954), Stover (1968), Conquistador (1983), Suwannee (1983), and Blanc Du Bois (1987) being the most widely planted. Set against this backdrop, it is difficult to understand why there has been an explosion of wineries opening up of late. There were just six as recently as 2000, yet no fewer than 33 by 2004.

## GEORGIA

Georgia has cultivated grapes since 1733 and by 1880 was the sixth-largest wine-growing state. Even in modern times, its wines have been based on native Muscadine grapes until very recently, and they have been an acquired taste. Since the late 1990s, however, wineries such as Creekstone, Frogtown Cellars, Tiger Mountain, Three Sisters Vineyard, and Wolf Mountain Vineyards have used *vinifera* grapes planted at an altitude of 1,800 to 2,000 feet (540 to 600 meters) in the Northeast Georgia Mountains, where humidity is no problem, and cool nights preserve acidity.

## HAWAII

Only Alaska seems a less likely wine-producing state, but vines were first planted here in 1814. The first vines planted in modern times were at Tedeschi Vineyard on Maui in 1974, and the first wines made in 1980. Dozens of experimental varieties were grown, but only Carnelian was chosen for commercial production. The Carnelian is a rather rustic cross developed in the 1930s for use in the hot continental climate of California's Central Valley, but fares less well in Hawaii's tropical climate, where the vine is overvigorous, producing more leaves than fruit, and tends to crop several times a year. The vineyards have to be sprayed with salt to force the vines into some sort of winter rest. Further problems occurred in 1995, when the Carnelian vines were found to be infected with eutypa, or crown gall, a wasting disease that is difficult to control. In 1987 Volcano Vineyard on Hawaii island was planted with the Symphony cross, which appears to be more successful, and by 2004 the Hawaiian islands boasted five wineries in total, although most are producing tropical fruit wines, and one, Diamond Head Winery, is a DIY operation utilizing grape juice from the mainland.

## ILLINOIS

By 1847, there were over 600 acres (240 hectares) of vineyards on the banks of the Mississippi, supplying no fewer than 40 wineries in Nauvo. In 1851 the oldest Concord vineyard in Illinois was planted in Nauvo State Park, where the vineyard is still producing wine today, as is Baxter's, which was established in 1857. By 1868, Illinois was producing 225,000 gallons (852,000 liters) a year, which was very nearly as much as New York.

## IOWA

Hiram Barney established 100 acres (40 hectares) of vines at Keokuk in 1869, which he called White Elk Vineyards, and it produced 30,000 gallons (115,000 liters) of wine a year before succumbing to a lethal combination of disease and Prohibition. Most of Iowa's modern-day vineyards were destroyed in 1980 by "2, 4-D" pesticide used on neighboring crops, forcing wineries to truck in grapes from out of state, or to make fruit wine, although a number of new vineyards have been established since 2001. Norton is the most exciting variety currently grown, and although many of the better-known hybrids are not hardy enough to survive Iowa's winters, Maréchal Foch and La Crosse are two of the more successful ones. However, of the 27 wineries in this state, none has stood out so far.

# KANSAS

Kansas has never been a huge winemaking state, but it did produce as much as 110,000 cases of wine a year until it voted to go "dry" in 1880. Although no modern-day wineries existed until 1990, there were 12 wineries by 2004, and Norton is the best grape.

# KENTUCKY

In 1799, John James Dufour set up the Kentucky Vineyard Society, which expected to raise $10,000 in capital though the sale of 200 shares of $50 each. Without waiting for the subscriptions certificates to be printed, let alone sold, Dufour had purchased 633 acres (253 hectares) of land at Big Bend on the banks of the Kentucky River, and began planting the optimistically named First Vineyard in 1798. However, almost all the vines had failed by 1802. Like so many early ventures, the cause was probably Pierce's disease, phylloxera, or both. Another more successful early Kentucky venture was planted by Colonel James Taylor at Newport. This vineyard was described by John Melish, an English traveler, as "the finest that I have yet seen in America."

# LOUISIANA

Jesuit priests made altar wine here as early as 1750, and by 1775 an Englishman we know of only as Colonel Ball produced a wine from the banks of the Mississippi, north of New Orleans, that was considered worthy of sending to George III, but the vineyard died after the colonel and his family were massacred by Indians, according to the August 1822 and December 1826 issues of *American Farmer*. Louisiana's climate is unsuitable for any vine other than Scuppernong, so grapes imported from California, or other fruit such as oranges, were relied upon for winemaking. There are just seven wineries in this state today.

# MINNESOTA

Vineyards have to be buried beneath several feet of earth in soil to survive Minnesota's winters, which restricts cultivation to native varieties and hybrids, with a heavy dependence on fruit wines, which are preferable more often than not. One exception is Northern Vineyards, which makes some of Minnesota's most exciting, cutting-edge wines from own-grown *vinifera* varieties such as as Chardonnay, Pinot Noir, Pinot Gris, Gewürztraminer, and even St. Laurent. Of the other 18 wineries in this state, only Carlos Creek, Saint Croix Vineyards, and Whitehaven stand out.

# MISSISSIPPI

The pattern here is very similar to that in Kentucky. However, heavy and restrictive taxes were reduced in 1984, when the Mississippi Delta was granted its own AVA. By 2004 there were five wineries, but none outstanding at the time of writing.

## MISSISSIPPI DELTA AVA

A fertile alluvial plain with loess bluffs that abruptly rise 100 feet (30 meters) along the entire eastern side of the delta that also covers parts of Louisiana and Tennessee.

# MISSOURI

The first wines were produced in Missouri in the 1830s and the state had a flourishing wine industry in the mid-18th century. The wine industry has almost doubled since the turn of the 21st century, with the number of wineries increasing from 37 in 2000 to 67 in 2004. Norton is the king of Missouri grapes.

## AUGUSTA AVA

Grape-growing in Augusta, the country's first established AVA, dates from 1860. The bowl-like ridge of hills from west to east, and the Missouri River on the southern edge of the viticultural area, provide a microclimate that distinguishes Augusta from the surrounding areas.

## HERMANN AVA

In 1904, this area furnished 97 percent of the wine produced in Missouri. The soils are well drained, have a high water capacity, and provide good root development.

## OZARK HIGHLANDS AVA

Located within the much larger Ozark Mountain AVA, this area's climate is frost-free and relatively cool during spring and fall, compared with surrounding areas.

# MONTANA

Although the growing season is generally too short for grapes, and most of this state's 11 wineries produce wines from locally grown soft fruits, or grapes trucked in from Washington, Idaho, and California, vines have grown around Flathead Lake and in the Flathead Valley since 1979, when Dr. Thomas Campbell established Mission Mountain Winery on Flathead Lake's west shore. Although Mission Mountain remains the only winery to produce pure Montana-grown wines, and has to supplement them with wines made from out-of-state grapes, there are several other growers in this southwestern area of Montana who could start up their own boutique wineries, if the experience of other embryonic wine states is anything to go by. It seems that award-winning Mission Mountain Winery and the other growers all agree that the most successful *vinifera* varieties for Montana so far are Chardonnay, Gewürztraminer, Pinot Noir, and Pinot Gris.

# NEBRASKA

The earliest known producer in Nebraska was Peter Pitz, who cultivated 12 acres (5 hectares) of vines near Plattsmouth in the 1890s, and claimed to make red, white, and yellow wine! The first vineyard in modern times was planted at Pierce by Ed Swanson of Cuthills Vineyards, and there are 12 wineries today, although apart from the modest successes of Whiskey Run Creek Vineyard & Winery, and Cuthills itself, no producers stand out. Some wines are made from native varieties, but essentially Nebraska viticulture suits hybrids, of which Edelweiss is most highly regarded, and others found include Cayuga, Chambourcin, DeChaunac, LaCrosse, Marechal Foch, St. Croix, and Traminette.

# NEVADA

Even though the growing season in Nevada is theoretically too short for growing vines, the first experimental vines were planted here in 1992, and by 1994 there were three vineyards: two in the Carson Valley of southern Nevada, and one in southern Nevada's Pahrump Valley. Instrumental in these ventures were Rick and Kathy Halbardier of Churchill Vineyards, which changed its name to Tahoe Ridge Vineyards & Winery in 1994, and built a research winery in 1996, harvesting its first commercial crop in 2000. There are now four wineries, but as far as I am aware, only Tahoe Ridge Vineyards & Winery produces Nevada-grown *vinifera* wines (as well as wines from California grapes), but with eight Nevada vineyards growing various *vinifera* varieties to sell to Tahoe Ridge, the nucleus exists for a small wine industry to blossom in this desert state.

# NEW MEXICO

Only Florida can claim an older winemaking industry than New Mexico's, which dates back to the early 1600s, but was unknown to Americans until 1821, when the Santa Fe Trail (known then as the Rio del Norte) was opened, and reports of its vineyards filtered back to the East Coast.

## MESILLA VALLEY AVA

An area that follows the Mesilla Valley along the Rio Grande River from an area just north of Las Cruces, New Mexico (where most of its vineyards are situated) to El Paso, Texas. Soils are alluvial, stratified, deep, and well drained.

## MIDDLE RIO GRANDE VALLEY AVA

This narrow valley stretches along the Rio Grande River from Albuquerque to San Antonio. Franciscan missions grew vines here during the 17th century and winemaking existed until Prohibition. At an altitude of between 4,800 and 5,200 feet (1,465 and 1,585 meters), the climate is characterized by low rainfall and hot summers.

## MIMBRES VALLEY AVA

An area of the Mimbres River from the north of Mimbres to the south of Columbus.

# NORTH CAROLINA

Both the first and second colonies to settle this area were expected to produce wine, and although these hopes are documented, no evidence of any success exists. The hot climate dictates that most wines are produced from the hardy, native Scuppernong vine, which produces the most extraordinary, disturbingly exotic, and unusual wine from large, cherrylike grapes. It was these grapes that made North Carolina the largest wine-producing state in 1840. It was also from Scuppernong grapes that "Captain" Paul Garrett first made his notorious, best-selling Virginia Dare wine from a string of East Coast wineries in the 1900s. After

Prohibition, he created the first singing commercial for wine, and Virginia Dare once again became the country's biggest-selling wine. Scuppernong grapes were scarce, however, and despite successfully encouraging many growers in other southern states to grow this vine, he had to blend in more Californian wine, and in the process Virginia Dare lost its distinctive (and, by today's standards, not very attractive) character, so sales dropped. There are nine wineries in North Carolina, but it is still a hostile environment for anything other than Scuppernong.

### YADKIN VALLEY AVA

North Carolina's first official appellation, Yadkin Valley was recognized as an AVA in February 2003. This viticultural area comprises 1.4 million acres in the northwestern section of the Piedmont region, where it spans seven counties along the Yadkin River. There were fewer than 10 wineries at the time of writing, but more were awaiting approval. Most vines here are *vinifera*, with Chardonnay, Riesling, Cabernet Sauvignon, and Merlot faring best over the long, warm growing season, with mild winters, on the Yadkin Valley's gently rolling hills of well-drained clay and loam soils.

## NORTH DAKOTA

According to the TTB, there were six wineries in this state by 2004, but the only ones I know of are Maple River Winery in Casselton and Pointe of View in Burlington, both of which make own-grown fruit wines.

## OKLAHOMA

The first known Oklahoma wines were made by Edward Fairchild, who in 1890 moved from the viticultural paradise of New York's Finger Lakes to establish a vineyard and orchard near Oklahoma City. Fairchild made commercial quantities of Concord and Delaware wine between 1893 and 1907, when Oklahoma joined the US as a dry state.

## SOUTH CAROLINA

Winemaking began here as long ago as 1748, when Robert Thorpe was paid the handsome prize of £500 by the Commons of South Carolina for being "the first person who shall make the first pipe of good, strong-bodied, merchantable wine of the growth and culture of his own plantation." However, this state has never really recovered from Prohibition, with only six wineries in existence today. The grapes used are invariably Muscadine or hybrid varieties, and even these tend to be supplemented with local-grown fruit wines. No wineries really stand out, except for Montmorenci Vineyards, which has won numerous awards for hybrid wines.

## SOUTH DAKOTA

Valiant Vineyards was the first ever winery in South Dakota, established as recently as 1993, when Eldon and Sherry Nygaard planted a small vineyard overlooking Turkey Ridge Creek in Turner County. At the time it would have been illegal to build and operate a winery, so the Nygaards drew up a farm winery bill and caused it to be introduced by the South Dakota Legislature, which passed it into law in July 1996.

By 2004 there were seven wineries in this state, but none has stood out, although Prairie Berry Winery appears to be the most successful so far.

## TENNESSEE

The best-known episode in this state's wine history took place in the 1850s, when a French, German, and Italian Catholic community called Vineland or Vinona established terraced vineyards, and made wine, which was sold to the Scottish Presbyterians in the southern Appalachians. Unfortunately, the Civil War put an end to both the activity and the community. In the 1880s, so-called Victorian Utopians established themselves in Rugby, and German settlers did likewise in the Allardt community of Fentress County. Although Tennessee still has some "dry" counties, the state now has 29 wineries. *Vinifera* vines have been planted here, but they usually perish under severe winter conditions. Most producers purchase grapes (*vinifera*, hybrid, and native varieties such as Scuppernong and Concord) from both in-state and out-of-state sources. Fruit wines are commonly encountered, and some mixed grape and fruit wines are also made. There are even tomato wines! Pure Tennessee grape wines are produced, but authentic is not necessarily superior. The modest wines of Beachhaven Vineyards & Winery are the most successful from this state. I tasted a promising Chambourcin from Beans Creek in 2006.

## TEXAS

The Franciscan missions were making wines here at least 130 years before the first vines were grown in California and the first commercial Texan winery, Vel Verde, was established before the first California one. In 1880, Thomas Volney Munson saved the phylloxera-infected French wine industry by sending Texas rootstock to Charente, and was awarded the French Legion of Honor medal, only the second American recipient at that time (the first being Benjamin Franklin). By 1919 there were 19 wineries in Texas, and a Texas wine won a gold medal at the Paris Exposition that year, but Prohibition destroyed winemaking in Texas, as everywhere else. The revival of Texas wine began by accident in the mid-1950s, when Robert Reed, a professor of viticulture at Texas Tech University, took home some discarded vine cuttings. He planted them in his garden and was astonished at how well they grew. Reed and colleague Clinton McPherson planted an experimental vineyard of 75 grape varieties, which led to the founding of Llano Estacado winery in 1975. In 1987, Cordier, the famous Bordeaux *négociant*, invested in a massive 1,000-acre (405-hectare) vineyard called Ste. Geneviève, and by 2004 there were no fewer than 91 Texan wineries in existence. In 1983 Texas was the smallest wine-producing state in the US; today it is the fifth largest.

### BELL MOUNTAIN AVA

Located in Gillespie County, north of Fredericksburg (another subappellation of the Texas Hill Country AVA), this is a single-winery denomination consisting of some 55 acres (22 hectares) of vines, growing on the southern and southwestern slopes of Bell Mountain. Over a third of the vines are Cabernet Sauvignon, which has so far proved to be significantly better suited to this area than the Pinot Noir,

Sémillon, Riesling, and Chardonnay that also grow here. Bell Mountain is drier than the Pedernales Valley to the south and the Llano Valley to the north, and also cooler due to its elevation and its constant breezes. Its soils are sandy-loam, with light, sandy-clay subsoil.

### ESCONDIDO VALLEY AVA

Proposed by Cordier, the Escondido Valley AVA in Pecos County encompasses the Ste. Geneviève winery. Escondido is an upland valley formed by ranges of mesas to the north and south, the vines growing at an elevation of between 2,600–2,700 feet (795 and 825 meters).

### FREDERICKSBURG AVA

This AVA's full title is "Fredericksburg in the Texas Hill Country," but it is usually shortened to distinguish it from the massive Texas Hill Country appellation. Fredericksburg contained eight vineyards when established, but the area is primarily known for its peach orchards. Since the peach tree has proved as sensitive to soil and climate as *vinifera* vines, many peach farmers have experimented with grapes, and a number of these are now in commercial production. The soil is sandy loam over a mineral-rich reddish clay.

### TEXAS DAVIS MOUNTAIN AVA

Described as a mountain island, this Texas appellation is cooler, twice as wet, and climatically more diverse than the Chihuahua desert that surrounds it. Located in Jeff Davis County, Davis Mountain AVA covers 270,000 acres (108,000 hectares) in the Trans-Pecos region of western Texas that was formed during the glacially slow tectonic and volcanic catastrophe that formed the front range of the Rockies. This viticultural region ranges in height from 4,500–8,300 feet (1,350 to 2,490 meters), with about 50 acres (20 hectares) of vines currently growing on a porous, well-drained soil composed of granitic, porphyritic, and volcanic rocks, as well as limestone.

### TEXAS HIGH PLAINS AVA

This massive appellation in the northwest of Texas covers 12,500 square miles (32,400 square kilometers), encompassing 24 counties and 2,000 acres (800 hectares) of vineyards. Soils are generally brown clay loams to the north and fine sandy loam to the south. Rainfall ranges from 14 inches (36 centimeters) in the west to 20 inches (51 centimeters) in the east.

### TEXAS HILL COUNTRY AVA

A vast appellation, Texas Hill Country consists of the eastern two-thirds of the Edwards Plateau, encompassing two tiny AVAs (Bell Mountain and Fredericksburg), 40 commercial vineyards, and 10 wineries. Most of the hillsides are on limestone, sandstone, or granite, while the valleys contain various sandy or clayey loams.

## UTAH

Despite the enormous influence wielded by the powerful Mormon Church based in Salt Lake City, winemaking has a history in this state, ironically originating with the arrival of the seemingly abstemious Latter-Day Saints. Brigham Young, who led the Mormons to Utah in 1847, ordered vineyards to be planted and a winery to be built. He required one of his followers, an experienced German winemaker, to make as much wine as he could, and although he permitted Mormons to drink it for Communion (no longer allowed), he recommended that the bulk should be sold. His advice was not taken by the Dixie Mormons, who ran the winery and kept back their best wines for consumption. Winemaking peaked at the end of the 19th century, declining once the Church clamped down on drinking, and died out during Prohibition. Eight wineries now exist.

## WISCONSIN

The present-day Wollersheim Winery is the historic site selected by the famous Agoston

Haraszthy to plant his Wisconsin vineyard in the 1840s before moving on to San Diego, after experiencing several years of winter damage on his vines. The Haraszthy vineyard was taken over by Peter Kehl, a German immigrant to the US°, who built the existing winery during the Civil War period. Until relatively recently, this state had a rather more considerable reputation for its cherry, apple, and other fruit wines than for those made from grapes. Fruit wines still dominate in Wisconsin, but grape hybrids are beginning to gain ground, with some *vinifera* varieties, such as Riesling, just starting to emerge. The soils in the region are predominantly clayey loams.

### LAKE WISCONSIN

Wisconsin Lake and River moderate the climate locally, providing winter temperatures that are several degrees higher than those found to the north, south, and west of this region, while the good air circulation helps to prevent both frost and rot.

## WYOMING

Established in 1994, Terry Bison Ranch was this state's first winery, and by 2004 there were just three wineries, but grapes are trucked in from out of state, and true Wyoming wines are all fruit based.

OTHER WINE PRODUCERS OF
# THE UNITED STATES

## ARIZONA
**17 wineries in 2004**

### CALLAGHAN VINEYARDS
**Sonoita**
★ⓥ

Extraordinarily impressive wines have been made here for a number of years, with Syrah a particularly exciting addition to the range.

✓ *Classic red blend* (Back Lot Cuvee) • *Classic white blend* (Lisa's Selection) • *Syrah*

## COLORADO
**54 wineries in 2004**

### MOUNTAIN SPIRIT WINERY
**Salida**
★ⓥ

Grapes are trucked in from the Western Slope vineyards of Colorado.

✓ *Rosé* (Angel Blush)

### PLUM CREEK CELLARS
**Palisade**
★ⓥ

Founded in 1984, Plum Creek Cellars was one of the pioneers of what was then a fledgling Colorado wine industry, and, having won more than 325 medals, it is one of the most successful.

✓ *Cabernet Franc* • *Cabernet Sauvignon* • *Riesling*

## GEORGIA
**17 wineries in 2004**

### CREEKSTONE
**Helen**
★ⓥ

Habersham Winery's new premium label reserved for *vinifera* wines grown primarily in its Mossy Creek vineyard.

✓ *Cabernet Sauvignon* • *Chardonnay* (American Oak) • *Viognier*

### THREE SISTERS VINEYARD
**Dahlonega**
★ⓥ

A promising start from Sharon and Doug Paul, whose winery was opened as recently as 2000.

✓ *Cabernet Franc*

### TIGER MOUNTAIN VINEYARDS
**Tiger**
★ⓥ

In 1995, John and Martha Ezzard planted the All-American Norton and an eclectic bunch of *vinifera* varieties (Cabernet Franc, Malbec, Mourvèdre, Tannat, Tinta Cão, Touriga Nacional, and Viognier) on mineral-rich, well-drained slopes of their 100-acre (40-hectare) farm, at an altitude of 2,000 feet (600 meters) on the southern Blue Ridge Mountains.

✓ *Cabernet Franc*

## HAWAII
**5 wineries in 2004**

### TEDESCHI VINEYARDS
**Maui**

Still and sparkling wines are made here from Carnelian grapes grown on the Maui's volcanic slopes, although three-quarters of the production is pineapple wine. Blanc de Noirs was the first *méthode champenoise* wine and, although I have visited this winery just twice, the wines have been coarse and uninspiring on both occasions. The easy-going rosé-styled Rose Ranch Cuvée proved to be less ambitious, more successful, although I have not tasted it recently. Tedeschi's grape wines are all made from the same variety, Carnelian, but there are vague plans for growing other varieties, so quality may improve.

### VOLCANO WINERY
**Hawaii**
★

Veterinarian Doc McKinney planted this vineyard between two active volcanoes in preparation for his

retirement in 1992, when he "went from working six days a week to seven," as he puts it. Surrounded by continuous volcanic eruption, the winery is prone to acid rain of such a strength that, in years such as 1993, production can be halved.

✓ *Symphony* (Mele)

## ILLINOIS
**62 wineries in 2004**

### ALTO VINEYARDS
**Alto Pass**
★ⓥ

Retired college professor Guy Renzaglia planted Chardonnay and Riesling, as well as hybrids, but the *vinifera* vines did not survive. The Renzaglia family produces a large variety of hybrid wines, and has consistently excelled with Chambourcin and Vidal Blanc.

✓ *Chambourcin* • *Traminette*
**12 wineries in 2004**

### MACKINAW VALLEY VINEYARD
**Mackinaw**
★ⓥ

Established in 1998 by Paul and Jennie Hahn, whose tasting room did not open until 2003, by which time Mackinaw Valley Vineyard was already the fastest-rising star.

✓ *Classic red blend* (Alexander's Conquest)

## KANSAS

### HOLY-FIELD
**Basehor**
★ⓥ

With steadily improving performance over the last 10 years, Holy-Field demonstrates that parts of "fly-over America" are worth a stopover.

✓ *Chambourcin* • *Fortified* (St. Francis Dessert Wine—port style) • *Norton* (Cynthiana) • *Seyval Blanc* • *Vignoles* (Late Harvest)

## KENTUCKY
**31 wineries in 2004**

### CHRISMAN MILL
**Nicholasville**
★ⓥ

Kentucky's best own-grown *vinifera* winery. The First Vineyard Reserve is a thoughtful blend of Chambourcin and Cabernet Franc.

✓ *Cabernet Sauvignon* • *Classic red blend* (First Vineyard Reserve) • *Chambourcin* • *Vidal Blanc*

## MISSOURI
**67 wineries in 2004**

### ADAM PUCHTA
**Hermann**
★ⓥ

Originally established as Adam Puchta & Son Wine Company in 1855, this winery was put out of business during Prohibition, but was resurrected in 1990 by Adam Puchta's great-great-grandson Timothy. Best known for Norton, but probably best at port-style wines, particularly the Signature Port.

✓ *Fortified* (Signature Port, Vintage Port) • *Norton* • *Vignoles*

### AUGUSTA WINERY
**Augusta**
★ⓥ

Impressive Norton, known in this state as Cynthiana.

✓ *Chambourcin* • *Norton* (Cynthiana) • *Vignoles*

### CROWN VALLEY WINERY
**St. Genevieve**
★ⓥ

One of Missouri's fastest-rising stars, this winery was established as recently as 2000 by Joe and Loretta Scott, who planted the first vineyard on their 600-acre (240-hectare) estate in 1998. Crown Valley Winery now has a staggering

165 acres (66 hectares) of vines (Chambourcin, Chardonel, Concord, Frontenac, Norton, Traminette, and Vignoles) with further expansions planned.

✓ *Chambourcin* • *Norton* • *Vignoles*

## HEINRICHAUS
### St. James
★ⓥ

Heinrich and Gina Grohe have been making Missouri wine since 1978, prior to which they grew grapes for other wineries.

✓ *Norton* (Cynthiana)

## HERMANNHOF WINERY
### Hermann
★ⓥ

Purchased in 1978 by the Dierberg family, Hermannhof dates back to 1852, and is today one of Missouri's award-winning wineries.

✓ *Norton* • *Vignoles*

## MONTELLE
### Augusta
★ⓥ

Clayton Byers was one of Missouri's modern-day viticultural pioneers, establishing Montelle in 1970, when he made his first wines in a converted smokehouse.

✓ *Seyval Blanc* • *Vignoles* (Dry)

## MOUNT PLEASANT VINEYARDS
### Augusta
★ⓥ

A 19th-century winery resurrected in 1967 by Lucien Dressel, who in 1980 successfully proposed Augusta as the US's first AVA. This winery produces both Norton and Cynthiana! Wines are also sold under the Bethlehem label.

✓ *Classic red blend* (Claret) • *Fortified* (Vintage Port) • *Norton* • *Seyval Blanc*

## ST. JAMES WINERY
### St. James
★ⓥ

Established in 1970 by the late James Hofherr, one of Missouri's viticultural pioneers.

✓ *Classic white blend* (School House White) • *Norton* • *Vignoles* (Vintage Select)

## STONE HILL WINERY
### Hermann
★ⓥ

Established in 1847, Stone Hill is the oldest winery in Missouri. Its cellars were used as a mushroom farm during Prohibition, but were revived in 1965 by Jim and Betty Held, who flirted briefly with *vinifera* varieties but gave up, and are best for Norton, both as a red wine and a port style.

✓ *Fortified* (Cream Sherry, Port) • *Norton* • *Seyval Blanc* • *Vignoles* (Late Harvest)

# NEBRASKA
### 12 wineries in 2004

## CUTHILLS VINEYARDS
### Pierce
★ⓥ

Ed Swanson chose this location for Nebraska's first winery because of its rolling hills, which he planted with 50-odd varieties of wine grapes, mostly hybrids, in 1985.

✓ *Rosé* (Autumn Blush) • *Traminette*

# NEW MEXICO
### 29 wineries in 2004

## DOMAINE CHEURLIN
### Truth or Consequences
★ⓥ

Established in 1981 by Jacques Cheurlin, whose family makes Champagne in the Aube district. The wines have a fresh, crisp style.

✓ *Sparkling* (New Mexico Brut)

## GRUET
### Albuquerque
★ⓥ

The Gruet family established a cooperative in the Sézanne district of Champagne, but are prone to inconsistency in New Mexico, although some of their best wines have shown extraordinary acidity.

✓ *Sparkling* (Blanc de Blancs, Grande Reserve)

## MILAGRO VINEYARDS
### Corrales
★ⓥ

The Milagro family focuses on Chardonnay, Merlot, and Zinfandel, as these varieties have been the most successful since they first planted these vineyards in 1985.

✓ *Chardonnay* • *Classic red blend* (Carrales Red) • *Merlot*

# NORTH CAROLINA
### 48 wineries in 2004

## BILTMORE ESTATE WINERY
### Asheville
★ⓥ

French grape varieties were planted in 1979 by the grandson of George Washington Vanderbilt, who built the country's largest mansion (250 rooms) on this 8,000-acre (3,200-hectare) estate. At a height of 4,500 feet (1,400 meters) in the Blue Ridge Mountains, it is not only cool enough for *vinifera* varieties to grow, but it can sometimes be too cold for them to ripen. The American appellation on these Biltmore Estate wines is a clue to the grapes that are trucked in from California, and the wines are, I am sure, all the better for it.

✓ *Cabernet Sauvignon* (Signature) • *Sparkling*

# OKLAHOMA
### 23 wineries in 2004

## STONE BLUFF CELLARS
### Haskell
★ⓥ

Bob and Sandy McBratney purchased this property in 1994, but did not open their winery until 2000.

✓ *Classic white blend* (Cheval Blanc) • *Norton* (Cynthiana)

# TEXAS
### 91 wineries in 2004

## CAPROCK
### Lubbock
★

Formerly known as Teysha Cellars, but under new ownership since 1992, when its name was changed to CapRock.

✓ *Cabernet* (Reserve, Royale) • *Chenin Blanc* • *Sauvignon Blanc*

## FALL CREEK VINEYARDS
### Austin
★ⓥ

Named after the waterfall that feeds Lake Buchanan from an upper ridge of Ed Auler's ranch, Fall Creek is planted on land where he once used to raise prize cattle, and has thus been well fertilized for many years. The wines are fruity and quaffable.

✓ *Chenin Blanc*

## FLAT CREEK ESTATE
### Marble Falls
★ⓥ

It was only in 1998 that Rick and Madelyn Naber purchased this property, but they now have 18 acres (7 hectares) under vine in the Texas High Plains AVA, and are racking up the awards.

✓ *Cabernet Sauvignon* (Travis Peak) • *Classic red blend* (Super Texan) • *Muscat* (Moscato d'Arancia)

## LLANO ESTACADO WINERY
### Lubbock
★ⓥ

Llano Estacado Winery is the first Texan winery to be established in recent history. It is best for crisp, lively white wines, but the reds are improving.

✓ *Cabernet Sauvignon* • *Chardonnay* • *Chenin Blanc* • *Classic white blend* (Signature White)

## MESSINA HOF WINE CELLARS
### Bryan
★★ⓥ

Paul Bonnarrigo's family originally came from Messina in Italy, while his wife Merril has a German heritage, hence the name of this winery, the third to be founded in the recent history of Texas wine. Messina Hof can go shoulder-to-shoulder with many a West Coast winery in terms of quality.

✓ *Cabernet Sauvignon* (Barrel Reserve) • *Chardonnay* • *Chenin Blanc* • *Classic red blend* (Meritage Paulo) • *Merlot* (Private Reserve) • *Muscat Canelli* • *Riesling* (Johannisberg) • *Sauvignon Blanc* • *Sémillon*

## PHEASANT RIDGE WINERY
### Lubbock
★ⓥ

Robert Cox of Pheasant Ridge Winery produces one of the state's best red wines.

✓ *Cabernet Sauvignon*

## STE. GENEVIÈVE
### Fort Stockton
★ⓥ

The Ste. Geneviève winery was originally a Franco-Texan venture to cultivate 1,000 acres (400 hectares) of land that was leased from the University of Texas. However, the partnership dissolved and the French partner, Cordier, took full ownership. Much of the production is sold in bulk.

✓ *Cabernet Sauvignon* (Grand Reserve) • *Sauvignon Blanc*

# UTAH
### 8 wineries in 2004

## ARCHES VINEYARD
### Spanish Fork

The most up-and-coming of Utah's wineries.

✓ *Riesling*

# WISCONSIN
### 30 wineries in 2004

## CEDAR CREEK WINERY
### Cedarburg
★ⓥ

An award-winning winery in Wisconsin. And with a winemaker named after a French winepress, it is little wonder that Philippe Coquard is so successful.

✓ *Syrah* • *Vidal Blanc*

## WOLLERSHEIM WINERY INC.
### Prairie du Sac
★ⓥ

The Wollersheim Winery was built in 1858 by the Kehl family, from Nierstein in Germany, and then reestablished in 1972 by Robert and Joann Wollersheim. Both hybrid and *vinifera* grapes are grown here. Wines are also sold under the Domaine du Sac label.

✓ *Classic white blend* (Prairie Fumé) • *Riesling* (Dry) • *Rosé* (Prairie Blush)

# CANADA

*British Columbia hardly figured in Canada's wine industry when I wrote the first edition of this book, and Ontario was only just beginning to emerge. Now Ontario is old hat, and although it still produces more than 80 percent of all Canadian wine and, thus, much of the best, British Columbia is arguably the country's most exciting wine region, and wineries are popping up in Quebec, Saskatchewan, Manitoba, New Brunswick, Nova Scotia... even Newfoundland.*

WINE HAS BEEN commercially produced in Canada since at least 1860. For the first 100 years, Canadian palates preferred the sweet styles produced by the native *labrusca* grape varieties, although from 1913 the Horticultural Research Centre of Ontario at Vineland began its program to develop hybrids.

## ONTARIO

Ask most people, including many Canadians, if they were to trace a finger around a globe at the same latitude as Ontario, where it would point to in Europe, and they would say somewhere in Scandinavia. Some might think the Netherlands or Belgium, but few would imagine Tuscany, which is, in fact, correct. It is only Canada's snowbound winter temperatures that stop Niagara Peninsula, the province's most important viticultural area, from being another California.

At the 1988 launch party of the first edition, I served Inniskillin Pinot Noir and Château des Charmes Cabernet Sauvignon because few knew that

---

## THE VQA SEAL OF QUALITY

After 20 years of following appellation systems around the world, I am aware that none can guarantee quality, but whereas most legally imposed systems indicate mediocrity, the self-regulated VQA seal has driven Canadian producers to higher and higher standards.

***Look for the VQA seal, which guarantees:***
• Provincial appellations, such as Ontario, use 100 percent Canadian-grown grapes, a minimum of 85 percent from the province indicated, and contain a minimum ripeness level.
• Specific appellations (see maps, below and opposite), such as Okanagan Valley, are 100 percent from the province named, a minimum of 85 percent from the area named (95 percent in British Columbia), and contain only classic *vinifera* or preferred hybrid varieties of a minimum ripeness level.
• Estate-bottled wines are 100 percent from grapes owned or controlled by the winery that is specified.
• Wines that are designated by vineyard names are 100 percent from grapes grown in the particular vineyard indicated.

---

CANADA, ONTARIO, *see also p.463*
*There are still some 5,500 acres (2,200 hectares) of* labrusca *in Ontario and most of these vineyards are in the Lake Erie North Shore area, but they can be used only for fruit juice, fortified, and cheap sparkling-wine products. The premium* vinifera *area is the Niagara Peninsula.*

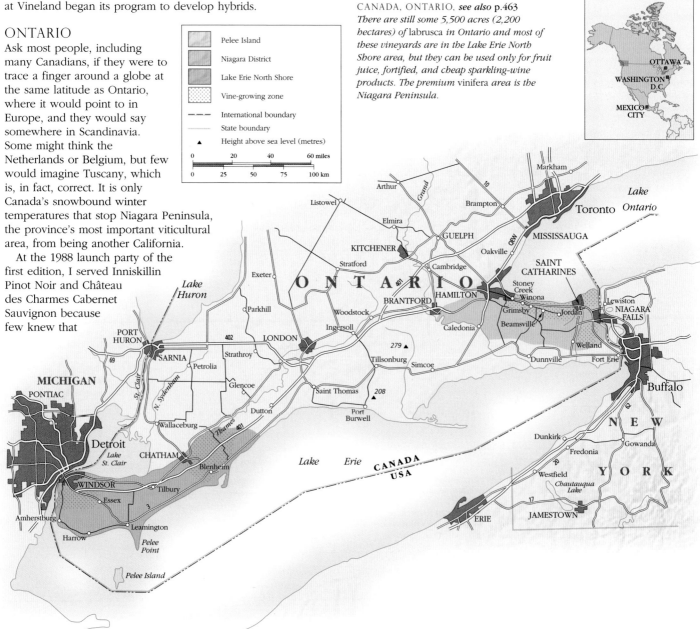

| | |
|---|---|
| | Pelee Island |
| | Niagara District |
| | Lake Erie North Shore |
| | Vine-growing zone |
| --- | International boundary |
| | State boundary |
| ▲ | Height above sea level (metres) |

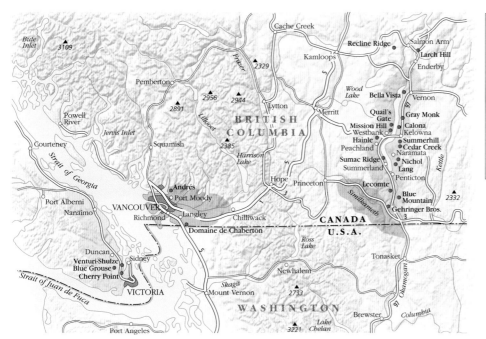

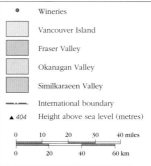

**CANADA, BRITISH COLUMBIA,** *see also* p.463
*British Columbia is rapidly closing the gap with Ontario. When NAFTA gave cheap California wines free access to the Canadian market, both regions had to upgrade their vineyards to survive. British Columbia's advantage was the smaller size of its vineyards and the tiny amount of* labrusca *planted, since this enabled the province rapidly to replace almost all of its hybrids with* vinifera *varieties, while Ontario still has 5,500 acres (2,200 hectares) of* labrusca *and 4,800 acres (2,000 hectares) of hybrids.*

Canada even grew vines,, let alone any of the classic varieties, and certainly no one imagined this country produced red wines. In fact, on my first visit to Niagara, I could find only three red wines made from *vinifera* grapes. Now there are hundreds.

Niagara's flagship wine is Icewine, and it is produced primarily from the Vidal Blanc hybrid, although there are plenty of Riesling Icewines, even Gewürztraminer and, most recently, Cabernet Franc and even sparkling Icewine. Ontario will always be the world's largest producer of this style of wine because the annual winter lows guarantees the process, but it is hardly everyday drinking and, despite the hype, represents only 5 percent of Ontario's total wine production. It might be more productive to focus on the juxtaposition of Ontario's seemingly northern vineyards being on the same latitude as Tuscany. It is no coincidence that Merlot and Cabernet Franc have proved to be among Ontario's most outstanding grapes, and wineries need to get the message across before British Columbia steals all its thunder.

## BRITISH COLUMBIA
The revolution in Ontario's wine industry over the last 10 years has acted like bait, luring British Columbia along the same premium-quality path. As in Ontario, winemaking here dates back to the 1860s, but the climate is more marginal and so the industry has always been smaller and—until recently—less adventurous. Large-scale plantings of *labrusca* varieties did not commence until

## FACTORS AFFECTING TASTE AND QUALITY

### LOCATION
The chief areas are the Niagara Peninsula of Ontario in the east and the Okanagan Valley of British Columbia 2,000 miles (3,200 kilometers) away to the west. Vines also grow in Nova Scotia and Quebec.

### CLIMATE
Eighty-five percent of vines are grown in Ontario at the same latitude as the French vineyards of Provence and the hills of Tuscany. In Ontario, the temperature-moderating influence of Lakes Erie and Ontario, the windbreak effect of the Niagara Escarpment, and the circular airflow from the lakes, protect the vines from winter wind and frost damage.

The Okanagan Valley of British Columbia is on a more northerly latitude, some 49° to 50°N and approximately in line with Champagne and the Rheingau, but the area is technically a desert, with as little as 6 inches (15 centimeters) of rain in the south. The summers have fierce daytime heat that rapidly builds up the grape sugars, followed by cold nights that allow the grapes to retain high acid levels. The glacial Okanagan Lake provides a moderating effect, but winter quickly sets in and grapes do not develop beyond mid-October.

### ASPECT
The vines in both Ontario and British Columbia are mostly grown on lakeside slopes. Those in Ontario are sheltered by the Niagara Escarpment, and the better grape varieties are grown on the steep north-facing slopes.

### SOIL
Ontario soils cover a wide range from sandy loams to gravel, sand, and clay. Soil is sandy loam to clay on the west bank at the centre of British Columbia's Okanagan Valley, but stony-sandy clay on the east bank, more rocky and gravelly to the south, and much lighter and sandier to the north.

### VITICULTURE AND VINIFICATION
The southern, red-wine producing end of the Okanagan Valley is undergoing the most extensive planting in Canada, although Niagara Peninsula's vineyards are still growing rapidly. Ontario's wine industry is mature by Canadian terms, while the smaller British Columbia industry is growing at an even more ferocious rate. The level of technology is high, but as in any young wine industry, methods and practices are changing all the time, as winemakers gain experience. Aside from Icewine production, techniques are in a state of flux.

### GRAPE VARIETIES
Auxerrois, Bacchus, Baco Noir, Cabernet Franc, Cabernet Sauvignon, Chambourcin, Chancellor, Chardonnay, Ehrenfelser, Gamay, Kerner, L'Acadie, Merlot, Pinot Blanc, Pinot Gris, Pinot Noir, Riesling, Sauvignon Blanc, Sémillon, Seyval Blanc, Shiraz, Vidal Blanc, Zweigelt

## RECENT CANADIAN VINTAGES

**2006** The hottest, driest growing season on record, preceded by a devastating frost, produced another great vintage in Ontario, albeit half the normal size and with the added bonus that the Icewines could even be better than in 2005. Great wines were also made across the board in British Columbia.

**2005** Simply sensational for all varieties in both Ontario and British Columbia. The wines show great intensity of fruit balanced by beautiful acids.

**2004** A mixed year for Ontario, where the white wines were excellent but, with the exception of some very good Pinot Noir, the reds were only good to average. Great all around in British Columbia.

**2003** Harsh weather reduced yields in Ontario by as much as half, but harvest conditions were good, and the quality excellent. British Columbia had one of its largest and possibly its greatest-ever vintage.

**2002** Very good-quality red and white wines in Ontario. British Columbia experienced such exceptional quality for both red and white wines that only 2003 vies with it so far.

the 1930s, and hybrids were not developed until the 1950s. The first *vinifera* varieties were planted in 1974, but they were not a significant presence until 1989, when two-thirds of the vineyards—all *labrusca* and the least fashionable hybrids—were transformed.

My first trip to British Columbia was in 1993, when the state of the industry was similar to that of Ontario in the mid- to late 1980s. There were only seven red wines made from premium varietals, although there were plenty made from hybrids. After seeing how rapidly Ontario changed from hybrid to *vinifera* wines, and how quickly this elevated the province's standing in the international wine community, British Columbia's winemakers managed the same transition even more rapidly.

Such has been the rate of progress in British Columbia that Chardonnay is now the only variety widely acknowledged as consistently better in Ontario, although perhaps its Cabernet Franc and Riesling are often hard to beat too. In British Columbia, some locals still love their Ehrenfelser, and although I have tasted some nice examples, it usually makes a lackluster wine, and even the best will mean absolutely nothing to customers outside that province. As for reds, the farther British Columbia pushes its vineyards into the hotter, southern Okanagan region, the greater the potential becomes. Those big southern reds are all the rage now.

# THE APPELLATIONS OF
# CANADA

## FRASER VALLEY VQA
### British Columbia

The Fraser Valley VQA comprises six small farm wineries that harvest hillside vineyards amid country lanes and historic towns, just one hour's drive from Victoria.

## LAKE ERIE
## NORTH SHORE VQA
### Ontario

In the southwest of Ontario, along the shoreline of Lake Erie (the shallowest and warmest of the five Great Lakes), the Lake Erie North Shore VQA has the most hours of sunshine in Canada and the grapes are picked weeks ahead of those of other areas. Its *vinifera* vineyards are just 2 percent of the total vines.

## MANITOBA

Manitoba is the easternmost of the three Prairie Provinces. On comparatively level land, plenty of soft fruits grow wild and abundant in Manitoba's rich soil and hot summers, but midwinter daytimes almost always remain well below freezing, making viticulture extremely difficult. However, some people are trying. Thomas and Ulrich Menold of Tobacco Creek Winery started experimenting with 600 vines, involving 20 varieties, in 2000, although it has yet to come to fruition. Valiant (*Fredonia* x *Wild Montana*) is supposed to be the most likely vine to survive in this province.

## NEW BRUNSWICK

This province is more ciders and fruit-wine country, with schnapps and liqueurs of every kind produced. There are wines made from berries, apples, honey, and maple syrup, not to mention so-called cider and apple "iced" wines. However, wine from New Brunswick grapes has existed since 2000, when Ferme Maury sold its first own-grown products. There are now seven wineries in this province, but none has stood out so far.

## NEWFOUNDLAND

Canada's most easterly province comprises the Island of Newfound and Labrador on the mainland. Viticulture would seem to be impossible in this province, which boasts five wineries, all on Newfoundland itself, and only fruit wines produced.

## NIAGARA PENINSULA VQA
### Ontario

On the south shore of Lake Ontario, Niagara Peninsula is where the lake-induced airflow is at its greatest, making viticulture most suitable, hence the area encompasses 97 percent of Ontario's vineyards. Most vines grow at a height of 300 feet (90 meters) above sea level, as the land gently slopes from the foot of the Niagara Escarpment to the lake. The escarpment rises to over 600 feet (180 meters) and contains a number of benches, about which there is increasing interest, especially in the Beamsville area.

## NOVA SCOTIA

Although the growing season here is short and cool, with very harsh winters, making vinegrowing more an act of faith than the result of hard work, Nova Scotia has had commercial vineyards since 1982 and today boasts 22 growers, who between them farm 400 acres (160 hectares) of vines. The southern tip is actually below the 45th parallel and its vineyards are to be found there, on the west coast, in the Annapolis Valley. The first varieties to show promise in Nova Scotia were French hybrids, such as Baco Noir, Castel, DeChaunac, Léon Millot, Marechal Foch, and Seyval Blanc. Two Russian hybrids, Mischurnitz and Severnyi, which are *Vitis amurensis* crosses, have also been successful early ripeners, with high sugar content and excellent winter hardiness. Another hybrid, L'Acadie, was specifically created for Nova Scotia at Vineland in Ontario. Grand Pré was the first commercial winery, established by the pioneering Roger Dial, and now owned by Jim Landry and Karen Avery, who added Chardonnay to the varieties grown.

## OKANAGAN VALLEY VQA
### British Columbia

The largest, oldest, and most important of BC's wine areas, this stretches 100 miles (160 kilometers), with some 2,400 acres (970 hectares) of vines: more than 96 percent of BC's vineyards. French and German varieties are planted at the northern end, but much activity is focused on the fast-expanding vineyards in the south, which receive less than 6 inches (152 millimeters) of rain and where classic red-wine varieties thrive.

## PELEE ISLAND VQA
### Ontario

This is the site of Canada's first commercial winery, established in 1866. It is located in Lake Erie, 15 miles (24 kilometers) off the mainland, where its 500 acres (200 hectares) are marginally closer to the equator than Rome is. Picking starts at the end of August and even late-harvested grapes are in by mid-October.

## QUEBEC

If Nova Scotia wines seem improbable, then many readers may wonder at the likelihood of vineyards in Quebec, where Arcticlike winters can bring bone-chilling temperatures along with several feet of snow. But it is not the figment of somebody's imagination or a scam to sell wines made from 100 percent imported grapes. Such vineyards do exist. It was here, after all, that the Jesuits, following in the wake of Jacques Cartier, made Canada's first wines circa 1564. But even if Quebec were at the North Pole, one gets the feeling that its French descendants would make an attempt to grow vines. It's in their blood. There are now 30 wineries in this province, all very small, and most located south of Montréal, near to the border with Vermont.

## SASKATCHEWAN

This province covers more than a quarter million square miles, half of which is covered by forest, and one-eighth with nearly 100,000 freshwater lakes. One-third of Saskatchewan is farmland, but while the hot summers provide numerous berry crops for the three local wineries to make fruit wine from, the long, bitterly cold winters make grape-growing seemingly impossible.

## SIMILKAMEEN VALLEY VQA
### British Columbia

To the southwest of the Okanagan Valley, in the high desert cattle country of the Similkameen Valley, Crowsnest Vineyards is leading a small band of pioneering wineries. The vines represent just over 2 percent of BC's vineyards, yet make this the province's second-largest appellation.

## VANCOUVER ISLAND VQA
### British Columbia

The province's newest wine area, Vancouver Island's wet and windy climate might not seem ideal for viticulture, yet Divino moved here from what some considered to be the finest vineyards in the Okanagan Valley. Vancouver Island is the second most important wine area in BC and shortly promises to overtake the Similkameen Valley as second-largest for vineyards.

THE WINE PRODUCERS OF
# CANADA

## BRITISH COLUMBIA

### ANDORA ESTATE
**Cobble Hill**
⭐

An exciting, new boutique winery growing *vinifera* varieties on Vancouver Island.

✓ *Classic red blend* (Vivace) • *Pinot Gris*

### ANDRÉS WINES
**Port Moody**

This is the winery that introduced Canada to the delights of "Baby Duck," a popular and much-imitated sweet pink or red fizzy *labrusca* wine. The original version was known in Germany as "Kalte Ente" or "Cold Duck," and was made from the dregs of both red and white wines, to which some Sekt was added. For anyone not used to foxy-flavored *labrusca* grapes, Andrés's commercial version was even more disgusting than the original concoction, but it took North America by storm. As *vinifera* wines gave Canada a wine industry to be proud of, even Andrés was forced to sell premium varietals. However, it dawned on Andrés that the sort of discerning customer most likely to buy premium varietals would be the least likely to buy from a firm that was synonymous with "Baby Duck." The Peller Estates label (named after Andrew Peller, the founder of Andrés) was thus launched to market exclusively VQA *vinifera* wines, and is a fast-improving winery today (see Peller Estates).

### BLUE MOUNTAIN
**Okanagan Falls**
⭐⭐

Ian Mavety's winery, located in a spectacular wilderness setting overlooking the Vaseux Lake, has come a very long way since 1992. He is a master of Pinot in all three formats, and under the guidance of Raphael Brisbois (formerly at Omar Khayyam in India and Iron Horse in California), he has refined his sparkling wines.

✓ *Pinot Blanc • Pinot Gris • Pinot Noir • Sparkling Wine* (Brut, Brut Rosé)

### BURROWING OWL
**Oliver**
⭐⭐

One of British Columbia's most up-and-coming wineries, Burrowing Owl vineyard lies at the tip of the Sonora Desert, near the north end of Osoyoos Lake, one of Canada's most exciting new wine regions. Improving Cabernet Sauvignon and Syrah should soon join the list of highly recommended wines.

✓ *Chardonnay • Classic red blend* (Meritage) • *Merlot • Pinot Gris*

### CALONA
**Kelowna**
⭐Ⓥ

Calona has been making wine since 1932. Its semisweet German-style Schloss Laderheim became Canada's best-seller in 1981, but Calona's wines improved, although resting on its relatively modest laurels of late.

✓ *Pinot Blanc* (Artist Series Reserve)

### CEDAR CREEK
**Kelowna**
⭐Ⓥ

This winery has come a long way over the last five years, and is now living up to its reputation, yet continues to improve.

✓ *Chardonnay* (Estate Select) • *Classic red blend* (Platinum Reserve) • *Merlot • Pinot Blanc • Pinot Gris • Pinot Noir* (Platinum Reserve) • *Riesling* (Dry)

### DOMAINE COMBRET
**Osoyoos**
⭐Ⓥ

With a reputation for Chardonnay and Cabernet Franc, Combret also produces a very good Gamay.

✓ *Cabernet Franc* (Saint Vincent) • *Chardonnay* (Saint Vincent) • *Gamay* (Reserve)

### DOMAINE DE CHABERTON
**Langley**
⭐Ⓥ

Owner Claude Violet has had winemaking experience in France and Switzerland and was the first to grow grapes in the Fraser Valley.

✓ *Bacchus • Gamay*

### GEHRINGER BROTHERS
**Oliver**
⭐Ⓥ

Gordon and Walter Gehringer's modern winery is tucked into the cleft of a spectacular amphitheater of immaculate vines.

✓ *Classic red blend* (Cabernet Merlot) • *Pinot Gris* (Private Reserve) • *Pinot Noir* (Private Reserve) • *Sauvignon Blanc*

### GRAY MONK CELLARS
**Okanagan Centre**
⭐Ⓥ

Gray Monk has a reputation for Gewürztraminer, but it is not this winery's best wine.

✓ *Pinot Blanc • Pinot Auxerrois* (Odyssey) • *Siegerrebe*

### HAINLE
**Peachland**
○⭐

I cannot fault Tilman Hainle's enthusiasm; he nearly always goes over the top, but can produce wonderfully exciting wines as a result, only to make a complete hash of the same *cuvée* in the following vintage.

✓ *Cabernet Franc • Gewürztraminer • Icewine* (Riesling)

### HAWTHORNE MOUNTAIN VINEYARDS
**Okanagan Falls**
⭐Ⓥ

This winery is owned by Albert and Dixie LeComte, with Dave Carson as winemaker.

✓ *Chardonnay* (Gold Label) • *Classic white blend* (Mountain Select White) • *Icewine* (See Ya Later Ehrenfelser) • *Merlot*

### HILLSIDE
**Penticton**

Vera Klokocka fled Czechoslovakia when the Soviets invaded in 1968. She has been growing grapes since the mid-1970s, and has been making some wonderfully gluggy wines since 1990.

✓ *Cabernet Franc* (CSPC) • *Pinot Blanc*

### INNISKILLIN OKANAGAN
**Oliver**
⭐

Ontario's premier publicist, Don Ziraldo, started making wines in 1994, when his winery became part of Vincor, but did not have his own premises until 1996, when Inniskillin acquired the former Okanagan Vineyards winery.

✓ *Icewine* (Dark Horse Vineyard Riesling) • *Pinot Noir* (Dark Horse Vineyard)

### JACKSON-TRIGGS
**Oliver**
⭐⭐Ⓥ

The original Jackson-Triggs winery started out by building a reputation for Icewine, but soon widened its scope, making it one of the country's top, all-around wine producers.

✓ *Classic red blend* (Proprietor's Grand Reserve: Cabernet-Shiraz, Meritage) • *Icewine* (Proprietor's Grand Reserve Riesling) • *Merlot* (Proprietor's Grand Reserve) • *Shiraz* (Proprietor's Grand Reserve) • *Viognier* (Proprietor's Reserve)

### LAKE BREEZE VINEYARDS
**Naramata**
⭐Ⓥ

Run by a bunch of former bankers and accountants, who now claim to have "dirty fingernails and new calluses." They've certainly got some good wines.

✓ *Chardonnay • Pinot Blanc • Pinot Gris • Sémillon*

### LANG VINEYARDS
**Naramata**
⭐Ⓥ

Owner Guenther Lang left Germany and in 1990 set up Lang Vineyards, the first boutique farm winery in the province, in 1990.

✓ *Maréchal Foch • Pinot Gris • Riesling* (Late Harvest, Reserve)

### MISSION HILL VINEYARDS
**Westbank**
⭐⭐

This operation has won more than its fair share of international medals since New Zealander John Simes took over as winemaker in 1992, including North America's only gold medal at the 2001 Chardonnay du Monde Competition, and being named Winery of the Year at the first ever Canadian Wine Awards..

✓ *Chardonnay* (Estate) • *Classic red blend* (Oculus) • *Merlot • Syrah* (Estate, Shiraz)

### NICHOL VINEYARD
**Naramata**
⭐

Alex and Kathleen Nichol have produced one of the Okanagan Valley's fastest-rising star wineries.

✓ *Cabernet Franc • Pinot Noir • Syrah*

### QUAILS' GATE
**Kelowna**
○⭐⭐Ⓥ

The Stewart family planted its vineyards in the 1960s, but there was an uncertain feel about these wines even until the early 1990s, when the arrival of Australian-born winemaker Jeff Martin rapidly turned the quality around. The current winemaker, Grant Stanley, hails from New Zealand, has an impressive resumé, and since the vintages of the early 2000s, has taken Quails' Gate up to a completely new quality level.

✓ *Cabernet Sauvignon* (Family Reserve) • *Chardonnay* (Family Reserve) • *Chenin*

**INNISKILLIN VINEYARD UNDER SNOW**
*Inniskillin made its first Icewine in 1984, but it was not until 1986 that the technique was perfected and started to attract international interest, which was sealed by the gold medal won at Vinexpo in 1991 for the 1989 Vidal Icewine.*

*Blanc* (Family Reserve) • *Gamay* (Family Reserve) • *Pinot Noir* (Family Reserve)

### SUMAC RIDGE
**Summerland**
★✰♥

Now part of Vincor, although still very much run by one of his former partners, Harry McWatters, and continuing to collect a gaggle of awards whenever the wines are entered into competitions.

☑ *Cabernet Sauvignon* (Black Sage Vineyard) • *Classic red blend* (Cabernet Merlot, Meritage) • *Icewine* (Pinot Blanc) • *Merlot* • *Pinot Blanc* (Reserve)

### SUMMERHILL ESTATE
**Kelowna**
◉✰

Whether the pyramid of Cheops on this property actually focuses pyramid-power is open to question, to put it mildly, but there is no doubt whatsoever that owner Stephen Cipes is eccentric. Famed for the world's only Pyramid-Aged "Champagne," Summerhill is appreciated locally for its Gewürztraminer, although far more consistent for its still wines made from Pinot varieties, particularly Meunier.

☑ *Pinot Blanc* • *Pinot Gris* (Platinum Series) • *Pinot Meunier*

### TOWNSHIP 7 VINEYARDS
**Langley**
★♥

Owners Corey and Gwen Coleman have already grabbed the attention of discerning consumers with their award-winning wines.

☑ *Merlot* (Reserve) • *Syrah*

### VINCOR
**Oliver**

Formerly called Brights-Cartier, this vineyard is the largest wine producer in Canada, owning Le Clos Jordanne, Jackson-Triggs, Inniskillin, Sumac Ridge, and Hawthorne Mountain, with wineries elsewhere, including R. H. Phillips and Hogue (US), Goundrey and Amberley Estate (Australia), and Kim Crawford Wines (New Zealand). Part of Constellation since 2006.

# NOVA SCOTIA

### JOST VINEYARDS
**Malagash**
★♥

When Jost Vineyards 1999 Vidal Icewine was named Canada's Wine of the Year 2000, it was the first time in the competition's 20-year history that the winning wine had come from outside Ontario and British Columbia.

☑ *Fortified* (Port) • *Icewine* (Muscat, Vidal) • *Léon Millot* • *Maréchal Foch* • *Michurinetz* (Premium Oak-Aged) • *Muscat* (Eagle Tree)

# ONTARIO

### 13TH STREET
**Jordan Station**
★✰

Established in 1998 by four friends (Ken Douglas, Gunther Funk, Herb Jacobson, and Irv Willms), who make wines from their own vines (Funk Vineyard, and the warmer Sandstone Vineyard), plus bought-in fruit for wines that are not vineyard-designated.

☑ *Gamay* (Unfiltered) • *Pinot Noir* (Reserve)

### CAVE SPRING CELLARS
**Jordan**
★✰

A large, ambitious venture founded in 1986 by Leonard Penachetti, whose vineyards are located on the Beamsville Bench, west of St. Catharines, and planted at twice the average density for this region. Something of a Chardonnay specialist, producing a rare Chardonnay exclusively from the Musqué clone, although the CSV is clearly the finest and most consistent of Cave Spring's Chardonnays.

☑ *Chardonnay* (CSV, Musqué, Reserve) • *Gamay* (Reserve) • *Icewine* (Riesling) • *Riesling*

### CHÂTEAU DES CHARMES
**St. Davids**
★✰

Established by Paul Bosc and run by his son Paul André, Château des Charmes excels with red-wine styles.

☑ *Cabernet Franc* (St David's Bench Vineyard) • *Chardonnay* (St David's Bench Vineyard) • *Classic red blend* (Equuleus, Paul Bosc Estate Vineyard) • *Icewine* (Riesling)

### LE CLOS JORDANNE
**Jordan**
★★✰

A joint venture between Vincor (now part of Constellation) and Boisset (Burgundy). The single-vineyard wines from Thomas Bachelder's first vintage (2004) are leaps and bounds better than any Pinot Noir produced in Canada up to that date.

☑ *Entire range* (so far!)

### COLIO WINES
**Harrow**
★♥

Colio Wines was founded by a group of Italian businessmen who wanted to import Italian wines from their town of Udine in Friuli-Venezia Giulia, but ultimately found that it was easier to build a winery and make their own.

☑ *Merlot* (CEV) • *Pinot Gris* (HE)

### DANIEL LENKO
**Vineland**
★♥

If you have ever wondered what the same wine tastes like in different oak, Lenko will help you out with its Old Vines Chardonnay, which you can buy in two flavors: American Oak or French Oak.

☑ *Cabernet Franc* • *Chardonnay* • *Merlot* (Old Vines) • *Rosé* (Cabernet Rosé) • *Viognier*

### FLAT ROCKS CELLARS
**Jordan**
★✰

A new winery perched on the brink of 75 acres of rolling vineyard located close to the top-performing Clos de Jordanne. South African Marlize Beyers is the winemaker, with Ann Sperling consulting.

☑ *Chardonnay* • *Pinot Noir* • *Riesling* (Nadia's Vineyard)

### HENRY OF PELHAM
**St. Catharines**
★

Established in 1988 by the Speck family, who have grown grapes in the area since 1974. After an initial period of inconsistency, this winery has settled to a high standard of quality. Hybrid enthusiasts should taste the Baco Noir, which is one of the best in the world.

☑ *Baco Noir* • *Icewine* (Riesling) • *Riesling* (Botrytis Affected) • *Sauvignon Blanc* • *Vidal* (Special Late Harvest)

### HILLEBRAND
**Niagara-on-the-Lake**
✰

Initially called Newark (the original name for Niagara-on-the-Lake), the title of this winery changed when it was purchased by Scholl & Hillebrand of Rüdesheim in 1983 and sold to Andre Wines in 1998. The best Hillebrand wines are not as outstanding as they used to be.

☑ *Chardonnay* (Trius) • *Classic red blend* (Trius)

### INNISKILLIN
**Niagara-on-the-Lake**
★✰♥

Founded by Don Ziraldo, an agronomist and one of Canada's greatest wine publicists, and the winemaker Karl Kaiser, a highly respected oenologist. You could not get two more contrasting characters, but the symbiotic relationship between extrovert Ziraldo and introvert Kaiser was essentially responsible for driving the Canadian wine industry from the backwaters to its present position on the international wine stage.

✓ *Cabernet Franc* (Reserve) • *Cabernet Sauvignon* (Klose Vineyard) • *Chardonnay* (Founder's Reserve, Reserve) • *Icewine* (Riesling) • *Pinot Noir* (Montagu Estate Vineyard, Reserve) • *Riesling* (Dry, Select Late Harvest)

## JACKSON-TRIGGS
### Niagara-on-the-Lake
★

Part of Vincor, Jackson-Triggs' new winery opened in Ontario in 2001, since when it has set new standards for future wineries, but it has not maintained this promise.

✓ *Chardonnay* (Proprietor's Grand Reserve) • *Classic red blend* (Proprietor's Grand Reserve Meritage) • *Icewine* (Proprietor's Grand Reserve: Gewürztraminer, Riesling) • *Riesling* (Delaine Vineyard)

## KONZELMANN
### Niagara-on-the Lake
★ ★ Ⓥ

Established in 1984 by Herbert Konzelmann, who introduced the vertical trellising of vines to Canada. Konzelmann is one of the most modest and gifted winemakers in Ontario and his vineyard has always displayed exceptional potential for Gewürztraminer. These wines sell out quickly every year.

✓ *Chardonnay* (Grand Reserve) • *Classic red blend* (Cabernet Merlot Reserve Unfiltered) • *Icewine* (Vidal) • *Merlot* (Barrel Aged) • *Riesling* (Select Late Harvest) • *Riesling Traminer* (Select Late Harvest)

## LAILEY VINEYARD
### Niagara-on-the-Lake
★ ★

English winemaker and part-owner Derrick Barnett has access to some of Canada's oldest *vinifera* vines, planted by the pioneering Donna Lailey almost 40 years ago.

✓ *Cabernet Sauvignon* • *Chardonnay* (Old Vines) • *Classic red blend* (Cabernet) • *Merlot* • *Pinot Noir*

## LONG DOG WINERY
### Milford
★

The most promising producer in Prince Edward County, Ontario's fastest-rising new wine district.

✓ *Pinot Noir* (The Otto)

## MAGNOTTA WINERY
### Mississauga
★ Ⓥ

This winery has vineyards on the Beamsville Bench, where it sources its top-performing Chardonnay and some interesting, often unusual, Icewine.

✓ *Cabernet Sauvignon* • *Carmenère* • *Chardonnay* • *Icewine* (Cabernet Franc, Riesling)

## MALIVOIRE
### Beamsville
Ⓞ ★ ★ Ⓥ

Owned by Martin Malivoire and Moira Saganski, whose choice of Ann Sperling as winemaker paid dividends in 2004, when she was named Winemaker of the Year at the Ontario Wine Awards (and they had not even entered any wines!). Sperling has since left to start up Southbrook's new winery, leaving her assistant, Shiraz Mottiar, to take over as winemaker.

✓ *Chardonnay* (Moira Vineyard) • *Gewürztraminer* (Moira Vineyard) • *Muscadet* (Estate Melon) • *Pinot Noir* (Estate)

## PELEE ISLAND
### Kingsville, Pelee Island
★

It takes an hour on a ferry to reach this island in Lake Erie, one of Ontario's VQA areas and the location of Canada's most southerly vineyards. With the longest growing season in the country and the warmest climate, it comes as no surprise that Vin Villa, Canada's first commercial winery, was established here in the 1860s.

✓ *Cabernet Franc* • *Icewine* (Cabernet Franc, Vidal) • *Pinot Gris* (Vendange Tardive) • *Riesling* (Late Harvest) • *Rosé* • *Sauvignon Blanc*

## PELLER ESTATES
### Niagara-on-the-Lake
★ Ⓥ

Large, successful, boutique winery owned by Andrés, the second-largest winery in Canada.

✓ *Icewine* (Founder Series Vidal) • *Merlot* (Signature Series Unfiltered)

## PENINSULA RIDGE
### Beamsville
★ ★ Ⓥ

Domaine Laroche's former winemaker Jean-Pierre Colas has very quickly established a reputation at Peninsula Ridge estate, not least for the purity of its stellar quality Chardonnays.

✓ *Chardonnay* (Inox) • *Icewine* (Vidal) • *Merlot* (Reserve)

## PILLITTERI ESTATES WINERY
### Niagara-on-the-Lake
★

The Pillitteri family has been growing grapes on the Niagara Peninsula for more than half a century, and selling wines under their own name since 1993. Although on average Icewine accounts for just 5 percent of Ontario's wine production, at Pillitteri Estates, it represents no less than one-third of its bottled wine.

✓ *Cabernet Franc* (Family Reserve) • *Merlot* (Family Reserve) • *Icewine* (Riesling) •

*Riesling* (Reserve) • *Sparkling* (Riesling Icewine)

## REIF ESTATE WINERY
### Niagara-on-the-Lake
★

Formerly one of Niagara's top wineries, the wines produced by Klaus Reif, just around the corner from Inniskillin, are 100 percent estate bottled and are often *barrique*-influenced.

✓ *Cabernet Sauvignon* (First Growth) • *Classic red blend* (Cabernet Merlot, Meritage) • *Merlot* • *Vidal* (Special Select Late Harvest)

## SOUTHBROOK FARMS
### Niagara-on-the-Lake
★ Ⓥ

Established in 1991, under the auspices of Brian Croser (of Petaluma in Australia), who also acted as consultant for the first vintage that year. The grapes came from Reif vineyard, and Klaus Reif was the winemaker initially. Since then owner Bill Redelmeier has hired Colin Campbell, who is obviously just as talented, from the awards he is picking up. In 2006, Southbrook relocated its winery to a 75-acre vineyard at Niagara-on-the-Lake and appointed Ann Sperling as the new winemaker.

✓ *Cabernet Franc* (Watson Vineyard) • *Cabernet Sauvignon* (Lailey Vineyard) • *Chardonnay* (Triomphe) • *Classic red blend* (Triomphe Cabernet-Merlot)

## STRATUS VINEYARDS
### Niagara-on-the-Lake
★ ★

Wines produced with "the philosophy of *assemblage*" by Loire-born J.L. Groux, in a completely pumpless, state-of-the-art, gravity-fed winery.

✓ *Classic red blend* (Stratus Red) • *Classic white blend* (Stratus White)

## TAWSE WINERY
### Vineland
★ ★

With a snazzy, six-story, state-of-the-art, gravity-fed winery powered by natural geo-thermal energy, Deborah Paskus the winemaker, and Pascal Marchand consulting, the strategy of the Tawse family cannot be faulted. This is the one to watch!

✓ *Chardonnay* • *Pinot Noir*

## VINELAND ESTATES
### Vineland
★

Formerly owned by Herman Weiss, whose family has a winery in the Mosel called St. Urban, Vineland Estates is now owned by Allan Schmidt, whose father had been one of the original partners in Sumac Ridge, while Allan's brother Brian is the winemaker.

✓ *Cabernet Franc* • *Icewine* (Vidal) • *Riesling* (Dry)

# QUEBEC
## CHAPELLE ST AGNÈS
### Sutton Mountains
❓

An exquisite amphitheater of terraced vines, owned by Henrietta Antony and dedicated to dessert wine, Chapelle St. Agnès cropped for the first time in 2003. One to watch.

## VIGNOBLE DIETRICH-JOOS
### Iberville
★ Ⓥ

This winery has won over 100 medals at international wine competitions since it was founded in 1986.

✓ *Cayuga* (Storikengold) • *Classic white blend* (Cuvée Spéciale) • *Icewine* (Sélection Impérial) • *Rosé* (Rosé d'Iberville)

## VIGNOBLE LES CHANTS DE VIGNES
### Magog
★ Ⓥ

One of Quebec's few gold medal winners, even though Vignoble les Chants de Vignes yielded its first crop as recently as 1999.

✓ *Classic red blend* (Le Canon Rouge)

## VIGNOBLE LES PERVENCHES
### Farnham
★ Ⓥ

The only producer of Chardonnay in Quebec, in 2004 Vignoble Les Pervenches became one of Quebec's first wineries to be awarded a gold medal, and won two for good measure.

✓ *Classic red blend* (Cuvée de Montmollin) • *Classic white blend* (Seyval-Chardonnay)

## VIGNOBLE DE L'ORPAILLEUR
### Frelighsburg
★ Ⓥ

Established in 1982, this vineyard produced its first crop in 1985. Since then Vignoble de L'Orpailleur has produced just 15,000 bottles a year, crafted into 10 artisanal cuvées.

✓ *Icewine* (Vendange de Glace) • *Seyval Blanc* (L'Orpailleur Blanc)

---

## OTHER CERTIFIED ORGANIC WINEMAKERS

**British Columbia**
A Very Fine Winery & Buried Treasure Vineyards (Abbotsford)
Beaumont Estate (Kelowna)
Hollywood & Wine (Summerland)
K & V Vineyards (Kelowna)
Knollvine Farm (Peniction)
Park Hill Vineyards (Oliver)
Stony Paradise (Kelowna)
Vispering Vines (Okanagan Falls)

# MEXICO

*The biggest obstacle to Mexico's success as a winemaking country is not its hot climate, nor the feared influx of cheaper American wines, let alone even cheaper Chilean imports, but the absence of wine drinking from the culture of its population.*

IT WAS THE SPANISH who brought wine to Mexico, the oldest wine-producing country in the Americas. By 1521, just one year after invading Mexico, the conquistadors had planted vines and soon afterward they began making wine.

In 1524 Hernán Cortés, the governor of New Spain (Mexico), ordered that all Spanish residents who had been granted land and given Indians for forced labor should annually plant "one thousand vines per hundred Indians" for a period of five years. By 1595 the country was almost self-sufficient in wine, and shipments of domestic Spanish wine had dwindled to such an extent that producers in the home country pressured Philip II into forbidding the planting of further vineyards in the New World.

## THE ORIGINAL "TEQUILA SUNRISE"

When the Spanish encountered a strange, milky-white Aztec "wine" called *pulque*, they were not impressed. However, in a bid to utilize this popular local product, they tried distilling it—the crystal-clear, colorless liquor that resulted was far more to their taste, and was named *tequila*, after *Agave tequilana*, the variety of succulent cactus used to make it (once thought to be part of the lily family). Today, tequila is one of Mexico's most important exports, and vast quantities of *pulque* are still made and consumed by Mexicans.

## MODERN MEXICAN WINE

There are 125,000 acres (50,000 hectares) of vines in Mexico, but almost 40 percent produce table grapes or raisins, and much of the wine produced is distilled into brandy.

It was not long ago that the best Mexican wines tasted little better than *pulque* but, by 1988, when the first edition of this encyclopedia was published, a combination of foreign investment and the demand from tourists for more sophisticated products had already led to significant improvements. At the time, many international oenologists were optimistic about Mexico's future as a producer of good-quality wines, but, unfortunately, although the potential remains the same, a lack of sales on the home market has seen more than half of Mexico's wineries close down. Most Mexicans drink beer or *pulque*, not wine. The consumption of wine *per capita* is less than one-thirtieth of that in the US, and

## MEXICAN LABEL LANGUAGE

Many terms found on Mexican wine labels are the same as, or similar to, those seen on Spanish labels (*see* Spanish Label Language, p.302). Some common terms are listed below:

**VINO TINTO**
Red wine

**VINO BLANCO**
White wine

**VARIEDAD**
Grape variety

**COMBINADOS**
Indicates a blend of different grape varieties.

**CONTENIDO NETO**
Contents

**COSECHAS SELECCIONADAS**
Special blend

**VIÑA**
Vineyard

**ESPUMOSO**
Sparkling

**SECO, EXTRA SECO**
Dry, Extra Dry

**VINO DE MESA**
Table wine

**BODEGA**
Winery

**HECHO EN MÉXICO**
Made in Mexico

## VINE-GROWING AREAS IN MEXICO

| STATE | NOTES |
|---|---|
| Sonora | Abutting Arizona, Sonora is by far the largest grape-growing state in Mexico, but much of the crop is for eating grapes or raisins, and virtually all of the wine grapes harvested go for distillation, although in isolated areas as much as 20–25 percent of the production is used for wine. L. A. Cetto owns 3,950 acres (1,600 hectares) of vines in Sonora. |
| Baja California | Baja California is the largest peninsula in the world, and the northern half, Baja California Norte, produces more than 90 percent of Mexico's wine, although it grows only 20 percent of Mexico's grapes. Indeed, just seven wineries in this state produce almost 80 percent of Mexico's wines. There are main quality districts: Valle de Calafia, Valle de Guadalupe, Ensenada, Tecate, San Antonio de la Minas, Valle de Santó Tomas, San Vincente, and Valle de Mexicali. |
| Aguascalientes | Just 7 percent of the vines yield wine grapes. |
| Zacatecas | Just 7 percent of the vines yield wine grapes, with vines growing on the Altiplano, at an altitude of 7,000 feet (2,000 meters), the highest wine region in Mexico. |
| Coahuila | This state and Durango together form La Laguna region, where three-quarters of the grapes grown are distilled, and much of the rest are table grapes, although quality wines are produced in the Valle de Parras. |
| Chihuahua | More famous for its cheddarlike cheese than wine. |
| Querétaro | Just 7 percent of the vines yield wine grapes, mostly sparkling from Finca Freixenet. |
| Durango | This state and Coahuila together form La Laguna region, where three-quarters of the grapes grown are distilled, and much of the rest are table grapes. |

## FACTORS AFFECTING TASTE AND QUALITY

**LOCATION**
Eight of the country's states grow grapes, from Baja California in the north to San Juan del Rio, just north of Mexico City in the south.

**CLIMATE**
Half of Mexico lies south of the Tropic of Cancer, but altitude moderates the temperature of the vineyards. Most are situated on the high central plateau and some are cooled by the nearby ocean. Principal problems include extreme fluctuation of day and night temperatures, and the fact that most areas have either too little or too much moisture. The dry areas often lack adequate sources of water for irrigation, and the wet districts suffer from too much rain during the growing season.

**ASPECT**
In the states of Aguascalientes, Querétaro, and Zacatecas, vines are grown on flat plateau lands and the sides of small valleys, at altitudes of 5,300 feet (1,600 meters), rising to nearly 7,000 feet (2,100 meters) in Zacatecas State. In Baja California, vines are located in valley and desert areas at much lower altitudes of between 330 and 1,100 feet (100 and 335 meters).

**SOIL**
The soils of Mexico can be divided into two wide-ranging categories: slope or valley soils are thin and low in fertility, while plains soils are of variable depth and

fertility. In the Baja California, the soils range from a poor, alkaline, sandy soil in Mexicali, to a thin spread of volcanic soil, which is intermixed with gravel, sand, and limestone to provide excellent drainage. In Sonora, the soils of Caborca are similar to those found in Mexicali, but those in Hermosillo are very silty and of alluvial origin. The high plains of Zacatecas have mostly volcanic and silty-clay soils. In the Aguascalientes, the soil in both the valley and the plains is of a scarce depth with a thin covering of calcium. The volcanic, calcareous sandy-clay soil in Querétaro has a good depth and drainage and is slightly alkaline, while in La Laguna the silty-sandy alluvium is very alkaline.

**VITICULTURE AND VINIFICATION**
Irrigation is widely practiced in dry areas such as Baja California and Zacatecas. Most wineries are relatively new and staffed by highly trained oenologists.

**GRAPE VARIETIES**
**Primary varieties:** Cabernet Sauvignon, Carignan, Chenin Blanc, Grenache, Mission, Palomino, Riesling, Ruby Cabernet, Sauvignon Blanc, Sémillon, Ugni Blanc, Zinfandel
**Secondary varieties:** Barbera, Cabernet Franc, Chardonnay, Colombard, Malbec, Merlot, Nebbiolo, Petit Sirah, Shiraz, Tempranillo, Viognier

BAJA CALIFORNIA, MEXICO
*Petite Sirah vines basking in the hot midday Mexican sunshine,
with the foothills of the Sierra San Pedro Mártir in the background.*

that in turn is less than one-tenth of the European average. The wine industry in the US is viable only because of the sheer scale of its economy, and the size and affluence of its middle classes, but in Mexico the middle classes are small in number and do not support the local wine industry. As Christopher Fielden put it in *The Wines of Argentina, Chile and Latin America,* "there is no national pride in the product; those who can afford to drink wine generally prefer to drink imported wine." This has been especially so since the North American Free Trade Agreement (NAFTA) and the Mexico-EU Free Trade Agreement (MEFTA), which have gradually lowered duty on imported wine. Imports now represent 60 percent of all the wines sold in Mexico, and this is set to increase. There may, however, be a silver lining in all this foreign infiltration because Mexico's wineries cannot compete in price with American or Chilean cheap wines, thus, they will have to focus on both quality and exports to survive. This will lead to a whittling down of its vineyards, so that in a decade's time, with only the best areas cultivated with site-specific clones, the full potential of Mexico as a wine producer might finally be realized.

## THE WINE PRODUCERS OF
# MEXICO

### BODEGAS DE SANTO TOMAS
Ensenada
★☆Ⓥ

This winery was founded by an Italian goldminer, who sold it to General Rodriguez in 1920. Rodriguez went on to become president of Mexico and the winery passed to Esteban Ferro. The winery now belongs to Elias Pando.

☑ *Cabernet Sauvignon • Classic red blend*
(Duetto, Gran Reserva Unico)

### CASA DE PIEDRA
San Antonio de las Minas
★

Hugo d'Acosta's expressive Tempranillo-Cabernet Sauvignon blend is a real treasure of a find.

☑ *Classic red blend* (Vino de Piedra Tinto)

### CASA MADERO
Monterey
★☆Ⓥ

The second-oldest winery on the continent, comprising 1,000 acres (400 hectares) of vineyards in the Valle de Parras. Flying winemaker John Worontschak has produced clean, easy-drinking wine here for British retailer Marks & Spencer.

☑ *Cabernet Sauvignon* (Gran Reserva Especial)
• *Chardonnay • Chenin Blanc • Classic
red blend* (San Lorenzo) • *Merlot*

### CAVAS VALMAR
Ensenada
☆

Owners Fernando and Yolanda Martain met when they worked together at Bodegas de Santo Tomás before establishing this boutique winery.

☑ *Cabernet Sauvignon*

### CHATEAU CAMOU
Ensenada
★Ⓥ

Owner Ernesto Alvarez-Morphy has *bordelais* aspirations, citing Château Margaux as his inspiration, and employing Bordeaux-trained Victor Torres as the winemaker at his state-of-the-art winery in the heart of the Valle de Guadalupe.

☑ *Classic red blend* (Cabernet Franc-Merlot)
• *Classic white blend* (Gran Vino Blanco)
• *Merlot* (Gran Vino) •

### FREIXENET MEXICO
San Juan del Rio
★Ⓥ

Freixenet was making a fine, light, fresh sparkling wine that was better than most authentic Spanish Cava as early as 1988. Promising developments with still wines, with young, entry-level wines sold under the Dolores Vivante label, and premium quality under the Viña Doña Dolores label.

☑ *Classic red blend* (Viña Doña Dolores
Tinto Gran Reserva) • *Classic white blend*
(Dolores Vivante) • *Sparkling* (Sala Vivé)

### LA CETTO
Tijuana
★Ⓥ

I visited this winery's facility in Mexico City when most of its products were still branded as Domecq and the Cetto wines were unknown internationally. Even back then, the quality here seemed more promising than at other producers.

☑ *Cabernet Sauvignon • Nebbiolo • Petite
Sirah • Zinfandel*

### MOGOR BADAN
Ensenada
☆

This has been dubbed the "virtual winery" because its wines are produced at other wineries.

☑ *Chasselas*

### MONTE XANIC
Ensenada
★☆Ⓥ

Pronounced Sha-nic, Xanic is Cora Indian for "the first bloom after the rain" and it certainly is blossoming well as the finest winery in Mexico.

☑ *Cabernet Sauvignon* (Calixa) • *Classic red
blend* (Cabernet Sauvignon Y Merlot) •
*Chardonnay* (Calixa) • *Classic red blend*
(Gran Ricardo) • *Merlot • Syrah*

### PEDRO DOMECQ
Mexico City
★Ⓥ

This winery's top wine, Château Domecq, produced in Baja California, is still one of Mexico's best Cabernet Sauvignons.

☑ *Chardonnay* (XA) • *Classic red blend*
(Château Domecq)

### VINAS DE LICEAGA
Ensenada
☆

Production began in 1993, but only now is the wine beginning to show promise.

☑ *Merlot* (Gran Reserva)

Other potentially interesting Mexican wineries include: Bodegas San Antonio, Cavas de Valmar, Casa Martell, and Vergel.

# SOUTH AMERICA

*The Spanish introduced viticulture to the Americas: first to Mexico in 1521, and then farther afield as the conquistadors opened up other areas of the southern continent. Relatively recently, Chile stood out for quality, and Argentina for quantity, but a growing number of ultrapremium*

*Argentinian wineries are slowly turning around this supertanker wine-producing country to take on Chile in the quality stakes, while Brazil and Uruguay continue to show some promise.*

SOUTH AMERICA'S WINE INDUSTRIES are inextricably linked to Spain's expansionist policies of the 16th century, although the conquistadors were not primarily concerned with the spread of viticulture. They were in South America to plunder gold for Ferdinand of Spain, and when the Indians grew tired of the colored glass beads traded for their treasures, the conquistadors took what they wanted by more direct and brutal means. In response, the Indians poured molten gold down the throats of captured soldiers, which no doubt quenched the Spanish thirst for the precious metal, but also served as a sardonic retort to the Christian missionaries, who had forced them to drink wine as part of the Sacrament.

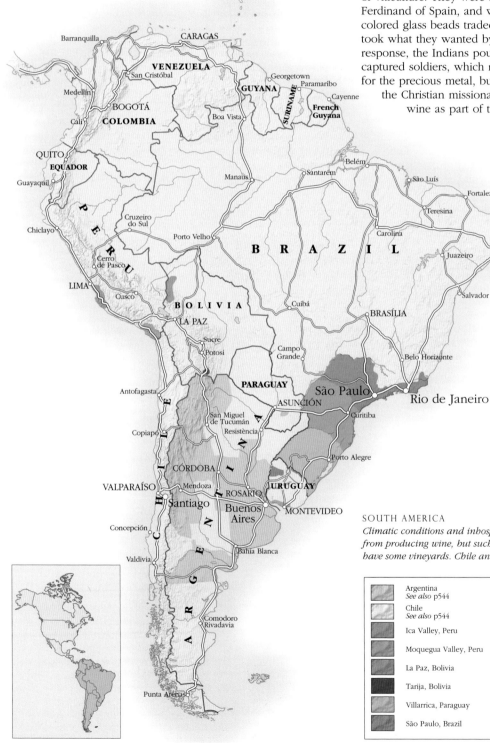

### HARVEST IN THE RIO GRANDE, BRAZIL
*Brazil's largest wine-producing region is Rio Grande do Sul. It borders the Atlantic and stretches down to Uruguay in the south.*

### SOUTH AMERICA
*Climatic conditions and inhospitable terrain prevent much of South America from producing wine, but such is the size of this continent that most countries have some vineyards. Chile and Argentina are the top producers.*

| | |
|---|---|
| Argentina *See also p544* | Santa Catarina, Brazil |
| Chile *See also p544* | Rio Grande do Sul, Brazil |
| Ica Valley, Peru | Salto, Uruguay |
| Moquegua Valley, Peru | Montevideo, Uruguay |
| La Paz, Bolivia | Rivera, Uruguay |
| Tarija, Bolivia | ★ Smaller winemaking areas |
| Villarrica, Paraguay | International boundary |
| São Paulo, Brazil | ▲ Height above sea level (meters) |

0      200      400      600      800 miles

0          400          800          1200 km

In more recent times, it has been the traditional beer-drinking culture of the local populations that has held back the development of South American wines as a whole. This phenomenon has even affected the two major wine-producing countries, Chile and Argentina. Brazil could be leading the way, however, as the switch from beer to wine among the younger generation makes this one of the few countries in the world where wine consumption is actually growing.

VINEYARDS OF SAN PEDRO AT MOLINA, CHILE
*Part of the largest single vineyard in Chile, at Molina in the Curicó district, 125 miles (200 kilometers) south of Santiago, with the Andes in the distance.*

## SOUTH AMERICAN COUNTRIES: AREA UNDER VINE AND YIELD

| COUNTRY | HECTARES | (ACRES) | HECTOLITERS | (CASES) | YIELD |
|---|---|---|---|---|---|
| ARGENTINA | 207,985 | (513,952) | 11,200,000 | (124,000,000) | 54 hl/ha* |
| CHILE | 108,570 | (268,287) | 5,750,000 | (63,900,000) | 53 hl/ha |
| BRAZIL | 80,000 | (148,260) | 4,000,000 | (33,000,000) | 50 hl/ha |
| URUGUAY | 11,000 | (27,181) | 710,000 | (7,900,000) | 65 hl/ha |
| PERU | 10,000 | (24,710) | 80,000 | (900,000) | 8 hl/ha** |
| BOLIVIA | 4,000 | (9,884) | 20,000 | (220,000) | 5 hl/ha** |
| COLOMBIA | 1,500 | (3,706) | | N/A | N/A |
| VENEZUELA | 1,000 | (2,470) | | N/A | N/A |
| ECUADOR | 250 | (618) | | N/A | N/A |
| PARAGUAY | | negligible | | N/A | N/A |

*\*This looks suspiciously low, almost half the expected yield, but the figures come from official statistics for the 2003 harvest.*

*\*\*These anomalies are because nearly all the wine is distilled into aromatic grape-brandy. Discounting this, yields can be as high as 700 cases/acre or 160 hl/ha.*

---

## THE WINE PRODUCERS OF
# SOUTH AMERICA

## BOLIVIA

### LA CONCEPCIÓN
**La Concepción**
★

This was Bolivia's first modern winery in 1978, and it remains the best.

✓ *Cabernet Sauvignon*

## BRAZIL

### AMADEU
**Bento Gonçalves**
★ ✪

An award-winning winery under the guidance of Mario Geisse, formerly of Chandon Brazil.

✓ *Cabernet Sauvignon • Merlot*

### COOPERATIVA VINICOLA AURORA
**Bento Gonçalves**

This cooperative has more than 1,000 members, who between them account for more than one-third of Brazil's vineyards, and supply 95 percent of the country's total wine exports. There are various labels, including Conde Foucolde and Clos de Nobles. Flying winemaker John Worontschak has made several wines here for British supermarkets. This might be Brazil's largest and, in a commercial sense, most successful winery, but in terms of quality this cooperative has the potential to do much better. Chardonnay has been the most consistent performer.

### CHANDON DO BRASIL
**Rio Grande do Sul**
★ ✪

The least impressive of Chandon's far-flung outposts, but at least the sparkling wines are no longer sold shamelessly on the Brazilian market as Champanha.

✓ *Classic red blend* (Grand Philippe) • *Sparkling* (Diamantina)

### LOVARA
**Rio Grande do Sul**
★ ✪

Despite its relatively ancient origins (established by Italian immigrants in the 1870s), Lovara is an up-and-coming winery that has been improving with each year since the 1990s.

✓ *Cabernet Sauvignon • Merlot*

### MIOLO
**Rio Grande do Sul**
★ ✪

Grapegrowers since 1897, the Miolo family built a winery in 1989. Since then their best, medal-winning wines have been some of the most exciting Brazilian wines made.

✓ *Classic red blend* (Lot 43, Quinta do Seival, RAR, Terranova Cabernet Sauvignon-Shiraz)

## ECUADOR
### CHAUPI ESTANCIA WINERY
**Yaruqui**
★ ✪

A boutique winery with 15 acres (6 hectares) of vineyard 25 milesx (25 miles) northeast of Quito, Chaupi Estancia Winery was established in 1989 to grow only *vinifera* grapes. Due to the rarefied altitude (8,100 feet; 2,440 meters) and equatorial latitude, viticulturist and winemaker Dick Handall has been experimenting with 32 different varieties and many styles and combinations of wine, with Chilean Hector Olivares Madrid consulting.

✓ *Palomino*

### VIÑA DAVELOS
**Mira**
❓

A relatively recent development by Uyama Farms, which are 100 miles (160 kilometers) north of Quito, and owned by Mauricio Davalos, a former Minister of Agriculture and ex-President of the Ecuadorian Central Bank. Viña Davelos has 60 acres (24 hectares) of vineyards, both table and wine grapes, located at a height of 6,270 feet (1,890 meters), and were planted between 1995 and 1998. Wine production started in 2003.

## THE LAW THAT NEVER WAS

In 1993 I asked Yves Bénard, then the head of Moët & Chandon in Champagne, how the *champenois* could justify court actions to prevent the use of the name Champagne or Champaña on any sparkling wine produced outside the officially delimited Champagne region, when Moët had been selling South American sparkling wine as Champaña for more than 30 years.

Bénard told me that they had been trying to get the name Champaña banned, but were required by local laws to use the term, and this raised the question of why any Champagne house would set up business in countries that undermined their own appellation. What prompted my original question was that I had been told no such law existed by Trevor Bell, who was managing director of Piper-Heidsieck. I put it to Bénard that as Piper produced Argentinian sparkling wine, Bell should know what he was talking about, and they could not both be right.

Bénard maintained "It is the law. I know, because every time the CIVC (Comité Interprofessionnel du Vin de Champagne) takes a case to court, this very question is always raised by the other side and I am called to give evidence in defense of my company's actions."

I asked Bénard to supply the text of the law he was referring to. He offered a translation used as evidence in a Canadian court, but I insisted on a copy of the law itself in original Spanish for Argentina and Portuguese for Brazil, as they would have to be independently translated if there were to be no question about their interpretation.

This was duly promised, but did not materialize. Eventually I received a letter dated June 25, 1993, admitting that "The law in that country requires that sparkling wine should be specified as either champagne, champaña, vino espumoso, or vino espumante. You should be aware that in Argentina to specify a wine as vino espumoso or vino espumante considerably depreciates the product in the mind of the consumer and nobody uses these terms." Yet this is precisely the argument used by sparkling wine producers worldwide, and the *champenois* take them to court to contest it.

No copy of the Brazil law turned up either, and Moët assured me "production is tiny, less than 200,000 cases, it is not really a problem." Yet when the *champenois* took Thorncroft to court over less than 3,000 cases of nonalcoholic Elderflower Champagne, they claimed it was "the thin-end of the wedge!".

The idea that sparkling wines in Argentina and Brazil must be labeled Champagne or Champaña by law has now been shattered. It is clear that the *champenois* involved were not legally obliged to use the term "Champaña" and the pity is that the court cases won by the *champenois* can now be challenged and, presumably, reversed. On a positive note, it might have taken a decade, but the shame that this publicity brought on the hypocritical Champagne houses involved has eventually forced them to drop all versions of Champagne and Champaña from the labels of their South American bubbly. Something it was not possible to state as recently as 2001 in that year's revise of this encyclopedia.

# PERU

## TACAMA
### Ica
### ★✓♥

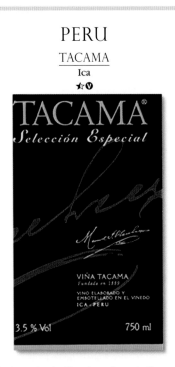

This is the only significant producer in the country and, although the wine is exported, only the Malbec is acceptable by international standards. Other reds are short or bitter, the whites are fresh but uninteresting, and the sparkling wines unpleasantly explosive. Bordeaux professors Peynaud and Ribéreau-Gayon have consulted here, and flying winemaker John Worontschak has made some quaffing wines (Malbec and Chenin) for British supermarkets.

✓ *Classic red blend* (Selección Especial 2000, Vino Tinto) • *Classic white blend* (Blanco de Blancos)

# URUGUAY

## ARIANO
### Las Piedras
### ★✓♥

Established in 1927 by Adelio and Amilcar Ariano, this winery has begun to shine since the 1990s.

✓ *Tannat*

## CASTILLO VIEJO
### San José
### ★✓♥

The winery of Castillo Viejo makes fresh, crisp whites and sharp, fruity reds from a private estate, which is 60 miles (100 kilometers) northwest of Montevideo. Flying winemaker John Worontschak has made wines here under the Pacific Peak label for British supermarket store Tesco.

✓ *Sauvignon Blanc* • *Tannat* (Reserve, Vieja Parcela)

## DE LUCCA
### El Colorado
### ★✓♥

De Lucca is an up-and-coming winery, run by passionate winemaker Reinaldo de Lucca. With vineyards situated 20 miles (30 kilometers) inland from the Atlantic coast, De Lucca is able to grow vines that do very well in Uruguay's relatively mild, maritime climate.

✓ *Classic red blend* (Tannat Syrah) • *Sauvignon Blanc*

## H. STAGNARI
### Canelones
### ★✓♥

Exclusively own-grown wines, with no bought-in fruit, the Tannat in particular benefits from the extremely high density of Stagnari's vineyards, which boast 4,000 vines per acre/10,000 vines per hectare.

✓ *Tannat* (Castel La Puebla Dayman, Stagnari Viejo)

## JUANICO
### Canelones
### ★✓♥

One of Uruguay's fastest-rising wineries, Juanico performs to international standards, thanks to a little help in the past from flying winemaker Peter Bright.

✓ *Chardonnay* (Reserve) • *Classic red blend* (Gran Classic Magrez) • *Classic white blend* (Don Pasqual Chardonnay-Viognier) • *Tannat* (Roble)

## PISANO
### Progreso
### ★✓♥

Established in 1924 by Don Cesare Secundino Pisano, the first generation of his Italian family to be born in Uruguay, the winery is now run by Eduardo Pisano, who has produced some of Uruguay's best wines in recent years. Around half of all the wine produced by this winery is sold abroad.

✓ *Merlot* (RPF) • *Pinot Noir* (RPF) • *Tannat* (RPF)

## TRAVERSA
### Montevideo
### ★✓♥

Carlos Domingo Traversa started off in 1937 as a grower of Isabela and Moscatel vines, and in 1956 he established a small winery, which has just started to blossom under his grandsons, who have produced some of Uruguay's greatest Tannat.

✓ *Tannat* (Gran Reserva, Roble)

# CHILE AND ARGENTINA

*Chile has always been the showcase of South America's wine-producing countries, and Argentina its bottomless vat. Yet a growing number of small, artisanal wineries have shown that Argentina can compete with Chile for quality, if its producers will only reduce their yields.*

## CHILE

The only problem with Chile is that most of its vineyards are in the wrong place. In such a long country it was natural for the population to live in or near the capital of Santiago, and to plant their vineyards thereabouts, especially as the melting snows of the nearby Andes provided an inexhaustible supply of irrigation.

As Chile became South America's best wine region, there was little incentive to look for better viticultural areas in uninhabited, less accessible parts of the country. New areas, such as the Casablanca Valley, are merely the fringe of the country's best wine area, the Secano region, a strip of coastal hills. Here, the cool maritime breezes temper the midday sun and sufficient rainfall permits viticulture without irrigation—if, that is, producers are content with lower yields. Casablanca nudges into the northern end of this future wine area, the greatest potential of which extends as far south as Concepcion. Ironically, the only people with vines here are peasants who cannot afford irrigation (hence its name, Secano, which means "unirrigated") and grow Pais for their own use, but a chainsaw and chip-budding could convert these vineyards overnight, while properly planted ones are laid

CABERNET SAUVIGNON, CHILE
*This Cabernet Sauvignon vine is more than 100 years old and grows on ungrafted roots in the Maipo Valley.*

## FACTORS AFFECTING TASTE AND QUALITY

### LOCATION
In Chile, vines are grown along 800 miles (1,300 kilometers) of Pacific coast and are most concentrated south of Santiago. In Argentina, vines grow mainly in the provinces of Mendoza and San. Juan, east of the Andes foothills, west of Buenos Aires.

### CLIMATE
Extremely variable conditions prevail in Chile, ranging from arid and extremely hot in the north to very wet in the south. The main wine area around Santiago is dry, with 15 inches (38 centimeters) of rain per year, no spring frosts, and clear, sunny skies. The temperature drops substantially at night due to the proximity of the snow-covered peaks of the Andes, enabling the grapes' acidity levels to remain high. Relatively new areas, such as the Casablanca Valley, are proving far more suitable for winegrowing, particularly for white wines, but inevitably the coastal range of hills will be Chile's fine-wine future, since they receive enough rainfall to allow viticulture at modest yields without irrigation. This is the area most affected by the ice-cold Humboldt Current, which supposedly brings a tempering Arctic chill to all Chilean vineyards, but is effectively blocked from flowing elsewhere in Chile by the coastal hills. In Argentina's intensively cultivated Mendoza district, the climate is officially described as continental-semidesertic and has even less rainfall than Chile, a mere 8–10 inches (20–25 centimeters) per year, although this is mercifully spread over the summer growing months, and temperatures range from 50°F (10°C) at night to 104°F (40°C) during the day.

### ASPECT
In both countries, most vines are grown on the flat coastal and valley plains extending into the foothills of the Andes. In Chile, the unirrigated hillside vineyards are found in the Central Zone, although irrigation is widely utilized in other parts of this country. In Argentina, by contrast, the hillside vineyards are usually levelled to a minimal slope in order to allow for more efficient use of water.

### SOIL
Vines are grown on a vast variety of soils in these countries. The deeper limestone soils of some parts of Chile are one reason for the generally better quality of wines from this country, but its most famous attribute is a total absence of phylloxera. In Argentina, the soils range from sandy to clay, with a predominance of deep, loose soils of alluvial and aeolian origin.

### VITICULTURE AND VINIFICATION
With no climatic challenges, Chile is almost uniquely suited to organic or biodynamic viticulture. While Chile uses traditional methods for most of its wines and often uses Bordeaux techniques, Argentina relies more on bulk-production methods, although high-tech methods are also used in Argentina for its growing production of higher-grade premium varietals. Modern equipment, stainless-steel vats, and improved technology are standard in most Chilean wineries today. The "native" Pais grape is banned from the label, but is allowed in wines. Wines are often distilled into pisco, which is Chile's local brandy, as well as Peru's.

### GRAPE VARIETIES
**Chile**
**Primary varieties:** Cabernet Sauvignon, Carmenère, Chardonnay, Merlot, Pinot Noir, Sauvignon Blanc, Syrah
**Secondary varieties:** Cabernet Franc, Carignan, Gewürztraminer, Malbec,Mourvèdre, Pais, Petit Verdot, Riesling, Sangiovese, Sauvignon Gris, Sauvignonasse, Viognier, Zinfandel
**Argentina**
**Primary varieties:** Bonarda, Cabernet Sauvignon, Chardonnay, Chenin Blanc, Malbec, Merlot, Petite Sirah, Sauvignon Blanc, Sémillon, Torrontés, Ugni Blanc
**Secondary varieties:** Barbera, Cabernet Franc, Cereza, Criolla, Greco Nero, Pinot Gris, Pinot Noir, Sangiovese, Sauvignon Gris, Tannat, Tempranillo, Viognier

and, most importantly, roads are built to connect these forgotten areas to the pan-American highway.

### *From red wines to white*
As Chile exported more wine during the 1980s, it became evident that, while it made some really good-value reds, its white wines left much to be desired. In the late 1970s, the quality of Chilean wines greatly improved, with the introduction of temperature-controlled, stainless-steel vats. The early to mid-1980s saw the removal from the winemaking process of *raule* wood, a native

variety of beech, which left a taint in the wines that the Chileans had got used to but that international consumers found unpleasant.

With the introduction of new oak *barriques*, mostly of French origin, the 1989 vintage saw a transformation in the quality of Chardonnay, and with this it was widely imagined that Chile had at long last cracked the secret to successful white-wine production. But it soon became evident that even the best producers could not improve their dismal Sauvignon Blanc. Why was this so?

### Non-existent Sauvignon

When I confronted producers, most confessed that virtually all the wine sold as Chilean Sauvignon Blanc was, in fact, Sauvignonasse. Sauvignonasse literally means "Sauvignon-like", but this variety is not related to Sauvignon and has no Sauvignon character whatsoever. Whenever I tried to get acreage figures for Sauvignon, the Chileans would lump it together with Sauvignonasse and Sémillon, because they seemed to think it was difficult to distinguish these varieties. When I tried to obtain a breakdown of the three varieties, the nearest to a firm figure I could squeeze out of any member of the

Chilean wine trade was at least 12,500 hectares (31,000 acres) of Sauvignonasse, no more than 2,000 hectares (5,000 acres) of Sauvignon Blanc, and between 2,500 and 4,000 hectares (6,000–10,000 acres) of Sémillon. Therefore, there was on average less than 12 per cent Sauvignon Blanc in virtually every supposed Chilean Sauvignon Blanc wine up until at least the early 1990s. Little wonder, then, that Chilean Sauvignon Blancs possessed little varietal character – they contained very little Sauvignon Blanc!

Doubting these statistics, I returned to Chile with the purpose of trying to locate and identify Sauvignon Blanc in its vineyards. I got my first clue to the true state of affairs while visiting Miguel Torres' vineyard at Curicó. He cocked his head and, with a little grin, asked, "So, Tom, tell me how you identify Sauvignon Blanc in the field?". I launched into the differences between the inferior and superior sinuses of the Sauvignon's leaf when compared with those of Sauvignonasse and Sémillon, and, having agreed with the ampelographic points I had churned out, Miguel Torres then set about pointing these out on the vines in front of us – only they were not there. He did not, in fact, have a pure strain of Sauvignon Blanc. We concluded that he probably had a mutated form of Sauvignon Blanc that was crossed with Sémillon. On that trip, I saw Sauvignonasse – lots of it – and what appeared to be mutations or crosses such as Sémillon with Sauvignon, Sauvignonasse with Sauvignon, and Sauvignonasse with Sémillon, but the only place I saw authentic Sauvignon Blanc was at Viña Canepa, and

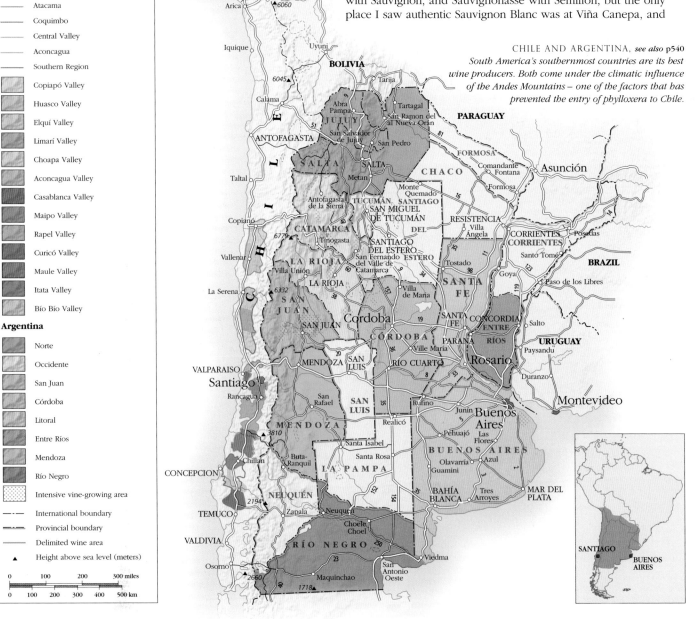

CHILE AND ARGENTINA, *see also* p540
*South America's southernmost countries are its best wine producers. Both come under the climatic influence of the Andes Mountains – one of the factors that has prevented the entry of phylloxera to Chile.*

**Chile**

— Atacama
— Coquimbo
— Central Valley
— Aconcagua
— Southern Region

　Copiapó Valley
　Huasco Valley
　Elquí Valley
　Limarí Valley
　Choapa Valley
　Aconcagua Valley
　Casablanca Valley
　Maipo Valley
　Rapel Valley
　Curicó Valley
　Maule Valley
　Itata Valley
　Bío Bío Valley

**Argentina**

　Norte
　Occidente
　San Juan
　Córdoba
　Litoral
　Entre Ríos
　Mendoza
　Río Negro

　Intensive vine-growing area

—·— International boundary
—··— Provincial boundary
—— Delimited wine area
▲ Height above sea level (meters)

0　100　200　300 miles
0　100　200　300　400　500 km

this was about the only producer engaged in making wine that actually tasted of the variety at that time.

After Chile's non-existent Sauvignon Blanc was exposed in an article in 1991, a number of Chilean wineries commissioned French experts to go through their vineyards with a fine toothcomb. They came to the same conclusion, and since then great swathes of vines have been chip-budded over to true Sauvignon Blanc. In the meantime, however, most wineries tried to make their Sauvignonasse more Sauvignon-like by harvesting early, picking unripe grapes, which resulted in wines that were green and mean. Many such wines still exist, but as the chip-budded vineyards mature, so Chile has begun to produce much better Sauvignon Blanc wines.

### And back to red again

Chile always has been red wine country, and over the last decade a concerted effort has been made to project Carmenère as its own unique variety, but at the moment this variety has a better story to tell than wine to make. Carmenère is a Bordeaux variety, but it had virtually died out over there when it was discovered in Chile, masquerading as Merlot. Here was an almost extinct, ancient *bordelais* grape that had been preserved in its pure, ungrafted format. A virtually unique grape variety of impeccable breeding with which to fly the flag for Chilean wines, unchallenged by major plantings anywhere else. So far, so good, but the wine, although rich, is all too often a one-dimensional parody of overripe blackcurrants. Who wants Chile to become known as the Ribena of the wine world? Not me, but Carmenère does deserve investigating – sifting through the natural clones that exist, testing them in different *terroirs,* and applying more thought to their production than the richness and ripeness that extended hang-time brings.

## ARGENTINA

This is the fifth-largest wine country in the world, and could be a major force in the premium-quality sector, if only its excessive yields could be curbed. While Chile has strengthened its position as South America's premier-quality wine-producing country by significantly reducing yields over the last ten years in order to concentrate on quality, Argentina has done the opposite. On the face of it, Argentina appears to have reduced production by some 10 per cent over the same period, but the fact is it has ripped up a third of its vineyards, thus its yield has actually increased from 66 to 88 hectolitres per hectare (297 to 396 cases per hectare).

Scarce rainfall dictates that Argentina's vineyards must depend on irrigation, but it is so cheap and plentiful that growers simply have to turn on the tap to increase the water supply in order to grow more grapes with which to make more wine, and this has killed the passion for quality among almost all the producers.

Initially, just a few wineries, such as Catena and Weinert, resolutely refused to go down this route, but as soon as they gave global consumers a glimpse of Argentina's true potential quality,

so others saw how much more profitable and prestigious it was to play the international field, and they have followed. However, such is the size of this wine-producing country that it requires an industry-wide change of heart to alter Argentina's image as a bottomless vat. That starts in the vineyards, which will take a generation to bring up to a desirable standard, selecting the right clones of the most appropriate varieties and planting them according to the *terroir* and in much higher densities, trained and pruned for quantity rather than volume. And the entire industry must agree on how to project a coherent, quality image, part of which will be to settle on a flagship variety or style. Malbec appears to be the logical choice. Then they must cooperate on and with major international markets. Until all this happens, even an imperfect Chile will have nothing to fear from Argentina.

### High and mighty

Argentina contains the greatest concentration of high-altitude vineyards in the world. Altitude has become such a status symbol for growers in Mendoza that they almost dare each other to plant slightly higher with each new vineyard, with the best wines boasting their altitude as if it were a *grand cru* classification. Vineyards are commonly found at 900 to 1,050 metres (3,000–3,500 feet), whereas in much of Europe 480 metres (1,600 feet) is considered the upper limit for ripening. Many vineyards have been planted at 1,500 metres (5,000 feet), while Donald Hess, not satisfied with his Colome vineyard at 2,250 metres (7,500 feet), has planted another at 3,000 metres (9,900 feet)! One advantage of growing grapes at such heights is that they benefit from extended hang-time without producing wines that are too big and alcoholic.

---

THE APPELLATIONS OF
# CHILE AND ARGENTINA

## CHILE

### ATACAMA VITICULTURAL REGION

**Wine districts** Copiapó Valley, Huasco Valley

The coastal hills are mountainous and join the Andes, with no central valley. Rainfall is virtually non-existent and viticulture is possible only with irrigation. In certain years, when there is rain, plants and insects awaken and what is one of the most arid deserts in the world suddenly

bursts into multi-coloured bloom. No quality wines are currently made from these vineyards, which produce mostly pisco and table grapes.

### CENTRAL VALLEY VITICULTURAL REGION

**Wine districts** Curicó Valley, Maipo Valley, Maule Valley (Claro Valley, Lontue Valley), Rapel Valley (Colchagua Valley, Cachapoal Valley, Curicó Valley, Tenue Valley)

The oldest, most central, and most traditional

wine region, the Central Valley Viticultural Region contains four wine districts encompassing seven wine areas. The Curicó Valley is situated 200 kilometres (120 miles) south of Santiago, and is home to such brand leaders as Caliterra, Montes, Torres, and Valdivieso. Curicó is known principally for Chardonnay, but also produces fine Cabernet Sauvignon, Merlot, and Pinot Noir. The Maipo Valley around Santiago itself is still the country's most intensively cultivated district and therefore its most famous wine appellation. It is one of the warmest growing districts in the

entrepreneur Eduardo Matte and Antinori of Tuscany. Located on Matte's stud farm in the Andean foothills, overlooking the Maipo Valley, Haras de Pirque is one of Chile's fastest-rising stars. Unlike some of this country's recently established boutique wineries, which are destined to go bust or be taken over, this operation exudes permanency.

✓ *Chardonnay* (Haras Character) • *Syrah* (Haras Character)

## LA FORTUNA
### Lontue
★

The Güell family has owned this winery for more than 50 years, but it has been seriously involved in export markets only since the mid-1990s. Winemaker Claudio Barrio has made some appallingly green Sauvignon Blanc (particularly in 1996), but consistently produces lovely, soft, violety-cherry Malbec.

✓ *Malbec*

## LA ROSA
### Cachapoal
★★✓

A 1,200-acre (500-hectare) vineyard and six-million-dollar winery owned by SOFRUCO, one of Chile's largest fruit producers.

✓ *Cabernet Sauvignon* • *Chardonnay* • *Merlot*

## LEYDA
### Leyda
★✓

This up-and-coming winery is proving that the Leyda Valley can produce some of Chile's fruitiest wines, especially Pinot Noir.

✓ *Pinot Noir* (Las Brisas Vineyard)

## LUIS FELIPE
### Colchagua
★★✓

These mature vineyards produce stunning-value Cabernet Sauvignon and deliciously ripe, tropical fruit-flavored Chardonnay. Part organic.

✓ *Cabernet Sauvignon* (especially Reserva) • *Chardonnay*

## MIGUEL TORRES
### Curicó
★★★✓

The reds produced by Spain's most innovative winemaker are often misunderstood, particularly in Chile itself, where their slow-evolving style is swamped by the immediacy of more flashy, up-front winemaking methods. Part organic.

✓ *Cabernet Sauvignon* (Manso de Velasco) • *Carignan* (Cordillera) • *Chardonnay* (Maquehua)

## MONTES
### Curicó
★★

The brainchild of Aurelio Montes, these wines started out as far too

oaky for all but lovers of two-by-fours. Their production has now moved from a heavy-handed use of primarily American oak to a more restrained application of French oak. Montes also makes some deliciously fruity unoaked wines. Part organic.

✓ *Cabernet Sauvignon* • *Chardonnay* • *Malbec* • *Merlot* • *Syrah* (Folly)

## MONTGRAS
### Colchagua
★★✓

Exciting quality from strict selection of 600 acres (250 hectares) of vineyards, made in a $15 million winery. Part organic.

✓ *Cabernet Sauvignon* (Ninquén Reserva) • *Classic red blend* (Ninquén Cabernet Merlot)

## PÉREZ CRUZ
### Paine
★★✓

Low-yield vineyards and well-ripened fruit are responsible for the intensity of flavor in this winery's Malbec.

✓ *Malbec* (Cot Reserva Limited Edition)

## SAN PEDRO
### Molina
★★✓

The wines of San Pedro, one of the pioneers that earned respect for Chilean wines on export markets, went through a patchy period, but are emerging better than before, thanks to an expensive ultramodern winery and consultancy from flying winemaker Jacques Lurton. Wines are also sold under the penny-saving Gato Blanco and Gato Negro brands. Santa Helena is an export brand.

✓ *Chardonnay* (Castillo de Molina Reserva)

## SANTA CAROLINA
### Santiago
★✓

Fresh, crisp, fruity whites are the best value here, although the reds are definitely the best quality. Santa Carolina owns Viña Casablanca.

✓ *Classic red blend* (VSC) • *Merlot* • *Sauvignon Blanc* • *Syrah*

## SANTA INÉS
### Isla de Maipo
◉

This small, quality-minded winery is owned by the De Martino family.

✓ *Carmenère*

## SANTA MONICA
### Rancagua
★

Owner-winemaker Emilio de Solminihac (a partner in Domaine Paul Bruno) makes wines with a fat, fruity style at his own winery.

✓ *Sauvignon Blanc*

## SANTA RITA
### Santiago
★★✓

These wines are fatter and riper than they have been in years, but the "120" range (so-called because Bernardo O'Higgins, the liberator of Chile, and his 120 men hid in these cellars after the battle of Rancagua in 1810) has remained reliable throughout. Santa Rita also owns the Carmen winery, and has a partnership with Lafite-Rothschild in Los Vascos.

✓ *Cabernet Sauvignon* ("120," Casa Real) • *Classic red blend* (Triple C) • *Sauvignon Blanc* (Casa Real) • *Merlot* (Medalla Real, Casablanca, Reserve)

## SEÑA
### Panquehue
★★

A joint-venture between Errázuriz and Robert Mondavi in 1996, Seña had established itself as one of Chile's *grands crus* when Errázuriz purchased Mondavi's share immediately prior to its takeover by Constellation Brands in 2004.

✓ *Classic red blend* (Seña)

## TERRANOBLE
### Talca
★

With Henri Marionnet, one of Touraine's best winemakers, consulting, Terranoble has fashioned an increasingly fine line of red wines.

✓ *Cabernet Sauvignon* • *Carmenère* (Reserva)

## UNDURRAGA
### Santiago
◉

This was the first Chilean winery to export to the US, and only remains in this encyclopedia for historic reasons, as I have seldom found any exciting wines from Undurraga. Having embarked upon a 1.5-million-dollar renovation and replanting program in 1997, it was hoped that this might bring about welcome changes for Undurraga's quality, but only the Late-Harvest Sémillon is recommendable, and even that could be an anomaly.

✓ *Sémillon* (Late Harvest)

## VALDIVIESO
### Santiago
★★✓

Originally called Champagne Alberto Valdivieso, this company still produces large quantities of ordinary Chilean fizz, but has moved into pure varietal, barrel-fermented table wines in a spectacularly successful fashion. Loco is Valdivieso's top-of-the-line red, a blend of different grape varieties from various vintages. To distinguish which batch is which (and to enable wine enthusiasts to cellar and follow the wines), they are numbered. I have tasted only Caballo Loco Number One, but it is

such a masterly wine that I have no hesitation ranking it as one of South America's finest wines. Cheaper wines are sold under the Casa label.

✓ *Caballo Loco* • *Cabernet Franc* • *Merlot* • *Pinot Noir*

## VILLARD
### Casablanca
★

This is a partnership between Thierry Villard (who in 1989 produced what was probably the first truly fine Chilean Chardonnay—Santa Emiliana—which is owned by Concha y Toro) and two growers, one of whom, Pablo Morandé, is Concha y Toro's winemaker.

✓ *Cabernet Sauvignon* • *Merlot* • *Pinot Noir*

## VIU MANENT
### Molina
★★✓

An old, established, family-owned winery that has moved away from bulk wines into more expressive, high-quality wines under its own label.

✓ *Cabernet Sauvignon* (Reserve) • *Malbec* (Single Vineyard)

# ARGENTINA
## ARCHÁVAL FERRER
### Luján de Cuyo
★★

Established as recently as 1998, low-yield vineyards and a dedication to quality have made this one of Argentina's fastest-rising, highest-flying wineries.

✓ *Classic red blend* (Quimera) • *Malbec* (Finca Altamira)

## ALTOS LAS HORMIGAS
### Cuidad
★★★

This vineyard was destroyed by a plague of ants (*hormigas*), hence its name, and had to purchase grapes until a new vineyard came into production.

✓ *Malbec*

## BODEGAS LOPEZ
### Buenos Aires
★

This family firm produces average-quality wines under the Château Montchenot label (known as Don Federico on some export markets).

## BODEGAS LURTON
### Buenos Aires
★

The Lurtons of Bordeaux originally came to Chile as flying winemakers for the British supermarket chain Tesco, but liked the potential so much that, together with the omnipresent Nicolas Catena, they purchased their own winery and are now firmly ensconced.

✓ *Malbec*

## BODEGAS NACARI
**La Rioja**

This small cooperative specializes in Torrontes.

## CATENA
**Córdoba**
★★

Argentina's greatest wine visionary, Nicolás Catena has produced some superb wines with the aid of his California winemaker Paul Hobbs, who helped to establish the Opus One winery before going to Argentina. Nicolas Catena Zapata is very much upmarket by local standards, while Caro is produced in conjunction with the Rothschilds of Château Lafite. Catena Alta are fine wines by any standard, and the basic Catena line is stylish, and far from basic. I should recommend the entire line, but have plucked out the very best below. Superb-value fine wines are also sold under the Alamos Ridge, Bodegas Esmerelda, and Libertad labels. Catena also owns Bodegas La Rural, and Cavas de Santa Maria. *See also* Luca and Tikal.

↳✓ *Cabernet Sauvignon* (Catena Alta) • *Chardonnay* (Catena Alta) • *Classic red blend* (Caro, Nicolás Catena Zapata) • *Malbec* (Catena Alta)

## CHANDON ARGENTINA
**Buenos Aires**

This long-established arm of Moët & Chandon makes mostly sparkling wines, which used to be sold shamelessly as Champaña, under the M Chandon and Baron B labels. The quality is fresh, clean, acceptable, and improving, but not special. More interesting is the increasing amount of good and improving still wine now being made with an eye on export markets (*see* Terrazas de Los Andes).

## CLOS DE LOS SIETE
**Tunuyán**
★

Tipped by some as potentially Argentina's greatest winery, Clos de los Siete is an ambitious project headed by Michel Rolland. The venture comprises of seven vineyards owned by seven French proprietors, who are expected to produce their own distinct wines within due course (look out for the

single vineyard names of Altamira, Lindaflor, Los Dassos, Miraflor, Primaflor, Rocaflor, and Monteviejo). Some critics claim that one investor has already backed out, and the scope of such a project will probably see others jumping ship before long. One partner, the late Jean-Michel Arcaute, tragically died before the first vintage (2002) was produced.

↳✓ *Classic red blend* (Clos de los Siete)

## COLOME
**Colome**
Ⓑ★★

This winery boasts the highest vineyards in the world, and Caifornia owners Hess Collection stand every chance of making Argentina's highest-quality wines here. Deliciously fruity, entry-level wines are sold under the Amalaya label.

↳✓ *Classic red blend* (Colme Estate)

## DOMINO DEL PLATA
**Luján de Cuyo**
★✪Ⓥ

One of Argentina's most exciting new wineries, Domino del Plata is owned by husband-and-wife team Pedro Marchevsky, the viticulturist, and Susana Balbo, the winemaker. The best wines are sold under the Susana Balbo and BenMarco labels, while excellent-value wines are sold in the Crios de Susana Balbo range.

↳✓ *Classic red blend* (Crios de Susana Balbo Syrah-Bonarda, BenMarco VMS) • *Malbec* (BenMarco)

## ETCHART
**Salta**
★✪Ⓥ

The very fresh, crisp, and dry Cafayate Torrontes, with its subtle, Muscat-like aromas, is a yardstick for this peculiarly Argentinian variety, but Cabernet Sauvignon is by far the best wine here. Etchart is now fully owned by Pernod-Ricard, with Michel Rolland consulting.

↳✓ *Cabernet Sauvignon* • *Torrontes* (Cafayate)

## FINCA LA ANITA
**Luján de Cuyo**
★✪Ⓥ

Established in 1992 by Antonio Mas, who has attained a very high quality, and continues to improve.

↳✓ *Malbec* • *Sémillon* • *Syrah* • *Tocai Friulano*

## FINCA FLICHMAN
**Mendoza**
✪

After considerable investment in stainless-steel vats and new French oak *barriques*, plus a certain amount of European technical assistance, the quality as well as quantity has increased. Furthermore, emphasis has moved to Latin grape

varieties such Barbera, Sangiovese, and Tempranillo, as the choice for blending with local favorites such as Malbec, Cabernet, and Merlot.

↳✓ *Cabernet Sauvignon* (Caballero de la Cepa) • *Sangiovese-Malbec* • *Syrah*

## HUMBERTO CANALE
**Rio Negro**
★Ⓥ

These are interesting, improving varietal wines from some of the most southerly vineyards in the world.

↳✓ *Malbec* • *Merlot* • *Pinot Noir*

## LUCA
**Mendoza**
★★

Stunning wines produced by Nicolas Catena's daughter Laura at her own winery, from her own vineyard, with typically Catena-like low yields and high altitude.

↳✓ *Cabernet Sauvignon* • *Chardonnay* • *Syrah*

## NORTON
**Buenos Aires**
✪

Although this firm dates back to 1895, it was not until 1989, when Austrian businessman Gernot Langes-Swarovski purchased the winery from its uninspiring English owners, that these wines started to show their true potential. Sangiovese and Barbera are the most interesting but, regrettably, the most variable as well.

↳✓ *Classic red blend* (Privada) • *Malbec*

## PEÑAFLOR
**Buenos Aires**
★Ⓥ

The quality here has been greatly improved in recent years by a magnum of flying winemakers, in the form of Peter Bright and John Worontschak. The Country Red is a cheap and cheerful blend. Peñaflor also sells wines under the Andean Vineyards, Fond de Cave, Parral, Tio Quinto, and Trapiche labels. *See also* Trapiche.

↳✓ *Classic red blend* (Cabernet-Malbec) • *Torrontes* • *Tempranillo*

## PIPER
**Buenos Aires**

When Englishman Trevor Bell was managing Charles Heidsieck and Piper-Heidsieck in France, he blew the whistle on those Champagne houses—including his own—that claimed they were forced by Argentinian law to use the word "Champaña" on their Argentinian sparkling wines. He considered it hypocritical and said that Piper for one would stop the practice. Bell was never heard of again. This is the only Champagne name that is still prostituting itself. Rémy-Cointreau, the owner of these two

Champagne houses, claims that it is not its responsibility, since it does not actually produce the wine. However, the company does admit to owning the brand, and licensing it out, which is just as reprehensible.

## SAN PEDRO DE YACOCHUYA
**Maipú**
★★✪

A joint venture between Michel Rolland and the Etchart family.

↳✓ *Malbec* (Yacochuya)

## TERRAZAS DE LOS ANDES
**Luján de Cuyo**
★✪Ⓥ

These still wines of Chandon Argentina are vastly superior to its sparkling wines.

↳✓ *Cabernet Sauvignon* (Gran Reserva) • *Classic red blend* (Cheval des Andes) • *Malbec* (Gran Reserva)

## TIKAL
**Mendoza**
★★

This winery and vineyard is owned by Ernest Catena, son of the famous Nicolas Catena.

↳✓ *Classic red blend* (Corazon, Júbilo) • *Malbec* (Altos de Mendoza Amorío)

## TRAPICHE
**Buenos Aires**
★✪Ⓥ

Part of Peñaflor, the quality of Trapiche has risen steadily in recent years. Michel Rolland consults. *See also* Peñaflor.

↳✓ *Cabernet Sauvignon* (Medalla) • *Classic red blend* (Iscay) • *Malbec* (Broquel) • *Syrah* (Oak Cask)

## VISTALBA
**Mendoza**
✪

This up-and-coming winery makes interesting reds from varieties such as Barbera and Syrah to complement Argentinian faithfuls such as Cabernet and Malbec.

↳✓ *Cabernet Sauvignon* • *Malbec* • *Syrah*

## WEINERT
**Buenos Aires**
★★

Although established as long ago as 1890, this winery emerged as one of Argentina's top two producers only under the present owner, Brazilian-born Bernardo Weinert. He renovated the winery in 1975 and shortly after became the first Argentinian producer to reduce yields in order to raise quality, inspiring others to follow.

↳✓ *Cabernet Sauvignon* • *Classic red blend* (Cavas de Weinert) • *Malbec*

# The WINES of
# AUSTRALIA, NEW ZEALAND, AND ASIA

WE TEND TO THINK OF AUSTRALIA AS THE older, more traditional winemaking country, with New Zealand being a much more recent phenomenon. Yet, just a 30-year gap separates the viticultural origins of these two countries. Australia's wine industry dates back to 1788, but New Zealand's started not much later, in 1819. In modern terms, they are just 10 years apart, Australia having won its spurs in the 1980s, with New Zealand assuming classic status in the 1990s. Australia is famous for its big, creamy-mellow, spicy-cedary Shiraz, while New Zealand leads with its fresh, crisp, exhilarating Sauvignon Blanc—but these are just the flagships. Both countries produce a large and diverse range of wine styles and are currently discovering a wealth of *terroirs* and the differences in expression that they bring. In Asia, Japan and China continue to dominate; India is treading water; and we are starting to see wines from Thailand, Korea, and even Bali.

HENSCHKE'S HILL OF GRACE VINEYARD, EDEN VALLEY
*This old Australian vineyard dates back to the 1860s. The Church of Gnadenberg can be seen in the background.*

# AUSTRALIA

*Having built its name on the consistent quality of its high-volume brands, which have been aggressively marketed through multibottle discount deals, "Brand Australia" has grown into the biggest success story in modern wine history. Yet some producers are beginning to wonder whether they will ever sell their wines for what they are really worth—rather than giving them away.*

IF ONLY THE AUSTRALIANS WERE as insecure and indecisive as this on the cricket field! They need not worry, however, since all the evidence suggests that their position will be consolidated over the medium term. The alarms are false, and merely the result of mixed messages generated by the two basic types of wine produced: brands and site-specific wines. It is no accident that the public perception of Australian wine is so dependent on the concept of branded wine. Australian brands have always been strong, but in 1996 their position was

formally promoted by the industry's 30-year plan to become the "world's most influential and profitable supplier of branded wines." Most people reading this for the first time will ask themselves why the word "branded" was inserted, and who could be the author of such a biased quest?

Australian brands have been criticized as overripe, over-alcoholic, formulaic wines that have no soul. Perhaps. However, the fact that so many might taste very similar is in itself an indication of their very consistent quality. They might not exude individuality, and wine lovers might wonder why this commercial category of wine has been singled out for official blessing in the 30-year plan, but Australia's branded wines are made in a soft, rich, consumer-friendly, fruit-driven style. They are nothing more than the equivalent of branded generic wines from, say, Bordeaux or Beaujolais, but infinitely more enjoyable. Certainly consumers think so. By 2003 Australia had become the second-largest exporter of wine to the US, and had even pushed out France from the number one position on the UK market.

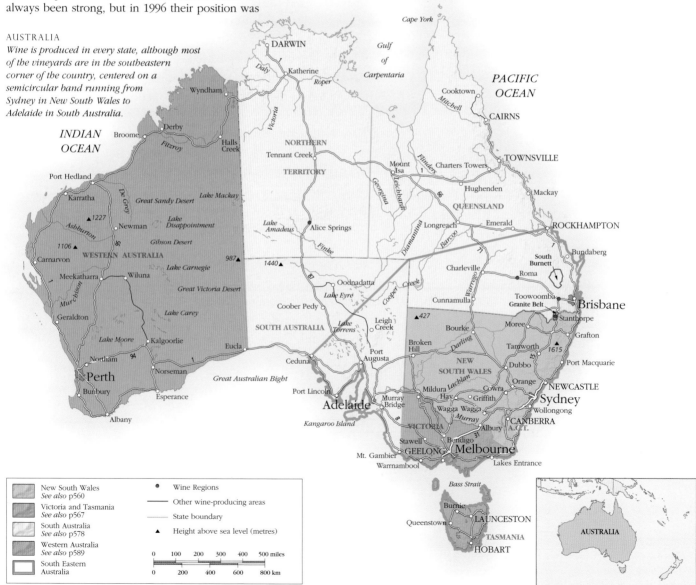

AUSTRALIA
*Wine is produced in every state, although most of the vineyards are in the southeastern corner of the country, centered on a semicircular band running from Sydney in New South Wales to Adelaide in South Australia.*

| | Wine Regions |
|---|---|
| | New South Wales *See also p560* |
| | Victoria and Tasmania *See also p567* |
| | South Australia *See also p578* |
| | Western Australia *See also p589* |
| | South Eastern Australia |

● Wine Regions
— Other wine-producing areas
State boundary
▲ Height above sea level (metres)

0   100   200   300   400   500 miles
0   200   400   600   800 km

While it might not seem so surprising that an up-and-coming wine country like Australia should appeal more to consumers, particularly younger ones, than an old and traditional producer such as France, it is an extraordinary feat considering the contrasting size of these two wine industries. France is nothing less than the largest wine producer in the world, responsible for 21 percent of global production, whereas Australia is a minnow, accounting for less than 4 percent. How on earth did the Aussies manage to pull this off?

## THE EXPORT TRAP
Did Australia achieve its export victories because its brands were sold at economically unsustainable prices, as some now fear? No. How could this be true when the country's largest wine groups have made handsome profits in the process? There has been much talk about falling sales, reduced profit margins, and ailing wine companies, but Australia did not achieve success overnight or, indeed, over just one year, and those ailing companies were all extremely profitable on the way up.

It is evident, therefore, that Australia's brands were not undersold, but if the industry is worried that there is a perception that its wines are too cheap, then it should ask itself a few questions. Should Australia concentrate its exports so heavily on two countries, the UK and the US, which between them take over 70 percent of all Australian wine exports? And should not the industry change its 30-year plan to become the "world's most influential and profitable supplier of geographically distinct wines"? There is nothing wrong with multistate blends, such as the all-encompassing Southeastern Australian appellation, which straddles 95 percent of the country's vineyards; but for their own sake, brand owners should concentrate less on such wines, and more on expressing some level of individuality.

## THE GROWTH OF AUSTRALIA'S WINE INDUSTRY
The first Australian vineyard was planted at Farm Cove in New South Wales in 1788, with vines originating not from France but from Rio de Janeiro and the Cape of Good Hope. These were collected by the first governor, Captain Arthur Phillip, *en route* to Sydney. The rich soil of Farm Cove and its humid climate proved fine for growing vines, but not for making wine. Phillip persevered, however, and planted another vineyard in Parramatta, just north of Sydney. Soil and climate were more suitable and the success of this new venture encouraged Phillip's official requests for technical assistance. England responded by sending out two French prisoners of war, who were offered their freedom in exchange for three years' service in New South Wales, in the belief that all Frenchmen knew something about making wine. This did not prove true: one was so bad at it that he was transported back to England; the other could make only cider, and mistakenly used peaches instead of apples! From these shaky beginnings an industry grew, but with no thanks to the British. At first, Australia's wine industry was monopolized by the needs of the British Empire, later the Commonwealth. It thus gained a reputation for cheap fortified wines—not because these were the only ones it could make, but because Britain wanted them. Unfortunately, Australians also acquired the taste. Although Australia made (and still makes) some of the world's finest dessert wines (botrytized as well as fortified), most wines were heavy, very sweet, and sluggish at a time when the rest of the world was drinking lighter and finer wines. Small quantities of truly fine table wine were produced but, until the 1960s, most of those exported were remarkably uniform in style.

## THE RENAISSANCE OF AUSTRALIAN WINES
Over the last 40 years, the technology used in Australian winemaking has made huge advances, taking with it the quality of the wines. Until the early 1980s, as much as 99 percent of all

CORIOLE VINEYARDS, MCLAREN VALE
*McLaren Vale is currently contesting Coonawarra's reputation as the best red wine region of South Australia, a state that accounts for almost 60 percent of Australia's total wine output.*

Australian wine was consumed domestically. When output dramatically increased, producers had to concentrate on exports, which increased tenfold in the 1980s, and a further tenfold in the 1990s. Today they represent more than 40 percent of the country's total production. If you thought you knew a bit about Australian wines in 1996, think again, since the number of wineries has doubled since then. There are now more than 1,800 wineries, and a new winery is born every 84 hours.

## THE WINE SHOW SYSTEM
Wine shows have been, and remain, a key factor in shaping the Australian wine industry, and, for better or worse, the "Australian style" of wine. The National Wine Show, held in Canberra, is considered to be the grand finale of the Australian wine show circuit, with entries restricted to wines that have previously been awarded a trophy or medal at other shows. Next in the hierarchy are the Australian Capital City Wine Shows (Adelaide, Sydney, etc.), followed by regional shows, such as the Australian Inland, Australian Small Winemakers, Ballarat, Barossa, Canberra Regional Wine Show, Clare Valley, Cowra, Griffith, Hunter Valley, Lilydale, Limestone Coast, McLaren Vale, Mount Barker, Mudgee, Riverland, Rutherglen, and Victorian Wines.

Most of these shows are run by Royal Agricultural Societies or are county fair-type shows. As such, wine is just one of the featured competitions. The societies organizing these wine shows are also responsible for other agricultural and horticultural competitions, judging everything from barley to lavender, cattle to goats, and wool to woodchopping. It is understandable how these shows originated, when a crop of grapes was very much like a crop of anything else, but since wine has evolved into such a diverse and sophisticated end product, there are good reasons to bring these competitions under specialized, independent control.

Not that the show system has had a negative effect. Indeed, the reverse has been true, particularly in the final two decades of the last century. The technical correctness demanded by judges raised quality levels across the board, and this was achieved, essentially, by Australian winemakers not being afraid to be very strict in scoring wines of their peers and, sometimes embarrassingly, wines of their own. Compare this with France, where there is reluctance among winemakers to mark down the wines of their peers, unless they are blatantly faulty, for fear of retaliation. In the 1990s, there was a move away from technical correctness, as allowances were made for the contribution of tiny faults to overall complexity.

# AUSTRALIAN GEOGRAPHICAL INDICATIONS (GIs)

Australia's new appellation system, which has been developing behind the scenes since 1993, but was enacted as recently as 2001, defines boundaries and nothing more. Thankfully, it does not attempt to dictate what varieties should be grown, how vines should be pruned or trained, or target yields, alcohol levels, or style of wine produced. Geographical Indications (GIs) were introduced to support the Label Integrity Program. Label Integrity is the simplest, sanest, nondraconian form of wine control invented: if the label states Coonawarra Cabernet Sauvignon, then at least 85 percent of the wine must be made from Cabernet Sauvignon grown in Coonawarra. But, while Cabernet Sauvignon is Cabernet Sauvignon, where does Coonawarra start and finish? Enter the GIs. The following table represents the complete list of existing GIs, all of which are mapped and described by this encyclopedia, plus those that are currently waiting in the wings (marked by an asterisk).

| State/Zones | Regions | Sub-regions |
|---|---|---|
| **SOUTHEAST AUSTRALIA**[1] | | |
| **NEW SOUTH WALES** Big Rivers | Lachlan Valley* Murray Darling Perricoota Riverina Swan Hill[3] | |
| Western Plains | | |
| Central Ranges | Cowra Mudgee Orange | |
| Southern New South Wales | Hilltops Canberra District Gundagai Tumbarumba | |
| South Coast | Shoalhaven Coast Southern Highlands Sydney* | |
| Northern Slopes | | |
| Northern Rivers | Hastings River | |
| Hunter Valley | Hunter | Allandale* Belford* Broke Fordwich Dalwood* Pokolbin* Rothbury* |
| **QUEENSLAND** | Granite Belt South Burnett | |
| **SOUTH AUSTRALIA** **ADELAIDE**[2] | | |
| Mount Lofty Ranges | Adelaide Hills | Lenswood Gumeracha* Piccadilly Valley |
| | Adelaide Plains | |
| | Clare Valley | Auburn* Clare* Hill River* Polish Hill River* Sevenhill* Watervale* |
| Barossa | Barossa Valley | |
| | Eden Valley | High Eden Springton* |
| Fleurieu | Currency Creek Kangaroo Island Langhorne Creek | |
| | McLaren Vale | Clarendon* |
| | Southern Fleurieu | |
| Limestone Coast | Bordertown* Coonawarra Mt Benson Padthaway Penola* Wrattonbully* Robe* | |
| Lower Murray | Riverland | |
| The Peninsulas | | |
| Far North | Southern Flinders Ranges* | |

| State/Zones | Regions | Sub-regions |
|---|---|---|
| **VICTORIA** North West Victoria | Murray Darling Swan Hill | |
| North East Victoria | Alpine Valleys | Kiewa River Valley* Ovens Valley* |
| | Beechworth Glenrowan* | |
| | King Valley[3] | Myrrhee* Whitlands* |
| | Rutherglen | Wahgunyah* |
| Central Victoria | Bendigo Central Victoria Mountain Country* | |
| | Goulburn Valley | Nagambie Lakes |
| | Heathcote | |
| | Strathbogie Ranges | |
| Western Victoria | Grampians | Great Western* |
| | Henty Pyrenees | |
| Gippslannd | | |
| Port Phillip | Geelong Macedon Ranges Mornington Peninsula Sunbury Yarra Valley | |
| **WESTERN AUSTRALIA** Greater Perth | Peel | |
| | Perth Hills | |
| | Swan District | Swan Valley |
| Central Western Australia | | |
| South West Australia | Blackwood Valley Geographe | |
| | Great Southern | Albany Denmark Frankland River Mount Barker Porongurup |
| | Manjimup[3] Margaret River Pemberton[3] Warren Valley* | |
| West Australian SE Coastal Eastern Plains, Inland and North of Western Australia | Esperance* | |
| **TASMANIA** | | |
| **AUSTRALIAN CAPITAL TERRITORY** | | |
| **NORTHERN TERRITORY** | | |

## AUSTRALIA AT A GLANCE

Australia produces a mere 4 percent of the world's wine, yet it is the fourth-largest wine-exporting country. Three states (South Australia, Victoria, and New South Wales) provide 95 percent of Australia's wine production. Just 20 of the country's 1,800 wineries account for 94 percent of Australia's wine production, and five of these (Southcorp, BRL Hardy, Orlando Wyndham, Beringer Blass, and McGuigan Simeon) represent 75 percent. Almost half of all Australian wine is sold as cask wine (bag-in-the-box). Chardonnay accounts for 48 percent of all Australian white wine, and is also the fastest-spreading variety of grape, black or white, with more than 12 acres (5 hectares) newly planted every day.

**Notes** [1]Superzone encompassing the whole of New South Wales, Victoria, and Tasmania, and only part of Queensland and South Australia
[2]Superzone encompassing Mount Lofty Ranges, Fleurieu, and Barossa.
**Notes** * Name included on listing pending determination by the GI Committee and inclusion in the Register of Protected Names.
[3] Not yet finalized, but sufficiently advanced to be mapped and described.

However, the winners of Australia's wine shows, like the winners of most wine competitions throughout the world, are invariably the biggest wines. The biggest wines are not always the best wines, and almost always never accompany food well. They are just so complete that to partner them with anything else is to detract from their glory. The only Australian wine competition I know of that actually deliberates over the concept of matching the wines to food, and also sets out to reward wine of finesse and elegance, is the Sydney International Wine Competition. In the second round, the judges even taste the wines with a platter of appropriate food. This competition also places a high emphasis on international judges to avoid the "cellar palate" and prejudices of the Australian wine industry and its homegrown commentators.

International judges do take part in the Royal Society shows, particularly the larger ones, but they are in a minority, and can do little against the unwritten rules. Of these, the one that troubles me the most concerns the Riesling class. Depending on the volume of Riesling entries, the trend is to judge the most recent vintage, and, possibly, the previous vintage, as classes on their own. Anything older will be lumped together under some sort of "museum" class, potentially judging a 3-year-old wine against one that may be 12 years old or more. One unwritten law among judges is to mark up lime aromas and flavors, and mark down any so-called "petrol" aromas (see Taste Chart and Glossary of Tasting and Technical Terms). This jars with many wine drinkers from northern climes, who enjoy the "petroly" bottle-aromas that accompany the honeyed richness of a fine, mature Riesling. However, when it is realized that so many Australian Rieslings, particularly the cheaper ones, develop an overwhelming gasoline

VINEYARDS IN MUDGEE
*Perhaps atypical of the area, these vineyards occupy flatland rather than the western slopes of the Great Dividing Range.*

character far too rapidly from a simplistic lime fruit base, it is easy to understand how gasoline aromas have acquired such a negative connotation in this country. It should be the job of the Australian wine show circuit to promote a better understanding. To recognize that the gasoline aroma is not negative *per se*. To mark down a gasoline character that is too dominant for a certain level and simplicity of fruit, but to mark up one that has taken ages to achieve a wonderfully complex nuance. This is particularly relevant now that Australia is making finer and finer Riesling. For these wines to increase will require not only a detailed examination of each new vintage, as is the current practice, but also encouragement of producers to enter Riesling in two distinct classes: 5 to 12 years, and 13 years and older.

## RECENT AUSTRALIAN VINTAGES

**2007** A small, very variable, and disappointing vintage, with the grapes in several areas tainted by smoke from bushfires. Excellent wines, however, can be found from the Margaret River, Hunter Valley, Tasmania, and southern Victoria, particularly Mornington Peninsula.

**2006** A great, classic red vintage; but with the exception of some good to very good Rieslings, not a very inspiring white-wine year.

**2005** This is the greatest Australian vintage of the 2000s—the best since 2002 and possibly 1998. It gave benchmark wines of all the classics: Rieslings in the Clare and Eden valleys, Sémillons in the Hunter Valley, Shiraz in the Barossa, Cabernet in Coonawarra, and Pinot Noir in Tasmania and the Yarra Valley. The whites proved outstanding, although the reds could be their equal; already, 2005 Pinot Noirs from the cooler southern districts have greatly impressed. Western Australia is the only real glitch: midvintage rain upset ripening, and winemakers were less enthusiastic than elsewhere. Some very good wines have already been released, however. Production equaled the 2004 record, although high yields in the high-quality regions were not a problem as in 2004.

**2004** Mixed weather produced a patchy vintage. It was a repeat of 2001 in the Hunter Valley, where the red wines were light and dilute, but some stunning Sémillon has been produced from old, low-yielding vineyards. Adelaide Hills was the best-performing region, and Shiraz the most successful variety.

**2003** If Australia is not blowing hot and cold on alternate vintages, it is veering from dry to wet. In 2003, it was very hot, with a nationwide drought. There were also widespread rains in February, which caused the berries to split, reducing yields further. Other problems included smoke-taint from the January bushfires, and unusually cool spring temperatures in the country's coolest wine areas, where yields were at their lowest. Originally thought to be a red wine year, 2003 has turned out to be far patchier, with best wines ranging from Shiraz in general throughout most of Victoria and South Australia to more specific, regionally distinct successes, such as Sauvignon Blanc in Adelaide Hills, Riesling in Eden Valley, and Cabernet Sauvignon in Coonawarra. Growers in Orange reported their best-ever vintage in 2003.

## GOING GREEN?

Taking the organic route in the vineyard is harder in some countries than others. Essentially, the more rain or humidity there is, the more rot affects the grapes, and the more difficult it becomes to control this by natural means. Some growers are game for the challenge, even in rain-soaked countries like England, whereas hardly any bother in sunny Australia. It should be pointed out that many good growers, and all the best, are "almost" organic the world over, since anyone who is interested in producing the best wine they possibly can will realize that it is in their own interest to ensure that their own viticulture is sustainable for the long term. However, the number of organic producers in a viticultural paradise like Australia is so pathetically small that I feel compelled to list all the wineries I know to be organic, in addition to the few specifically recommended in the following pages.

**Certified biodynamic**
Jeeleunup Gully Wines
(Mount Barker, Western Australia)
Kiltynane Estate
(Yarra Valley, Victoria)
Robinvale Wines
(Murray Darling, Vicoria)
Rosnay Wines
(Canowindra, New South Wales)
Streamville (Arthurs Creek, Victoria)
**Certified organic**
Captains Creek
(Macedon Ranges, Victoria)
Glenara Wines
(Adelaide Hills, South Australia)

Mabrook Estate
(Hunter Valley, New South Wales)
Martins Hill Wines
(Mudgee, New South Wales)
Petcheys Bay Vineyard (Tasmania)
Robinvale Wines
(Murray Darling, Victoria)
Temple Breuer
(Langhorne Creek, South Australia)
Serventy Wines
(Margaret River, Western Australia)
Thistle Hill Vineyard
(Mudgee, New South Wales)
Wilkie Estate Wines
(Adelaide, South Australia)

# AUSTRALIA'S WINE GROUPS

*There are a number of groups that cannot be usefully located under any one specific location; consequently, they have been collected together here for ease and completeness.*

## THE "BIG FIVE"

It used to the "Big Four," but with the merger between McGuigan and Simeon in 2002, and the swift expansion of this new group, four has turned into five, and these companies now account for more than 75 percent of Australia's total wine production.

## I. SOUTHCORP

Australia's largest wine group, Southcorp was created in 1993 after Penfolds had acquired Lindemans and was itself taken over by S. A. Brewing, which owned Seppelt at the time. That same year S. A. Brewing had sold off its brewing interests, and so a new name had to be found.

The origins of the twin pillars supporting this company are very much the story of two English doctors. Lindemans Wines dates back to 1843, when Dr. Henry John Lindeman planted his first vineyard, called Cawarra, on a tributary of the Hunter River. Lindeman had been a brilliant medical student at St. Barts, as evidenced by the fact that he had become a member of the Royal College of Surgeons in 1834 at the age of just 23, but he was rather carefree and footloose, opting for a career as a surgeon in the navy. On leave in England, he fell in love with Eliza Bramhall, and when they married in 1840 he left the navy, and the couple emigrated to Australia, where he established one of the country's most respected wineries, particularly for well-aged "Hunter Riesling" (Sémillon).

Just four years after Dr. and Mrs. Lindeman had arrived in Sydney, Dr. Penfold and his wife docked in Adelaide, where the Adelaide Register of August 8, 1844, recorded that they were "the fortunate purchaser of the delightfully situated and truly valuable Estate of Makgill at the sum of £1,200 (US$5,760)." This is known today as Magill Estate and was, of course, due to provide the primary element in the blending of Penfolds' Grange Hermitage (now simply Penfolds' Grange), the most famous and most expensive of all Australian wines. By the time Penfolds took over Lindemans, it had already acquired the Barossa Co-op Winery (Kaiser Stuhl), and Allied Vintners wineries (Glenloth, Seaview, Tulloch, and Wynns), while Lindemans had taken over Leo Buring and Rouge Homme. Along with Seppelt's specialized sparkling wine operation, these brands created a finely tuned portfolio that propelled Southcorp to the very top of the industry, yielding increasing profits year on year.

In 1996, the group purchased Coldstream Hills in the Yarra Valley, and Devil's Lair Winery and Vineyards in Margaret River. Its strategy to focus on premium-quality wines and increase the standard of its less expensive wines was the underlying factor for its sale in 1998 of 2,307 acres (934 hectares) of vineyards in Riverland to Simeon Wines. The proficient synergy went awry in 2001, when Southcorp Wines acquired the privately owned Rosemount Estates from the Oatley family. There were just too many similarities in the Lindemans and Rosemount products, particularly on export markets, and totally opposing management styles, not to mention the radically different winemaking regimes. When Penfolds' chief winemaker John Duval left after 28 years with the company amid rumors of a rift with Rosemount's Philip Shaw, and Shaw was appointed chief winemaker for the entire Southcorp group, the deal that saw Southcorp pay AU$1.5 billion (US$730 million) for the merger was billed by the press as a reverse takeover by the smaller Rosemount. In theory, the acquisition of Rosemount

**MAGILL ESTATE WINERY**
*Established by Dr. Christopher Rawson Penfold in 1844, Magill Estate is just 15 minutes from Adelaide. The winery often wins prizes for its tourist facilities.*

should have resulted in operational savings of up AU$50 million (US$24 million), plus, of course, a substantial increase in profits provided by the income from Rosemount's lucrative brands, but Southcorp made a loss of AU$923 million (US$554 million) in 2003, compared with a profit of AU$313 million (US$166 million) the year before. Excuses at the time included the surplus stock situation, which exacerbated the already aggressive policy on export markets to a point of unprofitability, and this was further compounded by unfavorable exchange rates. The market was indeed more difficult, but Australia's other three big wine groups faced the same conditions, and all of them posted healthy profits (BRL Hardy and Orlando Wyndham even managed to increase their profit over the previous 12 months).

Southcorp's problem was not so much the market, as the incompatability of its merger. This is borne out by the AU$645 million (US$387 million) in goodwill that was written off, and a drop of AU$240 (US$144 million) in the book value of the Rosemount name, which combined account for over 95 percent of Southcorp's loss in 2003. The best thing that Southcorp could do is divorce itself from Rosemount, as the two entities would be far more profitable on their own. Since it has been well known for a few years that the Oatley family would like to buy the company back, it might have been wiser to see what deal could have been made before writing down the Rosemount name. Whatever they can get now will be a quarter of a billion less than Southcorp could legitimately have expected prior to the write-down.

In 2002, when Southcorp was still blissfully ignorant of the massive loss it would soon endure, the company sold the Tulloch winery and brand, the Hungerford Hill brand, and the Rouge Homme winery. In June 2004, following the shockwave of almost a one billion Australian dollar loss, Southcorp analyzed its assets, and came up with various plans to rationalize its structure and operation. But although the first half of 2004 was profitable for the group, its plans are no more than the sort of integration procedures that should have been prepared prior to the merger. Specifically, they do not attend to the core problem of brand incompatibility: Lindemans and Rosemount are better apart, locked in genuine competition, than together.

The next few years will be interesting. Currently, Southcorp owns 20,000 acres (8,100 hectares) of vineyards, and its brands include Seven Peaks, Coldstream Hills, Devil's Lair, Edwards and Chaffey, Great Western, Hungerford Hill, Kaiser Stuhl, Killawarra, Leo Buring, Lindemans, Matthew Lang, Penfolds, Queen Adelaide, Rosemount Estate, Rouge Homme, Seaview, Seppelt, Tollana, Tulloch, Woodley, and Wynns.

## 2. BRL HARDY

BRL Hardy owns the second-largest wine producer in terms of volume in Australia and vies with Orlando Wyndham as number two in value. With the difficulties facing Southcorp, Australia's largest wine group, and BRL Hardy now part of Constellation, the largest wine group in the world, this company is in the best position to jump to the top of the Australian league. However, it would be quite a leap, and would require Southcorp's continuing decline.

BRL Hardy was established by Thomas Hardy, a farmworker who arrived in Adelaide on board the *British Empire* in 1850. He was 20 years of age, and had traveled with two cousins, the sisters Joanna and Mary Anna Hardy. They were also accompanied by a friend and fellow farmworker, John Holbrook. Hardy went to work for John Reynhill, who owned a cattle station in Normanville, and within 18 months he had made enough money driving cattle to feed miners at the Victorian goldfields to purchase 16.5 acres (7 hectares) of land next to the Torrens River, just outside Adelaide. He married Joanna, and John Holbrook married Mary Anna. Hardy called their homestead Bankside, and planted grapes, making his first wine in 1857, and exporting two hogsheads to London in 1859.

By 1865, the Bankside winery was producing 14,000 gallons (53,000 liters). Hardy's big break came in 1873, when he was the sole bidder for the Tintara Vineyards Company, which included a winery, cellars, vast stocks of wine, and 700 acres (280 hectares) of land a few miles northeast of McLaren Vale, where the vineyards had been planted in the 1850s and were thus mature. By selling the stocks, he recouped the entire cost of the bid, and set about extending the cellars and planting even more vineyards. In 1878 he converted a disused flour mill in McLaren Vale into a brand new winery, selling off the mill machinery to fund a large part of the construction. He might have been a farmworker in England, but he was evidently a natural-born businessman, and in Victorian Australia's land of opportunity, he had the freedom to express his talents, not least of which was grape growing and winemaking, although no one knows to this day how and where he learned those skills.

By 1895, Thomas Hardy was the largest wine producer in South Australia, a position Hardy's has maintained ever since. In 1976, Thomas Hardy and Sons purchased the Emu Wine Company, which was known primarily for exporting Kangaroo Red, but also owned a little gem called Houghton Wines. Chateau Reynella and Rhine Castle Wines were taken over in 1982. Perhaps its most innovative decision was made in 1990, when the company extended its wine holdings into France, where it acquired Domaine de La Baume on the outskirts of Béziers (sold off in 2003). The company's rationale for this move was that it believed the French had not exploited varietal wines, something the authorities in that country are only just recognizing 15 years later.

In 1992, Thomas Hardy and Sons merged with Berri-Renmano, becoming BRL Hardy, which listed itself on the Australian stock exchange. The funding that resulted helped the company to purchase 4,450 acres (1,800 hectares)—only 705 acres (285 hectares) of which was plantable—at Banrock Station in 1994. Over the next three years BRL Hardy purchased Yarra Burn, a one-third share in National Liquor Distributors (New Zealand), the Hunter Ridge brand (from McGuigan Wines), 50 percent of Brookland Valley Vineyards (which is certified organic) in Western Australia, and

HARDY'S ESTATE
*The company started by a British farmworker in the 1800s has developed into Australia's second-largest wine producer, BRL Hardy.*

announced plans for its ambitious Kamberra winery and vineyards in the Canberra region. In 1998 BRL Hardy increased its shareholding in National Liquor Distributors, which had by then merged with Nobilo Vintners, effectively taking control by 2000. Expansion continued as the company took a 50 percent shareholding in Barossa Valley Estates and, in 2001, entered a joint venture with the US-based Constellation Brands. This latter arrangement developed into a full merger in 2003 to form Constellation Wines, the largest wine group in the world. BRL Hardy owns 5,930 acres (2,400 hectares) of vineyards, and its brands include Banrock Station, Bay of Fires, Berri Estates, Brookland Valley, Crofters, Hardy's, Houghton, Hunter Ridge, Kamberra, Leasingham, Meeting Place, Moondah Brook, Omni, Renmano, Reynell, Stanley, Starvedog Lane, Stonehaven, Wicked Wines, and Yarra Burn.

## 3. ORLANDO WYNDHAM

Orlando Wyndham has been owned by the French Pernod-Ricard group since 1989. It produces, among many other wines, Jacob's Creek, which is Australia's leading export brand. Thus the French can be said not only to make a large proportion of Australian wine, but also—in delicious irony—the one brand that has done most damage to declining French wine exports. Furthermore, it was reported in February 2004 that France itself had started importing Jacob's Creek, so the enemy is now within.

Orlando Wyndham can trace its origins back to 1846, when a German immigrant, Johann Gramp, planted the Barossa Valley's first commercial vineyard, on the banks of Jacob's Creek, where he produced his first vintage in 1850. It was a white wine made in a Hock style, the forerunner of Gramp's popular Carte Blanche. The wine was sold under Gramp's label, and in 1953, the fourth generation established a milestone in Australian wine history by introducing temperature-controlled fermentation. In 1971, the UK company Reckitt and Colman, which had acquired Morris Wines of Rutherglen the year before, purchased Gramp's busines and, in 1976, released a Shiraz-Cabernet-Malbec from the 1973 vintage, naming it after Johann Gramp's first vineyard on the banks of Jacob's Creek.

It was not until 1989 that Pernod-Ricard bought Orlando Wines, and the following year the French beverages group purchased Wyndham Estate and its subsidiaries, including Hollydene Vineyards, Saxonvale Vineyards, Montrose, Craigmoor, and Amberton Wines, but there have been as many sales as purchases since then. In 1993 Orlando Wyndham took over the Leo Buring winery (not the brand) in Tanunda, and the Buronga Hill Winery, but the next year sold Buronga to Simeon Wines and the Richmond Grove winery (not the brand, which was switched to the old Leo Buring winery) to Brian McGuigan Wines (since that time McGuigan and Simeon have merged). In 1995 Orlando Wyndham acquired 765 acres (310 hectares) for planting at Langhorne Creek, but one year later sold Saxonvale Winery to Hill of Hope, and the Hunter Estate Winery and Vineyard to Brian McGuigan Wines. A year later, it sold Hollydene Vineyards to the Singapore Lian Huat Group.

Orlando Wyndham owns 5,435 acres (2,200 hectares) of vineyards. It is the third-largest wine group in terms of production, and vies with BRL Hardy as the second largest in terms of value. Considering that the volume of its leading brand, Jacob's Creek, is as high as 6.9 million cases (2003), over five million of which are exported to 70 countries, Orlando Wyndham has set itself up as a prime target for criticism. But the quality is consistent and better than could or should be expected, with some truly excellent wines sold under the Reserve label, not to mention a f ew stunning Limited Releases. All in all, Orlando Wyndham does a pretty good job of flying the flag for Australian wine. Its brands currently include Carrington, Coolabah, Craigmoor, Gramp's, Jacaranda Ridge, Jacob's Creek, Maison, Montrose, Morris Wines, Orlando, Poet's Corner, Richmond Grove, Steingarten, Wickham Hill, and Wyndham Estate.

## 4. BERINGER BLASS

The Australian half of Beringer Blass can trace its origins back to the original Mildara winery, which was established by the Chaffey Brothers in 1888 at the Jamieson's Run sheep station in Victoria. The real growth of this company dates from the mid-1980s, when Mildara Wines acquired Yellowglen Winery, Balgownie Winegrowers, and Krondorf Wines. At roughly the same time, another company, Wolf Blass Wines, purchased a share of Tim Knappstein Wines, and took over Quelltaler Wines, before merging with Mildara Wines in 1991 to become Mildara Blass in a deal worth AU$56 million (US$43 million). One year later, Mildara Blass sold Tim Knappstein Wines to Petaluma, before setting off on a spending spree that saw the acquisition of so many wineries, brands, and stocks that its greatly expanded portfolio made it one of the largest wine companies in Australia. This also left the publicly quoted company vulnerable to takeover, and in 1996 it was snapped up for AU$560 million (US$384 million) by Fosters Brewing, which had the funds to fuel another series of acquisitions in the late 1990s. In October 2000, Fosters acquired Beringer Wine Estates for AU$2.7 billion (US$1.7 billion), after which purchases of Australian wineries continued until June 2004, when it was reported that Beringer Blass intended to sell nine vineyards and three wineries worth an estimated AU$40 million (US$30 million). This is not so much a downsizing as a restructuring to create a leaner wine division in response to lower export profits experienced by the industry in general due to the increasing value of the Australian dollar.

However, Beringer Blass continues to be one of Australia's "Big Five" producers, with 9,300 acres (3,750 hectares) of vineyards. Although its output represents just 9 percent of Australian bottled wine, it allegedly accounts for 30 percent of the premium-quality market. Its brands include Andrew Garrett, Annie's Lane, Baileys of Glenrowan, Bayliss and Fortune, Bilyara, Black Opal, Blass, Clare Essentials, Eaglehawk, Greg Norman Estates, Half Mile Creek, Ingoldby, Jamieson's Run, Krondorf, Maglieri of McLaren

Vale, Mamre Brook, Metala, Mildara, Mt. Helen, Mt. Ida, Mt. Tanglefoot, Pepperjack, Quelltaler Estate, Robertson's Well, Rothbury Estates, Saltram, St. Huberts, Wolf Blass, Yarra Ridge, and Yellowglen.

## 5. McGUIGAN SIMEON

With the acquisition of Miranda Wines in September 2003, McGuigan Simeon moved up from fifth-largest producer to third, but much of the wine is sold in bulk and bottled by other wineries, thus in terms of shelf presence, it remains in fifth place. McGuigan Simeon controls (but does not own) the second-largest vineyard holding in the country, in excess of 12,350 acres (5,000 hectares), which is more than BRL Hardy and Orlando Wyndham combined. It farms even more vineyards—66,690 acres (27,000 hectares) in 2002—crushing no less than 12 percent of Australia's entire crop of grapes. All this from a zero start in 1992!

It was Brian McGuigan who founded Wyndham Estate (now part of Orlando Wyndham), based on the Dalwood Estate, which had been established by George Wyndham in 1830, and sold by Penfolds to its former cellar master, McGuigan's father, in the early 1960s. In 1992, Brian McGuigan set up McGuigan wines with the help of his wife, Fay, who was the export manager for Wyndham Estate in the 1980s. They listed the company on the Australian stock exchange, and by 2002 McGuigan Wines had become the sixth-largest wine producer in Australia, selling 1.2 million cases a year. Simeon Wines was established and listed on the Australian stock exchange in 1994, purchasing Buonga winery and vineyards from Orlando Wyndham the same year. In 1997 Simeon took over Australian Vintage, which included the Loxton winery, and the Coldridge and Manton's Run brands. The following year Simeon bought 2,307 acres (934 hectares) of Riverland vineyards from Southcorp, and Chateau Yaldara the year after that. In 2003, when market conditions and exchange rates were blamed for the others in the "Big Five" turning in a modest increase in profits at best, McGuigan Simeon announced a 27 percent jump in profits, and the acquisition of Miranda Wines. This increased its production in 2004 by 40 percent over the previous year. Brands include: Black Swan, Botany Creek, Cobweb, Conundrum Estate, Cowra Crossing, Ducks Flat, Earth's Portrait, Firefly, Fireside, Genus 4, Golden Gate, Hermitage Road, Howcroft Estate, Hunter Cellars, McGuigan, Miranda, Mirrool Creek, River Run, Silver Billet, Somerton, Tempus Two, The Drainings, and Vine Vale.

WOLF BLASS
*The flamboyant founder of the eponymous brand emigrated to Australia in 1961 with just £100 (US$280) in his pocket.*

## OTHER GROUPS
### CASELLA
Filippo Casella emigrated to Australia from Sicily in the 1950s, purchased a farm in 1965, planted vines, and made his first wine in 1969, but did so as a bulk supplier to other wineries. Consequently, the company he established went unnoticed until it started the transition to marketing wines under its own brand. In recent years, Casella has become a legend, thanks to the "Yellow Tail" phenomenon, which took Australia's biggest wine players by surprise. Yellow Tail went from zero to 5.9 million cases in just four years. In 2002, midway through this extraordinary growth, Yellow Tail had become the top-selling Australian wine in the US, and by 2004 Yellow Tail Shiraz was that country's best-selling bottled red wine, as well as being officially ranked as the fastest-growing export brand in the history of the Australian wine industry. Brands currently include Carramar Estate, Casella Estate, Cottlers Bridge, Crate 31, Yellow Tail, and Yenda Vale.

### LION NATHAN
This group was going down the tubes in 1997, when the self-confessed "aggressive, oppositional, demanding, and insensitive" Gordon Cairns took over, but as he rebuilt the business he went from an "in your face" type to Mr. Nice Guy. He also became a hypocrite, attributing it to the Buddhist principle that "you can hold two contradictory ideas in your mind at the same time." He declared that company would never get involved in the wine industry, but purchased Petaluma (including its Argyle operation in Oregon) and Banksia (Hillstowe, St. Hallett, and Tatachilla) in 2001. Unless the company philosophy changes, Lion Nathan will never challenge the "Big Five," since the strategy is to remain within a premium niche, where its wines are available only through independent outlets, and listed in hotels and restaurants. Lion Nathan currently brews 2½ billion gallons (one billion liters) of beer a year, while its Australian wine division includes Bridgewater Mill, Chainsaw, Croser, Enterprise Wines, Knappstein Wines, Mitchelton, Petaluma, Preece, Sharefarmers Vineyard, St. Hallets, Smithbrook, Stonier, Tatachilla, Thomas Mitchell, and Tim Knappstein.

### LVMH AUSTRALIA AND NEW ZEALAND
This small but formidable group began in 1986, when Moët & Chandon was intent on repeating the success of its Domaine Chandon operation in California. Under the watchful eye of Dr. Tony Jordan, this was not only achieved, but the quality level of its American counterpart was quickly overtaken; the US-based Domaine Chandon has been in the shadow of the Australian ever since.

The idea back then was to concentrate exclusively on sparkling wine and not to get involved with other brands, let alone build up any kind of group. However, in 1990, Veuve Clicquot acquired a substantial shareholding in Cape Mentelle. This was just three years after the merger between Louis Vuitton (in which Clicquot was the top Champagne house) and Moët-Hennessy (where Moët ruled supreme), and Clicquot enjoyed its independence, as it continued to do for much of the 1990s. Clicquot's stated goal not to get involved in sparkling wine in the southern hemisphere may have been a diplomatic stance (not wishing to step on Moët's toes by competing with Domaine Chandon), but Clicquot had to reconsider when it found out that Cloudy Bay, Cape Mentelle's New Zealand subsidiary, was five years down the line in its development of Pelorus sparkling wine, since David Hohnen (the founder of Cloudy Bay) had no intention of wasting all that effort. So Clicquot got into bubbly. Having achieved all his ambitions for Domaine Chandon, Jordan left to take over at Wirra Wirra, but returned when he was made an offer he could not refuse, to run all of LVMH's winemaking operations in Australia and New Zealand. Thus it was, in July 2003, that Jordan took up the position of Chief Executive Officer of Cape Mentelle, Cloudy Bay, and Mountadam (which Clicquot had purchased in 2001), in addition to Domaine Chandon Australia

CASELLA TANKS AT NIGHT
*Few wine drinkers have heard of the name Casella, although many know and drink Yellow Tail, Australia's top-selling brand.*

(Chandon and Green Point brands), and Moët developed an enthusiasm for table wine. Other brands include Mountadam's David Wynn and Eden Ridge.

### McWILLIAM'S
This company was established in 1877 by Samuel McWilliam, who planted his first vineyard at Corowa. In 1941, McWilliam's purchased the Mount Pleasant Estate, which was founded at Pokolbin by the legendary Maurice O'Shea. In 1989, McWilliam's took over Barwang Vineyard, which coincidentally had been established using cuttings from McWilliam's some 20 years earlier. Between 1990 and 1994, McWilliam's bought Brands Winery in Coonawarra, and Lillydale vineyards in the Yarra Valley. In 2000, this company won 13 trophies and 611 medals at Australian wine shows. It had also firmly established itself as the fifth-largest exporter of Australian wine by volume, and sixth by value. In 2001 McWilliam's entered into an international distribution agreement with Gallo Wines (US), and by 2002 had dropped to 15th largest exporter of Australian wine by volume, and 20th by value, yet there are still some great quality and amazing value wines produced by this group, whose brands include Barawang, Brands of Coonawarra, Hanwood, Lillydale, Maurice O'Shea, McWilliam's, Mount Pleasant, and Sunstone.

### RATHBONE FAMILY GROUP
A small but highly exclusive group of premium and superpremium wineries, including Yering Station in the Yarra Valley, Mount Langi Ghiran in the Grampians region, and the jewel in Rathbone's crown, Parker of Coonawarra.

### WINGARA GROUP
Majority-owned by the Spanish Freixenet group, Wingara owns 1,550 acres (630 hectares) of vineyards, over half of which are located on prime *terra rossa* soil in Coonawarra, and its brands include Katnook, the penny-saving Riddoch, and the penny-pinching Deakin Estate label.

### XANADU NORMANS WINE GROUP
This group was created in October 2001, when Xanadu Wines (formerly Chateau Xanadu) in Margaret River purchased the key premium brands and the business name of historic South Australian wine producer Normans Wines—founded in 1853—along with its Clarendon winery and vineyard and packaged stock of premium wines. These brands include Chais Clarendon, Lone Gum, and, of course, Normans. Xanadu is the best performing brand, although there are a few award-winning wines under the Normans labels. As well as the Xanadu label itself, there is the NXG label.

# NEW SOUTH WALES

*From the Hunter Valley's weighty Shiraz, through its honeyed, bottle-aged Sémillon, and the easy-drinking Riverina wines, to the fast-rising wines from areas such as Orange, Tumbarumba, and Hilltops—the wines of New South Wales are better in quality and more varied in style than they have ever been.*

ALTHOUGH VINES ARRIVED with the British First Fleet, and Australia's first governor, Captain Arthur Phillip, planted the country's first vineyard (at Farm Cove, known by the Aborigines as Woccanmagully and now the site of Sydney's Royal Botanic Gardens) in 1788, it was Gregory Blaxland who made Australia's first wine. Blaxland planted his vineyard at Ermington, a few miles down river from Phillip's second vineyard at Parramatta. In 1822, Blaxland also became the first person to export Australian wine, when he brandied a quarter pipe (36 gallons/137.5 liters) of red wine so that it might withstand the rigors of being shipped to London, where it won a Silver Medal from the Society for Encouragement of Arts, Manufactures, and Commerce (now the Royal Society of Arts).

## HUNTER SHIRAZ

The reputation of this state's wine industry will always revolve around the Hunter Valley, particularly the Upper Hunter, however much added value there is to gain from its newer regions. Because Australia has claimed Shiraz as its own, Hunter Shiraz will always play a pivotal role. But our perception of this wine has changed; it is hard to imagine that the Hunter was once famous for a huge, beefy style of Shiraz that gave off a strong, gamey, sweat-and-leather odor and possessed an earthy, almost muddy taste that was "chewed" rather than swallowed. Its "sweaty saddle" smell was supposed to derive from the Hunter Valley's volcanic basalt soil, until it was widely declared to be a defect. For quite some time, it was thought to be a mercaptan fault, but the sweaty saddle odor (also described as "horsey" or "stables") is now known to be ethyl-4-phenol, a specific volatile phenol defect caused by the Brettanomyces yeast.

NEW SOUTH WALES, *see also* p.552
*North of Sydney, the Lower and Upper Hunter Valley and the Mudgee area excel, while the Murrumbidgee Irrigation Area to the southwest proves that quantity can, to a certain extent, coexist with quality.*

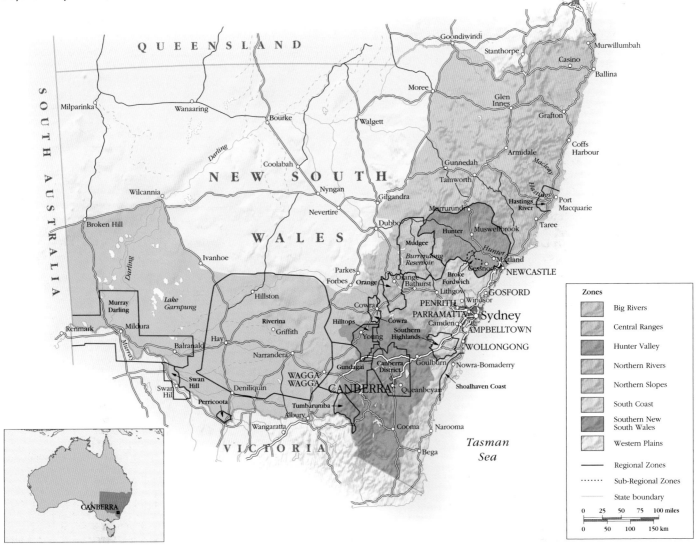

### Zones

- Big Rivers
- Central Ranges
- Hunter Valley
- Northern Rivers
- Northern Slopes
- South Coast
- Southern New South Wales
- Western Plains

— Regional Zones
····· Sub-Regional Zones
— State boundary

0  25  50  75  100 miles
0  50  100  150 km

## FACTORS AFFECTING TASTE AND QUALITY

 **LOCATION**
The southern part of Australia's east coast, between Victoria and Queensland.

**CLIMATE**
Temperatures during the growing season are similar to those of the Languedoc in southern France. Cloud cover can temper the heat in the Hunter Valley, but the accompanying rains often promote rot. The growing season is later, and the climate sunnier, in Mudgee, Orange, and Cowra, while it is hotter and drier in Riverina, and significantly cooler in Tumbarumba.

**ASPECT**
Vines are grown on generally low-lying, flat, or undulating sites, but also on steeper slopes such as the fringes of the Brokenback Range in the Lower Hunter Valley, where vines are grown at altitudes of up to 1,600 feet (500 meters); on the western slopes of the Great Dividing Range, where some vineyards can be found at an altitude of 2,600 feet (800 meters); and in Canberra at 2,706 feet (820 meters).

**SOIL**
Soils are varied, with sandy and clay loams of varying fertility found in all areas. Various other types of soil, such as the red-brown volcanic loams, are scattered about the Lower Hunter region and the fertile, but well-drained, alluvial sands and silts of the flat valley floors. Hilltops has a deep, gravelly, red soil, mixed with basalt and sandy granite, while Tumbarumba much farther south also has basalt and granite soils.

**VITICULTURE AND VINIFICATION**
Irrigation is practiced throughout the state, particularly in the mainly bulk-wine-producing inland area of Riverina. The range of grape varieties is increasing, and grapes are harvested several days earlier than they used to be, for a crisper style. Temperature-controlled fermentation in stainless-steel vats is common, but new oak is used judiciously.

**GRAPE VARIETIES**
**Primary varieties:** Cabernet Sauvignon, Chardonnay, Pinot Noir, Riesling, Sémillon, Shiraz
**Secondary varieties:** Cabernet Franc, Colombard, Grenache, Malbec, Merlot, Muscat Gordo Blanco, Petit Verdot, Ruby Cabernet, Sauvignon Blanc, Trebbiano, Verdelho

IRRIGATION CANAL AND DE BORTOLI WINERY
*A network of irrigation canals like this one enables Riverina wineries such as De Bortoli to produce vast amounts of modest, easy-drinking wines.*

THE APPELLATIONS OF
# NEW SOUTH WALES

### BIG RIVERS

This zonal GI encompasses the regional GIs of Lachlan Valley, Murray Darling, Perricoota, Riverina, and Swan Hill.

### BROKE FORDWICH

This subregion of Hunter centers in and around Broke, but also extends south and southwest, encompassing the catchment area of Wollombi Brook, and going north beyond Bulge. Chardonnay and Cabernet Sauvignon seem to be the most successful varieties grown here.

### CANBERRA DISTRICT

One of the quirkiest GI demarcations must be that of Canberra District, since most of the appellation is not even located within the Australian Capital Territory (ACT), but in New South Wales. In fact, prior to the arrival of BRL Hardy's Kamberra there were no wineries in ACT, and only 15 acres (6 hectares) of vines. However, the reason for this has nothing to do with any lack of viticultural potential within ACT. The absence of viticulture here was due solely to the fact that the concept of freehold property does not exist within ACT. This hardly makes Canberra an attractive option for anyone in the long-term business of establishing a vineyard, thus no vineyards or stylish new boutique wineries are within a stone's throw of the nation's capital. The altitude of most vineyards is 2,000 to 2,700 feet (600 to 820 meters), but most face north or northeast, so the sunshine hours are very high at 7.2 hours per day, enabling grapes to ripen on nearly all aspects. Although the climate is cool in Australian terms, it is not as cool as some local growers might like to boast. Summers are warm and dry, with three out of every four years yielding degree-day equivalents between those of the Médoc and Hermitage. The vineyards are dependent on irrigation, and water is a declining resource. All the usual grape varieties are grown, but snappy Rieslings, elegant Pinot Noir, and Rhône-style Shiraz excel.

### CENTRAL RANGES

A zonal GI that encompasses the regional GIs of Cowra, Mudgee, and Orange.

### COWRA

This is a small but growing viticultural area, which is situated some 120 miles (180 kilometers) inland and west from Sydney, and nearly the same distance north of Canberra. As in most of Australia's lesser-known wine areas, viticulture flourished here in the 19th century, and was reignited in the 1970s. But lesser known does not necessarily mean lesser quality, as demonstrated by the earliest vintages of Brian Croser's legendary Petaluma Chardonnay, which were sourced from Cowra.

### GUNDAGAI

It is surprising how many emerging wine regions in New South Wales happen to be conveniently located for tourist appeal, and Gundagai is no different, since it is touted as a near-perfect stopover between Sydney and Melbourne. Protected by the Snowy Mountains to the southeast, most vineyards are located at 1,640 to 3,280 feet (500 to 1,000 meters) in altitude, with Sémillon providing the most distinctive wines. Other varieties include Chardonnay, Sauvignon Blanc, Cabernet Sauvignon, Merlot, and Shiraz.

### HASTINGS VALLEY

This small region is located on the north coast of New South Wales, where the climate is maritime and subtropical, with high humidity and rainfall. The dominant grape variety is Chambourcin, a French hybrid that survives everything that the local squally weather can throw at it. Chambourcin was pioneered by John Cassegrain, formerly of Tyrrell's, who established a vineyard here in 1980, the first to be planted in the locality since the 1860s. Chardonnay and Sémillon are also supposed to perform well, but it is worth noting that Cassegrain now sources most of his grapes from elsewhere.

### HILLTOPS

Cool climatic conditions produce an elegant style of Chardonnay, and distinctive Sémillon, with red wines capable of a slow-building complexity, particularly Cabernet Sauvignon and Shiraz. This is essentially cherry orchard country, but the first vines were planted as long ago as the 1860s by Nichole Jaspprizza, a Croatian immigrant who made his money selling the wine he made to miners in the surrounding goldfields. More recently, Peter Robertson planted the first vines of the modern era at Barwang in 1969. Other varieties growing here include Merlot, Pinot Noir, Riesling, Sauvignon Blanc, and even Zinfandel. Vines grow at an elevation of 1,475 to 2,000 feet (450 to 600 meters) on a deep, gravelly, red soil, mixed with basalt and sandy granite. The climate is continental, cool, and dry with snow in winter and most rainfall occurring from mid-spring to mid-fall.

## HUNTER

**Subregions:**
*Broke Fordwich*

The Hunter sounds as if it should encompass the Hunter Valley, not the other way around. The Hunter covers the areas popularly known as the Lower Hunter Valley and the Upper Hunter Valley. *See* Lower Hunter Valley and Upper Hunter Valley.

## HUNTER VALLEY

This zonal GI encompasses the regional GI of Hunter.

## LOWER HUNTER VALLEY

Not an official GI, as yet, but the traditional practice of dividing the Hunter Valley into Lower and Upper regions must be formalized one day, if Australia's Geographical Indications are to be taken seriously. This is the "original" Hunter Valley. Its vineyards were pioneered in the 1820s by such growers as William Kelman of Kirkton and George Wyndham of Dalwood, over 130 years before the Upper Hunter Valley was opened up. The area has long been famous for its rich Sémillons (once sold as Hunter Riesling) and for its forceful Shiraz. The Lower Hunter Valley is not ideal grape country, being too hot and humid, although the nightly air-drainage from the Brokenback Range cools the vines and prevents the acidity of ripening grapes from dropping too rapidly. After a period of slow growth in the 1980s, the Hunter Valley has enjoyed the same rejuvenation as the Barossa Valley in South Australia.

## MUDGEE

With a continuous history of grape growing since 1856, this is the oldest district on the western side of the Great Dividing Range. Mudgee produces rich and succulent red wines, particularly from Shiraz and Cabernet Sauvignon, and is building a reputation as an excellent source for Sémillon.

## MURRAY DARLING

The Murray Darling GI straddles New South Wales and Victoria, and is essentially an industrialized wine-growing area. It has a hot and dry continental climate, with little rain, making it ideal for risk-free, large-scale, irrigated production of bag-in-the-box wines, although exceptional wines do exist, such as Tall Poppy's Petit Verdot. Almost every grape variety found in Australia grows here, but the most significant are Chardonnay and Cabernet Sauvignon, with Muscat Gordo Blanco, and clones of Sémillon and Colombard best suited to fortified styles.

## NORTHERN RIVERS

This zonal GI consists of New South Wales' northern coastal strip and encompasses the regional GI of Hastings Valley.

## NORTHERN SLOPES

Almost as barren as the Western Plains, this area is sandwiched between this area and the Northern Rivers GI.

## ORANGE

Orange continues to excel. When entering this town, the first thing you see is a huge sign saying "Welcome to Orange" with a large fruit underneath—an apple! That's right, Orange is famous for apples, and only very recently for grapes. As everywhere in the New World, the best potential vineyard areas have invariably turned out to be those that initially became famous for orchards. The vines grow 2,000 to 3,000 feet (600 to 900 meters) above sea level on an extinct volcano called Mount Canobolas, which is itself part of the Great Dividing Range. When I first visited the area in the late 1980s, the only local wine was Bloodwood, grown on a very small vineyard owned by Stephen Doyle, a lecturer at Orange Agricultural College. Now 22 vineyards market their own wine, with many more growers likely to follow suit when the University of Sydney's Orange Campus builds a winery on its Templer's Mill vineyard property, as this is intended to provide contract winemaking services for other vineyard owners. Orange is located between Cowra and Mudgee and, like most famous regions, it has expanded beyond its place of origin. Its most recent and most important plantings are found at Little Boomey, northeast of Molong. This extended region is best known for Cabernet Sauvignon and Chardonnay, but also grows Sauvignon Blanc and increasingly impressive Shiraz, although it could also succeed with Pinot Noir.

## PERRICOOTA

The Perricoota region is located in the Big Rivers zone on the Victoria border, with most wine production near or around the town of Moama, and only two significant producers. St. Anne is owned by the McLean family, whose vines are up to 30 years old, with Chardonnay, Cabernet Sauvignon, Merlot, and Shiraz the main varieties. The other producer is Riverview Estate, which was planted by the Morrison family as recently as 1996, and primarily grows Cabernet Sauvignon, Shiraz, Sauvignon Blanc, and Sémillon. Both also produce fortified wines.

## RIVERINA

The center of this region was formerly known as Murrumbidgee Irrigation Area, which was always a bit of a mouthful, or MIA, which sounded like an American military acronym. Riverina is a much more romantic name to see on a bottle of wine, although Murrumbidgee Irrigation Area accurately described a wine region that was made possible by the flooding and pumping of the Murrumbidgee River. This previously infertile land now cultivates rice and many fruits, including enough grapes to make one-tenth of all the wine in Australia. These wines are not all cheap plonk and include some of Australia's best botrytized wines.

## SHOALHAVEN COAST

An emerging region on the south coast of New South Wales, where the distinct maritime climate is responsible for Chambourcin being the primary grape, as it is farther up the coast at Hastings. Other varieties include Chardonnay, Gewürztraminer, Sauvignon Blanc, Sémillon, Verdelho, Cabernet Sauvignon, Merlot, and

Shiraz. The first vines were planted in the 1820s, by Alexander Berry, at Coolangatta Estate, which was revived in 1988, encouraging other vineyards to be established locally, although surprisingly it was not until 1996 that the first Chambourcin was planted (by Humphries Wines). There are now 10 wineries, and a further five vineyards owned by growers who supply others for the moment.

## SOUTH COAST

This zonal GI encompasses the regional GIs of Shoalhaven Coast and the Southern Highlands.

## SOUTHERN HIGHLANDS

The Southern Highlands is a little farther inland than Shoalhaven Coast, but still subject to a maritime climate. With its proximity to both Canberra and Sydney, one eye was obviously on the potential tourist trade when it was decided to plant vineyards in a region that had previously been devoted to sheep, dairy farming, and horse studs. The grapes grown here are primarily Chardonnay, Riesling, Sauvignon Blanc, Cabernet Sauvignon, Pinot Noir, and Shiraz.

## SOUTHERN NEW SOUTH WALES

This zonal GI encompasses the regional GIs of Canberra District, Gundagai, Hilltops, and Tumbarumba.

## SWAN HILL

This regional GI overlaps New South Wales and Victoria, with most producers located in the latter.

## TUMBARUMBA

One of Australia's coolest and most picturesque wine regions, Tumbarumba has an alpine climate that ripens grapes significantly later than in neighboring Gundagai region (late March to mid-April, as opposed to late February), making it one of the most exciting sources for producers of premium-quality sparkling wine. Still varietal wine successes include Chardonnay, Sauvignon Blanc, Cabernet Sauvignon, and Pinot Noir. The vineyards are in the foothills of the Australian Alps, growing at elevation of 1,640 to 2,600 feet (500 to 800 meters), on basalt or granite soils. Viticulture is relatively new in Tumbarumba, with the very first vines planted in 1983, but in keeping with much New World wine history, it was originally orchard country, and remains known today for its famous Batlow apples.

## UPPER HUNTER VALLEY

Not an official GI as yet, but the traditional practice of dividing the Hunter Valley into two appellations for the Lower and Upper Hunter must be formalized one day, if Australia's Geographical Indications are to be taken seriously. The Upper Hunter Valley was pioneered in the 1960s by Penfolds and put on the map internationally by the sensational performance of Rosemount Estate, whose Show Reserve Chardonnay took export markets by storm in the early 1980s. Although this district is just as hot as the Lower Hunter Valley and the growing season very similar, the climate is drier and the vineyards need irrigation. Despite fertile alluvial soils and high yields—two factors that do not augur well for quality—some very fine wines are made.

## WESTERN PLAINS

A virtual wilderness as far as wine today is concerned, this zonal GI covers more than one-third of the entire state.

THE WINE PRODUCERS OF
# NEW SOUTH WALES

## ALLANDALE
### Lower Hunter Valley
★☆Ⓥ

Amazingly good quality. Also uses grapes from Hilltops.

✓ *Cabernet Sauvignon •*
*Chardonnay • Sémillon •*
*Shiraz • Verdelho*

## ARROWFIELD WINES
### Upper Hunter Valley
★Ⓥ

This Japanese-owned estate dates back to 1824 when Governor Macquarie granted the land to one George Bowman, who named the huge fields on his property after variations of his family name, hence Arrowfield. Arrowfield primarily sources its grapes from the Hunter Valley and Cowra, tending to blend the wines for maximum effect, but the company has recently launched a regional range, defining the origin as either Hunter Valley or Cowra.

✓ *Chardonnay* (Show Reserve) •
*Classic white blend* (Sémillon Chardonnay)

## BARWANG VINEYARD
### Hilltops
★★Ⓥ

Part of the McWilliam's group, Barwang was established in 1969 by Peter Robinson, who planted the vineyards with cuttings that, as chance would have it, came from its future owner.

✓ *Cabernet Sauvignon • Merlot •*
*Shiraz*

## BLOODWOOD
### Orange
★☆Ⓥ

Owned by Stephen Doyle, a pioneer of Orange, Bloodwood's wines are made at the Reynolds Yarraman Estate in the Upper Hunter Valley.

✓ *Cabernet • Merlot*

## BOTOBOLAR VINEYARD
### Mudgee
ⓋⒷ

Good-quality, biodynamically produced wines come from the highest vineyard in the Mudgee district. Botobolar tends to use odd methods such as refermenting two-year-old Shiraz on the skins of freshly picked Shiraz. Low-preservative and preservative-free wines are a feature, but although low sulfur regimes are to be applauded, it has to be said that the preservative-free wines are not among Botobolar's best.

✓ *Marsanne • Shiraz*

## BRANGAYNE OF ORANGE
### Orange
★★☆Ⓥ

Don and Pamela Hoskins make supremely stylish wines, with the ubiquitous dynamic duo of Richard Smart and Simon Gilbert consulting.

✓ *Chardonnay • Classic red*
*blend* (The Tristan)

## BRIAR RIDGE
### Lower Hunter Valley
★★☆Ⓥ

Winemaker Steve Dodd joined Briar Ridge in December 2002, and partners Karl Stockhausen, one of the Hunter's legendary Sémillon stylists.

✓ *Chardonnay* (Hand Picked) •
*Sémillon* (Signature Stockhausen)

## BRINDABELLA HILLS
### Canberra District
★

Owner Dr. Roger Harris produces some of Canberra District's most elegant wines. The Shiraz is fleshy without being heavy, and a 1994 Riesling tasted in 2001 ranked as the best mature Australian Riesling I had ever tasted, with wonderful zesty-fresh aromas mingling with gasolinelike mature fruit.

✓ *Chardonnay • Cabernet*
*Sauvignon • Riesling • Shiraz*

## BROKENWOOD
### Lower Hunter Valley
★★★☆

This winery was established in 1970 by three partners, one of whom was none other that Australia's very own wine guru, James Halliday, but he has long since moved on. Iain Riggs has been winemaker here since 1983, and he is a driven man when it comes to Sémillon. The basic release is stunning, but bottle-age puts his ILR Aged Reserve Sémillon in a class of its own, demonstrating the potentially huge longevity and sheer quality of Hunter Sémillon. Brokenwood took over Yarra Valley's Seville Estate in 1997.

✓ *Cabernet Sauvignon*
(Graveyard Vineyard) •
*Sauvignon Blanc/Sémillon*
(Cricket Pitch) • *Sémillon •*
*Shiraz* (Graveyard Vineyard, Rayner Vineyard)

## CANOBOLAS-SMITH
### Orange
★

These hard-to-find, intensely ripe, complex wines show the great potential of Orange.

✓ *Chardonnay • Classic red*
*blend* (Alchemy)

## CASELLA WINES
### Riverina
★☆Ⓥ

Known primarily for its Yellow Tail brand, which went from zero to 5.9 million cases in just four years. The Yellow Tail range started with Chardonnay and Shiraz, but later included a Cabernet Sauvignon, Merlot, and a Verdelho. This success has attracted more than its fair share of adverse comments from various critics, quite often revolving around residual sugar levels (9 grams per liter in one of the Cabernet Sauvignons, for example). But Yellow Tail is a AU$10 (US$7.50) wine designed for mass appeal, and I have seen the analyses of supposedly higher-quality, medal-winning Australian wines with similar sugar levels—sometimes significantly higher. For its place in the market, ex-Southcorp winemaker Alan Kennet has done a remarkable job of churning out megavolumes of soft, clean, fresh, fruit-driven, consumer-friendly wines. The hard part will be in maintaining this standard. In August 2004, Casella announced that a premium Cabernet Sauvignon would be released at AU$45 (US$35). I cannot see how it will work myself, but who am I to question the marketing logic of the creators of Yellow Tail? What I can confidently predict, however, is that this commercial success will propel Casella into the major league, prompting takeovers, and will instill a desire to produce wines that attract critical acclaim at the highest level. Whether Yellow Tail is the brand to market premium quality through is doubtful, but an increased ranking in future editions of this encyclopedia is not. Brands currently include Carramar Estate, Casella Estate, Cottlers Bridge, Crate 31, Yellow Tail, and Yenda Vale.

✓ *Merlot* (Carramar Estate,
Cottlers Bridge) • *Petit Verdot*
(Yenda Vale) • *Sangiovese*
(Yenda Vale) • *Sémillon*
(Carramar Estate) •
*Tempranillo* (Yenda Vale)

## CASSEGRAIN VINEYARDS
### Hastings River

The Cassegrain family established this winery back in 1980. Some believe the maritime climate is far too marginal for viticulture, but despite the bracing sea breezes and lashing rain—which compelled John Cassegrain to plant the rot-resistant Chambourcin grape—some exciting wines are to be found amid the disappointments. Some of the early vintages of Cassegrain Brut show flashes of promise, but the quality, particularly the finesse, has lacked consistency, and requires considerable input from a top sparkling wine consultant to improve consistency. The Chambourcin is recommended within its class. Cassegrain purchased Hungerford Hill from Southcorp in 1992.

✓ *Chambourcin • Fortified*
(Old Yarras Tawny Port) •
*Fromenteau-Chardonnay*
(Reserve) • *Sémillon* (Reserve)
• *Verdelho*

## CHALKERS CROSSING
### Hilltops
★★

Established in 2000, Chalkers Crossing draws on grapes sourced from Tumbarumba and Gundagai to increase the range of wines available from its own 25-acre (10-hectare) vineyard. French-born Céline Rousseau produces regionally defined wines that combine ripe fruit with graceful lines, including a Sémillon to die for.

✓ *Cabernet Sauvignon* (Hilltops)
• *Chardonnay* (Tumbarumba)
• *Pinot Noir* (Tumbarumba) •
*Sémillon* (Hilltops)

## CHARLES STURT UNIVERSITY
### Wagga Wagga
★

Wagga Wagga is the oenological campus of Charles Sturt University, which has always sold the "students' wines" from its cellar door, but built a brand new commercial-scale winery in 2002.

✓ *Chardonnay* (Orange)

## CHATEAU PATO
### Lower Hunter Valley
★★

Tiny, family-owned estate producing one of the Hunter Valley's finest Shiraz wines.

✓ *Shiraz*

## CLONAKILLA
**Canberra District**
★★☆

Since taking over from his father, Tim Kirk has not only put his own stamp on Clonakilla, but has achieved fame above, beyond, and despite Canberra District's low profile. His Shiraz-Viognier has been recognized for more than a decade within Australia itself as one of the country's best reds, and will be known by many Australians who do not realize that Canberra District does, in fact, produce any wine. Any emerging region seeking recognition needs to be famous for something, and if other producers in this region had been quick enough, they might have been able to make Shiraz-Viognier Canberra District's signature wine.

 *Chardonnay • Classic red blend* (Shiraz-Viognier) *• Riesling • Shiraz • Viognier*

## COWRA ESTATE
**Cowra**
☆Ⓥ

Owned by South African businessman John Geber, who is obsessed with cricket and has thus introduced the new Classic Bat series of wines. He also magnanimously sells wines from other local wineries from his own cellar door. The wines are made by Simon Gilbert.

 *Chardonnay* (Classic Bat) *• Classic red blend* (Classic Bat Cabernet-Merlot) *• Pinot Noir* (Classic Bat)

## CRANSWICK ESTATE
**Riverina**
☆Ⓥ

Cash-strapped when acquired by Evans and Tate (*see* Western Australia) for AU$100 million (US$60 million) in March 2003, Cranswick Estate nevertheless increased its new parent company's profits by more than 40 percent, due to rolling its operations into the fold, and by in excess of 70 percent the second year. The attraction, however, was the inexpensive Barramundi range, which is Cranswick's top-selling export brand, and should open doors for Evans and Tate.

 *Sparkling wine* (Sparkling Shiraz)

## DE BORTOLI
**Riverina**
★☆Ⓥ

Founded in 1928, De Bortoli has always produced a vast amount of modest wines, as befits the reputation of Riverina. It won international acclaim with its Noble One Botrytis Sémillon, and has gone on to establish a wider reputation for quality with its outpost in Yarra Valley, Victoria. Quality has also risen at Riverina since the acquisition of vineyards in the Hunter Valley, whose wines are sold under the Black Creek label.

 *Chardonnay* (Black Creek, Deen De Bortoli Vat 7) *• Classic white blend* (Montage Sémillon-Chardonnay) *• Fortified* (Black Noble, Show Liqueur Muscat, Old Boys Tawny Port) *• Sémillon* (Noble One)

## DOONKUNA ESTATE
**Canberra District**
★

One of the most consistent Canberra District wineries, Doonkuna Estate was founded by the late Sir Brian Murray. It is now owned and run by Barry and Maureen Moran. The winemaker, Malcolm Burdett, likes high, ripe acidity and, although this winery has not produced a Riesling quite as special as Brindabella's 1994, it has been more consistent with this variety than Brindabella or any other Canberra District winery. Shiraz is the best red, but varies too much year on year to give a blanket recommendation.

 *Classic white blend* (Sauvignon Blanc-Sémillon) *• Riesling*

## EVANS FAMILY
**Lower Hunter Valley**
★★

The late indefatigable Len Evans established the famous Rothbury Estate, which is now part of Beringer Blass, leaving him to preside over his own vineyard, the top-quality, ageworthy wines of which are made under contract.

 *Chardonnay • Sémillon • Shiraz*

## ANDREW HARRIS
**Mudgee**
★★☆

One of Mudgee's fastest-rising stars in the 1990s, this winery has significantly increased production and sales. Second wines sold under Twin Beaks label.

 *Classic red blend* (Cabernet Merlot The Vision Shiraz Cabernet) *• Sémillon • Sparkling* (Double Vision Sparkling Shiraz)

## HELM WINES
**Canberra District**
★

Run by the irrepressible aspiring senator Ken Helms (he ran for the senate in 2001), Helm Wines is a microcosm of Canberra District itself, hallmarked by inconsistency, yet always capable of shining here and there. Among his best examples is a soft, smooth, easy-drinking 2000 Reserve Merlot, but Ken's hobbyhorse of the moment is his Riesling Classic Dry. This is picked at lower ripeness to avoid the typically high alcohol levels of most Australian Rieslings, in an attempt to achieve a more European balance. The 2001 is not a bad stab, with its light-bodied, refreshingly elegant, lime-free fruit.

 *Riesling* (Classic Dry, Premium)

## HILLBROOK ESTATE
**Canberra District**

Hillbrook Estate is a blueprint for any winery wanting to know how to manicure vineyards and set up tourist facilities, but the wines are not so outstanding, although I enjoyed its juicy-fruity 2000 Merlot.

## HUNGERFORD HILL
**Lower Hunter Valley**
★Ⓥ

Hungerford Hill was established in 1969 by John Parker, who quickly expanded his vineyards to more than 500 acres (200 hectares), before shrinking the estate to a fifth of its former size. In 1980, a vineyard in Coonawarra was acquired, and some of the wines were blended from these two regions, which was the geographical equivalent of blending Rioja in Spain with a wine from the Great Hungarian plains! Sales increased to 200,000 cases by the late 1980s, attracting the attention of Seppelt, which took over the company. Seppelt was part of SA Brewing, which acquired Penfolds the same year, thus Hungerford Hill soon became just another Southcorp brand, and wines ended up being sourced from even more diverse regions (Hilltops, Cowra, Gundagai, and Tumbarumba), although the results were equally good. In 2002, the Hungerford Hill brand was sold to the Kirby family, who also retained the services of Phillip John, the winemaker under Southcorp ownership. Members of the Kirby family are major shareholders in Cassegrain, thus the wines were made at that winery for the first year, while the stunning new complex at Pokolbin was being constructed. The wines are still sourced from wide and far, but are primarily pure regional, rather than blended bottlings, and the quality improves with each vintage.

 *Chardonnay* (Tumbarumba) *• Merlot* (Orange) *• Pinot Noir* (Tumbarumba) *• Riesling* (Clare Valley)

## HUNTINGTON ESTATE
**Mudgee**
★☆Ⓥ

Bob Roberts entered the business with a law degree and learned winemaking through a British-based correspondence course. Not the strongest base for success, perhaps, but his clean, fleshy, well-balanced, stylish wines regularly outshine wines made by highly qualified professionals. The same vintage of the same varietal is often released under different bin numbers, prefixed with MB for medium-bodied and FB for full-bodied, and while I might prefer one bin number to another, I have always enjoyed both. Some vintages of the Cabernet Sauvignon and Sémillon possess remarkable longevity.

 *Cabernet Sauvignon* (Special Reserve Bin) *• Sémillon • Shiraz*

## INGLEWOOD WINES
**Upper Hunter Valley**
★Ⓥ

Established as Inglewood Vineyards in 1988, this business initially built its profits selling grapes to Southcorp, an activity that continues under a long-term contract. It gradually moved into wines, eventually purchasing the Tulloch brand (but not winery) from Southcorp in 2002.

 *Chardonnay* (Two Rivers Lightning Strike) *• Sémillon* (Two Rivers Stone's Throw)

## JEIR CREEK
**Canberra District**
★

The 2000 Pinot Noir showed morello cherries with floral-menthol after-aromas, making an elegant wine, despite being the color of a full-bodied Shiraz, while the fresh, luscious 2000 Botrytis Sémillon-Sauvignon Blanc was the best dessert wine I encountered in the region on my last visit.

 *Botrytis wine* (Sémillon Sauvignon) *• Shiraz*

## KAMBERRA
**Canberra District**
★☆Ⓥ

The decision to name this winery Kamberra is because Canberra itself is a derivation of the Aboriginal word kamberra. Australia's capital occupies an area of land that Europeans discovered as recently as 1821, and which was granted to Lieutenant John Moore in 1824. Moore named his property Canberry after hearing local Ngunnawal Aborigines use the word *kamberra* for "meeting place" (which is this winery's second label). For more than 21,000 years the Ngunnawal have congregated at the kamberra in late spring to feast on *bogong*, a species of moth otherwise known as *Agrotis infusa*. These moths fly south to escape the coming summer heat, which is ironic for the thousands that end up cooked in sand and hot ashes by the Ngunnawal, who remove wings and legs to eat them straight, or mash and roast them into moth cakes. Except for 15 acres (6 hectares) belonging to Mount Majura, BRL

Hardy's new venture is the only winery to have vineyards that are actually located within the Australian Capital Territory part of the Canberra District GI. BRL Hardy had been purchasing fruit from the Canberra District and surrounds since 1995. This was initially blended into the company's other labels, but the company was sufficiently impressed with the quality to build a winery here, despite the obstacles (*see* Canberra District appellation). In fact, the Chardonnay purchased from Canberra in 1996 made up 30 percent of the Eileen Hardy label for that vintage, which won the Adelaide trophy for Best Table Wine of Show and a number of other trophies, including the inaugural Max Schubert Trophy. Little wonder that the company decided to invest so heavily in Canberra District! Meeting Place is Kambera's second label. In March 2007, BRL Hardy agreed to sell Kambera to the Elvin Group.

⬧✓ *Chardonnay* • *Shiraz* • *Sparkling* (Meeting Place, Pinot Noir Chardonnay)

## KYEEMA ESTATE
### Canberra District
★

Kyeema has won nearly 30 competition trophies and is renowned for its reds, particularly Shiraz and Merlot. I loved the rich, mellow, and classy reds up to and including 1998, but found a number of the wines from 1999 to be attenuated, with simplistic, bell-pepper flavors. Only after asking owner Andrew McEwin why there appeared to be a sea change, did I discover that he had had to change the source of his award-winning grapes and figured his new vines were too young and needed time to settle down. I hoped he was right, and the reds appear to have improved, with Merlot taking over from Shiraz as the very best, so I have rated Kyeema as if he is. Second wines are sold under the Blue Gum label.

⬧✓ *Chardonnay* • *Merlot* • *Shiraz*

## LAKE GEORGE
### Canberra District
✫

In its original incarnation as Cullarin Vineyard, this was the first winery in Canberra District, and you can still visit the wooden shed where Edgar Rieck made his wines. Rieck not only established this operation in 1971, but was also the driving force behind Canberra's National Wine Show, which is where I once met him and shared one of his remarkably long-lived wines. Lake George is now owned by the Karelas Family Trust, and much has changed since Rieck's days, not just the vineyards and winery, but also the lake that this property is named after and overlooks. Lake George is mostly dry (they even play cricket on it), yet it was once full,

highlighting the dire shortage of water this region faces.

⬧✓ *Merlot* • *Pinot Noir*

## LAKE'S FOLLY
### Lower Hunter Valley
★★✫

Surgeon Max Lake had no wine-making experience when he founded this property in 1963, hence the name. Yet he introduced the use of new oak to the region and consistently produced vivid, vibrant, and stylish wines. Lake's Folly was sold for US$5.3 million in 2000 to Peter Fogarty, a Perth businessman, who installed ex-McGuigan's winemaker Rodney Kempe, since when the quality has, if anything, become even better with each vintage.

⬧✓ *Chardonnay* • *Classic red blend* (Cabernet Blend)

## LARK HILL
### Canberra District
Ⓑ★★

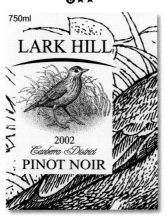

The highest vineyard in the Canberra District is one of its best, and where Pinot Noir is concerned it is the very best. I am also impressed by the richness, complexity, finesse, and length of Lark Hill's Shiraz—not quite in the Clonakilla league, but certainly the best pure Shiraz I have tasted from Canberra District. Readers will realize this is high praise indeed for a winery I first tried to visit in 1991, only to find a note tied to a tree, saying, "Sorry, but we had to go shopping." We had traveled half way around the world, and they had to go shopping. But in the years since, I have really come to like and respect David and Sue Carpenter. And they do make some very good wines.

⬧✓ *Chardonnay* • *Pinot Noir* • *Riesling* • *Shiraz*

## LAMBERT
### Canberra District
✫

Owner-winemakers Steve and Ruth Lambert planted their first vines in 1991, and studied winemaking and viticulture at Charles Sturt University in Wagga before they had their first crop. An impressive-looking winery, with a fine restaurant.

⬧✓ *Pinot Noir* • *Shiraz*

## LINDEMANS WINES
### Lower Hunter Valley

This brand is part of Southcorp, and its historic Hunter Valley home is now no more than a cellar door operation, bizarrely selling Lindemans wines from other areas. It's a shame that Lindemans' once-legendary Hunter Valley Sémillon wine is no longer produced. *See* Lindemans Wines, Victoria.

## LITTLE BRIDGE
### Canberra District
✫

Owned by four friends, who came up with the idea of planting a vineyard while out drinking a few beers together. The first vines were planted in 1997, and the first wines made in 2001. While passing through in 2006, I found Little Bridge's 2004 Merlot to be the best example of that varietal I had yet tasted from the Canberra District.

⬧✓ *Merlot*

## MADEW WINES
### Canberra District
✫

On the heels of Doonkuna when it comes to producing the most consistent Riesling. Lettuce-crisp, and limey-floral, it typically goes petrolly within 2 years.

⬧✓ *Riesling*

## MARGAN FAMILY
### Lower Hunter Valley
★

Although the vineyard was established in 1989, the winery was built in 1998, and the quality is very good.

⬧✓ *Botrytis* (Sémillon) • *Cabernet Sauvignon* • *Merlot* (House of Certain Views)

## McGUIGAN WINES
### Lower Hunter Valley
★★Ⓥ

Now part of McGuigan Simeon, this winery was established by Brian McGuigan as recently as 1992, yet was the precursor to the fifth-largest wine company. A two-star rating might appear controversially high to some critics, but McGuigan produces some superb wines at giveaway prices, performing at least as well as the two-star McWilliam's winery.

⬧✓ *Cabernet Sauvignon* (Genus 4 Old Vine, Hopcroft Estate) • *Chardonnay* (Bin 700, Genus 4 Old Vine) • *Petit Verdot* (Verdot Superior) • *Sémillon* (Bin 9000) • *Shiraz* (Genus 4 Old Vine)

## McWILLIAM'S
### Riverina
★★Ⓥ

The original McWilliam's winery might be based in Riverina, but most of its best wines are sourced from the classic regions.

⬧✓ *Botrytis* (Limited Release Botrytis Sémillon) • *Chardonnay* (Hanwood) •

*Classic white blend* (Margaret River Sémillon-Sauvignon Blanc) • *Fortified* (Amontillado, Family Reserve Tawny Port, Hanwood Fine Tawny, Show Reserve Liqueur Muscat) • *Riesling* (Clare, Eden Valley) • *Sémillon* (Hunter Valley)

## McWILLIAM'S MOUNT PLEASANT
### Lower Hunter Valley
★★Ⓥ

McWilliam's Mount Pleasant Elizabeth bottle-aged Sémillon is one of Australia's finest examples of this unique wine style, and one of its greatest bargains too. Look out for its museum releases.

⬧✓ *Chardonnay* (Maurice O'Shea) • *Classic red blend* ('1877' Cabernet Sauvignon-Shiraz) • *Sémillon* (Elizabeth, Lovedale) • *Riesling* (Collection) • *Shiraz* (Maurice O'Shea, OP & OH) • *Sparkling* (Brut)

## MIRAMAR WINES
### Mudgee
★Ⓥ

Ian McRae used to be seriously underrated, yet—ironically—the greatest of these wines has tapered off in quality since the mid-1990s. At their best, they can still be big and rich, in true Mudgee style.

⬧✓ *Botrytis* (Doux Blanc) • *Cabernet Sauvignon* • *Chardonnay* • *Sémillon* • *Shiraz* (Eljamar)

## MOUNT MAJURA
### Canberra District
★

The best wine has consistently been Mount Majura's rich, soft, and creamy Chardonnay, but I believe the vineyard will eventually produce greater Pinot Noir. It is also worth keeping an eye on the Cabernet Franc-Merlot blend and the Tempranillo. Second wines sold under the Woolshed Creek label.

⬧✓ *Chardonnay* • *Pinot Noir* • *Riesling* • *Tempranillo* (since 2005)

## MOUNT VIEW ESTATE
### Lower Hunter Valley
★✫Ⓥ

Established in 1971 by Harry and Anne Tulloch, who sold the property in 2000 to John and Polly Burgess. They have hired the talents of Keith Tulloch to maintain family traditions at the 40-acre (16-hectare) terraced estate.

⬧✓ *Cabernet Sauvignon* • *Chardonnay* (Reserve) • *Sémillon* (Reserve) • *Shiraz* (Reserve)

## MURRUMBATEMAN WINERY
### Canberra District
✫

The creamy-rich, black-pepper fruit in Murrumbateman's Reserve Shiraz just beats the menthol-laden Cabernet-Merlot for this winery's best wine. The juicy, rose-petal-infused fruit in the Rose of Australia makes a refreshingly enjoyable picnic wine, but blended from Traminer, Riesling, and Merlot, it should be relabeled Digger's Hodgepodge.

✓ *Barbera* • *Classic red blend* (Cabernet-Merlot) • *Pinot Noir*

## PANKHURST
### Canberra District
### ★❤

Since establishing this vineyard in 1986, Allan and Christine Pankhurst have built up a reputation for Pinot Noir. The wines are not made here, but at Lark Hill, where contract winemakers David and Sue Carpenter certainly have the expertise to maximize the potential of Pankhurst's excellent vineyard.

✓ *Chardonnay* • *Classic red blend* (Cabernet-Merlot) • *Pinot Noir*

## PETERSONS
### Lower Hunter Valley
### ★★

Petersons went through a difficult time in the early 1990s, but has returned to form, and even seems to be getting better with every new vintage.

✓ *Botrytis* (Sémillon) • *Cabernet Sauvignon* (Ian's Selection) • *Chardonnay* • *Sémillon* (Show Reserve) • *Shiraz* (Back Block, Glenesk, Glenesk Old Block Shiraz, Ian's Selection)

## POET'S CORNER
### Mudgee
### ★☆❤

The history of Poet's Corner is a bit like a reverse takeover, albeit one that is now confined within one of Australia's largest wine groups. Poet's Corner is housed in the old Craigmoor building, which was established in 1858. At one time, Craigmoor was the only winery in Mudgee, but was taken over in 1983 by Montrose, which owned three vineyards in the area, one of them being Poet's Corner, whence the brand was born. Montrose was purchased in 1988 by Wyndham Estate, which was itself purchased in 1990 by Orlando, to form Orlando Wyndham. Thus it is that Poet's Corner, which grew out of Montrose, which took over Craigmoor, is now the primary brand in the group's Mudgee outpost, with the older, once more famous brands of Montrose and Craigmoor effectively its second labels. However, while the Montrose label might be secondary, the quality of many of its wines most certainly is not.

✓ *Sémillon* (Henry Lawson) • *Shiraz* (Montrose Black)

## POTHANA
### Lower Hunter Valley
### ★★

The family-owned brand of well-traveled, former Lake's Folly winemaker David Hook.

✓ *Chardonnay* (Belford) • *Sémillon* (Belford) • *Shiraz*

## RAVENSWORTH
### Canberra District
### ★❤

The personal brand of Bryan Martin, the assistant winemaker at Clonakilla. Martin is also the vineyard manager and a partner in Rosehill Vineyards, which is where these wines are sourced from. Although he's busy doing these three jobs, he seems to spend more time in the kitchen, cooking for any passing wine journalist he can drag off the street. Despite being a graduate of Charles Sturt University, with a Bachelor of Applied Science (Wine Science) and an Associate Degree in Applied Science (Wine Growing), his background is in the food and hospitality industry. When he's not cooking, Martin teaches food at various institutes including the Australian International Hotel School.

✓ *Marsanne* • *Shiraz*

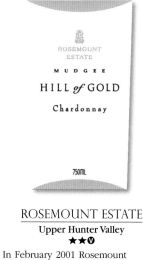

## ROSEMOUNT ESTATE
### Upper Hunter Valley
### ★★❤

In February 2001 Rosemount merged with Southcorp and, for a while, Philip Shaw became chief winemaker, pushing to one side—and eventually out—John Duval, Penfolds' illustrious winemaker. It was Shaw who made Rosemount's reputation, and maintained it even when production went stratospheric, so when he went, it left open the question of just how it might affect the future quality of this brand. However, the new winemaker, Matt Koch, has assisted Shaw since 1995, and there are just so many outstanding wines that I cannot see it all falling apart at the seams. So, if the ailing Southcorp can repair Rosemount's marketing, this brand should deserve at least a two-star rating. The best of the inexpensive Diamond range represents amazing value. To avoid confusion, I have also included here wines made at

the Rosemount Estate's winery in McLaren Vale, South Australia.

✓ *Cabernet Sauvignon* (Coonawarra Show Reserve, Diamond, Orange, Traditional) • *Chardonnay* (Giant's Creek, Orange, Show Reserve) • *Classic red blend* (Diamond Shiraz-Cabernet, GSM, Mountain Blue Shiraz-Cabernet) • *Merlot* (Orange) • *Pinot Noir* (Diamond) • *Sémillon* (Diamond, Show Reserve) • *Shiraz* (Diamond, Hill of Gold Mudgee, McLaren Vale, Orange, Show Reserve) • *Syrah* (Balmoral)

## ROTHBURY ESTATE
### Lower Hunter Valley
### ★★★❤

Once owned by the late Len Evans, who took the company public, and under his chairmanship it continued to produce wines of an extraordinarily high quality. Evans left in 1996, when Rothbury was taken over by Mildara Blass, now Beringer Blass. Quality is currently very high.

✓ *Chardonnay* (Brokenback) • *Merlot* (Neil McGuigan Series) • *Sémillon* (Brokenback, Neil McGuigan Series) • *Shiraz* (Brokenback)

## TALGA
### Canberra District
### ★★☆

Established in 1998 by the Richard family, and son-in-law Ian Little. The Chardonnay is a rich, oaky, designer wine, whereas the firm tannins in the Shiraz make it a much more serious long-term prospect—although it should also appeal to the same wealthy segment of the market.

✓ *Chardonnay* • *Shiraz*

## TOWER ESTATE
### Lower Hunter Valley
### ★★❤

Any joint venture involving Len Evans is bound to be noteworthy, and at Tower Estate, it is the relatively inexpensive price asked for such stunning quality that is so amazing.

✓ *Chardonnay* • *Riesling* • *Sémillon* • *Shiraz*

## TULLOCH
### Upper Hunter Valley
### ☆❤

Once one of the most traditional wineries in the Hunter Valley, it was little more than a brand under

Southcorp, which in 2002 sold the winery to People's Rock and the brand to Inglewood Wines. Southcorp kept the quality generally good, with the occasional star performer. Hopefully, Inglewood will do at least as well.

✓ *Verdelho*

## KEITH TULLOCH
### Lower Hunter Valley
### ★★

Eponymous brand established in 1997 by a former Lindemans and Rothbury Estate winemaker with a small, but expanding production. Five varietal wines made under the Per Diem label (Cabernet Sauvignon, Chardonnay, Merlot, Shiraz, and Verdelho) are produced exclusively for The Australian Wine Selectors club.

✓ *Chardonnay* • *Classic red blend* (Forres Blend) • *Sémillon* • *Shiraz* (Kester)

## TYRRELL'S VINEYARDS
### Lower Hunter Valley
### ★★

This long-established winery is still family-owned, and although in the 1990s some critics believed that Tyrrell's Chardonnay Vat 47 was not quite as outstanding as it was in the 1970s and 1980s, that was because the number of great Australian Chardonnay wines had increased, not because the quality of Vat 47 had dropped. It is still one of this country's exceptional white wines, although I have to say that what impresses me most here is the Sémillon, especially when aged in bottle. The Shee-Oak Chardonnay is unoaked. It refers to the name of the vineyard where the Chardonnay is grown, and it was so named because of the she-oak trees surrounding the vines. She-oak, or *Casuarina equisetifolia*, is not an oak as such, but an evergreen with red, termite-resistant wood.

✓ *Cabernet-Merlot* (Old Winery) • *Chardonnay* (Shee-Oak, Vat 47) • *Sémillon* (Belford, Lost Block, Steven's Reserve, Vat 1) • *Shiraz* (Old Winery, Vat 9)

## WYNDHAM ESTATE WINES
### Lower Hunter Valley
### ★☆❤

Part of the French-owned Orlando Wyndham group since 1990, Wyndham Estate offers a great range of good-value wines, particularly under the Show Reserve label.

✓ *Cabernet Sauvignon* (Mudgee Show Reserve) • *Fortified* (George Wyndham Old Tawny Port) • *Sémillon* (Show Reserve).

# VICTORIA AND TASMANIA

*Although Victoria is the smallest of Australia's mainland states, it is second only to South Australia for the volume of wine produced, and is by far the most diverse in terms of cool-climate terroirs and the styles of premium-quality wine made. And Tasmania is, of course, cool-climate personified.*

The wines of these two states range from deep-colored, cassis-flavored Cabernet Sauvignon to some surprisingly classy Pinot Noir; from light and delicate aromatic whites, to rich, oaky, yet finely structured Chardonnay and Sémillon; as well as fortified and sparkling wines of the highest reputation. Whereas Victoria is one of Australia's oldest winemaking states, and the most famous when it comes to the country's classic fortified specialties, especially its rich and sticky liqueur Muscat and Tokay, Tasmania is Australia's youngest winemaking state, and is better known for its potential than its actual quality: its greatest vineyards are probably not yet planted, and its finest wine styles possibly unimagined.

PIPERS BROOK VINEYARD, TASMANIA
*This world famous winery dominates Pipers Brook, the most successful wine-producing district of Tasmania.*

VICTORIA AND TASMANIA, *see also* p.552
*The relatively small state of Victoria lies beneath New South Wales and neighboring South Australia. The island of Tasmania lies due south, on the same latitude as New Zealand's South Island. This area covers a wide variety of climates, terrains, and wines.*

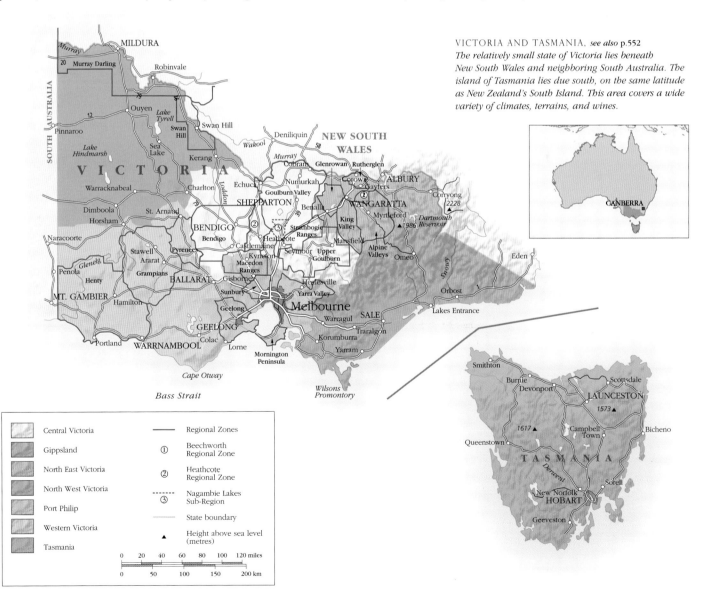

**CHÂTEAU TAHBILK, GOULBURN VALLEY**
*This well-known Victorian winery's huge output consists of traditionally made wines. Its Cabernets can be very tannic, requiring at least 10 years in the bottle.*

## VICTORIA

John Batman established Melbourne in 1834, and within four years, William Ryrie, a sheep farmer, planted the first Yarra Valley vineyard in a place that became known as Yering. The most important sequence of events in the viticultural history of the state began with the appointment of Swiss-born Charles La Trobe as Superintendent of Melbourne in 1839 and culminated in the arrival of 11 fellow Swiss *vignerons* from his home canton of Neufchâtel in 1846. They laid the foundation of Victoria's future wine industry when they settled in the Geelong district and planted vineyards around their homes.

## TASMANIA

Although this is really a new wine region, the first vines planted here were established in 1823 at Prospect Farm by Bartholomew Broughton, an extraordinary convict who had been granted a pardon and eventually came to own a substantial amount of property. By 1827 the quality of his wines had prompted the *Colonial Times* to contrast them with those of Gregory Blaxland, whose Parramatta River vineyard near Sydney had already produced Australia's first exported and first medal-winning wine. The paper reported that a Dr. Shewin, who had tasted Blaxland's famous wine, remarked that by comparison Broughton's was "as far superior as fine Port to Blackstrap."

Such was the cruelty of Britain's penal system in the colonies that it took its toll on Broughton's lifespan. His successful attempt to be

**GREAT DIVIDING RANGE, VICTORIA**
*Vines grow on the main upland areas of Victoria, a continuation of Eastern Australia's Great Dividing Range, which is up to 190 miles (300 kilometers) wide.*

pardoned suggests that he probably suffered less than most convicts at the time, yet it was sufficient to cut short the luxury of his freedom. He died in 1828, aged 32. Captain Charles Swanston purchased Broughton's property, and by 1865 there were no fewer than 45 different varieties of vines flourishing at various sites on the island. Yet, by the end of the same decade, virtually all the vineyards had disappeared. Except for an ephemeral resurgence in the 1880s, Tasmania's wine industry was nonexistent until the renaissance of the 1950s, led by a Frenchman named Jean Miguet.

Miguet was not a *vigneron* by profession; he came to Tasmania to work on the construction of a hydroelectric plant, but his new home at La Provence, north of Launceston, reminded him of his native Haute-Savoie and, since it was protected from ocean winds by trees, he believed that grapes might ripen there. In 1956 he cleared his bramble-strewn land and planted vines that grew successfully enough to encourage another European, Claudio Alcorso, to establish a vineyard on the Derwent River in 1958. Alcorso and his Moorilla Estate are still prospering, but after fifteen years, ill-health forced Miguet to abandon his vineyard and return to France, where he sadly died from leukemia in 1974.

The Tasmanian wine industry is still relatively tiny, but has undergone a rapid and exciting transformation over the past five years and the quality just gets better. It is an island whose destiny is to produce Australia's finest traditional-method sparkling wine. Tasmania produces some intensely flavored Chardonnay and Riesling, and as far as red wines are concerned, Pinot Noir offers the greatest potential.

## FACTORS AFFECTING TASTE AND QUALITY

**LOCATION**
Victoria is the smallest of Australia's mainland states, situated in the very southeastern corner of the continent. The island of Tasmania lies 100 miles (160 kilometers) due south of Victoria.

**CLIMATE**
Climates are extremely varied, ranging from the hot continental conditions of northwest Victoria around Mildura, to the temperate coastal climes of the Yarra Valley, and the cooler conditions of Tasmania.

**ASPECT**
Vines are grown on all types of land from the flat or undulating low-lying valley plains, mostly producing vast quantities of basic-quality wines, to the steeper, sloping sites favored for premium wines, where vineyards are planted to an altitude of 2,150 feet (650 meters).

**SOIL**
A wide variety of soils, ranging from the red loam of northeast Victoria that produces its famous fortified wines; through the sandy alluvial soils of the Murray Basin that produce mainly bulk wines; the gravelly soil mixed with quartz and shale on a clay subsoil found in the premium wine-producing Pyrenees area; and the rich, poorly drained, volcanic soils in Geelong, to the clay of Tasmania.

**VITICULTURE AND VINIFICATION**
Victoria is the only Australian state to have been totally devastated by phylloxera (1875–81) and so, unlike

neighboring South Australia, its vines all have to be grafted on to American rootstock. It generally utilizes high-quality wine-producing techniques. The northeast is traditionally dessert-wine country, but here, as elsewhere in Australia, winemakers have searched for cool-climate areas to expand the state's premium varietal industry since the 1970s. The famous traditional method sparkling wines of Victoria's Great Western region have suffered with competition from the new up-and-coming sparkling wine areas such as the French-influenced Bendigo district to the east. Tasmania has also taken to sparkling wine, and its cool climate has led to a varied cultivation of classic grape varieties. Viticulture and methods of vinification are in a constant state of flux as the tiny new wineries seek to establish a style.

**GRAPE VARIETIES**
**Primary varieties:** Cabernet Sauvignon, Chardonnay, Marsanne, Merlot, Muscat Blanc à Petit Grains, Muscadelle, Pinot Noir, Riesling, Sauvignon Blanc, Sémillon, Shiraz
**Secondary varieties:** Arneis, Barbera, Cabernet Franc, Carignan, Chasselas, Cinsault, Cortese, Crouchen, Dolcetto, Durif, Flora, Folle Blanche, Frontignan Blanc, Gamay, Gewürztraminer, Graciano, Grenache, Lagrein, Malbec, Marzemino, Mondeuse, Mourvèdre, Muscat d'Alexandrie, Nebbiolo, Orange Muscat, Petit Verdot, Pinot Gris, Pinot Meunier, Roussanne, Sangiovese, Tarrango, Tempranillo, Verduzzo, Viognier

## STICKY STUFF

Victoria's fortified wines are world class, with Liqueur Muscat and Liqueur Tokay its supreme classics: great wines that know no peers. The older these wines are, the sweeter they are likely to be, in addition to being richer and more complex. Since many of these products are exported to Europe, where most of the terminology evolved, the same wine will be available bearing a different designation, thus the current status of these wines under EU regulations is also provided. Many of these wines are being shipped to Europe as "Australian Fortified Wine" or "Fortified Wine of Australia" qualified by acceptable terms such as "ruby" or "tawny," but it is illegal to use the word "fortified" on any wine in the US, so there are designation complications for that market that are even more difficult to generalize about.

**Liqueur Muscat** The most luscious of Australia's fortified wines, the best Liqueur Muscat can be like liquid fruitcake. This wine is usually made from Brown Muscat (Muscat Blanc à Petits Grains), and has a minimum of 160g/l of residual sugar. While it is well worth paying a premium for a step or two up on a producer's entry-level Liqueur Muscat, there is no need to be seduced by ultrarare, superexpensive, extremely ancient bottlings, unless you just want a mind-blowing, tiny sip, since they are seldom drinkable in the ordinary sense. There

are no EU restrictions on the naming of this product. *See also* Classifications, below.

**Liqueur Port** Invariably made in a *rancio* style, to replicate a tawny rather than vintage or ruby port character. Traditionally, Australian port grape varieties include Shiraz, Grenache and Mataro (Mourvèdre). Under EU-Australian agreements, the name Liqueur Port is due to be phased out, but the date for this was supposed to have been agreed by the end of 1997, and by 2004 not even the phase-out date had been agreed. Until it is, Australian fortified wines may be labelled "Port" in Australia, and in any export market where this name is legally permitted as a generic style. In the long term, it seems likely that "Australian Vintage Port" will be replaced by "Australian Vintage", and "Australian Tawny Port" by "Australian Tawny", as inadequate as they may seem. Suggested future technical restrictions include a minimum of 18% alcohol, and a maximum of 72g/l of residual sugar. *See also* Classifications below.

**Liqueur Sherry** Traditionally the most important grapes for Australian Sherry-style wines are Muscat, Palomino and Pedro Ximenez. Until the EU phase-out date (*see above*) has been agreed and reached, it remains legal for Australian fortified wines to be labelled "Sherry" (qualified or not) in Australia, and in any export market where this name is legally

permitted as a generic style. In markets that do not allow "Sherry" on wines other than those from Jerez in Spain, "Australian Aperitif Wine" will be qualified by Pale Dry (for fino style with less than 10g/l residual sugar), and "Australian Dessert Wine" by Medium Dry (for amontillado style with less than 27g/l sugar), Medium Sweet (for oloroso style with 28–72g/l sugar), Sweet (over 72g/l), and Cream (over 90g/l).

**Liqueur Tokay** Australia's very own, unique fortified wine style, Liqueur Tokay is made exclusively from Muscadelle grapes and has a minimum of 158g/l of residual sugar. No restrictions so far under EU-Australian agreements, despite Hungary's membership of the EU and restrictions in EU winemaking areas such as Alsace. Strangely, Australian Liqueur Tokay was still available in EU markets in 2004, but it will inevitably have to change its name one day. *See also* Classifications below.

---

### Classifications
The following age-based classifications apply only to Australian Port, Muscat, and Tokay:

Classic: minimum 5 years
Grand: minimum 10 years
Rare: minimum 15 years

---

THE APPELLATIONS OF
# VICTORIA AND TASMANIA

## ALPINE VALLEYS
Most of the wineries and vineyards in the Alpine Valleys region are located in and around the upper reaches of the Ovens River, although vines grow as far north as the Kiewa Valley. This is a cool-climate region, with primarily Chardonnay, Sauvignon Blanc, Cabernet Sauvignon, Merlot, Pinot Noir, and Shiraz grapes growing on alluvial soils. The wines are ripe and well structured, although the Shiraz can be quite rustic.

## BEECHWORTH
This small GI region within the North West Victoria zone is former gold-digging country, where Ned Kelly once plied his trade as Australia's most infamous "bushranger." Beechworth is located in the foothills of the Victorian Alps, at the northeastern edge of the Alpine Valleys, of which it is geographically a part, but Beechworth contains wineries of superstar quality, such as Giaconda, and thus it has been accorded its own regional status. The soils vary from fertile sandy alluvium on the Ovens Valley flood plain to granitic loam over decomposed gravel and clay at higher elevations, and it is the latter that produces some of Australia's finest Chardonnay, not to mention some excellent Pinot Noir and Riesling. The size and structure of Giaconda's Chardonnay belie Beechworth's cool, sub-alpine, frosty climate. Fortified wine is a small but strong feature of this region.

## BENDIGO
Situated about 100 miles (160 kilometers) northwest of Melbourne, this part of the Central

Victoria zonal GI has a dry climate, although only some of its vines are irrigated. Bendigo is goldmining country, and viticulture began here during the 1850s Gold Rush. The vineyards tend to be small and scattered over three main growing areas: the Granite Slopes to the southeast; Loddon Valley to the northwest; and Marong and Golden Waters to the southwest. Bendigo is primarily known for its menthol-eucalyptus-tasting red wines. The sandy loam over red clay, quartz, and ironstone soil is well suited to producing top-quality Shiraz, but Cabernet Sauvignon and Chardonnay can also excel. More recent plantings have even included such contrasting varietals as Sauvignon Blanc and Viognier. And, as Domaine Chandon (known as Green Point on export markets) has shown, the potential for premium-quality sparkling wines also exists.

## CENTRAL VICTORIA
Also known as Victorian High Country, this zonal GI encompasses the regional GIs of Bendigo, Goulburn Valley, Heathcote, Strathbogie Ranges, and Upper Goulburn.

## GEELONG
Southeast of Ballarat, facing Melbourne across Port Phillip Bay, the vineyards of this district fan beyond the town of Geelong itself. Viticulture was established by Swiss immigrants in the mid-1800s, but came to a halt in 1875, when phylloxera struck, and the Victorian government ordered the removal of all vines. Geelong began its viticultural revival in 1966, somewhat earlier than other rediscovered areas of Australia, when Nini and Daryl Sefton planted the Idyll

vineyard. The cool climate and volcanic soil produce wines of fine acidity and varietal character, particularly from Chardonnay and Pinot Noir. Cabernet Sauvignon and Shiraz sometimes fare well. Bannockburn and Scotchman's Hill are the best producers.

## GIPPSLAND
Sometimes referred to as Coastal Victoria, this vast zonal GI encompasses two relatively small areas known locally as East Gippsland and South Gippsland, but has expanded well beyond these boundaries to give some sort of common thread to 20-odd wineries. Most vineyards are located in and around the towns of Bairnsdale, Loch, and Foster on the South Gippsland Highway.

## GLENROWAN
Part of the North East zone, this region was once better known outside Australia as Milawa, thanks to Brown Brothers, which used the name on its widely exported wines. Glenrowan has always, however, been more widely used by other winemakers. This is a classic dessert-wine area, but individual vineyards produce excellent Cabernet Sauvignon and other premium varietals, even Graciano (Brown Brothers 1974 Milawa Graciano was still in truly amazing form in 2004).

## GOULBURN VALLEY
**Subregion:**
*Nagambie Lakes*

Chateau Tahbilk (now known simply as Tahbilk) was the solitary exponent of fine wines in this traditional wine district 75 miles (120 kilometers) north of Melbourne, until the Mitchelton winery was established in 1969. Since then a number of new wineries have opened their doors, and begun to attract attention. At the heart of this region, qualitatively, or at its southern tip, geographically, is Nagambie Lakes, which has its own, well-deserved GI. Beyond this subregion, most Goulburn Valley vines are located to the north, in and around Mooroopna and Shepparton, but there are others farther north in Katunga, to the east between Cobram and Yarrawonga, and to the west near Echuca.

The region's climate is warm and dry in the summer, making it dependent on irrigation from the Goulburn River and aquifers. The wines are generally full-bodied, with Cabernet Sauvignon and Shiraz the best varieties, whether in their pure form or, more traditionally, blended together. Shiraz gets more attention than Cabernet Sauvignon these days, perhaps because of the Great Australian Shiraz Challenge, which has taken place here every year since 1995. Such an event obviously focuses attention on the locally grown Shiraz, although the competition is open to any Australian region. Chardonnay and Riesling can also be very good, and both Tahbilk and Mitchelton have produced excellent Marsanne.

## GRAMPIANS

The famous old sparkling-wine district of Great Western has been renamed Grampians under the GI scheme. Although it is still best known for sparkling wines, the dropping of Great Western should at least allow the region's finest varietal, Shiraz, to shine without being lumbered by a name that is linked historically and indelibly to the connotation of bubbly. Cabernet Sauvignon, Chardonnay, and Riesling can also be excellent. Top-performing wineries are Best's, Mount Langi Ghiran, and Seppelt.

## HEATHCOTE

Formerly considered by many to be part of Bendigo, Heathcote has been recognized by Australia's GI system as a wine region in its own right since 2002. This is due, in part, to its reputation as a premium Shiraz-producing area, which is well deserved, and has been built up slowly over 20 years of often outstanding vintages from the likes of Jasper Hill. However, it is perhaps no coincidence that the influential critic Robert Parker awarded Wild Duck Creek Estate 1997 Duck Muck Shiraz a perfect 100-point score, which not only propelled its owner, David "Duck" Anderson, from obscurity to international fame overnight, but also reflected well on the potential of the entire locality. This assessment was responsible for the US discovering Australian Shiraz in general, and a GI of its own was the least that Heathcote deserved in the circumstances. The region sits on the north side of the Great Dividing Range at elevations between 525 to 1,050 feet (160 to 320 meters). The soil is a rich, red volcanic type known as Cambrian, the mineral content of which is said to favour the production of red wine varietals, particularly Shiraz.

## HENTY

Formerly known as Drumborg, then Far South West and now a GI by the name of Henty, this remote region might have a changing identity, but is still best known for Seppelt's Drumborg winery. Henty takes its name from the Henty brothers, who in 1834 were the first to settle this part of the Portland Bay area, where they established a sheep station. In addition to the famous merino sheep, the Henty brothers also brought vines with them, plus "13 heifers, five pigs, four working bullocks, two turkeys, and six dogs." Grapes were more of an afterthought, and it seems that the idea of a vineyard literally withered on the vine.

The earliest truly commercial viticultural operation was not set up until much later, when Seppelt established its Drumborg winery in the 1960s. The company had been looking for new supplies of grapes to furnish its growing production of sparkling wines, and the grapes from this area have been very useful components in many an Australian bubbly blend ever since. The soil is volcanic and the climate so cool that some varieties did not ripen. It is surprising, therefore, that Cabernet Sauvignon and Merlot should be so successful here, but they can be excellent; Riesling and Pinot Noir are also very good. A number of other wineries have now opened up.

## KING VALLEY

Until 1989 Brown Brothers was the sole buyer of grapes in King Valley, but the fruit has since been sold far and wide, and other wineries have been built here. It has now become a full-fledged GI, but the boundaries were not finalized at the time of writing, thus the area depicted on the map should be considered as an approximate representation. Chardonnay, Riesling, and Cabernet are the most important varieties, but Barbera, Nebbiolo, and Sangiovese have shown the greatest potential. Sparkling wine is also produced.

## MACEDON RANGES

A developing district within the Central Victoria region, Macedon (plain and simple) was once considered to include Sunbury, but that has since been established as a GI in its own right, and this region is now referred to as Macedon Ranges. The good folk of Melbourne flock to the Macedon Ranges in summer to escape the heat, thus it has the reputation of an "icy-cold" climate. Cool, maybe, but icy, I think not. The Macedon Ranges are certainly cool enough for some sparkling winemakers to source grapes from here. Chardonnay and Pinot Noir are also good, but a whole range of grapes grows well here, if the site is carefully selected to maximize the number of hours of sunshine.

## MORNINGTON PENINSULA

After an early, but unsuccessful, start in the 1950s, a number of growers have established vineyards in this area overlooking Port Phillip Bay, south of Melbourne. Although only a handful established wineries initially, there are now more than 40 facilities in the area. Provided the vineyards are adequately protected from strong sea winds that whip up over the bay, Mornington Peninsula's cool, often wet, maritime climate shows great potential for first-class winemaking. Chardonnay and Pinot Noir are already exciting, with Viognier and Pinot Gris waiting in the wings. The red volcanic soils would seem to be ideal for premium Shiraz and, to a lesser degree, Cabernet Sauvignon, Malbec, and Merlot.

## MURRAY DARLING

This regional GI overlaps two zonal GIs: North West Victoria and Big Rivers, New South Wales. The region takes its name from the Murray and Darling rivers, two of Australia's great wine rivers. Farther upstream is the Rutherglen area while just downstream is Riverland. The Murray Darling region brings together several areas of mainly irrigated vineyards dotted along the banks of the middle section of the river. Vineyard plantings soared in the late 1990s, creating a major switch of emphasis from white to red, with some impressive and, frankly, unexpected results coming through.

## NAGAMBIE LAKES

The Nagambie Lakes subregion GI is part of the Goulburn Valley, where the Tahbilk and Mitchelton wineries are located. This is where the very best Goulburn Valley wines have traditionally been made. Its boundaries were determined on the basis of the Nagambie Lakes system, a large body of water made up of lakes, billabongs, lagoons, and streams of, and linked by, the Goulburn River. It is the only wine region in Australia where the climate is dramatically influenced by an inland water mass, which enables the vines to enjoy a milder, cooler climate than would otherwise be expected. This is a vivid illustration of man's role as the joker in the *terroir* pack, because these bodies of water are all man-made, as is the Goulburn River Weir, which created them, and was constructed in 1888 following a four-year drought (1877–81). Another factor in determining the Nagambie Lakes GI boundary was the rare soil type found in the area. Known as duplex 2.2, this soil is a red, sandy loam with a very high iron oxide content (hence the color), over a gravelly-sandy alluvium deposited by the river system, and this is said to give a certain distinctive regional character to the wines.

## NORTHEAST VICTORIA

This zonal GI encompasses the regional GIs of Alpine Valleys, Beechworth, Glenrowan, and Rutherglen.

## NORTHWEST VICTORIA

This zonal GI encompasses the Victorian parts of the regional GIs of Murray Darling and Swan Hill.

## PORT PHILLIP

This zonal GI encompasses the regional GIs of Geelong, Macedon Ranges, Mornington Peninsula, Sunbury, and Yarra Valley.

## PYRENEES

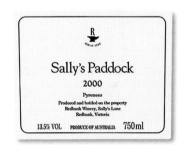

Formerly known as the Avoca district, the vineyards around Mount Avoca, Redbank, and Moonambel are now called Pyrenees, although the former name will no doubt remain in use for a while. Pyrenees, the name of a nearby mountain range, was chosen by local wine growers as an expressive marketing "hook" upon which to "hang" their wines. By whatever name, this area was originally perceived to be red-wine country, making wines of a distinctive and attractive minty character. There was a time in the early 1990s when white wine and even sparkling wine were thought to be the region's best prospects, but the original perceptions have since been proven right. Shiraz, Cabernet Sauvignon, and Merlot are the outstanding wines, with Chardonnay, and perhaps Pinot Noir, on the next rung of quality.

## RUTHERGLEN

Rutherglen was once considered by many to include also Glenrowan (or Milawa), but it has always been the heart of the Northeast region and the soul of Victoria's wine industry, and since 1997 its own boundaries have been determined by the GI process. Although there are other, arguably more exciting, regions in Victoria, it remains the hub around which the entire state's most traditional viticultural activities revolve. Rutherglen comprises a collection of wineries and vineyards on the south bank of the Murray River, around the town of Rutherglen, and farther south into the hinterland. This is Australia's greatest dessert-wine country, producing liqueur Muscats and Tokays that know no peers. However, in addition to these world-famous fortified wines, the cooler areas of Rutherglen have emerged as an innovative light wine-producing region. Chardonnay and Sémillon are clean, fresh, and vibrant; Gewürztraminer is performing relatively well; and Durif, Carignan, Shiraz, and Cabernet Sauvignon all show promise to one degree or another.

## STRATHBOGIE RANGES

Better known in Australia than abroad, this region was first planted in 1968 by Alan Plunkett, whose natural inclination was to grow cool-climate varieties, such as Riesling and Gewürztraminer. In the 1990s Dominion Wines drew attention to the area by establishing its winery at Avenel. Others followed and, in recent years, the Strathbogie Ranges has developed a growing reputation as a source for sparkling wine components, and for crisp, fresh white wines of excellent fruit intensity from a number of boutique wineries. The vineyards are located at varying altitudes, ranging from 500 to 2,130 feet (150 to 650 meters). This, plus the diversity of soil types throughout the region, suggests there may be an untapped potential for numerous styles of wine beyond the grape varieties already cultivated, which include Chardonnay, Pinot Gris, Riesling, Sauvignon Blanc, Cabernet Franc, Cabernet Sauvignon, Merlot, and Pinot Noir.

## SUNBURY

Sunbury is lower in altitude and much warmer in climate than the Macedon Ranges, which abut this region along the 1,310-foot (400-meter) contour line. It has alluvial soils on the plain and basalt-based loams on the slopes. Sunbury was lumped together with Macedon as part of the same region until it achieved its own GI in 1998. This status was deserved for historical reasons alone, Sunbury having been productive as a viticultural region as long ago as the 1860s. Indeed, it was Sunbury, not Macedon, that was established by the founders of Goona Warra in 1858 and Craiglee in 1864. Many Australians favor this region's Chardonnay and Shiraz, and these are definitely the best wines from its leading wine producer today, Craiglee. Other varieties grown include Sauvignon Blanc, Sémillon, Cabernet Sauvignon, and Pinot Noir. A number of new vineyards

were planted in the 1990s, and there are now 14 winemakers in the region.

## SWAN HILL

This regional GI overlaps New South Wales, extending to Kyalite, but most producers are located in Victoria. Swan Hill has a Mediterranean climate, with high temperatures and low summer rainfall, making viticulture dependent on irrigation from the Murray River. The region encompasses Brown Brothers' Mystic Park vineyard to the south, and a couple of other large wineries (Andrew Peace and R. L. Buller), but mainly comprises smaller boutique wineries. There are some very good red wines from Cabernet Franc, Cabernet Sauvignon, Shiraz, Durif, and Sangiovese; whites are less exciting, although Chardonnay and Riesling fare quite well. The Golden Mile Wine Trail runs from Goodnight in the north to Beverford in the south, with many of the wineries along the way offering lunch, as well as the inevitable cellar-door sales.

## TASMANIA

Tasmania is Australia's ultimate cool-climate location. The first vines were planted on Prospect Farm near Hobart in 1823 by Bartholomew Broughton, but viticulture did not last long on what was then Van Diemen's Land. The wine industry was gradually rekindled in the 1950s. Hopes of international recognition were raised in the late 1980s, when Champagne producer Louis Roederer invested in Heemskerk to produce a premium sparkling wine called Jansz, but Roederer pulled out in 1994 amid patently untrue rumors that the grapes would not ripen. Heemskerk was purchased by Dr. Andrew Pirie of Pipers Brook, Tasmania's largest and best winery. Pirie kept the vineyards, but sold the Jansz brand to Yalumba, since when his own bubbly, the eponymous Pirie, has established itself as one of the greatest sparkling wines in the world. When a winery goes public, success often breeds takeovers; Pipers Brook was taken over by a Belgian firm, and Pirie was asked to leave. In 2004 he had purchased back the right to use his own name, so it is difficult to tell whether the reputation of Tasmanian sparkling wine will be led by Pipers Brook or Pirie. Or Jansz perhaps? Or a different bubbly altogether?

Although Jansz's vintages in the 1990s have been disappointing, as have those of other aspiring Tasmanian fizz producers, they are understandable, predictable even, for three reasons. First, it is fair to say that the Australia is still getting to grips with the viticultural side of things when it comes to a climate as cool as Tasmania's (most of its vineyards are on the same latitude as Marlborough on New Zealand's South Island, some even farther south). Second, Tasmania is cut off from the rest of Australia, and many wineries lack the expertise that is readily available on the mainland. This results in a lack of sophistication in the winery, which can be great in the odd, outstanding example, but can lead to a certain rustic quality. Third, even the biggest wineries and most experienced winemakers have not been directly involved in Tasmanian winemaking that long—which brings me back to Jansz.

There is no doubt that Yalumba has the skill and determination to make Jansz an icon among New World sparkling wines, but the first vintage it can lay claim to is 1999, and we should not expect too much from the vintage of the year of the takeover. Nonetheless, it won a

gold medal at the local wine competition, whereas some of the previous vintages did not even chalk up a bronze. However, when the first releases of Jansz from the new millennium get some bottle age, they should start to show the true potential of Tasmanian sparkling wine. When they do, the plaudits they receive on international markets will form the locomotive that should drive other, smaller bubbly producers to higher and finer things.

The potential is great, but it probably won't be realized for another 10 years. Where Tasmania shows potential currently is in its intensely flavored Chardonnay, Riesling, and Pinot Noir. There has even been some fine Cabernet Sauvignon.

## UPPER GOULBURN

South of the more famous Goulburn Valley region, this GI covers the upper reaches of the river. Upper Goulburn encompasses the Lake Eidon area, between Alexander and Mansfield, and is set against the backdrop of the snow-capped Australian Alps, where the river begins its journey. This region makes crisp Chardonnay, which is better used as a component for sparkling wine production than as a still varietal wine, the best varieties for which are the more aromatic types, such as Riesling or Sauvignon Blanc. Some Gewürztraminer is also grown. Perhaps the best-known winery in this region is Delatite, just outside Mansfield.

## WESTERN VICTORIA

This zonal GI encompasses the regional GIs of Grampians, Henty, and Pyrenees.

## YARRA VALLEY

Considered by many to be Australia's answer to Burgundy, this recently rediscovered wine region benefits not only from the enriching aftereffect of earlier sheep farming, but also from a cool climate, a long growing season, relatively light yields, and some very talented winemakers. The vines grow on the gray-brown loams (to the south) and red volcanic soils (to the north). Viticulture began in 1837, when the three Ryrie brothers planted vines on their cattle ranch, Yering Station, and with the help of Swiss and German immigrants, Yering and two other wineries, St. Huberts and Yeringberg, achieved an international reputation for the Yarra Valley. This region declined in the depression of the 1890s and the situation was exacerbated by the consumer shift to fortified wines, so that by the 1920s the only surviving winery was forced to close down.

Viticulture in the Yarra Valley was revived in the 1960s by medical doctors who anticipated that consumers would return to table wines. Dr. John Middleton pioneered this revival, when he established the Mount Mary vineyard. The latest and most successful wave of interest in producing Yarra Valley wines came in the late 1980s. Wine critic James Halliday was responsible for much of this, after he established Coldstream Hills in 1985. It was Halliday more than anyone who made consumers believe in Yarra Valley Pinot Noir. It also helped that Moët & Chandon set up its Green Point/Domaine Chandon winery a few years later. Halliday has also produced some fine Chardonnay and Cabernet Sauvignon, but it was the Pinot Noir that caused the most excitement. Shiraz and Merlot are also very good and, of course, with the presence of Domaine Chandon, Yarrabank, and Devaux Yering Station, this is also sparkling wine country.

THE WINE PRODUCERS OF
# VICTORIA AND TASMANIA

### 2 BUD SPUR
**Tasmania**
★★ Ⓥ

Great Pinot Noir made under contract by Michael Vishacki, who does an even better job with it than at his own Panorama vineyard.
✓ *Pinot Noir*

### ALL SAINTS
**Rutherglen**
★★☆ Ⓥ

Established in 1864, All Saints was owned personally by the late Peter Brown of Brown Brothers fame, as was the nearby St. Leonards winery.
✓ *Durif* (Carlyle) • *Fortified* (all Liqueur Muscats, all Tokays, Vintage Port, Old Tawny Port, Show Reserve Amontillado) • *Shiraz* (Carlyle)

### APSLEY GORGE
**Tasmania**
★★☆ Ⓥ

Good Chardonnay, and starting to produce exciting quality Pinot Noir.
✓ *Pinot Noir*

### ARMSTRONG VINEYARDS
**Grampians**
★★

Limited quantity, top-performing Shiraz from former Seppelt Great Western winemaker, Tony Royal.
✓ *Shiraz*

### BALGOWNIE
**Bendigo**
★★☆

Balgownie went through a patchy period in the early 1990s, but now seems to be pulling out of it as far as the reds are concerned. The whites are disappointing.
✓ *Cabernet Sauvignon* (Estate) • *Shiraz* (Estate)

### BANNOCKBURN VINEYARDS
**Geelong**
★★

Winemaker Gary Farr's experience at Domaine Dujac in Burgundy shows through in the finesse of these wines, which are as appreciated in Europe as they are in Australia. The SRH Chardonnay and Serre Pinot Noir are ultra-premium limited releases.
✓ *Chardonnay* • *Classic red blend* (Cabernet-Merlot) • *Pinot Noir* • *Shiraz*

### BASS PHILLIP
**Gippsland**
★★ Ⓥ

Various stunning Pinot Noir in minuscule quantities.
✓ *Pinot Noir*

### BAY OF FIRES
**Tasmania**
★★☆ Ⓥ

BRL Hardy's specialist winery is the home of Arras, its premium sparkling wine, but its Bay of Fires and Tigress brands are equally exciting.
✓ *Sauvignon Blanc* (Tigress) • *Sparkling* (Arras from 2004, Bay of Fires Blanc de Blancs)

### BERRYS BRIDGE
**Pyrenees**
★★☆ Ⓥ

Established in 1990, but sold grapes initially, with 1997 the first vintage, and intense Shiraz the best and most consistent wine so far.
✓ *Shiraz*

### BEST'S WINES
**Great Western**
★★★

This historic winery boasts a large, superb range that includes many gems, such as the stunning Thomson Family Shiraz and the lovely zesty-fresh, lime-scented Riesling.
✓ *Cabernet Sauvignon* • *Chardonnay* • *Merlot* • *Riesling* • *Shiraz*

### BINDI WINE GROWERS
**Macedon Ranges**
★★

Fast-rising Chardonnay and Pinot Noir specialist of stunning quality and individuality.
✓ *Chardonnay* • *Pinot Noir*

### BLACKJACK VINEYARD
**Bendigo**
★

Blackjack Vineyard was named after an American sailor who caught gold fever in the 1850s and jumped ship, but this family-owned venture was established much more recently, in 1987. Everyday drinking Shiraz under the Chortle's Edge label.
✓ *Classic red blend* (Cabernet Merlot) • *Shiraz*

### BLUE PYRENEES
**Pyrenees**
★

The original winemaker here was Frenchman Vincent Gere, who tended to make his sparkling wines on the sweet side until the 1990

vintage, when they became more classic in style. He was succeeded by Kim Hart, who placed most emphasis on still wines. Then Greg Dedman, the current winemaker, gradually raised quality all around, resulting in Blue Pyrenees being sold to a Sydney-based syndicate in 2002. Second wines are sold under Fiddlers Creek and Ghost Gum labels.
✓ *Cabernet Sauvignon* • *Chardonnay* • *Classic red blend* (Reserve Red) • *Shiraz* • *Sparkling wine* (Midnight Cuvée)

### BROWN BROTHERS
**King Valley**
★★☆ Ⓥ

The size of this family-owned firm is deceptive until you visit Brown Brothers' so-called microvinification winery, which is bigger and better equipped than 70 percent of the wineries I regularly visit, with so-called microvinification tanks that are like a battery of boutique wineries. Brown Brothers' experimental wines are thus as polished as any commercially produced wine, which explains why this is one of Australia's most innovative wine producers. One of Brown Brothers' experiments has been with the Spanish Graciano grape, and that has demonstrated incredible longevity, with a 1974 vintage blowing away every example of the "genuine thing" put up by Rioja wineries at the London wine trade fair in 2004. The Tarrango might not be a fine wine, but if you like Beaujolais, it is made in that style, only better than 90 percent of wines bearing that appellation.
✓ *Botrytis* (Noble Riesling) • *Cabernet Sauvignon* (Patricia) • *Chardonnay* (Patricia) • *Classic red blend* (Shiraz Mondeuse Cabernet) • *Fortified* (Reserve Muscat, Very

Old Tokay) • *Graciano* • *Shiraz* (Banksdale) • *Sparkling* (Patricia, Pinot Noir, and Chardonnay, Vintaged Pinot Chardonnay)

### R L BULLER & SON
**Rutherglen**
★★☆

This firm dates back to 1921 and also has a winery at Beverford in Swan Hill. The most consistent table wines are Cabernet Sauvignon (Beverford), Durif (Sails), Sémillon (Beverford), and Shiraz (Beverford), but you can buy better, and cheaper, elsewhere. Best advice is to concentrate on the beautiful fortified wines, and if you see any of the final release of the 1978 Vintage Port, make every effort to get your hands on it. Judged on Fortified alone, R. L. Buller would deserve ★★★☆.
✓ *Fortified* (Calliope Rare Liqueur Muscat, Calliope Rare Liqueur Tokay, Fine Old Muscat, Fine Old Tawny)

### BY FARR
**Geelong**
★★★☆

The personal label of Bannockburn's turbocharged winemaker Gary Farr, from vines growing on the other side of the road to those of Bannockburn. So many puns could be made from "By Farr." Thankfully, none have so far, as the wine does all the talking.
✓ *Chardonnay* • *Pinot Noir* • *Shiraz*

### CAMPBELLS WINERY
**Rutherglen**
★★

This is one fortified wine specialist that has expanded into varietal wines with brilliant success.
✓ *Durif* (The Barkly) • *Fortified* (Allen's Port, Isabella Liqueur Tokay, Liquid Gold Tokay, Merchant Prince Liqueur Muscat) • *Shiraz* (Bobbie Burns)

### CHAMBERS
**Rutherglen**
★★

Bill Chambers is one of the all-time great producers of fortified wine. The Old Rare Muscat and Tokay have no peers.
✓ *Fortified* (all Liqueur Muscat, all Liqueur Tokay)

### COFIELD
**Rutherglen**
★

Cofield specializes in small quantities of high-quality red fizz, and produces a surprisingly good Merlot for Rutherglen.

✓ *Merlot* (Rutherglen) • *Shiraz* •
*Sparkling* (Shiraz)

## COLDSTREAM HILLS
### Yarra Valley
### ★★

James Halliday, the doyen of
Australia's wine writers, has sold
this property to Southcorp, but is
still involved with the winemaking
on a consultancy basis. Coldstream
is well-known for beautiful Pinot
Noir and classic Chardonnay, the
Reserves of which are well worth
the price for those with deep
enough pockets. However, the
Cabernet Sauvignon and, more
recently, the Merlot have been the
surprises, reflecting Halliday's
penchant for length, elegance, and
finesse in these Bordeaux varieties,
rather than mere weight or punch.

✓ *Cabernet Sauvignon* •
*Chardonnay* • *Merlot* • *Pinot
Noir*

## CRAIGLEE
### Sunbury
### ★☆

This famous 19th-century, four-story,
bluestone winery was reestablished
in 1976 by Pat Carmody, who
released his first wine, a 1980
Shiraz, in 1982.

✓ *Shiraz*

## CRAIGOW
### Tasmania
### ★☆ Ⓥ

Wines of exciting quality are
produced here by Hobart surgeon
Barry Edwards.

✓ *Pinot Noir* • *Riesling*

## CRAWFORD RIVER
### Western District
### ★★

This property was established in
1982 by John Thomson, who
quickly built a reputation for
Riesling, particularly in the botrytis
style, but is also very consistent
these days with Cabernet.

✓ *Cabernet Sauvignon* • *Classic
red blend* (Cabernet Merlot) •
*Classic white blend* (Sémillon
Sauvignon Blanc) • *Riesling*

## CRITTENDEN AT
## DROMANA
### Mornington Peninsula
### ★☆ Ⓥ

Garry Crittenden no longer has any
connection with Dromana Estate,
the public company he founded,
where his son Rollo is now chief
winemaker. Nor does he have any
involvement with any of Dromana
Estate's labels, not even its top-
performing Garry Crittenden "i" (for
Italian) range. All this seems a bit
strange, considering his new label is
Crittenden at Dromana, and he has
reclaimed the former Dromana
Estate winery and vineyard. He had
never sold these to the publicly
quoted company, although the
equipment inside the winery
belonged to Dromana Estate, and
this had to be relocated to its new
facility at Tuerong (*see* Dromana
Estate). He has always kept the
Schinus brand separate from the
public company, and continues with
that, as well as playing on his
reputation for Italian varietals by
releasing Arneis, Barbera, Rosato,
and Sangiovese under the
Pinocchio label, while Crittenden
at Dromana will focus on Pinot Noir
and Chardonnay. It is as safe as
houses to recommend in general
Crittenden's new wines, but too
early to specify which will be
the standouts. (If Michelin can do
it with *its* stars, I surely can
with mine!)

## CURLEWIS WINERY
### Geelong
### ★★

Established in 1998 by Rainer Brett,
who has very quickly established an
enviable reputation for great Pinot
Noir. His Shiraz is pretty damn good too.

✓ *Pinot Noir* • *Shiraz*

## CURLY FLAT
### Macedon Ranges
### ★☆

Owners Phillip and Jeni Moraghan's
production is relatively small,
but specializes in Burgundian
varietals, and the quality is
outstanding. A new winery was
built in 2002, and the old one
turned over to cellar sales.
Second wines are sold under the
Williams Crossing label.

✓ *Chardonnay* • *Pinot Noir*

## DALWHINNIE
### Pyrenees
### ★★

Intensely rich and well-structured
wines are consistently produced
from these vineyards adjacent
to Taltarni.

✓ *Cabernet Sauvignon*
(Moonambel) •
*Chardonnay* •
*Pinot Noir* •
*Shiraz*
(Moonambel)

## DE BORTOLI
### Yarra Valley
### ★★ Ⓥ

Riverina-based De Bortoli opened
up this "posh" operation in one of
Australia's most up-and-coming
premium-quality wine regions in
1987. Over the years, it has
gradually built up an outstanding
reputation, helped in no small
respect by the fact that it is
personally run by Leanne de
Bortoli, whose husband, Stephen
Webber, was Lindemans' winemaker
before taking up the post of the
chief winemaker here. Second
wines are sold under Gulf Station
and Windy Peak labels.

✓ *Cabernet Sauvignon* (Yarra
Valley) • *Chardonnay* (Gulf
Station, Yarra Valley) • *Classic
red blend* (Melba Barrel Select)
• *Pinot Noir* (Gulf Station,
Yarra Valley) • *Riesling* (Windy
Peak, Yarra Valley) • *Rosé*
(Cabernet) • *Shiraz* (GS
Reserve)

## DELATITE WINERY
### Central Victorian High Country
### Ⓥ

Situated on its own, in the Great
Divide, Delatite has produced some
very good value wines that always
show rich, tangy fruit. This winery
has a reputation for its Deadman's
Hill Gewürztraminer.

✓ *Chardonnay* • *Classic red
blend* (R. J. Cabernet-Merlot) •
*Pinot Noir* • *Riesling* (VS)

## DIAMOND VALLEY
## VINEYARDS
### Yarra Valley
### ★★

David Lance is well known for
Pinot Noir of great intensity yet
elegance, but his other wines
should not be overlooked.

✓ *Cabernet Sauvignon* •
*Chardonnay* • *Classic red
blend* (Cabernet-Merlot) •
*Pinot Noir* • *Sémillon-
Sauvignon*

## DOMAINE CHANDON
### Yarra Valley
### ★☆ Ⓥ

Moët & Chandon's Australian winery
was set up later than its California
venture, but quickly overtook it in
quality. Much of the credit should
go to Dr. Tony Jordan, who ran the
enterprise at that time, but even he
will admit that, with sources
stretching across an entire continent,
he had a wider choice of quality
components to draw on. Jordan left
to take over at Wirra Wirra, but has
returned to head all of LVMH's
winemaking operations in Australia
and New Zealand, including Western
Australia's Cape Mentelle. The Rosé
and Blanc de Noirs are both very
good, and would be recommended
under other producers, but I wanted
to showcase the very best bubbly
produced here. Conversely, the
nonvintage Brut still needs work.
In 2004, Chandon became the
first major producer to market a
sparkling wine sealed by a crown-
cap: Brut ZD (for Zero Dosage).
A pure Chardonnay blend, the
inaugural 2000 vintage, was one
of the few nondosaged wines that
could be consumed easily upon
purchase, but this was achieved by
the softness of the base wines, and
I found myself struggling to drink
more than one glassful. The wines
are known on export markets as
Green Point.

✓ *Chardonnay* (Reserve) • *Pinot
Noir* (Reserve) • *Sparkling
wine* (Blanc de Blancs,
Cuvée Riche, Pinot Shiraz,
Vintage Brut)

## DOMINIQUE PORTET
### Yarra Valley
### ★☆ Ⓥ

After 22 years as CEO at Taltarni,
Dominique Portet left to set up his
own venture in the Yarra Valley.
So far the Heathcote Shiraz is
the standout.

✓ *Cabernet Sauvignon*
(Heathcote) • *Sauvignon Blanc*
• *Shiraz* (Heathcote)

## DROMANA ESTATE
### Mornington Peninsula
### ★☆ Ⓥ

In 2004, this producer moved from
Dromana to Tuerong, as founder
Garry Crittenden reclaimed the
former Dromana Estate winery
and vineyard for his new label,
Crittenden at Dromana. It was
Crittenden who had established
Dromana Estate in 1982, but when
he took the company public in
2001, he retained ownership of
the property on which the
winery stood and its surrounding
vineyards. He also kept the rights
to the Schinus label. He is no
longer connected with the
company (*see* Crittenden of
Dromana), although his son Rollo
is now its chief winemaker, being
responsible not only for Dromana
Estate, but also Mornington Estate,
Yarra Valley Hills, and Garry
Crittenden "i" (for Italian) labels.
He is producing wines that are
every bit as good his father's and
he continues to improve. Director
and shareholder David Traeger
is the winemaker for Baptista,
Broken River, and, of course, his
eponymous brand.

✓ *Chardonnay* (Reserve) •
*Dolcetto* (Garry Crittenden "i")
• *Nebbiolo* (Garry Crittenden
"i") • *Pinot Noir* (Estate,
Reserve) • *Sangiovese* (Garry
Crittenden "i") • *Shiraz*
(Baptista)

## ELSEWHERE VINEYARD

**Tasmania**

★✰Ⓥ

Established by Eric and Jette Phillips in 1984, and sold to Kylie and Andrew Cameron in 1999, Elsewhere Vineyard continues to produce superb Pinot Noir from the Huon Valley, and very good Riesling too.

✓ *Pinot Noir* (Bay of Eight) • *Riesling*

## EVELYN COUNTY ESTATE

**Yarra Valley**

★✰Ⓥ

Everything here is design-driven, from the cellar door-cum-Tony Simbert gallery and restaurant, to the label. Even the wines appear to be designed for elegance.

✓ *Botrytized* (Sticky Black Paddock Chardonnay) • *Chardonnay* (Black Paddock) • *Merlot* (Black Paddock) • *Pinot Noir* (Black Paddock)

## FREYCINET

**Tasmania**

★✰

Geoff Bull makes a surprisingly big and beautiful Cabernet Sauvignon-Merlot, and various other fine wines, but his exquisitely crafted, sumptuous Pinot Noir surpasses all his other wines in quality and style.

✓ *Chardonnay* • *Classic red blend* (Cabernet Sauvignon Merlot) • *Pinot Noir* • *Riesling*

## GALLI ESTATE

**Sunbury**

★✰Ⓥ

Established in 1997 by Pam and Lorenzo Galli, who have swiftly built up a formidable reputation.

✓ *Cabernet Sauvignon* • *Pinot Grigio* • *Shiraz*

## GIACONDA

**Beechworth**

★★✰

Exquisitely crafted, highly sought-after wines, which only those on the mailing list have any chance of acquiring. The Pinot Noir is by far the best of an amazing range of wines.

✓ *Cabernet Sauvignon* • *Chardonnay* • *Classic white blend* (Les Deux) • *Pinot Noir* • *Roussanne* (Aeolia)

## HANGING ROCK

**Macedon Ranges**

★

This was once the largest winery in the Macedon area and specialized in bottle-fermented sparkling wine, but Shiraz is the best wine today. Although the Heathcote Shiraz is top of the range, and certainly best, the basic Victoria Shiraz can be very nearly as good at almost half the price.

✓ *Shiraz*

## HOLM OAK

**Tasmania**

★✰Ⓥ

Red wine specialist Nick Butler has always made one of Tasmania's best Cabernet Sauvignons, but his Pinot Noir is now every bit as good.

✓ *Cabernet Sauvignon* • *Pinot Noir*

## JASPER HILLⒷ

**Heathcote**

★★★

Not exactly known as the epitome of elegance, but there is no doubting the quality of Jasper Hill's biodynamic red wines in the big, muscular, complex style.

✓ *Classic red blend* (Emily's Paddock Shiraz-Cabernet Franc) • *Shiraz* (Georgia's Paddock)

## JINDALEE ESTATE

**Geelong**

★✰

Established as recently as 1997 by Vince and David Littoree, who own 1,400 acres (570 hectares) of vineyards in the Murray Darling region. The Jindalee label is for penny-pinchers, yet the Chardonnay can be very good indeed. The pricier Fettlers Rest label was launched in 2001, exclusively for estate-grown Geelong fruit.

✓ *Pinot Noir* (Fettlers Rest) • *Shiraz* (Fettlers Rest)

## JINKS CREEK

**Gippsland**

★✰Ⓥ

Although established in 1981, the winery was not built until 1992. Owner-winemaker Andrew Clark is a consultant viticulturist to 10 different vineyards, which gives him access to a wide range of fruit to supplement his own small Gippsland property. Winemaking practices include some wild yeast fermentations, no filtration, and a minimal sulfur regime.

✓ *Pinot Noir* (Fettlers Rest) • *Shiraz* (Heathcote, Longford Gippsland, Yarra Valley)

## KARA KARA

**Pyrenees**

★Ⓥ

At one time this winery seemed to be doing good things with Sauvignon Blanc, pure and blended, but excels today with its red wines.

✓ *Cabernet Sauvignon* • *Shiraz*

## KINGS CREEK WINERY

**Mornington Peninsula**

★✰Ⓥ

Some varietals are more consistent than others, but the Burgundian duo of Pinot Noir (particularly) and Chardonnay are always excellent quality.

✓ *Cabernet Sauvignon* • *Shiraz*

## KRAANWOOD

**Tasmania**

Not tasted, but I have heard very good things about the Pinot Noir produced from Frank van der Kraan's 1-acre (half-hectare) vineyard.

✓ *Pinot Noir*

## LILLYDALE VINEYARDS

**Yarra Valley**

★✰

Established in 1975, Lillydale has been owned by McWilliam's since 1994. I always thought of Lillydale as being best for white wines, but under McWilliam's the reds have outclassed everything except the elegantly rich and stylish Yarra Valley Chardonnay.

✓ *Chardonnay* • *Classic red blend* (Cabernet-Merlot) • *Shiraz*

## LINDEMANS WINES

**Murray Darling**

★✰Ⓥ

This vast winery is now part of Southcorp and produces wine from almost everywhere, although its historic home in the Hunter Valley has been reduced to cellar-door sales only. The Karadoc winery in the Murray Darling region churns out copious quantities of very respectable, sub-AU$10 (US$7.50) wines, including the good-value Cawarra range, and umpteen million of cases of Bin 65 Chardonnay, and would deserve a rating of no more than ★, and that would be for miraculous consistency, rather than quality *per se*. Lindemans' Coonawarra winery, which also makes the Padthaway wines, would however easily rate ★★, hence the compromise ★✰. Even at Coonawarra, regionality has gradually been replaced by state-wide blends, ripping the heart and soul out of the Lindemans heritage. The real pity is that under Southcorp, Lindemans no longer produces a modern equivalent of its legendary Hunter Riesling, some 70-year-old examples of which are still in amazing condition. The message to corporate Southcorp must be to reverse the decline of regionality in general, and reintroduce some form of ultrapremium bottle-aged Hunter Sémillon in particular.

✓ *Cabernet Sauvignon* (St. George) • *Chardonnay* (Padthaway) • *Classic red blend* (Limestone Ridge Shiraz-Cabernet, Pyrus Cabernet-

Merlot-Cabernet Franc) • *Fortified* (Macquarie Tawny Port) • *Pinot Noir* (Padthaway) • *Shiraz* (Padthaway)

## MEADOWBANK VINEYARD

**Tasmania**

★★✰

Classic black-cherry Pinot Noir from just north of Hobart, including the bright and brilliant Henry James Pinot Noir.

✓ *Cabernet Sauvignon* • *Chardonnay* (Grace Elizabeth) • *Pinot Noir*

## MERRICKS CREEK

**Mornington Peninsula**

★★✰

Established in 1998 by Peter and Georgina Parker, who are reputed to have a ridiculously high-density, low-canopy vineyard planted with a single variety, Pinot Noir, but this couple are not completely mad. They are indeed Pinot purists, but most of the 5-acre (2-hectare) vineyard is planted with vines 3 feet (1 meter) apart, and rows a very generous 8 feet (2.5 meters) apart, with the canopy a good 6½ feet (2 meters) high. However, a separate plot is planted with vines just 2 feet (600 millimeters) apart and row spacing at 3 feet (1 meter), with the fruiting wire just 8 inches (20 centimeters) above the ground—this plot must be frost-free. And only half crazy. The results are very impressive, with a helping hand from contract winemaker Nick Farr, who is the son of Pinot genius Gary (Bannockburn and By Farr), who acted as consultant viticulturist.

✓ *Pinot Noir* • *Sparkling wine* (Pinot Noir)

## MERRICKS ESTATE

**Mornington Peninsula**

★✰

Consistently stunning Shiraz. Owned by the Kefford family since 1977, with no connection to Merricks Creek above.

✓ *Shiraz*

## MÉTIER WINES

**Yarra Valley**

★★✰

Owner-winemaker Martin Williams is a Master of Wine with winemaking experience on three continents. He established Metier in 1995 and has shot to ★★✰ fame in a very short space of time with his single-vineyard masterpieces. Williams is also a partner in Master Winemakers, a premium contract winemaking business.

✓ *Chardonnay* (Trafford Vineyard) • *Classic red blends* (Manytrees Shiraz-Viognier) • *Pinot Noir* (Schoolhouse Vineyard, Trafford Vineyard)

## MITCHELTON VINTNERS

**Goulburn Valley**

★✰Ⓥ

Part of the Lion Nathan wine division since its takeover of

Petaluma. Innovative Rhône-style wines have added to Mitchelton's reputation as one of Australia's greatest value-for-money brands, although I find the whites such as Viognier and Airstrip (Marsanne-Roussanne-Viognier) too fat and soft.

✓ *Botrytis* (Blackwood Park Botrytis Riesling) • *Chardonnay* (Vineyard Series) • *Classic red blend* (Crescent Shiraz-Mourvèdre-Grenache) • *Merlot* (Chinaman's Ridge) • *Riesling* (Blackwood Park) • *Shiraz* (Print)

## MONTALTO VINEYARDS
### Mornington Peninsula
### ★★⯪

Pinot Noir is definitely the standout at Montalto, which was established as recently as 1998. Although the Pennon Hill range is effectively Montalto's entry-level label, some vintages of the Pennon Hill Pinot Noir are of such superb quality that they rank as one of the world's best bargains for this sought-after variety.

✓ *Chardonnay* • *Pinot Noir* • *Riesling*

## MOORILLA ESTATE
### Tasmania
### ★★

This pioneering Tasmanian winery still produces fabulous Chardonnay and exhilarating Riesling, but is now making top-notch red wines.

✓ *Cabernet Sauvignon* • *Chardonnay* • *Riesling* • *Syrah*

## MOOROODUC ESTATE
### Mornington Peninsula
### ★★

Richard McIntyre's well-established estate has long been reputed for its Chardonnay, but if anything the Pinot Noir is even better.

✓ *Chardonnay* • *Pinot Noir* • *Riesling*

## MORRIS WINES
### Rutherglen
### ★★ⓥ

While the table wines are decent enough (many of them being made at the parent company's Jacob's Creek winery), no one visits Morris Wines to taste anything other than

the fortifieds, the older and rarer blends of which are arguably the best of their type in the world. In fact, I was so eager not to miss an appointment to taste such nectar here in the early 1990s that I received an on-the-spot speeding ticket of AU$350 (US$250) from Victoria's finest, as I sped across the state line from New South Wales. The legendary Mick Morris was amazed at the size of the fine, asking what on earth I had done to deserve it, and I shall never forget that twinkle in his eye and the characteristic chuckle as I told him that my mind was so intent on getting to the winery that I hadn't realized that I had overtaken a police car in my haste!

✓ *Fortified* (entire range)

## MOUNT AVOCA VINEYARD
### Pyrenees
### ★

This winery was purchased by Barrington Estate in the Hunter Valley in 2002, and is currently performing better with red wines than white.

✓ *Cabernet Sauvignon* • *Classic red blend* (Arda's Choice) • *Merlot* • *Shiraz*

## MOUNT BECKWORTH
### Pyrenees
### ★⯪ⓥ

Established in 1984, although I've only just come across these wines, perhaps because the grapes were sold in bulk, and wines under the Mount Beckworth label did not appear until much more recently.

✓ *Chardonnay* • *Pinot Noir* • *Shiraz*

## MOUNT LANGI GHIRAN
### Grampians
### ★★ⓥ

This winery and vineyards were purchased by the Rathbone Family Group in 2002, but former owner Trevor Mast has stayed on as winemaker. Mast produces rich, ripe, complex reds (particularly Shiraz), and increasingly exciting Riesling.

✓ *Cabernet Sauvignon* (Joanna) • *Classic red blend* (Billi Billi, Cabernet Sauvignon-Merlot) • *Riesling* • *Shiraz* (Cliff Edge)

## MOUNT MARY VINEYARD
### Yarra Valley
### ★★⯪

Only small quantities of reds are made at Mount Mary, but these are outstanding with a well-deserved cult following.

✓ *Chardonnay* • *Classic red blend* (Quintet) • *Classic white blend* (Triolet) • *Pinot Noir*

## MURRINDINI
### Central Victorian High Country
### ★★⯪ⓥ

Owner-winemaker Hugh Cuthbertson makes wines of an extraordinary consistency and quality, from a tiny vineyard

between the Yarra Valley and the Strathbogie Ranges.

✓ *Chardonnay* • *Classic red blend* (Cabernets-Merlot)

## NICHOLSON RIVER
### Gippsland
### ★★

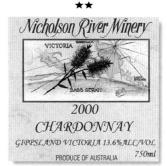

Great improvement over recent years from this well-established Gippsland producer. Second wines sold under the Mountview label.

✓ *Chardonnay* • *Classic red blend* (The Nicholson) • *Pinot Noir*

## NO REGRETS
### Tasmania
### ★★

An extremely promising start by Eric and Jette Phillips, who established this venture in 2000, just after they sold the nearby Elsewhere Vineyard.

✓ *Chardonnay* • *Classic white blend* (Triple S) • *Pinot Noir* • *Riesling* • *Sparkling* (Miss Otis)

## OAKRIDGE
### Yarra Yarra
### ★★

Stunning quality since the arrival of winemaker David Bicknell in 2001. The 864 Riesling is a manufactured icewine style, freezing the grapes in the winery, then pressing them in a refrigerated press!

✓ *Chardonnay* (864, Yarra Valley) • *Riesling* (864) • *Shiraz* (864, Yarra Valley)

## PANORAMA
### Tasmania
### ★★⯪

Since Michael and Sharon Vishacki purchased this relatively long-established vineyard (1974), they have built not only a new winery, but also a new, top-performing reputation, especially for Pinot Noir.

✓ *Pinot Noir*

## PARINGA ESTATE
### Mornington Peninsula
### ★★

Established in 1985, Lindsay McCall's Paringa Estate is well entrenched as one of the "*grands crus*" of Mornington Peninsula.

✓ *Pinot Noir* • *Shiraz*

## PASSING CLOUDS
### Bendigo
### ★★⯪ⓥ

Graeme Leith continues to produce classy, unirrigated red wines.

✓ *Classic red blend* (Graeme's Blend, Angel's Bland) • *Shiraz* (Reserve)

## PHILLIP ISLAND VINEYARD
### Tasmania
### ★★⯪

Established in 1994 by David Lance of Diamond Valley fame, Phillip Island must be the only vineyard within spitting distance of penguins and a seal colony.

✓ *Chardonnay* • *Pinot Noir* • *Riesling*

## PIPERS BROOK VINEYARD
### Tasmania
### ★

This winery was established in 1974 by Dr. Andrew Pirie, but was taken over in 2001 by the Belgian-owned Kreglinger Australia, a wool and sheepskin business that entered the wine industry as recently as 2000 (Norfolk Rise, Mount Benson). Wines are also sold under the Ninth Island label, but Ninth Island winery (formerly Rochcombe Vineyard) is now the site of BRL Hardy's Bay of Fires.

✓ *Pinot Noir* (Reserve) • *Chardonnay* (Estate, Reserve)

## PIRIE TASMANIA
### Tasmania
### ★★⯪ⓥ

After the winery he established, Pipers Brook, was taken over, Dr. Andrew Pirie did a bit of consulting with Parker Coonawarra Estates (since ended), and the more local Dalrymple (which is ongoing), before regaining the commercial rights to his own name. He has leased the "state-of-the-art" Rosevears winery in the Tamar Valley, and produced "substantial quantities of 2004 table wines including a top-end Pinot Noir." It looks as if his sparkling wine activities will be much smaller in the future, with the first wine due to be made in 2005, sourced from vineyards matched to "the old ones: same spacing, district, age and aspect." Tasmania is more suited to Pinot-Chardonnay sparkling wine than to Cabernet Sauvignon, although the latter is also grown. Pirie had experience of Cabernet Sauvignon at Pipers Brook, but his short spell at Parker Coonawarra left him uncertain that he was taking full advantage of the potential of this Bordeaux variety. He is reputed to be one of the best winemakers in Australia, but was humble enough to tell me that he was doing "one last masterclass with Vanya Cullen on Cabernet," and I cannot think of anyone better suited to pass on the necessary expertise. With the exception of an entry-level Pirie South range, Pirie intends to focus on "ultra-premium" estate wines.

✓ *Chardonnay* (Estate) • *Pinot Noir* (Estate) • *Riesling* (Estate) • *Sauvignon Blanc* (South)

## PONDALOWIE VINEYARDS
### Bendigo
★★🅥

Dominic and Krystina Morris have established Pondalowie Vineyards not only as the *"grand cru"* of Bendigo, but also as one of the best wineries in Australia. Look for the annually changing "Special Release"—I loved the delicious Sparkling Shiraz!

🗸 *Classic red blend* (Shiraz-Viognier, Vineyard Blend) • *Fortified* (Vintage Port) • *Tempranillo* (Mt Unwooded)

## PORT PHILLIP ESTATE
### Mornington Peninsula
★★☆

Established in 1987, this property was sold in 2000 to current incumbents Giorgio and Dianne Gjergja, who are making some stunning red wines.

🗸 *Pinot Noir* (Reserve) • *Shiraz* (Reserve)

## PRINCE ALBERT
### Geelong
★☆◉

Bruce Hyett produces tiny quantities of highly acclaimed Pinot Noir.

🗸 *Pinot Noir*

## PROVIDENCE VINEYARDS
### Tasmania
★★

Established as La Provence in 1956, with vines illegally removed from France, and smuggled into Tasmania, this estate eventually ran foul of Australia's agreement with the EU on controlled appellations, and was thus renamed Providence Vineyards in the 1990s. Contract winemaker Andrew Hood makes sensationally fine Pinot Noir, particularly under the Miguet Reserve label, which is widely recognized as one of Australia's best examples of Burgundy's great grape.

🗸 *Chardonnay* (Monet) • *Pinot Noir*

## PUNCH
### Yarra Valley
★★

Instantly established as iconic Pinot Noir, Punch is produced in minuscule volumes by James and Claire Lance from exactly the same fruit as Diamond Valley White Label Pinot Noir (produced by David Lane).

🗸 *Pinot Noir* (Close Planted)

## RED EDGE
### Heathcote
★★

Named after the red volcanic soil of the vineyard purchased in 1994 by Peter and Judy Dredge—and I don't think it is a coincidence that it is also almost an anagram of their surname. The vineyard was planted in 1971 by Vert Vietman, who originally named it Red Hill. Although the Dredges have expanded the vineyard, they still have quite a lot of mature vines to work with—this shows through in the intensity of some of their wines.

🗸 *Cabernet Sauvignon* • *Shiraz* (Heathcote, Degree)

## RED HILL ESTATE
### Mornington Peninsula
★★

Described by the president of the Australian Winemakers Federation as the "best view of any vineyard in the world," no wonder Red Hill's restaurant is packed. One of the peninsula's very best Pinot Noirs.

🗸 *Chardonnay* • *Pinot Noir*

## ROCHFORD WINES
### Yarra Valley
★☆

Part of this enterprise was formerly known as Eyton on Yarra. It was taken over in 2002 by Rochford Wines, whose winemaker, David Creed, coincidentally was a contract winemaker for Eyton on Yarra in 1993. The Rochford and Eyton wines have evolved into a three-tiered range, all under the Rochford label. The Rochford R Range is from the Macedon Ranges, and represents those wines formerly sold as Rochford; the Rochford E Range is from Yarra Valley, and is effectively the old Eyton wines; while the Rochford V Range is sourced from both wineries plus bought-in grapes, and consequently sold under the broader Victoria GI.

🗸 *Chardonnay* (R) • *Pinot Noir* (R)

## SCOTCHMAN'S HILL
### Geelong
★🅥

This winery is owned by David and Vivienne Browne, whose Burgundy-style specialist vineyard and winery overlook the Bellarine Peninsula and benefit from cool maritime breezes. Second wines sold under the Spray Farm label.

🗸 *Chardonnay* • *Pinot Noir*

## SEPPELT GREAT WESTERN
### Great Western
★★🅥

Part of the giant Southcorp group, this legendary sparkling wine producer makes everything from cheap but expertly made lime-and-lavender fizz under its most basic Great Western Brut label; through numerous exceptional-value, relatively inexpensive, genuinely premium *cuvées*; to the truly fine-quality, upmarket Salinger *cuvée*. And then there is the Show

Sparkling Shiraz, which is one of Australia's icons: the biggest, brashest, and most brilliant of sparkling "Burgundies," even though its massive, concentrated black-currant-syrup fruit is too much for many to swallow more than half a glass. But it is definitely a "show" wine in the biggest of senses. And just because this winery has a well-deserved reputation for sparkling wine, it would be wrong to overlook some of Seppelt's exceptionally fine table wines. A ★★ classification is not too high because some individual wines, both with and without bubbles, would rate ★★★☆ on their own.

🗸 *Cabernet Sauvignon* (Dorrien) • *Chardonnay* (Drumborg, Partalunga) • *Pinot Noir* (Drumborg, Sunday Creek) • *Shiraz* (Chalambar) • *Riesling* (Drumborg) • *Sparkling* (Blanc de Blancs, Original Sparkling Shiraz, Pinot Noir-Chardonnay, Salinger, Show Sparkling Shiraz, Sparkling Shiraz)

## SEVILLE ESTATE
### Yarra Valley
★★☆🅥

This winery made its name on minuscule releases of its superb botrytized Riesling, but has been owned by Brokenwood since 1997, and now concentrates on the more marketable premium varietals.

🗸 *Chardonnay* • *Pinot Noir* • *Shiraz*

## SHADOWFAX
### Geelong
★★☆

Shadowfax: is it some pun on email? No, it's from *The Lord of the Rings*, in which Shadowfax was chief among horses. Deep and meaningful, then? No, I suspect it was just named by some Tolkien nut. Shadowfax is not run by nuts, though. This ultramodern and stylish winery, which is located in Werribee Park, has its own award-winning, luxury hotel and restaurant, The Mansion Hotel, and makes wines that are as lush and as manicured as its surroundings.

🗸 *Cabernet Sauvignon* (Yarra Valley) • *Chardonnay* • *Pinot Noir* • *Shiraz* (McLaren Vale) • *Viognier* (Adelaide Hills)

## SHANTELL
### Yarra Valley
★☆🅥

An underrated producer of fine white wines, Shantell has recently started to make excellent reds.

🗸 *Cabernet Sauvignon* • *Chardonnay* • *Sémillon* • *Shiraz*

## SPRING VALE VINEYARDS
### Tasmania
★☆🅥

Established in 1986, but really took off from the late 1990s, particularly with Burgundian varietals.

🗸 *Chardonnay* • *Pinot Noir*

## STANTON & KILLEEN
### Rutherglen
★★🅥

Affectionately known as "Stomp It and Kill It," this famous old fortified wine producer also manages to make some excellent table wines.

🗸 *Classic red blend* (Shiraz Durif) • *Fortified* (entire Classic range, Grand Rutherglen Muscat) • *Shiraz* (Moodemere)

## STONIER WINES
### Mornington Peninsula
★★

Stonier has been owned by Lion Nathan since the takeover of Petaluma, but its Burgundy-style wines get even more stunning by the vintage under winemaker Geraldine McFaul, who has started specializing in the expression of single vineyards.

🗸 *Entire range*

## TAHBILK
### Goulburn Valley
★☆🅥

The oldest winery in Victoria was established in 1860, when it was known as Chateau Tahbilk, but dropped the pretension at the turn of the millennium. It still makes very traditional wines that always improve in bottle. Second wines are sold under the Dalfarras, Everyday Drinking, and Republic labels.

🗸 *Cabernet Sauvignon* • *Marsanne* • *Riesling* • *Sémillon* • *Shiraz*

## TALTARNI VINEYARDS
### Pyrenees
★★☆

Taltarni is Aboriginal for "red earth," the soil in this vineyard being an iron-rich siliceous clay and thus red in color. The wines have always been noticeably rich in extract, but they are no longer as austere, lean or—for reds—as tannic as they used to be under Dominique Portet (who now has his own label). The style has become more relaxed, and easier to access at a much earlier age. Clover Hill and Lalla Gulley are premium Tasmanian single-vineyard wines, whilst second wines are sold under the Fiddleback label.

✓ *Cabernet Sauvignon* (Taltarni) • *Chardonnay* (Lalla Gulley) • *Classic red blend* (Cephas) • *Merlot* (Taltarni) • *Sauvignon Blanc* (Fumé Blanc) • *Shiraz* (Taltarni) • *Sparkling* (Clover Hill, Taltarni Brut Taché)

## TAMAR RIDGE
### Tasmania
### ★★ ✪

Joe Chromy purchased Heemskerk and Rochecombe and sold them on to Pipers Brook in 1998. But he retained 125 acres (50 hectares) in the Tamar Valley, which formed the basis of Tamar Ridge, where he built a new winery. The wines have been excellent, particularly the Pinot Noir and Riesling (the Josef Chromy Selection was outstanding). After turning down offers to buy him out from two mainland wineries, Chromy sold Tamar Ridge to Gunns, Tasmania's largest timber company, for AS$14.8 million (US$9.7 million). Dr. Richard Smart, the "flying vine doctor," has consulted here from the beginning, but the new owners have persuaded him to move to Launceston to oversee the state's largest viticultural project, as Gunns invests a further AS$16 million (US$10.4 million) in new vineyards that will increase Tasmania's area under vine by more than 50 percent.

✓ *Pinot Noir* • *Riesling*

## TARRINGTON VINEYARDS
### Henty
### ★★

Beautiful, Burgundy-style Pinot Noir, and refreshing, unoaked Chardonnay.

✓ *Chardonnay* • *Pinot Noir*

## TEN MINUTES BY TRACTOR
### Yarra Valley
### ★★

You have to admire the ingenuity of such a name for a winery in country that thinks nothing of trucking grapes across several state lines. But it's not a gimmick. This venture is the combination of three separate family-owned vineyards (hence the three single-vineyard labels: Judd, McCutcheon, and Wallis), each of which is just 10 minutes by tractor from the other two. The wines are brilliant.

✓ *Chardonnay* • *Pinot Noir*

## VIRGIN HILLS VINEYARDS
### Macedon
### ★★

The creation of Hungarian-born Melbourne restaurateur Tom Lazar, this "one-wine-winery" has been one of Australia's hidden jewels for more than three decades. Lazar did not learn winemaking; he simply read a book, planted a vineyard, and made his wine. Virgin Hills has always consisted primarily of Cabernet Sauvignon, plus a dash of Syrah, Merlot, and Malbec. Lazar used to maintain approximately 75 percent Cabernet Sauvignon, but

over the years this has varied between 60 and 85 percent. When he retired, Mark Sheppard took over the winemaking, and continued in the Lazar fashion, making it one of the Australia's least-known, greatest wines. Sheppard left to join Vincorp, but returned when Vincorp owned Virgin Hills for a short while in 1998, after which it was purchased by Michael Hope, the current proprietor.

✓ *Virgin Hills*

## WARRABILLA
### Rutherglen
### ★☆✪

Great quality-price ratio from former All Saints owner-winemaker Alan Sutherland Smith.

✓ *Classic red blend* (Reserve Shiraz Durif) • *Durif* (Reserve) • *Fortified* (Reserve Muscat) • *Merlot* (Reserve) • *Shiraz* (Parola's Limited Release, Reserve)

## WARRENMANG VINEYARD
### Pyrenees
### ★★ ✪

The Grand Pyrenees does not indicate the nature of its blend on the label, but contains Merlot, Cabernet Franc, and Shiraz.

✓ *Cabernet Sauvignon* • *Chardonnay* • *Classic red blend* (Grand Pyrenees) • *Shiraz* (Puma)

## WATER WHEEL
### Bendigo
### ★★ ✪

Owner-winemaker Peter Cumming established this vineyard in 1972, and makes well-crafted wines at very reasonable prices, deserving its ★ rating on value alone.

✓ *Cabernet Sauvignon* • *Chardonnay*

## WATERTON ESTATE
### Tasmania
### ★★☆✪

Not tasted. Indeed, never seen! But comes highly recommended by a trusted colleague, and passed on.

## WEDGETAIL ESTATE
### Yarra Valley
### ★☆✪

This is a new one for me, although apparently established as long ago as 1994. Superb Burgundian varietals, and although the quality of the Cabernet (Cabernet Sauvignon-Shiraz blend) is vulnerable to change of vintage, it does hit the spot when the weather is right.

✓ *Chardonnay* • *Classic white blend* (Cabernet) • *Riesling*

## WELLINGTON
### Tasmania
### ★★ ✪

The own brand of consultant winemaker Andrew Hood (*see* Providence).

✓ *Chardonnay* • *Pinot Noir* • *Riesling* (Iced)

## WILLOW CREEK
### Mornington Peninsula
### ★

Willow Creek is housed in a historic building with magnificent views.

✓ *Cabernet Sauvignon* • *Chardonnay* (Tulum)

## WINSTEAD
### Tasmania
### ★★

Tiny production of extraordinary Pinot Noir courtesy of contract winemaker Andrew Hood.

✓ *Pinot Noir*

## YARRA BURN
### Yarra Junction
### ★

Established in 1975, but owned by BRL Hardy since 1995, the Yarra Burn range has been revamped, and the quality upped and still improving. I used to favor the Bastard Hill *cuvées* of Chardonnay and Pinot Noir, but the straight Yarra Burn label is often as good these days, and sometimes even a little better!

✓ *Chardonnay* • *Pinot Noir* • *Shiraz* • *Sparkling* (Pinot Noir-Chardonnay-Pinot Meunier)

## YARRA RIDGE
### Yarra Valley
### ★ ✪

Founded in 1982, but now owned by Beringer Blass, Yarra Ridge continues to make elegant red wines in a firm yet accessible style. Wines from other regions are sold under the Mount Tanglefoot range of the Yarra Ridge label.

✓ *Classic white blend* (Mount Tanglefoot Sémillon-Sauvignon Blanc) • *Pinot Noir*

## YARRA VALLEY HILLS
### Yarra Valley
### ★★☆✪

Owner-winemaker Terry Hill has turned out some truly fine, relatively inexpensive wines since he established Yarra Valley Hills in 1993.

✓ *Pinot Noir* • *Riesling*

## YARRA YARRA
### Yarra Valley
### ★★

Tiny production of superbly expressive wines from a vineyard that is so good, they named it twice!

✓ *Classic red blend* (Cabernets) • *Classic white blend* (Sémillon-Sauvignon Blanc) • *Cabernet Sauvignon* (Reserve)

## YARRA YERING
### Yarra Valley
### ★★

The first in a number of Yarra-named wineries, Yarra Yering was founded in 1969 by New Zealand botanist Dr. Bailey Carrodus, whose blended reds are legendary. Remarkably, 35 years later, he is still the day-to-day winemaker. Dry Red No.1 is Cabernet-based; Dry Red

No. 2 is Shiraz-based; Dry Red No. 3 is Cabernet-Tempranillo.

✓ *Cabernet Sauvignon* (Young Vines) • *Classic red blend* (Dry Red No.1, Dry Red No. 2) • *Merlot* • *Shiraz* (Underhill)

## YELLOWGLEN VINEYARDS
### Ballarat
### ★ ✪

This operation was started by Australian Ian Home and *champenois* Dominique Landragin, but is now owned by Beringer Blass. The wines have always shown excellent potential and have improved enormously, especially since the early 1990s. The nonvintage Pinot Noir-Chardonnay is often superior to the vintaged Brut. Wines also sold under Home and Landragin label.

✓ *Sparkling* (Cuvée Victoria, Hargrave, Pinot Noir-Chardonnay)

## YERING STATION
### Yarra Valley
### ★★

Part of the Rathbone Family Group since 1996, Yering Station sells table wines under its own name, and sparkling wines under the Yarrabank label. Its most prestigious sparkling wine is the Tibault and Gillet Cuvée, but I have to go back to the 1995 and 1994 vintages to find the real class that this wine once had, and it is amazing that these old Australian bubblies have aged so gracefully.

✓ *Chardonnay* (Reserve) • *Classic red blend* (Reserve Shiraz-Viognier) • *Merlot* • *Pinot Noir* (Reserve) • *Sparkling* (Yarrabank)

## YERINGBERG
### Yarra Valley
### ★★

The oldest winery in the Yarra Valley, Yeringberg was established in 1862 by Guillaume, Baron de Pury, and reestablished in 1969 by his grandson, Guillaume de Pury, who has consistently produced fine, sometimes exceptionally fine, wines. The Dry Red is a Bordeaux-style blend.

✓ *Chardonnay* • *Classic red blend* (Dry Red) • *Classic white blend* (Marsanne-Roussanne) • *Pinot Noir*

## ZILZIE
### Murray Darling
### ☆✪

A major supplier of grapes to Southcorp, the Forbes family established its own winery in 2000. With improving quality, and very reasonable prices, Zilzie is a name to watch. Second labels include Forbes Faily and Buloke Reserve.

✓ *Classic red blend* (Show Reserve GSM) • *Merlot* (Show Reserve) • *Tempranillo* (Buloke Reserve) • *Shiraz* (Show Reserve)

# SOUTH AUSTRALIA

*This is Australia's most productive and contradictory wine region, accounting for 42 percent of the country's vineyards, and over 50 percent of its total wine output, ranging from its cheapest to its most expensive wine.*

THE BEGINNINGS OF THIS VAST MARKET GARDEN of grapes can be traced back to John Barton Hack, who planted vines at Chichester Gardens, North Adelaide, in 1837, but they were removed in 1840 in order to make way for urbanization. Meanwhile, in 1839, Hack had purchased a 4,000-acre (1,600-hectare) property near Mount Barker called Echunga Springs, where he also planted vines, producing his first wine in 1843, and sending a case to Queen Victoria the following year. Hack's Echunga Springs is generally thought to have produced the first wine in South Australia, although George Stevenson had established a vineyard in 1838 at North Adelaide, and so could have made wine at least one year before

Hack, and possibly as early 1841. There is no documented evidence that he did or, at least, none that has surfaced. Nonetheless, it would be reasonable to assume that the records from this era are far from complete, because if Hack was indeed the first to make wine, in 1843, how come in the very same year *The South Australian Vigneron* was published? Where would be the demand? Furthermore, the author of this work, George McEwin, is credited on the cover as "Gardener to George Stevenson." What is on record, however, is that Stevenson won a prize for his "Burgundy" at the South Australian Agricultural and Horticultural Show in 1845.

## INCREASING REGIONAL DEFINITION
The paradox is that if consumers are asked what South Australia means to them as a winemaking state, they will probably say that it has a reputation for cheap wine, but ask them about Coonawarra, and they will say it is Australia's most famous, premium-quality wine region. Ask them about the Barossa Valley, and they will say that is where Australia's greatest Shiraz comes from. This state is an object lesson in the need to focus on

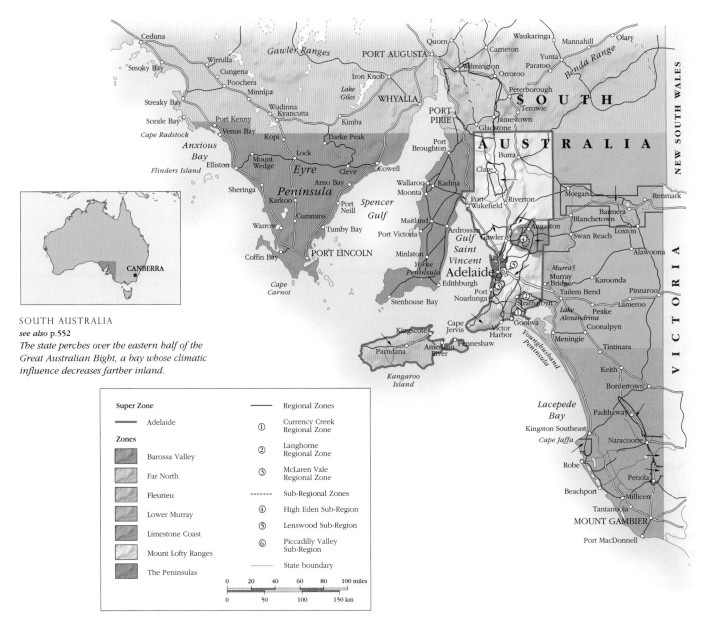

SOUTH AUSTRALIA
*see also p.552*
*The state perches over the eastern half of the Great Australian Bight, a bay whose climatic influence decreases farther inland.*

| Super Zone | | Regional Zones |
|---|---|---|
| ⎯⎯ Adelaide | ① | Currency Creek Regional Zone |
| **Zones** | ② | Langhorne Regional Zone |
| Barossa Valley | ③ | McLaren Vale Regional Zone |
| Far North | - - - - | Sub-Regional Zones |
| Fleurieu | ④ | High Eden Sub-Region |
| Lower Murray | ⑤ | Lenswood Sub-Region |
| Limestone Coast | ⑥ | Piccadilly Valley Sub-Region |
| Mount Lofty Ranges | | State boundary |
| The Peninsulas | | |

0   20   40   60   80   100 miles

0    50    100    150 km

## FACTORS AFFECTING TASTE AND QUALITY

### LOCATION
This is the southern central part of the country, with Australia's five other mainland states to the east, north, and west, and half of the Great Australian Bight forming the coastline to the south.

### CLIMATE
The climate varies greatly, from the intensely hot continental conditions of the largely cask-wine producing Riverland area, through the less extreme but still hot and dry Barossa Valley, to the cooler but still dry Coonawarra region. Sea breezes reduce humidity in the plains around Adelaide, which receives low annual rainfall, as does the whole region.

### ASPECT
Vines are grown on all types of land, from the flat coastal plain around Adelaide and flat interior Riverland district to the varied locations of the Barossa Valley, where vines are grown from the valley floor at 820 feet (250 meters), up to the slopes to a maximum of 1,970 feet (600 meters) at Pewsey Vale.

### SOIL
Soils are varied, ranging from sandy loam over red earth (*terra rossa*) on a limestone-marl subsoil in the Adelaide and Riverland areas (the latter having suffered for some time from excess salinity); through variable sand, loam, and clay topsoils, over red-brown loam and clay subsoils in the Barossa Valley, to the thin layer of weathered limestone, stained red by organic and mineral matter, over a thick limestone subsoil in the Coonawarra area.

### VITICULTURE AND VINIFICATION
This varies enormously, from the bulk-production methods of the large modern wineries that churn out vast quantities of clean, well-made, inexpensive wine from grapes grown in Riverland's high-yielding irrigated vineyards, to the use of new oak on restricted yields of premium-quality varietals by top estate wineries in areas such as Coonawarra, the Barossa Valley, and the up-and-coming Padthaway or Wrattonbully districts, which produce some of Australia's greatest wines.

### GRAPE VARIETIES
**Primary varieties:** Cabernet Franc, Cabernet Sauvignon, Chardonnay, Malbec, Merlot, Petit Verdot, Pinot Noir, Riesling, Sauvignon Blanc, Sémillon, Shiraz
**Secondary varieties:** Cinsault, Crouchen, Doradillo, Gewürztraminer, Grenache, Mourvèdre, Muscat à Petit Grains, Muscadelle, Muscat d'Alexandrie, Muscat Gordo Blanco, Palomino, Pedro Ximénez, Ruby Cabernet, Sangiovese, Taminga, Tinta Amarella, Touriga, Ugni Blanc, Viognier

REMUAGE, BAROSSA VALLEY
*Giant gyropalettes are indicative of the scale of the operation at the Southcorp-owned Barossa Valley cooperative.*

regional definition. Only by increasing the regional definition within South Australia will its wine industry be recognized for its true quality and future potential.

It is already happening, as the Adelaide Hills, for example, brings a breath of cool air to the hot-climate image of this state. And within the Adelaide Hills, smaller areas such as the Piccadilly Valley manage to express the notion that specific and different *terroirs* can and do exist side by side. Even the Mount Lofty Ranges zonal GI, encompassing the Adelaide Hills and Clare Valley, expresses a difference. No two Rieslings are more intrinsically Australian than those from the Clare and Eden valleys, yet how could you mistake one for the other? With winemaking of consistently high standards from such outstanding producers as Grosset, so the highly individual character and quality of subregions within the Clare Valley, such as Polish Hill, are starting to stand out. There are certainly plenty of top-notch producers in this state. How strange that South Australia should have such a generally inexpensive image when it produces some of Australia's finest and most expensive wines, from Grosset Polish Hill, to Henschke Hill of Grace, Rockford Black Shiraz, Petaluma Tiers Chardonnay, and, of course, Penfolds Grange.

---

THE APPELLATIONS OF
# SOUTH AUSTRALIA

### ADELAIDE
A superzonal GI that encompasses the regions of Barossa, Fleurieu, and the Mount Lofty Ranges.

### ADELAIDE HILLS
**Sub-regions:**
*Lenswood, Piccadilly Valley*

Petaluma country. This hilly region is just 9 miles (15 kilometers) from the coast, overlooking Adelaide, the Adelaide Plains, and McLaren Vale. It has two subregions of its own, Lenswood and Piccadilly Valley, which are determined by differing temperatures and soil types. Along with Clare Valley and Adelaide Plains, this region is part of the much larger Mount Lofty Ranges GI. Although the Adelaide Hills have a Mediterranean climate, this is by far the coolest of all South Australian wine regions, being strongly influenced by elevation ranging from 1,150–2,300 feet (350–700 meters), and the winds that sweep across St. Vincents Gulf. Undulating hills are interspersed with steep slopes, which drop into frost-prone gullies, creating many different kinds of *terroir* according to height, aspect, and the various soils, which range from (but are not restricted to) sandy alluvium on the valley floor, to yellow and red loams on the slopes. The first vines were planted here in the 1840s, but viticulture struggled for economic survival, finally succumbing to the Great Depression. Its revival finally came in the 1970s, when boutique wineries started to satisfy the demand of consumers who were switching from fortified to table wine. Chardonnay, Riesling, Pinot Noir, and bottle-fermented sparkling wines are now the classics here, with Cabernet Franc and Merlot faring better than Cabernet Sauvignon. Sauvignon Blanc and Sémillon are rising stars, with Sangiovese and the inevitable Shiraz showing promise.

### ADELAIDE PLAINS
The Adelaide Plains is described by James Halliday as "one of the least appealing, most frequently visited regions in Australia." It is, as he also states, "laser-flat and searingly hot in summer." Little surprise, then, that there are very few wineries here, and those that do exist mostly source their grapes from elsewhere. However, extraordinarily fine wines can be made from vines growing in these furnacelike conditions, as illustrated by some of the wines produced by the top-performing Primo winery from Joe Grilli's Virginia vineyard. Part of the Adelaide Plains has long since been consumed by the city's sprawling suburbs, which now surround Penfolds' legendary Magill vineyard. The grapes from this vineyard used to be the base for Penfolds' remarkable Grange Hermitage, but they now go to make The Magill Estate.

### BAROSSA
A zonal GI encompassing the Barossa Valley and Eden Valley regional GIs.

### BAROSSA VALLEY
This district is the oldest and most important of South Australia's premium varietal areas. With a hot, dry climate, the vines mostly grow on flatlands at an altitude of 800 to 1,000 feet (240 to 300 meters), although in some areas the altitude rises to 1,800 feet (550 meters), and the vines are cooled by ocean breezes. The Barossa Valley is heavily dependent on irrigation, but boreholes are metered, and the amount of water that may be drawn is strictly regulated. Big, brash Shiraz is king in this region, although a significant volume of white wine is also

produced. Chardonnay, Sémillon, and Riesling dominate, and depending on the climate and the soil (which may be limestone, clay, or sand), these white wines can range from full bodied to surprisingly delicate.

## CLARE VALLEY

Clare Valley is the most northerly vinegrowing district in South Australia and its climate is correspondingly hotter and drier. Many of the vineyards are not irrigated, however, and the result is a low yield of very intensely flavored, big-bodied, often strapping wines. Riesling is the valley's most important variety and botrytis-affected wines are rich, fine, and mellifluous. Other good wines are Cabernet Sauvignon (often blended with Malbec or Shiraz), Sémillon, and Shiraz.

## COONAWARRA

This famous district is the most southerly in South Australia. Coonawarra is Aboriginal for "wild honeysuckle"; it also happens to be easy on English-speaking tongues and this has been useful when it comes to marketing wine from the district in English-speaking countries. Consequently, this region achieved worldwide fame, which paradoxically held it back during the GI process, while other less well-known regions were demarcated relatively quickly. Everyone with the slightest chance of being considered part of Coonawarra wanted to be included within the boundaries, while the bureaucrats operating the GI scheme demonstrated little or no imagination, thus it took eight years to settle all the disputes. The crux of the matter revolved around Coonawarra's red earth, or *terra rossa*. Black soil areas are interspersed amongst the *terra rossa* and these soils produce quite different wines, even though they share the same limestone subsoil. The neatest solution would have been to have two appellations: a regional Coonawarra GI, within which there would be a subregional Coonawarra Terra Rossa GI. The Coonawarra ridge hardly stands out topographically, being just 194 feet (59 meters) above sea level, but it does stand out viticulturally, since the surrounding land is flat, frosty, and poorly drained. This, and the Mediterranean climate, which enjoys the cooling maritime influences off the Southern Ocean, make height-challenged Coonawarra superbly suited to viticulture, whether on black or red soils. It is just that those vineyards on *terra rossa* soils have historically been responsible for some of Australia's outstanding wines, particularly Cabernet Sauvignon. Vineyards on black soils can produce some very good wines, but those on *terra rossa* are demonstrably more expressive of their *terroir*. Cabernet Sauvignon might be king of

the *terra rossa*, but other varieties that perform well throughout Coonawarra include Shiraz, Petit Verdot, Pinot Noir, Malbec, and Merlot. Although Coonawarra is red wine country *par excellence*, successful white grapes include Chardonnay, Riesling, Sauvignon Blanc, and Sémillon.

## CURRENCY CREEK

This regional GI is located on the Fleurieu Peninsula, extending from Port Elliot in the west to the shores of Lake Alexandrina in the east, and includes three islands: Hindmarsh, Mundoo, and Long Islands. The proximity to Lake Alexandrina, and the mouth of the Murray River moderates the hot Mediterranean climate, making the area suitable for viticulture. Grapes growing include Cabernet Sauvignon, Chardonnay, Sauvignon Blanc, and Shiraz.

## EDEN VALLEY

**Subregions:**
*High Eden*

The Eden Valley has a rockier, more acid soil than that found in the neighboring Barossa Valley, with a cooler, much wetter climate. Vineyards are located at an altitude of 1,300–2,000 feet (400–600 meters) in the Mount Lofty Ranges, which form part of the Barossa Range. The Eden Valley GI is not a valley as such, but takes its name from the township of Eden Valley. While the preeminence of Henschke might suggest that the Eden Valley is world-class Shiraz country, that is very much due to one vineyard, Hill of Grace, and the 130-year-old Shiraz vines planted there. Eden Valley is best known for its quintessentially Australian (that is, limey) Riesling, and deservedly so. Chardonnay also fares well.

## FAR NORTH

Aside from the Southern Flinders Ranges GI in the far south, the vast Far North zonal GI is very much a viticultural wilderness.

## FLEURIEU

This zonal GI consists of the peninsula jutting out toward Kangaroo Island, and encompasses the regional GIs of Currency Creek, Kangaroo Island, Langhorne Creek, McLaren Vale, and Southern Fleurieu.

## HIGH EDEN

So named because, unsurprisingly, this subregional GI is located at the highest point in Eden Valley, which also makes it one of the coolest and most windy areas. The terrain is hilly, and rugged, with poor sandy soils that are well suited to Chardonnay, Riesling, and Shiraz, as is the rest of the Eden Valley. Cabernet Sauvignon is also grown.

## KANGAROO ISLAND

Located off the coast of South Australia, Kangaroo Island is renowned for its natural beauty, and an abundance of wildlife, including colonies of Australian sea lions, New Zealand fur seals, penguins, and the once-endangered Cape Barren goose. In recent years, Kangaroo Island has also been making a name for its Bordeaux-style blends. Most vines are grown on ruddy-colored ironstone or sandy loam soils on the north side of the island, near Kingscote, where the maritime climate is marked by strong winds and moderate humidity. In addition to Bordeaux varieties, Chardonnay and Shiraz are also grown.

THE HARVEST, BAROSSA VALLEY
*Many of the best premium varietal producers in South Australia have some sort of interest in the Barossa Valley, the state's most important wine area.*

## LANGHORNE CREEK

This once tiny, traditional area, located southeast of Adelaide on the Bremer River, has expanded rapidly since 1995, when Orlando started sourcing grapes from here for huge brands such as Jacob's Creek. This district was named after Alfred Langhorne, a cattle-herder from New South Wales, who arrived in 1841. The meager annual rainfall of 14 inches (35 centimeters) means that the vineyards require irrigation. This area is reputed for its beefy reds and for its dessert wines.

## LENSWOOD

This subregional GI is located north of Piccadilly, the other subregion in the Adelaide Hills. The vines grow on steep slopes and benefit from a cool climate, but at 1,300–1,840 feet (400–560 meters), thus lower than those in Piccadilly (up to 2,330 feet, 710 meters), and do not experience quite the same snap of coldness. The grape varieties that excel are the same— Chardonnay and Pinot Noir—and the quality can be equally exciting.

## LIMESTONE COAST

The naming of this zonal GI was a stroke of genius compared with all the hoo-ha over Coonawarra, when growers and bureaucrats alike could not see the wood for the trees. Not merely because Limestone Coast is so evocative of the one geological factor that links the regional GIs within its borders (Coonawarra, Mount Benson, Padthaway, and Wrattonbully), but also because, rightly or wrongly, limestone is one of the few soils known by even the casual wine drinker to have a positive influence over the growing of grapes.

## LOWER MURRAY

A zonal GI that encompasses the regional GI of Riverland.

## MCLAREN VALE

The rolling green hills of McLaren Vale's vineyards and orchards begin south of Adelaide and extend to south of Morphett Vale. With 22 inches (56 centimeters) of rain and a complex range of soils, including sand, sandy loam, limestone, red clay, and many forms of rich alluvium, there is great potential for quality in a range of styles from various grapes. This is perhaps why it is the most volatile wine district, attracting a lot of new talent, but also seeing wineries close or change hands. McLaren Vale produces big red wines of excellent quality from Shiraz and Cabernet Sauvignon (often blended with Merlot), with some increasingly fresh and vital white wines from Chardonnay, Sémillon, and Sauvignon Blanc. Fine dessert wines are also produced.

## MOUNT LOFTY RANGES

This zonal GI encompasses the regional GIs of Adelaide Hills, Adelaide Plains, and Clare Valley.

## PADTHAWAY

Once known as Keppoch, this area has been developed almost exclusively by the larger companies (Hardy's built Australia's largest winery for 20 years here in 1998). Provided the smaller businesses are not unreasonably prevented from buying land within the area, this should benefit all types of operation. The success of small ventures should be welcomed by the larger companies because it endorses the intrinsic quality potential of the district they are promoting.

## THE PENINSULAS

If the Far North zonal GI is a massive viticultural wilderness above an imaginary line, then the Peninsulas is that part of South Australia to the south of the same line where hardly any wineries exist. It is not as if there is no scope for viticulture here. There are plenty of gently undulating hills, with the right aspect and altitude. The subsoil is limestone, with everything from sandy-clayey loams to gravel for topsoil. There is even *terra rossa*. But there are only a couple of vineyards (Boston Bay and Decolline) in this zonal GI, and they are both confined to the Port Lincoln area on the Southern Eyre Peninsula.

## PICCADILLY

Subregion situated in the west of the Adelaide Hills GI, between Ashton and Bridgewater. The vines grow at altitudes of 1,300–2,300 feet (400–710 meters ), benefiting from a very cool, wet climate, which stretches the ripening process, yielding grapes with naturally high tartaric acid levels. Chardonnay and Pinot Noir excel.

## RIVERLAND

The wine areas that cluster around the Murray River in Victoria continue into Riverland, South Australia's irrigated answer to Riverina in New South Wales and Murray Darling in Victoria. Although a lot of cheap cask-wine is made in the Riverland district, rarely is a bad one encountered. Cabernet Sauvignon, Cabernet Sauvignon-Malbec, Chardonnay, and Riesling all fare well, and some relatively inexpensive wines are produced in the area.

## SOUTHERN FLEURIEU

This region GI is located at the southern end of the Fleurieu Peninsula, where its gentle, undulating coastal country benefits from cooling winds coming from both the west and south, and vines grow in sandy loam and gravelly-ironstone soils. An up-and-coming area for small, boutique wineries, where Shiraz grows best, but other varieties include Cabernet Sauvignon, Malbec, Riesling, and Viognier.

## SOUTHERN FLINDERS RANGES

Although the first grapes were grown here in the 1890s, it is only in the past 10 years that viticulture has become viable on a commercial scale, hence its regional GI status. This has been due to three factors: the so-called "Goyder's line of rainfall," which reduces demand on water supplies; an early harvest; and a ready market in the neighboring Barossa and Clare valleys. The Southern Flinders Ranges are divided by "Goyder's line of rainfall," which was named after the surveyor George W. Goyder, who first determined the "northernmost limits of feasible agriculture." Irrigation comes from underground water, but with an annual rainfall of 17–25 inches (450–650 millimeters), it is possible to grow grapes without it, which explains the focus on dry-grown, premium-quality grapes. The elevation extends from just 65 feet (20 meters) on the coast to 2,355 feet (718 meters) at Frypan Hill, but most vineyards are located on slopes at a height of 1,150–1,800 feet (350–550 meters), where the region's warm to hot climate is tempered by the cooling effects of altitude and winds crossing the gulf. The soils range from deep sandy loam on the coastal plains to the west of the Flinders Ranges, to deep loam over red clay to the east, around the Wild Dog Creek Land System, and more shallow, stony loam on the slopes. The best suited grapes are Cabernet Sauvignon, Merlot, and Shiraz.

## WRATTONBULLY

Surprisingly easy to pronounce for English-speaking tongues, despite the peculiar name, perhaps because it is itself an Anglo-Saxon interpretation of the Aboriginal expression (for "a place of rising smoke signals"). Wrattonbully was not the original name for this region, sandwiched between Coonawarra and Padthaway. It was formerly known as Koppamurra, but there is a vineyard of that name in the area, and there were trademark problems in using it for a GI, thus it was decided to rename the region Wrattonbully, presumably to send out a signal. The first commercial vineyard was established in 1968, and by the 1990s most of Australia's biggest wine groups were sourcing fruit from here. The climate is very similar to that of Coonawarra, but its slightly higher aspect provides better air drainage, therefore a reduced risk of frost, and lower humidity, thus fewer cryptogamic disease problems. The subsoil is limestone, of course, with various topsoils consisting of red-brown sandy and clayey loams, including some of the purest *terra rossa* soils, making this ideal *terroir* for Cabernet Sauvignon and Shiraz. Potentially, the reputation of Wrattonbully will be at least as great as Coonawarra's. We have barely begun to hear about these wines.

---

### THE WINE PRODUCERS OF
# SOUTH AUSTRALIA

### TIM ADAMS
**Clare Valley**
★★ Ⓥ

The Tim Adams style is very pure, deeply flavored, and bursting with fruit, no wine more so than the fabulous, pure lime-juice Sémillon.

✓ *Classic red blend* (The Fergus) • *Sémillon* • *Shiraz* (Aberfeldy)

### ANGOVE'S
**Riverland**
★ Ⓥ

Most wines are fairly cheap and usually rack up a bronze medal at wine competitions, thus the odds are that even those not specifically recommended below can be relied on for above average quality and very good value.

✓ *Cabernet Sauvignon* (Sarnia Farm) • *Chardonnay* (Classic Reserve) • *Classic red blend* (Agincourt Cabernet Sauvignon-Malbec-Merlot, Butterfly Ridge Shiraz-Cabernet) • *Fortified* (Premium Port)

### ANNIE'S LANE AT QUELLTALER ESTATE
**Clare Valley**
★★ Ⓥ

The winemaker since 2000 for this precious part of the Beringer Blass empire has been the talented Caroline Dunn, who in 1999 became the first woman to win the coveted Jimmy Watson Trophy, and in 2001 was awarded the Dux of the inaugural Len Evans Wine tutorial.

✓ *Classic red blend* (Cabernet-Merlot, Shiraz-Grenache-Mourvèdre) • *Riesling* • *Shiraz*

### ASHTON HILLS
**Adelaide Hills**
★★ Ⓥ

Owner-winemaker Stephen George has honed his style into one of great elegance. Wines are also sold under the Galah label.

✓ *Chardonnay* • *Classic red blend* (Cabernet Merlot) • *Pinot Noir* • *Riesling* • *Shiraz* (Lone Star) • *Sparkling* (Salmon Brut)

### BALNAVES OF COONAWARRA
**Coonawarra**
★★

Established in 1975 by Doug Balnaves, who sold his entire harvest as grapes until 1990, when he hired a contract winemaker to launch his own label. Quality and consistency surged upward in 1996, when Balnaves of Coonawarra got its own brand-new winery, with Wynns' former assistant winemaker Peter Bissell in charge.

✓ *Cabernet Sauvignon • Chardonnay • Classic red blend* (The Blend) • *Shiraz*

## BAROSSA VALLEY ESTATE
### Barossa Valley
★

Owned by BRL Hardy, Barossa Valley Estate continues to make E. & E. Black Pepper Shiraz, one of the biggest, oakiest sparkling Shiraz wines in the country from the low-yielding Barossa vineyards of Elmor Roehr and Elmore Schulz (whence the E. & E.). Recently introduced, Epiphany is a much cheaper, more accessible version of this varietal.

✓ *Classic red blend* (Monculta Cabernet Sauvignon-Merlot) • *Shiraz • Sparkling* (E. & E. Sparkling Shiraz)

## BERRI ESTATES
### Riverland
Ⓥ

The merger between Thomas Hardy and Sons and the huge, Berri-Renmano winery formed BRL Hardy, and this cooperative winery, servicing some 850 private grape-growers, was absolutely essential for the growth of that group. However, despite this pivotal role, and although Berri Estates is Australia's largest winery, processing up to 163,000 tons (this record set in 2004), neither its Berri Estates, nor its Renmano brand contribute much to the wealth and grandeur of BRL Hardy today. Most wines are bag-in-the-box and very cheap, although well made for what they are.

## BETHANY WINES
### Barossa Valley
★☆Ⓥ

Bethany produces some big, chewy, and often incredibly jammy red wines.

✓ *Chardonnay* (Barrel Fermented) • *Classic red blend* (Cabernet-Merlot) • *Grenache • Shiraz* (GR 6 Reserve)

## BOWEN ESTATE
### Coonawarra
★★

Doug Bowen continues to produce some truly exceptional wines.

✓ *Cabernet Sauvignon • Classic red blend* (Cabernet-Merlot) • *Shiraz* (Ampleton)

## BRAND'S OF COONAWARRA
### Coonawarra
★★  Ⓥ

This winery is sometimes known as Brand's Laira, because of its famous Laira vineyard in Coonawarra's *terra rossa* heartland, the original part of which is planted with 110-year-old Shiraz vines. The Brand family did not purchase the Laira vineyard until 1946, and the first wine sold under the Brand's Laira label was not until the 1966 vintage. In 1990, McWilliams purchased 50 percent of what was then known as Brand's Estate, buying up the other 50 percent in 1994, retaining Jim and Bill Brand as winemakers. Jim Brand is still one of this winery's two winemakers. The old Laira Vineyard Shiraz is sold today as Stentiford Old Vines Reserve. Other fruit from the extended Laira vineyard is also found in the Patron's Reserve Cabernet Sauvignon.

✓ *Cabernet Sauvignon* (Patron's Reserve) • *Riesling • Shiraz* (Stentiford Old Vines Reserve)

## BREMERTON WINES
### Langhorne Creek
★☆Ⓥ

Established in 1988, but the fact that rapidly expanding production in recent years has been matched with either constant or improved quality is something that the Wilson family should be proud of.

✓ *Cabernet Sauvignon* (Walter's) • *Classic red blend* (Tamblyn) • *Shiraz* (Old Adam)

## GRANT BURGE
### Barossa Valley
★★★☆Ⓥ

Although owner-winemaker Grant Burge launched this venture as recently as 1988, it quickly built up a reputation for richness, quality, and consistency, and he has not let his concentration lapse once. Grant Burge is probably best known for his icon Shiraz, Meshach, but the Filsell is probably just as outstanding at one-third the price, and there are numerous other wines, red and white, that are in a similar class. The Holy Trinity is a Grenache-Shiraz-Mourvèdre blend; MSJ2 is Shiraz-Cabernet; Balthasar is Shiraz-Viognier. The Lily Farm Frontignac is not a fortified wine, but is made in a wonderfully fresh, sweetish, late-harvest style.

✓ *Cabernet Sauvignon* (Cameron Vale) • *Chardonnay* (Summers) • *Classic red blend* (MSJ2, The Holy Trinity) • *Fortified* (20 Year Old Tawny) • *Frontignac* (Lily Farm) • *Riesling* (Thorn) • *Sémillon* (Barossa Vines, RBS2, Zerk) • *Shiraz* (Filsell, Meshach, Miamba)

## LEO BURING
### Eden Valley and Clare Valley
★★Ⓥ

Orlando took over the Leo Buring winery (which now operates as Richmond Grove), but Southcorp bought the Leo Buring name. Although just one of Southcorp's many brands, Leo Buring remains one of Australia's foremost Riesling producers. Indeed, the range is now reduced to this one varietal, and just three versions of that. On the one hand, this is a tragic end to a once great winery, but on the other, as an exclusive Riesling brand, Leo Buring must rate a good ★★.

✓ *Entire range!*

## CARDINHAM ESTATE
### Clare Valley
★★☆Ⓥ

Although these vineyards have been established since 1980, the Smith family sold grapes, not wine, and they did not launch their own label until as recently as 2000, since when the wines have rapidly achieved a brilliant reputation.

✓ *Classic red blend* (Cabernet-Merlot) • *Sangiovese • Shiraz* (Standbrooke)

## CHAIN OF PONDS
### Adelaide Hills
★★☆

Zar Brooks, the young man who put a smile on the face of D'Arenberg, was hired as CEO to put his impish ideas to work here, before he moved onto stranger things (Stranger & Stranger actually, a brand consultancy firm).

✓ *Chardonnay • Pinot Noir* (Jerusalem Selection) • *Sémillon* (Adelaide Hills) • *Shiraz* (Grave's Gate)

## CHAPEL HILL WINERY
### McLaren Vale
★★

This Chapel Hill has no connection with the Australian-made wines of the same name from Hungary, but instead derives its name from the deconsecrated, 19th-century hilltop chapel which is used as its winery. In December 2000, Chapel Hill was purchased by the Swiss Schmidheiny family, which also owns Cuvaison Winery in California, as well as vineyards in Argentina and Switzerland.

✓ *Cabernet Sauvignon • Chardonnay* (Reserve, Unwooded) • *Classic red blend* (The Vicar) • *Shiraz* (McLaren Vale) • *Verdelho*

## M. CHAPOUTIER
### Mount Benson
★★Ⓥ🅱

This famous Rhône Valley *négociant* established its presence in Australia in 1998, when it purchased land at Mount Benson, and began planting. It now has 90 acres (36 hectares) of Shiraz, Marsanne, Viognier, and Cabernet Sauvignon, plus two joint ventures in Victoria: one with Jasper Hill at Heathcote, the other with Mount Langi Ghiran in the Grampians region. Mount Benson is biodynamic, as is Jasper Hill, but Mount Langi Ghiran is not at the time of writing. Chapoutier's Mount Benson Shiraz is not your typical Australian blockbuster, claiming only 13 percent alcohol, with only 20 percent new oak.

✓ *Entire range, now and in the future*

## CLARENDON HILLS
### McLaren Vale
★★☆

Roman Bratasiuk strives for the biggest, most concentrated wines he can possibly extract from his old vines.

✓ *Grenache* (Romas Vineyard) • *Shiraz* (Piggott Range)

## COCKATOO RIDGE
### Barossa Valley
★Ⓥ

Although the Cockatoo Ridge wine label has been around since 1991, this company was not established until 2002, when it was launched on the Australian stock exchange, and now occupies Hardy's former Siegersdorf winery, which was built in 1920. Cockatoo Ridge took over International Australian Vintners (formerly Andrew Garrett Vineyard Estates) in May 2004 and in the process acquired various labels, including the founder's eponymous brand Andrew Garrett (export only; confusingly, almost exactly the same brand name as Garrett sold to Beringer Blass), Barossa Valley, Kelly's Promise (the Reserve restricted to the McLaren Vale fruit), Yarra Glen (Yarra Valley), Springwood Park (from various South Australian regions), and Ironwood.

✓ *Chardonnay* (Springwood Park) • *Classic red blend* (Yarra Glen Irma's Cabernet)

## CORIOLE
### McLaren Vale
★★

Full-throttle reds, including top-flight Shiraz and what was once the New World's best Sangiovese (still the same brilliant quality, but lots of top producers are now growing this and other Italian varieties). Redstone is a Shiraz-Cabernet blend, while Mary Kathleen is a Bordeaux-style blend.

✓ *Classic red blend* (Mary Kathleen, Redstone) • *Chenin Blanc • Nebbiolo • Sangiovese*

- *Sémillon* (especially the occasional Lalla Rookh) • *Shiraz*

### CRABTREE OF WATERVALE
**Clare Valley**
★★❶

Smallish, family-owned enterprise producing extraordinary-value, elegantly structured wines.

✓ *Grenache • Riesling • Shiraz*

### CROSER
*See* Petaluma

### D'ARENBERG WINES
**McLaren Vale**
★★★

The original vineyards were planted in the 1890s, and purchased in 1912 by teetotaller John Osborn, whose family has owned the business ever since. I have been tasting these wines since the 1970s, when the style of the reds was sort of dusty-dry, but could they age! The wines became more rounded in the 1980s, but the real revolution came in the 1990s, when the wines became more voluptuous. The 1990s also saw the arrival of Zar Brooks, whose marketing flair, and ability to dream up catchy names, woke this slumbering giant. All of D'Arenberg's Shiraz wines are stunning, but none more so than Dead Arm, which is a true Australian classic. Old Vine Shiraz and Footbolt Shiraz are almost in the same league, as is Sticks & Stones, the Rioja-style blend, and The Ironstone Pressings blend of Grenache, Mourvèdre, and Shiraz.

✓ *Botrytis* (Noble Riesling) • *Cabernet Sauvignon* (The Coppermine Road) • *Chardonnay • Classic red blend* (Bonsai Vine GSM, Sticks & Stones Tempranillo-Grenache, The Ironstone Pressings, The Laughing Magpie Shiraz-Viognier) • *Grenache* (The Custodian) • *Mourvèdre* (The Twentyeight Road) • *Shiraz*

### ELDERTON
**Barossa Valley**
★★❶

Established in 1984, Elderton has gained an enviable reputation for its high-quality, often highly oaked, wines since the early 1990s, with Cabernet Sauvignon king of this particular castle.

✓ *Cabernet Sauvignon* (Ashmead) • *Classic red blend* (CSM) •

*Merlot • Shiraz* (Command) • *Sparkling* (Pinot Pressings)

### ELDRIDGE
**Clare Valley**
★☆❶

The quality from Leigh and Karen Eldridge gets better with each vintage. Surprisingly good Gamay.

✓ *Cabernet Sauvignon • Classic white blend* (Sémillon-Sauvignon Blanc) • *Gamay • Riesling* (Watervale) • *Shiraz* (Blue Chip)

### GARTNER FAMILY VINEYARDS
**Coonawarra**
★☆❶

When you have over 1,000 acres (400 hectares), plus a shareholding in almost 500 acres (200 hectares) elsewhere, and supply other wineries with grapes, it's very easy to hold back something special for your own label.

✓ *Cabernet Sauvignon • Chardonnay • Shiraz*

### GLAETZER WINES
**Barossa Valley**
★★

Brilliant Shiraz, both still and sparkling.

✓ *Shiraz • Sparkling* (Shiraz)

### GROSSET
**Clare Valley**
★★★

Owner-winemaker Jeffrey Grosset is widely regarded as the king of Australian Riesling, but everything he produces is special. Gaia is a Bordeaux-style blend. Mesh is a Yalumba-Grosset collaboration.

✓ *Chardonnay* (Piccadilly) • *Classic red blend* (Gaia) • *Classic white blend* (Sémillon Sauvignon Blanc) • *Pinot Noir • Riesling* (Mesh, Polish Hill, Watervale)

### HAAN WINES
**Barossa Valley**
★☆❶

Established in 1993 by Hans and Fransien Haan. They are determined to make a name for their Merlot, thus have contracted James Irvine as winemaker.

✓ *Merlot • Sémillon • Viognier*

### HAMILTON
**McLaren Vale**
★☆❶

Richard Hamilton makes stunning wines, particularly reds. Hut Block Cabernets is a blend of Cabernet Sauvignon and Cabernet Franc. Hamilton also owns his late uncle's vineyard in Coonawarra, Leconfield.

✓ *Cabernet Sauvignon* (Hut Block) • *Classic red blend* (Hut Block Cabernets) • *Merlot* (Lot 148) • *Shiraz* (Gumpers' Block, Centurion 100 Year Old Vines)

### HARDY'S
**McLaren Vale**
★★❶

This large brand is the basis of the BRL Hardy group (*see* Australia's wine groups, p.556), which continues to produce a number of wines under various labels bearing the Hardy's name. This diverse selection ranges from penny-pinchers through penny-savers to premium-quality wines. Eileen Hardy Chardonnay (a wine named after the late but much-loved matriarch of the family for 40 years) consistently retains its reputation as one of Australia's very greatest wines.

✓ *Botrytis* (Padthaway Noble Riesling) • *Cabernet Sauvignon* (Padthaway, Thomas Hardy, Tintara) • *Chardonnay* (Eileen Hardy, Tintara) • *Fortified* (Ports: Show, Tall Ships, Tawny, Vintage, Whiskers Blake Tawny) • *Riesling* (Siegersdorf) • *Shiraz* (Eileen Hardy, Oomoo, Tintara) • *Sparkling* (Arras as from 1997 vintage, Banrock Station Sparkling Shiraz, Sir James, Nottage Hill, Omni)

### HEGGIES VINEYARD
**Eden Valley**
★★

Part of Yalumba, this winery has always been known for its Riesling, but has started to produce a fine Merlot in recent years.

✓ *Merlot • Riesling*

### HENRY'S DRIVE
**Padthaway**
★★

Established as recently as 1998, Henry's Drive was "discovered" by US critic Robert Parker and has quickly gained a reputation as one of Australia's finest red wine specialists.

✓ *Cabernet Sauvignon • Shiraz*

### HENSCHKE
**Eden Valley**
★★★

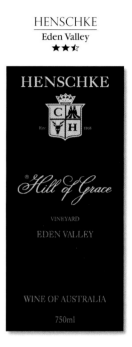

Founded in 1868, this is one of Australia's oldest and greatest wine-producing icons, with Hill of Grace Shiraz, and Cyril Henschke Cabernet Sauvignon lording it over the rest of the highly acclaimed range. Keyneton Estate used to be named Shiraz-Cabernet-Malbec, then Shiraz-Cabernet-Merlot, but is now labeled Euphonium, presumably to allow a certain varietal flexibility without advertising the fact. Henry's is a Shiraz-Grenache-Viognier blend, while Johann's Garden is a Grenache-Mourvèdre-Shiraz.

✓ *Cabernet Sauvignon* (Cyril Henschke) • *Chardonnay* (Crane's Eden Valley, Lenswood Croft) • *Classic red blend* (Keyneton Estate Euphonium, Henry's, Johann's Garden) • *Merlot* (Abbot's Prayer) • *Pinot Noir* (Giles) • *Riesling* (Green's Hill) • *Sémillon* (Julius Eden Valley, Louis Eden Valley) • *Shiraz* (Mount Edelstone, Hill of Grace)

### HEWITSON
**Adelaide**
★★★

Dean Hewitson was a winemaker at Petaluma for 10 years, where he achieved the impossible by shining even in the bright light of Brian Croser. During his time at Petaluma, he completed a vintage at that company's subsidiary in Oregon, the Argyle Winery, three harvests in

France, and picked up a Masters degree at UC Davis in California. Hewitson's specialty is to source grapes from very old, superbly sited vineyards in various regions. The Mourvèdre is the extreme example, coming from 150-year-old vines in Barossa.

☑ *Entire range*

## HILLSTOWE
### Adelaide Hills
★★ Ⓥ

Part of the Banksia group, thus now within the Lion Nathan portfolio.

☑ *Chardonnay* (Udy's Mill) • *Merlot* (The Pinchbowl) • *Shiraz* (Mary's Hundred)

## HOLLICK WINES
### Coonawarra
★ Ⓥ

Owner-viticulturist Ian Hollick set up his venture in 1983 and has produced some fresh, clean, well-focused wines, including a red Bordeaux-style blend that is simply sold by its Coonawarra appellation.

☑ *Cabernet Sauvignon* (Ravenswood) • *Chardonnay* (Reserve) • *Classic red blend* (Coonawarra Cabernet Sauvignon-Merlot)

## INGOLDBY
### McLaren Vale
★ Ⓥ

Now just another Beringer Blass brand, making mostly good-value wines, but with occasional standouts.

☑ *Cabernet Sauvignon* (McLaren Vale) • *Chardonnay* (McLaren Vale) • *Shiraz* (McLaren Vale Reserve)

## IRVINE
### Eden Valley
★★

Established in 1980 by the indefatigable James Irvine, whose name has become synonymous with Merlot. Cheaper wines sold under the Eden Crest range.

☑ *Classic red blend* (Eden Crest Merlot-Cabernet) • *Merlot* (James Irvine Grand Merlot)

## JAMIESONS RUN
### Coonawarra
★ Ⓥ

At one time, this was the most underrated brand in the Beringer Blass stable. It is not quite the treasure trove of inexpensive goodies it used to be, but can still come up with exceptional-value Chardonnay.

☑ *Classic red blend* (Winemakers Reserve Cabernet-Shiraz) • *Chardonnay*

## JIM BARRY WINES
### Clare Valley
★★ Ⓥ

Run by Mark and Peter, sons of the eponymous Jim Barry. Their top Shiraz, The Armagh, is one of

Australia's greatest wines. It is also one of the country's most expensive, and, at one-third of the price and almost as good quality as The Armagh, the McRae Wood Shiraz is better value. Virtually all other wines produced by Jim Barry are sold at bargain prices.

☑ *Cabernet Sauvignon* (McRae Wood) • *Chardonnay* (Unwooded) • *Fortified* (Old Walnut Tawny Port, Sentimental Bloke Port) • *Riesling* (Watervale) • *Shiraz* (Lodge Hill, McRae Wood, The Armagh)

## KAESLER WINES
### Barossa Valley
★★ Ⓥ

Toby and Treena Hauppauff have shone with Shiraz since purchasing the Kaesler vineyard in 1990, helped no doubt by a core of 110-year-old Shiraz vines. Now they are making top Cabernet Sauvignon.

☑ *Cabernet Sauvignon* • *Shiraz* (Old Vine, Stonehorse)

## KATNOOK ESTATE
### Coonawarra
★★

Part of the Wingara Group, which is majority-owned by Freixenet of Spain. With 815 acres (330 hectares) of vineyards in prime *terra rossa* soil, Katnook is an upmarket producer of intensely flavored wines that display remarkable finesse, the very best being Cabernet Sauvignon, Shiraz, and Sauvignon Blanc. Since 1979, when production began, Katnook wines have won a remarkable 14 trophies, plus 110 gold, 243 silver, and 645 bronze medals. Expensive wines are sold under the Riddoch label. This should not be confused with Wynns' John Riddoch, although some Riddoch reds are of almost the same outstanding quality. The penny-pinching label Deakin Estate (Murray Darling) has effectively replaced Katnook's cheaper Sunnycliff range.

☑ *Cabernet Sauvignon* (including Riddoch) • *Merlot* • *Riesling* • *Sauvignon Blanc* • *Shiraz* (including Riddoch)

## KAY BROTHERS
### McLaren Vale
★★ Ⓥ

A fast-rising star, thanks not only to the blessing of critic Robert Parker, but also to a block of incredibly low-yielding Shiraz vines planted in 1897.

☑ *Merlot* • *Shiraz* (Block 6, Hillside)

## KILIKANOON
### Clare Valley
★★ Ⓥ

Kilikanoon has been the talk of the town since 2002, when its Riesling, Shiraz, and Cabernet Sauvignon walked away with six out of seven trophies at the Clare Valley Wine Show.

☑ *Cabernet Sauvignon* (Blocks Road) • *Grenache* (Prodigal) • *Riesling* (Mort's Block) • *Shiraz* (Covenant, Oracle)

## KNAPPSTEIN
### Clare Valley
★★ Ⓥ

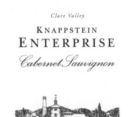

Part of Lion Nathan since the takeover of Petaluma. The wines continue going from strength to strength in the capable hands of Andrew Hardy, who trained under Brian Croser.

☑ *Cabernet Sauvignon* (Enterprise) • *Classic white blend* (Sauvignon Blanc-Sémillon) • *Riesling* (Hand Picked) • *Shiraz* (Enterprise) • *Sparkling* (Chainsaw Sparkling Shiraz)

## KNAPPSTEIN LENSWOOD VINEYARD
### Lenswood
★★★

Since selling off his original winery and vineyards to Petaluma, now owned by Lion Nathan, Tim Knappstein produces a fraction of his former output exclusively from his Lenswood vineyard in the Adelaide Hills, which he established in 1981. If anything, Knappstein's wines are more focused, and have greater finesse, than ever. The Palatine is a blend of Merlot, Malbec, and Cabernet Sauvignon.

☑ *Chardonnay* • *Classic red blend* (The Palatine) • *Pinot Noir* • *Sauvignon Blanc* • *Sémillon*

## LEASINGHAM
### Clare Valley
★★ Ⓥ

Part of the BRL Hardy group, Leasingham makes wines that offer outstanding quality and value. Bastion (sold on some export markets as Magnus) is a Shiraz-Cabernet blend, while Bin 56 is Cabernet-Malbec.

☑ *Cabernet Sauvignon* (Classic Clare) • *Classic red blend* (Bastion Shiraz Cabernet, Bin 56) • *Riesling* (Bin 7, Classic Clare) • *Shiraz* (Bin 61, Classic Clare, Domaine)

## LECONFIELD
### Coonawarra
★★

Owned by Richard Hamilton (*see* Hamilton), whose uncle, Sydney Hamilton, established Leconfield in 1974.

☑ *Cabernet Sauvignon* • *Merlot* • *Shiraz*

## PETER LEHMANN
### Barossa Valley
★★ Ⓥ

Often underrated in Australia itself, Peter Lehmann's range of always excellent-value, mostly brilliant-quality wines is highly regarded on international markets. The Mentor is a Cabernet Sauvignon-Malbec-Shiraz blend, while The Seven Surveys is Mourvèdre-Shiraz-Grenache.

☑ *Cabernet Sauvignon* • *Chardonnay* (The Barossa) • *Classic red blend* (The Mentor, The Seven Surveys) • *Fortified* (The King) • *Riesling* (Reserve) • *Rosé* (Grenache) • *Sémillon* (Reserve, The Barossa) • *Shiraz* (Mudflat, Stonewall)

## LINDEMANS WINES
### Coonawarra

Although this is the best-performing part of Lindemans' current operations, it is impossible to subdivide the brand according to location, particularly when Southcorp is progressively dropping Lindemans' regionality in favor of state blends. Consequently, all this brand's best wines can be found in the Victoria section, where the overall score is ★★, although the wines produced in Lindemans Coonawarra winery would easily rate ★★ at the moment. *See* Lindemans Wines, Victoria.

## MAGLIERI OF MCLAREN VALE
### McLaren Vale
★★ Ⓥ

Part of Beringer Blass since 1999. These extraordinary bargain wines are at last finding their way into mainstream outlets on export markets.

☑ *Barbera* • *Cabernet Sauvignon* • *Nebbiolo* • *Sangiovese* • *Sémillon* • *Shiraz*

## MAJELLA
### Coonawarra
### ★★

The Lynn family had kept merino sheep for four generations, when in 1968 George and Pat Lynn decided to invest in vineyards. The first 10 years were less than successful, with 30 tons or more of grapes left to rot on the vines in some years due to low demand. In 1980, however, they entered into an agreement to supply Wynns, a relationship that lasted for over 20 years, giving the Lynns confidence to strike out on their own. Cabernet Sauvignon and Shiraz are the standout wines here. The Malleea is a Shiraz-Cabernet Sauvignon blend.

✓ *Cabernet Sauvignon* • *Classic red blend* (The Malleea) • *Shiraz* • *Sparkling* (Sparkling Shiraz)

## MAXWELL WINES
### McLaren Vale
### ★☆Ⓥ

Founded in 1979, this fairly well-established winery became an Aladdin's cave of wonderful vinous treasures in the 1990s, but has settled down to two absolute standouts.

✓ *Cabernet Sauvignon* (Lime Cave) • *Shiraz* (Ellen Street)

## CHARLES MELTON
### Barossa Valley
### ★★Ⓥ

Most famous for his Châteauneuf-du-Pape-type blend, cheekily named Nine Popes, but all the reds produced here are highfliers, and Melton's sweet, seductive, sparkling Shiraz is regularly one of Australia's two or three finest. Rose of Virginia is a Grenache-Cabernet blend. If you want to see just how small, thus concentrated, a bunch of dry-farmed Shiraz is, then take a look at the website.

✓ *Cabernet Sauvignon* • *Classic red blend* (Nine Popes) • *Rosé* (Rose of Virginia) • *Shiraz*

## GEOFF MERRILL
### McLaren Vale
### ★☆Ⓥ

While Geoff Merrill was senior winemaker (1977–85) at Chateau Reynella, he started selling wines under his own name. He was appointed consultant red winemaker for Reynella's parent company, Thomas Hardy and Son, in 1985, but was actively searching for somewhere to make his own wines. That same year, Merrill came across the rundown Mount Hurtle Winery, which he purchased and restored, before leaving Hardy's in 1988 to concentrate on his own operation. At first, the emphasis was on the Mount Hurtle brand, but since 1993, when he took up the position as a consultant winemaker in Italy to UK supermarket Sainsbury and Gruppo Italiano Vini in Italy, the international fame of the moustachioed Merrill began to outshine that of Mount Hurtle, thus it was inevitable that his eponymous brand would one day take center stage. Merrill's style is for elegance and length over concentration and weight, with the occasional overoaking the only significant chink in his armor. Virtually all the wines offer value for money to one degree or another. The one obvious exception being the stunningly beautiful, but horrendously expensive, Henley Shiraz. Mount Hurtle survives, but as an exclusive brand for Liquorland.

✓ *Chardonnay* (Unwooded) • *Classic red blend* (Shiraz-Grenache-Mourvèdre) • *Classic white blend* (Sémillon-Chardonnay) • *Shiraz* (Henley, Reserve)

## MIRANDA WINES
### Barossa
### ★☆Ⓥ

Part of McGuigan Simeon since 2003, the origins of Miranda Wines date back to 1938, when Francesco Miranda arrived from Naples. There are three Miranda wineries, all producing and selling their own wines: the original and largest in Riverina, the latest (1998) in King Valley, and the best in Barossa. These wines are underrated, but since 1995, they have picked up more than 2,500 national and international awards, so they must be doing something right. The single most medal-laden wine is Golden Botrytis from the Riverina winery, but most of Miranda's best wines are made in the Barossa, where the value is great, and the quality constantly improving. The Emu Plains Colombard-Chardonnay is not a classic white blend, but it is a deliciously fresh one! An inexpensive range of night-harvested wines is sold under the Firefly label.

✓ *Botrytis* (Botrytis Sémillon, Golden Botrytis) • *Cabernet Sauvignon* (High Country) • *Classic red blend* (Reserve Shiraz Cabernet) • *Riesling* (Eden Valley) • *Rosé* (White Shiraz) • *Shiraz* (Family Reserve Old Vine, The Drainings)

## MITCHELL
### Clare Valley
### ★☆Ⓥ

A small winery, Mitchell produces one of Australia's classic examples of Riesling.

✓ *Riesling* (Watervale) • *Shiraz* (Pepper Tree Vineyard)

## MITOLO
### Adelaide Plains
### ★★

Fast-rising star with award-winning wine made by Ben Glaetzer. The wines are mostly sourced from McLaren Vale, with (so far) one from the Barossa Valley.

✓ *Cabernet Sauvignon* (Serpico) • *Shiraz* (G.A.M., Savitar)

## MOUNT HORROCKS
### Clare Valley
### ★★

The quality and definition in style of these wines have really shone since the late 1990s, especially in the Riesling wines, which are world class. All Rieslings are highly recommended, but one—the Cordon Cut—should be explained. Its beautifully balanced sweet style is achieved by cutting, but leaving in place the cordon, which disconnects the grape clusters from the vine's metabolism, artificially inducing *passerillage*.

✓ *Classic red blend* (Cabernet-Merlot) • *Riesling* • *Sémillon*

## MOUNTADAM VINEYARD
### Eden Valley
### ★☆

Recently purchased by LVMH, this estate produces wines that are rich, yet lean, and of excellent quality. They come from vineyards that once belonged to Adam Wynn, son of the founder of the almost legendary Wynns Coonawarra estate (now belonging to Southcorp). Adam Wynn is still very active in the day-to-day running of Mountadam. The Red is a Cabernet Sauvignon-Merlot blend. Other brands include David Wynn and Eden Ridge.

✓ *Classic red blend* (The Red) • *Pinot Noir* • *Riesling*

## MURDOCK
### Coonawarra
### ❓

I have not tasted the Cabernet Sauvignon from this relatively new producer (established 1998), but colleagues who have rave about its richness, ripeness, and elegance. To achieve elegance with richness and ripeness is, for me, the height of quality, thus I feel obliged to pass on the recommendation of this fast-rising producer.

## NEPENTHE VINEYARDS
### Adelaide Hills
### ★☆

In 1996 the Tweddall family became the second-ever vineyard owner to receive permission to build a winery in the Adelaide Hills (Petaluma being the first, almost 20 years earlier).

✓ *Chardonnay* • *Pinot Noir* • *Riesling*

## NOON WINERY
### McLaren Vale
### ★★

I don't know whether it's a trick of the mind, or if it really happened, but I have this memory of Drew Noon in 1991 at Cassegrain, where he was assistant winemaker, and he is telling me that he dropped the "e" from the end of his name because he didn't want to be "no one"! Since then, he has passed his Master of Wine examination, taken over his parents' winery and caused enough of a stir with his massive, superripe wine oddities to catch the attention of critic Robert Parker. Eclipse is a Grenache-Shiraz blend, and VP is a vintage port style.

✓ *Cabernet Sauvignon* (Reserve) • *Classic red wine* (Eclipse) • *Fortified* (VP) • *Shiraz* (Reserve)

## O'LEARY WALKER
### Clare Valley
### ★☆Ⓥ

David O'Leary and Nick Walker started this enterprise as recently as 2001, and so far the Rieslings have been splendid.

✓ *Classic red blend* (Cabernet Sauvignon Merlot) • *Riesling* (Watervale) • *Sémillon* (Watervale)

## ORLANDO
### Barossa Valley
### ★★Ⓥ

Orlando in general, and Jacob's Creek in particular, have propelled the French-owned Orlando Wyndham group to become one of Australia's top four wine companies. But there is a big difference between the Jacob's Creek basic range at AU$8 (US$6) a bottle, and various top-performing Jacob's Creek Reserve wines at twice the price (and 10 times the bargain). Even in the basic range, there are vintages that have been so stunning that they have run away with gold medals at Capital Shows, and have even taken trophies or top golds, much to the embarrassment of some judges. I am not ashamed to say that I have been impressed by bottom-line Jacob's Creek wines such as the 2003 Grenache-Shiraz, 2000 Merlot, 1998 Shiraz-Cabernet, 2000 Sémillon-Sauvignon Blanc, 2000 and 2002 Riesling. Even Jacob's Creek Chardonnay (the very thought of which normally makes my mouth water for a decent beer) enjoyed a remarkable run of quality between the 1999 and 2002 vintages, outclassing the Reserve in the last two of those years. Since being launched in 1983, Jacob's Creek core range Riesling alone has won 253 awards, including three trophies and 20 gold medals. The entire Jacob's Creek range has notched up 27 trophies and 169 golds, but is the wine the same everywhere? Is the same vintage of the same variety or blend exactly the same, not only in all parts of Australia, but on every market in the world? There is considerable variation in the awards, with supposedly the same wine winning a trophy and numerous golds, yet sometimes three times as many bronzes, but that happens to many other wines, and could equally be due to variation of judging panels or the precise stage at which the wines have developed in bottle when they are tasted. Until every wine at every competition is analysed, I do not suppose we will ever know. Note that JC below indicates Jacob's Creek.

✓ *Botrytis* (Sémillon) • *Cabernet Sauvignon* (Jacaranda Ridge, JC Reserve, St. Hugo) • *Chardonnay* (JC Limited Release, Russet Ridge Coonawarra, St. Hilary Padthaway) • *Classic red blend* (JC Grenache-Shiraz, JC Limited Release Shiraz-Cabernet) • *Riesling* (JC, JC Reserve) • *Shiraz* (Centenary Hill, JC Reserve, Lawson's Padthaway)

## PARACOMBE
### Adelaide Hills
### ★ ⓥ

Owner-viticulturist-winemaker Paul Drogemuller produces one of Australia's best-value Cabernet Franc wines.

✓ *Cabernet Franc* • *Chardonnay* • *Sauvignon Blanc*

## PARKER ESTATE
### Coonawarra
### ★★⯪

Acquired by the Rathbone Family Group in 2004, who utilized the consulting services of Dr. Andrew Pirie (*see* Pipers Brook, Tasmania) for a short while, the wines are now made by Peter Bissell of Balnaves. The estate's small, low-yielding vineyard produces superpremium wines, headed by First Growth, a blend of Cabernet Sauvignon and Merlot.

✓ *Cabernet Sauvignon* (Terra Rossa) • *Classic red blend* (Terra Rossa First Growth) • *Merlot* (Terra Rossa)

## PAULETT'S
### Clare Valley
### ★★

I have always enjoyed Neil Paulett's beautifully focused white wines, and am now rapidly becoming impressed with some of his reds.

✓ *Classic red blend* (Cabernet-Merlot) • *Riesling* • *Sauvignon Blanc* • *Shiraz*

## PENFOLDS WINES
### Barossa Valley
### ★★★⯪ ⓥ

Penfolds' superb Grange (formerly Grange Hermitage) is Australia's most famous wine, created by the late and legendary Max Schubert, and through this single masterpiece Penfolds itself has become a living legend. Naturally enough, Grange is a very expensive product—the price of a Bordeaux *premier cru*—but other far less expensive Penfolds wines are miniature masterpieces in their own right. However, some

wines, such as Bin 707 and The Magill, have become very pricey (though nowhere near as expensive as Grange), and The Magill is, in terms of its origin, more Grange than Grange has ever been, being sourced entirely from the vineyard that many people once believed to be the sole source of Grange. It is now part of Southcorp. RWT stands for Red Wine Trial, only the trial has long since stopped, and the name has stuck. Positioned between Grange and Magill, RWT is a Shiraz of incredible finesse for its size. Bin 707 is positioned as the Cabernet Sauvignon equivalent of RWT. Bin 138 is a Barossa Valley Shiraz-Mourvèdre-Grenache. Bin 389 is a Cabernet-Shiraz. Rawson's Retreat is the penny-pinching, decent-value label, but for just a little more, Koonunga Hill offers far better value for money, and even has the occasional real standout. Penfolds' Clare Valley operation is certified organic.

✓ *Cabernet Sauvignon* (Bin 407, Bin 707) • *Chardonnay* (Bin 00A, Bin 98A, Yattarna) • *Classic red blend* (Bin 138, Bin 389) • *Fortified* (Grandfather Port) • *Riesling* (Eden Valley Reserve) • *Sémillon* (Adelaide Hills) • *Shiraz* (Grange, Kalimna Bin 28, Magill Estate, RWT)

## PENLEY ESTATE
### Coonawarra
### ★★

Established in 1988 by Kym Tolley (whose mother was a Penfold and father a Tolley, hence the cheekily named Pen-ley). Penley Estates leans toward Penfolds in style, as Kym's penchant is clearly for red wines, but he has recently produced an excellent, rich, lush, toasty Chardonnay. However, Reserve and Phoenix Cabernet Sauvignons are the absolute standouts here.

✓ *Cabernet Sauvignon* • *Chardonnay* • *Classic red blend* (Shiraz-Cabernet) • *Sparkling* (Pinot Noir-Chardonnay)

## PETALUMA
### Adelaide Hills
### ★★★⯪ⓥ

This is still Brian Croser's domaine, even though Petaluma was the target of a hostile takeover by Lion Nathan. In the ensuing acrimony, Croser swore that he would not work for the new owner, but ended up in charge of Lion Nathan's entire wine group. Under Croser, Petaluma became a master of beautifully ripe, classically dry, top-quality Riesling that ages slowly and gracefully, and one of the best exponents of sparkling wine in the New World (*see* Argyle Winery, Oregon). Not to mention one of Australia's best Merlot wines, and a highly reputed Chardonnay too. Second wines are sold under Bridgewater Mill label.

✓ *Entire range*

## PEWSEY VALE
### Eden Valley
### ★★ ⓥ

Forget the Cabernet Sauvignon, there is only one reason to buy Pewsey Vale, and that is for its absolutely classic Eden Valley Riesling. Even the "basic" Riesling is superb, but The Contour is magnificent.

✓ *Riesling*

## PIKES
### Clare Valley
### ★★⯪ⓥ

Made by Neil Pike, formerly a winemaker at Mitchell, these excellent-quality red wines lean less on weight than subtlety and elegance to achieve complexity. The Luccio Red is a super-Tuscan-type blend of Sangiovese, Merlot, and Cabernet Sauvignon.

✓ *Classic red blend* (Luccio Red) • *Riesling* • *Shiraz*

## PRIMO
### Adelaide Plains
### ★★ⓥ

I cannot think why I was not wildly enthusiastic about these wines in previous editions. Owner-winemaker Joe Grilli produces some truly excellent wines, including the exquisitely rich, creamy-cedary Joseph sparkling red, its cult following being justified by the fact that it is regularly one of Australia's top two or three sparkling red wines. Although the best wines are sold under the Joseph label, don't ignore the basic Primo Estate white (La Biondina) and red (Il Briccone), which represent tremendous, everyday drinking value.

✓ *Botrytis* (Joseph La Magna Riesling) • *Classic red blend* (Il Briccone Shiraz-Sangiovese, Joseph Cabernet-Merlot) • *Colombard* (Il Biondina) • *Sparkling* (Joseph Red)

## PUNTERS CORNER
### Coonawarra
### ★★

This venture started life quite modestly in 1988, with 40 acres (16 hectares) of vineyards in Victoria

and Coonawarra, but now amounts to more than 370 acres (150 hectares), virtually all in Coonawarra, including 30 acres (12 hectares) surrounding the Punters Corner cellar sales (the wines are made under contract elsewhere). The basic Shiraz is stunning, but pales in comparison with the Spartacus Reserve. The Cabernet is almost entirely Cabernet Sauvignon, with just 9 percent (or thereabouts) of Merlot. Triple Crown is a blend of Cabernet Sauvignon, Shiraz, and Merlot.

✓ *Cabernet Sauvignon* • *Classic red blend* (Cabernet, Triple Crown) • *Shiraz*

## RESCHKE WINES
### Coonawarra
### ★★

The launch of the first wine, the 1998 Empyrean, caused something of a stir. First, because the asking price was AU$100 (US$65)for a wine with no track record. Second, because its big, porty character was praised to heaven and back by those who believe big is best. The next two vintages, however, saw a substantial drop down in alcohol level: virtually 1 percent per year, so that by 2000 Empyrean was a Bordeaux-like 12.9 percent alcohol. The wine is now more elegant, and possibly longer-lived, depending what you expect in a fully mature wine. The Vitulus is 100 percent Cabernet Sauvignon, whereas the Empyrean has always included 10 percent Merlot, but has also had 3 percent Cabernet Franc since 1999 (thus remains with the limit of a so-called pure varietal, which may include up to 15 percent of other grape varieties). The Taikurri is a blend of Cabernet Sauvignon, Merlot, Malbec, and Cabernet Franc.

✓ *Cabernet Sauvignon* (Empyrean, Vitulus) • *Classic red blend* (Taikurri) • *Shiraz*

## REYNELLA
### McLaren Vale
### ★★⯪

Formerly known as Chateau Reynella, this historic winery dates from 1838, but has belonged to BRL Hardy and its previous incarnations since 1982. Only two, so-called superpremium wines are made, both with the emphasis on traditional methods. Fruit is favored over oak, although the latter—both American and French—still plays a significant role.

✓ *Cabernet Sauvignon* (Basket Pressed) • *Fortified* (Vintage Port) • *Shiraz* (Basket Pressed)

## ROCKFORD WINES
### Barossa Valley
### ★★

The very traditional reds from low-yielding vines might be a bit soupy for some, but the Black Shiraz will be admired by anyone who enjoys Australia's wonderfully eccentric, show-style, sparkling Shiraz. Owner-winemaker Robert O'Callaghan has apparently made a number of onetime, single-vineyard Shiraz wines that are simply spectacular, but I have not, as yet, tasted them.

✓ *Cabernet Sauvignon* (Rifle Range) • *Grenache* (Moppa Springs) • *Sémillon* (Local Growers) • *Shiraz* (Basket Press) • *Sparkling* (Black Shiraz)

## ROSEMOUNT ESTATE
### McLaren Vale

*See* Rosemount Estate, New South Wales.

## ROUGE HOMME
### Limestone Coast
**Ⓥ**

Southcorp sold off the winery of this Lindemans brand in 2002, but not the name, thus it really is just another brand, albeit a good-value one. Rouge Homme could throw the odd curved ball, such as the truly excellent 1997 Coonawarra Pinot Noir. How on earth did they manage that? Coonawarra is hardly Burgundy; in fact, it is one of the last places on earth any sane person would plant that variety. In recent years, however, the provenance of these wines has been widened to the Limestone Coast, while the range has been reduced to a mere five wines. The Cabernet Sauvignon used to be the most reliable Rouge Homme, and some vintages were extraordinarily good, but 1999 was the last produced, unless Southcorp changes its mind. That leaves the Cabernet Merlot and Shiraz Cabernet as the safest bets.

## RYMILL
### Coonawarra
**★★⯪**

This property is owned and run by the descendants of John Riddoch, who planted the first Coonawarra vineyard in 1861. The MC² is so named because it is a blend of Merlot and two Cabernets (Sauvignon and Franc), but it is also half of Einstein's famous formula, $E=mc^2$, which demonstrates that energy equals mass and, as nuclear fission scientists would discover 30-odd years later, a minuscule mass can equal fabulously large amount of energy in some circumstances, so maybe there is also a more mystical meaning behind this label?

✓ *Cabernet Sauvignon* • *Classic red blend* (MC²) • *Shiraz*

## ST. HALLETT
### Barossa Valley
**★★**

Part of Banksia, which was taken over by Lion Nathan in 2001, this long-established winery still makes splendidly rich wines. Indeed, the quality has deepened over the last few years. GST is a blend of Grenache, Shiraz, and Touriga. It is also a pun on GST (Goods Services Tax), but that's only 10 per cent of the story.

✓ *Cabernet Sauvignon* • *Classic red blend* (GST) • *Merlot* • *Riesling* (Eden Valley) • *Shiraz* (Blackwell, Old Block)

## SALTRAM
### Barossa Valley
**★★**

Saltram has refocused on its red wines, for which it was once justifiably famous, and is again today.

✓ *Cabernet Sauvignon* (Mamre Brook) • *Chardonnay* (Mamre Brook) • *Classic red blend* (Barossa Cabernet-Merlot) • *Shiraz* (Mamre Brook, No.1 Reserve, The Eighth Maker)

## SEAVIEW WINERY
### McLaren Vale
**★⯪Ⓥ**

Now part of Southcorp, Seaview has the edge over its sister Seppelt brand with its entry-level wines, although Seppelt wins hands down in the premium category.

✓ Sparkling (Blanc de Blancs, Edwards & Chaffey, Pinot Noir-Chardonnay)

## SEPPELT
### Barossa Valley
**★★★⯪Ⓥ**

Seppelt Great Western in Victoria is Southcorp's sparkling wine specialist, while this Seppelt, in Seppeltsfield of the Barossa Valley, is its fortified wine specialist. Even though part of a corporate empire, Seppelt remains as priceless a piece of Australia's wine history as it has ever been, and Southcorp has emphasized that by restricting this winery and cellars exclusively to fortified wine. Table wines used to be made here, but no longer—they are all sourced from Victoria. The entire range of Seppelt's fortified wine is recommended, none more so than the Para range of liqueur ports. Yet it is with these wines that I have my only quibble. Or, more accurately, with the bottles that contain the wines. Worst of all is the Para 100 Year Old Liqueur Port, vintages of which easily fetch between AU\$1,000 and AU\$2,000 (US\$750–1,000) a bottle, and is

contained in a bottle that is a cross between a pretentious Cognac bottle and Mateus! What is wrong with a top-quality classic bottle shape?

✓ *Entire range*

## SHAW & SMITH
### Adelaide Hills
**★★Ⓥ**

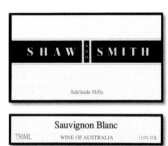

This up-and-coming venture was set up in 1989 by Martin Shaw, who is well known for his flying winemaker activities, and Michael Hill-Smith, the first Australian to become a Master of Wine. After squatting at Petaluma for a decade, Shaw & Smith built their own high-tech winery at Balhannah in 2000.

✓ *Chardonnay* (M3) • *Sauvignon Blanc* • *Merlot* • *Shiraz*

## SKILLOGALEE
### Clare Valley
**★★⯪Ⓥ**

Owner-winemaker David Palmer produces increasingly stylish wines from his 150-acre (60-hectare) property, particularly the Riesling.

✓ *Classic red blend* (The Cabernets) • *Riesling* • *Shiraz*

## TAPANAPPA WINES
### Wrattonbully
**❓**

This must be one to watch: a partnership formed between Brian Croser, Champagne Bollinger (which was a major shareholder in Petaluma before the takeover by Lion Nathan), and Jean-Michel Cazes of Château Lynch-Bages in Bordeaux. This high-powered trio has purchased Koppamurra Vineyard in Wrattonbully. Tapanappa is named after a sandstone formation near Croser's beach house. Apparently it is an Aboriginal word meaning "stick to the path"—and a lot of people will be watching to see if they live up to this!

## TATACHILLA
### McLaren Vale
**★★Ⓥ**

Part of Banksia, which was taken over by Lion Nathan in 2001, this long-established winery has increased tremendously its already excellent quality and value over the last five years or so. Keystone is a Grenache-Shiraz blend, while Partners is Cabernet Sauvignon-Shiraz.

✓ *Cabernet Sauvignon* (McLaren

Vale, Padthaway) • *Classic red blend* (Keystone, Partners) • *Merlot* (Adelaide Hills, Clarendon Vineyard) • *Shiraz* (Foundation, McLaren Vale) • *Sparkling* (Sparkling Malbec)

## TAYLORS
### Clare Vale
**★★⯪Ⓥ**

The basic Cabernet Sauvignon, Shiraz, and Riesling would probably be singled out at any other winery. They're not just some of the best bargains in Australia, but some of the country's greatest wines too. The St. Andrews range is, however, in a different league, as is part of the relatively new Jaraman range. The best classic red blend is the Promised Land Shiraz-Cabernet, but it too cannot live in the company of those recommended below. Wines also sold under the Wakefield label (the Cabernet Sauvignon and Merlot can be brilliant).

✓ *Cabernet Sauvignon* (Jaraman, St. Andrews) • *Chardonnay* (Jaraman) • *Riesling* (Jaraman, Clare, St. Andrews) • *Shiraz* (St. Andrews)

## TOLLANA
### Barossa Valley
**★★⯪Ⓥ**

Once entirely estate-produced, Tollana is now part of Southcorp, and I used to think this had not affected its identity, quality, or value, but is it my imagination or is this brand, which dates from 1888, disappearing before our very eyes? It is like watching a grand old ship steam into the horizon.

✓ *Botrytis* (Riesling)• *Cabernet Sauvignon* (Bin TR222) • *Shiraz* (Bin TR16)

## TORBRECK
### Barossa Valley
**★★★⯪Ⓥ**

The antithesis of Tollana, Torbreck is relatively young (1994), privately owned, and all of a sudden making headlines (thanks in part to US critic Robert Parker's gushing accolades). Both RunRig and Descendant are Shiraz-Viognier blends, but the former will set you back AU$200–250 (US$150–200), whereas the latter costs a mere AU$125–150 (US$100–120)—so what is the difference? Well, RunRig contains just 3 percent of Viognier, compared to 8 percent in Descendant. Furthermore, the Viognier is vinified separately for RunRig, whereas both grapes are crushed and fermented together for Descendant, which makes the cheaper wine (if it is possible to describe Descendant as cheaper) more classic in French terms. They are each from different vineyards, the Descendant vineyard having been planted from cuttings from RunRig, hence the name. Descendant spends 18 months in two- to three-year-old French oak, whereas RunRig is given 30 months in French oak, 60 percent of which is new. The Steading is Grenache, Mataro (Mourvèdre), and Shiraz, while Cuvée Juveniles is a full-throttle, fruit-driven, unoaked blend of Grenache, Shiraz, and Mataro. Juveniles is all old vines, but best drunk as young and as fresh as possible. VMR is a Viognier, Marsanne, and Roussanne blend, with winning acidity balance. The Bothie is Torbeck's interpretation of a Muscat de Beaumes-de-Venise.

✓ *Classic red blend* (Cuvée Juveniles, Descendant, RunRig, The Steading) • *Classic white blend* (VMR) • *Grenache* (Les Amis) • *Fortified* (The Bothie) • *Shiraz* (The Factor, The Struie)

## TURKEY FLAT
### Barossa Valley
### ★★ Ⓥ

Turkey Flat is a recently established, highflying winery producing several exceptionally rich, lush, complex red wines from superbly sited vineyards, the core of which are over 150 years old. Butcher's Block is a blend of Mataro (Mourvèdre), Shiraz, and Grenache.

✓ *Cabernet Sauvignon* • *Classic red blend* (Butcher's Block) • *Classic white blend* (Marsanne Sémillon) • *Fortified* (Pedro Ximénez) • *Grenache Noir* • *Rosé* • *Shiraz*

## GEOFF WEAVER
### Adelaide Hills
### ★★ Ⓥ

For four years Geoff Weaver was chief winemaker for the entire Hardys wine group, which effectively made him personally responsible for 10 percent of Australia's entire wine production. Not the sort of pressure that many of us would want to endure for too long, so little surprise that he left to pursue his own small wine operation in 1992. He had in fact planted his vineyard at Lenswood 10 years earlier, so it was nicely matured, and wines had been made on a part-time basis since 1986. Weaver's vineyard was also history in the making, as it was a pioneering venture into an untried region.

✓ *Chardonnay* • *Classic red blend* (Cabernet-Merlot) • *Pinot Noir* • *Riesling* • *Sauvignon Blanc*

## WENDOUREE
### Clare Valley
### ★★★ Ⓥ

One of Australia's icon wineries since the late 19th century. Wendouree's current CEO-winemaker, Tony Brady, has continued to produce some of this country's longest-lived reds since taking over in 1974. Shiraz is the jewel in Wendouree's crown, but given some bottle-age, Brady's wonderfully individual and expressive blended reds are near equals.

✓ *Cabernet Sauvignon* • *Classic red blend* (Shiraz-Malbec, Shiraz-Mataro, Cabernet Sauvignon-Malbec) • *Shiraz*

## WIRRA WIRRA
### McLaren Vale
### ★★

When Greg and Roger Trott took over Wirra Wirra in 1969, it was a wreck, literally. But the Trotts built it into a stylish winery making stylish wines, helped in the early days by that dynamic flying winemaker duo, Croser & Jordan (or should that be Jordan & Croser?). Croser returned for a stint as managing director, when he grew restless after having achieved everything he had set out to do at Domaine Chandon, but returned to that fold when LVMH made him an offer he couldn't refuse. Whoever Greg Trott has had around the place, Wirra Wirra has always had an excellent reputation, but over the last few years the quality has become more exciting and deepened across the range.

✓ *Cabernet Sauvignon* (The Angelus) • *Chardonnay* • *Classic red blend* (Grenache-Shiraz) • *Fortified* (VP Vintage Fortified Shiraz) • *Grenache* (McLaren Vale) • *Shiraz* (Church Block, McLaren Vale, RSW)

## WOLF BLASS
### Barossa Valley
### ★★ Ⓥ

This company is now part of Beringer Blass, but its range is still huge and the wines are marketed as aggressively as ever. Wolf Blass wines are mostly graded according to the color of their label, which works well enough, although the Yellow Label tends to be more cheap than cheerful these days (the last exception being the 1999 Yellow Label Cabernet Sauvignon, which really did punch above its weight). The Red Label is cheaper than the Yellow, and Eaglehawk cheaper still (but try the Riesling!). Contrary to what most people intuitively think, the pecking order after Yellow Label is Gold, Grey, Black, and, logically, at the very top comes Platinum. It is this role

reversal of what the colors really mean that has been the genius of Wolf Blass marketing, and no Australian winery is more marketing-driven than Wolf Blass, but its best wines have to be among the country's most prolific award-winners for this to work, and that has always been so. By 1990, the total number of awards that Wolf Blass had garnered stood at 2,575, including an amazing 135 trophies and no fewer than 712 gold medals. That was 15 years ago. Who knows what the total is these days, but I can safely say that at the upper end of the Wolf Blass range, the quality has never been better. The Grey Label, which has been around since 1967, has replaced the Brown Label, but I've retained the Brown Label recommendations as the wines will be around for some time to come.

✓ *Cabernet Sauvignon-Shiraz* (Black Label, Grey Label, Platinum Label, President's Selection) • *Classic red blend* (Black Label Cabernet Sauvignon-Shiraz, Grey Label Cabernet Sauvignon-Shiraz) • *Riesling* (Clare Valley, Eaglehawk, Gold Label, South Australia) • *Shiraz* (Brown Label, McLaren Vale Reserve, Platinum Label, President's Selection)

## WOODSTOCK
### McLaren Vale
### ★★

Doug and Mary Collett acquired a 25-acre (10-hectare), derelict vineyard and an old cottage named Woodstock in 1973. Apparently, the Townsend family had settled there in 1859, from Woodstock in Oxfordshire, England, which was the origin of the name. In fact I wrote the first and all successive editions of this encyclopedia in Witney, which is just a few miles from Woodstock. The Townsend name is still common in these parts. They are probably all distantly related to the original settlers of this property. The Colletts should try to get a local importer. The good folk of Woodstock would probably treat it as their house wine, making it as popular in its restaurants as Oxford Landing is in that city. Five Feet is a blend of Cabernet Sauvignon, Shiraz, Merlot, and Petit Verdot. The name supposedly comes from the wooden stocks found in English Woodstock, which had five holes for five feet—pull the other one!

✓ *Classic red blend* (Five Feet) • *Shiraz* (The Stocks)

## WYNNS
### Coonawarra
### ★★ Ⓥ

John Riddoch is supposed to be the top wine here, but, superb as it is, the straight Black Label Cabernet Sauvignon, although disappointingly thin during the 1980s, has been the epitome of elegance ever since, and, at half the price of John

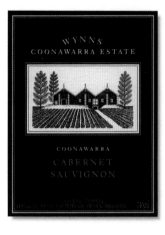

par with the John Riddoch, in terms of quality and price, but the basic Shiraz is not the equivalent of the Black Label Cabernet Sauvignon, neither is it meant to be, as its much cheaper price indicates. Wynns is part of Southcorp.

✓ *Cabernet Sauvignon* • *Chardonnay* • *Classic red blend* (Cabernet Shiraz-Merlot) • *Shiraz* • *Riesling*

## YALUMBA
### Barossa Valley
### ★★★ Ⓥ

This winery produces a vast range of styles and qualities, both still and sparkling. The Reserve and The Signature are both blends of Cabernet Sauvignon and Shiraz. Mesh is a Yalumba-Grosset collaboration. Oxford Landing is its penny-pinching, entry-level brand, offering very good value for money. Yalumba also owns Heggies Vineyard in Eden Valley, and Nautilus in New Zealand.

✓ *Cabernet Sauvignon* (The Menzies) • *Chardonnay* (Adelaide Hills, Heggies) • *Classic red blend* (Barossa Valley Shiraz-Viognier, Hand Picked Mourvèdre-Grenache-Shiraz, The Reserve, The Signature) • *Fortified* (all Museum Release wines) • *Pinot Noir* (Adelaide Hills) • *Riesling* (Hand Picked Eden Valley, Mesh) • *Shiraz* (The Octavius) • *Sparkling* (Cuvée One, Cuvée Two, D. since 1989, D. Black, N. V. Jansz, vintaged Jansz since 1997) • *Viognier* (Eden Valley, The Virgilius Eden Valley)

## ZEMA ESTATE
### Coonawarra
### ★★ Ⓥ

Established in 1982 by the Zema family, who currently cultivate 150 acres (60 hectares) of prime *terra rossa* land in Coonawarra. Cluny is a blend of Cabernet Sauvignon, Merlot, Cabernet Franc, and Malbec.

✓ *Cabernet Sauvignon* (Family Selection) • *Classic red blend* (Cluny) • *Shiraz* (Family Selection)

# WESTERN AUSTRALIA

*Much to the chagrin of winemakers in the rest of the country, Western Australia attracts a disproportionate amount of media attention for a state that possesses just 7 percent of Australia's vineyards. But it is no coincidence that from that 7 percent, Western Australia produces a mere 3 percent of the grapes crushed.*

WITHOUT WORLD-CLASS WINE REGIONS such as Margaret River, Western Australia could not produce world-class wines, but restricting yields enables those wines to stand out. Coonawarra might be Australia's most famous wine region, but South Australia is also a prolific producer of cheap wine. Apart from Western Australia, the only other state to harvest a smaller percentage of the country's crop than its vineyards represent is Victoria, and the best wines from that state's myriad top-performing wine regions also receive disproportionate publicity.

## HOW IT ALL BEGAN
The vineyards of Western Australia were established in 1829, by either Thomas Waters or Captain John Septimus Roe. If the founder was Roe, he would not have made any wine; his vines were grown to produce table grapes and raisins. Waters, on the other hand, bought 20 acres (8 hectares) of land that was to become Olive Farm. Waters was a botanist who had learned his winemaking skills from Boers in South Africa. He arrived in

**VASSE FELIX WINERY**
*A modern pioneering vineyard in the Margaret River region, Australia's first appellation of origin, Vasse Felix still produces a fine Cabernet Sauvignon.*

Australia with numerous seeds and plants, and by 1842 was making and bartering wine. In 1835, King William IV granted over 7,400 acres (3,000 hectares) of Swan Valley land to one Henry Revett Bland, who sold it to a trio of British army officers. These

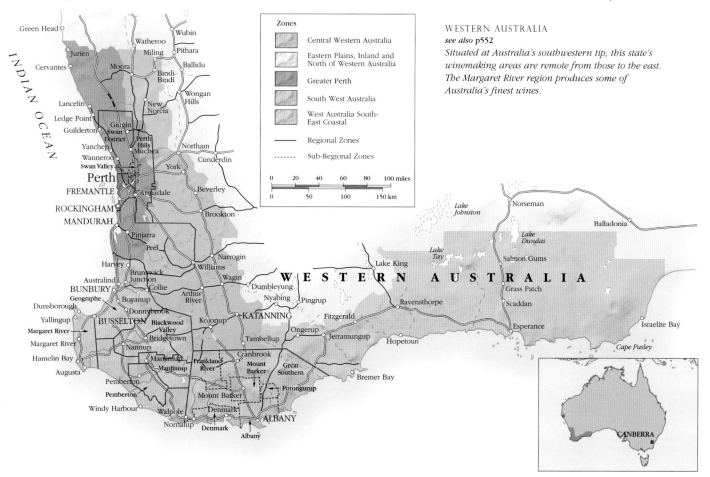

**WESTERN AUSTRALIA**
*see also* p552
*Situated at Australia's southwestern tip, this state's winemaking areas are remote from those to the east. The Margaret River region produces some of Australia's finest wines.*

**Zones**

- Central Western Australia
- Eastern Plains, Inland and North of Western Australia
- Greater Perth
- South West Australia
- West Australia South-East Coastal
- —— Regional Zones
- ······ Sub-Regional Zones

**SWAN VALLEY VINEYARDS**
*This flat plain belongs to one of the hottest winegrowing regions in the world, and the first of Western Australia's wine districts to be established.*

## FACTORS AFFECTING TASTE AND QUALITY

**LOCATION**
Western Australia's vine-growing areas sweep around the southwestern corner of Australia from Perth to Albany.

**CLIMATE**
This is very variable, from the long, very hot, dry summers and short, wet winters of the Swan Valley, one of the hottest winegrowing areas of the world, through the Mediterranean-type conditions of the Margaret River, with a higher rainfall and summer heat tempered by ocean breezes such as the "Fremantle Doctor" and "Albany Doctor", to the even cooler Lower Great Southern Area, which also has some light rainfall in summer. Ocean winds can exacerbate salinity problems and high coastal humidity helps with the development of botrytis.

**ASPECT**
Most vines are planted on the relatively flat coastal plain and river valley basins, but also on some rather more undulating, hilly areas, such as those around Denmark and Mount Barker near Albany in the south and east of the region. Vineyards generally grow at an altitude of between 295 and 820 feet (90 and 250 metres), but can be as high as 1,115 feet (340 metres) in the Blackwood Valley.

**SOIL**
Soils are fairly homogenous,
being mainly deep, free-draining, alluvial, sandy, gravelly, or clay loams over clay subsoils. Loam soils such as karri and marri are named after the gum trees that used to grow on them, and have significantly different properties. The Southwest Coastal area has a fine, white-grey topsoil called tuart sand, over a base of limestone with gravel in parts of the Margaret River.

**VITICULTURE AND VINIFICATION**
Drip irrigation is widespread because of the general lack of summer rain and the free-draining nature of the soil, although, ironically, winter water-logging due to clay subsoils is also a problem. Wide planting, mechanized harvesting, and the use of the most modern vinification techniques typify the area, which has generally concentrated on developing the cooler regions away from the Swan Valley in recent years. Well-equipped boutique wineries dominate the Margaret River wine regions.

**GRAPE VARIETIES**
**Primary varieties:** Cabernet Sauvignon, Chardonnay, Merlot, Riesling, Sauvignon Blanc, Sémillon, Shiraz
**Secondary varieties:** Cabernet Franc, Chenin Blanc, Malbec, Muscadelle, Muscat Gordo Blanco, Pinot Noir, Verdelho, Zinfandel

---

new owners, Messrs Lowis, Yule, and Houghton, were stationed in India, but Yule was despatched by the senior officer, Colonel Houghton, to run the property. Thus Houghton Wines, the first commercial winery in Western Australia, takes its name from a man who never set foot in the country.

The Swan Valley remained the hub of the state's wine industry and, with an influx of Europeans, all experienced in viticulture and winemaking, the expertise of this industry grew. Gradually, Mount Barker evolved as a wine area, then Frankland, and last, but certainly not least, Margaret River. For most non-Australian wine drinkers, it is the last of these appellations that has provided the greatest excitement and pleasure. Neither the climate, nor the soil, of the Margaret River is special in itself, but combined they produce grapes of unparalleled purity and finesse.

---

# THE APPELLATIONS OF
# WESTERN AUSTRALIA

## ALBANY

One of five sub-regional GIs within the Great Southern region, Albany has a Mediterranean climate that is moderated by sea breezes known locally as the "Albany Doctor". Soils suitable for viticulture are quite patchy, and mostly confined to the slopes. Pinot Noir has something of a reputation thanks, primarily, to Bill Wignall (Wignall Wines), but Cabernet Sauvignon, Chardonnay, and Sauvignon Blanc probably perform at least as well.

## BLACKWOOD VALLEY

This GI is the least known and one of the newest of Western Australia's wine regions, sandwiched between Manjimup and Geographe. The first vineyard was Blackwood Crest, planted by Max Fairbrass in 1976, and by 2004 there were over 50 vineyards and 10 wineries. The climate is Mediterranean, with dry summers and wet winters. Vines grow at an elevation of 100 to 330 to 1,115 feet (340 metres) on gravelly loam soils, which are thinner and more gravelly, with some red earths, on the steeper slopes. Cabernet Sauvignon is the most widely planted variety and the most successful, with Shiraz on the increase. Other grapes include Chardonnay, Riesling, Sauvignon Blanc, and Sémillon.

## CENTRAL WESTERN AUSTRALIA

This zonal GI covers a vast area of the Darling Ranges, from the Great Southern GI to north of the Swan District, but size is the only impressive aspect of what is currently a viticultural wasteland.

## DENMARK

The newest sub-region within the Great Southern GI, Denmark is situated some 60 kilometres (37 miles) along the coast from Albany. With its wet winters and warm to hot summers, the ocean's moderating influence, and a mix of marri and karri loam soils, the focus here has quite rightly been on Chardonnay and Pinot Noir. Other varieties grown include Cabernet Franc, Cabernet Sauvignon, Sauvignon Blanc, Sémillon, and Shiraz. The etymological origin of this Denmark had nothing to do with the Scandinavian country, but was named after Dr Alexander Denmark, an English naval surgeon.

## EASTERN PLAINS, INLAND AND NORTH OF WESTERN AUSTRALIA

Hardly rolls off the tongue, does it? I sincerely doubt that any wines will be sold under this zonal GI, which is the ultimate expression of bureaucratic logic, referring to all areas of Western Australia not already covered.

## FRANKLAND RIVER

A small area on the western edge of the Great Southern zone, Frankland River was put on the map by Houghton. This GI is, however, something of a misnomer, as four rivers converge in this sub-region: the Frankland, Gordon, Kent, and Tone. The climate is more Continental than Mediterranean, and, unlike the other sub-regions of the Great Southern zone, Frankland River has virtually no maritime influence. Surprisingly crisp Rieslings are made here. It is also good for Cabernet Sauvignon. Other grapes grown include Chardonnay, Sauvignon Blanc, and Shiraz.

## GEOGRAPHE

Formerly known as the Southwest Coastal Plains, this regional GI takes in the curve of land on Geographe Bay, where the somewhat Mediterranean climate is cooled and humidified by the Indian Ocean. The region extends inland, where it creeps eastward into the foothills of the Darling Range. Geographe has a limestone subsoil, and is dissected by four rivers, the Capel, Collie, Ferguson, and Harvey, which have deposited alluvial soils that have a much higher nutrient content than the deep sandy soils in the coastal areas. Chardonnay is perhaps the most successful variety, followed by Cabernet Sauvignon and Merlot, with Sémillon and Shiraz on the rise.

## GREAT SOUTHERN

**Sub-regions:**
*Albany, Denmark, Frankland River, Mount Barker, Porongurup*

This regional GI is the coolest of Western Australia's viticultural areas, and, although it has similar climatic influences to Margaret River, it has a lower rainfall. The vineyards are scattered throughout a vast area, and mostly consist of Riesling, Cabernet Sauvignon, Shiraz, Malbec, Pinot Noir, and Chardonnay.

## GREATER PERTH

This zonal GI encompasses the regional GIs of the Peel, Perth Hills, and Swan District.

## MANJIMUP

This GI is immediately north of Pemberton, on the same latitude as the Margaret River. Manjimup GI finalization was delayed because some producers wanted to be part of Pemberton, but the two regions differ in both soils and climate. Manjimup is warmer, with more sunshine and less humidity, while the marri loam is less fertile, having more sand and gravel than Pemberton's karri loam. In addition to wines produced by local boutique wineries, the region also sells a lot of its fruit to other wineries in the state. Chardonnay is the most widely planted variety, but Cabernet Sauvignon and Merlot fare best. There is more hope than promise for Pinot Noir, even though Picardy, the region's top producer, makes excellent wines from this grape. Other grapes grown include Sauvignon Blanc and Verdelho.

## MARGARET RIVER

This regional GI remains Australia's premier region for wine lovers who seek class and finesse, rather than weight and glory. Situated south of Perth, the Margaret River district attracted much attention in 1978 when it established Australia's first Appellation of Origin system. Like similar schemes, it was unsuccessful. The first vineyard was planted in the Margaret River area at Bunbury as long ago as 1890. However, it was a vineyard planted by Dr Tom Cullity at Vasse Felix in 1967 that was the first step in the Margaret River's journey to success. The region follows a ridge that runs along the coast from Cape Naturaliste to Cape Leeuwin in the south, with Margaret River flowing westward through its centre, while the Blackwood River flows southwest to Augusta. The land is undulating, with vines planted up to a maximum altitude of 90 metres (295 feet) on gravelly, sandy loams, with the majority of vineyards and wineries located in and around Wilyabrup. The warm maritime climate is cooled by ocean breezes, with most rain falling in autumn and winter. Relatively minor problems do exist in the area, notably powdery mildew, parrots, wind, and, most serious, dry summers. The powdery mildew seems to be under control, and the vineyard workers plant sunflowers to distract the parrots from the vines, while rye grass acts as a windbreak. A lot of vines experience water-stress, not a heat-related problem, but dry-summer induced, and one that is exacerbated by the wind factor. The greatness of Margaret River wines cannot be disputed. This quality of fruit is not bettered by any other Australian wine region. The best varieties are Cabernet Sauvignon, Chardonnay, Sauvignon Blanc, Sémillon, and Shiraz.

## MOUNT BARKER

A sub-region of the Great Southern zonal GI, where vines enjoy a Mediterranean climate, and grow at altitudes of 180 to 250 metres (590 to 820 feet) on gravelly-sandy loams over gently undulating hills. Growers avoid the valley floors due to the salinity of their soils. Mount Barker has a reputation for its lime-laden Riesling, and elegant red wines from Cabernet Sauvignon and Shiraz. Pinot Noir has also won awards. Other varieties grown include Cabernet Franc, Chardonnay, Malbec, Merlot, Sauvignon Blanc, Sémillon, and Shiraz.

## PEEL

This large region takes in the Peel Inlet just south of Mandurah, where the vines enjoy a Mediterranean climate that is cooled and moderated by this large body of water, backed up by the Indian Ocean, although this effect diminishes further inland. The soils are extremely diverse, and range from deep, free-draining tuart sand on the coast to sandy-alluvium on the plains, with marri-jarrah loams, yellow duplex soils, and gravel further inland. Although vines were planted at Pinjarra as early as 1857, and remained productive for 40 years, it was not until the 1970s that viticulture in this region underwent sustained development. Chenin Blanc and Shiraz are the primary varieties. Other grapes grown include Cabernet Sauvignon, Chardonnay, Merlot, Sémillon, Shiraz, and Verdelho.

## PEMBERTON

This GI south of Manjimup is one of Western Australia's less consistent wine regions, but with vineyards established in the 1980s and 1990s, it is still a young area and the locals are still confident. Pemberton is commonly known as "Karri country" after its magnificent forests of Karri gum trees, which give their name to the soil in which they grow. Karri loam is a deep, red, fertile soil that is too fertile for vines, causing excessive vigour problems, although growers overcome this by deliberate water-stressing and hard pruning to control the canopy. Pemberton was originally thought to be a Pinot Noir area, but Cabernet Sauvignon, Merlot, and Shiraz have been far more successful. Other varieties grown include Chardonnay, Sauvignon Blanc, Sémillon, and Verdelho.

## PERTH HILLS

This regional GI is adjacent to the Swan Valley and consists of a strip of the lower slopes of the Darling Ranges. Although this area has a hot climate, it is higher and cooler than the Swan Valley, with grapes ripening some two weeks later. Cabernet Sauvignon and Chardonnay are the most successful grapes, with Chenin Blanc, Shiraz, and Pinot Noir the other primary varieties grown.

## PORONGURUP

Set against a backdrop of the Porongurup Ranges, this picturesque region is one of five sub-regional GIs encompassed by the Great Southern region. The vines benefit from a Mediterranean climate, and grow on granite-based karri loam soils. The primary varieties are Cabernet Franc, Cabernet Sauvignon, Chardonnay, Merlot, Pinot Noir, Riesling, Sémillon, Shiraz, and Verdelho.

## SOUTH WEST AUSTRALIA

This zonal GI encompasses the majority of Western Australia's most exciting wine areas, including the regional GIs of Blackwood Valley, Geographe, Great Southern, Manjimup, Margaret River, and Pemberton.

## SWAN DISTRICT

**Sub-region:**
*Swan Valley*

This regional GI contains the Swan Valley itself, but also extends northwards from Perth, encompassing former unclassified areas such as Gingin and Moondah Brook.

## SWAN VALLEY

This sub-regional GI is located northeast of Perth, and represents the heart and soul of the Swan District zone. The Swan Valley has the dubious distinction of being one of the hottest viticultural regions in the world. Partly because of this, and partly as a reaction to the phenomenal success of the Margaret River, several producers have deserted the area and the number of vineyards is shrinking. What was once the traditional centre of Western Australia's wine industry is now a waning force, although the best areas are cooled by the so-called "Fremantle Doctor" wind, allowing the old-fashioned, foursquare wines to be replaced by lighter and fresher styles. If the Swan Valley can claim to make any classic wine whatsoever, it has to be fortified wines made from the Muscat Gordo Blanco and Muscadelle grapes. Other important varieties include Cabernet Sauvignon, Chardonnay, Merlot, Sémillon, and Shiraz.

## WEST AUSTRALIAN SOUTH EAST COASTAL

This zonal GI covers a large swathe of coastal area that lies immediately to the east of the Great Southern zone.

## THE WINE PRODUCERS OF
# WESTERN AUSTRALIA

### ALKOOMI WINES
**Frankland**
★★Ⓥ

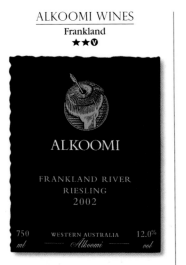

Sheep farmers Mervyn and Judy Lange established this venture in 1971, making their first wines five years later. They always used to produce fresh, fruity, and rich-flavoured wines that could be recommended with confidence, but were seldom special. However, since the mid-to-late 1990s the quality, style, and expressiveness has become ever more impressive. Blackbutt is a blend of Malbec, Cabernet Sauvignon, Cabernet Franc, and Merlot. Young, easy-drinking wines are sold under the Sutherlands label.

🖌 *Cabernet Sauvignon* (Frankland River) • *Classic red blend* (Blackbutt) • *Riesling* (Frankland River) • *Sémillon* (Wandoo) • *Shiraz* (Jarrah)

### AMBERLEY ESTATE
**Margaret River**
★ⓥ

Eddie Price, a former chief winemaker at Brown Brothers, is the managing director and winemaker at Amberley, where most wines offer good value, but Shiraz excels.

🖌 *Sémillon* (First Selection) • *Shiraz*

### ASHBROOK ESTATE
**Margaret River**
★★Ⓥ

Great quality, and even better value.

🖌 *Chardonnay* • *Classic red blend* (Cabernet-Merlot) • *Sémillon* • *Verdelho*

### BROOKLAND VALLEY
**Margaret River**
★★Ⓥ◉

Malcolm and Deirdre Jones established Brookland Valley in 1984, with BRL Hardy purchasing a 50 percent shareholding in 1997. Since then the quality has gone from good to excellent.

🖌 *Chardonnay* • *Classic red*

*blend* (Cabernet-Merlot, Verse 1 Cabernet-Merlot) • *Classic white blend* (Verse 1 Sémillon-Sauvignon Blanc) • *Merlot* • *Sémillon* (Verse 1)

### CAPE MENTELLE
**Margaret River**
★★★Ⓥ

Referred to by locals as the "Mentelle asylum", this is where David Hohnen started his cult-driven empire, which included New Zealand's Cloudy Bay phenomenon. He retired in 2003, to be succeeded by Dr Tony Jordan, who now oversees all of LVMH's operations in Australia and New Zealand. The quality remains exemplary, showing an uncanny ability to straddle both Old and New World styles, respecting tradition, and understanding restraint and finesse, yet revealing the best of Margaret River's ripe fruit flavours. This is the legacy of Hohnen's own philosophy, and it even applies to the Zinfandel, which under Cape Mentelle boasts infinitely more finesse than many a California icon of this variety. Marmaduke is primarily Shiraz-Grenache-Mataro (Mourvèdre), with a little Merlot and Pinot Noir. Trinders is Cabernet Sauvignon and Merlot, with a little Cabernet Franc and Petit Verdot. Georgina is Sauvignon Blanc and Chardonnay, with a little Sémillon and Chenin Blanc. Wallcliffe is a blend of Sauvignon Blanc and Sémillon.

🖌 *Cabernet Sauvignon* • *Chardonnay* • *Classic red blend* (Marmaduke, Trinders) • *Classic white blend* (Georgina, Sémillon-Sauvignon, Wallcliffe) • *Shiraz* • *Zinfandel*

### CAPEL VALE WINES
**Southwest Coastal Plain**
★★⯪

Owner Peter Pratten, a former radiologist, is the driving force behind this expanding brand, which is known for its delicious, vibrantly fruity wines.

🖌 *Cabernet Sauvignon* • *Classic white blend* (Sauvignon Blanc-Sémillon) • *Merlot* (Howecroft) • *Riesling* (Whispering Hill) • *Shiraz* (Kinnaird, Mount Barker Trifecta)

### CHATSFIELD
**Mount Barker**
★Ⓥ

Irish-born Dr Ken Lynch has a well-established record for producing easy-drinking wines, especially his ripe, peachy Riesling.

🖌 *Cabernet Franc* (Soft Red) • *Chardonnay* • *Riesling* • *Shiraz*

### CLAIRAULT
**Margaret River**
★⯪Ⓥ

The Martin family has expanded the vineyards, aiming to become biodynamic, and has taken the quality of the wines to new heights.

🖌 *Cabernet Sauvignon* • *Chardonnay* • *Classic red blend* (Claddagh Reserve) • *Classic white blend* (Sémillon-Sauvignon Blanc) • *Riesling* • *Sémillon*

### CULLEN WINES
**Margaret River**
★★⯪◉

Di Cullen passed away in 2003, leaving the winery that she and her late husband Kevin established in 1966 in the hands of her youngest daughter, Vanya. She could not have left the business in safer hands. Vanya Cullen has been the winemaker since 1989, and makes an outstanding range of wines, which get better with every vintage. If winemakers of the stature of Dr. Andrew Pirie are eager to subject themselves to a masterclass with her, it is little wonder that she was voted Australia's Winemaker of the Year in 2000. Cullen is an organic producer that is converting to biodynamic and, in 2006, became Australia's first carbon-neutral winery.

🖌 *Entire range*

### DEVIL'S LAIR
**Margaret River**
★★Ⓥ

Planted in 1981, and purchased by Southcorp in 1996, Devil's Lair takes it name from the nearby Devil's Lair cave, where the fossil remains of the so-called Tasmanian Devil have been discovered. The Cabernets blend of Cabernet Sauvignon, Cabernet Franc, and Merlot is deep, dark, and yet finely structured, showing great potential. The Fifth Leg wines are more for ready drinking, but they are fine, elegant wines nonetheless. The latest addition, Fifth Leg Rosé, a blend of Merlot and Cabernet Sauvignon, was introduced with the 2004 vintage, and had not been tasted by this author at the time of writing. But it got me thinking about the last bottle in my cellar of 1991 Devil's Lair Cabernet Sauvignon (no longer marketed as such), and it was in beautiful condition, with soft, sweet-tasting—although totally dry, of course—fruit of a freshness that belied its 13 years of age.

🖌 *Classic red blend* (Cabernet, Fifth Leg Red) • *Classic white blend* (Fifth Leg White)

### EVANS & TATE
**Margaret River**
★★⯪

This winery used to own vineyards in the Swan Valley as well as the Margaret River, but has sold off its Swan Valley holdings. In March 2003, Evans & Tate purchased the cash-strapped Cranswick Estates for A$100 million, but despite the latter's precarious financial situation, it fuelled Evans & Tate's profits by more than 40 per cent in the first year, and in excess of 70 percent the second year. The best wines at Evans & Tate combine richness with finesse.

✓ *Cabernet-Merlot* (Barrique 61) • *Chardonnay* • *Merlot* • *Sémillon* • *Sémillon-Sauvignon* • *Shiraz*

## FERMOY ESTATE
### Margaret River
★ ⓥ

The most consistent wines produced at the Fermoy Estate now are Chardonnay and Merlot. A new range has been launched under the Sentinel label, but has yet to make its mark.

✓ *Chardonnay* • *Merlot*

## FERNGROVE VINEYARDS
### Great Southern
★⯪ ⓥ

Murray Burton ordered the first vines to be planted in 1996, and now has over 1,000 acres (400 hectares) of vineyards, plus a brand-new winery built in 1999. Since then these wines have really taken off, reaching orbit with the 2002 Cossack Riesling, which won a record seven trophies and four golds.

✓ *Classic white blend* (Sémillon-Sauvignon Blanc) • *Riesling* (Cossack) • *Shiraz*

## FLINDERS BAY
### Margaret River
★ ⓥ

Established in 1995 as a joint venture between two families, the grape-growing Gillespies and wine-retailing Irelands.

✓ *Classic white blend* (Pericles Sauvignon-Sémillon Blanc) • *Merlot* • *Shiraz*

## FRANKLAND ESTATE
### Frankland
★ ⓥ

Frankland Estate is best for its blended red, which consists of Cabernets, Merlot, and Malbec. It is dedicated to the late Professor Olmo, California's famous grape breeder, not for creating varieties such as Ruby Cabernet, but because he was instrumental in selecting areas of Frankland best suited to viticulture in the early days of this wine region. Olmo's Reward is a blend of Cabernet Franc and Merlot primarily, supported by Malbec, Cabernet Sauvignon, and Petit Verdot. Poison Hill refers to the heartleaf plant growing there, which is poisonous to sheep and dogs, and thus was a threat to early settlers.

✓ *Classic red blend* (Olmo's Reward) • *Riesling* (Isolation Bridge, Poison Hill)

## GALAFREY
### Great Southern
★ ⓥ

Anyone who names a winery after the mythical planet of the Time Lords in *Dr Who* should be locked up in a dark place – preferably with a good supply of Galafrey wines.

✓ *Cabernet Sauvignon* • *Chardonnay* (Unoaked) • *Classic white blend* (Galafrey Art Label Semillon-Sauvignon Blanc) • *Riesling* • *Shiraz*

## GILBERTS
### Great Southern
★★⯪ ⓥ

The Gilberts have their wines made by contract at Plantagenet, which does a better job for them than it does with its own wines, which are good, but just not in the same class. This is a classic demonstration of the benefits of superior *terroir*. Best known to an informed few for their Riesling, which thrust the Gilberts into the limelight when it won Best of Show at the Qantas West Australian Wine Show in both 2000 and 2001, the class of these wines can also be seen throughout the range.

✓ *Entire range*

## GOUNDREY WINES
### Great Southern
★ ⓥ

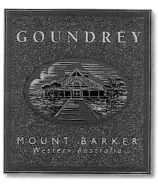

Owned by Perth-based US millionaire Jack Bendat, who has invested millions in Goundrey and has been intent on driving sales ever upwards, but only of late does there seems to be a more mature reflection as to increasing consistency of quality.

✓ *Cabernet Sauvignon* (Reserve) • *Chardonnay* (Unwooded) • *Chenin Blanc* • *Shiraz* (Reserve)

## GRALYN ESTATE
### Margaret River
★★

The style leans more towards size than finesse, but you cannot help being seduced by the lush quality of these wines.

✓ *Cabernet Sauvignon* • *Classic red blend* (Shiraz-Cabernet) • *Fortified* (Vintage Port) • *Shiraz* (Old Vine)

## HACKERSLEY
### Geographe
★★ ⓥ

These wines have come a long way in the short while since Hackersley was established as a joint venture between three families. The quality far exceeds the reasonable prices asked (so far), especially for such a tiny production.

✓ *Cabernet Sauvignon* • *Merlot* • *Shiraz*

## HAPPS VINEYARD
### Margaret River
★

Erl Happ makes several wines, all of which are eminently drinkable, but you can tell that he puts his heart into his reds, and of these Merlot is the most highly regarded. Charles Andreas is a blend of Cabernet Sauvignon, Merlot, Cabernet Franc, Malbec, and Petit Verdot.

✓ *Cabernet Franc* (Three Hills) • *Classic red blend* (Charles Andreas) • *Merlot* (Three Hills)

## HIGHER PLANE
### Margaret River
★★⯪

Venture by Craig and Cathie Smith that has rapidly hit the heights. Craig is a doctor (plastic surgeon), which is almost *de rigueur* for anyone starting a wine business in this part of the world, and Cathie has a Master of Business in Wine Marketing. Winemaking by Matt Wood.

✓ *Chardonnay* • *Classic red blend* (Cabernet-Merlot) • *Merlot*

## HOUGHTON WINES
### Swan Valley
★★⯪ ⓥ

Houghton wines are generally underestimated because of the winery's location in the under-performing Swan Valley, its huge production, and the fact that it is part of the even more gigantic BRL Hardy, but this winery is an exemplary instance of how big can be beautiful. Houghton's White Burgundy (sold as HWB in the EU) is a case in point: large-production and inexpensive, yet an award-winning wine of legendary reputation. However, if you have been impressed by the value of White Burgundy, you should try the White Burgundy Show Reserve, which is released when fully mature, and illustrates the potential quality of a wine that is mostly consumed within hours of purchase. As for its content, White Burgundy is primarily a blend of Chardonnay, Chenin Blanc, and Sémillon, with a mish-mash of other varieties, such as Verdelho, Sauvignon Blanc, Muscadelle, etc. These large-volume blends tend to evolve hand-in-hand with the development of Australia's vineyard mix. My notes from more than 20 years ago reveal that the 1981 was a 50/50 blend of Chenin Blanc and Muscadelle. From the

past to the future: one day this wine will have to be renamed, of course, as part of Australia's trading agreement with France. Top of the Houghton hierarchy is Jack Mann, a super-premium wine named after the late and legendary winemaker, Jack Mann MBE. Jack Mann is usually a blend of Cabernet Sauvignon with maybe Malbec one year, Shiraz another. At one time it was a blend that included both of those ancillary varieties, and occasionally it can be pure Cabernet Sauvignon (1998, for example). The Crofters is a blend of Cabernet Sauvignon and Merlot.

✓ *Cabernet Sauvignon* (Margaret River) • *Chardonnay* (Pemberton) • *Classic red blend* (Crofters, Jack Mann) • *Classic white blend* (Sémillon-Sauvignon Blanc, White Burgundy Show Reserve) • *Riesling* (Frankland River) • *Sauvignon Blanc* (Pemberton) • *Shiraz* (Frankland) • *Verdelho* (Show Reserve)

## HOWARD PARK
### Denmark
★★

Now owned by the Burch family, who also have vineyards in Margaret River, where they have built a new winery that has taken over some of the production. And lest the high rating misleads anyone, the production is very substantial indeed. Entry-level wines are sold under the Madfish label, of which the Chardonnay, Sémillon-Sauvignon Blanc, and Shiraz are all recommended as strongly as the Howard Park wines listed below.

✓ *Cabernet Sauvignon* • *Chardonnay* • *Classic red blend* (Cabernet Sauvignon-Merlot) • *Pinot Noir* (Scotsdale) • *Riesling* • *Shiraz* (Leston, Scotsdale)

## KARRIVIEW
### Great Southern
★★

Tiny production of expressive Burgundian varietals.

✓ *Chardonnay* • *Pinot Noir*

## KILLERBY
### Margaret River
★★⯪

This winery's move to the Margaret River has coincided with a noticeable increase in quality.

✓ *Cabernet Sauvignon • Chardonnay • Shiraz*

## LEEUWIN ESTATE
### Margaret River
★★⯪

Leeuwin Estate continues to produce lush, stylish, and very classy wines that belong with food.

✓ *Cabernet Sauvignon* (Art Series) • *Chardonnay* (Art Series) • *Classic red blend* (Prelude Vineyards Cabernet-Merlot) • *Classic white blend* (Sibblings Sauvignon Blanc-Sémillon) • *Pinot Noir* (Art Series) • *Riesling* (Art Series) • *Sauvignon Blanc* (Art Series)

## LENTON BRAE
### Margaret River
★⯪

Established in 1983 by Bruce Tomlinson, whose son Edward is the winemaker today.

✓ *Cabernet Sauvignon • Chardonnay • Classic red blend* (Cabernet-Merlot)

## MERUM
### Margaret River
★★

Tiny production of stunning Sémillon, and a beautiful Shiraz.

✓ *Sémillon • Shiraz*

## MOONDAH BROOK
### Swan District
★⯪ Ⓥ

This brand belongs to BRL Hardy and its good value, fruit-driven wines are made at the Houghton winery.

✓ *Cabernet Sauvignon • Chardonnay • Chenin Blanc • Shiraz • Verdelho*

## MOSS BROTHERS
### Margaret River
★⯪ Ⓥ

Established in 1984 by David Moss, who had been a viticulturist at Houghton and Moss Wood; Peter Moss, who actually built boutique wineries for a living; and Jane Moss,

who graduated from Roseworthy. With such experience, how could they fail? Well, they didn't, and Sémillon is this winery's flagship.

✓ *Classic red blend* (Cabernet Sauvignon-Merlot) • *Sémillon • Shiraz • Verdelho*

## MOSS WOOD
### Margaret River
★★

One of the very best Margaret River wineries, Moss Wood was the first in the area to perfect Pinot Noir, and arguably the best Sémillon outside the Hunter Valley.

✓ *Cabernet Sauvignon* (Glenmore Vineyard) • *Chardonnay* (Lefroy Brook Vineyard) • *Merlot* (Ribbon Vale) • *Pinot Noir • Sémillon*

## PIERRO
### Margaret River
★★⯪

Mike Perkin, who is a genius with white wines, makes one of the best examples of Chardonnay in Margaret River. His LTC is a blend of Sémillon and Sauvignon Blanc.

✓ *Chardonnay • Classic red blend* (Cabernet-Merlot) • *Classic white blend* (LTC)

## PLANTAGENET WINES
### Great Southern
★★⯪

A winery named after the shire in which it is situated, Plantagenet was the first to cultivate Mount Barker, and is the leading winery in the area today.

✓ *Cabernet Sauvignon • Chardonnay • Classic red blend* (Omrah Merlot-Cabernet) • *Pinot Noir • Riesling • Shiraz*

## SANDALFORD
### Margaret River
★★⯪

A historic winery dating back to 1840, Sandalford was purchased in 1991 by Peter and Debra Prendiville, who have successfully resurrected this great old name.

✓ *Cabernet Sauvignon* (Premium) • *Classic white blend* (Premium Sémillon-Sauvignon Blanc) • *Fortified* (Sandalera) • *Riesling • Shiraz* (Premium) • *Verdelho*

## SETTLERS RIDGE
### Margaret River
★ⓋⒸ

Wayne and Kaye Nobbs purchased this 40-hectare (100-acre) property in 1994. Originally part of a dairy farm in the heart of the Margaret River region, its gravelly loam soils were immediately planted with vines, which yielded a first crop in 1997. Since then, Settlers Ridge organic wines have won more than 50 medals at wine shows.

✓ *Cabernet Sauvignon • Shiraz*

## SMITHBROOK
### Manjimup
★⯪

Owned by Lion Nathan since the takeover of Petaluma, who used the Pinot Noir for its Croser sparkling wine before it was dug up.

✓ *Cabernet Sauvignon • Classic red blend* (The Yilgarn) • *Merlot • Sauvignon Blanc*

## SUCKFIZZLE
### Margaret River
★★⯪

The creation of two well-known Margaret River winemakers, Stuart Pym and Janice McDonald. The seemingly bizarre name was inspired by the Great Lord Suckfizzle from Rabelais's *Gargantua*, whereas the wines themselves are simply inspired.

✓ *Cabernet Sauvignon • Classic white blend* (Sauvignon Blanc-Sémillon) • *Muscat* (Stella Bella Pink) • *Sauvignon Blanc* (Stella Bella)

## VASSE FELIX
### Margaret River
★★⯪

One of the Margaret River's pioneering wineries of the modern era, Vasse Felix's speciality has always been its long-lived Cabernet Sauvignons. It remains so today, although since the change of ownership, and the move to a new winery in 1999, they are softer and easier to drink at a younger age than they used to be. Heytesbury is a Cabernet-Shiraz blend. Classic Dry White is a Sémillon-Sauvignon Blanc blend.

✓ *Cabernet Sauvignon • Chardonnay* (Heytesbury) • *Classic red blend* (Heytesbury) • *Classic white blend* (Classic Dry White)

## VOYAGER ESTATE
### Margaret River
★★

This property was purchased in 1991 by the current owner, Michael

Wright, the mining magnate.

✓ *Cabernet Sauvignon* (Tom Price) • *Chardonnay • Classic red blend* (Cabernet Sauvignon-Merlot) • *Classic white blend* (Sauvignon Blanc-Sémillon, Tom Price Sémillon-Sauvignon Blanc) • *Shiraz*

## WILLESPIE
### Margaret River
★

Kevin Squance continues to produce fine-quality Verdelho, but the expressiveness of his red wines, especially the Shiraz, has improved dramatically, which is a revelation.

✓ *Cabernet Sauvignon* (Reserve) • *Classic red blend* (Cabernets) • *Shiraz • Verdelho*

## WILLOW BRIDGE ESTATE
### Geographe
★★Ⓥ

Established as recently as 1997, when the Dewar family purchased this 180-hectare (445-acre) property in the Ferguson Valley. So far they have planted 150 acres (60 hectares), producing some immediately impressive wines in the process.

✓ *Cabernet Sauvignon* (Reserve) • *Classic white blend* (Winemaker's Reserve Sémillon Sauvignon Blanc) • *Shiraz* (The Black Dog, Winemakers Reserve)

## WOODY NOOK
### Margaret River
⯪

Neil Gallagher of Woody Nook has always made a lovely Cabernet Sauvignon, and is now starting to be noticed for his Sauvignon Blanc.

✓ *Cabernet Sauvignon • Sauvignon Blanc*

## XANADU
### Margaret River
★★⯪

Formerly Chateau Xanadu, this ex-boutique winery has expanded its annual production to 100,000 cases. Secession is a blend of Sémillon, Sauvignon Blanc, Chenin Blanc, and Chardonnay. Wines are also sold under the following brands (top-quality wines): Chais Clarendon (Shiraz), and Normans (Adelaide Hills Chardonnay, Encounter Bay Cabernet Sauvignon, Old Vines Shiraz). The Lagan Estate is a blend of Cabernet Sauvignon, Merlot, and Cabernet Franc. Wines are also produced under the NXG label, which stands for Next Generations wines, although they have yet to make their mark.

✓ *Cabernet Franc • Cabernet Sauvignon • Chardonnay • Classic red blend* (Lagan Estate) • *Classic white blend • Merlot • Sémillon*

# QUEENSLAND AND NORTHERN TERRITORY

*Queensland and Northern Territory cover nearly half of Australia, but contain just 15 percent of its population, the majority of whom live in Brisbane. The rest is a sparsely populated, swelteringly hot outback, yet there are at least two serious vine-growing areas, both in Queensland.*

## QUEENSLAND

One of the last places on Earth where one might expect to find a vineyard, Queensland actually has twice as much land planted with vines as Tasmania, Australia's most up-and-coming wine-producing state. There are some 70 wineries and a small wine industry dating back to the 1850s. Surprisingly, summers are much cooler in Queensland's high-altitude Granite Belt than in many other, far more famous Australian regions, which explains why this state's wine industry is enjoying a revival. South Burnett, where the climate is more tropical, is the latest, fastest-growing wine region.

## NORTHERN TERRITORY

A less likely location for a winemaking area than Queensland is hard to imagine, but its western neighbor, Northern Territory, was such a place until 2002. This state is swelteringly hot, with land ranging from desert to tropical forests with crocodile-infested swamps. (Tourists are advised to run in a zigzag if chased by a crocodile!) Curiously it is illegal to drink alcohol in a public place within 1 mile (2 kilometers) of a licensed bar, except, of course, inside one. Outback machismo might be expected to preclude wine drinking, bearing in mind the cooling properties attributed to some of Australia's beers, yet of all places the town of Alice Springs was home to Chateau Hornsby and its 7 acres (3 hectares) of vineyards until December 2002. Viticulture is made possible by drip-irrigation from wells, as water is plentiful throughout the desertlike plateau where Alice Springs is situated, if you dig deep enough.

The only reason the vineyard was abandoned by Denis Hornsby was that he had to move closer to Sydney so that Helen, his partner, could have access to long-term medical treatment. At the time of writing, it is unknown whether this vineyard will be resurrected, but it is not beyond the bounds of possibility that one of the larger wine companies might be attracted by Hornsby's one great marketing idea: every year he made the first *nouveau* in the world by harvesting his Shiraz at one minute past midnight on January 1. Since the harvest is normally in January, this was no problem. In fact, one year his Chardonnay ripened a month early, and the 1997 vintage was actually picked on December 7, 1996!

AN OUTBACK STATION IN ALICE SPRINGS
*The hot, dry climate means irrigation is necessary for the area's red-sand soil, but there is an abundant supply of water underground.*

## FACTORS AFFECTING TASTE AND QUALITY

### LOCATION
Queensland is situated in the northeastern corner of Australia, with the Coral Sea to the east, and the Northern Territory, the north-central state, to the west.

### CLIMATE
Annual rainfall at Roma is only 20 inches (51 centimeters), but the Granite Belt receives 31 inches (79 centimeters). Much of it tends to fall at vintage time and this can be a problem, but frost and hail pose a greater danger. Temperatures are high (similar to the Margaret River in Western Australia), but not unduly so, due to the tempering effect of altitude.

### ASPECT
The altitude of Stanthorpe in the Granite Belt, where the surrounding vineyards lie between 2,500–3,100 feet (750–940 meters) above sea level, helps to temper the otherwise scorching summer heat in both areas. The vines here are generally grown in the hilly area, on sloping sites, whereas at South Burnett vines grow at 990–1,459 feet (300–442 meters) on more rolling countryside.

### SOIL
The soils of Queensland are phylloxera-free. As the name suggests, they are granitic in the Granite Belt around Stanthorpe.

South Burnett varies from red granitic-sand with basalt on the plains and terraces, to basalt-based soils, light sandy soils, red-colored light, clayey soils, and heavier brown and black clayey soils elsewhere. The area around Alice Springs shares the same infertile, coarse, red, iron-rich sandy soil that is common to much of central Australia.

### VITICULTURE AND VINIFICATION
Irrigation is necessary to produce wines near Alice Springs and, indeed, at Roma. The most modern technology is used in these areas to combat the problems of heat and oxidation. As a result, quite good wines are produced.

### GRAPE VARIETIES
**Primary varieties:** Cabernet Sauvignon, Chardonnay, Riesling, Sauvignon Blanc, Sémillon, Shiraz, Verdelho
**Secondary varieties:** Barbera, Cabernet Franc, Chambourcin, Chenin Blanc, Gamay, Malbec, Marsanne, Merlot, Mourvèdre, Muscat, Nebbiolo, Petit Verdot, Pinot Gris, Pinot Noir, Ruby Cabernet, Sangiovese, Sylvaner, Tarrango, Tempranillo, Touriga Nacional, Viognier, Zinfandel

THE APPELLATIONS OF
# QUEENSLAND AND NORTHERN TERRITORY

## GRANITE BELT

Italian immigrants and their families pioneered viticulture and winemaking in the 1920s, selling to relations and friends in the Italian cane-growing communities to the north, but the current boutique-based industry started in the 1960s, when Shiraz was planted. The vines here are grown in an area that surrounds the town of Ballandean, on an elevated granite plateau 150 miles (240 kilometers) west of Brisbane. It is the altitude of this district, between 2,500 and 3,100 feet (790 and 940 meters), that provides a sufficiently cool climate. Indeed, at Felsberg, located at an altitude of 2,750 feet (850 meters), the grapes sometimes struggle to ripen. As can be imagined, the soil is granitic, with Riesling the most suitable variety, although the most successful individual wine is, believe it or not, Ballandean's late-harvest Sylvaner. Other varieties that do well include Cabernet Sauvignon, Chardonnay, Sémillon, and Shiraz.

## ROMA

Like Alice Springs, Roma is not a GI wine region, but viticulture in this hot and arid area of Queensland is almost equally as improbable, thus its inclusion as one of most bizarre locations to plant a vine. While this might not be classic wine country, there are some 62 acres (25 hectares) of vines, and the solitary wine estate, Romavilla, has not missed a vintage since 1866, which alone makes Roma worthy of mention. Indeed, there are not many producers in Australia's premium wine regions who can claim to have 140 consecutive vintages under their belt. If Roma is any sort of wine country, it is—or it is meant to be—fortified wine country, which is why I was so surprised to be greeted by a sign proclaiming "Welcome to Roma, Champagne Country," when I first visited the town. Apparently, in 1864 a certain Mayor Mitchell was so struck by Roma's resemblance to the Champagne area that he mentioned the fact in dispatches, and the description stuck. This can mean only one thing: that Mitchell had never visited Champagne in his life.

## SOUTH BURNETT

For anyone who has followed the tiny, emerging wine industry in Queensland, it might come as a surprise to discover that South Burnett was the first official wine region in this state. Observers might be forgiven for expecting that honor would go to the Granite Belt, which is Queensland's oldest and most famous wine region, yet it received GI status in 2002, almost two years after South Burnett. Vineyards in this regional GI were established in the early 1990s, and currently stretch from Goomeri in the north, through the Murgon region to the Bunya Mountains, Kingaroy, and south to Nanango. Not surprisingly, the climate is hot, humid, and subtropical, with high rainfall during the growing season. There are various soil types, from red granitic-sandy soils on the plains and terraces, to basalt-based soils, light sandy soils, red-colored, light clayey soils, and heavier brown and black clayey soils elsewhere. Grape varieties include Cabernet Sauvignon, Chardonnay, Merlot, Riesling, Sauvignon Blanc, Sémillon, and Shiraz.

---

THE WINE PRODUCERS OF
# QUEENSLAND AND NORTHERN TERRITORY

## ALBERT RIVER WINES
**Tamborine**
★❂ⓥ

Established in 1998, but the first pure Queensland wines were not produced until 2000. Very much early days, but the most consistent wines so far have been the reds.

↳✓ *Classic red blend* (Cabernet-Shiraz-Merlot) • *Shiraz* (Grand Masters)

## BALD MOUNTAIN
**Granite Belt**
❓

Owned by Denis and Jackie Parsons, whose vineyards are close to Girraween National Park. Not tasted recently, but Chardonnay and Shiraz used to be the most consistent wines here.

## BALLANDEAN
**Granite Belt**
★❂ⓥ

At AU$4,800 (US$3,700) for a single 75cl bottle, Ballandean's "Generation 3" Cabernet-Shiraz must be one of the world's most expensive wines, although it was bottle 001 of the first vintage, 2002, of this individually numbered line, and auctioned for charity. The same wine normally retails for a more modest AU$29.50 (US$22.50).

↳✓ *Chardonnay* (Black Label) • *Classic white blend* (Sémillon-Sauvignon Blanc) • *Fortified* (Liqueur Muscat) • *Shiraz* (Generation 3) • *Sylvaner* (Late Harvest)

## BARAMBAH RIDGE
**South Burnett**
★ⓥ

Owned by Tambarambah, a public company, Barambah Ridge was established in 1997, and quickly demonstrated the potential of Queensland's most exciting new wine region, South Burnett.

↳✓ *Cabernet Sauvignon* • *Chardonnay* (Unwooded) • *Classic white blend* (Chardonnay-Sémillon) • *Sémillon* • *Shiraz* (Reserve) • *Verdelho*

## BUNGAWARRA
**Granite Belt**
❓

Originally founded in the 1920s by Angelo Barbagello, this winery was reestablished in 1979 by Alan Dorr and purchased in 1993 by Jeff Harden, a Brisbane pharmacist, who upgraded the winery. Not tasted recently.

## ROBERT CHANNON
**Granite Belt**
★❂ⓥ

Queensland's most successful, medal-laden winery, Robert Channon's extraordinary-quality Verdelho is, however, the real standout.

↳✓ *Cabernet Sauvignon* (Reserve) • *Chardonnay* (Reserve) • *Classic red blend* (Shiraz-Cabernet Sauvignon) • *Merlot* (Reserve) • *Verdelho*

## CLOVELY ESTATE
**South Burnett**
★❂ⓥ

Ambitious 445-acre (180-hectare) project established in 1998.

↳✓ *Chardonnay* (Left Field, Reserve) • *Classic red blend* (Shiraz-Cabernet) • *Classic white blend* (Estate Sémillon-Chardonnay) • *Sémillon* (Left Field)

## FELSBERG WINERY
**Granite Belt**
★❂ⓥ

For a vineyard that could not ripen Chardonnay sufficiently, Felsberg has done surprisingly well with Cabernet Sauvignon and Shiraz.

↳✓ *Cabernet Sauvignon* • *Shiraz*

## GLASTONBURY VINEYARD
**Eumundi**
★❂ⓥ

Judged exclusively on the performance of Glastonbury's Emotion Cabernet Sauvignon, this winery would be rated ★★, but the other wines have to catch up.

↳✓ *Cabernet* (Emotion)

## GOLDEN GROVE ESTATE
### Granite Belt
★ ❶

Sam and Grace Costanzo have quickly made a name for themselves since establishing this winery in 1992. Best for Reserve Chardonnay, but doing well across the range.

☑ *Chardonnay* • *Classic red blend* (Cabernet-Merlot) • *Sémillon* (Reserve)

## GOVERNOR'S CHOICE
### Toowoomba
★ ❶

Established in 1999, Governor's Choice Cabernet-based blends have been the most successful wines so far.

☑ *Classic red blend* (Cabernet-Shiraz, Cabernet-Shiraz-Malbec)

## GOWRIE MOUNTAIN ESTATE
### Granite Belt
★

Established in 1998, four years later Gowrie Mountain Estate became the first Australian producer to sell wine in 250-milliliter aluminum cans, something that Stowell's of Chelsea did in the UK in the 1980s, but soon dropped the idea as soon as it was discovered that consumers did not take to wine in cans. However, times have changed; consumers would not have liked screw-top bottles back then, either, but do so now, so perhaps cans of wine might take off—literally, in planes, as an equally horrid, but much lighter alternative to glass splits? Wines include Tempranillo, Gamay, and Chambourcin, as well as the more regular varietals.

☑ *Chardonnay*

## GRANITE RIDGE WINES
### Granite Belt
★ ❶

Founded in 1995 by current owner-winemaker, Dennis Ferguson, who originally named this venture Denlana Ferguson Estate. The Ridge is a blend of Merlot and Cabernet Sauvignon.

☑ *Classic red blend* (The Ridge) • *Merlot* (Fergies Hill) • *Shiraz* (Granite Rock)

## HERITAGE WINES
### Granite Belt
★ ❶

Two very recently established ventures founded by Bryce and Paddy Kassulke, who have rapidly made a reputation for themselves.

☑ *Botrytis* (Chardonnay) • *Merlot* (Private Reserve) • *Shiraz* (Private Reserve)

## IRONBARK RIDGE
### Purga
★ ❶

This winery was established in 1984, in an isolated area between Brisbane and the Great Divide, where Robert Le Grand had planted vines in the late 19th century. His wines won acclaim in Europe in the 1890s. The Dick family took over and their wines also won awards in Europe in the early 1900s. Although best known for its Chardonnay, Ironbark Ridge has great hopes for its recent plantings of Dolcetto, Verdelho, and Nebbiolo.

☑ *Chardonnay*

## JIMBOUR STATION
### Jimbour
★ ❶

Interesting recent project to resurrect winemaking in Jimbour, with the not inconsiderable skills of consultants Michael von Berg, Peter Scudamore-Smith MW, and Geoff Weaver. Some of its best-received wines have not been made exclusively from Queensland fruit. Wines also produced under the Linkeith, Ludwig Leichhardt, and Old Monty labels.

☑ *Shiraz* (Darling Downs)

## LILYVALE
### Texas
★ ❶

Recently established venture located on a bend of the Dumaresq River on the southern border of Queensland, a 30-minute drive east of Texas.

☑ *Sémillon* • *Verdelho*

## MOUNTVIEW
### Granite Belt
❷

David and Linda Price, the founders of the tiny, immaculate, red-cedar barn that houses Mountview's winery, sold up in 2000. Not tasted recently, but some vintages of the Shiraz were extremely elegant, and brilliant value, thus hopefully the new owners will build on this legacy.

## PRESTON PEAK
### Granite Belt
★ ❶

One of the more successful Queensland operations, Preston Peak draws on fruit from two different vineyards, but as yet I have not seen any single-vineyard wines.

☑ *Cabernet Sauvignon* (Leaf Series) • *Chardonnay* (Leaf Series) • *Petit Verdot* (Leaf Series) • *Sauvignon Blanc* (Leaf Series) • *Sémillon* (Leaf Series) • *Shiraz* (Reserve)

## RIMFIRE
### MacLagan
★ ❶

Established in 1991 by the Connellan family, who have created a mysterious legend surrounding a dry white wine called 1893. This supposedly comes from a vineyard propagated from a single, 100-year-old vine found on their property, which they claim is "not listed on the Australian DNA grape vine data base."

☑ *Classic red blend* (Cabernet Franc-Ruby Cabernet) • *Muscat* (Dry White) • *Verdelho*

## RIVERSANDS VINEYARDS
### St. George
★ ❶

Established in 1990, and purchased by Alison and David Blacket in 1996, these vineyards are located on the banks of the Balbonne River in the southwest of Queensland. The fortified wines are the best.

☑ *Fortified* (Golden Liqueur Muscat, Stirlings Reserve Red Liqueur Muscat)

## ROBINSONS FAMILY
### Granite Belt
★ ❶

John Robinson got his passion for wine when living in France, close to the Beaujolais region, then studied wine science at Riverina College under Brian Croser.

☑ *Cabernet Sauvignon*

## ROMAVILLA WINERY
### Roma
★

Established in 1863, Romavilla is a living reminder of Queensland's wine history. However, although the recommended fortified wines are rich and intense, with a big finish, there are few other wines of interest.

☑ *Chardonnay* (Reserve) • *Classic red blend* (Old Tawny Port, Very Old Liqueur Muscat, Very Old Tawny)

## RUMBALARA VINEYARDS
### Fletcher
★ ❶

Rumbalara is Aboriginal for "end of the rainbow," but it is more likely to be a pot of bronze found here than the golds accumulated when there was much less competition.

☑ *Cabernet Sauvignon* • *Sémillon* • *Verdelho*

## SETTLERS RISE
### Montville
★ ❶

Another recently established Queensland winery that employs the contract winemaking skills of Peter Scudamore-Smith MW, Settlers Rise is located in the hinterland of Queensland's Sunshine Coast, one hour north of Brisbane. Shows promise.

☑ *Shiraz* (Reserve)

## SIRROMET WINES
### Mount Cotton
★

Established by the Morris family in 1998, Sirromet's *avant-garde* restaurant was recognized in 2004 with numerous awards, including Brisbane's Best Tourism Restaurant, Brisbane's Best Restaurant in a Winery, and Brisbane's Restaurant of the Year. If any Queensland winery has the potential to achieve a ★★ rating in this encyclopedia, it is Sirromet.

☑ *Cabernet Sauvignon* (Seven Scenes) • *Petit Verdot* (Vineyard Selection) • *Shiraz* (Seven Scenes, Vineyard Selection)

## STUART RANGE ESTATES
### South Burnett
★

A state-of-the art winery inside a historic butter factory built in 1907, Stuart Range Estates is one of South Burnett's rising stars.

☑ *Chardonnay* (Goodger) • *Classic red blend* (Goodger Cabernet-Merlot) • *Shiraz* (Goodger)

## SUMMIT ESTATE
### Granite Belt
★ ❶

Up-and-coming Granite Belt operation owned by Bill Ryan, Tim Galligan, and Martin Millard, who planted their vineyard in 1997. The Shiraz is most impressive.

☑ *Classic red blend* (Cabernet Sauvignon-Merlot, Merlot-Cabernet-Shiraz) • *Shiraz* (Reserve)

## WHISKEY GULLY WINES
### Granite Belt

Established in 1997 by John Arlidge, whose politically named wines definitely lean toward the left.

☑ *Cabernet Sauvignon* (Upper House) • *Shiraz* (Black Rod)

# NEW ZEALAND

*New Zealand's isolation and cool, maritime climate make it the most exciting place on Earth for wine, yet certain producers want to marginalize its most successful variety, Sauvignon Blanc. In the process they run the risk of ruining their unique reputation. While there is no doubt that New Zealand can and does produce top-class wines from numerous other grape varieties, only Sauvignon Blanc is undeniably a class apart from the same grape grown anywhere else in the world. No other country can make a similar claim for any other grape variety, and no other country has such an unassailable flagship for its wine industry. Why throw that away?*

MISSION VINEYARDS, NORTH ISLAND
*The Hawke's Bay winery has recently upgraded its wines.*

SOME PRODUCERS would also like to build a fresh reputation based on, of all grapes, Chardonnay. I am not an "anything but Chardonnay" man, but this is the last grape that any region should specialize in. New Zealand's producers should, of course, continue to make the finest Chardonnay possible, but only as part of an increasing range of world class wines. Chardonnay's place is alongside Pinot Noir, various Bordeaux varieties, Riesling, sparkling wine, and promising new grapes such as Syrah. All of these add to the breadth and depth of New Zealand's reputation.

So why would anyone in this industry want to marginalize Sauvignon Blanc? Embarrassment! They feel uncomfortable that New Zealand should be so famous for a grape of such obvious, upfront character. They long to have a more complex, classier wine to fly the flag. But it is nothing to be ashamed of: it is a refreshing, pure, vibrantly fruity wine. Sauvignon Blanc is the ideal choice to open up wider markets, whereas a more complex, more expensive wine would be restrictive.

NEW ZEALAND
*Although South Island has a younger wine industry, it boasts a slightly more favorable growing climate than North Island, having lighter rainfall.*

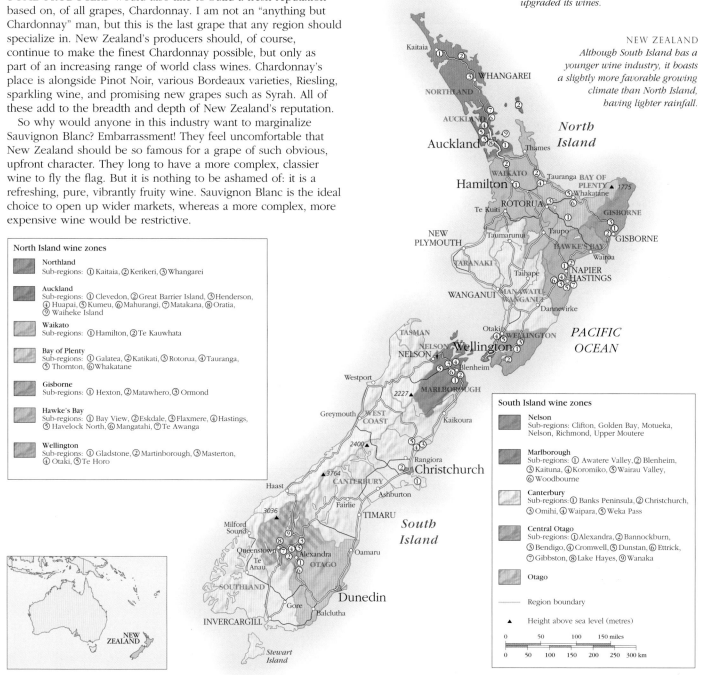

**North Island wine zones**

**Northland**
Sub-regions: ① Kaitaia, ② Kerikeri, ③ Whangarei

**Auckland**
Sub-regions: ① Clevedon, ② Great Barrier Island, ③ Henderson, ④ Huapai, ⑤ Kumeu, ⑥ Mahurangi, ⑦ Matakana, ⑧ Oratia, ⑨ Waiheke Island

**Waikato**
Sub-regions: ① Hamilton, ② Te Kauwhata

**Bay of Plenty**
Sub-regions: ① Galatea, ② Katikati, ③ Rotorua, ④ Tauranga, ⑤ Thornton, ⑥ Whakatane

**Gisborne**
Sub-regions: ① Hexton, ② Matawhero, ③ Ormond

**Hawke's Bay**
Sub-regions: ① Bay View, ② Eskdale, ③ Flaxmere, ④ Hastings, ⑤ Havelock North, ⑥ Mangatahi, ⑦ Te Awanga

**Wellington**
Sub-regions: ① Gladstone, ② Martinborough, ③ Masterton, ④ Otaki, ⑤ Te Horo

**South Island wine zones**

**Nelson**
Sub-regions: Clifton, Golden Bay, Motueka, Nelson, Richmond, Upper Moutere

**Marlborough**
Sub-regions: ① Awatere Valley, ② Blenheim, ③ Kaituna, ④ Koromiko, ⑤ Wairau Valley, ⑥ Woodbourne

**Canterbury**
Sub-regions: ① Banks Peninsula, ② Christchurch, ③ Omihi, ④ Waipara, ⑤ Weka Pass

**Central Otago**
Sub-regions: ① Alexandra, ② Bannockburn, ③ Bendigo, ④ Cromwell, ⑤ Dunstan, ⑥ Ettrick, ⑦ Gibbston, ⑧ Lake Hayes, ⑨ Wanaka

**Otago**

━━━ Region boundary

▲ Height above sea level (metres)

0    50    100    150 miles

0   50  100  150  200  250  300 km

## FACTORS AFFECTING TASTE AND QUALITY

### LOCATION
With the exception of Waiheke Island, all of New Zealand's grape-growing areas are on its two principal islands, North Island and South Island, stretched over 1,000 miles (1,600 kilometers) between latitudes 36°S and 45°S. Central Otago is the most southerly location.

### CLIMATE
North Island generally has a cool maritime climate, similar to that of Bordeaux in temperature but with much higher rainfall. The crucial fall periods are rarely dry; heavy rains and high humidity lead to problems of grape damage and rot. South Island is significantly cooler, but sunnier and drier. Marlborough is South Island's warmest area, and often has the country's most hours of sunshine. Rainfall is variable. Using the California heat summation system, the most important viticultural areas in both islands are all Region 1.

### ASPECT
Most vines are planted on flat or gently sloping land, and are easy to work. Some north-facing slopes have been planted in Auckland and Te Kauwhata; these provide better drainage and longer hours of intensive sunlight. Some steep vineyards are found in South Island's Central Otago district.

### SOIL
Soils are varied, mostly clay or loam based, often sandy or gravelly, with schistous loess over gravel in Central Otago, and volcanic subsoils in parts of Northland (Cottle Hill), and around Canterbury (Banks Peninsula).

### VITICULTURE AND VINIFICATION
Harvests begin in March and April, six months ahead of wine regions in the northern hemisphere. Canopy management has totally transformed New Zealand's wines, especially its reds, which no longer possess the excessive pyrazines that once gave them an unwelcome, ever-present herbaceousness. Most winemakers have studied oenology in Australia, and done at least one *stage* (internship) in Europe. This straddling of Old and New World, tradition and technique, has helped shape New Zealand's wine reputation. Many producers have adopted screwcap bottles.

### GRAPE VARIETIES
**Primary varieties:** Cabernet Sauvignon, Chardonnay, Merlot, Pinot Noir, Riesling, Sauvignon Blanc
*Secondary varieties:* Cabernet Franc, Chenin Blanc, Gewürztraminer, Malbec, Müller-Thurgau, Muscat, Pinotage, Pinot Gris, Sémillon, Syrah

COOPERS CREEK WINERY, NORTH ISLAND
*Situated in the Huapi Valley, this winery produces exceptionally stylish wines. Talented North Island winemakers use both traditional and high-tech methods.*

## PAST, PRESENT, AND FUTURE

Up to the 1980s, Cooks, Corbans, and Montana dominated the New Zealand wine scene, and the most popular product was Müller-Thurgau sweetened-up with *süssreserve* (now that was a wine to be embarrassed about). In 1987, Cooks took over Corbans, and both were consumed by Montana, then Sauvignon Blanc began its inexorable rise. Now Cooks and Corbans are little more than brand names without heart or soul, with wines that are seldom seen on export markets. And Montana itself has been taken over by the multinational beverage group Allied-Domecq.

Meanwhile, the number of individual wineries has ballooned from 100 in the mid-1980s to about 500. The range of varietals has blossomed in their wake, as boutique producers have sought something different with which to gain an edge. Nowhere has this been more evident than in red wine varieties. Just 15 years ago, almost all of New Zealand's red wines were noted for their herbaceous flavors, a result of excessive vigor in the vineyard; but this has been eradicated through better canopy management. Bordeaux varieties are now old hat, Pinot Noir has become one of the country's hottest wines, and even Syrah is excelling.

After Montana and Nobilo, the largest wine producer is Villa Maria, followed by a number of fairly big, well-known wineries; but the majority of wineries are very small operations. The large range of New Zealand brands available even on export markets like the UK makes it hard to believe that Montana processes more than half of the country's entire wine output. This is a heavy responsibility to bear, but one that rests lightly on Montana's shoulders, since it also produces many of the country's finest and best value wines. It is a role model that other large wine producers throughout the world should follow.

The future should be bright for New Zealand, if it can accept Sauvignon Blanc as the gift it is, and show restraint in yields, thereby consolidating quality, thus the reputation, of its wines.

This consolidation begins in the vineyard, getting to grips with where each variety grows best, and within these areas, selecting a compact range of site-specific clones and rootstock. It also means looking up from the valley floor to the surrounding hills, which is where the future lies. I cannot imagine that anyone has stood on the hills surrounding Marlborough and not wondered whether the vines are in the right place. Obviously they are not badly sited because quality speaks for itself, but some pretty special wines could be made in those hills. Irrigation is the problem, but not an insurmountable one. Besides, potential pioneers should not be thinking in terms of the irrigation required to churn out valley-floor yields. That would be defeating the object.

There are only two blots on New Zealand's winescape: one is brand disorientation; the other is a lack of a verifiable appellation system. Brand disorientation is when wines blended from two or more countries are sold under the same brand name as pure New Zealand wines. This is particularly dangerous when the name in question is globally famous. If this practice is not restricted to entirely different, easily distinguishable brands, it could undermine New Zealand's reputation as a premium wine producer.

As for a lack of a verifiable appellation system, I do not refer to a draconian system like the French AOC, which dictates what must be grown, how the vines should be trained, and what the style of wine should be. I mean simply a system that can guarantee that what is on the label is what is in the bottle—essentially that the grapes are of the variety claimed and were grown in the area indicated. New Zealand's core regions of Auckland, Bay of Plenty, Gisborne, Hawke's Bay, Northland, Waikato, and Wellington on North Island, and Canterbury, Central Otago, Marlborough, and Nelson on South Island are defined by the Local Government Act of 1974. However, the geographical appellations of Certified Origin status announced in 1996, and mentioned in the last edition of this book, have not been implemented. This was to be the wine industry's interpretation of the Geographical Indications Act 1994, an umbrella law designed to guarantee the origin of numerous products, not just wine. Certified Origin should have been done and dusted long ago, but as one New Zealand wine official put it, "let's just say it is very complicated, but I am hopeful of some action in the next year or so...although I am not holding my breath." Complicated or not, the New Zealand wine industry must get its act together, if it wants to steer clear of long-running boundary sagas like that in Coonawarra, Australia, and prevent a repeat of various labeling

## RECENT NEW ZEALAND VINTAGES

**2007** This small crop of good to excellent quality across the varietal board on both North Island and South Island has been overshadowed by the news that phylloxera has been found in Wairarapa (Wellington). With time, it is inevitable that phylloxera will spread, and with 25 percent of New Zealand's vines ungrafted, it will mean a massive replanting program.

**2006** Apart from the disappointing reds on North Island, this was a good vintage everywhere, and an excellent one for Marlborough Sauvignon Blanc.

**2005** A good to very good year for all North Island reds, the highlight of this vintage. Very good Marlborough Sauvignon Blanc, but forget Central Otago Pinot Noir!

**2004** Torrential rains in February threatened to dilute New Zealand's largest crop ever, but an Indian summer enabled growers who restricted yields and delayed harvesting to produce fine-quality wines. Central Otago was hit by frosts in spring and fall, reducing yields by one-third, but the quality should be high.

**2003** Spring frosts reduced yields by up to half in some regions. The quality was variable, with a number of disappointments, but the best producers got it right more often than not. South Island fared best, with fresh, elegant Sauvignon Blanc and Riesling produced in Marlborough standing out.

**2002** A massive crop of 118,700 tons rang alarm bells for some critics, but New Zealand's vineyards had grown by 35 percent since the previous all-time high of 80,100 tons in 2000. In terms of yield per hectare, 1999 and 1998 were both significantly higher, while 1996 and 1995 were higher still. By 1995 standards, the crop would have been 168,200 tons! Some Marlborough Sauvignon Blanc might have disappointed, but the best producers made brilliant wines, and the long, hot, dry fall easily ripened the weighty crop almost everywhere. Look for great reds from Hawke's Bay and, particularly, Central Otago. Also some exceptional Riesling from Central Otago.

NEUDORF VINEYARDS, SOUTH ISLAND
*Neudorf Vineyards on South Island produces 2,000 cases annually from its 11 acres (4.5 hectares) of land.*

scandals. Particularly as the current definition of origin does not hold water, let alone wine. As the same official source confirmed: subregions "are not defined in any legislation," but "they can be used if the grapes are derived from the named place," yet "the boundaries of each such subregion have not been defined" because they "are evolving over time as new vineyards are developed." And I thought the French were irrational.

THE APPELLATIONS OF

# NEW ZEALAND

## NEW ZEALAND

The New Zealand appellation is usually found on exported cask wines (bag-in-the-box) and inexpensive blended wines sold on the domestic market, such as Montana's Waimanu range and Corbans' White Label (if indeed the wine is from New Zealand at all!).

## NORTH ISLAND

Supporting some 70 percent of the population, North Island is where New Zealand's wine industry began and was confined to until as recently as 1973. North Island is technically an appellation in its own right, but seldom seen as such, although it has in the past been used by Azure Bay (Sauvignon Blanc-Sémillon).

### AUCKLAND
#### Subregions
*Brighams Creek, Clevedon, Drury, Glendene, Great Barrier Island, Henderson, Henderson Valley, Hobsonville, Huapai, Huapai Valley, Ihuamato, Karaka, Kumeu, Lincoln, Mahurangi, Mangatangi, Mangere, Matakana, Matua Valley, Oneroa, Onetangi, Oratia, Pukekohe, Putiki Bay,*
*Ranui, Riverhead, Riverlea, Sunnyvale, Swanson, Swanson Valley, Taupaki, Waiheke, Waiheke Island, Waimauku, Waitakere, Warkworth, West Auckland, Whitford, Woodhill*

In the 1960s, a decade before the first vines were planted in Marlborough, Auckland possessed more than half of New Zealand's vineyards. Even though the area under vine has doubled over the past 10 years, Auckland possesses just 3 percent of the country's vineyards today, such has been the rate of change throughout the rest of New Zealand. Despite this minuscule contribution in terms of vineyard land, Auckland remains the traditional center of its wine industry, primarily because it houses the headquarters of the largest wine companies: Montana and Villa Maria both bottle wines here from all over the country. And despite growth elsewhere, Auckland still has more wineries than any other region.

Auckland's various wine districts produce some of the country's very finest wines. Clevedon's vineyards are sited on steep, north-facing hillsides, where Cabernet Sauvignon, Malbec, Merlot, Syrah, and even Montepulciano vines are low-yielding and mostly handpicked. There is also a growing reputation for Chardonnay and Pinot Gris in dessert wine

styles. In the 1960s, the Henderson-Oratia district in West Auckland was second only to Hawke's Bay as the country's largest wine producing region, and is still the center of New Zealand's fortified wine industry. The Kumeu-Huapai district escapes some of the rain that falls on West Auckland, and has long been established as a source of premium varietal wines, including Chardonnay, Merlot, and Cabernet Sauvignon, although some wineries source their fruit from farther south. Matakana-Mahurangi is located on the east coast to the north of Auckland. A small, but fast-growing area, it is known for its pinkish-red, iron-rich, granulated clay soil, upon which the local wineries have built a certain red wine reputation and are beginning to show promise for full, fruity white wines. Waiheke Island is much drier and sunnier than mainland Auckland, and is one of New Zealand's most exciting districts for Bordeaux-style reds. Tiny quantities of Cabernet-Merlot have been produced on Great Barrier Island, which is way out in the Pacific, well beyond Waiheke Island. Transport costs have prevented this island from developing a wine industry with any aspirations for a national reputation. Although John Mellars, the largest of Great Barrier Island's two vineyards, with just 2.5 acres (1 hectare) of vines, has managed to survive on local trade since his first crop in 1993.

## BAY OF PLENTY
### Subregions
*Bethlehem, Galatea, Katikati, Murupara, Rotorua, Tauranga, Thornton, Whakatane*

Known more for its dairy products than for wine, the Bay of Plenty is a very large region containing relatively few wineries, and even fewer vineyards, as most of the producers source their fruit from Hawke's Bay or elsewhere. The most famous names here are Morton Estate and Mills Reef, but only Covell Estate has any significant area under vine (17 acres/7 hectares and growing).

## EAST COAST

This multiregional appellation straddles the eastern coast of both North Island and South Island, which effectively encompasses 90 percent of all the vines growing in New Zealand. It is used by high-volume wines where the brand name and flexibility of sourcing are more important than a specified provenance. Current users of the East Coast appellation include Azure Bay (Sauvignon Blanc-Sémillon), Babich (Chardonnay, Pinot Noir, and Pinotage), Montana (which owns the Azure brand, but also has an export-only East Coast range under the Montana label for Cabernet Sauvignon-Merlot, Chardonnay—usually Marlborough, Unwooded Chardonnay—usually Gisborne, and Pinotage), and Villa Maria (Gewürztraminer, Merlot-Cabernet, Müller-Thurgau).

## GISBORNE
### Subregions
*Bushmere, Hexton, Makaraka, Makauri, Manutuke, Matawhero, Mohaka, Muhaka, Muriwai, Ormond, Ormond Valley, Patutahi, Te Araroa, Te Karaka, Tolaga Bay, Waihirere, Waimata, Wairoa*

Gisborne is synonymous with Poverty Bay, and has been dubbed "carafe country" due to its once-enormous yields of Müller-Thurgau; but Gisborne Müller-Thurgau has become uneconomic for even the cheapest bag-in-the-box wines (which are now mostly blended with imported wines). Consequently, the amount of Müller-Thurgau grown has dropped dramatically.

Now Chardonnay is the region's major grape variety but Gisborne still has a reputation as a source of blending fodder. Most vineyards are located on the plains on each side of the Waipaoa River, and although the grape varieties grown have improved, this area is primarily flat and extremely fertile, thus it is inclined to churn out even the most classic of grapes at relatively high yields. Little wonder then that Gisborne regularly produces a higher tonnage of grapes than Hawke's Bay, despite having half the area under vine. There is no sense of place to most of the wines produced, since Gisborne Chardonnay averages over 440 cases per acre (100 hectoliters per hectare). It is, however,

ideal for bulking out young, easy-drinking multiregional blends, and this is one reason why only a small proportion ends up under the Gisborne appellation.

Another reason is the small number of wineries, although this is starting to change, having risen from 10 to 16 over the past two or three years. In the hands of quality-conscious growers, even vineyards on the flats can produce expressive Chardonnay. With moves into the hills overlooking the plains, we can expect to see more individual, higher quality Gisborne Chardonnay in future years.

More than one-third of Gisborne's vines are in flat-as-a-pancake Patutahi. To the south is Manutuke, the region's oldest winegrowing district (1894), where some of Gisborne's rare red wine varietals can be found, including Malbec and Pinot Noir. White grapes vary from Chenin Blanc (probably Gisborne's best) to Chardonnay, Muscat, and Riesling. Prior to the Chardonnay boom, Gisborne's only premium varietal was Gewürztraminer from around Matawhero, on the opposite bank of the Waipaoa. Although this was and still is justly famous by New Zealand's standards, its rendition is more floral than spicy, and Gewürztraminer from Montana's Patutahi estate has been every bit as impressive. North of Matawhero, radiating out from the suburbs of Gisborne itself, the Makauri district runs on both sides of the Taruheru River into Makaraka and Bushmere. Makauri grows some of the region's better Müller-Thurgau, along with Muscat, Sémillon, and Merlot. On the other side of the plain, at the foot of the Hexton Hills, some of this bulk-blending region's more exotic varieties can be found, including Gewürztraminer, Malbec, Merlot, and Viognier. Creeping farther northwest, around the edge of the foothills, is Waihirere, which is also referred to as the Golden Hills. This area has a reputation for Chardonnay, as does Ormond farther north. Corbans' late, lamented Cottage Block Chardonnay came from the Benson Vineyard in the Ormond region. It is now called Whitmore Vineyard, and in good years the grapes go into the Montana "O" Ormond Estate Chardonnay. Gisborne's northernmost vines are found at Tiritiri Organic Vineyard, in the back of beyond, on the upper reaches of the Waimata River.

In conclusion, Gisborne is essentially white wine country, where loose-cluster grapes perform best. Varieties with tightly packed clusters run the risk of rot, while most red varieties (less than 10 percent of all Gisborne vines) are difficult to ripen. This may change as more early-ripening clones of classic red wine varieties become available, and if growers plant a thirst-quenching cover-crop between the rows to mop up as much of the diluting rain as possible.

## HAWKE'S BAY
### Subregions
*Bay View, Clive, Crownthorpe, Dartmoor, Dartmoor Valley, Eskdale, Fernhill, Flaxmere, Gimblett Road, Greenmeadows, Hastings, Haumoana, Havelock North, Heretaunga, Korokipo, Mangatahi, Maraekakahoe, Matapiro, Meeanee, Mere Road, Mt Erin, Napier, Ngatarawa, Ngaruroro, Ohiti, Ohiti Road, Okawa, Omarunui, Pakuratahi Valley, Puketapu, Roy's Hill, Sherenden, Swamp Road, Taradale, Te Awanga, Te Mata, Tuki Tuki, Tutaekuri, Twyford, Waiohiki, Wharerangi, Woodthorpe*

Hawkes Bay or Hawke's Bay? As the *Encyclopaedia Britannica* and even official Hawke's Bay publications use both spellings,

even on the same page, each name is obviously in common usage. But since Captain Cook named the bay after the First Lord of the Admiralty, Lord Hawke, it should really be Hawke's Bay with an apostrophe. Hawke's Bay is the driest wine region in the country and has the most diverse range of soils, including but not restricted to fine alluvium over graywacke gravel, hard-pan clays, heavy silts, sandy loams, sandy loams over clay, sandy silt loams over gravel, stones over gravel, and stony gravels. Hawke's Bay has always offered more potential for Cabernet Sauvignon and its derivative blends than Marlborough or any other New Zealand region, but it is wrong to class this region as red wine country, let alone the sole province of Bordeaux varieties. It is at least as exciting for Chardonnay, and a handful of producers compete even with Marlborough's best Sauvignon Blancs, albeit in a richer, fuller style.

The two most important grape varieties are Chardonnay and Merlot, but the complex matrix of soils, the differences in aspect, and local variations in climate open up Hawke's Bay to myriad different grape varieties, some of which are yet to be planted. Gimblett Road is only just finding its feet for polished Syrah that is neither Australian nor Rhône in style, and seems likely to eclipse the already heady reputation of this designated district's Cabernet Sauvignon and Chardonnay. Roy's Hill is synonymous with Gimblett Road, although geographically Gimblett Road is located at the foot of Roy's Hill. Gimblett Gravels is a memorable, descriptive appellation invented by a number of wineries to market the superior qualities of their Gimblett Road vineyards. Adjacent to Gimblett Road, to the southwest, is Ngatarawa. (The "g" in Maori names beginning "Ng" is silent, thus Ngatarawa is pronounced "na-ta-rawaa.") This region is also known as the Redmetal Triangle, because the free-draining gravel deposits are known locally as "red metals" due to their color and metal content. However, what distinguishes Ngatarawa from the neighboring Gimblett Road is the different water-retention capacity of the gravel subsoil. In Ngatarawa, the gravels retain more moisture, giving the area a slight edge in hotter years, whereas Gimblett Road has the advantage in cooler vintages. Ngatarawa reds are generally softer than those from Gimblett Road, with Merlot the best-suited variety. It is also well known for its botrytized whites.

Dartmoor Valley could be called the Tutaekuri Valley, as its vineyards are laid out along its banks and in its hinterland, over the hills behind Taradale, leading up to Woodthorpe and beyond. This is indeed Bordeaux country, favoring Cabernet Sauvignon on the lower reaches, and Merlot farther upriver. Chardonnay also fares well, particularly on the upper reaches and at Swamp Road, north of Omahu, between the Ngaruroro and Tutaekuri rivers, and in the vineyards of Fernhill and Korokipo on the northern bank of the Tutaekuri. Eskdale is north of Napier, but the climate is cooler than the Hastings area due to sea breezes drawn up the Esk Valley, although nights can be warmer. Soils are relatively fertile, although more gravelly toward the coast, where the wines take on more finesse. Big, bold Bordeaux-type reds can be produced from Eskdale through the Esk Valley, and a little farther south at Bay View. Sheltered by Te Mata Peak, the north-facing slopes of Te Mata's famous Coleraine vineyard at Havelock North, southeast of Hastings, are sun-traps that have established over 25 years their ability to produce top class Cabernet Sauvignon.

To the east is Te Awanga, a coastal block of vines from the northern suburbs of Te Wanga to the mouth of the Tukituki River, where some surprising big, bold Chardonnay and Bordeaux-style blends are grown. To the west of Ngatarawa, on the bend of the Ngaruroro River is Maraekakahoe, while farther upriver and significantly cooler is the up-and-coming area of Mangatahi. Growers believe that Mangatahi's greater diurnal extremes of temperature will enable it to establish a reputation as Burgundy country, in both red and white formats. On the opposite, northern bank is the even newer Crownthorpe area, which is also known as Matapiro, and best suited to early-ripening varieties. Waipawa and Waipukurau are located at the center of Hawke's Bay itself, but way off the established Hawke's Bay viticultural map, to the southwest of Maraekakahoe. These new winegrowing areas are distinctly cool, offering the promise of crisper white wines than Hawke's Bay has previously been known for, and with hopes for sparkling wines and Pinot Noir.

## NORTHLAND
### Subregions
*Dargaville, Kaikohe, Kaitaia, Kerikeri, Kohukohu, Otaika, Raumanga, Ruakaka, Sweetwater, Te Hana, Whangarei*

It was in Kerikeri, Northland, that Samuel Marsden planted New Zealand's first vines in 1819. Shortly after, in 1833, James Busby, the so-called father of Australian viticulture, settled at Waitangi, where two years later he established his own vineyard. Despite these auspicious beginnings, local winemaking dwindled to almost nothing until very recently. Production has tripled over the past 10 years, but starting from a minuscule point. There are even now just seven wineries, and the vines planted do not represent even one percent of the country's vineyards. Currently most vines are located in three districts: Kaitaia on the far northwest, the Bay of Islands (which contains the appellation Kaikohe and Kerikeri) in the northeast, and around Whangarei, Northland's largest city. These areas boast the country's warmest climate, hence Cabernet Sauvignon, Merlot, and Chardonnay are the three most widely planted grape varieties. But they also have the highest rainfall and humidity, particularly on the west coast, and thus suffer fungal diseases and significant variations in yield. Sémillon, Pinot Gris, and Syrah are on the rise.

## WAIKATO
### Subregions
*Cambridge, Hamilton, Karangahake, Mangatawhiri, Ngahinepouri, Ohaupo, Paeroa, Pokeno, Pukeroro, Tamahere, Te Kauwhata, Thames*

Situated inland, south of Auckland, and dotted across various diverse locations, Waikato is

more cow country than a wine district. Indeed, the cows in this area are said to outnumber humans five-to-one, which is why the region is known as Mooloo to the locals. It encompasses the Te Kauwhata district, where yields are lower, and the climate is hotter and more humid, making it more suitable for botrytized wines.

## WELLINGTON
### Subregions
*East Taratahi, Gladstone, Kapiti, Longbush, Martinborough, Masterton, Otaki, Pirinoa, Ponatahi, Taratahi, Te Horo, Te Muna, Tuhitarata, Waingawa, Wairarapa*

This region can be divided into two distinctly different viticultural districts: Te Horo, a two-winery district to the west of the Taraua Range; and Wairarapa, which encompasses among other areas Martinborough, Wellington's most important district. It is extraordinary to think that Martinborough was only of minor importance in the first edition of this book, as it rapidly achieved a name in the early 1990s as a potentially exciting area for Pinot Noir. This mantle has since been taken over by Central Otago, which has turned out to be no bad thing for Martinborough, since it has always been at least as good for Chardonnay as for Pinot Noir, and is probably the best place to grow Sauvignon Blanc on New Zealand's North Island. But it does not stop there, as its Rieslings are among the best in the country, not to mention its reputation for Pinot Gris and Gewürztraminer, although this is more in a New World context than objectively defined.

Just a few miles east of the town of Martinborough is Te Muna, an up-and-coming subdistrict with great hopes for Pinot Noir, as evidenced by Larry McKenna's Escarpment vineyard. Craggy Range is also planting Sauvignon Blanc, Chardonnay, Pinot Gris, and Riesling in addition to Pinot Noir, and when all of its vineyards come on stream, it will double Martinborough's output, such is its belief in Te Muna. Other Wairarapa areas include East Taratahi, Gladstone, and Masterton. Gladstone is southwest of Masterton, north of Martinborough, where some the first Wairarapa vines were planted. Gladstone and the nearby East Taratahi area are well suited to Riesling and Sauvignon Blanc in the main, whereas Pinot Noir is grown on the sunniest, north-facing slopes. This area is attracting a lot of interest; so too is Masterton itself, where the same varieties are planted, though many of the vineyards are really quite young.

## SOUTH ISLAND

South Island has a much lower population than North Island and, due to transportation

difficulties, was not cultivated until 1973. It has quickly demonstrated exciting potential for premium varietals. Technically an appellation in its own right, it is seldom seen as such.

## CANTERBURY
### Subregions
*Akaroa, Amberley, Banks Peninsula, Burnham, Christchurch, Coutts Island, Halswell, Kaiapoi, Kaituna Valley, Lansdowne, Larcomb, Lincoln, North Canterbury, Omihi, Omihi Hills, Omihi Valley, School Road, Selwyn, Swannanoa, Taitapu, Tram Road, Two Chain Road, Waikari, Waipara, Waipara Valley, Weka Pass, West Melton*

Although the summer here can be as warm as in Marlborough, the fall is cooler and overall temperatures are lower. At just 24 inches (62 centimeters), the annual rainfall is substantially lower than in Marlborough and less than half of that received in Auckland. Most vineyards are located on the plains surrounding Christchurch, New Zealand's third-largest city, or at Waipara, a coastal area to the north. Quality is less consistent than it used to be, but this region still promises more than it gives. Anyone who has driven from Marlborough to Queenstown and back again knows just how flat and boring the plains around Christchurch are. It is depressing, after driving through some of the world's most spectacular scenery. There are one or two interesting producers on the plains, where the most successful wines are Pinot Noir and Chardonnay in an elegant style, but the best wineries have vineyards elsewhere.

Winegrowing in this region began as early as 1840 on the Banks Peninsula, but it has been stop-start here ever since. With just one winery and 7 acres (3 hectares) of vines, production is negligible. Waipara is the one classic winemaking area in the Canterbury region, with a variety of soils, including clays, gravels, and, in the promising Waikari-Weka Pass area to the north, brilliant-white, hard limestone. This encourages a number of different grapes to be planted. Currently, Pinot Noir, Chardonnay, Sauvignon Blanc, and Riesling fare best, but other varieties include Pinot Gris, Gewürztraminer, and Sémillon. Even Cabernet Sauvignon and Merlot are grown.

## CENTRAL OTAGO
### Subregions
*Alexandra, Ardgau Valley, Bannockburn, Bendigo, Central Otago, Cromwell, Dunstan, Earnscleugh, Ettrick, Gibbston, Hawea, Lake Hayes, Lowburn, Luggat, Omarama, Queenstown, Roxburgh, Tarras, Waitaki Valley, Wanaka*

Otago is the authentic regional name, but because the vineyards are located inland, the term Central Otago has evolved, and is more commonly used in a viticultural context than Otago itself. Central Otago is the fastest-developing wine region in New Zealand, having grown 20-fold over the past 10 years, and is the hottest, hippest, coolest place in New Zealand for vineyard investors. The cause of all this activity is the grape variety being grown. Ten years ago, no one knew what they should be growing in Central Otago. In fact, so confused was the issue that local growers would lobby every passing wine journalist for his or her opinion. With heat summation well below the supposed minimum for ripening grapes of 1,000°C degree-days, the growers assumed that it must be white wine country; but what variety, and whether to plump for sparkling, nobody was quite sure. If anything, there was a tendency to think of playing it safe with German varieties. No one ever imagined Central Otago could be red wine country, let alone a potential home for Pinot Noir, the Holy Grail of all red wine grapes. But since Central Otago Pinot Noir took off in the late 1990s, there has been no stopping it. A lesson, perhaps, for all those "fruit salad" regions throughout the world: find the right grape and create a reputation, rather than trying to be all things to all consumers.

So, what makes Pinot Noir work in heat summation-challenged Central Otago? Well, heat is not everything, and summation does not take account of the beneficial effect of diurnal temperature difference. Warm daytimes ripen the fruit, but the cooler it is at night, the more acidity is preserved, yielding brighter, more vibrant fruit. In Central Otago, the difference between the highest daytime and lowest nighttime temperatures can be as much as 55°F (30°C). Furthermore, the days this far south are long, with little cloud and low rainfall, thus exceptionally sunny and dry. At Bannockburn, in the heart of Central Otago's Pinot Noir country, the average annual precipitation is half that of rot-prone Burgundy. There are just 20 inches (50 centimeters) of rainfall, yet Milford Haven, only 75 miles (120 kilometers) away, can have nearly 30 feet (850 centimeters) in a single year. And finally, the schistous loess is a heavy-textured soil, which the Pinot likes, but schist tends to powder, rather than clay up, and thus provides excellent drainage. The fact that there is very little rot, due to low humidity (30 to 40 percent), is just the icing on the cake, keeping the vineyards clean and free from the chemicals that are often used to combat cryptogamic diseases.

Although trial blocks of vines had been planted as far south as Alexandra in the 1950s, it was not until 1976 that Central Otago's first commercial vineyard, Rippon, was established in Wanaka. And it took another five years for the first commercial vineyards to be planted in what would become Pinot country, between Gibbston (Gibbston Valley, 1981) and Alexandra (Black Ridge, 1981). Wanaka represents just three percent of Central Otago production and did not attract any other wineries until 1994, when Mount Maude started planting further north, halfway between Albert Town and Lake Hawea, and more recently when the Orpington Vineyard was established on the Ballantyne Road in Wanaka. Only time will tell whether these are just the first two in a last-minute rush. Alexandra is the most southerly established wine area in New Zealand; yet, counterintuitively, it is one of the warmest wine areas in Central Otago. Some claim it to be the very hottest, but it is an area of extremes. Whereas the sunny, north-facing sites are indeed among Central Otago's warmest, other parts are too cool for any sort of viticulture. By contrast, Gibbston is one of the coolest districts in the region, and its Pinot Noir wines are just beginning to shine. More than two-thirds of all the vines planted in Central Otago are found between Lowburn and the Cromwell Basin, including Bannockburn, the most intensively planted area in the region. It is much too early to make definitive statements as to which Central Otago area is best, but based on the wines produced so far, the warm north-facing sites in Bannockburn are definitely leading the pack for Pinot Noir. Bendigo is located at the northern end of Lake Dunstan in the Cromwell Basin. No wineries exist as yet, but many Central Otago wineries own vineyards or purchase fruit from here. Bendigo is the warmest of all the Central Otago wine areas, and even grows Syrah. Lake Hayes is located at the junction for Arrowtown and it boasts some of New Zealand's highest vineyards, which can only be considered a gamble at this southerly latitude. Bendemere is its highest and coldest vineyard, off the heat-summation viability scale, somewhere in the low 800s, which must be scary, even for a hardened gambler. The most southerly vines are found in the Margaret-John Vineyards at Ettrick, 25 miles (40 kilometers) south of Alexandra.

## MARLBOROUGH
### Subregions
*Awatere, Awatere Valley, Benmorven, Blenheim, Brancott, Brancott Valley, Conders Bend, Dillons Point, Dillons Point Road, Dog Point, Fairhall, Fairhall Valley, Hawkesbury, Kaituna, Koromiko, Lower Wairau, Marshlands, Omaka, Omaka Valley, Rarangi, Raupara, Renwick, Riverlands, Spring Creek, Waihopai, Waihopai Valley, Wairau, Wairau Valley, Woodbourne*

Allan Scott planted the first vines here as recently as 1973. At the time, Scott was opening up Montana's new Stoneleigh vineyard, but he set up his own winery and vineyards in 1990. Marlborough quickly became New Zealand's most famous wine region, and Marlborough Sauvignon Blanc its greatest asset. The part of Marlborough planted with vines is primarily the Wairau plains between the town of Blenheim and the Waihopai River. Protected by the Inland Kaikoura Range from cold, southerly winds, and by North Island from northeasterly winds, the combination of free-draining soils, abundant sunshine, cool nights, and a long growing season creates the ideal environment to produce wines that are marked by electrifyingly bright fruit flavors. Awatere Valley is located to the southeast, just over the Wither Hills, where grapes often take one or two weeks longer to ripen, and show intense flavor. The Lower Wairau and Spring Creek areas are immediately north of Blenheim, where irrigation is seldom necessary, and Sauvignon is giving way to Pinot Noir. Raupara is a warm, sheltered area west of Spring Creek, immediately north of the main Wairau plain, where the grapes are usually harvested first, with fruit-driven whites and some of Marlborough's ripest red wines. Vines have recently been planted north of the Wairau River, at the foot of the Richmond Range in Conders Bend, Kaituna, and further east, in areas that are becoming known for their Sauvignon Blanc and Pinot Noir. Benmorven, Brancott Valley, and Fairhall Valley are part of the Southern Valley, south of Raupara, nestling up to, but not yet climbing, the foothills. The climate is cooler and drier than Raupara, allowing Riesling and, to a certain extent,

Pinot Noir to compete with Chardonnay and Sauvignon Blanc. Further west is Omaka or Hawkesbury Valley, which includes Dog Point, where Pinot Noir shows promise, but frost can be a danger. Situated northeast of Blenheim, the up-and-coming areas of Marshlands and Rarangi are the closest to the sea, with vineyards on free-draining pea-gravel soils overlooking Cloudy Bay. This would be the obvious appellation name, although I think a certain winery might object. Koromiko is further north, along the Tuamarina River, but boasts only one producer, Johannishof, Marlborough's most northerly winery. Kaikoura Winery is Marlborough's most southerly winery, at Kaikoura, which is more famous for its seal colony than for vineyards, although there is a small block of vines.

## NELSON
### Subregions
*Appleby, Atawhai, Brightwater, Burkes Bank, Clifton, Golden Bay, Hope, Lower Moutere, Mahara, Mariri, Motueka, Motueka Valley, Moutere, Nelson, Neudorf, Rabbit Island, Redwood Valley, Richmond, Ruby Bay, Stoke, Tasman, Upper Moutere, Waimea, Waimea Plains, Wakapuaka, Wakefield*

Nelson is overshadowed by the fame of Marlborough, on the other side of Mount Richmond, but not because of any lack of quality potential. Nelson is known for its long warm summers, cool fall nights, and for being one of the sunniest places in New Zealand. The only negative factor is rainfall, although that is nowhere near as high as in Auckland. The low profile has been due simply to there being no parcels of land of sufficient size available to attract any of New Zealand's larger wineries. Nelson has thus never benefited from any significant marketing. The high price of land has not helped, either. However, over the past 10 years, the decline of Nelson's apple industry has resulted in many orchards being converted to vineyards, increasing the area under vine ninefold and quadrupling the number of wineries.

Many of Nelson's wineries, including most of the oldest established producers, are located on the Waimea plains to the east of Richmond, where rich, fruity wines are made. Similar wines are made to the south, at Brightwater, where most of the region's newest vineyards are located, and to the northwest, at Redwood Valley, which is used by Seifried Estate as a second label. Moutere runs north from Upper Moutere, on the edge of the Redwood Valley, to the southern outskirts of Motueka. Upper Moutere produces the more impressive wines, with a broad structure and a certain minerality of fruit, but most wines are marketed as Moutere plain and simple. The Motueka wine area north of Motueka itself is quite new, and capable of growing Sauvignon Blanc with an intense, passion fruit flavor. Golden Bay is well to the north of Motueka. Despite having produced wines in the late 19th century, it is generally considered much too wet for grape growing; but that has not stopped David Heraud from establishing Waiwera Estate at Clifton. At the time of writing there was just 2½ acres (1 hectare) of Pinot Noir and Riesling, and just one wine produced, a Pinot Noir in 2003 (not tasted).

THE WINE STYLES OF

# NEW ZEALAND

## BOTRYTIZED WINES

Botrytis, or noble rot, appears on an unpredictable basis throughout all of New Zealand's wine regions. The nearest that New Zealand has to a dedicated dessert-wine area is Te Kauwhata in Waikato, because of its high humidity. As such, it is a two-winery subdistrict. The one producer that specializes in the style is Rongopai. Riesling is, without doubt, the premier grape for this style in New Zealand, producing wines of the most vivid flavor enhanced by a scintillating acidity to deliver a razor-sharp sweetness. Chardonnay is, surprisingly, the second most successful variety, a chance discovery after Hunters produced the first Botrytis Chardonnay in 1987. All peaches and cream, it stunned those lucky enough to taste it, and encouraged other New Zealanders to perfect this unusual wine. Botrytized Sémillon has yet to make its mark, but should do so now that less grassy clones are coming into production.

ⓘ— *1–15 years*

🏆 *Dry River* (Botrytis Riesling) • *Fromm* (Auslese) • *Giesen* (Canterbury Late Harvest Riesling) • *Martinborough* (Late Harvest Riesling) • *Montana* (Virtu Noble Semillon) • *Rongopai* (Ultimo Late Harvest) • *Villa Maria* (Noble Reserve Riesling)

## CABERNET FRANC

Increasingly popular as a pure varietal wine, Cabernet Franc has always been considered a useful component in classic red wine blends. Hawke's Bay is the best region, and Gimblett Road the best subdistrict.

ⓘ— *2–5 years* (up to 15 for exceptional wines)

🏆 *Clearview* • *Kim Crawford* (Wicken)

## CABERNET SAUVIGNON
### Pure and Blended

Not so long ago, New Zealand suffered from a reputation for green, aggressive red wines. It was white-wine country, and its cool climate was thought to be too cool to ripen such thick-skinned grapes as Cabernet Sauvignon. Today, however, almost every wine region in New Zealand has become a goldmine for rich, ripe red wines of the most serious and sensual quality. Even volume-selling brands such as Montana Cabernet Sauvignon are big, full, and spicy, with more quality and character than you can find in Bordeaux for twice the price. The most exciting Cabernet Sauvignon wines are produced by strict selection from top vineyards or crafted by smaller boutique wineries. Hawke's Bay is the best region, and Gimblett Road the best subdistrict.

ⓘ— *2–5 years* (up to 15 for exceptional wines)

🏆 *Craggy Range* (The Quarry) • *Firstland* (Cabernet-Merlot-Malbec) • *Goldwater Estate* (Cabernet-Merlot) • *Montana* (Tom) • *Stonyridge* (Larose) • *Te Mata* (Coleraine) • *Trinity Hill* (Gimblett Road) • *Vidal* (Joseph Soler) • *Villa Maria* (Reserve Cabernet Sauvignon-Merlot)

## CHARDONNAY

The world's most widespread classic grape really does produce something special in New Zealand, which is why its cultivation has increased from 865 acres (350 hectares) in the late 1980s to more than 9,143 acres (3,700 hectares) today. It is generally less predictable, more expressive, and capable of a slower, more classic rate of maturation than its Australian equivalent. This is due not only to cooler climatic conditions, but also to handpicking, whole-bunch pressing, a wider use of natural (local) yeast fermentation, and less obvious oak, although some producers can spoil the natural elegance of these wines by various permutations of malolactic fermentation and lees-contact that turn out too heavy-handed. There is more weight and complexity in Hawke's Bay, greater finesse in Marlborough, lusher qualities in Nelson, and more upfront fruit in Gisborne. Central Otago still has to establish its style.

ⓘ— *1–4 years*

🏆 *Ata Rangi* (Craighall) • *Clearview* • *Kumeu River* (Maté's Vineyard) • *Matua Valley* (Ararimu) • *Morton Estate* (Coniglio) • *Neudorf* (Moutere) • *Nobilo* (Icon) • *Villa Maria* (Reserve Barrique Fermented Gisborne)

## CLASSIC WHITE-WINE BLENDS

Classic white-wine blends are one of New Zealand's slowest-developing niches, yet ultimately they could prove to be one of its most rewarding. The most logical partner for Sauvignon is Sémillon, of course; although until recently the only Sémillon vines cultivated in New Zealand were aggressively aromatic and unsuited for blending unless used in a covert way to emphasize the character of a seemingly pure Sauvignon Blanc wine. For classic blends, however, where a more neutral base is required, New Zealand's traditional late-ripening Swiss clone is much too grassy. The popular Australian Chardonnay-Sémillon blend is not a common combination in New Zealand, where Chardonnay does not need to be crisped up, but Chardonnay and Chenin Blanc have proved to be surprisingly good bedmates.

ⓘ— *1–3 years*

🏆 *Pegasus Bay* (Sauvignon-Sémillon) • *Villa Maria* (Private Bin Chardonnay-Chenin)

## CHENIN BLANC

New Zealanders should be able to show South Africa that their country can produce far more exciting Chenin Blanc than can the Cape. But the variety has never been widely planted here, and what there is has been declining of late. Pity; it would be great if, after Sauvignon Blanc, New Zealand could demolish the reputation of the Loire's other famous white grape. An opportunity missed?

ⓘ— *1–3 years*

🏆 *The Millton Vineyard* (Te Arai)

## GEWÜRZTRAMINER

This is one of New Zealand's potentially exciting niche wines. But the wrong vine stock, and little understanding of how to produce a classic dry Gewürztraminer with any real spice, results in typically wishy-washy wines, with rose-petal aromas and Turkish delight fruit. These are the best, but none of them truly excites me.

ⓘ— *1–3 years*

🏆 *Dry River* • *Lawson's Dry Hills* • *Margrain* • *Montana* ("P" Patutahi)

## MALBEC
### Pure and Blended

Increasing at a rate similar to Syrah, Malbec does not have the same single-varietal cachet. It

SAUVIGNON BLANC GRAPES, CLOUDY BAY
*Cloudy Bay makes one of Marlborough's greatest Sauvignon Blancs, and its cult following has benefited the reputation of the entire New Zealand wine industry.*

is judged more useful for its ability to add some midpalate smoothness to a classic red wine blends. The pure Malbecs of Fromm and Mills Reef are exceptions. Hawke's Bay is the best region, and Gimblett Road the best subdistrict.

🕒 *2–8 years*

🏆 *Esk Valley* (The Terraces) • *Fromm* (Reserve) • *Mills Reef* (Elspeth)

## MERLOT
### Pure and Blended

Ten years ago there was twice as much Cabernet Sauvignon growing in New Zealand as there was Merlot. Now the position has reversed, even though the area planted with Cabernet Sauvignon has increased eightfold. Merlot is much more lush than any of the Cabernet varieties, but with a more European structure than California Merlot. Some wines, such as the Goldwater Esslin, are not made every year. Hawke's Bay is the best region, and Gimblett Road the best subdistrict.

🕒 *2–8 years*

🏆 *Craggy Range* (Sophia) • *Esk Valley* (Reserve Merlot-Malbec-Cabernet Sauvignon) • *Matua Valley* (Bullrush) • *C. J Pask* (Gimblett Road Reserve) • *Sacred Hill* (Brokenstone) • *Selaks* (Founders Reserve) • *Sileni* (EV) • *Trinity Hill* (Gimblett Road) • *Unison Vineyard* (Unison Selection)

## PINOT GRIS

The most successful are closer to Pinot Grigio in style than to the spicy variety grown in Alsace, but it is distinctly superior Pinot Grigio, with more delicious, riper fruit.

🕒 *1–3 years*

🏆 *Ata Rangi* (Lismore) • *Chard Farm* • *Kim Crawford* (Boyzone) • *Dry River* • *Neudorf* (Moutere) • *Palliser Estate*

## PINOT NOIR

The Holy Grail of all grapes was first thought to excel in Martinborough. Although some excellent Pinot Noir wines have been and still are being made there, it certainly has not turned out to be a second Burgundy. South Island has produced most of the best Pinot Noir wines on a consistent basis. First it was Nelson that showed the most promise, particularly from the likes of Neudorf, whose Moutere Pinot Noir rarely fails to please. Then it was Canterbury, followed by Marlborough and, most exciting of all, Central Otago. However, as far as outside observers are concerned, Central Otago made its name on the 1998 vintage, and that was the year of the El Niño-induced drought, after which the region has enjoyed a string of good vintages. We have to remember that Central Otago's heat summation generally defies the viticultural textbooks. There are reasons other than heat summation why viticulture does work this far south, but I think it only prudent that we see what sort of Pinot Noir this region can produce throughout a series of cool vintages before we declare Central Otago to be the southern hemisphere's Burgundy.

🕒 *2–8 years*

🏆 *Akarua* • *Ata Rangi* • *Craggy Range* (Te Muna) • *Felton Road* (Block 3, Block 5) • *Martinborough Vineyard* (Reserve) • *Neudorf* (Moutere) • *Two Paddocks* (The Last Chance)

## RIESLING

Truly dry Riesling is still a minority product in New Zealand, where most renditions of this variety have some residual sugar, even if the result is not a distinctive sweetness. New Zealand Riesling seems to be generally crisper than its Australian counterpart, with more citrous finesse. It does not have the same simplistic lime fruit, and is not inclined to go gasolinelike very quickly either. In structure and style it leans closer to northern Europe, although not as close as the Riesling produced in Michigan or the Finger Lakes of the US.

🕒 *1–5 years*

🏆 *Kim Crawford* • *Dry River* (Craighall) • *Felton Road* • *Framingham* • *Grove Mill* • *Hunter's* (Stoneburn) • *Montana* (Stoneleigh) • *Neudorf* (Dry Moutere) • *Palliser Estate* • *Pegasus Bay* (Aria)

## SAUVIGNON BLANC

Why does New Zealand's Sauvignon Blanc have such vivaciously crisp and pure fruit character, while you have to scratch around to find any hint of fruit in most Loire versions of this wine? It is certainly not due to the use of a particularly expressive clone, as the clone in question is the UCD1, which was developed at the University of California, Davis; although it could be argued that the UCD1 has evolved into a more localized clone. Denis Dubourdieu of Bordeaux University is convinced it is the uniqueness of New Zealand's soil and climate that makes its Sauvignon Blanc so different. I might be able to give readers a more definitive answer in the next revision of this book, as the New Zealand government announced in 2004 that it was going to fund six years of research (at NZ$1.6 million per annum/US$1.15 million) into the factors affecting the aroma and flavor profile of New Zealand Sauvignon Blanc, and how the processes involved can be harnessed in the vineyard and during fermentation. This reflects the importance of New Zealand's flagship variety, the country's most widely cultivated grape, with no fewer than 13,600 acres (5,500 hectares) planted. There are now so many different techniques used to enhance various aspects of Sauvignon Blanc's style that it is no longer possible to say that it is made in any particular way. Though the secret to the earliest Marlborough successes with this grape was back-blending with a drop of early-harvested Sémillon, which is so grassy that it turbocharges the wine's varietal character. This country in general, but Marlborough in particular, has the rare capability of being able to slowly ripen Sauvignon Blanc to a near-perfect state, enabling a large number of wineries to produce very fresh wines with ripe gooseberry fruit and an electrifying balance of mouth-watering acidity. Some areas can produce such intensity of fruit that the flavors include passion fruit, even grapefruit; but asparagus and peas, especially canned peas, are characteristics to be avoided.

🕒 *1–2 years* (not older, unless you like the asparagus or canned-peas character that quickly develops with bottle-age in these wines, particularly when from the ripest vintages)

🏆 *Cloudy Bay* • *Craggy Range* • *Kim Crawford* • *Hunter's* • *Isabel Estate* • *Koura* (Whaleshack) • *Montana* (B. Brancott) • *Nobilo* (Icon) • *Palliser Estate* • *Villa Maria*

ATA RANGI, MARTINBOROUGH
*This estate produces consistent Pinot Noir.*

## SPARKLING WINES

At one time, Montana's Lindauer Brut and Rosé exemplified New Zealand's sparkling-wine industry. They are very good for creamy, easy-drinking bubbly made by the transfer method, but it took collaboration between Montana and Deutz to put this country on the bottle-fermented sparkling-wine map. However, it was *champenois* Daniel Le Brun who actually demonstrated Marlborough's true potential for serious sparkling wine. Le Brun's star shone so brightly in the early 1990s that he eclipsed even Montana. With the benefit of hindsight, however, we can see that his reputation was built on just three vintages: 1989, 1990, and 1991. It was the quality of these particular vintages and the speed with which Le Brun achieved this quality that grabbed the wine media's attention. Meanwhile, Cloudy Bay's Pelorus was slowly developing a cult following to match that of its Sauvignon Blanc. When Hunter's released its deliciously fresh and easy-drinking Miru Miru, the international wine press was willing to concede the potential of Kiwi bubbly, even though the Hunter's Brut is the superior wine. Quartz Reef now promises to put Central Otago on the sparkling-wine map, although Marlborough still reigns supreme.

🕒 *1–2 years* (from purchase)

🏆 *Kim Crawford* (Rory) • *Hunter's* (Hunter's Brut, Miru Miru) • *Montana* (Lindauer Special Reserve, Deutz Blanc de Blancs) • *Cloudy Bay* (Pelorus) • *Quartz Reef* (Chauvet NV, Chauvet vintage)

## SYRAH

This could be one of New Zealand's greatest wines. The quality of this grape has come a long way since the first commercial release of Stonecroft Syrah, the earliest vintages of which were tight and green. Hawke's Bay is definitely the right place for this variety, specifically in the Gimblett Road subdistrict, where the Syrah grows dark and deep, developing a truly lush style that is set off by the classic cracked-peppercorn character. The best examples are neither Rhône nor Australian in style.

🕒 *2–5 years* (up to 15 for exceptional wines)

🏆 *Craggy Range* (Le Sol) • *Kingsley Estate* (Gimblett Gravels) • *Te Mata* (Bullnose) • *Trinity Hill* (Gimblett Road) • *Vidal* (Soler)

# THE WINE PRODUCERS OF
# NEW ZEALAND

## AKARUA
### Central Otago
★★♥

This Bannockburn winery produces beautiful Pinot Noir at relatively inexpensive prices. I purchased a case of the 2002 to lay down, but drank it all and had to order another two cases! The Gullies, Akarua's entry-level Pinot Noir, is often better than most producers' top-of-the-line Pinot Noir.

✓ *Pinot Noir*

## ALPHA DOMUS
### Hawke's Bay
★★☆

Sometimes the wines have too much of a fruit-accentuated style, both reds and whites. They are never unfriendly; they just try too hard. Reds have become quite big in recent vintages. Now is the time for this producer to start thinking more about finesse than size.

✓ *Classic red blend* (The Aviator, The Navigator) • *Chardonnay* (AD) • *Pinot Noir* • *Sauvignon Blanc* • *Sémillon* (Leonarda)

## ALPINE PACIFIC WINES
### Canterbury
★

Formerly known as Chancellor Estates, these Waipara wines are sold under The Hanmer Junction and Mount Cass labels.

✓ *Pinot Noir* (Mount Cass)

## AMISFIELD
### Central Otago
☆

Wines of impressive acidity from vineyards in the Pisa Range foothills, just north of Lowburn. Only Riesling disappoints.

✓ *Pinot Gris* • *Pinot Noir*

## ATA RANGI
### Martinborough
★★♥

Clive Paton consistently demonstrates that Martinborough can hack it with Central Otago's very best Pinot Noirs. He also makes one of Martinborough's best Chardonnays. I am currently reserving my opinion on Ata Rangi's Célèbre. Since it has moved away from Cabernet toward more Merlot, and increased its Syrah content, so it has become more

blackcurranty and has displayed less complexity and finesse. Hopefully there is a swing back in the pipeline. Or maybe it's just a vintage thing?

✓ *Chardonnay* (Craighall) • *Pinot Gris* (Lismore) • *Pinot Noir*

## BABICH
### Henderson

★♥

The entry-level varietal wines of this large winery have never been exciting, but the Marlborough and Hawke's Bay Sauvignon Blanc came right by 2003, so hopefully this signals a revitalization of quality from the bottom up. The top-of-the-line Babich wines, such as Irongate and The Patriarch, always excel (they are ★★ wines in their own right). The Winemaker's Reserve is developing nicely as a middle-tier, best-value range. On the other hand, Joe Babich has sold his famed Irongate vineyard to Blake Family Vineyard. (The last Irongate wine was produced in 1997, after which the name became a trademark for wine sourced from a neighboring vineyard in Gimblett, albeit a damn good one.) In 2003, he pledged to increase overall Babich production fivefold by 2005, so we will have to wait to see if and how this affects the recent climb in quality.

✓ *Classic red blend* (Irongate) • *Cabernet Sauvignon* (The Patriarch) • *Chardonnay* (Irongate, The Patriarch) • *Sauvignon Blanc*

## BALDHILLS
### Central Otago

A young Pinot Noir and Pinot Gris vineyard with, it seems, excellent potential.

## BANNOCK BRAE
### Central Otago
★

Although its first vintage was as recent as 2001, Bannock Brae has produced some excellent Pinot Noir – with plenty of ripe, creamy fruit – from its vineyard on the shore of Lake Dunstan. Its entry-level Goldfields label is also recommended.

✓ *Pinot Noir*

## BENFIELD & DELAMARE
### Martinborough
★★☆

Minuscule quantities of high quality Bordeaux-style blends produced in Martinborough's Pinot Noir country.

✓ *Classic red blend* (Merlot-Cabernet Sauvignon-Cabernet Franc)

## BILANCIA
### Hawke's Bay
★

Bilancia is Italian for balance. This is the personal label of Trinity Hill's winemaker, Warren Gibson, and his partner, Lorraine Leheny, who is Bilancia's winemaker. Some excellent wines have been made from purchased grapes since 1997, with Syrah from its own vineyard the following year, and Viognier in 2000.

✓ *Merlot* • *Syrah*

## BLACK RIDGE
### Central Otago
★

You can rely on good quality Pinot Noir and Chardonnay from this Alexandra vineyard, and sometimes Riesling. Owner Verdun Burgess even grows Cabernet Sauvignon because he was told it would never ripen. "Hey Verdun, bet you'll never grow truffles!"

✓ *Pinot Noir*

## BLAKE FAMILY VINEYARD
### Hawke's Bay

This is definitely one to watch. Wine-loving San Francisco financier Mark Blake is on a mission: he wants to produce wine in the style of a great Bordeaux. Not just a good Bordeaux, or indeed an excellent Bordeaux, but a great Bordeaux. And he has the means to do so. In 2000, he purchased from Babich the famous 25-acre (10-hectare) Irongate vineyard (renamed "125"). Then, in 2002, he bought the Redd Gravels vineyard from Thornbury Wines. Mark Blake told me that, "The 2004 will be our first Blake Family Vineyard release, and it will be a Merlot-dominant wine from the Redd Gravels vineyard." I won't be in any position to judge the quality and style of these wines until the next revision, and nor will anyone else.

## BROOKFIELD
### Napier
★★☆

Impressive quality red wines, particularly in recent vintages.

✓ *Classic red blend* (Gold Label) • *Syrah* (Hillside)

## CABLE BAY
### Waiheke Island
★

It might seem strange that the best wine from this Waiheke Island producer is a very fine Marlborough Sauvignon Blanc, but even its Waiheke Merlot-Malbec-Cabernet is blended from various vineyards spread over the island. Winemakers Neil Culley and Briony Carnachan aim to produce the best wines they can, and they are not frightened to admit that this is not always achieved by restricting themselves to their own vineyards.

✓ *Sauvignon Blanc*

## CAIRNBRAE
### Marlborough
★★☆♥

Purchased by Sacred Hill in 2001. The quality here remains high, and the value is even better.

✓ *Chardonnay* • *Riesling* (Late Harvest, Reserve) • *Sauvignon Blanc* (The Stones)

## CANTERBURY HOUSE
### Waipara
★♥

Michael Reid's ambitious project started in 1994, with the first wines produced in 1997. Early wines were disappointing, particularly the dubious sparkling wine, but gradually the quality picked up, especially the Sauvignon Blanc. However, since the 2002 vintage, the quality at Canterbury House has been on a real roll under the helm of new winemaker Alan McCorkindale.

✓ *Chardonnay* (Reserve) • *Pinot Noir* • *Riesling* (Noble) • *Sauvignon Blanc*

## CARRICK
### Central Otago

This up-and-coming Bannockburn producer makes mainly Pinot Noir in a clean, rich, fruity, easy-drinking style.

✓ *Pinot Noir*

## CELLIER LE BRUN
### Marlborough

Daniel Le Brun has had no connection with his old company since 1996, when Allan McWilliams took over as winemaker and general manager. Allan has improved the quality of Cellier Le Brun's wines (confusingly sold under the Daniel Le Brun label) since the late-1990s. Second label wines are sold under Terrace Road brand.

✓ *Blanc de Blancs*

## CENTRAL OTAGO WINE COMPANY
### Central Otago

Affectionately known as CowCo, this custom winemaking company is owned by a group of investors, including actor Sam Neill and winemaker Dean Shaw. At the time of writing, in addition to Two Paddocks, Dean also makes the wines for Berridge, Clay Cliffs, Dry Gulley, Kawarau Estate, Maharg, Mount Maude, Mt. Rosa, Nevis Bluff, Penniket Vineyard, Rock 'n' Pillar, Sleeping Dogs, and Springvale.

## CHARD FARM
### Central Otago
★

Owned by Rob Hay, one of the earliest viticultural pioneers this far south, Chard Farm enjoys a dramatic location. It is approached along a rough-hewn track that bends around a mountainside, with a steep gorge on one side and barely enough room to drive a car. Some wines still have a tendency to rapidly develop a canned-pea character, but Redgate Pinot Noir is a banker.

✓ *Pinot Gris • Pinot Noir (Redgate) • Riesling*

## CLEARVIEW ESTATE
### Hawke's Bay
★★✫

Unashamedly bold-flavored wines from Tim Turvey, whose red wines have always benefited most from this approach. Some would claim the Chardonnay is one of New Zealand's very best. Production is set to rise due to a 55 percent increase in vineyard holdings.

✓ *Cabernet Franc • Chardonnay • Classic red blend* (Merlot-Malbec, Old Olive Block)

## CLIFFORD BAY
### Marlborough
★

An instant success from its very first vintage (1997), Clifford Bay's white wines have seduced critics and customers alike. They now seem set to repeat the experience with their very own Pinot Noir, as from the 2003 vintage.

✓ *Chardonnay • Pinot Noir • Sauvignon Blanc*

## CLOUDY BAY
### Marlborough
★★★✫

Cloudy Bay is a subsidiary of Cape Mentelle in Western Australia, which is now part of the French LVMH group. With 350 acres (140 hectares) supplying a fraction of its needs, even when newly planted vineyards come on stream, this is a big business. Yet it has developed the aura of a boutique winery, which has been essential to maintaining its perceived cult following and thus its relatively high prices (particularly on export markets). It has cleverly set up such a wide distribution for its Cloudy Bay Sauvignon Blanc that importers mail their clients saying, "Our allotment of seven cases has arrived," and it quickly sells out, giving the impression of a limited production. The Chardonnay is at least as good as the Sauvignon Blanc, but it is the latter that has made Cloudy Bay synonymous with Marlborough's marketing success. This is why the winery released its *barrique*-fermented Te Koko Sauvignon Blanc, rather than mess with the winning formula of its entry-level Sauvignon Blanc. I continue to have a strange, almost love-hate relationship with sparkling Pelorus. In tastings with other sparkling wines, I am invariably disappointed, finding it heavy by comparison, and lacking in finesse. Yet, whenever I order Pelorus in a restaurant, I am seldom disappointed. On its own, in the context of food, Pelorus is never heavy, and always has the finesse that is missing in the clinical ambience of a technical tasting. Sometimes it is the contradictory nature of a wine that makes it special.

✓ *Chardonnay • Pinot Noir • Sauvignon Blanc • Sparkling wine* (Pelorus)

## COLLARDS
### Henderson
★★✫Ⓥ

This winery, founded by English horticulturist J. W. Collard in 1910, is still in family ownership. Brothers Bruce and Geoffrey Collard have maintained the winery's reputation for consistency across the range. The wines have a rich vibrancy of fruit, notably the textbook Hawke's Bay Chardonnay, which displays a fine youthful complexity.

✓ *Chardonnay* (Hawke's Bay) *• Riesling • Sauvignon Blanc*

## COOPERS CREEK
### Huapai
★★✫Ⓥ

Despite a proliferation of silly names (Cat's Pee on a Gooseberry Bush Sauvignon, Fat Cat Chardonnay, etc.), the winemaking here is very serious.

✓ *Chardonnay* (Swamp Reserve) *• Classic red blend* (Merlot-Cabernet Franc) *• Pinot Noir* (Glamour Puss, Marlborough) *• Riesling* (Hawke's Bay, Marlborough Late Harvest, Nelson) *• Sauvignon Blanc* (Marlborough)

## COVELL ESTATE
### Galatea
✫Ⓑ

You have to be dedicated or mad, preferably both, to stick rigidly to a biodynamic regime. You also have to be dedicated or mad to plant a vineyard in the Bay of Plenty, where no one else has had the confidence to plant more than the odd acre of vines. Either way, Bob Covell makes a fine, steely, citrus-flavored Riesling.

✓ *Riesling*

## CRAGGY RANGE
### Hawke's Bay
★★★✫

The most ambitious wine project New Zealand has seen, the Craggy Range winery, with 700 acres (285 hectares) of vineyards, has so far cost US$36 million. It is owned by Terry Peabody, an American who has lived in Australia for more than 30 years. The winery is a mix of technology and tradition, and finely tuned to produce single-vineyard wines. One of New Zealand's top viticulturists, Steve Smith MW, is in overall charge, and Rod Easthorpe has been appointed winemaker following the tragic sporting accident that took the life of the young and talented Doug Wisor. All the wines show great finesse, from Sauvignon Blanc to Syrah, and everything between. Red Rock is Craggy Range's great-value second label, with interesting wines such as The Underarm Syrah and Gravel Pit Red.

✓ *Entire range*

## KIM CRAWFORD
### Hawke's Bay
★★

One of New Zealand's most experienced, talented, and award-winning winemakers, Kim Crawford has had his own winery since 1996. It was purchased by the Vincor group, Crawford's Canadian distributor, in 2004. The quality remains very good, and is climbing even higher. The Boyzone Pinot Gris has lovely fruit, but in true New World fashion, absolutely no spice.

✓ *Cabernet Franc* (Wicken) *• Chardonnay* (Tietjen, Unoaked) *• Classic red blend* (Tane) *• Pinot Gris* (Boyzone) *• Riesling • Sauvignon Blanc • Sparkling wine* (Rory)

## CROSSROADS
### Hawke's Bay
★★✫

The flagship wine here is a classic red blend called Talisman. Crossroads is happy to confirm it is comprised of six different black grape varieties, but refuses to divulge what they are, which has piqued many a New Zealand critic. The Destination Series is an entry-level range of 10 upfront, easy-drinking varietal wines, after which comes the Reserve range, and the Collectors Edition. The future focus will be on Merlot, Cabernet-Merlot, Syrah, and Chardonnay. And, of course, Talisman, whatever that is.

✓ *Chardonnay* (Reserve) *• Pinot Noir* (Collectors Edition) *• Classic red blend* (Talisman)

## DELEGAT'S
### Henderson
★★✫

The style is generally quite restrained, with more elegance than richness, but seldom lacking depth or length. Marlborough wines are sold under the Oyster Bay label.

✓ *Classic red blend* (Reserve Cabernet-Merlot) *• Merlot* (Reserve) *• Riesling* (Oyster Bay Botrytized) *• Sauvignon Blanc* (Oyster Bay)

## DRY RIVER
### Martinborough
★★

Neil McCallum sold Dry River to New York investment manager Julian Robertson and Napa Valley vineyard owner Reg Oliver (*see* Te Awa) in February 2003, but stayed on as winemaker. So, there is no real difference for the time being, except for Neil, who has NZ$11 million (US$8) in his pocket and, as he does not have to waste time running a business, more time to fish. Neil is known for his Gewürztraminer and Pinot Gris, but I have yet to be impressed beyond New World norms (i.e., the wines have no spice). He is, however, capable of producing one of New Zealand's most delicately perfumed dry Rieslings, his Pinot Noirs evolve beautifully, and his decadently rich botrytized wines are the stuff of legend.

✓ *Chardonnay* (Botrytized, Craighall) *• Gewürztraminer • Pinot Gris • Pinot Noir • Riesling* (Botrytized, Craighall) *• Syrah*

## DRYLANDS
### Marlborough
★Ⓥ

Selaks built this winery before the company was taken over by Nobilo,

which itself was purchased by BRL Hardy, now part of Constellation, the world's largest wine-producing group. Easy-drinking reds; much finer whites.

✓ *Riesling* (Winemakers Reserve) • *Sauvignon Blanc*

## ESCARPMENT
**Martinborough**
★★☆

If anyone put Martinborough Pinot Noir on the map, it was Larry McKenna, when he was the winemaker at Martinborough Vineyard. This is why his new venture (in partnership with the Kirby family) is so tantalizing for Martinborough Pinot Noir lovers.

✓ *Pinot Noir*

## ESK VALLEY
**Hawke's Bay**
★★☆ V

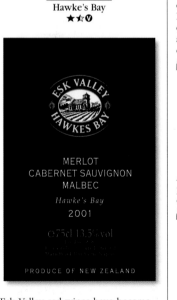

Esk Valley red wines have become increasingly impressive under the ownership of Villa Maria. The Terraces (Malbec-Merlot-Cabernet Franc) is one of New Zealand's most outstanding classic red blends.

✓ *Classic red blend* (Merlot-Malbec-Cabernet Sauvignon, Merlot-Cabernet Sauvignon,

The Terraces) • *Merlot* (Black Label) • *Verdelho*

## FAIRHILL DOWNS
**Marlborough**
★

This vineyard has been planted since 1982, but the Small family did not sell their own wine until 1996. Since then they have developed a reputation for their bold fruit, balanced by crisp, ripe acidity. So vivid was the fruit in the 2003 Pinot Gris that it was almost Sauvignon Blanc-like!

✓ *Pinot Gris* • *Sauvignon Blanc*

## FELTON ROAD
**Central Otago**
★★★☆

This is the producer of New Zealand's greatest Pinot Noir, and a stunning medium-sweet Riesling. Other labels include Cornish Point (good value, easy-drinking Drystone Pinot Noir). The difference between Felton Road's top-performing Block 3 and Block 5 Pinot Noirs has more to do with the clones than the soil. These vineyards are organic/biodynamic in part, but are not certified as such.

✓ *Chardonnay* • *Pinot Noir* (Block 3, Block 5) • *Riesling*

## FIRSTLAND
**Waikato**
★★

Originally known as De Redcliffe, this Waikato winery now excels at red winemaking, which had previously been its weakest area. Firstland was purchased in 2002 by Ed Astor, a wealthy former publisher from the US, whose decision to take the wines off the New Zealand market and focus on exports has been remarkably successful in boosting the reputation of this winery.

✓ *Cabernet Sauvignon* (Reserve) • *Classic red blend* • *Cabernet Sauvignon* (Cabernet-Merlot-Malbec) • *Sauvignon Blanc* (Marlborough)

## FORREST ESTATE
**Marlborough**
★★

An interesting range of fine wines is produced here, especially the soft, classic Sauvignon Blanc.

✓ *Classic red blend* (Cornerstone) • *Cabernet Sauvignon* (Cornerstone) • *Merlot* (Cornerstone) • *Riesling* (Botrytized, Late Harvest) • *Sauvignon Blanc*

## FOXES ISLAND WINES
**Marlborough**
★

John Belsham, Hunter's former winemaker, went on to establish Raupara Vintners, a designer-wine service that catered for the explosion of new labels for vineyards with no winery of their

own in the 1990s. He now focuses on his own wines, which invariably show a preference for finesse over weight, size, and overused vinification techniques. John specializes in the two classic Burgundian grapes. My only criticism is that he was so darn good with Sauvignon Blanc, he should add that variety.

✓ *Chardonnay* • *Pinot Noir*

## FRAMINGHAM
**Marlborough**
★★ V

Although Framingham produces a large and fascinating range of varietal wines, including a rare Montepulciano, its true specialty is Riesling in all its styles.

✓ *Riesling* • *Sauvignon Blanc*

## FROMM
**Marlborough**
★★

George and Ruth Fromm also own the George Fromm winery in Malans, Switzerland, where they currently live. The vineyards here are organic/biodynamic, but not certified as such. Winemaker Hätsch Kalberer believes in the minimum of intervention, regularly relying on wild yeasts and never filtering his red wines. Hätsch has carved out a cozy red-wine niche for Fromm, but his Riesling should not be overlooked, particularly the Auslese. All Fromm wines are sold under the La Strada label.

✓ *Malbec* (Reserve) • *Pinot Noir* (Fromm Vineyard) • *Riesling* (Auslese) • *Syrah* (Reserve)

## GIBBSTON VALLEY
**Central Otago**
★

Grant Taylor's Pinot Noirs are becoming increasingly fleshy, and this stylistic progression should continue as the new warmer vineyards in Alexandra and Bendigo come into production.

✓ *Pinot Noir* (Reserve)

## GIESEN WINE ESTATE
**Canterbury and Marlborough**
★★☆ V

Once the most important winery in Canterbury, the Giesen brothers have invested so heavily in a Marlborough winery and vineyards that this is now their primary location.

✓ *Pinot Noir* (Canterbury Reserve) • *Riesling* (Canterbury Reserve, Canterbury Late Harvest, Marlborough/Canterbury) • *Sauvignon Blanc* (Marlborough)

## GLADSTONE
**Wairarapa**
★☆

This small winery produced its first vintage in 1991, but the current owners took over in 1996. Some interesting reds, but intense Sauvignon is the best buy here.

✓ *Sauvignon Blanc*

## GOLDWATER ESTATE
**Waiheke Island**
★★★☆

Kim and Jeanette Goldwater produce one of New Zealand's greatest red wines, the Goldwater Cabernet-Merlot (sometimes with some Cabernet Franc). This is a wine of classic quality, which has the richness, finesse, longevity, and potential complexity to compete with the best wines that California, Australia, or Bordeaux can produce.

✓ *Classic red blend* (Cabernet-Merlot) • *Merlot* (Esslin) • *Sauvignon Blanc* (New Dog)

## GRAVITAS
**Marlborough**
★

This is a new, fast-rising star in Marlborough's brightly lit firmament, with intensely flavored, expressive white wines produced by Brian Bicknell.

✓ *Chardonnay* • *Sauvignon Blanc*

## GREENHOUGH
**Nelson**
★★☆

Established in 1991 by Andrew Greenhough and Jenny Wheeler, this small but growing vineyard produces wines that are brimming with fruit.

✓ *Chardonnay* (Hope Vineyard)
• *Pinot Noir* (Hope Vineyard)
• *Riesling* (Hope Vineyard) •
*Sauvignon Blanc*

### GROVE MILL
**Marlborough**
★ⓥ

Grove Mill is New Zealand's first carbon-neutral winery, thanks in part to its "smart cellar." This involves energy-efficient technology to draw cold night air into the winery and high-performance insulation to keep temperatures low during the day. There is also a heat-exchanger to supply the entire complex with hot water.

✓ *Chardonnay* • *Riesling* •
*Sauvignon Blanc*

### HARRIER RISE VINEYARD
**Kumeu**
★

The owner-winemaker is Tim Harris, an Auckland lawyer and *Metro Magazine* columnist. When he established this red wine specialist venture in 1986, he called it Waitakere Road Vineyard, and sold the wine under the Harrier Rise Vineyard label. He dropped the Waitakere Road name in 1997.

✓ *Cabernet Franc* (Monza) •
*Merlot* (Bigney Coigne)

### HERON'S FLIGHT
**Matakana**
★

David Hoskins and Mary Evans used to make splendid Cabernet Sauvignon, but they caught the Italian bug and started trialing Italian varieties in 1994. By 2004, they had replaced all the French varieties with Italian vines.

✓ *Sangiovese*

### HERZOG
**Marlborough**
★★✮

These wines might seem expensive, but if a Michelin-starred restaurant in a classic European wine region sold the wine, its customers would not blink at such prices. And that's not an unreasonable comparison, for while Hans Herzog makes the wines, his wife Therese runs the winery's restaurant, drawing on her Michelin-starred experience in Switzerland.

✓ *Classic red blend* (Spirit of Marlborough) • *Montepulciano*

### HIGHFIELD ESTATE
**Marlborough**
★

This Japanese-owned estate, with its brightly colored Tuscan-styled winery and restaurant overlooking the Omaka Valley, is perhaps best known for its improving sparkling wine, but rich, smooth Pinot Noir is the most consistent style here.

✓ *Pinot Noir* • *Sauvignon Blanc*
• *Sparkling wine* (Elstree)

### HUIA
**Marlborough**
✮

Claire and Mike Allan are white-wine specialists, making only one red, a Pinot Noir. The white wines are all handpicked and whole-bunch pressed, which works particularly well for Sauvignon Blanc and an improving sparkling wine.

✓ *Sauvignon Blanc*

### HUNTER'S
**Marlborough**
★★ⓥ

This large, established, and expanding winery is run by Jane Hunter, a gifted viticulturist whose medal-winning standards have earned her an OBE, the respect of her neighbors, and the very first IWS Women in Wine Award. Gary Duke is her longstanding winemaker.

✓ *Chardonnay* • *Riesling* (Stoneburn) • *Sauvignon Blanc* (Flax Mill, Marlborough, Winemaker's Selection) • *Sparkling wine* (Hunter's, Miru Miru)

### HYPERION
**Northland**
✮

In Greek mythology, Hyperion was one of the 12 Titans—the Titan of light. I'm not quite sure what the light is shining out of John Crone's winery, a former cowshed north of Auckland, but of all his wines, which are named after one Titan or another, his Gaia Merlot is the one that most deserves to be set free.

✓ *Merlot* (Gaia)

### ISABEL ESTATE
**Marlborough**
★★✮

This winery consistently produces one of New Zealand's most impressive Sauvignon Blancs. Watch out for the occasional release of Noble Sauvage, a botrytized version of Marlborough's famous varietal.

✓ *Pinot Gris* • *Pinot Noir* •
*Sauvignon Blanc*

### JACKSON ESTATE
**Marlborough**
★★✮ⓥ

At one time, Jackson Estate consistently produced Marlborough's greatest Sauvignon Blanc. The quality is still just as high, but a number of wineries now make Sauvignon Blanc that is at least as fine, and which of them produce the best of the crop varies from year to year. But Jackson Estate excels in quality and value throughout the range.

✓ *Chardonnay* • *Pinot Noir* •
*Riesling* • *Sauvignon Blanc*

### KAHURANGI ESTATE
**Nelson**
ⓥ

This is the original Seifried winery and 26-acre (10.5-hectare) vineyard. It was sold in 1998 to the current owners, Amanda and Greg Day, who renamed it Kahurangi, the Maori for "treasured possession." Kahurangi might be a new name, but it boasts the oldest commercial vineyard in the region. And with a new 30-acre (12-hectare) vineyard nearly a mile away (on the northwestern side of Upper Moutere, planted in 2001), production is expanding fast.

✓ *Chardonnay* • *Riesling* •
*Sauvignon Blanc*

### KAITUNA VALLEY
**Canterbury**
★

Owner-winemakers Grant and Helen Whelan specialize in Pinot Noir and Chardonnay.

✓ *Pinot Noir*

### KARAKA POINT
**Auckland**

Located on the Karaka Peninsula, southwest of Auckland, this winery is probably best known for its Chardonnay and Syrah (sometimes sold as Shiraz).

### KAWARAU
**Central Otago**
★◉

A restaurant-winery in an idyllic setting, with lovely, rich Pinot Noir.

✓ *Pinot Noir*

### KEMBLEFIELD
**Hawke's Bay**
★ⓥ

John Kemble produces excellent Chardonnay and Merlot-Cabernet. For a short while his 2001 Gewürztraminer showed some spicy potential, but a second tasting was disappointing, as were later vintages.

✓ *Chardonnay* (The Distinction) • *Classic red blend* (Merlot-Cabernet)

### KINGSLEY ESTATE
**Hawke's Bay**
Ⓑ★✮

Red-wine specialist Kingsley Tobin is one of only a few organic producers in Hawke's Bay.

✓ *Classic red blend* (Cabernet-Malbec, Cabernet Sauvignon-Merlot) • *Cabernet Sauvignon* • *Merlot* • *Syrah*

### KOURA BAY
**Marlborough**
★★✮

The Whalesback was probably the most delicious Sauvignon Blanc produced in 2003. There might be finer examples, but none that are more delicious.

✓ *Sauvignon Blanc* (Whalesback)

### KUMEU RIVER
**Auckland**
★★

Master of Wine Michael Brajkovich regularly produces one of New Zealand's greatest Chardonnays, but his reds are just as good. Excellent value, easy-drinking wines are sold under the Kumeu River Village label.

✓ *Chardonnay* (Maté's Vineyard) • *Classic red blend* (Melba) • *Merlot* • *Pinot Gris* • *Pinot Noir*

### LAKE CHALICE
**Marlborough**
★◉ⓥ

Lake Chalice opened its new winery in 2004. Called South Pacific Cellars, and sited at Riverlands for logistic rather than viticultural reasons, this is a clever joint venture with Waipara Hills and New Zealand Vineyards Ltd. It is clever because it means that both wineries can have a state-of-the-art winery with economies of scale and efficiencies that would not be possible on an individual basis. Top-of-the-range wines are sold under the Platinum label.

✓ *Chardonnay* (Platinum F. V.) • *Sauvignon Blanc* (Marlborough)

## LAWSON'S DRY HILLS
**Marlborough**
★★☆♥

This winery is capable of producing intensely flavored white wines. The Gewürztraminer is a bit too pretty-pretty, but highly regarded by New World standards. Sauvignon Blanc is my favorite.

✓ *Chardonnay •
Gewürztraminer • Riesling •
Sauvignon Blanc*

## LINCOLN
**Henderson**
☆

Most critics would put Lincoln's Chardonnay first, but I prefer the richer reds, with their minty finesse and fruitcake complexity. The Chardonnay Heritage Patricia is alarmingly overwhelmed by coconutty American oak.

✓ *Classic red blend* (Home Vineyards, Vintage Selection)

## LINDEN ESTATE
**Hawke's Bay**
★♥

This Esk Valley vineyard has been growing grapes since 1969, but making wine only since 1991. It has been under Canadian ownership since 2001, with a new winemaker, Emma Lowe, in 2003.

✓ *Classic red blend* (Dam Block)

## McCASHIN'S
**Nelson**
☆

When the McCashin family sold its famous Nelson brewery to Lion Breweries in 1999, it already had swapped horses, selling the first vintage (1998) of McCashin's wine, albeit from purchased grapes. Initially, wines were sourced from various different regions, but with the purchase of an established 100-acre (40-hectare) vineyard at Hope, this winery has begun to focus its efforts on Nelson.

✓ *Pinot Noir*

## MARGARET-JOHN
**Central Otago**
❷

John and Margaret May farm New Zealand's most southerly vineyard, at Ettrick, some 25 miles (40 kilometers) southeast of Alexandra.

## MARGRAIN
**Martinborough**
★

This vineyard was planted in 1992 by Graham and Daryl Margrain, who produced their first wine in 1995. In January 2000, the Margrains purchased the old Chifney vineyard. Margrain makes one of New Zealand's highest award-winning Gewürztraminers (again, by New World norms), but Pinot Noir is the better wine.

✓ *Chardonnay • Gewürztraminer • Pinot Noir • Riesling* (Botrytis Selection)

## MARTINBOROUGH VINEYARDS
**Martinborough**
★★

This winery's reputation was established by winemaker Larry McKenna, but his successor, Claire Mulholland (ex-Gibbston Valley), has proved more than a match.

✓ *Chardonnay • Pinot Noir* (Reserve) • *Riesling* (Jackson Block, Late Harvest)

## MATAKANA ESTATE
**Auckland**
☆

The quality at Matakana's most successful winery has been steadily improving since 2001. Wines are also sold under the Goldridge Estate label.

✓ *Chardonnay* (Goldridge Premium Reserve) • *Pinot Gris* (Matakana)

## MATARIKI
**Hawke's Bay**
★★☆

Although owners John and Rosemary O'Connor planted this vineyard as long ago as 1981, they did not start making and selling wines until 1997. Their mission statement is to produce "fruit-driven wines of elegance and complexity" using a "hands-off" approach to viticulture, and a "hands-on" approach in the winery. It has proved to be a very successful philosophy.

✓ *Chardonnay • Classic red blend* (Quintology) • *Merlot • Sauvignon Blanc • Syrah*

## MATAWHERO WINES
**Gisborne**
☆

Owner Denis Irwin was going to quit a few years ago, but ended up selling just half of his vineyards and refocusing his operation entirely on Bordeaux and Burgundy varieties. Gewürztraminer used to be his most consistent wine, and many believed it was New Zealand's finest example of that grape. But that was a reputation built on success at international competitions in the 1970s, when expectations were very different. I will not mourn the fact that Denis has sold his Gewürztraminer vineyards. However, if he wanted to reinvent himself as a specialist in Bordeaux grapes, why not move to Hawke's Bay? It is because Denis Irwin never takes the easiest route. So why change now? He has always cropped at a low level, hand-harvested, and used natural yeasts to express the individual *terroir* of his product long before they became fashionable. Occasionally this has produced something stunning, but the results have been inconsistent, which is why I cannot recommend anything specific. You will have to suck it and see, and sometimes you will be very pleased.

## MATUA VALLEY
**Waimauku**
★★

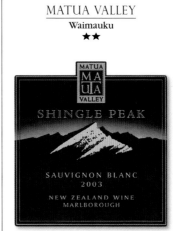

Owned by Beringer Blass since 2001, Matua Valley is located northwest of Auckland, but produces wine mainly from three other regions: Hawke's Bay, Gisborne, and Marlborough. This is a very large producer, with a high-tech winery that regularly produces a range of fine, expressive wines that are a pleasure to drink. The Ararimu label is reserved for Matua Valley's very best wines. At the other end of the price spectrum, the Settler Series concentrates on exceptional value, fruit-driven, entry-level wines. The Innovator series consists of commercial volumes of experimental wines. Excellent Marlborough wines are sold under the Shingle Peak label, and high quality, highly individual wines from the Ngatarawa triangle are sold under the Matheson Vineyard label.

✓ *Chardonnay* (Ararimu, Judd Estate) • *Classic red blend* (Ararimu Merlot-Cabernet Sauvignon) • *Grenache* (Innovator) • *Merlot* (Bullrush) • *Muscat* (Late Harvest) •

*Pinot Noir* (Wairarapa) • *Sauvignon Blanc* (Matheson Vineyard, Shingle Peak) • *Syrah* (Matheson Vineyard)

## DOMAINE GEORGE MICHEL
**Hawke's Bay**
★♥

Fine quality Chardonnay from a Beaujolais grower who now lives in New Zealand. There is also good Sauvignon and fairish Pinot Noir.

✓ *Chardonnay*

## MILLS REEF
**Hawke's Bay**
★★☆

Deliciously rich, fruity whites, and some stunning reds produced by father-and-son team Paddy and Tim Preston. Elspeth Preston, Paddy's mother, passed away in 2003 at the ripe old age of 94.

✓ *Classic red blend* (Elspeth) • *Malbec* (Elspeth) • *Merlot* (Elspeth) • *Syrah* (Elspeth)

## THE MILLTON VINEYARD
**Gisborne**
★❽

This biodynamic producer is justly famous for its award-winning, lightly botrytized, medium-sweet Opou Riesling. It also produces a stylish, barrel-fermented Chardonnay, and is appreciated locally for Chenin Blanc.

✓ *Chardonnay* (Essencia, Opou Vineyards) • *Chenin Blanc* (Te Arai) • *Pinot Noir* (Clos de Ste Anne)

## MISSION ESTATE WINERY
**Taradale**
★♥

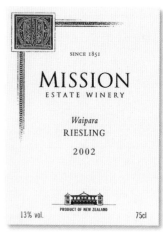

From a wine perspective, the Society of Mary fell into a rut until very recently, which is understandable considering it has been making wine here for more than 150 years. Now things are on the move, the quality is improving, and the best wines are extremely good value.

✓ *Cabernet Sauvignon* (Reserve)

• *Chardonnay* (Reserve) •
*Riesling*

## MORTON ESTATE
### Bay of Plenty
★✫

Well known for its white wines, particularly Chardonnay, and especially Black Label and the top-of-the-line Coniglio, Morton Estate also produces some great red wines. Black Label is the premium line, but the quality of White Label wines is not to be sniffed at. Cheaper wines are sold under the Mill Road brand.

✓ *Classic red blend* (Black Label Merlot-Cabernet, White Label, The Mercure) • *Chardonnay* (Black Label, Coniglio, Riverview) • *Sauvignon Blanc* (Stone Creek, White Label, Marlborough) • *Sparkling wine* (Black Label)

## MT. DIFFICULTY
### Central Otago
★

With no fewer than six vineyards and a heap of experience in South Africa, Italy, and Oregon, a lot is expected from father-and-son team Robin and Matt Dicey. At the time of writing, Matt Dicey was also

making wine for Alexandra Wine Company, Bannock Brae, and Mount Michael.

✓ *Pinot Noir*

## MOUNT EDWARD
### Central Otago
★

Owner-winemaker Alan Brady was the original proprietor of Gibbston Valley, where he was the first person to plant grapes in what is now the viticultural boom area of southern Central Otago. After selling his interest in Gibbston Valley, Brady set up this far smaller operation down the road, where he concentrates on producing rich, elegant Pinot Noir.

✓ *Pinot Noir*

## MOUNT RILEY
### Marlborough
★✫♥

This fast-expanding, fast-improving, award-winning winery has 250 acres (100 hectares) of vines spread over six vineyards, including the top-performing Seventeen Valley south of Blenheim.

✓ *Chardonnay* (Seventeen Valley) • *Pinot Noir* (Seventeen Valley) • *Sauvignon Blanc*

## MOUNTFORD
### Marlborough
★

Owners Michael and Buffy Eaton are attracting much well-deserved praise for the Pinot Noir and Chardonnay produced by their blind Taiwanese winemaker, Chung Pin Lin.

✓ *Pinot Noir*

## MUDDY WATER
### Waipara
★✫

Waipara is Maori for "muddy water," but there is nothing murky about the pure fruit in these wines. Belinda Gould's wines include Pinotage and the world's most southerly Syrah.

✓ *Chardonnay* • *Riesling* (James Hardwick, Unplugged)

## MURDOCH JAMES
### Martinborough
★

An up-and-coming, organic Martinborough producer, which now incorporates the old Blue Rock vineyard. An expanding range of wines includes Syrah and a rare, pure varietal Pinot Meunier. However, the 2003 Sauvignon Blanc was so green, it was mean!

✓ *Pinot Noir* (Fraser)

## NAUTILUS
### Marlborough
★

Owned by the Australian Yalumba group, Nautilus is improving on all fronts. It has invested heavily in developing its Pinot Noir program, which is showing progress, but the rich, ripe, Sauvignon Blanc is still its number one wine. Wines are also sold under the Twin Islands second label.

✓ *Pinot Gris* • *Pinot Noir* • *Sauvignon Blanc* • *Sparkling wine* (Marlborough Brut)

## NEUDORF VINEYARDS
### Nelson
★★

I have always enjoyed Tim and Judy Finn's creamy, Burgundian-style wines—particularly the Pinot Noir, which now benefits from its own winery. New vineyards should increase production by 50 percent.

✓ *Chardonnay* (Moutere) • *Pinot Gris* (Moutere) • *Pinot Noir* (Moutere) • *Riesling* (Dry Moutere, Late Harvest Moutere) • *Sauvignon Blanc*

## MONTANA WINERIES
### Auckland, Gisborne, Hawke's Bay, and Marlborough
★★♥

Although purchased by Allied-Domecq in 2001, and technically renamed Allied-Domecq Wines New Zealand in 2004, it is extremely doubtful that it will ever be known as anything other than Montana Wines. The company owns 7,400 acres (3,000 hectares) of vines, and accounts for 55 percent of all New Zealand's wines, making it the largest wine producer in the country, yet remarkable quality and consistency exist at all price points. Church Road is Montana's high-tech Hawke's Bay boutique winery, producing wines that combine the restrained exuberance of cool-climate New World fruit with the classic Old World structure. The top wine produced at Church Road is "Tom," Montana's icon red wine.

Corbans has been consumed, and is little more than just another label, but the wines are nonetheless well made, representing excellent value. Although Cooks swallowed Corbans in 1987, it no longer exists as a brand, even though its prey still does.

The only mistake made by Montana is one that other New Zealand wine producers have also made in recent years, and that is to create an uncertainty of origin for some of its lesser brands: Copperfields, Jackman Ridge, Murray Ridge, Riverlands, Robard & Butler, and Timara. Another label, Longridge, is described by Montana as "one of New Zealand's classic boutique wine ranges," yet the wines are often multi-regional blends. There's nothing wrong with that, but it is hardly the definition of a boutique winery, especially in years when yields are

**BRANCOTT WINERY**
*Montana's Brancott Winery was the first established in Marlborough, and opened in 1976.*

**KAITUNA**
*Wetlands neighbour the Kaituna vineyard, planted as recently as 2000 at the northern end of the Wairau Valley.*

low, and some Longridge wines are more than 50 percent Chilean! All duly declared, but not boutique, not classic, and not New Zealand. Saints is another mishmash brand, with some regional varietals, a pure imported Shiraz, and a multinational Cabernet Sauvignon-Merlot. Oaklands is a cask wine (bag-in-the-box) brand, which was relaunched as a varietal cask wine range in 2002, and includes imported wines.

Other Montana brands include Aquila (sweet, carbonated bubbly), Azure Bay, Bernadino (sweet, carbonated, multinational bubbly), Blenheimer, Brightstone, Cellarmans, Chardon (sweet, carbonated, multinational, low-alcohol), Chasseur, Country, Diva (*cuve close* sparkling), Emerald Peak, Huntaway, Italiano (sweet, carbonated, multinational, low-alcohol), Liebestraum, Lindauer, Montel, Oaklands, Ridge Estate, Riverlea, St. Arnaud, Seven Oaks, Sun Country, Velluto Rosso, Verde, Vineyard, Virtu, Waimanu, and Wohnsiedler. Ironically, since Allied-Domecq has purchased Montana, it is committed to selling Deutz Montana sparkling wines, although it owns Mumm and Perrier-Jouët!

✓ *Classic red blend* (Church Road, Tom) • *Cabernet Sauvignon* ("F" Fairhall, Marlborough) • *Chardonnay* (Church Road, Marlborough, "O" Ormand Estate, "R" Renwick Estate) • *Corbans* (Private Bin, Cottage Block) • *Gewürztraminer* ("P" Patutahi) • *Merlot* • *Pinot Noir* (Reserve, "T" Terraces) • *Riesling* (Reserve, Stoneleigh) • *Sauvignon Blanc* ("B" Brancott, Marlborough Reserve, Stoneleigh) • *Sémillon* (Virtu Noble) • *Sparkling Wines* (all Deutz *cuvées*, Lindauer Special Reserve)

## NGA WAKA VINEYARD
### Martinborough
### ★★

This is a small winery producing wines that boast intense, crisp fruit. All are now sealed by screwcap.

 *Riesling • Sauvignon Blanc*

## NGATARAWA WINES
### Hawke's Bay
### ★★

Founded by the Glazebrook family and Alwyn Corban in 1981. The Glazebrooks sold up in 1999, and Alwyn's cousin Brian Corban joined the company. This is a quality-conscious Hawke's Bay winery making its mark with distinctive red wines. But with the exception of Alwyn Riesling and Glazebrook Chardonnay, its whites are so understated that their subtlety is lost on me. Second wines are sold under the Stables brand.

 *Cabernet • Merlot* (Glazebrook) • *Chardonnay* (Glazebrook) • *Riesling* (Alwyn)

## NO. 1 FAMILY ESTATE
### Marlborough
### ★★

This brand is the result of Daniel Le Brun being unable to market wine under his own name for three years following the severing, in 1996, of his ties with Cellier Le Brun. In 1999, three years to the day after the split, Daniel cheekily opened up Le Brun Family Estate (since renamed No.1 Family Estate) around the corner. He produces three sparkling wines: Cuvée No.1 (nonvintage *blanc de blancs*), Cuvée Number Eight (nonvintage classic blend), and Cuvée Virginie (vintage classic blend).

 *Cuvée Number Eight*

## NOBILO
### Auckland
### ★

So much change in so little time. This was already a large wine producer before it purchased Selaks in 1998. That deal brought with it substantial additional vineyards, and the new Drylands winery in Marlborough, allowing Nobilo both to increase production and to develop its premium wine range. A new publicly listed company was formed, attracting investment from Australian giant BRL Hardy. The Aussies liked what they saw, invested more in the company, then effectively took it over in 2000, when the Nobilo family exchanged its remaining shareholding in the old family firm for shares in BRL Hardy (and did very nicely out of that when BRL Hardy was itself taken over by Constellation Brands in 2003). Nobilo is now the second-largest wine producer in New Zealand. Nobilo's Icon has replaced Dixon Vineyard as the company's best Chardonnay. There is also an exciting Icon Marlborough Sauvignon Blanc, which is a welcome addition to the basic, but consistently excellent, Marlborough Sauvignon Blanc. Nobilo needs to improve its red wines, but the premium Icon range is obviously the one to watch. Other labels include Fall Harvest, Fernleaf, and the new Station Road brand.

 *Chardonnay* (Icon) • *Sauvignon Blanc* (Marlborough, Icon)

## OKAHU ESTATE
### Northland
### ★

Established in 1984, Okahu Estate has started to earn more awards in recent years, so Monty Knight must be doing something right. Located 2 miles (3.5 kilometers) from Kaitaia on the road to Ahipara, at the southern end of the Ninety Mile Beach, this is the most northerly vineyard in New Zealand.

 *Cabernet* (Kaz) • *Chardonnay* (Clifton Proprietor's Reserve)

## OLSSENS
### Central Otago
### ★★

A Bannockburn star in the making, with complex Pinot Noir and a Sauvignon Blanc that is way too delicious for this far south!

 *Pinot Noir* (Sleepjack Creek)

## OMAKA SPRINGS
### Marlborough
### ★🅥

This estate is owned by Geoff and Robina Jensen, who were pioneers of the New Zealand olive industry, having planted 2,500 olive trees in 23 different varieties at Omaka Springs before venturing into the wine industry. They produce inexpensive, unpretentious wines from some 150 acres (60 hectares) of vineyards.

 *Sauvignon Blanc*

## PALLISER ESTATE
### Martinborough
### ★★🅥

This is a substantial producer of consistently classy wines. Even those under second label Pencarrow show some finesse.

 *Chardonnay* (including Pencarrow) *Pinot Gris • Pinot Noir • Riesling • Sauvignon Blanc* (including Pencarrow)

## C. J. PASK
### Hawke's Bay
### ★★

Kate Radburnd continues to churn out a wide range of classic quality, richly flavored wines. There are also good value, inexpensive wines sold under the Roy's Hill label.

 *Classic red blend* (Declaration, Gimblett Road Cabernet-Merlot) • *Chardonnay* (Gimblett Road) • *Merlot* (Gimblett Road Reserve, Reserve) • *Syrah* (Reserve)

## PEGASUS BAY
### Waipara
### ★★

The Donaldson family operate a very fine winery and restaurant south of Waipara. The style of wine produced is richly flavored with a classic structure.

 *Chardonnay* (Finale) • *Classic red blend* (Cabernet-Merlot) • *Pinot Noir* (especially Prima Donna) • *Riesling* (Aria) • *Classic white blend* (Sauvignon-Sémillon)

## PENINSULA ESTATE
### Waiheke Island
### ★

Brave or stupid, there is no doubting the viticultural risk taken by Doug Hamilton in planting this Cabernet-blend vineyard. It sticks out into the Pacific, exposed to salt-bearing sea breezes on three sides.

 *Classic red blend* (Island Red) • *Syrah* (Zeno)

## PEREGRINE
### Central Otago
### ★

Owned by Greg Hay, who helped his brother Rob establish Chard Farm before setting out on his own. Peregrine produces wines from grapes grown on the Wentworth Estates, under the banner "Wines with Altitude." Wentworth was set up as a cost-effective means of farming 75 acres (30 hectares) in an area close to Queenstown, where the price of land is high. It effectively involves selling off plots of land to build houses surrounded by vines, which are then managed by Wentworth. It provides the householder with an income from the meticulously manicured vines around it, and Peregrine with the grapes it needs.

 *Pinot Noir • Riesling*

## PROVIDENCE
### Matakana
### ★

This is a small, export-oriented, red wine specialist, whose wine often costs an arm and a leg, but the price can vary considerably from country to country.

 *Classic red blend* (Merlot-Cabernet Franc-Malbec)

## QUARTZ REEF
### Central Otago
### ★★

This estate is owned by Rudi Bauer and Clotilde Chauvet (who also makes Champagne in Rilly-la-Montagne). Rudi and Clotilde met at Rippon in the early 1990s, when Rudi was the winemaker. Clotilde took over as Rippon's winemaker when Rudi moved south, but they kept in touch, eventually establishing Quartz Reef together in 1996. They have pioneered vineyards at Bendigo and produce excellent Pinot Noir and sparkling wine. Rudi made the wines for Two Paddocks until the Central Otago Wine Company was set up, and Dean Shaw (who worked for Rudi at Rippon) took over. Rudi's consultancy work has gradually given way as Quartz Reef has taken off, but at the time of writing he was still making wines for Northburn, Pisa Range, and Rockburn.

 *Pinot Noir* (Reserve) • *Sparkling wine*

## RICHMOND PLAINS
### Nelson
### ★🅞

Also known as Holmes Brothers, this was the first vineyard on South Island to go organic.

 *Sauvignon Blanc* (Marlborough)

## RIPPON
### Wanaka
### ★

In 1974, against all advice, Lois and Rolfe Mills chose one of the most beautiful areas in the world to grow vines. They have certainly succeeded, although it took until 1989 to make their first commercial wine. Rippon is biodynamic, but not certified as such.

✓ *Pinot Noir • Riesling*

## ROCKBURN
### Central Otago
⭒

Greg Hay of Peregrine is the viticulturist, and Rudi Bauer of Quartz Reef the winemaker.

✓ *Pinot Noir*

## RONGOPAI WINES
### Te Kauwhata
⭒

The original Rongopai winery was established in 1932 by the Gordon family, and this continued until the death of Lou Gordon in 1954. The winery fell into disrepair until 1982, when it was resurrected by Dr. Rainer Eschenbruch and Tom Van Dam from the nearby Te Kauwhata Viticultural Research Station. They produced the first new Rongopai wines in 1985, attracting instant acclaim for their botrytized wines. But Eschenbruch left in 1993, and Van Dam retired in 2001. The current owner, Scottish businessman Derek Reid, had invested in Rongopai since 1991. In 1995, he purchased the old viticultural research station, which has since become Rongopai's winery. Reid's Rongopai is no longer confined to producing stickies, although they still excel. The range includes dry whites, reds, and a port style. The only wine not produced is sparkling, although I wonder if the winemaker, Emmanuel Bollinger, has thought of bringing one out under his own label.

✓ *Chardonnay* (Ultimo) • *Dessert wine* (Ultimo Late Harvest)

## SACRED HILL
### Hawke's Bay
★⭒

Since Sacred Hill produced its first wine in 1986, its reputation has been built on its vineyards in the Dartmoor Valley hills of Hawke's Bay. In 2001, the owners purchased Cairnbrae in Marlborough, and in addition to maintaining that brand, its vineyards now contribute to Sacred Hill's growing prestige, particularly its vibrantly fresh Sauvignon Blanc. Less expensive, early-drinking wines are sold under the Whitecliff label.

✓ *Chardonnay* (Rifleman's) • *Classic red blend* (Helmsman) • *Merlot* (Brokenstone) • *Riesling* (Halo Botrytis) • *Sauvignon Blanc* (Marlborough)

## SAINT CLAIR
### Marlborough
★★Ⓥ

This is a large vineyard that consistently produces fresh, crisp, expressive whites, including one of

New Zealand's best Sauvignon Blancs. There is also a rich, deliciously fresh, deep-flavored, fruit-driven Merlot.

✓ *Chardonnay* (Omaka) • *Merlot* (Reserve) • *Riesling* • *Sauvignon Blanc*

## ST. HELENA
### Canterbury
⭒

The nation's oldest Pinot Noir vines are found at St. Helena's vineyard near the Waimakirri River, which explains why this winery used to be one of New Zealand's leading Pinot Noir exponents. It was this winery that put Canterbury Pinot Noir on the map, with its legendary 1982 vintage. Those days are long gone, however. Although St. Helena occasionally manages to produce excellent wines from this variety under the Reserve label, the consistency is no longer there.

✓ *Pinot Noir* (Reserve)

## ST. JÉRÔME
### Henderson
★

The Ozich brothers have a well-deserved reputation for their Bordeaux-style blend, Matuka.

✓ *Classic red blend* (Matuka)

## DANIEL SCHUSTER
### Canterbury
★⭒

Danny Schuster co-authored *Grape Growing & Winemaking, A Handbook for Cool Climates* (1973), which has encouraged many New Zealanders to give it a go.

✓ *Chardonnay* (Omihi Hills) • *Pinot Noir* (Omihi Hills)

## ALLAN SCOTT
### Marlborough
★⭒

Allan Scott established Marlborough's very first vineyard in 1973, while working for Montana. He later became Corbans' chief viticulturist, but left to set up his own business in 1989. He produces a good, but not special, Pinot Noir, and has been persevering with a sparkling wine that frankly needs more finesse. But Scott truly excels at still white wines, which seem to have more fruit than wines from surrounding vineyards, particularly his Riesling.

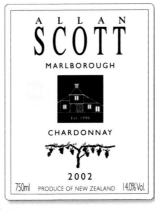

✓ *Chardonnay • Riesling • Sauvignon Blanc*

## SEIFRIED ESTATE
### Nelson
★⭒Ⓥ

Hermann Seifried's original winery and 26-acre (10.5-hectare) vineyard now belong to Amanda and Greg Day, who purchased and renamed it Kahurangi Estate in 1998. Two years earlier, the Seifried family had opened a brand new winery in closer proximity to most of its other vineyards, which now total 395 acres (160 hectares). Seifried always was Nelson's biggest wine producer, and still is. Consumers outside New Zealand will know these wines as Redwood Valley. Seifried is best for white wines, especially the superb botrytized Riesling and one of this country's better dry Rieslings.

✓ *Chardonnay* (Old Coach Road) • *Pinot Noir • Riesling* (Botrytis Dry Riesling)

## SELAKS
### Auckland
★★Ⓥ

This has been the award-winning division of the Nobilo group since it was taken over by the group in 1998. Selaks continues to produce fine quality, stylish wines by the barrel-load, with its red wines now notching up as many successes as its whites.

✓ *Chardonnay* (Founders Reserve, Premium Selection) • *Merlot* (Founders Reserve) • *Riesling* (Founders Reserve Noble) • *Sauvignon Blanc* (Premium Selection) • *Syrah* (Founders Reserve)

## SERESIN
### Marlborough
★⭒Ⓞ

The vines are all hand-tended, and some wines are fermented with wild yeasts. Winemaker Brian Bicknell is known for his flying winemaker exploits, but nothing he has made under contract compares with the wines from Seresin, some of which rank among the very best from Marlborough. The Seresin vineyard is certified organic. The Tatou and Raupo Creek vineyards were in the process of conversion at the time of writing, after which there are plans to go fully biodynamic. Future impetus will be toward polishing up the already impressive Pinot Noir.

✓ *Chardonnay* (Reserve) • *Pinot Gris • Pinot Noir • Riesling • Sauvignon Blanc* (Marama)

## SHERWOOD ESTATE
### Canterbury
⭒

Confusingly, wines solely from Sherwood Estate's own vineyards are sold under the Clearwater Vineyards label, while those under the Sherwood Estate label include purchased fruit. Other labels include Stratum, an entry-level range.

✓ *Sauvignon Blanc*

## SILENI
### Hawke's Bay
★★Ⓥ

Since crushing its first crop in 1998, this winery has quickly built up a reputation for wines of style and finesse. Wines in the EV range are made only in exceptional vintages, while those in the Estate Selection are premium wines from Sileni's own vineyards. Entry-level wines are sold under the Cellar Selection label, and often represent exceptional value.

✓ *Chardonnay* (Estate Selection) • *Classic red blend* (Estate Selection Merlot-Cabernets) • *Merlot* (EV) • *Sémillon* (Estate Selection)

## SLEEPING DOGS
### Central Otago
★⭒

Owned by film director Roger Donaldson, whose earliest work, *Sleeping Dogs* (1977), was the cornerstone of the New Zealand film industry. It gave his friend Sam Neill his first screen role. Donaldson's vineyard was the original other half of Two Paddocks, which he and Neill planted, but they are entirely separate operations. However, they both share the same winemaker—Dean Shaw.

✓ *Pinot Noir*

## SOLJANS
### Auckland
★

Tony Soljans can sometimes go over the top with the amount of VA lift he gives to the fruit in his wines, but it works well when it is understated.

✓ *Cabernet-Merlot* (Estate) • *Port-style wine* (10-Year-Old Tawny)

## SPENCER HILL
### Nelson
★

This estate was established in the Upper Moutere area in 1992 by Philip and Sheryl Jones, whose first release was in 1994. Production in the initial years was tiny, with no wine whatsoever made in 1999. Production was moved to its current location in the Coastal Ridge, north of Nelson, in 2000. Other labels include Mariner Vineyards (from own vineyards plus purchased fruit), and Tasman Bay.

✓ *Chardonnay* • *Pinot Noir* • *Sauvignon Blanc* (Tasman Bay)

## SPY VALLEY
### Marlborough
★❶

Owned by the Johnson family, Spy Valley is a name to watch out for. The name has its origins in the cold war: Spy Valley is what the locals have called the Waihopai Valley since the Americans built a listening station there. The grapes come from the 360-acre (145-hectare) Johnson Estate, which might sound vast for a relatively new winery, but the Johnsons have been growing for other wineries since 1992. Fresh, crisp, vibrantly fruity Sauvignon Blanc; sweet, ripe Pinot Noir; and classy Riesling are the best so far.

✓ *Chardonnay* • *Pinot Noir* • *Riesling* (Dry) • *Sauvignon Blanc*

## STAETE LANDT
### Marlborough
★❶

From the beginning (in 1997), Ruud Maasdam and Dorien Vermaas have aimed to produce single-vineyard wines. All, in fact, come from the same 52-acre (21-hectare) vineyard but they have been selected on a parcel-by-parcel basis according to which combination of variety and rootstock grows best. If there are differences, they are effectively what the Burgundians would call *climats* (individual block or plots), and it would be a good idea to name them.

✓ *Pinot Noir* • *Sauvignon Blanc*

## STONECROFT
### Hawke's Bay
★

Alan Limmer pioneered Syrah in New Zealand, but his has lacked the

lush character of other, more successful Syrahs that have been released of late. New plantations might re-energize this wine in the future. Meanwhile, Limmer makes better Chardonnay, and a classic red blend (Cabernet-Syrah-Merlot) called Ruhani.

✓ *Chardonnay* • *Classic red blend* (Ruhani)

## STONYRIDGE
### Waiheke Island
★★★

Since 1985, Stephen White has produced one of New Zealand's truly great red wines, Larose, which sells out within hours of being offered *en primeur* each year.

✓ *Classic red blend* (Larose)

## STRATFORD WINES
### Marlborough
★★

This is the personal label of Margrain's winemaker, Strat Canning, who first produced these wines in 1997. His best wine is, without doubt, Pinot Noir, but Strat's wonderfully racy Riesling should not be overlooked.

✓ *Chardonnay* • *Pinot Noir* • *Riesling*

## TE AWA
### Hawke's Bay
★

Sold in December 2002 to New York investment manager Julian Robertson and Napa Valley vineyard owner Reg Oliver (*see* Dry River), Te Awa remains under the same day-to-day control, with viticulturist Gus Lawson in overall charge. Winemaker Jenny Dobson worked at Domaine Dujac in Burgundy for 18 months before going over to the opposition—Bordeaux—where she was appointed winemaker at Château Sénéjac. Zone 10 and Boundary are both ★★ wines. Entry-level wines are sold under the Longlands label.

✓ *Cabernet Sauvignon* (Zone 10) • *Classic red blend* (Boundary)

## TE KAIRANGA
### Martinborough
★★

With 250 acres (100 hectares) under vine, Te Kairanga is no boutique winery, but its rich, creamy Pinot Noir is the sort of impressive quality

expected from the smallest, top-performing producer. Second label wines are sold under the Castlepoint brand.

✓ *Chardonnay* • *Pinot Noir* • *Syrah*

## TE MATA
### Hawke's Bay
★★

Te Mata Estate was purchased in 1978 by John Buck, who with the help of winemaker Peter Cowley has fashioned two of the country's greatest red wines, Awatea and Coleraine. However, in some years Awatea and/or Coleraine are too attenuated to deserve top billing. If John and Peter believe in their *terroir*, they should acknowledge that it is not possible for the vineyard to provide a top class wine every year, and declassify when necessary. Other labels include the entry-level Rymer's Change range.

✓ *Chardonnay* (Castle Hill, Elston) • *Classic red blend* (Awatea, Coleraine, Woodthorpe Syrah-Viognier) • *Sauvignon Blanc* (Cape Crest, Castle Hill) • *Syrah* (Bullnose) • *Viognier* (Woodthorpe)

## TE MOTU
### Waiheke Island
★

The Te Motu vineyard is just 60 meters from Stonyridge Vineyard, where Larose, one of New Zealand's true icon wines is produced. Currently just one style is marketed, a Cabernet-Merlot (which also includes a little Cabernet Franc and Malbec), with the same style appearing under the second label (Dunleavy).

✓ *Classic red blend* (Te Motu)

## TE WHARE RA
### Marlborough
★

In 1979, Te Whare Ra (Maori for "the house in the Sun") became the first Marlborough vineyard to be planted after Montana had paved the way. The present owners are Jason and Anna Flowerday. Under previous owners, Te Whare Ra was known principally for stickies and Gewürztraminer, but botrytized wines are now produced less often, and the Gewürztraminer has been a typical New World rose-petal-perfumed wimp. I hope the new owners know what a real Gewürztraminer tastes like. In the meantime, try the Sarah Jennings

blend of Cabernet Franc, Malbec, Merlot, and Cabernet Sauvignon. And look out for the 2004 inaugural vintage of Pinot Noir.

✓ *Classic red blend* (Sarah Jennings) • *Sémillon* (Noble)

## TORLESSE
### Waipara
★

Established in 1987 by 20-odd grower-suppliers, Torlesse soon went into receivership. It reemerged in 1990 as a new company that is now owned by several shareholders, also with vineyards dotted over Waipara. The spread of the vineyards should give winemakers Kym Rayner and Paul Hewett the opportunity to create a range of individual *terroir*-based wines, which is precisely their intention. So, watch this space. In the meantime, try the deliciously rich Sauvignon Blanc.

✓ *Sauvignon Blanc*

## TRINITY HILL
### Hawke's Bay
★★

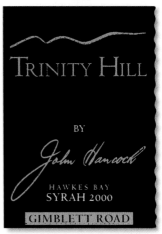

The trinity here consists of managing director John Hancock, who helped establish Morton Estate's reputation before setting up Trinity Hill; winemaker Warren Gibson, who assisted Hancock at Morton Estate; and viticulturist Michael Bell, who is a Gimblett Gravels expert, having tended the famed Irongate vineyard. The great thing about Hancock is that he insists on making beautiful wines even from grapes he dislikes, such as Sauvignon Blanc. However, Trinity Hill's most outstanding wines so far are Merlot and Syrah. The worst wine I could find at Trinity Hill was the High Country Pinot Noir, and that's a glugging wine full of strawberry fruit. The only thing I could fault it on was its straightforward, upfront, easy-drinking quality.

✓ *Cabernet Sauvignon* (Gimblett Road) • *Classic red blend* (Gimblett Road Cabernet Sauvignon-Merlot, Shepherds Croft Cabernet Sauvignon-Merlot, Shepherds Croft Merlot-CabernetFranc-Syrah) • *Merlot*

(Gimblett Road) • *Riesling* (Wairarapa) • *Roussanne* • *Syrah* (Gimblett Road) • *Tempranillo*

## TWO PADDOCKS
### Gibbston Valley
★★☆

This estate is owned by actor Sam Neill, who lives in Central Otago and loves Pinot Noir. The original 5-acre (2-hectare) Two Paddocks on the Gibbston Back Road is so called because it was one of two neighboring paddocks planted by Neill and friend Roger Donaldson in 1993. Donaldson has his own label (Sleeping Dogs), while Neill retains the name for the overall business, although this vineyard is now known as One Paddock. In 1998, Neill purchased Alex Paddocks in the Earnscleugh Valley, Alexandra, which is a warmer site, where 7 acres (3 hectares) have been planted. Alex Paddocks yielded its first crop in 2001, enabling the first truly *two-paddock* Two Paddocks to be produced that year. Then, in 2002, winemaker Dean Shaw made the stunning single-vineyard The Last Chance Pinot Noir. The latest addition has been Redbanks Paddock, also in the Earnscleugh Valley, but significantly warmer still. With potentially 60 acres (25 hectares) of vineyards, this is Neill's most ambitious project so far. Just a few acres have been planted, including a little Riesling, and he intends to expand the operation only as and when needs be. Since 2002, a soft, easy-drinking blend of all three paddocks has been produced under the Picnic Pinot Noir label.

✓ *Pinot Noir* (The Last Chance)

## UNISON VINEYARD
### Hawke's Bay
★★

A winery on the way up, Unison's high density, Gimblett Gravels vineyard produces just two reds, both of which blend Merlot, Cabernet Sauvignon, and Syrah. One is simply called Unison, the other Unison Selection. Both are brilliant. Now there is a refreshing rosé from the same varieties.

✓ *Classic red blend* (Unison, Unison Selection)

## VALLI
### Central Otago
★

This is the own label of Gibbston Valley's winemaker, Grant Taylor. It is named after a distant relative who emigrated to New Zealand in the 19th century. Taylor has two small vineyards at his disposal, one in Gibbston Valley, which is supposed to be better in cooler vintages, the other in Bannockburn, which excels in warmer years.

✓ *Pinot Noir* (Bannockburn Vineyard)

## VAVASOUR
### Marlborough
★★☆

Situated south of Blenheim, in the Awatere Valley, where the intense sun and dry winds are responsible for the intense fruit flavor of these well-structured wines. Excellent value wines are also sold under the Dashwood label.

✓ *Chardonnay* • *Pinot Noir* • *Sauvignon Blanc*

## VIDAL
### Hawke's Bay
★★☆ⓥ

Vidal was founded by a Spaniard, Anthony Vidal, but is now owned by George Fistonich, the son of a Dalmatian immigrant and proprietor of Villa Maria. This winery consistently produces some of the most exciting red wines in the Hawke's Bay area. The whites often lack finesse, although they are usually very easy to drink, and Vidal produces one of New Zealand's better Gewürztraminers.

✓ *Classic red blend* (Reserve Merlot-Cabernet Sauvignon) • *Cabernet Sauvignon* (Joseph Soler, Reserve) • *Chardonnay* (Reserve) • *Sauvignon Blanc* (Estate) • *Syrah* (Soler)

## VILLA MARIA
### Auckland
★★ⓥ

New Zealand's best all-around wine producer is the country's third-largest (after Montana and Nobilo), and the only one of the three that is still New Zealand owned. Villa Maria has a vast range of wines that are all beautifully crafted to enhance fruit and finesse. Where oak is used, the touch is light and impeccably integrated. For such a large company to have the level of quality and consistency that Villa Maria has is pretty remarkable. But some of the kudos must go to Montana for chasing Villa Maria on

quality and value at all price points, despite its production being considerably larger still. The very best Villa Maria wines deserve ★★★☆. Full marks to proprietor George Fistonich, who converted the entire production to screwcap bottling.

✓ *Entire range*

## VINO ALTO
### Auckland
❷

I have not tasted these wines, but I am passing on high praise from Bob Campbell MW and other critics I respect in New Zealand. Any readers who are curious how Italian varieties and styles might work in New Zealand should start at Vino Alto, where Margaret and Enzo Bettio grow, among others, Arneis, Barbera, Corvina, Montepulciano, Nebbiolo, and Sangiovese. The Retico is, apparently, well worth seeking out as an example of a rare Amarone-style wine, made from grapes that have been dried on racks for two months prior to fermentation.

## WAIPARA HILLS
### Canterbury
★ⓥ

An ambitious, young, up-and-coming venture that makes and sells wines from Canterbury and Marlborough, as well as Waipara.

✓ *Riesling*

## WAIPARA SPRINGS
### Waipara
★ⓥ

Owned by the Moore family, who tends the vineyard, and the Grants, who make and sell the wines, Waipara Springs produces a solid range of consistently fine quality wines.

✓ *Chardonnay* (Lightly Oaked) • *Pinot Noir* (Reserve) • *Sauvignon Blanc*

## WAIPARA WEST
### Canterbury
★ⓥ

This winery and vineyard is owned by a partnership called Tutton Sienko Hill. Paul Tutton is a London wine merchant, Olga Sienko is his wife, and Lindsay Hill is his sister-in-law, and the viticulturist who manages the Waipara West vineyard.

✓ *Chardonnay* • *Classic red blend* (Ram Paddock Red) • *Pinot Noir*

## WAIRAU RIVER
### Marlborough
★

Phil and Chris Rose have been growing grapes since 1978. In 1991, they decided to launch their own label, and now take the pick of the crop from their 310 acres (125 hectares) of vines spread over three vineyards. John Belsham (*see* Foxes Island Wines) has been the winemaker from the beginning.

✓ *Pinot Gris* • *Riesling* • *Sauvignon Blanc*

## WEST BROOK
### Auckland
★ⓥ

Founded by Mick Ivicevich in 1937 in what was rural Henderson. The estate was surrounded on all sides by urban sprawl by 2000, when grandson Anthony Ivicevich moved West Brook to its present location in the Ararimu Valley. Top wines are sold under the Blue Ridge label.

✓ *Chardonnay* (Blue Ridge) • *Riesling* (Marlborough) • *Sauvignon Blanc* (Blue Ridge)

## WHITEHAVEN
### Marlborough
★★☆

Sensational Riesling and Sauvignon Blanc, particularly the Single Vineyard Reserve.

✓ *Chardonnay* • *Riesling* • *Sauvignon Blanc*

## CHARLES WIFFEN
### Marlborough
★ⓥ

Charles Wiffen is based at Cheviot in North Canterbury, his vineyards are in Marlborough, and his wines are made in Auckland by Anthony Ivicevich of West Brook. Rieslings have been nothing less than stunning, especially the Late Harvest. Also very good are the Chardonnay and Sauvignon Blanc.

✓ *Chardonnay* • *Riesling* (Late Harvest) • *Sauvignon Blanc*

## WITHER HILLS
### Marlborough
★★☆ⓥ

In 2002, Wither Hills was purchased by Lion Nathan, the brewing giant that owns Australia's Petaluma. The vineyards are in South Island's Marlborough region, but the winery is at Henderson, Auckland, on North Island.

✓ *Chardonnay* • *Pinot Noir* • *Sauvignon Blanc*

# ASIA

*According to globetrotting Asian wine specialist Denis Gastin, there are no fewer than 700 wineries spread among 10 Asian countries. However, China and Japan are by far the most important, and the sheer scale of China's economy has seen that country take over from Japan as Asia's leading wine producer.*

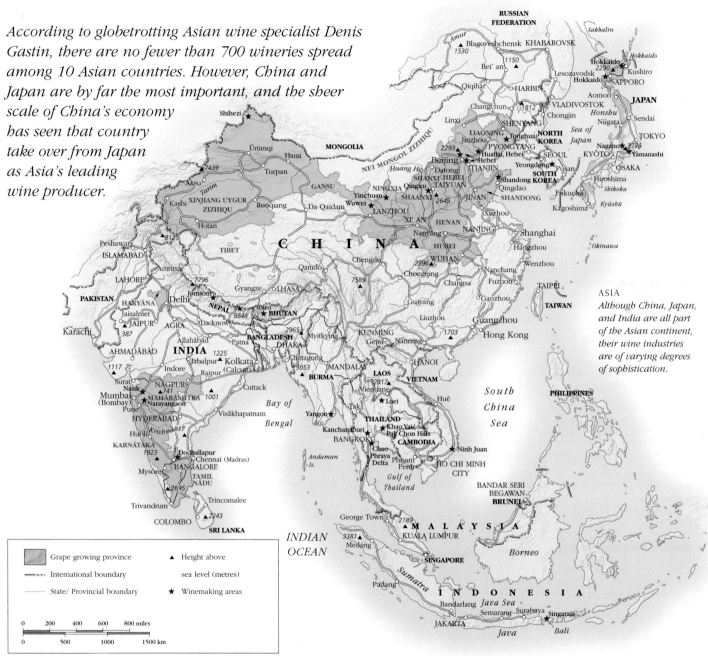

ASIA

*Although China, Japan, and India are all part of the Asian continent, their wine industries are of varying degrees of sophistication.*

**Legend:**

- Grape growing province
- - - - International boundary
- —— State/ Provincial boundary
- ▲ Height above sea level (metres)
- ★ Winemaking areas

0   200   400   600   800 miles
0   500   1000   1500 km

CHINA IS NOW THE SEVENTH-LARGEST wine-producing nation in the world, ahead of Germany, South Africa, Portugal, and Chile. After years of barely drinkable white plonk under labels such as Great Wall, China has started producing serious quality red wines, such as Dragon Seal's Syrah. For some, the most interesting phenomenon throughout Asia is the emergence of wines made from indigenous, non-*vinifera* varieties, but until the producers of these wines establish a consistent quality with international grapes, how are we to know whether a local variety wine is a true rendition?

## BALI

In 1994 Hatten Wines produced a rosé from Alphonse Lavallée table grapes. Local growers allow these grapes to crop as regularly as once a month, thus Hatten Rosé reached its 150th vintage by 2005! Hatten itself grows Chambourcin (on trial) and a Muscat-like variety called Belgia. The latter makes a semisweet, aromatic white wine called Alexandria, which won a bronze medal at the

International Wine and Spirit Competition in the UK in 2003. Its winemaker, French-born Vincent Desplats, also makes two traditional method wines, a rosé called Jepun and a white called Tungjung.

☑ *Hatten Wines* (Alexandria)

## BHUTAN

Taltarni of Victoria, Australia, consults for a vineyard established in the early 1990s at Paro, at an altitude of 7,500 feet (2,300 meters).

## BURMA

Myanmar Vineyard Estate was established in 1998 by Bert Morsbach at Loikaw, but moved in 1999 to Aythaya, where the vines grow on limestone slopes at 4,265 feet (1,300 meters). Varieties include Cabernet Sauvignon, Chenin Blanc, Dornfelder, Muscat, Sauvignon Blanc, Sémillon, Syrah, and Tempranillo. "Tropical" clones of Pinot Noir, Gewürztraminer, Chardonnay, and Barbera are under test. Red, white, and rosé wines are sold under the Aythaya label.

## FACTORS AFFECTING TASTE AND QUALITY

### ✳ LOCATION
One-third of the world!

### ▨ CLIMATE
**China** Vineyards are classified as "humid microthermal cool," a type similar to those of Austria and Hungary, where continental conditions are influenced by great water masses, creating hot, damp summers and very cold, dry winters. **India** Hot, with no real winter. Two harvests a year: one dry, one humid-monsoon (usually avoided). Altitude of Maharashtra and Dodballapur provides a relatively cool climate. **Japan** Extremes of climate: freezing winds in the winter, monsoon rains in the spring and fall, and typhoons in the summer. The temperature drops as one moves northward; humidity rises going southward. The climate of Miyazaki Prefecture on Kyushu, the most southerly of Japan's four main islands, has been likened to that of Florida!

### ◩ ASPECT
**China** Recent plantings have been on well-drained, south-facing slopes to overcome the earlier problem of high water-tables on the flatter sites. **India** Gentle east- and south-facing slopes at an altitude of 2,460ft (750m) in Narayangaon, and 1,980ft (600m) in Nasik and Dodballapur **Japan** In the most important wine area of Honshu Island, the best vineyards are planted on the south-facing valley slopes around Kofu.

### ▦ SOIL
**China** Soils are generally alluvial. **India** Vineyards at Narayangaon are on lime-rich soils, with sandy-clay loam at Nasik, and red-sandy loam at Dodballapur. **Japan** Predominantly acidic soils that are unsuitable for viticulture, except around Kofu, where the soil is gravelly and of volcanic origin.

### ⚏ VITICULTURE AND VINIFICATION
Generally the level of technology in wineries is good, but vineyard yields are too high, and sugar ripeness is seldom achieved—let alone physiological ripeness. In tropical regions, such as Bali, the grape vines never winter, and up to 15 vintages can be harvested. **China** Domestic consumption is increasing at 15 percent per annum, pushing the country's wine industry to the seventh largest in the world. Big, new wineries in the western provinces of Xinjiang, Gansu, and Ningxia are responsible for most of this expansion. Export-orientated wineries are driving quality upward and have had some great success with superpremium wines, such as Dragon Seal's Syrah, but attempts to raise standards across the board are held back by high-yielding varieties that crop up to 650 cases/acre (60 hl/hectare). So-called "Half Wine" (wines cut with water) have been banned in preparation to join OIV (Office International du Vin). **India** Vine training is moving from the Lenz Moser high system to more sophisticated high-trellis systems. **Japan** Recent developments have concentrated on the growing of top European varietals, and although this continues at an increasing pace, attention is also shifting to the Koshu grape. The biggest problem is still rain, which is frequently overcome by covering clusters of grapes with a waxed paper disk that acts as an umbrella, avoiding the rot that would otherwise be rampant. This is, however, a very expensive, labor-intensive operation.

### 🍇 GRAPE VARIETIES
**China** Beichun, Cabernet Franc, Cabernet Sauvignon, Carignan, Chardonnay, Chasan, Chenin Blanc, Cock's Heart, Dragon's Eye (*syn.* Longyan), Gamay, Gewürztraminer, Mare's Nipple, Marsanne, Muscat d'Hambourg, Muscat à Petits Grains, Merlot, Pinot Noir, Rkatsiteli, Saperavi, Sauvignon Blanc, Sémillon, Sylvaner, Syrah, Welschriesling **India** Anab-e-shahi, Arka Kanchan, Arka Shyam, Arkavti, Bangalore Blue, Cabernet Sauvignon, Chardonnay, Karachi Gulabi, Pinot Noir, Ruby Red, Thompson Seedless, Ugni Blanc **Japan** Cabernet Sauvignon, Campbell's Early, Chardonnay, Delaware, Koshu, Merlot, Müller-Thurgau, Muscat Bailey, Riesling, Sémillon **Vietnam** Cardinal

## CHINA

It is assumed that Chinese grape-winemaking (as opposed to rice-winemaking) began in 128 BC, when General Chang planted *vinifera* seeds at the Imperial Palace in Chang An (now Xian), which is 600 miles (1,000 kilometers) south of Beijing. But the first documented proof of wines, rather than vines, comes from AD 674, when a grape variety was sent to Emperor Tai-Tsung by a Turkish people known as the Yagbu. Called Mare's Nipple, this variety had purple grapes, with bunches up to 2 feet (60 centimeters) long, and the wine made from it was described as "fiery."

In 1892, Zhang Bishi, a Chinese businessman, brought cuttings of 10 *vinifera* grape varieties from Europe, and built the Zhang Yu Winery at Yantai in Shandong province. In 1910, a French priest opened a winery in Beijing called Shangyi (now Beijing Friendship Winery), and in 1914, a German company called Melchers set up a winery at Tsingtao (now Quindao) on the Shandong peninsula.

In more recent times, Rémy Martin was brought in to give expert technical assistance to the first Franco-Chinese joint venture. In 1980, this resulted in Dynasty, the first European-style wine produced in China, developed in conjunction with the Tianjin Winery. In 1987, the Pernod-Ricard group created the Dragon Seal brand in association with the Beijing Friendship Winery. This has been more of a success and has achieved much higher standards than Dynasty.

There are 350 wineries in China, with over 100 in the Shandong province alone, but many are small facilities. Most vineyards are either state-owned or cooperatives of several families in the same village. The area under vine has more than doubled since the late 1990s, and currently stands at 880,000 acres (360,000 hectares).

🍷 *Dragon Seal* (Syrah) • *Shanxi Grace Vineyard* (Cabernet Franc)

## INDIA

The vine has been growing in India for more than 6,000 years, and the country now has 113,000 acres (45,700 hectares) of vineyards, but wine production is so small that there are no official statistics. The best-known Indian wine story of modern times concerns self-made Bombay millionaire Sham Chougule. In 1982, Chougule asked Piper-Heidsieck to provide assistance for a project to create fine, traditional method Indian wines. The Champagne firm despatched a young oenologist called Raphael Brisbois, who chose a site at Narayangaon, west of Bombay and north of Pune, and constructed a $4.8-million, high-tech winery set into the side of the Sahyadri Mountains. The first wine exported under the Omar Khayyam label caused a stir in London, not least because few people believed that Chardonnay could be grown in India. I caught a plane and saw the vines with my own eyes. However, Brisbois later confessed that his first *cuvée* was made exclusively from sultana grapes! Although the wine is just as good today as it was then, it has not moved on, while the rest of the world's sparkling wines have. Brisbois has also moved on, and Chougule would be wise to lure him back.

Sula Vineyards is a more promising venture. It was established in 1993 by Rajeev Samant, a Stanford-trained engineer, who left his job in Silicon Valley and set up a 250-acre (100-hectare) vineyard and winery on his family's farm in Nasik. Sament lured Sonoma winemaker Kerry Damskey to India, and hired Rahul Mehrotra, one of Bombay's leading architects, to design his winery. Although Sula was not the first European-style winery on this subcontinent, it has pioneered Sauvignon Blanc and Chenin Blanc, not to mention Indian Blush Zinfandel. Red and sparkling wines are also produced.

However, the most exciting enterprise so far has to be Grover Vineyards, which germinated in 1979, when Kanwal Grover met *champenois* Georges Vesselle. After analyzing soil and weather data from all over India, they selected a site north of Bangalore, and by 1983 experiments had begun on 35 grape varieties. Within six years, this had been narrowed to nine varieties, all French, and in 1992, Grover Vineyards launched its first wine, a Cabernet Sauvignon. By 2004, it had expanded to 120 acres (50 hectares). Abhay Kewadkar, who trained as a winemaker under Brisbois at Indage, joined Grover in 1988. Michel Rolland has been consulting since 1995, and Veuve Clicquot took a small shareholding in 2001.

🍷 *Grover* (Cabernet Sauvignon-Shiraz, La Reserve Cabernet Sauvignon)

## JAPAN

**Wine districts** *Akita, Aomori, Hokkaido Kushiro, Honshu Aichi, Hyogo, Iwate, Kyushu Fukuoka, Nagano (the best area being the Kofu Valley), Niigata, Oita, Okayama, Osaka, Sapporo, Shimane, Yamagata, Yamanashi*

Japanese wine production was first documented by the Portuguese in the 16th century, but probably dates back to much earlier times. In the 17th century, under the all-powerful Tokugawa shogunate, which even controlled the emperor, Japanese wine virtually became extinct, and all things perceived as Christian or Western were condemned. Only after Yoshinobu, the last shogun, handed back military and civil powers to the emperor in 1867 were conditions right to rebuild Japan's wine industry. In 1875, the first commercial winery was established west of Tokyo in the Yamanashi district, which still accounts for 40 percent of Japanese vineyards today.

Due to this history, wine drinking was not felt to be natural in Japanese society, and it has been slow to take off, but Westernization led to a doubling of wine consumption throughout the 1980s, and it has doubled again since. This led the industry to improve quality and come clean on the provenance of its products. Once notorious for bottling imported bulk wine as "Produce of Japan," the industry now has a voluntary code that ensures the labeling of all imported wines as *yunyu san*, Japanese-fermented wines as *kokunai san*, and any blends of the two must be clearly indicated. This self-regulated system is adhered to by producers of any note, but *kokunai san* can still be fermented from imported grapes, grape juice, or concentrate.

Virtually all of Japan's best wines to date have been from classic grape varieties, mostly French (particularly Cabernet Sauvignon, Chardonnay, and Merlot), but there is renewed interest in Koshu, a variety this country has made its own. Though this grape originated in Asia Minor, arriving in China via the Silk Route and brought into Japan by Buddhists, it has been cultivated in the Yamanashi district since at least the 8th century. Until recently, the Koshu grape was used only to make sweet wine, or it would be lost in a blended "modern"-style wine. Since the turn of the millennium, however, some innovative Japanese producers have been honing a pure, dry style. Experimentation in production methods is going on, but the groundwork should first be figured out, by selecting the best sites, developing specialized clones, and reducing yields. When this is accomplished, the Koshu might even become Japan's flagship wine.

There are 170 commercial wineries in Japan, the largest of which are Chateau Mercian, Sapporo, and Suntory. Suntory operate four wineries (Yamanashi, Yamagata, Shiojiri in Nagano, and Seto in Okayama). The Yamanashi Winery, with its 370-acre (150-hectare) vineyard close to Mount Fuji, is the largest in Japan. These three producers lead the industry, but there are plenty of smaller wineries that compete in terms of quality, with others waiting in the wings.

✓ *Château Mercian* (Hokushin Reserve Chardonnay, Private Reserve Kikyogahara Merlot) • *Domaine Sogga* (Chardonnay) • *Grace* (Misawa Private Reserve Cabernet-Merlot) • *Hayashi Farm* (Kifugo) • *Kumamoto* (Night Harvest Chardonnay) • *Manns* (Solaris Chikumagawa Nagano Merlot) • *Okuizumo* (Shimane Chardonnay) • *Sapporo* (Grande Polaire Furusato Cabernet Sauvignon, Grande Polaire Nagano Furusato Vineyard Cabernet Sauvignon, Grande Polaire Yoichi Kifu) • *Suntory* (Tomi no Oka Cabernet Merlot, Tsutaishizaka Chardonnay) • *Tsuno* (Campbell's Early Rose)

## KOREA

Korea has 40,000 acres (16,000 hectares) of vineyards, primarily for table grapes and dried fruit. Winemaking dates back at least 2,000 years, but it was traditionally from rice and aromatized with herbs for medicinal purposes. A grape-based cooperative winery was set up in 1993 by Yoon Byeong-tae to make wine under the Chateaumani label. More recently, Roh Chong-ku established the East of Eden winery in a mountainous area of Pongwha County. He is a strong believer in Sanmaru, the local *amurensis* vine, and is Korea's only producer of such a wine, sold as Empery Cupid Wild Grapes Wine.

## KYRGYZSTAN

Situated between China and Kazakhstan, this country's vineyards amount to just 17,000 acres (7,000 hectares) and produce just over 1.5 million cases (135,000 hectoliters) of wine.

## TAJIKISTAN

There are more than 20 wineries in this central Asian state, most of which are found in Leninabad, Ghissar, and Vakhsh. In total, 90,000 acres (36,000 hectares) of vineyards produce 622,000 cases (56,000 hectoliters) of wine.

## THAILAND

A 12-year viticultural study ordered by King Bhumibol in the mid-1970s experimented with more than 400 types of grapes from Australia, Germany, and the US. In 1992, the Thai government officially allowed wine production, and in 1993 the country's first winery, Château de Loei, was established in the Phurua highlands of northeastern Thailand by the late Dr. Chaijudh Karnasuta. Château de Loei has been followed by Shala One, Siam Winery, PB Valley Khao Yai, Granmonte, and Village Farm.

The Siam Winery released its first wine as recently as 1997, but is already Thailand's biggest producer. Owned by the Yoovidhya family, its wines are marketed under the Chantemp and Monsoon labels. Grapes are grown on the famous "floating vineyards" around Damnoen Saduak in the Chao Phraya Delta. The vineyards do not actually float, but vines are grown on thin strips of land separated by canals, from which they are tended by growers in boats.

Shala One is located at King Amphur Dong Charoen in Pichit province and is best known for its Shiraz. The Khao Yai region, 109 miles (175 kilometers) northeast of Bangkok, is Thailand's most popular spot for vineyards: PB Valley Khao Yai; Village Farm, which sells wine under Château de Brumes and Village Thai labels; and Granmonte, Thailand's newest winery, are all located here.

✓ *Château de Loei* (Reserve Syrah) • *Granmonte* (Celebration Syrah)

## UZBEKISTAN

There are numerous wineries in Bukhara, Samarkand, and Tashkent. Together, 334,000 acres (135,000 hectares) of vineyards produce just over 11 million cases (990,000 hectoliters) of wine, mostly high-strength reds, dessert wines, and sparkling wines.

## VIETNAM

The first winery to be established in this country was the ill-fated Ninh Thuan joint venture, established by Allied-Domecq in 1995. The potential was thought to be very high, since under French rule the Vietnamese became the first Asians to acquire a taste for wine. However, the Vietnamese drink only Bordeaux, and tourists do not generally want to try Vietnamese wine. Or at least the former was the case until the Asian economies nose-dived in 1997, the same year that the Vietnamese government banned the advertising of all alcoholic products.

A VINEYARD IN THE YAMANASHI-KEN DISTRICT, JAPAN
*In the Yamanashi-Ken wine district, west of Tokyo on the island of Honshu, the vines are trained high on slightly sloping, south-facing slopes.*

# WINE AND FOOD

*There is only one golden rule when you are selecting a wine to accompany a dish. The more delicately flavored the dish, the more delicate the wine should be, whereas fuller-flavored foods can take fuller-flavored wines. It's as simple as that.*

THIS RULE IS VERY FLEXIBLE because it is capable of adapting to personal circumstances. We all have different ways of perceiving tastes and smells; if one person has a blind spot for, or is especially sensitive to, a particular characteristic such as acidity, sweetness, or bitterness, then their perception of the delicacy or fullness of a certain dish or wine will be somewhat different from other people's. The best approach is to start with conventional food-and-wine combinations, but use them as a launchpad for experimentation.

When using the food-and-wine combinations below to plan a menu, always aim to ascend in quality and flavor, serving white before red, dry before sweet, light-bodied before full-bodied, and young before old. The reason for this is twofold. Obviously, a step back in quality will be noticed. Equally, if you go straight to a reasonably fine wine, without first trying a lesser wine, you are likely to miss many of the better wine's subtle qualities.

Try also to make the sequence of wines proceed in some sort of logical order or according to a theme. The most obvious one is to remain faithful to the wines of one area, region, country, or grape variety. You could plan a dinner around the Pinot Noirs of the New World, or the Cabernet Sauvignons of Italy, for example. The theme could be one wine type or style, perhaps just Champagne or Sauternes, a popular ploy in those regions. It could be even more specific, such as different vintages of one specific grower's vineyard or a comparison of the "same" wine from different growers.

## APERITIFS

Whether you are serving a one-course supper, or a full dinner menu, you might like to start with an aperitif. This should not be an afterthought. Inevitably, the most delicate dishes in a meal arrive first and nobody will be able to appreciate them if palates have been saturated with strong spirits or highly flavored concoctions. Choose the most suitable aperitif according to your taste; do not offer a choice.

### SHERRY

*Fino* sherry is a traditional aperitif, but its use has been abused. If the first course is sufficiently well flavored, then sherry can be an admirable choice, and may sometimes be used as an ingredient. Mostly, however, even the lightest *fino* will have too much alcohol and flavor.

### PROPRIETARY APERITIFS AND SPIRITS

Proprietary brands of aromatized aperitifs, such as vermouths, inevitably also fall into the trap of being too alcoholic and too strong-tasting. All spirits, especially if they are not mixed, are too aggressive to allow the palate to appreciate the types of food usually served as a first course.

### WINES

It is customary in a few countries, notably France, to serve a sweet wine such as Sauternes as an aperitif. For most occasions, this choice would be inappropriate, but sometimes it can be effective. White wines that are light-bodied, dry or off-dry, still or sparkling, make perfect all-purpose aperitifs, although a rosé may be suitable if

### APPETIZERS

*When matching wines to appetizers, it is important to consider the next course and its accompanying wine.*

the first wine served with the meal is also a rosé or a light red wine. Excellent choices for a white-wine aperitif may include Mâcon Blanc or Mâcon Villages, good Muscadet, lighter Alsace wines such as Pinot Blanc or Sylvaner, new-wave Rioja, aromatic dry whites from northeastern Italy, many English wines, young Mosel (up to Spätlese) or Rhine (up to Kabinett), and light-bodied Chardonnay, Sauvignon, Chenin, or Colombard from California, Australia, New Zealand, or South Africa. The list is endless. If the choice is to be a rosé, try to select one from the same area, and preferably made from the same grape, as the first wine of the meal. The aperitif *par excellence* in every conceivable situation is Champagne, with Crémant de Bourgogne or Crémant d'Alsace making excellent alternatives.

☑️ **Budget choice** *Cava Brut*

## APPETIZERS

At one time, it was customary to get well into the first course before it was permitted to serve the wine. Nowadays, each stage of a meal is seen to play a vital part in the taste experience, leading onto the next taste, or following on from the previous one.

### ARTICHOKE

If artichoke is served with butter, a light but slightly assertive, dry Sauvignon Blanc from the Loire is best. The same wine might also accompany artichokes with Hollandaise sauce, although a dry rosé with a fairly high balance of acidity, such as a Coteaux d'Ancenis Rosé from the Loire, Arbois Rosé from the Jura, or Schilcher from Austria, is also suitable.

☑️ **Budget choice** *Sauvignon de Haut-Poitou*

### ASPARAGUS

Fine Champagne or a young Muscat d'Alsace are perfect accompaniments. Medium-weight white Burgundy and Californian or Pacific Northwest Chardonnay also work well.

☑️ **Budget choice** *Raimat Chardonnay Blanc de Blanc Brut*

### AVOCADO

Although many wines of excellent acidity, such as Champagne or Chablis, are extremely successful partners of this food, Alsace Gewürztraminer, which is naturally low in acidity, is the best choice.

☑️ **Budget choice** *Muscadet*

### CAVIAR

Champagne is the classic partner.

☑️ **Budget choice** *Mineral water*

### GARLIC BUTTER

Choose the general style of wine recommended for the main ingredient, but opt for one with more body and a more assertive flavor or higher acidity.

### PÂTÉS

Whether fish, fowl, or meat, pâté should be partnered according to its main ingredient or flavor. Look in the appropriate entry and choose a recommended wine. Foie gras is fabulous with a fine vintage Champagne or mature Sauternes and, although diverse in character, Alsace Gewürztraminer and Pinot Gris are both perfect partners.

### SALADS

Plain green salads need little more than a light, dry white such as a Muscadet, unless there is a predominance of bitter leaves, in which case something more assertive but just as light, such as a lesser Loire Sauvignon, should be chosen. A firm Champagne is the best accompaniment to salads that include warm ingredients.

☑️ **Budget choice** *Cava Brut*

SHELLFISH
*A variety of white wines including good Muscadet, Loire Sauvignon, and Mosel can accompany the Spanish dish paella.*

### SNAILS

Modest village Burgundy from the Côte d'Or, either red or white.

✓ **Budget choice** *Côtes de Roussillon*

### SOUPS

Champagne or any fine sparkling wine is ideal with most purée, velouté, or cream soups, especially with the more delicately flavored recipes. It is virtually essential with a chilled soup, whether a jellied consommé or a cold purée soup such as Vichyssoise. Most sparkling wines can match the flavor of a shellfish bisque, but a good pink Champagne makes a particularly picturesque partner. Rich-flavored soups can take full wines, most often red. A good game soup, for example, can respond well to the heftier reds of the Rhône, Bordeaux, Burgundy, and Rioja. The frothy character of Lambrusco cuts through the texture of a genuine minestrone. The sweet cherry flavor of Lambrusco also matches the soup's rich tomato tang.

✓ **Budget choice** *Blanquette de Limoux*

### TERRINES

Fish, shellfish, and meat terrines should be partnered with a wine according to their main ingredient or flavor (see appropriate entry). Most vegetable terrines go well with young, dry or off-dry, light-bodied, still, sparkling, or aromatic white wines from the Loire, Alsace, Germany, Austria, northeastern Italy, New Zealand, and England.

✓ **Budget choice** *Crémant d'Alsace*

### VINAIGRETTE

Appetizers with vinaigrette are difficult to partner. Conventional wisdom suggests a *fino* or *manzanilla* sherry, or Montilla, although many believe it best not to serve any wine with such a first course. I have found that an Alsace Gewürztraminer is one of the very few wines that can really take on vinaigrette and come out on top.

✓ **Budget choice** *Inexpensive Gewürztraminer*

### EGG, RICE, AND PASTA DISHES

Champagne is the perfect foil to the bland flavor of any egg dish, the texture of which is cut by the wine's effervescence. Dishes such as omelettes, quiches, soufflés, eggs cooked *en cocotte*, coddled, fried, scrambled, or poached can also be accompanied by any good sparkling wine. Savory mousses and mousselines, whether hot or cold, fish or fowl, should be partnered by a wine with slightly less body and at least as much acidity or effervescence (if this is applicable) than those suitable to accompany their main ingredient. Good sparkling wine is equally useful for many rice and pasta dishes, particularly the more delicately flavored ones, but light red wines —not too fruity and with nice grippy tannins—can make a surprisingly good accompaniment. Richer ingredients should be matched by the wine.

✓ **Budget choice** *Saumur Brut and Saumur Rouge*

# FISH

Most fish and shellfish go well with dry white wines, but red, rosé, sparkling, and sweet styles are all possible accompaniments in certain circumstances.

### FISH WITH SAUCES AND PAN-FRIED FISH

Whatever the fish, pan-fried, cream sauce, or butter sauce dishes require wines with more acidity or effervescence than normal. If the sauce is very rich, then consider wines with more intense flavors.

✓ **Budget choice** *Crémant de Loire*

### FISH STEWS

Although red wine and fish usually react violently in the mouth, dishes cooked in red wine, such as highly flavored Mediterranean fish stews, present no such problems.

### MACKEREL

An assertive but modest Loire Sauvignon is needed for mackerel, although a richer Sauvignon from various New World countries is preferable with smoked mackerel.

✓ **Budget choice** *Sauvignon de Touraine*

### RIVER FISH

Generally, most river fish go well with a fairly assertive rosé, since both the fish and the wine have a complementary earthiness, but an assertive white such as Sancerre is just as effective. Sancerre, white Graves, and Champagne are especially successful with pike. Champagne or Montrachet is classic with salmon or salmon-trout, whether baked, grilled, pan-fried, poached, or smoked, but any good-quality dry sparkling wine or white Burgundy will be excellent, as will top Chardonnay wines from California, the Pacific Northwest, New Zealand, Australia, and South Africa. Riesling, whether Alsace or German, is almost obligatory with trout, particularly when it is cooked *au bleu* (rapidly, in stock with plenty of vinegar).

✓ **Budget choice** *Pink Cava Brut*

### SARDINES

Vinho Verde is the ideal wine with sardines, especially if freshly caught and cooked on a beach in Portugal.

✓ **Budget choice** *Vinho Verde*

### SHELLFISH

Choose a top estate Muscadet, a Bourgogne Aligoté from a sunny vintage, a Loire Sauvignon, an English wine, or a Mosel with most modest forms of shellfish (shrimp, mussels, etc); a fine but assertive Sancerre or Pouilly Fumé with crayfish; a *grand cru* Chablis or a good Champagne with crab, lobster, oysters, and scallops. Choose a wine with more acidity or effervescence if the dish you are eating includes a cream sauce.

✓ **Budget choice** *Crémant de Bourgogne*

### SMOKED FISH

A good tip is oaked for smoked. For smoked fish, drink an oak-matured version of the wine you would drink with an unsmoked dish of the same fish. It does not work every time. Since some wines are not oak-matured, but oakiness in wine does blend well with the smokiness in food, so pick any oaked wine you think suitable.

✓ **Budget choice** *cheap Ryman-produced oaked Chardonnay from anywhere*

### WHITE FISH

White fish have the very lightest flavors and it would be a pity to overwhelm their delicate nuances with a dominant wine. Grilled sole, plaice, and mullet are enhanced by a youthful *blanc de blancs* Champagne, top-quality estate Muscadet, Savennières, Pinot Blanc from Alsace, Pinot Grigio from northeastern Italy, and fine estate Vinho Verde with authentically tart dryness and just the barest prickle. Haddock, hake, halibut, turbot, cod, and sea bream are good with all the wines mentioned above, but can take slightly richer dry whites.

✓ **Budget choice** *Crémant d'Alsace*

# MEAT DISHES

Few people have not heard the old maxim "red wine with dark meat, white wine with light," but it is quite acceptable to reverse the rule and have white wine with dark meat and red wine with light meat, provided that the golden rule in the introduction is observed.

### BEEF

Bordeaux is the classic accompaniment to roast beef. Choose a younger, perhaps lighter style if the meat is served cold. A good Cabernet Sauvignon from Australia, California, Chile, Italy, New Zealand, or South Africa would do just as well and would be preferable in the case of steaks that are charred on the outside and pink in the middle. For pure beef burgers, an unpretentious, youthful red Côtes-du-Rhône with an honest, peppery flavor is ideal. But, frankly, almost any drinkable red wine of medium, medium-full, or full body from anywhere will accompany all beef dishes with some degree of competence, as will most full-bodied and rich-flavored white wines.

✓ **Budget choice** *Bulgarian Cabernet Sauvignon*

### CASSEROLES, DARK

Dark meat casseroles require full-bodied red wines from Bordeaux, Burgundy, the Rhône, or Rioja. Chateau Musar from Lebanon and Chateau Carras from Greece are both also ideal, as are many Italian wines, from the Nebbiolo wines of Piedmont, through the fuller Sangiovese wines of Chianti, Carmignano, and Montalcino, to the Montepulciano wines of Abruzzi and the Aglianico del Vulture, not to mention the super *barrique* wines from Tuscany and northeastern Italy. The richer the casserole, the more robust can be the wine, and the more tannin needed.

**Budget choice** *Inexpensive Zinfandel*

## CASSEROLES, LIGHT

Light meat casseroles are best with young Beaujolais, Loire reds (e.g. Bourgueil or Chinon), various medium-bodied reds from south-western France and Coteaux du Languedoc, Pinot Noir from Alsace, and soft-styled Chianti. For the white-wine drinker, new-wave Rioja, Mâcon Blanc, Tokay d'Alsace, and inexpensive French Colombard or Chenin Blanc from California or South Africa are all worth trying.

**Budget choice** *Californian dry white jug wine*

## CHILLI CON CARNE

If it is a good chili, forget wine and stick to ice-cool lager or water.

## CHINESE DISHES

Good-quality German Riesling *Kabinett* wines are very useful for partnering many Chinese dishes, particularly those in black bean, ginger, or oyster sauces or with any gingery or bell pepper flavoring. Spare ribs require a *Spätlese*, sweet-and-sour an *Auslese*, chilies and other hotter flavors an Alsace Gewürztraminer, preferably *Vendange Tardive*. For duck or goose, try a good-quality Vouvray *demi-sec*, still or sparkling. If delicate or bland ingredients such as water chestnuts, bamboo shoots, or cashew nuts dominate, choose a fresh or soft white such as a light Australian Chardonnay. With egg rolls, choose a good dry fizz. Iced water makes a good substitute for any of the above.

## DUCK

Roast duck is very versatile, but the best accompaniments include certain *crus* Beaujolais such as Morgan or Moulin-à-Vent, fine red and white Burgundy, especially from the Côte de Nuits, and mature Médoc. With cold duck, a lighter *cru* Beaujolais such as Fleurie should be considered. Duck in orange sauce goes extremely well with softer styles of red and white Burgundy, southern Rhône wines, especially Châteauneuf-du-Pape, red Rioja, and Zinfandel.

**Budget choice** *Quinta da Bacalhôa*

## GAME

For lightly hung winged game, choose the same wines as for poultry. If it is mid-hung, try a fullish *cru* Beaujolais. Well-hung birds require a full-bodied red Bordeaux or Burgundy. Pomerol is the classic choice with well-hung pheasant. Treat lightly hung ground game in the same way as lamb and mid-hung meat in the same way as beef. Well-hung ground game can take the biggest Hermitage, Côte Rôtie, Cornas, Châteauneuf-du-Pape, red Rioja, or an old vintage of Château Musar. White-wine drinkers should opt for old vintages of Rhône or Rioja or an Alsace Pinot Gris *Vendange Tardive* (vinified dry).

**Budget choice** *Australian Shiraz*

## GOOSE

I find it hard to choose between Chinon, Bourgueil, Anjou Rouge, and (sometimes) Chianti on the red side, and Vouvray (still or sparkling), Riesling (preferably, but not necessarily, Alsace), and Champagne on the white. The one trait they all share is plenty of acidity, which is needed for this fatty bird. If the goose is served in a fruity sauce, stick to white wines; a little sweetness in the wine will do no harm.

**Budget choice** *South African Chenin Blanc*

## GOULASH

When on form, "Bull's Blood" is the obvious choice, otherwise any East European full-bodied, robustly flavored red wine will suffice.

**Budget choice** *Bulgarian Kadarka*

## HAM AND BACON

Ham can react adversely in the mouth with some red wines, particularly if it is unsmoked, but young Beaujolais, Loire Gamay, and Chianti are safe bets. Sparkling white wine is perhaps best of all, although I have known that to react strangely at times.

**Budget choice** *Cava Brut*

## INDIAN DISHES

Surprisingly enough, a light and slightly tannic red wine can go well with a number of Indian dishes, such as chicken tikka, korma, pasanda, tandoori, and even rogan josh. You need something fresh and crisp such as a Côtes de Gascogne or one of the lighter New Zealand Sauvignon Blancs to wash down a vegetable tikka or a Madras curry, something fruitier, such as German Riesling *Kabinett,* for a vindaloo.

**Budget choice** *Iced water*

## LAMB

Bordeaux is as classic with lamb as it is with beef, although Burgundy works as well, particularly when the meat is a little pink. It is well known in the wine trade that lamb brings out every nuance of flavor in the finest of wines, which is why it is served more often than any other meat when a merchant is organizing a special meal. Rack of lamb with rosemary seems to be a favorite. As with beef, almost any red wine can accompany lamb well, although this meat is perhaps best with slightly lighter wines.

**Budget choice** *Bourgogne Rouge* (Buxy)

## MEAT PIES

For hot pies and puddings, treat as for dark- or light-meat casseroles. Cold pork, veal-and-ham, or ham-and-turkey pies require a light- or medium-bodied red that has a firm acidity, such as Chinon or Bourgueil, while cold game pies call for something at least as rich, but softer, such as a New Zealand Cabernet Sauvignon.

**Budget choice** *Saumur Brut*

## MOUSSAKA

For romantic association, choose one of the better, medium- to full-bodied reds from Greece, such as Naoussa, Goumenissa, or Côtes de Meliton. White-wine drinkers require something of substance that is not too full or oxidative. A few Greek wines fit the bill (Lac des Roches from Boutari comes to mind), but something Spanish might be better, such as one of the "in-between" white Riojas.

**Budget choice** *Bulgarian Merlot*

## VARIETY MEATS

Kidneys go with full, well-flavoured, but round wines, such as a mature red or white Châteauneuf-du-Pape or a Rioja. But much depends on what sort of kidneys they are and how they are cooked. A ragout of lamb's kidneys, for example, needs something with the finesse of a mature *cru classé* Médoc. The finest livers go well with a good but not too heavy Syrah, such as a mature Côte Rôtie or Hermitage from a top producer in a medium-good vintage. Chicken livers are quite strong and require something with a penetrating flavor, such as a good Gigondas, Fitou, or Zinfandel. Pig and ox livers are the coarsest in texture and flavor, and require a full, robust, but not too fussy red— maybe a modest *vin de pays* from the Pyrénées-Orientales. Either red or dry- to- medium-dry white wine may be served with sweetbreads. Lamb's sweetbreads are the best, and take well to fine St-Émilion or St-Julien, if in a sauce, or a good white Burgundy if pan-fried.

**Budget choice** *Crémant de Bourgogne*

## PORK, POULTRY, AND VEAL

These meats are flexible and can take a diverse range of wines from modest traditional method sparkling, through almost every type of medium- or full-bodied dry or off-dry white wine, to light reds from Beaujolais, Champagne, Alsace, and Germany, literally any medium-bodied red wine, whatever its origin, and a large number of full-bodied ones too. For chops, cutlets, or escalopes, grilled, pan-fried, or in a cream sauce, it is advisable to choose something with a higher acidity balance or some sparkle. Beaujolais is perhaps the best all-round choice; it works well with roast pork, particularly served cold.

**Budget choice** *Gamay de Touraine*

## POT-ROAST

Consult the appropriate entry for meat, and choose a wine listed there. Because of the extra flavor from added vegetables, it is possible, though by no means necessary, to serve a slightly less fine wine than with the straight roast.

**Budget choice** *Côtes de Duras*

## STROGANOFF

An authentic Stroganoff requires a full red with a good depth of flavor, but with some finer characteristics, not too robust, and preferably well rounded with age. Try a modest Médoc, a good Cahors, or a Bergerac.

**Budget choice** *Bulgarian Cabernet Sauvignon-Merlot* (Oriahovica)

## THAI DISHES

Much spicier than Chinese, with a more intricate mix of flavors, these dishes are far more difficult to match wine to. For the very hottest chili-charged dishes, forget wine and stick to beer or, better still, iced water, but with mildly hot Thai dishes, you can get away with a New Zealand Sauvignon Blanc or a Champagne, which will also go

POULTRY
*Poultry has such a delicate flavor that how it is cooked will be the most important consideration when choosing a wine, particularly if it is served with a sauce, as even the most bland ancillary flavors can dominate.*

with dishes that include coconut milk. When lemongrass, lime, and other zesty ingredients dominate, try an unoaked Australian Sémillon.

✓ **Budget choice** *Iced water*

# DESSERTS

While a dessert wine can easily be drunk on its own, there is no reason why it has to be. There are those who believe that the finest points of a great dessert wine are lost or overshadowed by a sweet. But this happens only if the golden rule of partnering food and wine is broken.

### CAKES, GÂTEAUX, PUDDINGS, AND PASTRIES

Many cakes, sponges, and gâteaux do not require wine, but I have found that Tokaji enhances those with coffee or vanilla flavors, various Iberian Moscatels are very good when almonds or walnuts are present, and sweet sparkling Vouvray or Coteaux du Layon go well with fruit-filled, fresh cream gâteaux and fruit-flavored cheese-cakes. Iberian Moscatels are superb with Christmas or plum pudding and, on a similar theme, Asti is ideal with mince pies. Chocolate is more difficult, and although some people enjoy drinking wines ranging from Sauternes to *brut* Champagne with chocolate fudge cake or profiteroles, I am not one of them.

✓ **Budget choice:** *Iced water*

### CRÈME BRÛLÉE AND CRÈME CARAMEL

Something sweet and luxurious is required to accompany crème brûlée. German or Austrian wines would be too tangy, a top Sauternes or one of the richer Barsacs would be excellent, but perhaps best of all would be an Alsace Pinot Gris

Sélection de Grains Nobles or a great Malmsey Madeira.

✓ **Budget choice** *Australian Liqueur Muscat*

### FRUIT

A fresh peach, plump and juicy, makes the ideal partner for a Rheingau Riesling *Auslese* or *Beerenauslese*, or a late-harvest, botrytized Riesling from California or Australia. Asti, Californian Muscat Canelli, and Clairette de Die may also partner peaches, especially if they are served with strawberries or raspberries. These wines go well to one degree or another with virtually every other fruit, including fresh fruit salad. Lighter Sauternes and Barsacs, Coteaux du Layon, and sweet sparkling Vouvrays are also good with fruit salad and are the best choice for apple, pear, or peach pies, tarts, and flans.

An Austrian Grüner Veltliner or Gewürztraminer *Auslese* with strawberries and fresh coarse-ground black pepper (no cream) is a revelation. A fine Bordeaux or Burgundy with fresh raspberries that have been macerated in the same wine is liked by some, as is a top-quality Mosel *Auslese* with strawberries and fresh raspberry purée (no cream). Apple Strudel, Dutch Apple Pie, and other spicy fruit desserts need to be eaten with a Tokay, Iberian Moscatel, or an Austrian Gewürztraminer *Beerenauslese*. Pies made with dark, rich fruits require full Sauternes, Bonnezeaux, or Quarts de Chaume.

✓ **Budget choice** *Moscato Spumante*

### ICE CREAM

When ice cream is part of a dessert, the other ingredients should be considered when choosing a wine.

FRUIT PASTRIES
*Sweet wines, particularly Sauternes, are well suited to fruit pies, tarts, and pastries.*

Ice cream on its own rarely calls for any accompaniment, but there is one perfect combination—Muscat de Beaumes de Venise with Brown Bread Ice Cream.

✓ **Budget choice** *Moscatel de Valencia*

### MERINGUE

For meringue served as part of a vacherin or pavlova, choose a still or sparkling Moscato, Californian Muscat Canelli, a late-harvested botrytized Riesling, a top Mosel *Beerenauslese*, a sweet Vouvray, or a good Sauternes. For meringue desserts with nutty, coconutty, or biscuity ingredients, a Tokay Essencia, Alsace Pinot Gris Sélection de Grains Nobles, Torcolato from Veneto, or Malmsey Madeira would be equally successful. Lightly poached meringue served as floating islands or snow eggs needs something of less intensity, such as an Alsace Pinot Gris *Vendange Tardive*. An Eiswein is the perfect partner for lemon meringue pie—a dessert that demands luxury, acidity, and a vibrant sweetness.

✓ **Budget choice** *Iberian Moscatel*

# CHEESES AND CHEESE DISHES

There is a school of thought that decries the traditional concept of cheese and wine as ideal partners. I am not one of its pupils. Most cheeses are flattered by many wines; only the most delicate or the most powerful of either cheeses or wines require careful consideration before trying to partner them.

### BLUE-VEINED CHEESES

A good-quality blue cheese is best partnered by a sweet wine, which produces a piquant combination of flavors not dissimilar to that found in sweet-and-sour dishes. Many dessert wines will suffice, and the choice will often depend on personal taste, but I find that hard blues such as Stilton and Blue Cheshire are best with port, while soft blues are greatly enhanced by sweet white wines. Lighter Barsacs, Coteaux du Layon, German *Beerenauslese*, or a mature Sélection de Grains Nobles from Alsace for Bleu de Bresse cheeses, and Sauternes, Austrian Gewürztraminer *Trockenbeerenauslese* or Tokay are needed for the more powerfully flavored Roquefort and Gorgonzola.

✓ **Budget choice** *Moscatel de Valencia*

### SOFT AND SEMI-SOFT MILD CHEESES

A light Beaujolais Nouveau or an elegant Pinot Noir from Alsace (as opposed to the deep-colored, oak-aged reds that are now being made) will partner most soft and semi-soft cheeses of the mild type, although

something even more delicate, such as one of the many fragrant dry white wines of northeastern Italy or a soft-styled Champagne Rosé should be considered for double- and triple-cream cheeses.

✓ **Budget choice** *Blanquette de Limoux*

### SOFT AND SEMI-SOFT STRONG CHEESES

Munster demands a strong Gewürztraminer; and the most decadent way to wash down a perfectly ripe Brie de Meaux or Brie de Melun is with a 20-year-old vintage Champagne. Washed-skin cheeses (that have been bathed in water, brine, or alcohol while ripening) need an assertive red Burgundy or a robust claret.

✓ **Budget choice** *Young Côtes du Rhône*

### HARD CHEESES

Dry and off-dry English wines are ideal with Caerphilly, while the sweeter styles of English wine are perfect with Wensleydale served with a slice of homemade apple pie. Mature Cheddar and other well-flavored, hard English cheeses demand something full and red such as a fine Bordeaux or, if it has a bite, Châteauneuf-du-Pape or Château Musar. Sangiovese-based wines bring out the sweet flavor of fresh (but mature) Parmesan. Alsace Pinot Gris and Gewürztraminer are ideal with Gruyère, although something with a little more acidity, such as a Californian Sauvignon Blanc, is better with Emmental.

✓ **Budget choice** *New World Macération carbonique*

### GOAT CHEESES

These cheeses require an assertive, dry white wine such as Sancerre or Gewürztraminer, although a firm but light *cru* Beaujolais would also suit.

✓ **Budget choice** *Sauvignon de Haut-Poitou*

### CHEESE FONDUE

It is possible to drink a wide range of red, dry white, and sparkling wines with fondue, but it is fitting to serve a wine from the area of origin of the dish: Fendant from the Valais with a Swiss fondue, for example, and Apremont or Crépy with fondue Savoyarde.

✓ **Budget choice** *Edelzwicker*

### CHEESE SOUFFLÉ

This requires a good sparkling wine, preferably Champagne. If it is a very rich soufflé, such as soufflé Roquefort, then the wine must have the power to match it. A *blanc de noirs* such as Bollinger's "Vieilles Vignes" would be superb.

✓ **Budget choice** *Blanquette de Limoux*

# TASTE CHART

*A taste chart is a useful mind-jogging aid for identifying elusive aromas and flavors that you may have encountered in a wine, but cannot put a name to—something perhaps that leaps out of the glass and is instantly recognizable, yet, at the same time, is frustratingly hard to identify.*

EVEN THE MOST EXPERIENCED WINE TASTERS are prone to this baffling experience but, if we analyze the problem carefully, logic tells us that anything ringing bells of recognition in the brain must be well known to it, and the odds are it is an everyday aroma or flavor, rather than something obscure, rare, or esoteric. From this we can conclude that it is not, in fact, the aroma itself that is elusive, merely its name. This is not surprising, since we all have the sensory profile of more than a thousand everyday aromas locked away in our brains—the difficulty lies in accessing the information. I realized this long ago, which is why my personal tasting books always have a list of mind-jogging aromas and flavors. When I am on my travels and find that I cannot immediately identify a flower, fruit, or spice, I simply run my finger down the list until my brain connects with the aroma that is literally in front of my nose or the flavor that is on the tip of my tongue. This new edition of the encyclopedia seems the ideal opportunity to pass on the benefits of this system to readers.

## HOW TO USE THE CHART
If you instinctively know the category (flower, fruit, spice, etc.) of the aroma you are looking for, go straight to the appropriate section; otherwise start at the beginning. Take the glass in one hand, swirl the wine, and take a sniff. If it is a flavor you are seeking, take a sip, while methodically running a finger down through the following list, until one jogs your memory.

## THE ORIGIN OF EVERYDAY AROMAS IN WINE

Although no wines actually contain fruits (other than grapes, of course), flowers, vegetables, herbs, spices *et al.*, it is perfectly reasonable to use their aromas and flavors when describing wines. To the uninitiated it might sound rather fanciful to say that a wine is buttery, but diacetyl, which is used as an artificial flavoring to make margarine smell and taste buttery, is created naturally in wine as a by-product of the malolactic process. Wines, in fact, contain varying amounts of many chemical compounds that can be linked directly to a vast number of characteristic aromas or flavors.

Some of the compounds involved can evoke different aromas depending on the levels found and the presence of other compounds that can also exert an influence; and various unrelated compounds can induce a very similar aroma. The amount involved can be minuscule; a strong presence of the aromatic compounds responsible for peas and bell peppers or capsicums of the green variety can be detected, for example, at levels of one part in 100 billion!

Do not get carried away in the search for these aromas and flavors. It is far more important to concentrate on just one or two descriptors than to record a fruit cocktail or potpourri of aromas and flavors. When you read elaborate descriptions (not too many in this book, I hope), just ask yourself what such concoctions would actually smell like and whether it would be possible to discern any of their component parts.

**Note** Whether we perceive any of a wine's characteristics as aromas or flavors, technically they are all aromas (*see* p11). However, textural and tactile impressions made in the mouth, and true tastes sensed by the tongue (sweetness, acidity or sourness, bitterness, and saltiness), also influence our perception. Where specific chemical compounds are known to be responsible for an aroma or flavor, they are mentioned, and are italicized so that those who are interested can identify the possible cause, while those who are not can skim across without interruption to the text.

## FLOWERS

Floral aromas are primarily found in young white wines, and may be the major aromatic thrust of an agreeably modest wine or merely a component of finesse in a more complex product. Violet is the most significant floral anomaly in red wine.

### ACACIA
This is the flowery autolytic aroma on a recently disgorged sparkling wine. It can be found in other white wines (*paratolylmethyl ketone*).

### ELDERFLOWER
Found in wines made from aromatic grape varieties, elderflower is good only when the aroma is clean and fresh, and the fruit ripe, but can verge on cat pee when the grapes are unacceptably underripe.

### GERANIUM
Commonly a sweet wine fault (*2-ethoxyhexa-*3, 5-diene), but also the sign of an Asti that is too old (*geraniol* degradation), it is always distinctive (also *glycyrrhizin* or *hexanedienol*).

### LAVENDER
Lavender is often found with lime on Australian wines, particularly Riesling, Muscat, or sparkling wines, and occasionally in German Riesling and even Vinho Verde.

### ROSE
Rose petals can be found in many wines, particularly delicate Muscats and understated Gewürztraminers (*damascanone, diacetyl, geraniol, irone, nerol,* or *phenylethylic acid*).

### VIOLET
Violets can often be found as part of the finesse on the finish of Cabernet-based red wines, notably Bordeaux, especially from Graves. It is possibly more tactile-based than a volatile aroma.

## FRUITS

In general, fruitiness suggests riper grapes and more bottle-age than floral aromas and flavors, which often evolve into fruity characters. Fruitiness is enhanced by sweetness and acidity.

### APPLE
Apple is a white-wine aroma that ranges from green apple (*malic acid*) in underripe wines to soft, red-apple flavors in riper wines, where 50-some known compounds might or might not be responsible.

### APRICOT
A pithy apricot character is less ripe and more bottle-aged than peachiness, which is a finer, juicier, more succulent fruitiness. Apricot is often found in Loire or German whites (*4-decanolide*).

### BANANA
Banana is found in cool-fermented whites and reds made by carbonic maceration (*amyl acetate* or *isoamyl acetate*, also known as "banana oil" and "pear oil," which, in excess, can lead to a nail-polish aroma).

### BLACK CURRANT
Characteristic of classic Cabernet, black currant is also found in grapes such as Syrah, particularly when bottle-aged (*ethyl acetate, ethyl formate*, various acids and esters).

### CHERRY

Tart, red cherries are classic in cool-climate Pinot Noir, while black cherries can be part of the complexity of a great Cabernet or Syrah (*cyanbydrin benzaldehyde*).

### DRIED FRUIT

The aroma of dried currants is most commonly found in Italian Recioto or Amarone wines, whereas the aroma of raisins is characteristic of fortified Muscat.

### FIG

A figlike aroma is sometimes a characteristic of potential complexity in a youthful Chardonnay and may be found in combination with nuances of apple or melon.

### GOOSEBERRY

The classic aroma of a truly ripe, yet exceedingly fresh, crisp, and vibrant Sauvignon Blanc, gooseberry is most widely found in white wines from New Zealand, particularly Marlborough.

### GRAPE

Few wines are actually grapey, but grapiness is found in cheap German wines, young Gewürztraminer, and Muscat or Muscat-like wines (*ethyl caprylate, ethyl heptanoate,* and *ethyl perargonate*).

### GRAPEFRUIT

Grapefruit is found in the Jurançon Sec and Alsace Gewürztraminer, German or English Scheurebe and Huxelrebe, and Swiss Arvine wines (a combination of terpenes, such as *linalool* or *citronellal*).

### LEMON

Not as distinctive in wine as freshly cut lemon would suggest, many young white wines have simple, ordinary, almost mild lemony fruit or acidity (*limonene* or *citronellal*).

### LIME

A truly distinctive aroma and flavor found in good-quality Australian Sémillon and Riesling, in the latter often turning to lavender in bottle (*limonene, citronellal,* or *linalool*).

### LYCHEE

Fresh lychee is depicted as the classic varietal character of Gewürztraminer, but is not widely encountered, while canned lychee is commonly found in precocious white wines from off-vintages.

### MELON

A characteristic of young, cool-fermented, New World Chardonnay, melon may be found in combination with nuances of apple or fig (*limonene, citronellal,* or *linalool*).

### ORANGE

A good blind-tasting tip is that orange can be found in Muscat, but never Gewürztraminer. It is also found in some fortified wines and Ruby Cabernet (*limonene, citronellal,* or *linalool*).

### PEACH

Found in ripe Riesling and Muscat, very ripe Sauvignon Blanc, true Viognier, Sézannais Champagne, New World Chardonnay, and botrytized wines (*piperonal* or *undecalactone*).

### PEAR

Pear is found in cool-fermented whites and reds made by carbonic maceration (*amyl acetate* or *isoamyl acetate*, also known as "banana oil" or "pear oil," which, in excess, can lead to a nail-polish aroma).

### PINEAPPLE

Pineapple is found in very ripe Chardonnay, Chenin Blanc, and Sémillon, especially in the New World, and almost any botrytized wine. It implies good acidity for the ripeness (*ethyl caprylate*).

### RASPBERRY

This is sometimes found in Grenache, Loire Cabernet, Pinot Noir, and Syrah (evolving into black currant in bottle) (*ethyl acetate, ethyl formate,* various acids and esters).

### STRAWBERRY

Succulent, ripe strawberry fruit is found in classic Pinot Noir from a warm climate or top vintage. It is also found in Loire Cabernet (*ethyl acetate, ethyl formate,* various acids and esters).

### TOMATO

We tend to think of tomato as a vegetable, but it is really a fruit and, although not a common feature in wines, it is found in bottle-aged Sylvaner and, with blood-orange, in Ruby Cabernet.

## VEGETATIVE, HERBACEOUS

In small doses, vegetative and herbaceous aromas can add to a wine's complexity, but few are pleasant on their own; most are, in fact, faults.

### ASPARAGUS

Asparagus is common in Sauvignon Blanc made from overripe grapes or kept too long in bottle. Some people adore this style, but most do not. It can develop into canned pea aroma (*isobutyl* or *segbutyl*).

### BEETS

This fruity-vegetal earthiness may be found in some red wines, mostly Pinot Noir grown in unsuitable areas, and aged too long in bottle, or Cabernet Franc (*geosmin*).

### BELL PEPPER OR CAPSICUM

This can be found in a slightly grassy-herbaceous Sauvignon, a Loire Cabernet Franc, or a Cabernet Sauvignon from high-vigor vines. It used to be a big problem in New Zealand (*isobutyl* or *segbutyl*).

### CABBAGE OR CAULIFLOWER

The presence of cabbage or cauliflower usually denotes a Chardonnay wine or a wine from the Pinot family. Some people think mature unfiltered Burgundy should have this aroma, or even one that is farmyardy or evocative of manure (*methylmercaptan*).

### CUT GRASS

Can be aggressive, but if fresh, light, and pleasant, it is a positive attribute of deliberately early-picked Sauvignon Blanc or Sémillon grapes (*methoxy-pyrazine* or *hexanedienol*).

### HAY

Like dull, flat, or oxidized grassiness, the hay characteristic can be found in sparkling wines that have undergone a slight oxidation prior to their second fermentation (*linalool oxides*).

### MANURE

This aroma is a very extreme form of the "farmyardy" aroma, which some people (not this author) believe to be characteristic of great Pinot Noir (*see* Great Pinot Noir and Chardonnay, p136). Certain New World winemakers try to emulate this aroma in their wines, but it is probably a fixed-sulfur fault, and quite possibly a *mercaptan*.

### MUSHROOM

A beautifully clean mushroom aroma is an indication of Pinot Meunier in a fine old Champagne, but if the aroma is musty, it will be a contamination fault such as infected staves or a corked wine.

### ONION OR GARLIC

A serious wine fault created when ethyl alcohol reacts with hydrogen sulfide, another wine fault, to form a foul-smelling compound called *ethylmercaptan*.

### PEAS, CANNED

Common in Sauvignon Blanc made from overripe grapes or kept too long in bottle. Some people adore this style, but most do not. Can develop from an asparagus aroma (*isobutyl* or *segbutyl*).

### POTATO PEEL

More earthy and less fruity than beets, potato peel is found in a wide range of red wines, and could be an indication of infected staves or corkiness (*geosmin*).

## SPICY, HERBAL, RESINOUS

These aromas will be either a part of the varietal character of a grape or a component of the wine's complexity, but in both cases they are enhanced by dryness and masked by sweetness.

### CINNAMON

Part of the aged complexity of many fine red wines, especially Rhône, cinnamon is also found in oak-aged whites, particularly those made from botrytized grapes (*cinnamic aldehyde*).

### CLOVE

Clove is found in wines that have been matured or aged in new oak *barriques*, which gain this aroma during the process of being toasted (*see* p33). In addition, clove is found in Gewürztraminer from certain *terroirs*, such as Soultzmatt and Bergbieten in Alsace (*eugenol* or *eugenic acid*).

### CURRANT LEAF

Although associated with Sauvignon Blanc, this herbaceous character can be found in any wine made from underripe grapes or grapes from high-vigor vines. Can be green and mean on the finish.

### EUCALYPTUS

This aroma is noticeable in many Australian Cabernet Sauvignon and Shiraz wines, and could originate from leaves falling off eucalyptus trees into grape-pickers' baskets.

### GINGERBREAD

Found in mature Gewürztraminer of the highest quality, when the true spiciness of this variety is mellowed by bottle-age.

### LICORICE

This can be part of the complexity of red, white, and fortified wines of great concentration, particularly those that are made from late-harvested or sun-dried grapes (*geraniol* or *glycyrrhizin*).

## MINT

Although it is occasionally found in Bordeaux, mint is actually far more redolent in full-bodied New World reds, particularly Californian Cabernet (especially Napa) and Coonawarra Shiraz.

## PEPPERCORN

Many young reds have a basic peppery character, but Syrah evokes the distinctive fragrance of crushed black peppercorns, while for top-quality Grüner Veltliner it is ground white pepper.

## SPICY

Many wines have a hint of spiciness, which is more exotic than peppery, but, after a few years' bottle-age, the spiciness of Gewürztraminer should almost burn the palate.

## TAR

Like licorice with a touch of smoke, a tarry aroma in some full-bodied reds, typically Barolo and northern Rhône, could indicate a wine that has not been racked, fined, or filtered.

# OTHER AROMAS AND FLAVORS

These include oaky, smoky, creamy, nutty, biscuity, baked, roasted, and woody characteristics, all produced by the wine's aging. Other aromas and flavors defy classification.

## BISCUITY

Found in fine-quality, well-matured Champagnes, biscuitiness is the post-disgorgement bottle-aroma that typifies Pinot Noir, although many pure Chardonnay Champagnes develop a creamy-biscuitiness (*acetal*, *acetoin*, *diacetyl*, *benzoic aldehyde*, and *undecalactone*).

## BREADY

The second stage of autolysis, as the flowery acacia-like aromas take on more substance and a certain creaminess (*diacetyl*, *undecalactone*, or *paratolylmethyl ketone*).

## BUBBLEGUM

Found in cool-fermented whites and reds made by carbonic maceration (*amyl acetate* or *isoamyl acetate*, also known as "banana oil" or "pear oil," which, in excess, can lead to a nail-polish aroma).

## STRUCK MATCH

A struck match aroma is the clean, if somewhat choking, whiff produced by free sulfur. This is not a fault as such in a young or recently bottled wine, and it can be dispersed by swirling the wine around in the glass (*sulfur dioxide*).

## BURNED RUBBER

This is a serious wine fault created by the reaction between ethyl alcohol and hydrogen sulfide, another wine fault, which produces a foul-smelling compound called *ethylmercaptan*.

## BUTTER

This characteristic is usually found in Chardonnay, and is caused by *diacetyl*, an artificial flavoring that is used by the food industry, but it is also produced naturally during the malolactic process (also *undecalactone*). It is inappropriate for classic sparkling wine, so the *champenois* utilize special low-*diacetyl*-forming bacteria.

## BUTTERSCOTCH

Butterscotch is produced when very ripe, exotically fruity white wines are aged in well-toasted new oak *barriques*, and is most commonly found in New World wines (*cyclotene*, *diacetyl*, *maltol*, or *undecalactone*).

## CARAMEL

This may be either a midpalate flavor in young wines aged in new *barriques* or, as in tawny port, an aftertaste achieved through considerable aging in used barrels (*cyclotene* or *maltol*).

## CANDLE WAX

Candle wax is a more accurate descriptor for Sémillon wines than the more commonly employed lanolin, since lanolin possesses no smell, even though it has a connotation of one (*aprylate*, *caproate*, or *ethyl capryate*).

## CARDBOARD

This characteristic can literally be produced by storing glasses in a cardboard box. It may also be caused by heavy-handed filtration or by leaving a wine to mature for too long in old wood.

## CHEESE

Occasionally, a wine can have a clean cheese aroma (Emmental or blue-veined being most common), but a strong cheesy smell will be the result of a bacterial fault (*ethyl butryrate* or *S-ethythioacetate*).

## CHOCOLATE OR CHOCOLATE-BOX

This is the aroma or flavor typical of youngish Cabernet Sauvignon or Pinot Noir wines, when they are rich and soft with a high alcohol content and low acidity level. It may also be detected as part of the complexity of a mature wine.

## COFFEE

A sign of a great old Champagne, maybe 20- or 50-year-old or more, coffee is now increasingly found on the finish of inexpensive red wines made with medium- or high-toast American oak chips.

## COCONUT

This characteristic is another found in great old Champagne. Pungent coconutty aromas are also produced by various wood lactones that are most commonly found in American oak (could also be *capric acid*).

## EARTHY

Wines can have an earthiness on the palate that some people incorrectly attribute to the *terroir*, but this undesirable taste is unclean and not expressive of origin (*geosmin*).

## EGG, HARD-BOILED

Sulfur is added to wine in order to prevent oxidation, which it does by fixing itself to any oxygen that is present in the wine but, if it fixes with hydrogen, it creates *hydrogen sulfide*, which smells of hard-boiled or rotten eggs.

## FLINTY OR WET PEBBLES

This is a subjective connotation for the finest Sauvignon Blanc that only those who have been without water and had to suck a smooth pebble to keep the saliva going are likely to comprehend.

## FOXY

Foxy is the term used to describe the very distinctive, cloyingly sweet, and perfumed character of certain indigenous American grape varieties (*methyl anthranilate* or *ethyl anthranilate*).

## HONEY

Almost every fine white wine becomes honeyed with age, but particularly great Burgundy, classic German Riesling, and botrytized wines (*phenylethylic acid*).

## JAM

Any red wine can be jammy, but Grenache has a particular tendency toward raspberry jam, while Pinot Noir has a distinct tendency to evoke strawberry jam. A jammy flavor is not typical of a really fine wine, but can be characteristic of a wine that is upfront and lip-smacking.

## LEATHER

A suggestion of leather can be a complex element of many high-quality wines, but the "sweaty-saddle" aroma of old-fashioned Hunter Valley Shiraz is a *methylmercaptan* fault.

## MACAROONS

The almondy-coconutty taste of macaroons is a typical characteristic of a great old Champagne, being similar to a coconutty taste, but sweeter and more complex (*undecalactone* or *capric acid*).

## NAIL POLISH

Nail polish is the pungent, peardrop aroma produced by intensive carbonic maceration. It is found on the worst Beaujolais Nouveau (*amyl acetate* or *isoamyl acetate*, otherwise known as "banana oil" or "pear oil").

## NUTS

This ranges from the generic nuttiness of mature Burgundy, and the walnuts or hazelnuts in Champagne *blanc de blancs*, to the almondy fruit of young Italian red (*acetoin*, *diacetyl*, or *undecalactone*).

## GASOLINE

Anyone who has siphoned off gasoline will know that the classic "petroly" aroma of mature Riesling has nothing in common with the real thing. Yet for those who know and enjoy the zesty-honeyed richness of a great Riesling, "petroly" is one of the most evocative words in the wine-tasting vocabulary (various *terpenes*).

## SAUERKRAUT

The lactic smell of a wine that has undergone excessive malolactic, sauerkraut is actually even less acceptable in wine than the sour milk or sour cream aroma (*diacetyl* or *lactic acid*).

## SHERRY

This is the telltale sign of excessive *acetaldehyde*, which could turn a wine into vinegar unless it is sherry or another type of fortified wine, which will be protected by its high alcohol content.

## SMOKE

Smoke is a complexity that might be varietal, as in the case of Syrah, but can be induced by stirring less during barrel fermentation, suggesting that the wine has not been racked, fined, or filtered.

## SOUR MILK OR SOUR CREAM

The lactic smell of a wine that has undergone excessive malolactic, the sour-milk character may develop into a more pronounced sauerkraut aroma (*diacetyl* or *lactic acid*).

## TOAST

Toastiness is commonly associated with Chardonnay and mature Champagne, particularly *blanc de blancs*, but it can be found in many wines. Toastiness can either be a slow-developing bottle-aroma or an instant gift of new oak (*furanic aldehydes*). Current theory among research chemists is that the toastiness in Chardonnay wines is technically a fixed-sulfur fault, although it is a fault that many wine lovers have come to enjoy.

## VANILLA

Oak often adds a vanilla taste to wine due to vanillin, a substance that gives vanilla pods their aroma (also *lactone*s or *capric acid*).

# GUIDE TO GOOD VINTAGES

This chart provides a useful fingertip reference to the comparative performance of more than 950 vintages, covering 28 different categories of wine. As with any vintage chart, the ratings should merely be seen as "betting odds." They express the likelihood of what might reasonably be expected from a wine of a given year and should not be used as a guide to buying specific wines. No blanket rating can highlight the many exceptions that exist in every vintage, although the higher the rating, the fewer the exceptions; quality and consistency do to some extent go hand in hand.

### KEY TO VINTAGE RATINGS

| | |
|---|---|
| 90–100* | Excellent to superb |
| 80–89 | Good to very good |
| 70–79 | Average to good |
| 60–69 | Disappointing |
| 40–59 | Very bad |
| 0–39 | Disastrous |

100* No vintage can be accurately described as perfect, but those achieving a maximum score are truly great vintages.

Remember that some wines are not particularly enjoyable, nor even superior, in so-called "great years." Such wines, which are normally light-bodied, aromatic whites that are best drunk while young, fresh, and grapey (e.g. Muscat d'Alsace, German QbA, or *Kabinett,* etc), favor vintages with ratings of between 70 and 85, or lower.

| WINE CATEGORY | 2005 | 2004 | 2003 | 2002 | 2001 | 2000 | 1999 | 1998 | 1997 | 1996 | 1995 | 1994 | 1993 | 1992 | 1991 | 1990 | 1989 | 1988 | 1987 | 1986 | 1985 | 1984 |
|---|---|---|---|---|---|---|---|---|---|---|---|---|---|---|---|---|---|---|---|---|---|---|
| BORDEAUX—MÉDOC and GRAVES | 96 | 94 | 93 | 91 | 90 | 98 | 85 | 85 | 83 | 95 | 90 | 85 | 82 | 78 | 78 | 90 | 95 | 88 | 78 | 90 | 92 | 75 |
| BORDEAUX—ST-ÉMILION and POMEROL | 97 | 94 | 89 | 85 | 91 | 98 | 88 | 90 | 80 | 90 | 90 | 85 | 85 | 78 | 75 | 92 | 95 | 88 | 75 | 85 | 92 | 65 |
| BORDEAUX—SAUTERNES and BARSAC | 95 | 90 | 99 | 95 | 98 | 87 | 87 | 89 | 95 | 90 | 95 | 79 | 60 | 65 | 60 | 92 | 95 | 95 | 60 | 90 | 85 | 60 |
| BURGUNDY—CÔTE D'OR—red | 91 | 84 | 75 | 90 | 84 | 85 | 91 | 89 | 88 | 97 | 90 | 70 | 87 | 85 | 82 | 95 | 92 | 98 | 70 | 78 | 100 | 70 |
| BURGUNDY—CÔTE D'OR—white | 90 | 86 | 65 | 90 | 90 | 87 | 89 | 90 | 92 | 97 | 92 | 80 | 87 | 95 | 70 | 98 | 95 | 92 | 80 | 92 | 90 | 80 |
| BURGUNDY—BEAUJOLAIS—red | 90 | 80 | 90 | 85 | 80 | 87 | 88 | 83 | 85 | 90 | 85 | 90 | 85 | 92 | 85 | 90 | 90 | 85 | 78 | 85 | 90 | 70 |
| CHAMPAGNE | 84 | 86 | 50-95 | 88 | 35 | 80 | 80 | 87 | 85 | 98 | 90 | 70 | 87 | 85 | 80 | 98 | 89 | 90 | – | 80 | 95 | – |
| ALSACE | 88 | 87 | 80 | 88 | 90 | 85 | 85 | 85 | 90 | 90 | 90 | 90 | 85 | 80 | 75 | 90 | 95 | 90 | 78 | 75 | 90 | 65 |
| LOIRE—sweet white | 88 | 80 | 88 | 90 | 95 | 60 | 60 | 60 | 91 | 90 | 95 | 90 | 55 | 55 | 50 | 90 | 90 | 90 | 60 | 85 | 87 | 65 |
| LOIRE—red | 88 | 85 | 95 | 90 | 80 | 85 | 80 | 75 | 90 | 92 | 90 | 60 | 60 | 40 | 40 | 90 | 90 | 90 | 40 | 85 | 90 | 75 |
| RHÔNE—NORTHERN RHÔNE | 96 | 86 | 96 | 70 | 85 | 90 | 91 | 89 | 85 | 85 | 92 | 75 | 65 | 75 | 85 | 96 | 95 | 95 | 88 | 86 | 95 | 70 |
| RHÔNE—SOUTHERN RHÔNE | 96 | 90 | 95 | 55 | 89 | 92 | 88 | 96 | 70 | 85 | 90 | 80 | 80 | 75 | 70 | 90 | 95 | 92 | 70 | 88 | 90 | 70 |
| GERMANY—MOSEL | 96 | 91 | 85–97 | 92 | 90 | 80 | 87 | 75 | 90 | 85 | 92 | 92 | 94 | 92 | 88 | 100 | 98 | 95 | 75 | 93 | 95 | 50 |
| GERMANY—RHINE | 90 | 90 | 85–94 | 93 | 92 | 80 | 87 | 85 | 95 | 84 | 90 | 85 | 90 | 90 | 85 | 95 | 95 | 90 | 78 | 93 | 95 | 50 |
| ITALY—BAROLO | 86 | 91 | 90 | 75 | 94 | 90 | 95 | 94 | 92 | 94 | 90 | 88 | 85 | 75 | 80 | 93 | 95 | 95 | 88 | 82 | 95 | 55 |
| ITALY—CHIANTI | 85 | 93 | 89 | 75 | 91 | 87 | 89 | 85 | 93 | 80 | 88 | 90 | 85 | 75 | 80 | 90 | 65 | 90 | 83 | 80 | 93 | 60 |
| SPAIN—RIOJA | 90 | 90 | 80 | 70 | 93 | 85 | 84 | 80 | 85 | 75 | 87 | 95 | 87 | 85 | 85 | 78 | 85 | 80 | 80 | 80 | 80 | 75 |
| PORTUGAL—VINTAGE PORT | 80 | 88 | 92 | 70 | 86 | 94 | 75 | 80 | 90 | – | 88 | 95 | – | 85 | 95 | – | – | – | – | – | 95 | – |
| US—CALIFORNIA—red | 96 | 95 | 90 | 92 | 94 | 89 | 94 | 89 | 87 | 88 | 92 | 94 | 88 | 91 | 93 | 80 | 80 | 85 | 90 | 88 | 98 | 92 |
| US—CALIFORNIA—white | 96 | 90 | 90 | 91 | 90 | 89 | 90 | 89 | 88 | 88 | 92 | 88 | 89 | 92 | 85 | 80 | 82 | 88 | 85 | 90 | 84 | 95 |
| US—PACIFIC NORTHWEST—red | 85 | 89 | 88 | 93 | 89 | 90 | 95 | 92 | 85 | 90 | 88 | 88 | 87 | 89 | 85 | 85 | 85 | 85 | 85 | 86 | 96 | 50 |
| US—PACIFIC NORTHWEST—white | 82 | 84 | 85 | 90 | 90 | 90 | 90 | 88 | 85 | 90 | 85 | 75 | 69 | 85 | 85 | 88 | 80 | 80 | 85 | 90 | 96 | 70 |
| AUSTRALIA—HUNTER VALLEY—red | 95 | 82 | 98 | 70 | 70 | 88 | 80 | 90 | 65 | 95 | 85 | 70 | 90 | 65 | 95 | 80 | 85 | 80 | 88 | 95 | 90 | 80 |
| AUSTRALIA—HUNTER VALLEY—white | 90 | 89 | 98 | 95 | 85 | 88 | 80 | 90 | 65 | 95 | 85 | 85 | 90 | 75 | 90 | 75 | 90 | 90 | 90 | 95 | 90 | 80 |
| AUSTRALIA—BAROSSA VALLEY—red | 95 | 90 | 70 | 92 | 90 | 80 | 70-95 | 94 | 90 | 95 | 70 | 80 | 80 | 80 | 80 | 95 | 85 | 85 | 80 | 88 | 95 | 95 |
| AUSTRALIA—BAROSSA VALLEY—white | 90 | 86 | 70 | 88 | 75 | 85 | 80 | 90 | 90 | 90 | 95 | 80 | 80 | 70 | 80 | 90 | 90 | 70 | 80 | 80 | 90 | 95 |
| AUSTRALIA—MARGARET RIVER—red | 88 | 90 | 70 | 90 | 95 | 89 | 90 | 87 | 90 | 90 | 90 | 95 | 85 | 90 | 98 | 88 | 85 | 88 | 88 | 88 | 90 | 80 |
| AUSTRALIA—MARGARET RIVER—white | 89 | 87 | 70 | 90 | 90 | 88 | 85 | 85 | 85 | 95 | 93 | 93 | 85 | 88 | 86 | 85 | 88 | 88 | 88 | 88 | 90 | 80 |

## LOW-RATED VINTAGES

These should be treated with extreme caution, but not ignored. Although wine investors buy only great vintages of blue-chip wines, the clever wine drinker makes a beeline for unfashionable vintages at a tasting and searches for the exceptions. This is because no matter how successful the wine, if it comes from a modest year it will be relatively inexpensive.

## CLOSE-SCORING WINES

Obviously, the smaller the gap between two scores, the less difference one might expect in the quality of the wines, but many readers may think that to discriminate by as little as one point is to split hairs. Certainly, a one-point difference reveals no great divide but, on balance, it indicates which vintage has the edge.

## UNRATED VINTAGES

It is impossible to rate generally undeclared vintages of port and Champagne because the few wines released often prove to be truly exceptional anomalies. Take the Champagne vintage of 1951: this was one of the worst vintages in Champagne's history. According to almost everyone who remembers the harvest, no pure vintaged Champagnes were produced, yet my researches have uncovered three. If I were to rank 1951 on the two I actually tasted (Clos des Goisses and Salon), it would be one of the finest vintages of the century, which is clearly a nonsense. Port vintages pose a similar problem: should 1992 be judged on the basis of the superb Taylors, by the handful of other good, but distinctly lesser, 1992s, or by the majority of shippers, who did not produce good enough wine to declare a vintage?

| 1983 | 1982 | 1981 | 1980 | 1979 | 1978 | 1977 | 1976 | 1975 | 1974 | 1973 | 1972 | 1971 | PRE-1969 GREAT VINTAGES | |
|---|---|---|---|---|---|---|---|---|---|---|---|---|---|---|
| 88 | 98 | 82 | 78 | 85 | 90 | 45 | 80 | 90 | 60 | 80 | 40 | 83 | 1970, 1961, 1953, 1949, 1945, 1929, 1928, 1900 | BORDEAUX—MÉDOC and GRAVES |
| 85 | 98 | 82 | 75 | 85 | 80 | 45 | 80 | 90 | 60 | 78 | 40 | 83 | 1961, 1953, 1949, 1945, 1929, 1928, 1900 | BORDEAUX—ST-ÉMILION and POMEROL |
| 100 | 70 | 70 | 80 | 80 | 65 | 50 | 85 | 90 | 50 | 65 | 55 | 85 | 1962, 1959, 1955, 1949, 1947, 1945, 1937 | BORDEAUX—SAUTERNES and BARSAC |
| 88 | 80 | 75 | 60 | 75 | 85 | 40 | 88 | 20 | 70 | 65 | 85 | 90 | 1961, 1959, 1949, 1945, 1929, 1919, 1915 | BURGUNDY—CÔTE D'OR—red |
| 88 | 86 | 85 | 72 | 80 | 88 | 50 | 80 | 80 | 75 | 72 | 80 | 85 | 1962, 1928, 1921 | BURGUNDY—CÔTE D'OR—white |
| 90 | 72 | 74 | 55 | 60 | 90 | 55 | 90 | 50 | 55 | 82 | 70 | 85 | 1961, 1959, 1957, 1949, 1945, 1929 | BURGUNDY—BEAUJOLAIS—red |
| 90 | 92 | 90 | 70 | 90 | 80 | – | 90 | 90 | 60 | 88 | – | 95 | 1964, 1959, 1947, 1945, 1928, 1921, 1914 | CHAMPAGNE |
| 100 | 80 | 89 | 60 | 85 | 40 | 33 | 10 | 92 | 50 | 85 | 40 | 90 | 1969, 1961, 1959, 1953, 1949 1945, 1937, 1921 | ALSACE |
| 90 | 85 | 70 | 65 | 55 | 75 | 30 | 92 | 90 | 20 | 85 | 10 | 90 | 1969, 1961, 1959, 1949, 1945, 1921 | LOIRE—sweet white |
| 85 | 85 | 80 | 70 | 60 | 80 | 45 | 90 | 92 | 85 | 80 | 10 | 85 | 1969, 1961 | LOIRE—red |
| 98 | 92 | 75 | 78 | 81 | 100 | 50 | 85 | 72 | 78 | 85 | 90 | 86 | 1970, 1961 | RHÔNE—NORTHERN RHÔNE |
| 92 | 88 | 87 | 83 | 78 | 98 | 72 | 85 | 68 | 80 | 86 | 90 | 85 | 1970, 1967, 1961 | RHÔNE—SOUTHERN RHÔNE |
| 100 | 70 | 75 | 50 | 85 | 55 | 50 | 100 | 98 | 45 | 90 | 40 | 98 | 1969, 1959, 1953, 1949, 1945, 1921 | GERMANY—MOSEL |
| 98 | 73 | 75 | 50 | 88 | 55 | 50 | 98 | 100 | 40 | 88 | 40 | 100 | 1969, 1959, 1953, 1949, 1945, 1921 | GERMANY—RHINE |
| 90 | 95 | 80 | 60 | 85 | 100 | 40 | 80 | 70 | 83 | 50 | 20 | 90 | 1958, 1947, 1931, 1922 | ITALY—BAROLO |
| 85 | 90 | 80 | 70 | 85 | 88 | 75 | 40 | 85 | 75 | 70 | 65 | 98 | 1947, 1931, 1928, 1911 | ITALY—CHIANTI |
| 88 | 100 | 85 | 80 | 60 | 80 | 25 | 85 | 85 | 84 | 75 | 30 | 45 | 1970, 1968, 1964, 1962, 1942, 1934, 1924, 1920, 1916 | SPAIN—RIOJA |
| 95 | 80 | – | 85 | – | 80 | 99 | – | 75 | – | – | 78 | – | 1969, 1963, 1945, 1935, 1931, 1927, 1908 | PORTUGAL—VINTAGE PORT |
| 90 | 88 | 85 | 88 | 80 | 88 | 80 | 88 | 86 | 95 | 88 | 80 | 70 | 1970, 1968, 1951, 1946 | US—CALIFORNIA—red |
| 86 | 86 | 88 | 90 | 80 | 88 | 85 | 80 | 88 | 90 | 88 | 65 | 85 | 1970, 1967 | US—CALIFORNIA—white |
| 95 | 84 | 88 | 88 | 88 | 88 | 80 | 88 | 90 | 88 | – | – | – | | US—PACIFIC NORTHWEST—red |
| 95 | 83 | 80 | 87 | 80 | 88 | 80 | 88 | 88 | 88 | – | – | – | | US—PACIFIC NORTHWEST—white |
| 90 | 80 | 80 | 90 | 98 | 80 | 80 | 70 | 100 | 45 | 80 | 45 | 25 | 1965 | AUSTRALIA—HUNTER VALLEY—red |
| 90 | 80 | 85 | 98 | 90 | 70 | 70 | 80 | 70 | 80 | 88 | 80 | 20 | 1967 | AUSTRALIA—HUNTER VALLEY—white |
| 70 | 90 | 85 | 80 | 92 | 70 | 80 | 90 | 80 | 20 | 20 | – | – | | AUSTRALIA—BAROSSA VALLEY—red |
| 85 | 90 | 70 | 80 | 92 | 90 | 70 | 90 | 70 | 20 | 25 | – | – | | AUSTRALIA—BAROSSA VALLEY—white |
| 80 | 90 | 85 | 80 | 80 | 70 | 90 | 45 | 30 | 45 | – | – | – | | AUSTRALIA—MARGARET RIVER—red |
| 80 | 90 | 85 | 90 | 80 | 45 | 70 | 65 | 30 | 45 | – | – | – | | AUSTRALIA—MARGARET RIVER—white |

# TROUBLESHOOTER'S GUIDE

| SYMPTOM | CAUSE | REMEDY |
| --- | --- | --- |
| Pieces of floating cork | You are the cause, and this is not a corked wine! Tiny pieces of cork have become dislodged when opening the bottle. | Fish them out and drink the wine. If it happens frequently, buy a Screwpull corkscrew. |
| Sediment | All wines shed a deposit in time; most are drunk before they do. | Decant the bottle. |
| Coating on the inside of the bottle | Full-bodied reds from hot countries or exceptionally hot vintages in cool-climate countries are prone to shedding a deposit that adheres to the inside of the bottle. | You can check to see whether the wine pours clear. However, there is bound to be some loose sediment and, even when there is not, it is always safest to decant. |
| Cloudy haze | If it is not sediment, it will not drop out and is either a metal or protein haze. | Seek a refund. Home winemakers can try bentonite but, although this removes a protein haze, it could make a metal haze worse! |
| A film or slick on the surface | This is an oil slick caused by glasses or a decanter. Either they have not been properly rinsed or a minuscule amount of grease has come from the dish cloth used to polish them. | Use detergent to clean glasses and rinse them thoroughly in hot water. Never use a glass cloth for anything other than polishing glasses and never dry them with all-purpose tea towels. |
| Still wine with tiny bubbles clinging to the glass | An unwanted second fermentation or malolactic can make some still wines as fizzy as Champagne. | If the wine is really fizzy, then take it back but, if the fault is just a spritz or prickle, use a Vacu-vin to suck the gas out. |
| Asparagus or canned-peas aromas | Sauvignon Blanc from overripe grapes or kept too long in bottle. | No technical fault—buy a more recent vintage next time. |
| Cabbage, cauliflower, farmyard, or manure aromas | Technically a fault (methylmercaptan), but half the wine trade would argue it is part of the complexity of some wines, particularly Burgundy. | Some retailers will refund you, but those who have personally selected this "traditional" style may not. |
| Currant leaf aromas or flavors | Caused by underripe grapes or high-vigor vines, this may be deliberate if wine is from a hot country and green on the finish. | Not a fault as such, although it is not exactly good winemaking so, if you cannot force yourself to drink the wine, throw it away. |
| Bubblegum, peardrops, or nail polish aromas | Produced by cool-fermentation in white wines and carbonic maceration in reds, and found in the worst Beaujolais Nouveau. | This is not a fault, so drink the wine or give it away. |
| Burnt match aromas (or a tickle in the nose or throat) | The clean whiff of free sulfur, which protects the wine, as opposed to fixed-sulfur faults, which are pungent odors. | Swirl the glass or pour the wine vigorously into a jug and back into the bottle, to disperse the aroma through aeration. |
| Burnt rubber or skunk | A serious wine fault created when ethyl alcohol reacts with hydrogen sulphide, a fixed-sulphur fault, to form a foul-smelling compound called ethylmercaptan. | Take the wine back for a full refund. |
| Cardboard aromas | This can be due to storing glasses in a cardboard box, heavy-handed filtration, or leaving a wine too long in old wood. | If the wine is still cardboardy in a clean, untainted glass, you could seek a refund, but may have to put it down to experience. |
| Cheese aromas | Occasionally a wine has a clean cheese aroma (Emmental or blue-veined being most common), but a real cheesy smell will be a bacterial fault (ethyl butryrate or S-ethythioacetate). | Take the wine back for a full refund. |
| Earthy aromas | Unclean, but not exactly a known fault. | Since the wine was probably purchased by someone who thought it had a *goût de terroir*, you are unlikely to get a refund. |
| Hard cook or rotten-egg aromas | Sulfur is added to wine to prevent oxidation by fixing itself to any oxygen, but if it fixes with hydrogen it creates hydrogen sulfide, which is the stuff of stink-bombs. | Theoretically, if you put a brass or copper object into the wine, the smell should drop out as a very fine brown sediment, but frankly it is quicker and easier to ask for a refund. |
| Geranium aromas | In a sweet wine, this is a sorbic acid and bacterial infection fault. In Asti or any other Muscat wine, the geraniol that gives the wine its classic flowery-peach character has degraded with age. | Take the wine back for a full refund. |
| Maderized (in any wine other than Madeira) | Maderization is undesirable in any ordinary, light table wine. Such a wine will have been affected by light or heat, or both. | Take the wine back for a full refund, unless you have kept it under bad conditions yourself. |
| Mushroom aromas | A clean mushroom aroma indicates Pinot Meunier in a fine old Champagne but, if musty, it will be a contamination fault. | If a contamination fault, take the wine back for a full refund. |
| Musty aromas, as in an old church | The wine is corked (or at least it is suffering from a corky taint). | Smell the wine an hour later. A corked wine will get worse and you should seek a refund. Harmless bottle mustiness disappears. |
| Mousy aromas | Caused by *Brettanomyces* yeast and malolactic bacteria, this is feared in the New World but some Old World wineries use *Brettanomyces* yeast deliberately to add to a wine's complexity. | Give it to someone you do not like. |
| Onion or garlic aromas | A serious wine fault created when ethyl alcohol reacts with hydrogen sulfide, a fixed-sulfur fault, to form a foul-smelling compound called ethylmercaptan. | Take the wine back for a full refund. |
| Sauerkraut aromas | The smell of a wine that has undergone excessive malolactic, this is more unacceptable than sour milk or sour cream aromas. | Take the wine back for a full refund. |
| Sherry aromas (in any wine other than sherry) | Excessive acetaldehyde: the wine is oxidized. An ordinary wine with excessive acetaldehyde turns into vinegar, but sherry and other fortified wines are protected by a high alcohol content. | Take the wine back for a full refund. |
| Vinegar aromas | The distinctive aroma of acetic acid: the wine has oxidized. | Use it for salad dressing. |

# GLOSSARY OF TASTING AND TECHNICAL TERMS

Terms that are explained more comprehensively within the main body of the book are accompanied by a cross-reference to the appropriate page. Terms that appear within a Glossary entry and have their own separate entry appear set in bold type.

Key to abbreviations: Fr. = French; Ger. = German; Gr. = Greek; It. = Italian; Port. = Portuguese; Sp. = Spanish; S. Afr. = South African.

**ABC** An acronym for "Anything But Cabernet" or "Anything But Chardonnay," ABC was a more-than-acceptable term when originally conceived by Randall Grahm of Bonny Doon. Grahm was selling Cabernet at the time, but saw it as a rut that every California winery was trapped in. He wanted to explore the quality potential of other grapes, particularly the Rhône varieties, but was severely restricted by the public demand for Cabernet and Chardonnay. While Cabernet walked off the shelf, Grahm had to work hard at selling the virtues of anything more exotic. Compelled to sell Cabernet to fund other activities, he came up with the ABC term. Everyone loved it when Grahm invented it. It has since been hijacked by inverted snobs and myopic critics, however, who have been zealots in their crusade to rid the world of two great wine grapes.

**ABV** Abbreviation for alcohol by volume.

**AC** (Port., Gr.) Short for *Adega Cooperativa* in Portugal and Agricultural Cooperative in Greece, or other titles denoting a local or regional cooperative in these countries.

**ACCESSIBLE** Literally that the wine is easy to approach, with no great barriers of **tannin**, **acidity**, or undeveloped **extract** to prevent enjoyment of drinking. This term is often used for young, fine-quality wine that will undoubtedly improve with age but whose tannins are **supple** and thus approachable.

**ACETALDEHYDE** The principal **aldehyde** in all wines, but found in much greater quantities in sherry. In light, unfortified table wines, a small amount of acetaldehyde enhances the **bouquet**, but an excess is undesirable because it is unstable, halfway to complete **oxidation**, and evokes a sherrylike smell.

**ACETIC ACID** The most important **volatile acid** found in wine, aside from **carbonic acid**. Small amounts of acetic acid contribute positively to the attractive flavor of a wine, but large quantities produce a taste of vinegar.

**ACETIFICATION** The production of **acetic acid** in a wine.

**ACETOBACTER** The vinegar *bacillus* (rod-shaped bacterium), which can cause **acetification**.

**ACIDITY** Essential for the life and vitality of all wines. Too much will make wine too **sharp** (not sour—that's a fault), but not enough will make it taste **flat** and dull, and the flavor will not last in the mouth. *See also* **Total acidity** and **pH**.

**ACTIVE ACIDITY** Acids contain positively charged hydrogen ions, the concentration of which determines the **total acidity** of a wine. The **pH** is the measure of the electrical charge of a given solution (positive acidity hydrogen buffered by negative alkalinity hydrogen ions). Thus, the pH of a wine is a measure of its active acidity.

**ADEGA** (Port.) Cellar or winery. Often used as part of a firm's title.

**AEROBIC** Occurring in the presence of air.

**AFTERTASTE** A term for the flavor and **aroma** left in the mouth after the wine has been swallowed.

When the aftertaste is attractive, it could be the reason why you prefer one wine to a similar wine with no particular aftertaste.

**AGES GRACEFULLY** Describes wine that retains **finesse** as it matures and that sometimes may even increase in finesse.

**AGGRESSIVE** The opposite of **soft** and **smooth**.

**ALBANY DOCTOR** One of Western Australia's beneficially cooling sea breezes, the Albany Doctor provides similar relief to that of the famous **Fremantle Doctor**, only farther south and closer to the coast. *See also* **Canberra Doctor**.

**ALBARIZA** (Sp.) A white-surfaced soil formed by diatomaceous (decomposed deep-sea algae) deposits, which is found in the sherry-producing area of Spain. *See also* Sherry Country, p.321.

**ALCOHOL** In wine terms, this is **ethyl alcohol**; a colorless flammable liquid. Alcohol is essential to the flavor and **body** of alcoholic products, thus a de-alcoholized wine is intrinsically difficult to perfect.

**ALCOHOLIC** This term is usually employed in a pejorative rather than a literal sense and implies that a wine has too much **alcohol** to be in **balance**.

**ALDEHYDE** The midway stage between an **alcohol** and an **acid**, formed during the **oxidation** of an alcohol. **Acetaldehyde** is the most important of the common wine aldehydes, and forms as wine alcohol oxidizes to become **acetic acid** (vinegar). Small amounts of acetaldehyde add to the **complexity** of a wine, but too much will make a table wine smell like sherry.

**AMINO ACIDS** Proteins formed by a combination of fruit **esters**, amino acids are found naturally in grapes and are both created and consumed during **fermentation** and **autolysis**. They are essential precursors to the complexity and finesse of a sparkling wine. *See also* **Maillard Reactions**.

**AMPELOGRAPHER** An expert who studies, records, and identifies grapevines.

**AMYLIC** The peardrop, banana, or bubble-gum aromas of amyl or isoamyl acetate, excessive amounts of which can be produced in white wines if the fermentation is conducted at a very low temperature, and in red wines made by *macération carbonique*.

**ANAEROBIC** Occurring in the absence of oxygen. Most maturation processes that take place in a sealed bottle are considered to be anaerobic.

**ANBAUGEBIET** (Ger.) A wine region in Germany, such as Rheinpfalz or Mosel, that is divided into districts (*Bereiche*). All QbA and QmP wines must show their *Anbaugebiet* of origin on the label.

**ANTHOCYANINS** The second-most important group of phenolic compounds found in wine, anthocyanins are color pigments located in the grapes' skins.

**ANTIOXIDANT** Any chemical that prevents grapes, **must**, or wine from **oxidizing**, such as **ascorbic acid** or sulfur dioxide ($SO_2$).

**AOC** (Fr.) *Appellation d'Origine Contrôlée* is the top rung in the French wine-quality system, although in practice it includes everything from the greatest French wines to the worst; thus it is almost always better to buy an expensive *vin de pays* than a cheap AOC wine.

**APERITIF** Originally used exclusively to describe a beverage prescribed purely for laxative purposes, the term aperitif now describes any drink that is taken before a meal in order to stimulate the appetite.

**APPELLATION** Literally a name, this term is usually used to refer to an official geographically-based designation for a wine.

**APPELLATION D'ORIGINE CONTRÔLÉE** *See* AOC.

**AQUIFER** A water-retaining geological formation into which rainfall from the surrounding area drains.

**AROMA** This should really be confined to the fresh and fruity smells reminiscent of grapes, rather than the more winey or bottle-mature complexities of **bouquet**; but it is not always possible to use this word in its purest form, hence aroma and bouquet may be thought of as being synonymous.

**AROMATIC GRAPE VARIETIES** The most aromatic classic varieties are Gewürztraminer, Muscat, and Riesling, and they are defined as such because when ripe they possess high levels of various **terpenes** in their skins. Although attractive when young, these terpenes take a few years in bottle to develop their full varietal potential.

**AROMATIZED WINE** Usually fortified, these wines are flavored by as few as one, or as many as 50, aromatic substances and range from bittersweet **vermouth** to *retsina*. The various herbs, fruits, flowers, and other less-appetizing ingredients used include strawberries, orange peel, elderflowers, wormwood, quinine, and pine resin.

**ASCORBIC ACID** Otherwise known as Vitamin C, ascorbic acid is an **antioxidant**, which is often used in conjunction with sulfur. It has a more freshening effect than sulfur, which tends to dampen the aromatics in wine. It also enables less sulfur to be used in the **vinification** process. Not to be confused with **sorbic acid**.

**ASEPTIC** A particular characteristic of a substance such as **sorbic acid** or sulfur dioxide ($SO_2$) that can kill bacteria.

**ASPECT** The topography of a vineyard, including its altitude, the direction in which the vines face, and the angle of any slope.

**ASSEMBLAGE** (Fr.) A blend of base wines that creates the final *cuvée*.

**ATMOSPHERE** A measure of atmospheric pressure: 1 atmosphere = 15 pounds per square inch. The average internal pressure of a bottle of Champagne is six atmospheres.

**ATTACK** A wine with good attack suggests one that is **complete** and readily presents its full armament of taste characteristics to the **palate**. The wine is likely to be youthful rather than mature and its attack augurs well for its future.

**AUSLESE** (Ger.) A category of German **QmP** wine that is very sweet, made from late-harvested grapes, and may also contain some **botrytized** grapes.

**AUSTERE** This term is used to describe wine that lacks fruit and is dominated by harsh **acidity** and/or **tannin**.

**AUTOLYSIS** The enzymatic breakdown of **yeast** cells that increases the possibility of bacterial spoilage; the autolytic effect of aging a wine on its **lees** is therefore undesirable in most wines, exceptions being those bottled *sur lie* (principally Muscadet) and sparkling wines.

**AUTOLYTIC** With the aroma of a freshly disgorged brut-style sparkling wine, which is not "yeasty" at all, but has a flowery, often acacia-like, freshness.

**BACK-BLEND** To blend fresh, unfermented grape juice into a fully fermented wine, with the goal of adding a certain fresh, grapey sweetness commonly associated with German wines. Synonymous with the German practice of adding *Süssreserve*.

**BACKWARD** Describes a wine that is slow to develop (the opposite of precocious).

**BAKED** Applies to wines of high alcoholic content that give a sensory perception of grapes harvested in great heat—either from a hot country or from a classic wine area in a sweltering hot year. This characteristic can be controlled to some extent by the following methods: early harvesting, night harvesting, rapid transport to the winery, and modern cool-fermentation techniques.

**BALANCE** Refers to the harmonious relationship between acids, **alcohol**, fruit, **tannin**, and other natural elements. If you have two similar wines but you definitely prefer one of them, its balance is likely to be one of the two determining factors (**length** being the other).

**BAN DE VENDANGE** (Fr.) Official regional start of grape-picking for the latest vintage.

**BARREL-FERMENTED** Some white wines are still traditionally fermented in oak barrels—new for top-quality Bordeaux, Burgundy, and premium **varietal** wines; old for middle-quality wines and top-quality Champagnes. New barrels impart oaky characteristics; the older the barrels, the less oaky and more **oxidative** the influence. Barrel-fermented wines have more complex **aromas** than wines that have simply been matured in wood. *See also* Stainless Steel or Oak?, p.26.

**BARRIQUE** (Fr.) This literally means "barrel," but is used generically in English-speaking countries for any small **oak** cask and often denotes the use of new oak.

**BASIC** A marketing term for a quality category; *see* **Premium**.

**BAUMÉ** (Fr.) A scale of measurement used to indicate the amount of sugar in grape **must**.

**BEERENAUSLESE** (Ger.) A category of German QmP wine that comes above **Auslese** but beneath **Trockenbeerenauslese**, and is made from **botrytized** grapes. It has more **finesse** and **elegance** than any other intensely sweet wine, with the possible exception of *Eiswein*.

**BENCH** or **BENCHLAND** The flat land between two slopes, this term describes a form of natural, rather than artificial, terrace.

**BENTONITE** This is a fine clay containing a volcanic ash derivative called montromillonite, which is a hydrated silicate of magnesium that activates a precipitation in wine when used as a **fining** agent.

**BEREICH** (Ger.) A wine district in Germany, which contains smaller **Grosslagen** and is itself part of a larger **Anbaugebiet**.

**BIG VINTAGE, BIG YEAR** These terms are usually applied to great years, because the exceptional weather conditions produce bigger (i.e., fuller and richer) wines than normal. They may also be used literally to describe a year with a big crop.

**BIG WINE** This term describes a full-bodied wine with an exceptionally rich flavor.

**BIODYNAMIC** Wines produced biodynamically are grown without the aid of chemical or synthetic sprays or **fertilizers** and are vinified with natural **yeast** and the minimum use of **filtration**, sulfur dioxide ($SO_2$), and **chaptalization**.

**BISCUITY** A desirable aspect of **bouquet** that is found in some Champagnes—particularly in well-matured, Pinot-Noir-dominated blends (Chardonnay-dominated Champagnes tend to go toasty, although some top-quality Chardonnay Champagnes can slowly acquire a creamy-biscuitiness).

**BITE** A very definite qualification of **grip**. Bite is usually a desirable characteristic, although an unpleasant bite is possible.

**BITTERNESS** This quality may be an unpleasant aspect of a poorly made wine or an expected characteristic of an as-yet-undeveloped concentration of flavors that should, with maturity, become rich and delicious. The term is often applied to **tannin**.

**BLACKSTRAP** A derogatory term that originated when port was an unsophisticated product, colored by elderberries and very **coarse**.

**BLANC DE BLANCS** (Fr.) This literally means "white of whites," and describes a white wine made from white grapes. It is a term often, but not exclusively, used for sparkling wines.

**BLANC DE NOIRS** (Fr.) This literally means "white of blacks," and describes a white wine made from black grapes. It is a term that is often, but not exclusively, used for sparkling wines. In the New World, such wines usually have a tinge of pink (often no different from a full-fledged **rosé**), but a classic *blanc de noirs* should be as white as possible without artificial means.

**BLIND, BLIND TASTING** A winetasting at which the identity of the wines is unknown to the taster until after he or she has made notes and given scores. All competitive tastings are made blind.

**BLOWZY** An overblown and exaggerated fruity **aroma**, such as fruit jam, which may be attractive in a cheap wine, but would indicate a lack of **finesse** in a more expensive product.

**BLUSH WINE** A **rosé** wine that is probably cheap.

**BOB** An acronym for "Buyer's Own Brand," under which many retailers and restaurants sell wine of increasingly good value—particularly in the supermarket sector, in which the selection process has been increasingly honed to a fine art since the early 1980s.

**BODEGA** (Sp.) The Spanish equivalent of the Portuguese *adega* (i.e., a cellar or winery).

**BODY** The impression of weight in the mouth, which is brought about by a combination of the fruit **extract** and alcoholic strength.

**BOTA** (Sp.) A sherry butt (cask) with a capacity of between 600 and 650 liters (159 to 172 gallons).

**BOTRYTIS** A generic term for rot, but also often used as an abbreviation of *Botrytis cinerea*.

**BOTRYTIS CINEREA** The technically correct name for noble rot, the only rot that is welcomed by winemakers—particularly in sweet-wine areas, as it is responsible for the world's greatest sweet wines. *See also* Sauternes, p.98.

**BOTRYTIZED GRAPES** Literally "rotten grapes," but the term is commonly used for grapes that have been affected by *Botrytis cinerea*.

**BOTTLE-AGE** The length of time a wine spends in bottle before it is consumed. A wine that has good bottle-age is one that has sufficient time to mature properly. Bottle-aging has a mellowing effect.

**BOTTLE-AROMAS** In Riesling and Gewürztraminer, these are richer aromatics as **terpenes** develop under **anaerobic** conditions. In sparkling wine, they are the mellowing aromas created after **disgorgement**.

**BOUQUET** This should really be applied to the combination of smells directly attributable to a wine's maturity in bottle—thus "aroma" for grape-related smells and "bouquet" for maturation-related smells. But it is not always possible to use these words in their purest form, hence aroma and bouquet may be considered synonymous.

**BOURGEOIS** (Fr.) *Cru Bourgeois* is a Bordeaux château classification beneath *Cru Classé*.

**BREATHING** A term used to describe the interaction between a wine and the air after a bottle has been opened and before it is drunk.

**BREED** The **finesse** of a wine that is due to the intrinsic quality of grape and *terroir* combined with the irrefutable skill and experience of a great winemaker.

**BRETTANOMYCES** A genus of yeast that can inhabit a winery or barrels that are sold from one winery to another. Brett (as it is commonly referred to) is a common spoilage organism that mainly, although not exclusively, affects red wines. It creates various **volatile phenols**, including ethyl-4-phenol, which is responsible for the "Brett" off-odors, such as the so-called sweaty saddles, barnyard, stables, and generally horsey smells.

**BRUT** (Fr.) Normally reserved for sparkling wines, *brut* literally means raw or bone dry. Even the driest wines, however, contain a little residual sugar.

**BURNT** Synonymous with **baked**, and marginally uncomplimentary.

**BUTT** See **BOTA**.

**BUTTERY** This is normally a rich, **fat**, and positively delicious character found in white wines, particularly those that have undergone **malolactic** fermentation.

**BUYER'S OWN BRAND** BOB for short, this is a brand that belongs to the wine buyer, which could be a wine merchant, supermarket, or restaurant (the buyer is the seller as far as the consumer is concerned). *See also* **BOB**.

**CA** (Sp.) Short for *Cooperativa Agrícola* and other titles denoting a local or regional cooperative.

**CANBERRA DOCTOR** An easterly evening wind from the coast that helps to cool Canberra, although it virtually blows itself out by the time it reaches Braidwood or Bungendore. *See also* **Albany Doctor** and **Fremantle Doctor**.

**CANOPY MANAGEMENT** The vine's canopy is comprised of the collective arrangement of its shoots, leaves, and fruit. Ideally, a canopy will have most of its leaves well-exposed to sunlight, as this promotes fruit ripening through **photosynthesis**, and air circulation will be good, which provides the least favorable environmental conditions for the development of fungal diseases. References to an excessive or too-vigorous canopy imply that the ratio of leaves to fruit is too high, causing **herbaceous** flavors in the wines produced from such vines.

**CANTINA** (It.) Winery.

**CANTINA SOCIALE** (It.) A grower's cooperative.

**CAP** The manta or layer of skins that rises to the top of the vat during *cuvaison*.

**CARBON DIOXIDE** See Carbonic gas.

**CARBONATE** A salt or ester of **carbonic** acid. Active or free carbonates increase the alkalinity of soil and are thus found in limestone soils, such as chalk.

**CARBONIC ACID** The correct term for carbon dioxide ($CO_2$) when it dissolves in the water content of wine (to become $H_2CO_3$). Although sometimes referred to as a **volatile acid**, it is held in equilibrium with the gas in its dissolved state and cannot be isolated in its pure form.

**CARBONIC GAS** Synonymous with carbon dioxide ($CO_2$), this gas is naturally produced during the **fermentation** process (when the sugar is converted into almost equal parts of **alcohol** and carbonic gas). It is normally allowed to escape during fermentation, although a tiny amount will always be present in its dissolved form (**carbonic acid**) in any wine, even a still one; otherwise, it would taste dull, **flat**, and lifeless. If the gas is prevented from escaping, the wine becomes sparkling.

**CARBONIC MACERATION** The English term for *Macération carbonique*.

**CASEIN** A milk protein sometimes used for **fining**.

**CASK-FERMENTED** The same as barrel-fermented.

**CASSIS** (Fr.) Literally "blackcurrant." If "*cassis*" is used by winetasters in preference to "blackcurrant," it probably implies a richer, more concentrated, and viscous character.

**CEDARWOOD** A purely subjective word applied to a particular **bouquet** associated with the bottle-maturity of a wine previously stored or fermented in wood, usually **oak**.

**CELLAR DOOR** A sales point at a winery. This is often a sophisticated retail operation in the New World, with sales of wine accessories, books, and T-shirts as well as the wines. For small growers in the Old World, however, purchases are more-often-than-not conducted in the producer's kitchen!

**CENTRIFUGAL FILTRATION** Not **filtration** in the pure sense, but a process in which unwanted matter is separated from wine or grape juice by so-called "centrifugal force."

**CÉPAGE** (Fr.) Literally "grape variety," this is sometimes used on the label immediately prior to the variety, while in the plural format (*cépages*) it is used to refer to the **varietal** recipe of a particular *cuvée*.

**CERAMIC FILTRATION** An ultrafine depth filtration that utilizes **perlite**.

**CHAI, CHAIS** (Fr.) Building(s) used for wine storage.

**CHAPTALIZATION** The addition of sugar to fresh grape juice in order to raise a wine's alcoholic potential. Theoretically, it takes 1.7 kilograms of sugar per hectoliter (4 pounds per 27 gallons) of wine to raise its alcoholic strength by 1 percent, but red wines actually require two kilograms (4½ pounds) to allow for evaporation during the *remontage*. The term is named after Antoine Chaptal, a brilliant chemist and technocrat who served under Napoleon as minister of the interior from 1800 to 1805 and instructed winegrowers on the advantages of adding sugar at pressing time.

**CHARM** This is a subjective term; if a wine charms, it appeals without attracting in an obvious fashion.

**CHARMAT METHOD** Invented in 1907 by Eugène Charmat, this is a bulk-production method of making inexpensive sparkling wine through a natural **second fermentation** inside a sealed vat. Also known as the Tank Method or *Cuve Close*.

**CHÂTEAU** (Fr.) Literally "castle" or "stately home." Whereas many château-bottled wines do actually come from magnificent buildings that could truly be described as châteaux, many are modest one-story villas; some no more than functional *cuveries*; and a few merely tin sheds! The legal connotation is the same as for any *domaine*-bottled wine.

**CHEESY** This is a characteristic element in the **bouquet** of a very old Champagne, although other wines that have an extended contact with their lees—possibly those that have not been racked or filtered—may also possess it. It is probably caused by the production during **fermentation** of a very small amount of butyric acid that may later develop into an **ester** called ethyl butyrate.

**CHEWY** An extreme qualification of **meaty**.

**CHIP-BUDDING** A method of propagating vines in which a vine bud with a tiny wedge-shape of phloem (live bark) and xylem (inner wood) is inserted into a **rootstock** in an existing root system.

**CHLOROSIS** A vine disorder caused by mineral imbalance (too much active lime; not enough iron or magnesium) that is often called "green sickness."

**CHOCOLATY, CHOCOLATE-BOX** This is a subjective term often used to describe the odor and flavor of Cabernet Sauvignon or Pinot Noir wines. Sometimes "chocolate-box" is used to describe the **bouquet** of fairly mature Bordeaux. The fruity character of a wine may also be described as chocolaty in wines with a **pH** above 3.6.

**CHRISTMAS CAKE** A more intense version of the tasting term **fruitcake**.

**CIGAR-BOX** A subjective term often applied to a certain complex **bouquet** in wines that have been matured in **oak** and have received good bottle-age (usually in relation to red Bordeaux).

**CITROUS** This describes **aromas** and flavors of far greater **complexity** than mere **lemony** can suggest.

**CLAIRET** (Fr.) A wine that falls somewhere between a dark rosé and a light red wine.

**CLARET** An English term for a red Bordeaux wine. Etymologically, it has the same roots as the French term *clairet*.

**CLASSIC, CLASSY** These are subjective words to convey an obvious impression of quality. They are applied to wines that not only portray the correct characteristics for their type and origin, but also possess the **finesse** and **style** of top-quality wines.

**CLASSICO** (It.) This term may be used only for wines produced in the historic, or classic, area of an **appellation**—usually a small, hilly area at the center of a DOC.

**CLEAN** A straightforward term applied to any wine devoid of unwanted or unnatural undertones of **aroma** and flavor.

**CLIMAT** (Fr.) A single plot of land with its own name, located within a specific vineyard.

**CLONE** A vine that has developed differently to other vines of the same variety due to a process of selection—either natural, as in the case of a vine adapting to local conditions, or artificial. *See also* Clones and Cloning, p.36.

**CLOS** (Fr.) Synonymous with *climat*, except that this plot of land is, or was, enclosed by walls.

**CLOSED** Refers to the **nose** or **palate** of a wine that fails to show much character (or "open"). It implies the wine has some qualities—even if "hidden"—that should open up as the wine develops in bottle.

**CLOVES** Often part of the complex **bouquet** found on a wine fermented or matured in **oak**, the **aroma** of cloves is actually caused by eugenic acid, which is created during the toasting of oak barrels.

**CLOYING** Describes the sickly and sticky character of a poor sweet wine, where the **finish** is heavy and often unclean.

**CO₂** *See* **Carbonic gas**.

**COARSE** Applies to a "rough and ready" wine, not necessarily unpleasant but certainly not fine.

**COATES LAW OF MATURITY** Master of Wine Clive Coates claims that a wine remains at its **peak** for as long as it took to arrive at this point in its maturity. This law is infinitely variable according to both the wine and individual consumers. If you find a specific wine to your liking in, say, its fifth month, year, or decade, it will remain within the bounds of this taste profile until its tenth month, year, or decade. If you think about it, however, "Coates Law of Maturity" has a logic—and whereas I do not let it influence my optimal drinking recommendations in this book, I have yet to find an anomaly serious enough to debunk the theory.

**COCONUTTY-OAK** Coconutty aromas are produced by various wood lactones that are most commonly found in American **oak**.

**COMMERCIAL** A commercial wine is blended to a widely acceptable formula. At its worst it may be bland and inoffensive, at its best it will be fruity, quaffable, and uncomplicated.

**COMPACT FRUIT** This term suggests a good weight of fruit with a correct **balance** of **tannin** (if red) and **acidity** that is presented on the **nose** and palate in a distinct manner that is opposite to **open-knit**.

**COMPLETE** Refers to a wine that has everything (fruit, **tannin**, **acidity**, **depth**, **length**, and so on) and thus feels satisfying in the mouth.

**COMPLEXITY** An overworked word that refers to many different nuances of smell or taste. Great wines in their youth may have a certain complexity, but it is only with maturity in bottle that a wine will achieve its full potential in terms of complexity.

**CONCOCTION** Usually a derogatory term, but can be used in a positive sense for a medley of flavors in an inexpensive wine.

**COOKED** Similar to **baked**, but may also imply the addition of grape concentrate to the wine during **fermentation**.

**COOL-FERMENTED** An obviously cool-fermented wine is very **fresh**, with simple aromas of apples, pears, and bananas.

**CORKED** Originally believed to be the result of penicillin or aspergillus mold in the cork, but such infections are extremely rare, while the "corked" phenomenon is relatively common (believed to affect up to 8 percent of all wines). Various chloroanisoles are now deemed responsible, with 2,4,6-trichloroanisole (commonly referred to as TCA) the main culprit. Initially thought to be exclusively the unwanted by-product of sterilizing corks with chlorine, TCA has since been identified at source in cork oak trees, in oak barrels, wooden pallets, and wooden roofs. Other compounds that may also be responsible include **geosmin**, which gives beets their earthy taste and can be found in reservoir water.

**CORRECT** This word describes a wine with all the correct characteristics for its type and origin, but not necessarily an exciting wine.

**CÔTE, CÔTES** (Fr.) Slope(s) or hillside(s) of one contiguous slope or hill.

**COTEAUX** (Fr.) Slopes and hillsides in a hilly area, not contiguous.

**COULURE** (Fr.) A physiological disorder of the vine that occurs as a result of alternating periods of warm and cold, dry and wet conditions after bud-break. If this culminates in a flowering during which the weather is too sunny, the sap rushes past the embryo bunches to the shoot-tips, causing a vigorous growth of foliage, but denying the clusters an adequate supply of essential nutrients. The barely formed berries thus dry up and drop to the ground.

**COUPAGE** (Fr.) Blending by cutting one wine with another.

**CREAMY** A subjective term used to convey the impression of a creamy flavor that may be indicative of the variety of grape or method of vinification. I tend to use this word in connection with the fruitiness or oakiness of a wine. Dr. Tony Jordan believes that creaminess in a sparkling wine is probably a combination of the **finesse** of the **mousse** (created by the most minuscule of bubbles and their slow release) and an understated **malolactic** influence, the combined effect of which is picked up at the back of the throat on the finish of the wine, and this is most apparent in Chardonnay-based wines.

**CREAMY-OAK** A more subtle, lower-key version of the vanilla-oak character that is most probably derived from wood lactones during maturation in small **oak** barrels.

**CRÉMANT** (Fr.) Although traditionally ascribed to a Champagne with a low-pressure and a soft, creamy **mousse**, this term has now been phased out in Champagne as part of the bargain struck with other producers of French sparkling wines who have agreed to drop the term *Méthode Champenoise*. In return they have been exclusively permitted to use this old Champagne term to create their own appellations, such as Crémant de Bourgogne and Crémant d'Alsace.

**CRISP** A clean wine, with good **acidity** showing on the **finish**, yielding a refreshing, clean taste.

**CROSS** A vine that has been propagated by crossing two or more varieties within the same species (within *Vitis vinifera* for example). In contrast, a hybrid is a cross between two or more varieties from more than one species.

**CROSSFLOW FILTRATION** A relatively new, high-speed form of microfiltration in which the wine flows across (not through), a **membrane filter**, thus avoiding build-up.

**CROWN-CAP** The common beer-bottle cap, which is now widely used as the temporary closure while a sparkling wine undergoes its **second fermentation**.

**CRUSH** Grapes are often crushed so that the juice can **macerate** in the skins prior to and during **fermentation**—to obtain color for red wines, and aromatic qualities for white wines. In the US and Australia, "the crush" is synonymous with the harvest in general, and the crushing/pressing in particular.

**CRYPTOGAMIC** Refers to a fungus-based disease such as gray rot.

**CRU** or **CRÛ** (Fr.) Literally means growth, as in *Cru Bourgeois* or *Cru Classé*.

**CRU BOURGEOIS** (Fr.) A nonclassified growth of the Médoc.

**CRU CLASSÉ** (Fr.) An officially classified French vineyard.

**CS** (It.) Short for *Cantina Sociale* and other titles denoting a local or regional cooperative.

**CULTIVAR** A term used mainly in South Africa for a cultivated variety of wine grape.

**CUT** 1. In blending, a wine of a specific character may be used to cut (mix with) a wine dominated by an opposite quality. This can range from a bland wine that is cut by a small quantity of very acidic wine, to a white wine that is cut with a little red wine to make a **rosé**, as in pink Champagne. The most severe form of cutting is also called stretching and involves diluting wine with water, an illegal practice. 2. A cut in pressing terms is a point at which the quality of juice changes, the term deriving from the days of old vertical presses when the lid of the press would be lifted and workers would cut up the compacted mass with sharp spades, piling it in the middle so that more juice may be extracted. 3. In matching food and wine, a wine with high acidity may be used to cut (balance) the **organoleptic** effect of grease from a grilled or fried dish or an oily fish, just as the effervescence of a fine sparkling wine cuts the creamy texture of certain soups and sauces.

**CUVAISON** (Fr.) The **fermentation** period in red-wine production, during which the juice is kept in contact with its skins.

**CUVE** (Fr.) Vat; a *cuve* should not be confused with *cuvée*.

**CUVE CLOSE** (Fr.) A method of producing sparkling wine that involves a **second fermentation** in a vat. *Cuve Close* is synonymous with the Charmat Method or Tank Method.

**CUVÉE** (Fr.) This originally meant the wine of one *cuve* or vat, but now refers to a specific blend or product which, in current commercial terms, will be from several vats.

**CUVERIE, CUVIER** (Fr.) The room or building housing the fermenting vats (*cuves*).

**CV** (Fr.) Short for *Coopérative de Vignerons* and various other titles that denote a local or regional cooperative.

**DEFINITION** A wine with good definition is one that is not just clean with a correct **balance**, but that also has a positive expression of its grape variety or origin.

**DÉGORGEMENT** (Fr.) *See* **Disgorgement**.

**DEGREE-DAYS** *See* **Heat summation**.

**DÉLESTAGE** (Fr.) Commonly known to anglophile winemakers as "**rack** and return." *Délestage* is a process designed to produce softer red wines by reducing harsh **tannins** from the grape seeds, and is particularly successful in areas where unripe seeds are common due to uneven ripening. The basic *délestage* procedure starts after a cold soak of juice and skins. The juice is drawn off into a separate tank, allowing the **cap** to fall to the bottom of the first tank, where it is left to drain for several hours. During this time, many seeds are loosened from the pulp and can be caught by a filter that allows free passage to the draining juice, which also goes to the second tank. Once the cap has drained out, the drain is closed off, and the juice from the second tank is pumped back into the first tank, where it is mixed with cap. This process is repeated daily until all the seeds and their harsh tannins are removed.

**DELICATE** Describes the quieter characteristics of quality that give a wine **charm**.

**DEMI-MUID** (Fr.) A large oval barrel with a capacity of 300 liters/80 gallons (600 liters/160 gallons in Champagne).

**DEMI-SEC** (Fr.) This literally means "semidry" but such wines actually taste quite sweet.

**DENDOMETER** A very accurate device that measures the minute swelling and shrinkage of the vine trunk in response to water use. It can be used to control the amount of irrigation water taken up by the vine, rather than the amount that goes into the ground.

**DENOMINAÇÃO DE ORIGEM CONTROLADA** (Port.) *See* **DOC**.

**DENOMINACIÓN DE ORIGEN** (Sp.) *See* **DO**.

**DENOMINACIÓN DE ORIGEN CALIFICADA** (Sp.) *See* **DOCa**.

**DENOMINAZIONE DI ORIGINE CONTROLLATA** (It.) *See* **DOC**.

**DENOMINAZIONE DI ORIGINE CONTROLLATA E GARANTITA** (It.) *See* **DOCG**.

**DÉPARTEMENT** (Fr.) A French geopolitical division, similar to a state in the US and a county in the UK.

**DEPTH** This refers primarily to a wine's depth of flavor and secondarily to its depth of interest.

**DEPTH FILTRATION** The separation of solids from a liquid solely inside a **filtration** medium such as kieselguhr (*see* **diatomaceous earth**). A Rotary Drum Vacuum or Plate and Frame filter is commonly used.

**DIATOMACEOUS EARTH** Also known as kieselguhr, this is a fine, powdered, silaceous earth evolved from decomposed deep-sea algae called diatoms. *See also* **Perlite**, **Ceramic filtration**, and **Polishing**.

**DIRTY** This applies to any wine with an unpleasant off-taste or off-smell, and is probably the result of poor vinification or bad bottling.

**DISGORGEMENT** This is part of the process of making a bottle-fermented sparkling wine such as Champagne. After **fermentation**, the **yeast** forms a deposit, which must be removed. To allow for this removal, the bottles are inverted in a freezing brine for just long enough for the sediment to form a semifrozen slush that adheres to the neck of the bottle. This enables the bottle to be reinverted without disturbing the wine. The temporary cap used to seal the bottle is removed and the internal pressure is sufficient to eject or "disgorge" the slush of sediment without losing very much wine at all. The wine is then topped off and a traditional Champagne cork is used to seal the bottle.

**DISTINCTIVE** Describes a wine with a positive character. All fine wines are distinctive to some degree or other, but not all distinctive wines are necessarily fine.

**DIURNAL DIFFERENCE** In **viticulture**, any reference to a diurnal or daily difference will invariably be a reference to temperature, comparing the highest daytime temperature with the lowest nighttime temperature—the greater the difference, the better the grapes' acidity retention. There can be a wide diurnal difference in relatively cool wine areas, such as Champagne, as well as in essentially hot ones, such as Idaho.

**DO** (Sp.) This stands for Spain's *Denominación de Origen*, which is theoretically the equivalent of the French **AOC**.

**DOBLE PASTA** (Sp.) Red wines macerated with double the normal proportion of grape skins to juice during fermentation. *See also* Spanish Label Language, p.302.

**DOC** (It., Port.) Short for Italy's *Denominazione di Origine Controllata* and Portugal's *Denominação de Origem Controlada*, which are theoretically the equivalent of the French AOC.

**DOCa** (Sp.) Abbreviation for Spain's *Denominación de Origen Calificada*, which is the equivalent of the Italian **DOCG**.

**DOCG** (It.) Italy's *Denominazione di Origine Controllata e Garantita* is theoretically one step above the French **AOC**. Ideally it should be similar to, say, a *Premier* or *Grand Cru* in Burgundy or a *Cru Classé* in Bordeaux, but in reality, it is almost as big a sop as Italy's *Denominazione di Origine Controllata* itself. *See also* Italy, p.262.

**DOPPELSTÜCK** (Ger.) A very large oval cask with a capacity of 2,400 liters (635 gallons).

**DOSAGE** (Fr.) Sugar added to a sparkling wine after *disgorgement*, the amounts of which are controlled by the terminology used on the label—**brut, demi-sec**, and so on.

**DOUX** (Fr.) Sweet, as applied to wines.

**DRIP IRRIGATION** Various forms exist, but at its most sophisticated, this is a computer-controlled watering system programmed with the vine's general water requirement and constantly amended by a continuous flow of data from soil sensors. The water is supplied literally drip-by-drip through a complex system of pipes with metered valves.

**DRYING UP** Describes a wine that has dried up and lost some of its freshness and fruit through

aging in the bottle. It may still be enjoyable, but remaining bottles should not be kept long.

**DUPLEX SOILS** So-called when two contrasting soil textures are found layered, with a sharp divide between the two. Duplex soils usually consist of a coarse soil over a fine-grained soil, and are commonly found in Western Australia, where they are invariably sand over clay. They are categorized by color (red, yellow, brown, dark, and gray duplex soils) based on the color of the subsoil, not the topsoil.

**DUSTY** Akin to "peppery" in a red wine; a blurring of **varietal** definition in a white wine.

**EARTH FILTRATION** This term can be synonymous with **depth filtration**.

**EARTHY** Describes a drying impression in the mouth. Some wines can be enjoyably earthy, but the finest-quality wines should be as clean as a whistle. When a wine is very earthy, it is usually due to a preponderance of **geosmin**, which can occur naturally in grapes, but in excess can give a wine a **corked** taste.

**EASY** This term is to a certain extent synonymous with **accessible**, but probably implies a cheaper, value-for-money wine, whereas "accessible" often applies to finer wines.

**EAU-DE-VIE** (Fr.) Literally, "water of life"; specifically, a grape-derived spirit.

**EDELFÄULE** (Ger.) The German term for noble rot; *see* **Botrytis cinerea**.

**EDELKEUR** (S. Afr.) The South African term for noble rot; *see* **Botrytis cinerea**.

**EDGE** Almost, but not quite, synonymous with **grip**; wine can have an edge of **bitterness** or **tannin**. Edge usually implies that a wine has the capacity to develop, while grip may be applied to a wine in various stages of development, including fully mature wine.

**EDGY** Synonymous with **nervy** or "nervous."

**EGG WHITE** A traditional **fining** agent that fines out negatively charged matter.

**EINZELLAGE** (Ger.) A single-vineyard wine area; the smallest geographical unit allowed under German wine law.

**EISWEIN** (Ger.) Originally a German concept but now used in the New World as well, this rare wine resulted from the tradition of leaving grapes on the vine in the hope of attracting **Botrytis cinerea**. The grapes are then frozen by frost or snow, harvested, and pressed while frozen. They are pressed while still frozen because the frozen ice rises to the top of the vat and it can be scraped off to leave a concentrated juice that produces a wine with a unique balance of sweetness, acidity, and extract.

**ELEGANT** A subjective term applied to wines that may also be termed "stylish" or "possessing **finesse**."

**ELEVATED FRUIT** Synonymous with **VA lift**.

**ÉLEVÉ EN FÛTS DE CHÊNE** Aged in oak barrels.

**ELEVEUR, ÉLEVAGE** (Fr.) Literally "bringing up" or "raising" the wine. Both terms refer to the traditional function of a *négociant*: namely to buy ready-made wines after the harvest and take care of them until they are ready to be bottled and sold. The task involves **racking** the wines and blending them into a marketable product as each house sees fit.

**EMBRYO BUNCHES** In spring, the vine develops little clusters of miniature green berries that will form a bloom a few weeks later. If a berry successfully flowers, it is capable of developing into a grape. The embryo bunch is thus an indication of the potential size of the crop.

**EN PRIMEUR** (Fr.) Classic wines such as Bordeaux are offered for sale *en primeur*, which is to say within a year of the harvest, before the final blending and bottling has taken place. For experienced buyers given the opportunity to taste, this is a calculated risk and the price should reflect this element of chance.

**ENCÉPAGEMENT** (Fr.) The relative proportions of the grape varieties in a blend.

**ENOLOGIST, ENOLOGY** (Am.) Spelling of **oenologist**, oenology often used in the US.

**ENTRY-LEVEL WINE** From the producer's point of view, this will be his cheapest, most basic quality of wine. From a critic's point of view, this will be the cheapest wine worth buying.

**ENZYME** A protein produced by living organisms (anything from **yeast cells** to human beings) that functions as a biochemical catalyst.

**ESTERS** Sweet-smelling compounds, formed during **fermentation** and throughout maturation, that contribute to a wine's **aroma** and **bouquet**.

**ESTUFAGEM** (Port.) The process whereby Madeira is heated in ovens called *estufas*, then cooled. *See also* Madeira, p.340.

**ETHANOIC ACID** Synonymous with **acetic acid**.

**ETHANOL** Synonymous with **ethyl alcohol**.

**ETHYL ALCOHOL** This main alcohol in wine is so important in quantitative terms that to speak of a wine's alcohol is to refer purely to its ethyl alcohol content.

**EU LOT NUMBER** Proposed by an EC directive in 1989 and implemented by all member states of the Community by 1992, this Lot Number must be indicated on every bottle of wine produced in or sold to the EU. Should a wine have to be removed from general distribution for any reason, this code can save unnecessary waste by pinpointing the shipment involved.

**EVERYDAY WINES** These are inexpensive, easy-drinking wines.

**EX-CELLARS** Wines offered *en primeur* are usually purchased "ex-cellars"; the cost of shipping the wine to the importer's cellars is extra, on top of which any duty and taxes will be added.

**EXPANSIVE** Describes a wine that is **big**, but open and **accessible**.

**EXPRESSIVE** A wine that is expressive is true to its grape variety and area of origin.

**EXTRACT** Sugar-free soluble solids that give **body** to a wine. The term covers everything from proteins and vitamins to **tannins**, calcium, and **iron**.

**FALL BRIGHT** A liquid that becomes limpid after cloudy matter falls as sediment to the bottom of the vessel is said to fall bright.

**FALL OVER** A wine that goes past its peak and starts to decline at a relatively young age, and at a faster than normal rate, is said to fall over.

**FARMYARDY** A term used by many people to describe a wine, quite often Chardonnay or Pinot, that has matured beyond its initial freshness of fruit, past the desired stage of roundness and the pleasing phase when it acquires certain vegetal undertones. The wine is still healthy and drinkable, and for some it is at the very peak of perfection.

**FAT** A wine full in body and extract. It is good for any wine to have some fat, but fat in an unqualified sense can be derogatory and no wine should be too fat, as it will be flabby or too blowzy.

**FATTY ACIDS** A term sometimes used for **volatile acids**.

**FEMININE** A subjective term used to describe a wine with a preponderance of delicately attractive qualities, rather than weight or strength. Decribes a wine of striking beauty, grace, and **finesse**, with a silky texture and exquisite style.

**FERMENTATION** The biochemical process by which **enzymes** secreted by **yeast** cells convert sugar molecules into almost equal parts of **alcohol** and **carbonic gas**. *See also* Fermentation, p.25.

**FERTILIZER** A chemical product used to enrich the soil with one or more of the three basic requirements for all plant life: potassium (for fruit development and general plant metabolism), phosphorus (for root development), and nitrogen (for leaf development). Technically the term also refers to manure, compost, and other natural means of soil enrichment.

**FEUILLETTE** (Fr.) A small Burgundian barrel with a capacity of 114 liters (30 gallons); in Chablis this is 132 liters (35 gallons).

**FIELD BLEND, FIELD MIX** The best description I have seen for this is "a wine recipe planted in the ground." It is not a homogenous vineyard planted to a single grape variety (of which there may be several different clones), but a vineyard planted with a collection of grape varieties that reflect traditional Old World practices of several generations ago. The advantage is that if a disease or disorder affected one variety, the others would probably pull through unscathed. The disadvantage, however, is that the different varieties do not ripen at the same time; this was not a problem in the old days, however, since it was common practice to make several *tries* or sweeps through the vineyards, picking only the ripe grapes and cutting out any rotten ones.

**FILTER, FILTRATION** The removal of suspended matter. There are four basic methods of filtration: **depth filtration** (also known as earth filtration); **pad filtration** (also known as sheet filtration), **membrane filtration** (also known as microporous filtration), and **crossflow filtration**. There is also centrifugal filtration, which is not filtration in the pure sense but achieves the same objective of removing unwanted particles suspended in wine or grape juice.

**FINESSE** That elusive, indescribable quality that separates a fine wine from those of lesser quality.

**FINE WINES** Quality wines, representing only a small percentage of all wines produced.

**FINING** The clarification of fresh grape juice or wine is often sped up by the use of various fining agents that operate by an electrolytic reaction to fine out oppositely charged matter. *See also* Fining, p.26.

**FINISH** The quality, and a person's enjoyment, of a wine's aftertaste.

**FIRM** Refers to a certain amount of **grip**. A firm wine is a wine of good constitution, held up with a certain amount of tannin and acidity.

**FIRST PRESSING** The first pressing yields the sweetest, cleanest, clearest juice.

**FIXED ACIDITY** This is the total acidity less the **volatile acidity**.

**FIXED SULFUR** The principal reason why $SO_2$ (sulfur dioxide) is added to grape juice and wine is to prevent oxidation, but only free sulfur can do this. Upon contact with wine, some $SO_2$ immediately combines with oxygen and other elements, such as sugars and acids, and is known as fixed or bound sulfur. What remains is free sulfur, capable of combining with molecules of oxygen at some future date.

**FLABBY** The opposite of **crisp**, referring to a wine lacking in acidity and consequently dull, weak, and short.

**FLASH PASTEURIZATION** A sterilization technique that should not be confused with full pasteurization. It involves subjecting the wine to a temperature of about 176°F (80°C) for between 30 and 60 seconds.

**FLAT** 1. A sparkling wine that has lost all of its *mousse*. 2. A term that is interchangeable with **flabby**, especially when referring to a lack of acidity on the finish.

**FLESHY** This term refers to a wine with plenty of fruit and extract and implies an underlying firmness.

**FLOR** (Sp.) A scumlike **yeast** film that naturally occurs and floats on the surface of some sherries as they mature in part-filled wooden casks. It is the flor that gives Fino Sherry its inimitable character.

**FLURBEREINIGUNG** (Ger.) A modern viticultural method of growing vines in rows that run vertically up and down slopes, rather than across in terraces.

**FLYING WINEMAKER** The concept of the flying winemaker was born in Australia, where due to the size of the country and the staggered picking dates, highly sought-after consultants Brian Croser (now Petaluma) and Tony Jordan (now Green Point) would hop by plane from harvest to harvest. Riding

on the success of Australian wines in the UK market, other Australian wine wizards began to stretch their wings, flying in and out of everywhere from Southern Italy to Slovakia, usually at the behest of British supermarkets. Like the spread of Chardonnay and Cabernet, the flying winemakers were at first welcomed by wine writers, then turned upon for standardizing wine wherever they went. The truth is that before the arrival of international grapes and international winemakers, the peasant cooperatives in these countries had no idea that they could even produce wines to compete on the international market. Now that they have established a certain standard with known grape varieties and modern technology, they are beginning to turn to their roots to see what indigenous varieties might have the potential to produce more expressive wines. Few winemakers do more flying than Moët & Chandon's Richard Geoffroy, but the term is usually attributed to the mercenaries of the trade, who work for a supermarket, a supplier to a supermarket, or more than one company. Well-known flying winemakers include Peter Bright, Nick Butler, Steve Donnelly, Michael Goundrey, Lynette Hudson, Jacques and François Lurton, Geoff Merril, Kym Milne, Martin Shaw, Brenden Smith, Adrian Wing, and John Worontschak. The late, famous Bordeaux professor Peynaud avoided the flying-winemaker tag, as has Ribereau-Gayon, despite the fact that they have each consulted for more companies in more countries over more years than the entire flock of flying winemakers listed above, perhaps because today's mercenaries have a more hands-on approach to their job than was traditional for consultants in the past.

**FOLIAR FEEDS** Plant nutrients that are sprayed directly onto, and are absorbed by, the foliage.

**FORTIFIED** Fortification with pure alcohol (usually very strong grape spirit of 77 to 98 percent) can take place either before **fermentation** (as in Ratafia de Champagne and Pineau des Charentes), during fermentation (as in port and Muscat de Beaumes de Venise), or after fermentation (as in sherry).

**FOUDRE** (Fr.) A large wooden cask or vat.

**FOXY** The very distinctive, highly perfumed character of certain indigenous American grape varieties that can be sickly sweet and cloying to unconditioned palates.

**FREE-RUN JUICE** *See Vin de goutte.*

**FREE SULFUR** The active element of sulfur dioxide ($SO_2$) in wine, produced by free sulfur combining with intruding molecules of oxygen.

**FREMANTLE DOCTOR** Also known as the "Freo Doctor," this afternoon sea breeze brings a cooling relief to better parts of the Swan Valley in Western Australia. *See also* **Albany Doctor, Canberra Doctor.**

**FRENCH PARADOX** In 1991, Morley Safer, host of the CBS show *60 Minutes*, screened a program about the so-called "French Paradox." This described how the high-cholesterol-consuming, high-alcohol-drinking, low-exercising French have a very low mortality rate from heart disease compared to health-conscious Americans, who have low-cholesterol diets, exercise frequently, and drink relatively little alcohol. Part of the explanation was attributed to the Mediterranean diet, in which milk plays a negligible role and wine—particularly red wine—a very important one. Although it is a complete food for the young, milk is unnatural for adults, who cannot digest it properly. The more milk an adult drinks (and Americans are particularly high consumers of milk), the greater the risk of cardiovascular disease, while three glasses of wine a day has a proven protective effect against cardiovascular disease. *See also* **Health benefits of wine.**

**FRESH** Describes wines that are clean and still vital with youth.

**FRIABLE** Term used to describe a soil structure that is crumbly or easily broken up.

**FRIZZANTE** (It.) Semi-sparkling.

**FRIZZANTINO** (It.) Very lightly sparkling, between still and semi-sparkling (i.e., *perlant*).

**FRUIT** Wine is made from grapes and must therefore be 100 percent fruit, yet a fruity flavor depends on the grapes used having the correct combination of **ripeness** and **acidity**.

**FRUITCAKE** This is a subjective term for a wine that tastes, smells, or has the complexity of the mixed dried-fruit richness and spices found in fruitcake.

**FUDER** (Ger.) A large oval cask with a capacity of 1,000 liters (265 gallons), more prevalent in Mosel areas than in those of the Rhine.

**FULL** This term usually refers to body, as in "full-bodied." However, a wine can be light in body yet full in flavor.

**FULLY FERMENTED** A wine that is allowed to complete its natural course of **fermentation** and so yield a totally dry wine.

**FÛT** (Fr.) A wooden cask, usually made of oak, in which wines are aged, or fermented and aged.

**GARRIGUE** (Fr.) A type of moorland found in Languedoc-Roussillon.

**GASOLINE, GASOLINE-LIKE** With some bottle-age, the finest Rieslings have a vivid **bouquet** that some call gasoline-like. This character has an affinity with various **zesty** and **citrussy** odors, but many **lemony**, citrussy, zesty smells are totally different from one another and the Riesling's gasoline character is both singular and unmistakable. As great Riesling matures, so it also develops a **honeyed** character, bringing a classic, honeyed-gasoline richness to the wine.

**GELATINE** A positively charged **fining** agent used for removing negatively charged suspended matter in wines, especially an excess of **tannin**.

**GENERIC** Describes a wine, usually blended, of a general **appellation**.

**GENEROUS** A generous wine gives its fruit freely on the palate, while an ungenerous wine is likely to have little or no fruit and, probably, an excess of **tannin**. All wines should have some degree of generosity.

**GENUS** The botanical family *Ampelidaceae* has 10 *genera*, one of which, *Vitis*, through the subgenus *Euvites*, contains the species ***Vitis vinifera***, to which all the famous wine-making grape varieties belong.

**GEOSMIN** A chemical compound sometimes found in wine; responsible for the characteristic earthiness of beets and the earthy taste of some potatoes.

**GLUGGY** Easy to guzzle.

**GOOD GRIP** A healthy structure of **tannin** supporting the fruit in a wine.

**GOUT DE TERROIR** (Fr.) Literally "taste of earth," a term that denotes a particular flavor imparted by certain soils—although not necessarily the taste of the soil itself—in a wine.

**GRANDE MARQUE** (Fr.) Literally a great or famous brand. In the world of wine, the term *Grande Marque* is specific to Champagne and applies to members of the *Syndicat de Grandes Marques*, which include, of course, all the famous names.

**GRAFT** The joint between the **rootstock** and the scion of the **producer vine**.

**GRAND CRU** (Fr.) Literally "great growth." In regions such as Burgundy, where the term's use is strictly controlled, it has real meaning (in other words, the wine should be great relative to the quality of the year), but in other winemaking areas where there are no controls, it will mean little.

**GRAND VIN** (Fr.) Normally used in Bordeaux, this term applies to the main wine sold under the château's famous name and it will have been produced from only the finest barrels. Wines excluded during this process go into second, third, and sometimes fourth wines that are sold under different labels.

**GRAPEY** This term may be applied to an **aroma** or flavor that is reminiscent of grapes rather than wine, and is a particular characteristic of German wines and wines made from various Muscat or Muscat-like grapes.

**GRASSY** Often used to describe certain Gewürztraminer, Scheurebe, and Sauvignon wines portraying a grassy type of fruitiness.

**GREEN** Young and tart, as in Vinho Verde. It can be either a derogatory term or simply a description of a youthful wine that might well improve.

**GREEN PRUNING** Pruning is a bit of a misnomer, as this is really a method of reducing yields by thinning out the potential crop when the grapes are green (unripe) by cutting off a certain percentage of the bunches, so that what remains achieves a quicker, greater, and more even ripening. Also called summer pruning.

**GRIP** This term applies to a **firm** wine with a positive **finish**. A wine showing grip on the finish indicates a certain bite of **acidity** in white wines and of **tannin** in red wines.

**GRIPPY** Good grippy **tannins** imply ripe tannins that have a nice tactile effect without seeming in the least **firm**, **harsh**, or **austere**.

**GROSSLAGE** (Ger.) A wine area in Germany that is part of a larger district or *Bereich*.

**GROWTH** *See* Cru.

**GUTSY** A wine full in **body**, fruit, **extract**, and—usually—**alcohol**. The term is normally applied to wines of fairly ordinary quality.

**GUZZLY** This term is synonymous with **gluggy**.

**HALBFÜDER** (Ger.) An oval cask with a capacity of 500 liters (132 gallons), more prevalent in Mosel areas than in those of the Rhine.

**HALBSTÜCK** (Ger.) An oval cask with a capacity of 600 liters (159 gallons).

**HARD** Indicates a certain severity, often due to excess **tannin** and **acidity**.

**HARSH** A more derogatory term than **coarse**.

**HEALTH BENEFITS OF WINE** Wine consumed in moderation flushes out the cholesterol and fatty substances that can build up inside the body's artery walls. It does this through the powerful **antioxidant** properties of various chemical compounds found naturally in wine (through contact with grapeskins), the most important of which are polyphenols such as procyanidins and rytoalexins such as reservatol. Most chloresterol in the body is carried around the body on LDLs (low density lipoproteins), which clog up the arteries. By contrast, HDLs (high density lipoproteins) do not clog the arteries, but take the cholesterol straight to the liver, where it is processed out of the system. The antioxidants convert LDL into HDL, literally flushing away the cholesterol and other fatty substances. Together with **alcohol** itself, these antioxidants also act as an anticoagulant on the blood, diminishing its clotting ability, which reduces the chances of a stroke by 50 percent in contrast with nondrinkers. (However, I would be equally as dishonest as the neoprohibitionists who make phoney health-danger claims if I did not point out the one true health danger of moderate drinking that has recently come to light. In 2002, the *British Journal of Cancer* published a study demonstrating that a woman's risk of contracting breast cancer increases by 6 percent if she consumes just one drink per day, and this rises to 32 percent if she has three or four drinks per day. The report concludes that 4 percent of all breast cancers are attributable to alcohol. It is, however, not cut-and-dried. In a summary of this report, Dr. Isabel dos Santos Silva of the International Agency for Research on Cancer wrote "Alcohol intake… is likely to account, at present, for a small proportion of breast cancer cases in developed countries, but for women who drink moderately, its lifetime cardioprotective effects probably outweigh its health hazards." And as Dr. Philip Norrie pointed out, 10 times the number of women die from vascular disease as from breast cancer.)

**HEAT SUMMATION** A system of measuring the growth potential of vines in a specific area in terms of the environmental temperature, expressed in degree-days. A vine's vegetative cycle is activated only above a temperature of 50°F (10°C). The time during which these temperatures persist equates to the vine's growing season. To calculate the number of degree-days, the proportion of the daily mean temperature significant to the vine's growth—the daily mean minus the inactive 50°F (10°C)—is multiplied by the number of days of the growing season. For example, a growing season of 200 days with a daily mean temperature of 59°F (15°C) gives a heat summation of 1,800 degree-days Fahrenheit (1,000 degree-days Celsius) based on the following calculation: (59 – 50) x 200 = 1,800.

**HERBACEOUS** A green-leaf or white-currant characteristic that is usually associated with too much **vigor** in the vine's canopy, which can cause underripeness. A herbaceous quality can also be the result of aggressive extraction techniques employed for red wines fermented in stainless steel.

**HERBAL, HERBAL-OAK** These terms apply to wines matured in cask, but unlike **vanilla-oak**, **creamy-oak**, **smoky-oak**, and **spicy-oak**, their origin is unknown. A herbal character devoid of oak is usually derived from the **varietal** character of a grape and is common to many varieties.

**HERBICIDE** A weedkiller that is usually, but not necessarily, a highly toxic concoction of chemicals.

**HIGH-DENSITY VINES** Vines planted close together compete with each other to yield higher-quality fruit, but less of it per vine, than vines planted farther apart. Initial planting costs are higher and more labor is required for pruning, but if the vineyard is in balance, the greater number of vines should produce the same overall volume per acre, even though the output per vine is reduced. Quantity can therefore be maintained while significantly raising quality, although there is a threshold density that vineyards must reach before real benefits appear. For example, more than half the vineyards in the New World are planted at less than 800 per acre (2,000 vines per hectare) and 500 to 600 (1,200 to 1,500 per hectare) is very common, whereas in Champagne, 2,666 vines per acre (6,666 per hectare) is the minimum allowed by law, 2,800 to 3,200 the average (7,000 to 8,000), and 4,400 (11,000) possible. In pre-**Phylloxera** times, it was something like 10,000 vines per acre (25,000 per hectare). Indeed, before California's vineyards were mechanized, the average density of vines was twice what it is now because every other row has been ripped up to allow for tractors. When Joseph Drouhin planted his vineyard in Oregon, he planted 2,980 vines per acre (7,450 per hectare) and brought over French tractors that straddled the rows of vines, rather than went between them. All of a sudden, high-density vineyards entered the American vocabulary, although Drouhin did not consider them to be high density—merely a matter of course.

**HIGH-TONE** A term used in this book to describe elements of the bouquet that aspire to elegance, but that can become too exaggerated and be slightly reminiscent of vermouth.

**HOGSHEAD** A barrel with a capacity of between 300 and 315 liters (79 and 83 gallons), commonly found in Australia and New Zealand.

**HOLLOW** A wine that lacks any real flavor in the mouth compared to the promise shown on the nose. Usually due to a lack of **body**, fruit, or **acidity**.

**HONEST** Applied to any wine, but usually to one of a fairly basic quality, honest implies it is true in character and typical of its type and origin. It also implies that the wine does not give any indication of being souped-up in any unlawful way. The use of the word honest is, however, a way of damning with faint praise, for it does not suggest a wine of any special or truly memorable quality.

**HONEYED** Many wines develop a honeyed character through **bottle-age**, particularly sweet wines and more especially those with some **botrytis** character. However, some dry wines can also become honeyed, a mature Riesling being the classic example.

**HORIZONTAL TASTING** A tasting of different wines of the same style or vintage, as opposed to a vertical tasting (different vintages of the same wine).

**HOT** Synonym for **baked**.

**HOUSE CLARET** An unpretentious, and not too expensive, everyday-drinking red Bordeaux.

**HYBRID** A cross between two or more grape varieties from more than one species.

**HYDROGEN SULFIDE** When hydrogen combines with sulfur dioxide ($SO_2$), the result is a smell of bad eggs. If this occurs prior to bottling and is dealt with immediately, it can be rectified. If allowed to progress, the hydrogen sulfide can develop into **mercaptans** and ruin the wine.

**ICEWINE** See **Eiswein**.

**ICON** A marketing term for a quality category; see **Premium**.

**INDICAÇÃO DE PROVENIÊNCIA REGULAMENTADA** (Port.) See **IPR**.

**INKY** Can refer either to a wine's opacity of color or to an inkiness of character indicating a deep flavor with plenty of supple **tannin**.

**IPR** (Port.) Short for *Indicação de Proveniência Regulamentada*, a Portuguese quality designation that falls between **DOC** and **VR**.

**IRON** This is found as a trace element in fresh grapes that have been grown in soils in which relatively substantial ferrous deposits are located. Wines from such sites may naturally contain a tiny amount of iron, which is barely perceptible on the palate. If there is too much iron, the flavor becomes medicinal. Above seven milligrams per liter for white and 10 milligrams per liter for red, there is a danger of the wine going cloudy. But wines of such high iron levels should have been blue-fined prior to bottling (*see* **fining**).

**ISINGLASS** A gelatinous **fining** agent obtained from the swim-bladder of freshwater fish and used to clear hazy, low-tannin wines.

**JAMMY** Commonly used to describe a **fat** and eminently drinkable red wine rich in fruit, if perhaps a bit contrived and lacking **elegance**.

**JUG WINE** California's mass-produced *vin de table*, synonymous with carafe wine.

**KABINETT** (Ger.) The first rung of predication in Germany's QmP range, one below *Spätlese*, and often drier than a QbA.

**KIESELGUHR** A form of **diatomaceous earth**.

**LACTIC ACID** The acid that develops in sour milk, and which is also created in wine during the **malolactic** fermentation.

**LAGAR** (Port.) A rectangular concrete receptacle in which people tread grapes.

**LAID-BACK** A term that has come into use since the arrival of California wines on the international scene in the early 1980s. It usually implies that a wine is very relaxed, easy to drink, and confident of its own quality.

**LANDWEIN** (Ger.) German equivalent of *vin de pays*.

**LATE DISGORGED** See **LD**.

**LD** A sparkling-wine term that stands for "late disgorged" and, paradoxically, means the same as "recently disgorged." The use of LD implies that the wine in question is of a mature vintage that has been kept on its **yeast** deposit for an extended period. *See also* **RD**.

**LEACHING** A term that may be used to refer to the deliberate removal of **tannin** from new oak by steaming—or when discussing certain aspects of soil, such as pH, that can be affected when **carbonates** are leached (removed) by rainwater.

**LEES** Sediment that accumulates in the bottom of a vat during the **fermentation** of a wine.

**LEMONY** Many dry and medium-sweet wines have a tangy, fruity acidity that is suggestive of lemons.

**LENGTH** A wine that has length is one whose flavor lingers in the mouth a long time after

swallowing. If two wines taste the same, yet you definitely prefer one, but do not understand why, it is probably because the one you prefer has a greater length. *See also* **Balance**.

**LIE** (Fr.) The French for **lees**: *sur lie* refers to a wine kept in contact with its lees.

**LIEU-DIT** (Fr.) A named site (plural: *lieux-dits*). This term is commonly used for wines of specific growths that do not have *Grand Cru* status.

**LIGHT VINTAGE** A light vintage or year produces relatively light wines. Not a great vintage, but not necessarily a bad one either.

**LIME** This is the classic character shared by both the Sémillon and Riesling grape varieties when grown in many areas of Australia, which explains why Sémillon from the Hunter Valley used to be sold as Hunter Riesling.

**LINALOOL** A compound found in some grapes, particularly the Muscat and Riesling varieties. It contributes to the peachy-flowery fragrance that is characteristic of Muscat wines.

**LINGERING** Normally applied to the finish of a wine—an aftertaste that literally lingers.

**LIQUEUR DE TIRAGE** (Fr.) Bottling *liqueur*: the mix of wine, **yeast**, and sugar added to still Champagne to induce the **mousse**.

**LIQUOREUX** (Fr.) Literally "liqueurlike," this term is often applied to dessert wines of an unctuous quality. (Sometimes also "liquorous.")

**LIQUORICE** A quality often detected in Monbazillac, but may be found in any rich sweet wine. The term refers to the concentration of flavors from heat-shriveled, rather than **botrytized**, grapes.

**LIVELINESS** A term that usually implies a certain youthful freshness of fruit due to good **acidity** and a touch of **carbonic gas**.

**LONGEVITY** Potentially long-lived wines may owe their longevity to a significant content of **tannin**, **acidity**, **alcohol**, and/or sugar.

**LUSCIOUS, LUSCIOUSNESS** Almost synonymous with **voluptuous**, although more frequently used to describe an unctuous, sweet white wine than a succulently rich red.

**MACERATION** A term that is usually applied to the period during the vinification process when the fermenting juice is in contact with its skins. This process is traditionally used in red-winemaking, but it is on the increase for white wines utilizing prefermentation maceration techniques.

**MACÉRATION CARBONIQUE** (Fr.) A generic term covering several methods of vinifying wine under the pressure of **carbonic gas**. Such wines, Beaujolais Nouveau being the archetypal example, are characterized by amylic aromas (peardrops, bubble-gum, nail-polish). If this method is used for just a small part of a blend, however, it can lift the fruit and soften a wine without leaving such telltale aromas. *See also* **Macération Carbonique**, p.29.

**MADERIZED** All Madeiras are maderized by the *estufagem*, in which the wines are slowly heated in specially constructed ovens, and then by cooling them. This is undesirable in all wines except for certain Mediterranean wines that are deliberately made in a *rancio* style. Any ordinary, light, table wine that is maderized will often be erroneously diagnosed as oxidized, but there is a significant difference in the symptoms: maderized wines have a duller **nose**, have rarely any hint of the sherrylike character of **acetaldehyde**, and are flatter on the **palate**. All colors and styles of wine are capable of maderizing and the likely cause is storage in bright sunlight or too much warmth.

**MAILLARD REACTIONS** Chemical interactions between **amino acids** created during **autolysis** and residual sugar added by *dosage*, which are responsible for many of the mellow, complex post-**disgorgement** aromas adored by drinkers of mature Champagne. Maillard Reactions also play an important role in the raisining of grapes.

**MALIC** A tasting term that describes the green apple **aroma** and flavor found in some young wines due to the presence of **malic acid**, the dominant acid found in apples.

**MALIC ACID** A very strong-tasting acid that diminishes during the fruit's ripening process, but still persists in ripe grapes and, although reduced by **fermentation**, in wine too. The quantity of malic acid present in a wine may sometimes be considered too much, particularly in a red wine, and the smoothing effect of replacing it with just two-thirds the quantity of the much weaker **lactic acid** is often desirable. *See also* Malolactic Fermentation, p.26.

**MALOLACTIC** The malolactic **fermentation** is often termed a secondary fermentation, but is actually a biochemical process that converts the hard **malic acid** of unripe grapes into soft **lactic acid** and **carbonic gas**. *See also* Malolactic fermentation, p.26.

**MANURE** A very extreme form of **farmyardy**.

**MANNOPROTEIN** Nitrogenous matter secreted from yeast during **autolysis**.

**MANTA** See **Cap**.

**MARC** 1. The residue of skins, seeds, and stalks after pressing. 2. The name given to a four-ton load of grapes in Champagne. 3. A rough brandy made from the residue of skins, seeds, and stalks after pressing.

**MARQUE** A brand or make.

**MATURE, MATURITY** Refers to a wine's development in bottle, as opposed to **ripe**, which describes the maturity of the grape itself.

**MEAN** An extreme qualification of **ungenerous**.

**MEATY** This term suggests a wine so rich in **body** and **extract** that the drinker feels almost able to chew it. Wines with a high **tannin** content are often meaty.

**MELLOW** Describes a wine that is **round** and nearing its peak of **maturity**.

**MEMBRANE FILTRATION** Use of a thin screen of biologically inert material, perforated with microsized pores that occupy 80 percent of the membrane, to filter wine. Anything larger than these holes is denied passage when the wine is pumped through during **filtration**.

**MERCAPTANS** Methyl and ethyl **alcohols** can react with **hydrogen sulphide** to form mercaptans, foul-smelling compounds that are often impossible to remove and can ruin a wine. Mercaptans can smell of garlic, onion, burnt rubber, or stale cabbage.

**MÉTHODE CHAMPENOISE** (Fr.) The process in which an effervescence is produced through a secondary **fermentation** in the same bottle in which the wine is sold (in other words, not *transvasage*). This procedure is used for Champagne and other good-quality sparkling wines. In Europe, the term is forbidden on the label of any wine other than Champagne, which never uses it itself.

**MÉTHODE GAILLAÇOISE** (Fr.) A variant of *Méthode Rurale* involving *disgorgement*.

**MÉTHODE RURALE** (Fr.) The precursor of *Méthode Champenoise*, this method involves no secondary **fermentation**. The wine is bottled before the first alcoholic fermentation has finished, and **carbonic gas** is produced during the continuation of fermentation in the bottle. There is also no *disgorgement*.

**METODO CHAMPENOIS** (It.) Italian for *Méthode Champenoise*.

**MICROCLIMATE** Due to a combination of shelter, exposure, proximity to mountains and/or water mass, and other topographical features unique to a given area, a vineyard can enjoy (or be prone to) a specific microclimate that differs from the standard climate of the region as a whole.

**MICROPOROUS FILTRATION** Synonymous with **membrane filtration**.

**MICROVINIFICATION** This term involves **fermentation** in small, specialized vats, which are seldom bigger than a washing machine. The process is often used to make experimental wines. There are certain dynamics involved in fermentation that determine a minimum optimum size of vat, which is why home-brewers seldom make a polished product and why most wines made in research stations are dull.

**MID-PALATE** 1. The center-top of your tongue. 2. A subjective term to describe the middle of the taste sensation when taking a mouthful of wine. It may be hollow if the wine is thin and lacking, or full if it is rich and satisfying.

**MILLERANDAGE** (Fr.) A physiological disorder of the vine that occurs after cold or wet weather at the time of the flowering. This makes fertilization very difficult, and consequently many berries fail to develop, remaining small and seedless even when the rest of the bunch is full-sized and **ripe**.

**MINERAL** Some wines have a minerally aftertaste that can be unpleasant. Vinho Verde has an attractive, almost tinny aftertaste when made from certain grape varieties.

**MISTELLE** (Fr.) Fresh grape juice that has been muted with **alcohol** before any **fermentation** can take place.

**MOELLEUX** (Fr.) Literally soft or smooth, this term implies a rich, medium-sweet style in most areas of France. In the Loire, however, it is used to indicate a truly rich, sweet **botrytis** wine, thereby distinguishing it from **demi-sec**.

**MONOPOLE** (Fr.) Single ownership of a vineyard.

**MOUSSE** (Fr.) The effervescence of a sparkling wine, which is best judged in the mouth because a wine may appear to be flat in one glass and vigorous in another due to the different surfaces. The bubbles of a good *mousse* should be small and persistent; the strength of effervescence depends on the style of wine.

**MOUSSEUX** (Fr.) Literally "sparkling."

**MOUTH-FILL** Literally meaning a wine that easily fills the mouth with a satisfying flavor. There is no holding back, but it does not quite imply anything too upfront or obvious.

**MUID** (Fr.) A large oval barrel with a capacity of 600 liters (159 gallons).

**MUST** Unfermented or partly fermenting grape juice.

**MUST WEIGHT** The amount of sugar in ripe grapes or grape **must**.

**MUTAGE** (Fr.) The addition of pure **alcohol** to a wine or to fresh grape juice either before **fermentation** can take place, as in the case of a *vin de liqueur*, or during fermentation, as in the case of a *vin doux naturel*. *See also* Mutage, p.31.

**NÉGOCIANT** (Fr.) Trader or merchant. The name is derived from the traditional practice of negotiating with growers (to buy wine) and wholesalers or customers (to sell it).

**NÉGOCIANT-ÉLEVEUR** (Fr.) A wine firm that buys in ready-made wines for *éleveur*. The wines are then blended and bottled under the *négociant's* label.

**NERVY, NERVOUS** A subjective term usually applied to a dry white wine that is **firm** and vigorous, but not quite settled down.

**NEUTRAL GRAPE VARIETIES** Such grapes include virtually all the minor, nondescript varieties that produce bland tasting, low-quality wines, but also encompass better known varieties such as the Melon de Bourgogne, Aligoté, Pinot Blanc, Pinot Meunier, and even classics such as Chardonnay and Sémillon. The opposite of **aromatic** grapes, these varieties are ideal for **oak**-maturation, bottling *sur lie*, and turning into fine sparkling wines because their characteristics are enhanced rather than hidden by these processes.

**NOBLE ROT** A condition caused by the fungus *Botrytis cinerea* under certain conditions.

**NOSE** The smell or odor of a wine, encompassing both **aroma** and **bouquet**.

**OAK** Many wines are **fermented** or aged in wooden casks and the most commonly used wood is oak.

There are two main categories of oak, French and American, and they are both used the world over. Although the French always use French oak, the greatest California wines are also usually made in French oak barrels. American oak is traditional in Spain, particularly Rioja, and Australia, although both these countries have a growing usage of French oak. Oak often gives a **vanilla** taste to wine because it contains a substance called **vanillin**, which also gives vanilla pods their vanilla aroma. French oak is perceived to be finer and more refined, while American oak is generally considered to have a more upfront, obvious character. This difference in character is due not to intrinsic qualities in the two types of oak (although American oak grows more quickly than French and has a bigger grain, which does have some influence), but to the traditional weathering of French oak in the open for several years, which leaches out the most volatile **aromatics**. American oak is kiln-dried (therefore not leached) and sawn (unlike French oak, which is split), which ruptures the grain, exposing the wine to the oak's most volatile elements in a relatively short time. If French oak were to be kiln-dried and sawn, and American weathered and split, I suspect our perception of the two forms of oak might well be reversed. American oak is often highly charred in the construction of a barrel (winemakers can order it lightly toasted, medium toasted, or highly charred), and this too has an effect, adding caramel, toffee, and smoky-toasty aromas to a wine. The toastiness in oak is different to any toastiness derived from the grape itself. Strangely, oak can produce a cedary taste, although this is probably confined to wines made from spicy black-grape varieties that are fermented and/or matured in relatively old wood. If you get a very strong impression of coconut, it's a good bet that the oak used was American. Oak barrels are very expensive to buy and labor intensive to work with, so if you find a very cheap wine with obvious oak character, it will inevitably be due to the use of oak chips or shavings, which are chucked into a huge, gleaming stainless-steel vat of wine. Cheating this may be, but it is legal, and if people like the taste of oak-aged wine, but cannot afford to pay much for a bottle, what is wrong with it? *See also* Stainless Steel or Oak, p.26.

**OECHSLE LEVEL** (Ger.) A system of measuring the sugar content in grapes for wine categories in Germany and Austria.

**OENOLOGIST, OENOLOGY** Pronounced "enologist" and "enology" (and usually spelled this way in the US), oenology is the scientific study of wine. It is a branch of chemistry, but with practical consequences, hands-on production experience, and an understanding of **viticulture**.

**OFF VINTAGE** An off vintage or year is one in which many poor wines are produced due to adverse climatic conditions, such as very little sunshine during the summer, which can result in unripe grapes, and rain or humid heat at the harvest, which can result in rot. Generally an off vintage is a vintage to be avoided, but approach any opportunity to taste the wines with an open mind because there are always good wines made in every vintage, and they have to be sold at bargain prices if a vintage has a bad reputation.

**OIDIUM** A fungal disease of the vine that turns leaves powdery grey and dehydrates grapes.

**OILY** A subjective term meaning **fat** and viscous, and often also **flat** and **flabby**.

**OLOROSO** (Sp.) A sherry style, naturally dry but usually sweetened for export markets.

**OPEN-KNIT** An open and enjoyable **nose** or **palate**, usually found in a modest wine that is not capable of much development.

**OPULENT** Suggestive of a rather luxurious **varietal** aroma; very rich, but not quite **blowzy**.

**ORGANIC WINES** A generic term for wines made using the minimum amount of $SO_2$ (sulfur dioxide), from grapes grown without the use of chemical **fertilizers**, **pesticides**, or **herbicides**.

**ORGANOLEPTIC** Affecting a bodily organ or sense, usually that of taste or smell.

**OSMOTIC PRESSURE** When two solutions are separated by a semipermeable membrane, water will leave the weaker solution for the more concentrated one in an endeavor to equalize the differing solution strengths. In winemaking, this is most commonly seen when **yeast** cells are put to work in grape juice with an exceptionally high sugar content. Since water accounts for 65 percent of a yeast cell, osmotic pressure causes the water to escape through the semipermeable cell membrane. The cell caves in (a phenomenon called plasmolysis), and the yeast dries up and eventually dies.

**OVERTONE** A dominating element of **nose** and **palate**; often one that is not directly attributable to the grape or wine.

**OXIDATION, OXIDIZED** These terms are ambiguous; as soon as grapes are pressed or crushed, oxidation sets in and the juice or wine will become oxidized to a certain and increasing extent. Oxidation is also an unavoidable part of **fermentation** and essential to the maturation process. In this case, however, in order not to mislead it is best to speak of a "mature" or, at the extreme, "**oxidative**" wine. This is because when the word oxidized is used, even among experts, it will invariably be in an extremely derogatory manner, to highlight the sherrylike odor of a wine that is in a prematurely advanced stage of oxidation.

**OXIDATIVE** A wine that openly shows the character of maturation on the **nose** or **palate**. This can range from buttery, biscuity, and spicy characteristics through to a hint of nuttiness.

**PAD FILTRATION** A **filtration** system utilizing a Plate and Frame filter with a series of cellulose, asbestos, or paper sheets through which wine is passed.

**PALATE** The flavor or taste of a wine.

**PARTIAL ROOTZONE DRYING** *See* PRD.

**PASSERILLAGE** (Fr.) Grapes without **noble rot** that are left on the vine become cut off from the plant's metabolic system as its sap withdraws into its roots. The warmth of the day, followed by the cold of the night, causes the grapes to dehydrate and concentrate in a process known as *passerillage*. The sweet wine produced from these grapes is prized in certain areas. A *passerillage* wine from a hot fall will be totally different to one from a cold fall.

**PASSITO** (It.) The Italian equivalent of *passerillage*. *Passito* grapes are semidried, either outside—on the vine or on mats—or inside a warm building. This concentrates the pulp and produces strong, often sweet wines.

**PASTEURIZATION** A generic term for various methods of **stabilization** and sterilization.

**PEAK** The ideal maturity of a wine. Those liking fresher, crisper wines will perceive an earlier peak in the same wine than drinkers who prefer mature wines. As a rule of thumb that applies to all extremes of taste, a wine will remain at its peak for as long as it took to reach it.

**PEARDROP** *See* **Amylic**; *Macération carbonique*.

**PEPPERY** A term applied to young wines whose components are raw and not yet in harmony, sometimes quite fierce and prickly on the **nose**. It also describes the characteristic odor and flavor of southern French wines, particularly Grenache-based ones. Syrah can smell of freshly crushed black pepper, while white pepper is the character of great Grüner Veltliner. Young ports and light red Riojas can also be very peppery.

**PERFUME** An agreeable scented quality of a wine's **bouquet**.

**PERLANT** (Fr.) Very slightly sparkling, less so than *crémant* and *pétillant*.

**PERLITE** A fine, powdery, light, lustrous substance of volcanic origin with **diatomaceous earth**-like properties When perlite is used for filtration, it is sometimes referred to as **ceramic filtration**.

**PESTICIDE** Literally a pest-killer, but more accurately a parasite-killer, the term pesticide infers a highly toxic concoction of chemicals capable of eradicating parasitic insects that attack the vine, including larvae, flies, moths, and spiders.

**PÉTILLANCE, PÉTILLANT** (Fr.) This term describes a wine with sufficient **carbonic gas** to create a light sparkle.

**PETIT CHÂTEAU** (Fr.) Literally "small château," this term is applied to any wine château that is neither a *Cru Classé* nor a *Cru Bourgeois*.

**pH** A commonly used chemical abbreviation of "potential hydrogen-ion concentration," a measure of the **active acidity** or alkalinity of a liquid. It does not give any indication of the **total acidity** in a wine, but neither does the human **palate**. When we perceive the acidity in wine through taste, it is more closely associated with the pH than with the total acidity.

**PHENOLS, PHENOLIC COMPOUNDS** Compounds found in the skin, seeds, and stalks of grapes, the most common being **tannin** and **anthocyanins**.

**PHOTOSYNTHESIS** The process by which light energy is trapped by chorophyll, a green chemical in the leaves, and is converted into chemical energy in the form of glucose. This is then carried around the plant in special tubes called phloem to grow shoots, leaves, flowers, and fruit.

**PHYLLOXERA** A vine louse that spread from America to virtually every viticultural region in the world during the late 19th century, destroying many vines. New vines had (and still have) to be grafted on to phylloxera-resistant American **rootstocks**.

**PIPE** (Port.) The most famous Portuguese barrel, a Douro pipe has a 550-liter (145-gallon) capacity.

**PIQUANT** (Fr.) Usually applied to a pleasing white wine with positive underlying fruit and **acidity**.

**PLAFOND LIMITÉ DE CLASSEMENT** *See* PLC.

**PLC** Plafond Limité de Classement, a legalized form of cheating whereby producers of **AOC** wines are allowed to exceed the official maximum limit by as much as 20 percent.

**PLUMMY** An elegant, juicy flavor and texture that resembles the fleshiness of plums.

**PLUM-PUDDING** A subjective term for a rich and spicy red wine; a more intense term than **Christmas cake**.

**POLISHED** Describes a wine that has been skillfully crafted, leaving no rough edges. It is **smooth** and refined to drink.

**POLISHING** The very last, ultrafine **filtration** of a wine, usually with kieselguhr (*see* **diatomaceous earth**) or perlite. It is so called because it leaves the wine bright. Many high-quality wines are not polished because the process can wash out natural flavors.

**POST-DISGORGEMENT AGING** The period between **disgorgement** and when the wine is consumed. With the sudden exposure to air after an extended period of aging under **anaerobic** conditions, the development of a sparkling wine after disgorgement is very different from its development before.

**POURRITURE NOBLE** (Fr.) Noble rot, which is caused by the fungus *Botrytis cinerea* under certain conditions.

**PRD** Partial rootzone drying, a clever way of fooling the vine into thinking that it is not being irrigated, when in fact it is. This is achieved by alternating irrigation between two separate parts of the root system. Part of the vine receives a carefully metered out drip irrigation, but the rest of the plant system is unaware of this and, not sensing the irrigation, believes that it is in fact experiencing a mild water stress. The vine thus diverts its metabolism (energy) from the leaves to the grape clusters, improving the quality of the fruit. When the water is drawn into the part of the vine that has shut down the metabolism of its leaves, this part of the vine reverses the metabolic process. This is the very

time that the drip irrigation is switched to that side of the vine, as it has already accepted the water's presence. However, by turning off the irrigation to the other side of the vine, that side now believes it is experiencing a mild water stress, and it is its turn to divert the vine's metabolism from the leaves to the grape clusters. And so it goes on, drip feeding either side of a vine that perpetually experiences a mild state of water stress. This conserves water, and while it does not increase yields per se, it does produce better quality at normal yields.

**PREFERMENTATION MACERATION** The practice of **maceration** of juice in grape skins prior to **fermentation**, to enhance the **varietal** character of the wine. This maceration is usually carried out cold and is normally employed for **aromatic** white varieties, but can be undertaken warm—or even quite hot for red wines.

**PREMIER CRU** (Fr.) Literally "First Growth," this term is of relevance only in those areas where it is controlled, such as in Burgundy and Champagne.

**PREMIUM** A marketing term for a quality category. So-called premium or premium-quality wine is not as expensive as you might think, and certainly not the top category of wine. Because of the differential in tax, duty, and shipping costs, it is actually possible to categorize wines by exactly the same unit price in dollars (US), pounds (UK), and Euros (rest of Eurozone): Basic: less than $3/£3/€3; Premium: $/£/€5–7; Superpremium: $/£/€7–14; Ultrapremium: $/£/€14–150; and Icon: in excess of $/£/€150.

**PRESS WINE** *See Vin de presse*.

**PRICKLE, PRICKLY** This term describes a wine with residual **carbonic gas**, but with less than the light sparkle of a *pétillant* wine. This characteristic can be desirable in some fresh white and **rosé** wines, but it is usually taken as a sign of an undesirable **secondary fermentation** in red wines, although it is deliberately created in certain South African examples.

**PRODUCER VINE** Vines are usually grafted on to **phylloxera**-resistant **rootstock**, but the grapes produced are characteristic of the above-ground producer vine or scion, which is normally a variety of *Vitis vinifera*.

**PROTEIN HAZE** Protein is present in all wines. Too much protein can react with **tannin** to cause a haze, in which case **bentonite** is usually used as a **fining** agent to remove it.

**PUNCHEON** A type of barrel that is commonly found in Australia and New Zealand and has a capacity of 450 liters (119 gallons).

**PVPP** Abbreviation for polyvinylpolypyrrolidone, a **fining** agent used to remove compounds sensitive to browning from white wines.

**PYRAZINES** One of the most important groups of aromatic compounds found in grapes (especially methoxypyrazines), pyrazines typically have green, leafy, grassy characteristics through to bell-pepper, green-pea, and asparagus. The more herbaceous pyrazine **aromas** are symptomatic of an excessively vigorous vine canopy, particularly in red wines. Although pyrazines become less abundant as grapes ripen, they are considered a vital element in the varietal character of Sauvignon Blanc.

**QUALITÄTSWEIN BESTIMMTER ANBAUGEBIETE** *See* QbA.

**QUALITÄTSWEIN MIT PRÄDIKAT** *See* QmP.

**QbA** (Ger.) Germany's *Qualitätswein bestimmter Anbaugebiete* is the theoretical equivalent of the French **AOC**.

**QmP** (Ger.) The abbreviation for *Qualitätswein mit Prädikat*. Literally a "quality wine with predication," this term is used for any German wine above **QbA**, from *Kabinett* upward. The predication carried by a QmP wine depends upon the level of ripeness of the grapes used in the wine.

**QUAFFING WINE** Describes an unpretentious wine that is easy and enjoyable to drink.

**QUINTA** (Port.) A wine estate.

**R2** A **yeast** strain (*Saccharomyces cerevisiae race bayanus*) discovered by Danish-born winemaker Peter Vinding-Diers.

**RACKING** The draining of a wine off its **lees** into a fresh cask or vat. *See also* Racking, p.26.

**RACY** Often applied to wines of the Riesling grape. The term racy accurately suggests the liveliness, vitality, and **acidity** of this grape.

**RANCIO** Description of a *vin doux naturel* stored in oak casks for at least two years, often with the barrels exposed to direct sunlight. This imparts a distinctive flavor that is popular in the Roussillon area of France.

**RATAFIA** A *liqueur* made by combining *marc* with grape juice, Ratafia de Champagne being the best-known.

**RD** A sparkling-wine term that stands for "recently disgorged," the initials RD are the trademark of Champagne Bollinger. *See also* LD.

**RECIOTO** (It.) A strong, sweet wine made in Italy from *passito* grapes.

**REDOX** The aging process of wine was originally conceived as purely **oxidative**, but it was then discovered that when one substance in wine is **oxidized** (gains oxygen), another is reduced (loses oxygen). This is known as a reductive-oxidative, or redox reaction. **Organoleptically**, however, wines reveal either oxidative or reductive characters. In the presence of air, wine is prone to an oxidative character, but shut off from a supply of oxygen, reductive characteristics begin to dominate, thus the bouquet of bottle-age is a reductive one and the aroma of a fresh, young wine is more oxidative than reductive.

**REDUCTIVE** The less exposure it has to air, the more reductive a wine will be. Different as they are in basic character, Champagne, Muscadet *sur lie*, and Beaujolais Nouveau are all examples of reductive, as opposed to **oxidative**, wines, from the vividly **autolytic** Champagne, through Muscadet *sur lie* with its barest hint of autolytic character, to the **amylic** aroma of Beaujolais Nouveau. A good contrast is between sherry and Madeira, the latter of which is reductive, while the former is oxidative. The term is, however, abused, as many tasters use it to describe a fault, when the wine is heavily reduced.

**REFRACTOMETER** An optical device used to measure the sugar content of grapes when out in the field.

**REMONTAGE** (Fr.) The pumping of wine over the **cap** (or manta) of skins during the *cuvaison* of red wine.

**REMUAGE** (Fr.) An intrinsic part of the *méthode champenoise*; deposits thrown off during **secondary fermentation** are eased down to the neck of the bottle and are then removed at *disgorgement*.

**RESERVE WINES** Still wines from previous vintages that are blended with the wines of one principal year to produce a balanced nonvintage Champagne.

**RETICENT** This term suggests that the wine is holding back on its **nose** or **palate**, perhaps through youth, and may well develop with a little more maturity.

**RICH, RICHNESS** A balanced wealth of fruit and depth on the palate, and a good **finish**.

**RIPASSO** (It.) **Refermentation** of wine on the **lees** of a *recioto* wine.

**RIPE** Grapes ripen; wines mature. However, the fruit and even the **acidity** in wine can be referred to as ripe. Tasters should be careful not to mistake a certain residual sweetness for ripeness.

**RIPE ACIDITY** The main acidic component in ripe grapes (**tartaric acid**) tastes refreshing and fruity, even in large proportions, whereas the main acidity in unripe grapes (**malic acid**) tastes hard and unpleasant.

**ROASTED** Describes the character of grapes subjected to the shriveling or roasting of **noble rot**.

**ROBUST** A milder form of **aggressive**, which may frequently be applied to a mature product. A

**VDT** (It.) Short for *vino da tavola*. Supposedly the lowest rung in Italy's appellation system, it does, however, in practice, encompass some of the country's greatest wines. *See* Italy, p.263.

**VEGETAL** Applied to wines of a certain maturity, often Chardonnay or Pinot, that are well rounded in style and have taken on a **bouquet** pleasingly reminiscent of vegetation, rather than fruit.

**VENDANGE TARDIVE** (Fr.) Late harvest.

**VÉRAISON** (Fr.) The ripening period, during which the grapes do not actually change very much in size, but do gain in color (if black) and increase in sugar and **tartaric acid**, while at the same time decreasing in unripe **malic acid**.

**VERMOUTH** An **aromatized wine**. The name vermouth originates from *Wermut*, the German for wormwood, which is its principal ingredient. The earliest examples made in Germany in the 16th century were for local consumption only, the first commercial vermouth being Punt-é-Mes, created by Antonio Carpano of Turin in 1786. Traditionally, Italian vermouth is red and sweet, while French is white and dry, but both countries make both styles. Vermouth is made by blending very bland base wines (they are two or three years old and come from Apulia and Sicily in Italy and Languedoc-Roussillon in France) with an extract of aromatic ingredients, then sweetening the blend with sugar and fortifying it with pure alcohol. Chambéry, a pale and delicately aromatic wine made in the Savoie, France, is the only vermouth with an official **appellation**.

**VERTICAL TASTING** *See* Horizontal tasting.

**VIERTELSTÜCK** (Ger.) A small oval cask with a capacity of 300 liters (80 gallons).

**VIGNERON** (Fr.) Vineyard worker.

**VIGNOBLE** (Fr.) Vineyard.

**VIGOR** Although this term could easily apply to wine, it is invariably used when discussing the growth of a vine, and particularly of its canopy. In order to ripen grapes properly, a vine needs about 8 square inches (50 square centimeters) of leaf surface to every gram of fruit, but if a vine is too vigorous (termed "high vigor"), the grapes will have an **overherbaceous** character, even when they are theoretically **ripe**.

**VIN DE CAFÉ** (Fr.) This category of French wine is sold by the carafe in cafés, bistros, and so on.

**VIN DE GARDE** (Fr.) Wine that is capable of significant improvement if it is allowed to age.

**VIN DE GLACE** (Fr.) French equivalent of *Eiswein*.

**VIN DE GOUTTE** (Fr.) Free-run juice. In the case of white wine, this is the juice that runs free from the press before the actual pressing operation begins. With red wine, it is fermented wine drained off from the manta or cap before this is pressed.

**VIN DE L'ANNÉE** (Fr.) This term is synonymous with *vin primeur*.

**VIN DE LIQUEUR** *See* VdL.

**VIN DE PAILLE** (Fr.) Literally "straw wine," a complex sweet wine produced by leaving late-picked grapes to dry and shrivel in the sun on straw mats. *See also* The Jura and Savoie, p.224.

**VIN DE PAYS** (Fr.) A rustic style of country wine that is one step above *vin de table*, but one beneath VdQS. *See also* Vin de Pays, p.248.

**VIN DE PRESSE** (Fr.) Very dark, tannic, red wine pressed out of the manta or **cap**, after the *vin de goutte* has been drained off.

**VIN DE TABLE** (Fr.) Literally "table wine," although not necessarily a direct translation. It describes the lowest level of wine in France and is not allowed to give either the grape variety or the area of origin on the label. In practice, it likely consists of various varieties from numerous areas that have been blended in bulk to produce a wine of consistent character, or lack thereof, as the case may be.

**VIN DÉLIMITÉ DE QUALITÉ SUPÉRIEURE** *See* VdQS.

**VIN DOUX NATUREL** *See* VdN.

**VIN D'UNE NUIT** (Fr.) A rosé or very pale red wine that is allowed contact with the manta or **cap** for one night only.

**VIN GRIS** (Fr.) A delicate, pale version of rosé.

**VIN JAUNE** (Fr.) This is the famous "yellow wine" of the Jura that derives its name from its honey-gold color that results from a deliberate **oxidation** beneath a **sherrylike** *flor*. The result is similar to an aged Fino sherry, although it is not **fortified**. *See also* The Jura and Savoie, p.224.

**VIN MOUSSEUX** (Fr.) This literally means "sparkling wine" without any particular connotation of quality one way or the other. But because all fine sparkling wines in France utilize other terms, for all practical purposes it implies a cheap, low-quality product.

**VIN NOUVEAU** (Fr.) This term is synonymous with *vin primeur*.

**VIN ORDINAIRE** (Fr.) Literally "an ordinary wine," this term is most often applied to a French *vin de table*, although it can be used in a rather derogatory way to describe any wine from any country.

**VIN PRIMEUR** Young wine made to be drunk within the year in which it is produced. Beaujolais Primeur is the official designation of the most famous *vin primeur*, but export markets see it labeled as Beaujolais Nouveau most of the time.

**VINHO REGIONAL** (Port.) *See* VR.

**VINIFERA** *See* Vitis vinifera.

**VINIFICATION** Far more than simply describing **fermentation**, vinification involves the entire process of making wine, from the moment the grapes are picked to the point at which the wine is finally bottled.

**VINIMATIC** This is an enclosed, rotating **fermentation** tank with blades fixed to the inner surface, that works on the same principle as a cement-mixer. Used initially to extract the maximum color from the grape skins with the minimum **oxidation**, it is now being utilized for **prefermentation maceration**.

**VINO COMARCAL** (Sp.) *See* VC.

**VINO DA TAVOLA** (It.) *Vin de table*, table wine.

**VINO DE LA TIERRA** (Sp.) *See* VDLT.

**VINO DE MESA** (Sp.) Table wine, *vin de table*.

**VINO NOVELLO** (It.) The same as *vin primeur*.

**VINOUS** Of, or relating to, a characteristic of wine. When used to describe a wine, this term implies basic qualities only.

**VINTAGE** 1. A wine of one year. 2. Synonymous with harvest: a vintage wine is the wine of one year's harvest only (or at least 85 percent according to EU regulations) and the year may be anything from poor to exceptional. It is, for this reason, a misnomer to use the term vintage for the purpose of indicating a wine of special quality.

**VITICULTURE** Cultivation of the vine. Viticulture is to grapes what horticulture is to flowers.

**VITIS VINIFERA** A species covering all varieties of vines that provide classic winemaking grapes.

**VIVID** The fruit in some wines can be so **fresh**, **ripe**, clean-cut, and **expressive** that it quickly gives a vivid impression of complete character in the mouth.

**VOLATILE ACIDS** These acids, sometimes called fatty acids, are capable of evaporating at low temperatures. Too much volatile acidity is always a sign of instability, but small amounts do actually play a significant role in the taste and **aroma** of a wine. Formic, butyric, and proprionic are all volatile acids that may be found in wine, but **acetic acid** and **carbonic acid** are the most important.

**VOLATILE PHENOLS** Almost one-third of all French wines tested have volatile **phenols** above the level of perception, so they are clearly not always bad. Some volatile phenols such as ethyl-4-guaiacol (smoky-spicy aroma) and, to a lesser degree, vinyl-4-guaiacol (carnation aroma) can actually contribute attractive elements to a wine's bouquet. However, volatile phenols are generally considered to be faults, and the amount of ethyl and vinyl phenols

present in a wine is increased by harsh methods of pressing (particularly the use of continuous presses), insufficient settling, use of particular strains of yeast, and, to a lesser extent, increased skin-contact. Ethyl-4-phenol is responsible for the so-called Brett off-aromas (stables, horsey, sweaty-saddles—*see* **Brettanomyces**), while vinyl-4-phenol has a Band-Aid off-aroma.

**VOLUPTUOUS** A term used to describe a succulently rich wine, often a red wine, which has a seductive, mouthfilling flavor. *See also* **luscious**.

**VQPRD** A common abbreviation for *vin de qualité produit dans une région délimitée*.

**VR** (Port.) The abbreviation for *vinho regional*, the lowest rung in Portugal's **appellation** system. A VR can be compared to the regional *vin de pays* category in France.

**WARM, WARMTH** Terms suggestive of a good-flavored red wine with a high alcoholic content; if these terms are used with an accompanying description of cedary or **creamy**, they can mean well-matured in **oak**.

**WATERSHED** A term used for an area where water drains into a river system, lake, or some other body of water.

**WATERY** An extreme qualification of **thin**.

**WEISSHERBST** (Ger.) A single-variety rosé wine produced from black grapes only.

**WINE LAKE** A common term for the EU surplus of low-quality table wine.

**WINKLER SCALE** A term synonymous with the **heat summation** system.

**WOOD LACTONES** These are various **esters** that are picked up from new **oak**; they may be the source of certain creamy-oak and coconutty characteristics.

**WOOD-MATURED** This term normally refers to a wine that has been aged in new **oak**.

**YEAST** A kind of fungus that is absolutely vital in all winemaking. Yeast cells excrete a number of **yeast enzymes**, some 22 of which are necessary to complete the chain reaction that is known as **fermentation**. *See also* Yeast the Fermenter, p.25.

**YEAST ENZYMES** Each yeast **enzyme** acts as a catalyst for one particular activity in the **fermentation** process and is specific for that one task only.

**YEASTY** This is not a complimentary term for most wines, but a yeasty **bouquet** can sometimes be desirable in a good-quality sparkling wine, especially if it is young.

**YIELD** 1. The quantity of grapes produced from a given area of land. 2. How much juice is pressed from this quantity of grapes. Wine people in Europe measure yield in hl/ha (hectoliters per hectare—a hectoliter equals 1,000 liters), referring to how much juice has been extracted from the grapes harvested from a specific area of land. This is fine when the amount of juice that can be pressed from grapes is controlled by European-type **appellation** systems, but in the New World, where this seldom happens, they tend to talk in terms of tons per acre. It can be difficult trying to make exact conversions in the field, particularly after a heavy tasting session, when even the size of a ton or gallon can become quite elusive. This is why, as a rough guide, I multiply the tons or divide the hectoliters by 20 to convert one to the other. This is based on the average extraction rates for both California and Australia, which makes it a good rule-of-thumb. Be aware that white wines can benefit from higher yields than reds (although sweet wines should have the lowest yields of all) and that sparkling wines can get away with relatively high yields. For example, Sauternes averages 25 hl/ha, Bordeaux 50 hl/ha, and Champagne 80 hl/ha.

**ZESTY** A lively characteristic that is suggestive of a **zippy** tactile impression combined, maybe, with a distinctive hint of citrus **aroma**.

**ZING, ZINGY, ZIP, ZIPPY** Terms that are all indicative of something that is noteworthy for being refreshing, lively, and vital in character, resulting from a high balance of ripe fruit **acidity** in the wine.

# INDEX